双语美辞书是登
上翻译殿堂的必由之
路，是从事国际交流事
业的指路明灯。

黄友义

丁亥
正月

国际翻译家联盟副主席、中国翻译家协会
副会长兼秘书长黄友义为本书题词

目　录

CIPG

China International Publishing Group

新汉英词典

A New Learner's Chinese-English Dictionary

主　编　潘熙祥

副主编　齐晓燕

编　委　樊英波　郝黎明　马玉学
　　　　刘　跃　郭宝安　何冬雨
　　　　董全中　于　健　于明善
　　　　潘熙祥　齐晓燕

中国国际出版集团

华语教学出版社

图书在版编目(CIP)数据

新汉英词典/潘熙祥主编. —北京：华语教学出版社，2008
ISBN 978-7-80200-357-6

Ⅰ. 新… Ⅱ. 潘… Ⅲ. ①英语—词典②词典—汉、英 Ⅳ. H316

中国版本图书馆 CIP 数据核字（2008）第 014678 号

新汉英词典

说词解字系列工具书

出　版　人　　王君校
选题策划　　说词解字辞书研究中心
编　　　者　　潘熙祥
责任编辑　　肖　华
装帧设计　　赵佳阳
印刷监制　　佟汉冬
出　　　版　　华语教学出版社
社　　　址　　北京百万庄大街 24 号
邮政编码　　100037
电　　　话　　(010)68320585
传　　　真　　(010)68326333
读者热线　　(010)86226518
网　　　址　　www. sinolingua. com. cn
电子邮箱　　fxb@sinolingua. com. cn
印　　　刷　　北京外文印刷厂
经　　　销　　全国新华书店
开　　　本　　64 开（880×1230）
字　　　数　　2985（千）
版　　　次　　2009 年 8 月第 1 版第 3 次印刷
书　　　号　　ISBN 978-7-80200-357-6
定　　　价　　26.80 元

前　言

　　这是一部颇具时代特色的中型汉英词典，它将与我们生活、学习密切相关的电子信息、经济、金融、法律、财务、医药等词汇都足数收录。本词典集数十位长期从事英语教学工作的专家、教授和学者的劳动结晶，编写过程中充分吸收当前英语教学的优秀成果，借鉴了不同版本的国内外优秀的同类辞书。本词典能够满足大中学生、中学英语教师、广大英语爱好者在学习和工作中的需求，是一本新颖、实用的精品辞书。以下是这部词典特有的亮点：

　　一、收词广泛，选词量大。本词典兼收语文词汇及百科词汇，与同类词典相比，收词较多，单字条目6,500余条，多字条目85,000余条。对所收录的汉语字词完全着眼于实用，不贪多求全。本词典不给汉语释义，也不提供汉语语法与语用信息，从而省出了大量篇幅用于更多的词条。

　　二、广收新词新义。本词典力求与时俱进，尽可能多地收录新词。例如"粉丝""博客""网恋"等等，此类新词遍见于整部词典，数量上千，不胜枚举。真正做到了资讯量大，实用性强。

　　三、词义精当，译文流畅。本词典释义不考虑意义的引申脉络而按汉语的词类相对集中，能"译"的一般不"释"，只有极少数无对应词语的才给出英语解释，义项准确，用语浅显易懂。

　　四、双色印刷，体例新颖，美观大方，适宜检索、阅读。

　　词典的编写工作，难度极大，参编人数和花费的时间，非业外人士所能想象。一部优秀的词典，要经过诸多学者、编者长期伏案、连篇累牍、字斟句酌地审阅；要通过环环相扣、一丝不苟的出版流程方能与读者见面。这部词典的编写内容，认真贯彻执行了国家有关部门颁布的有关语言文字的标准与规范。编著者虽初衷良好，但囿于水平，疏漏之处在所难免，诚望读者朋友能把使用中发现的错误和疏漏及时告诉我们，以便我们加以修正，使本词典更臻完善。

《新汉英词典》编委会

体例说明

一、条目

1. 本词典所收条目分单字条目和多字条目；单字条目以大号黑体排印，多字条目以小号黑体按第一个字母分别列在领头的单字条目之下。

2. 单字条目按汉语拼音字母顺序排列。同音节（以汉语拼音字母和注音符号表示）的字依阴平、阳平、上声、去声、轻声的顺序排列。同音同调的字按起笔笔形横（一）、直（丨）、撇（丿）、点（、）、折（乙フ乚）的顺序排列。

3. 单字条目中字形相同而音或调不同者分立条目，分别排列于相应位置，并以 ➡ 指示"另见"。

4. 同一个单字条目下的多字条目不止一条时，先按字数的多少排列，少的在前，多的在后。再按第二个字的汉语拼音字母顺序和笔画多少排列。第二个字相同时，按第三个字排列，依此类推。

5. 成语习语以多字条目形式出现，内容包括常用成语、习语、俚语、谚语、动词短语及百科性词语等。

6. 多字条目领头单字在后时，第一个词前标有◇。

二、注音

1. 本词典单字条目以汉语拼音字母注音，置于方括号［］内。

2. 本词典依据《汉语拼音方案》注音，声调符号标在音节的主要母音上，轻声不标。

3. 有异读的词和有异读的作为"语素"的字依据《普通话异读词审音表》标注读音。

4. 轻声词凡列入《普通话异读审音表》的一律标注轻声，未列入该表的则依据《现代汉语词典》标注。

三、释义

1. 释义用白正体排印。

2. 单字条目标注词类，置于方框□内。具有多个词类的用罗马数字Ⅰ、Ⅱ、Ⅲ等表明。多字条目不标词性。条目词的语体标签与学科标签均置于尖括号〈〉内。适于整个条目各义项的，标在第一义项之前；只适于个别义项的，标在有关义项数码之后。

3. 释义一般用对应的英语词语，无对应的词语时用英语解释。一个条目有两个或两个以上义项时用①②③等数码标出顺序。同一义项下有两个或两个以上解释时，用分号";"隔开。

4. 释义中的可替换词语放在圆括号"（）"内，前面加 or。

5. 释义须用英语加注补充性或限制性说明的，用白斜体排印。

6. 某些条目先用英语作字面翻译，然后释义，二者之间加破折号"—"。

四、例证

1. 例证排在释义之后，其前加冒号"："。例证与例证之间用斜线号"/"隔开。

2. 例证中可替换部分及其英译放在圆括号内，前面加 *or*。

略语表

（一）

名	名词	副	副词
动	动词	介	介词
形	形容词	连	连词
数	数词	助	助词
量	量词	叹	感叹词
代	代词	象	象声词

（二）

〈贬〉	贬义	〈骂〉	骂人话
〈粗〉	粗俗词语	〈蔑〉	轻蔑用词
〈儿〉	儿童用语	〈昵〉	亲昵用词
〈方〉	方言	〈谦〉	谦辞
〈反〉	反语	〈诗〉	诗歌用语
〈废〉	废词，废义	〈书〉	书面语
〈讽〉	讽刺	〈缩〉	缩略语
〈古〉	古词，古义	〈套〉	客套语
〈罕〉	罕用	〈婉〉	委婉语
〈诙〉	诙谐语	〈文〉	文学语言
〈忌〉	忌讳用	〈学〉	学生用语
〈敬〉	敬畏语	〈谑〉	戏谑词语
〈旧〉	旧时用	〈谚〉	谚语
〈口〉	口语中用	〈喻〉	比喻
〈俚〉	俚语	〈尊〉	尊称

音 节 表

（音节右边的号码指正文的页码）

A

ā	1	bǎo	26	bǔ	59	chāo	91
á	1	bào	29	bù	60	cháo	93
ǎ	1	bēi	31			chǎo	94
à	1	běi	32			chào	94
a	1	bèi	33	cā	71	chē	94
āi	2	bei	35	cǎ	71	chě	95
ái	2	bēn	35	cāi	71	chè	95
ǎi	3	běn	35	cái	71	chēn	95
ài	3	bèn	36	cǎi	73	chén	96
ān	4	bēng	37	cài	74	chěn	97
ǎn	7	béng	37	cān	74	chèn	97
àn	7	běng	37	cán	75	chen	98
āng	9	bèng	37	cǎn	76	chēng	98
áng	9	bī	37	càn	77	chéng	98
àng	9	bí	38	cāng	77	chěng	103
āo	9	bǐ	38	cáng	77	chèng	103
áo	10	bì	40	cāo	78	chī	103
ǎo	10	biān	42	cáo	78	chí	104
ào	10	biǎn	44	cǎo	78	chǐ	105
		biàn	45	cè	79	chì	106
		bian	47	cēn	80	chōng	107
B		biāo	47	cén	80	chóng	108
		biǎo	48	cēng	81	chǒng	109
bā	12	biào	50	céng	81	chòng	109
bá	13	biē	50	cèng	81	chōu	109
bǎ	14	bié	50	chā	81	chóu	110
bà	14	biě	50	chá	82	chǒu	111
ba	15	biè	51	chǎ	84	chòu	111
bāi	15	bīn	51	chà	84	chū	111
bái	15	bìn	51	chāi	84	chú	115
bǎi	17	bīng	51	chái	85	chǔ	116
bài	19	bǐng	53	chān	85	chù	117
bān	20	bìng	54	chán	85	chuāi	118
bǎn	21	bō	55	chǎn	86	chuái	118
bàn	21	bó	57	chàn	87	chuǎi	118
bāng	23	bǒ	58	chāng	87	chuài	118
bǎng	24	bò	58	cháng	87	chuān	118
bàng	24	bo	59	chǎng	90	chuán	119
bāo	24	bū	59	chàng	90	chuǎn	120
báo	26	bú	59	chang	91	chuàn	121

chuāng	121		
chuáng	121		
chuǎng	121		
chuàng	122		
chuī	122		
chuí	123		
chūn	123		
chún	124		
chǔn	125		
chuō	125		
chuò	125		
cī	125		
cí	125		
cǐ	127		
cì	127		
cōng	128		
cóng	128		
còu	129		
cū	129		
cú	130		
cù	130		
cuān	131		
cuán	131		
cuàn	131		
cuī	131		
cuǐ	132		
cuì	132		
cūn	132		
cún	132		
cǔn	133		
cùn	133		
cuō	133		
cuó	134		
cuò	134		

C

D

dā	135
dá	135
dǎ	136
dà	139

da 146
dāi 146
dǎi 146
dài 146
dān 148
dǎn 151
dàn 151
dāng 152
dǎng 153
dàng 154
dāo 154
dáo 155
dǎo 155
dào 156
dē 158
dé 158
de 159
děi 160
dèn 160
dēng 160
děng 161
dèng 161
dī 162
dí 163
dǐ 164
dì 165
diǎ 169
diān 169
diǎn 169
diàn 171
diāo 174
diǎo 175
diào 175
diē 176
dié 176
dīng 177
dǐng 177
dìng 178
diū 180
dōng 180
dǒng 181
dòng 181
dōu 183
dǒu 183
dòu 183
dū 184
dú 185
dǔ 187
dù 187
duān 188
duǎn 188
duàn 189
duī 190
duì 190
dūn 192
dǔn 193
dùn 193
duō 193
duó 196
duǒ 196
duò 196

E

ē 197
é 197
ě 198
è 198
e 199
ēn 199
èn 199
ér 199
ěr 200
èr 201

F

fā 203
fá 205
fǎ 206
fà 207
fān 207
fán 208
fǎn 209
fàn 211
fāng 212
fáng 213
fǎng 215
fàng 216
fēi 217
féi 220
fěi 220
fèi 220
fēn 222
fén 225
fěn 225
fèn 225
fēng 226
féng 230
fěng 230
fèng 230
fó 231
fǒu 231
fū 231
fú 232
fǔ 235
fù 237

G

gā 243
gá 243
gǎ 243
gà 243
gāi 243
gǎi 243
gài 244
gān 245
gǎn 247
gàn 248
gāng 249
gǎng 250
gàng 250
gāo 251
gǎo 254
gào 255
gē 255
gé 256
gě 258
gè 258
gěi 259
gēn 260
gén 260
gěn 260
gèn 261
gēng 261
gěng 262
gèng 262
gōng 262
gǒng 269
gòng 269
gōu 270
gǒu 271
gòu 271
gū 272
gǔ 273
gù 276
guā 278
guǎ 278
guà 279
guāi 279
guǎi 280
guài 280
guān 280
guǎn 283
guàn 284
guāng 284
guǎng 286
guàng 287
guī 287
guǐ 288
guì 289
gǔn 290
gùn 290
guō 290
guó 290
guǒ 294
guò 295
guo 297

H

hā 298
há 298
hǎ 298
hà 298
hāi 298
hái 298
hǎi 299
hài 301
hān 302
hán 302
hǎn 303
hàn 303
hāng 305
háng 305
hàng 306
hāo 306
háo 306
hǎo 307
hào 309
hē 310
hé 310
hè 314
hēi 315
hén 316
hěn 316
hèn 317
hēng 317
héng 317
hèng 318
hōng 318
hóng 319
hǒng 321
hòng 321
hóu 321
hǒu 322
hòu 322
hū 324
hú 324
hǔ 326
hù 326
huā 328
huá 330
huà 331
huái 333
huài 334
huān 334
huán 334
huǎn 336
huàn 336
huāng 337
huáng 338
huǎng 340
huàng 340
huang 340
huī 340
huí 341
huǐ 343
huì 344
hūn 346
hún 347
hùn 347
huō 348
huó 348
huǒ 349
huò 350

J

jī 353
jí 358
jǐ 362
jì 363
jiā 368

jiá	372	kài	437	lǎ	461	lìn	495	mán	523
jiǎ	372	kān	437	là	461	líng	495	mǎn	523
jià	373	kǎn	437	la	462	lǐng	498	màn	524
jia	375	kàn	438	lái	462	lìng	499	máng	525
jiān	375	kāng	439	lài	463	liū	499	máng	525
jiǎn	377	káng	439	lán	464	liú	500	mǎng	526
jiàn	380	kàng	439	lǎn	465	liǔ	503	māo	526
jiāng	384	kāo	440	làn	465	liù	503	máo	526
jiǎng	385	kǎo	440	láng	466	lo	503	mǎo	527
jiàng	386	kào	441	lǎng	466	lóng	504	mào	527
jiāo	387	kē	441	làng	466	lǒng	505	me	529
jiáo	390	ké	442	lāo	466	lòng	505	méi	529
jiǎo	390	kě	443	láo	467	lōu	505	měi	531
jiào	392	kè	444	lǎo	468	lóu	505	mèi	532
jiē	394	kēi	446	lào	471	lǒu	506	mēn	533
jié	396	kěn	446	lè	471	lòu	506	mén	533
jiě	399	kèn	446	le	472	lou	506	mèn	534
jiè	400	kēng	446	lēi	472	lū	507	men	534
jie	402	kōng	447	léi	472	lú	507	mēng	534
jīn	402	kǒng	448	lěi	473	lǔ	507	méng	534
jǐn	405	kòng	449	lèi	473	lù	508	měng	535
jìn	406	kōu	449	lei	473	lǘ	509	mèng	535
jīng	409	kǒu	449	léng	474	lǚ	510	mī	536
jǐng	414	kòu	451	lěng	474	lǜ	511	mí	536
jìng	415	kū	451	lèng	475	luán	512	mǐ	537
jiōng	417	kǔ	452	lī	475	luǎn	512	mì	537
jiǒng	417	kù	452	lí	475	luàn	512	mián	539
jiū	418	kuā	453	lǐ	477	lüě	513	miǎn	539
jiǔ	418	kuǎ	453	lì	478	lüè	513	miàn	540
jiù	420	kuà	453	li	483	lūn	513	miāo	542
jū	422	kuài	454	liǎ	483	lún	513	miáo	542
jú	423	kuān	455	lián	483	lùn	514	miǎo	542
jǔ	423	kuǎn	455	liǎn	485	luō	514	miào	542
jù	424	kuāng	456	liàn	486	luó	515	miē	543
juān	426	kuáng	456	liáng	486	luǒ	516	miè	543
juǎn	427	kuàng	456	liǎng	488	luò	516	mín	543
juàn	427	kuī	457	liàng	489	luo	517	mǐn	545
juē	427	kuí	457	liāo	490			míng	546
jué	428	kuǐ	458	liáo	490	**M**		mǐng	549
juè	430	kuì	458	liǎo	491			mìng	550
jūn	430	kūn	458	liào	491	mā	518	miù	550
jùn	432	kǔn	458	liē	492	má	518	mō	550
		kùn	458	liě	492	mǎ	519	mó	550
K		kuò	459	liè	492	mà	520	mǒ	552
				lie	493	ma	520	mò	552
kā	433	**L**		līn	493	mái	520	mōu	554
kǎ	433			lín	493	mǎi	521	móu	554
kāi	433	lā	460	lǐn	495	mài	521	mǒu	555
kǎi	437	lá	461			mān	523		

mú	555	niú	576	pèn	596	qiàn	634	ráo	665
mǔ	555	niǔ	577	pēng	596	qiāng	635	rǎo	665
mù	556	niù	577	péng	597	qiáng	635	rào	666
N		nóng	577	pěng	597	qiǎng	637	rě	666
nā	559	nòng	579	pèng	597	qiàng	638	rè	666
ná	559	nú	580	pī	598	qiāo	638	rén	668
nǎ	559	nǔ	580	pí	599	qiáo	638	rěn	673
nà	560	nù	580	pǐ	601	qiǎo	639	rèn	673
na	560	nǚ	580	pì	601	qiào	640	rēng	675
nǎi	560	nuǎn	581	piān	602	qiē	640	réng	675
nài	561	nüè	581	pián	603	qié	640	rì	675
nān	562	nún	582	piàn	603	qiě	640	róng	676
nán	562	nuó	582	piāo	604	qiè	641	rǒng	678
nǎn	564	nuò	582	piáo	604	qie	641	róu	678
nàn	564	**O**		piǎo	605	qīn	641	ròu	679
nāng	564	ō	583	piào	605	qín	643	rú	679
náng	564	ó	583	piē	605	qǐn	643	rǔ	681
nǎng	564	ǒ	583	piě	605	qìn	644	rù	681
nāo	564	ò	583	pīn	605	qīng	644	ruá	683
náo	564	ōu	583	pín	606	qíng	648	ruǎn	683
nǎo	565	ǒu	583	pǐn	607	qǐng	649	ruǐ	684
nào	565	òu	584	pìn	607	qìng	650	ruì	684
nè	566			pīng	607	qióng	650	rùn	684
ne	566	**P**		píng	607	qiū	651	ruó	684
něi	566	pā	585	pō	611	qiú	652	ruò	684
nèi	566	pá	585	pó	611	qiǔ	653	**S**	
nèn	568	pà	585	pǒ	611	qū	653	sā	686
néng	569	pāi	586	pò	612	qú	655	sǎ	686
ní	569	pái	586	pōu	613	qǔ	655	sà	686
nǐ	570	pǎi	588	póu	613	qù	656	sāi	687
nì	570	pài	588	pǒu	613	qu	657	sài	687
niān	571	pān	588	pū	613	quān	657	sān	687
nián	571	pán	589	pú	614	quán	657	sǎn	690
niǎn	573	pàn	590	pǔ	615	quǎn	660	sàn	691
niàn	573	pāng	590	pù	616	quàn	660	sāng	691
niáng	573	páng	590	**Q**		quē	661	sǎng	691
niàng	573	pǎng	591	qī	617	qué	661	sàng	691
niǎo	574	pàng	591	qí	619	què	661	sāo	692
niào	574	pāo	591	qǐ	621	qūn	662	sǎo	692
niē	574	páo	592	qì	624	qún	662	sào	692
nié	575	pǎo	592	qiā	627	**R**		sè	693
niè	575	pào	593	qiá	627	rán	664	sēn	694
nín	575	pēi	593	qiǎ	627	rǎn	664	sēng	694
níng	575	péi	594	qià	627	rāng	664	shā	694
nǐng	576	pèi	595	qiān	628	ráng	665	shá	696
nìng	576	pēn	596	qián	631	rǎng	665	shǎ	696
niū	576	pén	596	qiǎn	633	ràng	665	shà	696

shāi	696	shuǎng	762	tào	797	**W**		xiàn	888
shǎi	696	shuǐ	762	tè	797			xiāng	891
shài	696	shuì	766	téng	799	wā	835	xiáng	893
shān	697	shǔn	766	tī	799	wá	835	xiǎng	894
shǎn	699	shùn	766	tí	800	wǎ	835	xiàng	895
shàn	699	shuō	767	tǐ	801	wà	836	xiāo	896
shāng	700	shuò	769	tì	802	wa	836	xiáo	898
shǎng	702	sī	769	tiān	803	wāi	836	xiǎo	898
shàng	702	sǐ	772	tián	806	wǎi	836	xiào	902
shang	706	sì	773	tiǎn	807	wài	836	xiē	903
shāo	707	sōng	775	tiāo	807	wān	840	xié	903
sháo	707	sǒng	776	tiáo	807	wán	840	xiě	905
shǎo	707	sòng	776	tiǎo	809	wǎn	841	xiè	905
shào	708	sōu	777	tiào	809	wàn	842	xīn	907
shē	709	sǒu	777	tiē	810	wāng	843	xìn	911
shé	709	sòu	777	tiě	810	wáng	844	xīng	913
shě	709	sū	777	tiè	812	wǎng	844	xíng	914
shè	710	sú	778	tīng	812	wàng	845	xǐng	917
shéi	713	sù	778	tíng	813	wēi	846	xìng	917
shēn	713	suān	780	tǐng	814	wéi	848	xiōng	918
shén	716	suàn	780	tìng	814	wěi	851	xióng	919
shěn	717	suī	781	tōng	814	wèi	852	xiòng	920
shèn	718	suí	781	tóng	816	wēn	855	xiū	920
shēng	718	suǐ	782	tǒng	819	wén	856	xiǔ	921
shéng	723	suì	782	tòng	820	wěn	858	xiù	921
shěng	723	sūn	783	tōu	820	wèn	859	xū	922
shèng	724	sǔn	783	tóu	821	wēng	859	xú	924
shī	725	suō	783	tòu	823	wéng	859	xǔ	924
shí	729	suǒ	784	tū	824	wěng	859	xù	924
shǐ	735	**T**		tú	824	wō	859	xu	925
shì	736			tǔ	826	wǒ	860	xuān	925
shi	744	tā	786	tù	827	wò	860	xuán	926
shōu	744	tǎ	786	tuān	827	wū	861	xuǎn	927
shǒu	745	tà	786	tuán	827	wú	862	xuàn	928
shòu	749	tāi	787	tuǎn	828	wǔ	867	xuē	928
shū	751	tái	787	tuàn	828	wù	869	xué	929
shú	754	tài	788	tuī	828			xuě	930
shǔ	755	tān	789	tuí	829	**X**		xuè	930
shù	756	tán	790	tuǐ	829	xī	872	xūn	931
shuā	758	tǎn	791	tuì	830	xí	875	xún	932
shuǎ	758	tàn	792	tūn	831	xǐ	876	xùn	933
shuà	759	tāng	793	tún	831	xì	878		
shuāi	759	táng	793	tǔn	832	xiā	879	**Y**	
shuǎi	759	tǎng	794	tùn	832	xiá	880		
shuài	760	tàng	795	tuō	832	xià	881	yā	935
shuān	760	tāo	795	tuó	834	xia	884	yá	937
shuàn	760	táo	795	tuǒ	834	xiān	884	yǎ	937
shuāng	760	tǎo	796	tuò	834	xián	886	yà	938
						xiǎn	887	ya	939

yān	939	yóu	996	zàng	1030	zhě	1051	zhuǎng	1098
yán	940	yǒu	999	zāo	1031	zhe	1051	zhuàng	1098
yǎn	944	yòu	1003	záo	1031	zhèi	1051	zhuī	1098
yàn	946	yū	1005	zǎo	1031	zhēn	1051	zhuì	1100
yāng	948	yú	1005	zào	1032	zhěn	1053	zhūn	1100
yáng	948	yǔ	1008	zé	1033	zhèn	1054	zhǔn	1100
yǎng	950	yù	1010	zè	1034	zhēng	1055	zhuō	1101
yàng	951	yuān	1014	zéi	1034	zhěng	1057	zhuó	1101
yāo	952	yuán	1015	zěn	1035	zhèng	1058	zī	1102
yáo	953	yuǎn	1018	zèn	1035	zhī	1062	zǐ	1104
yǎo	954	yuàn	1019	zēng	1035	zhí	1065	zì	1106
yào	954	yuē	1019	zèng	1036	zhǐ	1068	zi	1111
yē	956	yuě	1020	zhā	1036	zhì	1070	zōng	1112
yé	956	yuè	1020	zhá	1037	zhōng	1075	zǒng	1113
yě	956	yūn	1022	zhǎ	1037	zhǒng	1080	zòng	1114
yè	957	yún	1022	zhà	1037	zhòng	1081	zōu	1115
yī	959	yǔn	1023	zhāi	1038	zhōu	1083	zǒu	1115
yí	968	yùn	1023	zhái	1038	zhóu	1084	zòu	1116
yǐ	971	**Z**		zhǎi	1038	zhǒu	1084	zū	1116
yì	974			zhài	1039	zhòu	1084	zú	1117
yīn	980	zā	1026	zhān	1039	zhū	1085	zǔ	1117
yín	982	zá	1026	zhǎn	1040	zhú	1086	zuān	1119
yǐn	983	zǎ	1027	zhàn	1040	zhǔ	1087	zuǎn	1119
yìn	986	zāi	1027	zhāng	1043	zhù	1089	zuàn	1119
yīng	986	zǎi	1027	zhǎng	1044	zhuā	1092	zuǐ	1119
yíng	988	zài	1028	zhàng	1044	zhuǎ	1093	zuì	1120
yǐng	989	zān	1029	zhāo	1045	zhuāi	1093	zūn	1121
yìng	990	zán	1029	zháo	1047	zhuǎi	1093	zǔn	1122
yōng	991	zǎn	1029	zhǎo	1047	zhuài	1093	zùn	1122
yóng	992	zàn	1030	zhào	1047	zhuān	1093	zuō	1122
yǒng	992	zan	1030	zhē	1049	zhuǎn	1095	zuó	1122
yòng	993	zāng	1030	zhé	1049	zhuàn	1096	zuǒ	1122
yōu	994	zǎng	1030	zhě	1050	zhuāng	1097	zuò	1123

部首检字表

（一）部首目录

（部首右边的号码指检字表的页码）

（二）检字表

（字右边的号码指词典正文的页码）

一部

一 959

一至二画

丁 177
七 617
三 687
干 245
　 248
于 1005
下 881
　 884
丈 1044
兀 869
与 1008
　 1010
才 71
万 842
上 702
　 706

三画

丰 226
井 414
开 433
夫 231
　 232
天 803
无 550
　 862
专 1093
丐 244
廿 573
五 867
丏 539
卅 686
不 60
尤 527
友 999
屯 831
互 326
牙 937
币 40
丑 111

四画

末 552
未 853
击 353
正 1055
　 1058
甘 246
世 737
本 35
可 443
　 444
丙 53
左 1122
丕 598
右 1004
布 68
平 607
东 180
且 422
　 640
丘 651
册 79
丝 769

五画

考 440
共 269
亚 938
亘 261
吏 481
更 1028
再 1028
在 17
百 1004
有 999
而 200
存 132
死 772
夹 243
　 370
　 372
夷 968
尧 953
并 54
丞 100

六画

严 941
巫 861
甫 235
更 261
　 262
束 756
两 488
丽 481
来 462
求 652

七画

奉 230
武 868
表 48
忝 807
画 332
事 739
枣 1032
建 397
函 360
　 626

八画

奏 1116
毒 185
韭 419
甚 718
巷 306
柬 895
歪 378
甭 836
面 37
昼 540
　 1084

九画

艳 946
秦 643
泰 789
菁 272
哥 255
鬲 482
孬 564
夏 884

十画以上

馘 940
爽 762
棘 361
酾 41
赖 464
暨 368
赜 1034
矗 199
整 1057
臻 1053

丨部

二画

也 956

三画

中 1075
　 1081
内 566
引 983
书 751

四画

卡 433
　 627
北 32
凸 824
旧 420
归 287
甲 372
申 713
电 171
由 996
史 735
央 948
冉 664
凹 9
半 835
出 111

五画

师 727
曳 958
曲 654
　 655
　 679

六画

肉 888
县 121
串 284

七画

非 218
果 294
畅 90
肃 778

八画以上

临 494
幽 995
将 384
　 386
　 635
冀 368

丿部

一至二画

九 418
乜 38
乃 560
千 628
乞 621
川 118
义 974
及 358
久 419
么 529
丸 840

三画

午 868
壬 673
升 718
夭 952
长 87
　 1044
反 209
父 953
乏 205
氏 736
丹 148
乌 861

四画

生 719
失 725
乍 1037
甩 759
氐 164
处 116
　 117
冬 181
务 869
尔 200
乐 471
　 1021

五画

年 571
朱 1085
先 885
丢 180
乔 638
乒 607
乓 590
向 895
囟 911
后 322
杀 694
兆 1047
余 832
危 846

六画

我 860
每 531
囱 128
希 873
龟 287
　 431
卵 512
系 366

丿部

七画
- 垂 123
- 乖 279
- 卑 32
- 阜 239
- 所 784
- 肴 953
- 氽 163（878）

八画
- 拜 19
- 牲 723
- 舌 81
- 重 108、1082
- 复 239

九画以上
- 玺 877
- 甥 723
- 弑 743
- 舞 869
- 睾 254
- 疑 971
- 孵 232
- 萧 562
- 靠 441

、部

二至三画
- 丫 935
- 之 1062
- 为 848、853

四画
- 主 1087
- 头 821
- 必 40
- 永 992

五画以上
- 州 1083
- 农 577
- 良 486
- 卷 427
- 亲 642、650
- 举 423

乙部

- 乙 971

一至三画
- 刁 174
- 了 472、491
- 乜 543
- 卫 852
- 飞 217
- 刃 673
- 习 875
- 子 396
- 乡 891
- 尹 983
- 尺 105
- 巴 12、15
- 以 972
- 予 1006、1009
- 孔 448

四画
- 司 769
- 民 543
- 弗 232
- 发 203、207

五画
- 尽 405、406
- 买 521

六至九画
- 乱 512
- 君 431
- 即 359
- 甬 993
- 乳 681
- 隶 482
- 虱 728
- 承 100
- 函 303
- 既 367
- 咫 1070
- 矜 405、643

十画以上
- 乾 633
- 豫 1014

二部

- 二 201
- 亏 457
- 元 1015
- 云 1022
- 互 375
- 些 903
- 亟 1017

十部

- 十 729

二至五画
- 支 1063
- 卉 344
- 古 273
- 叶 903、958
- 协 903
- 毕 40
- 早 1031
- 华 330
- 孝 902
- 克 444
- 孛 33

六画
- 直 1066
- 丧 691
- 卖 522
- 卓 1101
- 卒 1117

七至十画
- 南 559、562、1052
- 真 785
- 索 783
- 隼 693
- 啬 1043
- 章 511
- 率 760
- 博 57、303
- 韩 93
- 朝 1046
- 辜 273

十一画以上
- 献 890
- 斡 861
- 兢 413
- 翰 304
- 蠡 118

厂部

- 厂 90

二至六画
- 厅 812
- 仄 1034
- 历 479
- 厄 198
- 厉 479
- 压 935、939
- 厌 946
- 库 710
- 厕 79

七至八画
- 厘 475
- 厚 323
- 厝 134
- 原 1015

九至十画
- 厢 893
- 厩 420
- 厨 116
- 厦 696
- 雁 947
- 厥 429

十一画以上
- 厮 771
- 愿 1019
- 魇 946
- 厣 947

匚部

二至四画
- 区 653
- 匹 601
- 巨 424
- 匝 611
- 匜 1026
- 匡 968
- 匠 456、386

五画以上
- 匣 880
- 医 967
- 甋 288
- 匼 441
- 匿 571
- 匪 220
- 匮 458
- 匾 45

卜部

- 卜 59
- 占 1039、1040
- 卢 507
- 外 836
- 贞 1051
- 志 791
- 卦 279
- 卧 860
- 桌 1101
- 睿 684

刂部

二至三画
- 刈 975
- 刊 437

四画
- 刑 914
- 列 492
- 划 330、332
- 刚 249
- 则 1033
- 创 121、122
- 刎 858
- 刘 500

五画
- 刬 87
- 别 50、51
- 利 481
- 删 698
- 刨 30、592
- 判 590
- 刭 414

六画
- 刺 125、127
- 到 451
- 刿 156
- 制 289
- 刮 1071
- 例 278
- 刽 482
- 刹 289、84
- 剀 695
- 剁 196
- 剂 367
- 刻 445
- 刷 758、759

七画
- 荆 412
- 剋 446
- 剌 461
- 削 896、928
- 剐 278
- 剑 382
- 前 631
- 剃 802

八画
- 剖 134
- 剔 799
- 剖 613
- 剐 944
- 剜 840
- 剥 26、56
- 剧 425
- 剜 195

九画以上
- 副 240
- 喇 461
- 剩 725
- 割 256
- 剽 604
- 剿 93、392
- 劓 638

冂部

- 冈 249
- 同 816

网部（续）

(820)
网　844
罔　417
罓　845

亻部

一画
亿　974

二画
仁　673
什　716　730
仃　177
仆　613　614
仇　110
化　331
仍　675
仂　471
仅　405　406

三画
仨　686
仕　738
仗　1044
代　146
付　237
仙　884
仪　968
们　534
他　786
仞　674
仔　1027　1105

四画
伕　231
伟　851
传　119　1096
休　920
伍　868
伎　365
伏　232
伛　1009
优　994
伢　95
伐　205
仳　601
伣　937
仲　1081
件　381
作　868
任　674
伤　700
伥　87
价　373　401　402
伦　513
份　225
伧　77　98
仰　950
伉　439
仿　215
伙　350
伪　851
伫　1089
伊　967
似　739　774

五画
佞　576
佉　654
估　272
体　799　801
何　311
佐　1123
伾　598
佑　1004
伻　37
但　151
伸　713
佃　174　806
佚　977
作　1122　1123
伯　18　57
伶　495
佣　991　994
低　162
佝　270
彼　39
你　570
住　1090
位　854
伴　23
佗　834
伺　127　775
倪　570
佛　231
伽　243　370　640

六画
佳　370
侍　740
佬　471
供　268　270
使　735
侑　1004
侉　453
侠　880
侥　391
侄　1067
侦　1052
侗　182　818
侣　510
侃　438
侧　79　1038
侏　1085
俚　814
侨　638
侩　455
佻　807
佩　595
侈　106
侪　85
佼　391
依　968
佯　949
侬　579

七画
俦　110
俨　944
便　46　603
俪　483　489
修　482
俏　920
俚　640
保　477
傅　27
促　607
俐　130
俄　482
侮　197
俭　869
俗　378
俘　778
信　234
悦　912
侵　830
侯　642
俑　321
俟　993
俊　775　432

八画
俸　231
倩　634
债　1039
俵　50
借　401
偌　685
值　1067
倏　561
倚　974
俺　7
倾　646
倒　156
候　753
倘　794
俱　425
倡　87　91
候　324
倭　859
倪　570
俾　40
倜　802
俯　236
倍　34
倦　427
偾　790
倌　282
健　382
倨　425
倔　429　430

九画
做　1126　946
偃　904
偕　90
偿　584
偶　367
偈　399　847
偎　288
傀　458　820
偷　813
停　510
偻　602
偏　373
假　374

十画
(146)
傣　10
傲　169
慎　241
傅　795
傥　24
傍　51
傧　117
储　605

十一画
僄　131
催　696
傻　896
像　896

十二画
僖　875
僎　415
僚　490
僭　384
僬　422　694

十三画
僵　385
儇　926
僻　602

十四画以上
儒　680
儡　473

八部
八　12

二画
兮　872
分　222　225
公　264

三至六画
兰　464
关　280
兴　913　917
兵　52
兑　192
弟　167
其　619
具　425
典　169
券　661　928
单　85　149

七至八画
叛　590
酋　653
首　748
兹　1103
总　1113
益　978
兼　377

九画以上
黄　338
兽　751
尊　1121
孳　1104
曾　81　1035
舆　1008

人（入）部
人　668
入　681

读 184
186
诽 220
课 446
诿 852
谡 1007
谁 713
谂 718
调 175
808
诣 87
谅 490
谆 1100
译 782
谈 790
谊 978

九画

谋 554
谌 97
谍 176
谎 340
谏 383
谐 905
谑 931
谒 959
谓 854
谕 1013
谖 926
诤 85
谙 6
谚 947
谛 168
谜 536

十画

谟 550
说 154
谡 779
谢 906
谣 953
谤 24
谥 743
谦 630
谧 538

十一画

谨 406
谩 523
524
谪 1050

谬 550

十二画以上

谮 1035
谯 639
谰 465
谱 615
谲 429
谴 634
谶 1039

卩部

叩 451
印 986
卯 527
爷 956
却 661
卲 708
卺 405
卸 906
卿 646

阝(在左)部

二至四画

队 190
阡 629
阱 414
阮 683
阵 1054
阳 949
阶 394
阴 980
防 213

五画

陆 508
际 366
阿 1
197
陈 96
陉 174
阻 1117
附 238
陀 834
陂 31

六至八画

陋 506
陌 553
降 386
894

限 889
183
陛 41
陨 1073
隈 1023
除 115
险 888
院 1019
陵 496
陲 123
陴 601
陶 796
陷 890
陪 594

九画

随 781
隅 1008
隍 339
隆 505
隐 985

十画以上

隔 257
隙 879
隘 4
障 1045
隧 783

阝(在右)部

二至四画

邓 161
邦 23
邪 904
那 560
566
568

五画

邮 996
邻 493
邸 164

六画

耶 956
郁 1011
郅 1071
郊 389
郑 1061
郎 466

七画

郭 234

郡 432

八画

都 183
184
郭 290
部 69

十一画

鄙 40

凵部

凶 918
凼 154

刀(⺈)部

刀 154
色 693
696
切 640
641
795
叨 115
刍 237
负 1055
争 896
象 379
剪 235
剿 399
劈 905
599
601

力部

力 478

二至四画

办 21
劝 660
功 267
夯 305
加 368
幼 1004
动 181
劣 492

五至六画

劫 397
励 481
助 1089
劬 655
努 580

勖 708
劲 408
415
劼 397
势 740
劲 312

七至九画

勃 57
勋 931
勉 540
勇 993
勚 648
258
勘 437
勒 472

十画以上

勤 643
勰 905

厶部

去 656
657
45
弁 787
台 554
牟 770
私 974
矣 74
参 80
朵 714
垒 877
畚 473
36
能 569

又(又)部

又 1003

一至四画

叉 81
82
84
双 760
圣 724
对 191
戏 878
观 281
284
欢 334

六至八画

取 656
叔 752
贤 887
受 749
艰 376
竖 757
叟 777
叙 924
爱 1015
难 563
564

十一画以上

叠 177
聚 426
矍 430

廴部

廷 813
延 940
建 382

工部

工 262
巧 639
巩 269
贡 270
攻 268
汞 269
缸 250
肛 385

土部

土 826

二至三画

圩 849
922
圬 861
圭 287
寺 774
至 1070
圪 255
圳 1054
353
圾 456
圮 601
坏 968
地 159

165
场　89
　　90
　　91

四画
坛　790
坏　334
址　1069
坝　14
圻　619
坂　21
坎　437
坍　789
均　431
坞　870
坟　225
坑　446
坊　215
　　214
块　454
坚　376
坌　36
坠　1100

五画
坩　246
坯　599
坪　610
坫　174
垆　507
坦　791
坤　458
坼　95
坻　105
垃　460
幸　918
坨　834
坡　611
坳　10
垄　505

六画
型　917
垭　936
垣　1015
垮　453
垯　146
城　101
垤　176
垱　154

垌　182
垲　437
埏　698
垢　272
垛　196
垝　289
垓　949
垟　82
垠　982
垩　198
埌　174
垫　205
垦　446

七画
埂　261
埕　102
埋　520
　　523
埚　290
埙　931
埒　492
埘　661
埚　924
垸　1019
埃　2

八画
堵　187
埴　1067
域　1013
埼　620
埯　7
堨　978
堌　278
埵　196
堆　190
堋　601
　　602
埠　70
埻　1101
培　594
堉　1013
壶　458
埽　693
堀　452
基　356
堑　634
堂　793

堕　196

九画
堵　124
堪　437
堞　176
塔　786
塂　338
堰　947
堤　163
塅　190
塆　840
堡　29
　　60

十画
填　807
　　257
塌　1018
塬　786
塌　794
塘　24
塝　558
墓　779
塑

十一画
墙　637
墟　923
墁　524
境　417
碣　641
墅　758
塾　754

十二画以上
墩　193
墙　700
增　1035
墀　105
壁　42
壕　307
壑　315
　　385
壤　665

士部
士　736
吉　358
壮　1098
壳　442
　　640
志　1071
声　722
壶　325
壹　1030
　　1098
壴　905
喜　877
鼓　276
嘉　372
熹　875
馨　911
蠹　188

扌部
一至二画
扎　1026
　　1036
打　135
　　136
扑　613
扒　13
　　585
扔　675

三画
扦　304
扛　249
　　439
扣　451
扞　629
托　832
执　1065
扩　459
扪　534
扫　692
扬　948

四画
扶　232
抚　840
抚　235
抟　828
技　365
抔　613
抠　449
扰　665
扼　198
拒　425
抻　160
找　1047
批　598
扯　95
抄　91
折　709
　　1049
抓　1092
扳　20
抢　513
扮　23
抢　635
　　637
拐　1021
抵　1069
抑　977
抛　591
投　822
扐　45
拉　858
抗　439
抖　183
护　327
抉　428
扭　577
把　14
报　29
拟　570
抒　752

五画
抹　518
　　552
　　553
拓　786
　　834
拢　505
拔　13
抨　596
拣　378
拼　627
拈　571
担　149
　　151
押　936
抻　95
抽　109
拐　280
柞　1037
拖　832
拊　236
拍　586
拆　71
　　84
拎　493
拥　992
抵　164
拘　422
抱　30
拄　1089
拉　460
　　461
拦　464
拌　23
拧　575
　　576
抿　546
拂　233
拙　1101
招　1045
披　599
拨　55
择　1034
　　1038
拚　590
抬　788
拇　556
拗　10
　　577
拭　742
挂　279

六画
持　105
拮　397
拷　440
拱　269
挜　939
挎　453
挞　787
挟　904
挠　564
挝　1093
挡　153
搜　1093
挺　814
括　459
挢　391
拴　760
拾　712
　　734

挑 807
　 809
指 1069
挣 1057
　 1062
挤 363
拼 605
挖 835
按 7
挥 341
挦 887
挪 582
拯 1057
捯 1026
　 1029

七画

捞 466
捕 60
捂 869
振 1054
捎 707
　 708
捍 304
捏 574
捉 1101
捆 458
捐 426
损 783
挹 978
捡 378
挫 134
捋 510
　 514
授 683
　 684
换 336
挽 841
捣 156
挠 833
捃 432
捅 819
挨 2
捘 1122

八画

捧 597
捫 956
措 134
描 542

捺 560
掎 363
掩 944
捷 399
捯 155
排 586
　 588
捐 446
掉 176
掳 507
捆 280
捶 123
推 828
掉 18
掀 886
授 750
捻 573
掏 795
掐 627
捌 423
掠 513
掂 169
掖 956
　 959
捽 1122
搭 613
接 395
掷 1074
掸 151
　 699
控 449
捩 493
捐 633
探 792
据 423
　 425
掘 429
掺 77
　 85
　 699
掇 195
掼 284

九画

揍 1116
揳 903
揩 1055
揲 177
搭 135

搽 84
揸 1036
揞 939
揩 436
揽 465
提 163
　 800
揖 968
揭 396
揣 118
揖 325
揪 644
插 82
揪 418
搜 777
揄 1008
援 1017
揎 85
揸 7
搁 256
　 257
搓 133
搂 505
　 506
揾 379
搅 392
揎 926
搭 443
握 860
摒 55
揸 692
揉 678
掾 1019

十画

摄 713
摸 550
搏 58
搋 754
搵 199
摆 18
携 905
揳 118
搬 20
摇 953
搞 254
搪 794
搒 24
搒 597

搐 117
搛 377
搠 769
摈 51
搌 1040
搦 582
摊 790
操 691

十一画

摽 48
　 50
撇 605
摺 492
擦 517
摧 132
撄 987
摭 1068
摘 1038
摔 759
摺 1050

十二画

撺 573
撷 905
撕 772
撒 686
撅 427
撩 490
　 491
撑 98
撮 1123
　 133
撬 640
播 56
擒 643
撸 507
撤 193
撞 1098
撤 95
搏 1122
撺 131
撰 1096

十三画

擀 248
撼 305
擂 472
　 473
操 78
撒 640

擅 700
擞 777
擗 601

十四画

擂 681
攇 917
擦 71
擢 1102

十六画以上

攉 348
攒 1029
　 131
攘 665
撷 169
攫 430
攥 1119
攮 564

艹部

一至三画

艺 975
艾 3
　 975
节 394
　 396
芄 560
芋 1011
芍 707
茇 353
芒 525
芝 1063
芎 891

四画

芙 232
芜 866
芫 1015
　 941
苇 851
芸 1023
芰 365
苣 425
芘 600
芽 937

芬 224
苍 77
芪 619
苈 870
苁 634
芡 698
芰 45
芳 213
苎 1089
芦 507
芯 909
　 912
劳 467
芭 13
苏 777
苡 974
苧 1089
　 924
芤 449

五画

茉 553
苦 452
苯 36
昔 873
苟 441
茎 605
若 666
　 684
茂 527
荜 610
苫 698
　 699
苜 557
苗 542
英 987
苒 664
苻 233
茶 575
茚 986
苟 271
茆 527
苑 1019
苞 25
范 212
苧 575
茇 929
茔 988
荩 651

（艹部　续）

字	页	字	页
苗	1101	茹	680
茄	370	荔	482
	640	荮	1084
苕	707	药	954
	808	荪	783
茎	409	**七画**	
苔	787	莰	438
	788	莩	38
茅	527	莽	526
六画		恭	268
茸	676	莱	463
茜	634	莲	484
茬	82	莫	553
荐	382	莳	743
荚	372	莴	859
荑	800	莉	482
	969	莠	1003
荛	665	莓	530
草	78	荷	313
茧	378		314
苘	818	莜	998
茵	981	莅	482
苘	343	荼	825
莛	813	莝	134
荞	639	莛	781
茯	234	莘	234
茌	673	莎	605
荃	660		351
荟	345	获	998
茶	82	莸	163
茗	549	荻	714
荠	367	莘	783
	620	莎	282
茭	389		841
荒	337		988
茨	125	莹	987
茫	526	莺	124
荡	154	**八画**	
荣	676	菁	412
荤	346	著	1091
荦	516		1102
荧	988	菶	37
荨	631	菱	497
	933	萁	620
茛	261	菘	776
荩	408	董	406
荫	986	萘	561
莰	639	萎	618

字	页	字	页
菲	219	萱	471
	220	葭	515
菝	753	葵	516
萌	534		926
萜	810		372
萝	515		457
菌	431	**十画**	
萎	432	蒜	780
萸	852	蓐	683
菂	1007	蓝	464
菜	168	幕	558
萄	74	蓍	553
菊	796	蒽	199
萃	423	蓓	35
菩	132	蒗	41
葵	614	蓬	597
萍	792	襄	784
菹	611	蒿	306
菠	1117	蒌	362
菅	56	蓄	925
菀	377	蒴	769
萤	841	蒲	615
营	1013	蓉	677
萦	988	蒙	534
萧	988		535
萨	989	蒸	1057
菇	898	**十一画**	
菰	687	蔫	571
	273	蔷	637
	273	蔌	780
九画		蕹	829
葚	718	蔽	41
葫	325	暮	558
葸	666	摹	550
葳	87	慕	558
葬	1030	蔓	523
葺	627		524
募	558		843
葛	257	蔑	543
萼	199	蔸	183
董	181	蓰	878
葆	29	蔗	1051
葩	585	蔟	130
葡	614	蓿	925
葱	128	蔼	3
蒂	168	蔚	855
蒎	588	蓼	491
落	461		509

字	页
十二画	
蕙	346
斠	809
蕨	429
蕉	390
蕃	208
蕊	684
蔬	754
蕴	1025
十三画	
蕲	321
蕾	473
薯	756
薨	319
薐	474
薇	848
薪	911
薤	859
薮	777
薄	26
	58
	306
十四画	
藉	362
	402
	77
	1031
薰	932
藐	542
十五画	
藕	584
藜	476
藤	799
藩	207
十六画以上	
蘖	575
蘑	552
藻	1032
蘸	1042

卄部

字	页
异	976
弄	423
弃	46
异	42
彝	971

寸部

字	页
寸	133
寻	932
导	155
寿	749
时	731
封	228
耐	561
酎	1084
辱	681
射	712
尉	855

大部

字	页
大	139
	146
一至四画	
太	788
夸	453
夺	196
尖	375
夜	483
夹	336
五画	
奈	561
奔	35
	36
奇	355
	619
奄	944
奋	225
六画	
契	627
奎	457
奓	135
牵	629
类	473
奖	386
七至八画	
套	797
奘	874
奢	709
九画以上	
奥	10
奠	174

尢部

字	页
尤	996

以下为六列"字—页码"对照（部首检字表），按列排出。

第一列

字	页
尣	491
尬	243
忧	995
尴	247
弋部	
弋	974
式	739
鸢	1014
贰	202
小部	
小	898
一至三画	
少	707
	708
尕	243
尘	96
当	152
	154
孙	783
四至六画	
肖	902
尚	706
省	723
	917
尝	89
八画以上	
雀	640
	661
常	89
辉	341
棠	794
赏	702
掌	1044
景	415
裳	90
裳	706
耀	956
口部	
口	449
二画	
叮	177
号	306
	309
卟	59
只	1063

第二列

字	页
	1068
叱	106
叽	353
叼	174
叫	392
另	499
叹	792
句	424
召	1047
三画	
吁	1005
吁	1011
吁	922
吐	827
吓	314
	884
吕	510
吊	175
吃	103
吸	873
吖	1
吗	518
	520
呙	952
吆	258
各	259
名	546
四画	
吞	831
吾	866
否	231
	601
呈	100
呋	231
呓	977
呆	146
吱	1063
	1102
吠	220
呕	583
呃	198
	199
吨	192
吡	39
	601
呀	936
	939
吵	92

第三列

字	页
	94
呐	560
员	1015
呗	35
呲	197
听	812
吟	982
吩	224
呛	635
	638
吻	858
吹	122
呜	861
吭	305
	447
吣	644
吧	13
	15
邑	977
呓	766
吼	322
告	255
齐	495
启	622
五画	
味	854
哎	2
咕	272
呵	310
哑	1026
呸	593
咙	504
咋	433
咀	423
呻	714
呷	879
咒	1084
咋	1027
	1034
	1036
咐	239
呱	272
	278
呼	324
呤	499
鸣	549
咆	592
咛	575

第四列

字	页
咏	993
呢	566
	569
咄	195
咴	564
咖	243
	433
	995
咝	771
知	1064
周	1083
咎	420
六画	
哉	887
咸	456
哐	835
哇	836
哄	319
	321
哑	936
	937
唎	492
	493
咦	969
哓	896
呲	125
咣	286
虽	781
品	607
咽	939
	946
	959
哕	345
	1020
咮	1084
咻	920
哗	330
咱	1029
	1030
咿	968
响	894
哈	298
咣	795
咯	255
	433
	503
	516

第五列

字	页
哆	106
	195
唪	367
咬	954
咳	298
	442
咩	543
咪	536
哚	1037
哏	260
哪	559
	560
	566
	554
咨	1103
七画	
唇	124
哲	1050
唪	505
哮	902
唠	468
	471
哺	60
哽	261
唔	866
哨	708
唢	785
哩	475
	483
哭	451
哦	197
	583
唏	873
唑	1125
唤	337
唁	947
哼	317
唧	355
啊	1
唉	2
	3
唆	783
唐	793
八画	
喷	1034
喏	582
喵	542
啉	494

第六列

字	页
啄	1102
啪	585
啦	462
啡	220
啃	446
唛	575
唬	326
唱	91
啰	515
	517
唾	834
唯	850
	852
啤	601
啥	696
喃	796
啐	132
喽	696
啴	87
唉	151
喉	482
啸	903
啜	125
售	751
九画	
喷	596
喋	177
嗒	135
	787
喳	82
	1036
喊	303
喱	476
喟	992
	1008
喝	310
	315
喂	855
喟	458
喘	120
嗖	777
喉	321
喻	1013
嗲	947
啼	801
嗟	396
喽	505
	506

彰 1043
影 989

犭部

二至四画

犰 652
犯 211
犷 287
狂 456
犹 997
狈 33
狙 577

五至六画

狨 599
狙 422
狎 880
狌 723
狐 324
狗 271
狍 592
狞 575
狄 1004
狒 221
狭 880
狮 728
独 185
狰 1057
狡 391
狩 750
狱 1012
狠 316
狲 783

七画

狲 1074
狸 475
猯 427
猁 482
狼 466

八画

猜 71
猪 1086
猎 493
猫 526
　 527
猗 968
猖 87
猡 515

———

猞 709
猝 130
猕 536
猛 535

九画

猢 325
猹 84
猩 914
猥 852
猬 855
猾 330
猴 321

十画以上

猿 1018
獐 1043
獭 786
獾 334

夕部

夕 872
舛 120
多 193
怨 1019
智 1014
鸳 1014
梦 535
飧 783
夥 350

夂部

条 807
备 33
惫 35

饣部

二至四画

饥 353
饧 916
饩 878
饪 675
饫 1011
饬 107
饭 211
饮 985
　 986

五至六画

饯 382
饰 740

———

饱 26
饲 775
饴 969
饵 201
饶 665
蚀 735
饷 894
饺 391
饼 53

七至八画

馇 56
馄 184
馅 198
馆 566
馈 347
馊 890
馋 283

九画以上

馌 82
馍 458
馎 777
馏 85
馐 959
馑 550
馒 502
　 503
　 523
　 1097
馔 564

广部

广 286

二至五画

庀 601
庄 1097
庆 650
庑 868
床 121
庋 288
库 452
庇 41
应 986
　 990
庐 507
序 924
庞 590
店 174

六至八画

庙 543
府 236
底 164
庖 592
庚 261
废 221
庤 1073
度 188
　 196
庭 813
麻 921
庳 894
席 876
座 1125
庶 757
庵 6
庼 650
廊 466
庸 992
康 439

九画以上

廒 261
廑 10
廓 459
廉 485
腐 236
膺 988
鹰 988
鏖 10

忄（小）部

一至四画

忆 975
忖 133
忏 87
忙 525
忱 868
怀 333
怄 584
忡 108
忤 868
忾 437
怅 90
忻 909
松 1079
怆 122
忮 886
怃 45
忧 96
快 454
忸 577

五画

怔 1057
　 1061
怯 641
怙 327
怵 117
怖 69
怗 810
怦 596
怛 136
怏 951
性 918
怍 1125
怕 585
怜 484
怩 569
怫 233
怊 92
怿 978
怪 280
怡 969

六画

恸 820
恃 743
恒 317
恢 939
恍 341
恫 340
　 183
　 814
　 437
恺 80
恻 806
恬 924
恤 627
恰 933
恂 919
恪 445
恼 565
恨 317

七画

悖 34
悚 776
悟 871
悭 630
悄 638
　 639
悍 304
悝 478
悒 978
悔 343
　 546
悯 1021
悦 802
悌 657

八画

情 648
惬 641
悻 918
惜 874
惭 76
悱 220
悼 157
惝 90
惧 425
惕 802
惘 845
悸 367
惟 850
惆 110
惚 324
惊 412
惇 193
惦 174
惮 151
惋 842
惨 76
愣 125
惯 284

九画

愤 226
惵 177
慌 338
　 340
惰 196
愠 1024
惺 914
愦 458
愕 199
惴 1100

十画
愣 475
愎 41
惶 340
愧 458
愉 1008
慨 437

十画
愫 780
慑 713
慎 718
慊 635
　 641

十一画
慢 524
慵 992
慷 439

十二画
懂 181
憭 491
憬 415
憔 639
懊 11
懔 131
憧 108
憎 1036

十三画以上
懵 118
懒 465
憾 305
懈 906
懦 582

门部

门 533

一至四画
闩 760
闪 699
闭 40
问 859
闯 121
闰 684
闱 850
闲 886
间 376
　 381
闷 533
　 534

五至六画
闸 1037
闹 565
闺 288
闻 858
闾 510
阃 437
阀 205
阁 257
阂 313

七至八画
阉 418
阅 1021
阈 1013
阉 940
阇 944
阆 199
阐 87

九画以上
阑 464
阔 459
阒 662
阖 314
阙 661
　 662

氵部

二画
汁 1063
汇 344
汀 812
汉 303

三画
汗 302
　 304
污 861
江 384
汕 146
汔 626
汲 359
汐 873
汛 933
池 104
汝 681
汤 793
汊 84

四画
汪 843
沄 1023
沐 557
沛 595
汰 789
沤 583
　 584
沥 481
沏 617
沚 1069
沙 695
　 696
　 274
汩 684
汭 626
汽 860
沃 513
沦 919
汹 212
泛 77
沧 228
沨 270
沟 529
没 553
　 306
　 96
沆 717
沉 644

五画
沫 553
浅 633
法 206
泔 247
泄 905
沽 272
河 312
沾 1039
沮 423
泪 473
油 997
决 948
泗 653
泅 775
泊 57
　 611
渗 482
泠 496

沿 943
泡 592
　 593
注 1090
泣 626
泫 928
泮 590
泞 576
沱 834
泻 906
泌 537
泳 993
泥 569
　 570
泯 546
沸 221
泓 321
沼 1047
波 55
泼 611
泽 1034
泾 409
治 1073

六画
洼 835
洁 397
洪 321
洒 686
浒 862
洌 492
浃 370
浇 389
洮 127
浊 1102
洞 182
洄 343
测 80
洗 876
活 348
洑 234
涎 887
洎 367
洫 924
派 588
洽 627
洵 933
洚 387
洛 516

浏 500
济 363
　 367
洋 949
洲 1084
浑 347
浒 326
浓 579
津 404
浔 933

七画
涛 795
涝 471
浦 615
酒 419
涟 484
涉 712
消 896
涅 575
涩 1102
涓 426
涡 859
湢 978
涔 81
浩 309
海 299
浜 24
涂 825
浴 1012
浮 234
换 337
涣 532
涤 163
流 501
润 684
涧 382
涕 802
浣 337
浪 466
浸 409
涨 1044
　 1045
涘 693
涩 573
　 108
涌 993
浚 432

八画
清 646
渍 1111
添 806
渚 1089
鸿 321
淋 495
淅 874
渎 187
涯 937
淹 940
渠 655
渐 377
　 383
淑 753
淖 566
淌 795
混 347
涸 314
淆 898
渊 1015
淫 983
渔 1007
淘 796
淳 124
液 959
淬 132
淤 1005
滗 23
淡 151
淙 129
淀 174
深 715
涮 760
渗 718
涵 303
浼 860

九画
湛 1042
港 250
溇 906
滞 1075
湖 325
渣 1036
湮 940
渺 542
湿 728
温 855

渴	444
渭	855
溃	458
湍	827
溅	383
滑	330
湃	588
湫	392
	652
渝	1008
湾	840
淳	813
渡	188
游	998
溪	532
滋	1104
渲	928
溉	245
渥	861
湄	530
渭	924

十画

滟	947
满	523
漠	553
滇	169
溥	615
溆	683
源	1018
滤	512
滥	465
滉	340
溻	786
潊	848
滗	41
溴	922
滔	795
溪	875
溜	499
	503
漓	476
滚	290
溏	794
滂	590
溢	979
溯	780
滨	51
溶	677

淬	1106
溟	549
溺	571
	574
滩	790

十一画

潢	340
潇	898
漆	618
漱	758
漂	604
	605
漫	524
潍	132
潋	486
漉	509
滴	163
漩	927
漾	952
演	946
漏	506
潨	491

十二画

潜	633
澍	758
澎	597
渐	772
潮	93
潽	699
潭	791
潦	471
	491
涌	709
潟	879
澳	10
澈	95
澜	465
澄	614
潞	86
澄	102
	162

十三画以上

濠	535
濑	464
濒	51
澡	1032
激	358

濡	681
瀤	307
瀍	1102
瀑	616
瀚	305
灌	284

宀部

二至四画

宁	575
	576
它	786
宇	1009
守	747
宅	1038
安	4
字	1111
完	840
宋	776
宏	320
牢	468
灾	1027

五至六画

宝	26
宗	1112
定	179
宕	154
宠	109
宜	969
审	717
宙	1084
官	281
宛	841
实	732
宓	537
宣	925
宦	336
宬	101
室	743
宫	268
宪	890
客	445

七画

害	301
宽	455
宧	969
宸	97
家	370
	375
	402
宵	897
宴	947
宾	51
容	677
宰	1027
案	8

八画

寇	451
寅	983
寄	367
寂	368
宿	779
	921
	922
密	537

九至十一画

寒	303
富	241
寓	1014
寐	533
塞	687
	693
	553
寞	1075
寝	643
寨	1039
赛	687
寡	278
瘟	871
察	84
蜜	538
寥	491

十二画以上

寮	491
寰	336
蹇	380

辶部

二至四画

边	42
	47
辽	490
迂	1005
达	135
迈	521
过	295
	297
迁	629
迄	626
迅	933
巡	932
进	407
远	1018
违	849
运	1023
还	298
	334
连	483
迤	939
迎	868
近	408
返	211
迓	988
这	1051
远	305
迟	105

五画

述	756
迪	163
迥	417
迭	176
迮	1034
迤	969
	974
迫	588
迩	201
迢	808

六画

选	927
适	742
追	1098
迺	324
逃	795
迹	367
迸	37
送	776
迷	536
逆	570
退	830
逊	934

七画

逋	59
速	779
逗	184
逦	478
逐	1087
逝	743
逑	653
逍	896
逞	103
造	1032
透	823
途	825
逛	287
逖	802
逢	230
递	168
通	814
	820
逡	662

八画

逵	457
逻	515
逶	847
逸	978
逮	146
	148

九画

逼	37
遇	1013
遏	199
遗	855
	970
遑	339
遁	193
逾	1008
道	157
遂	782
遍	47
遐	880

十画

遨	10
遢	786
遣	634
遥	953
遛	503

十一画以上
遭　1031
遮　1049
遴　495
遵　1121
遽　426
邀　952
邂　906
避　42
邈　542
邋　461

彐(彑彐)部
灵　496
录　508
彖　828
彗　345
雪　930

尸部
尸　725
二画
尼　569
尻　440
四至六画
层　81
屁　601
尾　851
　　974
局　423
尿　574
　　781
　　802
屉　422
居　401
届　37
屎　654
屋　862
屐　175
屏　53
　　611
屙　736
七画以上
展　1040
屑　906
屦　356
屠　826
犀　875
属　1089
　　755
屡　510
孱　86
屦　878
履　511
屡　426

己(巳)部
己　362
巳　773
已　971

弓部
弓　264
弘　319
弛　105
张　1043
弢　14
弧　325
弥　536
弦　887
弨　92
弩　580
弮　657
弭　537
躬　269
弹　152
　　791
弼　41
强　387
　　635
　　637
粥　1014
　　1084
彀　272

子(孑)部
孑　1104
　　1111
二至五画
孕　1023
李　477
孚　233
孜　1103
学　929
孟　535
孤　273
孢　26
六画以上
孳　1105
孵　1105
孩　299
孺　681

女部
女　580
二至三画
奶　561
奴　580
妆　1097
奸　375
如　679
妁　769
妇　238
妃　218
她　786
好　307
　　309
妈　518
四画
妍　942
妩　868
妓　366
妪　1011
妣　39
妙　542
妊　675
妖　952
姊　1105
妨　215
妒　187
妞　576
姒　775
五画
妻　617
　　626
委　851
妾　641
妹　532
姑　272
姐　399
姍　1084
姓　918
姗　698
始　736
姆　556
六画
威　847
耍　758
娄　505
姿　1103
娃　835
姥　471
　　556
娅　453
姨　969
娆　665
　　666
姻　982
姝　753
娇　389
姤　272
姣　389
姘　606
姹　84
娜　582
七画
姬　356
娠　715
娌　478
娱　1007
娉　607
娟　427
娥　197
娩　540
娴　887
娘　573
娓　852
婀　197
八画
娶　656
婴　987
婆　611
婧　416
婊　49
婳　333
婕　87
婢　41
婚　346
婵　85
婶　718
婉　842
九画
媒　530
媟　906
媪　10
嫂　692
媛　1019
媚　533
婿　925
十画
媾　272
媸　104
媳　876
媲　602
嫉　362
嫌　887
嫁　375
嫔　607
十一画
嫣　940
嫱　637
嫩　568
嫖　604
嫦　90
嫚　523
　　525
嫡　164
十二画以上
嬉　875
嫽　491
嬗　700
嬬　762

纟部
二至三画
纠　418
纤　1005
红　319
纣　1084
纤　634
　　885
级　359
约　952
　　1019
纨　840
纪　365
纫　675
四画
纬　851
绂　321
纯　124
纰　599
纱　695
纲　249
纳　560
纴　675
纵　1114
纶　514
纷　224
纸　1069
纹　858
纺　215
纼　1090
纽　577
纾　1054
　　752
五画
线　889
绀　249
绁　906
绂　234
练　486
组　1118
绅　714
细　878
织　1065
终　1079
绉　1084
绊　23
绋　234
绌　117
绍　708
绎　978
经　410
　　416
六画
绑　24
绒　677
结　395
　　398
绔　453
绕　666
绗　305
绘　345

给　259
　　363
绚　928
绛　387
络　516
绝　428
绞　391
统　819

七画

绠　261
绡　898
绢　427
绣　922
绥　781
绦　795
继　367

八画

绩　368
绪　924
绫　497
续　925
绮　624
绯　220
绰　92
　　125
绳　723
维　850
绵　539
绶　751
绷　37
绸　110
绺　503
绻　660
综　1036
　　1112
绽　1042
绿　508
　　511
缀　1100
缁　1104

九画

缄　377
缅　540
缆　465
缈　542
缊　1024
缉　357

缎　190
缲　47
　　603
缑　270
缒　1100
缓　336
缔　169
缕　511
编　43
缘　1017

十画

缜　1054
缚　242
缛　683
缝　230
　　231
缟　254
缠　86
缡　476
缢　979
缣　377
缤　51

十一画

缥　604
　　605
缦　525
缨　987
缩　784
缪　550
　　555

十二画以上

缬　905
缭　491
缮　700
縢　799
缰　385
缱　634
缲　638
缳　336
缴　392
　　1102
缵　1119

马部

马　519

二至四画

驭　1011
驮　196
　　834
驯　933
驰　105
驱　654
驵　676
驳　57
驴　509
驽　580
驾　374

五画

驵　1030
驶　736
驸　775
驷　239
驹　423
驺　1115
驻　1091
驼　834
驿　978

六至十画

骂　520
骁　896
骊　982
骄　389
骆　516
骇　301
骈　603
骊　476
骋　103
验　947
骍　914
骏　432
骐　620
骑　620
骒　446
骓　1099
骖　871
骗　604
骚　692
骛　10
骝　502
骟　700

十一画以上

骠　605
骡　515
骦　87
骤　1085
骥　368

幺部

幺　952
幻　336

巛部

巢　93

王部

王　844
　　845

一至四画

玉　1010
玎　177
玑　353
弄　505
　　579
玖　419
玛　520
玩　840
环　334
现　888
玫　530
玥　1021

五画

珂　441
珐　174
珀　612
珍　1052
玲　496
珊　698
珈　370
玻　56

六画

珥　153
珠　1085
珞　516
班　20

七画

球　653
琐　785
理　478
琉　502
琅　466

八画

琵　601
琴　643
琶　585
琪　620
琳　495
琦　620
琢　1102
　　1122
琥　326
琼　651
斑　20
琮　129
琛　95

九画

瑟　693
瑚　325
瑁　528
瑞　684
瑰　288
瑜　1008
瑕　880
瑙　565

十画以上

瑶　954
璃　476
瑾　406
璜　340
璀　132
璨　77
璎　1032
璧　42

韦部

韦　848
韧　675
韨　234
韫　1024
韬　795

木部

木　556

一画

术　756
　　1086
札　1037

二画

朽　921
朴　612
　　615
机　353
权　657
朵　196
杂　1026

三画

杆　246
　　247
杜　187
杠　249
　　250
杖　1045
杓　167
杌　870
材　72
村　132
杏　917
极　359
杞　622
杨　949
权　81
　　84

四画

枉　845
林　493
枝　1064
杯　31
枢　752
枥　482
柜　289
枇　600
杪　542
杳　954
柄　684
杵　116
枚　530
枨　100
析　873
板　21
枞　128
松　775
枪　635
枫　228
构　271
杭　305
枋　213
杰　397
枕　1054

字	页	字	页	字	页	字	页	字	页	字	页
杷	585	架	374	梵	212	禁	405	**十二画**		殚	150
杼	1090	柔	678	婪	464		409	橱	116	殡	51
枭	896	**六画**		梗	261	楂	84	橛	429	**车部**	
五画		栽	1027	梧	866		1037	橇	638	车	94
某	555	框	457	梢	693	楝	486	樵	639		422
标	47	梆	24		707	楷	396	橹	507	**一至四画**	
栈	1041	栻	743	梏	278		437	橦	819	轧	243
奈	561	桂	289	梅	530	楫	362	樽	1122		938
柑	247	桔	399	检	378	楬	399	橥	875		1037
枯	451	栲	441	桷	429	楞	474	橙	103	轨	288
栉	1073	桠	936	梓	1105	椴	190	橘	423	轩	925
柯	441	栖	617	梳	753	槐	333	**十三画以上**		轫	675
柄	53	桡	665	梯	799	槌	123	檬	535	轰	318
柘	1051	桎	1073	棂	497	榆	1008	檄	876	转	1093
栊	504	桢	1053	桶	819	榇	97	檐	944		1095
枢	420	桃	286	梭	783	榈	510	檀	791		1096
柈	611		287	梨	476	楼	505	檗	59	轭	198
栋	182	档	154	梁	487	楦	928	檫	84	斩	1040
栌	507	桐	818	**八画**		概	245	麓	509	轮	514
查	83	桤	617	棒	24	楣	530	**犬部**		软	683
相	891	株	1085	楮	117	**十画**		犬	660	**五画**	
	895	梃	814	棱	474	榖	276	状	1098	轱	273
柙	880	栝	278	棋	620	榛	1053	戾	482	轳	507
枵	896	桥	639	椰	956	模	551	臭	111	轴	1084
柚	998	栿	234	植	1068		555		922	轵	1069
	1004	柏	420	森	694	槛	384	焱	48	轶	978
枳	1069	桦	333	棼	225		438	葵	10	轸	1054
柞	1125	栓	760	楼	187	榥	340	**歹部**		轹	482
柏	18	桧	289	椅	974	榻	787	歹	146	轻	645
	57	桃	796	椒	390	榫	783	**三至六画**		**六画**	
	58	桅	850	棵	442	榭	906	歼	375	载	1027
枰	496	格	257	棍	290	榴	502	殁	553		1029
柢	165	桩	1097	棰	123	榜	24	残	75	轼	743
枸	271	校	393	椎	123	槟	51	殂	130	轾	1074
	423		902		1099	榨	1038	殃	948	轿	393
栅	698	核	313	棉	539	榕	677	殇	701	较	393
	1037		325	棚	597	槊	769	殆	148	**七至八画**	
柳	503	样	951	楮	347	**十一画**		殊	753	辄	1050
枹	26	桉	6	棬	657	横	317	殉	934	辅	236
栎	482	根	260	棕	1112		318	**七画以上**		辆	490
柱	1091	栩	924	棺	282	樯	637	毙	41	辇	573
柿	742	桑	691	棣	169	槽	78	殡	1023	辋	845
栏	464	柴	85	椭	834	槭	627	殓	486	暂	1030
样	23	桌	575	椠	634	樱	987	殍	605	辍	125
柠	575	桀	399	**九画**		樊	208	殖	1068	辎	1104
枷	370	桨	386	楔	903	橡	896			辈	34
树	756	**七画**		椿	124	樟	1043				
染	664	械	906	楠	564	橄	248				

车部（续）

九至十画

毂	276
辐	235
辑	362
输	754
辕	1018
辖	880
辗	1040

十一画以上

辘	509
錾	1030
辙	1050
辚	495

戈部

戈	255

二画

戎	676
戍	756
成	98

三至七画

戒	401
或	350
戗	635
	638
战	1041
戚	618
戛	372
盛	102
	724

八至九画

裁	73
戟	363
惑	352
戢	437

十画以上

截	399
戬	380
臧	1030
戮	509
戴	148
戳	125

比部

比	38
昆	458
皆	395

毖	41

瓦部

瓦	835
	836
瓯	583
瓮	859
瓴	496
瓶	611
瓷	126
甄	1053

止部

止	1068
此	127
步	69
歧	620
肯	446

攴部

敲	638

日部

日	675

一至三画

旦	151
旭	924
旬	932
旨	1069
旱	304
旰	249
旷	456

四画

者	1050
旺	846
昙	790
杲	254
昃	1034
昌	87
昕	909
明	547
易	977
昀	1023
昂	9
昏	346
沓	136
	787

五画

春	123
昧	532
是	742
昽	504
显	887
映	990
星	913
昳	176
昨	1122
昱	1012
昡	928
昵	570
昭	1046
昶	90

六画

晋	409
晒	696
晓	901
晃	340
晔	959
晌	702
晏	947
晖	341
晕	1022
	1024

七画

晢	1050
匙	105
	744
晡	59
晤	871
晨	97
晦	345
晚	841

八画

替	802
晴	649
暑	755
晰	874
晶	412
晷	289
晾	490
晬	1120
智	1074
普	615

九画

暖	581
暗	8
暄	926
暇	880

十至十二画

暧	4
暝	549
题	801
暴	31
暾	831

十三画以上

矇	535
曙	756
曛	932
曜	956
曝	31
	616
曦	875

曰部

曰	1019
曷	313
曹	78
曼	524
冕	540
最	1120

水部

水	762
泵	37
泉	660
浆	385
黎	476
膝	875
黏	572

贝部

贝	33

三至四画

财	72
责	1034
败	19
账	1045
贩	212
贬	44
购	272
贮	1090
货	351
质	1072
贪	789
贫	606
贯	284

五画

贲	35
贳	742
贵	289
贱	382
贴	810
贻	969
贷	148
贸	528
费	221
贺	314

六至七画

贾	276
赀	1103
贼	1034
贿	345
赂	508
赃	1030
赅	243
赆	409
赁	495
资	1103
赉	464
赈	1055
赊	709

八画

赍	357
赋	241
赌	187
赎	754
赐	128
赔	594

十画以上

赟	231
赘	1100
赙	242
罂	987
赚	1096
	1119
赠	1036
赞	1030
赜	1022
赡	700

见部

见	380

四至七画

规	287
觅	537
视	741
砚	946
觇	85
览	465
觉	393
	428
觊	367
舰	383
觋	876

八画以上

靓	416
	490
觎	164
舰	807
觍	1008
觐	272
觑	409
	655
	657

牛部

牛	576

二至四画

牝	607
牡	556
牤	525
牦	527
牧	557
物	870

五至六画

牯	276
特	797
牺	873

七画以上

牾	869
牿	278
犁	476
犊	187
犄	357
犍	377
犒	441
犟	387

手部

手	745

掣　641
挚　1073
拳　660
挲　686
　　784
掌　95
掰　15
擎　649
擘　59
攀　588

毛部
毛　526
毡　1039
耗　309
毫　528
蚝　306
毯　792
毽　383

气部
气　624
氕　605
氘　155
氚　561
氙　886
氖　225
氟　234
氢　646
氩　939
氨　301
氧　951
氦　6
氪　446
氰　649
氮　152
氯　512

攵部
二至五画
收　744
改　243
攸　20
放　216
政　1061
故　277
六至七画
敖　10
致　1073
敌　163
效　903
敉　537
赦　713
教　390
　　393
敕　107
救　420
敝　41
敏　546
敛　485
敢　247
八画以上
散　690
　　691
敬　416
敞　90
敦　192
　　193
数　755
　　757
　　769
敷　232
复　920

片部
片　602
　　603
版　21
牍　187
牌　587
牒　177

斤部
斤　402
斥　106
欣　909
斧　236
斫　910
斩　620
断　189
斯　771
斮　1102
新　910

爪（爫）部
爪　1047
　　1093
妥　834
采　73
　　74
爬　585
舀　954
爱　3
爵　429

父部
父　235
　　237
爸　14
釜　236
爹　176

月部
月　1020
二至三画
肋　473
肝　246
肟　860
肚　187
肛　249
肘　1084
肠　89
四画
肾　718
肼　414
肤　231
肺　221
肢　1065
肽　789
肱　268
肫　1100
肿　1080
服　233
　　237
　　1045
胀　597
朋　633
肷　274
股　9
肮　215
肪　220
肥　904
五画
胡　325
背　32
　　33
胃　854
胄　1084
胧　655
胚　593
胨　504
胖　433
胫　507
胆　151
胛　372
胂　718
胜　723
胙　724
胍　278
胗　1052
胞　26
胖　589
　　591
脉　522
　　553
胫　416
胎　787
胥　922
六画
胯　453
胰　969
脩　921
胱　286
胴　183
胭　939
胳　455
脆　809
脂　132
胸　1065
脍　919
脏　255
　　1030
脐　620
胶　389
脑　565
胲　244
　　299
胼　603
朕　1055
脒　537
脓　579
朔　769
脊　363

七画
脖　57
脯　236
　　614
脚　391
脲　718
脶　831
腩　515
脢　530
脸　485
脬　592
脱　833
脉　574
望　846

八画
期　357
　　618
腈　413
腊　461
腌　1
　　940
腓　220
腆　807
腴　1008
腋　601
腑　959
腙　236
腔　1113
　　180
腕　635
腱　843
　　383

九画
腻　571
腰　952
腼　540
腥　914
腮　687
腭　199
腹　241
腺　890
腽　1100
腧　757
鹏　597
腾　991
　　799

朗　466
腿　829

十画
膜　551
膊　58
膈　258
　　259
膀　24
　　590
　　591

十一画
膘　48
膛　794
膣　118

十二画
膨　597
膳　700

十三画以上
臌　276
朦　535
臊　692
　　693
臆　979
臃　992
臀　831
臂　35
　　42
臁　352

欠部
欠　634
三至七画
欤　1006
欧　583
欲　1013
八画以上
款　455
欺　618
歆　438
歇　903
歃　696
歉　1008
歌　911
　　256
欢　635

风部
风　226

飒 229
飓 686
飔 426
飕 777
飘 604
飙 48

殳部

殳 751
殴 583
段 189
殷 939
　 982
　 985
般 20
　 56
　 589
毁 343
殿 174
毅 979

文部

文 856
虔 632
蚊 858
紊 858
斐 220
斓 465

方部

方 212
於 861
施 728
舫 216
旅 510
旌 412
族 1117
旋 927
　 928
旒 502
旗 621

火部

火 349

一至三画

灭 543
灰 340
灯 160
灶 1032
灸 419

灿 77
灼 1101

四画

炜 852
炅 417
炙 1072
炬 425
炖 193
炒 94
炝 638
炊 122
炆 858
炕 440
炎 943
炉 507
炔 661

五画

炳 53
炼 486
炽 107
炯 418
炸 1037
炮 26
　 592
　 593
烁 769
炷 1091
炫 928
烂 465
烃 812

六画

耿 261
烤 441
烘 319
烜 928
烦 208
烧 707
烛 1087
烟 939
烨 959
烩 345
烙 471
　 516
烊 950
　 952
烬 409
烫 795

七至八画

焐 871

焊 304
烯 874
焕 337
烽 229
焖 534
烷 841
焗 423
焌 655
㶷 913
焰 947
焙 35
焱 947

九画

煲 26
煤 530
煜 1014
煨 848
煅 190
煌 340
煖 926
煊 926
煸 44
煺 831
煣 678

十至十一画

熄 875
熘 500
熔 677
煽 699
熨 1025

十二画以上

燎 491
燃 664
燧 783
燥 1033
爆 31

斗部

斗 183
科 441
料 491
斟 1053

灬部

五至八画

点 169
烈 492
热 666

羔 254
烹 596
煮 1089
焦 390
然 664

九画以上

煦 925
照 1048
煞 696
煎 377
熬 9
　 10
熙 875
熏 931
　 934
熊 920
熟 754
燕 947

户部

户 327
肩 376
房 215
扁 44
　 602
扄 417
扇 698
　 699
扉 220
雇 278

礻部

一至四画

礼 477
初 675
社 710
祀 775
祎 968
祉 1069

五画

祛 655
被 234
祖 1118
神 716
祝 1091
祚 1125
祇 620
祠 125

六画以上

祯 1053
祥 894
祷 156
祸 351
祺 621
禅 85
　 700
禄 508
福 235
禧 878
禳 665

心部

心 907

三至四画

忑 797
忒 797
　 828
忌 366
忍 673
态 789
忠 1079
怂 776
念 573
忿 226
忽 324

五画

思 771
怎 1035
急 360
怒 580
怠 148

六画

恚 345
恐 448
恶 198
　 862
　 871
　 511
虑 199
恩 568
恁 873
恋 486
恙 952
恣 1111
恳 446

恕 757

七至八画

悬 926
患 337
悠 996
您 575
悉 874
恿 993
惠 346
悲 32
惩 102

九至十画

想 894
感 247
愚 1008
愁 110
愈 1014
慈 126

十一画

慧 346
憋 50
慭 546
憨 302
慰 855

十二画以上

憩 627
懑 192
懿 534
戆 979

聿（肀）部

肆 775
肄 978
肇 1049

彐部

彖 635
彘 1030

毋（母）部

毋 555
毐 866

示部

示 736
祟 782
票 605
祭 367

石部

石 152
（730）

二至四画

矶 355
矸 246
矿 456
码 520
研 943
砖 1094
砗 95
砘 193
砒 599
砌 627
砑 939
砂 695
砟 1102
砭 43
砍 438

五画

砝 207
砹 3
砸 1027
砺 482
砰 596
砧 1053
砷 714
砥 165
砾 482
砬 461
础 116
破 612
砼 447
砻 504

六至七画

硅 288
硕 769
硇 565
硌 259
（516）
砦 1039
硬 991
硝 898
硷 379
确 661
硫 502

八画

碛 627
碍 4
碘 170
碓 192
碑 32
碉 175
碎 782
碰 597
碇 180
碗 842
碌 503
（508）
碜 97

九画

碧 41
碟 177
碴 82
（84）
碱 380
碣 399
碨 855
碳 793
磋 190
磁 169
磙 133
碹 126
磲 928

十画

磕 442
磊 473
磉 290
磅 24
（591）
碾 573
磐 589

十一画以上

磬 650
磺 340
礁 390
礅 193
磷 495
礓 162
礞 385
礤 472
礴 71
（58）

龙部

龙 504
胧 504
聋 504
龚 1050
袭 876
龛 437

业部

业 957
虚 922
凿 1031

目部

目 557

二至四画

盯 177
盱 922
眍 449
盹 193
眇 542
盼 590
眨 1037
冒 528
看 437
（438）
盾 193
眉 530

五至七画

眩 928
眠 539
眙 107
眶 457
眭 781
眦 1111
眺 809
睁 1057
眯 536
眼 945
眸 554
眷 427
睐 464
睑 379
睄 709
睇 169
睨 178
鼎 784

八画

督 185
睛 413
睹 187
睦 558
睃 475
瞄 542
睚 937
睫 399
睡 766
睥 602
睬 74

九至十画

瞅 111
瞍 777
睽 457
瞌 442
瞒 523
瞎 879
瞑 549

十一画以上

瞥 605
瞟 605
瞠 98
瞰 439
瞭 492
瞧 639
瞬 767
瞳 819
瞵 495
瞩 1089
瞪 162
瞿 426
瞻 1039

田部

田 806

二至三画

町 814
男 562
甾 1027

四画

禺 1007
畎 660
畏 854
毗 600
畋 806
畈 212
界 401

五至六画

畛 1054
畔 590
留 500
畦 620
略 513
累 472
（473）

七画以上

畴 110
畸 357
疃 828

罒部

三至八画

罗 515
罚 205
罡 250
罢 14
罟 276
罨 483
署 755
置 1075
罱 946
罪 1120
罩 1048
蜀 755

九画以上

罴 601
罹 476
羁 358

皿部

皿 545

三至五画

盂 1006
盅 1080
盆 596
盈 988
盏 1040
盐 943
盍 313
监 376
（382）
盔 9

六画以上

盔 457
蛊 276
盘 589
盖 244
盗 157
盟 535
盥 284

钅部

一至二画

钇 973
针 1051
钉 177
（179）
钋 611
钊 1045
钌 491

三画

钎 629
钏 121
钐 699
钓 175
钗 85

四画

钙 244
钚 69
钛 789
钜 425
钝 193
钞 92
钟 1080
钡 34
钢 251
（250）
钠 560
钣 21
钤 631
钥 956
（1021）
钦 641
钩 431
钨 861
钩 270
钫 213
钬 350
钮 577

（钅）五画
钯 14
钰 1012
钱 632
钲 1057
钳 633
钴 276
钵 56
钶 442
钜 612
钹 57
钺 1021
钻 1119
钼 558
钽 792
钾 373
铀 998
钿 174
806
铁 810
铂 57
铃 496
铅 630
铆 527
铄 769
铈 743
铉 928
铊 786
铌 570
铎 196

六画
铐 441
铗 372
铙 565
铛 98
153
铝 510
铜 818
铠 437
铡 1037
铢 1086
铣 877
888
铤 180
814
铧 330
铪 298
铬 259

铭 549
铮 1057
1062
铯 693
铰 391
铲 87
铳 109
铵 7
银 982

七画
铸 1092
锊 468
铺 614
616
铼 463
链 486
铿 447
销 898
锁 785
锃 1036
锄 116
锂 478
锅 290
锈 922
锉 134
锋 229
锌 910
锏 379
383
锐 684
锑 800
银 466
锎 1

八画
锗 1050
错 134
锚 527
锡 875
锢 278
锣 515
锤 123
锥 1099
锦 406
锨 886
锩 427
锭 180
键 384
锯 426

镏 1104

九画
锲 641
锴 437
锹 638
锻 190
镀 188
镁 532
镂 506
锵 635

十画
镊 575
镇 1055
镒 427
镍 575
镏 503
镐 254
镑 24
镕 678

十一画
镖 48
镘 525
镛 992
镜 417
镝 164

十二画
镣 492
镦 193
镧 465
镨 616
镪 131
镫 635
638
161
162

十三画以上
镭 472
镯 1102
镰 485
镱 51
镳 48
镶 893

矢部
矢 735
矩 423
矫 390
391
短 188
矬 134
矮 3
雉 1075

禾部
禾 310

二至三画
秀 921
秆 247
和 312
314
324
348
350
秉 53
季 366

四画
秕 39
秒 542
香 892
种 1080
秭 1082
秋 1105
乘 651
102
724

五画
秣 553
秫 754
秤 103
租 1116
积 356
秧 948
秩 1074
称 97
98
秘 537

六至七画
秸 396
稆 510
移 346
稞 969
稃 579
稣 777
稍 707
709
程 102
稀 874
黍 755
税 766
稂 466

八画
稙 1065
稚 1075
稗 20
稔 673
稠 110
颓 829
颖 989

九至十画
稳 858
穀 276
稽 357
稷 368
稻 158
稿 254
稼 375

十一画以上
穆 558
穗 783
馥 242
黐 477

白部
白 15

二至八画
皂 1032
帛 57
的 159
162
163
167
皇 338
皈 288
皋 251
昑 496
皑 3
皎 391
皓 310
皙 875

九画以上
魄 613
皛 10
皞 132
皦 392
皭 394

瓜部
瓜 278
瓞 176
瓟 835
瓠 604
瓣 23
瓢 665

用部
用 993

鸟部
鸟 175
574

二至四画
鸠 418
鸡 355
鸥 583
鸦 936
鸧 29
鸪 1054

五画
鸺 507
鸭 936
鸮 896
鸶 948
鸵 834

六至七画
鸽 256
鹁 58
鹂 476
鹃 427
鹄 276
325
鹅 197

八画
鹉 869
鹊 662
鹤 7
鹑 124

九画
鹗 199

鹔　127
鹏　531
鹜　871

十画
鹣　956
鹞　859
鹧　377
鹤　315

十一画以上
鹦　987
鹨　1051
鹫　503
鹭　422
鹬　1014
鹮　509
鹳　284

广部

二至四画
疗　177
疖　395
疔　490
疟　581
　　954
疠　482
疝　699
疙　255
疚　420
疡　949
疬　482
疣　998
疥　401
疮　121
疯　229
疫　978
疾　97
疤　13

五画
症　1057
　　1062
痄　247
疴　442
病　54
疳　698
疸　423
疽　151
疹　361
疹　1054

疼　799
疱　593
痊　1091
痂　370
疲　600
痉　416

六至七画
痔　1074
瘐　970
疵　125
痊　660
痒　951
痕　316
痣　1075
痨　468
痘　184
痞　601
痢　483
痤　134
痪　337
痛　820

八画
瘃　1087
痱　222
痹　41
瘤　278
痴　104
瘘　852
瘁　132
瘀　1005
痰　791
瘆　718

九至十画
瘌　462
瘟　856
瘦　751
瘘　506
瘙　693
瘪　50
瘢　21
瘤　503
瘠　362
瘫　790

十一画以上
瘿　990
瘴　1045
癌　986
瘸　661

瘳　110
癌　3
癫　464
瘢　756
癣　601
癣　928
癫　169

立部

立　479

四至六画
站　1042
翊　978
翌　978

七画以上
竦　776
童　818
竣　432
靖　417
意　978
竭　399
韶　707
端　188

穴部

穴　929

二至六画
究　418
穷　650
空　447
　　449
帘　484
穹　651
突　824
穿　118
窃　641
窍　640
窄　1038
窈　954
窒　1074
窑　953
宛　809

七画以上
窜　131
窝　860
窖　394
窗　121
窨　418

窥　457
窦　184
窟　452
窭　426

衤部

二至五画
补　59
初　114
衬　97
衫　698
衩　84
袆　341
衲　560
衽　675
袄　10
衿　405
袂　533
袜　836
祛　655
祖　792
袖　922
袗　1054
袍　592
被　34

六至八画
祜　399
裆　153
袱　235
裢　485
裕　1014
裤　453
裥　379
裙　662
褛　49
褂　279
褚　1089
裸　516
裨　41
　　601
褫　195

九至十画
褡　135
褙　35
褐　315
褓　29
褊　45
褪　831

　　832
褥　683
褴　465
褟　786
褾　50
褶　1050

十一画以上
襕　465
襁　638
襟　405
襻　590

疋(正)部

蛋　152
疏　753
楚　117

皮部

皮　599
皱　1084
皲　431
颇　611
皴　58
皱　132

矛部

矛　527

耒部

耕　261
耘　1023
耖　94
耙　14
　　585
耢　471
耥　793
耦　584
耧　506
耩　386
耪　591

老部

老　468
耆　271
耋　176

耳部

耳　200

二画
耵　177

四画
耻　106
耽　150
耸　776

五至九画
职　1067
聆　496
聊　490
聍　575
聒　290
联　484
聘　607
聩　458
聪　128

臣部

臣　96

西(覀)部

西　872
栗　482
粟　779
要　952
　　955
覆　242

页部

页　958

二至三画
顶　177
顷　649
预　302
项　895
顺　766
须　922

四画
顽　841
顾　277
顿　193
颁　20
颂　777
颃　306
预　1012

五至七画
颅　507
领　498
颈　414
颊　372

衣部

衣　967

四至六画

袅　574
袋　148
裂　372
裂　492
　　493
装　1097

七画以上

裘　653
裔　978
裴　696

羊(⺷⺶)部

羊　948

三至六画

差　81
　　84
　　85
　　125
美　531
养　950
羞　921
着　1046
　　1047
　　1051
　　1102
姜　385
羖　276
羚　497
羝　163
羟　637
善　699
翔　894
羡　890

七画以上

羧　784
群　662
羯　399
羹　261

米部

米　537

三至六画

籼　886
粉　225
粑　13
粝　482
粘　1039
粗　129
粕　613
粒　482
粜　809
粪　226
粞　874

七至十画

粲　77
粳　413
粮　487
粱　488
精　413
粼　495
粹　132
粽　1115
糁　691
　　716
糊　324
　　326
　　328
糌　1029
糍　127
糈　924
糅　678
糙　78
糗　653
糖　794
糕　254

十一画以上

糟　1031
糠　439
糵　387
糯　582

艮部

艮　260

羽部

羽　1009

四至八画

翅　107
翊　321
翁　859
翎　497
翘　639
　　640
翡　220
翠　132

九画以上

翩　603
翱　315
翼　979
翻　207

糸部

四至六画

素　778
紧　405
絷　1068
紫　1105
絮　925

八画以上

綦　621
繁　208
纂　1119

麦部

麦　521
麸　231

走部

走　1115

二至五画

赴　239
赳　418
赶　247
趄　699
起　622
越　1021
趄　641
趁　97
趋　655
超　92

六画以上

趔　493
趣　657
趟　793
　　795
趱　803

赤部

赤　106
赧　564
赪　879

赫　315
赭　1050
赯　794

豆部

豆　184
登　160
豌　840

酉部

酉　1003

二至五画

酊　177
　　178
酐　247
酌　1102
配　595
酏　974
酝　1024
酞　789
酗　924
酚　225
酣　302
酤　273
酢　130
　　1126

六至七画

酮　818
酯　1070
酪　471
酩　549
酬　110
酱　387
酵　394
酷　453
酶　531
酹　473
酿　573
酸　780

八至十画

醋　130
醇　124
醉　1121
醅　594
醡　1100
醛　660
醐　326
醒　801
醒　917

醚　536
醑　924

十一画以上

醵　59
醺　394
醾　932

辰部

辰　96

豕部

豕　735
貊　336

卤部

卤　507

里部

里　477
　　483
野　957
量　487
　　490

足(⻊)部

足　1117

二至四画

趴　585
趸　193
趵　30
　　56
跋　786
趼　378
跌　232
趺　620
　　627
距　425
趾　1070
跃　1021
跄　638

五画

践　383
跖　1068
跋　13
跕　176
跌　176
跗　232
跚　699
跑　592

踩　482
跎　834

六画

跬　458
跨　453
跶　146
跷　638
跐　125
　　127
　　1093
踅　888
跳　809
踩　196
跪　289
路　508
跻　357
跤　390
跟　260

七至八画

踅　930
踌　111
踉　490
踊　993
踆　132
踝　333
踢　800
踟　105
踬　860
蹀　1075
踩　74
踮　171
踣　58
蹄　1068
踪　1113
踞　426
踏　786
　　787

九至十画

蹅　84
蹉　169
蹁　118
踵　1081
蹀　196
蹄　801
蹉　133
蹁　603
蹂　678
蹑　575

足部（续）

字	页
蹒	589
蹟	169
蹋	787
蹈	156
蹊	619
	875
蹻	500
	503
蹼	573

十一画

字	页
蹩	131
蹐	50
蹡	116
蹦	37
蹯	1068

十二画以上

字	页
蹰	116
蹶	430
蹼	616
蹴	131
蹻	193
蹲	133
	193
蹭	81
蹿	131
蹬	161
躁	1033

身部

字	页
身	714
躯	655
躲	196
躺	795

采部

字	页
番	207
釉	1005
释	743

谷部

字	页
谷	274
豁	348
	352

豸部

字	页
豺	85
豹	30
貂	175
貉	307
	314
貌	529

角部

字	页
角	390
	428
觚	273
觥	269
触	117
解	399
	402
	906

言部

字	页
言	941
訄	653
詟	1104
	1106
誉	799
誊	1014
誓	743
謇	380
警	415
譬	602

辛部

字	页
辛	909
辟	41
	599
	602
辣	462
辨	47
辩	47
辫	47

青部

字	页
青	644
静	417
靛	174

雨部

字	页
雨	1009
	1011

三至七画

字	页
雯	1007
雱	482
雰	590
雷	472
零	497
雾	871
雹	26
需	923
霆	813
震	1055
霄	898
霉	531

八画以上

字	页
霖	495
霏	220
霓	570
霍	352
霎	696
霜	761
霞	881
霭	3
霸	15
露	506
	509
霹	599

齿部

字	页
齿	106
龀	97
龁	314
龃	424
龄	497
龅	26
龇	1104
龈	983

隹部

字	页
隹	1098
隼	427
雄	919
雅	938
集	361
雏	116
雌	127
雕	175
雠	111

金部

字	页
金	403
鉴	383
銎	590
鋬	871
	503
鑫	911

鱼部

字	页
鱼	1006

四至七画

字	页
鲁	507
稣	778
鲜	886
	888
鲠	261
鲤	478
鲫	368
鲨	696

八至十画

字	页
鲭	648
	1057
鲮	497
鲳	87
鲸	414
鳃	687
鳄	199
鳊	44
鳎	38
鳌	10
鳍	621
鳔	282
鳎	954

十一画以上

字	页
鳖	50
鳘	546
鳔	50
鳗	523
鳝	700
鳞	495
鳟	1122

革部

字	页
革	256
	360

二至四画

字	页
靬	177
靰	871
靸	686
靴	929
靶	14

五画

字	页
鞅	948
鞒	956

六画

字	页
鞋	905
鞑	136
鞍	7

七画以上

字	页
鞘	640
	707
鞠	423
鞟	459
鞭	44
鞣	679

骨部

字	页
骨	273
	275
骪	852
骱	402
骷	452
骶	165
骼	258
骸	299
髁	442
髅	506
髂	628
髋	591
髌	455
髓	782

鬼部

字	页
鬼	289
魂	347
魁	457
魅	533
魍	845
魉	104
魔	552

食部

字	页
食	734
	775
飨	894
餐	75

音部

字	页
音	981
韵	1024
黯	9

髟部

字	页
鬏	664
鬈	660
鬃	1113
鬓	51

麻部

字	页
麻	518
磨	551
	554
摩	518
	551
麾	341
縻	536
糜	536
靡	536
	537
蘑	582

鹿部

字	页
鹿	508
麂	363
麒	621
麝	713
麟	495

黑部

字	页
黑	315
墨	553
默	554
黔	633
黜	151
黝	118
	1003
黛	148
黠	881
黢	655
黩	187
黥	649

鼠部

字	页
鼠	755
鼬	1005

鼻部

字	页
鼻	38
鼾	302

ā（ㄚ）

吖 [ā]

吖嗪 azine

阿 ➡ē

阿爸 dad
阿爹 daddy
阿斗 A Dou—a weak-minded and ne'er-do-well person；a failure（or fool）
阿飞 young street rowdy；(teenager) hoodlum（or hooligan）
阿哥 elder brother
阿公 ①husband's father ②grandfather ③respected term for elderly man
阿訇 ahung；imam
阿妈 ①mom ②woman servant；amah
阿妹 little sister
阿门 amen
阿片 opium
阿婆 ①husband's mother ②granny ③respected term for elderly woman
阿姨 ①aunt ②auntie ③nursemaid（in a family）；childcare worker（in a nursery school or kindergarten）
阿米巴 amoeba
阿尔法粒子 alpha particle
阿尔法射线 alpha ray
阿富汗战争 Afghan War
阿拉伯半岛 the Arabian Peninsula；Arabia
阿拉伯国家 Arab countries（or states）
阿拉伯树胶 gum arabic；gum acacia
阿拉伯数字 Arabic numerals
阿米巴痢疾 amoebic dysentery
阿尔卑斯山脉 the Alps
阿尔法磁谱仪 alpha magnetic spectrometer
阿拉伯国家联盟 the League of Arab States；the Arab League
"阿帕奇"武装直升机 Apache helicopter

啊 [ā] 叹（expressing surprise or admiration）oh：啊，下雨了！ Oh，it's raining！ /啊，这些苹果多大呀！ How big these apples are！ ➡á；ǎ；à；a

锕 [ā] 名 actinium（Ac）

锕系元素 actinides

腌 [ā] ➡yān

腌臢 filthy；dirty

á（ㄚˊ）

啊 [á] 叹（expressing doubt or demanding a repetition of sth just said）hey；eh；what：啊？ 她真病了吗？ What！ It's she really ill？ /啊？ 她在讲什么？ Hey，what's she talking about？ ➡ā；ǎ；à；a

ǎ（ㄚˇ）

啊 [ǎ] 叹（expressing doubt or asking for an answer）well：啊？ 你今天晚上到底来不来吃晚饭？ Well，are you coming to have supper with us or not？ /啊？ 你怎么啦？ Hey！ What's the matter with you？ ➡ā；á；à；a

à（ㄚˋ）

啊 [à] 叹 ①（expressing consent）well；yes：啊，就照你说的办吧！ Well，let's do it according to what you say，then！ ②（expressing realization）oh；aha：啊，原来是他干的这事儿呀！ Ah，so it's he who did this！ ③（expressing admiration）oh：啊，伟大的母爱！ Oh，the great mother love！ ➡ā；á；ǎ；a

a（·ㄚ）

啊 [a] 叹 ①（used at the end of a sentence to indicate admiration or doubt）：多深刻的教训啊！ What a profound lesson！ /你喝不喝

啊? Do you want to drink or not? ②(*used at the end of a sentence to show approval or self-defence or to urge sb*):行啊,就这么办吧! Okey,so be it! /我没去是因为我没空啊! I didn't go, because I was fully occupied. /快点! 跟上我啊! Quick,keep up with me! /加油干啊! Work harder! /看见你妈可别哭啊! Do not cry when you see your mother! ③(*used in the middle of a sentence making a deliberate pause to draw attention to what is to be said next*):你啊,真自私! Look! How selfish you are! ④(*used after a list of items*):面包啊,黄油啊,鸡蛋啊,牛奶啊,香肠啊,摆满了一桌子。 The table is covered full of bread,butter,eggs,milk and sausages. ➡ā;á;ǎ;à

āi (ㄞ)

哎 [āi]
囡 ①(*showing surprise or dissatisfaction*)why;hey;ouch:哎! 真想不到是你啊! Why,it never occurs to me that it is you! /哎,你怎么能这样说话呢? But how could you speak in such a way? ②(*used as a reminder or warning*)hey;look out:哎,这儿可不许吸烟呀! Hey, it's not allowed to smoke here! /哎,别把盘子碰掉了! Look out! Don't knock off the plate!

哎呀 Ah; Oh, my! Dear me! My word! Oh dear!:哎呀,好大的雨呀! Oh,my,what a down pour! /哎呀,我的手机丢了! Oh dear! I've lost my mobile phone!

哎哟 Oh,dear! Ouch! Ow!:哎哟,我的左脚真疼啊! Ow! My left foot really hurts!

哀 [āi]
Ⅰ 图 ①grief;sorrow ②mourning ③pity;compassion Ⅱ 勔 mourn;lament;grieve over;be in sorrow Ⅲ 形 sorrowful;sad;doleful

哀愁 be distressed

哀辞 a formal expression of sorrow or mourning,esp. in verse;elegy

哀悼 mourn for the deceased;grieve over sb's death;lament sb's death

哀告 beg piteously;supplicate

哀歌 ①dirge;elegy ②croon plaintively

哀鸽 mourning dove

哀号 cry piteously;wail

哀乐 [āilè] grief and joy

哀怜 feel compassion for;pity

哀鸣 whine plaintively

哀求 entreat;implore

哀伤 be grieved and heartbroken

哀思 sad memories (of the deceased);grief

哀诉 whine;whimper;bleat

哀叹 sigh sorrowfully for;lament;bewail;bemoan

哀痛 mourn sorrowfully;grieve deeply for;la-

ment

哀怨 aggrieved;resentful

哀乐 [āiyuè] funeral music;dirge

哀兵必胜 A bullied and enraged army is bound to win.

哀兵政策 policy of building an army burning with righteous indignation

哀而不伤 sorrow without self-injury

哀鸿遍野 famished refugees swarming over the land;disaster victims moaning everywhere

哀其不幸 have pity on sb for his misfortune

埃 [āi]
图 ①dust ②angstrom (Å)

埃博拉病毒 Ebola virus

挨 [āi]
Ⅰ 阀 in the order of;one after another;by turns;one by one:挨人通知 inform one person after another Ⅱ 勔 ①be close to;be next to:挨肩坐着 sit shoulder to shoulder ②press ③be one's turn ➡ái

挨次 take turns (doing sth);do sth one after another or in turn

挨近 get close to;be near to

挨不上 have no relations;be irrelevant;be extraneous;be unrelated

挨个儿 do sth by turns or one by one

挨排儿 in proper sequence;one by one

挨门挨户 from house to house;from door to door

唉 [āi]
囡 ①(*sound indicating response*) yes;right;well:唉,来了! Yes,(I'm) coming! ②(*sound of sighing sadly*)Ah! alas:唉,我真倒霉! Ah! how unlucky I am! (*or* What bad luck!) ➡ài

唉声叹气 heave deep sighs (of grief,worry or anguish);moan and groan

ái (ㄞ)

挨 [ái]
勔 ①suffer;endure:挨打 get a beating ②go through hard time;suffer day after day;drag out a miserable existence ③delay;put off;dawdle;stall;play for time ➡āi

挨打 ①take a beating;get a thrashing ②come under attack

挨冻 endure (*or* suffer from) cold

挨斗 be criticized and denounced

挨饿 go hungry;be starved

挨罚 be fined;get (*or* catch) it in the neck

挨浇 be caught in the rain

挨骂 be given a telling-off;get a scolding

挨批 be criticized;be denounced

挨整 be in for criticism and denunciation

挨揍 ①take a beating ②be defeated

挨板子 get the caning;be punished

挨呲儿 get a talking-to；get a dressing down
挨日子 suffer day after day；drag out a miserable existence
挨时间 stall for time
挨雨淋 be caught in the rain
挨打受骂 be beaten and cursed；put up with blows and scoldings
挨冷受冻 endure the cold
挨欺受辱 be subjected to bullying and humiliations
挨揍儿童综合征 battered child syndrome

皑 [ái]
形 pure white；snow white
皑皑 (of snow，frost，etc.) pure white

癌 [ái]
名 cancer；carcinoma
癌变 canceration；metabolic change of cancer
癌症 cancer
癌肿 cancerous swelling
癌恐怖 cancerphobia
癌扩散 metastasis (or proliferation) of cancer
癌细胞 cancer cell
癌转移 cancerometastasis
癌切除术 carcinectomy；carcinomectomy

ǎi (ㄞ)

嗳 I 叹 belch II 叹：嗳，不是这样的。No，it's not like that.
嗳气 belch；eructation
嗳酸 eruct acid；have an acid belch

矮 [ǎi]
形 ①short：他比我矮。He's shorter than me. ②low：矮墙 a low wall ③be lower than；be inferior to
矮凳 low stool
矮林 coppice；brushwood
矮领 moat collar
矮胖 short and stout；squat；dumpy；roly-poly
矮人 ① short person；dwarf ② Pigmy (or Pygmy)
矮小 short and small；low and small；undersized
矮星 dwarf star；dwarf
矮子 short person；dwarf
矮半截 be inferior to (or worse than) others
矮墩墩 pudgy；dumpy；stumpy
矮个子 low-built person；short person
矮壮素 cycocel
矮秆品种 short-stalked variety；short-straw variety
矮秆作物 short-stalked plant
矮腰皮鞋 loafer
矮子里拔将军 choose a general from among the dwarfs—pick the best out of a mediocre bunch

蔼 [ǎi]
形 friendly；affable；amiable
蔼然可亲 amiable and endearing

霭 [ǎi]
名 mist；haze
霭滴 mist droplet

ài (ㄞ)

艾 I 名 Chinese mugwort；moxa II 动 halt；end III 形 pretty；beautiful ➧ yì
艾蒿 felon herb
艾虎 fitch
艾灸 moxibustion
艾绒 moxa
艾条 moxa stick；moxa-cigar
艾炷 moxa cone
艾米奖 Emmy
艾窝窝 steamed cone-shaped cake made of glutinous rice with or without filling
艾滋病 AIDS (acquired immune deficiency syndrome)
艾艾难言 stutter and speak with difficulty；speak haltingly (from embarrassment，etc.)
艾滋病毒 AIDS virus
艾滋病患者 person with AIDS (PWA)
艾滋病新药 new medicine for AIDS
艾滋病疫苗 vaccine for AIDS
艾滋病之友 buddy
艾滋病相关症 AIDS related complex
艾滋病携带者 AIDS carriers

砹 [ài]
名 astatine (At)

唉 [ài]
叹 (used to express sadness or regret)：唉，我早怎么没想到! My goodness，why didn't I think of that earlier? /唉，当时买下它来就好了! Oh! If only I had bought it then. ➧ āi

爱 [ài]
动 ①love ②cherish；treasure；hold dear；take good care of ③like；be fond of；be keen on；enjoy ④be apt to；be in the habit of
爱才 love for scholars (or talents)；thirst for talents
爱财 be covetous；be greedy for money
爱巢 love nest
爱称 term of endearment；pet name
爱畜 pet；favourite；household animal
爱戴 love and esteem
爱抚 show tender care for
爱国 love one's country；be patriotic
爱好 ① take great pleasure in；have sth as a hobby；be keen on ②interest；hobby
爱河 river of love
爱护 cherish；treasure；take good care of

爱怜 show tender affection for
爱恋 be in love with;feel deeply attached to
爱侣 lovers;sweethearts
爱女 beloved daughter
爱美 set great store by one's appearance;love to make up and wear beautiful clothes
爱慕 adore;admire
爱妻 beloved wife
爱情 love;amour
爱人 ①husband;wife ②sweetheart;lover
爱神 god of love;Cupid
爱窝 love nest
爱惜 value highly and use prudently;treasure
爱小 be greedy about petty gains;go after fringe advantages
爱心 love;sympathy;compassion
爱子 beloved son
爱国粮 excess grain contributed to the government;grain delivered to the state
爱国心 patriotic feeling;patriotism:唤起爱国心 arouse patriotism
爱国者 patriot
爱好者 lover (of art, sports, etc.);enthusiast;fan
爱面子 be concerned about face-saving;be sensitive about one's reputation
爱民月 Love-the-people Month
爱鸟周 Bird Protection (or Cherishing) Week
爱情结 love knot
爱情片 love film
爱情热 love fever
爱童癖 pedophilia
爱牙日 Teeth-cherishing Day
爱不释手 be so fond of sth that one will not let it out of one's hand
爱才若渴 One's love for scholars is equal to one's thirst for water.
爱财如命 love money as one loves one's life;love money as much as life itself;be greedy for money;be a money-grubber
爱答不理 look cold and indifferent;be stand-offish
爱国爱教 love for the country and the church;patriotic religious believers
爱国华侨 Patriotic Oversea Chinese
爱国人士 patriotic personage
爱国主义 patriotism
爱好倾向 predisposition
爱恨交织 be overwhelmed by mixed love-hate feelings
爱民如子 love the people as one's children
爱莫能助 be willing to help but unable to do so
爱慕虚荣 be vain
爱钱如命 love money as dearly as one's very life;love money more than dear life;money rather than life
爱情不专 fickle;wolfish;changeable in love

爱情歌曲 love song
爱情镜头 love scene
爱情小说 romance novel;love story
爱如己出 cherish a child as one's own
爱屋及乌 love for a person extends even to the crows on his roof;love me,love my dog
爱校如家 love the school as dearly as one does one's own home
爱心工程 Loving Care Project
爱婴医院 baby-friendly hospital
爱憎分明 understand what to love and what to hate;know whom to love and whom to hate
"爱国者"导弹 Patriot missile
爱情纪念品 love token
爱情伦理学 ethics of love
爱情心理学 love psychology
爱斯基摩人 Eskimo
爱尔兰共和军 Irish Republican Army (IRA)
爱国统一战线 the patriotic united front
爱国卫生运动 the patriotic health campaign
爱国主义教育 patriotic education;education in patriotism
爱国主义教育基地 base for patriotic education
爱美之心,人皆有之 Loving beauty is part of human nature.
爱国卫生运动委员会 Patriotic Health Campaign Committee

隘 [ài]
I 名 pass.II 形 narrow:林深路隘 narrow path in the depth of a forest
隘口 mountain pass
隘路 defile;narrow passage

碍 [ài]
动 hinder;obstruct;be in the way of
碍口 be too embarrassing to mention
碍难 find it difficult (or inconvenient) (to do sth)
碍事 ①be in the way;be a hindrance ②be of consequence;matter
碍眼 be unpleasant to look at;offend the eye;be an eyesore
碍面子 spare sb's feelings
碍手碍脚 be in the way;be a hindrance
碍于情面 for fear of hurting sb's feelings;out of consideration for sb's sensibilities

暧 [ài]
形 (of daylight) dim
暧昧 ①ambiguous;equivocal ②shady;dubious

ān（ㄢ）

安 [ān]
I 形 ① safe; secure; in good health ② peaceful;quiet;tranquil;calm;at ease II 动 ①cause to calm down;set at ease ②be satisfied;rest content ③place in a suitable position;find a place for ④install;fix;fit ⑤harbour;be up to ⑥bring (a charge against sb);

give (sb a nickname) Ⅲ 〔代〕 ①where：而今安在？ Where is it now？（*or* Where are they today?）②how：安能袖手旁观？ How can one stand by and do nothing？ Ⅳ 〔名〕（short for 安培）A：13 安 13A

安瓿 ampoule

安插 ①place (sb) in a certain position；assign (sb) to a job ②insert (an episode，etc.) into a story，play，article，etc.

安抵 arrive safely；arrive safe and sound

安定 ①stable；quiet；settled ②stabilize；maintain

安顿 ①help settle down（*or* in）；get sth or everything arranged；find a place for ② peaceful；undisturbed

安放 put in a proper place；lay

安分 not go beyond one's bounds；be law-abiding；know one's place

安抚 aid and comfort（*or* console）；reassure and pacify；appease

安好 safe and sound；well

安家 ①settle down ②set up a home；get married

安检 security check

安静 ①quiet；peaceful ②calm；undisturbed ③ quiet down

安居 settle down（in a place）

安康 in good health

安拉 Allah

安乐 peaceful and happy；free from worry

安谧 peaceful；tranquil

安眠 sleep peacefully

安民 pacify the people；reassure the public

安宁 ① peaceful；tranquil ② calm；composed；free from worry

安排 arrange (matters)；plan in detail；dispose (manpower)

安培 ampere

安全 safe；secure

安然 ①safe ②be free from worry；feel at ease

安设 install；set up

安身 have a roof over one's head；take shelter

安神 ①calm（*or* soothe) the nerves ②relieve uneasiness of body and mind

安生 [ānshēng] peaceful；restful

安生 [ānsheng] quiet；still；untroublesome

安适 quiet and comfortable

安泰 ①Antaios ②safe and sound

安危 safety and danger；safety

安慰 ①be comforted；feel encouraged ②comfort；console ③consolation；comfort

安稳 smooth and steady；sedate；calm and poised

安息 ①rest；go to sleep ②rest in peace；at rest

安闲 peaceful and carefree；relaxed；leisurely

安详 serene；composed；unruffled

安享 enjoy

安歇 go to bed；retire for the night

安心 ① feel at ease；be relieved；set one's mind at rest ②keep one's mind on sth

安逸 easy and comfortable；easy

安营 pitch a camp；camp

安于 be content or satisfied with a state of affairs

安葬 bury（the dead）

安置 find a suitable place，position，job，etc. for；arrange for the placement of

安装 install；fix；set up

安坐 sit idly

安魂曲 requiem

安家费 allowance for setting up a home in a new place；settling-in allowance；family allowance

安居房 affordable housing

安乐死 mercy killing；euthanasia

安乐窝 cosy nest

安乐椅 easy chair

安理会 the Security Council

安眠药 sleeping pill（*or* tablet)；soporific

安培计 ammeter；amperemeter

安琪儿 angel

安全带 safety belt；seat belt

安全岛 safety island；pedestrian island

安全灯 ①safety lamp ②safelight

安全阀 safety valve；emergency valve；escape valve

安全法 safety regulations

安全感 sense of security

安全奖 accident reduction bonus

安全帽 safety helmet

安全门 emergency exit

安全期 safe period

安全锁 safety lock

安全套 condom

安全梯 emergency staircase；fire escape

安全网 safety netting

安全月 Safety Month

安神药 sedative；tranquillizer

安慰剂 placebo

安慰奖 consolation prize

安慰赛 consolation event（*or* match，tournament)

安息日 Sabbath（day）

安息香 benzoin

安置费 placement or settlement allowance

安邦定国 (of a ruler) bring peace and stability to the country

安不忘危 mindful of possible danger in times of peace

安步当车 stroll over instead of riding in a carriage；walk rather than ride

安常处顺 stick to the status quo；go along with things as they are

A

安定团结 stability and unity
安度时光 pass one's time in peace
安度晚年 spend one's remaining years in comfort
安分度日 lead a sober life
安分守法 abide by the law and behave oneself
安分守己 abide by the law and behave oneself; be content with one's lot and act one's part; know one's place
安家立业 settle down to business; settle down and start one's career
安家落户 make one's home (or take up residence) in a new place; settle
安居工程 affordable housing project; Comfortable Housing Project
安居乐业 live and work in peace and contentment
安民告示 notice to reassure the public
安民恤众 improve the conditions of the people and maintain order
安内攘外 maintain internal security and repel foreign invasion
安培小时 ampere-hour
安贫乐道 be contented in poverty and devoted to things spiritual; be happy to lead a simple, virtuous life
安贫乐贱 glory in one's dignified poverty
安贫守贱 be content with poverty and keeping to humbleness
安全玻璃 safety glass
安全车距 safe distance behind the car in front
安全措施 safety measures
安全管理 safety management
安全合作 cooperation on security
安全检查 security check
安全认证 safety certification
安全设施 safety devices
安全生产 safety in production
安全剃刀 safety razor
安全系数 safety coefficient (or factor)
安然长逝 expire calmly
安然入睡 go to sleep peacefully
安然脱险 get oneself out of trouble without injury; be out of danger
安然无恙 safe and sound; (escape) unscathed
安然自愉 take the rough with the smooth
安如磐石 as firm (or solid) as a rock
安如泰山 as solid as Mount Tai; as firm (or solid) as a rock
安身立命 settle down and get on with one's work
安土重迁 love one's homeland and not wish to leave it; hate to leave one's native land
安危与共 share together danger and safety; stick together through thick and thin
安闲自在 be leisurely and carefree
安享清福 enjoy blessing of quiet, peaceful life

安享太平 enjoy times of peace; enjoy the present tranquility
安享天年 be comfortable all the rest of one's life
安营扎寨 pitch a camp; camp
安于患难 reconcile oneself with adversity
安于现状 be content with things as they are; be satisfied with the existing state of affairs; take things as they are
安于职守 stay at one's post
安枕无忧 lie peacefully on the pillow; sleep in peace; rest without anxiety
安之若命 submit to one's fate; bend to one's fate
安之若素 ① bear (hardship, etc.) with equanimity ② regard (wrongdoing, etc.) with indifference
安装调试 installation and trial run
安坐待毙 sit (or wait) passively for one's end
安全保障权 right to safety
安全经济学 economics of safety
安全数据库 safety data bank
安全通行证 safe-conduct
安全技能训练 safety skill training
安全技术主管 safety supervisor
安全文明小区 safety and civilized living quarter
安全生产责任制 responsibility system for safety in production
安非他明类兴奋剂 amphetamine-type stimulants
安理会常任理事国 permanent member of the Security Council

桉 [ān]
〈名〉 eucalyptus
桉树 eucalyptus
桉油 volatile oil extracted from eucalyptus' leaves or twigs

氨 [ān]
〈名〉 ammonia; hydrogen nitride(NH_3)
氨化 ammoniation
氨基 amino; amino-group
氨气 ammonia
氨水 ammonia solution; ammonia (water); aqua ammonia
氨茶碱 aminophylline
氨基酸 amino acid
氨碱法 ammonia soda process
氨硫脲 thiacetazone
氨溶液 ammonia solution
氨苯磺胺 sulfanilamide

庵 [ān]
〈名〉 ①hut ②nunnery; Buddhist convent
庵堂 nunnery; Buddhist convent

谙 [ān]
〈动〉〈书〉know well; be well-versed
谙练 be conversant; be skilled; be proficient
谙熟 be proficient in; be conversant with

A

鹌 [ān]

鹌鹑 quail

鞍 名 saddle

鞍鼻 saddle nose
鞍部 a ridge connecting two higher elevations;saddle (of a hill or mountain)
鞍点 saddle point
鞍垫 panel
鞍环 handle;pommel
鞍架 saddle
鞍马 ①pommelled horse;side horse ②saddle and horse;life on horseback
鞍子 saddle
鞍点定理 saddle point theorem
鞍马劳顿 be fatigued by a long journey (*or* a battle);travel-worn;toot-wearly
鞍前马后 (of a faithful attendant) fuss around the master

ǎn (ㄢ)

俺 [ǎn]
代 I;we;my;our;me;us

埯 [ǎn]
I 名 hole to dibble Ⅱ 动 dig a hole to dibble seeds Ⅲ 量:一埯豆 a cluster of beam

铵 [ǎn]
名 ammonium

铵矾 ammonium alum

揞 [ǎn]
动 apply (medicinal powder to a wound)

àn (ㄢ)

岸 [àn]
I 名 land along a river,lake,sea,etc. Ⅱ 形 ①tall;high ②haughty;arrogant;proud;lofty

岸边 shoreside;side
岸线 waterfront
岸上交货价格 landed price

按 [àn]
I 动 ①press;push down ②leave aside;shelve ③restrain;control ④check;refer to ⑤ (of an editor or author) add a note or comment (to an article,report etc.) Ⅱ 介 according to;in accordance with

按成 according to percentage;proportionately
按键 button
按揭 mortgage
按例 as a rule
按脉 feel (*or* take) the pulse
按摩 massage
按捺 restrain;control
按钮 push button
按期 on schedule;on time
按时 on time;on schedule

按说 in the ordinary course of events;ordinarily;normally
按位 step-by-step;positional
按蚊 anopheles;malarial mosquito
按弦 stopping
按序 according to the order of sequence
按压 ①press down with one's hand ②suppress;restrain
按语 note (*or* comment) (by an author or editor on a piece of writing or certain parts of it)
按照 according to;in accordance with;in the light of;on the basis of
按比例 pro rata;in proportion
按理(说) according to principle or reason;in the ordinary course of events;normally
按摩床 massage couch
按摩法 massage method
按摩机 massager
按摩女 massage lady
按摩器 massager
按摩师 massager;massagist
按摩室 massage parlour
按摩术 lomilomi
按摩霜 massage cream
按兵不动 ①hold one's troops where they are;not throw one's troops into battle ②take no action;bide one's time
按部就班 follow the prescribed order;keep to conventional ways of doing things
按股分红 share profits according to contributions
按价收购 buy up in accordance with published rates
按件计工 reckon by the piece
按件生产 jobbing production
按揭贷款 mortgage loan
按揭购房 buy a house on mortgage;mortgage a house;housing mortgage
按劳分配 distribution according to work
按摩技师 chiropractor
按摩疗法 massotherapy
按摩手法 massage manipulation
按摩水床 massage water bed
按摩医师 massotherapist
按摩浴缸 massage bath tub
按摩诊所 massage clinic
按摩中心 massage centre
按捺不住 cannot control oneself;be unable to contain (one's anger) any longer
按年摊付 yearly installments
按钮控制 push-button control;dash control
按钮战争 push-button warfare
按图索骥 look for a steed with the aid of its picture—①try to find sth by following up a clue ②deal with (*or* handle) a matter in a mechanical way

按位操作 step-by-step operation
按位开关 bit switch
按需分配 distribution according to need
按质分等 grade according to the quality
按键式电话 keyphone, push-button phone; Touch-Tone
按摩推拿法 massage
按摩振动器 massager vibrator
按下葫芦浮起瓢 hardly has one gourd been pushed under water when another bobs up—solve one problem only to find another cropping up

案 [àn]
②　① old-fashioned wooden saucer for serving meals ②long narrow table; desk ③record; file ④plan submitted for consideration; proposal ⑤ incident; event ⑥law (*or* legal) case; case
案板 kneading (*or* chopping) board (usu. rectangular)
案秤 counter scale
案底 file (*or* record) of previous offences
案牍 official documents (*or* correspondence)
案犯 case criminal
案件 law case; case
案卷 records; files; archives
案例 case
案情 details of a case; case
案头 on the table or desk
案验 investigate the evidence of a case
案由 the main points (*or* a brief summary) of a case; brief
案值 property and money involved in a case
案子 ① long, narrow table (*or* long board) (propped up to serve as a table or counter) ②law case; case
案例分析 analysis of case
案例汇编 case reporter (*or* reports, book)
案例研究 case study
案情大白 details of a case have come out

暗 [àn]
Ⅰ 形 ①dark; dim; dull ② muddled; confused; hazy; unclear; vague ③ hidden; secret　Ⅱ 副 secretly　Ⅲ 名 dark
暗暗 secretly; inwardly; to oneself
暗坝 underwater dam
暗堡 bunker
暗补 invisible (*or* hidden) subsidy
暗藏 hide; conceal
暗层 blindstory
暗娼 an underground prostitute
暗嘲 laugh in secret; ridicule
暗潮 undercurrent
暗处 ①a dark place ②a secret place; a covert place; cover; obscure corner
暗袋 camera bag (for changing film)
暗淡 dim; faint; dismal; gloomy

暗道 blind pass; covered way; postern
暗房 darkroom
暗沟 underground drainage ditch; underground drain
暗管 concealed piping; covered conduit
暗害 ①kill secretly ②stab in the back
暗含 imply
暗号 a secret signal (*or* sign); countersign; watchword
暗合 be in complete agreement without prior consultation; (happen to) coincide
暗河 underground river
暗盒 magazine; cassette; holder
暗红 dark red
暗湖 under current
暗火 fire without flame; smouldering fire
暗疾 a disease one is ashamed of; unmentionable disease
暗键 sunk key
暗箭 an arrow shot from hiding—an attack by a hidden enemy; stab in the back
暗礁 ①submerged reef (*or* rock) ②latent obstacle
暗井 winze
暗亏 hidden loss
暗里 in the dark; on the sly
暗恋 love sb in one's heart
暗流 undercurrent
暗盘 secretly negotiated price
暗泣 ① weep without sound ② weep behind others' backs
暗器 hidden weapon (as darts hidden inside sleeves)
暗青 dull black
暗弱 ① (of light) dim; faint ② stupid and weak
暗杀 assassinate
暗沙 shoal
暗伤 ①internal (*or* invisible) injury ②internal (*or* invisible) damage; dark burn
暗哨 secret sentry; hidden sentry duty
暗射 insinuate
暗示 ① drop a hint; hint; suggest ② suggestion; intimation; insinuation
暗事 clandestine (*or* illicit) action
暗室 darkroom
暗算 plot against
暗榫 blind mortise; dowel
暗锁 built-in lock
暗滩 hidden shoal
暗探 secret agent; spy
暗贴 invisible subsidy
暗喜 feel pleased but not show it
暗匣 camera obscura
暗下 on the sly; surreptitiously
暗线 buried wiring; dark lane; hidden conductor

暗箱 camera bellows;camera obscura
暗想 muse;ponder;turn over in one's mind
暗销 dowel
暗笑 laugh in one's sleeve;snigger;snicker
暗影 ①shadow ②umbra
暗语 code word
暗喻 metaphor
暗指 ①insinuation;hint at ②infer
暗中 ① in the dark ② in secret;on the sly;
　　stealthily;surreptitiously
暗转 blackout (in the middle of a scene or act
　　to indicate either a change in time,or,with
　　a quick change of setting, a change in
　　place)
暗自 inwardly;to oneself;secretly
暗灰色 dull grey
暗记儿 secret mark
暗间儿 inner room
暗扣儿 snap fastener
暗码锁 combination lock
暗门子 unlicensed whore
暗适应 dark adaptation
暗物质 dark matter
暗地(里) secretly;inwardly;on the sly
暗渡陈仓 do one thing under cover of another
暗访民情 make secret inquires into the condi-
　　tion of the people
暗箭难防 hidden arrows are difficult to guard
暗箭伤人 stab sb in the back;injure sb by un-
　　derhand means
暗送秋波 make eyes at sb;give sb the glad
　　eye;ogle;make secret overtures to sb
暗无天日 complete darkness—total absence of
　　justice
暗线光谱 dark-line spectrum
暗箱操作 black case work;do sth on the sly
暗中摸索 grope in the dark; search about
　　blindly
暗中行贿 cross sb's hand with silver
暗自发笑 laugh in one's sleeve;give a snicker
　　over sth (*or* at sb)
暗自庆幸 congratulate oneself;consider one-
　　self lucky
暗示教学法 suggestive teaching method

黯 [àn]
　形 dim;obscure;gloomy
黯淡 dim;faint
黯黑 ①swarthy ②dim;gloomy
黯然 ①dark and dim-looking ②dejected;low-
　　spirited;downcast;gloomy
黯然神伤 feel dejected (*or* depressed)
黯然失色 be cast into the shade;be overshad-
　　owed; be eclipsed; become insignificant in
　　comparison

āng（尢）

肮 [āng]

肮脏 ①dirty;filthy ②vile;mean;foul;dirty
肮脏外交 dirty diplomacy

áng（尢）

昂 [áng]
　Ⅰ 动 hold (one's head) high Ⅱ 形 high;
soaring;expensive
昂昂 high-spirited;brave-looking
昂奋 in high spirits;buoyant;be full of zest
昂贵 expensive;costly
昂然 chin up and chest out;upright and una-
　　fraid
昂首 hold one's head high
昂扬 high-spirited
昂首阔步 stride along with one's chin up;
　　stride proudly ahead
昂首挺胸 square one's shoulders and throw
　　back one's head

àng（尢）

盎 [àng]
　Ⅰ 名 ancient vessel with a big belly and a
small mouth Ⅱ 形 vigorous;full of life
盎然 abundant;full;exuberant
盎司 ounce

āo（幺）

凹 [āo]
　形 concave;hollow;sunken;dented ➡wā
凹岸 concave bank
凹版 intaglio;gravure
凹槽 beard;fillister
凹地 concave ground;depression
凹度 concavity
凹进 cave in
凹面 camber concave;concave surface
凹凸 concave-convex
凹下 depress
凹陷 cave in;sink
凹字 characters cut in bas-relief
凹版纸 plate paper
凹面镜 concave mirror
凹透镜 concave lens
凹版印刷 intaglio (*or* gravure) printing
凹版制版 gravure plate-making
凹凸不平 full of bumps and holes;uneven
凹凸轧花 embossing
凹凸印刷 embossing;die stamping
凹纹轮胎 well base tyre
凹版印刷机 intaglio (*or* gravure) press
凹凸印刷机 embossing (*or* die stamping)
　　press

A

熬 [áo]
〔动〕cook in water;boil ➡áo

áo (ㄠ)

敖 [áo]

敖包 *aobao*,pile of stones,earth or grass used by Mongolians as a sign for road or boundary

遨 [áo]
〔动〕stroll;saunter
遨游 go on a pleasure tour;travel;roam

嗷 [áo]
嗷嗷 sound of crying (of certain birds or animals,or of human beings in pain or suffering)
嗷嗷待哺 cry piteously for food

廒 [áo]
〔名〕storehouse for grain,etc.;granary;barn

獒 [áo]
〔名〕mastiff

熬 [áo]
〔动〕①cook into gruel,gravy or thick soup;boil;stew ②decoct sth by boiling;boil down ③endure (pain or a hard life) ➡āo
熬煎 suffering;torment;torture
熬心 vexed;upset;depressed
熬夜 stay up late (*or* all night)
熬不过 be unable to sustain;be unable to endure
熬出头 have gone through all sorts of ordeal
熬头儿 hope for a better life after years of suffering;good days to look forward to
熬更守夜 keep night-long vigil

螯 [áo]
〔名〕chela;pincers (of crustaceans)

翱 [áo]
〔动〕take wing
翱翔 ①hover;soar ②soaring
翱翔机 sailplane

鳌 [áo]
〔名〕huge legendary sea-turtle

鏖 [áo]
〔动〕engage in fierce battle
鏖战 fight hard;engage in fierce battle

ǎo (ㄠ)

拗 [ǎo]
〔动〕bend;twist and break ➡ào;niù

袄 [ǎo]
〔名〕short Chinese-style coat or jacket

媪 [ǎo]
〔名〕old woman

ào (ㄠ)

坳 [ào]
〔名〕depression in a mountain range

拗 [ào]
〔形〕①hard to read ②disobedient;intractable;refractory ➡ǎo;niù
拗口 hard to pronounce (esp. rapidly)
拗口令 tongue twister

傲 [ào]
Ⅰ〔形〕proud;unyielding;haughty;arrogant
Ⅱ〔动〕refuse to yield to;brave;defy
傲岸〈书〉proud;haughty
傲骨 unbending backbone—lofty and unyielding character
傲慢 arrogant;haughty;overbearing
傲气 ①air of arrogance;haughtiness ②arrogant;haughty
傲然 lofty and proud-looking;unyielding
傲视 regard with disdain;turn up one's nose at;show disdain for
傲岸不群 haughty and standoffish;proud and aloof
傲慢无礼 insolent and rude;disrespectful

奥 [ào]
Ⅰ〔形〕profound;abstruse;difficult to comprehend Ⅱ〔名〕①southwest corner of a house;innermost recess of a building ②(short for 奥地利) Austria ③(short for 奥斯特) Oe
奥纶 orlon
奥秘 profound mystery
奥妙 profoundity and subtlety
奥赛 International Discipline Olympiad
奥校 training course for discipline Olympiad contestants
奥氏体 austenite
奥斯特 oersted (Oe)
奥陶纪 the Ordovician Period
奥委会 Olympic Committee
奥运村 Olympic Village
奥运会 Olympic Games
奥匈帝国 Austro-Hungary Empire
奥运圣火 the Olympic holy flame
奥姆真理教 Aum Shinrikyo Sect
奥斯曼帝国 the Ottoman Empire
奥运会标志 Olympic Games logo
奥斯卡金像奖 Oscar (*or* the Academy Award)
奥运会吉祥物 mascot of the Olympic Games
奥运火炬传递 Olympic torch relay
奥运实况转播 telecast live on TV for the Olympic Games
奥林匹克运动会 Olympic Games

骜 [ào]
Ⅰ〔名〕fine horse;steed Ⅱ〔形〕arrogant;haughty

澳 [ào]

澳抗 Australia antigen; hepatitis-associated antigen (HAA)
澳门币 Macao pataca
澳人治澳 Macao people manage all of Macao's affairs.
澳门特别行政区 the Macao Special Administrative Region
澳门特别行政区基本法 Basic Law of the Macao Special Administrative Region

懊 [ào]
I 形 regretful; remorseful; annoyed; vexed
II 动 regret; repent
懊悔 feel remorse; repent; regret
懊恼 be annoyed, vexed or upset; fret
懊丧 feel dejected (or depressed)

bā （ㄅㄚ）

八 [bā]
〈数〉eight
八成 ①eighty percent ②most probably；most likely
八度 octave
八方 eight points of the compass；all directions
八股 ①eight-part essay ②stereotyped writing
八卦 the Eight Trigrams；interfering busybody
八角 ①anise；star anise ②aniseed ③octagonal
八开 octavo；8vo
八旗 the "Eight Banners"
八折 20 per cent discount
八珍 eight delicacies
八字 Eight Characters，used in fortune-telling
八宝菜 eight-treasure pickles；assorted soy-sauce pickles
八宝饭 eight-treasure rice pudding
八宝粥 eight-treasure congee
八辈子 of long standing；of the worst kind
八倍体 octoploid
八次方 eight power
八哥儿 crested myna
八级工 eight-grade worker（highest on the eightgrade wage scale）；top-grade worker
八角枫 alangium
八角帽 octagonal cap
八角形 octagon
八开本 octavo
八路军 the Eighth Route Army
八仙桌 Eight Immortals table—an old-fashioned square table for eight people
八音盒 music box；musical box
八月节 the Mid-Autumn Festival（the 15th day of the 8th lunar month）
八字胡 forked beard
八字脚 splayfoot
八字眉 slanted eyebrows

八端网络 octopole
八方呼应 responses from every direction；co-operation from all
八分音符 quaver；eighth note
八国联军 the Eight-Power Allied Forces
八进位制 octal（number）system
八面玲珑 be smooth and slick（in establishing social relations）；make oneself pleasant to people all around
八面威风 aura of awesome might；commanding presence
八旗子弟 ① descendants of the privileged families ②profligate children of privileged families
八人赛艇 octuple scull shell
八字贴儿 a card with the horoscope of a boy or girl sent as a proposal for betrothal
八九不离十 most correct；about right；pretty close；very near
八分之一决赛 eighth-finals
八竿子打不着 far-fetched；unrelated
八小时工作制 eight-hour day
八色联合印花机 8-colour combined printing machine
八字还没一撇儿 things aren't even starting to take shape yet；there's not the slightest sign of success（or of anything happening）yet
八仙过海,各显神通 like the Eight Immortals crossing the sea，each one showing his or her special prowess

巴 [bā]
Ⅰ〈动〉①long for；await anxiously for；hope earnestly ②cling to ③stick to ④〈方〉open；spread；split；crack；break up ⑤be close to；be next to Ⅱ〈名〉①crust ②bus
巴斗 round-bottomed basket
巴豆 （purging）croton
巴结 fawn on；curry favour with；make up to
巴士 bus（a transliteration）
巴望 ①look forward to；hope in real earnesty ②good prospects

巴掌 palm;hand
巴比伦 Babylon
巴不得 be only too anxious (to do sth);eagerly look forward to;earnestly wish;be itching to do sth
巴豆霜 defatted croton seed powder
巴儿狗 pekingese;sycophant;toady
巴黎绿 Paris green
巴高枝儿 ①play up to people of power and influence ②marry above one's station
巴黎公社 Paris Commune
巴士底狱 the Bastille
巴比特合金 babbitt (metal)
巴尔干半岛 the Balkan Peninsula
巴尔干国家 Balkan states;the Balkans
巴拿马运河 the Panama Canal
巴勒斯坦解放组织 the Palestine Liberation Organization (PLO)

扒 [bā]
动 ①hold on to;stick to;cling to ②dig up;rake;pull down ③push aside ④strip off;take off;peel off;skin ➡ pá
扒车 climb onto a slow-going train,etc.
扒钉 cramp
扒分 work in spare time for money
扒拉 push lightly
扒皮 exploit;take advantage of

芭 [bā]
名 ①fragrant plant;rush ②flower
芭蕉 plantain;Chinese banana
芭蕉扇 palm leaf fan
芭蕾舞 ballet
芭比娃娃 barbie girl
芭蕾舞剧 ballet
芭蕾舞迷 balletomane
芭蕾舞裙 tutu
芭蕾舞团 ballet ensemble
芭蕾舞设计 choreography
芭蕾舞男演员 ballet dancer
芭蕾舞女演员 ballerina

吧 [bā]
Ⅰ 动 〈方〉draw on (or pull at) one's pipe,etc. Ⅱ 名 bar ➡ ba
吧嗒 [bādā] patter;splatter
吧嗒 [bādā] ①smack one's lips ②pull at (a pipe,etc.)
吧娘 female owner of a bar
吧女 barmaid;bar girl
吧台 bar counter

疤 [bā]
名 ①scar;cicatrix ②a scar-like mark
疤痕 scar;sore;spot;pit
疤瘌 scar;sore;spot;pit

笆 [bā]
名 basketry;basket
笆斗 round-bottomed basket
笆篓 basket
笆篱子 prison;gaol

粑 [bā]
名 cake
粑粑 griddle cake

bá（ㄅㄚˊ）

拔 [bá]
动 ①pluck;draw ②draw;suck out ③stand out among;surpass ④choose;select;pick;promote ⑤capture;seize ⑥〈方〉cool in water
拔除 pull out;remove
拔萃 stand out from one's fellows;be out of the common run
拔毒 draw out pus (by applying a plaster to the affected part);draw out poison
拔高 ①raise ②deliberately boost (sb or sth);play up
拔河 tug-of-war
拔火 draw the fire
拔节 jointing
拔锚 weigh anchor
拔取 choose;select;drawing off
拔染 discharge
拔丝 ①wire drawing ②candied floss
拔腿 ①lift the foot (and begin to run,chase,etc.);take (or make) a step ②leave (one's work);get away;free oneself
拔销 pull pin
拔牙 extract teeth;put out a tooth
拔秧 pull up seedlings (for transplanting)
拔营 strike camp
拔钉锤 claw hammer
拔份儿 ①show off one's strength or power ②dominate;act violently
拔罐子 cupping
拔尖儿 ① tiptop; top-notch; outstanding ② push oneself forward;be pushy
拔刀相助 draw one's sword to help;unsheathe one's sword and go to the rescue of another (for the sake of justice);take up the cudgels against an injustice
拔火罐儿 detachable stove chimney
拔尖人才 tiptop talent
拔苗助长 try to help the shoots grow by pulling them upward—spoil things by excessive enthusiasm

跋 [bá]
Ⅰ 动 cross mountains Ⅱ 名 postscript (to a book,article,painting,etc.,mostly as appraisal,commentary or textual criticism)
跋扈 domineering;bossy
跋涉 trudge;trek
跋文 postscript (to a book)
跋语 postscript
跋山涉水 scale mountains and ford streams—travel afar under difficult conditions

bǎ（ㄅㄚˇ）

把 [bǎ]
Ⅰ〔动〕①hold；grip；grasp；handle ②control；monopolize；dominate ③guard；watch；keep ④keep close to；near；lean on；lean against ⑤hold sth together；lock；chain；attach closely ⑥hold Ⅱ〔名〕①handle ②bundle；bunch：草把 bundle of straw Ⅲ〔量〕①a；a pair of：一把茶壶 a teapot/一把雨伞 an umbrella ②a bundle；a handful of：一把稻草 a bundle of rice straw/一把雪 a handful of snow ③a bunch of：一把菠菜 a bunch of spinach/一把筷子 a bunch of chopsticks ④（用于抽象事物）：一把劲儿 great strength/努把力 make an effort；step up one's efforts ⑤（用于同手有关的动作）：洗一把脸 wash one's face ⑥（用于同手的动作有关的事物）：拉他一把 to pull him with a jerk ⑦（引申用法）：过把瘾 to one's heart's content Ⅳ〔介〕①（宾语是后面动词的受事者，表示处置）：把头一扭 toss one's head；turn around/我把那件事忘了。I've forgotten it. ②（后面是动词"忙，累，急，气"等并带有表示结果的补语，表示致使）：把我乐坏了。It excited me very much（or I'm overwhelmed with joy）./他说了个笑话，把我肚子都笑疼了。He told a joke, and I laughed until my side ached. ③（宾语是后面动词的施事者，表示不如意的事）：正在比赛的节骨眼上偏偏把我们队的主教练累病了。Of all people the main trainer of our team fell ill at this juncture of competition. Ⅴ〔动〕about；or so；some；over；around：个把月 a month or so；about a month；over a month；more than a month/丈把高 over 10 feet high ➡bà

把柄 handle

把持 ①dominate；monopolize ②control（one's feelings，etc.）

把舵 hold the rudder；hold（or take，be at）the helm；steer

把风 keep watch；be on the lookout

把关 ①guard a pass ②check on

把酒 ①raise one's wine cup ②fill a wine cup for sb

把脉 feel the pulse

把门 guard a gate

把式 ① wushu；martial arts ②person skilled in wushu；person skilled in a trade ③skill；technique

把守 guard

把手 ① shake hands ② handle；grip；knob；holder

把头 labour contractor；gangmaster

把稳 trustworthy；dependable

把握 ① hold；grasp；seize ② assurance；certainty

把戏 ① acrobatics；jugglery ② cheap trick；game

把兄弟 sworn brothers

把水搅浑 muddy the water—create confusion

钯 [bǎ]
〔名〕palladium（Pd）

靶 [bǎ]
〔名〕①target ②bridle；halter；reins

靶场 shooting range；range

靶船 target ship

靶壕 marking pit；pit

靶机 target drone

靶心 centre of a target；bull's-eye

靶纸 target sheet

靶子 target

靶理论 target theory

bà（ㄅㄚˋ）

坝 [bà]
〔名〕①dam ②dyke；embankment ③sandbar；sandbank；shoal ④flatland；plain

坝基 foundation of a dyke

坝面 dam face

坝塘 small reservoir in hill areas

坝田 flat farmland at the foot of a mountain

坝子 flatland（in southwestern China）

把 [bà]
〔名〕①grip；handle ②stem；peduncle；petiole ➡bǎ

把子 handle

弝 [bà]
〔名〕① middle of a bow（for the hand to grasp）②handle

爸 [bà]
〔名〕pa；dad；father

爸爸 papa；dad；father

耙 [bà]
Ⅰ〔名〕harrow Ⅱ〔动〕harrow；draw a harrow over（a field）➡pá

罢 [bà]
〔动〕①stop；cease ②dismiss；relieve；remove from office ③complete；finish ④let it be（or pass）

罢黜 ①dismiss from office ②ban；reject

罢工 strike；go on strike

罢官 dismiss from office

罢教 teachers' strike

罢课 students' strike

罢了 [bàle] that's all；nothing else

罢了 [bàliǎo] let it pass；be done with it

罢免 recall；remove from office

罢市 shopkeepers' strike；merchants' strike

罢手 give up

罢休 give up；let the matter drop

罢职 dismiss from office；remove from a position

罢免权 right of recall；recall

霸 [bà]　I 名 ①chief of feudal princes；overlord ② tyrant；despot；bully ③ hegemonistic power； hegemony Ⅱ 动 dominate；lord it over

霸道 [bàdào] ①rule by force ②overbearing；high-handed；unreasonable

霸道 [bàdao]（of liquor, medicine, etc.） strong，potent

霸气 arrogant

霸权 hegemony；supremacy

霸王 overlord；despot

霸业 hegemonist achievements；hegemony

霸占 forcibly occupy；seize；usurp

霸主 ①powerful leader of feudal lords ②overlord

霸王鞭 ①rattle stick used in folk dancing ② rattle stick dance

霸权主义 hegemonism

ba （·ㄅㄚ）

巴 [ba]

◇干巴 dried up；wizened；shrivelled

结巴 ①stammer；stutter ②stammerer；stutterer

尾巴 ①tail ②tail-like part ③servile adherent

下巴 ①lower jaw ②chin

哑巴 dumb person；mute

盐巴 salt；common（or table）salt

嘴巴 mouth

吧 [ba]　I 助 ①（*used at the end of a sentence to indicate agreement or approval*）：好吧 OK ②（*used at the end of a sentence to indicate consultation, suggestion, request, or command*）：快点儿吧。 Hurry up, will you？/去吧！ Well, go！③（*used at the end of a sentence to indicate doubt or surmise*）：你就是李先生吧？ You are Mr. Li, I suppose. ④（*used at the end of a sentence to indicate probability*）：大概是昨天吧。 Perhaps yesterday. ⑤（*used in a sentence to indicate a pause after suppositions, concessions, or conditions*）：温度高了吧，不行；温度低了吧，也不行。 If the temperature is too high or too low，it won't grow properly. Ⅱ 图 cracking：吧的一声，树枝断了 。 The twig broke off with a snapping sound. ➡bā

bāi （ㄅㄞ）

掰 [bāi]　动 ①break off with the fingers and thumb ②break up（relationship）；sever；fall apart；fall out ③analyse；study；examine

掰味 analyse；study；examine

掰腕子 hand wrestling

bái （ㄅㄞ）

白 [bái]　I 形 ①white ②bright；light ③clear ④ pure；plain；blank；unmixed ⑤White（as a symbol of counter-revolution or unsound political orientation）⑥funeral ⑦（of Chinese characters） wrongly written or mispronounced Ⅱ 副 ①in vain；for nothing ②free of charge；gratis：白吃 get a free meal Ⅲ 动 ① give a supercilious or unfriendly look ②state； explain；clear up Ⅳ 名 ①spoken part（in opera，etc.）②dialect ③vernacular；spoken language

白白 in vain；to no purpose；for nothing

白班 day shift

白醭 mould（on the surface of vinegar, soy sauce，etc.）

白边 white edge

白布 plain white cloth；calico

白菜 Chinese cabbage

白痴 ①idiocy ②idiot；oaf

白炽 white heat；incandescence

白醋 light-coloured vinegar

白搭 have no use；no good

白带 leucorrhoea；whites

白道 moon's path

白度 degree of whiteness

白丁 commoner；common man；illiterate person

白垩 chalk（a type of limestone）

白发 white hair；grey hair

白矾 alum

白匪 White bandit；White soldier

白费 waste

白宫 the White House

白果 ginkgo；gingko

白鹤 white crane

白喉 diphtheria

白狐 arctic fox

白话 [báihuà] vernacular

白话 [báihua] talk big；talk nonsense；be blah-blah；make empty talk

白桦 white birch

白芨 the tuber of hyacinth bletilla

白金 platinum

白净 （of skin）fair and clear

白酒 spirit；white spirit

白卷 a blank examination paper；an examination paper unanswered

白军 White Army

白蜡 white wax；insect wax

白痢 ①dysentery characterized by white mucous stool ②husbandry white diarrhoea

白鲢 silver carp

白脸 white face，face painting in Beijing oper-

a,etc.,traditionally for the villain
白磷 white phosphorus
白蛉 sand fly
白领 white-collar
白鹭 egret
白鹿 white deer
白茅 cogongrass
白煤 ①anthracite;hard coal ②white coal;waterpower
白米 (polished) rice
白面 wheat flour;flour
白描 ① line drawing in traditional ink and brush style ②simple,straightforward style of writing
白砒 white arsenic;arsenic trioxide
白热 white heat;incandescence
白人 white person
白刃 naked sword
白扔 spend without proper return;waste
白肉 plain boiled pork
白色 ①white (colour) ②White (as a symbol of reaction)
白芍 root of herbaceous peony
白食 free food;free meal
白事 funeral affairs;funeral
白首 hoary head;old age
白薯 sweet potato
白水 ①plain boiled water ②clean water
白糖 (refined) white sugar
白陶 white pottery
白体 lean type
白天 daytime;day
白条 ①unofficial receipt (in financial transactions);IOU note ②slaughtered poultry or animal (stripped of hairs or feathers, or with head,feet and entrails removed)
白铁 galvanized iron
白铜 copper-nickel alloy
白头 ① hoary head; old age ② unsigned; anonymous
白兔 white rabbit
白皙 (of skin) fair and clear
白鲜 shaggy-fruited dittany
白鹇 silver pheasant
白相 〈方〉play
白熊 polar bear;white bear
白絮 ①white cotton (fibre) ②cotton fluff—snowflake
白鳕 white hake
白鲟 Chinese paddlefish
白眼 supercilious look
白杨 white poplar
白页 white page
白夜 white night
白蚁 termite;white ant
白银 silver
白鱼 whitefish

白芋 taro
白种 white race
白昼 daytime;day
白字 incorrectly written or mispronounced character
白矮星 white dwarf stars
白报纸 newsprint
白大褂 white gown (worn by medical personnel)
白蛋白 albumin
白癜风 vitiligo
白垩纪 the Cretaceous Period
白粉病 powdery mildew
白姑鱼 white Chinese croaker
白骨精 ①White Bone Demon ②sinister and ruthless woman
白果松 lacebark pine
白化病 albinism
白话诗 free verse written in the vernacular
白话文 writings in the vernacular
白暨豚 flag dolphin
白僵蚕 the larva of a silkworm with batrytis
白菊花 feverfew
白开水 plain boiled water
白口铁 white iron
白蜡虫 wax insect
白兰地 brandy
白莲教 White Lotus Society
白蛉热 sandfly fever
白榴石 leucite (a mineral)
白茫茫 a vast expanse of whiteness
白茅根 cogongrass rhizome
白毛风 snowstorm;blizzard
白棉纸 stencil tissue paper
白面儿 heroin
白名单 white list
白木耳 tremella;phytin
白内障 cataract
白皮书 white paper;white book
白皮松 lacebark pine
白啤酒 white beer
白屈菜 greater celandine
白热化 turn white-hot
白刃战 bayonet charge;hand-to-hand combat
白色体 leucoplast
白砂糖 refined white (granulated) sugar
白铁皮 tinplate;galvanized iron sheet
白头翁 ①Chinese bulbul ②the root of Chinese pulsatilla
白钨矿 scheelite
白细胞 white blood cell;leucocyte
白鲜皮 the root bark of shaggy-fruited dittany
白血病 leukaemia
白血球 white blood cell;leucocyte
白眼狼 ingrate;treacherous and ruthless person
白眼珠 white of the eye

白云母 muscovite；white mica（a mineral）
白云石 dolomite（a mineral）
白噪声 white noise
白璧微瑕 slight flaw in white jade—a minor blemish in a thing of beauty；a slight defect in a person of integrity
白璧无瑕 flawless white jade—impeccable moral integrity
白炽电灯 incandescent lamp
白费心机 scheme in vain；draw water with a sieve；make futile efforts
白黑分明 make a clear distinction between black and white（*or* right and wrong）
白驹过隙 a glimpse of a white colt flashing past a chink in a wall—fleeting passage of time
白领犯罪 white-collar crime
白领工人 white-collar worker
白领文化 white-collar culture
白马王子 prince riding a white horse—Prince Charming
白面书生 pale-faced scholar；pasty-faced bookworm ·
白葡萄酒 sherry
白日做梦 spin daydreams；indulge in wishful thinking；build castles in the air
白色恐怖 white terror
白色农业 white agriculture
白色人种 the white race
白色收入 white income
白色污染 white pollution；pollution caused by white plastic waste
白色消费 white consumption
白手起家 build up from nothing；start from scratch
白头偕老 reach old age together；live in conjugal bliss to a ripe old age；remain a devoted couple to the end of their lives；remain happily married to a ripe old age
白衣天使 nurse
白衣战士 warrior in white；medical worker
白纸黑字 （written）in black and white
白字连篇 reams of wrong characters；（of speech or writing）full of mispronounced or wrong words
白话文运动 the Vernacular Movement
白猫黑猫论 theory that it doesn't matter if a cat is black or white as long as it catches mice

bǎi（ㄅㄞ）

百 [bǎi]
Ⅰ 〔数〕 hundred：几百个人 several hundred people Ⅱ 〔形〕 all；numerous；all kinds of Ⅲ 〔副〕 very；always
百般 in a hundred and one ways；in every possible way；by every means
百倍 a hundredfold；a hundred times
百病 all kinds of diseases and ailments
百出 full of；innumerable
百合 lily
百花 all sorts of flowers
百货 general merchandise
百灵 lark
百年 ①a hundred years；a century ②lifetime
百十… a hundred or so
百万 million
百姓 common people
百叶 louver
百分比 percentage
百分点 percentage point
百分率 percentage；per cent；percentage point
百分制 hundred-mark system
百合病 lily disease
百花奖 Hundred-flowers Award
百家姓 the Book of（China's）Family Names
百老汇 Broadway
百里香 thyme
百忙中 in the thick of things；while fully engaged
百慕大 Bermuda
百日咳 whooping cough；pertussis
百事通 ①knowledgeable person ②know-all
百叶窗 shutter；blind；jalousie
百叶箱 thermometer screen
百子莲 African agapanthus
百般刁难 create obstructions of every description；put up innumerable obstacles；raise all manner of difficulties
百弊丛生 all kinds of corruptions creep in
百步穿杨 shoot an arrow through a willow leaf at a hundred paces；split a willow wand at a hundred paces；shoot with great precision
百川归海 all rivers flow to the sea—all things tend in one direction；everyone turns to sb for guidance
百端待举 A hundred things remain to be done；Numerous tasks wait to be undertaken.
百发百中 A hundred shots, a hundred bull's-eyes；Every shot hits the target；shoot with unfailing accuracy；be a crack shot
百废俱兴 All neglected tasks are being undertaken；All that was left undone is now being undertaken.
百分之百 hundred-percent；out and out；absolutely
百感交集 have mixed feelings；all sorts of feelings well up in one's heart
百花齐放 let a hundred flowers bloom—free development of different forms and styles in the arts
百花盛开 All flowers are in full bloom.
百花争妍 A hundred flowers contend in beau-

ty；The flowers are a riot of colour.
百货公司 department store
百货商店 general store；department store
百科全书 encyclopaedia
百孔千疮 riddled with gaping wounds；afflicted with all ills
百口难辩 difficult to get at the truth
百里挑一 one in a hundred；cream of the crop
百炼成钢 be tempered into steel
百米赛跑 100-metre dash
百慕大人 Bermudan
百年不遇 not seen once in a hundred years
百年大计 matter of fundamental importance for generations to come；project of vital and lasting importance；major project
百年树人 It takes a hundred years to make education bear fruit.
百年偕老 live together to be a hundred—be happily married and together reach an old age
百思不解 still puzzled after pondering a hundred times；remain perplexed despite much thought
百听不厌 worth hearing a hundred times
百万吨级 megaton
百万富翁 millionaire
百万雄师 a million bold warriors；a mighty army
百无禁忌 all taboos in abeyance
百无聊赖 bored to death；bored stiff；overcome with boredom
百无一失 no danger of anything going wrong；no risk at all；perfectly safe；surefire
百无一是 Absolutely nothing is correct.
百业凋敝 all business declining
百依百顺 docile and obedient；all obedience
百用不厌 never get tired of using；worth using a hundred times
百战百胜 fight a hundred battles，win a hundred victories—emerge victorious in every battle；be ever-victorious
百折不回 pushing forward despite repeated frustrations；advance bravely and never withdraw；keep on fighting in spite of all setbacks；be undaunted by repeated setbacks
百折不挠 keep on fighting in spite of all setbacks；be undaunted by repeated setbacks；be dauntless；be indomitable；be unrelenting
百慕大三角 Bermuda Triangle；Devil's Triangle
百周年纪念 centenary；centennial；centenary celebration；one hundredth anniversary
百动不如一静 To be still is effective.
百闻不如一见 It is better to see once than to hear a hundred times；Seeing for oneself is better than hearing from others.

百尺竿头，更进一步 make still further progress；further improve one's work
百花齐放，百家争鸣 let a hundred flowers blossom and a hundred schools of thought contend
百花齐放，推陈出新 let a hundred flowers blossom，weed through the old to bring forth the new
百问不厌，百拿不烦 patiently reply to customers' every question and be ready to show them the goods for the hundredth time；offer excellent service
百足之虫，死而不僵 A centipede does not topple over even when dead；A centipede dies but never falls down；Old institutions die hard.

伯 [bǎi]
名 uncle ➡bó

柏 [bǎi]
名 cypress；cedar；tree of cypress family ➡bó；bò
柏树 cypress
柏油 pitch；asphalt；bitumen
柏子仁 the seed of Oriental arborvitae

捭 [bǎi]
动 open；separate

摆 [bǎi]
Ⅰ 动 ①put；lay；place；set in order ②display；put on；assume；show off ③sway；swing；wave；wag ④set forth；state clearly；speak Ⅱ 名 ①pendulum ②lower hem（of a jacket，skirt or gown）
摆布 ①decorate；arrange ②order about；manipulate
摆动 swing；sway
摆渡 ①cross a river by boat；ferry ②ferryboat；ferry
摆放 lay；place；put in a certain place
摆好 enumerate sb's merits；commend；praise
摆件 pieces of furniture for display than for use
摆阔 parade one's wealth；be ostentatious and extravagant
摆轮 balance（of a watch or clock）；balance wheel
摆弄 ①move back and forth；fiddle with ②order about；manipulate
摆盘 balance（of a watch or clock）；balance wheel
摆平 ①be fair to；be impartial to ②punish；deal with
摆设[bǎishè] furnish and decorate（a room）
摆设[bǎi she] ①ornaments；decorations ②objects or articles merely for show
摆式 pendulum；pendulous
摆手 ①shake one's hand（in admonition or disapproval）②beckon；wave

摆脱 shake off; cast off; break away from; free (*or* extricate) oneself from
摆尾 wag the tail
摆针 pointer (on a meter, scales, etc.)
摆振 hunt; sway
摆钟 pendulum clock
摆轴 balance staff (of a balance wheel)
摆子 malaria
摆地摊 set up a temporary stall (*or* simply lay out various items on a newspaper, cloth, etc.) to sell on the street
摆动额 swing limit
摆架子 put on airs; give oneself airs
摆擂台 ① make open challenges to fights ② make challenges to a contest
摆矛盾 lay bare the contradictions
摆门面 put up a front; maintain an outward show; keep up appearances
摆谱儿 ① keep up appearances; show off ② put on airs; throw one's weight about
摆摊儿 set up a stall (on roadside or in a market)
摆摊子 ① set up a stall (on roadside or in a market) ② lay things out in preparation for work ③ maintain a large staff (*or* organization)
摆条件 lay down terms; offer conditions
摆威风 display power (*or* prestige); give oneself airs; put on airs
摆样子 do sth for show
摆荡吊环 swinging rings
摆动信贷 swing credit
摆动账户 swing account
摆老资格 strike the pose of an elder; flaunt one's seniority
摆龙门阵 chat; gossip; spin a yarn
摆迷魂阵 lay out a scheme to bewitch sb; set a trap
摆脱困境 extricate oneself from predicament
摆事实,讲道理 present the facts and reason things out

bài（ㄅㄞˋ）

败 [bài]
Ⅰ 动 ① be defeated; lose ② defeat; beat ③ fail ④ spoil; ruin ⑤ counteract; relieve; eliminate Ⅱ 形 decayed; withered
败北 suffer defeat; lose a battle
败笔 ① faulty stroke (in calligraphy or painting) ② faulty expression (in writing)
败兵 defeated army; army in flight; defeated troops
败毒 relieve internal heat (*or* fever)
败坏 ruin; corrupt; undermine
败火 relieve inflammation (*or* internal heat)
败绩 be utterly defeated; be routed

败家 dissipate a family fortune
败将 defeated general
败局 lost game; losing battle
败类 scum of a community; degenerate
败露 (of a plot, etc.) fall through and stand exposed
败落 decline (in wealth and position)
败诉 lose a lawsuit
败退 retreat in defeat
败胃 spoil one's appetite
败兴 have one's spirits dampened; feel disappointed; frustrated
败仗 lost battle; defeat
败阵 be defeated on the battlefield; be beaten in a contest
败家子 spendthrift; wastrel; prodigal
败血症 septicaemia
败兴而归 come back disappointed
败絮其中 Inside is the cotton waste; foul inside

拜 [bài]
动 ① do obeisance (to sb) ② extend greetings (on meeting people); congratulate ③ make a courtesy call; visit ④ entitle sb with ceremony ⑤ acknowledge sb as one's master, teacher, etc.; formally establish a relationship ⑥ (*used before some verbs to show respect*)
拜别 take leave of; bid farewell to
拜辞 take leave; say goodbye
拜倒 prostrate oneself; fall on one's knees; grovel
拜读 read with respect; have the pleasure of reading (an essay, etc.)
拜访 pay a visit; call on
拜佛 prostrate oneself before the image of Buddha; worship Buddha
拜服 greatly admire
拜会 pay an official call; call on
拜见 ① pay a formal visit; call to pay respects ② meet one's senior (*or* superior)
拜客 pay visits; make calls
拜领 accept with thanks
拜年 pay a New Year call; wish sb a Happy New Year
拜神 worship a deity
拜师 formally become a pupil to a master
拜寿 congratulate an elderly person on his birthday; offer birthday felicitations
拜帅 be appointed supreme commander
拜堂 (of bride and groom) make ceremonial obeisance—perform the marriage ceremony
拜托 request sb to do sth
拜相 be made chief minister by the emperor
拜谢 express one's sincere thanks; humbly thank
拜谒 ① pay a formal visit; call to pay respects ② pay homage (at a monument, mausole-

um,etc.)
拜把子 become sworn brothers
拜火教 Zoroastrianism;Mazdaism
拜街坊 visit one's neighbours (on moving into a neighbourhood)
拜物教 fetishism
拜祖先 ancestor worship
拜金主义 money worship

稗 [bài] Ⅰ 名 barnyard grass Ⅱ 形 insignificant;unofficial
稗子 barnyard grass;barnyard millet
稗官野史 books of anecdotes

bān（ㄅㄢ）

扳 [bān] 动 ①pull;turn ②win back what has been lost
扳机 trigger
扳平 equalize the score;draw a match
扳手 ①spanner;wrench ②lever (on a machine)
扳子 spanner;wrench
扳道员 pointsman;switchman
扳不倒儿 tumbler;roly-poly
扳成平局 equalize the score;manage to draw a match
扳手劲儿 have a wrist-wrestling (or arm-wrestling) contest

攽 [bān] 动 issue;distribute

班 [bān] Ⅰ 名 ①class;grade;team ②shift;duty ③squad ④troupe;theatrical company Ⅱ 量 (a) gathering;staff;troop;group;class：一班青年人 a gathering of young people/一班飞机 an airplane flight Ⅲ 形 regularly-run;scheduled Ⅳ 动 (of troops) move;redeploy
班车 regular bus (service)
班次 ①order of classes (or grades) at school ②number of runs (or flights)
班底 ① ordinary members of a theatrical troupe ②core members of an organization
班房 jail
班费 activities fee (for school classes)
班会 class meeting (in schools)
班机 airliner;regular air service
班级 classes and grades in school
班轮 regular passenger (or cargo) ship;regular steamship service
班期 schedule
班师 withdraw troops from the front;return after victory
班长 ① class monitor ② squad leader ③ (work) team leader
班子 ①theatrical troupe ②organized group
班组 teams and groups;working team (or group)

班主任 teacher in charge of a class;class adviser
班禅喇嘛 the Panchen Lama
班门弄斧 show off one's skill with the axe before Lu Ban,the master carpenter—display one's slight skill before an expert

般 [bān] Ⅰ 名 sort;kind;way Ⅱ 副 as,like,alike in ➡bō;pán
般配 be well matched (as in marriage);match each other

颁 [bān] 动 promulgate;issue;publish
颁布 promulgate;issue;publish
颁发 ①issue;promulgate ②award
颁奖 give out an award
颁行 issue for enforcement
颁令嘉奖 issue an order of commendation

斑 [bān] Ⅰ 名 spot;speck;speckle;stripe Ⅱ 形 spotted;striped
斑白 grey;grizzled
斑斑 full of stains (or spots)
斑鬓 greying hair on the temples
斑点 spot;stain;speckle
斑痕 mark;trace
斑鸠 turtledove
斑斓 gorgeous;bright-coloured;multi-coloured
斑羚 goral
斑驴 zebrass
斑马 zebra
斑猫 tabby
斑蝥 Chinese blister beetle;cantharides
斑纹 stripe;streak
斑鹟 spotted flycatcher
斑岩 porphyry
斑疹 macula
斑竹 mottled bamboo
斑马线 zebra crossing
斑铜矿 bornite
斑驳陆离 of many colours;many-hued
斑翅山鹑 partridge
斑疹伤寒 typhus

搬 [bān] 动 ①move;carry;remove (usu. sth heavy or big) ②move (house);migrate ③apply indiscriminately;copy mechanically
搬兵 call in reinforcements;ask for help
搬家 ①move (house) ②remove;move
搬弄 ① move sth about;fiddle with ② show off;display ③instigate;sow discord
搬迁 move;transfer;remove
搬运 carry;transport
搬迁户 relocated unit (or household)
搬家公司 home-moving company
搬弄是非 sow discord;tell tales;make mis-

chief

搬起石头砸自己的脚 lift a rock only to drop it on one's own feet

瘢 [bǎn] 名 scar
瘢痕 scar

bǎn（ㄅㄢˇ）

坂 [bǎn] 名 slope

板 [bǎn] Ⅰ 名 ①board；plank；plate ②blackboard ③clappers ④accented beat（in music or traditional Chinese opera）；time；measure ⑤shutter；door plank Ⅱ 形 ①stiff；rigid；unnatural ②hard like a plate or plank Ⅲ 动 put on a grave expression；look stern；look grave

板壁 wooden partition
板锉 flat file
板凳 wooden bench（or stool）
板斧 broad axe
板钢 slab
板鼓 a small drum for marking time
板规 plate gauge
板胡 a bowed stringed instrument with a thin wooden soundboard
板结 harden
板锯 hand plate saw
板块 plate；sector
板栗 Chinese chestnut
板坯 slab；plaque
板皮 slab
板球 ①cricket ②cricket ball
板书 ①write on the blackboard ②words written on the blackboard；blackboard writing
板刷 scrubbing brush
板条 lath
板鸭 pressed（or dried）salted duck
板牙 ①front tooth；incisor ②molar ③screw die；threading die
板烟 plug（of tobacco）
板岩 slate
板眼 ①accented and unaccented beats in traditional Chinese music；measure；time ②orderliness；system；method
板油 leaf fat；leaf lard
板纸 paperboard；board
板滞 stiff；dull
板桩 sheet pile
板子 ①board；plank ②bamboo（or birch）for corporal punishment
板擦儿 blackboard eraser
板儿车 a flatbed cart
板儿寸 bush-top
板儿爷 pedicab man
板蓝根 radix isatidis；isatis root
板梁桥 plate girder bridge

板条箱 crate
板牙架 stock；die handle；holder for die
板羽球 ①battledore and shuttlecock ②shuttlecock
板牙扳手 stock and die
板儿板儿的 No problem.
板块构造(学) platetectonics

版 [bǎn] 名 ①printing plate；block ②edition ③page（of a newspaper）④board frame for making an earthen wall

版本 edition（as in different forms，bindings，etc. or by different publishers）
版次 the order in which editions are printed
版画 engraving；etching
版刻 carving；engraving
版权 copyright
版式 format
版税 royalty（on books）
版图 domain；territory
版权法 copyright law（or act）
版权页 copyright page；colophon
版权保护 copyright protection
版权收入 income from royalties
版权诉讼 copyright law suit
版权所有 all rights reserved

钣 [bǎn] 名 metal plate

舨 [bǎn]
◇舢舨 dingey；pulling-boat

bàn（ㄅㄢˋ）

办 [bàn] 动 ①do；handle；manage；attend to ②set up；carry out；run ③purchase；get sth ready；penalize ④punish（by law）；bring（an offender）to justice；penalize

办案 ①handle a legal case ②apprehend（a criminal）
办报 run a newspaper
办法 way；means；measure
办公 handle official business；work（usu. in an office）
办理 handle；conduct；transact
办事 handle affairs；work
办学 run a school
办罪 punish sb（for a crime）
办公费 administrative expenses
办公室 office
办公厅 general office
办公桌 desk；bureau
办教育 undertake educational work
办酒席 prepare a feast；cater
办实事 do the actual work；put into actual practice
办事处 office；agency

办事员 office worker
办事组 administrative group
办喜事 manage a wedding;prepare for a happy occasion
办事机构 administrative body;working body
办事章程 by-law
办福利事业 do welfare work
办公室终端 office terminal
办公自动化 office automation (OA)
办公室信息系统 office information system
办公制度公开化 open up office system
办公自动化系统 office automation system

半 [bàn]
Ⅰ 图 ①half;semi- ②in the middle;halfway ③very little;the least bit;不值半文钱 not worth a farthing Ⅱ 副 partly;about half;窗户半开着。The window is half open.
半百 fifty
半边 half of sth;one side of sth
半场 ①half of a game (*or* contest) ②half-court
半岛 peninsula
半点 the least bit
半蹲 parallel squat;half kneebend
半费 half the fee
半价 half price
半截 half (a section)
半径 radius
半拉 half
半路 halfway;midway;on the way
半票 half-price ticket;half fare
半旗 half-mast
半球 hemisphere
半圈 half-turn;semicycle
半生 half a lifetime
半数 half the number;half
半死 half-dead
半天 ① half of the day ②long time;quite a while
半途 halfway;midway
半夏 the tuber of pinellia
半夜 midnight;in the middle of the night
半音 semitone
半影 penumbra
半圆 semicircle
半月 half-moon
半载 half load
半包装 semi-packed
半辈子 half a lifetime
半闭合 semi-closure
半边莲 Chinese lobelia
半边天 ①half of the sky ②women of the new society;womenfolk
半成品 semi-manufactured goods;semi-finished articles (*or* products)
半导体 semiconductor
半道儿 halfway;midway

半吊子 ① dabbler;smatterer ② tactless and impulsive person
半封建 semi-feudal
半公开 semi-overt;more or less open
半官方 semi-official
半决赛 semi-final
半空中 in midair;in the air
半劳力 one able to do light manual labour only;semi-ablebodied or part-time (farm) worker
半流体 semifluid
半瓶醋 half a bottle of vinegar—dabbler;smatterer
半山腰 halfway up a hill
半身像 ①half-length photo (*or* portrait) ② bust
半失业 semi-employed;partly employed;underemployed
半熟练 semi-skilled
半衰期 half-life
半透明 translucent;semitransparent
半脱产 partly released from productive labour;partly released from one's regular work
半文盲 semiliterate
半元音 semivowel
半月板 meniscus
半月瓣 semilunar valve
半月刊 semimonthly (a periodical);fortnightly
半支莲 sun plant
半制品 semi-manufactured goods;semi-finished articles (*or* products)
半中间 middle;halfway
半周期 semiperiod;half cycle
半自动 semi-automatic
半字节 nibble (*or* nybble)
半半拉拉 incomplete;unfinished
半壁江山 half of the country (usu. referring to the unoccupied part of an invaded country)
半地下室 semi-basement
半工半读 part work and part study;work-study program
半饥半饱 half-starving;underfed
半斤八两 six of one and half a dozen of the other;not much to choose between the two;two of a kind
半老徐娘 woman of fading charms
半路出家 become a monk or nun late in life—switch to a job one was not trained for
半路夫妻 couple married halfway through life
半卖半送 sell goods at rock-bottom prices
半明半暗 half-light and half-dark;dim
半耐用品 semi-durable goods
半人半鬼 half man, half ghost—an inhuman person or one living in conditions that are

inhuman
半身不遂 hemiplegia
半生不熟 ① half-cooked; underdone ② unskilled
半说半噎 hesitate in speech; mutter and mumble
半死不活 half dead; more dead than alive
半通不通 know (*or* understand) a little
半透明体 translucent body
半透明纸 onionskin
半途而废 give up halfway; leave sth unfinished
半推半就 yield with a show of reluctance; give way after making a show of declining
半吞半吐 hesitate to speak one's mind; be mealy-mouthed; hum and haw
半文半白 semi-literary, semi-vernacular
半心半意 half-hearted; lukewarm
半新不旧 neither modern nor obsolete
半信半疑 half-believing, half-doubting; not quite convinced
半醒半睡 half aware and half asleep
半夜三更 in the depth of night; late at night
半真半假 ① half-genuine, half-sham; partly true, partly false ② half in jest, half in earnest
半殖民地 semi-colony
半主权国 half-sovereign state
半自动化 semi-automatization
半自耕农 semi-tenant peasant; semi-owner peasant
半拉子工程 uncompleted project
半日制学校 half-day (*or* double-shift) school
半自动步枪 semi-automatic rifle
半自动车床 semi-automatic lathe
半自动信息转接站 semi-automatic message switching centre

扮 ［bàn］
动 ①play the part of; disguise oneself as ② put on (an expression)
扮酷 play it cool
扮靓 beautify
扮相 the appearance of an actor or actress in costume and makeup
扮演 play the part of; act
扮装 (of an actor, etc.) put on makeup; make up

伴 ［bàn］
I 名 companion; partner Ⅱ 动 accompany
伴唱 ①vocal accompaniment ②accompany (a singer)
伴读 accompany one's spouse who is studying abroad
伴侣 companion; mate; partner
伴娘 bridesmaid
伴生 accompanying; associated
伴随 accompany; follow
伴舞 ①accompanying dancer ②(hired) dancing girl; escort
伴星 companion (star)
伴奏 accompany (with musical instruments)
伴生气 associated gas
伴音信号 sound signal

拌 ［bàn］
动 ①mix ②quarrel; bicker
拌和 mix and stir; blend
拌面 noodles served with soy sauce, sesame butter, etc.
拌种 seed dressing
拌嘴 bicker; squabble; quarrel
拌泥工 pugger
拌种机 seed dresser

绊 ［bàn］
动 (cause to) stumble; trip; trip over
绊腿 trip; tie up person's movements
绊脚石 stumbling block; obstacle

桦 ［bàn］
名 big piece of fire wood
桦子 chopped wood

淉 ［bàn］
名 mud; slush

瓣 ［bàn］
I 名 ①petal ②segment; clove (of garlic) ③fragment; piece ④valve; lamella Ⅱ 量 petal, clove, segment: 一瓣儿蒜 a clove of garlic
瓣膜 valve

bāng（ㄅㄤ）

邦 ［bāng］
名 nation; state; country
邦交 relations between two countries; diplomatic relations
邦联 confederation

帮 ［bāng］
I 动 ① help; assist ② be in paid labour service; be hired; work Ⅱ 名 ①side (of sth) ②outer leaf (of cabbage, etc.) ③gang; band; clique ④ secret society; underworld gang; band; clique; association Ⅲ 量 gang; group; gathering; band: 一帮小朋友 a group of children
帮办 ①assist in managing ②deputy
帮厨 help in the mess kitchen
帮扶 support
帮工 ①help with farm work ②casual labourer (in pre-liberation countryside); seasonal labourer; helper
帮会 secret society; underworld gang
帮教 help and educate
帮困 support those in difficulty
帮忙 help; give (*or* lend) a hand; do a favour; do a good turn
帮派 faction
帮腔 ① vocal accompaniment in some traditional Chinese operas ②speak in support of

B

sb；echo sb；chime in with sb
帮拳 help one of fighters
帮手 helper；assistant
帮闲 ①hang on to and serve the rich and powerful by literary hack work，etc. ②literary hack
帮凶 accomplice；accessary
帮助 help；assist；aid
帮子 ①outer leaf（of cabbage，etc.） ②upper（of a shoe）
帮倒忙 be more of a hindrance than a help；do sb a disservice
帮困资金 poverty alleviation funds；help-the-poor fund
帮派活动 factionalism；gang activities
帮派思想 factionalist；ideas
帮派体系 factional setup（or system）

梆 [bāng]
Ⅰ 名 watchman's bamboo（or wooden）clapper Ⅱ 拟 rat-tat；rat-a-tat：有人在梆梆地敲门。Somebody is giving a rat-tat at the door.
梆子 ①watchman's clapper ②wooden clappers with bars of unequal length

浜 [bāng]
名 creek；streamlet

bǎng（ㄅㄤˇ）

绑 [bǎng]
动 tie（up）；bind；truss（up）
绑匪 kidnapper
绑架 ①kidnap ②stake
绑票 kidnap（for ransom）
绑腿 leg wrappings；puttee
绑线 wiring；binding wire

榜 [bǎng]
名 ①list of names posted up ②horizontal inscribed board ③announcement；notice
榜额 horizontal inscribed board
榜首 the top candidate of an examination
榜文 notice
榜样 example；model
榜上无名 not on the list of successful candidates
榜上有名 listed for acceptance to sth

膀 [bǎng]
名 ①arm；upper arm ②wing（of a bird） ③shoulder ➡pāng；páng
膀臂 ①upper arm；arm ②capable assistant；reliable helper；right-hand man
膀爷 topless guy
膀子 ①upper arm；arm ②wing（of a bird）

bàng（ㄅㄤˋ）

蚌 [bàng]
名 freshwater mussel；clam

棒 [bàng]
Ⅰ 名 stick；club；cudgel Ⅱ 形 terrific；topping；superb；strong；excellent
棒槌 ①wooden club ②layman；non-professional
棒喝 blow and shout to waken one from error
棒球 baseball
棒杀 "kill with the club"—cause sb to fail by open attack
棒糖 lollipop；sucker
棒舞 club dance
棒针 thick knitting needle
棒子 ①stick；club；cudgel ②maize；corn ③ear of maize（or corn）；corncob
棒磨机 rod mill
棒子面 cornmeal；corn flour

傍 [bàng]
动 ①draw near；be close to ②（of time）towards；nearly；be close to ③follow；lean on；rely on or accompany（a rich person）
傍晚 toward evening；at nightfall；at dusk
傍系 coset；subset of a mathematical group
傍大款 accompany a rich man；have an intimate relationship with a rich man
傍家儿 ①lover；mistress ②friend；partner；assistant ③couple；husband and wife

谤 [bàng]
动 slander；defame；vilify；smear；calumniate

塝 [bàng]
名 edge of a ditch，ridge，etc.，in field

榜 [bàng]
动 paddle；row ➡péng
榜船 row a boat

磅 [bàng]
Ⅰ 量 pound Ⅱ 名 ①scales ②point；type Ⅲ 动 weigh ➡páng
磅秤 platform scale；platform balance

镑 [bàng]
量 pound

艕 [bàng]
动 ①（of ships，boats，etc.）draw close and moor with each other；row side by side ②paddle；row

bāo（ㄅㄠ）

包 [bāo]
Ⅰ 动 ①wrap ②surround；encircle；envelop ③include；contain ④undertake to fulfil an assignment；be responsible for the whole job ⑤assure；guarantee ⑥hire；charter Ⅱ 名 ①bundle；parcel；package；pack ②bag；sack ③protuberance；swelling；lump ④yurt Ⅲ 量 packet；sack；bag；box；bale：一包火柴 a pack of matches；a box of matches／一包货 a sack of goods
包办 ①take care of everything concerning a job ②run the whole show；monopolize eve-

rything

包庇 shield;harbour;cover up

包藏 contain;harbour;conceal

包产 make a production contract;take full responsibility for output quotas

包场 book a whole theatre (*or* cinema);make a block booking

包车 chartered bus (*or* car)

包抄 out flank;envelop

包乘 charter (a plane,ship,etc.)

包饭 ①get (*or* supply) meals at a fixed rate; board ②meals thus arranged

包房 ①rent a hotel room for a period of time ②hotel room thus rented

包扶 fully responsible for contracted aiding quotas

包袱 ①cloth-wrapper ②a bundle wrapped in cloth ③millstone round one's neck;load; weight;burden

包干 be responsible for a task until it is completed

包工 undertake to perform work within a time limit and according to specifications;contract for a job

包管 assure;guarantee

包裹 ①wrap up;bind up ②bundle;package; parcel

包含 ①contain;embody;include ②inclusion; encompassment;subsumption

包涵 excuse;forgive;bear with

包换 guarantee to accept the exchange

包机 ①charter a plane ②chartered plane

包金 cover with gold leaf;gild

包茎 phimosis

包括 include;consist of;comprise;incorporate

包揽 undertake the whole thing;take on everything

包料 contract for material supply;material included

包罗 include;cover;embrace

包络 envelope

包赔 guarantee to pay compensations

包皮 ① wrapping;wrapper ② prepuce;foreskin

包票 guarantee;warranty

包容 ① pardon;forgive;tolerate ② contain; hold

包退 money back guarantee

包围 surround;encircle

包厢 box (in a theatre or concert hall)

包销 ①have exclusive selling rights ②be the sole agent (for a production unit or a firm)

包养 give fully financial support

包扎 wrap up;bind up;pack

包装 pack (commodities);package

包子 steamed stuffed bun

包租 ①rent land or a house for subletting ② fixed rent for farmland (to be paid no matter how bad the harvest might be) ③hire (a car,boat,etc.) for a period of time; charter

包庇罪 offence of covering up the criminal

包乘制 responsible crew system

包乘组 (responsible) crew

包虫病 echinococcosis;hydatid disease

包二奶 have a concubine

包干制 a system of payment partly in kind and partly in cash

包工头 labour contractor

包裹单 parcel form

包活儿 undertake to perform work within a time limit and according to specifications; contract for a job

包身工 indentured labourer

包围圈 ring of encirclement

包线制 responsibility system by line

包圆儿 ①buy the whole lot (*or* the remainder) ②finish up (*or* off)

包装箱 packing box (*or* case)

包装纸 wrapping (*or* packing) paper

包办代替 take away sb else's work;run things all by oneself without consulting others

包办婚姻 arranged marriage

包藏祸心 harbour evil intentions

包产到户 fixing of farm output quotas for each household

包干到户 the fixed quota system based on individual farmer

包工包料 contract for labour and materials of work contracted;fixing the amount of materials in accordance with the amount

包购包销 exclusive right to purchase and sell

包价旅游 inclusive tour;package tour

包揽词讼 engage in pettifoggery

包揽选票 deliver votes

包罗万象 all-embracing;all-inclusive

包络检波 envelope detection

包团旅游 package tour

包退包换 guarantee change of article or refund if unsatisfactory;refund or change for a better one; guarantee exchange if returned as unsuitable

包治百病 guarantee a cure for all ills;be guaranteed to cure all ills

包装标志 packing mark

包装标准 standardization of packing

包装车间 packing department

包装多样 diversified packing

包装设计 packing design

包皮环切术 circumcision

包扎艺术品 empaquetage

苞 [bāo] I 名 bud II 形 luxuriant;profuse;thick

苞谷 maize;corn

B

苞米 maize；corn

孢 ［bāo］
〔名〕spore
孢子 〔名〕spore
孢子生殖 sporogony
孢子植物 cryptogam

枹 ［bāo］
〔名〕glandbearing oak；oaklet

胞 ［bāo］
〔名〕①afterbirth；placenta ②fellow country-men；compatriot
胞壁 cell wall
胞核 karyon
胞浆 endochylema；kytoplasm
胞妹 full sisters
胞衣 (human) afterbirth

炮 ［bāo］
〔动〕① quick-fry；sauté ② dry by heat ➡ páo；pào
炮羊肉 quick-fried mutton

剥 ［bāo］
〔动〕peel；shell；skin ➡ bō
剥皮 skin；peel off the skin
剥蕉抽茧 like peeling a banana or unwinding a cocoon—press on an inquiry step by step

龅 ［bāo］
龅牙 bucktooth；gagtooth

煲 ［bāo］
Ⅰ〔名〕cooking pot；boiler；cooker Ⅱ〔动〕cook with boiler (or cooker)
煲粥 cook porridge in a boiler
煲电话粥 chat too long on the phone；boil (or cook) porridge of phone

褒 ［bāo］
Ⅰ〔动〕praise；commend；extol；honour Ⅱ〔形〕(of garment) loose；large；ample
褒贬 ［bāobiǎn］ pass judgment on；appraise
褒贬 ［bāobian］ speak ill of；cry down
褒奖 praise and honour；commend and award
褒扬 praise；commend
褒义 commendatory (or complimentary) sense
褒义词 commendatory term
褒善贬恶 praise virtue and censure vice
褒旧贬新 glorify the old and belittle the new
褒衣博带 loose robe with a broad waistband

báo（ㄅㄠ）

雹 ［báo］
〔名〕hail；hailstone
雹暴 hailstorm
雹害 damage caused by hail
雹灾 disaster caused by hail
雹子 hail；hailstone

薄 ［báo］
〔形〕①thin；flimsy ②infertile；poor ③with-out depth；coldly；shabbily；lacking in warmth

④weak；thin；light ➡ bó；bò
薄板 sheet metal；sheet
薄被 light (or thin) cotton-wadded quilt
薄饼 thin pancake
薄布 flimsy cloth
薄脆 crisp fritter
薄地 poor land；infertile land
薄呢 woollenette
薄片 thin piece (or sheet)
薄纱 chiffon
薄脆饼 wafer；waffle；snap
薄钢板 sheet steel
薄页纸 ①tissue paper ②flimsy
薄壳结构 shell structure

bǎo（ㄅㄠ）

饱 ［bǎo］
Ⅰ〔形〕①full；replete：半饱 half full ②full；plump Ⅱ〔副〕fully；to the full Ⅲ〔动〕①satisfy ②fatten (one's purse)；embezzle
饱餐 eat one's full；feast one's eyes on
饱尝 ①enjoy to the full ②experience；suffer
饱和 saturation
饱满 full；plump
饱暖 well-fed and well-clad；more than enough to eat and wear
饱学 learned；erudite；scholarly
饱嗝儿 belch；burp
饱满度 plumpness (of seeds)
饱和轰炸 saturation bombing
饱经沧桑 have experienced many vicissitudes of life；have seen much of the changes in human life
饱经风霜 weather-beaten；having had one's fill of hardships；endure all the hardships
饱食暖衣 be well-fed and well-clad
饱学之士 an erudite person；a learned scholar；a man of learning
饱汉不知饿汉饥 The well-fed don't know how the starving suffer.
饱食终日,无所用心 eat all day without exerting one's mind；eat three square meals a day and do no work；be sated with food and lead an idle life

宝 ［bǎo］
Ⅰ〔名〕① treasure；treasured object；valua-bles；riches ②currency；coin ③a kind of gam-bling device ④darling；precious one ⑤funny fellow；a bit of clown Ⅱ〔形〕①precious；treas-ured ②your
宝宝 (a pet name for a child) darling；baby
宝贝 ① treasured object；treasure ② darling；baby ③good-for-nothing；queer character
宝刹 ①pagoda in a temple ②your temple (or monastery)
宝典 a treasured book；a revered book
宝贵 ① valuable；precious ② value；treasure；

set store by
宝盒 jewel casket;treasure box;magical box
宝号 your shop
宝剑 a double-edged sword;a treasured sword
宝眷 your (esteemed) family
宝库 treasure-house
宝石 precious stone;gem
宝塔 pagoda
宝物 treasure
宝藏 precious (mineral) deposits
宝珠 precious pearl
宝座 throne
宝宝装 infant clothes
宝石蓝 sapphire blue
宝石学 gemology
宝塔菜 Chinese artichoke
宝塔诗 pyramid
宝贝疙瘩 darling child; parent's favourite child
宝刀不老 The man is old,but not his sword;A good sword remains always sharp; The treasured sword is not yet blunt.
宝塔筒子 cone

保 [bǎo]
I 动 ①protect;defend;safeguard ②keep; maintain in good condition;preserve ③guarantee;ensure ④ bail;stand guarantor for II 名 ①guarantee ②guarantor ③division under former household registration system
保安 ①ensure public security ②ensure safety (for workers engaged in production) ③ guard
保本 keep the capital intact;protect any investment (or deposit) against possible loss
保镖 bodyguard
保藏 keep in store;preserve
保持 keep;maintain;preserve
保存 preserve;conserve;keep
保单 guarantee slip;warranty
保底 ① protect an investment (or deposit) against currency depreciation ②guarantee a minimum sum;ensure a basic figure
保兑 confirm;confirmation
保费 insurance fee
保管 ①take care of;put sth under one's custody ②certainly;surely
保函 letter of guarantee (L/G)
保驾 escort the Emperor
保荐 recommend sb (for a job) with guarantee
保健 health protection;health care
保洁 keep the environment clean;do sanitation work
保留 ① continue to have;retain ②hold (or keep) back;reserve
保媒 be a matchmaker (or go-between);arrange a match

保密 maintain secrecy;keep sth secret
保苗 keep a full stand of seedlings
保姆 ① housemaid; housekeeper ② (children's) nurse
保全 ① save from damage;preserve;assure the safe of ②maintain;keep in good repair
保释 release on bail;bail
保守 ①guard;keep;hold on ②conservative
保税 bonded
保送 recommend sb for admission to school (without taking the entrance examination),etc.
保胎 prevent miscarriages
保卫 defend;safeguard
保温 heat preservation
保鲜 keep vegetables, fruit, etc. fresh; preserve freshness
保险 ①insurance ②safe ③be sure;be bound to
保修 guarantee (to keep sth in good condition or to repair)
保养 ①take good care of (or conserve) one's health;keep fit ② maintain; keep in good repair
保佑 bless and protect
保育 child care;child welfare
保障 ensure;guarantee;safeguard
保证 pledge;guarantee;assure;ensure
保值 value-guaranteed; be inflation-proof in value
保重 take care of oneself
保不住 most likely;more likely than not;may well
保存期 retention period
保管费 storage charges;storage fee
保管室 storeroom
保管员 warehouseman;storeman;storekeeper
保护地 protectorate;dependent territory
保护国 protectorate
保护剂 protectant;preservative
保护价 protective pricing;price set to protect the manufacturers (or producers)
保护钱 protection money
保护区 reserve;conservation area
保护人 guardian
保护伞 protective umbrella (a protecting power)
保护色 protective coloration
保护性 protective;protectiveness
保皇党 royalists
保监会 China Insurance Regulatory Commission
保健操 setting-up exercises
保健费 health subsidies
保健所 clinic
保健网 health care network
保健箱 medical kit

保健员 health worker
保健站 health station (*or* centre)
保洁箱 litter-bin
保龄球 ① bowling；tenpins；tenpin bowling ② bowling ball
保留地 reservation
保密码 secret code
保释金 surety
保释人 bailsman
保守党 Conservative Party (as in Britain)
保守派 conservatives
保税区 bonded zone；bonded area
保卫科 security section
保温杯 thermos mug
保温层 (thermal) insulating layer
保温车 refrigerator wagon (*or* car)
保温瓶 vacuum flask (*or* bottle)；thermos
保鲜袋 freshness protection package
保鲜膜 plastic wrap
保鲜期 length for preservation
保险带 safety belt
保险刀 safety razor
保险费 insurance premium
保险粉 sodium hydrosulphite
保险杆 bumper bar
保险杠 bumper (on a car)
保险柜 strongbox；safe
保险盒 fuse box
保险机 safety catch (of a firearm)
保险金 insurance amount；insurance money
保险期 insurance period
保险人 the insurer；assurer
保险丝 fuse；fuse-wire
保险箱 strongbox；safe
保修期 guarantee period
保养费 maintenance cost；upkeep
保养工 maintenance worker
保育箱 incubitor
保育员 child-care worker；nurse
保育院 nursery school
保真度 fidelity
保证金 ① earnest money；cash deposit ② bail
保证人 ① guarantor ② bail
保证书 written pledge；guarantee；guaranty；letter of guarantee
保质期 quality guarantee period
保安措施 security measures
保安公司 security company
保安开关 safety cut-off
保安人员 security personnel
保持不变 remain unchanged
保兑文句 confirming clause
保兑银行 confirming bank
保付支票 certified check
保国安民 defend the country and ensure a peaceful life for the people
保护措施 protection；protection measures；co-cooning
保护关税 protective tariff
保护涂剂 protective coating
保护现场 preserve the scene undisturbed
保护主义 protectionism
保健按摩 keep-fit massage
保健产品 health products
保健产业 health industry
保健食品 health food；health protecting food
保健饮料 health drink
保健珍品 health treasure
保健组织 health organizations
保龄球馆 bowling alley
保留工资 retained salaries
保留剧目 repertory；repertoire
保留条款 reservation clause
保密级别 security classification
保密条例 security regulations
保密通信 secret communication
保密文件 classified document
保姆市场 the house-maid market
保暖防风 warm and windproof
保守疗法 conservative treatment
保守势力 conservative force
保守主义 conservatism
保税仓库 bonded warehouse (*or* store)
保税货场 bonded goods
保税加工 bonded processing
保税制度 bonded system
保熟保甜 ripeness and sweetness (of watermelons) guaranteed
保外就医 medical parole；be released on bail for medical treatment；remain out of custody and obtain medical treatment
保外执行 let serve a sentence on bail
保卫部门 public security bodies
保卫工作 security work
保温材料 thermal insulation material
保息股票 guaranteed stock
保鲜包装 fresh-keeping package
保险单据 insurance documents
保险范围 insurance coverage
保险公司 insurance company
保险合同 insurance contract
保险回扣 insurance rebate
保险金额 insurance amount
保险客户 insurance policy holder
保险类别 branch of insurance
保险凭证 certification of insurance (CT)
保险契约 contract of insurance
保险索赔 insurance claim
保险弹簧 relief spring
保险系数 factor of safety
保险险别 coverage
保险种类 kinds of benefits
保险装置 safety device
保养周期 maintenance period

保证单位 guarantor unit
保证合同 contract of guaranty
保值储蓄 inflation-proof savings deposit; value-ensured savings deposit
保值公债 inflation-proof government bonds
保值增值 preserve or increase the value
保质保量 guarantee both quality and quantity
保持低姿态 maintain a low profile
保单持有人 policy holder
保兑信用证 confirmed letter of credit
保护 protect; safeguard
保护性反应 protective reaction
保护性关税 protective duty
保护性价格 protective price
保护性拘留 protective custody; protective detention
保护性贸易 protective trade
保护性投资 protective investment
保释保证书 bail bonds
保险代理人 insurance agent
保险国有化 nationalization of insurance
保险经纪人 insurance broker
保险赔偿金 insurance indemnity
保险证明书 insurance certificate
保护关税政策 policy of protective tariffs
保护贸易政策 policy of protection
保护知识产权 protect intellectual property rights

鸨 [bǎo]
名 ①bustard ②procuress
鸨母 a woman running a brothel; procuress; madam

葆 [bǎo]
Ⅰ 动 preserve; maintain; keep; nurture Ⅱ 名 luxuriant growth

堡 [bǎo]
名 small fort; walled village ➡bǔ
堡礁 barrier reef
堡垒 fort; fortress; stronghold; blockhouse
堡垒战 blockhouse warfare

褓 [bǎo]
名 cloth for baby; blankets

bào（ㄅㄠ）

报 [bào]
Ⅰ 动 ①report ②tell; announce ③reply; respond; reciprocate ④recompense; requite ⑤retaliate; revenge Ⅱ 名 ①newspaper; paper ②periodical; journal ③telegram; cable ④reportage; bulletin; report ⑤retribution
报案 report a case to the security authorities
报表 forms for reporting statistics, etc.; report forms
报偿 repay; recompense
报仇 revenge; avenge
报酬 reward; remuneration; pay
报答 repay; requite

报单 taxation form; declaration form
报到 report for duty; check in; register
报道 ①report (news); cover ②news report; story; information
报恩 pay a debt of gratitude
报贩 news dealer
报废 ①report sth as worthless ②discard as useless; reject; scrap
报分 call the score
报复 make reprisals; retaliate
报告 ①report; make known ②report; speech; talk; lecture
报关 declare sth at customs; apply to customs
报馆 general office of a newspaper; newspaper office
报国 dedicate oneself to the service of one's country
报价 quoted price
报捷 report a success; announce a victory
报界 the press; journalistic circles; the journalists
报警 ①report (an incident) to the police ②give an alarm
报刊 newspapers and periodicals; the press
报考 enter oneself for an examination
报名 enter one's name; sign up
报幕 announce the items on a (theatrical) programme
报盘 offer
报批 submit to a higher authority for approval
报社 general office of a newspaper; newspaper office
报失 report the loss of sth to the authorities concerned
报时 give the correct time
报数 number off
报税 declare dutiable goods; make a statement of dutiable goods
报摊 news-stand; news stall
报头 masthead (of a newspaper, etc.); nameplate
报喜 announce good news; report success
报销 ①submit an expense account; apply for reimbursement ②hand in a list of expended articles ③write off; wipe out; be destroyed
报晓 (of a cock, bell, etc.) herald the break of day; be a harbinger of dawn
报效 render service to repay sb's kindness
报谢 express appreciation (for sb's kindness or hospitality); acknowledge
报信 notify; inform
报修 report to the relevant office and request the repair of sth
报业 the press as a profession
报应 ①retribution; judgment ②due punishment
报章 newspapers

B

报账 render an account;submit an expense account;apply for reimbursement
报纸 ①newspaper ②newsprint
报春花 fairy primrose
报到处 check in
报告会 public lecture meeting
报关表 declaration form;customs declaration
报关单 quotation list
报关费 customs clearing fee
报关行 customs agency
报关人 declarant
报户口 apply for a residence permit
报话机 handie-talkie
报火警 raise the fire alarm
报价单 quotation of prices
报价人 tenderer
报价日 offering date
报警灯 alarm lamp
报警铃 emergency alarm bell
报警器 alarm;warner;warning device
报盘人 offerer
报时器 chronopher
报时台 (telephone) time inquiry service
报税单 taxation form
报务员 telegraph operator;radio operator
报表生成 reports generation
报仇雪恨 avenge oneself;take revenge
报复关税 retaliatory duties
报复行为 vindictive act
报告文学 reportage
报关手续 customs formalities
报关证书 customs clearance certificate
报警电话 alarm call
报警信号 alerting signal
报时信号 time signal
报销凭证 expense-account certificate
报业巨子 press baron
报以白眼 give sb a supercilious (*or* disdainful) look
报以嘘声 hiss sb;greet sb with boos and catcalls
报以一笑 respond with a smile (*or* laugh)
报复陷害罪 revengeful circumvention
报关代理行 customs house broker;customs agency
报关代理人 customs agent
报喜不报忧 report the good news but not the bad;hold back unpleasant information;report only what is good while with holding what is unpleasant
报复性军事行动 retaliatory military action

刨 [bào]
Ⅰ 名 ①plane ②planer;planing machine Ⅱ 动 plane smooth;plane;shave ➡páo
刨冰 water ice
刨程 planing length
刨齿 gear-shaping

刨床 planer;planing machine;facing machine
刨刀 ①planer tool ②plane iron
刨工 ①planing ②planing machine operator;planer
刨花 wood shavings
刨子 plane (a carpenter's tool)
刨花板 shaving board
刨刃儿 plane iron
刨式磨床 planer-type grinder
刨式铣床 planer-type miller

抱 [bào]
Ⅰ 动 ①hold (*or* carry) in the arms;clasp in the arms;embrace;hug ②cherish;nourish;harbour ③ carry on;burdened with ④have one's first child (*or* grandchild) ⑤adopt (a child) ⑥hang together ⑦(of shoes,clothing, etc.)fit well ⑧ hatch (eggs);brood Ⅱ 量 armful:一抱柴火 an armful of firewood
抱病 be ill;be in bad health
抱负 aspiration;ambition;lofty aim
抱恨 have a gnawing regret
抱愧 feel ashamed
抱歉 be sorry;feel apologetic;regret
抱屈 feel wronged
抱窝 sit (on eggs);brood;hatch
抱养 adopt (a child)
抱怨 complain;grumble
抱闸 band-type brake
抱不平 be outraged by an injustice (done to sb else)
抱粗腿 latch on to the rich and powerful;throw oneself under the protection of someone of influence or power
抱佛脚 clasp Buddha's feet—profess devotion only when in trouble;make a hasty last-minute effort
抱残守缺 cherish the outmoded and preserve the outworn—be conservative;be an anachronism
抱恨终天 feel bitter regret to the end of one's days;have an aching void in one's heart
抱头鼠窜 cover the head and sneak away like a rat;scurry (*or* scamper) off like a frightened rat
抱头痛哭 weep in each other's arms;cry on each other's shoulders
抱薪救火 carry faggots to put out a fire—adopt a wrong method to save a situation and end up by making it worse;do sth counterproductive

趵 [bào]
名 spring forth;bounce ➡bō

豹 [bào]
名 leopard;panther
豹猫 leopard cat
"豹"式主战坦克 Leopard main battle tank

B

暴 [bào]
Ⅰ 形 ①sudden and violent ②cruel;savage; fierce;tyrannical ③hot-tempered;short-tempered Ⅱ 副 suddenly and fiercely Ⅲ 动 ①spoil;ruin;waste ②expose;reveal ③stick out;protrude;stand out;bulge Ⅳ 名 the cruel and ruthless

暴病 sudden attack of a serious illness

暴跌 steep fall (in price);slump

暴动 ①rebellion;riot ②uprising;insurrection;outbreak

暴发 ①break out ②suddenly become rich or important;get rich quickly

暴风 ①storm wind ②storm (force 11 wind)

暴富 suddenly become rich;get rich quickly; bonanza

暴汉 bully

暴君 tyrant;despot

暴力 violence;force

暴利 sudden huge profits;exorbitant profit; excessive profit

暴戾 ruthless and tyrannical;cruel and fierce

暴烈 violent;fierce

暴露 expose;reveal;lay bare

暴乱 riot;rebellion;revolt

暴民 mob;mobster

暴怒 violent rage;fury

暴虐 brutal;tyrannical

暴食 eat too much at one meal

暴徒 ruffian;thug

暴行 savage act;outrage;atrocity;unruly conduct;brutality

暴雨 torrential rain;rainstorm

暴躁 irascible;irritable

暴涨 (of floods, prices, etc.) rise suddenly and sharply

暴政 tyranny;despotic rule

暴卒 die of a sudden illness;die suddenly

暴发狂 raptus

暴发户 rich instant;arriviste;nouveau riche

暴风雪 snowstorm;blizzard

暴风雨 rainstorm;storm;tempest

暴力片 splatter film

暴性子 irascible temper

暴风骤雨 violent storm;hurricane;tempest

暴力工具 means of violence

暴力镜头 carnography

暴戾恣睢 cruel and despotic;tyrannical

暴露思想 unbutton one's thoughts; unfurl one's ideas

暴露文学 literature of exposure (exposing the dark side of a society)

暴露无遗 be thoroughly exposed

暴殄天物 a reckless waste of the products of nature

暴跳如雷 stamp with fury;fly into a rage

曝 [bào]
➡ pù

曝丑 expose disgraceful affairs

曝光 ①exposure ②make (sth bad) public;expose;lay bare

曝光表 exposure meter

爆 [bào]
动 ①explode;burst ②quick-fry;quick-boil ③appear or occur unexpectedly;crop up

爆炒 ①quick-fry and stir ②feeding frenzy; speculation

爆发 erupt;burst out;break out

爆管 cartridge igniter;squib

爆花 ①snuff (of a wick) ②popcorn

爆冷 a surprise

爆裂 burst;crack

爆满 ①(of a theatre, cinema, etc.) have a full house;house full ②(of a stadium, etc.) be filled to capacity

爆鸣 detonation

爆破 blow up;demolish;dynamite;blast

爆棚 filled to capacity;sensational

爆音 sonic boom;shock-wave noise

爆炸 explode;blow up;detonate

爆竹 firecracker

爆肚儿 quick-fried tripe

爆发力 explosive force

爆冷门 (of a contest, etc.) produce an unexpected winner;dark horse bobbing up

爆破弹 blasting cartridge

爆破手 dynamiter

爆破筒 bangalore (torpedo)

爆破组 demolition team

爆炸物 explosive

爆米花儿 ①puffed rice ②popcorn

爆破英雄 demolition hero;ace dynamiter

爆破炸弹 demolition bomb

爆炸极限 explosive limit

爆炸性新闻 startling news

bēi (ㄅㄟ)

陂 [bēi]
名 ①pond ②waterside;bank;shore ③mountain slope

陂塘 pond

杯 [bēi]
Ⅰ 名 ①cup ②trophy;(prize) cup Ⅱ 量 glass;cup;mug;tankard

杯赛 Cup

杯子 cup;glass

杯弓蛇影 mistake the reflection of a bow in the cup for a snake—beset with imaginary fears;extremely suspicious

杯盘狼藉 wine cups and dishes strewn in disorder (after a feast)

杯水车薪 try to put out a blazing cartload of faggots with a cup of water—an utterly inadequate measure

卑 [bēi]

Ⅰ 形 ①low-lying; low ②of low rank ③of low character; inferior in quality ④humble; modest Ⅱ 动 belittle; despise; look down on; take sth lightly

卑鄙 base; mean; contemptible; despicable; inferior

卑辞 modest words

卑贱 ①lowly; humble ②mean and low

卑劣 base; mean; despicable

卑怯 mean and cowardly; abject

卑微 lowly; inferior; humble

卑下 base; low

卑鄙无耻 base and shameless

卑躬屈节 bow and scrape; cringe; act servilely (or obsequiously)

卑劣行径 base conduct; dishonourable behaviour

背 [bēi]

Ⅰ 动 ①carry on the back ②bear; shoulder Ⅱ 量 bundle; 一背柴火 a bundle of firewood ⇒bèi

背包 ① knapsack; rucksack; infantry (or field) pack; backpack ②blanket roll

背带 ①braces; suspenders ②sling (for a rifle) ③straps (for a knapsack)

背负 bear; carry on the back; have on one's shoulder; tote

背篓 a basket carried on the back

背头 swept-back hair

背债 be in debt; be saddled with debts

背包袱 carry baggage—have a weight (or load) on one's mind

背负式 backpack

背黑锅 be made a scapegoat; be unjustly blamed

背负式喷雾器 knapsack sprayer

悲 [bēi]

Ⅰ 形 ①sad; sorrowful; melancholy ②compassionate Ⅱ 动 feel pity Ⅲ 名 sorrow; feeling of sadness; grief

悲哀 grieved; sorrowful

悲惨 miserable; tragic

悲悼 mourn; grieve over sb's death

悲愤 grief and indignation

悲歌 ① sad melody; stirring strains; sad tune ②elegy; dirge; threnody ③sing with solemn fervour

悲哽 choke with grief

悲观 pessimistic

悲剧 tragedy

悲鸣 utter sad calls; lament

悲泣 weep with grief

悲切 mournful; moanful

悲伤 sad; grieved; sorrowful

悲叹 sigh mournfully; lament

悲恸 weep loudly from sorrow

悲痛 grieved; sorrowful

悲壮 solemn and stirring; moving and tragic

悲喜剧 tragicomedy

悲不自胜 be overcome with grief

悲从中来 feel sadness welling up

悲愤填膺 be filled with grief and indignation

悲观情绪 pessimism

悲欢离合 joys and sorrows, partings and reunions—vicissitudes of life

悲天悯人 bemoan the state of the universe and pity the fate of mankind

悲喜交集 mixed feelings of grief and joy; grief and joy intermingled; joy tempered with sorrow

碑 [bēi]

名 upright stone tablet; stele

碑额 the top part of a tablet

碑记 a record of events inscribed on a tablet

碑林 a large collection of ancient stone tablets

碑帽 stone sculpture on top of a stele

碑身 body of a stele

碑帖 a rubbing from a stone inscription

碑文 a inscription on a tablet

běi (ㄅㄟˇ)

北 [běi]

Ⅰ 名 north Ⅱ 形 be defeated

北辰 Polaris

北国 the northern part of the country; the North

北货 delicacies from north China (such as dried persimmons, etc.)

北极 ①North Pole; Arctic Pole ②north magnetic pole

北约 the North Atlantic Treaty Organization (NATO)

北半球 the Northern Hemisphere

北冰洋 the Arctic (Ocean)

北大荒 the Great Northern Wilderness (in northeast China)

北斗星 the Big Dipper; the Plough

北伐军 the Northern Expeditionary Army

北寒带 the North Frigid Zone

北极光 northern lights; aurora borealis

北极狐 arctic fox

北极圈 the Arctic Circle

北极星 Polaris; the North Star; the polestar

北极熊 polar bear

北美洲 North America

北温带 the North Temperate Zone

北伐战争 Northern Expedition

北国江南 southlike area in the north; Riviera in the north

北回归线 the Tropic of Cancer

北京烤鸭 Peking roasted duck

北京猿人 Peking Man

B

北欧海盗 Viking
北洋军阀 Northern Warlords
北约东扩 eastward expansion of NATO
北约主义 Natoism
北极圈探险队 Arctic Circle Exploration Team
北约维和部队 NATO peacekeeping force
北美自由贸易区 the North American Free Trade Zone
北极圈科学考察团 Arctic Circle Scientific Investigation Group

bèi (ㄅㄟ)

贝 [bèi]
　[名] ①mollusk;shellfish;scallop ②cowrie
贝雕 shell carving
贝介 shellfish
贝壳 shell (of shellfish)
贝类 shellfish;molluscs
贝母 the bulb of fritillary
贝丘 shell mound
贝叶 pattra leaves
贝雷帽 beret
贝叶经 Buddhist scripture written on pattra leaves

孛 [bèi]
　[名] comet

狈 [bèi]
◇狼狈 in an awkward position;in a dilemma

备 [bèi]
　Ⅰ[动] ①have;be equipped with;possess ②prepare;get ready;provide with ③provide (or prepare) against;take precautions against Ⅱ[名] equipment Ⅲ[副] all;fully;in every possible way
备案 put on record (or on file);enter (a case) in the records
备查 for future reference
备份 back up;backup
备耕 make preparations for ploughing and sowing
备荒 prepare against natural disasters
备件 spare parts;repair parts
备考 (an appendix,note,etc.) for reference;prepare for examinations
备课 (of a teacher) prepare lessons
备料 ①get the materials ready ②prepare feed (for livestock)
备品 ①spares;repair piece;reserve part ②choice
备取 be on the waiting list (for admission to a school)
备选 be an alternative;be on the short list (for further screening)
备用 reserve;spare;alternate
备战 ①prepare for war ②be prepared against war

备至 to the utmost;in every possible way
备注 remarks
备降物 alternate airport
备忘录 ① memorandum; aide-mémoire ② memorandum book
备注栏 remarks column
备尝艰辛 experience untold hardships and difficulties
备而不用 have sth ready just in case;keep sth for possible future use
备受欺凌 be browbeaten and bullied in every way
备受拥戴 enjoy full support
备有现货 in stock
备战备荒 be (or get) prepared against war and natural disasters

背 [bèi]
　Ⅰ[名] ①back of the body;dorsum ②backside of an object Ⅱ[动] ①with the back towards ②turn away ③act contrary to;violate;break ④leave;go away ⑤hide sth from;do sth behind sb's back ⑥recite from memory;learn by heart or by rote Ⅲ[形] ①out-of-the-way:背街 back street;side street ②hard of hearing ③unlucky ➡bēi
背风 out of the wind;on the lee side;leeward
背光 be in a poor light;do sth with one's back to the light;stand in one's own light
背后 ①behind;at the back;in the rear ②behind sb's back
背景 background;backdrop
背静 quiet and secluded
背离 deviate from;depart from
背理 against good reason (or conscience)
背面 the back;the reverse side;the wrong side
背叛 betray;forsake
背弃 abandon;desert;renounce
背时 ①behind the times ②unlucky
背手 hands at the back
背书 ①recite a lesson from memory;repeat a lesson ②endorsement (on a cheque)
背诵 recite;repeat from memory
背心 sleeveless garment
背阴 in the shade;shady
背影 view of sb's back;figure viewed from behind
背约 break an agreement;go back on one's word;fail to keep one's promise
背运 ①bad luck;ill luck ②have bad luck;be out of luck
背地里 behind sb's back;privately;on the sly
背靠背 ①back to back ②criticize (or expose) sb without his knowledge
背阴处 shady spot
背城借一 make a last-ditch stand before the city wall;fight to the last ditch;put up a

desperate struggle

背道而驰 run in the opposite direction; run counter to

背合铰链 counter-flap hinge

背井离乡 leave one's native place (esp. against one's will); be away from home

背景音乐 background music

背山面海 with hills behind and sea in front

背水一战 fight with one's back to the river—fight to win or die

背信弃义 break faith with sb; be perfidious

背包式核弹 backpack nuke

背对背信用证 back-to-back letter of credit

钡 [bèi]
名 barium (Ba)

钡餐 barium meal

钡中毒 barium poisoning

钡餐检查 barium meal examination

倍 [bèi]
I 名 times; fold; 3 的 2 倍是 6。 Two times three is six. II 形 double; redouble

倍数 multiple

倍增 redouble

倍加器 dupler; doubler

倍频器 frequency multiplier

倍增器 multiplier

倍加努力 double one's effort

倍加小心 be especially careful; be doubly careful

倍塔粒子 beta particle

倍塔射线 beta ray

悖 [bèi]
I 动 be contrary to; go against; revolt against II 形 ①erroneous; perverse ②puzzled; confused; muddleheaded

悖德 against moral values; immoral

悖理 contrary to reason

悖礼 implite

悖谬 absurd; preposterous

悖逆 disloyal; treasonable; rebellious

悖入悖出 ill-gotten, ill-spent

被 [bèi]
I 名 quilt II 动 ①cover ②meet with; encounter III 助 (*used to form a passive verbal phrase*): 那房子被烧毁了。 The house was burnt down. IV 介 (*used in a passive sentence to introduce the agent or doer*): 玻璃杯被她的孩子打破了。 The glass was broken by her child.

被捕 be arrested; be under arrest

被袋 bedding bag

被单 (bed) sheet

被动 passive

被服 bedding and clothing (esp. for army use)

被俘 be captured; be taken prisoner

被告 defendant; the accused

被控 controlled; manipulated

被里 the underneath side of a quilt

被面 the facing of a quilt

被难 be killed in a disaster, political incident, etc.; suffer from a disaster

被迫 be compelled; be forced; be constrained

被褥 bedding; bedclothes

被套 ①bedding bag ②(bag-shaped) quilt cover; slipcover for a quilt ③cotton wadding for a quilt

被灾 be hit by disaster

被罩 (bag-shaped) quilt cover; slipcover for a quilt

被子 quilt

被乘数 multiplicand

被除数 dividend

被单布 sheeting

被动式 passive form

被服厂 clothing factory

被告席 defendant's seat; dock

被害人 the injured party; the victim

被加数 summand

被减数 minuend

被窝儿 a quilt folded to form a sleeping bag

被保护国 protectorate

被保护人 insurant; the insured; insured person

被保险人 ①the insured ②policy holder

被传出庭 be summoned to appear in court

被担保人 guaranteed person

被动吸烟 passive (*or* secondhand) smoking

被动语态 passive voice

被管制人 person under public surveillance

被叫用户 called party

被侵略者 victim of aggression

被请求方 requested party

被驱逐者 deportee

被上诉人 appellee

被索赔人 claimee

被统治者 the ruled

被选举权 the right to be elected; right to stand for election

被寻地址 addressee

被占领区 the occupied territories

被指定人 assignee; nomine

被转让人 transferee

被子植物 angiosperm

被保护文件 protected file

被剥削阶级 exploited class

被存储数据 stored data

被调用程序 called program; called procedure

被告辩护人 defence attorney

被压迫民族 oppressed nation

辈 [bèi]
名 ①generation; seniority ②people of a certain kind; the like; familiar circle ③lifetime

辈出 come forth in large numbers

辈分 order of seniority in the family (*or*

B

clan)；position in the family hierarchy
辈子 all one's life；lifetime

惫 [bèi]
形 exhausted；fatigued

焙 [bèi]
动 bake over a slow fire
焙茶 prepare and cure tea
焙烧 roast；bake
焙药 make herb medicine by drying it in the sun (*or* over a fire)
焙干研碎 dry sth over a fire and grind it into powder

蓓 [bèi]
蓓蕾 bud

褙 [bèi]
动 stick cloth (*or* paper) one piece on top of another with paste or glue

bei （·ㄅㄟ）

呗 [bei]
助 ①(*used to show that sth is self-evident*)：不会做就学着做呗。If you don't know how to do it，well，learn now. ②(*used to express reluctant agreement or concession*)：唱就唱呗。Well，sing if you like.

臂 [bei] ➡bì
◇胳臂 arm

bēn （ㄅㄣ）

奔 [bēn]
动 ①run quickly；dash；(of a horse) gallop ②flee；run away ③elope ④hurry；hasten；rush about；rush to ➡bèn
奔波 rush about；be busy running about
奔驰 run quickly；speed
奔窜 run helter-skelter
奔放 bold and unrestrained；untrammelled
奔赴 hurry to (a place)；rush to
奔流 ①flow at great speed；pour ②racing current；swift flow
奔马 galloping horse
奔忙 be busy rushing about；bustle about
奔命 rush about on errands；be kept on the run
奔跑 run
奔丧 hasten home for the funeral of a parent (*or* grandparent)
奔逃 flee；run away
奔腾 ①gallop ②surge forward；roll on in waves
奔袭 long-range raid
奔泻 (of torrents) rush down；pour down
奔走 ①run ②go around；rush about；be busy running about
奔腾芯片 Pentium chip
奔走呼号 go around crying for help (*or* cam-

paigning for a cause)
奔走相告 run around spreading the news；lose no time in telling each other the news

贲 [bēn]
动 run
贲门 cardia

běn （ㄅㄣˇ）

本 [běn]
I 名 ①root (*or* stem) of a plant ②foundation；basis；origin ③book ④edition；version ⑤memorial presented to the emperor ⑥script ⑦capital；principal II 形 ①original ②main；chief；central III 代 ①one's own；native ②current；this；present IV 副 originally；initially V 介 according to；based on；in line with VI 量 ①(of books of various kinds)：五本儿书 five books (*or* copies) ②(of traditional operas or their scripts)：头本《西游记》first part of the dramatized *Pilgrimage to the West* ③(of films)：这部电影有六本。This movie has 6 reels.
本币 basic monetary unit (of a country's currency)
本埠 this city；local
本部 headquarter
本草 a class of traditional Chinese medical literature consisting of herbals which focus on descriptions of individual drugs
本当 should have；ought to have
本底 background
本地 this locality
本分 ①one's duty；one's role；obligation ②honest；decent
本国 one's own country
本行 one's line；one's own profession
本家 member of the same clan；distant relative with the same family name
本届 current；this year's
本金 capital；principal
本科 (as distinguished from a preparatory course，a correspondence course，etc.) regular college course；undergraduate course
本来 ①original ②originally；at first ③it goes without saying；of course；naturally
本垒 home base；home plate；home；the plate
本利 principal and interest
本领 skill；ability；capability
本路 home road
本末 ①the whole course of an event from beginning to end；ins and outs ②the fundamental and the incidental
本能 instinct
本票 cashier's cheque
本钱 ①capital ②what is capitalized on；sth used to one's own advantage
本人 ①I (me，myself) ②oneself；in person ③

B

'principal
本色 [běnsè] true (*or* inherent) qualities; distinctive character
本色 [běnshǎi] natural colour
本身 itself; in itself
本事 [běnshì] source material; original story
本事 [běnshi] skill; ability; capability
本题 subject under discussion; point at issue
本体 ① noumenon; thing-in-itself ② body; main part of a machine (*or* a project)
本土 ①one's native country (*or* land) ②metropolitan territory
本位 ① standard; basic unit ② one's own department or unit
本文 ① this text; this article ② the original text; the original
本息 principal (*or* capital) and interest
本性 natural instincts (*or* character, disposition); nature; inherent quality
本业 ① agriculture; farming ② original occupation
本义 original meaning; literal sense
本意 original idea; real intention
本影 umbra
本源 origin; source
本着 in line with; in conformity with; in the light of
本职 one's job (*or* duty)
本质 essence; nature; innate character; intrinsic quality
本子 ①book; notebook ②edition
本科生 undergraduate
本命年 every 12th year after the year of one's birth; this animal year
本年度 this year; current year
本色布 unbleached and undyed cloth; grey cloth
本生灯 Bunsen burner
本体论 ontology
本土化 indigenization
本位号 natural
本族语 native language; mother tongue
本本主义 book worship; bookishness; pedantry
本草纲目 Compendium of Materia Medica
本底噪声 background noise
本地新闻 local items
本固枝荣 When the root is firm, the branches flourish.
本来面目 true colours; true features
本末倒置 take the branch for the root; put the incidental before the fundamental
本能行为 instinctive behaviour
本轻利重 the capital is small, but the profit remarkable; low cost great profit; the cost being low but the profit being great
本体感受 proprioception
本位货币 basic monetary unit of a country's currency
本位利益 localized interests
本位主义 selfish departmentalism; departmental selfishness
本乡本土 native soil; native land; home village
本小利微 small capital and little gain—a small business
本性难移 It is hard to change one's nature; The leopard can't change his spots.
本初子午线 the first meridian; the prime meridian

苯 [běn]
【名】 benzene; benzol
苯胺 aniline
苯酚 phenol
苯核 benzene nucleus
苯胺革 aniline leather
苯胺紫 mauve
苯丙烯 propenyl benzene
苯甲酸 benzoic acid
苯乙烯 styrene
苯胺染料 aniline dyes
苯胺印刷 aniline printing; flexography

畚 [běn]
Ⅰ【名】 dustpan; bamboo (*or* wicker) scoop
Ⅱ【动】 scoop with a dustpan
畚箕 ①bamboo (*or* wicker) scoop ②dustpan

bèn (ㄅㄣˋ)

坌 [bèn]
Ⅰ【名】 dust Ⅱ【动】 ①spread with powder ②gather; collect ③dig; turn up Ⅲ【形】 crude and inferior; shoddy
坌地 dig the ground; turn up the soil

奔 [bèn]
Ⅰ【动】 ① make straight for; head for; go straight to ②go about (some business); be after; be busy running about ③(of one's age) approach; get close to; get on for or towards
Ⅱ【介】 towards: 奔码头走 walk towards the wharf ➡bēn
奔命 be in a desperate hurry
奔头儿 sth to strive for; prospect
奔小康 strive to prosper; strive to become well-to-do

笨 [bèn]
【形】 ① cumbersome; heavy; awkward; unwieldy ② stupid; foolish; dull; dense ③ clumsy; awkward
笨蛋 fool; idiot
笨人 stupid person; simpleton; fool; dunce
笨重 heavy; cumbersome; unwieldy
笨拙 clumsy; awkward; stupid
笨口拙舌 awkward in speech; slow of speech; inarticulate
笨鸟先飞 clumsy birds have to start flying early—the slow need to start early (usu.

said self-depreciatingly)

笨手笨脚 clumsy;awkward

笨头笨脑 stupid;blockhead;with a wooden head

bēng (ㄅㄥ)

伻 [bēng] 名 envoy

崩 [bēng] 动 ①collapse ②burst;crack;split ③breakdown;collapse;crash ④ be hit by sth bursting;hit and smash ⑤shoot to death;execute by shooting ⑥(of an emperor) die

崩岸 burst

崩溃 ①collapse;crumble;fall apart ②crash

崩裂 burst (or break) apart;crack

崩漏 uterine bleeding

崩盘 stock market crash

崩塌 collapse;crumble

崩陷 fall in;cave in

绷 [bēng] Ⅰ 动 ①(of a dress,a piece of cloth,etc.) tight;taut ②stretch tight;strain ③be barely able to subsist;manage with difficulty ④spring;bounce ⑤baste;tack;pin Ⅱ 名 ①embroidery frame ②frame matting (for a bed) ➡ běng;bèng

绷带 bandage

绷簧 spring

绷子 embroidery frame;hoop;tambour

嘣 [bēng] 名 bang:嘣的一声响,提琴弦断了。The violin's string snapped.

béng (ㄅㄥˊ)

甭 [béng] 副 don't need to:甭再说了。Don't say any more.

běng (ㄅㄥˇ)

葑 [běng] **葑葑** luxuriant;exuberant

绷 [běng] 动 ①pull (a long face) ②strain oneself; stifle one's temper ➡ bēng;bèng

bèng (ㄅㄥˋ)

泵 [bèng] 名 pump

泵房 pump house

泵油 pump oil

泵站 pump station

泵排量 pumpage;pump delivery

迸 [bèng] 动 ①spout;spurt;burst forth;gush forth; blurt out ②break to pieces suddenly

迸发 burst forth;burst out

迸裂 split;burst (open)

迸碎 burst suddenly into fragments;break to pieces all of a sudden

绷 [bèng] Ⅰ 动 split open;burst open;crack Ⅱ 副 very ➡ bēng;běng

绷亮 exceedingly bright

绷硬 hard as rock

绷直 very straight

蹦 [bèng] 动 hop;leap;jump;spring

蹦床 trampoline

蹦迪 disco dancing

蹦蹦车 small motorized three-wheel transport vehicles

蹦豆儿 ①roasted broad beans ②little child

蹦极(跳) bungee jumping

蹦蹦跳跳 bouncing and vivacious

bī (ㄅㄧ)

屄 [bī] 名 vaginal orifice;vulva

逼 [bī] Ⅰ 动 ①press on towards;press up to;advance on;close in on ②force;compel;drive; press;threaten ③ press for;extort Ⅱ 形 close;narrow

逼宫 (of ministers,etc.) force the king (or emperor) to abdicate

逼供 extort a confession

逼近 press on towards;close in on;approach; draw near

逼迫 force;compel;coerce

逼人 pressing;threatening

逼视 look at from close-up;watch intently

逼死 hound sb to death

逼问 ①force sb to answer ②question closely

逼肖 bear a close resemblance to;be the very image of

逼债 press for payment of debts;dun;hound a debtor

逼真 ①lifelike;true to life;almost real ②distinctly;clearly;very much alike

逼租 press for payment of (land) rent

逼供信 obtain confessions by compulsion and give them credence

逼真度 fidelity

逼良为娼 force a girl of good family (or woman of virtue) to engage in prostitution;force an honest person to do sth dishonest

逼人太甚 press (or push) people too hard

逼入困境 drive sb into a corner;pull sb to the wall;get sb cornered

逼上梁山 be driven to revolt

鳊 [bī]
名 slipmouth

bí (ㄅㄧˊ)

荸 [bí]
荸荠 water chestnut

鼻 [bí]
名 ①nose ②pioneer；origination；start
鼻儿 ①hole in an implement，utensil，etc.，for sth to be inserted into；eye ②whistle
鼻窦 paranasal sinus
鼻尖 tip of the nose
鼻镜 rhinoscope
鼻孔 nostril
鼻梁 bridge of the nose
鼻毛 vibrissa
鼻腔 nasal cavity
鼻塞 have a stuffy nose
鼻饲 nasal feeding
鼻涕 nasal mucus；snivel
鼻烟 snuff
鼻炎 rhinitis
鼻翼 alae of the nose
鼻音 nasal sound
鼻渊 nasosinusitis
鼻子 nose
鼻祖 earliest ancestor；originator（of a tradition，school of thought，etc.）
鼻窦炎 nasosinusitis
鼻咽癌 nasopharyngeal carcinoma
鼻烟盒 snuffbox
鼻烟壶 snuff bottle
鼻中隔 nasal septum
鼻青脸肿 bloody nose and swollen face；badly battered
鼻针疗法 nose-acupuncture therapy
鼻吸避孕剂 sniffing contraceptive

bǐ (ㄅㄧˇ)

匕 [bǐ]
名 ①bi a type of ancient spoon ②dagger ③arrowhead
匕首 dagger

比 [bǐ]
Ⅰ 动 ①close together；next to ②depend on；collude with；gang up with；attach oneself to ③compare；contrast；emulate；compete ④be like；be similar to；match ⑤ratio；proportion ⑥to（in a score）⑦copy；do according to；model after ⑧draw an analogy；liken to；compare to ⑨gesture；gesticulate ⑩aim at；direct towards Ⅱ 名 ratio，proportion Ⅲ 介 than；（superior or inferior）to：我考得比他好。I did better in the examination than he. Ⅳ 副 ①recently；of late ②by（then）；by the time

比方 ①analogy；instance ②suppose ③同"比如"
比分 score
比划 gesture；gesticulate
比及 till；until；by the time；when
比价 ① price relations；parity；rate of exchange ②compare bids（or prices）
比较 ①compare；contrast ②fairly；comparatively；relatively；quite；rather
比例 ①proportion ②scale
比量 ① take rough measurements（with the hand，a stick，string，etc.）②make gestures
比邻 ① neighbour；next-door neighbour ② near；next to
比率 ratio；rate
比美 compare favourably with；rival
比拟 ①compare；draw a parallel；match ②analogy；metaphor
比拼 compete fiercely；go all out to win；rivalry
比丘 monk
比热 specific heat
比容 specific volume
比如 for example；for instance；such as
比赛 math；competition
比试 ①have a competition ②make gestures
比特 bit
比武 take part in a *wushu* contest
比翼 fly wing to wing
比喻 metaphor；analogy；figure of speech
比照 ①according to；in the light of ②contrast
比值 ratio；rate.
比重 ①specific gravity ②proportion
比干劲 enthusiastically compete with each other
比基尼 bikini
比较法 comparative method；comparative approach
比较级 comparative degree
比例尺 ①scale ②architect's scale；engineer's scale
比例税 proportional tax
比目鱼 flatfish；flounder
比丘尼 nun
比萨饼 pizza
比色计 colourimeter
比翼鸟 fabulous birds that had only one wing each and thus had to fly in pairs
比重计 hydrometer
比比皆是 can be found everywhere；such is the case everywhere
比肩而立 stand shoulder to shoulder
比较文学 comparative literature
比例失调 be out of proportion；lopsided development
比例税率 flat rate
比萨斜塔 Leaning Tower of Pisa

比赛项目 event
比翼双飞 fly wing to wing; fly side by side; pair off wing to wing
比较语言学 comparative linguistics
比学赶帮超 emulate, learn from, catch up with, help and in turn surpass each other; compare, learn from, try to catch up, help each other and then surpass (*or* supercede)
比着葫芦画瓢 draw a gourd ladle on a calabash
比上不足，比下有余 not up to those above, but above those below—middling; passable; tolerable

吡 [bǐ] ➡ pǐ

吡啶 pyridine
吡咯 pyrrole

佊 [bǐ] 形 evil

妣 [bǐ] 名 deceased mother

彼 [bǐ] 代 ①that; those; the other; another ②other party; one's opponent

彼岸 ①Faramita ②other side (*or* bank) of a river; opposite shore
彼此 ①each other; one another ②me too; you too
彼端 the other end of

秕 [bǐ] 形 ①(of grain) not plump; blighted ②evil; bad

秕糠 ①chaff ②worthless stuff
秕政 bed government policy
秕子 blighted grain

笔 [bǐ] I 名 ①pen ②technique of writing, calligraphy or drawing ③handwriting ④stroke in Chinese painting (*or* calligraphy) II 动 write; pen III 量 ①几笔收入 several items of income/一笔债 a debt ②一笔得意之作 a work one is proud of

笔触 brush stroke in Chinese painting and calligraphy; brushwork
笔答 give a written answer; answer in writing
笔调 (of writing) tone; style
笔伐 attack in writing
笔法 technique of writing (*or* calligraphy, drawing)
笔锋 ①the tip of a writing brush ②vigour of style in writing; stroke; touch
笔耕 make living by writing; drive a pen
笔供 written confession
笔画 strokes of a Chinese character
笔会 ①forum in writing ②association (*or* club) of writers
笔记 ①take down (in writing) ②notes ③pen jottings (a type of literature consisting mainly of short sketches)

笔迹 person's handwriting; hand
笔架 pen rack; penholder
笔尖 ①nib; pen point ②the tip of a writing brush or pencil
笔力 vigour of strokes in calligraphy (*or* drawing); vigour of style in literary composition
笔录 ①put down (in writing); take down ②notes; record
笔路 style; technique of calligraphy
笔帽 cap of a pen (*or* pencil, writing brush)
笔名 pen name; pseudonym
笔墨 pen and ink; words; writing
笔试 written examination
笔顺 order of strokes observed in calligraphy
笔算 ①do a sum in writing ②written calculation
笔谈 ①conversation by writing ②comment in writing; give a written statement ③pen conversations ④sketches and notes
笔套 ①cap of a pen ②sheath of a pen
笔体 writing style; calligraphy; handwriting; hand
笔挺 ①(standing) very straight; straight as a ramrod; bolt upright ②well-ironed; trim
笔筒 pen container; brush pot; tubular penrack
笔误 ①make a slip in writing ②slip of the pen
笔洗 writing-brush washer
笔下 ①ability to write ②wording and purport of what one writes
笔芯 ①pencil lead ②refill (for a ball-point pen)
笔译 written translation
笔友 pen-friend; pen pal
笔战 written polemics; war between writers; pen war
笔者 present writer; author
笔直 perfectly straight; straight as a ramrod; bolt upright
笔底下 ability to write
笔杆子 ①the shaft of a pen (*or* writing brush); penholder ②pen ③facile writer; literary spokesman
笔记本 notebook
笔头儿 ①nib; pen point ②ability to write; writing skill ③written; in written form
笔触输入 pen touch input
笔记小说 literary sketches; sketchbook
笔迹鉴定 handwriting verification
笔迹证据 proof of handwriting
笔墨官司 written polemics (*or* controversy); a battle of words
笔下留情 be charitable in writing critical comments
笔记本电脑 notebook computer; laptop

B

俾 [bǐ]
囵 in order to;so as to;so that
俾众周知 so as to make sth known to all;for the information of all

舭 [bǐ]
名 bilge

鄙 [bǐ]
I 名 out-of-the-way place;remote area Ⅱ 形 ①low;mean;vulgar ②my Ⅲ 囵 despise;disdain;scorn;look down
鄙薄 despise;scorn
鄙陋 superficial;shallow
鄙弃 disdain;loathe
鄙人 your humble servant;I
鄙视 despise;disdain;look down upon
鄙俗 vulgar;philistine
鄙笑 jeer;scoff at
鄙意 my humble opinion

bì (ㄅㄧ)

币 [bì]
名 money;currency
币市 special purpose currency market
币值 currency value
币制 currency (or monetary) system
币值改革 monetary reform;currency reform
币值坚挺 firm currency value
币值调整 currency realignment
币制改革 currency (or monetary) reform
币重言甘 much money and sweet words

必 [bì]
I 副 ①certainly;surely ②necessarily Ⅱ 囵 must;ought to;have to
必备 must prepare for
必得 must;have to
必定 ①must;have to ②be bound to;be sure to
必将 will certainly;surely will
必然 ①inevitable;certain ②be bound to;be sure to ③necessity
必须 must;have to
必需 essential;indispensable
必要 necessary;essential;indispensable
必然性 necessity;inevitability;certainty
必修课 required (or obligatory) course
必需品 necessities;necessaries
必要性 necessity
必不可少 absolutely necessary;indispensable;essential
必然规律 inexorable law
必然趋势 inexorable trend
必然王国 realm of necessity;realm of inevitability
必要产品 necessary product
必要带宽 necessary bandwidth
必要劳动 necessary labour
必要前提 prerequisite;precondition

必由之路 the road one must follow or take;only way
必需脂肪酸 essential fatty acid

毕 [bì]
I 囵 finish;complete;conclude Ⅱ 副 fully;altogether;completely
毕竟 after all;all in all;when all is said and done;in the final analysis
毕生 all one's life;lifetime
毕肖 resemble closely;be the very image of
毕业 graduate;finish school
毕业班 graduating class
毕业生 graduate
毕恭毕敬 reverent and respectful;extremely deferential
毕业典礼 graduation (ceremony);commencement
毕业分配 job assignment on graduation;graduates assignment
毕业教育 graduating education
毕业论文 graduation thesis (or dissertation)
毕业设计 graduation project
毕业实习 graduation field work
毕业献词 valedictory
毕业证书 diploma;graduation certificate
毕业生去向 student placement
毕其功于一役 accomplish the whole task at one stroke

闭 [bì]
囵 ①shut;close ②stop;end ③stop up;block up;obstruct
闭店 close up shop and stop business
闭关 ①block a pass;close a city gate ②close the border ③stay secluded meditating and studying scriptures for a period of time
闭合 close
闭环 closed loop;closed cycle
闭会 lose (or end,adjourn) a meeting
闭经 amenorrhoea
闭卷 closed-book
闭路 closed-circuit (television)
闭幕 ①the curtain falls;lower the curtain ②close;conclude
闭气 ①stop breathing ②hold one's breath
闭塞 ①stop up;close up ②hard to get to;out-of-the-way;inaccessible ③unenlightened ④blocking;blockage;occlusion
闭锁 shutting;bottoming;interlock
闭门羹 deny (or be denied) entrance
闭幕词 closing address (or speech)
闭幕式 closing ceremony
闭音节 closed syllable
闭元音 closed vowel
闭关锁国 cut off one's country from the outside world
闭关政策 closed-door policy;exclusion policy;policy of "closed-door"

B

闭关自守 close the country to international intercourse; follow a policy of national isolation; adopt a closed-door policy; isolate from other countries; cut oneself off from the outside world; close the door to the outside world

闭合电路 closed circuit

闭合生态 closed ecology

闭卷考试 closed-book examinition

闭口不谈 refuse to say anything about; avoid mentioning

闭口无言 remain silent; be tongue-tied; be left speechless

闭路电视 closed-circuit television; closed circuit

闭路系统 closed-circuit system

闭门思过 shut oneself up and ponder over one's mistakes; ponder over one's mistakes in seclusion

闭门谢客 close the door to visitors; stop receiving visitors

闭门造车 make a cart behind closed doors—work behind closed doors; divorce oneself from the masses and from reality; act blindly

闭目塞听 shut one's eyes and stop one's ears—cut oneself off from reality

闭目养神 refresh one's spirit by closing one's eyes

闭月羞花 (of feminine beauty) outshine the moon and put the flowers to shame

闭关自守经济 autarky; closed economy

闭路报警装置 closed-circuit alarm device

庀 [bǐ]
动 shelter; cover; protect; shield; screen

庀护 shelter; shield; put under one's protection; take under one's wing

庀荫 ①give shade ②shield; protect; conceal

庀护权 right of give asylum; right to asylum

庀护所 sanctuary; asylum

庀善罚恶 bless the good and punish the evil

惫 [bǐ]
动 ①caution; be cautious ②guard against; provide against

陛 [bì]
名 flight of steps leading to a palace hall

陛下 ①Your Majesty ②His or Her Majesty

毙 [bì]
动 ①fall; drop; collapse ②die; get killed ③kill; execute; shoot dead; shoot

毙命 meet a violent death; get killed

敝 [bì]
I 形 ① shabby; worn-out; ragged ② my; our; this II 动 decline; worsen

敝厂 our factory; this factory

敝处 my place

敝人 your humble servant; I

敝屣 worn-out shoes

敝校 my school

敝姓 my surname

敝衣恶食 wear shabby clothes and eat poor food; lead a hard life

敝帚自珍 value one's own old broom—cherish sth of little value simply because it is one's own

婢 [bì]
名 slave girl; servant girl

婢女 slave girl; servant girl

萉 [bì]
数 two hundred

筚 [bì]
名 bamboo or wicker fence

筚门 bamboo (*or* wicker) door—poor man's hut

筚路褴褛 drive a cart in ragged clothes to break fresh ground—endure hardships in pioneer work

愊 [bì]
形 wilful; self-willed

弼 [bì]
动 assist

蓖 [bì]

蓖麻 castor-oil plant

蓖麻蚕 castor silkworm

蓖麻油 castor oil

蓖麻子 castor bean

痹 [bì]
名 arthralgia; arthritis

滗 [bì]
动 decant; strain; drain

裨 [bì]
名 benefit; advantage ➡ pí

裨益 benefit; advantage; profit

辟 [bì]
I 名 monarch; sovereign II 动 ①(of a sovereign) summon sb and confer on him an official post ② ward off; keep away; remove ➡ pī; pì

辟谷 refrain from eating grain; live without eating grain

辟邪 exorcise evil spirits

碧 [bì]
I 名 green jade II 形 bluish green; blue

碧波 bluish waves

碧空 a clear blue sky; an azure sky

碧蓝 dark blue

碧绿 dark green

碧瓦 green, glazed tile

碧血 blood shed in a just cause

碧玉 jasper

碧云 bluish clouds

碧草如茵 carpet of green grass

碧海青天 blue sea merging with the azure sky

碧血丹心 loyalty unto death

蔽 [bì]
动 cover; shelter; hide

B

弊 [bì]
名 ① disadvantage；harm ② fraud；abuse；malpractice
弊病 ①malady；evil；malpractice ②drawback；disadvantage
弊端 malpractice；abuse；corrupt practice
弊多利少 more disadvantages than advantages；the disadvantages outweigh the advantages

篦 [bì]
Ⅰ名 double-edged fine-tooth comb Ⅱ动 comb with a double-edged fine-tooth comb
篦头 comb one's hair
篦子 double-edged fine-toothed comb

壁 [bì]
名 ① wall ② sth resembling a wall ③ cliff ④ rampart；breastwork
壁报 wall newspaper
壁橱 built-in wardrobe（or cupboard）；closet
壁灯 wall lamp；bracket light
壁挂（wall）hanging
壁厚 wall thickness
壁虎 gecko；house lizard
壁画 mural（painting）；fresco
壁垒 rampart；barrier
壁立（of cliffs, etc.）stand like a wall；rise steeply
壁炉 fireplace
壁球 squash rackets；squash
壁虱 ①tick ②bedbug
壁毯 tapestry
壁纸 wallpaper
壁炉架 mantel pick-up；mantel shelf
壁炉台 mantelpiece
壁细胞 parietal cell
壁垒森严 ① closely guarded；strongly fortified；strong defense preparations ②sharply divided；rival camps confronting each other

避 [bì]
动 ① avoid；evade；shun ② prevent；keep away；repel
避风 ①take（or seek）shelter from the wind ②lie low；stay away from trouble
避讳 [bìhuì] avoid a taboo（on the personal names of emperors，one's elders，etc.）
避讳 [bìhui] ① word（or phrase）to be avoided as taboo；taboo ②evade；dodge
避乱 run away from social up heaval
避免 avoid；refrain from；avert
避难 take refuge；seek asylum
避匿 lie in hiding；hide away
避让 avoid；dodge；get out of the way；make way
避世 retire from the world；withdraw from society
避暑 ① be away for the summer holidays；spend a holiday at a summer resort ②prevent sunstroke

避税 tax avoidance；evade tax
避嫌 avoid doing anything that may arouse suspicion；avoid arousing suspicion
避邪 avoid evil spirits
避孕 contraception
避弹坑 foxhole
避弹衣 flak jacket
避风港 haven；harbour
避风头 lie low until the wind blows over；stay away from trouble
避雷器 lightning arrester
避雷针 lightning rod
避难港 port of refuge
避难所 refuge；sanctuary；haven
避暑药 medicine for preventing sunstroke；preventive against sunstroke
避蚊剂 mosquito repellent
避孕栓 contraceptive suppository
避孕套 condom
避孕丸 the pill
避而不见 avoid meeting（sb）；steer clear of（sb）
避坑落井 dodge a pit only to fall into a well；out of the frying pan into the fire
避难就易 shirk the difficult and take the easy；take the easier way out；choose the easier of the two alternatives
避人耳目 avoid being noticed；elude observation
避实就虚 stay clear of the enemy's main force and strike at his weak points
避暑胜地 summer resort
避孕药膏 contraceptive jelly
避孕药具 contraceptive agents and devices
避孕用品 contraceptives
避重就轻 evade major responsibility and take minor；avoid the important and dwell on the trivial

臂 [bì]
名 ①arm ②upper arm ③sth resembling an arm ➡bei
臂膀 arm
臂纱（black）armband
臂章 ① armband；armlet ② shoulder emblem（or patch）

璧 [bì]
名 round flat piece of jade with a hole in the middle
璧还 ① return（a borrowed object）with thanks ②decline（a gift）with thanks
璧谢 decline（a gift）with thanks

biān（ㄅㄧㄢ）

边 [biān]
Ⅰ名 ①margin；side；edge；brim ② by the side of；close by ③ part；side ④ frontier；boundary；border ⑤hem；border；edge（as an

ornament) ⑥side ⑦limit;bound Ⅱ〔副〕along;while:边走边想 walk along thinking to oneself

边隘 frontier pass
边白 margin
边鄙 frontier region;remote district
边城 border (*or* frontier) town
边陲 border area;frontier
边带 sideband
边地 border district;borderland
边防 frontier (*or* border) defence
边关 frontier pass
边花 ray flower
边际 limit;bound;boundary
边疆 border area;borderland;frontier;frontier region
边界 boundary;border
边境 border;frontier
边框 frame;rim
边门 side door;wicket door (*or* gate)
边民 people living on the frontiers;inhabitants of a border area
边卡 border checkpoint
边区 border area (*or* region)
边塞 frontier fortress
边线 ①sideline ②foul line
边沿 border;edge;fringe
边音 lateral (sound)
边缘 ①border;edge;fringe;verge;brink;periphery ②marginal;borderline
边远 far from the centre;remote;outlying
边寨 borderland village
边防军 frontier force
边防哨 border sentry
边角料 leftover bits and pieces (of industrial material)
边界层 boundary layer
边界线 boundary line
边心距 apothem
边缘海 marginal sea
边缘化 decentring
边缘人 fringe group
边防部队 frontier guards
边防检查 frontier inspection
边防警察 frontier police
边防战士 frontier guard
边际成本 fixed cost;marginal cost
边际企业 marginal enterprises
边际效益 marginal benefit
边界划定 boundary delimitation
边界贸易 border trade
边界事件 border incident
边界谈判 border talks;boundary negotiations
边界现状 status quo on the border;status quo of the boundary
边界协定 boundary agreement
边界争端 boundary dispute

边界走向 alignment of the boundary line
边境城市 border cities
边境冲突 border clash (*or* conflict)
边境管制 border control;frontier control
边境交货 delivered at frontier (D.A.F.)
边境贸易 frontier trade;border trade
边境市镇 border town
边境事件 border incident
边境搜查 border search
边缘地区 border district;borders
边缘科学 frontier science;borderline science;bi-disciplinaty (*or* frontier, boundary, borderline) science
边缘团体 borderline group
边防检查站 border checkpoint;frontier inspection station
边际效用论 theory of marginal utility
边界通行证 frontier pass
边境贸易额 border trade volume
边线裁判员 linesman
边境贸易市场 border trade market
边境贸易中心 border trade centre
边境易货贸易 border barter trade
边界实际控制线 line of actual control on the border
边境经济合作区 border economic cooperative zone

砭 〔biān〕 Ⅰ〔名〕stone needle Ⅱ〔动〕①use stone needles in acupuncture ②pierce;castigate

编 〔biān〕 Ⅰ〔动〕①weave;plait ②organize;group;arrange ③edit;compile ④write;compose ⑤fabricate;invent;make up;cook up Ⅱ〔名〕①copy;book ②part of a book;volume ③authorized or stipulated strength or size;establishment

编班 group (*or* organize) into classes
编程 program
编次 order of arrangement
编档 filing
编导 ①write and direct (a play,film,etc.) ②playwright-director (of a play);choreographer director (of a ballet);scenarist-director (of a film)
编订 compile and edit
编队 ①form into columns;organize into teams ②formation (of ships or aircraft)
编发 edit and release (manuscript, news, etc.)
编号 ①number ②serial number
编辑 ①edit;compile ②editor;compiler
编校 edit
编剧 ①write a play, scenario, etc. ②playwright ③screenwriter;scenarist
编码 coding
编目 ① catalogue; list ② make a catalogue;

catalogue
编内 in-staff
编排 arrange;lay out
编审 ①read and edit ②senior editor
编外 (of personnel) not on the permanent staff;not on the regular payroll
编委 editorial member
编写 ①compile ②write;compose
编选 select and edit;compile
编演 write and produce (a play,etc.)
编译 ①translate and edit ②translator-editor
编印 compile and print;publish
编造 ① compile;draw up;work out ② fabricate;invent;concoct;make up;cook up ③ create out of the imagination
编者 editor;compiler
编织 weave;knit;plait;braid
编制 ① weave;plait;braid ② work out;draw up ③authorized strength of a unit;establishment
编制 authorized staff;authorized force;fixed number of personnel of a unit;authorized strength of a unit
编钟 a set of bells;chimes
编著 compile;write
编撰 compile;write
编组 ①marshalling ②organize into groups
编纂 compile
编程序 write program
编程员 programmer
编法儿 try every means;do everything possible
编辑部 editorial department
编辑机 editor;collector
编码机 code machine
编码盘 coding disk
编码器 coder
编码员 coder
编目部 cataloguing department
编目员 cataloguer
编年史 annalistic history;annals;chronicle
编年体 annalistic style (in historiography)
编者按 editor's note;editorial note
编组站 marshalling station
编队飞行 formation flight (or flying)
编队轰炸 formation bombing
编辑人员 editorial staff
编辑终端 editing terminal
编码程序 builder
编码指令 coded order
编外人员 non-permanent staff;unofficial personnel;extra-organizational personnel
编译程序 compiling routine;compiler program;compiler
编余人员 personnel left over after reorganization;surplus personnel
编造假账 falsification of account

编制预算 budget presentation;prepare budget
编辑委员会 editorial board
编译计算机 compiling computer
编译自动化 compiling automation

煸 [biān]
〔动〕 stir-fry before stewing:干煸鳝鱼 dry fried eel section

蝙 [biān]

蝙蝠 bat
蝙蝠衫 an upper outer garment with batwing sleeves

鳊 [biān]

鳊鱼 bream

鞭 [biān]
Ⅰ〔名〕①whip;lash ②sth resembling a whip ③ iron nodular staff ④ string of small firecrackers ⑤ penis of certain male animals Ⅱ〔动〕 flog;whip;lash
鞭策 spur on;urge on
鞭笞 flog;lash
鞭虫 whipworm
鞭打 whip;lash;flog;thrash
鞭痕 welt;whip scar;lash mark
鞭毛 flagellum
鞭炮 ① firecrackers;maroon ② a string of small firecrackers
鞭挞 lash;castigate
鞭子 whip
鞭击法 fustigation
鞭毛虫 flagellate
鞭长莫及 beyond the reach of one's power (or authority);too far away to be helped
鞭辟入里 penetrating;trenchant;incisive

biǎn (ㄅㄧㄢˇ)

贬 [biǎn]
〔动〕 ① devalue;reduce;depreciate ② demote;relegate;degrade ③ censure;belittle;play down
贬斥 ①demote ②denounce
贬低 belittle;depreciate;play down;disparage
贬价 reduce the price;mark down
贬义 derogatory sense
贬抑 belittle;depreciate
贬谪 banish from the court;relegate
贬值 devaluation;depreciation of value;devalue,depreciate (a currency)
贬职 demote
贬义词 derogatory term;expression of censure
贬为庶民 be degraded to the status of a commoner
贬值货币 depreciated money

扁 [biǎn]
〔形〕 flat ➡piān

B

扁虫 flatworm
扁蝽 flat bug
扁锉 flat file;mill file
扁担 carrying pole;shoulder pole
扁豆 hyacinth bean
扁骨 flat bone
扁簧 flat spring
扁坯 slab
扁桃 ①almond tree ②almond ③flat peach
扁圆 oblate
扁钢条 flat steel bar
扁平足 flatfooted
扁桃体 tonsil
扁形动物 flatworm;platyhelminth
扁桃体肥大 hypertrophy of tonsils
扁桃体切除术 tonsillectomy

匾 [biǎn]
〈名〉①horizontal inscribed board ②silk banner embroidered with words of praise ③ *bian*,big round shallow basket made from bamboo strips (for raising silkworms or holding grain)
匾额 horizontal inscribed board

褊 [biǎn]
〈形〉narrow;cramped
褊急 narrow-minded and short-tempered
褊狭 narrow;cramped

biàn (ㄅㄧㄢˋ)

弁 [biàn]
〈名〉① *bian*,man's cap worn in ancient times ②low-ranking military officer
弁言 foreword;preface

苄 [biàn]
〈名〉benzyl
苄胺 benzylamine;aminotoluene
苄醇 benzyl alcohol
苄基 benzyl

抃 [biàn]
〈动〉clap (one's hands);applaud
抃跃 jump and dance for joy

忭 [biàn]
〈形〉glad;happy
忭颂 happily celebrate with song;felicitate

变 [biàn]
Ⅰ〈动〉①become different;change ②change into;turn into;become ③change;transform;turn ④sell off (one's property) ⑤flexible Ⅱ〈名〉unexpected turn of events Ⅲ〈形〉changeable;changed
变产 sell off one's property
变场 variable field
变成 change into;turn into;become;transform into
变蛋 preserved egg
变调 ① tone sandhi ② transposition;modulation
变动 alteration;change;oscillation

变法 introduce institutional reforms
变干 exsiccation
变革 transform;change
变更 change;alter;modify
变工 exchange work (*or* labour)
变故 unforeseen event;accident;misfortune
变卦 go back on one's word;break an agreement
变化 change;vary
变幻 change irregularly;fluctuate
变换 vary;alternate;commutation
变价 appraise at the current rate
变节 make a political recantation;turn one's coat
变脸 ① suddenly turn hostile;take on a new look ② rapidly change facial expression (dramatic technique in play performance, esp. in Sichuan opera)
变量 variable
变卖 sell off (one's property)
变频 frequency conversion
变迁 changes;vicissitudes
变热 get hot;warming
变色 ① change colour;discolour ② change countenance;become angry
变式 variant;version
变数 variable
变速 speed change;gearshift
变态 ① metamorphosis ② abnormal;anomalous
变体 variant;version
变天 ①change of weather ②change of heavens—restoration of reactionary rule
变通 be flexible;accommodate (*or* adapt) sth to circumstances
变现 realization;liquidation
变相 ①in disguised form;covert ②phasing
变心 cease to be faithful;change loyalties;break faith
变星 variable (star)
变形 be out of shape;become deformed
变型 modification
变性 ①denaturation ②change sex
变样 change in shape (*or* appearance)
变异 variation;heteromorphosis
变址 indexed address;index;modifying
变质 ①go bad;deteriorate ②metamorphism
变种 ①mutation;variety ②variety;variant
变奏 variation
变把戏 perform conjuring tricks;conjure;juggle
变电站 (transformer) substation
变分法 calculus of variations
变工队 work-exchange team
变化率 rate of change;slewing rate
变换器 convertor
变迹器 apodizer

变流器 converter
变码器 transcoder
变频管 converter tube
变频器 converter
变色镜 light-sensitive glasses
变色龙 ①chameleon ②changeable (or fickle) person (esp. in politics)
变速比 gear ratio
变速器 gearbox;transmission
变速箱 change speed gear box
变温层 troposphere
变温性 poikilothermism
变戏法 perform conjuring tricks;conjure;juggle
变形虫 amoeba
变形体 plasmodium
变性人 transsexual
变性术 sex reassignment
变压器 transformer
变质岩 metamorphic rock
变阻器 rheostat
变本加厉 become aggravated; be further intensified
变动预算 sliding (or variable) budget
变废为宝 change waste material into things of value;recycle waste material
变分方程 variation equation
变分原理 variation principle
变更记录 change record
变更资本 capital punishment; capital amendment
变幻莫测 changeable;unpredictable
变换电子 conversion electron
变节分子 turncoat
变节投敌 turn traitor and go over to the enemy
变频增益 conversion gain
变色汽车 colour-changing car
变速车道 speed change lane
变速运动 variable motion
变态反应 allergy
变态心理 abnormal psychology
变通办法 accommodation;adoption
变温动物 poikilothermal (or coldblooded) animal
变相集资 disguised irregular fund raising
变相涨价 disguised price increase; disguised increase in price; camouflaged price hike; raise price in a disguised form;raise prices by deceptive means
变形金刚 transformer
变形镜头 anamorphic lens
变形能力 deformability
变性酒精 denatured alcohol
变性手术 transsexual operation
变种杂交 intervarieted cross
变焦距镜头 zoom lens

变色滤光器 variable-colour filter; metachromatic filter
变态心理学 abnormal psychology (a science)
变形虫痢疾 amoebic dysentery
变性蛋白质 denatured protein
变更商业登记 amendment of registration
变更注册事项 alternation on entires in the register
变速传动装置 speed transforming transmission;variable-speed drive device
变相通货膨胀 disguised inflation

昇 ［biàn］
形 ①bright ②joyful;merry

便 ［biàn］
Ⅰ 形 ① convenient; handy ② informal; plain;ordinary;simple　Ⅱ 名 ①convenience; ease ②piss or shit;urine or stool　Ⅲ 动 excrete;relieve oneself　Ⅳ 副 just;simply;then; in that case　Ⅴ 连 even if;even though ➡ pián

便车 sb's car in which one may have a ride
便池 urinal
便当 ①convenient;handy;easy ②fast food in box
便道 ① shortcut ② pavement; sidewalk ③ makeshift road
便饭 ordinary meal;simple meal;potluck
便服 ①everyday clothes;informal dress ②civilian clothes
便函 informal letter sent by an organization
便壶 (bed) urinal;chamber pot
便捷 ①convenient ②quick;nimble
便裤 casual slacks
便览 brief guide
便利 ① convenient; easy ② facilitate; accommodate
便路 shortcut
便帽 cap
便门 side door;wicket door
便秘 constipation
便民 for the convenience of the people
便溺 urinate or defecate;relieve oneself
便盆 bed pan
便桥 temporary (or makeshift) bridge
便人 somebody who happens to be on hand for an errand
便士 penny
便溏 loose stool
便条 (informal) note
便桶 chamber pot
便鞋 cloth shoes;slippers
便血 have (or pass) blood in one's stool
便宴 informal dinner
便衣 ①civilian clothes; plain clothes ②plainclothesman
便于 easy to;convenient for
便纸 toilet tissue;toilet paper

B

便中 at one's convenience；when it's convenient
便步走 march at ease；route step
便笺儿 ①(informal) note ②notepaper；memo；memo pad
便利店 convenience store
便携式 portable；man-pack
便饭招待 treat sb with an ordinary meal
便民服务 handy service for the people
便民商店 convenience store；variety store
便士股票 penny stock
便宜行事 (authorized to) act at one's discretion；act as one sees fit
便酌候教 I request your gracious presence at an informal dinner. (or I'll give an informal dinner in your honour.)
便携式计算机 laptop computer
便携式录像机 portable videotape recorder
便携式摄像机 portable video camera
便携式终端装置 portable terminal
便携式电视接收机 portable television receiver

遍 [biàn]
I 副 all over；everywhere Ⅱ 量 once through；a time：改了一遍 correct it(once)/写一遍 write it once
遍布 be found everywhere；spread all over
遍地 all over the place；everywhere
遍及 extend (or spread) all over
遍地开花 blossom everywhere；spring up all over the place
遍体鳞伤 be covered all over with cuts and bruises；be beaten black and blue；be a mass of bruises

缏 [biàn]
◇草帽缏 sennit

艑 [biàn]
名 boat；ship

辨 [biàn]
动 differentiate；distinguish；discriminate
辨别 differentiate；distinguish；discriminate
辨认 identify；recognize
辨析 differentiate and analyse；discriminate
辨正 determine and rectify
辨别力 ability to see things in their true light；discerning power
辨证施治 diagnosis and treatment based on an overall analysis of the illness and the patient's condition

辩 [biàn]
动 argue；dispute；debate
辩白 offer an explanation；plead innocence；try to defend oneself
辩驳 dispute；refute
辩才 eloquence
辩词 explanation；argument
辩护 ①speak in defence of；argue in favour of；defend ②plead；defend

辩解 provide an explanation；try to defend oneself
辩论 argue；debate
辩赛 debate contest
辩手 debater
辩证 ①investigate；authenticate ②dialectical
辩护权 right to defence
辩护人 defender；counsel；barrister；legal counsel of the defendant
辩护士 apologist
辩论会 debate
辩证法 dialectics
辩护律师 defence counsel；defence lawyer
辩论比赛 debate contest
辩诉交易 plea bargain
辩证逻辑 dialectical logic
辩证唯物主义 dialectical materialism

辫 [biàn]
I 名 ①plait；braid；pigtail ②sth resembling a braid Ⅱ 动 plait (into a braid)：辫辫子 plait one's hair
辫子 ① plait；braid；pigtail ② a mistake or shortcoming that may be exploited by an opponent；handle

bian (· ㄅㄧㄢ)

边 [bian]
◇北边儿 in the north
东边儿 in the east
后边儿 rear；back
里边儿 inside
那边儿 there；that place
南边儿 in the south
前边儿 in front
上边儿 above；over；on top of
外边儿 outside
西边儿 in the west
下边儿 ① below；under，underneath ② next；following
右边儿 on the right
这边儿 here
左边儿 on the left

biāo (ㄅㄧㄠ)

标 [biāo]
I 名 ①tip (or top) of a tree；treetop ② outward sign；symptom；superficiality ③ mark；sign ④ prize；award ⑤ standard；requirement；quota ⑥ tender；bid Ⅱ 动 put a mark，tag or label on；mark；label Ⅲ 量：一标人马 a detachment of troops；a group of soldiers
标榜 ①flaunt；advertise；parade ②boost；excessively praise
标本 ①specimen；sample ②the root cause and

symptoms of a disease

标兵 ①parade guards (usu. spaced out along parade routes) ②example; model; pacesetter

标程 beacon course

标尺 ①surveyor's rod; staff ②staff gauge ③rear sight

标灯 ①beacon light; beacon ②sign lamp

标底 base number of a tender; highest price the project owner could possibly accept; bottom price of the bid

标的 ①target ②aim; purpose ③common objectives of both parties to a commercial contract with regard to their rights and duties in the execution of the project

标点 ①punctuation ②punctuate

标定 ①demarcate calibration ②standardize ③check according to set standards ④standard; standardized

标杆 ①surveyor's pole; sign post ②model; example; pacesetter

标高 elevation; level

标号 grade

标记 sign; mark; symbol

标价 ①mark a price ②marked price

标量 scalar quantity

标明 mark; indicate

标牌 breastplate; label

标签 label; tag

标枪 javelin

标书 ①(papers for) invitation to bidding ②bidding papers

标题 title; heading; headline; caption

标音 transcription

标语 slogan; poster

标志 ①sign; mark; symbol ②indicate; mark; symbolize

标识 sign; mark; symbol

标致 (usu. of women) beautiful; handsome

标注 mark

标桩 (marking) stake

标准 ①standard; criterion ②serving as (or conforming to) a standard

标本虫 spider beetle

标题词 headword

标引词 index term

标语牌 placard

标志层 marker bed

标准版 standard edition

标准层 key bed

标准差 standard deviation

标准化 standardization; standardize

标准级 standard level

标准间 standard room

标准局 bureau of standards

标准时 standard time

标准像 official portrait

标准型 normalized form; standard form

标准音 standard pronunciation

标准语 standard speech (or language)

标本兼治 seek both temporary and permanent solutions; treat both the incidental and fundamental aspects simultaneously

标点符号 punctuation mark

标定数据 rating data; nominal data

标记文件 tab file

标题新闻 the headlines; headline news

标题音乐 programme music

标新立异 start sth new just in order to be different; do sth unconventional (or unorthodox); create sth new and original

标准测试 standard testing

标准代号 standard code

标准合同 model contract

标准样品 standard sample

标准大气压 standard atmosphere

标准工资率 standard wage rate

标准化考试 standard test

标准集装箱 standard container

标准大气压力 standard atmospheric pressure

标准化考试题 standardization test

标准普尔指数 Standard & Poor's Composite Index

标准作业程序 standard operation procedure

彪 [biāo] 名 ①stripes of a tiger ②literary talent ③young tiger

彪炳 shining; splendid

彪悍 intrepid; doughty; valiant

彪炳千古 shine through the ages

彪形大汉 burly chap; husky fellow; hefty fellow

猋 [biāo] 形 rapid

摽 [biāo] 动 ①wave off ②abandon; cast aside ➡ biào

膘 [biāo] 名 fat (of an animal)

飙 [biāo] 名 violent wind; hurricane; whirlwind

飙车 drive a car at top speed; speed

飙升 skyrocket; rise quickly

镖 [biāo] 名 lance

镖局 professional establishment which provided armed escorts

镖客 armed escort

镖师 armed escort

镳 [biāo] 名 bit (of a bridle); curb bit

biǎo (ㄅㄧㄠˇ)

表 [biāo] I 名 ①surface; outside; external; outward

appearance ②table; form; list ③memorial to an emperor (usu. on an important event or matter) ④relationship between the children or grandchildren of a brother and a sister or of sisters ⑤pole used as a sun dial ⑥meter; gauge ⑦watch; clock ⑧model; example Ⅱ 劢 ① show; express; demonstrate ② administer medicine to bring out the cold

表白 express or state clearly; explain; clarify; explain oneself

表报 statistical tables and reports

表册 statistical forms; book of tables (*or* forms)

表层 surface layer; skin layer

表差 difference

表尺 rear sight

表达 express; convey; voice

表带 watchband; watch strap

表弟 younger male cousin; cousin

表高 indicated altitude

表哥 older male cousin; cousin

表格 form; table

表功 ①brag about one's deeds ②praise; commend

表观 apparent

表汗 induce perspiration (by medication); bring about perspiration

表记 sth given as a token; souvenir; token

表姐 older female cousin; cousin

表决 decide by vote; vote

表里 ①outside and inside; one's outward show and inner thoughts ②exterior and interior

表链 watch chain

表露 show; reveal

表妹 younger female cousin; cousin

表面 ① surface; face; outside; appearance ② dial plate; dial

表明 make known; make clear; state clearly; indicate

表盘 dial plate; dial

表皮 epidermis; cuticle

表亲 ①cousin ②cousinship

表情 ① expression; countenance; look ② express one's feelings

表示 ①show; express; indicate ②expression; indication

表叔 male cousins of one's father

表述 explain; state

表率 example; model

表态 make known one's position; declare where one stands; commit oneself

表现 ①show; display; manifest ②expression; manifestation; display ③ behaviour; performance ④show off

表象 idea; image; presentation

表兄 older male cousin; cousin

表演 ① perform; act; play ② demonstrate ③ performance; exhibition

表扬 praise; commend

表语 predicative

表彰 cite (in dispatches); commend

表尺座 rear sight base

表决权 right to vote; voting power

表决心 express one's determination

表蒙子 watch glass; crystal

表面光 attractive on the surface; cheaply showy

表面化 come to the surface; become apparent

表面性 acrotic; superficialness

表现型 phenotype

表象论 presentationism

表演唱 singing with actions

表演赛 exhibition match; demonstration show

表演者 performer

表扬信 commendatory letter

表白心迹 lay bare one's true feeling

表观运动 apparent motion

表观质量 apparent mass

表决程序 voting procedure

表决机器 voting machine

表决通过 be voted through

表决议案 vote on the bills and proposals

表里不一 think one way and act another

表里如一 think and act in one and the same way

表里相济 mutual complementary; the outside and the inside supplement each other

表面处理 surface treatment

表面文章 show; ostentation

表面价值 face value

表面现象 superficial phenomenon

表面硬化 case-hardening

表面张力 surface tension

表情障碍 dysmimia

表示遗憾 express regret over

表现手法 technique of expression

表现形式 form of expression; manifestation

表现主义 expressionism

表演项目 demonstration event

表意文字 ideograph; ideogram; ideography

表音文字 phonography

表决指示牌 vote indicator

表面消费量 apparent consumption

表态性发言 statement of one's position

表壮不如里壮 Inner strength counts more than outward prowess.

婊 [biǎo]

婊子 prostitute; whore

裱 [biǎo]

劢 ①mount (a picture, etc.) ②paste paper on (a wall, ceiling, etc.); paper

裱褙 mount (a picture, etc.)

裱糊 paper (a wall, ceiling, etc.)

褾 [biǎo]
名 ①cuff of sleeve ②trimming on clothing, braid, hemming

biào（ㄅㄧㄠ）

俵 [biào]
动 distribute

摽 [biào]
动 ①fasten together; tie fast ②arm in arm ③cling to one another; locked together; be glued to ④fall ⑤hit; strike ⟹ biāo
摽劲儿 (of competitors) strain every muscle; exert oneself to emulate or excel

鳔 [biào]
Ⅰ名 ①swimming bladder; air bladder ②fish glue Ⅱ动 stick with (fish) glue
鳔胶 isinglass

biē（ㄅㄧㄝ）

瘪 [biē]
⟹ biě
瘪三 wretched-looking tramp who lives by begging or stealing

憋 [biē]
动 ①suppress; hold back; bottle up; shut up ②suffocate; stifle ③mull over; brew ④snap; break
憋闷 feel oppressed; be depressed; be dejected
憋气 ① feel suffocated (or oppressed) ② choke with resentment; feel injured and resentful

鳖 [biē]
名 (Chinese) soft-shelled turtle
鳖甲 turtle shell
鳖裙 calipash

bié（ㄅㄧㄝ）

别 [bié]
Ⅰ动 ①leave; part ②differentiate; distinguish ③fasten with a pin or clip ④stick in; insert in order to hinder the movement of sth or sb ⑤turn round; change ⑥cause to stumble by a swinging movement of one's leg; trip up ⑦deliberately hinder the advance (of a bike or car with one's own) Ⅱ代 other; another Ⅲ名 ①difference; distinction ②classification; category Ⅳ副 ①don't: 别客气。Don't stand on ceremony. (or Make yourself at home.) ②(usu. followed by 是, indicating conjecture of sth against one's own wish): 他已经答应来了，别是变卦了呀。He agreed to be here by now, and I hope he hasn't changed his mind. ⟹ biè
别车 stop an advancing bike (or car) with one's own
别称 another name; alternative name
别处 other places; elsewhere

别的 other
别管 no matter (who, what, etc.)
别号 another name; alias
别家 other stores, shops, factories, etc.
别看 in spite of; despite
别离 take leave of; leave
别论 another (or different) matter
别名 another name; alternative name
别人 other people; others; people
别史 privately compiled history
别墅 villa
别说 to say nothing of; not to mention; let alone
别提 no need to mention; you can well imagine
别腿 stick one's leg out to trip sb up
别绪 sorrow of separation
别针 ①safety pin; pin ②brooch
别致 unique; unconventional
别字 ① incorrectly written (or mispronounced) character ②another name; alias
别动队 ①special detachment; commando ②an armed secret agent squad
别出心裁 have an unconventional idea; try to be different (from the usual pattern)
别具匠心 have great originality; show ingenuity
别具一格 have a style of one's own; have a unique (or distinctive) style
别开生面 start sth new (or original); break a new path; break fresh ground
别来无恙 I trust all has been well with you since we last saw each other.
别其真伪 determine whether it's true or false
别树一帜 set up a new banner; found a new school of thought; have a style of one's own
别无长物 have nothing other than
别无出路 There is no other way out.
别无二致 without the slightest difference; just the same; identical
别无他图 have no other intentions
别有风味 have a distinctive flavour
别有所指 There is an implication here.
别有天地 a place of unique beauty; scenery of exceptional charm; an altogether different world
别有用心 have ulterior motives; have an axe to grind

蹩 [bié]
动 sprain (one's ankle or wrist)
蹩脚 inferior; shoddy
蹩脚货 inferior goods; poor stuff; shoddy work; third-rate goods

biě（ㄅㄧㄝ）

瘪 [biě]
Ⅰ形 shrivelled; shrunken; deflated Ⅱ动 ①become hallow; sink down ②be on a spot;

B

be (*or* put) in difficulty ➡ biē

bié（ㄅ丨ㄝ）

别 [bié]
囵 sway; bring round; change（sb's opinion）➡ bié

别扭 ① awkward; difficult; uncomfortable ② not see eye to eye; disagree ③（of speech or writing）unnatural; awkward

bīn（ㄅ丨ㄣ）

宾 [bīn]
囵 guest
宾词 predicate
宾格 the objective case
宾馆 guesthouse
宾服 admire; be convinced
宾客 guests; visitors
宾朋 friends and guests; guests
宾语 object
宾主 host and guest
宾客盈门 house always full of visitors
宾至如归 where guests feel at home; home away from home

彬 [bīn]
囵 refined; urbane
彬彬 refined; urbane
彬彬有礼 refined and courteous; urbane; be polite and respectful; be well-mannered

傧 [bīn]
傧相 ① usher（for quests）② attendant at a wedding

滨 [bīn]
Ⅰ 囵 water's edge; bank; shore Ⅱ 囵 be close to（the sea, a river, etc.）; border on
滨江路 river-side road; bund

缤 [bīn]
缤纷 in riotous profusion

槟 [bīn]
槟榔 betel palm; areca
槟子 species of apple which is slightly sour and astringent

濒 [bīn]
囵 ① be close to（the sea, a river, etc.）; border on ② be on the point of; be on the brink of
濒别 on the eve of parting
濒临 be close to; border on; be on the verge of
濒灭 on the verge of extinction
濒死 on the brink（*or* verge）of death
濒危 ① be in imminent danger; near death ② be critically ill; near death
濒行 about to leave; before setting out
濒于 be on the brink of

濒临灭绝 be on the verge（*or* brink）of extinction
濒危物种 endangered species
濒于破产 be on the brink of bankruptcy; be about to go to rack and ruin
濒危植物群 endangered flora
濒危植物物种 endangered plant species

bìn（ㄅ丨ㄣ）

摈 [bìn]
囵 abandon; discard; reject
摈斥 reject; dismiss
摈除 discard; get rid of; dispense with
摈弃 abandon; discard; cast away

殡 [bìn]
Ⅰ 囵 coffin Ⅱ 囵 ① lay a coffin in a memorial hall ② carry a coffin to the burial place
殡车 hearse
殡殓 corpse and carry it to the grave
殡葬 funeral and interment
殡仪馆 the undertaker's; funeral parlour（*or* home）

髌 [bìn]
囵 ① kneecap; patella ② chop at the kneecaps
髌骨 kneecap; patella

鬓 [bìn]
囵 temples; hair at the temples
鬓发 hair over the temples
鬓角 temples; hair on the temples

bīng（ㄅ丨ㄥ）

冰 [bīng]
Ⅰ 囵 ① ice ② sth resembling ice Ⅱ 囵 ① feel cold ② put sth on the ice（*or* in cold water）; ice
冰棒 ice-lolly; popsicle; ice-sucker; frozen sucker
冰雹 hail; hailstone
冰场 skating（*or* ice）rink; ice stadium; ice arena
冰川 glacier
冰镩 ice chisel
冰袋 ice bag
冰蛋 frozen eggs
冰刀 （ice）skates
冰灯 ice lantern
冰点 freezing point
冰雕 ① ice carving ② carved ice; ice sculpture
冰冻 ① freeze ② ice
冰斗 cirque
冰毒 drug "ice"—a deadly stimulant drug
冰帆 ① iceboat ② iceboating
冰封 ①（of a river, lake, etc.）freeze over; be blocked up with ice ② icebound
冰盖 ice sheet
冰糕 ice cream

B

冰镐 ice axe
冰柜 freezer;refrigerator
冰壶 ①curling ②curling stone
冰河 glacier
冰花 ① frost（on windows）;frostwork ② (soft) rime
冰窖 icehouse
冰晶 ice crystal
冰景 icescape
冰冷 ice-cold
冰凉 ice-cold
冰排 ice raft;ice floe
冰片 borneol
冰瀑 ice cascade
冰期 glacial epoch;ice age
冰碛 moraine
冰橇 led;sledge;sleigh
冰球 ①ice hockey ②puck
冰人 matchmaker;go-between
冰山 ① icy mountain ② iceberg;ice-capped mountain ③individual（or group）not to be relied upon for long
冰释 （of misgivings,misunderstandings,etc.） disappear;vanish;be dispelled
冰霜 ①ice and frost;②moral integrity ③austerity
冰塔 serac
冰糖 crystal sugar;rock candy
冰隙 crevasse
冰箱 icebox;refrigerator;freezer
冰鞋 skating boots;skates
冰心 moral purity
冰雪 ice and snow
冰镇 iced
冰柱 icicle
冰砖 ice-cream brick
冰锥 icicle
冰川湖 glacial lake
冰川期 glacial epoch;ice age
冰川学 glaciology
冰醋酸 glacial acetic acid
冰灯展 ice lantern show
冰冻区 frost zone
冰封区 icebound
冰棍儿 ice-lolly; popsicle; ice-sucker; frozen sucker
冰激凌 ice cream
冰晶石 cryolite
冰晶云 ice-crystal cloud
冰凝器 cryophorus
冰洲石 Iceland spar
冰川作用 glaciation
冰雕艺术 art of ice carving
冰冻季节 freezing season
冰冻疗法 ice therapy
冰冻食物 frozen foods
冰魂雪魄 pure and noble

冰河时代 glacial epoch;ice age
冰肌玉骨 flesh of ice and bones of jade—①a beautiful woman ②noble and unsullied
冰酿啤酒 ice beer
冰清玉洁 pure-hearted;pure and noble
冰染染料 azoic dyes
冰上表演 ice show
冰上溜石 curling
冰上赛车 icekhana
冰上舞蹈 skate dancing
冰上运动 ice-sports
冰糖葫芦 candied haws on a stick
冰天雪地 world of ice and snow
冰消瓦解 melt like ice and break like tiles—disintegrate;dissolve;be dispelled
冰雪聪明 extremely intelligent; remarkably bright;brilliant
冰点测定器 cryoscope
冰炭不相容 as incompatible（or irreconcilable）as ice and hot coals
冰箱保鲜膜 saran wrap;handi-wrap
冰雪橄榄球 ski football
冰冻三尺,非一日之寒 it takes more than one cold day for the river to freeze three *chi* deep—the trouble has been brewing for quite some time

兵 [bīng]
图 ①weapons;arms ②army;troops ③soldier;serviceman ④about war or military affairs ⑤(of Chinese chess) pawn
兵变 mutiny
兵车 war chariot;military vehicle
兵船 man-of-war;naval vessel;warship
兵法 art of war;military strategy and tactics
兵符 ①(in former times) military tally ②a book on the act of war
兵戈 ①weapons;arms ②fighting;war
兵家 ① military strategist ② military commander;soldier
兵舰 warship
兵谏 forced remonstration
兵力 military strength;armed forces;troops
兵乱 turmoil caused by war
兵马 troops and horses;military forces
兵痞 army riffraff; army ruffian; soldier of fortune
兵器 weaponry;weapons;arms;armament
兵权 military leadership;military power
兵戎 arms;weapons
兵士 rank-and-file soldier;private
兵书 book on the art of war
兵团 ①large（military）unit;formation;corps ②army
兵械 ordnance;armament
兵役 military service
兵营 military camp;barracks
兵员 soldiers;troops

B

兵源 manpower resources; sources of troops
兵站 army service station; military depot
兵种 combat branch; of one of the armed forces; arm
兵卒 soldiers
兵工厂 munitions (*or* ordnance) factory; arsenal; arms plant
兵马俑 terracotta soldiers and horses
兵役法 military service law
兵役制 system of military service
兵不血刃 with blades innocent of blood—win victory without shedding a drop of blood (*or* firing a shot)
兵不厌诈 There can never be too much deception in war; All's fair in war; War allows deceit.
兵多将广 a very large army with many able generals—very powerful military forces
兵贵神速 Speed is what counts in war; In war it's speed that counts.
兵荒马乱 the turmoil and chaos of war
兵精粮足 have well-trained troops and abundant supplies
兵连祸结 ravaged by successive wars; wartorn; war-ridden; One battle followed another, and the end never came.
兵临城下 The enemy host has reached the city gates; The city is under siege.
兵强马壮 strong soldiers and sturdy horses—a well-trained and powerful army
兵戎相见 appeal to arms; open hostilities; cross swords with; meet on the battleground
兵败如山倒 A rout is like a landslide.
兵贵勇不贵多 The strength of an army lies in its morale, not its numbers.
兵来将挡,水来土掩 confront soldiers with generals and stem water with earth—take such measures as the situation calls for
兵马未动,粮草先行 food and fodder should go ahead of troops and horses—proper preparations should be made ahead of time

bǐng（ㄅㄧㄥˇ）

丙 [bǐng]
I 数 third II 名 fire
丙等 third grade; grade C
丙纶 polypropylene fibre
丙酮 acetone
丙烯酸 acrylic acid
丙酮树脂 acetone resin
丙型肝炎 hepatitis C; viral hepatitis type C
丙种射线 gamma ray

秉 [bǐng]
动 ①hold; grasp ②control; preside over
秉笔 wield a brush
秉承 take (orders); receive (commands)

秉公 justly; impartially
秉性 natural disposition
秉正 fairminded; honest; upright
秉政 be at the helm of the state; be in power; be in office
秉直 honest; upright
秉烛 hold a candle
秉公办理 handle a matter impartially; act with justice
秉烛待旦 sit with the light in one's hand till morning
秉烛夜游 wander about at night carrying a lamp—make merry while one may

柄 [bǐng]
I 名 ①handle ②stem (of a flower, leaf or fruit) ③opportunity that may serve as evidence against sb; handle ④power; authority II 动 be in control; be in power III 量：两柄大刀 two broadswords
柄臣 powerful minister (of a monarchy)
柄国 be in control of the government; govern
柄权 be in power; exercise control
柄政 be in power

饼 [bǐng]
名 ①round flat cake ②sth shaped like a cake
饼铛 baking pan
饼肥 cake (fertilizer)
饼干 biscuit; cracker
饼子 (maize or millet) pancake

炳 [bǐng]
I 形 bright; splendid; remarkable II 动 illuminate; shine
炳耀 ①brilliant ②illuminate; shine

屏 [bǐng]
动 ①reject; get rid of; exclude ②hold (one's breath) ➡píng
屏除 get rid of; dismiss; brush aside
屏绝 dismiss; brush aside; abandon
屏气 hold one's breath
屏弃 discard; abandon; reject; throw away
屏息 hold one's breath
屏黜奸佞 get rid of crafty sycophants
屏绝往来 break off intercourse
屏气凝神 hold one's breath in concentration
屏退左右 dismiss one's attendants

禀 [bǐng]
I 动 ①give to grant; bestow; untrust ②report; petition; written report to one's superior ③receive (orders, commands, etc.); be endowed with II 名 documents (*or* papers) in ancient times
禀报 report
禀承 take orders from; act in accordance with
禀复 report back
禀赋 ①possess; be endowed with ②natural endowment; gift
禀告 report (to one's superior or senior)

禀明 explain (to one's superior or senior)
禀报上级 bring (a matter) to the attention of the leadership

bìng（ㄅㄧㄥˋ）

并 [bìng]
Ⅰ 动 ①combine; merge; incorporate ②side by side; parallel with Ⅱ 副 ①simultaneously; equally ②actually; definitely Ⅲ 连 and, besides：会议讨论并通过了这个报告。The meeting discussed and adopted the report.
并不 not; not at all; by no means; in no sense
并存 exist side by side
并发 be complicated by; erupt simultaneously
并非 really not
并股 reverse stock split
并轨 combination of two（methods, systems, etc.）
并激 shunt excitation
并肩 shoulder to shoulder; side by side; abreast
并进 advance side by side
并举 carry on（two things）at the same time; develop concurrently
并立 exist side by side; exist simultaneously
并联 parallel connection
并列 stand side by side; be juxtaposed; concatenation
并拢 close up; join together
并排 side by side; abreast
并且 ①and also; and... as well; in addition ②besides; moreover; furthermore
并入 merge into; incorporate into
并纱 doubling
并条 drawing
并吞 swallow up; annex; absorb
并网 merge and synchronize two or more power grids
并行 ①walk abreast; run side by side ②carry on（two things）at the same time ③parallel
并用 use two things simultaneously
并重 lay equal stress on; pay equal attention to
并蒂莲 twin lotus flowers on one stalk—devoted married couple
并发症 complication
并卷机 ribbon lap machine
并列句 compound sentence
并激绕组 shunt winding
并驾齐驱 run neck and neck; keep abreast of sb; keep pace with sb; be on a par with sb
并肩而行 walk shoulder to shoulder
并肩作战 fight side by side; fight shoulder to shoulder
并联谐振 parallel resonance
并列分句 coordinate clause

并行不悖 both can be accomplished without coming into conflict; not be mutually exclusive
并行操作 concurrent operation
并行处理 parallel processing
并行权力 concurrent power
并行主权 concurrent sovereignty
并激电动机 shunt motor

病 [bìng]
Ⅰ 名 ①illness; disease ②secret passion; syndrome; sore point; wrong ③fault; defect Ⅱ 动 ①be ill; be sick ②do harm to; injure ③blame; be displeased with
病案 medical record; case history
病变 pathological changes; lesion
病程 course of disease
病床 ①hospital bed ②sickbed
病倒 be down with an illness; be laid up
病毒 virus
病笃 be critically ill; be terminally ill
病房 ward（of a hospital）; sickroom
病夫 sick man
病根 ① incompletely cured illness; old complaint ②the root cause of trouble
病故 die of illness
病害 （plant）disease
病号 sick personnel; person on the sick list; patient
病患 disease; illness; sickness
病家 ①patient and his family ②patient
病假 sick leave
病句 faulty sentence
病菌 pathogenic bacteria; germs
病况 state of an illness; patient's condition
病理 pathology
病历 medical record; case history
病例 case（of illness）
病魔 the demon of disease—serious illness
病期 stadium
病情 state of an illness; patient's condition
病人 ①sick person; invalid ②patient
病容 sickly look
病弱 sick and weak
病史 medical history; case history
病势 degree of seriousness of an illness; patient's condition
病逝 die of illness
病室 sickroom; ward
病死 die of illness
病榻 sickbed
病态 morbid（or abnormal）state
病痛 slight illness; indisposition; ailment
病退 retire for being sick
病危 be critically ill; be terminally ill
病象 symptom（of a disease）
病休 be on sick leave
病因 cause of disease; pathogeny

病友 friend made in hospital;people who become friends in hospital
病愈 recover (from an illness)
病员 sick personnel;person on the sick list; patient
病原 cause of disease;pathogeny
病院 specialized hospital
病灶 focus
病征 symptom (of a disease)
病症 disease;illness
病重 be seriously ill
病株 diseased (*or* infected) plant
病状 symptom (of a disease)
病包儿 person who is always falling ill;chronic invalid
病虫害 plant diseases and insect pests
病毒病 virosis
病毒学 virology
病号饭 patient's diet;special food for patients
病假条 certificate for sick leave
病理学 pathology
病原菌 pathogenic bacteria
病原体 pathogen
病原学 aetiology
病病歪歪 weak (*or* unsteady) from illness;in bad shape
病毒感染 virus infection
病国殃民 injure both the state and the people
病假工资 sick pay;sick benefits
病其无能 deplore sb's incompetence
病入膏肓 the disease has attacked the vitals—beyond cure
病态心理 morbid psychology (*or* mentality)
病毒性肺炎 viral pneumonia
病毒性肝炎 viral hepatitis
病毒性感冒 virus flu
病急乱投医 men at death's door will turn in desperation to any doctor—men in a desperate plight will try anything
病态建筑物综合征 sick building syndrome
病从口入,祸从口出 Disease goes in by the mouth and trouble comes out of the mouth; Illness comes from food and trouble from speech;A closed mouth catches no flies.
病来如山倒,病去如抽丝 Sickness comes like an avalanche but goes like reeling silk;Illness strikes like a landslide, recovery is as slow as reeling silk;Agues come on horseback,but go away on foot.

摒 [bìng]
囫 get rid of;brush aside;dismiss
摒除 get rid of;renounce
摒绝 get rid of;dismiss;brush aside
摒弃 discard;reject;throw away;abandon
摒之门外 keep sb away

bō （ㄅㄛ）

拨 [bō]
I 囫 ①stir;poke;turn;pluck ②allocate; assign;appropriate ③turn round II 囵 group; batch;party：一拨儿顾客 a group of customers
拨出 ①dial-out ②appropriate
拨发 transfer;deliver;set aside;appropriate
拨付 appropriate (a sum of money)
拨号 dial a number;dial
拨开 push aside
拨款 ①appropriate money ②money appropriated
拨门 move the door bolt
拨弄 ①fiddle with;move to and fro ②stir up
拨冗 find time in the midst of pressing affairs
拨送 pull over
拨正 set right;correct
拨子 ①plectrum;pick ②(for people) group; batch
拨奏 pizzicato
拨改贷 replace government appropriations with loans
拨号盘 (telephone) dial
拨火棍 poker
拨浪鼓 drum-shaped rattle;rattle-drum
拨乱反正 right wrongs;bring order out of chaos;set to rights what has been thrown into disorder;restore things to order
拨弄是非 stir things up;stir up trouble;sow dissension;tell tales
拨弦乐器 plucked string (*or* stringed) instrument;plucked instrument
拨云见日 dispel the clouds and see the sun

波 [bō]
囵 ①wave ②unexpected turn of events ③glance;wink
波长 wavelength
波荡 heave;surge
波导 waveguide;duct
波道 radio frequency channel; wave canal; wave duct
波动 ①undulate;fluctuate ②wave motion
波段 wave band
波峰 wave crest
波幅 amplitude
波谷 trough
波及 spread to;involve;affect
波澜 great waves;billows
波浪 wave
波谱 spectrum
波束 beam
波斯 Persia
波速 wave velocity
波涛 great waves;billows
波纹 ①ripple ②corrugation

波形 wave form；wave shape；wave pattern
波音 ①mordent ②Boeing
波折 twists and turns
波波族 bobo
波长计 wavemeter；cymometer
波导管 wave guide
波动说 wave theory
波尔卡 polka（a dance）
波辐射 wave radiation
波美度 Baumé degrees
波斯菊 coreopsis
波斯猫 Persian cat
波斯湾 Persian Gulf
波斯语 Persian（language）
波特码 baudot code
波纹管 bellows；corrugated pipe
波纹铁 corrugated iron
波状热 undulant fever；brucellosis
波状云 undulatus
波长常数 wave-length constant
波导通信 waveguide tube
波动汇率 fluctuating rate
波段覆盖 band coverage
波段划分 band division
波段选择 band select
波尔多液 Bordeaux mixture
波澜起伏 （of a piece of writing）with one cli-max following another
波澜壮阔 surging forward with great momen-tum；unfolding on a magnificent scale
波罗的海 the Baltic（Sea）
波束展宽 beam-broadening
波束转换 beam switching
波纹纸板 corrugated cardboard
波茨坦公告 Potsdam Proclamation
波浪式前进 advance wave upon wave
波美比重计 Baumé hydrometer
波束制导计算机 beam-controlling computer

玻 [bō]

玻璃 ①glass ②nylon；plastic
玻璃板 glass plate；plate glass；glass top（of a desk）
玻璃版 collotype
玻璃杯 glass；tumbler
玻璃布 glass cloth
玻璃厂 glassworks
玻璃刀 glass cutter；glazier's diamond
玻璃粉 glass dust
玻璃钢 glass fibre reinforced plastic
玻璃棉 glass wool
玻璃膜 glass-film
玻璃片 sheet glass
玻璃纱 organdy
玻璃丝 glass silk
玻璃体 vitreous body
玻璃纸 cellophane；glassine

玻璃砖 glass block
玻璃幕墙 glass curtain wall
玻璃纤维 glass fibre
玻意耳定律 Boyle's law

趵 [bō]

〈动〉kick ➡bào

钵 [bō]

〈名〉①earthen bowl ②alms bowl（of a Bud-dhist monk）
钵盂 alms bowl（of a Buddhist monk）

般 [bō]

➡bān；pán
般若 highest wisdom

饽 [bō]

〈名〉steamed bun；cake
饽饽 ①pastry ②（steamed）bun；cake

剥 [bō]

➡bāo
剥夺 deprive；expropriate；strip
剥离 come off；peel off；be stripped；peel off
剥落 ①come off；peel off ②exfoliation
剥蚀 ①denude；corrode；erode；wear away ② erode
剥削 exploit
剥采比 stripping-to-ore ratio；stripping ratio
剥削者 exploiter
剥夺权利 divest（*or* deprive）sb of his rights
剥茧抽丝 reel silk from a cocoon—seek out a clue from a confused or chaotic situation
剥蚀作用 denudation
剥削阶级 exploiting class
剥削收入 income from exploitation
剥削思想 exploiting outlook

菠 [bō]

菠菜 spinach
菠萝 pineapple

播 [bō]

〈动〉①sow（seeds）②spread；broadcast ③ move；remove；migrate；exile
播发 broadcast
播放 ①broadcast ②broadcast a TV（*or* ra-dio）programme
播幅 width of furrows for sowing
播讲 talk over the radio
播客 podcast
播迁 migrate
播送 broadcast；transmit；beam
播音 transmit；broadcast
播映 broadcast on television
播种 [bōzhǒng] sow seeds；sow；seed
播种 [bōzhòng] sowing；seeding
播音室 broadcasting studio
播音员 announcer
播种机 seeder；planter；grain drill
播种期 sowing（*or* seeding）time
播音装置 broadcaster
播种面积 sown area；seeded area

bó（ㄅㄛˊ）

伯 [bó]
名 ①the first（*or* eldest）of brothers ② uncle ③earl；count ➡bǎi
伯伯 uncle
伯父 uncle
伯爵 earl；count
伯乐 ①*Bo Le*，a legendary connoisseur of horses ②good judge of talent
伯母 wife of father's elder brother；aunt
伯仲 the first and the second brother—not much difference
伯爵夫人 countess
伯仲叔季 eldest，second，third and youngest of brothers；order of seniority among brothers
伯仲之间 almost on a par；about the same；equally matched

驳 [bó]
Ⅰ 形 parti-coloured；variegated Ⅱ 动 ①refute；contradict；reject；gainsay ②transport by lighter Ⅲ 名 barge；lighter
驳岸 low stone wall built along the water's edge to protect an embankment；revetment
驳斥 refute；rebut；contradict；denounce
驳船 barge；lighter
驳倒 demolish sb's argument；refute；argue sb down；outargue
驳回 reject（an appeal，request，proposal，etc.）；turn down；overrule
驳卸 unload by lighter
驳运 transport by lighter；lighter
驳杂 multifarious；heterogeneous
驳子 tow；barge
驳壳枪 Mauser pistol
驳面子 not spare sb's sensibilities；not show due respect for sb's feelings
驳运费 lighterage
驳回案件 turn down a case；dismiss a case
驳回起诉 reject a complaint
驳回上诉 reject an appeal
驳回请求 overrule a claim

帛 [bó]
名 silks
帛画 painting on silk
帛书 book copied on silk

泊 [bó]
动 ①cast anchor；moor；berth；be at anchor ②stay for a time ③park（vehicles）➡pō
泊岸 anchor alongside the shore
泊车 park a car
泊位 berth（for a ship）；parking stall
泊位费 berthage

柏 [bó]
➡bǎi；bò
柏林蓝 Berlin blue

勃 [bó]
Ⅰ 形 vigorous；thriving；flourishing Ⅱ 副 suddenly
勃勃 thriving；vigorous；exuberant
勃发 ①thrive；prosper ②break out
勃起 have an erection；erect；erection
勃然 ①agitatedly；excitedly；suddenly ②vigorously
勃兴 rise suddenly；grow vigorously
勃郎宁 Browning
勃然大怒 fly into a rage；flare up
勃然而起 spring into life；burst into activity

钹 [bó]
名 cymbals

铂 [bó]
名 platinum（Pt）

舶 [bó]
名 ocean-going ship
舶来品 imports

脖 [bó]
名 ①neck ②sth shaped like a neck
脖子 neck
脖梗儿 back of the neck；nape
脖领儿 collar

博 [bó]
Ⅰ 形 ①rich；plentiful；abundant ②big；loose ③universal Ⅱ 动 ①erudite；be knowledgeable and well informed ②win；gain ③gamble
博爱 universal fraternity（*or* brotherhood）；universal love
博彩 gambling
博导 tutor of a Ph. D. student；supervisor of Ph. D. candidates
博得 win；gain
博古 ①conversant with things of the past ②paintings of ancient objects
博客 Blog
博览 read extensively（*or* widely）
博取 try to gain；court
博识 learned；erudite
博士 ①doctor ②learned scholar
博徒 gambler
博物 old general name for zoology，botany，mineralogy，physiology，etc.
博学 learned；erudite
博雅 learned
博弈 play chess；have a game of chess
博引 quote extensively
博彩税 betting duty；gambling tax
博彩业 triads congregate
博览会 （international）fair
博士后 ①postdoctoral student（*or* researcher）②postdoctoral study（*or* research）③postdoctoral；postdoctorate ④postdoctoral
博士帽 mortarboard
博士生 doctoral candidate
博物馆 museum

B

博物院 museum
博采众议 adopt good advice from all quarters
博大精深 have extensive knowledge and profound scholarship
博而不精 have wide but not expert knowledge;know something about everything
博古通今 possess a wide knowledge of things ancient and modern—erudite and informed
博识洽闻 experienced and knowledgeable;erudite
博士学位 doctor's degree;doctorate
博闻强记 possessed of wide learning and a powerful memory; have encyclopaedic knowledge
博闻强志 possessed of wide learning and a powerful memory; have encyclopaedic knowledge
博物馆学 museology
博学多才 learned and versatile
博学之士 learned scholar;man of great erudition
博鳌亚洲论坛 Bo'ao Forum for Asia
博士后流动站 centre for post-doctorate studies;post-doctorate position

鹁 [bó]

鹁鸽 pigeon
鹁鸪 wood-pigeon

搏 [bó]

动 ①wrestle;fight;struggle ②jump upon;pounce on ③beat;pulsate;throb
搏动 (of the heart, the blood, or the pulse) beat rhythmically;throb;pulsate
搏斗 wrestle;fight;struggle
搏击 struggle with;fight with
搏杀 ① fight with a weapon ② (in chess games) be locked in a fierce contest

箔 [bó]

名 ①screen ②frame for silkworms;bamboo tray for rearing silkworms;silkworm tray ③foil;tinsel ④paper tinsel burnt as offerings to the dead
箔材 foil
箔片 chaff

膊 [bó]

名 arm

踣 [bó]

动 fall down;tumble

薄 [bó]

Ⅰ 形 ①slight;meagre;small ②unkind;ungenerous; mean; stingy ③ frivolous ④ thin;flimsy;light;weak Ⅱ 动 ①despise;belittle;look down ②approach;near ➡báo;bò
薄产 a small property
薄酬 small reward;token (or meagre) remuneration
薄待 treat sb ungenerously
薄厚 (treat) casually or with kindness

薄技 my slight skill
薄酒 light wine (said by a host of his own wine)
薄礼 meagre present; modest present; my small (or unworthy) gift
薄利 small profits
薄命 (usu. of women) born under an unlucky star;born unlucky
薄膜 ①membrane ②film
薄暮 dusk;twilight
薄片 thin slice;thin section
薄情 inconstant in love;fickle
薄弱 weak;frail
薄识 my humble opinion
薄雾 mist;haze
薄幸 inconstant in love;fickle;heartless
薄葬 simple burial
薄油层 oil sheet
薄海同欢 All within the four seas (or People all over the country) will rejoice together.
薄利多销 small profits and quick returns; more sales at a lower profit
薄膜电阻 film resistor
薄片分析 thin section analysis
薄弱环节 weak link;vulnerable spot
薄胎瓷器 eggshell china

礴 [bó]

◇磅礴 boundless;majestic

bǒ (ㄅㄛˇ)

跛 [bǒ]

形 lame;limping
跛脚 lame
跛行 walk with a limp;limp along
跛子 lame person;cripple
跛鳖千里 a lame tortoise can walk a thousand *li*—success can be gained by steady continuous effort

簸 [bǒ]

动 ①winnow;fan ②toss up and down ➡bò
簸荡 roll;rock
簸动 ①jolt;bump;toss ②strike (a gong)
簸箩 shallow basket
簸扬 winnow

bò (ㄅㄛˋ)

柏 [bò]

➡bǎi;bó
◇黄柏 the bark of a cork tree

薄 [bò]

➡báo;bó
薄荷 field mint;peppermint
薄荷脑 menthol;peppermint camphor
薄荷糖 peppermint drops

薄荷酮 menthone
薄荷油 peppermint oil

檗 [bò]

◇黄檗 the bark of a cork tree

擘 [bò]

名 thumb
擘划 plan;arrange

簸 ➡bǒ [bò]

簸箕 ①dustpan ②winnowing fan ③loop (of a fingerprint)

bo (·ㄅㄛ)

卜 ➡bǔ [bo]

◇萝卜 radish

bū (ㄅㄨ)

逋 [bū]

I 动 ①flee ②owe;delay;be behind in payment;be in arrears;default II 形 scattered
逋遁 flee;disappear;abscond
逋客 ①fugitive ②recluse
逋欠 default;be behind in payment
逋逃 flee from justice

峬 [bū]

峬峭 charming;beautiful

晡 [bū]

名 late afternoon;period of the day from 3 to 5 pm

bú (ㄅㄨ)

醭 [bú]

名 whitish mould

bǔ (ㄅㄨ)

卜 [bǔ]

I 动 ① divine; tell fortunes ② select; choose ③ foretell; predict II 名 divination; fortune-telling ➡bo
卜辞 oracle inscriptions of the Shang Dynasty on tortoiseshells (or animal bones)
卜卦 system of divination
卜居 choose a place for one's home
卜邻 choose a neighbourhood
卜筮 divination;fortune-telling

吓 [bǔ]

吓吩 porphine
吓啉 porphyrin

补 [bǔ]

I 动 ①mend;patch;repair ②fill;supply; make up for ③nourish II 名 benefit;help;use
补白 filler (in a newspaper or magazine)
补报 ①make a report after the event;make a

supplementary report ②repay a kindness
补编 supplement
补仓 variation call;margin call;cover
补差 make up a deficiency;make up pay for difference between former pay and retirement
补偿 compensate;make up
补充 ① replenish; supplement; complement; add ② additional; complementary; supplementary
补丁 patch
补发 supply again (sth lost,etc.);reissue;pay retroactively
补过 make amends for one's faults
补花 appliqué
补给 supply
补剂 tonic
补假 days off for having worked overtime
补角 supplementary angle
补救 remedy
补考 make-up examination
补课 ①make up a missed lesson ②do over again sth not well done
补亏 the state subsidizing deficit enterprises
补漏 fill (or plug) the leak
补炉 fettling
补码 complement
补苗 fill the gaps with seedlings
补票 buy one's ticket after the normal time
补品 tonic
补缺 fill a vacancy;supply a deficiency
补色 complementary colour
补税 ①pay a tax one has evaded ②pay an overdue tax
补台 help sb strengthen his position;boost sb
补体 complement (in blood serum)
补贴 ①subsidize ②subsidy;allowance
补习 take lessons after school or work;take a make-up course
补休 take a deferred leave or holiday
补选 by-election;supplementary election
补血 build (or enrich) the blood
补牙 fill a tooth;have a tooth stopped
补养 take a tonic (or nourishing food) to build up one's health
补药 tonic
补液 ①fluid infusion ②(liquid) tonic
补遗 addendum;supplement
补益 ①benefit;help ②be of help (or benefit) ③tonic;tonifying
补语 complement
补种 reseed;replant
补助 ①help financially;subsidize ②subsidy; allowance
补缀 mend (clothes);patch
补足 bring up to full strength; make complete;make up a deficiency;fill (a vacancy,

gap,etc.)
补偿费 compensatory payment;compensation
补偿金 compensatory amounts
补给点 supply point
补给品 supplies
补给线 supply line
补给站 depot
补习班 make up class;remedial group
补血剂 blood (*or* haematic) tonic
补助金 grant-in-aid;subsidy
补偿报酬 compensation payment
补偿差额 make up a deficiency
补偿贷款 compensatory financing
补偿关税 compensation tariff
补偿贸易 compensation trade
补偿项目 offset item
补充规定 supplementary provision (*or* regulation)
补充协议 supplementary agreement
补发工资 back pay;retroactive wage
补救措施 remedial measures (*or* actions)
补码操作 complementary operation
补偏救弊 remedy defects and rectify errors;rectify a deviation and correct an error
补其不足 make up a deficiency
补缺选举 by-election
补习学校 continuation school
补偿电容器 compensation condenser

捕 [bǔ]
　动 catch;seize;arrest
捕俘 capture enemy personnel
捕获 catch;capture;seize
捕快 constable for catching criminals;sheriff
捕捞 fish for (aquatic animals and plants);catch
捕猎 catch (wild animals);hunt
捕拿 arrest;apprehend;capture;catch
捕杀 catch and kill
捕蛇 catch snakes
捕食 ①(of an animal) hunt for food;prey ②(of an animal) hunt and eat (another animal);prey on
捕鱼 catch fish;fish
捕捉 hunt;chase;catch;seize
捕虫叶 insect-catching leaf
捕获法 law of prize
捕获量 catch (of fish,etc.)
捕获物 prisal
捕鲸船 whaler;whale catcher
捕食链 predator chain
捕鼠器 mousetrap
捕蝇器 flytrap
捕鱼权 fishing right;fishery
捕捉器 raquet organ
捕风捉影 chase the wind and clutch at shadows—speak (*or* act) on hearsay evidence
捕捞控制 fishing control

捕捞能力 fishing capacity

哺 [bǔ]
　Ⅰ 动 feed (a baby);nurse　Ⅱ 名 food in one's mouth
哺乳 breast-feed;suckle;nurse
哺养 feed;rear
哺育 ①feed ②nurture;foster;develop
哺乳室 nursing room
哺乳动物 mammal;mammality

堡 [bǔ]
　名 bourg;village ➡ bǎo
堡子 village (with earthen walls)

bù (ㄅㄨˋ)

不 [bù]
　Ⅰ 副 ①(*used before verbs, adjectives, and other adverbs to indicate negation*) not;no ②(*inserted between repeated to show one's carelessness or indifference*) ③(*used as a negative prefix before a noun or noun-equivalent to form an adjective*):不法 illegal;lawless ④(*used as a negative reply to a question*):"你回家,是不是?""不,我不回家。""You're going home,aren't you?" "No,I am not." ⑤(*used as a question tag*):你喝茶不? Would you care for some tea? ⑥ either (... or):天气坏透了,不是刮风,就是下雨。The weather can't be worse. If it's not windy then it's raining. ⑦ needn't;don't:不送。Don't bother to come out.　Ⅱ 助 (*used in between a verb and its complement to indicate negation*):拿不动 cannot carry it
不安 ①intranquil;unpeaceful;unstable ②uneasy;disturbed;restless ③sorry
不备 unprepared;off guard
不比 unlike
不必 need not;not have to
不便 ①inconvenient ②inappropriate;unsuitable ③short of cash
不才 Ⅰ ("without ability")
不测 accident;mishap;contingency
不成 ① won't do ②(*used at the end of a rhetorical question beginning with* 难道 *or* 莫非)
不曾 never (have done sth)
不齿 despise;hold in contempt
不啻 ①not less than ②as;like;as good as
不错 ①correct;right ②yes ③not bad;pretty good
不大 ①not very;not too ②not often;seldom
不单 ①not the only ②not merely;not simply
不但 not only
不当 unsuitable;improper;inappropriate
不得 [bùdé] must not; may not; not be allowed
不得 [bùde] must not;can not
不等 ①vary;differ;in variety ②unequal

不迭 ①cannot cope;find it too much ②incessantly;profusely
不定 ①hard to say;hard to predict ②indefinite;indeterminate
不独 not only
不端 improper;dishonourable
不断 unceasing; uninterrupted; continuous; constant
不对 ①incorrect;wrong ②no ③amiss;abnormal;queer ④be in disagreement;be at odds
不乏 there is no lack of
不法 lawless;illegal;unlawful
不凡 out of the ordinary;out of the common run
不妨 there is no harm in;might as well
不服 refuse to obey (*or* comply);refuse to accept as final;remain unconvinced by;not give in to
不符 not agree (*or* tally,square) with;not conform to;be inconsistent with
不复 no longer
不甘 unreconciled to;not resigned to;unwilling
不敢 ①dare not;not dare ②I really don't deserve this;it's too much of an honour;I'm overwhelmed;I'm much obliged;you flatter me
不公 unjust;unfair
不恭 disrespectful
不苟 not lax;not casual;careful;conscientious
不够 not enough; insufficient; inadequate; short of
不顾 in spite of;regardless of;in defiance
不关 have nothing to do with
不管 regardless of; no matter (what, who, etc.);disregard;whether... or...
不光 ①not the only one ②not only
不轨 against the law (*or* discipline)
不过 ① only; just; merely; no more than ② but;however;only
不和 ①not get along well;be on bad terms;be at odds ②discord
不合 ①not conform to;be unsuited to;be out of keeping with ②should not;ought not ③ not get along well;be on bad terms
不会 ① be unlikely; will not (act, happen, etc.) ②have not learned to; be unable to ③(*used to express reproach for the non-performance of an action*)
不讳 ①without concealing anything ②die
不惑 be free from doubts
不及 ①not as good as;inferior to ②find it too late
不济 no good;of no use
不检 be indiscreet (in one's speech and conduct); be careless (about one's words and acts)

不见 not see;not meet
不解 ①not understand;be puzzled ②indissoluble
不仅 ①not the only one ②not only
不禁 can't help (doing sth);can't refrain from
不久 ① soon; before long; near future ② not long after;soon after;shortly after
不拘 ①not stick to;not confine oneself to ② no matter (what,who,etc.);whatever
不倦 tireless;untiring;indefatigable
不堪 ① cannot bear; cannot stand ② utterly; extremely ③extremely undesirable
不可 ①cannot;should not;must not ②must
不克 be unable to;cannot
不快 ① be unhappy; be displeased; be in low spirits ② be indisposed; feel under the weather;be out of sorts
不愧 be worthy of;deserve to be called;prove oneself to be
不赖 not bad;good;fine
不理 refuse to acknowledge; pay no attention to;take no notice of;ignore
不力 not do one's best;not exert oneself
不利 ① unfavourable; disadvantageous; harmful;detrimental ②unsuccessful
不良 bad;harmful;unhealthy
不了 without end
不料 unexpectedly;to one's surprise
不吝 not stint;not grudge;be generous with
不灵 not work;be ineffective
不论 ① no matter (what, who, how, etc.); whether... or... ② regardless of; irrespective of
不满 resentful;discontented;dissatisfied
不忙 there's no hurry;take one's time
不免 cannot avoid;cannot help but
不妙 (of a turn of events) not too encouraging;far from good;anything but reassuring
不明 ① not clear; unknown ② fail to understand
不能 cannot;must not;should not
不佞 I
不怕 be not afraid of;not fear
不配 ① be unworthy of; not deserve; be unqualified for ②not match
不平 ①injustice;unfairness;wrong;grievance ②indignant;resentful
不巧 unfortunately;as luck would have it
不屈 unyielding;unbending
不然 ①not so;not the case ②or else;otherwise;if not so ③no
不仁 ①not benevolent;heartless ②numb
不忍 cannot bear to
不日 within the next few days;in a few days' time
不容 not tolerate;not allow;not brook

不如 ①not equal to; not as good as; inferior to ②it would be better to

不善 ①bad; ill ②not good at

不胜 ①cannot bear (*or* stand); be unequal to ②(*used between two identical verbs to indicate difficulty or impossibility of fulfilment*) ③(*used in expressing feelings*) very; extremely

不时 ①frequently; often ②at any time

不是 [búshi] fault; blame

不适 unwell; indisposed; out of sorts

不爽 ①not well; out of sorts; in a bad mood ②without discrepancy; accurate

不送 don't bother to see me out

不通 ① be obstructed; be blocked up; be impassable ②not make sense; be illogical; be ungrammatical

不同 not alike; different; distinct

不图 ①not seek; not strive for ②unexpectedly; contrary to expectation

不妥 not proper; inappropriate; not the right way

不问 ①pay no attention to; disregard; ignore ②let go unpunished; let off

不惜 ①not stint; not spare ②not hesitate (to do sth); not scruple (to do sth)

不暇 have no time (for sth); be too busy (to do sth)

不详 ①not well known; not quite clear ②not in detail; unspecified

不祥 ominous; inauspicious

不孝 be an unfilial son or daughter; act contrary to filial piety

不肖 (of children) unworthy

不谢 don't mention it; not at all

不懈 untiring; unremitting; indefatigable

不兴 ①out of fashion; outmoded ②impermissible; not allowed ③can't

不行 ①not be allowed; won't do; be impossible ②be no good; won't work ③not be good; be poor ④awfully; extremely; deeply

不幸 ① misfortune; adversity ②unfortunate; sad ③unfortunately

不休 endlessly; ceaselessly

不朽 immortal; eternity

不许 ①not allow; must not ②can't

不逊 rude; impertinent

不厌 not mind doing sth; not tire of; not object to

不扬 not good-looking

不要 don't

不一 vary; differ

不依 ①not comply; not go along with ②not let off easily; not let sb get away with it

不宜 not suitable; inadvisable

不已 endlessly; incessantly

不意 ①unexpectedly ②unawareness

不用 need not

不由 can't help; cannot but

不予 not grant

不育 sterility

不悦 displeased; annoyed

不在 not be in; be out

不再 no longer; not any more

不争 indisputable

不值 not worth

不止 ① incessant; without end ② more than; not limited to

不只 not only; not merely

不致 not in such a way as to; not likely to

不忠 disloyalty

不周 not attentive and satisfactory; thoughtless; inconsiderate

不准 not allow; forbid; prohibit

不足 ①not enough; insufficient; inadequate ②not worth ③cannot; should not

不成材 good-for-nothing; worthless; ne'er-do-well

不出庭 default of appearance; non-appearance

不待说 needless to say; it goes without saying

不倒翁 self-righting doll; tumbler; roly-poly

不导电 non-conducting

不道德 immoral; unethical

不得不 have no choice (*or* option) but to; cannot but; have to

不得劲 ①awkward; unhandy ②be indisposed; not feel well ③feel embarrassed

不得了 ① terrible; horrible; serious ② extremely; exceedingly

不得已 act against one's will; have no alternative but to; have to

不等号 sign of inequality

不等式 inequality

不定度 uncertainty

不定根 adventitious root

不定式 infinitive

不定芽 adventitious bud

不动产 real estate; immovable property; immovables

不动心 showing no interest

不冻港 ice-free port; open port

不二价 fixed prices; uniform prices

不发育 agensis

不妨碍 get out of the (sb's) road

不干涉 noninterference; nonintervention

不干预 disintermediation; nonintervention

不甘心 not reconciled to; not resigned to

不敢当 I really don't deserve this; it's too much of an honour; I'm overwhelmed; I'm much obliged; you flatter me

不更事 have not seen the world; have not experienced life; be inexperienced

不辜负 be worthy of; live up to

不光彩 disgraceful; dishonorable; ignominious

不归零　non-return-to-zero
不归位　nonhoming
不规则　irregular
不过问　keep aloof from; not inquire into; not look into
不过意　be sorry; feel apologetic
不含糊　① unambiguous; unequivocal; explicit ②not ordinary; really good ③not be afraid of
不好惹　not to be trifled with; not to be pushed around; stand no nonsense
不合格　unqualified; substandard
不合理　unreasonable; irrational
不合作　uncooperative; noncooperative
不和谐　incompatibility; disharmony; discord
不及格　fail; flunk; disqualified
不济事　no good; of no use; not of any help
不简单　①not simple; fairly complicated ②remarkable; marvellous; unusual
不见得　not necessarily; not likely
不结盟　nonalignment
不进位　not-carry
不经意　carelessly; by accident
不精确　inaccuracy; out-of-true
不景气　① depression; recession; slump ② depressed state
不拘束　let loose; turn loose up
不客气　①impolite; rude; blunt ②You're welcome; Don't mention it; Not at all ③Please don't bother; I'll help myself.
不理解　incomprehension
不灵敏　insensitive
不留意　careless
不买账　not buy it; not go for it
不名誉　disreputable; disgraceful
不明智　unwise; ill-advised
不能不　have to; cannot but
不匹配　mismatching
不平衡　disequilibrium
不起诉　nonprosecution
不起眼　not attract attention; not be noticeable; not be attractive
不确切　inexact
不人道　inhuman
不善于　not good at
不胜任　incompetent; unfit on the post
不失为　can yet be regarded as; may after all be accepted as
不适应　not adapted to; not suited to; not fit to
不受理　①reject a complaint ②refuse to entertain (a proposal)
不顺眼　be on eyesore; give bad impression
不死心　unwilling to give up
不透明　opaque
不透气　airtight
不透水　waterproof; watertight; impermeable
不外乎　not beyond the scope of; nothing more than

不喜欢　dislike
不下(于)　①as many as; no less than ②not inferior to; as good as; on a par with
不相干　be irrelevant; have nothing to do with
不相容　incompatible
不像话　① unreasonable ② shocking; outrageous
不像样　①in no shape to be seen; unpresentable ②beyond recognition
不协调　inharmonious; discordant; out of tune
不屑于　disdain to do sth; think sth not worth doing; feel it beneath one's dignity to do sth
不信邪　not believe in heresy; refuse to be taken in by fallacies; not be scared by evil forces
不行了　on the point of death; dying
不锈钢　stainless steel
不雅观　offensive to the eye; unbecoming
不亚于　not second to; as good as
不要紧　①it's not serious ②it doesn't matter; never mind ③it looks all right, but
不要脸　have no sense of shame; shameless; brazen
不夜城　city with lights turned on all night
不由得　can't help; cannot but
不育性　incompatibility; sterility
不育症　sterility; barrenness
不允许　not allow; inadmissibility
不在乎　not mind; not care; immaterial
不在意　① pay no attention to; take no notice of; not mind ②negligent; careless
不怎么　not very; not particularly
不争气　be disappointing; fail to live up to expectations
不整合　unconformity; disagreement
不知足　insatiable; greedy
不至于　cannot go so far; be unlikely
不中用　unfit for anything; no good; useless
不周延　undistributed
不自爱　not have self-respect
不自量　not take a proper measure of oneself; overrate one's own abilities
不足道　not worth mentioning; inconsiderable; of no consequence
不作为　omission
不做声　keep silent; not say a word
不白之冤　unrighted wrong; unredressed injustice
不败之地　invincible position
不卑不亢　neither humble ourselves nor show disrespect
不避艰险　shrink (*or* flinch) from no difficulty or danger; make light of difficulties and dangers
不变成本　constant cost
不变函数　invariant function

B

不变价格 fixed price;constant price

不变资本 constant capital

不辨菽麦 be unable to tell beans from wheat—have no knowledge of practical matters

不成体统 most improper;downright outrageous

不成文法 unwritten (*or* customary) law

不成问题 be no problem at all;be out of question

不逞之徒 desperado;the unruly

不耻下问 not feel ashamed to ask one's subordinates (*or* people below)

不出所料 as expected

不揣冒昧 I venture to;may I take the liberty of

不辞而别 go away without taking leave;leave without saying goodbye

不辞辛苦 spare no effort;take pains;take the trouble to;go to the trouble of doing sth

不打自招 confess without being pressed;make a confession without duress;give oneself away

不大不小 neither too big nor too little

不大离儿 ① pretty close;just about right ② not bad

不得而知 unknown;unable to find out;can make nothing

不得人心 not enjoy popular support;be unpopular

不得上诉 not subject to cassation

不得要领 fail to grasp the main point;not see what sb is driving at

不丁点儿 very few;very small

不定变异 indeterminate variation

不定方程 indeterminate equation

不定冠词 indefinite article

不定积分 indefinite integral

不定收入 transitory income

不动产税 real estate tax

不动声色 maintain one's composure;stay calm and collected;not turn a hair;not bat an eyelid;not to change one's voice and expression because of emotion

不二法门 the one and only way;the only proper course to take

不乏其人 such people are not rare;there is no lack of such people

不乏先例 there is no lack of precedents

不法分子 law-breakers;lawless elements

不法收益 illegal interest

不法之徒 lawless person

不分彼此 make no distinction between one's own and sb else's;share everything;be on very intimate terms

不分敌我 not to distinguish between the enemy and ourselves

不分高低 be equally matched

不分你我 making no distinction between "you" and "me"

不分亲疏 irrespective the degree of intimacy

不分胜负 tie;draw;come out even

不孚众望 not inspire popular confidence

不服水土 not accustomed to the climate of a new place;not acclimatized

不干不净 unclean;filthy

不甘寂寞 hate to be neglected or overlooked

不甘落后 not content to lag behind

不甘示弱 unwilling to be outshone;not to be outdone

不敢苟同 beg to differ;cannot agree

不敢问津 not dare to inquire;be beyond the means of

不攻自破 collapse of itself

不共戴天 will not live under the same sky (with one's enemy)—absolutely irreconcilable

不苟言笑 reserved;reticent;taciturn;sober;sedate

不关痛痒 of no consequence;immaterial

不过尔尔 not better than that—only just so-so;merely mediocre;just middling

不过如此 only just so-so

不含油腻 greaseless;without grease

不含脂肪 fat free;no fat

不寒而栗 shiver all over though not cold—tremble with fear;shudder

不好意思 ①feel embarrassed;be ill at ease ② find it embarrassing (to do sth)

不合时宜 be out of keeping with the times;be incompatible with present needs;be inopportune or inappropriate

不怀好意 harbour evil designs;not with the best of intentions

不欢而散 part on bad terms

不慌不忙 unhurried;calm;leisurely

不即不离 be neither familiar nor distant;keep sb at arm's length

不急之务 a matter of no great urgency;business requiring no immediate attention

不计其数 countless;innumerable

不计后果 ignore the possible consequences;without respect to the results

不假辞色 look at sb with a solemn mien and speak harshly;be severe in speech and countenance

不假思索 (act,respond,etc.) without thinking;without hesitation;readily;offhand

不兼容性 incompatibility

不减当年 just like one's old self (in appearance,bearing,etc.)

不见不散 (let's) not leave without seeing each other

不见经传 not to be found in the classics—not authoritative;unknown

不见世面 not to know anything about the world

不骄不躁 not conceited or rash;free from arrogance and rashness

不解之谜 an unsolved riddle (*or* puzzle);enigma;mystery

不解之缘 indissoluble bond;irrevocable commitment

不进则退 move forward,or you'll fall behind

不近人情 not amenable to reason;unreasonable

不经之谈 absurd statement;cock-and-bull story

不胫而走 get round fast;spread like wildfire

不咎既往 forgive sb's past misdeeds;not censure sb for his past misdeeds

不拘小节 not bother about trifles;not niggling

不拘形迹 without formality;not standing on ceremony

不拘形式 not particular about form;informal

不拘一格 not stick to one pattern;not limited to one type (*or* style)

不绝于耳 can be heard without end

不堪回首 cannot bear to look back on;find it unbearable to recall

不堪入耳 intolerable to the ear;revolting;disgusting

不堪入目 most unsightly;not fit to be seen;revolting;disgusting

不堪设想 too ghastly (*or* dreadful) to contemplate

不堪一击 cannot withstand a single blow;collapse at the first blow

不堪造就 be not worth getting an education;cannot be trained

不可多得 hard to come by;rare

不可分割 inseparable

不可告人 not to be divulged;hidden

不可估量 inestimable;incalculable;immeasurable;beyond measure

不可忽视 assignable;not to be neglected

不可或缺 indispensable;absolutely necessary

不可救药 incurable;incorrigible;hopeless

不可开交 cannot avoid (*or* finish)

不可抗力 force majeure;act of god

不可理喻 be impervious to reason;won't listen to reason

不可弥补 irretrievable; irrecoverable; irredeemable

不可名状 beggar description; be indescribable;be beyond description

不可磨灭 indelible

不可逆转 irreversible

不可偏废 cannot do one thing and neglect the other

不可企及 matchless;inimitable

不可胜数 countless;innumerable

不可收拾 irremediable;unmanageable;out of hand;hopeless

不可思议 inconceivable; unimaginable; unthinkable

不可一世 consider oneself unexcelled in the world; be overwhelmingly (*or* insufferably) arrogant

不可逾越 impassable; insurmountable; insuperable

不可证实 unverifiability

不可知论 agnosticism

不可终日 be unable to carry on even for a single day;be in a desperate situation

不可转让 non-assignable; non-transferable; unalienable

不可捉摸 difficult to ascertain;unpredictable; elusive

不稂不莠 useless;worthless;good-for-nothing

不劳而获 reap without sowing;profit by (*or* reap) the fruits of other people's toil

不良贷款 non-performing loan

不良风气 unhealthy ways and customs;unhealthy tendency

不了了之 settle a matter by leaving it unsettled;end up with nothing definite

不吝赐教 not be stinting with comments or criticism;Please don't refuse to offer your kind advice!

不留情面 not spare sb's sensibilities;be not afraid to hurt sb's feelings

不留缺口 leave no loopholes

不留余地 leave no room;make no allowance

不露声色 not show (*or* betray) one's feelings,intentions,etc.

不伦不类 neither fish nor fowl;nondescript

不落窠臼 not follow the beaten track;have an original style; show originality; be unconventional

不落人后 not to lag behind;yield to none

不落俗套 conform to no conventional pattern; depart from convention

不毛之地 barren land;desert

不眠之夜 sleepless night;white night

不名一文 without a penny to one's name;penniless

不明不白 obscure;doubtful;dubious

不谋而合 agree without prior (*or* previous) consultation;happen to hold the same view

不能自拔 unable to extricate oneself (from one's plight)

不能自已 cannot control oneself;lose self-control;can't help;be beside oneself

不念旧恶 not bear a grudge;forgive and forget

不偏不倚 even-handed;impartial;unbiased

不平则鸣 Injustice provokes outcry; Where there is injustice,there will be protest.

不破不立 There is no construction without destruction; There's no making without breaking; make you must break

不期而遇 meet unexpectedly (*or* by chance); have a chance encounter

不切实际 unrealistic; unpractical; impracticable

不求甚解 read without thorough understanding; not seek deep understanding; be content with a superficial understanding; not seek to understand things thoroughly

不屈不挠 unyielding; indomitable; dauntless

不忍坐视 cannot bear to stand idly by

不容分说 allowing no explanation

不容讳言 There is no denying the fact that…; It is no secret that…

不容置辩 indisputable; incontestable

不容置疑 allow (*or* admit) of no doubt; not be open to doubt; be beyond doubt

不三不四 ① dubious; shady ② neither one thing nor the other; neither fish nor fowl; nondescript

不擅辞令 lack facility in polite speech

不上不下 be suspended in mid air; be in a fix

不甚了了 not know much (about sth); not be too clear (about sth)

不声不响 quiet; silent

不胜枚举 too numerous to mention individually (*or* one by one)

不胜其烦 be pestered beyond endurance

不失时机 not let the opportunity slip; seize the opportune moment; lose no time

不时之需 a possible period of want (*or* need)

不识大体 fail to see the larger issues; ignore the general interest

不识好歹 cannot tell good from bad; not to know what is good for one; not to know chalk from cheese

不识时务 ① show no understanding of the times ② lack judgment

不识抬举 fail to appreciate sb's kindness; not know how to appreciate favours

不是味儿 ① not the right flavour; not quite right; a bit off ② fishy; queer; amiss ③ feel bad; be upset; be vexed

不收小费 no gratuities accepted

不死不活 neither dead nor alive; half dead; lifeless; lethargic

不速之客 uninvited (*or* unexpected) guest; gatecrasher

不随意肌 involuntary muscle

不碎玻璃 shatterproof (*or* safety) glass

不同凡响 (usu. of literary and artistic works) outstanding; out of the ordinary; out of the common run

不痛不痒 scratching the surface; superficial; perfunctory

不透明色 body colour

不透明体 opaque body

不透明性 opacity

不透气性 gas-proofness; gas-tightness

不透水层 impermeable stratum; impervious bed

不完全叶 incomplete leaf

不畏强暴 defy brute force

不闻不问 not bother to ask or to listen; show no interest in sth; be indifferent to sth

不稳平衡 unstable equilibrium

不无小补 not be without some advantage; be of some help

不务正业 ① not do honest work; not live by honest labour ② ignore one's proper occupation; not attend to one's duties

不惜工本 spare no expense

不相上下 equally matched; about the same; almost on a par

不相适应 be out of keeping with; ill-adapted to the need to develop

不祥之兆 an ill (*or* evil) omen

不肖子孙 unworthy descendants

不屑一顾 will not spare a glance for; regard as beneath one's notice

不懈努力 unremitting efforts

不信任案 no-confidence motion

不省人事 lose consciousness; be unconscious; be in a coma

不幸言中 The prophecy unfortunately comes true.

不修边幅 not care about one's appearance; be slovenly

不锈钢管 stainless steel tube

不虚此行 The journey has not been made in vain; The journey has been well worthwhile; It's been a worthwhile journey.

不宣而战 open hostilities without declaring war; start an undeclared war

不学无术 have neither learning nor skill; be ignorant and incompetent

不言不语 not say a word; keep silent

不言而喻 it goes without saying; it is self-evident

不厌其烦 not mind taking the trouble; take great pains; be very patient

不厌其详 go into details; dwell at length upon

不一而足 no isolated case; numerous

不遗余力 spare no pains (*or* effort); do one's utmost

不以为耻 not to think it as shameful; not to be ashamed of

不以为然 not to regard it as right; object to; not to agree with

不以为意 pay no attention to; take no notice of; not mind

不义之财 ill-gotten wealth (*or* gains)

不亦乐乎 extremely; awfully

不易之论 perfectly sound proposition；undeniable truth；irrefutable argument
不翼而飞 ①（of an object）disappear without trace；vanish into thin air ②spread fast as if on wings；spread like wildfire
不阴不阳 neither *yin* nor *yang*—assume an ambiguous（*or* equivocal）attitude
不由分说 without listening to sb's protests
不由自主 can't help；involuntarily
不远千里 make light of travelling a thousand *li*；make light of travelling from afar；go to the trouble of travelling a long distance
不约而同 do（*or* think）the same without prior consultation；happen to coincide
不在话下 be nothing difficult；be a cinch
不赞一词 not say a word；keep silent；make no comment
不择手段 by fair means or foul；by hook or（by）crook；unscrupulously
不怎么样 not up to much；very indifferent
不战不和 no war，no peace
不折不扣 ①hundred-percent；to the letter；no discount ②out-and-out
不正之风 unhealthy tendency；malpractice
不知不觉 unconsciously；unwittingly
不知分寸 lack tact；have no sense of propriety
不知好歹 can't tell good from bad；not know what's good for one
不知进退 have no sense of propriety；not know where to stop
不知就里 not to know the inside story；not to know the inner reason
不知死活 act recklessly；do sth regardless of danger
不知所措 be at a loss；be at one's wits' end
不知所云 ①scarcely know what one has said ②not understand what sb is driving at
不值一驳 not worth refuting
不值一提 not worth mentioning
不值一文 utterly worthless
不治之症 incurable disease
不置可否 decline to comment；not express an opinion；be noncommittal；hedge
不着边际 not to the point；wide of the mark；neither here nor there；irrelevant
不着痕迹 leave no trace
不自量力 not have a proper measure of oneself；overrate one's own abilities；overreach oneself
不足挂齿 not worth mentioning；nothing to speak of
不足轻重 worthless；negligible
不足为凭 cannot be taken as evidence；afford little or no evidence
不足为奇 not at all surprising；nothing to be surprised at
不足为训 not fit to serve as a model；not to be taken as an example；not an example to be followed；not to be taken as authoritative
不足与谋 not worth consulting with
不足征信 not be taken as credible and reliable
不安定因素 factors leading to social instability
不承认主义 policy of "non-recognition"
不打不成器 spare the rod and spoil the child
不打不相识 out of blows friendship grows；no discord，no concord
不等额选举 voting from a large number of candidates
不等价交换 exchange of unequal values
不抵抗政策 non-resistance policy
不抵抗主义 policy of non-resistance
不定额抵押 open-end mortgage
不定期航班 nonregular service
不动产保险 immovables insurance
不动产抵押 real estate mortgage；pledge of immovable
不对称管制 dissymmetry control
不发达国家 underdeveloped country
不干涉政策 policy of noninterference（*or* nonintervention）
不公开公司 close corporation
不公平竞争 unfair competition
不管部部长 minister without portfolio
不规则动词 irregular verb
不含咖啡因 noncaffein；containing no caffein
不活跃市场 thin market
不及物动词 intransitive verb
不记名票据 blank bill；bearer paper
不记名投票 secret ballot
不间断电源 uninterruptable power supply（UPS）
不结盟国家 nonaligned countries
不结盟运动 non-aligned movement
不结盟政策 non-alignment policy
不可比因素 incomparable factor；factor not subject to comparison
不可侵犯权 inviolability
不可视物质 invisible matter
不可知一代 Generation X
不可转移性 untransferability
不明飞行物 unidentified flying object（UFO）；the flying saucer
不平等贸易 unfair trade；discriminative trade
不平等条约 unequal treaty
不上市股票 unlisted stock
不上市证券 unlisted securities
不设防城市 open city
不是…而是 not... but...
不是玩儿的 it's no joke
不溯及既往 non-retroactivity
不同工同酬 equal rewards for unequal work
不完全家庭 incomplete family
不完全统计 incomplete statistics
不完全中立 imperfect neutrality

不稳定市场 queasy market
不稳定因素 destabilizing factor;unstable factor
不信任投票 vote of no-confidence
不正当竞争 illicit competition;unfair competition
不正当收入 illegitimate income
不正当手段 dishonest methods
不正当职业 illegitimate occupation
不着陆飞行 nonstop flight
不保兑信用证 unassignable letter of credit
不变美元价值 constant-dollar values
不得其门而入 can't find the door and get in;can't find one's way in;can't gain admission
不得已而为之 do sth against one's will;have no alternative but to do sth
不登大雅之堂 too low to enter polite company;not appeal to refined taste;be unrefined;be unpresentable
不等边三角形 scalene triangle
不动产所有权 title to real estate
不费吹灰之力 as easy as blowing off dust;as easy as falling off a log
不分青红皂白 make no distinction between right and wrong;indiscriminately
不景气综合征 depression syndrome
不可兑换货币 inconvertible currency
不可更新资源 non-renewable resources
不可同日而语 cannot be mentioned in the same breath;there's no comparison between them
不可望其项背 can't (or not be fit to) hold a candle to sb
不亏不盈价格 breakeven price
不良债务问题 bad debt issue
不食人间烟火 not interested in (or out of touch with) mundane affairs;above the material attractions of the world
不同工不同酬 unequal rewards for unequal work
不完全的信托 imperfect market
不稳定性投资 destabilizing speculation
不知天高地厚 not know the height of the heavens or the depth of the earth—have an exaggerated opinion of one's abilities;not understand things
不足法定人数 insufficient quorum
不足为外人道 This is not to be mentioned to outsiders;This is strictly between ourselves.
不怕官,只怕管 It is not the official,but the clerk,that is to be feared;It is the person in direct control,however low his position,that has to be reckoned with;Fear no officials,except those who officiate over you.
不为名,不为利 seek neither fame or gain;not work for fame or gain

不自由,毋宁死 Give me liberty,or give me death.
"不采取行动"动议 "no action" motion
不到长城非好汉 One who fail to reach the Great Wall is not a hero.
不到黄河心不死 not stop until one reaches the Yellow River—not stop until one reaches one's goal;refuse to give up until all hope is gone
不得已而求其次 have to be content with the second best
不动产投资信托 real estate investment trusts
不敢越雷池一步 not dare to go one step beyond the limit
不管三七二十一 casting all caution to the winds;regardless of the consequences;recklessly
不见棺材不落泪 not shed a tear until one sees the coffin—refuse to be convinced until faced with grim reality
不看僧面看佛面 not for the monk's sake,but for the Buddha's—(do sth for a person) out of deference to sb else
不可撤销信用证 irrevocable letter of credit
不是冤家不聚头 Only the ones with mutual bonds will be thrown together;Enemies and lovers are destined to meet.
不行使应享权利 non-exercise of entitlements
不扩散核武器条约 the Treaty on the Non-proliferation of Nuclear Weapons
不经一事,不长一智 You can't gain knowledge without practice;Wisdom comes from experience.
不入虎穴,焉得虎子 how can you catch tiger cubs without entering the tiger's lair;nothing venture,nothing gain (or have)
不在其位,不谋其政 He who holds no rank in a state does not discuss its policies.
不结盟国家首脑会议 the Summit Meeting of Non-aligned Countries
不比不知道,一比吓一跳 If you don't compare,you're in the dark.(or The moment you do,you get a shock.)
不怕不识货,就怕货比货 Don't worry about not knowing much about the goods;Just compare them and you will see which is better.

布 [bù]
I 名 ①cloth ②ancient Chinese copper coin
II 动 ① declare;announce;publish;proclaim ②spread;disseminate ③dispose;arrange;deploy
布帛 cloth and silk;cotton and silk textiles
布道 preach the Gospel;evangelize
布店 cloth store;draper's;piece-goods store
布丁 pudding
布防 place troops on garrison duty;organize a defence

布岗 deploy sentinels
布告 notice;bulletin;proclamation
布景 ①composition (of a painting) ②setting
布局 ① overall arrangement; layout; distribution ② composition (of a picture, piece of writing, etc.) ③ position (of pieces on a chessboard)
布控 have (sb) under surveillance
布雷 lay mines;mine
布料 cloth
布面 cloth cover (of a book)
布匹 cloth;piece goods
布票 cloth coupon;clothing coupon
布设 lay;make arrangement
布施 alms giving;charity
布头 ①leftover of a bolt of cloth ②odd bits of cloth
布网 spread a net
布线 wiring
布鞋 cloth shoes
布衣 ①cotton clothes ②commoner
布艺 fabric art
布展 set up an exhibition
布置 ① fix up;arrange;decorate ② assign; make arrangements for; give instructions about
布告栏 notice board;bulletin board
布谷鸟 cuckoo
布雷区 minefield
布网船 netlayer
布纹纸 wove paper
布线器 wiring unit
布线图 wiring diagram
布政司 Chief Secretary (Hong Kong)
布帛菽粟 cloth, silk, beans and grain—food and clothing;daily necessities
布达拉宫 Potala Palace
布尔乔亚 bourgeoisie (a transliteration)
布朗运动 Brownian movement
布雷舰艇 minelayers
布鲁氏菌 brucella
布匹染色 piece dyeing
布衣蔬食 coarse clothes and simple fare—a thrifty and simple life
布尔什维克 Bolshevik
布莱尔盲字 Braille
布鲁氏菌病 brucellosis;undulant fever
布面精装本 clothbound de luxe edition
布尔什维克主义 Bolshevism

步 [bù]
Ⅰ 图 ① step; pace ② stage ③ condition; situation; state ④ *bu*, ancient unit for measurement of length,equivalent to five *chi* (or about two yards) Ⅱ 劢 ①walk;go on foot ② tread ③pace off
步兵 ①infantry ②infantryman;rifleman;foot soldier

步步 step by step;at every step
步测 measure by paces;pace out
步长 step;step length;step width;step size
步道 pavement;sidewalk;footpath
步调 pace;step
步伐 step;pace
步法 footwork (in dancing,sports,etc.)
步进 step-by-step
步犁 walking plough
步履 walk
步枪 rifle
步哨 sentry;sentinel
步行 go on foot;walk
步韵 use the rhyme sequence of a poem
步骤 step;move;measure
步子 step;pace
步话机 walkie-talkie
步进式 marching type
步进制 step-by-step system
步行虫 ground beetle
步行机 walking machine
步行街 vehicle free promenade (or street); pedestrian street
步步为营 advance gradually and dig in at every step;consolidate at every step;act cautiously
步调一致 march in step;keep in step;act in unison
步履蹒跚 walk haltingly;hobble along
步履维艰 have difficulty walking;walk with difficulty
步人后尘 follow in sb's footsteps
步入歧途 take the wrong turning

怖 [bù]
劢 fear;be afraid of

钚 [bù]
图 plutonium (Pu)

部 [bù]
Ⅰ 图 ① part; section ② unit; ministry; board;department ③headquarters (of military forces) ④troops;armed forces Ⅱ 量 a) (of movies,books,etc.):一部电影 a film b) (of machines or vehicles):五部机床 five lathes
部队 ①army;armed forces ② troops;force; unit
部分 part;section;share
部件 parts;components;assembly
部将 officers under one's control
部类 category;division
部落 tribe
部门 department;branch
部首 radicals by which characters are arranged in traditional Chinese dictionaries
部属 ①同"部下" ②affiliated to a ministry
部署 dispose;deploy
部委 ministries and commissions
部位 position;place

B

部下 ①troops under one's command ②subordinate
部优 good quality (of a product) designated by a ministry
部员 clerks (*or* staff) members in a department
部长 minister;head of a department
部颁标准 ministry standard
部队代号 code designation (of a military unit)
部分赔付 partial settlement
部级机构 agency at the ministerial level
部落社会 tribal society
部门经理 line (*or* department) manager
部门主管 department manager
部优产品 ministry prize product
部长会议 Council of Ministers
部长助理 assistant minister
部件分解图 exploded view

部门经济学 departmental economics
部长级会议 conference at ministerial level
部门不正之风 malpractice in government department

埠 [bù]
名 ①wharf;pier;town (*or* city) with a port ②trading port;port city ③city;metropolis
埠头 wharf;pier

簿 [bù]
名 book
簿册 books for taking notes (*or* keeping accounts)
簿记 bookkeeping
簿籍 account books,registers,records,etc.
簿子 notebook;book
簿记员 bookkeeper;ledger clerk

 Cc

cā（ㄘㄚ）

拆 [cā]
动 discharge (faeces or urine); shit or piss ➡chāi

擦 [cā]
动 ①rub; scratch: 擦火柴 strike a match ② brush past; approach; touch; shave: 滑翔机擦着山坡飞过。The glider shaved the mountain slopes. ③towel; wipe with rags: 擦地板 mop (*or* scrub) the floor/擦黑板 clean the blackboard ④apply; spread on; put on: 擦唇膏 apply lip stick ⑤shred (vegetables or melons)
擦布 wiping rag; wiper
擦亮 scour
擦伤 abrasion; gall; scotch; scratch
擦拭 wipe clean; cleanse
擦洗 clean (with water or alcohol)
擦音 fricative
擦澡 rub oneself down with a wet towel
擦棒球 foul tip (in baseball, soft ball, etc.)
擦边球 edge ball; touch ball
擦屁股 clear up the mess left by sb else
擦网球 net ball
擦鞋油 shoe polish
擦亮眼睛 remove the scales from one's eyes; sharpen one's vigilance

嚓 [cā]
名 scraping sound: 嚓的一声,汽车停住了。The car stopped with a screech. ➡chā

cǎ（ㄘㄚˇ）

礤 [cǎ]
名 coarse stone

cāi（ㄘㄞ）

猜 [cāi]
动 ①suspect; be doubtful ②guess; speculate; conjecture
猜测 guess; conjecture; surmise
猜度 surmise; conjecture
猜对 ①guess ②call
猜忌 be suspicious and jealous
猜奖 guessing game with prizes for winners
猜拳 finger-guessing
猜透 guess right
猜想 ①suppose; guess; suspect ②conjecture
猜疑 harbour suspicions; be suspicious; have misgivings
猜中 guess right
猜不透 unable to guess; unable to make out
猜谜儿 ①guess a riddle ②guess

cái（ㄘㄞˊ）

才 [cái]
Ⅰ名 ①ability; talent; gift ②capable person; talent Ⅱ副 ①(*used to indicate sth new has happened*): 听了他的解释,我才知道是怎么回事。Only after I had heard his explanation did I understand what it was all about. ②(*used to indicate that sth has just happened*): 他才回来,又出去了。He left again right after he returned. ③(*used to indicate that by comparison sth is small in amount or low in frequency, or that sb is weak in ability*): 这个孩子才四岁。This child is only four. ④(*used for emphatic assertion*): 我才不相信他的话呢。I'll be damned if I believe him! ⑤(*used to indicate that sth happens later than is expected*): 昨天他一直忙到十二点才睡。Yesterday he was kept up until midnight. ⑥(*used to indicate that sth happens only on certain conditions*): 只有齐心协力,才能完成任务。The task can only be completed when everybody works in close concert.
才干 ability; competence
才华 literary (*or* artistic) talent
才略 ability and sagacity (in political and military affairs)
才貌 talent and appearance
才能 ability; capability; talent

才女 gifted female scholar
才气 literary (*or* artistic) talent
才情 brilliant expression of emotions
才识 ability and insight
才思 imaginative power and creativeness (in writing)
才学 talent and learning;scholarship
才艺 talent and skill
才智 ability and wisdom
才子 talented scholar
才高八斗 be endowed with unusual literary talents
才华出众 talents and ability above the average
才貌出众 of exceptional talent and distinguished appearance
才貌双全 be endowed with both beauty and talent
才疏学浅 have little talent and less learning
才思敏捷 have a facile imagination
才子佳人 genius and beauty

材 [cái]
〈名〉① timber ② raw materials ③ material; matter ④ ability;talent;aptitude ⑤ person of a certain type
材积 volume of timber
材料 ① material ② data;material ③ makings; stuff
材质 material quality
材料科学 material science
材料力学 mechanics of materials

财 [cái]
〈名〉 wealth;money
财宝 money and valuables
财帛 wealth;money
财产 property
财东 ① shopowner;store owner ② moneybags
财阀 financial magnate;plutocrat;tycoon
财富 wealth;riches
财经 finance and economics
财力 financial resources (*or* capacity)
财路 means to acquire wealth
财贸 finance and trade (*or* commerce)
财迷 moneygrubber;miser
财气 luck in making big money
财权 ① ownership of property;property right ② economic rights;financial power;control over money matters
财势 wealth and influence
财税 finance and taxation
财团 financial group
财务 financial affairs
财物 money and goods;property (estate not included)
财险 property insurance
财源 financial resources;source of revenue
财运 luck in making money
财政 (public) finance

财主 rich man;moneybags
财产权 property right
财产税 property tax
财神爷 ① the God of Wealth ② very wealth man
财务科 finance section
财政部 the Ministry of Finance
财产保全 property preservation
财产变卖 sales of property
财产估价 assessment
财产管理 administration of assets
财产继承 inheritance of property
财产目录 inventory list;list of property
财产转让 transfer of property
财大气粗 He who has wealth speaks louder than others.
财经纪律 fiscal and economic discipline
财迷心窍 be mad about money; be money-grubbing
财务包干 responsibility for financial surpluses or deficits
财务报告 financial statement
财务补偿 financial indemnity
财务调查 financial investigation
财务管理 financial management
财务混乱 general chaos in book keeping
财务监督 financial supervision
财务会计 financial accounting
财务审计 financial audit
财务状况 financial position
财运亨通 Road to wealth is wide open;Wealth is prosperous.
财政包干 fiscal responsibility system
财政拨款 financial allocations
财政补贴 financial subsidies;financial subsidy
财政赤字 financial deficits
财政关税 financial duty
财政公开 make public the administration of finance
财政基金 financial funds
财政监督 financial supervision
财政紧缩 fiscal austerity
财政困难 in financial difficulties
财政年度 financial (*or* fiscal) year
财政实力 financial strength (solvency)
财政收入 financial revenue
财政体制 financial system
财政透支 fiscal overdraft
财政危机 financial crisis
财政预算 financial budget
财政援助 financial assistance
财政支出 fiscal expenditure
财政职能 functions of public finance
财政资本 financial capital
财产抵押权 encumbrance
财产留置权 possessory lien;encumbrance
财产使用权 right to the use of property

财产转让书 assurance
财务大检查 general financial inspection
财富全球论坛 Fortune Global Forum
财务会计制度 financial and accounting rules
财政复式预算 fiscal double entry budgeting
财政收支差额 the imbalance between revenue and expenditure

裁 [cái]
I 动 ①cut (paper, cloth, etc.) into parts ②reduce; cut down; dismiss ③control; check ④judge; decide; determine II 名 ①size of paper cut ②type of writing ③control; check
裁并 cut down and merge (organizations)
裁撤 dissolve (an organization)
裁处 consider and solve; decide and take action
裁刀 cut-off knife
裁定 decide (*or* declare) judicially; rule
裁断 consider and decide
裁夺 consider and decide
裁缝 tailor; dressmaker
裁剪 cut out (a garment)
裁减 reduce; cut down
裁决 adjudicate; rule
裁军 reduce armaments
裁判 ① judge ② act as referee ③ referee; judge; umpire
裁衣 cut cloth for making dress
裁员 cut down the number of persons employed; reduce the staff
裁决权 umpirage
裁判权 jurisdiction
裁判员 referee; judge; umpire
裁判长 head referee; head judge
裁纸刀 paper cutter; paper knife
裁纸机 paper cutter; (paper) trimmer

cǎi (ㄘㄞˇ)

采 [cǎi]
I 动 ①pick; pluck; gather ②adopt; select ③collect; gather ④mine; extract II 名 spirit; complexion; colour and facial expression ➡ cài
采办 select and purchase on a considerable scale (esp. for a special occasion)
采编 gather and edit (news material)
采场 stope
采伐 cut timber; lumber
采访 ①hunt for and collect ②gather news; cover
采风 collect folk songs and tales
采购 make purchases for an organization or enterprise; purchase
采光 (natural) lighting; daylighting
采集 gather; collect
采掘 excavate
采矿 mining

采录 collect and record
采买 ①select and purchase ②purchasing agent
采煤 coal mining; coal extraction; coal cutting
采纳 accept (opinions, suggestions, requests, etc.)
采暖 heating
采取 adopt; assume or take
采认 admit; acknowledge
采撷 ①pick; pluck ②gather
采信 accept
采样 sampling
采用 select and use; adopt
采油 oil extraction; oil recovery
采摘 pick (fruit, flowers, leaves, etc.); pluck
采制 gather and process
采种 collect seed
采伐量 cutting; yield from felling
采购价 procurement price
采购员 purchasing agent
采购站 purchasing station
采矿场 stope
采棉机 cotton picker (farming machine)
采石场 stone pit; quarry
采油队 oil production crew
采伐迹地 cutover
采购计划 procurement program
采取行动 take action
采取主动 take the initiative
采油平台 oil recovery platform
采购授权书 procurement authorization

彩 [cǎi]
名 ①colour ②coloured silk; colour festoons ③ variety; splendour ④ prize ⑤ applause; cheer ⑥ blood from a wound ⑦ stage craft used in traditional opera to achieve a special effect; jugglery
彩蚌 painted clam shell (a clam shell with a colour painting done on its inside)
彩笔 colour pencil; crayon
彩车 ①colourful float (in a parade) ②bridal car
彩池 lottery pool
彩绸 coloured silk
彩带 coloured ribbon (*or* streamer)
彩蛋 ①painted eggshell (an emptied eggshell with a colour painting done on its outside, with or without decorative silk tassels) ② preserved egg
彩灯 coloured lights
彩电 colour television set; colour TV
彩号 a soldier wounded in action
彩虹 rainbow
彩画 colour painting
彩绘 coloured drawing (*or* pattern)
彩金 prize money; award
彩卷 colour film

彩扩 make enlargements of 135 colour films
彩礼 betrothal gifts (from the bridegroom to the bride's family);bride-price
彩练 coloured ribbon
彩迷 lottery enthusiast
彩民 lottery buyer
彩排 dress rehearsal
彩棚 decorated tent
彩票 lottery ticket
彩旗 coloured banner;bunting
彩喷 colour ink jet printer
彩评 lottery review
彩球 coloured silk ball (for decorative purposes)
彩券 lottery ticket
彩色 multicolour;colour
彩市 lottery market
彩塑 colour modelling;painted sculpture
彩陶 painted pottery (of a Neolithic culture)
彩条 colour bar
彩头 good luck (in business,contests or lotteries)
彩霞 rosy (or pink) clouds
彩页 colour page
彩印 colour printing
彩照 colour picture;colour photo
彩纸 ①coloured paper ②colour photographic paper
彩砖 azulejo
彩釉陶 glazed coloured pottery
彩弹游戏 paintball
彩色玻璃 stained glass
彩色胶卷 colour film
彩色扩印 make enlargements of 135 colour films
彩色平衡 colour balance
彩色失真 colour distortion
彩色印刷 colour printing
彩色编码器 colour coder
彩色电视机 colour television set;colour TV
彩色解码器 colour decoder
彩色摄像机 colour video camera
彩色显像管 colour display tube
彩色显示屏幕 colour display screen

睬 [cǎi]
〔动〕pay attention to;take notice of

踩 [cǎi]
〔动〕①step on;trample ②belittle;trample on ③track down bandits (or robbers);investigate a criminal case
踩缉 hunt down bandits (or robbers)
踩水 tread water
踩线 ①foot-fault ②commit a foot-fault;step on the line
踩高跷 walk on stilts

cǎi (ㄘㄞ)

采 [cǎi]
➡cǎi

采地 fief;vassalage
采邑 fief;vassalage

菜 [cài]
〔名〕①vegetable;greens ②(non-staple) food ③dish;course ④wild herb
菜板 chopping board
菜帮 outer leaves (of a cabbage,etc.)
菜场 food market
菜虫 cabbageworm
菜畜 livestock (raised for meat)
菜单 menu;bill of fare;list of service items
菜刀 kitchen knife
菜地 vegetable plot
菜豆 kidney bean
菜瓜 snake melon
菜馆 restaurant
菜花 ①cauliflower ②rape flower
菜窖 vegetable cellar
菜牛 beef cattle
菜农 vegetable grower
菜品 dish
菜圃 vegetable garden;vegetable farm
菜谱 ①menu;bill of fare ②cookery book
菜畦 small sections of a vegetable plot;vegetable bed
菜青 dark greyish green
菜色 sickly pallor of one living on wild herbs;famished (or emaciated) look
菜市 food market;vegetable market
菜蔬 ① vegetables;greens ②(vegetable and meat) dishes prepared for a meal (or a feast)
菜摊 vegetable stall
菜汤 vegetable soup
菜心 heart (of a cabbage,etc.)
菜肴 cooked dishes
菜油 rapeseed oil;rape oil
菜园 vegetable garden;vegetable farm
菜籽 ①vegetable seeds ②rapeseed
菜墩儿 chopping board
菜粉蝶 cabbage butterfly
菜篮子 ① shopping basket (for food);food basket ②food supply
菜青虫 cabbage caterpillar
菜籽饼 rapeseed cake
菜籽油 rapeseed oil;rape oil
菜篮子工程 shopping basket programme—a programme for increasing food production

cān (ㄘㄢ)

参 [cān]
〔动〕①join;enter;take part in;participate ②refer;consult ③call to pay one's respects;pay homage to ④impeach an official before the emperor ⑤explore and grasp (the meaning,significance,etc.) ➡cēn;shēn
参拜 ① pay one's respects to (a superior);

present oneself to ②pay homage to sb（before his tomb or image）

参半 half；half-and-half

参禅（of Buddhists）sit in deep meditation

参股 purchase of shares in enterprises；equity participation

参观 visit；have a look around

参加 ①join（a group，organization，etc.）；take part in（an activity）②give（advice，suggestion，etc.）

参见 ①see ②pay one's respects to（a superior，etc.）

参军 join the army；join up；enlist

参看 ①see ②read sth for reference；consult

参考 ①consult；refer to ②reference

参谋 ①staff officer ②give advice

参拍 ①be auctioned；be put up for auction ② motion-picture making join the shooting crew；play a part

参评 be sent in for public appraisal or competitive selection

参赛 participate in a match or contest

参事 counsellor；adviser

参试 ①take part in an experiment ②take（*or* sit for）an exam

参数 parameter

参天（of trees，etc.）reach to the sky；tower

参选 ①enter into an election contest；run in an election ②enter a contest for public appraisal

参谒 ①pay one's respects to（a superior）② pay homage to sb

参议 counsel；advise

参与 participate in；have a hand in；involve oneself in

参赞 ①counsellor；councillor ②participate in planning；serve as an adviser

参展 supply exhibits for an exhibition；participate in an exhibition

参战 enter a war；take part in a battle

参照 consult and follow

参政 ①participate in government and political affairs ②counsellor；advisor

参酌 consider（a matter）in the light of actual conditions；deliberate

参观团 visiting group

参考书 reference book

参考值 reference value

参谋长 chief of staff

参议员 senator

参议院 senate

参战国 belligerent state

参照物 object of reference

参政党 party playing a role in state affairs

参政权 the right to participate in public affairs

参观游览 go on a sightseeing tour

参考价格 reference price

参考书目 a list of reference books；bibliography

参考资料 reference material

参天大树 towering trees

参与放款 participation loan

参与意识 sense of participation

参政议政 participate in the deliberation and administration of state affairs

参与式管理 management by participation

餐 [cān]

Ⅰ 动 eat Ⅱ 名 food；meal Ⅲ 量（for meals）

餐叉 fork

餐车 restaurant car；dining car；diner

餐匙 tablespoon

餐馆 restaurant

餐盒 dining box；dinner pail

餐巾 table napkin

餐具 tableware；dinner service；dinner set

餐盘 service plate

餐厅 ①dining room；dining hall ②restaurant

餐位 seating in a restaurant or dining hall

餐饮 food and drink

餐桌 dining table

餐巾纸 napkin paper；paper napkin；serviette

餐饮业 catering industry（*or* trade）

餐风宿露 eat in the wind and sleep in the open—endure the rigours of travel or outdoor living

餐桌台布 dinner cloth

餐桌转盘 Lazy Susan

cán （ㄘㄢˊ）

残 [cán]

Ⅰ 动 injure；damage Ⅱ 形 ①oppressive；savage；barbarous；ferocious ②remnant；remaining ③incomplete；deficient；disabled

残败 ①wreak ②wipeout

残暴 cruel and ferocious；brutal；savage

残本 incomplete text

残部 remnants of sb's defeated troops

残次 defective or substandard

残存 be left alive；survive

残敌 remnants of the enemy forces

残冬 last days of winter

残废 ①become disabled；be crippled ②disabled person；cripple

残骸 remains（of a person or animal）；wreckage（of a building，machine，vehicle，etc.）

残害 cruelly injure（*or* kill）

残货 damaged（*or* substandard）goods；shopworn goods

残疾 deformity；physical disability

残迹 remaining trace，sign，etc.；vestiges

残局 ①final phase of a game ②situation after the failure of an undertaking（*or* after social unrest）

残酷 cruel；brutal；ruthless

残留 remain;be left over
残年 ①the evening of life;declining years ②the last days of the year
残品 damaged article;defective goods
残破 broken;dilapidated
残缺 incomplete;with parts missing
残忍 cruel;ruthless
残杀 murder in cold blood;slaughter
残生 ①one's remaining years ②one's wretched life
残损 damaged;spoiled
残阳 the setting sun
残夜 end of night
残余 remnants;remains;survivals;vestiges
残月 ①the waning moon ②the setting moon
残照 sunset glow;evening glow
残障 disabled
残肢 stump
残奥会 Paralimpic Games
残废证 certificate of disability
残疾人 disabled (or handicapped) person;deformed man
残杯冷炙 crumbs which fall from one's master's table;leftovers from a rich man's table
残兵败将 remnants of a routed army
残茶剩饭 remains of a meal;leftovers
残废军人 disabled armyman
残花败柳 faded flowers and withered willows—fallen women
残花落叶 withered flowers and fallen leaves
残酷竞争 dog-eat-dog competition
残篇断简 stray fragments of text
残破建筑 dilapidated building
残缺不全 incomplete;fragmentary
残垣断壁 broken walls
残渣余孽 dregs of the old society
残疾人奥运会 Paralympics
残疾人联合会 association of physically challenged persons
残疾人福利事业 welfare services for the disabled

蚕 [cán]
〈名〉silkworm
蚕箔 bamboo tray for breeding silkworms
蚕床 rearing shed
蚕蔟 a small bundle of straw,etc.,for silkworms to spin cocoons on
蚕豆 broad bean (the plant,the pod or the seed)
蚕蛾 silk moth
蚕茧 silkworm cocoon
蚕卵 graine
蚕眠 inactive state of the silkworm before it sheds its skin
蚕农 silkworm breeder;sericulturist
蚕桑 silkworm breeding and mulberry growing (as an industry)
蚕沙 silkworm excrement
蚕山 a cone-shaped bundle of straw,etc.,for silkworms to spin cocoons on
蚕师 sericulturist
蚕食 nibble
蚕丝 natural silk;silk
蚕蚁 newly-hatched silkworm
蚕蛹 silkworm chrysalis
蚕纸 silkworm egg sheet (a sheet of paper on which silk moths have laid eggs)
蚕子 silkworm egg
蚕食鲸吞 nibble away like a silkworm or swallow like a whale—seize another country's territory by piecemeal encroachment or wholesale annexation
蚕食行动 nibbling operation
蚕食政策 the policy of nibbling at another country's territory
蚕食鲸吞政策 policy featuring nibbling and gorging

惭 [cán]
〈形〉feel ashamed
惭愧 be ashamed

cǎn (ㄘㄢˇ)

惨 [cǎn]
Ⅰ〈形〉①cruel;savage;inhuman ②disastrous ③miserable;pitiful;tragic Ⅱ〈副〉roundly;terribly;exceedingly;冻惨了 suffer terribly from the cold
惨案 massacre
惨白 deathly pale
惨败 be crushingly (or disastrously) defeated
惨惨 dull;melancholy;somber
惨淡 ①gloomy;dismal;dim ②labourious;arduous ③drearly;miserable
惨祸 horrible disaster;frightful calamity
惨叫 give a horrible shriek;give a blood-curdling scream
惨境 extremely miserable condition;dire straits
惨剧 dreadful,fatal event;tragic event;calamity;disaster
惨苦 miserable
惨然 saddened;grieved
惨杀 massacre;murder
惨死 die a tragic death
惨痛 distressingly grievous;excruciatingly painful;bitter;agonizing
惨笑 sad smile
惨重 heavy;grievous;disastrous
惨状 miserable condition;pitiful (or horrible) sight
惨不忍睹 be too horrible (or tragic) to look at
惨不忍闻 be too horrifying to hear
惨淡经营 keep (an enterprise,etc.) going by

painstaking effort; take great pains to carry on one's work under difficult circumstances

惨绝人寰 tragic beyond comparison in this human world; extremely tragic

惨无人道 inhuman; brutal

惨遭不幸 die a tragic death; meet a sad end; be killed in an accident; meet with a tragic death

惨遭杀戮 be massacred in cold blood

càn（ㄘㄢ）

灿 [càn]
形 bright; resplendent; dazzling

灿烂 magnificent; brilliant; resplendent; splendid

灿然 bright; brilliant; resplendent

灿若云锦 bright as brocade

掺 [càn]
名 a kind of ancient drum music ⇒ chān; shǎn

粲 [càn]
Ⅰ 形 bright; beaming Ⅱ 动 smile beamingly

粲然一笑 give a beaming smile; grin with delight

璨 [càn]
Ⅰ 名 beautiful jade Ⅱ 形 bright; beaming

cāng（ㄘㄤ）

仓 [cāng]
名 warehouse; storeroom; storehouse

仓储 keep grain, goods, etc. in a storehouse; warehouse

仓促 hurried; hasty

仓房 warehouse; storehouse

仓皇 in a flurry; in panic

仓库 warehouse; storehouse; depository

仓鼠 hamster

仓位 ratio of an investor's securities against the total volume of capital in his or her possession

仓租 warehouse storage charges

仓储成本 carrying cost

仓储管理 warehousing management

仓皇失措 be scared out of one's wits; be panic-stricken

仓储式超市 warehouse-type supermarket

仓储式销售 warehouse selling

仓储式商店 warehouse store

仓库保管员 warehouseman

伧 [cāng]
形 rude; uncouth; boorish ⇒ chen

伧俗 vulgar

苍 [cāng]
Ⅰ 形 ①green; blue ②grey; ashy Ⅱ 名 heaven; sky

苍白 ①pale; pallid; wan ②lifeless; flat

苍苍 ①grey ②dark blue ③luxuriant

苍翠 (of trees, grass, etc.) green; verdant

苍耳 Siberian cocklebur

苍黄 ①greenish yellow ②black or yellow— changeable

苍劲 ①(of trees) old and hardy ②(of calligraphy or painting) vigorous; bold

苍老 ①old (in appearance); hoary; (of an old man's voice) hoarse ②(of calligraphy or painting) vigorous; forceful

苍凉 desolate; bleak

苍鹭 heron

苍茫 ①vast; boundless ②indistinct

苍穹 the vault of heaven; firmament

苍髯 grey beard

苍生 common people

苍术 ①Chinese atractylodes ②the rhizome of Chinese atractylodes

苍天 ①Heaven ②blue sky

苍鹰 goshawk

苍蝇 fly; housefly

苍郁 verdant and luxuriant

苍蝇拍 flyswatter

苍劲有力 vigorous and forceful

苍穹浩渺 heaven's wide

苍松翠柏 verdant pines and cypresses

沧 [cāng]
形 (of water) dark blue

沧海 the deep blue sea; the sea

沧桑 from seas into mulberry fields and from mulberry fields into seas—time brings great changes to the world

沧海横流 the seas in turbulence—the country or the world in chaos

沧海桑田 from seas into mulberry fields and from mulberry fields into seas—time brings great changes to the world

沧海一粟 a drop in the ocean

沧桑变化 interchange of sea and land

舱 [cāng]
名 cabin; hold; module

舱底 bottom of a ship's hold

舱口 hatchway; hatch

舱门 hatch door; cabin door

舱面 deck

舱室 cabin

舱位 ① cabin seat (or berth) ② shipping space

舱口盖 hatch door; hatch cover

舱面货 deck cargo

舱内货 underdeck cargo

cáng（ㄘㄤ）

藏 [cáng]
动 ①hide; conceal ②collect; store; lay by

藏躲 go into hiding; hide oneself; conceal oneself

藏奸 ①harbour evil intentions ②be unwilling

to help others
藏匿 conceal;hide;go into hiding
藏品 object
藏身 hide oneself;go into hiding
藏书 ①collect books ②a collection of books;library
藏掖 ①try to cover up ②cover-up
藏拙 hide one's inadequacy by keeping quiet
藏踪 conceal one's tracks
藏书楼 bibliotheca;library
藏书票 exlibris
藏衣室 wardrobe
藏粮于民 store grain among the people
藏头露尾 hide the head but show the tail—hide one part of sth only to reveal another
藏污纳垢 shelter evil people and countenance evil practices
藏龙卧虎之地 place where dragons and tigers are hiding—place where people of unusual ability are to be found
藏污纳垢之所 club of evils

cāo （ㄘㄠ）

操 I 动 ①grasp;hold;wield ②act;do;operate ③speak (a language or dialect) ④drill;exercise II 名 ①drill;exercise ②conduct;behaviour
操办 manage affairs;make preparations (or arrangements) for
操场 playground;sports ground;drill ground
操持 manage;handle
操典 drill regulations;drill manual;drill book
操舵 steel;conn
操控 control
操劳 ①work hard ②take care;look after
操练 drill;train
操切 rash;hasty
操守 discretion in conduct;integrity;virtue
操心 worry;take trouble;take pains
操行 behaviour;conduct (usu. of a student at school)
操演 drill
操纵 ①operate;control ②manipulate;rig
操作 operate;manipulate
操舵室 wheelhouse;pilothouse;steering room
操纵杆 operating lever;control rod;control stick
操纵面 control surface
操纵室 control room
操纵台 control panel
操作杆 action bars;operating arm
操作码 command code;operational code;function code
操之过急 act with undue haste
操纵价格 control the price

操纵市场 play (or rig) the market
操纵选举 rig the election
操纵政局 manipulate the political situation
操作程序 operation sequence
操作代码 operation code
操作规程 operating rules and regulations
操作顺序 operations sequence
操作系统 operating system
操作性能 serviceability
操作程序图 flow diagram;flow chart

糙 [cāo] 形 rough;coarse
糙粮 coarse food grain
糙米 brown rice;unpolished rice
糙纸 rough paper
糙皮病 pellagra

cáo （ㄘㄠ）

曹 [cáo] 名 department of government under the monarch

嘈 [cáo] 形 noise;din
嘈杂 noisy

槽 I 名 ①trough;manger ②groove;slot;rabbet II 量 ①(of doors, windows, etc.);一槽窗户 a window ②time taken to raise a piglet until it is big enough for sale;两槽猪 two litters of piglets
槽板 frid
槽床 troughstand
槽坊 brewery;distillery
槽钢 channel iron
槽谷 trough valley
槽距 slot pitch
槽口 notch
槽榫 chase mortise
槽探 trenching
槽头 trough (in a livestock shed)
槽牙 molar

螬 [cáo]
◇蛴螬 grub

cǎo （ㄘㄠ）

草 I 名 ①grass ②straw ③the wild;the country ④rapid, cursive style of writing ⑤draft II 动 draft;起草文件 draft a document III 形 ①careless;hasty;sloppy;字写得很草。The handwriting is very sloppy. ②female (of certain domestic animals or fowls)
草案 draft (of a plan,law,etc.)
草包 ①straw bag;straw sack ②bungling oaf
草本 herbaceous
草编 straw plaited article

草草 carelessly;hastily
草测 make a preliminary survey
草叉 pitch-fork
草场 meadow;pasture;grassland
草创 start (an enterprise,etc.)
草丛 a thick growth of grass
草袋 straw bag
草地 ①grassland;meadow;meadowland;pasture ②lawn;grassplot
草垛 haystack;hayrick
草房 thatched cottage
草肥 weed fertilizer
草稿 rough draft;preliminary draft
草菇 straw mushroom
草荒 neglected farmland with more weeds than crops
草灰 ①plant ash ②ash grey
草浆 straw pulp (for making paper)
草芥 trifle;mere nothing;trash
草寇 robbers in the greenwood;brigands
草捆 bale
草兰 cymbidium;orchid
草料 forage;fodder
草绿 grass green
草马 mare
草莽 ①a rank growth of grass ②uncultivated land;wilderness
草帽 straw hat
草莓 strawberry (the plant or the fruit)
草棉 the cotton plant
草民 common herd;vulgar people
草木 grass and trees;plants and trees
草拟 draw up;draft
草棚 thatched shack;a thatched shed
草皮 sod;turf
草坪 lawn
草签 initial;tentative signature
草人 scarecrow
草绳 straw rope
草食 herbivorous
草书 (in Chinese calligraphy) cursive script
草率 sloppy;careless;slapdash;perfunctory
草酸 oxalic acid
草堂 humble cottage
草图 sketch
草屋 thatched hut
草席 straw mat
草鞋 straw sandals
草药 herbal medicine
草叶 grass-blade
草鱼 grass carp
草原 grasslands;prairie;steppe
草约 draft treaty;draft agreement;protocol
草纸 ①rough straw paper ②toilet paper
草子 grass seed
草甸子 grassy marshland
草垫子 straw mattress;pallet

草履虫 paramecium
草帽缏 sennit;braided straw;plaited straw
草木灰 plant ash
草裙舞 hula;hula-hula
草石蚕 ①Chinese artichoke ②the plant's pagoda-shaped stem tuber
草头王 king of the bushes—bandit chief
草本植物 herbs
草草了事 get a job done hastily
草草收场 hastily wind up a matter
草场退化 grassland degeneration
草地网球 lawn tennis
草根阶层 people at the grass roots;people of lower classes
草菅人命 treat human life as if it were not worth a straw;act with utter disregard for human life
草莽英雄 a hero of the greenwood
草木皆兵 every bush and tree looking like an enemy soldier—a state of extreme suspicion and fear
草签合同 sign a referendum contract
草签文本 initialed text
草率从事 act rashly;take hasty action
草原退化 grassland erosion

cè（ちさ）

册 [cè] Ⅰ 名 volume;book Ⅱ 动 confer a title:册为太子 make (sb) the crown prince Ⅲ 量 copy:这本词典印了一万册。Ten thousand copies of this dictionary have been printed.
册封 (of a king,emperor,etc.) confer a title upon sb;grant honorific title to sb
册页 album of paintings (or calligraphy)
册子 book;volume

厕 [cè] Ⅰ 名 lavatory;toilet;washroom;restroom;WC Ⅱ 动 be mixed up in;be mingled with;be involved in;place oneself in
厕所 lavatory;toilet;W.C.

侧 [cè] Ⅰ 名 side;lateral Ⅱ 动 lean;incline ➡ zhāi
侧耳 incline the ear;strain one's ears
侧翻 turn on one's side
侧根 lateral root
侧航 crabbing
侧击 make a flank attack
侧记 sidelights
侧力 side force;lateral force
侧门 side door;side entrance
侧面 side;flank;aspect
侧目 cast sidelong glances (with fear or indignation)
侧鳍 lateral fin
侧身 turn (or move) sideways
侧石 kerbstone;kerb

侧视 look sideways
侧室 side room—a concubine
侧卫 flank guard
侧卧 lie on one's side
侧线 lateral line (of fishes, amphibians, round worms, etc.)
侧向 side direction; crossrange
侧旋 sidespin; cut a sidespin
侧芽 axillary bud
侧翼 flank
侧影 profile; silhouette
侧泳 sidestroke; do the sidestroke
侧枝 lateral branch; side shoot; off shoot
侧重 lay special emphasis on
侧面像 profile
侧视图 side view; profile
侧手翻 cartwheel; turn a cartwheel
侧压力 lateral pressure
侧吹转炉 side-blown converter
侧目而视 look askance at sb (with fear or indignation)
侧身而卧 lie on one's side

测 [cè]
〔动〕① survey; fathom; measure ② conjecture; infer; predict
测定 ascertain by measuring or surveying; determine
测度 estimate; infer
测杆 surveying rod; measuring staff
测候 astronomical and meteorological observation
测绘 survey and drawing; mapping; cartography
测井 well logging
测量 survey; measure; gauge
测漏 track down a leak
测评 observe and evaluate
测时 time study
测试 ① test (a machine, meter or apparatus) ② test (a student's proficiency)
测算 measure and calculate
测验 ① put to the test; test ② test; quiz
测字 fortune-telling by analysing the component parts of a Chinese character; glyphomancy
测爆计 explosimeter
测程仪 mileage meter; (navigation) log
测电笔 test pencil (for detecting and measuring electricity)
测高计 height finder; altimeter
测候网 reseau
测谎器 polygraph; lie detector
测绘员 surveyor-draftsman; cartographer
测角器 angle meter; goniometer
测距仪 range finder
测力计 dynamometer
测量学 surveying

测量员 surveyor
测气温 measure the temperature
测深仪 fathometer; depth-sounder
测体温 take sb's temperature
测向仪 goniometer
测斜仪 inclinometer
测云器 nephoscope
测震仪 vialog; ride meter
测震学 seismometry
测醉器 drunkometer
测定结果 result of determination
测风气球 pilot balloon
测幅射仪 holometer
测绘飞机 airmapping plane
测绘卫星 cartographic satellite
测试报告 test report
测试程序 test program
测试技术 testing technique
测云气球 ceiling balloon
测字先生 glyphomancer
测风经纬仪 pilot balloon theodolite

恻 [cè]
〔形〕 sorrowful; sad
恻隐 feel compassion for sb
恻隐之心 compassion

策 [cè]
Ⅰ 〔名〕① bamboo or wooden slips used in ancient China for writing on ② type of essay in ancient China ③ riding-crop; hunting-crop Ⅱ 〔动〕① plan; scheme; strategy ② engineer; plan; arrange ③ use such a crop to urge a horse on
策动 instigate; engineer; stir up
策反 instigate rebellion within the enemy camp; incite defection
策划 plan; plot; scheme
策励 encourage; spur on
策略 ① tactics ② tactful
策论 essay on current affairs presented to the emperor as advice on government policy
策马 spur the horse
策士 counsellor
策应 support by coordinated action
策划人 sponsor; plotter; schemer
策源地 place of origin; source (of a war or a social movement)

cēn （ㄘㄣ）

参 [cēn]
➡ cān; shēn
参差 uneven; not uniform
参差不齐 uneven; not uniform

cén （ㄘㄣˊ）

岑 [cén]
〔名〕 high hill
岑寂 quiet; still; lonely

岑楼 high tower

涔 [cén]
形 rainy 名 puddle

cēng (ㄘㄥ)

噌 [cēng]
Ⅰ 图：麻雀噌的一声飞上了房。 The sparrow whizzed up onto the roof. Ⅱ 动 scold; shout at; rebuke

céng (ㄘㄥˊ)

层 [céng]
Ⅰ 形 one on top of another; overlapping Ⅱ 名 one of several overlapping layers (or tiers) Ⅲ 量 ①layer; tier; stratum: 一层奶油 a layer of cream ②storey; floor: 三层楼 three-storey building ③ component part (in a sequence): 这个词有几层意思。 This word has several shades of meaning.
层报 report a matter to the higher authorities level by level
层层 layer upon layer; ring upon ring
层次 ① arrangement of ideas (in writing or speech) ② administrative levels ③ gradation
层叠 one on top of another
层高 the number of stories and the height of a building
层级 hierarchy
层理 bedding; stratification
层流 laminar flow
层峦 range upon range of hills
层面 level
层压 lamination
层云 stratus
层子 straton
层层把关 check at each level
层层加码 increase the quotas at each level
层层筛选 be chosen through competition and elimination at various levels
层层设防 set up defences in depth
层层转包 multi-level contracting
层出不穷 emerge in an endless stream
层级组织 hierarchical organization
层见叠出 occur frequently; appear repeatedly
层峦叠嶂 peaks rising one upon another; range upon range of hills
层子模型 straton model
层次随机取样 stratified random sampling

曾 [céng]
副 once ➡zēng
曾经 once; formerly; at one time
曾经沧海 have sailed the seven seas—have much experience of life; have seen much of the world
曾经沧海难为水 one who has seen the ocean thinks nothing of mere rivers—to a sophis-

ticated person there is nothing new under the sun

嶒 [céng]
◇ 崚嶒 highness of a mountain

cèng (ㄘㄥˋ)

蹭 [cèng]
动 ①rub; grind; scratch ②be smeared with ③get sth free (of charge); scrounge ④dawdle; dillydally; loiter
蹭儿 ①sth one gets for free ②freeloader
蹭车 get a lift; take a bus or train without paying
蹭吃蹭喝 scrounge meals and drinks

chā (ㄔㄚ)

叉 [chā]
Ⅰ 名 ① fork ② cross Ⅱ 动 work with a fork; fork ➡chá; chǎ; chà
叉车 forklift
叉路 fork of a road
叉烧 grill (marinated pork)
叉手 raise one's folded hands to one's chin to salute sb
叉腰 akimbo
叉子 fork

杈 [chā]
Ⅰ 名 wooden fork; hayfork; pitchfork Ⅱ 动 work with a fork; fork ➡chà

臿 [chā]
Ⅰ 名 spade; shovel Ⅱ 动 thresh

差 [chā]
Ⅰ 名 ① difference; discrepancy ② mathematics difference Ⅱ 副 a little; somewhat; slightly ➡chà; chāi; cī
差别 difference; disparity
差池 ①accidents ②error
差错 ①mistake; error; slip ②mishap; accident
差动 differential
差额 difference; differential; balance; margin
差价 price difference
差距 ①gap; disparity ②difference
差频 difference frequency
差误 mistake; error; slip
差异 difference; divergence; discrepancy; diversity
差额税 variable levies
差别关税 differential rates of duty; differential duties
差别汇率 discriminatory cross-rates (or exchange rates)
差别阈限 difference limen (or threshold)
差错控制 error control
差错文件 error file
差额补贴 deficiency payment
差额选举 multi-candidate election; contested

election;competitive election
差价关税 variable import levy
差可告慰 barely consolable
差强人意 just passable
差之毫厘,谬以千里 An error the breadth of a single hair can lead you a thousand *li* astray.

C

插 [chā]
⟼ ①insert;stick in ②interpose;insert
插班 enroll late in class
插队 ①jump a queue;crash a queue ②go to live and work in a production team
插管 intubate
插花 ① arrange flowers (in a vase, basket, etc.) ②insert sth amidst things of another kind;mix;mingle
插话 ①interpose a remark,etc.;chip in ②a remark interposed ③digression;episode
插口 socket;jack
插屏 table plaque
插曲 ①interlude ②song in a film (*or* play) ③episode;interlude
插入 ①insert ②plug in ③interpolation
插身 ①squeeze in;edge in ②take part in;get involved in
插手 ①take part;lend a hand ②have a hand in;poke one's nose into;meddle in
插锁 mortise lock
插条 ①transplant a cutting ②cutting
插头 plug
插图 illustration (artistic or scientific in nature);plate
插销 ①bolt (for a door,window,etc.) ②plug
插叙 narration interspersed with flashbacks
插秧 transplant rice seedlings (*or* rice shoots)
插页 insert;inset
插足 put one's foot in
插嘴 interrupt;chip in
插座 socket;outlet
插班生 late enrollee
插杠子 poke one's nose into sb's business;meddle;butt in
插管法 intubation
插入语 parenthesis
插图本 illustrated edition
插楔子 drive a wedge
插秧机 rice transplanter
插播广告 plugola;commercial insertion;put in a plug
插翅难飞 unable to escape even if given wings
插队落户 go down to the countryside and become members of production teams;settle down in a production brigade
插科打诨 (of actors) make impromptu comic gestures and remarks;make gags
插入程序 plugged program

插入镜头 cut-in;interscene
插一杠子 have a hand in...at a wrong time;interfere;interrupt
插入式耳机 insert earphone
插入式存储器 plug-in type memory

喳 [chā]
⟼ zhā
喳喳 [chāchā] whispering sound
喳喳 [chācha] whisper

馇 [chā]
⟼ ①cook and stir (feed for pigs) ②cook porridge;cook gruel
馇粥 cook porridge
馇猪食 cook feed for pigs

碴 [chā]
⟼ chá
胡子拉碴 unshaven;stubbly beard

嚓 [chā]
⟼ cā
◇喀嚓 crack;snap
啪嚓 crash

chá (ㄔㄚˊ)

叉 [chá]
⟼ block;jam ⟼ chā;chǎ;chà
垞 [chá]
名 earthen mound
茬 [chá]
I 名 ①stubble ②stubbly moustache ③sth just said;sth just mentioned II 量 crop：一茬庄稼 a crop
茬口 ①crops for rotation ②soil on which a crop has been planted and harvested ③chance;opportunity

茶 [chá]
名 ①tea;tea leaves ②betrothal gift ③dark brown ④ certain kinds of drinks or liquid foods ⑤tea-oil tree;oil-tea camellia ⑥oil-tea camellia
茶杯 teacup
茶场 tea plantation
茶匙 teaspoon
茶袋 tea bag
茶点 tea and pastries;refreshments
茶饭 tea and rice—food and drink;food
茶房 waiter
茶倌 teahouse waiter
茶馆 teahouse
茶盒 caddy
茶壶 teapot
茶花 camellia
茶会 tea party
茶几 tea table;teapoy;side table
茶晶 citrine;yellow quartz
茶镜 tawny glasses;yellow coloured glasses
茶具 tea set;tea-things;tea service
茶客 ①customer of a teahouse ②tea dealer;

tea merchant
茶楼 teahouse with two or more storeys
茶末 tea dust
茶农 tea grower
茶钱 ①payment for tea (in a teahouse) ②tip
茶色 dark brown
茶食 cakes and sweetmeats
茶树 tea shrub; tea tree
茶水 tea or plain boiled water (supplied to walkers, trippers, etc.)
茶摊 roadside tea-stall
茶亭 tea-booth; tea-kiosk
茶托 saucer (for holding a teacup)
茶碗 (handleless) teacup; tea-bowl
茶锈 tea stain
茶叶 tea leaves; tea
茶油 tea-seed oil; tea oil
茶园 ①tea plantation ②place where tea and soft drinks are served; tea garden
茶盅 handleless teacup
茶砖 tea brick
茶座 ① tea-stall with seats ② seats in a teahouse (or tea garden)
茶碟儿 saucer (for holding a teacup)
茶缸子 mug
茶褐色 dark brown
茶话会 tea party (at which the participants chat or give talks)
茶盘儿 tea tray; teaboard
茶水站 tea-stall set up for an occasion
茶文化 tea culture
茶叶蛋 tea eggs
茶叶罐 tea caddy; tea canister
茶叶箱 tea chest
茶色玻璃 amber-yellow glass
茶余饭后 over a cup of tea or after a meal
茶来伸手,饭来张口 have a living without doing any work

查 [chá]
① check; examine; inspect ②look into; investigate ③look up; consult
查案 investigate a case
查办 investigate and deal with accordingly
查抄 make an inventory of a criminal's possessions and confiscate them
查处 investigate and prosecute
查档 consult the files
查点 check the number (or amount) of; make an inventory of
查对 check and verify
查房 (of doctors, nurses, etc.) make (or go) the rounds of the wards
查访 go around and make inquiries; investigate
查封 seal up; close down
查获 hunt down and seize; ferret out; track down

查禁 ban; prohibit; suppress
查究 investigate; try to ascertain (cause, responsibility, etc.); look into and find out
查勘 survey; prospect; explore
查看 look over; examine
查考 investigate; try to ascertain; do research on
查控 surveillance; investigate and control; monitor
查明 prove through investigation; find out; ascertain
查尿 have a urine test
查票 examine (or check) tickets
查铺 go the rounds of the beds (in barracks) at night; bed check
查讫 checked
查清 make a thorough investigation of; check up on
查哨 go the rounds of guard posts; inspect the sentries
查收 check and accept (what is sent herewith)
查税 make a tax inspection
查私 suppress smuggling
查问 ①inquire about ②question; interrogate
查血 have a blood test
查询 inquire about
查验 check; examine
查夜 ①go the rounds at night ②night patrol
查阅 consult (books, magazines, papers, etc.); look up
查账 check (or audit) accounts
查找 look for
查照 please note (and act accordingly)
查证 investigate and verify; check
查词典 look up (a word) in a dictionary; search in the dictionary; consult a dictionary; refer to a dictionary
查电表 read the electricity meter
查号台 directory inquiries; information operator
查户口 check residence cards; check on household occupants
查卫生 check sanitary conditions; make a sanitation check (or inspection)
查询台 query station
查禁贩毒 curb trade in drugs; ban traffic in drugs
查禁卖淫 prohibit prostitution
查禁嫖娼 prohibit going whoring; forbid prostitute visiting
查禁吸毒 prohibit drug-taking; prevent drug abuse
查无实据 Investigation reveals no evidence (against the suspect).
查封违禁品 seal up contraband goods

C

搽 [chá]
动 put on (*or* rub into) the skin; apply

猹 [chá]
名 badger-like animal

楂 [chá]
名 short, bristly hair (*or* beard); stubble ➡zhā

碴 [chá]
动 be cut (by broken glass, chinaware, etc.) ➡chā

碴儿 ① broken pieces; fragments ② sharp edge of broken glass, china, etc. ③ feeling of animosity; grudge, cause of quarrel

碴架 fight; engage in a gang fight

察 [chá]
动 examine; look into; scrutinize

察访 make firsthand observations and inquiries; make an investigation trip

察觉 be conscious of; become aware of; perceive

察勘 examine; survey

察看 watch; look carefully at; observe; inspect

察探 investigate; detect; scout

察言观色 carefully weigh up a person's words and closely watch his expression; watch a person's every mood

察其言,观其行 examine his words and watch his deeds; check what he says against what he does

檫 [chá]
名 sassafras

chǎ

叉 [chǎ]
动 part so as to form a fork; fork ➡chā; chá; chà

衩 [chǎ]
➡chà

◇裤衩 underpants; undershorts; underwear

蹅 [chǎ]
动 trudge (in mud, snow, etc.)

chà

叉 [chà]
➡chā; chá; chǎ

◇劈叉 do the splits

汊 [chà]
名 branch of a river; tributary

杈 [chà]
名 branch (of a tree) ➡chā

杈子 (tree) branch

岔 [chà]
I 动 ①branch off ②turn off (from the original direction); diverge ③change the topic or subject of conversation ④stagger II 名 accident; mistake III 形 be hoarse; lose one's voice

岔开 ①branch off; diverge ②diverge to (another topic); change the subject (of conversation) ③stagger

岔口 fork (in a road)

岔路 branch road; byroad; side road

岔气 feel a pain in the chest when breathing

岔子 ①branch road; byroad; side road ②accident; trouble; sth wrong ③fault

刹 [chà]
名 Buddhist temple; Buddhist monastery ➡shā

刹那 instant; split second

衩 [chà]
名 vent (*or* slit) in the side of a garment ➡chǎ

诧 [chà]
动 be surprised

诧异 be surprised; be astonished

差 [chà]
I 动 ①differ ②be wanting; fall short of; short a little II 形 ①wrong; mistaken ②not up to standard; poor; inferior ➡chā; chāi; cī

差劲 (of quality, ability, etc.) no good; disappointing

差生 slow student; poor student

差不多 ①about the same; similar ②just about right; just about enough ③almost; nearly; just about

差得多 ①very different; entirely different ②way below

差点儿 ①not quite up to the mark; not good enough ②almost; nearly; on the verge of

姹 [chà]
形 beautiful

姹紫嫣红 deep purples and bright reds—beautiful flowers

chāi (彳男)

拆 [chāi]
动 ①(tear) open; take apart; undo ②pull down; dismantle; demolish ➡cā

拆除 dismantle; tear down; demolish

拆穿 expose; unmask

拆掉 take down

拆封 open up a seal (of a door, a letter, etc.)

拆股 dissolve a partnership

拆毁 demolish; pull down; tear down

拆伙 dissolve a partnership; part company

拆建 tear down and build; rebuild after tearing

拆借 short-term loan (made at a daily interest)

拆开 take apart; open; separate

拆迁 have an old building pulled down and its occupants move elsewhere

拆散 [chāisǎn] break (a set)

拆散 [chāisàn] break up (a marriage, family, group, etc.)

拆台 cut the ground from under sb's feet; pull

away a prop
拆违 demolish squatter buildings
拆洗 wash after removing the padding or lining;take apart and clean
拆线 take out stitches (in surgery)
拆卸 dismantle;disassemble;dismount
拆阅 open and read
拆白党 gang of swindlers
拆迁户 households (*or* units) relocated due to building demolition
拆墙脚 undermine;pull away a prop
拆线刀 seam ripper
拆迁补偿 compensation for demolishing real estates
拆迁费用 removal expense
拆穿西洋镜 strip off the camouflage;expose sb's tricks
拆东墙,补西墙 tear down the east wall to repair the west wall—reinforce one place at the expense of another;rob Peter to pay Paul

钗 [chāi]
图 hairpin (formerly worn by women for adornment)

差 [chāi]
Ⅰ劢 send on an errand;dispatch Ⅱ图①one sent on such an errand;errand-boy;hireling ②job;official post ➡chā;chà;cī
差遣 send sb on an errand or mission;dispatch;assign
差使 send;dispatch;assign
差事 official post;billet;commission;job
差役 ①corvée ②runner (*or* bailiff) in a *yamen*
差旅费 allowances for a business trip

chái (ㄔㄞ)

侪 [chái]
图 peers;fellows;associates

柴 [chái]
Ⅰ图 firewood Ⅱ形 ①bony;not fleshy ②poor;shoddy;inferior;lousy
柴草 faggot;firewood
柴扉 wicker gate
柴胡 ①Chinese thorowax ②the root of Chinese thorowax
柴火 faggot;firewood
柴鸡 small-bodied chicken
柴油 diesel oil
柴油机 diesel engine
柴火妞儿 country girl
柴米夫妻 couple who live from hand to mouth;pair who got married for financial reasons
柴米油盐 fuel, rice, oil and salt—chief daily necessities

豺 [chái]
图 jackal
豺狗 jackal
豺狼 jackals and wolves—cruel and evil people
豺狼当道 jackals and wolves hold sway—the cruel and the wicked are in power

chān (ㄔㄢ)

觇 [chān]
劢 observe;survey

掺 [chān]
劢 mix;adulterate ➡càn;shǎn
掺兑 mix different substances (esp. liquids)
掺和 ①mix ②meddle;disturb;cause trouble
掺假 adulterate;mix... with fake stuff
掺杂 mix up;jumble up;mingle
掺假货 adulterated goods
掺水股 water (*or* watering, watered) stock

搀 [chān]
劢 help by the arm;support with one's hand
搀扶 support sb by the arm

chán (ㄔㄢ)

单 [chán]
➡dān
单于 *chanyu*, title of the chief of the Xiongnu people in ancient China

谗 [chán]
Ⅰ劢 accuse, slander (sb behind his back);backbite Ⅱ图 false accusations;slanderous talk;calumny
谗害 calumniate (*or* slander) sb in order to have him persecuted;frame sb up
谗言 slanderous talk;calumny;slander

婵 [chán]
婵娟 ①(of a woman) lovely;beautiful ②moon

馋 [chán]
形 greedy;gluttonous
馋嘴 ①gluttonous ②glutton;greedy eater
馋涎欲滴 mouth drooling with greed

禅 [chán]
图 ①prolonged and intense meditation (for cleansing the mind);*dhyana*;*Chan* ②related to Buddhism (*or* Buddhist) ➡shàn
禅床 bed for meditation
禅定 lost in Buddhist meditation
禅房 ①Buddhist monks' living quarters ②Buddhist temple
禅机 Buddhist allegorical word (*or* gesture)
禅林 Buddhist temple
禅师 honorific title for a Buddhist monk
禅堂 room (*or* hall) in a Buddhist monastery set apart for meditation;meditation room (*or* hall)

禅心 meditative mind
禅杖 Buddhist monk's staff
禅宗 Chan sect;Dhyana;Zen

屏 [chán]
〔形〕 weak;frail
屏弱 ①frail (of physique);delicate in health ②weak and incompetent ③insubstantial;thin

缠 [chán]
〔动〕 ①twine;wind ②tangle;tie up;pester;trouble ③deal with;cope with
缠绵 ①(of an illness or emotion) be lingering ②melodious and moving
缠磨 pester;bother
缠绕 ① twine;bind;wind ② pester;bother;harass;worry
缠身 be delayed;be held up by (*or* burdened with) sth
缠手 (of a matter) be troublesome;be hard to deal with;(of an illness) be hard to cure
缠足 foot-binding
缠绵悱恻 (of a story,poem,etc.) exceedingly sentimental;full of pathos
缠绕植物 twining plant;twiner

蝉 [chán]
〔名〕 cicada
蝉联 continue to hold (a post or title)
蝉蜕 ①cicada slough (used as a Chinese medicine) ②free (*or* extricate) oneself
蝉翼 cicada's wings
蝉翼纱 organdie

潺 [chán]
潺潺 murmur;babble;purl

蟾 [chán]
蟾蜍 ①toad ②the fabled three-legged toad in the moon ③the moon
蟾宫 Toad Palace—the moon
蟾酥 dried venom of toads;toad-cake
蟾宫折桂 pluck the laurel branch from Toad Palace—obtain a *jinshi* degree

chǎn (彳ㄢ)

产 [chǎn]
I 〔动〕 ①give birth to;be delivered of;bear;breed ②produce;manufacture;yield Ⅱ 〔名〕 ①product;produce ②property;estate
产床 obstetric table
产地 place of production (*or* origin);producing area
产犊 calving
产儿 ①newborn baby ②result;product
产房 delivery room
产妇 lying-in woman;woman in childbirth;puerpera
产羔 lambing;kidding

产后 postnatal;postpartum
产假 maternity leave
产驹 foaling
产科 ①obstetrical department;maternity department ②obstetrics
产量 output;yield
产卵 (of birds) lay eggs;(of fishes, frogs, etc.) spawn;(of insects) oviposit
产品 product;produce
产婆 midwife
产前 antenatal;prenatal;antepartum
产钳 obstetric forceps
产权 property right
产生 give rise to; bring about; evolve; emerge;come into being
产物 outcome;result;product
产销 production and marketing
产业 ①estate;property ②industry
产值 value of output;output value
产仔 (of a mammal) give birth to its young
产蛋鸡 laying hen;layer
产卵期 spawning period
产褥期 puerperium
产褥热 puerperal fever;childbed fever
产业界 industrial circles
产业军 the army (*or* body) of industrial workers
产业税 industrial tax
产后出血 postpartum haemorrhage
产科病房 obstetrical ward;maternity ward
产粮大省 granary province
产品包装 packaging of product
产品定型 type approval
产品返销 product buy-back
产品积压 stockpiling
产品检验 product inspection
产品结构 product structure
产品设计 product design
产品信息 product-availability information
产品责任 product responsibility
产品专利 product patent
产前检查 antenatal (*or* prenatal) examination
产权登记 registration of property rights
产权拍卖 equity auctioning
产权转让 transfer of property right
产销见面 link production with sale
产销结合 coordination between production and marketing
产需平衡 production-demand balance
产业革命 the Industrial Revolution
产业工人 industrial worker
产业结构 industrial structure; structure of production
产业循环 business cycle
产业政策 industrial policy
产业资本 industrial capital
产地证明书 certificate of origin

产品保证书 product warranty
产品附加值 added value of product
产品合格率 product percent of pass
产品商品化 product commercialization
产业后备军 industrial reserve army; reserve army of labour
产地检验证书 inspection certificate of origin
产供销一条龙 with production, distribution and sales as one series
产品质量认证 product quality authentication
产权交易市场 property rights exchange; equity market
产业结构重组 reorganization of an industrial structure
产业结构升级 upgrading of an industrial structure
产业结构调整 readjustment of the industrial structure

谄 ［chǎn］
［动］flatter; fawn on
谄媚 fawn on; toady to; curry favour with
谄笑 give an ingratiating smile; force smile in order to curry favour with sb; smile obsequiously; fawning smile
谄上欺下 be servile to one's superiors and tyrannical to one's subordinates; fawn on those above and bully those below

啴 ［chǎn］
［形］lenient; relaxed
啴缓 mild and lenient

铲 ［chǎn］
Ⅰ ［名］shovel Ⅱ ［动］①lift (*or* move) with a shovel; shovel ②solve; handle
铲车 forklift truck
铲除 root out; uproot; eradicate
铲斗 basket; scraper pan
铲子 shovel; spade
铲土机 spading machine; earth-scraper
铲运机 carry-scraper; scraper

阐 ［chǎn］
［动］explain; expatiate
阐发 elucidate
阐明 expound; clarify
阐释 explain; expound; interpret; clarify
阐述 expound; elaborate; set forth
阐扬 expound and propagate
阐述者 exponent

蒇 ［chǎn］
［动］finish; complete
蒇事 finish the work; be through with the job

骣 ［chǎn］
［动］ride an unsaddled horse
骣骑 ride a horse without a saddle

chàn （彳ㄢ）

忏 ［chàn］
［动］①repent; be penitent ②confess (one's sins)
忏悔 ①repent; be penitent ②confess (one's sins to God or to a priest to ask for forgiveness)

划 ［chàn］
◇一划 all; without exception

颤 ［chàn］
［动］quiver; tremble; vibrate
颤动 vibrate; quiver
颤抖 shake; tremble; quiver; shiver
颤音 ①trill ②trill; shake
颤悠 shake; quiver; flicker
颤巍巍 (usu. of aged people) tottering; faltering
颤动信号 dither signal

chāng （彳尢）

伥 ［chāng］
伥鬼 ghost of a man devoured by a tiger

昌 ［chāng］
［形］① prosperous; flourishing ② proper; meet; fair and proper
昌明 (of government, culture, etc.) flourishing; thriving; well-developed; advanced
昌盛 prosperous; flourishing
昌言 proper words; speak openly

倡 ［chāng］
［名］professional entertainer in singing and dancing or playing musical instruments ⇒ chàng

猖 ［chāng］
［形］ferocious; fierce; savage
猖獗 rampant; raging; running wild
猖狂 savage; furious
猖獗一时 be rampant for a while; run wild for a time

娼 ［chāng］
［名］prostitute
娼妇 bitch; whore
娼妓 prostitute; streetwalker
娼门淫窟 bawdy houses; whoredom

鲳 ［chāng］
［名］butterfish; silvery pomfret
鲳鱼 silvery pomfret; butterfish

cháng （彳尢）

长 ［cháng］
Ⅰ ［形］①long ②spare; surplus; extra ③forever; lasting Ⅱ ［名］①length ②strong point; forte Ⅲ ［动］be strong in; be good at Ⅳ ［副］often ⇒ zhǎng
长波 long wave
长城 ①the Great Wall ②impregnable bulwark
长处 good qualities; strong points
长传 (in ball games) throw a long pass
长存 live forever

长凳 backless bench
长笛 flute
长度 length
长短 ①length ②accident; mishap ③right and wrong; strong and weak points
长吨 long ton
长杆 stock; pole
长工 farm labourer hired by the year; long-term hired hand
长骨 long bone
长鼓 long drum (narrowing towards the middle, used by the Korean and Yao ethnic group)
长号 trombone
长河 long river; endless flow; long process
长假 long leave of absence; resignation
长江 the Changjiang (*or* Yangtze) River
长久 for a long time; permanently
长考 ponder
长空 vast sky
长裤 trousers; slacks; pants
长廊 ①covered corridor (*or* walk); long gallery ②Long Corridor (of the Summer Palace in Beijing)
长龙 long queue
长矛 long spear; lance
长眠 have an eternal sleep; be dead
长年 all the year round
长跑 long-distance running; long-distance race
长期 over a long period of time; long-term; long-lasting
长枪 ①spear ②long-barrelled gun; rifle
长驱 (of an army) make a long drive; push deep
长裙 longuette
长衫 unlined long gown
长舌 long tongue—gossipy person; gossip-monger
长石 feldspar (a mineral)
长逝 pass away; be gone forever
长寿 long life; longevity
长丝 filament
长叹 deep sigh
长途 ① long distance ② long-distance telephone call
长物 ①surplus ②presentable thing
长线 (of products) be in oversupply; long line; longterm
长项 sth one is good at; strong point
长销 (of merchandise) have strong market potential; be likely to be in demand in the long run
长效 enduring effect
长夜 ①eternal night ②all night
长缨 long rope; long string
长于 be good at; be adept in
长圆 oval; egg-shaped

长远 long-term; long-range
长斋 Buddhist's permanent abstention from meat, fish, etc.
长征 ① expedition; long march ② the Long March
长住 live in a place for long; settle
长足 leaps and bounds
长臂猿 gibbon
长大衣 redingote
长方体 rectangular parallelepiped; cuboid
长方形 rectangle
长颈鹿 giraffe
长距离 long distance
长靠椅 settee
长面包 streusel
长袍儿 long gown (worn by men)
长披风 inverness
长披肩 liripipe
长披巾 pelerine
长舌妇 gossip monger; garrulous woman
长蛇阵 single-line battle array
长蛇座 Hydra
长生果 peanut
长筒袜 stocking
长围巾 rebozo
长须鲸 finback (a whale)
长元音 long vowel
长波通讯 long-wave communication
长此以往 if things go on like this; if things continue this way
长话短说 make a long story short
长久之计 long-term plan; permanent solution
长命百岁 life of a hundred years; live to a ripe old age
长年累月 year in year out; over the years
长篇大论 lengthy speech (*or* article)
长篇小说 novel
长期保险 long-term insurance
长期贷款 long-term loan
长期亏损 run at a loss for years
长期利率 long-term interest rate
长期债券 long-term bond
长驱直入 drive straight in
长生不老 live forever and never grow old
长筒皮靴 high boots
长筒袜裤 pantyhose
长途跋涉 make a long, arduous journey; trudge a long distance; trek a long way
长途奔袭 make a long-distance raid
长途电话 long-distance telephone call
长途贩运 long-distance trade journey; grand business tour
长途汽车 long-distance bus; coach
长途运输 long-distance transport
长线产品 over stocked goods; goods in excessive supply
长吁短叹 utter sighs and groans; moan and

groan

长征火箭 Long March launch vehicle

长治久安 a long period of peace and order; lasting political stability

长途电话局 long-distance telephone exchange

长途电信局 long-distance telecommunications bureau

长江三峡工程 the Three Gorges Projects

长期市场前景 long-term market outlook

长期共存,互相监督 long-term coexistence and mutual supervision

场 ［cháng］
Ⅰ 名 ①level open space; threshing ground ②country fair; rural market Ⅱ 量 (*used to indicate a process*):一场大雪 a heavy snow-fall ➡ chǎng; chang

场院 threshing ground

肠 ［cháng］
名 ①intestines ②sausage

肠断 heartbroken

肠瘘 intestinal fistula

肠胃 intestines and stomach; stomach; belly

肠炎 enteritis

肠衣 casing for sausages

肠子 intestines

肠穿孔 intestinal perforation

肠梗阻 intestinal obstruction

肠激酶 enterokinase

肠结核 tuberculosis of the intestines

肠扭转 volvulus

肠套叠 intussusception

肠胃炎 enterogastritis

尝 ［cháng］
Ⅰ 动 ①try (food); taste; have a taste of ②experience; be aware of Ⅱ 副 ever; once:我何尝不想去呢,只是没时间。 I meant to go; only I didn't have time.

尝试 attempt; try

尝受 have a personal experience of (hardship, misery, etc.); taste (the bitterness of life, etc.)

尝味 try the flavour; taste; savour

尝鲜 have a taste of a delicacy; have a taste of what is just in season

尝新 have a taste of what is just in season

尝鼎一脔 try one morsel and you'll know the whole potful—get to know the whole from sampling a part

常 ［cháng］
Ⅰ 形 ①ordinary; common; normal ②invariable; constant Ⅱ 副 often; frequently; usually Ⅲ 名 morality; mores

常常 frequently; often; many a time; more often than not

常规 ①convention; common practice; routine ②routine

常轨 normal practice (*or* course)

常衡 avoirdupois (weight)

常会 regular meeting; regular session

常见 be common

常客 frequent guest (*or* customer); frequenter (of a theatre, restaurant, ballroom, etc.)

常理 general rule; what is normal

常例 common practice

常量 constant

常年 ① throughout the year ② year in year out ③an average year

常青 evergreen

常情 reason; sense

常人 ordinary person; man in the street

常任 permanent; standing

常山 ①antipyretic dichroa ②the root or leaves of antipyretic dichroa

常设 (of an organization) standing; permanent

常识 ① general knowledge; elementary knowledge ②common sense

常数 constant

常态 normal behaviour or conditions; normality; normalcy

常委 member of the standing committee

常温 ①normal atmospheric temperature (between 15° and 25℃) ②homoiothermy

常务 day-to-day business; routine

常销 (of merchandise) in constant demand

常言 saying

常用 in common use

常住 ①permanently reside at a place ②(佛教) changeless; permanent

常驻 resident; permanent

常备军 standing army

常春藤 Chinese ivy

常青树 hemlock

常备不懈 always be on the alert; be ever prepared (against war)

常规部队 conventional forces

常规裁军 conventional disarmament

常规疗法 routine treatment

常规能源 conventional source of energy

常规武器 conventional weapons

常规战争 conventional war

常来常往 pay frequent calls on each other

常绿植物 evergreen plants; evergreens

常任理事 permanent council member

常设机构 standing body; permanent organization

常胜将军 an ever-victorious general

常态分布 normal distribution

常态曲线 normal curve

常温动物 homoiothermal animal; homoiotherm

常务董事 managing director

常务理事 managing director

常务委员 member of the standing committee

常用词语 everyday expressions

常住户口 permanent registered residence

C

常驻大使 resident ambassador
常驻代表 permanent representative
常驻记者 resident correspondent
常务委员会 standing committee

偿 [cháng]
囝 ①repay;redeem;compensate ②satisfy; meet the need of;fulfil
偿付 pay back;pay
偿还 repay;pay back
偿命 pay with one's life (for a murder);a life for a life
偿清 pay back in full;clear (a debt)
偿债 pay a debt;redeem a debt
偿清债务 liquidate a debt;clear off debt
偿债高峰 debt repayment peak; peak period for debt repayment
偿债基金 sinking fund

徜 [cháng]
徜徉 wander about unhurriedly;roam leisure-ly

裳 [cháng]
囝 skirt ➡ shang

嫦 [cháng]
嫦娥 the Lady in the Moon

cháng (彳尢)

厂 [chǎng]
囝 ① factory;mill;plant;works ② yard;depot
厂标 emblem mark
厂房 ①factory building ②factory workshop
厂风 overall management and working style of a factory
厂规 factory rules and regulations
厂家 factory;mill
厂价 producer price;ex-factory price
厂矿 factories and mines
厂商 ①factory owner ②factories and stores
厂休 factory's day of rest
厂长 factory director
厂址 site (or location) of a factory
厂主 factory owner;millowner
厂矿企业 factories,mines and other enterpri-ses;industrial enterprises
厂校挂钩 establish a hookup between a school and a factory
厂长负责制 responsibility system of factory directors

场 [chǎng]
Ⅰ 囝 ① place where people gather for a specific purpose ② stage ③ scene ④ spot;scene ⑤field Ⅱ 量:一场球赛 a ball game ➡ cháng;chang
场次 the number of showings of a film,play,etc.

场地 space;place;site
场合 occasion;situation
场记 ①log (for film shooting,theatrical per-formance,etc.) ②log keeper
场景 ①scene ②sight;scene;picture
场面 ①scene (in drama,fiction,etc.);specta-cle ② occasion;scene ③ appearance;front; facade
场所 place;arena
场磁铁 field magnet
场界灯 boundary lights (in an airfield)
场面话 polite platitude for the occasion;civil banalities;unctuous words
场面人 man about town;very sociable person; person of prestige;celebrity
场面上 on social occasions;in social life
场效益 field effect
场效应 field effect
场地选择 site selection
场内交易 transaction on exchange
场外交易 ex-pit;kerb transaction
场外下注 off-track betting
场外指导 sideline coaching
场地使用权 right to the use of site
场内经纪人 floor broker;board broker
场外交易市场 over the counter market
场外交易证券 off-board securities

昶 [chǎng]
Ⅰ 囝 long day Ⅱ 囮 relaxed and easy;un-impeded;unblocked

惝 [chǎng]
囮 ① upset;unhappy;depressed ② hazy;vague

敞 [chǎng]
Ⅰ 囮 (of houses,yards,etc.) spacious;roomy Ⅱ 囝 open;uncovered
敞车 ①open wagon;open freight car ②a rail-way flatcar
敞怀 have one's shirt unbuttoned;bare one's chest
敞开 open wide
敞亮 ①light and spacious ②(of one's think-ing) clear
敞领衫 cutter shirt
敞篷车 open car
敞开思想 think in broader terms (or more o-penly)
敞胸露怀 bare one's chest

chàng (彳尢)

怅 [chàng]
囮 disappointed;sorry
怅然 disappointed;upset
怅惘 distracted;listless

畅 [chàng]
囮 ①smooth;unimpeded ②free;uninhibit-ed

C

畅达 fluent;smooth
畅快 free from inhibitions and happy;carefree
畅谈 talk freely and to one's heart's content
畅通 unimpeded;unblocked
畅想 pamper imagination;give free rein to one's imagination
畅销 sell well;best-selling;have a ready market;be in great demand
畅叙 chat cheerfully
畅饮 drink one's fill
畅游 ①have a good swim ②enjoy a sightseeing tour
畅销书 best seller
畅所欲言 pour out all that one wishes to say;speak without any inhibitions;speak one's mind freely;speak out freely
畅通工程 Smooth Traffic Project
畅通无阻 pass unimpeded;go unhindered;proceed without hindrance

倡 [chàng] 囵 initiate;advocate ➡chāng
倡导 initiate;propose
倡始 initiate;start;found
倡首 initiate;propose
倡言 propose;initiate
倡议 propose;initiate
倡导者 initiator;pioneer
倡始人 initiator;founder
倡议权 diplomacy initiative
倡议书 written proposal;proposal
倡议者 initiator

唱 [chàng] Ⅰ 囵 ①sing ②call;cry Ⅱ 図 song or singing part of a Chinese opera
唱本 libretto (or script) of a ballad-singer
唱词 libretto;words of a ballad
唱段 aria
唱歌 sing (a song)
唱功 art of singing;singing
唱好 hail;applause;cheer loudly
唱和 ①one singing a song and the others joining in the chorus ②an exchange of poems
唱机 phonograph;record player;gramophone
唱名 ①read out a list of names ②sol-fa syllables
唱片 phonograph (or gramophone) record;disc
唱票 call out the names of those voted for while counting ballot-slips
唱腔 vocal music in a Chinese opera
唱头 pickup (of a phonograph)
唱戏 sing and act in a traditional opera
唱针 gramophone needle;stylus
唱白脸 wear the white mask of the villain—play the villain;pretend to be harsh and severe
唱反调 sing a different tune;speak (or act) contrary to
唱高调 use high-sounding words;say fine-sounding things;affect a high moral tone
唱红脸 wear the red mask of the hero—play the hero;pretend to be generous and kind
唱老调 sing the same old song;beat over the same old ground
唱名法 sol-fa;solmization
唱票人 teller
唱诗班 choir
唱双簧 ①give a two-man comic show ②collaborate with each other
唱主角 play the leading role
唱独角戏 put on a one-man show;go it alone;do a thing alone
唱对台戏 put on a rival show;enter into rivalry with sb
唱空城计 perform The Stratagem of the Empty City—present a bold front to conceal a weak defence;have an absentee staff
唱名表决 vote by roll call;roll-call vote
唱念做打 singing, gesticulating, elocution and acrobatics—elements of the art of acting in traditional opera
唱收唱付 voice the amount in receiving and paying
唱片收藏家 discophile

chang （ㄔㄤ）

场 [chang] ➡cháng;chǎng
◇ 排场 ①grand style;ostentation;extravagance ②extravagant ③dignified;respectable

chāo （ㄔㄠ）

抄 [chāo] 囵 ① copy;transcribe ② copy;plagiarize;lift ③search and confiscate;make a raid upon;pinch ④ take a shortcut;outflank ⑤ fold (one's arms) in the sleeves ⑥grab
抄本 hand-copied book;transcript
抄道 ①take a shortcut ②shortcut
抄获 search out;ferret out
抄家 search sb's house and confiscate his property
抄件 duplicate;copy
抄录 make a handwritten copy of;copy
抄身 search a person;frisk
抄送 make a copy for;send a duplicate to
抄网 dip net
抄袭 ① plagiarize;lift ② copy;borrow indiscriminately (from other people's experience) ③launch a surprise attack on the enemy by making a detour
抄写 copy (by hand);transcribe
抄后路 outflank and attack (the enemy) in the

rear；turn the enemy's rear
抄近儿 take a shortcut
抄写员 copyist

吵
［chǎo］
➡chǎo

吵吵 make a row；kick up a racket；twitter

怊
［chāo］
〔形〕grieved and indignant

弨
［chāo］
Ⅰ〔形〕loosened bow Ⅱ〔名〕bow

钞
［chāo］
〔名〕paper money；banknote
钞票 bank note；paper money；bill

绰
［chāo］
〔动〕grab ➡chuò

超
［chāo］
Ⅰ〔动〕①exceed；surpass；overtake ②transcend；go beyond ③leap over；stride over Ⅱ〔形〕ultra-；super-；extra-

超薄 ultra-thin
超编 over-staffed
超标 surpass the set standard；exceed a quota
超产 overfulfil a production target (*or* quota)
超常 be above average；be above the common run
超车 overtake
超出 overstep；go beyond；exceed
超导 superconduction
超等 of superior grade；extra fine
超度 redeem lost souls by making offerings and saying prayers
超额 above quota
超凡 ①transcend the worldly ②out of the ordinary；extraordinary；uncommon
超过 outstrip；surpass；exceed
超级 super
超假 overstay one's leave
超绝 unique；superb；extraordinary
超龄 overage
超前 ①ahead of times；aiming at the future ② surpassing past generations ③lead
超群 head and shoulders above all others；pre-eminent
超然 aloof；detached
超人 ①be out of the common run ②superman (as defined by Nietzsche)
超生 ①（佛教）be reincarnated ②spare sb's life；be merciful ③ unplanned birth；give unplanned births
超市 supermarket
超速 ①exceed the speed limit ②hypervelocity
超脱 ① unconventional；original ② be detached；stand (*or* hold，keep) aloof
超线 superstring
超逸 unconventionally graceful；free and natural
超员 exceed seating capacity；be overloaded

超越 surmount；overstep；transcend；surpass
超载 overload
超支 overspend
超值 exceed the real value
超重 ①overload ②overweight
超轴 over haulage
超子 hyperon
超导体 superconductor
超低温 ultralow temperature
超短波 ultrashort wave
超短裤 hot pants
超短裙 miniskirt
超负荷 excess load；overload
超高频 ultrahigh frequency (UHF)
超高温 superhigh temperature
超高压 ① superhigh pressure ② extrahigh voltage (*or* tension)
超巨星 supergiant star
超空间 hyperspace
超链接 hyperlink
超媒体 hypermedia
超声波 ultrasonic (wave)；supersonic (wave)
超声学 ultrasonics
超外差 superheterodyne；superhet
超现实 go beyond reality；be unrealistic
超新星 supernova
超星团 supercluster
超音速 supersonic speed
超自然 supernatural
超(自)我 super-ego
超编单位 over-staffed units
超常儿童 supernormal child
超常记忆 hypermnesia
超尘拔俗 avoid earthly concerns and hold oneself aloof from the vulgar
超导材料 superconductor
超导电性 superconductivity
超导技术 superconducting technology
超导现象 superconductive phenomena
超额保险 excess insurance
超额利润 superprofit
超额预算 excess budget
超购加价 additional prices for above quota purchase
超级磁泡 superbubble
超级大国 superpower
超级大学 megaversity
超级公路 superhighway
超级间谍 superspy
超级市场 supermarket
超级油轮 supertanker
超龄团员 overage Youth League member
超平彩电 hyperplane colour TV
超期服役 extended active duty；extended service in the army
超前分配 divide and distribute far ahead of time

超前消费　excessive consumption
超然科学　pataphysics
超然物外　hold oneself aloof from the world; be above worldly considerations; stay away from the scene of contention
超人哲学　philosophy of a superman
超速粒子　hypervelocity particle
超小型管　subminiature tube
超铀元素　transuranic (*or* transuranium) element
超越射击　overhead fire
超越职权　overstep one's authority; exceed one's powers
超重量级　super-heavy weight
超导存储器　superconductivity memory
超低空飞行　minimum altitude flying; hedge-hopping
超负荷运转　overloading operation
超高层建筑　high-rise building
超级计算机　super computer
超计划生育　have more children than what the plan allows
超经济剥削　extraeconomic exploitation
超声波疗法　ultrasonic therapy
超声物理学　ultrasonic physics
超视距空战　over-the-horizon air action
超微粒胶片　superfine grain film
超现实主义　surrealism
超级 301 条款　"Super 301" clause
超额剩余价值　excess surplus value
超声波探伤仪　supersonic detector
超小型计算机　microminicomputer
超音速喷气机　superjet
超音速战斗机　supersonic fighter-plane; supersonic fighter
超重量级拳击　super heavy weight boxing
超重量级柔道　super weight judo
超外差式收音机　superheterodyne (radio set)
超文本传输协议　hypertext transfer protocol (http)
超大规模集成电路　very large scale integration (VLSI)
超高速巨型计算机　giant ultra-high-speed computer

剿　[chāo]
〔动〕plagiarize; copy ➡jiǎo

cháo（彳幺）

巢　[chāo]
〔名〕nest
巢菜　common vetch
巢蛾　ermine moth
巢居　live on trees
巢鼠　harvest mouse
巢穴　lair; den; nest; hideout

朝　[chāo]
Ⅰ〔名〕①court; government; governing party ②dynasty ③emperor's reign; ruling period of a monarch Ⅱ〔动〕have an audience with (a king, emperor, etc.); make a pilgrimage to Ⅲ〔介〕facing; towards ➡zhāo
朝拜　①make obeisances to (a sovereign) ②pay religious homage to; worship
朝代　dynasty
朝服　court dress
朝贡　(of envoys from a vassal state or a foreign country) present tribute to an emperor
朝见　have an audience with a sovereign
朝觐　①have an audience with a sovereign ②make a pilgrimage to a shrine (*or* a sacred place)
朝山　(of Buddhists) make a pilgrimage to a temple on a famous mountain
朝圣　(of religious people) make a pilgrimage to a sacred place
朝廷　①royal (*or* imperial) court ②royal (*or* imperial) government
朝向　turn towards; face
朝阳　[cháoyáng] ①exposed to the sun; face the sun ②with a sunny aspect; have a sunny aspect
朝野　①the court and the commonalty ②the government and the public
朝政　(in imperial times) court administration; affairs of state
朝鲜族　the Koreans
朝山进香　go on a pilgrimage to offer incense at the temple

嘲　[cháo]
〔动〕ridicule; deride; sneer
嘲讽　sneer at; taunt
嘲弄　mock; poke fun at
嘲笑　ridicule; deride; jeer at; laugh at

潮　[cháo]
Ⅰ〔名〕①tide ②large-scale social upsurge; current; tide; rise and fall of a campaign Ⅱ〔形〕①damp; moist ②of low (*or* inferior) quality; poor; bad ③not skilled; not skilful; awkward
潮解　deliquescence
潮金　impure gold ingot
潮流　①tide; tidal current ②trend
潮气　moisture in the air; humidity
潮热　hectic fever
潮湿　moist; damp
潮水　tidewater; tide
潮位　the level of the tidal current at its flow or ebb; tidemark
潮汐　morning and evening tides
潮汛　spring tide
潮银　inferior silver ingot
潮涌　roll like the tide
潮呼呼　damp; dank; clammy
潮汐表　tide table

潮汐能 tidal energy
潮流常数 current constant
潮汐测站 tide station
潮汐电站 tidal power stations

chǎo (彳幺)

吵 [chǎo]
〔动〕①make a noise ②quarrel; squabble; wrangle; argue; have words with ➡chāo
吵架 quarrel; have a row; wrangle
吵闹 ①wrangle; kick up a row ②harass; disturb ③din; hubbub
吵嚷 make a racket; shout in confusion; clamour
吵嘴 quarrel; bicker

炒 [chǎo]
〔动〕① stir-fry; fry; *sauté* ② speculate illegally; promote; sensationalize; fire ③ sack; fire; dismiss
炒饼 fried shredded pancake
炒菜 ①make dishes ②stir-fried dish
炒更 moonlight; take on a second job for added cash
炒股 profiteer with stocks; speculate in stocks
炒汇 buying and selling foreign currency; arbitrage
炒货 roasted seeds and nuts
炒家 speculator
炒米 ①parched rice ②millet stir-fried in butter (staple food of the Mongolians)
炒面 ①fried noodles with shredded meat and vegetables ②parched flour
炒勺 round-bottomed frying pan; wok
炒作 profiteering activities; sensationalize; speculate
炒地皮 speculate in real estate
炒瓜子 roasted melon seeds
炒鸡蛋 scrambled eggs
炒鸡丁 stir-fried chicken cubes
炒冷饭 do sth again and again; repeat doing the same things
炒米粉 fried rice-flour noodles
炒米花 puffed rice
炒明星 make a person famous; create a star through publicity
炒肉片 stir-fried sliced pork
炒鱿鱼 give sb the sack; sack; fire; dismiss
炒鱼片 *sautéed* fish slices
炒买炒卖 stir-fry in buying and selling

chào (彳幺)

耖 [chào]
Ⅰ〔名〕harrow-like implement for pulverizing sods Ⅱ〔动〕level land with such an implement
耖田 level land with a harrow

chē (彳ㄜ)

车 [chē]
Ⅰ〔名〕①vehicle ②wheeled machine or instrument ③machine Ⅱ〔动〕①lathe; turn ②lift water by waterwheel ③carry in a vehicle ④sew clothes with a sewing machine ⑤turn (one's body or limb) ➡jū
车把 handlebars (of a bicycle, motor cycle, etc.); shaft (of a wheelbarrow, handcart, etc.)
车本 general term for a driver's licence
车秤 cart balance
车床 lathe
车次 ①train number ②coach number (indicating order of departure)
车刀 lathe tool; turning tool
车道 (traffic) lane; roadway
车灯 general name for lights on a vehicle (e.g. headlights, bicycle lamp, etc.)
车笛 vehicle horn
车队 motorcade
车费 (passenger's) fare
车夫 carter; driver; rickshaw puller; chauffeur
车工 ①lathe work ②turner; lathe operator
车钩 coupling
车号 license number (of a vehicle)
车祸 traffic accident; road accident
车技 trick-cycling
车间 workshop; shop
车库 garage
车辆 vehicles
车流 ①traffic ②rate of traffic flow
车轮 wheel (of a vehicle)
车扒 pickpocket on bus (*or* train)
车牌 license plate
车篷 awning for a vehicle
车皮 railway wagon (*or* carriage); flatcar (*or* freight) car
车票 train (*or* bus) ticket; ticket
车钱 fare
车身 the body of a vehicle
车市 car market
车速 speed of a motor vehicle
车胎 tyre
车体 car body
车头 ①the front of a vehicle ②engine (of a train); locomotive
车帏 curtain in a carriage
车位 parking place; parking stall
车险 car insurance
车厢 railway carriage; railroad car
车削 turning
车辕 shaft (of a cart, etc.)
车闸 brake (of a car, bicycle, etc.)
车展 car exhibition

车站 station；depot；stop
车照 driving license
车辙 rut
车轴 axletree；axle
车子 ①a small vehicle ②bicycle
车座 saddle
车把式 cart-driver；carter
车轱辘 wheel（of a vehicle）
车架(子) frame（of a car，bicycle，etc.）
车轮战 tactic of several persons taking turns in fighting one opponent to tire him out
车马费 travel allowance
车臣战争 Chechen War
车匪路霸 train and highway bandits and robbers；railway and highway bandits
车轱辘话 repetitious talk；keep saying the same thing
车间主任 workshop director
车水马龙 an incessant stream of horses and carriages—heavy traffic
车载斗量 enough to fill carts and be measured by the bushel—common and numerous
车辆周转率 average turnround rate of rolling stock
车座安全带 shoulder harness；shoulder belt
车到山前必有路 the cart will find its way round the hill when it gets there—things will eventually sort themselves out
车辆购置附加费 surcharge over the purchase of motor vehicles

伡［chē］
名 ①engine driver ②chief engineer of a ship

砗［chē］
砗磲 giant clam

chě（ㄔㄜˇ）

扯［chě］
动 ①pull；drag ②tear；tear off ③chat；gossip
扯淡 talk nonsense；bullshit
扯谎 tell a lie or fib；lie
扯开 avulsion
扯了 plenty；too much；a lot
扯皮 wrangle；dispute over trifles；argue back and forth；bicker
扯平 evening up
扯碎 tear to pieces
扯后腿 hold sb back（from action）；be a drag on sb；be a hindrance to sb
扯家常 talk about everyday matters；engage in small talk；chitchat；chat about everyday family affairs
扯闲话 gossip

chè（ㄔㄜˋ）

彻［chè］
形 thorough；penetrating；complete
彻底 thorough；thoroughgoing
彻骨 penetrate to the bone
彻夜 all night；all through the night；from dusk to dawn
彻里彻外 out and out；through and through；downright
彻头彻尾 out and out；through and through；downright

坼［chè］
动 split open；crack
坼裂 split open；crack

撦［chè］
动 ①pull；tug；drag ②draw ③flash past
撦签 draw lots
撦肘 hold sb back by the elbow—impede sb from doing sth

撤［chè］
动 ①remove；take away ②withdraw；retreat；evacuate ③（of smell，weight，etc.）reduce；take off
撤兵 withdraw troops
撤除 remove；dismantle
撤防 withdraw a garrison；withdraw from a defended position
撤换 dismiss and replace；recall；replace
撤回 ①recall；withdraw ②revoke；retract；withdraw
撤火 （of cooking）put out the fire；stop heating
撤军 withdraw troops
撤离 withdraw from；leave；evacuate
撤诉 （of the plaintiff）withdraw an accusation；drop a lawsuit；revoke a court action
撤退 withdraw；pull out
撤席 clear the table（after a feast）
撤销 cancel；rescind；revoke
撤职 dismiss（or discharge）sb from his post；remove sb from office
撤资 withdraw investment；withdraw funds
撤走 withdraw；leave
撤味儿 reduce the smell
撤销条款 cancellation clause

澈［chè］
形 （of water）clear；limpid

chēn（ㄔㄣ）

抻［chēn］
动 pull out；stretch
抻面 ①hand-pulled noodles ②make noodles by drawing out the dough by hand

琛［chēn］
名 treasure

嗔 [chēn]
动 ①angry;displeased ②be annoyed (with sb);blame;be dissatisfied with
嗔诟 vilify;berate angrily
嗔怪 blame;rebuke
嗔怒 get angry
嗔色 angry (*or* sullen) look

chén (ㄔㄣˊ)

臣 [chén]
名 ① official under a feudal ruler;subject ②your vassal;I
臣服 ①submit oneself to the rule of;acknowledge allegiance to ②serve a ruler as his subject
臣民 subjects of a feudal ruler
臣子 an official in feudal times

尘 [chén]
名 ①dust;dirt ②this world;worldly affairs ③trace
尘埃 dust
尘暴 dust storm
尘肺 pneumoconiosis
尘封 be covered with dust;be dust-laden
尘垢 dust and dirt;dirt
尘世 this world;this mortal life;mundane world
尘事 worldly affairs
尘俗 ①this world;this mortal life ②mundane affairs
尘土 dust
尘烟 ①a cloud of dust ②smoke and dust
尘缘 bonds of this world;carnal thoughts
尘埃传染 dust infection
尘埃落定 end up with

辰 [chén]
名 ①celestial bodies ②any of the traditional twelve two-hour periods of the day ③time;day;occasion
辰砂 cinnabar;vermillion
辰时 the period of the day from 7 a.m. to 9 a.m.

沉 [chén]
Ⅰ 动 ①sink ②subside;sink;keep down ③keep down;lower;sink ④feel heavy or uncomfortable Ⅱ 形 ①(of degree) deep;profound ②heavy
沉沉 ①heavy ②deep
沉淀 form a sediment;precipitate
沉浮 ①sink and rise;bob on water ②ups and downs of fortune;vicissitudes
沉积 ①deposit ②sedimentation
沉寂 ①quiet;still ②no news
沉降 ①subside;settle ②sedimentation
沉浸 be immersed in;be steeped in;be permeated with
沉井 open caisson

沉静 ①quiet;calm ②calm;serene;placid
沉沦 sink into vice, degradation, depravity, etc.
沉闷 ①(of weather,atmosphere,etc.) dreary;gloomy;oppressive;depressing ②depressed;in low spirits ③not outgoing;withdrawn
沉迷 be confused;be bewildered
沉湎 indulge in;wallow in;be given to
沉没 ①sink;founder ②submergence
沉默 ①reticent;taciturn;uncommunicative ②silent
沉溺 wallow;indulge in (vices,etc.)
沉睡 be sunk in sleep;be fast asleep;be sound asleep
沉思 ponder;meditate;be lost in thought
沉痛 ① with a deep feeling of grief or remorse;heavy at heart ②deeply felt;bitter
沉稳 ① steady;staid;sedate ② untroubled;sound
沉陷 ①sink;cave in ②settlement
沉香 agalloch eaglewood
沉箱 caisson
沉毅 steady and strong
沉吟 mutter to oneself, unable to make up one's mind
沉郁 depressed;gloomy
沉冤 gross injustice
沉渣 ①sediment;dregs ②dregs of society
沉重 ①heavy ②serious;critical
沉着 cool-headed;composed;calm;steady
沉子 sinker
沉醉 get drunk;become intoxicated
沉甸甸 heavy
沉淀池 precipitating tank
沉淀剂 precipitating agent
沉淀器 settler;sump;deposit gauge
沉淀物 sediment;precipitate
沉积物 deposit;sediment
沉积岩 sedimentary rock
沉降缝 settlement joint
沉默权 right of silence
沉砂池 grit chamber
沉住气 keep calm;keep cool;be steady
沉默寡言 reticent;taciturn;uncommunicative
沉思凝想 think deeply or profoundly
沉吟不决 hesitate;be irresolute;be undecided
沉鱼落雁 (of feminine beauty) make fish sink and birds alight
沉冤莫白 grievous wrongs that can never be redressed

忱 [chén]
名 true sentiment;sincere feeling;hearty feeling

陈 [chén]
Ⅰ 动 ①lay out;put on display ②state;explain;narrate;tell Ⅱ 形 old;stale

陈兵 mass (*or* deploy) troops
陈醋 mature vinegar
陈腐 old and decayed；stale；outworn
陈规 outmoded conventions；established practice
陈货 old stock；shopworn goods
陈迹 a thing of the past
陈酒 old wine；mellow wine
陈旧 outmoded；obsolete；old-fashioned；out-of-date
陈列 display；set out；exhibit
陈年 of long standing；preserved for a long time
陈酿 ①ageing ②old wine；mellow wine
陈皮 dried tangerine (*or* orange) peel
陈设 ①display；set out ②furnishings
陈述 state
陈说 state；explain
陈诉 state；recount
陈废率 rate of obsolescence
陈列窗 sample window
陈列馆 exhibition hall
陈列柜 showcase
陈列架 frame；stand
陈列品 exhibits；articles on display
陈列室 exhibition room；showroom
陈述句 declarative sentence
陈兵百万 deploy a million troops
陈陈相因 follow a set routine；stay in the same old groove
陈词滥调 hackneyed and stereotyped expressions
陈规陋习 outmoded regulations and irrational practices；bad customs and habits

宸 ［chén］ 图 ①mansion ②emperor's residence (during the feudal era) ③emperor
宸居 emperor's residence
宸宇 great mansion
宸章 emperor's writing

晨 ［chén］ 图 morning
晨操 morning exercises
晨风 morning breeze
晨光 light of the early morning sun；dawn
晨练 morning exercise；morning practice
晨夕 morning and evening
晨曦 the first rays of the morning sun
晨星 ①stars at dawn ②morning star
晨光曦微 the first faint rays of dawn

谌 ［chén］ I 囫 believe in；trust II 副 truly；naturally；admittedly

chěn（ㄔㄣˇ）

碜 ［chěn］ 圈 ①gritty (food) mixed with sand ②ugly；unsightly；hideous

chèn（ㄔㄣˋ）

衬 ［chèn］ I 囫 ①line；place sth underneath ②serve as a contrast to；set off II 图 cloth lining；liner III 圈 sth worn underneath
衬布 lining cloth
衬裤 underpants；pants
衬里 lining
衬领 collar lining
衬裙 underskirt；slip；petticoat
衬衫 ①shirt ②blouse
衬托 set off；serve as a foil to
衬衣 ①underclothes；undergarments ②shirt
衬纸 slip sheet；interleaving paper
衬字 word inserted in a line of verse for balance or euphony
衬衫式夹克 bush jacket

疢 ［chèn］ 图 ill；sick
疢疾 disease

龀 ［chèn］ 囫 (of a child) grow permanent teeth

称 ［chèn］ 囫 fit；match；suit ⇒ chēng
称身 (of a garment) fit
称心 find sth satisfactory；be gratified
称愿 be gratified (esp. at the misfortune of a rival)
称职 prove oneself competent at one's job；fill a post with credit；be well qualified for a piece of work
称心如意 have sth as one wishes after one's own heart；very gratifying and satisfactory

趁 ［chèn］ I 囫 ①take advantage of；avail oneself of ②own；possess；be rich in ③chase；pursue II 矜 while
趁便 when it is convenient；at one's convenience
趁机 take advantage of the occasion；seize the chance
趁空 use one's spare time；avail oneself of leisure time
趁钱 have lots of money；be rich
趁势 take advantage of a favourable situation
趁早 as early as possible；before it is too late；at the first opportunity
趁火打劫 loot a burning house—take advantage of sb's misfortune to do him harm；fish in troubled waters
趁热打铁 strike while the iron is hot
趁人之危 take advantage of another's perilous state

榇 ［chèn］ 图 coffin

C

chen（·ㄔㄣ）

伧 [chen]
➡cāng
◇寒伧 ①ugly；unsightly；shabby ②shameful；disgraceful ③ridicule；make fun of；put to shame

chēng（ㄔㄥ）

称 [chēng]
Ⅰ动 ①call；style ②say；speak；state ③praise；commend ④weigh ⑤raise Ⅱ名 name ➡chèn
称霸 seek hegemony；dominate
称便 find sth a great convenience
称病 claim to be ill；offer illness as an excuse；plead illness
称臣 declare oneself a vassal or subject；acknowledge one's allegiance to a ruler
称大 show off one's status（or rank）；put on airs
称道 speak approvingly of；praise；acclaim
称帝 proclaim oneself emperor
称号 title；name；designation
称呼 ①call；address ②form of address
称快 express one's gratification；express joy and jubilation
称量 weigh
称奇 speak admiringly of；regard as amazing
称说 name sth when speaking
称颂 praise；extol；eulogize
称王 proclaim oneself king
称为 call；be called；be known as
称谓 appellation；title
称羡 express one's admiration or envy
称谢 express one's thanks；thank
称雄 hold sway over a region；rule the roost
称许 praise；commendation
称誉 sing the praises of；praise；acclaim
称赞 praise；acclaim；commend
称重 weigh；weighing；scalage
称得起 deserve to be called；be worthy of the name of
称量器 weighter
称霸世界 dominate the world
称孤道寡 style oneself king—act like an absolute monarch
称量体重 weigh in
称觞祝寿 raise one's drinking vessel to toast sb's health；drink a toast to sb's health
称王称霸 act like an overlord；lord it over；domineer
称贤举能 commend the virtuous and promote the capable
称兄道弟 call each other brothers；be on intimate terms

蛏 [chēng]
名 razor clam
蛏干 dried razor clam
蛏子 razor clam

铛 [chēng]
名 pan ➡dāng

撑 [chēng]
Ⅰ动 ①prop up；support ②move（a boat）forward with a long pole pushed against the bottom of the river ③maintain；keep up ④open；unfurl ⑤fill to the point of bursting Ⅱ名 brace；stay
撑臂 brace
撑持 prop up；shore up；sustain
撑竿 vaulting pole
撑架 strut
撑伞 open an umbrella
撑条 stay
撑腰 support；back up；bolster up
撑场面 keep up appearances
撑窗杆 adjuster for windows
撑高杆 adjuster for windows
撑门面 keep up appearances
撑死了 ①at the utmost；to the end；finally ②too full；stuffed to the gills
撑竿跳高 pole vault；pole jump
撑腰打气 bolster and pep up

瞠 [chēng]
动 stare
瞠目 stare（in alarm, embarrassment, confusion, etc.）
瞠乎其后 stare helplessly at the vanishing back of the runner ahead—despair of catching up
瞠目结舌 stare tongue-tied；stare dumbfounded

chéng（ㄔㄥ）

成 [chéng]
Ⅰ动 ①accomplish；succeed ②help sth to materialize；help sb to achieve sth ③become；turn into ④achievement；result；yield ⑤OK；all right Ⅱ形 ①fully developed；fully grown ②established；ready-made；finalized；existing ③in considerable numbers（or amounts）④able；capable Ⅲ量 one tenth；ten per cent；八
成新 eighty per cent new
成败 success or failure
成本 cost
成才 become a useful person
成材 ①grow into useful timber ②become a useful person
成虫 adult insect；imago
成簇 in-line；cluster
成堆 form a pile；be in heaps
成对 twinning；pairing
成方 set prescription

成分 ①composition;component part;ingredient ②one's class status;one's profession or economic status

成风 become a common practice;become the order of the day

成功 succeed;be a success

成规 established practice;set rules;groove;rut

成果 achievement;fruit;gain;positive result

成婚 get married

成活 survive

成绩 result (of work or study);achievement;success

成家 (of a man) get married

成见 preconceived idea;prejudice

成交 strike a bargain;conclude a transaction;clinch a deal

成教 adult education

成就 ①achievement;success;attainment;accomplishment ②achieve;accomplish

成考 adult higher education enrollment examination

成立 ①found;establish;set up ②be tenable;hold water

成例 precedent;existing model

成眠 fall asleep;go to sleep

成名 become famous;make a name for oneself

成命 an order already issued

成年 ①grow up;come of age ②all year

成批 group by group;in batches

成品 end product;finished product

成器 grow up to be a useful person

成亲 get married

成全 help sb achieve his aim

成群 in groups;in great numbers

成人 ①be grown up;become full-grown ②adult;grown-up

成仁 die for a righteous cause

成色 ①percentage of gold or silver in a coin, etc.;relative purity of gold or silver ②quality

成事 ①accomplish sth;succeed ②thing that is past (or finished)

成书 ①be published in book form ②a book already in circulation

成熟 ①ripe;mature ②maturation;adultness;grown

成双 form a pair

成说 accepted theory (or formulation)

成诵 be able to recite;be able to repeat from memory

成俗 become social custom

成算 preconceived idea (or plan)

成套 form a complete set

成天 all day long;all the time

成为 become;turn into

成文 ①existing writings ②written

成仙 become an immortal

成像 formation of image;imagery

成效 effect;result

成心 intentionally;on purpose;with deliberate intent

成形 ①take shape ②shaping;forming

成型 (of workpieces or products) be in finished form

成性 by nature;become sb's second nature

成药 pharmacist-prepared medicine;patent medicine

成衣 ①tailoring ②ready-made clothes;ready-to-wear

成议 agreement already reached

成因 cause of formation;contributing factor

成瘾 habituation

成鱼 adult fish

成语 set phrase (usu. composed of four characters);idiom

成员 member (of a group or family)

成约 signed treaty (or agreement);existing agreement

成灾 cause disaster;result in disaster

成长 grow up;grow to maturity

成本法 law of cost

成本账 cost accounts

成材林 standing timber;mature timber

成个儿 ①grow to a good size ②be well formed;be in the proper form

成活率 survival rate

成绩单 school report;report card;transcript

成交额 volume of business;turnover

成气候 make good;attain a position full of promise;be in power;become popular

成人日 coming of age

成熟林 mature forest

成熟期 mature period;maturity

成文法 written laws;statute law;statutory law

成问题 be a problem;be open to question (or doubt, objection)

成衣铺 tailor's shop;tailor's;dress-maker's

成员国 member state

成本分摊 cost assignment

成本核算 cost accounting

成本价格 cost price

成本会计 cost accounting

成本膨胀 cost inflation

成本效率 cost performance

成本指数 cost index number

成簇处理 in-line processing

成分输血 blood component transfusion

成果分享 gain sharing

成绩报告 score reporting

成绩评定 achievement evaluation

成家立业 marry and embark on a career

成交价格 transaction price

成角透视 angular perspective
成矿作用 mineralization
成龙配套 fill in the gaps to complete a chain (of equipment, construction projects, etc.); link up the parts to form a whole
成名成家 establish one's reputation as an authority in one's field
成年累月 year in year out; for years on end
成批处理 batch processing
成批生产 serial production; produce sth in batches
成千上万 thousands and tens of thousands; thousands upon thousands
成群结队 in crowds
成人电影 adult film
成人高考 entrance examination to institute of higher education for adults
成人高校 institution of higher education for adults
成人教育 adult education
成人之美 help sb to fulfil his wish; aid sb in doing a good deed
成双成对 make a pair of; join into pairs
成套设备 complete plant (or sets) of equipment
成本回收期 period of cost recovery
成交通知书 advice note
成人高等教育 adult higher education
成本加运费价格 cost and freight (C. & F.)
成人高等学历教育 certificate-oriented adult education
成事不足,败事有余 unable to accomplish anything but liable to spoil everything; never able to achieve, always able to ruin; never make, but always mar
成则为王,败则为寇 The winner is the king, the loser a bandit. (or Losers are always in the wrong; Nothing succeeds like success.)

丞 [chéng]
图 assistant; assistant officer
丞相 prime minister (in ancient China); chief minister

呈 [chéng]
I 动 ①assume (form, colour, etc.); manifest ②submit; present II 名 petition; memorial
呈报 submit a report; report a matter (to a superior)
呈递 present; submit
呈览 submit sth to a higher authority for perusal
呈请 apply (to the higher authorities for consideration or approval)
呈文 a document submitted to a superior; memorial; petition
呈现 present (a certain appearance); appear; emerge
呈献 respectfully present
呈交诉状 file a petition

枨 [chéng]
动 touch

诚 [chéng]
I 形 sincere; honest II 副 actually; really
诚笃 sincere and earnest
诚服 submit oneself willingly (to sb)
诚恳 sincere
诚朴 honest; sincere and simple
诚然 ①truly; really ②no doubt; to be sure; it is true; certainly
诚实 honest
诚心 ①sincere desire; sincerity; whole-heartedness ②sincere and earnest; devout
诚信 faith; honesty; integrity; creditability
诚意 good faith; sincerity
诚挚 sincere; cordial
诚非易事 be by no means an easy task
诚惶诚恐 with reverence and awe; in fear and trepidation
诚恳待人 treat others with earnestness
诚心诚意 earnestly and sincerely

承 [chéng]
动 ①hold; bear; carry ②bear; undertake; assume; contract (to do a job) ③be indebted (to sb for a kindness); be granted a favour ④continue; go on; carry on ⑤accept (orders, instructions, advice, etc.)
承办 undertake
承包 contract
承保 undertake to provide insurance; accept insurance
承担 bear; undertake; assume
承当 ①bear; take on ②agree (to do sth); promise
承兑 honour; accept
承继 ①be adopted as heir to one's uncle ②adopt one's brother's son (as one's heir)
承建 contract to construct (or build)
承接 ①hold out a vessel to have liquid poured into it ②continue; carry on ③undertake the task of; contract to accept
承揽 contract to do a whole job; undertake an entire project
承蒙 be accorded (a kindness); be granted (a favour)
承诺 promise to undertake; undertake to do sth
承情 be much obliged; owe a debt of gratitude
承认 ①admit; acknowledge; recognize ②give diplomatic recognition; recognize
承受 ① bear; support; endure ② inherit (a legacy, etc.)
承袭 ①adopt; follow (a tradition, etc.) ②inherit (a peerage, etc.)

承销 act as sales agent
承运 ①(of a ruler) be ordained by Heaven ② undertake the transportation of (goods)
承载 bear the weight of
承重 load-bearing;bearing
承转 assume the responsibility of forwarding (a document) to the level above or below
承办者 contractor
承包商 contractor
承包制 contract system;contracting out system
承保单 open cover
承保人 insurer
承兑人 acceptor
承诺人 accepter;acceptor
承销人 sales agent;salesman
承运人 carrier
承重墙 bearing (*or* load-bearing) wall
承租人 tenantry;lessee;tenant
承包合同 contract
承保范围 insurance coverage
承担风险 acceptance of risk;bear the risks
承担责任 shoulder (*or* bear) the responsibility
承兑交单 documentary against acceptance
承兑票据 acceptance bill
承兑银行 accepting bank
承揽合同 contract for work; contractor's agreement
承蒙不弃 meet with your gracious consent
承诺服务 guaranteed service
承前启后 inherit the past and usher in the future;serve as a link between past and future
承上启下 form a connecting link between what comes before and what goes after (as in a piece of writing,etc.)
承受能力 capability of adapting oneself to
承先启后 inherit the past and usher in the future;serve as a link between past and future
承包责任制 responsibility system of operation on contracting basis
承保通知书 cover note
承兑信用证 acceptance letters
承担法律责任 bear legal liability
承担经济责任 bear financial responsibility
承担民事责任 bear civil responsibility
承包经营责任制 managerial responsibility system of contractor

城 〔chéng〕
〔名〕①city ②city wall ③town
城邦 city-state
城堡 castle
城池 city wall and moat;city
城防 city defence
城府 mind hard to fathom;subtle thinking

城郭 inner and outer city walls;city walls
城根 sections of a city close to the city wall
城关 area just outside a city gate
城壕 moat
城隍 town god
城际 intercity
城郊 outskirts of a town
城里 inside the city;in town
城楼 tower over a city gate;gate tower
城门 city gate
城墙 city wall
城区 city proper
城市 town (*or* city)
城头 ①the top of the city wall ②gate tower
城外 outside the city;outside the city wall
城乡 town and country;urban and rural areas; city and countryside
城镇 cities and towns
城隍庙 town god's temple
城市学 urbanology
城际快车 intercity express (*or* buses,trains, etc.)
城市布局 city pattern
城市发展 urban development
城市建设 urban construction;city building
城市垃圾 municipal refuse
城市绿化 urban landscaping
城市贫民 urban poor;city poor
城市污染 municipal pollution
城下之盟 treaty concluded with the enemy who have reached the city wall;terms accepted under duress;treaty signed under coercion
城乡结合 integration of town and country
城乡贸易 urban and rural trade
城镇居民 urban residents
城镇污水 town sewage
城市社会学 urban sociology
城市学专家 urbanologist
城市运动会 city sports meet
城乡结合部 fringe; town-country bordering areas
城市高速铁路 rapid transit
城市旧区改造 renovate an old area of the city
城市热岛效应 urban heat island effect
城市综合开发 urban comprehensive development;city building
城市公共设施规划 urban public facilities planning
城市与区域计划学 ekistics
城门失火,殃及池鱼 when the city gate catches fire,the fish in the moat come to grief—innocent people suffering from what happens to others

宬 〔chéng〕
〔名〕archives

C

埕 [chéng]
〔名〕① razor clam bed; razor clam farm ② wine jar

乘 [chéng]
Ⅰ〔动〕①ride ②make use of (an opportunity); avail oneself of (a chance); take advantage of ③multiply Ⅱ〔名〕(佛教) main division of Buddhism ⟹ shèng

乘便 when it is convenient; at one's convenience
乘车 riding
乘法 multiplication
乘方 ①involution ②power
乘号 times sign; multiple sign
乘机 seize the opportunity
乘积 product
乘警 train police
乘客 passenger
乘凉 enjoy the cool; relax in a cool place
乘幂 power
乘胜 exploit (or follow up) a victory
乘数 multiplier
乘隙 take advantage of a loophole; turn sb's mistake to one's own account
乘兴 while one is in high spirits
乘虚 take advantage of a weak point (or an opening) in an opponent's defence; act when sb is off guard
乘法表 multiplication table
乘务员 ①crew member ②attendant on a train
乘风破浪 ride the wind and cleave the waves; brave the wind and the waves
乘龙快婿 excellent or ideal son-in-law
乘人不备 take sb by surprise
乘人之危 take advantage of sb's precarious position
乘胜前进 advance on the crest of a victory; push on in the flush of victory
乘兴而来 arrive in high spirits; set out cheerfully
乘虚而入 break through at a weak point; act when one's opponent is off guard; exploit one's opponent's weakness

盛 [chéng]
〔动〕①fill; ladle ②hold; contain ⟹ shèng
盛殓 be encoffined

程 [chéng]
Ⅰ〔名〕① rule; regulation ② order; procedure; course; sequence; schedule ③ journey; leg of a journey ④ distance; journey Ⅱ〔动〕measure; estimate
程度 ①level; degree ②extent; degree
程控 programmed control
程式 form; pattern; formula
程序 ①order; procedure; course; sequence ②automation program
程仪 gift (of money) for a friend going on a journey

程控网 program-controlled network
程式化 stylize
程序包 routine package
程序法 procedural law
程序化 routine package
程序库 program library
程序块 brick; program block
程控电话 program-controlled telephone
程控机床 program-controlled machine tool
程序教学 programmed instruction (or learning)
程序控制 programmed control
程序设计 automation programming
程序装入 program loading
程序存储器 program memory
程序分析员 analyst-programmer
程序化决策 programmed decision
程序计算器 program counter
程序流程图 program flow chart
程序设计员 programmer
程控电话网络 programme-controlled phone network
程序设计语言 programming language; program language

惩 [chéng]
〔动〕① punish; penalize ② guard against; warn; exhort
惩办 punish
惩处 penalize; punish
惩罚 punish; penalize
惩戒 punish sb to teach him a lesson; discipline sb as a warning; take disciplinary action against
惩治 punish; mete out punishment to
惩恶劝善 punish evil-doers and encourage people to do good
惩罚税率 penalty rate
惩忿窒欲 suppress one's anger and check one's desire
惩前毖后 learn from past errors to avoid future mistakes
惩一儆百 punish one to warn a hundred; make an example of sb
惩治腐败 fight against corruption
惩治贪污条例 Regulation for Suppression of Corruption

澄 [chéng]
Ⅰ〔形〕(of water, etc.) clear; transparent; limpid Ⅱ〔动〕clear up; clarify ⟹ dèng
澄碧 clear and blue
澄澈 clear
澄清 ①clear; transparent ②clear up; clarify ③be clear about
澄心 purify the heart
澄清事实 clarify some facts; clear up facts

橙 [chéng]
[名] ①orange ②orange (colour)
橙黄 orange colour
橙树 orange tree
橙子 orange (the fruit)

chěng (ㄔㄥˇ)

逞 [chěng]
[动] ①show off;flaunt ②carry out (an evil design);succeed (in a scheme) ③spoil;indulge;give free rein to
逞能 show off one's skill or ability;parade one's ability
逞强 flaunt one's superiority
逞凶 act violently;act with murderous intent
逞本事 flaunt one's abilities
逞威风 show off one's strength or power;swagger about
逞英雄 pose as a hero
逞性妄为 be reckless in doing evil
逞凶霸道 throw one's weight about

骋 [chěng]
[动] ①gallop ②give free rein to
骋目 look as far the eye can see;look into the distance
骋望 look as far as one's eyes can see

chèng (ㄔㄥˋ)

秤 [chèng]
[名] balance;steelyard
秤锤 sliding weight of a steelyard
秤杆 arm (or beam) of a steelyard
秤钩 steelyard hook
秤盘 ①pan or dish of a steelyard ②either of the pans or dishes of a balance;scale
秤台 weighing platform
秤砣 sliding weight of a steelyard
秤星 gradations marked on the beam of a steelyard

chī (ㄔ)

吃 [chī]
[动] ①eat;take ②have one's meals;eat (at a restaurant or by a certain standard);dine ③live off;live on;scrounge off ④absorb;soak up ⑤take in (sth) ⑥annihilate;wipe out;take (in a chess game) ⑦grasp;understand ⑧endure;withstand;take ⑨suffer;incur ⑩exhaust;consume ⑪stammer;stutter
吃饱 eat one's fill;be full
吃茶 drink tea
吃穿 food and clothing
吃醋 be jealous (usu. of a rival in love)
吃刀 (of the cutting tool on a lathe, etc.) penetrate a certain depth into a workpiece
吃饭 ①eat;have a meal ②keep alive;make a living
吃光 eat up;finish all the food
吃荤 eat meat
吃紧 be critical;be hard pressed
吃惊 be startled;be shocked;be amazed;be taken aback
吃苦 bear hardships
吃亏 ①suffer losses;come to grief;get the worst of it ②be at a disadvantage;be in an unfavourable situation
吃力 ①entail strenuous effort;be a strain ②tired;fatigued
吃奶 (of a baby) take milk from its mother;suck at its mother's breast
吃请 accept an invitation to dinner (extended as a bribe)
吃食 (of animals or birds) feed
吃水 ①drinking water ②absorb water ③have a draught (or draft) of
吃素 abstain from eating meat;be a vegetarian
吃透 understand thoroughly;have a thorough grasp of sth
吃香 be very popular;be much sought after;be well-liked
吃药 take medicine
吃斋 practise abstinence from meat (as a religious exercise);be a vegetarian for religious reasons
吃重 ① arduous;strenuous ② carrying (or loading) capacity
吃白食 eat food that isn't earned;not earn an honest living;live off others
吃败仗 suffer a defeat;be defeated in battle
吃不饱 ①not have enough to eat ②(of factories,etc.) cannot operate at full capacity;operate under capacity
吃不得 not good to eat;not edible
吃不开 be unpopular;won't work
吃不来 not be fond of certain food
吃不了 cannot finish (all the food)
吃不上 ①be unable to get sth to eat ②miss a meal
吃不下 not feel like eating;be unable to eat any more
吃不消 be unable to stand (exertion,fatigue,etc.)
吃不住 be unable to bear or support
吃大户 mass seizure and eating of food in the homes of landlords during famines (as in pre-liberation China)
吃大亏 suffer a great deal;inflict incalculable damage
吃得开 be popular;be much sought after
吃得来 be able to eat;not mind eating
吃得上 ①be able to get sth to eat;can afford to eat ②be in time for a meal;be able to get a meal

吃得下 be able to eat
吃得消 be able to stand (exertion, fatigue, etc.)
吃得住 be able to bear or support
吃豆腐 ①flirt with a woman ②crack a joke ③visit the bereaved to offer one's condolences
吃独食 not to share profit with others
吃耳光 get a slap in the face
吃父母 live off one's parents
吃官司 get into trouble with the law; serve a jail term
吃馆子 eat in a restaurant; dine out
吃喝风 practice of dining and wining on public funds
吃花酒 go to a dinner party with singsong girls in attendance
吃皇粮 be paid by government; live on the regular pay by the government
吃回扣 get commission; receive a kickback
吃劳保 live on labour security funds
吃老本 live off one's past gains; rest on one's laurels
吃利息 live on interest
吃零食 take snacks between meals
吃偏饭 eat better-than-average meals in the mess; enjoy special privilege
吃软饭 live off a woman
吃食堂 dine in a canteen
吃水线 waterline
吃素的 easygoing; easy to deal with
吃喜酒 go to wedding feast
吃闲饭 lead an idle life; be a loafer or sponger
吃小灶 eat at a small mess where better food is served—enjoy some privelege
吃早饭 eat (or have, take) breakfast
吃吃喝喝 wine and dine (with sb)
吃大锅饭 ①eat in the cafeteria the same as everyone else; mess together ②eat from the same big pot—get the same reward or pay as everyone else regardless of one's performance in work
吃喝嫖赌 go dining, wining, whoring and gambling—lead a dissipated life
吃喝玩乐 eat, drink and be merry—idle away one's time in pleasure-seeking
吃黑枣儿 eat a black date—get shot
吃后悔药 feel remorse; regret
吃苦耐劳 endure hardships; bear hardships and stand hard work
吃里扒外 live off one person while secretly helping another
吃太平饭 enjoy a peaceful life
吃现成饭 eat what is already prepared—enjoy the fruits of others' work
吃眼前亏 accept a present loss; suffer loss under one's nose

吃饱了撑的 restless from overeating (said of sb doing sth silly or senseless)
吃力不讨好 do a hard but thankless job; work hard but get little result
吃软不吃硬 be open to persuasion, but not to coercion
吃硬不吃软 be open to coercion, but not to persuasion
吃不了兜着走 ① take one's leftovers back home ②get more than one bargained for; land oneself in serious trouble
吃一堑，长一智 A fall into the pit, a gain in your wit.
吃苦在前，享乐在后 be the first to bear hardships and the last to enjoy comforts
吃得苦中苦，方为人上人 Only by standing the hardest of hardships can you hope to rise in society.

笞 ［chī］
囝 beat with a whip (or cane, split bamboo, etc.)
笞刑 flogging as a punishment
笞责 censure; severe criticism

嗤 ［chī］
囝 sneer
嗤笑 laugh at; sneer at
嗤之以鼻 give a snort of contempt; turn up one's nose at; despise

痴 ［chī］
Ⅰ 囮 ①silly; idiotic; stupid; foolish ②deranged; insane; crazy Ⅱ 囝 be infatuated; be crazy about; have a fancy for
痴呆 ①dull-witted; stupid ②dementia
痴楞 dumbstruck; in a daze; in a trance
痴迷 infatuated; obsessed; crazy
痴情 ①unreasoning passion; infatuation ②be infatuated
痴想 wishful thinking; illusion
痴笑 giggle; silly smile; titter
痴心 infatuation
痴愚 moronity; moronism
痴人说梦 idiotic nonsense; lunatic ravings
痴心妄想 wishful thinking; fond dream

媸 ［chī］
囮 ugly; unsightly

螭 ［chī］
囵 hornless dragon (a decorative motif)

魑 ［chī］
囵 (of ancient folklore) evil spirits dwelling in mountains
魑魅魍魉 evil spirits; all sorts of evil spirits; demons and monsters

chí (彳)

池 ［chí］
囵 ① pond; pool ② depression; low-lying land ③stalls (in a theatre) ④moat
池塘 pond; pool

池蛙 green frog
池盐 lake salt
池沼 large pond
池子 ①pond ②bathing pool ③dance floor ④ stalls;orchestra
池座 stalls (in a theatre);orchestra
池鱼之殃 a disaster for the fish in the moat— trouble not of one's own making

弛 [chí]
囝 loosen;relax;slacken
弛垂 sag
弛缓 relax;calm down
弛张热 remittent fever

驰 [chí]
囝 ① race; gallop; speed ② disseminate; popularize;promulgate;spread ③ desire;as- pire;crave
驰骋 gallop
驰离 depart
驰名 be known far and wide;be famous;be re- nowned
驰驱 ①gallop ②do one's utmost in sb's serv- ice
驰援 rush to the rescue
驰名商标 famous trademark; well-known trademark

迟 [chí]
Ⅰ 囫 ①slow;tardy ②late;delayed;belated Ⅱ 囝 fall behind schedule
迟迟 slow;tardy
迟到 be (or come,arrive) late
迟钝 slow (in thought or action);obtuse
迟发 tardy;tardive
迟付 delay payment
迟缓 slow;tardy;sluggish
迟脉 retarded pulse (less than 60 beats per minute)
迟误 delay;procrastinate
迟延 delay;retard
迟疑 hesitate
迟早 sooner or later
迟滞 ① slow-moving; sluggish ② de- laying (action)
迟疑不决 hesitate to make a decision; be irresolute;be undecided

坻 [chí]
囝 sand bar

持 [chí]
囝 ①hold;grasp ②support;maintain;keep ③manage;run;handle ④control;hold under duress;take advantage of sb's weakness and control them ⑤oppose;confront
持仓 wait for one's chance by refraining from selling and buying stocks
持家 run one's home;keep house
持久 lasting;enduring;protracted
持论 present an argument;put a case;express a view

持平 be in balance;keep...in balance
持球 holding
持续 continue;sustain
持有 hold
持重 prudent;cautious;discreet
持久力 staying power;stamina;endurance
持久战 protracted war;protracted warfare
持票人 bearer (of a cheque,etc.)
持币待购 wait to buy with cash in hand
持币抢购 rush to buy with cash in hand
持股公司 holding company
持论公平 state a case fairly
持平之论 fair argument;unbiased view
持枪抢劫 commit gun robbery
持续农业 sustainable agriculture
持续升温 persisted overheating
持续增长 increase continuously
持之以恒 persevere
持之有故 have grounds for one's views
持不同政见者 dissident
持久性有机污染物 persistent organic pollutant

匙 [chí]
図 spoon ➡ shi
匙子 spoon

墀 [chí]
図 landing (on top of a flight of steps); steps

踟 [chí]
踟蹰 hesitate;waver
踟蹰不前 hesitate to move forward

chǐ (彳)

尺 [chǐ]
図 ① chi, a unit of length equalling one third of a metre ②rule;ruler ③tool for draw- ing ④ sth shaped like a ruler ⑤ one of the three points where the pulse is felt
尺寸 [chǐcùn] ① measurement;dimensions; size ②proper limits for speech or action; sense of propriety
尺牍 ①a model of epistolary art ②correspon- dence (of an eminent writer)
尺度 scale;measure;yardstick
尺骨 ulna
尺蠖 looper; inchworm; measuringworm; ge- ometer
尺码 size;measures;footage
尺子 rule;ruler
尺动脉 ulnar artery
尺蠖蛾 geometrid moth
尺短寸长 sometimes a foot may prove short while an inch may prove long—everyone has his strong and weak points
尺幅千里 a thousand-mile view on a one-foot scroll—rich content within a small compass
尺有所短,寸有所长 sometimes a foot may

prove short while an inch may prove long—everyone has his strong and weak points

齿 [chǐ]
Ⅰ 名 ① tooth ② tooth-like part of an object;tooth;dentate ③ toothed ④ age Ⅱ 动 ① stand side by side;regard as of one's own ② speak of;mention
齿痕 indentation
齿冷 laugh sb to scorn
齿轮 gear wheel;gear
齿条 rack
齿音 dental sound
齿龈 gums
齿德俱尊 command respect on account of both one's age and one's moral integrity

侈 [chǐ]
形 ① wasteful;extravagant ② exaggerate
侈谈 talk glibly about;prate about;prattle about
侈言 exaggerated terms;exaggeration

哆 [chǐ]
动 open (one's mouth) ➡ duō
哆口 open one's mouth;talk

耻 [chǐ]
名 ① shame ② disgrace;humiliation;ignominy;insult;infamy
耻骨 pubic bones;pubis
耻辱 shame;disgrace;humiliation
耻笑 hold sb to ridicule;sneer at;mock
耻于人后 be ashamed to lag behind
耻与为伍 feel ashamed to associate with sb

chì（彳）

叱 [chì]
动 denounce or rebuke loudly;roundly rebuke;shout at
叱喝 shout at;bawl at
叱骂 scold roundly;curse;abuse
叱责 scold;upbraid;rebuke
叱咤 shout or bawl angrily
叱咤风云 commanding the wind and the clouds;shaking heaven and earth;all-powerful

斥 [chì]
Ⅰ 动 ① scold;upbraid;reprimand;denounce ② repel;exclude;dismiss;drive away ③ pay;spend ④ expand;enlarge;open up Ⅱ 名 ① scout;reconnoitre ② saline soil;alkaline soil
斥力 repulsion
斥骂 reproach;upbraid;scold
斥骑 mounted scout
斥退 ① dismiss sb from his post ② expel from a school ③ shout at sb to go away
斥责 reprimand;rebuke;denounce
斥逐 expel;oust;drive away
斥资 furnish funds for;fund
斥退左右 dismiss one's entourage

赤 [chì]
Ⅰ 名 a kind of red slightly lighter than vermillion Ⅱ 形 ① red ② revolutionary;Communist ③ loyal;devoted;faithful ④ bare;naked ⑤ empty ⑥ pure (gold)
赤背 barebacked
赤潮 red tide
赤诚 absolutely sincere
赤道 ① equator ② celestial equator
赤豆 red bean
赤红 crimson
赤脚 barefooted;barefoot
赤金 pure gold;solid gold
赤痢 dysentery characterized by blood in the stool
赤磷 red phosphorus
赤露 bare
赤裸 ① bare ② undisguised
赤贫 in abject poverty;utterly destitute
赤日 red sun;scorching sun
赤芍 (unpeeled) root of herbaceous peony
赤身 naked
赤松 Japanese red pine
赤陶 terra-cotta
赤心 sincere heart;genuine sincerity;whole-hearted devotion
赤子 ① newborn baby ② the people
赤字 deficit
赤足 barefooted;barefoot
赤道面 equatorial plane
赤道仪 equatorial telescope
赤褐色 russet
赤裸裸 ① without a stitch of clothing;stark naked ② undisguised;naked;out-and-out
赤条条 have not a stitch on;be stark naked
赤铁矿 red iron ore;hematite
赤铜矿 red copper ore;cuprite
赤卫队 Red Guard
赤血盐 potassium ferricyanide;red prussiate of potash
赤眼蜂 trichogramma
赤膊上阵 go into battle stripped to the waist—throw away all disguise;come out into the open
赤胆忠心 utter devotion;whole-hearted dedication;ardent loyalty
赤地千里 a thousand *li* of barren land—a scene of utter desolation (after a drought or an insect plague)
赤脚医生 barefoot doctor
赤贫如洗 as poor as if everything had been washed clean
赤色政权 Red power;revolutionary government
赤身裸体 stark naked;not wearing a stitch
赤手空拳 bare-handed;unarmed
赤子之心 heart of a newborn babe—utter in-

nocence
赤字财政 deficit financing
赤道无风带 the equatorial calm belt

饬 [chì] I 动 ①put in order;readjust;rectify ②order;instruct II 形 prudent
饬令 order
饬拿 issue order to arrest
饬其照办无误 order sb to act in conformity with the demand

炽 [chì] 形 burning;flaming;ablaze
炽烈 burning fiercely;flaming;blazing
炽热 ①red-hot;blazing ②passionate
炽盛 flaming;ablaze;flourishing
炽碳 burning charcoal
炽焰 raging flames

翅 [chì] 名 ①wing ②samara's wings ③shark's fin ④wing-like part of an object
翅膀 wing
翅果 samara
翅脉 vein (of the wings of an insect)

眙 [chì] 动 ①stare;gaze ②stare in surprise;gaze in shock

敕 [chì] 名 imperial edict
敕封 appoint sb to a post;confer a title on sb by imperial order
敕令 imperial order;edict
敕命 decree by imperial edict

啻 [chì] 副 only;merely

chōng (ㄔㄨㄥ)

冲 [chōng] I 名 ①thoroughfare;important place ②stretch of flatland in a hilly area ③opposition II 动 ①charge;rush;dash ②clash;collide ③pour boiling water on ④rinse;flush;wash away ⑤develop ⑥offset;cancel out;counteract III 形 young ➡chòng
冲茶 make tea
冲程 stroke
冲冲 in a state of excitement
冲出 ①rush out ②wash away
冲刺 spurt;sprint
冲淡 ① dilute ② water down;weaken;play down
冲顶 header;climb up to the summit;final spurt
冲动 ①impulse ②get excited;be impetuous
冲犯 offend;affront
冲锋 charge;assault
冲服 take (medicine) after mixing it with water,wine,etc.
冲毁 destroy by rush of water

冲击 ①lash;pound ②charge;assault
冲积 alluviation
冲剂 medicine to be taken after being mixed with boiling water,wine,etc.
冲决 burst;smash
冲垮 burst;shatter
冲浪 ① surfing; surfboarding ② surf (the web);surfing
冲力 impulsive force;momentum
冲凉 have a shower
冲量 impulse
冲年 childhood;infancy
冲破 break through;breach
冲散 break up;scatter;disperse
冲杀 charge;rush ahead
冲晒 develop and print
冲蚀 washout;ablation
冲刷 ①wash and brush;wash down ②erode;wash away
冲塌 (of floodwater,etc.) cause to collapse;burst
冲天 towering;soaring
冲突 conflict;clash
冲洗 ①rinse;wash ②develop
冲要 (of a place) strategically important
冲澡 take a shower
冲账 ①strike a balance ②reverse an entry
冲撞 ① collide; bump; ram ② give offence;offend;contradict
冲断层 thrust fault
冲锋号 bugle call to charge
冲锋枪 submachine gun;tommy gun
冲击波 shock wave;blast wave
冲积层 alluvium
冲积土 alluvial soil
冲咖啡 make (instant) coffee
冲浪板 board
冲浪者 surfer
冲奶粉 pour boiling water in powdered milk
冲沙闸 scouring sluice
冲锋陷阵 charge and shatter enemy positions;charge the enemy lines;charge forward
冲昏头脑 turn sb's head
冲积平原 alluvial plain
冲口而出 say sth unthinkingly;blurt out
冲水厕所 water closet
冲销坏账 write off uncollectible account
冲动性购买 impulse buying
冲出亚洲,走向世界 Break Asian records and set sights on world level in sports.

充 [chōng] I 形 sufficient;full II 动 ①fill;stuff ②assume office;serve as;act as ③pretend to be;pose as
充斥 flood;congest;be full of
充磁 magnetizing
充当 serve as;act as;play the part of

充电 ①charge (a battery) ②study to acquire new knowledge

充分 ①full;ample;abundant ②to the full;as fully as possible

充公 confiscate

充饥 allay (*or* appease) one's hunger

充军 be transported to a distant place for penal servitude;banish

充满 ①fill ②be filled with;be full of;brim with;be permeated (*or* imbued) with

充沛 plentiful;abundant;copious

充气 pump air (into sth)

充任 fill the post of;hold the position of

充塞 fill (up);cram

充实 ① substantial; rich ② substantiate; enrich;replenish

充数 make up the number;serve as a stopgap

充血 hyperaemia;congestion

充氧 oxygenate

充溢 be full to the brim; be exuberant; be overflowing

充裕 abundant;ample;plentiful

充足 adequate;sufficient;abundant;ample

充行家 pretend to be an expert

充其量 at most;at best

充耳不闻 stuff one's ears and refuse to listen; turn a deaf ear to

充分就业 full employment

充气电池 aeration (*or* oxygen) cell

充气建筑 inflatable building

忡 [chōng] 形 restless with anxiety

忡忡 laden with anxiety;careworn

涌 [chōng] 名 branch (of a river) ➡ yǒng

舂 [chōng] 动 pound;pestle

舂米 husk rice with mortar and pestle

舂药 pound medicinal herbs in a mortar

憧 [chōng]

憧憧 flickering;moving to and fro

憧憬 yearn for;long for;look forward to

chóng（ㄔㄨㄥˊ）

虫 [chóng] 名 ①insect;worm ②certain sort of people

虫草 Chinese caterpillar fungus

虫害 insect pest

虫胶 shellac

虫媒 entomophily

虫蚀 worm-eaten;moth-eaten

虫牙 dental caries;decayed tooth

虫眼 small holes caused by worms

虫瘿 gall (on plants)

虫灾 a plague of insects

虫子 insect (*or* worm)

虫媒花 entomophilous flower

虫胶清漆 shellac (varnish)

重 [chóng]
Ⅰ 动 ①repeat;duplicate ②pile up;stack up;overlap Ⅱ 副 again;once more Ⅲ 量 layer:双重领导 dual leadership ➡ zhòng

重版 ①(of books,periodicals,etc.) be republished ②republication

重播 ①rebroadcast a programme (from the same station) ②resow (the same field)

重唱 an ensemble of two or more singers, each singing one part

重重 layer upon layer;ring upon ring

重叠 one on top of another;overlapping

重返 return

重犯 repeat (an error or offence)

重逢 meet again;have a reunion

重复 repeat;duplicate

重估 re-evaluate;re-estimate;re-calculate

重合 coincide

重婚 (commit) bigamy

重建 rebuild;reconstruct;reestablish;rehabilitate

重码 coincident code

重申 reaffirm;reiterate;restate

重审 retrial

重孙 son's grandson;great-grandson

重提 bring up again

重围 tight encirclement

重温 review

重现 reappear

重新 again;anew;afresh

重修 ①rebuild;repair again ②retake a course after failing to pass examination

重檐 double-eaved roof

重演 ①put on an old play,etc. ②recur;reenact;repeat

重洋 seas and oceans

重译 retranslate

重印 reprint

重整 reform;reforming

重置 resetting

重奏 an ensemble of two or more instrumentalists,each playing one part

重组 reorganize;reshuffle;regroup;realign

重发球 let service;let

重入码 reentrant code

重孙女 son's granddaughter; great-granddaughter

重印本 reprint

重操旧业 resume one's old profession;take up one's old trade again

重蹈覆辙 follow the track of the overturned cart—follow the same old road to ruin

重返家园 go back to one's homeland;return to one's homeland

重复建设 duplicated project

重复利用 recycle
重复引进 overlapping of imports; duplication of imports
重见天日 once more see the light of day—be delivered from oppression or persecution
重开谈判 resume the talks
重起炉灶 begin all over again; make a fresh start
重入程序 reentrant program
重施故技 play the same old trick; repeat a stock trick
重算程序 rerun routine
重算方式 roll back system
重温旧梦 review an old dream; relive an old experience
重温旧情 review one's friendship
重新安顿 remount
重新组合 recombination
重修旧好 renew cordial relations; become reconciled; bury the hatchet
重振军威 restore the prestige of an army; make an army's might felt once again
重整旗鼓 rally one's forces (after a defeat)
重置资产 replacement assets
重返大气层 reentry (of a spaceship, rocket, etc.)
重新启动键 reset button (*or* key)

崇 [chóng]
Ⅰ 形 high; lofty; sublime Ⅱ 动 esteem; worship; respect
崇拜 worship; adore
崇奉 believe in (a religion); worship
崇高 lofty; sublime; high
崇敬 esteem; respect; revere
崇尚 uphold; advocate
崇实 practical; pragmatic; realistic; down-to-earth
崇山峻岭 lofty ridges and towering mountains
崇尚勤俭 advocate industry and thrift
崇尚正义 uphold justice
崇洋媚外 worship foreign things and toady to foreign powers

chǒng (ㄔㄨㄥˇ)

宠 [chǒng]
动 dote on; bestow favour on; indulge
宠爱 make a pet of sb; dote on
宠儿 pet; favourite; darling
宠物 pet (e.g. a cat or a dog)
宠信 be specially fond of and trust unduly (a subordinate)
宠遇 treat as a favourite
宠物店 pet shop
宠辱不惊 remain indifferent whether favoured or humiliated

chòng (ㄔㄨㄥˋ)

冲 [chòng]
Ⅰ 形 ①vigorous; with plenty of dash; blunt ②(of smell) strong Ⅱ 动 ①scold; tell off ②face ③punch Ⅲ 介 ①facing; towards: 冲北走 go north ②on the strength of; on the basis of; because of ➡chōng
冲床 punch (press); punching machine
冲孔 ①punching ②punched hole
冲模 die
冲切 die-cut; die cutting; punching
冲头 drift; punch pin
冲压 stamping; punching
冲子 punching pin (a tool)
冲劲儿 ①vim and vigour; dash ②strength (of liquor); kick
冲压机 punch (press); punching machine
冲模插床 die slotting machine

铳 [chòng]
名 blunderbuss; shotgun

chōu (ㄔㄡ)

抽 [chōu]
动 ①take out from in between; draw out ②take a part from a whole ③(of certain plants) put forth (buds, etc.) ④obtain by drawing; draw; absorb ⑤shrink ⑥lash; whip; thrash; flog
抽彩 raffle
抽测 spot check
抽查 carry out selective examinations; make spot checks; spot-check
抽出 draw out; extract; withdraw; select from a lot
抽搐 ①twitch ②tic
抽打 lash; whip; thrash
抽搭 sob
抽调 transfer (personnel or material)
抽动 twitch; have a spasm; jerk spasmodically
抽风 ① convulsions ② go crazy; lose one's senses
抽检 spot check
抽奖 draw lots (to give out prizes); draw a winning number (for lottery, etc.); lottery draw
抽筋 ①pull out a tendon ②cramp
抽考 make sample examination
抽空 manage to find time
抽气 breathe in; inhale
抽泣 sob
抽签 draw (*or* cast) lots
抽球 drive
抽取 draw; collect
抽纱 drawnwork
抽身 leave one's work; extricate oneself; get

away
抽水 ①draw (*or* pump) water ②shrink
抽税 levy a tax
抽丝 reel off raw silk from cocoons
抽穗 (of cereal plants) put forth ears;ear
抽缩 shrink;contract
抽薹 (of garlic,chives,rape,etc.) bolt
抽逃 flight
抽提 extraction
抽屉 drawer
抽头 ①take a percentage (*or* cut) of the winnings in gambling ②tap
抽闲 manage to find time
抽象 ①abstract ②form a general idea from particular instances
抽芽 put forth buds;bud;sprout
抽烟 smoke (a cigarette or a pipe)
抽验 sample testing;spot check
抽样 sampling (in statistics and research)
抽噎 sob
抽资 bailout
抽印(本) offprint
抽气机 air exhauster;air extractor;air pump
抽水机 water pump
抽水站 pumping station
抽穗期 earing stage (*or* period);heading stage (*or* period)
抽象派 abstractionist school
抽象数 abstract number
抽烟斗 draw (*or* pull) at a pipe;smoke a pipe
抽油泵 oil-well pump
抽肥补瘦 take from the fat to pad the lean;take from those with much and give to those with little
抽水马桶 flush toilet;water closet
抽逃资金 spirit one's money away
抽象劳动 abstract labour
抽象名词 abstract noun
抽象思维 abstraction
抽象艺术 abstract art
抽薪止沸 take out the fuel to stop the pot boiling—take drastic measures to stop sth
抽样调查 sample survey;sampling
抽样分布 sampling distribution
抽样分析 sampling analysis
抽样误差 sampling error
抽油烟机 range hood;cooker hood;smoke-dispelling machine
抽象表现派 action painting
抽象派画家 abstractionist

瘳 [chōu]
囷 ①recover from illness ②harm;injure

chóu (彳又)

仇 [chóu]
名 ①enemy;foe ②hatred;enmity;grudge
仇敌 foe;enemy

仇恨 ①hatred;enmity;hostility ②feel great enmity towards;hate
仇家 enemy;foe
仇人 personal enemy;foe
仇杀 kill in revenge
仇视 regard as an enemy;look upon with hatred;be hostile to
仇隙 bitter quarrel;feud
仇怨 hatred;enmity;hostility
仇人相见,分外眼红 when enemies come face to face,their eyes blaze with hate

俦 [chóu]
名 ①companion ②likes;peers;class;generation

帱 [chóu]
名 ①bed curtains ②carriage curtains ➡ dào

惆 [chóu]
形 disappointed;aggrieved
惆怅 sad;disconsolate;melancholy

绸 [chóu]
名 silk fabric;silk
绸布 silk fabric
绸缎 silks and satins
绸巾 silk scarf
绸料 silk fabric;silk
绸缪 be sentimentally attached
绸伞 silk parasol
绸子 silk fabric

畴 [chóu]
名 ①farmland ②kind;division ③domain
畴辈 people of the same generation
畴壁 domain wall (*or* boundary)

酬 [chóu]
Ⅰ 动 ①propose a toast;toast ②fulfil;realize ③repay a kindness Ⅱ 名 ①pay;payment;remuneration ②social intercourse
酬报 requite;reward;repay;recompense
酬宾 bargain sales;sell at a discount
酬答 ①thank sb with a gift ②respond with a poem or speech
酬对 reply;answer
酬金 monetary reward;remuneration
酬劳 ①repay;reward;recompense ②repayment;reward;recompense
酬谢 thank sb with a gift
酬宾展销 show for sale with gifts to customers

稠 [chóu]
形 ①thick ②dense
稠密 dense
稠粥 thick porridge
稠人广众 large crowd;big gathering

愁 [chóu]
Ⅰ 动 be worried;be anxious Ⅱ 名 melancholy;sadness;sorrow
愁苦 anxiety;distress
愁眉 knitted brows;worried look

C

愁闷 feel gloomy; be in low spirits; be depressed
愁容 worried look; anxious expression
愁思 deep longing; melancholy
愁绪 gloomy mood
愁云 a cloud of sorrow; depressing clouds; heavy clouds
愁肠百结 with anxiety gnawing at one's heart; weighed down with anxiety
愁眉不展 with a worried frown; with knitted brows
愁眉苦脸 wear a worried look; pull a long face
愁眉锁眼 with knitted brows and lowered eyes; wearing a deep frown on one's face

筹 [chóu]
Ⅰ 名 ① chip; counter ② resource; way; means Ⅱ 动 prepare; plan; raise
筹办 make preparations; make arrangements
筹备 prepare; arrange
筹措 raise (money)
筹划 plan and prepare
筹集 accumulate; raise (money)
筹建 prepare to construct or establish sth
筹款 raise funds; raise money
筹码 chip; counter
筹募 collect (funds)
筹商 discuss; consult
筹饷 raise funds for troops' pay and provisions
筹资 fund raising
筹备费 organization cost; start-up cost
筹委会 preparatory committee
筹备工作 preparatory work; preparations
筹措资金 raise funds; build up funds
筹备委员会 preparatory committee

踌 [chóu]
踌躇 hesitate; shilly-shally
踌躇不决 hesitating; irresolute
踌躇不前 hesitate to move forward; hesitate to make a move
踌躇满志 enormously proud of one's success; smug; complacent

雠 [chóu]
动 compare texts; collate

chǒu （彳ㄡ）

丑 [chǒu]
Ⅰ 形 ① ugly; unsightly; hideous ② disgraceful; shameful; scandalous; unpleasant ③ bad; not good Ⅱ 名 clown; comedian
丑恶 ugly; repulsive; hideous
丑化 uglify; defame; smear; vilify
丑话 ① vulgar language; abusive words ② blunt words
丑剧 farce
丑角 ① comic role ② (in real life) clown; comedian; buffoon

丑类 evil person; vile creature
丑陋 ugly
丑事 disgraceful affair; scandal
丑态 ugly (or ludicrous) performance; buffoonery
丑闻 scandal
丑星 clown; buffoon
丑八怪 very ugly person
丑表功 brag shamelessly about one's deeds; claim undeserved credit
丑小鸭 ugly duckling
丑恶灵魂 ugly soul
丑恶面目 ugly features
丑态百出 act like a buffoon
丑媳妇总得见公婆 an ugly daughter-in-law will have to face her parents-in-law sooner or later—whatever its faults or shortcomings, one's work must be shown to others

瞅 [chǒu]
动 look at
瞅见 see

chòu （彳ㄡ）

臭 [chòu]
Ⅰ 形 ① smelly; foul; stinking ② disgusting; disgraceful ③ inferior; poor; bad ④ (of a bullet) dud Ⅱ 副 harshly; severely; relentlessly Ⅲ 名 bad spell; notoriety ➡ xiù
臭虫 bedbug
臭椿 tree of heaven
臭骂 curse roundly; scold angrily and abusively
臭美 show off shamelessly; be disgustingly smug
臭气 bad (or offensive) smell; stink
臭氧 ozone
臭鼬 skunk
臭豆腐 strong-smelling preserved bean curd
臭烘烘 stinking; foul-smelling; smelly
臭鸡蛋 rotten egg
臭氧层 ozonosphere; ozone layer
臭氧洞 ozone layer hole
臭不可当 give off an unbearable stink
臭名昭著 of ill repute; notorious
臭味相投 be birds of a feather; be two of a kind
臭氧层损耗 ozone layer depletion

chū （彳ㄨ）

出 [chū]
Ⅰ 动 ① go or come out ② come; arrive; be at (an event) ③ exceed; go beyond ④ issue; put up; offer; give ⑤ produce; yield; turn out ⑥ arise; emerge; happen; occur; produce ⑦ publish ⑧ put forth; vent; emit; release ⑨ be quoted from ⑩ emerge; appear; show ⑪ (of

rice,etc.) rise well (with cooking) ⑫ pay out;spend;expend Ⅱ 〔名〕 dramatic piece;chapter in a romance:一出戏 a play;an opera

出版 come off the press; publish; put (*or* come) out

出榜 ①publish a list of successful candidates or examinees ②put up a notice

出奔 leave one's home or country under compulsion;run away;flee

出殡 carry a coffin to the cemetery;hold a funeral procession

出兵 dispatch (*or* send) troops

出彩 do brilliant things

出操 go out for drill or a workout

出差 go (*or* be) away on official business;go (*or* be) on a business trip

出产 ①yield;manufacture;produce ②product

出厂 (of products) be dispatched from the factory

出场 ① come on the stage; appear on the scene ②enter the arena

出超 favourable balance of trade;export surplus

出车 ①dispatch a vehicle ②be out driving a vehicle

出丑 make a fool of sb or oneself

出处 source (of a quotation or allusion)

出错 ①make a mistake ②malfunction;error

出道 (formerly of an apprentice) start working as a journeyman after serving one's apprenticeship;make one's début in society; embark on one's career;become known

出动 ①set out;start off ②send out;dispatch

出发 ①set out;start off ②start from;proceed from

出饭 rise well (with cooking)

出访 go abroad on an official visit

出伏 the *fu* days end;the hottest days of the year are over

出钢 tap molten steel;produce steel

出港 clear a port;leave port

出阁 (of a girl) get married;marry

出格 ①be out of the ordinary;be outstanding ② overstep the bounds; exceed what is proper

出工 show up for work;go to work

出恭 go to the lavatory (for a bowel movement)

出轨 ①go off the rails;be derailed ②overstep the bounds;exceed what is proper

出国 go abroad

出海 go to sea;put out to sea

出汗 perspire;sweat

出航 (of a ship or plane) set out on a voyage or flight

出活 yield results in work;get a lot done

出击 ①launch an attack;hit out;make a sally

②fight against (evil,crime,etc.)

出家 renounce the family (to become a monk or nun)

出价 offer a price;bid

出嫁 (of a woman) get married;marry

出界 out-of-bounds;outside;out

出借 lend (things other than money)

出警 dispatch policemen to the scene of a crime or accident

出境 ①leave the country ②leave a certain region

出镜 on camera

出局 be out; be eliminated; unload one's stocks;out (in baseball,soft ball,etc.)

出口 ①speak;utter ②(of a ship) leave port ③export ④exit

出来 ①come out ②emerge;arise;appear

出力 put forth one's strength;exert oneself

出列 leave one's place in the ranks

出猎 go on a hunting trip

出笼 ① come out of the steamer ② come forth;appear ③put forth in large quantities

出炉 come out of the stove—make sth known to the public

出路 ①way out;outlet ②outlet for goods

出落 (of a young person,esp. a young girl) grow (prettier,etc.)

出马 go into action;take the field

出卖 ①offer for sale;sell ②sell out;betray

出煤 produce coal

出门 ①go out ②leave home;go on a journey ③(of a woman) get married;marry

出面 appear personally;act in one's own capacity or on behalf of sb

出苗 (of seedlings) emerge;come out;sprout

出名 ①be famous;be well known ②lend one's name (to an occasion or enterprise); use the name of

出没 appear and disappear;haunt

出纳 ①receipt and payment of money or bills ② cashier; teller ③ lending and receiving books

出品 ①make;produce;manufacture ②product

出奇 unusual;extraordinary

出气 ① give vent to one's anger; vent one's spleen ②air out;gassing

出钱 offer money

出勤 ①turn out for work ②be or go out on business

出去 go out;get out

出缺 (of a high post) fall vacant

出让 sell (one's own things)

出任 take up the post of

出入 ①come in and go out ②discrepancy;divergence

出赛 take part in a sports competition

出色 outstanding;remarkable;splendid

出山 ①leave a hilly region ②enter politics as a government official; take up a post or task
出身 ①be descended from; come of (*or* from) ② family background; (class) origin ③ one's previous experience or occupation
出神 be spellbound; be in a trance; be lost in thought
出生 be born
出声 make a sound; utter
出师 ①complete one's apprenticeship ②dispatch troops to fight; send an army to battle
出使 serve as an envoy abroad; be sent on a diplomatic mission
出示 ①show; produce ②put up a notice
出世 ①come into the world; be born; come into being ②renounce the world; keep aloof from worldly affairs ③rise high above the world
出事 meet with a mishap; have an accident
出仕 become an official
出手 ① get (hoarded goods, etc.) off one's hands; dispose of; sell ② give out ③ skill displayed in making opening moves (in *wushu*, chess, etc.)
出售 offer for sale; sell
出书 publish books
出台 ①appear on the stage ②make a public appearance ③unveil
出逃 flee
出题 ①set a question; set a test paper ②set a topic
出挑 ①(of a young person, esp. a young girl) grow (prettier, etc.) ②develop (in skill, etc.)
出铁 tap molten iron; tap a blast furnace
出庭 appear in court
出头 ①hold up one's head; free oneself (from misery, persecution, etc.) ②appear in public; come forward ③a little over; odd
出土 ①be unearthed; be excavated ②come up out of the ground
出脱 ① manage to sell; dispose of ② (of a young person, esp. a young girl) grow (prettier, etc.) ③acquit; absolve
出亡 flee from one's home or country; go into exile
出席 be present; attend
出息 [chūxi] ①prospects; bright future ② make good progress
出险 ①be or get out of danger ②(of dykes, dams, etc.) be in danger; be threatened
出现 appear; arise; emerge
出线 qualify for the next round of competition
出项 item of expenditure; expenses; outlay
出血 ① lose blood; bleed ② haemorrhage; bleeding
出巡 go on an inspection tour

出芽 put forth buds; bud; sprout
出演 ① perform for an audience ② play the part of; act
出洋 go abroad
出迎 go (*or* come) out to meet
出油 yield oil
出游 go on a sightseeing tour
出于 start from; proceed from; stem from
出狱 be released from prison
出院 (of an inpatient) leave hospital
出账 ①enter an item of expenditure in the accounts ②items of expenditure
出诊 (of a doctor) visit a patient at home; pay a home visit; make a house call
出征 go on an expedition; go out to battle
出众 be out of the ordinary; be outstanding
出资 provide funds or capital
出走 leave one's home or country under compulsion; run away; flee
出租 hire out; rent; let
出版社 publishing house; press
出版物 publication
出布告 post an announcement; put up a notice
出厂价 factory invoice price; ex-factory price; producer price
出场费 presence fee; performance fee
出成果 yield results
出点子 offer advice; make suggestions
出发点 ① the starting point of a journey ② starting point (in a discussion, argument, etc.); point of departure
出发港 port of departure
出风头 seek (*or* be in) the limelight
出港证 clearance papers; clearance
出国热 craze of going abroad
出节目 give a performance
出口额 value of export
出口货 exported goods; exports; outbound freight; exportation
出口量 export volume
出口商 exporter
出口税 export duties
出娄子 get into trouble; go wrong
出乱子 go wrong; get into trouble
出满月 be over one month old
出毛病 be or go out of order; malfunction
出门子 marry; get married
出苗率 the rate of emergence
出纳台 ①cashier's (*or* teller's) desk ②circulation desk (in a library)
出纳员 cashier; teller
出难题 set difficult questions; pose a difficult problem
出票日 date of draft
出气口 gas outlet; air vent
出气筒 punching bag
出勤率 attendance rate; attendance

出入境 exit and entry
出入证 pass（identifying a staff member, etc.）
出生地 birthplace
出生率 birthrate
出生证 birth certificate
出数儿（of rice）rise well with cooking
出天花 have smallpox；contract smallpox
出铁口 taphole；iron notch
出头鸟 the head of a bird first appeared；someone who stands out from the crowd or who leads a flock
出问题 go wrong；go amiss
出洋相 make an exhibition of oneself；make a spectacle of oneself
出油井 producing well
出渣口 slag notch；cinder notch
出疹子 have measles
出主意 offer advice；make suggestions
出租车 taxi
出单公司 issuing company
出多入少 more-out-than-in method
出尔反尔 go back on one's word；contradict oneself
出发信号 starting signal
出乖露丑 make an exhibition of oneself
出国镀金 study abroad in order to improve one's social status
出国考察 investigation trip abroad
出乎意料 exceeding one's expectations；contrary to one's expectations；unexpectedly
出境签证 exit visa
出口包装 export packing
出口报单 entry outward
出口补贴 export subsidy
出口成章 words flow from the mouth as from the pen of a master；talk in literature
出口创汇 earn foreign exchange through export
出口刺激 export incentives
出口代理 export agent
出口单据 export documents
出口发票 export invoice
出口管制 export control
出口货物 export commodities
出口价格 export price
出口检验 export inspection
出口检疫 export quarantine
出口净值 net export value
出口贸易 export trade
出口伤人 say things that will hurt others' feelings；speak bitingly
出口商品 export commodities
出口收入 export earnings
出口推销 export drive
出口信贷 export credit
出口证书 export certification

出类拔萃 stand out from one's fellows；be out of the common run；be pre-eminent
出谋划策 give counsel；mastermind
出其不意 take sb by surprise；catch sb unawares
出奇制胜 defeat one's opponent by a surprise move
出人头地 rise head and shoulders above others；stand out among one's fellows
出人意料 exceeding all expectations；beyond all expectations
出入手续 entry and exit procedures
出神入化 reach the acme of perfection；be superb
出生低谷 baby bust
出生高峰 baby boom
出生入死 go through fire and water；brave untold dangers；at the risk of life and limb
出手不凡 make skilful（or masterly）opening moves（in *wushu*, chess, etc.）
出双入对 go with each other all the time as lovers；go to places together as a couple
出庭作证 take the witness stand；serve as a witness at court
出头露面 appear in public；be in the limelight
出土文物 unearthed object；archeological finds
出言不逊 make impertinent remarks；speak insolently
出以公心 keep the public interest in mind；act without selfish considerations
出于无奈 as it cannot be helped；there being no alternative
出港呈报表 bill of clearance
出境许可证 exit permit
出口加工区 export processing zones
出口特许证 special permission export
出口退税制 export tax refund system；system of export tax refunds
出口许可证 export permit；export license
出口转内销 export goods for sale
出资证明书 investment certification
出污泥而不染 emerge unstained from the filth
出租车计价器 taximeter
出口商品交易会 Export Commodities Fair

初 ［chū］
I ［名］ beginning（of sth）；early part（of sth）
II ［形］①first（in order）②elementary；rudimentary ③original III ［副］ for the first time；only just begun
初版 ①first edition ②be first published
初步 initial；preliminary；tentative
初潮 first menses
初创 newly established
初春 early spring；first spring month（i.e. the first month of the lunar year）
初次 the first time
初等 elementary；primary

初冬 early winter; first winter month (i.e. the tenth month of the lunar year)
初犯 ①first offender ②first offence
初伏 ① the first *fu*—the first of the three ten-day periods of the hot season ② first day of the first *fu* (falling in mid-July)
初稿 first draft; draft
初会 first encounter; first meeting
初婚 ①first marriage ②newly married
初级 elementary; primary
初交 new acquaintance
初亏 first contact
初恋 ① first love ② first stage of falling in love
初年 first years of a historical period
初评 preliminary appraisal; first round of evaluation
初期 initial stage; early days
初晴 just cleared
初秋 early autumn; first autumn month (i.e. the seventh month of the lunar year)
初赛 preliminary contest; preliminary
初审 trial of first instance; first trial
初时 at the beginning
初始 initial; first; primary
初试 ①first try ②preliminary examination
初夏 early summer; first summer month (i.e. the fourth month of the lunar year)
初选 primary election
初学 begin to learn; be a beginner
初雪 first snow
初叶 early years (of a century)
初夜 ①early evening ②wedding night
初诊 one's first visit to a doctor or hospital
初值 initial value
初中 junior middle school
初衷 one's original intention
初产妇 primipara
初级班 junior class; elementary course
初加工 preliminary working
初速度 initial velocity
初学者 beginner; learner in the first stage
初夜权 right of first night
初装费 initial installation charge
初步方案 tentative programs
初步设想 tentative ideas
初步知识 rudimentary knowledge
初出茅庐 just come out of one's thatched cottage—at the beginning of one's career; young and inexperienced
初次见面 first meeting
初等教育 elementary education
初级产品 primary products
初级阶段 primary stage
初级线圈 primary coil
初级小学 lower primary school
初级中学 junior middle school

初见成效 achieve an initial success; begin to take effect
初具规模 begin to take shape
初露锋芒 display one's talent for the first time; begin to display one's talent
初露头角 begin to show ability or talent
初入世途 embark on one's career in life
初生之犊不怕虎 newborn calves are not afraid of tigers—young people are fearless

chú（ㄔㄨˊ）

刍 [chú] I 〔名〕 hay; fodder Ⅱ 〔动〕 cut grass; weed Ⅲ 〔代〕 my
刍秣 fodder; forage
刍议（my）modest proposal;（my）tentative suggestion

除 [chú] I 〔动〕 ①get rid of; eliminate; abolish; remove ②divide：二除八得四。Two goes into eight four times. ③confer; appoint（sb to an official position）Ⅱ 〔介〕 except; not including Ⅲ 〔名〕 step
除草 remove weeds; weed
除法 division
除非 ① only if; only when ②（not）… unless ③must needs; necessarily
除根 dig up the roots; cure once and for all; root out
除号 division sign（÷）
除了 ①except ②besides; in addition to ③either… or…
除名 remove sb's name from the rolls; strike sb's name off the rolls; expunge sb's name from a list
除权 ex right
除湿 dehumidification
除数 divisor
除霜 defrost
除外 ①except; not counting; not including ② besides; apart from; other than; in addition to; otherwise than; on（the）top of
除夕 New Year's Eve
除息 ex dividend
除锈 rust cleaning; rust removal
除斑剂 stain remover
除草机 weeder
除草剂 weed killer; herbicide
除尘器 dust remover
除臭剂 deodorant
除霜器 defroster
除四害 eliminate the four pests（usu. referring to rats, bedbugs, flies and mosquitoes）
除雪机 snow remover; snow breaker
除莠剂 herbicide
除暴安良 get rid of bullies and bring peace to good people

C

除恶务尽 One must be thorough in exterminating an evil.
除旧布新 get rid of the old to make way for the new; do away with the old and set up the new
除旧更新 replace the old with the new
除外条款 exceptive clause
除外责任 exclusions

厨 [chú]
名 ①kitchen ②cook; chef
厨房 kitchen
厨工 ①kitchen work ②cook
厨师 cook; chef
厨艺 culinary art

锄 [chú]
Ⅰ 名 hoe Ⅱ 动 ①work with a hoe; hoe ②uproot; eliminate; wipe out
锄地 hoe the fields; do hoeing
锄奸 eliminate traitors; ferret out spies
锄头 ①pickaxe ②hoe
锄强扶弱 suppress the strong and aid the weak

蜍 [chú]
◇蟾蜍 toad

雏 [chú]
形 young (bird)
雏儿 ①young bird; nestling ②young, inexperienced person; fledgling
雏鸟 nestling; fledgling
雏形 ①rudimentary, undeveloped form of an organism; embryonic form ②miniature; model
雏鸭 duckling
雏莺乳燕 young orioles and swallows

橱 [chú]
名 cabinet; closet
橱窗 ①show (or display) window; showcase; shopwindow ②glass-fronted billboard
橱柜 ①cupboard ②cupboard that also serves as a table; sideboard
橱窗广告 glass-fronted billboard

躇 [chú]
◇踌躇 ①hesitate; shilly-shally ②sojourn ③self-satisfied

蹰 [chú]
◇踟蹰 demur; hesitate; be uncertain about whether to move or not

chǔ (ㄔㄨˇ)

处 [chǔ]
动 ①dwell; live; inhabit ②get along (with sb) ③be situated in; be in a certain condition ④manage; handle; deal with ⑤punish; sentence ➡ chù
处罚 punish; penalize

处方 ①write out a prescription; prescribe ②prescription; recipe
处分 ①take disciplinary action against; punish ②handle; manage; deal with
处警 (of public security department) deal with emergencies and dangerous situations
处境 unfavourable situation; plight
处决 ①put to death; execute ②manage and make decisions
处理 ①handle; deal with; dispose of ②treat (a workpiece or product) by a special process ③sell at reduced prices
处女 virgin; maiden
处身 place oneself; settle
处士 recluse
处世 conduct oneself in society
处事 handle affairs; deal with matters
处暑 ①End of Heat—the 14th of the 24 solar terms ②day marking the beginning of the 14th solar term
处死 put to death; execute
处刑 condemn; sentence
处于 be (in a certain condition)
处治 punish
处置 ①handle; deal with; manage; dispose of ②punish
处子 virgin
处方药 prescription drug; prescription medicine
处理机 processor
处理价 reduced price; bargain price
处理品 goods (usu. shopworn or substandard) sold at reduced prices
处女地 virgin land (or soil)
处女航 maiden voyage or flight
处女膜 hymen
处女作 maiden work; first effort
处罚条款 penal terms
处理程序 processing design
处世之道 ways of life; way of conducting oneself in society
处心积虑 deliberately plan (to achieve evil ends); incessantly scheme
处以罚金 impose a penalty
处以重刑 inflict a harsh sentence
处之泰然 take things calmly; remain unruffled

杵 [chǔ]
Ⅰ 名 ①pestle ②wooden club used to pound clothes in washing Ⅱ 动 poke
杵臼 mortar and pestle
杵药 pestle medicinal herbs

础 [chǔ]
名 plinth
础润而雨 a damp plinth predicts rain—sign that sth serious is going to happen; portent of what is going to happen

楮 [chǔ]
名 ①paper mulberry ②paper

储 [chǔ]
I 动 store up；save；keep in reserve II 名 heir to the throne
储备 ①store for future use；lay in；lay up ②reserve
储藏 ①save and preserve；store；keep ②deposit
储存 lay in；lay up；store；stockpile；deposit
储放 store；leave in sb's care
储户 depositor
储积 ①store up；save ②stock；savings
储集 store up；save
储君 crown prince
储款 savings
储量 reserves
储气 gas storage
储蓄 save；deposit
储油 oil storage
储运 store up and transport
储备粮 grain reserves
储藏量 reserves
储藏室 storeroom
储存器 reservoir
储集层 reservoir bed
储金会 saving society
储气罐 gas tank
储蓄额 total savings deposits
储蓄所 savings bank
储油罐 oil storage tank；oil tank
储值卡 stored-value card
储备寸头 reserve position
储备基金 reserve fund
储备银行 savings bank
储粮备荒 store up grain against natural disasters
储气构造 gas-bearing structure
储蓄存款 savings deposit
储蓄存折 savings pass-book
储油构造 oil-bearing structure
储蓄代办所 savings agency
储蓄存款实名制 person savings accounts system by registering true name

楚 [chǔ]
I 形 clear；neat II 名 pang；pain；suffering
楚楚 ①tidy；neat；spotlessly clean ②delicate；dainty
楚材晋用 the talents of Chu used by Jin—the intellectual resources of one country used by another
楚楚可怜 (of a young woman) delicate and charming

chù (彳ㄨ)

处 [chǔ]
I 名 ①place ②part；point ③division；of-fice；department II 置：一处别墅 a villa ➡ chù
处处 everywhere；in all respects
处所 place；location
处长 head of a department or office；section chief

怵 [chù]
动 fear；fright；be afraid
怵目惊心 strike the eye and rouse the mind；be shocked at the sight of

绌 [chù]
动 inadequate；insufficient

畜 [chù]
名 domestic animal；livestock ➡ xù
畜肥 animal manure
畜栏 corral
畜类 domestic animals
畜力 animal power
畜群 herd of livestock
畜生 ①domestic animals ②beast；dirty swine
畜疫 epidemic disease of domestic animals

搐 [chù]
动 twitch；jerk

触 [chù]
动 ①contact ②hit；strike ③touch ④move sb；stir up sb's feelings
触电 get an electric shock；begin work in film or television
触动 ①touch sth，moving it slightly ②move sb；stir up sb's feelings
触发 detonate by contact；touch off；spark；trigger
触犯 offend；violate；go against
触击 ①strike ②bunt
触及 touch
触礁 run (up) on rocks；strike a reef (or rock)
触角 antenna；feeler
触觉 tactile (or tactual) sensation；sense of touch
触雷 hit a mine；run into a mine
触媒 catalyst；catalytic agent
触摸 touch；feel
触目 ①meet the eye ②eye-catching；striking；conspicuous
触怒 make angry；infuriate；enrage
触手 tentacle
触痛 ①touch a tender (or sore) spot；touch sb to the quick ②tenderness
触网 touch net
触须 cirrus
触针 contact pilotage
触诊 palpation
触发器 trigger
触摸屏 touch screen
触杀剂 contact insecticide
触发地雷 contact mine
触发电路 trigger circuit

触犯刑律 break the criminal law; violate the criminal law
触及灵魂 touch one to his very soul
触景生情 the sight strikes a chord in one's heart
触觉器官 tactile organ
触类旁通 grasp a typical example and you will grasp the whole category; comprehend by analogy
触目惊心 startling; shocking

憷 [chù] 动 fear; flinch; shrink from
憷场 be timid on a public occasion

黜 [chù] 动 remove or dismiss sb from office; reject; discharge
黜免 dismiss (a government official)

矗 [chù] 动 stand tall and upright; be perpendicular
矗立 stand tall and upright; tower over sth

chuāi (ㄔㄨㄞ)

揣 [chuāi] 动 ①hide or carry in one's clothes; tuck ②(of animals) be pregnant ➡ chuǎi; chuài
揣手儿 tuck each hand in the opposite sleeve

搋 [chuāi] 动 ①rub; knead ②clear a drain with a suction pump

chuái (ㄔㄨㄞ)

膗 [chuái] 形 fat and flabby; overweight

chuǎi (ㄔㄨㄞ)

揣 [chuǎi] 动 estimate; speculate; conjecture; surmise ➡ chuāi; chuài
揣测 guess; conjecture
揣度 estimate; appraise; conjecture
揣摩 try to fathom; try to figure out
揣想 guess; think

chuài (ㄔㄨㄞ)

揣 [chuài] ➡ chuāi; chuǎi
◇囊揣 ①cowardly; feeble ②pork near the pig's nipples

嘬 [chuài] 动 bite; eat ➡ zuō

踹 [chuài] 动 ①kick (forward with sole and heel) ②trample; tread; stamp; step in

chuān (ㄔㄨㄢ)

川 [chuān] 名 ①river ②plain; flat land

川贝 tendril-leaved fritillary bulb of Sichuan origin
川芎 rhizome of *chuanxiong*
川资 travelling expenses
川流不息 flowing past in an endless stream; never-ending

穿 [chuān] 动 ①pierce through; penetrate ②*used after certain verbs to indicate thoroughness or completeness* ③go through; pass through; cross ④thread ⑤wear; put on; be dressed in; have... on
穿帮 give the game away; let the cat out of the bag; be exposed; reveal one's true colours
穿插 ①alternate; do in turn ②weave in; insert ③subplot; interlude; episode ④thrust deep into the enemy forces
穿刺 puncture
穿戴 apparel; dress
穿过 go across; pass through; cross; penetrate
穿孔 ①bore (*or* punch) a hole; perforate ②perforation
穿梭 shuttle back and forth
穿透 pierce through; run through
穿孝 be in mourning; wear mourning
穿越 pass through; cut across
穿凿 give a farfetched (*or* strained) interpretation; read too much into sth
穿针 thread a needle
穿着 dress; apparel
穿插营 deep-thrust battalion
穿甲弹 armour-piercing projectile; armour-piercing shell or bullet; armour piercer
穿卡机 punched-card machine
穿孔机 punch; perforator
穿箔机 reeding machine
穿山甲 ①pangolin ②pangolin scales
穿堂风 draught
穿堂门 passageway; alley gate
穿小鞋 give sb tight shoes to wear—make things hard for sb by abusing one's power; make it hot for sb
穿心莲 creat
穿衣镜 full-length mirror
穿梭外交 shuttle diplomacy
穿凿附会 give strained interpretations and draw farfetched analogies
穿针引线 act as a go-between
穿耳式耳环 pierced earring
穿一条裤子 share the same pair of trousers—band together; collude; gang up
穿新鞋，走老路 tread the same old path in new shoes—do sth old in a new form; old wine in a new bottle

chuán (ㄔㄨㄢˊ)

传 [chuán]
勋 ① pass; convey; hand down ② pass on (knowledge, skill, etc.); impart; teach ③ spread ④ transmit; conduct; transfer ⑤ convey; express ⑥ summon; demand the presence of sb ⑦ infect; be contagious ➡ zhuàn

传播 ① disseminate; propagate; spread ② propagation

传布 disseminate; propagate; spread

传抄 make private copies of (a manuscript, document, etc. which is being circulated)

传达 ① pass on (information, etc.); transmit; relay; communicate ② reception and registration of callers at a public establishment ③ janitor

传代 pass on from generation to generation

传单 leaflet; handbill

传导 ① conduct (heat, electricity, etc.) ② transmit

传道 ① deliver a sermon; preach ② propagate Confucianist doctrines

传递 transmit; deliver; transfer

传电 conduct electricity

传动 transmission; drive

传粉 pollination

传呼 (of a trunk-line operator or public telephone custodian) pass on a telephone message or call sb to answer the phone

传话 pass on a message

传唤 summon to court; subpoena

传教 do missionary work

传戒 initiate sb into monkhood or nunhood

传令 transmit (or dispatch) orders

传媒 ① mass media; the media ② media; vehicle

传票 ① (court) summons; subpoena ② accounting voucher

传奇 ① tales of the marvellous (short stories of the Tang-Song period, written in the literary style ② a form of drama of the Ming-Qing period, immensely long with an average of forty or more scenes ③ legend; romance

传情 express amorous feelings

传球 pass the ball to a teammate

传染 infect; be contagious

传热 transmit heat

传神 vivid; lifelike

传审 summon sb to court

传世 be handed down from ancient times

传授 pass on (knowledge, skill, etc.); impart; teach

传输 transmission

传述 it is said; they say

传说 ① pass from mouth to mouth; it is said; they say ② legend; tradition

传诵 be widely read; be on everybody's lips

传送 convey; deliver

传颂 be told from mouth to mouth with approbation; be on everybody's lips

传统 tradition

传闻 ① it is said; they say ② hearsay; rumour; talk

传销 multi-layer transit sale or a method of direct marketing; direct distribution; pyramid selling

传讯 summon for interrogation (or trial); subpoena; cite

传言 ① hearsay; rumour ② pass on a message

传扬 spread (from mouth to mouth)

传译 translate one language into another

传阅 pass round (or circulate) for perusal

传真 ① portraiture ② facsimile; fax

传旨 deliver an imperial order

传帮带 (of experienced people) pass on experience, help and guide new hands (in their work)

传达室 reception office; janitor's room

传动比 drive ratio; ratio of transmission; transmission ratio

传动带 transmission belt

传动箱 transmission case

传动轴 transmission shaft

传感器 sensor; transducer

传呼机 beeper; wireless pager

传话筒 voice tube; speaking tube

传家宝 ① family heirloom ② cherished tradition (or heritage)

传教士 missionary

传经验 pass on the experience

传口信 convey (or pass on) an oral message

传染病 infectious (or contagious) disease

传染性 infectiousness; contagion

传染源 source of infection

传声器 microphone

传声筒 ① megaphone; loud hailer ② one who parrots another; sb's mouthpiece

传手艺 teach the skill

传输线 transmission line; transmission control

传送带 conveyer belt

传真机 facsimile equipment; fax

传证人 summon a witness

传播媒介 mass media; the media

传出神经 efferent nerve

传单广告 flysheet

传动齿轮 transmission (or drive) gear

传动装置 gearing

传呼电话 neighbourhood telephone service

传呼服务 paging service

传染病院 hospital for infectious diseases; isolation hospital

传入神经 afferent nerve
传统产业 traditional industries
传统观念 traditional ideas
传统教育 traditional education
传统商品 traditional commodities
传为佳话 become a favourite topic or a much-told tale
传为美谈 pass from mouth to mouth with approbation
传谣信谣 spread rumours and give them credence
传真电报 phototelegraph
传真信号 facsimile signal
传真照片 wirephoto; radiophoto
传真装置 picture unit
传宗接代 produce a male heir to continue the family line
传播性病罪 crime of transmitting venereal diseases
传声清晰度 articulation
传真记录法 facsimile recording
传统安全威胁 traditional threats to security

船 [chuán]
名 ship; boat
船板 deck of a small wooden boat
船帮 ①side of a boat; shipboard ②merchant fleet
船舶 shipping; boats and ships
船埠 wharf; quay
船舱 ①ship's hold ②cabin
船次 ①number indicating a ship's order of departure ② number of voyages taken by a ship
船东 owner of the vessel; shipowner
船队 fleet; flotilla
船舵 rudder; helm
船帆 sail
船方 the ship
船费 cost of a boat ticket
船夫 boatmen
船工 ①boatman; junkman ②boatwright
船级 ship's classification (or class)
船籍 nationality of a ship
船家 one who owns a boat and makes a living as a boatman; boatman
船检 inspect ships
船脚 ①boatman; junkman ②shipping freight
船壳 hull
船龄 age of vessel; vessel age
船篷 ①the mat or wooden roofing of a boat ② sail
船票 steamer ticket
船期 sailing date
船桥 (ship's) bridge
船蛆 shipworm
船艄 stern
船身 hull (of a ship)

船首 stem; bow; prow
船索 ship's rigging
船台 (building) berth; shipway; slipway; slip
船体 body of a ship; hull
船尾 stern
船位 ①accommodation on a ship ②ship's position
船坞 dock; shipyard
船舷 side (of a ship or boat)
船员 (ship's) crew
船运 shipping; transportation by sea
船闸 (ship) lock
船长 captain; skipper
船只 shipping; vessels
船主 ①captain of a vessel; shipmaster ②owner of a boat (or ship)
船夫曲 boatmen's song
船级社 (ship's) classification society
船籍港 port of registry; home port
船老大 ①the chief crewman of a wooden boat ②boatman
船期表 sailing schedule
船首楼 forecastle
船尾部 quarter
船尾楼 poop
船坞费 dockage
船形帽 fore-and-aft cap
船用油 bunker oil
船边提货 alongside delivery; shipside delivery
船舶证书 ship's papers
船级证书 ship's classification certificate
船台周期 berth period
船形军帽 garrison cap
船边交货(价) free alongside ship (F.A.S.)
船上交货(价) free on board (F.O.B.)
船小好调头 it is easier for a small boat to turn round—it is easier for a small enterprise to change its line of products or a small company to change its business orientation
船舶登记证书 ship's certificate of registry
船到桥头自然直 You will cross the bridge when you get to it.

chuǎn (ㄔㄨㄢˇ)

舛 [chuǎn]
Ⅰ 名 ①error ②mishap Ⅱ 形 unfortunate Ⅲ 动 run counter to
舛驰 run in the opposite direction

喘 [chuǎn]
Ⅰ 动 breathe rapidly; gasp for breath; pant Ⅱ 名 asthma
喘气 ①breathe (deeply); pant; gasp ②take a breather
喘息 ① pant; gasp for breath ② breather; breathing spell; respite
喘粗气 puff and blow
喘吁吁 puff and blow

chuàn （ㄔㄨㄢˋ）

串 ［chuàn］
Ⅰ 〔动〕①string together ②conspire；gang up ③get things mixed up；connect wrongly ④go from place to place；go about；rove ⑤play a part（in a play）；act Ⅱ 〔名〕string of things Ⅲ 〔量〕string；stick；bunch；cluster：一串葡萄 a cluster of grapes ➡ guàn

串案 conspiracy

串供 act in collusion to make each other's confessions tally

串行 ［chuànháng］（in reading or typing）skip a line；confuse two lines

串换 exchange；swap

串讲 ①explain a text sentence by sentence ②give a summing-up of a text after going over it paragraph by paragraph

串联 ①establish ties；contact ②series connection

串骗 gang up to swindle（sb）

串气 gang up；collude with

串通 gang up；collaborate；collude

串演 play（*or* act）the role of

串音 babble

串珠 a string of beads

串并联 series-parallel connection

串门儿 call at sb's home；drop in on sb

串亲戚 go visiting one's relatives

串味儿 absorb the smell of sth；become tainted inflavour

串烤羊肉 skewered mutton

串亲访友 go visiting one's relatives and friends

串通一气 gang up；collaborate；work hand in glove；collude

串处理语言 string processing language

钏 ［chuàn］
〔名〕bracelet

chuāng （ㄔㄨㄤ）

创 ［chuāng］
〔名〕wound；trauma ➡ chuàng

创痕 scar

创口 wound；cut

创面 surface of a wound

创伤 wound；trauma

疮 ［chuāng］
〔名〕①sore；skin ulcer ②wound

疮疤 scar

疮痂 scab

疮口 open part of a sore

疮痍 wounds；traumata—devastation caused by a war or a natural calamity

窗 ［chuāng］
〔名〕window

窗洞 opening in a wall（to let in light and air）

窗户 window；casement

窗花 paper-cut for window decoration

窗口 ①window ②wicket ③medium；showpiece ④hatch ⑤aperture

窗框 window frame

窗帘 window curtain

窗膜 fenestrated membrane

窗纱 gauze for screening windows；window screening

窗扇 casement

窗台 windowsill

窗沿 windowsill

窗子 window

窗玻璃 windowpane

窗插销 window bolt；angle catch

窗格子 window lattice

窗户纸 window paper

窗口行业 service trades；"window" industry

窗明几净 with bright windows and clean tables；bright and clean

chuáng （ㄔㄨㄤˊ）

床 ［chuáng］
Ⅰ 〔名〕①bed；couch ②sth shaped like a bed Ⅱ 〔量〕（of sth that covers a bed）：两床铺盖 two sets of bedding

床边 bedside

床单 sheet；bedclothes

床垫 mattress

床架 bedstead

床铺 bed

床身 lathe bed

床头 head of a bed；bedside

床位 berth；bunk；bed

床沿 edge of a bed

床罩 bedspread；counterpane

床笫 bed mat—the bed as a place of conjugal intimacies

床上戏 bed show

床头灯 bedside lamp

床头柜 bedside cupboard

床头箱 headstock

床上用品 bedclothes；bedding

床笫之言 private talk between husband and wife；pillow talk

噇 ［chuáng］
〔动〕eat or drink without restraint；guzzle

幢 ［chuáng］
〔名〕① pennant；streamer ②stone pillar inscribed with Buddha's name or Buddhist incantation ➡ zhuàng

幢幢（of shadows）flickering；dancing

chuǎng （ㄔㄨㄤˇ）

闯 ［chuǎng］
〔动〕①rush；dash；charge ②temper oneself（by battling through difficulties and dangers）

③go around (in order to accomplish certain goals); be busy running about ④get into or bring on (sth undesirable); incur

闯荡 make a living away from home

闯祸 get into trouble; bring disaster

闯将 daring general; pathbreaker

闯劲 spirit of a pathbreaker; pioneering spirit

闯练 leave home to temper oneself; be tempered in the world

闯入 force on entrance; burst into; inbreak

闯关东 take a risky journey to the Northeast to eke out a living

闯红灯 ① go against a red light; jump a red light ② violate law and discipline; break down a barrier or limit

闯江湖 make a living wandering from place to place (as a fortune-teller, acrobat, quack doctor, etc.)

闯乱子 get into trouble; bring on a disaster

chuàng (ㄔㄨㄤˋ)

创 [chuàng] 动 start (doing sth); begin (to do sth); achieve (sth for the first time); create ➡ chuāng

创办 establish; set up

创导 initiate; propose

创汇 earn foreign exchange

创见 original idea

创建 found; establish

创举 pioneering work (*or* undertaking)

创刊 start publication

创立 found; originate

创利 make or earn a profit

创设 ①found; create; set up ②create (conditions, etc.)

创始 originate; initiate; found

创收 create income

创新 bring forth new ideas; blaze new trails

创业 start an undertaking; do pioneering work

创意 original idea

创优 create excellence; create new ideas

创造 create; produce; bring about

创制 formulate; institute; create

创作 ① create; produce; write ② creative work; creation

创高产 achieve a high yield

创刊号 first issue; first number

创奇迹 create miracles; work wonders; achieve prodigious feats

创始国 founding country

创始人 founder; originator; initiator

创新说 found a new theory

创造力 creative power (*or* ability)

创造性 creativeness; creativity

创汇产品 foreign exchange-earning export products

创新精神 enterprising spirit

创业资金 start-up funds; risk capital; venture capital

创业板市场 growth enterprise board

怆 [chuàng] 形 sorrowful; sad; mournful

chuī (ㄔㄨㄟ)

吹 [chuī] 动 ①blow; puff ②play (wind instruments) ③(of wind) blow; puff; strike ④boast; brag; exaggerate ⑤flatter; laud to the skies; compliment ⑥break off; break up; fall through; fail

吹风 ① be in a draught; catch a chill ② dry (hair, etc.) with a blower; blow-dry ③ blow-dryer; blower (for drying hair) ④ let sb in on sth in advance

吹拂 ①(of a breeze) sway; stir ②praise and recommend sb

吹管 blowpipe

吹号 blow a bugle; blare the call

吹炼 blowing

吹牛 boast; brag; talk big

吹捧 flatter; laud to the skies; lavish praise on

吹哨 blow a whistle

吹塑 blow molding; blowing

吹嘘 lavish praise on oneself or others; boast

吹奏 play (wind instruments)

吹打乐 ensemble of Chinese wind and percussion instruments

吹风会 briefing

吹风机 ① blower (for drying hair); blow-dryer ②air-blower; blower

吹鼓手 ①music makers at old-time weddings or funerals ②eulogist

吹口哨 whistle

吹喇叭 wind a trumpet

吹冷风 blow a cold wind over; throw cold water on; make discouraging remarks

吹奏乐 band music; wind music

吹吹打打 beating drums and blowing trumpets; piping and drumming

吹吹拍拍 boasting and toadying

吹灰之力 effort needed to blow away a speck of dust; just a small effort

吹拉弹唱 blow, bow, pluck, and sing—be very musical

吹毛求疵 find fault; pick holes; nitpick

吹牛拍马 boast and flatter

吹胡子瞪眼 froth at the mouth and glare with rage; foam with anger

炊 [chuī] 动 cook a meal

炊饼 steamed cake

炊具 cooking utensils

炊事 cooking; kitchen work
炊烟 smoke from kitchen chimneys
炊帚 brush for cleaning pots and pans
炊事班 cookhouse (*or* mess, kitchen) squad
炊事员 cook; kitchen staff
炊事用具 cooking utensils

chuí (ㄔㄨㄟˊ)

垂 [chuí]
Ⅰ 〔动〕 ① hang down; droop; let fall ② spread; hand down; go down in history; bequeath to posterity Ⅱ 〔副〕 ① (*used of kind action of other people , usu. one's seniors*) ②nearing; on the verge of; almost
垂钓 fish with a hook and line; go angling
垂柳 weeping willow; drooping willow
垂落 hang down; drop down; fall
垂暮 dusk; towards sunset; just before sundown
垂念 show kind concern for
垂青 show appreciation for sb; look upon sb with favour
垂手 ①obtain sth with hands down ②let the hands hang by the sides
垂死 moribund; dying
垂询 condescend to inquire
垂体 hypophysis; pituitary body (*or* gland)
垂头 hang (*or* bow) one's head
垂危 ①be critically ill; be at one's last gasp ② (of a nation) be in great peril
垂问 condescend to inquire
垂涎 drool; slaver; covet
垂直 perpendicular; vertical
垂耳犬 alco
垂盆草 stringy stonecrop
垂帘听政 (of an empress regent) sit behind a screen to receive ministerial reports; hold court from behind a screen (an empress regent was supposed to be concealed from the sight of ministers at audience)
垂示后世 set a shining example for posterity
垂手可得 extremely easy to obtain
垂死挣扎 be in one's death throes; put up a last ditch (*or* deathbed) struggle
垂头丧气 be crestfallen; be dejected
垂涎三尺 spittle three feet long—drool with envy
垂直传播 vertical transmission
垂直起落飞机 vertical takeoff and landing aircraft

陲 [chuí]
〔名〕 frontier; border

捶 [chuí]
〔动〕 beat (with a stick or fist); thump; pound
捶打 beat; pound; thump
捶胸顿足 beat one's breast and stamp one's feet (in sorrow, etc.)

棰 [chuí]
Ⅰ 〔名〕 short wooden club; cudgel Ⅱ 〔动〕 beat with a cudgel; strike
棰楚 caning (as a form of punishment in the past)

椎 [chuí]
Ⅰ 〔名〕 tool with a heavy head and handle, used for breaking or beating Ⅱ 〔动〕 beat; thump; pound ➡zhuī
椎鼓 beat drums
椎杀 kill with a hammer

槌 [chuí]
〔名〕mallet; beetle; pestle

锤 [chuí]
Ⅰ 〔名〕①metal ball with a chain or long handle; hammer ② hammer ③ sth shaped like a hammer Ⅱ 〔动〕 hammer into shape; knock with a hammer
锤骨 malleus; hammer
锤光 planish
锤炼 ①temper oneself; steel oneself ②refine; polish ③hammer into shape
锤子 hammer

chūn (ㄔㄨㄣ)

春 [chūn]
〔名〕①spring ②year; a year's time ③love; lust ④vital energy; vitality; life
春饼 spring pancake
春播 spring sowing
春分 ①Spring Equinox—the 4th of the 24 solar terms ② day marking the beginning of the 4th solar term
春风 ① spring breeze ② kindly and pleasant countenance
春耕 spring ploughing
春宫 ①living quarters of the crown prince ② pornographic pictures
春灌 spring irrigation
春光 sights and sounds of spring; spring scenery
春寒 spring chill; cold spell in spring
春化 vernalization
春季 spring; springtime
春假 spring holidays
春节 Spring Festival
春景 scenery of springtime
春卷 spring roll
春困 feeling of lethargy that comes over many people in spring
春雷 spring thunder
春联 Spring Festival couplets; New Year couplets
春令 ①spring ②spring weather
春梦 spring dream—transient joy
春情 stirrings of love
春秋 ①spring and autumn; year ②age ③ *The*

Spring and Autumn Annals

春色 ①spring's colours; spring scenery ②joyful look; wine-flushed face

春笋 bamboo shoots in spring

春天 spring; springtime

春宵 spring night

春心 thoughts of love; stirrings of love; budding love

春汛 ①spring flood ②spring (fishing) season

春药 aphrodisiac

春意 ① spring in the air; the beginning (*or* awakening) of spring ②thoughts of love

春游 spring outing

春运 spring transportation; transportation during the Spring Festival

春招 university enrolment in Spring

春种 spring sowing

春装 spring clothing; spring costume

春秋衫 jacket suitable for spring or autumn

春小麦 spring wheat

春风得意 be flushed with success

春风化雨 life-giving spring breeze and rain—salutary influence of education

春风满面 beaming with satisfaction; radiant with happiness

春福寿草 oxeye

春光明媚 sunlit and enchanting scene of spring

春寒料峭 there is a chill in the air in early spring

春华秋实 spring flowers and fall fruit—literary talent and moral integrity

春蕾计划 Spring Bud Program

春暖花开 spring has come and the flowers are in bloom

春去秋来 with the change of seasons; with the passage of time

春色满园 spring's colours fill the garden

春雨贵如油 rain in spring is as precious as oil

春运高峰期 spring peak transport period

春节文艺晚会 spring festival entertainment show

堵 ［chūn］
［名］ stone wall along the edge of fields against dust storms, etc.

椿 ［chūn］
［名］ ①Chinese toon ②tree of heaven

椿象 stinkbug; shieldbug

蝽 ［chūn］
［名］ stinkbug; shieldbug

chún （ㄔㄨㄣˊ）

纯 ［chūn］
［形］ ① pure; unmixed ② simple; pure and simple ③skilful; practised; well versed; fluent

纯白 pure white

纯粹 ①pure; unadulterated ②purely; sheerly; wholly

纯度 degree of purity

纯黑 all black

纯化 purification

纯碱 soda ash; sodium carbonate

纯洁 ①pure; clean and honest ②purify

纯金 pure gold; fine gold

纯净 pure; clean

纯棉 pure cotton

纯朴 honest; simple; unsophisticated

纯熟 skilful; practised; well versed

纯损 net loss

纯一 single; simple

纯音 pure (*or* simple) tone

纯真 pure; sincere

纯正 pure; unadulterated

纯种 thoroughbred; purebred

纯净水 purified water

纯利润 net profit

纯收入 net income

纯文学 pure literature; belles-lettres

纯血统 full blood; pure blood

纯羊毛 pure wool

纯平彩电 pure complanate colour TV

纯属污蔑 sheer slander

纯羊毛标志 woolmark

莼 ［chún］

莼菜 water shield

唇 ［chún］
［名］ lip

唇彩 lip gloss

唇膏 lipstick

唇裂 harelip; cleft lip

唇舌 words; argument

唇吻 ①lips ②eloquence; one's words

唇音 labial (sound)

唇齿音 labiodental (sound)

唇枪舌剑 cross verbal swords; engage in a battle of words

唇亡齿寒 If the lips are gone, the teeth will be cold; If one (of two interdependent things) falls, the other is in danger; share a common lot

淳 ［chún］
［形］ pure; honest

淳白 pure; clear

淳厚 pure and honest; simple and kind

淳朴 honest; simple; unsophisticated

鹑 ［chún］
［名］ quail

醇 ［chún］
I ［名］ ①strong alcoholic drink; liquor ②alcohol II ［形］ pure; unmixed; unadulterated; mellow

醇和 (of quality, taste, etc.) mellow; pure

醇厚 ①mellow; rich ②pure and honest; simple and kind

醇化 ①refine;purify;perfect ②alcoholization
醇解 alcoholysis
醇酿 liquor;spirits
醇酸 alcohol (*or* alcoholic) acid
醇化物 alcoholate
醇中毒 alcoholism;alcoholic poisoning
醇酸树脂 alkyd resin

chǔn (ㄔㄨㄣˇ)

蠢 [chǔn] Ⅰ 动 wriggle;squirm Ⅱ 形 ①stupid;foolish;dull ②clumsy;awkward
蠢笨 clumsy;awkward;stupid
蠢材 idiot;fool
蠢动 ① wriggle ② create disturbances;carry on disruptive activities
蠢话 foolish words;rubbish;nonsense
蠢货 blockhead;dunce;idiot
蠢驴 idiot;donkey;ass
蠢人 fool;blockhead
蠢事 stupid thing
蠢猪 idiot;stupid swine;ass
蠢蠢欲动 ready to start wriggling—ready to make trouble
蠢头蠢脑 stupid-looking

chuō (ㄔㄨㄛ)

戳 [chuō] Ⅰ 动 ①jab;poke;stab ②get sprained;blunted ③stand sth on end;stand erect Ⅱ 名 stamp;seal
戳穿 ①puncture ②lay bare;expose;explode
戳记 stamp;seal
戳伤 stab;stab wound
戳子 stamp;seal

chuò (ㄔㄨㄛˋ)

啜 [chuò] 动 ①sip;suck ②sob
啜茗 sip tea
啜泣 sob
啜粥 have porridge
啜菽饮水 live on coarse grain and drink plain water—live a simple life

惙 [chuò] 名 ①anxiety;worry ②fatigue

绰 [chuò] 形 ample;spacious ➡chāo
绰号 nickname
绰约 (of a girl) graceful
绰绰有余 more than sufficient;enough and to spare
绰约多姿 graceful and attractive

辍 [chuò] 动 stop;cease
辍笔 stop in the middle of writing (*or* painting)
辍学 discontinue one's studies;drop out of school
辍演 stop staging

cī (ㄘ)

刺 [cī] 象 wham:他刺的一声滑倒了。Wham! He slipped and fell. ➡cì

呲 [cī] 动 give a talking-to *or* a tongue-lashing (to sb);scold

差 [cī] ➡chā;chà;chāi
◇参差 uneven;not uniform

疵 [cī] 名 fault;flaw;defect;blemish
疵点 flaw;fault;defect
疵品 defective goods;bad work

跐 [cī] 动 slip;slide ➡cǐ

cí (ㄘˊ)

词 [cí] 名 ①speech;statement;lines of plays ②*ci*,a type of classical Chinese poetry ③word;term
词典 dictionary
词法 morphology
词干 stem
词根 root
词汇 vocabulary;words and phrases
词句 words and phrases;expressions
词类 parts of speech
词库 lexicon;word bank
词频 frequency of a word's use within a defined scope of language
词头 prefix
词尾 ①suffix ②inflectional ending
词形 morphology
词性 syntactical functions and morphological features that help to determine a part of speech
词序 word order
词义 meaning (*or* sense) of a word
词语 words and expressions;terms
词源 origin of a word;etymology
词缀 affix
词组 word group;phrase
词典学 lexicography
词汇表 word list;vocabulary;glossary
词汇学 lexicology
词不达意 The words fail to convey the idea.

茨 [cí] 名 ①thatched roof ②puncture vine

祠 [cí] 名 ancestral hall (*or* temple);memorial

C

temple
祠堂 ancestral hall (*or* temple); memorial temple

瓷 [cí]
名 porcelain; china
瓷雕 porcelain carving
瓷婚 china wedding
瓷漆 enamel paint; enamel
瓷器 porcelain; chinaware
瓷实 solid; firm; substantial
瓷土 porcelain clay; china clay
瓷牙 porcelain tooth
瓷砖 ceramic tile; glazed tile
瓷饭碗 porcelain bowl; unsecured position (*or* job)

辞 [cí]
I 名 ① diction; phraseology ② genre of classical Chinese literature:《楚辞》*The Songs of Chu* ③ form of classical Chinese poetry:《木兰辞》*The Ballad of Mulan* II 动 ① take leave ② resign; hand in one's resignation ③ dismiss; discharge ④ shirk; evade; dodge; decline
辞别 bid farewell (to); say goodbye (to); take one's leave (of)
辞呈 (written) resignation
辞典 dictionary
辞工 ①dismiss (a labourer or employee); discharge ②quit one's job; resign
辞官 resign one's government post
辞令 language appropriate to the occasion
辞让 politely decline
辞世 depart this life; pass away
辞书 dictionary; lexicographical work (e.g. wordbook, etc.)
辞岁 bid farewell to the outgoing year; see the old year out; celebrate the Lunar New Year's Eve
辞讼 legal cases; lawsuit
辞退 dismiss; discharge
辞谢 politely decline; decline with thanks
辞行 say goodbye (to one's relatives, friends, etc.) before setting out on a journey
辞藻 flowery language; rhetoric; ornate diction
辞章 ①poetry and prose; prose and verse ② art of writing; rhetoric
辞职 resign; hand in one's resignation
辞旧迎新 ring out the Old Year and ring in the New Year

慈 [cí]
I 形 kind; loving II 动 (*usu. of a senior person*) love III 名 mother
慈爱 love (of an older person for a younger one); affection; kindness
慈悲 mercy; benevolence; pity
慈父 loving father

慈姑 arrowhead (the plant or its edible corm)
慈和 kindly and amiable
慈母 loving mother; mother
慈亲 mother
慈善 charitable; benevolent; philanthropic
慈祥 kindly
慈善家 philanthropist
慈善堂 house of mercy
慈眉善目 benign countenance
慈善机构 charitable institution/organization
慈善事业 charities; good works; philanthropy

磁 [cí]
名 ①magnetism ②porcelain; china
磁暴 magnetic storm
磁北 magnetic north
磁场 magnetic field
磁带 (magnetic) tape
磁道 track
磁钢 magnet steel
磁化 magnetization
磁极 magnetic pole
磁卡 magnetic card; magnetic stripe card
磁力 magnetic force
磁疗 magnet therapy
磁盘 magnetic disk
磁石 ①magnetite ②magnet
磁体 magnetic body; magnet
磁铁 magnet
磁头 magnetic head (of a recorder)
磁心 (magnetic) core
磁性 magnetism; magnetic
磁选 magnetic separation
磁针 magnetic needle
磁子 magneton
磁感应 magnetic induction
磁化杯 magnetic cup (cup made of magnetic material, said to be good for health)
磁化率 magnetic susceptibility
磁化器 magnetizer
磁卡锁 magnetic card lock
磁力线 magnetic line of force
磁力仪 magnetometer
磁偏角 magnetic declination
磁铁矿 magnetite
磁通量 magnetic flux
磁场强度 magnetic field intensity
磁带文件 magnetic tape file
磁极强度 magnetic pole strength
磁卡电话 card phone
磁盘文件 disk file
磁性水雷 magnetic mine
磁性炸弹 magnetic bomb
磁带存储器 (magnetic) tape storage; tape-memory
磁带录音机 tape recorder
磁力探矿仪 magnetic detector (for ore deposits)

C

磁力探伤器 magnetic.flaw detector;magnetic fault finder
磁盘存储器 computer magnetic disk memory
磁盘格式化 disk formatting
磁盘驱动器 disk drive
磁石发电机 magneto
磁石检波器 magneto detector
磁头清洗带 head cleaning cassette tape
磁心存储器 core memory
磁悬浮列车 magnetic suspension train;maglev train
磁盘操作系统 disk operating system (DOS)
磁盘存储装置 magnetic storage device

雌 [cí] 形 female
雌花 female (*or* pistillate) flower
雌黄 ① orpiment ② make irresponsible remarks;wag one's tongue too freely
雌鹿 female deer
雌蕊 pistil
雌狮 lioness
雌兔 female rabbit
雌性 female
雌雄 ①male and female ②victory and defeat
雌孔雀 peahen
雌老虎 tigress
雌雄同体 hermaphroditism;monoecism
雌雄同株 monoecism
雌雄异体 gonochorism;dioecism
雌雄异株 dioecism

鸬 [cí]
◇鸬鹚 cormorant

糍 [cí]
糍粑 cooked glutinous rice pounded into paste;glutinous rice cake

Cǐ(ㄘ)

此 [cǐ] 代 ①this ②now;then;here
此岸 （佛教）this shore;temporality
此辈 people of this type;such (sort of) people
此次 this time
此地 this place;here
此后 after this;hereafter;henceforth
此间 around here;here
此刻 this moment;now;at present
此人 this person
此时 this moment;right now
此外 besides;in addition;moreover
此种 this kind
此呼彼应 as one calls out,another responds;echo and reecho
此路不通 dead end;blind alley
此起彼伏 as one falls,another rises;rise one after another

此时此地 here and now
此时此刻 at this very moment;this hour and moment
此一时,彼一时 that was one situation,and this is another;times have changed
此地无银三百两 no 300 taels of silver buried here (the sign put up by the man in a folk tale over the place where he had hidden some money)—a clumsy denial resulting in self-exposure

泚 [cǐ] Ⅰ 形 bright;clear;limpid Ⅱ 名 sweat Ⅲ 动 dip (one's brush in ink);wet

跐 [cǐ] 动 ①step on ②walk on tiptoe ➡cī

Cì(ㄘ)

次 [cì] Ⅰ 名 ① order;sequence ② stopping place on a journey;stopover ③middle Ⅱ 形 ①second;next ② shoddy;second-rate;inferior ③ hypo- Ⅲ 量 time;occasion：十三次列车 No. 13 train
次布 shoddy cloth
次等 second-class;second-rate;inferior
次第 ①order;sequence ②one after another
次货 inferior goods;substandard goods;throwout;second quality goods
次女 second daughter
次品 substandard products;defective goods;defective products
次生 secondary
次数 number of times;frequency
次序 order;sequence
次要 less important;secondary;subordinate;minor
次于 ①next to ②inferior to
次之 take second place
次大陆 subcontinent
次道德 hypo-moral
次氯酸 hypochlorous
次声波 infrasonic sound;infrasonic wave
次音速 subsonic
次级方案 subprogram
次级市场 secondary market
次级线圈 secondary coil
次轻量级 featherweight
次声武器 infrasonic weapon
次要问题 side issue
次中音号 tenor horn

伺 [cì] ➡sì
伺候 wait upon;serve

刺 [cì] Ⅰ 动 ①stab;prick;pierce ②irritate;stimulate ③ assassinate ④ spy;detect;pry;make roundabout or secret inquiries ⑤criticize Ⅱ 名 ① sting;thorn;splinter ② visiting card;

calling card ➡cī
刺柏 Chinese juniper;Taiwan juniper
刺刀 bayonet
刺耳 grating on the ear;jarring;ear-piercing; harsh
刺骨 piercing to the bones;piercing;biting
刺槐 locust (tree)
刺激 ① stimulation; stimulus; incentive ② stimulate;urge on;encourage ③ provoke; irritate;upset
刺客 assassin
刺杀 ①assassinate ②bayonet charge
刺伤 stab and wound;puncture
刺探 make roundabout or secret inquiries; pry;spy
刺网 gill net
刺猬 hedgehog
刺绣 ①embroider ②embroidery
刺眼 dazzling;offending to the eye
刺痒 itchy
刺字 ① tattoo ②(in former times) brand a criminal by tattooing
刺激物 stimulus;stimulant
刺绣品 embroidery
刺刺不休 talk incessantly;chatter on and on
刺耳的话 harsh words;sarcastic remarks
刺激反应 stimulus-response
刺激经济 stoke up/stimulate economy
刺激性毒剂 irritant agent

赐 [cì]
动 ①(of a senior person) confer;bestow ②(of the person addressed) grant;favour ③ gift;favour
赐福 blessing
赐复 please favour me with a reply
赐教 condescend to teach;grant instruction
赐予 grant;bestow

cōng（ㄘㄨㄥ）

匆 [cōng]
副 hastily;hurriedly
匆匆 hurriedly;in a rush;in haste
匆促 hastily;in a hurry
匆忙 hastily;in a hurry

囱 [cōng]
◇烟囱 chimney;funnel;stovepipe

枞 [cōng]
名 fir

葱 [cōng]
Ⅰ 名 onion;scallion Ⅱ 形 green
葱白 very light blue
葱翠 fresh green;luxuriantly green
葱花 chopped green onion
葱茏 verdant;luxuriantly green
葱绿 pale yellowish green; light green; ver- dant

葱头 onion
葱郁 verdant;luxuriantly green
葱白儿 scallion stalk
葱花饼 green onion pancake

聪 [cōng]
Ⅰ 名 ①faculty of hearing ②acute hearing
Ⅱ 形 bright;clever;intelligent
聪慧 bright;intelligent
聪明 intelligent;bright;clever
聪颖 intelligent;bright;clever
聪明才智 intelligence and wisdom
聪明伶俐 clever and sensible; clever and quick-witted
聪明反被聪明误 clever people may be victims of their own cleverness;cleverness may overreach itself
聪明一世,糊涂一时 clever all one's life but stupid this once;smart as a rule,but this time a fool

cóng（ㄘㄨㄥˊ）

从 [cóng]
Ⅰ 动 ① follow ② comply with; conform with;follow;obey ③join;be engaged in ④act in a certain manner or according to a certain principle Ⅱ 名 ①follower;attendant ②rela- tionship between cousins,etc. of the same pa- ternal grandfather,great-grandfather or a yet earlier common ancestor Ⅲ 形 secondary;ac- cessary Ⅳ 介 ① from;从今以后 from now on;in the future ②through;by;从空中 by air Ⅴ 副 ever;从来没有一件事使我生气。 Nothing ever makes me angry.
从此 from this time on; from now on; from then on;henceforth;thereupon
从动 driven
从而 thus;thereby
从犯 accessary criminal;accessary
从缓 be in no hurry;put sth off till a later time
从简 conform to the principle of simplicity
从教 be engaged in the teaching profession;be a teacher
从句 subordinate clause
从军 join the army;enlist
从来 from the past till the present;always;at all times;all along
从良 (of a prostitute) get married and start a new life
从略 be omitted
从命 do sb's bidding;comply with sb's wish; obey an order
从前 before;formerly;in the past
从权 as a matter of expediency
从戎 join the army;enlist
从容 ①calm;unhurried;leisurely ②plentiful
从事 ①go in for;be engaged in ②deal with

从属 subordinate
从俗 follow the general custom
从速 as soon as possible; without delay
从头 ① from the beginning ② anew; once again
从小 from childhood; as a child
从刑 accessary punishment
从严 on strict side (of punishment/criticism/etc.)
从业 obtain employment
从政 go into politics
从中 out of; from among; therefrom
从众 follow the populace; follow public opinion
从价税 ad valorem duties
从量税 specific duties
从兄弟 cousin of the same clan; cousin
从长计议 give the matter further thought and discussion; take one's time in reaching a decision
从古到今 from ancient times to the present; from ancient to modern times
从井救人 jump into a well to save sb who's fallen in—(originally) try to do a good deed in the wrong way; try to save sb's life at the risk of one's own
从宽处理 treat sb with leniency; be lenient in punishment
从难从严 extremely demanding and strict
从轻发落 let sb off lightly
从容不迫 calm and unhurried
从善如流 follow what is right as a stream follows its course; readily accept good advice
从上到下 from top to bottom; from the higher levels to the grass roots
从天而降 descend from heaven
从头到脚 from head to foot
从头至尾 from A to Z; from beginning to end; from cover to cover; from head to foot
从严治党 place high demands on the Party; administer the Party with strict discipline; be strict with Party members; run the Party strictly; tighten Party discipline
从严治政 run the government by high standards
从业人员 the employed; people with jobs
从一而终 be faithful to one's husband to the end; be faithful unto death
从中渔利 profit from; cash in on
从中作梗 hinder sb from carrying out a play; place obstacles in the way; put a spoke in sb's wheel
从众心理 group/mass psychology
从属信用证 subsidiary credit
从群众中来,到群众中去 come from the masses, go among the masses

丛 [cóng]
I 动 crowd together; cluster II 名 ① clump; thicket; grove ② crowd; collection III 量 bush; clump: 一丛玫瑰 a bush of rose
丛集 ① crowd together; pile up ② collected writings; a series of books
丛刊 a series of books; collection
丛林 jungle; forest
丛生 ①(of plants) grow thickly ②(of diseases, evils, etc.) break out
丛书 a series of books; collection
丛杂 motley
丛林热 jungle fever

淙 [cóng]
淙淙 gurgling

琮 [cóng]
名 long hollow piece of jade with rectangular sides

CÒU (ㄘㄡˋ)

凑 [còu]
动 ① gather together; pool; collect ② happen by chance; take advantage of ③ move close to; press near
凑合 ① gather together; collect; assemble ② improvise ③ make do ④ passable; not too bad
凑集 gather together
凑钱 pool money
凑巧 luckily; fortunately; as luck would have it
凑手 at hand; within easy reach
凑数 make up the number (*or* amount); serve as a stopgap
凑份子 club together (to present a gift to sb)
凑趣儿 ①join in (a game, etc.) just to please others ②make a joke about; poke fun at
凑热闹 ①join in the fun ②add trouble to
凑集资金 club resources

CŪ (ㄘㄨ)

粗 [cū]
I 形 ① wide (in diameter); thick ② wide (in breadth); broad; thick ③ coarse; crude; rough ④ gruff; husky ⑤ rough; unrefined ⑥ careless; negligent ⑦ rude; unpolished; vulgar II 副 slightly; roughly
粗暴 rude; rough; crude; brutal
粗笨 clumsy; unwieldy
粗鄙 vulgar; coarse
粗布 ①coarse cloth ②homespun cloth
粗糙 ①coarse; rough ②crude
粗大 ①thick; bulky ②loud
粗放 ①free and easy ②careless; slipshod ③ extensive
粗犷 ①rough; rude; boorish ②straightforward and uninhibited; bold and unconstrained; rugged
粗豪 ①forthright; straightforward ②raucous;

C

gruff;strident
粗话 vulgar language
粗活 heavy manual labour;unskilled work
粗粮 coarse food grain (e. g. maize,sorghum, millet,etc. as distinct from wheat flour and rice)
粗劣 of poor quality;cheap;shoddy
粗陋 coarse and crude
粗鲁 rough;rude;boorish
粗略 rough;sketchy
粗眉 thick (or heavy) brows
粗浅 superficial;shallow;simple
粗人 ①rough fellow;rash person ②unrefined person;boor
粗沙 coarse sand;grit
粗纱 roving
粗筛 riddle;bull screen;hurdle
粗疏 careless;inattentive
粗率 rough and careless;ill-considered
粗俗 vulgar;coarse
粗算 rough estimate or calculation
粗通 have a rough idea;know a little
粗细 ①(degree of) thickness ②crudeness or fineness;degree of finish;quality of work
粗心 careless;thoughtless
粗野 rough;boorish;uncouth
粗轧 roughing (down)
粗重 ①(of voice,etc.) loud and jarring ②big and heavy; bulky ③ thick and heavy ④ strenuous;heavy
粗壮 ① sturdy;thickset;brawny ② thick and strong ③deep and resonant
粗拙 crude;coarse
粗花呢 tweed
粗加工 rough machining;roughing
粗麻布 burlap;gunny;sacking
粗毛羊 coarse-wooled sheep
粗呢子 woolen suiting
粗纱机 fly frame
粗饲料 coarse fodder;roughage
粗线条 ① thick lines;rough outline ②rough-and-ready;slapdash
粗轧机 roughing mill
粗支纱 coarse yarn
粗制品 semifinished product
粗茶淡饭 plain tea and simple food;homely fare
粗放经营 extensive (or poor) management; low technology production of cheap products
粗具规模 be roughly in order;be roughly in shape
粗眉大眼 bushy eyebrows and big eyes;heavy features
粗声粗气 deep,gruff voice
粗梳毛纺 woollen spinning
粗梳棉纱 carded yarn

粗纹唱片 coarse groove record
粗心大意 negligent;careless;inadvertent
粗言恶语 dirty words
粗枝大叶 crude and careless;sloppy;slapdash
粗制滥造 crudely made; manufacture in a rough and slipshod way
粗中有细 there is finesse in sb's roughness; usually careless, but sometimes sharp; crude in most matters,but subtle in some
粗加工制成品 roughly processed products; simple-to-manufacture products

CÚ(ㄘㄨˊ)

徂 [cú]
勶 ①go;get ②pass;elapse ③begin;start

殂 [cú]
名 death;demise

CÙ(ㄘㄨˋ)

促 [cù]
Ⅰ 形 (of time) short;urgent;hurried Ⅱ 勶 ①urge; promote; hurry ② be close to; come near (to)
促成 help to bring about;facilitate
促进 promote;advance;accelerate
促销 promote the sale (of goods);sales promotion
促使 impel;urge;spur;precipitate
促进派 promoter of progress
促退派 promoter of retrogression
促膝谈心 sit side by side and talk intimately; have a heart-to-heart talk

猝 [cù]
形 sudden;abrupt;unexpected
猝毙 die suddenly;drop dead
猝变 sudden change
猝发 burst
猝然 suddenly;abruptly;unexpectedly
猝死 sudden death
猝倒病 damping off
猝不及防 be taken by surprise

酢 [cù]
➡ zuò
酢浆草 creeping oxalis

蔟 [cù]
名 small bundle of straw, etc. for silkworms to spin cocoons on

醋 [cù]
名 ① vinegar ② jealousy (particularly in love affairs)
醋精 vinegar concentrate
醋栗 gooseberry (the plant or its fruit)
醋酸 acetic acid
醋味 ①smell of vinegar ②feeling of jealousy
醋意 (feeling of) jealousy
醋罐子 jealous person
醋劲儿 (feeling of) jealousy;very jealous

C

醋酸酐 acetic oxide
醋酸盐 acetate
醋海生波 waves in a sea of jealousy—storms raised by a jealous woman
醋酯纤维 acetate fibre

憷 [cù] 形 uneasy; disturbed

簇 [cù] Ⅰ 动 form a cluster; pile up Ⅱ 名 cluster; pile Ⅲ 量 cluster; bunch; 一簇桃花 a bunch of peach blossoms
簇居 live in a community
簇射 shower
簇生 (of plants, flowers, etc.) grow in clusters
簇新 brand new
簇拥 cluster round

蹙 [cù] Ⅰ 形 pressed; cramped Ⅱ 动 knit (one's brows)
蹙额 frown
蹙眉 knit one's brows

蹴 [cù] 动 ①kick ②tread; strike the ground with foot
蹴鞠 kick the ball

cuān (ㄘㄨㄢ)

汆 [cuān] 动 ①quick-boil ②boil water in a small cylindrical iron pot thrust into a fire
汆子 a small, cylindrical metal pot which can be thrust into a fire to boil water quickly
汆丸子 quick-boiled meat balls with soup

攛 [cuān] 动 ①throw; fling ②jump in; throw oneself in ③do in a hurry ④fly into a rage; get into a temper; be infuriated
攛掇 urge; egg sb on
攛弄 urge; egg sb on (to do sth)

镩 [cuān] Ⅰ 名 ice pick; ice chisel Ⅱ 动 cut (or break) (ice) with an ice pick (or chisel)
镩子 ice pick

蹿 [cuān] 动 ①leap up; leap forward ②spurt; gush
蹿红 meteoric rise to stardom; become a star overnight; become instantly popular
蹿火 flare up; burn with anger
蹿升 climb sharply; soar; rise quickly
蹿稀 have loose bowels
蹿房越脊 (of swordsmen, robbers, etc. in old Chinese novels) leap from roof to roof

cuán (ㄘㄨㄢ)

攒 [cuán] 动 gather together; collect; assemble ➡ zǎn

攒聚 gather closely together; congregate
攒三聚五 (of people) gather in knots; gather in threes and fours

cuàn (ㄘㄨㄢ)

窜 [cuàn] 动 ①(of bandits, enemies, animals, etc.) flee; scurry; skedaddle ②exile; expel; banish ③change (the wording in a text, manuscript, etc.); alter
窜犯 raid; make an inroad into
窜改 alter; tamper with; falsify
窜扰 harass
窜逃 flee in disorder; scurry off
窜逐 send sb into exile
窜改账目 falsify accounts; manipulate accounts

篡 [cuàn] 动 usurp; seize illegally
篡党 usurp the leadership of a party
篡夺 usurp; seize
篡改 distort; misrepresent; tamper with; falsify
篡国 usurp state power
篡位 usurp the throne
篡夺政权 usurp state power
篡改历史 distort history

cuī (ㄘㄨㄟ)

崔 [cuī] 崔巍 lofty; towering

催 [cuī] 动 ①urge; hurry; press ②hasten; expedite; speed up
催办 press sb to do sth
催逼 press (for payment of debt, etc.)
催产 expedite child delivery; hasten parturition; induce labour (by artificial means)
催促 urge; hasten; press
催肥 fatten
催化 catalysis
催眠 lull (to sleep); hypnotize; mesmerize
催命 press sb to death
催奶 stimulate the secretion of milk; promote lactation
催青 hasten the hatching of silkworms (by adjusting temperature and humidity)
催情 induce oestrus
催生 ①(of an expectant mother's family) send gifts over to convey best wishes ②expedite child delivery; hasten parturition; induce labour (by artificial means)
催熟 accelerate the ripening (of fruit)
催泻 purgation
催债 press for payment of debt
催租 press tenant to pay rent; press for payment of rent

C

催产药 oxytocic
催化剂 catalyst；catalytic agent
催款单 prompt；prompt-note
催泪弹 tear bomb；tear-gas grenade；tear-gas bomb；tear-gas shells
催眠曲 lullaby；cradlesong
催眠术 hypnotism；mesmerism
催奶剂 galactagogue
催吐剂 emetic
催醒剂 analeptic
催泪瓦斯 CS gas
催收贷款 call in a loan

摧 [cuī] 动 break；destroy
摧残 wreck；destroy；devastate
摧毁 destroy；smash；wreck
摧折 ①break；snap ②setback
摧枯拉朽 (as easy as) crushing dry weeds and smashing rotten wood
摧眉折腰 bowing and scraping

cuǐ（ㄘㄨㄟˇ）

灌 [cuǐ] 形 ①(water) deep ②streaming with tears and snivel

璀 [cuǐ]
璀璨 bright；resplendent

皠 [cuǐ] 形 pure white；white and clean

cuì（ㄘㄨㄟˋ）

脆 [cuì] 形 ①fragile；brittle ②crisp；crunchy ③(of voice，sound，etc.) clear；crisp ④neat；tidy；crisp
脆骨 gristle (as food)
脆弱 fragile；frail；weak
脆性 brittleness

萃 [cuì] I 动 come together；assemble II 名 gathering of people；collection of things
萃集 gather；assemble
萃聚 gather；assemble
萃取 extraction
萃萃蝇 tsetse fly

啐 [cuì] 动 spit；expectorate

淬 [cuì] 动 temper by dipping (hot metal) in water，oil，chemicals，etc.；quench
淬火 quench
淬砺 temper oneself through severe trials
淬火剂 hardening agent；quenching liquid

瘁 [cuì] 形 overworked；exhausted

粹 [cuì] I 形 pure II 名 essence；the best

粹美 perfect；flawless
粹而不杂 pure and unadulterated

翠 [cuì] I 形 emerald green；green II 名 ①kingfisher ②jadeite
翠菊 China aster
翠蓝 bright blue；azure
翠绿 emerald green；jade green
翠鸟 kingfisher

cūn（ㄘㄨㄣ）

村 [cūn] I 名 ①village；hamlet ②populated area II 形 rustic；boorish；村风乡俗 customs of a rustic community
村夫 villager；countryman
村姑 village girl；country wench
村口 entrance to a village
村落 village；hamlet
村民 villager；village people
村舍 cottage
村野 ①villages；countryside ②rustic；countrified；rough
村寨 stockaded village；village
村长 village head
村镇 villages and small townships
村庄 village；hamlet
村子 village；hamlet
村办企业 village industry；village-run enterprise
村务公开 disclosure of village affairs；publicize village affairs；make public village affairs
村民委员会 villagers'committee；village committee
村民自治制度 system of self-government of villagers
村民代表会议制度 system of villagers' meetings

皴 [cūn] I 动 (of skin) be chapped (from the cold)；cracked II 名 dirt accumulated on the skin
皴裂 (of skin) be chapped from the cold

踆 [cūn] 动 ①kick ②retreat；stop；move back

cún（ㄘㄨㄣˊ）

存 [cún] 动 ①exist；live；survive ②store；preserve；keep ③accumulate；gather；collect ④deposit；save ⑤leave (for safekeeping)；check ⑥reserve；retain ⑦remain on balance；be in stock ⑧cherish；harbour
存案 register with the proper authorities
存查 file for reference
存储 memory；storage
存单 deposit receipt
存档 keep in the archives；place on file；file

存放 ①leave with;leave in sb's care ②deposit（money）
存根 counterfoil;stub
存户 depositor
存货 ① stock up ② goods in stock;existing stock;remainder
存款 deposit money（in a bank）;deposit;bank savings
存栏 livestock on hand
存盘 save
存身 take shelter;make one's home
存食 suffer from indigestion
存亡 live or die;survive or perish
存项 credit balance;balance
存心 ①cherish certain intentions ②intentionally;deliberately;on purpose
存续 exist and continue
存疑 leave a question open;leave a matter for future consideration
存在 exist;be
存折 deposit book;bankbook
存执 counterfoil;stub
存车处 parking lot（for bicycles）;bicycle park（or shed）
存储器 storage,memory
存底儿 keep the original draft;keep a file copy
存活率 survival rate
存款单 certificate of deposit
存储按钮 store key
存储程序 stored（or saved）program
存储技术 storage technology
存而不论 leave the question open
存取方式 access mode
存取控制 access control
存取周期 access cycle
存款不足 insufficient funds
存款利息 interest on deposit
存粮于民 store up grain among the people
存心不良 cherish evil designs（or intentions）

蹲 [cún]
动 hurt（one's legs or feet）while jumping ➡️ dūn

cǔn（ㄘㄨㄣˇ）

忖 [cǔn]
动 turn over in one's mind;ponder;mull over
忖度 speculate;conjecture;surmise
忖量 ①think over;turn over in one's mind ②conjecture;guess

cùn（ㄘㄨㄣˋ）

寸 [cùn]
Ⅰ 量 cun,a unit of length（1/30 metre）
Ⅱ 形 very little;very short;very small Ⅲ 副 just right（timing, exertion, way of doing, etc. for sth good or bad）;coincidentally;as luck would have it Ⅳ 名 the three places at the wrist where the pulse is taken
寸步 tiny step;single step
寸进 a little progress;small advance
寸劲 ①appropriate strength ②coincidence
寸心 ①feelings ②heart;mind
寸步不离 follow sb closely;keep close to sb;be always at sb's elbow
寸步不让 refuse to yield an inch;not budge an inch
寸步难行 be unable to move even a single step—be unable to do anything
寸草不留 leave not even a blade of grass;be devastated
寸土必争 fight for（or contest）every inch of land
寸金难买寸光阴 Money can't buy time;Time is more precious than gold.

cuō（ㄘㄨㄛ）

搓 [cuō]
动 ①rub with the hands ②twist with both hands ③chop
搓板 washboard
搓球 chopping
搓揉 rub;knead;twist
搓澡 give（or get）a rubdown with a damp towel
搓麻(将) play mahjong
搓手顿脚 wring one's hands and stamp one's feet—get anxious and impatient

磋 [cuō]
动 ①grind ivory,or other bones or horns,into utensils,implements,wares,etc. ②consult;deliberate;discuss
磋商 consult;exchange views

撮 [cuō]
Ⅰ 动 ①gather;bring together ②scoop up（with a dustpan or shovel）③pick up（powdery stuff）with fingers ④extract;summarize ⑤have a meal;eat Ⅱ 名 unit of capacity（= millilitre）Ⅲ 量 ①（of sth powdery one can pick up with one's fingers）:一撮儿芝麻 a pinch of sesame seeds/一撮白发 a tuff of white hair ②（used to indicate a tiny number）:一小撮坏人 a handful of evildoers/一小撮流氓 a small gang of gangsters ➡️ zuǒ
撮合 make a match;act as go-between
撮弄 ①make fun of;play a trick on;tease ②abet;instigate;incite
撮要 ① make an abstract;outline essential points ②abstract;synopsis;extracts

蹉 [cuō]
蹉跌 trip and fall—make a slip

蹉跎 waste time
蹉跎岁月 let time slip by accomplishing noth-
ing；idle away one's time

cuó（ㄘㄨㄛˊ）

矬 [cuó]
Ⅰ 形 short Ⅱ 动 ①bend down（the body）；
lower one's body；crouch ②cut；dock；reduce

痤 [cuó]
痤疮 acne（a skin disease）

cuò（ㄘㄨㄛˋ）

剉 [cuò]
动 cut；reap

莝 [cuò]
Ⅰ 动 chop（grass（or hay）Ⅱ 形 chopped
grass（or hay）

厝 [cuò]
Ⅰ 动 ①lay；place ②place a coffin in a temporary shelter pending burial Ⅱ 名 house
厝火积薪 a fire beneath a pile of faggots—a
hidden danger

挫 [cuò]
动 ①defeat；frustrate ②subdue；lower；de-
flate
挫败 frustrate；foil；defeat
挫伤 ① contusion；bruise ② dampen；blunt；
discourage
挫折 setback；reverse

措 [cuò]
动 ①arrange；manage；conduct；handle ②
make plans
措辞 wording；diction
措施 measure；step
措置 handle；manage；arrange
措手不及 be caught unprepared；be caught unawares
措置得当 handle properly

锉 [cuò]
Ⅰ 名 file Ⅱ 动 make smooth with a file
锉刀 file

锉屑 filing

错 [cuò]
Ⅰ 形 ① interlocked and jagged；in-
termeshed；intricate ②wrong；mistaken；erro-
neous ③bad，poor Ⅱ 动 ①grind；rub ②move
out of the way；make way；miss ③alternate；
stagger ④inlay（or plate）with gold，silver，
etc. ⑤ polish jade Ⅲ 名 ① mistake；error；
fault；demerit ②grindstone for polishing jade.
Ⅳ 介 except；but for
错爱 undeserved kindness（or favour）
错案 misjudged case
错车 one vehicle gives another the right of
way
错处 fault；demerit
错怪 blame sb wrongly
错过 miss；let slip
错会 understand wrongly
错角 alternate angle
错金 inlay with gold
错觉 illusion；misconception；wrong impression
错开 stagger
错乱 in disorder；in confusion；deranged
错落 in disorderly profusion
错失 ①let sth good slip through；lose. ②mis-
take；slip；fault
错位 dislocation；displacement
错误 ① wrong；mistaken；erroneous ② mis-
take；error；blunder
错杂 mixed；jumbled
错字 ①wrongly written character ②misprint
错综 crisscross；intricate
错别字 wrongly written（or mispronounced）
characters
错层公寓 split-level apartment
错误分析 error analysis
错误校正 error correction（EC）
错综复杂 intricate；complex
错层式住宅 split-level house
错误校正码 error correcting code

Dd

dā（ㄉㄚ）

耷 [dā]
Ⅰ 名 big ear Ⅱ 动 droop；hang down
耷拉 droop；hang down

搭 [dā]
动 ①put up；build ②hang over；lay over；put over ③join together；lap over ④throw in more（people，money，etc.）；add ⑤mixed together；in combination ⑥lift sth together ⑦take（a ship，bus，plane，etc.）；travel or go by（plane，train，etc.）
搭伴 join sb on a trip；travel together
搭车 take advantage of sth
搭乘 travel by（plane，car，ship，etc.）
搭档 ①cooperate；work together ②partner
搭话 ①make conversation；get a word in ②send word
搭伙 ①join as partner ②eat regularly in（a mess，etc.）
搭肩 ①help to shoulder sth heavy ②stand on another's shoulders
搭界 ①border on；have a common border ②have sth to do with；have connection with
搭救 rescue；go to the rescue of
搭客 ①passenger ②take on passengers
搭理 acknowledge（sb's greeting，etc.）；respond；answer
搭配 ①arrange in pairs（or groups）②collocation
搭腔 ①answer；respond ②talk to each other
搭桥 build bridge；act as a go-between
搭讪 strike up a conversation with sb；say sth to smooth over an embarrassing situation
搭售 pair unsalable goods up with goods that sell well，making the purchase of the former compulsory for anyone who wants to buy the latter
搭班子 set up a（work）team（or group）
搭架子 ①build a framework；get（an undertaking，etc.）roughly into shape ②put on airs；assume great airs
搭卖法 tie-in sale

搭桥引线 act as a go-between；bring（people，etc.）into contact

嗒 [dā]
象 clatter：马蹄嗒嗒 hoofbeats of a horse；clatter of horses' hoofs／机枪嗒嗒地响着。The machine-gun rattled away. ➡tà

答 [dā] ➡dá
答碴 put in a word
答理 respond；acknowledge sb's greeting
答腔 answer；respond
答应 ①answer；reply；respond ②agree；promise；comply with

褡 [dā]
褡包 long，broad girdle
褡裢 ①long，rectangular bag sewn up at both ends with an opening in the middle（usu. worn round the waist or across the shoulder）②jacket，made of several layers of cloth，worn by wrestlers

dá（ㄉㄚˊ）

打 [dá]
量 dozen ➡dǎ

达 [dá]
Ⅰ 动 ①go through to；extend ②reach；attain；arrive at；achieve；amount to ③understand thoroughly；be understanding ④express；convey；communicate Ⅱ 形 eminent；prominent；distinguished
达标 reach a set standard；target-hitting；up-to-standard
达成 reach（an agreement）
达旦 until dawn
达到 achieve；attain；reach
达观 take things philosophically
达人 ① intelligent，well-informed person ② person who takes everything philosophically
达意 express（or convey）one's ideas
达因 dyne
达姆弹 dumdum（bullet）
达官贵人 high officials and noble lords；VIPs

达斡尔族 Daur
达尔文主义 Darwinism

沓 [dá]
量 pile (of paper, etc.); stack ➡ tà
沓子 pile (of paper, etc.); pad

怛 [dá]
Ⅰ 形 sad; in deep sorrow; miserable Ⅱ 动 fear; be afraid
怛伤 saddened; in deep sorrow

笪 [dá]
名 ① bamboo mat ② hemp rope; tow line (for boats)

答 [dá]
动 ① answer; reply; respond ② return (a visit, etc.); repay; reciprocate ➡ dā
答案 answer; solution; key
答拜 pay a return visit (or call)
答辩 reply (to a charge, query or an argument)
答词 thank-you speech; answering speech; reply
答对 [dáduì] answer sb's question; reply
答复 answer; reply
答话 answer; reply
答卷 ① answer the questions or solve the problems in a test paper ② answer sheet ③ completed test paper
答数 answer (to an arithmetic problem)
答问 ① answer a question ② question-and-answer form of writing
答谢 express appreciation (for sb's kindness or hospitality); acknowledge
答疑 (of a teacher, speaker, etc.) answer questions
答题卡 response card
答谢词 speech of thanks; thank-you speech
答非所问 give an irrelevant answer
答记者问 press interview
答谢宴会 return banquet

鞑 [dá]
鞑靼 Tartar

dǎ (ㄉㄚˇ)

打 [dǎ]
Ⅰ 动 ① strike; hit; knock ② break; smash ③ beat; fight; attack; batter ④ deal with; come into contact with ⑤ construct; build ⑥ make (as in a smithy); forge ⑦ mix; stir; beat ⑧ tie up; pack ⑨ knit; weave ⑩ apply (sth to sth else); draw; paint; make a mark on ⑪ open; dig ⑫ raise; hoist; hold up ⑬ send; project; dispatch ⑭ issue or receive (a certificate, etc.) ⑮ remove; get rid of ⑯ ladle; draw ⑰ buy ⑱ catch; hunt: 打鱼 go fishing; catch fish ⑲ gather in; collect; reap ⑳ draw up; work out; calculate; reckon ㉑ do; engage in: 打零工 take odd jobs; be (or work as) an odd jobber / 打夜班 be on night shift ㉒ play: 打扑克 play cards ㉓ go through: 打跟跄 stagger (along) ㉔ adopt; use: 打比方 draw an analogy ㉕ label; charge: 被打成反革命 be labelled a counter-revolutionary ㉖ (as of a riddle) be about; concern: 这个谜语打一物。 The riddle is about a thing. Ⅱ 介 from; since: 打心眼里 from the bottom of one's heart ➡ dá
打靶 target (or shooting) practice
打败 ① defeat; beat; worst ② suffer a defeat; be defeated
打扮 ① dress up; make up; deck out ② way or style of dressing
打包 ① bale; pack ② unpack
打苞 (of wheat, sorghum, etc.) form ears; ear up
打杈 prune
打岔 interrupt; cut in
打场 thresh grain (on the threshing ground)
打车 take a taxi
打倒 ① knock down to the ground ② overthrow
打的 go by taxi; take a taxi
打底 ① eat sth before having a drink ② feel secure ③ lay a foundation ④ bottoming
打点 ① get (luggage, etc.) ready ② bribe officials
打掉 destroy; knock out; wipe out
打动 move; touch
打赌 bet; wager
打断 ① break ② interrupt; cut short
打发 ① send; dispatch ② dismiss; send away ③ while away (one's time)
打翻 overturn; strike down
打非 combat illegal publishing activities
打分 give a mark; mark students' papers, etc.
打稿 work out a draft
打更 sound the night watches
打埂 ridging
打工 hire out for work; do manual work (for sb temporarily); work part-time; job; odd-job
打钩 tick
打鼓 ① beat a drum ② feel uncertain (or nervous)
打拐 crack down on the abduction of women and children
打滚 roll about
打鼾 snore
打夯 ramming; tamping
打黑 ① crack down on evil forces ② combat black whistles
打滑 ① skid around ② slip (on slippery ground)
打诨 (as of a clown in a traditional opera) make a joke

打火 strike sparks from a flint;strike a light
打击 hit;strike;attack
打假 mount an attack on producers of counterfeit products;crack down on counterfeit goods; make public the dishonesty; take strong measure against fake and shoddy products
打架 come to blows;fight;scuffle
打价 bargain
打尖 ①stop for refreshment when travelling; have a snack (at a rest stop) ② topping; pinching
打浆 paper making beating
打搅 disturb;trouble
打劫 rob;plunder;loot
打结 tie a knot
打卡 punch the card
打开 ①open;unfold ②turn on;switch on
打垮 defeat completely;rout
打捞 ①get out of the water;salvage ②fishing
打雷 thunder
打擂 join in an open competition (or contest)
打理 arrange;manage
打量 ①measure with the eye;look sb up and down;size up ②think;suppose;reckon
打猎 go hunting
打乱 throw into confusion;upset
打磨 polish;burnish;shine
打牌 ①play cards or mahjong ② (in international or domestic politics) exploit for one's own end
打拼 struggle
打破 break;smash
打气 ① inflate; pump up ② bolster up (or boost) the morale;encourage;cheer up
打钎 drill a blasting hole in rock with a hammer and a drill rod
打趣 banter;tease;make fun of
打拳 shadowbox
打扰 disturb;trouble
打散 break up;scatter
打扫 sweep;clean
打闪 (of lightning) flash
打食 ①(of birds and beasts) seek food ②use medicine to aid digestion or ease constipation
打手 hired roughneck (or thug);hatchet man
打私 crack down on smuggling
打算 plan;intend
打碎 break into pieces;smash;destroy
打胎 have an (induced) abortion
打铁 forge iron;work as a blacksmith
打听 ask about;inquire about
打通 get through;open up
打头 take the lead
打退 beat back (or off);repulse
打围 encircle and hunt down (animals)

打响 ①start shooting;begin to exchange fire ②win initial success
打消 give up (an idea,etc.);dispel (a doubt, etc.)
打压 suppress
打眼 ①punch (or bore) a hole;drill ②catch the eye;attract attention
打烊 (of shops) put up the shutters;close for the night
打样 ①draw a design ②make a proof
打印 ① put a seal on; stamp ② cut a stencil and mimeograph;mimeograph ③print out
打援 attack (or ambush) enemy reinforcements
打造 forge
打战 shiver;tremble;shudder
打仗 fight;go to war;make war
打针 give (or have) an injection
打制 make (by hammering,chipping,etc.)
打中 hit the mark (or target);hit
打住 come to a halt; (in speech or writing) stop
打转 spin;rotate;revolve
打桩 pile driving;piling
打字 typewrite;type
打坐 (of a Buddhist or Taoist monk) sit in meditation
打靶场 target range
打白条 write IOUs (instead of paying cash)
打摆子 suffer from malaria
打包机 baling press
打包票 vouch for;guarantee
打冲锋 ① charge (in a battle) ② be in the vanguard
打虫药 parasiticide
打虫子 get rid of intestinal parasites or worms by taking medicine
打蛋器 egg-whisk;whisk
打底机 padding machine
打底子 ①sketch a plan, picture, etc. ② lay a foundation
打地铺 sleep on the floor;have a shakedown on the floor (or ground)
打点滴 (in nursing) put on a drip
打短工 work as a day or seasonal labourer;be a temporary worker;engage in temporary job
打盹儿 doze off;take (or have) a nap
打耳光 box sb's ears;slap sb in the face
打榧子 snap the fingers
打嗝儿 ①hiccup ②belch;burp
打工妹 employed female worker (usu. referring to a rural girl working in a city);jobber girl;casual girl labourers
打工仔 employed labourer (usu. referring to a rural young man working in a city);jobber boy

打谷场 threshing ground (*or* floor)
打官腔 speak in a bureaucratic tone; talk like a bureaucrat; stall with official jargon
打官司 ①go to court (*or* law); engage in a lawsuit ②sue squabble; resort to litigation
打光棍 remain a bachelor
打棍子 beat with a big stick—criticize unsparingly or unfoundedly; punish by harsh beating or hitting
打哈哈 make fun; crack a joke
打哈欠 yawn
打夯机 ramming machine; rammer; tamper
打火机 lighter
打江山 fight to win state power
打交道 come into (*or* make) contact with; have dealings with
打结器 fibre knotter
打瞌睡 doze off; nod
打孔机 card punch
打冷枪 ①shoot from a hiding-place; snipe ②attack in a sly way
打冷战 shudder; shiver
打卤面 noodles served with thick gravy as sauce
打埋伏 ①lie in ambush; set an ambush; ambush ②hold sth back for one's own use; keep sth in reserve
打闷棍 ①(of a robber) give sb a staggering blow with a cudgel ②give sb a stunning blow
打屁股 take sb to task; get punished
打气筒 inflater; tyre pump
打前失 (of horses or mules) stumble
打前站 act as an advance party; set out in advance to make arrangements
打秋风 try to sponge on people
打圈子 circle
打群架 engage in a gang fight
打算盘 ①calculate on an abacus ②calculate; scheme
打天下 ①(of rebels) seize state power ②win success in a big enterprise
打头炮 fire the first shot; be the first to speak or act
打头阵 fight in the van; spearhead the attack; take the lead
打下手 act as assistant
打先锋 fight in the van; be a pioneer
打雪仗 have a snowball fight; throw snowballs
打掩护 provide cover for
打样机 proof press
打夜作 work late into the night
打印件 mimeographed copy
打印机 printer
打油诗 doggerel; ragged verse
打游击 ①fight as a guerrilla ②operate like a guerrilla—work, eat, sleep, etc. at no fixed place

打圆场 mediate a dispute; smooth things over
打杂儿 do odds and ends
打砸抢 beating, smashing and looting
打招呼 ①greet sb; say hello ②notify; let sb in on sth ③warn; remind
打折扣 ①sell at a discount; give a discount ②fall short of a requirement or promise; allow a discount detract; sell at a discount
打主意 ①think of a plan; evolve an idea ②try to obtain; seek
打桩机 pile driver
打字带 typewriter ribbon
打字稿 typescript
打字机 typewriter
打字员 typist
打字纸 typing-paper
打嘴巴 slap sb's face
打嘴仗 quarrel
打抱不平 take up the cudgels for the injured party; defend sb against an injustice; be the champion of the oppressed
打草惊蛇 beat the grass and startle the snake—act rashly and alert the enemy
打成一片 become one with; identify oneself with; merge with
打打闹闹 have boisterous fun; horseplay
打得火热 be very thick with each other; be as thick as thieves
打躬作揖 bow and raise one's clasped hands in salute; fold the hands and make deep bows; bow and scrape
打击报复 retaliate; take revenge; make vindictive attacks on sb; strike back and seek revenge
打击乐器 percussion instrument
打家劫舍 loot; plunder
打假斗争 anti-fakery campaign
打捞工程 refloating (*or* salvage) operation
打捞公司 salvage company; wrecking company
打乱计划 disrupt a plan; upset a scheme
打落水狗 beat a drowning dog—completely crush a defeated enemy
打马虎眼 pretend to be ignorant of sth (in order to gloss it over); act dumb
打破常规 break away from conventions; break through conventionalities; leave the beaten track
打破僵局 break the impasse (*or* stalemate)
打破平衡 upset (*or* break) a balance
打破"三铁" break the "three iron's": iron armchairs, iron rice bowl and iron wages
打情骂俏 fool around and banter in flirtation
打入冷宫 banish (a queen or an imperial concubine) to the cold palace—consign to limbo; put on the back shelf
打水漂儿 play ducks and drakes; squander

打通关节 bribe officials in charge
打通思想 straighten out one's thinking;talk sb round
打退堂鼓 retreat;withdraw
打小报告 be an informer;whistle blowing;tell on sb
打小算盘 show petty shrewdness
打印格式 print format
打预防针 have a preventive injection—take precautions against sth;caution against
打砸抢者 smash-and-grabber
打制石器 chipped stone implement
打印机接口 printer port
打印机终端 typewriter terminal
打肿脸充胖子 slap one's face until it's swollen in an effort to look imposing—puff oneself up to one's own cost
打开天窗说亮话 frankly speaking;let's not mince matters;let's be frank and put our cards on the table
打破沙锅问到底 insist on getting to the bottom of the matter
打入十八层地狱 banish to the lowest depths of hell—condemn to eternal damnation
打印机驱动程序 printer driver
打出水平,打出风格 be at one's best in skill and style of play

dà(ㄉㄚˋ)

大 [dà]
Ⅰ 形 ①big;large;great ②(of age) old ③heavy;strong ④main;major;important;general ⑤loud;high ⑥eldest ⑦adult;major;elder ⑧your Ⅱ 副 ①to a great extent (or degree);greatly;fully ②not very;not often Ⅲ 名 ①father ②uncle ③size ➡dài

大案 major case;legal case of grave nature;serious criminal cases
大白 ①whiting ②come out;become known
大败 ①defeat utterly;put to rout ②suffer a crushing defeat
大班 ①big boss (a term for the manager of a foreign firm in old China);compradore;taipan ②top class in a kindergarten
大办 go in for sth in a big way (or on a big scale)
大半 ① more than half;greater part;most;more often than not ②most probably;most likely
大便 ①defecate;have a bowel movement;shit ②stool;human excrement;shit;faeces
大兵 common soldier
大饼 a kind of large flatbread
大伯 ①father's elder brother;uncle ②uncle (a polite form of address for an elderly man)

大部 greater part
大菜 ①last course of a feast (usu. a whole chicken or duck,or a leg of pork) ②Western-style food
大肠 large intestine
大氅 overcoat;cloak;cape
大潮 spring tide
大车 ①cart ②respectful term for an engine driver or the chief engineer of a ship
大臣 minister (of a monarchy)
大乘 Great Vehicle (a school of Buddhism);Mahayana
大虫 tiger
大锤 sledgehammer
大词 major term
大葱 green Chinese onion
大大 greatly;enormously
大胆 bold;daring;audacious
大刀 broadsword
大道 ①broad road ②way to the bright future
大灯 headlight (of a car)
大敌 formidable enemy;archenemy
大抵 generally speaking;in the main;on the whole
大地 earth;mother earth
大典 ① grand ceremony ② body of classical writings;canon
大调 major
大都 [dàdōu] mostly;for the most part
大豆 soybean;soya bean
大度 magnanimous
大端 main aspects (or features);salient points
大队 ①a military unit corresponding to the battalion or regiment;group ②production brigade (of a rural people's commune);brigade ③large body of
大多 for the most part;mostly
大鳄 big fish
大发 [dàfa] excessive;beyond the proper limits
大法 fundamental laws and principles (of a state);constitution
大凡 generally;in most cases
大方 ①expert;scholar ②generous;liberal ③natural and poised;easy;unaffected ④in good taste;tasteful
大粪 human excrement;night soil
大风 ①fresh gale ②gale;strong wind
大夫 senior official in feudal China
大副 first (or chief) mate;mate;chief officer
大概 ①general idea;broad outline ②general;rough;approximate ③probably;most likely;presumably
大干 work energetically;go all out;make an all-out effort
大纲 outline

大哥 ①eldest brother ②elder brother (a polite form of address for a man about one's own age)
大公 grand duke
大功 great merit;extraordinary service
大鼓 ① bass drum ② *dagu*, versified story sung to the accompaniment of a small drum and other instruments
大褂 unlined long gown
大观 grand sight;magnificent spectacle
大过 serious offence
大寒 Greater Cold—the last of the 24 solar terms
大好 very good;excellent
大号 ①large size;king size;large ②tuba;bass horn ③your (given) name
大亨 big shot;bigwig;magnate
大红 bright red;scarlet
大户 ① rich and influential family ② large family ③ (formerly) big clans such as wealthy,landlord families ④(now) households or units with large-scale enterprises; large-scale purchasers
大话 random remarks; big (or tall) talk; boast;bragging
大会 ① plenary session; general membership meeting ②mass meeting;mass rally
大计 major programme of lasting importance; matter of fundamental importance
大蓟 setose thistle
大家 ① great master; authority ② all; everybody
大驾 you
大奖 grand prize;top prize;big award or prize
大将 ①senior general ②high-ranking officer
大街 main street;street
大节 political integrity
大捷 great victory
大姐 ①eldest sister ②elder sister
大解 go to the lavatory (to defecate);have a bowel movement
大襟 front of a Chinese garment which buttons on the right
大净 Ghusl
大局 overall (or general, whole) situation; situation as a whole
大举 carry out (a military operation) on a large scale
大军 ①main forces;army ②large contingent
大卡 kilocalorie;large (or great) calorie
大楷 ① regular script in big characters, as used in Chinese calligraphy exercises ② block letters
大考 end-of-term examination;final exam
大课 lecture given to a large number of students;enlarged class
大款 tycoon;moneybags

大牢 prison;jail
大力 energetic;vigorous
大殓 encoffining ceremony
大梁 ridgepole;ridgepiece
大量 ① a large number; a great quantity ② generous;magnanimous
大料 aniseed
大溜 main current;main trend;greater number (of persons);majority (of the people)
大楼 multi-storied building
大路 main road
大陆 continent;mainland
大略 ①general idea;broad outline ②bold vision
大妈 ①father's elder brother's wife;aunt ② aunt (an affectionate or respectful form of address for an elderly woman)
大麻 ①hemp ②marijuana
大麦 barley
大忙 very busy
大门 entrance (or front) door;gate
大米 (husked) rice
大名 ① one's formal personal name ② your (given) name
大螟 pink rice borer
大拿 ①person with power;boss ②expert;authority
大难 catastrophe;disaster
大脑 cerebrum
大内 imperial palace
大鲵 giant salamander
大年 ① good year; bumper year; (for fruit trees) on-year ②lunar year in which the last month has 30 days ③Spring Festival
大娘 ①wife of father's elder brother;aunt ② aunt (a respectful form of address used for an elderly woman)
大牌 big wig;big name
大盘 market
大炮 ①artillery; big gun; cannon ②one who speaks boastfully or forcefully; one who noisily overstates things
大批 ① large quantities (or numbers, amounts) of ②mass
大片 blockbuster; great film; vent movie; hit movie;grand, big-budget movie;big-budget film
大气 ①atmosphere;air ②heavy breathing
大庆 ① grand celebration of an important event;great occasion ② birthday of an old person who commands respect
大秋 ①harvest season in autumn ②crops harvested in autumn;autumn harvest
大曲 ① yeast for making hard liquor ② hard liquor made with such yeast
大权 power over major issues;authority
大人 ① *used in a letter to address one's*

parents or people of an older generation ②adult;grown-up ③Your (*or* His) Excellency

大肉 pork

大厦 ①large building ②mansions (*used in names of large buildings*)

大嫂 ①eldest brother's wife;sister-in-law ②elder sister (a polite form of address for a woman about one's own age)

大赦 amnesty;general pardon

大师 ①great master;master ②Great Master (a courtesy title used to address a Buddhist monk)

大使 ambassador

大事 ①great (*or* major) event;important matter;major issue ②overall (*or* general) situation ③in a big way

大势 general trend of events

大叔 ①younger brother of one's father;uncle ②uncle (a polite form of address for a man about one's father's age)

大暑 Greater Heat—the 12th of the 24 solar terms

大水 flood;floodwater

大肆 without restraint;wantonly

大蒜 garlic

大堂 lobby (of a hotel)

大体 ①cardinal principle;general interest ②roughly;more or less;on the whole;by and large;approximately

大田 land for growing field crops

大厅 hall

大同 Great Harmony (an ideal or perfect society)

大头 ①head mask ②bigger end;main part ③spendthrift;wastrel

大腿 thigh

大王 ①magnate (*or* tycoon) of a monopoly ②master

大尉 senior captain

大喜 ①great rejoicing ②wedding

大戏 ① full-scale traditional opera ② Beijing opera

大虾 prawn

大小 ①big or small ②size ③degree of seniority ④adults and children

大校 senior colonel

大写 ①capital form of a Chinese numeral ②capitalization

大兴 go in for sth in a big way

大型 large-scale;large

大姓 ①clan ②common surname

大选 general election

大学 university;college

大雪 ①Greater Snow—the 21st of the 24 solar terms ②heavy snow

大修 overhaul;heavy repair

大牙 ①molar ②front tooth

大雅 elegance;refinement;good taste

大烟 opium

大盐 crude salt

大雁 wild goose

大洋 ①ocean ②silver dollar

大样 ①full-page proof ②detail drawing

大要 main points;gist

大爷 [dàyé] arrogant and wilful male lazybones

大爷 [dàye] ①father's elder brother;uncle ②uncle (a respectful form of address for an elderly man)

大业 great cause;great undertaking

大衣 overcoat;topcoat

大姨 mother's eldest sister;aunt

大义 cardinal principles of righteousness;righteous cause

大意 ①general idea;main points;gist;tenor ②careless;negligent;inattentive

大印 great seal—the seal of power

大油 lard

大有 ①there is much ②abundance

大雨 heavy rain

大员 high-ranking official

大院 courtyard;compound

大约 ①approximately;about ②probably

大月 greater month—a solar month of 31 days;a lunar month of 30 days

大灶 ordinary mess

大战 war;great battle

大指 thumb

大志 high aim; lofty aim; exalted ambition; high aspirations

大治 great order

大致 roughly;approximately;more or less

大众 masses; people; general public; broad masses of people

大洲 continent

大宗 ①a large amount (*or* quantity) ②staple

大作 ①your writing ②spring up;break out

大白菜 Chinese cabbage

大白话 colloquial speech

大白天 broad daylight;daytime

大板车 large flatbed tricycle

大包干 all-round contract system; lump-sum appropriation operation; contract on large scale

大包装 economy size

大本营 ①supreme headquarters ②base camp

大变样 a sea change

大辩论 great (*or* mass) debate

大兵团 large troop formation

大不了 ①at the worst; if the worst comes to the worst ②alarming;serious

大部头 voluminous work

大车店 inn for carters

大酬宾 sale with big discount; give big discount or preferential treatment on a large scale

大出血 ① massive hemorrhage ② bargain sale; big spending

大袋鼠 kangaroo

大道理 ① major principle; general principle; great truth ②empty talk; extravagant talk

大订单 maxi-order

大动脉 ① main artery; aorta ② main line of communication; main communications artery

大毒枭 drug baron

大多数 great majority; vast majority; the bulk

大法官 justice

大方向 general orientation

大风子 chaulmoogra

大幅度 by a wide margin; by a big margin; substantially

大腹贾 potbellied merchant; rich merchant

大哥大 ①cellular phone; mobile phone ②man with power; boss; rich person; powerful person

大革命 great revolution

大公国 grand duchy

大公司 corporate giant; conglomerate

大功率 high-power

大姑子 husband's elder sister; sister-in-law

大规模 large-scale; extensive; massive; mass

大锅饭 food prepared in a large canteen cauldron; mess

大合唱 cantata; chorus

大后方 ①rear area ②areas under KMT rule during the War of Resistance Against Japan

大后年 three years from now

大花脸 ①character with painted facial makeup in traditional Chinese opera, specializing in singing ②dirty funny face; besmirched face

大环境 overall situation; social, political and economic environment

大黄蜂 hornet

大黄鱼 large yellow croaker

大茴香 anise; star anise

大伙儿 we all; you all; everybody

大集体 big collective

大家庭 big family; extended family; community

大减价 sale; sale price; big bargain price; inflation busters; grand (*or* opening) sales; radical reduction; great reduction in price

大奖赛 prize-giving competition; contest with big awards

大教堂 cathedral

大姐大 woman with power; female boss

大静脉 vena cava

大救星 great liberator; saviour

大舅子 wife's elder brother; brother-in-law

大块头 fat person; person of big build; fatty

大括弧 brace

大老粗 uncouth fellow; uneducated person; rough and ready fellow

大礼拜 two-day weekend (in contrast with one day off)

大礼堂 big assembly hall; auditorium

大理石 marble

大力士 man of unusual strength, esp. a weight-lifter

大丽花 dahlia

大路货 popular goods of dependable quality

大陆货 generic stuff; goods of average quality; popular goods of dependable quality; popular and inexpensive commodities; run-of-the-mill goods

大陆架 continental shelf

大陆桥 continental bridge; land bridge

大满贯 Grand Slam

大忙人 busy bee

大帽子 big hat—an exaggerated epithet used to categorize a person; unwarranted charge; political label

大面儿 general appearance; surface

大拇指 thumb

大脑脚 cerebral peduncle

大年夜 Lunar New Year's Eve

大农业 greater agricultural industry; macro-agriculture; multi-form agriculture

大拍卖 sell at a bargain

大排档 side walk snack eatery; roadside food stall or restaurant

大棚菜 vegetables grown in big plastic tents

大篷车 ①(covered) wagon ②covered truck or lorry (for carrying goods); caravan

大披肩 (in ancient Greece or Rome) pallium

大谱表 great stave

大气层 atmospheric layer; atmosphere

大气电 atmospheric electricity

大气候 general tendency; general political climate; macroclimate

大气压 atmospheric pressure; atmosphere

大前年 three years ago

大前提 major premise

大前天 three days ago

大趋势 general trend of events

大犬座 Canis Major

大人物 important person; great personage; big shot; VIP

大容量 large capacity

大撒把 totally laissez-faire

大扫除 general cleaning; thorough cleanup

大少爷 ① eldest son (of a rich family) ② spoilt son of a rich family; spendthrift

大舌头 a thick-tongued person; one who lisps; lisper

大赦令 Act of Oblivion
大婶儿 aunt（an affectionate or respectful form of address for a woman about one's mother's age）
大牲口 draught animal
大师傅 cook；chef
大使馆 embassy
大使衔 ambassadorial rank
大事记 chronicle of events；record of important events
大手笔 ①work of a well-known writer ②well-known writer
大手术 major operation
大苏打 sodium thiosulfate；sodium hyposulfite；hypo
大踏步 in big strides
大特写 big close-up（BCU）
大提琴 violoncello；cello
大头菜 rutabaga
大头针 pin
大团圆 ①happy reunion ②happy ending
大腕(儿) ①star（usu. referring to actors, singers, etc.）②past master；master-hand
大问题 major issue；big problem
大无畏 dauntless；utterly fearless；indomitable
大五码 BIG-5 code
大西北 Northwest China；the great, vast Northwest
大西洋 Atlantic（Ocean）
大协作 large-scale cooperation；major pooling of efforts
大猩猩 gorilla
大行星 major planet
大熊猫 giant panda
大熊座 Ursa Major；the Great Bear
大学生 university（or college）student
大循环 systemic circulation
大烟鬼 opium addict
大洋洲 Oceania；Oceanica
大姨子 wife's elder sister；sister-in-law
大音阶 major scale
大元帅 generalissimo
大运河 the Grand Canal
大杂烩 hodgepodge；hotchpotch
大丈夫 true man；real man；man
大中型 large-and-medium-sized
大众化 popularize
大主教 archbishop
大自然 nature
大字报 big-character poster
大作家 major（or important）writer
大案要案 major cases
大笔一挥 with one stroke of the pen
大病统筹 comprehensive arrangement for serious disease
大步流星 with vigorous strides
大材小用 large material put to small use—

one's talent wasted on a petty job；not do justice to sb's talents
大操大办 make large-scale arrangements（for a marriage or funeral）
大肠杆菌 colon bacillus
大吵大闹 make a scene；set up a terrific racket
大吃大喝 eat and drink to one's heart's content；eat and drink extravagantly；belly-worship；extravagant wining and dining；gulp and glut
大吃一惊 be greatly surprised；be quite taken aback
大处落墨 concentrate on the key points
大吹大擂 make a great fanfare；make a big noise；beat the drum；completely mistaken；drop the ball；be all wet；make a gross error
大醇小疵 sound on the whole though defective in details
大慈大悲 infinitely compassionate and merciful
大错特错 completely mistaken；absolutely wrong
大打出手 come to blows；get into a fight；all-out fistfight；get into a free-for-all
大大咧咧 careless；casual
大胆创新 dare to innovate
大刀阔斧 bold and resolute；drastic
大堤溃决 breaching of the main dike；dyke burst
大敌当前 faced with formidable foe
大动干戈 go to war；get into a fight
大动肝火 fly into a rage；be furious；be very angry
大而无当 large but impractical；unwieldy
大发雷霆 be furious；fly into a rage；bawl at sb angrily
大放厥词 talk a lot of nonsense；spout a stream of empty rhetoric
大放异彩 yield unusually brilliant results
大风大浪 wind and waves；great storms
大腹便便 potbellied；big-bellied
大干快上 get going and go all out
大公无私 ①selfless；unselfish ②perfectly impartial
大功告成 be brought to successful completion；be accomplished；be crowned with success
大骨节病 Kaschin-Beck disease
大国外交 great-power politics
大海捞针 fish for a needle in the ocean；look for a needle in a haystack
大喊大叫 ①shout at the top of one's voice ②conduct vigorous propaganda
大好河山 beautiful rivers and mountains（of a country）；one's beloved country
大轰大嗡 make a terrific din；raise a hue and cry

大祸临头 disaster is imminent; disaster is hanging over one; a calamity is about to happen

大惑不解 be extremely puzzled; be unable to make head or tail of sth

大吉大利 good luck and great prosperity (an expression of good wishes)

大家闺秀 girl from a good family; well-bred girl; lady

大检查官 procurator

大街小巷 streets and lanes

大惊失色 turn pale with fright

大惊小怪 be surprised or alarmed at sth quite normal; make a fuss about nothing

大跨径桥 long-span bridge

大块文章 lengthy article

大快人心 (usu. of the punishment of an evil-doer) affording general satisfaction; most gratifying to the people; to the immense satisfaction of the people

大力扣杀 hammer

大量订购 huge order

大量生产 mass production

大龄青年 adult single; single youth above the normal matrimonial age

大陆板块 continental margin

大陆漂移 continental drift

大麻文化 pot culture

大马哈鱼 chum salmon; dog salmon

大名鼎鼎 famous; celebrated; well-known

大鸣大放 free airing of views

大谬不然 entirely wrong; grossly mistaken

大模大样 in an ostentatious manner; with a swagger

大难临头 with great disaster hanging over one; be faced with imminent disaster (or catastrophe)

大脑半球 cerebral hemisphere

大脑皮层 cerebral cortex

大逆不道 treason and heresy; worst offence; greatest outrage

大年初一 first day of the lunar year; Lunar New Year's Day

大陪审团 grand jury

大批定货 extension order

大起大落 great fluctuations; drastic fluctuations; sharp fluctuations; sharp rise and fall; marked ups and downs

大气臭氧 atmospheric ozone

大气干扰 atmospheric interference

大气环流 atmospheric circulation; general circulation of atmosphere

大气科学 atmospheric sciences

大气磅礴 of great momentum; powerful; grand and magnificent

大气污染 air (or atmospheric) pollution

大气折射 atmospheric (or astronomical) refraction

大器晚成 great vessels take years to produce—great minds mature slowly

大千世界 boundless universe

大秋作物 crops sown in spring and reaped in autumn; autumn-harvested crops

大权独揽 centralize power in one person's hands; have sole power; arrogate all authority to oneself

大权旁落 lose one's power to others (usu. one's subordinates); power has fallen into the hands of others

大权在握 with power in one's hands; wield the scepter

大厦将倾 a great mansion on the point of collapse—the situation is hopeless

大煞风景 utterly spoil the fun

大声疾呼 raise a cry of warning; loudly appeal to the public

大失所望 greatly disappointed; to one's great disappointment

大是大非 major matters of principle; cardinal questions of right and wrong

大势所趋 trend of the times; general trend; the situation is hopeless; the game is as good as lost; it's all up with sb

大势已去 the situation is hopeless; the game is as good as lost; it's all up with sb

大手大脚 wasteful; extravagant

大书特书 record in letters of gold; write volumes about; write elaborately

大肆挥霍 be flush with money; splash one's money out; launch out

大肆宣扬 indulge in unbridled propaganda for; give enormous publicity to

大肆渲染 enormously exaggerate; play up

大田作物 field crop

大庭广众 (before) a big crowd; (on) a public occasion

大同小异 much the same but with minor differences; alike except for slight differences; very much the same; similar with minor differences; much the same but with minor (or slight) differences

大喜过望 be delighted that things are better than one expected

大显身手 display one's skill to the full; give full play to one's abilities; distinguish oneself; give a good account of oneself

大显神通 give full play to one's remarkable skill (or abilities); display one's prowess

大相径庭 widely divergent; entirely different; poles apart

大写锁定 caps lock

大兴水利 large-scale building of water conservancy

大兴土木 go in for large-scale construction; be

busy putting up buildings
大型会议 bull session
大型客机 airliner
大型企业 large enterprises
大雪封山 heavy snow has sealed the mountain passes
大言不惭 brag unblushingly; talk big
大摇大摆 strutting; swaggering
大义凛然 inspiring awe by upholding justice; with stern righteousness
大义灭亲 uphold righteousness above family; place righteousness above loyalty to one's family; sacrifice ties of blood to righteousness
大有可为 be well worth doing; have bright prospects
大有人在 there are plenty of such people; such people are by no means rare
大有文章 there's sth behind all this; there's more to this than meets the eye
大有作为 have full scope for one's talents; be able to develop one's ability to the full; have great possibilities
大鱼大肉 plenty of meat and fish
大杂院儿 compound occupied by many households
大张旗鼓 on a grand scale; in a big way
大政方针 fundamental policy (of a state); major policy
大智若愚 a man of great wisdom often seems slow-witted
大众传播 mass communication
大众媒体 mass media
大专院校 universities and colleges; institutions of higher education
大赚一笔 grab the biz
大地测量学 geodesy
大地构造学 tectonics
大地水准面 geoid
大规模集成 large scale integration
大规模开发 large-scale development
大规模生产 mass (or large-scale, full-scale) production
大汉族主义 Han chauvinism
大旱望云霓 long for a rain cloud during a drought—look forward to relief from distress
大经贸战略 broadly-based foreign trade and economic cooperation strategy; comprehensive strategy of foreign trade and economic cooperation
大陆法体系 civil law system; continental legal system; continental law system
大陆性气候 continental climate
大面积丰收 bumper harvest over an extensive area
大面积滑坡 wide-spread decline

大民族主义 big-nationality chauvinism; great-nation chauvinism; great-nationality chauvinism
大男子主义 male chauvinism
大农业观念 think in terms of the greater agricultural industry
大使级会谈 talks at ambassadorial level; ambassadorial talks
大踏步前进 march forward with long strides; make great strides (or progress)
大巡回法庭 Grand Assize
大中型企业 large and medium-sized enterprises
大众消费品 large-scale goods
大白天说梦话 daydream talk; sheer nonsense
大爆炸宇宙论 Big Bang Theory; big bang cosmology
大国沙文主义 great-nation chauvinism; great-power chauvinism; big-nation chauvinism
大国一致原则 principle of unanimity of the Five Powers (i.e. the five permanent members of the Security Council of the United Nations)
大楼封顶仪式 topping-out ceremony of a building
大屏幕电视机 large-screen monitor
大气监测系统 atmospheric monitoring system
大兴问罪之师 angrily point an accusing finger at; scathingly condemn
大型促销活动 large-scale promotion activities
大学生运动会 university games; Universiade
大亚湾核电站 the Daya Bay Nuclear Power Plant
大中华经济区 Greater China Economic Zone
大众汽车公司 (Germany) Volkswagen Automobile Plant
大宗商品出口 export of commodities in large amounts
大规模改造工程 large-scale revamping
大规模集成电路 large-scale integrated circuit; LSI circuit
大黄蜂式战斗机 Hornet jet
大树底下好乘凉 a big tree affords good shade; an influential friend, relative or mentor provides protection and help
大型电视系列片 max-series; full-length TV series; long-running series
大棒加胡萝卜政策 stick-and-carrot policy; policy of stick and carrot
大规模杀伤性武器 weapons of mass destruction; mass-kill weapons
大屏幕投影电视机 large-screen television projector
大学英语六级考试 CET-6 (College English Test Band Six)
大学英语四级考试 CET-4 (College English Test Band Four)

大处着眼，小处着手 keep the general goal in sight while taking hold of the daily tasks

大难不死，必有后福 After surviving a great disaster, one is bound to have good fortune in later years.

大事化小，小事化了 reduce major issues to minor ones and minor ones to nothing; turn big problems into small ones and small ones into no problems at all

D

汰 [dà]
㊛ wash; rinse

da（·ㄉㄚ）

垯[da]
◇垃垯 ①mound; knoll ②pimple; lump; knot

跶[da]
◇蹦跶 bounce about; jump about

dāi（ㄉㄞ）

呆 [dāi]
Ⅰ ㊝ ① slow-witted; dull; dumb; blunt ② blank; wooden; dumbstruck Ⅱ ㊛ stay
呆板 stiff and awkward; rigid; not natural; inflexible
呆傻 mentally sluggish
呆账 doubtful account; dead loan; uncollectible account; doubtful debt; bad loan; bad debt; bad account
呆滞 ①dull ②idle; sluggish; slack; stagnant
呆子 idiot; simpleton; blockhead
呆小症 cretinism
呆若木鸡 dumb as a wooden chicken; dumbstruck; transfixed (with fear or amazement)
呆头呆脑 stupid-looking
呆性物质 inert material
呆滞贷款 dead loan; bad loan
呆滞存货 inactive stock; slow-moving inventory
呆滞库存 inert inventory; inactive stock
呆滞商品 unsalable commodity; drug on the market
呆滞市场 stagnant market; sluggish market
呆滞资产 slow assets

dǎi（ㄉㄞ）

歹 [dǎi]
㊝ bad; evil; vicious
歹毒 sinister and vicious
歹人 villain; gangster or robber; criminal
歹徒 scoundrel; ruffian; evildoer
歹心 malice; malicious intent
歹意 malice; malicious intent

逮 [dǎi]
㊛ capture; catch ⇒dài

傣 [Dǎi]
傣族 Dai ethnic group; the Dais

dài（ㄉㄞ）

大 [dài]
⇒dà
大夫 doctor; physician
大黄 Chinese rhubarb
大王 [dàiwang] great king (a term of address for a king or a bandit chief)

代 [dài]
Ⅰ ㊛ ①take the place of; be in place of; be a substitute for ②act for Ⅱ ㊐ ①historical period or era ②dynasty ③generation ④era
代办 ①do sth for sb; act on sb's behalf; manage on behalf of another ②chargé d'affaires
代笔 write (a letter, etc.) for sb; be a ghost writer
代表 ①deputy; delegate; representative ②represent; stand for ③ on behalf of; in the name of
代步 ride instead of walk
代词 pronoun
代沟 generation gap
代购 buy on sb's behalf; act as a purchasing agent
代管 manage on behalf of another
代号 code name
代价 price; cost
代课 take over a class for an absent teacher
代劳 do sth for sb; take trouble on sb's behalf
代理 ①act on behalf of sb in a responsible position ②act as agent (or proxy, procurator)
代码 code
代庖 do what is sb else's job; act in sb's place
代培 train on contract; be commissioned to train
代签 per pro (per procuration)
代售 be commissioned to sell sth (usu. as a sideline); sale on commission/by proxy; sell goods on a commission basis; act as a commission agent
代数 algebra
代替 replace; substitute for; take the place of
代为 on behalf of; for (sb)
代销 sell goods (for the state) on a commission basis; be commissioned to sell sth (usu. as a sideline); act as a commission agent
代谢 ①supersession ②metabolize
代行 act on sb's behalf
代序 article used in lieu of a preface (or by way of introduction)

代用 substitute
代孕 surrogacy
代职 hold a position in an acting capacity
代办处 Office of the Chargé d'Affaires
代办所 agency
代表权 representation
代表团 delegation;mission;deputation
代表性 representativeness
代表作 representative work
代价券 scrip
代金券 coupons
代理权 agency right;procuration;power of attorney;franchise;dealership
代理人 agent;deputy;proxy;procurator;attorney;mandatory
代理业 factorage
代理制 agent system
代培生 student recruited or trained for an organization;trainee on contract;student enrolled on contract with a work unit
代乳粉 milk powder substitute
代收款 agency receipt,collection for others
代谢病 metabolic disease
代谢期 metabolic stage
代谢物 metabolite
代言人 spokesman;mouthpiece
代议制 representative system (of government)
代用品 substitute;ersatz;stand-in
代字号 swung dash (～)
代办进口 importing on customer's behalf
代办律师 commission merchant
代表大会 congress;representative assembly (or conference)
代表人物 representative figure (or personage);typical representative;leading exponent
代表样本 representative sample
代表资格 qualifications of a representative
代垫款项 advance money for
代际公平 intergenerational equity
代理厂长 acting manager of a factory
代理关系 agency relation
代理贸易 commission trade
代理业务 agent service
代码检验 code check (or inspection)
代码图像 code image
代码文件 code file
代码系统 coding system
代内公平 generational equity
代人受过 suffer for the faults of another;bear the blame for sb else;be made a scapegoat
代数方程 algebraic equation
代位继承 succession by deceased heir's descendants
代谢作用 metabolism
代行职权 function in acting capacity

代孕母亲 surrogate mother
代购代销点 purchasing and marketing agency;commission agency;supply and marketing centre
代理人酬金 agent's remuneration
代理委托书 power of attorney
代表资格审查委员会 (delegates') credentials committee

带 [dài]
Ⅰ 图 ① belt; band; ribbon; girdle; tape ② tyre ③ zone; area; belt ④ leucorrhoea; whites Ⅱ 动 ① take; bring; carry ② do in passing or by the way; do incidentally ③ bear; have; reveal; show ④ contain; hold; have sth attached ⑤ lead; head; supervise ⑥ look after; bring up; raise ⑦ drive; promote; give impetus to
带病 in spite of illness
带材 strip
带操 gymnastics with ribbons
带电 electrified; live; charged
带动 ① drive; put in motion ② spur on; bring along
带钢 strip steel
带劲 ① energetic; forceful ② interesting; exciting; wonderful
带锯 band saw
带宽 bandwidth
带累 implicate; involve; get sb into trouble
带领 lead; guide
带路 show (or lead) the way; act as a guide
带速 tape speed
带头 take the lead; be the first; take the initiative; set an example
带音 voiced
带鱼 hairtail
带职 retain one's post during absence from duty
带子 belt; girdle; ribbon; band; tape
带电体 charged (or electrified) body
带菌者 carrier
带路人 guide
带头人 foregoer; person who plays a leading role or sets an example
带头羊 bellwether
带徒弟 train (or take on) an apprentice
带信儿 take or bring a message
带穿孔机 tape punch
带电粒子 charged particle
带电作业 live-wire work
带头科学 pioneering science
带薪产假 paid maternity leave
带研究生 direct postgraduates; be a tutor of postgraduates
带状疱疹 herpes zoster; zoster
带处理装置 tape processing unit
带式干燥器 belt drier; band drier
带式提升机 belt elevator; band elevator

D

殆 [dài]
I 名 danger II 副 almost;nearly

贷 [dài]
I 名 loan;credit II 动 ①borrow;lend ② shift (responsibility);shirk ③pardon;mercy
贷方 bookkeeping credit side;credit
贷款 ①provide (or grant) a loan;extend credit to;make an advance to ②loan;credit
贷记卡 credit card
贷款人 accommodator;credit receiver
贷学金 loan for students;student loan
贷款担保 security of loan
贷款规模 volume of credit
贷款结构 loan mix
贷款利率 lending rate
贷款凭单 credit memo
贷款期限 length of maturity;terms of a loan
贷款条件 conditions for a loan
贷款投放 deployment of loans
贷款拖欠 loan delinquency
贷款限额 credit quota/ceiling;basic credit line ceiling;maximum of loan;highest amount to lend or to be lent out
贷款协议 loan agreement
贷款业务 lending programme
贷款余额 outstanding bank credit/loans
贷款种类 types of loans
贷款诈骗罪 crime of loan frauds

待 [dài]
动 ①treat;deal with ②entertain ③wait for;await ④need ⑤be going to;be about to
待到 by the time;when
待岗 be on a waiting post;unemployed and waiting for a new post;job-waiting
待考 need checking;remain to be verified
待客 receive guests;entertain guests
待命 await orders;stand-by
待聘 await appointment;position wanted
待续 to be continued
待业 job-waiting;unemployed;waiting for job assignment
待遇 ①treatment;reception ②remuneration; pay;wages;salary
待机时间 standby time
待机行事 wait for an opportunity to act
待价而沽 wait to sell at a good price;wait for the highest bid
待聘人员 members waiting for engagement
待人处世 way one treats people and conducts oneself in society
待人接物 way one gets along with people
待业保险 unemployment insurance;insurance for awaiting occupation;employment-pending insurance
待业青年 job-seeking (or awaiting) youth
待字闺中 (of a girl) staying in the boudoir waiting to be betrothed—not yet betrothed

怠 [dài]
形 ①idle;lax;slack;negligent ②slighting; disrespectful;rude
怠惰 idle;lazy;indolent
怠工 slow down;go slow
怠慢 ①cold-shoulder;slight ② used by the host at the end of a reception, etc.:怠慢了! I'm afraid I have been a poor host!

袋 [dài]
I 名 bag;sack;pocket,pouch II 量 sack; bag;packet;一袋白糖 a bag (or packet) of sugar
袋兽 marsupial
袋鼠 kangaroo
袋装 in bags
袋子 sack;bag
袋泡茶 teabag
袋传送器 pocket conveyor
袋装奶粉 milk powder in bags

逮 [dài]
动 ①reach ②arrest ➡dǎi
逮捕 arrest;take into custody;make an arrest
逮捕证 arrest warrant
逮捕法办 arrest and deal with according to law;bring to justice

戴 [dài]
动 ①put on;wear;don ②respect;honour; esteem;support
戴胜 hoopoe
戴孝 wear mourning for a parent, relative, etc.;be in mourning
戴绿帽 be a cuckold
戴帽子 be branded as;be labelled
戴高帽子 ①flatter;lay it on thick;receive flattery ②wear a tall paper hat (as a mark of shame);wear a dunce's cap
戴帽下达 tasks/quotas assigned for a specific purpose or to a specific person or institution
戴罪立功 atone for one's crimes by doing good deeds;redeem oneself by good service; atone for mistake by meritorious service

黛 [dài]
名 black pigment used by women in ancient times to paint their eyebrows
黛绿 dark green

dān (ㄉㄢ)

丹 [dān]
I 形 red II 名 ①cinnabar ②pellet;powder pill
丹毒 erysipelas
丹方 folk prescription;home remedy
丹枫 red maple
丹凤 red phoenix
丹桂 orange osmanthus
丹麦 Denmark

D

丹皮 the root bark of the tree peony
丹青 red and green colours—painting
丹田 the pubic region
丹心 a loyal heart;loyalty
丹顶鹤 red-crested crane;red-crowned crane
丹凤眼 slanting eyes
丹麦人 Dane
丹麦语 Danish (language)

担 [dān]
⽥ ①carry on a shoulder pole ②take on;undertake;shoulder ➡ dàn
担保 assure;guarantee;vouch for
担待 ①be magnanimous;be tolerant ②bear the responsibility
担当 take on;undertake;assume
担负 bear;shoulder;take on;be charged with
担纲 play a major role
担架 stretcher;litter
担任 assume the office of;hold the post of
担心 worry;feel anxious
担忧 worry;be anxious
担保金 bail;bond
担保期 period of guarantee
担保人 guarantor;guarantee
担保书 deed of security;letter of indemnity
担不起 ①be unable to shoulder (the responsibility);be unequal to (a task) ②I really don't deserve this;you flatter me
担不是 take the blame
担风险 run risks
担责任 shoulder responsibility;take the blame
担重担 bear a heavy burden;carry the ball
担保承兑 acceptance on security
担保抵押 guaranteed/secured mortgage;loan mortgage
担保公司 bonding company
担保企业 guarantor enterprise
担保信贷 secured credit
担当罪名 bear the guilt
担惊受怕 feel alarmed;be in a state of anxiety
担任公职 hold public posts;be a civil servant

单 [dān]
Ⅰ 形 ① one;single ② odd ③ simple ④ weak;thin ⑤ unlined or unpadded (clothes) Ⅱ 副 ①singly;alone ②only;alone;solely Ⅲ 名 ①sheet ②bill;list ➡ chán
单摆 simple pendulum
单板 veneer
单帮 a travelling trader working on his own
单边 unilateral
单薄 ①(of clothing) thin ②thin and weak;frail ③insubstantial;flimsy;thin
单产 per unit area yield
单车 bicycle
单程 one way
单纯 ①simple;pure ②alone;purely;merely
单词 ① individual word;word ② single-mor-

pheme word
单打 singles
单单 only;alone
单刀 ① short-hilted broadsword ② single-broadsword event
单调 monotonous;dull;drab
单独 alone; by oneself; on one's own; single-handed;independent
单发 single shot
单方 folk prescription;home remedy
单飞 solo flight
单幅 single width
单干 ①work on one's own;go it alone;work by oneself;do sth single-handed ②individual farming
单杠 ①horizontal bar ②horizontal bar gymnastics
单轨 single track
单号 odd numbers (of tickets,seats,etc.)
单价 ①unit price ②univalent
单键 single bond
单句 simple sentence
单据 documents attesting to the giving or receiving of money,goods,etc.,such as receipts,bills,vouchers and invoices
单卡 single cassette deck
单跨 single span
单利 simple interest
单恋 unrequited love
单亲 single parent
单日 odd-numbered days (of the month)
单弱 thin and weak;frail
单色 monochromatic
单身 ①unmarried;single ②not be with one's family;live alone
单式 bookkeeping single entry
单数 ①odd number ②singular number
单丝 monofilament
单瘫 monoplegia
单糖 monose;monosaccharide
单体 monomer
单条 a vertically-hung scroll of painting or calligraphy (not in a set);wall scroll
单位 ①unit (as a standard of measurement) ②unit (as an organization,department,division,section,etc.)
单线 ①single line ②one-way (contact);single-line (link) ③single track
单相 single-phase;monophase
单向 one-way;unidirectional
单项 individual event
单斜 monocline
单选 single choice
单眼 simple eye
单叶 simple leaf
单一 single;unitary
单衣 unlined garment

单赢 win-lose
单元 unit
单子 ①list；bill；form ②bed sheet
单字 ① individual character（of the Chinese language）② separate word（of a foreign language）
单倍体 monoploid；haploid
单纯词 single-morpheme word
单打一 ① concentrate on one thing only ② have a one-track mind
单方面 one-sided；unilateral
单峰驼 one-humped camel；dromedary；Arabian camel
单个儿 ①individually；alone ②an odd one
单簧管 clarinet
单季稻 single cropping of rice
单间儿 separate room（in a hotel，restaurant，etc.）
单脚跳 hop
单晶硅 monocrystalline silicon
单晶体 monocrystal
单孔目 Monotremata
单宁酸 tannic acid
单片机 single-chip microcomputer
单人床 single bed
单人房 single-bed room
单人舞 solo dance
单色光 monochromatic light
单色画 monochrome（painting）
单身汉 unmarried man；bachelor；bachelor quarters
单生花 solitary flower
单位圆 unit circle
单位制 system of unit
单细胞 unicellular
单相思 unrequited love
单行道 single track
单行本 ①separate edition ②offprint
单行线 one-way road
单性花 unisexual flower
单眼皮 single-edged eyelid
单一税 single tax
单翼机 monoplane
单音词 monosyllabic word；monosyllable
单元楼 apartment building；block of flats
单本位制 monometallic standard；monometallism
单边废除 unilateral denunciation
单边贸易 unilateral trade
单边条约 unilateral treaty
单刀直入 come straight to the point；speak out without beating about the bush
单方行为 unilateral transaction，unilateral juristic act
单级火箭 single-stage rocket
单口相声 one-man comic talk
单轮射箭 single round archery

单门独户 house（or apartment）for one family
单片眼镜 monocle
单枪匹马 single-handed；all by oneself；alone
单亲家庭 one-parent family；single-parent family
单人牢房 cell
单身贵族 single aristocrat；single noble
单身母亲 bachelor mother
单身宿舍 quarters for unmarried men or women
单位犯罪 crimes committed by organizations
单位会员 work-unit/group member
单位价值 unit profit
单位利润 unit profit
单向否决 item veto
单向付费 pay for the air time for either incoming calls or outgoing calls
单行法规 special（or separate）regulations
单行条例 specific regulations
单性生殖 parthenogenesis；parthenogenetic propagation（or reproduction）
单一汇率 unified（or single）foreign exchange rate
单一货币 single currency
单一经济 single-product economy
单一市场 single market
单一种植 monoculture；one-crop farming；single cropping
单渣操作 single-slag practice
单座飞机 single-seater（aeroplane）
单程清棉机 single process scutcher
单独关税区 separate customs territory
单方面裁军 unilateral disarmament
单克隆抗体 monoclonal antibody
单片处理机 single-chip processor
单色胶印机 single-colour offset press
单体计算机 all-in-one computer
单细胞动物 unicellular animal
单子叶植物 monocotyledon
单一标志商店 only shop
单一分配制度 single-mode system of wealth distribution
单丝不成线，孤树不成林 one strand of silk doesn't make a thread；one tree doesn't make a forest

耽 ［dān］
〔动〕①delay ②abandon oneself to；indulge in
耽搁 ①stop over；stay ②delay
耽酒 be a heavy drinker；indulge in（or be addicted to）drinking
耽误 delay；hold up
耽于游乐 indulge in merry-making

殚 ［dān］
〔动〕devote；exhaust
殚力 spare no effort；stint no effort
殚心 devote oneself heart and soul to；be dedi-

cated to

殚精竭虑 tax one's ingenuity; rack (*or* cudgel) one's brains

dǎn (ㄉㄢˇ)

胆 [dǎn]
〈名〉① gallbladder ② courage; guts; bravery ③ bladder-like inner container
胆大 bold; audacious
胆矾 chalcanthite; blue vitriol
胆敢 dare; have the audacity to
胆管 bile duct
胆寒 be terrified; be struck with terror
胆碱 choline
胆量 courage; guts; pluck; spunk
胆略 courage and resourcefulness
胆囊 gallbladder
胆怯 timid; cowardly
胆石 cholelith; gallstone
胆识 courage and insight
胆酸 cholic acid
胆小 timid; cowardly
胆汁 bile
胆子 courage; guts; nerve
胆固醇 cholesterol
胆管炎 cholangitis
胆红素 bilirubin
胆囊炎 cholecystitis
胆石病 cholelithiasis
胆大包天 heaven-daring; with desperate daring
胆管造影 cholangiography
胆量过人 be bolder than all the rest
胆小如鼠 as timid as a mouse; chicken-hearted
胆战心惊 tremble with fear

疸 [dǎn]
◇黄疸 jaundice

掸 [dǎn]
〈动〉brush lightly; whisk ➡ shàn
掸子 duster (usu. made of chicken feathers or strips of cloth)

黕 [dǎn]
Ⅰ〈名〉filth; stain Ⅱ〈形〉pitch-black; jet-black

dàn (ㄉㄢˋ)

担 [dàn]
Ⅰ〈名〉① carrying pole and the loads on it; load; burden ② *dan*, a unit of weight (= 50 kilograms) Ⅱ〈量〉(of things carried on a shoulder pole) bucket; bundle ➡ dān
担子 ① carrying (*or* shoulder) pole and the loads on it; load; burden ② task; burden to bear; responsibility to shoulder
担担面 street vendor's noodles (served with sauce only)

旦 [dàn]
〈名〉① dawn; daybreak ② day ③ female character type in Beijing opera, etc. ④ denier
旦夕 this morning or evening—in a short while
旦夕祸福 unexpected good or bad fortune; sudden changes of fortune
旦夕之间 between morning and evening—in a day's time; overnight

但 [dàn]
Ⅰ〈副〉① merely; only; just Ⅱ〈连〉but; yet; still; nevertheless
但凡 in every case; without exception; as long as
但是 but; yet; still; nevertheless
但书 proviso
但愿 if only; I wish
但愿如此 be it so; I hope so; I hope that's right

诞 [dàn]
Ⅰ〈名〉① birth ② birthday Ⅱ〈形〉absurd; fantastic
诞辰 birthday
诞生 be born; come into being; emerge
诞生地 birthplace

啖 [dàn]
〈动〉① eat; feed ② entice (*or* lure) with profit

惮 [dàn]
〈动〉fear; dread

淡 [dàn]
〈形〉① thin; light ② tasteless; weak ③ (of colour) light ④ indifferent; cool; with little enthusiasm ⑤ dull; slack ⑥ meaningless; unimportant; trivial
淡泊 not seek fame and wealth; living tranquilly without seeking fame and wealth
淡薄 ① thin; light; not dense ② tasteless; weak ③ faint; dim; hazy ④ cool down; lessen; abate
淡菜 mussel
淡出 fade out
淡淡 ① thin; light; pale ② indifferent; cool ③ (of ripples) undulating gently
淡化 desalinate
淡季 slack (*or* dull, off) season (*or* period)
淡漠 ① indifferent; apathetic; nonchalant ② faint; dim; hazy
淡墨 light ink
淡青 light greenish blue
淡然 indifferent; cool
淡入 fade in
淡市 bear market
淡水 fresh water
淡忘 fade from one's memory
淡雅 simple but elegant; quietly elegant; unadorned and in good taste
淡竹 henon bamboo
淡妆 be lightly made up

淡积云 cumulus humilis
淡水湖 freshwater lake
淡水鱼 freshwater fish
淡味烟 mild-strength tobacco
淡泊明志 show high ideals by simple living
淡出淡入 fade over
淡然处之 treat with indifference; regard coolly
淡水资源 freshwater resources
淡于名利 be indifferent to fame and wealth; care little about fame and fortune

弹 [dàn]
名 ① ball; pellet ② bullet; shell; bomb; crump ➡ tán
弹道 trajectory
弹弓 catapult; slingshot
弹痕 bullet or shell hole; shot mark
弹夹 (cartridge) clip; charger
弹壳 shell case; cartridge case
弹坑 (shell) crater
弹盘 cartridge drum; magazine
弹片 shell fragment (*or* splinter); shrapnel
弹膛 chamber (of a gun)
弹头 bullet; projectile nose; warhead
弹丸 ①pellet; shot; bullet ②(of a place) very small; tiny
弹匣 magazine
弹药 ammunition; cartridge; ammo
弹着 impact
弹子 ①pellet ②marble ③billiards
弹道学 ballistics
弹药库 ammunition depot (*or* storehouse)
弹药手 ammunition man (*or* bearer)
弹药所 ammunition supply (*or* refilling) point
弹药箱 ammunition chest; cartridge box
弹道弧线 ballistic curve
弹道火箭 ballistic rocket
弹道导弹 ballistic missile
弹尽粮绝 run out of ammunition and provisions
弹丸之地 a tiny little place; tiny piece of land

蛋 [dàn]
名 ①egg ②egg-shaped thing; ball
蛋白 ①egg white; albumen ②protein
蛋粉 powdered eggs; egg powder
蛋糕 cake
蛋羹 egg custard
蛋黄 yolk
蛋鸡 laying hen; layer
蛋壳 eggshell
蛋品 egg products
蛋青 pale blue
蛋清 egg white
蛋子 egg-shaped thing
蛋白石 opal
蛋白质 protein
蛋用鸡 layer (a hen)

蛋白疗法 protein therapy

氮 [dàn]
名 nitrogen (N)
氮肥 nitrogenous fertilizer
氮当量 nitrogen equivalent

石 [dàn]
名 *dan*, a unit of dry measure of grain (=1 hectolitre) ➡ shí

dāng（ㄉㄤ）

当 [dāng]
I 动 ① equal; match ② ought to; should; must ③face; confront; be in sb's presence ④ serve as; act as; work as; be ⑤deserve; bear; accept ⑥manage; be in charge of; direct; administer; control ⑦stop; prevent; obstruct II 介 just at (a time or place) III 名 tip; top IV 拟 sound made by striking metals; 铃声当当响了。 The bell goes ding-dong. ➡ dàng
当班 be on a shift
当兵 be a soldier; serve in the army
当场 on the spot; then and there
当初 ①at the beginning; originally; at the outset; in the first place ②at that time; in the past
当代 present age; contemporary era
当道 ①blocking the way ②be in power; hold sway
当地 at the place in question; in the locality; local
当归 Chinese angelica
当红 in vogue
当即 at once; right away
当家 manage (household) affairs
当街 ①facing the street ②in the street
当今 ①now; at present; nowadays ②〈旧〉the emperor on the throne; the reigning emperor
当局 authorities
当空 high above in the sky
当啷 clank; clang
当量 equivalent (weight)
当令 in season
当面 to sb's face; in sb's presence
当年 ①in those years (*or* days) ②prime of life
当前 ①before one; facing one ②present; current
当权 be in power; hold power
当然 ①without doubt; certainly; of course; to be sure ②natural ③ex officio
当时 then; at that time
当事 ① be in charge; be in control ② concerned; involved ③ authorities or parties concerned
当头 ① right overhead; right on sb's head; head on ②facing (*or* confronting) one; im-

D

minent

当下 instantly; immediately; at once
当先 in the van; in the front ranks; at the head
当心 take care; be careful; look out
当选 be elected
当政 be in power; be in office
当中 ①in the middle; in the centre ②among
当众 in the presence of all; in public
当家的 ①head of a family ②husband
当口儿 this or that very moment
当枪使 be a tool; be cannon fodder
当事国 state directly involved; country concerned
当事人 ①party (to a lawsuit); litigant ②person (*or* party) concerned; interested parties
当头炮 direct criticism
当下手 work as sb's subordinate or assistant
当腰儿 middle
当场出彩 ① make a spectacle of oneself ② give the show away on the spot
当场交货 spot delivery
当代文化 contemporary culture
当代意识 modernism
当地公司 domestic corporation
当断不断 fail to make a decision when one should; hesitate when decision is needed
当机立断 decide quickly; make a prompt decision
当家作主 be master in one's own house; be the master of one's own affairs (*or* destiny)
当面对质 challenge sb face to face
当期成本 period cost
当前用户 active user
当仁不让 not decline to shoulder a responsibility; not leave to others what one ought to do oneself; not pass on to others what one is called upon to do
当头棒喝 a blow and a shout—a sharp (*or* severe) warning
当头一棒 head-on blow
当务之急 most pressing matter of the moment; top priority task; urgent matter
当之无愧 fully deserve (a title, an honour, etc.); be worthy of
当众出丑 make an exhibition of oneself
当日交易人 day trade
当地法律豁免 exemption from local law
当面锣对面鼓 direct confrontation and face-to-face argument
当局者迷;旁观者清 the spectators see the chess game better than the players; the onlooker sees most of the game
当一天和尚撞一天钟 go on tolling the bell as long as one is a monk—do the least that is expected of one; take a passive attitude towards one's work

当面说好话,背后下毒手 say nice things to sb's face, then stab him in the back

珰 [dāng] 名 ①earring ②eunuch

铛 [dāng] 象 clank; clang ➡chēng

裆 [dāng] 名 ①crotch of trousers; rise ②crotch

dǎng(ㄉㄤˇ)

挡 [dǎng] Ⅰ 动 ①keep off; ward off; withstand ② shelter from; block; keep out Ⅱ 名 ①fender; blind ② gear ③ (of some apparatuses and measuring instruments) indentation; gauge; grading
挡车 be in charge of looms and check the quality and quantity of the products
挡驾 turn away a visitor with some excuse; decline to receive a guest
挡横儿 intervene; interfere; get in the way
挡箭牌 ①shield ②excuse; pretext
挡泥板 mudguard (of a car); fender
挡土墙 retaining wall
挡风玻璃 windshield; wind screen

党 [dǎng] Ⅰ 名 ①political party; party ②the Communist Party of China ③clique; faction; gang ④ kinsfolk; relatives Ⅱ 动 be partial to; take sides with
党报 ①party newspaper (*or* organ) ②organ of the Chinese Communist Party; Party organ
党费 party membership dues
党风 party's work style; party member's conduct
党纲 party programme
党棍 dirty politician who uses his party membership as a means in promoting self-interest
党籍 party membership; party affiliation
党纪 party discipline
党建 Party building
党课 Party class; Party lecture
党魁 party chieftain (*or* chief, boss)
党龄 party standing
党内 within (*or* inside) the party; inner-party
党派 political parties and groups; party groupings
党旗 party flag
党人 ①members of a political party ②partisans
党徒 ①member of a clique or a reactionary political party ②henchman
党团 ① political parties and other organizations ②Chinese Communist Party and Chinese Communist Youth League; the Party

and the League ③parliamentary group of a political party

党外 outside the party
党委 Party committee
党务 party work;party affairs
党校 Party school
党性 Party spirit;Party character
党羽 members of a clique;adherents;henchmen
党员 party member
党章 party constitution
党证 party card
党组 leading Party member's group (in a state organ,of ministerial level)
党八股 stereotyped Party writing;Party jargon
党代表 Party representative (a political worker of the Chinese Communist Party in the Red Army before 1929)
党代会 Party Congress
党小组 Party group (a small group under a branch committee in the Party)
党支部 Party branch
党中央 Party Central Committee;central leading body of the Party
党总支 general Party branch
党风建设 the building of a fine Party style of work;the improvement of the Party's work style
党纪国法 party discipline and the law of the land (or state)
党内监督 supervision within the Party;supervision by Party organizations and members;inner-Party supervision
党内民主 inner-party democracy;democracy inside a party
党同伐异 defend those who belong to one's own faction and attack those who don't;be narrowly partisan
党政分开 separation of the functions of the Party and the government
党政机关 Party and government organs
党的基本路线 Party's basic line
党内民主生活会 inner-party criticism and self-criticism meeting

说 [dǎng]
形 (of advice or comment) honest;unbiased

dàng(ㄉㄤˋ)

当 [dàng]
I 形 proper;right;appropriate Ⅱ 动 ①be equal to;match ②treat as;regard as;take for ③think ④pawn Ⅲ 代 that very (day, year, etc.) Ⅳ 名 pawn;pledge ➡ dāng
当成 regard as;treat as;take for
当当 pawn things;put things in pawn

当年 same year;that very year
当票 pawn ticket
当铺 pawnshop
当日 same day;that very day
当时 right away;at once;immediately
当天 same day;that very day
当夜 same night;the very night
当真 ①take seriously ②(really) true ③really;sure enough
当作 treat as;regard as;look upon as

凼 [dàng]
名 shallow lake;pit;pond

宕 [dàng]
I 动 delay Ⅱ 形 with abandonment;freedom from restraint;indulgent

垱 [dàng]
名 embankment built for irrigation

荡 [dàng]
I 动 ①swing;sway;wave ②loaf about ③rinse ④clear away;sweep off Ⅱ 形 ①vast;broad and level ②loose in morals;debauched;licentious Ⅲ 名 ① shallow lake; marsh ② pond;pit;pool
荡除 clear away;get rid of
荡船 swingboat
荡涤 cleanse;clean up;wash away
荡妇 ①loose woman ②prostitute
荡平 wipe out;quell;stamp out
荡漾 ripple;undulate
荡气回肠 (of music, poems, etc.) soul-stirring;thrilling;inspiring
荡然无存 all gone;nothing left

档 [dàng]
名 ① shelves (for files); pigeonholes ②files;archives;records ③crosspiece (of a table,bed, etc.) ④ grade ⑤ open-air booth or stall
档案 files;archives;record;dossier
档次 grade
档期 session
档案馆 archives
档案柜 filing cabinet

dāo(ㄉㄠ)

刀 [dāo]
I 名 ① knife; sword; any kind of cutting tool ②sth shaped like a knife Ⅱ 量 (used with sheets of paper);一刀纸 one hundred sheets (of paper)
刀背 back of a knife blade
刀笔 writing of indictments, appeals, etc.;pettifoggery
刀兵 ①weapons;arms ②fighting;war
刀柄 hilt;knife handle
刀叉 knife and fork
刀豆 sword bean (the plant or the pods it bears)

D

刀锋 point or edge of a knife
刀痕 mark or scar left by a knife-cut
刀架 tool carrier；tool carriage
刀具 cutting tool；tool
刀口 ①edge of a knife ②where a thing can be put to best use；crucial point；right spot ③ cut；incision
刀片 ①razor blade ②（tool）bit；blade
刀枪 sword and spear；weapons
刀鞘 sheath；scabbard
刀刃 ①edge of a knife ②where a thing can be put to best use；crucial point
刀伤 wound inflicted with a knife or sword；gash；stab
刀鱼 ①hairtail ②long-tailed anchovy
刀把子 ①handle of a knife ②（sword）hilt ③ military power；power ④sth that may be used against one；handle
刀斧手 executioner；headsman
刀耕火种 slash-and-burn cultivation
刀光剑影 glint and flash of daggers and swords
刀枪不入 （of a human body）arms-proof
刀山火海 mountain of swords and sea of flames—most dangerous places；most severe trials
刀下留人 hold the execution
刀子嘴,豆腐心 （have）a sharp tongue but a soft heart
刀枪入库,马放南山 put the weapons back in the arsenal and graze the war horses on the hillside—relax vigilance against war

氘 ［dāo］
〔名〕deuterium（H²,D）
氘核 deuteron

dáo（ㄉㄠ）

捯 ［dáo］
〔动〕① pull（yarn, thread or string）hand over hand；wind round and round ②step（or stride）along（with alternating feet）③ look into；find out；investigate
捯饬 dress up；make up
捯老账 rake up（or look into）an old score

dǎo（ㄉㄠ）

导 ［dǎo］
〔动〕①lead；guide；channel ②transmit；conduct ③instruct；give guidance to ④direct（a performance, etc.）
导播 compile and broadcast（a program on radio or TV）；direct broadcast；programme director
导弹 guided missile
导电 transmit electric current；conduct electricity

导读 guide to reading
导购 provide guidance for purchase；shopping guide；guide to the shoppers
导管 ①conduit；pipe；duct ②vessel；duct
导轨 slide；guide
导航 navigation
导览 guide to visitors
导流 diversion
导轮 guide pulley；pilot wheel
导论 introduction（to a thesis, etc.）；introductory remarks
导尿 catheterization
导盘 godet
导热 conduct heat；transmit heat
导师 ① tutor；teacher ② guide of a great cause；teacher
导数 derivative
导体 conductor
导线 lead；（conducting）wire
导向 ①direct sth towards ②direct the course of sth；guide
导言 introduction（to a piece of writing）；introductory remarks
导演 ①direct（a film, play, etc.）②director
导医 hospital guide
导游 ① conduct a sightseeing tour ② tourist guide ③guidebook
导源 ①（of a river）have its source ②originate；derive
导展 exhibition guide
导致 lead to；bring about；result in；cause
导风板 baffle
导火索 （blasting）fuse
导火线 ①（blasting）fuse ② small incident that touches off a big one
导演椅 director's chair
导弹基地 missile base
导弹试验 missile tests
导轨磨床 slideway grinder
导流明渠 water diversion canal
导游证书 tourist guide certificate
导播控制室 production control room
导弹发射场 missile（launching）site；launching site
导弹发射井 launching silo
导弹发射器 missile launcher
导弹发射台 （missile）launching pad
导弹核潜艇 nuclear submarine armed with guided missiles
导弹护卫舰 （guided）missile frigate
导弹驱逐舰 guided missile destroyer
导弹巡洋舰 guided missile cruiser
导演控制台 production control desk

岛 ［dǎo］
〔名〕island
岛国 country consisting of one or more islands；island country

D

岛屿 islands and islets；islands

捣 ［dǎo］
囫 ①pound with a pestle，etc.；beat；smash ②beat；strike ③harass；disturb

捣蛋 make (*or* cause) trouble

捣动 ①turn over ②stir up；incite

捣固 make firm by ramming or tamping

捣鼓 ①fiddle with；meddle with ②move back and forth；buy in and sell out；trade in

捣鬼 play tricks；do mischief

捣毁 smash up；demolish；destroy

捣乱 make (*or* cause) trouble；create a disturbance

捣碎 pound to pieces

捣乱分子 trouble-makers；saboteurs

倒 ［dǎo］
Ⅰ 囫 ①fall；topple；tumble down ②collapse；fail；go bankrupt；go out of business ③overthrow；overturn；bring down ④(of voice) become hoarse；(of a singer) lose one's voice ⑤spoil (appetite) ⑥change；exchange；transfer ⑦move around；make room for ⑧sell out (a business，etc.) ⑨speculate；profiteer Ⅱ 呂 scalper；profiteer ➡dào

倒把 engage in profiteering；speculate

倒班 change shifts；work in shifts；work by turns

倒闭 close down；go bankrupt；go into liquidation

倒毙 drop dead

倒伏 (of crops) lodging

倒戈 change sides in a war；turn one's coat；transfer one's allegiance

倒换 ①rotate；take turns ②rearrange (sequence，order，etc.)；replace

倒汇 deal illegally in foreign currency；resell the foreign exchange at a profit

倒卖 resell at a profit；scalp

倒霉 have bad luck；be out of luck；be down on one's luck

倒嗓 (of a singer) lose one's voice

倒手 ①shift (*or* move) from one hand to the other ②change hands

倒塌 collapse；topple down

倒台 fall from power；downfall

倒腾 ①rummage；move；shift ②replace；exchange；rearrange ③buy in and sell out；deal in；trade in

倒头 touch the pillow；lie down

倒休 (of workers and staff) exchange working days and holidays；stagger holidays

倒爷 profiteer

倒运 ①have bad luck；be out of luck；be down on one's luck ②profiteer by buying cheap and selling dear

倒账 bad debt

倒计时 countdown；count backwards

倒胃口 spoil one's appetite

倒买倒卖 speculative buying and selling

倒卖票证 trade in coupons

祷 ［dǎo］
囫 ①pray ②long for；hope for；ask earnestly；beg

祷告 pray；say one's prayers

祷文 prayer

祷祝 pray and make a wish

蹈 ［dǎo］
囫 ① tread；step ② move up and down；skip；trip

蹈海 throw oneself into the sea

蹈袭 follow slavishly

蹈常袭故 go on in the same old way；get into a rut；follow a set routine

dào（ㄉㄠ）

到 ［dào］
Ⅰ 囫 ①arrive；reach ②go to；leave for ③ *as the complement of a verb indicating the result of an action*：说到做到 do what one says；be as good as one's word Ⅱ 疒 up till；until；up to；by：从一到十 from one to ten Ⅲ 形 considerate；thoughtful；thorough：不到之处请原谅。I hope you will forgive me if I have not been thoughtful enough.

到场 be present；show up；turn up

到处 at all places；everywhere

到达 arrive；get to；reach

到底 ①to the end；to the finish ②at last；in the end；finally ③after all；in the final analysis

到顶 reach the summit (*or* peak，limit)；cannot be improved

到会 be present at a meeting；attend a meeting

到家 reach a very high level；be perfect；be excellent

到来 arrival；advent

到期 become due；mature；expire

到任 take office；arrive at one's post

到手 in one's hands；in one's possession

到头 to the end；at an end

到位 attain a predetermined position；in position；specifically fulfill a policy (*or* measure)

到职 take office；arrive at one's post

到头来 in the end；finally

到岸价格 cost，insurance and freight (CIF)；CIF price

到货通知 arrival note

到期付款 payable at maturity

到期利息 interest due

帱 ［dào］
囫 cover ➡chóu

倒 [dào]
I 囫 ①move backward；turn upside down；reverse；invert ②tip；pour；dump II 形 ①inverted；inverse ②reverse；obverse；converse III 副 ① *contrary to what is expected or thought*：原想省点钱，不料倒花多了。I meant to be frugal but spent more than I had expected. ② *used to indicate contrast*：说说倒容易，做起来可不那么简单。It's easier said than done. ③ *used to indicate concession*：东西是贵，倒还值得买。It is expensive but still worth the money. ④ *used to urge sb to respond quickly, indicating impatience*：你倒快点呀，我们要晚了。Hurry up or we'll be late. ➡ dǎo

倒彩 booing；hooting；catcall
倒车 back a car
倒刺 hangnail；agnail
倒带 rewind(REW)
倒挡 reverse gear
倒飞 inverted (*or* upside down) flight
倒钩 overhead hook
倒挂 ①hang upside down ②be contrary to the natural order of things；be in an inverted order
倒灌 (of flood waters，tidal currents，etc.) flow from a lower to a higher place；(of smoke) pour in down a chimney
倒睫 trichiasis
倒经 vicarious menstruation
倒立 ①stand upside down ②handstand
倒流 flow backwards
倒赔 lose money instead of making money
倒片 film rewind
倒数 [dàoshǔ] count from bottom to top or from rear to front；count backwards
倒数 [dàoshù] reciprocal
倒算 seize back confiscated property
倒锁 lock sb in
倒贴 ①pay instead of getting paid ②(of a woman) pay for the upkeep of her paramour；keep a gigolo
倒退 go backwards；fall back
倒像 inverted image
倒叙 flashback
倒悬 hang by the feet—be in sore straits
倒影 inverted image；inverted reflection in water
倒置 place upside down；invert
倒转 turn the other way round；reverse
倒背手 with one's hands behind one (when pacing to and fro or strolling)
倒不如 it would be better to
倒插门 (of a man) marry into the wife's family
倒春寒 cold wave coming after the onset of warm spring weather

倒相器 inverted amplifier unit；phase reverser
倒栽葱 fall head over heels；fall headlong
倒背如流 can recite sth backwards—know sth by heart
倒打一耙 make unfounded counter-charges；put the blame on one's victim；recriminate
倒放速度 reverse speed
倒飞筋斗 inverted loop
倒挂金钟 fuchsia
倒立转体 handstand turn
倒摄遗忘 retroactive (*or* retrograde) amnesia
倒摄抑制 retroactive inhibition
倒收付息 negative interest
倒数计时 countdown
倒行逆施 ①go against the trend of the times；try to put the clock back；push a reactionary policy ②perverse acts
倒序词典 reversal dictionary
倒因为果 take cause for effect
倒置汽缸 inverted cylinder
倒装词序 inverted word order

盗 [dào]
I 囫 steal；rob；burgle；burglarize II 名 thief；robber；burglar
盗版 illegal copy；pirate copy；piracy
盗采 illegal mining
盗伐 fell trees unlawfully
盗匪 bandits；robbers
盗汗 night sweat
盗猎 illegal hunting
盗卖 steal and sell (public property)
盗墓 rob a tomb (*or* grave)
盗窃 steal
盗印 pirate
盗用 embezzle；usurp
盗贼 robbers；bandits
盗窃犯 thief
盗窃罪 larceny
盗版光盘 pirate CD
盗版侵权 piracy and inflicting damage on other's copyright
盗版音像制品 pirate audio-video material

悼 [dào]
囫 mourn；grieve
悼词 memorial speech
悼念 mourn；grieve over

道 [dào]
I 名 ①way；road；path ②course；channel ③orientation；way；justice ④morality；virtue ⑤technique；skill；art ⑥(academic，religious，or ideological) doctrine；principle ⑦Taoism；Taoist ⑧superstitious sect：会道门 superstitious sects and secret societies ⑨line：画道儿 draw a line/斜道儿 slanting line II 量 (*for long and narrow things*)：万道霞光 myriads of sun rays/上最后一道菜 serve the last course of a meal III 囫 ①say；talk；speak ②

D

express;extend ③say ④think;suppose
道白 spoken parts in an opera
道班 railway or highway maintenance squad
道别 bid farewell;say goodbye
道岔 railway switch;points
道场 ①Taoist or Buddhist rites (performed to save the souls of the dead) ②place where such rites are performed
道床 railway roadbed
道德 morals;morality;ethics
道钉 railway (dog) spike
道服 robe worn by a Taoist priest
道姑 Taoist nun
道观 Taoist temple
道号 Taoist name
道贺 congratulate
道家 Taoist school;Taoists
道教 Taoist religion;Taoism
道具 stage property;prop
道理 ①principle;truth;hows and whys ②reason;argument;sense
道路 road;way;path
道袍 Taoist robe
道破 point out frankly;lay bare;reveal
道歉 apologize;make an apology
道士 Taoist priest
道谢 express one's thanks;thank
道行 attainments of a Taoist priest
道学 ①Confucian school of idealist philosophy of the Song Dynasty;Neo-Confucianism ②affectedly moral
道义 morality and justice
道砟 railway ballast
道道儿 way;method
道德经 Classic of the Virtue of the Tao
道林纸 glazed printing paper
道不拾遗 no one picks up what's left by the wayside—honesty prevails throughout society
道德法庭 court of conscience
道德沦丧 moral degradation/backsliding
道貌岸然 pose as a person of high morals;be sanctimonious
道听途说 hearsay;rumour;gossip
道琼斯指数 Dow Jones Index
道不同,不相为谋 there is no point in people taking counsel together who follow different ways
道高一尺,魔高一丈 as virtue rises one foot, vice rises ten; the more illumination; the more temptation
道琼斯工业平均指数 Dow-Jones industrial average index
道琼斯商品行情指数 Dow Jones commodity index
道琼斯股票价格平均数 Dow Jones stock average

稻 [dào]
〔名〕 rice;paddy
稻草 rice straw
稻谷 paddy
稻糠 rice chaff
稻壳 rice husk (or hull)
稻田 (rice) paddy;rice field;paddy field
稻秧 rice seedlings;rice shoots
稻子 rice;paddy
稻苞虫 rice plant skipper
稻草人 scare crow
稻烂秧 seedling blight of rice
稻螟虫 rice borer
稻瘟病 rice blast
稻田皮炎 paddy-field dermatitis
稻纹枯病 sheath and culm blight of rice
稻鱼兼作 rice-fish cultivation
稻白叶枯病 bacterial blight of rice

dē（ㄉㄜ）

嘚 [dē]
〔象〕 clatter of a horse's hoofs

dé（ㄉㄜˊ）

得 [dé]
Ⅰ〔动〕 ①get;obtain;gain;win ②(of a calculation) equal;result in;make ③fit;proper ④satisfied;be complacent ⑤(*used before other verbs, indicating permission*)：未经许可，不得入内。 No admittance without permission. ⑥(*used before other verbs, usually in the negative, indicating probability*)：谈判没有一星期不得完。 The negotiation will last for over a week. ⑦be finished;be done; be ready:饭得了吗？ Is dinner ready? Ⅱ〔叹〕①(*used in ending a statement to indicate agreement or prohibition*)：得，就这么办。 OK! Just go ahead. ②(*used in a bad situation indicating helplessness*)：得，我又忘带钥匙了。 Oh, shoot! I forgot the key again. ➡de;děi
得便 when it's convenient
得病 fall ill;contract a disease
得逞 have one's way;prevail;succeed
得宠 find favour with sb; be in sb's good graces
得出 reach (a conclusion);obtain (a result)
得当 apt;appropriate;proper;suitable
得到 get;obtain;gain;receive
得法 do sth in the proper way;get the knack
得分 score
得计 succeed in one's scheme
得奖 win (or be awarded) a prize
得劲 ①feel well ②fit for use;handy
得救 be saved (or rescued)
得空 have leisure;be free

得了 ① *expressing a suggestion* ② that's enough;that's that

得力 ①benefit from ②get help from ③capable;competent

得胜 win a victory;triumph

得失 ① gain and loss;success and failure ② advantages and disadvantages;merits and demerits

得势 ①be in power ②get the upper hand;be in the ascendant

得手 go smoothly;come off;do fine;succeed

得体 befitting one's position or suited to the occasion;appropriate

得悉 hear of;learn about

得闲 have leisure;be free

得宜 proper;appropriate;suitable

得以 so that... can (*or* may)...

得益 benefit;profit

得意 proud of oneself;pleased with oneself;complacent

得志 achieve one's ambition;have a successful career

得罪 offend;displease

得人心 have the support of the people;be popular

得不偿失 the loss outweighs the gain;The game is not worth the candle.

得寸进尺 reach for a yard after getting an inch;give him an inch and he'll take a yard (*or* a mile,an ell);be insatiable

得过且过 get by however one can; muddle along;drift along

得陇望蜀 covet Shu after getting Long—have insatiable desires

得天独厚 be richly endowed by nature;abound in gifts of nature;enjoy exceptional advantages

得心应手 ①with facility;with high proficiency ②serviceable;handy

得意门生 favourite pupil

得意忘形 grow dizzy with success;have one's head turned by success

得意洋洋 be immensely proud;look triumphant

得鱼忘筌 forget the trap as soon as the fish is caught;forget the means by which the end is attained;forget the things or conditions which bring one success

得道多助,失道寡助 a just cause enjoys abundant support while an unjust cause finds little;a just cause gains great support,an unjust one gains little

德 [dé]（名） ①morality;virtue;moral character ②mind;heart ③kindness;favour

德国 Germany

德行 ①moral integrity;moral conduct ②disgusting;shameful

德语 German (language)

德育 moral education;education in ethics

德政 benevolent rule

德治 rule of virtue

德比战 Derby

德国人 German

德才兼备 have both ability and integrity

德高望重 (of an old person) be of noble character and high prestige;enjoy high prestige and command universal respect

德智体美全面发展 be all-round in moral,intellectual, physical and aesthetical developments

<h2 style="text-align:center">de(·ㄉㄜ)</h2>

地 [de]（助） *used after an adjective or a phrase to form an adverbial adjunct before the verb*：雪花轻轻地落在树叶上。 Snow flakes fell gently on the leaves. ➡dì

的 [de]（助） ①（*used after an attribute*）（a）（*when the attribute modifies the noun in the usual way*）：担心的事情 worrisome problem（b）（*when the attribute indicates possession*）：我的一位同事 a colleague of mine（c）（*when the attribute is a personal pronoun or a name，and the modified noun indicates role or position*）：今天是我的东。 It's my treat today.（d）（*when the attribute is a personal pronoun or a noun standing for a person，and the modified noun indicates the action received by the former*）：别尽看我的笑话,帮帮我。 Don't just stand by and laugh at me. Give me a hand. ②（*used at the end of a nominal structure equivalent to a noun phrase*（a）*to substitute for sth or sb already mentioned*）：这张票是我的,那张票是你的。 This ticket is mine while that one is yours.（b）（*to indicate a class or category of people or things*）：送信的 postman;messenger（c）（*to emphasize what precedes it*）：这里用不着你,你只管干你的去。 You have no business to be here. Go and get down to your own work. ③（*used between identical verbs，adjectives，etc. to constitute a sequence of contrasts*）：说的说,笑的笑。 Some talk while others laugh. ④（*used between a verb of past time and its object for emphasis of the subject，time，way，etc. of an action*）：她是上个月结的婚。 It was last month that she got married. ⑤（*used at the end of a statement to indicate certainty*）：熊猫一般是不吃肉的。 As a rule, pandas don't eat meat;Pandas are usually not carnivorous. /你

真够精明的！ You are really smart! ⑥(*used after words or phrases belonging to the same part of speech to imply further enumeration*)：破铜烂铁的,他捡来一大筐。He picked up a basketful of scrap iron and stuff. ⑦(*used between two numerals to indicate multiplication*)：两米的四米,是八平米。Two metres by four is eight square metres. ➡dī;dí;dì

D

得 [de]
〔劢〕①(*used after certain verbs to indicate possibility*)：这种蘑菇吃得。Mushrooms of this kind are edible. ②(*used between a verb and its complement to indicate possibility*)：办得到 can do sth ③(*used after a verb or an adjective to introduce a complement of result or degree*)：辣得狠 be terribly hot ④(*after a verb to indicate the completion of an action*)：出得门来 have come out of the house ➡dé;děi

děi(ㄉㄟˇ)

得 [děi]
Ⅰ〔劢〕①need;require;take ②must;have to ③will;be sure to Ⅱ〔形〕comfortable;cozy;contented ➡dé;de

dèn(ㄉㄣˋ)

扲 [dèn]
〔劢〕①pull (at both ends,or at one end with the other fixed);tug;yank ②grasp tightly;pull hard;tug hard

dēng(ㄉㄥ)

灯 [dēng]
〔名〕①lamp ②burner ③valve;tube
灯标 beacon light;beacon;light buoy
灯彩 ① coloured-lantern making ② coloured lanterns
灯草 rush
灯船 lightship;light vessel
灯光 ① light of a lamp;lamplight ②(stage) lighting
灯花 snuff (of a candlewick)
灯火 lights
灯节 Lantern Festival (the 15th of the first lunar month)
灯具 lamps and lanterns
灯笼 lantern
灯谜 riddles written on lanterns;lantern riddles
灯泡 (electric) bulb;light bulb
灯饰 decorations comprising lamps;decorative lamps
灯丝 filament (in a light bulb or valve)
灯塔 lighthouse;beacon

灯台 lampstand
灯头 ① lamp holder;electric light socket ② holder for the wick and chimney of a kerosene lamp ③number of lamps
灯箱 illuminated advertisement
灯心 lampwick;wick
灯油 lamp-oil;kerosene;paraffin oil
灯语 lamp signal
灯座 lampstand
灯笼裤 knee-length or ankle-length sports trousers;knickerbockers
灯心草 rush
灯心绒 corduroy
灯光球场 floodlit (*or* illuminated) court;field;etc.
灯光夜市 lamplit night market
灯红酒绿 red lanterns and green wine— feasting and revelry
灯火管制 blackout (enforced during wartime)
灯火辉煌 brilliantly illuminated;blaze with lights

登 [dēng]
〔劢〕①climb;ascend;mount;scale (a height) ②publish;record;enter ③(of grain) ripen (so that it may be harvested and taken to the threshing ground) ④tread;step;stand ⑤put on;wear (shoes or trousers) ⑥press down with the foot;pedal treadle
登岸 go ashore;land
登报 publish in the newspaper
登场 ①be gathered and taken to the threshing ground ②come on stage
登顶 reach the summit
登高 ① ascend a height ② climb up hills or mountains on the Double Ninth Festival (重阳节)
登基 ascend the throne;be enthroned
登记 register;check in;enter one's name
登临 ① climb a hill;tall building,etc. which commands a broad view ② visit famous mountains;places of interest,etc.
登陆 land;disembark
登录 entry;log on
登门 call at sb's house
登山 mountain-climbing;mountaineering
登时 immediately;at once;then and there
登台 mount a platform;go up on the stage
登载 publish (in newspapers or magazines);carry
登革热 dengue fever
登广告 advertise
登机牌 boarding card
登记簿 register;registry
登记处 registration (*or* registry) office
登陆场 beachhead
登陆车 lander
登陆舰 landing ship

D

登陆艇 landing craft
登山鞋 climbing（*or* mountaineering）boot
登山员 mountaineer
登月舱 lunar module
登场人物 characters in a play；dramatis personae
登峰造极 reach the peak of perfection；have a very high level（of scholastic attainment or technical skill）；reach great heights
登机入口 boarding gate
登记股东 stockholder of record
登陆部队 landing force
登陆地点 debarkation（*or* landing）point
登陆母舰 landing-craft carrier
登陆作战 landing operations
登山运动 mountaineering
登堂入室 pass through the hall into the inner chamber—reach a higher level in one's studies；become more proficient in one's profession
登月飞船 lunar excursion vehicle
登月行走 moon walk；moonwalk

噔 ［dēng］
〔图〕 thump；thud：他噔噔噔地走上楼梯来。He came thumping up the stairs.

镫 ［dēng］
〔名〕①vessel for meat food ②oil lamp ➡ dèng

簦 ［dēng］
〔名〕bamboo or straw hat with a conical crown，broad rim and handle

蹬 ［dēng］
〔动〕①step on；tread ②put on；wear（shoes or trousers）③press down with the foot；pedal ➡ dèng
蹬技 juggling with the feet
蹬腿 ①kick one's legs ②kick the bucket；turn up one's toes

děng（ㄉㄥˇ）

等 ［děng］
Ⅰ〔名〕①class；grade；rank ②kind；sort；type Ⅱ〔形〕equal：高矮相等 equal in height Ⅲ〔动〕wait；await：等车 wait for a bus，train，etc. Ⅳ〔介〕by the time when；till：等雨停了再走。Wait till the rain stops. Ⅴ〔助〕①（*used after a personal pronoun or a noun referring to people to indicate plural number*）：我等三人 the three of us ②and so on；and so forth；etc.：加点葱、姜、蒜等 add some scallion，ginger，garlic and so on ③（*used to end an enumeration*）：小提琴、钢琴、单簧管等乐器 musical instruments such as violin，piano and clarinet
等差 place in a series；grade
等次 place in a series；grade
等待 wait；await

等到 by the time；when
等等 ①and so on；and so on and so forth；etc. ②wait a minute
等份 equal divisions；equal portions
等号 equal-sign；equality sign
等候 wait；await；expect
等级 ① grade；rank ② order and degree；graded standards；social estate；social stratum
等价 of equal value；equal in value
等式 equality
等同 equate；be equal
等外 substandard
等闲 ①ordinary；unimportant ②easily；casually；lightly ③for nothing
等效 equivalent
等音 enharmonic
等于 ①equal to；equivalent to ②amount to；be tantamount to；be the same as
等高线 contour（line）
等价物 equivalent
等距离 equidistance
等深线 isobath
等同语 equivalent word；equivalent
等温线 isotherm
等压面 isobaric surface；constant pressure surface
等压线 isobar；isobaric line
等震线 isoseismal line；isoseismal；isoseismic line
等值线 isopleth；isoline；isogram
等待状态 wait state
等额选举 single-candidate election
等而下之 from that grade down；lower down
等风速线 isotach
等级证书 grading certificate
等级制度 hierarchy；social estate system
等价交换 equivalent exchange；exchange of equal values
等离子体 plasma
等量齐观 equate；put on a par
等日照线 isohel
等闲视之 regard as unimportant；treat lightly（*or* casually）
等雨量线 isohyet
等边三角形 equilateral triangle
等距离外交 equidistant diplomacy
等离子彩电 plasma TV
等腰三角形 isosceles triangle
等额分期付款 equal amount instalment payment
等离子体物理学 plasma physics

dèng（ㄉㄥˋ）

邓 ［dèng］

邓小平理论 Deng Xiaoping Theory

凳 [dèng]
名 stool; bench
凳子 stool

嶝 [dèng]
劲 path up a hill

澄 [dèng]
劲 ① (of liquid) become clear; settle ② strain; decant ➡chéng
澄清 (of a liquid) settle; become clear

磴 [dèng]
I 名 stone steps II 量 *used of steps and stairs*: 那段楼梯有十一磴。There are eleven steps on that flight of stairs.

瞪 [dèng]
劲 ① open one's eyes wide ② glare (*or* stare) with displeasure
瞪眼 ① open one's eyes wide; stare; glare ② glare (*or* glower) at sb; get angry with sb

镫 [dèng]
名 stirrup ➡dēng
镫骨 stapes; stirrup bone

dī (ㄉㄧ)

的 [dī]
名 taxi ➡de; dí; dì
的哥 taxi driver brother; male taxi driver
的姐 taxi driver sister; female taxi driver
的士 taxi
的站 taxi station; taxi stop

低 [dī]
I 形 ① at a small distance from the ground; low ② below average; low ③ low in grade or rank: 低年级学生 students of the junior years; lower-division students II 劲 hang down; droop
低保 minimum subsistence security for urban residents
低产 low yield
低潮 low tide; low ebb
低沉 ① overcast; lowering ② (of voice) low and deep ③ low-spirited; downcast
低垂 hang low
低挡 low gear
低档 low grade
低地 lowland
低调 ① low-key ② low-pitched tune
低端 low end
低飞 low-altitude flight
低估 underestimate; underrate
低谷 all-time low; at low ebb
低耗 low cost; low operation cost
低回 ① pace up and down ② linger; be loath to part; yearn
低级 ① elementary; rudimentary; lower ② vulgar; low; coarse
低价 floor price
低贱 low and degrading; humble

低井 stripper well; stripped well
低空 low altitude; low level
低栏 low hurdles
低廉 cheap; low
低劣 inferior; low-grade
低龄 young in age (compared to the norm); lower than normal age; under age
低落 low; downcast
低迷 stagnant
低能 mental deficiency; feeble-mindedness
低频 low frequency
低聘 person who had had a high professional position being hired for an inferior position; lower one's position when recruiting
低烧 low fever; slight fever
低声 in a low voice; under one's breath; with bated breath
低头 ① lower (*or* bow, hang) one's head ② yield; submit
低洼 low-lying
低微 ① (of a voice or sound) low ② low; little; meagre ③ lowly; humble
低温 ① low temperature ② microtherm ③ hypothermia
低下 (of status or living standards) low; lowly
低压 ① low pressure ② low tension; low voltage ③ depression ④ minimum pressure
低云 low clouds
低标准 low level
低成本 low cost
低利率 low interest rate; low cost of money
低龄化 become lower in age
低能儿 imbecile; retarded child
低气压 low pressure; depression
低声波 infrasonic wave
低碳钢 low-carbon steel
低温学 cryogenics
低消耗 low consumption (of raw materials, fuel, etc.)
低血糖 hypoglycemia
低血压 hypotension
低血脂 hypolipemia
低压槽 trough
低层住宅 low housing
低等动物 lower animal; invertebrate
低调演说 low-keyed address
低度啤酒 nonalcoholic beer
低合金钢 low-alloy steel
低级趣味 vulgar interests; bad taste
低级娱乐 cheap entertainment
低空导弹 low-level missile; low-altitude missile
低空飞行 low-altitude (*or* low-level) flying
低空轰炸 low-level bombing
低空扫射 low-level strafing; ground strafing
低眉顺眼 be submissive and servile
低人一等 inferior to others

低三下四 ①lowly；humble；degrading ②servile；obsequious；cringing
低声下气 speak humbly and under one's breath；be meek and subservient；be obsequious
低首下心 bow and scrape；be obsequiously submissive
低头认罪 hang one's head and admit one's guilt；plead guilty
低息贷款 low-interest loan
低音控制 bass control
低音提琴 double bass；contrabass
低工资职工 low-paid workers
低轨道卫星 lower-orbiting satellite
低频扬声器 woofer
低温恒温器 cryostat
低温生物学 cryobiology
低腰紧身裤 hip-huggers
低度开发国家 underdeveloped countries
低成本高收益投资 low-cost high-return investment

羝 [dī] 名 ram；billy goat

堤 [dī] 名 dyke；embankment
堤岸 embankment
堤坝 dykes and dams
堤防 dyke；embankment
堤防加固工程 embankment reinforcement project

提 [dī] ⇒tí
提防 take precautions against；be on guard against；beware of
提溜 carry

嘀 [dī] ⇒dí
嘀嗒 tick；ticktack；ticktock

滴 [dī] I 动 ①drip ②let drop；drip II 名 drop；bead III 量 (of dripping liquid)：两滴墨水 two drops of ink
滴虫 trichomonad
滴答 drip
滴定 titration
滴管 dropper
滴灌 drip irrigation；trickle irrigation
滴漏 water clock；clepsydra；hourglass
滴鼻剂 nose drops；collunarium
滴虫病 trichomoniasis
滴滴涕 DDT (dichloro-diphenyl-trichloroethane)
滴滤池 trickling filter
滴色画 drip painting
滴水石 dripstone
滴水瓦 drip-tile (placed at either end of an eaves)
滴眼剂 eye drops

滴水不漏 ①watertight ②tightly packed or completely enclosed
滴水成冰 (so cold that) the water freezes as it drips；freezing cold
滴入式经济 trickle-down economy

dí(ㄉㄧ)

迪 [dí] 动 enlighten；guide
迪厅 disco
迪斯科 disco (a transliteration)
迪斯科酒吧 discopub
迪斯科女郎 discogirl
迪斯科乐队 discoset
迪斯尼乐园 Disneyland

的 [dí] 副 truly；really ⇒de；dī；dì
的确 indeed；really
的确良 dacron；terylene

籴 [dí] 动 buy in (grain)

荻 [dí] 名 a kind of reed

敌 [dí] I 名 enemy；foe II 动 ①oppose；resist；stand up to ②be equal in strength；match；rival the wealth of a state
敌稗 Stam F-34 (dichloropropionanilide)
敌对 hostile；antagonistic
敌国 enemy state
敌后 enemy's rear area
敌机 enemy plane
敌军 enemy troops；enemy；hostile forces
敌情 enemy's situation
敌人 enemy；foe
敌视 be hostile (or antagonistic) to；adopt a hostile attitude towards
敌手 ①match；opponent；adversary ②enemy hands
敌台 enemy broadcasting station
敌探 enemy spy
敌特 enemy spy；enemy agent
敌伪 enemy and the puppet regime (during the War of Resistance Against Japan)
敌意 hostility；enmity；animosity
敌敌畏 DDVP；dichlorvos
敌占区 enemy-occupied territory
敌对观念 awareness of the enemy's presence
敌对势力 hostile forces
敌对状态 state of hostility
敌强我弱 with the enemy stronger than we are；facing the enemy's stronger forces
敌我矛盾 contradictions between ourselves and the enemy

涤 [dí] 动 wash；cleanse
涤除 wash away；do away with；eliminate

涤荡 wash away;clean up;cleanse
涤纶 polyester fibre
涤瑕荡垢 remove the stains and cleanse the filth—eradicate bad habits and customs

笛 [dí]
名 ①bamboo flute;flute ②whistle
笛子 bamboo flute

觌 [dí]
动 see;meet

嘀 [dī]
➡ dí
嘀咕 ①whisper;talk in whispers ②be apprehensive;have qualms;be unsettled

嫡 [dí]
Ⅰ 名 legal wife (as distinguished from a concubine under the feudal-patriarchal system) Ⅱ 形 ①of lineal descent;closely related ②orthodox;authentic
嫡传 be handed down in a direct line from the master
嫡派 ①legal or official branch of a family tree ②disciples taught by the master himself
嫡亲 blood relations;close paternal relations
嫡堂 relationship between cousins of the same paternal grandfather
嫡系 ① direct line of descent ② one's own clique

镝 [dí]
名 arrowhead;arrow

dǐ（ㄉㄧ）

氐 [dǐ]
名 foundation;base

邸 [dǐ]
名 residence of a high official

诋 [dǐ]
动 speak ill of;slander;defame
诋毁 slander;vilify;calumniate;defame

抵 [dǐ]
动 ①support;prop;hold;sustain ②resist;withstand ③compensate for;make good;make up for ④mortgage ⑤balance;set off ⑥be equal to;match ⑦arrive at;reach
抵偿 compensate for;make good;give sth by way of payment for
抵触 conflict;contradict
抵达 arrive;reach
抵挡 keep out;ward off;check;withstand
抵换 substitute for;take the place of
抵抗 resist;stand up to
抵赖 deny;disavow
抵命 pay with one's life (for a murder,etc.);give a life for a life
抵数 make up the number;serve as a stopgap
抵消 offset;cancel out;counteract
抵押 mortgage
抵御 resist;withstand
抵债 pay a debt in kind or by labour

抵制 resist;boycott
抵罪 be punished for a crime
抵销权 right of set-off
抵销税 countervailing duty
抵押法 law of mortgages
抵押品 security;pledge
抵押权 mortgage holdings
抵押险 hypothecation insurance
抵近射击 point-blank firing
抵销记入 cross entry
抵押承包 mortgage to contract
抵押放款 mortgage loan;secured loan;loan on security
抵押负债 mortgage debt
抵押合同 mortgage contract
抵押贷款 mortgage financing;mortgage loan
抵押市场 mortgage market
抵押诉讼 mortgage action
抵押条款 mortgage clause
抵押银行 mortgage bank
抵押债券 mortgage bond
抵押资产 mortgage assets
抵押经纪人 mortgage middleman

底 [dǐ]
Ⅰ 名 ①bottom;base ②origin or bottom of sth;heart of the matter;ins and outs ③rough draft;draft text ④end of a year or month ⑤background;foundation ⑥base number Ⅱ 动 end up with;end up in;come to
底版 photographic plate;negative
底本 ①copy for the record or for reproduction;master copy ②text against which other texts are checked;original text
底册 bound copy of a document kept on file
底层 ①(British) ground floor;(American) first floor ②bottom;lowest rung ③basement
底肥 base fertilizer
底稿 draft;manuscript
底火 ①fire in a stove before fuel is added ②primer;ignition cartridge
底价 base price
底架 chassis
底孔 bottom outlet
底牌 cards in one's hand;hand
底盘 chassis (of a car)
底片 photographic plate;negative
底漆 priming paint;primer
底气 lung power
底色 bottom
底墒 soil moisture (before sowing or planting)
底数 ①truth or root of a matter;how a matter actually stands ②base number;radix;base
底霜 cream base
底图 base map
底细 ins and outs;exact details;unapparent

details (of a matter); unknown background (of a person)

底下 ① under; below; beneath ② next; later; afterwards

底线 ① end line ② under thread ③ planted agent; baseline

底薪 base salary

底子 ① bottom; base ② foundation ③ rough draft or sketch ④ copy kept as a record ⑤ remnant

底座 base; pedestal; foundation

底视图 bottom view

底栖生物 benthon

柢 [dǐ]
名 root (of a tree)

砥 [dǐ]
名 (formerly also pronounced zhǐ) whetstone

砥砺 ① temper ② encourage

砥柱 mainstay

骶 [dǐ]

骶骨 sacrum

dì(ㄉㄧˋ)

地 [dì]
名 ① earth ② land; soil ③ fields; land ④ ground; floor ⑤ place; locality; area ⑥ position; situation; room ⑦ background; ground ⑧ distance: 二十里地 distance of twenty *li* → de

地板 ① floor board ② floor

地堡 bunker; blockhouse; pillbox

地表 earth's surface

地步 ① condition; plight ② extent; degree ③ room for action

地蚕 ① cutworm ② grub

地槽 geosyncline

地层 stratum; layer

地产 landed estate; landed property; real estate

地秤 weighbridge

地磁 terrestrial magnetism; geomagnetism

地带 district; region; zone; belt

地道 [dìdào] tunnel

地道 [dìdao] ① from the place noted for the product; genuine ② real; pure; typical ③ well-done; thorough

地点 place; site; locale

地电 terrestrial electricity

地动 earthquake; quake

地洞 a hole in the ground; burrow

地段 a sector (*or* section) of a town, etc.; area

地盾 shield

地方 [dìfāng] ① locality (as distinct from the central administration) ② local

地方 [dìfang] ① place; space; room ② part; respect

地瓜 ① sweet potato ② yam bean

地光 ashes of light preceding an earthquake

地核 the earth's core

地黄 glutinous rehmannia

地基 ① ground ② foundation

地极 terrestrial pole

地价 land price; rock-bottom price

地脚 lower margin (of a page)

地窖 cellar

地界 the boundary of a piece of land

地块 massif

地蜡 earth wax; ozocerite

地牢 dungeon

地雷 (land) mine

地垒 horst

地理 ① geographical features of a place ② geography

地力 soil fertility

地利 ① favourable geographical position; topographical advantages ② land productivity

地量 lowest amount

地裂 the ground cleaves

地龙 earthworm

地漏 floor drain

地幔 (the earth's) mantle

地貌 the general configuration of the earth's surface; landforms

地面 ① the earth's surface; ground ② ground; floor ③ region; area; territory

地名 place name

地膜 plastic sheets used for covering the ground in agriculture

地盘 territory under one's control; domain

地陪 local tourist guide

地皮 ① land for building ② ground

地痞 local ruffian; local riffraff

地铺 shakedown

地契 title deed for land

地堑 graben

地壳 the earth's crust

地勤 ground service

地球 the earth; the globe

地区 ① area; district; region ② prefecture

地权 land ownership

地热 the heat of the earth's interior; terrestrial heat

地声 earthquake sounds

地势 physical features of a place; relief; terrain; topography

地税 land tax; local duty

地摊 roadside stall

地毯 carpet; rug

地铁 underground (railway); tube; subway

地头 ① edge of a field ② destination ③ the

place
地图 map
地位 ① position; standing; place; status ② place (as occupied by a person or thing)
地委 prefectural Party committee
地温 ground (*or* earth) temperature
地物 surface features (usu. man-made features of a region)
地峡 isthmus
地下 ① underground; subterranean ② secret (activity); underground ③on the ground
地线 ground (*or* earth) wire
地心 the earth's core
地形 topography; terrain
地衣 lichen
地狱 hell; inferno
地域 region; district
地缘 geographical
地震 earthquake; seism
地址 address
地质 geology
地轴 the earth's axis
地主 ①landlord ②host
地砖 floor tile
地租 land rent; ground rent; rent
地巴唑 dibazol
地板革 plastic flooring
地板蜡 floor wax
地板砖 tiles for indoor flooring
地表水 surface water
地鳖虫 ground beetle
地层学 stratigraphy
地产税 tax on urban land
地磁暴 geomagnetic storm
地磁极 geomagnetic pole
地磁仪 magnetometer
地道战 tunnel warfare
地动仪 seismograph as invented
地方病 endemic disease
地方化 localization
地方税 local taxes
地方戏 local opera; local drama
地方志 local chronicles; annals of local history
地滚球 ① baseball ground ball; grounder ② bowling
地级市 prefecture-level city
地老虎 cutworm
地雷场 minefield
地雷战 (land) mine warfare
地理学 geography
地沥青 asphalt; bitumen
地龙墙 sleeper wall
地貌图 geomorphologic map
地貌学 geomorphology
地面砖 floor tile
地名学 toponomy; toponymy
地平线 horizon

地球村 global village
地球日 Earth Day (April 22)
地球仪 (terrestrial) globe
地热学 geothermics
地史学 historical geology
地头蛇 a snake in its old haunts—local villain (*or* bully)
地图集 atlas
地图学 cartography
地温表 ground (*or* earth) thermometer
地文学 physical geography; physiography
地下茎 subterranean stem
地下室 basement
地下水 groundwater
地形图 topographic map; relief map
地形学 topography
地形雨 orographic rain
地形云 orographic cloud
地应力 crustal stress
地震波 seismic (*or* earthquake) wave
地震带 seismic belt
地震区 seismic area (*or* region)
地震学 seismology
地震仪 seismograph
地志学 topology
地质图 geologic map
地质学 geology
地中海 the Mediterranean (Sea)
地槽学说 theory of geosyncline
地产公司 real estate agency
地产市场 market of real estate; real estate market
地处闹市 be located in the downtown area
地磁异常 magnetic anomaly
地大物博 vast territory and abundant resources; vast land with rich resources; a big country abounding in natural wealth
地地道道 out-and-out; outright; hundred-percent
地方财政 finance of local administration; local public finance; local finance
地方法规 lex loci; regional regulations
地方分权 decentralization
地方工业 local industry
地方国有 state-owned but locally-administered
地方气候 microclimate
地方时间 local time
地方主义 regionalism; localism
地方自治 regional autonomy
地广人稀 a vast but thinly populated area; a vast territory with a sparse population
地价测算 land price estimating
地脚螺栓 foundation bolt
地理先生 geomancer
地理坐标 geographical coordinates
地利人和 favourable terrain and friendly people

地貌学家 geomorphologist
地面部队 ground forces
地面沉降 surface subsidence
地面辐射 terrestrial surface radiation
地面灌溉 surface irrigation
地膜覆盖 covering with ground sheeting
地平经度 azimuth
地平纬度 altitude
地平坐标 horizontal coordinates
地壳均衡 isostasy
地壳运动 crustal movement
地球化学 geochemistry
地球环境 global environment
地球科学 geoscience
地球卫星 earth satellite
地区壁垒 regional barriers
地区差别 regional disparity
地区差价 regional price differences
地区冲突 regional conflict
地区封锁 barriers between the regions
地区合作 regional cooperation
地区经济 regional economy
地热电厂 geothermal power plant
地热电力 geothermal power
地热能源 geothermal energy resources
地热资源 geothermal resources
地图投影 map projection
地外文明 extraterrestrial civilization
地位平等 equal in status; on an equal footing
地温梯度 geothermal gradient
地下餐馆 caveteria; basement restaurant
地下车间 subterranean garage
地下工厂 underground factories
地下构造 subsurface structure
地下管道 underground piping
地下河流 subterranean river (*or* stream)
地下交易 covert transaction
地下刊物 underground publications; illegal publications
地下渗流 underground percolation
地下水位 groundwater level (*or* depletion); water table
地下铁道 underground (railway); tube; subway
地心引力 terrestrial gravity; gravity
地震海啸 seismic sea wave; tsunami
地震烈度 earthquake intensity
地震台站 seismograph (*or* seismic) station
地震预报 earthquake prediction; earthquake forecasting
地震震级 (earthquake) magnitude
地址变数 address modifier
地址常数 address constant
地址空间 address space
地质构造 geological structure
地质勘探 geological prospecting
地质力学 geomechanics

地质时代 geologic age (*or* period)
地主阶级 the landlord class
地产经纪人 real estate broker
地磁记录仪 magnetograph
地对地导弹 ground-to-ground (guided) missile; surface-to-surface missile
地对空导弹 ground-to-air (guided) missile; surface-to-air missile
地平经纬仪 altazimuth
地球保护日 Earth Day
地球物理学 geophysics
地毯式轰炸 carpet bombing
地下出版物 underground publications
地下发射井 underground launching silo
地下核试验 underground nuclear test
地下人行道 underground pedestrian walk ways
地下水漏斗 cone of groundwater
地下停车场 subterranean parking
地缘政治学 geopolitics
地震检波器 geophone
地址存储器 addressed memory
地址计数器 address counter
地质年代学 geochronology
地方保护主义 local (*or* regional) protectionism
地方民族主义 local nationalism; local-nationality chauvinism
地面通讯设备 ground communication equipment (GCE)
地面(卫星)站 ground satellite station
地面遥测装置 ground telemetering equipment
地球探测火箭 geoprobe
地球同步卫星 geostationary satellite; synchronous satellite
地球资源卫星 earth resources satellite
地区霸权主义 regional hegemonism
地区保护主义 regional protectionism
地区间经济协调 economic coordination among regions

杕 [dì] 〔劲〕 (of a tree) grow in isolation; stand alone

弟 [dì] 〔名〕 ①younger brother ②younger brother-in-law; (male) cousin ③I
弟弟 younger brother; brother
弟妹 ①younger brother and sister ②younger brother's wife; sister-in-law
弟媳 younger brother's wife; sister-in-law
弟兄 brothers
弟子 ①disciple; pupil ②follower

的 [dì] 〔名〕 bull's-eye; target ➡ de; dǐ; dí

帝 [dì] 〔名〕 ①Supreme Being; the Divine ②emperor; monarch ③(short for 帝国主义) imperialism

帝俄 tsarist Russia
帝国 empire
帝王 emperor；monarch
帝制 autocratic monarchy；monarchy
帝国主义 imperialism
帝国主义列强 imperialist powers

递 [dì]
Ⅰ〔动〕hand over；pass；deliver Ⅱ〔副〕successively；in the proper order
递补 fill vacancies in the proper order
递加 progressively（*or* successively）increase；increase by degrees
递减 decrease progressively（*or* successively）；decrease by degrees
递交 hand over；present；submit
递解 escort（a criminal）from one place to another
递进 ①go forward one by one ②increase progressively；increase by degrees
递送 send；deliver
递增 increase progressively；increase by degrees
递眼色 tip sb the wink；wink at sb
递增率 increasing rate
递归程序 recursive program
递交国书 present credentials；present letter of credence
递推公式 recurrence formula
递延贷款 deferred credit
递延股息 deferred dividends
递减累进税 degressive tax；regressive tax；degressive taxation
递交抗议书 lodge a protest

莳 [dì]
〔名〕lotus seed

第 [dì]
Ⅰ（前缀）（*indicating ordinal numbers*）：宪法第三条 Article 3 of the Constitution Ⅱ〔名〕①grades in which successful candidates in the imperial examinations were placed ②residence of a high official Ⅲ〔副〕①but；however ②only；alone
第一 first；primary；foremost
第二审 second instance
第二性 secondary
第三纪 the Tertiary Period
第三者 ①third party（to a dispute）②person having an affair with either the husband or the wife ③the other person
第四纪 the Quaternary Period
第一审 first instance
第一手 firsthand
第一线 forefront；front line
第一性 primary
第二产业 secondary industry
第二课堂 the second classroom—referring to teaching activity outside the classroom

第二世界 the second world
第二梯队 second echelon；the second echelon-referring to middle-aged leaders
第二学历 second degree
第二职业 a second occupation，the second job；second job；spare-time work
第六感觉 the sixth sense
第三产业 tertiary industry；the service sector
第三世界 the third world
第三梯队 the third echelon-referring to young cadres who will be future leaders
第三状态 third state；sub-health state
第四产业 quarternary（*or* information）industry
第四官员 the fourth official
第四媒体 fourth media
第五纵队 fifth column
第一把手 first in command；number one man；a person holding primary responsibility
第一产业 primary industry
第一夫人 the First Lady（wife of head of state）
第一家庭 First Family（family of head of state）
第一时间 to be the first
第一世界 the first world
第一梯队 the first echelon-referring to veteran leaders
第二优先股 second-preferred
第三次浪潮 the Third Wave
第一轮投票 first round of voting
第一生产力 primary productive force；the most important factor that stimulates economic development
第一手材料 first-hand material；primary sources
第一线飞机 first-line aircraft
第二信号系统 the second signal system
第二宇宙速度 second cosmic velocity
第四宇宙速度 fourth cosmic velocity；galaxy exit velocity
第一信号系统 the first signal system
第二步战略目标 the second step of the country's strategic plan for accomplishing modernization
第二次打击能力 second-strike capability
第二次世界大战 the Second World War；World War Ⅱ
第二次鸦片战争 the Second Opium War
第一次世界大战 the First World War；Word War Ⅰ
第一优先留置权 first and paramount lien

谛 [dì]
Ⅰ〔副〕attentively；carefully Ⅱ〔名〕meaning；significance
谛视 examine closely
谛听 listen attentively

蒂 [dì]
名 base of a fruit

棣 [dì]
名 ①kerria ②younger brother

睇 [dì]
动 ①look askance;cast a sidelong glance ②look;glance
睇视 look askance;cast a sidelong glance (at sb)

缔 [dì]
动 form;establish;conclude
缔交 ①establish diplomatic relations ②form a friendship;contract a friendship
缔结 conclude;establish
缔盟 form an alliance
缔约 conclude (*or* sign) a treaty
缔造 found;create
缔约国 signatory (state) to a treaty;party to a treaty;(high) contracting party
缔约各方 each of the contracting parties

碲 [dì]
名 tellurium (Te)

踶 [dì]
动 kick;tramp

diǎ(ㄉ丨ㄚˇ)

嗲 [diǎ]
动 act or speak like a pampered child;speak or act in an arch,or coquettish manner
嗲声嗲气 in an affectedly childish voice;in a coquettish manner

diān(ㄉ丨ㄢ)

掂 [diān]
动 weigh in the hand
掂量 ①weigh in the hand ②think over;weigh up
掂算 estimate;calculate;weigh
掂斤播两 engage in petty calculations;be calculating in small matters

傎 [diān]
形 confused;disordered

滇 [diān]
名 another name for Yunnan (Province)
滇池 Dianchi Lake
滇藏公路 Yunnan-Tibet highway

颠 [diān]
Ⅰ 名 ①crown (of the head) ②top;peak;summit Ⅱ 动 ①jolt;bump ②fall;turn over;topple down ③jump up and run;run;make off
颠簸 jolt;bump;toss
颠倒 ① put (*or* turn) upside down;transpose;reverse;invert ② confused;disordered
颠覆 overturn;subvert
颠连 ①hardship;trouble;difficulty ②peak upon peak
颠茄 belladonna

颠倒黑白 confound black and white;confuse right and wrong;stand facts on their heads
颠倒是非 confound (*or* reverse) right and wrong;confuse truth and falsehood;turn things upside down
颠来倒去 over and over
颠沛流离 drift from place to place,homeless and miserable;wander about in a desperate plight;lead a vagabond life
颠扑不破 be able to withstand heavy battering;irrefutable;indisputable
颠三倒四 incoherent;disorderly;confused
颠扑不破的真理 incontestable truth

蹎 [diān]
动 fall down
蹎仆 fall over

攧 [diān]
动 fall;drop

巅 [diān]
名 mountain top;peak;summit
巅峰 summit;peak;pinnacle

癫 [diān]
形 mentally deranged;insane
癫狂 ①demented;mad;insane ②frivolous
癫痫 epilepsy

diǎn(ㄉ丨ㄢˇ)

典 [diǎn]
Ⅰ 名 ① standard;canon;law ② standard work of scholarship;definitive work;code ③ allusion;literary quotation ④ceremony Ⅱ 动 ①be in charge of ②pawn;lease;mortgage
典当 mortgage;pawn
典范 model;example;paragon
典故 allusion;literary quotation
典籍 ancient codes and records;ancient books and records
典礼 ceremony;celebration
典卖 mortgage
典契 deed of mortgage
典试 act as chief examiner
典型 ① typical case (*or* example);model;type ②typical;representative
典押 mortgage;pawn
典雅 (of diction,etc.) refined;elegant
典衣 pawn clothes
典狱 prison warden
典章 institutions;decrees and regulations
典质 mortgage;pawn
典制 laws and institutions
典当商 pawn operator
典狱官 custodial officer

点 [diǎn]
Ⅰ 名 ①drop (of liquid) ②stain;spot;dot;speck ③dot stroke (in Chinese characters) ④point ⑤decimal point;point ⑥mark (of a given degree or level);point (bearing a given

D

characteristic);place (distinguished by a certain trait) ⑦aspect (*or* the whole);point;feature ⑧iron bell or clapper used to announce the hour or rally the people:敲点 strike an iron clapper or bell to announce the hour ⑨unit of time during the night (1/5 of 更,or about 24 minutes) ⑩o'clock:十一点见。See you at eleven. ⑪appointed time:正点到达 arrive on schedule (*or* time)/快到点了。It's almost time. ⑫refreshments;snack;cake Ⅱ 量 ①a little;a bit;some:大一点儿 a little bigger ②(*used in counting items*):两点不成熟的意见 two tentative proposals (*or* comments) ③point,a unit of measurement (about 3.5 millimetres) for type and matrix Ⅲ 动 ①put a dot:点三个点表示省略 put three dots to indicate an omission ②touch on briefly;mention in passing;skim:船夫用篙轻轻一点,船就离岸了。The boatman pushed the boat off with only a shove of the pole. ③incline one's head or hand briefly ④drip:点眼药 put drops in the eyes ⑤plant in holes;dibble ⑥check one by one;count one by one ⑦select;choose ⑧make clear directly or indirectly;hint;point out ⑨light;kindle;ignite ⑩embellish;ornament;adorn ⑪stain;spot

点播 request a programme from a radio station

点拨 give directions;show how (to do sth);coach

点菜 choose dishes from a menu;order dishes (in a restaurant)

点唱 (of an audience) request a number (a song,an aria from a traditional opera,etc.)

点穿 bring sth out into the open;lay bare

点滴 ①a bit ②intravenous drip

点定 make corrections in a piece of writing

点焊 spot (*or* point) welding

点火 ①light a fire ②ignition ③stir up trouble

点货 check over goods;tally the cargo;take stock

点饥 have a snack to stave off hunger

点击 click

点将 ①(in traditional operas) call the muster roll of officers and assign them tasks ②name a person for a particular job

点交 hand over item by item

点睛 bring a picture of a dragon to life by putting in the pupils of its eyes—add the touch that brings a work of art to life;add the finishing touch;add an apt word to clinch the point

点名 ①call the roll ②mention sb by name

点明 point out;put one's finger on

点炮 detonate (*or* ignite) a charge;cause a blowup

点评 ①make comments on;discuss. ②comment (spoken or written)

点破 bring sth out into the open;lay bare;point out bluntly

点钱 check (*or* count) the money

点燃 light;kindle;ignite

点染 ①add details to a painting ②touch up a piece of writing;polish a piece of writing

点射 ①fixed fire ②firing in bursts

点收 check and accept

点数 check the number (of pieces, etc.);count

点题 bring out the theme

点头 nod one's head;nod

点心 light refreshments;pastry

点穴 (in Chinese boxing) touch vital points on the adversary's body to cause internal injury

点烟 light a cigarette

点验 examine item by item

点阵 lattice

点种 dibble in the seeds

点缀 ①embellish;ornament;adorn ②use sth merely for show

点字 braille

点子 ①drop (*or* liquid) ②spot;dot;speck ③beat (of percussion instruments) ④key point ⑤idea;pointer

点钞机 money-counting machine (for bills only)

点火圈 ignition coil

点击率 page view

点名册 roll book;roll

点播节目 program on-demand

点火试验 firing run

点金成铁 touch gold and turn it into iron—miscreate a piece of writing

点名攻击 attack sb by name

点石成金 touch a stone and turn it into gold—turn a crude essay into a literary gem

点头哈腰 bow unctuously;bow and scrape

点头之交 nodding (*or* bowing) acquaintance

点子公司 ideas company

点对点传输 point to point transmission

点阵打印机 dot-matrix printer

点面结合,以点带面 combine work on key points with work in other areas;promote work in all areas by drawing upon experience gained in the work on key points;link work at selected spots with that in the entire field

碘 [diǎn]
名 iodine (I)

碘酊 tincture of iodine

碘仿 iodoform

碘酒 tincture of iodine

碘盐 iodized salt

碘值 iodine number (*or* value)

碘化银 silver iodide
碘试验 iodine test
碘中毒 iodism

踮 [diǎn] 动 stand on tiptoe

diàn(ㄉㄧㄢˋ)

电 [diàn] Ⅰ 名 ①electricity; electric power ②telegram; cable Ⅱ 动 ①give or get an electric shock ②send a cable; cable; send a telegram; telegraph
电霸 electricity tyrants
电棒 (electric) torch; flashlight
电报 telegram; cable
电表 ①any meter for measuring electricity, such as ammeter or voltmeter ②kilowatt-hour meter; watt-hour meter; electric meter
电波 同"电磁波"
电铲 power shovel
电场 electric field
电车 ①tram; tramcar; streetcar ②trolleybus; trolley
电池 (electric) cell; battery
电传 telex
电磁 electromagnetism
电大 college courses broadcast on television
电导 conductance
电灯 electric lamp; electric light
电动 motor-driven; power-driven; electric
电镀 electroplate
电感 inductance
电工 ①electrical engineering ②electrician
电光 light produced by electricity; lightning
电棍 eletric prod
电焊 electric welding
电荷 electric charge; charge
电贺 telegraph one's congratulations to sb; cable a message of congratulations
电弧 electric arc
电话 ①telephone; phone ②phone call
电汇 telegraphic money order; remittance by telegram; telegraphic transfer
电机 electrical machinery
电积 electrodeposition
电极 electrode
电键 telegraph key; key; button
电教 education with electrical audio-visual aids; audio-visual education programme
电解 electrolysis
电锯 electric saw
电抗 reactance
电缆 electric cable; cable
电离 ionization
电力 electric power; power
电疗 electrotherapy
电料 electrical materials and appliances
电铃 ①electric bell ②doorbell
电流 electric current
电炉 ①electric stove; hot plate ②electric furnace
电路 (electric) circuit
电码 (telegraphic) code
电门 (electric) switch
电木 bakelite
电纳 susceptance
电脑 "electronic brain"—computer
电钮 push button; button
电瓶 storage battery; accumulator
电气 electric
电器 electrical equipment (*or* appliance)
电热 electric heat; electrothermal
电容 electric capacity; capacitance
电扇 electric fan
电石 calcium carbide
电视 television; TV
电枢 armature
电刷 brush
电台 ① transmitter-receiver; transceiver ② broadcasting station; radio station
电烫 permanent hair styling (*or* waving); permanent wave; perm
电梯 lift; elevator
电筒 (electric) torch; flashlight
电网 electrified wire netting; live wire entanglement
电位 (electric) potential
电线 (electric) wire
电信 telecommunications
电刑 ①torture by electricity ②electrocution; electric chair
电学 electricity (as a science)
电讯 ①(telegraphic) dispatch; telecommunications ②radio telecommunication signals
电压 voltage
电唁 send a telegram (*or* message) of condolence
电椅 the electric chair
电影 film; movie; motion picture
电泳 electrophoresis
电源 power supply; power source; mains
电灶 electric cooking stove (*or* range)
电闸 main switch; master switch
电钟 electric clock
电子 electron
电阻 resistance
电钻 electric drill
电报机 telegraph
电报局 telegraph office
电冰箱 (electric) refrigerator; fridge; freezer
电唱机 electric gramophone (*or* phonograph); record player
电唱头 pickup (of a record player)

D

D

电唱针 (gramophone) stylus; needle
电磁波 electromagnetic wave
电磁炮 eletromagnetic gun
电磁铁 electromagnet
电磁学 electromagnetics
电灯泡 electric (light) bulb
电动机 (electric) motor
电动势 electro-motive force (EMF)
电度表 kilowatt-hour meter; watt-hour meter; electric meter
电饭煲 (electric) rice cooker
电风扇 同"电扇"
电工学 electrical engineering; electrotechnics
电功率 electric power
电灌站 electric pumping station (or house)
电焊工 electric welder
电焊条 welding electrode; welding rod
电化学 electrochemistry
电话簿 telephone directory (or book)
电话机 telephone (set)
电话间 telephone box (or booth, kiosk); call box
电话局 telephone office (or exchange)
电话卡 telephone card
电话亭 telephone booth; telephone kiosk; call box
电火花 electric spark
电机车 electric locomotive
电吉他 electric guitar
电价键 electrovalent bond
电教馆 the hall for education with electrical audio-visual aids (or A/V) centre
电解质 electrolyte
电介质 dielectric
电老虎 electricity tiger
电烙铁 ① electric iron ② electric soldering iron
电离层 ionosphere
电力网 power network
电力线 power line; electric line of force
电流表 同"安培计"
电流计 galvanometer
电路图 circuit diagram
电木粉 phenolic moulding powder
电脑盲 computer illiteracy
电脑迷 computerite
电瓶车 storage battery car; electromobile
电气化 electrify
电气石 tourmaline
电器店 electric appliances shop
电热杯 electric heating jug
电热器 electric heater
电热丝 heating wire
电热毯 electric blanket
电容器 condenser; capacitor
电熔炼 electric smelting
电渗析 electrodialysis

电石气 acetylene; ethyne
电视车 TV jeep; television car
电视剧 TV drama; TV play
电视片 telefilm
电视塔 television tower
电视台 television station
电视套 TV set cover
电视网 television network
电信局 telecommunication bureau
电压表 voltmeter
电冶金 electrometallurgy
电影节 film festival
电影界 film (or movie) circles
电影院 cinema; movie (house)
电影周 film week
电玉粉 urea-formaldehyde moulding powder
电源线 power cord
电渣炉 electroslag furnace
电铸版 electrotype
电子秤 electronic-weighing system
电子管 electron tube; valve
电子枪 electron gun
电子琴 electronic organ; electronic keyboard
电子束 electron beam
电子雾 electronic fog
电子学 electronics
电子眼 electronic eyes
电子云 electron cloud
电子战 electronic combat (EC); electronic warfare (EW)
电报等级 telegram message precedence
电报挂号 cable address; telegraphic address
电磁辐射 electromagnetic radiation
电磁感应 electromagnetic induction
电磁兼容 electromagnetic compatibility
电磁污染 electromagnetic pollution
电动力学 electrodynamics
电动剃刀 electric shaver
电动玩具 battery operated toy
电光工艺 schreinering
电弧焊接 (electric) arc welding
电化当量 electrochemical equivalent
电化教育 education with electrical audio-visual aids; audio-visual education programme
电话传真 telefacsimile
电话分机 extention (telephone)
电话号码 telephone number
电话会议 telephone conference; teleconference
电话银行 telephone bank
电话用户 telephone subscriber
电离层暴 ionospheric storm
电力捕鱼 electrofishing
电力机车 eletric locomotive
电脑病毒 computer virus
电脑犯罪 computer crime
电脑顾问 computer adviser

电脑红娘 computer dating
电脑排版 computer composition
电脑文化 cyberculture
电脑验光 computer optometry
电脑游戏 computer game
电脑中心 electronic computer centre
电热针灸 electrothermal acupuncture
电视大学 TV university
电视电话 video telephone；video-phone
电视电影 tele cine
电视购物 teleshopping
电视广播 television broadcasting；telecasting；videocast
电视广告 television advertising
电视会议 video conference
电视机柜 television board
电视讲座 telecourse
电视教育 screen education
电视录像 television recording
电视频道 television channel
电视屏幕 television screen
电视商场 TV home shopping
电视文化 TV culture
电视文学 literature TV
电视小品 TV comic skit
电视信号 television signal
电视直销 TV home shopping
电视制导 television guidance
电视转播 television relay
电影胶片 cinefilm；motion-picture film
电影剧本 scenario
电影明星 film star；movie star
电影演员 film actor (*or* actress)
电影字幕 (film) caption
电针疗法 acupuncture with electric stimulation；galvano-acupuncture
电针麻醉 galvano-acupuncture anaesthesia
电子病历 electronic medical record
电子宠物 virtual pet
电子传递 electron transfer
电子词典 electronic dictionary
电子对抗 electronic countermeasures
电子防御 electronic defence
电子伏特 electron-volt
电子干扰 electronic jamming
电子光学 electron optics
电子函件 e-mail；electronic mail
电子贺卡 electronic card
电子汇款 electronic remit
电子货币 e-money；electronic money
电子进攻 electronic attack
电子警察 electronic police
电子竞技 cyber athletic
电子壳层 electron shell
电子媒体 electronic medium
电子排版 computer composition
电子签名 electronic signature

电子钱包 electronic wallet
电子商务 electronic commerce；e-business
电子世界 electronic world
电子图书 e-book；electronic book
电子玩具 electronic toys
电子伪装 electronic camouflage
电子信箱 electronic mail box；electronic mailbox
电子音乐 electronic music
电子银行 electronic banking
电子邮件 e-mail；electronic mail
电子邮箱 e-mail box
电子游戏 electronic game；video game；TV game
电子侦察 eletronic reconnaissance
电子政务 electronic government affair
电报音响器 telegraph sounder
电池充电器 battery charger
电动计分器 electric scoring apparatus
电话交换机 telephone switch board
电话交换台 telephone exchange (*or* switchboard)
电话增音机 telephone repeater
电脑记事簿 personal digital assistant；PDA
电脑恐惧症 cyberphobia
电容传声器 condenser microphone
电视大奖赛 grand TV prix
电视发射机 television transmitter
电视接收机 television receiver；television set
电视连续剧 TV series；television serial；TV play series
电视摄影机 television camera；telecamera
电视收视率 TV audience rating；TV viewership
电视转播车 telecruiser；outside broadcast van
电影放映机 (film) projector；cineprojector
电影剪辑机 film editing machine
电影摄像机 cinecamera；film camera
电影摄影师 cinematographer；cameraman
电影说明书 film synopsis
电影招待会 film reception
电源变压器 power transformer；mains transformer
电子出版物 electronic publications
电子公告栏 bulletin board system (BBS)
电子计时器 electronic timer
电子计算机 electronic computer
电子计算器 electronic calculator
电子刻版机 electronic engraving machine
电子图书馆 electronic library
电子望远镜 electron telescope
电子物理学 electron physics
电子显微镜 electron microscope
电子游艺厅 arcade
电子游戏机 video game player；TV game player
电视实况转播 live television coverage；live

telecast
电视卫星中继 television relay by satellite
电视转播卫星 television transmission satellite
电子百科全书 electronic encyclopedia
电子点火装置 electric ignition device
电子对抗系统 electronic warfare system
电子管收音机 valve radio set
电子监测仪器 electronic surveillance instrument
电子警报系统 electronic alarm system
电传打字电报机 teletypewriter;teleprinter
电视雷达导航仪 teleran
电子回旋加速器 betatron
电子现金出纳机 electronic cash register

佃 ［diàn］
勋 rent land (from a landlord) ➡tián
佃户 tenant (farmer)
佃农 tenant peasant;tenant farmer
佃租 land rent

甸 ［diàn］
名 open country outside a town

阽 ［diàn］
勋 close on the verge of (danger)

站 ［diàn］
名 ①indoor earthen platform (for food and wine vessels) ②protective screen or barrier

店 ［diàn］
名 ①inn ②shop;store
店铺 shop;store
店堂 the business quarter of a shop (or store);commodity section
店员 shop assistant;salesclerk;clerk;salesman (or saleswoman)

玷 ［diàn］
Ⅰ 名 flaw in a piece of jade Ⅱ 勋 tarnish;disgrace;blemish
玷辱 bring disgrace on;be a disgrace to
玷污 stain;sully;tarnish

垫 ［diàn］
Ⅰ 勋 ①put sth under sth else to raise it;spread sth over sth else;make level by filling up;pad ②fill in gap;insert ③pay for sb and expect to be paid back later Ⅱ 名 pad;cushion;mattress;mat
垫背 act as a cushion—bear the blame for others;be made a scapegoat
垫付 pay for sb and expect to be repaid later
垫肩 shoulder pad (or padding)
垫路 repair a road by filling the holes
垫圈 ［diànjuàn］ bed down the livestock;spread earth in a pigsty,cowshed,etc.
垫款 money advanced for sb to be paid back later
垫球 under pass;under toss
垫片 ①spacer ②shim
垫平 level up
垫圈 ［diànquān］ washer
垫子 mat;pad;cushion

垫脚石 stepping-stone
垫密片 gasket
垫上运动 mat tumbling;mat work

钿 ［diàn］
名 flower-patterned ornament made of gold foil;shell-inlaid flower pattern on wooden or lacquer ware ➡tián

淀 ［diàn］
Ⅰ 勋 form sediment;settle;precipitate Ⅱ 名 shallow lake
淀粉 starch;amylum
淀粉酶 amylase
淀积作用 illuviation

惦 ［diàn］
勋 be concerned about;keep thinking about
惦记 remember with concern;be concerned about;keep thinking about
惦念 keep thinking about;be anxious about;worry about

奠 ［diàn］
勋 ①establish;settle ②make offerings to the spirits of the dead
奠定 establish;settle
奠都 establish (or found) a capital
奠基 lay a foundation
奠仪 a gift of money made on the occasion of a funeral
奠基仪式 foundation stone laying ceremony

殿 ［diàn］
Ⅰ 名 hall;palace Ⅱ 勋 march at the rear;march in the rear
殿后 bring up the rear
殿军 ①rearguard ②last winner in a contest;last among the winners
殿堂 palace or temple hall
殿下 Your Highness;His (or Her) Highness

靛 ［diàn］
名 ①indigo ②indigo-blue
靛蓝 indigo
靛青 ①indigo-blue ②indigo

diāo（ㄉㄧㄠ）

习 ［diāo］
Ⅰ 形 sly;wily;cunning;tricky Ⅱ 勋 ①create difficulties;make things difficult ②take (things from others) by force ③be picky about food
刁悍 cunning and fierce
刁滑 cunning;crafty;artful
刁民 unruly people
刁难 create difficulties;make things difficult
刁钻 cunning;artful;wily
刁钻古怪 sly and capricious

叼 ［diāo］
勋 hold in the mouth

凋 ［diāo］
勋 wither
凋敝 ①(of life) hard;destitute ②(of busi-

ness) depressed
凋零 withered, fallen and scattered about
凋落 wither and fall
凋谢 ①wither and fall ②die of old age

貂 [diāo]
名 marten; ermine
貂皮 fur or pelt of marten; marten
貂裘 marten coat
貂熊 glutton

碉 [diāo]
名 pillbox; blockhouse
碉堡 pillbox; blockhouse
碉楼 watchtower

雕 [diāo]
Ⅰ 动 ①carve; engrave; sculpt ②decorated with coloured drawings Ⅱ 名 ① carving; sculpture ②eagle; vulture
雕花 ① carve patterns or designs on woodwork ②carving
雕刻 carve; engrave
雕漆 carved lacquerware
雕塑 sculpture
雕像 statue
雕琢 ①cut and polish (jade, etc.); carve ② write in an ornate style
雕虫小技 insignificant skill (esp. in writing); the trifling skill of a scribe; literary skill of no high order
雕花玻璃 cut glass
雕梁画栋 carved beams and painted rafters—a richly ornamented building

diǎo(ㄉㄧㄠˇ)

鸟 [diǎo]
形 fucking; damned ⇒niǎo

屌 [diǎo]
名 penis

diào(ㄉㄧㄠˋ)

吊 [diào]
Ⅰ 动 ①hang; suspend; dangle ②lift up or let down with a rope, etc.; haul ③drop (the ball or shuttle) where one's rival or rivals find it hard to retrieve ④put in a fur lining; line ⑤revoke; withdraw ⑥condole; mourn Ⅱ 名 ①crane ②(monetary unit in ancient China) a string of 1,000 cash
吊钹 suspension cymbal
吊车 crane; hoist
吊床 hammock
吊打 hang up and beat sb
吊灯 pendent lamp
吊斗 cableway bucket
吊杆 ①well-sweep; sweep ②boom; jib
吊杠 trapeze
吊钩 (lift) hook; hanger
吊古 visit a historical site and muse over the

past
吊环 rings
吊架 hanger
吊景 drop scene
吊雷 hanging mine
吊链 chain sling; sling chain
吊楼 house projecting over the water
吊铺 hanging bed; hammock
吊桥 ①suspension bridge ②drawbridge
吊丧 visit the bereaved to offer one's condolences; pay a condolence call
吊扇 ceiling fan
吊死 hang by the neck; hang oneself
吊索 sling
吊桶 well-bucket; bucket
吊慰 offer condolences
吊线 plumb-line
吊销 revoke; withdraw
吊孝 visit the bereaved to offer one's condolences; pay a condolence call
吊唁 condole; offer one's condolences
吊装 hoisting
吊膀子 (of a man) try to get fresh with a woman; flirt
吊货盘 platform (*or* tray) sling
吊货网 cargo net
吊嗓子 train (*or* exercise) one's voice
吊袜带 garters; suspenders
吊胃口 tantalize
吊钟花 fuchsia
吊儿郎当 careless and casual; slovenly
吊销签证 cancel a visa already issued
吊销许可证 revoke a license
吊销营业执照 revoke the business license

钓 [diào]
Ⅰ 动 ①fish with a hook and line; angle ② fish for; angle for; hunt for; seek Ⅱ 名 fishhook
钓饵 bait
钓竿 fishing rod
钓钩 fishhook
钓具 fishing tackle
钓丝 fishline; fishing-line
钓鱼 go fishing; angle

调 [diào]
Ⅰ 动 ①transfer; shift; move ②investigate; enquire into ③ allot; allocate ④ exchange Ⅱ 名 ①accent; tone ②argument; view; tone (of one's words) ③key ④air; tune; melody ⑤tone; tune ⇒tiáo
调包 stealthily substitute one thing for another
调拨 allocate and transfer (goods or funds); allot
调查 investigate; inquire into; look into; survey
调档 transfer the files; examine sb's record

调动 ①transfer；shift ②move（troops）；manoeuvre；muster ③bring into play；arouse；mobilize

调度 ①dispatch（trains，buses，etc.）②dispatcher ③manage；control

调防 relieve a garrison

调号 ①tone mark ②key signature

调换 exchange；change；swop

调回 recall（troops，etc.）

调集 assemble；muster

调离 be transferred from one place or job（to another）

调令 transfer order

调派 send；assign

调配 allocate；deploy

调遣 dispatch；assign

调任 be transferred to another post

调式 mode

调研 investigation and research；survey and study

调演 assemble theatrical companies or actors and actresses to give performances

调用 transfer（under a unified plan）

调运 allocate and transport

调值 tone pitch

调职 be transferred to another post

调子 ①tune；melody ②tone（of speech）；note

调拨价 price for re-allocated products；price at appropriation or when appropriated

调查会 fact-finding meeting

调车场 switchyard

调度室 dispatcher's office；control room

调度员 dispatcher；controller

调门儿 ①pitch ②point of view；argument

调研员 investigator and researcher

调兵遣将 ① dispatch officers and men；move troops；deploy forces ②muster and organize manpower（according to needs）

调查户口 census-taking

调查问卷 questionnaire

调度程序 dispatcher；scheduler

调虎离山 lure the tiger out of the mountains—lure the enemy away from his base

调换债券 refunding bonds

调用程序 calling program

调用序列 calling sequence

掉 [diào] 动 ①fall；drop；shed；come off ②fall behind；lag behind ③lose；be missing ④reduce；cut down；drop；lower ⑤wag；wave；shake ⑥turn；turn round；turn back；spin；swing ⑦change；exchange；swap ⑧show off；vaunt ⑨(*used after some verbs，indicating the result of an action*)：把没用的东西扔掉 throw away the junk

掉包 stealthily substitute one thing for another

掉队 drop out（*or* off）；fall behind

掉魂 be frightened out of one's wits

掉价 fall（*or* drop）in price；go down in price

掉色 lose colour；fade

掉头 turn round；turn about

掉转 turn round；make a U-turn

掉书袋 a walking satchel—a person who lards his speech with quotations and allusions

掉头发 one's hair is thinning

掉眼泪 shed tears

掉以轻心 lower one's guard；relax one's vigilance；treat sth lightly

diē（ㄉㄧㄝ）

爹 [diē] 名 father；dad；pa

跕 [diē] 动 fall；tumble；land；descend

跌 [diē] 动 ①fall；tumble ②drop；fall；go down；plummet

跌宕 ①free and easy；bold and unconstrained ②flowing rhythm

跌倒 fall；tumble

跌幅 size of decrease；range of decrease

跌价 fall（*or* drop）in price；go down in price

跌跤 ①trip（*or* stumble）and fall；fall ②make a mistake；meet with a setback；suffer a setback

跌落 fall；drop

跌势 decline

跌停板 limit down

跌打损伤 injuries from falls，fractures，contusions and strains

跌跌撞撞 dodder along；stagger along

dié（ㄉㄧㄝ）

迭 Ⅰ 动 ①alternate；replace；change Ⅱ 副 ①repeatedly；time and again ②in time

迭次 repeatedly；again and again

迭起 occur repeatedly；happen frequently

迭代操作 iterative operation

垤 [dié] 名 mound

映 [dié] 名 (of the sun) incline to the west

瓞 [dié] 名 small melon

谍 [dié] 名 ① espionage ② intelligence agent；undercover agent；spy

谍报 information obtained through espionage；intelligence report；intelligence

堞 [dié] 名 battlements

D

耋 [dié]
名 age of seventy or eighty; old age

揲 [dié]
动 fold up

喋 [dié]
喋血 bloodshed; bloodbath
喋喋不休 chatter away; rattle on; talk endlessly

慄 [dié]
名 fear; terror
慄息 hold one's breath in fear; be struck dumb with terror

牒 [dié]
名 ① official document; certificate ② record; book; volume

叠 [dié]
动 ① pile up; repeat ② fold
叠句 reiterative sentence
叠韵 rhyming compound
叠字 reduplicated word; reduplication
叠罗汉 pyramid
叠床架屋 pile one bed upon another or build one house on top of another—needless duplication

碟 [dié]
名 (small) dish; saucer
碟子 small dish; small plate

蝶 [dié]
名 butterfly
蝶骨 sphenoid bone
蝶泳 butterfly stroke
蝶形花 papilionaceous flower

dīng (ㄉㄧㄥ)

丁 [dīng]
Ⅰ 名 ① male adult; man ② members of a family; population ③ person engaged in certain types of labour ④ small cube (of meat or vegetable) Ⅱ 动 meet; encounter
丁当 ding-dong; jingle; clatter
丁级 fourth grade; grade D
丁零 tinkle; jingle
丁烷 butane
丁烯 butene
丁香 ① lilac ② clove
丁字 T-shaped
丁点儿 a tiny bit
丁克族 DINKS (a short term for "dual income, no kids")
丁字尺 T-square
丁字钢 T-steel
丁字街 T-shaped road junction
丁字形 T-shaped
丁克家庭 DINK family
丁零当郎 cling-clang
丁种维生素 Vitamin D
丁是丁，卯是卯 keep *ding* (a Heavenly Stem) distinct from *mao* (an Earthly Branch)—be meticulous; be precise; be unaccommodating

仃 [dīng]
◇ 伶仃 left alone without help; lonely

叮 [dīng]
动 ① sting; bite ② urge again and again; exhort; admonish ③ say or ask again to make sure
叮咛 urge again and again; warn; exhort
叮嘱 urge again and again; warn; exhort

玎 [dīng]
玎玲 clink; jingle; tinkle

盯 [dīng]
动 fix one's eyes on; gaze at; stare at
盯防 close-marking defence; man-for-man defence
盯梢 shadow sb; tail sb

钉 [dīng]
Ⅰ 名 nail; tack Ⅱ 动 ① follow closely; shadow; tail ② urge; press; keep asking or reminding ⇒ dìng
钉锤 nail hammer; claw hammer
钉螺 oncomelania (a kind of freshwater snail, which is the intermediate host of the blood fluke); snail
钉帽 the head of a nail
钉耙 (iron-toothed) rake
钉人 watch (*or* mark) an opponent in a game
钉鞋 spiked shoes; spikes
钉子 ① nail ② snag
钉齿耙 spike-tooth harrow
钉子户 tartar; recalcitrant; household difficult to deal with
钉子精神 spirit of the nail—make the best use of one's time and work persistently to achieve one's purpose

疔 [dīng]
名 malignant boil or furuncle
疔疱 miliary vesicle under the nose or on either side of the mandible

耵 [dīng]
耵聍 earwax; cerumen

酊 [dīng]
名 tincture ⇒ dǐng
酊剂 tincture

靪 [dīng]
动 repair or mend sole of a shoe

dǐng (ㄉㄧㄥ)

顶 [dǐng]
Ⅰ 名 top; peak; crown (of the head)：到顶 reach the peak (*or* limit) Ⅱ 动 ① hold or carry on the head ② push from below or behind; push up ③ gore; butt ④ prop up; sustain; sup-

D

port ⑤go against ⑥answer back;retort;rebuff ⑦undertake;cope with;stand up to ⑧equal;be equivalent to ⑨take the place of;substitute;replace ⑩transfer business licence,or lease of real estate;sublease Ⅲ 图 (of sth that has a top):一顶帽子 a cap;a hat Ⅳ 副 ①most;very;extremely:顶有用 most useful ②at a specified time:顶下午两点你再来吧。 You can come at, say, two o'clock in the afternoon.

顶班 ①work on regular shifts;work full time ②work as a substitute for sb absent

顶板 roof

顶吹 top-blown

顶灯 dome light (of a car)

顶点 ①apex;zenith;acme;pinnacle ②vertex; apex

顶端 ①top;peak;apex ②end

顶多 at (the) most;at best

顶风 ①against the wind ②head wind ③in defiance of

顶峰 peak;summit;pinnacle

顶骨 parietal bone

顶好 ①very good ②had better;it would be best

顶级 top

顶尖 topmost;top level;tip-top

顶交 top cross

顶角 vertex angle

顶礼 prostrate oneself before sb and press one's head against his feet (a Buddhist salute of the highest respect)

顶命 give a life for a life;pay with one's life (for a first-degree murder)

顶盘 highest quotation

顶棚 ceiling

顶球 head (a ball)

顶少 at (the) least

顶事 be useful;serve the purpose

顶替 ① take sb's place;replace ② displacement

顶头 ①coming directly towards one ②top; end

顶芽 terminal bud

顶用 be of use (or help);serve the purpose

顶针 thimble

顶住 withstand;stand up to;hold out against

顶撞 contradict (one's elder or superior)

顶嘴 reply defiantly (usu. to one's elder or superior);answer back;talk back

顶呱呱 tip-top;first-rate;excellent

顶门儿 the front top of the head

顶牛儿 lock horns like bulls;clash;be at loggerheads

顶礼膜拜 prostrate oneself in worship;make a fetish of;pay homage to

顶天立地 of gigantic stature; of indomitable

spirit;dauntless

顶头上司 one's immediate (or direct) superior

顶部掘进法 top cut method

顶住外界压力 withstand outside pressure

酊 [dǐng] ➡dīng
◇酩酊 be dead drunk

鼎 [dǐng]
Ⅰ 名 ①ding—ancient cooking vessel with two loop handles and three (sometimes four) legs ②throne;state power ③pot;pan Ⅱ 形 great;grand Ⅲ 副 just when;at the very time

鼎沸 like a seething cauldron;noisy and confused

鼎革 change of dynasty or regime;dynastic change

鼎力 your kind effort

鼎立 (of three antagonists confronting one another) stand like the three legs of a tripod;tripartite confrontation;tripartite balance of forces

鼎盛 in a period of great prosperity;at the height of power and splendour

鼎新 make innovations

鼎足 the three legs of a tripod—three rival powers

鼎鼎大名 famous;celebrated;well-known

鼎足之势 tripartite balance of forces;triangular balance of power

dìng(ㄉㄧㄥˋ)

订 [dìng]
动 ①conclude;draw up;agree on:订条约 conclude a treaty ②subscribe to (a newspaper,etc.);book (a seat,ticket,etc.);order (merchandise, etc.) ③make corrections;revise ④staple together;bind

订单 order for goods;order form

订费 subscription (rate)

订购 order (goods);place an order for sth

订户 ①subscriber (to a newspaper or periodical) ②a person or household with a standing order for milk,etc.

订婚 be engaged (to be married); be betrothed

订货 order goods;place an order for goods

订交 pledge friendship;establish friendly relations with each other

订金 an initial payment;earnest

订立 conclude (a treaty, agreement, etc.); make (a contract,etc.)

订约 conclude a contract or treaty

订阅 subscribe to (a newspaper, periodical, etc.)

订正 make corrections;emend

订货单 order list

订货会 meeting for the placement of orders;

order-placing meeting

订货量 quantity (*or* size) of order

订书机 ① stapler; stapling-machine ② book-binding machine

订货付款 cash with order (CWO)

订货合同 goods-ordering contract; order contract

订货代理人 indent agent

钉 [dìng]
　　动 ①nail ②sew on ➡ dīng

定 [dìng]
Ⅰ 形 ① calm; still; stable ② determined; settled; established ③ stipulated; provided; fixed Ⅱ 动 ①fix; set ②decide; fix; set; make certain ③ subscribe to (a newspaper, magazine, etc.); book (seats, tickets, etc.); order (merchandise, etc.) Ⅲ 副 surely; certainly; definitely

定案 ①decide on (*or* pass) a verdict; reach a conclusion on a case ②verdict; final decision

定都 choose a site for the capital; establish a capital

定夺 make a final decision; decide

定额 quota; norm

定岗 set work requirements for a position

定稿 ①finalize a manuscript, text, etc. ②final version or text

定购 ①order (goods); place an order for sth ②a system of fixed quotas for purchasing

定规 ①established rule or practice; set pattern ②be bent on; be determined

定级 decide grade and level

定计 devise a stratagem; work out a scheme

定价 ①fix a price ②fixed price ③list price

定见 definite opinion; set view

定界 determination of boundaries

定金 deposit (put down on sth for future purchase)

定睛 fix one's eyes upon

定居 settle down

定局 ① foregone conclusion; inevitable outcome ②settle finally

定理 theorem

定例 usual practice; set pattern; routine

定量 ①fixed quantity; ration ②determine the amounts of the components of a substance

定律 (scientific) law

定论 final conclusion

定苗 final singling (of seedlings)

定名 name; denominate

定期 ①fix (*or* set) a date ②regular; at regular intervals; periodical

定钱 deposit; earnest (money)

定亲 engagement (usu. arranged by parents); betrothal

定情 pledge love

定然 certainly; definitely

定神 ①collect oneself; compose oneself; pull oneself together ②concentrate one's attention; take a grip on oneself; collect one's thoughts

定位 ①fixed position; location; orientation ②orientate; position; fix position

定息 fixed interest

定弦 ①tune a stringed instrument ②make up one's mind

定向 directional

定心 ①centering ②feel relieved; feel at ease

定形 ①fibre setting ②knitting boarding

定型 finalize the design; fall into a pattern

定性 ①determine the nature (of an offence or a case) ②determine the chemical composition of a substance

定义 definition

定影 fixing; fixation

定语 attribute

定员 fixed number of staff members or passengers

定则 rule

定植 field planting (*or* setting)

定址 addressing

定制 ①have sth made to order; have sth custom-made ②an established rule or practice

定子 stator

定罪 declare sb guilty; convict sb (of a crime)

定做 have sth made to order (*or* measure)

定点厂 designated factory; factory designated by the state to make a particular product

定调子 set the tone (*or* keynote)

定购粮 quota grain to be sold by peasants to the state at fixed price; list price

定冠词 definite article

定居点 settlement (of herdsmen, fishermen, etc.)

定时器 timer

定位器 positioner

定向仪 direction finder

定心丸 sth capable of setting sb's mind at ease

定音鼓 kettledrums; timpani

定比定律 the law of definite (*or* constant) proportions

定点企业 a specialized enterprise

定点运算 fixed-point arithmetic

定额管理 quota management

定高气球 constant-level balloon

定格镜头 freeze shot

定购定销 fixed quotas for purchasing and marketing

定量分析 quantitative analysis

定期班车 routine car

定期保险 term insurance

定期存款 fixed deposit; time deposit

定期贷款 term loan; time loan; time money

D

定期抵押 term mortgage
定期付款 periodical payments; payment on terms
定期汇票 date draft; time draft; time bill
定期贷款 time mortgage loan
定期债券 fixed-maturity bonds; term bond
定期租船 time charter
定时开关 time switch
定时炸弹 time bomb
定向爆破 directional blasting
定向地雷 oriented mine
定向培训 target training; job-oriented training
定向培育 directive breeding
定向天线 directional antenna
定向招生 targeted recruitment; recruitment with a fixed target enroll students who are pre-assigned specific posts or areas
定向分配 fixed direction allocation
定向培养 train professional personnel for a certain area or work unit
定向销售 fixed direction marketing
定向招生 directed recruitment of students; enroll students who are pre-assigned specific posts or areas
定性分析 qualitative analysis
定址方式 addressing mode
定额分配制 the quota system
定期信用证 time letter of credit
定向能武器 beam weapon
定活两便存款 either-time-or-savings deposit
定量供应商品 goods on ration
定量考核制度 quantitative appraisal system

铤 [dìng]
图 pig iron or crude copper

腚 [dìng]
图 buttocks

碇 [dìng]
图 heavy stone used as an anchor; killick

锭 [dìng]
Ⅰ 图 ① spindle ② (of medicine, Chinese ink, etc.) ingot-shaped tablet Ⅱ 圉 (of sth like an ingot): 一锭银子 a silver ingot
锭剂 lozenge; pastille; troche
锭模 ingot mould
锭墨 ink stick
锭钳 ingot dogs (or tongues)
锭铁 ingot iron
锭子 spindle

diū (ㄉ丨ㄡ)

丢 [diū]
劻 ① lose; mislay ② throw; cast; toss ③ put or lay aside; shelve
丢丑 lose face; be disgraced
丢掉 ① lose ② throw away; cast away; discard
丢脸 lose face; be disgraced
丢弃 abandon; discard; give up
丢人 lose face; be disgraced
丢失 lose
丢手 wash one's hands of; give up
丢饭碗 lose one's job
丢面子 lose face
丢眼色 wink at sb; tip sb the wink
丢盔卸甲 throw away one's helmet and coat of mail; throw away everything in headlong flight
丢人现眼 make a fool of oneself; make a spectacle of oneself
丢三落四 forget this and that; be always forgetting things
丢卒保车 give up a pawn to save a chariot—sacrifice minor things to save major ones

dōng (ㄉㄨㄥ)

东 [dōng]
图 ① east ② master; owner ③ host
东北 ① northeast ② northeast China; the Northeast
东城 eastern part of the city
东道 one who treats sb to a meal; host
东方 ① the east ② the East; the Orient
东风 ① east wind; spring wind ② driving force of revolution
东海 the Donghai Sea; the East China Sea
东家 a form of address formerly used by an employee to his employer or a tenant-peasant to his landlord; master; boss
东郊 eastern suburbs
东经 east longitude
东盟 the Association of Southeast Asian Nations (ASEAN)
东南 ① southeast ② southeast China; the Southeast
东欧 Eastern Europe
东西 [dōngxī] ① east and west ② from east to west
东西 [dōngxi] ① thing ② (referring to a person or animal) thing; creature
东亚 East Asia
东半球 the Eastern Hemisphere
东北虎 Manchurian tiger
东风带 easterlies
东南亚 Southeast Asia
东正教 the Orthodox Eastern Church
东奔西跑 run around here and there; bustle about; rush about (or around)
东窗事发 the plot has come to light; the secret is out
东倒西歪 leaning; unsteady; tottering
东方明珠 oriental pearl
东方文化 the Oriental/Occidental Culture
东郭先生 Master Dongguo (the soft-hearted scholar who narrowly escaped being eaten

by a wolf which he had helped to hide from a hunter)—a naive person who gets into trouble through being soft-hearted to evil people

东拉西扯 drag in irrelevant matters; talk at random; ramble

东鳞西爪 odds and ends; bits and pieces; fragments

东跑西颠 rush here and hurry there; rush about

东拼西凑 scrape together; knock together

东山再起 stage a comeback; resume one's former position

东施效颦 Dongshi, an ugly woman, knitting her brows in imitation of the famous beauty (西施), only to make herself uglier—crude imitation with ludicrous effect

东西对话 East-West dialogue

东张西望 gaze (*or* peer) around; glance this way and that; look in every direction

东风吹马耳 like the east wind blowing at the ear of a horse—go in one ear and out the other

东方航空公司 China Eastern Airlines; (US) Eastern Air Lines Inc.

"东突"恐怖分子 East Turkistan terrorist

东南亚国家联盟 the Association of Southeast Asian Nations (ASEAN)

冬 [dōng]
I 名 winter II 象 dub-a-dub; rat-tat; 战鼓
冬冬 booming (*or* dub-a-dub) of war drums
冬菜 preserved, dried cabbage or mustard greens
冬储 store away in winter
冬耕 winter ploughing
冬菇 dried mushrooms (picked in winter)
冬瓜 wax gourd; white gourd
冬灌 winter irrigation
冬烘 shallow but pedantic
冬季 winter
冬眠 winter sleep; hibernation
冬青 Chinese ilex
冬笋 winter bamboo shoots
冬天 winter
冬汛 winter fishing season
冬衣 winter clothes
冬泳 winter outdoor swimming
冬至 the Winter Solstice—the 22nd of the 24 solar terms
冬装 winter dress (*or* clothes)
冬候鸟 winter bird
冬虫夏草 Chinese caterpillar fungus
冬季施工 winter construction
冬季作物 winter crops
冬季体育运动 winter sports

dǒng（ㄉㄨㄥˇ）

董 [dǒng]
I 动 direct; superintend; supervise II 名 director; trustee
董理 manage
董事 director; trustee
董其成 supervise a project until its completion
董事会 board of directors (in an enterprise); board of trustees (in an educational institution)
董事长 chairman (*or* president) of the board of directors

懂 [dǒng]
动 understand; know
懂得 understand; know; grasp
懂行 know the business; know the ropes
懂事 sensible; intelligent

dòng（ㄉㄨㄥˋ）

动 [dòng]
I 动 ① move; stir ② act; get moving ③ change; alter ④ use; wield ⑤ touch (one's heart); arouse ⑥ be moving; be touching ⑦ eat; drink II 副 easily; often
动笔 take up the pen; start writing
动产 movable property; movables; personal property
动词 verb
动荡 turbulence; upheaval; unrest
动工 ① begin construction; start building ② construct
动火 get angry; flare up
动机 motive; intention
动静 ① the sound of sth astir ② movement; activity; happenings; events
动力 ① motive power; power ② motive (*or* driving) force; impetus
动量 momentum
动令 command of execution
动乱 turmoil; disturbance; upheaval; turbulence
动脉 artery
动漫 cartoon and comic
动能 kinetic energy
动怒 lose one's temper; flare up
动气 take offence; get angry
动迁 relocate
动情 ① get worked up; become excited ② become enamoured; have one's (sexual) passions aroused
动人 moving; touching
动身 go (*or* set out) on a journey; leave (for a distant place)
动手 ① start work; get to work ② touch; handle ③ raise a hand to strike; hit out

D

动态 ① trends；developments ② dynamic state；dynamic condition
动弹 move；stir
动听 interesting or pleasant to listen to
动土 break ground；start building
动窝 start moving；make a move
动武 use force；start a fight；come to blows
动物 animal
动向 trend；tendency
动销 begin to sell
动心 one's mind is perturbed；one's desire，enthusiasm or interest is aroused
动刑 subject sb to torture；torture
动摇 shake；vacillate；waver
动议 motion
动因 cause
动用 put to use；employ；draw on
动员 mobilize；arouse
动辄 easily；frequently；at every turn
动作 ①movement；motion；action ②act；start moving
动不动 easily；frequently；at every turn
动电学 electrokinetics
动肝火 get angry；flare up
动画片 animated cartoon（or drawing）；cartoon
动力学 dynamics；kinetics
动脉弓 arch of aorta
动名词 gerund
动脑筋 use one's head
动能弹 kinetic energy missile
动迁户 household to be relocated
动手术 ①perform an operation；operate on sb ②have an operation；be operated on
动土层 layer of frozen earth；permafrost
动物胶 animal size（or glue）
动物学 zoology
动物油 animal oil
动物园 zoo；zoological garden
动物志 fauna
动员令 mobilization order
动作片 action film
动宾词组 verb-object word group
动产抵押 chattel mortgage
动荡不安 turbulent；in turmoil
动力机械 motive power machine
动脉血压 arterial pressure
动脉脉炎 arteritis
动脉硬化 arteriosclerosis
动能武器 kinetic energy weapon
动人心弦 tug at one's heartstrings；be deeply moving
动如脱兔 move like a hare
动手动脚 get fresh with sb
动态范围 dynamic range
动态分析 dynamic analysis
动态平衡 dynamic equilibrium

动态特性 dynamic characteristic
动弹不得 cannot move
动物区系 fauna
动眼神经 oculomotor nerve
动员报告 mobilization speech
动员大会 mobilization meeting
动辄得咎 be constantly taken to task；be blamed for whatever one does
动力反应堆 power reactor；power pile
动态经济学 dynamic economics
动态再定位 dynamic relocation
动物生态学 animal ecology
动植物检疫 quarantine of animals and plants
动产和不动产 movable and immovable property
动量守恒定律 the law of conservation of momentum
动脉粥样硬化 atherosclerosis
动态数据互换 dynamic data exchange（DDE）
动物蛋白因子 animal protein factor
动植物保护区 fauna and flora reserve
动物权益维护者 animal rightist

冻 ［dòng］ I 动 ①freeze ②feel very cold；freeze；be frostbitten Ⅱ 名 jelly
冻冰 freeze
冻疮 chilblain
冻害 freeze injury
冻僵 frozen stiff；numb with cold
冻结 ① freeze；congeal ②（of wages，prices，etc.）freeze
冻凝 congeal
冻伤 frostbite
冻死 freeze to death；freeze and perish；die of frost
冻土 frozen earth（or ground，soil）
冻雨 sleet
冻原 tundra
冻豆腐 frozen bean curd
冻土学 cryopedology
冻结存款 blocked/frozen deposits
冻结账目 frozen account
冻结资金 frozen fund；blocked fund
冻手冻脚 freezing（or ice）cold

侗 ［dòng］ 名 Dong nationality ➡ tóng

垌 ［dòng］ 名 field

栋 ［dòng］ I 名 ridgepole Ⅱ 量 used of housing：一栋楼房 a building
栋梁 ridgepole and beam—pillar of the state
栋梁之材 one with the makings of a statesman

洞 ［dòng］ I 名 hole；cavity 小洞不补，大洞吃苦。A stitch in time saves nine. Ⅱ 副 penetratingly；thoroughly Ⅲ 动 penetrate；pierce：弹洞其腹。A bullet pierced his belly. Ⅳ 区（ used

in speaking to stand for the number "0")
洞察 see clearly;have an insight into
洞彻 understand thoroughly;see clearly
洞穿 ①pierce ②have an insight into;understand fully
洞达 understand thoroughly
洞房 bridal (*or* nuptial) chamber
洞天 cave heaven—fairyland; a heavenly abode
洞悉 know clearly;understand thoroughly
洞箫 a vertical bamboo flute
洞晓 have a clear knowledge of
洞穴 cave;cavern
洞烛 see through;discern clearly
洞察力 insight;discernment
洞穴蟇 catacomb
洞房花烛 wedding festivities;wedding
洞若观火 see sth as clearly as a blazing fire
洞烛其奸 see through sb's tricks

恫 [dòng]
〔动〕 fear;fright;terror ➡ tōng
恫吓 threaten;intimidate

胴 [dòng]
〔名〕①trunk;body;torso ②large intestine

dōu（ㄉㄡ）

都 [dōu]
〔副〕①all;both;every ②*used together with*
是 *to indicate cause* ③even ④already ➡ dū

兜 [dōu]
Ⅰ〔名〕pocket;bag Ⅱ〔动〕①wrap up or hold
as if in a bag ②move round;go in a circle;
make a detour ③canvass;solicit ④take upon
oneself;take care of;assume responsibility for
⑤disclose all the details of the matter
兜捕 surround and seize;round up
兜抄 close in from the rear and both flanks;round up
兜底 reveal all the details (of a person's disreputable background, etc.);disclose the whole inside story
兜风 ①catch the wind ②go for a drive,ride or sail;go for a spin
兜揽 ① canvass;solicit ② take upon oneself (sb else's work,etc.)
兜售 peddle;hawk;tout for
兜子 pocket;bag
兜兜裤 sunsuit
兜圈子 ① go around in circles;circle ② beat about the bush
兜生意 canvass business;solicit customers

苑 [dōu]
Ⅰ〔名〕root and lower stem of some plants Ⅱ
〔量〕piece;clump;一苑白菜 a head of Chinese cabbage

篼 [dōu]
〔名〕bamboo (*or* cane,wicker) basket

dǒu（ㄉㄡ）

斗 [dǒu]
〔名〕① *dou*, a unit of dry measure for grain
(now about a decalitre) ② *dou*，a measure
square or drum-like,made of wood or bamboo
③ sth shaped like a *dou* measure; object
shaped like a cup or a dipper ④ whorl (of a
fingerprint) ⑤ancient wine vessel ⑥Big Dipper ➡ dòu
斗车 trolley (in a mine or at a construction site);tram
斗胆 make bold;venture
斗箕 fingerprint
斗架 ladder
斗笠 bamboo hat
斗篷 ①cape;cloak ②bamboo hat
斗渠 lateral canal
斗室 a small room
斗子 ① coal tub ② container made of tree branches or wood
斗烟丝 pipe tobacco
斗式提升机 bucket elevator

抖 [dǒu]
〔动〕 ① tremble; shiver; quiver；浑身直抖
tremble all over ②shake;jerk;flick;抖掉衣
服上的土 shake the dirt off one's clothes ③
disclose the inside story;expose ④ rouse;
muster up;stir up ⑤ throw one's weight
about;preen oneself;get on in the world
抖颤 shiver;quiver;tremble
抖动 shake;tremble;vibrate
抖搂 ①shake off;shake out of sth ②expose;bring to light
抖擞 enliven;rouse
抖空竹 play with a diabolo
抖威风 throw one's weight about
抖擞精神 brace up;pull oneself together

陡 [dǒu]
Ⅰ〔形〕steep;precipitous Ⅱ〔副〕suddenly;abruptly
陡变 change suddenly (*or* abruptly)
陡槽 chute
陡度 gradient
陡峻 high and precipitous
陡立 rise steeply
陡坡 steep slope;heavy gradient;brow;abrupt slope
陡峭 precipitous
陡然 suddenly;unexpectedly;abruptly
陡沿 sharp edge;steep side

蚪 [dǒu]
◇蝌蚪 tadpole

dòu（ㄉㄡˋ）

斗 [dòu]
㓰 ① fight; tussle ② struggle against; denounce; fight ③ make animals fight (as a game) ④compete with; contend with; contest with ⑤ come together; fit together; put together ➡ dǒu
斗法 ① exercise magic powers against each other ②use stratagems
斗鸡 ①game fowl; game cock ②cockfighting
斗牛 bullfight
斗殴 fight; scuffle
斗气 quarrel or contend with sb on account of a personal grudge
斗士 fighter; warrior
斗争 ① struggle; fight; combat ② accuse and denounce at a meeting ③ strive for; fight for
斗志 will to fight; fighting will
斗智 fight a battle of wits
斗嘴 ①quarrel; bicker; squabble ②banter
斗牛士 bullfighter; matador
斗蟋蟀 cricket fight; cricket duel
斗争性 fighting spirit; militancy
斗心眼儿 fight a battle of wits
斗智斗勇 contest of wits and courage

豆 [dòu]
名 ①ancient stemmed cup or bowl ② legumes; pulses; beans; peas ③ sth like a bean; bean-like thing
豆包 steamed bun stuffed with sweetened bean paste
豆饼 soyabean cake; bean cake
豆豉 fermented soyabeans, salted or otherwise
豆腐 bean curd
豆荚 pod
豆浆 soyabean milk
豆秸 beanstalk (left after threshing)
豆科 the pulse family; bean family; pea family
豆蔻 round cardamom (Amomum cardamomum)
豆绿 pea green
豆面 bean flour
豆苗 bean seedling
豆奶 soya milk
豆娘 damselfly
豆萁 beanstalk
豆蓉 fine bean mash, used as stuffing in cakes
豆乳 ①soyabean milk ②fermented bean curd
豆沙 sweetened bean paste
豆象 bean weevil
豆雁 bean goose
豆油 soyabean oil
豆渣 residue from beans after making soyabean milk; bean dregs
豆汁 ①a fermented drink made from ground beans ②soyabean milk
豆子 ①pod-bearing plant or its seeds ②bean-shaped thing
豆瓣酱 thick broad-bean sauce
豆腐房 bean-curd plant
豆腐干 dried bean curd
豆腐皮 skin of soyabean milk
豆腐乳 fermented bean curd
豆角儿 fresh kidney beans
豆芽儿 bean sprouts
豆制品 bean products
豆腐脑儿 jellied bean curd
豆科植物 legume; leguminous plant
豆蔻年华 (of a girl) in one's early teens
豆腐渣工程 construction project with building materials like bean dregs; project built with skimped materials; jerry-built project

逗 [dòu]
Ⅰ **㓰** ①tease; tantalize; play with ②entice; attract; provoke; amuse Ⅱ **形** amusing; funny Ⅲ **名** ① stay; stop; sojourn ② short pause in reading a Chinese sentence
逗哏 provoke laughter with funny remarks (esp. in a comic dialogue)
逗号 comma (，)
逗留 stay; stop
逗弄 tease; kid; make fun of
逗引 tease
逗趣儿 set people laughing (by funny remarks, etc.); amuse
逗笑儿 set people laughing
逗嘴皮子 cross words with sb; quarrel with sb

读 [dòu]
名 short pause in reading a Chinese sentence ➡ dú

饾 [dòu]
饾版 black block printing
饾饤 ①food for display ②load one's writing with fancy phrases

痘 [dòu]
名 ①smallpox; variola ②vaccine (lymph) ③smallpox pustule
痘疮 smallpox; variola
痘痕 pockmark
痘浆 vaccine lymph
痘苗 (bovine) vaccine

窦 [dòu]
名 ① hole; opening; aperture ② sinus; antrum
窦刀 antrotome
窦囊 antral pouch

dū（ㄉㄨ）

都 [dū]
Ⅰ **名** ①capital ②big city; metropolis ③local government between the county and town-

ship levels Ⅱ 形 beautiful;lovely ➡ dōu
都城 capital (of a country)
都督 ①commander-in-chief in ancient China ②provincial military governor in the early Republican period who was also in charge of civil administration
都会 a big city;metropolis
都市 a big city;metropolis
都市化 urbanization
都市化地区 urbanized areas
都市间高速列车 metroliner

督 [dū]
勋 superintend and direct
督办 ①supervise and direct ②supervisor
督工 supervisor;overseer
督察 ①superintend;supervise ②supervisor
督促 supervise and urge
督导 supervise and direct
督军 provincial military governor in the early Republican period
督励 urge and encourage
督学 educational inspector
督察警 supervisory police

嘟 [dū]
Ⅰ 象 toot;honk Ⅱ 动 pout
嘟噜 ①bunch;cluster ②hang down in a bunch ③trill
嘟囔 mutter to oneself;mumble

dú （ㄉㄨˊ）

毒 [dú]
Ⅰ 名 ①poison;toxin ②anything pernicious to the mind ③narcotics;drugs Ⅱ 形 ①poisonous;noxious;poisoned;toxic ② vicious;malicious;cruel;fierce Ⅲ 动 kill with poison;poison
毒案 criminal narcotics cases
毒草 ① poisonous weeds ② harmful speech,writing,etc.
毒蛾 tussock moth
毒饵 poison bait
毒犯 drug criminal
毒贩 drug trafficker
毒谷 poison grains (planted with seeds to kill harmful insects)
毒害 ①murder by poisoning;poison ②poison (sb's mind)
毒化 poison;spoil
毒计 venomous scheme;deadly trap
毒剂 toxic;toxicant
毒辣 sinister;diabolic
毒瘤 malignant tumour;cancer
毒品 narcotics;(narcotic) drugs
毒气 poisonous gas;poison gas
毒区 contaminated area (in chemical warfare);gassed area
毒杀 kill with poison;poison

毒蛇 poisonous snake;venomous snake;viper
毒手 violent treachery;murderous scheme
毒死 kill with poison;poison
毒素 ①toxin ②poison
毒物 poisonous substance;poison
毒腺 poison gland
毒枭 big drug trafficker
毒刑 cruel corporal punishment;horrible torture
毒性 toxicity;poisonousness
毒蕈 poisonous fungus;toadstool
毒牙 poison fang;venom fang
毒药 poison;toxicant
毒液 venom
毒瘾 drug addiction
毒爪 poison claw
毒汁 venom
毒资 money involved in drug deals
毒扁豆 calabar bean
毒气弹 gas shell;gas bomb
毒气室 gas chamber
毒杀芬 toxaphene
毒瓦斯 poisonous gas;poison gas
毒扁豆碱 physostigmine;eserine
毒刺导弹 Stinger missile
毒品贩子 trafficker in drugs; drug pedlar; drugpusher
毒品买卖 drug biz(business)
毒素武器 toxin weapons
毒品走私者 narco
毒化社会风气 debase social morality

独 [dú]
Ⅰ 形 ①one;single;only;sole ②selfish;egoistic and not tolerant;standoffish Ⅱ 名 old people without offspring;the old and childless Ⅲ 副 ①alone;by oneself;on one's own;in solitude ②only;alone
独霸 dominate exclusively;monopolize
独白 soliloquy;monologue
独步 be unrivalled
独裁 dictatorship;autocratic rule
独唱 (vocal) solo
独创 original creation
独到 original
独断 arbitrary;dictatorial
独家 sole;the only one;exclusive
独居 live in solitude
独揽 arrogate;monopolize
独力 by one's own efforts;on one's own
独立 ①stand alone ②independence ③independent;on one's own
独苗 only son and heir
独身 ①separated from one's family ②unmarried;single
独特 unique;distinctive
独吞 take exclusive possession of sth
独舞 solo dance

独占 have sth all to oneself；monopolize
独资 exclusive investment
独自 alone；by oneself
独奏 （instrumental）solo
独裁者 autocrat；dictator
独唱会 recital （of a vocalist）
独词句 one-member sentence
独角戏 monodrama；one-man show
独立国 independent state
独立性 independent character；independence
独联体 Commonwealth of Independent States （CIS）
独轮车 wheelbarrow
独木桥 ① single-plank bridge；single-log bridge ②difficult path
独木舟 dugout canoe
独幕剧 one-act play
独生女 only daughter
独生子 only son
独眼龙 a person blind in one eye；one-eyed person
独奏会 recital （of an instrumentalist）
独霸一方 lord it over a district；be a local despot
独辟蹊径 open a new road for oneself；develop a new style or a method of one's own
独出心裁 show originality；be original
独此一家 the only authentic one （brand，store，etc.）
独当一面 take charge of a department or locality；assume responsibility for a certain sector
独到之处 distinctive qualities；specific characteristics
独断专行 make arbitrary decisions and take peremptory action；act arbitrarily
独家采访 exclusive interview with sb
独家出口 the sole export
独家代理 sole agency
独家经销 exclusive sell
独家经营 engage in a line of business without competition
独家新闻 journalism exclusive；exclusive news report
独家主顾 monopsony
独具匠心 show ingenuity；have originality
独具只眼 be able to see what others cannot；have exceptional insight
独来独往 coming and going all alone—unsociable；aloof
独揽大权 arrogate all powers to oneself
独立成分 independent element
独立董事 independent director
独立法人 independent legal person
独立核算 keep separate accounts；practise independent accounting
独立王国 independent kingdom

独立自主 maintain independence and keep the initiative；act independently and with the initiative in one's own hands
独门独院 a single house which has its own entrance and courtyard
独木难支 one log can't prop up a tottering building—one person alone can't save the situation
独善其身 maintain one's own integrity
独身主义 celibacy
独生子女 only child
独树一帜 fly one's own colours—develop a school of one's own
独行其道 go one's own way
独行其是 do what one thinks is right regardless of others' opinions
独一无二 unique；unparalleled；unmatched
独占鳌头 come out first；head the list of successful candidates；be the champion
独占资本 monopoly capital
独资经营 single proprietorship；sole proprietorship；business run as single venture（by foreigners）
独资企业 exclusive investment in enterprises；enterprises solely owned by sb
独家采访权 right to exclusive interview
独家代理人 sole agent
独立关税区 separate customs territory
独立检察官 independent counsel
独木不成林 one tree doesn't make a forest—one person alone can't accomplish much
独生子女费 the only-child allowance
独生子女证 single certificate；one-child certificate
独立的司法权 independent judicial power
独立核算单位 independent accounting unit
独立的经济实体 independent economic entities
独立的政治实体 independent political power
独立经营承包商 independent contractor
独立核算自负盈亏 independent accounting and assume sole responsibility for its profits losses
独立经营，自负盈亏 engage in independent management and assume sole responsibility for profits and losses
独立自主的和平外交政策 independent foreign policy of peace

读 ［dú］
动 ①read out；read aloud ②read ③attend （school）④pronounce ➡dòu
读本 reader；textbook
读秒 read the seconds
读取 fetch
读入 read-in
读书 ①read；study ②attend school
读数 reading；indication；registration；numeri-

cal reading
读图 interpret blueprints; interpret drawings
读物 reading matter; reading material
读音 pronunciation
读者 reader (of a book, newspaper, etc.)
读后感 reaction to a book or an article
读卡机 card reader
读书班 study class
读出装置 reading machine; readout unit
读取速度 reading speed
读入程序 read-in program
读书笔记 reading notes
读写磁头 read (*or* write) head
读者来信 readers' letters; letters to the editor
读者文摘 *Reader's Digest*
读写存储器 read (*or* write) memory

渎 [dú] I 动 show disrespect or contempt II 名 ditch; drain
渎职 malfeasance; dereliction of duty; malversation
渎职者 malfeasant
渎职罪 crime of misconduct in office; offence of dereliction of duty
渎职行为 malfeasance; malpractice; dereliction of duty

椟 [dú] 名 casket; case; box

犊 [dú] 名 calf

牍 [dú] 名 ①wooden tablets or slips for writing (in ancient times) ②documents; archives; correspondence

黩 [dú] 动 ①sully; defile ②act wantonly
黩武 militaristic; warlike; bellicose
黩武主义 militarism

dǔ (ㄉㄨˇ)

肚 [dǔ] 名 tripe ➡dù
肚子 [dǔzi] tripe

笃 [dǔ] 形 ①faithful; earnest; sincere ②seriously ill, in a critical condition
笃厚 sincere and magnanimous
笃实 ①honest and sincere ②solid; sound
笃信 sincerely believe in; be a devout believer in
笃学 diligent in study; devoted to study; studious
笃志力行 earnestly resolving to carry it out; work diligently without feeling tired

堵 [dǔ] I 动 ①stop up; block; plug up ②be stifled; be suffocated; be oppressed II 名 wall III 量 (of walls): 一堵墙 a wall

堵击 intercept and attack
堵截 intercept
堵塞 stop up; block up
堵嘴 gag sb; silence sb
堵塞漏洞 plug loopholes; close loopholes

赌 [dǔ] 动 ①gamble ②bet
赌本 ①money to gamble with ②resources for risky ventures
赌博 gambling
赌场 gambling house; gambling playground; casino
赌风 the common and unhealthy practice of gambling; penchant for gambling
赌棍 hardened gambler; professional gambler
赌局 gambling party; gambling joint
赌具 gambling paraphernalia; gambling device
赌客 gambler
赌窟 gambling-den
赌气 feel wronged and act rashly
赌钱 gamble
赌球 gamble on ball games
赌徒 gambler
赌友 gambling companions
赌债 a gambling debt
赌咒 take an oath; swear
赌注 stake
赌博罪 crime of betting
赌博性投资 go-go fund

睹 [dǔ] 动 see
睹物思人 seeing the thing one thinks of the person—the thing reminds one of its owner

dù (ㄉㄨˋ)

杜 [dù] 动 block; stop; forestall
杜衡 wild ginger
杜鹃 ①cuckoo ②azalea
杜绝 stop; put an end to
杜康 ①legendary figure who first distilled liquor ②wine; liquor
杜梨 birch-leaf pear
杜宇 cuckoo
杜仲 the bark of eucommia (Eucommia ulmoides)
杜撰 fabricate; make up
杜鹃花 azalea
杜仲胶 gutta-percha
杜松子酒 gin

肚 [dù] 名 belly; abdomen; stomach ➡dǔ
肚带 bellyband; girth
肚量 tolerance; magnanimity
肚皮 belly
肚脐 navel; belly button
肚痛 collywobbles

肚子 （dùzi） ① belly；abdomen ② a belly-shaped thing

妒 [dù] 动 be jealous of；be envious of；envy
妒忌 be jealous of；be envious of；envy
妒意 feeling of jealousy；jealousy
妒贤嫉能 be jealous of the worthy and the able

度 I 名 ①linear measure ②degree of intensity，hardness，heat，concentration，density or humidity ③extent；degree ④limit；bound；extent；degree ⑤ rule；standard；criterion ⑥ cross-over point （between quantitative and qualitative change） ⑦tolerance；magnanimity ⑧ temperament；bearing；mien；attitude ⑨ space or time of a given extent ⑩calculation；consideration II 量 ① （for arcs and angles）：四十五度角 an angle of 45 degrees② （for latitude or longitude）：北纬三十二度 latitude 32°N. ③ （for kilowatt-hours）：两度电 2 kilowatt-hours ④ （for temperature，percentage of alcohol，etc.）：这种酒是三十八度。 This liquor contains 38 percent alcohol. ⑤ occasion；time：一年一度 once a year；annually／再度声明 state once again；reaffirm；reiterate III 动 ①spend；pass：欢度春节 joyously celebrate the Spring Festival ② （of Buddhists or Taoists） （try to） convert ➡ duó
度过 spend；pass （of time）
度荒 tide over a lean year
度假 spend one's holidays；spend one's vacation；go vacationing
度量 tolerance；magnanimity
度日 subsist （in hardship）；eke out an existence
度数 number of degrees；reading
度假村 vacational village；holiday village
度量衡 length，capacity and weight；weights and measures
度蜜月 honeymoon
度量衡学 metrology
度日如年 one day seems like a year；the days drag on like years

渡 [dù] I 动 ①go across；cross：渡河 cross a river ②tide over；pull through ③ ferry （people，goods，etc.） across II 名 ferry crossing
渡槽 aqueduct
渡场 crossing site
渡船 ferryboat；ferry
渡口 ferry crossing
渡轮 ferry steamer；ferryboat
渡鸦 raven
渡河点 point of crossing
渡过难关 tide over a crisis；tide over a difficulty；ride out a storm；pull through

镀 [dù] 动 plate
镀槽 coating bath
镀金 ①gold-plating；gilding ②get gilded
镀锡 tin-plating；tinning
镀锌 zinc-plating；galvanizing
镀银 silver-plating；silvering
镀锌铁 galvanized iron

蠹 [dù] I 名 insect that eats into books，clothing，etc.；moth II 动 （of moths or worms） eat
蠹虫 ①a kind of insect that eats into books，clothing，etc.；moth ②a harmful person；vermin
蠹鱼 silverfish；fish moth

duān （ㄉㄨㄢ）

端 [duān] I 名 ① tip；end；extremity ② beginning；start；source ③reason；cause；occasion ④aspect；point；item II 形 upright；proper III 动 hold sth level with both hands；carry
端丽 comely；graceful
端量 look sb up and down
端倪 ①clue；inkling ②predict
端线 end line
端详 ①details ②dignified and serene ③look sb up and down
端绪 inkling；clue
端正 ①upright；regular ②proper；correct ③rectify；correct
端庄 dignified；sedate
端子 terminal；post
端午节 the Dragon Boat Festival （the 5th day of the 5th lunar month）
端点用户 an end user
端端正正 straight；regular （features）
端正党风 rectify Party style
端正思想 correct one's thinking；straighten out one's ideas
端正学习态度 take a correct attitude towards study

duǎn （ㄉㄨㄢˇ）

短 [duǎn] I 形 short；brief II 动 lack；owe III 名 shortcoming；deficiency；fault
短波 shortwave
短程 short distance；short range
短处 shortcoming；failing；fault；weakness
短传 short pass
短促 of very short duration；very brief
短笛 piccolo
短吨 short ton
短工 casual labourer；seasonal labourer
短骨 short bone
短号 cornet

短见 ①short-sighted view ②suicide
短剑 dirk;dagger;half-sword
短裤 shorts
短路 short circuit
短命 die young;be short-lived
短跑 short-distance run;dash;sprint
短片 short film;short
短评 short commentary;brief comment
短期 short term
短浅 narrow and shallow
短欠 ①owe;be in arrears ②be short of
短枪 short arm;handgun
短缺 shortage
短少 deficient;short;missing
短视 ①near-sightedness;myopia ②lack foresight;be short-sighted
短寿 be short-lived;die young
短途 short distance
短袜 socks
短线 under-supplied;short-term
短项 weak point
短小 short and small;short;small
短效 short-term effects
短卸 short-landed
短信 short message (SM)
短讯 news in brief;brief dispatch
短训 short-term training;short training
短语 phrase
短暂 of short duration;transient;brief
短装 be dressed in a Chinese-style jacket and trousers
短不了 ①cannot do without ②cannot avoid;have to
短大衣 short overcoat;car coat
短距离 short distance
短平快 short,adaptable and fast
短统靴 ankle boots
短尾猴 stump-tailed macaque (*or* monkey)
短纤维 ①short staple ②staple (fibre)
短训班 short-term course;short-term class
短元音 short vowel
短兵相接 fight at close quarters; engage in hand-to-hand fighting (*or* close combat)
短斤缺两 short-weight;short on the catty and lacking on the ounce;give short measure (*or* weight)
短篇小说 short story
短期保险 short-term insurance
短期公债 short-term public loan
短期汇率 short quotation;short exchange
短期趋势 short swings
短期投资 short-term investment; liquid investment
短期行为 acts and efforts for expediency; short-sighted behaviour;short-term behaviour;short-term action
短期预测 short-term forecasting

短期债务 quick liabilities;floating debt;short-term debt
短时记忆 short-term memory
短途贩卖 short-distance trade and sales
短线产品 goods in short supply;goods in great demand;under-supplied product
短线专业 major (*or* speciality) in urgent (*or* bad) need
短小精悍 ①not of imposing stature but strong and capable ②full of pith and point;short and pithy;terse and forceful
短程小客机 air taxi
短距离赛跑 short-distance run;dash;sprint
短期国库券 short-term treasury bond
短信息服务 short message service (SMS)

duàn （ㄉㄨㄢˋ）

段 [duàn]
Ⅰ 量 section; segment; part; paragraph; passage:一段衣料 a length of suiting Ⅱ 名 ① rank (in *weiqi*):九段国手 rank as level 9 *weiqi* master (the highest in *go*);ninth-dan *go* master ② section (as an administrative level in a mine or factory)
段表 segment table
段落 ①paragraph ②phase;stage

断 [duàn]
Ⅰ 动 ①cut (sth long) in two or more sections;break;snap:断砖 broken brick ②break off;cut off;stop:断电 cut off the supply of electrical power;cut power ③intercept:他把球断了下来,传给前锋。He intercepted the ball and passed it to the forward. ④quit;give up; abstain from:断酒 keep off alcohol ⑤ judge;decide:我断他不敢这样做。I just don't think he has the nerve to take such a course. Ⅱ 副 (*often used in the negative*) absolutely;utterly;decidedly:断不可轻信这类谣言。You must never give credence to such rumours.
断案 ①settle a lawsuit ②conclusion (of a syllogism)
断壁 ① dilapidated walls ② cliff; precipice; steep
断层 fault;break
断肠 heartbroken
断炊 run out of rice and fuel;can't keep the pot boiling;go hungry
断代 division of history into periods
断档 be out of stock;be sold out
断点 breakpoint;breaking point
断电 interrupt;interruption of power supply
断定 conclude;form a judgment;decide;determine
断断 absolutely
断顿 can't afford the next meal;go hungry
断根 ①be completely cured;effect a perma-

nent cure ②have no heir;have no progeny
断后 ①bring up the rear;cover a retreat ② have no progeny
断乎 absolutely
断火 cutoff
断交 ①break off a friendship ②sever (or break off) diplomatic relations
断句 ①make pauses in reading unpunctuated ancient writings ②punctuate
断绝 break off;cut off;stop;sever
断粮 run out of grain (or food)
断流 dry up
断路 ①open circuit;broken circuit ②waylay; hold up
断面 section;plane of fracture
断奶 ①wean ②cut off financial support
断片 part;passage;extract;fragment
断气 ①breathe one's last;die ②cut off the gas
断然 ①resolute;drastic ②absolutely;flatly; categorically
断乳 ①ablactation ②weaning
断水 water-break
断送 forfeit (one's life,future,etc.);ruin
断头 ①broken end ②end breaking
断弦 snap the lute string—lose one's wife
断线 ①breakage ②disconnect;sever;break off
断言 say (or state) with certainty;assert categorically;affirm
断语 conclusion;judgment
断层湖 fault lake
断层山 fault mountain
断代史 dynastic history
断流器 cutout
断头台 guillotine
断编残简 stray fragments of text
断不能信 absolutely incredible;beyond belief
断层地震 fault earthquake
断断续续 off and on;intermittently
断然措施 resolute measures
断然否认 categorically deny
断然拒绝 outright refuse;flatly refuse
断无可能 absolutely impossible;decidedly untrue
断线风筝 a kite with a broken string—gone beyond recall
断章取义 quote out of context;garble a statement,etc.
断肢再植 replantation of a severed limb
断子绝孙 may you die sonless (or without sons);may you be the last of your line

塅 [duàn]
名 vast plain area

缎 [duàn]
名 satin
缎带 silk ribbon

缎面 satin face
缎纹 satin weave
缎子 satin

椴 [duàn]
名 (Chinese) linden

煅 [duàn]
动 calcine
煅烧 calcine

碫 [duàn]
名 whetstone;grindstone

锻 [duàn]
动 forge
锻锤 forging hammer
锻工 ①forging ②forger;blacksmith;hammer-smith
锻件 forging
锻接 forge welding
锻炼 ①take exercise;have physical training ②temper;steel;toughen
锻裂 forge crack;forging bursting
锻炉 forge
锻烧 roasting
锻铁 ①wrought iron ②forge iron
锻造 forging;smithing
锻工钳 band jaw tongs
锻压机 forging press
锻压机械 metal forming machine

duī （ㄉㄨㄟ）

堆 [duī]
Ⅰ 动 pile (up);heap (up);stack (up) Ⅱ 名 ①heap;pile;stack:瓦砾堆 (pile of) debris ② hillock;mound Ⅲ 量 heap;pack;pile;crowd: 一堆灰烬 a heap of ashes
堆存 store up
堆放 pile up;stack
堆肥 compost
堆积 ①pile up;heap up ②accumulation
堆砌 ①pile up (hewn rocks,etc. to build sth) ②load one's writing with fancy phrases
堆笑 put on a smile;wear a grin from ear to ear
堆栈 storehouse;warehouse
堆置 bank up
堆垛机 (hay) stacker
堆谷场 stackyard
堆石坝 rock-fill dam
堆垒数论 additive theory of numbers

duì （ㄉㄨㄟ）

队 [duì]
Ⅰ 名 ①row of people;line;queue:站队 line up;queue up;stand in line ② team;group; band ③Chinese Young Pioneers:少先队歌 Young Pioneers' song Ⅱ 量 file;column;line: 一队士兵 a column of soldiers
队部 the office or headquarters of a team,etc.

队列 formation
队旗 team pennant
队伍 ①troops ②ranks;contingent
队形 formation
队友 fellow player;fellow member of a group or team
队员 team member
队长 ①captain ②team leader

对 [duì]
Ⅰ 动 ①reply;answer ②treat;cope with;counter ③be trained on;be directed at ④bring into coordination or contact;fit one into another;match ⑤suit;agree;fit ⑥compare;check;identify ⑦set;adjust ⑧add;mix;adulterate ⑨face each other:面对面 face to face;vis-à-vis ⑩divide into halves Ⅱ 形 ①opposite;opposing:偏和我作对 be set specifically against me ②right;correct;normal Ⅲ 名 (antithetical) couplet Ⅳ 量 pair;couple:一对石狮子 a pair of stone lions/一对青年夫妇 a young married couple Ⅴ 介 concerning;regarding:对老人表示尊重 show respect for the elderly
对岸 the opposite bank;the other side of the river
对案 diplomacy counterproposal
对白 dialogue
对半 ①half-and-half;fifty-fifty ②double
对比 ①contrast;balance ②ratio
对策 the way to deal with a situation;countermeasure;countermove;solution
对唱 musical dialogue in antiphonal style;antiphonal singing
对称 symmetry
对答 answer;reply
对待 treat;approach;handle
对等 reciprocity,equity
对调 exchange;swop
对方 the other (or opposite) side;the other party
对付 ①deal with;cope with;counter;tackle ②make do
对歌 singing in antiphonal style
对光 set (or focus) a camera
对过 opposite;across the way
对号 ①check the number ②fit;tally ③check mark(√);tick
对话 dialogue
对换 change or exchange
对接 ①link up ②dock
对襟 a kind of Chinese-style jacket with buttons down the front
对局 play a game of chess,etc.
对决 fight to the finish
对开 ①(of trains, buses or ships) run from opposite directions ② divide into two halves;go fifty-fifty ③folio

对抗 ① antagonism;confrontation ② resist;oppose
对口 ①(of two performers) speak (or sing) alternately ②be geared to the needs of the job;fit in with one's vocational training (or speciality) ③counterpart
对垒 stand facing each other,ready for battle;be pitted against each other
对立 oppose;set sth against;be antagonistic to
对联 antithetical couplet (written on scrolls, etc.)
对流 convection
对路 ①satisfy the need ②be to one's liking;suit one
对门 ①(of two houses) face each other ②the building or room opposite
对面 ① opposite ② right in front ③ face to face
对内 internal;domestic;at home
对偶 ①antithesis ②dual
对瓶 a twin vase
对齐 alignment;align;aline;register
对生 opposite
对手 ①opponent;adversary ②match;equal
对数 logarithm
对头 [duìtóu] ① correct; on the right track ②(usu. used in the negative) normal; right ③(usu. used in the negative) get on well;hit it off
对头 [duìtou] ① enemy ② opponent;adversary
对外 external;foreign
对位 counterpoint
对虾 prawn
对象 ①target;object ②boy (or girl) friend
对消 offset;cancel each other out
对眼 cross-eye
对应 corresponding;homologous
对照 contrast;compare
对折 50% discount
对证 verify;check
对质 confrontation (in court)
对峙 stand facing each other;confront each other
对准 ①aim at ②alignment
对子 ①a pair of antithetical phrases,etc. ② antithetical couplet (written on scrolls, etc.)
对暗号 exchange code words
对比度 contrast ratio;contrast
对比剂 contrast medium
对不起 ①I'm sorry;sorry;excuse me;pardon me;I beg your pardon ②let sb down;be unworthy of;do a disservice to;be unfair to
对策论 game theory
对称性 symmetrical characteristic
对得起 not let sb down;treat sb fairly;be

worthy of

对顶角 vertical angles

对话框 dialogue box

对讲机 walkie-talkie;intercom

对奖券 raffle ticket;lottery ticket

对角线 diagonal (line)

对接焊 butt welding

对劲儿 ① be to one's liking;suit one ② normal;right ③ get along (well)

对抗刺 opposition thrust;time thrust

对抗赛 dual meet

对抗性 antagonism

对口唱 musical dialogue in antiphonal style; antiphonal singing

对口疮 a boil on the nape

对口词 rhymed dialogue

对口赛 emulation between counterpart organizations

对口型 lip-sync

对立面 opposite;antithesis

对流层 troposphere

对流雨 convective rain

对日照 counterglow

对手戏 perform together

对数表 logarithmic table

对台戏 rival show

对味儿 ① to one's taste;tasty ②(*usu. used in the negative*) seem all right

对撞机 collider

对着干 ① adopt a confrontational approach;set oneself against ② compete with sb in work ③ do the very opposite of what sb is doing; try to beat sb at what he is doing

对冲操作 sterilization operation;sterilization hedging

对冲基金 hedge fund

对答如流 answer fluently;answer questions without hesitation

对等裁军 reciprocal disarmament

对等货样 counter sample

对等贸易 counter-trade

对等谈判 negotiation on a reciprocal basis;on an equal footing

对等条件 reciprocal terms

对调工作 exchange jobs

对股分成 go halves in profits

对讲电话 intercommunicating telephone set

对奖活动 hold a raffle

对进突击 two-pronged assault from opposite directions

对空射击 antiaircraft firing

对口单位 counterpart

对口会谈 counterpart talks;talks between representatives of similar organizations(of two countries)

对口相声 cross talk;comic dialogue

对口支援 unit-to-unit aid programme

对立统一 unity of opposites

对内政策 domestic (*or* internal) policy

对牛弹琴 play the lute to a cow—address the wrong audience;talk over sb's head

对偶原理 principle of duality

对外开放 open to the outside world

对外贸易 foreign trade

对外投资 investment abroad

对外宣传 international communications

对应原理 correspondence principle

对症下药 suit the medicine to the illness;suit the remedy to the case;prescribe the right remedy for an illness

对开信用证 reciprocal credit;counter credit

对抗性矛盾 antagonistic contradiction

对口型录音 lip-synchronization

对事不对人 concern oneself with facts and not with individuals (when trying to settle a question)

对外贸易额 value of foreign trade

对方付费电话 collect call;transferred charge call

对立统一法则 law of the unity of opposites

对内搞活经济 enliven the domestic economy

对外承包工程 contract for foreign projects; contract for construction projects abroad

对外经济体制 foreign economic system

对外劳务合作 provision of labour services abroad

对外清偿能力 external liquidity

对外文化交流 cultural exchanges with foreign countries

对外贸易资金融通 foreign trade financing

对内搞活,对外开放 revitalize domestic economy,open up to the outside world

对外贸易仲裁委员会 (China) Foreign Trade Arbitration Commission (FTAC)

兑 [duì]
〔动〕① exchange (old for new);convert ② honour (a bill,etc.);cash (a money order, cheque,etc.) ③ pour from one container into another;mix;mingle

兑付 cash (a cheque,etc.)

兑换 exchange;convert

兑现 ① cash (a cheque,etc.);pay cash ② honour (a commitment,etc.);fulfil;make good

兑换率 rate of exchange (between two currencies)

兑换券 bank draft;money order;foreign exchange certificates

兑换现金 exchange for cash;exchange for ready money

兑现支票 cash check

敦 [duì]
〔名〕ancient grain container ➡ dūn

碓 [duì]
名 treadle-operated tilt hammer for hulling rice; stone mortar

憝 [duì]
I 名 resentment; grudge II 形 evil; wicked

dūn (ㄉㄨㄣ)

吨 [dūn]
量 ① ton (t) ② register ton ③ (in shipping) tonnage
吨时 ton hour
吨位 tonnage
吨公里 ton kilometre
吨海里 ton sea (*or* nautical) mile

惇 [dūn]
形 honest and sincere

敦 [dūn]
形 sincere; honest ➡ duì
敦促 urge; press
敦厚 honest and sincere
敦睦 promote friendly relations
敦聘 sincerely invite
敦请 cordially invite; earnestly request
敦实 stocky
敦煌学 study of the Dunhuang Caves
敦煌石窟 the Dunhuang Caves

墩 [dūn]
I 名 ① mound ② block of stone or wood; foundation made of brick or cement ③ squat stool or cushion II 动 mop (the ground, etc.) III 量 cluster
墩布 mop; swab
墩木 block
墩子 a block of wood or stone

撴 [dūn]
动 catch hold of; seize

礅 [dūn]
名 large stone

镦 [dūn]
动 ① stamping; punching ② castrate

蹾 [dūn]
动 lay down heavily; put down with force; dump

蹲 [dūn]
动 ① squat on the heels ② be idle; stay ➡ cún
蹲膘 (of cattle, etc.) fatten in the shed
蹲点 work at a selected spot for investigation and study; work in a selected basic-level unit to gain experience; (of cadres) stay at a selected grass-roots unit to help improve its work and gain firsthand experience for guiding overall work
蹲苗 restrain the growth of seedlings (for root development)
蹲守 undercover
蹲班房 be put in jail; be imprisoned
蹲大狱 serve time in jail; lie in prison

蹲点采访 participant observation

dǔn (ㄉㄨㄣˇ)

旽 [dǔn]
名 doze; take a nap

趸 [dǔn]
I 名 wholesale II 动 buy wholesale (for retail trading)
趸船 landing stage; pontoon
趸货 buy goods wholesale
趸批 wholesale

dùn (ㄉㄨㄣˋ)

囤 [dùn]
名 grain bin ➡ tún

炖 [dùn]
动 ① stew ② warm sth by putting it in a container in boiling water

砘 [dùn]
动 ram loose soil with a stone-roller after sowing

钝 [dùn]
形 ① blunt; dull ② stupid; dull-witted
钝化 passivation; inactivation
钝角 obtuse angle
钝性物质 inactive substance
钝刀子割肉 cut flesh with a blunt knife

盾 [dùn]
名 ① shield; buckler ② shield-shaped object ③ money unit of Holland (*guilder*), Vietnam (*dong*), Indonesia (*rupiah*), etc.
盾牌 ① shield ② pretext; excuse
盾背椅 shield back

顿 [dùn]
I 动 ① pause ② (in Chinese calligraphy) pause in writing in order to reinforce the beginning or ending of a stroke ③ kowtow; stamp ④ arrange; handle II 副 suddenly; immediately III 量 (*used to indicate frequency*): 一日三顿饭 three meals a day IV 形 tired
顿挫 pause and transition in rhythm or melody
顿号 a slight-pause mark used to set off items in a series (、)
顿河 the Don
顿时 suddenly; immediately; at once
顿首 yours humbly
顿悟 insight
顿止 suddenly stop
顿足 stamp one's feet
顿开茅塞 suddenly see the light; be suddenly enlightened
顿悟学习 insight learning
顿钻钻井 churn drilling; percussion drilling; cable tool drilling

遁 [dùn]
动 ① escape; flee; run away ② hide; lie low; disappear
遁词 subterfuge; quibble

遁入空门 become a monk or nun

duō（ㄉㄨㄛ）

多 I 形 ①many;much;more;a lot of ②excessive II 动 ①exceed the original,correct or required number or amount;be or have too many or too much:恰恰多了一个人。There is one person too many. III 动 (*used after a numeral*) more;over;odd:二百多人 more than (*or* over) two hundred people IV 副 ① much more;much less;far more;far less:前景好多了。The prospects are much brighter. ②(*used in questions to indicate degree or extent*):这孩子多大了? How old is the boy? ③(*used in exclamations to indicate a high degree or great extent*):多好的年轻人啊! What a fine young man! ④(*used to indicate a certain degree or extent*):多复杂的算术题他也能做出来。He could work out even the most difficult math problem.

多半 ① the greater part;most;more often than not ②most probably;very likely

多边 multilateral

多变 changeable;changeful;varied

多产 ①prolific ②multiparity

多次 many times;time and again;repeatedly; on many occasions

多多 a lot of

多方 in many ways;in every way

多寡 number;amount

多管 multibarrel

多极 multipolar

多孔 porous

多跨 multispan

多亏 thanks to;luckily

多么 ①(*used in exclamations*) to what an extent ②to an unspecified extent

多盘 multiple-disc

多情 full of tenderness or affection (for a person of the opposite sex)

多色 polychrome

多少 [duōshǎo] ①number;amount ②somewhat;more or less;to some extent

多少 [duōshao] ①how many;how much ② (expressing an unspecified amount or number)

多时 a long time

多事 ①meddlesome ②eventful

多数 majority;most

多速 multi-speed

多肽 polypeptide

多糖 polysaccharide;polysaccharose

多头 ①(on the stock exchange) bull;long ② many chiefs or bosses

多相 heterogeneous

多谢 many thanks;thanks a lot

多心 oversensitive;paranoid

多选 multiple-choice

多样 diversified

多疑 suspicious;oversensitive

多赢 benefit multilaterally

多余 unnecessary; surplus; superfluous; uncalled-for

多云 cloudy

多嘴 speak out of turn;shoot off one's mouth

多倍体 polyploid

多臂机 dobby

多边形 polygon

多层次 multiple echelons (of administration); different levels (of combination)

多弹头 multiple warhead

多党制 multiparty system;multi-party system

多动症 hyperkinesis;hyperactivity

多发病 frequently-occurring disease

多方面 many-sided;in many ways

多功能 multi-functional; multi-purpose; all-purpose

多铧犁 multishare (*or* multifurrow) plough

多会儿 ①when ②ever;at any time

多极化 multipolarization

多晶硅 polycrystalline silicon

多晶体 polycrystal

多孔砖 porous brick;perforated brick

多媒体 multimedia

多面手 generalist; cross-functional; many-sided man;man of many parts (*or* accomplishments);all-rounder;Jack of all trades

多面体 polyhedron

多幕剧 a play of many acts;a full-length drama

多瑙河 the Danube

多年生 perennial

多尿症 polyuria

多偶制 polygamy

多妻制 polygyny;polygamy

多任务 multitasking;multitask

多神教 polytheism

多数党 the majority party;the majority

多数票 majority vote

多项式 multinomial;polynomial

多学科 multidisciplinary

多样化 diversify;make varied

多义词 polysemous word

多元论 pluralism

多元酸 polybasic acid

多源的 multi-source

多边合作 multilateral cooperation

多边条约 multilateral treaty

多边外交 multilateral diplomacy

多边协定 multilateral agreement

多才多艺 versatile;gifted in many ways

多层住宅 multi-storey housing

D

多吃多占 eat or take more than one is entitled to;grab more than one's share
多重处理 multiprocessing
多愁多病 be laden with sorrow and illness;be prone to anxiety and illness
多愁善感 sentimental and susceptible
多此一举 make an unnecessary move
多党合作 system of multiparty cooperation
多刀切削 multiple cut
多道程序 multiprogramming
多多益善 the more the better
多国公司 multinational corporation
多级导弹 multiple stage missile
多级管理 multiple management
多级火箭 multistage rocket
多极世界 multipolar world
多孔动物 porifera
多口相声 cross talk (*or* comic dialogue) performed by more than two persons
多快好省 more, faster, better, cheaper—achieve greater,faster,better and more economical results
多买多送 buy more and get more free
多谋善断 resourceful and decisive;sagacious and resolute
多难兴邦 Much distress regenerates a nation. *or* Deep distress resurrects a nation.
多刃刀具 multiple-cutting-edge tool;multi-point tool
多如牛毛 as many as the hairs on an ox;countless;innumerable
多式联运 multimodal transport
多事之秋 an eventful period or year;troubled times
多数表决 decision by majority
多听少说 give every man thine ear,but few thy voice
多头对外 multi-channel management in foreign trade
多头市场 long market;bull market
多头政治 polyarchy
多退少补 (in subscribing to sth or doing business) refund for any overpayment or demand a supplemental payment for any difference in price
多芯电缆 multicore cable
多学科的 multidisciplinary
多元分析 multivariate analysis
多元模式 plural patterns
多元文化 multiculturalism
多中心论 polycentrism
多种多样 varied;manifold
多种经济 diversified economy
多种经营 diversified economy;diversification;multiple (*or* diversified) operation
多足动物 myriopod
多层次推销 multilevel marketing

多弹头导弹 multiple warhead missile
多极化趋势 move toward multipolarity;multi-polarization;trend toward multipolarity
多路转换器 multiplexer
多媒体电脑 multimedia computer
多媒体通信 multimedia communication
多米诺骨牌 dominoes
多民族国家 a multinationality country
多品牌战略 multi-brand strategy
多普勒效应 Doppler effect
多任务程序 multitask program
多数党领袖 the majority leader
多细胞生物 multicellular organism
多项变压器 polyphase transformer
多项选择题 multiple-choice question
多元文化的 multicultural
多中心主义 polycentrism
多边关税谈判 multilateral tariff negotiations (MTN)
多边贸易协定 multilateral trade agreement
多边税务条约 multilateral tax treaty
多功能显示器 multifunctional display
多国维和部队 multinational peace-keeping force
多媒体教学法 multimedia approach
多种经济成分 diversified economic sectors;diverse sectors of the economy
多弹头分导导弹 multiple independently targetable missile (MTTM)
多媒体信息中心 multimedia information centers
多米诺骨牌理论 the domino theory
多米诺骨牌效应 domino effect
多元化投资主体 a diversity of (major) investors
多种所有制经济 different types of ownership;economic sectors under diversified ownership;the economy with diverse forms of ownership
多种所有制形式 diverse (*or* multiple) forms of ownership
多声道盒式录音机 multi-channel cassette recorder
多一事不如少一事 the less trouble the better;avoid trouble whenever possible
多劳多得,少劳少得 more pay for more work and less pay for less work

咄 ［duō］
Ⅰ 叹 *used to show amazement or to berate* Ⅱ 动 berate;be shocked
咄咄逼人 overbearing;aggressive
咄咄怪事 monstrous absurdity

哆 ［duō］
➡chǐ
哆嗦 tremble;shiver

剟 ［duō］
动 ①stab;attack ②cut down and take;de-

lete ③cut down and take

掇 [duō]
囫 ①pick up ②hold with both hands (a chair,stool,etc.);carry
掇弄 ①fix up ②stir up (trouble,etc.);incite;manipulate

裰 [duō]
囫 ①mend;patch ②loose robe worn by a Buddhist monk or Taoist priest

duó（ㄉㄨㄛˊ）

夺 [duó]
Ⅰ囫 ①take by force;seize;wrest ②contend for;compete for;strive for ③overwhelm;defeat;surpass ④deprive ⑤lose ⑥decide Ⅱ囵 omission (in a text)
夺标 ①win the championship ②have one's tender accepted
夺佃 eviction of peasants from land leased to them by landlords or rich peasants
夺冠 carry off the first prize;win first place;win the championship
夺回 recapture;retake;seize back
夺魁 carry off the first prize;win first place;win the championship
夺目 dazzle the eyes
夺取 ①capture;seize;wrest ②strive for
夺权 seize power;take over power
夺高产 strive for high yields
夺冠战 title decider

度 [duó]
囫 surmise;estimate ➡dù
度德量力 estimate one's own moral and material strength;make an appraisal of one's own position

铎 [duó]
囵 big bell used in ancient China in times of war or when a proclamation was issued

踱 [duó]
囫 pace;stroll

duǒ（ㄉㄨㄛˇ）

朵 [duǒ]
量 (of flowers, clouds, etc.):一朵花 a flower／一朵白云 a whitish cloud
朵儿 flower

垛 [duǒ]
Ⅰ囵 crenel;battlements Ⅱ量 (of a window,wall,etc.):砌一垛砖墙 build a brick wall ➡duò
垛口 crenel
垛子 ①buttress ②battlements

埵 [duǒ]
囵 hard soil

躲 [duǒ]
囫 ①go into hiding;hide (oneself) ②avoid;dodge;steer clear of
躲避 ①hide (oneself) ②avoid;elude;dodge
躲藏 ①hide (or conceal) oneself;go into hiding ②avoid;dodge
躲懒 shy away from work;shirk
躲闪 dodge;evade
躲债 avoid a creditor
躲躲闪闪 be evasive;hedge;equivocate

duò（ㄉㄨㄛˋ）

驮 [duò]
➡tuó
驮子 ①a load carried by a pack animal;pack ②used of caravan goods

剁 [duò]
囫 chop;cut

垛 [duò]
Ⅰ囫 pile up neatly Ⅱ囵 pile;stack ➡duǒ

舵 [duò]
囵 rudder;helm
舵工 steersman;helmsman
舵轮 steering wheel
舵手 steersman;helmsman

堕 [duò]
囫 fall;sink
堕地 fall on the ground
堕落 degenerate;sink low
堕入 sink (or lapse) into;land oneself in
堕胎 ①induced abortion ②have an abortion
堕胎药 aborticide
堕落场所 vice spots

惰 [duò]
形 lazy;idle;indolent
惰性 inertia
惰性气体 inert gas
惰性元素 inert element

跺 [duò]
囫 stamp (one's foot)

E e

ē（さ）

阿 [ē]
Ⅰ 劲 play up to; pander to; cater to Ⅱ 名 ①big hill; large mound ②twist in terrain; turn in terrain; bend ➡ā

阿胶 E-gelatin
阿魏 asafoetida
阿弥陀佛 ① Amitabha; Amitayus Buddha ② may Buddha preserve us; Buddha be praised
阿谀奉承 flatter; toady to

婀 [ē]

婀娜 （of a woman's carriage） be lithe and graceful; be supple and graceful

é（さ）

讹 [é]
Ⅰ 形 erroneous; wrong; mistaken Ⅱ 劲 blackmail; extort; bluff
讹传 false （or unfounded） rumour
讹钱 extort money by blackmail
讹人 blackmail sb; bluff sb
讹误 error （in a text）
讹诈 extort under false pretences; blackmail
讹字 wrong words （in a text）
讹言讹语 erroneous and irresponsible comments

吡 [é]
劲 ①move; act ②change; teach; cultivate; educate; train

俄 [é]
Ⅰ 副 shortly; presently; suddenly Ⅱ 名 ①Russian Empire ②Russian Soviet Federated Socialist Republic ③Union of the Soviet Socialist Republics ④Russian Federation
俄顷 in a moment; presently
俄语 Russian （language）
俄罗斯族 ① the Russian nationality ② the Russians （of Russia）
俄罗斯帝国 the Russian Empire
俄罗斯联邦 the Russian Federation
俄罗斯"和平"号空间站 Russian Mir space station

哦 [é]
劲 softly chant ➡ó; ò

峨 [é]
形 high; lofty; towering

娥 [é]
名 pretty young woman

鹅 [é]
名 goose
鹅黄 light yellow
鹅毛 ①goose feather ②sth as light as a goose feather
鹅绒 goose down
鹅颈管 gooseneck
鹅口疮 thrush
鹅卵石 cobblestone; cobble
鹅掌楸 Chinese tulip tree
鹅行鸭步 waddle along like a duck （or a goose）

蛾 [é]
名 moth
蛾子 moth

额 [é]
名 ①forehead ②horizontal tablet ③specified number, sum, volume, or amount
额度 specified number or amount; quota
额骨 frontal bone
额角 frontal eminence
额数 specified number, figure or amount
额头 forehead
额外 extra; additional; added
额定功率 rated power
额定马力 rated horsepower
额定人数 maximum member of persons allowed
额定输出 nominal output
额手称庆 raise one's hand to one's forehead in joy—be overjoyed
额外负担 added burden
额外所得 perquisite

ě(ㄜ)

恶 [ě]
➡è;wū;wù
恶心 ①feel like vomiting;feel nauseated;feel sick ②nauseating;disgusting;repugnant ③rotten;lousy

è(ㄜ)

厄 [è]
Ⅰ 名 ①strategic point ②disaster;catastrophe;adversity;hardship Ⅱ 动 be in distress;be stranded
厄境 a difficult situation;adversity
厄难 disaster;distress
厄运 adversity;misfortune
厄尔尼诺 El Niño
厄尔尼诺现象 El Niño phenomenon

扼 [è]
动 ①clutch;grip ②guard;control
扼杀 strangle;smother;throttle
扼守 hold (a strategic point);guard
扼死 strangle;throttle
扼要 to the point
扼制 control;restrain;check;bring under control
扼流圈 choke
扼腕叹息 sigh and wring one's hands
扼杀新生事物 stifle new things
扼制经济过热 curb an overheated economy

呃 [è]
叹 used to express an exclamation, a reminder, etc.：呃,你还在这里啊! Why, so you're still here. ➡e
呃逆 hiccups

轭 [è]
名 yoke

垩 [è]
Ⅰ 名 chalk Ⅱ 动 ①apply (fertilizer) ②whiten with chalk
垩墙 whitewash the wall

恶 [è]
Ⅰ 名 guilt;wickedness Ⅱ 形 ①fierce;ferocious;vicious ②bad;evil;wicked ➡ě;wū;wù
恶霸 local tyrant (or despot)
恶报 retribution for evildoing;judgment
恶变 grow from benign to malignant
恶补 cram for
恶炒 feeding frenzy
恶臭 a foul smell;stench
恶毒 vicious;malicious;venomous
恶感 ill feeling;malice
恶鬼 ①evil spirit ②devil
恶棍 ruffian;scoundrel;bully
恶果 evil consequence;disastrous effect
恶化 worsen;deteriorate;take a turn for the worse

恶疾 a foul (or nasty) disease
恶狼 ferocious wolf
恶浪 ①surging waves;crashing waves;torrential waves ②evil forces
恶劣 odious;abominable;disgusting
恶露 lochia
恶名 a bad name;a bad reputation;infamy
恶魔 demon;devil;evil spirit
恶评 unfavorable comments
恶气 ①a bad odor;a foul smell ②insult;humiliation;outrage ③grievance;resentment ④anger;fury
恶人 an evil person;a vile creature;villain
恶少 a young ruffian
恶习 a bad (or pernicious) habit
恶性 malignant;pernicious;vicious
恶言 rude language;abusive language
恶意 evil (or ill) intentions;ill will;malice
恶战 fierce battle;savage fight
恶兆 ill (or bad) omen
恶浊 foul;filthy
恶病质 cachexia (general ill health with emaciation,due to a serious chronic disease like cancer)
恶狠狠 fierce;ferocious
恶势力 vicious power;underworld/vicious forces
恶作剧 a practical joke;a mischievous prank;mischief
恶霸地主 despotic landlord
恶贯满盈 be guilty of countless crimes and deserve to come to judgment;be steeped in evil and deserve damnation
恶眉恶眼 a very fierce expression
恶声恶气 angry voices and hard words
恶性案件 pernicious case;case of disastrous consequences
恶性贫血 pernicious anaemia
恶性循环 vicious circle
恶性肿瘤 malignant tumour
恶衣菲食 poor clothing and meagre food
恶意接收 hostile takeover
恶意诉讼 malicious action
恶语中伤 viciously slander;calumniate
恶人先告状 the villain sues his victim before he himself is prosecuted;the guilty party files the suit
恶事传千里 bad news spreads far and wide
恶性通货膨胀 hyperinflation;galloping inflation;runaway inflation

饿 [è]
Ⅰ 形 hungry Ⅱ 动 starve
饿饭 go hungry;go without food
饿殍 bodies of the starved
饿虎扑食 like a hungry tiger pouncing on its prey
饿殍遍野 the fields strewn with the bodies of

the starved

阏 [è]
I 动 block; stop; close up II 名 sluice (gate)

萼 [è]
名 calyx
萼片 sepal

遏 [è]
动 check; restrain; prohibit
遏抑 suppress; restrain
遏止 check; hold back; restrain
遏制 keep within limits; contain
遏制政策 policy of containment

愕 [è]
形 stunned; dazed; astounded
愕然 stunned; astounded

腭 [è]
名 palate
腭裂 cleft palate

鹗 [è]
名 osprey; fish hawk; sea eagle

颚 [è]
名 ① mandible (of an arthropod); jaw ② palate

噩 [è]
形 shocking; frightening
噩耗 terrible news of the death of a beloved person
噩梦 a frightening (or horrible) dream; nightmare

鳄 [è]
名 crocodile; alligator
鳄鱼 crocodile; alligator
鳄鱼眼泪 crocodile tears

e （·ㄜ）

呃 [e]
助 (placed at the end of a sentence to express admiration, surprise, etc.): 红霞多美呃! How beautiful the rosy clouds are! ➡ è

ēn （ㄣ）

恩 [ēn]
名 kindness; favour; grace
恩爱 be deeply in love with each other
恩赐 ① bestow (favours, charity, etc.) ② favour; charity
恩德 benevolence; favour; kindness; grace
恩典 ① favour; grace ② bestow (favours)
恩惠 a favour bestowed or received; bounty
恩情 loving kindness
恩人 benefactor
恩师 esteemed teacher; honourable master
恩怨 ① feeling of gratitude or resentment ② resentment; grievance; old scores
恩断义绝 (of feeling) be estranged
恩将仇报 requite kindness with enmity; return

hate for love; bite the hand that feeds one
恩深义重 great debt of gratitude
恩同再造 favour tantamount to giving sb a new lease of life
恩威并用 make a combined use of favour and disfavour (as in controlling one's subordinates); use both the mailed fist and the velvet glove
恩怨分明 kindness and hatred are clearly distinguished
恩重如山 sb's great kindness is as weighty as a mountain
恩格尔系数 Engel's coefficient

蒽 [ēn]
名 anthracene

èn （ㄣ）

摁 [èn]
动 press (with the hand or finger)
摁钉儿 drawing pin; thumbtack
摁扣儿 snap fastener
摁快门 press the shutter; click the shutter

ér （ㄦ）

儿 [ér]
I 名 ① child; baby ② youngster; youth; young man ③ son II 形 male III 后缀① (used as a noun suffix): (a) (added to a noun to indicate smallness): 帽儿 hat; cap/零碎儿 odds and ends/小车儿 small cart (b) (added to a verb or an adjective to turn it into a noun): 吃儿 eatables; food/亮儿 light/热闹儿 fun (c) (added to a concrete noun to turn it into an abstract noun): 摸到了办这件事的门儿 get the knack of doing the work/这生意油水儿不大。You cannot make much profit from this business. (d) (added to a noun to change its original meaning): 老家儿 one's parents and other members of the old generation ② (used as suffix of a limited number of verbs): 我不玩儿了。I don't want to play any more./他火儿了。He blew up.
儿茶 ① Acacia catechu ② catechu
儿歌 children's song; nursery rhymes
儿科 (department of) paediatrics
儿郎 son
儿马 stallion
儿女 ① sons and daughters; children ② young man and woman (in love)
儿孙 children and grandchildren; descendants; posterity
儿童 children
儿戏 trifling matter
儿子 son
儿皇帝 puppet emperor

儿童节 （International) Children's Day (June
1)
儿童剧 children's drama
儿童团 the Children's Corps
儿科医生 paediatrician
儿女情长 love between man and woman is
long
儿童教育 education for children
儿童文学 children's (*or* juvenile) literature
儿童医院 children's hospital
儿媳妇儿 daughter-in-law
儿不嫌母丑 A mother never looks ugly to her
son.
儿童不宜片 X-rated movie; R-rated movie; AA
(Adult Audience)category
儿童心理学 child psychology
儿童学步车 go-car; walker; babywalker
儿童娱乐中心 Children's Amusement Centre

而 [ér]
〔连〕 ①(*used to express coordination*) (a)
(*by joining two parallel adjectives or other
elements*):朴素而大方 simple but with good
taste (b) (*by joining two elements that
form a sequence in meaning*):战而胜之
fight and defeat sb; defeat sb (c) (*by joining
an affirmative and a negative element
that complement each other*):忙而不乱
busy but not disorderly/艳而不俗 colourful
and in good taste (d) (*by joining two elements opposite in meaning that show a
contrast*):大而不甜 big but not sweet/有其
名而无其实 in name but not in reality (e)
(*by connecting cause and effect or aim and
means*):因病而辞职 resign on health
grounds ②(*used to indicate change from
one state to another*):由上而下 from top to
bottom/由远而近 approach from afar ③
(*used to connect an adverbial phrase of
time or manner with a verb*):日出而作
start working at sunrise ④(*inserted between
subject and predicate to indicate a condition*):科学研究而无进取精神，是不会有所
成就的。 Scientific research would never get
anywhere without the pioneering spirit.
而后 after that; then
而今 now; at the present time
而且 ①and also ②but also
而已 that is all; nothing more
而立之年 the age of thirty

ěr （儿）

尔 [ěr]
I 〔代〕 ①you ②that:尔时 at that time II 〔助〕
①only; just; merely:无他，但手熟尔。 It is
just that I am familiar with this. ②(*used after an adjective*):率尔 hastily; rashly III 〔副〕
like that; so

尔格 erg
尔后 thereafter; subsequently; henceforth
尔代节 Lesser Bairam; the Festival of Fast-
breaking
尔虞我诈 each trying to cheat the other

耳 [ěr]
I 〔名〕 ①ear ②sth in the shape of an ear ③
side II 〔助〕 only; just:此戏言耳。 I am only
joking.
耳背 be hard of hearing
耳病 otopathy
耳沉 be hard of hearing
耳垂 earlobe
耳朵 ear
耳福 the good fortune of hearing sth rare or
beautiful
耳垢 earwax
耳鼓 eardrum; tympanum
耳光 slap in the face; box on the ear
耳郭 pinna; auricle
耳环 earrings
耳机 earphone; earpiece
耳镜 otoscope
耳孔 earhole
耳聋 be deaf
耳轮 helix
耳鸣 have a ringing sensation in the ears; tin-
nitus
耳膜 tympanic membrane; eardrum
耳目 ①what one sees and hears; knowledge;
information ②one who spies for sb else
耳屏 tragus
耳塞 earplug
耳生 unfamiliar to the ear; strange-sounding
耳屎 earwax
耳熟 familiar to the ear
耳痛 earache; otalgia
耳闻 hear of (*or* about)
耳蜗 cochlea; acoustic labyrinth
耳穴 ear acupuncture point
耳语 whisper in sb's ear; whisper
耳罩 ear muffs
耳按摩 otomassage
耳边风 a puff of wind passing the ear—un-
heeded advice
耳朵软 credulous; easily influenced; susceptible to flattery
耳刮子 box on the ear; slap in the face
耳挖子 earpick
耳咽管 Eustachian tube; auditory tube
耳坠子 eardrops
耳鼻喉科 ① ear-nose-throat (ENT) department; otolaryngological department ② oto-
laryngology
耳鬓厮磨 ear to ear and temple to temple—
(of a boy and a girl) have close childhood
friendship

耳聪目明 have good ears and eyes—have a clear understanding (of the situation)
耳根清净 peace of heart or mind attained by staying away from, or shutting one's ears to, worldly discord
耳目闭塞 ill-informed; uninformed; ignorant
耳目所及 from what one sees and hears; from what one knows
耳目一新 find everything fresh and new
耳濡目染 be imperceptibly influenced by what one sees and hears
耳软心活 credulous and pliable
耳熟能详 What's frequently heard can be repeated in detail.
耳提面命 pour earnest advice into sb's ears; give earnest exhortations; give an earful of advice
耳闻目睹 what one sees and hears
耳鼻喉科医生 ENT specialist; otolaryngologist
耳闻不如目见 Seeing for oneself is better than hearing from others.
耳听为虚,眼见为实 What you hear may be false, what you see is true.

迩 [ěr]
形 near

饵 [ěr]
Ⅰ 名 ①cakes; pastry ②bait Ⅱ 动 entice; tempt
饵敌 set a trap for the enemy
饵子 (fish) bait

èr (儿)

二 [èr]
Ⅰ 数 two Ⅱ 形 different
二八 sixteen
二茬 regrowth of hair (*or* harvest)
二等 second-class; second-rate
二副 second mate; second officer
二胡 *erhu*, a two-stringed bowed instrument with a lower register than *jinghu*
二话 demur; objection
二黄 *erhuang*, one of the two chief types of music in traditional Chinese operas
二审 second trial
二手 ①assistant ②secondhand
二心 ①disloyalty; half-heartedness
二元 ①duality ②binary
二月 ①February ②the second month of the lunar year; the second moon
二职 second job
二把手 second in rank; No. 2 position; second fiddle; cadre who is second in command
二百五 ①stupid person ②dabbler
二等舱 second-class cabin
二等分 bisection; halve
二等功 Merit Citation Class Ⅱ
二等奖 second prize
二等品 second-class (*or* inferior) goods; seconds
二分点 the equinoxes
二锅头 strong, colourless liquor distilled from sorghum
二化螟 striped rice borer
二婚头 remarried woman
二级风 force 2 wind; light breeze
二极管 diode
二尖瓣 mitral valve
二进宫 ①detained (*or* sentenced) for a second time; in and out of prison twice ②do sth for a second time
二进码 binary code
二进制 binary system
二郎腿 a sitting posture with the legs crossed and one foot poised in the air
二愣子 a rash fellow
二流子 loafer; idler; bum
二面角 dihedral angle
二名法 binomial nomenclature
二年生 biennial
二人转 song-and-dance duet
二手房 second-hand house
二手货 second-hand (*or* used, pre-owned) goods
二手烟 second-hand smoking
二四滴 2,4-D; 2,4-dichlorophenoxyacetic acid
二踢脚 double-kick (popular name for 双响)
二五眼 ①of inferior ability or quality ②an incompetent person
二项式 binomial
二象性 dual property; duality
二性子 bisexual person
二元论 dualism
二至点 the solstices
二重唱 (vocal) duet
二重性 dual character (*or* nature); duality
二重奏 (instrumental) duet
二次创业 start a new undertaking
二次方程 quadratic equation
二次曲线 conic section
二次污染 secondary pollution
二道贩子 person who resells at inflated prices; secondhand dealer; two-way merchant
二等秘书 diplomacy Second Secretary
二级市场 secondary (*or* parallel) market
二阶环路 second-order loop
二进制数 binary number
二流选手 scrub, second-rater
二硫化物 bisulphide
二全音符 breve
二人世界 two people's world
二十四史 ①the Twenty-Four Histories (dynastic histories from remote antiquity till the Ming Dynasty) ②a long intricate story

E

二氧化硅 silicon dioxide；silica
二氧化碳 carbon dioxide
二氧化物 dioxide
二级子程序 second-order subroutine
二尖瓣狭窄 mitral stenosis
二进制标度 binary scale
二进制数字 binary digit
二年生植物 biennial plant
二十四节气 the twenty-four solar terms
二一添作五 go halves；go fifty-fifty

二级反馈系统 second order feedback system
二极管检波器 diode detector
二者必居其一 either one or the other
二氧化硫控制区 SO_2 control district

贰 [èr] Ⅰ 数 two Ⅱ 动 transfer one's allegiance；turn one's coat Ⅲ 形 disloyal

贰臣 official who retains his position after capitulating to the new dynasty；turncoat official

E

Ff

fā（ㄈㄚ）

发 [fā] I 刼 ①issue；send（out）；give out；distribute ②launch；discharge；shoot；fire；project ③ generate；produce；bring or come into existence ④speak；utter；express；convey；voice ⑤ develop；expand ⑥ become rich；make a fortune ⑦（of foodstuffs）rise or expand when fermented or soaked ⑧ disperse；diffuse；diverse ⑨open up；discover；expose ⑩get into a certain state；become；turn；appear ⑪ show （one's feeling）；elicit ⑫ feel；sense；perceive ⑬start on a journey；set out；depart ⑭begin （an action）；start Ⅱ 量（for ammunition）：五发炮弹 five shells ➡fà

发案（of a case）occur；take place

发榜 publish a list of successful candidates （or applicants）

发包 award contract；issue contract；put out to contract；contract out

发报 transmit messages by radio，telegraphy，etc.

发标 issue of bidding documents

发表 publish；issue

发病（of a disease）come on

发布 issue；release

发财 get rich；make a fortune；make a pile

发潮 become damp

发车 send off a car（or truck，bus）；dispatch a car（or truck，bus）

发愁 worry；be anxious

发出 issue；send out；give out

发憷 feel timid；grow apprehensive

发达 ① developed；flourishing ② promote；develop

发呆 stare blankly；be in a daze；be in a trance

发电 generate electricity（or electric power）

发动 ①start；launch ②call into action；mobilize；arouse

发抖 shiver；shake；tremble

发端 make a start

发放 provide；grant；extend

发奋 ①work energetically ②make a firm resolution；make a determined effort

发愤 make a firm resolution；make a determined effort

发疯 go mad；go crazy；become insane；be out of one's mind

发福（usu. said to older people）grow stout；put on weight

发付 send；dispatch；dismiss；send away

发糕 steamed sponge cake

发稿 ① distribute news dispatches ② send manuscripts to the press

发给 issue；distribute；grant

发光 ①give off light；shine；be luminous ②luminescence

发汗 induce perspiration（as by drugs）；diaphoresis

发行 [fāháng] sell wholesale

发狠 ①make a determined effort ②be angry

发花（of the eyes）grow dim；see things in a blur

发还 return sth（usu. to one's subordinate）；give（or send）back

发慌 feel nervous；get flustered；get flurried

发挥 ①bring into play；give play to；give free rein to ②develop（an idea，a theme，etc.）；elaborate

发昏 ① feel giddy（or dizzy）② lose one's head；become confused

发火 ①catch fire；ignite ②detonate；go off ③ get angry；flare up；lose one's temper

发货 send out goods；deliver goods

发迹（of a poor man）gain fame and fortune；rise to power and position

发急 become impatient or excited

发家 build up a family fortune

发奖 award prizes

发酵 ferment

发觉 find；detect；discover；realize

发掘 excavate；unearth；explore

发狂 go mad;go crazy
发困 feel sleepy (*or* drowsy)
发懒 feel lazy (*or* sluggish)
发楞 stare blankly;be in a daze;be in a trance
发冷 feel cold (*or* chilly)
发亮 shine
发令 ①issue an order;give orders ②give a
　password
发落 deal with (an offender)
发霉 go mouldy;become mildewed
发面 ①leaven dough ②leavened dough
发明 ①invent ②invention ③expound
发难 ①rise in revolt;launch an attack ②raise
　difficult questions for discussion
发怒 get angry;flare up;lose one's temper
发排 send a manuscript to the compositor
发盘 offer
发胖 put on (*or* gain) weight;get fat
发配 be transported to a distant place for pe-
　nal servitude
发票 invoice
发起 ①initiate;sponsor ②start;launch
发情 ①oestrus ②be in heat
发球 serve a ball
发热 ①have (*or* run) a fever;have (*or* run)
　a temperature ② give out heat;generate
　heat ③be hotheaded;be impetuous
发散 ①(of rays,etc.) diverge ②disperse the
　internal heat with sudorifics
发丧 ①announce a death;send out an obituary
　②arrange a funeral
发烧 have (*or* run) a fever;have (*or* run) a
　temperature
发射 ① launch;project;discharge;shoot;fire
　②transmit;emit
发生 happen;occur;take place
发声 sound production
发誓 vow;pledge;swear
发售 sell;put on sale
发水 flood
发送 ①transmit by radio ②dispatch (letters,
　etc.)
发馊 spoil and turn sour
发酸 ①turn sour;taste sour ②feel a tingle in
　one's eyes or nose (when about to break
　down and weep) ③ache slightly
发条 spiral power spring;clockwork spring
发文 outgoing message;dispatch
发问 ask (*or* pose,raise) a question
发现 ① discover; find ② discovery; find ③
　find;realize;perceive;notice
发笑 burst into laughter;laugh
发泄 give vent to;let off
发信 post a letter
发行 [fāxíng] issue; publish; distribute; put
　on sale
发虚 ①feel apprehensive;feel diffident ②feel

feeble and weak
发芽 germinate;sprout
发言 speak;make a statement or speech;take
　the floor
发炎 inflammation
发扬 ① develop; carry on (*or* forward) ②
　make the most of;make full use of
发音 pronounce;enunciate
发育 grow;develop
发源 rise;originate
发晕 feel dizzy (*or* giddy)
发展 ① develop; expand; grow ② recruit; ad-
　mit
发胀 ① swell ② feel distended (under acu-
　puncture treatment)
发作 ①break out;show effect ②have a fit of
　anger;flare up
发案率 incidence (of criminal cases)
发报机 transmitter
发病率 incidence (*or* rate) of a disease
发车场 departure track;departure yard
发电厂 power plant;power station
发电机 generator;dynamo
发电站 power station
发动机 engine;motor
发光漆 luminous paint
发光体 luminous body;luminary;luminophor
发汗药 sudorific;diaphoretic
发火点 ignition point
发货单 dispatch list
发货人 consignor;shipper
发酒疯 get drunk and behave sillily;have a
　drunken fit
发刊词 foreword (*or* introduction) to a peri-
　odical
发牢骚 grumble;complain;grouse
发令枪 starting gun (*or* pistol)
发令员 starter
发明权 patent rights of an inventor
发疟子 have an attack of malaria;suffer from
　malarial fever
发脾气 lose one's temper;get angry
发票机 invoice machinery
发起国 sponsor nation
发起人 initiator;sponsor
发情期 heat period;oestrus
发球器 service robot
发球区 service area
发球权 right to serve
发热量 calorific capacity
发烧友 fancier;zealot;(enthusiastic) fan
发射场 launching site
发射架 launcher
发射井 launching silo
发射台 launching stand;launching (*or* firing)
　pad
发神经 go mad;go crazy;be out of one's mind

发生器 generator
发祥地 matrix; cradle; place of origin; birth-place
发行量 circulation figures
发言权 right to speak
发言人 spokesman; spokeswoman
发源地 source; birthplace; place of origin; womb; nidus; seedbed; seminary
发展权 right to development
发包单位 the contract letting unit
发包工程 contract project
发达国家 developed country
发愤图强 work with a will to make the country strong
发号施令 issue orders; order people about
发挥潜力 bring potential into play
发挥正常 play to form
发挥专长 give full play to one's professional knowledge or skill
发家致富 build up a family fortune
发奖仪式 victory ceremony
发酵饲料 fermented feed
发明创造 inventions and other creations; innovations and inventions
发情周期 oestrous cycle
发球擦网 service touching the net
发球次序 service order
发球犯规 fault
发球失误 missed service
发人深省 set people thinking; call for deep thought; provide food for thought
发散思维 divergent thinking
发射光谱 emission spectrum
发射基地 launching base
发射时限 launch window
发射中心 launch centre
发行公债 issue of government (*or* public) bonds
发行股票 issue stocks
发行银行 bank of issue
发扬光大 carry forward; develop; enhance
发扬民主 develop a democratic style of work
发扬正气 encourage healthy trends (*or* practices); encourage standing up for what is right
发音部位 points of articulation
发音困难 dysphonia
发音器官 vocal organs; speech organs
发育不全 hypoplasia
发育异常 dysplasia
发展势头 growth momentum
发货通知书 consignment note
发盘附样品 offer sample
发上手旋球 overhand float serve
发展不平衡 disparate development; uneven development
发展经济学 development economics

发展生产力 develop productive forces
发展中国家 developing country
发扬优良传统 carry forward the fine traditions
发展科学技术 develop science and technology; promote the development of science and technology
发展外向型经济 develop an export-oriented economy
发展经济,保障供给 develop the economy and ensure the supply

fá（ㄈㄚˊ）

乏 [fá]
动 lack; be short of Ⅱ 形 ①tired; weary ②poor ③exhausted; worn-out; useless
乏力 lacking in strength; weak
乏味 dull; insipid; drab; tasteless

伐 [fá]
动 ①fell; cut down ②attack; strike; send an expedition against ③sing one's own praises; boast about oneself
伐木 lumbering; felling; cutting
伐区 cutting area; felling area
伐木业 lumbering

罚 [fá]
动 punish; penalize; fine; forfeit
罚单 ticket
罚金 fine; forfeit
罚酒 be made to drink as a forfeit
罚款 ①impose a fine (*or* forfeit) ②fine; forfeit; penalty
罚球 (in basketball) foul shot; free throw; (in football) penalty kick
罚站 make (a pupil, etc.) stand as punishment
罚出场 be ordered off the field for foul play; foul out
罚球点 penalty spot
罚球区 penalty area
罚球线 penalty line
罚不当罪 the punishment exceeds the crime; be punished too severely
罚界外球 throw-in
罚款收入 fines; forfeits and penalty receipt
罚饮一杯 (make sb) drink a cup of wine as a forfeit

垡 [fá]
Ⅰ 动 turn up soil Ⅱ 名 upturned soil

阀 [fá]
名 ①powerful person or family ②valve
阀门 valve
阀套 valve bush; valve pocket

筏 [fá]
名 raft
筏道 log chute; logway
筏运 rafting

筏子 raft

fǎ (ㄈㄚˇ)

法 [fǎ] I 〔名〕①law; statute ②way; method; mode; means ③ standard; criterion; model ④ dharma; the Law; the Way ⑤ magic; trick; magic arts ⑥(short for 法拉)farad (F) II 〔动〕follow; emulate; pattern or model after

法案 proposed law; bill

法办 deal with according to law; punish by law; bring to justice

法宝 ① the Sutras ② magic weapon; magic key; treasured tricks; talisman

法场 execution ground

法槌 judicial mallet

法典 code; statute book

法定 legal; statutory

法官 judge; justice

法规 laws and regulations; statutes

法纪 law and discipline

法警 bailiff

法拉 farad

法兰 flange

法郎 franc

法理 legal principle; theory of law

法力 ①power of the Buddhist doctrine; dharma power ②magic power

法令 laws and decrees; decree

法律 law; statute

法螺 ①triton (shell) ②conch

法盲 legal illiteracy; person ignorant of the law; one who lacks legal knowledge

法门 ①gateway to the Law ②way; method

法名 religious name (the name one adopts on becoming a Buddhist monk or nun)

法袍 judge's robe

法器 musical instruments used in a Buddhist or Taoist mass

法人 legal (or juridical, artificial) person; corporation

法师 Master of the Law (a title of respect for a Buddhist or Taoist priest)

法书 ①model calligraphy ②your calligraphy

法术 magic arts

法庭 court; tribunal

法统 legally constituted authority

法网 the net of justice; the arm of the law; dragnet of law; meshes of law

法系 genealogy of law

法学 the science of law; law

法眼 ①a mind which perceives both past and future ②mental discernment (or perception); insight; acumen

法衣 garments worn by a Buddhist or Taoist priest at a religious ceremony

法医 legal medical expert

法语 French (language)

法院 court of justice; law court; court

法则 ① rule; law ② laws and regulations ③ model

法制 legal system; legal institutions; legality

法治 rule by law

法子 way; method

法兰盘 flange plate

法兰绒 flannel

法理学 jurisprudence

法人股 institutional shares; corporate shares; legal-person shares; shares held by the legal person

法塔赫 AL Fatah

法西斯 fascist

法先王 (political slogan for looking into the past for model government) follow the ancient kings

法学家 jurist

法医学 medical jurisprudence; forensic medicine

法不阿贵 The law does not bend before the powerful.

法不徇情 The law does not yield to personal considerations. or The law is impartial.

法定贬值 official devaluation

法定股本 authorized stock

法定汇率 official rate (of exchange); pegged rate of exchange; pegged exchange parity

法定货币 legal tender

法定继承 inheritance through operation of the law; statutory succession

法定假期 official holiday

法定年龄 lawful (or legal) age; the age of majority

法定期限 prescription

法定人数 quorum

法定税率 national tariff; statutory tariff

法国梧桐 plane tree

法律保障 legal protection

法律承认 de jure recognition

法律程序 legal procedure

法律顾问 legal adviser (or counsel)

法律监督 supervision by the law

法律实体 judicial entity

法律诉讼 judicial proceedings; litigation

法律体系 legal system; statutory framework

法律条件 legal provision

法律推定 presumption of law

法律行为 legal activities

法律意识 law awareness

法律援助 legal aid

法律制裁 legal sanction

法轮常转 the ever-turning Dharma wheel

法人身份 status of a legal person

法人实体 corporate entities

法人团体 body corporate; corporate body; juridical entity
法人资格 legal personality
法庭保释 court bail; court bond insurance
法庭调查 court investigation
法制观念 awareness of the legal system; understanding of law; sense of law
法制国家 state with an adequate legal system
法制建设 building of the legal system; legal construction; improvement (or development, strength) of the legal system
法制教育 legal education; education in legality
法治国家 a country under the rule of law
法定代理人 legal representative
法定继承人 heir at law
法定监护人 statutory guardian
法国大革命 the French Revolution
法拉第定律 Faraday's law
法兰西银行 La Banque de France
法西斯主义 fascism
法制宣传日 free legal advice day
法定汇兑平价 official par of exchange
法律援助制度 legal assistance system
法律援助中心 legal aid centre
法定最低资本额 minimal capital required by law

砝 [fǎ]

砝码 weight (*used on a balance*)

fà（ㄈㄚˋ）

发 [fà] 〔名〕 hair ➡fā

发辫 plait; braid; pigtail
发髻 hair worn in a bun or coil
发夹 hairpin; bobby pin
发胶 hair spray
发蜡 pomade
发廊 hairdresser's; beauty parlour (for women); barber's or barbershop (for men)
发卡 hairpin
发乳 hair cream; pomade
发刷 hairbrush
发网 hairnet
发屋 hairdresser's; beauty parlour (for women); barber's or barbershop (for men)
发型 hairstyle; hairdo; coiffure
发癣 ringworm of the scalp; tinea capitis
发油 hair oil
发指 one's hair bristling up with anger
发型师 hairtician

fān（ㄈㄢ）

帆 [fān] 〔名〕 ①sail ②sailing boat; sailboat
帆板 windsurfer; sailboard

帆布 canvas
帆船 sailing boat (*or* ship); sailboat; junk
帆布裤 ducks
帆布鞋 plimsoll; canvas shoe
帆板运动 windsurfing; sailboarding
帆布背包 knap sack
帆船运动 sailing

番 [fān] Ⅰ〔形〕 foreign; barbarian; aboriginal Ⅱ〔量〕 ①kind; sort ②time; -fold
番号 the designation of a military unit
番茄 tomato
番人 foreigner; alien; barbarian
番薯 sweet potato
番芋 sweet potato
番木瓜 papaya (the tree or its fruit)

幡 [fān] 〔名〕 long narrow flag; streamer
幡儿 funeral streamer

藩 [fān] 〔名〕 ①fence; hedge ②protective screen; barrier; defence ③vassal state; feudatory
藩篱 hedge; fence; barrier
藩属 vassal state

翻 [fān] 〔动〕 ① turn (over, up, upside down, inside out, etc.) ② rummage; search; look through ③reverse; overturn ④climb over; cross; get over ⑤multiply; double ⑥translate; interpret ⑦fall out; quarrel; break up
翻案 reverse a verdict; overturn the original decision
翻版 reprint; reproduction; refurbished version
翻场 turn over the grain on the threshing ground
翻车 ①(of a car) overturn ②run into difficulties; fail in doing sth
翻地 turn up the soil; plough up the fields
翻斗 tipping bucket; skip bucket
翻番 increase by a specified number of times
翻覆 ① turn over; turn upside down ② toss and turn
翻改 remake (old clothes)
翻盖 rebuild or renovate (a house)
翻供 withdraw a confession; retract one's testimony
翻滚 ①seethe; churn ②roll about; toss about
翻悔 back out (of a commitment, promise, etc.)
翻检 glance through and check
翻浆 (of road surfaces) burst and become muddy when a thaw sets in
翻脸 fall out; suddenly turn hostile
翻领 turndown collar
翻录 pirate recordings
翻砂 ①founding ②moulding; casting
翻身 ①turn (the body) over ②free oneself;

stand up; be liberate ③ thoroughly change the backwardness of sth

翻腾 ①tuck dive ②seethe; rise; churn; surge ③turn sth over and over

翻胃 have a gastric disorder; feel nauseated; feel queasy

翻新 renovate; recondition; make over

翻修 rebuild or renovate

翻译 ① translate; interpret ② translator; interpreter

翻印 reprint; reproduce

翻阅 leaf through; thumb through; look over; glance over

翻白眼 show the whites of one's eyes (as from emotion or illness)

翻车机 tipper; dumper; tipple

翻斗车 skip car; tipcart

翻杠子 do gymnastics on a horizontal bar (or on parallel bars)

翻跟头 turn a somersault; loop the loop

翻老账 rake up old scores (or grievances)

翻两番 quadruple

翻砂工 foundry worker; caster

翻身仗 improvement in performance

翻译本 translation

翻译机 electronic translator; translation machine

翻译片 dubbed film

翻译器 interpreter

翻斗卡车 tipping lorry; tip lorry; tip truck

翻江倒海 holding back rivers and overturning seas—overwhelming; tremendous; earth-shaking

翻来覆去 ① toss and turn; toss from side to side ②again and again; repeatedly

翻脸无情 turn against a friend and show him no mercy; be treacherous and ruthless

翻牌公司 government-body-turned company

翻然悔悟 wake up to one's error; make an effort to atone for one's misdeeds

翻砂车间 foundry shop

翻山越岭 cross over mountain after mountain; tramp over hill and dale

翻天覆地 earth-shaking; world-shaking

翻箱倒柜 rummage through chests and cupboards; ransack boxes and chests

翻云覆雨 produce clouds with one turn of the hand and rain with another—be given to playing tricks; keep shifting one's ground

翻盖式移动电话 flip phone

fán (ㄈㄢ)

凡 [fán]
I 形 commonplace; ordinary II 副 ① all; every; any ② altogether; in all; all inclusive III 名 ① this mortal world; the earth ② out-line; gist

凡尘 this world; this mortal life

凡例 notes on the use of a book etc.; guide to the use of a book, etc.

凡人 ①ordinary person ②mortal

凡事 everything

凡是 every; any; all

凡庸 (usu. of humans) commonplace; ordinary

凡士林 vaseline; petrolatum

凡是派 Whatever Faction

凡夫俗子 ordinary people; the common herd

烦 [fán]
I 形 ①vexed; upset; irritated; annoyed ② fed up (with); tired of ③superfluous and confusing II 动 trouble

烦交 kindness of sb; care of sb

烦劳 ①trouble (sb to do sth) ②depressed; feeling low

烦闷 be unhappy; be depressed; be moody

烦恼 vexed; worried

烦扰 ①bother; disturb ②feel disturbed

烦人 annoying; vexing; troubling

烦冗 ①(of one's affairs) diverse and complicated ②(of speech or writing) lengthy and tedious; prolix

烦神 spend time and energy; take great trouble

烦琐 loaded down with trivial details

烦嚣 noisy and annoying

烦心 annoying; vexatious; troublesome

烦躁 fidgety; agitated

烦琐哲学 ①scholasticism ②over-elaboration; hairsplitting

蕃 [fán]
I 形 (of grass, trees, etc.) luxuriant; lush; growing in abundance II 动 reproduce rapidly; multiply; proliferate

樊 [fán]
名 fence

樊篱 ①fence ②barriers; restriction

樊笼 bird cage

繁 [fán]
I 形 in great numbers; numerous; manifold; complicated II 动 propagate; procreate; multiply

繁多 various

繁复 heavy and complicated

繁华 flourishing; bustling; busy

繁丽 rich and flowery

繁忙 busy

繁茂 lush; luxuriant

繁密 dense

繁难 hard to tackle; troublesome

繁荣 ① flourishing; prosperous; booming ② make sth prosper

繁盛 thriving; flourishing; prosperous

繁琐 many and miscellaneous with trifles

繁细 overloaded with details;excessively detailed

繁星 an array of stars

繁衍 multiply;increase gradually in number (*or* quantity)

繁育 breed

繁杂 many and diverse;miscellaneous

繁殖 breed;reproduce;propagate

繁重 heavy;strenuous;onerous

繁分数 complex fraction

繁体字 the original complex form of a simplified Chinese character

繁殖力 reproductive capacity;fecundity;fertility

繁殖率 rate of reproduction;breeding rate

繁荣昌盛 thriving and prosperous

繁荣兴旺 brisk and flourish;flourishing;prosperous;rich and vigorous;thriving

繁文缛节 unnecessary and overelaborate formalities;red tape

fǎn (ㄈㄢˇ)

反 [fǎn] I 副 ①in an opposite direction;inside out ②on the contrary;instead II 动 ①turn over;turn;reverse ② return;counter ③ oppose;combat;be against ④ rebel;revolt ⑤ analogize;reason by analogy III 名 ①reverse side ②counter-revolutionaries;reactionaries

反霸 ①struggle against local despots (in land reform) ②oppose hegemonism

反绑 bind sb's arms behind him (*or* her)

反比 inverse relation;inverse proportion

反驳 refute;rebut

反哺 repay

反差 contrast

反常 unusual;abnormal;strange

反超 turn the tide

反衬 set off by contrast;serve as a foil to

反冲 recoil;kick

反刍 ruminate;chew the cud

反串 temporarily play part other than one's customary role

反倒 on the contrary;instead

反帝 oppose imperialism;be anti-imperialist

反动 ①reactionary ②reaction

反对 oppose;be against;fight;combat

反而 on the contrary;instead

反方 (as of a debate) con side

反讽 sarcastic retort

反复 ① repeatedly;again and again ② back out;chop and change ③reversal;relapse

反感 be disgusted with;be averse to;dislike;take unkindly to

反攻 launch a counteroffensive;counterattack

反顾 look back;turn back

反观 conversely

反光 ①reflect light ②reflection of light

反话 ironic remark;irony

反悔 go back on one's word (*or* promise)

反击 strike back;beat back;counterattack

反剪 ① have one's hands tied behind one's back ②hold one's hands behind one's back

反间 sow distrust or dissension among one's enemies;set one's enemies at odds (by spreading rumours,etc.)

反诘 ask in retort;counter with a question

反抗 revolt;resist

反恐 crack down on terrorism

反馈 ①feedback ②feedback (a response)

反面 ① reverse side;wrong side;back ② the reverse side of a state of affairs,a problem,etc. ③opposite;negative side

反目 (*usu. of husband and wife*) fall out;have a falling-out

反派 villain (in drama,etc.);negative character

反叛 revolt;rebel

反聘 rehire after retirement;be employed after one's retirement

反扑 pounce on sb again after being beaten off;launch a counteroffensive to retrieve lost ground

反潜 defend (maritime space) against enemy submarines

反射 ①reflect (light,heat,sound,etc.) ②reflex

反手 backhand

反水 turn one's coat;defect

反思 self-examination;rethink

反诉 countercharge;counterclaim

反贪 combat graft

反弹 rebound;spring (*or* bounce) back;return to the original state

反特 prevent or thwart enemy espionage;engage in counterespionage

反题 antithesis

反胃 have a gastric disorder;feel nauseated;feel queasy

反问 ①ask a question in reply ②rhetorical question

反响 repercussion;echo;reverberation

反向 opposite direction;reverse

反省 engage in introspection,self-examination or soul-searching;introspection

反应 ① response;repercussion ② react;respond ③reaction

反映 ①reflect;mirror ②report;make known

反语 irony

反正 ① in any case;at any rate;anyway ② come over from the enemy's side ③since;as

反证 disproof;counterevidence

反之 whereas; on the other hand; conversely
反殖 anti-colonialist
反转 reverse
反坐 sentence the accuser to the punishment facing the person he falsely accused
反比例 inverse ratio; inverse proportion
反潮流 go against the tide; swim against the stream
反冲锋 counterattack
反冲核 recoil nucleus
反冲力 recoil
反倒退 oppose retrogression
反动派 reactionaries
反对党 opposition party; the Opposition
反对派 opposition faction
反对票 dissenting vote; negative vote; opposing vote
反封建 anti-feudal; against feudalism
反腐败 combat corruption; fight (*or* battle) corruption; anti-corruption
反干扰 anti-jamming
反革命 ① counter-revolutionary ② a counter-revolutionaries
反光灯 reflector lamp
反光镜 reflector
反过来 ① conversely; the other way round ② in turn; versa
反函数 inverse function
反核子 antinucleon
反季节 out-of-season
反间计 a stratagem of sowing distrust or discord among one's enemies
反科学 anti-science; opposition to science, scientific research or the scientific method
反空降 anti-airborne defence
反恐怖 anti-terrorism
反例证 counter-example
反粒子 antiparticle; any constituent particle of antimatter
反批评 counter-criticism
反气旋 anticyclone
反潜机 antisubmarine plane
反窃听 debug
反侵略 resist aggression
反倾销 anti-dumping
反人民 anti-popular
反射比 reflectance
反射波 reflected wave; return wave; echo
反射光 reflected light; reverberation; catoptric light
反射弧 reflex arc
反射计 reflectometer
反射镜 reflector
反射炉 reverberatory furnace
反围盘 reverse repeater (*used in steel rolling*)
反物质 anti-matter

反向铲 backhoe
反斜面 reverse slope; rear slope
反信风 antitrades
反宣传 ① counterpropaganda ② slander campaign
反要求 cross-demand
反义词 antonym
反应堆 reactor
反应塔 reaction tower
反应物 reactant
反映论 theory of reflection
反证法 reduction to absurdity; reductio ad absurdum
反政变 countercoup
反质子 antiproton
反中子 antineutron
反转片 reversal film
反作用 counteraction; reaction
反败为胜 turn defeat into victory; turn the tide; bring about a complete turnabout
反刍动物 ruminant
反唇相讥 answer back sarcastically
反党分子 diversionist
反导系统 ABM system, anti-ballistic missile system
反动分子 reactionary element; reactionary
反对堕胎 anti-choice; antiabortion
反法西斯 fight against fascism
反腐倡廉 combat corruption and advocate a clean government
反复无常 behave capriciously; blow hot and cold; chop and change
反戈一击 turn one's weapon around and strike—turn against one's own side
反攻倒算 (of members of an overthrown reactionary class) counterattack to settle old scores; launch a vindictive counterattack; retaliate
反躬自问 examine oneself; examine one's conscience
反光照明 reflect lighting
反华势力 anti-China forces
反华提案 anti-China motion
反季销售 off-season sale
反客为主 reverse positions of host and guest; turn from guest into host—gain the initiative
反馈信息 feedback information
反馈抑制 feedback inhibition
反面教材 negative example which may serve as a lesson; bad experience which teaches us what not to do
反面教员 teacher by negative example
反面人物 villain; negative character; negative role
反面意见 the other side of the coin
反潜导弹 antisubmarine missiles

反潜舰艇 antisubmarine vessels
反倾销法 anti-dumping law;anti-dumping act
反倾销税 anti-dumping duty; countervailing duty
反身代词 reflexive pronoun
反守为攻 turn from the defensive to the offensive;turn the tables on the attackers
反坦克炮 antitank gun
反向电流 reverse current
反向购买 counter purchase
反向兼并 reverse takeover
反向卫星 retrograde satellite
反咬一口 trump up a countercharge against one's accuser;make a false countercharge
反应本领 reaction capacity
反映民意 reflect the people's will
反右运动 anti-rightist campaign
反作用力 reacting force
反病毒软件 anti-virus (software)
反导弹导弹 antimissile missile
反对特殊化 oppose privileges
反腐败斗争 the fight against corruption
反汇编程序 disassembler
反季节蔬菜 vegetables grown out of season; out-of-season vegetables
反恐怖主义 counterterrorism
反射测云器 reflecting nephoscope
反射望远镜 reflecting telescope
反铁电现象 antiferroelectricity
反卫星武器 satellite active nullifier
反主流文化 counterculture
反走私运动 anti-smuggling drive
反馈控制系统 feedback control systems
反其道而行之 act in a diametrically opposite way;do exactly the opposite
反向技术转让 reverse transfer of technology
反弹道导弹条约 Anti-Ballistic Missile Treaty (ABMT)
反电子对抗措施 electronic counter-counter-measures

返 [fǎn]
囫 return;come or go back
返潮 get damp
返程 back tracking
返防 return to stations
返岗 return to original job
返工 do poorly done work over again
返航 (of ships, planes, etc.) return to base (or port)
返回 return;come or go back
返贫 slide back into poverty
返聘 re-employ after retirement
返青 (of winter crops or transplanted seedlings) turn green
返销 (of state-purchased grain) be sold back to a grain-producing area (in cases of natural disaster,etc.)

返校 (of students) return to school
返修 refix (or repair again) at the same repair shop
返回卫星 recoverable satellite;return satellite
返回指令 link order
返老还童 renew one's youth;become young again
返璞归真 one's original simplicity;return to one's original nature
返祖现象 atavism;reversion

fàn (ㄈㄢˋ)

犯 [fàn]
I 动 ①encroach on; violate; go against; offend (against the law, etc.) ②attack; violate;assail;invade ③have a recurrence of (an old illness);revert to (a bad habit) ④commit (a mistake, crime, etc.) II 名 criminal; offender;culprit
犯案 (of a criminal) be found out and brought to justice
犯病 have an attack of one's old illness
犯愁 worry;be anxious
犯法 violate (or break) the law
犯规 ①break the rules ②foul
犯忌 violate a taboo
犯戒 break into forbidden ground; break monk's vows
犯禁 violate a ban (or prohibition)
犯人 prisoner;convict
犯上 go against the king or emperor (in former times); defy one's elders, superiors, etc.
犯疑 become suspicious
犯罪 commit a crime (or an offence)
犯糊涂 become confused;get mixed up
犯忌讳 offend a person's sensitivity; touch a person's sore spot;break taboos
犯脾气 flare up;fly off the handle;be in a bad mood
犯死罪 commit a capital crime;incur the death penalty
犯嫌疑 arouse suspicion;come under suspicion
犯校规 violate school regulations
犯上作乱 defy one's superiors and start a rebellion;rebel
犯罪集团 crime syndicate
犯罪未遂 criminal attempt;attempted (or inchoate) crime
犯罪嫌疑人 criminal suspect
犯罪侦查学 criminalistics

饭 [fàn]
名 ①cooked rice or other cereals ②meal
饭菜 ①meal;repast ②dishes to go with rice, steamed buns,etc.
饭店 ①hotel ②restaurant
饭馆 (small) restaurant;eating house

饭锅 ① pot for cooking rice; rice cooker ② means of living; livelihood
饭盒 lunch-box; mess tin; dinner pail
饭局 dinner party; feast
饭量 appetite
饭票 meal ticket; mess card
饭铺 (small) restaurant; eating house
饭食 food provided by a canteen, restaurant, boarding house, etc. (esp. with regard to its quality); fare
饭厅 dining hall; dining room; mess hall
饭桶 ① rice bucket ② a big eater; a piggish eater ③ fathead; good-for-nothing
饭碗 ① rice bowl ② job; means of livelihood
饭庄 (big) restaurant
饭桌 dining table
饭后服 be taken after meals
饭前服 be taken before meals
饭后茶余 after meal hours or in leisure time
饭来张口, 衣来伸手 have only to open one's mouth to be fed and hold out one's arms to be dressed—lead an easy life, with everything provided; be waited on hand and foot
饭后百步走, 活到九十九 Walk a hundred paces after meals and you will live to ninety-nine.

泛 〔fàn〕 I 〔动〕 ① float ② emerge; turn; spread out; send forth; be suffused with ③ flood; inundate II 〔形〕 ① extensive; general; nonspecific ② superficial; shallow ③ pan-
泛称 general term
泛读 extensive reading
泛滥 be in flood; overflow; inundate
泛音 overtone; harmonic
泛指 make a general reference; be used in a general sense
泛舟 go boating; float on a boat
泛光灯 floodlight
泛神论 pantheism
泛音列 harmonic series
泛泛而谈 speak in general terms; talk in generalities
泛泛之交 casual acquaintance
泛泛之论 mere generalities
泛非主义 Pan-Africanism
泛函分析 functional analysis
泛滥成灾 flood; run rampant; run wild
泛美主义 Pan-Americanism
泛非主义者 Pan-Africanist

范 〔fàn〕 〔名〕 ① pattern; mould; matrix ② model; criterion; example ③ limits; range ④ restrictions; limits
范本 a model for calligraphy or painting
范畴 ① category ② type; scope
范例 example; model

范式 canonical form; normal form
范围 limits; scope; range
范文 model essay; anthology piece

贩 〔fàn〕 I 〔动〕 buy to resell II 〔名〕 trader; monger; pedlar; vendor
贩毒 traffic in narcotics; traffic drugs; drug traffic; push dope; traffic in drugs
贩黄 trafficking of obscene publications; porno peddling
贩卖 traffic; peddle; sell
贩私 traffic in smuggled goods; trafficking of smuggled goods
贩运 transport goods for sale; traffic
贩子 trader; monger
贩粮食 buy grain for resale
贩鸦片 traffic in opium
贩卖人口 traffic in human beings; human traffic

畈 〔fàn〕 〔名〕 land; field

梵 〔fàn〕 〔名〕 ① Sanskrit ② Buddhist ③ (in Hinduism) Brahman; Supreme Being
梵文 Sanskrit
梵语 Sanskrit
梵蒂冈 the Vatican

fāng （ㄈㄤ）

方 〔fāng〕 I 〔名〕 ① square ② involution; power ③ direction ④ side; party ⑤ place; region; locality ⑥ method; means; way ⑦ prescription II 〔量〕 ① (for square things): 三方图章 three seals/ 五方石碑 five stone tablets/ 一方砚台 an inkstone ② (short for 平方 or 立方) square metre; cubic metre: 一方地板 a square metre of floor III 〔形〕 morally square; upright; honest IV 〔副〕 ① then; just at the time; just then ② only; just; just now
方案 scheme; plan; programme
方便 ① convenient ② make things convenient for sb ③ have money to spare or lend ④ go to the lavatory
方步 measured steps
方才 ① just now ② (only) just; not until
方材 lumber; square-edged timber
方程 equation
方寸 ① square *cun* (= 1/9 square decimetre) ② heart
方凳 square stool
方法 method; way; means
方钢 square steel
方格 a pattern of squares; check
方根 root
方剂 prescription; recipe
方孔 square hole

方块 diamond;block
方框 square frame
方略 general plan
方面 respect;aspect;side;field
方士 ①necromancer ②alchemist
方式 way;fashion;pattern
方糖 sugar cube;lump sugar
方位 ①points of the compass ②direction and position;bearings
方向 direction;orientation
方形 square-shaped;square
方言 dialect
方圆 ① neighbourhood;vicinity ② circumference
方丈 [fāngzhang] ① Buddhist abbot ② abbot's room
方针 policy;guiding principle
方正 ①upright and foursquare ②straightforward;upright;righteous
方志 local records
方子 ① prescription ② directions for mixing chemicals;formula
方便米 instant rice
方便面 instant noodles
方程式 ①equation ②(chemical) equation
方法论 methodology
方尖碑 obelisk
方解石 calcite (a mineral)
方块字 square-shaped characters—Chinese characters
方括号 square brackets ([ ])
方面军 front army
方铅矿 galena
方位词 noun of locality;localizer
方位角 azimuth
方位物 topographic marker
方向舵 rudder (of an airplane)
方向盘 steering wheel
方言学 dialectology
方钻杆 kelly (bar)
方便食品 convenience food
方便之门 convenience
方法工程 methods engineering
方济各会 the Franciscan Order
方位罗盘 surveying azimuth compass
方兴未艾 be fast unfolding;be in the ascendant
方程式赛车 formula;formula racing car
方位天文学 positional astronomy
方向整流器 direction rectifier

坊 [fāng]
<名> ① lane;alley ② memorial archway or gateway ➡fáng
坊本 block-printed edition prepared by a bookshop
坊间 ①on the street stalls ②in the bookshops

芳 [fāng]
Ⅰ <形> ①sweet-smelling;aromatic;fragrant ②good (name or reputation);virtuous ③your Ⅱ <名> flowers and plants
芳草 fragrant grass;green grass
芳菲 ①the fragrance of flowers and plants ② flowers and plants
芳龄 the age of a young woman
芳名 ①the name of a young woman ②a good reputation
芳烃 aromatic hydrocarbon
芳香 (esp. of flowers or plants) fragrant
芳心 the heart of a young woman
芳族 aromatics
芳香剂 an aromatic drug;aromatic

枋 [fāng]
<名> ①tree whose timber is good for making vehicles ② square-shaped lumber;squared timber ③ square timber placed horizontally between two pillars;crossbeam

钫 [fāng]
<名> ①francium (Fr) ②bronze round-bellied wine vessel with a square mouth ③ cooking utensil;pot

fáng（ㄈㄤ）

防 [fáng]
Ⅰ <动> ① prevent; guard against; provide against ② defend; protect Ⅱ <名> dyke;embankment
防暴 riot protection
防备 guard against;take precautions against
防潮 ①dampproof;moistureproof ②give protection against the tide
防尘 dustproof
防磁 protect against magnetization;be anti-magnetic
防弹 bulletproof;shellproof
防盗 guard against theft; take precautions against burglars
防地 defence sector;station (of a unit)
防冻 prevent frostbite
防毒 protect (men or animals) against poisonous substances;protect against poison gas
防范 be on guard;keep a lookout
防风 protect against the wind;provide shelter from the wind
防腐 antiseptic
防旱 take precautions against drought
防洪 prevent or control flood
防护 protect;shelter
防火 ①prevent fires ②fireproof
防空 air defence
防涝 prevent waterlogging
防凌 reduce the menace of ice run
防区 defence (*or* garrison) area
防身 defend oneself against violence

F

防守 defend;guard
防暑 prevent heatstroke (*or* sunstroke)
防水 waterproof
防缩 shrinkproof
防特 guard against enemy agents
防卫 defend
防伪 false-proof
防务 matters pertaining to defence;defence
防线 line of defence
防锈 rust-resist;rustproof
防汛 flood prevention or control
防疫 epidemic prevention
防御 defend;guard
防灾 take precautions against natural calamities
防震 ①shockproof ②take precautions against earthquakes
防止 prevent;guard against;forestall;avoid
防治 provide prevention and cure;administer prophylaxis and treatment
防皱 crease-proof;crease-resistant
防暴车 antiriot vehicle
防暴队 riot protection team
防波堤 breakwater;mole
防潮层 dampproof course;damp course
防尘圈 dust ring
防尘罩 dust cover
防弹车 bubble car
防盗门 anti-theft door;security door;burglar-proof door
防盗锁 pick-proof lock
防冻剂 antifreezing agent;freeze proof agent
防冻液 antifreeze solution
防风林 windbreaks;wind break forest
防辐射 protect against radiation
防腐剂 antiseptic;preservative
防寒服 cold-resistant clothing;winter outerwear;warm clothing;eiderdown outerwear
防洪坝 flood dam
防护堤 (protection) embankment
防护林 shelter-forest
防滑链 tyre chain;skid chain
防化兵 antichemical warfare corps
防空洞 air-raid shelter
防空壕 air-raid dugout
防染剂 resist
防沙林 sand-break forests
防晒油 suntan lotion
防水层 waterproof layer
防坦克 antitank defence
防污染 anti-pollution
防锈剂 rust inhibitor;antirust agent
防疫站 epidemic prevention station
防疫针 (prophylactic) inoculation
防雨布 waterproof cloth;tarpaulin
防御区 defensive area
防御战 defensive warfare

防震棚 temporary shelter for earthquake
防暴警察 riot police;riot squad
防病治病 prevention and cure of diseases
防不胜防 hard to guard against;cannot reckon with all eventualities
防潮火药 moistureproof powder;nonhygroscopic powder
防弹玻璃 bulletproof glass
防弹汽车 bulletproof car
防毒面具 gas mask
防洪防汛 flood combating
防洪工程 flood control works;flood retarding (*or* prevention) project
防洪设施 flood control installations
防洪治涝 flood prevention and water-logging control
防护林带 shelter belt
防空部队 air defence forces
防空警报 air-raid warning;air-raid siren
防微杜渐 nip in the bud;check at the outset
防卫过当 excessive defence;act in undue self-defence
防卫力量 defense capabilities
防伪标记 false-proof seal
防汛抗旱 flood control and drought relief
防御部队 defending force (*or* troops,unit)
防御部署 defensive disposition
防御措施 defensive measure
防御工事 defences; fortifications; defence works
防御武器 weapons of defence
防御阵地 defensive position;defended post
防灾救灾 prevent natural disasters and relieve people in the stricken areas
防灾抗灾 prevent and fight natural adversities
防抱死系统 anti-lock braking system (ABS)
防护林工程 the shelter forest project
防患于未然 take preventive measures;provide against possible trouble
防火隔离墙 fire wall
防火隔离线 fire lane
防窃听电话 scrambler phone
防卫厅长官 Director General of the Defence Agency
防止核扩散 nonproliferation of nuclear weapons
防治病虫害 prevention and elimination of diseases and pests
防卫作战能力 defense capabilities and combat effectiveness
防治工业污染 prevent and control industrial pollution
防御性的国防政策 national defense policy that is defensive in nature
防范和化解金融风险 guard against and defuse (*or* eliminate) financial risks;take precautions against and reduce financial risks

坊 [fáng]
名 workshop;mill;shop ➡ fāng

妨 [fáng]
动 hinder;hamper;impair;harm
妨碍 hinder;hamper;impede;obstruct
妨害 impair;jeopardize;be harmful to
妨碍公务 interference with public function
妨害健康 harm one's health
妨害名誉 offences against personal reputation
妨害公务罪 crime of interference with public function
妨害婚姻家庭罪 crimes of interference with the family

肪 [fáng]
◇脂肪 fat

房 [fáng]
I 名 ①house;building ②room;chamber ③house-like structure ④branch of an extended family ⑤shop;store II 量 (for branches of an extended family):有三房儿媳妇 have three daughters-in-law
房舱 passenger's cabin in a ship
房产 house property
房车 luxury car;caravan
房贷 housing loan
房顶 roof
房东 the owner and lessor of a house or room; landlord or landlady
房改 housing reform;reform of the housing problem;housing system reform;dwelling house reform
房管 real estate management
房荒 housing shortage
房基 foundations (of a building)
房价 house (or apartment) purchase price
房间 room
房客 tenant (of a room or house);lodger
房契 title deed (for a house)
房市 property market;housing market
房事 sexual intercourse (usu. between a married couple)
房贴 rental allowance
房屋 house (or building);housing
房型 type of apartment
房檐 eaves
房展 property exhibition
房主 house owner
房子 ① house;building ② room,apartment, etc.
房租 rent (for a house,flat,etc.);rental
房产证 property ownership certificate
房地产 real estate;realty
房改房 housing reform houses
房管所 urban real estate management organs
房权证 property right certificate
房地产热 craze for real estate grabbing;real estate rush
房地产税 housing and land tax;real estate tax
房改方案 housing reform program
房屋出租 premises to let;house for rent
房屋装修 house improvement and betterment
房地产公司 real estate agency
房地产交易 real estate transaction
房地产经营 real estate business
房地产开发 real estate development
房地产市场 real estate market
房地产交易中心 real estate exchange centre
房地产经营管理 real estate operation and management

fǎng (ㄈㄤˇ)

仿 [fǎng]
I 动 ①imitate;model on;copy ②resemble;be like II 名 characters written after a calligraphy model
仿单 instructions for use (of a commodity, esp. a medicine)
仿佛 ①seemingly;as if ②be more or less the same;be alike
仿古 modelled after an antique;in the style of the ancients
仿冒 copy;counterfeit
仿效 imitate;follow the example of
仿形 profile modelling
仿造 copy;be modelled on
仿照 imitate;follow
仿真 simulation;emulation;phantom
仿制 copy;imitate;be modelled on
仿生耳 mimicry"ear"
仿生学 bionics
仿制品 an imitation;replica;copy;pastiche
仿生建筑 bionic architecture
仿生机器人 bio-robot
仿生计算机 bionic computer

访 [fǎng]
动 ①pay a visit;visit;call on ②seek by inquiry or search;try to get or gather
访查 go about making inquiries;investigate
访求 search for
访谈 interview and discuss
访问 visit;call on;interview;access;visiting
访演 visiting performance
访谈录 record of an interview discussion
访古寻幽 search for scenes of historical interests and sights of scenic beauty
访亲问友 call on one's relatives and friends
访问学者 visiting scholar

纺 [fǎng]
I 动 spin II 名 thin silk fabric
纺车 spinning wheel
纺绸 a soft plain-weave silk fabric
纺锤 spindle
纺机 frame

纺纱 spinning
纺丝 fibre spinning
纺织 spinning and weaving
纺织娘 katydid; long-horned grasshopper
纺织品 textile; fabric
纺纱织布 spin yarn and weave cloth; spinning and weaving

舫 [fǎng]
〈名〉boat

fàng（ㄈㄤˋ）

放 [fàng]
〈动〉① let go; set free; free; release ② let oneself go; act with abandon; give way to ③ put out to pasture; let off for prey ④ stop (work, etc.); knock off; have a holiday ⑤ show; play; turn on ⑥ light; fire; kindle; ignite ⑦ set; set off; give out ⑧ send away; banish; exile ⑨ lend (money) at interest; loan ⑩ (of flowers) blossom; bloom; open ⑪ let out; expand; enlarge; make larger ⑫ leave alone; lay aside; put aside; keep ⑬ fell; cause to fall to the ground ⑭ put in; add ⑮ put; place ⑯ readjust or moderate (one's attitude, behaviour, etc.)

放大 enlarge; magnify; amplify
放胆 act boldly and with confidence
放诞 wild in speech and behaviour
放荡 ①dissolute; dissipated ②unconventional
放电 (electric) discharge; eye up
放刁 make difficulties for sb; act in a rascally manner
放毒 ①put poison in food, water, etc.; poison ②make vicious remarks; spread poisonous ideas
放风 ①let in fresh air ②let prisoners out for exercise (or relieve themselves) ③leak certain information; spread news or rumours
放工 get out of work; knock off
放过 let sb off; let sth slip by
放火 ①set fire to; set on fire; commit arson ②create disturbances
放假 have a holiday or vacation; have a day off
放箭 shoot an arrow
放开 have a free hand in doing sth
放宽 relax restrictions; relax
放款 make loans; loan
放浪 ①unrestrained ②dissolute
放疗 radiotherapy
放牧 put out to pasture; graze; herd
放排 ①set a raft going (downstream) ②rafting (a way of transporting logs)
放盘 (of a shop) sell at reduced prices or buy in at raised prices
放炮 ① fire a gun ② set off firecrackers ③ blast ④ (of a tyre, etc.) blow out ⑤ shoot off one's mouth

放屁 ①break wind; fart ②talk nonsense
放弃 abandon; give up; renounce
放情 to one's heart's content; as much as one likes
放晴 clear up (after rain)
放权 delegate power to the lower levels; forsake one's power; transfer power to a lower level
放热 exothermic
放任 ①not interfere; let alone ②noninterference; laissez-faire
放散 (of smoke, scent, etc.) diffuse; disperse; dissipate
放哨 be on sentry or on patrol
放射 radiate
放生 free captive animals; (of Buddhists) buy captive fish or birds and set them free; free wildlife from captivity
放手 ①let go; let go one's hold ②have a free hand; go all out ③release one's control; hand over to sb else
放树 fell trees; cut down trees
放水 ① turn on the water ② draw off some water (from a reservoir, etc.) ③false play on purpose
放肆 unbridled; wanton
放松 relax; slacken; loosen
放送 broadcast; send out (over a loudspeaker, etc.)
放下 lay down; put down
放心 ①set one's mind at rest; be at ease; rest assured; feel relieved ②have confidence in sb; trust sb
放行 let sb or sth pass
放学 ① classes are over; school lets out ② have a holiday or vacation
放血 phlebotomy; bloodletting
放眼 take a broad view; scan widely
放羊 ①graze sheep; pasture sheep; look after sheep ②be reinless; throw (the) reins off; drift along
放养 put (fish, insects, etc.) in a suitable place to breed
放样 laying off; lofting; setting-out
放鹰 ①go hawking; hunt with falcons ②lose everything; lose completely
放映 show (a film); project
放债 lend money at interest
放账 lend money at interest
放置 lay up; lay aside
放逐 send into exile; exile; banish
放纵 ① let sb have his own way; indulge ② self-indulgent; undisciplined
放走 release; set free; let go
放爆竹 light firecrackers; let off firecrackers
放大尺 pantograph

放大机 enlarger
放大镜 magnifying glass;magnifier
放大率 magnifying power
放大器 amplifier
放大纸 enlarging paper;bromide paper
放电视 turn on the TV
放电影 show a film
放风筝 fly a kite
放火犯 arsonist
放空炮 talk big;spout hot air;indulge in idle boasting
放空气 drop a hint;spread word;create an impression
放录像 play a video tape
放录音 play a recording
放牧期 grazing season
放气球 let go a balloon
放射病 radiation sickness
放射线 radioactive rays
放射性 radioactivity
放线菌 actinomyces
放心菜 quality-assured vegetables
放心肉 rest-assured meat; quality-assured meat
放焰火 set off fireworks
放映队 film projection team
放映机（film）projector
放映室 projection room
放映员 projectionist
放大照片 enlarged photograph;enlargement; blowup
放荡不羁 unconventional and unrestrained
放高利贷 lend money at an excessively high rate of interest;practise usury
放虎归山 set a tiger free;set free a tiger free back to the mountains;lay by trouble for the future
放开搞活 open up and invigorate;adopt a flexible policy to enliven the economy
放开价格 relax price control;lift price controls
放宽条件 soften the terms
放宽限制 relaxation of restrictions;ease curbs on
放宽政策 introduce more flexible policies; adopt more liberal（or flexible）policies; implement policies more flexibly
放浪形骸 refuse to be bound by convention;be defiant of convention
放弃管理 drifting management; permissive management
放权让利 delegation of power and concession of profit;grant power to enterprises and allow them to keep a bigger share of profits
放热反应 exothermic reaction
放任管理 drifting（or permissive）management

放任自流 let things drift（or slide）
放射疗法 radiotherapy
放射现象 radioactivity
放松警惕 relax one's vigilance
放松银根 ease monetary policy
放眼世界 have the whole world in view;open one's eyes to the whole world
放弃核威慑 renounce（or abandon）nuclear deterrence
放弃索赔权 waive right of claim
放任式领导 laissez-faire（or permissive）leadership
放射性衰变 radioactive decay
放射性微尘 radioactive dust;fallout
放射性污染 radioactive contamination;radioactive pollution
放射性物质 radioactive materials
放射性元素 radioactive element;radioelement
放射性沾染 radioactive contamination
放射性制剂 radioactive agent
放纵走私罪 crime of unbridling smugglers
放射性同位素 radio isotope
放长线,钓大鱼 throw a long line to catch a big fish—adopt a long-term plan to secure sth big
放之四海而皆准 universally applicable; valid everywhere
放活国有小型企业 adopt a flexible policy toward small state-owned enterprises
放射性碳素断代法 radiocarbon dating
放下屠刀,立地成佛 drop one's cleaver and become a Buddha—achieve salvation as soon as one gives up evil

fēi（ㄈㄟ）

飞 [fēi]
Ⅰ 动 ①（of birds, etc.）fly; flit ②（of plane,etc.）fly ③hover or flutter in the air ④volatilize; disappear through volatilization or vapourization Ⅱ 副 ①swiftly; rapidly; speedily ②very;extremely Ⅲ 形 unexpected; accidental;unfounded;groundless
飞奔 run at full speed;run like the wind;run like mad
飞镖 ①a dart-like weapon ②darts（a game）
飞驰（of trains, cars, horses, etc.）speed along
飞虫 winged insect
飞船 ① airship; dirigible ② spaceship; spacecraft
飞弹 ①missile ②stray bullet
飞刀 fly-cutter
飞地 ① land of one province or county enclosed by that of another ②enclave;exclave
飞碟 ①skeet shooting;skeet; trapshooting ② flying saucer;UFO

飞过 fly past;fly across;fly over
飞花 ① cotton bits that fly about in the process of weaving or fluffing
飞蝗 migratory locusts
飞机 aircraft;aeroplane;plane
飞溅 splash
飞快 ① very fast;at lightning speed ② extremely sharp
飞轮 ①flywheel ②free wheel (of a bicycle)
飞盘 Frisbee disk;Frisbee
飞泉 cliffside spring
飞人 ①trapeze ②fastest runner;best sprinter;best athlete
飞散 ①(of smoke,mist,etc.) disperse;dissipate ②(of birds) fly away in different directions;scatter;disperse
飞逝 flight;fleet away;pass away swiftly
飞鼠 flying squirrel
飞速 at full speed
飞腾 fly swiftly upward;soar
飞天 flying Apsaras
飞艇 airship;dirigible
飞腿 fly kick
飞吻 blow a kiss
飞舞 dance in the air;flutter
飞翔 circle in the air;hover
飞行 (of an aircraft,missile,etc. or of a pilot) fly;make a flight
飞檐 upturned eaves
飞眼 make eyes;ogle
飞扬 fly upward;rise
飞鱼 flying fish
飞跃 ①jump;leap ②leap
飞灾 unexpected disaster
飞贼 ①a burglar who makes his way into a house over walls and roofs ②an intruding enemy airman;air marauder (or pirate)
飞涨 (of prices,water level,etc.) soar;shoot up;skyrocket
飞碟学 ufology
"飞鸽"牌 ①Flying Pigeon ②person ready to shift from one job to another
飞机场 airfield;airport;aerodrome
飞机库 hangar
飞毛腿 ① fleet-footed;swift of foot ② fleet-footed runner
飞行服 flying suit
飞行帽 aviator's helmet
飞行器 aircraft
飞行员 pilot;aviator;flyer
飞车走壁 acrobatics stunt cycling,driving or motorcycling on the inner surface of a cylindrical wall
飞短流长 spread embroidered stories and malicious gossip
飞蛾投火 a moth darting into a flame—bring destruction upon oneself;seek one's own doom

飞黄腾达 make rapid advances in one's career;have a meteoric rise
飞机修理 aircraft repair
飞来横祸 an unforeseen disaster (or misfortune)
飞沫传染 infection through breathing in flying particles of the saliva or phlegm of a sick person
飞沙走石 sand flying about and stones hurtling through the air (as in a windstorm)
飞行半径 flying radius
飞行管制 air traffic control
飞行人员 aircrew;aircrewman
飞行事故 flight accident
飞行药检 spot check
飞檐走壁 (of swordsmen,etc. in old Chinese novels) leap onto roofs and vault over walls
飞扬跋扈 arrogant and domineering
"飞鱼"导弹 Exocet missile
飞针走线 ply one's needle nimbly;do skilful needlework
飞机制造业 aircraft industry;aviation industry
"飞毛腿"导弹 Scud missile
飞行记录簿 flight log
飞机乘客保险 aircraft passenger insurance
飞机上交货价 free on plane;free on aircraft

妃 [fēi] 〈名〉 ① imperial concubine ② wife of a prince,etc.
妃红 light pink
妃色 light pink
妃子 imperial concubine

非 [fēi] I 〈名〉 ① wrong;wrongdoing;error;evil ② (short for 非洲) Africa II 〈动〉 ①not conform to;go against;run counter to ② censure;blame;oppose;find fault with ③deteriorate;degenerate ④not;non-;un-;in-:非人生活 inhuman life III 〈副〉 ①have got to;simply must ②(used to indicate wilfulness or determination):不让他唱,他非要唱。 We didn't want him to sing,but he insisted.
非常 ① extraordinary;unusual;special ② very;extremely;highly
非但 not only
非得 have got to;must
非独 not merely
非法 illegal;unlawful;illicit
非凡 outstanding;extraordinary;uncommon
非分 overstepping one's bounds;assuming;presumptuous
非礼 assault
非命 an unnatural death;a violent death
非难 blame;censure;reproach
非人 ①not the right person ②inhuman
非刑 brutal torture (not permitted by the

law)
非议 reproach;censure
非洲 Africa
非常任 nonpermanent
非官方 unofficial
非金属 nonmetal
非晶质 noncrystalline;amorphous
非卖品 (articles) not for sale
非物质 nonmaterial
非正式 unofficial;informal
非正统 unorthodox
非比寻常 unusual;out of the ordinary
非病原菌 nonpathogenic bacteria
非常时期 time of emergency
非处方药 over-the-counter (OTC) medicine (*or* drug)
非此即彼 either this or that;one or the other; either-or
非对抗性 nonantagonistic
非法传销 illegal pyramid selling
非法倒卖 profiteering;illegal buying and selling
非法交易 illegal deal
非法结社 illegal association
非法经商 unlawful trade
非法拘禁 illegal (*or* unlawful) custody
非法刊物 illegal publication
非法取证 obtaining evidence in unlawful way
非法收入 illegally derived income;illicit income
非法同居 illicit cohabitation
非法销售 illicit sale of sth
非分之想 inordinate ambitions
非公莫入 no admittance except on business
非建交国 country that has no diplomatic relations with China;countries that have no diplomatic relations(with each other)
非交战国 nonbelligerent
非军事化 demilitarize
非军事区 demilitarized zone (DMZ)
非驴非马 neither ass nor horse—neither fish, flesh,nor fowl
非农产业 non-agricultural industries
非亲非故 neither relative nor friend;neither kith nor kin
非生产性 unproductive;nonproductive
非同小可 no small (*or* trivial) matter
非刑拷打 put sb to the torture
非正规军 irregular troops;irregulars
非常设机构 ad hoc organizations
非对称作战 asymmetric warfare
非法出版物 illegal publications
非法拘禁罪 crime of illegal confinement
非法生产线 illegal production lines
非法行医罪 crime of practicing medicine illegally
非公有成分 non-public sector

非挂牌股票 unlisted stock
非挂牌证券 unlisted securities
非官方消息 information from unofficial sources
非会员银行 nonmember bank
非婚生子女 children born out of wedlock;illegitimate children;child of illegitimate birth
非婚性行为 extra-marital sexual activity
非技术支援 non-technical backstopping
非接触作战 noncontact warfare
非借入储备 non-borrowed reserves
非军事人员 civilian personnel
非牟利机构 non-profit making organization
非生产部门 nonproductive departments
非生产劳动 nonproductive labour
非条件反射 unconditioned reflex
非线性分析 nonlinear analysis
非银行背书 non-bank endorsement
非再生资源 unrenewable resource
非战斗人员 noncombatant
非正常死亡 irregular death;unnatural death
非正义战争 unjust war
非政府机构 non-governmental organization
非职务发明 non-service invention
非致命武器 nonlethal weapon
非智力因素 non-intelligence factor
非重点开支 expenditures for less important areas;non-essential disbursement
非主要矛盾 non-principal contradiction
非保兑信用证 unconfirmed letter of credit
非典型性肺炎 Severe Acute Respiratory Syndrome (SARS)
非公有制经济 economy under nonpublic ownership;non-public sector of the economy
非歧视性待遇 non-discriminatory treatment
非生产性投资 investment in non-productive projects
非统首脑会议 Summit of the Organization of African Unity
非约束性条款 permissive provision
非洲统一组织 the Organization of African Unity (OAU)
非专属经济区 non-exclusive economic zone
非传统安全威胁 non-traditional threats to security
非法持有毒品罪 carrying drugs illegally
非法集资 illegal collection of funds
非贸易外汇收入 foreign exchange earned from sources other than trade
非银行金融机构 non-bank financial institutions
非歧视性普遍优惠制 general nondiscriminatory system of preferences

菲 [fēi]
Ⅰ 形 (of flowers and grass) luxuriant and rich with fragrance Ⅱ 名 phenanthrene ➡fěi
菲菲 ①luxuriant and beautiful ②richly fra-

grant
菲迪克条款 FIDIC conditions

啡 [fēi]
◇ 咖啡 coffee
吗啡 morphine

绯 [fēi]
[形] red
绯闻 amorous affair;sex scandal;scandal
绯衣 red dress

扉 [fēi]
[名] door leaf
扉页 title page

霏 [fēi]
I [形] (falling) thick and fast II [动] flutter; disperse;diffuse
霏霏 (of rain, snow, mist, cloud, etc.) thick and fast;heavy

féi (ㄈㄟˊ)

肥 [féi]
I [形] ①fat;greasy ②fertile;rich ③lucrative; profitable ④ loose-fitting; loose; loose and large II [动] ①make fertile;fertilize ② feather one's nest;line one's pocket or purse; enrich by illegal income III [名] ①fertilizer;manure;compost ②benefit;profit
肥大 ①loose;large ②fat;plump;corpulent ③ hypertrophy
肥分 (the percentage of) nutriment in a fertilizer
肥厚 ①plump;fleshy ②thick and fertile
肥力 fertility (of soil)
肥料 fertilizer;manure
肥美 ① fertile; rich ② luxuriant; plump; fleshy;fat
肥胖 fat;corpulent
肥缺 a lucrative post;gravy train
肥肉 fat meat;speck;fat
肥实 ①fat;stout ②rich in fat
肥水 rich water
肥硕 ①(of fruit) big and fleshy ②(of limbs and body) large and firm-fleshed
肥田 ①fertile land ②fertilize (or enrich) the soil
肥沃 fertile;rich
肥效 fertilizer efficiency (or effect)
肥育 fatten
肥圆 tubbiness
肥源 source of manure
肥皂 soap
肥猪 fat pig
肥壮 stout and strong
肥胖病 obesity
肥胖症 obesity
肥田粉 ammonium sulphate
肥育期 stage of fattening

肥皂粉 soap powder
肥皂剧 soap opera
肥皂片 soap flakes
肥皂水 soapsuds
肥水不流外人田 No rich water should be let out of one's own fields. or One should always keep all benefits for one's own people.

腓 [féi]
I [名] calf (of the leg) II [动] become diseased;wilt;wither

fěi (ㄈㄟˇ)

匪 [fěi]
I [名] bandit; robber; brigand; gangster II [副] not
匪帮 bandit gang;a felonious political gang
匪巢 bandits' lair
匪患 the evil of banditry;banditry
匪军 bandit troops
匪窟 bandits' lair
匪首 bandit chieftain (or chief)
匪徒 gangster;bandit
匪穴 bandits' den
匪夷所思 (of ideas) unimaginably queer;fantastic

诽 [fěi]
[动] slander;calumniate
诽谤 slander;calumniate;libel
诽谤罪 crime of defamation (or slander)

菲 [fěi]
I [名] radish or red turnip II [形] humble; poor;unworthy ➡fēi
菲薄 ①humble;poor ②belittle;despise
菲材 my humble (or unworthy) talent
菲敬 my small (or unworthy) gift
菲礼 my humble gift
菲仪 my small (or unworthy) gift

悱 [fěi]
[动] be at a loss for words;not know what to say
悱恻 laden with sorrow;sad at heart

斐 [fěi]
[形] rich with literary grace;of striking literary talent
斐然 striking;brilliant;splendid
斐然成章 show striking literary merit
斐然可观 strikingly;stately

翡 [fěi]
[名] halcyon
翡翠 ①halcyon (a bird) ②jadeite (a mineral)

篚 [fěi]
[名] round bamboo basket

fèi (ㄈㄟˋ)

吠 [fèi]
[动] bark;yap;yelp
吠影吠声 when one dog barks at a shadow all

the others join in—blindly follow others

肺 [fèi]

〈名〉lung

肺癌 carcinoma of the lungs；lung cancer
肺病 pulmonary tuberculosis（TB）
肺腑 the bottom of one's heart
肺火 lung fire
肺痨 consumption；tuberculosis
肺泡 pulmonary alveolus
肺炎 pneumonia
肺叶 lobe of the lung
肺脏 lungs
肺活量 vital capacity
肺结核 pulmonary tuberculosis（TB）
肺静脉 pulmonary vein
肺脓肿 pulmonary abscess
肺气肿 pulmonary emphysema
肺吸虫 lung fluke
肺循环 pulmonary circulation
肺腑之言 words from the bottom of one's heart
肺切除术 pneumonectomy

狒 [fèi]

狒狒 baboon

废 [fèi]

Ⅰ〈动〉①give up；abandon；reject；abolish ②lie waste；decline ③depose；dethrone Ⅱ〈形〉①waste；useless；disused ②disabled；maimed；crippled

废材 mill waste；refuse wood；clash
废弛 （of a law，custom，discipline，etc.）cease to be binding；become lax
废除 abolish；abrogate；annul；repeal
废黜 dethrone；depose
废话 superfluous words；nonsense；rubbish
废疾 disability；cripplehood
废料 waste material；waste scrap
废票 ①invalidated ticket ②invalidated ballot；invalidated vote
废品 ①waste product；reject ②scrap；waste；spoiled products；seconds；rejects
废气 waste gas（or steam）；exhaust gas
废弃 discard；abandon；cast aside
废汽 spent steam
废热 waste heat
废人 ①disabled person ②good-for-nothing
废水 waste water；liquid waste
废丝 waste silk
废铁 scrap iron
废物 [fèiwù] waste material；trash
废物 [fèiwu] good-for-nothing
废渣 waste residue
废止 nullify；annul；abolish（a law，decree，regulation，etc.）
废纸 waste paper
废置 put aside as useless

废物袋 litter bag
废话连篇 pages of nonsense；reams of rubbish
废旧物资 waste materials；scrap
废料处理 waste treatment
废料艺术 junk art
废品回收 waste recovery；waste recycle；salvage of waste material
废寝忘食 forget to eat and sleep
废物回收 waste recovery
废物交换 waste exchange
废物利用 make use of scrap material；turn scrap material to good account
废品雕塑家 junk sculpture
废品收购站 salvage station
废水处理场 waste water processing station
废水处理池 purification tank for liquid waste
废气净化设备 gas-cleaning facilities
废物循环利用 cyclic utilization of "waste"

沸 [fèi]

〈动〉boil；bubble

沸点 boiling point
沸泉 near-boiling spring
沸水 boiling water
沸腾 ①boiling；ebullition ②seethe with excitement；boil over
沸水堆 boiling water reactor（BWR）
沸沸扬扬 bubbling and gurgling；in a hubbub

费 [fèi]

Ⅰ〈名〉fee；charge；expenses；fare Ⅱ〈动〉①cost；spend；expend ②be wasteful；consume too much；expend too quickly

费工 take a lot of work；require much labour
费话 take a lot of talking or explaining
费解 hard to understand；obscure；unintelligible
费劲 need（or exert）great effort；be strenuous
费力 need（or exert）great effort；be strenuous
费率 premium rate
费钱 cost a lot；be costly
费神 ①need（or exert）great mental effort ②may I trouble you（to do sth）；would you mind（doing sth）
费时 take time；be time-consuming
费事 give or take a lot of trouble
费心 ①give a lot of care；take a lot of trouble ②may I trouble you（to do sth）；would you mind（doing sth）
费用 cost；expenses
费改税 tax-for-fee；transform administrative fees into taxes
费工夫 take time and energy；be time-consuming；be exacting；be demanding
费口舌 require a lot of talking；require a lot of arguing
费手脚 take much hand work and footwork；

take much physical labour

费尽心机 rack one's brains (in scheming);tax one's ingenuity

费力不讨好 ①work hard but get little result; do a hard but thankless job ②arduous but fruitless

痱 [fèi]
[名] prickly heat
痱子 prickly heat
痱子粉 prickly-heat powder

fēn（ㄈㄣ）

分 [fēn]
Ⅰ [动] ①divide;separate;split;part ②distribute;assign;allot ③tell;distinguish;differentiate Ⅱ [名] ①branch (of an organization) ②fraction Ⅲ [量] ①(*used in fractions and percentages*):五分之三 three fifths ②one-tenth;有一分热,发一分光 give as much light as the heat can produce;exert every bit of one's energy ③*fen*,a unit of length (= 1/3 centimetre):一尺二寸三分 one *chi* and two *cun* and three *fen* ④*fen*,a unit of area (one tenth of a *mu*, = 66.666 square metres):一亩三分地 1.3 *mu* of land ⑤*fen*,a unit of weight (one tenth of a *qian*, = 1/2 gram):这条金项链重一两二钱五分。 This gold necklace weighs one *liang* and two and a half *qian*. ⑥*fen*,a fractional unit of money in China (= 1/100 of a *yuan* or 1/10 of a *jiao*):八元八角八分 eight *yuan* and eighty-eight *fen* ⑦minute (= 1/60 of an hour):现在是差五分六点。 It is five minutes to six. ⑧minute (= 1/60 of a degree):北纬 60 度 13 分 60 degrees and 13 minutes (60°13′) north latitude ⑨of interest rate:月利 10 分 a monthly interest of 10% ⑩point;mark:这次英语考试他得 92 分。 He got 92 marks out of 100 in the English exam. ➡fèn

分保 reinsurance

分贝 decibel (db)

分辨 ①distinguish;differentiate;tell ②resolution ③defend oneself (against a charge); offer an explanation

分辩 defend oneself (against a charge);offer an explanation

分别 ①part;leave each other ②distinguish; differentiate ③difference ④in different ways;differently ⑤separately;individually;respectively

分兵 divide forces

分布 be distributed (over an area);be dispersed;be scattered

分册 separately published part of a book;fascicle

分权 ①branching ②branch

分成 divide into tenths;share

分词 participle

分寸 proper limits for speech or action;sense of propriety;sense of proportion

分担 share responsibility for

分道 lane

分等 grade;classify

分店 branch (of a shop)

分队 a troop unit corresponding to the platoon or squad;element

分发 ①distribute;hand out;issue (to individuals) ②assign to a post;appoint to a job

分赴 leave for different destinations

分肥 divide up the spoils;share out ill-gotten gains;divide booty

分割 cut apart;break up;carve up

分隔 separate;divide

分工 division of labour

分管 be assigned personal responsibility for; be put in charge of;separate management; put under different jurisdiction

分行 [fēnháng] branch (of a bank,business firm,etc.)

分毫 fraction;iota

分号 ①semicolon (;) ②branch (of a shop, firm,etc.)

分红 draw (*or* receive) dividends;share profits;share out bonus;distribute dividends; draw extra profits

分洪 flood diversion

分化 ①become divided;break up ②split up ③ (of cells or tissues) differentiate

分会 branch (of a society,committee,association,etc.);chapter

分机 (telephone) extension

分家 ①divide up family property and live apart;break up the family and live apart ② separate;break up

分解 ①resolve ②decompose;resolve ③explain

分界 ①have as the boundary;be demarcated by ②dividing line;line of demarcation

分居 ①(of family members) live apart ②(of husband and wife) live separately;separate

分局 branch office;sub-bureau

分句 clause

分开 ①come apart;separate;part ②cause to separate;sort

分块 piecemeal;block;partitioning

分类 classify

分离 ①(of things) separate;sever ②(of people) leave;part;separate

分力 component (of force)

分裂 ①fission ②split;divide;break up

分流 ①distributary;split-flow ②split-flow of human resources ③(of communications and transport) split-flow;diversion ④(in economic restructuring) repositioning of re-

dundant personnel
分馏　fractional distillation; fractionation
分路　①go along separate routes or from several directions ②shunt
分袂　leave each other; part company; part
分米　decimetre (dm.)
分泌　secrete
分娩　childbirth; parturition
分秒　every minute and second; instant
分明　①be clear; be distinct; be unmistakable ②clearly; evidently; obviously
分母　denominator
分蘖　tiller
分派　assign (to different persons or groups); apportion
分配　①distribute; allot ②assign; dispose ③distribution
分批　in batches; group by group; in turn
分屏　split screen
分期　by stages
分歧　difference; divergence
分清　distinguish; draw a clear distinction between; draw a clear line of demarcation between
分权　a division of power or authority
分群　(of bees) hive off
分散　①scattered; dispersed; diverted; decentralized ②disperse; distribute
分身　spare time from one's main work to attend to sth else
分神　give some attention to
分时　time-sharing
分手　part company; say good-bye
分数　①fraction ②mark; grade
分说　defend oneself (against a charge); explain matters
分送　send; distribute
分摊　apportion; share
分头　①separately; severally ②parted hair
分文　a single cent (or penny)
分析　analyse
分享　share (joy, rights, etc.); partake of
分相　split phase
分晓　①outcome; solution ②sth seen or understood clearly
分校　a branch school
分心　①divert (or distract) one's attention ②may I trouble you (to do sth); would you mind (doing sth)
分野　dividing line
分忧　share sb's cares and burdens; help sb to get over a difficulty
分赃　divide the spoils; share the booty (or loot)
分针　minute hand (of a clock or watch)
分支　subdivision; branch
分装　split charging

分子　①numerator (in a fraction) ②molecule
分组　divide into groups
分包商　sub-contractor
分保险　cede insurance
分贝计　decibel meter; level-measuring set
分辨率　resolution ratio
分餐制　separate eating; eating together but from separate dishes
分公司　branch office (or company)
分光计　spectrometer
分光镜　spectroscope
分洪区　flood-diversion area
分洪闸　flood-diversion sluice
分户账　ledger
分级机　grader; sorter
分拣器　sorter
分解剂　disintegrant
分解热　decomposition heat
分解物　analyte
分界线　line of demarcation; boundary
分镜头　story board
分类法　classification
分类机　sequencer; sorter
分类学　taxology; taxonomy; systematics
分类账　ledger
分离器　separator
分理处　a small local branch (of a bank)
分列式　march-past
分馏塔　fractionating tower; fractional column
分泌物　secretion
分蘖节　tillering node
分蘖期　tillering stage
分配律　distributive law
分权制　system featuring divided power
分散剂　dispersing agent
分色机　colour scanner
分数线　minimum passing score; passing grade; passing line
分水岭　①watershed; divide ②line of demarcation; dividing line
分税制　a system of tax distribution; tax distribution system; revenue-sharing system; system whereby tax revenues are shared by central and local authorities
分析语　analytical language
分线规　dividers
分相器　phase splitter
分销店　retail shop
分压器　voltage divider
分子病　molecular disease
分子量　molecular weight
分子筛　molecular sieve
分子式　molecular formula
分子束　molecular beam
分包合同　sub-contract
分崩离析　disintegrate; fall to pieces; come apart

分不开身 too busy to attend to anything else
分道扬镳 go different ways;part company
分店经理 branch manager
分而治之 divide and rule
分工负责 division of labour with individual responsibility
分工合作 share out the work and cooperate with one another;share out the work and help one another;have division of labour as well as cooperation
分工协作 farm-out
分光吃光 total distribution and total consumption
分洪工程 flood-diversion project
分化瓦解 disintegrate;divide and demoralize
分级管理 manage by different levels
分级核算 business accounting at different levels
分解代谢 catabolism
分解反应 decomposition reaction
分进合击 concerted attack by converging columns
分居协议 deed of separation
分类程序 sorter
分类广告 classified advertisement;classified advertising
分类数字 breakdown figures
分类索引 classified index
分类折旧 classified depreciation
"分裂分治" "two split sides with separate administration"
分裂主义 splittism
分门别类 put into different categories;classify
分秒必争 seize every minute and second;every second counts;not a second is to be lost
分配不公 maldistribution
分配方式 forms of distribution
分配结构 distribution structures
分配渠道 distribution channel
分片包干 divide up and assign work;divide up the work and assign a part to each individual or group;allot work and responsibility to several individuals or groups
分期分批 by stages and in groups
分期付款 payment by installments;installment payment;hire purchase
分期交货 delivery by instalments
分清职责 define the duties incumbent on each person or post
分散染料 disperse dyes
分散学习 dispersed learning
分水闸门 bifurcation gate
分摊成本 apportioned cost
分庭抗礼 stand up to sb as an equal;act independently and defiantly
分文不取 not take (*or* charge) a cent;free of charge

分析方法 analytical method
分析化学 analytical chemistry
分析试剂 analytical reagent
分析天平 analytical balance
分析研究 analytical investigation
分支程序 branched program
分子结构 molecular structure
分子溶液 molecular solution
分保接受人 reinsurer
分层开采法 bench method;slicing
分级 grade;classify
分阶段撤军 phaseout;phased withdrawal of troops
分镜头剧本 continuity;shooting script
分居赡养费 separate maintenance
分散主义者 decentralist
分体式空调 split-type room air conditioner
分蓄洪工程 flood diversion and storage project
分子仿生学 molecular bionics
分子生物学 molecular biology
分子遗传学 molecular genetics
分而治之政策 divide-and-rule policy
分类财务报表 classified financial statement
分裂主义分子 secessionists;separatists
分配制度改革 reform of the distribution system
分清大是大非 draw clear distinctions concerning cardinal issues of right and wrong;distinguish (*or* discern) between right and wrong on cardinal issues
分散数据处理 decentralize data processing
分时电脑系统 time-sharing computer system
分流企业富余人员 resettle (*or* redirect) the surplus labour force of enterprises;disperse redundant employees of enterprises
分配结构和分配方式 the structure and mode of distribution

芬 [fēn]
[名] sweet smell;fragrance
芬芳 ① sweet-smelling; fragrant ② sweet smell;fragrance

吩 [fēn]
吩咐 ①tell;instruct ②instructions

纷 [fēn]
[形] ①confused;tangled;chaotic;disorderly ②many and various;diverse;numerous;profuse
纷繁 numerous and complicated
纷纷 ①one after another;in succession ②numerous and confused
纷乱 numerous and disorderly;helter-skelter;chaotic
纷扰 confusion;turmoil
纷纭 diverse and confused
纷争 dispute;wrangle
纷纷出笼 swarm out

F

纷至沓来 come in a continuous stream;come thick and fast;keep pouring in

氛 [fēn]
名 atmosphere
氛围 atmosphere

酚 [fēn]
名 phenol
酚醛 phenolic aldehyde
酚酞 phenolphthalein
酚醛树脂 phenolic resin
酚醛塑料 phenolic plastics
酚酞试纸 phenolphthalein test paper

fén (ㄈㄣˊ)

坟 [fén]
名 grave;tomb
坟场 graveyard;cemetery
坟地 graveyard;cemetery
坟墓 grave;tomb
坟头 grave mound
坟茔 ①grave;tomb ②graveyard;cemetery

焚 [fén]
动 burn
焚风 foehn (wind)
焚化 incinerate;cremate
焚火 stoking
焚毁 destroy by fire;burn down
焚烧 burn;set on fire
焚香 burn incense
焚化炉 incinerator;cremator
焚尸扬灰 burning the corpse and scattering the ashes
焚书坑儒 burning books and burying Confucian scholars alive

fěn (ㄈㄣˇ)

粉 [fěn]
I 名 ①powder ②powdered cosmetics ③noodles or vermicelli made from flour,bean,sweet potato starch,etc. II 动 ①crush to powder ②turn to powder ③whitewash III 形 ①white (with white powder) ②pink
粉笔 chalk
粉彩 arts and crafts mixed glaze
粉刺 pimple;acne
粉蝶 white butterfly
粉红 pink;rosy
粉剂 ①powder ②dust
粉瘤 sebaceous cyst
粉煤 powdered coal;pulverized coal
粉末 powder
粉皮 sheet jelly made from bean or sweet potato starch
粉扑 powder puff
粉墙 plaster wall
粉饰 gloss over;whitewash
粉刷 ①whitewash ②plaster

粉丝 ①vermicelli made from bean starch,etc. ②fans
粉碎 ①broken to (or into) pieces ②smash;shatter;crush
粉条 noodles made from bean or sweet potato starch
粉头 prostitute
粉线 tailor's chalk line
粉友 junkie mate
粉笔画 chalk drawing;crayon
粉底霜 foundation cream
粉领族 pink-collar (tribe)
粉碎机 pulverizer;grinder;kibbler
粉尘浓度 dust concentration
粉墨登场 make oneself up and go on stage—embark upon a political venture
粉身碎骨 have one's body smashed to pieces and one's bones ground to powder;die the most cruel death
粉饰太平 simulate peace and prosperity;present a false picture of peace and prosperity
粉妆玉琢 silvery white (said of a snow scene)
粉碎性骨折 comminuted fracture

fèn (ㄈㄣˋ)

分 [fèn]
I 名 ①component;element ②extent of one's duty or rights ③friendly feeling;affection II 动 expect;think;know ➡ fēn
分量 weight
分内 one's job or duty
分外 ①particularly;especially ②not one's job (or duty)
分子 member;element

份 [fèn]
I 名 share;portion;part II 量 ①set;两份儿快餐 two sets of fast food/一份儿咖啡 a coffee/一份儿饮料 a drink ②copy:一份报纸 a copy of newspaper/合同一式两份。The contract was done in duplicate. ③(*used for certain abstract things*):瞧他那份儿神气！Look what airs he puts on!
份额 share;portion
份子 ①one's share of expenses for a joint undertaking,as in buying a gift for a mutual friend ②a gift of money
份儿饭 table d'hote;set meal

奋 [fèn]
动 ①brace up;exert oneself;act vigorously ②take up;raise;lift;wave
奋斗 struggle;fight;strive
奋发 rouse oneself;exert oneself
奋进 advance bravely
奋力 do all one can;spare no effort
奋勉 make a determined effort
奋起 ①brace up;exert oneself;rise with force and spirit ②raise or lift sth with all one's

strength
奋勇 summon up all one's courage and energy
奋战 fight bravely;work strenuously
奋笔疾书 take up a pen and write swiftly; wield one's (writing) brush energetically
奋臂高呼 raise one's arms and hail
奋不顾身 dash ahead regardless of one's safety
奋发图强 go all out to make the country strong;work hard for the prosperity of the country
奋起直追 do all one can to catch up

F

忿 [fèn]
◇不忿 refuse to obey;refuse to accept as final; not give in to

粪 [fèn]
I 名 excrement;faeces;dung;droppings II 动 ① apply manure ② clear away;have a cleaning
粪便 excrement and urine;night soil
粪车 dung-cart;night-soil cart
粪池 manure pit
粪除 thoroughly clean (a place);wipe out
粪堆 dunghill;manure pile (or heap)
粪肥 muck;manure;dung
粪坑 manure pit
粪箕 manure basket
粪耙 muck-rake
粪桶 night-soil bucket;manure bucket
粪土 dung and dirt;muck

愤 [fèn]
名 anger;fury;indignation;resentment
愤恨 indignantly resent;detest
愤慨 (righteous) indignation
愤懑 depressed and discontented;resentful
愤怒 indignation;anger;wrath
愤不欲生 so angry one does not wish to live
愤愤不平 be indignant;feel aggrieved;be resentful
愤世嫉俗 detest the world and its ways;be cynical

fēng (ㄈㄥ)

丰 [fēng]
形 ① rich;plentiful;abundant ② great ③ good (looks);fine (appearance);graceful (carriage)
丰碑 ①tall stone tablet ②monument ③monumental work
丰产 high yield;bumper crop
丰登 bumper harvest
丰富 ①rich;abundant;plentiful ②enrich
丰厚 ①thick ②rich and generous
丰满 ① plentiful ② full and rounded;well-developed;full-grown
丰茂 luxuriant;lush

丰美 lush
丰年 a bumper harvest year;a good year
丰饶 rich and fertile
丰润 plump and smooth-skinned
丰盛 rich;sumptuous
丰收 bumper harvest
丰硕 plentiful and substantial;rich
丰盈 ①full and round;well-developed ②rich; plentiful
丰裕 well provided for;in plenty
丰韵 graceful bearing
丰足 abundant;plentiful
丰产田 high-yield plot
丰富多彩 rich and varied;rich and colourful
丰功伟绩 great achievements;signal contributions
丰厚回报 fat payoffs
丰衣足食 have ample food and clothing;be well-fed and well-clothed

风 [fēng]
I 名 ① wind;breeze;gale ② practice;custom;atmosphere ③ scene;view ④ attitude; style ⑤ news;information ⑥ section in *The Book of Songs* (诗经) consisting of ballads II 动 put out to dry;winnow:晒干风净 sun-dried and well winnowed III 形 ①air-dried ② rumoured;groundless IV 副 as swift as wind; speedily
风暴 ① windstorm; storm ② violent commotion;storm;tempest
风泵 ①air pump ②air compressor
风痹 wandering arthritis
风标 weathercock;weather vane
风波 wind and waves;disturbance;storm
风采 ① elegant demeanour;graceful bearing ②literary grace
风潮 agitation;unrest
风车 ①windmill ②winnower;winnow ③pinwheel
风尘 ①wind and dust—travel fatigue ②hardships or uncertainties in an unstable society ③the life of a prostitute
风传 (of news or rumours) get about (or round);be rumoured (or said);they say
风锤 pneumatic hammer;air hammer
风挡 automobile windscreen;windshield
风笛 bagpipes;pipes
风洞 wind-tunnel
风斗 wind scoop
风度 demeanour;bearing
风发 ①swift as the wind ②energetic
风帆 ①sail ②sailing boat (or ship)
风范 ① demeanour; bearing; poise ② style; manner;air
风干 air-dry
风镐 pneumatic pick;air pick
风格 style;manner;mode

风骨 ①strength of character ②vigour of style
风光 ① scenery; scene; view; sight ② grand; impressive; in style
风害 damage caused by a windstorm
风寒 chill; cold
风华 elegance and intellectual brilliance
风化 ① morals and manners; decency ② weathering; air-slake ③efflorescence
风级 wind scale
风纪 conduct and discipline; discipline
风井 ventilating shaft; air shaft
风景 scenery; landscape
风镜 goggles
风口 ①a place where there is a draught ② wind gap ③(blast) tuyere
风浪 ①stormy waves; storm ②hardship; difficulties
风雷 wind and thunder; tempest
风力 ①wind-force ②wind power
风凉 cool
风铃 wind-bells (hung on the eaves of pagodas or temple buildings)
风流 ①outstanding; distinguished and accomplished ② talented and free-spirited ③ romantic; amorous; licentious; dissolute; loose
风帽 ①a cowl-like hat worn in winter ②hood
风貌 ①style and features ②view; scene ③elegant appearance and bearing
风门 ①air door; ventilation door ②storm door
风靡 be fashionable
风磨 windmill (for grinding grain)
风能 wind energy source
风派 timeserver; trimmer
风气 general mood; atmosphere; common (or established) practice
风琴 organ
风情 ①information about wind direction, wind force, etc. ② bearing; demeanour ③ feelings ④amorous feelings; flirtatious expressions ⑤local conditions and customs
风趣 humour; wit
风圈 solar or lunar halo
风骚 ① literary excellence ② coquettish; flirtatious
风色 ① how the wind blows ② how things stand
风沙 sand blown by the wind
风扇 electric fan; fan
风尚 prevailing custom (or practice, habit)
风声 ①the sough of the wind ②rumour
风湿 rheumatism
风蚀 wind erosion; deflation
风霜 wind and frost—hardships of a journey or of one's life
风水 the location of a house or tomb, supposed to have an influence on the fortune of a family; geomantic omen

风俗 custom
风速 wind speed; wind velocity
风瘫 paralysis
风头 [fēngtóu] the way the wind blows
风头 [fēngtou] ①the trend of events (as affecting a person) ② the publicity one receives
风土 natural conditions and social customs of a place
风味 special flavour; local colour (or flavour)
风闻 learn through hearsay; get wind of
风险 risk; hazard
风箱 bellows
风向 wind direction
风行 be in fashion (or vogue); be popular
风选 selection by winnowing (or wind)
风压 wind pressure
风雅 ①literary pursuits ②elegant; refined
风衣 windcheater; windbreaker; wind-jacket
风雨 wind and rain; trials and hardships
风云 wind and cloud—stormy or unstable situation
风韵 (usu. a woman's) graceful bearing; charm
风灾 disaster caused by a windstorm
风闸 pneumatic brake
风障 windbreak
风疹 nettle rash; urticaria
风筝 kite
风姿 graceful bearing; charm
风钻 pneumatic drill
风光片 scenic film
风景画 landscape painting
风景林 scenic forest
风景区 scenic spot
风景线 scenic view; attractive scenery or phenomenon; long and narrow landscape; scene
风凉话 irresponsible and sarcastic remarks
风媒花 anemophilous flower
风俗画 genre painting; genre
风速表 anemometer
风速计 anemograph; registering anemometer
风速器 wind gauge
风味菜 typical local dishes; local delicacies
风向标 wind vane
风向袋 wind sleeve; wind sock; wind cone
风向计 registering weather vane
风向图 wind rose
风向仪 anemoscope
风信子 hyacinth
风选机 winnowing machine; winnower
风油精 essential balm
风雨衣 rainproof windcheater; mackintosh
风采动人 cut quite a figure
风餐露宿 eat in the wind and sleep in the dew—endure the hardships of an arduous journey

F

风尘仆仆 have endured the hardships of a long journey; be travel-stained; be travel-worn and weary

风尘女子 woman amidst winds and dust; prostitutes; courtesans

风驰电掣 swift as the wind and quick as lightning

风吹草动 the rustle of leaves in the wind—a sign of disturbance or trouble

风吹浪打 be beaten by wind and waves; be battered by a storm

风吹雨打 be buffeted by wind and rain; be exposed to the weather

风动工具 pneumatic tools

风度翩翩 (of a young man) have an elegant and smart carriage

风风雨雨 disturbances

风和日丽 bright sun and gentle breeze; warm and sunny weather

风花雪月 ①wind, flowers, snow and the moon ②love affairs

风华正茂 at life's full flowering; in one's prime

风卷残云 strong wind scattering the last clouds—make a clean sweep of sth

风口浪尖 where the wind and the waves are highest—where the struggle is fiercest

风雷激荡 storm raging in all its fury

风流云散 dispersed by the wind and scattered like the clouds—(usu. of old companions) separated and scattered

风流韵事 romance between man and woman

风媒传粉 wind pollination

风靡一时 become fashionable for a while; be all the rage at the time

风平浪静 the wind has dropped and the waves have subsided; calm and tranquil

风起云涌 winds rising and clouds scudding; rolling on with full force; surging forward

风清月朗 The breeze is fresh and the moon bright.

风水先生 geomancer

风俗喜剧 comedy of manners

风调雨顺 good weather for the crops; favourable weather

风土人情 local conditions and customs

风土驯化 acclimatization

风味小吃 local delicacies

风险报酬 risk premium

风险补贴 danger money

风险抵押 risk mortgage

风险分担 allocation of risks

风险管理 venture management

风险合同 risk contract

风险基金 risk fund

风险评估 risk assessment

风险企业 venture business

风险投资 risk investment; venture capital; venture investment

风险意识 risk awareness; risk consciousness; sense of risk

风险资本 venture capital; risk capital

风险资金 risk capital; risk assets; venture capital

风行一时 be popular for a while; be all the rage for a time

风言风语 groundless talk; slanderous gossip

风雨交加 It's raining and blowing hard or It's wet and windy.

风雨飘摇 swaying in the midst of a raging storm; precarious; tottering

风雨如晦 wind and rain sweeping across a gloomy sky—a grim situation

风雨同舟 in the same storm-tossed boat—stand together through thick and thin

风雨无阻 stopped by neither wind nor rain—regardless of the weather; rain or shine

风云变幻 constant change of events; changeable situation

风云人物 man of the hour

风云突变 a sudden change in the situation

风烛残年 old and ailing like a candle guttering in the wind

风姿绰约 charming appearance and personality; graceful figure

风力发电机 wind-driven generator; windmill generator

风力发电站 wind power station

风力输送机 pneumatic conveyor

风力提水机 wind-driven water pump; wind pump

风险抵押金 risk deposit

风马牛不相及 have nothing to do with each other; be totally unrelated

风云二号卫星 Fengyun Ⅱ satellite

风声鹤唳,草木皆兵 scared by the moan of the wind and the cry of the cranes, and seeing the enemy in every bush and tree (said of the extreme nervousness of a fleeing army)

沨 [fēng] 〖形〗 sound of flowing water; gurgle

枫 [fēng] 〖名〗 ①Chinese sweet gum ②maple

枫树 Chinese sweet gum

枫叶 leaves of Chinese sweet gum, maple, etc. which turn red in autumn

封 [fēng] Ⅰ〖动〗①confer (a title, territory, etc.) upon ②seal; close; cap Ⅱ〖名〗①boundary; scope; limit ②feudalism ③envelope; wrapper Ⅲ〖量〗:

一封电报 a telegram

封笔 seal off one's writing or painting brush

封闭 ①seal ②seal off; close

封存 seal up for safekeeping

封底 back cover
封地 fief;feud;manor
封顶 ①(of a plant) cease growing any taller;(of the terminal bud) stop growing ②impose a ceiling (on prices,wages,bonuses,etc.);the top-out (of a building)
封冻 (of a river,the ground,etc.) freeze
封二 inside front cover (also called 封里)
封港 close a port or harbour
封火 bank a fire
封建 ①the system of enfeoffment ②feudalism ③feudal;feudalistic
封疆 ① boundary;frontier ② governors or commanders of border provinces
封镜 finish making a film
封口 ①seal ②heal ③say sth definitive so as to prevent further discussion
封蜡 sealing wax
封里 ①inside front cover ②inside back cover
封面 ①the title page of a thread-bound book ②the front and back cover of a book ③front cover
封泥 ①sealing clay ②lute
封皮 ①paper wrapping ②envelope
封三 inside back cover
封杀 strangle;smother;ban
封山 seal (or close) a mountain pass
"封圣" canonization of "Saints"
封四 back cover
封锁 block or seal off (through military or other compulsory means);blockade
封套 big envelope
封条 strip of paper used for sealing (doors,drawers,etc.);paper strip seal
封网 block
封信 seal (up) a letter
封一 front cover
封印 seal (on mail)
封嘴 ①speak with a tone of finality ②seal sb's lips
封闭层 confining bed
封闭港 closed port
封袋机 bag seating machine;bagger
封冻期 a period of freezing weather;freeze
封建主 feudal lord
封锁线 blockade line;blockade
封闭疗法 block therapy
封官许愿 hand out official posts and make lavish promises;promise high posts and other favours
封建割据 feudal separationist rule
封建社会 feudal society
封建势力 feudal influence
封建主义 feudalism
封面女郎 cover girl
封妻荫子 (of the emperor) confer titles of honour on the wife of a deserving official

and hereditary ranks on his descendants
封杀出局 force out
封山育林 forest conservation (or reservation);close hillsides to facilitate afforestation;seal the mountain to cultivate forests
封锁市场 corner the market;deny market access
封锁消息 block the passage of information;news embargo (or blackout)
封闭式公司 closed corporation
封闭式基金 closed-end fund
封建专制主义 feudal autocracy

砜 ［fēng］
名 sulphone

疯 ［fēng］
Ⅰ 形 mad;deranged;insane;crazy ② without restraint Ⅱ 动 (of a grain crop,plant,etc.) spindle
疯狗 mad dog;rabid dog
疯狂 ①insane ②frenzied;unbridled
疯玩 enjoy oneself with abandon
疯长 overgrowing;spindling
疯子 lunatic;madman
疯牛病 mad cow disease (or syndrome)
疯人院 madhouse;lunatic asylum
疯疯癫癫 mentally deranged;acting like a lunatic;flighty
疯嚷疯闹 shout and fool around like mad

峰 ［fēng］
Ⅰ 名 ① peak;summit ② peak-like thing;hump Ⅱ 量 (of camels):一峰骆驼 a camel
峰巅 mountain peak;summit
峰会 summit meeting (or conference)
峰峦 ridges and peaks
峰年 peak year
峰态 kurtosis
峰位 peak point
峰值 peak value;crest value
峰回路转 amidst surrounding elevations and winding roads

烽 ［fēng］
名 beacon
烽火 ①beacon-fire;beacon ②flames of war
烽烟 beacon-fire;beacon
烽火台 beacon tower
烽火连天 flames of battle raging everywhere
烽烟滚滚 The flames of war are raging.

锋 ［fēng］
名 ① sharp point or cutting edge of a sword,knife,etc. ② (as of an army,etc.) van;forefront;leading edge ③front
锋钢 high-speed steel;rapid steel
锋利 ①sharp;keen ②incisive;sharp;poignant
锋芒 ① cutting edge;spearhead ② talent displayed;abilities
锋面 frontal surface
锋芒毕露 make a display of one's abilities
锋面低压 frontal low

蜂 [fēng] I 〈名〉 ①wasp ②bee II 〈副〉 in swarms
蜂巢 honeycomb
蜂刺 the sting of a bee (*or* wasp)
蜂毒 bee venom
蜂房 any of the six-sided wax cells in a honey-comb
蜂糕 steamed sponge cake (made of wheat or rice flour)
蜂蜡 beeswax
蜂蜜 honey
蜂鸟 hummingbird
蜂群 (bee) colony
蜂乳 royal jelly
蜂王 ①queen bee ②queen wasp
蜂窝 ① honeycomb ② honeycomb-like thing; honeycomb
蜂箱 beehive; hive
蜂拥 swarm; flock
蜂鸣器 buzzer
蜂王精 royal jelly
蜂窝炉 honeycomb briquet stove
蜂窝煤 honeycomb briquet (*or* briquette)
蜂窝织炎 cellulitis; phlegmon; phlegmona
蜂窝组织 cellular tissue; areolar tissue
蜂拥而来 come swarming; swarm forward
蜂窝式移动电话 cellar mobile telephone

féng (ㄈㄥˊ)

逢 [féng] 〈动〉 meet; encounter; come across
逢集 market day
逢迎 make up to; fawn on; curry favour with
逢场作戏 join in the fun on occasion
逢年过节 on New Year's Day or other festivals
逢凶化吉 ill luck turns into good
逢迎拍马 unctuous
逢山开路,遇水搭桥 cut paths through mountains and build bridges across rivers

缝 [féng] 〈动〉 stitch; sew ➡ fèng
缝补 sew; mend (by sewing)
缝合 suture; sew up
缝纫 sewing; tailoring
缝线 suture
缝合线 suture
缝纫机 sewing machine
缝缝补补 sew up

fěng (ㄈㄥˇ)

讽 [fěng] 〈动〉 ①satirize; mock ②chant; intone
讽刺 ①satirize ②ridicule; taunt; mock
讽示 hint (at sth); allude euphemistically (to sth)
讽诵 read with intonation and expression
讽喻 parable; allegory
讽刺画 caricature
讽刺诗 satirical poem
讽喻诗 allegorical poem
讽刺文学 satire
讽刺小品 satirical essay
讽一劝百 satirize one person in order to teach a lesson to others

fèng (ㄈㄥˋ)

凤 [fèng] 〈名〉 phoenix
凤凰 phoenix
凤梨 pineapple (the plant and its fruit)
凤凰木 royal poinciana (Delonix regia); flamboyant (tree)
凤凰竹 hedge bamboo (Bambusa multiplex)
凤凰座 Phoenix
凤求凰 like a male phoenix seeking its mate
凤尾鱼 anchovy
凤仙花 garden balsam; balsam
凤冠霞帔 phoenix coronet and robes of rank; chaplet and official robes
凤毛麟角 (precious and rare as) phoenix feathers and unicorn horns; rarity of rarities

奉 [fèng] 〈动〉 ①give (*or* present) with respect; submit; offer; dedicate ②receive (orders, etc.) ③regard with respect; esteem; revere ④believe in; espouse (a religion) ⑤wait upon; attend to
奉承 flatter; fawn on; toady to
奉佛 believe in Buddhism
奉告 let sb know; inform
奉公 perform official duties
奉还 return sth with thanks
奉命 receive orders; act under orders
奉陪 keep sb company
奉劝 may I offer a piece of advice
奉上 have the honour to send
奉送 offer as a gift; give away free
奉托 request sb to sth
奉献 offer as a tribute; present with all respect
奉行 pursue (a policy, etc.)
奉养 support and wait upon (one's parents, etc.)
奉召 be summoned
奉旨 by order of the emperor; by imperial decree
奉承话 flattery
奉公守法 be law-abiding
奉命唯谨 obey orders scrupulously
奉陪到底 have the honour of keeping sb company until the end
奉若神明 worship sb or sth; make a fetish of

sth
奉为经典 regard as a classic
奉为楷模 hold up (*or* look upon) as a model
奉献精神 spirit of utter devotion
奉行故事 follow established practice

俸 [fèng]
名 salary；stipend；pay
俸禄 an official's salary；government salary

赗 [fèng]
I 动 help with a funeral by presenting gifts or money to the bereaved family II 名 gift for a funeral

缝 [fèng]
名 ①seam ②chink；crack；crevice ➡féng
缝口 kiss；stitch closure
缝隙 chink；crack；crevice

fó（ㄈㄛˊ）

佛 [fó]
名 ①Buddha ②Buddhism ③image or statue of Buddha ④ *Amitabha*；Buddhist scripture or sutra；Buddhist sacred literature
佛法 ①Buddha dharma；Buddhist doctrine ② power of Buddha
佛骨 relic (*or* remains) of Buddha
佛光 flammule；glory；Brocken bow
佛海 the wide-open church of Buddhist
佛教 Buddhism
佛经 Buddhist Scripture；Buddhist sutra；Buddhist sacred literature
佛龛 a niche for a statue of Buddha
佛门 Buddhism
佛事 Buddhist ceremony (*or* service)
佛手 Buddha's hand；fingered citron
佛塔 pagoda
佛堂 family hall for worshipping Buddha
佛陀 Buddha—a title for Sakyamuni or a person who has attained enlightenment
佛像 an image of Buddha；Buddha
佛学 Buddhist philosophy
佛牙 sacred tooth relic of Buddha
佛爷 the Buddha
佛珠 beads；rosary
佛祖 Buddhist patriarch
佛法僧 Buddha-dharma-sangha
佛教徒 Buddhist
佛口蛇心 a Buddha's mouth but a viper's heart—honeyed words but evil intent
佛头着粪 smear Buddha's head with dung—desecrate
佛争一炷香，人争一口气 As Buddha needs incense，so man needs self-respect.

fǒu（ㄈㄡˇ）

缶 [fǒu]
名 ①long-necked earthen jar；amphora-like jar ②clay musical instrument

否 [fǒu]
I 动 negate；deny II 副 ① not；nay ② (*used at the end of a question*)：此物可得一见否? May we look at it? ③(*used after* 是，能，可，*etc. to indicate a choice or question*)：明日能否出发，尚待最后决定。Whether or not we will start off tomorrow is yet to be decided. ➡pǐ
否定 ①negate；deny ②negative ③negation
否决 vote down；veto；overrule
否认 deny；repudiate
否则 otherwise；if not；or else
否证 falsify
否决权 veto power；veto

F

fū（ㄈㄨ）

夫 [fū]
名 ①husband ②man ③person engaged in manual labour ④person served in forced labour ➡fú
夫妇 husband and wife
夫妻 husband (*or* man) and wife
夫权 authority of the husband
夫人 ①a lady of high rank；the wife of a feudal lord；the wife of a high official ② the wife of a diplomat ③ Mrs.；Madame (Mme)；Lady ④wife
夫婿 husband
夫子 ①master ②my husband ③pedant
夫妻店 small shop run by husband and wife
夫唱妇随 the husband sings and the wife follows—domestic harmony；conjugal felicity
夫子自道 what the Master says is a description of himself (said of a person criticizing others when he himself is open to the same charge)
夫妻共有财产 community property

伕 [fū]
名 person served in forced labour

呋 [fū]
呋喃 furan

肤 [fū]
名 skin
肤泛 superficial；shallow
肤功 outstanding service；great achievement
肤觉 dermal sensation
肤浅 superficial；shallow；skin-deep
肤色 colour of skin
肤纹学 dermatoglyphics
肤皮潦草 cursory；casual；perfunctory

麸 [fū]
名 (wheat) bran
麸皮 (wheat) bran
麸子 (wheat) bran
麸皮面包 whole wheat bread；brown bread

跗 [fū]
〔名〕①instep ②pedestal of a stone tablet

跗 [fū]
〔名〕instep
跗骨 tarsus;tarsal bones
跗面 instep
跗关节 hock;tarsal joint

孵 [fū]
〔动〕hatch;brood;incubate
孵出 hatch;brood
孵化 hatch;incubate
孵卵 brood;hatch;incubate
孵育 hatch;incubation
孵化场 hatchery (for poultry,etc.)
孵化池 hatchery (for fish,etc.)
孵化器 incubator
孵卵期 incubation period
孵卵器 incubator
孵窝鸡 broody (hen)

敷 [fū]
〔动〕① apply (powder, ointment, etc.) ② spread;lay out ③suffice
敷层 coating;backing;blanket
敷料 dressing
敷设 ①lay (pipes,etc.) ②lay (mines)
敷衍 ① act in a perfunctory manner; go through the motions;do just enough to satisfy sb ②barely get by;just manage
敷药 apply ointment
敷用 apply;application
敷着(作用) apposition
敷衍了事 muddle through one's work
敷衍塞责 perform one's duty in a perfunctory manner

fú（ㄈㄨˊ）

夫 [fú]
I 〔代〕①this;that ②he II 〔助〕① *used at the beginning of a sentence*：夫青年者，国家之精华也。 The youth are the cream of a nation. ② *used at the end of a sentence or of a pause in a sentence to express an exclamation*：逝者如斯夫! 不舍昼夜。 Thus do things flow away,day in and day out! ➡fū

弗 [fú]
〔副〕not
弗如 not as good as;not equal to

伏 [fú]
I 〔动〕①lean or bend over;lie prostrate ②fall;subside; go down ③hide ④yield;admit (defeat, guilt, etc.); surrender ⑤subdue; overcome;vanquish II 〔名〕①any of the three nine-day periods constituting the hottest season of the year;dog days ②(short for 伏特) volt
伏安 volt-ampere
伏案 bend (*or* lean) over a table
伏笔 a hint foreshadowing later developments in a story,essay,etc.;foreshadowing
伏兵 troops in ambush;ambush
伏地 prostrate (on the ground)
伏法 be executed;be put to death
伏获 waylay
伏击 ambush;still-hunt
伏流 subterranean drainage; underground stream
伏暑 the torrid weather of the year's hottest days
伏特 volt
伏天 hottest days of the year
伏贴 close fit;adhere fully
伏卧 lie prostrate;take a prone position;lie on one's stomach
伏羲 fúxī, a legendary ruler of great antiquity,the first of the Three August Ones （三皇）,credited with the invention of hunting and fishing and the domestication of animals
伏休 fishing-off in hot season
伏汛 summer flood (*or* freshet)
伏诛 be executed
伏击圈 ambush ring
伏特计 voltmeter
伏特加 vodka
伏地请罪 throw oneself on the ground to apologize or ask for punishment (for one's faults)

凫 [fú]
I 〔名〕wild duck II 〔动〕swim
凫水 swim
凫翁 water cock
凫趋雀跃 in high spirits;jubilant;elated
凫燕难明 hard to distinguish between high-flying wild ducks and swallows—things easily confused

芙 [fú]
芙蓉 ①cottonrose hibiscus ②lotus
芙蓉出水 lotus appearing above the water

扶 [fú]
〔动〕①place a hand on sb or sth for support; support with the hand ②hold up;straighten up ③lend a hand;help;assist
扶病 (do sth) in spite of illness
扶持 ①support sb with one's hand;help sb to stand or walk ②help sustain;give aid to; support
扶贫 aid-the-poor programme (a government programme for providing assistance for poor areas of the country);poverty alleviation
扶手 ①handrail;rail;banisters ②armrest
扶疏 luxuriant and well-spaced
扶梯 ①staircase ②ladder
扶养 ①provide for;support and assist ②bring

up;foster;raise

扶植 foster;prop up

扶助 help;assist;support

扶手椅 armchair

扶养费 payment for support and assistance (for one's former spouse);alimony

扶持生产 foster production

扶持先进 help advanced units

扶持正气 help sustain a healthy atmosphere; encourage healthy trends (in a society, etc.)

扶老携幼 holding the old by the arm and the young by the hand;bringing along the old and the young

扶贫工作 the poverty alleviation drive;aid to poor regions help to eliminate poverty in rural areas

扶贫攻坚 effort to alleviate absolute poverty

扶贫脱贫 aid poverty-stricken regions to shake off poverty

扶贫专款 special fund for aiding poor regions

扶弱抑强 help the weak and restrain the powerful;assist the weak and curb the violent

扶危济困 help those in distress and aid those in peril

扶摇直上 soar on the wings of a cyclone;rise steeply;skyrocket

扶杖而行 walk with (the support of) a stick

扶正祛邪 fight for justice against evil

扶植新生力量 foster new rising forces

孚 [fú] 勔 inspire confidence (in sb)

苻 [fú] 名 membrane inside a rush stalk

拂 [fú] 勔 ① stroke;caress;touch ② whisk;flick; brush off ③ run counter to;go against (sb's wishes)

拂尘 horsetail whisk

拂动 brush against;stroke;caress

拂过 whip;wash

拂拭 whisk or wipe off

拂晓 daybreak;dawn

拂煦 bring warmth

拂袖而去 leave with a flick of one's sleeve— go off in a huff

服 Ⅰ 名 ① clothes;garments;dress;attire ② mourning (apparel) Ⅱ 勔 ① wear (clothes) ② take (medicine) ③ serve ④ obey;submit (oneself to);be convinced ⑤ convince ⑥ be accustomed to;be used to;be acclimatized to ➡ fù

服从 obey; submit (oneself) to; be subordinated to

服毒 take poison

服法 ① submit to the law ② directions about how to take a medicine

服气 be convinced

服丧 be in mourning (for the death of a kinsman,etc.)

服式 style of dress;line

服饰 dress and personal adornment;dress

服侍 wait upon;attend

服输 admit (or acknowledge) defeat

服帖 ①docile;obedient;submissive ②fit perfectly ③at ease;content;comfortable

服务 give service to; be in the service of; serve

服孝 wear mourning clothes (or be in mourning) for one's parent (or husband)

服刑 serve a sentence

服药 take medicine

服役 ①be on active service;enlist in the army ②(in former times) do corvée labour

服用 ①clothing and articles for daily use ② take (medicine)

服装 dress;clothing;costume

服罪 plead guilty;admit one's guilt

服兵役 serve in the army

服务费 service fee

服务器 server

服务台 service desk (or counter);information and reception desk

服务员 attendant

服务站 service centre

服装店 clothes shop;clothing store

服务程序 service routine

服务行业 service industry; service trades; service sectors;services

服务忌语 service taboo wards

服务经济 service economy

服务贸易 service trade;trade in service

服务热线 helpline;service hotline

服务商标 service trademark

服务上门 door-to-door service

服务态度 attitude in attending to customers; attitude in waiting on guests

服务育人 educate students through service

服务质量 quality of service

服务周到 courteous service

服装表演 fashion show

服装工业 the clothing industry

服装模特 fashion model

服装设计 dress designing

服务性租赁 service leases

服装裁剪师 cutter

服装模特儿 mannequin

服务行业承诺制 system of offering guarantees to consumers in service industry

怫 [fú] 形 ① gloomy;depressed;worried ② indignant;angry;glowering

F

绂 [fú] 名 silk ribbon used to tie a seal in ancient China

绋 [fú] 名 big (hemp) rope; cord tying the coffin or leading the hearse

韨 [fú] 名 ①ceremonial gown in ancient China ② silk ribbon tying the imperial seal

茯 [fú]
茯苓 fuling

氟 [fú] 名 fluorine (F)
氟石 fluorite; fluorspar (a mineral)
氟化氢 hydrogen fluoride
氟化物 fluoride
氟利昂 freon
氟氯烷 chlorinated and fluorinated hydrocarbon
氟缺乏症 fluorine deficiency

俘 [fú] I 动 capture; seize; take prisoner of war II 名 prisoner of war; captive
俘获 ①capture; seize ②capture; trapping
俘虏 ①capture; take prisoner ②captive; captured personnel; prisoner of war (POW)

郛 [fú] 名 outer wall of a city
郛郭 outer wall of a city

洑 [fú] I 动 〈of water〉spin round; turn round II 名 whirlpool; eddy; vortex

祓 [fú] 名 ① offer sacrificial ceremony to banish misfortune and pray for blessings; exorcistic ceremony ②general cleaning or cleansing

莩 [fú] 名 thin membrane inside a rush stalk → piǎo

栿 [fú] 名 beam

浮 [fú] I 动 ①float; emerge ②swim ③exceed; be surplus or redundant II 形 ①on the surface; superficial ②movable; portable ③temporary; provisional; transient ④ flighty; frivolous; shallow; superficial; impetuous ⑤ hollow; empty; inflated
浮报 give inflated figures in a report
浮标 buoy
浮冰 floating ice; (ice) floe
浮尘 floating dust; surface dust
浮沉 now sink, now emerge; drift along
浮船 pontoon
浮荡 float in the air
浮雕 relief (sculpture)
浮吊 floating crane
浮动 ①float; drift ②be unsteady; fluctuate ③ float
浮泛 ①float about ②reveal; display ③superficial; too abstract
浮华 showy; ostentatious; flashy
浮记 keep a tally of a transaction before entering it in the regular accounts; keep a temporary account
浮夸 boastful; exaggerating
浮雷 floating mine
浮力 buoyancy
浮面 surface
浮名 empty name
浮萍 duckweed
浮签 note pasted on the margin of a page
浮浅 superficial; shallow
浮桥 pontoon bridge; floating bridge
浮石 pumice (stone)
浮筒 float; pontoon; buoy
浮屠 ①Buddha ②a title applied by Buddhists to a monk ③Buddhist pagoda or stupa
浮土 dust collected on furniture, clothing, etc.; surface dust
浮文 verbiage; padding
浮坞 floating dock
浮现 appear before one's eyes
浮想 ①thoughts flashing across one's mind ② recollections
浮选 flotation
浮游 ①swim; float ②go on a pleasure trip
浮云 floating clouds
浮躁 impetuous; impulsive
浮渣 dross
浮肿 dropsy; edema
浮子 ①float (in fishing) ②carburettor float (in automobile)
浮尘子 leafhopper
浮船坞 floating dock; floating dry dock
浮动轴 floating axle
浮夸风 common practice of exaggeration; proneness to boasting and exaggeration; atmosphere of inflated exaggeration; tendency toward boasting and exaggeration
浮码头 floating pier
浮皮儿 ①outer skin ②surface
浮选剂 flotation agent
浮出水面 emerge
浮动工资 floating wage; wage in sliding scale
浮动汇率 floating (or flexible) exchange rate
浮动价格 floating prices
浮动利率 floating interest rate
浮法玻璃 float glass
浮光掠影 skimming over the surface; hasty and casual; cursory
浮皮蹭痒 scratching the surface; superficial
浮生若梦 this fleeting life of ours is like an empty dream
浮想联翩 thoughts thronging one's mind

浮游生物 plankton
浮游资金 floating fund
浮动钻井台 floating oil drilling platform
浮翼水上飞机 float-wing seaplane

符 [fú]
Ⅰ 名 ①tally ②symbol；mark；sign ③magic drawing or sign traced by a Taoist priest to invoke or expel spirits and bring good or ill fortune Ⅱ 动 match；tally with；accord with
符号 ①symbol；mark ②insignia
符合 ①accord with；tally with；conform to；be in keeping with ②coincidence
符咒 Taoist magic figures or incantations
符号化 signifying
符号学 semiology
符合摆 coincidence pendulum
符号地址 symbolic address
符合标准 be up to the standard
符合客观规律 conform to the objective laws

匐 [fú]
◇匍匐 ①crawl；creep ②(of plants) grow along the ground；creep；trail

袱 [fú]
名 cloth-wrapper；covering cloth

艴 [fú]
形 angry；offended
艴然 be angry；be offended

幅 [fú]
Ⅰ 名 ①width (of cloth，etc.) ②breadth (in general)；size Ⅱ 量 (for cloth，pictures，scrolls，etc.)：两幅布 two pieces of cloth
幅度 range；scope；extent
幅面 width of cloth
幅员 the area of a country's territory；the size of a country
幅值 amplitude
幅员辽阔 have a vast territory

辐 [fú]
名 spoke
辐散 divergence
辐射 ①radiate (from a central point) ②radiation
辐条 spoke (of a wheel)
辐照 irradiation
辐射波 radiation wave；radiated wave；outgoing wave
辐射带 radiation zone
辐射计 radiometer
辐射能 radiant energy
辐射体 radiant body
辐射学 radiology
辐射源 radiant
辐照度 irradiance
辐射电阻 radiation resistance
辐射防护 radiation protection
辐射剂量 radiation dosage
辐射频率 radiation frequency

辐射强度 radiation intensity
辐射育种 radioactive breeding

蜉 [fú]
蜉蝣 mayfly

福 [fú]
Ⅰ 名 ①good fortune；luck；blessing；happiness ②(short for 福建) Fujian Province Ⅱ 动 (of a woman) make a curtsy：福了一福 make a curtsy
福彩 welfare lottery
福分 good luck；good fortune；a happy lot
福橘 tangerine produced in Fujian Province
福利 material benefits；well-being；welfare
福气 good luck；good fortune；a happy lot
福相 a face showing good fortune
福星 lucky star；mascot
福音 ①Gospel ②glad tidings
福利房 welfare-oriented public housing
福利费 welfare funds
福利彩票 welfare lottery
福利分房 welfare housing allocation system；welfare-oriented public housing distribution system
福利国家 welfare state
福利基金 welfare fund
福利设施 welfare facilities
福利事业 welfare project (or services)
福如东海 happiness as boundless as the eastern seas (a stock term of congratulations)
福至心灵 When good fortune comes，the mind works well.
福兮祸之所伏 In good fortune lurks bad luck.
福无双至，祸不单行 Blessings never come in pairs；misfortunes never come singly.

蝠 [fú]
名 bat

fǔ (ㄈㄨˇ)

父 [fǔ]
名 respectful term for an elderly man ⇒fù

甫 [fǔ]
副 just；only；only just

抚 [fǔ]
动 ①comfort；console ②protect；nurture；foster ③press lightly；stroke
抚爱 caress；fondle
抚孤 bring up the orphaned
抚摩 stroke；caress
抚弄 stroke；fondle
抚慰 comfort；console；soothe
抚恤 comfort and compensate a bereaved family
抚养 foster；raise；rear；bring up
抚育 foster；nurture；tend
抚掌 clap one's hands
抚恤金 pension for the disabled or for the

family of the deceased; pension for the disabled and for survivors

抚养费 payment for the upbringing of one's children

抚今追昔 recall the past and compare it with the present; reflect on the past in the light of the present

拊 [fǔ]
劂 clap; slap; strike
拊掌 clap hands

斧 [fǔ]
名 ①axe; hatchet ②battle-axe
斧头 axe; hatchet
斧正 (please) make corrections
斧子 axe; hatchet

F

府 [fǔ]
名 ① seat of government; government office ②archive or treasury of (local) government ③ official residence; mansion ④ your home; your house ⑤prefecture
府城 prefectural city
府绸 poplin
府第 mansion (of nobles, high officials, big landlords, etc.); mansion house
府库 government repository (in former times)
府上 ①your home; your family ②your native place

俯 [fǔ]
劂 ① bow (one's head); bend forward or down ②deign; condescend
俯察 ①look down ②deign to examine
俯冲 nose dive
俯伏 lie prostrate; lie prone
俯角 angle of depression
俯就 ①condescend to accept (a job) ②adapt oneself to; make the best of; make do with
俯瞰 look down at; overlook
俯临 overlook
俯拍 take a crane (*or* boom) shot
俯冗 condescend to grant; deign to approve
俯身 bend over; bend down
俯视 look down at; overlook
俯首 bow one's head; stoop
俯卧 lie prostrate; lie face down (on the ground)
俯仰 bending or lifting of the head—simple move or action
俯冲角 dive angle
俯视图 vertical view
俯卧撑 push-up
俯仰角 angle of pitch
俯冲飞行 diving flight
俯冲轰炸 dive-bombing
俯瞰摄影 crane shot; boom shot
俯拾即是 be found everywhere; be extremely common
俯首帖耳 be docile and obedient; be all obedience; be servile

俯言听命 bow down to obey submissively; be at sb's beck and call
俯仰由人 be at others' beck and call
俯仰运动 pitching movement
俯仰之间 in the twinkling of an eye; in an instant; in a flash
俯首甘为孺子牛 head bowed, like a willing ox, I serve the children—serve the people heart and soul

釜 [fǔ]
名 *fu*, a kind of cauldron used in ancient China
釜底抽薪 take away the firewood from under the cauldron—take drastic measures to deal with an emergency
釜底游鱼 fish swimming in the bottom of a cauldron—person whose fate is sealed
釜中之鱼 fish in the kettle; (like) a fish in the pot—without hope of escape; (like) fish in the cauldron

辅 [fǔ]
I 劂 assist; help; complement; supplement
II 名 areas round a national capital
辅币 fractional currency (*or* money)
辅导 give guidance in study or training; coach
辅机 auxiliary engine; donkey
辅课 subsidiary course
辅路 side road
辅修 minor; take up a course as a sideline
辅翼 assist a ruler in governing a country
辅音 consonant
辅助 ①assist ②supplementary; auxiliary; subsidiary
辅佐 assist a ruler in governing a country
辅导班 tutorial class
辅导员 (political and ideological) assistant; instructor
辅车相依 as dependent on each other as the jowls and the jawbone; as close as the jowls and the jaws
辅助机构 auxiliary body
辅助舰船 auxiliary vessels
辅助人员 auxiliary staff members
辅助设备 auxiliary equipment
辅助授粉 supplementary pollination
辅助存储器 auxiliary memory
辅助性任务 attaching task
辅助性贸易政策 complementary trade policy

脯 [fǔ]
名 ①dried meat ②preserved fruit ➡pú

腑 [fǔ]
◇肺腑 the bottom of one's heart

腐 [fǔ]
I 形 rotten; putrid; corroded; stale II 劂 turn bad; decay III 名 beancurd
腐败 ①rotten; putrid; decayed ②corrupt; rot-

ten;degenerate
腐臭 emitting a smell of decay;decaying and stinking;smelly
腐化 ①degenerate;become corrupt,dissolute or depraved ②rot;decay;decompose
腐烂 ①decompose;become putrid (*or* rotten) ②corrupt;rotten
腐米 rotten rice
腐乳 fermented tofu (*or* beancurd)
腐生 living on nonliving organic matter;saprophytic
腐蚀 ①corrode;etch ②corrupt;corrode
腐朽 ①rotten;decayed ②decadent;degenerate
腐鱼 rotten (*or* putrid) fish
腐竹 dried rolls of bean milk cream
腐蚀版 etched plate
腐蚀机 etching machine
腐蚀剂 corrosive;corrodent
腐殖煤 humic coal
腐殖酸 humic acid
腐殖土 humus soil
腐殖质 humus
腐败分子 corrupt element;degenerate
腐败透顶 rotten to the core
腐败无能 corrupt and incompetent
腐败现象 corruption
腐化堕落 degenerate and decadent;leading a dissolute (*or* dissipated) life
腐化分子 degenerate;a depraved person
腐化官僚 corrupt bureaucrat
腐朽生活方式 degenerate way of life;decadent life style

fù（ㄈㄨˋ）

服 [fù] 量 dose;一服中药 a dose of Chinese herbal medicines ➡fú

父 [fù] 名 ① father ② male relative of a senior generation ➡fǔ
父辈 people of father's generation
父本 male parent
父党 father's kinsfolk
父老 elders (of a country or district)
父母 father and mother;parents
父亲 father
父系 ①paternal ②patrilineal
父兄 ①father and elder brothers ②head of a family
父执 father's friends
父子 father and son
父权制 patriarchy
父父子子 Fathers do their duties as fathers and sons do their duties as sons.
父老乡亲 fellow countrymen
父母之命,媒妁之言 the command of parents

and the good offices of a go-between
讣 [fù] I 动 announce sb's death II 名 obituary
讣电 telegraphed obituary notice
讣告 ①announce sb's death ②obituary
讣文 obituary

付 [fù] 动 ①hand (*or* turn) over;commit;give ②pay
付出 pay;expend
付方 credit side;credit
付刊 send to the press;put into print
付款 pay a sum of money
付排 send to the compositor
付讫 (of a bill) paid
付清 pay in full;pay off;clear (a bill)
付托 put sth in sb's charge;entrust
付息 pay interest
付现 pay in cash
付印 ①send to the press ②turn over to the printing shop (after proofreading)
付邮 send by post;take to the post;post;mail
付与 take out;give
付账 pay a bill
付定金 pay earnest money
付款人 payer;drawee
付费电视 pay TV;pay-as-you-see television
付款方式 type of payment
付款凭单 warrant;paying certificate
付款凭证 payment voucher
付款条件 terms of payment
付款通知 advice of payment;payment order
付款银行 paying bank
付之一炬 commit to the flames
付之一笑 dismiss with a laugh
付诸东流 thrown into the eastward flowing stream—all one's efforts wasted;irrevocably lost
付诸实施 put into practice;carry out
付诸行动 put into practice
付款保证银行 certifying bank

负 [fù] I 动 ①carry on the back (*or* shoulder);shoulder ②bear;take up;shoulder ③rely on;have at one's back ④suffer;sustain ⑤enjoy ⑥owe;be indebted;bear debt ⑦fail (in one's duty, obligation, etc.);disappoint;betray ⑧lose (a battle,game,etc.);be defeated II 形 ①minus;negative ②negative
负案 filed criminal case
负担 ①bear (a burden);shoulder ②burden;load;encumbrance
负电 negative electricity
负号 negative sign
负荷 ① carry on one's back and shoulder;bear;shoulder ②load (that a person or machine is expected to perform);work load

负极 negative pole
负疚 feel apologetic;have a guilty conscience
负片 negative
负气 do sth in a fit of pique
负伤 be wounded;be injured
负数 negative number
负像 negative image
负心 ungrateful (esp. in love);untrue;heartless
负约 ① break a promise;go back on one's word ②fail to keep an appointment
负载 load
负责 ①be responsible for;be in charge of ② conscientious
负债 ①be in debt;incur debts ②liabilities
负重 ① carry a heavy load on one's back ② shoulder a heavy task
负罪 bear the blame
负电荷 negative (electric) charge
负电极 negative electrode;cathode
负电子 electron;negatron
负电阻 negative resistance
负反馈 negative feedback
负分数 negative fraction
负函数 negative function
负离子 anion
负责人 person in charge;leading cadre
负增长 negative growth
负资产 negative asset
负担系数 dependency coefficient
负加速度 negative acceleration
负荆请罪 proffer a birch and ask for a flogging—offer a humble apology
负面效应 negative effects
负隅顽抗 (of an enemy or a robber) fight stubbornly with one's back to the wall;put up a desperate struggle
负债经营 manage an enterprise with a loan
负债累累 be heavily in debt;be up to one's ears in debt
负重训练 weight training
负重致远 bear a heavy burden and go a long way—shoulder heavy responsibilities
负连带责任 be held jointly liable
负债证明书 certificate of indebtedness

妇 [fù]
名 ①woman ②married woman ③wife
妇科 (department of) gynaecology
妇女 woman
妇人 married woman
妇孺 women and children
妇婴 women and infants;mothers and babies
妇幼 women and children
妇产科 (department of) gynaecology and obstetrics
妇女病 gynaecological (or women's) disease
妇产医院 a hospital for gynaecology and obstetrics
妇道人家 women;womenfolk
妇科医生 gynaecologist
妇人之见 views of woman;shortsighted views not to be taken seriously
妇女联合会 the Women's Federation
妇女代表大会 conference of women representatives;women's conference
妇女自身修养 women's self-improvement
妇女权益保障法 the Law on Protection of Women's Rights and Interests

附 [fù]
动 ① add;attach;append;enclose ② get close to;be close by;be near ③attach oneself to;depend on;comply with;agree to
附笔 additional remarks (in a letter, document,etc.)
附带 ①in passing ②attach ③subsidiary;supplementary
附点 dot
附耳 move close to sb's ear
附睾 epididymis
附和 echo;chime in with
附会 draw wrong conclusions by false analogy;strain one's interpretation
附加 ①add;attach ②additional;attached;appended
附笺 docket
附件 ①appendix;annex ②enclosure ③accessories;attachment
附近 ①nearby;neighbouring ②in the vicinity of;close to
附录 appendix (to a book)
附上 be enclosed herewith
附设 have as an attached institution
附属 subsidiary;auxiliary;attached;affiliated
附图 attached map (or drawing);figure
附言 postscript (PS)
附议 second a motion;support a proposal
附庸 ①dependency;vassal ②appendage
附有 accompany
附则 supplementary articles (appended to a treaty,decree,etc.)
附中 attached middle school
附注 notes appended to a book,etc.;annotations
附着 adhere to;stick to
附子 monkshood
附睾炎 epididymitis
附加费 extra charge;surcharge
附加税 surtax;additional tax;supertax
附属国 dependency
附属品 accessory;appendage
附着力 adhesive force;adhesion
附带成本 incidental cost
附带提议 subsidiary motion
附带条款 additional article;memorandum (or

institute) clause
附加成本 additional paid-in capital
附加罚款 surcharge
附加工资 supplemental wage;extra wage
附加条款 additional article; memorandum clause
附加文件 diplomacy appended document
附生植物 epiphyte;air plant
附属公司 affiliated company;subsidiary company
附属小学 attached primary school
附属中学 attached middle school
附息贷款 lend money on interest
附庸风雅 (of landlords,merchants,etc.) mingle with men of letters and pose as a lover of culture
附赘悬疣 swelling tumours and protruding wens—superfluities
附加议定书 diplomacy additional protocol
附带民事诉讼 incidental civil action; subsidiary civil action

咐 [fù]
◇吩咐 ①tell;instruct ②instructions
嘱咐 enjoin;tell;exhort

阜 [fù]
I 名 earthen mound II 形 abundant; wealthy

驸 [fù]
名 horse harnessed by the side of a team
驸马 husband of an emperor's daughter or sister;emperor's son-in-law or brother-in-law

赴 [fù]
动 go to;be bound for;attend;leave for
赴会 attend a meeting;keep an appointment (to meet sb)
赴难 go to the aid of one's country;go to help save the country from danger
赴任 go to one's post;be on the way to one's post
赴宴 go to a feast;attend a banquet
赴约 keep an appointment
赴汤蹈火 go through fire and water;defy all difficulties and dangers

复 [fù]
I 形 ① repeated;duplicate ② compound; complex;complicated II 动 ① turn round; turn over ②answer;reply ③recover;return to;resume ④revenge III 副 again;repeatedly
复本 duplicate
复辟 restore a dethroned monarch (or the old order)
复波 complex wave
复查 check;reexamine
复仇 revenge;avenge
复出 resumption of work;resume to work;reappear

复电 ①send a telegram in reply ②telegram in reply
复读 (students destined to graduate from elementary or secondary schools) repeat the last year of schooling due to the next level
复发 have a relapse;recur
复方 ①prescription composed of two or more recipes of herbal medicines ② medicine made of two or more ingredients;compound
复岗 resume one's post
复根 compound radical
复耕 reclaim wasteland
复工 return to work (after a strike or layoff)
复古 restore ancient ways; return to the ancients
复关 rejoin the General Agreement on Tariff and Trade (GATT); re-enter GATT; resume GATT membership
复合 compound;complex;composite
复核 ① check ② (of the Supreme People's Court) review a case in which a death sentence has been passed by a lower court
复会 resume a session
复婚 (of a divorced couple) remarry each other
复活 ①come back to life;revive ②resurrection
复机 answer the paging call
复激 compound excitation
复交 ①resume (once broken) relations ②diplomacy reestablish (*or* resume) diplomatic relations
复旧 restore (*or* revive) old ways;return to the past
复句 a sentence of two or more clauses
复刊 (of magazines or newspapers) resume publication
复课 resume classes
复垦 reclamation
复利 compound interest
复明 recover lost eyesight
复命 report back after carrying out an order
复牌 relist
复赛 intermediary heat;semi-finals
复审 ①reexamine ②review a case
复生 come back to life
复式 double entry
复试 reexamination;final examination
复述 ①repeat ②retell (in language learning)
复数 ①plural (number) ②complex number
复丝 fibre multifilament
复苏 ①come back to life or consciousness;resuscitate ②recovery;resurgence
复位 ①reduce ②be restored to the throne
复吸 revert to take drugs
复习 review;revise
复现 recurrent

F

复线 multiple track
复写 make carbon copies;duplicate
复信 ①write a letter in reply;reply ②letter in reply
复兴 revive;rejuvenate
复姓 compound surname;two-character surname
复学 go back to school (after prolonged absence for health reasons, etc.); resume one's interrupted studies
复盐 double salt
复眼 compound eye (of insects)
复业 ①take up one's old trade again ②reopen or restart business
复叶 compound leaf
复议 reconsider (a decision)
复音 complex tone
复印 xerox;duplicate
复元 recover from an illness
复员 ①return to peacetime conditions ②(of servicemen) be demobilized
复原 ①be restored;be rehabilitated ②recover from an illness;be restored to health
复圆 fourth contact of a total eclipse;last contact of a partial eclipse;end of an eclipse
复杂 complicated;complex
复照 a note in reply
复诊 further consultation (with a doctor); subsequent visit
复职 resume one's post;be reinstated
复制 duplicate;reproduce;make a copy of
复种 multiple cropping
复背斜 anticlinorium
复穿孔 pang-punch
复读机 replayer
复读生 student retaking classes after failing a college entrance examination
复分数 complex fraction
复合词 compound word;compound
复合句 compound or complex sentence
复活节 Easter
复进口 re-import
复卷机 papermaking rewinding machine;rewinder
复位术 reduction
复向斜 synclinorium
复写纸 carbon paper
复音词 disyllabic (or polysyllabic) word
复印机 xerox (machine);duplicator;duplicating photocopy machine;photocopier
复印纸 duplicating paper
复员费 demobilization pay
复员令 demobilization order
复制片 duplicated film;copy of a film
复制品 replica;reproduction
复本位制 bimetallism
复仇心理 vindictiveness;desire for revenge

复仇主义 revanchism
复调音乐 polyphony
复古主义 the doctrine of "back to the ancients"
复关谈判 negotiation on the resumption of China's contracting party status of the GATT
复合材料 compound material
复合磁头 combined record
复合电路 compound circuit
复合肥料 compound fertilizer
复合量词 compound classifier
复合元音 diphthong (as ei,uo) or triphthong (as uai,iao)
复式车床 double lathe
复式预算 double-entry budget
复式住宅 a type of residential housing that maximizes usage space by increasing the number of two-storey buildings; duplex apartment;compound apartment
复习提纲 outline for review
复线铁路 double-tracking railways
复员军人 a demobilized serviceman; an ex-serviceman
复种面积 multiple cropping area
复种指数 multiple crop index
复分解反应 double decomposition reaction
复合型人才 comprehensive talent; multi-faceted talent;all round person;double personnel (or talent);cross field talent
复边贸易关系 plurilateral trade relations
复查平反冤假错案 review and redress past frame-ups and false and erroneous cases

副 [fù]
Ⅰ 〔形〕①deputy;assistant;vice- ②complementary;auxiliary;subsidiary;secondary Ⅱ〔名〕assistant post or position Ⅲ〔动〕correspond to;fit Ⅳ〔量〕①set;pair:一副对联 a pair of antithetical couplets ②*used to indicate facial expression*:一副黑里透红的脸膛 a suntanned ruddy face
副本 duplicate;transcript;copy
副词 ①adverbial word,any of a class of words that are used mainly to modify a verb or an adjective ②adverb
副歌 refrain
副官 adjutant;aide-de-camp
副虹 secondary bow
副件 duplicate
副井 auxiliary shaft
副刊 supplement
副品 substandard goods
副券 coupon
副食 non-staple food
副手 assistant
副署 countersign
副业 sideline;side occupation

副翼 aileron
副职 deputy position; the position of a deputy to the chief of an office, department, etc.
副轴 countershaft; layshaft
副标题 subheading; subtitle
副产品 by-product
副产物 by-product
副处长 deputy section (*or* division) chief
副代表 deputy representative (*or* delegate)
副导演 assistant director
副教授 associate professor
副经理 assistant manager
副热带 subtropical zone; subtropics; semitropics
副伤寒 paratyphoid (fever)
副神经 accessory nerve
副食品 non-staple food (*or* foodstuffs)
副司长 deputy director of the department
副油箱 ①auxiliary tank ②drop tank
副总理 vice-premier
副总统 vice-president
副作用 ① side effect; by-effect ② secondary action
副赤道带 subequatorial belt
副驾驶员 copilot; second pilot; kid
副食补贴 state subsidy to make up for price rise in non-staple foodstuffs; special allowance for supplementary food
副食商店 grocer's; grocery
副系主任 associate dean of the department
副研究员 associate professor
副交感神经 parasympathetic nerve
副食品价格补贴 subsidy to offset the increased prices of non-staple foodstuffs; special allowance for making up the price hike on non-staple food

赋 ［fù］
Ⅰ 名 ① natural endowment ② agricultural tax ③ *fu*; rhyme prose; poetic prose; prose poem Ⅱ 动 ① bestow on; endow with; vest with ②compose (verse); write (poetry) ③ levy; impose
赋税 taxes
赋闲 be out of office; be out of employment
赋性 inborn nature
赋役 taxes and corvée
赋有 be endowed with (qualities or characteristics)
赋予 entrust (an important task) to sb
赋值 assignment; evaluation
赋格曲 fugue
赋形剂 excipient
赋税减免 tax remission

傅 ［fù］
Ⅰ 动 ① teach; instruct; assist ② attach; stick to; adhere to ③ lay on; apply Ⅱ 名 teacher; instructor

傅彩 lay on colours
傅粉 apply powder
傅科摆 Foucault pendulum

富 ［fù］
Ⅰ 形 ① rich; wealthy ② rich; abundant Ⅱ 动 enrich Ⅲ 名 wealth; resource
富贵 riches and honour; wealth and rank
富国 ①rich nation ②make a nation rich and powerful
富豪 rich and powerful people
富矿 rich ore; high-grade ore
富民 make the people rich and prosperous
富农 rich peasant
富强 (of a country) prosperous and strong
富饶 richly endowed; fertile; abundant
富庶 rich and populous
富翁 man of wealth; moneybags
富有 ①rich; wealthy ②be rich in; be full of
富于 be rich in; be full of
富余 have more than needed; have enough and to spare
富裕 prosperous; well-to-do; well-off
富源 natural resources
富足 plentiful; abundant; rich
富贵病 rich man's disease (i.e. one which calls for a long period of rest and an expensive diet)
富矿体 ore shoot
富士山 Fujiyama
富国利民 enrich the nation and bring benefits to the people
富国强兵 enrich the nation and strengthen the military; make one's country rich and build up its military might
富丽堂皇 beautiful and imposing; in majestic splendour; sumptuous
富民政策 policy of enriching people; policy to enrich people
富商大贾 plutocrat
富营养化 eutrophication
富于表情 with vivid expression
富于幻想 full of imagination
富于水分 rich in moisture
富含维生素 vitamin-enriched
富于创造性 be highly creative
富于独创性 abound in originality
富余人员分流 reposition of redundant personnel; finding jobs in other trades for redundant workers

腹 ［fù］
名 ① belly; abdomen; stomach ② in the heart; innermost feelings ③ empty and protruding part in the middle of a vessel or a vase
腹地 hinterland
腹诽 unspoken criticism
腹稿 draft worked out in one's mind
腹面 underside

F

腹膜 peritoneum
腹鳍 ventral fin
腹腔 abdominal cavity
腹水 ascites
腹痛 abdominal pain
腹泻 diarrhoea
腹议 keep one's criticism or opinion to oneself
腹胀 abdominal distension
腹足 abdominal leg; proleg
腹股沟 groin
腹膜炎 peritonitis
腹腔镜 peritoneoscope
腹足类 gastropod
腹背受敌 be attacked front and rear
腹有鳞甲 have scales and shells of reptiles and arthropods in the heart—be evil; be sinister

缚 [fù]
动 tie up; bind fast

赙 [fù]
动 present a gift to a bereaved family

蝮 [fù]
蝮蛇 Pallas pit viper

覆 [fù]
动 ① cover; envelop ② overturn; capsize; upset
覆盖 ① cover ② plant cover; vegetation ③ overwrite
覆灭 destruction; complete collapse
覆没 ①(of a ship) capsize and sink ②(of an army) be overwhelmed; be annihilated
覆土 earthing
覆亡 fall (of an empire, nation, etc.)
覆辙 the track of an overturned cart
覆盖层 overburden
覆盖率 coverage rate
覆盆子 Korean raspberry
覆盆之冤 a wrong that can never be righted; irremediable wrong
覆水难收 spilt water can't be gathered up—what is done can't be undone
覆巢无完卵 when the nest is overturned no egg stays unbroken—when disaster befalls a family, etc. , no member can escape unscathed

馥 [fù]
名 fragrance
馥郁 strongly fragrant; heavy perfume; sweet-scented; sweet-smelling

Gg

gā（ㄍㄚ）

夹 [gā]
➡jiā；jiá
夹肢窝 armpit

伽 [gā]
➡jiā；qié
伽马刀 gamma knife
伽马射线 gamma ray

咖 [gā]
➡kā
咖喱 curry

嘎 [gā]
〔象〕screech
嘎巴 [gābā] crack；snap
嘎巴 [gāba] ①form into a crust ②crust
嘎嘎 quack
嘎吱 creak

gá（ㄍㄚˊ）

轧 [gá]
〔动〕①press hard against each other；squeeze ②make friends with；associate with ③check
➡yà；zhá
轧账 check the accounts
轧朋友 make friends with sb

gǎ（ㄍㄚˇ）

尕 [gǎ]
〔形〕small；little
尕娃 small child

gà（ㄍㄚˋ）

尬 [gà]
◇尴尬 ①(of the situation one is in) awkward；hard to deal with ②embarrassed

gāi（ㄍㄞ）

该 [gāi]
Ⅰ〔动〕①ought to；should ②fall to sb；be sb's turn (to do sth)：该你试了。It's your turn to try now. ③deserve；merit ④owe Ⅱ〔副〕①probably；most likely ②(*used in exclamatory sentences for emphasis*)：我要能跟你一块儿去，那该多好哇！If only I could go with you! Ⅲ〔代〕this；that；the above-mentioned；the said：该项 this item
该当 ①deserve ②should
该账 be in debt
该着 [gāizháo] predestined by fate；unavoidable

垓 [gāi]
〔数〕one hundred million

赅 [gāi]
Ⅰ〔动〕serve as (sth else)；include Ⅱ〔形〕complete；comprehensive；all-inclusive

gǎi（ㄍㄞˇ）

改 [gǎi]
〔动〕①change；convert；transform ②alter；revise；polish ③correct；rectify；remedy；put right ④change (*or* switch) over to
改版 corrected edition；(of a newspaper，etc.) get a face-lift；have a new face (*or* look)；revise an existing edition
改编 ①adapt；rearrange；revise ②reorganize；redesignate
改变 change；alter；transform
改道 ① change one's route ②(of a river) change its course
改掉 give up；drop
改订 reformulate；rewrite
改动 change；alter；modify
改革 reform；restructuring；perestroika
改观 change the appearance (*or* face) of
改过 mend one's ways；correct one's mistakes
改行 change one's profession (*or* occupation，trade)
改换 change over to；change
改悔 repent
改嫁 (of a woman) remarry
改建 reconstruct；rebuild

改进 improve;make better

改口 withdraw or modify one's previous remark;correct oneself

改良 ①improve;ameliorate ②reform

改判 change the original sentence;commute; amend a judgment

改期 change the date (usu. to a later date); postpone

改任 change to another post

改日 another day;some other day

改善 improve;ameliorate

改写 rewrite;adapt

改选 (hold) a new election;reelect

改元 change the designation of an imperial reign;change the title of a reign

改造 transform;reform;remould;remake

改正 correct;amend;put right

改制 reform of the system of ownership

改装 ①change one's costume or dress ②repackage;repack ③reequip;refit

改锥 screwdriver

改组 reorganize;reshuffle;shake-up

改革派 reformers; reformists; reform party (or faction,group,advocator)

改正液 correction fluid

改变现状 change the status quo

改朝换代 change of dynasty (or regime);dynastic changes

改道行驶 detour;alternate route;by-pass;take some other road;use the bypath

改恶从善 abandon evil and do good;turn over a new leaf;mend one's ways

改革攻坚 tackle hard issues in the reform

改革进程 the course of reform

改革开放 reform and open

改革力度 intensity of reform

改革试点 reform experimentation; pilot reform (or restructuring)

改革学制 reform educational (school) system

改过自新 correct one's errors and make a fresh start;mend one's ways;turn over a new leaf

改良主义 reformism

改天换地 transform heaven and earth;change the world

改头换面 change the appearance but not the essence;dish up the same old stuff in a new form

改弦更张 adopt new ways;make a fresh start

改弦易辙 change one's course;strike out on a new path

改邪归正 give up vice and return to virtue; turn over a new leaf

改造旧城 remold the old city

改制上市 reorganize an enterprise according to modern corporate system so that it will get listed on the stock market

改组内阁 reshuffle the cabinet;cabinet shake-up

改造老企业 transform outmoded enterprises

改革开放时代 era of reform and opening-up

改建扩建工程 projects for renovation and expansion

改进工作作风 improve the work style

改善经营管理 improve management and administration

改善居住条件 better (or improve) people's living conditions

改善人权状况 improve human rights situation

改善投资环境 improve the environment for investment

改造客观世界 transform the objective world

改组政府部门 reshuffle the government departments

改革开放的龙头 bellwether (or dragon head) of economic reform and opening to the outside world

改善出口商品结构 improve the export product mix

改革开放的总设计师 the chief architect of China's reform and opening up

胲 [gǎi]
　[名] cheek flesh

gài （《ㄞ）

丐 [gài]
　I [动] ①beg ②give;grant;bestow II [名] beggar

芥 [gài]
　➡jiè

芥菜 leaf mustard

芥蓝 cabbage mustard

钙 [gài]
　[名] calcium (Ca)

钙化 calcify

钙镁磷肥 calcium magnesium phosphate

盖 [gài]
　I [名] ①lid;cover;cap ②shell;carapace ③canopy II [动] ①cover;put (over...) ②affix (a seal) ③overwhelm;surpass;drown ④build;put up (housing) III [形] excellent;terrific;tops IV [副] approximately;about;around V [连] for;because;in fact

盖布 drop cloth

盖菜 leaf mustard (a vegetable)

盖戳 affix one's seal;put a stamp on

盖世 unparalleled;matchless;peerless

盖头 bridal veil

盖章 affix one's seal;seal;stamp

盖子 ①lid;cover;cap;top ②shell (of a tortoise,etc.)

盖钢印 affix the steel (or embossing) seal (to sth)

盖公章 put the official seal (on sth);apply the

official seal (to sth)

盖帽儿 ① block a shot (in basketball) ② great;bad;totally awesome;fantastic;marvellous

盖然性 probability

盖盅儿 teacup with a lid

盖棺论定 no final verdict can be pronounced on a man until after his death;one's deserts can only be judged after death

盖世太保 Gestapo

盖世英雄 a peerless (*or* matchless) hero

盖洛普民意测验 Gallup poll

溉 ［gài］
勋 water;irrigate

概 ［gài］
I 副 ①generally;approximately ②without exception;absolutely;categorically II 名 ① manner of carrying oneself;bearing;deportment ②scene;situation;circumstances

概况 general situation;survey

概括 ① summarize;generalize;epitomize ② brief and to the point

概览 general survey

概率 probability

概略 outline;summary

概论 outline;introduction

概貌 general picture

概念 concept;conception;notion;idea

概然 probable

概述 give a brief account of (an event,etc.)

概数 approximate number;round number

概算 budgetary estimate

概要 essentials;outline

概括性 generality

概率论 probability

概念车 concept car

概念股 concept stock

概念化 deal in generalities;write or speak in abstract terms

概言之 generally speaking;all told

概率预算 probabilistic budget

概莫能外 admit of no exception whatsoever

概念艺术 conceptual art

gān（《ㄢ）

干 ［gān］
I 名 ①shield ②edge of a body of water ③ dried food II 勋 ①offend;affront ②have to do with;be concerned with;be preoccupied with; be implicated in ③ seek (official position, official's salary,etc.);pursue ④embarrass or annoy by complaining or making offensive remarks III 量 *used of people*:那一干子人 that gang;those people IV 形 ①dry;arid ②without resort to water ③empty;hollow ④without substance;empty;dry ⑤rude;blunt;impolite V 副 vainly;helplessly ➡gàn

干白 dry white wine

干板 dry plate

干杯 drink a toast

干贝 dried scallop (adductor)

干瘪 ①dry ②shriveled;wizened ③(of writing) dull;drab;dryasdust

干冰 dry ice

干菜 dried vegetable

干草 hay

干柴 dry firewood

干醋 jealousy about sth that is none of one's business;vicarious jealousy

干脆 ① clear-cut;straightforward ② simply; just;altogether

干爹 (nominally) adoptive father;godfather

干犯 offend;encroach upon

干饭 cooked rice

干纺 dry spinning

干戈 weapons of war—arms;war

干股 shares that do not require payment of a unit price and that can earn a free dividend

干果 ①dry fruit (e.g. nuts) ②dried fruit

干旱 (of weather or soil) arid;dry

干涸 dry up;run dry

干红 dry red wine

干花 dehydrated flower

干货 dried food and nuts (as merchandise)

干季 dry season

干结 dry and hard

干净 ①clean;neat and tidy ②complete;total

干咳 have a dry cough

干枯 dried-up;withered;shriveled;wizened

干酪 cheese

干冷 dry and cold (weather)

干粮 solid food (prepared for a journey);field rations;rations for a journey

干裂 crack because of dryness;be dry and cracked

干馏 dry distillation

干妈 (nominally) adoptive mother;godmother

干呕 retch

干啤 dry beer

干亲 nominal kinship

干扰 ①disturb;interfere;obstruct ②interference;jam

干涩 ①not lenitive;not smooth ②(of voice) raucous ③blunt;affected

干涉 ①interfere;intervene;meddle ②relation ③interference

干瘦 skinny and wizened;bony

干洗 dry-clean;dry cleanse

干系 responsibility;implication

干笑 laugh hollowly;force a smile

干薪 salary drawn for a sinecure

干选 dry separation

干预 intervene;interpose;meddle

干燥 ①dry;arid ②dull;uninteresting

干租 dry lease

干巴巴 dull and dry; insipid; dryasdust; dull as ditchwater

干瞪眼 stand by anxiously, unable to help; look on in despair

干电池 dry cell

干儿子 (nominally) adopted son

干酪素 casein

干女儿 (nominally) adopted daughter

干扰弹 jamming bomb

干鞣法 leather dry tannage

干涉仪 interferometer

干湿表 psychrometer

干细胞 stem cell

干燥剂 drier; drying agent; desiccating agent

干燥器 desiccator

干着急 be anxious but unable to do anything

干柴烈火 dry wood near a fierce fire—① a man and a woman burning with passion ② an explosive situation

干净利落 neat and tidy; neat; efficient

干鲜果品 composite term for dried and fresh fruit

干预政策 intervention policy

干粉灭火器 dry-chemical fire extinguisher

干旱与热浪 droughts and heat waves

干红葡萄酒 claret

干细胞移植 stem cell transplantation

干打雷，不下雨 all thunder but no rain—much noise but no action

甘 [gān]
I 〔形〕 sweet; honeyed; pleasant II 〔副〕 willingly; voluntarily; readily; of one's own accord

甘草 licorice root

甘汞 calomel; mercurous chloride

甘结 (in former times) a written pledge given to the government authorities

甘苦 ① sweetness and bitterness; joys and sorrows; weal and woe ② hardships and difficulties experienced in work

甘蓝 wild cabbage

甘霖 a good rain after a long drought; timely rainfall

甘露 ① sweet dew ② manna

甘美 sweet and refreshing

甘薯 sweet potato

甘甜 sweet

甘心 ① do sth willingly; be ready and willing ② be reconciled to; resign oneself to; be content with

甘休 be willing to give up

甘油 glycerine

甘于 be willing to; be ready to; be happy to

甘愿 do sth willingly; be ready and willing

甘蔗 sugarcane

甘蔗板 cane fibre board

甘拜下风 candidly acknowledge one's inferiority (in knowledge, ability, etc.); bow to sb's superiority

甘居中游 be resigned to mediocrity; be content to stay mediocre

甘苦与共 share the joys and sorrows with sb; cast one's lot with sb

甘守清贫 be ready to lead a poor but honest life

甘心情愿 willingly and gladly

甘言美语 honeyed words

甘油炸药 dynamite

甘愿效劳 be glad to offer one's services; be glad to do sth for sb

甘之如饴 enjoy sth bitter as if it were malt sugar—gladly endure hardship

甘薯黑斑病 sweet potato black rot

甘薯软腐病 sweet potato soft rot

杆 [gān]
〔名〕 pole; staff ➡ gǎn

杆子 pole

肝 [gān]
〔名〕 liver; hepar

肝癌 cancer of the liver

肝肠 liver and bowels

肝胆 ① open-heartedness; sincerity ② heroic spirit; courage

肝管 common hepatic duct

肝火 irascibility

肝气 ① diseases with such symptoms as costal pain, vomiting, diarrhoea, etc. ② irritability

肝素 heparin

肝炎 hepatitis

肝脏 liver

肝蛭 liver fluke

肝功能 liver function

肝泰乐 glucurolactone; glucurone

肝吸虫 liver fluke

肝硬变 cirrhosis (of the liver)

肝硬化 cirrhosis (of the liver)

肝肿大 hepatomegaly

肝肠寸断 be heartbroken; be deeply grieved

肝胆过人 far surpass others in daring

肝胆相照 (of friends) treat each other with all sincerity; be devoted to each other heart and soul

肝脑涂地 spill one's liver and brains on the ground—lay down one's life (in fighting for one's sovereign)

肝胆相照，荣辱与共 treat each other with all sincerity and share weal and woe; be open with each other and share good and ill alike

坩 [gān]
〔名〕 earthenware

坩埚 crucible

坩埚炉 crucible furnace

矸 [gān]

矸石 waste (rock)
矸子 common name for 矸石

汈 [gǎn]

汈水 swill; slops; hogwash

柑 [gān]

〈名〉 mandarin orange
柑橘 ①oranges and tangerines ②citrus
柑子 mandarin orange
柑橘酱 marmalade

竿 [gān]

〈名〉 pole; staff; rod
竿子 bamboo pole

酐 [gān]

〈名〉 anhydride

疳 [gān]

〈名〉 infantile malnutrition due to digestive disturbances or intestinal parasites

尴 [gān]

尴尬 ①(of the situation one is in) awkward; hard to deal with ②embarrassed

gǎn《ㄍㄢˇ》

杆 [gǎn]

Ⅰ〈名〉 shaft (*or* arm) of sth Ⅱ〈量〉 (for implements with a shaft): 一杆笔 a pen ➡gān
杆秤 steelyard
杆菌 bacillus

秆 [gǎn]

〈名〉 stalk; stem

赶 [gǎn]

Ⅰ〈动〉 ①run after; chase; pursue; catch up ②try to catch; make a dash for; rush for; hurry ③go (to a place) ④drive ⑤drive out; drive away; expel ⑥encounter; come across; run into; find oneself in (a situation) Ⅱ〈介〉 by; till; until
赶场 ①go to the village fair or market ②(of a performer) hurry from one performance to a second one in another place
赶超 catch up with and surpass
赶车 drive a cart
赶集 go to market; go to a fair
赶紧 hastily; without losing time
赶考 take the imperial examinations
赶快 at once; quickly
赶路 hurry on with one's journey
赶忙 hurriedly; hastily
赶巧 happen to; it so happened that
赶上 ① overtake; catch up with; keep pace with ②run into (a situation); be in time for
赶不及 there's not enough time (to do sth); it's too late (to do sth)
赶不上 ① be unable to catch up with; be unable to meet with or chance upon ② there's not enough time (to do sth); it's too late (to do sth)

赶得及 there is still time; be able to do sth in time; be able to make it
赶得上 ①be able to catch up ②there is still time; be able to do sth in time; be able to make it
赶浪头 follow the trend
赶时髦 follow the fashion; try to be in style
赶趟儿 be in time for
赶尽杀绝 kill all; wipe out the whole lot; spare none; be ruthless
赶前不赶后 it's better to hurry at the beginning than to rush at the last moment
赶鸭子上架 drive a duck onto a perch—try to make sb do sth entirely beyond him
赶超世界水平 catch up with and finally overtake the highest world level

敢 [gǎn]

Ⅰ〈形〉 brave; bold; courageous; daring Ⅱ〈动〉 ①dare ②be sure; be certain ③make bold; take the liberty; venture Ⅲ〈副〉 boldly
敢莫 can it be that; is it possible that
敢是 can it be that; is it possible
敢于 dare to; be bold in; have the courage to
敢死队 dare-to-die corps; suicide squad
敢想敢干 have the courage to think and act; dare to use one's head and dare to act
敢作敢当 have the courage to take the blame for what one does; be bold and decisive in action
敢作敢为 bold and decisive in action
敢怒而不敢言 be forced to keep one's resentment to oneself; choke with silent fury
敢闯敢试的劲头儿 the vigor of daring to blaze a new trial and make experiments

感 [gǎn]

Ⅰ〈动〉 ① feel; sense; be aware ② move; touch; affect ③ be thankful; be grateful; be obliged ④be affected (by cold); catch (cold) ⑤ sensitize Ⅱ〈名〉 sense; sensation; feeling; impression
感触 thoughts and feelings; feeling
感到 feel; sense
感动 move; touch
感恩 feel grateful; be thankful
感奋 be moved and inspired; be fired with enthusiasm
感官 sense (*or* sensory) organ
感光 sensitize
感荷 be thankful for; feel gratitude for
感化 help (a misguided or erring person) to change by persuasion, setting an example, etc.
感怀 ① recall with emotion ② reflections; thoughts; recollections
感激 feel grateful; be thankful; feel indebted
感觉 ①sense perception; sensation; feeling ② feel; perceive; become aware of

G

感慨 sigh with emotion
感抗 inductive reactance
感冒 ① common cold ② be interested in; be enthusiastic about
感念 remember with gratitude; recall with deep emotion
感情 ① emotion; feeling; sentiment ② affection; attachment; love
感染 ①infect ②influence; infect; affect
感人 touching; moving
感伤 sad; sorrowful; sentimental
感受 ①be affected by ②experience; feel
感叹 sigh with feeling
感悟 come to realize
感想 impressions; reflections; thoughts
感谢 thank; be grateful
感性 (sense) perception
感应 ①response; reaction; interaction ②irritability ③induction
感召 move and inspire; impel
感知 mental perception through sensory organs
感恩节 Thanksgiving Day
感光纸 sensitive paper
感觉论 sensualism
感情线 heart line
感染力 appeal; power to move the feelings
感染区 infected area
感受器 receptor
感叹词 interjection; exclamation
感叹号 exclamation mark (*or* point) (!)
感叹句 exclamatory sentence
感谢信 letter of thanks
感应场 induction field
感应灯 sensitive light; sensor light
感应率 inductivity
感应圈 induction coil; inductor
感应箱 induction-box
感恩不尽 be everlastingly grateful
感恩戴德 be deeply grateful; be overwhelmed with gratitude
感恩图报 be grateful to sb and seek ways to return his kindness
感光材料 photosensitive material
感光测定 sensitometry
感激不尽 be exceedingly thankful; be extremely grateful
感激涕零 shed grateful tears; be moved to tears of gratitude
感觉器官 sense (*or* sensory) organ
感觉神经 sensory nerve
感觉阈限 sense limen (*or* threshold)
感慨万端 all sorts of feelings well up in one's mind
感慨系之 sigh with deep feeling
感情投资 invest in human relations
感情用事 be swayed by one's emotions; act impetuously

感人肺腑 touch one to the depths of one's soul; move one deeply
感同身受 I shall appreciate it as a personal favour (often said when making a request on behalf of a friend)
感物伤怀 be deeply affected at seeing sth; touched to the heart
感性认识 perceptual knowledge
感性运动 nastic movement
感性知觉 sense impressions
感应电流 induced current
感觉艺术品 feelie
感应电动机 induction motor
感应电压调节器 induction-voltage regulator

橄 [gǎn]

橄榄 ①Chinese olive; the fruit of the canary tree ②olive
橄榄绿 olive green
橄榄球 rugby; American football
橄榄石 olivine (a mineral)
橄榄岩 peridotite
橄榄油 olive oil
橄榄枝 olive branch—a symbol of peace

擀 [gǎn]

劢 ①roll (dough, etc. with a rolling pin) ②polish; shine
擀面杖 rolling pin

gàn（ㄍㄢ）

干 [gàn]

Ⅰ 名 ①trunk; stem; main part ②(short for 干部) cadre Ⅱ 动 ①do; act; work ②undertake (a job, etc.); hold the post of; assume the office of Ⅲ 形 competent; capable; able; talented ➡ gān
干部 cadre; public functionary or servant; government or Party employee
干才 ① ability; capability ② a capable (*or* able) person
干掉 kill; get rid of; put sb out of the way
干活 work; work on a job
干家 capable person
干架 ①quarrel ②come to blows
干将 capable person; go-getter
干劲 drive; vigour; enthusiasm
干警 police officers; cadres and police
干练 capable and experienced
干流 trunk stream; mainstream
干路 primary road
干吗 ①why on earth; whatever for ②what to do
干渠 trunk canal; main canal
干事 a secretary (*or* clerical worker) in charge of sth
干线 main line; trunk line; artery

干休所 sanatorium for retired cadres

干部交流 exchanges of cadres; transferring cadres from one job to another as appropriate

干部考核 assessment of cadres

干部下放 arrange for cadres to go to work at grassroots units or participate in physical labour

干部学校 a school for cadres; cadre school

干劲冲天 show great enthusiasm; work with untiring energy

干群关系 relations between cadres and the masses; cadre-mass relations

干部离退休制 cadre retirement system

干部双向交流 two-way exchange among the cadres

干部要能上能下 see that our cadres are ready to go up and equally ready to come down; see that our cadres are ready to take a lower as well as a higher post

干部领导职务终身制 life-long tenure of leading posts

干部任期目标责任制 responsibility system with a specified tenure and goal for the cadres to observe

干部队伍革命化、年轻化、知识化、专业化 make the ranks of cadres more revolutionary, younger in average age, better educated and professionally more competent

旰 [gàn] 名 night; evening

绀 [gàn] 名 dark purple

绀青 dark purple; prune purple

gāng （ㄍㄤ）

冈 [gāng] 名 (low and flat) ridge (of a hill)

扛 [gāng] 动 ① lift with both hands ②（of two or more people）carry sth together ➡ káng

刚 [gāng] I 形 firm; strong; hard; staunch Ⅱ 副 ① just; exactly; precisely ② barely; just; no more than ③ just; only a short while ago Ⅲ 连 hardly ... when... ; no sooner than; just as

刚才 a moment ago; just now

刚刚 ① just; only; exactly ② a moment ago; just now

刚好 ① just; exactly ② by chance; by coincidence

刚架 rigid frame

刚健 vigorous; energetic; robust

刚劲 bold; vigorous; sturdy

刚烈 fiery and forthright; upright and unyielding

刚强 firm; staunch; unyielding

刚体 rigid body

刚性 rigidity; inflexible

刚毅 resolute and steadfast

刚玉 corundum（a mineral）

刚正 upright; honourable; principled

刚直 upright and outspoken

刚…就 as soon as; no sooner than; immediately

刚愎自用 self-willed; headstrong; opinionated

刚劲有力 （the calligraphy）be powerful and vigorous

刚柔相济 couple hardness with softness（in dealing with people）; temper toughness with gentleness

刚正不阿 upright and above flattery

杠 [gāng] 名 ① bridge ② flagpole; flagstaff

肛 [gāng] 名 anus

肛裂 anal fissure

肛瘘 anal fistula

肛门 anus

纲 [gāng] 名 ① headrope of a fishing net ② key link; guiding principle; outline; programme ③ class

纲纪 law and order; discipline

纲领 programme; guiding principle

纲目 detailed outline（of a subject）; outline; compendium

纲要 ① outline; sketch ② essentials; compendium

纲举目张 once the headrope of a fishing net is pulled up, all its meshes open—once the key link is grasped, everything falls into place

纲领性文件 programmatic document; principal document

钢 [gāng] 名 steel ➡ gàng

钢板 ① steel plate; plate ② spring（of a motorcar, etc.）③ stencil steel board

钢笔 pen; fountain pen

钢材 steel products; steels; rolled steel

钢尺 steel rule

钢锤 steel hammer

钢锭 steel ingot

钢管 steel tube（or pipe）

钢轨 rails（for trains, etc.）; tracks

钢号 steel grade

钢花 spray（or sparks）of molten steel

钢筋 reinforcing bar

钢精 aluminium

钢锯 hacksaw

钢盔 （steel）helmet

钢坯 billet

钢钎 drill rod; drill steel

钢琴 piano

钢水 molten steel
钢丝 (steel) wire
钢铁 ①iron and steel; steel ②strong; firm; staunch
钢印 ①steel seal; embossing seal ②embossed stamp
钢珠 steel ball (in a ball bearing); ball bearing; ball
钢笔画 pen-and-ink drawing
钢笔水 ink
钢结构 steel structure
钢片琴 celesta
钢丝床 spring bed
钢丝锯 fret saw
钢丝钳 combination pliers; cutting pliers
钢丝绳 steel cable; wire rope
钢丝网 hardware cloth; steel wire gauze
钢骨水泥 reinforced concrete
钢化玻璃 toughened glass
钢筋铁骨 body strong as iron; muscles of steel
钢铁长城 powerful bulwark; bastion of iron
钢轨探伤仪 rail flaw detector
钢筋混凝土 reinforced concrete
钢丝录音机 wire recorder

缸 [gāng]
〈名〉①vat; jar; bowl; crock ②earthenware with crude glaze ③sth shaped like a jar or vat
缸管 earthen pipe
缸盆 glazed earthen basin
缸瓦 a compound of sand, clay, etc. for making earthenware
缸砖 clinker (tile); quarry tile
缸子 mug; bowl

罡 [gāng]
罡风 ① Taoism winds in the empyrean ② strong winds

gǎng（ㄍㄤˇ）

岗 〈名〉①hillock; mound ②ridge; welt; wale ③sentry; post
岗警 policeman on point duty
岗楼 watchtower
岗哨 ①lookout post ②sentry; sentinel
岗亭 sentry box; police box
岗位 post; station
岗子 ①hillock; mound ②ridge; wale; welt
岗峦起伏 undulating hills
岗位工资 basic post wage (*or* pay)
岗位津贴 subsidy appropriate to a particular job; extra compensation for doing certain job; special allowance for special posts
岗位培训 on-the-job training; professional skill training
岗位责任 post responsibility
岗位责任制 system of personal responsibility

(for each section of a production line, etc.)
岗位定编定员 fix the number of posts and employees

港 [gǎng]
〈名〉①port; harbour ②airport ③tributary of a river ④(short for 香港) Hong Kong; HK ⑤ Hong Kong style
港币 Hong Kong dollar
港汊 branching stream
港督 governor of Hong Kong
港府 Hong Kong government
港客 visitors and guests from Hong Kong region
港口 port; harbour
港区 Hong Kong Special Administrative Region (HKSAR)
港人 Hong Kong residents
港商 Hong Kong businessman
港式 Hong Kong style
港台 Hong Kong and Taiwan
港湾 harbour
港域 harbour region
港章 port's regulation
港务费 harbour dues
港务局 port office
港澳同胞 compatriots from (*or* in) Hong Kong and Macao
港口工程 port engineering
港口建设 port construction
港人治港 Hong Kong people governing Hong Kong
港台文学 literature of Hong Kong and Taiwan
港务监督 harbour superintendency administration
港口吞吐量 port capacity; volume handled at coastal ports
港至港提单 port to port bill of landing
港澳出入境签证 visa for exit (*or* entry) from (*or* into) Hong Kong and Macao
港澳居留权问题 problems of resident rights in Hong Kong and Macao

gàng（ㄍㄤˋ）

杠 [gàng]
Ⅰ〈名〉① thick stick or club ② bar ③ rod-shaped spare part (of a machine) ④ stout poles used to carry a coffin ⑤thick line drawn beside or under words as a mark ⑥standard; criterion Ⅱ〈动〉cross out; delete ➡ gāng
杠棒 stout carrying pole
杠杆 lever
杠铃 barbell
杠销 lever pin
杠子 ①thick stick; stout carrying pole ②thick line (drawn beside or under words in reading, correcting papers, etc.)

钢 [gàng]

动 ① sharpen; grind; whet; strop ② reinforce the edge (of a knife, etc.) by adding steel and retempering ➡gāng

钢菜刀 sharpen a kitchen knife

钢刀布 (razor) strop

钢剪刀 grind scissors

钢镰刀 whet a sickle

钢剃刀 strop a razor

gāo (《幺)

皋 [gāo]

名 highland on the riverside

高 [gāo]

Ⅰ 形 ①tall; high ②advanced; superior ③of a high or higher rank ④loud ⑤your; his; their

Ⅱ 名 ①height ②altitude

高矮 height

高昂 ①hold high (one's head, etc.) ②high; elated; exalted ③ dear; expensive; exorbitant

高傲 ① supercilious; arrogant; haughty ② proud; self-respecting; high-minded

高产 high yield; high production

高唱 ① sing loudly; sing with spirit ② talk glibly about; call out loudly for

高超 superb; excellent

高潮 ①high tide; high water ②upsurge; high tide ③(of fiction, drama and films) climax

高大 ①tall and big; tall ②lofty

高档 high (*or* top) grade; superior quality

高等 higher

高低 ①height ②relative superiority or inferiority ③sense of propriety; discretion

高地 ①highland; upland; elevation ②height

高调 ① lofty tone; high-sounding words ② high tone

高度 ①altitude; height ②a high degree

高端 high-end

高发 frequent

高峰 peak; summit; height

高干 high-ranking official; senior cadres

高工 senior engineer

高贵 ①morally elevated; magnanimous; noble ②highly privileged; elitist

高级 ① senior; high-ranking; high-level; high ②high-grade; high-quality; advanced

高价 high price

高见 your brilliant idea; your opinion

高洁 noble and unsullied

高就 move up to a higher position (usu. in another place)

高举 hold high; hold aloft

高踞 stand above; set oneself above; lord it over

高峻 high and steep

高亢 ① loud and sonorous; resounding ② (of terrain) high ③ supercilious; arrogant; haughty

高考 college entrance examination

高空 high altitude; upper air

高栏 high hurdles

高粱 *kaoliang*; Chinese sorghum

高龄 advanced age (usu. over 60); venerable age

高炉 blast furnace

高论 enlightening remarks; brilliant views

高迈 advanced in years

高妙 ingenious; masterly

高明 ①brilliant; wise ②a wise person

高难 (of technology) high caliber and high degree of difficulty

高能 high energy

高攀 make friends or claim ties of kinship with someone of a higher social position

高票 landslide

高频 high frequency

高聘 be appointed to a high position; promote sb when recruiting

高强 excelling in

高跷 stilts

高球 high ball; lob

高热 high fever

高人 ① a man of noble character; a man of great sanctity ②a man of superior attainments; past master; master-hand

高僧 eminent monk

高尚 ①noble; lofty ②meaningful; not in poor taste ③elegant and fashionable

高烧 high fever

高深 advanced; profound; recondite

高升 be promoted

高声 ①aloud ②bark ③in a loud voice

高手 past master; master-hand; ace

高寿 ① longevity; long life ② your venerable age

高耸 (stand) tall and erect; towering

高速 high speed

高汤 ①soup-stock ②thin soup

高堂 ①big hall; main hall ②one's parents

高危 high and dangerous

高温 high temperature

高校 institutions of higher learning; institutions of higher education; colleges and universities

高薪 high salary; high pay

高兴 ①glad; happy; cheerful ②be willing to; be happy to

高压 ① high pressure ② high tension; high voltage ③maximum pressure ④highhanded (persecution)

高雅 refined; elegant

高原 plateau; highland; tableland

高涨 rise; upsurge; run high

G

高知　higher intellectual
高职　vocational higher education institution
高专　technical college
高足　your brilliant disciple；your pupil
高祖　(paternal) great-great-grandfather
高保真　high fidelity；hi-fi
高标号　high grade
高才生　a brilliant (or outstanding) student
高层云　altostratus
高蛋白　high protein
高低杠　uneven (parallel) bars
高低角　angle of site
高度表　altimeter
高度差　altitude difference
高分子　high polymer；macromolecule
高个儿　a tall person
高跟鞋　high-heeled shoes
高工资　higher income
高官会　Senior Officials Meeting (SOM)
高积云　altocumulus
高技术　high-technology；high-tech；high tech-nology；sophisticated technology
高架路　elevated road；overhead road
高架桥　viaduct；elevated highway
高精度　high accuracy；high precision；pinpoint accuracy
高精尖　high-grade, precision and advanced (industrial products)；high-class, refined, and top most
高聚物　high polymer
高科技　high technology；high-level science and technology
高空病　altitude sickness
高丽参　Korean ginseng
高利贷　usury；usurious loan
高粱酒　spirit distilled from sorghum
高粱米　husked *kaoliang*
高粱饴　sweets (or candy) made of sorghum syrup；sorghum candy
高岭石　kaolinite
高岭土　kaolin
高氯酸　perchloric acid
高帽子　①tall paper hat (worn as a sign of hu-miliation)；dunce's cap ②flattery
高品位　high-grade
高气压　high atmospheric (or barometric) pressure
高强度　high strength
高山病　high altitude sickness；mountain sick-ness
高射炮　antiaircraft gun (or artillery)
高水平　advanced level
高速挡　top gear；high gear
高速钢　high-speed steel；rapid steel
高碳钢　high-carbon steel
高纬度　high latitudes
高消费　high level of consumption；excessive consumption

高血压　hypertension；high blood pressure
高压泵　high-pressure pump
高压锅　pressure cooker
高压脊　ridge of high pressure；pressure ridge
高压线　high-tension line (or wire)
高眼鲽　plaice
高招儿　clever move；brilliant idea
高指标　high targets in production
高质量　superior (or top) quality
高姿态　high profile；lofty stance；magnani-mous attitude
高祖母　(paternal) great-great-grandmother
高不可攀　too high to reach；unattainable
高层管理　top management
高层互访　high-profile visit
高层建筑　high-rise housing
高层往来　high-level exchanges
高层住宅　high-rise apartment building
高产稳产　high and stable yield；stable high yield
高产作物　high-yield crop；highly productive crop
高超音速　hypersonic speed
高档商品　expensive commodities, high-grade products
高等教育　higher education
高等数学　higher mathematics
高等学校　institutions of higher learning；insti-tutions of higher education；colleges and u-niversities
高低贵贱　lowliness and nobleness
高度评价　speak highly of sb；pay high tribute to；be loud in praise of
高度自治　high degree of autonomy
高额利润　huge profit
高尔夫球　①golf ②golf ball
高分辨率　high resolution
高分低能　high scores and low ability
高风亮节　noble character and sterling integri-ty
高峰会议　summit meeting
高峰时间　peak-hour；rush hour
高高在上　set oneself high above the masses；be far removed from the masses and real-ity；remote from masses
高歌猛进　stride forward singing songs of tri-umph；advance triumphantly
高歌一曲　sing a song loudly；chant a melody
高官厚禄　high position and handsome salary；high position with high pay
高级干部　senior cadre
高级官员　high-up
高级会晤　summit talk
高级经理　senior manager
高级小学　higher primary school
高级语言　high-level language

高级职称 senior academic or professional rank
高级中学 senior middle school
高价出售 sell sth at a high price
高价购买 give a long price for; take over bid (TOB); buy over at a high price
高价收购 offer high price for sth
高价招聘 offer an attractive remuneration to invite applications for a job
高架铁道 overhead railway; elevated railway
高架铁路 aerial railway; elevated railroad
高空跳水 high-diving
高空作业 work high above the ground
高楼大厦 high buildings and large mansions; high-rise
高锰酸钾 potassium permanganate
高难动作 difficult movements that require superior skills
高难技巧 a superior and difficult technique
高能燃料 high-energy fuel
高朋满座 a great gathering of distinguished guests
高频电波 high-frequency electric wave
高清晰度 high definition
高人一等 be a cut above other people
高入云霄 tower high above the level of the clouds; reach towards the sky
高山大川 high mountains and great rivers
高山反应 altitude reaction
高山滑雪 alpine skiing
高山流水 high mountains and flowing waters—① sublime music ② understanding friends
高山植物 alpine plant
高深莫测 unfathomable; enigmatic
高视阔步 carry oneself proudly; strut; swagger; prance
高速公路 freeway; motorway; expressway; autostrada; autoput; autobahn; autoroute; high-speed highway (*or* road); fast highway; superhighway
高速火车 bullet train
高速扫描 high-speed sweep; high-velocity scanning
高速摄影 high-speed photography
高抬贵手 be magnanimous; be generous; not be too hard on sb
高谈阔论 indulge in loud and empty talk; talk volubly or bombastically
高温切削 high-temperature machining
高温作业 high-temperature operation
高屋建瓴 pour water off a steep roof—sweep down irresistibly from a commanding height; operate from a strategically advantageous position
高息集资 raise funds by offering high interest
高下难分 very hard to tell which is better
高效节能 energy-efficient

高新技术 advanced high technology; hi-tech; high and new technology
高薪阶层 high-salary stratum
高压电缆 high-tension cable
高压手段 high-handed measures
高压水龙 water cannon
高雅艺术 art of refined taste and style
高音喇叭 tweeter
高瞻远瞩 stand high and see far; take a broad and long view; show great foresight
高枕无忧 shake up the pillow and have a good sleep; sit back and relax
高档消费品 high-grade consumer goods
高级商务师 Certified Business Executive
高级消费品 luxury goods
高级斜纹呢 himalaya
高级研究员 senior research fellow
高技术产品 high-tech products
高技术产业 high-tech industry
高技术领域 fields of high technology
高技术战争 high-tech warfare
高加索山脉 the Caucasus Mountains
高科技板块 high-tech sector
高科技产品 high-tech products
高科技企业 high-tech enterprises
高空气象学 aerology
高能物理学 high-energy physics
高抛式发球 high toss service
高频放大器 high-frequency potency amplifier; radio-frequency amplifier
高射机关枪 antiaircraft machine gun
高速存储器 high-speed memory
高速打印机 high-speed printer (HSP)
高压灭菌器 autoclave
高不成，低不就 ①be unfit for a higher post but unwilling to take a lower one ②be unable to achieve one's heart's desire but unwilling to accept less
高层决策早餐 power breakfast
高档建筑项目 the construction of more expensive housing projects
高度通货膨胀 hyperinflation
高分子化合物 macromolecular compound; high-molecular compound
高分子聚合物 high polymer
高级人民法院 higher people's court
高级神经活动 higher nervous activity
高级特技飞行 advanced aerobatics
高级知识分子 higher intellectual
高价位魅力股 high flying glamour stock
高清晰度电视 high definition television (HDTV)
高效低毒农药 highly effective and low-toxic pesticides
高性能战斗机 high performance fighter
高增长、低通胀 high economic growth rate with low inflation

高保真度接收机 high fidelity receiver

高档耐用消费品 high-priced consumer durables

高技术局部战争 hi-tech regional (*or* local) war

高速电影摄影机 high-speed motion picture camera

高速缓冲存储器 cache; cache memory

高校后勤社会化 system of commercialized university logistics

高新技术产业化 use of new and high technologies in all types of industrial production

高产优质高效农业 agriculture featuring high yields, fine quality and high efficiency; high-yield, high-quality and high-efficiency agriculture; highly efficient farming to provide greater and better yields

高等教育自学考试 higher education examinations for self-study students

高等学校招生考试 college entrance examination

高科技开发试验区 high-tech industrial development and experimental zone

高清晰度兼容数码 high definition compatible digital

高新技术工业开发区 New and High-Tech Industry Development Zone

高投入、低产出、高消耗、低效益 high input, low output; and high cost, low efficiency

高附加值、优质和高新技术产品 high-value-added, high-quality and new and high-tech products

羔 [gāo]
名 lamb; kid; fawn

羔皮 lambskin; kidskin; kid

羔羊 lamb—an innocent and helpless person or a scapegoat

羔子 lamb; kid; fawn

睾 [gāo]

睾丸 testis; testicle

睾丸炎 orchitis

膏 [gāo]
I 名 ①fat; grease; oil ②paste; cream; ointment; plaster II 形 fertile ➡ gào

膏剂 medicinal extract; electuary

膏粱 fat meat and fine grain; rich food

膏壤 fertile land

膏药 medicated plaster; plaster

膏腴 fertile

膏粱子弟 good-for-nothing sons of the idle rich

篙 [gāo]
名 punt-pole

糕 [gāo]
名 cake; pasty; pudding

糕点 cake; pastry

糕干 sweetened rice flour (sometimes fed to infants as a substitute for powdered milk)

糕点叉 pastry fork

gǎo（《ㄠ）

杲 [gǎo]
形 bright

搞 [gǎo]
动 ①do; go in for; carry on; be engaged in ②make; produce; work out ③make sb suffer; fix sb ④set up; start; organize ⑤get; get hold of; secure; wangle ⑥(followed by a complement) produce a certain effect or result; cause to become

搞错 mistake

搞定 work it

搞鬼 play tricks; be up to some mischief

搞好 make a good job of; do well

搞活 vitalize; enliven

搞垮 collapse; break down; get down; do in

搞乱 confuse; muddle; mess up

搞笑 amuse

搞对象 go steady

搞试点 make experiments at selected points; launch a pilot project; conduct an experiment

搞活经济 invigorate the economy; enliven the economy

搞活流通 simulate commodity circulation

搞活企业 enliven enterprises; invigorate enterprises

搞特殊化 use ones position to pursue personal perquisites and privileges

搞通思想 straighten out one's ideas (*or* thinking)

搞山头主义 form small factions within the Party or an organization

搞活商品流通 invigoration of commodity circulation

缟 [gǎo]
I 名 thin white silk used in ancient China II 形 white

缟素 white mourning apparel

镐 [gǎo]
名 pick; pickaxe

镐头 pick; pickaxe

稿 [gǎo]
名 ①stalk of cereal crops; straw ②draft; sketch; manuscript

稿本 manuscript (of a book, etc.)

稿费 payment for an article or book published; contribution fee; author's remuneration

稿件 manuscript; contribution

稿约 notice to contributors (to a magazine, etc.)

稿纸 standardized writing paper with squares or lines

稿子 ①draft；sketch ②manuscript；contribution ③idea；plan

gào（《ㄠ）

告 [gào]
囫 ①tell；inform；report；notify ②sue；bring an action or a case against；accuse ③ask for；request；solicit ④declare；announce ⑤announce or declare the completion of sth

告白 a public notice or announcement
告别 ①leave；part from ②bid farewell to；say good-bye to
告病 ask for sick leave
告成 (of a major task or project) be completed (or accomplished)
告吹 fizzle out；fail
告辞 take leave (of one's host)
告贷 ask for a loan
告发 report (an offender)；inform against；lodge an accusation against
告急 ①be in a state of emergency ②report an emergency；ask for emergency help
告假 ask for leave
告捷 ①win victory (in war or games) ②report a victory
告诫 warn；admonish；exhort
告警 report an emergency；give (or sound)an alarm
告老 retire on account of age
告密 inform against sb
告破 announce that sth has been unearthed，or ferreted out
告罄 run out；be exhausted
告缺 be short of；lack
告饶 beg for mercy；ask pardon
告示 ①notify；announce ②official notice；bulletin；placard ③slogan；poster
告诉 tell；let know
告退 ask to withdraw from a meeting；resign from office
告知 inform；notify
告终 come to an end；end up
告状 ①go to law against sb；bring a lawsuit against sb ②lodge a complaint against sb with his superior
告别词 farewell speech；valediction
告御状 accuse sb before the emperor；complain or report to the higher authorities (over one's immediate bosses，etc.)
告别宴会 farewell banquet
告别仪式 farewell ceremony
告老还乡 (of a government official) retire and return to one's native place
告一段落 come to end of a stage；be brought to temporary close
告枕头状 complain (about sb or sth) to one's

spouse when in bed；pillow-talk；give a curtain lecture

诰 [gào]
囵 ①order；enjoin ②written admonition ③imperial mandate

诰封 the conferment of honorary titles by imperial mandate
诰命 ①imperial mandate ②a titled lady

膏 [gào]
囫 ①lubricate；grease；oil ②dip a brush in ink and smooth it on an inkstone before writing ➡ gāo

膏笔 moisten and smooth a brush
膏机器 lubricate the axle (or conveyer) of the machine

gē（《ㄜ）

戈 [gē]
囵 ancient Chinese weapon with a long shaft and a horizontal blade；dagger-axe

戈壁 ①Gobi ②the Gobi Desert

圪 [gē]

圪垯 ①swelling on the skin；pimple；lump ②lump；knot ③a knot in one's heart；hang-up ④mound；knoll

疙 [gē]

疙瘩 ①a swelling on the skin；pimple；lump ②lump；knot ③a knot in one's heart；hang-up
疙疙瘩瘩 rough；knotty；bumpy

咯 [gē]
➡ kǎ；lo；luò

咯噔 click
咯咯 ①the sound made by a hen；cluck；chuckle；cackle ②the sound of laughing；chuckle；titter
咯吱 creak；groan

哥 [gē]
囵 ①elder brother ②form of address for the elder male relative of one's generation ③friendly way of addressing males of approximately one's age

哥哥 (elder) brother
哥儿们 ①brothers ②buddies；pals
哥特式 Gothic
哥特体 gothic (type)
哥德巴赫猜想 Goldbach's conjecture

胳 [gē]

胳臂 arm
胳膊 arm
胳膊腕子 wrist
胳膊肘儿 elbow
胳膊扭不过大腿 the arm is no match for the thigh—the weaker can't contend with the stronger
胳膊肘儿往外拐 one's elbow turns to the

wrong side; side with outsiders instead of one's own people

鸽 [gē]
名 pigeon; dove
鸽棚 pigeon shed or loft; dovecote
鸽哨 a whistle tied to a pigeon
鸽子 pigeon; dove

搁 [gē]
动 ① put; place; lay ② add; put in ③ put aside; leave over; shelve ➡ gé
搁板 shelf
搁笔 lay down the pen or brush; stop writing or painting
搁浅 ① run aground; be stranded ② reach a deadlock
搁置 shelf; shelter; table; hang up; go by the wayside; lay aside; pigeonhole
搁置争议,共同开发 Shelve disputes and go in for joint development. *or* Put aside disputes and engage in joint exploitation.

割 [gē]
动 ①cut; sever; mow ②divide; give up
割爱 give up what one treasures; part with some cherished possession
割除 cut off; remove; excise
割掉 cut off; get rid of
割断 sever; cut off
割胶 tap rubber
割炬 cutting torch
割据 set up a separatist regime by force of arms
割开 cut open; rip open
割礼 circumcision
割裂 cut apart; separate; isolate
割破 cut; gash; slash
割让 cede
割肉 (of stock market dealing) sell sth at a price lower than its original price
割舍 give up; part with
割线 secant
割草机 mower
割捆机 self-binder; binder
割晒机 windrower
割让领土 cession of territory

歌 [gē]
Ⅰ 名 song Ⅱ 动 sing; chant
歌本 songbook
歌唱 ①sing ②praise (through songs, poems, etc.)
歌词 words of a song
歌带 cassette tape of recorded songs
歌喉 (singer's) voice; singing voice
歌后 most accomplished female singer; singing queen
歌剧 opera
歌诀 formulas or directions put into rhyme
歌迷 song fan or devotee

歌女 singsong girl
歌谱 music score of a song; music of a song
歌曲 song
歌声 sound of singing; singing
歌手 singer; vocalist
歌颂 sing the praises of; extol; eulogize
歌坛 circles of vocal music; vocal music circles; the circle of singers
歌厅 karaoke hall
歌舞 song and dance
歌星 a singing star
歌谣 ballad; folk song; nursery rhyme
歌咏 singing
歌片儿 song sheet
歌舞伎 kabuki (a popular Japanese dramatic form)
歌舞剧 song and dance drama
歌舞片 musical
歌舞团 song and dance ensemble (*or* troupe)
歌功颂德 eulogize sb's virtues and achievements; sing the praises of sb
歌台舞榭 places of amusement; halls for the performance of songs and dances
歌舞升平 sing and dance to extol the good times—put on a show of peace and prosperity

gé（ㄍㄜˊ）

革 [gé]
Ⅰ 名 leather; hide Ⅱ 动 ① change; alter; transform ② remove from office; expel; get rid of ➡ jí
革除 ①abolish; get rid of; eliminate ②expel; dismiss; remove sb from office
革履 leather shoes
革命 ①cause great social change; rise in revolt; take part in revolution ②revolution
革新 innovate; improve
革职 discharge; remove sb from office; dismiss sb from his post; cashier
革命化 revolutionize; do things in a revolutionary way
革命家 revolutionary; revolutionist
革命性 revolutionary character (*or* quality, spirit)
革制品 leather goods
革故鼎新 discard the old and introduce the new
革命老区 old revolutionary base
革命晚节 lofty ethics of an revolutionary
革职为民 reduce an official to the ranks of the people
革命回忆录 reminiscences of earlier revolutionary times
革命接班人 revolutionary successors
革命浪漫主义 revolutionary romanticism

革命人道主义 revolutionary humanitarianism
革命现实主义 revolutionary realism
革命英雄主义 revolutionary heroism
革命事业接班人 successors in the revolutionary cause
革命化、现代化、正规化的人民军队 revolutionary, modernized and standardized (*or* regularized) people's army

阁 [gé]

名 ① pavilion (usu. two-storeyed) ② woman's chamber; boudoir ③ cabinet ④ rack; shelf

阁僚 member of a cabinet
阁楼 attic; loft; garret
阁下 Your (*or* His, Her) Excellency
阁员 member of a cabinet

格 [gé]

I 名 ① square (formed by crossed lines); check ② standard; rule; pattern; style ③ character; manner; style ④ case II 劢 ① resist; hinder; obstruct; impede ② probe; delve into; study thoroughly ③ fight; hit ➡ gē

格调 ① (literary or artistic) style ② one's style of work as well as one's moral quality
格斗 grapple; wrestle; fistfight
格局 pattern; setup; structure
格律 rules and forms of classical poetic composition
格式 form; pattern
格外 ① especially; particularly; all the more ② additionally
格物 study physical nature; study the world
格言 maxim; motto; aphorism
格子 squares formed by crossed lines; check; chequer
格陵兰 Greenland
格式化 format
格子布 checked fabric; check
格子窗 lattice window
格格不入 incompatible with; out of tune with; out of one's element; like a square peg in a round hole
格莱梅奖 Grammy; Grammys (*or* Grammies)
格杀勿论 kill on the spot with the authority of the law
格物致知 to investigate things is to attain knowledge
格于成例 be barred by accepted practice
格子花呢 tartan
格式化磁盘 format a diskette; a formatted diskette
格林尼治平均时 Greenwich Mean Time (GMT)

葛 [gé]

名 ① ko-hemp; kudzu ② poplin

葛布 ko-hemp cloth
葛根 the root of kudzu vine

葛麻 ko-hemp; kudzu

搁 [gé]

劢 bear; stand; sustain; endure ➡ gē

蛤 [gé]

① clam ② gecko ➡ há

蛤蚧 gecko
蛤蜊 clam

颌 [gé]

名 mouth ➡ hé

隔 [gé]

I 劢 ① separate; partition; divide; stand or lie between ② be at a distance from; space II 形 following; next-door

隔壁 next-door
隔断 ① cut off; separate; obstruct ② partition (wall, board, etc.)
隔阂 ① estrangement; misunderstanding ② barrier
隔绝 cut off; separate; obstruct
隔离 keep apart; isolate; segregate
隔膜 ① lack of mutual understanding ② be unfamiliar with
隔片 spacer
隔墙 partition (wall)
隔热 insulate against heat
隔扇 partition board
隔声 insulate against sound
隔夜 of the previous night
隔音 give sound insulation
隔离带 dividing strip, specifically the lines separating fast and slow lanes on a road
隔离栅 isolated gate
隔音室 soundproof room
隔岸观火 watch a fire from the other side of the river—look on at sb's trouble with indifference
隔代抚养 raise removedly
隔江相望 face each other across the river
隔离病房 isolation ward
隔离审查 (during political movements) isolate and interrogate
隔离医院 isolation hospital
隔墙有耳 walls have ears; beware of eavesdroppers
隔靴搔痒 scratch an itch from outside one's boot—fail to get to the root of the matter; fail to strike home; take totally ineffective measures
隔音符号 syllable-dividing mark
隔行如隔山 different trades are separated as by mountains (i.e. the outsider knows no more of the secrets of the craft than he knows of another country)

塥 [gé]

名 sandy field; sandlot

嗝 [gé]

名 ① belch ② hiccup; hiccough

膈 [gé]
名 diaphragm ➡gè

骼 [gé]

◇骨骼 skeleton

gě（《ㄜ）

个 [gě]
➡gè
◇自个儿 oneself；by oneself

合 [gě]
Ⅰ 量 unit of dry measure for grain（＝1 decilitre）Ⅱ 名 measuring container for 1 decilitre of grain ➡hé

各 [gě]
形 unusual；peculiar ➡gè

舸 [gě]
动 approve；regard as worthy

舸 [gě]
名 barge

gè（《ㄜ）

个 [gè]
Ⅰ 量 ①（usually used before a noun having no particular classifier）：第四个年头 fourth year ②（used before an approximate figure）：每周都要来个一两趟 come once or twice every week ③（used after a verb which is followed by an object）：吃了个大亏 suffer a great loss/上了个大当 be grievously deceived（or taken in）④（used between a verb and a complement）：把敌人打得个落花流水 put the enemy to rout Ⅱ 形 individual Ⅲ 助 ①used as suffix to the classifer 些 ②（used after 昨儿，今儿，明儿，etc.）：昨儿个你去哪儿了？ Where did you go yesterday? ➡gě

个案 （individual or special）case
个儿 size；height
个把 one or two；a couple of
个别 ①individual；specific ②very few；one or two
个唱 solo concert
个个 each and every one；all
个股 individual share；share
个例 individual case；exceptional case
个人 ①individual（person）②I
个体 individual
个险 personal insurance
个性 individual character；individuality；personality
个展 individual exhibition
个中 therein
个子 height；stature；build
个体户 individual entrepreneur；self-employed individual or household；privately owned small enterprise

个头儿 size；height
个中人 a person in the know
个别差异 individual differences
个别辅导 individual coaching
个别情况 isolated cases
个人崇拜 deify and worship an individual（national leader，etc.）；individual superstition；personality cult
个人储蓄 personal savings
个人存款 individual deposits
个人电脑 PC（personal computer）
个人冠军 individual championship
个人会员 individual member（as contrasted with）
个人技术 personal skill
个人迷信 cult of the individual；personality cult
个人通信 personal communication
个人投资 individual investment
个人项目 individual events
个人信用 personal credit
个人野心 personal ambition
个人主义 individualism
个人专断 arbitrary decision-making by one person
个体经济 individual economy；individual economic activity；self-employed business
个体经营 individually-owned business
个体企业 private enterprise；private firm；individual enterprise
个体商贩 individual traders and peddlers；businessman
个体商业 trade run by individuals
个中原因 the whys and wherefores of...
个别教学法 individualized introduction
个别许可证 individual licence
个人财产税 personal property tax
个人说了算 one person alone have the final say
个人所得税 income tax from individuals（or personal）income tax
个体工商户 self-employed businessmen individuals；individual industrial and commercial households
个体劳动者 self-employed labourer；independent businessmen；person who works on his own
个体生产者 individual producer
个体所有制 individual（or private）ownership
个性转变期 identity crisis
个人分工负责 division of work marked with individual responsibility
个人数字助理 personal digital assistant（PDA）
个人信用制度 credit rating system
个人英雄主义 individualistic heroism
个人住房贷款 loans extended to the individual housing purchasers

个人自由行动 individuals acting their own way
个体工商业者 individual industrialists and businessmen
个体劳动协会 self-employed laborer's association
个人收入调节税 individual income regulatory tax
个人收入申报制度 system of the declaration of personal incomes for tax payment
个人收入应税申报制度 system of the declaration of individual incomes for tax payment

各 Ⅰ〔代〕all;every;each:各兵种 all arms of the services Ⅱ〔形〕various;different ➡gě
各半 half and half;fifty-fifty
各别 ①distinct;different ②out of the ordinary;peculiar ③odd;eccentric;funny
各个 ①each;every;various ②one by one
各级 all (*or* different) levels
各界 all walks of life;all circles
各色 of all kinds;of every description;assorted
各位 ①everybody (a term of address) ②every
各自 each;respective
各就位 (word of command) on your marks
各奔前程 each pursues his own course;each goes his own way
各不相让 neither is willing to give ground;each is trying to outdo the other
各不相同 differ from each other;have nothing in common with each other
各持己见 each sticks to his own view
各得其所 each is in his proper place;each is properly provided for;each has a role to play
各行各业 all trades and professions;all walks of life
各怀鬼胎 each with his or her own axe to grind
各级政府 government at all levels
各界群众 people of all circles;people from all walks of life;a cross section of people
各尽所能 let each person do his best;from each according to his ability;each doing his best
各取所需 each takes what he needs
各抒己见 each airs his own views
各司其职 each does his or her duty;each performs his or her own functions
各显神通 each trying for all one is worth;each showing his special skill
各向同性 isotropy
各向异性 anisotropy
各行其是 each does what he thinks is right;each goes his own way

各有千秋 Each has something to recommend him;each has his strong points.
各有所长 each has his own strong points
各有所好 each has his likes and dislikes;each follows his own bent
各执一词 each sticks to his own version or argument
各自为政 each does things in his own way;everyone goes his own way;be lack of coordination
各族人民 people of all nationalities
各打五十大板 punish the wronged and the wrong-doer alike;punish the guilty and the innocent alike;blame both sides without discrimination
各人自扫门前雪 each one sweeps the snow from his own doorstep—each one minds his own business
各尽所能,按劳分配 from each according to his ability,to each according to his work—the socialist principle of distribution
各尽所能,按需分配 from each according to his ability,to each according to his needs—the communist principle of distribution
各兵种联合作战演习 joint training

硌 〔动〕 (of sth hard or bulging) press or rub against one ➡luò
硌牙 hurt one's teeth

铬 〔名〕chromium (Cr)
铬钢 chromium steel;chrome steel
铬鞣 chrome tanning
铬铁 ferrochrome
铬镍钢 chrome-nickel steel
铬镍线 chrome-nickel wire
铬铁矿 chromite

膈 ➡gé
膈膜 diaphragm

gěi（《ㄟ）

给 Ⅰ〔动〕①give;present;grant ②let;allow (a) (*used to ask the other party to do sth*) (b) (*used to indicate permission*) (c) (*used to show what has happened*) Ⅱ〔介〕①to;with ②for;for the benefit of ③(*used to introduce the recipient of an action,same as* 同) Ⅲ〔助〕(*used directly before the verb of a passive sentence,etc. to show emphasis*) ➡jǐ
给脸 do sb a favour;save sb's face
给以 give;grant
给出路 give sb a way out
给方便 accommodate
给小鞋穿 give sb tight shoes to wear—make

things difficult for sb by abusing one's power；make sb feel the pinch

给颜色看 make it hot for sb

给脸不要脸 be fool enough to reject a face-saving offer

给企业放权让利 pass power down and concede profits to enterprises

gēn（ㄍㄣ）

根 [gēn]
I 名 ①root (of a plant) ②offspring；progeny ③root；foot；base ④cause；origin；source；root ⑤foundation；basis ⑥（short for 方根）root ⑦solution of an algebraic equation ⑧radical II 副 thoroughly；completely；entirely III 量 long thin piece：几根粉笔 several pieces of chalk

根本 ①foundation；base ②basic；fundamental；essential；cardinal ③at all；simply ④radically

根除 thoroughly do away with；eradicate；root out；eliminate

根底 ①foundation ②cause；root

根雕 tree-root carving (a handicraft)

根冠 root cap

根号 radical sign

根基 ①foundation；basis ②property accumulated over a long time；resources

根茎 rhizome

根究 make a thorough investigation of；get to the bottom of；probe into

根据 ①on the basis of；according to；in the light of；in line with ②basis；grounds；foundation

根距 root distance

根绝 stamp out；eradicate；exterminate

根瘤 root nodule

根毛 root hair

根苗 ①root and shoot ②source；root ③（usu. male）offspring

根式 radical (expression)

根由 cause；origin

根源 ①source；origin；root ②originate；stem from

根植 take root

根治 effect a radical cure；cure once and for all；bring under permanent control

根子 ① root (of a plant) ② cause；origin；source；root

根本法 fundamental law

根腐病 root rot

根据地 base area；base

根瘤菌 nodule bacteria

根轴系 root system

根本好转 fundamental turn for the better

根本原因 basic reason；root cause

根本原则 cardinal principle

根深蒂固 deep-rooted；ingrained；inveterate

根深叶茂 have deep roots and luxuriant leaves—be well established and vigorously developing

根外追肥 foliage dressing；foliage spray

根治手术 radical operation

根本性逆差 fundamental deficit

根本政治制度 fundamental political system

跟 [gēn]
I 名 heel II 动 ①follow ②（of a woman）marry sb III 介 with；to；from：跟他学手艺 learn craftsmanship from him IV 连 ①as；from ②and

跟班 ①join a regular shift or class ②footman

跟风 follow the trend

跟脚 ①（of shoes）fit well ②close upon sb's heels ③wait upon one's master when going out ④（of children）not be willing to leave one's parents

跟进 follow suit

跟前 the area in front of sb or sth

跟上 keep pace with；catch up with；keep abreast of

跟随 ①follow ②retinue

跟帖 follow-up post

跟头 ①tumble；fall ②somersault

跟踪 follow the tracks of

跟读生 casual drop-in auditor with special permission

跟屁虫 persistent follower；shadow；pest

跟头虫 wiggler；wriggler

跟单承兑 documentary acceptance

跟单汇兑 documentary remittance

跟上潮流 keep up to date；keep abreast with the times

跟踪程序 tracing routine

跟踪审计 follow-up auditing

跟踪搜索 track-while-scan

跟单信用证 documentary credit

跟上形势的发展 keep up with the changing situation

gén（ㄍㄣˊ）

哏 [gén]
形 amusing；comical；farcical；funny 名 clownish speech or behaviour；clowning；antics

gěn（ㄍㄣˇ）

艮 [gěn]
形 ①（of character or speech）brusque；blunt；stiff；sharp ②（of food）tough；hard ➡ gèn

艮萝卜 leathery turnips

gèn（《ㄣˋ）

亘 [gèn]
Ⅰ 动 extend;stretch;span Ⅱ 介 from
亘古未有 no such things from days of old—unheard-of;unprecedented

茛 [gèn]
◇毛茛 buttercup

gēng（《ㄥ）

更 [gēng]
Ⅰ 动 ①change;alter;replace ②experience Ⅱ 名 one of the five two-hour periods into which the night was divided;watch ➡ gèng
更迭 alternate;change
更动 change;alter
更番 by turns;alternately
更夫 night watchman
更改 change;alter
更换 change;replace
更生 ①regenerate;revive ②renew
更事 experienced in the affairs of the world
更替 replace
更新 ①replace ②(of forest,plants,etc.) renew;rejuvenate
更衣 change one's clothes
更正 make corrections (of errors in published statements or articles)
更年期 climacteric or menopause;change of life
更新伐 regeneration felling (or cutting)
更衣室 changing room;locker room
更改支票 alter a cheque
更名改姓 change one's whole name;assume a false name
更仆难数 too many to count;innumerable;countless
更深人静 deep is the night and all is quiet
更生霉素 actinomycin D
更新观念 change one's concepts;renew ideas
更新换代 replace sth old with sth new;replace a product with one of new generation
更新设备 replace the equipment
更新投资 replacement investment
更新造林 reforestation
更正通知 correction advice;advice to correction
更年期综合征 climacteric syndrome
更新发展思路 change ideas about development
更新改造项目 projects of equipment renewal and technological transformation

庚 [gēng]
名 age

耕 [gēng]
动 ①plough;till;cultivate ②work (for a living);do

耕畜 farm animal
耕地 ①plough;till ②cultivated land;cropland
耕具 tillage implements
耕牛 farm cattle
耕耘 plough and weed;cultivate
耕种 till;cultivate
耕作 tillage;cultivation;farming
耕地面积 cultivated area;area under cultivation
耕作方法 methods of cultivation;farming methods
耕作机械 tillage machinery
耕作技术 farming technique
耕作制度 cropping system
耕者有其田 land to the tiller
耕作园田化 garden-style cultivation of farmland;gardenization

賡 [gēng]
动 continue;go on

羹 [gēng]
名 thick soup;jelly-like food (such as custard)
羹匙 soup spoon;tablespoon
羹汤 broth

gěng（《ㄥˇ）

埂 [gěng]
名 ①low bank ②long, narrow mound ③earth dike (or embankment)
埂堰 earth embankment

耿 [gěng]
Ⅰ 形 bright;brilliant Ⅱ 名 honest and just;upright
耿耿 ①bright ②devoted;dedicated ③having sth on one's mind;worried
耿光 bright light
耿直 honest and frank;upright
耿耿于怀 brood on (an injury,one's neglected duty,etc.);take sth to heart

哽 [gěng]
动 ①choke ②choke with emotion;feel a lump in one's throat
哽咽 choke with sobs

绠 [gěng]
名 rope for drawing up water (from a well,stream,etc.);well rope

梗 [gěng]
Ⅰ 名 stalk; stem Ⅱ 动 ① straighten;stiffen;hold stiff ②hinder;obstruct;block Ⅲ 形 ① straightforward; frank ② obstinate;stubborn
梗概 broad outline;main idea;gist
梗塞 ①block;obstruct;clog ②infarction
梗死 infarction
梗阻 ①block;obstruct;hamper ②obstruction

鲠 [gěng]
Ⅰ 名 fishbone Ⅱ 动 (of a fishbone) get caught in one's throat Ⅲ 形 upright

gèng《ㄍㄥˋ》

更 [gèng]

〔副〕① more；even more；still more ② further；furthermore；what is more

更加 more；still more；even more

更进一步 go a step further

更胜一筹 even better；be better by one tally

更添新愁 add to one's worries

更有甚者 what is more

gōng《ㄍㄨㄥ》

工 [gōng]

Ⅰ〔名〕① worker；workman；labourer；working class ② work；labour ③ (construction) project；construction；building ④ industry ⑤ engineer ⑥ man-day ⑦ skill；craftsmanship；workmanship Ⅱ〔动〕be expert in (or at)；be versed in；be good at Ⅲ〔形〕exquisite；excellent；delicate

工本 cost (of production)

工笔 traditional Chinese realistic painting characterized by fine brushwork and close attention to detail

工兵 engineer (in an army)

工部 the Board of Works

工长 section chief (in a workshop, or on a building site)；foreman

工厂 factory；mill；plant；works

工场 workshop

工潮 workers' demonstration or protest movement；strike movement

工程 ①engineering ②project

工尺 a traditional Chinese musical scale

工党 the Labour Party

工地 building site；construction site

工段 ①a section of a construction project ② workshop section

工蜂 worker (bee)

工夫 ①time ②at that time ③workmanship；skill；art；gongfu ④effort；work

工会 trade union；labour union

工件 workpiece；work

工匠 craftsman；artisan

工具 tool；instrument；implement；means

工卡 employee's name badge

工科 engineering course

工力 ① skill；craftsmanship ② manpower (needed for a project)

工料 labour and materials (for a building project)

工龄 length of service；standing；seniority

工贸 industry and trade

工农 workers and peasants

工棚 ①builders' temporary shed ②work shed

工期 time limit for a project

工钱 ①money paid for odd jobs；charge for a service ②wages；pay

工巧 exquisite；fine

工区 work area (a grass-roots unit of an industrial enterprise)

工人 worker；workman

工日 work day

工伤 injury suffered on the job；industrial injury

工时 man-hour

工事 fortifications；defence works

工头 foreman；overseer

工委 working committee

工效 work efficiency

工行 the Industrial and Commercial Bank

工序 working procedure；process

工业 industry

工艺 technology；craft

工友 a manual worker such as janitor, cleaner, etc. in a school or government office

工贼 scab；blackleg

工整 careful and neat

工致 exquisite；delicate

工种 type of work in production

工资 wages；pay

工作 ①work；operate ②work；job

工本费 production cost

工程兵 engineering corpsman；engineer (in an army)

工程车 machineshop car

工程队 engineer corps；construction brigade

工程师 engineer

工程院 academy of engineering

工尺谱 a traditional Chinese musical notation

工段长 section chief

工间操 work-break exercises

工具袋 kit bag；workbag

工具房 toolhouse；tool storeroom

工具钢 tool steel

工具书 reference book

工具箱 toolbox；tool kit；workbox

工商界 business community；industrial and commercial circles；the world of industry and commerce

工商联 association of industry and commerce

工商税 industrial and commercial (income) tax

工商业 industry and commerce

工薪族 wage-earners

工休日 day off；holiday

工业病 professional diseases of industrial workers

工业国 industrialized (or industrial) country

工业化 industrialize

工业品 industrial products；manufactured goods

工艺品 handicraft article；handiwork；handicraft

工转干 change of one's status from worker to cadre

工装裤 overalls

工资表 payroll;pay sheet

工资袋 pay packet

工资率 wage rate

工资制 wage system

工字钢 I-steel

工字形 I-shaped

工作本 working copy

工作表 worksheet

工作餐 working dinner;staff meal

工作队 work team;working force

工作服 work clothes;boiler suit

工作狂 workaholic;work freak

工作量 amount of work;work load

工作面 ①face ②working surface

工作日 workday;working day

工作台 working table;bench

工作站 ①working station;working centre ② workstation

工作者 worker

工作证 employee's card

工程贷款 financing of projects

工程公司 engineering company

工程塑料 engineering plastics

工程下马 discontinue (or suspend) a project

工程验收 acceptance of work

工程造价 cost of construction

工读学校 reform school;approved school

工间休息 coffee break

工具车床 toolmaker lathe

工联主义 (trade) unionism

工龄工资 pay based on years of service;seniority pay

工贸结合 co-ordination between industry and foreign trade; integrating industry and trade

工农差别 the difference between industry and agriculture

工农联盟 alliance of workers and peasants; worker-peasant alliance

工人贵族 labour aristocracy;aristocrats of labour

工人阶级 the working class

工人运动 labour (or workers') movement

工伤保险 worker's compensation for injuries; industrial injury insurance; insurance against injury at work

工伤事故 industrial accident

工商法规 commercial and industrial law and regulations

工商硕士 Master of Business Administration (MBA)

工商银行 the Industrial and Commercial Bank

工诗善画 be well versed in painting and poet-

ry

工团主义 syndicalism

工效挂钩 link pay to performance

工薪阶层 salariat; wage-earners; wage-and-salary class;salaried persons

工业布局 distribution of industry

工业产品 manufactured products

工业产权 industrial property (right)

工业废气 industrial waste (or exhaust) gas

工业废水 industrial waste water

工业废物 industrial wastes;industrial refuse

工业粉尘 industrial dust

工业革命 the Industrial Revolution

工业公害 industrial nuisance

工业基地 industrial base

工业酒精 industrial alcohol

工业气压 technic atmosphere

工业企业 industrial enterprise

工业体系 industrial system

工业危机 industrial crisis

工业萧条 industrial recession

工业园区 industrial park

工业噪声 man-made noise

工艺流程 technological process

工艺美术 industrial art;arts and crafts

工艺设计 technological design

工艺水平 technological level

工艺要求 technological requirements

工于心计 adept at scheming;very calculating

工资标准 wage rate

工资档次 salary range

工资冻结 pay pause

工资改革 reform of the wage system;reform of work scale;reformation of wage

工资级别 wage scale

工资普加 blanket wage increase

工作报告 work report

工作标兵 pace-setter;pioneer

工作单位 an organization in which one works; place of work

工作分配 job assignment

工作会议 working conference

工作母机 machine tool

工作人员 working personnel; staff member; functionary

工作午餐 working luncheon; business luncheon

工作样片 film rushes

工作语言 working language

工作周期 action cycle

工厂自动化 factory automation

工程地质学 engineering geology

工程经济学 value engineering; engineering economics

工程语言学 engineering linguistics

工人纠察队 workers' pickets

工商税收入 industrial and commercial tax rev-

G

enue

工商统一税 universal tax for all the industry and commerce sector

工业化国家 industrialized countries; industrial countries; developed countries

工业排放物 industrial emissions

工业总产值 gross value of industrial output

工资外收入 off-the-book income

工程技术人员 engineers and technicians

工程监理公司 construction supervision company

工程监理制度 the supervising system for projects

工农业总产值 gross output value of industry and agriculture; gross value of industrial and agricultural output/production

工商业联合会 association of industry and commerce

工业经济效益 economic performance of industrial enterprises

工业质量管理 industrial quality control

工资制度改革 reform of the wage system

工作获得好评 get credit for one's work

工作人员超编 feather-bedding

工贸一体化企业 integrated industrial and trade enterprises

工商管理学硕士 Master of Business Administration (MBA)

工业控制一体化 integrated industrial control; industrial control of integration

工作场所程序图 workplace chart

工农业产品之间的比价 price parities between industrial and agricultural products

工欲善其事,心先利其器 a workman must first sharpen his tools if he is to do his work well

工商行政等执法监督部门 law-enforcing and supervisory departments of industrial and commercial administration

工资总额与经济效益挂钩 link total payroll with economic performance; total wages tied to economic performance

弓 [gōng]
I [名] ① bow ② anything bow-shaped ③ ancient wooden bow-shaped divider for measuring land II [量] unit of length for measuring land, equal to five *chi* (尺) III [动] bend; arch; bow

弓箭 bow and arrow

弓弦 bowstring

弓形 ① segment of a circle ② bow-shaped; arched; curved

弓腰 bend over; bend down

弓子 ① bow (of a stringed instrument) ② anything bow-shaped

弓箭步 forward lunge

弓弩手 crossbowman

弓弦乐器 bowed stringed (*or* string) instrument; bowed instrument

弓腰驼背 hunchbacked

公 [gōng]
I [形] ① public; state-owned; collective ② common; general ③ international; metric ④ equitable; impartial; fair; just ⑤ (of animals) male II [名] ① public affairs; official business ② duke ③ respectful term of address for an aged or elderly man ④ husband's father; father-in-law III [动] make public

公安 public security

公案 ① court table ② a complicated legal case ③ a much discussed issue; a sensational affair

公办 government administered; state-run

公报 communiqué; bulletin

公布 promulgate; announce; publish; make public

公厕 public conveniences; public latrine; public toilets

公差 [gōngchā] ① common difference ② tolerance

公差 [gōngchāi] ① public errand; official business; noncombatant duty ② a person on a public errand (*or* noncombatant duty)

公产 public property

公车 ① public (as opposed to private) vehicles ② (in Taiwan) buses

公称 nominal

公尺 metre (m.)

公出 be away on official business

公畜 male animal

公担 quintal (q.)

公道 [gōngdào] justice

公道 [gōngdao] fair; just; reasonable; impartial

公德 public morality; social ethics

公敌 public enemy

公地 ① public domain ② common land

公牍 official document

公断 ① arbitrate ② consider and decide impartially

公吨 metric ton (MT)

公法 public law

公方 state ownership

公费 (at) public (*or* state) expense

公分 ① centimetre (cm.) ② gram (g.)

公愤 public indignation; popular anger

公干 official business

公告 announcement; proclamation

公公 ① husband's father; father-in-law ② (paternal) grandfather ③ (maternal) grandfather ④ (a respectful term of address for an elderly man) grandpa; grandad ⑤ a form of address for a court eunuch

公共 public; common; communal

公股 government share (in a joint state-

private enterprise)
公关 public relations
公馆 residence;mansion
公国 duchy;dukedom
公海 high seas
公害 public nuisance; social effects of pollution;environmental pollution
公函 official letter
公侯 dukes and marquises
公鸡 cock;rooster
公祭 public memorial ceremony
公家 the state;the public;the organization
公斤 kilogram (kg.);kilo
公爵 duke
公开 ① open;overt;public ② make public; make known to the public
公筷 serving chopsticks; chopsticks for serving food
公款 public money (or fund)
公里 kilometre (km.)
公理 ① generally acknowledged truth;self-evident truth ②axiom
公历 the Gregorian calendar
公立 established and maintained by the government;public
公粮 agricultural tax paid in grain;grain delivered to the state;public grain
公量 conditioned weight
公了 settle according to law or policy
公路 highway;road
公论 public opinion;verdict of the masses
公民 citizen
公亩 are (a.)
公墓 cemetery
公牛 bull
公派 be sent (abroad to study,to work,etc.) by the state
公平 fair;just;impartial;equitable
公婆 husband's father and mother;parents-in-law
公仆 public servant
公顷 hectare (ha.)
公权 public rights
公然 openly;undisguisedly;brazenly
公认 generally acknowledge (or recognize); (universally) accept;establish
公设 postulate
公社 ① primitive commune ② commune ③ people's commune
公审 public (or open) trial
公升 litre
公使 envoy;minister
公示 public notification
公式 formula
公事 public affairs;official business (or duties)
公署 government office

公司 company;corporation
公私 public and private
公诉 public prosecution
公摊 shared by the public;shared by all
公堂 ① law court; tribunal ② ancestral hall (or temple);memorial temple
公推 recommend by general acclaim
公文 official document
公务 public affairs;official business
公物 public property
公休 sabbatical leave; sabbatical; paid holidays;general holiday
公选 open selection
公演 perform in public;give a performance
公羊 ram
公议 have a public or mass discussion
公益 public good;public welfare
公意 public will;will of the public
公营 publicly-owned;publicly-operated;public
公用 for public use;public;communal
公有 publicly-owned;public
公寓 ①block of flats;apartment house ②lodging house
公元 the Christian era
公园 park
公约 ①convention;pact ②joint pledge
公允 just and sound;fair and equitable;even-handed
公债 government bonds
公章 official seal
公正 just;fair;impartial;fair-minded
公证 notarization
公职 public office;public employment
公制 the metric system
公众 the public
公猪 boar
公主 princess
公转 revolution
公子 son of a feudal prince or high official
公安部 the Ministry of Public Security
公安局 public security bureau
公倍数 common multiple
公德心 public spirit
公断人 umpire;arbitrator
公共课 common required course
公关部 public relations department
公积金 accumulation funds;public funds;common funds
公检法 public security organs, procuratorial organs and people's courts
公开化 come out into the open;be brought into the open
公开赛 open tournament
公开信 open letter
公路桥 highway bridge
公民权 civil rights;citizen's rights
公平秤 fair scales—scales provided by mar-

kets for consumers to verify accuracy of purchase weight

公切线 common tangent

公使馆 legation

公式化 ①formulism (in art and literature) ② formulistic；stereotyped

公事包 briefcase；portfolio

公事房 office (room or building)

公诉人 public prosecutor；the prosecution

公文包 portfolio

公文袋 document envelope

公文纸 paper for copying official documents

公务车 service car

公务员 government office worker；civil (*or* public) functionary (*or* officer, servant, employee)

公信力 public confidence

公益金 public welfare fund (of a socialist economic collective)

公因数 common factor

公因子 common factor

公有化 transfer to public ownership；socialize

公有制 public ownership (of means of production)

公约数 common divisor

公债券 government securities debentures；government bond

公证处 notary (public) office

公证人 notary public；notary

公证书 notarial deed (*or* document) certificate

公安干警 public security police

公报私仇 avenge personal wrongs in the name of public interests；abuse public power to retaliate against a personal enemy

公而忘私 so devoted to public service as to forget private interests；selfless

公房出售 sale of public-sector housing

公费旅游 travel at public expense

公费医疗 free medical service (*or* care)；public health services；socialized medicine

公共厕所 public conveniences；public latrine；public toilets

公共道德 public morality

公共关系 public relations

公共积累 common accumulation；accumulation fund

公共汽车 bus

公共权力 public rights

公共卫生 public health (*or* hygiene)

公共秩序 public order

公关手腕 public-relation gimmick

公关先生 public relations practitioner

公关小姐 public relations girl (*or* lady)；Miss Public Relations

公交系统 public transit system；mass transit system

公教人员 government employees and teachers

公爵夫人 duchess

公开报价 public order；public offer

公开答辩 reply (*or* answer) in public

公开法庭 open court

公开哄抢 open plunder

公开竞标 competitive bidding

公开买卖 market overt

公开拍卖 public auction；sell by public auction

公开上市 open listing

公开投标 open bidding；public bidding

公开招标 competitive bidding；competitive tender

公开招聘 recruit through public examination；publicly engage

公款吃喝 enjoy banquet on public funds

公款私存 deposit public funds in personal accounts

公路容量 highway capacity

公路养护 highway maintenance

公买公卖 be fair in buying and selling；buy and sell at reasonable prices

公民投票 plebiscite vote；referendum；plebiscite

公民义务 civil duty；civil obligation

公平合理 fair and reasonable；fair and square

公平交易 fair transactions

公平竞争 fair play；fair competition

公平原则 equitable principles

公仆意识 public servant consciousness

公勤人员 service personnel in an office；office attendants

公事公办 business is business；do official business according to official principles；not let private affairs interfere with public duty；not let personal considerations interfere with one's execution of public duty

公司改组 reorganization of a corporation

公司模型 company models

公司债券 corporate bond

公司章程 articles of association；articles of incorporation；corporation by-laws；charter；articles of incorporation

公私分明 be scrupulous in separating public from private interests

公私合营 joint state-private ownership (the principal form of state capitalism adopted during the socialist transformation of capitalist enterprises in China)

公私兼顾 advantageous to both public and private interest

公务护照 service passport

公务人员 government functionary

公益公告 public service announcement；public-interest ads；public-interest advertisement

公益劳动 labour for public good；volunteer labour

公益事业 cause of public good
公用事业 public utilities
公用语言 common language
公有住房 state-owned apartment
公债发行 public subscription
公证财产 notarize the properties
公证手续 notarial acts
公之于世 make known to the world；reveal to the public
公之于众 reveal to the public
公职人员 civil servant
公制螺纹 metric thread
公众人物 public figure
公诸同好 share enjoyment with those having similar tastes
公诸于世 make known to the world；reveal to the public
公子哥儿 a pampered son of a wealthy or influential family
公安派出所 public security police stations
公告板服务 Bulletin Board Service (BBS)
公共关系学 the study of public relations
公关部主任 public relations manager
公开招投标 open bidding；public bidding；competitive bidding
公路检查站 check-point；checkpost；inspection station
公派留学生 government-appointed student；students sent out by the government
公司加农户 company + peasant household
公司所得税 corporate income tax
公益性单位 welfare services
公约缔约国 state parties to the convention；signatory state to the pact
公证委托书 letter of commitment
公费留学人员 government-funded personnel studying abroad
公共管理硕士 Master of Public Administration (MPA)
公共责任保险 public liability insurance
公开办事制度 an open administrative system
公开审判制度 public trial system
公开市场业务 open-market operation
公民投票自决 referendum for self determination
公司组织大纲 memorandum of association
公正、公平、公开 just，fair and open
公民的人格尊严 the personal dignity of citizens
公民的人身自由 citizen's personal freedom
公益性文化事业 public cultural facilities
公共英语等级考试 Public English Testing System (PETS)
公民的义务和权利 rights and duties of citizens
公有制的主体地位 dominant position of public ownership
公正与全面的解决 just and comprehensive so-lution
公认的国际关系准则 accepted norms of international relations
公民的基本权利和义务 fundamental rights and duties of citizens
公民的劳动权利和义务 citizen's right and duty to work
公有制的多种实现形式 various forms for materializing (*or* realizing) public ownership
公说公有理，婆说婆有理 each says he (*or* she) is right；both parties claim to be in the right
公民私人所有的合法财产 citizen's lawfully-owned private property

功 ［gōng］
名 ① meritorious service or deed；achievement；merit；exploit ② effect；success；result ③ skill；technique ④ qigong；breathing exercise ⑤ effort；work
功臣 a person who has rendered outstanding service
功德 ① merits and virtues ② charitable and pious deeds；benefaction；beneficence；works
功底 grounding in basic skills
功过 merits and demerits；contributions and blunders
功绩 merits and achievements；contribution
功课 ① schoolwork；homework ② a school subject
功劳 contribution；meritorious service；credit
功利 utility；material gain
功率 power
功名 scholarly honour or official rank
功能 function
功效 efficacy；effect
功勋 exploit；meritorious service
功业 exploits；achievements
功用 function；use
功夫片 martial arts movie
功劳簿 record of merits
功能法 functional approach
功能键 function key
功败垂成 fail on the verge of success；suffer defeat when victory is within reach
功标青史 cause one's fame to glow in the pages of history
功成不居 claim no credit for one's service
功成名就 be successful and famous
功成身退 retire after winning merit
功成业就 (of a person's career) be crowned with success
功德无量 boundless beneficence；great service
功德圆满 come to a successful issue；round it off
功过是非 merits and demerits, right and wrong
功亏一篑 fail to build a mound for want of one

final basket of earth—fall short of success for lack of a final effort

功利主义 utilitarianism

功名利禄 position and wealth

功难掩过 the merit is not enough to redeem the offenses

功能各异 different in function

功能失调 functional disturbance

功到自然成 constant effort yïelds sure success

功在当代,利在千秋 (a historical event that) contributes to contemporary times and brings benefits for future centuries

G

攻 [gōng]

动 ①attack;assault;take or go onto the offensive ②accuse;refute;charge ③study;specialize in

攻打 attack;assault

攻读 ①assiduously study;diligently study ②specialize in

攻关 ①storm a strategic pass ②tackle key problems

攻击 ①attack;assault;launch an offensive ②accuse;charge;vilify

攻坚 storm fortifications;assault fortified positions

攻克 capture;take

攻破 make a breakthrough;breach

攻取 storm and capture;attack and seize

攻势 offensive

攻丝 tapping

攻下 capture;overcome

攻陷 capture;storm

攻心 ①attack the mind;make a psychological attack ②be in a coma or remain in a stupor,or be in danger of dying

攻占 attack and occupy;storm and capture

攻击机 attack plane

攻坚战 storming of heavily fortified positions

攻城略地 attack cities and seize territories

攻其不备 strike where or when the enemy is unprepared;take sb by surprise;catch sb unawares

攻守同盟 conspiracy of silence;offensive and defensive alliance

攻无不克 all-conquering;ever-victorious

攻心为上 psychological offensive is the best of tactics

攻击型选手 aggressive player(s)

攻击性言论 attack line

攻击型核潜艇 nuclear powered attack submarine

攻其一点,不及其余 pounce on one point and ignore all others—attack sb for a single fault without considering his other aspects

供 [gōng]

动 ① supply;furnish;provide ② for (the use or convenience of) ➡ gòng

供电 supply electricity;supply power

供货 supply of material

供给 supply;provide;furnish

供暖 heating

供气 air feed

供求 supply and demand

供销 supply and marketing

供养 provide for (one's parents or elders);support

供应 supply

供不上 run out;be in short supply

供电局 power supply bureau

供给制 the supply system—a system of payment in kind

供销社 supply and marketing cooperative

供应点 supply centre

供应线 supply line

供不应求 be in short supply;supply falls short of demand;demand exceeds supply

供电系统 power network

供过于求 supply exceeds demand

供暖系统 heating system

供求关系 supply-demand situation

供求流动 supply-and-demand flow

供销合作社 supply and marketing cooperative

供需见面,双向选择 graduates and companies meeting face to face and choosing as both see fit

肱 [gōng]

名 upper arm;arm

肱骨 humerus

肱动脉 brachial artery

肱静脉 brachial vein

宫 [gōng]

名 ①palace ②(celestial) palace;residence of immortals ③temple ④place for cultural activities and recreation ⑤womb;uterus

宫灯 palace lantern

宫殿 palace

宫调 modes of ancient Chinese music

宫女 a maid in an imperial palace;maid of honour

宫阙 imperial palace

宫廷 ①palace ②royal or imperial court;court

宫闱 palace chambers

宫刑 castration

宫苑 palatial garden

宫外孕 ectopic pregnancy;extrauterine pregnancy

宫廷秘方 imperial secret recipe,palace recipe

宫廷政变 palace coup

宫内节育器 intrauterine device (IUD)

恭 [gōng]

形 respectful;courteous;reverent

恭贺 congratulate

恭候 await respectfully

恭谨 respectful and cautious

恭敬 respectful
恭请 invite respectfully
恭顺 respectful and submissive
恭桶 closestool;nightstool;commode
恭维 flatter;compliment
恭喜 congratulate
恭迎 welcome respectfully
恭敬不如从命 it is better to accept deferentially than to decline courteously (on accept-ing gifts,etc. from one's elders)

蚣 [gōng]

◇蜈蚣 centipede

躬 [gōng]

I 副 in person;personally Ⅱ 动 bend forward;bow;stoop Ⅲ 名 oneself
躬亲 attend to personally
躬身 bend at the waist
躬逢其盛 be present in person on the grand occasion
躬身下拜 bow down and worship;bend the knee in obeisance
躬体力行 attend personally

觥 [gōng]

名 ancient wine vessel made of bronze
觥筹交错 wine cups and mora chips lying about in disorder—a hilarious party

gǒng《ㄍㄨㄥˇ》

巩 [gǒng]

动 consolidate;strengthen;solidify
巩固 ① consolidate;strengthen;solidify ② consolidated;strong;solid;stable
巩膜 sclera
巩膜炎 scleritis

汞 [gǒng]

名 mercury;hydrargyrum (Hg)
汞化 mercurate;mercurize
汞柱 mercury;mercury column
汞弧灯 mercury-arc lamp
汞溴红 mercurochrome

拱 [gǒng]

I 动 ①cup one hand in the other before the chest ②encompass;encircle;surround ③ hunch up;hump up;arch ④(of people) push with one's body;(of pigs,etc.) dig with the snout;(of earthworms,etc.) wriggle through ⑤sprout up through the earth Ⅱ 名 arch
拱坝 arch dam
拱抱 surround
拱道 archway
拱点 apsis;apse
拱顶 vault
拱门 arched door
拱桥 arch bridge
拱手 make an obeisance by cupping one hand in the other before the chest

拱卫 surround and protect
拱券 arch
拱式涵洞 arch culvert
拱手称谢 join one's hands together in salute and thank
拱手让人 surrender sth submissively;hand sth over on a silver platter
拱形建筑 arch;arched construction

gòng《ㄍㄨㄥˋ》

共 [gòng]

I 形 common;general;universal Ⅱ 动 share Ⅲ 副 ①in company;together ②altogether;in all;all told
共处 coexist
共存 coexist
共度 spend (an occasion) together
共轭 conjugate
共犯 accomplice
共管 condominium
共和 republicanism;republic
共计 amount to;add up to;total
共价 covalence
共聚 copolymerization
共勉 encourage each other
共鸣 ①resonance ②sympathetic response
共栖 commensalism
共生 ①intergrowth;paragenesis ②symbiosis
共识 common understanding;consensus
共事 work together;be fellow workers
共通 applicable to both or all
共同 ①shared;common ②together;jointly
共析 eutectoid
共享 enjoy together;share
共性 general character;generality
共赢 all win;win for all
共振 resonance
共轴 coaxial
共产党 the Communist Party
共电制 common-battery system
共轭点 conjugate point
共轭角 conjugate angles
共轭象 conjugate image
共和党 the Republican Party (in U.S.)
共和国 republic
共患难 go through hardships together
共基极 common base
共生矿 mineral intergrowth
共同点 common ground
共同体 community
共产国际 the Communist International;Comintern
共产主义 communism
共担风险 joint adventure
共渡难关 tide over the difficulties;weather the hard times

G

共发射极 common emitter
共进午餐 have lunch together
共聚一堂 gather in the same hall; gather together
共青团员 member of the Communist Youth League; League member
共生次序 paragenesis
共同保险 co-insurance
共同过失 joint negligence
共同配额 common quotas
共同市场 the Common Market
共同投标 joint bidding
共为唇齿 help each other to make an undertaking successful; provide each other with assistance
共享软件 shareware
共用天线 common antenna
共同承兑人 co-acceptor
共产主义信念 communist conviction; faith (*or* belief) in communism
共同对外关税 common external tariff (CET)
共产主义青年团 the Communist Youth League

贡 [gòng] 〔动〕①tribute ②recommend a person to the imperial court
贡金 tribute; aid
贡品 articles of tribute; tribute
贡士 person recommended for national service
贡税 tribute and taxes
贡献 ①contribute; dedicate; devote ②contribution; dedication; devotion

供 [gòng] Ⅰ〔动〕①lay (offerings) ②confess; admit; own up Ⅱ〔名〕①offerings ②confession; deposition ➡ gōng
供车 buy a car in instalments
供词 confession; statement made under examination
供奉 ①enshrine and worship; consecrate ②actors who gave command performances
供具 sacrificial vessel
供楼 buy property in instalments
供品 offerings
供认 confess
供事 take a post
供职 hold office
供状 written confession; deposition
供桌 altar table
供认不讳 candidly confess; confess everything

gōu〈ㄍㄡ〉

勾 [gōu] Ⅰ〔动〕①tick off; check; cross out; strike out ②delineate; sketch; draw ③fill up the joints of brickwork with mortar or cement; point ④thicken ⑤induce; evoke; arouse; call to mind ⑥collude with; gang up with; entice Ⅱ〔名〕 shorter leg of a right triangle ➡ gòu
勾搭 ①gang up with ②carry on (*or* have a carry-on) with sb
勾动 stir up (sb's feeling); move; arouse; cause
勾兑 curry favour with
勾画 draw the outline of; delineate; sketch
勾魂 captivate sb's soul—enchant; bewitch
勾结 collude with; collaborate with; gang up with
勾勒 ①draw the outline of; sketch the contours of ②give a brief account of; outline
勾通 collude with; work hand in glove with
勾引 tempt; entice; seduce
勾股定理 the Pythagorean theorem (*or* proposition)
勾魂摄魄 (of a woman) have the power to bewitch men; cast a spell (on); lay an enchantment (on)
勾起愁绪 arouse sorrow
勾起回忆 evoke memory
勾结外国反华势力 collaborate with foreign anti-Chinese forces

佝 [gōu]
佝偻病 rickets

沟 [gōu] 〔名〕① ditch; drain; channel; trench ② groove; rut; gutter; furrow ③ waterway; gullet; gully
沟灌 furrow irrigation
沟壑 gully; ravine
沟渠 irrigation canals and ditches
沟通 link up
沟沿儿 banks of a ditch or canal
沟通思想 promote mutual understánding

钩 [gōu] Ⅰ〔名〕①hook ②hook stroke ③spoken form of the numeral 九 Ⅱ〔动〕①check; mark; tick ②secure with a hook; hook ③explore; search after ④crochet ⑤sew with large stitches
钩虫 hookworm
钩吻 elegant jessamine
钩形 hook-type; hooked
钩针 crochet hook
钩子 ①hook ②hook-like things
钩虫病 hookworm disease; ancylostomiasis
钩花边 crochet lace; tat
钩贴边 sew on an edging
钩深致远 seek the profound truth
钩心斗角 intrigue against each other; jockey for position
钩端螺旋体病 leptospirosis

缑 [gōu] 〔名〕string round the hilt of a sword (*or* knife)

篝 [gōu] 〔名〕cage

篝火 bonfire；campfire

gǒu（《ㄡˇ）

苟 ［gǒu］
Ⅰ 〔形〕 casual；careless；thoughtless；negligent Ⅱ 〔连〕provided；if

苟安 seek a moment's peace however one can；be content with temporary ease and comfort

苟合 illicit sexual relations

苟活 drag out an ignoble existence；live on in degradation

苟且 ① drift along；be resigned to circumstances ② perfunctory；careless ③ illicit（sexual relations）；improper

苟全 aimlessly preserve（one's own life）

苟同 agree without giving serious thought；readily subscribe to（sb's view）

苟安一隅 seek momentary ease in an isolated place

苟且偷安 seek a moment's peace however one can；be content with temporary ease and comfort

苟且偷生 drag out an ignoble existence

苟全性命 barely manage to survive

苟延残喘 be on one's last legs；linger on in a steadily worsening condition

狗 ［gǒu］
〔名〕 dog

狗宝 the stone of a dog's gallbladder，kidney or bladder

狗洞 doghole

狗獾 badger

狗屁 horseshit；rubbish；nonsense

狗屎 dog's droppings—worthless stuff

狗窝 kennel；doghouse

狗熊 ①black bear ②coward

狗蝇 dog louse fly

狗鱼 pike（a fish）

狗蚤 dog flea

狗吃屎 fall flat on the face；fall down heavily

狗东西 cur；son of a bitch

狗脊蕨 chain fern

狗食袋 doggy bag

狗腿子 hired thug；lackey；henchman

狗尾草 green bristlegrass

狗咬狗 dog-eat-dog

狗崽子 son of a bitch

狗仔队 dog packs；paparazzo

狗胆包天 monstrously audacious

狗苟蝇营 shamelessly seek personal gain

狗急跳墙 a cornered beast will do sth desperate

狗皮膏药 ①dogskin plaster ②quack medicine

狗屁不通 unreadable rubbish；mere trash

狗偷鼠窃 petty theft

狗头军师 ①a person who offers bad advice；inept adviser ②villainous adviser

狗尾续貂 a dog's tail joined to sable—（of a literary work）a wretched sequel to a fine work

狗血喷头 let loose a stream of abuse against sb；pour out a flood of invective against sb

狗仗人势 like a dog threatening people on the strength of its master's power—be a bully with the backing of a powerful person

狗彘不如 worse than a cur or a swine

狗眼看人低 be a bloody snob

狗咬吕洞宾 snarl and snap at Lü Dongbin（one of the eight immortals in Chinese mythology）—wrong a kind-hearted person

狗嘴里吐不出象牙 no ivory issues from the mouth of a dog；a filthy mouth can't utter decent language；what can you expect from a dog but a bark

狗拿耗子，多管闲事 a dog trying to catch mice—poke one's nose into other people's business

耇 ［gǒu］
〔名〕 old age；long life；longevity

枸 ［gǒu］ ➡ jǔ

枸骨 Chinese holly

枸杞子 the fruit of Chinese wolfberry

笱 ［gǒu］
〔名〕 basket trap for fish

gòu（《ㄡˋ）

勾 ［gòu］
➡ gōu

勾当 business；deal

构 ［gòu］
Ⅰ 〔动〕 ①construct；form；build；compose ②fabricate；invent；make up Ⅱ 〔名〕 ①literary composition ②paper mulberry

构成 constitute；form；compose；make up

构词 form a word

构架 framework；establish

构件 ①（structural）member；component ②component（part）

构建 compose

构拟 work out；design；conceive

构思 （of a writer or artist）work out the plot of a story or the composition of a painting

构图 composition of a picture

构想 idea；conception；concept

构造 ① structure；construction ② tectonic；structural

构筑 construct（military works）；build

构词法 word-building；word-formation

构筑物 structures

构木为巢 construct a wooden hutch on a tree

构造地震 tectonic earthquake

构造运动 tectonic movement

构造地质学 structural geology

购 [gòu]
⑤ purchase;buy
购单 buying order
购买 purchase;buy
购销 purchase and sale;buying and selling
购置 purchase (durables)
购股单 stock purchase warrant
购货单 order form;order
购货券 a purchase coupon
购进量 volume of purchase
购买力 buying (*or* purchasing) power
购买税 purchase tax
购物袋 shopping bag;carrier bag
购货合同 purchase contract
购买动机 buying motive
购物天堂 a shopping kingdom
购物指南 shopping guide
购物中心 shopping centre
购销两旺 brisk buying and selling
购买力平价 purchasing power parity
购物手推车 push cart
购销价格倒挂 inverted purchasing and selling prices;selling prices are lower than purchasing prices

垢 [gòu]
I ⑮ soiled;dirty;filthy Ⅱ ⑧ ①dirt;filth; stain ②insult;disgrace;humiliation

诟 [gòu]
I ⑤ meet;encounter Ⅱ ⑧ virtue;benevolence

篝 [gòu]
⑧ depths of a mansion (*or* palace)

够 [gòu]
I ⑮ enough;sufficient;adequate Ⅱ ⑩ quite;rather;really Ⅲ ⑤ ① reach (sth by stretching) ② reach or be up to (a certain standard,etc.)
够本 ①make enough money to cover the cost; break even ②the gains balancing the losses
够格 be qualified;be up to standard
够呛 unbearable;terrible
够数 sufficient in quantity;enough
够标准 make the grade
够劲儿 ① (of an onerous task,etc.) almost too much to cope with ②strong (in taste, strength,etc.)
够朋友 deserve to be called a true friend;be a friend indeed
够瞧的 really awful;too much
够受的 quite an ordeal;hard to bear
够条件 reach the standard;be qualified
够味儿 just the right flavour;just the thing; quite satisfactory
够意思 ①really sth;terrific ②generous;really kind

彀 [gòu]
⑤ draw a bow to the full

媾 [gòu]
⑤ ① wed ② reach an agreement;make peace;become reconciled ③copulate
媾和 make peace

觏 [gòu]
⑤ meet

gū（《ㄨ）

估 [gū]
⑤ estimate;assess;appraise;reckon
估产 ①estimate the yield ②appraise the assets;assess
估计 estimate;appraise;reckon
估价 ①appraise;evaluate ②appraised price
估量 appraise;estimate;assess;reckon
估摸 reckon;guess
估税 tax assessment
估算 estimate;appraise;reckon
估值 value of assessment;appraisement
估税人 assessor
估计残值 estimated scrap value
估价惯例 valuation convention

咕 [gū]
⑧ (of hens,etc.) cluck;(of turtledoves, etc.) coo
咕咚 the sound of a heavy thing falling down; thud;splash;plump
咕嘟 ①bubble;gurgle ②boil for a long time ③purse (one's lips)
咕叽 ①a squelching sound ② whisper;murmur
咕隆 rumble;rattle;roll
咕噜 rumble;roll
咕哝 murmur;mutter;grumble

呱 [gū]
➡guā
呱呱 the cry of a baby
呱呱坠地 (of a baby) come into the world with a cry;raise the first cry of life;be born

沽 [gū]
⑤ ①purchase;buy ②sell
沽酒待客 buy wine to entertain a guest
沽名钓誉 fish for fame and compliments

姑 [gū]
I ⑧ ① father's sister;aunt ② husband's sister; sister-in-law ③ husband's mother; mother-in-law ④nun;priestess Ⅱ ⑩ just;for the time being
姑表 the relationship between the children of a brother and a sister;cousinship
姑夫 the husband of one's father's sister
姑父 uncle
姑姑 aunt
姑妈 (married) aunt
姑母 (married) aunt
姑娘 ①girl ②daughter
姑且 tentatively;for the moment

姑嫂 a woman and her brother's wife;sisters-in-law
姑息 appease;indulge;tolerate
姑嫜 a woman's parents-in-law
姑丈 uncle
姑老爷 a form of address for a man used by members of his wife's family
姑奶奶 ①married daughter ②grandaunt
姑妄听之 see no harm in hearing what sb has to say
姑妄言之 tell sb sth for what it's worth
姑息疗法 palliative treatment
姑息养奸 to tolerate evil is to abet it
姑息政策 appeasement
姑置勿论 leave it for the time being

孤 [gū] I 形 ①(of a child) fatherless;orphaned ② lone;solitary;isolated;alone Ⅱ 代 I
孤傲 proud and aloof
孤本 the only copy extant;the only existing copy
孤残 the orphaned and disabled
孤单 ①alone;lonely ②weak
孤胆 fighting single-handed
孤岛 an isolated island
孤独 lonely;solitary
孤儿 ①a fatherless child ②orphan
孤寡 ①widow and her child ②lonely;solitary
孤寂 lonely
孤军 an isolated force
孤立 ①isolated ②isolate
孤僻 unsociable and eccentric
孤身 alone
孤雁 solitary wild goose
孤独症 autism
孤儿院 orphanage
孤老院 old folks' home;home for the aged
孤零零 solitary;lone;all alone
孤独无援 alone and with no help
孤儿寡母 widow and her child
孤芳自赏 a solitary flower in love with its own fragrance;alone soul admiring his own purity;indulge in self-admiration
孤家寡人 a person who is utterly isolated
孤酒难饮 hard to drink alone
孤军深入 an isolated force penetrating deep into enemy territory
孤军作战 fight in isolation;fight a lone battle
孤苦伶仃 orphaned and helpless;alone and uncared for;friendless and wretched
孤立主义 isolationism
孤陋寡闻 ignorant and ill-informed
孤行己见 follow one's bigoted course
孤云野鹤 the solitary clouds and wild cranes
孤掌难鸣 it's impossible to clap with one hand—it's hard to succeed without support
孤注一掷 stake all on a single throw;risk everything on a single venture;put all one's eggs in one basket
孤儿监护养育 rearing under guardianship offered to orphans

轱 [gū]
轱辘 ①wheel ②roll
轱辘鞋 roller skates

骨 [gū] ➡ gǔ
骨碌 roll
骨朵儿 flower bud

菇 [gū] 名 mushroom

菰 [gū] 名 ①wild rice whose stem is eaten as vegetable ②mushroom

辜 [gū] I 名 guilt;crime Ⅱ 动 abandon;betray
辜负 let down;fail to live up to;be unworthy of;disappoint
辜恩背义 perfidious;unfaithful

酤 [gū] I 名 weak wine Ⅱ 动 ①buy (wine) ②sell (wine)

觚 [gū] 名 ①wine vessel;goblet;beaker ②wooden writing tablet ③edges and corners

箍 [gū] I 动 fasten round;bind fast;hoop Ⅱ 名 hoop;band
箍桶匠 cooper;hooper

gǔ(《ㄨˇ)

古 [gǔ] 形 ①ancient;age-old ②of ancient style ③ simple and sincere
古奥 (usu. of writing) archaic and abstruse
古板 old-fashioned and inflexible
古刹 an ancient temple
古城 ancient city;early city
古代 ①the period in Chinese history from remote antiquity down until the mid-19th century ②the age of slave society;ancient times;antiquity
古典 ①classical allusion ②classical
古董 ①antique;curio ②old fogey
古都 ancient capital
古风 ①ancient customs;antiquities ②a form of pre-Tang poetry, usu. having five or seven characters to each line,without strict tonal patterns or rhyme schemes
古怪 eccentric;odd;strange
古画 ancient painting
古话 old saying
古籍 ancient books
古迹 historic site;place of historic interest
古旧 antiquated;archaic

古柯 coca
古庙 ancient temple; old temple
古老 ancient; age-old
古朴 (of art, architecture, etc.) simple and unsophisticated; of primitive simplicity
古人 the ancients; our forefathers
古诗 ancient poetry
古书 ancient books
古玩 antique; curio
古文 ①prose written in the classical literary style; ancient Chinese prose ② Chinese script before the Qin Dynasty
古物 ancient objects; antiquities
古稀 seventy years of age
古雅 (of material things, literary works, etc.) of classic beauty and in elegant taste; of classic elegance
古装 ancient costume
古汉语 archaic Chinese
古柯碱 cocaine
古兰经 the Koran
古生代 the Palaeozoic Era
古生界 Palaeozoic Erathem
古塔胶 gutta-percha
古体诗 a form of pre-Tang poetry, usu. having five or seven characters to each line, without strict tonal patterns or rhyme schemes
古铜色 bronze-coloured; bronze
古文字 ancient writing
古装戏 costume play
古道热肠 warm-hearted and compassionate
古典文学 classical literature
古典音乐 classical music
古典主义 classicism
古动物学 palaeozoology
古尔邦节 Corban
古今中外 ancient and modern, Chinese and foreign; at all times and in all lands
古木参天 Ancient trees touch the sky. *or* The old trees reach into skies.
古人类学 palaeoanthropology
古色古香 antique; quaint
古生物学 palaeontology
古往今来 throughout the ages; from time immemorial
古为今用 make the past serve the present
古文字学 paleography
古植物学 palaeobotany
古为今用,洋为中用 Make the past serve the present and foreign things serve China.

谷 [gǔ] 名 ①valley; ravine; gully; gorge ②cereal; grain ③millet ④unhusked rice
谷仓 granary; barn
谷草 ①millet straw ②rice straw
谷底 bottom; bottom of a valley

谷蛾 grain moth
谷坊 check dam
谷壳 husk (of rice)
谷粒 corn; grain
谷物 cereal; grain
谷雨 Grain Rain—the 6th of the 24 solar terms
谷子 ①millet ②unhusked rice
谷氨酸 glutamic acid
谷蛋白 glutelin
谷穗儿 ears of millet
谷贱伤农 low prices for grain hurt the peasants; cheap grain harms the peasants
谷物干燥机 grain dryer
谷物交易所 corn exchange
谷子白发病 downy mildew of millet

汩 [gǔ] 形 (of running water) gurgle
汩汩 gurgle

诂 [gǔ] 动 explain archaic or dialectal words in current language

股 [gǔ] Ⅰ 名 ①thigh ②section (of an office, enterprise, etc.) ③strand; ply ④share of stock (in a company); one of several equal parts ⑤ longer leg of a right triangle Ⅱ 量 ①(*used to indicate sth long and narrow*): 一股棉线 a skein of cotton thread ②(for gas, smell, strength, etc.): 一股臭味 a whiff of offensive odour/一股劲 a burst of energy/一股热气 a stream (*or* puff) of hot air ③(*used to indicate a group of people*): 小股敌军 small groups (*or* bands) of enemy troops
股本 capital stock; share capital; equity
股长 section chief
股东 shareholder; stockholder
股份 share; stock
股肱 right-hand man
股骨 thighbone; femur
股海 fluctuating stock market
股金 money paid for shares (in a partnership or cooperative)
股民 person who buys and sells stocks; shareholder
股票 share certificate; share; stock
股评 stock review
股权 stock ownership; stockholder's right; shareholder's right
股市 stock market
股事 stock market affairs
股息 dividend
股线 plied yarn
股灾 stock market crisis
股指 stock market index
股子 ①share in a company ②(for strength, smell, etc.)

股本金 equity capital
股份制 joint stock (*or* share) system;shareholding system
股静脉 femoral vein
股评家 stock reviewer
股本折价 stock discount;discount on capital stock
股东产权 shareholder equity
股东大会 general meeting of share holders;shareholder's general meeting
股东大会 stockholders' meeting
股东权益 stockholder's equity
股份保险 joint stock insurance
股份分割 split up shares
股份公司 joint-stock company;stock company
股份红利 dividend on shares;stock dividend;stick bonus
股份转让 transfer of shares;changing hands of shares;exchange of shares
股份资本 share capital
股票发行 bond issue;stock issue;issuance
股票分割 stock split
股票过户 stock transfer
股票行情 stock quotation
股票行市 current prices of stocks;quotations on the stock exchange
股票交易 buying and selling of stocks
股票上市 be listed on the stock market
股票升水 premium on capital stock
股票市场 stock market
股票指数 stock index
股票转让 transfer of shares
股权出售 rights offering
股市指数 stock exchange indexes
股息限度 dividend limitation
股东分户账 stock ledger
股份合作制 joint stock cooperative system;joint stock partnership
股份制经济 share economy
股份制企业 shareholding enterprise
股票持有人 shareholder
股票交易所 stock exchange
股票经纪人 stockbroker;stockjobber
股市分析员 quant
股份有限公司 limited-liability company;limited company (Ltd.)
股票抵押借款 stock collateral loans
股票行情看跌 beating tendency
股票行情看涨 bullish tendency
股票价格限制 stock price restraint
股票价格指数 stock price index
股票票面价值 face value of share
股票平均价格 stock price averages
股票投资信托 stock investment trust
股东优先认购权 privileged allocation of insurance to stockholders
股份不定投资公司 open-end investment company

骨 [gǔ]
[名] ①bone;os ②skeleton;structure;framework ③character;quality;spirit ➡ gū
骨刺 spur
骨粉 bone meal;bone dust
骨感 bony
骨干 ①diaphysis ②backbone;mainstay
骨骼 skeleton
骨骺 epiphysis
骨化 ossify
骨灰 ①bone ash ②ashes of the dead
骨架 skeleton;framework
骨胶 bone glue
骨节 joint
骨科 (department of) orthopaedics
骨刻 bone sculpture (*or* carving)
骨痨 tuberculosis of bones and joints
骨料 aggregate
骨龄 bone age
骨瘤 osteoma
骨膜 periosteum
骨牌 dominoes
骨盆 pelvis
骨气 strength of character;moral integrity;backbone
骨器 bone object;bone implement
骨肉 flesh and blood;kindred
骨髓 marrow
骨炭 bone black;animal charcoal
骨头 ①bone ②moral character ③sharpness;bitterness
骨学 osteology
骨折 fracture
骨子 frame;ribs
骨骼肌 skeletal muscle
骨灰盒 cinerary casket
骨灰林 cinerary grove
骨结核 bone tuberculosis;TB bone
骨膜炎 periostitis
骨软化 osteomalacia
骨髓炎 osteomyelitis
骨子里 in the bones—beneath the surface;in one's innermost nature;in substance
骨干分子 backbone (*or* core,key) elements (*or* member)
骨干工程 backbone projects;major projects
骨干企业 key (*or* elite,backbone) enterprise
骨鲠在喉 having a fishbone caught in one's throat
骨科医生 orthopaedist
骨牌效应 domino effect
骨肉团聚 a family reunion
骨肉相残 fratricidal fighting
骨肉相连 as closely linked as flesh and blood
骨肉兄弟 blood brothers;one's own brothers
骨肉之亲 blood relations

骨瘦如柴 lean as a rake;worn to a shadow;a mere skeleton;a bag of bones
骨瘦形销 grow greatly emaciated
骨髓移植 bone marrow transplantation
骨头架子 ①skeleton ②a very thin person
骨质疏松 osteoporosis

牯 [gǔ] 名 bull
牯牛 bull

贾 [gǔ] Ⅰ 名 merchant Ⅱ 动 ①trade;do business ②buy;purchase ③incur;invite;ask for ④sell
贾害 court disaster
贾马 purchase a horse
贾勇 with courage to spare

罟 [gǔ] Ⅰ 名 fishing net;fishnet Ⅱ 动 catch fish with a net;net

钴 [gǔ] 名 cobalt (Co)
钴合金 cobalt alloy
钴同位素 cobalt isotope

羖 [gǔ] 名 ram

蛊 [gǔ] 名 legendary venomous insect
蛊惑 poison and bewitch
蛊惑人心 confuse and poison people's minds;resort to demagogy

鹄 [gǔ] 名 target (for archery) ➡hú

鼓 [gǔ] Ⅰ 名 ①drum ②drum-shaped object Ⅱ 动 ①beat;strike;play;sound ②blow with a bellows;fan ③rouse;agitate;stir up ④bulge;swell
鼓板 clappers
鼓吹 ①advocate ②preach;advertise;play up
鼓槌 drumstick
鼓捣 ①tinker with;fiddle with ②egg on;incite
鼓动 ①agitate;arouse ②instigate;incite
鼓风 (air) blast
鼓劲 rouse one's enthusiasm
鼓励 encourage;urge
鼓楼 drum tower
鼓膜 tympanic membrane;eardrum
鼓弄 fiddle with;play with
鼓瑟 play the *se*;play the Chinese harp
鼓室 tympanum
鼓手 drummer
鼓舞 inspire;encourage;hearten
鼓翼 (of a bird) flap its wings;wing its way
鼓乐 strains of music accompanied by drumbeats
鼓噪 make an uproar;raise a hubbub;clamour
鼓掌 clap one's hands;applaud
鼓点子 ① drumbeats ② clapper beats which set the tempo and lead the orchestra in traditional Chinese operas
鼓风机 air-blower;blower
鼓鼓囊囊 bulging
鼓膜穿孔 perforation of the tympanic membrane
鼓起精神 pluck up (*or* summon) one's spirit
鼓舞人心 inspiring;heartening
鼓乐喧天 a great din of drums and pipes
鼓掌表决 roll-call vote;vote by roll call (*or* acclamation)
鼓足干劲 go all out
鼓励性价格 incentive price

毂 [gǔ] 名 hub of a wheel

榖 [gǔ] 名 paper mulberry

穀 [gǔ] Ⅰ 形 good;lucky Ⅱ 名 official's salary
穀旦 auspicious day;lucky day

臌 [gǔ] 名 tympanites
臌胀 distension of abdomen caused by accumulation of gas or fluid due to dysfunction of liver and spleen;tympanites

gù（ㄍㄨˋ）

固 [gù] Ⅰ 形 ①firm;strong;solid ②hard;solid ③superficial;ignorant Ⅱ 动 solidify;consolidate;strengthen Ⅲ 副 ①resolutely;persistently;firmly ②originally;in the first place;just;as a matter of course ③admittedly;no doubt
固本 make the stem strong;strengthen the body
固定 ①fixed;regular ②fix;regularize
固防 strengthen (*or* consolidate) defence
固化 solidify
固件 computer firmware
固井 well cementation
固留 firmly ask sb to stay;insist on sb's stay
固请 request sb resolutely (to do sth);invite persistently
固然 though of course;admittedly;no doubt;it is true
固沙 stabilize sand dunes
固守 ① defend tenaciously;be firmly entrenched in ②stick to
固态 solid state
固体 solid body;solid
固有 intrinsic;inherent;innate
固执 ①obstinate;stubborn ②persist in;cling to
固氮菌 nitrogen-fixing bacteria;azotobacter
固沙林 sand-fixation forest;dune-fixing forest
固体水 solid water

固步自封 stand still and refuse to make progress;be complacent and conservative
固氮作用 nitrogen fixation
固定程序 fixed routine;fixed program
固定负债 fixed liability
固定汇率 fixed (exchange) rate
固定机库 permanent hangar
固定基金 fixed fund
固定价格 fixed (or regular) price
固定平价 fixed parity
固定收入 fixed income;regular income
固定投入 fixed input
固定资本 fixed capital
固定资产 fixed assets;permanent assets
固若金汤 strongly fortified;impregnable
固体废物 solid waste
固体酱油 solidified soy sauce
固体燃料 solid fuel
固体水库 solid reservoir
固执己见 stubbornly persist in one's opinions
固执如驴 be as stubborn as mules
固定工资制 fixed-wage system
固定式平炉 stationary open-hearth furnace
固态物理学 solid-state physics
固定资产投资 fixed investments; fixed-assets investment
固定资产增长 appreciation of fixed assets
固体燃料火箭 solid-propellant rocket; solid rocket
固体燃料发动机 solid propellant engine;solid engine

故 [gù] I 名 ①incident; accident ②reason; cause ③friend;acquaintance II 副 intentionally;deliberately;on purpose III 连 hence;therefore; consequently; for this reason IV 形 of the past;former;old V 动 die
故此 therefore
故地 an old haunt
故都 onetime capital
故而 and so;therefore;hence
故宫 the Imperial Palace
故国 native land;native soil;native place
故伎 stock trick;old tactics
故旧 old friends and acquaintances
故居 former residence (or home)
故里 native place;hometown
故且 tentatively;for the moment
故去 (of one's elders) die;pass away
故人 an old friend
故杀 premeditated (or wilful) murder
故事 ①story;tale ②plot
故土 native land; native place; birthplace; hometown
故乡 old home;native place;birthplace
故意 intentionally; wilfully; deliberately; on purpose

故障 hitch;breakdown;stoppage;trouble
故事会 a gathering at which stories are told; story-telling session
故事片 feature film
故纸堆 a heap of musty old books (or papers)
故步自封 stand still and refuse to make progress;be complacent and conservative
故伎重演 be up to one's old tricks; play the same old trick
故弄玄虚 purposely make a mystery of simple things;be deliberately mystifying
故态复萌 slip back into one's old ways
故土难移 it is hard to leave one's native land
故意刁难 deliberately place obstacles;deliberately make things difficult for others
故意犯规 intentional foul
故意杀人 intentional homicide
故作高深 pretend to be learned and profound
故作姿态 strike a pose;put on airs
故宫博物院 the Palace Museum
故障自动分析 automatic malfunction analysis

顾 [gù] I 动 ①turn round and look at; look at ②take care of;attend to;take into consideration (or account) ③pay a visit;visit;call on II 名 customer III 连 ①but; however; nevertheless ②on the contrary;instead
顾及 take into account;attend to;give consideration to
顾忌 scruple;misgiving
顾家 look after one's family
顾客 customer;shopper;client
顾虑 misgiving;apprehension;worry
顾盼 look around
顾全 show consideration for and take care to preserve
顾问 adviser;consultant
顾惜 value;care for
顾主 customer;client;patron
顾面子 ①save face;keep up appearances ②spare sb's feelings
顾此失彼 cannot attend to one thing without neglecting the other;have too many things to take care of at the same time
顾客至上 consumer's sovereignty
顾虑重重 have no end of worries;be full of misgivings
顾名思义 seeing the name of a thing one thinks of its function;just as its name implies;as the term suggests
顾盼生姿 look around charmingly
顾盼自雄 look about complacently
顾全大局 take the interests of the whole into account;consider the situation as a whole
顾问公司 consulting firm
顾影自怜 ①look at one's reflection and admire oneself ②look at one's shadow and la-

G

ment one's lot

顾客心理学 consumer psychology

顾前不顾后 drive ahead without considering the consequences;act rashly

顾问委员会 consultative (*or* advisory) committee

顾大局,识大体 bear the overall situation in mind and put the general interest above all else

堌 [gù] 名 dyke

梏 [gù] 名 ancient wooden handcuffs

崮 [gù] 名 mountain with a flat top surrounded by cliffs

牿 [gù] 名 ①cross wood tied to ox horns to prevent them from butting people ②cattle shed;horse stable;barn

雇 [gù] 动 hire;employ;engage

雇工 ①hire labour;hire hands ②hired labourer (*or* hand,worker) ③farmhand;farm labourer

雇农 farmhand;farm labourer

雇佣 employ;hire

雇员 employee

雇主 employer

雇佣军 mercenary army (*or* troops);mercenaries

雇佣关系 employer-employee relationship

雇佣观点 hired-hand mentality—the attitude of one who won't do more than he is paid for

雇佣合同 employment contract

雇佣奴隶 wage slave

雇佣兵役制 mercenary system

雇佣劳动者 wage labourer

锢 [gù] 动 ①plug with molten metal;run molten metal into cracks ②hold in custody;imprison;jail

锢囚 occlusion

痼 [gù] 形 chronic;enduring;inveterate

痼疾 chronic (*or* obstinate) illness

痼癖 addiction

痼习 inveterate (*or* confirmed) habit

guā（《ㄨㄚ）

瓜 [guā] 名 melon;gourd

瓜分 cut up a melon—carve up;dismember; partition;divide up

瓜葛 connection;implication;association

瓜果 melon and fruit

瓜棚 melon hut

瓜藤 melon (*or* gourd) vine

瓜子 melon seeds

瓜葛亲 distant relatives

瓜皮帽 a kind of skullcap resembling the rind of half a watermelon;skullcap

瓜熟蒂落 when a melon is ripe it falls off its stem—things are easily settled once conditions are ripe

瓜田李下 in a melon patch or under a plum tree—in suspicious circumstances or surroundings

呱 [guā] ➡ gū

呱嗒 clip-clop;clack

呱呱 the quacking of a duck;the croaking of a frog;the cawing of a crow

呱唧 the sound of hands being clapped

呱呱叫 tiptop;top-notch

刮 [guā] 动 ①scrape;scratch;shave ②smear with (paste,etc.) ③plunder;fleece;rob;extort ④scold;give a dressing down ⑤(of wind) blow

刮刀 scraping cutter;scraper

刮宫 dilatation and curettage (D. and C.)

刮脸 shave (the face)

刮痧 a popular treatment for sunstroke by scraping the patient's neck,chest or back

刮削 scrape

刮地皮 scrape off the earth—(of reactionary rulers) extort money from the people

刮脸刀 razor

刮脸皮 rub the forefinger against one's own cheek;point the finger of scorn at sb

刮垢磨光 scrape and polish—①take pains to teach and train a person or to improve oneself ②be meticulous and painstaking

刮目相看 look at sb with new eyes;treat sb with increased respect

胍 [guā] 名 guanidine

栝 [guā] 名 ①Chinese juniper ②nock of an arrow

guǎ（《ㄨㄚˇ）

剐 [guǎ] 动 ①cut to pieces;dismember ②cut;slit

寡 [guǎ] 形 ①few;scarce;scant ②tasteless;thin; bland ③widowed

寡妇 widow

寡人 I,your unworthy king

寡头 oligarch

寡言 taciturn

寡不敌众 be hopelessly outnumbered;fight against hopeless odds

寡见少闻 poorly informed and ignorant

寡廉鲜耻 lost to shame;shameless

寡头政治 oligarchy
寡欲清心 have few desires and cleanse the heart

guà (《ㄨㄚˋ)

卦 [guà]
〈名〉 one of the Eight Trigrams as a divinatory symbol

挂 [guà]
Ⅰ〈动〉①hang; put up; suspend ②leave sth outstanding; be pending ③ring off; hang up ④call up; ring up; put sb through to ⑤hitch; get caught ⑥ be anxious; be concerned about; have sth weighing on one's mind ⑦be covered with; be coated with ⑧register (at a hospital); make an appointment (with a doctor) Ⅱ〈量〉 a set or string (of sth): 一挂珠子 a string of pearls
挂表 pocket watch
挂彩 ①decorate with coloured silk festoons; decorate for festive occasions ② be wounded in action
挂车 trailer
挂齿 mention
挂挡 put into gear
挂钩 ①couple (two railway coaches); articulate ②link up with; establish contact with; get in touch with
挂冠 resign from office
挂号 ①register (at a hospital, etc.) ②send by registered mail
挂花 be wounded in action
挂记 worry about; be anxious about; keep thinking about
挂靠 be attached (or affiliated) to; be subordinate to; be linked with; become attached to another unit
挂历 monthly calender hung up on the wall; wall calender
挂零 odd
挂虑 be anxious about; worry about
挂面 fine dried noodles; vermicelli
挂名 titular; nominal; only in name
挂念 worry about sb who is absent; miss
挂拍 end a career as player of one of the racket games; end of a racket game competition
挂牌 hang out one's shingle; put up one's brass plate; open; go public; announce the transfer list
挂屏 a set of hanging scrolls of painting (or calligraphy)
挂失 report the loss of (identity papers, cheques, etc.)
挂帅 be in command; assume (or take) command; assume leadership
挂锁 padlock
挂毯 tapestry

挂图 ①wall map ②hanging chart
挂心 be on one's mind
挂靴 (of a footballer) retire
挂账 buy or sell on credit suspend repayment
挂职 suspend duties; retain one's position while working temporarily elsewhere
挂钟 wall clock
挂轴 hanging scroll
挂壁式 wall-hanging
挂不住 lose control of one's feelings (in embarrassment)
挂号处 registration office
挂号费 registration fee
挂号信 registered letter (or mail)
挂衣钩 clothes-hook
挂招牌 display a signboard; put up a signboard
挂靠单位 support (or sponsor) group; lack-up organization; work-unit attached to some other group
挂名董事 nominal director; dummy director
挂名夫妻 husband and wife in name only; false couple
挂名股东 nominal partner; ostensible partner
挂牌公司 company listed on a stock exchange; listed company
挂牌股票 listed stock
挂牌证券 quoted securities
挂线疗法 ligating method for treating anal fistula
挂一漏万 for one thing cited, ten thousand may have been left out—the list is far from complete
挂职下放 transfer (a cadre) to lower units with one's post retained
挂牌上市公司 listed company; quoted company
挂羊头,卖狗肉 hang up a sheep's head and sell dogmeat—try to palm off sth inferior to what it purports to be

褂 [guà]
〈名〉 traditional-style garment (or jacket); gown
褂子 a Chinese-style unlined upper garment; short gown

guāi (《ㄨㄞ)

乖 [guāi]
〈形〉①well-behaved; obedient; good ②clever; smart; alert ③contrary (to reason); variant; contradictory ④(of one's character, behaviour, etc.) perverse; abnormal; headstrong
乖乖 ①well-behaved; obedient ②(to a child) little dear; darling ③good gracious
乖觉 alert; quick
乖戾 perverse; unreasonable; disagreeable
乖谬 absurd; abnormal
乖僻 eccentric; odd
乖巧 ①clever; ingenious ②cute; lovely

乖张 eccentric and unreasonable；perverse；recalcitrant

掴 [guāi]
劢 slap；smack

guǎi （《ㄨㄞˇ）

拐 [guǎi]
Ⅰ 劢 ①change direction；turn ②limp ③swindle；make away with ④kidnap；abduct Ⅱ 名 ①corner；turning ②crutch Ⅲ 数 seven：洞拐（07）zero，seven

拐带 kidnap (women or children)；abduct
拐点 point of inflection
拐棍 walking stick
拐角 corner；turning
拐卖 kidnap and sell；engage in slavery
拐骗 abduct；swindle
拐弯 ①turn a corner；make a turn ②change one's opinion to another point of view；pursue a new course ③corner；turning
拐杖 walking stick
拐子 ①cripple ②I-shaped spool (or reel) ③crutch ④abductor；swindler
拐脖儿 elbow (of a stove pipe)
拐弯抹角 talk in a roundabout way；beat about the bush
拐卖人口罪 crime of abducting and selling people
拐卖妇女儿童 abduction of women and children；abduct and sell women and children

guài（《ㄨㄞˋ）

怪 [guài]
Ⅰ 形 strange；odd；queer；eccentric Ⅱ 劢 ①find sth strange；wonder at；be surprised ②blame；reproach Ⅲ 副 rather；quite Ⅳ 名 monster；fiend；demon；evil spirit

怪病 strange (or rare) disease
怪诞 weird；strange
怪话 cynical remark；grumble；complaint
怪癖 eccentric
怪圈 strange phenomenon which is hard to explain；vicious circle
怪事 strange thing
怪胎 monster；teratism
怪物 ①monster；monstrosity；freak ②an eccentric person；a queer bird；oddball
怪异 ①monstrous；strange；unusual ②strange phenomenon；portent；prodigy
怪罪 blame sb
怪不得 ①no wonder；so that's why；that explains why ②not to blame
怪诞不经 weird and uncanny；fantastic
怪喊怪叫 bawl and squall
怪里怪气 eccentric；peculiar；queer
怪模怪样 queer-looking；grotesque

怪声怪气 (speak in) a strange voice or an affected manner
怪石嶙峋 queer rocks of rugged beauty

guān （《ㄨㄢ）

关 [guān]
Ⅰ 劢 ①shut；close ②turn off；switch off ③lock up；shut in ④close down；shut down ⑤involve；implicate；concern Ⅱ 名 ①mountain pass ②area just outside the city gate ③(door) bolt；(door) bar ④tax-collector's checkpoint；customs；customs house ⑤barrier；critical juncture ⑥gear；joint；key

关爱 concern and care；love and care
关隘 (mountain) pass
关闭 ①close；shut ②(of a shop or factory) close down；shut down
关东 east of the Pass
关防 ①security measures ②government or army seal
关怀 show loving care for；show solicitude for
关键 ①door bolt；door bar ②key；hinge；crux
关节 ①joint ②a key (or crucial) link；a key (or crucial) point
关口 ①strategic pass ②juncture
关联 be related；be connected
关卡 an outpost of a tax office；checkpoint
关门 ①(of a shop, etc.) close ②(of a business) close down ③refuse discussion (or consideration)；slam the door on sth ④be behind closed doors
关内 inside the Pass
关切 ①considerate；thoughtful ②be deeply concerned；show one's concern over
关税 customs duty；customs；tariff
关头 juncture；key moment
关外 outside the Pass
关系 ①connections；relations；relationship ②relevance；bearing；influence；significance ③usu. used with 由于 or 因为 to indicate cause or reason ④credentials showing membership in or connection with an organization ⑤concern；affect；have a bearing on；have to do with
关饷 get paid
关心 be concerned about；show solicitude for；care for；be interested in
关押 lock up；put under detention；put in prison
关于 about；on；with regard to；concerning
关张 (of a shop) close down；go out of business
关照 ①look after；take care of；keep an eye on ②notify by word of mouth；tell
关注 follow with interest；pay close attention to；show solicitude for

关东糖 a kind of malt candy
关键词 vogue word;keyword
关节炎 arthritis
关税法 tariff act
关系户 parties of connection;connections
关系网 network of social connections;system of interconnected and cooperating individuals or units
关系学 art (*or* skill) of cultivating good relations with people
关怀备至 show the utmost solicitude
关进牢房 put sb behind bars
关联产业 related properties
关门打狗 bolt the door and beat the dog—block the enemy's retreat and then destroy him
关门大吉 (of a factory, business, etc.) close down for good
关门主义 advocacy of getting the door closed;isolationism
关门捉贼 catch the thief by closing his escape route
关税壁垒 tariff wall;tariff barriers
关税负担 incidence of duty
关税国境 customs frontier
关税豁免 exemption from customs duties
关税减让 tariff diminution;tariff concession
关税配额 customs quota;tariff quota
关税评估 customs evaluation
关税升级 tariff escalation
关税水平 tariff level
关税税则 customs tariff;tariff schedule
关税谈判 tariff bargaining
关税同盟 customs (*or* tariff) union
关税优惠 tariff preference
关税政策 tariff policy;customs policy
关税制度 tariff system
关税自主 tariff autonomy
关停并转 shutting down, suspension, amalgamation,and switching;shift to a different line of production, merge with others, suspend operations or simply close down
关系协调 harmonious relations
关贸总协定 General Agreement on Tariffs and Trade (GATT)
关税自主权 tariff autonomy
关税保证制度 system of customs security
关税最高限额 tariff ceiling
关税普遍优惠制 general preferential duties system
关贸总协定缔约国 a contracting party to GATT

观 [guān]
Ⅰ〈动〉look;see;watch;observe Ⅱ〈名〉① sight;spectacle;view ② outlook;view;concept;conception ➡guàn

观测 ①observe and survey ②observe;watch
观察 observe;watch;survey
观点 point of view;viewpoint;standpoint
观风 be on the lookout;serve as a lookout
观感 impressions;observations
观光 go sightseeing;visit;tour
观看 watch;view
观礼 attend a celebration or ceremony
观摩 inspect and learn from each other's work;view and emulate
观念 sense;idea;concept
观赏 view and admire;enjoy the sight of
观望 ①wait and see;look on (from the sidelines) ②look around
观音 Guanyin; the Goddess of Mercy; (Sanskrit) *Avalokitesvara*
观瞻 the appearance of a place and the impressions it leaves;sight;view
观战 ① watch a battle; watch other people fight ②watch a match (*or* contest)
观照 observe
观众 spectator;viewer;audience
观测站 observation station
观察机 observation aircraft
观察家 observer
观察所 observation post
观察员 observer (who has the right to make a speech,but not to vote)
观潮派 a person who takes a wait-and-see attitude;onlooker;bystander
观光团 touring group; visiting group; sightseeing party
观礼台 reviewing stand;visitors' stand
观摩会 meeting to view and emulate
观赏鱼 fishes for display (e.g. goldfish)
观通站 observation and communication post (of the naval service)
观象台 observatory
观众席 auditorium (of a theatre);grandstand (of a stadium)
观风驶舵 veer with the wind;trim one's sails
观光农业 tourist agriculture
观摩演出 trial performance before fellow artists
观赏艺术 the visual arts
观赏植物 ornamental (*or* decorative) plant
观望态度 wait-and-see attitude;laissez-fair attitude
观云知天 watch clouds and know signs in the sky
观察员身份 observer status
观赏动物保留地 game preserve

官 [guān]
Ⅰ〈名〉① government official; military officer;office holder ②organ Ⅱ〈形〉① official;government-run; state-owned; government-sponsored ②public

官办 run by the government;operated by official bodies
官兵 ①officers and men ②government troops
官厕 public toilet;public lavatory
官场 officialdom;official circles
官尺 official ruler
官倒 official black-marketing;profiteering official; bureaucratic profiteer; official-speculator
官邸 official residence;official mansion
官方 of the government;official
官府 ①local authorities ②feudal official
官宦 government official
官价 official price (*or* rate)
官阶 official's rank
官吏 government officials
官僚 bureaucrat
官了 settle according to policy and law
官迷 a person who hankers after public office; office seeker
官能 (organic) function;sense
官气 bureaucratic airs;bureaucratism
官腔 bureaucratic tone;official jargon
官商 ①government commerce;state-operated commerce ② government merchant;a bureaucratic operator of a commercial enterprise
官司 lawsuit
官衔 official title
官盐 salt sold by the government
官瘾 love for public office;anxiety to be an official
官员 official
官运 official career;fortunes of officialdom
官职 government post;official position
官本位 official rank or status taken as the only criterion for judging one's social worth;official rank standard;official rank standard
官架子 the airs of an official;bureaucratic airs
官能团 functional group
官能症 functional disease
官卑职小 petty official;be merely a petty official
官本位制 predominance of bureaucratic hierarchy;system of ranking of officials
官逼民反 people revolt against official exploitation; oppressive government drives the people to rebellion
官场得意 successful in one's official career
官场语言 bureaucratese;language used by the government agencies;language used in the officialdom
官督商办 government-supervised, merchant-run (enterprises)
官方口径 official version;official account
官方牌价 official market quotation; official listed price;official exchange rates

官方统计 official statistics
官方文件 official documents;patent
官方注册 official register
官复原职 restore an official to his original post;be reinstated
官官相护 bureaucrats shield each other;officials protect each other
官居极品 official of the highest rank
官僚机构 bureaucratic apparatus
官僚主义 bureaucracy;bureaucratism
官僚资本 capital owned by the bureaucrat-capitalist class;bureaucratic capital
官商分开 separate government from commercial undertakings
官商勾结 illegal hookup between government officials and businessmen
官商合营 be jointly run (*or* operated, managed) and/or owned by government and individual businessmen
官商作风 bureaucratic business style
官样文章 mere formalities;officialese;bureaucratic red tape;officialese
官运亨通 have a successful official career
官本位意识 rank consciousness
官方外汇市场 official exchange market
官方外汇资产 official foreign assets
官僚资产阶级 the bureaucrat-capitalist class

冠 [guān]
② ①cap;hat ②sth like a cap or at the top of sth else;corona;crest;comb ➡ guàn
冠冕 ① royal crown; official hat ② stately; ceremonious
冠子 crest;comb
冠心病 coronary heart disease
冠周炎 pericoronitis
冠盖如云 a large gathering of high officials
冠盖相望 constant exchange of high officials' visits between two nations
冠冕堂皇 highfalutin;high-sounding
冠状动脉 coronary artery
冠状静脉 coronary vein
冠状动脉硬化 coronary arteriosclerosis

莞 [guān]
② a long-stem water grass ➡ wǎn

倌 [guān]
② ① stockman; herdsman; livestock keeper;keeper of domestic animals ② hired hand (in certain trades)

棺 [guān]
② coffin
棺材 coffin
棺床 coffin platform
棺椁 inner and outer coffins
棺架 bier
棺木 coffin

鳏 [guān]
⑰ wifeless
鳏夫 an old wifeless man;bachelor (*or* wid-

ower)
鳏夫寡妇 the widows and the widowers
鳏寡孤独 widowers, widows, orphans and the childless—those who have no kith and kin and cannot support themselves

guǎn （ㄍㄨㄢˇ）

馆 [guǎn]
名 ①accommodation for guests; mansion; building ②embassy, legation or consulate ③term for certain service establishments ④place for cultural activities ⑤old-style private school
馆子 restaurant; eating house

管 [guǎn]
Ⅰ 名 ①tube; pipe; conduit; duct ②wind instrument ③valve; tube Ⅱ 量：一管笔 a pen/一管猎枪 a shotgun/一管牙膏 a tube of toothpaste Ⅲ 动 ①manage; run; control ②have jurisdiction over; administer ③subject sb to discipline ④be in charge of; undertake ⑤concern oneself with; bother about; mind; care about ⑥provide; ensure; guarantee ⑦call ⑧involve; concern Ⅳ 介 from; to; towards：管我借东西 borrow sth from me Ⅴ 连 no matter who, how, what, etc.; despite
管保 guarantee; assure
管道 pipeline; piping; conduit; tubing; channel
管护 care for
管家 ①manage a household; run a house ②steward; butler ③manager; housekeeper
管见 my humble opinion; my limited understanding
管教 discipline (children or students); correct
管界 ①area (or land) under control; sphere of jurisdiction; jurisdiction zone ②border of a jurisdiction zone
管井 tube well
管控 management and control
管窥 look at sth through a bamboo tube—have a restricted view
管理 ①manage; run; administer; govern; take care of ②control (people or animals)
管路 pipeline
管片 ①area (or land) under control; sphere of jurisdiction; jurisdiction zone ②border of a jurisdiction zone
管事 ①run affairs; be in charge ②of use; effective ③manager; steward
管束 restrain; check; control
管辖 have jurisdiction over; exercise control over; administer
管线 line pipe
管押 take sb into custody; keep in custody; detain
管涌 sand boil
管用 of use; effective

管制 ①control ②put (a criminal, etc.) under surveillance
管子 tube; pipe
管不了 be unable to control (or manage)
管不着 have no right to interfere; (it's) none of your concern (or business)
管得宽 make everything one's own business
管风琴 pipe organ; organ
管教所 reformatory
管卡压 control, manipulate and suppress
管理处 administrative (or management) office
管理费 management expenses; costs of administration
管理员 a person managing some aspect of daily work within an organization
管辖权 jurisdiction
管闲事 be meddlesome; be a busybody
管弦乐 orchestral music
管乐队 wind band; band
管乐器 wind instrument
管制股 controlled stock
管状花 tubular flower
管子工 plumber; pipe fitter
管吃管穿 provide food and clothing
管家公司 household management corporation (or company)
管窥蠡测 look at the sky through a bamboo tube and measure the sea with a calabash—be restricted in vision and shallow in understanding
管理不善 poor management
管理程序 supervisory routine
管理当局 routine management process
管理方法 office procedure
管理阶层 management echelon
管理经验 management expertise
管理决策 managerial decision
管理科学 management science
管理模式 management model; management pattern
管理系统 management system
管理要素 elements of management
管理艺术 managerial art
管理职能 management function
管弦乐队 orchestra
管修管换 guarantee to repair or exchange (substandard products)
管制价格 controlled price
管制商品 controlled commodity
管理委员会 administrative (or management) committee; board of management
管理专业化 professionalization of management
管中窥豹,可见一斑 look at one spot on a leopard and you can visualize the whole animal; conjure up the whole thing through seeing a part of it

guàn （ㄍㄨㄢ）

串 ［guàn］
名 ① habit ② one's dear ones; one's relatives ➡chuàn

观 ［guàn］
名 Taoist temple ➡guān

贯 ［guàn］
I 动 ① pass through; penetrate; pierce ② be connected; proceed in succession; follow in a continuous line II 名 ① a string of 1,000 cash: 十五贯（title of a traditional opera）*Fifteen Strings of Cash* ② ancestral home; native place ③precedent; existing model

贯彻 carry out; carry through; go through with; put into effect; implement

贯穿 ①run through; penetrate ②permeate

贯串 spread through; run through; permeate

贯通 ①have a thorough knowledge of; be well versed in ②link up; thread together

贯众 ①the rhizome of cyrtomium ②cyrtomium fortunei

贯珠 a string of pearls

贯注 ① concentrate on; be absorbed in ② be connected in meaning or feeling

贯彻始终 prosecute to the end; stick to（a task）to the bitter end

贯穿辐射 penetrating radiation

贯彻民主集中制 carry out the system of democratic centralism

贯彻以预防为主的方针 carry out the policy of putting prevention first

冠 ［guàn］
I 名 ① wear（*or* put on）a hat ② first place; the best; champion II 动 precede; crown with ➡guān

冠词 article

冠军 champion

冠军赛 championship contest; championships

冠名权 right to name

冠绝一时 be the best for a time

掼 ［guàn］
动 ① throw; fling; hurl; toss ② thresh ③ fall; tumble; throw on the ground

掼纱帽 throw away one's official's hat in a huff; resign in resentment; quit office

惯 ［guàn］
动 ① be used（*or* accustomed）to; be inured to; be in the habit of ② indulge; spoil; pamper; coddle

惯常 usualness

惯犯 habitual offender; hardened criminal; recidivist; repeater

惯匪 hardened bandit; professional brigand

惯技 customary tactic; old trick

惯例 convention; usual practice; conventional practice; universal practice; accepted practice

惯量 inertia

惯偷 hardened thief

惯性 inertia

惯用 ①habitually practise; consistently use ② habitual; customary

惯例集团 managerial body

惯性定律 the law of inertia

惯性领航 inertial navigation

惯用语手册 phrase book

惯性飞行导弹 coasting missile; coaster

盥 ［guàn］
I 动 wash（the hands or face）II 名 toilet articles

盥漱 wash one's face and rinse one's mouth

盥洗 wash one's hands and face

盥洗室 washroom

盥洗台 washstand

灌 ［guàn］
动 ① irrigate; water ② fill; pour; cram ③ record（sound or music on a tape or disc）

灌溉 irrigate

灌浆 ①grout ②（of grain）be in the milk ③ form a vesicle

灌录 make a recording

灌木 bush; shrub

灌区 irrigated district

灌输 ① divert running water for use elsewhere ②instil into; inculcate; imbue with

灌音 have one's voice recorded

灌制 tape-record; record

灌注 pour into

灌醉 make sb drunk; fuddle

灌溉渠 irrigation canal

灌溉网 irrigation network

灌米汤 lay it on thick; butter sb up

灌溉面积 area under irrigation; irrigated area

灌溉系统 irrigation system

灌迷魂汤 try to ensnare sb with honeyed words

鹳 ［guàn］
名 stork

罐 ［guàn］
名 ①jar; pot; tin; tank; pitcher ②coal tub

罐车 tank car; tank truck; tanker

罐笼 cage

罐头 ① pot; jar; pitcher; jug ② tinned（*or* canned）food

罐装 canning

罐子 pot; jar; pitcher; jug

罐焖牛肉 roast; pot roast

罐头食品 tinned（*or* canned）food（*or* goods）

guāng （ㄍㄨㄤ）

光 ［guāng］
I 名 ① light; ray ② scenery; landscape; sight ③ honour; glory; credit ④ good; advan-

tage;benefit ⑤ *used of what the other party does for one* Ⅱ 动 ① shine upon; glorify; bring honour to ② use up; finish Ⅲ 形 ① smooth; glossy ② bright; shiny ③ bare; naked Ⅳ 副 solely; merely; only; alone

光斑 facula
光泵 optical pump
光笔 light pen
光标 cursor
光波 light wave
光彩 ①lustre; splendour; radiance ②honourable; honoured; glorious
光大 ① glorify; carry forward; develop ② wide; extensive
光点 light spot
光电 photoelectricity
光碟 optical disc
光度 luminosity
光复 recover (lost territory); restore (old glory, etc.)
光谷 optical valley; Photon Valley
光顾 patronize
光棍 ①ruffian; hoodlum ②a clever (*or* wise) person
光华 brilliance; splendour
光滑 smooth; glossy; sleek
光化 ①actinic ②photochemical
光环 ①a ring of light (round a planet) ②halo (round the head of a holy person)
光辉 ①radiance; brilliance; glory ②brilliant; magnificent; glorious
光洁 bright and clean
光景 ①scene ②situation; circumstances; conditions ③about; around
光刻 photoetching
光缆 fiber-optic cable; optical cable
光亮 bright; luminous; shiny
光疗 phototherapy
光临 (of a guest or visitor) honour sb with one's presence
光芒 rays of light; brilliant rays; radiance
光敏 photosensitive
光明 ① light ② bright; promising ③ open-hearted; guileless
光年 light-year
光盘 optical disk; compact disc (CD)
光票 clean bill; clean draft
光谱 spectrum
光气 phosgene
光球 photosphere
光驱 optical disc driver
光圈 diaphragm; aperture; stop
光荣 ①honourable; honoured; glorious ②honour; glory; credit
光润 (of skin) smooth
光渗 irradiation
光束 light beam

光速 velocity of light
光头 ①bare one's head ②shaven head
光纤 light guide; optical fibre
光线 light; ray
光学 optics
光焰 radiance; flare
光耀 ① brilliant light; brilliance ② honour; glory; credit ③ glorify; carry forward; develop
光阴 time available; time
光源 light source; illuminant
光泽 lustre; gloss; sheen
光栅 grating
光照 illumination
光制 finishing
光子 photon
光板儿 ①worn-out fur ②(in former times) a copper coin without a distinctive stamp
光电管 photocell; phototube
光电子 photoelectron
光度计 photometer
光辐射 ray radiation
光杆儿 ① a bare trunk (*or* stalk) ② a man who has lost his family ③a person without a following
光洁度 smooth finish
光介子 photomeson
光溜溜 ①smooth; slippery ②bare; naked
光谱学 spectroscopy
光荣榜 honour roll; roster of honour
光荣花 rosette
光荣院 institutes for the glorious; nursing homes
光扫描 photoscanning; optical scanning
光通量 luminous flux
光通信 optical communication
光秃秃 bare; bald
光污染 light pollution
光行差 aberration
光质子 photoproton
光彩夺目 shine with dazzling brilliance
光导纤维 light guide; optical fibre
光电导体 photoconductor
光电效应 photoelectric efficiency
光杆司令 a general without an army; a leader without a following
光怪陆离 grotesque in shape and gaudy in colour; bizarre and motley
光合作用 photosynthesis
光滑如玉 as smooth as jade
光化作用 photochemical action
光辉灿烂 glorious and magnificent; brilliant and dazzling
光芒四射 radiate brilliant light
光芒万丈 shining with boundless radiance; gloriously radiant; resplendent
光敏电阻 photoresistance

G

光明磊落 open and aboveboard
光明正大 just and honourable; open and aboveboard
光盘杂志 CD-ROM magazine
光票托收 collection on clean bill
光谱分析 spectrum (*or* spectral) analysis
光荣之家 an honourable family
光山秃岭 bare hills and mountains
光说不做 only talk and not to act
光天化日 broad daylight; the light of day
光物理学 photophysics
光纤通信 optical fiber communication
光纤通讯 fibre communication optical
光学玻璃 optical glass
光学录音 optical recording
光学容限 optical tolerance
光学纤维 light guide; optical fibre
光学仪器 optical instrument
光阴似箭 time flies like an arrow; how time flies
光植物学 photobotany
光宗耀祖 bring honour to one's ancestors
光电子技术 photoelectronic technology
光幅度调制 light amplitude modulation
光敏二极管 photodiode
光盘驱动器 CD-ROM driver; disc drive
光谱比较仪 spectrocomparator
光打雷不下雨 all thunder and no rain; all bark and no bite; all words and no action
光机电一体化 optical, mechanical and electronic integration

呪 [guāng]
〔拟〕bang; crash: 呪的一声，关上了门 slam the door shut; shut the door with a bang

桄 [guàng]
⇒ guàng
桄榔 gomuti palm

胱 [guāng]
◇膀胱 (urinary) bladder

guǎng （《ㄨㄤ）

广 [guǎng]
Ⅰ〔形〕①(of area, scope, etc.) wide; vast; extensive ②numerous; many Ⅱ〔动〕expand; spread; extend
广板 largo
广播 ①broadcast; be on the air ②broadcast; air
广博 (of a person's knowledge) extensive; broad; wide
广场 public square; square
广大 ①(of an area or space) vast; wide; extensive ②large-scale; wide-spread ③(of people) numerous
广度 scope; range
广泛 broad; extensive; wide-ranging; wide-spread
广告 advertisement
广阔 vast; wide; broad
广漠 vast and bare
广延 extension
广义 ①broad sense ②generalized
广播稿 broadcast script
广播剧 radio play
广播室 broadcast
广播网 rediffusion (*or* broadcasting) network
广播员 (radio) announcer; broadcaster
广播站 broadcasting station (of a factory, school, etc.); rediffusion station
广告费 advertising expenses; advertising fee
广告画 poster
广告界 adland
广告栏 advertisement column (in a newspaper, etc.)
广告牌 billboard
广告片 advertising film
广告色 poster colour
广寒宫 the Moon Palace (the mythical palace in the moon)
广交会 the Guangzhou Export Commodities Fair
广木香 costusroot
广域网 wide area network (WAN)
广播电台 broadcasting (*or* radio) station
广播讲话 broadcast speech; radio talk
广播教学 distance teaching
广播节目 broadcast (*or* radio) programme
广播喇叭 loudspeaker
广播时间 air time
广播体操 setting-up (*or* callisthenic) exercises to radio music
广播卫星 broadcasting satellite
广播找人 page
广而告之 give extensive publicity; spread far and wide
广而言之 speaking generally; in a general sense
广告策划 advertisement scheme
广告歌曲 commercial song
广告公司 advertising firm
广告价格 advertising rates
广告文化 advertisement culture
广告预算 advertising budget
广见博闻 widely experienced
广角镜头 wide-angle lens
广开才路 open all avenues for people of talent
广开财源 open up new financial sources
广开言路 provide wide opportunities for airing views; encourage the free airing of views
广厦高楼 high and big buildings; skyscrapers
广为流行 be very popular
广种薄收 extensive cultivation with low yield
广告代理人 advertising agent

广播电视大学 radio and television university; college on the air
广告电话直销 direct response advertising
广开就业门路 create employment opportunities;open up new avenues (*or* channels) of employment;offer more job openings
广域信息服务系统 wide area information server（WAIS）

犷 ［guǎng］
形 rustic;uncouth;boorish
犷悍 tough and intrepid

guàng （ㄍㄨㄤˋ）

桄 ［guàng］
Ⅰ 动 reel (thread or wire) on a revolving frame Ⅱ 名 reel Ⅲ 量 (*of thread or wire*): 两桄电线 two reels of wire ➡ guāng

逛 ［guàng］
动 stroll;roam;saunter;ramble
逛荡 loiter;loaf about
逛窑子 visit a brothel

guī （ㄍㄨㄟ）

归 ［guī］
动 ①return;go or come back ②give back; return sth to sb ③converge;come together; group together ④be in sb's charge;put under sb's care ⑤belong to ⑥(*used between identical verbs to indicate uselessness or irrelevance of the action*):玩笑归玩笑,你欠的钱到期还得还。 Never mind the joke, you'll have to repay the debt punctually all the same. ⑦divide (on the abacus) with a one-digit divisor
归案 bring to justice
归并 ① incorporate into; merge into ② lump together;add up
归程 return journey
归档 place on file;file away
归队 ①rejoin one's unit ②return to the profession one was trained for
归附 submit to the authority of another
归功 give the credit to;attribute the success to
归国 return to one's country
归航 homing
归还 return;revert
归结 ①come to a conclusion;sum up;put in a nutshell ②end (of a story,etc.)
归咎 impute to;attribute a fault to;put the blame on
归类 sort out;classify
归拢 put together
归纳 induce;conclude;sum up
归期 date of return
归侨 returned overseas Chinese
归入 classify;include

归属 belong to;come under the jurisdiction of
归顺 come over and pledge allegiance
归宿 a home to return to;a permanent home;a final settling place
归天 pass away;die
归途 homeward journey;one's way home
归降 surrender
归于 ①belong to;be attributed to ②result in; end in
归置 put in order;tidy up
归巢儿 boomerang kid
归谬法 reduction to absurdity;reduction ad absurdum
归纳法 the inductive method;induction
归费收入 income from the payment of stipulated fees
归根结底 in the final analysis;fundamentally
归国华侨 returned overseas Chinese
归口部门 competent department;department in charge
归口管理 management through specialized authorities; centralized management by specific department; subject to control by competent authorities
归心似箭 with one's heart set on speeding home;impatient to get back;anxious to return
归真返璞 return to original purity and simplicity

圭 ［guī］
名 ① tapering jade tablet ② sundial (consisting of an elongated dial and one or two gnomons) ③ancient measurement of volume,about ten microlitres
圭表 an ancient Chinese sundial consisting of an elongated dial (gui) and one or two gnomons (biao)
圭臬 criterion;standard

龟 ［guī］
名 ①tortoise;turtle ②cuckold ➡ jūn
龟板 tortoise plastron
龟背 curvature of the spinal column
龟甲 tortoise-shell
龟缩 huddle up like a turtle drawing in its head and legs; withdraw into passive defence;hole up
龟头 glans penis

规 ［guī］
Ⅰ 名 ①dividers;compasses ②rule;regulation;convention ③gauge Ⅱ 动 ①admonish; counsel;advise ②plan;devise;map out
规避 evade;dodge;avoid
规程 rules;regulations
规定 ① stipulate; provide; prescribe ② rule; regulation;stipulation
规范 standard;norm
规费 state-set fees

G

规格 specifications;standards;norms
规划 ① programme; plan ② make a programme;draw up a plan
规矩 ①rules of a community or organization; established practice; custom ② customary rules of good behaviour; social etiquette; manners ③ proper in behaviour; well-behaved;well-disciplined
规律 law;regular pattern
规模 ① scale; scope; extent; dimensions ② large-scale
规劝 admonish;advise
规约 stipulations of an agreement
规则 ①rule;regulation ②regular
规章 rules;regulations
规范化 standardize
规律性 regularity;law
规避战术 evasion tactics
规定动作 compulsory exercise
规定数额 quota
规费收入 income from the payment of stipulated fees
规划目标 object of planning
规矩准绳 compasses, set square, spirit level and plumb line—standards;norms;criteria
规模经济 economy of scale
规行矩步 ① behave correctly and cautiously ②stick to established practice; follow the beaten track
规章制度 regulatory framework
规模不经济 diseconomy of scale
规范市场行为 standardize market activities

皈 〔guī〕
皈依 ①the ceremony of proclaiming sb a Buddhist ②be converted to Buddhism or some other religion

闺 〔guī〕
闺 名 ①arch-topped door ②boudoir
闺房 lady's chamber;boudoir
闺女 ①girl;maiden ②daughter

硅 〔guī〕
硅 名 silicon (Si)
硅尘 siliceous dust;silica dust
硅肺 silicosis
硅钢 silicon steel
硅谷 Silicon Valley
硅华 siliceous sinter;silica sinter
硅胶 silica gel
硅片 silicon wafer;silicon chip
硅石 silica
硅酸 silicic acid
硅铁 ferrosilicon
硅藻 diatom
硅砖 silica brick
硅单晶 single crystal silicon
硅铝带 sial

硅镁带 sima
硅锰钢 silico-manganese steel
硅酸铝 aluminium silicate
硅酸钠 sodium silicate
硅酸盐 silicate
硅藻土 diatomaceous earth;diatomite
硅二极管 silicon detector;silicon diode
硅可控整流器 silicon-controlled rectifier;thyristor

傀 〔guī〕
傀 形 ① unusual; strange; odd ② stand all by oneself ➡ kuǐ
傀奇 unusual;peculiar

瑰 〔guī〕
瑰 I 名 jade-like stone II 形 rare; marvellous;magnificent
瑰宝 rarity;treasure;gem
瑰丽 surpassingly beautiful;magnificent
瑰玮 ①(of one's character) remarkable ②(of language or style) ornate

guī 《ㄍㄨㄟ》

轨 〔guī〕
轨 I 名 ①rail ②track ③course; orbit; rule; order II 动 abide by;adhere to
轨道 ①track ②orbit; trajectory ③the proper way of doing things;a proper course
轨范 standard;criterion
轨迹 ①locus ②orbit
轨距 gauge
轨枕 sleeper;tie
轨道衡 track scale
轨迹球 trackball
轨道变换 orbital transfer
轨道火箭 orbital rocket
轨道交角 orbit inclination
轨道平面 orbit plane
轨道运动 orbital motion
轨于法令 abide by law
轨道空间站 orbital space station

庋 〔guī〕
庋 I 名 shelf II 动 keep;preserve;shelve
庋藏 store up;preserve
庋之高阁 have sth shelved

匦 〔guī〕
匦 名 folder;box;casket

诡 〔guī〕
诡 形 ① deceitful; tricky; sly; cunning ② weird;uncanny;eerie
诡辩 ①quibble; indulge in sophistry ②sophistry;sophism;quibbling
诡称 falsely allege;pretend
诡计 a crafty plot; a cunning scheme; trick; ruse
诡谲 ①strange and changeful ②weird;eccentric;odd ③crafty;cunning;treacherous
诡雷 booby mine;booby trap

诡秘 furtive;surreptitious;secretive
诡异 strange;abnormal
诡诈 crafty;cunning;treacherous
诡辩术 sophistry
诡计多端 have a whole bag of tricks;be very crafty

块 [guǐ] 〔形〕 collapsed
块垲 dilapidated wall;wall in ruins

鬼 [guǐ] Ⅰ〔名〕① ghost;phantom;spirit;apparition ②derogatory term for a person with a certain vice or problem ③sinister plot;dirty trick Ⅱ〔形〕① stealthy;clandestine;surreptitious ② terrible;wretched;damnable ③clever;smart;quick
鬼怪 ghosts and monsters;monsters of all kinds;forces of evil
鬼话 false words;lies
鬼魂 ghost;spirit;apparition
鬼混 lead an aimless (or irregular) existence;fool around
鬼火 phosphorescent light;will-o'-the-wisp;jack-o'-lantern
鬼脸 ① funny face;wry face;grimace ② a mask used as a toy
鬼魅 ghosts and goblins;forces of evil
鬼胎 sinister design; ulterior motive; dark scheme
鬼蜮 evil spirit;demon;treacherous person
鬼子 devil (a term of abuse for foreign invaders)
鬼把戏 sinister plot;dirty (or underhand) trick
鬼点子 wicked idea;devilish trick
鬼门关 the gate of hell—a danger spot;a trying moment
鬼天气 vile weather;terrible weather
鬼针草 beggar-ticks
鬼主意 evil plan;wicked idea
鬼斧神工 uncanny workmanship;superlative craftsmanship
鬼鬼祟祟 sneaking;furtive;stealthy
鬼话连篇 a pack of lies;lies from start to finish
鬼哭狼嚎 wail like ghosts and howl like wolves;let loose wild shrieks and howls
鬼迷心窍 be possessed;be obsessed
鬼使神差 doings of ghosts and gods—unexpected happenings;a curious coincidence
鬼头鬼脑 thievish;stealthy;furtive
鬼蜮伎俩 a devilish stratagem; evil tactics; dirty underhanded tricks

晷 [guǐ] 〔名〕①shadow cast by the sun;time ② sundial;gnomon

guì《ㄍㄨㄟˋ》

柜 [guì] 〔名〕① cupboard;cabinet ② cashier's office;cashier's desk;cashier's
柜房 cashier's office in a shop;shop cashier
柜台 counter;bar
柜员 counter clerk;teller
柜子 cupboard;cabinet
柜员机 automated teller machine (ATM)
柜台交易 over-the-counter

刿 [guì] 〔名〕 wound;cut;stab

刽 [guì] 〔动〕 cut off;chop off
刽子手 ①executioner;headsman ②slaughterer;butcher

贵 [guì] 〔形〕①high-priced;expensive;costly;dear ② valuable; highly valued; precious ③ of high rank;exalted;noble ④your
贵宾 honoured guest;distinguished guest
贵妃 highest-ranking imperial concubine
贵干 honourable business;noble errand
贵客 honoured guest
贵人 ①a high official ②a high-ranking imperial concubine
贵重 valuable;precious
贵族 noble;aristocrat
贵宾室 VIP room
贵宾席 seats for distinguished guests;distinguished visitors' gallery
贵金属 noble (or precious) metal
贵客盈门 The house was full of distinguished guests.
贵族学校 schools for privileged students
贵宾休息室 reserved lounge (for honoured guests)
贵人多忘事 a man of your eminence has a short memory;important people have short memories

桂 [guì] 〔名〕①cassia;cinnamon ②sweet-scented osmanthus ③laurel;bay tree ④cassia-bark tree
桂冠 laurel
桂花 sweet-scented osmanthus
桂皮 ① cassia-bark tree; Chinese cinnamon tree ② cassia;cassia bark;Chinese cinnamon
桂鱼 mandarin fish
桂圆 longan
桂枝 cassia twig
桂花酒 wine fermented with osmanthus flowers

桧 [guì] 〔名〕 Chinese juniper

跪 [guì] 〔动〕 kneel;go down on one's knees

跪拜　worship on bended knees; *kowtow*
跪倒　throw oneself on one's knees; prostrate oneself; grovel
跪射　kneeling fire
跪姿　kneeling position

gǔn （ㄍㄨㄣˇ）

衮　[gǔn]
〈名〉ceremonial dress for royalty
衮衮　①continual ②numerous
衮冕　emperor's ceremonial dress and hat
衮衮诸公　① high-ranking officials; government dignitaries ②Your Excellencies

滚　[gǔn]
〈动〉①roll; trundle; tumble ②get away; beat it ③ boil; seethe ④ roll along or about (in snow or flour); get bigger and bigger; snowball ⑤bind; trim
滚蛋　beat it; scram
滚刀　hobbing cutter; hob
滚动　roll; trundle; rolling
滚翻　roll
滚滚　roll; billow; surge
滚开　beat it; scram
滚雷　rolling mine
滚轮　gyro wheel; hoop
滚热　piping hot; burning hot; boiling hot
滚水　boiling water
滚烫　boiling hot; burning hot
滚梯　escalator
滚筒　cylinder; roll
滚圆　round as a ball
滚轧　rolling
滚珠　ball
滚槽机　channelling machine
滚齿机　gear-hobbing machine; hobbing machine
滚刀肉　unreasonable troublemaker; annoying person; nuisance
滚水坝　overflow dam
滚雪球　(of a business, project, etc.) get bigger and bigger as it proceeds; snowball
滚子链　roller chain
滚存费用　deferred charge
滚存利益　accumulated profit
滚存资金　deferred assets
滚动摩擦　rolling friction
滚动轴承　rolling bearing
滚瓜烂熟　(recite, etc.) fluently; (know sth) by heart
滚滚而来　roll in; come in torrents
滚汤热菜　boiling soup and hot dishes; hot food
滚针轴承　needle bearing
滚珠轴承　ball bearing
滚柱轴承　roller bearing
滚装码头　ro-ro dock; roll-on-roll-off dock
滚筒印刷机　cylinder press

磙　[gǔn]
Ⅰ〈名〉roller Ⅱ〈动〉level (ground) with a roller
磙子　①stone roller ②roller

gùn （ㄍㄨㄣˋ）

棍　[gùn]
〈名〉①rod; stick; cane; cudgel ②scoundrel; rascal; ruffian
棍棒　①club; cudgel; bludgeon ②a stick (or staff) used in gymnastics
棍术　art (or skill) of cudgel playing
棍子　rod; stick

guō （ㄍㄨㄛ）

埚　[guō]
◇坩埚　crucible

郭　[guō]
〈名〉①outer wall of a city ②rim; frame

聒　[guō]
〈形〉noisy
聒耳　grate on one's ears
聒噪　noisy; clamorous

锅　[guō]
〈名〉①pot; pan ②cooker ③bowl (of a pipe, etc.)
锅巴　crust of cooked rice; rice crust
锅铲　slice
锅盖　the lid of a cooking pot
锅炉　boiler
锅台　the top of a kitchen range
锅子　①bowl (of a pipe, etc.) ②chafing dish
锅炉房　boiler room
锅贴儿　lightly fried dumpling
锅驼机　portable steam engine; locomobile
锅烟子　soot on the bottom of a pan
锅炉防垢剂　boiler compound

蝈　[guō]
蝈蝈儿　katydid; long-horned grasshopper

guó （ㄍㄨㄛˊ）

国　[guó]
Ⅰ〈名〉country; state; nation Ⅱ〈形〉①of the state; national ② best in the country ③ of China; Chinese
国宝　national treasure
国标　state standard; international standard social dance
国宾　state guest
国策　the basic policy of a state; national policy
国产　domestically produced; made in our country; made in China
国耻　national humiliation
国粹　the quintessence of Chinese culture
国道　state highway; national road; national

highway
国都 national capital;capital
国度 country;state;nation
国法 the law of the land;national law;law
国防 national defence
国父 father of a republic
国歌 national anthem
国格 national prestige (*or* image, quality, character,dignity)
国号 the title of a reigning dynasty
国花 national flower (as an emblem)
国画 traditional Chinese painting
国徽 national emblem
国会 parliament;(in the U.S.) Congress;(in Japan) the Diet
国魂 the soul of a nation;the national genius
国货 China-made goods;Chinese goods
国籍 nationality;citizenship
国际 international
国家 country;nation;state
国交 diplomatic relations
国脚 national football team star (*or* player); player of the national football team;footballer of the national team
国教 state religion
国界 national boundaries
国境 national territory
国君 monarch
国库 the public purse; national (*or* state) treasury;exchequer
国力 national power (*or* strength,might)
国立 state-maintained;state-run
国门 the gateway of a country
国民 a member of a nation;national;the people of a nation
国难 national crisis
国内 internal;domestic;home
国旗 national flag
国企 state enterprise;state-owned enterprise
国情 the condition (*or* state) of a country; national conditions
国人 compatriots;fellow countrymen; countrymen
国事 national (*or* state) affairs
国手 top-notch person in the country (in chess,medicine,etc.);member of the national team;national champion (in chess, etc.);grand master
国书 letter of credence;credentials
国术 traditional Chinese martial arts
国税 national tax;central tax
国体 ①state system ②national prestige
国土 territory;land
国外 external;overseas;abroad
国王 king
国威 international prestige of a state;national power and influence

国务 state affairs
国玺 ①imperial seal ②national seal
国学 studies of Chinese ancient civilization
国宴 state banquet
国营 state-operated;state-run
国优 (of a product) national best
国有 belonging to the nation (*or* the state); state-owned
国语 the national language used by the people at large
国运 the fortunes (*or* destiny) of a nation
国葬 state funeral
国债 government bond;national debts
国嘴 a top-ranking broadcaster in the country
国奥队 the National Olympics Team
国宾馆 state guesthouse
国产化 production domestication (*or* signification)
国产品 national (*or* domestic, China-made, home-made) products
国防部 the Ministry of National Defence
国防军 national defence troops (*or* forces)
国防线 national defence line
国际歌 the Internationale
国际化 internationalize
国家队 national squad;national team
国家法 constitutional law;the law of the state
国家级 state-level;state-class
国境线 the boundary (line) of a country
国库券 state treasury bonds;exchequer bond; treasury bonds;treasury bill
国民党 the Kuomintang (KMT)
国庆节 National Day
国税局 National Tax Bureau
国务卿 (in the U.S.) Secretary of State
国务院 the State Council
国有股 state-owned shares
国有化 convert to national ownership;nationalize
国子监 the Imperial College (the highest educational administration in feudal China)
国产汽车 homebred autos
国耻纪念 commemoration of national humiliation
国定关税 national tariff
国法不容 not allowed by law; punishable by law
国防教育 education about national defense; defense education
国防经费 outlays for national defence
国防前哨 national defence outpost
国防实力 national defence capabilities
国防支出 expenditure on national defence;defence spending
国计民生 the national economy and the people's livelihood
国际财团 consortium

国际裁判 international referee
国际驰名 world-famous
国际大赦 Amnesty International
国际地位 international standing
国际法院 the International Court of Justice; the World Court
国际分工 international division of labour
国际公法 (public) international law; the law of nations
国际公约 international convention
国际公制 the metric system
国际共管 condominium
国际关系 international relations
国际惯例 international practices (*or* norms, conventions)
国际航道 international waterway (*or* sea-lane)
国际货币 convertible foreign exchange; international currency
国际机场 international airport
国际机构 international machinery
国际结算 international clearing
国际礼让 comity of nations
国际联盟 the League of Nations
国际列车 international train
国际贸易 international trade (*or* commerce); world trade
国际社会 the international community
国际市场 international market
国际事务 international (*or* world) affairs
国际收支 balance of (international) payments
国际水道 international waterway; international watercourse
国际水域 international waters
国际私法 private international law
国际象棋 chess
国际刑警 Interpol (International Criminal Police Commission)
国际音标 the International Phonetic Symbols (*or* Alphabet)
国际游资 hot money
国际友人 foreign friends
国际舆论 world (public) opinion
国际争端 international dispute
国际制裁 international sanctions
国际主义 internationalism
国家裁判 state (*or* national) referee
国家大事 national affairs; state affairs
国家典礼 state functions
国家公园 national park
国家机关 state organs; government offices
国家机器 state apparatus; state machinery
国家决算 final accounts of state revenue and expenditure; final state accounts
国家牌价 national price; price fixed by the highest national administrative office
国家赔偿 state compensation

国家权力 state power
国家统购 centralized state-operated procurement
国家学说 theory of the state
国家银行 state bank
国家预算 state budget
国家元首 head of state
国家政权 state power
国家职能 functions and powers of the state
国家主权 state sovereignty
国家主席 (Chinese) president
国将不国 the nation is in peril
国库盈余 treasury surplus
国力雄厚 have solid national strength
国民待遇 national treatment (NT)
国民经济 national economy
国民收入 national income
国难深重 serious national calamity
国破家亡 country conquered and family ruined
国情教育 education about national conditions
国情咨文 (in the U.S.) State of the Union Message
国色天香 ethereal colour and celestial fragrance (said of the peony or a beautiful woman)
国事访问 state visit
国泰民安 the country is prosperous and the people live in peace
国土规划 national land-use planning
国土资源 land and resources
国务会议 state conference
国务委员 a member of the State Council; State Councillor
国营经济 state sector of the economy; state-owned economy
国营农场 state farm
国营牌价 state set prices
国营企业 state enterprise
国优产品 quality products designated by the state; the nation's best products; state-recognized quality products; state-level quality product; quality products which have received national awards
国有经济 state-owned sector of the economy; state-owned economy
国有企业 state-owned enterprise
国有资产 state-owned assets; state assets
国债市场 market of national bonds; market of T-bonds; state treasure bond market
国防科工委 the Commission of Science Technology and Industry for National Defence
国防委员会 the National Defence Council
国际博览会 international fair; international exhibition
国际单位制 international system of units
国际儿童节 International Children's Day (June 1)

国际妇女节 International Women's Day (March 8)
国际和平年 International Year of Peace
国际环境日 World Environment Day
国际空间站 international space station
国际劳动节 International Labour Day; May Day (May 1)
国际扫盲年 International Literacy Year
国际住房年 International Year of Shelter for the Homeless
国家标准局 National Bureau of Standards (NBS)
国家储备金 state reserve funds
国家副主席 (Chinese) vice-president
国家公务员 civil servant
国家领导人 state leaders
国家所有制 state ownership
国家统计局 the State Statistic Bureau
国民生产力 per capita productivity
国民总储蓄 gross national savings
国民总供给 gross national supply
国民总收入 gross national income
国民总需求 gross national expenditure (GND)
国防动员体制 mobilization for national defense
国防后备力量 reserves for national defense; reserve force for defense
国际安全合作 international security cooperation
国际标准规格 international standards
国际标准书号 international standard book number (ISBN)
国际储备货币 international reserve currency
国际电信联盟 International Telecommunication Union (ITU)
国际关系准则 norms of international relations; standards for international relations
国际黄金总库 international gold pool
国际货币政策 international monetary policy
国际技术转让 international transfer of technology
国际金融中心 international financial centre
国际经济合作 international economic cooperation
国际经济秩序 international economic order
国际军火市场 the world munitions market
国际垄断同盟 international monopoly combines
国际垄断组织 international monopoly
国际贸易政策 international trade policy
国际贸易中心 international trade centre
国际人权领域 human rights in the world arena
国际人权组织 international human rights organization
国际商业机器 International Business Machine Corporation (IBM)
国际市场价格 world (*or* international) market price
国际双重征税 international double taxation
国际铁路联运 international railway through transport
国际通信卫星 Intelsat (International Telecommunications Satellite)
国际通用商标 international brand
国际刑警组织 interpol
国际资本市场 international capital market
国家安全利益 national security interests
国家创新能力 national innovation capacity
国家创新体系 national innovation system
国家工作人员 personnel of organs of state; state personnel
国家开发银行 National Development Bank
国家控股公司 state-controlling company
国家权力机关 organs of state power
国家特殊津贴 special state allowance
国家外汇储备 state (*or* national) foreign exchange reserves
国家行政机关 administrative organs of the state
国家一级企业 state first-level enterprises
国家整体实力 overall national strength
国家重点工程 the country's key projects
国家资本主义 state capitalism
国民待遇标准 the standard of national treatment
国民经济命脉 life-blood of the national economy
国民生产净值 net national product (NNP)
国民生产总值 gross national product (GNP)
国内生产总值 gross domestic product (GDP)
国内消费水平 domestic consumption level
国内直拨电话 domestic direct dial (DDD)
国外反华势力 anti-Chinese abroad
国外引进项目 projects whose equipment and technology are introduced from abroad
国有大型企业 large state-owned enterprise
国有控股企业 state-owned enterprise
国有商业银行 commercial state banks
国有资产流失 drain (*or* loss) of state-owned assets
国债专项资金 special fund for treasury bond
国定及协定税则 national and conventional tariff
国际标准化组织 International Organization for Standardization
国际公认的标准 universally (*or* internationally) accepted (*or* recognized) standards
国际日期变更线 international date line (IDL)
国际原子能组织 International Atomic Energy Agency (IAEA)
国家奥林匹克队 the National Olympics Team
国家公共信息网 national public information network
国家公务员制度 system of public services

国家技术发明奖 national technical invention award

国家技术监督局 the State Bureau of Technical Supervision

国家科技进步奖 national scientific and technological progress award; national award for progress in science and technology

国家认可的学历 state-designated standard of formal schooling

国家自然保护区 state nature reserves

国家自然科学奖 national natural science award

国有大中型企业 state-run large and medium-sized enterprises

国际共产主义运动 the international communist movement

国际货币基金组织 International Monetary Fund (IMF)

国际经济通行规则 generally accepted international practices in the economic field

国际人权法律文书 international legal instruments on human rights

国家经济建设大局 the overall interests of national economic development

国家垄断资本主义 state monopoly capitalism

国家重点建设项目 state (*or* national) key construction project

国民收入超额分配 excessive distribution of national income; earmark an excessive proportion of the national income for consumption

国务院稽查特派员 special inspector appointed by the State Council

国有经济主导作用 leading role of the state-owned sector of the economy

国有企业技术改造 technical upgrading of state-owned enterprise

国家兴亡，匹夫有责 every man has a share of responsibility for the fate of his country

国际奥林匹克委员会 the International Olympic Committee (IOC)

国际政治经济新秩序 new international political and economic order

国家普通话水平考试 National Proficiency Test of Putonghua

国民经济市场化进程 process of building a complete market system in the national economy; the market-oriented process of the national economy

国有资产经营责任制 system of responsibility for the management of state assets

国有资产评估与管理 assessment and management of state assets

国家经济体制改革委员会 the State Commission Restructuring the Economic Systems

国家语言文字工作委员会 State Language Work Committee

国民经济整体素质和效益 the quality and performance of the national economy as a whole; the overall quality and performance of the national economy

国务院直属机构与办事机构 offices and agencies directly under the State Council

国务院香港和澳门事务办公室 the Hong Kong and Macao Affairs Office under the State Council

帼 [guó]

◇ 巾帼 ①ancient woman's headdress ②woman

guǒ （ㄍㄨㄛˇ）

果 [guǒ] I 名 ①fruit; nut ②result; consequence; outcome; effect II 形 strong-willed; resolute; determined III 副 really; as expected; sure enough

果茶 ①fruit drinks ②hawthorn juice

果冻 jelly

果断 resolute; decisive; determined

果脯 preserved fruit; candied fruit

果腹 fill the stomach; satisfy one's hunger

果敢 courageous and resolute; resolute and daring

果酱 jam (as made of preserves)

果酒 fruit wine

果木 fruit tree

果农 fruit grower

果盘 fruit bowl; fruit tray

果皮 the skin of fruit; peel; rind

果品 fruit

果然 ①really; as expected; sure enough ②if indeed; if really

果肉 the flesh of fruit; pulp

果实 ①fruit ②gains; fruits

果树 fruit tree

果糖 fructose; levulose

果味 fruity

果园 orchard

果真 ①really; as expected; sure enough ②if indeed; if really

果珍 a kind of powdered fruit drink

果汁 fruit juice

果枝 ① fruit-bearing shoot; fruit branch ② boll-bearing branch (of the cotton plant)

果子 fruit

果料儿 raisins, kernels, melon seeds, etc. used in making cakes, buns, etc.

果木园 orchard

果皮箱 litterbin

果仁儿 ① kernel ② shelled peanut; peanut kernel

果子酒 fruit wine

果子狸 gem-faced civet

果子露 fruit syrup

果不其然 just as expected; sure enough
果如其言 if this is true; if such is the case

裹 Ⅰ 〔动〕 ① tie up; wrap; bind ② press into service; round up; make away with ③ suck Ⅱ 〔名〕 bundle; parcel; package
裹腿 puttee; leggings
裹胁 force to take part (in bad things); coerce
裹脚布 bandages used in binding women's feet in feudal China
裹足不前 hesitate to move forward

guò （《ㄨㄛˋ）

过 Ⅰ 〔动〕 ① go through or across; cross; pass ② spend (time); pass (time) ③ transfer; adopt ④ undergo; go through; go over ⑤ go over (with one's eyes or in one's mind); read over; call to mind ⑥ visit ⑦ pass away; die ⑧ infect; be contagious ⑨ exceed; go beyond; be over Ⅱ 〔名〕 fault; mistake; demerit Ⅲ 〔助〕 (used after a verb plus 得 or 不 to indicate superiority or inferiority, success or failure, etc.): 我说不过她。 I can't outargue her. / 这样的干部我们信不过。 We have no confidence in such cadres. Ⅳ（前缀）per-; super-; over- ➡ guo
过半 more than half
过磅 weigh (on the scales)
过场 ① interlude ② cross the stage ③ do sth as a mere formality; go through the motions; do sth perfunctorily or superficially
过程 course; process
过秤 weigh (on the steelyard)
过从 have friendly intercourse; associate
过错 fault; mistake
过道 passageway; corridor
过冬 pass the winter; winter
过度 excessive; undue; over-
过渡 transition; interim
过分 excessive; undue; over-
过高 overtop
过关 ① pass a barrier; go through an ordeal ② pass a test; reach a standard
过后 afterwards; later
过户 transfer of names (or ownership); change the name of the owner in a register
过话 ① exchange words; talk with one another ② send word; pass on a message
过火 go too far; go to extremes; overdo
过激 too drastic; extremist
过继 ① adopt a young relative ② have one's child adopted by a relative
过奖 overpraise; give undeserved compliment
过节 〔guòjié〕 celebrate a festival
过境 pass through the territory of a country; be in transit

过客 passing traveller; transient guest
过来 ① come over; come up ② used after a verb plus 得 or 不 to indicate the sufficiency or insufficiency of time, capability or quantity ③ used after a verb to indicate motion towards the speaker ④ used after a verb to indicate turning around towards the speaker ⑤ used after a verb to indicate a return to the normal state
过冷 supercooling
过礼 present gifts to the bride's family before marriage
过梁 lintel
过量 excessive; over-
过路 pass by on one's way
过虑 be overanxious; worry overmuch; worry unnecessarily
过滤 filter; filtrate
过门 (of a woman) go over to a man's house—get married
过敏 allergy
过目 look over (papers, lists etc.) so as to check or approve
过牧 overgraze
过年 celebrate the New Year or the Spring Festival; spend the New Year or the Spring Festival
过期 exceed the time limit; be overdue
过谦 too modest
过去 ① (in or of) the past; formerly; previously ② go over; pass by ③ used after a verb to indicate motion away from the speaker ④ used after a verb to indicate turning away from the speaker ⑤ used after a verb to indicate a departure from the normal state
过热 overheated
过人 surpass; excel
过熔 superfusion
过少 too little
过甚 exaggerate; overstate
过剩 excess; surplus
过失 ① fault; slip; error ② negligence
过时 out-of-date; outmoded; obsolete; antiquated; out of fashion
过世 die; pass away
过手 take in and give out (money, etc.); receive and distribute; handle
过数 take a count; count
过头 go beyond the limit; overdo
过往 ① come and go ② have friendly intercourse with; associate with
过问 concern oneself with; take an interest in; bother about
过午 afternoon
过细 meticulous; care too much

过夜 ①pass the night; put up for the night; stay overnight ②of the previous night

过瘾 satisfy a craving; enjoy oneself to the full; do sth to one's heart's content

过硬 have a perfect mastery of sth; be really up to the mark; be able to pass the stiffest test

过于 too; unduly; excessively

过载 ①transship ②overload

过早 premature; untimely

过账 transfer items (as from a daybook to a ledger); post

过重 (of luggage, letters, etc.) overweight

过半数 plurality

过饱和 supersaturation

过不去 ①cannot get through; be unable to get by ②be hard on; make it difficult for; embarrass ③feel sorry

过得去 ①be able to pass; can get through ②passable; tolerable; so-so; not too bad ③feel at ease

过电影 go over past scenes in one's mind; recall; recollect; bring to mind

过家家 play house (a children's game)

过节儿 [guòjiér] grudge; hard feelings; ill will

过境权 right of passage

过境税 transit duty

过来人 a person who has had some experience

过劳死 die from prolonged overwork

过滤器 filter

过滤嘴 filter tip (of a cigarette)

过门儿 ①opening bars ②short interlude between verses

过日子 live; get along

过筛子 sift out

过堂风 wind coming through a passageway; draught

过度捕捞 overfishing

过度放牧 overgrazing

过度竞争 over-competition

过度开发 overexploitation

过度开垦 excess reclamation/tillage

过度砍伐 overcut

过度疲劳 overfatigue

过渡措施 interim measures

过渡飞行 transition flight

过渡过程 transient process

过渡内阁 caretaker cabinet or government

过渡时期 interim; transitional period

过关思想 attitude of just getting by or scraping past

过关斩将 overcome all the difficulties in the way

过河拆桥 pull down the bridge after crossing the river—drop one's benefactor once his help is not needed; kick down the ladder

过火政策 excessive policy; policy executed to excess

过激言论 extremist opinions

过街老鼠 a rat crossing the street—a person or thing that provokes a hue and cry

过街天桥 overhead pedestrian crossing; overpass

过紧日子 belt-tightening; pass through lean years; lead a thrifty (or austere) life

过境货物 transit cargo

过境旅游 cross-border tourism

过境贸易 transit trade

过境签证 transit visa

过境手续 transit formalities

过境外交 stop-over diplomacy

过磷酸钙 calcium superphosphate

过磷酸盐 superphosphate

过路财神 a temporary God of Wealth—a person temporarily handling large sums of money

过目不忘 learn sth by heart after reading it once; have a photographic (or very retentive) memory

过目成诵 be able to recite sth after reading it once; have a photographic (or very retentive) memory

过硼酸盐 perborate

过期胶卷 expired film

过期提单 stale bill of lading

过期杂志 back number of a magazine

过期债权 overdue credit

过期账款 past due account

过期支票 overdue (or out-of-date, stale) check

过甚其词 give an exaggerated account; overstate the case

过失犯罪 crimes of negligence; unintentional crime; unpremeditated crime; offence through negligence

过失杀人 manslaughter

过时不候 no waiting after the set time

过时商品 obsolete merchandise

过水面积 discharge area

过水能力 discharge capacity

过眼云烟 as transient as a fleeting cloud

过氧化物 peroxide

过意不去 feel apologetic; feel sorry

过犹不及 going too far is as bad as not going far enough

过早乐观 count one's chickens before they are hatched

过渡性融资 bridging financing

过敏性反应 allergic reaction

过剩生产能力 surplus capacity

过屠门而大嚼 start munching when passing the butcher's—feed on illusions

过境对外开放城市 opening border (or frontier) cities

guo(·ㄍㄨㄛ)

过 [guo]
　助 ① (*used after a verb to indicate the* *completion of an action*)：账已经付过了。 The bill has been paid. ② (*used after a verb to indicate past action or experience*)：他当过水手。 He has been a sailor. ➡ guò

Hh

hā (ㄏㄚ)

哈 [hā]
Ⅰ 动 breathe out (with the mouth open); blow one's breath：哈了一口气 breathe out a breath Ⅱ 象 (*usu. reduplicated and used to describe laughter*) Ⅲ 叹 (*usu. reduplicated and used to indicate complacency or satisfaction*)：哈哈，我说对了。Aha, so I was right. /哈，球进了! Aha, it's in! *or* Aha, he's scored a goal! ➡ hǎ;hà

哈韩 craze for S. Korean pop culture

哈吉 haji (a title of honour for a Moslem who has made a pilgrimage to Mecca)

哈欠 yawn

哈日 craze for Japanese pop culture

哈腰 ①bend one's back；stoop ②bow slightly

哈哈镜 distorting mirror

哈喇子 dribble；drivel；drool

哈里发 caliph

哈密瓜 Hami melon (a variety of muskmelon)

哈哈大笑 roar with laughter；laugh heartily

哈雷彗星 Halley's Comet；the Halley Comet

铪 [hā]
名 hafnium (Hf)

铪板 hafnium plate

铪锭 hafnium ingot

há (ㄏㄚˊ)

蛤 [há]
名 clam ➡ gé

蛤壳 clamshell

蛤蟆 ①frog ②toad

hǎ (ㄏㄚˇ)

哈 [hǎ]
动 scold ➡ hā;hà

哈达 *hada*, a long piece of silk (usu. white in colour) used as a greeting gift among the Tibetan and Mongolian nationalities

哈巴狗 ①Pekinese (a breed of dog) ②toady；sycophant

hà (ㄏㄚˋ)

哈 [hà]
➡ hā;hǎ

哈什蚂 Chinese forest frog

哈什蚂油 the dried oviduct fat of the forest frog

hāi (ㄏㄞ)

咳 [hāi]
叹 (*used to express sorrow, regret, surprise, etc.*)：咳，我怎么忘得一干二净! Damnit! How could I have forgotten all about it! ➡ ké

咳声叹气 heave deep sighs；sigh in despair；moan and groan

嗨 [hāi]

嗨哟 heave ho；yo-heave-ho；yo-ho

hái (ㄏㄞˊ)

还 [hái]
副 ①still；yet；nevertheless ②even more；still more ③also；too；as well；in addition ④passably；fairly；rather ⑤even ⑥ *used for emphasis*：他还真有办法。He is really resourceful. *or* How resourceful he is! /这还假得了! It can't be a fake! *or* There isn't the slightest doubt that it's true (*or* genuine). ⑦ (*used to indicate that sth quite unexpected has happened*)：下这么大雪，你还骑车来了。We did not expect that you would come by bike in such heavy snow. ⑧as early as ➡ huán

还好 ①not bad；passable ②fortunately

还是 ①still；yet ②(*expressing a preference for an alternative*) ③(*expressing realization or discovery*) ④or ⑤no matter what, how etc.；whether... or...；regardless of

孩 [hái]
名 child
孩提　early childhood；infancy
孩子　①child ②son or daughter；children
孩儿参　caryophyllaceous ginseng
孩子话　silly childish talk
孩子气　childish

骸 [hái]
名 ①bones of the body；skeleton ②body
骸骨　bones of the dead

hǎi（《ㄞ）

胲 [hǎi]
名 hydroxylamine

海 [hǎi]
Ⅰ 名 ①sea；lake ②great number of people or things coming together；expanse；sea Ⅱ 形 ①extra large；of great capacity；immense ②from overseas；foreign ③(*usu. followed by* 了，啦，*etc.*) numerous；countless Ⅲ 副 ①at random；aimlessly；everywhere ②with no limit (*or* restraint)
海岸　seacoast；coast；seashore
海拔　height above sea level；elevation
海报　playbill
海豹　seal
海边　seafront；seaside
海滨　seashore；seaside
海波　sodium thiosulfate；sodium hyposulfite；hypo
海菜　edible seaweed
海产　marine products
海潮　(sea) tide
海程　distance travelled by sea；voyage
海船　seagoing vessel
海带　kelp
海胆　sea urchin
海岛　island (in the sea)
海盗　pirate；sea rover
海堤　sea wall
海底　the bottom of the sea；seabed；sea floor
海防　coast defence
海风　sea breeze；sea wind
海港　seaport；harbour
海沟　(oceanic) trench
海狗　fur seal；ursine seal
海关　custom house；custom office；customs
海归　returned students
海龟　green turtle；sea turtle
海涵　be magnanimous enough to forgive or tolerate (sb's errors or shortcomings)
海货　marine products
海鲫　Japanese seaperch
海疆　coastal areas and territorial seas
海角　cape；promontory
海禁　ban on maritime trade or intercourse with foreign countries

海景　seascape
海警　maritime police
海鸠　guillemot
海军　navy
海口　① seaport ②(*usu. used in* 夸海口) boast about what one can do；talk big
海葵　sea anemone
海蓝　sea green；sea blue
海狸　beaver
海里　nautical mile；sea mile
海量　①magnanimity ②great capacity for liquor
海流　ocean current
海龙　①sea otter ②pipefish
海路　sea route；sea-lane；seaway
海轮　seagoing (*or* oceangoing) vessel
海螺　conch
海马　sea horse
海鳗　conger pike
海米　dried shrimps
海绵　①sponge ②foam rubber or plastic
海面　sea surface
海难　perils of the sea
海内　within the four seas；throughout the country
海鲇　sea catfish
海牛　manatee；sea cow
海鸥　sea gull
海区　sea area
海撒　a kind of sea-burial
海鳃　sea pen；sea feather
海上　at sea；on the sea
海蛇　sea snake
海参　sea cucumber；sea slug；trepang
海狮　sea lion
海事　maritime affairs
海水　seawater；brine；the sea
海损　sea damage；average
海獭　sea otter
海滩　seabeach；beach
海棠　Chinese flowering crabapple
海塘　seawall
海退　regression
海豚　dolphin
海外　overseas；abroad
海湾　bay；gulf
海味　choice seafood
海峡　strait；channel
海鲜　seafood
海相　marine (*or* sea) facies
海象　walrus；morse
海啸　tidal wave；tsunami；seismic sea wave
海蟹　sea crab
海星　starfish
海熊　fur seal；ursine seal
海选　mass election
海寻　nautical fathom

海牙 The Hague
海盐 sea salt
海蜒 dried anchovy
海燕 (storm) petrel
海洋 seas and oceans; ocean
海妖 siren
海邮 by sea; sea mail
海域 sea area; maritime space
海员 seaman; sailor; mariner
海运 sea transportation; ocean shipping
海葬 sea-burial
海枣 date palm; date
海藻 marine alga; seaweed
海战 sea warfare; naval battle
海蜇 jellyfish
海震 seaquake
海岸炮 coast gun
海岸线 coastline
海百合 sea lily; crinoid
海盗船 pirate (ship); sea rover
海底矿 submarine mine
海底山 seamount
海防艇 coastal defence boat
海魂衫 sailor's striped shirt
海基会 the Straits Exchange Foundation (SEF)
海军呢 navy cloth
海狸鼠 coypu; nutria
海洛因 heroin
海绵垫 foam rubber cushion
海绵铁 sponge iron
海盘车 starfish
海泡石 sepiolite; sea-foam (a mineral)
海平面 sea level
海群生 hetrazan
海商法 maritime law
海水浴 seawater bath; sea bathing
海桐花 tobira
海豚泳 dolphin butterfly; dolphin fishtail; dolphin
海外版 overseas edition
海王星 Neptune
海协会 the Association for Relations Across the Taiwan Straits (ARATS)
海洋法 law of the sea
海洋权 marine rights
海洋学 oceanography; oceanology
海运业 sea-carrying trade; shipping industry
海蜘蛛 sea spider
海吃海喝 eat and drink to one's heart's content
海底采矿 undersea mining; offshore mining
海底电报 submarine telegraph; cablegram
海底电缆 submarine cable
海底勘察 submarine exploration
海底捞月 try to fish out the moon from the bottom of the sea—strive for the impossible or illusory
海底捞针 fish for a needle in the ocean; look for a needle in a haystack
海底水雷 ground mine (or torpedo)
海底隧道 seabed tunnel
海底峡谷 submarine canyon
海底油田 offshore oilfield
海底资源 seabed resources; submarine resources
海防部队 coastal defence force
海关仓库 customs warehouses
海关担保 customs guarantee
海关登记 customs entry
海关发票 customs invoice
海关放行 customs clearance
海关官员 customs house officer
海关监管 superintendent of customs
海关检查 customs inspection (or examination)
海关检疫 customs quarantine control
海关手续 customs formalities
海关税则 customs tariff
海关统计 customs statistics
海关退税 (customs) drawback; rebate
海关总署 customs head office
海关组织 customs organization
海角天涯 the ends of the earth; the remotest corners of the earth
海军基地 naval base
海军武官 naval attaché
海军学校 naval academy
海枯石烂 (even if) the seas run dry and the rocks crumble
海阔天空 as boundless as the sea and the sky; unrestrained and far-ranging
海蓝宝石 aquamarine
海绵球拍 foam-rubber (or sponge) table-tennis bat
海难救助 salvage at sea
海内无双 unequalled (or peerless) in the whole country
海上保险 marine (or maritime) insurance
海上补给 sealift; seaborne supply
海上封锁 naval blockade
海上交通 maritime traffic
海上贸易 marine trade
海上油井 offshore oil well
海上油田 offshore oil field
海上运输 marine transportation
海上作业 offshore operation; operation on the sea
海市蜃楼 ①mirage ②illusion
海事法庭 admiralty court; maritime court
海事仲裁 maritime arbitration
海誓山盟 (make) a solemn pledge of love
海水淡化 desalination sea water
海水工业 marine industry

H

海水入侵 saline water intrusion
海水养殖 mariculture;sea farming
海天一色 The sea and the sky merged into one. *or* The sea melted into the sky.
海外兵团 overseas force
海外关系 overseas connections;relatives (*or* friends) living abroad
海外捐赠 donations from overseas
海外奇谈 a strange story from over the seas;a traveller's tale;a tall story
海外市场 overseas market
海外投资 investment from overseas;investment overseas (*or* abroad)
海湾国家 Gulf states
海湾战争 Gulf War
海峡群岛 channel islands
海相沉积 marine deposit
海洋动物 marine animal
海洋工程 oceanics industries
海洋公约 maritime convention
海洋国土 marine territory
海洋环境 marine environment
海洋生物 marine organisms
海洋石油 offshore oil
海洋渔业 sea fishery
海洋资源 marine resources
海运合同 contract of ocean carriage
海运事业 shipping interest
海岸警卫队 coast guard
海岸线效应 coastline effect
海关监督区 customs supervision zone
海关检查站 customs inspection post
海关申报单 customs declaration
海关通行证 customs pass
海军航空兵 naval air force (*or* service)
海军陆战队 marine corps;marines
海上补给船 underway replenishment ship
海上缉私队 sea patrol team
海上自卫队 maritime self-defence force
海事审判权 admiralty jurisdiction
海洋气象船 ocean weather ship
海洋气象学 marine meteorology
海洋性冰川 marine glacier
海洋性气候 maritime (*or* marine) climate
海运保险商 underwriter;underwriting agent
海运承运人 ocean carrier
海运代理商 ocean shopping agents
海草床保护区 seaweed beds protected area
海关缉私官员 customs preventive officer
海关检查人员 customs examiner;surveyor of customs
海军舰艇编队 formation of naval vessels
海上遇险信号 signal of distress;GMDSS
海上钻井平台 offshore drilling platform
海水不可斗量 the sea cannot be measured with a bushel—great minds cannot be fathomed

海外工程承包 overseas project contracting
海外留学人员 Chinese students and scholars studying abroad
海峡两岸关系 relations between the two sides of the Taiwan Straits;relations across the Taiwan Straits;inter-Straits relations
海洋权益划分 delimitation of maritime rights and interests
海洋水位上涨 sea level rise
海岸潟湖保护区 coastal lagoons protected area
海湾战争综合征 Gulf War syndrome;the complexities of the Gulf War
海洋科学考察船 ocean scientific ship
海洋特别保护区 special marine protection area;special marine reserve
海运货物保险单 cargo policy
海洋自然资源保护区 marine nature conservation area;marine nature reserve
海阔凭鱼跃,天高任鸟飞 the sea's vastness allows the fish to leap;the sky's loftiness lets the birds fly
海内存知己,天涯若比邻 if in this world an understanding friend survives,then the ends of the earth seem like next door;a bosom friend afar brings a distant land near

hài （ㄏㄞˋ） 

亥 [hài]
［名］last of the twelve Earthly Branches
亥时 the period of the day from 9 p.m. to 11 p.m.

骇 [hài]
［动］frighten;shock;astonish;amaze
骇怪 be shocked;be astonished
骇惧 be frightened;be terrified
骇然 gasping with astonishment;struck dumb with amazement
骇异 be shocked;be astonished
骇人听闻 shocking;appalling

氦 [hài]
［名］helium (He)
氦龄 helium age
氦闪 helium flash
氦族 helium group
氦循环 helium cycle

害 [hài]
Ⅰ ［名］harm;injury;damage;evil Ⅱ ［形］harmful;destructive;injurious Ⅲ ［动］① do harm to;cause trouble to;impair ②kill;murder ③contract (an illness);suffer from ④feel (ashamed,afraid,etc.)
害病 fall ill
害虫 injurious (*or* destructive) insect;pest
害处 harm
害鸟 harmful (*or* destructive) bird
害怕 be (*or* feel) afraid;be scared
害臊 feel ashamed;be bashful;be shy

害兽　destructive animal;vermin
害羞　be bashful;be shy
害眼　have eye trouble
害疟疾　suffer from malaria;be taken ill with malaria
害人虫　an evil creature;pest;vermin
害群之马　an evil member of the herd;one who brings disgrace on his group;a black sheep
害人不浅　no small harm is done;do people great harm
害人之心不可有,防人之心不可无　one should never intend to harm others,nor should one forget to guard against others' evil intentions

嗐 [hài]
　囡 *used to express sorrow or regret*:嗐,你怎么不早点告诉我! Oh,why didn't you tell me earlier?

hān (ㄏㄢ)

顸 [hān]
　彤 thick

蚶 [hān]
　名 blood clam
蚶子　blood clam

酣 [hān]
　副 ①(drink) to one's heart's content ② heartily;merrily;to one's heart's content
酣畅　①merry and lively (with drinking) ② sound (sleep) ③with ease and verve;fully
酣歌　sing lustily;sing to one's heart's content
酣梦　a sweet dream
酣睡　sleep soundly;be fast asleep
酣饮　drink to the full;carouse
酣战　hard-fought battle
酣醉　be dead drunk
酣畅淋漓　heartily;to one's heart's content

憨 [hān]
　彤 ① foolish;silly ② straightforward;naive;ingenuous;innocent
憨痴　idiotic
憨厚　straightforward and good-natured;simple and honest
憨笑　smile fatuously;simper
憨直　honest and straightforward
憨态可掬　charmingly naive
憨头憨脑　with a stupid head and a dull brain;foolish-looking

鼾 [hān]
　名 snore
鼾声　sound of snoring
鼾睡　be sound asleep and snoring
鼾声如雷　snore thunderously

hán (ㄏㄢ)

汗 [hán]
　名 Khan ➡hàn

含 [hán]
　动 ①keep (*or* hold) in the mouth ②contain;bear ③nurse;cherish;harbour
含苞　in bud
含恨　nurse a grievance or hatred
含糊　①ambiguous;vague ②careless;perfunctory
含混　indistinct;ambiguous;vague
含泪　with tears in one's eyes
含量　content
含怒　be in anger
含片　lozenge
含权　with dividend right
含水　containing water (*or* moisture)
含息　with dividend
含笑　have a smile on one's face
含羞　with a shy look;bashfully
含蓄　①contain;embody ②implicit;veiled ③reserved
含义　meaning;implication
含有　contain;have;import
含冤　suffer a wrong
含怨　bear a grudge;nurse a grievance
含金量　①gold content ②real worth (*or* value)
含硫量　sulphur content
含氯量　chlorinity
含漱剂　gargle
含水层　water-bearing stratum;aquifer
含水率　moisture content
含碳量　carbon content;temper
含羞草　sensitive plant
含油层　oil-bearing formation;oil-bearing stratum
含苞待放　bud just ready to burst
含悲饮泣　sob pitifully
含尘气体　dusty gas
含垢忍辱　endure contempt and insults;bear shame and humiliation
含毫吮墨　moisten the tip of the writing brush with one's lips—pause to think while writing
含糊其辞　talk ambiguously;equivocate
含泪告别　say goodbye with tears in one's eyes
含煤地层　coal-bearing stratum
含铅汽油　leaded gasoline
含情脉脉　(soft eyes) exuding tenderness and love
含沙射影　innuendo;insinuations
含笑九泉　smile in the underworld
含辛茹苦　endure suffering;bear hardships
含血喷人　make slanderous accusations;make vicious attacks
含饴弄孙　play with grandchildren with candy in mouth—enjoy happy old age
含英咀华　relish the joys of literature
含油岩石　oil-bearing rock

含铀废水 uraniferous waste water

函 [hán]
名 ①case;casket;envelope ②letter
函电 letters and cables
函复 reply by letter;write a letter in reply
函告 inform by letter
函购 purchase by mail;mail order
函件 letters;correspondence
函售 sale by post
函授 teach by correspondence;give a correspondence course
函数 function
函索 request by letter
函诊 diagnosis by correspondence
函授大学 correspondence university
函授教学 correspondence instruction
函授学校 correspondence school

涵 [hán]
Ⅰ 动 contain;embody Ⅱ 名 culvert
涵洞 culvert
涵盖 cover;contain completely;contain;embody
涵养 ①ability to control oneself;self-restraint ②conserve
涵义 connotation;meaning;implication

韩 [Hán]
韩流 South Korea trend

寒 [hán]
Ⅰ 形 ①cold;frigid;chilly ②poor;needy ③my humble Ⅱ 动 be stricken with terror;tremble with fear
寒痹 arthritis (aggravated by cold)
寒潮 cold wave;cold spell
寒碜 ①ugly;unsightly ②shabby;disgraceful ③ridicule;make fun of;put to shame
寒窗 a cold window—the difficulties of a poor student
寒带 frigid zone
寒风 cold wind
寒假 winter vacation
寒噤 shiver (with cold or fear)
寒冷 cold;frigid
寒流 cold current
寒门 ①poor and humble family ②my family
寒气 cold air;cold draught;cold
寒热 chills and fever
寒儒 needy scholar
寒舍 my humble home (or abode)
寒湿 cold-dampness
寒士 poor scholar
寒暑 ①cold and heat ②winter and summer—a year
寒酸 shabby and miserable
寒腿 rheumatism in the legs
寒心 ①be bitterly disappointed ②be afraid;be fearful
寒星 stars on a cold night

寒暄 exchange of conventional greetings;exchange of amenities (or compliments)
寒鸦 jackdaw
寒夜 cold night;chilly night
寒衣 winter clothing
寒意 a nip (or chill) in the air
寒战 shiver (with cold or fear)
寒症 symptoms caused by cold factors (e.g. chill,slow pulse,etc.)
寒暑表 thermometer
寒冬腊月 severe winter;dead of winter
寒光闪闪 (a sword) glittered like frost and snow
寒来暑往 as summer goes and winter comes—as time passes;with the passage of time

hǎn (ㄏㄢˇ)

罕 [hǎn]
副 rarely;seldom
罕觏 rarely seen
罕见 seldom seen;rare
罕事 a rare event
罕物 a rare thing
罕用 seldom used
罕有 very rare

喊 [hǎn]
动 ①shout;cry out;yell ②call ③address
喊话 shout propaganda to enemy troops across the frontline
喊叫 shout;cry out
喊声 yell;hubbub
喊话器 megaphone
喊冤叫屈 cry out about one's grievances;complain loudly about an alleged injustice

hàn (ㄏㄢˋ)

汉 [hàn]
名 ①Han nationality ②Chinese (language) ③man ④Milky Way
汉化 Chinese localization
汉奸 traitor (to China)
汉人 ①the Hans;the Han people;Chinese ②people of the Han Dynasty
汉显 showing Chinese characters on the screen (of a pager)
汉学 ① the Han school of classical philology ②Sinology
汉语 Chinese (language)
汉子 ①man;fellow ②husband
汉字 Chinese character
汉族 the Han ethnic group,China's main nationality, or the Hans, distributed all over the country
汉白玉 white marble
汉堡包 hamburger
汉字编码 encoding of Chinese characters

汉字显示 showing Chinese characters on the screen（of a pager）
汉语拼音方案 the Scheme for the Chinese Phonetic Alphabet
汉语拼音字母 the Chinese phonetic alphabet
汉语水平考试 HSK；Hanyu Proficiency Test；Test of Chinese Language Ability for Foreigners
汉字操作系统 Chinese characters disk operating system（CCDOS）
汉字处理软件 Chinese character processing software
汉字简化方案 Scheme for Simplifying Chinese characters
汉字信息处理 Chinese character coding
汉字五笔字型输入系统 five-stroke input system for Chinese characters

扞 ［hàn］
扞格 conflict

汗 ［hàn］
名 sweat；perspiration ➡hán
汗斑 ①sweat stain ②tinea versicolour
汗碱 sweat stain
汗脚 feet that sweat easily；sweaty feet
汗孔 pore
汗毛 fine hair on the human body
汗青 ①sweating green bamboo strips—completion of a literary undertaking（reference to the ancient practice of drying green bamboo strips on the fire before writing on them）②historical records；chronicles；annals
汗衫 ①undershirt；T-shirt ②shirt
汗水 sweat（esp. in large amounts）
汗味 stink with perspiration
汗腺 sweat gland
汗颜 blush with shame；feel deeply ashamed
汗液 sweat；perspiration
汗渍 ①sweat stain ②be soaked with sweat
汗背心 sleeveless undershirt；vest；singlet
汗淋淋 dripping with perspiration；soaked with sweat
汗珠子 beads of sweat
汗流浃背 sweat streaming down and drenching one's back；soaked with sweat
汗马功劳 ①distinctions won in battle；war exploits ②one's contributions in work；render great services
汗牛充栋 enough books to make the pack-ox sweat or to fill a house to the rafters—an immense collection of books
汗如雨下 dripping with perspiration

旱 ［hàn］
Ⅰ 名 ①dry spell；drought ②dryland；land ③on land；by land Ⅱ 形 dry；arid
旱冰 roller skating

旱船 land boat，a model boat used as a stage prop in some folk dances
旱稻 upland rice；dry rice
旱地 nonirrigated farmland；dry land
旱季 dry season
旱井 ①water-retention well ②dry well
旱柳 dryland willow
旱路 overland route
旱年 year of drought
旱桥 viaduct；overpass；flyover
旱情 drought；damage caused by a drought；ravages of a drought
旱伞 parasol
旱獭 marmot
旱田 dry farmland；dry land
旱象 signs of drought
旱烟 tobacco
旱灾 drought
旱冰场 roller rink
旱冰鞋 roller skates
旱金莲 nasturtium
旱鸭子 ①ducks raised on dry land as opposed to ducks raised by rivers and ponds ②nonswimmer
旱涝保收 ensure stable yields despite drought or excessive rain；make gains no matter what happens；ensure a safe income
旱情严重 in the grip of a dry spell；serious drought
旱三角洲 dry delta
旱生动物 xerophilous animal
旱生植物 xerophyte
旱作农业 dry-land farming
旱地滑雪场 mock skiing park

捍 ［hàn］
动 defend；guard
捍卫 defend；guard；protect

悍 ［hàn］
形 ① doughty；dauntless；brave；bold ② fierce；ferocious；unreasonable
悍妇 shrewish woman；hot-tempered woman；shrew
悍将 brave warrior
悍然 outrageously；brazenly；flagrantly

焊 ［hàn］
动 weld；solder
焊点 soldered dot；welding spot
焊缝 soldering seam；weld joint；weld bead
焊工 ①welding；soldering ②welder；solderer
焊接 weld；solder
焊料 solder
焊枪 welding torch；（welding）blowpipe
焊条 welding rod
焊锡 soldering tin；tin solder
焊液 welding fluid；soldering fluid
焊油 soldering paste

翰 ［hàn］
名 ①writing brush ②writing；letters

翰林 member of the Imperial Academy
翰墨 brush and ink—writing, painting, or calligraphy
翰林院 the Imperial Academy (in feudal China)

撼 [hàn] 动 shake
撼动 shake; vibrate
撼天动地 shake heaven and earth

憾 [hàn] 名 regret
憾事 matter for regret

瀚 [hàn] 形 vast; immense
瀚海 big desert
瀚瀚 vast; boundless

hāng(ㄏㄤ)

夯 [hāng] Ⅰ 名 rammer; tamper Ⅱ 动 ①ram; tamp ②pound; buffet; thrash ③carry on one's shoulder with effort
夯歌 rammers' work chant
夯具 rammer; tamper
夯土机 rammer; tamper
夯土墙 loam wall

háng(ㄏㄤ)

行 [háng] Ⅰ 名 ①line; row ②seniority among brothers and sisters: 大排行 seniority among siblings of a clan ③ trade; profession; line of business ④business firm Ⅱ 量 (*used to refer to anything that forms a line*): 两行杨树 two rows of poplars ➡héng; xíng
行帮 trade association
行标 rower
行当 [hángdang] ①trade; profession; line of business ②type of role (in traditional Chinese operas)
行道 trade; profession
行贩 pedlar
行规 guild regulations
行风 tendencies in a particular social domain
行话 professional jargon; cant
行会 guild
行家 ①expert; connoisseur ②be expert at sth
行间 ① in the ranks ② between lines ③ between rows
行键 line unit
行距 row spacing
行列 ranks
行频 TV line frequency
行情 quotations (on the market); prices
行市 quotations (on the market); prices
行伍 the ranks
行长 president (of a bank)

行业 trade; profession; industry
行打印 line printing
行列式 determinant
行倾斜 line tilt
行情表 quotations list
行扫描 line scanning; horizontal scanning
行输出 line output
行业语 professional jargon; cant
行语句 line statement
行市标准 basis of quotation
行市记录 quotation record
行市坚稳 firm in the undertone
行市上涨 higher in quotation
行市下降 lower in quotation
行业亏损 loss incurred by an industry; industry loss
行业协会 business association
行行出状元 every profession produces its own leading authority
行同步脉冲 horizontal synchronization pulse
行业不正之风 malpractices in trades and professions; unhealthy tendency in a certain trade

吭 [háng] 名 throat ➡kēng

迒 [háng] 名 ①(of animals or wheels) track ②path; trail

杭 [háng]
杭纺 a silk fabric produced in Hangzhou
杭育 heave ho; yo-heave-ho; yo-ho

绗 [háng] 动 sew with long stitches

航 [háng] Ⅰ 名 boat; ship Ⅱ 动 navigate; sail; fly
航班 scheduled flight; flight number
航标 navigation mark
航测 air survey
航程 voyage; passage; range
航船 boat that plies regularly between inland towns
航次 ①the sequence of voyages (*or* flights); voyage (*or* flight) number ②the number of voyages (*or* flights) made
航道 channel; lane; course
航海 navigation
航迹 flight path; track
航空 aviation
航路 air route; sea route
航模 ①model airplane ②model of a ship
航拍 aerial photography
航区 navigation area
航速 speed of a ship (*or* plane)
航天 spaceflight
航图 chart
航务 navigational matters
航线 air (*or* shipping) line; route; course

航向 course (of a ship or plane)
航行 ①navigate by water;sail ②navigate by air;fly
航运 shipping
航空版 airmail edition
航空兵 ①air arm ②airman
航空病 airsickness
航空法 air law
航空港 air harbour
航空器 aerial craft;airborne craft;aircraft;air vehicle
航空信 airmail letter;air letter;airmail
航空学 aeronautics;aviation
航天舱 space capsule
航天服 spacesuit
航天器 spacecraft;space vehicle
航天站 spaceport
航行灯 navigation light
航行法 sailing
航行权 right of navigation
航道疏浚 water way dredging
航海法规 navigation law
航海罗盘 mariner's compass
航海日志 logbook;log
航空保险 aviation insurance
航空标塔 airway beacon
航空测量 aerial survey
航空磁测 aeromagnetic survey
航空地图 aeronautical chart;aerial map
航空公司 airline company;airways
航空技术 aeronautical technology
航空力学 aeromechanics
航空联运 through air transport
航空模型 model airplane
航空母舰 aircraft carrier
航空日志 aircraft logbook
航空探矿 mineral exploration aviation;aerial prospecting
航空协定 air transport agreement
航空学校 aviation school;flying school
航空学院 aeronautical engineering institute
航空照相 aerial photography
航天飞机 space shuttle
航天技术 space technology
航行半径 navigation radius
航运保险 shipping insurance
航运公司 shipping company
航海天文历 nautical almanac
航海天文学 nautical astronomy
航海望远镜 long glass
航空电子学 avionics
航空气象台 air weather station;aeronautical meteorological station
航空气象学 aeronautical meteorology
航空天文历 air almanac
航天器对接 spacecraft docking
航空航天部队 aerospace forces

航空快递信件 air express
航空体育运动 air sports;flying sports
航空母舰战斗群 aircraft-carrier battle group;carrier battle group
航天器运载火箭 space launch vehicle
航空人身意外保险 aviation personal accident insurance

颃 [háng]
◇ 颉颃 ① (of bird) fly upward ② equally matched

hàng（ㄏㄤˋ）

沆 [hàng]
名 vast expanse of water
沆瀣 evening mist
沆瀣一气 ①be congenial to each other ②act in collusion with;wallow in the mire with

巷 [hàng]
名 tunnel ➡xiàng
巷道 tunnel

hāo（ㄏㄠ）

蒿 [hāo]
名 wormwood;artemisia
蒿草 wormwood
蒿目 gaze into the distance
蒿子 wormwood;artemisia
蒿目时艰 watch the country's ills with deep concern
蒿子秆儿 crown daisy chrysanthemum (as a vegetable)

薅 [hāo]
动 ①pull up (weeds,etc.);weed by hand ②pull;tug;grab
薅草 weeding
薅锄 small short-handled hoe

háo（ㄏㄠˊ）

号 [háo]
动 ①howl;yell;bawl ②wail ➡hào
号叫 howl;yell
号哭 wail;cry loudly
号啕 cry loudly;wail
号天哭地 bewail loudly;weep to the very Heaven and to the very Earth

蚝 [háo]
名 oyster
蚝油 oyster sauce

毫 [háo]
Ⅰ 名 ①fine tapering hair ②writing brush ③loop for balancing a steelyard (from the user's hand) Ⅱ 副 in the least;at all Ⅲ 量 ① milli-,a thousandth of certain units of measurement ② hao,a unit of measure in weight or in length
毫安 milliampere

毫巴 millibar
毫发 a hair;the least bit;the slightest
毫法 millifarad
毫伏 millivolt
毫克 milligram（mg.）
毫厘 the least bit;an iota
毫毛 soft hair on the body
毫米 millimetre（mm.）
毫秒 millisecond
毫升 millilitre（ml.）
毫微米 millimicron
毫微秒 nanosecond;millimicrosecond
毫不迟延 without（the slightest）delay;immediately;at once
毫不动摇 unswervingly;not waver in the least
毫不逊色 not the least bit inferior;by no means worse;every bit equal;second to none
毫不犹豫 without the slightest hesitation
毫不在乎 do not care a cuss（or farthing）;could not care less
毫发不爽 not deviating a hair's breadth;without the slightest error
毫微程序 nanoprogram
毫无诚意 without the least sincerity
毫无二致 without the slightest difference;just the same;identical
毫无可能 out of the question
毫无例外 admit of no exception
毫无疑问 as sure as eggs are eggs;beyond（all）question
毫不利己,专门利人 utter devotion to others without any thought of self

嗥 ［háo］
动 （of a jackal or wolf）howl

貉 ［háo］
➡hé
貉绒 racoon dog fur
貉子 racoon dog

豪 ［háo］
I 名 person of extraordinary powers or endowments II 形 ①bold and unconstrained;magnanimous and forthright;unrestrained ② rich and powerful ③despotic;bullying;coercive
豪赌 play for high stakes;unrestrained gambling
豪夺 secure（sb's belongings,right,etc.）by force
豪放 bold and unconstrained
豪富 ①powerful and wealthy ②the rich and powerful
豪横 despotic;bullying
豪华 luxurious;sumptuous;splendid
豪杰 person of exceptional ability;hero
豪举 ①bold move ②munificent act
豪迈 bold and generous;heroic

豪门 rich and powerful family;wealthy and influential clan
豪气 heroism;heroic spirit
豪强 ①despotic;tyrannical ②despot;bully
豪情 lofty sentiments
豪商 wealthy and powerful merchant;merchant prince
豪绅 despotic gentry
豪爽 bold and uninhibited
豪侠 ①gallant ②gallant man
豪兴 exuberant spirits;exhilaration;keen interest
豪饮 drink with abandon;drink heavily
豪雨 torrential rain
豪语 brave words;bold promise
豪宅 luxury house
豪猪 porcupine
豪壮 grand and heroic
豪放不羁 bold and uninhibited
豪华别墅 luxury（or deluxe,posh）villa
豪华轿车 top-of-the-line car
豪华住宅 mansion;magnificent residential building
豪情满怀 full of pride and enthusiasm;full of spirit
豪情壮志 lofty sentiments and high aspirations
豪言壮语 brave words;proud words

壕 ［háo］
名 ①moat ②trench
壕沟 ①trench ②ditch
壕堑 trench;entrenchment

嚎 ［háo］
动 ①howl;yell;bawl ②wail;cry loudly
嚎天哭地 weep and wail

濠 ［háo］
名 moat

hǎo（ㄏㄠ）

好 ［hǎo］
I 形 ①good;fine;nice ②in good health;well ③friendly;kind ④（*used after a verb to indicate the completion of an action*）:我穿好衣服就去。I'll go after I get dressed. ⑤ easy（to do）;convenient:这地方真不好找。It was difficult to find the place. II 副 ①for the purpose of;in order to;so that ②（*used before certain time or numeral indicators to suggest a large number or a long time*）:今天下午好几个人来找过你。Quite a few people came in looking for you this afternoon. ③（*used before adjectives or verbs for emphasis and with exclamatory force*）:街上好热闹。What a bustling（or busy）street! ④ （*used before adjectives*）to what extent;how:电影要放好长时间? How long will the film last? III 叹 ①（*used to express approval,agreement,conclusion,etc.*）ok:好,就

照你的意见做吧。OK, let's do it according to your suggestion. ② (*used ironically to express dissatisfaction*) well; now: 你要爬上去, 好, 看你怎么爬? So you want to climb it; well, let us see how you do it. ③ *used as a polite formula*: 你好! How do you do? *or* Hello! *or* Hi! Ⅳ 囝 may; can; should; ought to: 我明天好去你家吗? May I come to your house tomorrow?　➡ hào

好办 easy to handle

好比 can be compared to; may be likened to; be just like

好不 very; quite; so

好处 ① good; benefit; advantage ② gain; profit

好歹 ① good and bad; what's good and what's bad ② mishap; disaster ③ in any case; at any rate; anyhow ④ no matter in what way; anyhow

好多 ① good many; a good deal; a lot of ② how many; how much

好感 good opinion; favourable impression

好汉 brave man; true man; hero

好话 ① good word; word of praise ② fine words

好久 ① a long time ② how long

好看 ① good-looking; nice ② interesting ③ honoured; proud ④ in an embarrassing situation; on the spot

好评 favourable comment; high opinion

好球 well played; good shot; bravo

好人 ① good (*or* fine) person ② healthy person ③ soft person who tries to get along with everyone (often at the expense of principle)

好生 ① quite; exceedingly ② carefully; properly

好使 be convenient to use; work well

好事 ① good deed; good turn ② an act of charity; good works ③ happy event; joyous occasion

好手 good hand; past master

好受 feel better; feel more comfortable

好说 ① *used in answer to praises or thanks* ② no problem

好似 seem; be like

好听 pleasant to hear

好闻 smell good; smell sweet

好戏 ① good play ② great fun

好像 seem; be like

好笑 laughable; funny; ridiculous

好心 good intention

好意 good intention; kindness

好在 fortunately; luckily

好转 take a turn for the better; take a favourable turn; change for better

好走 goodbye

好处费 pickings; favour fee; kickback; commissions; brokerage; brokerage offer in return; rebate; tips

好端端 in perfectly good condition; when everything is all right

好好儿 ① well; all out; to one's heart's content ② in perfectly good condition; when everything is all right

好家伙 good god; good lord; good heavens

好莱坞 Hollywood (centre of US movie industry located close to Los Angeles)

好日子 ① auspicious day ② wedding day ③ good days; happy life

好容易 with great difficulty; have a hard time (doing sth)

好天儿 fine day; lovely weather

好玩儿 amusing; interesting

好下场 good end

好些个 quite a lot; a good deal of

好一个 what a

好意思 how can one have the face (*or* nerve) to do sth

好不容易 not at all easy; very difficult

好好先生 one who tries not to offend anybody; Mr. Agreeable; Mr. Goody-goody

好借好还 make it a point to return or repay what one has borrowed

好景不长 good times don't last long

好人好事 good people and good deeds; fine people and fine deeds

好人主义 seek good relations with all and sundry at the expense of principle

好声好气 in a kindly manner; gently

好事多磨 ① the road to happiness is strewn with setbacks ② the course of true love never did run smooth

好说歹说 try every possible way to persuade sb

好说话儿 good-natured; open to persuasion

好样儿的 (of a man or woman) fine example; great fellow

好自为之 look out for yourself

好莱坞大片 Hollywood blockbuster

好钢用在刀刃 use the best steel to make the knife's edge—use material where it is needed most; use the best material at the key point

好男不跟女斗 a gentleman doesn't fight women

好死不如赖活 even a good death is not like a wretched existence

好汉不吃眼前亏 a wise man will not fight when the odds are obviously against him; a wise man doesn't fight against impossible odds

好汉不提当年勇 a hero is silent about his past glories

好汉做事好汉当 a true man has the courage to

accept the consequences of his own actions

好了疮疤忘了疼 forget the pain once the wound is healed—forget the bitter past when released from one's suffering

好心当作驴肝肺 take an honest man's heart for a donkey's liver and lungs—take sb's goodwill for ill intent

好话说尽，坏事做绝 say every fine word and do every foul deed

好事不出门，坏事传千里 good news never goes beyond the gate，while bad news spreads far and wide

hào（ㄏㄠ）

号 [hào]　Ⅰ〖名〗①name；title ②alias；assumed name；alternative name ③business house；firm ④mark；sign；signal ⑤order；sequence ⑥size ⑦kind；sort；type ⑧person of a given type ⑨ordinal number：（a）order；sequence：第五号简报 Bulletin No. 5 （b）date：六月八号 June 8th ⑩anything used as a horn ⑪any brass-wind instrument ⑫bugle call；any call made on a bugle　Ⅱ〖量〗（*used to indicate numbers*）：①of people：有三百多号人在这个食堂用餐。Over three hundred people eat in this canteen. ②of business deals：一会儿工夫，就做了几号买卖。Several deals were made in no time.　Ⅲ〖动〗①put a mark on；give a number to：号房子 mark out houses (as billets，etc.) ②feel (the pulse) ③order ➡hǎo

号兵 bugler；trumpeter for troops
号称 ①be known as ②claim to be
号角 ①bugle；horn ②bugle call
号令 verbal command；order
号码 number
号脉 feel the pulse
号手 bugler；trumpeter
号筒 trumpet
号外 extra (of a newspaper)
号型 size (of shoes，clothes，etc.)
号衣 livery or army uniform
号召 call；appeal
号子 ①mark；sign；signal ②cell ③work song sung to synchronize movements，with one person leading
号码机 numbering machine
号召书 appeal

好 [hào]　〖动〗①like；love；be fond of ②be liable to：好发脾气 be apt (*or* liable) to lose one's temper/好晕船 easily get seasick ➡hǎo

好恶 likes and dislikes；taste
好客 be hospitable；keep open house
好奇 be curious；be full of curiosity
好强 eager to do well in everything
好色 love woman's beauty；be fond of women

好胜 love to outshine others；seek to keep others down
好事 meddlesome；officious
好学 be fond of learning；be eager to learn
好战 bellicose；warlike
好奇心 curiosity
好吃懒做 be fond of eating and averse to work；be gluttonous and lazy
好大喜功 be ambitious for great achievements；crave for greatness and success；have a fondness for the grandiose
好斗分子 militant
好高骛远 reach for what is beyond one's grasp；aim too high
好色之徒 lecher；libertine
好事之徒 busybody
好为人师 like to lecture people；be given to laying down the law；know-it-all
好逸恶劳 love ease and hate work
好整以暇 remain calm and composed while handling pressing affairs

耗 [hào]　Ⅰ〖动〗①consume；take；cost ②waste time；dawdle　Ⅱ〖名〗bad news

耗电 consume electricity
耗费 consume；expend
耗竭 exhaust；use up
耗尽 exhaust；use up
耗散 dissipation
耗神 take up one's energy
耗损 consume；waste；lose
耗资 cost (a large sum of money)
耗子 mouse；rat
耗电量 power consumption
耗能量 quantity of energy consumption
耗时间 waste time；dawdle
耗油量 oil consumption
耗子药 ratsbane
耗减优惠 depletion allowance

浩 [hào]　〖形〗①great；vast；grand ②many；much；numerous

浩博 extensive；wide-embracing
浩大 very great；huge；vast
浩荡 vast and mighty
浩繁 vast and numerous
浩瀚 vast
浩劫 great calamity；catastrophe
浩淼 (of water) extending into the distance；vast
浩气 noble spirit
浩叹 ①heave a deep sigh；sigh deeply ②be greatly touched
浩浩荡荡 vast and mighty
浩然之气 noble spirit；moral force
浩如烟海 vast as the open sea—a tremendous amount (of literature，data，etc.)

皓 [hào]

形 ①white ②bright;luminous

皓齿 white teeth
皓矾 zinc sulphate
皓鬐 white beard
皓首 hoary head
皓月当空 The bright moon hung in the sky.

hē（ㄏㄜ）

诃 [hē]

劢 scold

诃子 myrobalan

呵 [hē]

劢 ①breathe out (with the mouth open) ②scold

呵斥 berate;excoriate
呵叱 rebuke angrily;shout angrily at;bawl at
呵呵 the sound of laughing
呵护 ①bless ②take good care of;baby sb
呵欠 yawn
呵责 berate;excoriate
呵护备至 baby (or be babied) in every possible way

喝 [hē]

劢 ①drink ②drink alcoholic liquor ➡hè

喝水 drink water
喝汤 eat soup
喝闷酒 drink alcohol alone when one is unhappy
喝墨水 drink ink—go to school
喝西北风 drink the northwest wind—live on air;have nothing to eat
喝水不忘掘井人 when you drink the water, think of those who dug the well

嗬 [hē]

叹 (used to indicate astonishment) ah;oh

hé（ㄏㄜ）

禾 [hé]

名 ①standing grain (esp. rice) ②foxtail millet

禾场 threshing floor
禾苗 seedlings of cereal crops
禾本科 the grass family
禾草类 grass

合 [hé]

Ⅰ劢 ①close;shut ②come together;join; combine ③conform with;suit;agree ④be equal to;add up to Ⅱ形 ①proper;appropriate;理应如此。We deem it appropriate to do so.②whole;entire Ⅲ量 round;bout:大战三十余合 fight thirty-odd rounds Ⅳ名 conjunction ➡gě

合办 operate (or run jointly)
合瓣 sympetalous;gamopetalous
合璧 (of two different things) combine harmoniously;match well
合编 ①compile in collaboration with ②merge and reorganize (army units,etc.)
合并 ①merge;amalgamate ②(of an illness) be complicated by another illness
合唱 chorus
合成 ①compose;compound ②synthetize;synthesize
合村 entire (or whole) village
合法 legal;lawful;legitimate;rightful
合格 qualified;up to standard
合股 ① pool capital; form a partnership ② plying
合乎 conform with (or to);correspond to;accord with;tally with
合欢 ① conjoined happiness—sexual pairing ②silk tree
合伙 form a partnership
合击 make a joint attack on
合计 [héjì] amount to;add up to;total
合计 [héji] ①think over;figure out ②consult
合剂 mixture
合家 the whole family
合金 alloy
合刊 combined issue (of a periodical)
合口 ①(of a wound) heal up ②(of a dish) be to one's taste
合理 rational;reasonable;equitable
合力 ①join forces;pool efforts ②resultant of forces
合流 ①flowing together;confluence ②collaborate;work hand in glove with sb
合龙 ①closure (of a dam,dyke,etc.) ②join the two sections of a bridge,etc.
合谋 ① conspire; plot together; connive ② conspiracy
合拍 in time;in step;in harmony
合群 ①get on well with others;be sociable ② be gregarious
合身 fit
合十 put the palms together before one (a Buddhist greeting)
合时 fashionable;in vogue
合适 suitable;appropriate;becoming;right
合算 ①paying;worthwhile ②reckon up
合题 synthesis
合同 contract
合围 surround
合演 appear in the same play,dance,etc.;co-star
合页 hinge
合宜 suitable;appropriate;becoming;right
合意 suit;be to one's liking (or taste)
合营 jointly owned;jointly operated
合影 ① take a group photo (or picture) ② group photo (or picture)
合用 ①share ②of use

合约 contract
合葬 （of husband and wife） be buried in the same grave
合账 make up accounts；figure out accounts
合辙 ①in rhyme ②in agreement
合资 pool capital；enter into partnership
合奏 instrumental ensemble
合族 whole clan
合作 cooperate；collaborate；work together
合不来 not get along well；be incompatible
合唱曲 （music for） chorus
合唱团 chorus （a group of singers）
合成氨 synthetic ammonia
合成词 compound word
合成革 synthetic leather
合成酶 synzyme
合成器 synthesizer
合得来 get along well；be compatible
合订本 one-volume edition；bound volume
合法化 legalize；legitimize
合格证 certificate of inspection （or quality, conformity，competency）
合金钢 alloy steel
合理化 rationalize
合霉素 syntomycin
合气道 aikido
合情理 fitness
合同法 contract law
合同工 contract worker
合同制 contract system
合议庭 full court；collegiate bench （or panel）；collegiate body of judges
合议制 collegiate system （a judicial system according to which justice is administered by a collegiate bench of judges, or by a judge and people's assessors）
合众国 federated country
合作化 （a movement to） organize cooperatives
合作社 cooperatives；co-op
合并程序 merging program
合并分类 merge sort
合成树脂 synthetic resin
合成纤维 synthetic fibre
合成橡胶 synthetic rubber
合二而一 two combine into one
合法程序 legal program
合法经营 lawful operation
合法权益 lawful （or legitimate，legal） rights and interests
合法收入 lawfully earned income
合法手段 lawful means
合法席位 lawful seat
合股公司 joint-stock company
合股企业 joint stock enterprises
合伙经营 run a business in partnership
合伙企业 enterprise in partnership；partnership enterprise
合伙契约 partnership agreement；articles of co-partnership
合金元素 alloying element
合理涨价 justified raise
合情合理 fair and reasonable；fair and sensible
合署办公 （of related offices） handle official business together in the same building
合同婚姻 contract marriage
合同纠纷 contract dispute
合同满期 termination of the contract
合同期限 contract period
合同授权 contract authorization
合同医院 assigned hospital
合资经营 jointly owned；jointly operated
合作经营 cooperative business operations；jointly operated；cooperative management；cooperative business operated
合作开发 joint exploitation
合作项目 cooperative projects；cooperative project
合作医疗 cooperative medical service
合作银行 cooperative bank
合成洗涤剂 synthetic detergent
合法持票人 lawful bearer
合法继承人 rightful heir
合理化建议 rationalization proposal
合同用工制 contract employment
合法上市证券 securities eligible for market operations
合格技术人员 qualified technicians
合理引导消费 guide rational consumption
合同管理制度 the contract system for governing projects
合同有效时间 duration of contract
合同仲裁机构 contract arbitration committee
合资经营各方 parties to a venture
合作伙伴关系 cooperative partnership
合作经营企业 cooperatively managed enterprise
合作医疗制度 pooled medical system；cooperative medical system
合成结晶牛胰岛素 synthetic crystalline bovine insulin
合乎国情,顺乎民意 conform with the national conditions and the will of the people

何 [hé]
Ⅰ 代 （used in specific questions） who；what；which Ⅱ 副 ①where；why；how come ② （used in rhetorical questions）：有何不可？ Why not?
何必 there is no need；why
何不 why not
何尝 ever so
何等 ①what kind ②what；how
何妨 why not；might as well
何干 what relation

何故 why
何苦 why bother;is it worth the trouble
何况 ①much less;let alone ②moreover;besides;in addition
何其 what;how
何如 ①how about ②wouldn't it be better
何谓 what is meant by;what is the meaning of
何须 what is the need
何许 what kind of;what
何以 how;why
何在 where
何止 far more than
何首乌 the tuber of multiflower knotweed (Polygonum multiflorum)
何去何从 what course to follow
何足挂齿 not worth mentioning;don't mention it
何乐而不为 why not do it;one would be only too glad to do it
何其相似乃尔 what a striking likeness (*or* similarity)

和 [hé] I 形 ①gentle;mild;kind:性情温和 have a gentle disposition/对敌狠,对己和 ruthless to one's enemy and kind to one's own people ② harmonious;on good terms Ⅱ 名 ①peace ② sum ③Japan;Japanese Ⅲ 动 (棋)draw;tie Ⅳ 介 ①(together) with:这药丸要和姜汤一起服下。 The pills are to be swallowed with ginger water. ②(*used to indicate relationship*, *comparison*, *etc.*):这件事和他无关。 It has nothing to do with him. Ⅴ 连 and ⇒ hè;hú;huó;huò
和蔼 kindly;affable;amiable
和畅 (of a wind) gentle and pleasant
和风 ①soft (*or* gentle) breeze ②moderate breeze
和服 kimono
和好 become reconciled
和缓 ①gentle;mild ②ease up;relax
和会 peace conference
和奸 commit adultery
和解 become reconciled
和局 drawn game;draw;tie
和美 harmonious and happy
和睦 harmony;concord;amity
和暖 pleasantly warm;genial
和平 ①peace ②mild
和棋 a draw in chess (*or* other board games)
和气 ①gentle;friendly;polite;amiable ②harmony;friendship
和亲 (of some feudal dynasties) make peace with rulers of minority nationalities in the border areas by marriage
和善 kind and gentle;genial
和尚 Buddhist monk
和声 harmony

和数 sum
和谈 peace negotiations;peace talks
和弦 chord
和谐 harmonious
和煦 pleasantly warm;genial
和衣 (sleep) with one's clothes on
和约 peace treaty
和平队 Peace Corps
和平鸽 dove of peace
和尚头 shaven head
和事老 peacemaker (esp. one who is more concerned with stopping the bickering than settling the issue)
和为贵 harmony is most precious;nothing is more precious than peace;peace is the best option
和蔼可亲 affable;amiable;genial
和风细雨 like a gentle breeze and light rain—in a gentle and mild way
和光同尘 soften one's glare and move along old ruts—swim with the tide
和盘托出 reveal everything;hold nothing back
和平贩子 peacemonger
和平攻势 peace offensive;peaceful offensive
和平共处 peaceful coexistence;coexist with someone peacefully;live with someone in peace
和平过渡 peaceful transition
和平竞赛 peaceful competition
和平谈判 peace negotiations;peace talks
和平演变 peaceful evolution (from socialism back to capitalism)
和平主义 pacifism
和气生财 amiability begets riches (a motto for businessmen)
和颜悦色 have a kind face;have a genial expression
和衷共济 work together with one accord (in time of difficulty);work together with one heart
和解新迹象 new signs of reconciliation
"和平号"空间站 the Mir
和平行为守则 code of peaceful conduct
和平中立政策 policy of peace and neutrality
和平共处五项原则 the Five Principles of Peaceful Coexistence (mutual respect for territorial integrity and sovereignty,mutual non-aggression,non-interference in each other's internal affairs,equality and mutual benefit,and peaceful coexistence)
和平统一,一国两制 peaceful reunification and one country,two systems

劾 [hé] 动 expose sb's misdeeds or crimes

河 [hé] 名 ①river ②Milky Way system ③Yellow River

河岸 river bank
河滨 streamside
河川 rivers and creeks
河床 riverbed
河道 river course
河堤 river embankment
河底 river bottom
河防 flood-prevention work done on rivers, esp. the Huanghe River
河港 river port
河沟 brook; stream
河谷 river valley
河口 river mouth; stream outlet
河狸 beaver
河流 rivers
河柳 dryland willow
河马 hippopotamus; hippo; river horse
河鳗 river eel
河泥 river silt; river mud
河曲 bend (of a river); meander
河渠 rivers and canals; waterways
河山 rivers and mountains; land; territory
河套 ①the bend of a river ②the Great Bend of the Huanghe River
河豚 globefish; balloonfish; puffer
河湾 ancon; cove; hook; river bend
河网 a network of waterways
河虾 river prawn; shrimp
河蟹 river crab
河源 river head (*or* source)
河运 river transport
河滩地 flood land
河东狮吼 the roar of the lioness from the east side of the River (said of sb's dominating wife in a temper)
河流沉积 fluvial (*or* fluviatile) deposit
河流疏浚 river dredging
河流污染 stream pollution
河流袭夺 river capture; river piracy
河清海晏 the Yellow River is clear and the sea is calm—the world is at peace
河外星系 extragalactic nebula

曷 [hé]
圖 ①how; why ②when

阂 [hé]
圖 cut off from; be not in communication with

盍 [hé]
圖 why not

荷 [hé]
圖 lotus ➡hè
荷包 ①small bag (for carrying money and odds and ends); pouch ②pocket (in a garment)
荷花 lotus
荷叶 lotus leaf
荷包蛋 poached eggs; fried eggs

荷尔蒙 hormone

核 [hé]
Ⅰ 图 ① pip; stone; 无 核 葡 萄 pipless grapes; seedless grapes ② nucleus ③ atomic nucleus; nuclear energy; nuclear weapon Ⅱ 動 examine; check Ⅲ 形 faithful; true; real ➡hú
核查 examine and verify; check; verification
核尘 nuclear dust
核定 check and ratify; appraise and decide
核对 check
核发 approve and issue
核苷 nucleoside
核果 drupe
核计 assess; calculate
核价 verify prices
核能 nuclear energy
核仁 ①nucleolus ②kernel (of a fruit-stone)
核实 verify; check
核素 ①nuclein ②nuclide
核酸 nucleic acid
核算 ①examine and calculate; assess ②business accounting
核糖 ribose
核桃 walnut
核销 cancel after verification
核心 nucleus; core; kernel
核验 check; examine
核准 examine and approve; check and approve
核资 verify capital or asset
核子 nucleon
核安全 nuclear security; nuclear safety
核爆炸 nuclear explosion
核备战 preparation for nuclear war
核裁军 nuclear disarmament
核大国 nuclear power
核弹头 nuclear warhead; uranium warhead
核蛋白 nucleoprotein
核导弹 nuclear missile
核电站 nuclear power plant
核冬天 nuclear winter
核动力 nuclear power
核讹诈 nuclear blackmail
核反应 nuclear reaction
核废料 nuclear waste; N-waste
核辐射 nuclear radiation
核黄素 riboflavin; lactoflavin
核火箭 nuclear rocket
核聚变 nuclear fusion
核扩散 nuclear proliferation
核理论 nuclear theory
核裂变 nuclear fission
核垄断 nuclear monopoly
核潜艇 nuclear-powered submarine
核燃料 nuclear fuel
核事故 nuclear accident
核试验 nuclear test; nuke test

核衰变 nuclear disintegration
核桃仁 walnut meat
核威胁 nuclear threat
核武库 nuclear weapon;arsenal weapon
核武器 nuclear weapon
核优势 nuclear superiority
核战争 nuclear war (*or* warfare)
核装置 nuclear device
核子学 nucleonics
核保护伞 nuclear umbrella
核不扩散 nonproliferation
核磁共振 nuclear magnetic resonance (NMR)
核定概算 approve estimates
核定股本 authorized stock
核对账目 verify account;check account
核反应堆 nuclear reactor
核算单位 accounting unit
核糖核酸 ribonucleic acid (RNA)
核心家庭 nuclear family
核心课程 core curriculum
核心内阁 inner cabinet
核心人物 key figure
核心小组 core group
核子废料 nuclear decay;nuclear waste
核子武器 nucleonic weapon;nuclear weapon
核爆幸存者 hibakusha
核爆炸装置 nuclear explosive device
核打击力量 nuclear strike capability (*or* force)
核禁试条约 nuclear (*or* nuke) test ban treaty
核军备竞赛 nuclear arms race
核威慑力量 nuclear deterrent power
核微粒沾染 contamination from nuclear fallout
核定承兑汇票 approved acceptance
核算生产成本 work out the cost of production
核材料非法贩卖 illicit trafficking of nuclear materials
核爆炸放射性危害 radiological hazard of nuclear explosions

龁 [hé]
劲 bite

盒 [hé]
名 ①box;case ②box-shaped fireworks
盒带 video cassette tape
盒饭 box lunch
盒子 box;case;casket
盒子枪 Mauser pistol
盒式磁带 cassette tape
盒式磁带录像机 video cassette recorder
盒式磁带录音机 cassette tape recorder

涸 [hé]
劲 dry up;run dry
涸竭 dried up;exhausted
涸井 dry well
涸辙 dry rut
涸辙之鲋 a fish stranded in a dry rut—in a desperate situation

颌 [hé]
名 jaw ➡gé
颌痛 gnathalgia
颌畸形 jaw abnormality

貉 [hé]
名 racoon dog ➡háo

阖 [hé]
I 形 entire;whole II 劲 shut;close
阖城 entire city
阖村 whole village
阖第 your whole family
阖府 your whole family
阖家 the whole family
阖门 close the door
阖眼 close one's eyes

hè(ㄏㄜˋ)

吓 [hè]
I 劲 threaten;intimidate II 叹 (*used to express disapproval or resentment*):吓，你也太不像话了! Humph, how impudent you are! ➡xià

和 [hè]
劲 ①join in the singing ②compose a poem of the same theme and rhyme scheme as one by someone else；write a poem in reply (to sb's poem) ➡hé;hú;huó;huò
和以笔墨 chime in with tendentious articles

贺 [hè]
劲 congratulate;felicitate;celebrate
贺匾 congratulatory plaque
贺词 speech (*or* message) of congratulation;congratulations;greetings
贺电 message of congratulation;congratulatory telegram
贺卡 greeting card
贺礼 congratulatory gift;handsel
贺年 extend New Year greetings (*or* pay) a New Year call
贺岁 celebrate the new year
贺喜 congratulate sb on a happy occasion (e.g. a wedding, the birth of a child, etc.);offer congratulations
贺信 congratulatory letter;letter of congratulation
贺年片 New Year card
贺岁片 New Year greeting film

荷 [hè]
I 劲 ①carry on one's shoulder (*or* back) ②bear;take on II 名 burden;responsibility III 形 obliged;grateful ➡hé
荷负 bear;shoulder
荷载 load
荷重 the weight a building can bear;load
荷担而行 carry a load on a shoulder-pole
荷枪实弹 (of soldiers or policemen) carry loaded rifles—ready for an emergency

荷重能力 loading capacity

喝 [hè]
囫 shout loudly ➡ hē
喝彩 acclaim；cheer；shout "bravo!"
喝令 shout an order (*or* command)
喝问 shout a question to
喝倒彩 make catcalls；hoot；boo

赫 [hè]
I 囫 conspicuous；distinguished；grand Ⅱ 囵 (short for 赫兹)hertz
赫赫 illustrious；very impressive
赫然 ① impressively；awesomely ② terribly (angry)
赫兹 hertz
赫哲族 the Hezhen (*or* Hoche) nationality
赫赫有名 distinguished；illustrious

褐 [hè]
I 囵 coarse cloth (*or* clothing) Ⅱ 囫 brown
褐煤 brown coal；lignite
褐色 brown；tan
褐藻 brown alga
褐斑病 brown spot
褐黄斑 chloasma；cloasma
褐色土 drab soil
褐铁矿 brown iron ore；limonite

鹤 [hè]
囵 crane
鹤年 crane's age—longevity
鹤嘴 jumper
鹤嘴镐 pick；pickaxe；mattock
鹤发童颜 white hair and ruddy complexion—healthy in old age；hale and hearty
鹤立鸡群 like a crane standing among chickens—stand head and shoulders above others

鹖 [hè]
囫 (of bird's feather) white and sleek

壑 [hè]
囵 gully；big pool

hēi(ㄏㄟ)

黑 [hēi]
I 囫 ① black ② dark；dusky ③ secret；illegal；shady；clandestine；unlawful ④ wicked；sinister；evil；vicious ⑤ reactionary Ⅱ 囫 do sth unlawful or unethical
黑暗 dark；without light
黑疤 black scar
黑白 ① black and white ② right and wrong
黑板 blackboard
黑帮 reactionary gang；sinister gang；cabal
黑潮 black stream；Kuroshio；Japan Current (*or* Stream)
黑车 unlicensed vehicle；unlicensed car，tricycle，etc
黑船 ships used for smuggling and other illegal acts
黑道 ① dark road ② dark deeds；illegal activi-

ties ③ underworld organizations
黑点 stain；blemish；smirch
黑店 clip joint；customers' trap；gangster inn；inn run by brigands
黑貂 sable
黑鲷 black porgy
黑洞 black hole；collapsar
黑豆 black soya bean
黑粪 melaena
黑光 black light
黑海 the Black Sea
黑户 ① family without residence permit；unregistered household；unregistered resident ② a shop without a license；an illegal shop；private business without a licence
黑话 ① (bandits') argot；(thieves') cant ② double-talk；malicious words
黑货 smuggled goods；contraband；sinister stuff；trash
黑鲩 black carp
黑会 a clandestine meeting
黑金 black money
黑客 hacker(person who tampers with other people's computers through the Internet)；e-guerrilla；cyber intruder；cyber punk
黑牢 dark prison cell
黑领 black-collar worker
黑瘤 melanoma
黑马 dark horse—little-known person who unexpectedly becomes successful or prominent
黑麦 rye
黑幕 inside story of a plot，shady deal，etc.
黑钱 black money；ill-gotten money；money obtained by unlawful means
黑枪 ① illegally possessed firearms ② shot fired from a hiding-place
黑人 Black people；Black
黑色 black (colour)
黑纱 black armband
黑哨 black whistle
黑市 black market；illicit market
黑手 vicious person manipulating sb or sth from behind the scenes；evil backstage manipulator
黑桃 spade (in cards)
黑陶 black pottery
黑体 ① blackbody ② boldface
黑天 night；nightfall
黑土 ① chernozem；black earth ② opium
黑箱 black box
黑心 black heart；evil mind
黑信 poison-pen letter
黑熊 black bear
黑夜 night
黑鱼 snakehead
黑云 black clouds；dark clouds

黑枣　dateplum persimmon
黑痣　pigmented naevus
黑子　①black mole (on the skin) ②sunspot
黑字　surplus
黑白片　black-and-white film
黑斑病　black spot
黑板报　blackboard newspaper；blackboard bulletin
黑板擦　(blackboard) eraser
黑洞洞　pitch-dark
黑非洲　Black Africa
黑钙土　black earth；dark soil
黑孩子　off-the-book baby
黑乎乎　① black；blackened ② rather dark；dusky ③indistinctly observable in the distance
黑胡椒　black pepper (Piper nigrum)
黑胶布　black tape；friction tape
黑里俏　a dark beauty
黑面包　black bread；brown bread；rye bread
黑名单　blacklist
黑木耳　edible black fungus
黑啤酒　dark beer；black beer；stout
黑热病　kala-azar
黑色素　melanin
黑社会　gangsterdom；secret societies；the underworld；Mafia-style organizations；gangland
黑市价　black rate
黑市票　scalping ticket
黑手党　Mafia
黑死病　the plague
黑穗病　smut
黑窝点　hideout；hiding place；underground workshop (or factory，mill，joint)
黑钨矿　wolframite
黑匣子　black box (as used in planes or cars)
黑心棉　inferior cotton；substandard cotton
黑猩猩　chimpanzee
黑压压　a dense (or dark) mass of
黑眼镜　sunglasses
黑眼珠　iris
黑曜岩　obsidian
黑影儿　a dark shadow；shadow
黑油油　jet-black；shiny black
黑黝黝　dim；dark
黑云母　black mica；biotite
黑芝麻　black sesame
黑白电视　black-and-white television
黑白分明　with black and white sharply contrasted；in sharp contrast
黑不溜秋　swarthy
黑灯瞎火　dark；unlighted
黑咕隆咚　very dark；pitch-dark
黑货市场　fence (market)
黑加工点　underground processing joint；hideout (or hideaway) of an illegal processing factory
黑色火药　black powder
黑色金属　ferrous metal
黑色经济　black economy
黑色人种　the black race
黑色食品　black food
黑色收入　black income；irregular (or abnormal) income；income with no identifiable source
黑色幽默　black humour
黑市汇兑　black market exchange
黑市交易　off-the-books deal；trading illegally on the black market
黑陶文化　the black pottery culture
黑箱操作　black case work
黑箱理论　black box theory
黑衣法官　football referee
黑里康大号　helicon
黑色星期一　Black Monday
黑社会头目　gang leader；chieftain of the underworld
黑市投机买卖　black market；speculative trading
黑社会性质组织　mafia

嘿 [hēi]

〔叹〕①(*used as a form of greeting or to call attention*)Hey：嘿，你倒是上啊！Hey, you! Go ahead! ②(*used to express satisfaction or self-congratulation*)Hey：嘿，咱们这篇文章写得真不错呀！Hey! Our article is really well-written. ③(*used to express surprise*)Ah：嘿，原来你在这儿！Ah, there you are!

hén（ㄏㄣˊ）

痕 [hén]

〔名〕mark；trace
痕迹　①mark；trace ②vestige
痕量　trace
痕量分析　trace analysis

hěn（ㄏㄣˇ）

很 [hěn]

〔副〕very；quite；awfully
很可能　very likely

狠 [hěn]

Ⅰ〔形〕①ruthless；relentless ②firm；resolute；stern；vigorous Ⅱ〔动〕suppress (one's feelings)；make a painful effort；harden (one's heart，etc.)；狠着劲止住眼泪 fight back one's tears Ⅲ〔副〕very；quite；awfully
狠毒　vicious；venomous
狠命　go all out
狠心　①harden one's heart；make a painful decision ②cruel；heartless；callous；pitiless；ruthless
狠狠地　brutally；cruelly；in cold blood；merci-

lessly

hèn (ㄏㄣˋ)

恨 动 ①hate;resent ②regret;remorse
恨事 matter for regret;regrettable things
恨不得 one wishes one could;one would if one could;be dying to
恨透了 hate to the utmost degree
恨得要命 hate with all one's soul
恨之入骨 hate sb to the marrow of one's bones;bear a bitter hatred for sb;bitterly hate
恨铁不成钢 wish that iron could turn straight into steel—be anxious for sb to improve
恨不相逢未嫁时 How sorry I am that I met you (my true love) only after my marriage.

hēng (ㄏㄥ)

亨 I 动 go smoothly (*or* well) Ⅱ 名 Henry
亨利 Henry
亨通 go smoothly;be prosperous

哼 动 ①snort;groan ②hum;croon
哼哧 puff hard
哼唧 mutter;hum
哼声 groaning
哼唷 heave ho;yo-heave-ho;yo-ho
哼儿哈儿 hem and haw
哼哈二将 a pair of fierce men serving one master or acting in collusion with each other

héng (ㄏㄥˊ)

行 ➡háng;xíng
◇**道行** the attainments of a Taoist priest

恒 I 形 ①lasting;permanent ②usual;common;constant Ⅱ 名 perseverance;constancy (of purpose)
恒齿 permanent tooth
恒等 identically equal;identical
恒定 constant
恒久 permanent;lasting;enduring
恒量 constant
恒生 Hang Sang
恒速 constant speed
恒态 usual (*or* normal) appearance
恒温 constant temperature
恒心 perseverance;constancy of purpose
恒星 (fixed) star
恒言 common saying
恒温箱 incubator;thermostatted container

恒星年 sidereal year
恒星日 sidereal day
恒星时 sidereal time
恒星系 stellar system;galaxy
恒星月 sidereal month
恒星云 star cloud
恒压器 barostat
恒河沙数 as numerous as the sands of the Ganges;innumerable;countless
恒生银行 Hang Seng Bank,Ltd.
恒生指数 Hang Seng Index (HIS)
恒温动物 homoiothermal (*or* warm-blooded) animal
恒阻网络 constant resistance network
恒流调节器 constant current regulator
恒星天文学 stellar astronomy
恒星望远镜 star telescope
恒星物理学 stellar physics

横 [héng] I 形 ①horizontal;transverse ②from east to west;from west to east ③across;crosswise;sideways ④at a right angle (to sth) Ⅱ 动 place crosswise or horizontally Ⅲ 副 ①unrestrainedly;turbulently ②violently;fiercely;flagrantly ③in any case;anyhow;anyway ④probably;(most) likely Ⅳ 名 horizontal stroke (in a Chinese character) ➡hèng
横波 transverse wave
横穿 cross
横担 cross arm
横档 crosspiece (of a table,etc.)
横笛 bamboo flute
横渡 cross a river;sail across
横队 rank;row
横幅 ①horizontal scroll of painting or calligraphy ②banner;streamer
横杆 cross bar;beam
横亘 lie across;span
横贯 pass through from east to west or from west to east;traverse
横过 cross;across;transverse
横祸 unexpected calamity;sudden misfortune
横加 do sth to sb unreasonably,forcibly,wilfully,etc.
横跨 stretch over (*or* across)
横梁 ①crossbeam ②cross member (of a car)
横眉 frown in anger;scowl
横批 a horizontal scroll bearing an inscription
横披 a horizontal wall inscription;a horizontal hanging scroll
横切 crosscut
横肉 fierce-looking
横扫 ①sweep across;sweep away;make a clean sweep of ②glance quickly from side to side
横生 ①grow wild ②be overflowing with;be full of ③happen unexpectedly

横式 horizontal type
横竖 in any case;anyway
横向 horizontal;crosswise
横巷 crosscut
横心 steel one's heart;become desperate
横行 run wild;run amuck;be on a rampage
横移 sidesway
横溢 ①(of a river) overflow;be in flood ②(of talent, enthusiasm, etc.) brimming;overflowing;abundant
横越 traverse;overstep
横轴 cross axle (*or* shaft)
横断面 cross section;transverse section
横格纸 lined paper
横隔膜 diaphragm
横结肠 transverse colon
横剖面 cross (*or* transverse) section
横尾翼 tail plane;horizontal stabilizer
横纹肌 striated muscle
横坐标 abscissa
横冲直撞 push one's way by shoving or bumping;jostle and elbow one's way;dash around madly;barge about;charge about
横刀夺爱 draw one's sword to seize what sb cherishes;take away sb's woman (*or* valued possession) by force
横倒竖歪 in disorder;higgledy-piggledy
横加干涉 flagrantly interfere
横加指责 make unfounded (*or* unwarranted) charges;hurl abuses
横眉怒目 with frowning brows and angry eyes;darting fierce looks of hate
横眉竖眼 glare in anger
横拍握法 tennis grip;handshake grip
横七竖八 in disorder;at sixes and sevens;higgledy-piggledy
横生枝节 raise unexpected difficulties;deliberately complicate an issue
横向合并 horizontal combination;merger combination;lateral integration
横向交流 lateral communication;lateral exchange
横向扩散 horizontal proliferation
横向联合 horizontal linkage
横向联系 lateral ties;horizontal connections (*or* association,integration,linkage)
横行霸道 ride roughshod over;trample on;tyrannize;domineer
横行无忌 run wild;run amuck
横行一时 run wild for a time
横征暴敛 extort excessive (*or* heavy) taxes and levies;levy exorbitant taxes
横向经济协作 lateral (*or* horizontal) economic cooperation
横挑鼻子,竖挑眼 nitpick;find fault in a petty manner;pick holes in sth
横眉冷对千夫指,俯首甘为孺子牛 fierce-browed,I coolly defy a thousand pointing fingers;head bowed, like a willing ox, I serve the children

衡 [héng]
Ⅰ 名 ① graduated arm of a steelyard ② weighing apparatus Ⅱ 动 weigh;measure;judge Ⅲ 形 levelled;balanced
衡量 ①weigh;measure;judge ②consider;deliberate
衡器 weighing apparatus
衡平权 equitable interest
衡量得失 weigh up the gains and losses
衡情度理 considering the circumstances and judging by common sense;all things considered

hèng(ㄏㄥˋ)

横 [hèng]
形 ①rude;rough;fierce and brutal;harsh and unreasonable;perverse ② inauspicious;unexpected;ominous ➡héng
横暴 perverse and violent
横财 ill-gotten wealth (*or* gains)
横祸 sudden misfortune;unexpected calamity
横事 untoward accident
横死 die a violent death;meet with a sudden death
横议 comment without reserve;make unbridled criticism

hōng(ㄏㄨㄥ)

轰 [hōng]
Ⅰ 拟 bang;boom:轰！轰！轰！礼炮鸣放二十一响。Boom! Boom! Boom! Twenty-one salvoes were fired. Ⅱ 动 ①rumble;bombard;explode ②shoo away;drive (off):轰牲口 drive draught animals
轰动 cause a sensation;create a sensation;make a stir;create a furore
轰赶 shoo away;drive off
轰击 ①shell;bombard ②bombard
轰隆 rumble;roll
轰鸣 thunder;roar
轰撵 force out;expel
轰然 with a loud crash (*or* bang)
轰响 roar;rumble
轰炸 attack with bombs;bomb
轰炸机 bomber
轰动效应 shocking effect;resounding effect
轰动一时 create a furore;make a great stir;cause a great sensation
轰轰烈烈 on a grand and spectacular scale;vigorous;dynamic
轰炸雷达 blind bombing radar
轰炸误差 bombing error
轰炸瞄准具 bombsight

哄 [hōng]
I 叹 (*used to describe roars of laughter or uproarious talk*) guffaws; roars of laughter or noise: 众人哄的一声大笑起来。All burst into uproarious laughter. II 动 hubbub; din; noise; uproar ➡ hǒng; hòng

哄传 (of rumours) circulate widely

哄抢 (of a crowd of people) make a mad rush for; make a scramble for (public property, goods, etc.)

哄然 boisterous; uproarious

哄抬 drive up (prices)

哄笑 go off into laughter

哄抬价格 inflate (*or* bid up, jack up, drive up, force up) price

哄堂大笑 The whole room is rocking with laughter.

訇 [hōng]
名 ①loud noise ②imam

訇然 with a loud crash (*or* bang)

烘 [hōng]
动 ①dry; warm; bake ②set off

烘焙 cure (tea or tobacco leaves)

烘干 ①dry over heat ②stoving

烘缸 dryer

烘烘 sound of a roaring fire

烘烤 toast; bake

烘炉 oven; oast

烘漆 baking finish; stoving finish

烘托 ① (in Chinese painting) add shading around an object to make it stand out ②set off by contrast; throw into sharp relief

烘箱 oven

烘干机 drying machine; dryer

烘丝机 cut-tobacco drier

烘相器 print drier

烘云托月 paint clouds to set off the moon; provide a foil for a character or incident in a literary work

薨 [hōng]
动 (of feudal lords or high officials) die; pass away

薨逝 die; pass away

hóng (ㄏㄨㄥˊ)

弘 [hóng]
动 enlarge; expand

弘扬 carry forward; develop; enhance

弘扬正气 encourage healthy trends

弘扬主旋律 give full scope to the theme of our times

弘扬爱国主义精神 promote patriotic spirit

弘扬民族优秀文化 advance and enrich the fine cultural heritage of the nation

红 [hóng]
I 形 ①red ②revolutionary; red II 名 ① red cloth, bunting, etc. ②bonus; dividend ③ symbol of success; luck; popularity

红斑 erythema

红榜 honour roll (*or* board)

红包 (neutral) red paper containing money as a gift; (derogative) covert payment; under-the-table cash gift

红茶 black tea

红场 Red Square

红潮 ①blush; flush ②red tide; red water

红尘 the world of mortals; human society

红丹 red lead; minium

红豆 ①red bean shrub ②love pea

红粉 ①rouge and powder ②women; the fair sex

红汞 mercurochrome

红股 bonus issue

红果 the fruit of large Chinese hawthorn; haw

红鹳 ibis

红狐 red fox

红花 safflower

红火 flourishing; prosperous

红货 pearls and jewels; jewelry

红军 ① the Chinese Workers' and Peasants' Red Army; the Red Army ②Red Army man ③Soviet Union army

红利 bonus; dividends earned; extra dividend

红脸 ①blush ②flush with anger; get angry ③ red face, face painting in Beijing opera, etc., traditionally for the heroic or the honest

红磷 red phosphorus

红麻 bluish dogbane

红媒 matchmaker; go-between

红霉 erythromycin

红焖 stew in soy sauce

红米 red rice

红木 mahogany

红娘 go-between; matchmaker

红牌 red card

红盘 red listing

红旗 red flag or banner

红壤 red soil (*or* earth)

红人 a favourite with sb in power; fair-haired boy

红润 ruddy; rosy

红色 ①red ②revolutionary; red

红杉 Chinese larch

红烧 braise in soy sauce

红事 happy occasion

红树 mangrove

红松 Korean pine

红糖 brown sugar

红桃 heart (in cards)

红陶 red pottery; terra-cotta

红心 a red heart—a heart loyal to the cause of proletarian revolution

红星 red star

红学 studies of *A Dream of Red Mansions*; Redology
红颜 pretty face; beautiful woman
红眼 ①become infuriated; see red ②be envious; be jealous of
红叶 red autumnal leaves (of the maple, etc.)
红鱼 (red) snapper
红雨 blood-rain
红运 good luck
红晕 blush; flush
红枣 red date
红藻 red alga
红肿 red and swollen
红装 ①gay feminine attire ②young woman
红宝石 ruby
红菜头 beetroot
红绸舞 red silk dance
红筹股 red chips
红丹漆 red lead paint
红灯区 red-light district; specially-sectioned-off area for prostitution houses
红骨顶 moorhen
红脚鹬 redshank
红角儿 popular actor; popular actress
红利股 bonus stock; bonus share; bonus dividend
红铃虫 pink bollworm
红领巾 ①red scarf (worn by Young Pioneers) ②Young Pioneer
红领章 red collar tab (as formerly on PLA uniforms)
红绿灯 traffic light; traffic signal
红墨水 red ink
红模子 a sheet of paper with red characters printed on it, to be traced over with a brush by children learning calligraphy
红娘鱼 sea robin; red gurnard
红喷喷 reddish; with a red tint
红皮书 red paper; red book
红扑扑 flushed
红旗手 red-banner pacesetter; model worker; advanced worker
红三叶 red clover
红彤彤 bright red; glowing
红外线 infrared; infrared ray
红细胞 red blood cell; erythrocyte
红小豆 red bean
红血球 red blood cell
红眼病 ①bloodshot eye; pinkeye ②envy; jealousy
红艳艳 brilliant red
红药水 mercurochrome
红缨枪 red-tasseled spear
红蜘蛛 red spider (mite); spider mite
红柱石 andalusite
红白喜事 weddings and funerals
红斑狼疮 lupus erythematosus

红得发紫 (of a person) extremely popular
红电气石 rubellite
红粉佳人 young beauty; gaily dressed beauty
红光满面 one's face glowing with health; in the pink
红极一时 be well-known for a time; enjoy popularity for a time
红利分配 profit sharing
红男绿女 young men and women in love
红旗单位 red-banner unit; advanced unit
红色警戒 red alert
红色网站 redweb
红十字会 the Red Cross (Society)
红头文件 document issued by a party or government office (usu. with the title printed in red, hence the name); official document
红颜薄命 beautiful women suffer unhappy fates
红眼航班 red-eye flight
红衣主教 cardinal
红装素裹 clad in white, adorned in red (said of a sunlit snow scene)
红外线辐射 infrared radiation
红外线照相 infrared photography
红外报警装置 infrared warning device
红外线探测器 infrared detector
红细胞生成素 erythropoietin (EPO)
红领巾助残活动 Young Pioneers Helping the Disabled Activity
红外线扫描装置 infrared scanner
红外线遥感技术 infrared remote sensing technique

宏 [hóng]
形 great; grand; magnificent
宏辩 well-supported argument; eloquent contention
宏大 grand; great
宏观 ①macroscopic ②macro
宏论 informed opinion; intelligent view
宏图 great plan; grand prospect
宏伟 magnificent; grand
宏业 great achievement
宏愿 great aspirations; noble ambition
宏旨 main theme; leading idea of an article
宏变量 macro-variable
宏代码 macro-code
宏指令 macro instruction
宏观结构 macrostructure
宏观决策 policy-making in a macrocosmic sense; macro-level policy making
宏观世界 macrocosm
宏观调控 macroeconomic control; macro-control
宏程序设计 macroprogramming
宏观经济学 macroeconomics
宏观紧缩力度 depth of macro-economic retrenchment

宏观经济管理 macro-economic management; macro-economic control
宏观经济调控 macro-economic regulation and control
宏观经济调整 macro-economic regulation; macro-economic adjustment
宏观经济效益 macro-economic results
宏观经济政策 macro economic policy
宏观调控能力 capacity for macroeconomic regulation and control
宏观调控体系 macro-economic control system
宏观经济调控机制 macro-economic control mechanism; macro-economic regulation mechanism

纮 [hóng]
名 lace on a hat in ancient times

泓 [hóng]
I 形 (of water) deep II 量 *used of clear water*：一泓秋水 an expanse of limpid water in autumn

虹 [hóng]
名 rainbow ➡ jiàng
虹膜 iris; irides
虹桥 rainbow-shaped bridge; arched bridge
虹雉 monal
虹吸管 siphon
虹吸现象 siphonage

洪 [hóng]
I 形 big; vast; grand II 名 flood
洪波 turbulent waves
洪才 great talent
洪大 loud
洪峰 flood crest; flood peak; the highest point of a flood
洪荒 chaotic state; primeval times
洪亮 loud and clear; sonorous
洪量 ①magnanimity; generosity ②great capacity for liquor
洪流 mighty torrent; powerful current
洪炉 great furnace
洪脉 pulse beating like waves; full pulse
洪水 flood; floodwater
洪涛 big waves
洪讯 flood information; flood message
洪灾 a big flood; inundation
洪钟 large bell
洪泛区 flood plain; flooded area
洪福齐天 limitless blessing
洪水猛兽 fierce floods and savage beasts-great scourges; deluge

翃 [hóng]
动 fly

鸿 [hóng]
I 名 ①swan goose; Chinese goose ②letter II 形 great; grand
鸿笔 great pen; great literary style
鸿沟 wide gap; chasm; gulf
鸿鹄 ①swan ②a person of noble aspirations; a person with lofty ideals
鸿毛 goose feather—sth very light or insignificant
鸿儒 learned scholar; erudite person
鸿雁 swan goose
鸿运 good luck
鸿门宴 *Hongmen* feast—a meeting contrived as a trap
鸿鹄之志 lofty ambition; high aspirations
鸿篇巨制 a monumental work

蕻 [hóng]
◇雪里蕻 potherb mustard

hǒng(ㄏㄨˇ)

哄 [hǒng]
动 ①fool; humbug; kid ②keep in good humour; coax; humour ➡ hōng; hòng
哄逗 keep (esp. a child) in good humour; coax
哄骗 cheat; humbug; hoodwink; cajole
哄劝 coax

hòng(ㄏㄨˋ)

讧 [hòng]
动 quarrel; discord

哄 [hòng]
名 uproar; clamour; horseplay ➡ hōng; hǒng
哄场 make catcalls; hoot

蕻 [hòng]
形 luxuriant; exuberant

hóu(ㄏㄡˊ)

侯 [hóu]
名 ①marquis; marquess ②nobleman; high official
侯爵 marquis
侯门 mansion of the nobility
侯爵夫人 marquise
侯门似海 the gate of a noble house is like the sea—impassable to the common man

喉 [hóu]
名 larynx; throat; gullet
喉病 laryngeal disease
喉风 sore throat
喉结 Adam's apple
喉镜 laryngoscope
喉咙 throat
喉痧 scarlet fever
喉舌 mouthpiece
喉头 larynx; throat
喉炎 laryngitis
喉擦音 guttural fricative
喉塞音 glottal stop

猴 [hóu]
I 名 monkey II 形 smart; clever; mischievous III 动 squat (like a monkey)

猴拳 monkey boxing
猴市 monkey market
猴头 hedgehog hydnum
猴戏 show by a performing monkey; monkey show
猴子 monkey
猴儿急 very impatient; feel anxious; feel worried
猴儿精 ① astute; shrewd; smart ② clever and mischievous person; mischief-maker
猴面包树 monkey-bread tree; baobab
猴年马月 impossible date; day that will never come
猴皮筋儿 rubber band

hǒu (ㄏㄡˇ)

吼 [hǒu]
劢 ① (of large animals) roar; growl ② (of angry or excited people) shout; roar ③ (of wind, siren, cannon, etc.) howl; boom
吼叫 roar; howl; shout
吼声 roaring cry; shrill cry

hòu (ㄏㄡˋ)

后 [hòu]
Ⅰ 名 ① back; rear ② offspring; progeny; posterity ③ empress; queen ④ emperor; monarch; sovereign Ⅱ 形 ① hind ② back Ⅲ 副 ① behind ② after; later; afterwards
后备 reserve
后背 ① back (of the body) ② at the back; in the rear
后辈 ① younger generation; juniors ② posterity
后步 room for manoeuvre
后场 backcourt
后尘 dust kicked up by sb walking in front
后代 ① later periods (in history); later ages ② later generations; descendants; posterity ③ progeny
后灯 taillight (of a car); tail lamp
后爹 stepfather
后盾 backing; backup force
后方 ① rear ② behind
后妃 empress and imperial concubines
后福 ① future blessings ② blessings in one's old age
后跟 heel (of a shoe or sock)
后宫 ① imperial harem; palace of imperial concubines ② imperial concubines
后顾 ① turn back (to take care of sth) ② look back (on the past)
后果 consequence; aftermath
后话 part of a story to be recounted later; part of a story that is to come
后患 future trouble

后悔 regret; repent
后记 postscript (added to a finished book, etc.)
后继 succeed; carry on
后脚 ① the rear foot (in walking) ② close behind
后襟 the back of a Chinese robe (or jacket)
后进 ① lagging behind; less advanced; backward ② juniors
后劲 ① delayed effect; aftereffect ② reserve strength; stamina; sustaining power; staying power; ability to make further advances
后景 background (of a picture)
后来 afterwards; later
后路 ① communication lines to the rear; route of retreat ② room for manoeuvre; a way of escape
后轮 rear wheel
后妈 stepmother
后门 ① back door (or gate) ② backdoor (or backstairs) influence
后面 ① at the back; in the rear; behind ② later
后母 stepmother
后脑 hindbrain; rhombencephalon
后年 the year after next
后娘 stepmother
后怕 fear after the event
后排 back row
后坡 back slope; adverse grade
后期 later stage; later period
后起 (of people of talent) of new arrivals; of the younger generation
后桥 rear (or back) axle (of a car)
后勤 rear service; logistics
后人 ① later generations ② posterity; descendants
后任 successor (to a post)
后身 ① the back of a person ② the back of a garment
后生 ① young man; lad ② having a youthful appearance
后世 ① later ages ② later generations
后市 latter market
后事 ① what happened afterwards ② funeral affairs
后视 back vision
后手 ① successor ② defensive position (in chess) ③ room for manoeuvre; a way of escape
后嗣 offspring; descendant
后送 evacuation
后台 ① backstage ② backstage supporter; behind the scenes backer
后天 ① day after tomorrow ② postnatal; acquired
后头 ① at the back; in the rear; behind ②

later；future
后腿 hind legs
后退 draw back；fall back；retreat
后卫 ①rear guard ②full back；defender ③ guard
后项 consequent
后续 ①follow-up ②remarry after the death of one's wife
后悬 rear overhang (of a car)
后腰 the small of the back
后裔 descendant (of a dead person)；offspring
后影 the shape of a person or thing as seen from the back
后援 reinforcements；backup force；backing
后院 backyard
后者 the latter
后肢 hind legs (of an animal)
后轴 rear axle
后缀 suffix
后半生 the latter half of one's life
后半天 afternoon
后半叶 latter half of a century
后半夜 ①the second half of the night ②the small hours
后备队 backup team
后备军 reserves；reserve force
后背箱 rear trunk
后处理 ①aftertreatment ②finishing
后滚翻 backward roll
后花园 back garden
后脊梁 backbone；spine
后空翻 backward somersault
后来人 successors
后掠角 sweep angle；sweepback
后掠翼 swept-back wing
后视镜 rearview mirror；rear-vision mirror
后视图 back view；rearview
后手翻 back handspring
后遗症 ①sequelae ②aftereffect；aftermath
后肘子 hind shank
后坐力 recoil
后备部队 reserve units
后备干部 reserve cadre；cadres in support
后发制人 gain mastery by counterattacking；gain masters by striking only after the enemy has struck
后方空虚 leave the defense exposed
后工业化 postindustrialism
后顾之忧 trouble back at home；fear of disturbance in rear or on home front
后患无穷 no end of trouble for the future
后悔莫及 too late to repent
后会有期 we'll meet again some day
后继无人 leave no successor (to carry on a tradition，transmit an art or craft，etc.)
后继有人 there is no lack of successors；there's another generation to carry on

后决条件 condition subsequent
后来居上 come from behind；the late comers surpass the old-timers
后力不济 lack the strength to continue
后脑勺儿 the back of the head
后起之秀 an up-and-coming youngster；a promising young person
后勤保障 logistical support
后生成本 after-cost
后生可畏 A youth is to be regarded with respect.
后台程序 background program
后台老板 moneyman；backstage supporter；boss supporter；behind-the-scenes backer
后续服务 follow-up service
后续投资 follow-up investment
后座议员 backbencher
后工业社会 post-industrial society
后浪推前浪 the waves behind drive on those before
后三角队形 V formation
后现代主义 post-modernism
后天免疫缺损综合征 acquired immunodeficiency syndrome；acquired immune deficiency syndrome (AIDS)

厚 [hòu]
Ⅰ 形 ① thick ② deep；profound ③ kind；magnanimous ④large；generous；handsome ⑤ rich (*or* strong) in flavour ⑥ well-off；well-to-do；wealthy Ⅱ 名 thickness
厚爱 your kind thought；your kindness
厚薄 thickness
厚待 treat kindly and generously；kindhearted
厚道 honest and kind
厚度 thickness
厚礼 generous gifts
厚利 large profits
厚禄 handsome salary；high government pay
厚漆 paste paint
厚实 ①thick ②abundant；rich
厚望 great expectations
厚意 kind thought；kindness
厚葬 ①bury with full honours ②lavish funeral
厚重 ① thick and heavy ② rich and generous ③kind and dignified
厚薄规 feeler (gauge)
厚墩墩 very thick
厚脸皮 thick-skinned；brazen；cheeky
厚此薄彼 favour one and be prejudiced against the other；favour one and discriminate against the other
厚古薄今 stress past and slight present
厚积薄发 be versed in a subject；be well-grounded；be well-prepared
厚今薄古 stress the present，not the past
厚利多销 large profits and quick turnover

厚人薄己 treat others well but be frugal with oneself
厚颜无耻 impudent;brazen;shameless
厚以待人 be magnanimous to people

逅 [hòu]

◇邂逅 meet (a relative,friend,etc.) unexpectedly;run into sb;meet by chance

候 [hòu]

Ⅰ 动 ①wait;await ②inquire after Ⅱ 名 ①time;season ②pentad;period of five days ③condition;state
候补 be a candidate (for a vacancy);be an alternate
候车 wait for a train,bus,etc.
候教 await your instructions
候鸟 migratory bird;migrant
候审 pending trial;await trial
候诊 wait to see the doctor
候车室 waiting room (in a railway or bus station)
候机室 airport lounge or waiting room
候选人 candidate (nominee)
候诊室 waiting room (in a hospital)
候补委员 alternate member

hū (ㄏㄨ)

呼 [hū]

Ⅰ 动 ①breathe out;exhale ②shout;cry out ③call Ⅱ 象 howl:大北风呼呼地吹。A cold northerly was howling.
呼哧 the sound of panting
呼斥 berate;excoriate;shout at (sb)
呼喊 call out;shout
呼号 [hūháo] wail;cry out in distress
呼号 [hūhào] ① call sign;call letters ② catchword (of an organization)
呼唤 call;shout to
呼机 beeper;pager
呼叫 ①call out;shout ②telecommunications call
呼救 call for help;send out SOS signals
呼噜 snore
呼请 call for (a doctor)
呼扇 ①shake ②fan
呼哨 whistle
呼声 cry;voice
呼吸 breathe;respire
呼啸 whistle;scream;whizz
呼应 echo;work in concert with
呼吁 appeal;call on
呼口号 shout slogans
呼啦圈 hula hoop
呼吸道 respiratory tract
呼吸率 respiratory rate
呼吸器 respirator
呼吁书 letter of appeal;appeal

呼爹叫娘 cry "mamma" in distress
呼风唤雨 summon wind and rain—exercise magic powers;stir up trouble
呼呼大睡 snore loudly in one's sleep;snore away
呼朋引类 gang up
呼声甚高 there are wide speculations
呼天抢地 lament to heaven and knock one's head on earth—utter cries of anguish
呼吸器官 respiratory apparatus
呼吸系统 respiratory system
呼吸相通 share the same sentiments and fate;be bound together by common interests
呼兄唤弟 call each other brothers
呼之欲出 (of lifelike figures in pictures or vivid characters in novels) ready to come out at one's call—be vividly portrayed
呼之即来,挥之即去 have sb at one's beck and call

忽 [hū]

Ⅰ 动 neglect;overlook;ignore Ⅱ 副 ①suddenly ②now... now...
忽而 now... ,now...
忽略 neglect;overlook;lose sight of
忽然 suddenly;all of a sudden
忽闪 (of the eyes,etc.) sparkle;flash
忽视 ignore;overlook;neglect
忽闻 hear suddenly;learn of sth unexpectedly
忽悠 flicker
忽忽悠悠 indifference to the passing of time;careless
忽左忽右 suddenly left, suddenly right—now one extreme,now the other

惚 [hū]

◇恍惚 ① in a trance;absentminded ② dimly;faintly;seemingly

糊 [hū]

动 plaster ➡hú;hù

hú (ㄏㄨ)

囫 [hú]

囫囵 whole
囫囵吞枣 swallow a date whole—lap up information without digesting it;read without understanding

和 [hú]

动 win in a game of mahjong (or cards) ➡hé;hè;huó;huò

狐 [hú]

名 fox
狐猴 lemur;lemuroid
狐臭 body odour;bromhidrosis
狐狸 fox
狐媚 bewitch by cajolery;entice by flattery
狐裘 fox-fur robe

狐仙 fairy fox
狐疑 doubt;suspicion
狐步舞 foxtrot (a ballroom dance)
狐狸精 fox spirit—a seductive woman
狐假虎威 the fox borrows the tiger's fierce-
　·ness (by walking in the latter's compa-
　ny)—bully people by flaunting one's pow-
　erful connections
狐狸尾巴 fox's tail—sth that gives away a
　person's real character or evil intentions;
　cloven hoof
狐群狗党 a pack of rogues;a gang of scoun-
　drels

弧 [hú]
　图 ①arc ②bow
弧度 radian
弧光 arc light;arc
弧角 arc angle
弧菌 vibrio
弧线 pitch arc
弧形 arc;curve
弧圈球 loop drive

胡 [hú]
　Ⅰ 副 recklessly;wantonly;outrageously Ⅱ
　图 moustache;beard;whiskers
胡扯 talk nonsense;chatter idly
胡吹 boast outrageously;talk big
胡匪 bandit
胡蜂 wasp;hornet
胡干 do things recklessly;go it blindly
胡搞 ① mess things up;meddle with sth ②
　carry on an affair with sb;be promiscuous
胡话 ravings;wild talk
胡混 fool around;loaf around
胡椒 pepper
胡搅 ①pester sb;be mischievous ②argue te-
　diously and vexatiously;wrangle
胡来 ① mess things up;fool with sth ② run
　wild;act irresponsibly (or recklessly)
胡乱 carelessly;casually;at random
胡闹 run wild;be mischievous;make trouble
胡说 ①talk nonsense;drivel ②nonsense
胡同 lane;alley
胡须 beard;moustache;whiskers
胡杨 diversiform-leaved poplar
胡诌 fabricate wild tales;cook up
胡子 ①beard,moustache or whiskers ②bandit
胡椒鲷 grunt
胡萝卜 carrot
胡枝子 shrub lespedeza
胡吃海塞 recklessly stuff oneself with food
胡搅蛮缠 argue tediously and vexatiously;
　plague sb with unreasonable demands;pes-
　ter endlessly
胡萝卜素 carotene
胡说八道 talk nonsense;sheer nonsense;rub-
　bish

胡思乱想 go off into flights of fancy;give way
　to foolish fancies;let one's imagination run
　away with one
胡言乱语 talk nonsense;rave
胡子工程 long-drawn-out project;project that
　drags on for years;unduly long project
胡子拉碴 stubbly beard;bristly unshaven chin
胡作非为 act wildly in defiance of the law or
　public opinion; commit all kinds of
　outrages;ran amuck
胡萝卜加大棒政策 a carrot-and-stick policy

壶 [hú]
　图 ①kettle;pot;can ②bottle;flask

核 [hú]
　图 pip;stone ➡hé
核儿 ① stone; pip; core ② sth resembling a
　fruit stone

葫 [hú]
葫芦 bottle gourd;calabash

搰 [hú]
　动 ①dig ②stir up;make muddy

鹄 [hú]
　图 swan ➡gǔ
鹄发 gray hair;white hair
鹄候 await respectfully;expect
鹄立 stand erect
鹄望 eagerly look forward to

猢 [hú]
猢狲 macaque;monkey

湖 [hú]
　图 lake
湖笔 writing brush produced in Huzhou (湖
　州),Zhejiang Province
湖滨 lakeside
湖面 lake surface
湖泊 lakes
湖色 light green
湖水 lake water
湖田 land reclaimed from a lake;shoaly land
湖盐 lake salt
湖泽 lakes and marshes
湖心亭 a pavilion in the middle of a lake
湖沼学 limnology
湖光岚影 shimmering light of the lake and
　hazy atmosphere of the mountain
湖光山色 a beautiful scenery of lakes and
　mountains
湖上泛舟 boating on the lake
湖上人家 lake-dwellers

瑚 [hú]
◇ 珊瑚 coral

蝴 [hú]
蝴蝶 butterfly
蝴蝶花 fringed iris

蝴蝶髻 hair worn in a butterfly-shaped bun
蝴蝶结 bowknot；bow
蝴蝶衫 butterfly-sleeved top
蝴蝶效应 butterfly effect

糊 [hú] Ⅰ 囫 stick（paper，cloth，etc.）with paste；paste Ⅱ 彤 burnt ➡hū；hù
糊精 dextrin；artificial gum
糊口 keep body and soul together；make a living to feed the family
糊涂 ① muddled；confused；bewildered ② blurred；indistinct
糊墙纸 wall paper
糊涂虫 blunderer；bungler
糊涂官 muddle magistrate
糊涂账 chaotic accounts；a mess
糊里糊涂 muddle-headed；mixed up

醐 [hú]
◇醍醐 clarified butter；ghee

hǔ（ㄏㄨˇ）

虎 [hǔ] Ⅰ 名 tiger Ⅱ 彤 brave；vigorous Ⅲ 囫 put on a fierce（or angry）look
虎胆 as brave as a tiger
虎将 a brave general
虎劲 dauntless drive；dash
虎口 ①tiger's mouth—jaws of death ②part of the hand between the thumb and the index finger
虎狼 tiger and wolf—cruel and ruthless
虎钳 jaw vice
虎鲨 bullhead shark
虎市 tiger market
虎势 strong
虎威 (of a military officer) valiant and awe—inspiring
虎穴 tiger's den—a danger spot
虎牙 protruding canine teeth
虎骨酒 tiger-bone liquor
虎背熊腰 have a back like a tiger's and a waist like a bear's—tough and stocky
虎口拔牙 pull a tooth from the tiger's mouth—dare the greatest danger
虎口余生 be saved from the tiger's mouth—have a narrow escape from death；be snatched from the jaws of death
虎狼之兵 ferocious soldiers（or troops）
虎里虎气 strong and vigorous；strapping
虎视眈眈 glare like a tiger eyeing its prey；eye covetously or menacingly
虎头虎脑 looking strong and good natured
虎头蛇尾 tiger's head and a snake's tail—a fine start and a poor finish；in like a lion, out like a lamb
虎虎有生气 be full of vim and vigour

浒 [hǔ] 名 waterside
唬 [hǔ] 囫 bluff
琥 [hǔ]
琥珀 amber

hù（ㄏㄨˋ）

互 [hù] Ⅰ 副 mutually Ⅱ 代 each other；one another
互爱 love one another
互补 mutually complementary
互导 mutual conductance；transconductance
互调 intra-office transfer
互动 mutual；reciprocal；interact
互访 exchange visits
互感 mutual inductance
互换 exchange
互惠 mutually beneficial；reciprocal
互见 ①cross-reference ②(of two contrasting things) exist side by side
互利 mutually beneficial；of mutual benefit
互让 yield to each other；give in to each other
互生 alternate
互相 ①mutually ②each other
互赢 mutual benefit
互助 help each other
互联网 Internet；interconnection network
互助会 credit union（financial aid society organized by workers or staff members on a voluntary basis）
互助组 ①mutual aid group ②mutual aid team（an elementary form of organization in China's agricultural cooperation）
互不侵犯 mutual non-aggression
互不退让 neither side is willing to retreat
互持股权 mutual holding；reciprocal holding
互动广告 interactive advertisement
互换协定 swap agreement
互惠待遇 reciprocal treatment
互惠关税 mutually preferential tariff；reciprocal tariff；reciprocal duty
互惠合作 mutual benefit and collaboration
互惠贸易 trade with mutual benefit；fair trade；mutual trade with fairness as the major concern
互惠条约 reciprocal treaty
互惠原则 principle of reciprocity
互利合作 mutually-beneficial cooperation
互利互惠 mutual benefit and reciprocity；offer mutual benefit and achieve common progress
互派大使 exchange ambassadors；exchange of ambassadors
互调干扰 intermodulation interference
互通音信 communicate（or correspond）with

each other
互通有无 each supplies what the other needs; supply (*or* meet) each other's needs
互为因果 interact as both cause and effect
互相扯皮 buck-passing; will not serve as a precedent; engage in endless haggling and shifts of responsibility
互相配套 support and complement each other
互致问候 extend greetings to each other
互助资金 mutual fund
互不干涉内政 non-interference in each other's internal affairs
互不侵犯条约 non-aggression treaty (*or* pact)
互惠互利协议 reciprocal and mutually advantageous arrangement
互惠贸易协定 reciprocal trade agreement
互惠通商政策 bargaining policy
互惠协定关税 bargaining tariff
互相参股的企业 enterprises with shares pooled by different localities, departments and enterprises
互不把核导弹瞄准对方 not to target nuclear missiles at each other

户 [hù]
名 ① door ② household; family ③ family status ④(bank) account
户籍 ①census register; household register ②registered permanent residence
户均 per household; per family
户口 ①number of households and total population ②registered permanent residence
户头 (bank) account
户外 outdoor
户型 type of apartment
户主 head of a household
户籍警 policeman in charge of household registration
户口本 household certificate; permanent residence booklet
户口簿 (permanent) residence booklet
户口清册 census record
户枢不蠹 door hinge never becomes worm-eaten—constant activity staves off decay
户限为穿 a threshold worn low by visitors—an endless flow of visitors
户口管理制度 domicile system; residence registration system

冱 [hù]
Ⅰ 动 freeze Ⅱ 形 out-of-the-way
冱寒 freezing cold; icy cold
冱涸 be worried and pent-up

护 [hù]
动 ①protect; guard; shield ②be partial to; shield; shelter
护岸 bank revetment
护庇 shield; put under one's protection; take under one's wing

护兵 military guards
护持 shield and sustain
护短 shield a shortcoming (*or* fault)
护耳 earmuffs
护封 book jacket; jacket
护工 carer
护航 escort; convoy
护肩 shoulder pad (*or* padding)
护颈 camail
护壳 protective case (*or* shell)
护理 nurse; tend and protect
护林 protect a forest
护路 ①patrol and guard a road or railway ② road maintenance
护绿 protect green land
护面 mask
护青 keep watch over the ripening crops
护秋 keep watch over the autumn harvest
护士 (hospital) nurse
护送 escort; convoy
护腿 shinguard
护腕 wristlet; bracer
护卫 ①protect; guard ②bodyguard
护膝 kneepad; kneecap
护胸 chest protector
护袖 oversleeve
护养 ①cultivate; nurse; rear ②maintain
护运 armed escort
护照 passport
护肘 elbow guard
护岸林 protective belt (of trees) along an embankment
护城河 city moat
护发素 hair conditioner
护肤霜 face cream
护肤液 skin moisturizer
护林员 forest ranger
护路林 protective belt (of trees) along a road
护目镜 goggles
护身符 ①amulet; protective talisman ② person or thing that protects one from punishment or censure; shield
护士长 head nurse
护手盘 hand guard
护田林 farmland shelter belt
护卫舰 escort vessel; corvette
护卫艇 escort boat; patrol gunboat
护发用品 hair care articles
护理人员 nursing staff
护身法宝 amulet
护士学校 nurses' school

岵 [hù]
名 mountain covered by vegetation

怙 [hù]
动 rely on
怙恶不悛 be steeped in evil and refuse to repent; remain impenitent

糊 [hù]
〔名〕paste;porridge-like food ➡hū;hú
糊弄 ① fool; deceive; palm sth off ② go through the motions;be slipshod in work
糊弄局 be slipshod in work; muddle through one's work

huā(ㄏㄨㄚ)

花 [huā]
Ⅰ〔名〕① flower; blossom; bloom ② ornamental plant;decorative plant ③anything resembling a flower ④ cotton ⑤ fireworks ⑥ particles; drops ⑦ pattern; design ⑧ young, pretty woman ⑨flower;cream;essence;quintessence ⑩young of certain animals ⑪smallpox ⑫ wound Ⅱ〔形〕① multicoloured; coloured; variegated ② blurred; dim; bleary ③ showy;tricky;false;fancy;flowery ④decorated with flowers or decorative patterns ⑤romantic（in love）; promiscuous; lascivious ⑥ threadbare Ⅲ〔动〕① spend; expend ② prostitute;be related to prostitutes
花白 (of hair or beard) grey;grizzled
花斑 piebald
花瓣 petal
花苞 (flower) bud
花被 perianth;floral envelope
花边 ①decorative border ②lace ③fancy borders in printing
花布 cotton print;print
花菜 cauliflower
花草 ① flowers and plants ② Chinese milk vetch
花插 any container for cut flowers
花茶 scented tea
花厂 flower shop;florist's
花车 festooned vehicle
花虫 pink bollworm
花丛 flowering shrubs;flowers in clusters
花旦 female role in traditional opera
花道 ikebana
花灯 festive lantern (as displayed on the Lantern Festival)
花店 flower shop;florist's shop
花缎 figured satin;brocade
花朵 flower
花萼 calyx
花房 greenhouse
花肥 fertilizers for potted flowers
花费 ① spend; expend; cost ② money spent; expenditure;expenses
花粉 pollen
花梗 pedicel
花工 worker employed in a plant nursery; flower grower
花鼓 flower-drum,a folk dance popular in the Changjiang valley

花冠 ①corolla ②an ornamental crown worn by a bride on her wedding day in former times
花光 wipe out
花红 ①Chinese pear-leaved crabapple ②gift for a wedding,etc. ③bonus
花候 flowering season
花环 garland;floral hoop
花卉 ①flowers and plants ②painting of flowers and plants in traditional Chinese style
花会 flower fair
花鸡 bramble finch;brambling
花季 adolescence
花甲 a cycle of sixty years
花剑 foil
花键 spline
花匠 gardener
花椒 Chinese prickly ash
花轿 bridal sedan chair
花秸 chopped straw
花镜 presbyopic glasses
花酒 dinner party with singsong girls in attendance
花卷 fancy-shaped（ or plaited, twisted）steamed roll;steamed twisted roll
花魁 ① the plum flower ② the most popular courtesan
花篮 ①a basket of flowers ②gaily decorated basket
花蕾 (flower) bud
花鲢 variegated carp
花脸 male character in Chinese opera with a painted face
花露 (medicinal) liquid distilled from honeysuckle flowers or lotus leaves
花猫 spotted kitten
花蜜 nectar
花苗 flower seedling
花木 flowers and trees
花呢 fancy suiting
花鸟 painting of flowers and birds in traditional Chinese style
花农 flower grower
花盘 ①flower disc ②disc chuck;faceplate
花炮 fireworks and firecrackers
花盆 flowerpot
花瓶 flower vase;vase
花圃 flower nursery
花期 florescence
花旗 star-spangled banner—the United States
花枪 ①short spear used in ancient times ② trickery
花腔 ①florid ornamentation in Chinese opera singing;coloratura ②guileful talk
花墙 lattice wall
花青 cyanine
花圈 (floral) wreath

花蕊 stamen (*or* pistil)
花色 ①design and colour ②(of merchandise) variety of designs,sizes,colours,etc.
花哨 ① garish;gaudy ② full of flourishes; flowery
花生 peanut;groundnut
花市 flower market
花饰 ornamental design
花鼠 Siberian chipmunk;chipmunk
花束 a bunch of flowers;bouquet
花丝 ①filament ②filigree
花坛 (raised) flower bed;flower terrace
花毯 dimity;tapestry
花厅 reception room or parlour (usu. in a garden or side courtyard)
花筒 tube-shaped fireworks
花托 receptacle
花纹 decorative pattern;figure
花线 ①coloured thread ②flexible cord;flex
花香 fragrance of a flower
花销 cost;expense
花心 lecherous
花序 inflorescence
花絮 titbits (of news);interesting sidelights
花芽 (flower) bud
花眼 ①presbyopia ②be dazzled
花样 ①decorative pattern;variety ②trick
花药 anther
花艺 flory culture
花园 flower garden;garden
花账 padded accounts (*or* bills)
花招 ①showy movement in *wushu*;flourish ②trick;game
花轴 floral axis
花烛 candles with dragon and phoenix patterns used in the bridal chamber on the wedding night
花柱 style
花砖 ornamental slab for paving the floor
花子 [huāzi] beggar
花把式 gardener;experienced florist
花斑癣 tinea versicolour
花插着 crisscross
花池子 flower bed
花搭着 interspersed;diversified
花大姐 potato ladybird
花灯戏 local opera popular in Yunnan and Sichuan Provinces
花岗岩 ①granite ②incorrigibly obstinate
花格窗 lattice window
花骨朵 flower bud
花鼓戏 flower-drum opera,popular in Hunan, Hubei and Anhui
花蝴蝶 variegated butterfly
花架子 showy postures of martial arts—thing that is showy but of no practical use
花柳病 venereal disease (V. D.)

花露水 toilet water
花面狐 masked civet;gem-faced civet
花名册 pseudonym list;register;membership roster
花瓶儿 pretty and coquettish woman
花纱布 collective name for cotton,cotton yarn and cloth
花生饼 peanut cake
花生酱 peanut butter
花生米 shelled peanut;peanut kernel
花生仁 shelled peanut;peanut kernel
花生糖 peanut brittle
花生衣 peanut coat
花生油 peanut oil
花椰菜 cauliflower
花叶病 mosaic (disease)
花衣服 bright-coloured clothes
花子儿 [huāzǐr] seed
花边新闻 sidebar;titbits (of news);interesting sidelights
花粉食品 pollen food
花岗岩化 granitize
花好月圆 blooming flowers and full moon—perfect conjugal bliss
花红柳绿 red flowers and green willows—a beautiful spring scene
花花肠子 ①cunning,trickery;deceit ②a cunning person
花花公子 playboy;dandy;coxcomb;fop
花花绿绿 brightly coloured;colourful
花花世界 the dazzling human world with its myriad temptations; this mortal world; world of sensuality
花花事儿 (extramarital) affair;sex scandal
花街柳巷 streets of ill repute;red-light district
花里胡哨 ① gaudy;garish;showy ② without solid worth
花旗银行 the First National City Bank of New York
花前月下 amidst flowers and in the moonlight—ideal setting for amorous dalliance
花拳绣腿 showy but not practical martial arts; any showy but not practical skill
花容月貌 flower-like features and moonlike face—great beauty
花色品种 variety of colours and designs;product variety and design
花生豆儿 shelled peanut;peanut kernel
花式跳水 fancy diving
花式游泳 fancy synchronized swimming
花天酒地 indulge in dissipation;lead a life of debauchery
花团锦簇 bouquets of flowers and piles of silks—rich multi-coloured decorations
花言巧语 sweet words; fine words; flattery; blandishments

花样翻新 ①innovations in pattern (*or* design) ②old things in a new guise
花样滑冰 figure skating
花样滑水 figure water skiing;acrobatic water skiing
花样游泳 water ballet; synchronized swimming
花园城市 garden city
花枝招展 be gorgeously dressed
花腔女高音 coloratura soprano;coloratura
花生黑斑病 cercospora black spot of peanut
花冤枉钱财 pay for a dead horse;spend money to no avail
花钱少,见效大 require less money,earn more profit

哗 [huā]
拟 gurgle;clan：雨哗哗地下。The rain came down in torrents. ➡huá

huá(ㄏㄨㄚˊ)

划 [huá]
动 ①paddle;row ②be to one's profit;pay ③scratch;cut the surface of ④scratch;strike ➡huà
划船 paddle (*or* row)a boat
划桨 paddle;row
划拉 [huálɑ] ①sweep;brush away ②look for
划拳 play the finger-guessing game
划水 strike water with one's arms in swimming
划算 ①calculate;weigh ②be to one's profit;pay
划艇 canoe
划行 paddle;row
划子 small rowboat
划不来 be not worth it;do not pay
划得来 be worth it;pay
划得着 it pays;it's profitable
划船运动 boating
划艇运动 canoeing

华 [huá]
I 形 ①radiant;magnificent;splendid ②prosperous;flourishing ③luxurious;extravagant;flashy ④grizzled;grey II 名 ①corona ②best part;cream;essence ③time;years ④Chinese (language) ⑤China III 代 your
华北 North China, area including Hebei, Shanxi and the municipalities of Beijing and Tianjin
华表 ornamental columns erected in front of palaces,tombs,etc.
华诞 glorious birthday
华灯 colourfully decorated lantern;light
华发 grey hair
华服 splendid dress;magnificent clothes
华盖 ①canopy (as over an imperial carriage) ②ancient name for a certain star considered unlucky
华贵 ①luxurious; sumptuous; costly ②wealthy
华丽 magnificent;resplendent;gorgeous
华美 magnificent;resplendent;gorgeous
华侨 overseas Chinese
华人 Chinese
华文 Chinese
华屋 magnificent house
华裔 foreign citizen of Chinese origin
华语 Chinese (language)
华宗 your namesake
华达呢 gabardine
华尔街 Wall Street
华尔兹 waltz
华灯初上 when the evening lights are lit
华而不实 flashy and without substance;superficially clever
华沙条约 the Warsaw Treaty (1955)
华氏温度计 the Fahrenheit thermometer
华夏系构造 Cathaysian (structural) system

哗 [huá]
动 make noise;clamour ➡huā
哗变 mutiny
哗然 in an uproar;in commotion
哗笑 uproarious laughter
哗众取宠 try to please the public with claptrap

铧 [huá]
名 ploughshare

猾 [huá]
形 cunning;crafty;sly

滑 [huá]
I 形 ①slippery; smooth; glossy ②cunning; crafty; oily; slippery II 动 slip; slide; glide
滑板 ①slide ②feint play ③skateboard
滑冰 ice-skating;skating
滑道 chute;slide;ski run
滑动 slide
滑竿 a kind of litter
滑稽 ①funny;amusing;comical ②comic talk
滑键 feather key;sliding key
滑精 involuntary emission;spermatorrhoea
滑熘 sauté with starchy sauce;stir-fry with thick gravy
滑溜 slick;smooth;slippery
滑轮 pulley;block
滑脉 smooth pulse
滑面 sliding surface;slide face
滑腻 (of the skin) satiny;velvety;creamy
滑坡 ①landslide;landslip ②be on the slippery slope;decline;come down;drop
滑撬 skidding;runner
滑润 smooth;well-lubricated
滑石 talcum;talc
滑水 water skiing

滑梯 (children's) slide
滑头 ①slippery fellow; sly customer ②slippery; shifty; slick
滑下 slipping; sliding; glide; gliding
滑翔 glide
滑行 slide; coast
滑雪 skiing
滑移 slide; slip
滑音 ①glide ②portamento
滑板车 scooter
滑冰场 skating rink
滑旱冰 roller-skate
滑稽戏 farce
滑轮组 assembly pulley
滑石粉 talcum powder
滑水板 aquaplane; hydro-ski
滑膛枪 smoothbore (gun); musket
滑翔机 glider; sailplane
滑脂枪 grease gun
滑车神经 trochlear nerve
滑动关税 sliding tariff
滑动摩擦 sliding friction
滑动轴承 sliding bearing
滑动闸门 slide gate
滑天下之大稽 be the biggest joke in the world; be the laughing stock of the world; be the object of universal ridicule

huà (ㄏㄨㄚˋ)

化 [huà]
Ⅰ 动 ①change; turn; transform ②convert; influence ③ melt; dissolve ④ digest; eliminate; dispel; remove ⑤ burn up ⑥ (of monks and priests) pass away; die ⑦ (of Buddhist monks or Taoist priests) beg for alms Ⅱ 名 (short for 化学) chemistry
化除 eliminate; dispel; remove
化冻 thaw; melt
化肥 chemical fertilizer
化工 chemical industry
化合 chemical combination
化解 ease off; reconcile; resolve
化境 sublimity; perfection
化疗 chemotherapy
化名 ① use an assumed name ② assumed name; alias
化脓 fester; suppurate
化身 incarnation; embodiment
化石 fossil
化食 help digestion
化痰 reduce phlegm
化纤 chemical fibre
化学 ①chemistry ②celluloid
化验 chemical examination; laboratory test
化缘 (of Buddhist monks or Taoist priests) beg alms

化斋 (of Buddhist monks or Taoist priests) beg a vegetarian meal
化妆 ①(of actors) make up ②put on make-up; make up
化装 ①(of actors) make up ②disguise oneself
化粪池 septic tank
化工厂 chemical plant
化合价 valence
化合物 chemical compound
化尸炉 cremator; cinerator
化铁炉 cupola furnace
化油器 carburettor
化妆品 cosmetics
化妆室 dressing room
化妆水 beauty water
化装师 makeup man
化装室 dressing room
化敌为友 convert an enemy into a friend
化工仪表 chemical instrument
化工原料 industrial chemicals
化公为私 turn public property into private property; line one's pocket with public funds; embezzle public property
化解矛盾 resolve contradictions
化为乌有 melt into thin air; vanish; come to naught
化险为夷 turn danger into safety; head off a disaster
化学变化 chemical change
化学成分 chemical composition
化学处理 chemical treatment
化学弹头 chemical warhead
化学当量 chemical equivalent
化学反应 chemical reaction
化学肥料 chemical fertilizer
化学符号 chemical symbol
化学工业 chemical industry
化学疗法 chemotherapy
化学平衡 chemical equilibrium
化学试剂 chemical reagent
化学武器 chemical weapons
化学纤维 chemical fibre
化学性质 chemical property
化学元素 chemical element
化学炸药 chemical explosive
化学战争 chemical warfare
化学作用 chemical action
化验样品 assay sample
化整为零 break up the whole into parts
化装舞会 fancy dress ball; masked ball; masquerade
化学方程式 chemical equation
化悲痛为力量 turn grief into strength (usu. used in a memorial speech)
化腐朽为神奇 turn the foul and rotten into the rare and ethereal—①turn bad into good ②

change waste material into things of value
化干戈为玉帛 bury the hatchet; turn swords into plough shares
化解社会不稳定因素 eliminate factors contributing to social instability

划 [huà]
〔动〕① delimit; differentiate ② transfer; assign ③plan ➡huá
划拨 ①transfer ②assign; allocate
划定 delimit; designate
划分 ①divide ②differentiate
划归 put under (sb's administration, etc.); incorporate into
划价 have a prescription priced (in a hospital dispensary)
划界 description; demarcation; bracketing
划清 draw a clear line of demarcation; make a clear distinction
划线 delineate (esp. into political camps during the Cultural Revolution)
划一 ①standardized; uniform ②standardize
划账 transfer accounts
划等号 equate one thing with another
划范围 delimit the sphere
划框框 set limits; place restrictions
划时代 epoch-making
划成右派 be stigmatized as a rightist
划清界限 draw a clear line of demarcation
划清界线 make a clear distinction between; make a clean break with sb
划线支票 crossed check
划一不二 fixed; unalterable; rigid

画 [huà]
Ⅰ〔动〕①draw; paint ②draw a line or write a character as a mark; 画线 draw a line ③describe; portray; depict; draw; paint Ⅱ〔名〕① drawing; painting; picture ②stroke (of a Chinese character) ③ sth decorated with paintings or pictures
画板 drawing board
画报 illustrated magazine (or newspaper); pictorial
画笔 painting brush; brush
画布 canvas (for painting)
画册 an album of paintings; picture album
画出 draw up
画法 technique of painting or drawing
画舫 gaily-painted pleasure-boat
画风 style of painting
画符 draw magic figures
画幅 ①picture; painting ②size of a picture
画稿 rough sketch (for a painting)
画工 artisan-painter
画家 painter; artist
画夹 painting folder
画架 easel
画匠 ①artisan-painter ②inferior painter

画境 picturesque scene
画具 painter's paraphernalia
画卷 ①picture scroll ②magnificent scenery; stirring battle scene
画绢 silk for drawing on; drawing silk
画刊 ①pictorial section of a newspaper ②pictorial
画框 frame (for a picture)
画廊 ①painted corridor ②(picture) gallery
画眉 ①a kind of thrush ②blacken eyebrows; draw eyebrows
画面 ① general appearance of a picture; tableau ②film frame
画谜 picture puzzle
画皮 disguise or mask of an evildoer
画片 miniature reproduction of a painting
画屏 painted screen
画谱 a book on the art of drawing (or painting)
画师 ①painter; artist ②artisan-painter
画室 studio
画坛 art circle
画帖 a book of model paintings (or drawings)
画图 ①draw designs, maps, etc. ②picture
画线 setting-out; cross
画像 ① draw a portrait; portray ② portrait; portrayal
画押 make one's cross (or mark); sign
画页 page with illustrations (in a book or magazine); plate
画展 art exhibition; exhibition of paintings
画纸 drawing paper
画轴 painted scroll; scroll painting
画作 painting
画句号 finish; end; complete; put an end to
画圈儿 draw a circle round one's name on a document submitted for approval to show that one has read it
画十字 ① mark a cross (on a document in place of a signature by sb who cannot write) ②cross oneself
画外音 film offscreen voice
画像石 stone relief (on ancient Chinese tombs, shrines, etc.)
画饼充饥 draw cakes to allay hunger—feed on illusions
画地为牢 draw a circle on the ground to serve as a prison—restrict sb's activities to a designated area or sphere
画龙点睛 bring a picture of a dragon to life by putting in the pupils of its eyes—add the touch that brings a work of art to life; add the finishing touch; add an apt word to clinch the point
画蛇添足 draw a snake and add feet to it—ruin the effect by adding sth superfluous
画中画功能 picture-in-picture capability

画虎不成反类犬 try to draw a tiger and end up with the likeness of a dog—attempt sth over-ambitious and end in failure

画龙画虎难画骨 in drawing a tiger or dragon, it is easy to show its skin or scales, but not its bones

话 [huà] I 名 words;talk;remark II 动 talk about; speak about

话本 printed versions of the prompt-books used by popular storytellers in Song and Yuan times

话别 say a few parting words;say good-bye

话柄 subject for ridicule;handle

话费 telephone bill

话锋 thread of discourse;topic of conversation

话旧 talk over old times;reminisce

话剧 modern drama;stage play

话梅 preserved plum

话说 (The story) says...

话题 subject of a talk;topic of conversation

话亭 telephone booth;telephone kiosk;telephone box;call box

话筒 ① microphone ② telephone transmitter ③megaphone

话头 thread of discourse

话音 ①one's voice in speech ②tone;implication

话语 what one says;words

话把儿 subject for ridicule;handle

话茬儿 ①thread of discourse ②tone of one's speech ③a cause for dispute;quarrel

话家常 chitchat;exchange small talk

话剧团 modern drama troupe;theatrical company

话务员 (telephone) operator

话匣子 ① gramophone ② radio receiving set ③chatterbox

话语权 speech right

话里有话 the words mean more than they say; there's more to it than meets the ear

话题作文 topic composition

话中有刺 (there are) hidden barbs in one's words;have a sting in the tail;sarcastic remark

话不投机半句多 If there's no common ground, a single word is a waste of breath.

桦 [huà] 名 birch

桦木 birch wood

桦树 birchwood

桦木林 birch grove

桦皮舟 birchbark

桦树皮 birch bark

婳 [huà] 形 quite and nice

huái(ㄏㄨㄞˊ)

怀 [huái] I 名 ① chest;bosom ② mind;heart II 动 ① think of;yearn for;miss ② conceive (a child) ③keep in mind;cherish;harbour;nurse

怀抱 ①hold (or carry) in the arms ②bosom ③cherish

怀表 pocket watch

怀春 harbour the amorous thoughts of spring—(of a young girl) have thoughts of love

怀古 recall antiquity;meditate on the past (often used in titles of poems which are reflections on historical events)

怀恨 nurse hatred;harbour resentment

怀旧 remember past times or old acquaintances

怀恋 think fondly of (past times,old friends, etc.);look back nostalgically

怀炉 handwarmer (small aluminum box burning a special kind of coal for warming the hands or stomach)

怀念 cherish the memory of;think of

怀柔 (of feudal rulers) make a show of conciliation in order to bring other nationalities or states under control

怀胎 be (or become) pregnant

怀疑 doubt;suspect

怀孕 be pregnant

怀着 be filled with;cherish;harbour

怀鬼胎 have evil intentions;harbour sinister designs

怀旧热 retro boom

怀乡病 nostalgia;homesickness

怀疑论 scepticism

怀才不露 refrain from showing one's abilities; sheathe (or hide) one's talents;be modest about one's learning

怀才不遇 have unrecognized talents

怀旧情结 retrocomplex

怀旧文化 retroculture

怀柔政策 policy of control through conciliation;policy of mollification

怀乡之情 yearning for one's native place; homesickness;nostalgia

怀有私心 have selfish motives

槐 [huái] 名 Chinese scholartree

槐花 sophora flower

槐角 the pod of Chinese scholartree

槐树 pagoda-tree;locust tree

踝 [huái] 名 ankle;malleolus

踝骨 anklebone

踝关节 ankle;ankle joint

huài (ㄏㄨㄞˋ)

坏 [huài]
Ⅰ 形 ①bad; poor; defective ②evil; wicked Ⅱ 动 ①go bad; break down ②spoil; ruin Ⅲ 名 evil idea; dirty trick Ⅳ 副 badly; awfully; very
坏处 harm; disadvantage
坏蛋 bad egg; scoundrel; bastard
坏话 ①malicious remarks; vicious talk ②unpleasant words
坏疽 gangrene
坏人 bad person; evildoer; scoundrel
坏事 ①bad thing; evil deed ②ruin sth; make things worse
坏水 evil trick; deceit; craft and guile
坏死 necrosis
坏账 dead account; uncollectible account; bad account
坏东西 bastard; scoundrel; rogue
坏分子 bad element; evildoer
坏良心 heartless; depraved conscience
坏血病 scurvy
坏人当道 evildoers hold sway
坏心眼儿 evil intention; ill will

huān (ㄏㄨㄢ)

欢 [huān]
Ⅰ 形 joyous; merry; happy; jubilant Ⅱ 副 vigorously; with great drive; with a vengeance; in full swing Ⅲ 名 lover; sweetheart
欢畅 thoroughly delighted; elated
欢唱 sing merrily
欢度 spend (an occasion) joyfully
欢呼 hail; cheer; acclaim
欢聚 happy get-together; happy reunion
欢快 cheerful and light-hearted; lively
欢乐 happy; joyous; gay
欢庆 celebrate joyously
欢送 see off; send off
欢腾 great rejoicing; jubilation
欢喜 ①joyful; happy; delighted ②like; be fond of; delight in
欢笑 laugh heartily
欢心 favour; liking; love
欢颜 happy looks; happy appearance
欢宴 entertain sb to dinner on some happy occasion
欢迎 ①welcome; greet ②be well received
欢愉 happy; joyous; joyful
欢送会 farewell meeting; send-off meeting
欢蹦乱跳 healthy-looking and vivacious
欢呼雀跃 shout and jump for joy; be elated
欢聚一堂 happily gather under the same roof
欢声雷动 cheers resound like peals of thunder
欢声笑语 happy laughter and cheerful voices

欢天喜地 with boundless joy; wild with joy; overjoyed
欢喜冤家 quarrelsome and loving couple; quarrelsome lovers
欢欣鼓舞 be filled with exultation; be elated

獾 [huān]
名 badger
獾油 badger fat (for treating burns)

huán (ㄏㄨㄢˊ)

还 [huán]
动 ①go back; come back; return; restore ②give back; return; repay ③give (or do) sth in return ➡hái
还本 repayment of principal (or capital)
还耕 restore abandoned land to cultivation; reclaim
还魂 revive after death; return from the grave
还击 ①fight back; return fire; counterattack ②fencing riposte
还家 go back home; return home
还价 counter-offer; counter-bid
还口 answer back; retort
还礼 ①return a salute ②send a present in return; present a gift in return
还迁 move back
还钱 repay; pay back
还清 pay off
还情 repay a favour
还手 strike (or hit) back
还书 return a book
还俗 (of Buddhist monks and nuns or Taoist priests) resume secular life
还席 give a return banquet or dinner
还乡 return to one's native place
还原 ① return to the original condition or shape; restore ②reduction
还愿 ①redeem a vow to a god ②fulfil one's promise
还债 pay one's debt; repay a debt
还账 pay one's debt; settle accounts
还嘴 answer (or talk) back; retort
还乡团 landlord's restitution corps; homegoing legion
还本付息 repayment of principal and interest; reimbursement for both capital and interest; pay principal and interest; repay capital with interest
还债基金 sinking fund
还政于民 hand (state) power back to the people; restore or establish democracy
还款信用状 reimbursement letter of credit
还债高峰期 peak period of dept repayment; peak debt repayment period; debt repayment peak

环 [huán]
Ⅰ 名 ①ring; hoop; loop ②ring ③link Ⅱ 形

cyclic;cyclo- Ⅲ劢 surround;encircle;hem in
环胺 cyclamine
环靶 round target
环保 environmental protection
环抱 surround;encircle;hem in
环城 around the city
环醇 cyclic alcohol;ring alcohol;cyclitol
环带 clitellum
环岛 rotary island;roundabout
环顾 look about (*or* round)
环海 be surrounded by sea
环化 cyclization
环礁 atoll
环节 ①link;sector ②segment
环境 environment; surroundings; circumstances
环流 circulation
环路 roundabout;traffic circle;ring highway; circular road
环球 ① round the world ② the earth; the whole world
环绕 surround;encircle;revolve around
环山 ①around a mountain ②be surrounded by mountains
环蛇 krait
环食 annular eclipse (of the sun)
环视 look around
环烃 cyclic hydrocarbon
环酮 cyclic ketone;cyclone
环烷 cycloparaffin
环线 circular road; circular track; belt; loop line
环行 going in a ring
环形 annular;ringlike
环游 tour around (a place)
环状 cyclic;annular;ring-like;loop-like
环子 ring;link
环保局 environmental protection bureau
环颈雉 ring-necked pheasant
环境权 environmental right
环境战 environment warfare
环绕声 surround sound
环形山 ring structure;lunar crater
环保产业 environmental protection industry
环比指数 chain index
环城公路 ring road;loop road;belt line
环湖公路 road winding round a lake
环环相扣 each linked with another; closely linked with one another
环节动物 annelid
环境保护 environmental protection
环境壁垒 environmental barrier
环境标志 environmental labelling
环境标准 environmental standard
环境风险 environmental risk
环境激素 environmental hormone
环境建设 environmental improvement; environmental construction
环境净化 depollution of environment
环境科技 environmental science and technology
环境科学 environmental science
环境枯竭 environmental depletion
环境伦理 environmental ethics
环境难民 environmental refugee
环境容量 environmental capacity
环境试验 environmental test
环境退化 environment degradation
环境卫生 environmental sanitation; general sanitation
环境污染 pollution of the environment; environmental pollution
环境无害 environmentally friendly (*or* positive,sound)
环境效益 environmental benefits
环境要素 environmental element
环境意识 environmental awareness; awareness of the importance of the environment
环幕电影 panorama film;circular movie
环球飞行 circumaviation
环绕速度 circular (*or* orbital) velocity;first cosmic velocity
环太平洋 Pacific Rim;circum-Pacific
环行天线 loop antenna
环形公路 ring road;beltway;belt highway;the orbital;circular road
环形联合 circular integration
环形铁路 circular railway
环氧树脂 epoxy resin
环渤海地区 the rim of Bohai Bay;areas around the perimeter of Bohai Bay
环境保护法 law of environmental protection
环境承载力 environmental carrying capacity
环境生态学 environmental ecology
环境脏乱差 the environment which is polluted,disorderly and poor in some places
环渤海经济圈 the Bohai Economic Sphere
环境标志认证 environmental label certification
环境法律体系 environmental statutory framework
环境监测系统 environmental monitoring system
环境空气标准 ambient air standard
环境空气质量 ambient air quality
环境系统工程 environmental systems engineering
环境行动纲领 framework for environmental action
环境友好材料 environmentally friendly material
环境质量标准 environmental quality standards
环球定位系统 global positioning system (GPS)

环太平洋地区 Pacific Basin; Pacific Rim; circum-Pacific region

环境影响评价制度 Environmental Impact Assessment (EIA)

环境保护目标责任制 the target responsibility system for environmental protection

豰 [huán]
名 ①cub of the racoon dog ②porcupine

寰 [huán]
名 extensive region

寰球 the earth; the whole world

寰宇 the earth; the whole world

缳 [huán]
Ⅰ 名 noose Ⅱ 动 hang

缳首 be hanged

缳首之罪 crime punishable by hanging

huǎn (ㄏㄨㄢˇ)

缓 [huǎn]
Ⅰ 形 ①slow; unhurried; sluggish ②relaxed; not tense Ⅱ 动 ①delay; postpone; put off ②revive; recuperate; come to

缓步 walk unhurriedly

缓冲 buffer; cushion

缓付 delay payment; defer payment

缓和 ①relax; ease up; mitigate; alleviate ②détente

缓急 ①pressing or otherwise; of greater (*or* lesser) urgency ②emergency

缓减 abate; relieve; ease; subside

缓建 postpone construction

缓解 relieve; alleviate; ease

缓慢 slow

缓聘 defer employment

缓坡 gentle slope

缓期 postpone a deadline; suspend

缓气 get a breathing space; have a respite; take a breather

缓刑 temporary suspension of the execution of a sentence; reprieve; probation

缓行 ①move (*or* drive, walk) slowly ②put off; postpone

缓议 defer the discussion

缓役 deferment (of service)

缓征 postpone the imposition of a tax (*or* levy)

缓滞 moderate; abate

缓冲国 buffer state

缓冲器 buffer; bumper

缓冲区 buffer area; buffer zone

缓和剂 moderator

缓兵之计 measures to stave off an attack; a stratagem to gain a respite

缓不济急 slow action cannot save a critical situation

缓冲地带 buffer zone

缓冲文化 buffer culture

缓冲作用 buffer action; buffer effect; cushioning effect

缓急相助 help each other in time of need

缓冲存储器 buffer storage

缓冲放大器 buffer amplifier

缓冲国际紧张局势 ease international tension

huàn (ㄏㄨㄢˋ)

幻 [huàn]
形 ①unreal; imaginary; illusory ②magical; chargeable

幻灯 ①slide show ②slide projector

幻化 magically change

幻景 illusion; dream

幻境 dreamland; fairyland

幻觉 hallucination; illusion

幻梦 illusion; daydream

幻灭 vanish into thin air

幻视 photism

幻术 magic, conjuring

幻听 phonism

幻想 ①imagine; dream ②illusion; fancy; fantasy

幻象 mirage; phantom; phantasm

幻影 unreal image

幻肢 phantom limb

幻灯机 slide projector; epidiascope

幻灯片 (lantern) slide

幻想曲 fantasia

幻觉重现 (hallucination) flashback

幻影式战斗机 Mirage

奂 [huàn]
形 ①numerous; plentiful ②(of writing or diction) bright; brilliant

宦 [huàn]
名 ①official ②hold a public office; be an official ③eunuch

宦官 eunuch

宦海 officialdom; official circles

宦途 official career

宦游 leave home and take up government employment

宦者当道,国运必衰 With the eunuchs holding real power, the nation would certainly suffer.

换 [huàn]
动 ①exchange; barter; trade ②change; substitute ③convert; cash

换班 ①change shift ②relieve a person on duty ③changing of the guard

换房 exchange houses

换岗 relieve a sentry (of guard)

换工 exchange labour

换股 exchange of share; exchange of stock

换汇 earn foreign exchange; exchange for foreign currencies

换货 exchange goods; barter

换季 change garments according to the season; wear different clothes for a new season; out of season

换肩 shift the carrying pole onto the other shoulder

换届 replace (a leading group whose term has expired)

换气 take a breath (in swimming)

换钱 ①change money (*or* bills) ②sell

换亲 take each other's daughters as daughters-in-law

换取 exchange (*or* barter) sth for; get in return

换人 substitution (of players)

换算 conversion

换文 change of notes (*or* letters)

换洗 exchange clothes (for washing)

换向 changing-over; change; jibe

换型 change the model (of a product); remodel; replace the old model by a new one

换休 change the day off

换血 change blood; reshuffle (usu. sports team)

换牙 (of a child) grow permanent teeth

换样 vary

换药 change bandage; use fresh dressing for a wound

换羽 moult

换约 exchange of notes (*or* letters)

换脑筋 ① remould one's ideology ② change habitual ways of thinking; change one's mindset

换能器 transducer

换气扇 ventilation fan

换衣服 change one's clothes

换装站 transshipment station

换代产品 brand-new product; product of a new generation

换俘协定 agreement for exchange of prisoners; cartel

换汇成本 costs in terms of foreign exchange

换机放映 film changeover

换届选举 election at expiration of office terms

换句话说 in other words

换人暂停 time-out for substitution

换位思考 put oneself in another's shoes and think in his or her terms; think in sb else's perspective

换汇申请书 application for conversion

换汤不换药 the same medicine with a different name—the same old stuff with a different label; a change in form but not in content (*or* essence)

换季减价销售 end-of-season sale

唤
[huàn]
劻 call (out); summon

唤起 ①arouse ②call; recall

唤醒 wake up; awaken

涣
[huàn]
劻 dissolve; dissipate; vanish

涣然 (of misgivings, doubts, etc.) melt away; clear up

涣散 lax; slack

涣然冰释 melt away; clear up

浣
[huàn]
Ⅰ 劻 wash; rinse Ⅱ 名 any of the three 10-day periods of a month

浣纱 rinse yarn

浣熊 racoon

浣衣 wash clothes

患
[huàn]
Ⅰ 名 ① trouble; peril; disaster ② anxiety; worry Ⅱ 劻 contract; suffer from (an illness)

患病 suffer from an illness; fall ill; be ill

患处 affected part (of a patient's body)

患难 trials and tribulations; adversity; trouble

患者 sufferer; patient

患得患失 worry about personal gains and losses; be swayed by considerations of loss and gain

患难夫妻 husband and wife who have gone through difficult times together

患难与共 go through thick and thin together; share weal and woe

患难之交 friends in adversity; tested friends

患难见真情 a friend in need is a friend indeed; prosperity makes friends

焕
[huàn]
形 shining; glowing

焕发 shine; glow; irradiate

焕然一新 take on an entirely new look (*or* aspect); look brand-new

痪
[huàn]
◇瘫痪 ①paralysis; palsy ②(of transportation, etc.) be paralysed; break down; be at a standstill

huāng（ㄏㄨㄤ）

肓
[huāng]
◇病入膏肓 The disease has attacked the vitals—beyond cure.

荒
[huāng]
Ⅰ 形 ①waste; uncultivated ②desolate; barren; wild ③unreasonable; fantastic; absurd ④ uncertain; unverified Ⅱ 名 ① famine; crop failure ② wasteland; uncultivated land; leftover area ③shortage; scarcity Ⅲ 劻 ①neglect; be out of practice ②indulge; be addicted

荒草 weeds

荒村 a deserted village

荒诞 fantastic; absurd; incredible

荒岛 desert (*or* uninhabited) island

荒地 wasteland; uncultivated (*or* undevel-

oped) land
荒废 ①leave uncultivated;lie waste ②fall into disuse;fall into disrepair ③waste (time) ④neglect;be out of practice
荒瘠 wild and barren;desolate and infertile
荒郊 desolate place outside a town;wilderness
荒凉 bleak and desolate;wild
荒乱 in great disorder;in turmoil
荒谬 absurd;preposterous
荒漠 ① desolate and boundless ② bleak and boundless desert;wilderness
荒年 famine (or lean) year
荒僻 desolate and out-of-the-way
荒歉 crop failure;famine
荒沙 barren sand
荒山 a barren hill
荒疏 out of practice;rusty
荒数 rough figure;approximate number
荒唐 ① absurd;fantastic;preposterous ② dissipated;loose;intemperate
荒芜 lie waste;go out of cultivation
荒信 unconfirmed news or information;rumour
荒野 wilderness;the wilds
荒淫 dissolute;licentious;debauched
荒原 wasteland;wilderness
荒置 leave unused;desert;abandon
荒冢 abandoned grave;uncared-for grave
荒漠化 desertification
荒诞不经 preposterous;fantastic;absurd
荒诞无稽 fantastic;absurd;incredible
荒地造林 afforestation
荒谬绝伦 utterly absurd;absolutely preposterous
荒时暴月 time of dearth;lean year;hard times
荒无人烟 desolate and uninhabited
荒淫无耻 shamelessly dissipated
荒于游乐 indulge in pleasure-seeking

塃 [huāng]
名 ore

慌 [huāng]
形 flurried;confused;panicky
慌乱 flurried;alarmed and bewildered
慌忙 in a great rush;in a flurry;hurriedly
慌张 flurried;flustered;confused
慌神儿 be scared out of one's wits;panic
慌不择路 flee along any path one stumbles upon;seize on any solution when hard pressed
慌了手脚 be thrown into a panic;be alarmed and confused;become panicky
慌里慌张 in a hurried and confused manner;all in a fluster;in a flurry
慌手慌脚 in a rush;in a flurry

huáng（ㄏㄨㄤ）

皇 [huáng]
Ⅰ 形 grand;magnificent Ⅱ 名 emperor;
sovereign
皇朝 feudal dynasty
皇储 crown prince;designated heir to the throne
皇帝 emperor
皇都 imperial capital
皇宫 (imperial) palace
皇冠 imperial crown
皇后 empress
皇家 imperial family (or house)
皇历 almanac
皇粮 public grain funds,goods,etc. provided by the government;salary paid by the state
皇陵 imperial mausoleum
皇权 imperial power (or authority)
皇上 ①the emperor;the throne;the reigning sovereign ②Your Majesty;His Majesty
皇室 imperial family (or house)
皇天 Heaven (personified);High Heaven
皇族 people of imperial lineage;imperial kinsmen
皇带鱼 oarfish
皇太后 empress dowager
皇太子 crown prince
皇亲国戚 relatives of the emperor
皇天后土 Heaven and Earth;great heaven and sovereign earth;heaven above and earth below
皇天不负苦心人 Providence doesn't let down a man who does his best.

黄 [huáng]
Ⅰ 形 ① yellow;sallow;xanthic ② pornographic Ⅱ 名 ①gold ②yolk ③pornography ④Yellow River ⑤ Huangdi;Yellow Emperor Ⅲ 动 fizzle out;fall through;be off
黄柏 bark of a cork tree
黄斑 ① yellow spot;macula lutea retinae ② yellow stain;fox mark
黄榜 imperial edict
黄檗 the bark of a cork tree
黄疸 jaundice
黄道 ecliptic
黄帝 Huangdi;Yellow Emperor
黄鲷 yellow porgy
黄豆 soya bean;soybean
黄毒 pornographic items;evil of pornography;pornography
黄蜂 wasp
黄瓜 cucumber
黄花 ①chrysanthemum;gold flower ②day lily ③virgin
黄昏 dusk
黄酱 salted and fermented soya paste
黄金 gold
黄荆 five-leaved chaste tree
黄精 sealwort
黄酒 yellow rice or millet wine;Shaoxing（绍

兴）wine
黄鹂 oriole
黄历 almanac
黄连 ①Coptis chinensis ②coptis
黄磷 yellow phosphorus
黄栌 smoke tree
黄麻 jute
黄米 glutinous millet
黄泥 yellow mud
黄鸟 canary
黄牛 ①ox；cattle ②scalper of tickets，etc.
黄牌 yellow card
黄芪 the root of membranous milk vetch；astragalus base
黄芩 the root of large-flowered skullcap
黄泉 the Yellow Springs；the world of the dead；the underworld；the nether world
黄雀 siskin
黄壤 yellow earth；yellow soil
黄色 ① yellow ② decadent；obscene；pornographic
黄鳝 finless eel
黄熟 yellow maturity
黄鼠 ground squirrel；suslik
黄体 corpus luteum
黄铜 brass
黄土 loess
黄癣 favus
黄羊 Mongolian gazelle
黄杨 Chinese little-leaf box
黄页 Yellow Page
黄莺 oriole
黄油 ①butter ②grease
黄鼬 yellow weasel
黄鱼 yellow croaker
黄玉 topaz（a mineral）
黄源 source of pornography；supplier of pornography
黄种 the yellow race
黄包车 rickshaw
黄灿灿 bright yellow；golden
黄澄澄 glistening yellow；golden
黄、赌、毒 pornography，gambling and drug abuse and trafficking
黄刺玫 yellow rose
黄道带 zodiac
黄泛区 areas formerly flooded by the Huanghe River；the Yellow River Inundated Area
黄姑鱼 spotted maigre
黄褐斑 chloasma
黄褐色 yellowish-brown；tawny
黄花菜 day lily
黄花鱼 yellow croaker
黄昏恋 love of the elderly；twilight love；evening love
黄金周 golden week
黄连木 Chinese pistache

黄梅季 the rainy season，usu. in April and May，in the middle and lower reaches of the Changjiang River
黄梅雨 intermittent drizzles in the rainy season in the middle and lower reaches of the Changjiang River
黄热病 yellow fever
黄鼠狼 yellow weasel
黄水疮 impetigo
黄体酮 progesterone
黄铁矿 pyrite
黄铜矿 chalcopyrite
黄土区 loess area
黄萎病 verticillium wilt
黄白之物 gold and silver；money
黄疸指数 icterus index；icteric index
黄道吉日 propitious（or auspicious）date；lucky day
黄花闺女 virgin；maiden
黄金地带 golden area
黄金分割 golden section
黄金海岸 Gold Coast
黄金时代 golden age
黄金时段 prime time；peak viewing time
黄金时间 prime time；peak viewing time
黄金市场 gold market
黄金水道 gold water route—referring to much-used water route
黄金外流 gold drain；gold outflow
黄粱美梦 Golden Millet Dream；pipe dream
黄毛丫头 a chit of a girl；a silly little girl
黄牌警告 a yellow card warning
黄袍加身 be draped with the imperial yellow robe by one's supporters—be acclaimed emperor；seize political power after a coup
黄色工会 yellow union；scab union
黄色人种 the yellow race
黄色书刊 decadent books and periodicals；pornographic books and magazines
黄色网站 pornographic website
黄色炸药 trinitrotoluene（TNT）；trinol
黄土高原 loess plateau
黄道十二宫 the 12 signs of the zodiac；zodiacal signs
黄金非货币化 demonetization of gold
黄金外汇储备 gold and foreign exchange reserves
黄金的货币作用 monetary functions of gold
黄金双重价格制 two-time gold price system
黄鼠狼给鸡拜年，没安好心 The weasel goes to pay his respects to the hen—not with the best of intentions.

凰 [huáng]
名 female phoenix

隍 [huáng]
名 dry moat outside a city wall

遑 [huáng]
名 leisure
遑论其他 let alone the other points

徨 [huáng]
◇彷徨 walk back and forth, not knowing which way to go; hesitate

惶 [huáng]
形 fearful; afraid; anxious
惶惶 in a state of anxiety; on tenterhooks; alarmed
惶惑 perplexed and alarmed; apprehensive
惶遽 frightened; scared
惶恐 terrified
惶惶不安 be greatly upset
惶恐不安 in a state of alarm (*or* trepidation)
惶惶不可终日 be in a constant state of anxiety; be on tenterhooks

煌 [huáng]
形 bright; brilliant
煌绿 brilliant green
煌斑岩 lamprophyre

潢 [huáng]
Ⅰ 名 pond; pool Ⅱ 动 dye paper; colour paper

璜 [huáng]
名 semicircular jade pendant

蝗 [huáng]
名 locust
蝗虫 locust; grasshopper
蝗蝻 the nymph of a locust
蝗灾 plague of locusts

磺 [huáng]
名 sulphur
磺胺 sulphanilamide (SN)
磺化 sulphonate
磺酸盐 sulphonate
磺酰胺 sulphonic acid amide

蟥 [huáng]
◇蚂蟥 leech

簧 [huáng]
名 ① reed (in a musical instrument) ② spring
簧片 reed
簧风琴 reed organ; harmonium
簧乐器 reed instrument
簧舌扬声器 moving armature loud-speaker

huǎng(ㄏㄨㄤˇ)

恍 [huǎng]
副 ① all of a sudden; suddenly ② seemingly; as if
恍惚 ① in a trance; absentminded ② dimly; faintly; seemingly
恍然大悟 suddenly see the light; suddenly realize what has happened
恍如隔世 There seems to be an interval of a whole generation. (said on finding things greatly changed)
恍如梦境 as if in a dream

晃 [huǎng]
动 ① dazzle ② flash past ➡ huàng
晃眼 ① dazzle ② twinkling

谎 [huǎng]
名 lie; falsehood
谎报 lie about sth; give false information; start a canard
谎称 falsely claim to be; pretend to be
谎话 lie; falsehood
谎骗 deceive; cheat; dupe
谎言 lie; falsehood
谎花儿 fruitless flower
谎报军情 make a false report about the (military) situation

幌 [huǎng]
名 heavy curtain
幌子 ① shop sign; signboard ② pretence; cover; front

huàng(ㄏㄨㄤˋ)

晃 [huàng]
动 shake; sway ➡ huǎng
晃荡 rock; shake; sway
晃动 rock; sway
晃梯 balancing on an upright ladder
晃悠 shake from side to side; wobble; stagger
晃晃悠悠 swaying; unstable

潢 [huàng]
形 (of water) deep and wide

榥 [huàng]
名 curtain; screen

huang(・ㄏㄨㄤ)

慌 [huang]
副 unbearably; awfully

huī(ㄏㄨㄟ)

灰 [huī]
Ⅰ 名 ① ash ② dust; powder ③ lime; (lime) mortar Ⅱ 形 ① grey ② disheartened; discouraged
灰暗 murky grey; gloomy
灰白 greyish white; ashen; pale
灰尘 dust; dirt
灰度 grey scale; gradation
灰分 ash content
灰鹤 grey crane
灰浆 mortar
灰烬 ashes
灰客 greyhacker
灰泥 plaster
灰墙 plastered wall
灰雀 bullfinch
灰壤 podzol

灰色 ① grey；ashy ② pessimistic；gloomy ③ obscure；ambiguous
灰沙 dust and sand
灰鼠 squirrel
灰土 dirt；dust
灰心 lose heart；be discouraged
灰渣 ash；lime-ash
灰质 grey matter
灰沉沉 gloomy·leaden
灰姑娘 Cinderella
灰口铁 grey (pig) iron
灰溜溜 ① dull grey ② gloomy；dejected；crestfallen
灰蒙蒙 dusky；overcast
灰沙燕 sand martin
灰指甲 ringworm of the nails
灰飞烟灭 become ashes and smoke；vanish like so much smoke
灰领工人 gray-collar worker
灰色市场 grey market (unofficial market in shares before regular distribution)
灰色收入 ① grey income；irregular income ② income from moonlighting
灰心丧气 be disheartened；get discouraged；lose heart
灰色系统理论 grey systems theory

诙 [huī]
劻 ① banter；tease good-humouredly ② mock；ridicule
诙谐 humorous；jocular
诙谐曲 humoresque
诙谐百出 jeer with hundred jokes；break a lot of jests

挥 [huī]
劻 ① wave；wield；brandish；shake ② wipe off ③ command (an army) ④ scatter；disperse
挥动 brandish；wave
挥发 volatilize
挥戈 brandish one's weapons
挥汗 wipe off one's sweat
挥毫 wield one's writing brush；write (or draw) a picture (with a brush)
挥霍 spend freely；squander
挥泪 wipe away tears；wipe one's eyes
挥拳 shake one's fist (at sb)
挥手 wave one's hand；wave
挥舞 wave；wield；brandish
挥发物 volatile matter
挥发油 volatile oil
挥刀舞枪 brandish swords and rifles
挥汗如雨 dripping with sweat
挥霍公款 squander public funds
挥金如土 throw money about like dirt；spend money like water
挥军前进 command an army to march forward；order one's army to push forward
挥泪如雨 in a storm of tears

挥旗示意 wave a flag as a signal
挥之即去 leave (or depart) at a motion of one's hand

恢 [huī]
形 vast；broad；extensive
恢复 ① resume；renew；return to ② recover；regain；revive ③ restore；reinstate；rehabilitate
恢宏 ① broad；extensive；magnanimous ② develop；carry on (or forward)
恢恢 extensive；vast
恢复期 convalescence
恢复正常生产 be back to normal production
恢复对香港行使主权 resume the exercise of sovereignty over Hong Kong
恢复中国的缔约国地位 restore China's status as a contracting state

祎 [huī]
名 sacrificial robe for the queen (or empress)

晖 [huī]
名 sunshine；sunlight

辉 [huī]
Ⅰ 名 brightness；radiance；splendour；glow；brilliance Ⅱ 劻 shine；glow
辉光 glow
辉煌 brilliant；splendid；glorious；magnificent
辉石 pyroxene；augite
辉映 shine；reflect
辉长岩 gabbro
辉光灯 glow lamp
辉绿岩 diabase
辉钼矿 molybdenite
辉锑矿 stibnite
辉铜矿 chalcocite
辉银矿 argentite

麾 [huī]
Ⅰ 名 standard of a commander Ⅱ 劻 command
麾下 ① under sb's command ② (a respectful title) general；commander

徽 [huī]
Ⅰ 名 emblem；badge；insignia Ⅱ 形 fine；glorious
徽标 emblem；badge；insignia
徽带 kummerbund
徽号 title of honour；good name
徽记 mark；sign；logo；insignia
徽章 badge；insignia

huí（ㄏㄨㄟ）

回 [huí]
劻 ① circle；wind ② return；go or come back ③ turn round ④ answer；reply；respond ⑤ report (to higher authorities, etc.) ⑥ decline；cancel；dismiss Ⅱ 量 ① (*used to indicate frequency of occurrence*) time ② chapter；section；session

H

回拜 pay a return visit
回报 ①report back on what has been done ② repay;requite;reciprocate ③ retaliate; get one's own back
回避 ① evade;dodge;avoid (meeting sb) ② withdraw
回禀 report back (to one's superior)
回波 echo
回驳 refute
回采 stoping;extraction
回肠 ①ileum ②worried;agitated;anxious
回潮 ①(of dried things) get damp again ②resurgence;reversion
回程 ①return trip ②return (or back) stroke
回春 ①return of spring ②bring back to life
回答 answer;reply;response
回荡 resound;reverberate
回电 ①wire back ②a telegram in reply
回跌 (of prices) go down after a rise
回动 reverse
回读 repeat the last year of schooling
回访 pay a return visit
回放 instant replay
回风 return air
回复 ①reply (to a letter) ②return to normal state
回购 buy-back;counter purchase
回顾 look back;review;retrospect
回灌 recharge;water recharge
回归 ①regression ②return ③draw back;fall back;retreat
回锅 ①heat up (a cooked dish) ②cook again
回国 return to one's country (or native land)
回航 return to base (or port)
回合 round;bout
回话 reply;answer
回火 ①tempering ②flareback
回击 fight back;return fire;counterattack
回家 go home;be home;return home
回见 see you later (or again);cheerio
回交 backcross
回教 Islam
回敬 ①return a compliment;do (or give) sth in return ②give sb tit for tat
回绝 decline;refuse
回空 (of vehicles and ships) make the return trip empty (without passengers or cargo)
回扣 commissions;rebate;brokerage;kickback;netback
回馈 repay;feedback
回来 ① return;come back;be back ②(used after a verb) back (here)
回廊 winding corridor
回礼 ①return a salute ②send a present in return;present a gift in return
回笼 ①steam again ②withdrawal (of currency) from circulation

回炉 ①melt down ②bake (cakes,etc.) again
回路 return circuit;return;loop
回落 (of water levels,prices,etc.) fall after a rise
回骂 answer back and scold in return
回民 the *Hui* people
回眸 (of a woman) glance back
回暖 get warm again after a cold spell
回聘 engage again (retired people, usu. by their former work units);re-employ
回迁 (of those who have been removed to make way for a project,or evacuated during an emergency) move back;return
回青 (of winter crops or transplanted seedlings) turn green
回请 return hospitality;give a return banquet
回去 ①return;go back;be back ②(used after a verb) back (there)
回扫 flyback
回升 rise again (after a fall);pick up
回生 ① bring back to life ② forget through lack of practice;get rusty
回声 echo
回收 retrieve;recover;reclaim
回手 ①turn round and stretch out one's hand ②hit back;return a blow
回首 ① turn one's head; turn round ② look back;recollect
回赎 redeem pawned articles
回水 ascent;damming;backwater;return water
回顺 roll back and rationalize
回溯 recall;look back upon
回填 backfill
回条 short note acknowledging receipt of sth;receipt
回帖 money order receipt to be signed and returned to the sender
回头 ① turn one's head;turn round ②repent ③later
回味 ①aftertaste ②call sth to mind and ponder over it
回乡 return to one's home village;return home
回响 reverberate;echo;resound
回想 think back;recollect;recall
回信 ①write in reply;write back ②letter in reply ③verbal message in reply;reply
回修 return sth for repairs
回旋 ①circle round ②(room for) manoeuvre
回忆 call (or bring) to mind;recollect;recall
回音 ①echo ②reply ③turn
回应 answer;respond
回赠 send a present in return;present a gift in return
回涨 (of water levels,prices,etc.) rise again after a fall

回执 short note acknowledging receipt of sth; receipt;acknowledgment of receipt
回注 recycle
回柱 prop drawing
回转 turn round
回族 the Hui nationality;the Huis
回嘴 answer (*or* talk) back;retort
回潮率 (moisture) regain
回车键 return key;enter key
回风道 air return way
回顾展 retrospective exhibition
回归年 tropical year;solar year
回归热 relapsing fever
回归线 tropic
回锅肉 twice-cooked pork (often with chilli seasoning)
回老家 ①revisit one's native town ②(usu. jocular or mocking) die;be no more
回笼觉 fall asleep again after waking up in the morning
回马枪 back thrust
回娘家 ①(of a married woman) return to her mother's house ②go back to one's old job
回扫率 retrace ratio
回扫描 flyback retrace;return trace
回扫期 flyback time;retrace time
回收率 rate of recovery (*or* reclamation)
回收塔 recovery tower
回收站 (waste materials) collection depot
回头见 see you later (*or* again);cheerio
回头客 frequenter;regular (*or* repeat, second-time) customer
回头路 the road back to one's former position; the road of retrogression
回头率 rate of second glance
回乡证 home visit certificate
回形针 clip
回旋曲 rondo
回忆录 reminiscences;memoirs;recollections
回音壁 the Echo Wall (in the Temple of Heaven,Beijing)
回转炉 rotary furnace
回转体 solid of revolution
回转仪 gyroscope;gyro
回避制度 avoidance system; challenge system;system of withdrawal
回差现象 backlash phenomena
回肠荡气 (of music, poems, etc.) soul-stirring;thrilling;inspiring
回肠九转 with anxiety gnawing at one's heart;weighed down with grief
回灌能力 water recharge capacity
回光返照 ①the last radiance of the setting sun ②momentary recovery of consciousness just before death;a sudden spurt of activity prior to collapse
回归分析 regression analysis

回降价格 roll back price
回笼货币 recall part of the currency issued; withdraw currency from circulation;withdraw surplus paper money
回笼资金 backward flow of capital; capital flowing back
回收投资 recoup the investment
回收卫星 recover satellites
回收装置 retrieving device
回天乏术 unable to save the situation
回天之力 power capable of saving a desperate situation;tremendous power
回头是岸 turn the head and the shore is at hand—repent and be saved
回心转意 change one's mind; come around; have a change of heart
回旋余地 room for freedom of action;room for manoeuvre;leeway;latitude
回忆对比 recall the past and contrast it with the present
回邮信封 self-addressed stamped envelop (SASE)
回转半径 radius of gyration
回旋加速器 cyclotron
回转工作台 rotary table
回转式钻床 rotary drill
回避要害问题 evade the crucial question

茴 [huí]

茴香 ①fennel ②aniseed

洄 [huí]

动 (of water) whirl

蛔 [huí]

蛔虫 roundworm;ascarid

huǐ(ㄏㄨㄟˇ)

悔 [huǐ]

动 regret;repent
悔改 repent and mend one's ways
悔过 repent one's error;be repentant
悔恨 regret deeply;be bitterly remorseful
悔婚 break a pledge of marriage;break off an engagement
悔棋 retract a false move in a chess game
悔悟 realize one's error and show repentance
悔罪 show repentance;show penitence
悔不当初 regret having done sth
悔过自新 repent and turn over a new leaf;repent and make a fresh start
悔之晚矣 it is now too late to repent;be too late to regret
悔之无及 too late to repent; too late for regrets
悔之无益 no use crying over spilt milk

毁 [huǐ]

动 ① destroy; ruin; demolish; damage ②

burn up ③defame；slander ④refashion；make over
毁谤 slander；malign；calumniate
毁害 destroy；damage
毁坏 destroy；damage
毁林 deforest
毁灭 destroy；exterminate
毁弃 scrap；annul
毁容 disfigure one's face
毁伤 injure；hurt；damage
毁损 damage；impair
毁形 unmake
毁誉 praise or blame；praise or condemnation
毁约 ①break one's promise；go back on one's word ②scrap a contract（or treaty）；annul a contract（or treaty）
毁家纾难 give the family fortune to the state in a time of crisis
毁于一旦 be destroyed in one day；be destroyed in a moment
毁誉参半 be as much censured as praised；get both praise and blame；find a mixed reception

huì（ㄏㄨㄟˋ）

卉 ［huì］
名（usu. decorative）grass

汇 ［huì］
I 动 ①converge ②gather together；collect ③remit Ⅱ 名 ①things collected；assemblage；collection ②foreign exchange
汇报 report；give an account of
汇编 compilation；collection；corpus
汇单 money order；remittance slip
汇兑 remittance
汇费 remittance fee
汇付 pay by remittance
汇合 converge；join
汇集 ①collect；compile ②come together；converge；assemble
汇寄 remit
汇价 conversion rate；exchange rate
汇款 ①remit money；make a remittance ②remittance
汇流 converge；flow together
汇拢 ① come together；gather；assemble ② collect；compile
汇率 exchange rate
汇票 draft；bill of exchange；money order
汇市 foreign exchange market；foreign exchange quotations
汇算 settle accounts；wind up an account
汇演 joint performance
汇映 film festival
汇总 gather；collect；pool
汇报会 report-back meeting
汇流点 confluence

汇流条 busbar
汇报工作 report to sb on one's work
汇报演出 report-back performance
汇编程序 assembler program；assembler；assembly routine
汇编语言 assembler language
汇编指令 assembler instruction
汇兑管理 exchange control
汇兑银行 exchange bank
汇丰银行 Hongkong and Shanghai Banking Corporation
汇率并轨 unification of exchange rates；merge or combine the exchange rates；introduce a single exchange rate
汇率波动 exchange rate fluctuations
汇率牌价 market exchange rate
汇率调整 exchange rate adjustments
汇算清缴 make the final settlement

会 ［huì］
Ⅰ 动 ① get together；gather；assemble；meet；congregate ② meet；see ③ happen to；coincide with ④ understand；comprehend；grasp ⑤ be acquainted with；have knowledge of ⑥ can；be able to ⑦ be well versed in；be good at；be conversant ⑧ be likely to；be sure to ⑨ foot（or pay）a bill Ⅱ 名 ① meeting；party；conference；convention；congregation ② association；society；union；organization；foundation ③ temple fair ④ pilgrimage；religious festival；village thanksgiving festival ⑤ association of people who contribute regularly to a common fund and draw from it by turns；rotatory credit club ⑥ major city；large city；capital ⑦opportunity；occasion；chance ⑧ moment ➡ kuài
会标 logo；mascot
会餐 dine together；have a dinner party
会操 joint drill；joint practice
会场 meeting-place；conference（or assembly）hall
会费 membership dues
会风 style of meeting
会歌 anthem of the games
会馆 guild hall；provincial or county guild
会海 sea of meetings—numerous meetings
会合 join；meet；converge；assemble
会话 conversation（as in a language course）
会徽 emblem of a sports meet，etc.
会集 assemble；gather together
会籍 membership（of an association）
会见 meet with（esp. a foreign visitor）
会聚 assemble；flock together
会刊 ①proceedings of a conference，etc. ② the journal of an association，society，etc.
会考 general examination for students from various schools
会客 receive a visitor（or guest）

会面 meet
会期 ① the time fixed for a conference; the date (*or* time) of a meeting ② the duration of a meeting
会齐 get together; assemble
会旗 the banner of a meeting
会签 (of two or more than two units) jointly sign an official document; joint signature; co-sign
会商 hold a conference (*or* consultation)
会审 ① joint hearing (*or* trial) ② make a joint checkup
会师 join forces; effect a junction
会所 the office of an association
会谈 talks
会堂 assembly hall; hall
会同 (handle an affair) jointly with other organizations concerned
会务 day-to-day work of a conference; routine affairs of a conference
会晤 meet
会心 understanding; knowing
会演 joint performance (by a number of theatrical troupes, etc.)
会厌 epiglottis
会议 ① meeting; conference ② council; congress
会意 combined meaning; associative compound
会阴 perineum
会员 member
会战 ① meet for a decisive battle ② launch a mass campaign; join in a battle
会章 ① the constitution (*or* statutes) of an association, society, etc. ② the emblem of an association, society, etc.
会长 the president of an association (*or* society)
会账 pay (*or* foot) a bill
会诊 consultation of doctors; (group) consultation
会址 ① the site of an association (*or* society) ② the site of a conference (*or* meeting)
会道门 superstitious sects and secret societies
会合点 meeting point; rallying point; rendezvous
会客室 reception room
会员国 member state (*or* nation)
会员证 membership card
会聚透镜 convergent lens
会谈纪要 memorandum of meeting
会员资格 the status of a member; membership
会展经济 exhibition economy

讳 〔huì〕
I 劢 avoid as taboo II 名 ① taboo; forbidden word ② name of emperor, high official, head of a family, or elder of a clan
讳言 dare not (*or* would) not speak up
讳疾忌医 hide one's sickness for fear of treatment—conceal one's fault for fear of criticism
讳莫如深 closely guard a secret; not breathe a word to a soul; not utter a single word about sth

荟 〔huì〕
名 luxuriant growth (of plants)
荟萃 gather together; assemble
荟集 gather; assemble; collect

哕 〔huì〕
劢 (of birds) chirp; cry ➡ yuě

诲 〔huì〕
劢 teach; instruct
诲人不倦 be tireless in teaching; teach with tireless zeal
诲淫诲盗 propagate sex and violence; stir up the base passions

绘 〔huì〕
劢 paint; draw
绘画 drawing; painting
绘图 charting; map-making; drafting
绘制 draw (a design, etc.)
绘图板 drawing board
绘声绘色 vivid; lively

恚 〔huì〕
名 hate; resentment; grudge

贿 〔huì〕
名 ① money and property; goods; valuables ② bribe
贿金 bribe
贿款 bribe
贿赂 ① bribe ② bribery; offer a bribe; resort to bribery
贿买 buy over; suborn
贿选 practise bribery at an election; get elected by bribery
贿赂费 hush money
贿赂行为 corrupt transaction

烩 〔huì〕
劢 ① braise ② cook (rice, etc.) with meat, vegetables and water
烩饼 shredded pancakes cooked with meat, vegetables and water
烩豆腐 bean curd braised in soy sauce

彗 〔huì〕
名 broom
彗头 cometary head
彗尾 the tail of a comet
彗星 comet

晦 〔huì〕
I 名 ① last day of a lunar month ② night II 形 dark; dim; obscure; gloomy III 劢 cover up; hide
晦暗 dark and gloomy
晦明 night and day; gloomy and bright
晦匿 retire into obscurity
晦气 unlucky

晦涩 (of literary writing, music, etc.) hard to understand; obscure

秽 [huì]
〔形〕①dirty ②ugly; abominable
秽乱 debauched ways; immoral conduct
秽气 stink; bad (*or* offensive) smell
秽土 rubbish; refuse; dirt
秽闻 ill repute (referring to sexual behaviour); reputation for immorality
秽亵 ① filthy; foul ② obscene; salacious; bawdy
秽行 debauched behaviour; immoral conduct
秽语 obscene words; lewd speech

惠 [huì]
I 〔名〕favour; kindness; benefit II 〔形〕kind; generous III 〔动〕favour; give
惠存 please keep (this photograph, book, etc. as a souvenir); to so-and-so
惠风 gentle breeze; soft breeze
惠顾 your patronage
惠鉴 be kind enough to read (the following letter)
惠临 your gracious presence
惠书 your letter
惠而不费 beneficial and not costly

喙 [huì]
〔名〕①bill; beak (of a bird); snout (of an animal) ②mouth

慧 [huì]
〔形〕intelligent; bright; clever
慧根 root of wisdom that can lead to truth
慧黠 clever and artful; shrewd
慧心 wisdom
慧眼 ①a mind which perceives both past and future ② mental discernment; mental perception; insight; acumen
慧中秀外 intelligent within and beautiful without; both intelligent and beautiful

蕙 [huì]
〔名〕orchid
蕙兰 a species of orchid
蕙心 pure heart of a woman

<h2 align="center">hūn（ㄏㄨㄣ）</h2>

昏 [hūn]
I 〔名〕dusk II 〔形〕①dark; dim; murky ②confused; muddled; dizzy III 〔动〕lose consciousness; faint
昏暗 dim; dusky
昏沉 ①murky ②dazed; befuddled
昏呆 stupor; narco
昏倒 fall into a swoon; go off into a faint; fall unconscious; faint
昏黑 dusky; dark
昏花 dim-sighted
昏黄 pale yellow; faint; dim
昏厥 faint; swoon

昏君 fatuous and self-indulgent ruler
昏聩 decrepit and muddleheaded
昏乱 ①dazed and confused; befuddled ②benighted and disorderly
昏迷 stupor; coma
昏睡 lethargic sleep; lethargy
昏死 faint; fall into a coma
昏星 evening star
昏眩 dizzy; giddy
昏庸 fatuous; muddleheaded; stupid
昏昏欲睡 drowsy; sleepy
昏天黑地 ①heaven and earth in darkness ② be in a state of delirium; lose consciousness ③dissipated ④dark rule and social disorder
昏头昏脑 dizzy; muddle-headed; absent-minded

荤 [hūn]
I 〔名〕①meat or fish ②odorous vegetables II 〔形〕filthy; indecent
荤菜 meat dish
荤腥 meat or fish
荤油 lard
荤笑话 dirty joke
荤素搭配 balanced diet of meat and vegetables

婚 [hūn]
〔动〕wed; marry
婚变 divorce; extramarital affair (that disrupts a marriage)
婚假 marriage leave
婚嫁 marriage
婚检 physical check-up before marriage; premarital checkup
婚介 matchmaking
婚礼 wedding ceremony; wedding
婚恋 fall in love and get married
婚龄 (legally) marriageable age
婚配 married
婚期 wedding day
婚庆 wedding ceremony
婚娶 (of a man) get married; take a wife
婚事 marriage; wedding
婚书 marriage certificate
婚姻 marriage; matrimony
婚约 marriage contract; engagement
婚外恋 extramarital love affair; sexual relationship outside of marriage
婚外情 extramarital affair
婚姻法 marriage law
婚育期 marriageable and child-bearing age
婚内强奸 rape inside marriage; rape committed by spouse
婚前检查 premarital (physical) checkup; medical examination before marriage
婚纱摄影 photograph featuring wedding gown; taking pictures for wedding couples
婚生子女 children born in wedlock; legitimate children
婚姻状况 marital status

婚姻介绍所 match-making agency;matrimoni-
al agency

椿
[hūn]
名 albizzia

hún(ㄏㄨㄣˊ)

浑
[hún]
形 ①muddy;murky;turbid ②foolish;stu-
pid;addle-brained ③simple and natural;unso-
phisticated ④whole;full;complete;all over

浑厚 ① simple and honest ②(of writing,
painting,etc.) simple and vigorous
浑话 impudent remark
浑朴 simple and honest
浑身 from head to foot;all over
浑象 celestial globe
浑仪 armillary sphere
浑圆 perfectly round
浑浊 muddy;turbid;murky
浑天仪 ①armillary sphere ②celestial globe
浑浑噩噩 muddle-headed and ignorant
浑然一体 one integrated mass;a unified entity;an integral whole
浑身是胆 be every inch a hero;be the embodiment of valour
浑水摸鱼 fish in troubled waters

馄
[hún]
馄饨 wonton;dumpling soup

混
[hún]
形 ①muddy;turbid ②foolish;stupid ➡hùn
混蛋 blackguard;wretch;scoundrel;bastard;
skunk
混球儿 rascal;wretch;skunk;son of a bitch

魂
[hún]
名 ①soul ②mood;spirit ③lofty spirit of a
nation,army,etc.
魂灵 soul
魂魄 soul
魂不附体 feel as if one's soul had left one's
body
魂不守舍 be scared out of one's wits;have lost
one's mind
魂飞魄散 be scared out of one's wits;be half
dead with fright
魂牵梦萦 miss very much;pine for

hùn(ㄏㄨㄣˋ)

诨
[hùn]
名 joke;jest
诨号 nickname
诨名 nickname

圂
[hùn]
名 lavatory;privy

混
[hùn]
I 动 ①mix;mingle;confuse ②pass for;
pass off as;palm off as ③muddle along;mud-

dle on;drift along ④get along with II 副
carelessly;thoughtlessly;recklessly;at random;irresponsibly ➡hún
混播 mixed seeding;mixture sowing
混充 pass oneself off as;palm sth off as
混沌 ①Chaos(the primeval state of the universe according to folklore)②ignorant;
simple-minded;muddle-headed
混纺 blending
混合 mix;blend;mingle
混迹 unworthily occupy a place among
混进 infiltrate;sneak into;worm one's way into
混乱 confusion;chaos
混入 infiltrate;sneak into;worm one's way into
混说 speak thoughtlessly
混同 confuse;mix up
混响 reverberation
混淆 obscure;blur;confuse;mix up
混一 amalgamation
混杂 mix;mingle
混战 tangled warfare
混账 scoundrel;bastard;son of a bitch
混浊 muddy;turbid;cloudy
混子 one who fools around in a respectable
profession;quack
混饭吃 engage in a job for the sake of making
a living(without having any real interest in
it)
混合器 mixer
混合色 secondary colour
混合物 mixture
混合岩 migmatite
混混儿 rascal;scoundrel
混交林 mixed forest
混凝剂 coagulant
混凝土 concrete
混频管 mixer tube
混频器 mixer
混日子 drift along aimlessly
混响室 reverberation chamber
混血儿 a person of mixed blood;half-breed
混账话 impudent remark
混不过去 unable to fool others
混不下去 can no longer permit oneself to drift
along
混合编队 composite formation
混合授粉 mixed pollination
混合双打 mixed doubles
混声合唱 mixed chorus
混世魔王 world-wrecking demon king—an
evil man who disturbs the peace of the
world;human fiend;devil incarnate
混为一谈 lump(or jumble) together;confuse
sth with sth else
混淆黑白 mix up black and white;confound

right and wrong
混淆视听 confuse the public opinion; mislead the public opinion; call black white
混淆是非 confuse right and wrong
混装货物 consolidated cargo
混合所有制经济 the economic sector of mixed ownership

huō（ㄏㄨ）

嚄 [huō]
〔叹〕 wow ➡ǒ

豁 [huō]
〔动〕①split; crack; breach ②pay a high price (for sth one must do); give up; sacrifice ➡ huò
豁口 opening; break; breach
豁嘴 ①harelip ②a harelipped person
豁出去 go ahead regardless; be ready to risk everything

攉 [huō]
〔动〕 shovel (coal, ore, etc.) from one place to another
攉煤工 coal shoveller
攉煤机 coal shovel

huó（ㄏㄨㄛˊ）

和 [huó]
〔动〕 add liquid to powder and stir or knead to make viscous ➡ hé; hè; hú; huò
和面 knead dough
和面机 flour-mixing machine

活 [huó]
Ⅰ〔动〕①live ②save (the life of a person); feed; keep alive Ⅱ〔形〕①alive; living; live ② movable; flexible; moving ③ vivid; lively; quick Ⅲ〔副〕exactly; simply Ⅳ〔名〕①work; job ②product; finished product
活靶 manoeuvring target
活版 typography; letterpress
活瓣 valve
活宝 a bit of a clown; funny fellow
活动 ① move about; exercise ② shaky; unsteady ③movable; mobile; flexible ④activity; manoeuvre ⑤ use personal influence (or irregular) means ⑥behaviour
活度 activity
活泛 flexible
活佛 ①Living Buddha ②Buddha incarnate
活该 it serves sb right
活化 activation
活话 indefinite, vague, or open-ended remark; non-committal words
活活 while still alive
活计 ① handicraft work; manual labour ② handiwork; work
活结 knot that can be undone by a pull; slip-knot

活剧 living drama; drama in real life
活口 ①survivor of a murder attempt ②prisoner who can furnish information ③ keep body and soul together; eke out an existence ④flexible tone; flexible words
活力 vigour; vitality; energy
活路 ① means of subsistence; way out ② workable method
活络 ①loose ②noncommittal; indefinite
活埋 bury alive
活门 valve
活命 ①earn a bare living; scrape along; eke out an existence ②save sb's life ③life
活泼 ①lively; vivacious; vivid ②reactive
活期 current
活气 lively atmosphere
活人 the living
活塞 piston
活水 flowing water; running water
活现 appear vividly; come alive
活像 look exactly like; be the spit and image of; be an exact replica of
活性 active; activated
活血 invigorate the circulation of blood
活页 loose-leaf
活用 apply flexibly; apply with imagination and ingenuity
活跃 ① brisk; active; dynamic ② enliven; animate; invigorate
活捉 capture alive
活字 type; letter
活罪 (endure) hardships, tortures, etc. , while alive; bitter sufferings
活靶子 live target
活报剧 living newspaper; skit; street performance
活标本 living specimen
活茬儿 farm work
活地图 walking map
活地狱 hell on earth
活动坝 movable dam
活动家 activist; public figure
活动桥 movable bridge
活工资 fluctuating (or conditional, sliding, adjustable, unfixed) wage
活广告 stand messenger
活荷载 live load
活化石 living fossil
活火山 active volcano
活见鬼 sheer nonsense; utterly impossible; simply absurd
活教材 persons or things that can serve to educate people; vivid examples for education
活扣儿 knot that can be undone by a pull; slip-knot
活菩萨 living Bodhisattva—an epithet for a person who is full of compassion for the

needy and the suffering
活钱儿 ①ready money;cash ②extra income
活神仙 living immortal—an epithet for a man noted for his longevity or supposed to have clairvoyance
活生生 ①real;living ②while still alive
活受罪 suffer a living hell;have a hell of a life
活死人 living corpse—slow-witted, clumsy person
活头儿 [huótour] interest to live for
活性炭 active (or activated) carbon
活阎王 devil incarnate;tyrannical ruler
活样板 live model
活字典 a walking dictionary
活版印刷 typographic printing; typography; letterpress printing
活蹦乱跳 skip and jump about;gambol;frolic
活不长了 One's days (or hours) are numbered.
活动扳手 adjustable spanner (or wrench)
活动房屋 detachable house;make-shift house
活动资本 liquid capital
活而不乱 dynamic but not chaotic
活佛转世 reincarnation of Living Buddha
活结领带 four-in-hand
活灵活现 vivid;lifelike
活期储蓄 current saving
活期存款 demand deposit;current deposit
活期放贷 demand loan
活期利息 current interest
活体解剖 vivisection
活性酵母 activated dry yeast
活性染料 reactive dyes
活学活用 live learning,live usage
活页乐谱 sheet assets
活跃产品 dynamic product
活跃市场 buoyant market;live up the market
活跃的需求 buoyant demand
活到老,学到老 one is never too old to learn; keep on learning as long as you live

huǒ(ㄏㄨㄛˇ)

火 [huǒ] Ⅰ 图 ①fire ②firearms; ammunition; firing;fire ③internal heat,one of the six causes of disease ④ anger; temper Ⅱ 形 ①red as fire;fiery;flaming ②urgent;pressing ③prosperous;thriving;flourishing Ⅲ 动 get angry; lose one's temper
火把 torch
火棒 lighted torch (used in acrobatics)
火暴 fiery;impatient;irritable
火爆 prosperous;exuberant;thriving
火并 open fight between factions
火柴 match
火场 the scene of a fire

火车 train
火攻 fire attack (using fire as a weapon against enemy personnel and installations)
火光 flame;blaze
火锅 chafing dish
火海 a sea of flames
火红 red as fire;fiery;flaming
火候 ①duration and degree of heating,cooking,smelting,etc. ②level of attainment
火狐 red fox
火花 spark
火化 cremate
火鸡 turkey
火急 urgent;pressing
火碱 caustic soda
火箭 rocket
火警 fire alarm
火炬 torch
火炕 heated *kang*;heated brick bed
火坑 fiery pit;pit of hell;abyss of suffering
火力 firepower;fire
火龙 ①fiery dragon—a procession of lanterns or torches ②air channel from a brick kitchen stove to a chimney;flue
火炉 (heating) stove
火棉 guncotton;pyroxylin
火苗 a tongue of flame;flame
火捻 ①kindling ②fuse
火炮 cannon;gun
火盆 fire pan;brazier
火拼 open fight between factions
火漆 sealing wax
火气 ①internal heat (as a cause of disease) ②anger;temper
火器 firearm
火枪 firelock
火墙 wall with flues for space heating
火情 the condition of a fire
火热 ①burning hot;fervent;fiery ②intimate
火绒 tinder
火山 volcano
火伤 burn (caused by fire)
火烧 baked wheaten cake
火舌 tongues of fire
火绳 rope of plaited plants burnt as a mosquito repellent
火石 flint
火势 the intensity of a fire
火速 at top speed;posthaste
火炭 burning charcoal (or faggot)
火头 ①flame ②duration and degree of heating, cooking, smelting, etc. ③ anger ④ house where a fire started
火腿 ham
火网 network of fire;fire net
火险 fire insurance
火线 ① battle (or firing, front) line ② live

wire
火硝 common name for 硝酸钾
火星 ①Mars ②spark
火眼 pinkeye
火焰 flame
火药 gunpowder;powder
火印 mark burned on bamboo (*or* wooden) articles;brand
火油 kerosene
火源 burning things which may cause a fire disaster
火灾 fire (as a disaster);conflagration
火葬 cremation
火种 ① kindling material;kindling;tinder ② live cinders kept for starting a new fire
火烛 things that may cause a fire
火主 the owner of the house where a fire started;the person responsible for the starting of a fire
火砖 refractory brick;firebrick
火嘴 nozzles
火柴盒 matchbox
火车头 (railway) engine;locomotive
火车座 booth (in a restaurant)
火成岩 igneous rock
火电厂 heat-engine plant
火罐儿 upping jar (*or* glass)
火花塞 sparking plug;spark plug;ignition plug
火化炉 cremator;crematory
火箭弹 rocket projectile;rocket shell
火箭炮 rocket gun
火箭筒 rocket launcher (*or* projector);bazooka
火辣辣 burning
火力网 network of fire;fire net
火烈鸟 flamingo
火流星 bolide;fireball
火山尘 volcanic dust
火山岛 volcanic island
火山灰 tephra
火山口 crater;volcanic vent
火山学 volcanology
火山锥 volcano;cone
火烧云 red clouds (at sunset or sunrise)
火树石 flint
火头军 army cook
火药库 powder magazine
火药味 the smell of gunpowder
火葬场 crematorium;crematory
火爆大片 smash hit
火车轮渡 train ferry
火法冶金 pyrometallurgy
火箭喷焰 exhaust
火炬计划 Torch Programme,a plan to develop new and high technology
火力发电 thermal power generation
火冒三丈 fly into a rage;flare up

火伞高张 fully spread umbrella of fire—scorching sunlight in summer
火山地震 volcanic earthquake
火上加油 pour oil on the flames;add fuel to the flames
火烧火燎 ① feeling terribly hot ② restless with anxiety
火烧眉毛 the fire is singeing the eyebrows—desperate situation
火烧油层 combustion (of oil) in situ
火险隐患 potential fire hazards
火星卫星 Martian satellite
火眼金睛 fiery eyes and diamond pupils—discerning eyes
火焰光谱 flame spectrum
火中取栗 pull sb's chestnuts out of the fire;be a cat's-paw
火车交货价 free on rail
火车时刻表 railway timetable
火警报警器 fire alarm
火焰喷射器 flamethrower
火炬点燃仪式 flame-lighting ceremony

伙 [huǒ]
I 〈名〉 ①mess;board;meals;food ②partner;mate ③partnership;company II 〈量〉 group (of people);band;gang:一伙强盗 a band of robbers III 〈动〉 combine;join;club
伙伴 partner;companion
伙犯 accomplice
伙房 kitchen (in a school,factory,etc.)
伙夫 mess cook
伙计 ① partner ② fellow;mate ③ salesman;salesclerk;shop assistant;farm labourer
伙买 club together to buy sth
伙食 mess;food;meals
伙同 in league with;in collusion with
伙用 share in the use of sth
伙食科 catering office
伙伴关系 partnership

钬 [huǒ]
〈名〉 holmium (Ho)

夥 [huǒ]
〈形〉 much;many;a great deal of;numerous

huò(ㄏㄨㄛˋ)

或 [huò]
I 〈副〉 ①perhaps;maybe;probably ②slightly;a little bit II 〈连〉 or;either… or… III 〈代〉 somebody;some one;some people
或然 probable
或许 perhaps;maybe
或则 or;either… or…
或者 ①perhaps;maybe ②or;either… or… ③ no matter what,how,etc.

和 [huò]
I 〈动〉 mix;blend;mix powder (*or* particles) with water II 〈量〉 (number of) rinses:床单已

经洗了两和。The bed-sheet has been given two rinses. ➡hé;hè;hú;huó

和弄 ① stir;agitate;mix ② instigate;incite;sow discord

和稀泥 try to mediate differences at the sacrifice of principle;try to smooth things over

货 [huò] I 名 ①currency;money ②goods;commodity;product ③ *used in reference to a person* II 动 sell

货币 money;currency

货舱（cargo）hold;cargo bay（of a plane）

货场 goods（*or* freight）yard

货车 ①goods train;freight train ②goods van（*or* wagon）;freight car（*or* wagon）③lorry;truck

货船 freighter;cargo ship;cargo vessel

货单 manifest;waybill;shipping list

货柜 ①counter;bar ②another name for 集装箱

货机 cargo aircraft（*or* plane）;air freighter

货价 commodity price;price of goods

货款 money for buying（*or* selling）goods;payment for goods

货郎 itinerant pedlar;street vendor

货轮 freighter;cargo ship;cargo vessel

货品 kinds（*or* types）of goods

货色 ①goods ②stuff;trash;rubbish

货摊 stall;stand

货物 goods;commodity;merchandise

货箱 packing box

货样 sample goods;sample

货源 source of goods;supply of goods

货运 freight transport

货栈 warehouse

货主 owner of cargo

货币化 monetization

货币战 monetary war

货架子 goods shelves

货郎担 street vendor's load（carried on a shoulder pole）

货物税 commodity tax

货运单 waybill

货运费 shipping cost;freight（charges）

货运量 volume of goods transported;volume of rail freight;volume of road haulage

货比三家 shop around to get a good buy

货币贬值（currency）devaluation;（currency）depreciation

货币存量 money stock

货币单位 monetary unit

货币地租 money rent

货币工资 money wages

货币回笼 withdrawal of currency from circulation

货币交换 exchange through money

货币经济 monetary economy

货币疲软 currency weakness

货币平价 currency parity;par value of currency

货币升值（currency）revaluation;（currency）appreciation

货币投放 currency put into circulation;currency issue

货币危机 monetary crisis

货币信用 confidence in the currency

货币政策 monetary policy

货币主义 monetarism

货币资本 money-capital

货币总量 monetary aggregates

货不对路 unwanted goods

货到付款 cash on delivery（COD）

货款拖欠 overdue obligations to suppliers

货源基地 base of cargo source

货运列车 goods train;freight train

货真价实 ① genuine goods at a fair price ② through and through;out-and-out;dyed-in-the-wool

货币发行量 amount of money issued;amount of currency in circulation

货币供应量 money supply

货币流通量 currency（*or* money）in circulation;money supply

货币一体化 monetary integration

货好客自来 First-rate goods advertise themselves. *or* Good wine needs no bush.

货物集散地 entrepot

货物吞吐量 cargoes loaded and unloaded

货运周转量 rotation volume of goods（*or* freight）transport

货币超量发行 over-issuance of currency

货币流量分析 money flow analysis

获 [huò] 动 ① capture;catch;seize ② get;obtain;win ③harvest;reap

获得 gain;obtain;acquire;win;achieve

获奖 win a prize;be awarded a prize

获救 be rescued

获利 make a profit;reap profits

获取 procure;obtain;gain;reap

获赦 be pardoned

获胜 win victory;be victorious;triumph

获释 be released（from prison）

获悉 learn（of an event）

获选 be elected;win an election

获知 learn

获准 secure approval;get permission

获得性 acquired character

获冠军 win the championship（*or* gold medal）

获胜率 average of wins

获益匪浅 reap no little benefit

获得性免疫 acquired immunity

祸 [huò] I 名 misfortune;disaster;calamity II 动

bring disaster upon; ruin; injure; damage

祸端 the source of the disaster; the cause of ruin

祸根 the root of the trouble; the cause of ruin; bane

祸害 ①disaster; curse; scourge ②damage; destroy

祸患 disaster; calamity

祸乱 disaster; curse

祸事 disaster; calamity; mishap

祸首 chief culprit (*or* offender)

祸水 person (esp. a woman) who is the source of trouble

祸胎 the root of the trouble; the cause of the disaster

祸心 evil intent; malice

祸殃 disaster; calamity; catastrophe

祸不单行 misfortunes never come singly; it never rains but it pours

祸从口出 trouble comes out of the mouth; all one's troubles were caused by his tongue

祸从天降 A disaster comes from the sky.

祸国殃民 bring calamity to the country and the people

祸及百姓 play (*or* wreak) havoc among the people

祸起萧墙 trouble arises behind the walls of the home; trouble arises within the family; there is internal strife afoot

祸兮福所倚,福兮祸所伏 good fortune lieth within bad, bad fortune lurketh within good

惑 [huò]
Ⅰ 形 puzzled; bewildered Ⅱ 动 delude; mis-

lead

惑乱 delude and confuse

惑众 delude people; confuse people

膔 [huò]
名 meat soup

霍 [huò]
副 suddenly; quickly

霍地 suddenly

霍霍 ① the sound of sharpening knives etc. ②flash

霍乱 ①cholera ②acute gastroenteritis

霍然 suddenly; quickly

豁 [huò]
Ⅰ 形 open; clear; open-minded; generous Ⅱ 动 exempt; remit ➡ huō

豁达 sanguine; optimistic

豁亮 ① roomy and bright ② sonorous; resonant

豁免 exempt (from taxes or from customs inspection, etc.); remit

豁免权 immunity; charter; right of immunity

豁达大度 open-minded and magnanimous

豁免条款 escape clause; exemption clause

豁免债务 remit a debt

豁然贯通 suddenly see the whole thing in a clear light

豁然开朗 suddenly see the light; be suddenly enlightened

嚯 [huò]
Ⅰ 叹 oh; wow: 嚯! 你穿这套衣服真漂亮! Oh, how smart you look in this suit! Ⅱ 象 laugh boisterously: 嚯嚯大笑 guffaw

Jj

jī（ㄐㄧ）

几 [jī]
Ⅰ 名 ①small table ②slight sign (*or* trace)
Ⅱ 副 nearly;almost;practically：几近于零 virtually nothing ➡ jǐ
几乎 almost;nearly;practically
几近 be close to;be on the verge of
几率 probability
几维鸟 kiwi

讥 [jī]
动 ridicule;deride;mock;satirize
讥讽 ridicule;satirize
讥笑 ridicule;jeer;sneer at;deride

击 [jī]
动 ① beat；hit；knock；strike ② attack；assault;assail ③come in contact with；bump into；collide with
击败 defeat；beat；vanquish
击毙 shoot dead
击沉 bombard and sink；send (a ship) to the bottom
击穿 puncture；breakdown
击发 ①pull the trigger (of a gun) ②percussion
击毁 smash；wreck；shatter；destroy
击剑 fencing
击溃 rout；put to flight；defeat utterly
击落 shoot down；bring down；down
击破 break up；destroy；rout
击球 batting (in baseball or softball)
击伤 wound (a person)；damage (a plane, tank,etc.)
击退 beat back；repel；repulse
击掌 clap one's hands
击中 hit the target
击剑场 fencing strip
击剑服 fencing clothes
击剑馆 fencing gall
击剑裤 fencing breeches
击乐器 percussion instrument
击鼓助兴 beat a drum to add to the festive at-mosphere
击剑上衣 fencing jacket
击剑手套 fencing glove
击弦乐器 hammered string instrument
击掌为号 clap hands as a signal
击中要害 hit the nail on the head；hit sb's vital point；hit home
击剑运动员 fencer

叽 [jī]
象 sharp sound of small birds；小鸟叽叽叫。Little birds chirp.
叽咕 talk in a low voice；whisper；mutter
叽叽喳喳 the sound of birds chirping or of people talking rapidly and indistinctly
叽里咕噜 the sound of sb talking indistinctly or of sth rolling around
叽里呱啦 the sound of loud talk or chatter

饥 [jī]
Ⅰ 形 hungry；starving；famished Ⅱ 名 famine；crop failure
饥肠 empty stomach
饥饿 hungry；starved
饥荒 ①famine；crop failure ②be hard up；be short of money ③debt
饥渴 hunger and thirst
饥民 famine victim；famine refugee
饥不择食 a hungry person is not picky and choosy
饥肠辘辘 one's stomach rumbling with hunger
饥寒交迫 suffer from hunger and cold；live in hunger and cold；be poverty-stricken

玑 [jī]
名 ①pearl that is not quite round ②ancient astronomical instrument

圾 [jī]
◇垃圾 rubbish；garbage；refuse

芨 [jī]
芨芨草 splendid achnatherum

机 [jī]
Ⅰ 名 ① machine；engine ② aircraft；aeroplane；plane ③crucial point；pivot；key link ④

chance；occasion；opportunity ⑤important affairs ⑥ intention；idea Ⅱ 〔形〕 flexible；quick-witted；clever

机变 ①flexible ②sly
机播 machine sowing of crops
机舱 ①engine room（of a ship）②passenger compartment（of an aircraft）；cabin
机插 machine transplanting of rice；mechanical rice transplanter
机场 airport；airfield；aerodrome
机车 locomotive；engine
机船 motor vessel
机床 machine tool
机电 mechanical and electrical equipment
机动 ① power-driven；motorized ② flexible；expedient；mobile ③ in reserve；for emergency use
机断 act on one's own judgment in an emergency
机房 ①generator（or motor）room ②engine room（of a ship）
机耕 tractor-ploughing
机工 mechanic；machinist
机构 ① mechanism ② organization；setup ③ the internal structure of an organization
机关 ①mechanism；gear ②machine-operated ③office；organ；body ④stratagem；scheme；intrigue
机会 chance；opportunity
机件 parts；works
机井 motor-pumped well
机警 alert；sharp-witted；vigilant
机具 machines and tools
机库 hangar
机理 mechanism
机灵 clever；smart；sharp；intelligent
机米 machine-processed rice
机密 ① secret；classified；confidential ② sth secret；secret
机敏 alert and resourceful
机能 function
机票 passenger ticket
机器 machine；machinery；apparatus
机枪 machine-gun
机巧 adroit；ingenious
机群 a group of planes
机身 fuselage
机师 ①engineer ②air pilot
机头 nose（of an aircraft）
机尾 tail（of an aircraft）
机械 ① machinery；machine；mechanism ② mechanical；inflexible；rigid
机心 ①diabolical scheme；cunning idea ②inner works（of a watch，etc.）
机型 ①type（of an aircraft）②model（of a machine）
机要 confidential

机宜 principles of action；guidelines
机翼 wing（of an aircraft）
机油 engine oil；machine oil
机遇 favourable circumstances；opportunity
机缘 good luck；lucky chance
机长 aircraft（or crew）commander
机罩 bonnet（of an aircraft）
机制 ① machine-processed；machine-made ② mechanism
机智 quick-witted；resourceful
机组 ①unit；set ②aircrew；flight crew
机车组 locomotive crew
机顶盒 set-top box
机动车 motor vehicle；automotive vehicle
机动粮 grain reserve for emergency use
机动性 mobility；flexibility
机帆船 motor sailboat；motorized junk
机耕船 boat tractor；wet-field tractor
机关报 newspaper of a government organ
机关炮 cannon
机关枪 machine gun
机灵鬼 a clever person
机器码 machine code
机器人 robot
机器油 lubricating oil；lubricant
机枪手 machine gunner
机头炮 nose gun（of a fighter）
机务段 locomotive depot
机械功 mechanical work
机械化 mechanize
机械能 mechanical energy
机械师 machinist
机械手 manipulator
机电产品 electromechanical products
机动财力 financial resources for unforeseen expenditures；contingency reserve（or fund）
机动力量 reserve force
机动灵活 flexible
机构改革 institutional（or organizational，structural）reform；streamlining of organizations；institutional restructuring
机构庞大 unwieldy organization
机构臃肿 bloated bureaucracy；inflated departments；over-expansion of organizations
机构重叠 organizational overlapping
机构重组 institutional reorganization
机关干部 government functionary；office worker
机关刊物 official journal of an organization
机会成本 opportunity cost
机会均等 equal opportunities
机会主义 opportunism
机器翻译 machine translation
机器语言 machine language（ML）
机上导弹 air-launched missile
机务人员 ①maintenance personnel ②ground

crew
机械工业 machine building
机械加工 machining
机械运动 mechanical movement
机械制图 mechanical drawing
机要秘书 confidential secretary
机载导弹 air-launched missile
机场建设费 airport construction fee
机电一体化 integration of machinery with electronics
机器脚踏车 motorcycle
机器人技术 robotics
机械动力学 mechanical kinetics
机械工程学 mechanical engineering
机械化部队 mechanized force (*or* troops, unit)
机动车辆保险 motorcar insurance; automobile insurance
机会成本价值 opportunity cost value
机械唯物主义 mechanical materialism
机会与挑战并存 opportunity and challenge co-exist
机不可失，时不再来 don't let slip an opportunity as it may never come again; opportunity knocks but once

肌 [jī] 名 muscle
肌肤 (human) skin and muscle
肌腱 tendon
肌理 skin texture
肌肉 muscle
肌体 human body; organism
肌萎缩 muscular dystrophy; amyotrophy
肌肉肿瘤 muscle tumour
肌肉注射 intramuscular injection

矶 [jī] 名 rock projecting over the water

鸡 [jī] 名 chicken; fowl
鸡巴 penis; cock
鸡蛋 (hen's) egg
鸡冠 cockscomb
鸡奸 sodomy; buggery
鸡肋 chicken ribs—things of little value or interest
鸡毛 chicken feather
鸡肉 chicken (as food)
鸡舍 barton; pheasantry
鸡食 chicken feed
鸡汤 chicken broth
鸡瘟 chicken pest
鸡窝 chicken coop; henhouse; roost
鸡心 ① chicken's heart ② heart-shaped ③ a heart-shaped pendant
鸡胸 pigeon breast; chicken breast
鸡眼 corn; clavus
鸡杂 chicken giblets

鸡蛋糕 (sponge) cake
鸡冠花 cockscomb (a flower)
鸡冠石 realgar
鸡霍乱 fowl cholera
鸡内金 the membrane of a chicken's gizzard
鸡尾酒 cocktail
鸡血藤 reticulate millettia
鸡飞蛋打 the hen has flown away and the eggs in the coop are broken—all is lost
鸡零狗碎 in bits and pieces; fragmentary
鸡毛掸子 feather duster
鸡毛蒜皮 chicken feathers and garlic skins—trifles; trivialities
鸡鸣狗盗 (ability to) crow like a cock and snatch like a dog—get up to mean or petty tricks
鸡鸣犬吠 the crowing of cocks and the barking of dogs—country sounds
鸡皮疙瘩 gooseflesh
鸡皮鹤发 wrinkled skin and white hair—advanced in age
鸡犬不留 even fowls and dogs are not spared—ruthless mass slaughter
鸡犬不宁 even fowls and dogs are not left in peace—general turmoil
鸡犬升天 fowls and dogs turn immortals—relatives and followers of a high official got promotion after him
鸡尾酒会 cocktail party
鸡鸭鱼肉 chicken and duck, fish and meat; fine dishes
鸡嘴猴腮 thrust out one's lips and have a chin like an ape's
鸡蛋碰石头 (like) an egg striking a rock—attack sb far stronger than oneself; court destruction
鸡毛当令箭 make a fuss about a casual remark dropped by one's superior
鸡蛋里挑骨头 look for a bone in an egg—look for a flaw where there's none to be found; find fault; nitpick
鸡窝里飞出金凤凰 a golden phoenix flying out of a henhouse—a person of humble origin rising to prominence

奇 [jī] Ⅰ 形 odd (number) Ⅱ 名 fractional amount; odd lots ➡ qí
奇偶 odd and even numbers
奇日 odd-numbered days (of a month)
奇数 odd number
奇偶校验 parity check

唧 [jī] 动 spurt; squirt
唧唧 the sound of insects chirping
唧咕 talk in a low voice; whisper
唧筒 pump

积 [jī]
Ⅰ〔动〕amass; gather; store up; accumulate Ⅱ〔形〕accumulated; long-standing; long-pending; age-old Ⅲ〔名〕①indigestion ②product
积案 a long-pending case
积弊 age-old malpractice; long-standing abuse
积储 store up; lay up; stockpile
积存 store up; lay up; stockpile
积德 accumulate merit (by good works)
积淀 accumulate and take form (usu. the gradual formation of ideology, culture, customs, etc.); accumulate; accretion
积肥 collect (farmyard) manure
积分 ①integral ②accumulated points
积极 ①positive ②active; energetic; vigorous
积久 accumulate in the course of time
积聚 gather; accumulate; build up
积累 ① accumulate ② accumulation (for expanded reproduction)
积木 building blocks; toy bricks
积欠 ①have one's debts piling up ②outstanding debts; arrears
积善 accumulation of good deeds; performance of one good deed after another
积习 old habit; long-standing practice
积蓄 ①put aside; save; accumulate ②savings
积雪 accumulated snow
积压 keep long in stock; overstock
积怨 accumulated rancour; piled-up grievances
积云 cumulus
积攒 save (*or* collect) bit by bit
积分学 integral equation
积分学 integral calculus
积分仪 integrator
积极性 zeal; initiative; enthusiasm
积雨云 cumulonimbus
积不相能 have always been at variance; have never been on good terms; be always at loggerheads
积非成是 wrong idea passed down from over a long time can be mistaken for truth
积谷防饥 store up grain against famine
积毁销骨 repeated calumny can bring about one's ruin
积极分子 activist; active element; enthusiast
积极稳妥 active and cautious efforts
积劳成疾 fall ill from constant overwork
积年累月 for years on end; year after year
积少成多 many a little makes a mickle
积习难改 Old habits die hard.
积压产品 piled-up products; accumulated products; overstocked commodities; overstocked inventories
积压严重 heavy stockpile; excessive inventory
积压滞销 overstocking and sluggish sales
积玉堆金 store up gems and pile up gold
积重难返 bad old practices die hard; ingrained

habits are hard to change
积铢累寸 save every tiny bit; accumulate bit by bit
积极财政政策 pro-active fiscal policy
积极吸引外资 boldly absorb foreign investment

笄 [jī]
〔名〕*jī*, a large pin that women used to hold their hair in ancient China

屐 [jī]
〔名〕①clogs ②shoes in general

姬 [jī]
〔名〕① complimentary term for women in ancient China ②name used in ancient China for a concubine ③professional female singer
姬蜂 ichneumon wasp

基 [jī]
Ⅰ〔名〕① base; foundation ② radical; base; group Ⅱ〔形〕basic; fundamental; primary; cardinal
基本 ① foundation ② basic; fundamental; elementary ③ main; essential ④ basically; in the main; on the whole; by and large
基层 basic level; primary level; grass-roots unit
基础 ① foundation; base; basis ② economic base; economic basis
基带 base band
基地 ①base ②centre
基点 ①basic point; starting point ②base point (BP)
基调 ①fundamental key; main key ②keynote ③key tone
基督 Christ
基肥 base manure; base fertilizer
基干 backbone; hard core
基极 base
基价 base price
基建 capital construction
基金 fund
基坑 ground pit
基期 base period
基色 primary colours
基石 foundation stone; cornerstone
基数 ①cardinal number ②statistics base
基线 datum line
基业 property, inheritance, family estate, etc., considered as a foundation on which to build
基因 gene
基音 fundamental tone
基于 because of; in view of
基站 base station
基准 ①datum ②standard; criterion
基座 foundation bed; foundation support
基本法 basic law
基本费 minimum fare
基本功 basic training; basic skill; essential

technique
基础课 basic courses (of a college curriculum)
基督教 the Christian religion; Christianity
基督徒 Christian
基金会 foundation; fund
基因库 gene bank; gene pool
基因组 genome
基准兵 guide; base marker
基本词汇 basic vocabulary; basic word-stock
基本工资 base pay; basic wage
基本规则 ground rule; primitive rule
基本国策 basic policy of the country
基本国情 fundamental realities of the country
基本建设 capital construction
基本粒子 elementary particle
基本路线 basic line
基本矛盾 fundamental contradiction
基本人权 basic (or fundamental, substantive) human rights
基本事实 underlying and fundamental fact
基本投资 capital investment; investment in capital construction
基层单位 grass-roots unit; basic unit
基层干部 basic-level cadre
基层民主 democracy at the grass-roots level
基层组织 organizations at the grass-roots level
基础产品 products of key projects
基础产业 basic industries; basic sectors of industry
基础代谢 basal metabolism
基础工业 basic industry
基础教育 elementary education
基础科学 basic science
基础理论 basic theory
基础设施 infrastructure; infrastructural (or basic) facilities
基础研究 basic research; research in basic science
基础知识 rudimentary (or elementary) knowledge
基尼系数 gini coefficient
基因工程 genetic engineering
基因芯片 gene chip
基因学说 gene theory
基因移植 gene transplantation; implantation of genes
基因增殖 gene amplification
基因诊断 gene diagnosis
基因治疗 gene therapy
基因转换 gene transfer
基因组合 gene combination
基因组学 genome science
基因作用 action of a gene; genetic effect
基准测试 benchmark test
基准汇率 benchmark exchange rate
基本生活费 basic allowances

基层党组织 grassroots party cells
基本建设投资 investment for infrastructure (or capital) construction
基督教青年会 the Young Men's Christian Association (YMCA)
基本建设项目审批权限 power to examine and approve construction projects

赍 [jī]
〔动〕①cherish; harbour ②give as a present

期 [jī]
〔名〕one whole year (or month) ➡ qī

犄 [jī]
犄角 ①horn ②corner

缉 [jī]
〔动〕seize; arrest; apprehend ➡ qī
缉捕 seize; arrest
缉查 search; ransack
缉毒 drug control
缉拿 seize; arrest; apprehend
缉私 suppress smuggling; seize (or search) for smugglers (or smuggled goods)
缉毒队 narcotics squad
缉私船 revenue cutter; anti-smuggling patrol boat
缉私官 revenue officer
缉拿归案 bring to justice
缉私力量 anti-contraband forces; forces engaged in the fight against smuggling
缉私人员 anti-contraband personnel

畸 [jī]
Ⅰ〔形〕①lopsided; unbalanced ②irregular; eccentric; abnormal Ⅱ〔名〕fractional amount; odd lots
畸变 distortion
畸恋 abnormal love
畸胎 monster
畸形 ①deformity; malformation ②lopsided; unbalanced; abnormal
畸轻畸重 attach too much weight to this and too little to that; lopsided; now too much, now too little
畸形发展 deformed development
畸形消费 abnormal consumption; irregular consumption

跻 [jī]
〔动〕ascend; climb (up); mount
跻身 ascend; mount

箕 [jī]
〔名〕①dustpan ②loop (of a finger print) ③winnowing basket; winnowing fan ④one of the 28 constellations in ancient Chinese astronomy

稽 [jī]
〔动〕①check; examine; scrutinize; investigate ②argue; dispute ③delay; linger; procrastinate
稽查 ①check (to prevent smuggling, tax evasion, etc.) ②an official engaged in such

J

work;customs officer
稽核 check;examine
稽考 ascertain;verify
稽留 delay;detain
稽留热 continued fever
稽查特派员 special supervisor

激 〔jī〕 I 动 ①(of water,etc.) swash;splash;dash ②(cause to) fall ill from getting wet;(cause to) catch a chill ③chill (by putting in ice water,etc.) ④ arouse;evoke;stimulate;incite ⑤feel stirred (or moved) Ⅱ 形 radical;drastic;fierce;violent
激昂 excited and indignant;roused
激变 change violently
激辩 heated argument
激波 shock wave
激荡 agitate;surge;rage
激动 excite;stir;agitate
激发 ①arouse;stimulate;set off ②excite
激奋 rouse sb to action
激愤 wrathful;indignant
激光 laser
激化 sharpen;intensify;become acute
激活 activation;activate;stimulate
激进 radical
激励 ①encourage;impel;urge ②drive;excitation
激烈 intense;sharp;fierce;acute
激流 torrent;rapids;turbulent current
激怒 enrage;infuriate;exasperate
激起 arouse;evoke;cause;stir up
激切 (of language) impassioned;vehement
激情 intense emotion;fervour;passion;enthusiasm
激素 hormone
激扬 ①drain away the mud and bring in fresh water;drive out evil and usher in good ② excited and high-spirited;vehement ③ encourage;urge
激越 intense;vehement;loud and strong
激增 increase sharply;soar;shoot up
激战 fierce fighting
激子 exciton
激光刀 laser scalpel
激将法 prodding (or goading) sb into action (as by ridicule,sarcasm,etc.)
激进派 radicals;militants
激发电流 excitation current
激发电压 excitation voltage
激光唱片 compact disc (CD)
激光电视 laser television
激光扫描 laser scanning
激光视盘 video compact disc (VCD)
激光武器 laser weapon
激光照排 laser phototypesetting
激进政策 militant policy

激励因素 motivator
激烈竞争 cut-throat (or keen,fierce,strong) competition
激流险滩 turbulent rivers and treacherous shoals
激起公愤 arouse public indignation;provoke general rage;stir up a hornet's nest
激束炸弹 cluster bomb
激于义愤 be stirred by righteous indignation
激浊扬清 drain away the mud and bring in fresh water—drive out evil and usher in good;eliminate vice and exalt virtue
激光打印机 laser printer
激烈的枪战 wild gun battle
激光致盲武器 blinding laser weapons
激励和制约机制 incentive and restrain (or control) mechanisms

羁 〔jī〕 I 名 bridle;headstall;halter Ⅱ 动 ①control;restrain;restrict ②stay;delay;hamper;detain
羁绊 trammels;fetters;yoke
羁留 ①stay (in a strange place);stop over ② keep in custody;detain
羁旅 stay long in a strange place;live in a strange land
羁押 detain;take into custody

jí〔ㄐㄧˊ〕

及 〔jí〕 I 动 ①reach;come up to;attain ②catch up with;be in time for ③match;be equal to ④ think of by analogy;take into account;give consideration to Ⅱ 连 (used to join two or more nouns or noun phrases, usu. with the one following 及 subordinate in meaning):张氏夫妇及子女 the Zhangs and their children
及第 pass an imperial examination
及格 pass a test,examination,etc.;pass
及时 ①timely;in time;seasonably ②promptly;without delay
及早 at an early date;as soon as possible;before it is too late
及至 by the time;as soon as
及格赛 qualification contest
及时雨 fertile showers;heaven-sent rain
及时行乐 enjoy life while yet may
及物动词 transitive verb
及早回头 mend one's ways without delay

吉 〔jí〕 形 lucky;auspicious
吉利 lucky;auspicious;propitious
吉庆 an auspicious occasion;a happy occasion
吉日 auspicious day;lucky day
吉他 guitar
吉祥 lucky;auspicious;propitious

吉凶 good or ill luck
吉言 auspicious remarks;blessing
吉兆 good omen;propitious sign
吉普车 jeep
吉祥物 mascot
吉光片羽 fragment of a highly treasured relic
吉庆有余 auspicious happiness in overmeasure
　（*or* in superabundance）
吉人天相 Heaven stands by the good man.
吉祥如意 be as lucky as desired;good fortune
　as one wishes
吉星高照 be blessed by a lucky star
吉凶未卜 one's fate is in the balance;fate un-
　known
吉尼斯世界纪录 Guinness World Records
吉尼斯世界纪录大全 Guinness Book of World
　Records

岌 ［jí］
形 (of a mountain) high;lofty;towering
岌岌可危 in imminent danger

汲 ［jí］
动 draw (water)
汲取 draw;derive

级 ［jí］
I 名 ①level;rank;grade ②(of a school)
course;grade;class;form ③step ④degree II
量 step;stage
级别 rank;level;grade;scale
级数 progression;series
级别工资 rank salary
级差地租 differential (land) rent
级间分离 stage separation

极 ［jí］
I 名 ①utmost point;extreme ②pole II 动
do one's utmost;reach the limit III 形 last;ul-
timate;highest IV 副 extremely;exceedingly;
utterly
极板 plate
极大 maximum
极地 polar region
极点 the limit;the extreme;the utmost
极度 ①extremely;exceedingly;to the utmost
　②the limit;the extreme;the utmost
极端 ①extreme ②extremely;exceedingly
极光 aurora;polar lights
极化 polarization
极力 do one's utmost;spare no effort
极量 maximum dose
极目 look as far as the eye can see
极品 best quality;highest grade;highest offi-
　cial rank
极谱 polarogram
极其 most;extremely;exceedingly
极圈 polar circle
极盛 the highest (point of development)
极限 ①the limit;the maximum ②limit
极刑 capital punishment;the death penalty
极夜 polar night

极右 ultra-Right
极值 extreme value
极昼 polar day
极"左" ultra-"Left"
极乐鸟 bird of paradise
极坐标 polar coordinate
极尽能事 do everything possible to ...
极乐世界 Pure Land; Western Paradise; the
　Land of Ultimate Bliss
极目远眺 gaze into the distance;strain one's
　eyes to look at the distance
极权主义 totalitarianism
极限概率 limiting probabilities
极限运动 extreme sports
极地考察船 polar research ship
极端民主化 ultra-democracy
极端个人主义 ultra-individualism;out-and-out
　egoism
极端狂热主义 far-out fanatic
极诽谤之能事 spare no slander whatsoever;
　stop at nothing to slander

即 ［jí］
I 动 ①approach;reach;be close to;be in
contact ②attain;assume;undertake ③be;
mean II 副 ①presently;at present;in immediate future ②at once;immediately;in no
time III 连 even if;even though;though
即便 even;even if;even though
即将 be about to;be on the point of;soon
即景 (of a literary or artistic work) be in-
　spired by what one sees
即刻 at once;immediately;instantly
即令 even;even if;even though
即期 immediate;spot
即日 ①this (*or* that) very day ②within the
　next few days
即时 immediately;forthwith
即使 even;even if;even though
即位 ascend the throne
即席 ① impromptu; extemporaneous ② take
　one's seat (at a dinner table,etc.)
即兴 impromptu;extemporaneous
即景诗 extempore verse
即食面 instant noodles
即兴曲 impromptu
即兴诗 extempore verse
即将成行 about to start off (*or* set out)
即景生情 the scene touches a chord in one's
　heart
即期承兑 immediate acceptance
即期存款 deposit at call;demand deposit
即期债务 debt at call
即时重播 instant replay
即食麦片 granola
即席反驳 spontaneous retort;talk back imme-
　diately
即席赋诗 write poems in the course of a din-

ner party;improvise a poem
即兴表演 extemporaneous performance
即兴买主 impulse buyer
即开式奖券 scratch-open ticket
即期信用证 deposit at call;demand deposit; sight letter of credit
即以其人之道,还治其人之身 deal with a man as he deals with you;pay a person back in his own coin

亟 [jí]
〔副〕urgently;promptly;anxiously;earnestly
⇒ qì
亟待解决 have to be settled urgently;demand prompt solution call for immediate solution
亟盼复函 earnestly look forward to your reply
亟须纠正 must be speedily put right
亟须注意 call for immediate attention
亟欲成行 desire most ardently to make the journey;want very much to set out

革 [jí]
〔形〕(of wound or illness) fatal;critical ⇒ gé

笈 [jí]
〔名〕①book chest ②book;record

急 [jí]
I 〔形〕①impatient;anxious;restless;hasty ②irritable;annoyed;nettled ③fast;rapid; sudden;violent ④urgent;compelling;pressing II 〔动〕①make restless (or anxious);worry ② be eager to help III 〔名〕urgent matter;urgency;exigency;emergency
急板 presto
急病 acute disease
急促 ①hurried;rapid ②(of time) short; pressing
急电 urgent telegram;urgent cable
急件 an urgent document (or dispatch)
急救 first aid;emergency treatment
急剧 rapid;sharp;sudden
急遽 rapid;sharp;sudden
急流 ①torrent;rapid stream;rapids ②jet stream;jet flow
急忙 in a hurry;in haste;hurriedly;hastily
急迫 urgent;pressing;imperative
急切 ①eager;impatient ②in a hurry;in haste
急速 very fast;rapid
急湍 swift (or rushing) current;gurgling rapids
急弯 sharp turn
急务 urgent task
急性 acute
急需 ①be badly in need of ②urgent need
急眼 be taken aback;feel anxious
急用 urgent need
急于 eager;anxious;impatient
急雨 pelting rain
急躁 ①irritable;irascible ②impetuous;rash; impatient

急诊 emergency call;emergency treatment
急症 sudden attack (of illness);acute disease; emergency case
急智 nimbleness of mind in dealing with emergencies;quick-wittedness
急腹症 acute abdominal disease;acute abdomen
急惊风 acute infantile convulsions
急救包 first-aid dressing
急救车 breakdown van;emergency ambulance
急救站 first-aid station
急就章 hurriedly-written essay;hasty work; improvisation
急刹车 ①slam the brakes on ②bring to a halt
急先锋 ①daring vanguard ②most aggressive, adventurous henchman
急行军 rapid march;forced march
急性病 ①acute disease ②impetuosity
急性子 ①of impatient disposition;impetuous ②an impetuous person
急诊室 emergency room
急转弯 sudden turnabout
急不可待 too impatient to wait;extremely anxious
急不容缓 too urgent to allow of delay
急风暴雨 violent storm;hurricane;tempest
急公好义 zealous for the common weal;public-spirited
急功近利 eager for instant success and quick profits
急救电话 first-aid phone;emergency phone
急救人员 first-aid personnel
急救药品 first-aid medicine
急救药箱 first-aid kit
急救中心 first-aid centre
急流勇进 forge ahead against a swift current; press on in the teeth of difficulties
急流勇退 resolutely retire at the height of one's official career
急起直追 rouse oneself to catch up;do one's utmost to overtake
急人之难 help people in trouble;be eager to help those in need
急如星火 extremely pressing;most urgent; posthaste
急于成名 career-hungry
急于求成 undue haste for success;overanxious for success;impatient for success
急诊病人 emergency case
急中生智 hit upon a plan in desperation;show resourcefulness in an emergency;suddenly hit on a way out of a predicament
急转直下 (of the march of events,etc.) take a sudden turn and then develop rapidly
急得团团转 so agitated that one was like an ant on a hot pan
急来抱佛脚 clasp Buddha's feet when in trou-

ble—seek help at the last moment; make a frantic last-minute effort

疾 [jí] Ⅰ 图 ①disease; malady; sickness; illness ② suffering; pain; distress; difficulty Ⅱ 动 hate; loathe; abhor Ⅲ 形 swift; fast; quick; vigorous
疾病 disease; illness
疾风 ①strong wind; gale ②moderate gale
疾苦 sufferings; hardships
疾驶 (of vehicles) speed along
疾病保险 sickness insurance
疾病缠身 be eaten up with diseases
疾恶如仇 hate evil like an enemy
疾首蹙额 with aching head and knitted brows—frowning in disgust; with abhorrence
疾似流星 swift as a shooting star; very quick
疾言厉色 harsh words and stern looks
疾风扫落叶 like a strong wind sweeping away dead leaves—carrying everything before one
疾风知劲草,烈火见真金 sturdy grass withstands high winds; true gold stands the test of fire—strength of character is tested in a crisis

棘 [jí] 图 ①sour jujube ②thorn bushes; brambles ③prick; puncture
棘齿 wolf teeth
棘刺 caltrops; caltrops spine
棘轮 notch wheel; paw wheel
棘手 thorny; troublesome; knotty
棘爪 pawl; detent
棘皮动物 echinoderm

集 [jí] Ⅰ 动 gather; collect; assemble Ⅱ 图 ①market; fair ② collection; anthology ③ volume; book; part ④(short for 集合) set; assemblage
集材 logging; skidding; yarding
集藏 collect
集成 ①collection ②integration
集萃 fine collection
集股 collect capital; form a stock company
集管 header
集合 gather; assemble; muster; call together
集会 assembly; rally; gathering; meeting
集结 (esp. of troops) mass; concentrate; build up
集锦 a collection of choice specimens
集句 a poem made up of lines from various poets
集聚 gather; collect; assemble
集刊 collected papers (of an academic institution)
集纳 gather; assemble
集权 centralization of power; centralized power

集群 colony; schooling
集日 market day
集市 country fair; market
集束 ① tied in a bundle ② compile; compilation; collection
集体 collective
集团 group; clique; circle; bloc
集训 assemble for training
集邮 stamp collecting; philately
集约 intensive
集运 transport sth containerized
集镇 town; market town
集中 concentrate; centralize; focus; amass; put together
集注 ①focus ②collected commentaries; variorum
集资 raise funds; collect money; pool resources
集子 collection; collected works; anthology
集尘器 dust arrester; dust collector; duster
集大成 gather together all that is good; synthesize; be the culmination of; be a comprehensive expression of
集电极 collecting electrode; collector
集电器 collector; collector electrode
集合号 bugle call for fall-in; assembly
集合论 set theory
集合体 aggregate
集流环 slip ring
集散地 entrepot; point (or centre) of collection and distribution; collecting and distributing centre
集散港 feeder port
集体户 ① collective ownership of an enterprise ②living place of a group of educated youth settled in the countryside (during the Cultural Revolution)
集体化 collectivize
集体舞 group dancing
集团军 group army; army
集训队 team of athletes in training
集邮簿 stamp-album
集约化 intensification; intensify
集中营 concentration camp
集注本 variorum edition
集装箱 container
集资房 houses built on the funds collected from the buyers
集资热 fund-raising drive; craze of capital accumulation; craze in raising capital money
集成电路 integrated circuit
集合名词 collective noun
集结地域 assembly area
集贸市场 fair trade market—a town or country market at which various products are sold and bought
集散市场 terminal market

集市贸易 country fair trade; open market
集束炸弹 cluster bomb
集思广益 draw on collective wisdom and absorb all useful ideas; pool the wisdom of the masses
集体辞职 resign in mass
集体婚礼 web-in; collective (*or* group) wedding ceremony
集体经济 collective economy; collectively-owned sector of the economy
集体领导 collective leadership
集体农庄 collective farm
集体企业 collectively-owned enterprise
集体宿舍 dormitory
集体提留 retention of common funds by collectives; amount of profit retained by collectives
集体主义 collectivism
集团购买 institutional purchase
集团消费 institutional spending
集腋成裘 the finest fragments of fox fur, sewn together, will make a robe—many a little makes a mickle
集约经济 intensive economy
集约投资 intensive investment
集中采购 centralized purchasing; central buying
集中供热 central heating
集中轰炸 mass bombing
集资办学 raise money to set up new schools
集成电路卡 integrated circuit card
集体所有制 collective ownership
集团购买力 the purchasing power of institutions; institutional purchases
集邮爱好者 stamp-collector; philatelist
集约型增长 intensive mode of economic development
集资诈骗罪 crime of fund-raising frauds
集体生产劳动 collective productive labour
集体主义教育 education to foster a community spirit
集中全部财力 pool all its resources
集中力量办大事 concentrate our resources to get big jobs done
集中过多,统得过死 overcentralization and rigid control
集中和统一,组织和纪律 centralization and unity, organization and discipline
集中精力把国内事情办好 concentrate on doing a good job in domestic affairs; concentrate on our domestic affairs
集中力量发展社会生产力 concentrate efforts to develop the productive forces
集中性检查和经常性检查 general reviews and routine inspection
集中精力把经济建设搞上去 go all out for economic development

蒺 [jí]
蒺藜 puncture vine

楫 [jí]
名 oar

辑 [jí]
I 动 collect; gather; compile; edit II 名 part; volume; division
辑集 collect and edit; compile
辑录 compile
辑要 summary; abstract

嶍 [jí]
名 ridge of a mountain (*or* hill)

嫉 [jí]
动 ①jealous; envious; covetous ②hate; detest
嫉妒 be jealous (*or* envious) of; envy
嫉恨 envy and hate; hate out of jealousy
嫉贤妒能 be envious of people of worth and ability

瘠 [jí]
形 ①lean; emaciated; thin and weak ②barren; poor
瘠田 infertile land

藉 [jí]
动 tread on; trample underfoot; insult ➡ jiè

籍 [jí]
名 ①book; record; register ②place of origin; native place; hometown ③membership
籍贯 the place of one's birth (*or* origin); native place; origin and parentage

jǐ(ㄐㄧˇ)

几 [jǐ]
数 ①how many ②a few; several; some ➡ jī
几分 a bit; somewhat; rather
几何 ①how much; how many ②geometry
几经 several times; time and again
几时 ①what time; when ②any time; when
几何学 geometry
几边协定 plurilateral agreement
几次三番 time and again; repeatedly
几番风雨 the devastation of a few storms and gusts
几何级数 geometric progression; geometric series
几何失真 geometric distortion
几何图形 geometric figure

己 [jǐ]
代 self; oneself; one's own
己方 one's own side
己任 one's duty
己不正,难正人 one who lacks moral integrity cannot expect to correct others' misdeeds; a person lacking moral integrity is in no position to help others correct their behaviour
己所不欲,勿施于人 do not impose on others what you yourself do not desire; do not unto

others as you would not have them do unto you

虮 〔jǐ〕

虮子 the egg of a louse；nit

挤 〔jǐ〕

〔动〕①crowd；throng；cram；pack ②jostle；push；squeeze ③squeeze；press ④exclude；squeeze out；push out

挤兑 a run on a bank
挤奶 milk (a cow，etc.)
挤提 squeeze；run on a bank
挤压 extruding
挤眼 wink
挤占 occupy
挤奶机 milking machine；milker
挤牙膏 squeeze toothpaste out of a tube—be forced to tell the truth bit by bit
挤眉弄眼 make eyes；wink
挤占挪用 unwarranted diversion of resources from designated uses

济 〔jǐ〕 ➡jì

济济 (of people) many；numerous
济济一堂 gather together under the same roof

给 〔jǐ〕

Ⅰ〔动〕supply；provide；furnish Ⅱ〔形〕ample；abundant；well-provided for：家给户足。Every household is well provided for. ➡gěi

给水 ①water-supply ②feed water
给养 provisions；victuals
给予 give；render

脊 〔jǐ〕

〔名〕①spine；backbone；vertebra ②sth like a spine；ridge

脊背 back (of a human being or any other vertebrate)
脊梁 back (of the human body)
脊檩 ridgepole
脊鳍 dorsal fin
脊髓 spinal cord
脊索 notochord
脊柱 spinal column；vertebral column；backbone；spine
脊椎 vertebra
脊梁骨 backbone；spine
脊神经 spinal nerve
脊髓炎 myelitis
脊椎骨 vertebra；spine
脊索动物 chordate (animal)
脊椎动物 vertebrate
脊髓灰质炎 poliomyelitis；polio

掎 〔jǐ〕

〔动〕①pull；pin down ②tow；pull；draw

戟 〔jǐ〕

Ⅰ〔名〕halberd Ⅱ〔动〕stimulate；excite

麂 〔jǐ〕

〔名〕muntjac

麂皮 chamois (leather)；chammy
麂子 muntjac

jì〔чì〕

计 〔jì〕

Ⅰ〔动〕①count；compute；calculate；number ②make plans；design；aim；intend ③consider；concern oneself；care；bother about Ⅱ〔名〕①meter；gauge ②idea；ruse；stratagem；plan

计策 stratagem；plan
计酬 work out (*or* calculate) payment
计划 ①plan；project；programme ②map out；plan
计价 valuate
计件 reckon by the piece
计较 ①haggle over；fuss about ②argue；dispute ③think over；plan
计量 measure；calculate；estimate
计谋 scheme；stratagem
计时 reckon by time
计数 count
计算 ①count；compute；calculate ②consideration；planning ③scheme；plot
计议 deliberate；talk over；consult
计程表 taximeter；meter
计程车 taxi
计程仪 log
计划外 in excess of planned quotas；outside the plan
计价器 fare meter；indicator (of fare)
计生委 family planning commission
计时工 time-worker
计时器 hour meter；hour counter
计数器 counter
计算尺 slide rule
计算机 computer；calculating machine
计算器 electronic calculator
计出万全 make a perfectly safe plan
计划调拨 planned allocation
计划供应 planned supply
计划经济 planned economy
计划生产 planned production
计划生育 family planning；birth control；planned parenthood
计件工资 piece rate wage
计件工作 piecework
计尽智穷 be at one's wits' end；at a loss for a good plan
计日程功 estimate exactly how many days are needed to complete a project；have the completion of a project in sight
计时工资 payment by the hour；time wage
计时工作 timework
计算报酬 remunerate；calculate payment
计算中心 computing centre
计划内投资 planned investment；investment

J

under the plan
计划外生育 unplanned birth
计划外用工 labour needed (*or* used) beyond the general plan
计划外资金 extra-budgetary revenue
计件工资制 piece-rate system
计时工资制 time-rate system
计算机安全 computer security
计算机病毒 computer viruses
计算机程序 computer program
计算机代码 computer code
计算机动画 computer-animation
计算机犯罪 computer crime;cyber crime
计算机教育 education for computer
计算机科学 computer science
计算机控制 computer control
计算机模拟 computer simulation
计算机排字 computer typesetting
计算机配置 computer configuration
计算机软件 computer software
计算机网络 computer network
计算机文化 computer culture
计算机系统 computer centre
计算机效益 computer utility
计算机应用 computer application;computer utility
计算机硬件 computer hardware
计算机语言 computer language
计算机知识 computeracy;computer literacy
计算机指令 computer instruction
计算机专家 computernik
计算语言学 computational linguistics
计划评审技术 program evaluation and review technique
计算机存储器 computer memory; computer storage
计算机化战争 computerized war
计算机恐惧症 cyberphobia
计划生育责任制 responsibility system of family planning
计划体制 planning system
计算机程序设计 computer programming
计算机等级考试 band test of computer
计算机断层扫描 computer tomography; computer laminography
计算机辅助教学 computer-aided (*or* assisted) instruction (CAI)
计算机辅助设计 computer-aided (*or* assisted) design (CAD)
计算机辅助制造 computer-aided (*or* assisted) manufacturing (CAM)
计算机监控系统 computer supervisory control system
计算机情报检索 information retrieval by computer
计算机体层成像 computer tomography; computer laminography

计算机网络设备 computer network facilities
计划外怀孕及生育 pregnancy and childbearing outside the plan;unplanned (*or* unscheduled) pregnancy and childbearing
计算机动画片制作 computer animation
计算机中央处理器 central processing unit (CPU)
计划生育的基本国策 the basic state family planning policy
计算机辅助语言教学 computer-aided (*or* assisted) language learning (CALL)
计算机集成制造系统 computer integrated manufacturing system (CIMS)
计划经济与市场调节相结合 combine (*or* integrate) planned economy with market regulation;integrate economic planning with regulation by market forces

记 [jì]

Ⅰ 〔动〕 ①remember; recall; bear in mind; commit to memory ②write down; record; jot down;take down Ⅱ 〔名〕 ①note;record;narrative;account ②mark;stamp;sign ③birthmark Ⅲ 〔量〕 (usu. of certain actions):一记耳光 a slap in the face
记仇 bear grudges;harbour bitter resentment
记得 remember
记分 ①keep the score;record the points (in a game) ②register a student's marks ③record workpoints
记功 cite sb for meritorious service;record a merit
记挂 be concerned about; keep thinking about;miss
记过 record a demerit;record a serious offence
记号 mark;sign
记恨 bear grudges
记录 ①take notes; keep the minutes; record ②minutes;notes ③notetaker ④record
记名 put down one's name (on a cheque,etc. to indicate responsibility or claim);sign
记取 remember;bear in mind
记事 ①keep a record of events;make a memorandum ②account; record of events; chronicles
记述 record and narrate
记诵 commit to memory and be able to recite; learn by heart
记性 memory
记叙 narrate
记忆 ①remember;recall ②memory
记载 ①put down in writing ②record;account
记账 ①keep accounts ②charge to an account
记者 reporter;correspondent;newsman;journalist
记住 remember;learn by heart;bear in mind
记大功 record a merit

记分牌 scoreboard
记分员 scorekeeper；scorer；marker
记录本 minute book
记录片 documentary film；documentary
记录器 describer；recorder apparatus
记录员 notetaker；stenographer；reporter
记谱法 musical notation
记时仪 chronograph
记事儿 (of a child) begin to remember things
记叙文 narrative writing
记忆力 the faculty of memory；memory
记者席 press box；press gallery
记者证 press card
记录在案 be put on record；be a matter of record
记名股票 inscribed stock certificate；registered certificate of shares
记名票据 bill to order；order bill；note to order
记名债券 registered bond
记名证券 inscribed security
记名支票 order cheque
记忆所及 as far as one can recollect；anything that one can remember
记忆犹新 remain fresh in one's memory
记账交易 transaction for account
记者协会 journalists' association
记账式国债 registered T-bond；national bond
记账式债券 boot-entry bond
记者招待会 press conference
记账式国库券 registered (*or* inscribed) treasury bond

伎 [jì] 名 ① skill；ability；trick ② professional female dancer (*or* singer)
伎俩 trick；intrigue；manoeuvre

齐 [jì] 名 ①seasoning；flavouring；condiment ②alloy ➡ qí

纪 [jì] I 名 ① discipline ② twelve years' cycle (*or* period)；(now of longer period) age；epoch ③period II 动 put down in writing；write down；record
纪检 inspect discipline
纪录 ① take notes；keep the minutes；record ②minutes；notes；record ③notetaker ④record
纪律 discipline
纪年 ① a way of numbering the years ② chronological record of events；annals
纪念 ① commemorate；mark ② souvenir；keepsake；memento ③commemoration day；anniversary
纪实 record of actual events；on-the-spot report
纪委 commission for inspecting discipline
纪行 travel notes

纪要 summary of minutes；summary
纪元 ① the beginning of an era (e.g. an emperor's reign) ②epoch；era
纪录片 documentary film；documentary
纪念碑 monument；memorial
纪念币 commemorative coin
纪念册 autograph book；autograph album
纪念封 (stamp collecting) commemorate envelope
纪念馆 memorial hall；museum in memory of sb
纪念品 souvenir；keepsake；memento
纪念日 commemoration day
纪念塔 memorial tower；monument
纪念堂 memorial hall；commemoration hall
纪念章 souvenir badge
纪传体 history presented in a series of biographies
纪律处分 take disciplinary action against sb
纪律监督 disciplinary supervision
纪律检查 discipline inspection
纪律严明 observe strict discipline；be highly disciplined
纪念邮票 commemorative stamp
纪实文学 documentary literature
纪实小说 fiction based on actual events
纪念品商店 souvenir shop
纪律检查委员会 commission for inspecting discipline
纪律面前人人平等 All members are equal before discipline.

荙 [jì] 名 water caltrop；water chestnut

技 [jì] 名 skill；ability；trick
技法 skill and technique (in painting，sculpture，etc.)
技改 technical upgrading；technological change
技工 ①skilled worker ②mechanic；technician
技能 technical ability；mastery of a skill (*or* technique)
技巧 skill；technique；craftsmanship
技穷 exhaust one's whole bag of tricks；come to the end of one's rope
技师 technician
技术 technology；skill；technique
技痒 itch to exercise one's skill
技艺 skill；artistry
技术性 technical；of a technical nature
技术员 technician
技改投资 investment in technological upgrading
技高一筹 more skilful
技工学校 technical school
技巧运动 acrobatic gymnastics
技术壁垒 technical barriers

技术兵种 technical forces; technical military services
技术创新 technology innovation
技术等级 technical rank
技术服务 technical service
技术改造 technical transformation; technological transformation
技术革命 technological revolution
技术革新 technological innovation; technical innovation
技术工人 skilled worker
技术攻关 technical attack in terms of innovation and renovation
技术管理 technical management
技术规范 technical specification; technological specification
技术鉴定 technical appraisement; technical expertise
技术诀窍 technical know-how
技术开发 technological development
技术科学 applied science
技术力量 technical force; technical personnel
技术名词 technical term
技术评估 technological assessment
技术人员 technical personnel (or staff); technician
技术入股 technology invested as capital stock; technology investment
技术市场 technology exchange market
技术手册 technical manual; technological manual
技术下乡 spread technological knowledge to farmers; take technology to the countryside
技术学校 technical school
技术依托 technical backstopping
技术移民 skill immigration (or migration); skill immigrant (or migrator)
技术援助 technical assistance
技术知识 technological know-how; technical knowledge
技术职称 (academic or professional) title for technical personnel
技术指导 ①technological (or technical) guidance ②technical adviser
技术转让 transfer of technology; technology transfer
技术装备 technical plant; technological plant
技术咨询 technical advice
技术资料 technical data; technological data
技术合同法 technological contract law
技术化社会 technopolis
技术密集型 technology intensive
技术推广站 technical advice station
技术研究所 technological research institute
技术革新能手 dab at technical innovation
技术诀窍协议 technical know-how agreement
技术有偿转让 transfer of technology with compensation
技术专业人才 professional technicians; technical professionals
技术产权交易所 technology equity market; technology property right exchange
技术密集型产业 technology-intensive industry
技术先进型企业 enterprises using advanced technology
技术性贸易壁垒 technical barriers to trade

系 [jì] 劢 tie; fasten; do up; button up ➡ xì
系泊 moor (a boat)
系留 moor (a balloon or airship)
系绳 tether
系船索 mooring rope; mooring line
系留塔 mooring mast; mooring tower
系泊浮筒 mooring buoy

忌 [jì] 劢 ① be jealous of; envy ② fear; dread; scruple ③ avoid; shun; abstain from; refrain from ④quit; give up
忌辰 the anniversary of the death of a parent, ancestor, or anyone else held in esteem
忌惮 dread; fear; scruple
忌妒 be jealous (or envious) of; envy
忌讳 ① taboo ② avoid as taboo ③ avoid as harmful; abstain from
忌刻 jealous and mean; jealous and malicious
忌口 avoid certain food (as when one is ill); be on a diet
忌日 the anniversary of the death of a parent, ancestor, or anyone else held in esteem
忌食 ①avoid certain food for health reasons or because of medical treatment ② avoid certain food out of religious beliefs
忌嘴 avoid certain food (as when one is ill); be on a diet
忌贤妒能 be jealous of the worthy and able

际 [jì] Ⅰ 名 ①border; boundary; edge ②occasion; moment; time ③one's experiences (or lot); circumstances Ⅱ 劢 be on the occasion of Ⅲ 介 ①in; inside ②between; among
际会 chance; opportunity
际涯 boundary; limit
际遇 favourable turns in life; spells of good or bad fortune
际会风云 riding on the crest of success

妓 [jì] 名 prostitute; whore
妓女 prostitute; hooker; street girl
妓院 brothel

季 [jì] 名 ①season ②period of time that has a distinctive characteristic; season ③last period of (a dynasty) ④last month of a season ⑤fourth (or youngest) among brothers
季报 quarterly reports

季弟 fourth (*or* youngest) brother
季度 quarter (of a year)
季风 monsoon
季节 season
季军 third place (in sports contest,etc.)
季刊 quarterly publication;quarterly
季风雨 monsoon rain
季节工 seasonal worker
季节性 seasonal
季风气候 monsoon climate
季节差价 seasonal price difference; parities according to season;seasonal variations in price
季节回游 seasonal migration (of fish,etc.)
季节失业 seasonal unemployment

剂 [jì]
Ⅰ [名] ① pharmaceutical (*or* chemical) preparation ②agent ③a small piece of dough Ⅱ [量] (of concoctions of herbal medicine):连服三剂 take three doses in a row
剂量 dosage;dose
剂型 the form of a drug (e.g. liquid,powder, pill,etc.)
剂子 small pieces cut from a long strip of dough for making dumplings and buns

荠 [jì] ➡qí
荠菜 shepherd's purse

哜 [jì]
[动] taste

迹 [jì]
[名] ①mark;trace ②remains;ruins;vestige ③outward sign;indication
迹象 sign;indication

洎 [jì]
[介] up to (a point or period of time):自古洎今 from ancient times up to the present

济 [jì]
[动] ① ferry; cross a river; go across a stream ②relieve;aid;help ③be helpful;be of no help ➡jǐ
济贫 aid the poor;relieve the poor;administer the poor
济事 be of help (*or* use)
济人之急 relieve sb from distress; aid (*or* help) sb in his hour of need
济弱扶贫 help the weak and the distressed
济危扶困 help people with money and rescue men from danger

既 [jì]
Ⅰ [副] already Ⅱ [连] ①as;since;now that ② both...and...;as well as Ⅲ [形] finished;done
既定 set;fixed;established
既然 since;as;now that
既是 since;as;now that
既遂 accomplished offence
既成事实 accomplished fact
既得利益 vested interest

既得权利 acquired right
既定方针 fixed policy
既往不咎 forgive sb's past misdeeds;not censure sb for his past misdeeds;let bygones be bygones
既得利益集团 vested interests
既经济又实惠 inexpensive and substantial
既来之,则安之 since you are here,you may as well stay and make the best of it;since we have come,let us stay and enjoy it

觊 [jì]
[动] hope for;try to get
觊觎 covet;cast greedy eyes on

继 [jì]
Ⅰ [动] continue; succeed; inherit; follow Ⅱ [副] then;afterwards
继承 ①inherit ②carry on
继而 then;afterwards
继父 stepfather
继进 go on;continue the process
继母 stepmother
继女 stepdaughter
继任 succeed sb in a post
继嗣 ①adopt a son ②heir
继位 succeed to the throne
继续 ①continue;go on ②continuation
继子 stepson
继承法 law of succession; succession act; inheritance law
继承权 right of succession; right of inheritance
继承人 heir;successor;inheritor
继承税 succession inheritance
继电器 relay
继往开来 carry forward the (revolutionary) cause and forge ahead into the future
继续教育 continuing education

偈 [jì]
[名] libretto in Buddhist scripture ➡jié

徛 [jì]
[动] stand up

祭 [jì]
[动] ①offer sacrifices to ②hold a memorial ceremony for ③wield (sth magic)
祭奠 hold a memorial ceremony for
祭礼 ①sacrificial rites ②memorial ceremony ③sacrificial offerings
祭品 sacrificial offerings;oblation
祭器 sacrificial utensil
祭祀 offer sacrifices to gods (*or* ancestors)
祭坛 sacrificial altar
祭文 funeral oration;elegiac address
祭献 sacrifice

悸 [jì]
[动] (of the heart) throb with terror
悸动 palpitate from nervousness

寄 [jì]
Ⅰ [动] ①send by post;post;mail ②entrust;

—deposit;place;park ③depend on;attach oneself to Ⅱ 〔形〕 adopted

寄存 deposit;leave with;check
寄儿 adopted son
寄放 leave with;leave in the care of
寄费 postage
寄居 live away from home
寄卖 consign for sale on commission;put up for sale in a secondhand shop
寄生 ①parasitism ②parasitic
寄售 consignment sales
寄宿 ①lodge ②(of students) board
寄托 ①entrust to the care of sb;leave with sb ②place (hope,etc.) on;find sustenance in
寄销 commission sale;sell on commission
寄养 entrust one's child to the care of sb;ask sb to bring up one's child
寄予 ①place (hope,etc.) on ②show;give;express
寄语 send word
寄主 host (of a parasite)
寄存器 computer register
寄父母 foster parents
寄件人 sender
寄居蟹 hermit crab
寄卖品 consignment merchandise
寄生虫 parasite
寄宿生 resident student;boarder
寄信人 sender
寄卖商店 commission shop;secondhand shop
寄情山水 abandon oneself to nature
寄人篱下 live under another's roof;depend on sb for a living
寄生虫病 parasitic disease;parasitosis
寄生虫学 parasitology
寄生动物 parasitic animal
寄生植物 parasitic plant
寄售合同 agreement on consignment;consignment contract
寄售商店 consignment store
寄宿学校 boarding school;residential college
寄托哀思 give expression to one's grief over sb's death

寂 [jì]
〔形〕 ①still;quiet;calm;silent ②lonely;lonesome;solitary
寂静 quiet;still;silent
寂寥 solitary;lonesome
寂寞 ①lonely;lonesome ②quiet;still;silent
寂然无声 solitary and noiseless

绩 [jì]
〔名〕 ①twist hempen thread ②achievement;accomplishment;contribution;merit
绩效 performance
绩差股 bad performance stock
绩优股 blue chip stocks;good performance stock

暨 [jì]
Ⅰ 〔连〕 and;as well as Ⅱ 〔介〕 to;up to

稷 [jì]
〔名〕 ①(broomcorn) millet ②god of grains worshipped by ancients

鲫 [jì]
〔名〕 crucian carp
鲫鱼 crucian carp

冀 [jì]
〔动〕 hope;long for;yearn for;look forward to
冀望 hope for;long for

骥 [jì]
〔名〕 ① thoroughbred horse ② virtuous and competent person

jiā(ㄐㄧㄚ)

加 [jiā]
〔动〕 ① add ② increase;rise;raise;augment ③put in;add;append ④(same as 加以 but used generally after a monosyllabic adverb):不加干涉 not interfere/横加阻挠 wilfully obstruct
加班 work overtime;work an extra shift
加倍 double;redouble
加餐 snack
加车 (put on) extra buses (or trains)
加成 addition
加多 add;increase
加法 addition
加封 grant additional titles and territories (to the nobles)
加高 heighten
加工 ① process ② machining;working ③ improve;polish (writings);put final touches to
加固 reinforce;consolidate
加害 injure;do harm to
加号 plus sign (+)
加黑 (粗体字) boldface
加厚 thicken
加价 price markup
加紧 step up;speed up;intensify
加劲 put more energy into;make a greater effort
加剧 aggravate;intensify;exacerbate
加快 quicken; speed up; accelerate; pick up speed
加宽 broaden;widen
加力 thrust augmentation;afterburning
加料 ①feed in raw material ②reinforced
加仑 gallon
加码 ① raise the price of commodities; overcharge ② raise the stakes in gambling ③raise the quota
加盟 become a member of an alliance (or union);join
加密 ①encrypt;encryption ②set up a secret

number (*or* code)
加冕 coronation
加捻 twisting
加气 air entrainment
加强 ① strengthen; enhance; augment; reinforce ②reinforced
加氢 hydrogenization; hydrogenation
加热 heating
加入 ①add; mix; put in ②join; accede to
加上 ①add; give ②moreover; in addition
加深 deepen
加试 add (more items) to an examination
加数 addend
加速 quicken; speed up; accelerate; expedite
加温 heat up; raise the temperature; stimulate (economy, etc)
加线 ledger line; leger line
加薪 increase the salary; raise the pay
加压 pressurization; compression; pressure
加以 ① *used before a disyllabic verb to indicate that the action is directed towards sth or sb mentioned earlier in the sentence* ②in addition; moreover
加意 with special care; with close attention
加油 ①oil; lubricate ②refuel ③make an extra effort
加重 ① make (*or* become) heavier; increase the weight of ② make (*or* become) more serious; aggravate
加班费 pay for extra shift; overtime pay
加碘盐 iodized salt
加法器 adder
加冕日 Coronation Day
加农炮 cannon; gun
加入国 acceding (*or* adhering) state
加入书 instrument of accession
加塞儿 push into a queue out of turn; jump a queue
加湿器 humidifier
加时赛 play-off competition
加速度 acceleration
加速器 accelerator
加压舱 compressing chamber
加油车 refuelling truck; refueller
加油站 filling (*or* petrol, gas) station
加班加点 work extra shifts or extra hours; put in extra hours
加工出口 export processing
加工订货 place orders with enterprises for processing materials or supplying manufactured goods
加工贸易 processing trade
加官晋爵 be promoted to a higher office and rank
加密电路 encrypted circuit
加强普法 enhance the nationwide awareness of law

加油飞机 tanker aircraft
加工出口区 processing and export zone
加大打假力度 launch a more vigorous attack on counterfeiters
加急电 urgent telegram; urgent cable
加快改革步伐 quicken the pace of reform; accelerate reform; speed up reform
加快资金周转 increase the turnover rate of capital
加勒比共同体 the Caribbean Community (CARICOM)
加强党风建设 improve the Party's style of work; redouble our efforts to improve the Party's work style
加强优生、优育 improve prenatal and postnatal care
加强舆论监督 ensure that the correct orientation is maintained in public opinion
加强重点建设 give priority to the key construction projects
加大反腐败力度 increase the intensity of combating corruption
加大结构调整力度 intensify efforts on structural adjustment
加强国际人权合作 strengthen international cooperation in the field of human rights
加强精神文明建设 promote cultural and ideological progress
加强农业基础地位 strengthen agriculture as the foundation of the economy
加强勤政廉政建设 make greater efforts to keep government functionaries honest and industrious; make greater efforts to build an honest, clean and industrious government; step up the building of an honest and industrious government
加强人大执法检查 strengthen (*or* reinforce) the inspection of law-enforcement of the People's Congress
加强社会主义法制 strengthen the socialist legal system
加强税收征管稽查 enhance tax administration
加强思想道德建设 raise people's ideological and moral standards; enhance ideological education and political work
加强思想政治工作 strengthen ideological and political work
加强物质文明建设 work for material improvement
加快老企业技术革新 accelerate the technological innovation of old enterprises
加快现代化建设步伐 accelerate the construction of modernization
加强税收和税务管理 reinforce tax levy and management
加强物价和市场管理 tighten price and market
加强预算外资金管理 set up management of

extrabudgetary funds

加大改革的分量和力度 step up reform; increase the impact and momentum of reform; increase the scale and momentum of reform

加强对农民的科技培训 strengthen scientific and technical training for the peasants

加强执法检查监督工作 tighten inspection of and supervision over law enforcement

加强中央宏观调控能力 enhance the central government's power in macro-control

加强个体零散税收的征管 improve the collection and control of income taxes from private businesses

夹 [jiā] I 动 ①press from both sides; clip; pinch ②carry (sth) under one's arm ③place (or stay) in between ④mix; mingle; intersperse II 名 clip; clamp; folder ➡gā; jiá

夹板 ① boards for pressing sth or holding things together ②splint

夹层 double layer

夹持 clamp; grip; grasp

夹带 ①carry secretly; smuggle ②notes smuggled into an examination hall

夹道 ①a narrow lane; passageway ②line both sides of the street

夹缝 a narrow space between two adjacent things; crack; crevice

夹攻 attack from both sides; converging attack; pincer attack

夹击 converging attack; pincer attack

夹剪 tweezers; tongs

夹具 clamping apparatus; fixture; jig

夹克 jacket

夹钳 grab; pliers

夹生 (of food) half-cooked; (of a job) not well done; (of facts or knowledge) not quite assimilated

夹馅 stuffed (pastry, etc.)

夹心 with filling

夹杂 be mixed up with; be mingled with

夹注 interlinear notes

夹子 ①clip; tongs ②folder; wallet

夹生饭 ① half-cooked rice ②a job not thoroughly done

夹杂物 inclusion

夹竹桃 (sweet-scented) oleander

夹鼻眼镜 pince-nez

夹七夹八 incoherent; confused; cluttered (with irrelevant remarks)

夹心饼干 sandwich biscuits

夹叙夹议 narration interspersed with comments

夹着尾巴 run away with one's tail between one's legs

伽 [jiā] 名 gal ➡gā; qié

茄 [jiā] 名 ①stem of lotus ②cigar ➡qié

佳 [jiā] 形 good; fine; excellent; beautiful

佳宾 welcome guest

佳话 deed praised far and wide; a story on everybody's lips; a much-told tale

佳绩 accomplishment

佳节 happy festival time; festival

佳境 the most enjoyable (or pleasant) stage

佳句 beautiful line (in a poem); well-turned phrase

佳丽 ①(of looks, scenery, etc.) beautiful ②beautiful woman

佳偶 a happily married couple

佳品 excellent product; famous produce

佳期 wedding (or nuptial) day

佳人 beautiful woman; beauty

佳肴 delicacies

佳音 welcome news; good tidings; favourable reply

佳作 a fine piece of writing; an excellent work

珈 [jiā] 名 ornament worn by ancient Chinese women

枷 [jiā] 名 cangue—wooden yoke for a prisoner

枷锁 yoke; chains; shackles; fetters

浃 [jiā] 动 soak through; spread all over

痂 [jiā] 名 scab; crust

痂病 scall

痂皮 crust; crusta

家 [jiā] I 名 ①family; household ②home ③place where one belongs (e.g. officer at a barracks, official in his office, etc.) ④person or family engaged in a certain trade ⑤specialist in a certain field; expert ⑥school of thought; school ⑦referring to one of the opposite parties II 代 my III 形 ①domestic; tame; cultivated ② tamed; domesticated; broken IV 量 (used for families or enterprices); 四家人家 four families ➡jia; jie

家财 family property

家蚕 silkworm

家产 family property

家常 the daily life of a family; domestic trivia

家丑 family scandal; the skeleton in the cupboard (or closet)

家畜 domestic animal; livestock

家传 handed down from the older generations of the family

家当 family belongings; property

家道 family financial situation

家底 family property accumulated over a long time;resources
家电 electrical home appliances; electrical household appliances
家法 ①theory and methods of academic studies handed down from a master to his disciples ②domestic discipline exercised by the head of a clan (or household) ③rod (or stick) for punishing children (or servants) in a traditional household
家访 a visit to the parents of schoolchildren (or young workers)
家风 family custom and style;family tradition
家鸽 pigeon
家规 domestic discipline and family rules
家伙 ①tool;utensil;weapon ②fellow;guy
家计 family livelihood
家教 ①family education;upbringing ②private tutor (for a school child,etc.); private tutoring
家境 family financial situation;family circumstances
家居 ①residence②family life③living space
家具 furniture
家眷 ①wife and children;one's family ②wife
家里 in the family;at home
家门 ①house gate;home ②family ③member of the same clan ④family background
家培 cultivate
家谱 family tree;genealogical tree;genealogy
家禽 domestic fowl;poultry
家人 ①family member ②servant
家史 family history
家事 family matters;domestic affairs
家室 ①wife ②family
家什 [jiāshi] utensils,furniture,etc.
家书 ①a letter home ②a letter from home
家属 family members;(family) dependents
家私 family property
家庭 family;household
家兔 rabbit
家务 household duties
家乡 hometown;native place
家小 ①wife and children ②wife
家信 ①a letter home ②a letter from home
家宴 ①family reunion feast ②family feast
家燕 house swallow
家业 family property;property
家蝇 housefly
家用 family expenses;housekeeping money
家园 home;homeland
家贼 thief within a house
家长 ①the head of a family;patriarch ②the parent (or guardian) of a child
家珍 family heirloom
家政 ① household management ② home economics

家装 home decoration
家族 clan;family
家常菜 home cooking
家常话 small talk;chitchat
家乡话 native dialect
家长式 patriarchal
家长制 patriarchal system
家政学 home economics
家常便饭 ①homely food;simple meal ②common occurrence;routine;all in the day's work
家畜繁育 animal breeding
家传秘方 a secret recipe handed down in the family
家大业大 big household,lots of work
家给人足 each family is provided for and every person is well-fed and well-clothed; all live in plenty
家家户户 each and every family;every household
家贫如洗 utterly destitute;penniless
家破人亡 with one's family broken up,some gone away,some dead
家属工厂 factory run by family members of workers,cadres,armymen,etc.
家庭暴力 domestic violence
家庭背景 family background
家庭病床 hospital bed at home;home bed
家庭成员 family member
家庭出身 class status of one's family;family origin
家庭服务 domestic help;servant;maid
家庭妇女 housewife
家庭副业 household sideline production
家庭顾问 home consultant
家庭观念 attachment to one's family
家庭教师 private teacher;tutor
家庭教育 family education;home education
家庭经济 family economy;household economy
家庭纠纷 family quarrel;domestic discord
家庭生活 home life;family life
家庭舞会 home party
家庭影院 home theatre;family cinema
家庭作业 homework
家徒四壁 have nothing but the bare walls in one's house—be utterly destitute
家用电器 electrical home appliances;electrical household appliances
家喻户晓 known to every household;widely known;known to all
家贼难防 a thief within a house is hard to guard against
家长学校 parents' school
家长作风 high-handed way of dealing with people;patriarchal behaviour
家政服务 home management service;home-making service

J

家族企业 family firm
家和万事兴 if the family lives in harmony, all affairs will prosper; harmony in the family leads to prosperity in all undertakings
家书抵万金 a letter from home is worth ten thousand pieces of gold
家丑不可外扬 the disgrace of a family should never be spread without; do not give publicity to family scandals; don't wash your dirty linen in public
家庭财产保险 household property insurance
家庭服务公司 family service company
家家有本难念的经 every family has some sort of trouble; every family has its own hard nut to crack
家庭联产承包责任制 household contract responsibility system with remuneration linked to output

袈 [jiā]
袈裟 kasaya (a patchwork outer vestment worn by a Buddhist monk)

葭 [jiā]
名 young shoot of a reed; young reed

嘉 [jiā]
Ⅰ 形 good; nice; fine Ⅱ 动 praise; laud; commend
嘉宾 honoured guest; welcome guest
嘉奖 commend; cite
嘉礼 wedding ceremony
嘉勉 praise and encourage
嘉许 praise; approve
嘉言 nice words
嘉奖令 citation
嘉年华 carnival
嘉谋善政 excellent achievements in one's official post

jiá(ㄐㄧㄚˊ)

夹 [jiá]
形 double-layered; lined ⇒ jiā; gā
夹袄 lined jacket
夹被 double-layered quilt

荚 [jiá]
名 pod
荚果 pod; legume

戛 [jiá]
动 knock gently; tap
戛然 the loud cry of a bird
戛然而止 (of a sound, etc.) cease abruptly; come to an abrupt end
戛玉敲金 sonorous and pleasant tone

铗 [jiá]
名 ①pincers; pliers; tongs ②sword; sabre ③handle of a sword; hilt

颊 [jiá]
名 cheek
颊骨 cheekbone
颊囊 cheek pouch

jiǎ(ㄐㄧㄚˇ)

甲 [jiǎ]
Ⅰ 名 ①first of the ten Heavenly Stems ② (*used to refer to an unspecified person or thing*): 甲方与乙方 party A and party B ③ shell; carapace ④nail ⑤armour ⑥administrative unit of 10 households Ⅱ 区 A; first: 甲等 first-rate; first class
甲板 deck
甲苯 toluene; methylbenzene
甲虫 beetle
甲醇 methyl alcohol; methanol; wood spirit; wood alcohol
甲酚 cresol
甲基 methyl
甲壳 crust
甲醛 formaldehyde
甲酸 formic acid; methanoic acid
甲烷 methane
甲癣 onychomycosis; ringworm of the nails
甲鱼 soft-shelled turtle
甲胄 armour
甲子 a cycle of sixty years
甲紫 gentian violet
甲睾酮 methyltestosterone
甲沟炎 paronychia
甲骨文 inscriptions on bones or tortoise shells of the Shang Dynasty
甲级股 Alpha Stock
甲醛水 formalin
甲氧胺 methoxamine
甲状腺 thyroid gland
甲A联赛 Division One Group A soccer league
甲级联赛 major league
甲级战犯 top war criminal
甲壳动物 crustacean
甲午战争 the Sino-Japanese War of 1894 — 1895
甲型肝炎 hepatitis A
甲状腺素 thyroxine
甲状腺炎 thyroiditis; strumitis
甲状腺肿 goitre
甲基纤维素 methylcellulose
甲种活期存款 demand deposit A
甲状腺切开术 thyroidectomy
甲状腺功能亢进 hyperthyroidism

岬 [jiǎ]
名 ①cape; promontory; headland; ness ② space between two mountains; narrow passage between mountains; col
岬角 cape; promontory

胛 [jiǎ]
胛骨 shoulder blade

钾 [jiǎ]
〈名〉potassium（K）.
钾肥 potash fertilizer
钾碱 potash
钾盐 sylvite

假 [jiǎ]
I 〈形〉false；fake；bogus；counterfeit；sham；phoney II 〈动〉①suppose；presume；assume ②borrow；avail oneself of；make use of III 〈连〉if；in case ➡ jià
假案 fabricated case；slanderous case
假扮 disguise oneself as；dress up as
假币 counterfeit（ or bad, fake, fraudulent, queer）money；false coin
假唱 lip-synch
假钞 counterfeit money
假充 pretend to be；pose as
假道 via；by way of
假定 ① suppose；assume；grant；presume ② hypothesis
假发 wig
假根 rhizoid
假果 pseudocarp；spurious fruit
假花 artificial flower
假话 lie；falsehood
假货 fake goods；fake products
假借 make use of
假冒 pass oneself off as；palm off（a fake as genuine）
假寐 catnap；doze
假名 ①pseudonym ②kana（Japanese syllabic script）
假漆 varnish
假球 false play
假如 if；supposing；in case
假若 if；supposing；in case
假山 rockery
假设 ① suppose；assume；grant；presume ② hypothesis
假声 falsetto
假使 if；in case；in the event that
假释 parole；release on probation
假手 do sth through sb else；make a cat's-paw of sb
假摔 simulation
假说 hypothesis
假死 ① suspended animation ② play dead；feign death；play possum
假托 ① on the pretext of ② under sb else's name ③ by means of；through the medium of
假想 ① imagination；hypothesis；supposition ②imaginary；hypothetical；fictitious
假象 ①false appearance ②pseudomorph
假牙 dental prosthesis；false tooth；denture
假眼 ocular prosthesis；artificial eye；glass eye
假药 imitation medicine；fake medicine

假意 ①unction；insincerity；hypocrisy ②pretend；put on
假造 ①forge；counterfeit ②invent；fabricate
假账 false entry
假肢 artificial limb
假植 heel in
假装 pretend；feign；simulate；make believe
假大空 exaggeration and empty talk；boasting and empty talk；talk big and utter hollow words
假动作 deception；feint；dummy
假、恶、丑 the false，the bad and the ugly
假发票 provisional invoice；forged invoice
假分数 improper fraction
假合资 bogus joint venture
假离婚 fake divorce；sham divorce
假面具 mask；false front
假嗓子 falsetto
假释犯 parolee
假想敌 imaginary enemy；hypothetical foe
假小子 tomboy
假惺惺 hypocritically；unctuously
假正经 be hypocritical；pretend to be a saint
假支票 forged check；stumer
假传圣旨 deliver a false imperial edict—give a fake order
假公济私 use public office for private gain；practice jobbery；work for one's own ends in public affairs
假冒产品 fake products；phony products
假冒商标 counterfeit trademarks
假冒商品 counterfeit goods；fraudulent goods；phony goods
假面舞会 masked ball；masquerade
假仁假义 pretended benevolence and righteousness；hypocrisy
假设成交 assumptive close（of a deal）
假手于人（achieve one's end）through the instrumentality of sb else
假性近视 pseudomyopia
假冒伪劣产品 fake quality commodity
假破产、真逃债 evade payment of debts by declaring bankruptcy

jià（ㄐㄧㄚˋ）

价 [jià]
〈名〉①price ②value ③valence ➡ jiè；jie
价拨 undersell；sell at a reduced price；discount
价差 price differential
价格 price
价款 money paid for sth purchased or received for sth sold；cost
价码 listed price；marked price
价目 marked price；price
价钱 price

价位 price standing; current price; current standing of price; level of a price
价值 ①value ②worth; value
价格战 price war
价目表 price list
价值量 magnitude of value
价格标签 price tag
价格标准 price standards
价格波动 price volatility; price fluctuation
价格补贴 price subsidies; state subsidies to offset price
价格差别 price discrimination
价格大战 price war
价格倒挂 selling prices going below purchasing prices
价格低廉 low in price
价格反弹 rebound in price; price rebound
价格放开 price liberalization; price decontrol; relax rice control
价格公道 fair price; reasonable price
价格结构 price mechanism
价格扭曲 price distortion
价格趋涨 price tend upwards
价格双轨 double-track system in commodity price
价格弹性 price elasticity
价格体系 price system
价格体制 price system
价格调整 price readjustment; price regulation
价格同盟 price cartel
价格稳定 price steadiness
价格协定 price cartel
价格指数 price index number
价廉物美 bargain buy; (of a commodity) cheap but good; inexpensive but elegant
价值尺度 measure of value
价值工程 value engineering
价值观念 values
价值规律 law of value
价值决定 determination of value
价值取向 value orientation
价值形态 form of value
价格剪刀差 price scissors; scissors movement of price
价格可比性 price comparability
价格伸缩性 price flexibility
价格上涨因素 factors for price hike
价格调控目标责任制 responsibility system to attain objective in price readjustment and control

驾 [jià]
Ⅰ 勔 ①harness; draw (or pull) (a cart, etc.) ②drive; pilot; sail; ride Ⅱ 名 ①vehicle; carriage ②you ③emperor's carriage; emperor
驾崩 (of an emperor) pass away; die
驾到 arrival of a visitor

驾临 your arrival; your esteemed presence
驾龄 number of years of experience or service as car driver, airplane pilot, etc.
驾驶 drive (a vehicle); pilot (a ship or plane)
驾驭 ①drive (a cart, horse, etc.) ②control; master
驾辕 be harnessed in the shafts; be hitched up
驾驶舱 control cabin; cockpit; pilot's compartment
驾驶杆 control stick (or column); joystick
驾驶盘 steering wheel
驾驶室 driver's cab
驾驶台 bridge (of a ship)
驾驶员 driver (of a vehicle); pilot (of an airplane)
驾轻就熟 drive a light carriage on a familiar road—handle a job with ease because of previous experience; do a familiar job with ease
驾驶学校 driving school
驾驶执照 driving (or driver's) license

架 [jià]
Ⅰ 名 frame; shelf; hanger; stand; rack Ⅱ 勔 ①prop up; put up; erect ②fend off; ward off; withstand ③kidnap; abduct; take sb away forcibly ④support; help along ⑤fight; quarrel Ⅲ 量 (of sth with a stand or mechanism): 两架钢琴 two pianos/一架飞机 an airplane/一架葡萄 a cluster of grapes; a trellis of grapes
架次 sortie
架空 ①built on stilts ②impracticable; unpractical ③make sb a mere figurehead
架设 erect (above ground or water level, as on stilts or posts)
架势 posture; stance; manner
架子 ①frame; stand; rack ②framework; skeleton; outline ③airs; haughty manner ④posture; stance
架不住 ①cannot sustain (the weight); cannot stand (the pressure); cannot stand up against ②be no match for; cannot compete with
架得住 be able to bear (or endure)
架子车 handcart; two-wheeled cart pushed or pulled by one person
架子工 scaffolder
架空管道 overhead pipe
架子十足 put on airs of greatness; overbearing; on one's high horse

假 [jià]
名 ①holiday; vacation ②leave of absence; furlough ➡ jiǎ
假期 vacation; holiday; period of leave
假日 holiday; day off
假条 ①application for leave ②leave permit
假日经济 holiday economy

J

嫁 [jià]
劻 ①（of a woman）marry ②（of blame, loss,etc.）shift;transfer
嫁接 grafting;graft
嫁娶 marriage
嫁人 （of a woman）get married;marry
嫁妆 dowry;trousseau
嫁祸于人 shift the misfortune onto sb else;put the blame on sb else
嫁鸡随鸡,嫁狗随狗 follow the man you marry,be he fowl or cur

稼 [jià]
Ⅰ 劻 sow（grain）Ⅱ 名 cereals;crops
稼穑 sowing and reaping;farming;farm work

jiɑ (·ㄐㄧㄚ)

家 [jiɑ]
①used after certain nouns, indicating the category they come under：小孩子家别插嘴! You kids,stop cutting in! ②used after a man's name, referring to his wife：老二家 second son's wife/祥子家 Xiangzi's wife
➡ jiā;jie

jiān (ㄐㄧㄢ)

戋 [jiān]
形 small

尖 [jiān]
Ⅰ 形 ①pointed; tapering; sharp ②shrill; sharp; piercing ③sharp; acute; keen ④stingy; miserly; calculating ⑤sharp-tongued; caustic Ⅱ 劻 make（one's voice,etc.）shrill or sharp：尖着嗓子 in a shrill voice Ⅲ 名 ①point; tip; tapering end：钢笔尖儿 tip of a pen;point of a pen;pen-point ②best of its kind;pick of the bunch;cream of the crop：拔尖儿的 top-notch;pick of the bunch
尖兵 ①point ②trailblazer;pathbreaker;pioneer;vanguard
尖刀 sharp knife;dagger
尖顶 pinnacle
尖端 ①pointed end;acme;peak ②most advanced;sophisticated
尖叫 shriek;scream;yell;whoop
尖刻 acrimonious;caustic;biting
尖利 ①sharp;keen;cutting ②shrill;piercing
尖脐 ①the narrow triangular abdomen of a male crab ②male crab
尖锐 ①sharp-pointed ②penetrating;incisive; sharp;keen ③shrill;piercing ④intense;acute;sharp
尖酸 acrid;acrimonious;tart
尖子 ①the best of its kind; the pick of the bunch; the cream of the crop ②a sudden rise in pitch（in opera singing）
尖括号 angle brackets（〈〉）
尖锐化 sharpen;intensify;become more acute

尖子班 class of top students;class of talents
尖嘴钳 long flat nose pliers; nipper pliers; sharp-nose pliers
尖端产品 highly sophisticated products
尖端技术 sophisticated technology; cutting-edge technology
尖端科学 advanced science; most advanced branches of science;acme of science;frontiers of science;top-most science;the latest achievement of science
尖端武器 sophisticated weapons
尖声尖气 in a shrill voice
尖酸刻薄 tart and mean;bitterly sarcastic
尖嘴薄舌 have a caustic and flippant tongue
尖嘴猴腮 have a mouth that sticks out and a chin like an ape's—have a wretched appearance

奸 [jiān]
Ⅰ 形 ①wicked; evil; false; treacherous ②betray one's country（or monarch）;traitorous ③crafty; self-seeking and wily Ⅱ 名 ①traitor：为国除奸 rid the country of traitors（or collaborators）②illicit sexual relations;adultery
奸臣 treacherous court official
奸党 clique（or people）disloyal to the country（or monarch）;cabal
奸夫 adulterer
奸妇 adulteress
奸猾 treacherous;crafty;deceitful
奸计 an evil plot
奸佞 ①crafty and fawning ②crafty sycophant
奸情 adulterous affair
奸人 evildoer;malefactor
奸商 profiteer;dishonest trader;unscrupulous merchant
奸尸 necrophilia
奸徒 crafty person
奸污 rape（or seduce）
奸细 spy;enemy agent
奸险 wicked and crafty;treacherous;malicious
奸笑 sinister（or villainous）smile
奸邪 ①crafty and evil;treacherous ②a crafty and evil person
奸雄 a person who achieves high position by unscrupulous scheming;arch-careerist
奸淫 ①illicit sexual relations;adultery ②rape（or seduce）
奸贼 traitor;conspirator
奸诈 fraudulent;crafty;treacherous
奸淫掳掠 rape and loot

歼 [jiān]
劻 annihilate;wipe out;destroy
歼击 attack and wipe out
歼灭 annihilate;wipe out;destroy
歼击机 fighter plane;fighter;pursuit plane

坚 [jiān]
I 〔形〕 solid; hard; firm; strong II 〔名〕 armour; heavily fortified point; fortification; stronghold III 〔副〕 firmly; flatly; determinedly; resolutely

坚城 strongly defended city

坚持 persist in; persevere in; uphold; insist on; stick to; adhere to

坚定 ①firm; staunch; steadfast ②strengthen

坚固 firm; solid; sturdy; strong

坚果 nut

坚拒 flatly refuse; categorically reject

坚决 firm; resolute; determined

坚强 ①strong; firm; staunch ②strengthen

坚忍 steadfast and persevering (in face of difficulties)

坚韧 ①tough and tensile ②firm and tenacious

坚实 ①solid; substantial ②strong; robust

坚守 stick to; hold fast to; stand fast

坚挺 strong; firm

坚信 firmly believe

坚毅 firm and persistent; with unswerving determination; with inflexible will

坚硬 hard; solid

坚贞 faithful; constant

坚牢度 fastness

坚壁清野 strengthen defence works, evacuate noncombatants, and hide provisions and livestock; strengthen the defences and clear the fields

坚不可摧 indestructible; impregnable; indomitable

坚不能破 impregnable

坚持不懈 unremitting; persistent

坚持不渝 persistent; persevering

坚定不移 firm and unshakable; unswerving; unflinching

坚甲利兵 equipped with strong armour and sharp weapons; good armour and weapons

坚忍不拔 firm and indomitable; persistent and dauntless

坚如磐石 solid as a rock; rock-firm

坚守岗位 stand fast at one's post; stick to one's guns

坚信不移 firmly believe; have not the slightest doubt

坚贞不屈 remain faithful and unyielding

坚贞不渝 loyal through thick and thin

坚持改革开放 persevere in reform and opening policy

坚持四项基本原则 adhere to the four cardinal principles

间 [jiān]
I 〔名〕 ①space between ②(within) a definite time (or space) ③room II 〔量〕 used of smallest units of housing: 两间卧室 two bedrooms ➡jiàn

间架 ①framework of a house ②form of a Chinese character ③structure of an essay

间距 interval; separation; spacing

间冰期 interglacial stage; interglacial

间奏曲 ①entr'acte ②intermezzo

间不容发 not a hair's breadth apart or away—extremely critical

肩 [jiān]
I 〔名〕 shoulder II 〔动〕 ①undertake; shoulder; sustain; bear ②carry on the shoulder; shoulder

肩膀 shoulder

肩负 take on; undertake; shoulder; bear

肩头 ①on the shoulders ②shoulders

肩章 ①shoulder loop; shoulder strap ②epaulet

肩胛骨 scapula; shoulder blade

肩周炎 periarthritis

肩摩毂击 shoulder to shoulder and hub to hub—crowded with people and vehicles

艰 [jiān]
〔形〕 difficult; arduous; hard

艰巨 arduous; formidable

艰苦 arduous; difficult; hard; tough

艰难 difficult; hard

艰涩 involved and abstruse; intricate and obscure

艰深 difficult to understand; abstruse

艰危 difficulties and dangers (confronting a nation)

艰险 hardships and dangers

艰辛 hardships

艰苦备尝 have experienced all hardships; have suffered untold hardships

艰苦创业 start undertakings with painstaking efforts

艰苦朴素 hard work and plain living

艰苦卓绝 showing the utmost fortitude

艰难困苦 difficulties and hardships

艰难曲折 difficulties and setbacks

艰难险阻 difficulties and obstacles

艰难的历程 rough passage

艰苦创业精神 hardworking and enterprising (or pioneering) spirit

艰苦奋斗、勤俭建国 work hard and build the country through diligence and thrift

艰苦朴素的工作作风 style of hard work and plain living

监 [jiān]
I 〔动〕 supervise; inspect; watch; control II 〔名〕 prison; jail ➡jiàn

监测 monitor

监察 supervise; control

监场 invigilate (or monitor) at an examination

监督 ①supervise; superintend; control ②supervisor

监犯 prisoner;convict
监工 ①supervise;oversee ②overseer;supervisor
监管 supervise;keep watch on
监护 guardianship
监禁 take into custody;imprison;put in jail (*or* prison)
监考 ①invigilate ②invigilator
监控 monitor and control
监牢 prison;jail
监理 ①supervise and manage an engineering project ②supervisor
监事 supervisor;member of board of supervisors
监视 keep watch on;keep a lookout over
监守 have custody of;guard;take care of
监听 listen in;monitor;wiretapping
监狱 prison;jail
监制 supervise the manufacture of
监测器 monitor
监察员 supervisor;controller
监督权 authority to supervise;supervise role; watchdog role;right of supervision
监督员 intendant;supervisor;monitor
监护人 guardian
监票员 controller of ballots
监事会 board of supervisors
监视器 monitor
监视人 guard;sentinel
监视哨 lookout post;lookout
监听器 monitor
监狱长 warden
监察制度 supervisory system
监督部门 supervisory department;watchdog
监督程序 monitor program
监督电话 complaint telephone number
监督机关 supervisory institution
监督劳动 do penal labour under surveillance
监视雷达 surveillance radar
监守自盗 steal what is entrusted to one's care;embezzle;defalcate
监外就医 undergo medical treatment outside the prison under surveillance
监外执行 serve a sentence outside jail;execute (a sentence) outside prison
监狱暴动 prison riot
监察委员会 control commission;supervisory committee
监听无线电台 monitoring station

兼 [jiān]
Ⅰ 形 double;twice Ⅱ 副 simultaneously; concurrently
兼备 have both...and...
兼并 annex (territory,property,etc.)
兼程 travel at double speed
兼顾 give consideration to (*or* take account of) two or more things

兼管 be also in charge of
兼课 ①do some teaching in addition to one's main occupation ②hold two or more teaching jobs concurrently
兼任 ①hold a concurrent post ②part-time
兼容 compatible
兼优 be good in more than one field
兼之 furthermore;besides;moreover;in addition
兼职 ①hold two or more posts concurrently ②concurrent post;part-time job
兼容机 compatible computer
兼容性 compatibility
兼而有之 have both at the same time
兼容并包 all-embracing;all-inclusive
兼收并蓄 incorporate things of diverse nature;take in everything
兼职教师 part-time teacher
兼容信息系统 compatible information system
兼听则明,偏信则暗 listen to both sides and you will be enlightened;heed only one side and you will be benighted

菅 [jiān]
名 villous themeda

笺 [jiān]
名 ①annotation;commentary ②writing paper ③letter
笺注 notes and commentary on ancient texts

渐 [jiān]
动 ①soak;be saturated with;imbue ②flow into ➡ jiàn

犍 [jiān]
名 bullock;castrated bull
犍牛 bullock

缄 [jiān]
动 seal;close
缄口 keep one's mouth shut;hold one's tongue;say nothing
缄默 keep silent;be reticent

搛 [jiān]
动 pick up (with chopsticks)

煎 [jiān]
Ⅰ 动 ①fry in shallow oil ②simmer in water;decoct Ⅱ 量 decoction
煎熬 suffering;torture;torment
煎饼 thin pancake made of millet flour,etc.

缣 [jiān]
名 fine silk

鹣 [jiān]
名 pair of lovebirds—fabulous birds each with one eye and one wing and always having to fly together
鹣鲽情深 be deeply in love

jiǎn (ㄐㄧㄢˇ)

囝 [jiǎn]
名 ①son ②child

拣 [jiǎn]

〔动〕①choose；select；pick ②collect；gather
拣选 select；choose
拣便宜 get a bargain；gain a small advantage

茧 [jiǎn]

〔名〕①cocoon ②callus
茧绸 pongee
茧丝 bave
茧衣 husks；frison
茧子 silkworm cocoon

柬 [jiǎn]

〔名〕card；note；letter
柬帖 note；short letter

俭 [jiǎn]

〔形〕thrifty；frugal
俭朴 thrifty and simple；economical
俭省 economical；thrifty
俭约 economical；thrifty；frugal；sparing

捡 [jiǎn]

〔动〕pick up；collect；gather
捡漏儿 repair the leaky part of a roof；plug a leak in the roof
捡破烂儿 pick odds and ends from refuse heaps
捡拾压捆机 pick-up bale；pick-up press
捡了芝麻，丢了西瓜 pick up the sesame seeds but overlook the watermelons—concentrate on minor matters to the neglect of major ones

检 [jiǎn]

〔动〕①check up；inspect；examine ②restrain oneself；be careful in one's conduct ③pick up；collect
检波 detection
检测 test；examine；check up
检查 ① check up；inspect；examine ② self-criticism
检察 procuratorial work
检点 ①examine；check ②be cautious (about what one says or does)
检定 examine and determine
检获 search and seize；capture；root out
检举 report (an offence) to the authorities；inform against (an offender)；accuse
检控 ①investigate (criminal activities) ②inform against；accuse；charge
检漏 leak hunting
检票 ①examine tickets (or ballots)；counting of ballots ②check in
检试 (of machines, facilities, installations, etc.) test；examine；inspect
检视 check up；examine
检索 refer to；look up
检讨 ①self-criticism ②examine；inspect
检修 examine and repair；overhaul
检验 test；examine；inspect
检疫 quarantine
检阅 review (troops, etc.)；inspect

检查哨 checkpost
检查团 inspection party
检查站 checkpoint；checkpost；inspection station
检察官 public procurator (or prosecutor)
检察院 procuratorate
检察长 chief procurator；public procurator-general
检举人 informant；accuser
检举箱 a box for accusation letters
检举信 letter of accusation；written accusation
检视窗 inspection window
检视孔 peep hole；sight hole；sight stop
检验费 survey fees
检验师 labouratorian
检验室 checkout room
检验员 inspector；inspecting officer
检疫旗 quarantine flag；yellow flag
检疫员 quarantine officer
检疫站 quarantine station
检阅台 reviewing stand
检字表 word index (in a dictionary)
检字法 the way in which Chinese characters are arranged and are to be located (as in a dictionary)；indexing system for Chinese characters
检察机关 procuratorial organ
检疫证明书 quarantine certificate；vaccination certificate；yellow book

趼 [jiǎn]

〔名〕callus

减 [jiǎn]

〔动〕①subtract；deduct；minus ②reduce；diminish；decrease；cut
减半 reduce by half
减编 staff reduction
减仓 sell shares
减产 reduction of output；drop in production
减低 reduce；lower；bring down；cut
减法 subtraction
减肥 reduce weight；slim；lose weight；downsize
减幅 range of decrease；decrease；amount of cut
减负 alleviate burdens on sb；lighten the burden
减号 minus sign (-)
减河 distributary
减缓 retard；slow down
减价 reduce (or lower) the prices；mark down
减亏 reduce a deficit；deficit reduction
减免 ①mitigate or annul (a punishment) ②reduce or remit (taxation, etc.)
减摩 antifriction
减轻 lighten；ease；alleviate；mitigate
减让 reduce；offer discounts

减弱 weaken;abate
减色 lose lustre;impair the excellence of;detract from the merit of
减少 reduce;decrease;lessen;cut down
减数 subtrahend
减税 tax reduction
减速 slow down;decelerate;retard
减缩 reduce;cut down;retrench
减退 drop;go down
减薪 reduce salary
减刑 reduce a penalty;reduce a sentence;commute (*or* mitigate) a sentence
减压 reduce pressure;decompress
减员 depletion of numbers (in the armed forces,etc.)
减灾 reduce natural disasters;disaster reduction;disaster alleviation
减震 shock absorption;damping
减肥操 slimming exercises
减肥茶 weight-reducing tea
减肥药 weight-reduction medicine;loss medicine
减色法 subtractive process (in cinematography)
减声器 muffler
减速度 deceleration
减速剂 moderator
减速伞 drag (*or* deceleration) parachute
减肥中心 health spa;weight-control centre
减亏增盈 reduce losses and increase profits
减免税收 exempt sb from taxation
减税让利 reduce tax burden and give more benefits to enterprises;reduce tax on enterprises and allow them to retain more profits
减速副翼 deceleron
减速火箭 retro-rocket
减速运动 retarded motion
减员增效 downsize for efficiency;cut payroll to improve efficiency;increase efficiency by reducing staff
减少流通环节 cut down on circulation intermediaries
减少盲目投资 reduce blind investment
减少税收流失 reduce tax losses
减少关税和非关税壁垒 reduce tariff and non-tariff barriers

剪 [jiǎn]
Ⅰ 图 ①scissors;shears;clippers ②scissor-shaped tool Ⅱ 动 ①cut (with scissors);clip;trim ②wipe out;exterminate
剪报 newspaper cutting (*or* clipping)
剪裁 ①cut out (a garment);tailor ②cut out unwanted material (from a piece of writing);prune
剪彩 cut the ribbon at an opening ceremony
剪除 wipe out;annihilate;exterminate

剪床 shearing machine
剪刀 scissors;shears
剪掉 cut off;scissor off
剪断 cut off;nip;snip
剪发 have one's hair cut
剪辑 ①film montage;film editing ②editing and rearrangement
剪接 film montage;film editing
剪开 cut open
剪毛 shearing;clipping
剪票 punch a ticket
剪切 shearing
剪贴 ①clip and paste (sth out of a newspaper,etc.) in a scrapbook (*or* on cards) ②cutting out (as school-children's activity) ③cut and paste
剪影 ①paper-cut silhouette ②outline;sketch
剪纸 paper-cut;scissor-cut
剪子 scissors;shears;clippers
剪边机 end shears;squaring shears;trimming machine
剪草机 grass mower;grass-mowing machine;lawn mower
剪窗花 cut paper for window decoration
剪刀差 scissors movement of prices;scissors differential (*or* difference);price scissors
剪票铗 conductor's punch
剪贴板 clipboard
剪贴簿 scrapbook
剪应力 shearing stress
剪烛谈心 snuff the candles and converse freely

碱 [jiǎn]
图 alkali;soda

捡 [jiǎn]
动 cut off;separate

睑 [jiǎn]
图 eyelid
睑腺炎 sty

锏 [jiǎn]
图 mace ➡jiàn

裥 [jiǎn]
图 folds (in clothes,etc.)

简 [jiǎn]
Ⅰ 形 simple;succinct;terse;brief Ⅱ 动 ①simplify;abridge;make sth simpler ②select;choose Ⅲ 图 ①bamboo slip ②note;letter
简拔 select and promote
简报 bulletin;brief report
简本 concise edition
简编 short course;concise edition
简便 simple and convenient;handy
简称 the abbreviated form of a name;abbreviation
简单 ①simple;uncomplicated ②oversimplified;casual
简短 brief
简化 simplify

J

简洁 succinct;terse;pithy
简捷 simple and direct;forthright
简介 brief introduction;synopsis;summarized account
简括 brief but comprehensive;compendious
简历 biographical notes;curriculum vitae (cv);résumé
简练 terse;succinct;pithy
简陋 simple and crude
简略 simple (in content);brief;sketchy
简慢 negligent
简明 simple and clear;concise
简朴 simple and unadorned;plain
简谱 numbered musical notation
简图 sketch;diagram
简写 ①write a Chinese character in simplified form ②simplify a book for beginners
简讯 news in brief
简要 concise and to the point;brief
简仪 abridged armilla
简易 ①simple and easy ②simply constructed;simply equipped;unsophisticated
简约 brief;concise;sketchy
简章 general regulations
简直 simply;at all
简装 simple packing
简单化 oversimplify
简分数 common fraction;single fraction
简体字 simplified Chinese character
简写本 simplified edition
简易房 lightly constructed and simply equipped building
简易楼 economy building
简单多数 simple majority;bare majority
简单明了 simple and clear;brief and clear
简而言之 in brief;in short;to put it in a nutshell
简化汉字 ① simplify Chinese characters ② simplified Chinese characters
简化手续 simplify the formalities (or procedures);cut red tape
简明扼要 brief and to the point;concise
简明新闻 news in brief
简谐运动 simple harmonic motion
简易病房 simply equipped ward
简易读物 easy reader
简易公路 simply-built highway
简易机场 airstrip
简易仲裁 arbitration by summary procedure
简政放权 simplify (or streamline) the administration and delegate more decision-making powers to lower levels
简单再生产 simple reproduction
简化审批环节 streamline (or simplify) the procedures for examination and approval

戬 [jiǎn]
I 动 get rid of;wipe out II 形 lucky;propitious

碱 [jiǎn]
I 名 ①alkali;base ②soda II 动 alkalinize;base
碱地 alkaline land
碱化 alkalization;basification
碱性 basicity;alkalinity
碱处理 alkali treatment
碱金属 alkali (or alkaline) metal
碱式盐 basic salt
碱土金属 alkaline-earth metal
碱性反应 alkaline reaction

蹇 [jiǎn]
I 形 ①lame;crippled ②not smooth-going;unlucky;hapless II 名 donkey;inferior horse

謇 [jiǎn]
I 动 stutter;stammer II 形 upright

jiàn（ㄐㄧㄢˋ）

见 [jiàn]
I 动 ①see;behold;witness;catch sight of ②meet with;be exposed to ③show evidence of;appear (or seem) to be ④refer to;see;vide ⑤meet;receive;call on;see II 名 view;opinion;依我之见 in my opinion;to my mind III 助 ①(used before a verb to express the passive idea):见重于当时 be held in esteem by his contemporaries ②(used before a verb to express the request that others would do sth for one)
见报 appear in the newspapers
见长 [jiàncháng] be good at;be expert in
见地 insight;judgment
见方 square
见怪 mind;take offence
见鬼 ①fantastic;preposterous;absurd ②go to hell
见好 (of a patient's condition) get better;mend
见机 as the opportunity arises;as befits the occasion;according to circumstances
见教 favour me with your advice;instruct me;ask to benefit from sb's advice
见解 view;opinion;understanding
见老 be aged
见谅 excuse me;forgive me
见面 meet;see
见弃 be rejected;be discarded
见俏 saleable
见上 see above;vide supra
见识 [jiànshi] ①widen one's knowledge;enrich one's experience ②experience;knowledge;sensibleness
见外 regard sb as an outsider
见旺 sell well
见闻 what one sees and hears;knowledge;information

见习 learn on the job;be on probation
见下 see below;vide infra
见笑①laugh at（me or us）②incur ridicule（by one's poor performance）.
见效 become effective;produce the desired result
见长 [jiànzhǎng] grow perceptibly
见证 witness;testimony
见不得①not to be exposed to;unable to stand ②not fit to be seen or revealed
见分晓 be clear;be sorted out;clear up（a matter or doubts）;find a solution
见面礼 a present given to sb on first meeting him
见面熟 hail-fellow-well-met
见上帝 go to see God—go the way of all flesh;die
见世面 see the world;enrich one's experience
见习生 probationer
见证人 eyewitness;witness
见财起意 entertain evil thoughts at the sight of money
见多识广 experienced and knowledgeable
见风是雨 take wind as the forerunner of rain—jump to hasty conclusions
见风转舵 trim one's sails
见缝插针 stick in a pin wherever there's room—make use of every bit of time or space
见过世面 have seen much of life;have seen the world;have experienced life
见机行事 act according to circumstances;do as one sees fit;use one's discretion
见景生情 have one's emotion aroused by the scene
见利思义 remember what is right at the sight of profit
见利忘义 forget what is right at the sight of profit
见猎心喜 thrill to see one's favourite sport and itch to have a go
见马克思 go to see Marx—breathe one's last;pass away
见票即付 payable at sight;payable to bearer
见钱眼开 be wide-eyed at the sight of money—greedy
见人就问 ask everybody one meets
见仁见智 different people, different views;opinions differ
见势不妙 see the danger of what is being done
见数就晕 be poor in accounting
见死不救 not try to save sb who is in mortal danger;be impervious to other people's misfortunes（or disasters）
见所未见 see what one has never seen before
见危授命 be ready to die for one's country when it is in danger

见微知著 from the first small beginnings one can see how things will develop;from one small clue one can see what is coming
见闻广博 well-informed; have extensive knowledge
见习领事 student consul
见习医生 intern
见贤思齐 when you meet someone better than yourself, turn your thoughts to becoming his equal
见血封喉 upas
见义勇为 have the courage to do righteous things;defy（or brave）danger to fight with evil;run the risk to uphold or defend whatever one thinks is right
见异思迁 change one's mind the moment one sees sth new;be inconstant
见树不见林 not see the wood for the trees
见物不见人 see things but not people;see only material factors, not human ones
见习技术员 technician on probation
见不得人的勾当 under-the-table deal
见怪不怪,其怪自败 face the fearful with no fears, and its fearfulness disappears

件 [jiàn] I 量 piece II 名 ① things that can be counted:大件儿 big piece ②letter;correspondence;paper;document

间 [jiàn] I 名①space（or time）in between;break;opening ②enmity;estrangement;discord:团结无间 united as one II 动①separate;intersperse:晴雨相间 wet days alternated with fine days ② sow discord ③ thin out（seedlings）➡jiān

间谍 spy
间断 be disconnected;be interrupted
间隔 interval;intermission
间或 occasionally;now and then;sometimes;once in a while
间接 indirect;secondhand
间苗 thin out seedlings（or young shoots）
间隙 ①interval;gap;space ②clearance
间歇 intermittence;intermission
间杂 be intermingled;be mixed
间作 intercropping
间谍网 espionage network
间断性 discontinuity
间隔号 separation dot
间接税 indirect tax
间歇泉 intermittent spring
间歇热 intermittent fever
间谍飞机 spy plane
间谍卫星 spy satellite
间接宾语 indirect object
间接地址 indirect address
间接肥料 indirect fertilizer

J

间接接触 mediate contacts
间接经验 indirect experience
间接贸易 indirect trade
间接损害 indirect damage
间接推理 mediate inference
间接消费 indirect consumption
间接选举 indirect election
间接引语 indirect speech
间接原因 remote cause
间接证据 circumstantial evidence
间歇喷泉 geyser
间作套种 interplanting
间接分摊法 step down method; step-ladder method

饯 [jiàn]
Ⅰ 〔动〕 give a farewell dinner Ⅱ 〔名〕 candy (fruit)
饯别 give a farewell dinner
饯行 give a farewell dinner

建 [jiàn]
〔动〕 ①build; construct; erect ②establish; set up; found ③propose; put forward; advocate
建材 building materials
建仓 buy in
建策 offer advice; give counsel
建党 ①found (*or* form) a political party ② build up the Party
建点 lay foundations; set up (an organization); do pioneering work
建都 found a capital; make (a place) the capital
建功 do a deed of merit; perform meritorious service
建构 frame; construct
建国 ①found (*or* establish) a state ②build up a country
建交 establish diplomatic relations
建军 ①found an army ②build up the army
建兰 sword-leaved cymbidium
建立 build; establish; set up; found
建设 build; construct
建树 make a contribution; contribute
建议 ①propose; suggest; recommend ②proposal; suggestion; recommendation
建造 build; construct; make
建账 keep accounts
建制 organizational system
建筑 ①build; construct; erect ②building; structure; edifice ③architecture
建军节 Army Day
建设性 constructive
建筑群 architectural complex
建筑师 architect
建筑物 building; structure
建筑学 architecture
建筑业 building industry
建成投产 be up and running

建设公债 public bonds for construction
建设银行 China Construction Bank
建设周期 construction cycle
建议价格 suggested price
建筑材料 building materials
建筑工地 building site; construction site
建筑工人 building worker; builder
建筑红线 property line
建筑面积 built-up area; floorage
建筑设计 architectural design
建筑造价 construction costs
建设性意见 constructive suggestions
建筑工程学 architectural engineering
建设性的战略伙伴关系 constructive strategic partnership
建设有中国特色的社会主义 build socialism with Chinese characteristics

荐 [jiàn]
Ⅰ 〔动〕 ①recommend; introduce ②sacrifice; devote Ⅱ 〔名〕 ①grass; straw ②straw mat
荐举 propose sb for an office; recommend
荐贤 recommend persons of virtue and ability
荐引 recommend; introduce
荐优 recommend the excellent

贱 [jiàn]
Ⅰ 〔形〕 ① low-priced; inexpensive; cheap ② lowly; common; humble ③ low-down; mean; base; despicable ④my Ⅱ 〔动〕 look down upon; despise; contemn
贱货 ① cheap goods ② miserable (*or* contemptible) wretch
贱民 ① people of the lowest social strata ② untouchables
贱内 my (humble) wife
贱人 slut
贱骨头 miserable (*or* contemptible) wretch
贱相毕露 One's bad countenance is flatly revealed.

剑 [jiàn]
〔名〕 sword; sabre
剑客 chivalrous swordsman (in old novels)
剑麻 sisal hemp
剑眉 straight eyebrows slanting upwards and outwards; dashing eyebrows
剑术 swordsmanship; fencing skill
剑侠 chivalrous swordsman (in old novels)
剑拔弩张 with swords drawn and bows bent; at daggers drawn
剑眉倒竖 peak one's eyebrows
剑桥商务英语证书考试 Cambridge Business English Certificate

涧 [jiàn]
〔名〕 ravine; gully; mountain cleft

监 [jiàn]
〔名〕 imperial office ➡jiān

健 [jiàn]
Ⅰ 〔形〕 healthy; robust; strong Ⅱ 〔动〕 ① strengthen; toughen; fortify; invigorate ② be

strong in；be good at
健步 walk with vigorous strides
健儿 ①valiant fighter ②good athlete
健饭 healthy appetite
健将 master sportsman；top-notch player
健康 ①health；physique ②healthy；sound
健美 ① strong and handsome；vigorous and graceful ②body-building
健脑 be good for the brain
健全 ①sound；perfect ②strengthen；amplify；perfect
健商 health quotient
健身 keeping fit；body-building
健肾 invigorate the function of the kidney
健谈 be a good talker；be a brilliant conversationalist
健体 be healthy and strong；strengthen the body
健忘 forgetful；having a bad memory
健旺 healthy and vigorous
健羡 admire very much
健在（of a person of advanced age）be still living and in good health
健壮 healthy and strong；robust
健美操 aerobics dancing；aerobic dance
健身操 calisthenics；body-building exercises；figure-gymnastics；circuit
健身房 palaestra；gymnasium；gym
健身器 fitness（or body-building）equipment
健忘症 amnesia
健胃药 stomachicus；stomachic tonic
健步如飞 walk as if on wings；walk fast and vigorously
健美比赛 body-building championship；body-building competition
健美体操 callisthenics
健美运动 body-building
健脾益肺 strengthening spleen and tonifying lung
健全法制 improve the legal system
健身路径 workout path
健身运动 body-building
健身中心 fitness centre
健康证明书 health certificate
健全交易秩序 ensure orderly transactions

舰 [jiàn]
名 warship；naval vessel；man-of-war
舰船 ships and warships
舰队 fleet；naval force
舰艇 naval ships and boats；naval vessels
舰载 carrier-borne；carrier-based；ship-based
舰长 captain（of a warship）
舰只 warships；naval vessels
舰首炮 bow chaser
舰尾炮 stern chaser
舰载机 carrier-based aircraft
舰载飞机 carrier-borne aircraft；carrier air-craft
舰对空导弹 ship-to-air missile

渐 [jiàn]
副 gradually；little by little；by degrees ➡jiān
渐次 gradually；one after another
渐渐 gradually；by degrees；little by little
渐进 advance gradually；progress step by step
渐显 fade in
渐隐 fade out
渐缩管 reducing pipe
渐入佳境（of a situation）be improving；be getting better

谏 [jiàn]
动 expostulate with（one's superior or friend）；admonish

践 [jiàn]
动 ①trample；tread ②act on；carry out；execute
践诺 keep one's promise；keep one's word
践踏 tread on；trample underfoot
践言 keep one's promise；keep one's word
践约 keep a promise；keep an appointment

锏 [jiàn]
名 iron protection for a wheel axle ➡jiǎn

毽 [jiàn]
名 shuttlecock
毽子 shuttlecock

腱 [jiàn]
名 tendon
腱鞘 tendon sheath
腱子（beef or mutton）shank
腱鞘炎 tenosynovitis

溅 [jiàn]
动 splash；spatter；splatter
溅落（of a space vehicle，etc.）splash down
溅落点 splash point

鉴 [jiàn]
Ⅰ 名 ①ancient bronze mirror ②warning；forewarning；object lesson Ⅱ 动 ①reflect；mirror ② inspect；survey；scrutinize；examine；赏鉴 appreciate（an artistic work，etc.）③form of address at the very beginning of a letter
鉴别 distinguish；differentiate；discriminate
鉴定 ① appraisal（of a person's strong and weak points）②appraise；identify；authenticate；determine ③expert evaluation
鉴戒 warning；object lesson
鉴评 appraise；judge
鉴认 authenticate；verify
鉴赏 appreciate
鉴于 in view of；seeing that
鉴证 appraise and verify
鉴别器 discriminator
鉴定会 appraisal meeting
鉴定书 testimonial；written appraisal
鉴戒会 appraising meeting

键 [jiàn]

〔名〕①key ②metal bolt（of a door）③key（of a typewriter, piano, etc.）④bond

键槽 keyway; key slot; key seat
键盘 keyboard; fingerboard
键入 key in
键控穿孔 key-punch
键盘乐器 keyboard instrument
键钮式电话 touch-tone phone

槛 [jiàn]

〔名〕①banister; balustrade ②cage ➡kǎn

槛车 prisoner's cage-van

僭 [jiàn]

〔动〕exceed one's responsibility of office; usurp

僭号 adopt an illegal title
僭位 usurp the throne
僭越 overstep one's authority; go beyond proper bounds

箭 [jiàn]

〔名〕①arrow ②distance covered by a flying arrow

箭步 a sudden big stride forward
箭杆 arrow shaft
箭号 arrow
箭翎 arrow horn; vane
箭楼 an embrasured watchtower over a city gate
箭筒 quiver (for arrows)
箭头 ①arrowhead ②arrow (as a sign)
箭猪 porcupine
箭镞 metal arrowhead
箭靶子 target for archery
箭不虚发 every shot tells
箭如雨下 a shower of arrows; a storm of arrows
箭无虚发 No arrow is shot in vain. or Not a single arrow missed its target.
箭在弦上, 不得不发 an arrow fitted to the bowstring cannot avoid being discharged—one cannot but go ahead; one has reached the point of no return

jiāng（ㄐㄧㄤ）

江 [jiāng]

〔名〕①river ②the Changjiang（or Yangtze）River

江岸 river bank
江北 north of the River—a region including parts of Jiangsu and Anhui which are north of the Changjiang River
江湖 ① rivers and lakes—all corners of the country; the wide world ② rivers and lakes—people wandering from place to place and living by their wits, e.g. fortune-tellers, quack doctors, itinerant entertainers, etc., considered as a social group

江轮 river steamer
江米 polished glutinous rice
江南 south of the River—a region in the lower Changjiang River valley, including southern Jiangsu and Anhui and northern Zhejiang
江山 ① rivers and mountains; land; landscape ② country; state power
江豚 black finless porpoise
江珧 pen shell
江湖气 worldly-wise; slippery; sleek
江米酒 fermented glutinous rice
江珧柱 the dried adductor of a pen shell
江河日下 go from bad to worse; be on the decline
江湖好汉 a good fellow of the rivers and lakes; a bravo of river and lake
江湖骗术 quackery; quack methods
江湖骗子 swindler; charlatan
江湖医生 quack; mountebank
江湖艺人 itinerant entertainer
江郎才尽 a writer written out
江洋大盗 a great robber
江山易改, 本性难移 it's easy to change rivers and mountains but hard to change a person's nature

将 [jiāng]

Ⅰ〔动〕①support; take; bring ②take care of（one's health）③（animals）give birth to; breed ④do sth; deal with; handle（a matter）⑤（in chess）check ⑥put sb on the spot ⑦incite; challenge; spur; prod Ⅱ〔介〕① with; by means of; by ②（used to introduce the object before the verb）: 将精华与糟粕分开 separate the essence from the dross Ⅲ〔副〕① going to; about to; will; shall ② besides; also Ⅳ〔助〕（used between a verb and an objective complement）: 哭将起来 begin to weep ➡jiàng; qiāng

将近 close to; nearly; almost
将就 make do with; make the best of; put up with
将军 ① general ②（Chinese chess）check ③ put sb on the spot; embarrass; challenge
将来 future
将养 rest; recuperate
将要 going to; will; shall
将军肚 pot belly; big belly; beer belly
将错就错 leave a mistake uncorrected and make the best of it
将功补过 atone for faults by good deeds; make amends for one's faults by good deeds
将功赎罪 atone for a crime by good deeds; expiate one's guilt by good deeds
将功折罪 expiate one's crime by good deeds
将己比人 compare oneself to another
将计就计 meet plot with plot; turn sb's trick against him; beat sb at his own game

将勤补拙 make up for lack of skill with (*or* by) industry

将心比心 put oneself in sb's shoes; think of others; be empathic

将心换心 to win other people's hearts by one's sincerity

将信将疑 half believing, half doubting

将欲取之，必先与之 give in order to take

姜 [jiāng] 名 ginger

姜黄 turmeric

姜汤 ginger tea

姜片虫 fasciolopsis

姜还是老的辣 old ginger is hotter than new—veterans are abler than recruits

豇 [jiāng]

豇豆 cowpea

浆 [jiāng] Ⅰ 名 thick liquid Ⅱ 动 starch

浆果 berry

浆纱 sizing

浆洗 wash and starch

浆纸机 papermaking coating machine

僵 [jiāng] Ⅰ 形 ①stiff; rigid; numb ②deadlocked Ⅱ 名 impasse; stagnation Ⅲ 动 stop smiling; look stern

僵持 (of both parties) refuse to budge

僵化 become rigid; ossify; stereotyped

僵局 deadlock; impasse; stalemate

僵尸 corpse

僵死 dead; ossified

僵卧 lie stiff and motionless

僵硬 ①stiff ②rigid; inflexible

僵直 stiff and rigid

僵化思想 fossilized thinking

缰 [jiāng] 名 reins; halter

缰绳 reins; halter

礓 [jiāng]

◇砂礓 conglomerate

疆 [jiāng] 名 boundary; border; frontier

疆场 battlefield

疆界 boundary; border

疆土 territory

疆域 territory; domain

jiǎng（丩一ㄤ）

讲 [jiǎng] Ⅰ 动 ① speak; talk; say; tell ② explain; make clear; interpret ③ discuss; negotiate ④ stress; pay attention to; consider; be particular about Ⅱ 介 as to; concerning; with regard to

讲法 ①the way of saying a thing; wording ② statement; version; argument

讲稿 the draft (*or* text) of a speech; lecture notes

讲和 make peace; settle a dispute; become reconciled

讲话 ①speak; talk; address ②speech; talk ③ talks

讲价 ①haggle over the price; bargain ②negotiate the terms; insist on the fulfilment of certain conditions

讲解 explain

讲究 ①be particular about; pay attention to; stress; strive for ② exquisite; tasteful ③ careful study

讲课 teach; lecture

讲理 ①reason with sb; argue ②listen (*or* be amenable) to reason; be reasonable; be sensible

讲明 explain; make clear; state explicitly

讲评 comment on and appraise

讲情 intercede; plead for sb

讲求 be particular about; pay attention to; stress; strive for

讲师 lecturer

讲授 lecture; instruct; teach

讲述 tell about; give an account of; narrate; relate

讲台 platform; dais; rostrum

讲坛 ①(speaker's) platform; rostrum ②forum (for public discussion)

讲堂 lecture room; classroom

讲题 topic of a lecture

讲习 lecture and study

讲学 give lectures; discourse on an academic subject

讲演 ①give a speech (*or* lecture) ②speech; lecture

讲义 (mimeographed or printed) teaching materials

讲桌 lectern

讲座 a course of lectures

讲大局 stress the overall (*or* general) interests (*or* situation); take the overall interests (*or* situation) into account

讲解员 guide; announcer; narrator; commentator

讲排场 go in for ostentation and extravagance; put up a show; be ostentatious

讲师团 lecturers' group; teaching corps; lecturing team

讲习班 study group

讲习所 institute

讲义气 set store by personal loyalty (*or* friendship)

讲究效益 pay close attention to results

讲求实效 stress practical results; strive for practical results

讲诚信，反欺诈 honour credibility and oppose

cheating

讲党性,讲原则 stress Party spirit and principles

讲学习,讲政治,讲正气 emphasis on three things: study, politics and integrity; stress the need to study, to be politically minded and to be honest and upright; stress study, politics and healthy tendencies; place emphasis on study, politics and healthy tendencies

奖 [jiǎng]
I 动 praise; commend; encourage; reward
II 名 award; bonus; prize; reward
奖杯 cup (as a prize)
奖惩 rewards and punishments; rewards and penalties
奖级 grade of prizes (*or* awards)
奖金 bonus; incentive pay; incentive compensation; money award; bonus; premium
奖励 encourage and reward; award; reward
奖牌 medal
奖品 prize; award; trophy
奖旗 banner (as an award)
奖券 lottery ticket
奖赏 award; reward
奖售 encourage sales to the state
奖台 temporary platform (*or* stage) on which prizes are awarded to the winners; presentation stage (*or* platform)
奖项 prize
奖掖 reward and promote; encourage by promoting and rewarding
奖章 medal; decoration
奖状 certificate of merit
奖学金 scholarship; exhibition
奖惩制度 system of reward and penalty
奖励工资 incentive pay; premium wages; reward wages
奖励制度 system of reward
奖勤罚懒 reward the diligent and punish the lazy
奖优罚劣 reward the good and punish the bad
奖金分配制度 reward distribution system

桨 [jiǎng]
名 oar

耩 [jiǎng]
动 sow with a drill

jiàng (ㄐㄧㄤ)

匠 [jiàng]
名 ① craftsman; artisan ② person of remarkable achievements in a particular field; master
匠气 unimaginative craftsmanship
匠人 artisan; craftsman
匠心 ingenuity; craftsmanship
匠心独具 have great originality

降 [jiàng]
动 ① go down; fall; drop; lose ② lower; reduce ➡ xiáng
降低 reduce; cut down; drop; lower
降调 falling tune; falling tone
降幅 (of prices, profits, income, etc.) range of decrease
降格 lower one's standard or status
降号 flat (b)
降耗 reduce consumption; cut down on consumption
降级 ① reduce to a lower rank; demote ② send (a student) to a lower grade
降价 reduce (*or* lower) the prices
降临 befall; arrive; come
降落 descend; land
降旗 lower a flag
降生 (of the founder of a religion, etc.) be born
降水 precipitation
降温 ① lower the temperature (as in a workshop) ② drop in temperature
降雪 fall of snow
降压 step-down
降雨 a fall of rain; rainfall
降旨 issue an imperial edict
降半旗 hoist a flag at half-mast
降落场 landing field
降落伞 parachute
降水量 precipitation
降压片 hypertension pill
降雨量 rainfall
降低成色 debasement
降低能耗 reduce (*or* lower) the consumption (*or* use) of energy
降格录取 admit sb by lowering the standard
降格以求 fall back on sth inferior to what one hoped for; settle for a second best
降级留用 degrade in rank but retain in office
降低关税总水平 bring down the overall tariff level

虹 [jiàng]
名 another pronunciation of 虹 (hóng) when it is used separately ➡ hóng

将 [jiàng]
I 名 ① general; commander; military officer ② King (chief piece in Chinese chess) II 动 command; lead ➡ jiāng; qiāng
将才 a man with military talent; a man born to command troops
将官 general
将领 high-ranking military officer; general
将令 order (issued by the commanding general)
将士 officers and men
将帅 high commanding officer
将相 generals and ministers of state

将门虎子 capable young man from a distinguished family

将遇良材 meet one's equal; find one's own match; diamond cuts diamond

将门无犬子 a general's family will not produce a mongrel of a son

将在外，君命有所不受 general in the field is not bound by orders from his sovereign

浒 [jiàng] 动 overflow; inundate

浒水 overflow of water; flood

绛 [jiàng] 形 deep red; crimson

绛紫 dark reddish purple

强 [jiàng] 形 stubborn; obdurate; unyielding ➡ qiáng; qiǎng

强嘴 reply defiantly; answer back; talk back

酱 [jiàng] I 名 ①thick sauce (or paste) made from soya beans, flour, etc. ②things cooked (or pickled) in soya sauce ③sauce; paste; jam II 动 cook (or pickle) things in soy sauce

酱菜 vegetables pickled in soy sauce; pickles

酱缸 jar or vat for making or keeping soybean paste, pickled vegetables, etc.

酱肉 pork cooked in soy sauce; braised pork seasoned with soy sauce

酱色 dark reddish brown

酱油 soy sauce; soy

酱园 a shop making and selling sauce, pickles, etc. ; sauce and pickle shop

酱紫 dark reddish purple

酱豆腐 fermented bean curd

犟 [jiàng] 形 obstinate; stubborn; self-willed; headstrong

犟劲 obstinacy; stubbornness

糨 [jiàng] 形 thick

糨糊 paste

jiāo (ㄐㄧㄠ)

交 [jiāo] I 动 ①hand in; hand (or turn) over; pass on; deliver ②reach; set in; come ③meet; join ④cross; intersect ⑤associate with; befriend: 交朋友 make friends ⑥have sexual intercourse; copulate; mate; breed II 形 mutual; reciprocal III 副 together; simultaneously IV 名 ① friend; acquaintance; friendship; relationship; relation ② deal; bargain; business transaction

交班 hand over to the next shift

交保 release on bail

交兵 (of two or more parties) be at war; wage war

交叉 ①intersect; cross; crisscross ②overlapping ③alternate; stagger

交差 report to the leadership after accomplish-ing a task

交出 surrender; hand over

交存 deposit; hand in for safekeeping

交错 ①interlock; crisscross ②staggered

交代 ① hand over ② explain; make clear; brief; tell ③account for; justify oneself ④ confess

交单 surrender documents

交底 tell sb what one's real intentions are; put all one's cards on the table

交点 ①point of intersection ②node

交恶 fall foul of each other; become enemies

交锋 cross swords; engage in a battle (or contest)

交付 ①pay ②hand over; deliver; consign

交割 complete a business transaction

交工 hand over a completed project

交公 hand over to the collective (or the state)

交媾 sexual intercourse; copulation

交好 (of people or states) be on friendly terms

交互 ① each other; mutual ② alternately; in turn

交还 give back; return

交换 exchange; swop

交会 intersection; rendezvous

交火 exchange shots; fight

交货 delivery

交集 (of different feelings) be mixed; occur simultaneously

交际 social intercourse; communication

交加 (of two things) accompany each other; occur simultaneously

交角 angle of intersection

交接 ① join; connect ② hand over and take over ③associate with

交界 (of two or more places) have a common boundary

交警 traffic police; traffic policeman

交卷 ①hand in an examination paper ②fulfil one's task; carry out an assignment

交困 beset by difficulties

交流 exchange; interflow; interchange

交纳 pay (to the state or an organization); hand in

交配 mating; copulation

交情 friendship; friendly relations

交融 blend; mingle

交涉 negotiate; make representations

交手 fight hand to hand; be engaged in a hand-to-hand fight; come to grips

交售 sell (to the state)

交税 pay tax

交谈 talk with each other; converse; chat

交替　① supersede; replace ② alternately; in turn
交通　①be connected; be linked ②traffic; communications ③liaison; liaison man
交往　association; contact
交尾　mating; pairing; coupling
交心　lay one's heart bare; open one's heart to
交验　hand over for examination (*or* checking)
交椅　①an ancient folding chair ②armchair
交易　business; deal; trade; transaction
交谊　friendship; friendly relations
交游　make friends
交战　be at war; fight; wage war
交账　①hand over the accounts ②account for
交织　interweave; intertwine; mingle
交白卷　① hand in a blank examination paper ②completely fail to accomplish a task
交杯酒　mutual toasting by bridegroom and bride by drinking from each other's cup at a wedding ceremony
交叉点　intersection
交割日　pay (*or* settlement) day
交互式　interactive
交换器　converter
交货单　delivery order
交货港　port of delivery
交货期　date of delivery
交际花　social butterfly; society woman
交际舞　ballroom dance; social dance
交流电　alternating current (AC)
交配期　mating season
交通部　the Ministry of Communications
交通车　special bus (service)
交通壕　communication trench
交通警　traffic police
交通量　volume of traffic
交通图　traffic map
交通网　network of communication lines
交通线　communication lines; communication routes
交通员　liaison man; underground messenger
交响曲　symphony
交响诗　symphonic poem; tone poem
交响乐　symphony; symphonic music
交学费　① pay tuition fees ② price paid for mistakes or losses
交易池　trading pit; trading pool
交易会　trade fair; commodities fair
交易量　volume of business; volume of trade
交易日　market day
交易税　trade tax; transaction tax
交易所　exchange
交谊舞　"friendship dance"—social dance; ballroom dance
交战国　belligerent countries (*or* states, nations)

交叉发价　cross offer
交叉反应　cross reaction
交叉感染　cross infection
交叉汇率　cross rate
交叉火力　cross fire
交叉科学　intersecting sciences
交付表决　put to the vote
交付使用　be made available to the users; be turned over to the users
交感神经　sympathetic nerve
交互处理　interactive processing
交互系统　interactive system
交换齿轮　change gear
交换分保　exchange of reinsurance
交换技术　swapper
交换价值　exchange value
交换意见　commune; compare notes; exchange views
交货收据　delivery receipt
交口称誉　unanimously praise
交流经验　swap experience
交流学者　visiting scholar under an exchange program
交浅言深　have a hearty talk with a casual acquaintance; give sincere advice to people one knows only slightly
交通安全　traffic safety
交通标线　traffic marking
交通标志　traffic sign
交通干线　main line of communication; main communications artery
交通高峰　traffic peak; rush hour; peak hour
交通工具　means of transportation
交通管理　traffic control
交通规则　traffic regulations
交通流量　traffic flow
交通事故　traffic (*or* road) accident
交通信号　traffic signal
交通要道　vital communication line
交通运输　communications and transportation
交通阻塞　traffic jam (*or* congestion, block, impedance, ponding, hold-ups)
交头接耳　speak in each other's ears; whisper to each other
交相辉映　enhance each other's beauty
交响乐队　symphony orchestra; philharmonic orchestra
交易市场　the trading market
交运价格　shipment price
交叉报酬率　intersection rate of return
交叉型人才　person with crossed (*or* mixed) talent; all-round person
交割延期费　backwardation
交互式电视　interactive television (ITV); multifunctional television; multimedia television
交货前付款　cash before delivery

交流发电机 alternating current generator; alternator

交易所术语 stock exchange expression; stock exchange parlance

"交钥匙"工程 "turn-key" project

交易所经纪人费用 exchange brokerage

交战国和非交战国 belligerents and non-belligerents

郊 [jiāo] 名 suburbs; outskirts

郊区 suburban district; suburbs; outskirts

郊外 the countryside around a city; outskirts

郊县 suburbs and counties under the jurisdiction of a large city

郊游 outing; excursion

茭 [jiāo] 名 dry grass as fodder

茭白 wild rice stem

浇 [jiāo] Ⅰ 动 ①pour (liquid on sth); sprinkle (water on sth) ②irrigate; water ③cast Ⅱ 形 unkind; harsh; mean

浇版 casting

浇灌 ①water; irrigate ②pour

浇口 runner

浇勺 pony ladle

浇桶 ladle pot

浇注 ① pour (melted metal, cement mixed with water, etc.) into a mould ② devote (one's energies, etc.) to

浇铸 casting; pouring

浇冷水 cast a damper over; pour cold water on others' enthusiasm

娇 [jiāo] Ⅰ 形 ① tender; delicate; lovely; charming ②squeamish; finicky; fragile; frail Ⅱ 动 pamper; spoil

娇嗔 grumble in a flirtish manner

娇惯 pamper; coddle; spoil

娇贵 ①spoiled; coddled ②delicate and fragile

娇憨 lovely and innocent

娇客 ①son-in-law ②a pampered person

娇媚 ① coquettish; flirtatious ② sweet and charming

娇嫩 ①tender and lovely ②fragile; delicate

娇娘 beautiful young lady

娇妻 a beloved wife; a pretty young wife

娇气 ①fragile; delicate ②squeamish; finicky

娇娆 enchantingly beautiful

娇弱 tender and delicate; frail and delicate

娇态 sweet and charming manner

娇小 petite; delicate

娇艳 delicate and charming; tender and beautiful

娇纵 indulge (a child); pamper; spoil

娇滴滴 delicately pretty; affectedly sweet

娇生惯养 have been delicately brought up; be pampered and spoiled

娇声嫩语 in a sweet voice

娇小玲珑 delicate and exquisite; petite and dainty

姣 [jiāo] 形 beautiful; handsome

姣好 beautiful and charming

骄 [jiāo] 形 ①proud; arrogant; supercilious; conceited ②intense; fierce; violent; vigorous

骄傲 ①arrogant; conceited ② be proud; take pride in ③pride

骄横 arrogant and imperious; overbearing

骄矜 self-important; proud; haughty

骄气 overbearing airs; arrogance

骄人 proud

骄阳 blazing sun

骄躁 arrogant and rash

骄子 favourite son

骄纵 arrogant and wilful

骄傲自大 self-important; conceited and arrogant

骄傲自满 conceited and self-satisfied; arrogant and complacent

骄兵必败 an army puffed up with pride is bound to lose

骄奢淫逸 lordly, luxury-loving, loose-living and idle; wallowing in luxury and pleasure; extravagant and dissipated

骄阳似火 The sun is blazing like a ball of fire.

胶 [jiāo] Ⅰ 名 ①glue; gum ②rubber Ⅱ 动 stick with glue; glue Ⅲ 形 gluey; sticky; gummy

胶版 offset plate

胶布 ①rubberized fabric ②adhesive plaster

胶带 rubberized tape; adhesive tape

胶合 glue together; veneer

胶结 glued; cemented

胶卷 roll film; film

胶轮 rubber tyre

胶木 bakelite

胶囊 capsule

胶泥 ①clay ②daub

胶皮 ①(vulcanized) rubber ②rickshaw

胶片 film

胶乳 latex

胶水 mucilage; glue

胶体 colloid

胶鞋 rubber overshoes; galoshes; rubbers

胶靴 high rubber overshoes; galoshes

胶着 deadlocked; stalemated

胶版纸 offset paper

胶布带 rubberized tape; adhesive tape

胶合板 plywood; veneer board

胶结剂 cementing agent

胶粘剂 adhesive

胶版印刷 offset printing; offset lithography; offset

J

胶结材料 cementing material
胶凝作用 gelation
胶漆相投 intimate and complete meeting of minds
胶体化学 colloid chemistry
胶版打样机 offset proof press
胶片阅读器 film reader

教 [jiāo]
〔动〕 teach;instruct ➡jiào
教书 teach school;teach
教学 teach
教书匠 pedagogue
教书先生 school teacher
教书育人 impart knowledge and educate people
教然后知不足 Teaching others will make you realize your own ignorance.

椒 [jiāo]
〔名〕 any of several hot spice plants
椒盐 a condiment made of roast prickly ash and salt;spiced salt

蛟 [jiāo]
〔名〕 flood dragon, a mythical creature capable of invoking storms and floods

焦 [jiāo]
I 〔形〕 ① burnt;scorched;charred ② worried;anxious II 〔名〕 ① coke ② certain parts of the body III 〔量〕 joule
焦比 coke ratio
焦脆 ①(of food) turn crisp after being baked (or fried) ② (of a voice, sound, etc.) clear;crisp
焦点 ①focal point;focus ②central issue;point at issue
焦耳 joule
焦黑 burned black
焦化 coking
焦黄 sallow;brown
焦急 anxious;worried
焦痂 eschar
焦距 focal distance;focal length
焦渴 terribly thirsty;parched
焦枯 shrivelled;dried up;withered
焦虑 feel anxious;have worries and misgivings
焦煤 coking coal
焦肉 carbonado
焦炭 coke
焦土 scorched earth—ravages of war
焦味 smell of burning;burnt smell
焦心 feel terribly worried
焦油 tar
焦躁 restless with anxiety;impatient
焦灼 deeply worried;very anxious
焦头烂额 in a sorry plight;in a terrible fix;in bad shape
焦土政策 scorched-earth policy

跤 [jiāo]
〔动〕 tumble;fall

蕉 [jiāo]
〔名〕 any of several broadleaf plants
蕉麻 abaca;Manila hemp

礁 [jiāo]
〔名〕 reef;rock
礁石 reef;rock

jiǎo (ㄐㄧㄠˇ)

矫 [jiǎo]
〔形〕 argumentative;contentious;quarrelsome ➡jiǎo
矫情 wilfully make trouble;use lame arguments

嚼 [jiáo]
〔动〕 masticate;chew;munch ➡jué
嚼烂 poltophagy
嚼舌 ① wag one's tongue;chatter;gossip ② argue meaninglessly;squabble
嚼烟 chewing tobacco
嚼子 bit (of a bridle)

jiǎo (ㄐㄧㄠˇ)

角 [jiǎo]
I 〔名〕 ①horn ②bugle;horn ③horn-shaped things ④cape;promontory;headland ⑤corner ⑥angle ⑦first of the 28 constellations II 〔量〕 ①quarter ② *jiao*, a fractional unit of money in China (= 1/10 of a *yuan* or 10 *fen*):五元六角 five *yuan* and six *jiao* ➡jué
角尺 angle square
角度 ①angle ②point of view
角阀 angle valve
角钢 angle iron
角规 angle gauge
角楼 a watchtower at a corner of a city wall;corner tower;turret
角落 corner;nook
角马 gnu
角门 side gate
角膜 cornea
角球 football corner (kick)
角鲨 spiny dogfish
角铁 angle iron
角质 cutin
角动量 angular momentum
角度计 goniometer;angle gauge
角砾岩 breccia
角膜炎 keratitis
角闪石 hornblende
角速度 angular velocity
角柱体 prism
角锥体 pyramid
角弓反张 opisthotonos
角巾私第 live as a recluse in one's hometown;live in retirement

角膜混浊 opacity of the cornea
角膜移植术 keratoplasty; corneal transplantation

侥 [jiǎo]

侥幸 lucky; by luck; by a fluke
侥幸心理 try-your-luck mentality

佼 [jiǎo]

形 beautiful; handsome; pretty
佼佼 above average; outstanding
佼人 beauty

挢 [jiǎo]

动 lift; raise

狡 [jiǎo]

形 crafty; foxy; cunning; sly
狡辩 quibble; indulge in sophistry
狡猾 sly; crafty; cunning; tricky
狡计 crafty trick; ruse
狡赖 deny (by resorting to sophistry)
狡黠 sly; crafty; cunning
狡诈 deceitful; crafty; cunning
狡兔三窟 a wily hare has three burrows—a crafty person has more than one hideout

饺 [jiǎo]

名 a kind of dumpling
饺子 dumpling

绞 [jiǎo]

Ⅰ 动 ①(of two or more strands) twist into one; entangle ②twist; wring ③ream ④hang by the neck ⑤wind; 用绞盘机把锚绞起来 wind (or raise) the anchor up by turning the capstan Ⅱ 量 skein; hank
绞棒 lease rods
绞车 winch; windlass
绞刀 reamer; drift
绞架 gallows
绞盘 capstan
绞杀 strangle
绞纱 skein
绞碎 rubbing; trituration
绞索 (the hangman's) noose
绞痛 angina
绞刑 death by hanging
绞肠痧 dry cholera
绞肉机 meat mincer; mincing machine
绞尽脑汁 rack one's brains

铰 [jiǎo]

动 ①cut with scissors ②bore with a reamer; ream ③hinge
铰车 lift winch
铰接 join with a hinge; articulate
铰孔 ream a hole
铰链 hinge

矫 [jiǎo]

Ⅰ 动 ①rectify; remedy; straighten out; correct ② pretend; feign; counterfeit Ⅱ 形 strong; powerful; brave ➡ jiáo
矫健 strong and vigorous

矫捷 vigorous and nimble; brisk
矫情 be affectedly unconventional
矫饰 feign in order to conceal sth; dissemble
矫俗 rectify a bad practice
矫形 orthopaedics
矫诏 counterfeit an imperial edict; take unauthorized action in the name of an emperor
矫正 correct; put right; rectify
矫形术 orthopaedics
矫直机 straightening machine
矫揉造作 affected; artificial
矫如脱兔 be swift of foot like a hare; as fast as an escaped hare
矫枉过正 exceed the proper limits in righting a wrong; overcorrect
矫邪归正 turn over a new leaf
矫形外科 orthopaedic surgery
矫形医生 orthopaedist

皎 [jiǎo]

形 clear and bright; white and luminous
皎皎 very clear and bright; glistening white
皎洁 (of moonlight) bright and clear
皎月东升 A luminous moon is rising in the east.

脚 [jiǎo]

名 ①foot ②base; foot ③dregs; residue ④ (*used in connection with carrying and transporting manually*)
脚背 instep
脚本 script; scenario
脚步 step; pace
脚灯 footlights
脚凳 cripple; ottoman
脚垫 callus on the sole (of the foot)
脚法 kicking skill
脚夫 ①porter ②one who hires out his donkey or horse to riders and leads or follows it on foot
脚跟 heel
脚光 footlight
脚尖 the tip of a toe; tiptoe
脚劲 strength of one's legs
脚力 strength of one's legs
脚镣 fetters; shackles
脚炉 foot warmer; foot stove
脚轮 castor (on furniture, luggage, etc.)
脚面 instep
脚盆 a basin for washing feet
脚蹼 flippers
脚气 ①beriberi ②athlete's foot
脚心 the underside of the arch (of the foot); arch
脚癣 ringworm of the foot; tinea pedis; athlete's foot
脚印 footprint; footmark; track
脚掌 sole (of the foot)
脚趾 toe

脚注 footnote
脚镯 ankle bangle
脚脖子 ankle
脚蹬子 pedal;treadle
脚底板 sole (of the foot)
脚后跟 heel
脚刹车 service brake
脚手架 scaffold;scaffolding
脚踏板 treadle (of a sewing machine,etc.)
脚踏车 bicycle
脚丫子 foot
脚指甲 toenail
脚指头 toe
脚踏实地 in a down-to-earth way;have one's feet planted on solid ground—earnest and down-to-earth
脚踏游艇 pedal boat
脚底板抹油 hotfoot;go fast;flee quickly
脚踏两只船 straddle two boats—have a foot in either camp;sit on the fence
脚踏脱粒机 pedal thresher
脚正不怕鞋歪 a straight foot is not afraid of a crooked shoe—an upright man fears no gossip

搅 [jiǎo]
劻 ①stir;mix;mingle ②disturb;upset;annoy
搅拌 stir;agitate;mix
搅棒 string rod
搅动 mix;stir
搅浑 stir and make muddy;deliberately create confusion
搅混 mix;blend;mingle
搅和 ①mix;blend;mingle ②mess up;spoil
搅局 upset the apple cart;make a mess of sth
搅乱 confuse;throw into disorder
搅扰 disturb;annoy;bother
搅拌机 mixer
搅拌器 stirrer;agitator
搅碎机 pulper

筊 [jiǎo]
名 bamboo rope

湫 [jiǎo]
形 low-lying ⇒qiū

剿 [jiǎo]
劻 send armed forces to suppress;put down;quell ⇒chāo
剿除 exterminate;wipe out
剿匪 suppress bandits
剿灭 exterminate;wipe out
剿尽杀绝 exterminate once and for all

徼 [jiǎo]
劻 beg;request ⇒jiào
徼福 beg good fortune;request a blessing

缴 [jiǎo]
劻 ① pay;hand over;hand in ② capture (arms);缴了他们的武器 have captured their arms;have them disarmed ⇒zhuó

缴获 capture;seize
缴纳 pay
缴枪 ①(of enemy) hand over arms;surrender ②capture the enemy's guns
缴销 hand in for cancellation
缴械 ①disarm ②surrender one's weapons;lay down one's arms

皦 [jiǎo]
形 ① (of jade, pearls, etc.) pure white;brilliant ②pure;clean;clear
皦日 bright sun

jiào (ㄐㄧㄠˋ)

叫 [jiào]
Ⅰ 劻 ①cry;shout;yell ②greet;call;ask ③hire;order;get ④ name;call;designate ⑤make;order;ask ⑥ allow;permit;let Ⅱ 名 male (animal or fowl) Ⅲ 介 (*used to introduce the doer of an action*)：玻璃杯叫儿子打碎了。The glass was broken by my son.
叫板 challenge;ask for trouble;pick a quarrel
叫菜 choose dishes from a menu;order dishes (in a restaurant)
叫车 hire a taxi;call a taxi
叫喊 shout;yell;howl
叫好 applaud;shout "bravo!";shout "well done!"
叫号 ①call a number ②sing a work song to synchronize movements, with one person leading ③provoke by words;challenge
叫唤 ①cry out;call out ②(of animals, birds, insects,etc.) cry;call
叫鸡 cock
叫价 bid;quoted price;offer
叫劲 ① challenge;have a competition ② oppose;dispute
叫绝 applaud as the very best (one has seen, etc.);shout "bravo!"
叫苦 complain of hardship (*or* suffering);moan and groan
叫驴 jackass
叫骂 shout curses
叫卖 cry one's wares;peddle;hawk
叫门 call at the door to be let in
叫牌 make a bid at bridge;bid
叫屈 complain of being wronged;protest against an injustice
叫嚷 shout;howl;clamour
叫嚣 clamour;raise a hue and cry
叫醒 wake up;awaken
叫阵 challenge an opponent to a fight when two armies meet
叫座 draw a large audience;draw well;appeal to the audience;be a box-office success
叫做 be called;be known as
叫倒好 hoot
叫花子 beggar

叫苦不迭 complain incessantly; pour out endless grievances
叫苦连天 complain to high heaven; complain bitterly

峤 [jiào]
名 mountain path

觉 [jiào]
名 sleep ➡jué

校 [jiào]
动 ① check; proofread; collate ② compare; contest ➡xiào

校次 number of times a proof is read before publishing
校订 check against the authoritative text
校读 proofreading
校对 ① proofread; proof ② proofreader ③ check against a standard; calibrate
校改 read and correct proofs
校勘 collate
校验 check; proof; inspection
校样 proof sheet; proof
校阅 read and revise
校正 proofread and correct; rectify
校准 calibration
校对机 collator
校勘学 textual criticism
校对符号 proofreader's mark

轿 [jiào]
名 sedan (chair); litter

轿车 ①(horse-drawn) carriage ②bus; car
轿夫 sedan-chair bearer
轿子 sedan (chair)

较 [jiào]
Ⅰ 动 ①compare ②haggle; quibble; dispute
Ⅱ 形 clear; obvious; marked; evident

较比 comparatively; relatively; fairly; quite
较劲 match strength
较量 ① measure one's strength with; have a contest; have a trial (or test) of strength ②haggle; argue; dispute
较为 comparatively; relatively; fairly
较真 ①argue; wrangle ②be finicky; be inflexible; be conscientious and meticulous
较强的互补性 substantial complementarity

教 [jiào]
Ⅰ 动 teach; instruct Ⅱ 名 religion ➡jiāo

教案 ①teaching plan; lesson plan ②〈史〉missionary case
教本 textbook
教鞭 (teacher's) pointer
教材 teaching material
教参 reference material used in teaching
教程 ①course of study ②(published) lectures
教导 ①instruct; teach; give guidance ②teaching; guidance
教德 teaching ethics; ethics of the teaching profession
教范 manual

教父 godfather
教改 educational reform
教工 teaching and administrative staff (of a school)
教官 drillmaster; instructor
教规 rules of a religion; canon
教化 transform by instruction; enlighten by education
教皇 pope; pontiff
教会 (the Christian) church
教诲 teaching; instruction
教籍 teaching post
教具 teaching aid
教练 ①train; drill; coach ②coach; instructor; trainer
教龄 length of service as a teacher
教母 godmother
教女 goddaughter
教派 religious sect; denomination
教区 parish; diocese
教师 teacher; schoolteacher
教士 priest; clergyman; Christian missionary
教室 classroom; schoolroom
教授 ①professor ②instruct; teach
教唆 instigate; abet; put sb up to sth
教堂 church; cathedral
教条 dogma; doctrine; creed; tenet
教廷 the Vatican; the Holy See
教头 coach
教徒 believer (or follower) of a religion
教委 commission of education
教务 educational administration
教学 ① teaching; education ② teaching and studying ③teacher and student
教训 ①lesson; moral ②chide; teach sb a lesson; give sb a talking-to; lecture sb (for wrongdoing, etc.)
教养 ① bring up; train; educate ②breeding; upbringing; education; culture
教义 religious doctrine; creed
教益 benefit gained from sb's wisdom; enlightenment
教育 ①education ②teach; educate; inculcate
教员 teacher; instructor
教长 religion imam; dean
教主 the founder of a religion
教导员 (battalion) political instructor
教科书 textbook
教练车 learner-driven vehicle
教练船 training ship
教练弹 practice projectile; dummy projectile; dummy
教练机 trainer aircraft; trainer
教练员 coach; instructor; trainer
教师节 Teacher's Day (Sept. 10, initiated in 1985)
教授法 teaching methods; pedagogics

教唆犯 abettor;instigator
教唆罪 guilt of instigation to a crime
教务处 Dean's Office
教务长 Dean of Studies
教学法 teaching methods;pedagogics
教研室 teaching and research section
教研组 teaching and research group
教养所 penitentiary where those who have committed misdemeanors that are not serious enough for a jail sentence are reeducated through labour
教养员 kindergarten teacher
教养院 correctional; indoctrination centre; house of correction
教友会 the Society of Friends;the Quakers
教育家 educationist;educator
教育界 educational circles
教育学 pedagogy;pedagogics;education
教长国 imamate
教职员 teaching and administrative staff
教导有方 skilful in teaching and able to provide guidance
教皇通谕 papal encyclical
教会学校 missionary school
教条主义 dogmatism;doctrinairism
教廷大使 nuncio
教廷公使 internuncio
教学测试 instructional testing
教学大纲 teaching programme;syllabus
教学方针 principles of teaching
教学改革 transformation of education;reform in education;educational reform
教学节目 teaching program
教学设计 instructional design
教学相长 teaching benefits teacher and student alike;teaching benefits teachers as well as students
教育程度 level of education
教育创新 education innovation
教育贷款 education loan
教育电视 educational television
教育方针 policy for education;educational policy
教育扶贫 aid a poverty-stricken area by promoting education there
教育革命 revolution in education
教育投资 educational investment
教育哲学 educational philosophy
教育制度 system of education
教条式理解 dogmatic interpretations
教育心理学 educational psychology
教员休息室 teacher's lounge;faculty lounge; staff room;common room
教学参考资料 reference material used in teaching
教育体制改革 reform of the educational structure;reform of the management system of education

教学、科研、生产三结合 three-in-one combination of teaching,research and production
教育质量的评估和检查 assessment of and check-up of educational quality

窖 [jiào]
Ⅰ 〈名〉 cellar (*or* pit) for storing things;cellar Ⅱ 〈动〉 store (sth) in a cellar (*or* pit)
窖藏 store sth in a cellar (*or* pit)

酵 [jiào]
〈动〉 ferment;leaven
酵母 yeast
酵素 ferment;enzyme
酵母菌 saccharomyces

徼 [jiào]
Ⅰ 〈名〉 boundary Ⅱ 〈动〉 patrol ➡jiǎo

醮 [jiào]
〈名〉 ①libation at wedding ceremony ②Taoist sacrificial ceremony

皭 [jiào]
〈形〉 pure white;spotlessly clean

jiē (ㄐㄧㄝ)

节 [jiē]
➡jié
节骨眼 critical juncture;vital link

阶 [jiē]
〈名〉 ①steps;stairs ②rank
阶层 (social) stratum
阶地 terrace
阶段 ①stage;phase ②level
阶级 ①steps;stairs ②(social) class
阶梯 a flight of stairs;ladder
阶级性 class character;class nature
阶下囚 prisoner;captive
阶级报复 class vengeance
阶级本能 class instinct
阶级本质 class nature
阶级成分 class status
阶级斗争 class struggle
阶级队伍 class ranks
阶级分化 class polarization
阶级分析 class analysis
阶级感情 class feeling
阶级根源 class origin
阶级观点 class viewpoint
阶级教育 class education
阶级觉悟 class consciousness
阶级烙印 brand of a class
阶级立场 class stand
阶级路线 class line
阶级矛盾 class contradictions
阶级社会 class society
阶级阵线 class alignment
阶梯教室 lecture theatre
阶段性成果 achievements of the current stage;relatively obvious achievement

阶段性就业 periodic employment
阶级异己分子 alien-class element; individual from an alien class

疖 ［jiē］

疖子 furuncle; boil

皆 ［jiē］

〔副〕all; each and every
皆大欢喜 everybody is happy; to the satisfaction of all

结 ［jiē］

〔动〕bear (fruit); form (seed); produce ⇒ jié
结巴 ①stammer; stutter ②stammerer; stutterer
结果 bear fruit; fructify
结实 ①solid; sturdy; durable ②strong; sturdy; tough
结子 seed

接 ［jiē］

〔动〕①come into contact with; come close to; be in touch with ②connect; join; link up; put together ③catch; take hold of ④receive; take; accept ⑤meet; welcome ⑥take over; succeed
接班 take one's turn on duty; take over from; succeed; carry on
接办 accept and handle
接产 ①practise midwifery ②deliver animals of their young
接触 ①come into contact with; get in touch with ②engage ③contact
接待 receive; admit
接地 ①ground connection; grounding; earthing ②touchdown; ground contact
接点 contact
接防 relieve a garrison; relieve
接风 give a dinner of welcome (to a visitor from afar)
接羔 deliver lambs
接骨 set a (broken) bone; set a fracture
接管 take over control; take over
接轨 bring in line with; join tracks with; be in line with; be in agreement with; integrate
接柜 receive at the counter
接合 joint
接活 accept work; receive an order
接火 ①start to exchange fire ②energize
接获 receive
接济 give material assistance to; give financial help to
接见 receive sb; grant an interview to
接近 be close to; near; approach
接警 receive a crime report
接客 ①(of a hotel, etc.) receive lodgers (or guests) ②(of a prostitute) receive (or sleep with) a patron
接口 interface

接力 work by relays
接连 on end; in a row; in succession
接龙 (in cards or dominoes) build up a sequence
接木 grafting
接纳 admit (into an organization)
接片 splicing (of pieces of film)
接气 coherent
接洽 take up a matter with; arrange (business, etc.) with; consult with
接壤 border on; be contiguous to; be bounded by
接任 take over a job; replace; succeed
接生 deliver a child; practise midwifery
接收 ①receive ②take over (property, etc.); expropriate ③admit
接手 ①take over (duties, etc.) ②catcher
接受 accept
接送 pick up
接穗 scion
接替 take over; replace
接听 answer the phone
接通 put through
接头 ①connect; join; joint ②piecing; tying-in ③contact; get in touch with; meet ④have knowledge of; know about
接吻 kiss
接线 wiring
接续 continue; follow
接应 ①come to sb's aid; coordinate with; reinforce ②supply
接站 meet sb at the station
接诊 (of a doctor) see and treat patients; be consulted by patients
接枝 grafting
接种 have an inoculation; inoculate
接踵 following on sb's heels
接着 ①catch ②follow; carry on ③after that; and then
接班人 successor
接触炉 contact furnace
接待日 open day; reception day
接待室 reception room
接待站 reception centre
接发球 receive; return of service
接合点 junction point
接合器 splicer; contact maker; connector; articulator
接力棒 relay baton
接目镜 eyepiece; ocular
接生婆 midwife
接生员 midwife
接收站 receiving station; accepting station
接受国 accepting state; receiving state
接受书 instrument of acceptance
接物镜 objective lens; objective
接线生 switch board operator

接触传染 contagion
接触眼镜 contact lens
接触政策 policy of engagement
接待单位 host organization
接待人员 reception personnel
接二连三 one after another; in quick succession
接颈交臂 be very intimate with
接力赛跑 relay race; relay
接收信号 receipt signal
接收性能 receptivity
接受监督 subject oneself to the supervision of
接受条款 acceptance clause
接物待人 attend a matter and receive a person
接踵而至 follow hard at heel

秸 [jiē]
名 grain stalk after threshing; straw
秸秆 straw
秸秆还田 return crop stocks to the field

J

揭 [jiē]
动 ①tear off; remove; take off ②uncover; lift (the lid, etc.) ③expose; show up; make public; bring to light ④raise; hoist
揭榜 ①announce the results of an examination ②tear off (or take off) a notice inviting applications for jobs, etc., from a wall as a sign of accepting the invitation
揭标 bid opening
揭穿 expose; lay bare; show up
揭底 reveal the inside story
揭短 rake up sb's faults (or shortcomings, weaknesses)
揭发 expose; unmask; bring to light
揭开 uncover; reveal; open
揭露 expose; unmask; ferret out
揭秘 break a secret; unveil a mystery
揭幕 unveil (a monument, etc.); inaugurate
揭牌 open
揭示 ①announce; promulgate ②reveal; bring to light
揭帖 notice; poster
揭晓 announce; make known; publish
揭盖子 take the lid off sth; bring sth into the open
揭老底 reveal the inside story; disclose sb's unsavoury past; dredge up embarrassing facts about sb's past
揭幕式 unveiling ceremony
揭不开锅 have nothing in the pot; having nothing to eat; go hungry
揭发检举 expose and denounce
揭发同伙 expose one's accomplices
揭竿而起 raise the standard of revolt; start an uprising; rise in rebellion
揭人隐私 expose another person's secrets; expose sb's shameful secret

嗟 [jiē]
叹 sigh; lament
嗟来之食 food handed out in contempt; handouts

街 [jiē]
名 ①street ②country fair; market
街道 ① street ② residential district; neighbourhood
街灯 street lamp
街坊 [jiēfang] neighbour
街景 scenic street
街垒 street barricade
街貌 appearance of streets
街区 block
街市 downtown streets
街头 street corner; street
街舞 hip hop
街头剧 street-corner skit; street performance
街道妇女 housewives of the neighbourhood
街道工厂 neighbourhood factory
街道企业 neighbourhood enterprise; street-enterprises
街面儿上 ①(activities, etc.) in the street ② neighbourhood
街谈巷议 street gossip; the talk of the town
街头乞讨 beg for food in the streets
街头巷尾 streets and lanes
街心公园 parks at the intersections
街道办事处 street administration office; sub-district office
街道服务站 street service stations
街道委员会 neighbourhood committee
街头采访节目 man-in-the-street program
街头时装表演 street fashion show
街道居民委员会 neighbourhood committee; resident's committee

楷 [jiē]
名 Chinese pistache ⇒kǎi

jié(ㄐㄧㄝ́)

孑 [jié]
形 lonely; all alone
孑然 solitary; lonely; alone
孑然一身 all alone in the world

节 [jié]
I 名 ①joint; node; knot ②division; section; part ③festival; red-letter day; holiday ④item ⑤moral integrity; chastity ⑥knot Ⅱ 量 section; length: 第三章第二节 Section Two, Chapter Three Ⅲ 动 ①abridge ②economize; save; restrain; control ⇒jiē
节哀 restrain one's grief
节本 abridged edition; abbreviated version
节操 high moral principle; moral integrity
节点 node; panel point
节电 save electricity
节徽 emblem (or motif) of a festival (or spe-

cial occasion)
节汇 save foreign exchange
节俭 thrifty;frugal
节节 successively;steadily
节理 joint
节令 climate and other natural phenomena of a season
节流 ①reduce expenditure ②throttle
节录 extract;excerpt
节律 the rhythm and pace of moving things
节目 programme;item (on a programme);number
节能 save energy
节拍 metre
节气 solar term (or period)
节庆 red-letter days
节日 festival;red-letter day;holiday
节省 economize;save;use sparingly;cut down on
节食 be moderate in eating and drinking;be (or go) on a diet
节饰 knuckle
节水 save water
节选 excerpts;extracts
节译 abridged translation
节余 ①save ②surplus (as a result of economizing)
节育 birth control
节欲 restrain one's carnal desires;check one's selfish desire
节约 practise thrift;economize;save
节支 ①cut down expenses;reduce expenses;retrench ②balance;money saved
节制 ①control;check;be moderate in ②temperance;abstinence
节资 economize the use of funds;use funds conservatively
节奏 ①rhythm ②tempo
节假日 public holidays;festivals and holidays
节目单 programme;playbill
节能灯 energy-saving stove
节能灶 energy-saving stove
节拍器 metronome
节食者 dieter
节水器 water-saving device
节油器 fuel economizer
节育环 intrauterine device (IUD);the loop
节制闸 check gate
节节败退 retreat one step after another;suffer one defeat after another
节目导演 program director (PD)
节目预告 program reminder;program parade
节能技术 energy-saving technology;energy-efficient technology
节水农业 water-efficient agriculture;agriculture with good water-saving results
节外生枝 ① side issues (or new problems)

crop up unexpectedly ②raise obstacles;deliberately complicate an issue
节衣缩食 economize on food and clothing;live frugally
节育手术 birth control surgery
节肢动物 arthropod
节目主持人 host (of a radio or TV show);compère;master of ceremonies
节水灌溉系统 water-saving irrigation system
节约用地,少占或不占耕地 economization on land use and little or no occupation of cultivated land

讦 [jié]
〔动〕 chide (sb for his faults);expose (sb's hidden misdeeds)

劫 [jié]
Ⅰ〔动〕①rob;loot;plunder;raid ②coerce;compel Ⅱ〔名〕calamity;adversity;disaster;misfortune
劫持 kidnap;hold under duress;hijack
劫道 waylay;hold up;mug
劫夺 seize (a person or his property) by force
劫匪 highwayman;robber
劫机 hijack an aeroplane;engage in air piracy;hijack a plane
劫掠 plunder;loot
劫难 disaster;calamity
劫数 inexorable doom;predestined fate
劫营 raid the enemy camp
劫狱 break into a jail and rescue a prisoner
劫机犯 hijacker
劫富济贫 rob the rich to give to the poor
劫后余生 be a survivor of a disaster

劼 [jié]
〔形〕①prudent;cautious ②hard-working;diligent

杰 [jié]
Ⅰ〔名〕outstanding person;hero Ⅱ〔形〕outstanding;prominent;distinguished
杰出 outstanding;remarkable;prominent
杰作 masterpiece

迒 [jié]
〔形〕very fast;quick;rapid

诘 [jié]
〔动〕closely question;interrogate
诘问 closely question;interrogate;cross-examine
诘责 censure;rebuke;denounce

拮 [jié]
拮据 [jiéjū] in straitened circumstances;short of money;hard up

洁 [jié]
〔形〕clean;pure;clear
洁白 spotlessly white;pure white
洁净 clean;spotless
洁具 sanitary ware
洁癖 unhealthy obsession with cleanliness;

J

mysophobia
洁肤霜 cleansing cream
洁身自好 ①refuse to be contaminated by evil influence; preserve one's purity ② mind one's own business in order to keep out of trouble ③maintain one's integrity

结 [jié]
Ⅰ 动 ① tie; knit; knot; weave ② congeal; form; forge; associate ③ settle; finish; conclude Ⅱ 名 ①knot：把结打紧一点 make a tight knot; make a knot tight ②written guarantee; affidavit ③junction ④node ➡ jiē

结案 wind up a case; close a case; settle a lawsuit
结疤 become scarred
结拜 become sworn brothers or sister
结伴 go with
结冰 freeze; ice up; ice over
结彩 adorn (or decorate) with festoons
结肠 colon
结成 form
结仇 start a feud; become enemies
结存 ① cash on hand; balance ② goods on hand; inventory
结点 intersection
结构 ① structure; composition; construction ②texture
结关 customs clearance
结果 ①result; outcome ②kill; finish off
结合 ① combine; unite; integrate; link ② be united in wedlock
结核 ①tubercle ②tuberculosis ③nodule
结喉 Adam's apple
结悔 settlement of exchange
结汇 settlement of exchange; surrender of exchange
结婚 marry; get married; be married
结伙 gang
结集 ① concentrate; mass ② collect articles, etc. into a volume
结痂 form a scab; crust
结茧 cocooning
结交 make friends with; associate with
结节 tubercle; node
结晶 ①crystallize ②crystal ③crystallization
结局 final result; outcome; ending
结块 agglomerate; curdle
结论 ①conclusion (of a syllogism) ②conclusion; verdict
结盟 form an alliance; ally; align
结膜 conjunctiva
结欠 balance due
结亲 ① marry; get married ②(of two families) become related by marriage
结清 settle; square up
结舌 unable to say anything because of terror (or lack) of argument; tongue-tied

结社 form an association
结绳 tie knots
结石 stone; calculus
结识 get acquainted with sb; get to know sb
结束 end; finish; conclude; wind up; close
结算 settle accounts; close (or wind up) an account
结为 enter into a specified relationship
结尾 ①ending; winding-up stage ②coda
结业 complete a course; wind up one's studies
结余 cash surplus; surplus; balance
结缘 form ties (of affection, friendship, etc.); become attached to
结怨 contract enmity; incur hatred
结扎 ligation; ligature
结账 settle (or square) accounts; balance the books
结转 ①carry-over ②carry down
结肠炎 colitis
结对子 become a partner of; partner sb; associate with; cooperate as pairs; mutually help each other
结构钢 structural steel
结构式 structural formula
结构图 structural drawing
结关费 customs clearing charges
结关证 clearance; clearance papers
结核病 tuberculosis
结节虫 nodular worm
结晶学 crystallography
结膜炎 conjunctivitis
结束语 concluding remarks
结业证 certificate of completion
结草衔环 pay a debt of gratitude
结党营私 form a clique to pursue selfish interests; band together for selfish purposes
结缔组织 connective tissue
结发夫妻 husband and wife by the first marriage
结构调整 structural readjustment
结构力学 structural mechanics
结构主义 structuralism
结果管理 management by results; results management
结核杆菌 tubercle bacillus
结核菌素 tuberculin
结婚登记 marriage registration
结婚证书 marriage certificate; marriage lines
结晶化学 crystal chemistry
结球甘蓝 cabbage
结社自由 freedom of association
结算价格 settlement price
结构工资制 structural wage system
结构流程图 structure flow chart
结构心理学 structural psychology
结构语言学 structural linguistics
结秦晋之好 marriage between two families;

untied in matrimony
结售汇制度　the system of exchange，settlement and sales
结构主义学派　structuralists
结构主义语法　structural grammar

桔 [jié]
桔梗　the root of balloon flower

桀 [jié]
[名] Jie，name of the last ruler of the Xia Dynasty，traditionally considered a tyrant
桀骜不驯　stubborn and intractable；obstinate and unruly
桀犬吠尧　the tyrant Jie's cur yapping at the sage-king Yao—the underling of an evil man will attack whoever he is told to attack
桀黠暴戾　cruel and ferocious

捷 [jié]
I [形] prompt；agile；nimble；quick II [名] victory；triumph；success
捷报　news of victory；report of a success
捷径　shortcut
捷报频传　news of victory keeps pouring in
捷足先登　the swift-footed arrive first；the early bird catches the worm

偈 [jié]
[形] valiant ➡ jì

袺 [jié]
[动] hold (*or* carry) sth in the front of one's jacket

絜 [jié]
[形] clean ➡ xié

楬 [jié]
[名] stake used as a mark；marking stake

睫 [jié]
[名] eyelash；lash
睫毛　eyelash；lash
睫毛油　mascara

截 [jié]
I [动] ①cut；separate；sever ②stop；check；intercept；stem II [名] section；chunk；length：一截儿绳子 a (length of) rope III [介] by (a specified time)；up to
截断　①cut off；block ②cut short；interrupt
截稿　stop accepting incoming articles or contributions
截获　intercept and capture
截击　intercept
截留　intercept and hold on to；retain for one's own use；withhold
截流　dam a river
截面　section
截取　cut off a section of sth
截然　sharply；completely
截瘫　paraplegia
截肢　amputation
截止　①end；close ②cut-off
截至　by (a specified time)；up to

截击机　interceptor
截流井　catch basin
截煤机　coalcutter；cutter
截长补短　take from the long to add to the short；draw on the strength of each to offset the weakness of the other
截击导弹　interceptor missile；interception missile
截金雕玉　cut gold and carve jade
截流工程　project of damming a river
截流合龙　river enclosure；river closing
截然不同　completely different；different as black and white；poles apart
截留上缴利润　withhold profits that should be turned over to the state

碣 [jié]
[名] stone tablet

竭 [jié]
[动] ①exhaust；use up ②run out
竭诚　wholeheartedly；with all one's heart
竭尽　use up；exhaust
竭力　do one's utmost；use every ounce of one's energy；try by every possible means
竭尽全力　spare no effort；do one's utmost；do all one can
竭泽而渔　drain the pond to get all the fish；kill the goose that lays the golden eggs

羯 [jié]
羯羊　wether

jiě（ㄐㄧㄝˇ）

姐 [jiě]
[名] ①elder sister；sister ②elder female relative ③general term for young women
姐夫　elder sister's husband；brother-in-law
姐姐　elder sister；sister
姐妹　①sisters；pals ②brothers and sisters
姐妹城　sister cities
姐妹学校　sister schools；sister universities

解 [jiě]
I [动] ①separate；divide；split ②untie；undo；unbutton ③relieve；remove；dispel；dismiss ④explain；construe；clear up；interpret ⑤understand；comprehend；be clear ⑥relieve oneself II [名] solution ➡ jiè；xiè
解表　induce sweat；diaphoresis
解馋　satisfy a craving for good food
解嘲　try to explain things away when ridiculed
解除　remove；relieve；get rid of
解答　answer；explain
解冻　①thaw；unfreeze ②unfreeze (funds，assets，etc.)；relax tension；loosen control
解毒　①detoxify；detoxicate ②relieve internal heat (*or* fever)
解读　decode

解饿 satisfy one's hunger
解乏 ①recover from fatigue ②refreshing
解法 solution
解放 ①liberate；emancipate ②Liberation
解构 deconstructionism；deconstruct
解雇 discharge；dismiss；fire
解恨 vent one's hatred；have one's hatred slaked
解惑 resolve (*or* remove，dispel) doubts
解禁 lift a ban；lift a restriction
解救 save；rescue；deliver
解决 ①solve；resolve；settle ②dispose of；finish off
解开 untie；undo
解渴 quench one's thirst
解扣 trip
解困 relieve sleepy feeling；overcome difficulties
解码 decipher；decode
解闷 divert oneself (from boredom)
解密 declassify；deciphering；decrypt
解囊 open one's purse (to help sb with money)
解聘 dismiss an employee
解剖 dissect
解气 vent one's spleen；work off one's anger
解热 allay a fever
解散 ①dismiss ②dissolve；disband
解释 explain；expound；interpret
解手 relieve oneself；go to the toilet (*or* lavatory)
解说 explain orally；comment
解送 send under guard
解算 resolving；calculating
解锁 deblocking；clear
解套 unlocking
解题 solve a (mathematical，etc.) problem
解体 disintegrate
解痛 alleviate pain
解脱 ①free (*or* extricate) oneself ②absolve；exonerate
解危 head off danger
解围 ①force an enemy to raise a siege；rescue sb from a siege ②help sb out of a predicament；save sb from embarrassment
解析 analysis；resolution；resolving
解严 declare martial law ended；lift a curfew
解译 decipher；decode；figure out a message
解约 terminate an agreement；cancel (*or* rescind) a contract
解职 dismiss from office；discharge；relieve sb of his post
解放军 ① liberation army ② the Chinese People's Liberation Army ③PLA man
解放区 liberated area
解疙瘩 solve a problem that is on sb's mind；get rid of a hang-up

解雇费 severance pay
解扣儿 ① unbutton；undo a button ② sink a feud；get rid of a hang-up；remove ill will；overcome difficulties
解困房 houses for the poor；lower housing project；welfare apartments；problem-solving houses
解剖刀 scalpel
解剖学 anatomy
解释权 power (*or* right) of interpretation；right to interpret
解释性 explanatory；interpretative
解说词 (oral) commentary；(written) caption
解说员 announcer；narrator；commentator
解疑心 dispel doubts (*or* suspicions)
解油腻 cut the grease of a rich meal (as with a cup of tea，etc.)
解职金 severance pay；separation allowance；compensation for being laid off (*or* termination of job)
解除合同 terminate a contract
解除警报 ①sound the all-clear ②all-clear
解除契约 discharge a contract
解放思想 emancipate the mind；free oneself from old ideas
解放战争 ① war of liberation ② China's War of Liberation
解甲归田 take off one's armour and return to the land；be demobilized
解禁期间 open season；open time
解决争端 settle a dispute
解困资金 anti-poverty funds；poverty-relief funds
解囊相助 help sb generously with money
解剖麻雀 dissect a sparrow—analyze a typical case
解忧消愁 dissipate sorrow；allay grief；relieve sb from anxiety
解放生产力 emancipate (*or* release) productive forces
解雇通知书 pink slip
解析几何学 analytic geometry
解除劳动关系 sever labour relations
解冻银行存款 release of bank account
解决温饱问题 achieve food security
解铃还须系铃人 let him who tied the bell on the tiger take it off—whoever started the trouble should end it

jiè（ㄐㄧㄝˋ）

介 [jiè]
Ⅰ 动 ① be situated between；interpose ② introduce ③ remain；have in mind Ⅱ 名 armour；shell Ⅲ 形 upright；high-minded
介虫 beetle
介词 preposition

介壳 shell (of oysters, snails, etc.)
介入 intervene; interpose; get involved
介绍 ①introduce; present ②recommend; suggest ③let know; brief
介意 take offence; mind
介质 medium
介子 meson; mesotron
介壳虫 scale insect
介绍人 ① introducer; recommender; sponsor ②matchmaker
介绍信 letter of introduction; reference
介形虫 mussel-shrimp
介电常数 dielectric constant
介入疗法 interventional therapy
介绍贿赂罪 crime of introducing bribery

价 [jiè]
图 messenger; errand boy ➡jià; jie

戒 [jiè]
Ⅰ 动 ① guard against; be on the alert against; be prepared against ②exhort; admonish; caution; warn ③give up; drop; stop Ⅱ 图 ①abstinence; taboo ②Buddhist monastic discipline; religious preception or commandment ③(finger) ring
戒备 guard; take precautions; be on the alert
戒尺 teacher's ruler for beating pupils
戒除 give up; drop; stop
戒毒 quit drug abuse; abstain from poison
戒赌 stop gambling
戒酒 give up drinking; swear off drinking
戒律 religious discipline; commandment
戒心 vigilance; wariness
戒烟 give up smoking; swear off smoking
戒严 enforce martial law; impose a curfew; cordon off an area
戒指 (finger) ring
戒毒所 drug rehabilitation centre; narcotic house; narcotic detention centre
戒严令 proclamation of martial law
戒备森严 tight security is in force
戒毒中心 drug rehabilitation centre
戒骄戒躁 guard against arrogance and rashness; be on one's guard against conceit and impetuosity

芥 [jiè]
图 ①mustard ②small grass—tiny and trivial things ➡gài
芥菜 leaf mustard
芥蒂 ill feeling; unpleasantness; grudge
芥末 mustard
芥子 mustard seed
芥子气 mustard gas
芥菜疙瘩 rutabaga

届 [jiè]
Ⅰ 动 fall due Ⅱ 量 session; class
届满 (term of office) expire
届期 when the day comes; on the appointed date
届时 when the time comes; at the appointed time; on the occasion

界 [jiè]
图 ①boundary; border ②scope; range; extent ③walks of life; circles ④primary division in nature; kingdom ⑤primary division in stratigraphy; group ⑥bound
界碑 boundary tablet; boundary marker
界标 boundary mark
界尺 ungraduated ruler
界定 specify the limits; delimit; define
界段 area under a person's administration
界河 boundary river
界面 interface; user interface
界石 boundary stone (or tablet)
界限 ①demarcation line; dividing line; limits; bounds ②limit; end
界线 ①boundary line ②demarcation line; dividing line; limits; bounds
界址 location of a dividing line (of land)
界桩 boundary marker
界内球 in bounds; in
界外球 out-of-bounds; out

疥 [jiè]
图 scabies
疥虫 sarcoptic mite
疥疮 scabies
疥螨 itch mite
疥癣 mange
疥蛤蟆 toad

诫 [jiè]
图 warning; admonish; advise

蚧 [jiè]
◇ 蛤蚧 gecko

借 [jiè]
动 ①borrow ②lend; loan ③use as a pretext ④make use of; take advantage of; rely on
借词 loanword; loan
借贷 ①borrow (or lend) money ②debit and credit sides
借调 be on secondment to another post temporarily; transfer to a different work unit; temporarily transfer; loan
借读 study as an adopted (or guest) student; study at a school on a temporary basis
借端 use as a pretext
借方 debit side; debit
借故 find an excuse
借光 excuse me
借火 ask for a light
借鉴 use for reference; draw lessons from; draw on the experience of
借据 receipt for a loan; IOU
借口 ①use as an excuse (or pretext) ②excuse; pretext
借款 ①borrow (or lend) money; ask for (or

offer) a loan ②loan
借脑 brain import
借宿 stay overnight at sb else's place;put up
for the night
借条 receipt for a loan;IOU
借位 borrow ten (in subtraction)
借问 may I ask
借以 so as to;for the purpose of;by way of
借用 ①borrow;have the loan of ②use sth for
another purpose
借阅 borrow and read;lend
借债 borrow money;raise (or contract) a
loan
借支 ask for an advance on one's pay
借重 rely on for support;enlist sb's help
借住 stay at sb else's place
借助 have the aid of;draw support from
借东风 taking advantage of the east wind;
with sb's help
借记卡 debit card
借书处 loan desk (of a library)
借书证 library card
借贷股票 lending stock;loan stocks
借贷资本 loan capital
借刀杀人 kill sb by another's hand;make use
of one person to get rid of another
借东补西 borrow from one to pay another;cut
out one piece to mend another
借风使船 sail the boat with the help of the
wind—achieve one's purpose through the
agency of sb else
借公肥私 enrich oneself by performing public
services
借古讽今 use the past to disparage the present
借花献佛 present Buddha with flowers given
by another—make a gift of sth given by another
借鸡下蛋 borrow a hen to lay an egg—use external conditions to advance one's own project
借景抒情 take advantage of a scene to express
one's emotion
借酒浇愁 drown one's sorrows in liquor
借壳上市 go public through borrowing a shell.
借款契约 loan agreement
借入资本 debt capital;borrowed capital;loan
capital
借尸还魂 (of a dead person's soul) find reincarnation in another's corpse—(of sth evil)
revive in a new guise
借水行舟 sail the boat with the help of the
current—achieve one's purpose through
the agency of sb else
借题发挥 make use of the subject under discussion to put over one's own ideas;seize
on an incident to exaggerate matters
借债抵押品 security for a loan

骱 [jiè]
名 joint

解 [jiè]
动 carry (or take) under guard;escort ➡
jiě;xiè
解款 take money (to a bank)
解送 send under guard

藉 [jiè]
I 名 pad;cushion;mat II 动 ①fill up;pad
②make use of ➡ jí

jie(·ㄐㄧㄝ)

价 [jie]
I 助 (used for emphasis after a negative
adverb):不价。No! ➡ jià;jiè

家 [jie]
(后缀):整天家 all day long ➡ jiā;jia

jīn(ㄐㄧㄣ)

巾 [jīn]
名 piece of cloth (used as a towel,scarf,
tie,muffler,kerchief,etc.)
巾帼 ①ancient woman's headdress ②woman
巾夹 towel clip
巾帼须眉 women who act and talk like a man
巾帼英雄 a heroic woman;heroine
巾帼建功标兵 woman pacesetter

斤 [jīn]
I 量 jin,unit of weight (= 1/2 kilogram)
II 名 ancient instrument (or tool) for felling
trees
斤斗 ①fall ②somersault
斤斤 be particular (about small matters)
斤两 weight
斤斤计较 haggle over every ounce;be calculating

今 [jīn]
名 ①modern;present-day;now ②today ③
this
今后 from now on;in the days to come;hence-
forth;hereafter;in future
今年 this year
今日 ①this day;today ②present;now
今生 this life
今世 ①this life ②this age;the contemporary
age
今天 ①this day;today ②the present time (or
age);today
今晚 this evening;tonight
今昔 the present and the past;today and yesterday
今夜 this evening;tonight
今译 modern translation;modern-language
version
今朝 ①today ②the present;now
今非昔比 no comparison between past and
present;The past cannot be compared with

the present.

今古奇谈 modern and ancient strange talks

今日要闻 Today's Contents; Today's Section; Inside (Today)

今胜于昔 The present is superior to the past.

今是昨非 today right, yesterday wrong (i.e. what I do today is right, what I did yesterday was wrong; said of repentance and reformation)

今昔对比 contrast the past with the present

今朝有酒今朝醉 drink today while drink you may

金 [jīn] I 名 ① metal ② money ③ ancient metal percussion instrument; gong ④ gold II 形 ① precious; dignified ② golden

金榜 a list of successful candidates in the imperial examinations

金杯 golden cup; gold cup

金笔 (quality) fountain pen

金币 gold coin

金箔 goldleaf; gold foil

金疮 metal-inflicted wound; incised wound

金殿 imperial palace

金额 amount (*or* sum) of money

金粉 ①lead powder ②pollen ③gold bits

金刚 Buddha's warrior attendant

金工 metalworking; metal processing

金股 golden share

金光 golden light (*or* ray)

金龟 tortoise

金衡 troy weight; troy

金红 golden red

金黄 golden yellow; golden

金婚 golden wedding

金鸡 golden pheasant

金奖 gold medal; highest award; first prize

金匠 goldsmith

金橘 kumquat

金卡 gold card

金库 national (*or* state) treasury; exchequer

金块 gold bullion

金矿 goldmine

金领 gold-collar

金牌 gold medal

金漆 gold lacquer

金器 gold vessel

金钱 money

金秋 golden autumn

金曲 great hit; song hit; hit song

金融 finance; banking

金色 golden

金哨 gold whistle

金石 ① metal and stone—a symbol of hardness and strength ②inscriptions on ancient bronzes and stone tablets

金饰 gold ornament

金属 metal

金条 gold bar

金文 inscriptions on ancient bronze objects

金星 ①Venus ②golden star (an object or figure) ③flashes of light that one seems to see (as from dizziness or a blow on the head)

金鱼 goldfish

金玉 gold and jade—valuable; precious

金元 gold dollar; U.S. dollar

金针 ① acupuncture needle ② dried day lily flower

金子 gold

金本位 gold standard

金不换 not to be exchanged even for gold; invaluable; priceless

金唱片 golden disc; gold record

金翅雀 greenfinch

金饭碗 golden rice bowl; secure and well-paid job

金刚砂 emery; corundum; carborundum

金刚石 diamond

金刚钻 diamond

金箍棒 golden cudgel

金龟婿 rich son-in-law

金龟子 scarab

金合欢 sponge tree

金红石 rutile

金花菜 bur clover

金鸡奖 the Gold Rooster Award—the Chinese film award

金交椅 extremely important post (*or* position)

金銮殿 the Hall of Golden Chimes

金霉素 aureomycin

金牛座 Taurus

金钱豹 leopard

金枪鱼 tuna

金桥网 gbnet

金融家 financier

金融界 financial circles

金三角 Golden Triangle (an area between Burma, Thailand and Laos, notorious for its drug production and trafficking)

金嗓子 beautiful voice; sweet, mellow voice

金石学 the study of inscriptions on ancient bronzes and stone tablets; epigraphy

金属模 metal pattern

金丝猴 golden monkey; snub-nosed monkey

金丝雀 canary

金丝绒 pleuche

金丝燕 esculent swift

金线鱼 red coat; golden thread

金相学 metallography

金小蜂 tiny golden wasp

金钥匙 golden key—the best solution to a problem

J

金银花 honeysuckle
金樱子 the fruit of Cherokee rose
金鱼缸 goldfish bowl；goldfish basin
金云母 phlogopite
金盏花 pot marigold
金针菜 day lily
金针虫 wireworm
金字塔 pyramid
金榜题名 have passed the examination；succeed in the imperial examination
金本位制 gold standard
金碧辉煌 （of a building，etc.） looking splendid in green and gold；resplendent and magnificent
金边债券 gilt-edged bonds
金边证券 gilt-edged securities；gilts
金蝉脱壳 slip out of a predicament like a cicada sloughing its skin；escape by cunning manoeuvring
金城汤池 ramparts of metal and a moat of boiling water—an impregnable fortress
金刚怒目 glare like a temple door-god—be fierce of visage
金戈铁马 golden spears and armoured horses—war or warriors
金鼓齐鸣 All the gongs and drums are beating.
金光大道 golden road；bright broad highway
金鸡独立 standing on one leg like a cock （a posture in Chinese boxing）
金鸡纳树 cinchona
金鸡纳霜 quinine
金降落伞 golden parachute
金科玉律 golden rule and precious precept
金口玉言 a golden mouth and pearly words—precious words；utterances that carry great weight
金兰之交 intimate friendship；sworn brotherhood
金缕玉衣 jade clothes sewn with gold wire；the jade suit sewn with gold thread
金绿宝石 chrysoberyl
金瓯无缺 territorial integrity unimpaired
金瓶掣签 Drawing Lots from the Gold （or Golden） Urn
金钱挂帅 money （money-making） in command
金钱万能 money talks
金融财团 financial syndicate
金融脆弱 financial fragility
金融动荡 financial turbulence
金融风波 financial disturbulance
金融改组 financial reorganization
金融寡头 financial oligarch （or magnate）
金融汇率 financial rate
金融机构 financial organ （or facilities，institution）

金融集团 financial clique
金融巨头 financial magnate；shark of high finance；financial tycoon
金融恐慌 financial panic
金融媒介 financial intermediation
金融市场 money （or financial） market
金融体制 monetary system；banking system
金融投机 monetary speculation
金融危机 financial crisis；monetary crisis
金融违纪 financial indiscipline
金融业务 financial business
金融诈骗 financial fraud
金融政策 financial policy
金融中心 financial （or banking） centre
金融资本 financial capital
金属加工 metal processing；metal working
金属结构 metal structure
金属疲劳 metal fatigue
金属探伤 metal defect detection；crack detection
金属陶瓷 cermet
金属涂料 metallic paint
金丝镶嵌 gold filigree
"金税"工程 Golden Tax Project
金童玉女 the Golden Boy and the Jade Maiden
金乌玉兔 crow of gold and hare of jade—the sun and the moon
金屋藏娇 live with one's young concubine in a plush house；keep a mistress in a love nest；take a concubine
金无足赤 Gold can't be hundred percent pure.
金银财宝 gold，silver，treasures，and jewels—riches
金银花露 distilled liquid of honeysuckle
金玉良言 golden sayings；invaluable advice
金玉满堂 a hall filled with gold and jade—wealthy；learned
金枝玉叶 golden branches and jade leaves—people of imperial lineage；royalty
金字招牌 a gold-lettered signboard—a vainglorious title
金汇兑本位 gold exchange standard
金球制胜法 golden goal
金融电子化 computerize financial services
金属工艺品 metal handicrafts
金融监管制度 financial supervision system
金融信息中心 financial information centre
金字塔式推销 pyramid selling
金字塔式控制股权 pyramid golding
金要足赤，人要完人 gold must be pure and man must be perfect—perfectionism
金玉其外，败絮其中 rubbish coated in gold and jade；fair without，foul within

津 [jīn]
Ⅰ 名 ① saliva ② sweat ③ ferry crossing；ford Ⅱ 形 moist；humid；damp
津贴 ① financial aid；subsidy；allowance ②

give financial aid;subsidize

津要 ①key place ②key post

津液 ①body fluid ②saliva

津津乐道 take delight in talking about;dwell upon with great relish

津津有味 with relish;with gusto;with keen pleasure

衿 [jīn]
名 belt;girdle

矜 [jīn]
Ⅰ 动 pity;sympathize with;have compassion for Ⅱ 形 ①self-conceited;self-important;singing one's own praise ②prudent;restrained;reserved ➡ qín

矜持 restrained,reserved

矜夸 conceited and boastful

矜重 reserved and dignified

矜而不争 firm but not quarrelsome

矜功自伐 be fond of bragging about one's contributions;ring one's own bell;blow (or sound) one's own horn

筋 [jīn]
名 ①muscle ②tendon;sinew ③veins that stand out under the skin ④anything resembling a tendon or vein

筋道 ①(of food) tough and chewy ②sturdy (old man)

筋斗 ①somersault ②fall,tumble (over)

筋骨 bones and muscles—physique

筋肉 muscles

筋疲力尽 exhausted;played out;worn out;tired out;all in;dead-beat;dog-tired

禁 [jīn]
动 ①bear;stand;endure ②hold back;contain oneself;restrain oneself ➡ jìn

禁受 bear;stand;endure

禁不起 be unable to stand (tests,trials,etc.)

禁不住 ①be unable to bear (or endure) ②can't help (doing sth);can't refrain from

禁得起 be able to stand (tests,trials,etc.)

禁得住 be able to bear (or endure)

襟 [jīn]
名 ①front of a garment ②brothers-in-law whose wives are sisters

襟弟 husband of one's wife's younger sister;brother-in-law

襟怀 bosom;(breadth of) mind

襟兄 husband of one's wife's elder sister;brother-in-law

襟翼 (wing) flap

襟怀坦白 open-hearted and aboveboard;honest and straightforward

jǐn（ㄐㄧㄣˇ）

仅 [jǐn]
副 only;merely;barely;just ➡ jìn

仅仅 only;merely;alone

仅供参考 just for reference;for reference only

尽 [jǐn]
Ⅰ 副 ①to the greatest extent (or degree possible) ②furthest;most ③keep on doing sth Ⅱ 介 within the limit (or bounds,time) Ⅲ 动 give priority (or precedence) to ➡ jìn

尽管 ①feel free to;not hesitate to ②though;even though;in spite of;despite

尽快 as quickly (or soon,early) as possible

尽量 to the best of one's ability;as far as possible

尽先 give first priority to

尽早 as soon as possible

尽可能 as far as possible;to the best of one's ability

卺 [jǐn]
名 nuptial wine cup

紧 [jǐn]
Ⅰ 形 ①tight;taut;close ②fast;firm;close ③close;too tight ④urgent;pressing;following (each other) closely ⑤hard up;hard pressed;short of money Ⅱ 动 tighten;fasten

紧逼 press hard;close in on

紧凑 compact;terse;well-knit

紧跟 follow closely;keep in step with;hard on heels

紧急 urgent;pressing;critical

紧紧 closely;firmly;tightly

紧邻 close neighbour;next-door neighbour

紧密 ①close together;inseparable ②rapid and intense

紧迫 pressing;urgent;imminent

紧俏 (of consumer goods) in great demand but short supply

紧缺 in short supply;badly needed

紧缩 reduce;retrench;tighten

紧要 critical;crucial;vital

紧张 ①nervous;keyed up ②tense;intense;strained ③in short supply;tight

紧追 in hot pursuit

紧巴巴 ①tight ②hard up;short of money

紧绷绷 ①tightly drawn ②(of one's facial expression) taut

紧箍咒 the Incantation of the Golden Hoop—inhibition;inhibiting magic phrase

紧急闸 emergency brake

紧迫感 a feeling of urgency;a sense of urgency

紧日子 an austere life

紧身衣 tights

紧跟形势 keep abreast of the situation

紧急拨款 emergent appropriations

紧急出口 emergency exit

紧急措施 emergency measures;stringent effort

紧急法令 emergency act

紧急会议 emergency meeting

紧急集合 emergency muster
紧急降落 emergency landing
紧急警报 emergency (air-raid) alarm
紧急起飞 scramble
紧急提议 urgent motion
紧急信号 emergency (*or* distress) signal
紧急援助 bailout; emergency aid
紧急状态 emergency; state of emergence
紧急着陆 emergency landing
紧锣密鼓 a wild beating of gongs and drums—an intense publicity campaign
紧俏产品 products that sell well and are in short supply; hard-to-get commodity; scarce commodity; commodity in short supply; plum catches
紧俏商品 hard-to-get commodities; high demand merchandise
紧缩编制 reduce staff
紧缩措施 austerity measures
紧缩开支 retrench; curtail spending; curtail outlay; cut down expenses
紧缩通货 currency deflation
紧缩政策 austerity policies; tight financing policies
紧缩支出 retrenchment of expenditure; curtail financial outlays
紧急停车带 emergency parking bay
紧身短上衣 coatee
紧急特别联大 emergency special session of UN General Assembly
紧缩货币投放 tighten up the money supply
紧缩银根政策 tight money policy
紧跟时代的步伐 keep in step with the times
紧密型企业集团 tightly-knit groups of enterprises
紧缩财政和信贷 tighten control over finance, credits and loans

堇 [jǐn]

堇菜 violet
堇色 violet (colour)
堇青石 cordierite

锦 [jǐn]

Ⅰ 名 brocade Ⅱ 形 bright and gorgeous
锦标 prize; trophy; title
锦缎 brocade
锦鸡 golden pheasant
锦葵 high mallow
锦纶 polyamide fibre
锦旗 silk banner (as an award or a gift)
锦绣 as beautiful as brocade; beautiful; splendid
锦标赛 championship contest; championships
锦囊妙计 instructions for dealing with an emergency; wise counsel
锦上添花 add flowers to the brocade—make what is good still better

锦绣河山 a land of splendours; a land of charm and beauty; a beautiful land
锦绣前程 a glorious future
锦衣玉食 live in an luxury

谨 [jǐn]

Ⅰ 形 careful; cautious; prudent; circumspect Ⅱ 副 solemnly; sincerely
谨防 guard against; beware of
谨上 yours respectfully
谨慎 prudent; careful; cautious; circumspect
谨严 careful and precise
谨赠 with the compliments of
谨防假冒 beware of imitations
谨小慎微 overcautious (in small matters)
谨言慎行 speak and act cautiously; be discreet in word and deed

瑾 [jǐn]

名 beautiful jade
瑾瑜匿瑕 Flaws are hidden in a beautiful gem; Even a beautiful gem has flaw.

jìn (415)

仅 [jìn]

副 approaching; approximately; near ➡ jǐn

尽 [jìn]

Ⅰ 动 ① exhausted; finished; devoid ② die; pass away ③ to the utmost; to the limit ④ use up; exhaust ⑤ try one's best; do all one can; put to the best use Ⅱ 形 all; entire ➡ jǐn
尽处 terminal point; end
尽瘁 do one's utmost; spare no effort; do all one can
尽欢 enjoy oneself to the full
尽力 do all one can; try one's best
尽量 (drink or eat) to the full
尽情 to one's heart's content; as much as one likes
尽然 exactly like this
尽是 full of; all; without exception
尽头 end
尽心 with all one's heart
尽孝 be filial to one's parents; be a filial son (*or* daughter)
尽兴 to one's heart's content; enjoy oneself to the full
尽责 do one's duty; discharge one's responsibility; try one's best to fulfil one's responsibility
尽职 fulfil one's duty
尽忠 ① be utterly loyal ② be faithful unto death
尽人事 do what one can (to save a dying person, etc.); do all that is humanly possible (though with little hope of success)
尽义务 ① do one's duty; fulfil one's obligation ② work for no reward
尽力而为 do one's best; do everything in one's

power
尽其所有 give everything one has; give one's all
尽人皆知 be known to all; be common knowledge
尽如人意 just as one wishes; entirely satisfactory
尽善尽美 the acme of perfection; perfect
尽收眼底 have a panoramic view
尽心竭力 (do sth) with all one's heart and all one's might

进 [jìn]

Ⅰ 囫 ① advance; move forward; march ahead; press onward ② enter; come into; go into; get into ③ receive; take ④ submit; present ⑤ eat; drink; take ⑥ into; in Ⅱ 图 any of the several rows of houses within an old-style residential compound

进逼 close in on; advance on; press on towards
进兵 dispatch troops to attack (a place); (of troops) march on (a place)
进补 take tonic; take extra nourishment
进步 ① advance; progress; improve ② (politically) progressive
进餐 have a meal
进场 ① march into the arena ② approach
进城 go into town; go to town
进程 course; process; progress
进尺 footage
进出 ① pass in and out ② (business) turnover
进度 ① rate of progress (or advance) ② planned speed; schedule
进而 and then; after that
进发 set out; start
进犯 intrude into; invade
进攻 attack; assault; offensive
进宫 ① (in feudal times) enter imperial palace ② be detained (or imprisoned) by police
进贡 ① pay tribute (to a suzerain or emperor) ② grease (or oil) sb's palm
进化 evolution
进货 stock (a shop) with goods; lay in a stock of merchandise; replenish one's stock
进击 advance on (the enemy)
进见 call on (sb holding high office); have an audience with
进京 go to the capital of the country
进军 march; advance
进口 ① entrance ② enter port ③ import
进款 income; receipts
进来 ① come (or get) in; enter ② in (here)
进料 feedstock; charging; charge-in
进门 ① go in; pass the gate ② learn the rudiments of sth; cross the threshold ③ (of a woman) get married and move into the bridegroom's family
进球 goal

进取 keep forging ahead; be eager to make progress; be enterprising
进去 ① go in; get in; enter ② in (there)
进入 enter; get into
进食 take food; have one's meal
进士 a successful candidate in the highest imperial examinations
进退 ① advance and retreat ② sense of propriety
进位 carry (a number, as in adding)
进献 offer (or present) (to one's superior)
进香 (of Buddhists or Taoists) go on a pilgrimage to a temple; offer incense; worship
进项 income; receipts
进行 ① be in progress; be underway; go on ② carry on; carry out; conduct ③ be on the march; march; advance
进修 engage in advanced studies; take a refresher course
进言 give word of advice; go a step further; further
进展 make progress; make headway
进占 march on and take (a place)
进站 (of a train) get into (or draw into, pull into) a station
进账 income; receipts
进驻 ① enter and be stationed in; enter and garrison ② (of a working group) sent by a higher authority (to investigate or resolve problems)
进出口 ① exits and entrances; exit ② imports and exports
进度表 progress chart
进风井 downcast (shaft)
进化论 the theory of evolution; evolutionism
进局子 be taken into custody by police; go to prison; be taken to prison
进军号 bugle to advance
进口港 port of entry
进口货 imported goods; imports
进口商 importer
进口税 import duties
进取心 enterprising spirit; initiative; gumption; push
进水闸 intake work; intake
进香客 Buddhist pilgrim
进行曲 march
进修班 class for advanced studies
进修生 graduate student
进口报单 import declaration; consumption entry
进口报关 customs entry
进口壁垒 import barrier
进口补贴 import subsidy
进口承诺 import commitment
进口管制 import control
进口检疫 import quarantine

J

进口结构 import structure；import mix
进口配额 import quota
进口申报 declaration for import
进口渗透 import penetration
进口替代 import substitution
进口限额 import quota
进口原料 imported materials
进取精神 enterprising spirit；go-aheadism
进入角色 get inside the character that one is playing；enter into the spirit of a character；live one's part
进入系统 log in（on）
进身之阶 stepping-stone（in one's official career）
进退两难 find it difficult to advance or to retreat—be in a dilemma
进退维谷 in a dilemma；between the devil and the deep blue sea
进退自如 proceed or step back freely；be free to advance or retreat
进贤举能 recommend properly qualified persons for service
进展顺利 proceed smoothly
进出口贸易 import and export trade；foreign trade
进出口商会 chamber of import and export trade
进刀 feed
进攻性武器 offensive weapon
进口代办行 import commission
进口代理商 import agent
进口附加税 import surcharge；import surtax
进口许可证 import license
进出口经营权 import-export operation right；power to engage in import and export trade
进出口许可证 import-export licence
进出口自营权 self-determining rights to import and export
进出口商品检验 import-export commodity inspection
进出口商品结构 structure of imports and exports
进口替代型产品 import substitute
进出口许可证制度 import and export license system

近 ［jìn］
［形］① near；close；immediate ② approaching；nearly；approximately；close to ③ intimate；closely related ④ easy to understand；simple and obvious
近便 close and convenient
近程 short range
近处 vicinity；place nearby
近代 modern times
近道 shortcut
近东 the Near East
近海 coastal waters；inshore；offshore

近乎 ① close to；little short of ② intimate；friendly
近郊 outskirts of a city；suburbs；environs
近景 close shot
近况 recent developments；how things stand
近来 recently；of late；lately
近邻 near neighbour
近路 shortcut
近年 in recent years
近旁 nearby；near
近期 in the near future
近前 nearby；near
近亲 close relative；near relation
近日 ①recently；in the past few days ②within the next few days
近似 approximate；similar
近因 immediate cause
近于 bordering on；little short of
近战 fighting at close quarters；close combat
近地点 perigee
近日点 perihelion
近视(眼) myopia；nearsightedness；shortsightedness
近似商 approximate quotient
近似值 approximate value
近体诗 modern-style poetry
近义词 near synonym
近月点 perilune
近海工程 offshore engineering
近海渔业 offshore fishery
近亲繁殖 inbreeding；nepotism
近亲婚姻 consanguineous marriage
近视眼镜 spectacles for nearsighted person
近水楼台 waterside pavilion—a favourable position
近似读数 approximate reading
近似计算 approximate calculation
近台防守 close-table defence
近台快攻 close-table fast attack
近在咫尺 close at hand；well within reach
近水楼台先得月 a waterside pavilion gets the moonlight first—a person in a favourable position gains special advantages
近朱者赤,近墨者黑 he who stays near vermilion gets stained red,and he who stays near ink gets stained black—one takes on the colour of one's company

劲 ［jìn］
［名］① strength；powers；energy ② spirit；mood；gusto；drive ③ air；manner；look；expression ④ interest；relish；savour；gusto ➡ jìng
劲头 ① strength；energy ② vigour；spirit；drive；zeal

荩 ［jìn］
Ⅰ［名］hispid arthraxon Ⅱ［形］loyal；faithful
荩草 hispid arthraxon

晋 [jìn]
<动> ①enter; advance ②promote
晋级 rise in rank; be promoted
晋见 call on (sb holding high office); have an audience with
晋升 promote to a higher office
晋谒 call on (sb holding high office); have an audience with

赆 [jìn]
<名> money presented at parting

烬 [jìn]
<名> cinder; ashes

浸 [jìn]
I <动> ① soak; dip; steep; immerse ② be soaked (in liquid); be steeped; (of liquid) ooze; leak II <副> gradually; bit by bit
浸膏 extract
浸灌 ①(as of floodwater) come in; spread out; flood ②irrigate
浸剂 infusion
浸礼 Christianity baptism; immersion
浸没 ① submerge; flood; immerse ② be immersed in; be permeated with
浸泡 soak; immerse
浸染 ① be contaminated; be gradually influenced ②soak; infiltrate ③dip-dye
浸软 macerate
浸润 (of liquid) soak; infiltrate
浸透 soak; saturate; steep; infuse
浸种 seed soaking (in water)
浸渍 soak; ret; macerate
浸礼会 the Baptist Church; the Baptists

禁 [jìn]
I <动> ① prohibit; forbid; ban ② put behind bars; imprison; detain II <名> ① what is forbidden by law (*or* custom); taboo ② forbidden area ➡ jīn
禁闭 confinement (as a punishment)
禁地 forbidden area; restricted area; out-of-bounds area
禁毒 ban drugs; drug control
禁赌 ban gambling
禁方 secret medicinal recipe
禁放 firework control
禁锢 ① debar from holding office (in feudal times) ②keep in custody; imprison ③confine
禁果 forbidden fruit; sex for the first time
禁忌 ①taboo ②avoid; abstain from ③contraindication
禁酒 prohibition on alcoholic drinks
禁绝 totally prohibit; completely ban
禁例 prohibitory regulations; prohibitions
禁猎 prohibit hunting
禁令 prohibition; ban
禁鸣 horn-blowing control
禁区 ① forbidden zone; restricted zone ② (wildlife or plant) preserve; reserve; natural park ③ football penalty area ④ basketball restricted area
禁赛 ban from competition; suspend
禁食 fast
禁书 banned book
禁线 restraining line
禁烟 ban on opium-smoking and the opium trade
禁渔 prohibit fishing; fishing ban
禁欲 be ascetic
禁运 embargo
禁止 prohibit; ban; forbid
禁阻 prohibit; ban; forbid; prevent; stop
禁伐林 forest reserve where lumbering is prohibited
禁飞区 no fly zone; no-flight area
禁卫军 imperial guards
禁烟区 no-smoking area
禁运品 contraband
禁制品 articles the manufacture of which is prohibited except by special permit; banned products
禁食疗法 fasting treatment; starvation cure
禁欲主义 asceticism

觐 [jìn]
<动> ①present oneself before (a monarch) ②go on a pilgrimage
觐见 present oneself before (a monarch); go to court; have an audience with

jīng (ㄐㄧㄥ)

茎 [jīng]
<名> ①stem (of a plant); stalk ②anything like a stem or stalk
茎病 stem disease

京 [jīng]
<名> ①capital of a country ②Beijing ③ten million
京城 the capital of a country
京都 ①the capital of a country ②Kyoto
京官 government officials in the capital of the country
京剧 Peking opera
京腔 Beijing accent
京味 of special Beijing flavour; with Beijing characteristics
京戏 Beijing opera
京族 the Jing nationality; the Ching nationality
京剧票友 Peking Opera fan
京韵大鼓 story-telling in Beijing dialect with drum accompaniment
京剧人物脸谱 types of facial make-up in Peking Opera

泾 [jīng]
<名> brook; stream
泾渭不分 fail to distinguish between the good

J

and the bad
泾渭分明 as different as the waters of the Jinghe and the Weihe—entirely different

经 [jīng]
I 名 ① warp ② channels ③ longitude ④ scripture;canon;classics ⑤ menses;menstruation II 动 ①manage;rule;deal in;engage in ②hang ③pass through ④stand;bear;endure III 形 constant;regular;normal IV 介 via;by way of ⇒jìng
经办 handle;deal with
经闭 amenorrhoea
经编 warp knitting
经常 ① day-to-day;everyday;daily ② frequently;constantly;regularly;often
经典 ①classics ②scriptures ③classical
经度 longitude
经费 funds;outlay
经管 be in charge of
经过 ①pass;go through;undergo ②as a result of;after;through ③process;course
经纪 ①manage (a business) ②manager;broker
经济 ① economy ② of industrial (or economic) value;economic ③financial condition;income ④economical;thrifty
经久 ①prolonged ②durable
经理 ①handle;manage ②manager;director
经历 go through;undergo;experience
经络 channels and subsidiary channels
经脉 passages through which vital energy circulates,regulating bodily functions
经贸 economy and trade
经密 warp density;ends per inch
经期 (menstrual) period
经纱 ①warp ②end
经商 engage in trade;be in business
经手 handle;deal with
经受 undergo;experience;withstand;stand;weather
经售 sell on commission;deal in;distribute;sell
经丝 organzine
经纬 ①meridian and parallel (lines) ②main threads;orderliness;reason ③plan and administer
经文 scripts;passages from the Confucian classics or religious scriptures
经线 ①warp ②meridian (line)
经心 careful;mindful;conscientious
经验 ①experience ②go through;experience
经营 manage;operate;run;engage in
经由 via;by way of
经轴 warp beam
经传 [jīngzhuàn] ①Confucian classics and commentaries on them;Confucian canon ② classical works;classics

经常化 become a regular practice
经纪人 broker;middleman;agent
经济舱 economy class
经济林 cash trees;economic forest
经济圈 economic circle
经济学 economics
经济战 white war
经济账 financial considerations
经商热 upsurge in doing business
经手人 person handling particular task
经纬度 latitude and longitude
经纬仪 theodolite;transit
经销商 distributor
经营权 power of management;managerial authority
经常费用 overhead charges;current expenditure
经典力学 classical mechanics
经典作家 author of a classic;classic
经费包干 take full responsibility for one's surpluses and deficits under an approved budget;contract for one's outlays
经费困难 wear a fiscal straitjacket
经国之才 ability to administer a state
经济报酬 financial reward
经济崩溃 economic breakdown;economic bust
经济布局 economic layout;economic patterns;geographical distribution of the different sectors of the economy
经济成分 economic sector
经济成分 sector of the economy;economic sector
经济刺激 economic stimulus;economic incentive
经济倒退 economic adversity
经济动物 economic animal
经济法规 laws and regulations pertaining to the economy;economic statutes
经济法庭 economic tribunal
经济法则 economic statutes;economic legislation;economic laws and decrees
经济繁荣 economic prosperity
经济犯罪 economic crime
经济封锁 economic blockade
经济复苏 economic resurgence;economic recovery;economic rehabilitation
经济改革 economic reform;economic restructuring
经济杠杆 economic lever
经济规律 economic law;canon of economics
经济过热 overheated economy
经济合同 economic contract
经济核算 business accounting;economic accounting
经济滑坡 economic decline
经济环境 economic environment
经济活力 economic vitality

经济基础 economic base;economic basis
经济拮据 be in reduced circumstances
经济恐慌 economic panic
经济宽裕 be in easy circumstances
经济昆虫 economic insects
经济立法 economic legislation
经济命脉 economic lifeline;economic arteries;key branches of the economy
经济模式 economic mould
经济汽车 econobox
经济起飞 economic takeoff
经济侵略 economic infringement
经济渗透 economic penetration;economic infiltration
经济失调 economic ailment;dislocation of economy
经济实力 economic strength
经济实体 economic entity
经济素质 economic quality
经济态势 economic situation
经济特区 Special Economic Zone(SEZ)
经济腾飞 economic take-off
经济体制 economic structure
经济危机 economic crisis
经济萎缩 economic contraction
经济萧条 economic depression (*or* slump)
经济效益 economic performance;economic results;economic effectiveness
经济援助 economic aid
经济杂交 commercial crossbreeding
经济责任 financial responsibility
经济振兴 vigorous economic growth
经济支柱 economic pillars
经济植物 economic plants
经济指数 economic index number
经济制裁 economic sanctions
经济制度 economic system
经济秩序 economic order
经济仲裁 economic arbitration
经济主义 economism
经济总量 total supply and demand
经济作物 industrial crop;cash crop
经久不息 prolonged
经理助理 assistant manager;aide of the manager
经年累月 for years and years;year in year out
经销品牌 dealer brand
经验之谈 the wise remark of an experienced person;remark made by one who has had experience
经验主义 empiricism
经营方向 management direction
经营方针 managerial principles
经营思想 management philosophy
经营资金 operation fund;floating capital
经营作风 management style
经院哲学 scholasticism

经常性贷款 commercial lending
经常性支出 running expenses
经济百强县 top 100 counties in economic strength
经济地理学 economic geography
经济多元化 economic pluralization
经济法制化 manage economic affairs according to law;put economic operation on a legal basis
经济活跃区 economically dynamic area
经济开发区 business improvement district;business development zone
经济开放区 open(ed) economic region
经济联合体 economic association;
经济全球化 economic globalization
经济适用房 economic houses
经济协作区 economically coordinated region;economic coordination region;economic cooperation zone
经济一体化 economic integration
经济优惠装 economy pack
经济增长点 economic growth point;economic growth area;growth engines
经济增长率 the economic growth rate
经济自由化 economic liberalization;liberalization of the economy
经理席会议 joint executive meeting
经销专业户 households specializing in marketing
经营承包制 management contract system
经营管理权 the right of operation and management
经营决策权 making decisions on operation and management
经营性亏损 losses of a management nature;operational deficit;operational loss
经营责任制 responsibility system for operation
经营自主权 independent managerial right;right to make its own managerial decision
经常项目顺差 favourable balance of current account;surplus of current account
经济发展后劲 staying power of economic development
经济发展速度 the rate of economic development
经济发展战略 strategy for the development of economy;the economic development strategy
经济犯罪行为 economic crime
经济紧缩政策 economic austerity policy;business restraining policy
经济扩张政策 expansionary policy
经济失调指数 misery index
经济实用住房 economic and functional buildings
经济体制改革 economic restructuring;reform

the economic structure

经济协调发展 coordinated development of the economy

经济循环不畅 circulation in the economy is not smooth

经济运行机制 economic mechanism; economic operation mechanism

经济运行效益 operational efficiency of the economy

经济增长模式 the mode of economic growth

经济总量平衡 balance between total demand and total supply

经风雨，见世面 face the world and brave the storm; see life and stand its tests

经常性财政开支 day-to-day expenditures from government

经济承包责任制 economic responsibility system with contracted jobs

经济互助委员会 the Council of Mutual Economic Assistance (CMEA); Comecon (now dissolved)

经济技术开发区 Economic and Technological Development Zone (ETDZ)

经济技术协作区 economic and technical assistance

经营权与所有权分离 separation of the right of management from the right of ownership

荆 [jīng]
名 ① chaste tree ② rot for flogging

荆棘 thistles and thorns; brambles; thorny undergrowth

荆树 wattle

荆条 twigs of the chaste tree

荆棘载途 a path overgrown with brambles—a path beset with difficulties

荆天棘地 thistles and thorns everywhere—a very difficult situation (with one barrier after another in one's path)

菁 [jīng]
Ⅰ 名 ① chives flower ② turnip ③ water weeds Ⅱ 形 lush; luxuriant

菁华 essence; cream; quintessence

旌 [jīng]
Ⅰ 名 flag Ⅱ 动 honour officially

旌德 honour the virtuous

旌旗 banners and flags

惊 [jīng]
动 ① start; get alarmed; be frightened ② surprise; shock; alarm; amaze ③ shy; stampede

惊诧 surprised; amazed; astonished

惊呆 stunned; stupefied

惊动 ① alarm ② alert ③ disturb

惊愕 stunned; stupefied

惊风 infantile convulsions

惊骇 frightened; panic-stricken

惊呼 cry out in alarm

惊慌 alarmed; scared; panic-stricken

惊惶 trepidation

惊悸 palpitate with fear

惊叫 cry in fear; scream; give a cry of alarm; scream with fear

惊厥 ① faint from fear ② convulsions

惊恐 alarmed and panicky; terrified; panic-stricken; seized with terror

惊雷 frightening thunder; loud clap of thunder; thunderous warning (or awakening)

惊奇 wonder; be surprised; be amazed

惊扰 alarm; agitate

惊人 astonishing; amazing; alarming

惊叹 wonder at; marvel at; exclaim (with admiration)

惊悉 be shocked to learn

惊喜 pleasantly surprised

惊吓 frighten; scare

惊险 alarmingly dangerous; breath-taking; thrilling

惊醒 [jīngxǐng] ① wake up with a start ② rouse suddenly from sleep; awaken

惊醒 [jīngxing] sleep lightly; be a light sleeper

惊讶 surprised; amazed; astonished; astounded

惊疑 surprised and bewildered

惊异 surprised; amazed; astonished; astounded

惊叹号 exclamation mark (!)

惊堂木 (in former times) a wooden block used by a magistrate to strike the table in calling for attention or order

惊险片 thriller

惊弓之鸟 a bird that starts at the mere twang of a bow-string—a badly frightened person

惊慌失措 frightened out of one's wits; seized with panic; panic-stricken

惊魂未定 not yet recovered from a fright; still badly shaken

惊恐万状 in a great panic; convulsed with fear

惊人之举 masterstroke; coup de maitre

惊世骇俗 astound the world with an extraordinary idea, etc.

惊涛骇浪 terrifying waves; a stormy sea

惊天动地 shaking heaven and earth; earth-shake; world-shake

惊心动魄 soul-stirring; profoundly affecting

晶 [jīng]
Ⅰ 形 bright; shiny; glittering; brilliant Ⅱ 名 ① quartz; (rock) crystal ② any crystalline substance

晶格 (crystal) lattice

晶粒 crystalline grain; grain

晶面 crystal face; lattice plane

晶石 spar

晶体 crystal

晶莹 sparkling and crystal-clear; glittering and translucent

晶体管 transistor

晶状体 crystalline lens

腈 [jīng]
名 nitrile
腈纶 acrylic fibres

睛 [jīng]
名 eyeball

粳 [jīng]
粳稻 japonica rice
粳米 polished round-grained nonglutinous rice

兢 [jīng]
兢兢业业 cautious and conscientious

精 [jīng]
I 形 ①refined; polished; picked; choice ② perfect; excellent; essential ③ fine; delicate; exquisite; superb ④ smart; sharp; clever; astute; shrewd ⑤ skilled; versed; conversant; proficient II 名 ① essence; spirit; concentrate; extract ② energy; vigour; spirit ③ sperm; semen; seed ④goblin; spirit; demon ⑤ fundamental substance which maintains the functioning of the body; essence of life III 副 extremely; very; awfully
精兵 picked troops; crack troops
精彩 brilliant; splendid; wonderful
精巢 spermary; testis; testicle
精诚 absolute sincerity; good faith
精虫 spermatozoon
精纯 consummate; superb
精粹 succinct; pithy; terse
精当 precise and appropriate
精读 ①read carefully and thoroughly ②intensive reading
精度 precision
精干 ① (of a body of troops, etc.) small in number but highly trained; crack ② keen-witted and capable
精光 ①with nothing left ②bright and clean; shiny
精悍 ① capable and vigorous ② pithy and poignant
精华 cream; essence; quintessence
精简 retrench; simplify; cut; reduce
精讲 present briefly and succinctly
精金 fine gold
精矿 concentrate
精力 energy; vigour; vim
精练 refine
精炼 ①refine; purify; reduce to a pure state ②concise; succinct; terse
精良 excellent; superior; of the best quality
精料 refined fodder
精灵 ① spirit; demon ② (of a child) clever; smart; intelligent
精馏 rectification
精煤 clean coal
精美 exquisite; elegant
精米 polished rice

精密 precise; accurate
精明 astute; shrewd; sagacious
精囊 seminal vesicle
精辟 penetrating; incisive
精品 ①fine works (of art) ②quality goods; articles of fine quality
精巧 exquisite; ingenious
精确 accurate; exact; precise
精肉 lean meat
精锐 crack; picked
精深 profound
精神 ①spirit; mind; consciousness ②essence; gist; spirit ③vigour; vitality; drive ④lively; spirited; vigorous; smart
精瘦 skinny; skin and bones
精梳 combing
精髓 marrow; pith; quintessence
精通 be proficient in; have a good command of; master
精细 meticulous; fine; careful
精心 meticulously; painstakingly; elaborately
精选 ① concentration ② carefully chosen; choice
精盐 refined salt; table salt
精液 seminal fluid; semen
精英 elite; person of outstanding ability; the best and brightest
精轧 finish rolling
精湛 consummate; exquisite
精制 make with extra care; refine
精致 fine; exquisite; delicate
精装 (of books) clothbound; hardback; hardcover
精壮 able-bodied; strong
精准 accurate; perfect
精子 sperm; spermatozoon
精加工 finish machining; precision work; fine finishing
精密度 precision
精品屋 store selling quality products only
精饲料 concentrated feed; concentrate
精装本 hardback edition; deluxe edition
精子库 sperm bank
精兵简政 crack troops and streamlined administration; better staff and streamlined administration
精打细算 careful calculation and strict budgeting
精雕细刻 work at sth with the care and precision of a sculptor; work at sth with great care
精耕细作 intensive and meticulous farming; intensive cultivation
精简会议 cut down the number of meetings and make them short
精简机构 trim the administrative structure; streamline organizations; make operations

J

leaner
精简开支 cut down the outlay; retrench expenses
精力充沛 full of vim and vigour; vigorous; energetic
精明强干 intelligent and capable; able and efficient
精疲力竭 exhausted; worn out; tired out; spent
精品商店 up-market store
精品意识 awareness of creating excellent works
精品战略 refined works strategy; strategy of creating excellent works
精气神儿 vigour; energy; drive
精确轰炸 pinpoint bombing
精锐部队 an elite battalion
精深加工 fine and further processing
精神产品 intellectual products
精神错乱 mentally deranged; insane
精神抖擞 full of energy (*or* vitality); vigorous
精神分析 psychoanalysis
精神公害 public spiritual poison
精神鼓励 moral encouragement
精神贵族 intellectual aristocrats
精神焕发 be in high spirits; one's spirits rise
精神枷锁 ideological shackles; mental yoke
精神空虚 be spiritually barren
精神疗法 psychotherapy
精神面貌 mental attitude; mental outlook
精神生活 cultural life
精神失常 have bats in the belfry; have lost one's marbles; have a screw loose; be deranged
精神食粮 spiritual food; (mental) pabulum; food for thought; mental food; mental nourishment; nourishment for the mind
精神世界 inner world; mental world
精神衰弱 psychasthenia
精神文明 ethical and cultural progress; spiritual civilization
精神污染 spiritual contamination; cultural contamination; ideological pollution
精神鸦片 mental or spiritual opium (sth that corrupts people's mind)
精神支柱 anchorage; spiritual prop; ideological prop
精神状态 state of mind; mental outlook
精卫填海 the mythical bird *jingwei* trying to fill up the sea with pebbles—dogged determination to achieve one's purpose
精细化工 fine chemicals
精心炮制 elaborately concoct
精益求精 constantly improve sth; keep improving
精神分裂症 schizophrenia
精神损失费 damages for emotional distress

精加工制成品 products requiring high-precision techniques
精诚所至，金石为开 Complete sincerity can affect even metal and stone.

鲸 [jīng] 名 whale
鲸肉 whalemeat
鲸鲨 whale shark
鲸吞 swallow like a whale; annex (territory)
鲸须 baleen; whalebone
鲸油 whale oil; blubber
鲸鱼 whale
鲸仔 whale calf
鲸目动物 cetacean

jǐng (ㄐㄧㄥˇ)

井 [jǐng] I 名 ① well ② sth in the shape of a well ③ settlement; village II 形 in good order; orderly; neat
井场 well site
井底 ① the bottom of a well ② shaft bottom; pit bottom
井灌 well irrigation
井架 ① derrick ② headframe; headgear
井口 ① the mouth of a well ② pithead ③ wellhead
井栏 brandreth
井喷 blowout
井然 orderly; neat and tidy; shipshape; methodical
井台 a raised platform around a well
井筒 pit shaft
井下 in the pit; under the shaft
井斜 well deflection; well deviation
井盐 well salt
井眼 borehole; well
井灌区 well-irrigated area
井底之蛙 a frog in a well—a person with a very limited outlook
井井有条 in perfect order; shipshape; methodical
井然有序 in good order; orderly; methodical
井水不犯河水 well water does not intrude into river water—I'll mind my own business, you mind yours

阱 [jǐng] 名 trap; pitfall; pit

刭 [jǐng] 动 cut the throat

肼 [jǐng] 名 hydrazine

颈 [jǐng] 名 ① neck ② anything shaped like the neck
颈项 neck
颈椎 cervical vertebra
颈动脉 carotid

景 [jǐng]

Ⅰ 名 ① view; sight; scene; landscape; scenery ② situation; condition; circumstance ③ scenery (of a play or film); setting ④ scene (of a play) Ⅱ 动 admire; esteem; revere; respect

景点 scenic spot
景观 landscape
景况 situation; circumstances
景慕 esteem; revere; admire
景片 a piece of (stage) scenery; flat
景气 prosperity; boom
景色 scenery; view; scene; landscape
景深 depth of field
景天 red-spotted stonecrop
景物 scenery
景象 scene; sight; picture
景仰 respect and admire; hold in deep respect
景遇 circumstances; one's lot
景致 view; scenery; scene
景泰蓝 cloisonné enamel; cloisonné
景气产业 thriving business; thriving industries

儆 [jǐng]

动 warn; admonish
儆戒 warn; admonish; exhort

憬 [jǐng]

动 wake up to reality; come to see the truth
憬悟 awaken; wake

警 [jǐng]

Ⅰ 形 ① alert; vigilant ② sharp; acute; keen Ⅱ 动 ① guard against ② warn; admonish; alarm Ⅲ 名 ① alarm; emergency; accident ② police; policeman

警报 alarm; warning; alert
警备 guard; garrison
警察 police; policeman
警车 police car; police van
警笛 ① police whistle ② siren
警服 police uniform
警告 ① warn; caution; admonish ② warning (as a disciplinary measure)
警官 police officer
警棍 policeman's baton; truncheon
警花 policewoman
警徽 police emblem
警戒 ① warn; admonish ② be on the alert against; guard against; keep a close watch on
警句 aphorism; epigram
警觉 vigilance; alertness
警力 police force; police power; guards; police strength
警铃 alarm bell
警犬 police dog
警嫂 a policeman's wife
警示 lesson; warning
警世 caution against impending disasters

警探 police detective; police-spy
警惕 be on guard against; watch out for; be vigilant
警亭 police box
警卫 (security) guard
警务 police affairs; police service
警衔 police rank
警醒 be a light sleeper
警钟 alarm bell; tocsin
警报器 siren; alarm
警察局 police headquarters; police station
警匪片 "cops and robbers" feature film; crime action movie
警戒色 warning (or aposematic) coloration
警戒线 warning line; cordon; security line
警告信号 warning signal
警号标志 cautionary mark
警戒水位 warning water level; warning stage
警戒状态 state of alert
警民共建 police and civilians working together to build a society with a high cultural and ideological level
警察巡逻车 patrol car

jìng (ㄐㄧㄥˋ)

劲 [jìng]

形 strong; vigorous; powerful; sturdy →jìn
劲敌 formidable adversary; strong opponent (or contender)
劲风 a strong wind
劲歌 pop song characterized by a strong beat
劲旅 strong contingent; crack force
劲射 sudden shot at the goal
劲升 rocket
劲舞 rap dancing; strong dance

径 [jìng]

Ⅰ 名 ① footpath; path; trail; track ② way; road; means ③ diameter Ⅱ 副 directly; straight; straightaway

径迹 track
径流 runoff
径赛 track
径庭 very unlike
径线 radial line
径向 radial
径直 straight; directly; straightaway
径自 without leave; without consulting anyone
径情直遂 as smoothly as one would wish

净 [jìng]

Ⅰ 形 ① clean ② with nothing left; completely ③ net; pure Ⅱ 动 wipe (sth) clean Ⅲ 副 nothing but; only; merely Ⅳ 名 "painted face", a character type in Peking opera, etc.

净菜 cleaned vegetables (readied for market)
净额 net amount
净高 clear height
净化 purify

净货 clean cargo
净价 net price
净街 close a street to traffic
净空 headroom;clearance
净身 (of a man) be castrated
净桶 nightstool;closestool;commode
净土 Pure Land;Paradise of the West
净心 ①free from care ②have a peaceful and quiet mind;feel completely at ease
净余 net balance;remainder;surplus
净增 net increase;net growth
净值 net worth;net value
净重 net weight
净赚 make a net profit of;clear
净菜社 clean vegetable shop
净产量 net production
净产值 net output value
净成本 pure cost
净出口 net export
净存货 net inventory
净荷载 net load
净进口 net import
净收入 net income
净水厂 water treatment plant
净现值 net present value
净支出 net disbursement

经 [jīng]
［名］warping ➡jīng

胫 [jìng]
［名］shin
胫骨 shin bone;tibia

痉 [jìng]
痉挛 convulsion;spasm

竞 [jìng]
Ⅰ［动］compete;contest;contend;vie Ⅱ［形］strong;powerful
竞标 competitive bidding;competitive tender
竞猜 compete to answer (in contest)
竞渡 ①boat race ②swimming race
竞岗 employment by competition
竞技 sports;athletics
竞价 bid (in auction);bid against each other
竞买 compete to buy
竞卖 compete to sell
竞拍 auction;bid against each other
竞聘 employment by competition
竞赛 contest;competition;emulation;race
竞投 compete in bidding (for a contract,etc.)
竞相 compete;vie
竞选 enter into an election contest;campaign for (office);run for
竞争 compete
竞走 heel-and-toe walking race
竞选团 race group;campaigning group
竞争力 competitiveness;competitive power
竞争性 competitiveness

竞技状态 form (of an athlete)
竞选演说 campaign speech;stumping speech
竞争机制 competitive mechanism;mechanism of competition
竞争价格 competitive price
竞争上岗 employment through competition
竞争主体 competitor;principal in competition
竞选委员会 election committee;election board
竞争性贬值 competitive depreciation;competitive devaluation
竞争淘汰机制 mechanism of selection through competition

竟 [jìng]
Ⅰ［动］①end;finish;complete ②investigate Ⅱ［形］from beginning to end;throughout;whole Ⅲ［副］①in the end;finally;eventually ②unexpectedly;actually ③ go so far as to;have the impudence to
竟敢 actually dare;have the audacity;have the impertinence
竟然 ①unexpectedly;to one's surprise;actually ②go so far as to;go to the length of;have the impudence (or effrontery) to
竟自 unexpectedly;to one's surprise;actually
竟夜无眠 lay awake the whole night (or throughout the night)

婧 [jìng]
［名］talented woman

靓 [jìng]
Ⅰ［动］decorate;make up Ⅱ［形］motionless ➡liàng
靓衣 beautiful dress;beautiful clothing

敬 [jìng]
Ⅰ［名］respect;honour;esteem;revere Ⅱ［副］respectfully;reverently Ⅲ［动］offer politely
敬爱 respect and love
敬茶 serve tea
敬辞 term of respect;polite expression
敬奉 ①piously worship ②offer respectfully;present politely
敬告 beg to inform
敬贺 congratulate with respect;send respectful greetings to
敬候 await respectfully
敬酒 propose a toast;toast
敬礼 salute;give a salute
敬慕 respect and admire
敬佩 esteem;admire
敬请 invite respectfully
敬上 (*used after the signature in a letter to one's senior or superior*) yours respectfully;yours sincerely
敬挽 (*used on funeral scrolls*) with deep condolences from sb
敬畏 hold in awe and veneration;revere
敬献 present politely;offer respectfully
敬仰 revere;venerate

敬业 dedicate oneself to one's studies
敬意 respect;tribute
敬语 words spoken out of respect or courtesy; respectful remarks
敬赠 (*used when sending a gift*) with compliments
敬重 deeply respect;revere;honour
敬祝 (*used at the end of a letter*) I wish you
敬老节 Day for Respecting the Aged;Day for the Old
敬老院 home of respect for the aged;old folks' home
敬而远之 stay at a respectful distance from sb
敬老爱幼 respect the aged and cherish the young
敬请斧正 Please make whatever corrections you like.
敬请光临 request the honour of your presence
敬请指教 humbly request your advice
敬业精神 professional dedication;professional ethics;spirit of devotion to work
敬鬼神而远之 keep one's distance from the gods and spirits while showing them respect—stay at a respectful distance from sb
敬酒不吃吃罚酒 refuse a toast only to drink a forfeit—submit to sb's pressure after first turning down his request;be constrained to do what one at first refused to

靖 [jìng]
I 名 peace;tranquility II 动 pacify;suppress
靖边 pacify the border regions
靖国神社 (Japan) Yasukuni Shrine;Yasukuni Jinjia

静 [jìng]
I 形 ①still;calm;motionless ②silent;quiet;noiseless II 动 calm;quieten
静电 static electricity
静观 watch quietly
静候 quietly await
静立 stand still
静脉 vein
静谧 quiet;still;tranquil
静默 ①become silent ②mourn in silence;observe silence
静穆 solemn and quiet
静水 still water
静态 static state
静听 listen attentively and quietly
静卧 lie motionless
静物 still life
静养 rest quietly to recuperate;convalesce
静止 static;motionless;at a standstill
静坐 ①sit quietly ②sit still as a form of therapy ③sit-down;sit-in
静荷载 dead load
静力学 statics

静脉炎 phlebitis
静悄悄 very quiet
静待时机 lie low and bide one's time
静脉点滴 intravenous drip
静脉曲张 varix;varicosity
静脉注射 intravenous injection
静以制动 beat action by inaction
静止图像 still picture
静坐罢工 sit-down
静电复印机 xerox;electrostatic copier
静态经济学 static economic

境 [jìng]
名 ①border;boundary ②place;area;land;territory ③condition;situation;circumstances
境地 condition;circumstances
境界 ①boundary ②extent reached;plane attained;state;realm
境况 (financial) condition;circumstances
境域 ①condition;circumstances ②area;realm
境遇 circumstances;one's lot
境外企业 business (enterprises) outside national boundary

镜 [jìng]
I 名 ①looking glass;mirror ②lens;glass;mirror II 动 ①mirror ②perceive ③use for reference
镜框 ①picture frame ②spectacles frame
镜面 mirror face;mirror plate;mirror surface
镜片 lens
镜台 dressing table
镜头 ①camera lens ②shot;scene
镜匣 a wooden case with a looking glass and other toilet articles;dressing case
镜像 image;mirror image
镜子 ①mirror;looking glass ②glasses;spectacles
镜花水月 flowers in a mirror or the moon in the water—an illusion
镜面电视 flat TV

jiōng (ㄐㄩㄥ)

扃 [jiōng]
I 名 ①bolt;hook;bar (for fastening a door from outside) ②door;door leaf II 动 shut a door
扃户 shut the gate

jiǒng (ㄐㄩㄥˇ)

冏 [jiǒng]
I 名 light II 形 bright
冏冏秋月 bright autumn moon

炅 [jiǒng]
I 名 sunlight;heat II 形 bright

迥 [jiǒng]
I 形 remote;far away II 副 widely different
迥然 far apart;widely different

迥异 totally different
迥然不同 utterly different; not in the least a- like

炯 [jiǒng]
形 bright; shining
炯炯 (of eyes) bright; shining
炯炯发光 One's eyes shot fire.
炯炯有神 (of eyes) bright and piercing

窘 [jiǒng]
Ⅰ 形 ① in straitened circumstances; short of money; hard up ② awkward; embarrassed; ill at ease Ⅱ 动 embarrass; upset; disconcert
窘境 awkward situation; predicament; plight
窘况 awkward situation; predicament; plight
窘迫 ① poverty-stricken; very poor ② hard pressed; embarrassed; in a predicament
窘态 an embarrassed look
窘口无言 distressed mouth said nothing

jiū （ㄐㄧㄨ）

纠 [jiū]
动 ① entangle; involve ② gather together; assemble ③ inform against (sb); supervise ④ correct; rectify; right
纠察 ① maintain order at a public gathering ② picket
纠缠 ① get entangled; be in a tangle ② nag; worry; pester
纠纷 dispute; issue
纠风 rectify unhealthy tendencies
纠葛 entanglement; dispute
纠合 gather together
纠集 get together; muster
纠结 intertwine; entangle
纠举 accuse; inform against
纠偏 rectify a deviation; correct a political error
纠正 correct; put right; redress
纠众 incite mob
纠错码 Error Correction Code (ECC)
纠缠不清 too tangled up to unravel
纠举要犯 denounce an arch criminal (to the authorities)
纠谬绳违 rectify mistakes and punish law breakers according to law
纠正党风 rectify Party style
纠正冤假错案 redress the wrongs done to people who were unjustly, falsely or wrongfully accused
纠正行业不正之风 rectify unhealthy tendencies in various trades; rectify malpractice in various trades

鸠 [jiū]
名 turtledove
鸠形鹄面 gaunt and emaciated

究 [jiū]
Ⅰ 动 study carefully; probe into; investigate

Ⅱ 副 actually; really; after all
究办 investigate and deal with
究竟 ① outcome; what actually happened ② (*used in questions to press for an exact answer*) actually; exactly ③ after all; anyway; finally
究其根源 trace sth to its source; search to the bottom

赳 [jiū]
赳赳 valiant; gallant
赳赳武夫 a stalwart, martial man

阄 [jiū]
名 lot

揪 [jiū]
动 ① hold tight; grab; seize ② pull; tug; drag
揪出 uncover; ferret out
揪痧 a popular treatment for sunstroke or other febrile diseases by repeatedly pinching the patient's neck, etc. to achieve congestion
揪心 ① anxious; worried ② heartrending; agonizing; gnawing
揪辫子 seize sb's queue—seize upon sb's mistakes or shortcomings; capitalize on sb's vulnerable point

jiǔ （ㄐㄧㄨ）

九 [jiǔ]
Ⅰ 数 nine Ⅱ 名 beginning from the day of the Winter Solstice, each of the following nine nine-day periods is called a "nine" Ⅲ 形 numerous; many
九段 ninth-dan (highest grade in go or *weiqi*)
九泉 the Nine Springs—the nether world; grave
九天 the highest heavens; heaven
九月 ① September ② the ninth month of the lunar year; the ninth moon
九折 ten percent discount
九州 ① the nine divisions of China in remote antiquity ② a poetic name for China
九边形 nonagon; enneagon
九级风 force 9 wind; strong gale
九节狸 zibet; large Indian civet
九九表 multiplication table
九大行星 nine principal planets
九九重阳 the 9th day of the 9th lunar month
九九归一 when all is said and done; in the last analysis; after all
九流三教 the nine schools of thought and three religions; people in various trades; people of all sorts
九牛一毛 a single hair out of nine ox hides—a drop in the ocean
九死一生 a narrow escape from death; survival after many hazards

九五攻关 State Key Task 95
九霄云外 beyond the highest heavens—far, far away
九曲十八弯 hard; strenuous; twists and turns
九牛二虎之力 the strength of nine bulls and two tigers—tremendous effort

久 [jiǔ] 副 ①for a long time; long ②of a specified duration
久等 wait for a long time
久后 long afterwards; in the future
久久 for a long, long time
久留 stay long
久违 how long it is since we last met; I haven't seen you for ages
久仰 I've heard about you for a long time (*used when meeting sb for the first time*); I've long been looking forward to meeting you; I'm very pleased to meet you.
久远 far back; ages ago; remote
久别重逢 meet again after a long separation; reunite after a long parting
久病成医 Prolonged illness makes a doctor of a patient.
久而久之 in the course of time; with the lapse of time; as time passes
久负盛名 have long enjoyed a good reputation
久假不归 put off indefinitely returning sth one has borrowed; appropriate sth borrowed
久经考验 long-tested; seasoned
久静思动 grow weary of being quiet for a long time
久闻大名 I've long heard about your great name.
久旱逢甘雨 have a welcome rain after a long drought—have a long-felt need satisfied
久病床前无孝子 In cases of chronic sickness, there are no dutiful children at the bedside.

玖 [jiǔ] 名 jade-like black stone

灸 [jiǔ] 名 moxibustion

韭 [jiǔ] 名 fragrant-flowered garlic; (Chinese) chives
韭菜 fragrant-flowered garlic; (Chinese) chives
韭黄 hotbed chives

酒 [jiǔ] 名 alcoholic drink; wine; liquor; spirits
酒保 bartender; barkeeper
酒杯 wine cup or glass
酒菜 ①food and drink ②food to go with wine or liquor
酒厂 brewery; winery; distillery
酒刺 acne
酒店 ①wineshop; public house ②hotel
酒饭 food and drink

酒疯 the silly behaviour of a person when drunk; a drunken fit
酒馆 public house; pub
酒鬼 ①drunkard; sot ②winebibber; toper
酒后 after drinking; under the influence of wine (or alcohol)
酒壶 wine pot; flagon
酒花 hops
酒会 cocktail party
酒家 ①wineshop; tavern ②restaurant
酒窖 wine cellar
酒精 ethyl alcohol; alcohol
酒具 drinking set
酒力 ① capacity for liquor ② stimulating effect of wine; influence of alcohol
酒量 capacity for liquor
酒令 drinker's wager game
酒楼 restaurant
酒蜜 girl who accompanies someone to drink in a bar or restaurant
酒酿 fermented glutinous rice
酒钱 tips
酒窝 dimple
酒席 feast; banquet
酒兴 elation caused by intoxicants; rapture with wine
酒醒 awake from a drunken sleep (or a drunken stupor)
酒宴 feast; banquet
酒药 yeast for brewing rice wine or fermenting glutinous rice
酒意 a tipsy feeling
酒糟 distillers' grains
酒盅 a small handleless wine cup
酒醉 be drunk
酒吧间 bar; barroom
酒精灯 spirit lamp; alcohol burner
酒精炉 alcohol heater
酒石酸 tartaric acid
酒糟鼻 acne rosacea; brandy nose
酒吧舞女 cabaret dancer
酒池肉林 lakes of wine and forests of meat—unbridled debauchery and licentiousness
酒过三巡 when the wine has been round three times; after three cups of wine; after three drinks
酒酣耳热 warmed with wine; mellow with drink
酒后开车 driving a car under the influence of alcohol; drunk driving
酒后滋事 provoke incidents after getting drunk
酒精发酵 alcoholic fermentation
酒精含量 alcohol content
酒精酵母 distillery yeast
酒精中毒 alcoholic intoxication; alcoholism
酒囊饭袋 wine skin and rice bag—a good-for-

nothing

酒肉朋友 wine-and-meat friends; fair-weather friends

酒色财气 wine, women, wealth, and temper—generally considered to be the four archevils of life

酒色之徒 debauchee; libertine

酒肆茶楼 wine shops and teahouses

酒足饭饱 have drunk and eaten to one's heart's content

酒后吐真言 wine in, truth out

酒精比重计 spirit gauge

酒心巧克力 liqueur

酒不醉人人自醉 Liquor does not intoxicate, one intoxicates oneself.

酒逢知己千杯少，话不投机半句多 For a congenial friend a thousand toasts are too few; In a disagreeable conversation one word more is too many.

jiù（ㄐㄧㄡˋ）

旧 ［jiù］
I 形 ① past; outdated; antiquated; old ② used; old; worn; secondhand ③ former; onetime II 名 old friendship; old friend; old acquaintance

旧案 ① a court case of long standing ② old regulations; former practice

旧部 former subordinate

旧地 place where one went or stayed before; once familiar place; old haunt

旧都 former capital

旧恶 old grievance; old wrong

旧观 former appearance; former state

旧货 secondhand goods; junk

旧交 old acquaintance; old friend

旧居 former residence; old home

旧历 the old Chinese calendar; the lunar calendar

旧年 ① the lunar New Year ② last year

旧情 old (or former) friendship; former affection

旧日 former days; old days

旧诗 old-style poetry; classical poetry

旧时 old times; old days

旧式 old type; old style

旧事 an old matter (or affair); a past event

旧书 ① secondhand book; used (or old) book ② ancient book; ancient text

旧俗 old customs

旧习 old habit and custom

旧业 ① old trade (or profession) ② ancestral estate; family fortune

旧约 the Old Testament

旧宅 old residence; old house

旧账 old debt; old score; old feud

旧址 site (of a former organization, building, etc.)

旧制 ① old system; old practice ② China's old system of weights and measures

旧货店 secondhand shop; junk shop

旧金山 San Francisco

旧书店 secondhand bookstore

旧病复发 ① have a recurrence of an old illness; have an attack of a recurrent sickness; have a relapse ② relapse into one's old bad habits; slip back into one's bad old ways

旧地重游 revisit a once familiar place

旧房改造 old housing renovation

旧恨新仇 new hatred piled on old

旧话重提 go over the matter of discussion before; repetition of the old tale

旧货商店 secondhand shop; junk shop

旧货市场 flea market; second-hand goods market

旧梦重温 renew a sweet experience of bygone days

旧知新交 old friends and new acquaintances

旧瓶装新酒 new wine in old bottles—new content in old form

旧石器时代 the Old Stone Age; the Paleolithic Period

臼 ［jiù］
名 ① mortar ② any mortar-shaped thing ③ joint (of bones)

臼齿 molar

咎 ［jiù］
I 名 ① fault; blame ② ill luck; bad fortune II 动 censure; punish; blame

咎由自取 have only oneself to blame

疚 ［jiù］
名 remorse; guilt; compunction

柩 ［jiù］
名 coffin with a corpse in it

柏 ［jiù］
名 Chinese tallow tree

厩 ［jiù］
名 stable; cattle-shed; pen

厩肥 barnyard manure

救 ［jiù］
动 ① rescue; save; salvage ② help; relieve; succour

救兵 relief troops; reinforcements

救国 save the nation

救护 give first-aid; rescue

救荒 send relief to a famine area; help to tide over a crop failure

救活 bring sb back to life; resuscitate

救火 fight a fire; try to put out a fire

救急 help sb to cope with an emergency; help meet an urgent need

救济 extend relief to; relieve the distress of

救驾 save the emperor from danger—save sb from an awkward situation

救命 save sb's life
救难 help sb out of distress
救球 follow the ball
救生 save life (esp. through the prevention of drowning)
救亡 save the nation from extinction
救星 liberator;emancipator;saviour
救援 rescue;come to sb's help
救灾 provide disaster relief;help people tide over a natural disaster;relieve victims of a disaster
救治 bring a patient out of danger;treat and cure
救助 help sb in danger or difficulty;succour
救护车 ambulance
救护船 ambulance ship
救护队 ambulance corps
救护所 medical aid station (*or* point)
救护站 first-aid station
救火车 fire engine
救火队 fire brigade
救济金 alms;relief fund
救济粮 relief food;relief grain
救生船 rescue craft
救生带 life belt
救生圈 life buoy
救生艇 lifeboat
救生衣 life jacket
救生员 lifeguard;lifesaver
救世主 the Saviour;the Redeemer
救险车 wrecking truck;wrecking car
救护飞机 ambulance aircraft
救火队员 fireman;fire fighter
救苦救难 help the needy and relieve the distressed
救命稻草 a straw to clutch at
救命恩人 saviour
救人济世 helping others and remaking the world
救生背心 survival vest
救死扶伤 heal the wounded and rescue the dying
救亡运动 national salvation movement
救援工作 rescue work
救援物质 relief supplies
救灾扶贫 provide disaster relief and help the poor
救助条款 salvage clause
救人一命胜造七级浮屠 Saving one life is better than building a seven-tiered pagoda.

就 [jiù]
Ⅰ 〔动〕①come near;move towards ②undertake;engage in;embark on ③accomplish;attain;make ④take advantage of;accommodate oneself to;suit;fit ⑤(of food,etc.) go with:花生米就酒 have peanuts to go with wine Ⅱ (*used in a passive sentence to introduce an action*) Ⅲ 〔副〕①at once;right away;in a moment ②as early as;already ③as soon as;no sooner... than;right after ④(*often with* 只要,要是,既然,*or similar phrase in the conditional clause,used to indicate that sth comes naturally under certain conditions or circumstances*):既然没事,就多坐一会儿吧。 Stay a little longer since you have nothing else to attend to. ⑤as much as;as many as ⑥(*used between two identical words or expressions to express tolerance (or resignation*)):去就去,怕什么? I'll go if I must. What's there to be afraid of? ⑦(*used to indicate that sth has been like this all along*):我本来就不想去,是你非拉我去的。 I never said I wanted to go. It was you that got me to. ⑧only;merely;just ⑨(*used to express resolve*):不去,不去,就不去! I won't go,never! ⑩exactly;precisely;very;right:这就是我最需要的。 This is precisely what I want. Ⅳ 〔连〕even if;even though Ⅴ 〔介〕with regard to;as far as;concerning;on:就目前情况来看 as matters now stand
就伴 keep sb company;accompany sb
就便 at sb's convenience;while you're at it
就餐 have a meal;eat;dine
就此 at this point;here and now;thus
就地 on the spot
就读 attend school
就范 submit;give in
就歼 be wiped out;be annihilated;be destroyed
就近 (do or get sth) nearby;in the neighbourhood;without having to go far
就擒 be arrested;be caught
就寝 retire for the night;go to bed
就让 even if
就任 take up one's post;take office
就势 making use of momentum
就是 ①(*used,usu. with* 了,*at the end of a sentence to give force to the statement*) ② yes,that's right;exactly;precisely ③(*used correlatively with* 也) even if
就手 while you're at it
就算 even if;granted that
就位 take one's place
就席 take one's seat (at a banquet,etc.);be seated at the table
就绪 be in order;be ready
就要 be about to;be going to;be on the point of
就业 obtain employment;take up an occupation;get a job
就医 seek medical advice;go to a doctor
就义 be executed for championing a just cause;die a martyr
就诊 see a doctor;seek medical advice

就正 solicit comments (on one's writing)
就职 assume office
就座 take one's seat; be seated
就是说 that is to say; in other words; namely
就地采购 local procurement
就地待命 stay where one is, pending further orders; stand by for orders
就地取材 draw on local resources; make use of indigenous materials; draw on local talents
就地视察 on-site-inspection
就地正法 execute (a criminal) on the spot
就事论事 consider sth in isolation or out of context; deal with a matter on its merits
就我所知 so far as I know; for all I know
就业安置 outplacement
就业保险 employment security
就业门路 job opportunities
就职典礼 inaugural ceremony; inauguration
就职演说 inaugural speech
就正于读者 solicit readers' criticism
就业服务中心 employment service centre
就业技能培训 pre-job training
就业培训中心 employment training centre
就业预备制度 pre-employment training system

舅 [jiù]
名 ① mother's brother; uncle ② wife's brother; brother-in-law ③ husband's father
舅父 mother's brother; uncle
舅舅 mother's brother; uncle
舅妈 wife of mother's brother; aunt
舅母 wife of mother's brother; aunt
舅子 wife's brother; brother-in-law

傀 [jiù]
动 rent; hire; lease
傀费 rent; rental
傀屋 rent a house

鹫 [jiù]
名 vulture

jū (ㄐㄩ)

车 [jū]
名 ① (of Chinese chess) chariot ② (of chess) castle; rook ➡ chē

且 [jū]
动 oh ➡ qiě

拘 [jū]
动 ①arrest; detain; take into custody ②restrain; constrain ③restrict; limit; bound ④adhere to rigidly; be inflexible
拘捕 arrest; take into custody
拘谨 overcautious; reserved
拘禁 take into custody; detain
拘礼 be punctilious; stand on ceremony
拘留 detain; hold in custody; intern
拘拿 arrest; take into custody
拘泥 be a stickler for (form, etc.); rigidly ad-

here to (formalities, etc.)
拘票 arrest warrant; warrant
拘守 ①hold fast to; stick to ②imprison
拘束 ①restrain; restrict ②constrained; awkward; ill at ease
拘押 take into custody; detain
拘役 criminal detention
拘留权 right of detain
拘留所 jailhouse; lockup; house of detention
拘留证 detention warrant
拘于形式 rigidly adhere to form; be formalistic

狙 [jū]
I 名 a kind of monkey II 动 be on watch for; spy
狙击 snipe
狙伺 watch in secret
狙击手 sniper
狙击战 sniping action

居 [jū]
I 动 ①reside; dwell; live ②be (in a certain position); occupy (a place) ③claim; assert ④save; store up; lay by ⑤stay put; be at a standstill II 名 residence; house; home
居多 be in the majority
居功 claim credit for oneself
居家 live at home; run a household
居间 (mediate) between two parties
居留 reside
居民 resident; inhabitant
居奇 hoard and speculate
居然 ① unexpectedly; actually; to one's surprise ②go so far as to
居室 room
居首 occupy first place; rank first
居心 harbour (evil) intentions
居右 be on the right side
居于 occupy (a certain position)
居中 ①(mediate) between two parties ②be placed in the middle
居住 live; reside; dwell
居左 be on the left side
居间人 intermediary; mediator
居留权 right of residence
居留证 residence permit
居民点 residential area
居委会 residents' committee; neighbourhood committee
居住证 residence permit
居安思危 think of danger in times of safety; be vigilant in peace time
居高临下 occupy a commanding position (or height)
居功自傲 become arrogant because of one's achievements; claim credit and put on airs; monopolize credit and become arrogant
居家办公 small office home office (SOHO)
居民储蓄 household savings

居心不良 harbour evil intentions
居心叵测 with hidden intent; with ulterior motives
居心险恶 be vicious in one's motives
居住面积 living space; floor space
居住期限 length of residence
居住小区 residential district
居民身份证 resident's identification card
居民委员会 neighbourhood committee; residents' committee
居民住房建设 residential construction

驹 ［jū］ 名 ①young horse; colt ②foal

疽 ［jū］ 名 subcutaneous ulcer; deep-rooted ulcer
疽毒 deep carbuncle
疽蝇 Cuterebridae

掬 ［jū］ 动 hold with both hands

据 ［jū］ ⇒jù
◇拮据 in straitened circumstances; short of money; hard up

鞠 ［jū］ Ⅰ 动 ①rear; bring up ②bend Ⅱ 名 a kind of ball
鞠躬 bow
鞠育 rear; bring up
鞠躬尽瘁 bend oneself to a task and exert oneself to the utmost; spare no effort in the performance of one's duty
鞠躬尽瘁,死而后已 bend one's back to the task until one's dying day; give one's all till one's heart stops beating

jú (ㄐㄩˊ)

局 ［jú］ 名 ①chessboard ②game; set; innings: 下一局棋 play a game of chess ③situation; position; state of affairs ④breadth of mind; magnanimity; tolerance ⑤gathering; party ⑥ruse; trap; trick ⑦restrain; constrain; restrict ⑧part; portion ⑨bureau; department ⑩functional office ⑪shop
局部 part
局促 ①narrow; cramped ②(of time) short ③feel (or show) constraint
局面 aspect; phase; situation
局势 situation
局限 limit; confine
局子 police station; cop shop
局内人 a person in the know; insider
局外人 outsider; person not in the know
局限性 limitations
局域网 local area network(LAN)
局部麻醉 local anaesthesia
局部认付 partial acceptance

局部要价 partial bid
局部战争 local war; partial war
局促不安 ill at ease

菊 ［jú］ 名 chrysanthemum
菊花 chrysanthemum
菊科 the composite family
菊展 chrysanthemum show

焗 ［jú］ 动 ①steam ②feel suffocated; be stifled
焗油 ①treatment of the hair with a cream to make it soft and shiny ② hair treatment cream; hair treatment with cream; hair treatment cream

橘 ［jú］ 名 tangerine; orange
橘红 ①tangerine (colour); reddish orange ②dried tangerine peel
橘黄 orange (colour)
橘皮 orange peel
橘树 tangerine tree
橘汁 orange juice
橘子 tangerine

jǔ (ㄐㄩˇ)

弆 ［jǔ］ 动 collect; preserve

咀 ［jǔ］ 动 chew
咀嚼 ①masticate; chew ② mull over; ruminate; chew the cud

沮 ［jǔ］ 动 ①stop; check; prevent ②turn gloomy; turn glum; feel dejected
沮丧 ①dejected; depressed; dispirited; disheartened ②depress; dispirit; dishearten

枸 ［jǔ］ ⇒gǒu
枸橼 citron
枸橼酸 citric acid
枸橼酸钠 sodium citrate

矩 ［jǔ］ 名 ①carpenter's square; square ②rules; regulations ③moment
矩臂 moment arm
矩尺 carpenter's square
矩形 rectangle
矩阵 matrix

举 ［jǔ］ Ⅰ 动 ①lift; raise; hold up ②start; begin; initiate; raise ③give birth (to a child) ④elect; choose ⑤cite; enumerate; take; give Ⅱ 名 ①act; work; deed; move ②(short for 举人) successful candidate in the imperial examinations at the provincial level in the Ming and Qing dynasties Ⅲ 形 all; whole; entire
举哀 ①wail in mourning ②go into mourning
举办 conduct; hold; run

举报 report (an offender);inform against;report (sth) to authorities;turn sb in
举步 take a step
举措 move;act
举动 movement;move;act;activity
举度 manner
举发 report (evildoer or evil doings) to the authorities concerned
举国 the whole nation
举家 whole family
举荐 recommend (a person)
举例 give an example
举目 raise the eyes;look
举世 throughout the world;universally
举手 raise (*or* put up) one's hand or hands
举行 hold (a meeting,ceremony,etc.)
举债 borrow money;raise (*or* contract) a loan
举证 put the proof;produce evidence show evidence
举止 bearing;manner
举重 weight lifting
举手礼 hand salute
举重台 platform
举案齐眉 holding the tray level with the brows—husband and wife treating each other with courtesy
举报电话 informants' hot-line telephone;telephone number for informing, accusing or complaining
举报信箱 box for accusation letters
举报制度 system of reporting offenses to law and discipline enforcement authorities
举报中心 report centre;centre for receiving accusatory information or petitioning visitors
举不胜举 too numerous to mention
举措失当 make an ill-advised move
举国上下 the whole nation from top to bottom;from the leaders of the nation to all the people
举国无双 have no parallel in the whole country
举目无亲 be away from all one's kin; be a stranger in a strange land;have no one to turn to (for help)
举棋不定 hesitate about (*or* over) what move to make;be unable to make up one's mind; vacillate;shilly-shally
举世闻名 of world renown;world-famous
举世无双 unrivalled;matchless
举世瞩目 attract world-wide attention;become the focus of world attention
举手表决 hand-show;with a show of hands; vote by a show of hands
举手之劳 lift a finger
举贤让能 recommend the worthy and give way to the able
举一反三 draw inferences about other cases from one instance
举债筹资 debt financing
举债经营 trading on the equity;operation with borrowed capital
举足轻重 hold the balance;prove decisive; count heavily
举证责任倒置 reversal of burden of proof
举世瞩目的成就 achievements of world attention
举行事务级谈判 hold working-level talks

龃 [jǔ]

龃龉 the upper and lower teeth not meeting properly—disagreement;discord

jù (ㄐㄩˋ)

巨 [jù]
形 huge;tremendous;colossal;gigantic
巨变 a great change;a tremendous change
巨擘 ①thumb ②authority in a certain field
巨大 huge; tremendous; enormous; gigantic; immense
巨额 a huge amount;a huge sum
巨富 ①immense wealth ②a man of immense wealth;multimillionaire
巨匠 great master;consummate craftsman;giant
巨款 a huge sum of money
巨浪 billow;surge;mountainous waves
巨流 a mighty current
巨轮 ①a large wheel ②a large ship
巨人 giant;colossus
巨商 big businessman;business tycoon
巨头 magnate;tycoon
巨细 big and small
巨星 giant;giant star;megastar
巨著 monumental work
巨子 magnate;tycoon;giant
巨人症 gigantism
巨无霸 the giant;the extra large
巨额债务 mountain of debt
巨幅画像 huge portrait
巨奸大猾 an arrant swindler
巨型超市 hypermarket

句 [jù]
I 名 sentence II 量 (of language):写了几句
句诗 write a few lines of verse
句读 [jùdòu] the period and the comma;sentences and phrases
句法 ①sentence structure ②syntax
句号 full stop;full point;period (。) (.)
句型 sentence pattern
句子 sentence
句子成分 sentence element;member of a sentence

诓 [jù]
圃 (*used to introduce a rhetorical question*)：诓料事情生变？ Who expected that things would suddenly change?

苣 [jù]
◇莴苣 lettuce

拒 [jù]
劢 ①resist；repel；ward off ②refuse；reject
拒捕 resist arrest
拒付 non-payment；dishonor；refuse to pay
拒绝 ①refuse ②reject；turn down；decline
拒聘 turn down an appointment；refuse an engagement
拒收 rejection
拒载 refuse to take passengers
拒发签证 refusal to issue a visa
拒腐防变 guard against corruption and degeneration；resist corruption and guard against deterioration
拒谏饰非 reject representations and gloss over errors；reject criticisms and whitewash one's mistakes
拒绝承兑 non-acceptance
拒狼防虎 guard against a tiger while repelling the wolf
拒敌于国门之外 block the enemy at the gate of our country
拒人于千里之外 keep people at a distance of 1000 *li*—be arrogant and unapproachable

具 [jù]
Ⅰ 名 ①utensil；tool；implement ②talent；ability Ⅱ 量：一具僵尸 a corpse Ⅲ 劢 ①be endowed with；possess；have ②provide；furnish；fix：应用之物毕具。 All the things required were ready. ③state；enumerate；write out：条具时弊 list (*or* enumerate) current malpractices
具备 possess；have；be provided with
具名 put one's name to a document，etc.；affix one's signature
具体 concrete；specific；particular
具文 mere formality；dead letter
具有 have (sth immaterial)；possess
具体而微 small but complete；miniature
具体劳动 concrete labour

炬 [jù]
名 torch；flame

钜 [jù]
名 ①hard iron ②hook

俱 [jù]
副 all；complete
俱全 complete in all varieties
俱乐部 club

倨 [jù]
形 haughty；overbearing；arrogant

剧 [jù]
Ⅰ 名 drama；play；show；opera Ⅱ 形 acute；sharp；severe；intense

剧本 ①drama；play ②script；scenario；libretto
剧变 a violent (*or* drastic) change
剧场 theatre
剧毒 hypertoxic
剧减 dramatic reduction
剧烈 violent；acute；severe；fierce
剧目 a list of plays (*or* operas)
剧评 a review of a play (*or* opera)；dramatic criticism
剧情 the story (*or* plot) of a play (*or* opera)
剧痛 a severe pain
剧团 theatrical company；opera troupe；troupe
剧务 ①stage management ②stage manager
剧院 theatre
剧增 increase drastically or sharply
剧照 stage photo；still
剧终 (play or opera) end
剧种 type (*or* genre) of drama
剧装 stage costume
剧组 cast，director and stage hands in a drama production
剧作 drama；play
剧中人 characters in a play or opera；dramatis personae
剧作家 playwright；dramatist

据 [jù]
Ⅰ 劢 ①occupy；hold；seize ②rely on；depend on Ⅱ 尒 according to；on the basis of；on the grounds of：据调查 on the basis of the investigation Ⅲ 名 evidence；proof；certificate ➡ jū
据称 it is said；they say；allegedly
据传 a story is going around that；rumour has it that
据此 on these grounds；in view of the above；accordingly
据点 strongpoint；fortified point；stronghold
据守 guard；be entrenched in
据说 it is said；they say；allegedly
据悉 it is reported
据理力争 argue strongly on just grounds
据实相告 tell according to facts
据为己有 take forcible possession of；appropriate
据杖而行 walk on a stick
据山险可久守 can defend the place for a long time by taking advantage of a mountain defile

距 [jù]
名 ①distance ②spur (of a cock，etc.)
距离 ①distance ②be apart (*or* away) from；be at a distance from

惧 [jù]
劢 fear；dread；frighten
惧内 henpecked
惧怕 fear；dread
惧色 a look of fear

J

飓 [jù]

飓风 hurricane

锯 [jù]

Ⅰ 名 saw Ⅱ 动 cut with a saw; saw

锯齿 sawtooth
锯床 sawing machine
锯末 sawdust
锯条 saw blade
锯屑 sawdust
锯子 saw
锯木厂 sawmill; lumber-mill

聚 [jù]

动 assemble; gather; get together

聚变 fusion
聚餐 dine together (usu. on festive occasions); have a dinner party
聚赌 group gambling; gamble in group; assemble for gambling; get together to gamble
聚合 ①get together ②polymerization
聚会 ①get together; meet ②get-together
聚积 accumulate; collect; build up
聚集 gather; assemble; collect
聚歼 round up and annihilate; annihilate en masse
聚焦 focusing
聚居 inhabit a region (as an ethnic group); live in a compact community
聚敛 amass wealth by heavy taxation
聚拢 gather together
聚首 gather; meet
聚星 multiple star
聚酯 polyester
聚众 assemble a crowd; gather a mob
聚氨酯 polyurethane
聚宝盆 treasure bowl—a place rich in natural resources; cornucopia
聚丙烯 polypropylene
聚光灯 spotlight
聚光镜 condensing lens
聚合物 polymer
聚甲醛 polyformaldehyde
聚居点 settlement
聚酰胺 polyamide
聚乙烯 polyethylene; polythene
聚苯乙烯 polystyrene
聚丙烯腈 polyacrylonitrile
聚才集贤 collect and keep men of talent
聚精会神 concentrate one's attention; be all attention
聚氯乙烯 polyvinyl chloride (PVC)
聚醛树脂 aldehyde resin
聚伞花序 cyme
聚沙成塔 many grains of sand piled up will make a pagoda—many a little makes a mickle
聚少成多 Many a little makes a mickle; A penny saved is a penny earned.
聚讼纷纭 argue back and forth without coming to an agreement; opinions differ widely; a welter of conflicting opinions
聚碳酸脂 polycarbonate
聚乙烯醇 polyvinyl alcohol
聚众斗殴 gather a crowd to engage in an affray
聚众滋事 gather a crowd to make disturbances
聚变反应堆 fusion reactor
聚四氟乙烯 polytetrafluoroethylene (PTFE)

窭 [jù]

形 poor; impoverished

窭而不能葬 be too poor to bury the dead

踞 [jù]

动 ①crouch; squat; sit ②be entrenched; occupy

屦 [jù]

Ⅰ 名 straw sandals Ⅱ 动 tread; step on; tramp over

遽 [jù]

Ⅰ 副 hurriedly; speedily; hastily Ⅱ 形 frightened; agitated; alarmed

遽然 suddenly; abruptly

瞿 [jù]

动 look at sth in surprise; look around in consternation

juān (ㄐㄩㄢ)

捐 [juān]

Ⅰ 动 ①relinquish; abandon; give up ②contribute; donate; subscribe Ⅱ 名 tax; levy

捐款 ①contribute money ②contribution; donation; subscription; donate funds to establish
捐弃 relinquish; abandon
捐躯 sacrifice one's life; lay down one's life
捐税 taxes and levies
捐献 contribute (to an organization); donate; present
捐赠 contribute (as a gift); donate; present
捐助 offer (financial or material assistance); contribute; donate
捐资 contribute funds to
捐忿弃瑕 forget about past resentment and become reconciled; bury the hatchet
捐弃前嫌 bury old grudges; overcome previous alienation
捐赠器官 donate organs
捐资办学 donate money for school
捐资兴建 construct through donated money (or capital)
捐资兴学 make donations for the setting up of schools
捐赠品义卖 rummage sale

涓 [juān]

名 tiny steam

涓涓 trickling sluggishly

涓滴归公 every bit goes to the public treasury;turn in every cent of public money

娟 [juān]
形 beautiful;graceful
娟秀 beautiful;graceful
娟好静秀 beautiful,modest and refined

圈 [juān]
动 ①shut in a pen;pen in;把猪圈起来 pen up the pigs ②lock up：他把男孩圈在家里。 He shut the boy up at home. ➡ juàn;quān

鹃 [juān]
◇杜鹃 ①cuckoo ②azalea

镌 [juān]
动 engrave;carve;inscribe
镌刻 engrave
镌石 engrave a stone
镌心铭骨 be engraved on one's bones and heart—a lasting memory

juǎn（ㄐㄩㄢˇ）

卷 [juǎn]
I 动 ①roll (up);curl;furl ②sweep along,up,or off;pull up;carry along II 名 ①cylindrical mass of sth;roll ②steamed roll III 量 roll;spool;reel ➡ juàn
卷布 batching
卷尺 tape measure;band tape
卷发 curly hair;wavy hair
卷绕 winding
卷刃 (of a knife blade) be turned (or twisted)
卷入 be drawn into;be involved in
卷逃 abscond with valuables
卷筒 reel
卷须 tendril
卷烟 ①cigarette ②cigar
卷云 cirrus
卷轴 reel
卷子 steamed roll
卷板机 veneer reeling machine
卷笔刀 pencil sharpener
卷层云 cirrostratus
卷发器 curler
卷积云 cirrocumulus
卷铺盖 ①pack up and quit ②get the sack
卷筒纸 web
卷尾猴 (weeping) capuchin;weeping monkey
卷心菜 cabbage
卷烟纸 cigarette paper
卷扬机 hoist;hoister
卷叶蛾 leaf roller
卷款潜逃 make off with money;abscond with money
卷舌辅音 retroflex consonant
卷舌元音 retroflex vowel
卷土重来 stage a comeback

锩 [juǎn]
动 (of the edge of a sword or knife) be turned

juàn（ㄐㄩㄢˋ）

卷 [juàn]
名 ①book ②volume ③examination paper ④file;dossier ➡ juǎn
卷轴 scroll
卷子 ①examination paper ②a handwritten copy in scroll form
卷宗 ①folder ②file;dossier

隽 [juàn]
形 meaningful
隽永 meaningful

倦 [juàn]
形 ①tired;worn out;weary ②be weary;be tired;be bored
倦容 a tired look
倦色 a tired look
倦意 a feeling of tiredness
倦游 weary of wandering and sightseeing

狷 [juàn]
形 ①impatient;impetuous ②upright;honest
狷忿 impatient and irritable
狷急 of impatient disposition;impetuous
狷洁 exercise self-control and keep away from immorality

圈 [juàn]
名 (of livestock) pen;fold;sty ➡ juān;quān
圈肥 barnyard manure
圈养 rear livestock in pens

绢 [juàn]
名 thin,tough silk
绢本 silk scroll
绢纺 silk spinning
绢花 silk flower
绢画 classical Chinese painting on silk
绢丝 spun silk (yarn)
绢网印花 screen printing

眷 [juàn]
I 名 family dependant II 动 have tender feeling for
眷恋 be sentimentally attached to (a person or place)
眷念 think fondly of;feel nostalgic about
眷属 family dependants

juē（ㄐㄩㄝ）

撅 [juē]
动 ①stick up;pout (one's lips) ②embarrass (sb) openly;contradict ③make (a fainted person) come to by massage,etc. ④break (sth long and narrow);snap

噘 [juē]
动 stick up;pout (one's lips)

啜嘴 pout (one's lips); thrust out (one's lips)

jué (ㄐㄩㄝ)

决 [jué]
I 㓝 ①make a decision; decide; determine ②decide the final result; win or lose ③execute (a person) ④ (of a dyke, etc.) be breached; burst II 副 (*used before negatives*) definitely; absolutely; certainly; under any circumstances
决标 select the winning tender; award
决策 ①make policy; make a strategic decision ②policy decision; decision of strategic importance; decision-making; policy-making
决出 contest (prizes); fight for
决堤 breach (*or* burst) a dyke
决定 ①decide; resolve; make up one's mind ②decision; resolution ③determine; decide ④decisive
决斗 ①duel ②decisive struggle
决断 ① make a decision ② resolve; decisiveness; resolution
决计 ① have decided; have made up one's mind ②definitely; certainly
决口 (of a dyke, etc.) be breached; burst
决裂 break with; rupture
决然 ①resolutely; determinedly ②definitely; unquestionably; undoubtedly
决赛 finals
决胜 decide the issue of the battle; determine the victory
决死 life-and-death
决算 final accounts; final accounting of revenue and expenditure
决心 determination; resolution
决议 resolution
决意 have one's mind made up; be determined
决战 decisive battle; decisive engagement
决策权 decision-making power; right to make decision; power to make decision
决策人 policy-maker
决策树 decision tree
决定论 determinism
决定权 power to make decisions
决定性 decisiveness
决胜局 deciding game (*or* set)
决胜球 deciding ball
决心书 written pledge; statement of one's determination
决不反悔 will under no circumstances go back on one's word
决不可能 absolutely impossible; no way
决策程序 procedure of decision
决策分析 decision analysis
决策机构 policy-making body; policy-making organ

决非偶然 in no case accidental
决无异言 have no disagreement whatsoever
决一雌雄 fight to see who is the stronger; fight it out
决一胜负 fight it out
决一死战 fight to the death; fight to a finish
决定性因素 determining factor; decisive factor
决非长久之计 not at all a permanent solution

诀 [jué]
I 名 ①rhymed formula ②knack; key to success; tricks of the trade II 㓝 bid farewell; part (when there is little chance of meeting each other again)
诀别 part; bid farewell
诀窍 secret of success; tricks of the trade; knack

抉 [jué]
㓝 pick out; single out
抉择 choose
抉摘 ①choose ②expose and censure

角 [jué]
I 名 ①role; part; character ②type of role ③actor or actress ④ancient, three-legged wine cup ⑤note of the ancient Chinese five-note scale, corresponding to 3 in numbered musical notation II 㓝 contend; struggle; fight ➡jiǎo
角斗 wrestle
角力 have a trial of strength; wrestle
角色 ①role; part ②type of role (in traditional Chinese drama)
角逐 contend; tussle; enter into rivalry
角斗场 wrestling ring
角斗士 wrestler
角色错位 role reversal; role deviation
角色扮演游戏 roles play games

觉 [jué]
I 名 sense; feel; sensation; perception II 㓝 ①sense; feel ②wake (up); awake ③become aware (*or* conscious); become awakened ➡jiào
觉察 detect; become aware of; perceive
觉得 ①feel ②think; feel
觉悟 ①consciousness; awareness; understanding ②come to understand; become aware of; become politically awakened
觉醒 awaken

绝 [jué]
I 㓝 ①cut off; break off; sever ②exhausted; spent; used up; finished; heartless ③stop breathing; die II 形 ①desperate; beyond help; hopeless ②unique; excellent; superb; matchless III 副 ①extremely; most ②(*used before negatives*) absolutely; in the least; in all circumstances; on any account IV 名 (short for 绝句) *jueju*, a poem of four lines, each containing five or seven characters, with a strict tonal pattern and rhyme scheme

绝版 out of print
绝笔 ①last words written before one's death ②the last work of an author or painter
绝壁 precipice
绝唱 the peak of poetic perfection
绝代 unique among one's contemporaries; peerless
绝地 ①a danger spot ②hopeless situation; dead end; impasse
绝顶 ①extremely; utterly ②peak; summit
绝对 ①absolute ②absolutely; perfectly; definitely
绝后 ①without offspring (*or* issue) ②never to be seen again
绝户 ① without offspring (*or* issue) ② a childless person
绝活 one's best skill; unique ability
绝迹 disappear; vanish; be stamped out
绝技 unique skill; consummate skill
绝交 break off relations (as between friends or countries)
绝经 menopause
绝境 ① isolated condition ② hopeless situation; impasse; blind alley; cul-de-sac
绝口 ①(*only used after* 不) stop talking ② keep one's mouth shut
绝路 ①block the way out; leave no way out ② road to ruin; blind alley; dead end; impasse
绝伦 unsurpassed; unequalled; peerless; matchless
绝密 top-secret; strictly confidential
绝妙 extremely clever; ingenious; excellent; perfect
绝灭 die out
绝情 heartless; cruel
绝热 heat insulation
绝色 (of a woman) exceedingly beautiful; of unrivalled beauty
绝食 go on a hunger strike; fast
绝收 total crop failure
绝望 give up all hope; despair
绝育 sterilization
绝缘 ①cut all ties with sth ②insulation
绝招 ①unique skill ②unexpected tricky move (as a last resort)
绝症 incurable disease; fatal illness
绝种 (of a species) become extinct; die out
绝对值 absolute value
绝命书 ①suicide note ②note written on the eve of one's execution; pre-execution note
绝缘层 insulation layer; insulating layer; insulating course; insulating barrier
绝处逢生 be unexpectedly rescued from a desperate situation
绝代佳人 a woman of beauty
绝对担保 absolute guaranty
绝对地租 absolute rent

绝对高度 absolute altitude
绝对观念 absolute idea
绝对量度 absolute measurement
绝对零度 absolute zero
绝对权威 absolute authority
绝对人权 absolute human rights
绝对湿度 absolute humidity
绝对温度 absolute temperature
绝对音乐 absolute music
绝对优势 absolute advantage
绝对真理 absolute truth
绝对主义 absolutism
绝非偶然 by no means fortuitous (*or* accidental)
绝无此意 have absolutely no such intentions
绝无仅有 the only one of its kind; unique
绝对继承权 absolute inheritance
绝对贫困化 absolute impoverishment
绝对平均主义 absolute equalitarianism

倔 [jué]
➡jué
倔强 stubborn; unbending

桷 [jué]
名 square rafter

掘 [jué]
动 dig; excavate
掘获 dig up
掘进 drive; tunnel
掘凿 drive
掘墓人 gravedigger
掘土机 excavator; power shovel
掘地三尺 dig to a depth of three feet; dig deep
掘壕据守 dig oneself in; entrench oneself

崛 [jué]
动 rise abruptly
崛起 ①(of a mountain, etc.) rise abruptly; suddenly appear on the horizon ②rise to prominence

厥 [jué]
Ⅰ 动 faint; swoon; lose consciousness; fall into a coma Ⅱ 代 his or her; its; their Ⅲ 副 only then
厥父 his or her father
厥功甚伟 Great are his services to the country.

谲 [jué]
Ⅰ 动 cheat; swindle Ⅱ 形 strange; odd
谲诈 cunning; crafty

蕨 [jué]
名 brake (fern)

橛 [jué]
名 short wooden stake; wooden pin; peg
橛子 a short wooden stake; wooden pin; peg

噱 [jué]
名 loud laughter

爵 [jué]
名 ①rank of nobility; peerage ②ancient wine vessel with three legs and a loop handle
爵禄 ranks and stipends; titles and stipends;

dignities and emoluments
爵士 ①knight ②Sir
爵位 the rank (*or* title) of nobility
爵士音乐 jazz

蹶 [jué]
〔动〕 fall;setback

矍 [jué]
〔形〕 look surprised
矍铄 hale and hearty

嚼 [jué]
〔动〕 masticate;chew ➡jiáo

攫 [jué]
〔动〕 seize;snatch;grab
攫取 seize;grab

juè (ㄐㄩㄝ)

倔 [juè]
〔形〕 gruff;blunt;surly;irascible ➡jué
倔驴 bullheaded mule
倔头倔脑 blunt of manner and gruff of speech

jūn (ㄐㄩㄣ)

军 [jūn]
〔名〕 ①armed forces;forces;army;troops ②army;corps
军备 armament;arms
军操 military drill
军车 military vehicle
军刀 soldier's sword;sabre
军队 armed forces;army;troops
军阀 warlord
军法 military criminal code;military law
军方 the military
军费 military expenditure
军服 military (*or* army) uniform;uniform
军港 naval port
军歌 army song
军工 ①war industry ②military project
军功 military merit;military exploit
军官 officer
军管 military control
军棍 (in former times) a cane for corporal punishment in the army
军号 bugle
军徽 army emblem
军婚 marriage of serviceman (*or* servicewoman)
军火 munitions;arms and ammunition
军机 ①military plan ②military secret
军籍 military status;one's name on the army roll
军纪 military discipline
军舰 warship;naval vessel
军阶 (military) rank;grade
军界 military circles;the military
军垦 reclamation of wasteland by an army unit
军礼 military salute

军力 military strength
军粮 army provisions;grain for the army
军列 military train
军龄 length of military service
军令 military orders
军旅 armies;troops
军马 army horse
军帽 army cap;service cap
军蜜 soldier's girlfriend
军民 the army and the people;soldiers and civilians;military and civilian
军品 military products;military goods
军旗 army flag;colours;ensign
军企 military-run enterprise
军情 military (*or* war) situation
军区 military region;(military) area command
军权 military leadership;military power
军犬 a police dog used for military purposes
军人 soldier;serviceman;armyman
军容 soldier's discipline,appearance and bearing
军嫂 a female soldier;the wife of a soldier;honorific appellation for the wives of military personnel;armyman's wife
军师 war counsellor;military adviser
军士 noncommissioned officer (NCO)
军事 ①military affairs ②military
军售 arms sale
军属 soldier's dependants;armyman's family
军团 army group
军威 military might
军委 the Military Commission of Central Committee of the Communist Party of China
军务 military affairs;military task
军衔 military rank;rank in the military forces
军饷 soldier's pay and provisions
军校 military school;military academy
军鞋 military footwear
军械 ordnance;armament
军心 soldier's morale
军需 ①military supplies ②quartermaster
军训 military training
军演 military exercise
军衣 military (*or* army) uniform;uniform
军医 medical officer;military surgeon
军营 military camp;barracks
军用 for military use;military
军援 military aid
军乐 martial (*or* military) music
军运 military transport
军长 army commander
军政 ①military affairs and politics ②military administration ③army and government
军职 official post in the army; military appointment
军种 (armed) services

军装 military (*or* army) uniform；uniform
军兵种 arms and services of the armed forces
军大衣 frock
军代表 military delegates；representatives from the military
军分区 military subarea
军风纪 soldier's bearing and discipline
军功章 medal for military merit
军管会 military control commission
军火库 arsenal
军火商 munitions merchant；arms dealer；merchant of death
军粮库 military grain depot；army granary
军令状 a promise to get a job done，which one is willing to accept a severe penalty if fails；pledge to obey military orders
军事化 militarize；place on a war footing
军事家 strategist
军事学 military science
军需库 military supply depot；
军需品 military supplies；military stores
军用品 military supplies and equipment；war materials；materiel
军乐队 military band
军政府 military government
军转民 turn military production into civilian production；conversion from military to civilian production
军备竞赛 armament (*or* arms) race
军阀主义 warlordism
军国主义 militarism
军令如山 Military orders are like mountains (i.e. are unalterable and must be obeyed).
军民结合 integrate military with civilian purposes
军民联防 army-civilian joint defence；community policing；team policing
军人政权 military junta
军事法庭 military tribunal (*or* court)
军事工业 war industry
军事管制 military control
军事过硬 militarily competent
军事基地 military base
军事科学 military science
军事冒险 military gamble
军事素质 military capability
军事态势 military posture
军事体育 military sports
军事条令 military manuals
军事学院 military academy (*or* institute)
军事演习 maneuver
军民鱼水情 The army and the people are as close to each other as fish and water.
军事分界线 militarized fault；militarized demarcation line
军中无戏言 Military orders must be carried out；There is no room for levity in the army.

均 ［jūn］
Ⅰ 形 equal；even Ⅱ 副 without exception；every one；all
均等 equal；impartial；fair
均分 divide equally；share out equally
均衡 balance；equilibrium
均价 average price
均势 balance of power；equilibrium of forces；equilibrium；parity
均摊 share equally
均线 average line
均一 even；uniform；homogeneous
均匀 even；well-distributed
均沾 share (interests，etc.) equally；have equal access to (advantages)
均值 average value
均衡论 the theory of equilibrium
均一性 homogeneity

龟 ［jūn］
➡ guī
龟裂 ①(of parched earth) be full of cracks ②(of skin) chap

君 ［jūn］
名 ①monarch；sovereign；supreme ruler ②gentleman；Mr.
君权 monarchical power；royal prerogative
君王 monarch；sovereign；emperor
君主 monarch；sovereign
君子 a man of noble character；a man of virtue；gentleman
君主国 monarchical state；monarchy
君主制 monarchy
君子国 the Land of Gentlemen (an imaginary land free from deceit and avarice)
君子兰 kaffir lily
君无戏言 The king's words are to be taken seriously.
君主立宪 constitutional monarchy
君主专制 autocratic monarchy；absolute monarchy
君子协定 gentlemen's agreement
君子之交淡如水 The friendship of a gentleman is insipid as water.

钧 ［jūn］
Ⅰ 量 ancient unit of weight (equal to 30 *jin*) Ⅱ 名 potter's wheel；throwing wheel Ⅲ 形 you；your

菌 ［jūn］
名 ①fungus ②bacterium ➡ jùn
菌核 sclerotium
菌苗 bacterial vaccine；vaccine
菌丝 hypha
菌细胞 bacterial cell
菌血症 bacteremia

皲 ［jūn］
皲裂 (of skin) chap

jùn（ㄐㄩㄣˋ）

俊 [jùn]
〈形〉① handsome; pretty; beautiful ② outstandingly talented
俊杰 a person of outstanding talent; hero
俊美 pretty
俊气 pretty
俊俏 pretty and charming
俊秀 pretty; of delicate beauty
俊雅 refined and elegant
俊男靓女 handsome men and beautiful women

郡 [jùn]
〈名〉①prefecture ②county（in the UK, Ireland, etc.）

捃 [jùn]
〈动〉pick up
捃其菁华 grasp the essence; skim the cream

峻 [jùn]
〈形〉①（of mountains）high ②harsh; hard; severe; stern
峻峭 high and steep

浚 [jùn]
〈动〉dredge
浚泥船 dredger

骏 [jùn]
〈名〉fine horse; steed
骏马 fine horse; steed

菌 [jùn]
〈名〉mushroom ➡ jūn
菌子 mushroom

竣 [jùn]
〈动〉complete; finish
竣工（of a project）be completed
竣工式 completion ceremony

箘 [jùn]
〈名〉① bamboo shoots ② a kind of bamboo mentioned in ancient books

J

K k

kā（丂丫）

咔 [kā]
拟 click；clack ➡kǎ

咖 [kā]
➡gā
咖啡 coffee
咖啡杯 coffee cup
咖啡豆 coffee bean
咖啡馆 coffee house；café
咖啡壶 coffee pot
咖啡色 coffee（colour）
咖啡因 caffeine
咖啡伴侣 coffee mate

喀 [kā]
拟（*indicating noise made in coughing or vomiting*）
喀嚓 a cracking（*or* snapping）sound
喀秋莎 katyusha rocket launcher
喀斯特 karst

kǎ（丂丫）

卡 [kǎ]
Ⅰ 量 calorie Ⅱ 名 ① card ② cassette ③ truck；lorry ➡qiǎ
卡车 lorry；truck
卡片 card
卡其 khaki
卡钳 callipers
卡通 ① caricature；cartoon ② another name for 动画片
卡巴胂 carbarsone
卡宾枪 carbine
卡丁车 kart；karting
卡介苗 BCG vaccine
卡拉 OK karaoke
卡路里 calorie
卡片柜 card cabinet
卡特尔 cartel
卡那霉素 kanamycin
卡介苗注射 BCG injection

卡片分类机 card sorter
卡式录像带 video cassette
卡片式分类账 card ledger

咔 [kǎ]
➡kā
咔唑 carbazole

胩 [kǎ]
名 carbylamine；isocyanide

咯 [kǎ]
动 cough up ➡gē；lo；luò
咯痰 cough up phlegm
咯血 spit blood；haemoptysis

kāi（丂历）

开 [kāi]
Ⅰ 动 ①open；turn on；be on ②make an opening；open up；reclaim ③ open out；come loose ④thaw；become navigable ⑤lift（a ban；restriction，etc.） ⑥ start；operate；drive；run ⑦（of troops，etc.） set out；move ⑧ set up；run ⑨begin；start ⑩hold（a meeting，exhibition，etc.） ⑪write out；make out ⑫pay（wages，fares，etc.） ⑬ kick out；fire；sack ⑭ boil ⑮serve（a meal，banquet，etc.） ⑯finish；eat up ⑰（*used after a verb or an adjective*）：（a） extend；expand；spread：这支歌儿很快便流行开了。The song soon became popular.（b） start and continue：一见到我她就哭开了。She began to cry as soon as she saw me.（c） apart；away：离开 go away Ⅱ 名 percentage；proportion（in round numbers）Ⅲ 量 division of standard size printing paper
开办 run（a factory，school，store，etc.）；set up；start
开本 format；book size
开编 begin the compilation of（books）
开标 bid opening；open sealed tenders；open sealed bids
开播 ①initiate broadcast ②start sowing
开采 mine；extract；exploit
开衩 vent（at the bottom of a coat at the sides or back）；branch；slit

开场 (of a performance,etc.) begin;start

开车 ①drive or start a car,train,etc. ②set a machine going

开秤 (of a purchasing station) start business

开除 expel;discharge

开锄 begin tilling land for the year

开船 set sail;sail

开创 start;initiate

开春 beginning of spring (usu. referring to the first month of the lunar year)

开刀 ① behead; decapitate ② perform (or have) an operation;operate;be operated on ③make sb the first target of attack

开导 help sb to see what is right or sensible; help sb to straighten out his wrong or muddled thinking;enlighten

开道 ①clear the way ②make way

开动 ①start;set in motion ②move;march

开冻 thaw;unfreeze

开端 beginning;start

开恩 show mercy;bestow favours

开发 develop;open up;exploit

开饭 serve a meal

开方 extraction of a root;evolution

开放 ①(of flowers) come into bloom ②lift a ban,restriction,etc. ③ open to traffic or public use ④be open (to the public) ⑤be open (to the outside world);

开缝 crack;fracture

开赴 move (or march) to;be bound for

开杆 start (game,e.g. billiard game)

开工 ①(of a factory,etc.) go into operation ②(of work on a construction project,etc.) start

开关 switch

开馆 open (library,art gallery,etc.) to the public

开锅 (of a pot) boil

开国 found a state

开航 ①become open for navigation ②set sail

开河 ①(of a frozen river) thaw out ②construct a canal

开户 open (or establish) an account (with a bank)

开花 ①blossom;bloom ②split (like a flower blooming) ③feel happy;smile happily

开化 ①become civilized ②thaw;unfreeze

开荒 open up (or reclaim) wasteland

开怀 to one's heart's content

开会 hold (or attend) a meeting

开荤 (esp. of a person with a religious belief) begin (or resume) a meat diet;end a meatless diet

开豁 ①open and clear ②with one's mental outlook broadened

开火 open fire

开伙 ①run a mess (or cafeteria) ②provide food

开机 ① start a machine ② start shooting a film,TV play,etc.

开价 state (or quote) a price

开架 open shelves (as in a supermarket,from which customers select goods)

开讲 begin lecturing (or story-telling)

开奖 draw lottery in public and announce winner

开胶 come unglued

开戒 break an abstinence (from smoking, drinking,etc.)

开禁 lift a ban

开镜 start shooting (film)

开局 opening (of a chess game,etc.);beginning

开具 write out (a certificate,etc.)

开卷 ①open a book;read ②(of examinations) open-book

开掘 dig

开课 ①school begins;begin classes ②(chiefly in college) give a course;teach a subject

开垦 open up (or reclaim) wasteland;bring under cultivation

开口 ①open one's mouth;start to talk ②put the first edge on a knife

开矿 open up a mine;exploit a mine

开阔 ① open; wide ② tolerant; broad-minded ③widen

开朗 ①open and clear ②sanguine;optimistic

开犁 start the year's ploughing

开镰 start harvesting

开脸 ①(of a girl on the eve of marriage) remove the fine hairs on the face and neck and tidy up hairline at temples ②carve the face of a statue

开练 ①start working ②fight;come to blows

开列 draw up (a list);list

开裂 crack;fracture

开溜 sneak away; slink off; make oneself scarce

开路 ①open a way;blaze a trail ②open circuit

开门 ①open the door ②(of a store) begin a day's business

开明 enlightened;open-minded

开幕 ①the curtain rises ②(of a meeting,exhibition,etc.) open;inaugurate

开拍 start shooting (a film,TV serial,etc.)

开盘 give the opening quotation (on the exchange);open

开炮 ① open fire with artillery; fire ② fire criticism at sb or sth

开辟 ①open up ②establish;start;set up

开篇 introductory song in fiddle ballad

开瓢 break one's head

开票 ①open the ballot box and count the ballots ②make out an invoice，receipt，voucher，etc.

开屏 (of a peacock) spread its tail；display its fine tail feathers

开启 open

开枪 fire with a rifle，pistol，etc.；shoot

开腔 begin to speak；open one's mouth

开窍 ①have one's ideas straightened out ②(of a child) begin to know things

开球 kick off (in soccer)

开山 ①cut into a mountain (for quarrying，etc.) ②unseal a closed mountain for a period of time ③build the first temple on a famous mountain

开哨 whistle for the start of a game

开设 ①open (a shop，factory，etc.)；set up ②offer (a course in college，etc.)

开审 start the trial；sit at session

开始 ①begin；start ②initial stage；beginning；outset

开市 ①(of a shop) reopen after a cessation of business ②conduct the first transaction of a day's business

开释 release (a prisoner)

开涮 make fun of；make a fool of

开水 ①boiling water ②boiled water

开锁 unlocking

开台 begin a theatrical performance

开膛 cut open the chest (of a pig，chicken，etc.)；draw

开庭 open a court session；call the court to order

开通 〔kāitōng〕 remove obstacles from；dredge；clear

开通 〔kāitong〕 open-minded；liberal；enlightened

开头 ①begin；start ②beginning；start

开脱 absolve；exonerate

开拓 ①open up ②developing；opening

开挖 excavate

开外 over；above

开往 (of a train，ship，etc.) leave for；be bound for

开胃 ①whet (or stimulate) the appetite ②amuse oneself at sb's expense；make fun of sb

开销 ①pay expenses ②expense

开心 ①happy；joyous；elated ②amuse oneself at sb's expense；make fun of sb

开学 school opens；term begins

开眼 open one's eyes；widen one's view (or horizons)；broaden one's mind；enrich one's experience

开演 (of a play，movie，etc.) begin

开业 ①(of a shop．etc.) start business ②(of a lawyer，doctor，etc.) open a private practice

开营 (of summer camp，etc.) open

开凿 cut (a canal，tunnel，etc.)

开斋 ①resume a meat diet ②come to the end of Ramadan

开展 ①develop；launch；unfold ②open-minded；politically progressive ③(of exhibition，etc.) open

开战 ①make war；open hostilities ②battle (against nature，conservative forces，etc.)

开绽 come unsewn

开张 ①open a business；begin doing business ②conduct the first transaction of a day's business ③(of certain activities) begin；start

开仗 make war；open hostilities

开账 ①make out a bill ②pay the bill (at a restaurant，hotel，etc.)

开诊 begin to treat patients

开征 begin to levy (or collect) taxes

开支 ①pay (expenses) ②expenses；expenditure；spending ③pay wages (or salaries)

开罪 offend；displease

开白条 give an IOU note instead of paying cash；pay with credit slips

开办费 start-up expenses；seed money

开场白 ①prologue (of a play) ②opening (or introductory) remarks

开裆裤 open-seat (or split) pants (for children)

开倒车 back the car—turn back the clock

开发区 Open Economic Zone

开方子 write out a prescription

开房间 rent a room in a hotel (esp. for a secret liaison)

开放型 open；export-oriented

开工率 utilization of capacity

开罐器 can opener

开合桥 bascule bridge；folding bridge

开红灯 give the red light to

开后门 back-door dealings to secure advantages for others；open green light for

开花期 florescence

开口销 split pin

开口子 ①(of a dyke) break；burst ②(of the skin) chap

开快车 step on the gas；speed up the work

开阔地 open terrain；open ground；unenclosed ground

开绿灯 give the green light；give the go-ahead

开门红 make a good beginning；get off to a good start

开幕词 opening speech (or address)

开幕式 opening ceremony

开盘价 opening rate

开刃儿 put the first edge on (a knife or a pair of scissors)；sharpen for the first time

开市价 opening quotation

开司米 cashmere
开天窗 ① syphilis nose start festering ② put in a skylight—leave a blank in a publication to show that sth has been censored
开条子 write slip requesting sth
开拓者 pioneer
开玩笑 crack a joke;joke;make fun of
开小差 ①（of a soldier）desert ② be absent-minded;be woolgathering
开小灶 kitchen where food is cooked in small quantities for a few people;special favour;special treatment;special consideration
开心果 pistachio
开洋荤 have a new experience;see（or eat）sth for the first time;enjoy a foreign lifestyle
开夜车 work late into the night;put in extra time at night;burn the midnight oil
开音节 open syllable
开元音 open vowel
开斋节 Lesser Bairam;the Festival of Fast-breaking
开诚布公 frank and sincere;open-hearted
开诚相见 deal with sb in all sincerity;treat sb open-heartedly;be frank and open
开除公职 dismiss from one's current office;remove from one's current post;discharge from public employment;take the name off the book
开顶风船 sail against the wind;run counter to the mainstream of thought or conduct
开发过度 overexploitation project
开发软件 develop software
开发市场 explore market
开发中心 development centre
开放城市 a city open to foreigners;open city
开放搞活 open up and stir thing up;relax control and enliven the economy
开放骨折 open（or compound）fracture
开工不足 operate under capacity;run under capacity
开工典礼 commencement ceremony;opening ceremony for project
开关灯头 switch socket
开国元勋 founding father of a country;the founder of the state
开户银行 bank where account has been opened
开花结果 blossom and bear fruit—yield positive results
开花馒头 split-top steamed bun
开怀畅饮 drink to one's content;drink freely with great joviality;have a hearty drink
开架书店 open-shelf book store
开局不利 make a slow start
开卷有益 Reading is always profitable.
开开眼界 broaden one's vision
开口闭口 every time one opens one's mouth;whenever one speaks
开阔眼界 broaden one's horizon;widen one's field of vision
开路先锋 pathbreaker;trail-blazer;pioneer
开门办学 open-door school management
开门见山 come straight to the point
开门揖盗 open the door to robbers—invite disaster by letting in evildoers
开门整风 open-door rectification of the style of work（a campaign aimed to rectify the Party's work style with the help of the masses）
开盘行市 opening quotation
开盘叫价 opening call
开球一方 service side
开山祖师 builder of the first temple on a famous mountain—the founder of a religious sect,a school of thought.etc.
开始生效 activate;take effect;set the seal on;go into force;come into operation;enter into effect;come into effect;go into effect
开题报告 opening speech;opening report
开天辟地 the creation of heaven and earth—the beginning of history
开拓进取 blaze new trails;make pioneering efforts;pioneer to make progress;make bold exploration
开拓市场 open up markets;explore markets
开学典礼 school-opening ceremony
开业大吉 commence the business auspiciously
开源节流 increase income and reduce expenditure;open up new sources of revenue and cut back on expenditure
开云见日 the clouds disperse and the sun shines forth—①darkness recedes and light dawns ②all misunderstanding has been dispelled
开宗明义 make clear the purpose and theme from the very beginning
开足马力 put into high gear;go full steam ahead;with the throttle wide open
开创新世纪 usher in a new age
开发性项目 exploration project
开放式基金 open-ended fund
开放式商店 free-standing stores
开放式系统 open system
开辟新财源 open up new sources of income
开拓型人才 talent of the developmental type;talented people with development potentials
开架销售商店 self-service store
开创现代化建设新局面 attain new heights in our modernization drive

揩 [kāi]
动 wipe;rub
揩拭 clean;wipe
揩油 get petty advantages at the expense of

other people (*or* the state);scrounge

kǎi（ㄎㄞˇ）

凯 ［kǎi］
彤 triumphant (strains)
凯歌 a song of triumph;paean
凯旋 triumphant return
凯旋门 ①triumphal arch ②Arc de Triomphe (in Paris);Arch of Triumph
凯恩斯政策 Keynesian policy

垲 ［kǎi］
彤 (of terrain) high and dry

阆 ［kǎi］
动 open

恺 ［kǎi］
Ⅰ 彤 happy;joyful;cheerful and resourceful
Ⅱ 名 triumphant strains

铠 ［kǎi］
名 armour
铠甲 (a suit of) armour
铠装 armour

慨 ［kǎi］
彤 ①indignant ②deeply touched ③generous
慨然 ①with deep feeling ②generously
慨叹 sigh with regret
慨允 readily consent;kindly promise

楷 ［kǎi］
名 ①model;pattern ②(of Chinese calligraphy) regular script ➡jiē
楷模 model;paragon;example
楷书 (in Chinese calligraphy) regular script
楷体 ①(in Chinese calligraphy) regular script ②block letter

锴 ［kǎi］
名 iron of good quality

kài（ㄎㄞˋ）

忾 ［kài］
名 hatred

kān（ㄎㄢ）

刊 ［kān］
Ⅰ 动 ① print; publish ② delete; correct
Ⅱ 名 periodical;publication
刊登 publish in a newspaper (*or* magazine);carry
刊发 publish (in a newspaper or magazine)
刊刻 inscribe
刊授 teach through publications;give courses through periodicals
刊头 masthead of a newspaper (*or* magazine)
刊物 publication
刊误 correct errors on printing
刊行 print and publish
刊印 ① cut blocks and print ② compose and print

刊载 publish (in a newspaper or magazine);carry
刊误表 errata;corrigenda

看 ［kān］
动 ①look after;take care of;tend ②keep under surveillance;keep watch over;guard ➡kàn
看场 guard the threshing floor (during the harvest season)
看管 ①look after;attend to ②guard;watch
看护 ①nurse ②a hospital nurse
看家 ①look after the house;mind the house ②outstanding (ability);special (skill)
看门 ①guard the entrance;act as doorkeeper ②look after the house
看青 keep watch over the ripening crops
看守 ①watch;guard ②jailer;warder
看押 take into custody;detain
看堆儿 keep an eye on sth;watch over sth
看家狗 watchdog—a person who takes care of the affairs and property of a landlord, high official, etc.
看守所 lockup for prisoners awaiting trial;detention house
看家本领 one's stock-in-trade; one's special ability
看守内阁 caretaker cabinet
看守政府 caretaker government;caretaker administration;watchdog administration

勘 ［kān］
动 ①read and correct the text of;collate ②investigate;survey
勘测 survey
勘查 look into;investigate
勘察 ①reconnoitre (an area for engineering or other purposes) ②prospecting
勘界 demarcation of boundaries
勘探 exploration;prospecting
勘误 correct errors in printing
勘误表 errata;corrigenda

龛 ［kān］
名 niche;shrine
龛影 niche (shown in an X-ray photograph)

堪 ［kān］
动 ①may;can ②bear;endure
堪称典范 set an example;be exemplary;be good enough to serve as a model
堪当重任 be capable of shouldering important tasks

戡 ［kān］
动 suppress;put down
戡乱 suppress (*or* put down) a rebellion

kǎn（ㄎㄢˇ）

坎 ［kǎn］
名 ①one of the Eight Trigrams (formerly used in divination) representing water ②

bank;ridge ③ depression;pit;hole ④ critical moment;crux;point of great importance ⑤ streak of bad luck;predicament ⑥(short for 坎德拉)candela

坎坷 ①bumpy;rough ②full of frustrations

坎子 mound;rise

坎肩儿 sleeveless jacket (usu. padded or lined)

坎儿井 an irrigation system of wells connected by underground channels used in Xinjiang;karez

侃 [kǎn] Ⅰ 形 ①upright and honest;straightforward ②joyful;cheerful;amiable Ⅱ 动 ①chat idly;tattle ②boast ③smoothly talk

侃价 bargain;haggle with a peddler

侃侃 with assurance and composure

侃星 ①chatterbox ②great boaster

侃爷 big talker

侃大山 ① chatter away;chat idly;gossip ② boast;brag

砍 [kǎn] 动 ①cut;chop;hack;fell ②reduce;cut ③throw (at sth or sb)

砍刀 chopper

砍伐 fell (trees)

砍价 bargain;cut (or beat) down the price

砍头 chop off the head;behead

莰 [kǎn] 名 camphane

歁 [kǎn] 形 ①not self-satisfied;not complacent ②frustrated;depressed

歁憾 be melancholy;feel frustrated (or depressed)

歁然 not look complacent

槛 [kǎn] 名 threshold ➡jiàn

kàn (ㄎㄢˋ)

看 [kàn] 动 ①look at;see;watch;read ②think;consider;view;judge ③call on;visit;go to see ④look upon;regard;treat ⑤treat (a patient or an illness) ⑥look after;attend to ⑦(used to show sth is going to happen, or as a warning) mind;watch out;look ⑧(used after a verb or verbal structure to indicate a tentative action) try and see;… and see what'll happen ⑨depend on;rely on ➡kān

看扁 underestimate;belittle

看病 ①(of a doctor) see a patient ②(of a patient) see (or consult) a doctor

看成 ①take sb or sth for;look upon as;regard as ②be able to see or watch

看出 make out;see

看穿 see through

看待 look on (or upon);regard;treat

看淡 slack trend;foresee a slack trend

看到 catch sight of;see

看低 look down on;belittle

看点 highlight

看跌 (of market prices) be expected to fall

看法 ①a way of looking at a thing;view ②an unfavourable (or critical) view

看惯 be accustomed to the sight of;get used to the sight of

看好 have a good prospect (of winning, gaining,etc.)

看见 catch sight of;see

看开 accept (or resign oneself to) an unpleasant fact (or situation)

看看 ① look carefully;examine ② soon;in a moment

看来 it seems (or appears);it looks as if

看破 see through

看齐 ①dress ②keep up with;emulate

看轻 underestimate;look down on

看清 ①see clearly ②realize

看上 take a fancy to;settle on

看台 bleachers;stands

看透 ①understand thoroughly ②see through

看头 [kàntou] sth worth seeing (or reading)

看旺 booming trend;foresee a booming trend

看望 call on;visit;see

看相 read fortune (by face,palm lines,etc.)

看涨 (of market prices) be expected to rise

看中 take a fancy to;settle on

看重 regard as important;value;set store by

看准 be certain about sth

看作 look upon as;regard as

看座 (said to a servant,waiter,etc.) find a seat for the guest

看不起 look down on;scorn;despise

看得起 have a good opinion of;think highly of

看风水 practise geomancy (for selecting a site for a tomb,house,etc.)

看起来 it seems (or appears);it looks as if

看情况 depending on circumstances

看热闹 watch the excitement;watch the fun

看手相 practice palmistry

看笑话 amuse oneself by watching other people make fools of themselves;watch the fun;have a good laugh at

看眼色 be ready to take hint

看医生 see a doctor;consult a doctor

看着办 size up situation and act accordingly;do as one sees fit

看不过去 cannot stand by and watch

看不顺眼 be disgusting;to one's dislike;not to one's taste

看得过去 passable;just presentable

看风使舵 steer according to the wind;trim

one's sails

看破红尘 see through the vanity of the world; be disillusioned with the mortal world

看人嘴脸 live on another's favour; depend on another

看图识字 learn to read with the aid of pictures

看人下菜碟儿 treat people according to their social status; be snobbish

看菜吃饭,量体裁衣 fit the appetite to the dishes and the dress (*or* clothes) to the figure—act according to actual circumstances

瞰 [kàn]
Ⅰ 动 ①look down from a height; overlook ②peep; look

kāng (丂尢)

康 [kāng]
形 ①healthy ②well-being; abundant; affluent

康复 restored to health; recovered

康健 healthy; in good health

康乐 happy and peaceful

康泰 in good health

康铜 constantan

康拜因 combine (harvester)

康采恩 conglomerate

康复车 public bus reserved for the disabled

康乐球 caroms

康乃馨 carnation (a transliteration)

康师傅 Chef Kang

康复训练 rehabilitation training

康复中心 rehabilitation centre; health recovery centre

康居工程 comfortable housing project

康乐中心 recreation centre

康庄大道 broad road; main road

慷 [kāng]

慷慨 ①vehement; fervent ②generous; liberal

慷慨悲歌 sing with solemn fervour

慷慨陈词 speak with fervour; speak with righteous indignation; present one's views vehemently

慷慨激昂 impassioned; vehement

慷慨解囊 help sb generously with money; give generously (of one's money)

慷慨就义 go to one's death like a hero; die a martyr's death

糠 [kāng]
名 ①chaff; bran; husk ②(*usu. of a radish*) spongy

糠秕 ①chaff ②worthless stuff

糠醛 furfural

káng (丂尢)

扛 [káng]
动 ①carry on the shoulder; shoulder ②deal

with; handle ③bear; stand; endure ⇒ gāng

扛竿 acrobatics on a bamboo pole

扛活 work as a farm labourer

扛长活 work as a farm labourer on a yearly basis

kàng (丂尢)

亢 [kàng]
形 ①high ②haughty; arrogant ③excessive; extreme

亢奋 extremely excited; stimulated

亢旱 severe drought

亢进 hyperfunction

伉 [kàng]
形 ①(of spouse) match; fit ②lofty; big and tall

伉俪 married couple; husband and wife

抗 [kàng]
动 ①resist; combat; fight ②refuse; defy ③contend with; be a match for

抗癌 anticancer

抗暴 fight against tyranny; fight against violent repression

抗爆 antiknock

抗辩 ①contradict ②counterplea; demurrer

抗病 disease-resistant

抗敌 fight the enemy

抗寒 resist the cold

抗旱 fight (*or* combat) a drought

抗衡 contend with; match

抗洪 anti-flood battle; fight against floods; battle against floods; struggle against floods

抗婚 refuse to marry the person chosen by one's family

抗击 resist and fight back

抗拒 resist; defy

抗菌 antibacterial

抗命 defy orders; disobey

抗扰 anti-interference; anti-jamming

抗渗 impervious

抗霜 frost-resistant

抗税 tax dodge; refuse to pay tax

抗诉 lodge protests

抗体 antibody

抗议 protest

抗御 resist and guard against

抗原 antigen

抗灾 fight natural calamities

抗战 ①war of resistance against aggression ②the War of Resistance Against Japan

抗震 ①anti-seismic capability ②take precautions against an earthquake; fight an earthquake ③antiknock

抗争 take a stand against; resist

抗皱 anti-wrinkle

抗冲击 shock-resistant

抗磁性 diamagnetism

抗倒伏 resistant to lodging;lodging-resistant
抗地震 earthquake-resistant;anti-seismic
抗毒素 antitoxin
抗毒药 antidote
抗干扰 anti-interference
抗静电 antistatic;anti-static electricity
抗菌素 antibiotic
抗老剂 antiager
抗霉素 antimycin;antitoxin
抗生素 antibiotic
抗水性 water-resistance; water-resisting property
抗体酶 abzyme
抗药性 resistance to poisons;resistance to the action of a drug
抗议书 written protest
抗震棚 quake-proof shelter
抗催化药 anticatalyst
抗毒血清 antitoxin serum
抗洪前线 flood-control front
抗洪抢险 flood-fighting and emergency rescues;combat a flood and rush to deal with an emergency;combat a flood and go to the rescue
抗坏血酸 ascorbic acid;vitamin C
抗拒从严 harsh punishment for those who resist
抗捐抗税 refuse to pay levies and taxes
抗拉强度 tensile strength
抗热合金 heat-resisting alloy
抗日战争 the War of Resistance Against Japan
抗弯强度 bending strength
抗压强度 compressive strength (*or* resistance)
抗议照会 note of protest
抗灾救灾 rescue and relief operation;fight calamities and provide relief;fight disasters and provide disaster relief
抗张强度 tensile strength
抗溶血球素 antihemolysin
抗美援朝战争 the War to Resist U. S. Aggression and Aid Korea

囥 [kàng]
囨 hide

炕 [kàng]
I 名 *kang*,a heatable brick bed II 劢 bake (*or* dry) by the heat of a fire
炕头 ①the warmer end of a *kang* ②the edge of a *kang*
炕席 *kang* mat
炕沿 the edge of a *kang*
炕桌儿 a small,short-legged table for use on a *kang*;a *kang* table

kāo（ㄎㄠ）

尻 [kāo]
名 buttocks;bottom;behind

kǎo（ㄎㄠ）

考 [kǎo]
I 劢 ①quiz;question ②give (*or* take) an examination (*or* test) ③check;inspect ④study;investigate;verify II 名 one's deceased father
考本 take the relevant exam in order to obtain a driver's license
考查 examine;check
考察 ①inspect;make an on-the-spot investigation ②observe and study
考场 examination hall (*or* room)
考点 location of an examination
考订 examine and correct;do textual research
考古 ①engage in archaeological studies ②archaeology
考官 examiner
考核 examine;check;assess (sb's proficiency)
考绩 efficiency evaluation
考级 grade examination
考究 ① observe and study;investigate ② be particular about;pay attention to;strive for ③exquisite;fine
考据 textual criticism;textual research
考卷 examination paper
考虑 think over;consider
考聘 recruit by examination
考评 check and evaluate (ranking, results, etc.)
考期 date of an examination
考勤 check on work attendance
考区 examination district
考取 pass an entrance examination;be admitted to school (after an examination)
考生 a candidate for an entrance examination;examinee
考试 ① take an examination ② examination;test
考题 examination questions;examination paper
考问 examine orally;question
考务 examination affairs (administration)
考研 take the graduate school entrance exam;take part in the entrance exams for graduate schools
考验 test;trial
考证 make textual criticism;do textual research
考中 pass an examination;be admitted to (a college,etc.) through examination
考古学 archaeology
考试晋升制 system of promotion through examination

拷 [kǎo]
劢 flog;beat;torture
拷贝 copy

拷打 flog；beat；torture (prisoner)
拷问 torture sb during interrogation；interrogate with torture
拷贝纸 copy (*or* copying) paper

栲 [kǎo]
名 evergreen chinquapin
栲胶 tannin extract

烤 [kǎo]
动 ①bake；roast；toast ②warm oneself (by a fire or some other heat source)
烤电 diathermy
烤火 warm oneself by a fire
烤焦 burned in roasting (*or* baking)
烤炉 oven
烤盘 ovenware
烤肉 roast meat；roast
烤箱 oven
烤鸭 roast duck
烤烟 flue-cured tobacco
烤鱼 grill；roast fish
烤炙 (sun or heat) scorch
烤面包 toast
烤肉叉 spit；skewer
烤羊肉串 mutton shish kebab

kào （ㄎㄠ）

铐 [kào]
I 名 handcuffs Ⅱ 动 put handcuffs on sb；handcuff

犒 [kào]
动 reward with food and drink
犒劳 reward with food and drink
犒赏 reward a victorious army, etc. with bounties

靠 [kào]
I 动 ①(of sb) lean ②(of sth) lean (*or* stand) against ③keep to；get near；come up to；near ④depend on；rely on ⑤trust Ⅱ 名 military officer's armour
靠岸 pull in to shore；draw alongside
靠背 back (of a chair)
靠边 ①keep to the side ②(be forced to) step down from one's post ③reasonable；sensible
靠垫 cushion (for leaning on)
靠近 ①be close to；be near ②draw near；approach
靠拢 draw close；close up
靠山 backer；patron；backing
靠手 armrest
靠枕 back cushion
靠背椅 chair
靠不住 unreliable；undependable；untrustworthy
靠得住 reliable；dependable；trustworthy
靠边儿站 stand aside；get out of the way；(be forced to) leave the post；lose power

靠天吃饭 depend on Heaven for good；rely on destiny
靠山吃山，靠水吃水 those living on a mountain live off the mountain，those living near the water live off the water—make use of local resources

kē （ㄎㄜ）

苛 [kē]
形 ①harsh；severe；rigorous；exacting ②overelaborate；tedious
苛待 treat (inferiors) harshly
苛刻 harsh；severe；exacting
苛求 make excessive demands；be overcritical
苛细 severe and exacting
苛性 causticity
苛杂 exorbitant taxes and levies
苛责 criticize severely；excoriate
苛政 harsh (*or* oppressive) government；tyranny
苛性钾 caustic potash
苛性碱 caustic alkali
苛性钠 caustic soda
苛捐杂税 exorbitant taxes and levies；multifarious and onerous taxes
苛政猛于虎 Tyranny is fiercer than a tiger.

匼 [kē]
名 kerchief

珂 [kē]
名 ①jade-like stone ②ornament on a bridle

柯 [kē]
名 ① stalk；branch；bough ② axe handle；helve

科 [kē]
I 名 ① branch of academic or vocational activity；subject of instruction or study；discipline；department ②administrative section ③ imperial civil examinations；subject in such examinations ④ old-type Chinese opera school；regular professional training ⑤family ⑥law；rule ⑦(in classical Chinese scenario or libretto) stage directions for actions Ⅱ 动 impose (a punishment，etc.)；pass (a sentence)
科班 ①old-type opera school ②regular professional training
科幻 science fiction
科技 science and technology
科举 imperial examinations
科盲 science-illiterate；person who is ignorant of science
科目 ①subject (in a curriculum)；course ②headings in an account book
科普 popular science
科室 administrative (*or* technical) offices
科学 ①science；scientific knowledge ②scientific
科研 scientific research

科员 a member of an administrative section; section member
科长 section chief
科罪 impose a punishment on sb; punish sb
科技馆 museum of science and technology
科教片 popular science film; science and educational film
科学家 scientist
科学院 academy of sciences
科班出身 be a professional by training
科幻影片 sci-fi film
科技奥运 Hightech Olympics
科技成果 scientific and technological achievements (or fruits, payoffs, advances, developments)
科技扶贫 support the poor areas with technology; relieve poverty by using science and technology; help (or aid) the poor by teaching them practical skills
科技攻关 tackle hard-nut (or key) problems in science and technology
科技含量 technology content
科技强军 strengthen the army by relying on science and technology
科技人员 scientist and technician
科教兴国 boost (or invigorate) the nation through science and education; rejuvenate (or revitalize) the nation developing science and education
科普活动 activity to propagate scientific knowledge
科学幻想 science fiction
科学技术 science and technology
科学假设 scientific hypothesis
科学普及 popular science
科学研究 scientific research
科研攻关 scientific research and tackle the key research project
科研活动 scientific pursuits
科研院所 research academies and institutes
科技示范户 model households in science and technology
科索沃战争 Kosovo War
科学讨论会 science symposium
科学无禁区 There is not out-of-bounds area as far as science is concerned.
科技体制改革 reform of the management system of science and technology; reform of the system for managing science and technology
科技咨询活动 scientific and technological consulting services
科学工业园区 science-based industrial park
科学共产主义 scientific communism
科学教育影片 popular science film; science and educational film
科学社会主义 scientific socialism

科学文化素质 cultural and scientific quality
科研生产联合体 integrated entity of research and production
科学技术是第一生产力 Science and technology constitute a primary productive force.

钶
[kē]
名 (now known as 铌) columbium (Cb)

疴
[kē]
名 (formerly pronounced ē) illness

棵
[kē]
量 (usu. of plants): 两棵树 two trees

嗑
[kē]
名 words; talk; chat ➡️ kè

颗
[kē]
量 (of grains and grain-like things): 颗颗汗珠 drops (or beads) of sweat
颗粒 ① anything small and roundish (as a bean, pearl, etc.); pellet ② a grain (of rice, wheat, etc.)
颗粒肥料 granulated fertilizer; pellet fertilizer
颗粒无收 No kernels or seeds are gathered; Not a single grain was reaped.
颗粒物质 particulate matter
颗粒细胞 granular cell

磕
[kē]
动 ① knock (against sth hard) ② knock (sth out of a container); knock out
磕碰 knock against; collide with; bump against
磕头 kowtow
磕磕绊绊 ①(of a road) bumpy; rough ②(of a person) limping
磕磕撞撞 walk unsteadily (when drunk or in a hurry); stumble (or stagger) along; reel
磕头赔罪 give sb a grand kowtow and apologize
磕头碰脑 bump against things on every side (as in a room full of furniture); push and bump against one another (as in a crowd)

瞌
[kē]

瞌睡 sleepy; drowsy
瞌睡虫 ① sleep-inducing insect ② a sleepy person

蝌
[kē]

蝌蚪 tadpole

髁
[kē]
名 condyle

ké (ㄎㄜˊ)

壳
[ké]
名 ①shell ②housing; casing; case ➡️ qiào

咳
[ké]
动 cough ➡️ hāi
咳嗽 cough
咳血 hemoptysis
咳嗽糖浆 cough syrup

搁 [kē]
劢 ① get stuck; wedge ② create difficulties; make things difficult

kě (ㄎㄜ)

可 [kě]
Ⅰ 劢 ① approve; agree ② can; may ③ (*often used with a monosyllabic verb to form an adjectival phrase*) need (doing); be worth (doing): 我没什么可说的。 I have nothing to say. ④ go as far as is possible; make the best (*or* most) of; make do: 可嗓子喊 shout at the top of one's voice ⑤ (*usu. used in the early vernacular*) be fully recovered (from an illness): 待你病可后商量。 We won't discuss it until you get well again. ⑥ fit; suit: 可人意 agreeable to one; just what one wants Ⅱ 副 ① about; some: 长可七尺 some seven *chi* in length ② (*used for emphasis*): 你可把钱带来了! So you've brought the money with you. ③ (*used in a rhetorical question for emphasis*): 这么大的北京城，可上哪儿去找他呀? Beijing is such a big city. Where on earth should we find him? ④ (*used in a question to emphasize doubt*): 你可曾跟父亲商量过? Have you actually discussed this with father? Ⅲ 连 but; yet: 我本想去，可天太冷。 I meant to go, but it was too cold. ➡ kè

可爱 lovable; likable; lovely

可悲 sad; lamentable

可比 comparable

可鄙 contemptible; despicable; mean

可变 variable

可不 exactly; right; that's just the way it is

可怖 horrible; frightful

可拆 removable; detachable

可耻 shameful; disgraceful; ignominious

可观 ① worth seeing ② considerable; impressive; sizable

可贵 valuable; praiseworthy; commendable

可好 as luck would have it; by a happy coincidence

可恨 hateful; detestable; abominable

可嘉 laudable; praiseworthy

可见 it is thus clear (*or* evident, obvious) that; it shows; that proves; so

可敬 worthy of respect; respected

可靠 reliable; dependable; trustworthy

可可 cocoa

可口 good to eat; nice; tasty; palatable

可乐 ① laughable; funny; amusing ② cola (a type of non-alcoholic drink)

可怜 ① pitiful; pitiable; poor ② have pity on; pity ③ (of quantity or quality) meagre; wretched; miserable; pitiful

可恼 annoying; irritating

可能 ① possible; probable; likely ② probably; maybe

可逆 reversible

可怕 fearful; frightful; terrible; terrifying

可欺 ① gullible; easily duped ② easily cowed (*or* bullied)

可气 annoying; exasperating; irritating

可巧 as luck would have it; by a happy coincidence

可亲 amiable; affable; genial

可取 desirable

可人 ① one with strong points worth recommending ② satisfactory; satisfying

可身 be a good fit; fit nicely

可是 ① but; yet; however ② (*used for emphasis*)

可叹 it is regrettable; it is a pity

可体 be a good fit; fit nicely

可调 adjustable

可谓 one may well say; it may be said; it may be called

可恶 hateful; abominable; detestable

可惜 it's a pity; it's too bad

可喜 gratifying; heartening

可笑 laughable; ridiculous; ludicrous; funny

可心 satisfying; likeable; to the satisfaction (*or* liking) of

可信 credible

可行 feasible

可疑 suspicious; dubious; questionable

可以 ① can; may ② be worth (doing) ③ passable; pretty good; not bad ④ terrible; awful

可憎 hateful; detestable; abominable

可的松 cortisone

可读性 readability

可锻性 malleability; forgeability

可兑换 convertible

可耕地 arable land; cultivable land

可见度 visibility

可见光 visible light

可卡因 cocaine

可控硅 silicon controlled rectifier (SCR); thyristor

可怜虫 pitiful creature; wretch

可怜相 pitiable look

可能性 possibility

可燃冰 combustible ice

可燃性 combustibility; flammability

可数性 countability

可塑性 plasticity

可行性 feasibility

可知性 knowability

可转换 convertible

可转让 ① transferable ② negotiable

可变资本 variable capital

可采储量 recoverable reserves (of petroleum)

可操左券 be sure to succeed; be certain of

success
可乘之机 an opportunity that can be exploited
可大可小 may be big or small; may be serious or light
可锻铸铁 malleable (cast) iron
可歌可泣 move one to song and tears
可加工性 machinability
可进可退 be free to press forward or back out; can either attack or retreat
可口可乐 Coca-Cola; coke
可怜巴巴 pitiable; pathetic
可逆反应 reversible reaction
可庆可贺 be worthy of congratulations
可圈可点 praiseworthy
可视电话 videophone; viewphone; picture telephone
可数名词 countable noun
可想而知 one can well imagine
可笑之至 be ridiculous in the extreme
可有可无 not essential; not indispensable
可造之才 a person suitable for training; a promising (*or* hopeful) young person; a person with great potentialities
可变电容器 variable capacitor (*or* condenser)
可变均衡器 variable equalizer
可撤销婚姻 voidable marriage
可持续发展 sustainable development
可兑换货币 convertible currency
可兑换债券 convertible bond
可更新资源 renewable resources
可过户证券 assignable instrument; negotiable instrument
可交割商品 deliverable supply
可靠性试验 fail-test
可裂变物质 fissile (*or* fissionable) material
可实现利润 realizable profit
可赎回股票 redeemable shares
可塑性炸药 plastic explosive
可贴现票据 bankable bill
可行性报告 feasibility report
可行性研究 feasibility study
可遇不可求 sth that can only be found by accident, and not through seeking
可再生能源 renewable energy; regenerative energy
可再生资源 renewable resource
可支配收入 disposable income
可转让财产 alienable property
可转让债券 negotiable securities
可兑换优先股 convertible preference share
可杀而不可辱 you can kill (sb) but not insult (him); (sb) would rather die than be humiliated
可视电话会议 videoconferencing
可望而不可即 within sight but beyond reach; unattainable
可吸入颗粒物 inhalable particle (IP)

可转让信用证 negotiable letter of credit; transferable letter of credit; assignable letter of credit
可变现金融工具 liquidable financial instruments
可行性研究报告 feasibility study report
可意会而不可言传 can be appreciated but not clearly defined; defy analysis (*or* description)
可依法强制执行的裁决 award enforceable at law

渴 [kě]
I 形 thirsty; dry II 副 yearningly; eagerly
渴念 long for; yearn for; miss sb very much
渴盼 eagerly look forward to; earnestly hope
渴求 eagerly desire; crave for
渴望 thirst for; long for; yearn for
渴想 long for; miss sb very much
渴仰 admire; look up to

kè (ㄎㄜ)

可 [kè]
➡ kě
可汗 khan

克 [kè]
I 动 ① can; be able to ② overcome; restrain ③ capture; conquer; subdue ④ digest ⑤ set a time limit II 量 ① gram (g): 五百克 500 grams; half a kilogram ② Tibetan unit of dry measure holding about 12.5 kilograms of barley ③ Tibetan unit of land area equal to about 1 *mu* or ⅙ of an acre
克服 ① surmount; overcome; conquer ② put up with (hardships, inconveniences, etc.)
克复 retake; recapture; recover
克己 restrain oneself
克扣 embezzle part of what should be issued
克拉 carat
克隆 clone (transliteration)
克期 set a date; set a time limit
克食 help digestion
克星 jinx; natural enemy
克制 restrain; exercise restraint
克当量 gram equivalent
克分子 gram molecule
克格勃 KGB, the former Soviet State Security Committee
克厘米 gram-centimetre
克丝钳 combination pliers; cutting pliers
克原子 gram atom
克敌制胜 vanquish (*or* conquer) the enemy and win victory
克己奉公 be wholeheartedly devoted to public duty; work selflessly for the public interest
克勤克俭 be industrious and frugal; be hard-working and thrifty
克分子浓度 molarity

克分子体积 gram molecular volume
克里姆林宫 the Kremlin
克服铺张浪费 eliminate extravagance and waste without fail
克服各种障碍与绊脚石 overcome all the barriers and stumbling blocks
克服官僚主义和形式主义 get rid of bureaucracy and formalism

刻 ［kè］
Ⅰ 动 ①carve; engrave; cut ②set a time limit Ⅱ 量 ①unit of time when the water clock or hourglass was used to measure time (with 100 such units is a day) ②quarter (of an hour) Ⅲ 名 moment; time Ⅳ 形 ①in the highest degree ②cutting; biting; harsh
刻板 ①cut blocks for printing; carve printing blocks ②mechanical; stiff; inflexible
刻版 cut blocks for printing; carve printing blocks
刻本 block-printed edition
刻薄 unkind; harsh; mean
刻刀 burin; graver
刻毒 venomous; spiteful
刻度 graduation (on a vessel or instrument)
刻骨 deeply ingrained; deep-rooted
刻痕 score; hack; nick; nicking
刻花 engraved designs; carved designs
刻画 depict; portray
刻记 cut (stencils)
刻苦 ①assiduous; hardworking; painstaking ②simple and frugal
刻意 be painstaking; be meticulous about; sedulously strive
刻印 stamp mark; mint-mark
刻字 carve (or engrave) characters (on a seal, slabstone, etc.)
刻度尺 dividing ruler
刻度盘 division circle; dial scale
刻录机 CD writer; disc-carving machine
刻字社 seal-engraving shop
刻版印刷 block printing
刻不容缓 brook no delay; demand immediate attention; be of great urgency
刻骨铭心 be engraved on one's bones and heart—be remembered with deep gratitude
刻画入微 describe even to the trifling point; portray to the life
刻苦耐劳 work hard without complaint; suffer hardship and persevere in toil
刻意求工 sedulously strive for perfection; be a scrupulous craftsman
刻舟求剑 nick the boat to seek the sword—take measures without regard to changes in circumstances

恪 ［kè］
副 scrupulously and respectfully; meticulously

恪守 scrupulously abide by (a treaty, promise, etc.)
恪尽职守 be whole-heartedly devoted to one's duty
恪守中立 observe a strict neutrality
恪守一个中国的立场 maintain the one China position

客 ［kè］
Ⅰ 名 ①guest; visitor ②passenger; traveller ③travelling merchant ④customer; patron; client ⑤person engaged in some particular pursuit requiring a certain amount of travelling and running around Ⅱ 量 (for food or drinks sold in portions): 两客冰激凌 two ice creams Ⅲ 动 live (or settle) in a strange place Ⅳ 形 independent of human consciousness; objective
客舱 passenger cabin
客场 (in basketball as between two competing teams) other team's home court; (in soccer) other team's home ground
客车 ①passenger train ②bus
客船 passenger ship (or boat)
客串 (of an amateur singer, actor, etc.) play a part in a professional performance; be a guest performer
客店 inn
客队 visiting team
客饭 ①a meal specially prepared for visitors at a cafeteria ②set meal; table d'hôte
客房 guest room
客观 objective
客户 customer
客机 passenger plane; airliner
客籍 ①a settler from another province ②the province into which settlers move
客家 the Hakkas
客居 live abroad; live away from home
客流 the flow of passengers
客轮 passenger ship (or liner)
客满 ①(of a theatre, cinema, etc.) have a full house; house full ②no vacancy (in a hotel)
客票 passenger ticket
客气 ①polite; courteous ②modest ③make polite remarks; act politely; be polite; be courteous
客人 ①visitor; guest ②guest (at a hotel, etc.); traveller ③travelling trader
客商 travelling trader
客室 guest room
客死 die in a strange land; die abroad
客套 ①polite formula; civilities ②make polite remarks; exchange greetings
客体 object
客厅 drawing room; parlour; living room; sitting room
客源 source of tourists; potential customers

（ or tourists）

客运 passenger transport；passenger traffic

客栈 inn

客座 ①seat（ or place）for a guest（ or client）②professional person invited to work temporarily in an institution

客货船 passenger-cargo vessel

客家话 Hakka（dialect）

客套话 polite expressions（ or formulas）

客场比赛 away match

客场获胜 get an away win .

客房服务 room service

客观规律 objective law（ or principle）

客观实在 objective reality

客观世界 objective world

客观真理 objective truth

客观主义 objectivism

客户定金 customer's deposit

客流高峰 peak passenger season

客随主便 A guest should suit the convenience of the host or hostess.

客运列车 passenger train

客座教授 guest professor；visiting professor

客房出租率 room occupancy rate

客观经济规律 objective law of economics

客观唯心主义 objective idealism

客货两用汽车 notchback

课 [kè] I [名] ①class；lecture ②subject；course ③class ④lesson ⑤subdivision of an administrative unit；section ⑥tax ⑦divination；fortune-telling II [动] levy；impose

课本 textbook

课程 course；curriculum

课间 break（between classes）

课件 courseware

课时 class hour；period

课税 ①levy（ or collect）taxes ②taxes

课堂 classroom；schoolroom

课题 ①a question for study（ or discussion）②problem；task

课外 extracurricular； outside class； after school

课文 text（of a lesson）

课业 lessons；schoolwork

课余 after school；after class

课桌 （school）desk

课程表 school timetable；class schedule

课间操 setting-up exercises during the break between classes

课税品 dutiable goods

课题组 research group（for an assigned topic）

课税单位 taxable unit

课税公平 tax equity

课税价值 taxable value

课外活动 extracurricular activities；after-class activities

氪 [kè] [名] krypton（Kr）

骒 [kè] [形] female（mule or horse）

骒骒 female mule

嗑 [kè] [动] crack sth between the teeth ⇒kē

kēi（ㄎㄟ）

剋 [kēi] [动] ①beat；fight ②scold；curse

kěn（ㄎㄣˇ）

肯 [kěn] I [名] flesh sticking to the bone II [动] ①agree；consent ②be willing（ or ready）（to do sth）；be agreeable（to doing sth）③be liable to；frequently occur

肯定 ① affirm；confirm；approve；regard as positive ②positive；affirmative ③definite；sure ④certainly；undoubtedly；definitely

肯干 ready to work；willing to do sth

肯德基 Kentucky Fried Chicken

垦 [kěn] [动] turn up（soil）；cultivate（land）；reclaim（wasteland）

垦荒 reclaim wasteland；bring wasteland under cultivation；open up virgin soil

垦区 reclamation area

垦殖 reclaim and cultivate wasteland

恳 [kěn] I [形] sincerely；earnestly II [动] request；entreat；beg

恳辞 sincerely decline；earnestly beg off

恳祈 beg fervently

恳切 earnest；sincere

恳请 earnestly request

恳求 implore；entreat；beseech

恳劝 persuade（ or admonish）earnestly

恳谈 talk sincerely；have a heart-to-heart conversation

恳谢 thank sincerely

恳挚 earnest；sincere

恳谈会 problem-solving talks；frank discussion meeting

啃 [kěn] [动] ①gnaw；nibble ②kiss

kèn（ㄎㄣˋ）

掯 [kèn] [动] ①push down hard；press ②deliberately make things difficult ③（of eyes）contain；hold

kēng（ㄎㄥ）

坑 [kēng] I [名] ① pit；depression；hollow ② tunnel；

hole;pit Ⅱ 动 ①bury alive ②harm by cunning (*or* deceit);cheat;hoodwink

坑道 ①gallery ②tunnel

坑害 lead into a trap;entrap

坑木 pit prop;mine timber

坑农 cheat the farmers

坑骗 entrap;cheat

坑人 ①entrap;cheat ②be upset (by a heavy loss)

坑子 pit;hollow

坑坑洼洼 full of bumps and hollows;bumpy;rough

坑蒙拐骗 swindle

吭 [kēng]
动 utter a sound (*or* word);speak ➡háng

吭哧 ①puff and blow ②work hard;toil ③hum and haw

吭声 utter a sound (*or* a word)

硁 [kēng]
名 sound of striking stones;clangour

铿 [kēng]
图 clang;clatter

铿锵 (of sound produced by the gong,piano, cymbals,etc.) rhythmic and sonorous

铿锵玫瑰 steel rose

kōng (ㄎㄨㄥ)

空 [kōng]
Ⅰ 形 empty;hollow;void;unoccupied Ⅱ 名 air;sky:对空射击 fire into the air Ⅲ 副 in vain;for nothing;to no avail:空欢喜 rejoice too soon;rejoice only to be let down ➡kòng

空靶 air (*or* aerial,airborne) target

空层 dead level

空肠 jejunum

空车 empty

空程 idle running;idle stroke

空带 blanking bar;empty band;empty tape

空挡 neutral gear

空调 ①air-conditioning ②air conditioner

空洞 ①cavity ②empty;hollow;devoid of content

空翻 somersault;flip

空泛 vague and general;not specific

空防 air defence

空腹 on an empty stomach

空港 airport

空喊 indulge in empty shouting

空话 empty talk;idle talk;hollow words

空怀 barren

空幻 visionary;illusory

空寂 quiet and deserted

空间 space

空降 land from the air;be airborne

空姐 air hostess

空警 air police

空军 air force

空口 eat dishes without rice or wine;eat rice or drink wine with nothing to go with it

空旷 open;spacious

空阔 open;spacious

空廓 open;spacious

空灵 free and natural;unconventionally graceful

空论 empty talk

空忙 make fruitless efforts

空门 Buddhism

空名 ① empty title;empty name ② undeserved reputation

空难 air disaster;air crash;plane crash;aviation accident

空气 ①air ②atmosphere

空前 unprecedented

空勤 air duty

空嫂 middle-aged female flight attendants;air lady;married stewardess

空身 carry no luggage;carry nothing

空手 empty-handed

空谈 ①indulge in empty talk ②empty talk;idle talk;prattle

空头 ① (on the stock exchange) bear;short seller ②nominal;phony

空投 air-drop;paradrop

空文 ineffective law (*or* rule,etc.)

空吸 suction

空袭 make an air attack (*or* raid)

空想 ①indulge in fantasy;daydream ②unrealistic thought;fantasy;daydreaming

空心 (of trees,vegetables,etc.) become hollow inside

空虚 hollow;void

空穴 hole

空邮 send a letter,etc. by airmail

空域 airspace

空援 air reinforcement;assistance from the air

空运 transport by air;airlift

空战 air battle;aerial combat

空中 in the sky;in the air;aerial;overhead

空重 empty weight

空竹 diabolo

空转 ①(of a motor,etc.) idle;race ②(of a wheel) turn without moving forward;spin

空包弹 blank cartridge

空舱费 dead freight

空城计 the stratagem of the empty city—presenting a bold front to conceal a weak defence

空荡荡 empty;deserted

空调病 air-conditioning syndrome;air-conditioning disease

空欢喜 rejoice too soon

空架子 mere skeleton (usu. referring to a piece of writing, an organization, etc.);

bare outline
空间波 space wave
空间站 space station
空降兵 airborne force;paratroops;parachuti-
sts
空气浴 air bath
空天战 space warfare
空心面 macaroni
空心砖 hollow brick
空巢家庭 empty nest
空洞无物 utter lack of substance;devoid of
content
空谷足音 the sound of footsteps in a deserted
valley—unexpected good news
空锅冷灶 empty pots and cold stove
空间点阵 space lattice;crystal lattice
空间技术 space technology
空间垃圾 space junk
空间速度 space velocity
空间医学 space medicine;aeromedicine
空间知觉 space perception
空空如也 absolutely empty
空口无凭 A mere verbal statement is no guarantee.
空气净化 air purification;air purge
空气冷却 air-cooling
空气力学 aeromechanics
空气调节 air-conditioning
空气污染 air pollution
空前绝后 unprecedented and unrepeatable;u-
nique
空谈主义 phrase-mongering
空天飞机 aerospacecraft
空头市场 bear market
空头政治 phony politics;empty politicizing
空头支票 ① dud (*or* rubber) cheque;bad
cheque ②empty promise;lip service
空袭警报 air raid alarm;air raid siren
空心长丝 fibre hollow filament
空穴来风 an empty hole invites the wind—
weakness lends wings to rumours
空运公司 air transport company
空运货物 air freight;air cargo
空运提单 air bill of lading
空中打击 air strike
空中发射 air-launched
空中飞人 flying trapeze
空中花园 Hanging Gardens of Babylon (one of
the ancient world's seven wonders)
空中加油 air refueling;in-flight refueling;air-
to-air refueling
空中劫持 aerial hijacking
空中客车 airbus;skylounge
空中楼阁 castles in the air
空中小姐 air hostess;air stewardess
空中优势 air superiority;strategic advantage
in air

空中预警 airborne early warning
空中走廊 air corridor;air lane
空地一体战 air-land battle
空对地导弹 air-to-surface missile;air-to-
ground missile
空对空导弹 air-to-air guided missile
空间探测器 space probe
空间天文学 space astronomy
空口说白话 make empty promises;pay mere
lip service
空气采样法 impingement
空气过滤器 air filter
空气加湿器 humidifier
空气净化器 air purifier
空气调节器 air conditioner
空气压缩机 air compressor
空头政治家 armchair politician
空战主动权 freedom of the air
空气动力试验 aerodynamic experiment or test
空气净化装置 air cleaner
空气污染指数 air pollution index (API)
空气质量预报 air quality prediction
空气质量指数 air quality index (AQI)
空想社会主义 utopian socialism
空中交通管制 air traffic control
空气质量和排放标准 air quality and emission
standards

kǒng (ㄎㄨㄥˇ)

孔 [kǒng]
I 名 hole;opening;aperture:多孔动物 po-
rifer II 量 (of caves):两孔砖窑 two brick-
lined cave-dwellings
孔道 a narrow passage providing the only
means of access to a certain place;pass
孔洞 opening (*or* hole) in a utensil,etc.
孔径 ①aperture ②bore diameter
孔庙 Confucian temple
孔桥 bridge
孔雀 peacock
孔隙 small opening;hole
孔型 pass
孔穴 hole;cavity
孔眼 eyelet;oillet
孔方兄 Brother Square Hole—money
孔雀绿 peacock green;malachite green
孔雀石 malachite (a mineral)
孔隙度 porosity
孔孟之道 the doctrine of Confucius and Mencius
孔雀开屏 peacock spreading its tail;peacock in
his pride

恐 [kǒng]
I 动 ① be afraid;fear;dread ② scare;
frighten;terrify;intimidate II 副 I'm afraid:
恐不容易。I'm afraid it's not that easy.
恐怖 terror;horror

恐吓 threaten;intimidate
恐慌 panic
恐惧 fear;dread
恐龙 dinosaur
恐怕 ①fear;dread;be afraid of ②perhaps;probably;maybe
恐怖症 phobia
恐高症 acrophobia
恐吓信 blackmailing letter;threatening letter
恐水病 hydrophobia;rabies
恐怖电影 horror film
恐怖分子 terrorist
恐怖主义 terrorism

kòng (ㄎㄨㄥ)

空 [kòng]
Ⅰ 动 leave empty (or blank);leave unoccupied;vacate Ⅱ 形 vacant;unoccupied;blank Ⅲ 名 ①unoccupied space;empty space;room ②free time;spare time;leisure time ➡ kōng
空白 blank space
空仓 hold capital,having sold all securities
空乘 ①services for passengers aboard a flight ②airline steward
空当 space;interval;gap
空地 vacant lot;open ground;open space
空额 vacancy
空格 blank space (on a form)
空行 null;null string
空缺 vacant position;vacancy
空隙 space;gap;interval
空暇 free time;spare time;leisure
空闲 ①idle;free ②free time;spare time;leisure
空心 on an empty stomach
空余 free;vacant;unoccupied
空置 empty;unoccupied
空子 ① unoccupied place (or time);gap;opening ② chance (or opportunity) (for doing sth bad)
空白点 blank spot;gap;blank
空格键 space key
空白承兑 acceptance in blank
空白收据 blank receipt
空白背书汇票 bill endorsed in blank

控 [kòng]
动 ①accuse;charge;denounce ②control;dominate ③keep (one's body or part of one's body) hanging in the air;keep unsupported ④turn (usu. a container) upside down to let the liquid trickle out
控编 control staff size
控办 group consumption control office
控告 charge;accuse;complain
控股 hold the controlling share
控盘 manipulate stock quotations
控诉 accuse;denounce

控制 control;dominate;command
控告信 letter of complaint
控制杆 joystick
控制论 math cybernetics
控制台 automation console
控股公司 holding company;controlling company;parent company
控制电路 control circuit
控制数字 control figure
控制武器转让 control arms transfers; curb arms transfers
控制现金投放 control currency issue; control currency supply
控制新开工项目 control the number of new projects

kōu (ㄎㄡ)

苁 [kōu]
名 onion;scallion

抠 [kōu]
Ⅰ 动 ① dig (out) with a finger or sth pointed;scratch ②carve;cut ③study punctiliously;be studious (or exacting) to the degree of being bookish; delve into Ⅱ 形 stingy;closefisted;penny-pinching
抠门儿 stingy;miserly
抠字眼儿 pay too much attention to wording;find fault with the choice of words

眍 [kōu]
动 (of the eyes) become (or be) sunken

kǒu (ㄎㄡˇ)

口 [kǒu]
Ⅰ 名 ①(of a human or animal) mouth ②one's taste ③people;population ④(of a container,etc.) sth resembling (or functioning) as a mouth ⑤opening;mouth;exit;entrance:胡同口儿 entrance of an alley ⑥(often used in place names) gateway of the Great Wall;pass ⑦cut;hole;crack;chip ⑧general category or division grouping organs,institutions or enterprises of similar nature loosely together under an umbrella administrative body; departments of such a category or division ⑨sharp edge of a knife,etc.;blade ⑩age of a draft animal Ⅱ 量:吃几口饭 have a few mouthfuls of food/讲一口流利的英语 speak fluent English/一口刀 a knife
口岸 port
口白 ①(in an opera) words spoken;spoken parts ②colourless lipstick (used to prevent the lips from being dry)
口碑 public praise
口才 eloquence
口彩 praise;extol;acclaim;commend
口吃 stutter;stammer
口齿 ①enunciation ②ability to speak

口臭 bad breath;halitosis
口传 instruct orally
口疮 aphtha
口袋 ①pocket ②bag;sack
口德 restraint in one's speech; propriety of words
口风 one's intention (*or* view) as revealed in what one says
口服 ①profess to be convinced ②take orally
口福 gourmet's luck;the luck to get sth very nice to eat
口腹 food
口干 dry;thirst
口感 texture (of foods)
口供 a statement made by the accused under examination
口号 slogan;watchword
口红 lipstick
口惠 lip service;empty promise
口技 vocal mimicry;vocal imitation
口角 [kǒujiǎo] corner of the mouth
口紧 close-mouthed;tight-lipped
口径 ① bore;calibre ② requirements;specifications;line of action
口诀 a pithy mnemonic formula (often in rhyme);mnemonic rhyme
口角 [kǒujué] quarrel;bicker;wrangle
口渴 thirsty
口粮 grain ration
口令 ①word of command ②password;watchword;countersign
口气 ① tone;note ② manner of speaking ③ what is actually meant;implication
口器 mouthparts (of an insect)
口腔 oral cavity
口琴 mouth organ;harmonica
口轻 ①not too salty ②be fond of food that is not too salty ③(of a horse,donkey,etc.) young
口舌 ①dispute (*or* misunderstanding) caused by gossip ②talking round
口实 a cause for gossip;handle
口试 oral examination;oral test
口授 ①teach (*or* instruct) orally ②dictate
口述 give an oral account
口水 saliva
口算 ①chant out the result while doing mental calculation;calculate orally ②poll tax
口条 pig's (*or* ox's) tongue (as food)
口头 oral
口腕 oral arm
口味 ① a person's taste ② the flavour (*or* taste) of food
口吻 ①muzzle;snout ②tone;note
口误 ①make a slip of the tongue ②a slip of the tongue;an oral slip
口小 (of a horse,donkey,etc.) young

口信 oral message
口形 degree of lip-rounding
口炎 stomatitis
口译 oral interpretation
口音 ①voice ②accent
口语 ①spoken language ②slander;calumny
口罩 gauze mask (worn over nose and mouth);surgical mask
口重 ①salty ②be fond of salty fond
口子 opening;hole;cut;tear
口袋书 pocket book
口服液 oral liquid
口腔学 stomatology
口哨儿 whistling sound made through rounded lips
口水战 war of words
口蹄疫 foot-and-mouth disease; hoof-and-mouth disease
口头禅 pet phrase;pet expression
口头交 a casual acquaintance
口头语 pet phrase;habitual turn of phrase
口香糖 chewing gum
口碑载道 be praised everywhere
口齿伶俐 have a ready tongue;good talker;be clever and fluent;fluent of speech
口出狂言 talk wildly
口传心授 Oral teaching inspires true understanding.
口福不浅 luck of having good food;lucky in having good things to eat
口腹之欲 the desire for good food
口干舌燥 mouth parched and tongue scorched
口口声声 say again and again;keep on saying
口蜜腹剑 honey-mouthed and dagger-hearted; honey on one's lips and murder in one's heart;hypocritical and malignant
口腔溃疡 canker sore
口腔医院 stomatological hospital
口若悬河 let loose a flood of eloquence;be eloquent;speak volubly
口舌之争 contention of mouth and tongue
口是心非 say yes and mean no;say one thing and mean another
口说无凭 Verbal statements are no guarantee;Oral agreement is not binding.
口头表决 voice vote;vote by "yes" and "no"
口头契约 oral contract;verbal contract
口头文学 folk tales,ballads,etc. handed down orally;oral literature
口眼歪斜 facial paralysis
口燥唇干 (talk until) the lips are dry and the mouth is parched
口诛笔伐 denounce orally and in writing;condemn both in speech and in writing
口服避孕药 the pill (Pill); birth (control) pill;oral contraceptive
口服心不服 pretend to be convinced

口述记录机 dictating machine
口惠而实不至 make a promise and not keep it; pay lip service
口对口呼吸 mouth-to-mouth breathing

kòu（ㄎㄡˋ）

叩 [kòu]
动 ① knock; tap; rap: 叩门 knock at the door ②kowtow ③inquire; ask
叩拜 kowtow
叩击 (usu.) knock; beat; tap
叩见 visit (one's superior); call on (one's superior)
叩首 kowtow
叩头 kowtow
叩问 make inquiries
叩谢 kowtow in thanks; offer earnest thanks
叩诊 percussion
叩头虫 click beetle; snapping beetle

扣 [kòu]
Ⅰ 动 ①button up; buckle; bolt ② place (a container, vessel, etc.) upside down; cover (with an inverted container, vessel, etc.) ③ accuse unjustly; brand groundlessly; frame (up) ④ take into custody; detain; arrest; apprehend ⑤ deduct; discount; dock ⑥ smash; spike Ⅱ 名 ①knot; loop ②button; buckle ③ circle of thread (of a screw)
扣除 deduct
扣发 withhold; hold
扣分 deduct mark; deduction of point
扣环 jump ring; cramp ring
扣缴 withhold
扣紧 fasten; secure
扣篮 basketball dunk shot; over-the-rim shot
扣链 bitch chain
扣留 detain; hold in custody; arrest
扣球 smashing; (to) smash
扣杀 smash; spike (a ball)
扣题 keep to the point; be relevant to the subject
扣压 withhold; pigeonhole
扣押 ①detain; hold in custody; sequester ② distrain; seize
扣眼 buttonhole
扣子 ①knot ②button ③an abrupt break in a story to create suspense; a point of high suspense
扣工资 cut wages; dock one's pay (*or* wages); deduct a part of one's pay
扣帽子 put a label on sb; hurl an epithet at sb
扣下领 bottom-down shirt collar
扣人心弦 exciting; thrilling; breath-taking

寇 [kòu]
Ⅰ 名 bandit; invader; enemy Ⅱ 动 (of an enemy) invade; overrun
寇仇 enemy; foe

筘 [kòu]
名 reed

kū（ㄎㄨ）

刳 [kū]
动 hollow out
刳木为舟 hollow a (dugout) canoe out of a tree trunk

枯 [kū]
Ⅰ 动 ①(of a plant, etc.) withered ②(of a well, river, etc.) dried up Ⅱ 形 ① thin and haggard ② dull; uninteresting Ⅲ 名 dregs; residue (from soybean, sesame or other oilseeds after the oil has been extracted)
枯肠 impoverished mind
枯干 dried-up; withered; wizened
枯槁 ①(of a plant, etc.) withered ②haggard
枯涸 (of the source of a river) dry up
枯黄 withered and yellow
枯寂 bored and lonely
枯竭 dried up; exhausted
枯井 a dry well
枯窘 dried up
枯涩 dull and heavy
枯瘦 emaciated; skinny
枯水 low water
枯萎 withered
枯朽 withered and rotten
枯燥 dry and dull; uninteresting
枯草热 hay fever
枯水期 dry season
枯叶蛾 lappet moth
枯木逢春 spring comes to the withered tree— get a new lease of life
枯燥无味 dry as dust; dry and dull
枯枝败叶 withered branches and dead leaves

哭 [kū]
动 cry; weep
哭闹 cry and scream
哭泣 cry; weep; sob
哭腔 ①(in traditional opera) sobbing tune ② speak with sobs (maybe pretending)
哭穷 poor-mouth; make a poor mouth; go about telling people how hard up one is; complain of being hard up
哭诉 complain tearfully; accuse while weeping; sob out
哭鼻子 snivel
哭丧棒 the stick which the son in mourning leans on
哭爹叫娘 yell inordinately
哭哭啼啼 weep and wail
哭丧着脸 put on (*or* wear) a long face; go around with a long face
哭天抹泪 wailing and whining; crying piteously
哭笑不得 not know whether to laugh or to

K

cry;find sth both funny and annoying

堀 [kū]
名 ①hole;cavity;cave;grotto ②dig a hole

窟 [kū]
名 ①hole;cave;cavern;grotto ②den;lair
窟窿 ①hole;cavity ②deficit;debt
窟窿眼儿 small hole

骷 [kū]
骷髅 ① human skeleton ② human skull;death's-head

kǔ (ㄎㄨˇ)

苦 [kǔ]
Ⅰ 形 bitter Ⅱ 名 hardship;suffering;misery Ⅲ 动 ①cause sb suffering;give sb a hard time ②suffer from;be troubled by Ⅳ 副 ①painstakingly;assiduously;doing one's utmost ②too much;to excess
苦艾 absinthium;wormwood
苦熬 go through years of suffering and hardship
苦差 a hard and unprofitable job
苦楚 suffering;misery;distress
苦处 suffering;hardship;difficulty
苦胆 gallbladder
苦干 work hard
苦工 ①hard (manual) work;hard labour ②a person doing hard (manual) work
苦功 hard work;painstaking effort
苦瓜 ①balsam pear ②bitter gourd
苦果 bitter fruit—evil consequence;disastrous effect;bitter pill
苦海 sea of bitterness;abyss of misery
苦寒 bitter cold
苦谏 do one's utmost to advise (or exhort) (the monarch)
苦口 ①(admonish) in earnest ②bitter to the taste
苦苦 strenuously;hard;persistently
苦劳 credit for hard work
苦乐 joy and sorrow;enjoyment and suffering;happiness and hardship
苦力 coolie
苦练 practise hard;drill diligently
苦闷 depressed;dejected;feeling low
苦命 cruel fate;ill-fated life
苦难 suffering;misery;distress
苦恼 vexed;worried
苦涩 ① bitter and astringent ② pained;agonized;anguished
苦水 ①bitter water ②gastric secretion,etc. rising to the mouth ③suffering (in the old society)
苦思 think hard;cudgel one's brains
苦痛 pain;suffering;agony
苦头 ①bitter taste ②suffering

苦夏 loss of appetite and weight in summer
苦想 think hard
苦笑 force a smile;make a wry smile
苦心 trouble taken;pains
苦行 religion ascetic practices
苦役 hard labour;penal servitude
苦于 ① suffer from (a disadvantage) ② be harder than;be worse off than
苦雨 continuous rain
苦战 ①hard fighting;bitter battle ②wage an arduous struggle;struggle hard
苦衷 difficulties that one is reluctant to discuss (or mention)
苦竹 bitter bamboo
苦主 the family of the victim in a murder case
苦肉计 the ruse of self-injury (inflicting an injury on oneself to win the confidence of the enemy)
苦味酸 picric acid
苦行僧 person who lives a life of self-denial and mortification;ascetic monk
苦杏仁 semen armeniacae amarae
苦不堪言 (of a person) suffer untold misery and hardship;(of sth) be indescribably painful (or miserable);The misery or hardship is beyond words.
苦尽甘来 The bitterness ends and the sweetness begins.
苦口婆心 (admonish) earnestly and maternally
苦苦哀求 entreat piteously;implore urgently
苦苦相逼 run hard;press hard
苦难深重 be in deep distress;be in the depth of misery
苦思冥想 think long and hard;cudgel one's brains (to evolve an idea);rack one's brains (to evolve an idea)
苦心孤诣 make painstaking efforts;work hard and get good results
苦心经营 take great pains to build up (an enterprise,etc.)
苦中作乐 seek joy amidst sorrow;try to enjoy oneself despite one's suffering
苦海无边,回头是岸 The sea of bitterness has no bounds,repent and the shore is at hand.

kù (ㄎㄨˋ)

库 [kù]
Ⅰ 名 ① warehouse;storehouse;storage;bank ②base;library Ⅱ 量 (short for 库仑) coulomb
库藏 have in storage
库存 stock;reserve
库房 storehouse;storeroom
库仑 coulomb
库区 the area covered by a reservoir;reser-

voir；dam area
库容 storage capacity（of a reservoir，ware-house，etc.）
库蚊 culex
库存管理 inventory control
库存商品 merchandise inventory
库存物资 stock in storage；goods kept in stock
库存现金 cash holdings；cash on hand；vault cash
库仑定律 Coulomb's law
库存管理系统 inventory control system

绔 ［kù］

◇**纨绔** silk clothes—a rich family

裤 ［kù］ 图 trousers；pants

裤衩 underpants；undershorts
裤裆 crotch（of trousers）
裤兜 trouser pocket
裤缝 seams of a trouser leg
裤脚 ①bottom of a trouser leg ②trouser legs
裤料 panting；trousering
裤筒 trouser legs
裤头 underpants；undershorts
裤腿 trouser legs
裤袜 panty hose
裤线 creases（of trousers）
裤腰 waist of trousers
裤子 trousers；pants
裤腰带 waist belt；band；girdle

酷 ［kù］ I 形 ①cruel；oppressive ②cool II 副 very；extremely

酷爱 ardently love
酷毙 very（or extremely）cool；the coolest；the best
酷寒 bitter cold
酷烈 ①cruel；fierce ②（of fragrance）very strong
酷评 trenchant comments
酷热 （of weather）extremely hot
酷暑 the intense heat of summer；high summer
酷似 be the very image of；be exactly like
酷刑 cruel（or savage）torture

kuā （ㄎㄨㄚ）

夸 ［kuā］ 动 ①exaggerate；overstate；boast；brag ②praise；compliment

夸大 exaggerate；overstate；magnify
夸奖 praise；commend
夸克 quark
夸口 boast；brag；talk big
夸脱 quart（one fourth of a gallon）
夸耀 brag about；show off；flaunt
夸赞 speak highly of；commend；praise
夸张 ①exaggerate；overstate ②hyperbole
夸大其词 make an overstatement；exaggerate
夸夸其谈 indulge in exaggeration；indulge in verbiage
夸夸其谈 indulge in exaggeration；indulge in verbiage
夸下海口 have boasted about what one can do；have talked big

婩 ［kuā］ 形 pretty；beautiful

婩容修态 beautiful look and graceful manner

kuǎ （ㄎㄨㄚˇ）

侉 ［kuǎ］ 形 ①（speak）with an accent（esp. a provincial one）②big and clumsy；unwieldy

垮 ［kuǎ］ 动 collapse；fall in；break down

垮塌 collapse
垮台 fall from power；collapse
垮掉的一代 beat generation

kuà （ㄎㄨ）

挎 ［kuà］ 动 ①carry on the arm ②carry over one's shoulder（or round one's neck，at one's side）

挎包 satchel
挎兜 satchel

胯 ［kuà］ 图 hip

胯骨 hipbone；innominate bone
胯部动作 hip movement
胯下之辱 crawl between another's legs—drain the cup of humiliation

跨 ［kuà］ 动 ①step；stride ②sit（or stand）astride；bestride；straddle ③cut across；go beyond ④attach to the side of sth

跨度 span
跨间 small side room
跨越 stride across；leap over；cut across；span
跨部门 trans-departmental
跨地区 trans-regional；inter-regional
跨行业 trans-sectoral
跨年度 go beyond the year
跨世纪 extending into the next century
跨线桥 flyover；overpass
跨学科 interdiscipline
跨院儿 （of a traditional Chinese compound house）house by the side of the main one；side house；side compound
跨国公司 transnational corporation；multinational corporation
跨国银行 multinational bank
跨鹤西去 （euphemistical of a deceased woman）go west astride a crane
跨栏赛跑 hurdle race；the hurdles

K

跨部门合作 interdepartmental cooperation
跨行业公司 conglomerate
跨领域问题 cross-cutting issues
跨年度工程 project to be carried on in the next year
跨年度预算 multi-year budgeting
跨世纪工程 project which will not be completed until the next century; a trans-century project
跨世纪人才 talent spanning this century and next; trans-century talent
跨文化交流 cross cultural communications; intercultural communications; trans-cultural communications
跨越式发展 great-leap-forward development; development by leaps and bounds
跨部门联合企业 interdepartmental complex
跨地区联合经营 joint undertakings embracing processing factories in one region and raw material producers in another
跨地区的经济区域 cross-regional economic zone
跨国犯罪和恐怖主义 international organized crime and terrorism
跨行业、跨地区经营 engage in inter-trade and trans-regional operations

kuài （ㄎㄨㄞ）

会 ［kuài］
形 grand total; total ➡ huì
会计 ①accounting ②bookkeeper; accountant
会计师 certified accountant; chief accountant; treasurer
会计年度 fiscal (or financial) year
会计制度 accounting system
会计事务所 accounting firm

块 ［kuài］
Ⅰ 名 ①lump; piece ②block Ⅱ 量 ①(of sth cubical or flat in shape); 一块菜地 a vegetable plot ②(a unit of money, such as dollar and yuan); 两块钱 two yuan
块根 root tuber
块规 slip gauge; gauge block
块茎 stem tuber
块垒 indignation; gloom; depression
块码 block code
块煤 lump coal
块头 (physical) build
块状 bulk; massive
块儿八毛 one yuan or slightly less

快 ［kuài］
Ⅰ 形 ① quick; fast; rapid; swift ② quick-witted; clever; nimble ③ sharp; keen ④ straightforward; forthright; plainspoken ⑤ pleased; happy; satisfied; gratified Ⅱ 副 ① soon; before long ② hurry (up); make haste Ⅲ 名 sheriff; constable (in a yamen)

快班 fast stream; accelerated class
快板 allegro
快报 wall bulletin; bulletin
快步 ①walk at a quick pace ②half step; trot
快餐 quick meal; fast food; snack
快车 express train (or bus)
快当 quick; prompt
快递 express delivery
快干 quick-drying
快感 pleasant sensation; delight
快攻 quick attack (in ball games)
快活 happy; merry; cheerful
快件 express delivery luggage (or goods, mail)
快捷 (of speed) quick; fast; nimble; agile
快乐 happy; joyful; cheerful
快慢 speed
快门 (camera) shutter
快人 straight person
快事 a happening that gives great satisfaction or pleasure; delight
快手 quick worker; deft hand
快书 quick-patter (rhythmic storytelling accompanied by bamboo or copper clappers)
快速 fast; quick; high-speed
快艇 speedboat; motor boat; mosquito boat
快慰 feel pleased with and derive comfort from sth; be pleased
快信 express letter
快婿 son-in-law after one's heart
快讯 newsflash; flash
快要 soon; before long
快意 pleased; satisfied; comfortable
快邮 express mail; special delivery
快照 snapshot
快针 swift insertion
快嘴 ①one who readily voices his thoughts; one who is quick to articulate his ideas; a straight person ② one who has a loose tongue
快板儿 kuaibanr, rhythmic comic talk or monologue to the accompaniment of bamboo clappers; clapper talk
快步舞 quickstep
快餐部 quick-lunch (or snack, fast-food) counter
快车道 fast traffic lane (on a street); highway
快动作 snap action
快镜头 snapshot
快慢针 regulator (in a clock or watch)
快中子 fast (or high-speed) neutron
快餐文化 fast food culture
快递业务 express delivery
快递邮件 express mail service
快捷方式 shortcut
快马加鞭 spur on the flying horse—at top speed; posthaste; whip and spur

K

快拍相机 candid camera
快人快语 straight talk from an honest man; straightforward talk from a straightforward person
快如闪电 quick as a flash of lightning
快如脱兔 swift as a fleeing hare
快速倒带 fast rewind
快速进带 fast forward
快速冷冻 flash freezing; snap freezing
快硬水泥 quick-hardening cement
快刀斩乱麻 cut a tangled skein of jute with a sharp knife; cut the Gordian knot
快速存储器 rapid memory
快照摄影机 pistolgraph
快速部署部队 rapid deployment forces
快速反应部队 rapid reaction force; rapid response force

侩 [kuài]
〈名〉go-between; middleman; broker

脍 [kuài]
Ⅰ〈名〉finely sliced meat (*or* fish) Ⅱ〈动〉cut into thin slices; slice
脍炙人口 (of a piece of good writing, etc.) win universal praise; enjoy great popularity

筷 [kuài]
〈名〉chopsticks
筷子 chopsticks

kuān（ㄎㄨㄢ）

宽 [kuān]
Ⅰ〈形〉①wide; broad ②generous; lenient ③comfortably off; well-off Ⅱ〈名〉width; breadth Ⅲ〈动〉①relax; relieve ②extend
宽敞 spacious; roomy; commodious
宽畅 free from worry; happy
宽绰 ① spacious; commodious ② relaxed; relieved ③comfortably off; well-off
宽大 ① spacious; roomy ② lenient; magnanimous ③show leniency (towards an offender)
宽带 broadband
宽贷 pardon; forgive
宽待 treat with leniency; be lenient in dealing with
宽度 width; breadth
宽泛 (of meaning) covering a wide range; broad
宽幅 (of cloth, etc.) wide; broad
宽广 broad; extensive; vast
宽轨 broad gauge
宽厚 ①thick and broad ②tolerant and generous; honest and kind
宽解 ease sb's anxiety; ease sb of his trouble
宽旷 extensive; vast
宽阔 broad; wide
宽饶 forgive; show mercy; give quarter
宽容 tolerant; lenient

宽舒 ① happy; entirely free from worry ② spacious and smooth
宽恕 forgive
宽松 ①(of clothes) loose and comfortable ② not crowded ③feel relieved; be free from worry ④comfortably off; ample; easy
宽慰 comfort; console
宽限 extend a time limit
宽心 feel relieved
宽衣 take off your coat
宽裕 well-to-do; comfortably off; ample
宽窄 width; breadth; size
宽带网 wideband network
宽面纸 broadsheet
宽限期 grace period
宽打窄用 budget liberally and spend sparingly
宽大为怀 be magnanimous (with an offender); be lenient
宽轨铁路 broad-gauge railway
宽宏大量 large-minded; magnanimous
宽体客机 wide-bodied airliner
宽心丸儿 anxiety-relief pills—words that set sb's mind at ease; reassuring words
宽衣解带 undress oneself; loosen one's tie (and fall asleep)
宽波段天线 broadband antenna
宽银幕电影 wide-screen film
宽带综合业务数字网 broadband integrated services digital network (BISDN)

髋 [kuān]
〈名〉hip
髋骨 hipbone; innominate bone

kuǎn（ㄎㄨㄢ）

款 [kuǎn]
Ⅰ〈形〉①sincere ②leisurely; slow Ⅱ〈动〉① receive with hospitality; entertain ②knock; tap Ⅲ〈名〉①section (of an article in a legal document, etc.); paragraph ②sum of money for a specific purpose; fund ③rich person; money bags ④name of author or recipient ⑤style; pattern (of fashion, etc.) Ⅳ〈量〉kind; type; style
款步 walk with deliberate steps
款待 treat cordially; entertain
款额 amount of money; sum of money
款哥 rich brother
款姐 rich sister
款客 entertain a guest
款留 cordially urge (a guest) to stay
款曲 heartfelt feelings
款式 pattern; style; design
款项 ①a sum of money; fund ②sections and items (in a legal document, etc.)
款型 style; fashion; model; design
款爷 moneybag; nouveau riche
款子 a sum of money

款酌慢饮 pour the wine in small cups and sip slowly

kuāng (ㄎㄨㄤ)

匡 [kuāng]
劢 ①rectify;correct ②assist;save ③calculate roughly;estimate ④(*usu. used in the early vernacular*) expect
匡复 save the state
匡救 deliver sb (from evil);rescue;save
匡谬 correct mistakes
匡算 roughly calculate;estimate
匡正 rectify;correct
匡助 help;assist

诓 [kuāng]
劢 deceive;cheat;hoax
诓骗 deceive;hoax;dupe

哐 [kuāng]
𡥧 crash;bang：锣哐地响了一声。 Bang, went the gong.
哐啷 crash

筐 [kuāng]
名 basket
筐子 small basket

kuáng (ㄎㄨㄤˊ)

狂 [kuáng]
形 ①mad;crazy;insane ②violent;fierce ③unrestrained;wild ④arrogant;overbearing;presumptuous
狂傲 wildly arrogant;presumptuous
狂暴 violent;wild
狂奔 run wildly;run like mad
狂飙 hurricane
狂草 wild scribble;excessively free cursive style
狂潮 turbulent tidewater
狂放 unruly;unrestrained
狂吠 bark furiously;howl
狂风 ①whole gale ②fierce wind
狂欢 revelry;carnival
狂澜 raging waves
狂怒 furious;mad with rage
狂热 fanaticism
狂人 ①madman;maniac ②an extremely arrogant person
狂妄 wildly arrogant;presumptuous
狂喜 wild with joy
狂想 ①fancy;fantasy ②vain hope;wishful thinking;illusion
狂笑 laugh wildly;laugh boisterously
狂言 ravings;wild language
狂野 violent and rough;wild and boorish
狂躁 rash and impatient;indiscreet and hot-headed;restless with anxiety
狂犬病 hydrophobia;rabies
狂想曲 rhapsody;fantasia

狂风暴雨 violent storms
狂轰滥炸 wanton and indiscriminate bombing
狂人呓语 ravings of a madman
狂涛巨澜 the angry waves;the raging tide
狂妄自大 arrogant and conceited

诳 [kuáng]
Ⅰ 劢 deceive;dupe;fool;hoodwink Ⅱ 名 lie;falsehood
诳骗 deceive;hoax;dupe
诳语 lies;falsehood

kuàng (ㄎㄨㄤˋ)

圹 [kuàng]
名 ①coffin pit;open grave ②open country;champaign

旷 [kuàng]
Ⅰ 形 ①open and empty;vast;spacious ②free from worries and petty ideas;relaxed;expansive ③loose-fitting;loose Ⅱ 劢 neglect (duty,work,etc.);waste (time,etc.)
旷达 broad-minded;big-hearted
旷费 waste
旷夫 unmarried man of marriageable age
旷工 stay away from (*or* miss) work without leave (*or* good reason)
旷古 from time immemorial
旷课 be absent from school without leave;cut school
旷世 unequalled in one's time;unrivalled;unique
旷野 wilderness
旷职 be absent from duty without leave (*or* good reason)
旷古未闻 unheard-of;unprecedented
旷离职守 desert one's post
旷日持久 long-drawn-out;protracted;prolonged
旷世无双 stand without peer in one's generation

况 [kuàng]
Ⅰ 名 condition;situation Ⅱ 劢 compare Ⅲ 连 ①moreover;besides ②much less;let alone
况且 moreover;besides;in addition

矿 [kuàng]
名 ①mineral (*or* ore) deposit ②ore ③mine
矿藏 mineral resources
矿层 ore bed;ore horizon;seam
矿产 mineral products;minerals
矿车 mine car;tub;tram
矿尘 mine dust
矿床 mineral (*or* ore) deposit;deposit
矿灯 miner's lamp
矿工 miner
矿井 mine shaft or pit
矿坑 (mining) pit

矿脉 mineral ore;mineral vein;lode
矿棉 mineral wool
矿苗 outcropping;outcrop;crop
矿难 mine disaster
矿泥 sludge;slime;slurry
矿区 mining area
矿泉 mineral spring
矿砂 ore in sand form
矿山 mine (with its accompanying shafts, buildings,etc.)
矿石 ore
矿田 ore field
矿物 mineral
矿样 sample ore
矿业 mining industry
矿渣 slag
矿柱 (ore) pillar
矿物学 mineralogy
矿物油 mineral oil
矿物质 mineral substance
矿质肥料 mineral fertilizer

框 [kuàng] I 名 ① frame; case ② (formerly pronounced kuāng) set pattern; convention; restriction II 动 ① draw a frame around ② restrict;restrain;confine
框定 pinpoint;delimit;isolate
框架 frame;framework
框框 ① frame; circle ② restriction; convention;set pattern
框子 frame;rim
框架公约 framework convention; framework treaty;framework agreement

眶 [kuàng] 名 socket of the eye

kuī (ㄎㄨㄟ)

亏 [kuī] I 动 ① lose (money, etc.); have a deficit ② deficient; short ③ treat unfairly II 副 ① fortunately;luckily;thanks to ② (used to indicate irony):亏你还有脸来见我! And you have the cheek to come and see me!
亏本 lose money in business;lose one's capital
亏仓 broken stowage
亏产 fail to fulfil a production target (or quota)
亏秤 ①give short measure ②lose weight
亏待 treat unfairly;treat shabbily
亏得 ① fortunately; luckily; thanks to ② (used to show sarcasm)
亏乏 short (of supplies);deficient
亏负 let sb suffer;let sb down
亏耗 loss by a natural process
亏空 ①lose money in business;be in debt ② debt;deficit
亏欠 have a deficit;be in arrears

亏蚀 ①eclipse of the sun (or the moon) ② lose money in business;lose one's capital ③ loss;wear and tear
亏损 ①loss;deficit ②general debility
亏心 have a guilty conscience
亏损企业 enterprises running in the red;enterprises running under deficit;debt-ridden enterprises; loss-making enterprises; money-losing enterprises; loss-incurring enterprises;unprofitable enterprises

岿 [kuī]
岿然 towering;lofty
岿然不动 steadfastly stand one's ground

盔 [kuī] 名 ①basin-like pottery container ②helmet ③any helmet-shaped hat
盔甲 suit of armour

窥 [kuī] 动 ①peep ②pry;spy
窥测 spy out
窥察 spy upon;pry about
窥见 get (or catch) a glimpse of;detect
窥器 speculum
窥视 peep at;spy on
窥伺 lie in wait for;be on watch for
窥探 spy upon;pry about
窥听 eavesdrop
窥望 peep at;spy on
窥视孔 peep hole
窥测方向 see how the land lies;see which way the wind blows

kuí (ㄎㄨㄟ)

奎 [kuí] 名 one of the Chinese zodiacal constellations
奎宁 quinine

逵 [kuí] 名 thoroughfare;road

葵 [kuí] 名 common name for certain herbaceous plants with big flowers
葵花 sunflower
葵扇 palm-leaf fan
葵花子 sunflower seeds

魁 [kuí] I 名 chief;head II 形 tall and burly;of stalwart build
魁首 a person who is head and shoulders above others;the brightest and best
魁伟 big and tall;stalwart
魁梧 big and tall;stalwart

睽 [kuí] 动 ①(of people) separate;part ②violate; go against;run contrary to
睽睽 stare;gaze

K

kuǐ (ㄎㄨㄟˇ)

傀 [kuǐ] ⇒ guī
傀儡 puppet
傀儡政权 puppet regime

跬 [kuǐ] 〔名〕 half a step

kuì (ㄎㄨㄟˋ)

匮 [kuì] 〔形〕 deficient; lacking
匮乏 short (of supplies); deficient

喟 [kuì] 〔动〕 heave a sigh; sigh

馈 [kuì] 〔动〕 make a present of; present (a gift)
馈电 feed
馈赠 present (a gift); make a present of sth
馈以珠宝 make a present of jewels

溃 [kuì] 〔动〕 ①(of floodwater, etc.) burst (a dyke or dam); break ②break through (an encirclement, etc.) ③be routed; fall to pieces ④fester; ulcerate
溃败 be defeated; be routed
溃决 (of flood waters) burst (a dyke, dam, etc.)
溃军 routed army
溃口 crevasse; breach; break
溃烂 fester; ulcerate
溃灭 (of a regime, etc.) crumble and fall
溃散 (of troops) be defeated and dispersed
溃逃 escape in disorder; fly pell-mell; flee helter-skelter
溃退 beat a precipitate retreat
溃疡 ulcer
溃不成军 (of troops) be utterly routed; break and scatter

愦 [kuì] 〔形〕 muddle-headed; befuddled; senile
愦乱 dazed and confused; befuddled

愧 [kuì] 〔形〕 ashamed; abashed; conscience-stricken
愧恨 ashamed and remorseful; remorseful
愧疚 feel remorseful and uneasy; be conscience-stricken
愧色 a look (or an expression) of shame
愧不敢当 I do not deserve such an honour (or gift); I am flattered.
愧恨交集 be ashamed and angry with oneself; overcome with shame and remorse

聩 [kuì] 〔形〕 deaf; hard of hearing

蒉 [kuì] 〔名〕 basket for carrying earth

kūn (ㄎㄨㄣ)

坤 [kūn] I 〔名〕 symbol for earth in the Eight Trigrams II 〔形〕 female; feminine
坤表 woman's watch
坤车 lady's (or woman's) bicycle
坤鞋 woman's shoes
坤宅 the bride's family

昆 [kūn] 〔名〕 ①elder brother ②offspring; progeny ③(short for 昆曲) Kunqu opera
昆布 kelp
昆虫 insect
昆仲 elder and younger brothers; brothers
昆虫学 entomology; insectology

kǔn (ㄎㄨㄣˇ)

捆 [kǔn] I 〔动〕 tie; bind; bundle up II 〔名〕 bundle; bunch III 〔量〕 (of sth bundled up)
捆绑 tie up (usu. a person); truss up; bind
捆缚 tie up; bind; bound
捆扎 tie up; bundle up
捆绑式 cluster
捆绑销售 bundling
捆绑式火箭 strap-on rocket

壸 [kǔn] 〔名〕 alley (or path) in a palace

kùn (ㄎㄨㄣˋ)

困 [kùn] I 〔动〕 ①be stranded; be stricken; be trapped ②surround; hold in check ③sleep II 〔名〕 difficulty; hardship III 〔形〕 ① tired; exhausted ② sleepy; drowsy
困顿 ①tired out; exhausted ②be in financial straits
困乏 ①tired; fatigued ②financially difficult; straitened economically
困惑 perplexed; puzzled
困境 difficult position; predicament; straits
困窘 ①in straitened circumstances; in a difficult position; embarrassed ② poverty-stricken; destitute
困倦 sleepy
困苦 (live) in privation
困难 ① difficulty ② financial difficulties; straitened circumstances
困扰 perplex; puzzle
困守 defend against a siege; stand a siege
困难户 ①low-income household; hard-up families ②bad looking; ugly; hard for sb to love
困苦劳顿 in great distress and weariness
困难补助 subsidy to those in financial difficulties

困难重重 beset with difficulties; in a fix; in deep water
困难行业 difficulty-ridden industries
困难职工 needy employees; the needy
困兽犹斗 Cornered beasts will still fight; beasts at bay will fight back.

kuò (ㄎㄨㄛˋ)

扩 [kuò]
〔动〕 extend; expand; enlarge; magnify
扩兵 increase the number of one's troops; recruit more soldiers
扩版 expansion of page volume (of a newspaper, etc.)
扩充 expand; strengthen; augment
扩大 enlarge; expand; extend
扩地 expand one's land; extend the territory
扩股 enlarge the number of shares
扩建 extend (a factory, mine, etc.)
扩军 engage in arms expansion
扩孔 reaming
扩权 expand enterprise autonomy
扩容 expand capacity; enlarge
扩散 spread; diffuse
扩印 make enlargements from a 135 (esp. colour) film
扩展 expand; spread; extend; develop
扩张 ①expand; enlarge; extend; spread ②dilate
扩招 to increase enrollment; expand enrolment
扩大化 magnify (or extend) wrongly (or unrealistically, unnecessarily)
扩胸器 chest expander; chest developer
扩音器 ①megaphone ②audio amplifier
扩展槽 expansion slot
扩张器 dilator
扩大会议 enlarged meeting (or session, conference)
扩大内需 expand domestic market; expand domestic demand; expand domestic need
扩建工程 extension (project)

扩军备战 arms expansion and war preparations
扩张政策 expansionist policy
扩张主义 expansionism
扩大再生产 reproduction on an extended scale; extended (or expanded) reproduction
扩大耕地面积 bring more land under cultivation
扩大国内需求 expand domestic demand
扩大后备储量 increase reserves
扩大企业自主权 expand the power of enterprises in management; give enterprises greater power to manage their own business affairs

括 [kuò]
〔动〕 ①tie (up); tighten up; contract (muscles, etc.) ②include; comprise ③bracket
括号 brackets (〔〕, ( ), 〈 〉)
括弧 parentheses
括注 an explanatory note in brackets
括约肌 sphincter

蛞 [kuò]
蛞蝓 slug

筈 [kuò]
〔名〕 arrow-tail

阔 [kuò]
〔形〕 ①wide; broad; vast ②wealthy; rich
阔别 long separated; long parted
阔步 take big strides
阔绰 ostentatious; liberal with money
阔斧 broad axe
阔佬 a rich (old) man
阔气 luxurious; extravagant; lavish
阔少 a rich man's son
阔叶树 broadleaf tree

廓 [kuò]
Ⅰ 〔形〕 wide; extensive; vast Ⅱ 〔动〕 expand; extend Ⅲ 〔名〕 outer features; outline
廓张 expand; enlarge; extend; spread

鞟 [kuò]
〔名〕 animal skin or hide without hair

LI

lā（ㄌㄚ）

垃 [lā]

垃圾 rubbish；garbage；refuse
垃圾场 landfill
垃圾车 dust cart
垃圾袋 litterbag；garbage bag
垃圾堆 rubbish heap；refuse dump；garbage heap
垃圾股 junk share
垃圾坑 dump pit
垃圾桶 ash can；garbage can
垃圾箱 dustbin；ash can；garbage can；trash can
垃圾处理 garbage disposal；refuse disposal
垃圾发电 garbage power
垃圾分类 refuse classification
垃圾时间 rubbish time
垃圾邮件 junk mail
垃圾债券 junk bond
垃圾袋装化 enclose garbage with plastic garbage bags
垃圾焚化炉 garbage furnace；refuse burner；incinerator；destructor
垃圾倾倒场 dumping ground
垃圾综合处理 integrated garbage treatment

拉 [lā]
I 〔动〕①pull；draw；drag；tug ②carry；convey by vehicles；transport by vehicle；haul ③move (troops to a place) ④play (certain musical instruments) ⑤drag out；draw out；space out ⑥bring up ⑦give (*or* lend) a hand；help；assist ⑧drag in；implicate；involve in ⑨draw in；drag in；win over ⑩canvass；solicit ⑪organize；set up；put together ⑫chat；engage in chitchat ⑬press；pressgang ⑭lift ⑮have a bowel movement；empty the bowels ⑯destroy；break；smash Ⅱ〔名〕 short for Latin America or Latin ➡lá；là
拉拔 drawing
拉扯 ①drag；pull ②take great pains to bring up (a child) ③help；support；promote ④gang up with；rope in ⑤implicate；drag in
拉床 broaching machine
拉刀 broach
拉倒 forget about it；leave it at that；never mind；let it go at that；drop it
拉动 promote
拉夫 pressgang；press people into service
拉杆 pull rod；drag link；draw bar；tension link
拉钩 pull each other's little fingers—making a promise or swearing to do sth
拉花 garland
拉环 ring-pull
拉簧 extension spring
拉架 try to stop people from fighting each other
拉脚 transport persons (*or* goods) by a cart at a charge
拉锯 ①work a two-handed saw ②be locked in a seesaw struggle
拉开 ①pull open；draw back ②increase the distance between；space out
拉客 ①(of inns，small restaurants，etc.) solicit guests (*or* diners) ②(of taxi drivers，pedicab riders，etc.) take on passengers ③(of prostitutes) solicit；solicit (for) customers
拉力 pulling force
拉链 zip fastener；zipper
拉拢 draw sb over to one's side；win over；rope in
拉门 sliding door
拉面 ①hand-pulled noodles ②make noodles by drawing out the dough by hand
拉模 drawing die
拉平 bring to the same level；even up
拉纤 ①tow (a boat) ②act as go-between
拉揪 ①draw in (*or* up) the net；haul in the net ②close in on (besieged forces)
拉屎 have a bowel movement；shit；empty the bowels
拉手 [lāshǒu] shake hands

拉手 [lāshou] handle（of a door, window, drawer, etc.）

拉条 brace; stay

拉稀 have loose bowels; have diarrhoea

拉线 act as go-between

拉削 broaching

拉秧 uproot plants after their edible portions have been harvested

拉杂 rambling; jumbled; ill-organized

拉账 be in debt; run into debt

拉出去 pull out; drag out

拉丁文 Latin（language）

拉肚子 suffer from diarrhoea; have loose bowels

拉队伍 raise a force（or contingent）; form a band

拉幅机 stenter; tenter

拉关系 cotton up to sb; establish underhand connections（for the sake of personal gain）; carry favour with; build connections for

拉广告 solicit advertisements（from companies, etc.）

拉后腿 hold sb back; be a drag on sb; be a hindrance to sb

拉火绳 lanyard

拉饥荒 be in debt; run into debt; owe a debt

拉家常 talk about everyday matters; engage in small talk; chitchat

拉交情 try to form ties with; cotton up to

拉锯战 seesaw battle

拉拉队 cheering squad; rooters

拉力器 chest-developer; chest-expander

拉力赛 rally

拉痢疾 suffer from dysentery

拉买卖 canvass business orders; drum up trade

拉皮条 act as a procurer（or pimp）

拉山头 form a faction

拉锁儿 zip fastener; zipper

拉团伙 form a gang

拉下脸 ①look displeased; pull a long face; put on a stern expression ②not spare sb's sensibilities

拉下水 pull sb into the water—get sb involved in one's scheme; drag sb into the mire; make an accomplice of sb; corrupt sb

拉选票 canvass for votes; canvass

拉赞助 canvass for contributions（or sponsors）; seek sponsorship

拉主顾 solicit customers（or clients）

拉壮丁 forcibly conscript; pressgang into military service

拉帮结伙 recruit people to form a faction; gang up; band together

拉不下脸 cannot do sth for fear of hurting another person's feeling

拉丁美洲 Latin America

拉丁民族 Latin peoples

拉丁字母 the Latin alphabet; the Roman alphabet

拉杆天线 telescopic antenna

拉家带口 be burdened with a family

拉拉扯扯 ① pull（or drag）sb about ② exchange flattery and favours; scratch each other's backs

拉拢腐蚀 win someone over and corrupt him; win people over to one's side and corrupt them

拉人力车 pull a rickshaw

拉线搭桥 pull strings and make contacts; go between; serve as a link

拉马克学说 Lamarckism

拉尼娜现象 La-Niña phenomenon

拉大旗作虎皮 use a great banner（of revolution, etc.）as a tiger-skin—deck oneself out and intimidate people

拉动经济增长 fuel economic growth

拉一派打一派 try to win over one faction while attacking another; draw in one faction and hit out at another

邋 [lā]

邋遢 slovenly; sloppy

lá（ㄌㄚˊ）

拉 [lá]
〔动〕slash; slit; cut; gash ➡lā; là

砬 [lá]
〔名〕big rock

lǎ（ㄌㄚˇ）

喇 [lǎ]

喇叭 ① laba, a woodwind instrument ② trumpet; horn ③loudspeaker

喇嘛 lama

喇叭花 （white-edged）morning glory

喇叭裤 flared trousers; bell-bottoms

喇嘛教 Lamaism

喇嘛庙 lamasery

喇叭式扬声器 horn

là（ㄌㄚˋ）

拉 [là]
➡lā; lá

拉拉蛄 mole cricket

剌 [là]
〔形〕perverse; disagreeable

落 [là]
〔动〕① leave out; be missing; omit ② leave behind; forget to bring ③ lag behind; fall behind ➡lào; luō; luò

腊 [là]
Ⅰ〔名〕ancient practice of offering sacrifices to the gods in the twelfth month of the lunar

year；(hence the) twelfth lunar month Ⅱ 形
(of fish，meat，etc.) cured in winter，esp. in
the twelfth lunar month

腊肠 sausage
腊梅 wintersweet
腊肉 cured meat；bacon
腊味 cured meat
腊鱼 cured fish
腊月 the twelfth month of the lunar year；the
　twelfth moon
腊八粥 porridge

蜡 [là]
名 ①wax ②candle
蜡版 mimeograph stencil (already cut)
蜡笔 wax crayon
蜡布 cerecloth；wax cloth
蜡虫 wax insect
蜡果 wax fruit
蜡花 snuff
蜡画 encaustic painting
蜡黄 wax yellow；waxen；sallow
蜡染 wax printing；batik
蜡人 wax figure；waxwork
蜡塑 wax sculpture
蜡台 candlestick
蜡丸 a wax-coated pill
蜡像 wax figure；waxwork
蜡印 wax seal
蜡纸 ①wax paper ②stencil paper；stencil
蜡烛 (wax) candle
蜡版术 cerography
蜡笔画 crayon drawing
蜡光纸 glazed paper
蜡头儿 stump of a candle
蜡像馆 waxworks museum
蜡嘴雀 hawfinch

痢 [là]
痢痢 favus of the scalp
痢痢头 ①affected with favus on the head ②
　person affected with favus on the head

辣 [là]
Ⅰ 形 ① peppery；hot；pungent ② vicious；
ruthless Ⅱ 动 (of smell or taste) burn；bite；
sting
辣根 horse radish
辣酱 thick chilli sauce
辣椒 hot pepper；chilli
辣手 ①ruthless method；vicious device ②vi-
　cious；ruthless
辣味 peppery taste；piquancy；pungency
辣子 hot pepper；cayenne pepper；chilli
辣酱油 pungent sauce (similar to Worcester-
　shire sauce)
辣椒粉 chilli powder
辣椒油 chilli oil
辣妹子 hot girl；a girl who is bold, hot and

quick-tempered with a sharp tongue
辣婆娘 impetuous and overbearing woman；
　termagant
辣丝丝 a little hot

la (·ㄌㄚ)

啦 [la]
助 (combination of 了 (le) and 啊 (a)
expressing exclamation， interrogation，
etc.)：上课啦! Hey! It's time for class.

lái (ㄌㄞ)

来 [lái]
Ⅰ 动 ①come；arrive ②crop up；take place；
come up ③(used as a substitute for a more
specific verb)：来一盘棋 have a game of
chess ④(used with 得 or 不 to indicate
possibility or capability，or the lack of it)：
合得来 get along well；hit it off ⑤(used before another verb to indicate an intended
or suggested action)：我来说几句。Let me
say a few words. ⑥(used after another
verb or verbal phrase to indicate what one
has come for)：他们给你贺喜来了。They've
come to offer you their congratulations. ⑦
(used between two verbs or verbal phrases
to indicate the purpose of the former)：你用
什么办法来解决这个问题? How are you go-
ing to solve the problem? Ⅱ 形 future；
coming；next：来春 coming spring；next spring
Ⅲ 助 ①(used after a verb or verbal expression to indicate motion towards the speaker)：出来 come out ②(used after a verb to
indicate the result or estimation)：此事说
来话长。It's a long story. ③(used to indicate what happened in the past)：这话你什
么时候说来? When did you say it? ④(used
after a time phrase or its equivalent to indicate a duration that lasts from the past
up to the present)：一年来 for the past year
⑤(used after round numbers like 十，百，
千 or after numerals plus measures to indicate approximation)：七十来岁 about (or
around) seventy/三米来深 about three metres
deep ⑥(used after numerals 一，二，三，to
enumerate reasons or points of argument)：退休后他开始练习书法，一来培养业
余爱好，二来有益于健康。He began to prac-
tise calligraphy after retirement. For one
thing，it was a good hobby to develop；for an-
other，it helped to keep fit. ⑦(used as fill-
er-word in a line of balladry，proverb or
vendor's pitch for rhythm and euphony)：
磨剪子来抢菜刀! (shouted by a tradesman
to solicit business) Scissors and knives sharp-
ened!

来宾 guest;visitor
来到 arrive;come
来电 ① incoming telegram (*or* telephone call);your telegram (*or* telephone call);your message ②send a telegram (*or* make a telephone call) here ③of both sexes fall in love with sb
来犯 come to attack us;invade our territory
来访 come to visit;come to call
来稿 incoming manuscript;your manuscript
来函 incoming letter;your letter
来回 ①make a round trip;make a return journey;go to a place and come back ②a round trip ③back and forth;to and fro
来件 communication or parcel received
来劲 ①full of enthusiasm;in high spirits ②exhilarating;exciting;thrilling ③jest with;annoy;offend
来客 guest;visitor
来历 origin;source;antecedents;background;past history
来临 arrive;come;approach
来路 ①incoming road;approach ②origin;antecedents
来年 the coming **year**;next year
来人 bearer;messenger
来日 the days to come;the future
来生 next life;afterlife
来世 next life;afterlife
来势 the force with which sth breaks out;oncoming force
来书 incoming letter
来头 ①connections;backing ②the motive behind (sb's words,etc.);cause
来往 [láiwǎng] come and go
来往 [láiwang] ① dealings;contact;intercourse ②have contact (*or* dealings)
来文 document received
来信 ①send a letter here ②incoming letter;your letter
来意 one's purpose in coming
来由 reason;cause
来源 ①source;origin ②(followed by 于) originate;stem from
来着 *used at the end of affirmative sentences or special questions, indicating a past action or state*
来宾席 seats reserved for guests
来不得 won't do;be impermissible
来不及 there's not enough time (to do sth);it's too late (to do sth)
来得及 there's still time;be able to do sth in time;be able to make it
来复枪 rifle
来复线 rifling
来回票 round-trip ticket;return ticket
来事儿 know how to deal with people

来电显示 calling identity delivery(CID)
来函照登 unabridged readers' letter
来回飞行 round-trip flight
来回来去 back and forth;over and over again
来件装配 assemble parts supplied by clients
来来往往 come and go;go to and fro
来历不明 (of things) of unknown origin;(of persons) of dubious background;of questionable antecedents
来料加工 process materials supplied by customers;accept customers' materials for processing;customers' own materials made up (notice outside tailor's shop)
来龙去脉 origin and development;the entire process
来路不明 unidentified of questionable origin
来去自由 have the freedom of entry and exit;be free to come and go
来日方长 there will be ample (*or* plenty of) time;there will be time for that
来样加工 process according to buyer's samples
来者不拒 refuse nobody;refuse nobody's request or offer
来之不易 not easily come by;hard-earned
来踪去迹 traces of sb 's movements;traces of sb's whereabouts
来得容易去得快 easy come,easy go
来电显示电话机 caller ID telephone
来而不往非礼也 it is impolite not to reciprocate—one should return as good as one receives
来者不拒的风度 welcome-all style
来者不善,善者不来 ① He who has come is surely strong or he'd never have come along. ②He who has come,comes with ill intent,certainly not on virtue bent.
来料、来样、来件加工产品 processed products with supplied materials,samples or components

莱 [lái]
名 ①lamb's-quarters ②fields lying fallow in rotation;wasteland outside a town
莱菔 radish
莱菔子 radish seed

铼 [lái]
⇒lài
◇招铼 solicit (customers or business);canvass

铼 [lái]
名 rhenium (Re)
铼酸 rhenic acid
铼合金 rhenium alloy
铼同位素 rhenium isotope

lài (ㄌㄞˋ)

徕 [lài]
动 send one's best wishes (*or* bring gifts)

in recognition of services rendered ➡ lái

赉 [lài] 囫 grant；bestow；confer

睐 [lài] 囫 ①squint ②look at；glance

赖 [lài] Ⅰ 囫 ① depend；rely；hinge ② drag out one's stay（beyond what is necessary or welcome）；hang on where one does not belong ③ deny one's error（*or* responsibility）；renege；shirk；go back on one's word ④put the blame on（sb else）；shift the blame onto（sb else）⑤ blame Ⅱ 囵 ①impudent；cheeky；brazen；rascally；shameless ②no good；poor
赖床 be feeling too lazy to get out of bed
赖婚 repudiate a marriage contract
赖皮 rascally；shameless；unreasonable
赖学 play truant；cut class
赖债 repudiate a debt
赖账 ① repudiate a debt ② go back on one's word

濑 [lài] 囶 rapids；swift current

癞 [lài] 囶 ①leprosy ②favus of the scalp
癞瓜 bitter gourd
癞子 ①favus ②person affected with favus of the scalp
癞蛤蟆 toad
癞皮狗 ①mangy dog ②loathsome creature
癞蛤蟆想吃天鹅肉 a toad lusting after a swan's flesh—aspiring after sth one is not worthy of

籁 [lài] 囶 ①ancient musical pipe ②sound；noise

lán（ㄌㄢˊ）

兰 [lán] 囶 ①cymbidium；orchid ②fragrant thoroughwort ③lily magnolia
兰草 fragrant thoroughwort
兰花 cymbidium；orchid
兰室 boudoir
兰花指 orchid fingers

岚 [lán] 囶 mountain haze or mist

拦 [lán] 囫 ①block；bar；hold back ②direct right at
拦挡 block；obstruct
拦击 ①intercept and attack ②volley
拦劫 waylay and rob；mug
拦截 intercept
拦路 block the way
拦网 block
拦蓄 retain（water）；impound
拦腰 （hold）by the waist；（cut across）in the middle
拦阻 block；hold back；obstruct

拦道木 road fence；roadblock
拦河坝 a dam across a river；dam
拦河闸 regulating dam
拦河栅 kiddle
拦洪坝 a dam for holding back floodwater；a dam for flood control；flood-control dam
拦路虎 a road-blocking tiger—obstacle；hindrance
拦鱼栅 fish screen
拦街阻路 block（*or* obstruct）traffic（in the streets）
拦路抢劫 waylay

栏 [lán] 囶 ① fence；railing；balustrade；hurdle ② pen；shed；barn ③column（in a newspaper or magazine）④column（of a form）⑤board（for putting up notices or newspapers）
栏杆 railing；banisters；balustrade
栏目 the heading（*or* title）of a column（in a magazine，etc.）

婪 [lán]
◇ 贪婪 avaricious；greedy；rapacious

阑 [lán] Ⅰ 囶 fence；railing Ⅱ 囫 ①bar；block ②do without authorization Ⅲ 囵 （of time）late
阑出 go out（*or* leave）without permission
阑干 ①across；crisscross ②railing
阑入 ①place that is forbidden to one；trespass ②interpolate；mix；mingle
阑珊 coming to an end；waning
阑尾 appendix
阑尾炎 appendicitis
阑尾切除术 appendectomy

蓝 [lán] Ⅰ 囵 blue Ⅱ 囶 indigo
蓝本 ① writing upon which later work is based；chief source ②original version
蓝靛 indigo
蓝矾 blue vitriol；cupric sulphate
蓝鲸 blue whale
蓝客 bluehacker
蓝领 blue-collar
蓝图 blueprint
蓝牙 blue tooth
蓝藻 blue green algae
蓝宝石 sapphire
蓝筹股 blue chip stocks；blue chips
蓝晶石 kyanite；disthene
蓝皮书 blue book
蓝铜矿 azurite；chessylite
蓝盔人员 blue helmet personnel；personnel of a UN peace-keeping force
蓝领工人 blue-collar worker
蓝色国土 blue territory
蓝色农业 blue agriculture
蓝牙技术 bluetooth technology

谰 [lán]
劻 ①calumniate；slander；malign ②deny；disavow；refuse to admit a guilt
谰词 slanderous remarks；calumny
谰言 calumny；slander

澜 [lán]
名 billows；waves

褴 [lán]
褴褛 ragged；shabby

篮 [lán]
名 ①basket ②goal；basket ③basketball
篮板 backboard；bank
篮球 basketball
篮圈 ring；hoop
篮坛 basketball circles
篮子 basket
篮板球 rebound
篮球场 basketball court
篮球队 basketball team；quintet
篮球架 basketball stands
篮球赛 basketball match
篮球队员 basketballer；basketball player

斓 [lán]
◇斑斓 gorgeous；bright-coloured；multi-coloured

镧 [lán]
名 lanthanum（La）
镧系 lanthanide series
镧族 lanthanide series
镧系元素 lanthanide

襕 [lán]
名 dress；overall

lǎn （ㄌㄢˇ）

览 [lǎn]
劻 ①look at；see；view ②read
览古 visit historic sites
览胜 visit scenic spots

揽 [lǎn]
劻 ①pull into one's arms；take into one's arms；clasp；hold ②fasten with a rope；tie rope around sth ③take on；take upon oneself；canvass ④grasp；seize；exercise control over；monopolize
揽承 agree（or contract）to do a job
揽储 solicit depositors
揽活 take on work
揽权 arrogate power to oneself
揽买卖 canvass for business orders
揽镜自照 hold up a mirror to look at oneself

缆 [lǎn]
Ⅰ名 ① hawser；mooring rope；cable ② thick rope；cable Ⅱ劻 moor（a ship）
缆车 cable car
缆道 cableway
缆绳 cable；rope
缆索 thick rope；cable
缆舟 moor the ship
缆车铁道 cable railway
缆索铁道 funicular railway；funicular

懒 [lǎn]
形 ①lazy；indolent；slothful ②sluggish；languid；listless
懒虫 lazybones
懒怠 ①lazy；indolent ②be disinclined to
懒得 not feel like（doing sth）；not be in the mood to；be disinclined to
懒惰 lazy
懒汉 sluggard；idler；lazybones
懒猴 slender loris
懒猫 eyra
懒散 sluggish；negligent；indolent
懒熊 sloth bear
懒骨头 lazybones
懒汉鞋 "lazy man's shoe"
懒洋洋 languid；listless

làn （ㄌㄢˋ）

烂 [làn]
Ⅰ形 ①sodden；pappy；mushy；soft ②worn-out；tattered ③ messy；confused ④ bright；shining Ⅱ劻 rot；fester；decay Ⅲ副 thoroughly；very
烂糊 （of food）mashed；pulpy
烂花 burn-out；burnt-out；burnt discharge
烂漫 ① bright-coloured；brilliant ② unaffected；natural
烂泥 mud；slush
烂熟 ①thoroughly cooked ②know sth thoroughly
烂醉 dead drunk
烂摊子 shambles；mess；situation difficult to rectify
烂尾楼 incomplete（or delayed）projects

滥 [làn]
Ⅰ劻 overflow；flood；inundate Ⅱ副 excessive；indiscriminate；without restraint
滥调 hackneyed tune；worn-out theme
滥伐 severe deforestation；denudation
滥交 choose friends indiscriminately
滥用 abuse；misuse；use indiscriminately
滥支 lavish expenditure
滥捕滥猎 fish and hunt excessively
滥发钞票 inflate the paper currency；issue bank notes recklessly
滥发奖金 indiscriminate distribution of bonuses；overissue of bonuses；give out extravagant bonuses
滥发钱物 indiscriminate issuing of bonuses in cash（or in kind）
滥发文凭 issue diplomas recklessly
滥伐树木 deforestation；denudation；deforest
滥印钞票 excessive print of bank notes
滥用职权 misfeasance；breach of privilege；a-

buse one's power; abuse one's authority; a-buse one's position

滥竽充数 pass oneself off as one of the players in an ensemble—be there just to make up the number

láng (ㄌㄤ)

郎 [láng]
名 ①title for certain officials ②(*used in forming nouns denoting a particular category of person usu. male*) ③darling; love ④son of another person ➡làng

郎当 ①unfit ②dejected; dispirited ③good-for nothing; worthless
郎舅 a man and his wife's brother
郎君 you
郎猫 tom-cat
郎中 a physician trained in herbal medicine; doctor
郎才女貌 a brilliant young scholar and a beautiful woman—a fine couple

狼 [láng]
名 wolf
狼狈 in a difficult position; in a tight corner
狼疮 lupus
狼狗 wolfhound
狼孩 wolf child
狼毫 a writing brush made of weasel's hair
狼嚎 the howl of a wolf
狼獾 glutton
狼藉 in disorder; scattered about in a mess
狼狈不堪 in an extremely awkward position; in a sorry plight; in sore straits
狼狈为奸 act in collusion (*or* cahoots) with each other
狼吞虎咽 wolf down; gobble up
狼心狗肺 rapacious as a wolf and savage as a cur; cruel and unscrupulous; brutal and cold-blooded; heartless and ungrateful
狼烟四起 smoke signals rising on all sides; war alarms raised everywhere
狼子野心 a wolf cub with a savage heart—have a wolfish nature; be full of wild ambitions

琅 [láng]
名 ①kind of jade ②pure white
琅琅 a tinkling (*or* jingling) sound; the sound of reading aloud

廊 [láng]
名 porch; corridor; veranda
廊檐 the eaves of a veranda
廊子 porch; corridor; veranda

锒 [láng]
锒铛 ①iron chains ②a clanking (*or* clanging) sound
锒铛入狱 be put in chains and thrown into

prison

稂 [láng]
名 Chinese pennisetum
稂莠 ①pennisetum and green bristlegrass ②scoundrel; bad people

螂 [láng]
名 (*used in the names of certain insects*)

lǎng (ㄌㄤˇ)

朗 [lǎng]
形 ①light; bright ②loud and clear; resonant
朗读 read aloud; read loudly and clearly
朗朗 the sound of reading aloud
朗声 in a clear loud voice
朗诵 read aloud with expression; recite; declaim
朗咏 narrate in a loud and clear voice
朗姆酒 rum (a transliteration)

làng (ㄌㄤˋ)

郎 [làng]
➡láng
◇屎壳郎 dung beetle

浪 [làng]
Ⅰ 名 ①wave; billow; breaker ②sth undulating like waves Ⅱ 形 ①unrestrained; dissolute ②(of women) flighty; frivolous Ⅲ 动 ramble; roam
浪潮 tide; wave
浪船 swingboat
浪荡 ①loiter about; loaf about ②dissolute; dissipated
浪费 waste; squander; be extravagant
浪花 ①the foam of breaking waves ②episodes in one's life
浪迹 wander about; roam about
浪漫 ①romantic ②unconventional; bohemian; loose
浪木 swing log
浪人 ①wanderer; vagrant ②ronin (in Japan)
浪涛 billows
浪头 ①wave ②trend
浪涌 surge
浪游 ramble; roam about aimlessly
浪子 prodigal; loafer; wastrel
浪漫史 romance
浪漫主义 romanticism
浪子回头 return of the prodigal son
浪漫主义运动 the Romantic Movement (in western Europe in the early 19th century)

lāo (ㄌㄠ)

捞 [lāo]
动 ①drag for; dredge up; fish for; scoop up

from the water ② get by improper means; wangle ③make off with sth in passing

捞本 win back lost wagers; recover one's losses;recoup oneself

捞饭 rice boiled,strained and then steamed

捞钱 make money (by quick or improper means)

捞取 ①scoop up from a liquid ②fish for;gain

捞着 get the opportunity (of doing sth)

捞稻草 (try to) take advantage of sth;(try to) make capital of sth

捞外快 get extra income

捞一把 reap some profit;gain some advantage

捞油水 make a side profit;get a squeeze

捞资本 make political and economic "capital"

捞钱工作 lubrication job

捞取外快 have sth as a perquisite

捞取政治资本 fish for political capital; seek political advantage

láo（ㄌㄠ）

劳 [láo] Ⅰ 动 ①work;labour ②may I trouble you; will you be so kind (as to do sth);will you please ③ express one's appreciation or thanks;reward Ⅱ 名 ①labourer;labour ②fatigue; toil ③ meritorious deed; service; exploits

劳保 ①labour insurance ②labour safety

劳动 ①work;labour ②physical labour;manual labour

劳顿 fatigued;wearied

劳方 labour (as opposed to capital or management)

劳改 reform (of criminals) through labour

劳工 labourer;worker

劳驾 excuse me;may I trouble you…; would you please…

劳军 award soldiers for their distinctive service

劳苦 toil;hard work

劳累 tired;run-down;overworked

劳力 ① labour;labour force ② labour with one's strength;work with one's brawn

劳碌 work hard;toil

劳模 model worker

劳神 be a tax on (one's mind);bother;trouble

劳师 take greetings and gifts to army units

劳损 strain

劳务 labour services

劳心 work with one's mind or brains

劳役 ① penal servitude; forced labour ② corvée

劳逸 work and rest

劳资 labour and capital

劳动布 denim

劳动法 labour law

劳动节 Labour Day (May 1)

劳动力 ①labour (or work) force;labour ② capacity for physical labour ③ able-bodied person

劳动权 the right to work

劳动日 workday;working day

劳动者 labourer;worker

劳改队 a group sentenced to reform through labour

劳改犯 a prisoner serving a sentence of reform through labour

劳什子 nuisance

劳务费 service charge;cost of service

劳动保护 labour safety

劳动保险 labour insurance

劳动报酬 payment for labour

劳动定额 work norm;production quota

劳动对象 subject of labour

劳动改造 reform (of criminals) through labour

劳动观点 labour viewpoint (i.e. to view labour,esp. manual labour,with respect);attitude towards labour

劳动号子 work song

劳动教养 reeducation (of juvenile delinquents,etc.) through labour;indoctrination through labour;undergo education through labour

劳动竞赛 labour emulation;emulation drive; emulation campaign

劳动立法 labour legislation

劳动模范 model worker

劳动强度 labour intensity;intensity involved in the labour

劳动人民 labouring people;working people

劳动手段 means (or instruments) of labour

劳动英雄 labour hero

劳动争议 labour dispute

劳动资料 means (or instruments) of labour

劳而无功 work hard but to no avail; work fruitlessly

劳改产品 prison labour products; products made under a reform-through-labour program

劳改农场 reform-through-labour farm

劳教人员 a person subjected to reeducation in a reform school

劳苦功高 have worked hard and performed a valuable service

劳民伤财 exhaust the people and drain the treasury;waste money and manpower

劳师动众 mobilize too many troops—drag in lots of people (to do sth)

劳师远征 tire the troops on a long expedition

劳务出口 export of labour services; service export

劳务合同 service contract;contract for services

劳务市场 labour market;market for labour service

劳务输出 export of labour services

劳燕分飞 the shrike and the swallow flying in different directions—part from each other

劳役地租 rent paid in labour;labour rent

劳逸不均 uneven allocation of work

劳逸结合 strike a proper balance between work and rest;alternate work with rest and recreation

劳资关系 relations between labour and capital;labour-capital relations;employee-employer relations;labour-management relations

劳资合同 contract between labour and capital

劳资纠纷 industrial dispute;industrial conflict;trouble between labour and management

劳资双方 labour and management

劳资谈判 labour-management talks

劳资协议 labour agreement

劳动合同制 labour contract system

劳动力不足 manpower shortage;labour famine

劳动力过剩 labour surplus;manpower surplus

劳动力资源 human resources;pool of labour power

劳动密集型 labour-intensive

劳动生产率 labour productivity;productivity

劳动者素质 professional competence of workers

劳保医疗制度 system of workers' benefits including medical care

劳动服务公司 labour service company;manpower contractor

劳动监察制度 labour supervision system

劳动预备制度 vocational training system

劳动仲裁制度 labour arbitration system

劳动力流动状况 degree of mobility within the labour force

劳动者权益的保障 protection of the rights and interests of workers

劳动制度和用工制度 labour and employment system

劳心者治人,劳力者治于人 Those who work with their brains rule and those who work with their brawn are ruled.

牢 [láo]
Ⅰ 名 ①animal enclosure;pen;fold;stables ②sacrifice ③prison;jail Ⅱ 形 firm;fast;durable

牢房 prison cell

牢固 firm;secure

牢记 keep firmly in mind;remember well

牢靠 ①firm;strong;sturdy ②dependable;reliable

牢牢 firmly;safely

牢笼 ①cage (for birds or animals);bonds ②trap;snare ③win over ④shackle

牢骚 ①complaint;grumble ②complain;grumble

牢实 firm and solid;secure and steady

牢头 jailer

牢稳 [láowěn] safe;reliable

牢稳 [láowen] (of objects) stable;secure;firm

牢狱 prison;jail

牢不可破 unbreakable;indestructible

唠 [láo]
→láo

唠叨 be garrulous;chatter

铹 [láo]
名 lawrencium (Lw)

铹化合物 lawrencium compound

铹同位素 lawrencium isotope

痨 [láo]
名 consumptive disease;consumption;tuberculosis;TB

痨病 tuberculosis;TB

lǎo（ㄌㄠˇ）

老 [lǎo]
Ⅰ 形 ①old;aged ②seasoned;experienced;veteran ③of long standing;old ④outdated;old-fashioned;obsolete ⑤original;former;same ⑥(of colour) dark ⑦overcooked;well done ⑧youngest ⑨overgrown Ⅱ 名 elderly person;senior person;old people Ⅲ 动 ①go the way of all flesh;die ②change in quality;age;deteriorate Ⅳ 副①for a long time;long ②always;constantly;frequently ③very;extremely;terribly ④(*used as prefix before a person to indicate order or before some animals and plants*):老刘 Lao Liu

老板 shopkeeper;proprietor;boss

老鸨 a woman running a brothel;procuress;madam

老本 principal;capital

老兵 old soldier;army veteran

老病 ①chronic illness;old trouble ②old and sick

老伯 uncle

老财 moneybags;landlord

老插 old re-educated youth

老巢 nest;den;lair

老成 experienced;steady

老粗 an uneducated person;a rough and ready chap

老大 ①number one (in order of seniority, i.e. the eldest son, daughter, brother, or sister) ②the captain of a boat ③metaphor for a head of a gang or a bandit chieftain ④greatly;very

老道 Taoist priest
老到 〔lǎodao〕 experienced; considerate; careful
老底 sb's past; sb's unsavoury background
老弟 (a familiar form of address to a man much younger than oneself) young man; young fellow; my boy
老调 hackneyed theme; platitude
老坟 ancestral grave
老夫 old I
老赶 ①amateur; layman; nonprofessional person ②ignorant; benighted; hillbilly
老公 husband; hubby
老光 presbyopic
老汉 ①old man ②I
老红 dark red
老虎 tiger
老花 presbyopic
老化 ①ageing ②(of cadres) become old ③(of knowledge, etc.) become outdated
老话 ①old saying; saying; adage ②remarks about the old days
老几 ①order of seniority among brothers or sisters ②(*used in rhetorical questions to express disparagement*)
老记 news hound
老家 〔lǎojiā〕 ①native place; old home ②birthplace
老茧 callosity; callus
老将 veteran; old-timer
老辣 shrewd and ruthless
老练 seasoned; experienced
老路 old road; beaten track
老绿 dark green
老迈 aged; senile
老衲 old monk
老年 old age
老娘 ①mother ②I, your old mother
老农 old farmer; experienced peasant
老牌 old brand
老派 ①antiquated; outmoded ②old fashioned person
老婆 wife
老气 ①mature and steady ②(of clothes) dark and old-fashioned
老区 the old areas; the Old Areas (as referred to the old revolutionary bases)
老人 ①old person; the aged; the old ②one's aged parents (*or* grandparents)
老弱 ①the old and the young ②the old and the weak
老少 the old and the young
老师 teacher
老实 ①honest; frank ②well-behaved; good ③simpleminded; naive; easily taken in
老式 old style
老是 always; all the time

老手 old hand; old stager; veteran
老鼠 mouse; rat
老外 ①layman ②foreigner; foreign enterprise
老翁 old man; greybeard
老窝 ①nest; den ②lair
老乡 ① fellow-townsman; fellow-villager ② a friendly form of address to a man in the countryside
老小 grown-ups and children; one's family
老兄 (a familiar form of address between male friends) brother; man; old chap
老朽 ①decrepit and behind the times ②I
老爷 ①master; bureaucrat; lord ②a respectful address to a master by a servant
老鹰 black-eared kite; hawk; eagle
老账 old debts; long-standing debts
老子 ①father ②I, your father (said in anger or in fun)
老总 ①Sir ②big chief; general
老百姓 common people; ordinary people; civilians
老板娘 shopkeeper's wife; proprietress
老半天 a long time
老伴儿 (of an old married couple) husband or wife
老帮子 old person; old fogy
老鼻子 ① much more; far more ② long time ago
老处女 old maid; spinster
老搭档 old partner; old workmate
老大哥 elder brother (a respectful form of address for a man older than oneself)
老大姐 elder sister (a respectful form of address for a woman older than oneself)
老大娘 (a polite form of address to an old woman, esp. a stranger) aunty; granny
老大爷 (a polite form of address to an old man, esp. a stranger) uncle; grandpa
老掉牙 very old; out of date; obsolete; antediluvian
老东西 unwelcome old creature (person)
老豆腐 ①firm tofu ②northern-style bean tofu
老方法 outmoded method
老夫子 ①private school teacher ②aide; advisor ③bookish person
老干部 veteran cadre
老公公 ①grandpa ②husband's father; father-in-law
老姑娘 old maid; spinster
老古董 old fogey; fuddy-duddy
老规矩 old rules and regulations; convention; established custom or practice
老好人 Mr. Goody-goody
老狐狸 old fox; crafty scoundrel
老虎凳 rack
老虎机 slot machine
老虎钳 ①vise ②pincer pliers

老花镜 presbyopic glasses
老花眼 presbyopia
老皇历 last year's calendar—ancient history; obsolete practice
老黄牛 willing ox—a person who is diligent and conscientious in serving the people
老家儿 [lǎojiār] parents; grandparent
老家贼 sparrow
老江湖 a well-travelled, worldly-wise person; a person who has seen much of the world
老交情 long-standing friendship; an old friend
老街坊 old neighbour
老来俏 an elderly woman who tries to make herself attractive
老脸皮 a thick-skinned person
老邻居 old neighbour
老龄化 aging of the population; greying of the population
老妈子 amah; maidservant
老毛病 old trouble; old weakness
老冒儿 country person; layman; hick; wooden spoon
老妹子 youngest sister
老面皮 cheeker; boldface; hussy
老奶奶 ① paternal great grandmother ② old granny
老脑筋 old (or outmoded) way of thinking
老蔫儿 slowpoke; slow, sluggish, slothful person
老年斑 senile plaque
老年人 old people; the old; the aged
老年学 gerontology
老婆婆 ① granny ② husband's mother; mother-in-law
老前辈 one's senior; one's elder
老人家 ① a respectful form of address to an old person ② parent
老人星 Canopus
老三届 senior high school graduates of the classes of 1966, 1967 and 1968
老师傅 master craftsman; experienced worker
老视眼 presbyopia
老思想 old-fashioned idea
老太太 ① old lady; (in direct address) Venerable Madam ② (a polite term) your mother; his mother; my mother (or grandmother)
老太爷 ① elderly gentleman; (in direct address) Venerable Sir ② (a polite term) your father; his father; my father (or grandfather)
老套子 out-of-date practices; outmoded ways of doing things
老天爷 God; Heavens
老同事 long-time colleague
老头儿 old chap
老头子 ① old fogey; old codger ② my old man

老顽固 old diehard; old fogey; old stick-in-the-mud
老学究 old pedant
老眼光 old ways of looking at things; old views
老爷兵 pampered soldier
老爷爷 ① great grandfather ② grandpa
老爷子 ① venerable, old man ② my old father; your old father
老一辈 older generation
老一套 the same old stuff; the same old story
老油条 wily old bird; old campaigner
老油子 wily old bird; old campaigner
老玉米 maize; Indian corn; corn
老丈人 father-in-law
老主顾 old customer; old client; regular customer
老资格 old-timer; veteran
老字号 old and famous shop or enterprise
老祖宗 ancestor; forefather
老蚌生珠 an old oyster yielding a pearl—have a son born in one's old age
老不死的 (swearword or intimate term) old fellow; old folk; old fogy
老厂改造 modernization and expansion of the existing plant
老成持重 experienced and prudent
老大不小 have grown up and be no longer a child
老当益壮 old but vigorous
老调重弹 harp on the same string; play the same old tune
老而弥笃 the older one gets, the deeper one's love
老奸巨猾 a past master of machination and manoeuvre; a crafty old scoundrel; a wily old fox; an old hand at trickery and deception
老老实实 honestly; conscientiously; in earnest
老泪纵横 (of an old person) be in tears
老马识途 An old horse knows the way; An old hand is a good guide.
老谋深算 circumspect and far-seeing; experienced and astute
老年大学 university for the elderly
老年公寓 grey-headed flat
老年医学 geriatrics
老娘们儿 married woman; housewife
老牛破车 an old ox pulling a rickety cart—making slow progress
老牛舐犊 an old cow licking her calf—a parent doting on his or her child
老气横秋 ① arrogant on account of one's seniority ② lacking in youthful vigour
老人政治 gerontocracy
老弱病残 the old, weak, sick and disabled
老弱残兵 old, weak and wounded troops; those

who on account of old age, illness, etc. are no longer active or efficient

老生常谈 commonplace; platitude; truism

老实巴交 soft-spoken and timid

老式汽车 jalopy

老态龙钟 senile; doddering

老羞成怒 fly into a rage out of shame; be shamed into anger

老眼昏花 dim-sighted from old age

老爷们儿 ①man ②husband

老幼咸宜 be suitable (or good) for people of all ages

老于世故 versed in the ways of the world; worldly-wise

老着脸皮 unabashedly; unblushingly

老龄化社会 the ageing society

老年性痴呆 senile dementia

老大难(问题) long-standing, big and difficult problems; lasting, complex and hard-to-solve problems

老虎头上蹭痒 scratch oneself against a tiger's head—court disaster

老死不相往来 grow old and die without having had any dealings with each other—never be in contact with each other

老爷式的态度 bureaucratic attitude

老中青三结合 three-in-one combination of the old, the middle-aged and the young; combination of the old, the middle-aged and the young in an undertaking (or in the leadership)

老子天下第一 think oneself the most important person in the world

老虎屁股摸不得 like a tiger whose backside no one dares to touch—not to be provoked

老骥伏枥，志在千里 an old steed in the stable still aspires to gallop a thousand *li*—an old hero still cherishes high aspirations

老将出马，一个顶俩 When a veteran goes into action, he can do the job of two.

老鼠过街，人人喊打 a rat running across the street, with everybody shouting, "Kill it!" (said of a person or thing hated by everyone)

老王卖瓜，自卖自夸 Lao Wang selling melons praises his own goods—praise one's own work or wares

老、少、边、穷地区 old revolutionary base areas, areas inhabited by minority ethnic groups, remote areas and poor areas; former revolutionary base areas, areas inhabited by ethnic minorities, remote and border areas and poverty-stricken areas

佬 [lǎo]
图 man; guy; fellow

姥 [lǎo]
➡mǔ

姥姥 ① maternal grandmother; grandma ② midwife

姥爷 maternal grandfather; grandpa

潦 [lǎo]
图 ① heavy rainfall ② running water (or water puddles) on the road ➡liáo

lào (ㄌㄠˋ)

唠 [lào]
动 speak; talk; say; chat ➡láo

烙 [lào]
动 ①brand; sear; iron ②bake in a pan ➡luò

烙饼 pancake

烙铁 ①flatiron; iron ②soldering iron

烙印 brand (on cattle)

涝 [lào]
I 动 waterlogging II 图 floodwater (on low-lying land); excessive water

涝灾 damage (or crop failure) caused by waterlogging

涝洼地 waterlogged lowland

落 [lào]
➡là; luō; luò

落槌 ①wind up a deal ②warp up; wind up

落汗 stop sweating

落价 fall (or drop) in price; go down in price

落炕 stay in bed with illness; be laid up

落色 discolour; fade

落枕 have a stiff neck (caused by cold or an awkward sleeping posture)

落不是 be blamed for doing sth wrong

耢 [lào]
I 图 leveller II 动 level (land)

酪 [lào]
图 ① junket ② fruit jelly; sweet paste (made from crushed nuts)

酪乳 buttermilk

酪素 casein

酪酸 butyric acid

酪氨酸 tyrosine

lè (ㄌㄜˋ)

仂 [lè]
图 remainder; surplus; fractional amount

乐 [lè]
I 形 happy; glad; cheerful; joyful II 动 ① be glad to; find pleasure in; enjoy ②laugh; be amused III 图 pleasure; enjoyment IV 副 gladly; happily; willingly ➡yuè

乐道 be happy to have the chance to; be only too glad to; readily take the opportunity to

乐得 readily take the opportunity to; be only too glad to

乐观 optimistic; hopeful; sanguine

乐趣 delight; pleasure; joy

乐事 pleasure; delight

乐天 carefree;happy-go-lucky
乐土 land of happiness;paradise
乐意 ①be willing to;be ready to ②pleased;
　happy
乐于 be happy to;take delight in
乐园 paradise;playground;amusement park
乐子 ①fun;pleasure ②a laughable matter
乐呵呵 buoyant;happy and confident
乐天派 optimist;a happy-go-lucky person
乐滋滋 contented;pleased
乐不可支 overwhelmed with joy;overjoyed
乐不思蜀 so happy as to forget home and duty
乐此不疲 always enjoy it;never be bored with
　it
乐观主义 optimism
乐极生悲 Extreme joy begets sorrow.
乐山大佛 the Giant Stone Buddha at Leshan
　Mountain
乐善好施 be given to doing charitable work
乐天知命 submit to the will of Heaven and be
　content with one's lot
乐于助人 be happy to help others;be eager to
　help people
乐观主义者 optimist

勒 [lè]
Ⅰ 名 ①headstall;halter;bridle ②lux Ⅱ 动
①rein in ②force;compel;coerce ③command
④carve;engrave;inscribe ➡lēi
勒碑 inscribe on a stone tablet
勒逼 force;coerce
勒捐 compel sb to make money contributions
勒令 compel (by legal authority) order
勒派 force sb to pay levies or do corvée labour
勒索 extort;blackmail
勒克司 lux
勒令停业 be closed down by order
勒索钱财 extort money (from sb) under false
　pretences

le（·ㄌㄜ）

了 [le]
助 ①(used after a verb or an adjective to
indicate the completion of a real or expected action or a change) ②(used at the end
of or in the middle of a sentence to indicate
a change or new circumstances) ③(used
for urging or dissuasion) ➡liǎo

lēi（ㄌㄟ）

勒 [lēi]
动 ①tie (or strap) tight ②force;compel;
coerce ➡lè
勒脚 plinth

léi（ㄌㄟ）

累 [léi]
➡lěi;lèi
累累 ①clusters of;heaps of ②haggard;gaunt
累赘 ① burdensome;cumbersome ② wordy;
　verbose ③encumbrance;burden;nuisance

雷 [léi]
名 ①thunder ②mine
雷暴 thunderstorm
雷达 radar
雷电 thunder and lightning
雷动 thunderous
雷公 Thunder God
雷汞 mercury fulminate
雷管 detonator;detonating cap;blasting cap;
　primer
雷击 be struck by lightning
雷鸣 ①thunder ②thunderous
雷鸟 white partridge
雷声 thunderclap;thunder
雷霆 ① thunderclap; thunderbolt ② thunder-
　like power (or rage);wrath
雷同 ①echoing what others have said ②du-
　plicate;identical
雷雨 thunderstorm
雷暴雨 thunderstorm rain
雷电计 ceraunograph
雷雨云 thundercloud
雷阵雨 thunder shower
雷达测距 radar range finding
雷打不动 not to be shaken by thunder—(of an
　arrangement or plan) not to be altered un-
　der any circumstances
雷厉风行 with the power of a thunderbolt and
　the speed of lightning—(carry out orders,
　policies,etc.) vigorously and speedily;vig-
　orously and resolutely
雷霆万钧 as powerful as a thunderbolt
雷雨大作 The storm bursts with a tremendous
　peal of thunder and a rush of rain.
雷声大,雨点小 loud thunder but small rain-
　drops—much said but little done; much
　talk,little action
雷公打豆腐,拣软的欺 the God of Thunder
　strikes the bean curd—bullies pick on the
　soft and weak

镭 [léi]
名 radium (Ra)
镭疗 radium therapy
镭射 laser
镭系 radium family
镭射气 radium emanation
镭化合物 radium compound
镭射影碟 laser videodisc
镭同位素 radium isotope

擂 [léi]
动 ①grind;pestle;pound ②hit;beat ➡lèi

礌 [léi] Ⅰ 名 huge stones to be pushed down from a height against an attacking enemy Ⅱ 动 beat; hit; strike; attack
礌敌 attack the enemy
礌击 throw stones upon the enemy from a height

嬴 [léi] 形 ① thin; skinny; emaciated ② tired out; exhausted
嬴瘠 haggard and thin

lěi (ㄌㄟˇ)

垒 [lěi] Ⅰ 动 build by piling up bricks, stones, earth, etc. Ⅱ 名 ①rampart; wall; fort; fortification ②base
垒球 softball

累 [lěi] Ⅰ 动 ①pile up; gather; accumulate ②implicate; involve Ⅱ 形 again and again; repeated; continuous; running ➡léi; lèi
累次 time and again; repeatedly
累犯 ①recidivism ②recidivist
累积 accumulate
累及 implicate; involve; drag in
累计 ①add up ②accumulative total; grand total
累加 accumulation; cumulation; summation
累进 progression
累累 ①again and again; many times ②innumerable; countless
累卵 a stack of eggs—liable to collapse any moment; precarious
累年 for years in succession; year after year
累世 for many generations; generation after generation
累积股本 cumulative capital stock
累积亏损 accumulated deficit
累积盈余 accumulated surplus
累积资本 accumulating capital
累进税率 progressive tax rate

磊 [lěi]
磊落 open and upright

蕾 [lěi] 名 flower bud; bud
蕾铃 cotton buds and bolls

偏 [lěi]
◇傀儡 puppet

lèi (ㄌㄟˋ)

肋 [lèi] 名 rib; costal region
肋骨 rib
肋膜 pleura

肋炎 pleurisy
肋木 stall bars
肋条 ①rib ②pork ribs; spareribs
肋间肌 intercostal muscle
肋骨切除术 costectomy

泪 [lèi] 名 tear; teardrop
泪痕 tear stains
泪花 tears in one's eyes
泪人 in tears; all tears
泪水 tear; teardrop
泪腺 lachrymal gland
泪眼 tearful eyes
泪液 tear
泪珠 teardrop
泪涟涟 in tears; tears keep coming to one's eyes
泪汪汪 (eyes) brimming with tears
泪盈盈 brimming with tears; tearful
泪如泉涌 tears welling up in one's eyes; tears gushing from one's eyes
泪如雨下 tears falling like rain

类 [lèi] Ⅰ 名 kind; type; class; category Ⅱ 动 resemble; be similar to
类比 analogy
类别 classification; category
类似 similar (to); analogous (to)
类推 analogize; reason by analogy
类型 type; category
类病毒 viroid
类毒素 toxoid
类人猿 anthropoid (ape)
类星体 quasi-stellar object
类型学 typology
类地行星 terrestrial planet
类木行星 Jovian planet
类义词典 lexicon; Thesaurus
类型语言学 typological linguistics; linguistic typology
类风湿性关节炎 rheumatoid arthritis

累 [lèi] Ⅰ 形 tired; fatigued; weary Ⅱ 动 ① tire out; fatigue; weary; strain ② work hard; toil ➡léi; lěi
累乏 tired out with too much exertion
累死累活 tire oneself out with backbreaking toil; work oneself to death

酹 [lèi] 动 pour a libation; libate

擂 [lèi] Ⅰ 名 ring (for martial contests); arena Ⅱ 动 beat (a drum) ➡léi
擂台 a platform for martial contests; ring; arena
擂台赛 arena contest; arena match

lei（·ㄌㄟ）

嘞 [lei]
〔助〕(*similar to the usage of* 喽 *but with a lighter tone*)Ok；All right ➡ lē

léng（ㄌㄥ）

棱 [léng]
〔名〕① edge；corner ② corrugation；ridge；raised angle
棱角 ①edges and corners ②edge
棱镜 prism
棱线 crest line
棱柱(体) prism
棱锥(体) pyramid

楞 [léng]
楞场 dump
楞堆 log pile
楞间通道 alley

薐 [léng]
〔名〕spinach

lěng（ㄌㄥ）

冷 [lěng]
Ⅰ〔形〕①cold；chilly ②cold in manner；frosty；frigid；icy ③ unfrequented；deserted；forlorn；out-of-the-way ④strange；rare；unusual；out-of-the-way ⑤ unwelcome；neglected；unpopular ⑥covert；underhanded；sudden Ⅱ〔动〕①(usu. of food) cool ②dishearten；discourage；dampen
冷拔 cold-drawing.
冷布 (cotton) gauze
冷菜 cold dish
冷餐 buffet
冷藏 refrigeration；cold storage
冷场 ①awkward silence on the stage (when an actor enters late or forgets his lines) ② awkward silence at a meeting
冷床 cold bed；cold frame
冷脆 cold short
冷待 treat coldly；cold-shoulder；slight
冷淡 ①cheerless；desolate ②cold；indifferent ③treat coldly；cold-shoulder；slight
冷岛 cool island
冷点 cold spot
冷碟 cold dish
冷冻 freeze
冷锻 cold forging；cold hammering
冷风 cold air blast；cold-blast air
冷锋 cold front
冷敷 cold compress
冷宫 ① cold palace—a place to which disfavoured queens and concubines were banished ②limbo

冷光 cold light
冷汗 cold sweat
冷焊 cold welding
冷荤 cold meat；cold buffet
冷货 goods not much in demand；dull goods
冷箭 an arrow shot from hiding；sniper's shot
冷静 sober；calm
冷觉 sensation of cold；sense of cold
冷峻 grave and stern
冷库 cold storage；freezer
冷酷 unfeeling；callous；grim
冷落 ①unfrequented；desolate ②treat coldly；cold-shoulder；leave out in the cold
冷铆 cold riveting
冷门 ① a profession (*or* trade，branch of learning) that receives little attention ②an unexpected winner；dark horse
冷漠 cold and detached；unconcerned；indifferent
冷凝 condensation
冷暖 changes in temperature—daily life
冷盘 cold dish；hors d'oeuvres
冷僻 ①deserted；out-of-the-way ②rare；unfamiliar
冷气 air conditioning
冷枪 sniper's shot
冷清 cold and cheerless；desolate；lonely；deserted
冷却 become (*or* make) cool
冷色 cool colour
冷杉 fir
冷射 make a sudden shot for the goal
冷食 cold drinks and snacks
冷霜 cold cream
冷水 ①cold water ②unboiled water
冷线 unfrequented route
冷销 unsaleable
冷笑 sneer；laugh grimly；grin with dissatisfaction (*or* helplessness，bitterness，etc.)
冷姓 rare surname
冷眼 ①(with) a cold eye；(with) cool detachment ②cold shoulder
冷饮 cold drink
冷遇 cold reception；cold shoulder
冷轧 cold rolling
冷战 ①cold war ②shiver
冷铸 chill casting
冷板凳 cold bench—an indifferent post or a cold reception
冷冰冰 ① cold in manner；frosty ②(of objects) ice-cold；icy
冷不防 suddenly；unexpectedly；without warning
冷菜间 pantry
冷藏车 (on a railway train) refrigerator car (*or* van)
冷藏库 cold storage；freezer

冷藏室 refrigerating compartment (in a refrigerator)
冷藏箱 refrigerator;fridge
冷处理 cold treatment;handle a matter after tempers have cooled
冷冻机 refrigerator;freezer
冷冻剂 refrigerant
冷冻室 freezer compartment (in a refrigerator);freezer
冷和平 cold peace
冷加工 cold working
冷凝点 condensation point
冷凝器 condenser
冷凝物 condensate
冷气管 cold air duct;cold air pipe
冷气机 air conditioner
冷气团 cold air mass
冷启动 cold start
冷却剂 coolant;cooler
冷却器 chiller;cooler
冷却塔 cooling tower
冷热病 ① malaria ② capricious changes in mood;sudden waxing and waning of enthusiasm
冷丝丝 a bit chilly
冷飕飕 (of wind) chilling;chilly
冷压机 cold press
冷藏汽车 cold storage truck
冷嘲热讽 with freezing irony and burning satire;with biting sarcasm
冷冻干燥 freeze-dry
冷冻疗法 cold therapy
冷冻食品 frozen food
冷冻手术 cryosurgery
冷酷无情 unfeeling;cold-blooded
冷冷清清 cold and cheerless;desolate
冷暖自知 one knows whether it's cold or warm without being told—one knows best by personal experience
冷却导管 cooling duct
冷若冰霜 (usu. of women) as cold as ice;have an icy (or chilly) manner
冷水浇头 splashing the head with cold water—a rude shock;a bitter disappointment
冷血动物 ① cold-blooded animal;poikilothermal animal ② an unfeeling person;a cold-hearted person
冷言冷语 sarcastic comments;ironical remarks
冷眼旁观 look on with a cold eye
冷战思维 Cold War mentality
冷暖式空调 dual-purpose air conditioner;cooling-heating air conditioner
冷餐(招待)会 buffet reception

lèng（ㄌㄥˋ）

愣 [lèng]
Ⅰ 形 ① distracted;stupefied;absent-minded;blank;dumbfounded ② blunt;rash;reckless;foolhardy Ⅱ 副 stubbornly;recklessly;wilfully
愣干 do things recklessly (or rashly);persist in going one's own way
愣说 insist;allege;assert
愣着 not moving;in a daze
愣劲儿 dash;pep;vigour
愣神儿 stare blankly;be in a daze
愣头愣脑 rash;impetuous;reckless
愣头儿青 rash (or brusque) fellow;hothead

睖 [lèng]
动 ① see directly ② stare ③ stare in dissatisfaction

lī（ㄌ丨）

哩 [lī]
➡ li
哩哩啦啦 scattered;sporadic
哩哩啰啰 verbose and unclear in speech;rambling and indistinct

lí（ㄌ丨ˊ）

厘 [lí]
Ⅰ 量 ① (of certain measurement) one hundredth ② li, as a measurement,(a) a unit of length (1/3 millimetre) (b) a unit of weight (= 0.05 grams) (c) a unit of area (= 0.666 square metres) ③ li, a unit of Chinese currency,equal to 0.1 fen (分) or 0.001 yuan (元) ④ li, a unit of monthly interest rate (= 0.1%) or annual interest rate (= 1%);月利率二厘一 monthly interest of 0.21%/年利率三厘二 annual interest of 3.2% Ⅱ 名 very small amount;fraction;the least Ⅲ 动 put in order;administer;regulate
厘定 collate and stipulate
厘米 centimetre (cm.)
厘升 centilitre (cl.)
厘米波 centimetre wave
厘米克秒单位 centimetre-gram-second unit (CGS unit)

狸 [lí]
名 ① leopard cat ② yellow weasel
狸猫 leopard cat
狸藻 bladderwort

离 [lí]
动 ① leave;part from;depart from;be away from ② off;away;from ③ without;independent of ④ go against ⑤ deviate from;shift from
离别 part (for a longish period);leave;bid farewell
离队 leave the ranks;leave one's post
离合 separation and reunion
离婚 divorce

离间 sow discord; drive a wedge between; set one party against another
离解 dissociation
离境 leave a country (*or* place)
离开 ① leave; depart from; deviate from ② check out
离谱 go beyond what is proper; be out of place
离奇 strange; odd; fantastic; bizarre
离弃 abandon; desert; forsake
离去 split; leave
离任 leave one's post
离散 (of relatives) be dispersed; be scattered about; be separated from one another
离题 digress from the subject; stray from the point
离心 ① be at odds with the community or the leadership ② centrifugal
离休 leave office for rest; retire with full pay
离异 divorce
离辙 off the track—off the beam; off the point
离职 ① leave one's job temporarily ② leave office; resign
离子 ion
离不开 ① can't do without ② too busy to get away
离格儿 go beyond what is proper; be out of place
离合器 clutch
离婚率 divorce rate
离间计 the scheme of sowing dissension
离心泵 centrifugal pump
离心机 centrifugal machine; centrifuge
离心力 centrifugal force
离子泵 ionic pump
离子束 ion beam
离子雾 ion-atmosphere
离岸价格 free on board (FOB)
离不开身 be fully occupied (*or* be very much needed) and unable to leave for a moment; cannot afford to get away for a moment
离婚赔偿 divorce compensation
离家出走 leave home to lead a vagrant life; abandon one's family
离经叛道 depart from the classics and rebel against orthodoxy
离境签证 exit visa
离群索居 live in solitude; live all alone
离散系数 coefficient of dispersion
离心离德 torn by dissension and discord
离职偿金 severance pay
离职工资 dismissal wage
离中趋势 statistics dispersion
离子交换 ion exchange
离子淌度 ionic mobility
离到任大使 outgoing and new ambassadors
离境许可证 exit permit
离退休老人 retirees

离退休人员 retired personnel; retiree; the retired

骊 [lí]
名 pure black horse

梨 [lí]
名 pear
梨膏 pear syrup (for the relief of coughs)
梨树 pear
梨园 the Pear Garden—the theatre
梨子 pear
梨园子弟 students of the Pear Garden—operatic actors

犁 [lí]
Ⅰ 名 plough Ⅱ 动 work with a plough; plough
犁壁 breast
犁刀 coulter; skim cutter
犁地 plough fields
犁沟 furrow
犁铧 ploughshare; share
犁头 coulter
犁把手 plough handle
犁底层 plough sole; plough pan

鹂 [lí]
◇黄鹂 oriole

喱 [lí]
◇咖喱 curry

蜊 [lí]
◇蛤蜊 clam

漓 [lí]
◇淋漓 ① dripping wet ② (of a piece of writing or a speech) free from inhibition

缡 [lí]
名 silk veil worn by women

璃 [lí]
◇玻璃 ① glass ② nylon; plastic
琉璃 coloured glaze

黎 [lí]
Ⅰ 名 ① the Li nationality ② multitude; host
Ⅱ 形 black
黎民 the common people; the multitude
黎明 dawn; daybreak
黎民百姓 common people
黎巴嫩真主党 Lebanese Hezbollah

罹 [lí]
动 suffer from
罹病 suffer from a disease; fall ill
罹难 ① die in a disaster (*or* an accident) ② be murdered
罹网 enmesh

篱 [lí]
名 fence; hedge
篱笆 bamboo (*or* twig) fence
篱牢犬不入 When the fence is strong, no dogs

can get in.

藜 [lí]
　名 lamb's-quarters
藜草 blite
藜芦 black false hellebore

黧 [lí]
　形 black; dark and sallow

lǐ (カǐ)

礼 [lǐ]
　名 ①ceremony; rite; ritual ②courtesy; etiquette; manners ③gift; present
礼拜 ①religious service ②week ③day of the week ④Sunday
礼兵 honour guard
礼单 a list of presents
礼服 ceremonial robe (*or* dress); full dress; formal attire
礼花 fireworks display
礼教 code of ethics; feudal ethics and rites
礼节 courtesy; etiquette; protocol; ceremony
礼金 a gift of money; cash gift
礼帽 hat that goes with formal dress
礼貌 ①courtesy; politeness; manners ②courteous; polite
礼炮 salvo; (gun) salute
礼品 gift; present
礼聘 invite sb cordially; enlist the service of sb with rich gifts
礼让 give precedence to sb out of courtesy (*or* thoughtfulness); comity
礼数 courtesy; etiquette
礼俗 etiquette custom
礼堂 assembly hall; auditorium
礼物 gift; present
礼仪 ceremony and propriety
礼遇 courteous reception
礼治 rule by rites
礼拜天 Sunday
礼宾司 the Department of Protocol; the Protocol Department
礼品部 gift and souvenir department (*or* counter) (in a shop)
礼品店 gift shop
礼品券 gift coupon; gift voucher; gift certificate; gift cheque; gift token
礼品电报 telegram message accompanied by a gift
礼品商店 gift and souvenir store
礼尚往来 ①courtesy demands reciprocity ②deal with a man as he deals with you; pay a man back in his own coin; give as good as one gets
礼贤下士 (of a ruler or a high minister) treat worthy men with courtesy
礼仪电报 etiquette telegram; protocol telegram; greeting telegram; telegram featu-

ring greetings, congratulations, condolences and other sentimental expressions or gestures
礼仪服务 courtesy service
礼仪公司 protocol company; etiquette company; business firm specializing in ceremonial activities
礼仪先生 ceremony boy
礼仪小姐 ceremony girl; ritual girl; ceremonial usherette; young lady serving at ceremonies
礼仪之邦 state of ceremonies; land of propriety and righteousness
礼义廉耻 propriety, righteousness, honesty, and a sense of shame
礼不下庶人 Rites do not extend to the common people.
礼多人不怪 Nobody will blame you for being too polite.
礼轻情意重 The gift is trifling but the feeling is profound; It's nothing much, but it's the thought that counts.

李 [lǐ]
　名 plum
李树 plum tree
李子 plum
李代桃僵 ①substitute one thing for another; substitute oneself for another person ②sacrifice oneself for another person; bear the blame for another person's mistake

里 [lǐ]
　名 ①lining; inside ②inner; inside ③neighbourhood ④home town; native place
里边 inside; in; within
里程 ① mileage ② course of development; course
里带 inner tyre; inner tube
里脊 tenderloin
里拉 lira
里弄 lanes and alleys; neighbourhood
里面 inside; interior
里圈 inner lane (of a running track)
里手 ①the left-hand side (of a running vehicle or machine) ②expert; old hand
里外 inside and outside
里屋 inner room
里子 lining
里程标 milepost
里程表 odometer
里程碑 milestone
里出外进 irregular; uneven
里勾外联 in collusion with forces within and without
里里外外 inside and outside
里通外国 have (*or* maintain) illicit relations with a foreign country
里应外合 act from inside in coordination with

forces attacking from outside; collaborate from within with forces from without

俚 [lǐ]
形 vulgar
俚歌 folk songs
俚俗 vulgar; rustic; unrefined
俚语 slang

逦 [lǐ]
◇迤逦 winding; tortuous; meandering

悝 [lǐ]
形 worry; sorrow

娌 [lǐ]
◇妯娌 wives of brothers; sisters-in-law

理 [lǐ]
Ⅰ 名 ① texture; grain (in wood, stone, skin, etc.) ② reason; logic; truth ③ natural science (esp. physics) Ⅱ 动 ① manage; run; administer ② put in order; tidy up ③ pay attention to; acknowledge
理财 manage money matters; conduct financial transactions
理财 manage money matters
理睬 pay attention to; show interest in
理当 ought to; should
理短 be in the wrong; have no justification
理发 ① (of men) get a haircut; (of women) go to the hairdresser's ② give a haircut; do sb's hair
理工 science and engineering
理化 physics and chemistry
理会 ① understand; comprehend ② take notice of; pay attention to
理货 freight forwarding; customs brokerage
理家 keep house; manage family affairs
理解 understand; comprehend
理科 ① science (as a field of study) ② science department in a college
理亏 be in the wrong
理疗 physiotherapy
理论 theory; principle
理念 notion
理赔 settle claims; claims settlement; settlement of claims
理事 member of an executive council (or of a board of directors); director; manager
理顺 rationalize
理想 ① an ideal ② be ideal
理性 ① rational ② the rational faculty; reason
理学 ① a rationalistic Confucian philosophical school that developed during the Song and Ming Dynasties, known to the West as Neo-Confucianism ② natural science
理应 ought to; should
理由 reason; ground; argument
理喻 reason with sb
理智 ① reason; intellect ② rational

理财家 financier
理舱费 stowage charges
理发馆 barbershop; barber's; hairdresser's
理发师 barber; hairdresser
理发员 barber; hairdresser
理货单 tally sheet
理货员 tallyman; tally clerk
理解力 faculty of understanding; understanding; comprehension
理论家 theoretician; theorist
理事国 a member of the UN Security Council
理事会 executive council; board of directors
理事长 chairman of a board of directors (or of an executive council); council chairperson
理想国 an ideal state; utopia
理学士 bachelor of science
理财公司 money management firm
理工学院 college of science and engineering
理亏心虚 feel that one is not on solid ground
理论科学 theoretical science; pure science
理清思路 get one's ideas into shape; put one's thoughts into shape
理屈词穷 fall silent on finding oneself bested in argument; be unable to advance any further arguments
理所当然 of course; as a matter of course; naturally
理通外国 have illicit relations with foreign country
理想气体 ideal gas
理想主义 idealism
理性认识 rational cognition; rational knowledge
理直气壮 With justice on one's side, one is bold and assured.
理论联系实际 link theory with practice; integrate theory with practice
理顺价格体系 rationalize the price system; balance price relationships
理论与实践脱节 theory divorced from practice

锂 [lǐ]
名 lithium (Li)
锂云母 lepidolite; lithia mica
锂(离子)电池 lithium ion battery

鲤 [lǐ]
名 carp
鲤鱼 carp
鲤鱼钳 slip-joint pliers

lì (力)

力 [lì]
Ⅰ 名 ① force; energy ② power; strength; ability ③ physical strength Ⅱ 动 do one's best; make every effort; exert oneself
力巴 [lìba] ① not adept; awkward; clumsy ② layman
力避 try hard to avoid (or avert)

力臂 arm of force
力场 field of force
力促 make every effort to promote
力挫 defeat (the best) after many efforts
力度 ①dynamics ②intensity of force ③depth of intension
力荐 recommend strongly
力谏 strongly counsel against (doing sth)
力戒 strictly avoid; do everything possible to avoid; guard against
力矩 moment of force; moment
力量 ① physical strength ② power; force; strength ③potency; efficacy; strength
力偶 couple
力气 physical strength; effort
力求 make every effort to; do one's best to; strive to
力劝 persuade earnestly
力士 a man of great strength; strong man
力图 try hard to; strive to
力行 be diligent in action; practise with earnestness
力学 mechanics
力邀 make effort to invite
力争 ①work hard for; do all one can to ②argue strongly; contend vigorously
力作 major piece of writing; major article; well-written influential writing
力气活 heavy work; strenuous work
力不从心 ability falling short of one's wishes; unable to do as much as one would like to
力不胜任 be unequal to one's task; incompetent
力持异议 insist on one's dissenting views
力持正义 uphold justice
力排众议 prevail over all dissenting views; override all objections
力所能及 in one's power
力挽狂澜 make vigorous efforts to turn the tide; do one's utmost to stem a raging tide (*or* save a desperate situation)
力争上游 aim high; strive for first place; strive for progress; strive for the best

历 [lì] I 动 go through; undergo; experience II 名 ①experience ②calendric system; calendar ③almanac III 形 all previous (years, occasions, sessions, etc.) IV 副 all over; all through; one by one; one after another
历程 course
历次 all previous (occasions, etc.)
历代 successive dynasties; past dynasties
历法 calendric system; calendar
历届 all previous (sessions, governments, etc.)
历尽 have gone through a lot of
历来 always; constantly; all through the ages

历历 distinctly; clearly
历年 ①over the years ②calendar year
历任 ① have successively held the posts of; have served successively as ②successive
历时 last (a period of time); take (a period of time)
历史 ①history ②history (as a course of study) ③personal records
历书 almanac
历数 count one by one; enumerate
历月 calendar month
历史观 view (*or* conception) of history
历史剧 historical play
历史性 historic; of historic significance
历届政府 all previous governments
历久弥坚 unshakable and ever firmer
历来如此 this has always been the case
历历在目 come clearly into view; leap up before the eyes
历史潮流 the tide of history; historical trend
历史地图 historical map (*or* atlas)
历史人物 historical personage; historical figure
历史使命 historic mission
历史缩影 sketch of history; epitome of history
历史文献 historical documents
历史小说 historical novel
历史学家 historian
历史遗产 legacy of history; historical heritage
历史博物馆 history (*or* historical) museum
历史唯物论 historical materialism
历史唯心论 historical idealism
历史循环论 historicism
历代班禅喇嘛 Panchen Lamas of successive generations
历史唯物主义 historical materialism
历史唯心主义 historical idealism
历史文化名城 historically and culturally famous city; city famous for both its history and culture
历史遗留问题 problem left over by history; question left over from the past
历史比较语言学 historical comparative linguistics

厉 [lì] 形 ① strict; rigorous; rigid; stringent ② stern; severe; grim; serious; fierce
厉鬼 an evil spirit
厉害 ①(of a wild animal or of one's temper, words, etc.) fierce; terrible ②(of a person) strict; stern; harsh ③(of illness, heat, cold, etc.) intense; severe; terrible
厉色 a stern countenance
厉声 in a stern voice
厉行 strictly enforce; rigorously enforce; make great efforts to carry out
厉声斥责 scold with an irritating voice

厉行节约 practise strict economy

立 I 囫 ①stand; remain in an erect position ②set up; stand up; erect; make upright ③set up; found; establish ④sign; conclude; draw up ⑤exist; live; grow ⑥ascend the throne ⑦appoint; designate; adopt II 圐 upright; erect; vertical III 圓 immediately; instantaneously; at once; right away

立案 ①register; put on record; set up a file ② place a case on file for investigation and prosecution

立碑 erect a monument

立场 position; stand; standpoint

立春 the Beginning of Spring

立等 wait for sth to be done immediately

立定 halt

立冬 the Beginning of Winter

立法 make (or enact) laws; legislate

立方 ①cube ②cubic metre; stere

立功 render a meritorious service; perform a meritorious service; do meritorious work

立柜 clothes closet; wardrobe; hanging cupboard

立国 found a state

立后 make sb queen

立候 wait for sth to be done immediately

立户 ① register for a household residence card; register for permanent residence ② (less common than 立户头) open an account with the bank

立即 immediately; at once; promptly

立决 summary execution

立刻 immediately; at once; right away

立论 ① set forth one's views; present one's arguments ② argument; position; line of reasoning

立名 gain distinction

立秋 the Beginning of Autumn

立射 fire from a standing position

立式 vertical; upright

立誓 take an oath; vow

立体 ①three-dimensional; stereoscopic ②solid

立夏 the Beginning of Summer

立宪 constitutionalism; establish a constitution

立相 appoint sb as prime minister

立项 put a project under an authorized plan; have a project plan approved

立言 expound one's ideas in writing; achieve glory by writing

立业 establish a business; have a respectable career

立意 ①be determined; make up one's mind ② conception; approach

立约 conclude a treaty; draw up an agreement (or a contract)

立账 open an account

立正 stand at attention

立志 resolve; be determined

立轴 ①vertical scroll (of painting or calligraphy); wall scroll ② vertical shaft; upright shaft

立传 glorify sb by writing his biography

立姿 standing position

立足 ① have a foothold somewhere ② base oneself upon

立标牌 put up a signboard

立德粉 lithopone

立法权 legislative power

立方根 cube root

立方米 cubic metre

立方体 cube

立合同 conclude a contract

立交桥 flyover; overpass; cloverleaf; grade separation bridge; over-bridge; overpass bridge

立马儿 immediately; at once; right away

立面图 elevation (drawing)

立体感 three-dimensional effect

立体角 solid angle

立体派 cubism

立体声 stereophony; stereo

立体图 hologram

立字据 sign a pledge

立足点 ①foothold; footing ②standpoint; stand

立党为公 build a party serving the interests of the people

立等可取 have sth ready while waiting; repairs done while you wait

立地成佛 become a Buddha immediately

立定跳远 standing long jump

立法机关 legislative body; legislature

"立法真空" "legislation vacuum"

立方厘米 cubic centimetre

立竿见影 set up a pole and you see its shadow—produce instant results

立功奖状 certificate for meritorious service; certificate of merit

立功赎罪 expiate crime by meritorious service

立国之本 fundamental to the building of the country; foundation underlying all efforts to build the country

立身处世 the way one conducts oneself in society

立式冰柜 vertical refrigerator

立体地图 three dimensional map

立体电视 three-dimensional film; stereoscopic mobile picture

立体电影 stereoscopic film; three-dimensional (or 3-D) film; cinerama

立体化学 stereochemistry

立体几何 solid geometry

立体交叉 grade separation

立体模型 space model
立体农业 three-dimensional agriculture
立体显示 three-dimensional display
立体战争 three-dimensional warfare; triphibious warfare
立体种养 stereo cultivation and stereo breeding; three dimensional farming and agriculture
立宪政体 constitutional government
立行停止 stop immediately
立锥之地 land just enough to stick an awl into; tiny bit of land
立足之地 foothold; footing
立克次氏体 rickettsia
立体式报道 overall report
立体显微镜 stereoscopic microscope; stereo-microscope
立体照相机 stereoscopic camera; stereo camera
立于不败之地 establish oneself in and unassailable position; be in an impregnable position; be invincible

吏 [lì]
名 ①government clerk; petty official ②official; mandarin
吏部 the Ministry of Official Personnel Affairs
吏治 the administration of local officials

丽 [lì]
Ⅰ 形 pretty; beautiful Ⅱ 动 attach oneself to; rely on; adhere to
丽人 beautiful woman; beauty
丽日 bright sun
丽质 beauty (of a woman)

励 [lì]
动 encourage; urge; exert oneself
励磁 excitation
励磁机 exciter
励精图治 (usu. of a ruler or prime minister) exert oneself to make the country prosperous
励磁式扬声器 excited-field loudspeaker

利 [lì]
Ⅰ 形 ① sharp; keen ② fluent; eloquent ③ favourable; convenient Ⅱ 名 ① advantage; benefit ②profit; interest Ⅲ 动 ①do good to; benefit ②sharpen; perfect
利弊 advantages and disadvantages; pros and cons
利钝 ① sharp or blunt ② smooth going or rough
利多 upside factors
利害 advantages and disadvantages; gains and losses
利空 downside factors
利禄 rank and wealth
利率 rate of interest; interest rate
利落 ①agile; nimble; dexterous ②neat; orderly ③settled; finished

利器 ①a sharp weapon ② good tool; efficient instrument
利钱 interest (on an investment)
利权 economic rights (esp. of a country)
利刃 a sharp sword
利润 profit
利市 ① good sign for business; prediction of business prosperity ②money given to children as lunar New Year gift; red envelope; bonus
利税 profit and tax
利息 interest (on an investment)
利益 interest; benefit; profit
利用 ①use; utilize; make use of ②take advantage of; exploit
利诱 lure by promise of gain
利于 be of advantage to; benefit
利改税 substitution of tax payment for profit delivery; switch from profit delivery to tax payments; replace handing over of profits with a tax system
利滚利 at compound interest
利尿剂 diuretic
利润率 profit margin
利润税 profits tax
利用率 utilization ratio
利多弊少 The advantages outweigh the disadvantages.
利害冲突 conflict of interest
利己主义 egoism
利令智昏 be blinded by lust for gain
利润分成 profits sharing
利润留成 proportional profit retention
利润提成 commission from profit; profit drawing; withhold or keep a certain percentage of profit
利税分流 payment of tax plus a percentage of profits to the state; pay tax plus a percentage of profits
利他主义 altruism
利息差额 interest spread
利息回扣 interest rebate
利息津贴 interest subsidization
利益集团 interest group
利益均沾 let everybody share the pie
利用外资 utilize foreign capital; utilize foreign investment; utilize foreign fund
利用系数 utilization coefficient; utilization factor
利欲熏心 be obsessed with the desire for gain; be overcome by covetousness; be blinded by greed
利息所得税 interest tax
利益约束机制 profit-control mechanism
利用非法手段 by hook; by crook

沥 [lì]
Ⅰ 动 drip; trickle Ⅱ 名 drop

沥干 drip-dry
沥涝 waterlogging
沥青 pitch;asphalt;bitumen
沥水 waterlogging caused by excessive rain-
　fall
沥青油毡 asphalt felt

枥 [lì] 〈名〉 manger

例 [lì] I 〈名〉①example;instance ②precedent ③
case ④rule;regulation II 〈形〉 regular;routine
例话 cliché;platitude
例会 regular meeting
例假 ①official holiday;legal holiday ②men-
　strual period;period
例句 illustrative sentence;example sentence
例如 for instance;for example (e. g.);such as
例示 illustration
例套 regular practice;routine
例题 a problem designed to illustrate a princi-
　ple or method (as in a mathematics book);
　example
例图 illustration
例外 ①be an exception ②exception
例言 introductory remarks;notes on the use
　of a book
例语 illustrative phrase;example word or
　phrase
例证 illustration;example;case in point
例子 example;case;instance
例行公事 ①routine;routine business ②mere
　formality

疬 [lì] 〈名〉①pestilence;plague ②ulcer;sore ③lep-
rosy

渗 [lì] 〈名〉①ill omen ②harm;hurt
渗气 bad omen (for disaster)

戾 [lì] I 〈名〉 crime;sin II 〈形〉①perverse;unrea-
sonable ②speedy ③stable

隶 [lì] I 〈动〉 be subordinate to;be affiliated to (or
with);be under II 〈名〉①person in servitude
②yamen runner
隶书 official script
隶属 be subordinate to;be under the jurisdic-
　tion (or command) of

荔 [lì]
荔枝 litchi;lichee

栎 [lì] 〈名〉 oak

轹 [lì] 〈动〉①crush with cartwheels;run over ②
bully by force;oppress

俪 [lì] I 〈形〉 paired;parallel II 〈名〉 husband and
wife;married couple

俪句 parallel sentences
俪影 a photograph of a couple

俐 [lì]
◇伶俐 clever;bright;quick-witted

疬 [lì]
◇瘰疬 scrofula;struma

莉 [lì]
◇茉莉 jasmine

莅 [lì] 〈动〉 arrive;be present
莅场 be present on the occasion
莅临 arrive;be present
莅席 be present at a banquet

鬲 [lì] 〈名〉 ancient cooking tripod with hollow legs

栗 [lì] I 〈名〉① chestnut tree ② chestnut II 〈形〉
tremble;shudder
栗果 acorn
栗色 chestnut colour;maroon
栗子 chestnut
栗钙土 chestnut soil

砺 [lì] I 〈名〉 whetstone;grindstone II 〈动〉 whet;
sharpen

砾 [lì] 〈名〉 gravel;shingle
砾煤 pebble coal
砾石 gravel;grail;dirt
砾岩 conglomerate

猁 [lì]
◇猞猁 lynx

蛎 [lì] 〈名〉 oyster
蛎黄 oyster meat

唳 [lì] 〈动〉 cry (of birds)

笠 [lì] 〈名〉 large bamboo (or straw) hat with a
conical crown and broad brim (worn by peasants or fishermen at work)
笠贝 limpet

粝 [lì] 〈名〉 coarse grain;brown rice;unpolished rice

粒 [lì] I 〈名〉 grain;granule;pellet;small particles
II 〈量〉(of granular objects):一粒种子 a grain
of seed
粒度 size
粒肥 granulated fertilizer
粒选 grain-by-grain seed selection
粒状 granular
粒子 particle;grain
粒子加速器 particle accelerator
粒子束武器 particle beam weapon

霹 [lì]
◇霹雳 thunderbolt;thunderclap

跞 [lì]
囫 walk about

罯 [lì]
囫 rebuke;scold;berate
罯骂 scold;abuse;curse

痢 [lì]
囵 dysentery
痢疾 dysentery

lǐ（·ㄌㄧ）

里 [lǐ]
①in;inside ②(*used after* 这,那,哪 *to indicate a location*):哪里 where

哩 [lǐ]
囵 (*used like* 呢 *but not in interrogative sentence*):山上的雪还没化哩。The snow on the mountain has not melted. ➡lī

liǎ（ㄌㄧㄚˇ）

俩 [liǎ]
囮 ①two ②a few;a little;some;several;我一月挣那俩钱儿,哪够哇! My monthly salary? Only a pittance. Far from enough! ➡liǎng

lián（ㄌㄧㄢˊ）

奁 [lián]
囵 toilet case used by women

连 [lián]
Ⅰ 囫 link;join;connect Ⅱ 囷 continuously;in succession;one after another;repeatedly Ⅲ 囹 ①including ②even Ⅳ 囵 company
连词 conjunction
连带 related
连队 company
连发 running fire
连杆 connecting rod
连亘 (of mountain ranges) continue;extend
连贯 link up;piece together;hang together;be coherent
连环 a chain of rings
连击 double hit (in table tennis);double contact (in volleyball)
连枷 flail
连接 join;link
连襟 husbands of sisters
连累 implicate;involve;get sb into trouble
连连 repeatedly;again and again
连忙 hastily;hurriedly;promptly
连绵 continuous;unbroken;uninterrupted
连年 in successive years;in consecutive years;for years running;for years on end

连皮 (weight of goods) including the packing;gross (weight)
连篇 ①throughout a piece of writing;page after page ②one article after another;a multitude of articles
连任 renew one's term of office
连日 for days on end;day after day
连射 running fire
连声 say repeatedly
连锁 linked together
连天 ①for several days in a row;for days on end ② continuously;incessantly ③ (of a mountain,the horizon,flames,etc.) touch the sky
连同 together with;along with
连续 continuously;successively;in a row
连夜 ① the same night;that very night;all through the night ②for nights on end
连用 use consecutively;use together
连载 publish in instalments;serialize
连长 company commander
连珠 like a chain of pearls or a string of beads—in rapid succession
连缀 ①join together;put together ②cluster
连奏 legato
连裆裤 child's pants with no slit in the seat
连根拔 tear up by the roots;uproot
连拱坝 multiple-arch dam;multi-arch dam
连拱桥 multiple-arch bridge;multi-arch bridge
连贯性 coherence;continuity
连锅端 remove or destroy lock,stock and barrel;get rid of the whole lot
连环画 a book (usu. for children) with a story told in pictures
连环计 a set of interlocking stratagems;a series of stratagems
连接号 hyphen
连接线 tie
连裤袜 panty hose
连谱号 accolade;brace
连体婴 Siamese twins
连续剧 serial
连续性 continuity;continuance
连衣裙 a woman's dress;dress
连阴天 cloudy weather for several days running
连阴雨 an unbroken spell of wet weather
连轴转 work day and night;work round the clock
连珠炮 continuous firing;drumfire
连字号 hyphen (-)
连本带利 both principal and interest;profit as well as capital;total sum including interest
连鬓胡子 whiskers;full beard
连成一片 join together
连带责任 joint responsibility;joint liability;responsibility jointly and severally bound

连环图画 comic strips;comics
连篇累牍 lengthy and tedious;at great length
连锁比例 chain relative
连锁反应 chain reaction
连锁商店 chain store;link store;multiple store
连锁涨价 chain rising spiral of prices
连续报道 follow-up story follow-up;development story follow-up
连续光谱 continuous spectrum
连续航次 consecutive voyages
连续轰炸 train bombing
连选连任 be reelected and serve another term
连战连北 be defeated in one battle after another
连环大撞车 mass line-up;chain collision
连带法律关系 joint legal relations

怜 [lián]
　动 ①sympathize with;pity ②love tenderly;have tender affection for
怜爱 love tenderly;have tender affection for
怜悯 pity;take pity on;have compassion for;empathy
怜惜 take pity on;have pity for;empathy
怜贫惜老 feel compassion for the aged and the poor
怜香惜玉 show pity and tenderness to women

帘 [lián]
　名 ①flag (or banner) used as shop sign ②curtain;(hanging) screen
帘布 cord fabric (in tyres)
帘幕 heavy curtain
帘子 (hanging) screen;curtain
帘栅管 screen-grid tube
帘栅极 screen grid
帘子布 cord fabric (in tyres)

莲 [lián]
　名 ①lotus ②lotus seed
莲房 ①lotus speed pod ②monk's bedroom
莲花 lotus flower;lotus
莲藕 the lotus plant;lotus root
莲蓬 seedpod of the lotus
莲台 a Buddha's seat in the form of a lotus flower;lotus throne
莲心 the heart of a lotus seed
莲子 lotus seed
莲花纹 lotus design
莲蓬头 shower nozzle

涟 [lián]
　名 ①ripples ②continual flow (of tears)
涟漪 wimpled waves;ripples

联 [lián]
　Ⅰ **动** ally oneself with;unite;combine;join
　Ⅱ **名** antithetical couplet
联邦 federation;union;commonwealth
联播 radio hookup;broadcast over a radio network
联单 receipts (or other documents) in duplicate

联动 chain effect;chain reaction
联队 wing (of an air force)
联防 ①joint defence;joint command of defence forces ②joint defence;neighbourhood watch
联合 ①unite;ally ②joint;combined ③combination;alliance;union;coalition ④symphysis
联欢 have a social gathering;have a get-together
联机 on-line
联结 join;connect;link;bind
联军 allied forces;united army
联络 ①start (or keep up) personal relations;make (or maintain) contact of liaison ②contact (between people);liaison
联袂 go (or come,etc.) together
联盟 alliance;coalition;league;union
联名 jointly signed;jointly
联翩 in close succession;together
联赛 circuit;league matches
联手 join hands;word hand in hand
联网 on line;be networked;be wired with
联系 ①contact;touch;connection;relation ②integrate;relate;link;get in touch with
联想 connect with mentally;associate with
联谊 keep up a friendship;strengthen the bonds of friendship
联姻 ally;(of two families) be related by marriage;form an alliance by marriage
联营 joint venture
联运 combined (multimodal) transportation
联展 joint exhibition
联邦制 federal system;federalism
联苯胺 benzidine
联管节 pipe union;pipe coupling;union joint
联管箱 header
联合国 the United Nations (U.N.)
联合会 federation;union
联合机 combine
联合体 an organic whole;association
联欢会 get-together;party;gala
联欢节 festival;carnival;fiesta
联络部 liaison department
联络处 liaison office
联络官 liaison officer
联络网 liaison net
联络员 liaison man
联络站 liaison station
联系人 liaison man;person to contact
联谊会 friendship association
联运票 through ticket
联轴节 shaft coupling;coupling
联邦基金 federal funds
联播节目 networked program
联产计酬 payment linked to output
联合办案 jointly work on a certain case

联合兵种 combined arms
联合词组 coordinative word group
联合公报 joint communiqué
联合公司 joint company
联合兼并 conglomeration and merger of enterprises
联合经营 joint venture
联合开发 joint exploitation
联合企业 an incorporated business enterprise
联合商标 unite band
联合声明 joint statement
联合投标 joint tender；syndicated tender
联合王国 the United Kingdom
联合行动 joint action；concerted action
联合宣言 joint declaration
联合演出 variety show；joint manoeuvre
联合演习 joint manoeuvre；joint exercise
联合战线 united front
联合招生 enroll students cooperatively
联合政府 coalition government
联合作战 combined operations
联欢晚会 (evening) party
联机测试 online testing
联机检索 on-line information retrieval
联立方程 simultaneous equations
联名上书 submit a joint letter；submit a joint petition
联锁机构 interlocking mechanism
联席会议 joint conference；joint meeting
联想集团 Legion Group Ltd.
联运提单 through bill of lading
联邦调查局 the (U.S.) Federal Bureau of Investigation (FBI)
联邦共和国 federal republic；federated republic
联合采煤机 cutter-loader；combine
联合大企业 conglomerate company
联合国大会 the United Nations General Assembly
联合国会费 United Nations assessments
联合国宪章 the United Nations Charter
联合收割机 combine (harvester)
联系汇率制 linked exchange rate system
联邦储备系统 Federal Reserve System
联合打击走私 joint crackdown on smuggling
联合股份公司 jointed-stock company
联合国秘书处 the United Nations Secretariat
联合联络小组 joint liaison group
联机实时系统 on-line real-time system
联产承包责任制 a system of contracted responsibility linking remuneration to output；a contract system with remuneration linked to output
联合国安全理事会 the United Nations Security Council
联合国宪章的宗旨和原则 the purposes and principles of the UN Charter

裢 [lián]

◇褡裢 ①a long, rectangular bag sewn up at both ends with an opening in the middle (usu. worn round the waist or across the shoulder) ②a jacket, made of several layers of cloth, worn by wrestlers

廉 [lián]

〖形〗①honest and clean ②low in price；inexpensive；cheap
廉耻 integrity and a sense of honour
廉价 low-priced；cheap
廉洁 honest and clean；incorruptible
廉明 (of officials) upright and incorruptible
廉政 honest and clean government
廉价部 bargain counter
廉内助 clean half；clean wife of an official
廉价出售 sell at a bargain；dispose of at a low price
廉价抛售 distress sale；distress selling
廉价商店 bargain shop；discount store；cheapie
廉洁奉公 be honest in performing official duties；perform one's official duties honestly
廉洁自律 be honest, clean and self-disciplined
廉政公署 commission against corruption；ombudsman commission
廉政建设 construction of a clean and honest administration；build a clean and honest government；construct clean politics；keep government honest and austere

镰 [lián]

〖名〗sickle
镰刀 sickle
镰鱼 Moorish idol (a fish)

liǎn (ㄌㄧㄢˇ)

敛 [liǎn]

〖动〗①hold back；keep back；restrain ②collect
敛步 check one's steps；hold back from going
敛财 accumulate wealth by unfair means
敛迹 temporarily desist from one's evil ways；lie low
敛钱 collect money illegally；raise money
敛容 assume a serious expression

脸 [liǎn]

〖名〗①face ②front ③sensibilities；credit ④countenance；facial expression
脸红 ①blush (with shame or embarrassment) ②flush with anger；get excited；get worked up
脸颊 cheeks；face
脸面 ①face ②self-respect；sb's feelings
脸盆 washbasin；washbowl
脸皮 face；cheek
脸谱 types of facial makeup in operas
脸色 ①complexion；look ②facial expression

脸形 the shape of one's face;facial features
脸蛋儿 (usu. children's) cheeks;face
脸盘儿 the cast of one's face
脸盆架 washstand
脸上无光 have lost face
脸红脖子粗 get red in the face from anger or excitement;flush with agitation

liàn （ㄌㄧㄢˋ）

练 [liàn]
Ⅰ 〈名〉 white silk Ⅱ 〈动〉 ①practise;train;drill ②boil and scour raw silk ③beat;thrash Ⅲ 〈形〉 experienced;skilled;seasoned
练笔 ①practise writing ②practise calligraphy
练兵 train troops;drill soldiers
练操 (of troops,etc.) drill
练达 experienced and wordly-wise
练队 drill in formation;drill for a parade
练功 do exercises in gymnastics, *wushu*, acrobatics,etc.;practise one's skill
练球 practise a ball game
练鹊 long-tailed flycatcher
练武 ① learn (*or* practise) martial arts ② learn (*or* practise) military skills
练习 ①practise ②exercise (in a book)
练兵场 drill ground;parade ground
练摊儿 set up a stall to sell goods;run a private stall
练习本 exercise-book
练习曲 étude
练习题 exercise problems;exercises
练好企业"内功" improve the quality (*or* "software") of an enterprise

炼 [liàn]
〈动〉 ① smelt;refine ② burn;temper with fire;test with fire ③polish;improve;refine
炼丹 (try to) make pills of immortality (as a Taoist practice)
炼钢 make steel;smelt steel
炼焦 make coke;coke
炼句 try to find the best turn of phrase;polish and repolish a sentence
炼乳 condensed milk
炼铁 smelt iron
炼油 ①refine oil ②extract oil by heat ③heat edible oil
炼狱 purgatory
炼制 refine
炼钢厂 steel mill;steelworks
炼钢炉 steelmaking furnace;steel-smelting furnace
炼焦厂 coking plant;cokery
炼焦炉 coke oven
炼焦煤 coking coal
炼金术 alchemy
炼铁厂 ironworks
炼铁炉 iron-smelting furnace;blast furnace

炼油厂 (oil) refinery
炼钢工人 steelworker

恋 [liàn]
〈动〉 ①love;love affair ②long for;feel attached to
恋爱 ① romantic love;love affair ② be in love;have a courtship
恋歌 love song
恋家 long for home;be reluctant to be away from home
恋旧 ①yearn for one's native place;be filled with nostalgia ② remember past times or old acquaintances
恋慕 have tender feelings towards;adore
恋情 romantic love
恋人 sweetheart;loved one;girlfriend (*or* boyfriend)
恋父情结 Electra complex
恋恋不舍 be reluctant to part from;hate to see sb go
恋母情结 Oedipus complex

殓 [liàn]
〈动〉 put a body into a coffin;encoffin
殓衣 graveclothes
殓葬 put (a dead body) in a coffin and bury it

链 [liàn]
Ⅰ 〈名〉 chain Ⅱ 〈动〉 chain;enchain Ⅲ 〈量〉 cable length
链钩 chain hook;sling
链轨 caterpillar track (of a tractor)
链接 interlinkage
链节 link;chain element
链锯 chain saw
链轮 chain wheel;sprocket (wheel)
链球 hammer
链套 chain case (of a bicycle)
链条 ①chain ②roller chain (of a bicycle)
链烃 chain hydrocarbon
链闸 chain brake
链罩 chain guard (of a bicycle);chain cover
链轴 chain axle
链子 ①chain ②roller chain (of a bicycle)
链扳手 chain wrench
链霉素 streptomycin
链球菌 streptococcus
链式反应 chain reaction
链式输送机 chain-linked conveyer

楝 [liàn]

楝树 chinaberry

潋 [liàn]

潋滟 ① overflowing;inundating ② billowing;rippling

liáng（ㄌㄧㄤ）

良 [liáng] Ⅰ 〔形〕 good; fine Ⅱ 〔名〕 good people Ⅲ 〔副〕 very; very much

良材 ①good timber ②able person

良策 good plan; sound strategy

良方 ①effective prescription; good recipe ② good plan; sound strategy

良港 a good harbour

良好 good; well

良机 good (or golden) opportunity

良家 good and decent family

良姜 galingale

良久 for a good while; a long time

良能 intuitive ability; inborn ability

良深 very deep; quite profound

良田 good farmland; fertile farmland

良心 conscience

良性 benign

良药 good medicine

良医 a skilful doctor

良友 good friend

良知 ①intuitive knowledge; innate knowledge ②conscience

良种 ①(fine) improved variety ②fine breed

良导体 good conductor

良种场 seed multiplication farm

良辰美景 a fine moment and a beautiful scene

良师益友 good teacher and helpful friend

良性循环 virtuous circle; normal circle; regular circle; beneficent cycle

良性肿瘤 benign tumour

良药苦口 Good medicine tastes bitter.

良莠不齐 The good and the bad are intermingled.

良种推广站 stations for popularizing better seed strains

凉 [liáng] Ⅰ 〔名〕 coolness; coldness Ⅱ 〔形〕 ①cool; cold ②disheartened; discouraged; disappointed ➡ liàng

凉拌 (of food) cold and dressed with sauce

凉菜 cold dish

凉粉 bean-starch noodles

凉快 ①nice and cool; pleasantly cool ②cool oneself; cool off

凉棚 mat-awning; mat shelter

凉气 cold air; chilly air

凉伞 sunshade; parasol

凉爽 nice and cool; pleasantly cool

凉水 ①cold water ②unboiled water

凉台 balcony; veranda

凉亭 wayside pavilion; summer house; kiosk

凉席 summer sleeping mat (of woven split bamboo, etc.)

凉鞋 sandals

凉意 slight chill in the air

凉丝丝 coolish; rather cool; a bit cool

凉飕飕 (of wind) chilly; chill

凉风习习 The clear breeze blows gently; A cool breeze is blowing.

梁 [liáng] 〔名〕 ①roof beam ②purlin ③bridge ④ridge

梁桥 beam bridge

梁子 ridge of a mountain

梁上君子 gentleman on the beam—burglar; thief

量 [liáng] 〔动〕 ①measure; weigh ②appraise; estimate; assess; size up ➡ liàng

量棒 length bar

量杯 measuring glass; graduate

量程 measurement range; measuring range; span

量度 measurement

量规 gauge; metric gauge

量具 measuring tool

量瓶 measuring flask; graduated flask; volumetric flask

量筒 graduated (or volumetric, measuring) cylinder; graduate

量尺寸 take sb's measurements

量角器 protractor

量热器 calorimeter

量日仪 heliometer

量体温 take sb's temperature

量体重 weigh oneself; take sb's weight

量图仪 map measurer

量雪尺 snow scale

量雪器 snow gauge

量油尺 oil dip rod; dipstick

量雨筒 precipitation gauge

粮 [liáng] 〔名〕 ① grain; food; provisions ② grain tax paid in kind; farm tax

粮仓 ①granary; garner ②rice bowl

粮草 army provisions; rations and forage (or fodder)

粮店 grain shop

粮库 grain depot

粮秣 army provisions; rations and forage; grain and fodder

粮票 food coupon; grain coupon

粮食 grain; cereals; food

粮油 grain and cooking oil

粮援 international grain aid

粮栈 wholesale grain store; grain depot

粮站 grain distribution station; grain supply centre

粮秣库 ration depot

粮食仓库 grain depot

粮食产量 grain yield

粮食储备 grain reserves; grain stock

粮食供应 staple food supply
粮食加工 grain processing
粮食配给 grain ration
粮食缺乏 food shortage;food deficit
粮食征购 grain purchases by the state
粮食作物 cereal crops;grain crops
粮油关系 grain and oil rationing registration
粮食收购价 grain procurement (*or* purcha-
　sing) prices
粮食储备制度 grain reserve system
粮食风险基金 risk fund for grains
粮食购销体制 grain purchasing and marketing
　system
粮食收购部门 government's grain procure-
　ment (*or* purchasing) agencies
粮棉购销体制改革 reform of the grain and
　cotton purchasing and marketing system
粮食流通体制改革 reform of the grain circula-
　tion (*or* distribution) system
粮食专项储备制度 system of storing grain for
　unforeseen needs

粱 [liáng]
　[名] ① fine strain of millet ② fine grain;
choice (staple) food

liǎng（ㄌㄧㄤ）

两 [liǎng]
　I [数] ① two ② a couple;a few;some II [名]
both (sides);either (side) III [量] *liang*,a unit
of weight (= 50 grams)
两边 ① both sides;both directions;both places
　② both parties;both sides
两便 be convenient to both;make things easy
　for both
两侧 both sides;either flank
两重 double;dual;twofold
两抵 balance or cancel each other
两湖 the Two Hus—Hubei and Hunan Prov-
　inces
两会 two Conferences;the National People's
　Congress and the Chinese Political Consult-
　ative Conference
两极 ① the two poles of the earth ② the two
　poles (of a magnet or an electric battery)
　③ two opposing extremes
两可 both will do;either will do;could go ei-
　ther way
两立 coexist
两利 benefit both sides;be convenient to both
　sides
两面 ① two sides;both sides;two aspects;both
　aspects ② having a dual (*or* double) char-
　acter;dual;double
两难 face a difficult choice;be in a dilemma
两旁 both sides;either side
两栖 amphibious
两讫 The goods are delivered and the bill is

cleared.
两全 be satisfactory to both parties;have re-
　gard for both sides
两手 dual tactics
两头 ① both ends;either end ② both parties;
　both sides
两相 two-phase
两厢 ① wing-rooms on either side of a one-
　storey house ② both sides
两性 ① both sexes ② amphiprotic;amphoteric
两翼 ① both wings ② both wings;both flanks
两用 dual purpose
两院 the Supreme People's Court and the Su-
　preme People's Procuratorate
两造 ① both parties in a lawsuit;both plaintiff
　and defendant ② two crops
两半儿 two halves;in half;in two
两边倒 lean now to one side,now to the oth-
　er;waver
两党制 two-party system;bipartisan system
两点论 doctrine that everything has two as-
　pects or that"one divides into two"
两分法 application of the Marxist law that
　"one divides into two"
"两国论" "two-state comments"; "two-state
　theory"
两回事 two entirely different things;two dif-
　ferent matters
两件套 two-piece dress
两脚规 ① compasses ② dividers
两口子 husband and wife;couple
两码事 two entirely different things;two dif-
　ferent matters
两面光 (try to) please both parties
两面派 double-dealer
两面性 dual nature;duplicity;ambivalence
两条心 in fundamental disagreement;not of
　one mind
两下子 ① a few times ② a few tricks of the
　trade
两性花 hermaphrodite flower
两性人 bisexual person;hermaphrodite
两用衫 jacket suitable for spring or autumn
两院制 two-chamber system;bicameral sys-
　tem;bicameralism
两岸关系 relations between the two sides of
　the Taiwan Straits
两岸三地 the Mainland, Taiwan and Hong
　Kong
两岸直航 cross-Straits direct transportation
　links
两败俱伤 both sides suffer;neither side gains
两边讨好 ingratiate oneself with both sides
两鬓斑白 greying at the temples;grey at the
　temples
两鬓苍苍 greying at the temples
两次三番 again and again;time and again;over

and over again
两次运球 double dribble
两弹一艇 A-bomb，H-bomb and nuclear-powered submarine
两弹一星 atomic bomb，hydrogen bomb and artificial satellite
两个"凡是" the "two whatevers"；whatever Mao directed (*or* ordered)
两个文明 material progress and cultural and ideological advancement；material and spiritual civilization
两极分化 polarization；gap between the rich and the poor
两可之间 ①either will do；not know which to choose ②both are possible；maybe，maybe not
两面夹攻 close in from both sides；make a pincer attack
两面三刀 double-dealing；double cross
两栖部队 amphibious forces；amphibious units
两栖动物 amphibious animal；amphibian
两栖演员 amphibian actor；amphibian actress；multi-functioning actor (*or* actress)
两栖植物 amphibious plant；amphibian
两栖作战 amphibious warfare；amphibious operations
两权分立 system of independent legislative and executive branches
两全其美 satisfy both sides；satisfy rival claims
两人世界 two people's world
两世为人 barely escape with one's life；be lucky to have escaped death
两头落空 fall between two stools
两相情愿 by mutual consent；both parties being willing
两小无猜 (of a little boy and a little girl) be innocent playmates
两性关系 sexual relations
两性胶体 amphoteric colloid；ampholytoid
两性生殖 bisexual reproduction
两袖清风 (of an official) have clean hands；remain uncorrupted
两伊战争 the Iran-Iraq War
两用人才 qualified personnel versed in both military and civilian affairs；people qualified for both military and civilian work
两院院士 academicians of both academies；academicians of the Chinese Academy of Science and the Chinese Academy of Engineering
两审终审制 the system of the court of second instance being the court of last instance
两条腿走路 walk on two legs；adopt two-pronged approach；do two interrelated things simultaneously
两性化合物 amphoteric compound

两岸人员往来 mutual visits of people between the two sides of the Taiwan Straits
两岸渔事纠纷 fishing disputes across the Taiwan Straits
两岸政治谈判 political negotiations between the two sides of the Taiwan Straits
两系法杂交稻 double-hybrid rice strains
两头小，中间大 small at both ends and big in the middle；a few at each extreme and many in between；a few advanced，a few backward，but the majority middling
两岸直航促进会 Association for Promotion of Cross-Straits Direct Transportation
两耳不闻窗外事 both ears shut to what goes on outside the window
两个文明一起抓 pay equal attention to material progress and cultural and ideological progress；place equal emphasis on material and ethical progress
两极格局终结 disintegration (*or* end) of the bipolar structure
两岸直接"三通" cross-Straits direct links (in mail，transportation and trade)
"两个国际法人" "two international legal persons"
两虎相斗，必有一伤 When two tigers fight，one is bound to get hurt.
两手抓，两手都要硬 promote socialist material and ethical progress simultaneously；place equal emphasis on material progress and ethical and cultural progress；do two types of work at the same time，attach equal importance to both；grasp two links at the same time and attach equal importance to both；work at two tasks and be steadfast with regard to both
"两个对等的政治实体" "two equal political entities"

俩 [liǎng]
⇒liǎ
◇伎俩 trick；intrigue；manoeuvre

liàng （ㄌㄧㄤˋ）

亮 [liàng]
I 形 ①bright；light ②loud and clear；clarion ③enlightened；clear II 动 ①shine；flash ②make loud and clear；lift (one's voice) ③show；lay open；make public III 名 light
亮底 reveal the whole story；disclose one's plan (*or* stand，views，etc.)；put one's cards on the table
亮点 shining point；bright spot；eye-catching
亮度 brightness；brilliance
亮分 marks given and shown by the panel of judges
亮光 light
亮丽 beautiful

亮色 bright colour
亮堂 ① light; bright ② (of voice) loud and clear ③ clear; enlightened
亮相 ① (in Beijing opera, dancing, etc.) strike a pose on the stage ② declare one's position; state one's views
亮底牌 show one's cards (*or* hand); reveal one's true intention
亮光漆 lacquer polish
亮红灯 show the red light; forbid
亮晶晶 glittering; sparkling; glistening

凉 [liàng] 动 make cool; become cool ⇒ liáng

跟 [liàng]
跟跄 stagger
跟跟跄跄 stumble along

谅 [liàng] 动 ① forgive; excuse; understand ② I think; I believe; I expect; presumably
谅必 most likely; probably
谅察 ask sb to understand and forgive oneself
谅解 understand; make allowance for
谅解备忘录 memorandum of understanding

辆 [liàng] 量 (of vehicles): 一辆自行车 one bicycle

靓 [liàng] 形 pretty; beautiful; handsome; good-looking ⇒ jìng
靓哥 handsome brother; good-looking man
靓歌 beautiful song
靓丽 pretty; beautiful
靓女 pretty girl
靓仔 handsome young man

量 [liàng] I 名 ① bulk measure ② capacity; capability ③ quantity; amount; number; volume II 动 estimate; appraise; measure ⇒ liáng
量变 quantitative change
量词 measure word; classifier
量纲 dimension
量化 quantization
量力 estimate one's own strength (*or* ability) (and act accordingly)
量项 quantifier
量刑 measurement of penalty
量子 quantum
量贩店 wholesale store
量子论 quantum theory
量才度德 estimate (*or* appraise) sb's moral character and abilities; take sb's measure morally and intellectually
量才录用 give sb work suited to his (*or* her) abilities; assign jobs to people according to their abilities
量力而行 do what one is capable of; act according to one's capability
量入为出 keep expenditures below income;

live within one's means; cut one's coat according to one's cloth
量体裁衣 cut the garment according to the figure—act according to actual circumstances
量子化学 quantum chemistry
量子力学 quantum mechanics
量子生物学 quantum biology

晾 [liàng] 动 ① dry in the air; air-dry; air ② dry in the sun; sun ③ make cool; become cool ④ ignore; slight; give the cold shoulder to
晾干 dry by airing
晾晒 air; sun; spread out to air
晾台 sun terrace (for drying clothes)
晾烟 ① air-curing of tobacco leaves ② air-cured tobacco
晾衣绳 clothesline

liāo (ㄌ丨ㄠ)

撩 [liāo] 动 ① hold (*or* lift) up (a curtain, skirt, etc. from the bottom) ② sprinkle (with one's hand) ⇒ liáo

liáo (ㄌ丨ㄠ)

辽 [liáo] 形 distant; faraway
辽阔 vast; extensive
辽落 open and spacious
辽远 distant; faraway

疗 [liáo] 动 treat; cure
疗程 course (*or* period) of treatment
疗法 therapy; treatment
疗饥 allay one's hunger
疗效 curative effect
疗养 recuperate; convalesce
疗养院 sanatorium; convalescent hospital (*or* home)
疗养胜地 health resort

聊 [liáo] I 副 ① barely; merely; just ② a little; somewhat; slightly II 动 ① rely; depend ② chat; chew the fat
聊赖 bored to death; bored stiff; overcome with boredom
聊且 tentatively; for the moment
聊天(儿) chat; gab
聊天室 (web) chat room
聊备一格 may serve as a specimen
聊表寸心 as a small token of my feelings
聊胜于无 better than nothing
聊以解嘲 make a feeble attempt to explain things away when ridiculed; in a feeble attempt to silence jeers
聊以解忧 just to assuage one's worry

聊以塞责 just to meet the bare requirements
聊以自慰 just to console oneself
聊以卒岁 just to tide over the year

僚 [liáo]
名 ①official ②associate in office
僚机 ①wing plane ②wingman
僚舰 consort
僚属 officials under sb in authority;subordinates;staff
僚友 colleague;associate in office

漻 [liáo]
形 (of water) clear and deep

寥 [liáo]
形 ①few;scanty;scarce ②silent;quiet;deserted ③broad and empty;vast
寥廓 boundless;vast;vague
寥戾 carrying far
寥寥 very few
寥落 few and far between;sparse;scattered
寥寥可数 very few
寥寥无几 very few
寥若晨星 as sparse as the morning stars;few and far between
寥无人烟 no trace of human habitation in sight

撩 [liáo]
动 tease;provoke;stir up;excite (emotions) ⇒liāo
撩拨 ①tease;banter ②incite;provoke
撩动 provoke;stir up
撩逗 tease;provoke
撩人 stirring;exciting;teasing
撩痒 tickle

嘹 [liáo]
嘹亮 resonant;loud and clear

潦 [liáo]
⇒lǎo
潦草 ①(of handwriting) hasty and careless;illegible ②sloppy;slovenly
潦倒 be frustrated;be down on one's luck

寮 [liáo]
名 small house;hut
寮棚 shed;hut

嫽 [liáo]
形 fine;lovely;charming

缭 [liáo]
动 ①entangled ②sew with slanting stitches
缭乱 confused;in a turmoil
缭绕 curl up;wind around
缭缝儿 stitch up a seam
缭贴边 stitch a hem;hem

燎 [liáo]
动 (of fire) spread;burn ⇒liǎo
燎泡 blister raised by a burn (or scald)
燎原 set the prairie ablaze
燎原计划 Prairie Fire Program
燎原烈火 blazing prairie fire

liǎo （ㄌㄧㄠˇ）

了 [liǎo]
I 动 ①end;finish;settle;dispose of ②can:做得了 can do it ③know clearly;understand II 副 entirely ⇒le
了得 horrible;terrible
了结 finish;settle;wind up;bring to an end
了解 ①understand;comprehend ②find out;acquaint oneself with ③understanding;comprehension
了局 ①end ②solution;settlement
了了 [liǎole] be over;end;finish
了却 settle;solve
了然 understand;be clear
了事 dispose of a matter;finish up sth;get sth over
了悟 comprehend;understand
了不得 ① wonderful; terrific ② extremely;awfully;terribly ③terrible;awful
了不起 amazing;terrific;extraordinary
了不相涉 have nothing whatever to do with it;be totally unrelated (or irrelevant)
了此一生 end this life
了如指掌 know sth like the palm of one's hand;have sth at one's fingertips
了无惧色 show no fear at all;look completely undaunted
了无生趣 without any joy of life
了无长进 make little progress

蓼 [liǎo]
名 knotweed ⇒lù
蓼科 polygonaceae
蓼蓝 indigo plant

憭 [liǎo]
形 comprehend;understand

燎 [liǎo]
动 singe ⇒liáo

liào （ㄌㄧㄠˋ）

尥 [liào]
尥蹶子 ①kick back;give a backward kick ②get angry;stir up trouble

钌 [liào]
钌铞儿 hasp and staple

料 [liào]
I 动 ①suppose;expect;anticipate ②take care of;manage II 名 ①material;stuff ②(grain) feed;forage;fodder ③synthetic jade;opaque coloured glass III 量 ①prescription:配一料药 make up a prescription ②liao,a former measure unit for timber (7 *chi* × 1 square *chi*)
料车 skip car;skip
料到 foresee;expect

料定 be certain;know for sure
料及 expect;anticipate
料酒 cooking wine
料理 ①arrange;manage;attend to;take care of ②cuisine;food;dish ③cuisine;cooking
料器 glassware
料峭 chilly
料想 expect;think;presume
料子 ①material for making clothes ②woollen fabric ③qualities;makings;stuff
料理后事 make arrangements for a funeral
料事如神 predict like a prophet;foretell with miraculous accuracy

撂 [liào]
动 ①put down;leave behind;shelve ②throw down;knock down;shoot down ③abandon;discard;cast aside;leave behind
撂挑子 put down the load—give up one's responsibilities;quit one's job

瞭 [liào]
动 watch (from a height or a distance);survey
瞭哨 go on sentry;stand guard
瞭望 watch from a height (or a distance);keep a lookout
瞭望哨 lookout post
瞭望台 observation tower;lookout tower

镣 [liào]
名 fetters;shackles
镣铐 fetters and handcuffs;shackles;irons;chains

liē (ㄌㄧㄝ)

咧 [liē]
⟹liě;lie
咧咧 ①gossip;talk nonsense;blabber;speak carelessly ②(of a child) cry

liě (ㄌㄧㄝˇ)

咧 [liě]
动 ①grin ②talk ⟹liē;lie
咧嘴 draw back the corners of the mouth;grin

裂 [liě]
动 part in the middle;sever;split (or break) open ⟹liè

liè (ㄌㄧㄝˋ)

列 [liè]
Ⅰ 动 ①arrange;line up ②enter in a list;list;rank Ⅱ 名 ①row;file;rank ②kind;sort;category Ⅲ 量 (of a series or row of things):一列火车 a train Ⅳ 形 various;each and every
列表 tabulation;entry;listing
列兵 private
列车 train
列当 broomrape

列岛 a chain of islands;archipelago
列队 line up
列国 the various countries (or states,kingdoms)
列举 enumerate;list
列强 the Great Powers
列位 all of you;gentlemen;ladies and gentlemen
列席 attend (a meeting) as an observer (or a nonvoting delegate);attend without voting rights
列阵 array
列传 biographies
列车员 attendant (on a train)
列车长 head of a train crew
列队相迎 line up to welcome
列宁主义 Leninism
列入计划 be listed in the plan
列入议程 place on the agenda;include in the agenda
列席代表 delegate without the right to vote;nonvoting delegate
列席会议 attend a conference without voting rights
列祖列宗 successive generations of ancestors;an array of ancestors
列车调度员 train dispatcher
列车时刻表 train schedule;timetable
列氏温度计 the Réaumur thermometer

劣 [liè]
形 ①bad;inferior;of low quality ②minor;smaller than some standard
劣币 sinker
劣等 of inferior quality;low-grade;poor
劣弧 minor arc
劣化 degradation
劣货 poor quality goods;goods of inferior quality
劣迹 misdeed;evil doing
劣马 ①inferior horse;nag ②vicious horse
劣绅 evil gentry
劣势 inferior position;unfavourable situation
劣质 of poor (or low) quality;inferior
劣种 inferior strain (or breed,stock)
劣根性 deep-rooted bad habits;an inherent weakness
劣质煤 inferior coal;faulty coal
劣迹昭彰 have a notorious record
劣质工程 shoddy projects

冽 [liè]
形 cold;chilly;icy

洌 [liè]
形 (of water or wine) clear;limpid

埒 [liè]
动 equal;be on a par with

烈 [liè]
Ⅰ 形 ①strong;fierce;intense ②staunch;upright;stern Ⅱ 名 ①person dying for a just

cause ②exploits;achievements
烈度 intensity
烈风 strong gale
烈火 raging fire;raging flames
烈酒 moonshine;hard drink;strong drink
烈马 savage horse;fiery steed
烈日 burning sun;scorching sun
烈士 ①martyr ②(in former times) a man of high endeavour;hero
烈属 members of a revolutionary martyr's family
烈性 ①spirited ②strong
烈焰 raging flames;roaring blaze
烈士墓 the tomb of a revolutionary martyr
烈士陵园 revolutionary martyrs' cemetery; martyrs' park
烈性大麻 high-potent cannabis
烈性炸药 high explosive
烈火见真金 pure gold proves its worth in a blazing fire—people of worth show their mettle during trials and tribulations;trials test character
烈士纪念碑 a monument to revolutionary martyrs

捩 [liè]
劢 twist;turn

猎 [liè]
Ⅰ 劢 hunt Ⅱ 形 hunting
猎豹 cheetah
猎场 hunting ground;hunting field
猎刀 hunting knife
猎狗 hunting dog;hound
猎户 hunter;huntsman
猎获 capture (or kill) in hunting;bag
猎奇 hunt for novelty;seek novelty
猎枪 shotgun;fowling piece;hunting rifle
猎区 hunting-field
猎取 ①hunt ②pursue;seek;hunt for
猎犬 hunting dog;hound
猎人 hunter;huntsman
猎手 hunter
猎头 headhunting;headhunter
猎物 prey;quarry;game
猎艳 ①rack one's brains for ornate diction ②chase after pretty women
猎鹰 falcon
猎装 hunting suit;hunting outfit
猎户座 Orion
猎获物 bag
猎狼犬 wolfhound
猎鹿犬 deerhound
猎潜艇 submarine chaser
猎头公司 headhunter; manhunters & Co.; headhunting agent (or agency,firm)

裂 [liè]
Ⅰ 劢 split;crack;rend Ⅱ 名 gap ➡lie
裂变 fission

裂缝 ①crack;split ②rift;crevice;crack;fissure
裂果 dehiscent fruit
裂痕 rift;crack;fissure
裂化 cracking (in the distillation of petroleum)
裂解 splitting decomposition;splitting
裂开 crack open;split open
裂孔 gap
裂口 ①crack;split ②breach;gap;crack;split ③vent (of a volcano)
裂伤 lacerated wound
裂纹 ①crack (the sides being still together) ②crackle (on pottery,porcelain,etc.)
裂隙 crack;crevice;fracture
裂化炉 cracking still (or furnace,heater)
裂化气 cracked gas
裂隙水 crevice water
裂殖菌 schizomycete
裂变产物 fission product
裂变武器 the fission type of weapon
裂解作用 splitting action
裂口火山锥 breached cone

趔 [liè]

趔趄 stagger;reel

lie（·ㄌㄧㄝ）

咧 [lie]
劢 (used like 了,啦 or 哩);好咧,我这就来。Ok,I'll be with you in a moment. ➡liě;liè

līn（ㄌㄧㄣ）

拎 [līn]
劢 carry;hold;lift
拎包 handbag;shopping bag;bag

lín（ㄌㄧㄣˊ）

邻 [lín]
Ⅰ 名 ① neighbour ② administrative unit covering five households Ⅱ 形 neighbouring; near;adjacent
邻邦 neighbouring country
邻村 neighbouring village
邻国 neighbouring country
邻海 adjacent sea
邻家 next-door family;next-door (or close) neighbour
邻角 adjacent angles
邻接 border on;be next to;be contiguous to; adjoin
邻近 ①be near;be close to;be adjacent to ② neighbourhood;vicinity
邻居 neighbour

邻里 ①neighbourhood ②people of the neighbourhood;neighbours
邻舍 neighbour
邻位 ortho-position
邻桌 adjacent table

林 [lín]

〔名〕①forest;woods;grove ②cluster of similar things;circles ③forestry
林产 forest products
林场 forestry centre (including tree nurseries,lumber camps,etc.);tree farm
林带 forest belt
林道 forest road
林地 forest land;woodland;timberland
林冠 crown canopy;crown cover
林海 immense forest
林间 woodland
林警 forest ranger
林垦 forestry and land reclamation
林立 (of masts,smokestacks,derricks,tall buildings,etc.) stand (in great numbers) like a forest
林龄 age of stand
林木 ①forest;woods ②forest tree
林檎 ①Chinese pear-leaved crabapple ②gift for a wedding,etc. ③bonus
林区 forest zone;forest region;forest
林涛 the soughing of the wind in forest trees
林业 forestry
林园 wooden land;a park of trees and vegetation
林子 woods;grove;forest
林产品 forest productor
林阴道 boulevard;avenue
林林总总 numerous;in great abundance
林业工人 forest worker;forester
林草植被率 forestry and grass coverage

临 [lín]

〔动〕①face;confront;overlook;be close to ②arrive;be present ③be about to;be on the point of;happen just before ④copy
临本 copy (of a painting,etc.)
临别 at parting;just before parting
临产 about to give birth;parturient
临场 ①when attending an examination;when participating in a contest ②come personally to the site (or spot)
临床 clinical
临到 ①just before;on the point of ②befall; happen to
临画 copy a painting
临机 face an emergency
临界 critical
临近 close to;close on
临了 finally;in the end
临门 ①come to the house ②facing the goal
临摹 copy (a model of calligraphy or painting)

临盆 be giving birth to a child;be confined;be in labour
临时 ①at the time when sth is needed (or is expected to happen) ②temporarily;for the time being ③temporary;provisional
临死 on one's deathbed
临头 befall;happen
临危 ①be dying (from illness) ②face death (or deadly peril)
临刑 just before execution
临战 just before going into battle
临终 approaching one's end;immediately before one's death;on one's deathbed
临床学 clinical medicine
临界点 critical point
临界角 critical angle
临界态 critical state
临时工 casual labourer;temporary worker
临别赠言 words of advice at parting;parting advice
临产阵痛 labour pains;birth pangs
临床表现 clinical manifestation
临床医生 clinician
临床应用 clinical practice
临界体积 critical size
临界温度 critical temperature
临渴掘井 not dig a well until one is thirsty—start acting too late;make an eleventh-hour attempt
临时船闸 temporary ship lock
临时代办 chargé d'affaires ad interim
临时动议 extempore motion
临时法庭 provisional court
临时费用 interim (or incidental) expenses
临时雇员 grass hand
临时户口 temporary residence permit
临时提议 incidental motion
临时协议 provisional agreement
临时证书 (in diplomacy) temporary credentials (or papers)
临时政府 provisional (or interim) government
临时执照 temporary license
临时主席 interim chairman
临危不惧 face danger fearlessly;betray no fear in face of danger
临危授命 be ready to give one's life in times of national danger
临渊羡鱼 stand by a pond longing for fish;One should take practical steps to achieve one's aims.
临阵磨枪 sharpen one's spear just before going into battle—start to prepare at the last moment
临阵脱逃 desert on the eve of a battle;sneak away at a critical juncture
临终关怀 hospice care

临终遗言 deathbed testament;last words
临海经济带 coastal economic belts
临时抱佛脚 embrace Buddha's feet in one's hour of need—seek help at the last moment;make a frantic last-minute effort
临时主教练 caretaker coach

啉 [lín]

◇喹啉 quinoline

淋 [lín]

动 ① pour;splatter;drench ② sprinkle;splash;spray ➡ lìn

淋巴 lymph
淋漓 ①dripping wet ②(of a piece of writing or a speech) free from inhibition
淋淋 dripping wet
淋湿 be soaked;be splashed wet
淋透 be drenched through
淋洗 drip washing
淋雨 get wet in the rain
淋浴 shower bath;shower
淋巴结 lymph node (or gland)
淋巴球 lymphocyte
淋巴液 lymph
淋巴结炎 lymphnoditis
淋巴肉瘤 lymphosarcoma
淋巴组织 lymphoma
淋漓尽致 vividly and incisively;in great detail

琳 [lín]

名 beautiful jade

琳琅 beautiful jade;gem
琳琅满目 a superb collection of beautiful things;a feast for the eyes

粼 [lín]

粼粼 (of water,stone,etc.) clear;crystalline

嶙 [lín]

嶙峋 ①(of mountain rocks,cliffs,etc.) jagged;rugged;craggy ②(of a person) bony;thin

遴 [lín]

动 choose carefully;select

遴选 select;choose

霖 [lín]

名 continuous heavy rain

霖雨 continuous heavy rain

辚 [lín]

辚辚 the sound made by a running cart,chariot,etc.

磷 [lín]

名 phosphorus (P)

磷肥 phosphate fertilizer
磷光 phosphorescence
磷化 parkerizing process
磷火 phosphorescent light;will-o'-the-wisp;jack-o'-lantern

磷酸 phosphoric acid
磷虾 euphausiid shrimp
磷脂 phosphatide
磷光体 phosphor
磷矿粉 ground phosphate rock
磷酸铵 ammonium phosphate
磷酸钙 calcium phosphate
磷酸盐 phosphate
磷脂酸 phosphatidic acid

瞵 [lín]

动 (of eagles) descry;gaze at

鳞 [lín]

Ⅰ 名 scale (of fish,etc.) Ⅱ 形 like the scales of a fish

鳞甲 scale and shell (of reptiles and arthropods)
鳞茎 bulb
鳞片 ①scale (on fish or insects' wings) ②bud scale
鳞伤 mass of bruise
鳞屑 scales of skin that peel off
鳞爪 scales and claws—small bits;fragments;odd scraps
鳞次栉比 (of buildings) like fish scales and comb teeth;in tight rows;row upon row

麟 [lín]

名 kylin;(Chinese) unicorn

麟凤龟龙 the unicorn, the phoenix, the tortoise,and the dragon—worthy men

lǐn (ㄌㄧㄣˇ)

凛 [lǐn]

形 ①cold;frigid ②strict;rigorous;stern;severe ③afraid;fearful

凛冽 piercingly cold
凛凛 ①cold ②stern;awe-inspiring
凛然 stern;awe-inspiring
凛若冰霜 look severe;have a forbidding manner
凛于夜行 dread going on a journey at night

lìn (ㄌㄧㄣˋ)

吝 [lìn]

形 stingy;miserly;mean;closefisted

吝啬 stingy;niggardly;miserly;mean
吝惜 grudge;stint
吝啬鬼 miser;niggard;skinflint

淋 [lìn]

动 strain;filter ➡ lín

淋病 gonorrhoea
淋滤 leaching
淋溶 leaching;eluviation
淋溶层 leached horizon;eluvial horizon;eluvium

赁 [lìn]

动 rent;hire;lease

赁费 rental fee;rent

赁金 rental fee;rent

líng (ㄌㄧㄥˊ)

伶 [líng]
［名］actor;actress
伶仃 left alone without help;lonely
伶俐 clever;bright;quick-witted
伶人 actor
伶牙俐齿 have the gift of the gab;have a glib tongue;have a ready tongue

灵 [líng]
Ⅰ［形］① quick;clever;bright;nimble;flexible ② efficacious;effective Ⅱ［名］① mind;soul;spirit;intelligence ②deity;fairy;sprite;elf ③bier;hearse;the deceased
灵便 ①nimble;agile ②easy to handle;handy
灵车 hearse
灵床 ①bier ②a bed kept as it was when the person was alive
灵动 agile
灵感 inspiration
灵怪 elf;goblin;sprite
灵光 ① miraculous brightness ② bright light around the head of a god (or Buddha)
灵魂 soul
灵活 ①nimble;agile;quick ②flexible;elastic
灵机 sudden inspiration;brainwave
灵柩 coffin;bier
灵快 nimble;agile
灵猫 civet (cat)
灵敏 sensitive;keen;agile;acute
灵牌 spirit tablet
灵气 anima
灵巧 dexterous;nimble;skilful;ingenious
灵寝 seat of a bier
灵台 ① the mind;the heart ② a platform on which a coffin (or a cinerary casket) is placed
灵堂 mourning hall
灵通 ① having quick access to information;well-informed ②be of use (or help)
灵童 soul boy
灵位 spirit tablet
灵犀 magic horn (i.e. rhinoceros horn with its threadlike white core, mentioned in old texts as having a high sensibility)
灵效 (usu. of drugs) effective;efficacious
灵性 intelligence (of animals)
灵验 ① efficacious;effective ②(of a prediction,etc.) accurate;right
灵芝 magic fungus—glossy ganoderma
灵长目 Primates
灵活性 flexibility;elasticity;mobility
灵敏度 sensitivity
灵丹妙药 a magic (or wonder) drug;a miraculous cure;panacea
灵魂深处 place in one's innermost soul

灵机一动 have a brainwave
灵巧炸弹 laser-guided bombs
灵魂工程师 engineers of the soul;teachers
灵活机动的战略战术 flexible strategy and tactics

囹 [líng]
囹圄 jail;prison

泠 [líng]
［形］cool and fresh

玲 [líng]
玲珑 ①(of things) ingeniously and delicately wrought;exquisite ②(of people) clever and nimble
玲珑剔透 exquisitely carved;beautifully wrought

梿 [líng]
［名］Eurya plant

瓵 [líng]
［名］water jar

铃 [líng]
［名］①bell ②bell-shaped things ③boll;bud
铃铛 small bell
铃鼓 tambourine
铃扣 bellpull
铃兰 lily of the valley
铃片 burr shale
铃碗 bell dome

皊 [líng]
［形］white

凌 [líng]
Ⅰ［动］①rise high;tower aloft ②approach;draw close ③insult;bully;violate Ⅱ［名］ice
凌波 ① dashing waves ② like treading the waves (said of a beautiful woman's graceful way of walking)
凌晨 in the small hours;before dawn
凌迟 (in imperial times) the punishment of dismemberment and the lingering death (for heinous crimes)
凌驾 place oneself above;override
凌空 be high up in the air;soar (or tower) aloft
凌厉 swift and fierce
凌乱 in disorder;in a mess
凌日 transit
凌辱 insult;humiliate
凌汛 spring flood caused by melting river ice
凌云 reach the clouds;soar to the skies
凌锥 icicle
凌波舟 surf boat
凌霄花 Chinese trumpet creeper
凌波仙子 fairy walking over ripples
凌云壮志 have a strong resolution to reach the clouds;have high aspirations;have lofty aspirations

陵 [líng]
［名］①hill;mound ②imperial tomb;mausole-

um
陵谷 hills and valleys
陵墓 mausoleum;tomb
陵寝 emperor's（*or* king's）resting place;
　mausoleum
陵园 funerary park;cemetery

聆 ［líng］
　囝 listen;hear
聆教 hear your words of wisdom
聆听 listen（respectfully）
聆悉 learn;hear;have learned from a letter
　that

菱 ［líng］
　名 ling;water caltrop
菱角 ling;waternut;water caltrop
菱形 diamond;rhombus;lozenge
菱镁矿 magnesite
菱锰矿 rhodochrosite
菱铁矿 siderite
菱锌矿 smithsonite
菱形队形 diamond formation
菱形六面体 rhombohedron
菱形无线网 multiple rhombic antenna

棂 ［líng］
　名（window）lattice;latticework

蛉 ［líng］
◇白蛉 sand fly

笭 ［líng］
　名 ①bamboo curtain ②rack

舲 ［líng］
　名 ①boat with windows ②small boat

翎 ［líng］
　名 ①plume;tail（*or* wing）feather;quill ②
peacock feather worn at the back of a Qing
Dynasty official's hat
翎毛 ① plume ② a type of classical Chinese
　painting featuring birds and animals

羚 ［líng］
　名 ①antelope ②antelope's horn
羚牛 takin
羚羊 antelope;gazelle
羚羊角 antelope's horn

绫 ［líng］
　名 damask silk
绫锦 silk brocade
绫子 damask silk
绫罗绸缎 silks and satins

零 ［líng］
Ⅰ 形 ①fractional;fragmentary ②odd Ⅱ 数
①（*placed between two numbers to indicate
a smaller quantity following a larger one*）
②zero;nought;nil ③zero sign;nought ④zero
（on a thermometer）Ⅲ 名 fraction;odd lot;ex-
tra Ⅳ 囝 ①wither and fall ②fall
零吃 between-meal nibbles;snacks
零档 zero span;zero step
零点 zero hour;midnight
零度 zero degrees

零分 zero;scoreless;goose egg
零工 ① odd job;short-term hired labour ②
odd-job man;casual labourer
零花 ① spend money on minor purchases ②
pocket money
零件 ① part（of a machine）② spare parts;
spares
零乱 in disorder;in a mess;all over the shop
零落 ①（of plants）withered;stripped of leaves ②desolate;wretched;in reduced circumstances ③scattered;sporadic
零卖 ① sell retail;retail ② sell by the piece
（*or* in small quantities）
零钱 ①small change ②pocket money
零散 scattered
零时 zero hour;midnight
零食 between-meal nibbles;snacks
零售 ① sell retail;retail ② sell by the piece
（*or* in small quantities）
零碎 ① scrappy;fragmentary;piecemeal ②
odds and ends;oddments;bits and pieces
零头 ① the remaining sum beyond the round
figure ②remnant（of cloth）
零位 zero;zero position
零星 ① fragmentary;odd;piecemeal ② scattered;sporadic
零用·① spend money on minor purchases ②
pocket money
零部件 spare parts;component parts
零对策 zero game
零对象 null object
零活儿 odd jobs
零距离 zero distance
零口供 zero confession
零库存 zero stock
零利率 zero rate
零售店 retail shop（*or* store）
零售额 turnover（from retail trade）
零售商 retail trader（*or* dealer）;retailer
零售网 retail network
零用费 petty cash
零用钱 pocket money
零用账 petty cash book;petty cash account
零增长 zero growth
零指数 zero exponent
零存整取 small deposits for lump withdrawal;
　instalment savings with the principal and
　interest obtainable at maturity
零担货运 less-than-car-load lot（L.C.L.）
零点方案 zero option
零七八碎 ① scattered and disorderly ② miscellaneous trifles;odds and ends
零敲碎打 do sth bit by bit（*or* off and on）;
　adopt a piecemeal approach
零售价格 retail price
零售市场 retail market
零售总额 total volume of retail sales

零点人口增长 zero population growth
零售物价总指数 general index of retail prices
零售物价上涨幅度 rate of retail price rise

龄 [líng]
名 ①age;years ②length of time (*or* service);duration ③instar;stadium

鲮 [líng]
名 dace

líng（ㄌㄧㄥˊ）

令 [líng]
量 ream:两令新闻纸 two reams of newsprint ➠ lìng

岭 [líng]
名 ① ridge of a mountain;mountain ② mountain range ③the Five Ridges

岭南 south of the Five Ridges——the area covering Guangdong and Guangxi

领 [líng]
Ⅰ 名 ① neck ② collar ③ outline;main point;collarband;neckband Ⅱ 动 ①lead;usher;take ②have jurisdiction over;be in possession of;own ③receive;draw;get ④accept ⑤ understand;comprehend;grasp Ⅲ 量（of a gown,coat,mat,etc.）:穿了一领新长袍 wear a new robe

领班 ①head a work group ②gaffer;foreman
领唱 ① lead a chorus ② leading singer (of a chorus)
领带 necktie;tie
领导 ① lead;exercise leadership ② leadership;leader
领地 ①manor (of a feudal lord);domain ② territory
领队 ①lead a group ②the leader of a group (*or* sports team,etc.)
领港 ① pilot a ship into (*or* out of) a harbour;pilot ②(harbour) pilot
领钩 hook and eye on the collar
领海 territorial waters;territorial sea
领航 ①navigate;pilot ②navigator;pilot
领会 understand;comprehend;grasp
领江 ①navigate a ship on a river ②river pilot
领奖 receive reward;receive prize
领教 ①receive instructions ②ask sb's advice (*or* opinion) ③used ironically
领结 bow tie
领巾 scarf;neckerchief
领进 usher into;lead to;introduce into
领军 bellwether
领空 territorial sky (*or* air);territorial air space
领口 ① collarband; neckband ② the place where the two ends of a collar meet
领扣 collar button;collar stud
领款 receive funds;draw money
领路 lead the way

领略 have a taste of;understand;appreciate
领情 feel grateful to sb;appreciate the kindness
领取 receive;draw;get
领圈 neckband
领事 consul
领受 accept (kindness,etc.);receive
领水 ①inland waters ②territorial waters
领头 take the lead;be the first to do sth
领土 territory
领舞 ①lead a dance ②leading dancer
领悟 comprehend;grasp
领先 be in the lead;lead
领衔 head list of signers (of a document); head list of actors
领袖 leader
领养 adopt (a child)
领有 possess;own
领域 ① territory; domain; realm ② field; sphere;domain;realm
领章 collar badge;collar insignia
领主 feudal lord;suzerain
领子 collar
领罪 admit one's guilt;plead guilty
领带卡 tie clasp;tie clip
领导权 leadership;authority;overall control
领导人 leader
领导者 leader
领队机 lead aircraft
领工资 get one's salary (*or* wages)
领航员 navigator;pilot
领款人 payee
领路狗 guide dog
领路人 guide
领事处 consular section
领事馆 consulate
领事团 consular corps (c.c.)
领水员 navigator;pilot
领头羊 bellwether
领袖欲 drive (*or* desire) to be a leader
领带扣针 tiepin
领导班子 the leadership;leading community; leading body;cast of leaders
领导潮流 lead the trend (tendency)
领导地位 a position of leadership;status as a leader
领导方法 method of leadership
领导干部 leading cadre
领导骨干 the backbone (*or* mainstay, key members) of the leadership
领导核心 the core of leadership;leading core
领导机关 leading body
领导水平 the level of leadership
领导小组 leading group
领导艺术 the art of leadership
领导有方 wise leadership
领导作风 the work style of the leadership;

leadership style
领导作用 leading role
领海主权 sovereignty over the territorial seas
领航飞机 pathfinder aircraft
领事条例 consular act
领事协定 consular agreement
领事证书 exequatur
领土割让 cession of territory
领土扩张 territorial expansion; territorial aggrandizement
领土完整 territorial integrity
领土要求 territorial claims
领土争端 territorial disputes
领土主权 territorial sovereignty
领衔主演 star in a film; be a featured actor (*or* actress)
领海管辖权 jurisdiction within territorial water
领事裁判权 consular jurisdiction
领事委任书 certificate of appointment of consul; consular commission
领土不可侵犯性 territorial inviolability
领导水平和执政水平 leading and governing ability; level of leadership and government
领土、领空、领海主权 sovereignty over territorial land, air and seas
领导干部任期经济责任审计制度 system auditing the economic responsibility of leading cadres during their terms of office

lìng （ㄌ丨ㄥˋ）

另 [lìng]
I 代 other; another II 副 besides; in addition III 形 separate
另案 a separate case
另册 the other register, a Qing Dynasty census book for listing disreputable people
另函 ①a separate letter ②write another letter
另寄 post (*or* mail) separately; post (*or* mail) under separate cover
另类 alternative
另外 ①in addition; besides ②different; other
另行 (do sth) separately
另页 separate sheet; separate page
另议 discuss (*or* negotiate) separately
另当别论 should be regarded as a different matter
另搞一套 go one's own way
另类时装 alternative fashion
另立门户 set up separate sect
另谋生路 find another way of earning a living
另起炉灶 make fresh start; set up a "new kitchen"
另请高明 find someone better qualified (than myself)

另眼相看 ①regard (*or* look up to) sb with special respect; give sb special treatment ②view sb in a new, more favourable light; see sb in a new light
另有安排 make separate arrangements
另有所图 have other fish to fry; have ulterior motives
另有想法 have other (*or* different) ideas

令 [lìng]
I 动 ①issue an order; order ②make; cause II 名 ① command; order; decree ② drinking game ③ ancient official title ④ season III 形 ①good; excellent ②your ⇒ lǐng
令爱 your daughter
令箭 an arrow-shaped token of authority
令郎 your son
令妹 your sister
令堂 your mother
令兄 your brother
令尊 your father
令出如山 Orders are like a mountain (i.e. cannot be changed and compel obedience).
令箭荷花 nopalxochia
令人齿冷 arouse scorn
令人发指 get one's hackles up; make one bristle with anger
令人费解 elude understanding
令人喷饭 side-splitting; screamingly funny
令人捧腹 set people roaring with laughter; make one burst out laughing
令人神往 fire one's imagination; have a strong appeal for one
令人生厌 make one feel disgusted
令人痛心 It really hurts to think of it!; cut one to the heart
令人作呕 make one sick; be nauseating; be revolting
令行禁止 Any order will be immediately carried out, and any prohibition will be heeded.

呤 [lìng]
◇嘌呤 purine

liū （ㄌ丨ㄡ）

溜 [liū]
I 动 ①slide; glide ②sneak off; slip away ③take a look; glance II 形 smooth III 副 ① along: 溜河边走 walk along the riverside ② very; extremely ⇒ liù
溜边 keep to the edge (of a road, river, etc.)
溜冰 ①skate ②roller-skate; go roller-skating
溜达 stroll; saunter; go for a walk
溜掉 slip; vanish; escape
溜光 very smooth; sleek; glossy
溜号 sneak away; slink off
溜滑 skid

溜尖 very sharp
溜净 extremely clean
溜圆 smooth and round
溜匀 very evenly
溜走 slip away；slink away；slope off
溜冰场 skating rink
溜肩膀 ①sloping shoulders ②lacking a proper sense of responsibility；irresponsible
溜须拍马 smooth sb's beard and pat his horse's hindquarters—lick sb's boots；toady to；fawn on
溜之大吉 sneak away；slink off；make oneself scarce

熘 [liū]
〔动〕sauté (with thick gravy)；quick-fry
熘腰花 kidney sauté

蹓 [liū]
〔动〕sneak off；slip away ➡liù

liú (ㄌㄧㄡ)

刘 [liú]
刘海儿 bang；fringe

浏 [liú]
〔形〕①(of water) clear；limpid ②(of wind) swift
浏览 glance over；skim through；browse
浏览器 browser

留 [liú]
〔动〕① remain；stay ② study abroad：留日 study in Japan ③ask sb to stay；keep sb where he is；detain；我留她吃晚饭。I ask her to stay for dinner. ④concentrate on sth ⑤reserve；keep；retain；save ⑥ let grow；grow；wear ⑦ accept；take；keep ⑧ leave behind；leave
留步 (said by departing guest to host) Don't bother to see me out；Don't bother to come any further.
留成 retain a portion (of earnings, profits, etc.)
留出 keep out；set apart；set aside
留存 ①preserve；keep ②remain；be extant
留待 wait till later
留底 office copy
留点 stationary point
留话 leave a message；leave word
留级 (of pupils, etc.) fail to go up to the next grade (or year)；repeat the year's work；stay behind
留客 detain a guest；ask a guest to stay
留空 leave a blank；leave a space in writing
留利 retained profits
留恋 ①be reluctant to leave (a place)；can't bear to part (from sb or with sth) ②recall with nostalgia

留量 allowance
留门 leave a door unlocked (or unbolted) (in expectation of sb during the night)
留名 leave behind a good reputation
留难 make things difficult for sb；put obstacles in sb's way
留念 accept (or keep) as a souvenir
留鸟 resident (bird)
留情 show mercy or forgiveness
留任 retain a post；remain (or continue) in office
留神 be careful；take care
留守 ①act for the emperor during his absence from the capital ②stay behind to take care of things；stay behind for garrison or liaison duty (after the main force has left)
留宿 ①put up a guest for the night ②stay overnight；put up for the night
留题 leave one's comments
留头 let the hair grow long
留下 leave；keep；stay；remain
留校 remain at a school (or university) after graduation as a faculty member
留心 be careful；take care
留学 study abroad
留言 leave one's comments；leave a message
留医 be hospitalized
留意 be careful；look out；keep one's eyes open
留影 ①take a photo as a memento；have a picture taken as a souvenir ②a picture taken as a souvenir
留用 continue to employ；keep on
留职 retain one's post
留种 reserve seed for planting；have seed stock
留长发 wear long hair
留底稿 keep the manuscript
留后路 keep a way open for retreat；leave a way out
留后手 leave room for manoeuvre
留胡子 grow a beard (or moustache)
留兰香 spearmint
留平头 have closely cropped hair
留声机 gramophone；phonograph
留守处 rear office
留尾巴 leave loose ends
留学生 student studying abroad；student abroad；returned student
留言簿 visitors' book
留一手 hold back a trick or two (in teaching a trade or skill)
留余地 allow for unforeseen circumstances；leave some leeway
留置权 lien
留种地 seed-breeding field
留座位 reserve a seat (for sb)
留党察看 be placed on probation within the

Party
留守人员 rear personnel
留校察看 be kept in school under surveillance
留学咨询 consulting on the study abroad
留用人员 personnel (of the old regime) who were kept on after liberation
留有余地 leave some leeway; leave a margin of safety; allow for unforeseen circumstances
留职停薪 take an unpaid leave; stop payment of salary but retain office; retain the job but suspend the salary
留得青山在,不怕没柴烧 As long as the green hills last, there'll always be wood to burn.

流 [liú]
I 动 ①flow ②move; drift; wander; migrate ③ spread; circulate; propagate ④ change for the worse; degenerate ⑤banish; send into exile Ⅱ 名 ①stream of water; current; torrent ②sth resembling a stream of water; current ③ class; rate; grade; 一流大学 first class university; leading university ④(short for 流明)lumen
流弊 corrupt practices; abuses
流标 abortive tender
流产 ①(of a woman) have a miscarriage; miscarry ②(of a plan, etc.) miscarry; fall through
流畅 (of writing) easy and smooth
流程 ①a distance travelled by a stream of water ②technological process ③circuit
流传 spread; circulate; hand down
流窜 flee hither and thither
流弹 stray bullet
流动 ①(of water, air, etc.) flow; circulate ②go from place to place; be on the move; be mobile
流毒 ①exert a pernicious (or baneful) influence ②pernicious (or baneful) influence
流放 ①banish; send into exile ②float (logs) downstream
流感 flu
流寇 ①roving bandits ②roving rebel bands
流浪 roam about; lead a vagrant life
流离 wander about as a refugee or vagrant
流利 fluent; smooth
流连 be reluctant to leave; linger on
流量 volume of flow; rate of flow; flow; discharge; flow capacity
流露 show unintentionally (one's thoughts or feelings); reveal; betray
流落 wander about destitute
流氓 ①rogue; hoodlum; hooligan; gangster ②immoral (or indecent) behaviour; hooliganism; indecency
流民 refugee; exiled person
流明 lumen

流年 ①fleeting time ②(in fortune-telling) prediction of a person's luck in a given year
流拍 abortive lot
流派 school; sect
流气 ①rascally ②rascally behaviour; hooliganism
流散 scatter; drift
流沙 shifting sands; drifting sands; quicksand
流失 ①run off; be washed away ②(of students) drop out
流食 liquid diet
流逝 (of time) pass; elapse
流水 ①flowing water ②turnover (in business)
流苏 tassels
流速 ①velocity of flow ②current velocity
流淌 (of liquid) flow
流体 fluid
流通 (of air, money, commodities, etc.) circulate
流亡 be forced to leave one's native land; go into exile
流网 drift net
流星 ①meteor; shooting star ②(in acrobatics) meteors
流行 popular; prevalent; fashionable; in vogue
流血 lose blood; shed blood; draw blood; bleed
流言 rumour; gossip
流域 river valley; river basin; drainage area
流质 liquid diet (for patients)
流转 ①wander about; roam; be on the move ②(of goods or capital) circulate
流鼻涕 have a running nose
流程图 flow chart; flow diagram
流窜犯 criminal on the run
流动哨 person (or soldier) on patrol duty; patrol
流动性 mobility; fluidity
流口水 make one's mouth water; run of the mouth; drool
流媒体 streaming media
流水号 serial number
流水席 feast at which guests are served as they come
流水线 assembly line
流水账 day-to-day (bookkeeping) account; current account
流速仪 current meter (for use in water conservancy)
流铁槽 iron runner
流通管 runner pipe
流通券 (in former times) paper money issued by a provincial bank to be circulated in a given area
流纹岩 rhyolite
流线型 streamlined
流星暴 star shower

流星尘 meteoric dust
流星群 meteor stream;meteor swarm
流星雨 meteor (*or* meteoric) shower
流行病 epidemic disease
流行色 fashionable colour
流行性 epidemic
流转税 turnover tax
流传甚广 spread far and wide
流动存款 float deposit
流动费用 floating charge
流动红旗 mobile red banner
流动货车 shop-on-wheels
流动人口 transient population;floating population;mobile population
流动商店 mobile shop
流动售货 mobile sale
流动支票 circulating cheque
流动资本 circulating capital;floating capital;working capital
流动资产 current assets;liquid assets;floating assets
流动资金 circulating fund;operating fund;revolving fund
流芳百世 leave a good name for a hundred generations;leave a good name to posterity;win immortal fame;leave one's mark on history
流离失所 become destitute and homeless;wander about homeless
流里流气 rascally
流连忘返 enjoy oneself so much as to forget to go home;linger on with no thought of leaving;cannot tear oneself away
流落江湖 live a vagabond life
流落他乡 lead a wretched life far from home;be stranded in a strange land
流氓集团 gang of hooligans (*or* hoodlums);criminal gang
流氓习气 hooliganism
流氓行为 indecent behaviour;hooliganism
流年不利 an unlucky year
流散人口 drifting population
流水作业 assembly line method;flow process;conveyer system;line production
流体力学 hydromechanics;fluid mechanics
流通费用 circulation costs
流通货币 currency
流通领域 the field of circulation
流通手段 medium (*or* means) of circulation
流通体系 circulation system
流通网络 circulation network
流通证券 negotiable instrument
流通秩序 the sequence of circulation
流亡政府 government in exile;government-in-exile
流星防护 meteoroid protection
流行病学 epidemiology

流行歌曲 pop song;pop music;pop
流行文化 pop culture
流行音乐 pop music
流言飞语 rumours and slanders
流于形式 become a mere formality
流动售票车 ticket-office-on-wheels
流动图书馆 travelling library
流氓活动罪 offense of indecent activities
流氓无产者 lumpen-proletariat
流体动力学 hydrokinetics;hydrodynamics
流体静力学 hydrostatics
流体压力计 manometer
流线型列车 streamlined train
流线型设计 airflow design
流行性感冒 influenza;flu
流通体制改革 reform of the circulation (*or* distribution) system
流行性腮腺炎 mumps
流言止于智者 Rumours find no credence with a wise man.
流动电影放映队 travelling film projection team;mobile cinema team
流行歌曲排行榜 best pop song list
流行性乙型脑炎 epidemic encephalitis B
流行性脑脊髓膜炎 epidemic cerebrospinal meningitis
流水不腐,户枢不蠹 Running water is never stale and a door-hinge never gets worm-eaten.

琉 [liú]

琉璃 coloured glaze
琉璃猫 ①glazed cat ②a metaphor for a mean person
琉璃塔 glazed pagoda
琉璃瓦 glazed tile
琉球群岛 the Ryukyu Islands

硫 [liú]

【名】 sulphur (S)
硫化 vulcanize
硫磺 sulphur
硫酸 sulphuric acid
硫胺素 thiamin(e)
硫化汞 mercuric sulphide
硫化剂 vulcanized agent;curing agent
硫化氢 hydrogen sulphide
硫化物 sulphide
硫磺泉 sulphur spring
硫酸铵 ammonium sulphate
硫酸盐 sulphate
硫化染料 sulphur dyes
硫化橡胶 vulcanized rubber;vulcanizate
硫磺温泉 solfatara
硫代硫酸钠 sodium thiosulphate

馏 [liú]

【动】 distil ⇒liù
馏份 fraction;cut

馏出油 distillate oil

旒 [liú] 名 ①flowing ribbon attached to a flag;tassels ②stringed jade attached to the imperial crown

骝 [liú] 名 red horse with black mane and tail

榴 [liú] 名 pomegranate
榴弹 high explosive shell
榴莲 durian
榴弹炮 howitzer
榴霰弹 shrapnel;canister (shot);case shot

镏 [liú] 动 ①gild ②kill ➡ liù
镏金 gold-plating

瘤 [liú] 名 tumour
瘤胃 rumen
瘤子 tumour
瘤胃膨胀 bloat

鎏 [liú] 名 fine gold

liǔ (ㄌㄧㄡˇ)

柳 [liǔ] 名 willow
柳林 osier bed
柳眉 arched eyebrows (of a woman)
柳木 willow
柳琴 a plucked stringed instrument
柳杉 cryptomeria
柳树 willow;osier
柳丝 fine willow branches;wicker
柳条 willow twig;osier;wicker
柳絮 willow catkins
柳腰 willowy (or slender) waist
柳阴 the shade of a willow tree
柳莺 willow warbler
柳枝 withy;willow branch
柳条筐 wicker basket
柳条帽 wicker safety helmet
柳条箱 wicker suitcase (or trunk)
柳暗花明 dark willows and blooming flowers—a beauteous scene;a new vista
柳条制品 wickerwork;wicker

绺 [liǔ] I 动 steal II 量 tuft;lock;skein:一绺胡子 a lock of a board/一绺毛线 a skein of wool

liù (ㄌㄧㄡˋ)

六 [liù] 数 six
六畜 the six domestic animals
六根 (in Buddhism) the six roots of sensation—eye,ear,nose,tongue,body and mind
六亲 the six relations (father, mother, elder brothers, younger brothers, wife, children);one's kin
六月 ①June ②the sixth month of the lunar year;the sixth moon
六边形 hexagon
六分仪 sextant
六角形 hexagon
六六六 benzene hexachloride(BHC)
六面体 hexahedron
六弦琴 guitar
六指儿 six-finger hand
六畜兴旺 The domestic animals are all thriving.
六道轮回 the six great divisions in the wheel of karma
六号房间 Room No. 6
六角车床 turret lathe
六亲不认 disown all one's relatives and friends
六亲无靠 have no relatives (or friends) to depend on
六神无主 all six vital organs failing to work properly—distracted;out of one's wits;at a loss what to do
六十四开 sixty-fourmo;64 mo

遛 [liù] 动 ①saunter;stroll ②walk (an animal)
遛狗 walk a dog
遛马 walk a horse
遛鸟 (of bird keepers) take caged birds out into the country (to eat insects or to listen to and learn the songs of their kind who are free to roam the skies)
遛大街 saunter in the street
遛弯儿 take a walk;go for a stroll

碌 [liù] ➡ lù
碌碡 stone roller (for threshing grain,levelling a threshing floor,etc.)

馏 [liù] 动 heat up (cold food in a steamer);warm ➡ liú

溜 [liù] I 名 ①swift current ②rainwater from the roof ③ eaves gutter ④ surroundings;neighbourhood II 形 swift;rapid;deft III 动 ① train;exercise ②fill (a crevice,fissure,etc.) IV 量 row:一溜儿脚印 a row of footsteps ➡ liū
溜缝 fill the cracks
溜子 scraper-trough conveyer
溜嗓子 train one's voice
溜窗户缝 seal the window cracks

镏 [liù] ➡ liú
镏子 [liùzi] ring

鹨 [liù] 名 pipit

蹓 [liù]
囮 walk slowly;stroll ➡ liū
蹓大街 stroll in the street
蹓公园 take a walk in the park

lo (·ㄌㄛ)

咯 [lo]
囮 (同"了" *but more emphatic*)：那就好咯！That would be much better! /走咯，走咯。Let's go. ➡ gē;kě;luò

lóng (ㄌㄨㄥˊ)

龙 [lóng]
Ⅰ 囝 ①dragon ②dragon as the symbol of the emperor;imperial ③anything shaped like a dragon or with the pattern of a dragon on it ④a kind of extinct reptile Ⅱ 囫 (of a bicycle rim)crooked;twisted
龙车 dragon float
龙船 dragon boat
龙床 imperial bed
龙胆 rough gentian
龙灯 dragon lantern
龙宫 the palace of the Dragon King
龙骨 ①a bird's sternum ②fossil fragments ③keel
龙井 Dragon Well tea
龙卷 spout
龙葵 black nightshade
龙脑 borneol;borneo camphor
龙旗 dragon flag
龙套 ①costume with dragon designs,worn by groups of soldiers or attendants in traditional opera ②actor playing a walk-on part in traditional opera;utility man
龙头 ①tap;faucet;cock ②handlebar (of a bicycle) ③in the lead;playing the key role;leading
龙王 the Dragon King
龙舞 dragon dance
龙虾 lobster
龙眼 longan
龙椅 emperor's seat
龙钟 decrepit;senile
龙舟 dragon boat
龙胆紫 gentian violet
龙骨车 dragon-bone water lift;square-pallet chain-pump
龙睛鱼 dragon-eyes
龙卷风 tornado
龙舌兰 century plant
龙头鱼 Bombay duck
龙涎香 ambergris
龙须菜 asparagus
龙须草 Chinese alpine rush
龙须面 dragon whiskers noodles—long, thin noodles
龙血树 dragon tree
龙牙草 hairy vein agrimony
龙爪槐 Chinese pagoda tree
龙飞凤舞 like dragons flying and phoenixes dancing—lively and vigorous flourishes in calligraphy;a flamboyant style of calligraphy
龙凤呈祥 the dragon and the phoenix bringing prosperity—excellent good fortune
龙驹凤雏 dragon colt or young phoenix—a brilliant young man
龙口夺粮 snatch food from the dragon's mouth—speed up the summer harvesting before the storm breaks
龙门铣床 planer-type milling machine
龙盘虎踞 a coiling dragon and a crouching tiger—a forbidding strategic point
龙蛇混杂 dragons and snakes jumbled together—good and bad people mixed up
龙潭虎穴 a dragon's pool and a tiger's den—a danger spot
龙腾虎跃 dragons rising and tigers leaping—a scene of bustling activity
龙头企业 leading enterprise;enterprise playing the leading role
龙争虎斗 fighting between a tiger and a dragon—a fierce struggle between well-matched opponents;a contest between giants
龙多不治水 Too much dragons won't control the flood.
龙门起重机 gantry crane
龙生龙,凤生凤 dragons beget dragons,phoenixes beget phoenixes—each after its own kind
龙游沟壑遭虾戏,凤入牢笼被鸟欺 The dragon in a puddle is the sport of shrimps,whereas the phoenix in a cage is mocked by small birds.

咙 [lóng]
◇ 喉咙 throat

栊 [lóng]
囝 ① window ② cage (for keeping animals);pen
栊槛 cage;pen

昽 [lóng]
◇ 曚昽 ① (of sunlight) dim;hazy ② obscure;dim;hazy

胧 [lóng]
◇ 朦胧 ① (of moonlight) dim;hazy ② obscure;dim

砻 [lóng]
Ⅰ 囝 rice huller (usu. made of wood) Ⅱ 囫 hull (rice)

眬 [lóng]

◇蒙眬 ①half asleep；drowsy；somnolent ②obscure；dim

聋 [lóng]

〔形〕deaf；hard of hearing

聋哑 deaf and dumb；deaf-mute

聋子 deaf person

聋哑人 deaf-mute

聋哑症 deaf-mutism

聋哑学校 school for deaf-mutes

笼 [lóng]

Ⅰ〔名〕①cage；coop；basket ②wooden framework for confining prisoners；cage ③(food) steamer Ⅱ〔动〕put each hand in the opposite sleeve ➡lǒng

笼鸟 cage bird

笼屉 bamboo (or wooden) utensil for steaming food (composed of several tiers)；food steamer

笼头 headstall；halter

笼养 cage culture

笼子 ①cage；coop ②basket；container

隆 [lóng]

Ⅰ〔形〕① grand；solemn ② prosperous；thriving ③intense；deep Ⅱ〔动〕swell；bulge；protrude

隆鼻 augmentation rhinoplasty

隆冬 midwinter；the depth of winter

隆隆 rumble；boom

隆起 swell；bulge

隆胸 augmentation mammoplasty

隆重 grand；solemn；ceremonious

隆准 high nose (bridge)

隆头鱼 wrasse

隆胸手术 breast-enlarging operation；breast enlargement surgery

lǒng（ㄌㄨㄥˇ）

垄 [lǒng]

〔名〕①ridge (in a field) ②raised path between fields ③ridge-like thing

垄断 monopolize

垄沟 field ditch；furrow

垄作 ridge culture

垄断集团 monopoly group

垄断价格 monopoly price；cartel price

垄断交易 ring trading

垄断利润 monopolist profits

垄断市场 hold the market；engross the market；monopolize the market

垄断资本 monopoly capital

垄断资本主义 monopoly capitalism

垄断资产阶级 monopoly capitalist class

拢 [lǒng]

〔动〕①close ②draw near；approach；reach ③ add up；sum up ④ hold together；gather together；keep close together ⑤comb (hair)

拢岸 come alongside the shore

拢共 altogether；all told；in all

拢头 comb hair

拢音 concentrate the sound

拢账 add up the accounts

拢子 a fine-toothed comb

笼 [lǒng]

Ⅰ〔动〕envelop；cover；enclose Ⅱ〔名〕large box；chest；trunk ➡lóng

笼络 win sb over by any means；draw over；rope in

笼统 general；sweeping

笼罩 envelop；shroud

笼络人心 cultivate people's good will (by dispensing charity，favours，etc.)

lòng（ㄌㄨㄥˋ）

弄 [lòng]

〔名〕lane；alley；alleyway ➡nòng

弄堂 lane；alley；alleyway

哢 [lòng]

〔动〕(of a bird) sing；chirp；tweet

lōu（ㄌㄡ）

搂 [lōu]

〔动〕①gather up；rake together ②hold up；tuck up；roll up ③grab；squeeze (money)；extort ④pull；draw ⑤check and calculate；assess ➡lǒu

搂钱 grab money

搂头 head-on；directly

搂扳机 pull a trigger

搂草机 rake

搂头盖脸 right in the face

lóu（ㄌㄡˊ）

娄 [lóu]

Ⅰ〔形〕frail；feeble；infirm Ⅱ〔动〕become overripe and decay；go bad

娄瓜 decayed melon

娄子 trouble；blunder

喽 [lóu]

➡lou

喽罗 ①the rank and file of a band of outlaws ②underling；lackey

楼 [lóu]

〔名〕①storeyed building；multi-storey house ② storey；floor ③ superstructure；tower ④ house；mansion

楼板 floor；floor slab

楼层 storey；floor

楼道 corridor；passageway

楼房 a building of two or more storeys

楼阁 building attic；house

楼花 forward delivery apartment

楼面 floor
楼盘 building
楼上 upstairs
楼市 property market;real-estate market
楼梯 stairs;staircase;stairway
楼下 downstairs
楼堂馆所 office buildings,auditoriums,hotels

耧 [lóu]
名 animal-drawn seed plough;drill barrow;drill

蝼 [lóu]
名 mole cricket
蝼蛄 mole cricket
蝼蚁 ①mole crickets and ants ②nobodies;nonentities

髅 [lóu]
◇骷髅 ① human skeleton ② human skull;death's-head

lǒu（ㄌㄡˇ）

搂 [lǒu]
Ⅰ 动 hold in one's arms;hug;embrace
Ⅱ 量 circular length when one's hands meet in stretching out one's arms：两搂粗的大树 large tree two arm-spans round ➡lōu
搂抱 hug;embrace;cuddle

嵝 [lǒu]
名 hilltop

篓 [lǒu]
名 basket
篓子 basket

lòu（ㄌㄡˋ）

陋 [lòu]
形 ①plain;ugly ②rough;coarse;crude ③(of a dwelling) rude;humble;mean ④vulgar;corrupt;undesirable ⑤(of knowledge) scanty;limited;shallow
陋规 objectionable practices
陋见 shallow (or superficial) views
陋居 one's rude dwelling;one's humble house
陋室 humble room
陋俗 undesirable customs
陋习 corrupt customs;bad habits
陋巷 mean alley

镂 [lòu]
镂花 ornamental engraving
镂刻 ①carve;engrave ②impress deeply (on the mind);engrave
镂空 pierced work; reticulated work; openwork;fretwork

瘘 [lòu]
名 ①fistula ②scrofula
瘘管 fistula

漏 [lòu]
Ⅰ 动 ①trickle;leak;seep ②(as of a container) leak ③divulge;let out;leak ④miss;

leave out Ⅱ 名 water clock;hourglass
漏报 non-disclosure;omission of declaration;fail to report;fail to declare
漏疮 anal fistula
漏电 leak electricity
漏洞 ①leak ②flaw;hole;loophole
漏兜 spill the beans;let the cat out of the bag
漏斗 funnel
漏风 ①leak air;not be airtight ②speak indistinctly through having one or more front teeth missing ③(of information,secrets) leak out
漏缝 crack;leak
漏光 leak light
漏壶 water clock;clepsydra;hourglass
漏孔 small opening;hole
漏勺 strainer;colander
漏失 ①leak and lose ②careless omission;oversight;slip;error
漏税 evade payment of a tax;evade taxation;tax evasion
漏网 slip through the net;escape unpunished
漏诊 fail to pinpoint a disease in diagnosis
漏征 tax default
漏子 ①funnel ②flaw;hole;loophole
漏嘴 let slip a remark; make a slip of the tongue
漏洞百出 full of loopholes
漏尽更残 The night is waning.
漏网之鱼 a fish that has slipped through the net—fugitive; runaway; sb who escapes punishment

露 [lòu]
露白 show one's money (or belongings)
露丑 make a fool of oneself in public
露底 let the secret out
露富 show one's wealth
露脸 ①show up;appear ②become known (by doing sth);be successful;shine
露面 show one's face;make (or put in) an appearance;appear (or reappear) on public occasions
露苗 come out
露怯 display one's ignorance;make a fool of oneself
露头 ①show one's head ②appear;emerge
露相 show one's true colours
露马脚 give oneself away;let the cat out of the bag
露脐装 crop top
露馅儿 let the cat out of the bag;give the game away;spill the beans
露一手 make an exhibition of one's abilities (or skills);show off

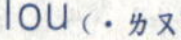

L

喽 [lou]

勋 ①(*used after a verb to refer to an anticipated or envisaged action*)：他要知道喽一定很高兴。I'm sure he'll be glad to hear it. ②(*used at the end or in the middle of a sentence to attract attention*)：下地喽！Look, it's time to go to the fields! ➡lóu

lū (ㄌㄨ)

撸 [lū]

勋 ①close one's hand around (sth long) and push; strip with the hand ②remove; dismiss ③scold; take to task; dress down

lú (ㄌㄨˊ)

卢 [lú]

卢比 rupee
卢布 rouble
卢沟桥事变 the Lugouqiao Incident

芦 [lú]

名 reed ➡lǔ
芦柴 reed stems
芦荡 reed marshes
芦丁 rutin
芦花 reed catkins
芦荟 aloe
芦笙 reed-pipe wind instrument
芦笋 asparagus
芦苇 reed
芦席 reed mat

庐 [lú]

名 hut; hovel
庐舍 house; farmhouse
庐山真面目 the true face of Lushan—the truth about a person or a matter

垆 [lú]

名 ①black earth ②earthen platform where wine jars are placed; wineshop
垆土 black soil

炉 [lú]

Ⅰ 名 stove; oven; furnace：围炉而坐 sit round a fire Ⅱ 量 (of what is made or contained in a furnace, stove or oven)：一炉钢 a heat of steel
炉衬 (furnace) lining
炉顶 furnace top; furnace roof
炉灰 stove ashes
炉料 furnace charge; furnace burden
炉龄 furnace life
炉门 the draft of a stove
炉盘 stone or metal plate for standing a stove on as a precaution against fire
炉身 (furnace) shaft; furnace stack
炉台 stove top
炉膛 the chamber of a stove (*or* furnace)
炉条 fire bars; grate

炉瓦 stove tiles
炉温 furnace temperature
炉灶 kitchen range; cooking range
炉渣 slag; cinder
炉子 stove; oven; furnace
炉箅子 fire grate
炉前工 blast-furnace man; furnaceman
炉火纯青 the stove fire (for making pills of immortality) begins to glow a pure blue— attain a high degree of perfection

栌 [lú]

◇黄栌 smoke tree

轳 [lú]

◇辘轳 well-pulley; windlass; winch

胪 [lú]

勋 state; set out; display

鸬 [lú]

鸬鹚 cormorant

颅 [lú]

颅骨 cranial bones
颅腔 cranial cavity
颅骨骨折 effracture
颅内出血 intracranial hemorrhage

lǔ (ㄌㄨˇ)

芦 [lǔ]

➡lú
◇油葫芦 a kind of field cricket

卤 [lǔ]

Ⅰ 名 ①bittern ②halogen ③thick gravy used as sauce for noodles, etc. ④thick infusion Ⅱ 勋 stew in salty water with spices (*or* in soy sauce)
卤菜 pot-stewed meat (*or* fowl)
卤蛋 spiced corned egg
卤化 halogenate
卤鸡 pot-stewed chicken
卤肉 pot-stewed meat
卤水 ①bittern ②brine
卤素 halogen
卤味 pot-stewed fowl (*or* meat, etc.) served cold
卤虾 salted shrimp gravy
卤族 halogen family
卤化物 halogenide; halide
卤虾油 shrimp sauce

虏 [lǔ]

Ⅰ 勋 take prisoner Ⅱ 名 ①captive; prisoner of war ②slave ③enemy
虏获 capture (men and arms)

掳 [lǔ]

勋 carry off; capture
掳掠 pillage; loot

鲁 [lǔ] 形 ① slow-witted; stupid; dull ② rash; rough; rude
鲁钝 dull-witted; obtuse; stupid
鲁莽 crude and rash; rash
鲁直 frank in an impetuous way

橹 [lǔ] 名 ①scull (at boat's stern) ②big shield

lù （ㄌㄨˋ）

陆 [lù] 名 land
陆稻 dryland rice; upland rice; dry rice
陆地 dry land; land
陆风 land breeze
陆军 ground force; land force; army
陆路 land route
陆相 land facies
陆续 one after another; in succession
陆运 land transportation
陆半球 the continental hemisphere; the land hemisphere
陆地棉 upland cotton
陆海空 land, sea, and air
陆连岛 land-tied island; tombolo
陆龙卷 tornado
"陆委会" "Mainland Affairs Council of the Executive Yuan"
陆战队 marine corps; marines
陆基导弹 land-based missile
陆军武官 military attaché
陆上油田 onshore oil fields; inland oil fields
陆生动物 terrestrial animal
陆相沉积 continental deposit
陆基巡航导弹 ground-launched cruise missile (GLCM)
陆海空三军仪仗队 guard of honour of the three services
陆地和海洋生态体系 terrestrial and marine e-cosystems

录 [lù] I 动 ①record; note (or write) down; copy ②tape-record ③use; employ; hire II 名 record; register; collection
录播 make a recorded broadcast
录放 record and play back
录供 take down a confession (or testimony) during an interrogation
录取 enroll; recruit; admit
录入 key in; input; enter (words, etc.)
录像 videotape; video
录音 ①tape-record (sound); record; tape ② sound-recording
录用 employ; take sb on the staff
录制 transcribe
录像带 ①videotape ②video cassette ③a videotape recording

录像机 video recorder; videotape recorder; video
录像片 video film; TV play
录音带 magnetic tape; tape
录音机 tape recorder; cassette recorder; recorder
录音棚 sound recording studio
录音师 recordist
录音室 recording room
录音报告 tape-recorded speech
录音打字 audiotyping
录音电话 answering machine; dictaphone
录音胶片 recording film
录取分数线 admission line; acceptable grade; minimum passing marks for admission; cut-off score for admission
录取通知书 admission notice
录音电话机 telegraphone
录音放大器 recording amplifier
录音摄影机 sound camera

赂 [lù] I 动 give money or goods as gifts; bribe II 名 (gift of) goods or money

鹿 [lù] 名 deer
鹿脯 dried venison
鹿角 deerhorn; antler
鹿圈 deer enclosure; deer pen
鹿皮 deerskin
鹿茸 pilose antler (of a young stag)
鹿肉 venison
鹿舌 deer's tongue
鹿尾 single; deer's tail
鹿苑 deer park
鹿角菜 siliquose pelvetia
鹿角胶 deerhorn glue
鹿死谁手 at whose hand will the deer die—who will win the prize; who will gain supremacy

绿 [lù] ⇒lǜ
绿林 the greenwood—brigands; outlaws
绿林好汉 greenwood hero—brigand; outlaw

禄 [lù] 名 official's salary (or stipend) in feudal China; emoluments
禄蠹 sinecurist
禄位 official rank and salary

碌 [lù] 形 ①commonplace; mediocre ②busy ⇒liù
碌碌 ① mediocre; commonplace ② busy with miscellaneous work
碌碌无能 devoid of ability; incompetent; mediocre
碌碌无为 lead a vain and humdrum life

路 [lù] 名 ①road; path; way ②way travelled; journey; distance ③way; means ④sequence; line;

logic ⑤region；area；district ⑥line；route ⑦sort；grade；class

路霸 highway overlord (person or unit illegally stopping passing vehicles and passengers and fraudulently charging tolls)

路标 ①road sign ②route marking；route sign

路程 distance travelled；journey

路单 waybill

路道 ①way；approach ②behaviour

路灯 street lamp；road lamp

路堤 embankment

路段 a section of a highway (or railway)

路费 travelling expenses

路风 work style of the railway workers；quality of the railway service

路轨 ①rail ②track

路过 pass by or through (a place)

路基 roadbed；bed

路检 road check

路劫 highway robbery；holdup；mugging

路警 railway police

路径 ①route；way ②method；ways and means

路口 crossing；intersection

路况 road conditions

路矿 railways and mines

路面 road surface；pavement

路牌 street nameplate

路堑 cutting (for a railway or highway)

路人 passerby；stranger

路上 ①on the road ②on the way；en route

路数 ①way；approach ②a movement in martial arts ③exact details；inside story

路途 ①road；way；path ②way；journey

路网 road network

路线 ①route；itinerary ②line

路向 direction

路演 road show

路由 route

路缘 curb

路障 roadblock；barricade

路子 ①way；approach；means ②social connections；pull

路边摊 roadside market

路路通 play both sides of the street；know the route like the back of one's hand

路透社 (UK) Reuter's News Agency；Reuters

路子野 be well-connected

路不拾遗 no one picks up and pockets anything left on the road—good social mores

路旁餐馆 drive-in

路旁阴沟 gutter

路线斗争 struggle between two lines；two-line struggle

路由选择 routing；route selecting

路中护栏 median barrier

路中安全岛 central refuge

路中林阴带 centre mall

路见不平，拔刀相助 see injustice on the road and draw one's sword to help the victim—take up the cudgels for the injured party

路遥知马力，日久见人心 As distance tests a horse's strength，so time reveals a person's heart.

蓼 [liǎo]

形 (of plants) tall and big；tall ➡liǎo

漉 [lù]

动 seep through；filter

漉网 vat-net

辘 [lù]

辘车 pole dolly

辘轳 well-pulley；windlass；winch

辘辘 the rumbling sound of cart wheels

戮 [lù]

动 ①kill；slay ②unite；join

戮力同心 unite in a concerted effort；make concerted efforts

篓 [lǒu]

名 ① woven bamboo trunk ②bamboo (or wicker) basket

鹭 [lù]

名 egret；heron

鹭鸶 egret

麓 [lù]

名 foot of a hill (or mountain)

露 [lù]

I 名 ① dew ② beverage distilled from flowers，fruit or leaves；drink mixed with fruit juice；syrup Ⅱ 形 in the open；outdoors Ⅲ 动 show；reveal；betray ➡lòu

露点 dew point

露骨 thinly veiled；undisguised；barefaced

露酒 alcoholic drink mixed with fruit juice

露水 dew

露宿 sleep in the open

露台 flat roof

露天 in the open (air)；outdoors

露头 outcrop；outcropping

露营 camp (out)；encamp；bivouac

露珠 dewdrop

露光计 exposure meter

露脊鲸 right whale

露天矿 opencut；opencast；open-pit；strip mine

露头角 (of a young person) beginning to show ability or talent；budding

露齿而笑 grin；present a toothpaste smile

露水夫妻 man and woman living together only for a short while without being married

露天电影 open-air cinema

露天堆栈 open-air repository；open-air depot

露天剧场 open-air theatre

露天开采 opencast mining

露天煤矿 opencut coal mine

露天市场 open market

露点湿度表 dew-point hygrometer
露天游泳池 outdoor (*or* open-air) swimming pool

lǘ （ㄌㄩˊ）

驴 [lǘ]
〈名〉 donkey；ass
驴脸 a donkey's face—a long face
驴骡 hinny
驴子 donkey；ass
驴打滚 snowballing usury
驴肝肺 ①donkey's internal organs ②ill intent
驴皮影 leather-silhouette show
驴鸣犬吠 asses braying and dogs barking—a poor style of writing
驴年马月 year of the donkey and month of the horse—a time that will never come (as there is no such year or month in the Chinese calendar)
驴唇不对马嘴 donkeys' lips don't match horses' jaws—•incongruous；irrelevant

闾 [lǘ]
〈名〉 ①gate (*or* entrance) to an alley (*or* lane) ②alley；lane；neighbourhood ③unit of twenty-five households
闾里 native village；home town
闾巷 alley；lane

榈 [lǘ]
◇棕榈 palm

lǚ （ㄌㄩˇ）

吕 [lǚ]
〈名〉 temperament

侣 [lǚ]
〈名〉 companion；associate

捋 [lǚ]
〈动〉 smooth out with the fingers；stroke ➡ luō

旅 [lǚ]
Ⅰ〈动〉 travel；journey；live away from home Ⅱ〈名〉 ①brigade ②troops；force Ⅲ〈副〉 together；jointly
旅伴 travelling companion；fellow traveller
旅程 route；itinerary；journey
旅店 inn
旅费 travelling expenses
旅馆 inn；hotel
旅居 live away from one's native place；sojourn
旅客 hotel guest；traveller；passenger
旅舍 hotel；hostel
旅途 journey；trip
旅行 travel；journey；tour
旅游 tour；tourism
旅长 brigade commander
旅资 travelling expenses
旅差费 travelling expenses on a business trip
旅行包 travelling bag
旅行车 station wagon
旅行袋 travelling bag
旅行剪 folding scissors
旅行社 travel service；travel agency
旅行团 touring party
旅行证 travel certificate
旅行装 safari suit
旅游车 tourist bus；touring.car
旅游船 houseboat
旅游热 travel fever；travel bug；travel craze
旅游团 touring party
旅游鞋 sneakers；walking shoes
旅游业 tourist industry；tourism
旅法侨胞 Chinese nationals living in the France
旅进旅退 always follow the steps of others, forward or backward—have no views of one's own
旅行结婚 destination wedding；tour wedding
旅行闹钟 travelling clock
旅行支票 traveller's cheque
旅行指南 guidebook
旅游背包 packsack
旅游结婚 have a honeymoon trip
旅游农业 tourism-oriented agriculture；tourist agriculture
旅游胜地 tourist attraction
旅游市场 tourist market
旅游特区 special tourist zone；special zone for tourism
旅游资源 tourism resources
旅客登记簿 hotel register
旅游度假区 tourist holiday zone
旅客、货物周转量 volume of passenger of freight transport
旅游搭台,经贸唱戏 with tourism paving the way for economic and trading activities

铝 [lǚ]
〈名〉 aluminium (Al)
铝箔 aluminium foil
铝锭 aluminium ingot；aluminium pig
铝胶 alumina gel
铝线 aluminium wire
铝导线 aluminium conductor
铝合金 aluminium alloy
铝热剂 thermite
铝土矿 bauxite
铝铸造 aluminium casting

稆 [lǚ]
Ⅰ〈动〉 (of grains) naturally grow Ⅱ〈形〉 wild
稆生 naturally-grown；self-sown

偻 [lǚ]
Ⅰ〈形〉 crooked (back) Ⅱ〈副〉 instantly；immediately；at once ➡ lóu

屡 [lǚ]
副 repeatedly;frequently;time and again
屡次 time and again;repeatedly
屡屡 time and again;repeatedly
屡败屡战 fight on despite repeated setbacks
屡次三番 again and again; over and over again;many times
屡见不鲜 common occurrence;nothing new
屡建战功 win one victory after another in battle;have many exploits to one's credit
屡教不改 refuse to mend one's ways despite repeated disciplinary action
屡禁不绝 continue despite repeated warnings
屡试不爽 time-tested; put to repeated tests and proved right

缕 [lǚ]
Ⅰ 名 thread Ⅱ 副 detailed;in fine detail Ⅲ 量 wisp;strand;lock：几缕头发 several locks of hair
缕解 explain in detail;go into particulars;elaborate
缕缕 continuously
缕述 state in detail;give all the details;go into details (or particulars)
缕析 analyse in detail; make a detailed analysis

履 [lǚ]
Ⅰ 名 ①shoe ②footstep Ⅱ 动 ①tread on;walk on ②fulfil;carry out;implement;honour
履带 caterpillar tread;track
履历 ①one's personal record (of education, work experience, and attainments);antecedents ②curriculum vitae (cv);résumé
履新 ①celebrate the New Year ②take up a new post
履行 perform;fulfil;carry out
履约 keep a promise (or pledge,agreement, appointment,etc.)
履历表 (British) curriculum vitae (cv);(American) résumé
履险如夷 go over a dangerous pass as if walking on level ground—cope with a crisis without difficulty
履行合同 comply with an agreement;fulfil a contract

lǜ （ㄌㄩˋ）

律 [lǜ]
名 ① law; statute; rule; regulation ② ancient Chinese standard of pitch; tone ③ name of a classical Chinese poetic form ④restrain;keep under control
律动 rhythm
律师 lawyer;barrister;solicitor;attorney
律诗 regulated verse
律师袍 attorney's robe
律师事务所 law firm; law office; legal firm;

solicitors' firm
律师资格考试 bar examination;the bar

虑 [lǜ]
Ⅰ 动 consider;ponder;mull (over);think over Ⅱ 名 concern;anxiety;worry

率 [lǜ]
名 rate;ratio;proportion ➡ shuài

绿 [lǜ]
形 green ➡ lù
绿茶 green tea
绿带 green belt
绿灯 ①green light (a traffic signal) ②green light;permission
绿地 greenery patches (in a town or city); green space
绿豆 mung bean;green gram
绿矾 green vitriol
绿肥 green manure
绿肺 green lung
绿化 make (a place) green by planting trees, flowers,etc.;afforest
绿卡 "green card"(USA);permit of permanent residence
绿篱 hedgerow;hedge
绿盘 green listing
绿色 green;green colour
绿条 issued by a post office (IOU)
绿茵 ①a carpet of green grass;greensward ② green meadow
绿藻 green alga
绿洲 oasis
绿菜花 (general term for) broccoli
绿宝石 emerald
绿豆糕 a pastry made of mung bean flour
绿豆芽 mung bean sprouts
绿蓝色 turquoise (blue)
绿帽子 a green hat or turban—the state of being a cuckold
绿内障 another name for 青光眼
绿泥石 chlorite
绿茸茸 lush green
绿视率 forest sight rate
绿松石 turquoise
绿头鸭 mallard
绿油油 fresh green
绿柱石 beryl
绿岛工程 green street island project
绿肥作物 green manure crop
绿化地带 greenbelt
绿化工程 landscape engineering
绿化荒山 planting trees on barren hills;afforesting barren hills and mountains
绿色奥运 Green Olympics
绿色包装 green package
绿色壁垒 green trade barriers
绿色标志 environmental labelling
绿色冰箱 green refrigerator; Freon-free re-

frigerator
绿色产品 green product
绿色革命 the Green Revolution
绿色和平 the Green Peace
绿色建筑 green building
绿色农业 green agriculture
绿色食品 green food;green foodstuffs
绿色通道 green channel
绿色网站 "green" website
绿色消费 green consumption
绿色营销 green marketing
绿色植物 green plants
绿地覆盖率 forest coverage rate
绿化覆盖率 rate of greening coverage
绿色和平组织 Greenpeace
绿色急救通道 emergency green path
"绿色证书"工程 "Green Certificate" Project

氯 [lù]
名 chlorine (Cl)
氯仿 chloroform
氯喹 chloroquine
氯纶 polyvinyl chloride fibre
氯气 chlorine
氯酸 chloric acid
氯丙嗪 chlorpromazine
氯化铵 ammonium chloride
氯化钾 potassium chloride
氯化钠 sodium chloride
氯化物 chloride
氯磷定 pyraloxime methylchloride
氯霉素 chloromycetin;chloramphenicol
氯噻酮 chlorthalidone
氯酸钾 potassium chlorate
氯丁橡胶 chloroprene rubber

滤 [lù]
动 strain;filter
滤器 filter
滤液 filtrate
滤纸 filter paper
滤波器 wave filter
滤光器 light filter;ray filter
滤色镜 (colour) filter
滤过性病毒 filterable virus

luán (ㄌㄨㄢˊ)

峦 [luán]
名 hills (or mountains) in a range
娈 [luán]
形 beautiful
孪 [luán]
名 twin
孪生 twin
孪子 twin sons
栾 [luán]
名 goldenrain tree
挛 [luán]
名 contraction
挛缩 contracture

鸾 [luán]
名 legendary bird like a phoenix
鸾凤 ①a married couple ②distinguished talents
鸾凤和鸣 be a happy couple;be blessed with conjugal felicity
鸾飘凤泊 ① free and powerful calligraphic style ②husband and wife separated ③men of worth neglected
鸾翔凤集 a gathering of talented men
銮 [luán]
名 ①small tinkling bell ②tinkling bells on the emperor's carriage;imperial carriage
銮驾 imperial carriage
銮铃 tinkling bells on a carriage
銮舆 imperial carriage

luǎn (ㄌㄨㄢˇ)

卵 [luǎn]
名 ①ovum;egg;spawn ②zygote ③ testicles;penis
卵白 white of an egg;albumen
卵巢 ovary
卵核 egg nucleus
卵黄 yolk
卵生 oviparity
卵石 cobble;pebble;shingle
卵翼 cover with wings as in brooding;shield
卵子 ovum;egg
卵磷脂 lecithin
卵胎生 ovoviviparity
卵细胞 egg cell;ovum
卵用鸡 a chicken raised for egg production; layer
卵生动物 oviparous animal;ovipara
卵胎生动物 ovoviviparous animal

luàn (ㄌㄨㄢˋ)

乱 [luàn]
I 形 ①in disorder (or chaos);in disarray; in a mess;in confusion ②confused;unsettled (state of mind);in a turmoil II 名 ①upheaval; rebellion; unrest; turmoil ② promiscuous sexual behaviour;promiscuity III 动 confuse; mix up;jumble IV 副 indiscriminate;random; arbitrary
乱兵 ① mutinous soldiers ② totally undisciplined troops
乱搞 ①bed-hop ②bed-hopping
乱来 act foolishly (or recklessly)
乱伦 commit incest
乱码 confusion code
乱民 common people in revolt;rebellious people
乱世 troubled times;turbulent days
乱说 speak carelessly (or foolishly);talk in a scatterbrained way;talk nonsense;make ir-

responsible remarks

乱套 muddle things up; turn things upside down

乱腾 confused; disorderly; restless

乱真 ①(of fakes) look genuine ②spurious

乱子 disturbance; trouble; disorder

乱拆借 irregular borrowing or taking loans

乱罚款 impose unjustified fines

乱纷纷 disorderly; confused; chaotic

乱坟岗 unmarked common graves; unmarked burial-mounds

乱哄哄 in noisy disorder; in a hubbub; tumultuous; in an uproar

乱集资 illegal fund-raising; unwarranted pooling of funds

乱了营 be thrown into confusion; be in disarray

乱蓬蓬 dishevelled; tangled; jumbled

乱弹琴 act (*or* talk) like a fool; talk nonsense

乱糟糟 ①chaotic; in a mess ②confused; perturbed

乱涨价 unauthorized price rise; illegal (reckless) price hike; wilfully raise commodity price

乱着装 practice of discriminate wearing of uniforms

乱臣贼子 rebels and traitors; traitors and villains

乱点鸳鸯 ① misarrangement of matches through wrong identification of couples ② misarrangement of personnel

乱喊乱叫 shout and scream madly

乱砍滥伐 fell trees indiscriminately; engage in destructive lumbering practices

乱七八糟 at sixes and sevens; in great disorder; in an awful mess

乱上项目 rashly launch new projects

乱世英雄 heroes in times of disorder

lüě（ㄌㄩㄝˇ）

掠 劻 grab; take up ➧ lüè

lüè（ㄌㄩㄝˋ）

掠 劻 ① rob; plunder; pillage; sack ② sweep past; brush past; graze; skim over ③hit with a club (*or* a whip); flog ➧ lüě

掠夺 plunder; rob; pillage

掠美 claim credit due another

掠取 seize; grab; plunder

掠影 ①impression gained after brief observation ②bird's-eye view; panorama

掠地飞行 minimum-altitude flight; treetop flight; hedgehopping

掠人之美 claim credit due to others

掠水飞行 wave-hopping

略 Ⅰ 形 brief; sketchy; rough Ⅱ 名 ①brief account; summary; outline; sketch ②plan; strategy; scheme Ⅲ 动 ①omit; delete; leave out ② capture (city or land); seize

略称 abbreviation; shortened form

略略 slightly; briefly

略图 sketch map; sketch

略微 slightly; a little; somewhat

略语 abbreviation; shortening

略表寸心 just to show my gratitude

略见一斑 catch a glimpse of; get a rough idea of

略胜一筹 slightly superior

略识之无 know only a few simple characters

略述一二 give a brief account

略有所知 have an inkling of the matter

略有盈余 with a small favorable balance

略知一二 have only a smattering of; know only a little

lūn（ㄌㄨㄣ）

抡 劻 ①swing; brandish ②hit; beat; slap one's face; fling; throw; scatter ➧ lún

抡锤 swing a hammer

抡刀 brandish a sword

抡拳 shake one's fist

抡圆了 exert all one's strength; swing one's arms with all one's might

lǔn（ㄌㄨㄣ）

仑 名 logical sequence; coherence

伦 名 ①human relations, esp. as conceived in terms of ethics ②logic; order ③peer; match

伦巴 rumba (a dance)

伦比 rival; equal

伦常 feudal order of importance (*or* seniority) in human relationships

伦次 coherence; logical sequence

伦理 ethics; moral principles

伦琴 rontgen (*or* roentgen)

伦理学 ethics

伦琴射线 rontgen (*or* roentgen) rays

伦敦金融时报指数 Financial Times Average

论 名 *The Analects of Confucius*: 上论 Volume One of the *Analects* / 下论 Volume Two of the *Analects* ➧ lùn

抡 劻 choose; select ➧ lūn

囵 ◇囫囵 whole

沦 [lún]
〔动〕①sink;subside ②fall;degenerate;be reduced to
沦落 fall low;come down in the world;be reduced to poverty
沦丧 be lost;be ruined
沦亡 (of a country) be annexed (*or* subjugated)
沦陷 ①(of territory,etc.) be occupied by the enemy;fall into enemy hands ②submerge;inundate;flood;drown
沦陷区 enemy-occupied area
沦落街头 be driven onto the streets;be reduced to beggary (*or* vagrancy,etc.)
沦入风尘 fall into professions not socially respectable
沦为奴隶 be reduced to slavery
沦于深渊 plunge into an abyss

纶 [lún]
〔名〕①black silk ribbon ②fishing line ③synthetic fibre

轮 [lún]
Ⅰ〔名〕①wheel ②sth resembling a wheel;disc;ring ③steamboat;steamer Ⅱ〔动〕take turns;do by turns Ⅲ〔量〕①(of the sun,the moon,etc.);一轮明月高挂半空。A bright moon was hanging in the sky. ②(of things or actions that rotate);赛罢首轮 after the first round (of matches)
轮班 in shifts;in relays;in rotation
轮唱 round
轮齿 teeth of a cogwheel
轮虫 wheel animalcule;rotifer
轮船 steamer;steamship;steamboat
轮次 ①order of turns ②number of turns (*or* rounds)
轮渡 ferry
轮番 take turns
轮辐 arm of wheel;wheel rib
轮换 rotate;take turns
轮回 samsara;transmigration
轮机 ①turbine ②motorship engine;engine
轮奸 (of two or more men) rape a woman in turn;gang-rape
轮距 track;tread
轮空 bye
轮廓 outline;contour;rough sketch
轮流 take turns;do sth in turn
轮牧 rotation grazing
轮盘 corona;body of wheel
轮生 verticillate
轮胎 tyre
轮辋 rim (of a wheel)
轮休 ①(of land) lie fallow in rotation ②have holidays by turns;rotate days off;stagger holidays
轮训 training in rotation

轮窑 annular kiln
轮叶 wheel blade
轮椅 wheelchair
轮种 rotate crops
轮轴 ①wheel and axle ②wheel axle
轮转 rotate
轮子 wheel
轮作 crop rotation
轮班制 rotation system;relay system
轮机室 engine room
轮机员 engineer
轮机长 chief engineer
轮训班 a training class operating on a rotating basis
轮番轰炸 bomb in waves
轮值主席 chairman on duty
轮式拖拉机 wheeled tractor
轮胎帘子线 tyre cord
轮胎压力计 tyre pressure gauge
轮转印刷机 rotary press

lùn（ㄌㄨㄣˋ）

论 [lùn]
Ⅰ〔动〕①comment;discuss;talk about ②speak of;mention;treat;consider ③measure;appraise;decide on;determine Ⅱ〔名〕①view;opinion;statement;essay ②theory;doctrine Ⅲ〔介〕by;in terms of ⇒lún
论辩 argue;debate
论丛 collection of commentaries;decide on sb's punishment;punish
论点 argument;thesis
论调 view;argument
论断 inference;judgment;thesis
论及 touch upon
论据 grounds of argument;argument
论理 ①reason (with sb) ②normally;as things should be ③logic
论述 discuss;expound
论说 ①exposition and argumentation ②normally;as things should be
论坛 forum;tribune
论题 proposition
论文 thesis;dissertation;treatise;paper
论战 polemic;debate
论争 debate;argument
论证 ①demonstration;proof ②expound and prove ③grounds of argument
论著 treatise;work;book
论罪 decide on the nature of the guilt
论说文 argumentation
论功行赏 dispense rewards (*or* honours) according to merit;give people awards according to their contributions
论文答辩 thesis defence;orals
论资排辈 arrange in order of seniority;give

top priority to seniority in promotion;go by seniority;stress seniority in promotion

luō（ㄌㄨㄛ）

捋 动 rub one's palm along（sth long）;strip sth by closing the palm around it and running one's hand along the length;hand-strip ➡ lǚ
捋胳膊 push up one's sleeve and show the arm
捋虎须 stroke the tiger's whiskers—do sth very daring;run great risks
捋袖子 roll up one's sleeve
捋榆钱儿 strip an elm branch of its seeds

啰 ➡ luo
啰唆 ① talkative; long-winded; wordy ② overelaborate;troublesome

落 ➡ là;lào;luò
◇**大大落落** natural and at ease

luó（ㄌㄨㄛ）

罗 Ⅰ 名 ①net for catching birds ②sieve;sifter;screen ③silk gauze Ⅱ 动 ①catch（birds）with a net ②collect;recruit;gather together ③display; set out; spread out ④ sieve; sift Ⅲ 量 （transliteration）gross;twelve dozen
罗锅 arched
罗汉 Arhat;Arhant
罗经 compass
罗口 rib cuff;rib collar;rib top（of socks）
罗列 ①spread out;set out ②enumerate
罗盘 compass
罗圈 the round frame of a sieve
罗裙 a skirt of thin silk;silk skirt
罗网 net;trap
罗帏 gauze curtain
罗纹 rib;whorl
罗帐 curtain of thin silk
罗织 frame up
罗致 enlist the services of;secure sb in one's employment;collect;gather together
罗布麻 bluish dogbane
罗锅儿 ①hunchbacked;humpbacked ②hunchback;humpback
罗汉果 mangosteen
罗汉松 yew podocarpus
罗马法 Roman law
罗盘赌 roulette
罗圈腿 ① bowlegs;bandy legs ② bowlegged; bandy-legged
罗马数字 Roman numerals
罗马语族 the Romance group of languages; Romance languages
罗曼蒂克 romantic（a transliteration）

罗织罪名 cook up charges; frame a case against sb
罗致人才 enlist the services of able people

萝 名 trailing plant;vine
萝卜 radish
萝芙木 devilpepper
萝卜干儿 dried radish

逻 动 patrol
逻辑 logic
逻辑学 logic
逻辑操作 logical operation
逻辑电路 logical circuit
逻辑记录 logical record
逻辑思维 logical thinking
逻辑主语 logical subject
逻辑数据库 logical database

脶 名 fingerprint;fingermark

猡
◇**猪猡** pig;swine

锣 名 gong
锣槌（gong）hammer
锣鼓 ① gong and drum ② traditional percussion instruments ③ ensemble of such instruments with gongs and drums playing the main part
锣鼓喧天 a deafening sound of gongs and drums

箩 名 square-bottomed bamboo basket
箩筐 a large bamboo（or wicker）basket

骡 名 mule
骡子 mule
骡马店 an inn with sheds for carts and animals

螺 名 ①spiral shell;snail ②whorl（in fingerprint）
螺钿 mother-of-pearl inlay
螺钉 screw
螺号 conch;shell trumpet
螺杆 screw;spiral;scroll;threaded rod
螺距（screw）pitch;thread pitch
螺帽 nut;blind nut
螺母（screw）nut
螺栓（screw）bolt
螺丝 screw
螺蛳 spiral shell;snail
螺纹 ①whorl（in fingerprint）②thread（of a screw）
螺旋 ①spiral;helix ②screw
螺丝刀 screwdriver
螺丝钉 screw
螺丝扣 thread（of a screw）

螺丝母 (screw) nut
螺旋桨 (screw) propeller；screw
螺旋式 spiral
螺旋体 spirochaeta
螺旋形 spirality；volution
螺口灯泡 screw-socket bulb；screw bulb
螺口灯头 screw socket
螺丝板牙 screw die；threading die
螺丝起子 screwdriver
螺纹刀具 threading tool；screw tool

luǒ（ㄌㄨㄛˇ）

裸 [luǒ]
〔形〕 bare；naked；nude；exposed
裸奔 streak
裸机 bare bones
裸鲤 naked carp
裸露 uncovered；exposed
裸麦 naked barley；highland barley
裸女 nude (or naked) woman
裸体 naked；nude
裸线 bare wire
裸眼 naked eye
裸泳 swim raw；skinny-dip；swim in the nude；
　swim in the raw
裸电线 bare (electric) wire
裸露癖 exhibitionism
裸体画 a painting of a nude (esp. a nude
　woman)
裸体像 nude figure (or statue)；nude
裸装货 nude cargo
裸背女裙 backless dress；sunback dress
裸子植物 gymnosperm

luò（ㄌㄨㄛˋ）

荦 [luò]
〔形〕 prominent；extraordinary；outstanding
荦荦 conspicuous；apparent；obvious
荦荦大端 major items；salient points

咯 [luò]
➡ gē；kǎ；lo
◇吡咯 pyrrole

洛 [luò]
洛氏硬度 Rockwell hardness
洛阳纸贵 Paper is dear in Luoyang.

骆 [luò]
〔名〕 white horse with a black name
骆驼 camel
骆驼刺 camel thorn
骆驼队 camel train；caravan
骆驼绒 camel hair cloth

络 [luò]
Ⅰ〔名〕①sth resembling a net ②collateral
channels in the human body through which vital energy and blood circulate Ⅱ〔动〕①hold sth
in place with a net ②twine；coil；wind

络合 complexing
络脉 branches of channels
络纱 doff
络盐 complex salt
络离子 complex ion
络筒机 (high speed) cone winder；winding
　machine；winder
络腮胡子 whiskers；full beard
络绎不绝 in an endless stream

珞 [luò]
◇赛璐珞 celluloid

烙 [luò]
➡ lào
◇炮烙 the hot pillar

硌 [luò]
〔名〕 big rock (or boulder) on a mountain ➡
gè

落 [luò]
Ⅰ〔动〕①fall；drop ②go down；descend；land；
set ③lower；let down ④decline；come down；
deteriorate ⑤lag behind；fall behind；fail ⑥
stay behind；remain ⑦fall onto；belong to；rest
with ⑧get；gain；receive ⑨write；put down
Ⅱ〔名〕①whereabouts ②settlement ➡ là；lào；
luō
落榜 flunk competitive exam for job (or
　school admission)
落笔 put pen to paper；start to write (or
　draw)
落标 fail to win a bid；fail in an election (or
　competition)
落泊 be in dire straits；be down and out
落差 ①drop in elevation (between two points
　in a stream) ②head drop (in hydroelectric
　power plants)
落草 take to the greenwood；take to the
　heather；become an outlaw
落潮 ebb tide
落成 (of a building，etc.) be completed
落锤 drop hammer
落得 get；end in
落底 ①the end of a year (or month) ②feel at
　ease；have one's mind set at rest
落地 ①fall to the ground ②(of a baby) be
　born
落第 fail in an imperial examination
落点 ①placement (of a ball) ②point of fall
落果 premature drop
落后 ① be behind；fall behind；lag behind ②
　backward；behind the times
落户 settle
落价 fall (or drop) in price
落脚 stay (for a time)；stop over；put up
落空 come to nothing；fail；fall through
落款 write the names of the sender and the
　recipient (on a painting，gift or letter)；in-

scribe (a gift, etc.)

落泪 shed tears; weep

落铃 shedding (*or* premature dropping) of cotton bolls

落马 ①fall off a horse ②be defeated; lose a race

落寞 lonely; desolate

落幕 the curtain falls; lower the curtain

落难 meet with misfortune; be in distress

落聘 not be hired (*or* recruited); be turned down in one's job application

落日 the setting sun

落实 ① practicable; workable ② fix (*or* decide) in advance; ascertain; make sure ③ carry out; fulfil; implement; put into effect

落水 ①fall into water ②fall into evil ways

落俗 show poor taste

落体 falling body

落拓 untrammeled by convention; casual; unconventional

落网 (of a criminal) fall into the net—be caught; be captured

落伍 ① fall behind the ranks; straggle; drop behind; drop out ② out of date; behind the times; backward

落线 line of fall

落选 also-ran; wash out; lose an election

落叶 ①fallen leaves ②deciduous leaf

落英 ① fallen (*or* falling) flowers ② new-bloomed flowers

落座 take a seat

落地窗 floor-to-ceiling window

落地灯 floor lamp; standard lamp

落地签 landing visa

落花生 peanut; groundnut

落脚点 stopover; underlying objective; basis

落水狗 dog in the water—a bad person who is down

落汤鸡 (of a person) like a drenched chicken; like a drowned rat; soaked through; drenched and bedraggled

落叶树 deciduous tree

落叶松 larch

落成典礼 dedication ceremony; inauguration ceremony

落地车床 face lathe

落地生根 ①air plant; life plant ②take root; strike root

落发为僧 shave one's head and become a Buddhist monk

落后分子 backward elements

落花流水 like fallen flowers carried away by flowing water—in a sorry plight

落花有主 be (*or* become) betrothed to someone

落荒而逃 plunge into the wilds and flee; be defeated and flee from the battlefield

落井下石 drop stones on someone who has fallen into a well—hit a person when he's down

落落大方 natural and at ease

落落寡合 standoffish; unsociable; aloof

落入圈套 fall into sb's snare (*or* trap)

落实政策 conscientiously implement the policies

落拓不羁 unconventional and uninhibited

落叶归根 the falling leaves settle on the roots—a person residing elsewhere finally returns to his ancestral home

落英缤纷 petals falling in riotous profusion

落地式收音机 console (radio) set

落花有意，流水无情 the waterside flower pining for love sheds petals, while the heartless brook babbles on—unrequited love

撺 [luǒ]
Ⅰ 动 pile up; heap up; stack up Ⅱ 量 pile; stack：一撺碗 a stack of bowls

luo（·ㄌㄨㄛ）

啰 [luo]
助 (*used at the end of a sentence to indicate affirmation*)：你放心好啰。You may just as well set your mind at rest. ➡luō

Mm

mā（ㄇㄚ）

妈 [mā]
〔名〕①ma；mom；mum；mother ②form of address for an elderly married woman or a married woman of the elder generation ③form of address for a housemaid or maidservant
妈妈 ma；mum；mummy；mother
妈祖 Goddess of the Sea

抹 [mā]
〔动〕①wipe；mop ②put sth down；slip sth off ➡ mǒ；mò
抹布 rag（to wipe things with）
抹脸 be strict with sb all of a sudden

摩 [mā]
➡ mó
摩挲 [māsɑ] ①gently stroke；smooth sth out with one's hands ②do sth in a careless and quick way ③coax；humour

má（ㄇㄚˊ）

吗 [má]
〔代〕what ➡ mǎ；ma

麻 [má]
Ⅰ〔名〕①(general term for) fibrous crops ② fibre of fibrous crops ③sesame ④pockmarks ⑤anaesthesia Ⅱ〔形〕①rough；rugged；coarse ②numb；dead ③speckled；dotted；spotted
麻包 gunnybag；gunnysack；burlap sack；sack
麻痹 ①paralysis ②benumb；lull；blunt ③lower one's guard；slacken one's vigilance
麻布 ①gunny（cloth）；sackcloth；burlap；hessian ②linen
麻袋 gunnybag；gunnysack；burlap sack
麻刀 hemp；hair
麻烦 ①troublesome；inconvenient ②put sb to trouble；trouble sb；bother
麻纺 the spinning of jute，hemp or flax
麻风 leprosy
麻花 ①fried dough twist ②(of clothes) wearing thin；worn out
麻黄 Chinese ephedra

麻将 mahjong
麻酱 sesame paste
麻利 ① quick and neat；dexterous；deft ② quick；fast
麻脸 pockmarked face
麻乱 confused（state of mind）；in a turmoil
麻木 ①numb ②apathetic；insensitive；lifeless
麻雀 (house) sparrow
麻纱 ①yarn of ramie，flax，etc. ②cambric
麻绳 rope made of hemp，flax，jute，etc.
麻糖 sesame candy
麻线 flaxen thread；linen thread
麻鸭 shelduck；sheldrake
麻药 anaesthetic
麻油 sesame oil
麻疹 measles
麻籽 flaxseed；linseed；hempseed；castor bean
麻子 ① pockmarks ② a person with a pockmarked face ③a person with a pockmarked face
麻醉 ① anaesthesia；narcosis ② anaesthetize ③corrupt（sb's mind）；poison
麻玻璃 frosted glass；ground glass
麻豆腐 cooking-starch residue
麻花钻 (fluted) twist drill
麻黄碱 ephedrine
麻辣辣 (of a pain) searing
麻酥酥 slightly numb；tingling
麻织品 fabrics of flax，hemp，etc.；linen fabrics
麻醉剂 anaesthetic；narcotic
麻醉品 narcotics；narcotic drugs
麻醉师 anaesthetist
麻醉药 anaesthetic；narcotic
麻痹大意 lower one's guard and become careless；be off one's guard
麻木不仁 apathetic；insensitive；unfeeling
麻婆豆腐 pockmarked grandma's beancurd—stir-fried beancurd in hot sauce

蟆 [má]
◇蛤蟆 ①frog ②toad

mǎ（ㄇㄚˇ）

马 **[mǎ]** Ⅰ 名 horse Ⅱ 形 big; great
马鞍 saddle
马帮 a train of horses carrying goods; caravan
马宝 bezoar of a horse
马鞭 horsewhip
马弁 officer's bodyguard; footman
马表 stopwatch
马鳖 leech
马槽 manger
马车 ①（horse-drawn）carriage ②cart
马刺 spur
马达 （electric）motor
马刀 sabre
马灯 barn lantern; lantern
马镫 stirrup
马队 ①a train of horses carrying goods; caravan ②a contingent of mounted troops; cavalry
马蜂 hornet
马夫 groom
马褂 mandarin jacket （worn over a gown）
马号 ①public stable ②long-tubed bugle
马虎 careless; casual
马会 jockey club
马甲 a sleeveless garment; vest
马脚 sth that gives the game away
马厩 stable
马具 horse harness; horse gear
马克 ① mark （German monetary unit）② markka （Finnish monetary unit）
马裤 riding breeches
马蓝 acanthaceous indigo
马力 horsepower （h. p.）
马蔺 Chinese small iris
马羚 roan antelope
马鹿 red deer
马路 road; street; avenue
马骡 mule
马奶 mare's milk
马匹 horses
马枪 carbine
马球 equestrian polo; polo
马群 manada
马肉 horsemeat; horseflesh
马上 ① at once; immediately; straight away; right away ②in the near future; soon
马勺 ladle
马梳 currycomb
马术 horsemanship
马蹄 ①horse's hoof ②water chestnut
马桶 ①nightstool; closestool; commode; chamber pot ②toilet
马戏 circus

马熊 brown bear
马靴 riding boots
马蝇 horse botfly
马贼 mounted gangsters
马扎 campstool; folding stool
马掌 ①cutin skin of a horse's hoof ②horseshoe
马桩 hitching post
马仔 gangster; accomplice
马子 girlfriend; lover
马鬃 horse's mane
马鞍形 the shape of a saddle—a falling-off between two peak periods
马鼻疽 glanders
马齿苋 purslane
马大哈 ①careless; forgetful ②a careless person; scatterbrain
马丁炉 Martin furnace; open-hearth furnace; open hearth
马兜铃 birthwort
马贩子 horse dealer; coper
马粪纸 strawboard
马蜂窝 hornet's nest
马海毛 mohair
马赫数 Mach number; Mach
马后炮 belated action; belated advice; "I told you so" remark
马驹子 foal; colt; filly
马口铁 tinplate; galvanized iron
马裤呢 whipcord
马拉犁 horse-drawn plough
马拉松 marathon
马铃薯 potato
马屁精 sycophant; flatterer; ass-kisser; boot licker
马前卒 pawn; cat's-paw
马钱子 vomiting nut; nux vomica
马赛克 mosaic
马蹄表 round （or hoof-shaped）desk clock （usu. an alarm clock）
马蹄铁 ①horseshoe ②U-shaped magnet; horseshoe magnet
马蹄形 the shape of a hoof; U-shaped
马头琴 a bowed stringed instrument with a scroll carved like a horse's head（used by the Mongolians）
马尾草 gulfweed
马尾松 masson pine
马缨丹 lantana
马缨花 ①conjoined happiness—sexual pairing ②silk tree
马不停蹄 a horse galloping without a stop; nonstop
马到成功 be victorious the moment the battle steeds arrive—win success immediately upon arrival; gain an immediate victory; win instant success

马革裹尸 be wrapped in horsehide after death—die on the battlefield
马关条约 the Treaty of Shimonoseki
马赫主义 Machism
马列主义 Marxism-Leninism
马路新闻 street gossip;hearsay
马马虎虎 ①careless;casual ②not very good; just passable;so-so;fair;not so bad
马失前蹄 make a mistake by accident;have an accidental setback
马首是瞻 take the head of sb's horse as guide—follow sb's lead
马克思主义 Marxism
马六甲海峡 the Strait of Malacca
马尔萨斯主义 Malthusianism
马克思主义者 Marxist
马尔萨斯人口论 Malthusian theory of population
马克思列宁主义 Marxism-Leninism
马克思主义哲学 Marxist philosophy
马克思主义人权观 Marxist outlook of human rights
马拉松式竞选活动 campaignathon
马克思主义政治经济学 Marxist political economy
马克思主义立场、观点、方法 Marxist stand, viewpoint and method

M

吗 [mǎ]
➡ má;ma
吗啡 morphine

玛 [mǎ]
玛瑙 agate
玛祖卡 mazurka

码 [mǎ]
Ⅰ ① sign (or thing) indicating number ② instrument (or device) used to indicate number ③ same thing;thing of the same category Ⅱ pile up;stack;put in order Ⅲ yard (yd):三码布 three yards of cloth
码表 speedometer
码布 plaiting
码尺 yard measure;yardstick
码头 ① wharf;dock;quay;pier ② port city; commercial and transportation centre
码洋 total price (of books)
码子 ①numeral ②counter;chip ③(in financial circles) cash under one's control
码长城 build the Great Wall—play mahjong
码头费 wharfage;dockage
码头税 pierage
码头工人 docker;stevedore;long-shore-man
码头交货 ex wharf (or pier,quay)

蚂 [mǎ]
蚂蟥 leech
蚂蚁 ant

蚂蚁缘槐 ants on the locust tree—little people inflated with pride
蚂蚁搬泰山 ants can move Mount Taishan—the united efforts of the masses can accomplish mighty projects
蚂蚁啃骨头 ants gnawing at a bone—a concentration of small machines on a big job; plod away at a big job bit by bit

mà(ㄇㄚˋ)

骂 [mà]
① abuse;curse;swear;call names ② chide;reproach;reprove;scold
骂架 quarrel;wrangle
骂街 shout abuses in public;call people names in public
骂名 bad name;infamy
骂娘 abuse;curse;swear
骂人 abuse;give a bad name to sb
骂人话 swearword;a word of abuse;abusive language
骂脏话 shout curses (or abuse)
骂不还口 do not return a curse with a curse
骂骂咧咧 intersperse one's talk with curses; be foul-mouthed;be grumbling and swearing

ma(·ㄇㄚ)

吗 [ma]
①(used at the end of a question):你听明白了吗? Did you get what I said? ②(used before a pause in the middle of a sentence to indicate the subject in question):这件事情吗,其实也不能怪他。 As regards the matter in question, he is not to blame indeed. ③(used at the end of a rhetorical question to indicate dissatisfaction or disagreement):你这些话不是自相矛盾吗? Aren't you being self-contradictory by saying all that? ➡ má;mǎ

嘛 [ma]
①(indicating that the reason is obvious):别责怪孩子,他才六岁嘛。 Don't blame the boy. He is only six years old. /有意见就提嘛。 Air your complaints if you have any. ②(used to indicate an expectation or an attempt at dissuasion):不让你去,就别去嘛! Since they don't want you to go, why don't you do as they say? ③(used within a sentence to mark a pause drawing attention to what is coming):其实嘛,这也并不神秘。 As a matter of fact, this is nothing mysterious.

mái（ㄇㄞˊ）

埋 [mái]
〈动〉① cover up（with earth, sand, snow, etc.）; bury ② conceal; hide ➡ mán

埋藏 lie hidden in the earth; bury
埋存 bury
埋单 "bury the bill"—pay the bill
埋伏 ① lie in ambush; ambush ② hide; lie low
埋名 conceal one's identity; keep one's identity hidden; live incognito
埋没 ① cover up（with earth, snow, etc.）; bury ② neglect; stifle
埋设 fit sth underground
埋汰 ① dirty ② insult; ridicule
埋头 immerse oneself in; be engrossed in
埋忧 hide one's sorrow
埋葬 bury（a dead person）
埋名隐姓 conceal one's name; live incognito
埋没人才 stifle real talents
埋头苦干 quietly immerse oneself in hard work; quietly put one's shoulder to the wheel
埋头铆钉 countersunk rivet
埋线疗法 catgut embedding therapy

mǎi（ㄇㄞˇ）

买 [mǎi]
〈动〉buy; purchase

买办 comprador
买单 pay a bill; check
买点 buying point
买断 buy out; buy the ownership of
买方 the buying party（of a contract, etc.）; buyer
买光 clear
买好 try to win sb's favour; ingratiate oneself with; play up to
买回 buy back
买家 purchaser; buyer; customer
买价 buying price
买进 buy in
买空 bull; buy long
买卖 ① buy and sell; business; deal; transaction ②（private）shop
买通 bribe; buy over; buy off
买账 acknowledge the superiority（or seniority）of; show respect for
买主 buyer; customer
买东西 go shopping
买关节 get round（law, rules, etc.）by bribery; offer bribes to facilitate one's operations
买路钱 ① paper money thrown on the road during a funeral procession ② toll money（formerly asked for by highwaymen）
买面子 have regard for sb's face; defer to sb

买期货 forward buying
买椟还珠 keep the glittering casket and give back the pearls—show lack of judgment; make the wrong choice
买方市场 buyers' market
买进卖出 trade
买壳上市 go public through buying a shell
买空卖空 fictitious transactions; buy long and sell short; speculate（in stocks, etc.）
买卖公平 be fair in buying and selling; buy and sell at reasonable prices; pay fairly for what you buy
买卖婚姻 mercenary marriage
买卖清淡 dull business; slack business
买卖兴旺 booming business; brisk business
买入汇率 buying rate
买一送一 two-for-one offer; buy one get one free
买办资产阶级 comprador bourgeoisie

mài（ㄇㄞˋ）

迈 [mài]
Ⅰ〈动〉walk; step; stride Ⅱ〈形〉advanced in age; old Ⅲ〈量〉mile

迈步 take a step; make a step; step forward
迈进 stride forward; forge ahead; advance with big strides
迈方步 walk with measured steps; stride leisurely forward

麦 [mài]
Ⅰ〈名〉wheat, barley, oats, rye Ⅱ〈量〉（short for 麦克斯韦）maxwell

麦茬 wheat stubble
麦冬 the tuber of dwarf lilyturf
麦蛾 gelechiid（moth）
麦粉 flour
麦麸 wheat bran
麦角 ergot
麦秸 wheat straw
麦精 malt extract
麦浪 rippling wheat; billowing wheat fields
麦芒 awn of wheat
麦苗 wheat seedling
麦片 oatmeal
麦秋 wheat harvest season
麦收 wheat harvest
麦穗 ear of wheat; wheat head
麦田 wheatland; wheat field
麦芽 malt
麦蚜 wheat aphid
麦种 wheat seeds
麦子 wheat
麦当劳 MacDonald's
麦地那 Medina
麦秆虫 skeleton shrimp
麦秸画 woven straw patchwork
麦克风 microphone; mike

M

麦粒肿 sty
麦门冬 the tuber of dwarf lilyturf
麦片粥 oatmeal porridge
麦淇淋 margarine
麦乳精 extract of malt and milk
麦芽糖 malt sugar;maltose
麦尔登呢 melton (cloth)
麦克斯韦 maxwell
麦红吸浆虫 wheat midge
麦卡锡主义 McCarthyism

卖 [mài]
I 〔动〕①sell ②betray;sell down the river ③do one's utmost;spare (or stint) no effort ④show off;vaunt II 〔量〕dish (a term used in old-time restaurants):一卖炒腰花 a dish of fried kidney
卖场 market place
卖唱 sing for a living
卖呆 ①pretend to be naive (or stupid);feign stupidity ②(of a woman) stand idly at the gate and watch what's going on in the street
卖点 selling point
卖掉 sell off;sell out
卖恩 do sb a favour for an ulterior motive
卖方 the selling party (of a contract,etc.); seller
卖功 parade one's merits;show off what one has done
卖乖 show off one's cleverness
卖国 betray one's country;turn traitor to one's country
卖好 curry favour with;ingratiate oneself with;play up to;fawn on
卖价 selling price
卖空 short sales;sell short
卖老 flaunt one's seniority;put on the airs of a veteran
卖力 exert all one's strength;spare no effort; do all one can
卖名 capitalize on one's reputation (or prestige)
卖命 ①work oneself to the bone for sb ②die (unworthily) for
卖弄 show off;parade
卖钱 sell for money
卖巧 show off one's petty cleverness
卖俏 play the coquette;coquette;flirt
卖身 ①sell oneself (or a member of one's family) ②sell one's body;sell one's soul
卖相 ①outward appearance;exterior;surface ②demeanour;bearing;manner
卖笑 (of a prostitute or a singing girl) show a smiling face and flirt
卖艺 make living oneself;make a living as a performer
卖淫 prostitute oneself;be a prostitute

卖友 betray one's friend
卖主 seller
卖嘴 show off one's ability (or good nature) by trying to talk cleverly
卖座 (of a theatre,etc.) draw large audiences;attract large numbers of customers
卖不动 not sell well;be unsalable
卖出价 selling rate
卖大户 (of a shop) profiteer by selling goods in great demand to individual buyers in batches
卖高价 sell at an exorbitant price
卖关子 (stop a story at a climax to) keep the listeners in suspense;keep people guessing
卖国贼 traitor (to one's country)
卖劲儿 exert all one's strength;spare no effort
卖空者 bears;short interest
卖力气 ①exert all one's strength;exert oneself to the utmost;do one's very best ②live by the sweat of one's brow;make a living by manual labour
卖破绽 (in a fight or combat) feign an opening in order to hoodwink the opponent
卖人情 show favours for one's own ends;win gratitude by favours
卖儿鬻女 sell one's children
卖方市场 sellers' market
卖官鬻爵 sell official posts and title
卖国集团 traitorous clique
卖国求荣 seek power and wealth by betraying one's country;turn traitor for personal gain
卖国条约 traitorous treaty
卖国行为 treasonable act
卖国主义 national betrayal
卖弄风情 play the coquette;flirt
卖弄噱头 play to the gallery
卖身投靠 barter away one's honour for sb's patronage;basely offer to serve some reactionary bigwig
卖主求荣 betray one's master for the sake of glory
卖狗皮膏药 sell quack remedies;practise quackery;palm things off on people

脉 [mài]
〔名〕①arteries and veins ②(short for 脉搏) pulse ③vein (of leaves or insects' wings) ④range;row;line ➡mò
脉搏 pulse
脉冲 pulse
脉动 pulsation
脉络 ①(general name for) arteries and veins ② veins (of a leaf,etc.) ③ train (or thread) of thought;sequence of ideas
脉石 gangue (a mineral);veinstone
脉速 rapid pulse
脉息 pulse

脉象 pulse condition；type of pulse
脉泽 maser
脉诊 diagnosis by feeling the pulse
脉搏计 sphygmometer
脉冲星 pulsar
脉动器 pulsator
脉动星 pulsating star
脉管炎 vasculitis
脉冲雷达 pulse radar
脉冲信号 pulse signal
脉动电流 pulsating current
脉冲发生器 pulser
脉冲计数器 pulse counter
脉冲编码调制 pulse-code modulation（PCM）

嫚 [mān]
名 girl
嫚子 girl ➡màn

mán（ㄇㄢˊ）

埋 [mán]
➡mái
埋怨 blame；complain；grumble

蛮 [mán]
Ⅰ 形 ①savage；fierce；unreasonable；boorish ②reckless；rash；brute Ⅱ 名 ancient derogatory name for China's southern nationalities Ⅲ 副 jolly；pretty；quite
蛮干 act rashly；act recklessly；be foolhardy
蛮悍 boorish；rough
蛮好 jolly good
蛮横 rude and unreasonable；arbitrary；peremptory；overbearing
蛮荒 ①barbarous ②remote and underdeveloped place
蛮劲 sheer muscle
蛮勇 impetuous；valiant；bold
蛮子 barbarian
蛮有趣 pretty interesting
蛮不讲理 be utterly unreasonable；be impervious to reason；persist in being unreasonable；be wilful；be obstinate
蛮横无理 rude and unreasonable；arbitrary；peremptory

谩 [mán]
动 cheat；deceive；hoodwink ➡màn
谩语 deceitful words
谩天谩地 try to deceive everybody

蔓 [mán]
➡màn；wàn
蔓菁 turnip

馒 [mán]
馒头 steamed bun；steamed bread

瞒 [mán]
动 hide the truth from；cover up；conceal
瞒报 make a deceptive report
瞒哄 deceive；pull the wool over sb's eyes

瞒上欺下 deceive those above and bully those below；hoodwink superiors and bully inferiors
瞒天过海 cross the sea by a trick—practise deception

鳗 [mán]
名 eel
鳗鲡 eel
鳗鱼苗 eel fry

mǎn（ㄇㄢˇ）

满 [mǎn]
Ⅰ 形 ①full；filled；brimful；packed ②satisfied；gratified；contented ③ proud；complacent；smug；conceited Ⅱ 动 ①fill；replenish ②expire；complete；reach a deadline（or quota，limit）Ⅲ 副 fully；completely；entirely；very
满仓 buy securities with all one's capital
满额 fulfil the quota
满分 full marks
满腹 be full of；have one's mind filled with
满贯 ①reach the limit ②（in mahjong，card games，etc.）perfect score；slam
满锅 panful
满怀 ①have one's heart filled with；be imbued with ②bump right into sb ③bear a full crop of young
满街 streetful
满口（speak）unreservedly；profusely；be full of
满门 the whole family
满面 have one's face covered with
满目 meet the eye on every side
满期 expire
满腔 have one's bosom filled with
满身 have one's body covered with；be covered all over with
满师（of an apprentice）finish serving one's time；serve out one's apprenticeship
满天 all over the sky
满心 have one's heart filled with
满眼 ①have one's eyes filled with ②meet the eye on every side
满意 satisfied；pleased；content
满员 ①be at full strength ②（of a train，etc.）have all seats taken
满月 ①a baby's completion of its first month of life ②full moon
满载 be loaded to capacity；be fully loaded；be laden with
满足 ①satisfied；content；contented ②satisfy；meet（needs，demands，etc.）
满嘴 entire mouth
满座 have a capacity audience；have a full house
满肚子 whirlpool
满负荷 full load；full-loaded

满脑子 have one's mind stuffed with

满世界 everywhere;all over;in all places;the world over

满堂彩 bring the house down;win great applause

满堂灌 (of a teacher) cram students;spoon-feed

满堂红 ①all-round victory;success in every field ②crape myrtle

满意度 degree of satisfaction

满编单位 full-staffed units

满不在乎 not worry at all;not care in the least;give (or take) no heed

满城风雨 (become) the talk of the town

满打满算 reckoning in every item (of income or expenditure);at the very most

满口答应 consent without much deliberation;readily promise

满满当当 full to the brim

满满登登 full

满面春风 beaming with satisfaction;radiant with happiness

满目疮痍 Misery and suffering greets the eyes everywhere.

满腔热忱 filled with ardour and sincerity

满腔热情 full of enthusiasm;whole-hearted·

满山遍野 all over the mountains and plains;over hill and dale

满身铜臭 the whole body smelling of copper;stinking with money;filthy rich

满天星斗 a star-studded sky

满头大汗 head covered with big drops of perspiration

满园春色 spring's colours fill the garden

满载而归 come back with fruitful results;return from a rewarding journey

满负荷工作 full-load work;operate at full capacity

满招损,谦受益 Haughtiness invites disaster, humility receives benefit.

螨 [mǎn] 名 mite;acarid

mmàn(ㄇㄢˋ)

曼 [màn] 形 graceful;gentle;exquisitely

曼妙 (of dancing) lithe and graceful

曼声 (sing or recite in) lengthened sounds

曼延 draw out (in length);stretch

曼陀林 mandolin

曼陀罗 datura

谩 [màn] 形 disrespectful;uncivil;rude ➡mán

谩骂 hurl invectives;fling abuse;rail

墁 [màn] 动 ①pave;surface;macadamize ②plaster a wall

蔓 [màn] 名 tendrilled vine ➡mán;wàn

蔓草 creeping weed

蔓延 spread;extend

蔓生植物 trailing plant

幔 [màn] 名 curtain;screen

幔帷 heavy curtain

幔帐 curtain;screen;canopy

幔子 curtain;screen

漫 [màn] Ⅰ 动 ①overflow;run over;brim over;flood;inundate ②have not Ⅱ 形 ①all over the place;in all places;everywhere ②broad;extensive;long ③without restraint (or purpose);casual;random

漫笔 literary notes

漫步 stroll;ramble;roam

漫长 very long;endless

漫道 let alone;say nothing of

漫灌 ① flood irrigation ② (of a flood) overflow (into an area)

漫画 caricature;cartoon

漫骂 use bad language against (sb);fling abuse

漫漫 very long;boundless

漫灭 wear away;efface;obliterate

漫射 diffusion

漫说 let alone;say nothing of

漫谈 (have an) informal discussion

漫天 ①filling the whole sky;all over the sky ②boundless;limitless

漫延 draw out (in length);stretch

漫溢 overflow;spill

漫野 all over the plains

漫游 ①go on a pleasure trip;roam;wander ② roaming

漫反射 diffuse reflection

漫射光 diffused light

漫射体 diffuser

漫不经心 careless;casual;negligent

漫山遍野 all over the mountains and plains;over hill and dale

漫天要价 ask (or demand) an exorbitant price

漫无边际 ①boundless ②straying far from the subject;rambling;discursive

漫无标准 without standard (or principle) to go by

漫无目的 aimless

漫无限制 without any restriction

漫无止境 know no bounds;be without limit

慢 [màn] Ⅰ 形 ①slow;sluggish;tardy ②cold and indifferent;supercilious;rude Ⅱ 动 ① take one's time;postpone;defer ②have not

慢车 slow train

慢待 treat rudely (*or* discourteously)
慢火 slow fire; gentle heat
慢件 package freight; ordinary mail
慢跑 jogging
慢坡 gentle slope
慢性 ①chronic ②slow (in taking effect)
慢走 ① don't go yet; stay; wait a minute ② (said by the host or hostess to a guest at departure) good-bye; take care
慢车道 slow (traffic) lane (on a street); inside lane
慢动作 slow motion
慢镜头 slow motion
慢腾腾 at a leisurely pace; unhurriedly; sluggishly
慢吞吞 irritatingly slow; languid; jog-trot
慢性病 chronic disease
慢性子 ① phlegmatic temperament ② slowpoke; slowcoach
慢悠悠 unhurried; leisurely
慢中子 slow neutron; low-speed neutron
慢藏诲盗 Failure to put things away properly is inviting theft.
慢慢腾腾 loiteringly slow
慢声细语 in a slow, soft voice
慢手慢脚 slow in doing sth; slow moving
慢速摄影 low-speed cinematography
慢条斯理 slowly; leisurely; unhurriedly
慢工出细活 Slow work yields fine products.
慢性通货膨胀 chronic inflation; creeping inflation; mild inflation
慢性支气管炎 chronic bronchitis

嫚 [màn]
勔 scorn; despise; humiliate ➡ mān

缦 [màn]
名 plain silk fabric

镘 [màn]
名 ①trowel ②back of a coin

māng (ㄇㄤ)

牤 [māng]
牤牛 bull

máng (ㄇㄤˊ)

芒 [máng]
名 ①Chinese silvergrass ②awn; beard; arista
芒果 mango
芒硝 mirabilite; Glauber's salt
芒种 ①Grain in Beard—the 9th of the 24 solar terms ②the day marking the beginning of the 9th solar term
芒刺在背 feel prickles down one's back—feel nervous and uneasy

忙 [máng]
Ⅰ 形 busy; fully occupied Ⅱ 勔 hurry; rush; hasten; make haste
忙乎 be busy; bustle about
忙活 [mánghuó] ①be busy with sth ②an urgent piece of work; an urgent job
忙活 [mánghuo] be busy; bustle about
忙碌 be busy; bustle about
忙乱 be in a rush and a muddle; tackle a job in a hasty and disorderly manner
忙人 busy person
忙音 engaged signal; busy tone (in telephone)
忙不迭 hastily; hurriedly; in a hurry
忙里偷闲 snatch a little leisure from a busy life
忙忙叨叨 busy and flustered
忙中有错 Haste makes waste.

盲 [máng]
Ⅰ 形 blind Ⅱ 名 one who lacks knowledge; illiterate
盲肠 caecum
盲从 follow blindly
盲打 touch system
盲道 blind track—grooved track for the blind (along the middle of a sidewalk)
盲点 blind spot; scotoma
盲动 act blindly; act rashly
盲干 act aimlessly (*or* rashly)
盲沟 french drain; blind drain
盲流 unchecked flow of population; jobless peasants in search of work
盲鳗 hagfish
盲目 blind
盲棋 blind chess
盲区 blind area; blind zone
盲人 blind person
盲文 ①braille ②braille publication
盲校 school for the blind
盲杖 blind man's stick
盲障 blindage
盲字 braille
盲肠炎 appendicitis; cecitis
盲椿象 plant bug
盲目性 blindness (in action)
盲人院 blind asylum
盲动主义 putschism
盲目崇拜 worship blindly
盲目发展 pell-mell development
盲目飞行 blind flight; instrument flying
盲目雇佣 buy a pig in a poke
盲目轰炸 blind bombing
盲目竞争 blind competition; unbridled competition
盲目乐观 be unrealistically optimistic
盲目排外 blind opposition to things foreign; oppose everything foreign indiscriminately
盲目着陆 blind landing
盲人摸象 a group of blind men trying to size up an elephant, each mistaking the part he

M

touches for the whole animal—take a part for the whole

盲人瞎马 a blind man on a blind horse—rushing headlong to disaster；in for trouble

盲哑教育 education for the blind and the deaf-mute

盲目上项目 rashly launch new projects

盲目铺新摊子 launch new projects without proper feasibility studies

氓 [máng]
➡ méng

◇流氓 ①rogue；hoodlum；hooligan；gangster ② immoral（*or* indecent）behaviour；hooliganism；indecency

茫 [máng]
形 ①（of water，etc.）vast；boundless；hazy ②unaware；ignorant；in the dark

茫茫 boundless and indistinct；vast

茫昧 ①dim；gloomy；blurred ②confused；uncomprehending；ignorant

茫然 ①ignorant；in the dark；at a loss ②frustrated；disappointed

茫无头绪 not know how to go about things；be in a hopeless muddle

mǎng（ㄇㄤˇ）

莽 [mǎng]
I 名 rank grass；thick undergrowth II 形 ① vast；colossal；boundless ② rude；crude；rash；reckless

莽苍 （of scenery）blurred；misty

莽汉 a boorish fellow；boor

莽莽 ①（of plant growth）lush；rank ②（of fields，plains，etc.）vast；boundless

莽原 wilderness overgrown with grass

莽撞 crude and impetuous；rash

蟒 [mǎng]
名 boa；python

蟒袍 official robe worn by ministers during Ming and Qing Dynasties，with gold designs of pythons

蟒蛇 boa；python

māo（ㄇㄠ）

猫 [māo]
I 名 cat；feline II 动 hide ➡ máo

猫步 cat's walk；catwalk

猫叫 mewing；purring

猫论 theory that it doesn't matter if it's a white cat or a black one so long as it can catch mice

猫熊 panda；giant panda

猫眼 peephole（fixed in a door）；spyhole

猫耳洞 air raid shelter；bomb shelter；foxhole

猫儿腻 cunning plot；illegal deal；underhand act；trick

猫头鹰 owl

猫眼石 cat's eye（a mineral）

猫哭老鼠 the cat weeping over the dead mouse—shed crocodile tears

máo（ㄇㄠˊ）

毛 [máo]
I 名 ①hair；feather；down ② wool ③ mildew；mould II 形 ①coarse；semifinished ② gross ③very young；raw ④careless；unthinking；crude；rash ⑤ flurried；nervous；scared III 动 ①（of currency）devalue；depreciate ② get angry；flare up IV 量 *mao*, fractional money unit in China（= *jiao* 角，= 1/10 *yuan* or 10 *fen*）；三块五毛 three *yuan* and five *mao*

毛笔 writing brush

毛病 ①trouble；mishap；breakdown ②defect；shortcoming；fault；mistake ③ bad habit；shortcoming ④illness

毛布 coarse cotton cloth；coarse calico

毛糙 rude；coarse；careless

毛虫 caterpillar

毛刺 burr

毛豆 young（*or* fresh）soya bean

毛发 hair（on the human body and head）

毛纺 wool spinning

毛感 the feel of wool

毛葛 poplin

毛茛 buttercup

毛蚶 blood clam

毛巾 towel

毛孔 pore

毛口 burr

毛裤 long woollen underwear；woollen pants

毛拉 mullah

毛梾 long-petioled dogwood

毛蓝 darkish blue

毛利 gross profit

毛料 woollen cloth；woollens

毛驴 donkey

毛毛 baby

毛呢 woollen cloth（for heavy clothing）；heavy woollen cloth；wool coating（*or* suiting）

毛坯 ①semifinished product ②blank

毛皮 fur；pelt

毛片 ①unprocessed film after shooting ②pornographic film（*or* telefilm）；blue film

毛票 banknotes of one，two or five *jiao*；denominations

毛渠 sublateral canal；sublateral

毛纱 wool yarn

毛石 rubble

毛刷 brush

毛丝 broken filament

毛损 gross loss

毛笋 the shoot of mao bamboo

毛毯 woollen blanket
毛桃 wild peach
毛虾 shrimp
毛线 knitting wool
毛象 woolly mammoth
毛样 galley proof
毛衣 woollen sweater; sweater; woolly
毛蚴 miracidium
毛躁 ① short-tempered; irritable ② rash and careless
毛贼 petty thief; pilferer
毛毡 felt
毛重 gross weight
毛猪 a live pig
毛竹 mao bamboo
毛白杨 Chinese white poplar
毛背心 woollen vest
毛边纸 writing paper made from bamboo
毛玻璃 frosted glass; ground glass
毛地黄 digitalis
毛纺厂 woollen mill
毛孩子 a small child; a mere child
毛烘烘 hairy; furry
毛巾被 towelling coverlet
毛巾布 towelling
毛巾架 towel rail (*or* rack)
毛毛虫 caterpillar
毛毛雨 drizzle
毛囊炎 folliculitis
毛茸茸 hairy; downy
毛瑟枪 Mauser
毛收入 gross income
毛细管 capillary
毛丫头 a chit of a girl
毛织品 ① wool fabric; woollens ② woollen knitwear
毛发倒竖 gruesomely; with one's hair standing on end—absolutely terrified
毛骨悚然 with one's hair standing on end—absolutely terrified
毛焦火辣 burning with impatience; in a nervous state
毛举细故 bring up trifling matters
毛皮大衣 fur coat
毛入学率 gross rate of school attendance
毛手毛脚 careless (in handling things)
毛遂自荐 offer one's services as Mao Sui
毛细管水 capillary
毛细现象 capillarity
毛细血管 blood capillary
毛发生长剂 hair-growing tonic
毛泽东思想 Mao Zedong Thought

矛 [máo]
　名 spear; lance; pike
矛盾 ① contradiction ② problem; conflict ③ contradict ④ contradictory
矛头 spearhead

矛盾律 the law of contradiction
矛盾上交 pass the buck upwards

茆 [máo]
　名 cogongrass

茅 [máo]
　名 cogongrass
茅草 cogongrass
茅厕 latrine; outhouse
茅房 latrine; outhouse
茅坑 ① latrine pit ② latrine; outhouse
茅庐 thatched cottage
茅舍 thatched cottage
茅屋 thatched cottage
茅草棚 thatched shed; thatched shack
茅膏菜 sundew
茅塞顿开 suddenly see the light; be suddenly enlightened

牦 [máo]

牦牛 yak

猫 [máo]
　➡ māo
猫腰 arch one's back

锚 [máo]
　名 anchor
锚地 anchorage
锚链 anchor chain; anchor cable
锚雷 mooring mine; moored buoyant mine
锚爪 fluke (of an anchor)
锚链孔 hawsehole

mǎo (ㄇㄠ)

冇 [mǎo]
　动 have not; not

卯 [mǎo]
　名 mortise
卯时 the period of the day from 5 a.m. to 7 a.m.
卯榫 mortise and tenon
卯眼 mortise

铆 [mǎo]
　动 fasten with a rivet; rivet
铆钉 rivet
铆工 ① riveting ② riveter
铆机 riveter
铆接 riveting; rivet joint
铆劲儿 ① make a sudden all-out effort ② have a trial of strength; compete; contest

mào (ㄇㄠ)

芼 [mào]
　动 pick; pull up (grass, vegetables, etc.)

茂 [mào]
　Ⅰ 形 ① luxuriant; exuberant; lush; flourishing ② rich and exquisite; splendid; excellent
　Ⅱ 名 cyclopentadiene
茂密 (of grass or trees) dense; thick
茂盛 (of plants) luxuriant; exuberant; flour-

M

ishing
茂林修竹 thick forest of trees and tall bamboos
茂竹繁花 luxuriant bamboos and gorgeous flowers

冒 [mào]
Ⅰ 动 ①emit;issue;give off;send out (*or* up,forth) ②run the risk of;risk;brave Ⅱ 副 ①imprudently;recklessly;boldly;rashly ②falsely;dishonestly
冒称 falsely claim
冒充 pretend to be (sb or sth else);pass (sb or sth) off as
冒顶 roof fall
冒渎 bother (*or* annoy) a superior
冒犯 offend;affront
冒富 become better off;become better than the average
冒汗 perspire;sweat
冒号 colon (:)
冒火 burn with anger;get angry;flare up
冒进 prematurely advance;advance rashly
冒口 rising head;riser
冒领 falsely claim as one's own
冒昧 make bold;venture;take the liberty
冒名 go under sb else's name;assume another's name
冒牌 falsely use a well-known trade mark;be an imitation;be a fake
冒失 rash;abrupt;reckless
冒头 begin to crop up
冒险 take a risk;take chances
冒烟 ①(of smoke) rise ②get angry;flare up
冒雨 braving the rain;in spite of the rain
冒充货 adulterated fake goods
冒尖儿 ①be piled high above the brim ②be a little over;be a little more than ③stand out;be conspicuous ④begin to crop up
冒尖户 uprising household;outstanding household;topnotch household;household sticking;household standing out
冒金星 see stars
冒牌货 imitation; fake goods; adulterated goods
冒傻气 do sth unwise;stupid
冒失鬼 harum-scarum
冒险家 adventurer
冒充包装 copycat packaging
冒充内行 charlatan
冒名顶替 pretend to be sb by assuming his or her name;take another's place by assuming his name;use other people's name
冒牌医生 a quack doctor
冒险政策 adventurist policy
冒用商标 infringement
冒名注册商标 register pirated trademark
冒牌社会主义 bogus (*or* sham) socialism

冒天下之大不韪 risk universal condemnation;defy world opinion;fly in the face of the will of the people

贸 [mào]
动 trade;commerce;exchange of goods
贸然 rashly;hastily;without careful consideration
贸易 trade
贸易额 volume of trade;turnover
贸易法 trade act
贸易港 trading port;commercial port
贸易战 trade war
贸易壁垒 trade barrier;trade wall
贸易差额 trade balance;trade gap;balance of trade
贸易赤字 trade deficit
贸易公司 trading corporation
贸易惯例 trade conventions;usual trade practices
贸易伙伴 trade partner
贸易禁运 commercial embargo
贸易摩擦 trade friction
贸易逆差 unfavourable balance of trade
贸易顺差 favourable balance of trade
贸易谈判 trade negotiation
贸易条件 term of trade
贸易往来 trade contacts;commercial intercourse
贸易协定 trade agreement
贸易中心 trade centre
贸易总额 total volume of trade
贸易议定书 trade protocol
贸工农一体化 integrated management of trade,industry and agriculture;integration of trade,industry and agriculture
贸易保护主义 trade protectionism
贸易和投资自由化 trade and investment liberalization

耄 [mào]
形 ①octogenarian ②advanced in years;aged
耄耋 advanced in years
耄耋之年 advanced in age

袤 [mào]
形 lengthwise (from north to south)

帽 [mào]
名 ①headgear;cap;hat ②cap-like cover
帽带 hatband
帽顶 crown
帽耳 earflaps (of a cap)
帽徽 insignia (*or* badge) on a cap
帽舌 peak (of a cap);visor
帽檐 the brim of a hat
帽子 ①headgear;hat;cap ②label;tag;brand
帽盔儿 skullcap
帽子戏法 hat trick

瑁 [mào]

◇玳瑁 hawksbill turtle

貌 [mào]
〔名〕 looks; look; appearance
貌似 seem to be; appear to be
貌不惊人 be unprepossessing (*or* unimposing) in appearance; be of undistinguished appearance
貌合神离 (of two persons or parties) be seemingly in harmony but actually at variance
貌慧心毒 bear the semblance of an angel but have the heart of a devil
貌似公正 pretend to be just and fair; put on an appearance of impartiality
貌似强大 be seemingly powerful; be outwardly strong
貌似有理 be apparently reasonable

me (·ㄇㄜ)

么 [me]
①(*used as suffix*):那么，他是无辜的了。 If so, he is innocent. ②(*used in a line of verse for balance or euphony*):金秋的北京美呀么美如花。 Beautiful as a garden of flowers is the city of Beijing in this golden season of autumn.

méi (ㄇㄟˊ)

没 [méi]
I 〔动〕①not have; there is not; be without ②be not so... as ③less than; not more than
II 〔副〕 have not; did not ➡ mò
没劲 ①weak ②uninteresting
没救 incurable; incorrigible; beyond remedy (*or* hope)
没脸 feel ashamed; feel embarrassed
没命 ①lose one's life; die ②recklessly; desperately; like mad; for all one's worth
没趣 feel put out; feel snubbed
没挑 faultless; perfect
没完 have not finished with sb (in quarrelling)
没戏 hopeless
没羞 have no shame; be unabashed
没辙 can find no way out; be at the end of one's rope
没治 ①incurable; beyond hope ②excellent; beyond description ③cannot do anything with sb
没出息 not promising; good for nothing
没词儿 ①can find nothing to say ②be at a loss for words; be stuck for an answer
没错儿 ①I'm quite sure; you can rest assured ②can't go wrong
没得说 ①be on intimate terms; be cronies ②really good; incomparably fine; perfect

没法儿 ①most unlikely; absolutely impossible ② beyond comparison ③ can do nothing about it; can't help it; there is no way out
没法子 can do nothing about it; can't help it; there is no way out
没骨头 weak-kneed; spineless
没关系 it doesn't matter; it's nothing; that's all right; never mind
没规矩 not observing proper rules (*or* manners); improper; inappropriate
没见识 inexperienced and ignorant; unlearned and provincial
没空(儿) have no time (for sth or sb)
没来由 without any cause; for no reason; without rhyme (*or* reason)
没良心 without conscience; unconscionable; ungrateful
没门儿 ① have no access to sth; have no means of doing sth ②no go; nothing doing
没跑儿 beyond doubt; undoubtedly
没谱儿 be unsure; have no idea
没商量 irretrievable; irredeemable; irrevocable
没什么 it doesn't matter; it's nothing; that's all right; never mind
没事儿 ①have nothing to do; be free; be at a loose end ②it doesn't matter; it's nothing; that's all right; never mind
没事人 not care in the least; give (*or* take) no heed; be indifferent
没想儿 hopeless
没心肝 heartless; ungrateful
没眼色 inconsiderate; unable to see the fitness of things
没样儿 have no manners; be ill-mannered
没意思 ①bored ②boring; uninteresting ③(of people) petty
没影儿 ①disappear without a trace ②groundless; unfounded; fantastic
没有种 gutless; cowardly
没主意 lose one's head; cannot make up one's mind
没大没小 show no respect for one's elders
没好气儿 be angry; be in a bad temper
没精打采 listless; in low spirits; out of sorts; lackadaisical
没老没少 overfamiliar (between old and young)
没皮没脸 have no sense of shame
没轻没重 (speak) tactlessly; indiscreetly
没深没浅 have no sense of propriety
没事找事 ①ask for trouble; ask for it ②try hard to find fault; cavil
没头案子 a criminal case without a clue for law enforcement officers to work on
没头没脑 without rhyme (*or* reason); abrupt
没完没了 endless; without end

没心没肺 ①simple-minded ②scatter-brained
没心眼儿 careless；frank
没羞没臊 be shameless；have no sense of shame
没有把握 not sure of；not confident
没有出路 find oneself in a blind alley；without a way out
没有的话 it's not true；nothing of the sort
没有结果 come to nothing；with no result
没有什么 nothing the matter；nothing wrong
没有说的 ①really good ②there's no need to say any more about it；it goes without saying ③there's no need arguing；indisputable
没有依靠 with no support；have no backing
没见过世面 green and inexperienced
没有的事儿 nothing of the sort；it's impossible
没有解决的问题 open question；suspended problem
没有什么了不起 not enough to；not so great；nothing to be impressed by

玫 〔méi〕
〔名〕 a kind of jade
玫瑰 rugosa rose；rose
玫瑰红 rose-red
玫瑰花茶 rose tea

枚 〔méi〕
〔量〕（of small objects）：两枚古币 two ancient coins

眉 〔méi〕
〔名〕①eyebrow；brow ②top margin of a page
眉笔 eyebrow pencil
眉端 ①the space between the eyebrows ②the top of a page；top margin
眉峰 brows
眉急 pressing need；matter of extreme urgency
眉尖 brows
眉睫 (as close to the eye as) the eyebrows and eyelashes
眉毛 eyebrow；brow
眉目 〔méimù〕①features；looks ②logic（of writing）；sequence of ideas ③prospect of a solution；sign of a positive outcome
眉目 〔méimu〕 sign of a positive outcome；prospect of a solution
眉批 notes and commentary at the top of a page
眉梢 the tip of the brow
眉头 brows
眉心 the space between the eyebrows
眉眼 appearance；looks
眉宇 forehead；appearance
眉月 eyebrow-shaped moon—the crescent moon；crescent
眉棱骨 superciliary ridge
眉飞色舞 with dancing eyebrows and radiant face—enraptured；exultant

眉高眼底 an expression on the face
眉开眼笑 be all smiles；beam with joy
眉来眼去 make eyes at each other；exchange amorous glances；flirt with each other
眉毛倒竖 raise the eyebrows
眉目传情 flash amorous glances；make eyes at sb
眉目不清 (of writing) not well organized
眉清目秀 have delicate features；have finely chiselled features
眉眼高低 an expression on the face
眉毛胡子一把抓 try to grasp the eyebrows and the beard all at once—try to attend to big and small matters all at once
眉头一皱，计上心来 knit the brows and a plan (or stratagem) comes to one's mind

莓 〔méi〕
〔名〕 certain kinds of berries

梅 〔méi〕
〔名〕 Chinese *mei* flower or its tree (Prunus mume)；Chinese plum
梅毒 syphilis
梅花 ①plum blossom ②wintersweet
梅干 prune
梅雨 plum rains
梅子 plum
梅红色 plum (colour)
梅花鹿 sika (deer)
梅花针 plum-blossom needle
梅童鱼 baby croaker
梅尼埃尔氏综合征 Meniere's syndrome；Meniere's disease

脢 〔méi〕
〔名〕 loin；tenderloin

湄 〔méi〕
〔名〕 river bank；waterside

媒 〔méi〕
〔名〕①matchmaker；go-between ②intermediary；vehicle；medium
媒介 intermediary；medium；vehicle
媒婆 a woman matchmaker
媒染 mordant dyeing
媒人 matchmaker；go-between
媒妁 matchmaker
媒体 medium；media
媒质 medium
媒染剂 mordant
媒染料 mordant dye
媒妁之言 the matchmaker's remarks

楣 〔méi〕
〔名〕 lintel (over a door)；house

煤 〔méi〕
〔名〕 coal
煤饼 coal cake
煤仓 coal bunker
煤层 coal seam；coal bed
煤铲 coal shovel
煤场 coal yard

煤尘 coal dust
煤斗 coal scuttle;scuttle
煤毒 carbon monoxide poisoning;gas poisoning
煤港 coal harbour
煤耗 coal consumption
煤化 carbonize
煤灰 coal ash
煤精 black amber;jet
煤矿 coal mine;colliery
煤轮 coal freighter
煤泥 slush;slurry;coal slime
煤气 coal gas;gas
煤球 (egg-shaped) briquet
煤炭 coal
煤田 coalfield
煤系 coal measures
煤屑 nickings
煤烟 ①smoke from burning coal ②coal soot;soot
煤窑 coalpit
煤油 kerosene;paraffin
煤渣 coal cinder
煤砖 (brick-shaped) briquet
煤矸石 gangue
煤核儿 partly-burnt briquet;coal cinder
煤焦油 coal tar
煤末子 coal dust
煤气表 gas meter
煤气厂 gasworks;gashouse
煤气灯 gas lamp;gas light
煤气管 gas pipe
煤气罐 gas tank;gas container
煤气机 gas engine
煤气炉 gas stove;gas furnace
煤气灶 gas range;gas cooker
煤油灯 kerosene lamp
煤油炉 kerosene stove
煤渣路 cinder road
煤砟子 a small piece of coal
煤气设备 gas fittings
煤气中毒 carbon monoxide poisoning;gas poisoning
煤气贮罐 gas (storage) holder
煤气总管 gas main
煤渣跑道 cinder track
煤酚皂溶液 cresol and soap solution
煤烟型污染 coal-smoke pollution

酶 [méi]
〈名〉 enzyme;ferment
酶原 zymogen;fermentogen
酶蛋白 zymoprotein;pheron

鹛 [méi]
〈名〉 babbler

霉 [méi]
Ⅰ〈名〉 mould;mildew Ⅱ〈动〉 go mouldy;become mildew

霉斑 mildew
霉变 become mildewy;go moldy
霉病 mildew
霉蠹 (of books) get mildewed and worm-eaten
霉菌 mould
霉烂 mildew and rot
霉天 early summer rains
霉头 bad luck
霉雨 intermittent drizzles in the rainy season in the middle and lower reaches of the Changjiang River
霉菌病 mycosis

měi(nǐ)

每 [měi]
Ⅰ〈代〉 every;each Ⅱ〈副〉 ① every time;whenever;per ②often
每次 at every turn
每当 whenever;every time
每每 often
每个角落 every nook and cranny
每况愈下 steadily deteriorate;go from bad to worse
每时每刻 all the time;at all times
每逢佳节倍思亲 On festive occasions more than ever we think of our dear ones far away.

美 [měi]
Ⅰ〈形〉 ① beautiful;pretty;handsome;attractive ② satisfactory;good;gratifying Ⅱ〈动〉 ① beautify ②be pleased with oneself;feel smug Ⅲ〈名〉 good deed;satisfaction
美餐 ① tasty food;table delicacies ②eat and drink one's fill;have an excellent dinner
美差 cushy job;plum job;pleasant task
美钞 U.S. banknote;greenback
美称 laudatory title;good name
美传 a story passed on with approval
美德 virtue;moral excellence
美吨 short ton
美发 give beauty treatment to hair (cut or perm);hair-styling
美感 aesthetic feeling;aesthetic perception;sense of beauty
美工 ①art designing ②art designer
美观 pleasing to the eye;beautiful;artistic
美国 the United States (U.S.A)
美好 fine;happy;glorious
美化 beautify;prettify;embellish
美金 American dollar;U.S. dollar ($)
美景 beautiful scenery (or landscape)
美丽 beautiful
美满 happy;perfectly satisfactory
美貌 ①good looks ②pretty;beautiful
美梦 fond dream
美妙 beautiful;splendid;wonderful

美名 good name;good reputation
美女 a beautiful-woman
美气 comfortable;easy
美缺 an ideal vacancy;a well-paid post
美人 a beautiful woman;beauty
美容 beauty treatment;cosmetology;art of fa-
　cial make-up
美食 good food;table delicacies
美术 ①the fine arts;art ②painting
美谈 a story passed on with approval
美体 body beautification
美味 ① delicious food;delicacy ② delicious;
　dainty
美学 aesthetics
美言 put in a good word for sb
美艳 beautiful and voluptuous;gorgeous;
　glamorous
美意 good intention;kindness
美育 aesthetic education;art education
美誉 good name;good reputation
美元 American dollar;U.S. dollar（$）
美展 art exhibition
美洲 America
美发厅 beauty shop
美国佬 Yankee（U.S. citizen）
美国人 American
美劲儿 ①outward expression of joy（or de-
　light）②joy;delight
美联储 FED,Federal Reserve System
美男子 a handsome man
美人计 sex-trap; sexual entrapment; beauty
　trap
美人蕉 canna;Indian shot
美人鱼 mermaid
美容师 beautician
美容术 cosmetic surgery; plastic surgery;
　beauty culture
美容厅 beauty parlour; beauty shop; beauty
　salon
美容院 beauty parlour;beauty shop
美食家 gourmet
美食街 cuisine variety street;food court;dain-
　ty street
美食节 gourmet festival
美术革 fancy leather
美术馆 art gallery
美术家 artist
美术片 film cartoons;puppet films
美术字 artistic calligraphy;art lettering
美洲虎 jaguar
美洲狮 cougar;puma
美滋滋 very pleased with oneself
美不胜收 so many beautiful things that one
　simply can't take them all in;more beauty
　than one can take in
美国本土 the conterminous United States;the
　Stateside

美籍华人 Chinese American
美酒佳肴 good wine and delicious dishes
美利奴羊 Merino（sheep）
美轮美奂 （of building） tall and splendid;mag-
　nificent
美目流盼 bewitching glances of a beauty
美其名曰 call it by the fine-sounding name of;
　describe it euphemistically as
美人迟暮 beauty in her old age
美容服务 creative cosmetology;esthetic serv-
　ices
美容手术 cosmetic surgery
美容专家 cosmetologist
美如冠玉 as beautiful as the jade ornament of
　a cap—a handsome man
美若天仙 pretty as a fairy;beautiful like a
　fairy
美声唱法 bel canto
美术人型 artist figurine
美术设计 artistic design
美术学校 art school
美术学院 academy of fine arts
美元冲击 dollar shock
美中不足 a blemish in an otherwise perfect
　thing;a blemish in a thing of beauty
美尼尔氏病 Ménière's syndrome（or disease）
美术爱好者 lover of arts
美术工作者 art worker;artist
美术明信片 picture（or pictorial）postcard
美术展览会 art exhibition
美元购买力 dollar's purchasing power
美化战争罪行 beautify war crimes
美术作品展览 art exhibition

浼 [měi]
〔动〕 ①pollute;contaminate ②ask and commit sth to sb's care

渼 [měi]
〔名〕 ripples

镁 [měi]
　镁光 magnesium light
镁砂 magnesia;magnesite
镁砖 magnesia brick

mèi（ㄇㄟˋ）

妹 [mèi]
〔名〕 ①younger sister ②junior female relative of the same generation ③young girl
妹夫 younger sister's husband;brother-in-law
妹妹 younger sister;sister
妹婿 younger sister's husband;brother-in-law
妹子 ①younger sister;sister ②a young girl

昧 [mèi]
Ⅰ〔形〕 ①ignorant;bewildered;confused ②
dim;dark;gloomy Ⅱ〔动〕 ①hide;conceal ②
offend;venture;risk
昧心 （do evil） against one's conscience
昧于 be ignorant of;fail to understand

昧心钱 filthy money;ill-gotten money
昧着良心 go against one's conscience

袂 [mèi]
图 sleeve

寐 [mèi]
动 sleep

媚 [mèi]
Ⅰ 动 fawn on;curry favour with;be servile to;toady to Ⅱ 形 charming;attractive;fascinating;lovely
媚敌 curry favour with (*or* toady to) the enemy
媚骨 obsequiousness
媚世 try to please the public;play to the gallery
媚俗 (of literary works) catering to the readership's poor taste
媚态 ①obsequiousness ②feminine charms
媚外 fawn on (*or* toady to) foreign powers
媚笑 a bewitching smile;an ingratiating smile
媚眼 seductive eyes
媚悦 curry favour with;ingratiate oneself;court
媚上骄下 fawn on and please superiors while to be proudly contemptuous to inferiors

魅 [mèi]
图 evil spirit;demons;monster
魅力 glamour;charm;enchantment;fascination
魅惑 charm;irresistible temptation;enchanting

mēn (ㄇㄣ)

闷 [mēn]
Ⅰ 形 ①stifling ②silent;speechless ③(of a sound) muffled;subdued Ⅱ 动 ①cover tightly ②shut oneself indoors ➡ mèn
闷气 stuffy;close
闷热 hot and suffocating;sultry;muggy
闷死 suffocated;stifle;smother
闷头儿 (work hard) quietly (*or* silently)
闷声不响 remain silent

mén (ㄇㄣ)

门 [mén]
Ⅰ 图 ①(of a building, vehicle, or vessel) entrance ② door;gate ③ any opening ④ valve;switch ⑤way to do sth;knack ⑥branch of a family (*or* clan);family ⑦sect;school of thought ⑧derived from the same master (*or* teacher) ⑨ class;category;branch ⑩ phylum ⑪position in a gambling game Ⅱ 量 ①(of artillery):一门大炮 a cannon;a piece of artillery ②(of field of study or technical training)
门把 door knob;door handle
门板 ①door plank ②shutter
门钹 gate cymbal (nailed onto old-fashioned gates,with a ring-shaped knocker attached to it)
门齿 front tooth;incisor
门窗 doors and windows
门道 [méndào] gateway;doorway
门道 [méndao] ①way to do sth;knack ②social connections;contacts
门第 family status
门吊 gantry crane
门丁 doorman;gatekeeper
门房 ① gate house; janitor's room; porter's lodge ② gatekeeper;doorman;janitor;porter
门风 ethics and moral standards that a family (*or* a clan) keeps
门缝 a crack between a door and its frame (*or* between) two doors
门岗 gate sentry
门户 ①door ② gateway;important passageway ③faction;sect ④family ⑤family status
门将 goalkeeper (soccer,hockey,etc.)
门警 police (*or* security guard) at an entrance
门禁 entrance guard
门径 access;key;way
门镜 peep-hole (in a door)
门槛 ①threshold ②way to do sth;knack
门客 hanger-on of an aristocrat
门口 entrance;doorway
门框 doorframe
门廊 porch;portico
门类 class;kind;category
门帘 door curtain
门联 gatepost couplet;scrolls pasted on either side of the door forming a couplet
门铃 doorbell
门楼 an arch over a gateway
门路 ①way to do sth;knack ②social connections (for securing jobs,etc.);pull
门楣 ①lintel (of a door) ②family status
门面 ①the facade of a shop;shop front ②appearance;facade
门钮 door knob;door handle
门牌 ①(house) number plate ②street number;house number
门票 entrance ticket;admission ticket
门桥 raft of pontoons;boat raft
门球 croquet
门人 ①pupil;disciple;follower ②a hanger-on of an aristocrat
门神 door-god
门生 pupil;disciple;follower
门市 retail sales
门闩 (door) bolt;(door) bar
门厅 entrance hall;vestibule
门庭 ①courtyard ②family status

M

门徒 disciple;follower;adherent
门卫 entrance guard
门下 ①hanger-on of an aristocrat ②disciple;follower;adherent
门牙 front tooth;incisor
门诊 outpatient service
门柱 doorpost
门鼻儿 bolt staple
门吊儿 hasp and staple
门洞儿 gateway;doorway
门环子 knocker
门静脉 portal vein
门脸儿 ①the vicinity of a city gate ②the facade of a shop;shop front ③shop
门面话 formal and insincere remarks;lip service
门市部 retail sales department;salesroom
门外汉 layman;the uninitiated
门诊部 clinic;outpatient department
门诊所 clinic
门插关儿 (door) bolt
门当户对 be well-matched in social and economic status (for marriage)
门户之见 sectarian bias;sectarianism
门可罗雀 you can catch sparrows on the doorstep—visitors are few and far between
门里出身 come from a craft family
门前三包 responsibility contract on the sanitation and greening of the area in front of a unit;be responsible for general sanitation, green covering and keeping good social order in a designated area outside the unit building
门庭若市 the courtyard is as crowded as a marketplace—①a much visited house ②the shop is doing booming business
门诊病人 outpatient;clinic patient
门诊时间 consulting hours
门户开放政策 open door policy
门捷列夫元素周期律 Mendeleev's law

扪 [mén]
动 touch;feel;stroke
扪诊 palpation
扪心自问 examine (or search） one's conscience

mèn（ㄇㄣˋ）

闷 [mèn]
形 ① bored;dejected;depressed; in low spirits ② tightly closed;shut up;sealed ➡ mēn
闷堵 suffocated;oppressed
闷棍 staggering blow
闷酒 drinks taken alone to drown one's sorrows
闷倦 bored and listless
闷雷 ① muffled thunder ② unpleasant surprise;shock
闷气 the sulks
闷沉沉 depressed;gloomy
闷葫芦 enigma;puzzle;riddle
闷子车 boxcar
闷闷不乐 depressed;in low spirits

焖 [mèn]
动 boil in a covered pot over a slow fire;braise:红焖牛肉 braised beef in soy sauce

懑 [mèn]
Ⅰ 动 feel vexed Ⅱ 形 angry;indignant

men（·ㄇㄣ）

们 [men]
助 ①(suffix used to form a plural number when added to a personal pronoun or a noun referring to a person)：孩子们 children ②(in personification, when added to a noun referring to an animal or thing)：小兔子们在树林里唱歌、跳舞。 The rabbits were singing and dancing in the wood. ③(when added to the name of a person to indicate people of the same kind or those who associate with him or her) ④(when added to a noun referring to a despised person)：大小霸权主义者们 hegemonists big or small

mēng（ㄇㄥ）

蒙 [mēng]
Ⅰ 动 ① cheat;deceive;fool;kid ② take a random guess;make a wild guess Ⅱ 形 unconscious;senseless ➡ méng;měng
蒙骗 deceive;cheat;hoodwink;delude
蒙蒙亮 first glimmer of dawn;daybreak
蒙头转向 lose one's bearings;be utterly confused

méng（ㄇㄥˊ）

氓 [méng]
名 common people;common herd ➡ máng
虻 [méng]
名 horsefly;gadfly
萌 [méng]
名 sprout;bud;germinate
萌动 ①(of plants) sprout;shoot forth;germinate;bud ②start
萌发 sprout;shoot forth;bud;germinate
萌生 come into being;arise
萌芽 ①sprout;shoot forth;bud;germinate ② rudiment;shoot;seed;germ

蒙 [méng]
Ⅰ 动 ① cover ② suffer;incur;encounter Ⅱ 名 ignorance ➡ mēng;měng
蒙蔽 hoodwink;deceive;hide the truth from;pull the wool over sb's eyes
蒙尘 be exposed to wind and dust
蒙垢 be subjected to humiliation;be humilia-

ted

蒙馆 private school

蒙哄 deceive;hoodwink;swindle;cheat

蒙混 deceive (*or* mislead) people

蒙眬 ①half asleep;drowsy;somnolent ②obscure;dim;hazy

蒙昧 ①barbaric;uncivilized;uncultured ②ignorant;benighted;unenlightened

蒙蒙 drizzly;misty

蒙难 (of a revolutionary) be confronted by danger;fall into the clutches of the enemy

蒙受 suffer;sustain

蒙学 private school

蒙冤 be wronged;suffer an injustice

蒙导法 mentor method

蒙汗药 a narcotic believed to have been used by highwaymen,etc. to drug their victims; knockout drops

蒙面盗 a masked bandit;a masked burglar

蒙太奇 montage

蒙昧无知 unenlightened;benighted;childishly ignorant

蒙昧主义 obscurantism

蒙头盖脸 cover one's head and face

蒙羞而亡 die an ignominious death

蒙在鼓里 be kept inside a drum—be kept in the dark

盟 [méng] I 名 ①alliance;coalition ②league II 动 take one's oath;swear

盟邦 an allied country;ally

盟国 an allied country;ally

盟军 allied forces

盟誓 ①an oath of alliance;a treaty of alliance ②take an oath;make a pledge

盟友 ally

盟员 a member of an alliance (*or* league)

盟约 an oath of alliance;a treaty of alliance

盟主 the leader (*or* chief) of an alliance

盟兄弟 sworn brothers

潆 [méng] 形 drizzling

檬 [méng]

◇柠檬 lemon

曚 [méng]

曚昽 ①(of sunlight) dim;hazy ②obscure;dim

朦 [méng]

朦胧 ①(of moonlight) dim;hazy ②obscure; dim;hazy

朦胧诗 obscure poems

měng (ㄇㄥˇ)

猛 [měng] I 形 fierce;violent;strong;vigorous II 副

①suddenly;abruptly ②with a spurt of force

猛地 suddenly;abruptly

猛攻 onslaught;fierce attack

猛虎 fierce tiger

猛将 valiant general

猛进 push ahead vigorously;advance in quick and big strides

猛力 with sudden force

猛厉 fierce;vigorous;violent

猛料 sensational news

猛烈 fierce;vigorous

猛犸 mammoth

猛禽 bird of prey

猛然 suddenly;abruptly

猛士 brave warrior

猛兽 beast of prey

猛醒 suddenly wake up (to the truth)

猛增 dramatic increase

猛鸷 hawk;eagle

猛追 give a hot pursuit

猛不防 by surprise;unexpectedly;unawares

猛劲儿 ①a spurt of energy;dash ②great vigour

猛吃猛喝 eat and drink one's fill

猛打猛冲 go full blast ahead

猛孤丁地 suddenly;abruptly

猛虎扑食 like a fierce tiger springing on the prey;with a quick and ferocious speed

猛将如云 a great many brave warriors

猛犬债券 bulldog bond

蒙 [měng] 名 Mongol (*or* Mongolian) nationality ➡ mēng;méng

蠓 [měng] 名 midge;biting midge

mèng (ㄇㄥˋ)

孟 [mèng] 名 ①first month of a season (of the Chinese lunar calendar) ②eldest (brother)

孟春 the first month of spring

孟冬 the first month of winter

孟浪 rash;impetuous;impulsive

孟秋 the first month of autumn

孟夏 the first month of summer

孟子 Mencius

梦 [mèng] 名 ①dream ②illusion

梦话 ①words uttered in one's sleep;somniloquy ②daydream;nonsense

梦幻 illusion;dream;reverie

梦见 see in a dream;dream about

梦境 dreamland;dreamworld;dream

梦寐 dream;sleep

梦乡 dreamland

梦想 ①vain hope;wishful thinking ②vainly hope;dream of

M

梦魇 nightmare
梦遗 nocturnal emission；wet dream
梦呓 ①sleeptalking；somniloquy ②rigmarole
梦游症 somnambulism；sleepwalking
梦笔生花 dream that one's brush is blooming—begin to show one's literary brilliance
梦幻泡影 pipe dream；bubble；illusion

mī (ㄇㄧ)

咪 [mī]

咪咪 mew；miaow

眯 [mī]

〔动〕①narrow (one's eyes) ②take a short sleep；nap；doze off ➡ mí

眯缝 narrow (one's eyes)
眯盹儿 doze off；take a nap

mí (ㄇㄧˊ)

弥 [mí]

Ⅰ〔动〕① be full of；overflow ②fill；cover Ⅱ〔副〕even more；still more

弥补 make up；remedy；make good
弥缝 plug up holes—gloss over faults
弥合 close；bridge
弥勒 Maitreya
弥留 be dying
弥漫 fill the air；spread all over the place
弥蒙 misty；foggy
弥撒 Mass
弥散 spread (or diffuse) in all directions
弥雾 atomizing；atomization
弥撒曲 Mass
弥补亏空 meet a deficit；make up (for) a loss
弥天大谎 monstrous lie；outrageous lie
弥天大罪 monstrous crime；heinous crime
弥望无际 boundless horizon

迷 [mí]

Ⅰ〔动〕①be confused；be lost ②be fascinated by；engrossed in；crazy about ③bewitch；fascinate；enchant；perplex Ⅱ〔名〕fan；enthusiast；buff

迷彩 camouflage；camouflage colours
迷瞪 [mídeng] muddle；confuse
迷宫 labyrinth；maze
迷航 (of a plane, ship, etc.) drift off course；lose one's course；get lost
迷糊 ①misted；blurred；dimmed ②dazed；confused ③muddleheaded
迷幻 hazy and illusionary；fantastic
迷惑 puzzle；confuse；perplex；baffle
迷津 miss the ferry—stray from the right path
迷离 blurred；misted
迷恋 be infatuated with；madly cling to
迷路 ①lose one's way；get lost ②go astray
迷乱 dazed and confused；befuddled

迷漫 boundless and indistinct；vast and hazy
迷茫 ①vast and hazy ②confused；perplexed；dazed
迷梦 pipe dream；fond illusion
迷你 mini
迷人 charming；fascinating；enchanting；bewitching
迷失 lose (one's way, etc.)
迷途 ①lose one's way ②wrong path
迷惘 be perplexed；be at a loss
迷雾 ① dense fog ② anything that misleads people
迷信 ①superstition；superstitious belief；blind faith；blind worship ②have blind faith in；make a fetish of
迷住 charm；entrance；fascinate
迷醉 be fascinated by；intoxicate；enchant
迷彩服 camouflage clothing；camouflage uniform；mottled camouflage jacket
迷幻剂 psychedelic drug
迷幻药 acid；LSD
迷魂汤 ①sth intended to turn sb's head；magic potion ②flattery
迷魂阵 a scheme for confusing (or bewildering) sb；maze；trap
迷你裙 miniskirt
迷不知返 go astray not knowing how to return
迷离惝恍 indistinct；blurred
迷迷糊糊 in a daze；difficult to make out
迷迷怔怔 dazed；confused
迷途知返 recover one's bearings and return to the fold；realize one's errors and mend one's ways
迷走神经 vagus (nerve)

眯 [mí]

〔动〕(of dust, etc.) get into one's eye ➡ mī

猕 [mí]

猕猴 macaque；macacus monkey；rhesus monkey

谜 [mí]

〔名〕①riddle；conundrum ②enigma；mystery；puzzle

谜底 ①answer (or solution) to a riddle ②truth
谜团 doubts and suspicions
谜语 riddle；conundrum

醚 [mí]

〔名〕ether

糜 [mí]

Ⅰ〔名〕gruel Ⅱ〔动〕rot Ⅲ〔形〕wasteful；extravagant

糜烂 ① rotten to the core；dissipated；debauched ②erosion
糜灭 rot away

縻 [mí]

〔动〕fasten；tie；do up

靡 [mǐ]
　形 wasteful;extravagant ⇒mí
靡费 waste

mǐ (nǐ)

米 [mǐ]
　Ⅰ 名 ①rice ②shelled (*or* husked seed) (usu. edible) ③anything like a grain of rice Ⅱ 量 metre
米波 metric wave
米尺 metre rule;metre scale;meterstick
米醋 rice vinegar
米饭 (cooked) rice
米粉 ①ground rice;rice flour ②rice-flour noodles
米糕 rice cake;rice pudding
米黄 cream-coloured
米价 the price of rice
米酒 rice wine
米糠 rice bran
米粒 grain of rice
米面 ①rice and wheat flour ②ground rice; rice flour ③rice-flour noodles
米色 cream-coloured
米汤 ①water in which rice has been cooked ②thin rice or millet gruel;rice water
米线 rice-flour noodles
米象 rice weevil
米纸 rice paper
米制 the metric system
米粥 congee;rice gruel
米袋子 rice sack;rice supply to the market
米粉肉 steamed rice flour pork
米泔水 water in which rice has been washed
米老鼠 Mickey Mouse;mickey mouse
米粮川 rich rice-producing area
米烛光 metre-candle;lux
米蛀虫 ①rice worm ②rice profiteer
米珠薪桂 rice is as precious as pearls and firewood as costly as cassia—exorbitantly high cost of living
"米袋子"省长负责制 system of the provincial governor's responsibility for the "rice bag"

弭 [mǐ]
　动 put down;quell;remove
弭谤 stop a slander
弭除 eliminate;dispel;remove;clear up
弭患 remove the source of trouble
弭乱 put down a rebellion;stop a civil war
弭战 quell a rebellion;stop a civil war

脒 [mǐ]
　名 amidine

敉 [mǐ]
　动 placate;pacify;appease

靡 [mǐ]
　Ⅰ 动 bend with the wind Ⅱ 形 fine;wonderful;excellent Ⅲ 副 no;not ⇒mí

靡丽 ①magnificent;resplendent ②luxurious; extravagant
靡然 universally;leaning to one side
靡衣 gorgeous dress
靡靡之音 decadent music
靡事不为 like to try one's hand at anything

mì (nì)

觅 [mì]
　动 look for;seek
觅句 seek a telling line (for a poem)
觅取 look for;hunt for;seek
觅索词句 strive for phrases and sentences
觅致人才 on the lookout for proper personnel

泌 [mì]
　动 secrete
泌尿科 urological department
泌尿学 urology
泌尿器官 urinary organs
泌尿系统 urinary system

宓 [mì]
　形 peaceful;tranquil;quiet

秘 [mì]
　Ⅰ 形 ①secret;confidential ②seldom seen; rare Ⅱ 动 make a secret of;keep sth secret; hold sth back
秘宝 a rare treasure
秘本 treasured private copy of a rare book
秘传 hand down (a recipe,formula,etc.) from generation to generation in the family as a closely guarded secret
秘方 secret recipe
秘诀 secret of success
秘密 ①secret;clandestine;confidential ②sth secret
秘史 secret history (as of a feudal dynasty); inside story
秘事 private affair;secret
秘书 secretary
秘闻 secret
秘书处 secretariat
秘书长 Secretary-General
秘而不漏 conceal;hide
秘而不宣 keep sth secret;not let anyone in on a secret
秘密报告 a secret report
秘密会议 secret meeting;closed-door session
秘密活动 clandestine activities
秘密警察 secret police
秘密渠道 back channel
秘密文件 secret papers;confidential document

密 [mì]
　形 ①dense;heavy;close;thick ②intimate; familiar;close ③fine;precise;meticulous ④secret;confidential
密报 ①secretly report;inform against sb ②a secret report

M

密闭 airtight；hermetic
密布 be densely covered
密电 ①secretly telegraph sb ②cipher telegram
密度 ①density；thickness ②density
密访 pay a secret visit；make investigation by travelling incognito
密封 seal up；seal airtight；seal hermetically
密告 secretly report；inform against sb
密集 concentrated；crowded together
密件 a confidential paper（or letter）；classified matter；classified material
密林 thick（or dense）forest
密令 ①give a secret order（or instructions）②secret order（or instructions）
密码 cipher；cipher code；secret code
密谋 conspire；plot；scheme
密切 ①close；intimate ②build（or forge，establish）close links（between two parties）③careful；intent；close
密商 hold private counsel；hold secret talks
密实 closely knit；dense；thick
密使 secret emissary；secret envoy
密室 a room used for secret purposes
密谈 have a secret（or confidential，private）talk；talk behind closed doors
密探 secret agent；spy
密位 mil
密文 ciphertext
密信 confidential letter；secret letter
密友 close（or fast）friend；bosom friend
密约 secret agreement；secret treaty
密召 recall secretly
密植 close planting
密电码 cipher code
密度计 densimeter
密封舱 sealed cabin；airtight cabin
密集型 intensive
密码机 cipher machine；cryptograph
密码术 cryptography
密码锁 trick lock
密码箱 code box；cipher suitcase
密码学 cryptography
密码员 cryptographer
密码子 codon
密陀僧 litharge；yellow lead
密匝匝 thick；dense
密不透风 airtight
密封包装 air-tight wrapping
密封保存 preserve sth by sealing it airtight
密封垫圈 sealing washer
密封机身 closed fuselage
密封投标 sealed bid；sealed tender
密封压盖 sealing gland
密函告知 inform one by means of confidential letters
密集队形 close formation；tight formation

密集轰炸 massive bombing
密集炮火 intensive bombardment；concentrated fire；massed fire；drumfire
密来暗往 secretly communicate with each other
密码电报 cipher telegram
密密层层 packed closely layer upon layer（or ring upon ring）；dense；thick
密密丛丛 （of grass or trees）dense；thick
密密麻麻 close and numerous；thickly dotted
密密匝匝 thick；dense
密如雨点 as thick as raindrops；as thick as hail
密通声息 pass on（or exchange）secret information；keep each other imformed（or posted）in secret
密纹唱片 long-playing record；microgroove record
密写情报 intelligence written in invisible ink，etc.
密语通信 crypto-communication
密云不雨 dense clouds but no rain—trouble is brewing
密闭集装箱 sealed container
密切联系群众 forge（or maintain）close links with the masses

幂 [mì]
名 ①cloth cover ②cover；hood ③power
幂乘积 power product
幂函数 power function
幂级数 power series

谧 [mì]
形 tranquil；peaceful
谧静 quiet；still；tranquil

嘧 [mì]
嘧啶 pyrimidine

蜜 [mì]
Ⅰ 名 ① honey ② honey-like thing Ⅱ 形 sweet；honeyed；luscious
蜜蜂 honeybee；bee
蜜柑 mandarin orange；tangerine orange
蜜罐 honey jar；comfortable living conditions
蜜剂 mellite
蜜饯 candied fruit；preserved fruit
蜜橘 tangerine
蜜蜡 beeswax
蜜露 honeydew
蜜鸟 honeycreeper
蜜色 light yellow
蜜桃 nectarine
蜜甜 as sweet as honey；very sweet
蜜腺 nectary
蜜源 nectar source
蜜月 honeymoon
蜜枣 candied date（or jujube）
蜜渍 candied；preserved in sugar
蜜丸子 a bolus made of powdered Chinese medicine and honey

蜜源区 (bee) pasture
蜜源植物 nectariferous (*or* bee,honey) plant

mián (ㄇㄧㄢˊ)

眠 I 劲 sleep II 名 dormancy
眠尔通 miltown
眠花宿柳 visit prostitutes;go whoring

绵 I 名 silk floss II 形 ①continuous;consecutive ②thin;weak;soft ③(of a person's temper) gentle;meek
绵薄 (my) meagre strength;humble effort
绵长 (of time) very long
绵绸 fabric made from waste silk
绵亘 (of mountains,etc.) stretch in an unbroken chain;continuous;unending
绵力 my limited power
绵绵 continuous;unbroken
绵邈 faraway;remote
绵软 ①soft ②weak
绵延 be continuous;stretch long and unbroken
绵羊 sheep
绵纸 tissue paper
绵白糖 fine white sugar
绵里藏针 a needle hidden in silk floss—a ruthless character behind a gentle appearance; an iron hand in a velvet glove
绵绵絮语 whisper continually

棉 I 名 ①(general term for) cotton and kapok ②cotton ③cotton-like material II 形 cotton-padded
棉袄 cotton-padded (*or* quilted) jacket
棉被 a quilt with cotton wadding;cotton-wedded quilt
棉布 cotton cloth;cotton
棉纺 cotton spinning
棉凫 cotton teal
棉婚 cotton wedding anniversary—the 2nd wedding anniversary
棉花 cotton
棉卷 lap
棉裤 cotton-padded trousers
棉铃 cotton boll
棉帽 cotton-padded cap
棉农 cotton grower
棉球 cotton ball
棉区 cotton region;cotton belt
棉绒 cotton velvet
棉纱 cotton yarn
棉毯 cotton blanket
棉桃 cotton boll
棉套 a cotton-padded covering for keeping sth warm
棉田 cotton field
棉条 sliver

棉线 cotton thread;cotton
棉鞋 cotton-padded shoes
棉絮 ①cotton fibre ②a cotton wadding (for a quilt,etc.)
棉衣 cotton-padded clothes
棉籽 cottonseed
棉纺厂 cotton mill
棉猴儿 hooded cotton-padded coat;anorak
棉花签 (cotton) swab
棉花蛆 pink bollworm
棉花胎 cotton wadding (for a quilt,etc.)
棉花糖 cotton candy
棉铃虫 bollworm
棉毛机 interlock (knitting) machine
棉毛裤 cotton (interlock) trousers (worn as underwear)
棉毛衫 cotton (interlock) jersey (worn as underwear)
棉袍子 cotton-padded robe
棉纱头 (cotton) waste
棉条桶 sliver can
棉蚜虫 cotton aphid
棉织品 cotton goods; cotton textiles; cotton fabrics
棉纺织品 cotton textiles
棉红铃虫 pink bollworm
棉红蜘蛛 two-spotted spider mite
棉花套子 cotton wadding (for a quilt)
棉枯萎病 fusarium wilt of cotton
棉毛衫布 cotton interlock (fabric)

miǎn (ㄇㄧㄢˇ)

丏 劲 cover;be out of sight

免 劲 ①excuse or free (sb from sth);exempt; dispense with ②remove from office;dismiss; sack;relieve ③avoid;avert;evade;escape ④ do not (do)
免除 ① prevent; avoid ② remit; excuse; exempt;relieve
免得 so as not to;so as to avoid
免费 free of charge;free;gratis
免冠 ①take one's hat off (in salutation) ② without a hat on;bareheaded
免检 exempt from inspection;inspection-free
免票 ①free pass;free ticket ②free of charge
免试 ①be exempted from an examination (for admission to college or for promotion) ②be exempted from a test
免税 ①exempt from taxation ② tax-free;duty-free
免俗 act contrary to common practice
免烫 easy-care;wash-and-wear;non-ironing
免刑 exempt from punishment
免修 waive a course requirement; be exempt from a required course

免验 exempt from customs examination
免役 exempt from military service
免疫 immunity (from disease)
免征 be exempt from taxation
免职 remove sb from office;relieve sb of his post
免罪 be exempt from punishment
免不了 be unavoidable;be bound to be
免税期 tax holiday
免验证 laissez-passer
免疫力 immunity (from disease);immune to unhealthy ideas
免疫体 immune body
免疫性 immunity
免战牌 a sign used in ancient times to show refusal to fight
免办签证 dispense with a visa
免耕农业 till-less agriculture
免开尊口 Please keep your mouth shut (i.e. not broach the ticklish topic).
免赔条款 franchise clause
免试外语 be exempted from the foreign language examination
免税货物 duty-free goods
免税利润 tax-free profits
免税商店 duty-free shop
免税投资 tax-free investment
免税物品 free goods
免税证券 tax-exempt securities
免提电话 hand-free phone
免验放行 pass without examination (P. W. E)
免疫证书 bill of health
免疫治疗 immunization therapy
免疫注射 inoculation
免于公诉 immunity from prosecution
免于体检 be excused from a physical examination
免予处罚 remit
免予罚款 be exempt from a fine
免予起诉 be exempt from prosecution;drop the case;be free from accusation (or suit)
免遭物议 so as to avoid public censure;so as not to incur criticism by the masses
免致后患 avoid causing future trouble
免签证协议 agreement on mutual exemption of visas
免疫球蛋白 immunoglobulin

勉 [miǎn]
劢 ①make an effort;exert oneself;strive ②encourage;spur;urge ③try to do what is almost beyond one's power (or act against one's will)
勉力 exert oneself;try hard;make great efforts
勉励 encourage;urge
勉强 ①manage with an effort;do with difficulty ②reluctant;grudging ③force sb to do sth ④inadequate;unconvincing;strained;farfetched ⑤barely enough
勉人为善 urge people to do good
勉为其难 undertake to do a difficult job as best one can;agree to do what one knows is beyond one's ability or power

娩 [miǎn]
◇分娩 childbirth;parturition

冕 [miǎn]
名 crown;coronet

缅 [miǎn]
I 形 remote;far back II 劢 roll up
缅怀 cherish the memory of;recall
缅邈 remote;far back
缅想 think of (past events);recall

腼 [miǎn]
腼腆 shy;bashful

miàn（ㄇ丨ㄢˋ）

面 [miàn]
I 名 ①face;visage ②surface;top;face ③right side;cover;outside ④surface ⑤side;aspect ⑥extent;range;scale;scope ⑦entire range or area (as distinct from particular points);overall situation ⑧wheat flour;flour;meal ⑨power ⑩noodles II 劢 face (a certain direction) III 量 ①(of for flat and smooth object):一面锣 a gong/两面镜子 two mirrors ②(used to indicate the times people meet one another):见过一次面 have met once IV 副 face-to-face;personally;directly V (*used as a suffix to form a noun of locality*) VI 形 (of food) soft and mealy:面倭瓜 mealy pumpkin
面包 bread
面禀 report (to one's superior) in person
面茶 seasoned millet mush
面陈 tell (*or* explain) in person
面呈 submit in person
面斥 give sb a talking-to;reprove
面辞 go to say good-bye to sb;take leave of sb
面的 minibus taxi
面点 snacks made from wheat (*or* rice) flour
面对 face;confront
面额 ①denomination ②forehead
面肥 ①leavening dough;leaven ②topdressing
面粉 wheat flour;flour
面革 upper leather
面糊 ①paste ②soft and floury
面积 area
面颊 cheek
面交 deliver personally;hand-deliver
面巾 towel
面筋 gluten
面具 mask

面孔 face
面盔 visor；vizor
面料 material for making the outside (of a garment)；material to make clothing
面临 be faced with；be confronted with；be up against
面聆 hear sb's words of wisdom in person
面貌 ① face；features ② appearance (of things)；look；aspect
面膜 face-pack；mask；facial mask
面目 ① face；features；visage ② appearance (of things)；look；aspect ③ self-respect；honour；sense of shame；face
面嫩 ① look younger than one's age ② shy；bashful；sensitive
面庞 contours of the face；face
面盆 ① washbasin；washbowl ② bowl for kneading dough
面皮 ① face；cheek ② rapper (of dumpling)
面洽 discuss with sb face to face；take up a matter with sb personally
面前 in (the) face of；in front of；before
面罄 explain in detail personally
面容 facial features；face
面色 ① complexion ② facial expression
面纱 veil
面善 ① look familiar ② affable；amiable
面商 discuss with sb face to face；consult personally
面上 general；overall
面生 look unfamiliar
面食 cooked wheaten food
面世 (of writing, product, etc.) come into existence；come out；be published
面试 oral quiz；audition；interview；viva
面首 keep man of noblewoman；handsome man who is kept by a noblewoman to play with
面授 instruct personally；classroom teaching
面熟 look familiar
面谈 speak to sb face to face；take up a matter with sb personally
面汤 ① water in which noodles have been boiled ② noodles in soup ③ hot water for washing face
面条 noodles
面团 dough
面向 ① turn one's face to；turn in the direction of；face ② be geared to the needs of；cater to
面相 facial features；looks；appearance
面谢 thank sb in person
面议 negotiate face to face；take up a matter with sb personally
面谕 (of superiors or elders) instruct (or tell) sb in person
面罩 face guard
面值 ① par value；face value；nominal value ② denomination
面砖 face brick
面子 ① outer part；outside；face ② reputation；prestige；face ③ feelings；sensibilities
面包车 minibus；small van
面包房 bakery
面包干 rusk
面包果 breadfruit
面包师 baker
面对面 facing each other；face-to-face；vis-à-vis
面粉厂 flour mill
面疙瘩 balls of dough
面巾纸 face tissue；kleenex；serviette
面面观 comprehensive survey；full overview
面人儿 dough figurine
面神经 facial nerve
面包酵母 baker's yeast
面包渣儿 bread crumbs；crumbs
面壁而立 stand facing the wall
面不改色 not change colour；remain calm；without turning a hair；without batting an eyelid
面部表情 facial expression
面从后言 say yes to sb's face but begin to carp the moment his back is turned
面带病容 one's face shows sickly countenance
面带愁容 with a sad air
面带笑容 have (or wear) a smile on one's face
面带笑意 one's face shows smiling mood
面对现实 face reality；come down to earth
面红耳赤 be red in the face；be flushed
面黄肌瘦 sallow and emaciated；lean and haggard
面貌一新 take on a new look
面面俱到 attend to each and every aspect of a matter
面面相觑 look at each other in blank dismay；gaze at each other in speechless despair
面目可憎 repulsive in appearance
面目全非 be changed beyond recognition
面目一新 take on an entirely new look；present a completely new appearance；assume a new aspect
面目狰狞 ferocious features；a vile visage
面南坐北 facing the south and with the north at one's back
面如死灰 look like dying embers—be deathly pale due to fright or poor health
面如土色 look ashen；look pale
面上无光 loss of prestige
面授机宜 give confidential briefing
面无表情 expressionless
面无惧色 one's face shows no fear
面无人色 look ghastly pale
面向大众 be geared to the needs of the popu-

M

lace at large
面向市场 market orientation;gear to the demand of the market
面有菜色 look famished
面有难色 show signs of reluctance (*or* embarrassment)
面誉背毁 praise sb to his face and abuse him behind his back;praise openly and slander secretly
面和心不和 remain friendly in appearance but estranged at heart
面向 21 世纪 gear to the 21st century;be oriented toward the 21st century

miāo (ㄇㄧㄠ)

喵 [miāo]
拟 mew;miaow

miáo (ㄇㄧㄠˊ)

苗 [miáo]
名 ①shoot;sprout;seedling;young plant ②offspring;male child;son ③young of some animals ④ vaccine ⑤ sth resembling a young plant
苗儿 symptom of a trend;suggestion of a new development
苗床 seedbed
苗木 forestry nursery stock
苗圃 nursery (of young plants)
苗期 seedling stage
苗条 (of a woman) slender;slim
苗头 symptom of a trend;suggestion of a new development
苗裔 progeny;descendants;offspring
苗子 ①young plant;seedling ②young successor ③symptom of a trend;suggestion of a new development
苗而不秀 put forth shoots that fail to flower—show great potentialities but fail to fulfil them

描 [miáo]
动 ①trace;copy ②touch up;retouch
描红 trace in black ink over characters printed in red (in learning to write with a brush)
描画 draw;paint;depict;describe
描绘 depict;describe;portray
描金 trace a design in gold
描眉 pencil one's eyebrows
描摹 depict;portray;delineate
描述 describe
描图 tracing
描写 describe;depict;portray
描图员 tracer
描图纸 tracing paper
描龙绣凤 do fine needlework
描写语言学 descriptive linguistics

瞄 [miáo]
动 aim;take aim
瞄准 take aim;aim;train on;lay;sight
瞄准环 ring sight
瞄准具 sighting device;(gun) sight
瞄准手 layer;pointer
瞄准市场 keep a close eye on the market

miǎo (ㄇㄧㄠˇ)

杪 [miǎo]
名 ①tip of a twig;top of a tree ②end (of a year,month or season)

眇 [miǎo]
形 ①blind ②tiny;minute

秒 [miǎo]
名 second (= 1/60 of a minute)
秒表 stopwatch;chronograph
秒针 second hand (of a clock or watch)
秒差距 parsec
秒立方米 cubic metre per second
秒数计数器 seconds counter

渺 [miǎo]
形 ①distant and indistinct;nebulous;vague ②tiny;insignificant;trivial
渺茫 ①distant and indistinct;vague ②uncertain
渺小 tiny;negligible;insignificant;paltry
渺远 faraway;distant;remote
渺不足道 not worth mentioning;insignificant;negligible
渺若烟云 as vague as mist;as obscure as mist
渺无声息 devoid of noise—still;quiet
渺无人迹 remote and uninhabited
渺无人烟 uninhabited;without a trace of human habitation
渺无音信 there has been no news whatsoever about sb;never been heard of since

缈 [miǎo]
◇ 缥缈 dimly discernible;misty

藐 [miǎo]
Ⅰ 形 small;petty Ⅱ 动 despise;slight;belittle
藐视 despise;look down upon
藐小 tiny;negligible;insignificant;paltry

邈 [miǎo]
形 remote;far away
邈远 faraway;distant;remote
邈不可见 too distant to be seen

miào (ㄇㄧㄠˋ)

妙 [miào]
形 ①wonderful;superb;excellent;marvellous ②ingenious;clever;abstruse;subtle
妙笔 ingenious (*or* exquisite) writing
妙策 excellent plan;brilliant scheme
妙处 ①ideal place;suitable location ②merit;advantage;fine point

妙计 an excellent plan;a brilliant scheme
妙境 fairyland;wonderland
妙句 beautiful sentence;well-turned phrase
妙诀 clever way;ingenious method
妙龄 youthfulness (of a girl)
妙论 ingenious remark;very clever remark
妙品 ①fine quality goods ②fine work of art
妙棋 clever (chess) move
妙算 wonderful foresight;accurate calculations
妙药 efficacious medicine;wonder drug
妙用 magical effect
妙语 witty remark
妙笔生花 write like an angel
妙不可言 too wonderful for words;most intriguing
妙龄女郎 young girl;young maiden
妙趣横生 full of wit and humour;very witty
妙手回春 (of a doctor) effect a miraculous cure and bring the dying back to life
妙手空空 ①petty (or sneak) thief;pilferer ②not own a thing in the world;not have a thing to one's name
妙语解颐 witty remarks that make people laugh;wisecracks that really tickle
妙语惊人 unsurpassed beauty of expression
妙语如珠 stream of witticism
妙语双关 very clever pun
妙在不言中 The charm lies in what is left unsaid.

庙 [miào]
〔名〕①temple;shrine ②imperial court ③late emperor ④temple fair
庙号 posthumous title of an emperor
庙会 temple fair;fair
庙讳 name of a late emperor
庙堂 ①the Imperial Ancestral Temple ②imperial court
庙议 deliberations in the imperial court;court conference
庙宇 temple
庙主 head priest of a temple
庙祝 temple attendant in charge of incense and religious service;acolyte

mié（ㄇㄧㄝ）

乜 [mié]
〔动〕squint
乜斜 ①squint ②(of eyes) half-closed

咩 [mié]
〔象〕baa;bleat

miè（ㄇㄧㄝˋ）

灭 [miè]
〔动〕①(of a light,fire,etc.) go out ②extinguish;put out;turn off ③submerge;drown ④perish;die out;wither away;become extinct

⑤destroy;exterminate;annihilate
灭茬 clean stubble (fields)
灭顶 be drowned
灭火 ①put out a fire;extinguish a fire ②cut out an engine
灭迹 destroy the evidence (of one's evildoing)
灭绝 ①become extinct ②completely lose
灭菌 sterilization;disinfection
灭口 do away with a witness (or accomplice)
灭门 exterminate an entire family
灭失 loss
灭亡 be destroyed;become extinct;die out
灭种 exterminate a race;commit genocide
灭族 extermination of an entire family (a punishment in ancient China)
灭草剂 herbicide
灭虫宁 bephenium
灭涤灵 niclosamide
灭火剂 fire-extinguishing chemical (or agent)
灭火器 fire extinguisher
灭音器 muffler
灭此朝食 will not have breakfast until the enemy is wiped out—be anxious to finish off the enemy immediately
灭顶之灾 getting drowned
灭尽天良 destroy utterly one's conscience
灭绝人性 inhuman;savage;cannibalistic
灭绝种族 genocide
灭门之灾 the calamity of exterminating a family

蔑 [miè]
Ⅰ〔形〕small;slight;petty;paltry Ⅱ〔副〕not;no;none;nothing
蔑称 ①call in contempt ②contemptuous name
蔑视 despise;show contempt for;scorn
蔑视法庭 contempt of court

篾 [miè]
〔名〕①thin bamboo strip ②husk or outer layer of reed or sorghum stalks
篾黄 the inner skin of a bamboo stem
篾匠 craftsman who makes articles from bamboo strips
篾片 ①thin bamboo strip ②old hanger-on;sycophant
篾青 the outer cuticle of a bamboo stem
篾条 bamboo strip
篾席 mat made of thin bamboo strips

mín（ㄇㄧㄣˊ）

民 [mín]
Ⅰ〔名〕①the people ②member of a nationality ③person of a certain occupation Ⅱ〔形〕①of the people;popular;folk ②civilian;civil Ⅲ〔代〕my
民办 be run by the local people
民变 mass uprising;popular revolt

民兵 ①people's militia;militia ②militiaman
民法 civil law
民防 civil defence
民房 house owned by a citizen;private house
民愤 popular indignation;the people's wrath
民风 folkways;local traits
民歌 folk song
民工 transient worker;labourer working on a public project
民国 the Republic of China
民航 civil aviation
民间 ①among the people;popular;folk ②nongovernmental;people-to-people
民警 people's police;policeman;policewoman
民居 local-style dwelling houses
民力 financial resources of the people
民氓 the masses of the people;the common people
民品 civilian products;civilian goods;products for civilian use
民气 the people's morale;popular morale
民情 ①condition of the people ②feelings of the people;public feeling
民权 civil rights; civil liberties; democratic rights
民生 the people's livelihood
民事 relating to civil law;civil
民俗 folk custom;folkways
民团 civil corps (formerly, reactionary local armed forces organized by landlords)
民心 popular feelings;common aspirations of the people;will of the people
民谚 common proverb
民谣 folk rhyme (esp. of the topical and political type)
民意 the will of the people;popular will
民营 run by private citizens
民用 for civil use;civil
民乐 music,esp. folk music,for traditional instruments
民运 ①civil transport ②the army's propaganda and organizational work among the civilians during the revolutionary wars led by the Chinese Communist Party ③ mass movement;mass campaign
民贼 traitor to the people
民宅 a private (*or* civilian) residence
民政 civil administration
民众 the masses of the people;the common people;the populace
民主 ①democracy;democratic rights ②democratic
民族 nation;nationality;ethnic group
民法典 civil code
民工潮 massive influx of migrant worker; massive flow of farmers into the city for casual jobs

民航机 civil aircraft;civil airplane
民进党 the Democratic Progressive Party
民俗学 folklore
民乐队 traditional instruments orchestra
民主党 the Democratic Party (in U.S.)
民族感 sense of peoplehood
民族学 ethnology
民安国泰 The masses are in peace and the country is prosperous.
民办大学 private university;university run by individuals but with the help of government
民办公助 run by the local people but subsidized by the state
民办机构 community-run institution
民办教师 citizen-managed teachers; teacher not on government payroll
民办科技 research institutes run by the non-state sectors
民办小学 a primary school run by the local people
民办学校 school run by the local people;non-government-run school
民不聊生 The people have no means of livelihood;The masses live in dire poverty;The people are destitute.
民粹主义 populism
民法通则 general provisions of the civil law
民风淳朴 The people are simple, honest and unspoiled.
民富国强 The people live in plenty and the country is strong.
民间传说 popular legend;folk legend;folklore
民间故事 folktale;folk story
民间机构 non-governmental bodies
民间疾苦 hardships of the people
民间交流 people-to-people exchange
民间纠纷 dispute among the people
民间来往 nongovernmental contact;people-to-people exchange
民间诗人 folk bard
民间团体 private organization; non-governmental organization
民间外交 non-governmental diplomacy
民间文学 folk literature
民间舞蹈 folk dance
民间协定 nongovernmental agreement
民间艺术 folk art
民间音乐 folk music
民间组织 nongovernmental organization
民康物阜 Products abound and the people live in peace.
民穷财尽 The people are impoverished and the nation's resources exhausted;The people are destitute and the national economy is in dire straits.
民权主义 the Principle of Democracy
民生凋敝 The people live in destitution.

民生主义 the Principle of the People's Livelihood
民事案件 civil case
民事调解 civil mediation
民事法庭 civil court
民事过失 civil negligence
民事警察 civil police
民事纠纷 civil litigation
民事立法 civil legislation
民事赔偿 civil compensation
民事上诉 civil appeal
民事诉讼 civil action
民事责任 civil liability; obligation relation to civil law
民心工程 projects corresponding to popular aspirations
民心所向 trend of public feeling; where the popular will inclines; common aspiration of the people
民心向背 will of the people; whether the people are for or against sb or sth
民意调查 poll; poll taking; public opinion poll
民营经济 nonpublic economy
民营企业 non-State sectors; non-governmentally operated enterprise
民用产品 products for civilian use
民用航空 civil aviation
民用市场 civilian market
民怨沸腾 The people are boiling with resentment; seething popular discontent.
民乐合奏 ensemble of traditional instruments
民政机关 civil administration organ
民脂民膏 fruits of the people's toil; flesh and blood of the people
民众团体 people's organization; mass organization
民主党派 democratic parties
民主改革 democratic reform
民主革命 democratic revolution
民主管理 democratic management
民主决策 democratic decision-making; make decisions in a democratic manner
民主人士 democratic personage
民主生活 democratic life
民主协商 democratic consultation
民主作风 democratic ways; democratic style of work
民族败类 scum of a nation
民族大义 supreme interests of the nation
民族动乱 ethnic unrest
民族独立 national independence
民族复兴 revival of nationhood; national rejuvenation
民族革命 national revolution
民族隔阂 national estrangement
民族精神 national spirit; national pride
民族歧视 ethnic discrimination

民族气节 national integrity
民族素质 nation's quality
民族特征 national traits
民族意识 national consciousness
民族英雄 national hero
民族政策 policy towards nationalities
民族之林 nations of the world; galaxy of nations; community of nations
民族主义 ①nationalism ②the Principle of Nationalism
民族自决 national self-determination
民族自治 autonomy of minority nationalities
民族尊严 national dignity
民事诽谤罪 civil libel
民事管辖权 civil jurisdiction
民事侵法权 law of tort
民事审判庭 the civil division of a people's court; civil court
民事诉讼法 law of civil litigation; law of civil procedure; civil procedure act
民以食为天 The masses regard food as their heaven (i.e. as their prime want).
民主共和国 democratic republic
民主集中制 democratic centralism
民族大家庭 the great family of nationalities
民族共同语 common national language
民族凝聚力 national cohesion
民族委员会 ethnic affairs commission
民族自信心 national confidence
民族自尊心 national pride; national self-respect
民事法律关系 civil legal relationship
民主党派人士 non-Communist political figures
民主法制建设 development (*or* improvement) of democracy and the legal system; efforts to develop democracy and improve the legal system
民主评议厂长 democratic appraisal on factory directors
民主政治建设 strengthen democracy and encourage democratic participation
民族解放运动 national liberation movement
民族利己主义 national egoism
民族民主革命 national-democratic revolution
民族区域自治 regional autonomy of minority nationalities; regional national autonomy
民族文化大省 province with rich ethnic culture
民族虚无主义 national nihilism
民族杂居地区 multi-national area
民族资产阶级 national bourgeoisie
民兵预备役部队 the militia and the reserves

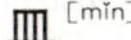

mǐn（ㄇㄧㄣˇ）

皿 [mǐn]

◇**器皿** household utensils; containers esp. for use in the house

抿 [mǐn]
动 ①smooth (hair, etc.) with a wet brush ②(of mouth, ear, wing, etc.) close lightly; tuck; furl ③sip
抿子 a small hairbrush

泯 [mǐn]
动 get rid of; lose; vanish; die out
泯灭 die out; disappear; vanish
泯没 vanish; sink into oblivion; become lost
泯弃宿怨 disregard old grievances

悯 [mǐn]
Ⅰ 动 pity; commiserate; sympathize Ⅱ 形 sorrow; grief
悯恻 feel compassion for; pity
悯惜 take pity on; have pity for
悯恤 feel compassion for; pity
悯然涕下 weep sadly
悯弱摧强 sympathize with the weak and overthrow the strong

敏 [mǐn]
形 ①quick; lithe; nimble; agile ②quick-witted; acute; keen; smart
敏感 sensitive; susceptible
敏化 sensitization
敏慧 bright; intelligent
敏捷 quick; nimble; agile
敏锐 sharp; acute; keen
敏感度 susceptibility
敏化剂 sensitizer
敏化纸 sensitized paper
敏感市场 sensitive market
敏感元件 sensitive element; sensor

憨 [mǐn]
形 smart and quick

鳘 [mǐn]
名 slate cod croaker

míng (ㄇㄧㄥˊ)

名 Ⅰ 名 ①name; appellation ②name; excuse; pretext ③fame; reputation; renown Ⅱ 动 ① given name ② express; describe ③ possess; have Ⅲ 形 famous; well-known; renowned; celebrated; noted Ⅳ 量 (of persons): 这个班有 30 名学生。There are 30 students in this class.
名菜 famous dish; speciality dish
名册 register; roll
名茶 famous brand of tea
名产 famous product
名称 name (of a thing or organization)
名城 a famous city
名厨 well-known chef
名词 ① noun; substantive ② term; phrase ③ name
名次 position in a name list; place in a competition

名单 name list
名额 the number of people assigned (or allowed); quota of people
名分 a person's status
名贵 famous and precious; rare
名号 person's official and courtesy names; person's name
名家 ①the School of Logicians ②a person of academic or artistic distinction; famous expert; master
名将 famous general; great soldier
名教 the Confucian ethical code
名节 reputation and integrity
名酒 vintage wine
名句 a well-known phrase; a much quoted line
名款 the name of the painter (or writer) inscribed on a painting or a piece of calligraphy
名利 fame and gain; fame and wealth
名流 distinguished personages; celebrities
名录 directory
名门 an old and well-known family; a distinguished family; an illustrious family
名模 famous model; celebrity model
名目 names of things; items
名牌 ①famous brand ②nameplate; name tag
名片 visiting card; calling card
名气 reputation; fame; name
名曲 a great musical composition; a masterpiece in music
名人 famous person; eminent person; celebrity; notable
名声 reputation; repute; renown
名胜 place famous for its scenery (or historical relics); scenic spot
名手 a famous artist (or player, etc.)
名数 ①concrete number ②numeral-classifier compound
名堂 ①variety; item ②result; achievement ③ what lies behind sth; reason
名头 reputation; repute; renown
名望 fame and prestige; good reputation; renown
名位 fame and position
名下 under sb's name; belonging (or related) to sb
名言 well-known saying; celebrated dictum; famous remark
名医 famous doctors
名义 ①name ②(usu. followed by 上) nominal; titular; in name
名优 famous actor (or actress)
名誉 ①fame; reputation ②honorary
名著 famous book; famous work
名状 give the right name for; describe
名字 ① name; given name ② name (of a

thing)
名嘴 popular anchorperson
名作 (literary) masterpiece
名利场 Vanity Fair
名片盒 cardcase
名不副实 The name falls short of the reality; be sth more in name than in reality; be unworthy of the name or title
名不虚传 have a well-deserved reputation; deserve the reputation one enjoys; live up to one's reputation
名从主人 name after originating person (*or* place)
名垂青史 go down in history; be crowned with eternal glory
名存实亡 cease to exist except in name; exist in name only
名孚众望 Prestige commands public confidence.
名副其实 The name matches the reality; be sth in reality as well as in name; be worthy of the name
名工巧匠 noted artisans and skilled craftsmen
名冠一时 overtop the age; well known in one's time
名过其实 be sth more in name than in reality; have an undeserved reputation
名缰利锁 the fetters of fame and wealth
名利双收 win fame and fortune; gain both fame and wealth
名列前茅 be among the best of the successful candidates
名落孙山 fall behind Sun Shan (who was last on the list of successful candidates)—fail in a competitive examination
名门闺秀 daughter of an illustrious family
名门望族 distinguished family; prominent family
名门之后 descendant of an illustrious family
名目繁多 a multitude of names (*or* items); names of every description
名人效应 socialite effect; celebrity effect
名山大川 famous mountains and great rivers
名山事业 commitment to literature
名升实降 kick sb upstairs
名胜古迹 places of historic interest and scenic beauty; scenic spots and historical sites
名士淑媛 the wit and the beauty of the town
名特产品 famous and special local products
名特商店 specialties shop
名特优新 famous, special, superior and new products
名闻中外 well-known both at home and abroad
名下无虚 deserve the reputation one enjoys; live up to one's reputation
名扬四海 become famous all over the world; be world-renowned

名义被告 nominal defendant
名义代理 ostensible agency
名义负债 nominal liability
名义工资 nominal wages
名义汇价 nominal rate (of exchange)
名义所得 nominal income
名义原告 nominal plaintiff
名誉董事 honorary director
名誉公民 honorary citizen
名誉会员 honorary member
名誉教授 professor emeritus
名誉主席 honorary chairman; honorary president
名噪一时 enjoy fleeting fame; gain considerable fame among contemporaries
名正言顺 the name is correct and what is said accords with reason—perfectly justifiable; fitting and proper
名师出高徒 A great teacher produces a brilliant student.
名义代理权 ostensible authority
名义当事人 nominal party
名义合伙人 nominal partner
名誉权官司 defamation suit
名牌优质产品 brand-name and quality products
名不正，言不顺 If names are not right, arguments will not be tenable.

M

明 [míng]

明 Ⅰ 形 ① bright; brilliant; light ② obvious; clear; distinct ③ open; plain; overt; explicit ④ sharp-eyed; clear-sighted ⑤ immediately following in time; next Ⅱ 名 ① brightness; light; honesty ② sight Ⅲ 动 ① understand; realize; know ② make known; make clear; demonstrate Ⅳ 副 obviously; plainly
明儿 ① tomorrow ② one of these days; some day
明暗 light and shade
明白 ① clear; obvious; plain ② open; unequivocal; explicit ③ sensible; reasonable ④ understand; realize; know
明补 direct subsidy (to compensate for price rise)
明畅 clear and lucid; lucid and smooth
明澈 bright and limpid; transparent
明处 ① where there is light ② in the open; in public
明达 sensible; understanding
明灯 bright lamp; beacon
明兜 patch pocket
明断 pass (fair) judgment
明矾 alum
明沟 open drain
明河 the Milky Way
明慧 intelligent; bright; clever
明火 ① flame ② carry torches (esp. in a rob-

bery)
明鉴 ① bright mirror; clear mirror ② your brilliant idea; your penetrating judgment
明胶 gelatin
明净 bright and clean; clear and bright
明镜 bright mirror; clear mirror
明快 ① lucid and lively; sprightly ② straightforward; forthright ③ bright
明朗 ① bright and clear ② clear; obvious ③ forthright; bright and cheerful
明理 ① sensible; reasonable ② an obvious truth or fact
明丽 bright and beautiful
明亮 ① well-lit; bright ② bright; shining ③ become clear
明了 ① understand; be clear about ② clear; plain
明令 explicit order; formal decree; public proclamation
明码 ① plain code ② with the price clearly marked
明媚 bright and beautiful; radiant and enchanting
明灭 now in view, now hidden; appearing and vanishing
明明 obviously; plainly; undoubtedly
明年 next year
明确 ① clear and definite; clear-cut; explicit; unequivocal ② make clear; make definite; clarify
明日 ① tomorrow ② the near future
明睿 wise and farsighted
明示 explicitly instruct; clearly indicate
明誓 ① an oath of alliance; a treaty of alliance ② take an oath; make a pledge
明说 speak frankly; speak openly
明天 ① tomorrow ② the near future
明文 (of laws, regulations, etc.) proclaimed in writing
明晰 distinct; clear
明虾 prawn
明显 clear; obvious; evident; distinct
明线 open-wire line; open wire
明效 obvious results; telling (or marked) effects
明星 ① Venus ② a famous performer; star ③ old society lady; social butterfly
明莹 sparkling and crystal-clear; glittering and translucent
明喻 simile
明早 ① tomorrow morning ② tomorrow
明证 clear proof
明知 know perfectly well; be fully aware
明志 show one's high ideals
明智 sensible; sagacious; wise
明珠 bright pearl; jewel
明子 pine torch

明摆着 obvious; clear; plain
明白人 perceptive person; sensible person
明打明 clear; obvious; plain
明矾石 alunite
明后天 tomorrow or the day after tomorrow
明晃晃 gleaming; shining
明太鱼 walleye pollack
明细账 subsidiary ledger
明信片 postcard
明眼人 a person with a discerning eye; a person of good sense
明白如话 as plain as ordinary speech; plain and easy to understand
明白事理 know what's what
明辨是非 make a clear distinction between right and wrong
明察暗访 observe publicly and investigate privately—conduct a thorough investigation
明察秋毫 have eyes sharp enough to perceive an animal's autumn hair—be perceptive of the minutest detail
明火执仗 carry torches and weapons (in a robbery)—do evil openly
明来暗往 have overt and covert contacts with sb
明令取缔 proscribe by formal decree
明码标价 attach price-tags (to prevent overcharging or short-changing)
明码实价 put goods on sale with wet prices clearly marked
明媒正娶 be legally and formally married
明眸皓齿 (of a beautiful woman) have bright eyes and white teeth
明眸善睐 the enticing glances of a beauty; shining eyes and attractive looks
明目张胆 brazenly; flagrantly
明弃暗取 take back secretly what one has openly discarded
明枪暗箭 spear thrusts in the open and arrows shot from hiding—both open and covert attacks
明日黄花 chrysanthemums after the Double Ninth Festival—things that are stale and no longer of interest
明若观火 as obvious as a glowing fire
明升暗降 a promotion in appearance but a demotion in fact; promote in appearance but demote in reality; kick upstairs
明十三陵 the Ming Tombs; Tombs of Thirteen Emperors of the Ming Dynasty to the north of Beijing
明文规定 proclaimed in writing; stipulate in explicit terms
明效大验 clinching proof of effectiveness; telling (or marked) effects
明星联队 all-star team
明星效应 celebrity's appeal

明哲保身 be worldly-wise and play safe
明争暗斗 both open strife and veiled struggle; overt contention and covert struggle
明正典刑 carry out a death sentence according to the law
明知故犯 knowingly violate (discipline, etc.); deliberately break (a rule, etc.); do sth one knows in wrong
明知故问 ask while knowing the answer
明珠暗投 a bright pearl cast into darkness— ①a person of talent or a thing of value unrecognized ② a good person fallen among bad company
明珠弹雀 shoot a pearl at the sparrow—the loss outweighs the gain; the game is not worth the candle
明暗对照法 chiaroscuro
明明白白消费 transparent consumption
明人不做暗事 An honest man does nothing underhand.
明枪易躲,暗箭难防 It is easy to dodge a spear thrust in the open, but difficult to guard against an arrow shot from hiding.
明修栈道,暗渡陈仓 pretend to advance along one path while secretly going along another; do one thing under cover of another
明于观人,暗于察己 good at knowing others but poor at knowing oneself
明于知人,昧于知己 have a good knowledge of others but a poor knowledge of oneself; understand others but not oneself
明(里)一套,暗(里)一套 act one way in the open and another way in secret
明知山有虎,偏向虎山行 go deep into the mountains, knowing well that there are tigers there—go on undeterred by the dangers ahead

鸣 [míng]
劢 ①(of birds, insects or small animals) chirp; cry ②ring; sound ③express; air; voice
鸣镝 whistling (or twanging) arrow
鸣放 ①fire a shot ②air one's views (through meetings, newspapers and other media)
鸣禽 songbird; singing bird
鸣哨 whistle for the start of a game
鸣谢 express one's thanks formally
鸣冤 voice grievances; complain of unfairness
鸣不平 complain of unfairness; cry out against injustice
鸣金收兵 beat the gong and recall the troops—call off a battle
鸣锣开道 beat gongs to clear the way (for officials in feudal times)—prepare the public for a coming event; pave the way for sth
鸣枪示警 fire a warning shot
鸣冤叫屈 complain and call for redress; voice grievances

茗 [míng]
名 tea

冥 [míng]
Ⅰ 形 ① dark; dim; obscure ② deep; abstruse; profound ③ dull; stupid; foolish Ⅱ 名 underworld; nether world
冥钞 paper made to resemble bank notes and burned for the dead
冥府 the nether world
冥间 nether world
冥器 funerary object; burial objects
冥思 be deep in thought; be immersed in meditation
冥顽 thickheaded; stupid
冥想 deep thought; meditation
冥王星 pluto
冥冥之中 in the unseen world
冥思苦想 think long and hard; cudgel (or rack) one's brains (to evolve an idea)
冥顽不灵 silly and clumsy; insensitive

铭 [míng]
Ⅰ 名 inscription Ⅱ 动 engrave
铭感 be deeply grateful
铭功 inscribe one's exploits
铭记 ①bear firmly in mind; always remember ②inscription; epigraph
铭刻 ① inscription ② be engraved on one's mind; be always remembered
铭牌 data plate; nameplate
铭文 inscription; epigraph
铭谢 show gratefulness
铭心 be engraved on one's heart—be remembered with gratitude
铭刻学 epigraphy
铭肌镂骨 be engraved on one's mind forever
铭诸肺腑 be engraved on one's mind (or memory); be borne firmly in mind

溟 [míng]
名 sea

暝 [míng]
Ⅰ 动 (of the sun) set; (of the sky) grow dark Ⅱ 名 dusk; evening twilight

瞑 [míng]
动 ① shut one's eyes ② be dim-sighted; have blurred vision
瞑目 close one's eyes in death—die content
瞑眩 dizziness, nausea, etc. as a side effect of drugs

螟 [míng]
名 snout moth's larva
螟虫 snout moth's larva
螟蛾 snout moth
螟蛉 ①corn earworm ②adopted son

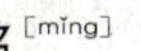

酩 [míng]
酩酊 be dead drunk

míng（ㄇㄧㄥˋ）

命 [míng] Ⅰ 名 ①life ②fate；destiny；lot Ⅱ 动 ①order；command；instruct ②assign（a name，title，etc.）；name

命案 a case involving the killing of a person；homicide case
命薄 doomed to a hapless life
命笔 take up one's pen；set pen to paper
命大 of extremely good fortune；very lucky
命定 be determined by fate；be predestined
命好 born under a lucky star
命苦 be doomed to a life of misfortunes；have a hard lot；be born under an unlucky star
命令 ①order；command ②order
命脉 lifeblood；lifeline
命门 the gate of vitality(the area between the kidneys，generally regarded as the source of vitality，the function of which is to promote respiration，digestion，reproduction and the metabolism of body fluid)
命名 name（sb or sth）
命数 destiny；fate；lot
命题 ①assign a topic；set a question ②proposition
命运 destiny；fate；lot
命中 hit the target（or mark）；score a hit
命根子 one's very life；lifeblood
命令句 imperative sentence
命名法 nomenclature
命名权 privilege to name
命数法 numeration
命中率 percentage of hits
命不该绝 not be destined to die（said of a person who has had a narrow escape）
命里注定 it is one's lot；be predestined
命令系统 command system
命若悬丝 life as if hanging by a thread
命途多舛 suffer many a setback during one's life
命意何在 where is the meaning
命在旦夕 Death may come any minute；be dying；be on one's last legs；One's life hangs in the balance.
命之所招 be caused by fate
命中注定 decreed by fate；predestined
命中目标 hit the target（or mark）
命中偏差 deviation of impact

miù（ㄇㄧㄡˋ）

谬 [miù] 形 false；wrong；erroneous；mistaken
谬传 a false report
谬见 ①a wrong view ②my humble opinion
谬奖 overpraise（me）
谬论 fallacy；false（or absurd）theory；falsehood
谬误 falsehood；error；mistake
谬种 ①error；fallacy ②scoundrel
谬种流传 the dissemination of error

缪 [miù] ➡ móu
◇纰缪 error；mistake

mō（ㄇㄛ）

摸 [mō] 动 ①feel；stroke；caress；touch ②grope；fumble ③try to find out；feel out；sound out ④grope in the dark
摸彩 draw lot to determine the prize winners in a raffle（or lottery）
摸底 ①know the real situation ②try to find out the real intention（or situation）；sound sb out
摸黑 grope one's way on a dark night
摸索 ①grope；feel about；fumble ②try to find out
摸透 get to know very well
摸瞎 grope one's way in the dark
摸不透 wonder；be puzzled
摸门儿 learn the ropes；get the hang of sth
摸到门路 have learned the ways of the trade
摸清底细 get to the bottom of the story；ascertain the actual situation
摸不着头脑 feel at a loss；be unable to understand what it is all about
摸着石头过河 grope one's way across the river；act with caution in handling uncertain issues；tread carefully
摸实情、办实事、求实效、讲实话 know the actual situation，do sth concrete，seek practical results and speak the truth

mó（ㄇㄛˊ）

无 [mó] ➡ wú
◇南无 [nāmó] Namah；Namo

谟 [mó] 名 plan

馍 [mó] 名 steamed bun；steamed bread

摹 [mó] 动 copy；trace
摹本 facsimile；copy
摹绘 draw；paint；depict；describe
摹刻 ①carve a reproduction of an inscription（or painting）②a carved reproduction of an inscription（or painting）
摹写 ①copy；imitate ②describe；depict
摹印 ①copy and print ②a style of characters（or lettering）on ancient imperial seals
摹状 depict；portray；delineate

模 [mó]

Ⅰ 名 ①pattern;standard ②model ③modulo;module Ⅱ 动 imitate ➡️mú

模本 calligraphy (*or* painting) model

模范 an exemplary person (*or* thing);model;fine example

模仿 imitate;copy;model oneself on

模糊 ①blurred;indistinct;dim;vague ②blur;obscure;confuse;mix up

模块 module

模量 modulus

模拟 imitate;simulate

模式 pattern;model

模数 modulus

模特 ①model ②model;dummy

模型 ①model ②mould;matrix;pattern

模拟战 sham fight

模范事迹 exemplary deeds;exemplary conduct;exemplary behaviour

模范作用 exemplary role

模糊理论 fuzzy theory

模糊逻辑 fuzzy logic

模糊数学 fuzzy mathematics

模糊语言 fuzzy language

模糊战略 indistinct strategy on the Taiwan question

模棱两可 equivocal;ambiguous

模拟程序 simulation program

模拟法庭 moot court

模拟飞行 simulated flight

模拟考试 simulated test;mock test;practice test;sample test

模拟设计 board design

模拟试验 simulated test

模拟通信 analogue communication

模特大赛 modeling competition;catwalk competition

模型展品 scale model;replica

模糊经济学 fuzzy economics

模式化栽培 standardized cultivation;systematic cultivation

模范共青团员 model member of the Communist Youth League

模拟移动电话 analogue mobile telephone

模拟－数字转换器 analogue-to-digital converters

膜 [mó]

名 ①membrane ②film;thin coating

膜拜 prostrate oneself (before an idol or person);worship

膜层 rete

膜法 membrane method

膜片 diaphragm

膜翅目 Hymenoptera

膜蛋白 membrane protein

摩 [mó]

Ⅰ 动 ①rub;scrape;touch ②caress;stroke ③mull over;study;fathom Ⅱ 名 (short for 摩尔)mole ➡️mā

摩擦 ①rub ②friction ③clash (between two parties);friction

摩登 modern;fashionable

摩尔 mole

摩丝 styling mousse;mousse

摩挲 stroke;caress

摩天 skyscraping

摩托 motor

摩擦力 frictional force;friction

摩擦音 fricative

摩擦桩 friction pile

摩电灯 dynamo-powered lamp (on a bicycle,etc.)

摩托车 motorcycle;motor bicycle;motorbike

摩托艇 motor boat

摩擦抛光 burnishing

摩登家具 fashionable furniture

摩登女郎 a fashionable girl

摩顶放踵 wear the whole body smooth from head to foot—serve the interests of others at great self-sacrifice

摩尔定律 Moore's Law

摩尔法则 Moore's Law

摩肩接踵 jostle each other in a crowd

摩拳擦掌 rub one's fists and palms—be eager for a fight;be itching to have a go

摩擦和纠葛 frictions and complications

摩尔根主义 Morganism

摩托化部队 motorized troops

磨 [mó]

动 ①rub;wear ②sharpen;whet;grind;polish ③torment;wear down ④keep nagging;plague;pester ⑤sink into oblivion;die out;erase;obliterate ⑥dawdle;waste (time);while away ➡️mò

磨边 edging

磨蹭 ①rub (lightly);stroke (gently) ②move slowly;dawdle ③pester;nag

磨床 grinding machine;grinder

磨革 buff (leather)

磨工 ①grinding work ②grinder

磨光 polish

磨耗 wear and tear

磨合 ①(of machines) grind in;wear in;mesh together ②adapt to each other

磨砺 go through the mill;steel oneself;harden oneself;discipline oneself

磨炼 put oneself through the mill;temper oneself;steel oneself

磨料 abrasive;abradant

磨灭 wear away;efface;obliterate

磨难 tribulation;hardship;suffering

磨片 abrasive disc

磨蚀 abrasion

磨损 wear and tear

磨洗 wear away;corrode;erode
磨削 grinding
磨牙 ①grind one's teeth (in sleep) ②indulge in idle talk;argue pointlessly
磨板机 graining machine
磨刀石 whetstone;grindstone
磨工夫 consume time
磨光机 polishing machine;glazing machine
磨木机 paper making (wood) grinder
磨舌头 indulge in idle talk;argue pointlessly
磨洋工 goldbrick;dawdle along;loaf on job
磨杵成针 if you work at it hard enough, you can grind an iron rod into a needle—perseverance spells success
磨穿铁砚 wear out an iron inkslab—study assiduously
磨光玻璃 polished glass
磨合过程 a period of adjustment
磨墨挥毫 grind the ink and flourish the brush to write
磨砂玻璃 frosted glass;ground glass
磨砂灯泡 frosted bulb
磨损留量 wear allowance
磨嘴皮子 ① jabber;blah-blah ② do a lot of talking ③indulge in idle talk;argue pointlessly
磨刀不误砍柴工 Sharpening the axe won't interfere with the cutting of firewood.

M

蘑 [mó] 名 mushroom;鲜蘑 fresh mushroom
蘑菇 ①mushroom ②worry;pester;keep on at ③dawdle;dillydally
蘑菇云 mushroom cloud (esp. from nuclear explosion)
蘑菇战术 the tactics of "wear and tear"

魔 [mó] I 名 evil spirit;demon;fiend;devil II 形 magic;occult;mystic
魔法 sorcery;witchcraft
魔方 magic square
魔怪 demons and monsters;fiends
魔鬼 devil;demon;monster
魔窟 den of monsters
魔力 magical power;magic;charm
魔球 magic ball
魔术 magic;conjuring;sleight of hand
魔毯 magic carpet
魔头 ①devil;demon;evil spirit ②wizard sorcerer
魔王 ①Prince of the Devils;erlking ②tyrant;despot;fiend
魔影 spectre
魔芋 Amorphophallus rivieri
魔掌 devil's clutches;evil hands
魔杖 magic wand
魔障 demon;evil spirit
魔爪 devil's talons;claws;tentacles

魔术师 magician
魔术演员 magician;conjurer

mǒ (ㄇㄛˇ)

抹 [mǒ] I 动 ①smear;apply;put on ②wipe;clean off ③cross out;delete;erase II 量 (of cloud, etc.):一抹浮云 a floating cloud ⇒mā;mò
抹刀 trowel
抹掉 erase;wipe away
抹粉 apply face powder;prettify;whitewash
抹黑 throw mud at;bring disgrace on;discredit
抹零 count the small change (in a payment)
抹杀 blot out;obliterate;write off;deny
抹音 erasure
抹子 trowel
抹鼻子 cry;weep
抹脖子 cut one's own throat;commit suicide
抹稀泥 try to mediate differences at the sacrifice of principle;try to gloss things over
抹香鲸 sperm whale
抹不下脸 unable to swallow one's pride;unwilling to stoop to
抹杀成绩 obliterate achievements
抹一鼻子灰 suffer a snub;meet with a rebuff

mò (ㄇㄛˋ)

末 [mò] I 名 ①point;tip;end ②nonessentials;trifles;minor details ③end;bottom ④powder;dust II 形 ①humble;petty;worthless②last
末代 the last reign of a dynasty
末端 end;bottom
末伏 ①the last or third fu—the third hottest period of the year (10 days) ②the first day of the last or third fu (falling in early or mid August)
末技 a trifling skill;an insignificant stunt
末节 minor details;nonessentials
末了 last;finally;in the end
末流 ① the later and decadent stage of a school of thought,literature,etc. ②inferior
末路 dead end;impasse
末年 last years of a dynasty or reign
末期 last phase;final phase;last stage
末日 ①doomsday;Day of Judgment;Judgment Day ②end;doom
末梢 tip;end
末世 last phase (of an age)
末尾 ①end ②fine
末席 the least prominent seat at a dinner table
末屑 bits;scraps;crumbs
末业 (in ancient times) industry and commerce
末叶 last years (of a century or dynasty)

末子 powder;dust
末座 the most inferior seat at table
末班车 ① last bus (*or* train) ② last chance (*or* turn)
末日论 eschatology
末制导 terminal guidance
末梢神经 nerve ending
末位淘汰 The person graded last in the performance evaluation will be laid off from his position.
末制导炮弹 terminal-guided shell

没 [mò] 动 ①sink;submerge ②overflow;rise higher than ③ hide;conceal;disappear ④ confiscate;impound;seize ⑤come to the end;come to the last ⑥die ➡méi
没齿 all one's life;life long
没顶 be drowned
没落 decline;wane
没世 all one's life;lifelong
没收 confiscate;expropriate
没药 myrrh
没奈何 be utterly helpless;have no way out;have no alternative
没齿不忘 will never forget to the end of one's days;remember for the rest of one's life
没收赃款 confiscate the money embezzled in bribes
没收非法所得 confiscate illegal income

茉 [mò]
茉莉 jasmine
茉莉花茶 jasmine tea

抹 [mò] 动 ①daub;plaster ②skirt;bypass ➡mā;mǒ
抹灰 plastering
抹不开 ① feel embarrassed;be put out ② unable to act impartially for fear of offending sb;afraid of impairing personal relations
抹得开 ①not feel embarrassed;be at ease ② not find it embarrassing (to do sth) ③be convinced;come round
抹浆机 grouting machine

殁 [mò] 动 die
殁而不朽 be immortal though dead

沫 [mò] 名 ①foam;froth ②saliva;spittle
沫子 foam;froth

陌 [mò] 名 ①footpath between fields (running east and west) ②road
陌路 stranger (whom one passes in the street)
陌生 strange;unfamiliar
陌头杨柳 roadside willows

脉 [mò]
➡mài
脉脉 affectionate;loving;amorous

莫 [mò] I 代 no one;none;nothing II 副 ①not;no ②don't ③(*indicating speculation or questioning*)
莫不 there's no one who doesn't (*or* isn't)
莫大 greatest;utmost
莫非 can it be that;is it possible that
莫怪 no wonder that ...
莫名 beyond description;indescribable;nameless
莫逆 very friendly;intimate
莫如 would be better;might as well
莫过于 nothing is more... than
莫须有 unwarranted;groundless;fabricated;trumped-up
莫测高深 unfathomable;enigmatic
莫此为甚 A more flagrant instance has yet to be found.
莫霍界面 Moho discontinuity;Moho
莫可名状 that cannot be described
莫可指数 beyond counting on one's fingers—countless;innumerable
莫名其妙 ①be unable to make head (*or* tail) of sth;be baffled ②without rhyme (*or* reason);inexplicable;odd
莫逆之交 bosom friends
莫衷一是 unable to agree (*or* decide) which is right
莫为子孙作牛马 do no slave for your children
莫信直中直,须防仁不仁 Don't believe the honesty of the honest,be wary of the unkindness of the kind.

秣 [mò] I 名 fodder;forage II 动 feed (animals)
秣马厉兵 feed the horses and sharpen the weapons—make preparations for war;prepare for battle

蓦 [mò] 副 suddenly
蓦地 suddenly;unexpectedly;all of a sudden
蓦然 suddenly

漠 [mò] I 名 desert II 形 indifferent;unconcerned
漠漠 ①misty;foggy ②vast and lonely
漠然 indifferent;apathetic;unconcerned
漠视 treat with indifference;ignore;overlook;pay no attention to
漠不关心 indifferent;unconcerned

寞 [mò] 形 lonely;solitary;deserted

墨 [mò] I 名 ①Chinese ink;ink stick ②pigment;ink ③calligraphy;painting ④learning;literacy ⑤line in a carpenter's ink marker—rules and regulations ⑥corruption;graft;embezzle-

M

ment ⑦ Mohist school; Mohism Ⅱ 形 black;
pitch-dark Ⅲ 动 tattoo the face (*or* forehead)
in ink
墨宝 ① treasured scrolls of calligraphy (*or*
painting) ②beautiful handwriting
墨斗 carpenter's ink marker
墨海 a big basin-like inkstone
墨盒 ink box (fox Chinese calligraphy or
painting)
墨黑 pitch-dark
墨迹 ① ink marks; ink stains ② sb's writing
(*or* painting)
墨家 Mohist School
墨晶 smoky quartz
墨镜 sunglasses
墨客 literary men; men of letters
墨吏 corrupt officials
墨绿 blackish green
墨囊 ink sac (of a cuttlefish)
墨水 ① prepared Chinese ink ② ink ③ book
learning
墨线 ①the line in a carpenter's ink marker ②
a line made by a carpenter's ink marker
墨鸦 cormorant
墨汁 prepared Chinese ink
墨渍 ink blot; ink spot
墨斗鱼 cuttlefish; inkfish
墨水池 inkwell
墨水瓶 ink bottle
墨水台 inkstand
墨迹未干 before the ink is dry
墨守成规 stick to convention; stay in a rut
墨守旧习 adhere to old customs

默 [mò] Ⅰ 形 silent; quiet; tacit Ⅱ 动 write from
memory
默哀 stand in silent tribute
默察 watch quietly
默祷 pray in silence; say a silent prayer
默悼 pay a silent tribute of memory (to the
dead)
默读 read silently
默记 make a mental note; learn by heart; commit to memory
默默 quiet; silent
默念 ①read silently ② think back; recollect;
recall
默契 ① tacit agreement; tacit understanding
②secret agreement
默然 silent; speechless
默认 give tacit consent to; tacitly approve; acquiesce in
默示 ①imply ②tacit declaration
默书 write out a text from memory
默诵 ①read silently ②read silently to oneself
from memory
默算 ①do mental arithmetic; do sums in one's

heart ②calculate; figure; plan
默想 think deeply; ponder over; reflect on
默写 write from memory
默许 tacitly consent to; acquiesce in
默页 preliminary pages
默坐 sit quietly
默默无闻 unknown to the public; without attracting public attention
默示承诺 implied promise
默示承认 implied recognition
默示担保 implied warrant
默示放弃 implied waiver
默示合同 implied contract
默示批准 implied ratification
默示条件 implied term
默示同意 implied consent
默示协定 implied agreement
默示信托 implied trust
默示异议 implied objection
默示特约条款 warranty implied

磨 [mò] Ⅰ 名 mill; millstones Ⅱ 动 ①grind; mill ②
turn round ➡má
磨坊 mill
磨轮 mill wheel
磨盘 ①nether (*or* lower) millstone ②mill;
millstones
磨棚 grinding shed; mill shed
磨扇 upper and lower millstone
磨头 grinding head
磨子 mill; millstone
磨豆腐 ①grind soya beans to make bean curd
②say sth over and over again; repeat again
and again
磨面机 flour-milling machine

mōu (ㄇㄡ)

哞 [mōu] 象 (of a cow) moo; low; bellow

móu (ㄇㄡˊ)

牟 [móu] 动 seek; try to gain
牟利 seek private (*or* selfish) interests; seek
personal gain
牟取 try to gain; seek; obtain
牟取暴利 reap staggering profits; obtain colos-
sal profits; seek exorbitant profits

眸 [móu] 名 pupil (of the eye); eye
眸子 pupil (of the eye); eye

谋 [móu] Ⅰ 名 design; plan; scheme; stratagem Ⅱ 动
①work for; seek; strive ②consult; deliberate
谋臣 emperor's counsellor
谋刺 plot to assassinate
谋反 conspire against the state; plot a rebel-

lion
谋害 ① plot to murder ② plot a frame-up against
谋和 sue for peace
谋划 plan;scheme;try to find a solution
谋利 make a profit;seek gain
谋虑 consider carefully;contemplate;deliberate
谋略 astuteness and resourcefulness;strategy
谋面 meet each other;be acquainted with sb
谋篇 plan a composition
谋求 seek;strive for;be in quest of
谋取 try to gain;seek;obtain
谋杀 murder
谋生 seek a livelihood;make a living
谋士 adviser;counsellor
谋事 ①plan matters ②look for a job
谋私 seek personal gain
谋算 ①plan;scheme;try to find a solution ② scheme against sb or for sth;plot ③ calculate;plan
谋图 premeditate
谋议 plan;scheme
谋职 seek employment;try to find a job
谋私利 have an eye to the main chance;seek personal gains
谋财害命 murder sb for his money
谋取私利 seek personal gain;play one's own game
谋章布局 plan the structure
谋职面试 be interviewed for a job
谋独立,求解放 seek independence and liberation
谋事在人,成事在天 The planning lies with man,the outcome with Heaven;Man proposes,God disposes.

缪 [móu]
➡ miù
◇绸缪 be sentimentally attached
未雨绸缪 repair the house before it rains;provide for a rainy day;take precautions

mǒu (ㄇㄡˇ)

某 [mǒu]
代 ①certain;some ②yours truly ③(*often used instead of sb's given name in an impolite way*):他李某实在太吝啬了。That fellow Li is a real skinflint.
某处 somewhere
某地 somewhere
某某 so-and-so
某年 in a certain year
某人 ①a certain person;someone ② (referring to oneself)
某日 at a certain date
某时 sometime
某物 somewhat

某些 certain;some

mú (ㄇㄨˊ)

模 [mú]
名 mould;die;matrix;pattern ➡ mó
模板 ①shuttering;formwork ②pattern plate
模具 mould;matrix;pattern;die
模压 mould pressing
模样 ①appearance;look ②indicating a rough estimate of time or age
模子 mould;matrix;pattern;die
模压机 moulding press

mǔ (ㄇㄨˇ)

母 [mǔ]
Ⅰ名 ①mother ②one's female elder ③nut ④origin;parent;mother Ⅱ形 female (animal)
母爱 mother love;maternal love
母版 mother set;master mask
母本 female parent
母畜 female animal;dam
母带 master tape
母鹅 goose
母蜂 queen bee
母狗 female dog;bitch
母机 ① machine tool ② mother aircraft;launching aircraft
母鸡 hen
母舰 mother ship
母狼 she-wolf
母鹿 doe
母驴 jenny
母马 female horse;mare
母牛 cow
母亲 mother
母乳 breast milk;mother's milk
母狮 lioness
母树 mother tree;seed tree
母体 the mother's body;the (female) parent
母兔 doe
母系 ①maternal ②matrilineal;matriarchal
母线 ①bus;bus bar ②generatrix;generator
母校 one's old school;Alma Mater
母性 maternal instinct
母鸭 duck
母羊 ewe
母液 mother liquor;mother solution
母音 vowel
母语 ①mother tongue ②parent language;linguistic parent
母株 maternal plant;mother plant
母猪 female pig;sow
母子 mother and son
母公司 parent company
母老虎 ①tigress ②vixen;shrew;termagant

M

母亲河 mother river
母权制 matriarchy
母山羊 she-goat;nanny goat
母夜叉 an ugly and fierce woman; an ugly shrew
母乳喂养 breast feeding

牡 [mǔ]
名 male
牡丹 tree peony;peony
牡蛎 oyster
牡牛 bull

拇 [mǔ]
拇指 ①thumb ②big toe

姆 [mǔ]
姆欧 mho
姆夫蒂 mufti

姥 [mǔ]
名 old lady ➡lǎo

mù (ㄇㄨˋ)

木 [mù]
I 名 ①tree ②timber;lumber;wood ③coffin II 形 ①made of wood;wooden ②simple; unsophisticated;dense ③numb;wooden
木板 plank;board
木版 block
木棒 stick;cudgel
木笔 lily magnolia
木材 wood;timber;lumber
木柴 firewood
木醇 methyl alcohol; methanol; wood spirit; wood alcohol
木锉 wood rasp;rasping file
木雕 wood carving
木钉 peg;wood nail
木牍 inscribed wooden tablet
木耳 an edible fungus
木筏 raft
木工 ①woodwork;carpentry ②woodworker; carpenter
木瓜 ①Chinese flowering quince ②papaya
木棍 stick;cudgel
木盒 tub
木婚 wood wedding
木屐 clogs
木简 inscribed wooden slip
木浆 wood pulp
木僵 numb;stiff
木匠 carpenter
木槿 rose of Sharon
木精 methyl alcohol; methanol; wood spirit; wood alcohol
木刻 woodcut;wood engraving
木兰 lily magnolia
木立 stand motionless

木料 timber;lumber
木马 ① vaulting horse; pommelled horse ② (children's) hobbyhorse;rocking horse
木棉 silk cotton;kapok
木讷 simple and slow (of speech)
木偶 ①puppet;marionette ②wooden image; carved figure
木排 raft
木盆 wooden basin;vat
木片 wood chip
木器 wooden furniture;wooden articles
木桥 wooden bridge
木琴 xylophone
木然 stupefied
木塞 tie plug
木石 a lifeless thing;a senseless being
木梳 wooden comb
木薯 cassava
木栓 phellem;cork
木丝 wood wool
木榫 dowel;wood plug
木炭 charcoal
木通 akebi
木头 wood;log;timber
木纹 wood grain
木屋 log cabin
木樨 ①sweet-scented osmanthus ②egg beaten and then cooked
木锨 wooden winnowing spade
木楔 chuck;wood key
木鞋 sabot
木屑 bits of wood;sawdust
木星 Jupiter
木俑 wooden figurine
木鱼 wooden fish
木贼 scouring rush
木砖 woodbox;block
木桩 wood pile;timber pile
木板床 plank bed
木版画 woodcut;wood engraving
木菠萝 jackfruit
木醋酸 pyroligneous acid
木蠹蛾 wood moth;carpenter moth
木芙蓉 cotton rose
木化石 petrified wood
木焦油 wood tar
木结构 timber structure;wood construction
木刻术 xylography
木马计 the stratagem of the Trojan horse; Trojan horse
木乃伊 mummy
木偶片 puppet film
木偶戏 puppet show;puppet play
木丝板 wood wool board
木炭画 charcoal drawing
木须肉 shredded pork and eggs with dried mushroom

木质部 xylem
木质素 lignin
木版印花 block printing
木版印刷 block printing
木本水源 the root of a tree and the source of a stream—the root of a matter
木本植物 woody plant
木雕泥塑 like an idol carved in wood or moulded in clay;as wooden as a dummy
木工机械 woodworking machinery
木管乐器 woodwind instrument;woodwind
木人石心 a body of wood and a heart of stone—insusceptible;unfeeling
木头木脑 wooden-headed;dull-witted
木头脑袋 numskull
木头人儿 woodenhead;blockhead;slow coach
木已成舟 the wood is already made into a boat—what is done cannot be undone

目 [mù]
Ⅰ 名 ①eye ②mesh;eye;hole ③item;number ④order ⑤list;catalogue ⑥name;title ⑦(in *weiqi* or *go*) eye Ⅱ 动 look;see
目标 ①target;goal;aim
目测 range estimation
目次 table of contents;contents
目的 purpose;aim;goal;objective;end
目睹 see with one's own eyes;witness
目光 ①sight;vision;view ②gaze;look
目击 see with one's own eyes;witness
目疾 eye trouble
目见 see for oneself
目镜 eyepiece;ocular
目力 vision;sight
目录 ① catalogue; list ② table of contents;contents
目前 at present;at the moment
目示 hint with a look
目送 follow sb with one's eyes;watch sb go;gaze after
目下 the present time;now
目眩 dizzy;dazzled
目语 communicate with the eyes
目的地 destination
目的港 port of destination
目的论 teleology
目击记 eyewitness account;eye-account;I-account
目击者 eyewitness;witness
目录学 bibliography (as a science)
目标程序 target program
目标管理 management by objectives(MBO);quota management
目标语言 object language
目不见睫 the eye can't see its lashes—lack self-knowledge
目不交睫 not sleep a wink
目不窥园 never take a peep into the garden—bury oneself in one's studies
目不忍睹 cannot bear to look at
目不识丁 not know one's ABC;be totally illiterate
目不暇接 the eye cannot take it all in;too many things for the eye to take in
目不斜视 not look sideways;refuse to be distracted
目不转睛 look with fixed gaze;regard with rapt attention
目瞪口呆 gaping;dumbstruck;stupefied
目光如豆 vision as narrow as a bean—of narrow vision;short-sighted
目光如炬 ①eyes blazing like torches—blazing with anger ②looking ahead with wisdom;far-sighted
目空一切 be supercilious;consider everybody and everything beneath one's notice
目迷五色 dazzled by a riot of colour—bewildered by a complicated situation
目视飞行 visual flight
目为奇迹 look on (*or* regard) as a miracle
目无法纪 disregard (*or* flout) law and discipline;show contempt for the law;have no regard for law
目无全牛 (of an experienced butcher) see an ox not as whole (but only as parts to be cut)—be supremely skilled
目无组织 disregard organizational discipline;defy the leadership of one's organization
目无尊长 with no regard for one's elders and betters
目中无人 consider everyone beneath one's notice;be supercilious;be overweening
目标跟踪雷达 target-tracking radar (TTR)
目标经济增长率 target economic growth rate

沐 [mù]
动 ① wash one's hair;wash;bathe ② receive;be given
沐恩 receive favour
沐浴 ①have (*or* take) a bath ②bathe;immerse
沐猴而冠 a monkey with a hat on—a worthless person in imposing attire
沐雨栉风 be combed by the wind and washed by the rain—travel or work in the open despite wind and rain

苜 [mù]
苜蓿 lucerne;alfalfa

牧 [mù]
Ⅰ 动 herd;tend Ⅱ 名 animal husbandry;livestock raising
牧鞭 stockwhip
牧草 herbage;forage grass
牧场 grazing land;pastureland;pasture
牧笛 reed pipe

牧放 herd;tend;put out to pasture
牧歌 ①pastoral song;pastoral ②madrigal
牧工 hired herdsman
牧民 herdsman
牧区 ①pastureland;pasture ②pastoral area
牧犬 shepherd dog;sheep dog
牧群 spread
牧人 herdsman
牧师 pastor;minister;clergyman
牧童 shepherd boy;buffalo boy
牧羊 tend sheep
牧业 animal (*or* livestock) husbandry;stock raising;livestock farming
牧主 herd owner (who owns livestock and pastures and hires herdsmen)
牧马人 herdsman (of horses)
牧羊犬 shepherd dog;collie
牧羊人 shepherd

钼 [mù]
名 molybdenum (Mo)
钼钢 molybdenum steel
钼酸 molybdic acid
钼酸铵 ammonium molybdate

募 [mù]
动 raise;collect;enlist;recruit
募股 raise capital by floating shares
募化 collect alms
募集 raise;collect
募捐 solicit contributions;collect donations
募款 raise money
募兵制 mercenary system
募集资金 raise a fund

墓 [mù]
名 grave;tomb
墓碑 tombstone;gravestone
墓道 ①path leading to a grave;tomb passage ②aisle leading to the coffin chamber of an ancient tomb
墓地 graveyard;burial ground;cemetery
墓群 cemetery;tombs
墓室 coffin chamber
墓穴 coffin pit;open grave
墓园 cemetery;graveyard
墓葬 grave
墓志 inscription on the memorial tablet within a tomb
墓志铭 inscription on the memorial tablet within a tomb;epitaph

幕 [mù]
名 ①canopy;tent ②curtain;screen ③office (*or* headquarters) of a general ④act:一出三幕七场的话剧 a play in three acts and seven scenes
幕宾 high official's house guest and adviser
幕布 ①(theatre) curtain ②(cinema) screen
幕府 office of a commanding general (in ancient China or Japan)

幕后 behind the scenes;backstage
幕僚 ①aides and staff ②assistant to a ranking official (*or* general) in old China
幕墙 screen wall (made of a series of screens, often with inlaid glass);curtain wall
幕友 a private assistant (attending to legal, fiscal or secretarial duties) in a local *ya-men*;private adviser
幕后管理 shadow-manage
幕后交易 backstage deal
幕间休息 interval (in a play, etc.);intermission
幕天席地 have the sky as one's tent and the earth as one's mat—①take one's ease out in the open air ②have great breadth of view

睦 [mù]
形 peaceful;harmonious
睦邻 good-neighbourliness
睦邻关系 good-neighbourly relations
睦邻政策 good-neighbour policy;policy of good-neighbourly and friendly relations

慕 [mù]
动 ①admire;envy ②long for;yearn for
慕名 out of admiration for a famous person (*or* a place)
慕尼黑协定 Munich Agreement

暮 [mù]
Ⅰ 名 dusk;sunset;evening Ⅱ 形 (of time) towards the end;late
暮霭 evening mist
暮齿 old age;one's later (*or* remaining) years
暮春 late spring (the third month of the lunar year)
暮景 ① sunset scene;twilight ② life in old age;evening of one's life
暮龄 old age;one's later years
暮年 declining years;old age;evening of one's life
暮气 lethargy;apathy
暮秋 late autumn (the ninth month of the lunar year)
暮色 dusk;twilight;gloaming
暮世 modern times;recent years
暮岁 ①towards the end of the year ②old age;one's later (*or* remaining) years
暮鼓晨钟 the evening drum and the morning bell (in a monastery)—exhortations to virtue and purity
暮色苍茫 deepening dusk;spreading shades of dusk

穆 [mù]
形 reverent;solemn
穆民 believers in Islam
穆斯林 Moslem;Muslim
穆罕默德 Mohammed,founder of Islam

Nn

nā（ㄋㄚ）

南 [nā]
➡ nán
南无 [nāmó] Namah；Namo

ná（ㄋㄚˊ）

拿 [ná]
Ⅰ 动 ①hold；take；bring；fetch ②seize；capture；catch；take over ③have a firm grasp of；control；manage ④put sb in a difficult position；make things difficult for sb ⑤pretend；put on ⑥get；receive；gain；win ⑦（as of a chemical agent）cause some change to；affect Ⅱ 介 ①with；by means of；by；in ②（*introducing the object of a following verbal phrase*）Ⅲ 名 massage
拿办 apprehend and punish by law；arrest and bring to justice
拿获 apprehend（a criminal）
拿开 take away
拿捏 ①be affectedly bashful ②make things difficult for；put pressure on；threaten
拿权 wield power；be in the saddle
拿人 make things difficult for others；raise difficulties
拿事 have the power to do sth（*or* to decide what to do）
拿手 adept；expert；good at
拿稳 hold steadily；predict with confidence
拿住 hold firmly；put under arrest
拿大顶 stand on one's hands
拿大头 ①take the lion's share ②take sb for a sucker；cheat sb out of his money；fleece sb
拿架子 put on airs；assume great airs；throw one's weight around
拿主意 make a decision；decide
拿不出手 not be presentable
拿不起来 cannot manage
拿刀动杖 take up swords and cudgels；start a fight with weapons
拿得起来 can manage；can do

拿定主意 make up one's mind
拿来主义 mechanical borrowing without thought of appropriateness
拿腔拿调 speak with an affected tone of voice
拿腔作势 be affected（*or* pretentious）；act affectedly；strike a pose
拿手好戏 ①the play that an actor does best ②one's speciality；one's forte
拿印把子 hold the seal of authority—be in an important position；be in power
拿得起，放得下 can take it up or put it down—be adaptable to circumstances
拿着鸡毛当令箭 take a chicken feather for a warrant to issue orders—treat one's superior's casual remark as an order and make a big fuss about it

nǎ（ㄋㄚˇ）

哪 [nǎ]
Ⅰ 代 ①which；what ②any Ⅱ 副 how can；how could；how is it possible ➡ na；něi
哪儿 ① where ② wherever；anywhere ③（*used in rhetorical questions to express negation*）
哪个 ①which ②who
哪里 ①where ②wherever；where ③（*used in rhetorical questions to express negation*）④（*used as a polite reply to a compliment*）
哪能 how can；how could
哪怕 even；even if；even though；no matter how
哪些 which（ones）；who；what
哪样 ① what kind；what ② whatever kind；whatever
哪知 who would have thought
哪会儿 ①when ②whenever；any time
哪门子 *used to emphasize a rhetorical question*
哪儿的话 what are you saying；you shouldn't say that

nà(ㄋㄚˋ)

那 [nà]
I 代 (*used to indicate sb or sth away from the speaker*) II 连 then; in that case ⇒ nè; nèi

那儿 ①that place; there ②that time; then
那边 there; over there
那个 ①that (one) ②(*used before a verb or adjective with exclamatory force*) ③(*used euphemistically as a predicative adjective*)
那里 that place; there
那么 ①like that; in that way; so ②about; or so ③then; in that case
那时 at that time; then; in those days
那些 those
那样 of that kind; like that; such; so
那程子 those days; that period
那达慕 Nadam Fair, a Mongolian traditional fair
那当儿 at that time; in those days
那会儿 at that time; then
那么些 so much; so many
那么着 do that; do so
那阵儿 during that period (of time); in those days; then
那么点儿 so little; so few

呐 [nà]
呐喊 shout loudly; cry out

纳 [nà]
I 动 ①receive; let in; admit ②accept; take ③enjoy ④bring into (a plan, a project, etc.) ⑤pay; give (as a duty required by the authorities) ⑥sew close stitches (over sth rather thick) II 名 noy

纳彩 (of the bridegroom-to-be's family) present gifts to the girl's family at time of betrothal
纳粹 Nazi
纳呆 indigestion and loss of appetite
纳福 (usu. of elderly people) enjoy a life of ease and comfort
纳贡 pay tribute (to a suzerain or emperor)
纳罕 be surprised; marvel
纳贿 ①take bribes ②offer bribes
纳谏 (of a sovereign, an elder or superior) accept an admonition; accept advice
纳款 surrender and pledge allegiance
纳凉 enjoy the cool (in the open air)
纳闷 feel puzzled; be perplexed; wonder
纳米 nanometre
纳聘 (of the bridegroom-to-be's family) present gifts to the girl's family at time of betrothal
纳妾 take a concubine

纳入 bring (or channel) into
纳税 pay taxes
纳头 bow one's head (in greeting)
纳降 accept the enemy's surrender
纳新 take in the fresh—take in new members
纳税人 taxpayer; tax payer
纳赂被控 be accused of receiving bribes
纳米材料 nanometre material
纳米技术 nanotechnology
纳米科学 nano science
纳入计划 bring sth into line with the plan
纳入正轨 put sth on the right track (or course); lead sth onto the correct path
纳纱制品 petit-point articles
纳税大户 big tax-payer
纳税对象 object of taxation
纳税年度 tax year
纳税凭证 tax payment receipt
纳税义务 tax obligation; tax liability; obligation to pay tax; duty to pay taxes
纳斯达克 National Association of Securities Deal Automated Quotations (NASDAQ)
纳税申报单 tax returns
纳税申报制 system of tax payment; (for tax payers) fill personal returns

衲 [nà]
I 动 patch up (esp. with close stitches)
II 名 vestment worn by a Buddhist monk

钠 [nà]
名 sodium (Na)
钠长石 albite (a mineral)
钠平衡 sodium balance
钠汽灯 sodium lamp; sodium vapor
钠缺乏 sodium deficiency

捺 [nà]
I 动 ①press; push; put ②hold back; press down; restrain II 名 right-falling stroke

na(·ㄋㄚ)

哪 [na]
助 (*used after a word ending in* n *to tone up what is being said*) ⇒ nǎ; něi

nǎi(ㄋㄞˇ)

乃 [nǎi]
I 动 be II 副 ①so; therefore ②only then; only thus III 代 you; your

乃尔 like this; to such an extent
乃是 be
乃翁 your father
乃兄 your brother
乃至 and even
乃兄乃弟 be tweedledum and tweedledee

芀 [nǎi]
◇ 芋芀 taro

奶 [nǎi]
Ⅰ 〈名〉 ① breast ② milk Ⅱ 〈动〉 breastfeed; nurse; suckle
奶茶 tea with milk
奶疮 mastitis
奶粉 milk powder; powdered milk; dried milk
奶糕 a baby food made of rice-flour, sugar, etc.
奶积 indigestion of suckling babies due to improper breast-feeding
奶酒 fermented (cow's or mare's) milk
奶酪 cheese
奶妈 wet nurse
奶毛 foetal hair
奶名 a child's pet name; infant name
奶奶 ① grandmother; grandma ② young mistress of the house
奶娘 wet nurse
奶牛 milch cow; milk cow; cow
奶皮 skin formed on boiled milk
奶品 milk products; dairy products
奶瓶 feeding bottle; nursing bottle; (baby's) bottle
奶水 milk
奶糖 toffee
奶头 ① nipple; teat ② nipple (of a feeding bottle)
奶昔 milk shake
奶牙 milk tooth
奶羊 milch goat
奶油 cream
奶罩 brassiere; bra
奶汁 milk
奶子 ① milk ② breasts ③ wet nurse
奶嘴 rubber nipple (of a feeding bottle)
奶油色 cream-coloured
奶子酒 fermented (cow's or mare's) milk
奶油蛋糕 cream cake
奶油泡夫 cream puff
奶油分离器 cream separator

氖 [nǎi]
〈名〉 neon (Ne)
氖灯 neon lamp; neon light; neon
氖管 neon tube
氖气 neon
氖闪光管 neon flash tube

㑷 [nǎi]
〈代〉 you

nài (ㄋㄞˋ)

奈 [nài]
Ⅰ 〈副〉 ① how; however ② be helpless; cannot but Ⅱ 〈动〉 bear
奈何 ① what alternative is there; what's to be done ② how; why ③ do sth to (a person); cope with; deal with
奈基－宙斯导弹 Nike-Zeus

奈基－X 反弹道导弹系统 Nike-X

柰 [nài]
〈名〉 a crab apple

耐 [nài]
〈动〉 stand; resist
耐穿 (of clothing) stand wear and tear; stand hard wear; be durable; can last long
耐烦 be patient
耐寒 cold-resistant
耐旱 drought-enduring
耐火 fire-resistant; refractory
耐久 lasting long; durable
耐看 have lasting appeal
耐苦 able to endure hardships
耐劳 able to stand hard work; able to endure heavy labour; industrious
耐力 endurance; staying power; stamina
耐磨 (of metals) wear-resisting; wear-proof
耐热 heat-resisting; heatproof
耐受 bear; stand; endure
耐酸 acid-proof; acid-resisting
耐洗 wash well (*or* bear washing)
耐心 ① patient ② patiently ③ patience
耐性 patience; endurance
耐用 durable; (of things) be durable; can last long
耐波力 seakeeping qualities (of a vessel)
耐不住 unable to bear; unable to stand
耐潮湿 humidity resistant
耐高温 heat-resistant
耐寒性 cold resistance
耐火砖 refractory brick; firebrick
耐磨性 wearability; wear resistance
耐热性 heat resistance
耐蚀钢 corrosion-resisting steel
耐印力 pressrun
耐寒作物 cold-resistant crop
耐旱植物 drought-enduring plant
耐航包装 seaworthy packing
耐火材料 refractory (material); fireproof material
耐火衬砌 refractory lining
耐火黏土 refractory clay
耐火水泥 refractory cement
耐磨硬度 abrasion hardness
耐热合金 heat-resisting alloy
耐人寻味 afford food for thought
耐水作物 water-tolerant crop
耐酸缸器 acid-proof stoneware
耐心烦儿 patience
耐磨合金钢 wear-resisting alloy steel
耐酸混凝土 acid-resisting concrete
耐用消费品 durable consumer items (*or* goods)

萘 [nài]
〈名〉 naphthalene
萘酚 naphthol

N

萘球 naphthalene ball;moth ball

鼐 [nài]
名 big tripod

nān (ㄋㄢ)

囡 [nān]
名 ①child ②daughter

nán (ㄋㄢˊ)

男 [nán]
名 ①man;male ②son;boy ③baron
男儿 man
男方 the bridegroom's (*or* husband's) side
男服 menswear
男家 the bridegroom's (*or* husband's) family
男爵 baron
男科 ①andrologic department (of a hospital) ②andrology
男篮 men's basketball game (*or* team)
男女 ① man and female;men and women ② sons and daughters
男排 men's volleyball team
男人 [nánrén] ①man ②menfolk
男人 [nánren] husband
男色 pederasty
男生 man student;boy student;schoolboy
男声 male voice
男士 man;gentleman
男式 men's
男相 (of a female) look (*or* behave) like a man
男性 ①the male sex ②man
男装 menswear;men's clothing
男子 man;male
男傧相 best man
男病房 men's ward
男厕所 ①men's lavatory (*or* toilet,room) ② Gentlemen;Men;Gents
男低音 bass
男高音 tenor
男孩儿 ①boy ②son
男角儿 male role;actor
男朋友 boyfriend
男青年 young man
男学生 male student;boy student
男演员 actor
男职工 male staff
男中音 baritone
男子汉 a manly man;man
男扮女装 men dressed as women;man disguised in female attire
男才女貌 the man is able and the woman is beautiful;an ideal couple
男盗女娼 behave like thieves and whores;be out-and-out scoundrels
男耕女织 The man works in the fields while the woman sits at the loom.
男婚女嫁 A man should take a wife and a woman a husband.
男爵夫人 baroness
男男女女 men and women
男女关系 relations between the two sexes
男女老少 men and women,old and young
男女平等 equality of men and women;equality of the sexes
男女有别 Males and females should be treated differently.
男主人公 hero (in a novel or play)
男子单打 men's singles (of tennis,table tennis,etc.)
男子双打 men's doubles (of table tennis,tennis,etc.)
男尊女卑 men superior to women
男性更年期 male climacterium
男性同性恋 urning;man homosexuality;male homosexuality
男女混合双打 mixed doubles
男女同工同酬 equal pay for equal work irrespective of sex
男权主义思想 male chauvinism
男士用品专卖店 men's store;store exclusively selling things used by men
男大当婚,女大当嫁 Upon growing up, every male should take a wife and every female should take a husband.

南 [nán]
名 ① south ② southern region; Yangtze River valley and areas south of the river
南北 ①north and south ②from north to south
南边 ①south;the southern side ② the southern part of the country,esp. the area south of the Changjiang River;the South
南部 southern part;south
南斗 the Southern Dipper
南方 ①south ②the southern part of the country,esp. the area south of the Changjiang River;the South
南非 South Africa
南风 south wind
南瓜 pumpkin;cushaw
南国 the southern part of the country; the South
南海 the Nanhai Sea;the South China Sea
南货 delicacies from south China
南极 ①the South Pole;the Antarctic Pole ② the south magnetic pole
南面 ①face south—be a ruler (from the fact that the emperor sat facing south when holding court) ②south;the southern side
南欧 Southern Europe
南曲 ①southern tunes ②opera sung in southern tunes
南式 (of) southern style

南纬 south (*or* southern) latitude
南味 of southern taste and flavour; food of southern taste and flavour
南席 banquet of southern cuisine
南下 go down south
南亚 South Asia
南音 southern music
南岳 the Southern Mountain
南针 ①compass ②a guide (to action)
南竹 mao bamboo
南半球 the Southern Hemisphere
南北朝 the Northern and Southern Dynasties
南方话 southern dialect
南方人 Southerner
南寒带 the south frigid zone
南极光 southern lights; aurora australis
南极圈 the Antarctic Circle
南极虾 euphausiid shrimp
南极洲 the Antarctic Continent; Antarctica
南美洲 South America
南冕座 Corona Australis
南天极 south pole; south celestial pole
南天竹 nandina
南温带 the south temperate zone
南北对话 North-South dialogue
南方风味 southern style; southern flavour
南方古猿 Australopithecus
南回归线 the Tropic of Capricorn
南箕北斗 sth which enjoys empty name but serves no practical purposes
南柯一梦 a Nanke dream—a fond dream; all illusory joy
南来北往 going north and south (said of heavy traffic or a bustling crowd)
南粮北调 supply grain to the north from the south
南南合作 South-South cooperation
南腔北调 (speak with) a mixed accent
南三角座 Southern Triangle
南沙群岛 the Nansha Islands
南十字座 Cross; Crux; South Cross
南水北调 South-to-North water diversion; divert water from the south to the north; divert water from the Yangtze River to North China; south water to north
南下政策 South-Heading Policy
南辕北辙 try to go south by driving the chariot north—act in a way that defeats one's purpose
南征北战 fight north and south; campaign all across the country
南亚次大陆 the South Asian Subcontinent
南极科学考察 scientific investigation in the Antarctic
南水北调工程 projects for diverting water from the south to the north

难 [nán]
Ⅰ 形 ①hard; difficult; troublesome ②uncertain; hardly possible; unlikely ③unpleasant; not good; bad Ⅱ 动 put sb in a difficult position ➡nàn
难熬 hard to bear
难办 difficult to manage; difficult to operate; hard to deal with
难保 ①there is no guarantee; one cannot say for sure; it's hard to say ②difficult to preserve (*or* protect, defend, etc.)
难缠 (of a person) unreasonable and hard to deal with
难产 ①difficult labour; dystocia ②(of a literary work, plan, etc.) be difficult to fulfil; be slow in coming
难吃 taste bad; be unpalatable
难处 [nánchǔ] hard to get along (*or* on) with
难处 [nánchu] difficulty; trouble
难当 ①find it hard to shoulder (a responsibility, etc.) ②hard to endure; unbearable; insufferable
难倒 daunt; baffle; beat
难道 surely it doesn't mean that...
难得 ①hard to come by; rare ②seldom; rarely
难点 a difficult point; difficulty; a hard nut to crack
难懂 hard to understand; difficult to comprehend
难度 degree of difficulty; difficulty
难怪 ①no wonder ②understandable; pardonable
难关 difficulty; crisis
难管 difficult to govern; hard to rule
难过 ① have a hard time ② feel sorry; feel bad; be grieved
难堪 ①intolerable; unbearable ②embarrassed
难看 ① ugly; unsightly ② shameful; embarrassing
难免 hard to avoid
难耐 hard to bear; unbearable
难人 ①difficult; delicate; ticklish ②a person handling a delicate matter
难色 a reluctant (*or* embarrassed) expression
难事 a difficult matter; sth not easy to manage
难受 ①feel unwell; feel ill; suffer pain ②feel unhappy; feel bad
难说 it's hard to say; you never can tell
难题 a difficult problem; a hard nut to crack; poser
难听 ①unpleasant to hear ②offensive; coarse ③scandalous
难忘 unforgettable; memorable
难为 ①embarrass; press ②be a tough job to
难闻 smell unpleasant; smell bad
难以 hard to; difficult to

N

难易 degree of difficulty
难于 hard to;difficult to
难字 uncommon word;rarely used word
难上难 extremely difficult;all the more difficult
难说话 be difficult to talk with (*or* deal with)
难为情 ①abashed;embarrassed ②embarrassing;disconcerting
难办之事 have a long row to hoe
难辨是非 difficult to discriminate between right and wrong
难辨真伪 hard to distinguish between the true and false
难打交道 hard to deal with
难度系数 degree-of-difficulty factor
难割难舍 find it hard to part with (a person,place,etc.);be loath to tear oneself away
难乎为继 hard to carry on (*or* keep up)
难解难分 ①be inextricably involved (in a dispute);be locked together (in a struggle) ② be sentimentally attached to each other;can't bear to part
难能可贵 difficult of attainment,hence worthy of esteem;deserving praise for one's excellent performance (*or* behaviour);estimable;commendable
难舍难分 loath to part from each other
难逃法网 be unable to escape the net of justice
难兄难弟 two of a kind;birds of a feather
难言之隐 a painful topic;sth which it would be awkward to disclose;sth embarrassing to mention
难以为继 hard to carry to (*or* keep up)
难于启齿 have a bone in the throat;difficult to speak out one's mind

楠 [nán]

楠木 *nanmu*
楠竹 phyllostachys pubescens

nǎn (ㄋㄢˇ)

赧 [nǎn]
形 blushing

赧红 (of one's face) blush for shame;crimson from shame
赧愧 ashamed
赧赧 blushing;shamefaced
赧然 blushing;shamefaced
赧颜 blush;be shamefaced

nàn (ㄋㄢˋ)

难 [nàn]
Ⅰ 名 trouble;disaster;calamity;catastrophe Ⅱ 动 blame;censure;take to task ➡nán
难胞 fellow countrymen in distress
难民 refugee

难侨 fellow countrymen in distress overseas
难友 fellow sufferer
难兄难弟 fellow sufferers
难民收容所 haven (*or* shelter) for refugees;refugee camp

nāng (ㄋㄤ)

囔 [nāng]

囔囔 speak in a low voice;murmur

náng (ㄋㄤˊ)

囊 [náng]
Ⅰ 名 ①bag;sack;pocket;purse ②anything shaped like a bag;bladder Ⅱ 动 put into a bag;bag
囊虫 cysticercus
囊括 ①include;embrace ②win all
囊瘤 cystoma
囊生 Tibetan household slave (*or* bondman,bondwoman)
囊肿 cyst
囊尾蚴 cysticercus
囊中物 sth which is in the bag—sth certain of attainment
囊空如洗 with empty pockets;penniless;broke

馕 [náng]
名 *nang*,a kind of crusty pancake ➡nǎng

nǎng (ㄋㄤˇ)

攮 [nǎng]
动 stab
饢 [nǎng]
动 cram food into one's mouth ➡náng

nāo (ㄋㄠ)

孬 [nāo]
孬种 coward

náo (ㄋㄠˊ)

呶 [náo]
动 clamour;talk noisily;shout
挠 [náo]
动 ① scratch ② hinder;obstruct;block ③ yield;flinch;give in
挠度 deflection
挠钩 long-handled hook
挠曲 bending;flexure
挠头 ①scratch one's head ②difficult to tackle
挠性 flexibility
挠秧 weed rice fields and loosen the soil around the seedlings
挠痒痒 scratch an itch
挠人清梦 disturb one's dream

硇 [náo]

硇砂 sal ammoniac

铙 [náo]

〔名〕 *nao*，big cymbal

蛲 [náo]

蛲虫 pinworm
蛲虫病 enterobiasis

nǎo（ㄋㄠˇ）

恼 [nǎo]

Ⅰ〔动〕 be angry；upset；irritate；annoy Ⅱ〔形〕 unhappy；vexed；worried

恼恨 resent；hate
恼火 annoyed；irritated；vexed
恼怒 angry；indignant；furious
恼人 irritating；annoying
恼羞成怒 fly into a rage from shame；be shamed into anger

脑 [nǎo]

〔名〕 ① brain；encephalon ② head ③ brains；mind ④ best part（of sth）；cream ⑤ bits；residue；odds and ends

脑儿 ① animal brains（as food）② brain-like jellied food
脑袋 ① head ② brains；mind
脑海 brain；mind
脑际 mind；memory
脑浆 brains
脑筋 ① brains；mind；head ② way of thinking；ideas
脑壳 ① skull ② head
脑库 think-tank
脑力 mental power；intelligence
脑瘤 brain tumour
脑颅 brainpan；cranium
脑膜 meninx
脑桥 pons
脑室 ventricles of the brain
脑髓 brains
脑瘫 brain failure；brain paralysis；stroke
脑学 encephalology
脑炎 encephalitis；cerebritis
脑汁 brains
脑子 ① brain ② brains；mind；head
脑充血 encephalemia
脑出血 cerebral hemorrhage
脑电波 brain wave
脑电图 electroencephalogram（EEG）
脑动脉 cerebral artery
脑瓜子 head
脑黄金 docosahexaenoic acid（DHA）
脑积水 hydrocephalus
脑脊膜 meninges
脑脊液 cerebrospinal fluid（CSF）
脑门子 forehead；brow

脑膜炎 meningitis
脑贫血 cerebral anaemia
脑上体 pineal body
脑勺子 the back of the head
脑神经 cranial nerve
脑死亡 brain death
脑损伤 cerebral injury
脑溢血 cerebral haemorrhage
脑震荡 cerebral concussion；concussion
脑袋瓜子 ① head ② brains；mind
脑脊膜炎 meningitis
脑脊髓炎 encephalomyelitis
脑筋迟钝 have a slow wit；have slow wits；be slow-witted
脑力劳动 mental work
脑满肠肥 heavy-jowled and potbellied
脑室造影 ventriculography
脑体倒挂 income of mental workers falling short of that of manual workers；irrational income differential between white and blue collar workers in favour of the latter；income of the manual labourers being higher than that of mental workers
脑下垂体 pituitary body；pituitary gland；hypophysis
脑力劳动者 mental worker；brain worker
脑血管造影 cerebral angiography

瑙 [nǎo]

◇ 玛瑙 agate

nào（ㄋㄠˋ）

闹 [nào]

Ⅰ〔形〕 noisy Ⅱ〔动〕 ① clamour；make a scene；stir up trouble ② give vent to（one's anger，resentment，etc.）；vent ③ suffer from；be troubled by ④ do；make；engage oneself in；go in for ⑤ crack jokes；tease

闹病 fall ill；be ill
闹场 a flourish of gongs and drums introducing a theatrical performance
闹翻 fall out with sb
闹房 （of friends and relatives）banter（*or* tease）the newlyweds on wedding night
闹鬼 ① be haunted ② play tricks behind sb's back；use underhand means
闹哄 ① make a noise；make a fuss ② （of a group of people）bustle about
闹荒 （of peasants in former times）start famine riots
闹剧 farce
闹猛 bustling
闹气 be cross with sb
闹嚷 clamour；make a racket；kick up a row
闹市 busy streets；busy shopping centre；downtown area
闹事 create a disturbance；make trouble

闹腾 ①make a noise；kick up a row ②talk and laugh boisterously

闹心 ①be vexed；be annoyed ②feel sick；feel queasy

闹钟 alarm clock

闹嘴 quarrel；bicker

闹别扭 be difficult with sb；be at odds with sb

闹不清 cannot tell；be unclear about

闹虫灾 suffer from insect pests

闹地位 clamour for position

闹洞房 (of friends and relatives) banter (or tease) the newlyweds on wedding night

闹肚子 have diarrhoea；be suffering from loose bowels

闹翻天 raise hell；raise a rumpus

闹风潮 carry on agitation；stage strikes, demonstrations, etc.

闹革命 carry out revolution；make revolution；rise in revolution

闹哄哄 clamorous；noisy

闹会场 stir up trouble at a meeting

闹饥荒 ①suffer from famine ②be hard up；be short of money

闹乱子 cause trouble

闹矛盾 be at odds with one another；clash with one another；fall out with one another

闹名誉 clamour for fame

闹脾气 vent one's anger; get into a huff; throw a tantrum; vent one's spleen; lose one's temper; be in a tantrum

闹情绪 be disgruntled；be in low spirits

闹嚷嚷 noisy

闹水灾 suffer from floods

闹笑话 make a fool of oneself；make a stupid mistake

闹新房 (of friends and relatives) banter or tease the newlyweds on wedding night

闹性子 lose one's temper；be in a tantrum

闹玄虚 purposely make a mystery of simple things；be deliberately mystifying

闹意见 be on bad terms because of a difference of opinion；be at odds；have difference of opinion

闹意气 feel resentful because something is not to one's liking；sulk

闹独立性 assert one's independence—refuse to obey the leadership

闹着玩儿 be joking；horse around

闹中取静 seek peace and quietness in noisy surroundings; enjoy peace and quietness from noisy surroundings

闹得鸡犬不宁 cause such utter confusion as to make everybody nervous

闹得满城风雨 cause a big scandal

闹得头昏脑胀 cause such utter confusion as to crave one crazy

淖 ［nào］
名 mire

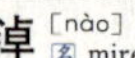

nè （ㄋㄜˋ）

讷 ［nè］
形 slow (of speech)

讷于言而敏于行 deliberate in speech but swift in action

那 ［nè］
代 that ➡nà；nèi

ne （·ㄋㄜ）

呢 ［ne］
助 ①(used at the end of an interrogative sentence)：我不去，你呢？ I'm not going. What about you? (or And you?) ②(used at the end of a statement to give emphasis)：我才不会告诉你呢! I am the last person to tell you that! Catch me telling you that! ③(used at the end of a statement to indicate continuation of action)：别吵！我忙着呢。 Be quiet. I'm pretty busy. ④(used to make a pause within a sentence usu. to show a contrast)：小孩子呢，算了，就别去了。 As for the children, well, they'd better not go. ➡ní

něi （ㄋㄟˇ）

哪 ［něi］
代 which；what ➡nǎ；na

馁 ［něi］
形 ①hungry；famished ②disheartened ③(of fish) putrid；rotten

馁怯 lose heart；lose courage；lose one's nerve

nèi （ㄋㄟˋ）

内 ［nèi］
I 名 ①inner; inside; interior; within ②one's wife (or her relatives) ③internal organs；heart ④of the imperial palace II 形 female

内白 words spoken by an actor from offstage

内嬖 favourite imperial concubine

内宾 Chinese guest (as distinguished from 外宾 foreign guest)

内部 ①inside；interior；within ②inside；restricted

内场 (baseball, softball) infield

内臣 ①chamberlain ②eunuch

内城 inner city

内存 memory

内地 inland；interior；hinterland

内弟 wife's younger brother；brother-in-law

内定 (of an official appointment) decided at the higher level but not officially announced

内耳 internal ear;inner ear
内封 title page
内锋 inside forward
内服 taken by the mouth;oral
内港 inner harbour
内阁 cabinet
内功 exercises to benefit the internal organs; quality and capability
内海 ①inland sea ②continental sea
内涵 intension;connotation
内行 ①be expert at;be adept in;know the ins and outs of ②an expert;a dab hand;master
内耗 in-fighting; inside consumption; losses suffered in internal strife; internal dissension;internal friction
内河 inland river (*or* waters,waterway)
内核 the crux of a matter
内讧 internal conflict;internal strife;internal dissension
内踝 the medial part of the ankle (where the lower end of the tibia is)
内急 have to go to the toilet
内奸 a secret enemy agent within one's ranks;a hidden traitor
内间 inner room
内监 eunuch
内角 interior angle;internal angle
内景 indoor setting;indoor scene;interior
内径 internal diameter;inside (*or* inner) diameter (ID)
内疚 compunction;guilty conscience
内眷 female members of a family
内科 (department of) internal medicine
内控 controlled from the inside (i.e.,not allowing those on the outside to take part)
内库 imperial treasury
内裤 briefs;knickers
内涝 waterlogging
内力 internal force
内敛 ① self-restraint; self-restrained; self-control; reserved; introvert ② implicit; intriguing
内陆 inland;interior;hinterland
内乱 civil strife;internal disorder
内妹 wife's younger sister
内幕 what goes on behind the scenes;inside story
内能 internal energy;intrinsic energy
内亲 relatives on one's wife's side;(a man's) in-laws
内勤 ①internal (*or* office) work (as distinguished from work carried on mainly outside the office) ②office staff
内情 inside information (*or* story)
内圈 inner circle
内热 internal heat—disorders due to predominance of the yang

内人 my wife
内容 content;substance
内嫂 wife of wife's elder brother
内伤 ①internal injury ②disorder of internal organs (caused by improper diet,fatigue,emotional strains,sexual excess,etc.)
内侍 eunuch
内室 inner room;bedroom
内水 inland waters
内胎 inner tube (of a tyre)
内廷 inner chambers in an imperial palace;imperial residence;imperial palace
内退 early retirement
内外 ①inside and outside;domestic and foreign ②around;about
内网 intranet
内务 ①internal affairs ②daily routine tasks to keep the barracks,etc. clean and tidy
内线 ①planted agent ②interior lines ③inside (telephone) connections
内详 name and address of sender enclosed
内向 introversion
内项 the second or third term (in a proportion of four terms);mean
内销 sold inside the country;for the domestic market
内心 ①heart;innermost being ②incentre (of a triangle)
内省 [nèixǐng] self-examination;introspection
内兄 wife's elder brother;brother-in-law
内秀 be intelligent without seeming so
内需 domestic demand (in a market);domestic market demand;domestic needs
内焰 inner flame
内衣 underwear;underclothes
内因 internal cause
内应 a person operating from within in coordination with outside forces;planted agent; plant
内苑 palace grounds
内在 inherent;intrinsic;internal;inner
内脏 internal organs;viscera
内宅 inner chambers (for the womenfolk of a household)
内债 internal debt;domestic loan
内战 civil war
内障 cataract of glaucoma
内招 recruit (personnel) inside the production group;recruitment from within
内争 internal strife
内政 internal affairs;domestic affairs;home affairs
内侄 son of wife's brother;nephew
内痔 internal piles;internal haemorrhoids
内中 the inside
内助 wife (considered as a helpful companion)

N

内资 domestic investment;domestic capital
内子 my wife
内阻 internal resistance;inherent resistance
内部价 cost-plus price
内场手 infielder
内出血 internal haemorrhage (*or* bleeding)
内当家 ①wife ②the wife of one's master (*or* employer,landlord)
内电阻 internal resistance
内毒素 endotoxin
内耳炎 otitis interna
内分泌 endocrine;internal secretion
内骨骼 endoskeleton
内果皮 endocarp
内画壶 a bottle with painted designs inside
内环线 inner-city beltway; inner-city ring road
内寄生 endoparasitism
内接形 inscribed figure
内径规 internal gauge
内聚力 cohesive force;cohesion
内卡钳 inside callipers
内窥镜 endoscope
内联网 intranet
内流河 continental river
内陆国 landlocked country
内陆海 inland sea
内陆河 continental river
内陆湖 inland lake
内切圆 inscribed circle (of a triangle)
内燃机 internal-combustion engine
内务部 Ministry of Internal Affairs
内吸磷 demeton
内向型 domestically-oriented
内斜视 esotropia;cross-eye
内应力 internal stress
内在美 inner beauty
内侄女 daughter of wife's brother;niece
内置式 built-in
内转外 export products and technologies originally targeted at the domestic market
内装修 interior decoration
内部参考 document to be read only by a certain circle of people
内部电影 film to be shown in limited circles
内部发行 (of newspapers, magazines or books) for restricted circulation; not publicly distributed
内部刊物 restricted publication; limited-readership publication
内部矛盾 inner contradictions
内部消息 inside information
内查外调 make investigations both within and without
内存储器 internal storage;internal memory
内方外圆 square internally and round externally

内分泌腺 endocrine glands
内阁大臣 cabinet minister
内阁会议 cabinet council
内顾之忧 domestic worries;trouble at home
内寄生物 endoparasite
内紧外松 be relaxed outwardly but vigilant (*or* alert) inwardly
内联企业 domestically-associated enterprise; enterprise with internal connections;internally-linked enterprise
内联外引 introduce investment from abroad and establish lateral ties at home
内陆边境 inland frontier area
内陆盆地 interior (*or* inland) basin
内幕交易 insider trading
内燃机车 diesel locomotive
内容提要 synopsis;résumé
内外夹攻 attack from both within and without
内外交困 beset with difficulties at home and abroad
内外有别 keep inside information from outsiders (*or* foreigners)
内销商品 commodities for home consumption
内忧外患 domestic trouble and foreign invasion; internal disturbance and foreign aggression
内在规律 inherent law
内在联系 inner link;internal relations
内在矛盾 inner (*or* inherent) contradictions
内在因素 internal factor
内部调拨价 transfer price
内分泌失调 endocrine imbalance;endocrinopathy
内分泌系统 endocrine system
内接多边形 inscribed polygon
内向型经济 domestically-oriented economy
内部参考资料 classified reference materials
内部职工股份 shares held by company employees
内耳眩晕综合征 Ménière's syndrome; Ménière's disease
内容与形式的统一 unity of content and form

那 [nèi]
囮 that ➡nà;nè

nèn (ㄋㄣˋ)

恁 [nèn]
囮 ①so;such ②that;those

嫩 [nèn]
形 ①tender;delicate;sensitive ②(of food) under-done;soft; tender ③(of colour) light ④inexperienced;immature;unskilled
嫩红 pink;apricot pink
嫩黄 light yellow
嫩绿 light green;soft green
嫩气 ①delicate (*or* dainty) looks; youthfulness ②dainty-looking;youthful-looking

嫩色 light colour;soft colour;pastel shade
嫩手 new hand;green hand;raw hand
嫩芽 bud
嫩叶 tender leaf
嫩枝 spray;twig
嫩黄瓜 young cucumber;gherkin
嫩生生 very tender;very delicate

néng（ㄋㄥˊ）

能 [néng] Ⅰ 名 ① ability;capability;competence ② energy Ⅱ 形 able;capable Ⅲ 动 can;may
能动 active;dynamic
能干 able;capable;competent
能够 can;be able to;be capable of
能耗 energy consumption
能级 energy level
能力 ability;capacity;capability
能量 ①energy ②capabilities
能耐 ability;capability;skill
能人 able person
能事 what one is particularly good at
能手 dab;expert;crackajack
能源 the sources of energy;energy resources;energy
能动性 dynamic role;activity;initiative
能见度 visibility
能歌善舞 good at both singing and dancing
能工巧匠 skilful craftsman;skilled artisan;dab hand
能攻能守 be able to take the offensive as well as hold one's ground
能官能民 be ready to serve as an official or to be one of the common people
能力倾向 aptitude
能力水平 ability level
能骑善射 expert at horseback riding and shooting arrow
能掐会算 tell fortunes;be able to predict the future course of events
能屈能伸 be able to stoop or to stand;submit or assert oneself as the occasion requires;be adaptable to circumstances
能上能下 be ready to work either at the top or at the grass roots;be ready to accept a higher or a lower post
能诗善画 having superior abilities to write poetry and good in painting
能说会道 have the gift of the gab;be a glib talker
能文能武 be versed in both polite letters and martial arts;be able to wield both the pen and the sword
能言快语 eloquent and frank in speech
能言善辩 eloquent, glib and quick-tongued in argument

能源短缺 energy shortage
能源危机 energy crisis
能愿动词 modal verb
能者多劳 Able people should do more work; The abler one is,the more one should do.
能者为师 let those who know teach
能量守恒律 the law of conservation of energy
能书不择笔 People good at calligraphy are not particular about the brush;A good workman does not complain about the tools.
能人背后有能人 For every able person there is always one still abler.
能源交通重点建设基金 construction funds for key energy and transport projects

ní（ㄋㄧˊ）

尼 [ní] 名 nun
尼庵 Buddhist nunnery
尼姑 Buddhist nun
尼龙 nylon
尼古丁 nicotine
尼罗河 the Nile
尼亚加拉瀑布 Niagara Falls

呢 [ní] 名 cloth made of wool;(heavy) woollen cloth ➡ne
呢帽 felt hat
呢喃 (of swallows) twitter
呢绒 woollen goods;wool fabric
呢子 woollen cloth (for heavy clothing);heavy woollen cloth;wool coating (or suiting)
呢大衣 woollen overcoat

怩 [ní]
◇忸怩 blushing;bashful

泥 [ní] 名 ①mud;silt;mire ②any paste-like matter;mashed vegetable or fruit ➡nì
泥巴 mud;mire
泥地 mud ground;quagmire
泥肥 sludge (used as manure)
泥封 lute
泥工 bricklayer;tiler;plasterer
泥垢 dirt;grime
泥浆 slurry;mud
泥金 coating material made of powdered gold or other metals;golden paint
泥坑 mud pit;mire;morass
泥疗 mud therapy
泥煤 peat
泥泞 ①muddy;miry ②mire;mud
泥鳅 loach
泥人 clay figurine
泥沙 silt
泥塑 clay sculpture
泥胎 an unpainted clay idol

N

泥潭 mire；morass；quagmire
泥炭 peat
泥塘 mire；bog；morass
泥土 ①earth；soil ②clay
泥洼 marsh；mire
泥污 mire
泥岩 mudstone
泥俑 clay figure buried with the dead；funerary clay figure；earthen figurine
泥浴 mud bath
泥沼 mire；swamp；morass；slough
泥醉 dead drunk
泥饭碗 clay rice bowl；insecure job
泥灰岩 marl
泥盆纪 the Devonian period（the 4th period of the Palaeozoic era，350，000，000—400，000，000 years ago）
泥盆系 the Devonian system
泥石流 mud-rock flow
泥水匠 bricklayer；tiler；plasterer
泥胎儿 unfired pottery
泥腿子 bumpkin；clodhopper
泥瓦匠 bricklayer；tiler；plasterer
泥牛入海 like clay oxen entering the sea— never to be heard of again；gone forever
泥沙俱下 mud and sand are carried along— there is a mingling of good and bad
泥足巨人 a colossus with feet of clay
泥菩萨过河，自身难保 like a clay idol fording a river—hardly able to save oneself（let alone anyone else）

铌 [ní] 〔名〕 niobium（Nb）
铌铁矿 columbite

倪 [ní] 〔名〕 ①clue；inkling ②prediction

霓 [ní] 〔名〕 secondary rainbow
霓虹灯 neon lamp；neon light；neon
霓虹灯广告牌 neon sign

nǐ （3ǐ）

拟 [nǐ] 〔动〕 ①draw up；draft ②plan；intend ③imitate；mimic；simulate ④ compare ⑤ conjecture；suppose；guess
拟订 draw up；draft；work out
拟稿 prepare a draft；make a draft
拟古 model one's literary（or artistic）style on that of the ancients
拟人 personification
拟态 mimicry；imitation
拟议 ①proposal；recommendation ②draw up；draft
拟作 a work done in the manner of a certain author
拟于不伦 draw inapt parallels

你 [nǐ] 〔代〕 ①you ②you；one；anyone
你好 how are you；hello
你们 you；your
你死我活 life-and-death；mortal
你追我赶 try to overtake each other in friendly emulation
你走你的阳关道，我过我的独木桥 you take the open road，I'll cross the log bridge—you go your way，I'll go mine

nì （3ì）

伲 [nì] 〔代〕 I；we

泥 [nì] I 〔动〕 cover（or daub，smear，coat）with plaster，putty etc.；plaster II 〔形〕 stubborn；obstinate；rigid；obdurate　➡ ní
泥古 have bigoted belief in the ancients；obstinately follow ancient ways
泥子 putty

昵 [nì] 〔形〕 close；intimate；confidential
昵称 a term of endearment；pet name
昵交 get along intimately；be on close terms

逆 [nì] I 〔形〕 ① counter；contrary；inverse ② adverse II 〔动〕 ①go against；disobey；resist；defy ②salute；greet；meet；welcome III 〔名〕 traitor IV 〔副〕 beforehand；in advance
逆差 adverse balance of trade；trade deficit
逆产 ①a traitor's property ②（of a baby）breech birth；breech delivery
逆耳 grate on the ear；be unpleasant to the ear
逆风 ①go against the wind ②contrary wind；head wind
逆光 backlighting
逆火 （of an internal-combustion engine）backfire
逆价 junk price
逆经 vicarious menstruation
逆境 adverse circumstances；adversity
逆客 greet guests
逆料 anticipate；foresee；prognosticate
逆流 ①go against the current ②adverse current；countercurrent
逆旅 inn；hotel
逆伦 the violation of proper human relationships（e. g. parricide）
逆市 reverse market tendency
逆事 ①untoward incidents；mishaps ②rebellious acts
逆水 （of a boat，etc.）go against the current
逆温 （temperature）inversion
逆向 opposite direction
逆行 ①（of vehicles）go in a direction not allowed by traffic regulations；go in the

wrong direction ②retrograde motion
逆序 backward sequence
逆运 adversity;misfortune;ill luck
逆证 a severe case with unfavourable prognosis
逆知 know sth before it happens
逆转 take a turn for the worse;reverse;deteriorate
逆子 unfilial son
逆颤音 inverted trill
逆定理 converse theorem
逆温层 inversion layer
逆反心理 antagonistic psychology;rebellious psychology
逆来顺受 resign oneself to adversity;meekly submit to oppression (*or* maltreatment, etc.)
逆水行舟 a boat sailing against the current

匿 [nì]
囵 hide;conceal;cache;bury
匿报 withhold information
匿藏 conceal;hide;go into hiding
匿伏 be in hiding;lurk
匿迹 go into hiding;stay in concealment
匿名 anonymous
匿名信 an anonymous letter
匿影藏形 hide from public notice;conceal one's identity;lie low
匿名 FTP 服务器 anonymous FTP server

腻 [nì]
Ⅰ 形 ①greasy;oily ②bored;tired of;fed up ③meticulous;scrupulous ④viscous;sticky;gummy;glutinous ⑤close;intimate Ⅱ 名 dirt;filth;grime;soil;soot
腻虫 aphid
腻烦 ①be bored;be fed up ②loathe;hate
腻人 ①be boring (*or* tedious) ②(of food that is too greasy or sweet) make one sick
腻味 ①be bored;be fed up ②hate;loathe
腻子 luting;putty;mastic

溺 [nì]
Ⅰ 囵 ①be submerged;be drowned ②be addicted to Ⅱ 形 obsessed;unduly ➡ niào
溺爱 spoil (a child);dote on (a child)
溺水 drowning;sinking
溺死 drowned
溺婴 infanticide by drowning
溺职 neglect of duty;dereliction
溺于酒色 given over to wine and women
溺于名利 be addicted to fame and gain;lust for fame and fortune

niān（ㄋㄧㄢ）

拈 [niān]
囵 pick up;pinch
拈香 burn incense sticks
拈阄儿 draw lots

拈花惹草 toy with flowers and grass—dally with women;philander
拈轻怕重 prefer the light to the heavy—pick easy jobs and shirk hard ones

蔫 [niān]
Ⅰ 囵 (of flower, tree, fruit, etc.) fade;wither;sag;shrivel up;droop Ⅱ 形 ①listless;spiritless;lethargic;languid ②(of temperament) slow;not open;not direct
蔫巴 fading;withering;shrivelling
蔫蔫 ①quiet;silent ②listless;droopy;sluggish
蔫呼呼 weak-willed and indecisive
蔫儿坏 inwardly vicious;behave in an underhand way
蔫不出溜 quiet;silent
蔫不唧儿 ①listless;droopy;sluggish ②quiet
蔫头耷脑 with head hanging—dejected;listless;droopy

nián（ㄋㄧㄢ）

年 [nián]
Ⅰ 名 ①year ②age ③period in one's life ④period (in history);time ⑤harvest ⑥New Year ⑦friendship between those who passed the imperial examinations in the same year Ⅱ 形 ①annual;yearly ②(of articles for use) related to the New Year
年报 ①annual (a book or magazine, often used in titles) ②annual report
年辈 one's age and generation
年表 chronological table
年菜 dishes prepared for the lunar New Year (*or* Spring Festival)
年成 the year's harvest
年初 the beginning of the year
年代 ①age;years;time ②a decade of a century
年底 the end of the year
年度 year (a yearly period fixed for a certain purpose)
年饭 family reunion dinner on the lunar New Year's Eve
年份 ①a particular year ②age;time
年俸 annual salary;yearly pay
年糕 New Year cake (made of glutinous rice flour)
年庚 the time (year,month,day and hour) of a person's birth;date of birth
年关 the end of the year (formerly time for settling accounts)
年光 ①time;years ②the year's harvest
年号 reign title (a designation for the years when an emperor was on the throne)
年华 time;years
年画 New Year (of Spring Festival) pictures
年会 annual meeting

N

年货 special New Year purchases
年级 grade;year
年纪 age
年假 ①New Year holidays ②winter vacation ③annual leave
年间 certain period (of a dynasty or reign)
年检 annual examination;annual checkup
年鉴 yearbook;almanac
年节 the lunar New Year Festival;the Spring Festival
年金 annuity
年景 ① the year's harvest ② holiday atmosphere of the Spring Festival
年均 annual average
年历 a calendar with the whole year printed on one sheet;single-page calendar
年利 annual interest
年龄 age
年轮 annual ring;growth ring
年迈 old;aged
年貌 age and appearance
年末 the end of the year
年年 every year;year after year
年谱 chronological life
年青 young
年轻 ①young ②younger
年少 ①young ②youngster;a young man
年时 last year
年事 age (of a person)
年岁 ①age ②years
年头 ① year ② years;a long time ③ days;times ④harvest
年息 annual interest
年限 fixed number of years
年薪 annual salary;yearly pay
年夜 the lunar New Year's Eve
年幼 young;under age
年月 ①days;years ②times
年长 older in age;senior
年中 the middle of the year
年终 the end of the year;year-end
年资 age and years of service;seniority
年产量 annual output;annual yield
年龄段 age group;age bracket
年龄群 age set
年龄组 age group
年平均 annual mean
年轻化 make... younger;become younger in average age
年收入 annual income
年同比 year-on-year;on an annual basis
年夜饭 family reunion dinner on the lunar New Year's Eve
年终奖 year-end bonus
年度报告 annual report
年度计划 annual plan
年度结算 annual account

年度收入 annual revenue
年复一年 year after year;year in year out
年富力强 in the prime of life;in one's prime
年高德劭 of venerable age and eminent virtue;of advanced years and known integrity;venerable
年高望重 aged and in high standing
年购买额 annual purchase (rate)
年关荏苒 the quick passing of time
年久失修 worn down by the years without repair
年龄结构 age structure
年少气盛 young and impetuous
年深日久 with the passage of time;as the years go by
年事已高 be advanced in years
年愈不惑 have passed 40
年终报告 year-end report
年终分配 year-end distribution
年终奖金 year-end bonuses
年终结存 annual balance
年终结账 year-end settlement of accounts
年终评比 year-end appraisal of work
年度决算表 annual statement
年度统计表 annual returns
年增长系数 annual improvement factor
年龄性别组成 age-sex structure

黏 [nián]
〔形〕 sticky;glutinous
黏儿 gum;resin
黏巴 sticky;gluey;gummy
黏虫 armyworm
黏度 viscosity
黏附 adhere
黏合 bind;bond;adhere
黏糊 ①sticky;glutinous ②languid;slow-moving
黏胶 viscose
黏结 cohere
黏菌 slime mould;slime fungus
黏米 ①glutinous rice ②broomcorn millet
黏膜 mucous membrane;mucosa
黏泥 foundry loam;slime
黏土 clay
黏性 stickiness;viscidity;viscosity
黏液 mucus
黏着 stick together;adhere
黏度计 viscosimeter
黏合剂 binder;adhesive;bonding agent
黏胶丝 viscose
黏膜炎 mucositis
黏土砖 clay brick
黏涎子 slaver;slobber tedious;dull
黏性油 viscous oil
黏着力 adhesion force
黏着语 agglutinative language
黏附作用 adhesion

N

黏胶长丝 viscose filament yarn
黏胶纤维 viscose fibre
黏性物质 stickum
黏胶短纤维 viscose staple fibre
黏液性水肿 myxoedema

niǎn （ㄋㄧㄢˇ）

涩 [niǎn]
形 sweating; perspiring

捻 [niǎn]
Ⅰ 动 ①twist with the fingers ②dredge up Ⅱ 名 sth made by twisting
捻度 number of turns (*or* twists); twist
捻针 twirling (*or* rotating) of the acupuncture needle
捻子 spill (for lighting candles, lamps, etc.); wick
捻河泥 dredge up silt (*or* sludge) from a river
捻线机 twisting frame

辇 [niǎn]
名 ①man-drawn carriage ②imperial carriage

碾 [niǎn]
Ⅰ 名 roller Ⅱ 动 ① grind with a roller; husk with a roller; crush ②cut and polish
碾场 thresh (*or* husk) grain on a threshing ground
碾槌 pestle
碾坊 grain mill
碾烂 crush to pieces; crush to powder
碾米 husk rice
碾磨 milling; pan milling
碾盘 millstone upon which a stone roller is used
碾平 flatten; level (with a roller); roll out
碾碎 pulverize; crush to pieces
碾砣 stone roller
碾压 roller compaction
碾玉 cut and polish jade
碾子 roller and millstone; roller
碾滚子 stone roller
碾米厂 rice-hulling mill
碾米机 rice mill (a machine)

撵 [niǎn]
动 ①drive out; oust; expel; banish ②catch up; run after; pursue
撵走 oust; kick out; drive away
撵出去 drive sb away; drive sb out

蹍 [niǎn]
动 step on; tread

niàn （ㄋㄧㄢˋ）

廿 [niàn]
数 twenty

念 [niàn]
Ⅰ 动 ①think of; long for; miss ②read aloud

③study; attend school Ⅱ 名 thought; idea
念白 spoken parts of a Chinese opera
念叨 ①talk about again and again in recollection (*or* anticipation); be always talking about ②talk over; discuss
念佛 chant the name of Buddha; pray to Buddha
念经 recite (*or* chant) scriptures
念旧 keep old friendships in mind; remember old friends
念书 ①read ②study
念诵 ①read aloud; chant ②talk about (in recollection or anticipation)
念头 thought; idea; intention
念咒 chant incantations
念珠 beads; rosary
念念不忘 bear in mind constantly
念念有词 ①mutter incantations ②mumble

niáng （ㄋㄧㄤˊ）

娘 [niáng]
名 ① ma; mum; mom; mother ② aunt ③ young woman
娘家 a married woman's parents' home
娘舅 brother of one's mother; uncle
娘娘 ①empress concubine; imperial concubine ②a name for certain guardian goddesses
娘亲 mother
娘胎 mother's womb
娘子 ①one's wife ②madam; ma'am
娘儿们 ① mother and son or daughter ② the womenfolk ③wife
娘娘庙 Temple of the Goddess of Fertility
娘子军 a detachment of women; any contingent entirely made up of women

niàng （ㄋㄧㄤˋ）

酿 [niàng]
Ⅰ 动 ① make (wine); brew (beer); ferment ②make (honey) ③lead to; result in ④ (method of cooking) fill (hollowed bell peppers, etc. with minced meat, etc.) and fry (*or* steam) Ⅱ 名 wine
酿成 lead to; bring on; breed
酿祸 create trouble; ferment disturbance
酿酒 make wine; brew beer
酿酶 zymase
酿蜜 make honey
酿造 make (wine, vinegar, etc.); brew (beer, etc.)
酿酒厂 winery; brewery
酿酒业 wine-making industry
酿母菌 yeast
酿热物 ferment material
酿成大祸 lead to a disaster

N

niǎo (ㄋㄧㄠˇ)

鸟 [niǎo]
〈名〉bird ⇒ diǎo
鸟儿 a small bird;birdie
鸟巢 nest
鸟粪 ①birds' droppings ②guano
鸟害 bird pest
鸟喙 beak;bill
鸟瞰 ①get a bird's-eye view ②a general survey of a subject;bird's-eye view
鸟类 birds (of any kind)
鸟笼 birdcage
鸟鸣 singing of birds
鸟枪 ①fowling piece ②air gun
鸟兽 birds and beasts;fur and feather
鸟窝 (bird's) nest
鸟葬 celestial burial (by which bodies are exposed to birds of prey)
鸟篆 bird script (an ancient form of Chinese written characters,resembling birds' footprints)
鸟嘴 beak;bill
鸟粪层 guano
鸟瞰图 a bird's-eye view;an aerial view
鸟类学 ornithology
鸟兽散 scatter;flee
鸟尽弓藏 cast aside the bow once the birds are all killed—cast sb aside when he has served his purpose
鸟笼经济 "bird cage economy"; market economy within socialist limits
鸟枪换炮 change from fowling pieces into guns—become much better equipped;have much better conditions;improve greatly;be better armed
鸟语花香 Birds sing and flowers give forth fragrance (as on a fine spring day).
鸟类保护区 bird reserves
鸟为食亡,人为财死 Birds die in pursuit of food and human beings die in pursuit of wealth.

袅 [niǎo]
〈形〉slender and delicate
袅袅 ①curl upwards ②wave in the wind ③linger
袅娜 ①(of plants) soft and slender ②(of a female figure) delicate and graceful;willowy
袅绕 linger
袅袅婷婷 lithe,slim and supple

niào (ㄋㄧㄠˋ)

尿 [niào]
Ⅰ〈名〉urine Ⅱ〈动〉urinate;make water;pass water;pee ⇒ suī
尿闭 anuria

尿布 diaper;napkin;nappy
尿池 urinal
尿床 bed-wetting
尿道 urethra
尿肥 urine used as manure
尿壶 chamber pot;urinal
尿检 urine testing
尿炕 wet the *kang*;wet the bed
尿尿 urinate;make water;pass water;pee
尿盆 chamber pot;urinal
尿频 frequent micturition
尿素 urea;carbamide
尿酸 uric acid
尿血 haematuria
尿崩症 diabetes insipidus
尿不湿 paper nappy;disposable diaper
尿胆素 urobilin
尿道炎 urethritis
尿毒症 uraemia
尿分析 urinalysis
尿少症 oliguria
尿失禁 urinary incontinence;incontinence of urine
尿潴留 retention of urine
尿素脱蜡 urea dewaxing

脲 [niào]
脲醛塑料 urea-formaldehyde plastics

溺 [niào]
Ⅰ〈名〉urine Ⅱ〈动〉urinate;make water;pass water ⇒ nì

niē (ㄋㄧㄝ)

捏 [niē]
〈动〉①hold between the thumb and other fingers;pinch ②knead with the fingers;mould ③bind together;put together;link ④fabricate;make up;frame up
捏合 ①put together;bring together ②fabricate;make up
捏积 a method of treating children's digestive disorders by kneading (or massaging) the muscles along the spine;chiropractic
捏弄 ①play with;fiddle with ②order about;manipulate ③discuss in private
捏造 fabricate;concoct;fake;trump up
捏闸 apply the handbrake
捏把汗 be breathless (with anxiety or tension);be keyed up;be on edge
捏合机 kneading machine
捏饺子 knead the wrappers when making dumplings
捏面人儿 mould clay figurines
捏橡皮泥 knead plasticine
捏造事实 invent a story;make up a story
捏造罪名 fabricate an accusation;trump up charges

nié（ㄋㄧㄝ´）

茶 [nié]
〔形〕 tired；listless；lethargic；languid

niè（ㄋㄧㄝˋ）

臬 [niè]
〔名〕 ① target（for arrows）② gnomon ③ standard；criterion

涅 [niè]
Ⅰ〔名〕alunite Ⅱ〔动〕dye black
涅白 opaque white
涅槃 nirvana

啮 [niè]
〔动〕gnaw
啮合 ①clench the teeth ②（of gears）mesh；engage
啮咬 nibble
啮齿目 Rodentia
啮齿动物 rodent

镊 [niè]
Ⅰ〔名〕 tweezers Ⅱ〔动〕 pick up sth with tweezers
镊子 tweezers

镍 [niè]
〔名〕nickel（Ni）
镍币 nickel coin；nickel
镍钢 nickel steel
镍黄铁矿 pentlandite（a mineral）
镍铬电池 NiCd battery

颞 [niè]
颞骨 temporal bone
颞颥 temple

蹑 [niè]
〔动〕① lighten（one's step）；walk on tiptoe ② follow；dog；track ③ tread；step on；walk with
蹑迹 follow the trace；track
蹑踪 follow the trail of；track
蹑足 ①walk with light steps ②participate in；join
蹑悄悄 softly；quietly
蹑手蹑脚 walk gingerly；walk on tiptoe
蹑足不前 not move a step forward
蹑足潜踪 walk stealthily

孽 [niè]
Ⅰ〔名〕①evil（or wicked）creature；monster ②evil；crime；sin Ⅱ〔形〕 unfaithful；treacherous；unfilial
孽报 retribution for sins
孽臣 traitorous vassal
孽根 root of evil；ruin；bane
孽海 sea of retribution
孽障 ①retribution in this life for the sins of a previous existence ②medium of retribution
孽种 ① the bane of one's existence ② vile spawn；unfilial son

孽子 ① son of a concubine；unfilial son ② an unfilial son；an unworthy descendant

nín（ㄋㄧㄣ´）

您 [nín]
〔代〕you
您好 How are you? *or* How do you do?

níng（ㄋㄧㄥ´）

宁 [níng]
Ⅰ〔形〕 peaceful；serene；tranquil Ⅱ〔动〕① pacify；appease ②pay a visit to（one's parents or elders） ⇒nìng
宁静 peaceful；tranquil；quiet；calm
宁日 peaceful days
宁馨儿 a lovely child
宁静致远 Still water runs deep；leading a quiet life

苧 [níng]
〔名〕limonene

拧 [níng]
〔动〕①twist；wring ②pinch；tweak ⇒nǐng；nìng
拧成一股绳 twist into a rope—stick together；make joint efforts

咛 [níng]
◇叮咛 urge again and again；warn；exhort

狞 [níng]
〔形〕ferocious；hideous
狞恶 fierce；ferocious
狞视 stare fiercely at；fix one's sinister eyes on
狞笑 grin hideously

柠 [níng]
柠檬 lemon
柠檬茶 lemon tea
柠檬黄 citrine；lemon-coloured
柠檬色 lemon yellow
柠檬水 lemonade；lemon squash
柠檬素 citrin；vitamin P
柠檬酸 citric acid
柠檬糖 lemon drops
柠檬油 lemon oil
柠檬汁 lemon juice
柠檬榨汁器 lemon squeezer

聍 [níng]
◇耵聍 earwax；cerumen

凝 [níng]
〔动〕①congeal；curdle；coagulate ②concentrate；focus
凝成 congeal into；solidify；cement
凝点 condensation point
凝冻 freeze
凝固 solidify

N

凝华 sublimate
凝集 (of fluids or gases) agglutinate
凝胶 gel
凝结 congeal;coagulate;curdle;condense
凝聚 ① (of vapour) condense;(of fluids) coagulate;curdle ②coacervation
凝练 (of writing) concise;condensed;compact
凝眸 fix (*or* focus) one's eyes on;look with a fixed gaze
凝神 with fixed (*or* concentrated, rapt) attention
凝视 gaze fixedly;stare
凝思 be lost in thought;meditate
凝听 listen attentively (*or* intently) listen with rapt attention
凝望 gaze (*or* stare) at
凝想 meditate
凝脂 congealed fat (said of a woman's skin)
凝滞 stagnant;unmoving;sluggish
凝重 ① dignified;imposing ② (of sound or voice) deep and forceful ③ deep;dense;thick
凝固点 solidifying point
凝固浴 coagulating bath
凝灰岩 tuff
凝集素 agglutinin
凝结剂 coagulant
凝结物 coagulum
凝聚层 coacervate
凝聚力 rallying power;cohesiveness
凝析油 condensate
凝血酶 thrombin;thrombase
凝血药 coagulant
凝固汽油 napalm
凝结尾迹 contrail;condensation trail
凝结作用 coagulation
凝固汽油弹 napalm bomb

nǐng (ㄋ丨ㄥˇ)

拧 [nǐng]
Ⅰ 动 ① twist;screw;turn ② differ;disagree;be at cross-purposes;be at odds Ⅱ 形 wrong;erroneous;mistaken ➡níng;nìng

nìng (ㄋ丨ㄥˋ)

宁 [nìng]
副 ① would rather;better ② could there be;could it be ➡níng
宁可 would rather;better
宁肯 would rather
宁愿 would rather;better;prefer to
宁缺毋滥 rather go without than have something shoddy—put quality before quantity
宁死不屈 rather die than submit (*or* surrender)
宁"左"勿右 mentality of those who always prefer being on the "left" to being on the right politically
宁为玉碎,不为瓦全 rather be a broken piece of jade than a whole tile—better to die in glory than live in dishonour
宁教我负天下人,休教天下人负我　Ⅰ would rather betray the world than let the world betray me.

佞 [nìng]
形 ① given to flattery;sycophantic ② able and wise;gifted
佞臣 a sycophantic official (*or* courtier)
佞人 sycophant;toady;toad-eater

拧 [nìng]
形 pigheaded;stubborn;obstinate;unbending ➡níng;nǐng

泞 [nìng]
名 mud;slush

niū (ㄋ丨ㄡ)

妞 [niū]
名 girl

niú (ㄋ丨ㄡˊ)

牛 [niú]
Ⅰ 名 ox;cattle Ⅱ 形 stubborn;proud
牛蒡 great burdock
牛车 ox cart;bullock cart
牛刀 butcher's knife
牛痘 ① cowpox ② smallpox pustule;vaccine pustule
牛犊 calf
牛顿 newton;large dyne
牛轭 oxbow;yoke
牛粪 cow dung
牛倌 cowherd;cowhand;oxherd;herd-boy
牛黄 bezoar
牛角 ox horn
牛劲 ① great strength;tremendous effort ② stubbornness;obstinacy;tenacity
牛圈 lair
牛栏 cattle pen
牛马 oxen and horses—beasts of burden
牛毛 ox hair
牛虻 gadfly
牛奶 milk
牛腩 sirloin;tenderloin
牛排 beefsteak
牛棚 cowshed
牛皮 ①cowhide;oxhide ② tough;tensile;pliable ③bragging
牛气 arrogant;overbearing
牛肉 beef
牛乳 cow's milk
牛虱 ox louse
牛市 bull market
牛蛙 bullfrog

牛尾 oxtail
牛瘟 rinderpest;cattle plague
牛膝 the root of bidentate achyranthes
牛性 pigheadedness;stubbornness
牛饮 drink gallons
牛蝇 gadfly
牛油 butter
牛蒡子 the achene of great burdock
牛鼻子 the nose (*or* muzzle) of an ox
牛痘苗 (bovine) vaccine
牛轭湖 oxbow lake
牛肺疫 pleuropneumonia (of cattle)
牛角画 horn mosaic
牛角尖 the tip of a horn—an insignificant or insoluble problem
牛郎星 altair
牛奶场 dairy
牛奶糖 toffee
牛皮糖 sticky candy
牛皮癣 psoriasis
牛皮纸 kraft (paper)
牛脾气 stubbornness;obstinacy
牛舌鱼 tonguefish;tongue sole
牛尾鱼 flathead
牛仔裤 jeans;levis;cowboy pants
牛仔帽 cowboy hat
牛刀小试 a master hand's first small display
牛鬼蛇神 monsters and demons—forces of evil;evil people of all descriptions
牛角制品 hornwork
牛郎织女 the Cowherd and the Weaver
牛毛细雨 drizzle;fine drizzling rain
牛奶咖啡 white coffee
牛溲马勃 cheap but useful things
牛头刨床 shaping machine;shaper
牛头马面 Ox Head and Horse Face
牛顿望远镜 Newtonian telescope
牛顿运动定律 Newton's law of motion
牛头不对马嘴 horses' jaws don't match cows' heads—incongruous;irrelevant
牛奶果仁巧克力 milk and nuts chocolate
牛顿万有引力定律 Newton's law of gravitation

niǔ (ㄋㄧㄡˇ)

扭 [niǔ]
Ⅰ 〔动〕① turn ② twist;contort;wrench ③ sprain;wrench;strain ④ swing;sway ⑤ seize;grapple Ⅱ 〔形〕 twisted;slanted
扭摆 (of one's body) sway
扭秤 torsion balance
扭打 wrestle;grapple
扭动 sway;writhe
扭干 wring dry
扭结 twist together;tangle up
扭亏 wipe out deficits;make up for losses
扭力 twisting (*or* torsional,torque) force

扭捏 walk affectedly with a swing
扭曲 twist;distort
扭伤 sprain;wrench
扭送 (of civilians) seize (a criminal,etc.) and deliver him to (the police)
扭头 ① turn one's head away;turn away ② turn (round)
扭转 ① turn round ② turn back;reverse
扭摆舞 twist
扭秧歌 do the yangko dance
扭亏为盈 turn loss into gain (*or* profit)
扭亏无望 no way to make up the deficit;no way to reverse the losing trend
扭亏增盈 make up deficits and increase surpluses;eliminate losses and increase profits
扭力天平 torsion balance
扭转局面 reverse the tide;turn the table
扭转局势 turn the tide;reverse a trend
扭转乾坤 change course of events;retrieve a situation
扭转企业亏损 eliminate enterprise losses

狃 [niǔ]
〔动〕 be bound by;be constrained by
狃于成见 bound by prejudice;prejudiced;biased
狃于陋习 accustomed to bad habits

忸 [niǔ]
忸怩 blushing;bashful
忸怩作态 behave coyly;be affectedly shy

纽 [niǔ]
〔名〕① handle;knob ② button ③ bond;tie;link ④ immature fruit
纽带 link;tie;bond
纽扣 button
纽襻 button loop
纽眼 buttonhole
纽子 button

钮 [niǔ]
〔名〕① handle;knob ② button ③ bond;tie;link ④ push button

niù (ㄋㄧㄡˋ)

拗 [niù]
〔形〕 stubborn;bigoted;obstinate;stiff-necked
➡ ǎo;ào
拗不过 be unable to dissuade;fail to talk sb out of doing sth

nóng (ㄋㄨㄥˊ)

农 [nóng]
〔名〕① agriculture;farming ② farmer;peasant
农产 ① agricultural production ② agricultural products;farm produce
农场 farm
农村 rural area;countryside;village

农贷 agricultural loans (*or* credits)
农夫 farmer
农妇 peasant woman
农工 peasants and workers
农户 peasant household
农活 farm work
农机 agricultural machinery;farm machinery
农家 peasant family
农具 farm implements;farm tools
农垦 land reclamation and cultivation
农历 the traditional Chinese calendar;the lunar calendar
农忙 busy season (in farming)
农民 peasant;peasantry
农膜 plastic film for agricultural use
农奴 serf
农渠 field ditch
农桑 farming and sericulture
农舍 farmhouse;cottage
农时 farming season
农事 farm work;farming
农田 farm land;crop land;arable land;cultivated land;agricultural fields
农隙 slack season (in farming)
农闲 slack season (in farming)
农械 farm chemical apparatus (e.g. sprayer, duster)
农学 agronomy;agriculture
农谚 farmer's proverb;farmer's saying
农药 agricultural chemical;farm chemical;pesticide
农业 agriculture;farming
农资 materials and equipment for agricultural production
农产品 agricultural products;farm produce
农机具 agricultural implements;farm implements
农技站 agrotechnical station
农家肥 farm manure;farmyard manure
农科所 institute of agricultural science
农忙假 rush period
农奴主 serf owner
农学院 agricultural college
农业国 an agricultural country
农业税 agricultural tax
农艺师 agronomist
农艺学 agronomy
农转非 change from rural to non-rural registration
农作物 crops
农村集市 village fair;rural market
农村经济 rural economy;rural relief
农村生活 rural life
农副产品 farm produce and sideline products;agricultural and sideline products
农贸市场 a market of farm produce (in urban areas);market for farm produce (in cities)

农民阶级 the peasantry
农民起义 peasant uprising;peasant revolt
农民协会 peasant association
农民意识 peasant mentality
农民战争 peasant war
农奴制度 serf system;serfdom
农田水利 irrigation and water conservancy
农业保险 agricultural insurance
农业化学 agricultural chemistry
农业机械 agricultural machinery;farm machinery
农业技术 agricultural technology
农业科研 agro-scientific research
农业人口 people engaged in agriculture;agricultural population
农业投入 agricultural input
农业银行 Agricultural Bank of China
农用薄膜 plastic sheets used for agricultural purposes
农用工业 agroindustry
农产品比价 parity rate of agricultural products
农村城市化 urbanization of villages
农村电气化 electrification of the countryside;rural electrification
农林牧副渔 farming,forestry,animal husbandry,sideline production and fishery
农民企业家 farmer-entrepreneur;peasant entrepreneur
农药残留物 pesticide residue
农业产业化 industrial management of agriculture
农业工程学 agricultural engineering
农业合作化 cooperative transformation of agriculture;agricultural cooperative (*or* cooperation) movement
农业集体化 the collectivization of agriculture
农业技术员 agrotechnician
农业技术站 agrotechnical station
农业气象学 agricultural meteorology;agrometeorology
农业生物学 agrobiology
农业现代化 modernization of agriculture;agricultural modernization
农业信息化 have an information-driven agriculture;apply IT extensively to agricultural development
农用拖拉机 agricultural tractor;agrimotor
农转非人员 persons who have changed from agricultural to non-agricultural status
农村商业网点 network of commercial establishments in rural areas;rural commercial establishments and networks
农工贸一体化 the integration of agriculture,industry and trade
农民家庭经营 farmer household operation
农田基本建设 capital construction on farm-

land;farmland improvement project

农田生态平衡 ecological equilibrium for farm-land

农田水利建设 construction of water conservancy works

农业集约经营 intensive management of agriculture

农业技术改造 the technical transformation of agriculture

农业抗灾能力 ability of agriculture to withstand natural disasters

农业区域经济 regional economy in agriculture

农业生态环境 agro-ecoenvironment;ecological environment in agriculture

农业综合开发 comprehensive agricultural development;comprehensive exploitation of agriculture;overall development of agriculture

农产品统购派购 unified purchasing of farm produce by the state according to fixed quotas

农村剩余劳动力 rural surplus labourers (or workers)

农工商联合企业 integrated farm-industry-commerce enterprise

农民土地使用权 peasants' right to land-use

农业技术推广站 station for popularizing agricultural technique

农业生产合作社 agricultural producers' cooperative

农村流通体制改革 reform of the rural circulation (or distribution) system

农村市场体系建设 building of rural market system

农业技术推广网络 agrotechnique popularization (or extension) network

农产品价格补贴政策 agricultural-support policy

农村居民人均纯收入 the average annual per-capita net income for rural residents

农村三级医疗保健网 three-level (or three-tiered) medicare network in the rural areas

农村社会化服务体系 rural community-run service system

农业技术联产责任制 system of output-related responsibility in agrotechnical service;the right of decision-making in enterprises

农业社会化服务体系 socialized rural network of services

农产品价格和流通体制 pricing and distribution system of farm produce

农业、农村、农民问题 issues of agriculture,countryside and peasants;the issues of agriculture,rural areas and farmers

侬 [nóng]
代 ①you ②I

浓 [nóng]
形 ① concentrated;thick;dense;heavy ② strong;great;deep

浓茶 strong tea

浓淡 deep or light—shade of colour

浓度 consistency;concentration;density

浓厚 ①dense;thick ②strong;pronounced

浓烈 strong;thick;heavy

浓眉 heavy (or bushy,thick) eyebrows

浓密 dense;thick

浓墨 thick ink

浓缩 concentrate;enrich

浓雾 heavy fog

浓香 ①giving off a strong fragrance ②strong fragrance

浓烟 dense smoke

浓艳 rich and gaudy

浓阴 dense leafy shade

浓郁 ①(of perfume,fragrance,etc.) strong;rich ②dense;thick

浓重 dense;thick;strong

浓妆 heavy makeup and gaudy dress

浓积云 cumulus congestus

浓缩铀 enriched uranium

浓眉大眼 with big eyes and bushy (or thick) eyebrows

浓云密布 be overcast

浓妆淡抹总相宜 (as of a woman) always look beautiful with either light or heavy makeup

脓 [nóng]
名 pus

脓包 ①pustule ②worthless fellow;good-for-nothing

脓疮 running sore

脓袋 pus-pocket

脓尿 pyuria

脓胸 pyothorax

脓肿 abscess

脓疱病 impetigo

秾 [nóng]
形 (of plants,trees,etc.) luxuriant

nòng (ㄋㄨㄥˋ)

弄 [nòng]
动 ①play with;fiddle with;fumble about (or with) ② do;make;fix;handle ③ get;fetch;wangle ④play (tricks);manoeuvre ⇒ lòng

弄臣 favourite courtier

弄错 make a mistake;misunderstand

弄鬼 play the devil—play tricks;hatch a plot

弄好 ①do well ②finish doing sth

弄坏 ruin;put out of order;make a mess of

弄假 practise fraud;resort to trickery

弄僵 bring to a deadlock;deadlock

弄清 make clear;clarify;gain a clear idea of;

understand fully
弄权 manipulate power for personal ends
弄死 put to death;kill
弄通 get a good grasp of
弄瓦 have a newborn daughter
弄脏 stain;soil;pollute;smudge;smear
弄糟 make a mess of;mess up;bungle;spoil
弄璋 have a newborn son
弄潮儿 seaman;beach swimmer
弄手段 play tricks
弄假成真 What was make-believe has become reality;What was said in fun is fulfilled in earnest.
弄巧成拙 try to be clever only to end up with a blunder;outsmart oneself
弄虚作假 practise fraud;employ trickery;resort to deception

nú（ㄋㄨˊ）

奴 [nú] Ⅰ 名 slave;bondservant Ⅱ 代 I;me Ⅲ 动 enslave;treat as a slave
奴婢 slave girls and maidservants
奴才 ①lackey ②serf
奴化 enslave
奴隶 slave
奴仆 servant;lackey
奴使 enslave;keep in bondage
奴性 servility;slavishness
奴役 enslave;keep in bondage
奴隶主 slave owner;slaveholder
奴化教育 enslavement education
奴隶起义 slave uprising
奴隶社会 slave society
奴隶主义 slavishness;slavish mentality
奴颜婢膝 subservient;servile
奴颜媚骨 bowing and scraping;sycophancy and obsequiousness

驽 [nú] Ⅰ 名 inferior horse;jade Ⅱ 形 incompetent;dull
驽才 incompetent（or slow-witted）person;dullard
驽钝 dull;stupid
驽马 inferior horse;jade

nǔ（ㄋㄨˇ）

努 动 ①exert;strive ②pout;bulge ③injure oneself through overexertion;strain oneself
努力 make great efforts;try hard;exert oneself
努目 stare with bulging eyes
努伤 sustain an injury through overexertion
努嘴 pout one's lips as a signal
努劲儿 put forth all one's strength

弩 [nǔ]
名 crossbow
弩弓 crossbow
弩箭 crossbow arrow

nù（ㄋㄨˋ）

怒 [nù] Ⅰ 名 anger;rage;fury;wrath Ⅱ 形 vigorous;flourishing
怒潮 ①(tidal) bore ②angry tide;raging tide
怒斥 angrily rebuke;indignantly denounce
怒放 in full bloom
怒号 howl;roar
怒吼 roar;howl
怒火 flames of fury;fury
怒骂 curse in rage
怒目 ①stare with anger ②glaring eyes;fierce stare
怒气 anger;rage;fury
怒容 angry look
怒色 angry look
怒视 glare at;glower at;scowl at
怒涛 furious（or raging）billows
怒族 the Nu nationality
怒冲冲 in a rage;furiously
怒不可遏 be beside oneself with anger;be in a towering rage;boil with rage
怒发冲冠 bristle with anger;be in a towering rage（or passion）
怒海扁舟 small boat on an angry sea
怒形于色 betray one's anger;look angrily

nǚ（ㄋㄩˇ）

女 [nǚ] 名 ①woman;female ②daughter
女伴 female companion
女车 woman's bicycle;lady's bicycle
女儿 daughter;girl
女方 the bride's side;the wife's side
女工 ①woman worker;female worker ②needlework
女红 needlework
女皇 empress
女监 prison for women criminals
女将 ①woman general ②female dab（or expert,mastermind）
女眷 the womenfolk of a family
女角 female role;actress
女郎 young woman;maiden;girl
女垒 women's softball team
女流 the weaker sex
女排 ①women's volleyball team ②women's volleyball
女气 effeminate
女权 women's rights
女人 woman;womenfolk

女色 woman's beauty; feminine charms; woman as a sexual partner
女神 goddess
女生 woman student; girl student; schoolgirl
女声 female voice
女甥 sister's daughter; niece
女士 lady; madam
女式 women's (clothing)
女孙 granddaughter
女王 queen
女巫 witch; sorceress
女性 ①the female sex ②woman
女婿 ①son-in-law ②husband
女贞 glossy privet
女装 women's clothing; women's costume
女子 woman; female
女傧相 bridesmaid
女厕所 ① women's lavatory (or toilet); ladies' room ②Ladies; Women
女低音 alto
女儿酒 daughter's wine—wine made at a daughter's birth and kept underground until her wedding feast
女儿墙 parapet
女高音 soprano
女孩儿 ①girl ②daughter
女教师 woman teacher
女民兵 militia woman
女能人 woman of exceptional ability; capable career woman
女朋友 girlfriend
女强人 woman of exceptional talent and ability; female power hitter
女演员 actress
女医生 woman doctor
女英雄 heroine
女招待 waitress
女贞子 the fruit of glossy privet
女职工 women staff members and women workers
女中音 mezzo-soprano
女主角 feminine lead; leading lady
女主人 hostess
女作家 woman writer; authoress
女扮男装 a woman disguised as a man
女发言人 spokeswoman
女飞行员 female pilot; aviatrix
女服务员 stewardess; waitress; woman attendant
女企业家 entrepreneuse; woman entrepreneur
女权运动 movement for women's rights
女权主义 feminism
女式衬衣 shimmy
女式上衣 women's jacket
女售货员 shopgirl; saleswoman
女修道院 convent
女运动员 sportswoman

女中尧舜 wise and virtuous woman
女中丈夫 as a man amongst the woman folks
女主人公 heroine
女子单打 women's singles
女子排球 women's volleyball
女子双打 women's doubles
女子项目 woman's event
女子学校 girl's school
女子足球 powder-puff football
女大十八变 There is no telling what a girl will look like when she grows up.
女子垒球队 women's softball team
女子排球队 women's volleyball team
女子团体赛 women's team event
女式贴身内衣 lingerie

nuǎn（ㄋㄨㄢˇ）

暖 [nuǎn]
　Ⅰ 形 warm; genial Ⅱ 动 warm up; heat
暖调 warm colour tone; warm tone
暖冬 warm winter
暖房 ①go to the bridal chamber on the eve of a wedding to offer congratulations ②call on sb who has moved into a new home to congratulate him ③greenhouse; hothouse
暖风 warm braw
暖锋 warm front
暖阁 a partitioned-off section of a large room with a heating stove
暖锅 chafing dish
暖壶 ①thermos flask; thermos bottle ②a teapot (or water pot) with a cosy ③a metal (or earthen) hot-water bottle
暖和 ① (of weather, environment, etc.) warm; nice and warm ②warm up
暖酒 warm (or heat) wine
暖帘 quilted door curtain
暖流 ①warm current ②warm feeling
暖瓶 thermos flask; thermos bottle
暖气 ①steam heat; central heating ②central heating equipment ③a warm gas; warm air
暖色 warm colour
暖低压 warm-core cyclone; warm-core low
暖烘烘 nice and warm
暖呼呼 warm; nice and warm
暖气片 heating radiator; radiator
暖气团 warm air mass
暖人心 warm the heart
暖融融 nice and warm
暖水瓶 thermos flask; thermos bottle
暖洋洋 warm

nüè（ㄋㄩㄝˋ）

疟 [nüè]
　名 malaria ➠ yào
疟疾 malaria; ague

疟蚊 malarial mosquito
疟原虫 plasmodium;malarial parasite

虐 [nüè]
I 形 cruel;ferocious;tyrannical II 名 disaster;calamity
虐待 maltreat;ill-treat;tyrannize
虐杀 cause sb's death by maltreating him;kill sb with maltreatment
虐政 tyrannical government;tyranny
虐待狂 sadism
虐待儿童 mistreatment of children

nún (ㄋㄨㄣˊ)

䴔 [nún]
名 fragrance;aroma

nuó (ㄋㄨㄛˊ)

挪 [nuó]
动 move;shift;change
挪动 move;shift
挪借 borrow money for a short time;get a short-term loan
挪开 move away
挪用 ①divert (funds) ②misappropriate;embezzle
挪窝儿 ① move to another place ② move house;move
挪东补西 make up deficiency at one place by drawing upon the surplus at the other
挪用公款 misappropriate (*or* embezzle) public funds
挪用救灾专款 embezzle relief funds

娜 [nuó]
◇婀娜 (of a woman's carriage) lithe and graceful;supple and graceful
袅娜 ①(of plants) soft and slender ②(of a female figure) delicate and graceful;willowy

nuò (ㄋㄨㄛˋ)

诺 [nuò]
I 动 promise;assent II 叹 yes;yeah
诺言 promise
诺诺连声 keep on saying "yes";eagerly agree
诺亚方舟 Noah's Ark
诺贝尔奖金 Nobel Prize

喏 [nuò]
叹 (*used to call attention to the matter or object one is mentioning*)look;see;there

搦 [nuò]
搦战 provoke sb into a fight;challenge sb to a fight
搦笔疾书 hold the brush and write swiftly

懦 [nuò]
形 cowardly;faint-hearted
懦夫 coward;craven;weakling
懦弱 cowardly;weak

糯 [nuò]
名 glutinous (cereal)
糯稻 glutinous rice
糯米 polished glutinous rice
糯米酒 glutinous rice wine
糯米纸 wafer;rice-paper

N

Ō (ㄛ)

噢 [ō] 叹 (*used to indicate understanding*) Oh：噢，原来是你干的。So it was you (who did it).

Ó (ㄛ)

哦 [ó] 叹 (*used to indicate doubt*) Really；What：哦，这件事我怎么没听说？Really? I haven't heard anything about it. ➡ é；ò

Ǒ (ㄛ)

嚄 [ǒ] 叹 (*used to indicate surprise*) What：嚄，他有两米高！What? He's two metres tall? ➡ huō

Ò (ㄛ)

哦 [ò] 叹 (*used to indicate realization or understanding*) Oh，Ah：哦，我想起来了。Ah，I remember. ➡ é；ó

ŌU (ㄡ)

讴 [ōu] I 动 sing II 名 folk songs；ballads
讴歌 sing the praises of；celebrate in song；eulogize
讴吟 sing；chant
讴歌颂德 praise one's merit

沤 [ōu] 名 ①water bubble ②gull ➡ òu

瓯 [ōu] 名 cup；bowl
瓯子 bowl；cup

欧 [ōu] 名 ①Europe ②ohm
欧化 Europeanize；westernize
欧姆 ohm

欧鸲 robin；redbreast
欧元 Euro (€)
欧洲 Europe
欧安会 the European Security Council
欧椋鸟 starling
欧姆表 ohmmeter
欧佩克 Organization of Petroleum Exporting Countries(OPEC)
欧氏管 Eustachian tube；auditory canal (named after B. Eustachio，an Italian anatomist)
欧元区 euro zone
欧姆定律 Ohm's Law
欧亚大陆 Eurasia
欧洲证券 Euro bond
欧罗巴人种 the Caucasoid race；the white race
欧亚大陆桥 the Eurasian Continental Bridge
欧洲中央银行 European Central Bank (ECB)
欧盟主席轮值制 rotating presidency of the EU
欧洲货币一体化 European monetary integration
欧洲经济共同体 European Economic Community (EEC)

殴 [ōu] 动 beat up；hit；strike
殴打 beat up；hit
殴斗 have a fist fight；have fisticuffs
殴辱 insult and beat up
殴杀 beat to death
殴伤 beat and injure；sustain an injury through a fist fight

鸥 [ōu] 名 gull
鸥鸟 hagdon

ŎU (ㄡ)

呕 [ǒu] 动 vomit；throw up；retch
呕乳 milk regurgitation
呕吐 vomit；throw up；be sick
呕心 exert one's utmost effort (in creative work)

呕血 haematemesis; spitting blood
呕心沥血 shed one's heart's blood; take infinite pains; work one's heart out

偶 [ǒu]
Ⅰ 名 ① figure; image; idol ② mate; spouse Ⅱ 形 even (number); in pairs Ⅲ 副 by chance; by accident; occasionally
偶尔 once in a while; occasionally; by chance; by accident
偶发 accidental; chance; fortuitous
偶犯 casual offence
偶感 ① random thoughts (often used in titles of articles) ② suddenly feel; occasionally feel
偶合 coincidence
偶或 occasionally; now and then; sometimes; once in a while
偶见 see by accident; happen to witness
偶然 ① accidental; fortuitous; chance ② accidentally; by accident; by chance ③ once in a while; occasionally
偶数 even number
偶闻 learn (*or* hear) by chance; happen to hear
偶像 image; idol
偶遇 meet by chance
偶氮基 azo group; azo radical
偶然性 contingency; fortuity; chance
偶数页 even page
偶蹄目 artiodactyla
偶氮染料 azo dyes
偶发事件 chance occurence; chance event

偶蹄动物 even-toed mammal; artiodactyl
偶一为之 do sth once in a while; do sth accidentally

耦 [ǒu]
动 two people plough side by side
耦合 coupling

藕 [ǒu]
名 lotus root
藕粉 ① lotus root starch ② lotus root paste (a semifluid food)
藕荷 pale pinkish purple
藕灰 pale pinkish grey
藕煤 honeycomb briquet
藕色 pale pinkish grey
藕节儿 joints of a lotus root
藕断丝连 the lotus root snaps but its fibres stay joined—(of lovers, etc.) still in contact though apparently separated; separated but still in each other's thoughts

Òu (ㄡ)

沤 [òu]
动 soak; steep; macerate ➡ōu
沤肥 ① make compost ② wet compost; water-logged compost
沤粪 make compost
沤麻 ret flax (*or* hemp)
沤田 a waterlogged plot (*or* field)

怄 [òu]
动 annoy; upset; irritate
怄气 be difficult and sulky

pā（ㄆㄚ）

趴 [pā]
囫 ①lie on one's stomach；lie prone ②bend over；lean

趴伏 lie on one's stomach；lie prone

趴架 (of houses) collapse；topple down

趴窝 ①be broken in health ②be sitting ③lie on the ground ready to give birth ④break down；be out of order

啪 [pā]
図 (*indicating the sound of clapping, striking or shooting*) bang；crackle；台下啪啪地鼓掌。The audience clapped loudly.

啪嚓 (the sound of sth crashing, hitting the ground, etc.)

啪嗒 patter

啪唧 patter

葩 [pā]
囵 flower

pá（ㄆㄚˊ）

扒 [pá]
囫 ①scrape together；rake up；gather up；spread out：扒草 rack up hey ②scratch；scrape ③steal ④stew；braise ➡bā

扒灰 ① scoop up ashes ②incest committed with one's daughter-in-law

扒鸡 braised chicken

扒拉 take a swallow of rice

扒窃 pick people's pockets

扒肉 stewed meat

扒手 pickpocket

扒痒 scratch an itch

扒鲍鱼龙须 braised abalone with asparagus

扒鱼肚菜心 braised fish maw with cabbage heart

杷 [pá]
◇ 枇杷 loquat (the tree and its fruit)

爬 [pá]
囫 ①crawl；creep ②climb；clamber ③sit up；stand up；get up

爬虫 reptile

爬竿 ①pole-climbing ②climbing pole

爬高 ①climb ②crawl；creep

爬犁 sledge；sleigh

爬坡 ①climb a mountain slope ②aim high

爬升 ascend；climb；gain altitude

爬绳 rope climbing

爬行 crawl；creep

爬泳 the crawl (stroke)

爬越 climb over

爬格子 take up writing as career；make a living by one's pen；slink ink

爬山虎 ①Boston ivy ②a sedan chair (*or litter*) to carry a person up a mountain

爬行动物 reptile

爬行主义 unwilling to take the initiative

耙 [pá]
Ⅰ 図 rake Ⅱ 囫 make smooth with a rake；rake ➡bà

耙出 rake-off

耙平 rake

耙子 rake

琶 [pá]

琶音 arpeggio

pà（ㄆㄚˋ）

帕 [pà]
図 ①kerchief；handkerchief ②(short for 帕斯卡) pascal

帕金森氏病 paralysis agitans；Parkinson's disease

帕米尔高原 the Pamirs

怕 [pà]
Ⅰ 囫 ①be afraid；fear；dread ②be worried；be anxious；be concerned ③be unable to bear；be unable to endure Ⅱ 副 I'm afraid (that)；I suppose；probably

怕人 ①dread to meet people；be shy ②frightening；terrifying；horrible

怕生 (of a child) be shy with strangers

怕事 be afraid of getting into trouble
怕是 I guess; I suppose; perhaps; maybe
怕头 sth to be afraid of
怕羞 coy; shy; bashful
怕老婆 be henpecked
怕麻烦 hate to put oneself to any trouble
怕死鬼 coward
怕得罪人 be afraid of offending others
怕三怕四 have all sorts of misgivings; be apprehensive of this and that
怕字当头 put fear before everything else

pāi（ㄆㄞ）

拍 Ⅰ 〔动〕①pound; pat; clap; beat ②(of waves) lash; strike; beat ③take (a photo); shoot (a film) ④send (a telegram, etc.) ⑤flatter; fawn on Ⅱ 〔名〕①bat; racket ②beat; time
拍案 strike (or bang) the table
拍板 ①clappers ②beat time with clappers ③rap the gavel ④have the final say; give the final verdict
拍打 pat; slap
拍档 partner
拍发 send (a telegram)
拍抚 pat; caress
拍号 time signature
拍击 (of waves) beat; run against
拍价 hammer price
拍节 breath-group
拍卖 ①auction ②selling off goods at reduced prices; sale
拍品 lot
拍摄 take (a picture); shoot
拍手 clap one's hands; applaud
拍拖 court
拍戏 make a film; shoot a scene; shoot a film (or a TV play)
拍掌 clap one's hands; applaud
拍照 take a picture; have a picture taken; photograph
拍子 ①bat; racket ②beat; time
拍巴掌 clap one's hands
拍翅膀 flap wings
拍电报 send a telegram
拍节器 metronome
拍马屁 lick sb's boots; flatter; soft-soap; play up to; fawn on
拍卖场 auction market
拍卖槌 gavel
拍卖行 auction house
拍卖品 lot
拍卖业 auctioneering
拍胸脯 ①vouch for ②chest thumping
拍纸簿 (writing) pad
拍案大怒 pound the table in great anger

拍案而起 smite the table and rise to one's feet in anger
拍案叫绝 thump the table and shout "bravo!"
拍板成交 strike a bargain; close a deal; clinch a deal
拍记录片 shoot (or make) a documentary
拍手称快 clap in high glee; clap and cheer (as on being avenged)

pái（ㄆㄞ）

排 Ⅰ 〔动〕①arrange in order; line up ②rehearse ③exclude; expel; eject; drain ④push Ⅱ 〔名〕①line; row ②platoon ③raft; floating bridge Ⅲ 〔量〕row; line; 两排牙齿 two rows of teeth ➡ pǎi
排班 arrange in order of shifts, runs, or classes and grades
排版 composing; typesetting
排比 parallelism
排笔 a broad brush comprising a row of pen-shaped brushes
排查 check up
排场 ①ostentation and extravagance; pomp and ceremony ②ostentatious and extravagant; sumptuous; lavish
排斥 repel; exclude; reject
排除 get rid of; remove; eliminate
排挡 gear; stall; stand
排队 form a line; line up; queue up
排筏 bamboo (or timber) raft
排放 ①place (things) in proper order ②discharge; let out; drain off
排废 waste discharge
排骨 spareribs; spines
排灌 irrigation and drainage
排行 seniority among brothers and sisters
排号 ①row number ②arrange in numerical order ③line up; queue up
排洪 discharge floodwater; drain off floodwater
排挤 push aside; push out; squeeze out; elbow out
排解 ①mediate; reconcile ②divert oneself (from loneliness or boredom)
排拒 reject; repel; exclude
排涝 drain flooded (or waterlogged) fields
排雷 removal of mines; mine clearance; mine removal
排立 stand in a line; line up
排练 rehearse
排列 ①arrange; range; put in order ②permutation
排卵 ovulate
排尿 urinate; micturate
排炮 ①(artillery) salvo; volley of guns ②suc-

cessive blastings（in mining，tunnelling，etc.）③remove（*or* defuse）a dud，or a charge of explosive that fails to explode when it should

排气 exhaust

排遣 divert oneself（from loneliness or boredom）

排枪 volley of rifle fire

排球 volleyball（the game or the ball）

排热 heat rejection；heat extraction

排射 volley（of fire）

排笙 a reed pipe wind instrument with a keyboard

排水 ①drain off（*or* away）water ②drainage

排送 dispatch（vehicle）

排坛 volleyball circles

排头 the person at the head of a procession（*or* formation）；file leader

排土 casting

排外 exclusive；antiforeign；xenophobic

排尾 the last person in a row（*or* procession，formation）；the person at the end of a row，etc.

排污 emit pollutants

排戏 rehearse a play

排险 eliminate a danger；remove danger

排箫 Pan's pipes

排泄 ①drain rainwater，waste water，etc. ②excrete

排序 sort；collate；rank；sequence；order

排烟 eject smoke；discharge smoke

排演 rehearse

排椅 seats in a row

排印 typesetting and printing

排运 rafting

排轧 push aside；squeeze out；outdo；get the best of

排长 platoon leader

排钟 chimes

排字 composing；typesetting

排队论 queuing theory

排风扇 ventilating fan

排行榜 ranking；(best-seller) list；chart

排节目 rehearse a performance programme

排卵期 period of ovulation

排名次 list the names in proper order（according to examination results，etc.）

排名单 arrange the order of names on a list

排气管 exhaust pipe

排球场 volleyball court

排球网 volleyball net

排球柱 volleyball post

排水管 drain pipe

排水量 ①displacement ②discharge capacity（of a spillway，etc.）

排酸肉 exclude acid meat

排他性 exclusiveness

排头兵 ①the soldier at the head of a formation ②pacesetter；pacemaker

排污权 dumping right

排泄物 excreta；excrement

排中律 the law of excluded middle

排坐次 arrange the seating order；make seating arrangements

排斥竞争 spurn competition

排斥异己 exclude outsiders；discriminate against those who hold different views；discriminate against anybody who does not belong to one's coterie；push aside people of different views；tolerate no dissenting voices

排除干扰 get rid of interference

排除万难 surmount every difficulty；conquer all obstacles

排除杂念 banish distracting thoughts from one's mind

排放标准 emission standards

排华政策 policy of discrimination against the Chinese

排列规则 queueing discipline

排门而出 throw open the door and walk out

排难解纷 clear up misunderstandings and mediate disputes

排尿困难 dysuria

排山倒海 topple the mountains and overturn the seas

排水工程 drainage works

排水沟渠 escape canal

排水管道 drainage pipeline

排外心理 xenophobia

排外政策 exclusive policy

排外主义 exclusivism；exclusionism

排泄器官 excretory organs

排忧解难 relieve sb of worries and help solve his problems；get rid of worries and overcome difficulties

排犹运动 anti-Semitic campaign

排他性集团 exclusive bloc

排他性条约 exclusive treaty

排污收费制度 pollutant discharge levy system

排他性区域合作 closed regional cooperation

徘 ［pái］

徘徊 ①loiter；walk up and down；pace back and forth ②dither；waver ③ebb and flow；rise and fall；hover

牌 ［pái］

名 ①board ②plate；sign；tablet ③brand；make；trademark ④cards，dominoes，etc. ⑤title（of a *ci* or *qu* tune）

牌匾 an inscribed board（fixed to a wall or the lintel of a door）；tablet；plaque

牌额 a horizontal inscribed board

牌坊 memorial archway（*or* gateway）

牌号 ①the name of a shop;shop sign ②trade-mark

牌价 ① list price;posted price ②（market）quotation

牌九 *paijiu*,a game of Chinese dominoes

牌局 a game at dominoes（*or* mah-jong, cards）;a gambling game

牌例 sample card hands used for demonstrating plays（usu. bridge）

牌楼 ① *pailou*,decorated archway ②temporary ceremonial gateway

牌品 personal style and attitude（of cardplayer）

牌情 the cards one holds;a hand at cards

牌示 bulletin;public notice

牌手 participants in a bridge game

牌位 memorial tablet

牌艺 skill（usu. at bridge）

牌照 license plate;license tag;license certificate;license

牌证 ①licence,certificate ②badge

牌子 ①plate;sign ②brand;trademark

簰 ［pái］
图 raft;floating bridge

pǎi（ㄆㄞˇ）

迫 ［pǎi］ ➡pò
迫击炮 mortar

排 ［pǎi］
动 stretch with a（shoe）last ➡pái

排子车 a large handcart

pài（ㄆㄞˋ）

派 ［pài］
Ⅰ 图 ①branch of a river ②group of people sharing identical views,style or tastes;sect;faction ③style;bearing;manner and air Ⅱ 形 stylish;graceful;handsome Ⅲ 量 ①（for parties,schools,factions,etc.）:这个问题两派学者之间有争论。This issue is controversial among scholars of the two schools. ②（*used with words indicating scenery, atmosphere, sound, voice, language, etc., and preceded by the word*）一:一派胡言 a pack of nonsense Ⅳ 动 ① send; dispatch; assign; appoint ②apportion;assign ③find fault;censure

派别 group;sect;school;faction

派对 party

派发 assign to deliver;distribute

派饭 meals in peasant homes arranged for cadres,students,etc. temporarily staying at a village;arranged meals

派购（of the state）prescribe purchases（of farm produce）;fix quantities for state pur-

chase

派活 assign jobs;assign sb a task（usu. manual work）

派款 impose levies of money

派遣 send;dispatch

派生 derive

派势 manner;momentum

派送 distribute giveaways

派头 style;manner

派系 groups;factions（within a political party,etc.）

派性 factionalism

派驻 ①post;station ②accredit to

派不是 put（*or* lay）the blame on sb

派出所 local police station;police substation

派力司 palace

派遣国 the sending state;the accrediting state

派生词 derivative

派用场 put to use;turn to account

派出机构 agency

派粮派款 levy grain and money

蒎 ［pài］
图 pinane

湃 ［pài］
◇ 澎湃 surge

pān（ㄆㄢ）

攀 ［pān］
动 ①climb;clamber ②cling;hold;grasp ③seek connections in high places ④involve;implicate

攀比 cite the cases of others in support of one's own claim;vie with;compete

攀冰 ice climbing

攀缠 climb and intertwine

攀扯 implicate（sb in a crime）

攀登 climb;clamber;scale

攀附 ①（of a plant）climb（a support）②seek connections with（people of power and influence）

攀高 ①climb to a higher point ②make friends（*or* claim ties of kinship）with someone of a higher social position

攀交 make friends with people of a higher social position

攀亲 ① claim kinship（with people in high places）②arrange a match

攀禽 scansorial birds

攀雀 penduline tit

攀升 climb;rise continuously

攀谈 engage in small talk;have a chat

攀岩 cliff-climbing as a competitive sport;rock-climbing

攀援 ①climb;clamber ②climb the social ladder through pull

攀缘 climb;climber

攀越 climb up and over;scale;surmount

攀折 pull down and break off (twigs,etc.)

攀比风 irrational vying (or competition) craze;craze to vie with each other

攀登架 jungle gym (a playground apparatus for children to climb on)

攀关系 seek powerful connections

攀高枝儿 make friends (or claim kinship) with somebody of a higher social status

攀龙附凤 play up to people of power and influence;put oneself under the patronage of a bigwig

攀亲道故 claim ties of blood or friendship

攀山越岭 trek over mountains and ridges

攀缘植物 climber;climbing plant

攀登科学高峰 scale the heights in science

pán (ㄆㄢ)

胖 [pán]
[形] easy and carefree;fit and happy ➡ pàng

般 [pán]
[名] joy;delight ➡ bān;bō

般乐 pleasure;enjoyment

盘 [pán]
I [名] ①washbasin ②tray;plate;dish ③sth shaped like or used as a tray, plate, etc. ④ market quotation;current price II [动] ①coil; wind;twist ②build with bricks ③check;examine;investigate;interrogate ④transfer;sell ⑤move;transfer III [量]:和了一盘 have ended in a draw

盘剥 practise usury

盘菜 ready-to-cook dish of meat,vegetables, etc. (sold at the food market);assorted cold dishes

盘查 interrogate and examine

盘缠 money for the journey;travelling expenses

盘秤 a steelyard with a pan

盘存 take inventory

盘道 winding mountain paths;bends

盘点 check;make an inventory of;take stock of

盘店 transfer the ownership of a shop with its merchandise and equipment to another person;transfer a business;sell a shop along with its stock,furniture and equipment

盘跌 slow,small fall

盘费 money needed on a journey

盘古 *Pan Gu*,creator of the universe in Chinese mythology

盘管 coil (pipe)

盘桓 ①stay;linger ②winding;coiling ③wind round and round;spiral up or down

盘簧 coil spring

盘活 liquidize

盘货 make an inventory of stock on hand;take stock

盘诘 cross-examine;interrogate

盘踞 illegally (or forcibly) occupy;be entrenched

盘炕 build a *kang*

盘库 make an inventory of goods in a warehouse

盘面 market situation of stock,ect. at a given point (or during a given period of time)

盘弄 play with;fiddle with;fondle

盘绕 twine;coil;spiral;wreathe

盘山 wind up a mountain

盘升 edge up

盘算 calculate;figure;plan

盘损 adjustment debit

盘梯 winding staircase;spiral staircase

盘条 wire rod

盘头 ①hair worn in a bun (or coil) ②turban

盘腿 cross one's legs

盘问 cross-examine;interrogate

盘膝 cross one's legs

盘香 incense coil

盘旋 ①spiral;circle;wheel ②linger;stay

盘羊 argali

盘灶 build a brick cooking range

盘账 check (or audit,examine) accounts

盘整 adjust slightly;regroup

盘桌 tray-top table

盘子 ① tray;plate;dish;programme ② the market rate

盘坐 sit cross-legged

盘整期 period of recovery,regrouping

盘根错节 with twisted roots and gnarled branches—complicated and difficult to deal with;deep-rooted

盘根究底 get to the heart of a matter;get to the bottom of things;inquire deeply into sth;ask about sth in great detail;try to get to the bottom of a matter

盘马弯弓 ride round and round bending one's bow—assume an impressive posture but take no action

盘山公路 winding mountain highway

盘活存量土地 efficiently use the available land

盘式录像磁带 reel videotape

盘式录音磁带 reel audiotape

盘式磁带录像机 reel videotape recorder

磐 [pán]
[名] huge rock

磐石 huge rock

磐石之固 the firmness of a rock

蹒 [pán]

蹒跚 walk haltingly;limp;hobble

蟠 [pán]
[动] coil;curl

蟠伏 lie curled up;coil

蟠桃 ① flat peach ② legendary peach in the land of immortals；peach of longevity
蟠桃会 meeting of immortals at which peaches of longevity are offered

pàn（ㄆㄢˋ）

判 [pàn]
Ⅰ 〔动〕 ① distinguish；differentiate；separate ② judge；decide；grade ③ sentence；condemn
Ⅱ 〔副〕 obviously（different）
判案 decide a case
判别 differentiate；distinguish
判处 sentence（sb）to；condemn（sb）to
判词 court verdict
判定 judge；decide；determine
判读 interpret；read and make a judgement
判断 ①judge；decide；determine ②judgment
判罚 penalize（in a sports event）
判分 give a mark；mark；score
判官 a judge in Hades
判据 criterion
判卷 mark（examination）papers
判决 pass judgment；pronounce（judgment）
判例 legal precedent；judicial precedent
判令 make a binding court decision on civil（or economic）cases
判明 clearly distinguish；ascertain
判然（of differences）noticeable；marked；striking
判刑 pass a sentence on；sentence sb to
判罪 declare guilty；convict
判别式 discriminant
判断词 a grammatical term for the character 是（used as a link word to form a compound predicate with a noun or pronoun）
判断力 the ability to judge correctly；judgment
判决书 court verdict；written judgment
判作业 grade students' homework
判若两人 have become quite a different person；no longer be one's old self
判若天渊 be as far removed as is heaven from earth；be poles apart
判若云泥 be as far removed as is heaven from earth；be poles apart

拚 [pàn]
拚命 defy death；do sth for all one's worth
拚弃 give up；cast

泮 [pàn]
〔动〕 thaw；melt；dissolve

盼 [pàn]
〔动〕 ① hope for；yearn for；long for；expect ②look
盼顾 look around；look left and right
盼念 look forward to seeing；long to see
盼头 sth hoped for and likely to happen；good prospects

盼望 hope for；long for；look forward to

叛 [pàn]
〔动〕 betray；revolt；rebel
叛变 betray one's country，party．etc．；turn traitor；turn renegade
叛党 turn renegade；betray one's party；turn traitor to one's party
叛敌 treachery
叛匪 rebel bandit；bandit rebels
叛国 betray one's country；commit treason
叛军 rebel army；rebel forces；insurgent troops
叛离 betray；desert；defect from；turn renegade
叛乱 armed rebellion
叛卖 betray；sell out
叛逆 ①rebel against；revolt against ②rebel
叛逃 desert and flee one's country；defect
叛徒 traitor；renegade；turncoat
叛教者 apostate；renegade

畔 [pàn]
〔名〕 ① side；bank ② boundary；border（of a field）；edge

鋬 [pàn]
〔名〕 handle of a utensil

襻 [pàn]
Ⅰ 〔名〕 ① loop for fastening a button ② sth shaped like a button loop（or used for a similar purpose）Ⅱ 〔动〕 fasten（as with a rope，string，etc．）；tie

pāng（ㄆㄤ）

乓 [pāng]
〔象〕 bang

雱 [pāng]
〔形〕 ① snow thick and fast ②（of water）overflowing；roaring and rushing

滂 [pāng]
〔动〕 ①（of water）overflowing ② gushing；rushing
滂湃（of water）roaring and rushing
滂沛 ①（of water）surging；rushing ②（of rain）torrential；pouring；pelting ③powerful；of great momentum
滂沱 torrential；streaming；pouring

膀 [pāng]
〔动〕 swell ➡ bǎng；páng
膀肿 swollen；bloated

páng（ㄆㄤˊ）

彷 [páng]
彷徨 walk back and forth，not knowing which way to go；hesitate
彷徨歧途 hesitate at the crossroads

庞 [páng]
Ⅰ 〔形〕 ① huge ② numerous and disordered
Ⅱ 〔名〕 face

庞大 huge;enormous;colossal;gigantic
庞杂 numerous and jumbled
庞然大物 huge monster;colossus;giant

旁 [páng]
Ⅰ 图 ① side ② lateral radical of a Chinese character (e.g. 亻,氵,etc.) Ⅱ 形 ① else;other ② extensive;wide-ranging
旁白 aside (in a play)
旁边 side
旁侧 side
旁顾 attend to other matters
旁观 look on;be an onlooker
旁及 take up (along with sth more important)
旁路 bypass
旁落 (of power,etc.) pass into other's hands
旁门 side door
旁人 other people
旁听 be a visitor (at a meeting or in a school class);audit a class
旁证 circumstantial evidence;collateral evidence
旁支 collateral branch (of a family)
旁族 collateral family
旁听生 auditor
旁听席 visitors' seats;public gallery (at a Congressional session,etc.)
旁通管 bypass pipe
旁压力 lateral pressure
旁观者清 The spectator sees most clearly;The onlooker sees the game best.
旁门左道 ① heretical sect;heterodox school ② heresy;heterodoxy
旁敲侧击 attack by innuendo;make oblique references
旁求俊彦 look for talents far and near
旁若无人 act as if there was no one else present—self-assured or supercilious
旁系亲属 collateral relatives (or kinsmen);collaterals
旁征博引 quote copiously to support one's thesis;be well documented

膀 [páng]
➡ bǎng;pāng
膀胱 (urinary) bladder
膀胱镜 cystoscope
膀胱炎 cystitis
膀胱结石 bladder calculi;vesical calculus
膀胱造影 cystography

磅 [páng]
➡ bàng
磅礴 ① boundless;majestic;vast ② fill

螃 [páng]
螃蟹 crab

pǎng (ㄆㄤˇ)

嗙 [pǎng]
动 sing one's own praises;boast;blow one's own trumpet;brag

耪 [pǎng]
动 loosen soil with a hoe
耪草 weed a field (with a hoe)
耪地 hoe the soil

髈 [pǎng]
图 thigh

pàng (ㄆㄤˋ)

胖 [pàng]
形 fat;stout;plump ➡ pán
胖子 a fat person;fatty
胖大海 the seed of boat-fruited sterculia
胖墩儿 (esp. referring to children) roly-poly;fatty
胖鼓鼓 fat;plump;full;bulging
胖乎乎 (of children) plump;chubby;pudgy;
胖头鱼 bighead;variegated carp
胖娃娃 chubby child;cherub

pāo (ㄆㄠ)

抛 [pāo]
动 ① throw;hurl;toss;fling ② leave behind;cast aside ③ expose;reveal;lay bare
抛出 ejection;cast;get out;expel
抛给 toss to
抛光 polishing;buffing
抛荒 ① (of cultivated land) go out of cultivation;lie waste ② (of one's studies) be neglected;(of one's professional knowledge or ability) be wasted through disuse;get rusty
抛空 sell short;sell against the box;short sale
抛离 abandon;leave behind
抛锚 ① drop anchor;cast anchor ② (of vehicles) break down
抛弃 abandon;forsake;cast aside
抛却 cast aside;throw away
抛洒 spill;shed;scatter
抛射 project;catapult;launch
抛石 rock rip-rap
抛售 sell (goods,shares,etc.) in big quantities(usu. in anticipation of or in order to bring about a fall in price);undersell;dump;sell in big quantities
抛掷 throw;cast
抛射体 projectile
抛物线 parabola
抛头露面 reveal one's head and show one's face (formerly said of a woman showing herself in public,which was considered unbecoming;now said of sb blatantly seeking publicity)

P

抛秧技术 seedling spraying method

抛砖引玉 cast a brick to attract jade—offer a few commonplace remarks by way of introduction so that others may come up with valuable opinions

抛物面天线 dish antenna

抛头颅，洒热血 shed one's blood and lay down one's life (for a just cause)

泡 [pāo]
Ⅰ 名 ① sth puffy and soft ② small lake Ⅱ 形 spongy; puffy and soft Ⅲ 量 (*used of excrement and urine*)：撒一泡尿 have a piss ➡ pào

脬 [pāo]
名 (urinary) bladder

páo (ㄆㄠ)

刨 [páo]
动 ① dig; excavate ② exclude; not counte; minus ➡ bào

刨除 exclude; subtract; not count

刨分 deduct marks (*or* points) (for errors in a student's work)

刨根 get to the root (*or* bottom) of the matter

刨煤机 coal plough

刨根问底 get to the root (*or* bottom) of things

咆 [páo]
动 (of beasts) howl

咆哮 ① (of beasts of prey) roar; howl ② (of humans) roar with rage ③ (of torrents) roar on; thunder away

狍 [páo]
名 roe (deer)

狍子 roe deer

庖 [páo]
名 ① kitchen ② cook

炮 [páo]
动 ① prepare (Chinese medicine) by roasting it in a hot iron pan ② bake; roast; toast ➡ bāo; pào

炮姜 roasted ginger

炮炼 parch and refine medicinal herbs

炮烙 the hot pillar (an ancient instrument of torture)

炮制 ① the process of preparing Chinese medicine, as by parching, roasting, baking, steaming, soaking, simmering, etc. ② concoct; cook up

炮炙 drug processing with supplementary materials

袍 [páo]
名 robe; gown

袍泽 fellow officers

袍子 robe; gown

袍罩儿 gown; robe

袍笏登场 dress up and go on stage (said con-

temptuously of an official or a political puppet taking office)

跑 [páo]
动 (of a beast) dig (the ground) with hoofs (*or* paws) ➡ pǎo

跑槽 (of draft animals, etc.) dig a trough (while feeding)

pǎo (ㄆㄠ)

跑 [pǎo]
动 ① run; race; gallop ② run away; escape; flee ③ walk; stroll ④ run about (doing sth); go about (for sth); busy oneself (with sth) ⑤ go away (*or* off); leak ⑥ (of a liquid) evaporate ⑦ give off ➡ páo

跑表 stopwatch

跑步 ① run; march at the double ② jogging (a form of physical exercise)

跑车 ① racing bicycle ② a trolley for conveying logs in a forest ③ sports car ④ (of train conductors) be on the job ⑤ (of trolleys for hoisting coal in a mine) accidentally slide down

跑弛 run errands; be on the run; hurry here and there

跑刀 racing skates

跑道 ① runway (on an airfield) ② track

跑电 leakage of electricity

跑肚 have loose bowels; have diarrhoea

跑光 (of a film) be exposed to light accidentally

跑街 travelling agent (*or* salesman)

跑马 ① have a ride on a horse ② horse racing

跑墒 loss of moisture in soil (through evaporation)

跑堂 waiter (in a wineshop, small restaurant, etc.)

跑题 digress from the subject; stray from the point

跑外 act as a travelling agent (*or* salesman)

跑鞋 track shoes (either with spikes for use outdoors or with rubber soles for use indoors)

跑材料 run about collecting material (*or* making inquiries)

跑单帮 travel around trading on one's own

跑旱船 boat that runs on land (a folk dance performed by a girl gliding about with a cloth boat and a man making rowing movements with an oar, singing a rude ditty as they dance)

跑江湖 wander about, making a living as a street-performer (e.g. an acrobat, fortune-teller, physiognomist, etc.)

跑警报 run for shelter during an air raid

跑垒员 base runner

跑龙套 play a walk-on part; play a bit role

跑马场 racecourse; the turf
跑码头 travel from port to port as a trader; be a travelling merchant
跑买卖 be a commercial traveller; chase after business
跑情况 run about gathering information
跑生意 chase after business
跑腿儿 run errands; do legwork
跑官要官 crave official positions
跑跑颠颠 bustle about; be on the go
跑跑跳跳 skip along
跑了和尚跑不了庙 the monk may run away, but the temple can't run with him—a fugitive must belong to some place that can provide clues

pào (ㄆㄠˋ)

泡 [pào]
Ⅰ 名 ①bubble ②sth shaped like a bubble
Ⅱ 动 ①steep; soak ②dawdle; loiter; dillydally ➡pāo
泡吧 kill time in the bar
泡菜 pickled vegetables; pickles
泡茶 make tea
泡饭 ①soak cooked rice in soup (or water) ②cooked rice reheated in boiling water
泡货 light but bulky goods
泡沫 foam; froth
泡妞 chase after girls
泡汤 ①fall flat; fall through ②dawdle; dillydally
泡桐 paulownia
泡影 visionary hope (or plan, scheme, etc.); bubble
泡枣 spongy dates
泡制 brew
泡子 bulb
泡病号 shun work on pretence of illness
泡沸石 zeolite
泡蘑菇 ①play for time; use delaying tactics; stall ②importune; pester
泡沫浴 bubble bath
泡泡纱 seersucker
泡泡糖 bubble gum; chewing gum
泡时间 dawdle away time
泡罩塔 bubble-cap tower (or column)
泡沫包装 bubble wrap
泡沫玻璃 foam glass; foamed glass
泡沫经济 bubble economy
泡沫塑料 foamed plastics
泡沫陶瓷 foamed ceramics
泡沫橡胶 air foam rubber
泡沫混凝土 foam concrete
泡沫灭火器 foam extinguisher

炮 [pào]
名 ①(big) gun; cannon; artillery piece ②

firecracker ③load of explosive ➡bāo; páo
炮兵 artillery; artillerymen
炮车 gun carriage
炮铳 fire cracker
炮弹 ①(artillery)shell ②cannon ball
炮轰 (of artillery) bombard; shell
炮灰 cannon fodder
炮火 artillery fire; gunfire
炮击 bombard; shell
炮架 gun carriage; gun mount
炮舰 gunboat
炮口 gun muzzle; cannon's mouth
炮垒 vallation
炮楼 blockhouse
炮钎 rock drill
炮声 report (of a big gun)
炮手 gunner; artilleryman
炮闩 breechblock; breech mechanism
炮栓 breechblock (of a big gun)
炮塔 gun turret; turret
炮台 a fortification with built-in cannons; battery
炮膛 bore (of a big gun)
炮艇 gunboat
炮筒 barrel (of a big gun)
炮尾 gun breech
炮位 emplacement
炮眼 ①porthole; embrasure ②dynamite hole; borehole
炮衣 gun cover
炮战 artillery action (or engagement)
炮仗 firecracker
炮座 gun platform
炮筒子 a person who shoots off his mouth
炮子儿 small shell; bullet
炮舰外交 gunboat diplomacy
炮舰政策 gunboat policy

疱 [pào]
名 blister; bleb
疱疹 ①bleb ②herpes
疱症 tetter

pēi (ㄆㄟ)

呸 [pēi]
叹 (*indicating contempt or censure*) pah; bah; pooh; pfui

胚 [pēi]
名 embryo
胚层 germinal layer
胚根 radicle
胚孔 blastopore
胚膜 embryonic membrane; blastoderm membrane
胚囊 embryo sac
胚盘 blastodisc; germinal disc
胚乳 endosperm
胚胎 ① embryo ② beginning; rudimentary

P

stage
胚芽 ① plumule ② an undeveloped thing; the bud
胚叶 germinal layer
胚珠 ovule
胚子 ① silkworm embryo ② egg; person
胚胎学 embryology

醅 [pēi]
〈名〉 unfiltered wine

péi（ㄆㄟˊ）

陪 [péi]
〈动〉① accompany; keep sb company ② assist; help
陪伴 accompany; keep sb company
陪绑 ① be taken to the execution ground together with those to be executed as a form of intimidation ② (of an innocent person) be criticized (or punished) together with the guilty
陪衬 ① serve as a contrast or foil; set off ② foil; setoff
陪床 (of an inpatient's family member, etc.) stay in the ward to look after the patient night and day; keep overnight bedside company in a hospital
陪吊 entertain the guests
陪都 an alternate (or secondary) capital; a provisional capital
陪读 accompany a person studying at school; accompany a spouse studying abroad; help one's children in study
陪护 stay with and nurse
陪嫁 dowry
陪酒 be a drinking partner
陪客 [péikè] accompany a guest
陪客 [péike] guest invited to a dinner party to help entertain the guest of honour
陪老 accompany old people
陪练 one who trains (or practices) with top athletes; practice athlete
陪审 ① act (or serve) as an assessor (in a law case) ② serve on a jury
陪送 ① give as a dowry; dower ② dowry ③ include as a gift ④ accompany
陪同 ① accompany ② a responsible official accompanying an important visitor or visiting delegation
陪夜 stay with patient at night
陪音 overtone; harmonic
陪葬 ① (of a wife, concubine or slave) be buried alive with the dead ② (of figurines or objects) be buried with the dead ③ (of a wife or concubine after her death) be buried by the side of her husband's grave
陪住 sleep in the ward to tend the patient; stay in the ward to look after a bedridden

patient
陪酒女 bar girl; B-girl; mixer
陪审团 jury
陪审席 jury box
陪审员 juror; juryman
陪审制 jury system
陪同团 hosting team; receptionist committee
陪葬品 funerary objects, figurines, etc.
陪同人员 entourage

培 [péi]
〈动〉① bank up (with earth); earth up ② cultivate; foster; train
培护 grow and protect
培土 hill up; earth up
培训 train (personnel)
培养 ① cultivate (plants); culture (microorganisms) ② foster; train; develop (a certain spirit, ability, etc.)
培育 ① help (young plants) grow by labour and care; cultivate; breed ② nurture and educate; bring up; rear
培植 ① cultivate (plants) ② foster; train
培智 educate mentally retarded children
培种 cultivate (plants)
培训班 training course
培养基 culture medium
培养皿 glass garden; culture dish
培养瓶 culture bottle
培育市场 cultivate the market

赔 [péi]
〈动〉① compensate; pay for; refund ② apologize ③ stand (or incur) a loss; lose
赔本 sustain losses in business; run a business at a loss
赔补 make good a loss; make up a deficit
赔偿 ① make good a loss; compensate; indemnify ② reparations
赔错 acknowledge a mistake; apologize for one's wrongdoing
赔垫 pay for sb
赔付 compensate
赔话 say a word in apology
赔款 ① pay an indemnity; pay reparations ② indemnity; reparations
赔礼 make (or offer) an apology; apologize
赔钱 ① sustain economic losses; lose money in business ② pay for a loss; pay damages
赔笑 smile obsequiously (or apologetically, appeasingly); smile an apologetic (or obsequious) smile
赔账 ① pay for the loss of cash or goods ② lose money in business
赔罪 apologize (for a wrong done to sb); ask forgiveness for one's wrongdoing
赔不起 be unable to make good a loss
赔不是 apologize
赔偿费 (compensatory) damages

赔偿人 compensator
赔偿物 indemnity
赔钱货 money-losing commodity
赔小心 behave with great caution;act warily
赔本买卖 losing business;run a business at a loss
赔偿损失 make amends to;indemnity for damage
赔偿条款 indemnity clause
赔了夫人又折兵 give one's enemy a wife and lose one's soldiers as well—pay a double penalty;instead of making a gain,suffer a double loss

pèi (ㄆㄟˋ)

沛 [pèi]
〔形〕copious;abundant

帔 [pèi]
〔名〕short embroidered cape (worn over a woman's shoulders)

佩 [pèi]
Ⅰ〔动〕①wear (at the waist,etc.) ②admire Ⅱ〔名〕pendant worn at the waist
佩带 wear (a pistol,sword,etc.) at the waist
佩戴 wear (a badge,insignia,etc.) on the chest,arm,or shoulder
佩刀 ①wear a sword at the waist ②a sword worn at the waist
佩服 esteem;admire
佩剑 sabre
佩兰 orchid
佩带式话筒 lapel mike;body mike

配 [pèi]
〔动〕①join in wedlock;make a couple ②spouse ③(of animals) mate ④blend;mix ⑤distribute according to plan;apportion;assign;allot ⑥replenish;find sth to fit (or replace) sth else;replace ⑦foil;set off ⑧match;go well together;harmonize with ⑨deserve;be worthy of;measure up to;be qualified ⑩exile for penal servitude;banish
配备 ①provide (manpower or equipment);equip;fit out ②dispose (troops,etc.);deploy ③outfit;equipment
配菜 ①garnish food ②garnishes
配餐 ①assorted foods for a meal ②prepared meal
配搭 supplement;match;accompany
配电 (power) distribution
配殿 side hall in a palace or temple
配对 ①pair;match ②(of animals) mate;pair
配额 quota
配发 ①allocate ②publish a related article
配方 ①fill (or make up) a prescription ②a formula for compounding a chemical (or metallurgical) product ③prescription
配房 wing (of a house)

配购 buy rations
配股 scrip issue;allotment of shares
配合 coordinate;cooperate;concert
配货 replenish the stocks (or supplies)
配给 ration
配件 ①parts;fittings;accessories ②replacement
配酒 mix drinks
配角 ①appear with another leading player;co-star with sb ②supporting role;supporting actor
配军 be deported to a remote place for penal servitude
配料 ①mix ingredients according to a recipe;get materials ready (for the manufacture of sth) in the right proportion ②burden
配马 mate horses
配偶 spouse
配器 orchestration
配色 [pèisè] mix colours in the right proportion
配色 [pèishǎi] match colours;harmonize colours
配售 ration (at state price)
配属 place part of one's troops temporarily under the command of a subordinate officer
配送 distribution
配套 ①form a complete set (or system) ②coordinated;complementary
配伍 compatibility of medicines
配戏 play a minor part (to support a leading actor)
配系 system of disposition
配演 perform supporting role in a play
配药 ①(of a pharmacist) make up a prescription;dispense a prescription ②have a prescription made up
配页 gather (leaves of a book) in proper sequence for binding
配音 dub (a film,etc.)
配乐 ①select passages to serve as background music (for a film,play,radio programme,etc.) ②dub in background music
配制 compound;make up
配置 dispose (troops,etc.);deploy
配种 breeding
配猪 mate pigs
配子 gamete
配餐室 pantry
配电盘 distributor
配电网 distribution network
配给制 ration system;allotment system
配偶权 spouse's rights
配拼盘 put together an assorted cold dish
配水闸 distribution structure
配眼镜 have a pair of glasses made
配钥匙 have a key made to fit a lock

配种站 breeding station
配子体 gametophyte
配佐料 mix condiments
配合饲料 mixed feed;compound feed
配套措施 supplementary measure
配套改革 coordinated reform; synchronized reform; supportive reform; corresponding reform; well-coordinated reform; overall reform;reform with all the related factors taken into consideration
配套工程 auxiliary project; conveyance system;parts and accessories for imported equipment
配套能力 ability to provide the auxiliary items
配套器材 necessary accessories
配套设备 complete set of equipment;chain of equipment
配套设施 accessory facilities
配套生产 form a complete production network
配套政策 supporting policies
配音演员 dubber
配乐广播 dubbed-in radio programme
配套政治体制改革 corresponding coordinative political restructuring

pēn (ㄆㄣ)

喷 [pēn]
动 ①spurt;gush ②spray;sprinkle ➡pèn
喷薄 gush out
喷灯 blowtorch;blowlamp
喷发 erupt;throw out
喷饭 laugh so hard as to spew one's food;split one's sides with laughter
喷放 spurt;spout
喷粪 utter foulmouthed abuse
喷灌 sprinkling irrigation;spray irrigation
喷壶 watering can;sprinkling can
喷溅 (of a liquid when being squeezed out) splash;spatter
喷浆 ①whitewashing ②guniting
喷漆 spray paint;spray lacquer
喷枪 spray gun;airbrush
喷泉 fountain
喷洒 spray;sprinkle
喷射 spray;spurt;jet
喷嚏 sneeze
喷桶 watering can;sprinkling can
喷头 ①shower nozzle ②sprinkler head
喷涂 spray paint
喷吐 shoot out (flames,light,gas,etc.)
喷雾 spray;atomize
喷泻 (of a liquid) shoot out;gush forth;spurt
喷子 sprayer;spraying apparatus
喷嘴 spray nozzle;spray head
喷出岩 extrusive rock;extrusive
喷粉器 duster

喷灌器 sprinkler
喷火器 flamethrower
喷气式 jet-propelled
喷水池 (artificial) fountain
喷丝头 spinning jet;spinning nozzle
喷雾器 sprayer;atomizer
喷薄欲出 (of the sun) emerge in all its splendour
喷气织机 air-jet loom
喷云吐雾 ①(of a smoker) puff away ②(of a chimney,etc.)belch out smoke
喷墨打印机 ink printer;in-jet printer
喷气发动机 jet engine
喷气式飞机 jet plane;jet aircraft;jet

pén (ㄆㄣˊ)

盆 [pén]
I 名 ①basin;tub;pot ②sth like a basin
II 量 (for things held in a basin or pot):两盆花 two pots of flowers
盆地 basin
盆花 potted flower
盆景 potted landscape;miniature trees and rockery
盆腔 pelvic cavity
盆浴 tub bath;tub
盆栽 ①grown (or cultivated) in a pot ②potted flowers;miniature trees
盆子 basin;pot
盆腔炎 pelvic infection
盆盆罐罐 pots and pans—household utensils

pèn (ㄆㄣˋ)

喷 [pèn]
I 名 in season II 量 (of flowering, fruit-bearing, or harvesting):豆子结二喷角了。 The string beans are bearing their second crop of pods. ➡pēn
喷红 crimson
喷香 fragrant;delicious

pēng (ㄆㄥ)

抨 [pēng]
动 impeach;censure;denounce
抨击 attack (in speech or writing); assail (with words);lash out at

怦 [pēng]
象 (of heart) pound;thump:他的心老是怦怦地跳。 His heart kept thumping;His heart pounded violently.

砰 [pēng]
象 thump;bang;zap;thunder
砰然 with a bang;with a thump

烹 [pēng]
动 ①cook;boil ②quick-fry in hot oil and stir in sauce

烹饪 cooking;culinary art
烹调 cook (dishes)
烹饪法 ①cuisine;cookery ②recipe (for cooking)
烹饪比赛 cook-off;cooking competition

嘭 [pēng]
象 bang;thump

péng (ㄆㄥ)

朋 [péng]
I 名 ①friend ②form a clique;gang up for evil purposes II 动 ①gang up ②match;equal
朋党 clique;cabal
朋克 punk
朋僚 colleagues;friends
朋友 ①friend ②boyfriend;girlfriend
朋比为奸 act in collusion;conspire;collude; gang up

棚 [péng]
名 ①awning of straw mats propped up with wooden or bamboo poles to keep off wind and rain ②shed;shack ③room ceiling ④trellis
棚车 ①box wagon;boxcar ②covered truck
棚户 shacks;family that live in shacks
棚架 trellis; frame for vines (or climbing plants)
棚圈 covered pen (for animals)
棚舍 sukkah;booth
棚子 shed;shack

蓬 [péng]
I 形 ①flourishing ②fluffy;dishevelled II 量 (of luxuriant flowers or grass) clump;tangle
蓬勃 vigorous;flourishing;full of vitality
蓬户 a wicker door—a humble house
蓬莱 a fabled abode of immortals
蓬乱 (of grasses,hair,etc.) fluffy and disorderly
蓬蓬 (of grasses, shrubs, hair, beard, etc.) thick and untidy;shaggy
蓬茸 luxuriant;exuberant
蓬松 fluffy;puffy
蓬筚增辉 lustre lent to a humble house (said in thanks for a visit or a gift such as a scroll)
蓬门筚户 (a house with) a wicker door—a humble abode
蓬头垢面 with dishevelled hair and a dirty face;unkempt
蓬头散发 shock-headed;with dishevelled hair

搒 [péng]
动 beat with a rod ➡bàng

鹏 [péng]
名 roc,a huge legendary bird
鹏程万里 (make) a roc's flight of 10,000 li— have a bright future

澎 [péng]

澎湃 surge
澎湖列岛 the Penghu Islands; (European name) the Pescadores

篷 [péng]
名 ①covering (or awning) on a car (or boat,etc.) ②sail (of a boat)
篷布 tarpaulin
篷车 ① covered truck; box wagon ② horse-drawn cart with an awning
篷帐 tent
篷罩 tilt
篷子 awning (for protection from the sun, rain,wind,etc.)

膨 [péng]
动 expand;swell
膨大 expand;inflate
膨化 popped;dilation
膨松 bulk
膨胀 expand;swell;dilate;inflate
膨松剂 leavening agent
膨体纱 bulk yarn
膨胀计 dilatometer
膨胀性 expansibility
膨化食品 dilated food;inflated food
膨胀系数 coefficient of expansion (or dilation)

蟛 [péng]

蟛蜞 amphibious crab;brackish-water crab

pěng (ㄆㄥ)

捧 [pěng]
I 动 ① hold in both hands; carry in both hands ②flatter;promote;boost II 量 (of what can be held in both hands):一捧花生 a double handful of groundnuts
捧杯 ①hold the cup (as a prize) ② win the championship;win an award
捧场 ①be a member of a claque ②boost;sing the praises of;flatter
捧读 have the pleasure of reading (your work)
捧腹 split (or shake,burst) one's sides with laughter
捧哏 supporting role (in a cross talk)
捧角 try to build up an actor
捧杀 kill with praise (over-praising leads to arrogance and complacency,and ultimately to failure)
捧献 offer with respect
捧臭脚 flatter;carry favour;lick sb's boots
捧腹大笑 be convulsed with laughter; split one's sides with laughter

pèng (ㄆㄥ)

碰 [pèng]
动 ① touch; knock; bump ② meet; come

across;run into ③have a try;take a chance;
try one's luck ④meet to discuss
碰杯 clink glasses
碰壁 run up against a stone wall;be rebuffed
碰到 meet with;run into
碰见 meet unexpectedly;run into
碰铃 a pair of hand-held bells played by striking together (*used as a percussion instrument in traditional opera* , etc.)
碰面 meet
碰巧 by chance;by coincidence
碰伤 be injured (*or* damaged) after being hit
by sth
碰锁 spring lock
碰头 meet and discuss;put (our, your, or
their) heads together
碰硬 boldly confront (*or* challenge) a powerful opponent;try to remove a formidable
obstacle
碰撞 ①collide;run into ②offend;affront ③
collision;impact
碰钉子 meet with a rebuff;hit (*or* strike,run
against) a snag
碰碰车 bumper car
碰碰船 bumper boat
碰碰舞 slam dance
碰头会 (of leaders) brief meeting
碰运气 try one's luck;take a chance
碰一鼻子灰 be snubbed;meet with a rebuff

pī (ㄆl)

丕 [pī]
形 big;great
丕变 immense change
丕业 great cause

P

批 [pī]
Ⅰ 动 ①slap ②scrape;peel;skin ③write
instructions (*or* comments) on (a report
from a subordinate,etc.) ④officially approve
⑤criticize;refute Ⅱ 副 (of buying and selling) batch;bulk Ⅲ 量 batch;lot;group Ⅳ 名
fibres of cotton,flax,etc. ,ready to be drawn
and twisted
批办 issue (certificates,credentials,etc.)
批驳 ①veto an opinion (*or* a request) from a
subordinate body ②refute;criticize;rebut
批捕 issue an arrest warrant;approve an arrest
批斥 refute;criticize
批次 batch (of aircraft,etc.)
批答 give an official,written reply to a subordinate body
批点 mark words and phrases for special attention with dots or small circles and write
comments
批斗 criticize and denounce sb (at a public
meeting)

批发 ①wholesale ②(of an official document)
be authorized for dispatch
批复 give an official,written reply to a subordinate body
批改 correct
批号 lot number;batch number
批颊 slap sb's face;box sb's ear
批件 an official,written reply to a subordinate
body
批量 ①(produce) in batches ②batch;lot
批判 ①criticize ②critique
批评 ①criticize ②criticism
批示 write instructions (*or* comments) on a
report (*or* memorandum,etc.) submitted
by a subordinate
批售 wholesale
批条 note bearing a superior's instructions
(*or* comments)
批文 document bearing an official written response from senior authorities
批销 wholesale
批语 ①remarks (on a piece of writing) ②
written instructions (*or* comments) on a
report (*or* memorandum,etc.) submitted
by a subordinate
批阅 read over (official papers);read and
comment on (writings,texts,etc.)
批注 ①annotate and comment on ②annota-
tions and commentaries;marginalia
批转 make comments (*or* give instructions)
on and transmit (a document or report);
write instructions (*or* comments) on a report submitted by a subordinate and refer it
to those concerned
批准 ratify;approve;sanction
批租 approve to rent
批处理 batch processing
批发部 wholesale department
批发商 jobber;wholesaler
批判地 critically;discriminatingly
批条子 (of an official) write instructions (*or*
comments) on a note (to approve a request
from a subordinate)
批文件 write instructions on documents
批准书 instrument of ratification;certificate
of approval
批发价格 wholesale price
批发市场 wholesale business
批发折扣 trade discount;distributor discount
批量生产 batch production;mass production;
job-lot manufacturing
批零差价 differences between wholesale and
retail prices;price parities between the
wholesale and retail trades
批准文号 sanction number
批处理文件 batch file
批评中前进 advance amid criticism

批判现实主义 critical realism

伾 [pī]

伾伾 strong;muscular

纰 [pī]

〔动〕(of cloth,silk thread,etc.) become un-woven (*or* untwisted);be spoilt

纰漏 a careless mistake;a small accident;slip

纰缪 error;mistake

坯 [pī]

〔名〕①base;blank ②unburnt brick;earthen brick;adobe ③semifinished product

坯布 unbleached and undyed cloth;grey cloth;grey

坯革 crust leather

坯件 ①blank ②breed;strain

坯模 mould

坯子 semifinished product;base;blank

披 [pī]

〔动〕① drape over one's shoulders;wrap around:披上节日的盛装 be brilliantly deco-rated for a festival ② open;unroll;unfold;spread out ③split open;crack

披读 open (a book) and read

披风 cloak

披拂 ①wave;sway ②(of a breeze) blow gen-tly

披挂 ①put on a suit of armour ②a suit of ar-mour

披红 drape a band of red silk over sb's shoul-ders (on a festive occasion or as a token of honour)

披甲 put on a suit of armour

披肩 ①cape ②shawl

披巾 shawl;tippet

披襟 loosen one's jacket

披露 ①publish;announce ②reveal;show;dis-close

披靡 ①(of grass,etc.) be swept by the wind ②be routed;flee

披散 (of hair,mane,etc.) hang down loosely

披阅 open and read (a book);peruse

披肩发 shoulder length hair

披头士 Beatles

披肝沥胆 open one's heart;be open and sin-cere;be loyal and faithful;lay bare one's heart

披红戴花 have red silk draped over one's shoulders and a big red flower pinned on one's breast (as a token of honour)

披坚执锐 buckle on one's armour and take up weapons—go forth to battle

披荆斩棘 break through brambles and thorns—hack one's way through difficulties

披麻戴孝 wear the hemp garments of mourn-ing

披沙拣金 sort out the fine gold from the sand—extract the essentials from a mass of material

披头散发 with hair dishevelled;with hair in disarray;unkempt

披星戴月 under the canopy of the moon and the stars—travel by night;work from be-fore dawn till after dark

披上"民主"的外衣 under the mantle of democ-racy

狉 [pī]

狉狉 (of a place wild animals) move about

砒 [pī]

〔名〕①arsenic (As) ②(white) arsenic

砒霜 (white) arsenic

辟 [pī]

⇒bì;pì

辟头 at the very beginning;at the very start

劈 [pī]

Ⅰ〔动〕① split;chop;cleave ② split;crack;break ③ hoarse ④ be right against (one's face,etc.) ⑤(of thunder) strike Ⅱ〔名〕wedge

⇒pǐ

劈刺 sabre or bayonet fighting

劈刀 ①chopper ②sabre fighting

劈开 rive;split

劈理 cleavage

劈脸 right in the face

劈裂 rip;separation

劈啪 the sound of crackling,etc.

劈杀 (usu. of a man on horseback) slash at sb (with a sword)

劈山 level off hilltops;blast cliffs

劈手 make a sudden snatch

劈头 ①straight on the head;right in the face ②at the very start

劈胸 right against the chest

劈波斩浪 cleave through the waves

劈风斩浪 brave the wind and the waves—slash one's way through difficulties

劈里啪啦 the successive sounds of crackling,etc.

劈头盖脸 right in the face

霹 [pī]

霹雷 thunderbolt;thunderclap

霹雳 thunderbolt;thunderclap

霹雳舞 break dance

pí (ㄆㄧ)

皮 [pí]

Ⅰ〔名〕①skin;cutis ②leather;fur;hide ③peel;rind ④ cover;wrapper ⑤ surface ⑥broad,flat piece (of some thin material);sheet ⑦rubber Ⅱ〔形〕① pliable;tough ②no longer crisp;soggy ③naughty;mischievous ④case-hardened;apathetic

皮袄 fur-lined jacket

皮板 dermatotome; fell
皮包 leather handbag; briefcase; portfolio
皮鞭 leather-thonged whip
皮草 leather and fur
皮层 ①cortex ②cerebral cortex
皮尺 tape measure; tape
皮带 ①leather belt ②(driving) belt
皮蛋 a kind of preserved egg
皮筏 skin raft
皮肤 skin
皮革 leather; hide
皮花 ginned cotton; lint
皮婚 leather wedding anniversary—the 3rd wedding anniversary
皮货 furs; peltry
皮匠 ①cobbler ②tanner
皮胶 hide glue
皮具 leather products; leatherware
皮脸 ①shameless ②naughty
皮毛 ① fur ② smattering; superficial knowledge
皮棉 ginned cotton; lint (cotton)
皮面 ①outer skin; surface; outside ②leather cover
皮囊 ①leather bag ②the human body
皮袍 furred robe
皮球 rubber ball; ball
皮肉 skin and flesh
皮实 ①sturdy ②durable
皮试 a test for allergies whereby allergens are injected into the skin; skin test
皮糖 a sticky candy
皮条 ①leather strap ②pimp
皮艇 ①kayaking ②kayak
皮线 rubber-insulated wire; rubber-covered wire
皮箱 leather suitcase; leather trunk
皮鞋 leather shoes
皮靴 leather boots
皮炎 dermatitis
皮衣 ①fur clothing ②leather clothing
皮张 hide; pelt
皮疹 rash
皮纸 tough paper made from bast fibre of the mulberry or paper mulberry, etc.
皮质 ①cortex ②cerebral cortex
皮重 tare
皮子 ①leather; hide ②fur
皮大衣 fur coat
皮带轮 (belt) pulley
皮垫圈 leather washer; leather packing collar
皮肤病 skin disease; dermatosis
皮肤科 dermatological department; dermatology
皮肤针 cutaneous acupuncture; needles used in cutaneous acupuncture
皮辊花 lap waste

皮猴儿 hooded fur overcoat; fur parka; fur anorak
皮划艇 canoeing (including kayaking)
皮夹子 wallet; pocketbook
皮筋儿 rubber band
皮内针 intradermal needling (acupuncture by embedding the needle subcutaneously for one or several days)
皮褥子 fur-lined mattress
皮条纤 procurer; pimp
皮桶子 fur lining (for a jacket or an overcoat)
皮鞋油 shoe polish
皮影戏 leather-silhouette show; shadow play
皮掌儿 outsole
皮脂腺 sebaceous glands
皮包公司 bogus company; briefcase company; bubble company; dummy company; fly-by-night company
皮包骨头 skinny
皮包生意 free riding
皮肤病学 dermatology
皮开肉绽 the skin torn and the flesh gaping
皮里阳秋 criticism kept to oneself
皮肉生涯 career of prostitution
皮下注射 subcutaneous (or hypodermic) injection
皮下组织 subcutaneous tissue
皮肤真菌病 dermatomycosis
皮笑肉不笑 put on a false smile; smile hypocritically
皮之不存,毛将焉附 with the skin gone, what can the hair adhere to—a thing cannot exist without its basis

苃 [pí]

苃基 pyrenyl

枇 [pí]

枇杷 loquat (the tree and its fruit)

毗 [pí]

劢 ①adjoin; be contiguous; be adjacent ②assist

毗连 adjoin; border on
毗邻 be adjacent to

蚍 [pí]

蚍蜉 large ant

疲 [pí]

形 ①tired; weary; exhausted ②weakened; slump

疲惫 ①tired out; exhausted ②tire sb out
疲顿 be tired out
疲乏 ① tired; fatigued; weary ② fatigue ③ weakening of material subjected to stress; fatigue
疲倦 tired and sleepy
疲困 ①tired ②slump
疲劳 ① tired; fatigued; weary ② fatigue ③

weakening of material subjected to stress
疲软 ①fatigued and weak ②weakened;slump
疲弱 tired and weak;frail and fatigued
疲沓 slack;negligent
疲态 weakness
疲劳战术 gruelling tactic
疲软股票 soft stock
疲于奔命 be tired out by too much running around;be kept constantly on the run;be weighed down with work
疲劳综合征 effort syndrome;exhaustion syndrome;fatigue syndrome

陴 [pí]
〈名〉parapet wall;parapet

埤 [pí]
I 〈动〉increase;augment II 〈名〉low wall ➡ pì

啤 [pí]
啤酒 beer
啤酒杯 blackpot
啤酒厂 brewery
啤酒肚 beer belly
啤酒罐 beer can;beer tin
啤酒花 hops
啤酒桶 beer barrel

琵 [pí]
琵琶 *pipa*,a plucked string instrument with a fretted fingerboard

脾 [pí]
〈名〉spleen
脾气 ①temperament;disposition ②bad temper
脾胃 taste
脾性 temperament;disposition;nature;habits and characteristics
脾虚 insufficiency of the spleen
脾脏 spleen
脾切除 splenectomy
脾肿大 splenomegaly
脾胃相投 have similar tastes;have similar likes and dislikes

裨 [pí]
〈形〉assistant;secondary ➡ bì

蜱 [pí]
〈名〉tick
蜱螨 mite

罴 [pí]
〈名〉brown bear

pǐ ㄆㄧˇ

匹 [pǐ]
I 〈动〉be equal to;be a match for;rival II 〈形〉alone;single III 〈量〉①(of horses,mules,etc.):一匹马 a horse/两匹骡子 two mules ②of bolts of silk or cloth:一匹布 a bolt of cloth
匹敌 be equal to;be well matched

匹夫 ①ordinary man ②ignorant person
匹配 ①mate;marry ②matching
匹染 piece dyeing
匹头 piece goods;dry goods;soft goods
匹夫有责 Every one has the duty.
匹夫之勇 reckless courage;foolhardiness

庀 [pǐ]
〈动〉①possess;be provided with ②administer;manage

圮 [pǐ]
〈动〉collapse;fall apart;be in ruin

仳 [pǐ]
〈动〉①part ②distinguish

否 [pǐ]
I 〈形〉bad;evil II 〈动〉censure;condemn ➡ fǒu
否极泰来 Out of the depth of misfortune comes bliss;The extreme of adversity is the beginning of prosperity.

吡 [pǐ]
〈动〉①slander;defame;calumniate ②reprimand;rebuke ➡ bǐ

痞 [pǐ]
〈名〉①lump in the abdomen ②ruffian;hooligan;riffraff
痞积 lump in the abdomen
痞块 lump in the abdomen
痞气 mass at the right hypochondrium
痞子 ruffian;riffraff

劈 [pǐ]
〈动〉①cut;split;divide ②break off;strip off ③open one's legs (*or* fingers) as wide as possible ➡ pī
劈叉 do the splits
劈柴 kindling;firewood
劈腿 trestle;tressel
劈账 share out proceeds according to a certain rate
劈一字腿 do the splits

擗 [pǐ]
〈动〉①break off ②beat one's breast
擗棒子 pick corn

癖 [pǐ]
〈名〉addiction
癖好 favourite hobby;fondness
癖嗜 addiction
癖习 old habit
癖性 natural inclination;proclivity;propensity

pì ㄆㄧˋ

屁 [pì]
〈名〉①wind (from bowels);fart ②damned;worthless and trivial thing ③(*often used in a negative sense or as a rebuke*) what;anything:你懂个屁！ What an idiot you are!
屁股 ① buttocks (of humans);bottom;behind;backside ② rump (of animals);haunch;hindquarters ③end;butt

屁话 shit; nonsense; rubbish

屁事 trifling matter; mere nothing; nothing worth speaking of

屁股蛋 buttocks

屁滚尿流 be scared shitless; be frightened out of one's wits (*or* life); piss in one's pants (in terror)

坤 [pì]
名 parapet wall ➡pí

辟 [pì]
I 动 ①open up (territory, land, etc.); reclaim ②refute; repudiate Ⅱ 形 penetrating; incisive Ⅲ 名 law ➡bì; pī

辟谣 refute a rumour; refute slanders; deny a rumour

睥 [pì]

睥睨 look sideways

媲 [pì]
动 be equal to; match

媲美 compare favourably with; rival; be on a par with

僻 [pì]
形 ①out-of-the-way; secluded ②eccentric; odd ③rare; uncommon

僻静 secluded; lonely

僻陋 secluded and desolate

僻壤 out-of-the-way place

僻性 eccentric character

僻远 remote and out-of-the-way

僻字 rare word

譬 [pì]
名 example; analogy

譬如 for example; for instance; such as

譬若 for example; for instance; such as

譬喻 metaphor; simile; analogy; figure of speech

piān (ㄆㄧㄢ)

片 [piān]
➡piàn

片窗 gate

片盒 film magazine

片花 film clips

片夹 film jacket

片孔 film perforation

片门 film gate

片盘 film spool; bobbin

片头 titles (of a film)

片尾 trailer; trail leader

片子 ①roll of film ②film; movie ③gramophone record; disc ④ the negative of a roentgenogram

扁 [piān]
➡biǎn

扁舟 small boat; skiff

偏 [piān]
I 形 ①inclined to one side; leaning to one side; slanting; diverging ②partial; prejudiced ③assistant; supplementary; supporting; auxiliary ④different (e. g. higher or lower) from a certain standard Ⅱ 副 persistently; wilfully; deliberately Ⅲ 动 move to one's side

偏爱 have partiality for sth; show favouritism to sb

偏安 (of a feudal regime) be content to retain sovereignty over a part of the country

偏差 deviation; error

偏磁 bias

偏方 folk prescription

偏房 ①wing-room ②concubine

偏废 do one thing and neglect another; emphasize one thing at the expense of another

偏航 going off course; off-course; yaw

偏好 [piānhǎo] it so happened that; as luck would have it

偏好 [piānhào] have a special fondness for sth; have a partiality for sth

偏护 be partial to and side with

偏激 extreme

偏见 prejudice; bias

偏将 assistant general

偏科 over-emphasize one or two subjects and thus neglect many other subjects

偏枯 ①hemiplegia ②lopsided (development)

偏劳 (*used when asking sb for help or thanking sb for his help*)

偏离 deviate; diverge

偏旁 character components (*or* basic structural parts) of Chinese characters

偏僻 remote; out-of-the-way

偏偏 ① wilfully; insistently; persistently ② contrary to expectations ③only; alone

偏颇 biased; partial

偏巧 it so happened that; as luck would have it

偏色 colour cast

偏师 auxiliary force

偏食 ①partial eclipse ②partiality for a limited variety of food; a one-sided diet

偏瘫 hemiplegia

偏袒 be partial to and side with; give unprincipled protection to

偏疼 favour one (child, etc.) more than the others

偏题 a catch (*or* tricky) question (in an examination)

偏西 (of the sun) move towards the west

偏向 ① erroneous tendency; deviation ② be partial to; give unprincipled support (*or* protection) to

偏斜 deflection; deviation; crab

偏心 ①partiality; bias ②eccentric

偏压 bias voltage; bias

偏移 shifting; excursion; offset

偏远 remote; faraway

偏振 polarization
偏执 stubbornly biased
偏重 stress one aspect at the expense of another
偏转 deflection
偏坠 swelling and hanging down of either of the testes (caused by orchitis, hernia, etc.)
偏口鱼 flatfish; flounder
偏头痛 migraine
偏心轮 eccentric wheel; eccentric
偏振光 polarized light
偏安一隅 be content to exercise sovereignty over only a part of the country
偏磁电流 bias current
偏听偏信 heed and trust only one side; listen only to one side; be biased
偏心眼儿 prejudiced; partial
偏振光镜 polariscope
偏正词组 word group consisting of a modifier and the word it modifies
偏振光显微镜 polarizing microscope

篇 [piān]
Ⅰ 名 ①piece of writing ②printed sheet (of paper, etc.) Ⅱ 量 (of writing, paper, or publication): 一篇论文 a thesis
篇幅 ①length (of a piece of writing) ②space (on a printed page)
篇目 table of contents; contents; list of articles
篇章 sections and chapters; writings
篇子 sheet

翩 [piān]
形 ①(of flying) rapidly ②(of flag) waving ③admirable and unrestrained ④fleeting
翩翩 ①lightly (dance, flutter, etc.) ②elegant
翩然 lightly; trippingly
翩跹 lightly; trippingly
翩翩起舞 rise and dance in a happy mood; dance trippingly
翩若惊鸿 (of a beautiful woman) tripping lightly like a startled swan

pián (ㄆㄧㄢˊ)

便 [pián]
形 quiet and comfortable ⇒ biàn
便便 bulging; swelling
便宜 ① cheap ② unmerited advantages; unearned gains ③ let sb off lightly
便宜货 cheapie; twofer

骈 [pián]
Ⅰ 形 parallel; antithetical Ⅱ 名 pair of horses Ⅲ 动 stand (or lie, go) side by side
骈丽 art of parallelism
骈文 parallel prose

胼 [pián]
胼胝 callosity; callus
胼胝体 corpus callosum

胼手胝足 callused hands and feet—a life of toil

缠 [pián]
动 stitch; sew ⇒ biàn

蹁 [pián]
Ⅰ 动 walk on the side of one's foot Ⅱ 名 knee
蹁跹 whirl about

piàn (ㄆㄧㄢˋ)

片 [piàn]
Ⅰ 名 ①flat, thin piece; slice; flake ②motion picture; TV film ③subarea; section of a place Ⅱ 形 incomplete; fragmentary; partial; brief Ⅲ 动 cut into slices; slice Ⅳ 量 ①(of things that are in the form of flat, thin pieces): 两片药 two tablets/一片黄瓜 a slice of cucumber/几片白云 patches of fluffy white clouds ②(of land, waters, etc.): 一大片水 a vast expanse of water/一大片庄稼 a vast stretch of crops ③(of scenery, atmosphere, sound, feeling, etc.): 一片新气象 a new atmosphere/一片真心 all sincerity ⇒ piān
片酬 remuneration for a movie actor (or actress); pay for making a film
片段 part; passage; extract; fragment
片断 ① part; passage; extract; fragment ② fragmentary; incomplete
片剂 tablet
片刻 short while; instant; moment
片流 laminar flow
片面 ①unilateral ②one-sided
片商 movie distributor
片石 slabstone; flagstone
片时 a short while; a moment
片言 a few words; a phrase or two
片岩 schist
片约 film contract (between an actor and a film producer)
片子 ①a flat, thin piece; slice; flake; scrap ②visiting card
片儿会 neighbourhood meeting; temporary group meeting
片假名 katakana
片儿警 policeman responsible for a specific neighbourhood; beat policeman
片麻岩 gneiss
片面性 one-sidedness
片艳纸 a machine-glazed paper (glossy on one side)
片儿医 neighbourhood doctor
片甲不存 not a single armoured warrior remains—the army is completely wiped out
片面观点 lopsided view; one-sided view
片面之词 account given by one party only
片梭织机 gripper loom
片瓦无存 not a single tile remains—be razed

to the ground
片言只语 (in) only a few words
片纸只字 fragments of writing

骗 [piàn]
劢 ①deceive;cheat;dupe;fool;hoodwink sb with lies ②cheat;gain by swindle ③mount;bestride;jump onto
骗保 insurance fraud
骗贷 loan fraud
骗供 trap (or trick) into making a confession
骗汇 foreign currency fraud
骗局 fraud;hoax;swindle
骗赔 fraudulent claim
骗钱 cheat sb of his money;swindle sb out of his money;get money by swindle
骗取 gain sth by cheating;cheat (or trick, swindle) sb out of sth;defraud
骗人 deceive people
骗术 deceitful trick;fraud;ruse
骗税 tax fraud;tax evasion
骗宿 trick a person into staying in a hotel, guest house,etc.
骗子 swindler;impostor;cheat;trickster
骗取钱财 cheat (or swindle) sb out of money;defraud sb of money
骗取荣誉 seek honour through deception
骗取信任 worm one's way into sb's confidence;obtain credit by fraud
骗取选票 wangle votes

piāo (ㄆ丨ㄠ)

剽 [piāo]
I 劢 rob;hijack;loot;plunder II 形 nimble;swift
剽悍 agile and brave;quick and fierce
剽疾 fierce and nimble
剽掠 plunder;loot
剽窃 plagiarize;lift;plagiarism
剽袭 plagiarize

漂 [piāo]
劢 ①float;stay afloat;drift ②move downstream (or in the direction of the wind) ⇒ piǎo;piào
漂儿 fishing float
漂泊 lead a wandering life;drift
漂浮 ①float ②hover before the eyes;float in the mind
漂砾 erratic;erratic boulder
漂流 ①be driven by the current;drift about ②rafting
漂移 drift
漂逸 possessing natural grace;elegant
漂溢 drift about
漂悠 drift leisurely
漂游 lead a wandering life;drift
漂族 floaters
漂泊者 vagabond

漂流瓶 drift bottle;messenger bottle
漂一代 floaters
漂洋过海 travel far across the ocean (or sea)

缥 [piāo]
⇒ piǎo
缥缈 dimly discernible;misty

飘 [piāo]
I 劢 wave;flutter;float (in the air);waft
II 形 ①weak;wobbly;feeble ②giddy;superficial;frivolous;flippant
飘尘 airborne dust;floating dust
飘带 streamer;ribbon
飘荡 ① drift;float;wave;flutter ② lead a wanderer's life;drift
飘动 float (in the air or upon the waves);flutter;drift
飘拂 float slowly
飘浮 (of style of work) superficial;showy
飘红 grow
飘忽 ①(of clouds,etc.) move swiftly;fleet ②mobile;uncertain
飘零 ①fading and falling;whirling and scattering ②wandering;adrift;homeless
飘落 drift and fall slowly;descend slowly and lightly
飘然 floating in the air
飘洒 [piāosǎ] float in the air;drift with the wind
飘洒 [piāosa] free and easy
飘散 (of smoke,mist,etc.) drift away
飘逝 ① float and disperse ② pass by;wear away;disappear
飘舞 wave in the wind
飘扬 wave;flutter;fly
飘摇 sway in the wind
飘曳 sway
飘移 drift
飘逸 ①graceful;free and easy ②float;scatter
飘溢 drift about
飘悠 drift leisurely
飘游 wander aimlessly
飘飘然 ①feel high ②feeling of floating in the air ③smug;self-satisfied;complacent

螵 [piāo]
螵蛸 the egg capsule of a mantis

piáo (ㄆ丨ㄠ)

嫖 [piáo]
劢 go whoring;visit prostitutes
嫖猖 whoring
嫖妓 visit prostitutes;go whoring
嫖客 brothel (or whorehouse) frequenter;whoremonger;whoremaster

瓢 [piáo]
名 gourd ladle;wooden dipper
瓢虫 ladybug;ladybird

瓢子 ①gourd ladle ②spoon
瓢泼大雨 heavy rain; torrential rain; downpour

piāo (ㄆㄧㄠ)

莩 [piāo]
〔动〕 die from starvation ➡fú

殍 [piāo]
Ⅰ〔动〕 die from starvation Ⅱ〔名〕 victim of starvation

漂 [piāo]
〔动〕①bleach ②rinse ➡piǎo; piào

漂白 bleach
漂染 bleaching and dyeing
漂洗 rinse
漂白粉 bleaching powder
漂洗槽 potcher

缥 [piāo]
〔名〕①pale green ②pale-green silk ➡piāo

瞟 [piāo]
〔动〕 look askance at; glance sideways at

piào (ㄆㄧㄠ)

票 [piào]
〔名〕① ticket; printed slip as certificate ②ballot ③bank note; bill ④person held for ransom by brigands; hostage ⑤amateur performance (of Beijing opera, etc.)
票额 the sum stated on a cheque or bill; denomination; face value
票房 booking office; box office value
票根 counterfoil; stub
票号 draft bank
票汇 send bank drafts
票价 the price of a ticket; admission fee; entrance fee
票据 ①bill; note ②voucher; receipt
票面 face (or par, nominal) value
票品 stamps, miniature sheets, first day covers, etc. collected by philatelists
票券 ticket; coupon
票箱 ballot box
票选 vote; elect (or vote) by ballot; vote for sb
票友 amateur performer
票源 supply of tickets
票证 coupons; ticket
票子 bank note; paper money; bill
票贩子 scalper; ticket tout; ticket shark; ticket broker
票房价值 box-office value; box-office intake; box-office receipts; box-office income
票房收入 box-office income (or returns, collections) at the booking (or ticket) office
票据贴现 discounting of bill
票面价值 face value; par (value)
票据交换所 clearinghouse

僄 [piào]
〔形〕①quick and nimble ②frivolous; flippant

嘌 [piào]
〔形〕 swift; quick
嘌呤 purine

漂 [piào]
〔动〕 come to nothing; fail; peter out ➡piāo; piǎo
漂亮 ①handsome; good-looking; pretty; beautiful ②remarkable; brilliant; splendid; beautiful
漂亮话 fine words; high-sounding words

骠 [piào]
〔形〕①(of horses) gallop fast ②brave; valiant; intrepid
骠悍 intrepid

piē (ㄆㄧㄝ)

氕 [piē]
〔名〕 protium (^{1}H)

撇 [piē]
〔动〕①cast aside; put aside; discard; leave behind; throw overboard ②skim ➡piě
撇开 leave aside; bypass
撇弃 cast away; abandon; discard
撇清 whitewash oneself; plead innocence
撇去 skim
撇油器 oil skimmer

瞥 [piē]
〔动〕 shoot a glance at; catch a glimpse of
瞥见 get a glimpse of; catch sight of
瞥视 cast a quick glance at
瞥眼 in the twinkling of an eye; in an instant; in a flash

piě (ㄆㄧㄝ)

苤 [piě]
苤蓝 kohlrabi

撇 [piě]
Ⅰ〔动〕①throw; fling; cast ②pout one's lips (in disdain or displeasure) Ⅱ〔名〕 left-falling stroke (in Chinese characters) Ⅲ〔量〕：两撇扫帚眉 two bushy brows ➡piē
撇号 accent (sign); prime
撇嘴 curl one's lip (in contempt, disbelief or disappointment); twitch one's mouth

pīn (ㄆㄧㄣ)

拼 [pīn]
〔动〕①put together; piece together ②risk all (in doing sth); exert one's utmost (in work); fight tooth and nail ③spell
拼版 makeup
拼搏 struggle hard; exert oneself to the utmost; go all out
拼刺 ①bayonet drill; bayonet practice ②bayo-

net charge
拼凑 piece together;knock together;rig up
拼接 piece together;join together
拼力 go all out;do one's utmost
拼命 ① risk one's life; defy death; go all out regardless of danger to one's life ② exerting the utmost strength; for all one is worth;with all one's might;desperately
拼排 compose and lay out
拼盘 assorted cold dishes;hors d'oeuvres
拼抢 scramble for;press on
拼杀 battle fiercely
拼死 risk one's life;defy death;fight desperately
拼写 spell;transliterate
拼音 ①combine sounds into syllables ②spell; phoneticize
拼攒 assemble (spare parts)
拼争 take on;face up to
拼装 assemble;fit together
拼缀 join together
拼刺刀 bayonet charge
拼到底 fight to bitter end;fight to the finish
拼劲儿 energy and determination
拼时间 race against time
拼体力 risk exhausting all one's physical strength
拼贴画 paste-up
拼写法 spelling;orthography
拼命工作 work with all one's might
拼命精神 the death-defying spirit
拼死拼活 put up a life-and-death fight; exerting one's utmost;for all one is worth; desperately
拼死挣扎 wage a desperate struggle
拼图游戏 jigsaw puzzle
拼写检查 spelling check
拼音文字 alphabetic (system of) writing
拼音字母 phonetic alphabet;phonetic letters

姘 [pīn]
劢 have illicit relations with
姘夫 (man) lover;paramour
姘妇 kept woman;mistress;paramour
姘居 live illicitly as husband and wife;cohabit
姘头 paramour

pín (ㄆㄧㄣˊ)

贫 [pín]
形 ① poor; needy; impoverished ② inadequate;deficient;poor ③garrulous;loquacious
贫乏 ① poor; needy; impoverished ② wretchedly lacking
贫寒 poor;poverty-stricken
贫化 dilution
贫瘠 barren;infertile;poor
贫贱 poor and lowly;in straitened and humble circumstances

贫苦 poor;poverty-stricken;badly off
贫矿 lean ore
贫困 impoverished; in pinching poverty; in straitened circumstances
贫民 poor people;paupers
贫气 ①stingy;niggardly ②annoyingly garrulous
贫穷 poor;needy;impoverished
贫弱 (of a country) poor and weak
贫水 water shortage
贫血 anaemia
贫油 oil-poor
贫嘴 garrulous;loquacious
贫骨头 ① a person keen on petty gain ② a stingy person;niggard ③an idle chatterer; windbag
贫化铀 depleted uranium
贫困户 poor family; family in poverty; destitute house hold (or family)
贫困县 impoverished county
贫困线 poverty line
贫民窟 slum
贫民区 slum area;slum district
贫铀弹 depleted uranium projectile; depleted uranium bomb
贫病交迫 suffer from both poverty and sickness;be plagued by poverty and ill heath
贫齿动物 edentate animal;edentate
贫富差距 disparities in wealth;polarization of rich and poor
贫富悬殊 a wide gap between the rich and the poor
贫贱之交 friends that have seen poverty together;friends in days of poverty
贫困地区 poverty-stricken area;impoverished area;destitute area;poor region
贫下中农 poor and lower-middle peasants
贫嘴薄舌 be garrulous and sharp-tongued
贫贱之交不可忘 A man should not forget the friends he made when he was poor.

频 [pín]
Ⅰ 形 frequent Ⅱ 副 frequently;repeatedly Ⅲ 名 frequency
频传 (of good news,etc.) keep pouring in
频次 frequency
频带 frequency band
频道 (TV) frequency channel;channel
频段 frequency range
频发 take place (or happen) frequently
频繁 frequently;often
频率 rate of recurrence;frequency
频密 frequent
频频 again and again;repeatedly
频谱 frequency spectrum
频仍 frequent;repeated
频数 frequent and continuous
频率函数 frequency function

频率理论 frequency theory
频率调制 frequency modulation（FM）
频率发生器 frequency generator

嫔 [pín]

[名] ①concubine of an emperor ②woman attendant at court；lady-in-waiting

颦 [pín]

[动] frown；knit one's brows
颦蹙 knit the brows；be worried
颦眉凝望 gaze with knitted brows

pǐn（ㄆㄧㄣˇ）

品 [pǐn]

I [名] ①article；product；goods ②character；quality ③grade；class；rank ④official ranks in dynastic times ⑤kind；type；variety II [动] ①taste sth with discrimination；sample；savour ②play
品尝 taste；sample；savour
品德 moral character
品第 ① appraise；rate；grade ② quality and style
品读 appreciate
品格 ① one's moral character ② quality and style（of literary or artistic works）
品红 ①magenta；fuchsine（a dye）②purplish red
品级 ①official rank in feudal times ②grade（of products，commodities，etc.）
品蓝 reddish blue
品类 category
品绿 malachite green；bamboo green
品貌 ① looks；appearance ② character and looks；personality and appearance
品名 the name of an article；the name（or description）of a commodity
品茗 sip tea（to judge its quality）；sample tea
品目 the names（or descriptions）of goods
品牌 brand（name）
品评 judge；appraise；comment on
品脱 pint
品位 ①grade ②quality（of products，literary works，etc.）③taste
品味 ① taste；sample；savour ② quality；flavour
品系 strain
品箫 blow a bamboo flute
品行 moral conduct；behaviour
品性 one's nature and moral character
品质 ①character；intrinsic quality ②quality（of commodities，etc.）
品种 ① breed；strain；variety ② variety；assortment
品牌机 brand-name computer
品头论足 ① make frivolous remarks about a woman's appearance ② find fault；be overcritical

品学兼优 be a good student of good character；be a student of good character and fine scholarship
品质因数 quality factor
品种齐全 complete range of articles；rich assortment of goods

pìn（ㄆㄧㄣˋ）

牝 [pìn]

[形] female
牝鸡 hen
牝马 mare
牝牛 cow

聘 [pìn]

[动] ①engage；employ；appoint ②visit ③betroth ④get married；be married off
聘金 betrothal money for the bride's family
聘礼 betrothal gifts
聘请 engage；invite
聘任 engage sb as；appoint sb to a position
聘书 letter of appointment；contract；formal letter of employment
聘问 visit a friendly country on behalf of one's government
聘用 employ；engage；appoint to a position
聘任制 system of appointment

pīng（ㄆㄧㄥ）

乒 [pīng]

I [象] ping，a short high-ringing sound：乒的一声枪响 crack of a gun shot II [名] table tennis；ping-pong
乒乓 ①rattling（or clattering）sound ②table tennis；ping-pong
乒坛 the table tennis circles
乒乓球 ①table tennis；ping-pong ②table tennis ball；ping-pong ball
乒乓球赛 table tennis match（or tournament）
乒坛老将 veteran table tennis player
乒乓球联合会 table tennis federation

俜 [pīng]

[动] let a lone

娉 [pīng]

娉婷（of a woman）have a graceful demeanour

píng（ㄆㄧㄥˊ）

平 [píng]

I [形] ①flat；level；smooth ②on the same level；equal ③ equal；just；fair；impartial ④calm；tranquil；peaceful；quiet ⑤common；average；ordinary；usual II [名] ①make the same score；draw ②level tone III [动] ①make even；level out；level up ②be on the same level；be on a par；equal；draw ③put down；quell；suppress ④ restrain one's anger；pacify；calm；soothe

P

平安 safe and sound; without mishap; well
平白 for no reason; gratuitously
平板 dull and stereotyped; flat
平版 planographic plate
平暴 suppress a rebellion
平辈 persons of the same generation
平布 plain cloth
平槽 rise as high as the banks; be level with the banks
平产 show no increases in output
平常 ① ordinary; common ② generally; usually; ordinarily; as a rule
平车 ① flatcar; platform wagon; platform car ② flatbed cart
平川 level land; flat, open country; plain
平淡 flat; insipid; prosaic; pedestrian
平等 equality
平底 ① flat-bottomed ② low-heeled
平地 ① level the land (or ground); rake the soil smooth ② level ground; flat ground
平电 ordinary telegram
平定 ① calm down ② suppress; put down
平峒 adit; tunnel
平凡 ordinary; common
平反 redress (a mishandled case); rehabilitate
平泛 (of writings) flat and superficial
平方 ① the second power (of a quantity); square ② square metre (sq. m.)
平房 ① single-storey house; one-storey house ② a house with a flat plastered roof
平分 divide equally; give (or take) equal shares; share alike
平伏 ① calm down; subside; be pacified ② lie prostrate; lie flat
平服 be convinced
平复 ① calm down; subside; be pacified ② be cured; be healed
平光 zero diopter; plain glass
平和 gentle; mild; moderate; placid
平衡 ① balance; equilibrium ② bring into (or keep in) equilibrium; balance
平滑 level and smooth; smooth
平话 popular story
平缓 ① (of the terrain, flow of water, etc.) gentle; smooth ② mild; placid; gentle
平毁 demolish
平击 flush hit; plain hit
平价 ① stabilize prices ② stabilized (or normalized, moderate) prices ③ par; parity
平角 straight angle; an angle of 180°
平静 calm; quiet; tranquil
平局 draw; tie
平均 ① average; mean ② equalize; go fifty and fifty
平旷 open and flat
平列 place side by side; place on a par with each other

平流 advection
平炉 open-hearth furnace; open hearth; Martin furnace
平乱 put down a revolt; suppress a rebellion
平落 drop to normal
平脉 normal pulse
平米 square metre (sq. m.)
平面 plane
平民 the common people; the populace
平明 day-break; dawn
平年 ① non-leap year; common year ② average year (in crop yield)
平疲 weak
平平 average; mediocre; indifferent
平权 (enjoy) equal rights
平日 on ordinary days; ordinarily; usually
平绒 velveteen
平射 flat (trajectory) fire
平身 ① stand up after kowtowing ② stand up (said by an emperor to a kowtowing subject)
平生 ① all one's life; one's whole life ② usually
平声 level tone
平实 simple and unadorned
平时 ① at ordinary times; in normal times ② in peacetime
平视 look squarely (or directly); look straight ahead
平手 draw
平顺 smooth-going; plain sailing
平素 usually
平台 ① terrace ② movable platform ③ platform ④ plateau
平坦 (of land, etc.) level; even; smooth
平添 add (or give) as an effect (or a result)
平头 ① crew cut ② full; round; complete
平纹 plain weave
平稳 smooth and steady; smooth; stable
平西 (of the sun) be setting
平昔 in the past
平息 ① calm down; quiet down; subside ② put down (a rebellion, etc.); suppress
平巷 drift; level
平信 ① ordinary mail ② surface mail
平行 ① of equal rank; on an equal footing; parallel ② simultaneous; concurrent
平衍 open and flat; plain and broad
平移 translation
平议 ① pass a fair judgment on ② appraise sth through discussion
平抑 stabilize
平易 ① unassuming; amiable ② (of a piece of writing) easy; plain
平庸 mediocre; indifferent; commonplace
平鱼 butterfish
平原 plain; flatlands

平月 February of a non-leap year
平匀 regular and steady;even and regular
平允 fair and just;equitable
平仄 ① level and oblique tones ② tonal patterns in classical Chinese poetry
平展 ①(of land,etc.) open and flat ② well smoothed out;unruffled;unwrinkled
平整 ①level (land) ②neat;smooth;level
平职 new position at the same administrative level as a former one
平装 paperback;paper-cover;paperbound
平足 flatfoot
平安险 free of particular average (F.P.A.)
平板车 flatbed tricycle;flatbed
平板仪 surveying panel
平舱费 trimming charges
平底机 land leveller;grader;road grader
平方根 square root
平方米 square metre (sq.m.)
平分线 bisector
平衡觉 sense of equilibrium
平衡力 equilibrant
平衡木 balance beam
平衡器 balancer
平滑肌 smooth muscle;involuntary muscle
平记录 equal a record
平价粮 grain bought and sold according to the government-stipulated price
平假名 hiragana
平均律 equal temperament
平均数 average;mean
平均值 average value;mean value;mean
平口钳 flat-nose pliers
平流层 stratosphere
平面波 plane wave
平面镜 plane mirror
平面人 two-dimentional person
平面图 plan;plane figure
平民愤 assuage popular indignation
平射炮 flat fire gun;flat trajectory gun
平水期 the period when a river is at its normal level
平头数 round figure
平行脉 parallel veins
平安无事 All is well.
平白无故 for no apparent reason
平板玻璃 plate glass
平步青云 rapidly go up in the world;have a meteoric rise
平淡无奇 commonplace;prosaic;pedestrian
平等待人 treat others as equal
平等互惠 reciprocal favoured treatment
平等竞争 fair competition;equal competition
平等协商 consultation on the basis of equality;consulation on an equal footing
平地风波 a sudden storm on a calm sea—unforeseen trouble

平地楼台 high buildings rise from the ground—start from scratch
平定叛乱 crush a rebellion
平方公里 square kilometre (sq.km.)
平分秋色 (of two parties) have equal shares (of honour,power,glory,etc.)
平衡常数 equilibrium constant
平衡价格 equilibrium price
平价商店 low-price shop;fair price shop
平价市场 bargain centre;market selling inexpensive goods at government-fixed price
平均利润 average profit
平均寿命 average life span;life expectancy
平均主义 equalitarianism;egalitarianism
平面几何 plane geometry
平面交叉 grade crossing;level crossing
平面磨床 surface grinding machine
平面直角 flat square
平平当当 done smoothly;without a hitch
平铺直叙 ① tell in a simple,straightforward way ②speak (or write) in a dull,flat style
平起平坐 sit as equals at the same table;be on an equal footing
平头正脸 have regular features
平稳过渡 smooth transition
平息暴乱 put down a riot
平心而论 in all fairness;give sb his due
平心静气 calmly;dispassionately
平行联机 peer-to-peer network
平行作业 parallel operations;simultaneous operations
平抑物价 level out the price;stabilize commodity prices;lower the price (artificially or by force)
平易近人 amiable and easy of approach
平装开关 flush switch
平地一声雷 a sudden clap of thunder—a sudden rise in fame and position;an unexpected happy event
平行六面体 parallelepiped
平行四边形 parallelogram
平均期望寿命 average life expectancy
平时不烧香,急来抱佛脚 never burn incense when all is well but clasp Buddha's feet when in distress—do nothing until the last minute

评 [píng]
囵 ①make comments;comment;criticize;review ②judge;assess;appraise
评比 appraise through comparison;compare and assess
评标 evaluation of bid
评定 pass judgment on;evaluate;assess
评断 judge;arbitrate
评分 give a mark;mark (students' papers,etc.);score
评功 appraise sb's merits

P

评估 assess
评级 ①grade (cadres,workers,etc.) according to work ②grade (products) according to quality
评价 appraise;evaluate
评奖 decide on awards through discussion; give awards after panel discussion
评介 review (a new book,etc.)
评卷 mark examination papers
评理 ①judge between right and wrong;decide which side is right ② reason things out; have it out
评劣 inferiority evaluation (evaluation to find out who or which is the worst)
评论 ①comment on;discuss ②comment;commentary;review
评判 pass judgment on;judge
评聘 assess and appoint to a position
评审 examine and appraise
评书 storytelling (by a professional storyteller)
评述 commentary
评说 comment on;appraise;evaluate
评委 jury; the judging panel;evaluation committee; evaluation committee member; member of a review committee
评析 comment and analyse
评选 choose through public appraisal
评议 appraise sth through discussion;deliberate (a question) in a formal meeting
评优 appraise and select the most outstanding (or the highest) quality; select the best through appraisal
评语 comment;remark
评阅 read and appraise (sb's writing,etc.)
评注 ①make commentary and annotation ② notes and commentary
评传 critical biography
评论家 critic;reviewer
评论员 commentator
评判员 judge (in sports or speech contests, etc.); adjudicator (in musical contests, etc.)
评职称 grant a technical (or professional) title (e.g. professor,associate professor,assistant professor; senior researcher, research fellow,etc.)
评定职称 evaluation process for granting a professional title;evaluate the title of a technical or professional post
评功摆功 extol; enumerate sb's merits; speak of sb in glowing terms
评功摆好 enumerate sb's merits; speak of sb in glowing terms
评价报告 evaluation report
评头论足 ① make frivolous remarks about a woman's appearance ② find fault; be overcritical
评议考核制 system of assessment and examination

坪 [píng]
　〔名〕①level ground ②ping,unit of area (= 3.3 square metres)
坪坝 a level open space
坪长 plateau length
坪斜 plateau stope

苹 [píng]
苹果 apple (the tree and its fruit)
苹果脯 preserved apple
苹果干 dried apple slices
苹果机 Apple
苹果酱 apple jam
苹果酒 cider;applejack
苹果绿 apple green
苹果蜜 apple honey
苹果泥 apple butter
苹果肉 apple grunt
苹果树 apple (tree)
苹果油 apple oil
苹果园 apple orchard
苹果汁 cider
苹果沙司 applesauce
苹果去皮机 apple peeler

凭 [píng]
　Ⅰ〔动〕①lean on;lean against ②rely on;depend on ③ go by; base on; act according to; take as the basis Ⅱ〔名〕evidence;proof;guarantee Ⅲ〔连〕no matter (what,how,etc.)
凭单 a certificate for drawing money (or goods,etc.);voucher
凭吊 visit (a historical site,etc.) and ponder on the past
凭借 rely on;depend on
凭据 evidence;proof
凭靠 rely on;depend on
凭空 out of the void;out of thin air;without foundation;groundless
凭栏 lean on a railing
凭恃 rely on;depend on
凭眺 gaze from a high place into the distance; enjoy a distant view from a height
凭险 rely on natural barriers
凭信 trust;believe
凭依 base oneself on; rely on; have sth to go by
凭倚 lean on;lean against
凭仗 rely on;depend on
凭照 certificate;permit;licence
凭证 proof;evidence;certificate;voucher
凭常识 by common sense
凭经验 by rule of thumb
凭良心 in all conscience;to be fair
凭手艺 by one's craftsmanship

凭瞎猜 by guess and by golly
凭窗远眺 stand at a window gazing into the distance
凭单付款 pay cash on presentation of documents
凭单支票 voucher check
凭据报销 refund by invoices
凭空捏造 make out of nothing；fabricate
凭身份证 by identity card
凭证供应 voucher supply system
凭证式国库券 certificate treasury bond

枰 ［píng］
名 chessboard；checkerboard

屏 ［píng］
Ⅰ 名 ①screen ②set of scrolls Ⅱ 动 shield sb or sth；screen ➡ bǐng
屏蔽 ①screen；shield ②protective screen ③ screen
屏风 screen
屏极 plate
屏幕 screen
屏条 set of vertically hung scrolls（usu. four in a row of painting or calligraphy）；a set of wall scrolls
屏障 ①protective screen ②provide a protective screen for
屏蔽线 shielding line
屏蔽天线 screened antenna
屏幕保护程序 screen-saver；screen saver

瓶 ［píng］
名 bottle；jar；flask；vase
瓶胆 glass liner（of a thermos flask）
瓶盖 cap
瓶颈 bottleneck
瓶口 bottleneck
瓶塞 bottle stopper；bottle plug；cork
瓶装 bottled
瓶子 bottle；vase；jar；flask
瓶装水 bottled water
瓶颈制约 "bottleneck" restrictions

萍 ［píng］
名 duckweed
萍踪 tracks（or whereabouts）of a wanderer
萍水相逢 （of strangers）meet by chance like patches of drifting duckweed
萍踪浪迹 leaving no traces like duckweed and waves（said of persons who wander from place to place）

pō（ㄆㄛ）

钋 ［pō］
名 polonium（Po）

坡 ［pō］
Ⅰ 名 slope Ⅱ 形 sloping；slanting
坡岸 a sloping bank
坡道 ramp
坡地 hillside fields；sloping fields；land on the slopes
坡度 the degree of an incline；slope；gradient
坡跟 wedgies（of woman's shoe）

泊 ［pō］
名 lake ➡ bó

泼 ［pō］
Ⅰ 动 sprinkle；splash；spill Ⅱ 形 ① rude and unreasonable；shrewish ②daring and resolute；bold
泼妇 shrew；vixen；virago
泼剌 the sound made by fish jumping in the water；splash；splosh
泼辣 ① rude and unreasonable；shrewish ② pungent；forceful ③bold and vigorous；daring and resolute
泼墨 splash-ink，a technique of Chinese ink-painting
泼皮 ruffian；knave；gangster；blackguard
泼洒 spill；splash
泼野 tough，fierce and unreasonable
泼冷水 pour（or throw）cold water on；dampen the enthusiasm（or spirits）of
泼水节 the Water-Splashing（or Water-Sprinkling）Festival（of the Dais（傣族）and some other minority nationalities）

颇 ［pō］
Ⅰ 形 inclined to one side；oblique；partial Ⅱ 副 quite；rather；considerably
颇丰 good
颇佳 quite good
颇为 rather
颇为费解 rather difficult to understand

pó（ㄆㄛ）

婆 ［pó］
名 ①old woman ②woman in a certain occupation ③husband's mother；mother-in-law
婆家 husband's family
婆母 husband's mother；mother-in-law
婆娘 ①married woman ②wife
婆婆 ① husband's mother；mother-in-law ② Grandmother ③ authorities（or leaders）who control their subordinate units too strictly ④supervisory unit
婆娑 whirling；dancing
婆姨 ①young married woman ②wife
婆子 ① married woman ② wife ③a middle-aged（or oldish）woman servant
婆罗门 Brahman
婆罗门教 Brahmanism
婆婆妈妈 ①like an old woman；old-womanish ②sentimental；mawkish；maudlin
婆娑起舞 start dancing；begin to trip a measure

P

pǒ （ㄆㄛˇ）

叵 [pǒ]
副 ①impossibly ②at once；right away
叵测 unfathomable；unpredictable
叵耐 can not put up with；can not tolerate
叵欲讨之 plan to launch an immediate punitive expedition

钷 [pǒ]
名 promethium（Pm）

筪 [pǒ]

筪篮 basket
筪箩 a shallow basket made of wicker（*or* thin bamboo）strips

pò （ㄆㄛˋ）

朴 [pò]
名 Chinese hackberry ➡pǔ
朴硝 mirabilite；Glauber's salt

迫 [pò]
I 动 ①compel；force；drive；press ②approach；go towards（*or* near）Ⅱ 形 urgent；critical；pressing ➡pǎi
迫促 ①short；pressing ②urge；press；bring pressure on（sb to do sth）
迫害 persecute；persecution
迫降 [pòjiàng] forced landing；distress landing
迫近 approach；get close to；draw near
迫临 approach；get close to
迫令 force sb to（do sth）
迫切 urgent；pressing；imperative
迫使 force；compel
迫视 look at from close-up；watch intently
迫降 [pòxiáng] force sb to surrender
迫害狂 crazed persecutor
迫切性 urgency
迫不得已 have no alternative（but to）；be forced（*or* driven，compelled）to；（do sth）against one's will
迫不及待 unable to hold oneself back；too impatient to wait
迫于形势 under the pressure of events；under the stress of circumstances
迫在眉睫 ①extremely urgent ②imminent

珀 [pò]
◇琥珀 amber

破 [pò]
I 动 ①be broken；be damaged ②destroy；break；damage ③split；break；cleave；cut ④break a banknote into small change ⑤break；break with；get rid of；do away with ⑥defeat（enemy）；capture（a city，etc.）⑦spend；expend ⑧not spare；risk ⑨expose the truth of；lay bare；show up Ⅱ 形 ①broken；cracked；

torn；worn-out ②poor；wretched；lousy
破案 solve（*or* clear up）a case；crack a criminal case
破败 ruined；dilapidated；tumbledown
破财 suffer unexpected personal financial losses；lose money
破产 ①bankruptcy ②go bankrupt；go broke；become insolvent ③come to naught；fall through；be bankrupt
破除 do away with；get rid of；eradicate；break with
破费 spend money；go to some expense
破格 break a rule；make an exception
破坏 ①destroy；wreck ②do great damage to；disrupt；sabotage ③change（a social system，custom，etc.）completely（*or* violently）④violate（an agreement，regulation，etc.）；break ⑤decompose；destroy（the composition of a substance）
破货 loose woman
破获 unearth；uncover
破击 attack and destroy；wreck；sabotage
破解 analyse and explain
破戒 ①break a religious precept ②break one's vow of abstinence
破旧 old and shabby；worn-out；dilapidated
破口 ①a cut（on one's hand，etc.）；a break（in a hedge，etc.）；a breach（in a wall，etc.）；a tear（in one's clothes，etc.）②get a cut（*or* break，breach，tear，etc.）
破烂 ①tattered；ragged；worn-out ②junk；scrap
破浪 cleave the waves；brave the waves
破例 break a rule；make an exception
破脸 turn against（an acquaintance or associate）；fall out
破裂 burst；split；rupture；crack
破陋 run-down；dilapidated
破落 decline（in wealth and position）；fall into reduced circumstances；be reduced to poverty
破门 ①burst（*or* force）open the door ②excommunicate sb ③score a goal
破灭 be shattered；fall through；evaporate
破身 lose one's virginity；have one's first sexual intercourse
破水 （of a woman about to give birth）one's water breaks
破碎 ①tattered；broken ②smash（*or* break）sth to pieces；crush
破损 damaged；worn；torn
破涕 stop crying
破土 ①break ground（in starting a building project，etc.）②start spring ploughing ③（of a seedling）break through the soil
破碗 broken bowl
破网 score a goal

破相 (of facial features) be marred by a scar, etc.;disfigure
破晓 dawn;daybreak
破鞋 loose woman;promiscuous woman
破颜 break into a smile
破译 decode;decipher
破约 break one's promise
破绽 ①a burst seam ②flaw;weak point
破冰船 icebreaker
破产法 insolvency law; law of bankruptcy; bankruptcy law
破坏力 destructive power
破烂货 worthless stuff;rubbish;trash
破落户 a family that has gone down in the world
破碎机 crusher;breaker
破碎险 risk of breakage
破伤风 tetanus
破体字 a non-standard (or corrupted) form of a Chinese character
破天荒 occur for the first time; be unprecedented
破袭战 sabotage operations
破衣服 worn-out clothes
破折号 dash(—)
破产申请 bankruptcy petition
破除迷信 do away with superstitions (or bland faith);topple old idols
破釜沉舟 break the cauldrons and sink the boats (after crossing)—cut off all means of retreat;burn one's boats
破格提拔 skip-promote;unconventionally promote;break a rule to promote sb;make accelerated promotion to sb
破关斩将 break through numerous strategic passes and kill many defending generals—overcome a lot of difficulties and vanquish many opponents
破罐破摔 smash a pot to pieces just because it's cracked—write off one's situation as hopeless and act recklessly
破坏分子 saboteur
破坏试验 destructive test;breaking test
破镜重圆 a broken mirror joined together—reunion of husband and wife after an enforced separation or rupture
破旧立新 destroy the old and establish the new
破口大骂 shout abuse; let loose a torrent of abuse
破私立公 overcome selfishness and foster public spirit
破涕为笑 one's tears giving way to smiles
破土春耕 start spring ploughing
破土动工 break ground
破衣烂衫 ragged clothes;rags;tatters
破绽百出 full of flaws (or holes)

破竹之势 an irresistible force
破坏选举罪 crime of interfering with election
破世界记录 break the world record
破题儿第一遭 the first time one ever does sth;the first time ever
破迷信,树新风 do away with superstition and establish new customs

粕 [pò] 名 dregs of rice
粕酒 arrack

魄 [pò] 名 ①soul ②vigour;energy;spirit
魄力 daring and resolution;boldness

pōu（ㄆㄡ）

剖 [pōu] 动 ①cut open;rip open ②analyse;examine
剖白 explain oneself;vindicate oneself
剖解 analyse;dissect
剖露 lay bare;strip bare;reveal
剖面 section
剖明 analyse and make clear
剖尸 autopsy;post-mortem examination
剖析 analyse;dissect
剖心 open one's heart; lay bare one's true feelings;be completely open and sincere
剖腹产 caesarean birth
剖面图 sectional drawing;section
剖视图 cutaway view
剖腹藏珠 rip (or cut) open the stomach to hide a pearl—die for the sake of gain
剖腹自杀 (commit) hara-kiri

póu（ㄆㄡˊ）

抔 [póu] 量 (of what can be held in both hands):—抔黄土 a handful of earth
掊 [póu] 动 ①amass;extort ②dig;excavate ➡pǒu

pǒu（ㄆㄡˇ）

掊 [pǒu] 动 ①strike;hit ②split;cut;cleave ➡póu

pū（ㄆㄨ）

仆 [pū] 动 fall forward;fall prostrate ➡pú
扑 [pū] 动 ①throw oneself on;pounce on;dash at;attack ②throw oneself (heart and soul) into; devote oneself to ③pat;flap;plop ④bend over
扑鼻 assail the nostrils
扑哧 the sound of snorting (or fizzing)
扑打 [pūdǎ] swat
扑打 [pūda] pat;beat

扑跌 ①wrestling ②fall forward
扑冬 the sound of sth heavy dropping on the ground；thump；thud
扑粉 ①face powder ②talcum powder ③apply powder
扑击 ① pounce on；fall on；set on ② lap against；beat against
扑救 ①put out a fire to save life and property ②(in volleyball，football，etc.) diving save
扑克 ①playing cards ②poker
扑空 fail to get (*or* achieve) what one wants；fail to find a person where he is supposed to be；come away empty-handed
扑拉 ①flap；spread (wings) ②pat；slap；whisk ③(of tears，sweat，etc.) roll down；trickle down
扑棱 [pūlēng] the sound of flapping of wings
扑棱 [pūleng] flap
扑落 ①shake off；shake out of sth ②be scattered about
扑满 earthenware money box；piggy bank
扑面 blow on (*or* against) one's face
扑灭 ①stamp out；put out；extinguish ②exterminate；wipe out
扑球 dive for the ball
扑杀 beat to death；kill
扑闪 ①blink ②flap；flutter
扑簌 (of tears) trickling down
扑腾 [pūtēng] the sound of a heavy fall；flop；thump；thud
扑腾 [pūteng] ① move one's legs up and down in the water；flop ② throb；palpitate ③ hustle；bustle；keep the ball rolling ④ spend freely；squander
扑通 the sound of sth heavy dropping into the water or to the ground；flop；thump；splash；pit-a-pat
扑翼 flapping wing
扑蝇 swat flies
扑尔敏 chlorpheniramine
扑朔迷离 bewildering；confusing

铺 [pū]
I 动 spread；lay；pave Ⅱ 量 of *kang*：一铺炕 a *kang* ➡ pù
铺衬 small pieces of cloth used for patches
铺床 make the bed
铺垫 ①bedding ②foreshadowing
铺盖 [pūgài] spread (evenly) over
铺盖 [pūgai] bedding；bedclothes
铺轨 lay a railway track
铺炕 spread out the bedclothes on the *kang*；prepare the *kang* for sleep
铺面 pavement；facing
铺排 ①put in order；arrange ②be extravagant
铺平 ① smooth out；spread sth out smoothly ②make the ground，etc. level (*or* even)；level

铺砌 pave
铺设 lay；build
铺叙 narrate in detail；elaborate
铺展 spread out；sprawl
铺张 ①extravagant ②exaggeration
铺植 sod；turf；plant
铺被褥 spread a quilt
铺草皮 turf；lay turf (*or* sod)
铺地砖 ①floor tile；paving tile ②tile the floor
铺管道 lay pipes
铺路机 paver
铺底资金 minimum capital；start-up fund；seed money
铺盖卷儿 bedding roll；bedroll；luggage roll
铺平道路 pave the way (for sth)
铺天盖地 blot out the sky and cover up the earth
铺新摊子 launch new projects；undertake new projects
铺张浪费 extravagance and waste；be extravagant and wasteful
铺张扬厉 ①praise extravagantly ②indulge in extravagance and ostentation
铺底流动资金 start-up capital

噗 [pū]
象 puff：她噗的一声把桌上的蜡烛吹灭了。With one puff，she blew out the candle on the table.

潽 [pū]
动 (as of water) boil over

pú (ㄆㄨˊ)

仆 [pú]
I 名 servant Ⅱ 谦 your humble servant ➡ pū
仆从 footman；retainer；henchman
仆妇 elderly woman servant
仆人 (domestic) servant
仆役 (domestic) servants
仆从国 vassal country

匍 [pú]
匍匐 ①crawl；creep ②(of plants) grow along the ground；creep；trail
匍匐茎 stolon
匍匐植物 creeper

菩 [pú]
菩萨 ①Bodhisattva ②Buddha；deity；god ③a term applied to a kindhearted person
菩提 bodhi，supreme wisdom or enlightenment，necessary to the attainment of Buddhahood
菩提树 pipal；bo tree；bodhi tree
菩萨心肠 the heart of a Bodhisattva—the bowels of compassion (*or* pity)；the bowels of mercy；kindheartedness；mercifulness

脯 [pú]
[名] chest；breast ➡fǔ

葡 [pú]
葡萄 grape
葡萄弹 grapeshot；grape
葡萄干 raisin
葡萄酒 grape wine；wine
葡萄胎 hydatidiform mole；vesicular mole
葡萄糖 glucose；grape sugar；dextrose
葡萄园 vineyard；grapery；vinery
葡萄汁 grape juice
葡萄球菌 staphylococcus

蒲 [pú]
[名] cattail；reed mace；club grass
蒲棒 the spike of cattail
蒲包 cattail bag；rush bag
蒲草 ①the stem (or leaf) of cattail (or reed mace，club grass) ②dwarf lilyturf
蒲黄 cattail pollen
蒲葵 Chinese fan palm
蒲柳 big catkin willow
蒲绒 cattail wool，used for stuffing pillows
蒲扇 Chinese fan；palm fan
蒲桃 rose apple
蒲团 cattail hassock used for kneeling；rush hassock
蒲苇 pampas grass
蒲席 cattail mat；rush mat
蒲公英 dandelion
蒲式耳 bushel (= 8 gallons)
蒲柳之姿 feel like a willow withering at the approach or autumn—suffer from poor health

pǔ（ㄆㄨ）

朴 [pǔ]
[形] simple；plain；honest ➡pò
朴厚 simple and honest
朴实 ① simple；plain ② sincere and honest；guileless
朴素 ①(of colour，style，language，etc.) simple；plain ②(of one's living) frugal；thrifty；plain and modest ③naive；undeveloped
朴直 honest and straightforward
朴质 simple and unadorned；natural
朴实无华 simple and unadorned
朴素唯物主义 naive materialism

圃 [pǔ]
[名] plot of land for growing plants；garden

浦 [pǔ]
[名] water's edge；river mouth

普 [pǔ]
[形] general；common；universal
普遍 universal；general；widespread；common
普查 ①general investigation (or survey) ②reconnaissance survey

普度 deliver all from torment
普法 popularize knowledge of national laws；law popularization；law dissemination
普及 ①be universalized in；be made popular among；be extensively spread ②popularize；disseminate；spread among the people
普降 (of rain or snow) fall over a large area
普教 general education
普调 make general readjustment (of price，wage，etc.)
普通 ordinary；common；average
普选 general election
普照 illuminate all things
普遍性 universality
普惠制 generalized system of preference (GSP)
普及本 popular edition
普通法 common law
普通股 ordinaries；ordinary share；common stock
普通话 *putonghua*；Mandarin Chinese；common speech (of the Chinese language)；standard Chinese pronunciation
普选权 universal suffrage
普选制 universal suffrage；general election system
普遍服务 universal service
普遍规律 universal law
普遍现象 commonplace phenomenon
普遍真理 universal truth
普度众生 deliver all living creatures from torment
普法教育 education of the populace about the law
普及教育 universal education
普及科学 popularize science
普天同庆 The whole world (or nation) joins in the jubilation；universal jubilation
普天之下 everywhere under the sun；all under heaven；all over the world；in every part of the world；in this wide world
普调工资 make general (or blanket) readjustment of wages
普通税则 general tariff
普通用户 domestic consumer
普通邮件 snail mail
普通照会 diplomacy verbal note
普遍优惠制 generalized system of preferences (GSP)；general preferential scheme
普通心理学 general psychology
普及义务教育 promote compulsory education
普通高级中学 regular senior middle school (different from a key senior middle school)

溥 [pǔ]
[形] ①broad；wide；vast ②common；universal
溥原 vast plains

溥天同庆 The whole world (*or* nation) joins in the jubilation;universal jubilation

谱 [pǔ]
Ⅰ 〔名〕 ① chronology;record;register ② manual;guide ③ music score;music ④ sth to count on;fair amount of confidence ⑤ airs Ⅱ 〔动〕 set to music;compose
谱斑 flocculus
谱表 stave;staff
谱号 clef
谱架 music stand
谱曲 set (words) to music;compose music for
谱术 spectrometry
谱系 pedigree
谱写 compose (music)
谱制 compose
谱子 music score;music

镨 [pǔ]
〔名〕 praseodymium (Pr)

蹼 [pǔ]
〔名〕 web (of the feet of ducks,frogs,etc.)
蹼趾 webbed toe
蹼足 webfoot;palmate foot

pù（ㄆㄨˋ）

铺 [pù]
〔名〕 ① shop;store ② plank bed ③ post (where couriers changed horses or rested);courier station ➡ pū
铺板 bed board;bed plank
铺保 guarantee for a person,given by a shop-keeper
铺底 shop fixtures
铺户 shop;store
铺面 shop front
铺位 bunk;berth
铺子 shop;store
铺面房 shop building

瀑 [pù]
〔名〕 waterfall
瀑布 waterfall;falls;cataract

曝 [pù]
〔动〕 expose to the sun ➡ bào
曝露 expose to the open air
曝晒 expose to the sun
曝气池 aeration tank

P

 Q q

qī（ㄑ丨）

七 [qī] 囝 ①seven ②seventh-day mourning period
七绝 seven syllable quatrain
七律 seven syllable regulated verse
七窍 the seven apertures in the human head (i.e. eyes, ears, nostrils and mouth)
七情 ① the seven human emotions（namely, joy, anger, sorrow, fear, love, hate and desire) ②the seven emotional factors
七夕 the seventh evening of the seventh month (when the Herd-boy and the Weaving-girl are supposed to meet)
七月 ①July ②the seventh month of the lunar year; the seventh moon
七边形 heptagon
七级风 force 7 wind; moderate gale
七级管 heptode
七巧板 seven-piece puzzle; tangram
七鳃鳗 lamprey
七色板 spectrum board
七叶树 Chinese Horsechestnut
七政仪 orrery
七步之才 seven-pace talent—literary talent in ready play
七长八短 be of uneven size
七颠八倒 at sixes and sevens; all upside down; topsy-turvy
七级浮屠 pagoda of seven stories
七零八落 scattered here and there; in disorder
七老八十 late seventies and early eighties—a very old person
七扭八歪 irregular; in a state of great disorder
七拼八凑 throw together; piece together; knock together; rig up
七七八八 mixed; assorted; miscellaneous
七窍生烟 fume with anger; foam with rage; be outraged
七情六欲 the seven emotions and six sensory pleasures
七上八下 seven buckets coming up and eight buckets going down—be agitated; be perturbed
七十二变 seventy-two transformations（or metamorphoses）—countless changes of tactics
七十二行 all sorts of occupations; every conceivable line of work
七手八脚 with everyone lending a hand
七折八扣 (with) various deductions（or cuts）
七嘴八舌 seven mouths and eight tongues—with everybody trying to get a word in; all talking at once
七十七国集团 Group of 77; G77

沏 [qī] 囫 infuse

妻 [qī] 囝 wife ⇒ qì
妻弟 wife's younger brother; brother-in-law
妻舅 wife's brother; brother-in-law
妻室 wife
妻小 wife and children
妻子 [qīzǐ] wife and children
妻子 [qīzi] wife
妻管严 henpecked; be tied to one's wife's apron strings
妻儿老小 parents, wife and children—a married man's entire family
妻离子散 breaking up（or scattering) of one's family

栖 [qī] 囫 ①（of birds) perch; rest ②dwell; live; stay
栖木 roost; perch
栖身 stay; sojourn
栖息 (of birds) perch; rest
栖息地 habitat

桤 [qī] 囝 alder

凄 [qī] 囮 ①chilly; freezing; cold ②bleak and desolate; dreary ③sad; wretched; dejected; melancholy
凄惨 wretched; miserable; tragic
凄恻 grieved; sad; sorrowful

凄楚 wretched;miserable
凄厉 sad and shrill
凄凉 dreary;desolate;miserable
凄迷 ①desolate and indistinct ②sad;distracted
凄切 plaintive;mournful
凄清 ①slightly cold;cool ②dreary;plaintive
凄然 sad;mournful
凄酸 grieved;distressed;sorrowful
凄婉 (of sound) plaintive but lovely;sadly moving
凄怨 sad;plaintive
凄风苦雨 ①wailing wind and weeping rain ②wretched circumstances;distress

萋 [qī]

萋萋 luxuriant;lush

戚 [qī]
〔名〕①relative;kin ②sorrow;grief ③a kind of ancient weapon,like an axe
戚属 kinsfolk;relatives
戚友 friends and relatives

期 [qī]
Ⅰ〔名〕①scheduled time;appointed day (or date) ② period of time;term;stage;phase Ⅱ〔副〕 referring to things done periodically Ⅲ〔动〕① appoint (a time);schedule ②await (sb by appointment);expect;anticipate;hope ➡ jī
期初 the beginning of the period
期待 expect;await;look forward to
期房 forward delivery housing
期股 option share
期汇 forward exchange
期货 futures
期冀 ardently hope (or expect)
期价 futures' price
期间 time;period;course
期刊 periodical
期考 end-of-term examination;final (or terminal) examination
期满 expire;run out;come to an end
期末 end of term;terminal
期盼 expect;await;look forward to
期票 promissory note;term bill
期求 hope to get (or obtain)
期权 option
期市 forward market
期望 ①ardently hope (or expect) ②expectation
期限 allotted time;time limit;deadline
期许 ardently hope (or expect)
期颐 a 100-year-old person;centenarian
期望值 expectations
期货交易 futures;futures transaction
期货市场 futures market;forward market;option market;terminal market

期期艾艾 stammer;stutter
期终考试 final examination;terminal examination

欺 [qī]
〔动〕① cheat;dupe;deceive ② bully;intimidate;take advantage of
欺负 ①bully;treat sb high-handedly;take advantage of sb ② take advantage of (sb's weakness,etc.)
欺凌 bully and humiliate
欺瞒 hoodwink;dupe;pull the wool over sb's eyes
欺蒙 deceive;cheat;dupe;defraud
欺弄 dupe;hoodwink
欺骗 deceive;cheat;dupe
欺辱 bully and humiliate;insult
欺生 ①bully (or cheat) strangers ②(of horses,mules,etc.) be ungovernable by strangers
欺侮 bully and humiliate;treat sb high-handedly
欺压 bully and oppress;ride roughshod over
欺诈 cheat;swindle
欺行霸市 bully fellow traders and dominate the market;bully others in the same trade and monopolize the market;monopolize the market by bullying and cheating others
欺瞒夹账 engage in fraud;falsify accounts;practise graft
欺人太甚 what a beastly bully;that's going too far;push people too hard
欺人之谈 deceitful words;deceptive talk
欺软怕硬 bully the weak and fear the strong
欺上瞒下 deceive one's superiors and delude (or dupe) one's subordinates
欺世盗名 gain fame by deceiving the public;fish for undeserved fame

缉 [qī]
〔动〕hem clothing,etc. in close and joint stitches ➡ jī

喊 [qī]

喊哩喀喳 quick and efficient;snappy and clear-cut
喊喊喳喳 the sound of chatter

漆 [qī]
Ⅰ〔名〕lacquer;paint Ⅱ〔动〕paint;cover with paint
漆布 varnished cloth
漆革 patent leather
漆工 ① lacquering;painting ②lacquerer;lacquer man;painter
漆黑 pitch-dark;pitch-black
漆画 lacquer painting
漆匠 ①lacquerware worker ②lacquerer;lacquer man;painter
漆皮 ①coat of paint ②shellac

漆片 a coating agent which has to be dissolved in alcohol before use
漆器 lacquerware;lacquerwork
漆树 lacquer tree;varnish tree
漆包线 enamel-insulated wire
漆黑一团 ①pitch-dark—utterly hopeless ②be entirely ignorant of;be in the dark

蹊 [qī]
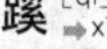 ➡ xī
蹊跷 odd;strange;fishy

qí (ㄑㄧˊ)

齐 [qí]
Ⅰ 形 ①neat;even;in order ②equal;identical Ⅱ 动 reach the same level;be of the same level Ⅲ 形 even out;cut close to Ⅳ 副 ①together;in unison ②all ready;in order ➡ jì
齐备 complete;all ready
齐唱 singing in unison;unison
齐楚 neat and smart
齐集 assemble;gather;collect
齐名 enjoy equal popularity;be equally famous
齐明 aplanatic
齐巧 by chance;fortunately;as chance would have it
齐全 complete;having everything that one expects to find;all in readiness
齐射 salvo;volley
齐声 in chorus;in unison
齐心 be of one mind (or heart)
齐整 neat;uniform
齐奏 playing (instruments) in unison;unison
齐步走 quick march
齐齿呼 a class of syllables with i as the final (韵母) or a final beginning with i
齐明点 aplanatic foci
齐明镜 aplanat
齐刷刷 even;uniform
齐东野语 what folks say;popular report;unreliable words
齐家治国 regulate the family and rule the state
齐明成像 aplanatic image formation
齐头并进 advance side by side;do two or more things at once
齐心协力 work as one;take concerted action;shoulder to shoulder

圻 [qí]
名 boundary

芪 [qí]
◇黄芪 the root of membranous milk vetch

岐 [qí]
岐黄 Chinese medicine
岐黄之术 Chinese traditional medical science

其 [qí]
Ⅰ 代 ①his;her;its;their ②he;she;it;they ③ that;such ④ (used as a functional word):大上其当 walk straight into the trap;play into sb's hands Ⅱ 助 ①(expressing conjecture or retort) ②(expressing an order or instruction)
其次 ①next;secondly;then ②secondary
其后 later;after;afterwards
其间 ①between (or among) them;of them;in it ②during this (or that) time
其实 actually;in fact;as a matter of fact
其他 other;else
其余 all the other (persons or things);the rest;the remainder
其中 among them;of them;in it
其乐融融 with happiness knowing no bounds;very cheerful
其乐无穷 find it a delight (or joy)
其貌不扬 be unprepossessing (or unimposing) in appearance;be of undistinguished appearance
其味无穷 have a marvellous flavour;be infinitely enjoyable

奇 [qí]
Ⅰ 形 ①strange;unusual;extraordinary ②unexpected;surprising Ⅱ 动 surprise;wonder;astonish Ⅲ 副 very;singularly ➡ jī
奇兵 an army suddenly appearing from nowhere;an ingenious military move
奇才 a rare talent;genius
奇功 outstanding service
奇怪 ①strange;surprising;odd ②feel surprised;wonder
奇观 marvellous spectacle;wonder
奇幻 fantastic;visionary
奇迹 miracle;wonder;marvel
奇景 wonderful view;extraordinary sight
奇妙 marvellous;wonderful;intriguing
奇谋 a very clever strategy;an ingenious plan
奇葩 exotic flowers
奇巧 ingenious;exquisite
奇缺 in great shortage
奇人 ①an eccentric person;eccentric ②a person of unusual ability
奇事 a strange affair;an unusual phenomenon
奇书 a remarkable book
奇谈 a strange tale;an absurd argument
奇特 peculiar;queer;singular
奇文 ①a remarkable piece of writing ②absurd writing
奇闻 sth unheard-of;a thrilling,fantastic story
奇袭 surprise attack;raid
奇效 extraordinary efficacy (of medicine)
奇痒 awfully itchy
奇异 ①unusual;strange;bizarre ②surprised;amazed;astonished;astounded

Q

奇遇 ①happy encounter；fortuitous meeting ②adventure

奇缘 relationship entered into unexpectedly；romance

奇珍 rarity；curio

奇志 high aspirations；lofty ideal

奇耻大辱 burning shame；burning disgrace；deep disgrace；crying shame

奇花异草 exotic flowers and rare herbs；exotic flowers and strange grasses

奇货可居 a rare commodity worth hoarding

奇谈怪论 a strange tale；an absurd argument

奇文共赏 share the pleasure of reading a rare piece of writing

奇形怪状 grotesque (*or* fantastic) in shape (*or* appearance)

奇珍异宝 rare treasures

奇装异服 exotic costume；bizarre dress；outlandish (grotesque) clothes；strange fashions；fancy clothes

歧 [qí] Ⅰ 名 fork；branch Ⅱ 形 divergent；varied；different

歧管 manifold

歧见 difference；divergent opinions；disagreement

歧路 branch road；forked road

歧视 discriminate against

歧途 wrong road

歧义 being capable of various interpretations；ambiguity

歧路亡羊 a lamb going astray at a fork in the road—go astray in a complex situation

祈 [qí] 动 ①pray ②request；entreat

祈祷 pray；say one's prayers

祈福 pray for a good fortune

祈年 pray for a good harvest

祈盼 ①look forward to；expect ②wish；expectation

祈求 earnestly hope；pray for

祈望 hope；wish

祈雨 pray for rain

祈使句 imperative sentence

衹 [qí] 名 god of the earth

荠 [qí] ⇒ jì

◇荸荠 water chestnut

脐 [qí] 名 ①navel；umbilicus ②abdomen of a crab

脐带 umbilical cord

脐风 umbilical tetanus

埼 [qí] 名 meandering coast (*or* bank)

萁 [qí] 名 stalk

畦 [qí] 量 rectangular pieces of land in a field surrounded by ridges：两畦白菜 two beds growing cabbages

畦灌 border method of irrigation

畦田 an embanked field

跂 [qí] 名 ①extra toe ②(of insects) crawl ⇒ qǐ

崎 [qí] 形 sloping；uneven；rugged

崎径 rugged path

崎岖 rugged

骐 [qí] 名 black horse

骑 [qí] Ⅰ 动 ①ride；sit (on a horse，etc.) ②straddle Ⅱ 名 ①horse or other animal one rides ②cavalryman；cavalry；horseman；rider

骑兵 cavalryman；cavalry

骑缝 a junction of the edges of two sheets of paper

骑警 horseback police

骑墙 sit on the fence

骑射 horsemanship and archery

骑士 knight；cavalier

骑手 rider；horseman

骑术 horsemanship；equestrian skill

骑马订 saddle stitching

骑兵部队 mounted troops；cavalry unit

骑虎难下 he who rides a tiger is afraid to dismount—irrevocably but unwillingly committed；unable to extricate oneself from a difficult situation

骑虎之势 a case of one riding a tiger—an awkward predicament that one can neither manage nor get rid of

骑马找马 ①sit on one horse and look for another—hold on to one job while seeking another ②sit on the very horse one is looking for—look for sth that's right under one's nose

骑士风度 knightly manner

琪 [qí] 名 fine jade

琪树 jade tree

琪花瑶草 jade flowers of a fairy land

琦 [qí] Ⅰ 名 fine jade Ⅱ 形 out of the ordinary run；uncommon

琦行 fine virtues；noble character

棋 [qí] 名 ①chess；board game ②piece；chessman

棋布 scattered all over like men on a chessboard；spread all over the place

棋锋 brilliance shown in playing chess

棋局 ①a game of chess as it develops ②chessboard

棋路 chess tactics

棋迷 chess fan;chess enthusiast
棋盘 chessboard;checkerboard
棋谱 chess manual
棋圣 champion chess player;grand master
棋手 chess player
棋坛 chess circles
棋艺 skill in playing chess
棋友 fellow chess player;chess friend
棋苑 chess circles
棋峙 be locked in a stalemate;each sticks to his own stand
棋子 piece (in a board game);chessman
棋逢对手 meet one's match in a game of chess—be well-matched in a contest
棋高一着 be superior to one's opponent (in chess or otherwise);outmatch one's opponent

蛴 ［qí］
蛴螬 grub

祺 ［qí］
名 good luck;blessing

綦 ［qí］
副 very;exceedingly;extremely

蟛 ［qí］
◇蟛蜞 amphibious crab;brackish-water crab

旗 ［qí］
名 ① flag;banner;pennant;standard ② "Eight Banners"（八旗）,military-administrative organizations of the Manchu nationality before and during the Qing Dynasty ③ of the "Eight Banners",esp. of the Manchu nationality ④ name of place where the troops of the "Eight Banners" ⑤ banner,an administrative division of county level in the Inner Mongolia Autonomous Region
旗杆 flagpole;flag post
旗号 banner;flag
旗舰 flagship
旗袍 a close-fitting woman's dress with high neck and slit skirt;cheongsam;mandarin gown
旗绳 halyard
旗手 standard-bearer
旗鱼 sailfish
旗语 semaphore;flag signal
旗帜 ①banner;flag ②stand;colours
旗子 flag;banner;pennant
旗鼓相当 be evenly matched in strength
旗开得胜 win victory the moment one's standard is raised;win victory in the first battle;win speedy success
旗帜鲜明 take (or have) a clear-cut stand

鳍 ［qí］
名 fin
鳍脚 clasper
鳍脚动物 Pinnipedia;pinniped

麒 ［qí］
名 kylin;(Chinese) unicorn
麒麟 kylin;(Chinese) unicorn
麒麟座 Monoceros

qǐ（ㄑ丨）

乞 ［qǐ］
动 beg (for alms,etc.);seek charity;supplicate
乞丐 beggar
乞怜 beg for pity (or mercy)
乞灵 resort to;seek help from
乞盟 sue for peace
乞免 beg for forgiveness
乞求 beg for;supplicate;implore
乞食 beg for food
乞恕 beg sb's pardon;ask sb for forgiveness
乞讨 beg;go begging
乞降 beg to surrender
乞援 ask for assistance;beg for aid
乞哀告怜 beg for mercy;piteously beg for help

屺 ［qǐ］
名 barren hill

岂 ［qǐ］
副 (used to introduce a rhetorical question):孩子落水,岂能见死不救? How could we stand by with folded arms when a child is drowning?
岂但 not only
岂非 (used to ask a rhetorical question)
岂敢 You flatter me;I don't deserve such praise (or honour).
岂能 (used to ask a rhetorical question)
岂止 not only
岂有此理 preposterous;outrageous;absurd

企 ［qǐ］
动 stand on tiptoe;look forward to;expect
企待 expect;await;look forward to
企鹅 penguin
企划 make an overall plan;plan
企及 hope to reach;hope to attain
企口 tongue-and-groove
企慕 admire;look up to
企盼 hope for;look forward to;long for
企求 desire to gain;seek for;hanker after
企图 attempt;try;seek
企望 hope for;look forward to
企羡 admire;look up to
企业 enterprise;business
企口板 matched board
企业化 run an enterprise on a commercial basis
企业家 entrepreneur;big businessman
企业标志 logo
企业重组 re-engineering of enterprises
企业倒闭 business failure
企业法规 business law and regulation

企业法人 legal entity
企业改组 reorganization(association, merger, leasing, contract operation, sell-off) of enterprises
企业管理 business management
企业集团 enterprise group
企业兼并 enterprise mergence; enterprise amalgamation
企业结构 the line-up of enterprises
企业精神 entrepreneurship; enterprise spirit
企业亏损 loss incurred in an enterprise; loss of an enterprise
企业实体 enterprise entity
企业文化 enterprise culture
企业形象 corporate image(CI); enterprise image
企业转产 conversion to the production of other goods
企足而待 wait on tiptoe—expect sth to happen soon
企事业单位 enterprises and institutions
企业孵化器 enterprise incubator
企业破产制 system of enterprise bankruptcy
企业所得税 enterprise income tax
企业自主权 decision-making power of enterprises; right of autonomy for enterprises
企业变更登记 enterprise alteration registration
企业规章制度 rules and regulations in enterprise
企业技术改造 updating of enterprise
企业技术进步 technological progress of enterprise
企业经营机制 managerial mechanism of enterprise
企业领导体制 system of leadership in enterprises
企业所得税制 income-tax system of enterprises
企业股份制改革 reform aimed at establishing a joint stock system in enterprises
企业自我约束机制 self-regulating mechanism of enterprises
企业自有流动资金 working capital of enterprises
企业组织管理制度 system of organization and management in enterprises
企业承包经营责任制 contract managerial responsibility system for enterprises; enterprise contracted production responsibility system; enterprise-related system of contracted managerial responsibilities

杞 [qǐ]

杞柳 purple willow; bitter willow
杞人忧天 like the man of Qi who feared that the sky might fall—entertain imaginary or groundless fears

启 [qǐ]

I 动 ①open ②enlighten; inspire; awaken ③start; begin; initiate ④state; declare; inform
II 名 letter; note

启程 set out; start on a journey
启齿 open one's mouth; start to talk about sth
启迪 enlighten; inspire
启碇 weigh anchor
启动 ①start (a machine, etc.); switch on ② boot up
启发 arouse; inspire; enlighten
启封 ①unseal; break (or remove) the seal ② open an envelop (or wrapper)
启航 set sail; weigh anchor
启蒙 ①impart rudimentary knowledge to beginners; initiate ②enlighten; free sb from prejudice or superstition
启示 enlightenment; inspiration; revelation
启事 notice; announcement
启衅 start a quarrel; provoke discord; provoke dispute
启行 set off on a journey
启颜 (of a person's face) light up; smile; beam
启用 start using (an official seal, etc.)
启运 start shipment (of goods)
启动区 boot sector
启发式 elicitation method (of teaching); heuristic method
启明星 Venus
启运港 port of departure
启动资金 starting capital; start-up money; seed money; initial fund (or investment) for starting a project
启蒙运动 the Enlightenment
启发式教学 heuristic teaching

起 [qǐ]

I 动 ① get up; rise; arise; stand up ② move; leave ③rise; go up ④get; appear ⑤remove; draw; extract; pull ⑥ crop up; rise; grow ⑦initiate; launch ⑧ draft; make; work out ⑨set up; put up; build ⑩obtain; secure; buy ⑪start; begin ⑫(*used after verbs to indicate the beginning or starting point*): 从头做起 start from the very beginning; start all over again from the beginning ⑬(*used before nouns of time and place to indicate the point of departure*): 您起哪儿来? Where did you come from? ⑭(*used before nouns of place to indicate movement*): 我看见一个人起窗户外走过去。 I saw a man passing by the window. ⑮(*used after verbs to indicate upward movement*): 抬起头来 raise one's head/鸟儿飞起又落下。 The bird took to its wings and then alighted. ⑯ (*used after verbs and often preceded by 不 or 得 to indicate whether it is within or beyond one's power to do sth*)：惹不起 cannot afford to offend sb /经得起考验 be able to stand the test ⑰（*used after verbs to indicate sth happening right after the action*）：点起篝火 light a bonfire/奏起国歌 play the national anthem ⑱（*used after verbs to indicate the person or thing involved in the action*）：他提起了这件事。He mentioned the event. Ⅱ 〔名〕①case；instance；前天发生一起火灾。A fire broke out the day before yesterday. ②batch；group；party：他们分三起上车。They boarded the train in three batches.

起岸 bring (cargo,etc. from a ship) to land

起爆 detonate

起笔 ①the first stroke of a Chinese character ②start a stroke in writing a Chinese character

起兵 dispatch troops

起驳 start shipment by lighter

起步 be in the initial stage；start；move

起草 make a draft；draft；draw up

起程 leave；set out；start on a journey

起初 originally；at first；at the outset

起床 get up；get out of bed

起点 ①starting point ②starting point (for a race)

起电 electrification；charge

起吊 lift by crane

起动 (of a train,machine,etc.) start

起端 origin；beginning (of an event,etc.)

起飞 ①(of aircraft) take off ②takeoff

起伏 rise and fall；undulate

起稿 make a draft；draft；draw up

起航 set sail；weigh anchor

起哄 ①(of a crowd of people) create a disturbance ②(of a crowd of people) jeer；boo and hoot；tease clamorously

起火 ①catch fire；be on fire ②cook meals

起伙 set up a mess

起货 take goods (from a warehouse)；unload (from a ship,etc.)

起获 track down and recover stolen goods，etc.

起急 get impatient；lose one's patience

起家 build up；grow and thrive；make one's fortune，name，etc.

起见 for the purpose of；in order to

起降 (of aircraft) take off and land

起劲 vigorous；energetic；enthusiastic

起敬 show respect

起居 daily life

起开 step aside；stand aside

起课 practise divination

起来 ①stand up；sit up；rise to one's feet ②get up；get out of bed ③rise；arise；revolt ④upwards；up ⑤start to；become ⑥(indicating completeness or effectiveness) ⑦

when one comes to ⑧（*forming a verbal topic*）

起立 stand up；rise to one's feet

起灵 move sb's coffin（*or* ashes）to the graveyard

起垄 ridge

起落 rise and fall

起码 ①minimum；rudimentary；elementary ②at least

起毛 (of woollen cloth) pill

起锚 weigh anchor；set sail

起名 give a name；name

起腻 ①feel sick ②pester；annoy

起拍 open the auction

起跑 start of a race

起泡 ①blister；bubble ②foam；bead

起讫 the beginning and the end

起圈 remove manure from a pigsty，sheepfold，etc.

起色 improvement；pickup

起身 ①get up；get out of bed ②leave；set out；get off

起始 ①originate；stem from ②at first；in the beginning

起事 start armed struggle；rise in rebellion

起誓 take an oath；swear

起首 at first；in the beginning；originally

起诉 prosecute；bring a suit against；bring an action against

起算 reckon from (a stated point)

起跳 take off

起头 ①start；originate ②at first；in the beginning ③beginning

起网 (net) hauling

起息 carry interest

起席 rise from the table

起先 at first；in the beginning

起心 cherish certain intentions

起薪 probationary salary

起行 leave；set out；start on a journey

起眼 attract attention

起夜 get up in the night (to urinate)

起疑 become suspicious

起义 rise in revolt；revolt

起意 conceive a design

起因 cause；origin

起用 ①reinstate (an official who has retired or been dismissed) ②call sb to office；appoint sb to an important position

起源 ①originate；stem from ②origin

起运 start shipment

起赃 track down and recover stolen goods

起止 start-stop

起皱 wrinkle；crease；crumple

起子 ① bottle opener ② baking powder ③ screwdriver

起搏器 pacemaker

Q

起步价 starting (*or* minimum) fare (of a taxi)

起床号 reveille

起道机 track jack

起钉钳 nail puller

起动机 starter

起居室 living room;sitting room

起落架 landing gear (of a plane); undercarriage

起跑线 starting point; jumping-off place; scratch line (for a relay race)

起诉人 suitor;prosecutor

起诉书 indictment; bill of complaint; bill of prosecution;statement of claim

起义军 insurrectionary army

起征点 starting point for taxation

起重车 derrick car

起重船 crane ship

起重机 hoist;crane;derrick

起步不公 unfair start

起承转合 introduction, elucidation of the theme,transition to another viewpoint,and summing up—the four steps in composing an essay

起点运费 minimum freight;minimum charge per bill of lading

起立表决 vote by sitting and standing

起死回生 (of a doctor's skill) bring the dying back to life;snatch a patient from the jaws of death;raise sb from the dead

起诉资格 standing to sue

起早贪黑 start work early and knock off late; work from dawn to dusk

起草委员会 drafting committee

起诉意见书 opinion recommending prosecution

绮 [qǐ]
Ⅰ 〈名〉 figured woven silk material;damask
Ⅱ 〈形〉 beautiful;exquisite

绮丽 beautiful;gorgeous

绮罗 figured woven silk material

绮札 letter written in flowery language (*or* ornate style)

绮年玉貌 pretty young girl;young and beautiful

qì〈气〉

气 [qì]
Ⅰ 〈名〉①gas ②air ③breath ④weather ⑤smell;odour ⑥mental state;spirit;morale ⑦momentum;drive;daring ⑧airs;manners ⑨*qi* or vital energy;life force ⑩certain symptoms Ⅱ 〈动〉①anger;rage ②enrage;make angry;provoke ③insult;ridicule;bully

气泵 air pump

气藏 gas pool

气喘 asthma

气窗 transom (window);fanlight

气锤 air-hammer;pneumatic hammer

气粗 ①rough;rude;boorish ②speak in a gruff voice

气促 gasp for breath;be out of breath

气灯 gas lamp

气笛 air whistle

气垫 air cushion

气顶 petroleum gas cap

气动 pneumatic

气度 ①bearing;manner ②tolerance;magnanimity

气短 ①short of breath;panting ②discouraged;disheartened

气氛 surrounding feeling;atmosphere

气愤 indignant;furious

气腹 pneumoperitoneum

气概 lofty quality;mettle;spirit

气缸 air cylinder;cylinder

气割 gas cutting

气功 *qigong*,a system of deep breathing exercises

气臌 distension of the abdomen caused by accumulation of gas due to dysfunction of the spleen (*or* to emotional factors)

气管 windpipe;trachea

气锅 steamer

气焊 gas welding

气候 ①climate ②situation;climate

气化 gasify

气话 words said in a fit of rage

气急 gasp for breath;be out of breath

气节 integrity;moral courage

气结 depressed;melancholy;gloomy

气井 gas well

气绝 stop breathing—die

气厥 faint away;lose consciousness

气孔 ①stoma ②spiracle ③gas hole ④air hole

气浪 blast (of an explosion)

气冷 air cooling

气力 effort;energy;strength

气量 tolerance;forbearance

气流 ①air current; airflow; airstream ②breath

气楼 a small ventilation tower on the top of a roof

气煤 gas coal

气门 ①(air) valve of a tyre ②spirácle;stigma

气闷 ①unhappy;worried;in low spirits ②feel suffocated (*or* oppressed)

气密 airtight;gastight;gasproof

气囊 ①(of birds) air sac ②gasbag (of an aerostat)

气恼 get angry;take offence;be ruffled

气馁 become dejected; be discouraged; lose heart

气逆 circulation of vital energy in the wrong direction
气派 imposing manner; dignified air
气泡 air bubble; bubble
气喷 gas blowout
气瓶 air bottle; gas cylinder
气魄 ① boldness of vision; breadth of spirit; daring ② imposing manner
气枪 air gun; pneumatic gun
气球 balloon
气圈 ① balloon ② aeroshpere
气色 complexion; colour
气盛 ① overbearing; arrogant; aggressive ② (of writing) forceful; vigorous
气势 momentum; imposing manner
气数 destiny; fate
气水 air water; air hydraulic
气态 ① gaseous state ② manner; bearing; air
气体 gas
气田 gas field
气艇 airship
气筒 inflator; bicycle pump
气团 air mass
气味 ① smell; odour; flavour ② smack; taste
气温 air temperature; atmospheric temperature
气雾 aerial fog
气息 ① breath ② flavour; smell
气象 ① meteorological phenomena ② meteorology ③ atmosphere; scene
气性 ① temperament; disposition ② bad temper
气胸 pneumothorax
气虚 deficiency of vital energy
气旋 cyclone
气压 atmospheric pressure; barometric pressure
气眼 ① air hole ② gas hole
气焰 arrogance; bluster
气宇 bearing; deportment
气郁 obstruction of the circulation of vital energy
气韵 the spirit, character, tone, or style (in the broadest sense) of a work of art (or literature)
气闸 air (or pneumatic) brake
气质 ① temperament; disposition ② qualities; makings
气滞 stagnation of the circulation of vital energy
气嘴 air cock; air faucet; air tap; fume cock
气昂昂 full of mettle; full of dash
气包子 a person who has a quick temper (or is quick to take offence)
气不公 be indignant over an injustice
气不过 cannot restrain one's anger; be beside oneself with rage

气不平 be indignant over an injustice
气冲冲 furious; beside oneself with rage
气垫车 hovercar
气垫船 hovercraft
气鼓鼓 fuming with anger; foaming with rage; furious
气管炎 tracheitis
气候带 climate zone
气候图 climate chart
气候学 climatology
气候志 climatography
气呼呼 in a huff; panting with rage
气门心 ① valve inside ② valve rubber tube
气生根 aerial root
气死人 driving one crazy; infuriating; exasperating
气头上 in a fit of anger; in a temper
气象台 meteorological observatory
气象图 meteorological map
气象学 meteorology
气象员 weatherman
气汹汹 fuming with anger; foaming with rage; furious
气压表 barometer
气吁吁 panting; gasping for breath
气肿疽 blackleg; black quarter
气冲牛斗 anger shooting up to the skies—in a towering rage; furious
气冲霄汉 dauntless; fearless
气功疗法 treatment with deep breathing exercises
气贯长虹 filled with a spirit as lofty as the rainbow spanning the sky; full of noble aspiration and daring
气候反常 extraordinary climate
气急败坏 flustered and exasperated; utterly discomfited
气流纺纱 open-end spinning; jet spinning
气流干扰 interference in airflow
气流畸变 flow distortion
气密结合 airtight joint
气密试验 air seal test (for an aircraft); leakage test
气平怒息 calm down and cease to be angry; with one's rage cooled down
气势磅礴 of great momentum; powerful
气势汹汹 fierce; truculent; overbearing
气体力学 pneumatics
气体燃料 gaseous fuel
气吞山河 imbued with a spirit that conquers mountains and rivers; full of daring
气味相投 congenial to each other; be two of a kind
气息奄奄 be breathing feebly; be at one's last gasp; be at the point of death; be sinking fast
气象火箭 meteorological rocket

Q

气象雷达 weather radar
气象万千 a scene majestic in all its variety
气象卫星 meteorological satellite; weather satellite
气象预报 weather forecast
气血辩证 analysing and differentiating the pathological condition according to the function of vital energy and the state of the blood
气血两亏 malfunction of vital energy complicated by anaemia; malfunction of vital energy and dificiency of blood
气压沉箱 pneumatic caisson
气焰嚣张 be puffed up with pride; insufferably arrogant
气宇轩昂 have a dignified appearance; have an impressive bearing
气壮如牛 fierce as a bull
气壮山河 full of power and grandeur; magnificent
气管切开术 tracheotomy
气体打火机 gas lighter
气体动力学 aerodynamics
气体发生器 gas generator
气体分离器 gas separator
气象观测船 weather observation ship
气象观测站 weather observation station
气不打一处来 be filled with anger
气可鼓而不可泄 Morale should be boosted, not dampened.

讫 [qì]
㓁 ① settled; accomplished; completed ② end

迄 [qì]
Ⅰ 介 up to; till; until Ⅱ 副 so far; yet
迄今 up to now; to this day; to date; so far

汔 [qì]
副 so that; so as to

Q

弃 [qì]
㓁 throw away; abandon; forsake; discard
弃官 give up one's office; abandon official life
弃绝 abandon; cast aside
弃权 ①abstain from voting ②waive the right (to play); forfeit
弃世 pass away; die
弃水 water spilling; water release
弃婴 ①abandon a baby ②foundling
弃置 discard; throw aside
弃暗投明 forsake darkness for light—leave the reactionary side and cross over to the side of progress
弃短取长 overcome one's shortcoming and make use of his strong points
弃官经商 cease to be an officer and start to do business; giving up one's life in the officialdom and begin trading
弃甲曳兵 (of routed troops) throw away armour and trail weapons

弃旧图新 turn over a new leaf
弃农经商 give up farm production and engage in trading; leave farm work behind to engage in trade
弃之可惜 hesitate to discard sth; be unwilling to throw away
弃舟登岸 leave the ship and go ashore
弃之如敝屣 cast away like a pair of worn-out shoes

汽 [qì]
名 ①gas; vapour ②water steam; steam
汽车 automobile; motor vehicle; car
汽船 steamship; steamer
汽锤 steam hammer
汽灯 gas lamp
汽笛 steam whistle; siren; hooter
汽阀 steam valve
汽缸 cylinder
汽锅 Yunnan steaming pot
汽化 vaporize
汽机 ①steam engine ②steam turbine
汽酒 light sparkling wine
汽碾 steamroller
汽水 aerated water; soft drink; soda water
汽提 petroleum strip
汽艇 motorboat
汽油 petrol; gasoline; gas
汽车吊 truck crane
汽车队 motor transport corps; fleet of cars (or trucks)
汽车库 garage
汽化器 ①carburettor ②vaporizer
汽轮机 steam turbine
汽车工业 auto industry
汽车旅馆 motel
汽车安全带 shoulder belt
汽车拉力赛 motor rally; automobile rally
汽车销赃店 chop shop
汽车制造厂 automobile factory; motor works
汽轮发电机 turbogenerator
汽车废气净化 purification of automobile exhaust gas
汽车废气排放 motor vehicle exhaust emission

妻 [qì]
㓁 marry a girl to (a man) ➡️ qī

泣 [qì]
Ⅰ 㓁 weep; sob Ⅱ 名 tears
泣诉 accuse while weeping; accuse amid tears
泣不成声 choke with sobs
泣涕涟涟 weep copious tears
泣下如雨 shed tears like rain; weep copious tears

亟 [qì]
副 repeatedly; time and again ➡️ jí
亟经洽商 after repeated consultation
亟来搅扰 come again and again to disturb sb,

契 [qì]
I 动 ① carve; engrave; chisel ② agree; match together II 名 ①carved inscriptions ② agreement; contract; deed
契合 agree with; tally with; correspond to
契机 ①moment ②turning point; juncture
契据 deed; contract; receipt
契友 close friend; bosom friend
契约 contract; deed; charter
契纸 contract; deed
契舟求剑 mark the moving boat to locate the place where the sword has dropped into the river—take measures without regard to changed circumstances

砌 [qì]
I 动 lay bricks (or stones) to build II 名 step

跂 [qì]
动 stand on tiptoe ➡qí
跂望 stand on tiptoe to look forward to sb or sth

葺 [qì]
I 名 cover of a roof with straw; thatch II 动 repair; fix; mend

碛 [qì]
名 ①moraine ②desert
碛北 north of the Gobi Desert
碛砾 gravel

槭 [qì]
名 maple

器 [qì]
I 名 ① instrument; implement; utensil; tool; ware ② organ ③ tolerance; forbearance ④talent; ability II 动 value; think highly of
器材 equipment; material
器官 organ; apparatus
器件 parts of an apparatus (or appliance)
器具 utensil; implement; appliance
器量 tolerance
器皿 household utensils; containers esp. for use in the house
器物 implements; utensils
器械 ① apparatus; appliance; instrument ② weapon
器乐 instrumental music
器重 think highly of (one's juniors or subordinates); regard highly
器质性 organic
器官移植 transplant organ; organ transplant
器械体操 gymnastics on (or with) apparatus
器宇轩昂 One's deportment is dignified.

憩 [qì]
动 rest
憩息 have a rest; rest

qiā 〈ㄑㄧㄚ〉

掐 [qiā]
I 动 ①pinch; nip; pick ②clutch; grip II 量

a pinch, bunch, handful, etc. of; 一大掐子韭菜 a big bunch of leeks
掐断 nip off; cut off
掐诀 calculate on one's fingers (while chanting incantations)
掐丝 wire inlay; filigree
掐算 count (or reckon) sth on one's fingers
掐腰 (of a dress) have a waistline
掐尖儿 ①topping; pinching ②oust sb from office ③scrounge; squeeze
掐头去尾 break off both ends; leave out the beginning and the end

qiá 〈ㄑㄧㄚˊ〉

揢 [qiá]
动 clutch (or grip) with both hands

qiǎ 〈ㄑㄧㄚˇ〉

卡 [qiǎ]
I 动 ①wedge; stick; get stuck ②withhold; hold back ③ strangle II 名 ① clip; clasp; fastener ②checkpost; post ➡kǎ
卡具 clamping apparatus; fixture
卡壳 ①(of cartridge or shell case) jam ②get stuck; be held up; have a temporary stoppage
卡盘 chuck
卡子 ①clip; fastener ②checkpost
卡钻 jamming of a drilling tool; sticking of a tool
卡脖子 ① seize sb by the throat; grip sb's throat ②have in a stranglehold; subdue
卡口灯泡 bayonet-socket bulb
卡口灯头 bayonet socket

qià 〈ㄑㄧㄚˋ〉

洽 [qià]
I 动 ①be in harmony; be in agreement ② consult; discuss; arrange II 形 wide; broad; extensive
洽办 arrange with sb to get sth done
洽购 arrange (or negotiate) a purchase
洽借 explore the possibility of borrowing sth (or of a loan)
洽商 make arrangements with; talk over with
洽谈 consult; discuss together
洽妥 have made an arrangement
洽谈会 talk; symposium
洽谈订货 consult about ordering goods

恰 [qià]
I 形 suitable; fitting; appropriate II 名 precisely; exactly
恰当 proper; suitable; fitting; appropriate
恰好 just right
恰恰 just; exactly; precisely
恰巧 by chance; fortunately; unfortunately

Q

恰如 just like
恰似 just like
恰恰舞 cha-cha (dance);cha-cha-cha
恰到好处 just right (for the purpose or occasion)
恰如其分 apt;appropriate;just right

髂 [qià]

髂骨 ilium

qiān (ㄑㄧㄢ)

千 [qiān]

（数）①thousand：拥有良田千顷 boast a thousand of hectares of fertile land ②large numbers of;innumerable
千乏 kilovar (KVAR)
千夫 numerous people
千伏 kilovolt (Kv.)
千古 ①through the ages;eternity;for all time ②(*used in an elegiac couplet or on wreaths dedicated to the dead*)
千赫 kilohertz
千斤 ①a thousand *jin*—very heavy;weighty ②hoisting jack;jack ③pawl
千金 ①a thousand pieces of gold;a lot of money ②daughter (other than one's own)
千卡 kilocalorie (Kcal.)
千克 kilogram (kg.)
千里 a thousand *li*—a long distance or a vast expanse
千米 kilometre (km.)
千秋 ①a thousand years;centuries ②birthday (other than one's own)
千瓦 kilowatt (KW)
千万 ①ten million;millions upon millions ②be sure to;must
千周 kilocycle (KC)
千层饼 multi-layer steamed bread
千层底 layers of cloth firmly stitched together for soles of cloth shoes
千分表 dial gauge;dial indicator
千分尺 micrometer
千分点 permillage point
千斤顶 hoisting jack;jack
千里光 climbing groundsel
千里驹 thousand-*li* colt—a son who is showing great promise
千里马 a horse that covers a thousand *li* a day;a winged steed
千里眼 ①farsighted person ②telescope;field glasses
千枚岩 phyllite
千年虫 millennium bug;Y2K (problem)
千日红 globe amaranth
千禧年 millennium year
千字节 kilobyte (KB)
千儿八百 a thousand or slightly less

千变万化 ever-changing
千差万别 differ in thousands of ways
千愁万恨 a thousand and one worries and hatreds;innumerable worries and hatreds
千疮百孔 riddle with gaping wounds;afflicted will all ills
千锤百炼 ① thoroughly tempered (*or* steeled); finely honed ②(of literary works) be polished again and again;be revised and rewritten many times;be a finished product
千刀万剐 be hacked to pieces;be made mincemeat of
千电子伏 kiloelectron-volt (KeV)
千恩万谢 express a thousand thanks; be eternally indebted
千方百计 in a thousand and one ways;by every possible (*or* conceivable) means;by hook;by crook
千古绝唱 (of poems) rank as a masterpiece throughout the ages
千古奇谈 a fantastic tale
千古罪人 evil person condemned through the ages
千呼万唤 a thousand calls;a thousand entreaties
千回百转 full of twists and turns
千家万户 innumerable households or families; every family
千娇百媚 (of a woman) bewitchingly charming
千金一诺 A promise is worth a thousand ounces of gold.
千军万马 thousands upon thousands of man and horses—a powerful army; a mighty force
千钧一发 a hundredweight hanging by a hair—in imminent peril
千钧重负 a grave responsibility
千里迢迢 from a thousand *li* away;from afar; (come) all the way from
千虑一得 ① The greatest fool, in a thousand schemes,must hit once on the truth;Even a fool occasionally hits on a good idea. ②My observations may contain a grain of truth.
千虑一失 The wisest man, in a thousand schemes,must make at least one mistake; Even the wise are not free from error.
千难万险 innumerable hazards and hardships
千篇一律 stereotyped;following the same pattern
千奇百怪 all kinds of strange things;an infinite variety of fantastic phenomena
千千万万 thousands upon thousands
千秋万代 throughout the ages;generation after generation;forever
千山万水 ten thousand torrents and a thou-

sand crags—the trials of a long and arduous journey

千丝万缕 countless ties; a thousand and one links

千头万绪 thousands of strands and loose ends; a multitude of things

千禧婴儿 millennium infant; millennium baby

千辛万苦 innumerable trials and tribulations; untold hardships

千言万语 thousands and thousands of words

千载难逢 not occurring once in a thousand years; very rare

千载一时 a chance that comes once in a thousand years—the chance of a lifetime; a rare opportunity

千真万确 absolutely true

千姿百态 in different poses and with different expressions; in thousands of postures

千里送鹅毛 a goose feather sent from a thousand *li* away (*or* from afar)

千年虫问题 millennium bug; millennium bomb; millennium glitch

千不该万不该 really should not have (done sth)

千里姻缘一线牵 Two beings destined to marry each other, though a thousand *li* apart, are tied together as if by a thread; People a thousand *li* apart may be linked by marriage.

千部一腔,千人一面 all of the same tone, all with the same feature—(usu. of literary compositions) stereotyped

千夫所指,无病而死 when a thousand people point accusing fingers at a man he will die even though not ill—it is dangerous to incur public wrath

千军易得,一将难求 simpler by far to raise a thousand troops than find a single general to lead them

千里之堤,溃于蚁穴 one ant-hole may cause the collapse of a thousand-*li* dyke—slight negligence may lead to great disaster

千里之行,始于足下 A thousand-*li* journey is started by taking the first step.

阡 [qiān]
名 ① footpath between fields, running north and south ② narrow path leading to a grave

阡陌 crisscross footpaths between fields

扦 [qiān]
Ⅰ 名 ①poker; pick ②sharp-pointed implement or prod Ⅱ 动 ①fasten; insert ② pedicure; peel

扦插 make a cuttage

扦子 ①a slender pointed piece of metal, bamboo, etc. ② a sharp-pointed metal tube (used to extract samples of grains, etc.

from sacks)

迁 [qiān]
动 ① move; remove ② change ③ change one's official post

迁厂 move a factory to another site

迁都 move the capital to another place

迁飞 (of birds) migrate

迁就 accommodate oneself to; yield to

迁居 change one's dwelling place; move (house)

迁离 move to another place

迁流 (of time) flow past

迁怒 vent one's anger on sb who's not to blame; take it out on sb

迁徙 move; migrate; change one's residence

迁延 delay; defer; procrastinate

迁移 move; remove; migrate

迁葬 move a grave to another place

迁户口 report to the local authorities for change of domicile; change one's residence registration

迁移性 animal migration

迁址公告 removal notice

金 [qiān]
形 whole; total

钎 [qiān]
名 drill rod; drill steel; borer

钎子 hammer drill (for making holes in rock); rock drill

牵 [qiān]
动 ①lead along; lead; pull ②involve; entangle

牵缠 involve; get entangled

牵扯 involve; implicate; drag in

牵掣 hold up; impede

牵动 affect; influence

牵挂 worry; care

牵合 make a match; act as go-between

牵累 ①tie down ②implicate; involve (in trouble)

牵连 ① involve (in trouble); implicate ② tie up with; integrate with

牵强 forced (interpretation, etc.); farfetched

牵涉 involve; drag in

牵伸 draft; drawing

牵手 join hands

牵头 ①take the lead; lead off; be the first to do sth ②act as a go-between ③go-between

牵系 link; join; connect

牵线 ①manipulate; control (from behind the scenes) ②act as a go-between

牵引 ①tow; draw ②traction

牵制 pin down; tie up; check; contain

牵鼻子 lead by the nose

牵牛花 (white-edged) morning glory

牵牛星 the Herd-boy star—Altair

牵切纺 tow-to-yarn direct spinning

牵线人 wire-puller; go-between

牵引车 tractor; tractor truck
牵引犁 trailed plough
牵引力 traction force; traction; pulling force
牵引炮 towed artillery
牵肠挂肚 feel deep anxiety; be very worried; be on tenterhooks
牵强附会 draw a forced analogy; make a far-fetched (*or* irrelevant) comparison; give a strained interpretation
牵丝攀藤 drag out affairs (*or* argument)
牵线搭桥 act as a go-between
牵引能量 haulage capacity (of a locomotive, etc.)
牵制战术 diversionary tactics
牵引式滑翔机 towed glider
牵一发而动全身 pull one hair and you move the whole body—a slight move in one part may affect the whole situation

铅 [qiān]
名 ①lead (Pb) ②lead (in a pencil); black lead
铅白 white lead
铅版 stereotype
铅笔 pencil
铅锤 plummet; plumb (bob)
铅丹 red lead; minium
铅粉 lead powder
铅封 lead sealing
铅球 shot
铅丝 ①galvanized wire ②lead wire
铅条 ① slug; lead ② lead (for a propelling pencil)
铅印 letterpress (*or* relief, typographic) printing; stereotype
铅直 vertical; plumb
铅坠 plummet
铅字 type; letter
铅笔刀 a small knife for sharpening pencils; pen-knife
铅笔盒 pencil-case
铅笔画 pencil drawing
铅笔心 lead (in a pencil); black lead
铅玻璃 lead glass
铅垂线 plumb line
铅灰色 leaden colour; lead gray
铅制品 leadwork; leading
铅中毒 lead poisoning; saturnism
铅刀一割 a leaden knife can cut—a mediocre person can be put to some use
铅字合金 type metal

悭 [qiān]
Ⅰ 形 miserly; parsimonious; stingy Ⅱ 动 lack
悭吝 stingy; miserly

谦 [qiān]
形 modest; unassuming
谦卑 humble; modest

谦诚 modest and sincere
谦辞 self-depreciatory expression; humble words
谦恭 modest and courteous
谦和 modest and amiable
谦让 modestly decline
谦慎 modest and prudent
谦顺 modest and deferential
谦虚 ① modest; self-effacing ② make modest remarks
谦逊 modest; unassuming
谦恭有礼 respectful and polite
谦谦君子 a modest gentleman
谦虚谨慎 modest and prudent

签 [qiān]
Ⅰ 动 ① write one's signature; sign; autograph ②make brief comments ③tack Ⅱ 名 ① bamboo slip ② label; sticker; tag ③ slender pointed chip of bamboo (*or* wood)
签呈 a brief document submitted to a superior; memorial
签单 sign a bill without paying cash after shopping and having a meal, leaving the accounts to be settled afterwards
签到 sign-in; register one's attendance (at an office or at a meeting)
签订 conclude and sign (a treaty, etc.)
签发 sign and issue (a document, certificate, etc.)
签名 sign one's name; autograph
签收 sign after receiving sth; sign to acknowledge the receipt of sth; sign for
签售 autographed copy sale
签署 sign
签条 docket
签筒 ① a tube-like holder of lot-sticks ② a sharp-pointed metal tube used to extract samples of grains, etc. from sacks
签退 sign-out
签押 put one's signature (*or* seal) on an official document
签约 sign a contract
签证 ①visa; visé ②grant a visa
签注 ① attach a slip of paper to a document with comments on it; write comments on a document (for a superior to consider) ② write comments (*or* points for attention) on a certificate, book of tables, etc.
签子 ① bamboo slips used for divination (*or* drawing lots) ②a slender pointed piece of bamboo (*or* wood)
签字 sign; affix one's signature
签到簿 attendance book
签合同 sign a contract; conclude a contract
签名盖章 sign and affix seal
签名歌手 signed singer
签名运动 signature drive; sign-in

签署条约 conclude a treaty;sign a treaty
签署意见 write comments and sign name(on document)
签字盖章 sign and affix one's seal;set one's hand and seal to
签字画押 sign one's name on a document

qián (ㄑ㊀ㄢ)

萼 [qián] ➡xún
萼麻 nettle

钤 [qián] 〈动〉①seal ②affix a seal to ③lock;control;restrict
钤束 keep under control;restrict

前 [qián]
Ⅰ〈名〉①first;top ②prospect;future ③battlefront;front Ⅱ〈动〉go forward;go ahead Ⅲ〈形〉①first;front ②before;ago ③former ④earlier than;prior to;pre-
前辈 senior (person);elder;the older generation
前臂 forearm
前边 in front
前部 forepart;front;nose
前叉 front fork (of a bicycle)
前尘 the past
前程 ①future;prospect ②a desired career;a high rank (sought after by an intellectual or official)
前池 forebay
前仇 old hatred;old grievance
前导 ①lead the way;march in front;precede ②a person who leads the way;guide
前敌 front line
前端 nose;front end;leading end
前额 forehead
前方 ①ahead ②the front
前锋 ①vanguard ②forward ③front
前夫 ① former husband (either divorced or dead);ex-husband ②late husband
前后 ①around (a certain time);about ②from beginning to end (in time) ③in front and behind ④the same kind in succession
前胡 the root of purple-flowered peucedanum
前脚 the forward foot in a step
前进 advance;go forward;forge ahead
前景 ①foreground (of a view,picture,photo, etc.) ②prospect;vista;perspective
前科 record of previous crime
前来 come
前例 precedent
前列 front row (or rank);forefront;van
前轮 front wheel (of a vehicle);nosewheel (of a plane)
前门 front door;front gate
前面 ①in front;at the head;ahead ②above; preceding
前母 father's former wife
前脑 forebrain
前年 the year before last
前排 front row
前炮 forward gun (on a ship);bow-piece
前妻 ① former wife (either divorced or dead);ex-wife ②late wife (dead)
前期 earlier stage;early days
前桥 front axle (of a car)
前情 ① antecedent;cause ② old friendship; former affection
前驱 forerunner;precursor;pioneer
前人 forefathers;predecessors
前任 predecessor
前日 the day before yesterday
前晌 before noon;morning
前哨 outpost;advance guard
前身 predecessor
前生 previous incarnation;previous existence
前世 previous incarnation;previous existence
前市 previous market
前束 toe-in (of a car)
前台 ① proscenium ② on the stage ③ front desk
前提 ① premise ② prerequisite;presupposition
前蹄 forehoof
前天 the day before yesterday
前厅 antechamber;vestibule
前庭 vestibule
前头 ①in front;at the head;ahead ②above; preceding
前途 future;prospect
前腿 foreleg
前往 go to;leave for;proceed to
前卫 ① advance guard;vanguard ② halfback ③fashionable;modern;avant-garde
前夕 eve
前嫌 previous ill will;old grudge
前线 frontline;front
前项 antecedent
前胸 corselet
前言 preface;foreword;introduction
前沿 forward position
前夜 eve
前阴 external genitalia
前缘 predestined ties (or relationship);fore-ordained affinity
前约 precontract
前院 front courtyard
前瞻 look ahead
前兆 omen;forewarning;premonition
前者 the former
前肢 forelegs (of an animal);forelimbs
前缀 prefix
前奏 prelude

前半场 first half (of a game, concert, etc.)
前半晌 before noon; morning
前半生 the first half of one's life
前半天 before noon; morning
前半夜 the first half of the night (from night-fall to midnight)
前儿个 the day before yesterday
前滚翻 forward roll
前臼齿 premolar teeth
前空翻 forward somersault in the air
前列腺 prostate (gland)
前掠翼 buzzard-type wing (of a plane)
前驱期 prodromal stage
前哨战 skirmish
前视图 front view
前苏联 former Soviet Union
前庭炎 vestibulitis
前卫派 avant garde
前装炮 muzzle-loading gun; muzzleloader
前奏曲 prelude
前车之鉴 warning taken from the overturned cart ahead; lessons drawn from others' mistakes
前程似锦 splendid prospects; a glorious future
前程万里 bright prospects
前度刘郎 the young Master Liu of those days—a person who revisits a place
前赴后继 advance wave upon wave
前功尽弃 all previous work undone; All that has been achieved is spoiled; All one's previous efforts are wasted.
前寒武纪 pre-Cambrian Period
前后夹击 make a simultaneous frontal and rear attack; attack from the front and the rear simultaneously
前后脚儿 almost simultaneously; one close behind another
前后矛盾 antilogy; inconsistent; inconse-cutive
前后左右 ①on all sides; all around ②in every direction
前呼后拥 with attendants crowding round
前倨后恭 first supercilious and then deferential; change from arrogance to humility
前列腺素 prostaglandin
前列腺炎 prostatitis
前仆后继 no sooner has one fallen than another steps into the breach; advance wave upon wave
前前后后 ①the whole story; the ins and outs ②from beginning to end (in time)
前哨阵地 outpost; advance guard camp
前世姻缘 fated marriage; connected in a former existence
前思后想 think over again and again
前所未闻 never heard of before
前所未有 never existed before; hitherto unknown; unprecedented; without parallel
前庭后院 front and back yards
前途茫茫 have a bleak future; have gloomy prospects
前途未卜 hanging in the balance; ambiguous future
前途无量 have boundless prospects; have unlimited possibilities
前无古人 without parallel in history; unprecedented
前沿科学 frontier science; front line science
前仰后合 rock (with laughter)
前因后果 cause and effect; the entire process
前敌委员会 front committee
前敌总指挥 frontline commander-in-chief
前列腺肥大 hypertrophy of the prostate
前资本主义 pre-capitalism
前进中有曲折 twists and turns on our way for advance
前言不搭后语 utter words that do not hang together; talk incoherently; babble disconnected phrases
前沿部署系统 forward-based system
前怕狼,后怕虎 fear wolves ahead and tigers behind—be full of fears
前不着村,后不着店 with no village ahead and no inn behind—be stranded in an uninhabited area
前车之覆,后车之鉴 The overturned cart ahead is a warning to the ones behind.
前门拒虎,后门进狼 drive the tiger from the front door and let a wolf in at the back—fend off one danger only to fall a prey to another
前人栽树,后人乘凉 one generation plants the trees in whose shade another generation rests—profiting by the labour of one's forefathers; sweating for the benefit of future generations
前事不忘,后事之师 Past experience, if not forgotten, is a guide for the future; Lessons learned from the past can guide one in the future.
前不见古人,后不见来者 I look back—I do not see the ancients; I look ahead—can't see the generations to come.

虔 [qián]
I 彤 pious, devout; sincere II 名 plunder; slaughter
虔诚 pious; devout
虔敬 reverent

钱 [qián]
I 名 ①coin; cash ②money ③fund; sum ④wealth ⑤anything that resembles a coin in shape II 量 qian, a unit of weight (= 5 grams)
钱包 wallet; purse

钱币 coin
钱财 wealth；money
钱袋 wallet；purse
钱柜 money box
钱夹 billfold
钱龙 millipede
钱庄 old-style Chinese private bank
钱币学 numismatics
钱迷心窍 be blinded by lust for money；money-grubbing
钱能通神 Money will move the gods；Money opens the gates of heaven.

钳 [qián]
Ⅰ 名 pincers；pliers；tongs Ⅱ 动 ①hold with pincers ②clamp；restrain
钳工 ①benchwork ②fitter
钳口 ①force sb into silence；prevent sb from talking ②shut up；keep silent
钳制 clamp down on；suppress
钳爪 chela（of a crab，lobster，etc.）
钳子 pliers；pincers；forceps
钳口结舌 keep one's mouth shut；hold one's tongue

乾 [qián]
乾坤 heaven and earth；the cosmos；the universe

㧀 [qián]
动 carry on the shoulder
㧀客 broker

潜 [qián]
Ⅰ 动 ① hide under water；submerge ② hide；be latent；lurk Ⅱ 副 secretly；stealthily；on the sly Ⅲ 形 potential；latent
潜藏 hide；go into hiding
潜返 return secretly
潜伏 hide；conceal；lie low
潜航 （of a submarine）submerge
潜亏 latent deficit
潜力 latent capacity；potential；potentiality
潜流 undercurrent；underflow
潜能 ①latent energy ②potential
潜匿 hide；go into hiding
潜热 latent heat
潜入 ① slip into；sneak into；steal in ② dive（into water）；submerge
潜师 move troops in secret
潜水 ①go under water；dive ②phreatic water
潜逃 abscond
潜艇 submarine
潜心 with great concentration
潜行 ①move under water ②move stealthily；slink
潜血 occult blood（in the faeces）
潜隐 ①hide；conceal ②withdraw from society and live in solitude；be a hermit
潜泳 underwater swimming
潜鱼 pearlfish

潜在 latent；potential
潜质 latent quality；potential
潜伏期 incubation period；latency period
潜科学 science of the human embryo to detect early signs of talent
潜水病 caisson disease；decompression sickness
潜水艇 submarine
潜水衣 diving suit
潜水员 diver；frogman
潜台词 ①unspoken words in a play left to the understanding of the audience（or reader）② what is actually meant（in one's speech）；implication
潜望镜 periscope
潜意识 the subconscious；subconsciousness
潜地导弹 submarine-launched missile aimed at objectives on land；sea-to-ground missile
潜移默化 exert a subtle influence on sb's character，thinking，etc.；imperceptibly influence
潜在力量 latent force；latent power
潜在市场 potential market
潜在需求 potential demand
潜滋暗长 grow and develop imperceptibly

黔 [qián]
形 black
黔驴技穷 the（proverbial）Guizhou donkey has exhausted its tricks—at one's wit's end；at the end of one's rope
黔驴之技 tricks of the（proverbial）Guizhou donkey—tricks not to be feared；cheap tricks

qiǎn（ㄑㄧㄢˇ）

肷 [qiǎn]
名 fur on the belly and breast

浅 [qiǎn]
形 ①shallow；of little depth ②simple；easy；not difficult ③superficial ④not familiar；not chummy ⑤（of colour）light ⑥not long in time；for a short while
浅薄 shallow；superficial；meagre
浅淡 ①（of colour）light；pale ②（of feeling）vague；faint
浅耕 shallow ploughing
浅海 shallow sea；epeiric sea；epicontinental sea
浅黄 pale yellow
浅见 ①superficial view ②humble opinion
浅近 simple；plain；easy to understand
浅陋 meagre；mean
浅明 simple；plain；clear；obvious
浅色 light colour
浅释 simple explanation
浅说 elementary introduction
浅滩 shoal；shallows

Q

浅谈 brief talk
浅显 plain; easy to read and understand
浅笑 smile
浅学 having superficial knowledge; of little learning; ill-educated
浅易 simple and easy
浅种 shallow sowing
浅成岩 hypabyssal rock
浅口鞋 shoes with low-cut uppers
浅蓝色 baby blue
浅水池 the shallow end of a swimming pool; shallow pool
浅棕色 light brown
浅尝辄止 stop after gaining a little knowledge; be satisfied with a smattering of knowledge
浅尝辄止 do sth cursorily
浅而易见 easy to understand; simple
浅斟低唱 drinking leisurely and singing softly—a cultured way of enjoying oneself

遣 [qiǎn] ① send; transmit; dispatch ② drive away; dispel; expel
遣返 repatriate
遣散 disband; dismiss; send away; lay off
遣送 send back; repatriate
遣散费 severance pay
遣词造句 choice of words and building of sentences; wording and phrasing
遣返难民 repatriation of refugees
遣返战俘 repatriation of prisoners of war

嗛 [qiǎn] ape's jaws

谴 [qiǎn] ① censure; reprimand; reproach ② (of officials) be demoted on account of wrongdoing
谴责 condemn; denounce; censure

缱 [qiǎn]
缱绻 lingering; abiding; deeply attached to each other

qiàn (ㄑㄧㄢˋ)

欠 [qiàn] I ① owe; be behind with; be in debt ② want; need ③ deserve to be punished ④ yawn ⑤ raise slightly (part of one's body); stretch II ① fidgety; troublesome ② not enough; insufficient; wanting
欠安 (of an aged person or a VIP) feeling unwell; indisposed; under the weather
欠产 fall short of the production target; have a shortfall in output
欠抽 need a good thrashing
欠单 accommodation bill or note; IOU
欠火 have not been cooked (or heated) long enough; undercooked
欠佳 not good enough; not up to the mark
欠据 a bill signed in acknowledgement of debt; IOU
欠款 ① owe a debt ② money that is owing; arrears; balance due
欠批 should be taken to task
欠情 owe sb a debt of gratitude; be indebted to sb
欠缺 ① be deficient in; be short of ② shortcoming; deficiency
欠伸 stretch oneself and yawn
欠身 raise oneself slightly; half rise from one's seat
欠税 default on (or be in arrears with) tax payments
欠条 a bill signed in acknowledgement of debt; IOU
欠妥 not proper
欠息 debit interest
欠项 liabilities
欠薪 ① delay paying a salary ② back pay; overdue salaries
欠债 owe a debt; run into debt
欠账 ① owe a debt; run into debt ② bills due; outstanding accounts
欠资 postage due
欠揍 need a spanking
欠人情 owe favours (which should be repaid)
欠付工资 back pay; back wages
欠发达地区 less developed areas

纤 [qiàn] rope for towing a boat; tow-rope ⇒ xiān
纤夫 boat tracker
纤路 towpath; towing path; track road
纤绳 towline; towrope

芡 [qiàn] ① Gorgon euryale ② starch

茜 [qiàn] ① madder ② alizarin crimson
茜草 madder
茜纱 red gauze
茜素染料 alizarin dyes

倩 [qiàn] I beautiful; attractive II ask sb to do sth on one's behalf
倩影 beautiful image (of a woman); picture (of a beautiful woman)
倩装 (a woman's) beautiful dress
倩男倩女 smartly dressed men and women
倩女离魂 The young lady died for love.
倩人相助 ask sb to give a helping hand

堑 [qiàn] moat; chasm; ditch
堑壕 trench; entrenchment

椠 [qiàn] ① wood block ② engraved edition of books

嵌 [qiàn]
动 inlay；embed；set
嵌石 inlaid stone pieces
嵌银 be set with silver pieces

慊 [qiàn]
动 regret；sorrow；hate ➡ qiè

歉 [qiàn]
Ⅰ 动 apology；regret Ⅱ 名 crop failure
歉疚 having a guilty conscience
歉年 lean year
歉然 apologetic
歉收 crop failure；poor harvest
歉意 apology；regret

qiāng（ㄑㄧㄤ）

抢 [qiāng]
动 ①knock；touch ②be in the opposite direction；go against ➡ qiǎng
抢断 steal
抢风 go against the wind；brave the wind

呛 [qiāng]
动 be unable to breathe because one's windpipe is blocked by sth；choke ➡ qiàng

枪 [qiāng]
Ⅰ 名 ① spear ② rifle；gun；firearm ③ any appliance which functions like a gun (or resembles) it in shape Ⅱ 动 serve as a substitute for sb at an examination
枪靶 (shooting) target
枪把 the small of the stock；pistol grip
枪版 pirated video disc
枪毙 execute by shooting
枪柄 stock
枪刺 bayonet
枪带 (rifle) sling
枪弹 ①cartridge ②bullet
枪法 marksmanship
枪管 barrel (of a gun)
枪机 rifle bolt
枪架 rifle rack
枪决 execute by shooting
枪口 muzzle
枪炮 firearms；arms；guns
枪杀 shoot dead
枪伤 bullet wound
枪声 report of a gun；shot；crack
枪手 [qiāngshǒu] ① marksman；gunner ② spearman
枪手 [qiāngshou] one who sits for an examination in place of another person
枪栓 rifle bolt
枪膛 bore (of a gun)
枪替 sit for an examination in place of another person
枪筒 metal；tube
枪托 (rifle) butt；buttstock
枪械 firearms

枪眼 ①embrasure；loophole ②bullet hole
枪药 small arms propellant
枪鱼 marlin
枪支 firearms
枪放下 (word of command) Order arms!
枪杆子 rifle；gun；arms
枪榴弹 rifle grenade
枪上肩 (word of command) Shoulder arms!
枪乌贼 squid
枪战片 shoot-'em-up
枪子儿 ①cartridge ②bullet；shot
枪林弹雨 a forest of guns and a hail of bullets—heavy fire

戗 [qiāng]
动 ①be in the opposite direction ②clash ➡ qiàng
戗风 against the wind
戗顺不吃 yield neither to coercion nor to persuasion

戕 [qiāng]
动 kill
戕害 injure；harm
戕贼 injure；undermine

将 [qiāng]
动 please；wish ➡ jiāng；jiàng

腔 [qiāng]
Ⅰ 名 ① cavity ② speech；talk ③ tune ④ tone；accent Ⅱ 量 carcass (of slaughtered sleep)：一腔羊 a mutton carcass
腔背 back lining；hollow
腔调 ①tune ②tone of voice ③accent；intonation
腔骨 spinal joints of pigs, sheep, etc. (for food)
腔肠动物 coelenterate

蜣 [qiāng]
蜣螂 dung beetle

锖 [qiāng]
象 clang；gong：锣声锖锖 continuous clanging of gongs

镪 [qiāng]
➡ qiǎng
镪水 strong acid

qiáng（ㄑㄧㄤ）

强 [qiáng]
Ⅰ 形 ①strong；mighty；powerful ②demanding；resolute ③ better；stronger ④ a little over；plus Ⅱ 副 forcibly；by force Ⅲ 动 strengthen；enhance ➡ jiàng；qiǎng
强半 more than half；greater part；most
强暴 ① violent；brutal ② ferocious adversary ③rape
强大 big and powerful；powerful；formidable
强档 prime time
强盗 robber；bandit

强敌 formidable opponent or enemy
强点 strong point
强调 stress;emphasize;underline
强度 intensity;strength
强渡 fight one's way across a river;force a river
强队 power house;the top team
强风 strong breeze
强干 capable and experienced
强攻 take by storm;storm
强固 strong;solid
强国 powerful (*or* strong) nation;power
强悍 fierce;intrepid;doughty
强横 rude and unreasonable;tyrannical;surly;arrogant
强化 strengthen;intensify;consolidate
强记 have a retentive memory
强加 impose;force
强奸 violate (a woman);rape
强碱 alkali;strong base
强健 strong and healthy
强劲 powerful;forceful
强梁 brutal;tyrannical;surly
强烈 ① strong; intense; violent ② clear-cut;distinct;striking;sharp
强令 arbitrarily give orders
强拍 strong beat;accented beat
强权 power;might
强人 ①strong man ②robber;bandit
强如 be better than;be superior to
强身 build up a good physique;improve one's health
强盛 (of a country) powerful and prosperous
强势 going strong;great force
强手 ① a very capable person ② a master player;a topnotch athlete;ace
强似 be better than;be superior to
强酸 strong acid
强袭 take by storm;storm
强项 ① resolute and unbending; upright and unyielding ②strong point (of an athlete or a team)
强行 force
强压 suppress;stifle
强毅 resolute and steadfast;staunch
强硬 strong;tough;unyielding
强于 be better than
强占 forcibly occupy;seize
强者 the strong and valiant;survivor
强震 strong shock
强直 rigidity
强制 force;compel;coerce
强壮 strong;sturdy;robust
强子 hadron
强化班 enrichment course;intensive training class
强击机 attack plane

强溶剂 strong solvent
强心剂 cardiac stimulant;cardiotonic
强行军 forced march
强硬派 hardliner
强有力 strong;vigorous;forceful
强壮剂 roborant;tonic
强兵猛将 strong men and fierce chieftains
强盗逻辑 gangster logic
强化机制 strengthening mechanism
强化基因 enhancer gene
强化食品 fortified food
强化学校 cram school
强加于人 impose (one's views,etc.) on others
强奸民意 defile public opinion;coerce public opinion;outrage public opinion
强劳动力 an able-bodied labourer
强力霉素 doxycycline
强力启动 jump-start
强烈反差 striking contrast
强弩之末 an arrow at the end of its flight—a spent force
强强联合 megamerger; association between strong enterprises
强权外交 power diplomacy
强权政治 power politics;Realpolitik
强势群体 the advantaged
强硬路线 the hard line
强硬外交 aggressive diplomacy
强制措施 coercive measures
强制破产 involuntary insolvency; involuntary bankruptcy
强制征购 compulsory purchase
强制执行 compulsory execution;enforce compulsory execution
强制性措施 compulsory measure; coercive measure
强制性制裁 mandatory sanction
强大精神动力 powerful ideological driving force
强大思想武器 powerful ideological weapon
强化法制观念 enhance the awareness of the law
强化市场机制 intensify the market force
强化税收征管 strengthen tax administration
强有力的后盾 strong backing
强将手下无弱兵 There are no poor soldiers under a good general.
强龙不压地头蛇 a powerful dragon cannot crush a snake in its old haunts—even a powerful man cannot crush a local bully
强制性绝育手术 compulsory sterilization operation
强中自有强中手 However strong you are, there's always someone stronger.
强化企业自我约束机制 strengthen the self-discipline of enterprises

墙 [qiáng]
名 ①wall ②anything that looks like a wall (*or serves the purpose of partitioning*)
墙报 wall newspaper
墙壁 wall
墙根 the foot of a wall
墙画 mural painting
墙基 bench-table;footing of wall
墙角 corner formed by two walls
墙脚 ①the foot of a wall ②foundation
墙裙 dado
墙头 ①the top of a wall ②a short,low enclosing wall
墙围 circummure
墙垣 wall
墙纸 wallpaper
墙倒众人推 when a wall is about to collapse, everybody gives it a shove—everybody hits a man who is down
墙头草,随风倒 grass atop a wall swaying in the wind—a person who follows the crowd
墙内开花墙外香 receive recognition only from outsiders

蔷 [qiáng]
蔷薇 rose

嫱 [qiáng]
名 lady-in-waiting

樯 [qiáng]
名 mast
樯折舟覆 The mast broke and the ship capsized.

qiǎng（＜lㄤ）

抢 [qiǎng]
动 ①rob;loot;snatch;grab ②vie for;compete for ③hurry;rush ④scrape;scratch;sharpen ➡qiāng
抢白 tell off;dress down;rebuff
抢答 vie for the opportunity of answering questions
抢点 ①(of a train,etc.) make up time (in order to keep on schedule) ②(of a football striker,etc.) race to a favourable position
抢渡 speedily cross (a river)
抢夺 snatch;wrest;seize
抢购 shopping rush;buying binge;panic buying;shop spree;rush to purchase
抢婚 marriage by capture
抢劫 rob;loot;plunder
抢截 intercept
抢救 rescue;save;salvage
抢掠 loot;sack;plunder
抢拍 seize the opportunity to take pictures; grab the photo opportunity;photograph real-life scenes;take a snapshot
抢亲 ①a marriage ceremony in which the bridegroom pretends to kidnap his bride ②steal,kidnap or force a woman to be one's wife
抢青 rush a harvest of ripening crops (in anticipation of bad weather)
抢墒 hurry to sow seeds while the soil is still moist
抢市 rush (goods) to the market (to get a better price);grab the market
抢收 rush in the harvest;get the harvest in quickly
抢手 (of goods) in great demand
抢滩 grab the market
抢先 try to be the first to do sth;anticipate; forestall
抢险 rush to deal with an emergency (e.g. a breach in an embankment,a cave-in,etc.)
抢修 rush to repair;do rush repairs;first-aid repair;rush-repair
抢眼 noticeable;conspicuous;spectacular;eye-catching
抢运 rush to transport
抢占 ①race to control;seize;grab ②unlawfully occupy
抢种 rush-plant;rushed planting
抢注 rush registration
抢嘴 ①try to get the first word in;try to be heard above the rest ②rush to eat up the food
抢答题 question to vie to answer
抢饭碗 fight for a job;snatch sb else's job
抢购风 panic purchasing;panic buying spree
抢镜头 ①(of a cameraman) fight for a vantage point from which to take a news picture ②steal the show;be fond of being in the limelight
抢生意 compete for business
抢时间 race against time
抢手货 hot item;popular goods;popular commodities; easy-to-sell goods;easy-to-sell commodities
抢劫一空 rob to the last pin
抢险救灾 do rescue and relief work

羟 [qiǎng]
名 hydroxyl (group)
羟基 hydroxyl (group)

强 [qiǎng]
动 make an effort;try hard;force ➡jiàng; qiáng
强逼 compel;force
强辩 defend oneself by sophistry; argue against all reason;argue stubbornly or obstinately
强留 force sb to stay on
强迫 compel;force;coerce
强求 insist on;impose
强使 compel;force

强笑 ①force a smile ②a forced smile
强词夺理 use lame arguments; resort to sophistry; reason fallaciously
强打精神 try hard to appear unperturbed; pull oneself together
强买强卖 buy and sell under coercion
强人所难 try to make sb do what he is unwilling (*or* unable) to
强颜欢笑 put on an air of cheerfulness; try to look happy
强作解人 pretend to be in the know
强作镇定 do one's best to keep a calm exterior
强迫交易罪 crime of coercive business transactions

镪 [qiǎng]
名 string of copper coins ➡qiāng

襁 [qiǎng]
名 belt to carry a baby on the back with
襁褓 swaddling clothes

qiàng (ㄑㄧㄤˋ)

呛 [qiàng]
动 irritate (respiratory organs) ➡qiāng

戗 [qiàng]
Ⅰ 名 ①prop ②wooden support Ⅱ 动 buttress; shore up ➡qiāng

炝 [qiàng]
动 ①boil sth in water for a while, and then dress it with soy sauce, vinegar, etc. ②fry sth quickly in hot oil, then cook it with sauce and water
炝黄瓜 boiled cucumber chips with soy source dressing
炝腰花 boiled and dressed pork kidney

跄 [qiàng]
动 walk
跄踉 stagger

Q

qiāo (ㄑㄧㄠ)

悄 [qiāo]
➡qiǎo
悄悄 quietly; on the quiet
悄悄话 whisperings (esp. between husband and wife, lovers, etc.)

跷 [qiāo]
Ⅰ 动 ①lift up (a leg); hold up (a finger) ②stand (*or* walk) on tiptoe ③limp; hobble Ⅱ 名 stilts
跷蹊 fishy; dubious
跷跷板 seesaw

锹 [qiāo]
名 spade; shovel

劁 [qiāo]
动 geld; castrate

敲 [qiāo]
动 ① knock; rap; beat; strike ② swindle money out of sb; force sb to pay through the nose; fleece
敲打 ①beat; rap; tap ②say sth to irritate sb ③pressurize and supervise sb
敲定 nail down; make the final decision
敲击 beat; rap; tap
敲诈 extort; blackmail; racketeer
敲边鼓 join bandwagon in support (*or* opposition); assist sb from the sidelines; back sb up
敲警钟 sound the alarm bell—sound a warning; ring warning bells
敲门砖 a brick picked up to knock on the door and thrown away when it has served its purpose—a stepping-stone to success
敲丧钟 sound the funeral bell
敲小鼓 beat a little drum—feel uneasy or nervous
敲诈者 racketeer
敲竹杠 ①fleece sb; daylight robbery ②blackmail
敲骨吸髓 break the bones and suck the marrow—suck the lifeblood; be a cruel, blood-sucking exploiter
敲锣打鼓 beat gongs and sound drums
敲诈勒索 extort; blackmail; racketeer

橇 [qiāo]
名 sledge; sled; sleigh

缲 [qiāo]
动 hem with invisible stitches

qiáo (ㄑㄧㄠˊ)

乔 [qiáo]
Ⅰ 形 tall Ⅱ 动 pretend to be; disguise
乔林 high forest
乔木 arbor; tree
乔迁 move to a better place get a promotion
乔装 disguise
乔其纱 georgette
乔迁会 house-warming party
乔模乔样 in an artificial (*or* affected) manner
乔迁之喜 happy occassion of moving into new home
乔装打扮 disguise; masquerade

侨 [qiáo]
Ⅰ 动 live abroad; reside in a foreign country Ⅱ 名 person living abroad; resident in a foreign country
侨胞 countrymen (*or* nationals) residing abroad; overseas compatriots
侨汇 overseas remittance; immigrant remittance
侨居 live abroad
侨眷 relatives of overseas Chinese who remain in the homeland
侨民 a national of a particular country residing abroad
侨生 ①children of overseas Chinese born abroad ②overseas Chinese studying in China

侨务 affairs concerning nationals living abroad;overseas Chinese affairs
侨乡 village (*or* town) inhabited by relatives of overseas Chinese and returned overseas Chinese
侨属 relatives of overseas Chinese who remain in the homeland
侨资 capital investments of overseas Chinese;overseas Chinese funds
侨汇券 overseas remittance coupon
侨务工作 work regarding overseas Chinese

荞 [qiáo]
荞麦 buckwheat

莜 [qiáo]
名 ①high mallow ②buckwheat

桥 [qiáo]
名 bridge
桥洞 bridge opening
桥墩 (bridge) pier
桥拱 bridge arch
桥涵 bridges and culverts
桥基 bridge group
桥架 crane span structure
桥孔 bridge opening
桥梁 bridge
桥面 road of bridge;bridge floor;deck
桥牌 bridge (a card game)
桥塔 bridge tower
桥台 abutment
桥头 either end of a bridge
桥堍 either end of a bridge
桥址 bridge site
桥桩 bridge pier
桥楼室 bridge house
桥头堡 ①bridgehead ②bridge tower
桥支座 bridge seat
桥式起重机 bridge crane;overhead travelling crane

翘 [qiáo]
动 ①raise (one's head);lift up ②become warped (*or* bent) ➡qiào
翘楚 talented person;outstanding person
翘面 warping
翘盼 eagerly look forward to
翘企 raise one's head and stand on tiptoe—eagerly look forward to
翘首 raise one's head and look
翘足而待 wait on tiptoe—expect sth to happen soon
翘足引领 stand on tiptoe and crane one's neck—eagerly look forward to

谯 [qiáo]
名 watchtower
谯楼 ①watchtower ②drum tower

憔 [qiáo]
憔悴 wan and sallow;thin and pallid

樵 [qiáo]
Ⅰ名 firewood Ⅱ动 gather firewood
樵夫 woodcutter;woodman

瞧 [qiáo]
动 look;watch;see
瞧病 ①(of a patient) see (*or* consult) a doctor ②(of a doctor) see a patient
瞧见 see;catch sight of
瞧上 ①have a chance to see ②to one's liking
瞧不起 look down on;despise
瞧得起 have a good opinion of;think highly of
瞧不上眼 consider beneath one's notice;turn one's nose up at
瞧哈哈儿 have a good laugh over (sb's misfortune);gloat over

qiǎo (ㄑ丨ㄠ)

巧 [qiǎo]
形 ①skilful;adept;ingenious;clever ②(of hand and tongue) deft;glib;clever ③opportune;accidental ④(of words) fine-sounding;sly;artful
巧辩 argue skilfully or plausibly
巧干 work ingeniously;do sth in a clever way
巧合 coincidence
巧计 clever device;artful scheme
巧匠 clever artisan;craftsman;skilled workman
巧妙 ingenious;clever
巧事 coincidence
巧手 a dab (*or* deft) hand;being clever with one's hands;dexterity
巧思 ingenious (*or* brilliant) conception
巧遇 encounter by chance
巧妇鸟 wren
巧劲儿 ①knack;trick ②coincidence
巧克力 chocolate
巧夺天工 wonderful workmanship (*or* superb craftsmanship) excelling nature
巧立名目 concoct various pretexts;invent all sorts of names (*or* excuses)
巧取豪夺 secure (sb's belongings, rights, etc.) by force or trickery
巧舌如簧 have a smooth tongue like the reed of a wind instrument—have a glib tongue
巧言令色 clever talk and ingratiating manner
巧干加实干 be both ingenious and down-to-earth in one's work
巧妇难为无米之炊 the cleverest housewife can't cook a meal without rice—one can't make bricks without straw

悄 [qiǎo]
形 ①quiet;silent ②sad;worried;grieved ➡qiāo
悄寂 quiet;still;silent
悄然 ①sad;worried;sorrowful ②quiet;soft
悄声 a low voice;whisper

悄没声儿 silent; low-voiced
悄然落泪 shed silent tears

雀 [qiǎo]
〔名〕sparrow ⇒ què
雀盲眼 night blindness; nyctalopia

qiào（ㄑㄧㄠˋ）

壳 [qiào]
〔名〕hard outer covering of sth; shell; crust ⇒ ké
壳菜 mussel
壳斗 acorn-cup; cupule
壳质 chitin

俏 [qiào]
Ⅰ〔形〕①stylish; handsome; good-looking ②fast-selling Ⅱ〔动〕seasoning
俏货 goods in great demand
俏丽 handsome; pretty
俏皮 ①good-looking; smart-looking ②witty; clever
俏销（of commodities）sell well; be in great demand; have a ready market
俏皮话 ①witty remark; witticism; wisecrack ②sarcastic remark ③a two-part allegorical saying, of which the first part, always stated, is descriptive, while the second part, sometimes unstated, carries the message

诮 [qiào]
〔动〕①blame; censure; reproach; upbraid ②sneer at; deride

峭 [qiào]
〔形〕①high and steep; abrupt; precipitous ②stern; harsh; severe
峭拔 ①（of a mountain）high and steep ②（of style of writing）vigorous
峭壁 cliff; precipice; steep
峭寒 （esp. of early spring）chilly
峭立 rise steeply
峭直 severe; stern

窍 [qiào]
〔名〕①aperture; orifice ②key to sth; knack
窍门 key（to a problem）; knack

翘 [qiào]
〔动〕stick up; hold up; turn upwards ⇒ qiáo
翘辫子 kick the bucket
翘舌音 cacuminal
翘尾巴 be cocky; get stuck-up

撬 [qiào]
〔动〕prize; pry; jimmy
撬棒 crowbar
撬杠 pinch bar; crowbar; pry
撬棍 pinch bar; crowbar; pry

鞘 [qiào]
〔名〕sheath; scabbard ⇒ shāo
鞘翅 elytrum
鞘细胞 sheath cell

撒 [qiào]
〔动〕beat from the sides

qiē（ㄑㄧㄝ）

切 [qiē]
〔动〕①cut; chop; slice ②tangency ⇒ qiè
切边 scrap edge; side cut
切变 shear
切槽 grooving
切除 excise; resect
切磋 learn from each other by exchanging views
切点 point of tangency; point of contact
切掉 cut; clear; dissect
切断 cut off
切换 cut
切糕 a kind of cake made of glutinous rice, sold in sliced pieces
切割 cut metal（by lathes, etc.）
切开 incise
切口 the side margin of a page in a book
切块 stripping and slicing（food）
切力 shearing force; shear
切面 ①cut noodles; machine-made noodles ②tangent plane ③section
切片 ①cut into slices ②section（of organic tissues）
切入 penetrate into
切伤 cut wound; incised wound
切线 tangent（line）
切削 cut
切牙 incisor; incisor teeth
切布机 paper making rag cutter（or chopper）
切菜机 vegetable-chopper; vegetable-cutter
切齿机 gear cutting machine
切分音 syncopation
切割器 sickle; knife bar
切片机 ①slicer ②chipper ③microtome
切纸机 paper cutting machine; paper cutter
切磋琢磨 carve and polish—learn from each other by exchanging views
切腹自杀 commit hara-kiri; commit seppuku

qié（ㄑㄧㄝˊ）

伽 [qié]
（used in transliteration of Sanskrit）⇒ gā; jiā

茄 [qié]
〔名〕eggplant; aubergine ⇒ jiā
茄泥 mashed eggplant（a dish）
茄子 eggplant; aubergine

qiě（ㄑㄧㄝˇ）

且 [qiě]
Ⅰ〔副〕①just; for the time being; for a while ②for a long time; for quite some time Ⅱ〔连〕①even ②also; and ⇒ jū
且慢 wait a moment; not so soon; not so fast

且不说 let alone
且惊且喜 be surprised but glad;pleasant surprise
且信且疑 half-believing and half-doubting;between belief and doubt

qiè（くlせ）

切 [qiè] I 动 correspond to;accord with;conform to（or with） II 形 ① close to; warm ② eager; keen; anxious III 副 be sure to; make sure that... ➡ qiē
切齿 gnash one's teeth（in hatred）
切当 proper;suitable;fitting;appropriate
切骨（of hatred）deep;bitter
切合 suit;fit in with
切己 of immediate concern to oneself
切记 be sure to keep in mind;must always remember
切忌 must guard against;avoid by all means
切近 ①close to ②close;near
切口 the secret language of underworld gangs（or of certain professions）
切脉 feel the pulse
切盼 eagerly look forward to;wait impatiently for
切切 ①be sure to ②eager;urgent;earnest
切身 ①of immediate concern to oneself or sb ②personal;first-hand
切实 ① feasible; practical; realistic ② conscientious;earnest
切题 keep to the point;be relevant to the subject
切望 on tiptoe
切诊 pulse feeling and palpation,one of the four methods of diagnosis
切中 hit（the mark）
切肤之痛 keenly felt pain
切切实实 make a determined effort;down to earth
切身体会 personal understanding; intimate knowledge
切中时弊 cutting into the present-day evils; criticise the current social evils sharply

妾 [qiè] 名 ① concubine ②（used by women in humble reference to themselves）

怯 [qiè] 形 ① timid; cowardly; chicken-hearted; nervous ②（used by people in Beijing to refer to all other northern dialects）：他的口音带点怯。He speaks with a northern accent. ③inelegant;outmoded;vulgar ④lacking in knowledge;superficial;shallow
怯场 have stage fright
怯懦 timid and overcautious
怯弱 timid and weak-willed

怯生 shy with strangers
怯阵 ①feel nervous when going into battle;be battle-shy ②have stage fright
怯生生 in a timid manner
怯声怯气 speak in a timid manner;speak haltingly
怯头怯脑 uncouth;lumpish;countrified

窃 [qiè] I 动 steal;pilfer;pinch II 副 secretly;furtively;stealthily;surreptitiously III 代（used to refer to oneself）：窃 以 为 不 可。In my humble opinion,this won't work.
窃案 larceny;burglary
窃盗 deathwatch
窃夺 usurp;grab
窃国 usurp state power
窃据 usurp;unjustly occupy
窃窥 peep
窃密 steal secret information;steal secrets
窃窃 low（voice）;whispering
窃取 usurp;steal;grab
窃听 eavesdrop;wiretap;tap;bug
窃笑 laugh secretly;laugh up one's sleeve
窃贼 thief;burglar;pilferer
窃听器 bug; hidden microphone; tapping device;listening-in device
窃窃私议 exchange whispered comments
窃窃私语 talk in whispers;whisper
窃钩者诛,窃国者侯 He who steals a belt buckle pays with his life;He who steals a state gets to be a feudal lord.

挈 [qiè] 动 ①lift;hoist;take up;raise ②take along
挈带 take along;carry

惬 [qiè] 动 gratify;satisfy
惬意 be pleased;be satisfied

慊 [qiè] 形 contented; satisfied; gratified; pleased ➡ qiàn

朅 [qiè] I 动 go;leave II 形 brave;courageous

锲 [qiè] 动 chisel;carve;engrave
锲而不舍 keep on chipping away—work with perseverance

箧 [qiè] 名 small suitcase;small box

qie（·くlせ）

趄 [qie] I 动 tilt II 形 slanting;inclined

qīn（くlㄣ）

钦 [qīn] I 动 admire; adore; respect II 副 by the emperor himself
钦差 imperial envoy;imperial commissioner

Q

钦赐 granted (*or* stowed) by the emperor
钦定 compiled and edited by imperial orders
钦服 esteem;admire
钦敬 admire and respect
钦佩 admire;esteem
钦羡 admire and respect
钦差大臣 ① imperial commissioner; imperial envoy ②a nickname for a representative of the higher authorities

侵 [qīn]
I 动 invade; intrude into; encroach on; infringe upon II 形 approaching
侵晨 approaching daybreak;towards dawn
侵犯 encroach on;infringe (upon);violate
侵害 encroach on;make inroads on
侵略 aggression;invasion
侵染 (of germs,bacteria,or viruses) infect
侵扰 invade and harass
侵入 invade;intrude into;make incursions into
侵蚀 ①corrode; erode ②seize (property) in secret and bit by bit
侵吞 ① embezzle; misappropriate ② swallow up;annex
侵袭 make inroads on;invade and attack;hit
侵晓 approaching daybreak;towards dawn
侵占 ①invade and occupy ②seize;embezzle
侵彻力 penetrativeness (of a bullet)
侵权案 infringement case
侵入岩 intrusive rock;irruptive rock
侵蚀土 eroded soil
侵占罪 crime of encroachment
侵犯版权 infringe a copyright
侵犯人权 violate human rights;infringe upon human rights
侵权行为 tort;act of tort
侵人犯规 (of basketball) personal foul
侵吞公款 graft;embezzle public funds;plunder the public treasury
侵犯商标权 trademark infringement
侵犯肖像权 infringe upon the right of portrait
侵犯专利权 infringe on the patent right
侵犯别国主权 infringe upon the sovereignty of other countries
侵犯人身自由 infringement of human freedom
侵犯领土和主权 violate a country's territorial integrity and sovereignty
侵犯商业秘密罪 crime of breaching business secrets

亲 [qīn]
I 名 ①parent ②one's own flesh and flood ③blood relations;next of kin ④kin;relative ⑤marriage;match ⑥bride II 形 close;intimate;near and dear III 副 in person;personally IV 动 ①in favour of;supporting ②kiss ➡ qìng
亲爱 dear;beloved

亲本 parent
亲笔 ①in one's own handwriting ②one's own handwriting
亲代 parental generation
亲等 degree of kinship
亲丁 blood relation
亲睹 see with one's own eyes;see for oneself
亲和 affable;genial
亲近 be close to;be on intimate terms with
亲眷 ①one's relatives ②family dependants
亲口 (say sth) personally
亲历 have a personal experience of sth
亲临 come (*or* go) to a place personally
亲聆 go in person to listen to (instructions)
亲密 close;intimate
亲昵 very intimate;affectionate
亲朋 relatives and friends;kith and kin
亲启 personal
亲戚 [qīnqi] relative
亲切 ①cordial;kind ②close;intimate;dear
亲情 affection between family members
亲热 affectionate;intimate;warmhearted
亲人 ①one's parents, spouse, children, etc.; one's family members ② dear ones; those dear to one
亲善 close and friendly (between countries)
亲身 personal;firsthand
亲生 ①be sb's own child (i.e. not an adopted one) ②one's own (children or parents)
亲事 marriage
亲手 with one's own hands;personally;oneself
亲疏 (of relatives or social connections) close or distant
亲属 kinsfolk;relatives
亲王 prince
亲吻 kiss
亲信 ①close and trustful ②trusted aide (*or* follower)
亲眼 with one's own eyes;personally
亲友 relatives and friends;kith and kin
亲缘 affinity
亲自 personally;in person;oneself
亲族 members of the same clan
亲嘴 kiss
亲骨肉 one's own flesh and blood (i.e. parents and children,brothers and sisters)
亲和力 affinity;attraction and seduction
亲临现场 be on the spot
亲临指导 come personally to give guidance
亲密无间 be on intimate terms
亲如手足 as close as brothers
亲如兄弟 as close as brothers
亲如一家 as dear to each other as members of one family
亲上加亲 be doubly related;choose a bride (*or* groom) from relatives
亲生父母 one's own parents

亲生子女 one's own children
亲水住宅 waterfront housing
亲子鉴定 identification in disputed paternity; parent-child test; paternity test; test to determine whether the child is one's own
亲者痛,仇者快 sadden one's own folk and gladden the enemy

衾 [qīn]
名 ①quilt ②pall

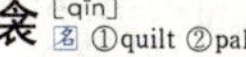

qín〈ㄑㄧㄣˊ〉

芹 [qín]
名 celery
芹菜 celery

矜 [qín]
名 handle of a spear ➡ jīn

秦 [qín]
秦艽 large-leaved gentian
秦皮 the bark of ash
秦腔 Shaanxi opera (popular in the northwestern provinces)
秦越 as far apart as Qin and Yue—have no dealings with each other
秦晋之好 the amity between Qin and Jin (sealed by a marriage alliance between the two royal houses)—a marriage alliance between two families
秦楼楚馆 towers of Qin and pavilions of Chu—quarters of pleasure; courtesans' quarters

琴 [qín]
名 ①*qin*, a seven-stringed plucked instrument in some ways similar to the zither ②(general name for) certain musical instruments
琴拨 plectrum
琴凳 music stool
琴键 key (on a musical instrument)
琴马 bridge (of a stringed instrument)
琴鸟 lyrebird
琴师 stringed instrumentalist
琴弦 string (of a musical instrument)
琴剑飘零 (of a scholar) wander from place to place
琴棋书画 lute-playing, chess, calligraphy, and painting—accomplishments of a scholar of the old school
琴瑟不调 the *qin* and the *se* are not in harmony—discord between husband and wife; an uncongenial marriage
琴瑟和谐 the *qin* and the *se* are in harmony—husband and wife living in harmony; wedded bliss
琴心剑胆 the sentiments of the lute (*qin*) and the spirit of the sword—a cultivated mind animated with a chivalrous spirit

禽 [qín]
名 ①birds; fowl ②fowls and animals
禽龙 iguanodon
禽兽 birds and beasts—inhuman
禽流感 bird flu
禽兽不如 be worse than a beast

勤 [qín]
I 形 ① diligent; assiduous; industrious; hardworking ② frequent II 名 ① work; duty ②(office, school, etc.) attendance
勤奋 diligent; assiduous; industrious
勤俭 hardworking and thrifty
勤恳 diligent and conscientious
勤快 diligent; hardworking
勤劳 diligent; industrious; hardworking
勤勉 diligent; assiduous
勤朴 industrious and thrifty
勤王 ①come to the rescue of the king ②do one's best to serve the throne
勤务 ①(public) duties; service ②a person who does logistic duties
勤务兵 orderly
勤务员 ① odd-job man (in an army unit or government office) ②a servant(of the people)
勤杂工 odd-job man; handyman
勤工俭学 part-work and part-study system; work-study programme
勤俭持家 be industrious and thrifty in running a household
勤俭建国 build up the country through thrift and hard work
勤俭节约 practise thrift and economy
勤劳勇敢 be industrious and courageous; valiant and industrious
勤劳致富 make a fortune by means of industry; achieve prosperity through industrial work
勤勤恳恳 work diligently and conscientiously; zealously and earnestly
勤学苦练 study diligently and train hard
勤杂人员 personnel regularly doing certain odd jobs (in an army unit or government office); odd-job man
勤政廉政 be diligent and honest in one's work
勤政为民 be assiduous in government affairs and serve the people

擒 [qín]
动 capture; catch; take; seize
擒拿 arrest; capture; catch
擒纵轮 escape wheel
擒贼先擒王 to catch brigands, first catch their king

qǐn〈ㄑㄧㄣˇ〉

寝 [qín]
I 动 ① sleep ② stop; cease; end II 名 ①

bedroom ②coffin chamber;tomb
寝车 sleeping car;sleeping carriage;sleeper
寝宫 ①sleeping quarters of the emperor and empress ②coffin chamber in an imperial mausoleum
寝具 bedding
寝食 eating and sleeping—daily life
寝室 room (in a dormitory)
寝食不安 feel uneasy even when eating and sleeping;be worried waking or sleeping

qìn（ㄑㄧㄣˋ）

呤 [qìn] 动 ①(of animals such as dogs and cats) vomit ②rail;yelp;spit out hogwash

沁 [qìn] 动 ①(of fragrance,liquid,etc.) ooze;exude ②lower one's head ③soak in liquid
沁人心脾 seep into the heart;gladdening the heart and refreshing the mind;feel comfortable when breathing fresh air (or having a cold drink)

揿 [qìn] 动 press;push

qīng（ㄑㄧㄥ）

青 [qīng] Ⅰ 形 ①blue;green ②black ③young in age Ⅱ 名 ① green grass;young crop ② youth;young people
青斑 blue spot;livedo
青布 black cloth
青菜 ①vegetable ②Chinese cabbage
青草 green grass
青春 youth;youthfulness
青瓷 celadon (ware)
青葱 verdant;fresh green
青翠 verdant;fresh and green
青豆 green soya bean
青工 young workers
青果 Chinese olive
青灰 graphite
青椒 green pepper
青筋 blue veins
青稞 ①highland barley ②the seed of highland barley
青睐 favour;good graces
青楼 blue mansions—pleasure quarters;courtesans' quarters
青绿 dark green
青盲 glaucoma
青梅 green plum
青苗 young crops;green shoots of (food) grains
青年 youth;young people
青鸟 ①messenger ②bird messenger of Fairy God-Mother

青山 green hills;blue mountains
青史 annals of history
青丝 black hair (of a woman or girl)
青松 pine
青蒜 garlic leaves
青苔 moss
青天 ①the blue sky ②the clear sky (a respectful sobriquet for a clean and upright official)
青铜 bronze
青蛙 frog
青虾 freshwater shrimp
青葙 feather cockscomb
青杨 Cathay poplar
青蝇 greenbottle (fly)
青鱼 black carp
青郁 verdant and luxuriant
青云 high official position;rapid official advancement
青贮 ensiling
青春饭 occupation for young persons only;pursue a profession on the strength of one's young age;job for young persons only
青春期 puberty;adolescence
青光眼 glaucoma
青花瓷 blue and white porcelain
青灰色 cinerous
青莲色 pale purple;heliotrope
青霉素 penicillin
青年期 adolescence
青纱帐 the green curtain of tall crops
青少年 teen-agers;youngsters
青饲料 greenfeed;green fodder
青铜器 bronze ware
青葙子 the seed of feather cockscomb
青云志 high aspirations
青出于蓝 blue comes from the indigo plant but is bluer than the plant itself—the pupil surpasses the master
青春焕发 be full of vigour;be bursting with youthful energy
青春偶像 adolescent idol
青红皂白 black and white;right and wrong
青黄不接 gap between the old and the young;temporary shortage gap in succession
青梅竹马 green plums and a bamboo horse—a girl and a boy playing innocently together;a man and a woman who had an innocent affection for each other in childhood
青面獠牙 green-faced and long-toothed—terrifying in appearance
青年工人 young workers
青山绿水 blue mountains and green waters—beautiful scenery
青天白日 ①bright and sunny ②broad daylight
青铜时代 the Bronze Age
青云直上 rapid advancement;a meteoric rise

青藏铁路 Qinghai-Tibet railway
青年劳教所 Youth Correctional Institute
青山不老,绿水常存 The blue mountains do not grow old, the green waters always remain.
青少年思想道德教育 education in ideology and ethics among the youth and youngsters

轻 [qīng]
Ⅰ 形 ①of little weight;light ②easy to carry;light;simple ③ small in number, degree, etc. ④relaxed;light ⑤not important;be of no significance ⑥ flighty;frivolous Ⅱ 动 regard sb or sth as of no importance;make light of; belittle Ⅲ 副 ①gently;softly ②rashly;impetuously
轻便 ①light;portable ②easy and convenient
轻薄 (usu. of a man towards a woman) given to philandering;frivolous
轻淡 ①faint;dim ②casual;random
轻敌 take the enemy lightly;underestimate the enemy
轻放 put down gently
轻风 light breeze
轻浮 frivolous;flighty;light
轻轨 light rail
轻核 light nucleus
轻活 light work;soft job
轻健 spry and light;nimble;brisk
轻捷 spry and light;nimble
轻看 look down upon;belittle
轻快 ①brisk;spry ②lighthearted;lively
轻狂 extremely frivolous
轻慢 treat sb without proper respect;slight
轻蔑 despise;scorn;disdain;be contemptuous
轻骑 ①light cavalry ②moped
轻巧 ① light and handy ②dexterous;deft ③ simple;easy
轻取 win an easy victory (in a game);beat easily;win hands down
轻柔 soft;gentle
轻纱 fine gauze
轻伤 slight (or minor) wound;flesh wound
轻生 make light of one's life—commit suicide
轻声 ①in a soft voice;softly ②neutral tone
轻视 belittle;look down on;underrate
轻率 rash;hasty;indiscreet
轻水 light water
轻松 light;relaxed
轻瘫 paresis
轻佻 frivolous;flippant;giddy
轻微 light;slight;trifling;to a small extent
轻闲 ① not busy; leisurely ② easy or light (work)
轻信 be credulous;readily place trust in;readily believe
轻型 light-duty;light
轻易 ①easily ②lightly;rashly
轻盈 ①slim and graceful;lithe;relaxed

轻油 light oil
轻重 ①weight ②degree of seriousness;relative importance ③propriety
轻舟 a small light boat;skiff
轻装 ①light packs ②light equipment
轻罪 misdemeanour; minor offence (or crime)
轻磅纸 lightweight paper
轻辅音 voiceless consonant
轻歌剧 light opera
轻工业 light industry
轻机枪 light machine gun
轻金属 light metal
轻量级 lightweight
轻泡货 light cargo
轻炮兵 light artillery
轻飘飘 light;buoyant
轻骑兵 light cavalry
轻武器 light arms;small arms
轻泻剂 laxative
轻音乐 light music
轻元音 light vowel
轻财重义 value friendship more than money; be generous and charitable
轻车简从 travel with minimum of pomp;travel with a modest staff;receive a simple reception
轻车熟路 drive in a light carriage on a familiar road—do sth one knows well and can manage with ease
轻度衰退 mild recession
轻而易举 easy to do
轻纺工业 textile and other light industries
轻歌曼舞 soft music and graceful dances
轻轨火车 light rail vehicle;light rail train
轻轨交通 light rail communication;light rail traffic
轻轨铁路 light railway
轻混凝土 lightweight concrete
轻举妄动 act rashly;take reckless action
轻口薄舌 ① speak unkindly;make caustic remarks;be sharp-tongued;have a caustic and sharp tongue ②make improper remarks
轻描淡写 touch on lightly;mention casually
轻诺寡信 make promises easily but seldom keep them
轻世傲物 full of conceit and defiant of convention
轻手轻脚 gently;softly
轻言细语 speak in a soft,gentle voice
轻于鸿毛 lighter than a goose feather
轻重倒置 put the trivial above the important; stress trifles and overlook matters of moment
轻重缓急 order of priority;in order of importance and urgency;order of priority;relative importance and urgency

Q

轻重量级 light heavyweight
轻妆淡抹 have a simple makeup
轻装简从 travel with light packs and few attendants
轻装上阵 join a movement without hesitation (*or* reservation)
轻水反应堆 light water reactor (LWR)
轻度通货膨胀 moderate inflation
轻重工业的比例失调 disproportion between light and heavy industries

氢 [qīng]
[名] hydrogen (H)
氢弹 hydrogen bomb
氢化 hydrogenation
氢气 hydrogen
氢氧 oxyhydrogen
氢弹头 hydrogen warhead; H-warhead
氢氟酸 hydrofluoric acid
氢离子 hydrogen ion
氢气球 hydrogen balloon
氢氰酸 hydrocyanic acid
氢燃料 hydrogen fuel
氢同位素 hydrogen isotope
氢氧吹管 oxyhydrogen blowpipe
氢氧化物 hydroxide

倾 [qīng]
I [动] ①slant; incline; bend ②collapse; topple ③overturn and pour out; dump; empty ④use up (all one's energy); exhaust ⑤overwhelm; overbear II [名] tendency; deviation
倾城 ① the whole city (*or* town) ②(of a woman) lovely enough to cause the fall of a city or a state; devastatingly beautiful; exceedingly beautiful
倾倒 [qīngdǎo] ①topple and fall; topple over ②greatly admire
倾倒 [qīngdào] tip; dump; empty; pour out
倾点 pour point; flow point
倾动 move and win admiration
倾耳 prick up one's ears
倾覆 overturn; topple; capsize
倾角 ①dip ②inclination ③dip angle
倾力 all out
倾慕 have a strong admiration for; adore
倾情 devoted
倾洒 (of snow, tears, etc.) pour down (*or* forth)
倾诉 pour out (one's heart, troubles, etc.)
倾谈 have a good, heart-to-heart talk
倾听 listen attentively to; lend an attentive ear to
倾吐 say what is on one's mind without reservation
倾向 ①tendency; trend; inclination; deviation ②be inclined to; prefer
倾销 sell goods at a very low price; dump; cutthroat sale

倾斜 tilt; incline; slope; slant; in favour of
倾泻 come down in torrents
倾卸 tip; dump; empty; pour out
倾心 ①admire; adore ②cordial; heart-to-heart
倾轧 engage in internal strife; jostle against each other
倾注 ①pour into ②throw (energy, etc.) into
倾向性 tendentiousness
倾斜度 gradient
倾斜计 inclinometer; tiltmeter; gradiometer
倾斜角 ①bank angle (of an airplane) ②dip; inclination; dip angle
倾斜面 inclined plane
倾巢出动 (of the enemy or bandits, etc.) turn out in full force (*or* strength)
倾国倾城 (of a woman) lovely enough to cause the fall of a city or a state; devastatingly beautiful; exceedingly beautiful
倾家荡产 lose a family fortune; be reduced to poverty and ruin
倾囊相助 empty one's purse to help; give generous financial assistance
倾盆大雨 heavy downpour; torrential rain; cloudburst
倾箱倒箧 turn out all one's boxes and suitcases—give away all one has
倾销政策 favorable policy; slanting policy; preferential policy; policy with special emphasis on one side; policy tilting toward whatever needs to be emphasized
倾斜政策 preferential policy; affirmative policy
倾卸汽车 dump truck; tipper
倾心吐胆 pour out one's heart; unburden one's heart; unbosom oneself
倾角测量仪 dipmeter

卿 [qīng]
[名] ①minister or senior official in ancient times ②(emperor's form of address for a court official) you ③term of endearment used between husband and wife or among close friends in ancient times
卿卿我我 (of lovers) whisper sweet nothings to one another; bill and coo

圊 [qīng]
[名] latrine
圊粪 manure from latrines
圊土 human excrement; night soil

清 [qīng]
I [形] ①(of liquids and gases) pure; clear ②quiet; silent; still ③honest and upright ④clear; lucid ⑤clear; plain II [动] ①clear up; purify; clean up ②settle accounts ③count; check
清白 pure; clean; stainless
清仓 ① make an inventory (*or* checkup) of warehouses ②sell all out one's securities

清册 detailed list

清茶 ① green tea ② tea served without refreshments

清查 ① check ② ferret out（counterrevolutionaries,etc.）;uncover;comb out

清偿 pay off;clear off

清场 clear out（*or* clean up）a gathering place（theatre,arena,athletic field,etc.）

清唱 sing opera arias（without makeup and acting）

清澈 limpid;clear

清晨 early morning

清除 clear away;eliminate;get rid of

清楚 ①clear;distinct ②be clear about;understand

清醇 pure（in taste or smell）

清脆 clear and melodious

清单 detailed list;detailed account

清淡 ①light;weak;delicate ②not greasy（*or* strongly flavoured）;light ③dull;slack

清党 purge（a political party）;carry out a purge

清道 ① sweep the streets ② clear the way（for a high official in imperial times）

清点 check;make an inventory;sort and count

清炖 boiled in clear soup（without soy sauce）

清芬 ①delicate fragrance;faint scent ②moral integrity;nobility of character

清风 cool breeze;refreshing breeze

清福 the happiness of a leisurely,retired life

清高 aloof from politics and material pursuits

清稿 ① make a fair（*or* clean）copy ② fair（*or* clean）copy

清关 customs clearance

清官 honest and upright official

清规 monastic rules for Buddhists

清寒 ① poor; in straitened circumstances ② cold and clear

清还 clear up and pay back（debts,etc.）

清火 relieve inflammation（*or* internal heat）

清剿 clean up;suppress;eliminate

清洁 clean

清结 ① settle（*or* square）accounts;balance the books ②bring to an end;wind up;settle

清净 peace and quiet

清静 quiet

清客 protégés of the powerful who stay with their benefactions like parasites

清口 tasty and refreshing

清苦 （esp. of scholars or teachers）poor;badly off

清蜡 paraffin removal

清朗 ①cool and bright ②loud and clear;resounding

清冷 ①chilly ②deserted;desolate

清理 put in order;check up;clear;sort out

清廉 honest and upright;free from corruption

清凉 cool and refreshing

清亮 clear and resounding;resonant

清棉 scutching

清明 ①clear and bright ②sober and calm ③（of government or administration）well ordered;well regulated ④Pure Brightness—the 5th of the 24 solar terms ⑤ the day marking the beginning of the 5th solar term

清盘 ①liquidation ②close out;go into liquidation

清贫 （usu. of scholars or teachers）poor;badly off

清平 peaceful;tranquil

清漆 varnish

清讫 payment received;paid

清泉 cool spring（water）

清扫 thoroughly clean up; give a thorough cleanup

清瘦 thin;lean;spare

清爽 ①fresh and cool ②relieved;relaxed ③ clean and tidy

清算 ①clear（accounts）;square ②settle accounts;expose and criticize

清谈 ① pure conversations—intellectual discussions on lofty and nonmundane matters ②idle talk;empty talk

清汤 clear soup;light soup;consommé

清婉 （of voice）clear and sweet

清晰 distinct;clear

清洗 ①rinse;wash;clean ②purge;comb out

清闲 at leisure;idle

清香 delicate fragrance;faint scent

清新 pure and fresh;fresh

清醒 ① clear-headed; sober ② regain consciousness

清秀 delicate and pretty

清雅 elegant;refined

清样 final proof;foundry proof

清夜 the stillness of night;quiet night

清音 voiceless sound

清幽 （of a landscape）quiet and beautiful

清油 boiled oils;edible vegetable oil

清越 （of sound）clear and melodious;clear and far-reaching

清运 clear;remove

清早 early in the morning;early morning

清账 square（*or* clear）an account

清真 ①simple and unadorned;plain ②Islamic;Muslim

清蒸 steamed in clear soup（usu. without soy sauce）

清整 level（land）

清正 upright and just

清浊 ① pure and impure; good and bad ② voiceless and voiced sounds

清唱剧 oratorio

清创术 débridement

清道夫 scavenger; street cleaner; street sweeper
清教徒 Puritan
清洁车 street sweeper; street vehicle
清洁袋 sick bag
清洁队 cleaning squad
清洁剂 cleanser; detergent
清劲风 fresh breeze
清凉油 cooling ointment; essential balm
清喷漆 clear lacquer
清热法 antipyretic method (using medicines of a cold nature to treat acute febrile diseases)
清热药 antipyretic
清水墙 dry wall
清晰度 ①(TV) clarity ②(sound) articulation
清选机 cleaner
清一色 ① all of one suit (in playing mahjong); flush ② all of the same colour; uniform; homogeneous
清真寺 mosque
清仓查库 make an inventory of warehouses
清仓处理 liquidation
清仓利库 make warehouse inventory and put the stocks to best use
清仓拍卖 clearance sale; rummage sale; clearing stock sale
清仓物资 old stock
清茶淡饭 coarse fare—living in poverty
清产核资 ①check-up of assets; general check-up on the fixed assets ②take inventory of property and make an accounting of funds; make a general check on the assets
清偿债务 pay off debts
清风亮节 clear breeze and bright principles—as of one's deportment
清歌妙舞 clear singing and exquisite dancing
清规戒律 ①regulations, taboos and commandments (for Buddhists or Taoists) ②restrictions and fetters
清锅冷灶 the pot is empty and the stove is cold—(of a house, restaurant, etc.) deserted; unfrequented
清洁工人 sanitation worker; street cleaner
清洁能源 clean energy
清洁燃料 clean fuel
清洁生产 clean production
清洁提单 clean bill of lading
清理欠税 clear up cases of arrear tax; clear up cases of taxes in arrears
清理文件 sort out documents
清理现场 sift through the wreckage
清清白白 be pure in mind and body; lead a clean life
清清楚楚 be crystal clear; be absolutely clear
清水衙门 plain water *yamen*
清算公司 clearing corporation; liquidation company
清算协定 clearing agreement
清算银行 clearing bank
清算账户 clearing account
清汤寡水 (of a dish) watery and tasteless; dishwater
清心寡欲 purify one's heart and reduce the number of one's desires; be pure of heart and have few desires
清夜扪心 examine one's conscience in the stillness of night
清夜自思 be deep in thought in the stillness of night
清仓大甩卖 clearance sale
清仓削价处理 sell goods at a clearance price
清理破产企业 wind up bankrupt businesses
清理整顿公司 screen and reorganize (*or* rectify) corporations
清官难断家务事 Even an upright official finds it hard to settle a family quarrel.
清洁高效的工艺 clean and efficient technologies

蜻 [qīng]

蜻蜓 dragonfly
蜻蜓点水 like a dragonfly skimming the surface of the water—just touch on sth lightly without going into it deeply

鲭 [qīng]

名 mackerel ➡zhēng

qíng ⟨ㄑㄧㄥˊ⟩

勍 [qíng]

形 powerful; strong
勍敌 powerful foe

情 [qíng]

名 ①feeling; emotion; affection; sentiment ②kindness; favour ③love; passion ④intense sexual desire; lust ⑤situation; circumstance; state; condition ⑥reason; sense
情爱 love (esp. between man and woman)
情报 intelligence; information
情变 break-up
情操 sentiment
情场 the arena of love; the tournament of love
情痴 love maniac
情敌 rival in love
情调 sentiment; emotional appeal
情分 mutual affection
情夫 an illicit lover of a married woman; lover
情妇 an illicit lover of a married man; mistress
情感 emotion; feeling
情歌 love song
情话 ①intimate words; heart-to-heart talk ② lovers' prattle; whispers of love; sweet nothings
情怀 feelings

情节 ①plot ②circumstances
情结 emotional ties; deep emotions associated with sth; complex
情景 scene; sight; circumstances
情境 circumstances; situation
情况 ① circumstances; situation; condition; state of affairs ②military situation
情郎（girl's) lover; sweetheart
情理 reason; sense
情侣 sweethearts; lovers
情面 feelings; sensibilities
情趣 ①temperament and interest ②interest; appeal
情人 sweetheart; lover
情杀 murder for love
情商 EQ; emotional quotient
情诗 love poem
情事 the facts; the phenomena
情势 situation; circumstances; trend of events
情书 love letter
情丝 affection; tender feelings
情思 ①tender regards; affection; goodwill ② state of mind; mood
情死 die for love
情愫 ①feeling; sentiment ②real sentiment; innermost feeling
情态 spirit; mood
情网 snares of love
情味 sentiment; interest
情形 circumstances; situation; condition; state of affairs
情绪 ① morale; feeling; mood; sentiments ② depression; moodiness; the sulks
情义 ties of friendship, comradeship, etc.
情谊 friendly feelings; friendly sentiments
情意 tender regards; affection; goodwill
情由 the hows and whys
情欲 sexual passion; lust
情愿 ①be willing to ②would rather; prefer
情致 interest; appeal
情种 person of the sentimental type, especially one who easily falls in love
情状 state of affairs; situation; condition
情报网 intelligence network
情侣表 his-and-hers watch
情人节 Valentine's Day
情报机关 intelligence agency
情报检索 information retrieval
情报人员 intelligence personnel; intelligence agent
情报系统 intelligence channel
情不可却 It would be ungracious not to accept.
情不自禁 cannot refrain from; cannot help (doing sth); be seized with a sudden impulse to
情窦初开（of a young girl) first awakening

(*or* dawning) of love
情感商品 emotional product
情感消费 emotional consumption
情急智生 hit on an idea in a moment of desperation
情见乎辞 sincerity shines through the words
情景交融（of literary works) feeling and setting happily blended
情景喜剧 sitcom; situation comedy
情理难容 inexcusable feelings; unacceptable sentiments
情深似海 One's feeling is as deep as the ocean; The affection is as deep as the sea.
情随事迁 Feeling change with circumstances.
情态动词 modal verb
情同手足 like brothers; with brotherly love for each other
情投意合 find each other congenial
情文并茂（of writing) excellent in both content and language
情有可原 excusable; pardonable
情有所钟 have already had a lover in one's heart
情景教学法 situational teaching method
情人眼里出西施 A lover sees a Xi Shi in his beloved; In the eyes of the lover, his beloved is a beauty; Beauty is in the eye of the beholder.

晴 [qíng]
　彤 sunny; fine; clear
晴好 warm and fine
晴和 warm and fine
晴朗 fine; sunny
晴丝 gossamer
晴天 fine day; sunny day
晴雨表 weatherglass; barometer
晴间多云 fine with occasional clouds
晴空万里 boundless stretch of blue skies; the vast clear skies
晴天霹雳 a bolt from the blue

氰 [qíng]
　名 cyanogen
氰化 cyaniding
氰酸 cyanic acid
氰化钾 potassium cyanide
氰化物 cyanide

擎 [qíng]
　动 raise; hold up; lift up
擎天柱 a man in a responsible position; mainstay

黥 [qíng]
　动 ①（as punishment for a criminal in ancient times) brand the face ②tattoo

qǐng（ㄑㄧㄥˇ）

顷 [qǐng]
　I 量 *qǐng*, unit of area equal to one hun-

dred *mu* or 6.66 hectares, or 16.47 acres
Ⅱ 名 short while; moment; instant Ⅲ 副 ①
just; just now ②(of time) about

顷刻 in a moment; in an instant; instantly

请 [qǐng]
动 ① request; ask; entreat ② invite; engage; send for ③ please ④ buy (incense, joss sticks, and various other accessories for religious worship); set out (image, statue, etc.) for worship

请安 pay respects to sb; wish sb good health

请便 do as you wish; please yourself

请调 ask to be transferred to another post

请功 ask the higher level to record sb's meritorious deeds

请假 ask for leave

请柬 invitation card

请见 request an audience; ask for an interview

请教 ask for advice; consult

请客 stand treat; invite sb to dinner; entertain guests; give a dinner party

请命 ①plead on sb's behalf ②ask (the higher authorities) for instructions

请求 ask; request

请示 ask for (*or* request) instructions

请帖 invitation card; invitation

请问 ①excuse me; please ②we should like to ask; it may be asked; one may ask

请勿 please don't

请降 beg to surrender

请缨 request a cord from the emperor (to bind the enemy)—submit a request for a military assignment

请援 ask for support (*or* aid)

请愿 present a petition; petition

请战 ask for a battle assignment

请罪 admit one's error and ask for punishment; apologize

请假条 written request for leave (of absence)

请愿书 petition

请战书 a written request for a battle assignment

请君入瓮 kindly step into the vat—have a taste of what you intended for others

请客送礼 invite guests and give them presents; give lavish dinner parties and presents

庼 [qǐng]
名 small hall (*or* chamber)

qìng 〈ㄑㄧㄥˋ〉

庆 [qìng]
Ⅰ 动 celebrate Ⅱ 名 occasion for celebration

庆典 celebration; a ceremony to celebrate

庆贺 congratulate; celebrate

庆幸 rejoice

庆祝 celebrate

庆功会 victory meeting; victory celebration; meeting to celebrate a victory

庆功酒 jungle juice

庆大霉素 gentamicin

庆功论赏 confer honours according to merits in service while celebrating victory

庆祝大会 celebration meeting

庆父不死,鲁难未已 until Qing Fu is dead, the crisis in (the state of) Lu will not end— there will always be trouble until the one who causes it is gone

亲 [qìng]
➡ qīn

亲家 ① parents of one's daughter-in-law or son-in-law ②relatives by marriage

亲家公 son's or daughter's father-in-law

亲家母 son's or daughter's mother-in-law

磬 [qìng]
名 ①ancient percussion instrument made of jade or stone, shaped like a carpenter's square ② Buddhist percussion instrument made of bronze and shaped like an alms bowl

罄 [qìng]
动 use up; consume; exhaust

罄尽 with nothing left; all used up

罄竹难书 (of crimes) too many (*or* numerous) to record

qióng 〈ㄑㄩㄥˊ〉

穷 [qióng]
Ⅰ 形 with little money; poor Ⅱ 动 ①end; limit ② exhaust; use up Ⅲ 副 ① thoroughly (investigate); through to the end ②utterly; extremely

穷尽 limit; end

穷寇 hard-pressed enemy; tottering foe

穷苦 poverty-stricken; impoverished

穷困 poverty-stricken; destitute; in straitened circumstances

穷期 termination; end

穷人 poor people; the poor

穷酸 (of a scholar) poor and pedantic

穷途 straitened circumstances; destitution

穷相 appearance (*or* manner) suggestive of abject poverty

穷追 go in hot pursuit

穷光蛋 pauper; poor wretch

穷讲究 strive for shabby genteel; be fastidious (*or* fussy) despite difficult conditions; be overly choosy (*or* picky)

穷开心 ① enjoy oneself despite poverty ② seek joy amidst sorrow; try to enjoy oneself despite one's suffering

穷日子 days of poverty; straitened circumstances

穷兵黩武 use all one's armed might to wage wars of aggression; wantonly engage in

military ventures
穷不夺志 remain firm in one's faith despite straitened circumstances
穷愁潦倒 be penniless and frustrated
穷当益坚 The greater the adversity, the stronger the will.
穷得可怜 be shockingly poor
穷极思变 think of change only when in extremity
穷极无聊 ① be utterly bored ② absolutely senseless;disgusting
穷家富路 One should be frugal at home but well equipped for a journey.
穷寇勿追 don't pursue a beaten enemy
穷困潦倒 fall on evil days;in a state of utter poverty;live a life of poverty
穷年累月 for years on end;year after year
穷山恶水 barren mountains and unruly rivers; barren hills and untamed rivers
穷奢极侈 (indulge in) luxury and extravagance;(live a life of) wanton extravagance
穷奢极欲 extremely extravagant and luxurious
穷途潦倒 at the end of one's tether;desperate
穷途末路 be in an impasse;have come to a dead end;at end of one's rope
穷乡僻壤 a remote, backward place; remote hinterland
穷形尽相 ①describe in minute, vivid detail ② appear in all one's ugliness
穷凶极恶 extremely vicious;utterly evil;atrocious;diabolical
穷原竟委 get to the bottom of the matter; make a thorough (*or* exhaustive) inquiry into sth;explore the origin of sth and follow its development;trace back
穷则思变 Poverty gives rise to a desire for change.
穷追猛打 hotly pursue and fiercely attack
穷国与富国 "have-nots"and"haves";poor and rich countries

茕 [qióng]
〔形〕①solitary;all alone ②worried;sad
茕茕 all alone;lonely
茕茕子立,形影相吊 standing all alone, body and shadow comforting each other

穹 [qióng]
〔名〕①vault;dome ②sky
穹苍 the vault of heaven; the firmament; the sky
穹顶 dome
穹隆 vault;arched roof
穹形 vaulted;arched

筇 [qióng]
〔名〕a kind of bamboo recorded in ancient literature

琼 [qióng]
①fine jade;exquisite thing ② Qiongya or Hainan Island

琼岛 Hainan Island
琼浆 jade-like wine;good wine
琼脂 agar-agar;agar
琼浆玉液 fine, delicious wine; top-quality wine;nectar
琼楼玉宇 a richly decorated jade palace; a magnificent building

qiū（ㄑㄧㄡ）

丘 [qiū]
Ⅰ〔名〕mound;hillock Ⅱ〔动〕cover with earth or bricks and stones prior to burial Ⅲ〔量〕plot (of paddy field bordered by ridges):一丘水田 a plot of paddy field
丘陵 hills
丘脑 cerebral ganglion
丘鹬 woodcock
丘疹 papule
丘比特 Cupid,Roman god of love

秋 [qiū]
〔名〕①autumn;fall ②harvest time ③year ④ (troubled) period of time;juncture
秋波 autumn ripples—the bright and clear eyes of a beautiful woman
秋播 autumn sowing
秋菜 autumn vegetable
秋地 fields waiting for autumn sowing
秋分 ①the Autumn Equinox—the 16th of the 24 solar terms ②the day marking the beginning of the 16th solar term
秋风 autumn wind
秋耕 autumn ploughing
秋毫 autumn hair or newly-grown—sth so small as to be almost indiscernible
秋季 autumn;fall
秋景 ①autumn scenery ②autumn harvest
秋凉 cool autumn days
秋粮 autumn grain crops
秋令 ①autumn ②autumn weather
秋千 swing (a seat for swinging)
秋色 autumn scenery
秋收 ①autumn harvest ②autumn crops
秋水 autumn waters—limpid eyes (of a woman)
秋天 autumn;fall
秋汛 autumn floods
秋鸭 fall duck
秋游 autumn outing
秋雨 autumn rains
秋装 autumn clothing
秋海棠 begonia
秋老虎 a spell of hot weather after the Beginning of Autumn
秋水仙 meadow saffron;autumn crocus
秋庄稼 autumn crops
秋风过耳 like autumn wind passing by the ear—unnoticed;unheeded

Q

秋高气爽 autumn (sky) high and air brisk—the autumn sky is clear and the air is bracing

秋毫无犯 (of highly disciplined troops) not commit the slightest offence against the civilians; not encroach on the interests of the people to the slightest degree

秋毫之末 the tip of an autumn hair—a minute, almost indiscernible particle

秋后算账 wait for an opportunity to settle accounts with sb; revenge in response to earlier grievance when the opportunity arises; settle accounts afterwards

秋水仙素 colchicine

秋风扫落叶 the autumn wind sweeping away fallen leaves—carry everything before one

秋后的蚂蚱 a grasshopper at the end of autumn—nearing its end

蚯 [qiū]

蚯蚓 earthworm

湫 [qiū]

[名] pond; pool ➡ jiǎo

qiú (く1ㄡ)

囚 [qiú]

I [动] imprison; jail II [名] prisoner; convict

囚车 prison van; prisoners' van

囚犯 prisoner; convict

囚房 prison cell

囚歌 prisoner's laments

囚禁 imprison; put in jail; keep in captivity

囚牢 prison; jail

囚笼 (wooden) prisoner's cage used in imperial China

囚室 prison cell

囚徒 prisoner; convict

囚衣 prison garb

囚首垢面 with unkempt hair and dirty face

犰 [qiú]

犰狳 armadillo

求 [qiú]

[动] ①ask; beg; request; entreat ②strive for ③try; seek; search ④demand

求爱 pay court to; court; woo

求才 search for talent; scout for talent

求成 hope for success

求告 implore; entreat; supplicate

求根 extract a root

求购 offer to purchase

求和 ① sue for peace ② (in ball games or chess) try to equalize the score; try for a draw ③summation

求婚 make an offer of marriage; propose

求见 ask to see (one's superior or a VIP); request an interview; beg for an audience

求教 ask for advice

求解 find the solution (of a mathematical problem); solve a problem

求借 ask sb for a loan

求救 ask sb to come to the rescue; cry for help

求名 seek publicity; court publicity

求偶 seek a spouse

求乞 beg

求签 divine by drawing lots in a temple

求亲 seek a marriage alliance

求情 plead; intercede; ask for a favour; beg for leniency

求全 ①demand perfection ②try to round sth off

求饶 beg for mercy; ask for pardon

求人 ask sb for help

求生 seek survival

求胜 strive for victory

求仙 ①seek immortality ②seek divine advice

求降 beg to surrender; hang out (or hoist) the white flag

求学 ① go to school; attend school ② pursue one's studies; seek knowledge

求医 seek medical advice; see a doctor

求雨 pray for rain

求援 ask for help; request reinforcements

求战 ①seek battle; provoke battle ②ask to go into battle

求证 seek to prove; seek evidence or verification

求知 seek knowledge

求值 evaluation

求职 look for a job; find a job; apply for a job

求助 turn to sb for help; seek help

求积仪 planimeter

求知欲 thirst for knowledge

求职者 office seeker; office hunter

求告无门 have nowhere to turn to for help

求亲告友 ask for favours (usu. loans) from relatives and friends

求全责备 demand perfection; nitpick

求神拜佛 pray to Buddha for help

求实精神 matter-of-fact attitude; realistic approach

求田问舍 desire nothing but a homestead—have no high aims in life

求同存异 seek common ground while put aside (or maintain, reserve) differences; explore common ground and narrow difference

求贤若渴 eagerly seek after men of worth and ability

求真务实 be realistic and pragmatic; seek truth and deal with concrete matters

求之不得 all one could wish for; most welcome

求助热线 helpline

求人不如求己 Self-help is better than help from others; God helps those that help themselves.

求爷爷告奶奶 beg grandpas and entreat grandmas—go about begging for help

求大同,存小异 seek common ground on major issues while reserving differences on minor ones

虬 [qiú] 〈形〉coiled;curled

泅 [qiú] 〈动〉float on water;swim

泅渡 swim across

泅水 swim

赇 [qiú] 〈动〉force;compel

酋 [qiú] 〈名〉①chief (of a tribe) ②chieftain (of bandits,aggressors,etc.)

酋长 ①chief of a tribe ②sheik(h);emir

酋长国 sheikhdom;emirate

逑 [qiú] 〈名〉spouse;consort;life mate

球 [qiú] 〈名〉①sphere;globe ②anything shaped like a sphere;ball ③ball game ④globe;world

球场 a ground where ball games are played;court;field

球胆 bladder (of a ball)

球队 (ball game) team

球风 sportsmanship shown in ball games

球罐 sphere

球果 cone

球茎 corm

球菌 coccus

球路 tactics in ball games

球门 goal

球迷 (ball game) fan

球面 spherical surface

球囊 saccule;sacculus

球拍 ①(tennis,badminton,etc.) racket ②(table-tennis) bat

球赛 ball game;match

球市 ball game market

球手 ball game player

球坛 the ball-playing world;ball-playing circles;ball-players

球探 scout

球体 spheroid

球王 "ball king",a champion or superstar in a certain ball game

球网 net (for ball games)

球鞋 gym shoes;tennis shoes;sneakers

球心 centre of sphere

球星 ball-game star;star;star player

球形 spherical;globular;round

球艺 skills in playing a ball game;ball game skills

球员 player

球蛋白 globin;globulin

球面镜 spherical mirror

球磨床 ball grinder

球磨机 ball mill

球团矿 pellet

球窝节 ball-and-socket joint

球轴承 ball bearing

球茎甘蓝 kohlrabi

球类运动 ball games

球迷协会 association of sports fans (*or* enthusiasts)

球面车床 spherical turning lathe

球面投影 stereographic projection

球墨铸铁 nodular cast iron

球面天文学 spherical astronomy

裘 [qiú] 〈名〉fur coat

qiǔ (ㄑㄧㄡˇ)

糗 [qiǔ] I 〈名〉solid food II 〈动〉(of rice or noodles) be clotted;cake together

qū (ㄑㄩ)

区 [qū] I 〈动〉distinguish; differentiate; classify; subdivide II 〈名〉①area; zone; district; region ②(as an administrative division) district;region;division

区别 ①distinguish; differentiate; make a distinction between ②difference

区分 differentiate;distinguish

区划 division into districts

区徽 regional emblem

区间 lap;section of a route,line

区块 block

区旗 flag of a certain administrative region

区区 trivial;trifling

区时 zone time

区位 geographical location

区域 region;area;district

区长 head of a district (as in a city)

区间车 a train (*or* bus) travelling only part of its normal route;shuttle bus (*or* train)

区位码 region-position code

区域性 pertaining to a region

区位结构 ecological structure

区位商业 location-based commerce

区域规则 regional planning

区域会议 regional conference; local conference

区域自治 regional autonomy

区域性公约 regional convention or pact

区域性同盟 regional alliance

区域性问题 matter of regional significance

区域性战争 regional war

区域经济合作 regional economic cooperation

Q

区域经济一体化 integration of regional economies

曲 Ⅰ 形 ①bent;crooked:山道盘曲 winding path in the mountains ②wrong;false;unjustifiable Ⅱ 动 bend;flex;curve;crook Ⅲ 名 ① bend ②leaven;yeast ➡qǔ

曲柄 crank
曲尺 carpenter's square
曲拱 arch
曲解 misinterpret(usu. deliberately);twist
曲径 winding path
曲流 meander
曲率 curvature
曲霉 aspergillus
曲面 curved surface;camber
曲奇 cookie
曲射 curved fire
曲室 secret chamber
曲线 ①curve ②sth,esp. a human body, or part of it having the shape of a curve
曲折 ①tortuous;winding ②complicated ③complications
曲直 right and wrong
曲衷 heartfelt emotion;inner feelings
曲轴 crankshaft;bent axle
曲别针 paper clip
曲柄钻 brace drill
曲棍球 ①field hockey;hockey ②hockey ball
曲颈甑 retort
曲率计 exometer
曲线板 curve ruler
曲线美 line of beauty
曲线球 curve ball
曲线图 diagram(of curves)
曲肱而枕 sleep with one's head resting on a bent arm
曲古霉素 trichomycin
曲解原意 distort the meaning
曲尽其妙 bring out(a quality,point,etc.)in a subtle and skilful way
曲径通幽 winding path leading to secluded place
曲里拐弯 winding;zigzag
曲曲弯弯 winding;meandering
曲突徙薪 bend the chimney and remove the fuel(to prevent a possible fire)—take precautions against a possible danger
曲线运动 curvilinear motion
曲意逢迎 go out of one's way to curry favour

岖 ［qū］
◇崎岖 rugged

佉 ［qū］ 动 expel;drive out

诎 ［qū］ 动 ①shorten;curtail ②slow of speech

驱 ［qū］ 动 ①drive(a horse,etc.);spur ②run quickly;drive ③expel;drive away;exorcise

驱策 ①drive;whip on ②order about
驱车 drive a vehicle
驱除 drive out;get rid of;repel
驱动 drive
驱赶 ①drive(a cart,etc.) ②drive away;brush away
驱寒 dispel cold;warm oneself up
驱迫 order about;force;compel
驱遣 ①drive away;banish;expel ②order about;drive ③dispel;get rid of
驱散 disperse;dispel;break up
驱使 ①order about ②prompt;urge;spur on
驱邪 exorcise(or drive out)evil spirits
驱逐 drive out;expel;banish
驱虫剂 insectifuge;anthelmintic
驱虫药 anthelmintic;vermifuge
驱动器 driver
驱蛔灵 piperazine citrate
驱逐舰 destroyer
驱逐出境 deport;expel;send away from a country

屈 Ⅰ 动 ①bend;bow;crouch;crook:屈腿 bend one's legs ②subdue;yield;submit ③wrong;treat unjustly Ⅱ 名 injustice;wrongful treatment Ⅲ 形 in the wrong

屈才 do work unworthy of one's talents
屈从 submit;yield
屈服 subdue;submit;yield;knuckle under
屈驾 condescend(or be kind enough)to make the journey
屈节 forfeit one's honour
屈就 condescend to take a post offered
屈居 be forced to accept a place(or position)
屈理 unreasonable;unfair;unjust
屈辱 humiliation;mortification
屈死 be wronged and driven to death;be persecuted to death
屈膝 go down on one's knees;bend one's knees
屈心 have a guilty conscience
屈指 count on one's fingers
屈尊 condescend
屈光度 dioptre
屈光仪 refractometer
屈氏体 troostite
屈折语 inflexional language
屈肢葬 flexed burial
屈打成招 confess to false charges under torture
屈膝投降 go down on one's knees in surrender;knuckle under
屈意奉承 be studious to please
屈指可数 can be counted on one's fingers—

very few

肷 [qū] I 名 (of human body) part between armpit and waist;flank Ⅱ 动 pry open
肷箧 prize open a trunk to steal

祛 [qū] 动 dispel;prevent;remove;ward off
祛除 dispel;get rid of;drive out
祛风 dispel the wind;relieve rheumatic pains, colds,etc.
祛寒 dispelling cold
祛暑 drive away summer heat
祛痰 make expectoration easy
祛邪 eliminate evil
祛疑 remove suspicion (*or* doubts)
祛热剂 antipyretic
祛病延年 prevent disease and prolong life
祛蠹除奸 get rid of harmful elements and evil-doers
祛风湿药 medicine for rheumatism
祛瘀活血 remove blood stasis and promote blood circulation

袪 [qū] 名 sleeve cuff

蛆 [qū] 名 maggot
蛆虫 ①maggot ②a shameless (*or* base) person

躯 [qū] 名 human body
躯干 trunk;torso
躯壳 the body (as opposed to the soul);outer form
躯体 body;stature

焌 [qū] 动 ①put sth burning in water;douse sth burning in water to extinguish the fire ②(of cooking method) stir-fry vegetables as soon as the condiments are mixed with the boiling oil

趋 [qū] 动 ①hasten;rush;hurry along ②tend towards;head for;tend to become ③(of a goose or snake) pop its head to bite at people;snap at
趋避 avoid;dodge
趋承 toady to;fawn on
趋奉 toady to;fawn on
趋附 ingratiate oneself with; curry favour with
趋冷 cool down
趋热 warm up
趋势 trend;tendency
趋同 converge
趋向 ①tend to;incline to ②trend;tendency; direction
趋新 trendy
趋性 taxis

趋迎 hasten forward to meet sb
趋光性 phototaxis
趋热性 thermotaxis
趋药性 chemotaxis
趋势平衡 dynamic equilibrium; mobile equilibrium
趋同消费 blind consumption to go with the fad
趋向动词 directional verb
趋炎附势 curry favour with the powerful;play up to those in power
趋之若鹜 go after sth like a flock of ducks; scramble for sth

蛐 [qū]
蛐蛐儿 cricket (an insect)

觑 [qū] 动 screw up one's eyes;squint ➡qù

黢 [qū] 形 black;dark
黢黑 pitch-black;pitch-dark

qú（ㄑㄩˊ）

劬 [qú] 形 ①very tired;fatigued ②diligent;industrious;hardworking

渠 [qú] I 名 canal;conduit;ditch;channel Ⅱ 形 great Ⅲ 代 he;him
渠辈 they;those people
渠道 ①irrigation ditch ②medium of communication;channel
渠灌 canal irrigation
渠首 leader
渠首工程 headwork

衢 [qú] 名 thoroughfare;main road
衢肆 business area;shopping centre

qǔ（ㄑㄩˇ）

曲 [qǔ] 名 ①*qu*,a type of verse for singing originated in folk ballads ②song;tune;melody ③music (of a song) ➡qū
曲调 tune (of a song);melody
曲剧 opera derived from ballad singing
曲牌 the names of the tunes to which *qu* are composed
曲谱 ①music score of Chinese operas ②a collection of tunes of *qu*
曲式 musical form
曲艺 *quyi*, folk art forms including ballad singing,story telling,comic dialogues,clapper talks,cross talks,etc.
曲子 song;tune;melody
曲高和寡 Highbrow songs find few singers; too highbrow to be popular
曲终人散 The music is over and people are

Q

gone.
曲终奏雅 a grand finale

取 [qǔ]
〔动〕① get；draw；collect；fetch ② aim at；gain；seek ③adopt；assume；select；choose
取保 go bail for one
取材 draw materials
取代 replace；substitute for；supersede；supplant
取道 by way of；via
取得 gain；acquire；obtain
取缔 outlaw；ban；suppress
取法 take as one's model；follow the example of
取经 ①go on a pilgrimage for Buddhist scriptures ②learn from sb else's experience
取景 find a view（to photograph，paint，etc.）
取决（usu. followed by 于）be decided by；depend on；hinge on
取乐 seek pleasure；find amusement；amuse oneself；make merry
取名 give a name to；be named
取闹 ①kick up a row；make trouble ②amuse oneself at sb's expense；make fun of
取暖 warm oneself（by a fire，etc.）
取平 make even；even up
取齐 ①make even；even up ②assemble；meet each other
取枪 take arms
取巧 resort to trickery to serve oneself or avoid a difficulty
取容 try to please；ingratiate oneself with sb
取舍 accept or reject；make one's choice
取胜 win victory；score a success
取向 orientation
取消 cancel；call off；abolish
取笑 ridicule；make fun of；poke fun at
取信 win the confidence（or trust）of the others
取样 take a sample
取悦 try to please；ingratiate oneself with sb
取证 collect evidence；taking of evidence
取景器 viewfinder（on a camera）
取力器 power takeoff（of a car）
取水口 water intake
取保候审 obtain a guarantor and pending trial
取保释放 be released on bail
取长补短 made up for each other's deficiencies；learn from others' strong points to offset one's own weaknesses
取而代之 replace sb；supersede sb
取精用宏 select the finest from a vast quantity
取快一时 derive momentary pleasure
取其精华 get the cream off；absorb what is best
取消合同 cancel a contract；rescind a contract
取消资格 disqualify

取信于民 win the people's support；obtain the people's confidence；not betray people's trust；not disappoint people（or let people down）
取代衍生物 substitution derivate
取消考试资格 be disqualified from an examination
取缔个人拥有枪支 outlaw private firearms
取法乎上，仅得乎中 aim high or you may fall below the average
取人之长，补己之短 overcome one's shortcoming by learning from other's strong points
取之不尽，用之不竭 inexhaustible
取之于民，用之于民 What is taken from the people is used for the people.

娶 [qǔ]
〔动〕marry（a woman）；take to wife
娶妻 take a wife
娶亲 （of a man）get married

qù （ㄑㄩˋ）

去 [qù]
Ⅰ〔动〕①go（from here to another place）；travel ②depart；leave；go（away）：一怒而去 leave in anger；storm out ③lose；forfeit ④remove；get rid of；shake off ⑤be away from；be apart from ⑥pass away；depart；die ⑦（used before another verb to indicate an action）：他去看电影了。He has gone to the cinema. ⑧（used after a verb-object structure to indicate an intention of doing sth）：我要浇花去。I'm going to water the flowers. ⑨（used between a verbal or a propositional structure，and a verb or a verbal structure to indicate the latter is the purpose of the former）：要从不同角度去考虑这些新措施。It is necessary to consider these new measures from different angles. ⑩ play the part（or role）of；act（the part of）：适合去正面人物 be fit for the part of a hero Ⅱ〔形〕past；of last year：去冬 last winter／去岁末 at the end of last year Ⅲ〔副〕very；extremely：他的话可多了去了。He is very loquacious.／他们劲头可大了去了。They are overflowing with enthusiasm. Ⅳ〔名〕falling tone ➡qu
去病 prevent（or cure）a disease
去臭 deodorizing
去除 dislodge
去处 ①place to go；whereabouts ②place；site
去磁 deperm；demagnetize；degauss
去火 reduce internal heat；relieve inflammation（or fever）
去壳 hull；shucking；dismantling；shell
去留 go or remain（or stay）
去路 the way along which one is going；outlet
去年 last year
去声 ① falling tone（the third of the four

tones in classical Chinese pronunciation) ② falling tone (the fourth of the four tones in modern standard Chinese pronunciation)

去世 (of grown-up people) die; pass away

去势 castrate; emasculate

去暑 drive away summer heat

去岁 last year

去向 the direction in which sb or sth has gone

去雄 emasculate; castrate

去职 no longer hold the post

去垢剂 detergent

去你的 Go to hell!; The hell you are!

去污粉 household cleanser; cleanser

去粗取精 discard the dross and select the essential

去恶从善 shun evil and follow good reform

去旧更新 do away with the old and change it for new

去伪存真 discard the false and retain the true

去杂去劣 roguing

趣 [qù]

I 名 ①interest; amuse; delight ②purport; inclination Ⅱ 形 interesting; amusing; diverting; pleasant

趣事 an interesting episode; an amusing incident

趣谈 interesting tale (usu. in title of book, article, etc.)

趣味 ①interest; delight ②taste; liking; preference

趣闻 interesting hearsay (or news)

趣味盎然 full of interest

趣味索然 dry as dust; insipid

觑 [qù]

动 look; stare; gaze ➡ qū

觑视 look; gaze

qu (‧ㄑㄩ)

去 [qu]

动 ①(used after a verb to indicate movement away from the speaker): 拍去身上的尘土 flick the dust off one's clothes ②(used after a verb to indicate continuation of an action): 一眼看去 look far ahead ➡ qù

quān (ㄑㄩㄢ)

桊 [quān]

名 crossbow

悛 [quān]

动 be penitent; repent; make amends

圈 [quān]

I 名 ① circle; ring; hoop: 吐烟圈 blow smoke rings ②circle; set; coterie Ⅱ 动 ①enclose; surround; encircle ②mark with a circle ➡ juān; juàn

圈闭 petroleum trap

圈点 ①punctuate (with periods or small cir-

cles) ②mark words and phrases for special attention with dots or small circles

圈定 draw a circle around sth to show approval (or selection))

圈梁 girth

圈数 number of turns; cylinder number

圈套 snare; trap

圈外 outside a circle

圈椅 round-backed armchair

圈阅 draw a circle around one's name on a document submitted for approval to show that one has read it; tick off one's name listed on a circular, notice, etc. after reading it

圈占 circle piece of land to stake out one's claim

圈子 circle; ring

圈外人 outsider; people out of the loop

圈内人士 in-group source

桊 [quān]

名 drinking vessel made of wood

quán (ㄑㄩㄢ)

权 [quán]

I 动 weigh; consider Ⅱ 名 ① counterpoise; sliding weight of a steelyard ②power; authority ③right ④advantageous (or favourable) position ⑤ expediency; adaptability Ⅲ 副 tentatively; provisionally; for the time being

权变 adaptability (or flexibility) in tactics; acting according to circumstances; tact

权便 expedient

权标 fasces

权柄 power; authority

权臣 powerful minister

权贵 influential officials; bigwigs

权衡 weigh; balance

权力 ① power; authority ② scope of power; extent of authority; jurisdiction

权利 right

权谋 (political) tactics; trickery

权能 powers and functions

权且 tentatively; for the time being

权势 power and influence

权术 statecraft; political trickery; shifts in politics

权威 ① authority; authoritativeness ② a person of authority; authority

权限 limits of authority; jurisdiction; competence

权宜 expedient

权益 rights and interests

权欲 a lust for power

权责 power and responsibility; rights and duties

权诈 trickery; craftiness

权杖 staff of authority (as carried by political or religious leaders)
权威性 authority; finality
权衡轻重 weigh the relative importance (of two or more things)
权力机构 organs of power; authorities
权力下放 devolution; decentralization; shift of power to the grassroots; delegate (or transfer) power to the lower levels
权其轻重 weigh up one thing against another; weigh the pros and cons
权钱交易 power-money deal; trade one's power for profits
权威人士 authoritative person; authoritative sources
权宜之计 an expedient measure; makeshift (device); stopgap
权欲熏心 be overcome with a lust for power
权责划分 division of authority and responsibility
权力过分集中 overconcentration of power; excessive concentration of power

全 [quán] I 形 ① all ready; complete ② whole; entire; all; full II 动 keep from harm (or damage); keep intact III 副 wholly; entirely; completely
全豹 the whole picture; the overall situation
全部 whole; complete; total; all
全才 versatile person; all-rounder
全长 overall length
全场 ① the whole audience; all those present ② full-court; all-court
全称 full name (of a thing)
全程 whole journey; whole course
全等 congruent
全都 all; without exception
全份 complete set
全副 complete; full
全国 ① the whole nation (or country) ② nationwide; countrywide; throughout the country
全乎 complete
全会 plenary meeting; plenary session; plenum
全集 complete works; collected works
全价 real price; full price
全歼 annihilate; wipe out
全景 panorama; a full view; a whole scene
全局 the overall situation; the situation as a whole
全军 ① the whole (or entire) army ② preserve military strength
全开 a standard-sized sheet
全力 with all one's strength; all-out; sparing no effort
全貌 a complete picture; a full view
全面 overall; comprehensive; all-round

全苗 a full stand
全民 the whole (or entire) nation; all the people
全名 full name
全能 all-round
全年 annual; yearly
全盘 whole; all; overall
全陪 guide the full tour; tour conductor
全票 ① full ticket ② all the votes; a unanimous vote
全勤 full work attendance
全球 the whole world
全权 ① full powers; plenary powers ② full responsibility
全然 completely; entirely
全色 panchromatic
全身 the whole body; all over (the body)
全胜 ① complete victory ② win every match; be all-victorious
全盛 (of a historical period) flourishing; in full bloom
全食 total eclipse
全数 total number; whole amount
全速 full (or maximum, top) speed
全损 total loss
全套 a complete set
全体 all; entire; whole
全托 full-time care; take care of the trusted full time (or around the clock); put child in boarding nursery
全文 full text
全线 ① all fronts; the entire length ② the whole line (of a railway or highway)
全新 completely new; brand-new
全休 ① a complete rest ② a long-term sick leave
全音 whole tone
全员 entire staff; all members
全责 all responsibility
全职 full-time
全反射 total reflection
全方位 comprehensive; all-inclusive; all-round
全国性 nationwide; countrywide; national
全家福 ① a photograph of the whole family ② hotchpotch (as a dish)
全景式 panorama
全屏幕 full screen
全勤奖 reward for perfect work attendance; reward for full attendance; full attendance bonus
全球化 globalization
全球通 Global System for Mobile Communication (GSM)
全日制 full-time; full-day
全身像 full-length picture
全视图 full view; general view
全损险 total loss only (T.L.O.)

全天候 all-weather
全新世 the Recent Epoch
全音符 whole note;semibreve
全自动 full automation
全动机翼 all-moving wing (of an aircraft)
全额保险 full insurance
全国普查 national census
全国上下 the whole nation from the leadership to the masses
全家收入 household income
全景电视 cinerama
全景电影 panoramic movie
全军覆没 the whole army overwhelmed—a complete failure
全科医生 general practitioner
全科医师 general practitioner
全科医学 general family medicine
全劳动力 an able-bodied farm worker
全力爬升 full climb (of an aircraft)
全力以赴 go all out;spare no effort
全面安排 all-round arrangement
全面崩溃 total collapse
全面大赦 blanket pardon
全面发展 full-scale development;develop in an all-round way;develop in full scale
全面合作 cooperation in all fields
全面进攻 an all-out attack
全面开展 go full steam ahead; get into full swing
全面投产 fully operational
全面展开 get into full swing
全面战争 full-scale war;total war
全民公决 referendum
全民教育 education for all
全民皆兵 an entire nation in arms;every citizen being a soldier
全民投票 popular vote
全能冠军 all-around winner
全能运动 decathlon;pentathlon
全盘否定 total repudiation
全盘接受 total and uncritical acceptance
全盘考虑 give overall consideration
全盘西化 total westernization;complete westernization
全球变暖 global warming
全球战略 global strategy
全权代表 plenipotentiary
全色胶片 panchromatic film
全身麻醉 general anesthesia
全神贯注 concentrate one's attention on; be absorbed (*or* engrossed) in;be preoccupied with
全始全终 see (*or* carry) sth through;stick to sth to the very end
全体辞职 resign en bloc
全维作战 full dimensional operations
全文发表 publish in full;report a text verba-

tim
全息电影 holographic movie
全息摄影 holography
全息照相 hologram
全心全意 whole-heartedly;heart and soul
全员承包 all-staff contractual responsibility system
全员培训 training program for all the staff members;all-member training
全员效率 output per man-shift(o. p. m. s.)
全知全能 omniscient and omnipotent
全脂奶粉 whole milk powder
全方位外交 multi-faceted diplomacy
全国一盘棋 coordinate all the activities of the nation like moves in a game of chess;take the whole country into account
全国运动会 the national games
全景摄影机 panoramic camera
全民所有制 ownership by the whole people
全屏幕编辑 full-screen editing
全屏幕方式 full-screen mode
全权代理人 universal agent
全日制教育 full-time schooling
全日制学校 full-time school
全托托儿所 boarding nursery
全息照相机 holocamera
全员合同制 all-member contract system
全国代表大会 national congress
全国健身运动 national fitness campaign
全面质量管理 total quality control(TQC)
全民健身计划 the National Fitness Program; the nationwide body-building campaign
全球财富论坛 Fortune Global Forum
全球定位系统 global positioning system (GPS)
全球经济秩序 global economic order
全球自由贸易 global free trade
全天候自动化 all weather capability and automation
全员抵押承包 all-member mortgage contract
全自动洗衣机 automatic linen washer; automatic laundry machine
全国文明礼貌月 National Socialist Ethics and Courtesy Month
全民所有制单位 state enterprises and institutions
全民所有制企业 enterprises owned by the whole people
全球经济一体化 integration with the global economy
全天候低空飞行 all-weather low-level flight
全国导弹防御系统 National Missile Defense (NMD)
全国人民代表大会 the National People's Congress (NPC)
全面对话伙伴关系 full dialogue partnership
全民健身计划纲要 outline of the nationwide

body-building plan
全球多边贸易体系 the global system of multilateral trade

诠 [quán]
I 动 expound; annotate; provide a gloss; interpret II 名 reason; logic; truth
诠释 annotate; give explanatory notes
诠注 provide notes and commentary

荃 [quán]
名 aromatic (*or* fragrant) plant

泉 [quán]
名 ①spring ②mouth of a spring ③ancient term of coin
泉币 ancient coin
泉华 sinter
泉水 spring water; spring
泉眼 the mouth of a spring; spring
泉涌 gush
泉源 ① fountainhead; springhead; wellspring ②source

拳 [quán]
I 名 ①fist ②boxing; pugilism II 动 curl; twist; warp; bend
拳击 boxing; pugilism
拳脚 Chinese boxing
拳曲 curl; twist; bend
拳拳 sincere
拳师 boxing coach; pugilist
拳术 Chinese boxing
拳坛 boxing circles; the boxing world
拳头 fist
拳王 boxing champion; lord of the ring
拳打脚踢 cuff and kick; beat up
拳拳服膺 ①always bear in mind ②have a sincere belief in
拳头产品 competitive products; knock-out products
拳王争霸赛 boxing championship decider; boxing match for a championship
拳不离手，曲不离口 The boxer's fist must stick to its task, and the singer's mouth no rest must ask; Practice makes perfect.

痊 [quán]
动 fully recover from an illness
痊愈 fully recover from an illness; be fully recovered

蜷 [quán]
动 coil (as a snake); curl up; huddle up
蜷伏 curl up; huddle up; lie with the knees drawn up
蜷曲 curl; coil; twist
蜷缩 roll up; huddle up; curl up

醛 [quán]
名 aldehyde
醛酸 aldehydic acid
醛糖 aldose
醛酯 aldehydo-ester

鬈 [quán]
形 ①curly; wavy ②(of hair) lovely
鬈曲 crimp; crinkle; curl

颧 [quán]
颧骨 cheekbone

quǎn (ㄑㄩㄢˇ)

犬 [quǎn]
名 dog
犬病 dog disease
犬齿 canine tooth
犬儒 cynic
犬牙 ①canine tooth ②fang (of a dog)
犬子 my son
犬马之劳 serve like a dog or a horse
犬儒主义 cynicism
犬牙交错 jigsaw-like; interlocking

畎 [quǎn]
名 ditch on a farm (*or* in the field)

绻 [quǎn]
◇**缱绻** lingering; abiding; deeply attached to each other

quàn (ㄑㄩㄢˋ)

劝 [quàn]
动 ①talk (sb) round by reasoning; try to persuade; advise; urge ②encourage; foster
劝导 try to persuade; advise; induce
劝返 persuade sb to return
劝服 prevail
劝告 ①advise; urge; exhort ②advice; exhortations
劝和 try to persuade two parties to become reconciled; mediate
劝化 ①urge to do good ②collect alms
劝驾 urge sb to accept an invitation or a post
劝架 try to reconcile parties in a quarrel (*or* to stop people from fighting each other); mediate
劝解 ①help sb to get over his worries, etc. ②mediate; make peace between; bring people together
劝诫 admonish; expostulate
劝酒 urge sb to drink (at a banquet)
劝勉 advise and encourage
劝募 solicit contributions by persuasions
劝善 encourage people to do good
劝说 persuade; advise
劝退 be persuaded to retire; persuade sb to resign from official position
劝慰 console; soothe
劝降 induce to capitulate
劝学 encourage learning
劝诱 induce; prevail upon
劝止 dissuade sb from; advise sb not to

劝阻 dissuade sb from;advise sb not to
劝业场 bazaar
劝业银行 industrial bank

券 [quàn]
名 certificate;ticket;voucher
券商 broker

què (ㄑㄩㄝ)

炔 [quē]
名 alkyne
炔雌醇 ethinyloestradiol

缺 [quē]
Ⅰ动 ①be short;be deficient;lack ②be not present;be absent Ⅱ名 unfilled position;vacancy;opening Ⅲ形 ①with parts missing;incomplete ②imperfect
缺编 ①understaffed ②vacant position;vacancy
缺档 be in short supply;be out of stock
缺德 mean;wicked;rotten
缺点 shortcoming;defect;weakness;drawback
缺额 vacant position;vacancy
缺乏 be short of;lack;be in want of
缺钙 calcium deficiency
缺憾 regrettable imperfection;regret
缺货 be in short supply;be out of stock;run short
缺课 be absent from school;miss a class
缺口 ①breach;gap ②notch
缺漏 gaps and omissions
缺门 gap (in a branch of learning,etc.)
缺欠 ①shortcoming;defect;weakness ②lack;be short of
缺勤 absence from duty (or work)
缺少 lack;be short of;be in want of
缺失 defect
缺市 in short supply
缺损 ① damaged;worn;torn ② physiological defect;physiological deficiency
缺位 ①(of a position) be vacant ②vacant position;vacancy
缺席 absent (from a meeting,etc.)
缺陷 defect;drawback;flaw;blemish
缺氧 anoxia;oxygen lack
缺页 the missing page
缺员 understaffing
缺阵 no-show
缺货单 want slips
缺刻叶 incised leaf
缺勤率 absence rate;absentee rate
缺编单位 under-staffed units
缺吃少穿 have not enough for food and clothing
缺乏后劲 unsustainable momentum
缺乏经验 lack experience
缺乏证据 want of proof
缺乏资源 be deficient in resources

缺斤短两 give short weight
缺席判决 default judgement;judgement by default
缺席审判 trial by default;try in absentia
缺席投票 absentee voting;absentee vote;absentee ballot
缺心眼儿 ①simple-minded;scatterbrained ②dull-witted;mentally deficient;retarded
缺医少药 shortage of physicians as well as medicine
缺铁性贫血 iron-deficiency anaemia

阙 [quē]
名 fault;error;mistake ➡ què
阙如 deficient;wanting;lacking
阙失 mistake;fault
阙疑 leave the question open

qué (ㄑㄩㄝ)

瘸 [qué]
动 be lame;(walk) with a limp
瘸腿 lame
瘸子 lame person;cripple

què (ㄑㄩㄝ)

却 [què]
Ⅰ动 ①fall back;retreat ②drive back;beat back;repulse ③ refuse;decline;reject;turn down ④lose;get rid of Ⅱ副 (used to indicate a transition, but somewhat weaker than 倒 or 可):今天下雪,却不冷。It's snowy,but not cold.
却病 prevent (or cure) a disease
却步 step back (in fear or disgust);hang back
却敌 repulse the enemy
却说 we were telling you... (a stock phrase used by traditional storytellers when resuming narration where they left off)
却病延年 prevent illness and prolong life
却之不恭 (said when receiving a gift) it would be impolite to decline

埆 [què]
名 infertile soil

雀 [què]
名 sparrow ➡ qiǎo
雀斑 freckle
雀鲷 damselfish
雀麦 bromegrass;brome
雀鹰 sparrow hawk
雀跃 jump for joy
雀噪 enjoy loud fame

确 [què]
名 ①true;reliable;authentic ②rock-solid;firm
确保 ensure;guarantee
确定 ①define;fix;determine ②definite
确乎 really;indeed
确立 establish

Q

确论 a sound assertion；a just argument
确切 ①definite；exact；precise ②true；reliable；sure
确认 affirm；confirm；acknowledge
确实 ①true；reliable ②really；indeed
确守 strictly (*or* scrupulously) abide by
确数 exact figures；exact amount
确信 ①firmly believe；be convinced；be sure ②reliable information
确凿 conclusive；authentic；irrefutable
确诊 make a definite diagnosis；diagnose
确证 ①prove conclusively (*or* positively) ②proof positive；conclusive (*or* irrefutable) evidence
确定性 determinacy；certainty；definiteness
确认书 letter of confirmation
确乎不拔 firm and unshakable；unswerving；unflinching
确确实实 for a certainty；beyond all doubt
确凿不移 well established and irrefutable

阕 [què]
Ⅰ 动 end Ⅱ 量 (*used in a Songci poem*)：一阕新词 a new *ci* poem Ⅲ 名 stanza (of a *ci* poem)

鹊 [què]
名 magpie
鹊报 the cry of the magpie—a good omen
鹊豆 Dolichos lablab
鹊起 ①act according to circumstances；do as one sees fit；use one's discretion ②(of fame) spread；rise
鹊桥 Magpie Bridge
鹊鸲 magpie robin
鹊雁 magpie goose
鹊巢鸠占 the turtledove occupies the magpie's nest—one person seizes another person's place，land，etc.

阙 [què]
名 ①watchtower on either side of a palace gate ②imperial palace ③stone carving erected in front of a temple or tomb ➡ quē

qūn (ㄑㄩㄣ)

逡 [qūn]
动 yield；give in；shrink from
逡巡 hesitate to move forward；hang back

qún (ㄑㄩㄣ)

裙 [qún]
名 ①skirt ②sth like a skirt
裙钗 woman
裙带 ①belt (as a decoration for a skirt or dress) ②connected through one's female relatives
裙裤 culottes
裙舞 skirt dance
裙子 skirt

裙带风 nepotism；petticoat influence
裙带关系 nepotism；connections through one's female relatives；networking through petticoat influence

群 [qún]
Ⅰ 名 ①crowd；group ②large numbers of people ③in groups；in large numbers Ⅱ 量 group；herd；swarm；flock：一群鸽子 a flock of doves
群邦 various countries
群唱 ensemble singing
群岛 islands；archipelago
群雕 a group of statues
群斗 gang fight
群芳 ①beautiful and fragrant flowers ②a group of beauties (*or* artists)
群峰 connected mountain peaks
群婚 group marriage；communal marriage
群集 gather；assemble
群件 groupware
群居 live in groups；live as a group
群落 ①community ②building complex；cluster of buildings
群氓 the common herd；the mob
群起 all rise (to do sth)
群青 ultramarine
群情 public sentiment；feelings of the masses
群山 connected hills (*or* mountains)
群书 all kinds of books；a wide variety of books
群体 ①colony ②groups
群贤 numerous persons of virtue and ability
群像 images of a group of characters
群众 ①the masses ②non-Party ③a member of the rank and file
群控制 group control
群言堂 allow everybody to air his view；let everyone have his say；speak one's mind freely
群英会 a gathering of heroes；a conference of outstanding workers
群众性 of a mass character
群策群力 pool the wisdom and efforts of everyone；work and pull together；work as a team
群芳之冠 the queen of flowers—the reigning beauty
群居动物 social animal
群居昆虫 social insect
群龙无首 a host of dragons without a head—a group without a leader
群魔乱舞 a host of demons dancing in riotous revelry—rogues of all kinds running wild
群轻折轴 a load of many light things can break the axle of a cart—minor offences unchecked may bring disaster
群体认同 group identification

群威群胆 mass heroism and daring
群雄割据 rivalry of the powerful
群众工作 mass work
群众关系 one's relations (*or* ties) with the masses
群众观点 the mass viewpoint
群众监督 supervision by the masses
群众路线 the mass line
群众生活 well-being of the masses
群众团体 mass (non-government) organization
群众运动 mass movement; mass campaign
群众组织 mass (non-government) organization; people's organization
群起而攻之 all rise (*or* turn) against sb
群众体育活动 mass sports exercises

Q

Rr

rán（ㄖㄢˊ）

然 [rán]
Ⅰ 形 right；correct；accurate Ⅱ 副 so；like that Ⅲ 连 but；yet；nevertheless；however Ⅳ (*used as an adjectival or adverbial suffix*)：举座哗然. The whole room burst into an uproar.
然而 but；however；yet
然后 then；after that；afterwards
然诺 promise；pledge
然则 in that case；then

髯 [rán]
名 whiskers；beard
髯口 artificial beard (*or* whiskers) worn by traditional opera actors

燃 [rán]
动 ①burn：燃为灰烬 be burned to ashes ② ignite；light；set fire to：点燃仇恨的火焰 kindle the flames of hatred
燃炽 burn；smolder
燃点 ①kindle；set fire to；light；ignite ②ignition (*or* burning，kindling) point
燃放 set off (fireworks，etc.)
燃耗 fuel consumption
燃料 fuel
燃煤 coal for fuel
燃烧 ①burn；kindle ②combustion；inflammation
燃油 fuel oil
燃料比 fuel ratio
燃料库 fuel depot；fuel reservoir
燃烧弹 incendiary bomb
燃烧剂 incendiary agent
燃烧瓶 frangible grenade；Molotov cocktail
燃烧室 combustion chamber；blast chamber；combustor
燃油泵 fuel pump
燃油炉 fuel burner
燃料电池 fuel cell
燃眉之急 as pressing as a fire singeing one's eyebrows—extremely urgent；overwhelming urgency

燃气轮机 gas turbine
燃料附加费 bunker surcharge
燃气热水器 gas water heater
燃料动力工业 fuel and power industry

rǎn（ㄖㄢˇ）

冉
冉冉 ①(of hair，twigs，etc.) hang down softly ②slowly；gradually

苒 [rǎn]
◇荏苒 (of time) elapse quickly (*or* imperceptibly)；slip by

染 [rǎn]
动 ①dye：染毛线 dye knitting wool ②catch (a disease)；acquire；contract (a bad habit，etc.)；be stained；be contaminated：染上流感 catch influenza (*or* the flu)
染病 catch (*or* contract) an illness；be infected with a disease
染毒 contaminate
染坊 dyehouse；dye-works
染缸 dye vat
染料 dyestuff；dye
染色 dye；colour
染液 dye liquor
染指 take a share of sth one is not entitled to；encroach on
染发剂 tint
染发水 rinse；hair dye
染色剂 colouring agent
染色体 chromosome
染色质 chromatin
染指甲 paint the fingernails
染指择肥 dip one's finger in the pie and claim the lion's share

rāng（ㄖㄤ）

嚷 [rāng]
⇒ rǎng
嚷嚷 ①make a noise；make an uproar ②make widely known

ráng (ㄖㄤ)

禳 [ráng]
〔动〕keep off evil；exorcise（spirits）
禳解 avert（a misfortune or disaster）by prayers
禳灾 avert a disaster by prayers，etc.

瓤 [ráng]
Ⅰ〔名〕①pulp；flesh；pith：红瓤的西瓜 watermelon with red flesh ②interior part of certain things：秫秸瓤 inside of a corn stalk Ⅱ〔形〕weak；bad
瓤子 pulp；flesh；pith

rǎng (ㄖㄤ)

壤 [rǎng]
〔名〕①soil；earth ②ground ③area；land；territory
壤土 loam

攘 [rǎng]
〔动〕①reject；resist expel ②seize；snatch；grab ③roll up（one's sleeves）④trouble；disturb
攘臂 push up one's sleeves and bare one's arms（in excitement or agitation）
攘除 get rid of；weed out；reject
攘敌 resist the enemy
攘夺 seize；grab
攘善 claim credit due to others
攘外 resist foreign aggression
攘袖 roll up one's sleeves
攘往熙来 coming and going in crowds；busy coming and going

嚷 [rǎng]
〔动〕①shout；yell ②argue heatedly（or noisily）③scold；reprimand；reproach ➡ rāng
嚷叫 shout；yell；make an uproar

ràng (ㄖㄤ)

让 [ràng]
〔动〕①give way；give in；give up；yield ②offer；invite；treat ③let sb have sth at a price；sell；transfer ④allow；let；give sb a free hand ⑤make way；make room ⑥（used in the passive voice to introduce the agent）：这杯子让我给打碎了。I am the one who broke the cup.
让步 make a concession；give in；give way；yield
让茶 offer sb tea
让渡 transfer the possession of；alienate
让价（of a seller）agree to reduce the price asked
让开 get out of the way；step aside；make way
让利 concession
让路 make way；give way；yield
让球 concede points（in ball games）
让权 give up power
让位 ①resign sovereign authority；give one's place to another abdicate ②offer（or give up）one's seat to sb ③yield to；give way to；change into
让贤 relinquish one's post in favour of sb better qualified
让账（of friends eating out）insist on paying the bill
让座 ①offer（or give up）one's seat to sb ②invite guests to be seated
让利促销 promote（or stimulate）sales by cutting profits
让利销售 cut-price sales
让枣推梨 offer dates and decline pears—show brotherly love

ráo (ㄖㄠ)

荛 [ráo]
〔名〕firewood；faggot
荛花 canescent wikstroemia

饶 [ráo]
Ⅰ〔形〕rich；abundant；plentiful Ⅱ〔动〕①throw in；give（or get）sth extra for nothing ②have mercy on；let sb off；forgive Ⅲ〔连〕although；despite
饶命 spare sb's life
饶舌 ① too talkative；garrulous ② say more than is proper；shoot off one's mouth
饶恕 forgive；pardon
饶头 a small item given away free（in business transactions）；extra
饶沃（of soil）fertile；rich
饶有风趣 full of wit and humour；very amusing；very witty

娆 [ráo]
➡ rǎo
◇娇娆 enchantingly beautiful
妖娆 enchanting；fascinating；bewitching

桡 [ráo]
〔名〕oar
桡骨 radius
桡动脉 radial artery

rǎo (ㄖㄠ)

扰 [rǎo]
Ⅰ〔动〕①harass；trouble；harry；molest ②give sb a good deal of bother Ⅱ〔名〕disorder；chaos；confusion
扰动 be in turmoil；be turbulent
扰乱 harass；disturb；create confusion
扰民 disturb the people；harass the people
扰攘 hustle and bustle；noisy confusion；tumult
扰频器 scrambler
扰乱民心 undermine the morale of the people；set the people's minds in a turmoil；sap

public confidence

扰乱市场 disrupt the market; rig the market

扰乱视听 confuse the public; mislead public opinion

扰乱治安 disturb public order; nuisance public peace

扰乱法庭秩序罪 offence of disturbance of court order

娆 [ráo]
名 tumult; perturbation ⟹ráo

ráo（ㄖㄠˊ）

绕 [rào]
动 ①wind; coil ②move (or go) round; circle; revolve ③make a detour; bypass; circumvent; go round ④confuse; baffle; confound

绕道 make a detour; go by a roundabout route

绕接 solderless wrapped connection

绕梁 (of the sound of singing) linger; reverberate

绕线 passing round; make a detour

绕行 ①make a detour; bypass ②move round; circle

绕组 winding

绕嘴 (of a sentence, etc.) not be smooth; be difficult to articulate

绕脖子 ①beat about the bush; speak or act in a roundabout way ②involved; knotty; tricky

绕口令 tongue twister

绕圈子 ① circle; go round and round; beat around the bush ②take a circuitous route; make a detour ③talk in a roundabout way; beat about the bush

绕弯儿 ①go for a stroll (or walk) ②talk in a roundabout way; beat about the bush

绕弯子 talk in a roundabout way; beat about the bush

绕远儿 go the long way round

绕场致意 (of winners) run a lap of honor

rě（ㄖㄜˇ）

若 [rě]
⟹ruò

◇般若 highest wisdom

惹 [rě]
动 ①bring upon oneself (sth unpleasant); incur ② offend; provoke; annoy; tease ③ attract; draw; cause

惹祸 court disaster; stir up trouble

惹恼 make sb angry; offend

惹气 get angry

惹事 stir up trouble; make trouble

惹眼 conspicuous; showy

惹不起 dare not provoke

惹得起 dare nettle; dare to offend

惹乱子 court disaster; stir up trouble

惹火烧身 stir up a fire only to burn oneself—court disaster; ask for trouble

惹是生非 provoke a dispute; stir up trouble; stir up conflict

rè（ㄖㄜˋ）

热 [rè]
I 名 ①heat ②fever; temperature ③(used after a noun, a noun phrase or a verb) craze; fever; fad; 网球热 tennis craze; intense popular interest in tennis II 形 ①hot ②in great demand; popular ③ ardent; chummy; deep; thick ④envious; keen; eager ⑤strongly radioactive; thermal; thermo- III 动 make hot; heat up; warm up

热爱 ardently love; have deep love (or affection) for

热拔 hot drawing

热病 acute disease accompanied by fever

热播 well-received programme

热补 vulcanize (tyre, etc.)

热潮 great mass fervour; upsurge

热炒 feeding frenzy

热忱 zeal; warm-heartedness; enthusiasm and devotion

热诚 warm and sincere; cordial

热带 the torrid zone; the tropics

热点 ①hot spot ②central issue; point at issue ③matter arousing general interest

热电 pyroelectricity; thermoelectricity

热度 ①degree of heat; heat ②fever; temperature

热敷 hot compress

热狗 hot dog

热管 heat pipe

热合 heat seal

热核 thermonuclear

热乎 [rèhu] ①nice and warm; warm ②warm and friendly; pally; chummy; thick

热货 hot commodity; commodities that command a ready market are in great demand and sell well

热火 [rèhuo] ①showing tremendous enthusiasm; exciting ② nice and warm; warm; warm and friendly; pally; chummy; thick

热和 [rèhuo] ① nice and warm; warm ② warm and friendly; pally; chummy; thick

热机 heat engine

热寂 heat death

热键 hot key

热辣 hot

热浪 heat wave; hot wave

热泪 hot tears; tears of joy, sorrow or gratitude

热力 heating power

热恋 be passionately in love; be head over heels in love
热量 quantity of heat
热烈 warm; enthusiastic; animated
热流 ①thermal current ②warm current
热卖 sell like hot cakes
热门 arousing popular interest; popular
热闹 ①lively; bustling with noise and excitement ② liven up; have a jolly time ③ a scene of bustle and excitement; a thrilling sight
热能 heat (*or* thermal) energy
热评 hot review
热气 steam; heat
热切 fervent; earnest
热情 ① enthusiasm; zeal; warmth ② warm; fervent; enthusiastic; warmhearted
热身 warm-up
热天 hot weather; hot season; hot days
热望 fervently hope; ardently wish
热线 ①(telephone) hot line ②busy passenger (*or* freight) route; busy route
热销 ① fast-selling; highly marketable ②(of goods) sell well; be in great demand
热心 enthusiastic; ardent; earnest; warmhearted
热学 heat (a branch of physics)
热血 warm blood—righteous ardour
热压 hot pressing
热药 medicines of a hot or warm nature; tonics and stimulants
热饮 hot drink
热映 well-received film
热源 heat source
热轧 hot-rolling
热战 hot war; shooting war
热障 heat barrier
热证 heat symptom-complex; febrile symptoms
热值 calorific value
热衷 ①hanker after; crave ②be fond of; be keen on
热处理 heat (*or* thermal) treatment
热传导 heat transfer
热传递 heat passage; thermal transmission
热脆性 hot-shortness; red-shortness
热带鱼 tropical fish
热导体 heat conductor
热得快 immersion heater; element
热电厂 heat and power plant
热电池 thermal cell
热电偶 thermocouple
热电学 pyroelectricity
热电子 thermoelectron
热电阻 thermal resistance
热对流 free convection; thermal convection
热反应 thermal response

热风炉 hot-blast stove
热辐射 heat (*or* thermal) radiation
热烘烘 very warm
热乎乎 warm
热加工 hot-working; hot work
热扩散 thermal diffusion
热辣辣 burning hot; scorching
热离子 thermion
热力学 thermodynamics
热量计 calorimeter
热裂化 thermal cracking
热门货 goods in great demand; popular ware; fast-selling products; hot item; hot goods; goods which sell well
热门书 active title
热喷喷 steaming hot
热膨胀 thermal expansion
热平衡 thermal equilibrium; heat balance
热启动 warm boot (*or* start)
热气球 fire balloon; hot air balloon
热气田 geothermal area
热身赛 tune-up; warm-up game; warm-up exercises; warm-up match
热释光 thermoluminescence (TL)
热水袋 hot-water bottle (*or* bag)
热水瓶 thermos bottle (*or* flask); thermos; vacuum bottle (*or* flask)
热水器 hot water heater; geyser
热塑性 thermoplasticity
热汤面 noodles in hot soup
热腾腾 steaming hot
热污染 thermal pollution; heat pollution
热像仪 thermal imaging system
热心肠 ①warm-heartedness ②a warmhearted (*or* sympathetic) and helpful person
热原子 hot atom
热真空 thermal vacuum
热中子 thermal neutron
热处理炉 heat-treated furnace
热带草原 savanna
热带风暴 tropical storm
热带气旋 tropical cyclone; tropical revolving storm
热带植物 tropical plant
热带作物 tropical crops
热岛效应 tropical island effect
热电效应 pyroelectric effect
热功当量 mechanical equivalent of heat
热固塑料 thermosetting plastic
热核爆炸 thermonuclear explosion
热核弹头 thermonuclear warhead
热核反应 thermonuclear reaction
热核武器 thermonuclear weapon
热火朝天 buzzing (*or* bustling) with activity; in full swing
热泪盈眶 one's eyes brimming with tears
热烈欢迎 warm welcome; welcome with open

R

arms
热门股票 blue chip
热门话题 heated topic
热门新闻 hot news
热门学科 hot subject
热敏电阻 thermal resistor; thermistor
热气腾腾 ①steaming hot ②seething with activity
热情奔放 bubbling with enthusiasm
热情洋溢 permeated (or brimming) with warm feeling; glowing with enthusiasm
热塑塑料 thermoplastic
热性肥料 hot manure
热血动物 warm-blooded animal; warm blood
热血沸腾 One's blood boils; burning with righteous indignation
热血青年 ardent youth
热核反应堆 thermonuclear reactor
热锅上的蚂蚁 an ant on a hot pan—restless

rén(ㄖㄣˊ)

人 [rén]
【名】①human being; man; person; people ②everybody; each; all ③adult; grown-up ④person engaged in a particular activity ⑤other people; people ⑥personality; character ⑦one's state of health or mind ⑧hand; manpower
人儿 ①figurine ②personality; character
人才 ①a person of ability; a talented person; talent; qualified personnel ②handsome appearance
人潮 stream of people
人臣 minister; subject
人称 ①person ②be called; be named
人次 person-time
人丛 crowd (of people)
人大 the National People's Congress
人道 ①humanity; human sympathy ②human; humane
人丁 population; number of people in a family
人犯 the accused; people implicated in a crime
人防 people's air defence; civil air defence
人份 person-portion; person-share
人格 ① personality; character; moral quality ②human dignity
人工 ① man-made; artificial ② manual work; work done by hand ③manpower; man-day
人海 a sea of faces; a huge crowd (of people)
人和 human unity; support of the people; unity and coordination within one's own ranks
人话 human speech; sensible talk
人寰 the human world; man's world; the world
人祸 man-made calamity
人迹 human footmarks (or footprints); traces of human presence

人家 [rénjiā] ①household; family ②the family of a girl's fiancé
人家 [rénjia] ① a person or persons other than the speaker or hearer ②(with the person or persons referred to in a near context, roughly equivalent to the third personal pronoun) ③(used before a nominal expression, usu. with liveliness of feeling) ④(used rhetorically in place of the first personal pronoun, often playfully expressing displeasure)
人间 the human world; man's world; the world
人杰 outstanding personality
人均 per capita
人孔 manhole
人口 ① population ② number of people in a family
人浪 Mexican wave
人类 mankind; humanity
人力 manpower; labour power
人流 ①stream of people ②induced abortion
人龙 long queue
人伦 human relations (according to feudal ethics)
人马 forces; troops
人们 people; men; the public
人民 the people
人命 human life
人偶 image; figure
人品 ①moral standing; moral quality; character ②looks; bearing
人气 popularity
人墙 wall
人情 ①human feelings; human sympathy; sensibilities ② human relationships ③ favour ④gift; present
人权 human rights; rights of man
人群 crowd; throng; multitude
人人 everybody; everyone
人蛇 illegal immigrant
人身 living body of a human being; person
人参 ginseng
人生 life
人声 voice
人士 personage; public figure
人氏 people native to a place
人世 this world; the world
人事 ① human affairs; occurrences in human life ② personnel matters ③ ways of the world ④consciousness of the outside world ⑤ what is humanly possible ⑥ sexual awareness (or passion); the facts of life
人手 manpower; hand
人梯 ①human ladder (as used in assaulting a fortress) ②a person who helps another to rise to success
人体 human body

人头 ①the number of people ②relations with people

人望 prestige;popularity

人为 artificial;man-made

人物 ①figure;personage ② person in literature;character

人像 portrait;image;figure

人心 ①popular feeling;public feeling;the will of the people ②human feelings;human reason

人性 [rénxìng] human nature;humanity

人性 [rénxìng] normal human feelings;reason

人熊 brown bear

人选 person selected

人烟 signs of human habitation

人样 ①proper human appearance;proper behaviour ②a successful person

人欲 human desires

人员 personnel;staff

人猿 anthropoid (ape)

人造 man-made;artificial;imitation

人证 testimony of a witness

人质 hostage

人治 rule by men

人中 the vertical groove on the median line of the upper lip;philtrum

人种 ethnic group;race

人才库 brain bank;brain trust;talent bank

人才学 talent studies

人代会 People's Congress at different levels (county,municipality)

人堆儿 crowd (of people)

人贩子 trader in human beings

人粪尿 night soil;human wastes (or excrement)

人格化 personify

人工岛 man-made island;artificial island

人工湖 man-made lake

人工林 artificial forest;man-made forest

人公里 passenger-kilometre

人来疯 (of a child) show off his liveliness before visitors

人类学 anthropology

人力车 ① a two-wheeled vehicle drawn (or pushed) by a man ②rickshaw

人马座 Sagittarius

人民币 Renminbi (RMB, Chinese monetary unit)

人民性 (in literary and artistic works) popular or folk character;feeling for the people;affinity to the people

人情礼 gift presented to obtain a favour

人情味 human touch;human interest

人情债 a debt of gratitude

人身权 personal rights

人身险 personal insurance

人生观 outlook on life

人世间 this world;the world

人事处 personnel division

人头费 fee per person

人头税 capitation taxes;poll tax;head tax

人味儿 humanness;humanity

人物表 a list of characters (in a play or novel);characters

人物画 figure painting

人物像 bust (sculpture)

人像靶 silhouette target

人行道 pavement;sidewalk

人性论 the theory of human nature

人影儿 ①the shadow of a human figure ②the trace of a person's presence;figure

人缘儿 relations with people;popularity

人造冰 artificial ice

人造革 imitation (or artificial) leather;leatherette

人造光 artificial light

人造浪 artificial wave

人造毛 artificial wool;man-made feather

人造棉 artificial cotton;staple rayon

人造肉 textured vegetable protein (TVP)

人造丝 artificial silk;rayon

人造土 artificial soil

人种学 ethnology

人字呢 herringbone

人本主义 humanism;human-centered thinking

人才辈出 no lack of talented persons;people of talent coming forth in large numbers

人才出众 a person of exceptional ability or striking appearance

人才断层 gap in talents;lack of talented persons;broken continuity of personnel

人才荟萃 a galaxy of talent

人才济济 an abundance of capable people;a galaxy of talent

人才交流 exchange of talent

人才结构 composition of trained personnel

人才竞争 talent scramble;scramble for talents

人才流动 flow of trained personnel;flow of talent

人才流入 brain gain

人才市场 talents market;employment market;human resources pool

人才外流 brain drain

人才招聘 personnel recruitment

人财两空 lose both a person and money

人称代词 personal pronoun

人大代表 a deputy to the National People's Congress

人道主义 humanitarianism

人地生疏 be unfamiliar with the place and the people;be a complete stranger

人丁兴旺 have a growing family;have a flourishing population

R

人定胜天 Man can conquer nature; man will triumph over nature; People are masters of their own fate.

人多势众 overwhelm with numerical strength; dominate by sheer force of numbers

人多嘴杂 many people, many words; the more people, the more talk

人防工程 people's air defense project

人非木石 man is not made of wood or stone—man is not feelingless

人浮于事 be overstaffed; have more staff (*or* hands) than needed

人工繁殖 artificial propagation

人工放顶 artificial caving

人工孵化 artificial incubation

人工更新 forestry artificial regeneration

人工呼吸 artificial respiration

人工基因 artificial gene

人工降水 artificial precipitation

人工降雨 artificial precipitation; artificial rainfall; man-made precipitation

人工流产 induced abortion

人工免疫 artificial immunity; artificial immunization

人工气腹 (artificial) pneumoperitoneum

人工气胸 (artificial) pneumothorax

人工器官 artificial organ

人工授粉 artificial pollination

人工授精 artificial insemination; artificial conception

人工选择 artificial selection

人工语言 artificial language

人工造林 artificial afforestation

人工智能 AI, artificial intelligence

人海战术 huge-crowd strategy; wave strategy; "tactics of human sea"—a big increase in the labour force

人欢马叫 people bustling and horses neighing—a busy, prosperous country scene

人机对话 man-machine interaction

人机交互 human-computer interaction

人机界面 man-machine interface; user's interface

人迹罕至 without human trace; uninhabited; untraversed

人际关系 human relationships; interpersonal relationships

人间地狱 hell on earth

人间天堂 heaven on earth

人杰地灵 Heroes bring glory to a place; The greatness of a man lends glory to a place.

人尽其才 make the best possible use of men

人均耕地 per capita cultivated (*or* arable) land; amount of farmland per capita

人均住房 per capita housing

人口爆炸 population explosion

人口分布 population distribution

人口过密 over-congested population

人口过剩 over population

人口基数 population base

人口结构 population structure

人口老化 aging of population

人口密度 density of population; population density

人口普查 population census

人口衰减 depopulation

人口素质 population quality

人口统计 population statistics

人口意识 awareness of population problem

人口增长 population growth

人口质量 population quality

人口专家 demographic experts; population expert

人口组成 population composition

人困马乏 the men weary, their steeds spent—tired out; exhausted

人力物力 man power and material resources

人力资源 human resources

人满为患 overcrowded with people; overstaffed

人面兽心 the face of a man but the heart of a beast—a beast in human form

人面桃花 her face and the peach-blossoms—the pinings of a lover

人民法院 people's court

人民防空 people's air defence; civil air defence

人民公仆 people's public servant

人民公社 people's commune

人民警察 the people's police

人民来信 letters from the masses

人民群众 the masses

人民日报 Renmin Ribao; the People's Daily

人民团体 mass organization; people's organization

人民武装 people's armed forces

人民战争 people's war

人民阵线 popular front

人民政府 the People's Government

人命关天 a case involving human life is one of supreme importance; matter of life and death

人莫予毒 no one dare harm me—be supercilious

人弃我取 I pick up what others discard; I have my own views and tastes.

人强马壮 both men and horses are strong—① a strong, combat effective army ② a strong working force

人琴俱亡 The man and his lute are both dead (a lament for the death of a friend).

人情冷暖 social snobbery

人情练达 experienced in the ways of the

world
人情世故 worldly wisdom
人穷志短 Poverty chills ambition.
人权法案 the Bill of Rights
人权立法 human rights legislation
人权宣言 Universal Declaration of Human Rights
人权外交 human rights diplomacy
人权卫士 human rights defenders
人权问题 the human rights issue
人人过关 Everyone must pass a test.
人人平等 Everyone is equal.
人人有责 Everyone is responsible.
人人自危 Everyone finds himself in danger; Everyone feels insecure.
人山人海 huge crowds of people; a sea of people
人身安全 personal safety (*or* security)
人身保险 life insurance; insurance against accidents
人身攻击 character assassination; personal attack; personal abuse; assault and battery
人身伤害 personal injury
人身事故 personal injury caused by an accident
人身侮辱 personal insult
人身自由 freedom of person; personal freedom
人神共愤 (of a great outrage) arouse the great indignation of both men and gods
人生如寄 Man's life is like a traveller's stay.
人生如梦 Life is but a dream.
人生朝露 Life is like the morning dew.
人生哲学 philosophy of life
人声鼎沸 a hubbub of voices
人世沧桑 tremendous changes in this world of ours
人事变动 personnel changes
人事档案 personal file (*or* dossier)
人事调动 transfer of personnel
人事关系 organizational affiliation
人事管理 personnel management
人事制度 personnel system
人手不足 be short of hands; be short-handed; be understaffed
人手一册 Everyone has a copy.
人寿保险 life insurance
人寿年丰 good harvests and good health; The land yields good crops and the people enjoy good health.
人梯精神 zeal to help others climb higher
人体克隆 human cloning
人体模特 mannequin
人体炸弹 human bomb
人微言轻 The words of the lowly carry little weight.
人为地貌 culture features
人为嬗变 artificial transmutation

人文奥运 People's Olympics
人文关怀 humanistic care
人文景观 humanistic sights; place of cultural interest
人文科学 the humanities; humane studies
人文主义 humanism
人五人六 be affected; strike poses
人心不古 Public morality is not what it used to be (i.e. has degenerated).
人心大快 to gratification of all
人心惶惶 popular anxiety
人心如面 Men's hearts are as different as their faces.
人心丧尽 lose (*or* forfeit) all popular sympathy
人心所向 popular sentiment; the feelings of the people
人心稳定 People are free from anxiety; tranquil mood of the general public
人心向背 whether the people are for or against; the feelings of the people
人行横道 pedestrian crosswalk; pedestrian crossing; zebra crossing
人烟稠密 densely populated; populous
人烟稀少 be sparsely populated; meagrely-populated
人言可畏 The voice of the people is something to fear; Gossip is a fearful thing.
人言啧啧 There is a good deal of unfavourable comment.
人仰马翻 men and horses thrown off their feet—badly battered; thrown into confusion
人欲横流 unbridled indulgence of human desires and passions; universal decadence
人员编制 staff quota; authorized strength; establishment strength
人员过多 overstaffed
人云亦云 echo the view of others; have no views of one's own; parrot other's words
人造黄油 margarine
人造卫星 man-made satellite
人造纤维 man-made fibre
人造橡胶 artificial rubber; synthetic rubber
人造血管 artificial blood vessel
人造羊毛 artificial wool
人证物证 human testimony and material evidence
人之常情 what is natural and normal (in human relationships)
人自为战 each man fighting all by himself
人才交流会 talent fair; the personnel exchange meeting
人大常委会 the Standing Committee of the National People's Congress
人盯人防守 man-to-man defence
人工心肺机 heart-lung machine
人口出生率 fertility rate

R

人口动态学 population dynamics
人口负增长 negative population growth
人口金字塔 population pyramid
人口老龄化 population aging; population greying
人口死亡率 mortality rate
人口统计学 demography
人类工程学 human engineering
人类语言学 anthropological linguistics
人民币汇率 exchange rates for the Renminbi against other currencies
人民大会堂 the Great Hall of the People
人民检察院 people's procuratorate
人民陪审员 people's assessor
人民武装部 people's armed forces department (of a county, etc.)
人勤地不懒 Where the tiller is tireless the land is fertile.
人穷志不短 poor but proud; poor but ambitious
人身保护令 habeas corpus
人生地不熟 be unfamiliar with the place and the people; be a stranger in a strange place
人事决定权 exercise the direction rights on personnel
人丝斜纹绸 rayon twill
人死如灯灭 A man dies the way a lamp goes out.
人体生物钟 biological clock
人心隔肚皮 different hearts in different breasts—it's hard to tell what's going on in the minds of other people; People should always be on guard against one another.
人不可以貌相 Never judge a person by his appearance; You can't judge people by appearances.
人才交流中心 personnel exchange centre; talent exchange centre
人道主义干涉 humanitarian intervention
人道主义精神 humanitarianism; the humanitarian spirit
人道主义援助 humanitarian aid
人工肾 artificial kidney
人居环境质量 environmental conditions for human settlements
人均实际收入 real income per capita
人均住房面积 per capita living space
人口动态统计 vital statistics
人口生育高峰 baby boom
人类基因图谱 human genome
人民币不贬值 not to devalue the Renminbi
人民代表大会 people's congress
人民民主专政 people's democratic dictatorship
人民内部矛盾 contradictions among the people
人身不可侵犯 inviolability of the person
人事制度改革 reform of the personnel system
人体特异功能 extrasensory perception (ESP); paranormal bodily ability

人为设置障碍 artificially imposed obstacles
人为万物之灵 Man of all creatures is the one endowed with intelligence.
人造地球卫星 artificial earth satellite; sputnik
人不知,鬼不觉 without a soul knowing anything about it
人心齐,泰山移 The people all working with one will can move Mount Tai; A people united can move mountains.
人要脸,树要皮 Face is as important to man as the bark is to the tree.
人有脸,树有皮 a man has a face just as a tree has bark—a man has a sense of shame
人逢喜事精神爽 Joy puts heart into a man.
人工合成蛋白质 synthetic protein
人均国内总产值 per capita gross domestic product
人口自然增长率 natural growth rate of population
人老珠黄不值钱 in old age, one is like a pearl whose lustre has faded—no longer held in esteem
人类基因组草图 draft of the human genome
人类基因组工程 Human Genome Project
人类基因组计划 human genome programme
人类灵魂工程师 engineers who shape human souls—teachers, writers, artists, etc.
人民币汇率并轨 single rate for the RMB
人民英雄纪念碑 the Monument to the People's Heroes
人怕出名猪怕壮 Fame portends trouble for men just as fattening does for pigs.
人配衣服马配鞍 Clothes make the man as the saddle makes the horse; Clothes make the man.
人生七十古来稀 Man's life from of old has rarely reached seventy; Men who reach the age of seventy have always been a rarity.
人心不足蛇吞象 A man who rests content with nothing is like a snake trying to swallow an elephant.
人不为己,天诛地灭 Unless a man looks out for himself, Heaven and Earth will destroy him; Everyone for himself and the devil take the hindmost.
人均国民生产总值 per capita gross national product
人类免疫缺陷病毒 Human Immunodeficiency Virus (HIV)
人身意外伤害保险 personal accidents insurance; insurance against accidents to one's physical existence
人不犯我,我不犯人 If others let me alone, I'll let them alone.
人而无信,不知其可 If a man does not keep his word, what is he good for?
人非圣贤,孰能无过 Men are not saints, how

can they be free from faults;To err is human.
人命危浅,朝不虑夕 be sinking fast;be dying
人人为我,我为人人 all for one and one for all
人生一世,草生一春 Man has but one life,grass sees but one spring;life is short.
人同此心,心同此理 On this matter people feel and think alike.
人为财死,鸟为食亡 Men will die for wealth,as birds for food.
人为刀俎,我为鱼肉 be meat on sb's chopping block—be at sb's mercy
人无远虑,必有近忧 He who gives no thought to difficulties in the future is sure to be beset by worries much closer at hand.
人之将死,其言也善 Good are the words of a dying man.
人工合成结晶胰岛素 synthetic crystalline insulin
人们关心的热点问题 focus of public interest and discussion
人民当家作主的权利 the rights of the people as the masters of the country
人民的生存权和发展权 the people's rights of subsistence and development;the people's rights to earn a living and develop
人民币经常项目下可兑换 convertibility of RMB under the current account;make the RMB convertible under current accounts

壬 [rén]
〔名〕ninth of the ten Heavenly Stem

仁 [rén]
Ⅰ〔名〕① benevolence;kindheartedness;humanity ② kernel;stone (of a peach, plum, etc.) Ⅱ〔代〕you;your
仁爱 kindheartedness;benevolence;humanity
仁慈 benevolent;merciful;kind
仁德 kindheartedness;benevolence;humanity
仁弟 my dear friend
仁厚 honest and kindhearted
仁心 kindheartedness
仁兄 my dear friend
仁义 benevolence and uprighteousness
仁政 benevolent government;policy of benevolence
仁人君子 benevolent gentlemen;public-spirited people
仁人志士 people with high ideals
仁义道德 humanity, justice and virtue;virtue and morality
仁至义尽 do everything called for by humanity and duty;do what is humanly possible to help;be magnanimous
仁者见仁,智者见智 the benevolent see benevolence and the wise see wisdom—different people have different views

rěn（ㄖㄣˇ）

忍 [rěn]
〔动〕① bear;endure;stand;tolerate ② have the heart to
忍冬 honeysuckle
忍耐 exercise patience;exercise restraint;restrain oneself
忍让 exercise forbearance;be forbearing and conciliatory
忍受 bear;endure;stand
忍痛 very reluctantly
忍心 have the heart to;be hardhearted enough to
忍者 ninja
忍住 bear;endure
忍饥挨饿 endure the torments of hunger
忍俊不禁 cannot help laughing
忍气吞声 swallow an insult;submit to humiliation;stifle one's indignation
忍辱负重 endure humiliation in order to carry out an important mission
忍辱偷生 bearing one's shame
忍痛割爱 part reluctantly with what one treasures
忍无可忍 be driven beyond (the limits of) forbearance;come to the end of one's patience

荏 [rěn]
Ⅰ〔名〕common perilla Ⅱ〔形〕weak;cowardly
荏苒 (of time) elapse quickly (or imperceptibly);slip by
荏弱 weak;feeble;delicate

稔 [rěn]
Ⅰ〔形〕①(of grain) ripe ②familiar;acquainted (usu. with people) Ⅱ〔名〕year

rèn（ㄖㄣˋ）

刃 [rèn]
Ⅰ〔名〕①edge of a knife,scissors,etc.;blade ② sword; knife Ⅱ〔动〕kill with a sword (or knife)
刃钢 shear-steel
刃具 cutting tool
刃口 the edge of a knife,sword,etc.

认 [rèn]
〔动〕①recognize;identify;distinguish;tell ② enter into a certain kind of relationship with;acknowledge;adopt ③admit;accept;recognize ④(followed by 了) resign oneself to a loss, etc.;accept as unavoidable
认出 recognize;make out;identify
认错 acknowledge a mistake;admit a fault;offer (or make) an apology
认得 know;recognize
认定 ① firmly believe;maintain;hold ② set one's mind on
认罚 admit that one deserves punishment;

R

submit to punishment; be ready to pay the penalty

认购 offer to buy; subscribe to buy; subscribe for

认捐 offer a donation

认可 approve

认领 claim

认命 accept fate; resign oneself (*or* be resigned) to fate

认赔 admit an obligation to pay (for damage done, etc.); agree to pay compensation

认亲 ①become related by marriage ②claim a family connection

认清 see clearly; recognize; get a clear understanding of

认人 (of a baby) can recognize people

认生 (of a child) be shy with strangers

认识 ①know; understand; recognize ②understanding; knowledge; cognition

认输 admit defeat; throw in (*or* up) the sponge; give up

认为 think; consider; hold; deem

认养 ①adopt and bring up ②assume the responsibility to raise flowers, trees, or animals with the approval of the departments concerned

认账 acknowledge a debt (*or* an account); admit what one has said or done

认真 ①conscientious; earnest; serious ②take seriously; take to heart

认证 ①legalize; attest; authenticate ②attestation; authentication

认准 set one's mind on

认字 know (*or* learn) how to read

认罪 admit one's guilt; plead guilty

认识论 theory of knowledge; epistemology

认敌为友 take a foe for a friend

认赔抛售 sacrifice sale

认识过程 process of cognition

认识能力 cognitive ability

认识水平 level of understanding

认死理儿 stubborn; as obstinate as a mule

认同危机 identity crisis

认贼作父 take the foe for one's father; regard the enemy as kith and kin

认证机构 certification bodies

认知科学 cognitive science

认知心理学 cognitive psychology

仞 [rèn] 量 ancient measure of length equal to seven or eight *chi*

讱 [rèn] 形 inarticulate; slow of speech

任 [rèn] Ⅰ 动 ①appoint; engage ②assume; undertake; hold; take up ③bear; face ④let; allow; permit; give rein to Ⅱ 名 office; official post

Ⅲ 量 term of office：当过两次委员会主席 have been chairman of the committee for two terms Ⅳ 连 no matter (how, what, etc.)

任便 as you like; as you see fit

任从 ①allow; let (sb do as he pleases) ②no matter (how, what, etc.) ③even if; even though

任何 any; whichever; whatever

任教 be a teacher; teach

任课 teach (at a school)

任满 at the expiration (*or* expiry) of one's term of office

任免 appoint and remove (*or* dismiss)

任命 appoint

任凭 ①allow; let (sb do as he pleases) ②no matter (how, what, etc.) ③even if; even though

任期 term of office; tenure of office

任情 let oneself go; to one's heart's content; as much as one likes

任人 let people (do sth without restrictions)

任事 ①have a job; be employed ②take up a task

任所 office

任务 assignment; mission; task; job

任性 wilful; self-willed; wayward; headstrong

任意 wanton; arbitrary; wilful

任用 assign sb to a post; appoint

任职 hold a post; be in office

任命状 letter of appointment; commission

任期制 tenure system

任意球 free kick; free throw

任劳任怨 work hard regardless of criticism; willingly bear the burden of office

任期届满 expiration of term

任其自流 leave sth to take its own course

任其自然 give free rein to; let nature take its course

任人唯亲 appoint people by favouritism; practise nepotism

任人唯贤 appoint people on their merit; appoint people according to their integrity and ability

任人宰割 (cannot but) allow oneself to be trampled upon

任务观点 get-it-over-and-done-with attitude; perfunctory attitude

任务提示 briefing

任贤用能 use the wise and the capable

任意常数 arbitrary constant

任重道远 the burden is heavy and the road is long—shoulder heavy responsibilities

任期目标责任制 system of responsibility for goals set for one's term of office; tenure-goal-responsibility system; system with tenure, goal and responsibility clearly defined (*or* specified)

任凭风浪起,稳坐钓鱼船 sit tight in the fishing boat despite the rising wind and waves— hold one's ground despite pressure or opposition

纫 [rèn] 劢 ①thread (a needle) ②sew;stitch ③be very grateful;be very much obliged
纫针 thread a needle

韧 [rèn] 形 pliable but strong;likely to bend but not to crack;tough
韧带 ligament
韧度 tenacity
韧劲 indomitableness;dauntlessness;tenacity; persevering spirit;perseverance
韧力 indomitable will;indomitable spirit;persevering spirit;unyielding will
韧性 toughness;tenacity
韧皮部 bast;phloem
韧皮纤维 bast fibre

靭 [rèn] 名 log used to stop wheels;发靭 lift the log to set the carriage going;commence an undertaking;start (*or* set) the ball rolling

饪 [rèn] 劢 cook

妊 [rèn] 劢 be pregnant
妊妇 pregnant woman
妊娠 gestation;pregnancy
妊娠期 period of gestation;gestational period
妊娠反应 morning sickness

纴 [rèn] 劢 weave

衽 [rèn] 名 ①one or two pieces making up the front of a Chinese gown ②sleeping mat
衽席 sleeping mat;place for sleeping

rēng (日ㄥ)

扔 [rēng] 劢 ①throw;cast;toss;fling ②throw away;cast aside
扔掉 throw away
扔弃 abandon;discard;cast aside
扔下 abandon;put aside;leave behind

réng (日ㄥˊ)

仍 [réng] Ⅰ 劢 remain Ⅱ 形 frequent Ⅲ 副 still;yet
仍旧 ①remain the same ②still;yet
仍然 still;yet

礽 [réng] 名 good fortune;blessing

rì (日ˋ)

日 [rì] Ⅰ 名 ①sun ②(short for 日本) Japan ③ daytime;day ④day ⑤time;period ⑥specified day Ⅱ 副 every day;daily;with each passing day
日班 day shift
日报 daily paper;daily
日本 Japan
日常 day-to-day;everyday;daily
日场 day show;daytime performance;matinée
日程 programme;schedule
日出 sunrise
日戳 ①date stamp;dater ②datemark
日珥 prominence
日工 ①daywork ②day labour ③day labourer
日光 sunlight;sunbeam
日晷 sundial
日后 in the future;in the days to come
日记 diary
日间 in the daytime;during the day
日见 grow conspicuous on a daily basis;with each passing day
日渐 with each passing day;day by day (slowly)
日久 with the passing of time;in (the) course of time
日均 average per day;daily average
日历 calendar
日落 sunset
日冕 (solar) corona
日暮 evening;nightfall;dusk
日内 in a few days;in a day or two;in a couple of days
日期 date
日前 a few days ago;the other day
日趋 with each passing day;gradually;day by day
日射 insolation
日食 solar eclipse
日坛 the Altar to the Sun (in Beijing)
日托 day care
日息 per diem interest;daily interest
日薪 daily wage;per diem
日夜 day and night;night and day;round the clock
日益 increasingly;day by day
日用 ①daily expenses ②of everyday (*or* daily) use
日语 Japanese (language)
日元 yen (Japanese monetary unit)
日月 ①life;livelihood ②the sun and the moon
日晕 solar halo
日杂 sundry goods;general merchandise;daily household supplies
日照 sunshine
日志 daily record;journal
日中 noon;midday
日子 ①day;date ②time ③life;livelihood
日本海 the Sea of Japan

R

日本人 Japanese
日程表 schedule
日光灯 fluorescent lamp;daylight lamp
日光浴 sunbath
日记本 diary
日记账 journal;daybook
日界线 international date line;date line
日冕仪 coronagraph
日射表 actinometer
日射病 sunstroke;insolation
日心说 heliocentric theory
日用品 articles of everyday use
日本料理 Japanese cuisine;Japanese restaurant
日薄西山 the sun is setting beyond the western hills—declining rapidly;nearing one's end
日不暇给 be fully occupied every day;be pressed for time
日复一日 day after day;day in and day out
日光疗法 heliotherapy
日积月累 accumulate over a long period
日经指数 Nikkei Index
日久年深 after a long lapse of time;with the passage of time
日久天长 after a considerable period of time
日就月将 achieve sth every day and make progress every month—many a little makes a mickle
日理万机 attend to numerous affairs of state every day;be occupied with a myriad of state affairs
日历手表 calendar watch
日暮途穷 the day is waning and the road is ending—approaching the end of one's days;be on one's last legs;be at the end of one's rope
日日夜夜 day and night;night and day
日上三竿 the sun is three poles high—it's late in the morning
日思夜想 long for day and night;have sb (or sth) daily and nightly in one's thoughts
日新月异 change with each passing day
日夜商店 shop open night and day;round-the-clock shop;day-and-night-service shop
日以继夜 night and day;round the clock
日用器具 household utensils;articles of everyday use
日月重光 the sun and the moon shining again—back to peace and prosperity after a dark period
日月如梭 the sun and the moon shuttle back and forth—how time flies
日月同辉 shine forever like the sun and the moon
日月星辰 the sun,the moon and the stars;the heavenly bodies

日久见人心 Time reveals a person's heart;It takes time to know a person.
日托托儿所 day nursery
日用必需品 daily necessities;household necessities
日用工业品 manufactured goods for daily use
日用小商品 small articles of everyday use
日本军国主义 Japanese militarism
日本协办银行 Japan Bank For International Cooperation (JBIC)
日本右翼势力 right-wing forces in Japan
日出而作,日入而息 begin work at sunrise and rest at sunset—life in primitive society
日经-道琼斯平均指数 Nikkei-Dow Jones Average
日美"新防务合作准则" Japan-US "new defense cooperation guidelines"
日间不做亏心事,半夜敲门不吃惊 He who has done nothing shameful by day need not be alarmed by a knock at the door by night.

驲 [rì]
名 carriage for a post station;post-chaise

róng(ㄖㄨㄥˊ)

戎 [róng]
名 ①arms;weaponry ②army;military affairs
戎马 army horse
戎装 martial attire
戎马倥偬 burdened with pressing military duties
戎马生涯 army life;military life

茸 [róng]
Ⅰ 形 (of grass) newly-grown,soft and fine;downy Ⅱ 名 young pilose antler
茸鞭 flimmer
茸长 long and untidy (hair,grass,etc.)
茸茸 (of grass,hair,etc.) fine,soft and thick;downy

荣 [róng]
Ⅰ 动 grow exuberantly (or luxuriantly);prosper;thrive;flourish Ⅱ 形 thriving;flourishing Ⅲ 名 honour;glory
荣光 honour;glory
荣归 return in glory
荣获 get (or win) sth as an honour
荣枯 ①(of plants) flourishing and withering ②rise and fall (or decline)
荣任 be honoured with a post
荣辱 honour or disgrace
荣升 be honoured by promotion to a higher post
荣退 ①retire from (or leave) a post with merit ②(general term for) army veterans
荣幸 be honoured
荣耀 honour;glory
荣膺 be honoured with a post (or decoration)

R

荣誉 honour;credit;glory
荣誉奖 honourable prize
荣华富贵 glory,splendour,wealth and rank;high position and great wealth
荣辱与共 (of friends) share honour or disgrace,weal or woe
荣誉称号 title of honor;honorary title
荣誉军人 disabled soldier

绒 [róng]
[名] ①fine soft hair;down ②nap (*or* pile) of cloth ③fine floss for embroidery
绒布 flannelette;cotton flannel
绒花 velvet flowers,birds,etc.
绒画 painting on velvet
绒裤 sweat pants
绒毛 ①fine hair;down;villus ②nap;pile
绒毯 flannelette blanket
绒线 ①floss for embroidery ②knitting wool
绒绣 woollen needlepoint tapestry;woollen embroidery
绒衣 sweat shirt
绒羽 fluff;down feather
绒面革 suède (leather)
绒头绳 ①wool (for tying pigtails) ②knitting wool

容 [róng]
Ⅰ [动] ①hold;contain ②tolerate;excuse;forgive ③permit;allow;let Ⅱ [副] perhaps;maybe;probably Ⅲ [名] ①facial expression;look ②facial features;looks;appearance ③appearance;look
容错 fault toleration
容光 facial expression;bearing
容华 features and complexion;looks
容积 volume
容量 capacity
容留 give shelter to;take sb in;keep
容貌 facial features;appearance;looks
容纳 hold;have a capacity of;accommodate
容器 container;vessel
容情 (*usu. used in the negative*) show mercy
容人 ①regard people with kind tolerance ②tolerant towards others;magnanimous;broad-minded
容忍 tolerate;put up with;condone
容色 facial expression;countenance
容身 take shelter
容受 ①hold;contain ②endure;put up with
容恕 tolerate;forgive
容物 tolerant;forbearing;magnanimous
容限 tolerance;allowance
容许 ①tolerate;permit;allow ②perhaps;possibly
容蓄 hold;contain;accumulate
容颜 appearance;looks
容易 ①easy ②likely;liable;apt

容重 unit weight
容装 appearance and dress
容电器 condenser;capacitor
容积吨 measurement ton
容错软件 fault-tolerant software
容光焕发 one's face glowing with health
容身之地 a place to stay
容许负载 allowable load
容许收缩量 shrinkage allowance

嵘 [róng]
◇峥嵘 ①lofty and steep;towering ②outstanding;extraordinary

蓉 [róng]
[名] mashed fruit (*or* seeds)

溶 [róng]
[动] dissolve;thaw;meet
溶洞 limestone cave
溶化 dissolve
溶汇 ①dissolve and mix ②mingle;merge
溶剂 solvent
溶胶 sol
溶解 dissolve
溶煤 solvent
溶没 fade into;become invisible;dissolve
溶溶 broad
溶蚀 corrosion
溶血 haemolysis
溶液 solution
溶质 solute
溶注 absorb
溶合词 fused vowel
溶解度 solubility
溶解热 heat of solution
溶解物 dissolved matter
溶菌素 bacteriolysin
溶性油 soluble oil

榕 [róng]
[名] small-fruited fig tree;banyan

熔 [róng]
[动] melt;fuse;smelt
熔池 (molten) bath
熔滴 molten drop
熔点 melting (*or* fusing,fusion) point
熔断 fusing
熔化 melt
熔剂 flux
熔接 weld
熔结 fuse;combine
熔解 fuse;fusion
熔炼 smelt
熔炉 ①smelting furnace ②crucible;furnace
熔融 melt
熔岩 lava
熔铸 found;cast
熔化炉 melting furnace
熔化期 melting stage
熔炼炉 smelting furnace

R

熔铸工 smelter
熔化速率 melting rate
熔融纺丝 melting spinning
熔融挤压法 extrusion by melting

蝾 [róng]

蝾螈 salamander;newt

镕 [róng]

劻 melt;fuse;smelt

融 [róng]

Ⅰ 劻 ①melt;thaw ②fuse;merge;blend;be in harmony Ⅱ 名 circulation
融合 mix together;fuse;merge
融和 pleasantly warm;genial
融化 (of ice,snow,etc.) melt;thaw
融会 mix together;fuse;merge
融解 melt;thaw
融洽 harmonious;on friendly (or good) terms
融融 ①happy and harmonious ②warm
融通 circulate
融资 finance;raise funds
融会贯通 achieve mastery through a comprehensive study of the subject;gain a thorough understanding of the subject through mastery of all relevant material
融通资金 put capital into circulation;circulate funds
融资渠道 financing channel
融资项目 financing project
融资租赁 financial lease

rǒng (ㄖㄨㄥˇ)

冗 [rǒng]

Ⅰ 形 ① redundant;superfluous ② loaded with trivial details Ⅱ 名 busy schedule
冗笔 superfluity in writing or painting;unnecessary touches or strokes
冗长 tediously long;lengthy;long-winded;prolix
冗词 superfluous words (in a piece of writing)
冗繁 (of affairs) many and diverse;miscellaneous
冗余 redundance;redundancy
冗员 redundant personnel
冗杂 ① (of writing) lengthy and jumbled ② (of affairs) miscellaneous
冗赘 verbose;diffuse
冗词赘句 redundant words and expressions

róu (ㄖㄡˊ)

柔 [róu]

Ⅰ 形 ①soft;supple;pliant;flexible ②gentle;tender;yielding;mild Ⅱ 劻 soften
柔板 adagio
柔肠 soft heart
柔道 judo
柔和 soft;gentle;mild
柔滑 soft and smooth;satiny;creamy
柔静 gentle and quiet
柔麻 soften jute,hemp,etc.
柔曼 ①soft;gentle ②soft and smooth;satiny;creamy ③good-looking;gorgeous
柔美 soft and graceful
柔媚 gentle and lovely;genial;lovable
柔绵 mellow (taste)
柔嫩 tender;delicate
柔懦 timid and overcautious;weak-willed
柔情 tender feelings;tenderness
柔韧 pliable and tough
柔软 soft;lithe
柔润 soft and smooth;delicate
柔弱 weak;delicate
柔桑 supple mulberry leaves
柔术 jujitsu
柔顺 gentle and agreeable;meek
柔婉 soft and mild
柔细 soft and fine
柔性 flexible
柔鱼 squid
柔软剂 softening agent;softener
柔肠寸断 brokenhearted;The heart breaks thinking of one's love.
柔能克刚 The soft can overcome the hard.
柔情似水 tender feelings like water—be deeply attached;be passionately devoted
柔情侠骨 a tender heart and a chivalrous spirit
柔茹刚吐 bully the weak and fear the strong
柔软体操 callisthenics
柔若无骨 soft as soap
柔荑花序 catkin;ament
柔心弱骨 soft heart and weak bone—soft;mild;meek
柔中有刚 firmness cloaked beneath gentleness;an iron hand in a velvet glove

揉 [róu]

劻 ①rub ②knead;crumple into a ball ③bend;reform
揉搓 rub
揉木为耒 make a farm tool out of a log

煣 [róu]

劻 bend (a piece of wood) on fire

糅 [róu]

劻 mingle;mix
糅合 form a mixture (usu. of things which don't blend well);mix

蹂 [róu]

劻 stamp;trample
蹂躏 trample on;trample upon;ravage;make havoc of;devastate
蹂踏 trample
蹂躏人权 gross violation of human rights
蹂躏别国主权 trample upon the sovereignty of other countries

鞣 [róu]
〔动〕tan
鞣料 tanning material
鞣酸 tannic acid；tannin
鞣皮子 tan hides

ròu（ㄖㄡˋ）

肉 [ròu]
Ⅰ〔名〕①flesh；meat ②pulp；flesh (of fruits)
Ⅱ〔形〕①not crisp；mushy ②phlegmatic
肉饼 ground-meat pie；meat pie
肉搏 fight hand-to-hand
肉畜 livestock raised for meat
肉垂 wattle
肉刺 corn
肉店 butcher's (shop)
肉丁 diced meat
肉冻 meat jelly；aspic
肉干 jerky
肉感 sex appeal；sexiness
肉鸽 meat pigeon；table pigeon
肉羹 bouillon
肉冠 comb
肉桂 cinnamon tree；Chinese cinnamon tree；cassia-bark tree
肉红 flesh-coloured；pale red
肉鸡 table hen；table chicken；broiler
肉酱 meat pulp；minced meat
肉瘤 sarcoma
肉麻 nauseating；sickening；disgusting
肉马 meat horse
肉末 minced meat；ground meat
肉牛 store cattle；beef cattle；meat cattle；stocker
肉排 steak
肉皮 pork skin
肉片 sliced meat
肉禽 table poultry
肉色 yellowish pink；flesh-coloured；flesh-tinted
肉身 the mortal body
肉食 [ròushí] carnivorous
肉食 [ròushi] meat
肉丝 shredded meat (esp. pork)
肉松 dried meat (esp. pork) floss
肉袒 strip off the upper garments (in begging forgiveness)—make a humble apology
肉汤 broth
肉体 the human body；the flesh
肉头 soft and fleshy
肉兔 table rabbit
肉馅 meat stuffing；chopped (*or* ground) meat
肉刑 corporal punishment
肉芽 granulation
肉眼 naked eye
肉羊 mutton sheep

肉欲 carnal desire
肉圆 meatball
肉汁 gravy；(meat) juice
肉猪 slaughter pig；hog；porker；pork pig
肉赘 wart
肉包子 steamed bun with meat stuffing
肉搏战 hand-to-hand fight (*or* combat)；bayonet fighting (*or* charge)
肉苁蓉 saline cistanche
肉豆蔻 nutmeg
肉嘟嘟 plump；chubby；pudgy
肉墩墩 stocky
肉泡眼 eyes with fleshy eyelids；pouchy eyes
肉皮儿 human skin；complexion
肉脾气 habitually slow
肉食品 meat product
肉丸子 meatball
肉星儿 tiny bits of meat
肉性子 phlegmatic temperament
肉制品 meat products
肉穗花序 spadix
肉眼凡胎 a very mundane person；a commonplace and ignorant person
肉眼泡儿 eyes with fleshy eyelids；pouchy eyes
肉用仔鸡 broiler
肉类加工厂 meat processing factory

rú（ㄖㄨˊ）

如 [rú]
Ⅰ〔动〕①according to；in conformity with ②like；as；as if ③(*used in the negative*) be as good as；can compare with ④be more than；surpass ⑤for example；for instance；such as；as ⑥go to；arrive at Ⅱ〔连〕if
如常 as usual
如此 so；such；in this way；like that
如次 be as follows
如故 ①as before ②like old friends
如果 if；in case (of)；in the event of
如何 how；what
如今 nowadays；now
如命 in compliance with your instructions
如期 as scheduled；by the scheduled time；on schedule
如其 if；in case (of)；in the event of
如若 if；in case (of)；in the event of
如上 as above
如实 go strictly by the facts
如数 exactly the number or amount
如同 like；as
如下 as follows
如像 like；as
如心 after one's own heart；to one's liking
如许 ①so；such；in this way；like that ②so much；so many

R

如意 ① find sth satisfactory (*or* as one wishes); be gratified ② *ruyi*, an S-shaped ornamental object, usu. made of jade, formerly a symbol of good luck

如愿 have one's wish fulfilled

如约 keep one's appointment appropriate

如云 cloudlike; many; full of

如臂使指 have a perfect command of sth

如痴如醉 delude one to folly; lose one's mind

如出一口 as if from one mouth—with one voice; unanimously

如出一辙 be exactly the same; be no different from each other; be cut from the same cloth

如此等等 and so on and so forth

如此而已 that's what it all adds up to

如此这般 thus and thus; thus and so

如堕烟海 as if lost on a misty sea; all at sea; completely at a loss

如法炮制 prepare herbal medicine by the prescribed method—follow a set pattern; follow suit

如鲠在喉 like a fishbone getting stuck in the throat—necessary to give vent to one's pent-up feelings

如虎添翼 like a tiger that has grown wings—with might redoubled

如花似锦 like flowers and brocade—① beautiful (scenery) ② bright (future)

如花似玉 like flowers and jade—(of a woman) young and beautiful

如火如荼 like a raging fire

如获至宝 like finding rare treasure; as if one had found a priceless treasure

如饥似渴 as if thirsting or hungering for sth; with great eagerness

如箭在弦 an arrow fitted to the bowstring cannot avoid being discharged—one cannot but go ahead; one has reached the point of no return

如胶似漆 stick to each other like glue or lacquer; remain glued to each other; be deeply attached to each other

如狼牧羊 like a wolf shepherding sheep—(of an oppressive official) ride roughshod over the people

如狼似虎 as ferocious as wolves and tigers; like cruel beasts of prey

如雷贯耳 reverberate like thunder

如临大敌 as if faced with a formidable foe; like confronting a mortal enemy

如梦初醒 as if awakening from a dream—beginning to see the light

如鸟兽散 scatter and flee like birds and beasts; flee helter-skelter; be utterly routed

如牛负重 like an ox carrying a heavy load

如泣如诉 (of music or singing) querulous and plaintive

如日方升 rising like the morning sun—have bright and boundless prospects

如日中天 like the sun at high noon—at the apex (*or* zenith) of one's power, career, etc.

如丧考妣 (look) as if one had lost one's parents—(look) utterly wretched

如上所述 as is mentioned above

如释重负 (feel) as if relieved of a heavy load

如数家珍 as if enumerating one's family treasures—show thorough familiarity with a subject

如汤沃雪 like melting snow with hot water—easily done

如同儿戏 be like child's play

如蚁附膻 like ants clinging to sth rank—swarming after unwholesome things or attaching oneself to influential people

如意算盘 smug calculations; wishful thinking

如影随形 like the shadow following the person—closely associated with each other

如鱼得水 like a stranded fish put back into water (said of one in his proper surroundings or having got a great aid)

如愿以偿 have one's wish fulfilled; achieve (*or* obtain) what one wishes

如之奈何 what's to be done

如醉如痴 as if intoxicated and stupefied

如坐针毡 feel as if sitting on a bed of nails; be on pins and needles; be on tenterhooks

如入无人之境 like entering an unpeopled land—smashing all resistance; meeting no resistance

如坠五里云雾中 as if lost in a thick fog; utterly mystified

如临深渊, 如履薄冰 as though on the brink of an abyss, as though treading on thin ice—acting with extreme caution

如闻其声, 如见其人 (so vividly described that) You seem to see and hear the person.

如入鲍鱼之肆, 久而不闻其臭 it's like staying in a fish market and getting used to the stink—long exposure to bad surroundings or bad company accustoms one to evil ways

如入芝兰之室, 久而不闻其香 it's like entering a room full of fragrant orchids and getting used to the sweet smell—associating with people of noble character accustoms one to good ways

茹 [rú]

动 eat

茹素 eat grain and vegetables only; be on a vegetarian diet

茹毛饮血 (of primitive man) eat the raw flesh of birds and beasts

儒 [rú]

名 ① Confucianism; Confucianist ② scholar;

learned man
儒艮 dugong
儒家 the Confucianist
儒将 scholar-general
儒商 scholarly merchant; scholarly business-man; scholar-like tradesman; well-educated business people
儒雅 scholarly and refined

嚅 [rú]
嚅嚅 hesitate in speech; hem and haw; mutter and mumble

濡 [rú] 〈动〉①immerse; dip in; moisten; catch ②stay; linger
濡缓 slow-moving
濡迹 (break off a journey to) stay; linger
濡染 immerse; imbue
濡润 make moist
濡湿 soak; make wet

孺 [rú] 〈名〉child
孺子 child
孺子牛 a herd boy's willing ox—a servant of the people
孺子可教 You could be taught, young man; The boy is worth teaching.

蠕 [rú] 〈动〉wriggle; squirm
蠕虫 worm; helminth
蠕动 ①wriggle; squirm ②peristalsis ③creep
蠕蠕 wriggling; squirming
蠕虫学 helminthology

rǔ（ㄖㄨˇ）

汝 [rǔ] 〈代〉you
汝等 you people

乳 [rǔ] I 〈动〉reproduce II 〈名〉①breast ②milk ③any milk-like liquid III 〈形〉newborn (animal); suckling
乳白 milky white; cream colour
乳钵 mortar (a vessel)
乳齿 milk tooth; deciduous tooth
乳畜 milch livestock
乳蛾 acute tonsillitis
乳儿 a nursing infant; suckling
乳房 ①breast; mamma ②udder
乳峰 (young women's) rounded breasts
乳膏 emulsifiable paste
乳化 emulsify
乳剂 emulsion
乳胶 emulsion
乳疽 intramammary abscess
乳酪 cheese
乳糜 chyle

乳名 infant name; child's pet name
乳母 wet nurse
乳牛 dairy cattle; milch cow
乳酸 lactic acid
乳糖 milk sugar; lactose
乳头 ①nipple; teat; mammilla ②papilla
乳腺 mammary gland
乳香 frankincense
乳臭 smelling of milk—childish
乳牙 primary teeth; milk teeth; temporary teeth
乳燕 young swallow
乳液 latex; milk; emulsion
乳罩 brassiere; bra
乳汁 milk (in general)
乳脂 butterfat
乳猪 sucking pig; suckling pig
乳化液 emulsion
乳剂层 emulsion layer
乳胶漆 emulsion paint; latex paint
乳糜尿 chyluria
乳牛场 dairy farm
乳品业 dairy husbandry
乳酸钙 calcium lactate
乳糖酶 lactase
乳腺癌 breast cancer
乳腺炎 mastitis
乳脂糖 toffee; taffy
乳制品 dairy products
乳浊液 emulsion
乳化原油 emulsified crude oil
乳头状瘤 papilloma
乳臭未干 still smell of one's mother's milk—be young and inexperienced; be wet behind the ears

辱 [rǔ] I 〈名〉disgrace; dishonour II 〈动〉①humiliate; insult ②bring disgrace (or humiliation); be unworthy of ③be honoured; be grateful
辱骂 abuse; call sb names; hurl insults
辱命 disgrace a commission; fail to accomplish a mission
辱没 bring disgrace to; be unworthy of
辱承指教 be honoured by your advice; thank you for giving me the benefit of your wise counsel

擩 [rǔ] 〈动〉thrust; tuck; put in

rù（ㄖㄨˋ）

入 [rù] I 〈动〉①enter; go in; come in ②join; become a member of ③agree with; conform to II 〈名〉①income ②entering tone
入仓 be stored in a barn; be put in storage
入场 entrance; admission
入超 unfavourable balance of trade; import

R

surplus
入党 join (*or* be admitted to) a political party
入档 file (away)
入定 sit in meditation (a technique for mental self-discipline)
入肚 swallow; consume
入耳 pleasant to the ear
入伏 the *fu* days begin; the hottest days of the year begin
入港 ① enter a port ② (of conversation) in full agreement; in perfect harmony
入股 buy a share; become a shareholder
入骨 to the marrow
入户 ① go to sb's place; call at sb's house ② obtain a residence permit
入画 suitable for a painting; picturesque
入会 join a society, association, etc.
入伙 ① join a gang; join in partnership ② have one's meals at a canteen or mess hall
入籍 be naturalized
入寂 (of Buddhist monks or nuns) pass away; die
入教 embrace a religion
入静 (of Taoists) sit still (a technique for achieving mental calm and conserving energy)
入境 enter a country
入口 ① enter the mouth ② (of foreign goods or goods from another place) be transported into; import ③ entrance
入寇 invade (a country); intrude
入库 be put in storage; be laid up
入款 income; receipts
入殓 put a corpse in a coffin; encoffin
入列 take one's place in the ranks; fall in
入流 qualified
入门 ① cross the threshold; learn the rudiments of a subject ② (*usu. used in book titles*) elementary course; ABC; primer
入梦 ① fall asleep ② (of a person) appear in one's dream
入迷 be fascinated; be enchanted
入魔 be infatuated; be spellbound
入暮 towards evening; at nightfall; at dusk
入鞘 inlayer; invagination
入侵 invade; intrude; make an incursion; make inroads
入神 ① be entranced; be enthralled ② superb; marvellous
入声 entering tone (the fourth of the four tones in classical Chinese pronunciation, still retained in certain dialects)
入时 (of clothes) fashionable; modish; à la mode
入世 entry to World Trade Organization
入室 become well advanced in scholarship; be highly proficient in a profession

入手 start with; begin with; proceed from; take as the point of departure
入睡 go to sleep; fall asleep
入土 be buried; be interred
入团 join (*or* be admitted to) the Chinese Communist Youth League
入托 start going to a nursery
入网 link with a telecommunication network
入微 in every possible way; in a subtle way
入围 enter (*or* be selected for) the next round of competition; qualify for
入味 ① tasty ② interesting
入伍 enlist in the armed forces; join up
入席 take one's seat at a banquet, ceremony, etc.
入选 be selected; be chosen
入学 ① start school ② enter a school
入眼 pleasing to the eye
入药 be used as medicine
入夜 at nightfall
入狱 be put in prison; be sent to jail
入院 be admitted to hospital; be hospitalized
入账 enter an item in an account; enter into the account book
入蛰 (of animals) go into hibernation
入住 move into
入赘 marry into and live with one's bride's family
入座 take one's seat (esp. at a feast)
入场费 door money; gate money; price of admission
入场券 (admission) ticket
入场式 march-in ceremony
入海口 estuary; entry to the sea
入射点 incidence point
入射角 angle of incidence; incident angle
入射线 incident ray
入眼货 sth (esp. goods) pleasant to the eye or to one's liking
入不敷出 income falling short of expenditure; unable to make ends meet
入党宣誓 oath on joining the Party; take the oath on being admitted to the Party
入国问禁 on entering a country, inquire about its prohibitions (*or* taboos)
入境登记 entrance registration
入境口岸 port of entry
入境签证 entry visa
入境问俗 on entering a country, inquire about its customs
入木三分 ① (of calligraphy) written in a forceful hand ② penetrating; profound; keen
入情入理 fair and reasonable
入世不深 lack experience of life; not be socially experienced
入室操戈 attack sb with his own spear in his own house—turn sb's words or argument

against himself
入土为安 have one's bones (*or* coffin) buried; Burial brings peace to the deceased.
入乡随俗 when in Rome do as Romans do
入主出奴 academic sectarianism (*or* bigotry)
入党志愿书 application form for Party membership
入世后的中国 post-WTO China

蓐 [rù]
名 straw mat (*or* mattress)

溽 [rù]
形 humid; damp
溽热 humid and hot; muggy
溽暑 sweltering summer weather

缛 [rù]
形 elaborate; intricate; cumbersome
缛礼 elaborate rules of etiquette

褥 [rù]
名 padded mattress
褥疮 bedsore
褥单 bed sheet
褥套 ①bedding sack ②mattress cover
褥子 cotton-padded mattress

ruá（ㄖㄨㄚˊ）

挼 [ruá]
动 ①(of cloth or paper) crumple; crease ②wear thin; be threadbare ➡ruó

ruǎn（ㄖㄨㄢˇ）

阮 [ruǎn]
名 plucked stringed instrument

软 [ruǎn]
形 ①soft; supple; pliable ②gentle; mild; soft ③weak; shaky; feeble ④poor in quality, ability, etc. ⑤easily moved; apt to be influenced
软币 ①paper money; paper currency; note ②soft currency
软蛋 ①soft-shelled egg ②coward
软缎 soft silk fabric in satin weave
软腭 soft palate
软风 light air
软钢 mild steel; soft steel
软膏 ointment; paste
软骨 cartilage
软管 flexible pipe (*or* tube); hose
软焊 soft soldering; soldering
软和 ①soft ②gentle; kind; soft
软化 ①soften ②win over by soft tactics ③bate (leather)
软话 soft words
软件 software; service, management and labour quality
软禁 put (*or* place) sb under house arrest
软款 soft; lithe
软媚 gentle and lovely; genial; lovable

软磨 use soft tactics
软木 cork (bark of the oak tree)
软泥 ooze
软盘 floppy disk
软片 (a roll of) film
软驱 floppy drive
软弱 weak; feeble; flabby
软食 soft diet; soft food; pap
软水 soft water
软糖 soft sweets; jelly drops
软梯 rope ladder
软席 soft seat (*or* berth); cushioned seat (*or* berth)
软线 flexible cord
软性 softness; gentleness; lightness
软语 soft words
软玉 nephrite (a mineral)
软炸 (in Chinese cooking) soft-fry
软脂 palmitin
软包装 foods sold in soft packages; flexible package
软处理 handle a matter in a calm atmosphere
软磁盘 diskette; floppy disk
软贷款 soft loan
软刀子 soft knife—a way of harming people imperceptibly
软钉子 soft nail—a mild (*or* tactful) refusal or refutation
软耳朵 soft ear—a credulous person
软腐病 soft rot
软骨病 osteomalacia
软骨头 a soft bone—a weak-kneed person; a spineless person; a coward
软骨鱼 cartilaginous fish
软罐头 foods packed in carton containers
软广告 soft advertisement
软环境 soft environment
软货币 soft currency
软技术 soft technology
软件包 software package
软件狗 software Dog
软件库 software library
软拷贝 soft copy (data not printed out on paper)
软科学 soft science
软锰矿 pyrolusite
软绵绵 ①soft ②weak
软能源 renewable energy
软杀伤 soft destruction
软设备 software; service, management and labour quality
软酥酥 limp; weak; soft
软通货 soft currency; weak currency; paper currency
软新闻 soft news
软饮料 soft drink
软脂酸 palmitic acid; palmic acid

R

软着陆 soft landing
软资源 soft resources
软组织 soft tissue
软件产业 software industry
软件工程 software engineering
软件公司 software house
软件维护 software maintenance
软件文件 software documentation
软件质量 software quality
软麻工艺 bruising (of flax); batching (of jute)
软弱涣散 signs of flabbiness and slack of unity; state of weakness and slackness
软弱可欺 be weak and easy to bully
软弱无能 weak and incompetent; effete; ineffectual
软式排球 soft volleyball
软式网球 soft tennis
软体动物 mollusk
软席卧铺 sleeping carriage with soft (or cushioned) berths
软硬不吃 yield neither to persuasion nor to coercion
软硬兼施 use both hard and soft tactics; couple threats with promises; use the stick and the carrot
软玉温香 soft fragrance and warmth—feminine charm
软件兼容性 software compatibility
软体动物学 malacology
软磁盘存储器 diskette storage

ruǐ(ㄖㄨㄟˇ)

蕊 [ruǐ] 名 stamen; pistil

ruì(ㄖㄨㄟˋ)

汭 [ruì] 名 ①river bend ②place where two rivers converge

枘 [ruì] 名 tenon

蚋 [ruì] 名 buffalo gnat; blackfly

锐 [ruì] I 形 ①sharp; keen; pungent; acute ②rapid; sharp; drastic II 名 vim; vigour; fighting spirit
锐减 sharp fall (or decline); sudden drop; plummet
锐角 acute angle
锐利 ① sharp-edged; sharp-pointed; sharp; keen ②penetrating; incisive; sharp; keen
锐敏 (of senses or insight) keen; sharp
锐气 dash; drive
锐舞 rave
锐眼 sharp eyes
锐意 firm; resolute; determined; bent on

锐不可当 can't be held back; be irresistible
锐意改革 reform with keen determination

瑞 [ruì] 形 auspicious; lucky
瑞香 winter daphne (Daphne odor)
瑞雪 timely snow; auspicious snow
瑞雪兆丰年 a timely snow promises a good harvest; a snow year, a rich year

睿 [ruì] 形 farsighted
睿哲 wise and farsighted
睿智 wise and farsighted

rùn(ㄖㄨㄣˋ)

闰 [rùn] 名 intercalary
闰年 leap (or intercalary) year
闰日 leap (or intercalary) day
闰月 intercalary month in the lunar calendar; leap month

润 [rùn] I 形 smooth and glossy; moist; sleek II 动 ①moisten; lubricate ②embellish; beautify; touch up III 名 profit; remuneration
润笔 ①(of a writing brush) dip in ink ②remuneration for a writer, painter or calligrapher
润肠 lubricate the intestines; ease constipation
润肺 moisten the lungs—make expectoration easy
润滑 lubricate
润色 polish (a piece of writing, etc.); touch up
润湿 ①moist; damp ②soak; infiltrate
润饰 polish (a piece of writing, etc.); touch up
润燥 moisten the respiratory tract, skin, etc.
润泽 ①moist; smooth; sleek ②moisten; lubricate
润肤露 skin lotion; skin moisturizer
润滑油 lubricating oil; lubrication oil
润滑脂 (lubricating) grease

ruó(ㄖㄨㄛˊ)

捼 [ruó] 动 finger; knead ➡ruá

ruò(ㄖㄨㄛˋ)

若 [ruò] I 动 like; seem; as if II 连 if III 代 you ➡ rě
若辈 you people
若虫 nymph
若非 if not; were it not for
若干 ①a certain number (or amount) ②how many; how much

若何 how;what
若是 if
若即若离 be neither close nor distant;maintain a lukewarm relationship;keep sb at arm's length
若明若暗 have an indistinct (*or* blurred) picture of;have a hazy (*or* vague) notion about
若无其事 as if nothing had happened—calm;indifferent
若隐若现 appear indistinctly
若有若无 not much,if any;faintly discernible;intangible;vague
若有所失 feel as if sth were missing;look distracted
若有所思 seem lost in thought;look pensive;look as if deep in thought
若要人不知,除非己莫为 If you don't wish anyone to know what you've done,it is better not to have done it in the first place.

偌 [ruò]
代 (*often used in the early vernacular*) such;so
偌大 of such a size;so big

弱 [ruò]
Ⅰ 形 ①weak;frail;delicate ②young;little ③inferior;not as good as ④(*coming after a number with a fraction*) a little less than Ⅱ 动 die
弱点 weakness;weak point;failing
弱冠 a young man of around twenty (an age when man in ancient China started wearing hats)
弱化 weaken; deplete; enfeeble; become weak;play down;downplay
弱碱 weak base
弱旅 weak team (esp. sports)
弱脉 weak pulse
弱拍 weak beat;unaccented beat
弱势 going weak;disadvantage
弱视 weak-sighted;weak vision;poor eyesight
弱手 ①unskilled;poor ability (of person) ② weak opponent
弱酸 weak acid
弱听 hard of hearing;hearing-impaired
弱项 event in which one does poorly esp. sports;weak point
弱小 small and weak
弱智 mentally deficient; retarded; feeble-mindedness
弱辅音 lenis
弱音器 mute
弱不禁风 too weak to withstand a gust of wind;extremely delicate;fragile
弱不胜衣 (of a woman) too frail to bear the weight of one's clothes
弱柳扶风 like willow branch trembling in the wind
弱肉强食 the weak are the prey of the strong—the law of the jungle
弱势群体 disadvantaged groups
弱智教育 education for the mentally retarded

S s

仁 [sā]
〔数〕 three
仁人 three people
仁瓜俩枣 three melons and two dates—only a few small things; mere trifles

挲 [sā]
⟹ suō
◇摩挲 [māsa] ①gently stroke; smooth sth out with one's hands ②do sth in a careless and quick way

撒 [sā]
〔动〕 ①cast; loosen; let go; let out ②throw off all restraint; let oneself go; run wild ⟹ sǎ
撒旦 Satan
撒刁 act in a slick and shameless way
撒疯 ①behave atrociously ②vent one's anger
撒谎 tell a lie; lie
撒娇 act like a spoiled child; act spoiled
撒赖 make a scene; act shamelessly; raise hell
撒尿 piss; pee
撒泼 be unreasonable and make a scene
撒气 ①(of a ball, tyre, etc.) leak; go soft; get a flat ②vent one's anger (or ill temper)
撒手 let go one's hold; let go
撒腿 take to one's heels; beat it
撒网 ①cast a net; pay out a net ②invite relatives and friends to weddings, funerals, etc. with the intention of collecting presents
撒野 act wildly; behave atrociously
撒欢儿 gambol; frisk
撒酒疯 be drunk and act crazy; be roaring drunk
撒手锏 an unexpected thrust with the mace—one's trump card
撒丫子 take to one's heels; beat it
撒手不管 wash one's hands of the business
撒手尘寰 pass away; leave this mortal world
撒哈拉沙漠 the Sahara (Desert)

洒 [sǎ]
〔动〕 ①sprinkle; spray ②spill; shed
洒家 (used by men) I
洒泪 shed tears
洒落 ①drip; trickle down ②(of one's speech, deportment, etc.) free and easy; unrestrained
洒扫 sprinkle water and sweep the floor; sweep
洒脱 (of one's speech, deportment, etc.) free and easy; unrestrained
洒水车 watering car; sprinkler
洒泪而别 part in tears

靸 [sǎ]
〔动〕 wear cloth shoes with the backs turned in; shuffle about with the counters of one's shoes trodden down

撒 [sǎ]
〔动〕 ①scatter; sprinkle; spread; broadcast ②spill; drop ⟹ sā
撒播 broadcast sowing; broadcast
撒粉 dusting
撒施 scatter (or spread) fertilizer over the fields; broadcast fertilizer
撒种 sow seeds
撒播机 broadcast seeder; broadcaster
撒肥机 fertilizer distributor; manure spreader
撒粉器 duster
撒种器 broadcaster

卅 [sà]
〔数〕 thirty

飒 [sà]
I 〔动〕 sough; rustle II 〔形〕 wither; wilted
飒然 soughing; whistling
飒飒 sough; rustle
飒爽 of martial bearing; valiant
飒爽英姿 valiant and heroic in bearing; bold and brave

萨 [sà]

萨克管 saxophone
萨克号 saxhorn
萨其马 a kind of Manchu candied fritter

sāi(ㄙㄞ)

腮 [sāi]
名 cheek

腮颊 cheek
腮托 chin rest (of a violin or viola)
腮腺 parotid gland
腮帮子 cheek
腮腺炎 parotitis;mumps

塞 [sāi]
I 动 stop;fill in;squeeze in;stuff up II 名 stopper ⇒ sài;sè

塞阀 plug valve;plug cock
塞规 plug gauge
塞环 ring of plug
塞满 fill up;stuff full
塞牙 (of food) get stuck between the teeth
塞子 stopper;plug;spigot;cork

噻 [sāi]

噻吩 thiophene
噻唑 thiazole

鳃 [sāi]
名 gill;branchia

鳃瓣 gill lamella
鳃盖 gill cover

sài(ㄙㄞ)

塞 [sài]
名 stronghold of strategic importance ⇒ sāi;sè

塞北 region north of the Great Wall
塞外 beyond the Great Wall
塞翁失马 the old frontiersman losing his horse—a blessing in disguise

赛 [sài]
I 名 ①match;game;tournament;competition ②old practice of offering a sacrifice to gods;worshiping gods II 动 ①compete ②be comparable to;surpass

赛场 competition ground;arena for competition
赛车 ①cycle racing;motorcycle race;automobile race ②racing vehicle
赛程 ①distance in a sports event ②competition schedule
赛池 competition pool
赛次 round of competition
赛地 venue of sports event
赛点 match point
赛段 leg of a long-distance race;section
赛风 sportsmanship;competition
赛过 overtake;be better than;surpass;exceed
赛季 competition season;playing season
赛况 the events during a competition;proceedings of a match
赛马 horse racing
赛跑 race
赛区 (of sports and other competitions) venue;playing area;playing zone
赛事 sports competition;match;game
赛势 proceedings of a competition
赛艇 ①rowing ②racing boat;shell
赛制 competition rules;competition system
赛力散 phenylmercuric acetate (PMA)
赛璐玢 cellophane
赛璐珞 celluloid

sān(ㄙㄢ)

三 [sān]
I 数 three II 形 more than two;several;many;numerous

三包 three guarantees (for repair, replacement and compensation of faulty products)
三宝 ①three treasures;three precious things ②Triratna;the triad of the Buddha, the dharma, and the Sangha
三北 Three Northern Regions (Northwest China, North China and Northeast China)
三产 tertiary industry;service industry
三春 the three spring months
三代 three generations (i.e. of father, son, and grandson)
三法 the three therapeutic methods of traditional Chinese medicine (i.e. diaphoresis, emetic measures, purgation and diuresis)
三方 tripartite
三防 triple prevention against fire, theft, and sabotage
三废 the three wastes;waste gas, waste water and industrial residue;factory fumes, polluted runoff water, and residue wastes;pollution from gaseous, liquid or solid waste
三分 ①30% ;a little;somewhat ②divided into three parts;split into three
三伏 ①the three *fu*—the three hottest periods of the year (i.e. 初伏、中伏、and 末伏;altogether 30 or 40 days) ②the third *fu* (another name for 末伏)
三副 third mate;third officer
三好 Triple A (A in ideology and moral character, A in studies, A in health)
三讲 teach the need to study, to be political-minded and to be honest and upright; "three emphases" education
三焦 the three visceral cavities housing the internal organs
三角 ①triangle ②trigonometry

三军 ①the three armed services ②the army

三乱 indiscriminate fines, charges and assessments

三昧 ①samadhi ②secret; knack

三七 pseudo-ginseng

三秋 ①the three autumn jobs (of harvesting, ploughing and sowing) ②the three autumn months ③three years

三生 the three lives—the present life, the previous life, and the next life

三思 think thrice—think carefully

三通 ①tee; tee joint ②direct links across the Taiwan Straits between mainland China and Taiwan Province for mail, trade, and air and shipping services; three direct links of mail, trade and air and shipping services across the Taiwan Straits

三围 body measurements; three vital measurements; measurements (of the chest, waist and hips)

三峡 Three Gorges

三夏 ①the three summer jobs (of planting, harvesting and field management) ② the three summer months

三鲜 three delicacies

三弦 *sanxian*, a three-stringed plucked instrument

三险 three social insurances

三相 three-phase

三薪 triple time

三月 ①March ②the third month of the lunar year; the third moon

三K党 Ku Klux Klan

三八式 38-rifle

三胞胎 triplets

三倍体 triploid

三边形 triangle

三不管 come within nobody's jurisdiction; be nobody's business

三部曲 trilogy

三叉戟 a three-pronged spear; trident

三大球 three games played with large balls (football, basketball and volleyball)

三等兵 (U.S. Army) basic private; (U.S. Navy) apprentice seaman; (U.S. Air Force) airman third class

三等品 third grade product

三点式 bikini

三叠纪 the Triassic Period

三叠系 the Triassic System

三段论 syllogism

三分球 three pointer; trey

三合板 three-ply board; plywood

三合土 a mixture of lime, clay, and sand to which water is added (used in building)

三合星 triple star

三化螟 yellow rice borer

三级风 force 3 wind; gentle breeze

三级片 blue film

三极管 triode

三季稻 triple cropping of rice

三家村 a three-family village—a very small remote village

三尖瓣 tricuspid valve

三角板 set square

三角鲂 triangular bream

三角枫 trident maple

三角肌 deltoid

三角巾 sling

三角裤 panties; briefs

三角旗 pennant; pennon

三角铁 ①triangle ②angle iron

三角湾 estuary

三角形 triangle

三角学 trigonometry

三角债 chain debts; debt chains; inter-company debts

三角洲 delta

三脚架 tripod

三脚猫 a jack of all trades

三节棍 a cudgel of three linked sections; three-section cudgel

三九天 the third nine-day period after the winter solstice—the coldest days of winter

三棱尺 three-square rule; triangular scale

三棱镜 (triangular) prism

三连冠 win the championship three times in succession; triple crown

三联单 triplicate form

三轮车 tricycle; pedicab

三秒区 3-second area or zone

三明治 sandwich

三陪女 professional escort

三色版 three-colour halftone; three-colour block

三色堇 pansy

三熟制 triple-cropping system

三通管 three-way pipe

三下乡 program under which officials, doctors, scientist and college students go to the countryside to spread scientific and literacy knowledge and offer medical service to farmers

三小球 three games played with small balls (table tennis, badminton and tennis)

三叶虫 trilobite

三只手 pickpocket

三趾鹑 button quail

三字经 three-character scripture

"三不"政策 "Three-no" policy

三槽出钢 three-trough steel tapping technique

三叉神经 trigeminal nerve

三岔路口 a fork in the road; a junction of three roads

三长两短 unexpected misfortune;sth unfortunate,esp. death

三朝元老 minister to three emperors—an official who stays in power under different regimes

三次方程 cubic equation

三从四德 the three obediences and four virtues (for a woman according to Confucian ethics)—obedience to father before marriage,to husband after marriage,and to son after husband's death; morality, proper speech,modest manner,and diligent work

三寸金莲 three-*cun* lily feet (formerly,men's laudatory term for women's bound feet)

三大差别 the three major distinctions (between town and country,industry and agriculture,physical and mental labour)

三等秘书 diplomacy third secretary

三度空间 three-dimensional space

三对六面 the presence of the two interested parties plus a third disinterested party as a witness

三番五次 again and again;time and again;over and over again;repeatedly

三纲五常 the three cardinal guides and the five constant virtues as specified in the feudal ethical code

三高农业 "three highs" agriculture (high yield,high quality and high efficiency agriculture)

三个代表 Three Represents Theory

三个面向 orient educational work to the needs of modernization, the world, and the future;gear education to the needs of modernization,the world and the future

三更半夜 in the dead of night

三宫六院 the three palaces and six chambers—the imperial harem

三姑六婆 women of dubious character making a living by dishonest means

三顾茅庐 make three calls at the thatched cottage—repeatedly request sb to take up a responsible post

三光政策 the policy of "burn all,kill all,loot all"

三好学生 Triple-A pupil (title of merit)

三核苷酸 trinucleotide

三级火箭 three-stage rocket

三级跳远 hop,step and jump;triple jump

三驾马车 ① a carriage drawn by a team of three horses ②troika;triumvirate

三缄其口 with one's lips sealed

三江平原 the Three-River Plain (referring to the vast alluvial plain formed by convergence of the waters from the three rivers Songhuajiang,Heilongjiang and Wusulijiang in Northeast China)

三角测量 triangulation; trigonometrical survey

三角关系 triangular relationship

三角函数 trigonometric function

三角恋爱 love triangle;eternal triangle

三教九流 ① the three religions and the nine schools of thought ②various religious sects and academic schools ③ people in various trades;people of all sorts

三来一补 business of toll processing with supplied materials, manufacturing after customer's samples, assembling with supplied parts and compensation trade

三连音符 triplet

三令五申 repeatedly give injunctions

三六九等 various grades and ranks

三轮汽车 three-wheeled automobile (*or* motorcar)

三民主义 the Three Principles of the People

三年五载 from three to five years—in a few years

三农问题 issues of agriculture, countryside and peasants; the issues of agriculture, rural areas and farmers

三陪服务 escort services

三朋四友 a lot of friends

三亲六故 relatives,friends and acquaintances

三权分立 separation of the three powers

三人成虎 the testimony of three men creates a tiger in the market—repeated false reports will lead one astray

三三两两 in twos and threes;in knots

三生有幸 consider oneself most fortunate

三十二开 thirty-two mo;32mo

三水铝矿 gibbsite

三思而行 think thrice before you act;look before you leap

三天两头 every other day;almost every day

三通一平 three supplies and one leveling;supply of water,electricity and road and leveled ground (conditions ready for further economic development)

三头对案 the confrontation of the three parties (i.e. the plaintiff, the defendant and the witness) in court

三头六臂 (with) three heads and six arms—superhuman powers

三头政治 triumvirate

三推六问 a good many interrogations

三网合一 the integration of three networks

三维电影 three-dimensional movie

三维动画 three-dimensional animation

三维空间 three-dimensional space

三位一体 ① the Trinity ② three forming an organic whole;three in one;trinity

三无产品 unbranded and dateless product by a nameless factory;three-no-products

三无企业 three-no-enterprises
三无人员 transients without proper work, lawful identification or permanent address
三五成群 in threes and fours;in knots
三峡工程 the Three Gorges Project;Three Gorges Dam Project
三心二意 be of two minds;be shilly-shally;be half-hearted
三言两语 in a few words;in one or two words
三氧化物 trioxide
三灾八难 (children's) various illnesses and ailments
三战两胜 the best of three games
三资企业 three kinds of foreign-invested enterprises or ventures; Sino-foreign joint ventures,cooperative businesses and exclusively foreign-owned enterprises in China
三八妇女节 March 8, International Women's Day
三八红旗手 female model worker;woman pacesetters
三百六十行 all trades and professions; all walks of life
三不管地区 area for which no one or no unit is responsible
三步走战略 the three-step development strategy
三叉戟飞机 Trident
三个有利于 three favorables
三尖瓣狭窄 tricuspid stenosis
三磷酸腺甙 adenosine triphosphate (ATP)
三轮摩托车 motor tricycle
三色版印刷 trichromatic printing
"三同时"制度 "three-simultaneous" regulation
三下五除二 three-down-five-reject-two—neat and quick
三相变压器 three-phase transformer
三硝基甲苯 trinitrotoluene (TNT)
三寸不烂之舌 a little lithe tongue;an eloquent tongue;a silver tongue
三分之二多数 two-thirds majority
三十二分音符 demisemiquaver; thirty-second note
三项全能运动 triathlon
三北防护林工程 the Three-North (Northeast, North and Northwest China) Shelterbelt Project
三级医疗保健网 three-tiered medical care network
三句话不离本行 can hardly open one's mouth without talking shop;talk shop all the time
三门峡水利枢纽 the Sanmenxia Key Water Control Project
三人行,必有我师 Where there are three men walking together,one of them is bound to be able to teach me something.
三级医疗防病体系 the three-tiered medical

and prevention network
三分像人,七分像鬼 look more like a ghost than a human being
三十六计,走为上计 Of the thirty-six stratagems,the only choice is to run away;The only thing to do now is to quit.
三天打鱼,两天晒网 go fishing for three days and dry the nets for two—work by fits and starts;lack perseverance
三个臭皮匠,赛过诸葛亮 three cobblers with their wits combined surpass Zhuge Liang the master mind—the wisdom of the masses exceeds that of the wisest individual

sǎn（ㄙㄢˇ）

伞 [sǎn]
名 ①umbrella ②sth shaped like an umbrella
伞兵 paratrooper
伞伐 shelterwood cutting
伞降 parachuting;chuting
伞投 drop by parachute;parachute;chute
伞齿轮 bevel gear
伞形科 carrot family
伞兵部队 parachute troops;paratroops
伞房花序 corymb
伞形花序 umbel

散 [sǎn]
Ⅰ 动 come loose;break up;fall apart;not hold together Ⅱ 形 loose;scattered Ⅲ 名 medicine in powder form;medicinal powder ➡ sàn
散兵 skirmisher
散打 a style of wrestling
散工 ① odd job;short-term hired labour ② odd-job man;casual labourer
散光 astigmatism
散户 individual investors
散货 bulk cargo
散记 random notes;sketches;sidelights
散剂 powder;pulvis
散架 fall apart;fall to pieces
散居 live scattered
散客 walk-in customer (or tourist);individual passenger
散乱 in disorder
散漫 ①undisciplined;lax in discipline;slack; careless and sloppy ② unorganized;scattered
散曲 non-dramatic songs
散砂 loose sand
散射 scattering
散套 a sequence of sanqu songs within a particular musical mode
散体 prose style free from parallelism;simple,direct prose style
散文 prose

散养 free-range raising of poultry,cattle,etc.
散装 unpackaged;loose packed;in bulk
散兵壕 fire trench
散兵坑 foxhole;pit
散兵线 skirmish line
散货船 bulk freighter
散射线 scattered rays
散文诗 prose poem
散兵游勇 stragglers and disbanded soldiers
散光眼镜 astigmatic glasses
散射粒子 scattering particles
散射通信 scatter communication
散装货物 bulk cargo;bulk freight
散装汽油 petrol (*or* gasoline) in bulk
散装水泥 bulk cement
散装运输 bulk transportation

糁 [sǎn]
名 grains of cooked rice ➡shēn

sàn(ㄙㄢˋ)

散 [sàn]
动 ① become separate;break up;disperse ②distribute;scatter;disseminate;give out ③ dispel;drive away;let out ④fire;sack;lay off ➡sǎn

散播 disseminate;spread
散布 ① spread; disseminate; distribute ② be scattered here and there
散步 take a walk;go for a walk;go for a stroll
散场 (of a show,performance,etc.) be over
散发 ① send out;send forth;diffuse;emit ② distribute;issue;give out
散会 (of a meeting) be over;break up
散伙 ①(of a group,body or organization) dissolve;disband ②(of lovers or a married couple) break up
散开 spread out (*or* apart);disperse;scatter
散落 ①fall scattered ②be scattered ③scatter and disappear
散闷 divert oneself from boredom
散热 ①dissipate heat ②radiate heat
散失 ①scatter and disappear;be lost;be missing ②(of moisture,etc.) be lost;vaporize; dissipate
散水 apron
散戏 (of a show,play,opera,etc.) be over
散心 drive away one's cares;relieve boredom
散佚 be scattered and lost;be no longer extant
散逸 ①(of a gas,etc.) escape;leak ②dissipation
散热管 cooling tube;radiating pipe
散热片 cooling fin;radiating fin (*or* rib)
散热器 radiator
散摊子 (of a group,body or organization) dissolve;disband;break up

sāng(ㄙㄤ)

丧 [sāng]
名 funeral;mourning ➡sàng
丧服 mourning apparel
丧家 family of the deceased
丧礼 obsequies;funeral
丧乱 disturbance and bloodshed;tragic disaster
丧事 funeral arrangements
丧葬 burial;funeral
丧钟 funeral bell;death knell;knell
丧门星 ①a woman who brings ill luck to her husband's family ②anyone who brings ill luck

桑 [sāng]
名 white mulberry;mulberry
桑巴 samba (a Brazilian dance)
桑蚕 silkworm
桑苗 mulberry sapling
桑葚 mulberry (the fruit)
桑树 white mulberry;mulberry (tree)
桑榆 ① waning day;evening ② the west (where the sun sets) ③the evening of life; old age
桑园 mulberry field
桑梓 one's native place
桑白皮 the root bark of white mulberry
桑寄生 parasitic loranthus
桑拿浴 sauna bath;Finnish bath;Turkish bath
桑皮纸 mulberry (bark) paper
桑榆暮景 the evening of life;old age

sǎng(ㄙㄤˇ)

搡 [sǎng]
动 push roughly;shove
嗓 [sǎng]
名 ①throat;larynx ②voice
嗓门 voice
嗓音 voice
嗓子 ①throat;larynx ②voice
嗓子眼儿 throat

sàng(ㄙㄤˋ)

丧 [sàng]
动 lose ➡sāng
丧胆 be terror-stricken;be smitten with fear
丧命 meet one's death;get killed;lose one's life
丧偶 be bereaved of one's spouse (esp. one's wife);have lost one's wife or husband
丧气 [sàngqì] feel disheartened;lose heart; become crestfallen
丧气 [sàngqi] unlucky;out of luck;unfortunate
丧生 meet one's death;get killed

S

丧失 lose;forfeit
丧亡 meet one's death
丧魂落魄 driven to distraction;shaken to the core
丧家之犬 a homeless dog;a stray cur
丧尽天良 utterly devoid of conscience;conscienceless;heartless
丧权辱国 humiliate the nation and forfeit its sovereignty;surrender a country's sovereign rights under humiliating terms
丧失立场 depart from correct stand
丧心病狂 frenzied;frantic;perverse

sāo (ㄙㄠ)

搔 [sāo]
动 scratch
搔首 scratch one's head
搔头 ①scratch one's head (in perplexity) ② perplexing ③hairpin;hair clasp
搔到痒处 scratch where it itches—hit the nail on the head
搔首踟蹰 scratch one's head in perplexity
搔首弄姿 (of a woman) stroke one's hair in coquetry;posture and preen oneself

骚 [sāo]
Ⅰ 动 disturb;disrupt;upset Ⅱ 形 ①coquettish;obscene ②(of certain domestic animals) male Ⅲ 名 smell of urine (or of a fox);foul smell;stench
骚动 ①disturbance;commotion;ferment ②be in a tumult;become restless
骚货 tart;bitch
骚客 poet
骚乱 disturbance;riot;unrest
骚马 male horse;stallion
骚扰 harass;molest
骚人 poet
骚人墨客 literary men;men of letters

臊 [sāo]
名 smell of urine (or of a fox);foul smell;stench ➡ sào
臊气 foul smell;stink

sǎo (ㄙㄠ)

扫 [sǎo]
动 ①sweep;clear away ②wipe out;eliminate;get rid of ③move along quickly;sweep ④all put together ➡ sào
扫边 play a minor role (in a traditional opera)
扫除 ① cleaning;cleanup ② clear away;remove;wipe out
扫荡 mop up
扫地 ①sweep the floor ②(of honour, credibility, etc.) reach rock bottom;reach an all-time low;be dragged in the dust
扫毒 anti-drug campaign

扫黄 anti-porn campaign
扫雷 de-mining; mine-sweeping (or clearance)
扫盲 eliminate (or wipe out) illiteracy
扫描 scanning
扫灭 mop up;wipe out
扫墓 sweep a grave—pay respects to a dead person at his tomb
扫平 put down;crush;suppress
扫清 clear away;get rid of
扫射 strafe
扫视 (of one's eyes or glance) sweep
扫数 the total number;the whole amount
扫榻 sweep the bed clean (in expectation of a visitor)
扫尾 wind up;round off
扫兴 have one's spirits dampened;feel disappointed
扫雷舰 minesweeper
扫雷器 mine-sweeping apparatus
扫雷艇 minesweeper
扫路车 street sweeper
扫盲班 literacy class
扫雪车 snow-plough
扫除文盲 eliminate (or wipe out) illiteracy
扫地出门 be deprived of one's belongings and evicted (or driven out);be swept out like rubbish
扫地以尽 be swept clean;be swept out
扫黄打非 eliminate pornography and illegal publications;wipe out pornographic publications and crack down on illegal publishing practices
扫清道路 clear the path;pave the way
扫尾工作 round-off work;wind-up work
扫除青壮年文盲 wipe out (or eliminate) illiteracy among youth and adults
扫除黄赌毒等社会丑恶现象 eradicate social evils such as pornography, gambling and drug abuse and trafficking

嫂 [sǎo]
名 ①elder brother's wife;sister-in-law ② (form of address for a married woman about one's own age) sister
嫂嫂 ① elder brother's wife;sister-in-law ② sister
嫂子 elder brother's wife;sister-in-law
嫂夫人 your wife

sào (ㄙㄠ)

扫 [sào]
➡ sǎo
扫帚 broom
扫帚眉 bushy eyebrows
扫帚星 ①comet ②a person (esp. a woman) who brings ill luck;jinx

埽 [sào]
〔名〕①cylindrical bundle formed by tying up tree twigs, sorghum stalks and stone for use to protect the dykes on the banks of the Yellow River from being washed by flood ②water conservancy structure made of many cylindrical bundles

梢 [sào]
〔名〕①conical shape ②coning; taper ➡ shāo

瘙 [sào]
〔名〕scabies
瘙痒 itch

臊 [sào]
〔形〕shy; bashful; diffident ➡ sāo

sè (ㄙㄜˋ)

色 [sè]
〔名〕① colour ② look; appearance; countenance; expression ③kind; sort; description ④view; scene; scenery ⑤(of precious metals, goods, etc.) quality ⑥ woman's beautiful looks ⑦erotism ➡ shǎi
色斑 stain; patch; coloured patches; colour spot
色标 colour code; shadeguide
色彩 ①colour; hue ②characteristic quality; flavour; colour
色差 ①chromatic aberration; chromatism ②off colour; off shade
色胆 the lengths to which one will go for sex
色淀 (colour) lake
色调 tone; hue
色光 chromatic light; coloured light
色鬼 lecher; sex maniac
色基 colour base
色觉 colour vision
色卡 coloured card
色拉 salad
色狼 man with excessive sexual desire; lecher
色盲 achromatopsia; colour blindness
色魔 satyr
色品 chroma; chromaticity
色谱 colour spectrum; chromatograph
色情 sex
色球 chromosphere
色散 chromatic dispersion
色色 every kind
色素 pigment
色相 ①form and aspect ②feminine charms ③the colours of the spectrum—red, orange, yellow, green, blue, indigo and violet
色艺 looks and skills (of a female entertainer)
色欲 sexual urge; lust
色泽 colour and lustre
色值 colour content
色纸 coloured paper
色痣 pigmented mole (*or* nevus)
色层谱 chromatogram
色度计 colourimeter
色盲表 colour test cards
色迷迷 look erotic; have lust in the eyes
色谱法 chromatography
色情狂 erotomania; sex mania
色素痣 mole
色织厂 yarn-dyed fabric mill
色厉内荏 fierce of mien but faint of heart; threatening in manner but cowardly at heart
色谱分析 chromatographic analysis
色情电话 dial-a-porn; phone sex
色情电影 blue movie; pornographic film
色情文学 erotica
色情文艺 erotology
色情作品 pornography
色授魂与 Beauty yields and passion quickens.
色衰爱弛 Passion cools as beauty fades.
色素沉着 pigmentation
色艺双绝 unrivalled (*or* peerless) in physical charm and skill
色觉检查表 colour test cards
色情文艺作者 erotologist
色不迷人人自迷 Lust does not blind, one blinds oneself; Good looks do not bewitch one; One bewitches oneself.

涩 [sè]
〔形〕① puckery; astringent ② rough; unsmooth; hard-going ③ (of writing) not smooth; obscure; difficult to read or understand
涩脉 a weak, thready, uneven pulse
涩味 astringent
涩滞 (of style of writing) not smooth

啬 [sè]
〔形〕miserly; stingy; mean; close-fisted
啬刻 stingy; miserly

铯 [sè]
〔名〕cesium (Cs)
铯光灯 cesium vapour lamp
铯原子钟 cesium-beam atomic clock (*or* oscillator)
铯源装置 cesium unit

瑟 [sè]
〔名〕*se*, a sixteen-string or twenty-five-string plucked instrument like the zither
瑟瑟 ①(of the wind) rustling ②(of a person) trembling
瑟缩 curl up and shiver with cold; cower

塞 [sè]
➡ sāi; sài
塞音 plosive; stop
塞责 not do one's job conscientiously; perform one's duties perfunctorily
塞擦音 affricate

S

sēn（ㄙㄣ）

森 [sēn]
形 ①trees growing thickly ②in profusion ③dark;gloomy

森林 forest

森然 ①(of tall trees) dense;thick ②awe-inspiring

森森 ①(of trees) dense;thick;luxuriant ②ghastly;eerie

森严 stern;strict;forbidding

森林学 forestry

森罗殿 the Hall of Darkness

森罗万象 all-embracing;all-inclusive

森林覆盖率 forest coverage rate;percentage of forest cover

sēng（ㄙㄥ）

僧 [sēng]
名 Buddhist monk;monk

僧道 Buddhist monks and Taoist priests

僧侣 monks and priests;clergy

僧尼 Buddhist monks and nuns

僧袍 frock;cowl;alb

僧人 Buddhist monk

僧俗 clergy and laity

僧徒 Buddhist monks

僧院 Buddhist temple;Buddhist monastery

僧多粥少 not enough to go around

僧侣主义 fideism

shā（ㄕㄚ）

杀 [shā]
Ⅰ 动 ①kill;slay;slaughter ②fight;battle;struggle with;go into battle ③weaken;lessen;reduce;abate ④end;wind up ⑤smart Ⅱ 副 in the extreme;intensely

杀笔 stop writing

杀敌 fight the enemy;engage in battle

杀毒 kill virus

杀害 murder;kill;slaughter

杀机 murderous intentions

杀价 drive a bargain;beat down the price;screw down the price;force down the price;slash price

杀戒 prohibition against taking life

杀菌 destroy harmful microorganisms;disinfect;sterilize

杀戮 massacre;slaughter

杀掠 massacre and plunder

杀灭 kill;wipe out;eliminate;exterminate;slay

杀气 ①an aura of death;a murderous look ②vent one's spleen

杀青 finalize a manuscript

杀人 ①homicide ②kill a person

杀伤 kill and wound;inflict casualties on

杀生 take animal life

杀手 killer

杀熟 fool friends (*or* acquaintances) in business

杀头 behead;decapitate

杀退 put to flight

杀婴 infanticide

杀虫剂 insecticide;pesticide

杀虫药 insecticide;pesticide

杀风景 spoil the fun;be a wet blanket

杀菌剂 germicide;bactericide

杀菌纸 antiseptic paper;bactericidal paper

杀卵剂 ovicide

杀螨剂 acaricide;miticide

杀人犯 homicide;murderer;manslayer

杀人狂 homicidal maniac

杀伤弹 fragmentation bomb; antipersonnel bomb

杀手锏 sudden thrust of the mace;one's trump or master card

杀鼠剂 rat poison;raticide

杀出重围 fight one's way out of a heavy encirclement

杀毒软件 KILL software

杀回马枪 make a backward thrust at one's pursuer;give sb a backward thrust;wheel around and hit back

杀鸡取卵 kill the hen to get the eggs;kill the goose that lays the golden eggs

杀鸡吓猴 kill the chicken to frighten the monkey—punish someone as a warning to others

杀精子剂 spermatocide

杀开血路 cut one's way out;fight one's way through the press

杀气腾腾 murderous-looking;ferocious

杀人成性 love to kill;be bloodthirsty

杀人放火 murder and arson

杀人如麻 kill people like flies

杀人越货 kill a person and seize his goods;rob and kill

杀身成仁 die to achieve virtue—die for a just cause

杀身之祸 fatal disaster

杀一儆百 execute one as a warning to a hundred;kill one to warn a hundred

杀人不见血 kill without spilling blood—kill by subtle means

杀人不眨眼 kill without batting an eyelid;kill without blinking an eye

杀伤性地雷 anti-personnel landmines

杀鸡焉用牛刀 why use an ox-cleaver to kill a chicken;why break a butterfly on the wheel

杉 [shā]
名 China fir ⇒shān

杉篙 fir pole

杉木 fir wood

沙 [shā]

Ⅰ 名 ① sand ② sth granulated (*or* pow-dered) Ⅱ 形 (of voice) hoarse;husky ➡ shà

沙岸 hurst
沙坝 sandbar
沙包 ①sand dune ②sandbag
沙暴 sandstorm
沙蚕 clam worm
沙场 battlefield;battleground
沙尘 dust and sand in the air
沙船 a large junk
沙袋 sandbag
沙堤 sand
沙地 sand;desert
沙雕 sand sculpture
沙发 sofa
沙岗 sand hill
沙锅 earthenware pot;casserole
沙果 Chinese pear-leaved crabapple
沙海 sea of sand;huge expanse of desert
沙狐 corsac (fox)
沙化 desertification
沙荒 sandy wasteland;sandy waste
沙皇 tsar;czar
沙鸡 sandgrouse
沙金 placer gold;alluvial gold
沙坑 ①sandpit ②jumping pit
沙拉 salad
沙梨 sand pear
沙砾 grit;gravel
沙龙 salon
沙漠 desert
沙盘 sand table
沙坪 sand flat
沙丘 (sand) dune
沙瓤 mushy watermelon pulp
沙沙 rustle
沙参 the root of straight ladybell
沙司 sauce
沙滩 sand beach
沙土 sandy soil;sand
沙哑 hoarse;husky;raucous
沙眼 trachoma
沙浴 ①sand bath (of birds) ②sand bath
沙枣 narrow-leaved oleaster
沙蚤 sand hopper
沙洲 sandbank
沙蠋 lugworm
沙柱 dust devil;sand column
沙锥 snipe
沙子 ①sand;grit ②small grains;pellets
沙嘴 sand-spit
沙尘暴 sand storm;dust storm
沙丁鱼 sardine
沙发床 studio couch;sofa bed
沙狐球 shovelboard

沙漠化 desert encroachment;desertification;desertization
沙滩车 dune buggy
沙滩椅 beach chair
沙里淘金 wash grains of gold out of the sands—extract the essential from a large mass of material;get small returns for great effort
沙漠气候 desert climate
沙漠植被 desert vegetation;desert cover
沙滩排球 beach volleyball
沙文主义 chauvinism

纱 [shā]

名 ①yarn ②sheer ③curtain-like products ④textile (*or* fabric) products

纱布 gauze
纱厂 cotton mill
纱橱 screen cupboard
纱窗 screen window;screen
纱灯 gauze lantern
纱锭 spindle
纱巾 gauze kerchief
纱罗 gauze
纱线 yarn
纱罩 ① gauze (*or* screen) covering (over food) ②mantle (of a lamp)
纱包线 cotton-covered wire

刹 [shā]

动 put on the brakes;brake;stop ➡ chà

刹把 brake crank
刹车 ①stop a vehicle by applying the brakes;put on the brakes ②stop a machine by cutting off the power;turn off a machine ③ bring to a halt ④the brakes
刹住歪风 check the unhealthy tendency;put an end to the unhealthy practice

砂 [shā]

名 sand;grit

砂布 emery cloth;abrasive cloth
砂带 abrasive band;sand belt
砂浆 mortar
砂礓 conglomerate
砂礁 sandbar
砂矿 placer deposit;placer
砂轮 emery wheel; grinding wheel; abrasive wheel
砂囊 gizzard (of birds)
砂糖 granulated sugar
砂箱 sandbox;moulding box
砂芯 core
砂型 sand mould
砂岩 sandstone
砂眼 sand hole;blowhole
砂样 drilling;mud cuttings
砂纸 abrasive paper;sand paper
砂轮机 grinder
砂壤土 sandy loam

砂质岩 arenaceous rock
砂型铸造 sand casting

煞 [shā]
Ⅰ 动 ① stop; halt; check; brake ② tighten Ⅱ 副 in the extreme; intensely ⟶ shà
煞笔 ① concluding lines of an article; ending of a piece of writing ② write the final line of an article, letter, etc.
煞车 ① firmly fasten a load (on a vehicle); lash down ② stop a vehicle by applying the brakes; put on the brakes ③ stop a machine by cutting off the power; turn off a machine ④ bring to a halt ⑤ the brakes
煞尾 ① finish off; round off; wind up ② final stage; end; ending

裟 [shā]
◇袈裟 kasaya

鲨 [shā]
名 shark
鲨鱼 shark

shá（ㄕㄚˊ）

啥 [shá]
代 what

shǎ（ㄕㄚˇ）

傻 [shǎ]
形 ① dull; stupid; muddle-headed ② bigoted ③ dumbfounded; stunned
傻蛋 fool; blockhead; simpleton
傻瓜 fool; blockhead; simpleton
傻话 stupid talk; foolish words; nonsense
傻乐 laugh foolishly; giggle; smirk
傻气 foolish; stupid
傻笑 laugh foolishly; giggle; smirk
傻眼 be dumbfounded; be stunned
傻样 foolish look
傻子 fool; blockhead; simpleton
傻呵呵 simple-minded; silly; foolish
傻乎乎 simple-minded; silly; foolish
傻劲儿 ① stupidity; foolishness ② sheer enthusiasm; doggedness
傻冒儿 ① fool; blockhead; idiot ② foolish; stupid
傻小子 silly lad
傻里瓜唧 foolish; stupid
傻头傻脑 ① foolish-looking ② muddle-headed
傻瓜照相机 point-and-shoot; user-friendly camera; fully automatic camera; fool-proof camera

shà（ㄕㄚˋ）

沙 [shà]
动 sift; sieve ⟶ shā

唼 [shà]
动 (of water birds, fish, etc.) eat noisily;

gnaw; suck

厦 [shà]
名 ① tall building; mansion ② back veranda; porch

嗄 [shà]
形 (of voice) hoarse

歃 [shà]
动 suck
歃血 smear the blood of a sacrifice on the mouth—an ancient form of swearing an oath
歃血为盟 swear an oath of alliance by smearing the mouth with the blood of a sacrifice

煞 [shà]
Ⅰ 名 evil spirit; devil; goblin Ⅱ 副 very ⟶ shā
煞白 ghastly pale; deathly pale; pallid
煞神 demon; fiend
煞费苦心 cudgel one's brains; take great pains
煞有介事 make a show of being in earnest; pretend to be serious

霎 [shà]
名 very short time; moment; instant
霎眼 in a moment; in a twinkling
霎时间 in a twinkling; in a split second; in a jiffy

shāi（ㄕㄞ）

筛 [shāi]
Ⅰ 名 sieve; sifter; screen; riddle Ⅱ 动 ① sieve; sift; screen; riddle ② eliminate through selection ③ warm a pot of rice wine over a slow fire (or in hot water) ④ pour (wine) ⑤ strike (a gong)
筛布 bolting cloth
筛法 sieve method
筛分 screening; sieving
筛管 sieve tube
筛号 screen size; screen mesh; mesh number
筛级 screen grading
筛浆 stock screening
筛糠 shiver
筛洗 dress and wash (coal, etc.)
筛选 ① screening ② select
筛子 sieve; sifter; screen

shǎi（ㄕㄞˇ）

色 [shǎi]
名 dice ⟶ sè
色子 dice

shài（ㄕㄞˋ）

晒 [shài]
动 ① (of the sun) shine upon ② dry in the sun; sun; bask ③ ignore; give the cold shoulder to
晒场 sunning ground (for drying grain, etc.)

晒垡 sun the earth which has been ploughed up；sun the upturned soil
晒干 dry in the sun
晒裂 sun crack
晒台 flat roof (for drying clothes，etc.)
晒图 make a blueprint；blueprint
晒烟 sun-cured tobacco
晒盐 evaporate brine in the sun to make salt
晒暖儿 get warm in the sun
晒太阳 sunbathe；bask in the sun
晒图员 blueprinter
晒图纸 blueprint paper
晒像框 printing frame

shān(ㄕㄢ)

[shān]

山 ㄖ ①hill；mountain ②anything resembling a mountain ③bushes in which silkworms spin cocoons ④gable
山坳 col
山包 a small hill
山崩 landslide；landslip
山茶 camellia
山产 mountain products
山城 mountain city
山川 mountains and rivers—land；landscape
山鹑 partridge
山村 mountain village
山丹 morningstar lily
山道 mountain pass
山地 ① mountainous region；hilly area；hilly country ②hillside field
山顶 the summit (*or* top) of a mountain；hilltop
山洞 cave；cavern
山风 mountain breeze
山峰 mountain peak
山冈 low hill；hillock
山歌 folk song (sung in the fields or in mountain areas during or after work)
山根 the foot of a hill
山沟 ①gully ②ravine；(mountain) valley ③a remote mountain area
山谷 mountain valley；ravine
山国 a mountainous country；a hilly region
山河 mountains and rivers—the land of a country
山洪 mountain torrents
山火 mountain fire
山货 ① mountain products (such as haws，chestnuts and walnuts) ②household utensils made of wood，bamboo，clay，etc.
山鸡 pheasant
山脊 ridge (of a mountain or hill)
山涧 mountain stream
山脚 the foot of a hill

山口 mountain pass；pass
山梁 ridge (of a mountain or hill)
山林 mountain forest；wooded mountain
山陵 ①hills ②tombs of emperors
山岭 a chain of mountains
山路 mountain path
山麓 the foot of a mountain；piedmont
山峦 a chain of mountains
山脉 mountain range；mountain chain
山猫 leopard cat
山门 ①the gate of a Buddhist temple ②Buddhism
山民 mountain people
山奈 cyanide
山炮 mountain gun；mountain artillery
山坡 hillside；mountain slope；hillslope
山墙 gable
山区 mountain area
山泉 mountain spring
山雀 tit
山人 recluse；hermit
山水 ① water from a mountain ② mountains and rivers；scenery with hills and waters ③ traditional Chinese painting of mountains and waters；landscape painting；landscape
山桃 mountain peach
山田 hillside plot
山头 ① hilltop；mountain top ② mountain stronghold；faction ③gable
山溪 mountain stream
山系 mountain system
山险 difficult mountain terrain
山乡 mountain village；mountain area
山响 deafening；thunderous
山魈 ①mandrill ②mountain elf
山鸦 chough
山崖 cliff
山羊 ①goat ②buck
山腰 halfway up the mountain
山药 Chinese yam
山野 mountains and plains
山芋 sweet potato
山峪 mountain valley
山鹬 woodcock
山岳 lofty mountains
山楂 ①(Chinese) hawthorn ②haw
山寨 mountain fastness；a fortified mountain village
山庄 ①mountain villa ②mountain village
山子 rockery
山嘴 spur
山苍子 the fruit of a cubeb litsea tree
山慈姑 edible tulip
山道年 santonin
山地车 mountain bicycle
山豆根 subprostrate sophora
山核桃 ①hickory ②hickory nut

S

山鸡椒 cubeb litsea tree (Litsea cubeba)
山椒鸟 minivet
山里红 large-fruited Chinese hawthorn
山毛榉 beech
山梅花 mock orange
山水画 mountains-and-waters painting; landscape painting; landscape
山水诗 scenic poem; painting poetry
山窝窝 an out-of-the-way mountain area
山羊绒 cashmere
山楂糕 haw jelly cake
山茱萸 the fruit of medicinal cornel
山崩地裂 mountains collapsing and the earth cracking up
山重水复 mountains multiply and streams double back
山顶洞人 Upper Cave Man
山东梆子 Shandong clapper opera
山东快书 Shandong clapper ballad
山旮旯儿 a faraway hilly area; an out-of-the-way place in the mountains; a remote mountain area
山高水长 (of nobility of character) as high as the hills and as long as the rivers—of lasting influence
山高水低 unexpected misfortune; sth unfortunate, esp. death
山高水远 ① the mountains are high and the rivers far away—a long distance ② unexpected misfortune; sth unfortunate, esp. death
山梗菜碱 lobeline
山光水色 the beauty of the rivers and mountains; landscape of mountains and lakes or rivers
山荒地瘦 barren mountains and sterile land
山盟海誓 lovers' vow to be true to each other forever
山姆大叔 Uncle Sam
山南海北 ① south of the mountains and north of the seas—far away; far and wide ② discursive; rambling
山清水秀 green hills and clear waters—picturesque scenery
山穷水尽 where the hills and streams end—at the end of one's rope (or tether, resources)
山区开发 development of mountain areas
山水画家 landscape painter
山水相连 be linked by common mountains and rivers
山头主义 mountain-stronghold mentality
山外有山 There's always a mountain beyond a mountain—there's always something better; Nothing can be perfect.
山西梆子 Shanxi clapper opera
山羊胡子 goatee

山肴野蔌 mountain meats and wild vegetables
山岳冰川 mountain glacier; alpine glacier
山珍海味 delicacies from land and sea; dainties of every kind
山高皇帝远 beyond reach of the government
山雨欲来风满楼 The wind sweeping through the tower heralds a rising storm in the mountains; The rising wind forebodes the coming storm.
山中无老虎，猴子称大王 When the tiger is away from the mountain, the monkey proclaims himself king.

芟 [shān]
〔动〕 ① mow (grass) ② weed out; get rid of; eliminate
芟除 ① mow; cut down ② delete

杉 [shān]
〔名〕 China fir ➡ shā

删 [shān]
〔动〕 delete; strike out; leave out
删除 delete; strike (or cut, cross) out
删改 delete and change; revise
删节 abridge; abbreviate
删略 leave out; omit
删削 delete; cut out; strike out
删节本 abridged edition; abbreviated version
删节号 ellipsis; suspension points; ellipsis dots
删繁就简 simplify sth by cutting out the superfluous

苫 [shān]
〔名〕 straw mat ➡ shàn

衫 [shān]
〔名〕 unlined upper garment

姗 [shān]
姗姗 walk slowly like a woman
姗姗来迟 be slow in coming; be late

珊 [shān]
珊瑚 coral
珊瑚虫 coral polyp; coral insect
珊瑚岛 coral island
珊瑚礁 coral reef

埏 [shān]
〔动〕 mix water with clay

栅 [shān]
➡ zhà
栅极 grid

舢 [shān]
〔名〕 sampan
舢板 sampan

痁 [shān]
〔名〕 malaria

扇 [shān]
〔动〕 ① fan ② hit with hands; box ③ incite; foment; stir up; whip up ➡ shàn
扇动 flap
扇风耳 protruding ears; flappy ears
扇风机 ventilating fan

扇阴风,点鬼火 fan the winds of evil and spread the fires of turmoil—foment trouble

跚 [shān]

◇蹒跚 walk haltingly;limp;hobble

煽 [shān]
㊅①fan (a fire) ②incite;foment;stir up;whip up
煽动 instigate;incite;stir up;whip up
煽惑 incite;agitate
煽情 ①incite (*or* stir up) emotions;sensationalize ②sensational
煽风点火 fan the flames;in flame and agitate people;stir up trouble

潸 [shān]
㊎ in tears;tearfully
潸然 in tears;tearful
潸潸 in tears;tearful

shǎn(ㄕㄢˇ)

闪 [shǎn]
I ㊅①move quickly to one side;dodge ② twist ③ sprain ④ flash ⑤ sparkle;shine ⑥ leave behind Ⅱ ㊅ lightning
闪避 dodge;sidestep
闪挫 sudden strain (*or* contusion) of a muscle;sprain
闪点 flash point
闪电 lightning
闪动 flash;twinkle;flicker
闪躲 dodge;evade
闪光 ①a flash of light ②gleam;glisten;glitter
闪击 launch (*or* make) a surprise attack
闪开 get out of the way;jump aside;dodge
闪亮 sparkling;glittering;glistening
闪念 an idea which flashes through one's mind
闪盘 flash memory disk
闪闪 sparkling;glistening;glittering
闪射 glitter;shine;radiate
闪身 ①dodge ②move sideways
闪失 mishap;accident
闪石 amphibole
闪烁 ① twinkle; glimmer; glisten ②evasive; vague;noncommittal
闪现 flash before one
闪眼 dazzling
闪耀 glitter;shine;radiate
闪熠 glitter;shine;radiate
闪音 flap
闪蒸 flash vaporization
闪爆弹 flash-band;stun grenade
闪长岩 diorite
闪电战 blitz;lighting war
闪光灯 ①flash lamp;flashlight;photo flash ② flashlight
闪击战 lightning war;blitzkrieg;blitz
闪锌矿 (zinc) blende;sphalerite

闪光同步 flash synchronization
闪烁其词 speak evasively;hedge
闪烁计数器 scintillation counter

搡 [shān]
㊅ hold;grasp ⇒càn;chān
搡手 shake hands

shàn(ㄕㄢˋ)

讪 [shàn]
I ㊅ mock; scorn; ridicule Ⅱ ㊎ embarrassed;discomfited;awkward;shamefaced
讪谤 slander;malign;calumniate
讪讪 embarrassed;awkward;shamefaced
讪笑 ridicule;mock;deride

苫 [shàn]
㊅ cover with a straw mat, tarpaulin, etc. ⇒shān
苫布 tarpaulin
苫席 mat cover

钐 [shàn]
㊅ cut with a sickle

疝 [shàn]
㊏ hernia
疝带 truss
疝气 hernia

赸 [shàn]
㊅ hide oneself;go away;vanish

扇 [shàn]
I ㊏① fan ② leaf Ⅱ ㊏ (of windows, doors,etc.):一扇窗户 a window ⇒shān
扇贝 scallop;fan shell
扇车 winnowing machine;winnower
扇形 ①fan-shaped ②sector
扇坠 fan pendants
扇子 fan
扇骨子 the ribs (*or* mount) of a folding fan
扇面儿 the covering of a fan
扇形齿轮 sector (*or* segment) gear

掸 [shàn]
㊏①reference in Chinese annals to the Dai nationality ② one of the Burmese nationalities,most of whom live in the state of Shan ⇒dǎn

善 [shàn]
I ㊎①good ②satisfactory ③friendly;kind ④familiar Ⅱ ㊅①make a success of;do well ②be good at;be expert in ③be apt (*or* liable) to Ⅲ ㊍ properly Ⅳ ㊏ benevolent act; good deed
善本 reliable text;good edition
善变 be apt to change;be changeable
善策 wise move;best policy
善处 deal discreetly with;conduct oneself well
善待 treat sb well;treat friendly
善感 (of a person) sensitive
善果 good fruit—the rewards of good deeds
善后 deal with problems arising from an accident,etc.

S

善举 a philanthropic act (*or* project)
善类 good people
善良 good and honest;kind-hearted
善邻 be a good neighbour
善人 philanthropist;charitable person;welldo-er
善事 charitable deeds;good deeds
善忘 be forgetful;have a short memory
善心 mercy;benevolence
善行 good conduct
善意 ①goodwill;good intentions ②bona fide
善于 be good at;be adept in
善战 be good at fighting;be skilful in battle
善终 ①die a natural death;die in one's bed ② end well
善罢甘休 leave the matter at that;let it go at that
善恶分明 distinguish good from evil
善后处理 after-math treatment;deal with problems arising from an accident
善后事宜 matters concerning reconstruction; rehabilitation works;problems arising from an accident,etc.
善男信女 Buddhist devotees;devotees of Bud-dha;the faithful
善始善终 start well and end well;do well from start to finish;see sth through
善为说辞 put in a good word for sb
善意合约 bona fide contract
善意买方 bona fide purchaser
善意原告 bona fide claimant
善于辞令 be gifted with a silver tongue
善于应对 be good at repartee
善于用人 know how to make proper use of personnel;know how to choose the right person for the right job
善自保重 take good care of oneself
善自为谋 know how to look after oneself;con-sider the matter carefully before making up one's mind
善意第三者 bona fide third party
善意执票人 bona fide holders
善有善报,恶有恶报 Good is rewarded with good,and evil with evil.

禅 [shàn]
动 abdicate (from) the throne in favour of another person ➡ chán
禅让 abdicate and hand over the crown to an-other person
禅位 abdicate the throne

骟 [shàn]
动 castrate;geld;spay
骟马 castrate (*or* geld) a stud;gelded horse

墡 [shàn]
名 white clay

缮 [shàn]
动 ①repair;fix;mend ②copy;write out

缮写 write out;copy

擅 [shàn]
动 ①do sth without the approval (*or* prior knowledge) of one's superior;act on one's own authority ②be good at;be versed in;be expert in
擅长 be good at;be expert in;be skilled in
擅自 do sth without authorization
擅离职守 unauthorized departure from official duty;be absent from one's post without permission;talk liberty with one's job
擅自提价 raise a price without permission
擅自行动 act presumptuously
擅作主张 act without authorization;make a decision without authorization

膳 [shàn]
名 meals;board
膳费 board expenses
膳食 meals;food
膳宿 board and lodging
膳务长 chief stewed

嬗 [shàn]
动 ①change;alternate;evolute ②abdicate the throne in favour of another person
嬗变 ①evolute ②transmutation

赡 [shàn]
Ⅰ 动 support;keep;provide for Ⅱ 形 ade-quate;sufficient;abundant
赡养 support;provide for
赡养费 payment for support of one's parents; alimony
赡家养口 support a family

鳝 [shàn]
名 eel;finless eel

shāng (ㄕㄤ)

伤 [shāng]
Ⅰ 名 wound;injury Ⅱ 动 ①injure;wound; hurt ②surfeit;overeat ③be harmful to;im-pair Ⅲ 形 sad;distressed
伤疤 scar
伤背 sad;sorrowful
伤兵 wounded soldier
伤残 wounded and disabled
伤悼 mourn (*or* grieve) over the deceased
伤风 catch cold;have a cold
伤感 sick at heart;sentimental
伤害 injure;harm;hurt
伤寒 ① typhoid fever;typhoid ② diseases caused by harmful cold factors;febrile dis-eases;fevers
伤耗 damage
伤痕 scar;bruise
伤怀 sad;grieved;broken-hearted
伤科 (department of) traumatology
伤口 wound;cut
伤力 overstrain

伤气 ①feel frustrated；feel disheartened ②sap one's vitality
伤情 ①the condition of an injury（*or* wound）②sick at heart；sentimental；sad；sorrowful ③hurt sb's feelings
伤人 ①hurt sb's feelings ②inflict injuries ③injure the health
伤神 ①overtax one's nerves；be nerve-racking ②sad；grieved
伤生 be injurious to life
伤食 dyspepsia caused by excessive eating or improper diet
伤势 the condition of an injury（*or* wound）
伤痛 ①grieved；distressed ②the pain of an injury（*or* wound）
伤亡 injuries and deaths；casualties
伤心 sad；grieved；broken-hearted
伤员（*usu.* used among army personnel）wounded personnel；the wounded
伤病员 the sick and wounded
伤残人 disabled person；handicapped person
伤脑筋 knotty；troublesome；bothersome
伤皮肉 injury of skin and superficial muscles
伤心事 a heartbreaking affair；a painful memory；an old sore
伤风败俗 corrupt public morals；offend public decency
伤痕文学 trauma literature
伤筋动骨 be injured in the tendons or bones
伤天害理 offend against Heaven and reason—atrocious；outrageous
伤亡报告 report of losses；casualty report
伤心惨目 too ghastly to look at；tragic（scene）

殇 ［shāng］
动 die young

商 ［shāng］
Ⅰ 动 talk over；discuss；consult Ⅱ 名 ①trade；commerce；transaction；business ②merchant；businessman；salesman；dealer ③quotient
商标 trademark；brand name
商埠 commercial（*or* trading）port
商场 market；bazaar；department store
商船 merchant ship；merchantman
商德 business ethics
商店 shop；store
商调（of one organization）negotiate with another organization for the transfer of one of its cadres
商定 decide through consultation；agree
商队 a company of travelling merchants；trade caravan
商法 commercial law
商贩 small retailer；pedlar
商港 commercial port
商贾 merchant
商海 business world

商行 trading company；commercial firm
商号 shop；store；business establishment
商会 chamber of commerce
商机 business opportunity；commercial opportunity
商计 have discussions（*or* consultations）
商检 commodity inspection
商界 business circles；commercial circles
商借 negotiate to borrow
商量 consult；discuss；talk over
商流 commodity circulation
商路 trade route
商旅 travelling merchants
商贸 commerce；trade
商棚 peddler's stall；makeshift stall for selling goods
商品 commodity；goods；merchandise
商气 market conditions
商洽 arrange with sb；take up（a matter）with sb
商情 market condition；market situation；business information
商圈 business district
商榷 discuss；deliberate
商人 businessman；merchant；trader
商嫂 a woman engaged in commerce
商厦 department store；emporium；large
商社 business organization
商数 quotient
商谈 exchange views；confer；discuss；negotiate
商讨 discuss；deliberate over
商亭 kiosk；stall
商务 commercial affairs；business affairs
商业 commerce；trade；business
商议 confer；discuss
商用 commercial use
商誉 goodwill；commercial standing；business reputation
商约 commercial treaty
商载 commercial transport（of passengers，cargo，etc.）
商展 commodity exhibition；commodity display；commodity show
商战 ①trade war ②business competition
商酌 discuss and consider；deliberate over
商标法 trademark law
商标权 trademark privileges；trademark rights；ownership of trademark
商船队 mercantile marine；merchant marine
商调函 letter for negotiated transfer；letter requesting transfer of personnel
商贸区 commercial and trading area
商品菜 market vegetables；（U. S.）truck vegetables
商品房 commercial housing；residential housing；commodity apartment；commodity

building;housing for sale
商品化 commercialization
商品粮 commodity grain;marketable grain
商业城 commercial city
商业街 shopping street
商业片 commercial film
商业区 business quarter;commercial district; business district
商业网 commercial network;network of trading establishments
商标注册 trademark registration
商检单位 commodity inspection agency
商品包装 commodity package
商品过剩 glut of goods
商品检验 commodity inspection
商品经济 commodity economy
商品流通 flow of commodities;circulation of commodities
商品生产 commodity production
商品条码 bar code
商品意识 commodity consciousness
商品住宅 commercial residential building
商事法院 commercial court
商务参赞 commercial counsellor;commercial attaché
商务代表 commercial representative;trade representative
商务旅行 business travel
商务秘书 commercial secretary
商务套房 service apartment
商务卫星 commercial satellite
商务午餐 business lunch
商务中心 business centre
商务专员 commercial attaché,multi-floor department store
商业广告 commercial advertising
商业秘密 business secret
商业网点 network of trading establishments; commercial network
商业文化 commercial culture
商业信贷 commercial credit;commercial loans and credits
商业演出 commercial performance
商业银行 commercial bank
商业用语 trade language
商业中心 commercial centre;trading centre; shopping centre
商业周期 business cycle
商业资本 commercial capital;merchant capital
商用电脑 business computer
商住住宅 commercial and residential housing
商标专有权 patent right of the trademark registration
商品拜物教 commodity fetishism
商品房空置 vacancy problem in commercial housing
商品交易会 trade fair;commodities fair

商品粮基地 area specialized in the production of commodity grain;base for the production of commodity grains
商品流通税 commodity circulation tax
商品推销员 commercial travellers (CT)
商情晴雨表 business barometer
商业交易法 law of commercial transactions
商业心理学 business psychology
商品流通体系 commodity circulation system
商品销售市场 outlet for goods
商务英语证书考试 Business English Certificate (BEC)

shǎng(ㄕㄤ)

上 [shǎng]
名 fall-rising tone → shàng;shang

晌 [shǎng]
名 ①part of the day ②noon
晌饭 ① midday meal;lunch ② extra meal in the daytime during the busy farming season
晌觉 afternoon nap
晌午 midday;noon

赏 [shǎng]
Ⅰ 动 ①grant (or bestow) a reward;award ②admire;enjoy;appreciate ③appreciate;recognize Ⅱ 名 reward;bounty;award
赏赐 ①grant (or bestow) a reward;award ② a reward;an award
赏罚 rewards and punishments
赏光 (used when requesting sb to accept an invitation)
赏鉴 appreciate and evaluate (a work of art)
赏金 money reward;pecuniary reward
赏脸 honour me with your presence
赏钱 tips
赏识 recognize the worth of;appreciate
赏玩 admire the beauty of sth;delight in;enjoy;fondle
赏析 appreciate and analyze;study carefully
赏雪 enjoy a beautiful snow scene
赏月 enjoy a beautiful full moon
赏罚分明 be fair in meting out rewards and punishments;be discriminating in one's rewards and punishments
赏罚严明 be strict and fair in meting out rewards and punishments
赏心乐事 happy moods and pleasurable things
赏心悦目 find the scenery pleasing to both the eye and the mind

shàng(ㄕㄤ)

上 [shàng]
Ⅰ 名 ①higher place ②superior;senior ③emperor Ⅱ 形 ①upper;upward ②higher;better ③first (part);preceding;previous Ⅱ 动 ①go up;mount;board;get on ②go to;leave for ③submit;send in;present ④forge ahead;

press on ⑤enter the court ⑥lay on the table ⑦fill;add;supply ⑧fix sth on sth else ⑨apply;paint;put on ⑩be put on record;be carried (in a publication);be published ⑪wind;tighten ⑫begin work (*or* study) at a fixed time ⑬be up to;be as many as ➡ shǎng;shang

上岸 go ashore;go on shore;land

上班 go to work;start work;be on duty

上绑 truss sb up

上榜 be on the list

上报 ①appear in the newspapers ②report to a higher body;report to the leadership

上辈 ① ancestors ② the elder generation of one's family;one's elders

上臂 the upper arm

上膘 (of animals) become fat;fatten

上表 wind a watch

上宾 distinguished guest;guest of honour

上菜 serve the dishes (of food)

上苍 Heaven;God

上操 go out to drill;be drilling

上策 the best plan;the best way out;the best thing to do

上层 upper levels;upper strata

上场 ①appear on the stage;enter ②enter the court (*or* field);join in a contest

上车 get on a bus

上乘 first-class

上传 upload

上船 go aboard a ship;go on board

上床 go to bed;get into bed

上次 last time

上达 reach the higher authorities

上代 the previous generation;former generations

上当 be taken in;be fooled;be duped

上灯 light the lamp;light up

上等 first-class;first-rate;superior

上帝 God (in Christianity)

上吊 hang oneself

上调 [shàngdiào] ①transfer sb to a post at a higher level ②transfer goods,funds,etc. to a unit at a higher level

上冻 freeze

上颚 ①mandible (of certain arthropods) ② the upper jaw;maxilla (of vertebrates)

上饭 serve a meal

上房 main rooms

上访 appeal to the upper level;seek an audience with the higher authorities to appeal for intervention;apply for an audience with the higher authorities to appeal for help

上肥 spread manure;apply fertilizer

上坟 visit a grave to honour the memory of the dead

上粪 apply manure to the fields

上风 ①windward ②advantage;superior position;upper hand

上峰 superior;boss

上浮 (salary or price) increase;go up

上纲 raise to the higher plane of principle

上岗 go to one's post;go on duty

上告 ①complain to the higher authorities;appeal to a higher court ②report to one's superior

上工 go to work;start work

上供 ① offer up a sacrifice;lay offerings on the altar ②give presents to the higher-ups expecting favours in return

上钩 rise to the bait;swallow the bait;get hooked

上古 ancient times;remote ages

上光 ①glazing;polishing ②ferrotyping

上好 first-class;best-quality;tip-top

上颌 the upper jaw;maxilla

上回 last time

上火 ①suffer from excessive internal heat ②get angry

上货 ①get in stocks;replenish stocks ②replenish the goods shelves

上机 operate computers

上级 ① higher level ② higher authorities;one's superior

上佳 excellent; good; admirable; first-class;praiseworthy

上家 the player whose turn comes just before

上浆 ①starching (of clothes) ②dressing (of yarn,fabrics,etc.)

上将 (U.S. & Brit. Army,U.S. Air Force,U.S. & Brit. Marine Corps) general;(U.S. & Brit. Navy) admiral;(Brit. Air Force) air chief marshal

上交 hand in (*or* over) to sb above oneself;pass on to the higher authorities

上胶 sizing

上焦 the part of the body cavity above the diaphragm housing the heart and lungs

上缴 turn over (revenues,profits,surplus materials,etc.) to the higher authorities

上街 ①go to the street;go shopping ②take to the streets;go on to the streets

上届 previous term (*or* session);last

上界 the world above;the abode of the gods

上紧 lose no time (in doing sth);hasten;speed up

上进 go forward;make progress

上劲 energetically;with gusto;with great vigour

上镜 on camera;telegenic

上卷 first volume;volume one

上课 ①attend class;go to class ②conduct a class;give a lesson (*or* lecture)

上空 in the sky;overhead

S

上口 ①be able to read aloud fluently ②be suitable for reading aloud; make smooth reading

上款 ①the name of the recipient (as inscribed on a painting or a calligraphic scroll presented as a gift) ②the name of the addressee (of a letter or package)

上蜡 waxing

上来 ①begin; get started ②sum up (the aforesaid) ③come up ④come up to a place or state regarded as higher or above ⑤up (here)

上联 the first line of a couplet

上梁 ①put the beams in place (in building a wooden house) ②(of bicycles) cross bar; top tube ③(of buildings) upper beam

上列 listed above; above-listed; the above

上流 ①upper reaches (of a river) ②belonging to the upper circles; upper-class

上路 set out on a journey; start off

上马 ①mount (or get on) a horse ②start (a project, etc.)

上门 ①come (or go) to see sb; call; drop in; visit ②shut the door (or lock up) for the night; bolt the door ③marry into and live with one's bride's family

上面 ①above; over; on top of; on the surface of ②above-mentioned; aforesaid; foregoing ③higher authorities; higher-ups ④aspect; respect; regard ⑤the elder generation of one's family; the elders

上年 last year

上盘 hanging wall

上皮 epithelium

上品 highest grade; top grade

上铺 upper berth

上漆 paint (sth)

上情 feelings (or wishes) of the higher authorities

上去 ①go up ②rise to a place or state regarded as higher or above ③up (there)

上任 ①take up an official post; assume office ②predecessor

上色 [shàngsè] best-quality; top-grade

上色 [shàngshǎi] colour (a picture, map, etc.)

上山 go up a hill; go uphill

上上 ①the highest; the very best ②before last

上士 (U. S. Army) sergeant first class; (Brit. Army) staff sergeant; (U. S. Navy) petty officer first class; (Brit. Navy) chief petty officer; (U. S. Air Force) technical sergeant; (Brit. Air Force) flight sergeant; (U. S. Marine Corps) technical sergeant or staff sergeant; (Brit. Marine Corps) colour sergeant

上身 ①the upper part of the body ②upper outer garment; shirt; blouse; jacket ③start wearing

上升 ①move upward ②rise (to a higher point, degree, rank, etc.); ascend

上市 ①go (or appear) on the market ②go to market ③(of companies) go public; be listed

上手 ①left-hand seat; seat of honour ②the player whose turn comes just before ③(of work, etc.) get started

上首 seat of honour

上书 submit a letter; submit a written statement to a higher authority; send in a memorial

上述 mentioned above; above-mentioned; aforementioned; aforesaid

上树 climb up a tree

上水 ①feed water to a steam engine, radiator (of an automobile), etc. ②upper reaches (of a river) ③sail upstream

上税 pay taxes

上司 superior; boss

上诉 appeal (to a higher court)

上溯 ①go upstream ②trace back

上算 paying; worthwhile

上锁 lock

上台 ①go up onto the platform; appear on the stage ②assume power; come (or rise) to power

上膛 ①(of a gun) be loaded ②palate

上套 ①harness a draught animal (to a cart, etc.) ②fall into a trap

上体 the upper part of the body

上天 ①go up to the sky; fly sky-high ②go to Heaven—die ③Heaven; Providence

上调 [shàngtiáo] raise (prices)

上头 [shàngtóu] go to head (of liquor)

上头 [shàngtou] ①above; over; on top of; on the surface of ②above-mentioned; aforesaid; foregoing ③higher authorities; higher-ups ④aspect; respect; regard ⑤the elder generation of one's family; the elders

上网 get on the Internet; go on-line; have access to the Net

上尉 (U. S. & Brit. Army, U. S. Air Force, U. S. & Brit. Marine Corps) captain; (U. S. & Brit. Navy) lieutenant; (Brit. Air Force) flight lieutenant

上文 foregoing paragraphs (or chapters); preceding part of the text

上午 morning; forenoon

上下 ①high and low ②from top to bottom; up and down ③relative superiority or inferiority ④(used after round numbers) about; or so; or thereabouts ⑤go up (or down)

上弦 ①tighten the spring of; wind (up) ②

first quarter (of the moon)

上限 the upper limit; the maximum permissible (*or* prescribed)

上线 ① raise ordinary matters to the higher plane of political struggle ② reach the admission test scores

上相 come out well in a photograph; be photogenic

上香 burn joss sticks (before an idol or a spirit tablet)

上校 (U. S. & Brit. Army, U.S. Air Force, U.S. & Brit. Marine Corps) colonel; (U. S. & Brit. Navy) captain; (Brit. Air Force) group captain

上心 set one's heart on sth

上星 television by satellite

上刑 put to torture; torture

上行 ① (of trains) going to the capital from any part of the country; up; upgoing ② (of boats) going upstream; upriver ③ (of documents) sent to the upper levels

上旋 top spin

上选 best choice; best select

上学 go to school; attend school; be at school

上旬 the first ten-day period of a month

上演 put on the stage; perform

上扬 go up

上衣 upper outer garment; jacket

上瘾 be addicted (to sth); get into the habit (of doing sth)

上映 show (a film); screen

上油 refuel

上游 ① upper reaches (of a river) ② advanced position

上谕 imperial decree

上载 upload

上灶 do the cooking

上涨 rise; go up

上账 make an entry in an account book; enter sth in an account

上阵 go into battle; take part in a match; pitch into the work

上肢 upper limbs

上装 ① make up (for a theatrical performance) ② upper outer garment; jacket

上座 the seat of honour

上班族 commuter; office (*or* factory) worker

上半场 first half (of a game, concert, etc.)

上半截 upper half

上半年 first half of a year

上半晌 morning

上半身 the upper part of the body; above the waist

上半天 forenoon; morning

上半夜 before midnight

上辈子 ① ancestors ② previous existence

上场门 entrance (of a stage)

上档次 upgrade a product

上等兵 private first class

上等货 prime quality; super-fine quality

上飞机 board a plane; go on board a plane

上古史 ancient history

上光机 glazing machine; glazer

上光蜡 wax polish

上轨道 get on the right track; begin to work smoothly

上进心 desire to do better; urge for improvement

上剧院 go to the theatre

上领子 fix a collar to a garment

上螺丝 tighten a screw

上年纪 be getting on in years; be stricken in years

上牌子 apply for a license

上皮癌 epithelioma

上坡路 ① an uphill road; an upward slope ② upward trend; steady progress

上圈套 be taken in; be entrapped; fall into sb's trap

上染率 dye-uptake

上纱窗 install a screened window

上升角 angle of climb (*or* ascent)

上市价 list price; listed price

上视图 top view

上水道 water-supply line

上诉权 right of appeal

上诉人 appellant

上岁数 be getting on in years

上台阶 ascend the steps; reach a new height (in social development, work, production, etc.)

上网卡 pre-paid Internet card

上西天 go to the Western Paradise—die

上下水 water supply and sewage

上下文 context

上弦月 the moon at the first quarter

上新世 the Pliocene Epoch

上压力 upward pressure

上药膏 apply ointment

上议院 upper house; (Brit.) the House of Lords

上周末 previous weekend

上嘴唇 upper lip

上座儿 ① (of restaurants) draw customers; (of theatres, etc.) draw an audience ② be a draw; be a box-office success

上座率 attendance rate; occupancy rate; attendance; occupancy; box office sales

上不封顶 unlimitedly upward; with no ceiling (*or* limitation) above

上层建筑 superstructure

上层路线 the upper-level line

上层领域 realm of the superstructure

上层社会 haut monde; upper strata of society;

upper-class society

上谄下骄 obsequious towards one's superiors and arrogant towards one's inferiors

上窜下跳 jump about; run around on sinister errands

上当受骗 swallow a gudgeon; be taken in; play sb false

上低音号 baritone

上方空间 superjacent air space

上岗培训 pre-job training

上呼吸道 the upper respiratory tract

上级机构 parent body; roof body

上级指示 instruction（or order）from the higher authorities

上缴利润 that part of profits turned over to the state; turn over part of the profits to the higher authorities

上届冠军 defending champion

上跨交叉 overpass

上流社会 high society; polite society; upper classes

上门服务 service to one's home; door-to-door business service; doorstep; make house calls; come to the customer's house to render service

上门女婿 live-in son-in-law

上门推销 knocking-the-door sale

上皮组织 epithelial tissue

上情下达 relay information from an upper to a lower level

上上下下 high and low; old and young; everybody

上升气流 ascending air; up current

上升失速 advance stall

上升转弯 pull-up turn

上市公司 listed company; quoted company

上市股票 listed stock; quoted share

上市债券 marketable securities; on board securities

上市证券 listed securities

上诉法庭 court of appeals

上诉法院 court of appeals; appellate court

上吐下泻 throw up on top and purge down below; suffer from vomiting and diarrhoea; have loose bowels and vomit

上推下卸 pass the buck both up and down; shift the blame on to one's superiors or on to one's subordinates

上下其手 practise fraud; manoeuvre for some evil end; get up to tricks

上新台阶 reach a new level; reach a higher stage of development

上行下效 Subordinates follow the example of their superiors; Those below follow the（usu. bad）example of those above; If a leader sets a bad example, it will be followed by his subordinates.

上游产品 fundamental produces; raw materials

上涨趋势 upward trend

上证指数 Shanghai Stock Exchange Index

上门推销员 knocker

上海合作组织 Shanghai Cooperation Organization（SCO）

上海五国机制 the Shanghai Five mechanism

上呼吸道感染 infection of the upper respiratory tract

上气不接下气 gasp for breath; be out of breath

上证综合指数 Shanghai Composite Index

上不上，下不下 be stranded halfway; be in awkward position

上有老，下有小 have both parents and young children to support and take care of

上梁不正下梁歪 if the upper beam is not straight, the lower ones will go aslant—when those above behave unworthily, those below will do the same

上不封顶，下不保底 impose "no ceiling or lower limit" on bonuses

上不着天，下不着地 touch neither the sky nor the ground—be suspended in midair

上天无路，入地无门 there is no road to heaven and no door into the earth—no way of escape; in desperate straits

上有天堂，下有苏杭 Up above there is Paradise, down here there are Suzhou and Hangzhou.

上有政策，下有对策 The higher authorities have policies and the localities have their counter measures.

上海五国第六次峰会 the sixth summit of Shanghai Five

上无片瓦，下无插针之地 have neither a tile above one's head nor an inch of land beneath one's feet—be utterly destitute

尚 ［shàng］
I 〔动〕 esteem; value; treasure; set great store by　II 〔名〕 prevailing custom, habits, etc. III 〔副〕 ①still; yet ②even

尚且 （not）even...（let alone...）

尚书 ①a high official in ancient China ②minister（in the Ming and Qing Dynasties）

尚武 encourage a military（or martial）spirit

尚方宝剑 the emperor's sword（the bearer of which is invested with discretionary powers）—a symbol of delegated power

尚武精神 a military（or martial）spirit

shang（·ㄕㄤ）

裳 ［shang］
⇒ cháng

◇衣裳 clothing; clothes

上 ［shang］
①（used after a verb indicating an upward movement）：爬上山顶 reach the sum-

mit (*or* the peak of the mountain) ② (*used after a verb indicating that an aim has been achieved*)：安上电话 have a telephone installed ③ (*used after a verb indicating the beginning and continuation of an action*)：踏上祖国的土地 set foot on the soil of one's motherland ④ (*used after a verb indicating the amount or extent reached or to be reached*)：花上一两天时间把这本书看完 spend a day or two finishing the book ⑤ (*used after a noun indicating the surface of an object*)：脸上 on the face ⑥ (*used after a noun indicating the scope of sth*)：报纸上 in the press ⑦ (*used after a noun, indicating an aspect of sth*)：技术上 technologically ➡ shǎng；shàng

shāo（ㄕㄠ）

捎 ［shāo］
囫 take sth to (*or* for) sb；bring sth to sb：捎包东西 take a parcel to sb ➡ shào
捎带 incidentally；in passing
捎话 take a message to sb
捎脚 pick up passengers (*or* goods) on the way；give sb a lift

烧 ［shāo］
Ⅰ 囫 ①set fire to；burn：壁炉烧木柴 burn logs in the fireplace ②cook；bake；heat：烧瓷器 bake (*or* fire) porcelain ③ (of culinary art or cooking) stew after frying；fry after stewing：红烧鲤鱼 carp stewed in brown source ④roast；braise：叉烧肉 grilled pork ⑤run a fever；have a temperature ⑥ damage；hurt (due to excessive use of fertilizer, drugs, etc.) ⑦one's head turned by newly acquired riches Ⅱ 图 fever
烧包 be drunken with success；have a swollen head
烧杯 beaker (in the laboratory)
烧饼 sesame seed cake
烧饭 do the cooking；cook food；prepare a meal
烧锅 (liquor) distillery
烧化 ①cremate ②burn (paper, etc. as an offering to the dead)
烧荒 burn the grass on waste land
烧毁 destroy by fire；burn up
烧火 make a fire；light a fire；tend the kitchen fire
烧鸡 roast chicken
烧碱 caustic soda
烧结 sintering；agglomeration；agglutination
烧酒 spirit；colourless spirit
烧烤 barbecue
烧料 imitation frosted glass
烧卖 a steamed dumpling with the dough gathered at the top
烧毛 singeing

烧瓶 flask
烧伤 burn (an injury)
烧蚀 ablation
烧香 burn joss sticks (before an idol)
烧心 ① heartburn ② (of cabbages) turn yellow at the heart
烧纸 ①burn paper money for the dead ②paper money burnt as an offering to the dead
烧炙 burn
烧灼 burn；scorch；singe
烧结厂 sintering plant
烧结法 sintering process
烧结剂 agglutinant
烧烤架 barbecue grill
烧伤疗法 medical burn therapy

梢 ［shāo］
图 tip；thin end of a twig, etc. ➡ sào
梢头 ①the tip of a branch ②top log

稍 ［shāo］
副 a little；a bit；a trifle；slightly ➡ shào
稍稍 a little；a bit；slightly；a trifle
稍微 a little；a bit；slightly；a trifle
稍为 a little；a bit；slightly；a trifle
稍许 a little；a bit；slightly；a trifle
稍加润色 touch up
稍事休息 take a breather
稍纵即逝 transient；fleeting

艄 ［shāo］
图 ①stern ②rudder；helm
艄公 ①helmsman ②boatman

鞘 ［shāo］
图 whiplash ➡ qiào

sháo（ㄕㄠ）

勺 ［sháo］
Ⅰ 图 spoon；scoop；ladle Ⅱ 量 shao, an old unit of capacity (= 1 centilitre)
勺子 ladle；scoop

芍 ［sháo］
芍药 Chinese herbaceous peony

苕 ［sháo］
图 sweet potato ➡ tiáo

韶 ［sháo］
形 beautiful；splendid；magnificent
韶光 ①beautiful springtime ②glorious youth
韶华 ①beautiful springtime ②glorious youth
韶丽 beautiful
韶秀 delicate and pretty

shǎo（ㄕㄠ）

少 ［shǎo］
Ⅰ 形 few；little；scanty；meagre Ⅱ 囫 ①be short of；lack；have not enough ②lose；be missing ③owe ④stop；cut out Ⅲ 副 a little while；a minute ➡ shào
少见 ① (a form of greeting) I haven't seen

S

you for a long time；I have seen very little of you these days—I'm very glad to see you again ②seldom seen；infrequent；rare

少刻 after a little while；a moment later

少量 a small amount；a little；a few

少陪 （an apology for taking leave of sb）if you'll excuse me；I'm afraid I must be going now.

少顷 after a short while；after a few moments；presently

少时 after a little while；a moment later；soon

少数 a small number；few；minority

少许 a little；a few；a modicum of

少有 rare；few and far between

少不得 cannot do without；cannot dispense with

少不了 ①cannot do without；cannot dispense with ②be bound to；be unavoidable ③can't be only a few （or a little）；must be a lot

少得了 （used in rhetorical questions）can do without；can dispense with

少而精 smaller in quantity but better in quality；fewer but better

少数党 a minority party；minority

少安毋躁 Keep calm，don't get excited；Don't be impatient，wait a while.

少出差错 make less mistakes

少见多怪 The less a man has seen，the more he has to wonder at；Ignorant people are easily surprised.

少慢差费 fewer，slower，poorer and more costly

少生优生 have fewer but healthier children （or births）

少数民族 minority nationality；ethnic minority

少说空话 make no empty promise

少花钱多办事 do more and better with less funds

少数民族地区 minority nationality regions；areas inhabited by the minority nationalities

少数民族干部 cadres from among minority ethnic groups

少走弯路，避免失误 avoid detours and mistakes

shào（ㄕㄠ）

少 [shào]
Ⅰ 〔形〕young；youthful Ⅱ 〔名〕son of a wealthy family；young master ➡ shǎo

少儿 children and early teenagers

少妇 young married woman

少将 （U. S. & Brit. Army，U. S. Air Force，U. S. & Brit. Marine Corps）major general；（U. S. & Brit. Navy）rear admiral；（Brit. Air Force）air vice marshal

少年 ①early youth （from about ten to sixteen）②boy or girl in early teens；juvenile

少女 young girl

少尉 （U. S. & Brit. Army，U. S. Air Force，U. S. & Brit. Marine Corps）second lieutenant；（U. S. Navy）ensign；（Brit. Navy）acting sublieutenant；（Brit. Air Force）pilot officer

少相 young-looking

少校 （U. S. & Brit. Army，U. S. Air Force，U. S. & Brit. Marine Corps）major；（U. S. & Brit. Navy）lieutenant commander；（Brit. Air Force）squadron leader

少爷 ①（a form of address formerly used by servants of the house）young master ②son

少壮 young and vigorous

少白头 ①be prematurely grey ②young person with greying hair

少东家 young master

少管所 correction institution for juveniles；reform school；juvenile penitentiary

少奶奶 ①young mistress ②daughter-in-law

少年班 juvenile college class

少年犯 juvenile delinquent

少年宫 Children's Palace

少先队 Young Pioneers

少壮派 the up-and-coming

少不更事 young and inexperienced；green

少男少女 unmarried young men and women

少年读物 books for young people；juvenile books

少年犯罪 juvenile delinquency

少年老成 ①an old head on young shoulders；young but mature ②an old young man；a young person lacking in vigour and drive

少年之家 Children's Centre；Children's Club

少女课堂 girl guide

少先队员 Young Pioneer

少爷脾气 behaviour of a spoilt boy

少年先锋队 Young Pioneers

少年犯管教所 correction institution for juveniles；reform school；juvenile penitentiary

少壮不努力，老大徒伤悲 If one does not exert oneself in youth，one will regret it in old age；Laziness in youth spells regret in old age.

卲 [shào]
〔形〕noble；admirable

劭 [shào]
Ⅰ 〔动〕encourage；admonish；exhort Ⅱ 〔形〕noble；admirable

绍 [shào]
〔动〕carry on；keep on；continue

绍复大业 inherit and carry on the great cause

捎 [shào]
〔动〕（of draught animals）draw back a step or two；shy ➡ shāo

哨 [shào]
Ⅰ 〔动〕①reconnaissance；patrol ②（of birds）

warble；chirp ③idle talk Ⅱ 名 ①sentry post；
post ②whistle Ⅲ 量 contingent；column
哨兵 sentry；guard
哨岗 sentry post
哨卡 a frontier sentry post；strategic sentry
　post
哨所 sentry post；post
哨位 sentry post
哨子 whistle

睄 ［shào］
动 cast a glance

稍 ［shào］
➡ shāo
稍息 stand at ease

潲 ［shào］
Ⅰ 动 ①(of rain) slant in ②sprinkle；spray
Ⅱ 名 hogwash；swill；slops

shē（ㄕㄜ）

奢 ［shē］
形 ①luxurious；extravagant；profligate ②
excessive；inordinate；undue
奢侈 luxurious；extravagant；wasteful
奢华 luxurious；sumptuous；extravagant
奢靡 extravagant and wasteful
奢念 unrealistic hopes；wild wishes
奢求 extravagant claims；excessive demands；
　unreasonable demands
奢望 extravagant hopes；wild wishes
奢想 extravagant hopes；wild wishes
奢侈品 luxury goods；luxuries
奢侈品税 luxury tax

赊 ［shē］
动 buy or sell on credit
赊购 buy on credit
赊欠 buy or sell on credit
赊销 installment purchase；sell on credit
赊账 ①a system of buying or selling on cred-
it；the credit system ②outstanding bills (or
accounts) ③have outstanding bills (or accounts)
赊购商店 tally shop

猞 ［shē］
猞猁 lynx

shé（ㄕㄜ）

舌 ［shé］
名 ①lingua；tongue ②sth shaped like a
tongue ③clapper
舌根 the root of the tongue
舌耕 make a living by teaching
舌尖 the tip of the tongue
舌鳎 tonguefish；tongue sole
舌苔 coating on the tongue；fur
舌头 ①tongue ②an enemy soldier captured
　for the purpose of extracting information

舌炎 glossitis
舌蝇 tsetse fly (or tzetze fly)；tsetse (or
　tzetze)
舌战 ①have a verbal battle with；argue heat-
edly with ②a hot dispute；a verbal battle
舌根音 velar
舌尖音 apical
舌下腺 sublingual gland
舌状花 ligulate flower
舌敝唇焦 talk till one's tongue and lips are
parched；wear oneself out in pleading，ex-
postulating，etc.
舌尖后音 blade-palatal
舌尖口快 sharp-tongued
舌尖前音 dental
舌尖中音 blade-alveolar
舌面后音 velar
舌面前音 dorsal
舌下神经 hypoglossal nerve

折 ［shé］
动 ①break；split；snap ②suffer losses；lose
money in business ➡ zhē；zhé
折本 lose money in business
折秤 damage and loss to goods in the course of
reweighing
折耗 damage and loss

蛇 ［shé］
名 snake；serpent ➡ yí
蛇胆 gall bladder of snake；gall bladder of pit
viper
蛇毒 snake venom
蛇莓 mock-strawberry
蛇丘 esker
蛇头 ①snake head ②coyote；ringleader of organized illegal immigration
蛇蜕 snake slough
蛇蝎 snakes and scorpions—vicious people
蛇行 move with the body on the ground；crawl
蛇形 snakelike；S-shaped
蛇足 feet added to a snake by an ignorant artist—sth superfluous
蛇皮管 flexible conduit
蛇纹石 serpentine (a mineral)
蛇蝎心肠 as venomous as snakes and scorpions
蛇无头不行 a snake cannot move without its
head—nothing can be accomplished without
a leader

shě（ㄕㄜ）

舍 ［shě］
动 ① give up；discard；abandon ② give
alms；dispense charity ➡ shè
舍宾 shaping
舍得 be willing to part with；not grudge
舍脸 cast aside considerations of one's face
舍命 risk one's life；sacrifice oneself
舍弃 give up；abandon

S

舍入 rounding off
舍身 give one's life;sacrifice oneself
舍不得 hate to part with or use;grudge;begrudge
舍本逐末 attend to trifles and neglect essentials
舍己救人 sacrifice oneself to save sb else
舍己为公 sacrifice one's interests for public good
舍己为人 sacrifice one's own interests for the sake of others
舍近求远 seek afar for sth close;seek from afar what lies close at hand;forgo what is close at hand and seek what is far afield
舍车保帅 give up a chariot to save the marshal (in Chinese chess)—make minor sacrifices to safeguard major interests
舍生取义 lay down one's life for a just cause
舍死忘生 disregard one's own safety;risk one's life
舍我其谁 if I can't do it,who can;who but myself can do it
舍命陪君子 I would throw in my lot with you,sir,at the risk of my life.
舍此别无他法 There is no other way out.
舍得一身剐,敢把皇帝拉下马 He who fears not being cut to pieces dares to unhorse the emperor.

shè（ㄕㄜ）

厍 [shè]
图 village

设 [shè]
I 动 ①set up;form;establish ②work out;design II 连 ①given;supposing;假设 suppose;assume ②if;in case;设有福,当共享。If fortune comes our way,we should share it among us.
设备 equipment;installation;facilities
设辞 excuse;pretext
设点 (of a firm) set up a retail outlet
设定 set
设法 think of a way;try;do what one can
设防 set up defences;fortify;garrison
设伏 lay an ambush
设岗 ①post a sentry ②create a post (job,position)
设计 ①design;plan ②work out a plan (or scheme)
设立 establish;set up;found
设如 if
设色 fill in colours on a sketch;lay paint on (canvas);colour
设施 installation;facilities
设想 ① imagine;envisage;conceive;assume ②tentative plan;tentative idea ③have consideration for

设宴 give a banquet;fête
设营 quarter;encamp
设障 place obstacles;make trouble;complicate matters
设置 ①set up;establish ②put up;install ③configuration;setup
设座 choose a place to give a banquet
设定值 set a value;set point
设计师 ①designer ②architect
设计图 design drawing
设计院 designing institute
设营地 camp site
设营队 quartering party
设备保养 equipment maintenance
设备更新 renewal of equipment;updating of equipment
设备检修 equipment examine and repair
设备齐全 fully equipped
设备租赁 equipment leasing
设计吃水 designed draft
设计洪水 design flood
设计能力 design capacity
设身处地 put oneself in sb else's position
设施农业 industrialized agriculture
设备利用率 utilization rate of equipment and installations
设备完好率 rate of equipment in good condition
设置贸易壁垒 erect trade barriers

社 [shè]
图 ①organization;agency;society ②some service units ③god of the land;sacrifices to the god;altars for such sacrifices
社保 social security
社工 ①social work ②social worker
社会 society;community
社稷 the altars to the gods of earth and grain—the state;the country
社交 social intercourse;social contact;social life
社论 editorial;leading article;leader
社评 editorial
社情 social conditions
社区 community
社群 community;social group;social
社团 mass organizations
社戏 village theatrical performance given on religious festivals in old times
社员 a member of a society,club,etc.
社会党 Socialist Party
社会化 socialization
社会学 sociology
社办企业 commune-managed enterprises
社会办学 all sectors of society giving support to school education;operate schools by all sectors of society
社会保险 social insurance

社会保障 social security
社会财富 wealth of society;public wealth
社会传真 reality show;reality program
社会地位 social position;social status
社会调查 social investigation;social survey
社会发展 social development;social growth
社会分工 division of labour in society
社会分配 distribution of social wealth
社会风气 social conduct;general trends in society
社会风尚 social morality
社会福利 social welfare;public welfare
社会工作 ① work outside one's regular job,done for the community;community work ②professional work ③social work
社会公德 social ethics;social morality;public morality;standards of social behaviour
社会公正 social justice
社会关系 ①human relations in society;social relations ② one's social connections;relatives and friends
社会环境 social environment
社会活动 social activities;public activities
社会基础 social base;social basis
社会集团 organized grouping;collective
社会集资 fund raising from various sectors of society;social money gathering
社会科学 social sciences
社会名流 noted public figures;socialite;social celebrity
社会青年 unemployed youth
社会生活 social activity
社会实践 social practice
社会统筹 centralized social system;overall social planning
社会团体 public organization;social organizations;social groups
社会稳定 social stability
社会效益 social benefits;social effects;social efficacy;social returns;social results
社会学家 sociologist
社会制度 social system
社会治安 public order
社会主义 socialism
社稷之臣 a loyal servant of the dynasty's sacred altars;a bulwark of the state
社情民意 community services; social conditions and public opinions;social atmosphere
社区发展 community development
社区服务 community service
社区文化 community culture
社区学院 community college
社区医院 community hospital
社会安全网 social safety net
社会发展史 history of social development;history of development of society
社会福利院 social welfare institute (orphanage,old people's home)
社会抚养费 social support fee
社会公众股 social public shares
社会活动家 social activist
社会民主党 Social Democratic Party
社会生物学 sociobiology
社会心理学 social psychology
社会语言学 sociolinguistics
社会总产品 aggregate social product
社会总产值 gross domestic product;GDP;total output value
社会总供给 total social supply
社会总需求 total social demand
社会总资产 the gross social assets
社会保障制度 social security system
社会分配不公 income disparities;unfair distribution of social wealth
社会服务组织 social service organization
社会福利彩票 lottery intended for the purpose of raising funds for social welfare
社会福利事业 social welfare undertakings
社会规范教育 education in standards of social conduct
社会化大生产 large-scale socialized production;socialized mass production
社会经济制度 socio-economic system
社会救济制度 social relief system
社会力量办学 run schools by non-government sectors
社会民主主义 social democracy
社会全面进步 all-round social progress
社会热点问题 hot spots of society
社会中介组织 social intermediary organization
社会主义道路 socialist road
社会主义法制 socialist legality;socialist legal system
社会主义方向 socialist orientation
社会主义改造 socialist transformation
社会主义革命 socialist revolution
社会主义建设 socialist construction
社会主义民主 socialist democracy
社会主义制度 socialist system
社区活动中心 community centre
社会集团购买力 institutional purchases
社会主义公有制 socialist public ownership
社会主义所有制 socialist ownership
社会商品零售总额 total amount of retailed social commodities
社会协商对话制度 a social system of consultation and dialogue (between groups of people with varied social interests)
社会治安综合管理 improvement of all facets of public security;improvement of public order with the help of comprehensive measures;maintain social public order in a comprehensive way;adopt an integrated approach to the maintenance and improve-

S

ment of public order

社会主义初级阶段 preliminary stage of social-
ism；the primary stage of socialism

社会主义法治国家 socialist country ruled by
law

社会主义精神文明 socialist spiritual civilization

社会主义市场经济 socialist market economy

社会主义物质文明 socialist material civilization

社会主义制度优越性 superiority of the socialist system

社会主义精神文明建设 development of advanced socialist culture and ideology

社会主义民主法制体系 socialist democratic legal system

社会主义思想道德建设 socialist ideological and
ethical progress

社会主义事业的领导核心 force at the core
leading the cause of socialism；the leading
core for the socialist cause

社会主义事业的建设者和接班人 builders of
and successors to the cause of socialism

舍 [shè]
Ⅰ 名 ①house ②hut ③shed Ⅱ 代 my Ⅲ 量
ancient unit of distance equal to 30 *li* ⇒ shě

舍间 my humble abode；my house；my place

舍监 the warden of a school dormitory

舍利 relics left after the cremation of Buddhas
or saintly monks

舍妹 my younger sister

舍亲 my relative；a relative of mine

舍下 my humble abode；my house；my place

舍营 billet

舍利塔 a pagoda for Buddhist relics；stupa

拾 [shè]
动 ascend in light steps ⇒ shí

射 [shè]
动 ①shoot；fire；eject ②discharge in a jet
③emit (light，heat，etc.) ④allude to sth or
sb；insinuate；intimate

射程 range (of fire)

射弹 projectile

射干 blackberry lily

射击 ①shoot；fire ②shooting

射箭 ①shoot an arrow ②an archery

射角 angle of fire

射界 area (*or* field) of fire；firing area

射精 ejaculation

射孔 perforation

射猎 hunting with bow and arrow or firearms

射流 efflux

射门 shoot (at the goal)

射频 radio frequency

射手 ①shooter；marksman；archer ②goal getter

射速 firing rate

射线 ray

射影 projection

射电源 radio source

射击场 shooting range

射击孔 embrasure

射精管 ejaculatory ducts

射门手 goal getter

射水鱼 archer fish

射线病 radiation sickness

射击地境 sector of fire

射流技术 fluidics

射线疗法 radiotherapy

射电天文学 radio astronomy

射电望远镜 radio telescope

射频放大器 radio frequency amplifier

涉 [shè]
动 ①wade；ford ②go through；undergo；ex-
perience ③involve；implicate

涉案 implicated in a case；related to the case；
involved in the case

涉笔 wet the brush—start writing or painting

涉毒 drug-related

涉赌 related to gambling activities；involved in
gambling activities

涉黑 deal with mafia organizations

涉黄 deal with pornography

涉及 involve；relate to；touch upon

涉老 concerning senior citizens

涉猎 do desultory reading；read cursorily

涉密 concerning security matters

涉农 concerning agriculture

涉禽 wading bird；wader

涉世 gain life experience

涉税 concerning taxes

涉讼 be involved in a lawsuit

涉外 concerning foreign affairs (*or* foreign
nationals)

涉嫌 be suspected of being involved；be a suspect

涉险 go through dangers；go through perils

涉足 set foot in

涉笔成趣 (of a writer or painter) produce
good work as soon as the brush touches paper (*or* as soon as he sets his brush to paper)

涉毒犯罪 drug-related crime

涉枪犯罪 crimes related to guns

涉世不深 have scanty experience of life；have
seen little of the world

涉水而过 wade across the water

涉外案件 case involving foreign nationals (*or*
firms)；foreign-related case；case with a
foreign element

涉外宾馆 hotels involved with foreign affairs；
hotels catering foreign guests

涉外部门 foreign-related authorities (*or* department)

涉外法规 foreign-related legal laws and regulations
涉外婚姻 marriage between Chinese and foreigners
涉嫌受贿 suspected of bribe-taking
涉外经济法规 laws and regulations governing
business relations with foreigners

赦 [shè]
动 remit (a punishment);pardon;absolve
赦令 order of pardon or amnesty
赦免 amnesty;remit(a punishment);pardon
赦罪 absolve sb from guilt;pardon sb

摄 [shè]
动 ① take in;absorb;assimilate ② take a
photo; photo; shoot ③ conserve (one's
health);keep fit ④act for
摄动 perturbation
摄理 hold an office in an acting capacity
摄取 ① absorb; assimilate; take in ② take a
photograph of;shoot
摄生 conserve one's health;keep fit
摄食 (of animals) feed
摄像 make a video recording (with a video
camera or TV camera)
摄行 act for another
摄影 ①take a photograph ②shoot a film;film
摄政 act as regent
摄制 film produce
摄谱仪 spectrograph
摄像机 video camera;television camera
摄影机 camera
摄影棚 film studio
摄影师 photographer;cameraman
摄影室 photographic studio;photo studio
摄政王 prince regent
摄制组 production unit (of film)
摄氏温标 Celsius (or centigrade) temperature scale
摄影记者 press photographer;cameraman
摄影展览 photographic exhibition;photo exhibition
摄氏温度计 centigrade thermometer;Celsius
thermometer

慑 [shè]
动 fear;dread;coerce
慑服 ①submit in fear;succumb ②cow sb into
submission

麝 [shè]
名 ①musk deer ②musk
麝牛 musk-ox
麝鼠 muskrat
麝香 musk

shéi(ㄕㄟˊ)

谁 [shéi]
Ⅰ 代 ①who ②nobody;no one ③somebody;
someone ④ anyone; anybody; everyone; everybody Ⅱ ①(used before 都 or 也):这东西
我们谁也不愿买。 None of us would buy it. /
谁来都欢迎。 Whoever comes will be welcome. ②(used to denote both the subject
and the object):他们俩谁也不服谁。 Nei-
ther of them thinks better of the other. ③
(used to refer to the same person):谁笑到
最后,谁笑得最好。 He who laughs last
laughs best.
谁边 where
谁个 who
谁人 who

shēn(ㄕㄣ)

申 [shēn]
动 state;expound;explain
申奥 bid for Olympic Games
申办 apply for permission to do sth;bid;bid
for
申报 ①report to a higher body ②declare sth
(to the Customs)
申辩 defend oneself;plead one's case
申购 request to purchase;apply for the purchase of
申令 issue orders
申论 expound and prove
申明 declare;state;avow
申请 apply for;file an application
申述 state;explain in detail
申诉 appeal;rebuke;reprimand
申讨 openly condemn;denounce
申谢 acknowledge one's indebtedness;express
one's gratitude
申雪 ①appeal for redress of a wrong ②re-
dress a wrong
申冤 ①redress an injustice;right a wrong ②
appeal for redress of a wrong
申请国 applicant country
申请人 applicant
申请书 (written) application;petition
申诉方 the claimant
申请执行 petition for enforcement
申办奥运会 bid for the Olympic Games

屾 [shēn]
名 two mountains standing side by side

伸 [shēn]
动 put out;stretch;extend
伸开 stretch out
伸手 ①stretch (or hold) out one's hand ②
ask for money,honour,gifts,etc. ③have a
hand in;poke one's nose into;meddle in
伸缩 ①stretch out and draw back;expand and
contract; lengthen and shorten ②flexible;
elastic;adjustable
伸腿 ①stretch one's legs ②step in (to gain
an advantage) ③kick the bucket;turn up
one's toes

伸延 extend;stretch
伸腰 straighten one's back;straighten oneself up
伸引 extend
伸展 spread;extend;stretch
伸张 uphold;promote
伸直 straighten
伸懒腰 stretch oneself
伸手派 sb who keeps asking superiors for help
伸缩缝 expansion joint
伸缩性 flexibility;elasticity
伸大姆哥 hold up one's thumb (in praise)
伸头探脑 stretch one's neck to see (*or* find out);peep;spy
伸张正义 uphold justice
伸缩三角架 extension tripod
伸手不见五指 so dark that you can't see your hand in front of you;pitch-dark

身 [shēn]
Ⅰ 名 ①body ②life ③oneself;personally ④ one's moral character and accomplishment ⑤ frame of a structure;body ⑥one's lifetime;all one's life Ⅱ 量 (of clothes) suit:一身西装 a Western-style suit
身板 body;bodily health
身边 ①at (*or* by) one's side ②(have sth) on one;with one
身材 stature;figure
身长 ①height (of a person) ②length (of a garment from shoulder to hemline)
身段 ①(woman's) figure ②(dancer's) posture
身份 ①status;capacity;identity ②honourable position;dignity ③the quality of a thing
身高 height (of a person)
身故 (of a person) die
身后 after one's death
身价 ①social status ②the selling price of a slave
身教 teach others by one's own example
身历 experience personally
身量 height (of a person);stature
身躯 body;stature
身上 ①on one's body ②(have sth) on one;with one
身世 one's (unfortunate) life experience;one's (hard) lot
身手 skill;talent
身受 experience personally
身体 ①body ②health
身心 body and mind
身形 figure (of person)
身影 a person's silhouette;form;figure
身孕 pregnancy
身姿 manner of holding oneself;carriage;posture;figure
身子 ①body ②pregnancy

身份证 identity card;identification card;ID card;ID
身败名裂 lose all standing and reputation; bring shame and ruin upon oneself;be utterly discredited
身不由己 involuntarily;under compulsion;in spite of oneself
身怀六甲 be with child;be pregnant
身家性命 man's life and family possessions
身价百倍 a meteoric rise in social status
身价倍增 rise in social status
身兼二任 take upon oneself both tasks
身经百战 have fought a hundred battles
身居要职 occupy an important position;hold an important post
身临其境 be personally on the scene
身强力壮 (of a person) strong;tough;sturdy
身首异处 be beheaded
身体力行 earnestly practise what one advocates (*or* preaches)
身体素质 fitness;physique;physical constitution;physical attribute
身外之物 external things;mere worldly possessions
身无长物 have nothing other than
身先士卒 lead one's men in a charge;charge at the head of one's men
身陷囹圄 be thrown into jail;be shut up in prison
身子骨儿 one's health;physique
身教胜于言教 Example is better than precept.
身在曹营心在汉 (of one's attitude) stand on one's side apparently but actually on another's
身在福中不知福 not appreciate the happy life one enjoys;Growing up in happiness,one often fails to appreciate what happiness really means.
身正不怕影子斜 a man standing straight doesn't worry about his shadow slanting— an upright man fears no gossip

呻 [shēn]
动 chant;recite
呻吟 groan;moan

参 [shēn]
名 ①general term for ginseng and dangshen,but often referring to ginseng ②one of the twenty-eight constellations ➡ cān;cēn

绅 [shēn]
名 ①sash;girdle (as worn by scholars and officials in feudal China) ②gentry
绅士 gentleman;gentry

莘 [shēn]
形 numerous
莘莘 numerous
莘莘学子 students;large number of students

砷 [shēn]
名 arsenic (As)

娠 [shēn]
㊊ be pregnant

深 [shēn]
Ⅰ 形 ①going far downward (*or* going well inward) from an outer surface;deep ②hard to comprehend;difficult ③ in-depth;incisive;penetrating ④close;intimate ⑤dark;rich ⑥late Ⅱ 名 depth Ⅲ 副 very;keenly;fully

深奥 abstruse;profound;recondite
深长 (of meaning,intention,etc.) profound
深沉 ① deep ② (of sound or voice) low-pitched;deep;dull ③ undemonstrative;reserved
深处 depths;recesses
深度 ①degree of depth;depth ②profundity;depth;thoroughness ③ advanced stage of development
深耕 deep ploughing
深广 deep and broad
深闺 boudoir
深海 deep sea
深厚 ①deep;profound ②solid;deep-seated
深化 deepen
深交 deep friendship
深究 go into (a matter) seriously;get to the bottom (of a matter)
深刻 deep;profound;deep-going
深空 deep space
深密 deep;thick;dense
深浅 ①depth ② shade (of colour) ③proper limits (for speech or action);sense of propriety
深切 ①heartfelt;deep;profound ②keen;penetrating;thorough
深情 deep feeling;deep love
深入 ① go deep into;penetrate into ② thorough;deep-going
深山 remote mountains
深深 deeply;keenly;profoundly
深水 deep water
深思 think deeply about;ponder deeply over
深邃 ①deep ②profound;abstruse;recondite
深谈 discuss thoroughly;go deeply into
深透 deep and thorough
深味 profound meaning or significance
深信 be deeply convinced;firmly believe
深省 wake up to a sharp awareness of the truth
深夜 late at night;in the small hours of the morning
深意 profound meaning
深渊 abyss
深远 profound and lasting;far-reaching
深造 take a more advanced course of study or training;pursue advanced studies
深湛 profound and thorough
深挚 deep and sincere

深重 very grave;extremely serious
深成岩 plutonic rock;plutonite
深度计 depth gauge
深海带 abyssal zone
深海鱼 deep-sea fish
深呼吸 deep breathing
深加工 more refined processing;deep processing;further processing;downstream processing;intensive processing
深水港 deepwater port
深闭固拒 obstinate and perverse
深不可测 unfathomable;enigmatic
深藏若虚 hide what one has and act as if one had nothing—be modest about one's talent or ability;not be given to boasting or showing off
深层结构 deep structure
深仇大恨 bitter and deep-seated hatred;profound hatred
深得人心 enjoy immense popular support
深度报道 in-depth reporting
深更半夜 at dead of night;in the depth (*or* dead) of night;in the middle of the night
深沟高垒 deep trenches and high ramparts;strong defence
深海捕捞 deep-sea fishing
深海采矿 deep-sea mining
深海测量 bathymetry
深海资源 deep-sea resources
深化改革 deepen reform;further reform;intensify reform
深居简出 live in the seclusion of one's own home
深明大义 be deeply conscious of the righteousness of a cause;be clear on matters of principle
深谋远虑 think deeply and plan carefully;be circumspect and far-sighted
深情厚谊 profound sentiments of friendship;profound friendship
深入基层 go down to the grass roots units
深入浅出 explain the profound in simple terms
深入群众 immerse oneself among the masses
深入人心 impress deeply upon everyone's mind;strike root in the hearts of the people
深水码头 deepwater wharf
深水炸弹 depth charge;depth bomb
深思熟虑 careful consideration
深文周纳 apply the law with the utmost severity and make sb appear guilty
深恶痛绝 hate bitterly;abhor;detest
深有同感 share a similar feeling
深宅大院 imposing dwellings and spacious courtyards
深层次矛盾 deep-seated contradiction;deep-rooted contradiction
深证综合指数 Shenzhen Composite Index

S

糁 [shēn]
名 ground cereal ➡ sǎn

shén (ㄕㄣ)

什 [shén]
➡ shí

什么 ① what ② something; anything ③ any; every ④ whatever ⑤ (*expressing anger, surprise, censure or negation*) ⑥ (*expressing disapproval or disagreement*) ⑦ things like; such as; and so on; and what not
什么的 things like that; and so on; and what not

神 [shén]
I 名 ①god; divine being; deity; divinity ②man with magic power; supernatural person ③spirit; mind; energy ④expression; appearance; look II 形 ① supernatural; magical; amazing ②smart; clever; incredible
神采 demeanour; mien; countenance
神道 ①the way of the gods ②gods; deities; divinities ③aisle leading to the coffin chamber of an ancient tomb; tomb passage ④Shinto; Shintoism
神殿 temple
神父 Father
神怪 gods and spirits
神乎 [shénhu] strange; odd; sensational; fantastic
神化 deify
神话 mythology; myth; fairy tale
神魂 state of mind; mind
神交 ①friends with mutual understanding and admiration ②friendship grown out of mutual admiration without the friends ever having met
神经 nerve
神龛 baldachin
神力 superhuman strength; extraordinary power
神聊 indulge in idle and empty talk
神灵 gods; deities; divinities
神秘 mysterious; mystical
神妙 wonderful; marvellous; ingenious
神明 gods; deities; divinities
神女 goddess
神品 ①sublime work ②holy orders
神奇 magical; mystical; miraculous
神气 ① expression; air; manner ② spirited; vigorous ③ putting on airs; cocky; overweening
神情 expression; look
神曲 medicated leaven
神权 ①religious authority; theocracy ②rule by divine right
神人 ①spiritual being; Taoist immortal ②a man of distinguished appearance

神色 expression; look
神社 ① place of worship; shrine; altar ② a Shinto shrine
神圣 sacred; holy
神思 state of mind; mental state
神似 be alike in spirit; be an excellent likeness
神速 marvellously quick; with amazing speed
神算 miraculous foresight; marvellous prediction
神态 expression; manner; bearing; mien
神通 magic power; remarkable ability
神童 child prodigy
神往 be carried away; be rapt; be charmed
神威 martial prowess; invincible might
神位 spirit tablet
神武 epithet of a great conquering general
神仙 ①supernatural being; celestial being; immortal ②a person who has the power of clairvoyance; person who is free from worldly cares
神像 the picture (*or* statue) of a god or Buddha
神效 magical effects; miraculous effect
神学 theology
神医 highly skilled doctor; miracle-working doctor
神异 ①gods and spirits ②magical; mystical; miraculous
神鹰 condor
神勇 extraordinarily brave; superhumanly brave
神游 make a spiritual tour; range in fancy
神韵 romantic charm (in literature and art)
神志 consciousness; senses; mind
神智 intelligence; mental ability
神州 the Divine Land (a poetic name for China)
神经病 ① neuropathy ② mental disorder; nervous disorder; neurosis ③ mentally disordered; neurotic
神经节 ganglion
神经索 nerve cord
神经痛 neuralgia
神经炎 neuritis
神经元 neuron; nerve cell
神经战 war of nerves
神经质 nervousness
神秘化 make a mystery of; mystify
神炮手 crack gunner
神枪手 crack shot; expert marksman; sharpshooter
神仙鱼 angelfish
神学院 theological seminary
神不守舍 be out of one's wits; be distracted
神采奕奕 glowing with health and radiating vigour
神出鬼没 come and go like a shadow; appear

and disappear mysteriously
神鬼莫测 be unpredictable
神乎其神 fantastic;wonderful;miraculous
神昏意乱 look distracted and confused
神魂不定 be distracted;be deeply perturbed
神魂颠倒 be infatuated
神机妙算 a superb strategy,a miracle of foresight;wonderful foresight in military operations,etc.
神经错乱 mental disorder
神经毒气 nerve gas;nerve agents
神经过敏 ①neuroticism ②neurotic;oversensitive
神经科学 neuroscience
神经末梢 nerve ending
神经衰弱 neurasthenia
神经外科 neurosurgery
神经系统 nervous system
神经细胞 neuron;nerve cell
神经纤维 nerve fibre
神经中枢 nerve centre
神来之笔 an inspired work;a stroke of genius
神秘主义 mysticism
神气活现 very cocky;high and mighty
神气十足 looking very dignified;putting on grand airs;looking triumphant
神色自若 be perfectly calm and collected;show composure and presence of mind
神神道道 odd;fantastic;bizarre
神圣权利 sacred right
神思恍惚 be distracted;be distraught;be in a trance
神通广大 have vast magic powers;possess unusual powers;be infinitely resourceful
神仙葫芦 chain block
神学博士 Doctor of Divinity (D.D.)
神职人员 clergy;clergymen
神州三号 "Shenzhou Ⅲ" unmanned spacecraft
神经官能症 neurosis
神经性皮炎 neurodermatitis
神经遗传学 neurogenetics
神经语言学 neurolinguistics
神不知鬼不觉 unknown to god or ghost—without anybody knowing it;with great secrecy
神州行电话卡 Shenzhou pre-paid card
神龙见首不见尾 move in and out with wizardly elusiveness;be secretive in one's movement and trace
"神州五号"载人飞船 "Shenzhou Ⅴ" manned spaceship

shěn（ㄕㄣˇ）

沈 [shěn] 名 juice

审 [shěn] Ⅰ 形 careful;circumspect Ⅱ 动 ① examine;check up;go over ② interrogate;try ③ know;be familiar;be aware Ⅲ 副 indeed;really

审办 try,hear (a case)
审标 comparison and review of bid
审查 examine (plans,proposals,credentials,etc.);investigate
审察 ①closely observe;closely examine ②investigate
审处 ①try and punish ②deliberate and decide
审订 examine and revise;revise
审定 examine and approve;examine and finalize
审读 read and evaluate (a manuscript);read
审度 study and estimate
审改 examine and revise (a manuscript);revise
审稿 go over a manuscript (draft)
审核 verify;check
审计 audit
审校 ①check and revise ②reviser
审结 complete legal proceedings;decide (a case);close a case
审看 ① view movies,TV and theatrical programmes,etc. (before public showing) ② scrutinize;examine carefully
审理 try;hear
审美 appreciation of the beautiful
审判 bring to trial;try
审批 examine and approve;examine and give instructions
审片 review of a film by the censor
审评 ① examine,appraise (quality of products) ②evaluate (performance)
审慎 cautious;careful;circumspect
审视 look closely at;examine closely
审听 review music programme or performance before public showing
审问 interrogate;question
审悉 know
审讯 ①hearing ②interrogate;hear;try
审验 examine and verify;inspect
审议 (of a deliberative body,a committee,etc.) review;deliberate
审阅 examine carefully and critically
审改本 a draft for examination and revision (before printing)
审计员 auditor
审计长 auditor general
审美观 aesthetic conceptions;aesthetic standards
审判权 judicial authority;jurisdiction
审判员 judge;judicial officer
审判长 presiding judge
审核预算 verify a budget
审计机构 auditing bodies
审计监督 supervision through auditing

审美能力 aesthetic judgment
审判程序 judicial procedure
审判机关 judicial organ
审时度势 judge the hour and size up the situation
审思明辨 discriminate with wisdom
审议机构 deliberative body

谂 ［shěn］
囫 ①know；be acquainted with ②advise；urge；exhort
谂熟 know sth or sb well；be familiar with；have an intimate knowledge of
谂知 know；be aware of

婶 ［shěn］
图 ①wife of father's younger brother；aunt ②form of address for a woman about one's mother's age；aunt；auntie
婶母 wife of father's younger brother；aunt
婶娘 wife of father's younger brother；aunt
婶子 wife of father's younger brother；aunt

shèn（ㄕㄣˋ）

肾 ［shèn］
图 ①kidney ②testis；testicle
肾亏 renal weakness
肾囊 scrotum
肾石 renal calculus；kidney stone
肾虚 deficiency of the kidney
肾炎 nephritis
肾盂 renal pelvis
肾脏 kidney
肾功能 nephritic function
肾结石 kidney stone；renal calculus
肾上腺 adrenal gland；adrenal
肾下垂 nephroptosis
肾移植 kidney transplant；renal transplant
肾盂炎 pyelitis
肾上腺素 adrenaline
肾盂肾炎 pyelonephritis
肾功能试验 kidney function test
肾功能衰竭 renal failure；kidney failure

甚 ［shèn］
Ⅰ 副 ①very；most；extremely ②more than Ⅱ 代 what
甚或 even；so far as to；so much so that
甚冷 extremely cold
甚为 very；extremely
甚于 surpass；exceed
甚高频 very high frequency（VHF）
甚至于 ①even to the extent that ②（go）so far as to；so much so that
甚为悲痛 be excessively grieved
甚为不安 feel very upset
甚为关切 be most concerned
甚嚣尘上 cause a temporary uproar；cause a great clamour

胂 ［shèn］
图 arsine

脤 ［shèn］
图 raw meat offered for sacrifice in ancient times

渗 ［shèn］
动 ooze；seep；leak
渗沟 sewer
渗坑 seepage pit
渗漏 seepage
渗滤 percolation filtration；percolation
渗入 ①permeate；seep into ②（of influence，etc.）penetrate；infiltrate
渗色 bleeding
渗碳 carburization；cementation
渗透 ①osmosis ②permeate；seep ③infiltrate
渗滤器 percolator
渗碳钢 carburizing steel
渗碳体 cementite
渗透性 permeability
渗透压 osmotic pressure
渗滤白土 percolation clay
渗透战术 infiltration tactics

葚 ［shèn］
◇ 桑葚 mulberry（the fruit）

蜃 ［shèn］
图 big clam；clam
蜃景 ①mirage ②illusion

瘆 ［shèn］
动 terrify；horrify

慎 ［shèn］
形 careful；cautious；prudent
慎密 cautious and meticulous
慎重 cautious；careful；prudent；discreet
慎言慎行 be cautious in speech and in conduct
慎之又慎 exercise maximum caution
慎重其事 be very careful；handle with care

shēng（ㄕㄥ）

升 ［shēng］
Ⅰ 动 ①rise；hoist；go up；climb；ascend ②promote；elevate；go up Ⅱ 量 ①litre（1.）：一升汽油 a litre of petrol（or gas）②sheng，a unit of dry measure for grain（＝1 litre）：十升为一斗。Ten sheng equals one dou. Ⅲ 图 （measure）sheng：用升量比用秤称方便。It's easier to weigh grain with a sheng than with a balance.
升班 go up（one grade in school）
升调 rising tune；rising tone
升幅 range of increase
升格 raise；promote；upgrade
升汞 mercuric chloride
升官 be promoted
升号 sharp（♯）
升华 ①sublimation ②raising of things to a higher level；distillation；sublimation

升级 ①go up one or more grades ②escalate ③(of product) update,upgrade
升降 go up and down
升空 lift-off;levitation
升力 lift
升幂 ascending power
升平 peace
升旗 hoist (*or* raise) a flag
升起 rise;takeoff;ascent;assurgent
升迁 be transferred and promoted
升任 be promoted
升势 rally;upswing
升水 premium
升腾 (of flames,gas,etc.) leap up;rise
升天 go up to Heaven——die
升位 expand digit
升温 ①rise in temperature;be booming ②rise in enthusiasm,etc.
升限 ceiling
升学 go to a school of a higher grade;enter a higher school
升压 step up;boost
升涨 rise;go up;shoot up
升值 ①appreciation ②upwardly revaluate
升班马 new promoter
升船机 ship lift
升降舵 elevator
升降机 elevator;lift
升水率 premium rate
升学率 proportion of students entering higher school
升压器 booster
升官发财 win promotion and get rich;(be out for) power and money
升华干燥 lyophilization
升级换代 (of manufactured goods) updating and upgrading
升降奖惩 promotion and demotion,reward and punishment
升堂入室 pass through the hall into the inner chamber——have profound scholarship;become highly proficient
升留级制度 system of promoting or holding students
升压变压器 step-up transformer

生 [shēng] I 动 ①grow ②give birth to;bear;deliver ③be born ④cause;engender;give rise to ⑤light (a fire) Ⅱ 名 ①existence;life ②living;livelihood ③ life ④ life span; life time; (throughout) one's life ⑤learned man;scholar;intellectual ⑥pupil;student ⑦male role in traditional opera Ⅲ 形 ① living; alive ② unripe; immature; green ③ raw; uncooked ④ crude;raw;unprocessed;rigid ⑤ unfamiliar; new; strange ⑥ stiff; unnatural; rigid Ⅳ 副 very:生怕同行批评 be very afraid of criti-

cism from one's colleagues Ⅴ ①(*suffix of certain nouns referring to people*) ②(*suffix of certain adverbs*):好生为难 be in an extremely embarrassing or difficult situation
生变 trouble arises
生病 fall ill
生财 develop financial resources;make money
生菜 ①romaine lettuce;cos lettuce ②lettuce ③row vegetable
生产 ①produce;manufacture ②give birth to a child
生长 ①grow ②grow up;be brought up
生辰 birthday
生成 ① come or bring into being;generate;produce ②be born with;be gifted with
生词 new and unfamiliar words (to the student)
生凑 mechanically put together (disconnected words and phrases); arbitrarily dish up (unrelated facts)
生存 subsist;exist;live
生地 ①the dried rhizome of rehmannia ②virgin soil;uncultivated land
生动 lively;vivid;vital
生分 estranged;not as close as before
生父 one's own father
生根 take root;strike root
生瓜 unripe melon
生光 third contact
生还 come back alive;survive
生荒 virgin soil;uncultivated land
生活 ①life ②live ③livelihood ④work
生火 make a fire;light a fire
生机 ①lease of life ②life;vitality
生计 means of livelihood;livelihood
生姜 ginger
生津 promote the secretion of saliva (*or* body fluid)
生境 habitat
生就 be born with;be gifted with
生客 an unfamiliar guest;stranger
生恐 be very much afraid;fear greatly
生来 from birth
生冷 raw or cold food
生理 physiology
生料 raw material
生灵 the people
生路 means of livelihood;way out
生猛 bold;lively;alive and jumping vigorously
生命 life
生母 one's own mother
生怕 be very much afraid;fear greatly
生皮 rawhide;(untanned) hide
生僻 uncommon;rare
生平 all one's life
生漆 raw lacquer
生气 ①take offence;get angry ②vim;vitality

生前 before one's death;during one's lifetime
生擒 capture alive
生趣 joy of life;pleasures of life
生人 ①stranger ②be born
生日 birthday
生色 add colour to;add lustre to;give added significance to
生涩 (of language) jerky;choppy;not smooth
生事 make trouble;create a disturbance
生手 new hand;green hand
生疏 ①not familiar ②out of practice;rusty ③ not as close as before
生水 unboiled water
生丝 raw silk
生死 life and death
生态 organisms' habits,modes of life and relation to their environment;ecology
生铁 pig iron
生土 immature soil
生物 living things;living beings;organisms
生息 ① bear interest ② live;exist ③ propagate;multiply;procreate
生肖 any one of the names of 12 symbolic animals associated with a 12-year cycle,often used to denote the year of a person's birth
生效 take effect;set the seal on;come into effect;go into effect
生性 natural disposition
生锈 get rusty
生涯 career;profession
生养 give birth to;bear (children)
生药 crude drug;dried medicinal herbs
生疑 be suspicious
生意 [shēngyì] tendency to grow;life and vitality
生意 [shēngyì] business;trade
生硬 ①(of writing) not smooth;not polished;crude ②stiff;rigid;harsh
生油 unboiled oil
生鱼 raw fish
生育 give birth to;bear
生源 source of students;number of applicants
生造 coin (words and expressions)
生殖 reproduction
生猪 live pig;pig;hog;pork on the hoof
生字 characters or words new to the student;new characters or words
生产队 production team
生产力 productive forces
生产率 productivity
生产税 production tax
生产线 production line;manufacturing line
生长点 growing point
生长率 growth rate
生长轮 growth ring
生长期 growth period;growing period
生成物 product;resultant

生存权 right of existence;right to subsistence;survival rights
生活费 living expenses;cost of living
生活关 the test of rigorous living conditions
生理学 physiology
生力军 ①fresh and combat-worthy troops ② fresh activists;new force
生命力 life-force;vitality
生命率 vital rates
生命线 lifeline;lifeblood
生牛奶 raw milk
生啤酒 draught beer
生石膏 plaster stone
生石灰 quick lime
生柿子 green persimmon;unripe persimmon
生态圈 ecosphere
生态群 cline
生态型 ecotype
生态学 ecology
生物层 biosphere
生物带 biozone
生物碱 alkaloid
生物量 biomass
生物膜 biomembrane
生物区 biotic division
生物圈 biosphere
生物体 organism
生物学 biology
生物岩 biogenic rock;biolith
生物战 biological warfare
生物钟 biological clock;biochronometer;living clock
生(橡)胶 raw rubber;caoutchouc
生药学 pharmacognosy
生意经 the knack of doing business;shrewd business sense
生油层 source bed
生鱼片 sashimi
生育率 fertility rate
生育权 right of bearing children
生源说 biogenesis
生造词 coinage
生长点 growing point
生殖孔 gonopore
生殖率 reproduction rate
生殖器 reproductive organs;genitals
生殖腺 gonad
生字表 list of new words (attached to a textbook)
生搬硬套 apply or copy mechanically;copy mechanically and apply indiscriminately
生不逢时 be born out of one's time;be born at the wrong time
生财有道 know how to make money;have the knack of making money
生财之道 the way to earn money;a means to make money

生产成本 cost of production; manufacturing cost
生产大队 production brigade
生产单位 production unit
生产方式 mode of production
生产工具 tool of production
生产关系 relations of production; production relations
生产过剩 overproduction
生产劳动 productive labour
生产能力 production capacity
生产手段 means of production
生产要素 production factors; essential factors of production; key elements of production
生产指标 production target (quota)
生产资料 means of production
生产总值 total output value
生长激素 growth hormone
生成语法 generative grammar
生存竞争 struggle for existence
生存空间 living space
生旦净丑 the male role, the female role, the painted-face role, and the comic role (the four main roles in traditional opera)
生动活泼 vivid and vigorous; lively
生而知之 be born wise; be born with knowledge; have innate knowledge
生花妙笔 a brilliant pen; a brilliant style of writing
生化效应 biochemical effect
生活补贴 living allowances
生活补助 extra allowance for living expenses
生活方式 life-style; mode of life; way of life
生活福利 welfare; welfare benefits
生活环境 surroundings; environment
生活经验 experience of life
生活救济 hardship relief assistance; relief
生活来源 source of income
生活能力 viability
生活水平 living standards
生活条件 living conditions
生活习惯 habits and customs
生活细节 trifling matters of everyday life; domestic trivia
生活周期 life cycle
生活资料 means of subsistence; means of livelihood
生活作风 ① life style ② behaviour with the opposite sex
生机盎然 full of life; overflowing with vigour; exuberant
生拉硬拽 ① drag sb along against his will ② stretch the meaning
生老病死 birth and old age, sickness and death—the lot of man
生离死别 part never to meet again; part for ever

生理反应 physiological reaction
生理缺陷 physiological defect; physiological deficiency
生理盐水 physiological saline; normal saline
生理作用 physiological action
生灵涂炭 The people are plunged into an abyss of misery.
生龙活虎 doughty as a dragon and lively as a tiger—brimming (or bursting) with energy; full of vim and vigour
生命科学 life science
生命特征 vital signs
生命现象 biological phenomena
生命银行 life bank; organ depository
生拼硬凑 dish up (or lump together) unrelated words or facts
生平事迹 one's life story; one's profile
生气勃勃 dynamic; vigorous; full of vitality
生擒活捉 capture alive; take prisoner
生杀予夺 hold power over sb's life and property; have sb completely in one's power
生杀之权 power over sb's life
生身父母 one's own parents
生生世世 generation after generation; for generations
生死存亡 life or death; critical juncture; survival or extinction; juncture when one's life is at stake; moment when one's fate hangs in the balance
生死关头 a juncture when one's life is at stake; a moment when one's fate hangs in the balance; a critical juncture
生死攸关 matter of life or death; of vital importance
生死与共 share a common destiny; go through thick and thin together
生死之交 friends that are ready to die for each other
生态爆炸 ecological explosion
生态变异 ecocline
生态工程 eco-engineering
生态环境 ecological environment
生态科学 ecological science
生态旅游 ecotourism
生态灭绝 ecocide
生态农业 eco-agriculture; eco-farming; environment(ally)-friendly agriculture
生态平衡 ecological balance; eco-equilibrium
生态屏障 ecological protective screen
生态破坏 ecocide
生态退化 ecological degradation
生态危机 ecological crisis; ecocrisis
生态系统 ecosystem
生态效益 ecological benefits
生态灾难 ecocatastrophe
生态住宅 ecological residence
生吞活剥 swallow sth raw and whole—accept

S

sth uncritically
生物安全 biosafety
生物电流 bioelectric current
生物电脑 biocomputer
生物防治 biological control
生物工程 bioengineering
生物固氮 biological nitrogen fixation
生物合成 biosynthesis
生物化学 biochemistry
生物技术 biotechnology; biological engineering
生物节律 biorhythm
生物疗法 biotherapy
生物群落 biocommunity
生物入侵 biotic intrusion
生物武器 bacteriological weapon
生物芯片 biochip
生物炸弹 biological bomb
生物制品 biological product
生息资本 interest-bearing capital
生意兴隆 booming business
生育低谷 baby bust
生育高峰 baby boom; peak population growth; birth peak
生造词语 forging new words and expressions; unnatural coinages
生殖洄游 breeding migration
生殖健康 reproduction health
生殖系统 reproductive system
生产合作社 producers' cooperative
生产许可证 production licence
生产责任制 production responsibility system
生活必需品 necessaries of life; daily necessities
生活方式病 life style disease
生命科学家 life scientist
生态经济学 eco-economics
生物传感器 biosensor
生物地理学 biogeography
生物多样性 biodiversity
生物发生律 biogenetic law; recapitulation theory
生物耗氧量 biological oxygen demand
生物伦理学 bioethics
生物气候学 bioclimatology
生物生态学 bioecology
生物天文学 bioastronomy
生物物理学 bio-physics
生物遥测器 biopack
生猪出栏率 slaughter rate of hogs
生产建设兵团 production and construction corps
生米煮成熟饭 the rice is cooked—what's done can't be undone
生态环境保护 protection of ecological environment
生态环境恶化 deterioration of the ecological environment
生态良性循环 benign ecological cycles
生物医学工程 bio-medical engineering
生殖泌尿系统 urogenital system
生态型经济开发区 ecological type economic development zone
生得光明,死得磊落 live honourably and die honourably
生得伟大,死得光荣 live a great life and die a glorious death

声 [shēng] Ⅰ 〔名〕①sound; voice; noise ②fame; reputation ③initial consonant (of a Chinese syllable) ④tone Ⅱ 〔动〕make a sound; state Ⅲ 〔量〕(of sounds): 听见了几声鸡叫 hear a cock crow several times
声辩 argue; justify oneself; explain away
声波 sound wave; acoustic wave
声部 part (in concerted music)
声称 profess; claim; assert
声带 ①vocal cords ②soundtrack (on a film)
声道 sound track; sound channel
声调 ①tone; note ②the tone of Chinese characters
声价 reputation
声控 sound-activated; sound-controlled
声浪 voice; clamour
声门 glottis
声名 reputation
声明 ①state; declare; announce ②statement; declaration
声母 the initial of a syllable
声囊 vocal sac
声呐 sonar
声频 audio frequency; sonic frequency
声谱 sound spectrum
声气 ①information ②voice; tone
声强 sound intensity
声色 voice and countenance
声势 prestige and power; fame and influence; impetus; momentum
声速 speed of sound
声讨 denounce; condemn
声望 popularity; prestige
声威 renown; prestige; fame and influence
声息 ①sound; noise ②information
声响 sound; noise
声学 acoustics
声言 profess; claim; declare
声音 sound; voice
声誉 reputation; fame; prestige
声冤 voice grievances; complain and call for redress
声援 express support for; support
声乐 vocal music; vocalist
声张 make public; disclose
声能学 sonics

声谱仪 sound spectrograph
声讨会 denunciation meeting
声韵学 phonology
声东击西 make a feint to the east and attack in the west
声控电视 voice-controlled TV
声泪俱下 shedding tears while speaking; in a tearful voice
声名狼藉 have a bad name; be notorious; be utterly discredited
声频信号 audio signal
声情并茂 (of a singer) be remarkable for both voice and expression
声色俱厉 stern in voice and countenance
声色犬马 music and women, keeping dogs and riding horses—sensual pleasures
声施千里 (enjoy) a widespread reputation
声势浩大 great in strength and impetus; powerful and dynamic; impressive display of power (or influence)
声嘶力竭 be hoarse and exhausted; shout oneself hoarse; shout oneself blue in the face
声威大震 gain great fame and high prestige
声震寰宇 become known far and wide; gain resounding fame
声音识别系统 sound recognition system

犰 [shēng]
　【名】 yellow weasel

牲 [shēng]
　【名】 ①domestic animal; live stock ②animal sacrifice (offering of an ox, sheep, pig, etc. as a sacrifice)
牲畜 livestock; domestic animals
牲粉 animal starch; glycogen
牲口 draught animals; beasts of burden; livestock
牲畜车 livestock wagon; stock wagon; stock car
牲畜肥 animal manure
牲口棚 stock barn; livestock shed
牲口贩子 cattle dealer

胜 [shēng]
　【名】 peptide ⇒ shèng

笙 [shēng]
　【名】 *sheng*, a reed pipe wind instrument
笙歌 music and singing

甥 [shēng]
　【名】 sister's son; nephew
甥女 sister's daughter; niece

shéng (ㄕㄥˊ)

绳 [shéng]
　Ⅰ【名】 rope; cord; string Ⅱ【动】 ①restrict; restrain; punish ②continue; carry on
绳操 rope exercise
绳技 rope walking or dancing; tightrope walking or slack rope walking

绳墨 ①carpenter's line marker ②rules and regulations
绳索 thick cord; rope
绳套 ①loop ②lasso
绳梯 rope ladder
绳头 fag end
绳子 cord; rope; string
绳鞭技 (doing) tricks with a whip; (performing) feats with a whip
绳锯木断 A rope can cut through a log; Little strokes fell great oaks.
绳捆索绑 truss up; bind; tie up
绳趋尺步 conform to every rule and regulation; toe the line
绳以纪律 enforce discipline
绳之以法 bring to justice; be dealt with according to the law; be punished according to the law

shěng (ㄕㄥˇ)

省 [shěng]
　Ⅰ【动】 ①economize; save; be frugal ②omit; delete; leave out ③shortened form (of words and expressions) Ⅱ【名】 ①province ②capital of a province ③(of Japan) ministry ⇒ xǐng
省便 convenient; timesaving or laboursaving
省城 provincial capital
省得 so as to save (or avoid)
省份 (*not to be used in names of provinces*) province
省府 provincial government
省会 provincial capital
省界 provincial boundaries
省劲 save effort; save labour
省力 save effort; save labour
省略 ①leave out; omit (on purpose) ②be understood
省钱 save money; be economical
省却 save
省事 save trouble; simplify matters
省属 directly under the jurisdiction of a provincial government
省委 provincial Party committee
省心 save worry; free from worry
省优 (of product) up to quality standards set by the province
省长 governor of a province
省直 directly under the Party committee (or government of a province)
省部级 at the provincial and ministerial level
省妇联 provincial women's federation
省略号 ellipsis; suspension points; ellipsis dots
省略句 elliptical sentence
省辖市 city under the jurisdiction of a province
省政协 provincial people's political consulta-

S

tive conference
省吃俭用 live frugally；pinch and scrape（*or* screw）；cut corners；scrape and screw；skimp and save
省工省钱 save both labour and money
省级机关 Party and government organizations at the provincial level
省级企业 provincial state-owned enterprises（*or* firms）
省时省力 save both time and labour
省优产品 quality products designated as such by a province；quality products of provincial-level standard
省油的灯 lamp that does not burn much oil；person who knows his place and stirs up no trouble（usu. in a negative sentence）

shèng（ㄕㄥˋ）

圣 I 〔形〕①holy；sacred ②holy II 〔名〕①sage；master ②sage；saint ③emperor
圣餐 the Lord's Supper；the Holy Communion；Eucharist
圣诞 Christmas（the birthday of Jesus Christ）
圣地 ①（宗教）the Holy Land（*or* City）②a sacred place；shrine
圣殿 Temple of God
圣恩 his（*or* her）majesty's kindness
圣父 ①Holy Father—God ②Holy Father（a title of the Pope）
圣火 sacred fire
圣驾 his（*or* her）majesty
圣洁 holy and pure
圣经 the Holy Bible；the Bible；Holy Writ；the（Holy）Scriptures
圣灵 the Holy Spirit；the Holy Ghost
圣庙 Confucian temple
圣明 august wisdom
圣母 ①female deity；goddess ②（基督教）the（Blessed）Virgin Mary；the Madonna
圣人 ①sage；wise man ②the Sage（a title of respect for Confucius）
圣上 Your Majesty；His Majesty
圣手 a master of a certain skill
圣水 ①sacred water credited with curative or exorcising powers ②holy water for religious uses
圣所 Holy Place
圣坛 chancel
圣体 holy bread
圣徒 believer；disciple；devotee
圣贤 sages and men of virtue
圣药 efficacious medicine
圣谕 imperial decree
圣战 jihad；holy war；crusade
圣旨 imperial edict

圣子 Holy Son—Jesus Christ
圣诞节 Christmas Day（Dec. 25）
圣诞卡 Christmas card；Xmas card
圣诞树 Christmas tree
圣公会 the Anglican Church
圣公宗 Anglicanism；the Anglican Church
圣灵节 Whitsunday
圣诞老人 Santa Claus
圣经贤传 Confucian classics
圣人无常师 Sages have no constant teachers；A sage has more than one teacher.
圣城耶路撒冷 Holy City of Jerusalem

胜 〔shèng〕
I 〔动〕①win victory over（sb or sth）；defeat ②surpass；be superior to；be better than；get the better of ③be equal to；can bear II 〔名〕① victory；success ② woman's hair ornament III 〔形〕superb；wonderful；beautiful；lovely ➡ shēng
胜败 victory or defeat；success or failure
胜出 outplay
胜地 a famous scenic spot
胜负 victory or defeat；success or failure
胜果 fruit of victory
胜过 be better than；be superior to
胜迹 a famous historical site
胜景 wonderful scenery
胜境 a scenic spot；a beautiful place
胜利 ①victory；triumph ②successful；triumphant
胜率 probability of win
胜面（in games such as *weiqi* or *go* chess）the chance of winning
胜券 confidence in victory
胜任 be competent；be qualified；be equal to
胜如 be better than；surpass
胜似 be better than；surpass
胜诉 win a lawsuit；obtain satisfaction of a claim
胜算 a stratagem which ensures success
胜友 good friends
胜于 outstrip；superior to
胜仗 victorious battle；victory
胜利者 victor；winner
胜利果实 fruits of victory
胜人一筹 have edge on sb
胜不骄，败不馁 not made dizzy with success，nor discouraged by failure
胜败乃兵家常事 For a military commander，winning or losing a battle is a common occurrence；Victory or defeat is a common thing for the soldier.

乘 〔shèng〕
〔名〕①historical works ②war chariot drawn by four horses in ancient times ➡ chéng

盛 〔shèng〕
I 〔形〕①flourishing；thriving；prosperous ②

vigorous; energetic; aggressive ③ magnificent; grand; solemn ④ rich; sumptuous ⑤ profuse; profound; abundant ⑥ popular; prevalent; extensive Ⅱ 副 greatly; deeply ➡ chéng
盛产 abound in; teem with
盛传 be widely known; be widely rumoured
盛大 grand; magnificent
盛典 a grand ceremony (*or* occasion)
盛服 full dress; splendid attire; rich dress
盛会 distinguished gathering; grand meeting
盛季 peak period; busy season
盛举 grand occasion (*or* event)
盛开 (of flowers) be in full bloom; flourish
盛夸 praise lavishly; laud to the skies
盛况 grand occasion; spectacular event
盛名 great reputation
盛年 the more robust years of one's life; the prime of life
盛怒 be very angry; be in a rage
盛情 great kindness; boundless hospitality
盛秋 the height of autumn
盛世 flourishing age; heyday
盛事 grand occasion; great event
盛暑 sweltering summer heat; very hot weather
盛衰 prosperity and decline; rise and fall; ups and downs
盛夏 the height of summer; midsummer
盛行 be current (*or* rife, rampant); be in vogue
盛宴 a grand banquet; a sumptuous dinner
盛意 great kindness; generosity
盛誉 great fame; high reputation
盛赞 highly praise; speak of sb in glowing terms
盛馔 feast; sumptuous meal
盛装 splendid attire; rich dress
盛极一时 be in fashion (*or* vogue) for a time; be all the rage
盛况空前 an exceptionally (*or* unprecedentedly) grand occasion
盛气凌人 domineering; arrogant; overbearing
盛情款待 treat sb with the utmost cordiality
盛情难却 It would be ungracious not to accept your kindness.
盛衰荣辱 prosperity and decline, glory and humiliation; rise and fall; ups and downs; vicissitudes of life
盛行一时 be in vogue; prevail for a time
盛名之下，其实难副 A high reputation is hard to live up to.

剩 ［shèng］
形 surplus; leftover; remnant
剩菜 leftover dishes
剩磁 residual magnetism
剩货 surplus wares
剩下 be left (over); remain

剩余 surplus; remainder
剩饭残羹 swill; leftovers; remains of food
剩余产品 surplus products
剩余价值 surplus value
剩余劳动 surplus labour
剩余物资 surplus materials
剩余资产 residual assets; surplus assets
剩余劳动力 surplus labour force

shī（尸）

尸 ［shī］
Ⅰ 名 ①corpse; dead body; carcass ②person who sat behind the altar, acting as the deceased during the performance of the sacrificial rites Ⅱ 动 hold a job without doing anything
尸骨 bones of the dead
尸骸 skeleton
尸检 autopsy
尸蜡 a dead body naturally dried and preserved
尸身 corpse; dead body; remains
尸首 a dead body of a human being
尸体 corpse; carcass
尸横遍野 a field littered with corpses
尸体解剖 autopsy; postmortem (examination)

失 ［shī］
Ⅰ 动 ①suffer loss of; lose ②lose hold of; let slip; miss ③get lost ④fail to achieve one's end ⑤deviate from the normal ⑥break (a promise); go back on (one's word) Ⅱ 名 mishap; defect; error
失败 ①be defeated; lose (a war, etc.) ②fail
失标 fail in bidding; fail to win the tender
失策 ① err (in tactics, scheming or planning); do sth unwise ②an error (in tactics, etc.)
失察 neglect one's supervisory duties
失常 not normal; odd
失宠 fall into disfavour; be out of favour; be in disgrace
失传 not be handed down from past generations; be lost
失聪 become deaf
失措 lose one's presence of mind; lose one's head
失单 a list of lost (*or* stolen) articles (*or* property)
失当 improper; inappropriate
失盗 be robbed or burgled
失地 lost territory
失掉 ①lose ②miss
失范 loss of standards; disobey standards
失分 (in competition) lose points
失和 fail to keep on good terms; become estranged
失衡 off balance; out of balance

失悔 regret; be remorseful
失婚 divorced; widowed
失火 catch fire; be on fire
失机 lose the opportunity; miss the chance
失计 wrong move; unwise decision
失记 forget
失检 be indiscreet
失脚 lose one's footing; slip
失节 ① forfeit one's integrity; be disloyal ② (of a woman, according to feudal morality) lose one's chastity
失禁 lose control over one's bladder or rectum functions; be unable to restrain one's natural discharges; suffer from incontinence
失惊 be startled; be shocked
失敬 sorry I didn't recognize you; excuse me for my lack of manners
失控 get out of control; get out of hand
失口 make a slip of the tongue
失礼 ① commit a breach of etiquette ② excuse me for my impropriety (*or* lack of manners, etc.)
失利 suffer a setback (*or* defeat)
失恋 be disappointed in a love affair; be jilted
失灵 (of a machine, instrument, etc.) not work; not work properly; be out of order
失落 lose; drop
失迷 lose one's way; lose one's bearings
失密 give away official secrets due to carelessness
失眠 (suffer from) insomnia
失明 lose one's sight; go blind
失陪 Excuse me, but I must be leaving now.
失窃 have things stolen; suffer loss by theft
失去 lose
失却 lose; miss
失群 stray from one's flock
失散 be separated from and lose touch with each other; be scattered
失色 ① be discoloured; lose colour ② turn pale
失闪 mishap; unexpected danger
失墒 (of soil) loss of moisture
失身 (of a woman) lose one's virginity (*or* chastity)
失神 ① inattentive; absent-minded ② out of sorts; in low spirits
失慎 ① not cautious; careless ② cause a fire through carelessness
失声 ① ejaculate (involuntarily); burst out ② lose one's voice
失时 miss the season; let slip the opportunity
失实 inconsistent with the facts; inaccurate
失事 (have an) accident
失势 lose power and influence; fall into disgrace
失手 ① lose control of one's hand; accidentally drop sth; accidentally hurt sb ② suffer de-

feat in competition
失守 (of a city, etc.) fall
失水 dehydration
失溲 lose control over one's bladder functions; incontinence of urine
失速 stall
失算 miscalculate; misjudge; be injudicious
失所 become homeless; be displaced
失态 lose control of oneself; misbehave; forget oneself
失调 ① imbalance; dislocation ② lack of proper care (after an illness, etc.) ③ maladjustment; detuning
失望 ① lose hope; lose heart ② disappointed
失物 lost article; lost property
失误 error; fault; muff
失陷 (of cities, territory, etc.) fall; fall into enemy hands
失笑 laugh in spite of oneself; cannot help laughing
失效 ① lose efficacy; lose effectiveness; cease to be effective ② be no longer in force; become invalid
失谐 detuning; mismatching
失信 break one's promise; go back on one's word
失修 (of houses, etc.) be in bad repair; fall into disrepair
失序 disorder; loss of order
失学 be deprived of education; be unable to go to school; be obliged to discontinue one's studies
失血 lose blood
失言 make an indiscreet remark; make a slip of the tongue
失业 ① lose one's job; be out of work; be unemployed ② idleness; unemployment
失仪 ① forget one's manners ② a breach of etiquette
失宜 inappropriate
失意 have one's aspirations (*or* plans, etc.) thwarted; be frustrated; be disappointed
失音 aphonia; loss of voice
失迎 fail to meet (a guest)
失约 fail to keep an appointment
失着 [shīzhāo] ① make a careless (*or* an unwise) move ② a careless move; an unwise move
失责 dereliction of duty
失真 ① (of voice, images, etc.) lack fidelity; not be true to the original ② distortion
失职 ① neglect one's duty ② dereliction of duty
失重 weightlessness; zero gravity
失主 owner of lost property
失踪 (usu. of people) be missing
失足 ① lose one's footing; slip ② take a wrong

step in life
失落感 sense of alienation; feeling of being lost or neglected
失业率 rate of unemployment
失业者 the unemployed; the jobless
失语症 aphasia
失败情绪 defeatist sentiments
失败主义 defeatism
失道寡助 An unjust cause finds scant (or little) support.
失而复得 lost and found; recover what one has previously lost
失魂落魄 driven to distraction
失信于民 lose the confidence of the people; lose credibility with the public
失学儿童 dropout
失业保险 unemployment insurance
失业救济 unemployment relief
失业人数 unemployed population
失之交臂 just miss (the person or opportunity)
失足青年 youth who took wrong step in life
失物招领处 Lost Property Office
失业保险金 unemployment insurance benefits; jobless insurance benefits
失业保险制度 unemployment insurance institutions
失败为成功之母 Failure is the mother of success.
失之东隅,收之桑榆 lose in the east and gain in the west—make up on the roundabouts what one loses on the swings

师 [shī]
Ⅰ 名 ①teacher; master ②model; example; guide ③person skilled in a certain profession or trade ④courtesy title for a Buddhist monk or Taoist priest ⑤of one's master or teacher ⑥division (of an army) ⑦troops; army Ⅱ 动 learn; follow
师表 person of exemplary virtue
师部 division headquarters
师承 ①have studied under (a teacher, usu. with reference to a particular school of thought or learning); be a disciple of ②transmission from master to disciple
师德 professional ethics of the teaching profession
师弟 ①junior (male) fellow apprentice ②the son of one's master (younger than oneself) ③father's (male) apprentice (younger than oneself)
师法 ①model oneself after (a great master); imitate ②knowledge (or technique) handed down by one's master
师范 ①teacher-training; school; normal school ②model to be followed
师父 ①master; teacher ②(a term of respect for a monk or nun) master; mother
师傅 ①master worker (a qualified worker as distinct from an apprentice) ②a respectful form of address for a skilled worker ③a form of address for any stranger
师公 ①master's master ②sorcerer
师古 take the ancients as one's model
师姐 ①senior (female) fellow apprentice ②the daughter of one's master (older than oneself) ③father's (female) apprentice (older than oneself)
师妹 ①junior (female) fellow apprentice ②the daughter of one's master (younger than oneself) ③father's (female) apprentice (younger than oneself)
师母 the wife of one's teacher (or master)
师娘 the wife of one's teacher (or master)
师生 teacher and student
师事 treat sb with the respect due to a teacher
师徒 master and apprentice
师团 division
师兄 ①senior (male) fellow apprentice ②the son of one's master (older than oneself) ③father's (male) apprentice (older than oneself)
师训 teacher's instructions
师爷 private assistant attending to legal, fiscal or secretarial duties in a local *yamen*; private adviser
师友 teachers and friends
师长 ①(a term of respect) teacher ②division commander
师专 teacher-training school; normal school; (two-year) teachers' college
师资 persons qualified to teach; teachers
师兄弟 male apprentices of the same master; fellow apprentices
师出无名 dispatch troops without just cause
师出有名 make trouble under a certain pretext
师道尊严 dignity of the teaching profession
师范学校 normal school
师老兵疲 an army worn-down and war-weary
师其所长 learn from sb's strong points
师心自用 be opinionated
师直为壮 An army fighting for a just cause has high morale.
师父领进门,修行在个人 The master initiates the apprentices, but their skill depends on their own efforts; The master teaches the trade, but the apprentice's skill is self-made.

诗 [shī]
名 poetry; verse
诗歌 poems and songs; poetry
诗话 ①poetry talks ②vernacular stories interspersed with poems
诗集 collection of poems; poetry anthology

诗经 *The Book of Songs*
诗句 verse;line
诗剧 drama in verse;poetic drama
诗律 prosody
诗篇 ①poems ②an inspiring story;epic
诗人 poet
诗社 poets' club
诗圣 poet-sage (an epithet for Du Fu 杜甫)
诗史 ①history of poetry ②epic
诗书 Confucian classics
诗坛 poetry circles;world of poetry;the circle of poets
诗文 poetic prose
诗仙 poet-immortal (an epithet for Li Bai)
诗兴 urge for poetic creation;poetic inspiration;poetic mood
诗选 collection of poems;poetry anthology
诗意 poetic quality or flavour
诗韵 ①rhyme (in poetry) ②rhyming dictionary
诗章 ①poem ②inspiring story
诗作 poetical works
诗礼之家 highly cultured household;a family of scholars
诗情画意 a quality suggestive of poetry or painting;poetic charm
诗穷而后工 Poverty makes for poetic excellence;Only a poet in adversity is apt to develop skill;An impoverished poet tends to attain skill;Adversity makes for (poetic) excellence.
诗中有画,画中有诗 There are pictures (i.e. a pictorial imagination) in poetry and poetry (i.e. a poetic imagination) in pictures;evoke painting in poetry and poetry in painting;There is painting in poetry just as there is poetry in painting.

虱 [shī]
〈名〉 louse
虱子 louse

狮 [shī]
〈名〉 lion
狮猴 lion monkey
狮子 lion
狮头鹅 lion-headed goose (a fine breed of goose)
狮子鼻 pug nose
狮子狗 pug-dog
狮子头 large meatball
狮子舞 lion dance (a popular folk dance)
狮子座 Leo
狮子搏兔 (like) a lion pouncing on a hare—go all out even when fighting a weaker enemy or tackling a minor problem
狮身人面像 sphinx
狮子大开口 open one's mouth wide;demand an exorbitant price

施 [shī]
〈动〉 ①execute;carry out;put into practice ②exert;exercise;impose ③ bestow;grant;hand out;give ④use;apply
施暴 ①lay violent hands on sb ②rape
施恩 bestow favour
施放 discharge;fire
施肥 spread manure;apply fertilizer
施工 carry out construction (*or* large repairs)
施计 play tricks
施加 exert;bring to bear on
施教 teach;educate;instruct
施礼 make a bow;salute
施舍 give alms;give in charity
施事 the doer of the action in a sentence;agent
施威 exhibit one's power;show severity
施洗 administer baptism
施行 ①put (laws,rules,regulations,etc.) into force;enforce;implement ②perform;administer;apply
施压 exert pressure
施药 ①prescribe ②give medicine to the poor free of charge
施用 use;employ
施与 grant (money,gifts,etc.) to sb;bestow (favours) on sb
施斋 provide (itinerant) monks with free food
施展 put to good use;give free play to
施政 administration;management of government affairs
施粥 provide free porridge for the poor
施主 (monks' or nuns' form of address for a layman) patron
施工缝 construction joint
施工图 working drawing
施力点 point of application
施脂粉 apply cosmetics
施不望报 bestow favours without expecting anything in return
施工现场 fabricating yard;construction site;job location
施政报告 Policy Address;administrative report
施政方针 administrative policy;policies (*or* principles) for running an institution or government
施政纲领 administrative programme

湿 [shī]
〈形〉 wet;moist;damp;humid
湿痹 arthritis with fixed pain caused by dampness
湿病 diseases caused by dampness
湿材 moist wood;green lumber
湿地 wet land
湿度 humidity;moisture
湿纺 wet spinning

湿敷 soak;hydropathic compress
湿寒 raw
湿气 ①eczema;fungus infection of hand or foot ②moisture;humidity
湿热 damp and hot
湿润 moist
湿贴 wet combining
湿透 wet through;drenched
湿土 wet soil
湿选 wet separation
湿疹 eczema
湿租 wet lease
湿答答 dripping wet
湿度表 hygrometer
湿度器 hygroscope
湿乎乎 damp;moist;humid
湿津津 moist with sweat;sweaty
湿淋淋 dripping wet;drenched
湿漉漉 moist;damp
湿蒙蒙 (of the air) damp;moist
湿水货 water-damaged goods
湿法冶金 hydrometallurgy

嘘 [shī]
囡 (*used to stop sb from doing sth or to drive sb or sth away*)hush!;sh;嘘,别出声! Sh (*or* Hush)! Be quiet! ➡ xū

shí(ㄕ)

十 [shí]
Ⅰ 颲 ten Ⅱ 形 topmost;highest
十方 the ten positions
十分 very;fully;utterly;extremely
十佳 ten best individuals or units
十戒 the Ten Prohibitions
十诫 the Ten Commandments;the Decalogue
十一 October 1,National Day of the People's Republic of China
十月 ①October ②the tenth month of the lunar year;the tenth moon
十足 ①pure ②100 per cent;out-and-out;sheer;downright;complete
十二分 more than 100 per cent;extremely
十二月 ①December ②the twelfth month of the lunar year;the twelfth moon
十级风 force 10 wind;whole gale
十进制 the decimal system
十六开 sixteenmo;16mo
十一月 ①November ②the eleventh month of the lunar year;the eleventh moon
十字镐 pick;pickaxe;mattock
十字架 the Cross
十字军 ①the Crusades (11th-13th centuries) ②crusade ③crusader
十足类 Decapoda;decapods
十八罗汉 18 arhats
十步芳草 fragrant grass is to be found within ten paces—talent is close at hand

十大功劳 Chinese mahonia (Mahonia fortunei)
十冬腊月 the tenth, eleventh and twelfth months of the lunar year;the cold months of the year
十恶不赦 guilty of unpardonable evil;unpardonably wicked;wicked beyond redemption
十二级风 force 12 wind;hurricane
十二门徒 the 12 apostles of Jesus Christ
十二生肖 the 12 symbolic animals associated with a 12-year cycle
十二指肠 duodenum
十行俱下 take in ten lines at a glance—read rapidly
十里长街 the Ten-*Li* long street
十六进制 hexadecimal system
十拿九稳 ninety per cent sure;practically certain;in the bag
十年寒窗 ten years' study at a cold window—a student's long years of hard study
十全十美 be perfect in every way;be the acme of perfection;leave nothing to be desired
十室九空 nine houses out of ten are stripped bare—the aftermath of war,natural calamities,etc.
十四行诗 sonnet
十万火急 most urgent;posthaste;express
十羊九牧 nine shepherds for ten sheep—too many bosses
十一级风 force 11 wind;storm
十有八九 in eight or nine cases out of ten;most likely
十月怀胎 ten month's pregnancy
十指连心 the fingers are linked to the heart—what happens to children is of vital interest to parents
十字花科 the mustard family
十字街头 crisscross streets;busy city streets
十字路口 crossroads;intersection
十八般武艺 skill in wielding the 18 kinds of weapons—skill in various types of combat
十八层地狱 the eighteenth hell—the lowest depths of hell
十二平均律 twelve-tone equal temperament
十佳排行榜 Top Ten
十六分音符 semiquaver;sixteenth note
十年九不遇 not occur once in ten years;be seldom seen
十万八千里 a distance of one hundred and eight thousand *li*;poles apart
十二指肠溃疡 duodenal ulcer
十项全能运动 decathlon
十个指头有长短 the fingers are unequal in length—you can't expect everybody to be the same
十目所视,十手所指 with many eyes watching and many fingers pointing—one cannot do

wrong without being seen

十年树木，百年树人 It takes ten years to grow trees, but a hundred to rear people.

什 [shí]
I 数 ten II 形 assorted; varied; sundry III 名 odds and ends; articles for everyday use; sundries ⇒shén

什百 tenfold or hundredfold

什锦 assorted; mixed

什九 nine tenths

什物 articles for daily use; odds and ends; sundries

什件儿 giblets

什叶派 Shiite sect (of Islam); Shiah; Shiites

石 [shí]
名 ①stone; rock; pebble ②stone inscription ③stone needle used in ancient times to cure diseases ⇒dàn

石板 ①slabstone; flagstone; flag ②slate (for writing on)

石版 stone plate

石碑 stone tablet; stele

石笔 slate pencil

石壁 cliff; precipice

石材 stone used in construction and masonry

石担 stone barbell

石堤 stone embankment (*or* dyke)

石雕 ①stone carving ②carved stone

石碓 a treadle-operated tilt hammer for hulling rice

石墩 a block of stone used as a seat

石方 cubic metre of stonework

石坊 stone memorial archway (*or* gateway)

石膏 ①gypsum; plaster stone ②(for a broken bone) plaster cast; cast

石工 ①masonry ②stonemason; mason

石棺 sarcophagus

石河 stone river; rock stream

石斛 ①noble dendrobium ②the stem of noble dendrobium

石化 petrochemistry

石灰 lime

石鸡 chukar (a partridge)

石级 a flight of stone steps

石匠 stonemason; mason

石经 inscriptions of classics (*or* scriptures) on stone

石刻 ①carved stone ②stone inscription

石窟 rock cave; grotto

石块 stone block; rock

石蜡 paraffin wax

石栗 candlenut tree

石料 stone as material

石林 stone forest

石榴 pomegranate

石绿 malachite green

石煤 bone coal

石棉 asbestos

石磨 millstones

石墨 graphite

石楠 Chinese photinia

石弩 onager; catapult

石女 a woman with a hypoplastic vagina

石器 ①stone implement; stone artifact ②stone vessel; stoneware

石墙 stone wall

石桥 stone bridge

石青 azurite blue

石蕊 ①reindeer moss ②litmus

石笋 stalagmite

石锁 a stone dumbbell in the form of an old-fashioned padlock

石炭 coal

石头 stone; rock

石像 figure in stone

石印 lithographic printing; lithography

石英 quartz

石油 petroleum; oil

石竹 China pink (Dianthus chinensis)

石柱 stone pillar

石作 masonry

石斑鱼 grouper (a fish)

石菖蒲 grass-leaved sweetflag

石刁柏 asparagus

石膏床 plaster bed

石膏像 plaster statue; plaster figure

石拱桥 stone arch bridge

石花菜 agar (a seaweed)

石花胶 agar-agar

石灰华 travertine; tufa

石灰浆 lime white

石灰石 limestone

石灰水 limewash

石灰岩 limestone

石灰窑 limekiln

石灰质 calcareous

石决明 the shell of abalone or sea-ear

石窟寺 cave temple

石砬子 crag; boulder; projecting rock

石榴红 garnet (colour)

石榴裙 ①garnet-red skirt ②feminine charms

石榴石 garnet

石龙子 skink

石棉板 asbestos board

石棉布 asbestos cloth

石棉瓦 asbestos shingle; asbestos tile

石棉纸 asbestos paper

石漠化 stony desertification

石脑油 naphtha

石牌坊 dolmen

石首鱼 sciaenoid; sciaenid

石炭纪 the Carboniferous Period

石炭酸 carbolic acid

石炭系 the Carboniferous System

石印机 lithographic press
石印石 lithographic stone
石印纸 lithographic paper
石英岩 quartzite
石英钟 quartz clock
石油气 petroleum gas
石钟乳 stalactite
石子儿 cobblestone；cobble；pebble
石沉大海 like a stone dropped into the sea—disappear for ever；never to be seen or heard of again
石膏绷带 plaster bandage
石膏夹板 plaster splint
石化作用 petrifaction
石灰砂浆 lime mortar
石硫合剂 lime sulfur
石棉衬里 asbestos lining
石墨铀堆 graphite-uranium pile
石墨炸弹 graphite bomb
石破惊天 heaven-shaking—（of a message, opinion，etc.）remarkably original and forceful
石器时代 the Stone Age
石人石马 stone figures and horses in front of a grave
石蕊试纸 litmus paper
石头子儿 cobblestone；cobble；pebble
石印油画 oleograph
石英玻璃 quartz glass
石油工业 oil industry；petroleum industry
石油管路 petroleum pipeline
石油化学 petrochemistry
石油勘探 petroleum prospecting
石油沥青 petroleum pitch
石油美元 petrodollars
石油运移 oil migration
石灰质砂岩 calcareous sandstone
石英电子表 quartz watch
石英凹钨灯 quartz tungsten halogen lamp
石油地质学 petroleum geology
石油化工厂 petrochemical works
石油输出国组织 the Organization of Petroleum Exporting Countries（OPEC）

时 ［shí］
Ⅰ 名 ① time；times；days ② fixed time ③ season ④ fashion ⑤ one of the 12 periods into which the day was divided in ancient times ⑥ hour ⑦ opportune moment；opportunity；chance ⑧ tense Ⅱ 形 current；present Ⅲ 副 ① occasionally；now and then；from time to time ②（used in pairs）now... now... ；sometimes... sometimes...
时弊 ills of the times
时标 ①time scale ②time mark；clock
时病 ①ills of the times ②seasonal disease
时差 ① differences of local time between places belonging to different time zones ②

equation of time
时常 often；frequently
时辰 ① one of the 12 two-hour periods into which the day was formerly divided before the introduction of western chronology ② the time for sth；opportunity
时代 ① times；age；era；epoch ② a period in one's life
时调 popular song；popular music
时段 time interval
时而 ① from time to time；sometimes ②（used reduplicatively）now... now... ；sometimes... sometimes...
时分 the time of；the time when
时光 ①time ②times；years；days
时候 ①（the duration of）time ②（a point in）time；moment
时货 goods of the season
时机 opportunity；an opportune moment
时计 chronometer
时价 current price；prevailing price；running prices
时间 ①（the concept of）time ②（the duration of）time ③（a point in）time
时角 hour angle
时节 ① season（marked by certain weather conditions，activities，etc.）② a particular time；occasion
时局 the current political situation
时刻 ①a point of time；hour；moment ②constantly；always
时控 time control
时令 season
时髦 fashionable；stylish；in vogue
时评 news commentary；editorial
时期 a particular period
时区 time zone
时日 time
时尚 craze；fashion；fad
时时 often；constantly
时世 times；age
时事 current events；current affairs
时势 the current situation；the trend of the times；the way things are going
时蔬 vegetables in season
时速 speed per hour
时态 tense
时务 current affairs；current situation；trend of the times
时下 at present；right now
时鲜 （of vegetables, fruits, fishes，etc.）in season
时限 time limit
时象 current social phenomena
时效 ① effectiveness for a given period of time ②prescription ③ageing
时新 stylish；trendy

时兴 fashionable;in vogue;popular
时宜 what is appropriate to the occasion
时疫 epidemic
时运 luck;fortune
时针 ①hands of a clock or watch ②hour hand (of a clock or watch)
时政 the political situation of the time
时值 duration;value
时钟 clock
时装 ①fashionable dress;the latest fashion ②contemporary costume
时不时 often;time and again
时代感 period feel;sense of contemporaneity
时代性 epochal character
时间表 timetable;schedule
时间差 time difference
时间词 time word
时间性 seasonality;timeliness;topicality
时刻表 timetable;schedule
时空观 notion (*or* conception) of time and space
时令病 seasonal disease
时尚迷 fashionista
时装店 fashion house
时不可失 Don't let slip an opportunity.
时不我待 Time and tide wait for no man.
时差反应 jet lag;jet fatigue
时代特征 features of the times
时断时续 on and off
时乖命蹇 be born under an evil star;have the hand of fate against one;fall on bad times
时过境迁 Things have changed with the lapse of time.
时间控制 time control;duration control
时间知觉 time perception
时间滞后 time lag
时快时慢 sometimes fast,sometimes slow
时来运转 one's luck turns in the fullness of time
时令不正 unseasonable weather
时令食品 seasonal food
时髦股票 glamour stock
时起时伏 now rise, now fall; have ups and downs;rise and fall at different times;have frequent ups and downs
时喜时忧 one's moods alternate between happiness and gloom
时效硬化 age-hardening
时效终止 lapse of time
时移俗易 customs change with the times
时运不济 have bad luck; have spell of bad luck;be down on one's luck
时运亨通 be quite fortunate
时至今日 at this late hour;even to this day
时装表演 fashion show;modelling
时装模特 fashion model;manikin
时穷节乃见 Integrity (*or* loyalty) shines out

in time of woe.
时势造英雄 The times produce their heroes.
时装博览会 fashion fair
时装模特儿 fashion model
时装设计师 fashion designer

识 [shí]
I 动 know II 名 knowledge;learning
识别 distinguish;discern;spot
识货 know all about the goods;be able to tell good from bad;know what's what
识记 memorize;memorization
识破 see through;penetrate
识趣 know how to behave in a delicate situation;be sensible;be tactful
识相 be sensible;be tactful
识羞 have a sense of shame
识字 learn to read;become literate
识别力 discernment
识字班 literacy class
识穷天下 (possess) infinite wisdom and intelligence
识事明理 show good sense
识途老马 an old horse who knows the way—a person of rich experience;a wise old bird
识文断字 be able to read;be literate
识字课本 reading primer;elementary reader
识大体,顾大局 have the cardinal principles in mind and take the overall situation into account; keep the whole situation in mind; have the fundamental principles and overall situation in mind
识时务者为俊杰 Whosoever understands the times is a great man;A wise man submits to circumstances.

实 [shí]
I 形 ①solid;full ②real;true;actual;sincere II 名 ①reality;actuality;fact ②fruit;seed
实诚 honest;trustworthy
实词 notional word;full word
实弹 ①(of a gun or cannon) be loaded ②live shell;live ammunition
实地 on the spot
实干 get right on the job;do solid work
实感 thoughts and feelings acquired from personal experience;true feelings
实话 truth
实惠 ①material benefit ②substantial;solid
实绩 actual results;tangible achievements
实际 ① reality;practice ② practical;realistic ③real;actual;concrete
实价 actual price
实践 ① practice ② put into practice;carry out;live up to
实景 actual setting;location (movies)
实据 substantial evidence;substantial proof
实况 what is actually happening

实力 actual strength;strength
实例 living example;example
实录 a faithful record
实脉 forceful pulse
实盘 firm offer
实情 the true state of affairs; the actual situation;truth
实权 real power
实施 put into effect;implement;carry out
实时 real-time
实事 practical things
实数 ①the actual amount ②real number
实说 to tell the truth;frankly speaking;frankly
实体 ①substance ②entity
实物 ①material object;object ②goods instead of money
实习 (of students or trainees) practise (what has been learnt in class); exercise one's skill in;do fieldwork
实现 realize;fulfil;carry out;bring about
实像 real image
实效 actual effect;substantial results
实心 ①sincere;honest ②solid
实行 put into practice (or effect);carry out; practise;implement
实学 real learning;sound scholarship
实言 truth
实验 experiment;test
实业 industry and commerce;a large-scale industry or business
实用 practical;pragmatic;functional
实在 [shízài] ①true;real;honest;dependable ②indeed;really;honestly ③in fact;as a matter of fact
实在 [shízai] (of work) well-done; done carefully
实则 actually;in fact;in reality
实战 actual combat
实证 authentic proof;substantial evidence
实症 a case of a physically strong patient running a high fever or suffering from such disorders as stasis of blood,constipation, etc.
实质 substance;essence
实字 full word;content word
实足 full;solid
实打实 hundred percent true; genuine; most assuredly;real;honest
实干家 man of action;one who is conscientious and down-to-earth;mover and shaker
实际价 real price
实践性 practicality
实力派 those who actually hold power
实名制 real name system for personal bank account
实权派 people who have real power

实生苗 seedling
实体法 substantive law
实物税 tax paid in kind
实习生 trainee
实心球 solid ball;medicine ball
实性人 an honest and sincere person
实验室 laboratory
实验田 experimental plot
实验员 laboratory technician
实验组 experimental group
实业家 industrialist
实用文 practical writing (as in official documents,notices,receipts,etc.)
实在论 realism
实质性 substantive;substantial
实报实销 reimburse the amount actually spent;be reimbursed for what one spends
实逼处此 be forced to do so by the circumstances;There's no alternative under the circumstances.
实不相瞒 tell you honestly;be candid with you
实地考察 field trip
实繁有徒 There is no lack of people of that ilk.
实干精神 down-to-earth
实话实说 not mince words;speak frankly;tell truth
实际工资 real wages
实际汇价 effective exchange rate
实际行动 practical action
实际增长 growth in real terms
实况广播 mike-racket
实况录音 on-the-spot recording;live recording
实况演出 an in-person performance
实况转播 televise live;live broadcast;live telecast
实力地位 position of strength
实力雄厚 fully reinforced
实力政策 policy of force;Realpolitik
实盘交易 firm bargain
实情实理 the actual situation and the real reason
实时操作 real-time operation
实时处理 real-time processing
实事求是 seek truth from facts; be practical and realistic
实体经济 the real economy
实物地租 rent in kind
实物工资 natural wages;wages in kind
实物交易 barter
实习工厂 a factory for training students in practical skills
实习教师 student teacher;trainee teacher
实习医生 intern
实心实意 honest and sincere
实心眼儿 ①honest and serious-minded ②an honest and serious-minded person

S

实验动物 animal used as a subject of experiment;experimental farm
实业银行 industrial bank
实用美术 applied fine arts
实用主义 pragmatism
实战演习 combat exercise with live ammunition
实证主义 positivism
实至名归 Fame follows merit.
实质外交 substantial diplomacy
实足年龄 exact age (i.e. age in completed years)
实际控制线 line of actual control
实践出真知 Genuine knowledge comes from practice.
实况转播车 outside broadcasting van
实时控制器 real-time controller
实物幻灯机 epidiascope
实验心理学 experimental psychology
实验性工厂 pilot plant
实用新技术 applied new technology
实弹军事演习 live-fire military exercises;military exercises with ammunition; military exercises using live fire
实际利用外资 foreign investment actually used
实验通信卫星 experimental communications satellite

拾 [shí]
动 ①pick up (from the ground);gather; collect ②put in order;clean;tidy up
拾掇 ①tidy up;put in order ②repair;fix ③settle with;punish
拾荒 glean and collect scraps (to eke out an existence)
拾零 news in brief;sidelights
拾取 pick up;collect
拾趣 collect interesting bits and pieces
拾声 pickup
拾物 a lost article found
拾遗 ①appropriate lost property ②make good omissions
拾波器 adapter
拾声器 (acoustical) pickup
拾音器 pickup;adapter
拾金不昧 not pocket the money one picks up
拾人牙慧 pick up phrases from sb and pass them off as one's own;steal others' ideas
拾遗补阙 make good omissions and deficiencies
拾物招领处 Lost and Found (Bureau);Lost-property Office

食 [shí]
I 动 ①eat ②have one's meal ③live on
II 名 ①food;meal ②feed ③edible;seasoning ④eclipse ➡ sì
食补 better health through good eating

食道 esophagus
食饵 (fish) bait
食分 magnitude of eclipse
食粪 coprophagy
食管 esophagus
食积 dyspepsia;indigestion
食既 the second contact of a total eclipse;the beginning of totality
食街 food street
食具 eating utensils;tableware
食客 ①a person sponging on an aristocrat;a hanger-on of an aristocrat ②a customer of a restaurant
食口 (of a family) number of people to provide for
食粮 grain;food
食量 capacity for eating;appetite
食疗 food therapy;diet therapy
食糜 chyme (the pulp to which the food is reduced in the stomach)
食品 foodstuff;food;provisions
食谱 cookbook;recipes
食甚 the maximum phase of an eclipse; the middle phase of an eclipse
食宿 board and lodging
食堂 dining room;mess hall;canteen
食糖 sugar
食物 food;eatables;edibles
食相 the phases of an eclipse
食性 feeding habits;eating patterns
食言 go back on one's word; break one's promise
食盐 table salt;salt
食用 ①used for food ②edible
食油 edible oil;cooking oil
食欲 appetite
食指 index finger;forefinger
食变星 eclipsing variable
食管癌 cancer of the esophagus
食管炎 esophagitis
食火鸡 cassowary
食品部 food department
食品厂 bakery and confectionery; food products factory
食品袋 plastic bag for storing food;doggy bag
食品街 food bazaar;restaurant row
食人俗 cannibalism
食蚊鱼 mosquito fish
食物链 food chain
食蚁兽 anteater
食茱萸 ailanthus prickly ash
食不甘味 eat without relish
食不果腹 have not enough food in one's belly; go hungry
食草动物 herbivorous animal;herbivore
食虫动物 insectivorous animal;insectivore
食虫植物 insectivorous plant;insectivore

食而不化 eat without digesting—read without understanding
食粪动物 coprophagous animal
食腐动物 saprophagous animal；scavenger
食古不化 swallow ancient learning without digesting it
食品安全 food safety
食品保藏 food preservation
食品工业 food industry
食品公司 food company
食品加工 food processing
食品结构 composition of diet
食品色素 food colouring
食品商店 provisions shop
食肉动物 carnivorous animal；carnivore
食肉寝皮 （want to）eat sb's flesh and sleep on his skin—（want to）see the person one hates destroyed
食肉植物 carnivorous plant；insectivorous plant；insectivore
食色性也 Appetite for food and sex is nature.
食少事烦 eat too little and does too much—cannot last long
食物摄入 food intake
食物污染 food pollution
食物中毒 food poisoning；food-borne intoxication
食血动物 sanguinorous animal
食言而肥 fail to make good one's promise；break faith with sb
食用期限 use-by date
食用色素 food colouring
食欲不振 ①have a jaded appetite；have a poor appetite ②anorexia
食租衣税 （of officials）live on taxes and levies
食品防腐剂 food antiseptic
食品添加剂 food additive
食用碘化盐 consume iodized salt
食而不知其味 eat without knowing the taste of what one is eating—read without understanding
食品质量管理 quality control of food
食不厌精，脍不厌细 eat no rice but is of the finest quality，nor meat but is finely minced—be very particular about one's food
食之无味，弃之可惜 hardly worth eating but not bad enough to throw away

蚀 ［shí］
　勋 ①erode；corrode ②lose
蚀本 lose one's capital
蚀财 lose money（*or* property）
蚀耗 loss；wear and tear
蚀刻 etching
蚀损 deteriorate；lose in value
蚀刻机 etching machine
蚀本生意 a business running at a loss；a losing

proposition；an unprofitable venture（*or* undertaking）

shǐ（ㄕ）

史 ［shǐ］
　名 ①history ②official in charge of historical records；official
史册 history；annals
史抄 extracts from history
史纲 survey
史官 official historian in ancient China；historiographer
史话 stories about historical events
史籍 history；historical records
史记 Records of the Historian
史迹 historical site or relics
史料 historical data；historical materials
史略 outline history；a brief history
史评 commentary on historical events（*or* historical records）
史前 prehistoric
史诗 epic
史实 historical facts
史书 history；historical records
史学 the science of history；historical science；historiography
史前学 prehistory
史实剧 documentary drama
史学家 historian；historiographer
史不绝书 History is full of such instances.
史无前例 without precedent in history；unprecedented
史前考古学 prehistoric archaeology

矢 ［shǐ］
　Ⅰ 名 ① arrow ② excrement；faeces　Ⅱ 勋 take an oath；vow；swear
矢量 vector
矢石 arrows and stones（ancient weapons）
矢志 pledge one's devotion（to a cause）
矢忠 vow one's allegiance
矢车菊 cornflower
矢量图 vectogram；vector diagram
矢口否认 flatly deny；deny stone and bone
矢口狡赖 quibble and prevaricate，refusing to admit one's guilt；persistently quibble and deny one's errors
矢量字库 vector font
矢死不二 pledge unswerving allegiance（*or* faith）unto death
矢志不渝 vow to adhere to one's chosen course

豕 ［shǐ］
　名 pig；hog；swine

使 ［shǐ］
　Ⅰ 勋 ① send；have（sb do sth）② make；cause；help；enable ③ use；employ；exert；apply　Ⅱ 连 if；supposing　Ⅲ 名 envoy；emissary；mes-

senger
使出 use;exert
使得 ①can be used;be usable ②be workable;
　　be feasible ③make;cause;render
使馆 diplomatic mission;embassy
使坏 be up to mischief;play a dirty trick
使唤 ①order about ②use;handle
使节 diplomatic envoy;envoy
使劲 exert all one's strength
使力 exert all one's strength
使命 mission
使女 maidservant; housemaid; chambermaid;
　　maid
使气 lose one's temper;get angry
使钱 spend money;use money
使徒 apostle
使团 diplomatic mission;diplomatic corps
使役 work (an animal)
使用 use;employ;apply
使者 emissary;envoy;messenger
使绊儿 ①trip sb up in wrestling ②injure sb
　　by underhand methods
使不得 ①cannot be used; be useless; be un-
　　serviceable ②be impermissible;be undesir-
　　able
使不惯 be not used to using
使不了 cannot use;be unable to use
使绝招 play one's best (or trump) card
使君子 the fruit of Rangoon creeper
使领馆 diplomatic and consular missions;em-
　　bassies and consulates
使性子 get angry;lose one's temper
使眼色 tip sb the wink;wink
使用额 the amount of disbursement
使用率 rate of utilization
使用权 right of use;right to use a thing
使用税 use tax
使用价值 use value
使用面积 usable floor area
使用手册 instruction manual
使用寿命 service life (of machines,etc.)
使用说明书 operation instructions; user's
　　manual
使出浑身解数 use all one's skill; do all that
　　one is capable of

始 ［shǐ］
Ⅰ 动 begin; commence; start Ⅱ 副 only
then;not... until
始创 initiate;originate
始而 at first;originally;at the start
始料 originally expected
始末 beginning and end—the whole story
始业 the beginning of the school year
始终 from beginning to end;from start to fin-
　　ish;all along;throughout
始祖 first ancestor;earliest ancestor
始发站 starting station;station of departure

始祖鸟 palaeontology archaeopteryx
始料不及 come as a surprise;be unexpected
始乱终弃 (of a man) seduce and then abandon
始终不懈 unremitting;untiring
始终不渝 unswerving;consistent;steadfast
始终如一 constant;consistent
始作俑者 the man who first made tomb fig-
　　ures—the creator of a bad precedent

驶 ［shǐ］
动 ①go quickly;pass quickly;speed ②sail;
drive;ride
驶离 bear off
驶向 bear in with

屎 ［shǐ］
名 ①excrement;faeces;dung;stool ② secretion (of the eye,ear,etc.)
屎尿 stool and urine
屎壳郎 dung beetle

shì（ㄕ）

士 ［shì］
名 ① bachelor ② social stratum between
senior officials and the common people in
ancient China ③ scholar; intelligentsia ④
(praiseworthy) person ⑤person trained in a
specified field ⑥ soldier; armyman; serviceman ⑦ noncommissioned officer ⑧ bodyguard,one of the pieces in Chinese chess
士兵 rank-and-file soldiers;privates
士官 non-commissioned officer
士女 young men and women
士气 morale
士绅 gentry
士卒 soldiers;privates
士大夫 scholar-officials (in imperial times)
士农工商 scholars,farmers,artisans and mer-
　　chants
士为知己者用,女为悦己者容 A gentleman acts
　　on behalf of an understanding friend, as a
　　woman makes herself beautiful for her lov-
　　er.

氏 ［shì］
名 ①family name;surname ②née ③(used
after famous persons such as scientists,
inventors,etc.)：陈氏定理 Chen Jingrun's
theorem ④one's kinsfolk
氏族 clan
氏族公社 clan commune
氏族社会 clan society

示 ［shì］
动 show;indicate;produce;notify;instruct
示范 set an example;demonstrate
示教 teach
示警 give a warning;warn
示例 give typical examples;give a demonstration
示人 show sth to others;let others have a look

at sth
示弱 give the impression of weakness; take sth lying down
示威 ①demonstrate; hold a demonstration ②put on a show of force; display one's strength
示意 signal; hint; motion
示众 publicly expose; put before the public
示波管 oscilloscope tube
示波器 oscillograph; oscilloscope
示分牌 flash card
示功器 indicator
示功图 indicator card; indicator diagram
示意图 ① sketch map ② schematic diagram; schematic drawing
示踪物 tracer
示威游行 demonstration; parade; march
示踪测定 tracer determination
示踪元素 tracer element
示踪原子 labelled atom; tagged atom; tracer

世 ［shì］
　图 ①generation ②from generation to generation ③form of address among people who maintain good family relations ④lifetime; life ⑤age; era; time ⑥world; society ⑦epoch
世伯 older friend of one's father
世仇 ①family feud ②ancient enemy
世传 be handed down through generations
世代 ① years; ages ② for generations; from generation to generation; generation after generation
世道 the manners and morals of the time
世弟 son of father's friend, younger than oneself
世风 public morals
世故 ［shìgù］ the ways of the world
世故 ［shìgu］ worldly-wise
世纪 century
世家 an old and well-known family; an aristocratic family
世间 ①in this world ②in society
世交 ①friendship spanning two or more generations ②old family friends; long-standing friendship between two families
世界 ①world ②the universe ③field; sphere; domain; realm
世局 the world situation
世面 various aspects of society; society; world; life
世情 worldly affairs; social trends
世人 common people
世上 in the world; on earth
世事 affairs of human life
世叔 younger friend of one's father
世俗 ①common customs ②secular; worldly
世态 the ways of the world
世途 experiences in life

世务 current affairs; the trend of the times
世袭 hereditary
世系 pedigree; genealogy
世象 variety of life
世兄 ①man who is a friend of the family or clan ②son of one's friend or teacher
世谊 friendship spanning generations
世纪末 end of the century; fin-de-siècle
世界波 goal of world class
世界观 world outlook
世界时 universal time
世界语 Esperanto; world language
世乒赛 World Table Tennis Championship
世代交替 alternation of generations
世代相传 pass on from generation to generation
世道人心 the ways of the world and public sentiment
世风日下 The world is going to the dogs.
世界大同 one world on equal basis; cosmopolitan; the world commonwealth
世界大战 world war
世界纪录 world record
世界末日 doomsday of the world; end of the world; the end of time on earth; Day of Last Judgment
世界音乐 world music
世界银行 World Bank
世界主义 cosmopolitanism
世世代代 age after age; for generations
世态炎凉 warmth or coldness is the way of the world—people are friendly or unfriendly, depending on whether one is successful or not
世外桃源 the Land of Peach Blossoms—a fictitious land of peace, away from the turmoil of the world; a haven of peace
世袭制度 hereditary system
世界博览会 World EXPO; World Exposition; World's Fair
世界多极化 global multi-polarization
世界无烟日 World No-Tobacco Day
世界华商大会 World Chinese Entrepreneurs Convention
世界科技前沿 fields on the cutting edge of science and technology in the world; world frontier sciences and technologies
世界贸易组织 World Trade Organization (WTO)
世界人权大会 the World Conference on Human Rights
世界人权法官 global (or world) judge of human rights
世界人权宣言 Universal Declaration of Human Rights (Dec. 10, 1948)
世界文学名著 classics of world literature
世界贸易自由化 liberalization of world trade

S

世界知识产权组织 the World Intellectual Property Organization（WIPO）
世界贸易组织总干事 Director-General of the World Trade Organization
世界人口与发展大会 the International Conference on Population and Development
世上无难事,只怕有心人 Nothing in the world is difficult for one who sets his mind on it.
世有伯乐,然后有千里马 A talented man will remain obscure unless somebody appreciates his talent and is in a position to help him.
世界贸易乌拉圭回合谈判 the Uruguay Round of world trade talks
世界贸易组织部长级会议 the ministerial conference of the World Trade Organization
世事洞明皆学问,人情练达即文章 A grasp of mundane affairs is genuine knowledge, and understanding of worldly wisdom is true learning.

仕 [shì]
Ⅰ 动 hold an official post; be an official Ⅱ 名 bodyguard, one of the pieces in Chinese chess
仕宦 be an official; be in government service
仕进 pursue an official career
仕路 official career
仕女 ① maid in an imperial palace; maid of honour ② painting traditional Chinese painting of beautiful women
仕途 official career
仕宦子弟 sons（or children）of officials

市 [shì]
Ⅰ 名 ① market ② business transaction ③ city; municipality ④ administrative units ⑤ pertaining to the Chinese system of weights and measures Ⅱ 动 buy; sell; deal in
市场 marketplace; market; bazaar
市秤 the traditional Chinese scale of weights
市府 the municipal government
市花 city flower
市话 local telephone call
市集 ①fair ②small town
市价 current price; market price; ruling price
市郊 suburb; outskirts
市井 marketplace; town
市侩 sordid merchant
市立 municipal
市面 market conditions; the state of trade; business situation
市民 city residents; townspeople; urban inhabitants
市内 city; urban
市情 ①special characteristics of a city ②market conditions
市区 city proper; urban district
市容 the appearance of a city

市售 available on the market
市委 municipal Party committee
市长 mayor
市镇 small towns; towns
市政 municipal administration
市值 market capitalization
市制 the traditional Chinese system of weights and measures
市属 directly under the jurisdiction of a municipal government
市盈率 price-earnings ratio
市政府 the municipal government
市政厅 town hall; guildhall
市中心 city centre; downtown area
市场饱和 market saturation; saturated market
市场导向 market orientation; market guide
市场调查 market survey; market research
市场调研 market survey
市场繁荣 the market is brisk
市场份额 market share
市场规则 market mechanism
市场行情 market quotation
市场机制 market mechanism
市场价格 market price
市场价值 market value
市场经济 market economy; commodity economy; exchange economy
市场竞争 market competition
市场疲软 weak market; sluggish market
市场取向 market orientation
市场容量 capacity of the market; market absorption capacity
市场渗透 market penetration
市场失效 market failure
市场调节 market regulation; regulation through market; regulation by market forces
市场信息 market information
市场需求 market requirement
市场业务 marketing functions
市场意识 market sense; market sensibility
市场预测 market forecasting
市场准入 market access; market entry
市井小人 philistine
市井之徒 philistine
市内电话 local telephone service; local（phone）call
市政工程 municipal works; municipal engineering
市政建设 municipal construction
市场多元化 multi-outlet market
市场透明度 market transparency
市场占有率 market share
市场杠杆作用 lever action of the market
市场供求关系 supply and demand
市场价格体制 market pricing system
市场价格调节 regulation by market price

市场竞争主体 market competitor; principal in market competition
市场信息调研 market information research
市场中介组织 intermediary market organization
市内公共汽车 intracity buses; incity buses
市场多元化战略 market diversification strategy

式 [shì]
〔名〕① type; style; fashion ② pattern; form; model ③ ceremony; celebration; ritual ④ formula ⑤ mood; mode
式样 style; type; model
式子 ① posture ② formula

似 [shì]
➡ sì
似的 be like; as... as...; as if

事 [shì]
Ⅰ〔名〕① matter; affair; thing; business ② trouble; difficulty; accident ③ job; task; work ④ responsibility; involvement Ⅱ〔动〕① attend upon; wait upon; serve ② go in for; be engaged in
事变 ① incident ② emergency; exigency ③ the course of events; events
事典 encyclopedia
事端 disturbance; incident
事功 achievement
事故 accident; mishap
事后 after the event; afterwards
事机 ① affairs that should be kept secret ② situation
事迹 deed; achievement
事假 leave of absence (to attend to private affairs); compassionate leave
事件 incident; event
事理 reason; logic
事例 example; instance
事略 biographical sketch; short biographical account
事前 before the event; in advance; beforehand
事情 affair; matter; thing; business
事实 fact
事事 ① everything ② be engaged in some work or business
事态 scenario; state of affairs; state of things; goings-on; conjunction
事体 matter; affair
事务 ① work; routine ② general affairs
事物 thing; object
事先 in advance; beforehand; prior
事项 item; matter
事业 ① cause; undertaking; career ② institution; facilities
事宜 matters concerned; arrangements
事由 ① the origin of an incident; particulars of a matter ② main content ③ job; work

事主 the victim of a crime
事实上 in fact; in reality; as a matter of fact; actually
事务所 office
事务员 office clerk
事业家 entrepreneur
事业心 dedication to one's work; devotion to one's work
事半功倍 get twice the result with half the effort
事倍功半 get half the result with twice the effort
事必躬亲 see (or attend) to everything oneself; take care of every single thing personally
事不宜迟 We must lose no time in doing it; We must attend to the matter immediately; This matter needs immediate attention.
事出有因 There is good reason for it; It is by no means accidental.
事到临头 when things come to a head; when the situation becomes critical; at the last moment
事关人命 A man's life is involved.
事过境迁 The affair is over and the situation has changed; The incident is over and the circumstances are different.
事后聪明 afterwit; hindsight; wise after the event
事后认可 after-the-fact approval
事实真相 truth of the matter; what's what; true state of affairs
事属两难 It is difficult either way; We are caught in a dilemma.
事无巨细 (take part in) all kinds of work, no matter how big or trivial; all matters, big and small; all matters, whether important or trivial
事务主义 routinism
事先声明 advance directive
事业单位 public institutions
事有凑巧 as luck would have it
事有蹊跷 sense sth fishy; smell a rat
事与愿违 Things turn out contrary to one's wishes.
事在人为 It all depends on human effort; Human effort is the decisive factor.
事故报告书 accidental report
事后诸葛亮 be a Zhuge Liang only after something unpleasant has happened—be wise after the event
事务主义者 pettifogger
事故多发地段 black spot; accident-prone area
事实胜于雄辩 facts are stronger than rhetoric; facts speak louder than words
事非经过不知难 You never know how hard a task is until you have done it yourself.

S

事无不可对人言 There is nothing we should hold back from others.

事物的正面和反面 obverse and reverse sides of a thing; both sides of a thing

事不关己,高高挂起 let things drift if they do not affect one personally; stand aloof from things on the ground that they are no concern of one's

势 [shì]

〔名〕① power; force; strength; influence ② tendency; momentum ③ outward appearance (of a natural object or phenomenon) ④ situation; state of affairs; circumstances; tendency ⑤sign; gesture ⑥male genitals

势必 certainly will; be bound to

势差 potential difference

势力 force; power; influence

势利 snobbish

势能 potential energy

势态 situation; state

势头 ① impetus; momentum ② tendency; the look of things

势焰 influence and power

势利眼 snobbish attitude; snobbishness; snob

势不可挡 irresistible

势不两立 be mutually exclusive; be extremely antagonistic; be irreconcilable

势成骑虎 like riding a tiger—a situation from which it is hard to extricate oneself

势均力敌 match each other in strength

势力范围 sphere of influence

势难从命 Circumstances make it difficult for me to comply with your request.

势如累卵 be in a very perilous position; hazardous like a pile of eggs

势如破竹 like splitting a bamboo; like a hot knife cutting through butter; with irresistible force

势所必然 inevitably; as a matter of course

势在必行 be imperative (under the circumstances)

侍 [shì]

〔动〕wait upon; attend on; serve

侍从 attendants; retinue

侍奉 support and wait upon (one's elders)

侍候 wait upon; look after; attend

侍立 be in attendance

侍弄 ① tend with care (crops, domestic animals, etc.) ②repair; fix

侍女 maidservant; maid

侍卫 ①guard ②imperial bodyguard

侍养 support and wait upon (one's elders)

侍者 attendant; servant; waiter

侍应生 a young attendant; odd-jobber (in banks, etc.)

侍茶侍水 serve tea and drink

侍从副官 aide-de-camp (A. D. C.); aide

饰 [shì]

Ⅰ〔动〕① adorn; dress up; polish ② hide ③ play the role of; act the part of (a dramatic character) Ⅱ〔名〕decoration; ornaments

饰材 decoration materials

饰词 excuse; pretext

饰品 ornaments; jewelry

饰物 ①articles for personal adornment; jewelry ②ornaments; decorations

饰演 play the role of; act the part of; play

试 [shì]

Ⅰ〔动〕try; attempt; test Ⅱ〔名〕examination; test

试办 run an enterprise, etc. as an experiment; run a pilot scheme

试笔 try one's hand at writing (or painting, calligraphy)

试表 take sb's temperature

试播 trial broadcast; trial telecast

试产 trial production; test run

试场 examination room

试唱 try out a song

试车 test run (of a machine, car, etc.); trial run

试穿 try on clothes; clothes fitting

试点 ①make (conduct) an experiment; make experiments; conduct tests at selected points; launch a pilot project ② a place where an experiment is made; experimental unit

试读 probationary study

试飞 test flight; trial flight

试岗 probation

试工 (of a worker or servant) be hired (or engaged) on a probational basis; be on probation

试管 test tube

试航 ① trial voyage or flight; shakedown cruise or flight; trial run ②shake down (a ship or an aeroplane)

试婚 trial marriage

试机 test-run a machine

试剂 reagent

试讲 give a trial lecture; dry run

试镜 screen test

试卷 examination paper; test paper

试刊 trial publication of a newspaper or periodical

试看 just see; try sth and see how it works

试射 fire for adjustment; trial fire; test-launch

试探 [shìtàn] probe (or explore) (a question)

试探 [shìtan] sound out; feel out

试题 examination questions; test questions

试图 attempt to (do sth); try to (do sth)

试问 we should like to ask; it may well be asked; may we ask

试想 just think
试销 ①place goods on trial sale ②trial sale
试行 try out
试演 ① trial performance; preview; trial run (of a play, etc.) ② give a trial performance; give a preview (of a play, etc.) have a trial run
试验 trial; experiment; test
试样 ① sample; specimen ② try on a partly finished garment ③try on
试映 preview (of a film)
试用 ①try out ②on probation
试纸 test paper
试制 trial-produce; trial-manufacture
试种 plant experimentally
试点班 experimental class (in a teaching experiment)
试电笔 test pencil
试金石 touch stone; lydian stone; litmus test
试试手 have a try at sth
试探性 trial; exploratory; probing
试验场 proving ground; testing ground
试验田 ① experimental plot; experimental field ②a trial undertaking
试营业 open on a trial basis; in trial operation (or service)
试用本 trial edition (an edition put out to solicit comments)
试用品 trial products
试用期 probation period; trial period
试运行 pilot run; test run
试运转 test run; running-in
试车投产 go into trial production
试管婴儿 test-tube baby
试选样品 pilot model
试验农场 experimental farm
试用人员 probational clerk
试探性攻击 probing attack
试探性气球 trial balloon
试探性谈判 exploratory talks
试验性工厂 pilot plant

视 [shì]

劢 ① look at; view ② regard; look upon; treat ③inspect; examine; watch
视差 parallax
视察 ①inspect ②watch; observe
视场 field of vision (or view)
视唱 sightsinging; sing from a musical score
视窗 Windows
视点 point of view; perspective
视感 visual sense; visibility
视角 angle of view; visual angle
视界 field of vision; visual field
视景 what comes into a driver's or a pilot's view as the vehicle or the craft proceeds; vista
视觉 visual sense; vision; sense of sight

视力 vision; sight
视盘 video disc
视频 video frequency
视事 (of officials) attend to business after assuming office; assume office
视听 seeing and hearing; what is seen and heard
视图 view
视线 line of vision; view; line of sight (in surveying)
视像 video
视学 educational inspector
视野 field of vision (or view)
视译 sight translation
视阈 visual threshold
视众 TV viewers
视察团 inspection team; inspectorate
视察员 inspector
视导员 inspector; supervisor
视地平 apparent horizon
视轨道 apparent orbit
视觉像 visual image
视力表 visual chart
视亮度 apparent brightness
视神经 optic nerve
视网膜 retina
视紫质 visual purple
视唱练耳 solfeggio
视而不见 look but see not; turn a blind eye to; close (or shut) one's eyes to
视觉污染 visual pollution
视觉印象 eye impressions; visual impressions
视觉暂留 persistence of vision
视频点播 video on demand
视频光盘 video compact disc(VCD)
视如敝屣 regard as worn-out shoes—cast aside as worthless
视如粪土 look upon as filth and dirt; consider as beneath contempt
视如寇仇 regard as an enemy
视若草芥 regard as worthless
视若无睹 take no notice of what one sees; shut one's eyes to; turn a blind eye to; ignore
视死如归 look upon death as going home; look death calmly in face; face death unflinchingly
视听教材 audio-visual materials; audio-visuals
视听教具 audio-visual aids
视听教学 audiovisual instruction
视同等闲 regard sb or sth as unimportant; treat lightly (or casually)
视同儿戏 treat (a serious matter) as a trifle; trifle with
视同路人 regard as a stranger; treat like a stranger
视网膜炎 retinitis
视为例外 make an exception of

视为畏途 regard as a dangerous road to take; be afraid to undertake

视网膜脱离 detachment of retina

视窗操作系统 Windows system; Windows software

视而不见,听而不闻 look but see not; listen but hear not; turn a blind eye to and a deaf ear to; take no notice of; pretend not to see or hear

贳 [shì]
〔动〕①hire; rent; let ②buy or sell on credit; give or get credit ③deal with leniently; remit (a punishment); pardon

贳酒 buy wine on credit

柿 [shì]
〔名〕persimmon

柿饼 dried persimmon

柿蒂 the calyx and receptacle of a persimmon

柿树 persimmon tree

柿霜 powder on the surface of a dried persimmon

柿子 persimmon

柿子椒 sweet pepper; bell pepper

拭 [shì]
〔动〕wipe away; wipe; remove

拭除 wipe (*or* brush) sth off

拭泪 wipe (away) one's tears

拭子 swab

拭镜纸 lens paper; lens tissue

拭目以待 wait and see; wait expectantly (for sth to happen)

是 [shì]
Ⅰ〔代〕this, that Ⅱ〔动〕①(*used like "be" before nouns or pronouns to identify, describe or amplify the subject*):《女神》的作者是郭沫若。*The Goddess*'s author is Guo Moruo. ②(*used to indicate the state or condition of the subject*):我是一片好心。I am of good intentions. ③(*used with* 的 *at the end of the sentence, to indicate category, characteristic, etc.*):这轿车是中国造的。This car was made in China. ④(*used after nouns denoting place or position to express existence*):房前是绿茵茵的草坪。There is a verdant lawn in front of the house. ⑤(*used in between two identical nouns or verbs in two or more similar patterns to indicate distinction*):你是你,我是我,我们谁也管不着谁。We have our own wills, you and I, neither is the other's master. /这个人言行不一,说是说,做是做。This man's deeds do not match his words; He never practises what he preaches. ⑥(*used to indicate concession*)even though:东西旧是旧,可还能用。Old as it is, it can still be used. ⑦(*used before a noun*)be just right:她来得正是时候。She's come just in the nick of time. ⑧(*used before a noun to indicate each and everyone of the kind*)all; everything; anything:是人都会犯错误。Every man is liable to error; No one is free from error. ⑨(*pronounced emphatically to indicate certainty*)really; truly:这件事他是不知道。He certainly doesn't know this. ⑩(*used before the subject for emphasis*):是谁告诉你的? Who told you? ⑪(*used in alternative, yes/no, or rhetorical questions*):你是看电视还是听音乐? Would you like to watch TV or listen to music? ⑫praise; justify; uphold Ⅲ〔形〕correct; right; true Ⅳ〔名〕(important) affairs Ⅴ〔叹〕yes; right

是的 yes; right; that's it

是凡 all; any; every

是非 ①right and wrong ②quarrel; dispute

是否 whether or not; whether; if

是荷 much obliged

是时 that time

是幸 much obliged

是个儿 equal; match

是味儿 ①(of food) have the right flavour; taste good ②(of a person) feel good

是样儿 look right; look good

是非得失 right and wrong, gain and loss

是非曲直 rights and wrongs; truth and falsehood

是非之地 a place where one is apt to get into trouble

是古非今 praise the past and condemn the present

是非自有公论 The public will judge the rights and wrongs of the case; Public opinion is the best judge.

是可忍,孰不可忍 If this can be tolerated, what else cannot?

适 [shì]
Ⅰ〔形〕①fit; suitable; appropriate; proper ②right; opportune ③comfortable; well; at ease Ⅱ〔动〕①go; follow; move towards ②(of a woman) get married; marry

适才 just now

适当 suitable; proper; appropriate

适度 appropriate measure; moderate degree

适合 suit; fit

适婚 of marriageable age

适间 just now; a moment ago

适口 agreeable to the taste; palatable

适量 an appropriate amount (*or* quantity)

适龄 of the right age

适时 at the right moment; in good time; timely

适销 salable

适宜 suitable; fit; appropriate; favourable

适应 suit; adapt to; adjust to; conform to

适用 be suitable; be applicable

适值 just when; as it happens

适中 ①moderate ②well situated

适耕地 arable land
适航性 airworthiness (of a plane); seaworthiness (of a ship)
适应性 adaptability
适应症 indication
适用性 applicability
适得其反 run counter to one's desire; be just the opposite to what one wished
适可而止 stop before going too far; know when or where to stop; not overdo it
适龄儿童 children of school age
适销对路 salable and in good demand; marketable
适者生存 natural selection; survival of the fittest
适当发展速度 moderate rate of growth
适度消费政策 policy of proper consumption
适度从紧的财政政策 moderately tight financial policy

恃 [shì]
I 动 rely on; depend on; count on II 名 mother
恃才傲物 be inordinately proud of one's ability; be conceited and contemptuous
恃强凌弱 use one's strength to bully the weak

室 [shì]
名 ①room ②administrative subdivision (of an agency, organization, institution, corporation, etc.); office ③shop (in a hotel, department store, etc.) ④wife ⑤family ⑥cavity
室内 indoor; interior
室女 unmarried girl; virgin
室外 outdoor; outside
室温 room temperature
室内剧 indoor drama; studio production
室内乐 chamber music
室女座 Virgo
室内环境 indoor environment
室内乐队 chamber orchestra
室内植物 house plant
室内装饰 interior decoration
室内运动场 xyst; xystus
室内空气污染 indoor air pollution
室内健身脚踏车 exercycle

莳 [shì]
动 ①transplant ②plant; cultivate
莳花 grow flowers
莳秧 transplant rice shoots

栻 [shì]
名 instrument for divination in ancient China

轼 [shì]
名 wooden handrail in the front of an ancient carriage

逝 [shì]
动 ①pass ②die; pass away
逝世 pass away; die

铈 [shì]
名 cerium (Ce)

舐 [shì]
动 lick
舐犊情深 the cow fondly licking her calf—parental love

弑 [shì]
动 murder (one's sovereign or parent)
弑父 murder one's own father
弑君 murder one's sovereign; commit regicide

释 [shì]
I 动 ①explain; expound; elucidate ②clear up; dispel; remove ③let go; be relieved of ④release; set free; put down II 名 Sakyamuni; Buddhism
释放 ①release; set free ②release
释怀 (usu. used in the negative) dispel from one's bosom; dismiss from one's mind
释卷 put a book aside; leave off reading
释门 Buddhism
释梦 dream interpretation
释然 feel relieved; feel at ease
释文 annotations
释疑 clear up (or remove) doubts; dispel suspicion
释义 explain the meaning (of a word, sentence, etc.)
释子 monk
释放令 order for discharge; order of acquittal
释迦牟尼 Sakyamuni, the founder of Buddhism

谥 [shì]
I 名 title given to an emperor, noble, minister, etc. after his death for his achievements II 动 call; name
谥号 posthumous title

嗜 [shì]
动 have a liking for; take to; be addicted to
嗜好 ①hobby ②addiction; habit
嗜睡 drowsiness; somnolence
嗜血 bloodthirsty; bloodsucking
嗜痂成癖 a depraved taste
嗜酒成性 be addicted to alcohol
嗜杀成性 bloodthirsty; sanguinary
嗜书成癖 be fond of reading to a fault

筮 [shì]
动 practise divination with alpine yarrow

誓 [shì]
I 动 take an oath; swear; vow; pledge II 名 solemn promise; oath; vow
誓词 oath; pledge
誓师 ①a rally to pledge resolution before going to war ②take a mass pledge
誓死 pledge one's life; dare to die
誓言 oath; pledge
誓愿 vow
誓约 vow; pledge; solemn promise
誓不罢休 swear not to stop; swear not to rest
誓不两立 swear not to coexist with sb; resolve

S

to destroy sb；be irreconcilable
誓死不二 pledge to be true to death
誓同生死 swear to share weal and woe with somebody

噬 ［shì］
　劲 bite
噬菌体 bacteriophage；phage
噬脐莫及 one cannot bite one's own navel—it is too late to repent

shì（·ㄕ）

匙 ［shi］
　⇒ chí
◇ 钥匙 key

shōu（ㄕㄡ）

收 ［shōu］
　劲 ①bring in；gather together；take in；put in proper place ②recover；retrieve ③collect (revenues)；charge (fees) ④reap；harvest；gather in ⑤receive；accept ⑥restrain；control ⑦arrest；take into custody；put in jail (or prison) ⑧bring to an end；stop
收编 incorporate into one's own forces
收兵 withdraw (or recall) troops；call off a battle
收藏 collect and store up
收操 bring drill to an end
收场 ①wind up；end up；stop ②end；ending；denouement
收车 return the vehicle to the garage，terminal，etc. and knock off
收成 harvest；crop
收存 receive and keep
收到 receive；get；achieve；obtain
收订 receive and process subscriptions
收发 ①receive and dispatch ②dispatcher
收方 debit side；debit
收费 collect fees；charge
收风 call prisoners in after letting them out for exercise
收服 subdue；reduce to submission
收抚 take in and console；take in and raise
收复 recover；recapture
收港 (of ships) return to harbour
收割 reap；harvest；gather in
收工 stop work for the day；knock off；pack up
收购 purchase；buy
收归 take back (rights，ownership，etc.)
收回 ①take back；call in；regain；recall；recover ②withdraw；countermand
收活 ①accept orders (for repairs or processing) ②stop work for the day；knock off；pack up
收获 ①gather (or bring) in the crops；harvest ②results；gains

收集 collect；gather
收监 take into custody；put in prison
收缴 take over；capture
收紧 tighten up
收进 incorporate；inning
收据 receipt
收看 watch (television)；look in
收口 ①(of a wound) close up；heal ②(in knitting) cast off；bind off
收揽 ①draw over to one's side ②keep in one's grasp
收礼 accept gifts
收敛 ①weaken；disappear ②restrain oneself ③convergence ④astringent
收镰 end the harvest season
收殓 lay a body in a coffin
收留 take sb in；have sb in one's care
收拢 ①draw sth in ②draw over to one's side
收录 ①employ；recruit；take on ②include ③listen in and take down；take down；record
收罗 collect；gather；enlist
收买 ①purchase；buy in ②buy over；bribe
收拿 put under arrest；arrest
收纳 receive；take in
收盘 closing；closing quotation (on the exchange，etc.)
收讫 ①payment received；paid ②(on a bill of lading，an invoice，etc.) all the above goods received；received in full
收起 pack up；cut out；stop
收清 received in full
收秋 gather in the autumn crops
收取 receive；collect
收权 retake the power
收容 take in；accept；house
收入 ① income；revenue；receipts；earnings；proceeds ②take in；include
收审 detain for interrogation
收生 midwifery
收尸 cremate the dead；bury the dead
收拾 ① put in order；tidy；clear away ② get things ready；pack ③repair；mend ④ settle with；punish
收市 (of markets or stores) close for the day
收受 receive；accept；take
收束 ① bring together；collect ② bring to a close ③pack (for a journey)
收缩 ① contract；shrink ② concentrate one's forces；draw back ③systole
收条 receipt
收听 listen (in)
收尾 ①bring to a conclusion；wind up ②ending (of an article，etc.)
收文 incoming dispatches
收效 yield results；produce effects；bear fruit
收心 ①get into the frame of mind (for work or study)；concentrate on more serious

things ②have a change of heart

收押 take into custody;detain
收养 take in and bring up;adopt
收益 income;profit;earnings;gains
收音 ①radio reception ②acoustics(of an auditorium,etc.)
收载 record
收摘 pick(fruit,etc.)
收展 take down the exhibits;collect and put away exhibits
收账 ①charge to an account ②collect debts
收针 (in knitting) decrease stitches;bind off;cast off
收支 revenue and expenditure;income and expenses
收执 ①(of a certificate,etc.) be issued to the person concerned for safekeeping ②receipt (issued by a government agency)
收治 accept for treatment
收住 hospitalize
收报机 telegraphic(or radiotelegraphic) receiver
收藏家 collector(of books,antiques,etc.)
收操号 a bugle call to dismiss;recall
收发报 transmit and receive telegrams
收发室 office for incoming and outgoing mail
收割机 harvester;reaper
收购站 purchasing station(or centre)
收货人 consignee
收获量 harvest yield;yield;crop
收件人 addressee;consignee
收据簿 receipt book
收款机 cash register
收款人 payee
收录机 radio-tape recorder;radio-cassette recorder
收盘价 closing price;price at closing time;price at closure
收票员 ticket collector
收容所 collecting post
收入税 income tax
收生婆 midwife
收视率 (of TV program) viewing rate;rating;watching rate
收缩压 systolic pressure
收摊儿 pack up the stall—wind up the day's business or the work on hand
收文簿 register of incoming dispatches
收信人 the recipient of a letter;addressee
收养人 adoptive parents
收益率 income rate
收音机 radio(set);wireless(set)
收银台 cash desk
收发报机 transmitter;receiver;transceiver
收费厕所 pay toilet
收费电话 toll call;pay phone
收费电视 subscription television;pay television

sion

收费公路 toll road
收复失地 recover lost territory
收购价格 purchasing price
收归国有 nationalize
收回成命 countermand(or retract) an order;revoke a command
收监候审 take into custody to await trial
收买人心 buy popular support
收拾残局 clear up the mess;pick up the pieces
收支包干 (of an enterprise) be responsible for one's own revenue and expenditure;be responsible for balancing one's budget
收支逆差 balance of payments deficit
收支两条线 separation between revenue and expenditure

shǒu(ㄕㄡˇ)

手 [shǒu]
Ⅰ 名 ①hand ②ability;stratagem ③expert (of some occupation or job) Ⅱ 形 handy;easy to carry Ⅲ 动 hold in one's hand;possess Ⅳ 副 personally;in person Ⅴ 量 of skill or proficiency:学一手真功夫 learn some genuine skill
手板 palm
手包 handbag
手背 the back of the hand
手笔 ①a famous person's own handwriting or painting ②literary skill
手臂 ①arm ②a reliable helper
手边 on hand;at hand
手表 wristwatch
手柄 hand lever;hand shank
手册 ① handbook;manual ② record book;workbook
手抄 ①write by hand;handwrite ②hand-written
手车 handcart;pushcart;barrow
手持 hand;in hand
手锤 light hammer
手戳 private seal;signet
手挡 (car) stick shift;manual transmission
手订 personally edit
手段 ① means;medium;measure;method ② trick;artifice ③skill;finesse
手法 ①skill;technique ②trick;gimmick
手斧 hand-adz
手感 feel
手稿 original(or holograph) manuscript;manuscript
手镐 pick;pickax
手工 ①handwork ②by hand;manual ③charge for a piece of handwork
手鼓 a small drum similar to the tambourine
手黑 be unscrupulous

手机 mobile phone;cellular phone

手记 ① write down notes (*or* records) ② written notes (*or* records)

手技 ①handicraft;craftsmanship ②acrobatics juggling;jugglery

手迹 sb's original handwriting (*or* painting)

手脚 ①movement of hands or feet;motion ② underhand method;devious device;trick

手巾 ①towel ②handker

手紧 ① closefisted;tightfisted ② be short of money;be hard up

手锯 handsaw

手卷 hand scroll

手绢 handkerchief

手铐 handcuffs

手控 manual control;hand control;switch insertion

手快 deft of hand

手辣 be vicious or unscrupulous

手雷 antitank grenade

手令 an order personally issued by sb in command

手笼 muff

手轮 handwheel

手锣 small gong

手慢 slow with one's hands; slow in movements;slow-moving

手面 the extent of one's spending

手模 fingerprint

手帕 handkerchief

手旗 semaphore flag

手气 luck at gambling (*or* card playing,etc.)

手钳 hand vice;pliers

手枪 pistol;handgun

手巧 skilful with one's hands;nimble-fingered;deft;dexterous;deft (*or* skilful) with one's hands

手勤 diligent;industrious;hardworking

手轻 have gentle hands;not use too much force;handle gently

手球 ① handball (a game) ② handball (the ball) ③handball (a foul in sports)

手刃 stab to death;kill with one's own hand

手软 be irresolute when firmness is needed; be softhearted

手生 lack practice and skill;be out of practice

手势 gesture;sign;signal

手书 ① write in one's own hand ② personal letter

手术 surgical operation;operation

手松 free with one's money; free-handed; open-handed

手套 ① gloves; mittens ② baseball gloves; mitts

手提 portable

手头 ①right beside one;on hand;at hand ② one's financial condition at the moment

手腕 ①trick;artifice ②skill;finesse;tactics

手纹 the lines of the palm

手下 ①under the leadership (*or* guidance,direction) of;under ②at hand ③at the hands of sb ④one's financial condition at the moment

手相 palmistry

手写 ① write by hand;handwrite;write in one's own hand ② handwritten;written in one's own hand

手心 ①the centre of the palm ②control

手续 procedures;formalities

手选 picking;picking out

手癣 tinea manuum;fungal infection of the hand

手痒 ①one's fingers itch ②have an itch to do sth

手艺 ①craftsmanship;workmanship ②handicraft;trade

手淫 ①masturbation;self-abuse ②masturbate

手印 ①hand print ②thumb print;fingerprint

手语 sign language;dactylology

手谕 personally written orders (*or* instructions)

手札 personal letter

手闸 hand brake

手章 private seal;signet

手掌 palm (of the hand)

手杖 walking stick;stick

手诏 order of a ruler in his personal writing

手折 ①a record book in accordion form ②an account book in accordion form ③notebook recording deliveries,orders,payments,etc.

手诊 diagnose by observing signs on a patient's palm

手植 personally plant (a tree,etc.)

手纸 toilet paper

手指 finger

手重 use too much force

手镯 bracelet

手足 ①movement ②brothers

手钻 hand drill

手把手 personally instruct;pass on one's own knowledge and skills

手抄本 handwritten copy

手倒立 handstand

手底下 ①under the leadership (*or* guidance, direction) of; under ② at hand ③ at the hands of sb ④ one's financial condition at the moment

手递手 hand to hand

手电筒 electric torch;flashlight

手风琴 accordion

手工业 handicraft industry;handicraft

手工艺 handicraft art;handicraft

手巾架 towel rack

手劲儿 muscular strength of the hand

手拉手 hand in hand
手榴弹 hand grenade;grenade
手模特 hand-model
手枪套 holster
手刹车 hand brake
手势语 sign language
手术包 surgical kit
手术刀 scalpel
手术室 operating room;operating theatre
手术台 operating table
手提包 handbag;bag
手提箱 suitcase
手推车 handcart;pushcart;barrow
手腕子 wrist
手下人 one's subordinate;servant
手携手 hand in hand
手写体 handwritten form;script
手续费 service charges; handling charges;
commission
手摇泵 hand pump
手摇钻 handdril
手艺人 craftsman
手掌心 ①the centre of the palm ②control
手指甲 finger nail
手指头 finger
手不释卷 always have a book in one's hand;be
very studious;be a diligent reader
手到病除 Illness departs at a touch of the hand
(said as a tribute to a doctor or a trouble-
shooter).
手到擒来 just stretch the hand and bring it
back—very easy
手工工具 hand tools
手工艺品 articles of handicraft art;handicrafts
手疾眼快 quick of eye and deft of hand
手拉葫芦 chain block
手忙脚乱 in a rush;in a flurry
手拿把掐 in the bag;a sure thing
手枪速射 rapid-fire pistol
手提电话 mobile phone;cellular phone
手提电脑 handheld computer; portable computer
手无寸铁 bare-handed;unarmed;defenceless
手舞足蹈 dance for joy
手下败将 one's vanquished foe;one's defeated
opponent
手下留情 show mercy;be lenient;make allowances for (when dealing out punishment to
sb)
手写电脑 pentop computer;handwriting computer
手眼通天 exceptionally adept in trickery
手指字母 manual alphabet;deaf-and-dumb alphabet
手足无措 all in a fluster;at a loss what to do
手扶拖拉机 walking tractor
手工艺工人 craftsman;artisan

手机入网费 mobile access fee
手脚不干净 sticky-fingered;dishonest in money matters
手力千斤顶 hand jack
手提打字机 portable typewriter
手推婴儿车 pushchair;light baby carriage
手摇发电机 hand generator
手指头肚儿 the inner side of the fingertip
手无缚鸡之力 lack the strength to truss a
chicken—physically very weak
手枪慢加速比赛 centre-fire pistol

守 [shǒu]

囡 ① guard; defend; garrison ② keep
watch;watch over;look after ③observe;abide
by;adhere ④be by the side of;be next to;be
near
守备 perform garrison duty; be on garrison
duty;garrison
守车 (British) guard's van;(American) ca-
boose
守成 maintain the achievements of one's predecessors
守敌 the enemy holding a fortress (or a strategic point)
守法 abide by (or observe) the law;be law a-
biding
守寡 remain a widow;live in widowhood
守恒 conservation
守候 ①wait for;expect ②keep watch
守护 guard;defend
守家 ① look after the house;mind the house
②maintain what has been achieved (or acquired) by one's forefathers
守节 (of a woman in former times) remain
unmarried after the death of her husband or
her betrothed
守旧 adhere to past practices;stick to old
ways;be conservative
守军 defending troops;defenders
守灵 stand as guards at the bier;keep vigil beside the coffin
守门 ①be on duty at the door (or gate) ②
keep goal
守丧 keep vigil beside the coffin
守时 be on time;be punctual
守势 defensive
守岁 stay up late (or all night) on New
Year's Eve;see the Old Year out and the
New Year in
守土 defend the territory of one's country
守望 keep watch
守卫 guard;defend
守孝 observe a period of mourning for one's
deceased parent
守信 keep one's word
守业 maintain what has been achieved by
one's forefathers (or predecessors);safe-

S

guard one's heritage

守夜 keep watch at night; spend the night on watch

守约 ①abide by an agreement ②keep an appointment

守则 rules; regulations

守职 stand fast at one's post; be faithful in the discharge of one's duties

守财奴 miser

守场员 fielder (in baseball, softball or cricket)

守法户 law-abiding firm

守护神 guardian spirit; tutelary spirit; patron saint

守活寡 be a grass widow

守旧派 old-liners; conservatives

守空房 stay home alone

守垒员 baseman (in baseball or softball)

守林人 forest guard

守门员 goalkeeper (in football, ice hockey, etc.)

守望台 watchtower

守备部队 garrison force; (holding) garrison

守恒定律 conservation law

守经达权 be mindful of principles but act according to circumstances; consider expediency as well as principle

守口如瓶 keep one's mouth shut; breathe not a single word; be tight-mouthed; be tight-lipped

守身如玉 keep oneself as pure as jade—preserve one's honour or integrity

守望相助 (of neighbouring villages, etc.) keep watch and help defend each other; give mutual help and protection

守正不阿 be strictly just and impartial

守株待兔 stand by a stump waiting for more hares to come and dash themselves against it—trust to chance and strokes of luck

首 [shǒu]
I 名 ① head ② head; boss; leader; chief: 以…为首 headed by sb; with sb as the leader II 形 ① first; foremost; supreme ② first of all; first (to do sth) III 动 bring charges against sb IV 量 (of poems and songs): 三首民歌 three folk songs/《唐诗三百首》300 Tang Poems

首播 broadcast (by TV or radio) for the first time

首倡 be the first to advocate; initiate; start

首车 first bus (of a regular bus service)

首创 originate; initiate; pioneer

首次 for the first time; first

首都 capital (of a country)

首恶 chief criminal; principal culprit

首发 first issue (of book, magazine, stamp, etc.); give out (*or* hand out) for the first time

首犯 chief criminal; principal culprit

首飞 first test-flight of a new model of aircraft; maiden flight

首府 ① (in former times) head prefecture (the prefecture in which a provincial capital was located) ②the capital of an autonomous region or prefecture ③the capital of a dependency (*or* colony)

首富 the wealthiest family in the locality; the richest person

首告 report (an offender); inform against (an offender); start court action by lodging a complaint

首功 the first-class merit

首航 maiden voyage (*or* flight)

首户 the wealthiest family in the locality; the richest person

首级 chopped-off head (in battle, etc.)

首届 the first occasion, term, session, etc.

首肯 nod approval; nod assent; approve; consent

首领 ① head and neck ② chieftain; leader; head

首脑 head

首任 the first to be appointed to an office

首饰 ① (originally) head ornaments ② jewels; jewelry

首位 the first place

首尾 ① the head and the tail; the beginning and the end ②from beginning to end

首乌 the tuber of multiflower knotweed

首席 ①seat of honour ②chief

首先 ① before all others; first ② in the first place; first of all; above all

首相 prime minister

首选 first choice

首演 the first (*or* opening) performance; premiere

首要 of the first importance; first; chief

首长 leading cadre; senior officer

首座 ①seat of honour (at a banquet) ②abbot

首播式 ceremony for the first broadcast (of a radio or TV); première program

首发式 ceremony celebrating the first publication of a book; inaugural ceremony for launching a publication; ceremony held for the first issuing (of books or magazines)

首日封 the first day cover

首饰店 jewelry store

首饰盒 jewel case

首陀罗 Sudra

首乌藤 the vine of multiflower knotweed

首映片 first-run movie

首映式 premiere; ceremony for a premiere; ceremony for the first show (of a film)

首创精神 creative initiation; pioneering spirit

首当其冲 be the first to be affected (by a dis-

aster,etc.);bear the brunt
首期按揭 down-payment
首屈一指 come first on the list;be second to none
首善之区 the best of places
首鼠两端 be in two minds;shilly-shally
首席代表 chief delegate;senior representative
首要分子 ringleader
首要问题 a matter of utmost importance
首战告捷 win in the very first battle or game
首长工程 project built according to a senior official's individual intention;project sheerly based on the leader's whimsical will with no other objective references
首席财务官 Chief Finance Officer (CFO)
首席沟通官 Chief Government Officer (CGO)
首席技术官 Chief Technology Officer (CTO)
首席检查官 chief inspector;chief procurator
首席商务官 Chief Business Officer (CBO)
首席信息官 Chief Information Officer (CIO)
首席运营官 Chief Operating Officer (COO)
首席执行官 chief executive officer (CEO)

舳 [shǒu]
〈名〉 stem;(of a ship) bows

shòu(ㄕㄡˋ)

寿 [shòu]
〈名〉①long life;longevity;old age ②life;age ③ birthday ④ (sth prepared before one's death) for burial
寿斑 senile plagues;black speckle on the face
寿板 coffin boards
寿材 a coffin prepared before one's death;coffin
寿辰 birthday (of an elderly person)
寿诞 birthday
寿酒 birthday wine;birthday feast
寿礼 birthday present (for an elderly person)
寿联 birthday couplets;birthday scrolls
寿面 birthday noodles;longevity noodles
寿命 life span;life
寿木 coffin prepared before one's death;coffin
寿数 person's destined age
寿司 sushi
寿桃 ①peaches offered as a birthday present ②peach-shaped birthday cakes
寿险 life insurance
寿星 ①the god of longevity ②an elderly person whose birthday is being celebrated
寿穴 a grave prepared before one's death
寿筵 birthday feast
寿衣 graveclothes;shroud;cerements
寿终 die of old age
寿同彭祖 be as old as Methuselah
寿终正寝 die in bed of old age;die a natural death
寿比南山,福如东海 May your age be as the southern mountain and your happiness as the eastern sea (said as birthday congratulations to an elderly person).

受 [shòu]
〈动〉① receive;accept ② suffer;sustain;be subjected to ③stand;endure;bear;tolerate ④ be pleasant;be agreeable
受病 catch a disease
受潮 be affected with damp
受吃 pleasant to the taste;tasty
受宠 be in sb's favour
受酬 accept a reward
受挫 be foiled;be baffled;be thwarted;suffer a setback
受敌 be attacked by the enemy
受罚 be punished
受粉 be pollinated
受过 bear the blame
受害 suffer injury;fall victim;be affected
受寒 catch a chill;catch cold
受旱 suffer from drought;be drought-stricken
受贿 accept (or take) bribes
受惠 receive benefits
受奖 be rewarded
受教 receive instruction;learn from sb;study under sb
受戒 be initiated into monkhood or nunhood
受尽 suffer enough from;suffer all kinds of; have one's fill of
受惊 be frightened;be startled
受精 be fertilized
受窘 be embarrassed;be in an awkward position
受看 ① pleasant to look at;good-looking ② honourable;creditable
受控 controlled
受苦 suffer (hardships);have a rough time
受累 [shòulěi] get involved on account of sb else
受累 [shòulèi] be put to much trouble;be inconvenienced
受冷 catch cold
受礼 receive gift
受理 ①accept (a case) ②deal with;handle
受凉 catch cold
受领 accept (an assignment,etc.);appreciate (kind thoughts,etc.)
受命 receive instructions (or assignments)
受难 suffer calamities (or disasters);be in distress
受盘 buy up a business
受骗 be deceived (or fooled,cheated,taken in)
受聘 ①(of a girl) accept betrothal gifts ②accept an appointment (to a post)
受气 be bullied;suffer wrong
受穷 suffer poverty;live in poverty

S

受屈 be wronged
受权 be authorized
受热 ① be heated ② be affected by the heat; have heatstroke (*or* sunstroke)
受辱 be insulted; be disgraced; be humiliated
受伤 be injured; be wounded; sustain an injury
受赏 be awarded
受审 stand trial; be tried; be on trial
受事 a word denoting the receiver of an action (not necessarily an object, as in 饭准备好了 "Dinner is ready," where 饭, the subject, denotes the receiver of the action)
受暑 suffer from heatstroke (*or* sunstroke)
受胎 become pregnant; be impregnated; conceive
受听 pleasant to the ear; sweet sounding
受托 be commissioned; be entrusted (with a task)
受洗 be baptized; receive baptism
受降 accept a surrender
受刑 be tortured; be put to torture
受训 receive (*or* undergo) training
受业 ① receive instruction ② (in letters to one's teacher) I, your pupil
受益 profit by; benefit from; be benefited
受用 [shòuyòng] benefit from; profit by; enjoy
受用 [shòuyong] (*usu. used in the negative*) feel comfortable
受援 receive aid
受阅 be reviewed
受孕 become pregnant; be impregnated; conceive
受灾 be hit by a natural adversity (*or* calamity)
受制 ① be controlled ② endure hardships (*or* tortures, rough conditions, etc.); suffer
受众 readers, listeners and viewers reached by the mass media; audience
受主 acceptor; audience
受助 aided
受阻 be obstructed; meet with obstruction
受罪 endure hardships, tortures, rough conditions, etc.; have a hard time
受不了 cannot stand (*or* endure)
受不起 dare not accept; not deserve
受得了 can stand (*or* endure)
受鼓舞 be inspired; be encouraged
受害者 victim; sufferer
受话器 (telephone) receiver
受话人 receiver (of telephone call)
受惠国 beneficiary country; beneficiary
受教育 receive an education
受精卵 zygote
受款人 payee
受冷落 out in the cold
受批评 under criticism; be criticized

受票人 drawee
受歧视 be subjected to discrimination; be discriminated against
受气包 a person whom anyone can vent his spite upon; one who always gets blamed (*or* takes the rap)
受让方 assignee
受让人 assignee
受伤害 sustain an injury
受胎率 conception rate
受托国 mandatory power
受托人 trustee; fiduciary
受委屈 suffer injustice; be wronged
受训斥 get a dressing down
受益人 beneficiary
受援国 recipient country
受责骂 get a scolding; be scolded
受重伤 be seriously wounded
受宠若惊 be overwhelmed by an unexpected favour; feel extremely flattered
受害不浅 suffer not a little; suffer a lot
受话号码 called number; receiving number
受夹板气 be blamed by both parties
受苦受难 live in misery; have one's fill of sufferings
受理案件 accept and hear a case; enter in the reference; take up a case
受用不尽 benefit from sth all one's life
受灾地区 disaster-hit area; disaster-affected area; disaster-stricken area; disaster-ravaged area; disaster-beleaguered area; distressed area; disaster area
受之有愧 I don't deserve it; I am not worthy of it.
受欢迎的人 persona grata

狩 [shòu]
〈名〉 hunting (esp. in winter)
狩猎 hunting

授 [shòu]
〈动〉 ① award; present; vest; confer; give ② teach; instruct; tell
授粉 pollination
授给 award; remunerate
授计 confide a stratagem to sb; tell sb the plan of action
授奖 award (*or* give) a prize
授精 insemination
授课 give lessons; give instruction
授命 ① give (*or* lay down) one's life ② give orders
授旗 present (sb with) flag
授权 empower; authorize; delegation of authority
授时 ① time service ② (formerly of the government or the emperor) issue the official calendar
授受 grant and receive; give and accept

授位 confer a degree
授衔 confer a title (*or* a military rank)
授勋 confer orders (*or* medals);award a decoration
授业 impart knowledge;give instruction
授艺 teach a trade;pass on skill
授意 incite (*or* get) sb to do sth;inspire
授予 confer;award
授权令 warrant
授权书 letter of authorization;letter of attorney;power of attorney
授予权 gift
授予人 grantor
授予物 grant
授助费 aid fund;"helping hand"payments
授权立法 delegated legislation
授时信号 time signal
授信额度 line of credit
授勋仪式 medal conferring ceremony

售 [shòu]
动 ① be on sale;sell ② carry out (intrigues,tricks,etc.);make (one's plan,etc.) work
售货 sell goods
售价 selling price;price
售卖 sell
售货车 wagon
售货机 vending machine
售货亭 kiosk;stall;stand
售货员 shop assistant;salesclerk
售票处 ① ticket office;booking office (at a railway station) ②box office (at a theatre,cinema,etc.)
售票口 wicket
售票台 ticket counter
售票员 ① ticket seller;conductor ② booking-office clerk ③box-office clerk
售后服务 after-sale service;post-sell service;service after sale
售后服务部 helpdesk
售台武器问题 question of arms sales to Taiwan

兽 [shòu]
I 名 beast;animal;brute II 形 beastly;bestial
兽环 animal-head knocker (on doors of old-type houses)
兽王 the king of beasts—the lion
兽行 brutal act;brutality
兽性 brutish nature;barbarity
兽穴 shed;den;lodge;lair
兽医 veterinary surgeon;veterinarian;vet
兽疫 epizootic disease;epizootic
兽欲 animal desire;bestial desire
兽力车 animal-drawn vehicle (*or* cart)
兽医师 veterinarian
兽医学 veterinary science;veterinary medicine
兽医站 veterinary station
兽疫学 epizootiology
兽聚鸟散 (as of a loosely assembled group) scramble and scatter like beasts and birds

绶 [shòu]
名 coloured silk ribbon
绶带 coloured silk ribbon
绶章 cordon
绶带鸟 paradise flycatcher

瘦 [shòu]
形 ①thin;slim;emaciated ②lean ③fitting too closely;tight ④not fertile;poor;barren
瘦长 long and thin;tall and thin;lanky
瘦果 achene
瘦煤 lean coal;meagre coal
瘦缺 an unprofitable post
瘦肉 lean meat
瘦弱 thin and weak;emaciated;frail
瘦身 slim
瘦田 poor soil;infertile land
瘦小 thin and small
瘦削 very thin;gaunt;bony
瘦子 a lean (*or* thin) person
瘦肉率 cutability
瘦肉型 animals bred for lean meat;lean meat species
瘦高挑儿 ①a tall and slender figure ②a tall,slender person
瘦骨嶙峋 all skin and bones
瘦猴似的 thin and shrivelled;skinny
"瘦肉精"中毒 Poisoning of Clenbuterol;Spiropent Poisoning

shū(ㄕㄨ)

殳 [shū]
名 ancient weapon made of bamboo

书 [shū]
I 动 write;record II 名 ①style of calligraphy;script ②book ③letter;epistle ④official paper;document
书包 satchel;schoolbag
书报 books,newspapers,and periodicals
书背 the back of a book;spine;backbone
书本 book
书场 a place of entertainment where *quyi* performances are given
书虫 pedant;bookworm
书橱 bookcase (often with glass doors)
书挡 bookend
书店 bookshop;bookstore;book-seller's
书法 penmanship;calligraphy
书坊 [shūfāng] bookshop
书房 study
书扉 title page
书稿 manuscript
书柜 bookcase (often with glass doors)

S

书函 ①slipcase ②letters;correspondence
书号 book number;call number
书后 postscript (by the author or sb else)
书画 painting and calligraphy
书籍 books;works;literature
书脊 spine (of a book);backbone
书记 ①secretary ②clerk
书架 bookshelf;bookcase
书简 letters;correspondence
书经 The Book of History
书局 publishing house;press;book company
书卷 books
书卡 book card
书刊 books and periodicals
书壳 slipcase
书口 fore-edge
书库 stack room
书林 a forest of books—a treasury of books
书录 bibliography
书眉 the top of a page;top margin
书面 written;in written form;in writing
书名 the title of a book;title
书目 booklist;title catalogue
书皮 ①book cover ②dust cover
书评 book review
书签 ①a title label pasted on the cover of a
  Chinese-style thread-bound book ② book-
  mark
书商 bookman
书社 ①literary club ②publishing house
书生 intellectual;scholar
书市 book fair;book market
书摊 bookstall;bookstand
书套 slipcase
书体 style of calligraphy
书亭 book-kiosk;bookstall
书童 page boy
书屋 study
书香 (of a family) having literary (or intellectual) fame
书写 write
书心 type area (of a book page)
书信 letter;written message
书业 book industry
书页 book page;printed page
书院 (in former times) academy of classical
  learning
书札 letters;correspondence
书斋 a study
书展 book exhibition
书证 evidence in writing;written evidence
  (that supports or verifies facts in a case)
书桌 desk;writing desk
书包带 book strap (used by schoolchildren)
书报亭 newsstand
书呆子 pedant;bookworm
书法家 calligrapher;calligraphist

书记处 secretariat
书卷气 (of an intellectual) air of cultivated
  refinement;cultured;polished
书面语 written language;literary language
书名号 punctuation marks used to enclose the
  title of a book or an article (《》)
书名页 title page
书皮纸 paper for covering books
书生气 bookishness;a bookish cast of mind
书写纸 writing paper
书信电 letter cable
书信体 epistolary style
书本知识 book learning
书不尽言 I have much more to say than I can
  write in this letter.
书法比赛 calligraphy competition
书面合同 contract in writing;written contract
书面声明 written statement
书面通知 written notice
书面形式 black and white;in written form
书生之见 a bookish approach;a pedantic view
书香门第 a literary (or intellectual) family;a
  family of scholars
书到用时方恨少 It is when you are using what
  you have learned from books that you wish
  you had read more books than you have.
书山有路勤为径 Diligence is the only way to
  acquire learning;There is no royal road to
  learning.

抒 [shū]
〔动〕 ①give voice to;express;convey ②relieve;relax;remove;alleviate
抒发 express;voice;give expression to
抒怀 pour out one's heart;unburden one's
heart
抒情 express (or convey) one's emotion
抒写 express in writing;write of;describe
抒情诗 lyric poetry;lyrics
抒情散文 lyric prose

纾 [shū]
Ⅰ〔动〕 ①relieve;alleviate;free from ②procrastinate;delay Ⅱ〔形〕 well-to-do;comfortably
off
纾死 slow death
纾人之忧 relieve sb from anxiety

枢 [shū]
〔名〕 ①hinge;pivot;hub ②centre of activity
③important position
枢机 ①(in former times) a key government
  post (or office) ②a vital element
枢纽 pivot;hub;axis;key position
枢要 the central administration
枢密院 privy council
枢机主教 cardinal

叔 [shū]
〔名〕 ①father's younger brother;uncle ②Un-
cle(form of address for a man about one's
father's age) ③husband's younger brother ④

third son in the family
叔伯 relationship between cousins of the same grandfather or great-grandfather
叔父 father's younger brother;uncle
叔公 ①husband's father's younger brother ② grandfather's younger brother; grand-uncle;great-uncle
叔母 wife of father's younger brother;aunt
叔婆 ① husband's father's younger brother's wife ② wife of grandfather's younger brother;grand-aunt;great-aunt
叔嫂 brother-in-law and sister-in-law
叔叔 ①father's younger brother; uncle ②(a child's form of address for any young man one generation its senior) uncle
叔子 husband's younger brother; brother-in-law
叔祖 (paternal) grandfather's younger brother;granduncle (*or* great-uncle)
叔祖母 wife of (paternal) grandfather's younger brother;grandaunt (*or* great-aunt)

姝 [shū] I 形 pretty;beautiful II 名 beauty;pretty girl

殊 [shū] I 形 ①different;divergent ②outstanding; special;unusual II 副 very much;exceedingly;really III 动 break off;cut off
殊功 distinguished service; outstanding achievement
殊荣 special honours
殊死 ①desperate;life-and-death ②the penalty of decapitation
殊勋 outstanding merit;distinguished service
殊誉 special honour
殊不知 little imagine;hardly realize
殊感悲痛 feel deeply grieved
殊深轸念 express deep solicitude;feel deeply concerned
殊途同归 reach the same goal by different routes

倏 [shū] 副 swiftly
倏地 suddenly;quickly
倏尔 suddenly;quickly
倏忽 suddenly;quickly
倏然 suddenly;abruptly

菽 [shū] 名 beans

梳 [shū] I 名 comb II 动 comb one's hair,etc.
梳理 ①card ②comb out (one's hair);dress (one's hair)
梳棉 comb and parallel cotton fibers prior to spinning
梳头 comb one's hair
梳洗 wash and dress
梳妆 dress and make up

梳子 comb
梳辫子 ①braid one's hair ②sort out matters, problems,etc.
梳棉机 carding machine
梳妆台 dressing table
梳洗用具 toilet articles
梳妆打扮 deck oneself out;dress smartly;be dressed up

淑 [shū] 形 chaste and mild-mannered; refined; pure;virtuous
淑德 female virtue
淑静 (of a woman) refined and gentle
淑美 virtuous and beautiful;refined and beautiful
淑女 fair maiden;virtuous maiden;noble lady

舒 [shū] I 动 stretch;relax;unfold;free from (oppressed feeling,etc.) II 形 easy;leisurely
舒步 walk unhurriedly
舒畅 happy;entirely free from worry
舒服 ①comfortable ②be well
舒缓 ①slow and unhurried;leisurely ②relaxed;mild ③(of a slope) gentle;gradual
舒卷 (of clouds or smoke) curl and uncurl; roll and unroll;roll back and forth
舒快 comfortable and relaxed;refreshed
舒气 ①get one's breath;catch one's breath ② relax; have a breathing space ③ relieve one's feelings;let off steam
舒散 ①stretch and flex ②shake off one's fatigue or cares
舒适 comfortable;cosy;snug
舒爽 comfortable and refreshed
舒松 relieved and relaxed
舒泰 free from worries;comfortable and at ease
舒坦 comfortable;at ease
舒心 comfortable;happy
舒展 ① unfold; extend; smooth out ② limber up;stretch
舒张 diastole
舒适带 comfort zone (the range of temperature considered comfortable for most people,generally 20°C—24°C)
舒张压 diastolic pressure
舒筋活络 stimulate the circulation of the blood and cause the muscles and joints to relax
舒筋活血 relax muscles and enliven blood
舒眉展眼 smiling eyes;a beaming face
舒舒服服 nice and cosy
舒腰伸臂 lean back and stretch one's arms

疏 [shū] I 动 ①dredge (a river,etc.) ②thin out; disperse; scatter ③ neglect II 形 ① thin; loose;sparse;scattered ②(of family or social relations) distant ③not familiar with ④negli-

gent; careless ⑤ scanty; inadequate; meagre Ⅲ 名 ①memorial to the emperor ②detailed annotation
疏导 dredge; persuasion
疏忽 carelessness; negligence; oversight
疏浚 dredge; sweep; scouring
疏漏 careless omission; oversight; slip
疏散 ①sparse; scattered; dispersed ②evacuate
疏松 ①loose; puff ②loosen
疏通 ①dredge ②mediate between two parties
疏远 keep at a distance; not in close touch
疏不间亲 Casual acquaintances should not come between near relatives.
疏导交通 direct the flow of traffic
疏而不漏 be loose but never miss
疏于职守 negligent of one's duties

摅 [shū] 动 ①express; set forth; give expression to ②gallop

输 [shū] 动 ①transport; transmit; convey ②make a gift of; contribute money; donate ③ lose; be beaten; suffer defeat
输出 ①send out ②export ③computer output
输电 transmit electricity
输家 loser (in a gambling game)
输将 contribute; donate
输理 be in the wrong
输钱 lose money (in gambling)
输入 ① bring in; introduce ②import ③computer input
输送 carry; transport; convey
输血 ①blood transfusion ②give aid and support; bolster up; give sb a shot in the arm
输氧 oxygen therapy
输液 infusion
输赢 ①victory or defeat ②winnings and losses (in gambling)
输电网 power transmission network; grid system
输精管 spermatic duct; seminal duct
输卵管 oviduct
输尿管 ureter
输入端 input end; input terminal; lead-in
输沙率 silt discharge
输送带 conveyor belt
输送机 conveyor
输血者 blood donor
输液器 transfusion system
输油管 petroleum pipeline
输电线路 transmission line
输精管炎 deferentitis
输尿管炎 ureteritis
输入－输出 input-output(I-O)
输精管结扎术 vasoligation

蔬 [shū] 名 vegetables
蔬菜 vegetables; greens; greenstuff
蔬果 vegetables and fruits
蔬菜基地 vegetable base

shú(ㄕㄨˊ)

秫 [shú] 名 kaoliang; (Chinese) sorghum
秫秸 kaoliang stalk; sorghum stalk
秫米 husked sorghum
秫秫 kaoliang; sorghum

孰 [shú] 代 ①who ②which; who ③what
孰得孰失 who wins and who loses
孰是孰非 which is right and which is wrong

赎 [shú] 动 ① redeem; ransom ② atone for (a crime)
赎当 redeem sth pawned; take sth out of pledge; redeem a pledge
赎价 ransom price; ransom
赎金 ransom money; ransom
赎买 redeem; buy out
赎身 (of slaves or prostitutes) redeem (or ransom) oneself; buy back one's freedom
赎刑 redeem sb from punishment by paying a ransom
赎罪 atone for one's crime
赎罪券 indulgence
赎罪日 Yom Kippur; Day of Atonement
赎买政策 policy of redemption

塾 [shú] 名 private school; family school
塾师 tutor at an old-style private school; private tutor

熟 [shú] 形 ① ripe ② cooked; done ③ processed; wrought ④ frequently seen or heard; well-known; familiar ⑤skilled; experienced; versed in ⑥deeply; profoundly
熟谙 be familiar with; be good at
熟菜 cooked food; prepared food
熟道 familiar road (or route)
熟地 ①cultivated land ②prepared rhizome of rehmannia
熟读 read carefully over and over again
熟化 cultivate (land); till
熟记 learn by heart; memorize; commit to memory
熟见 (of things) commonly seen
熟客 frequent visitor
熟练 skilled; practised; proficient
熟料 fired refractory material; grog; clinker
熟路 a familiar road (or route); a beaten track
熟年 a year of good harvests; bumper year

熟漆 lacquer
熟人 acquaintance;friend
熟稔 be familiar with;be conversant with
熟肉 cooked meat
熟食 prepared food;cooked food
熟识 be well acquainted with;know well
熟手 old hand;practised hand
熟睡 sleep soundly;be fast asleep
熟丝 boiled-off silk
熟思 ponder deeply;consider carefully;deliberate
熟铁 wrought iron
熟土 mellow soil
熟悉 know sth or sb well;be familiar with;have an intimate knowledge of
熟习 be skilful at;have the knack of;be practised in
熟油 stand oil;boiled oil
熟语 idiom;idiomatic phrase
熟知 know very well;know intimately
熟字 words already learned;familiar words
熟荒地 once cultivated land;abandoned cultivated land
熟石膏 plaster of Paris;plaster
熟石灰 slaked lime
熟橡胶 vulcanized rubber
熟门熟路 a familiar road and a familiar door—things that one knows well
熟能生巧 Skill comes from practice;Practice makes perfect.
熟视无睹 pay no attention to a familiar sight;turn a blind eye to;ignore

shǔ(ㄕㄨˇ)

暑 [shǔ]
名 summer heat;hot weather
暑假 summer vacation (or holidays)
暑期 summer vacation time
暑气 summer heat;heat
暑热 hot summer weather
暑天 hot summer days;dog days
暑瘟 febrile diseases in summer(including encephalitis B, dysentry, malignant malaria, etc.)
暑运 passenger flow in summer

黍 [shǔ]
名 broomcorn millet
黍子 broomcorn millet

属 [shǔ]
Ⅰ 名 ①category ②genus ③family members;dependants Ⅱ 动 ①be subordinate to ②belong to;be part of ③be ④be born in the year of (one of the 12 animals) ➡ zhǔ
属地 possession;dependency
属国 vassal state;dependent state
属实 turn out to be true;be verified
属下 subordinates

属相 any one of the names of 12 symbolic animals associated with a 12-year cycle,often used to denote the year of a person's birth
属性 attribute;property
属于 belong to;be part of

署 [shǔ]
Ⅰ 名 government office; office; workplace Ⅱ 动 ①make arrangements for;arrange;prepare ②stand proxy for;act as deputy;handle by proxy ③affix one's name to;sign
署理 handle by proxy;act as deputy
署名 sign;put one's signature to
署名权 right to express the author's name in the works
署名人 the undersigned
署名文章 signed article;byline story

蜀 [shǔ]

蜀锦 Sichuan brocade
蜀葵 hollyhock
蜀绣 Sichuan embroidery

鼠 [shǔ]
名 mouse;rat
鼠辈 mean creatures;scoundrels
鼠标 mouse
鼠疮 scrofula
鼠窜 scamper off like a rat;scurry away like frightened rats
鼠胆 as timid as a mouse;chicken-hearted
鼠害 a plague of rats;damage caused by rats
鼠耗 wastage of grain,etc. caused by rats
鼠夹 mousetrap
鼠笼 squirrel cage
鼠疫 the plague
鼠曲草 affine cudweed
鼠咬热 rat-bite fever
鼠肚鸡肠 petty;narrow-minded
鼠目寸光 A mouse can see only an inch;see only what is under one's nose;be short-sighted
鼠窃狗偷 filch like rats and snatch like dogs—play petty tricks on the sly
鼠笼式电动机 squirrel-cage motor

数 [shǔ]
动 ① count ② be particularly conspicuous by comparison ③enumerate;list ➡ shù;shuò
数伏 beginning of the three *fu*,the three hottest ten-day periods of the year;beginning of the hottest days of the year
数九 beginning of the nine nine-day periods following the Winter Solstice;beginning of the coldest days of the year
数落 ①scold sb by enumerating his wrongdoings;rebuke;reprove ②enumerate;cite one example after another
数秒 count the seconds
数说 ①enumerate ②scold;rebuke;reprove

S

数不清 countless;innumerable
数不上 not count as outstanding, important, etc.
数不着 not count as outstanding, important, etc.
数得上 be reckoned as outstanding, important,etc.
数得着 be reckoned as outstanding, important,etc.
数来宝 rhythmic story telling to clapper accompaniment
数数儿 count;reckon
数不过来 too many to be counted;innumerable
数不胜数 innumerable;incalculable;countless
数典忘祖 give all the historical facts except those about one's own ancestors; forget one's own origins;be ignorant of the history of one's own country
数黑论黄 talk irresponsibly;gossip
数黄道黑 talk irresponsibly;gossip
数九寒天 the coldest days of the year
数米而炊 count the grains of rice before cooking them—fuss over small things;be miserly
数一数二 count as one of the very best;rank very high
数葫芦道茄子 rattle on;talk endlessly

薯 [shǔ]
　名 potato;yam
薯莨 dye yam
薯蓣 Chinese yam
薯芋类作物 tuber crops

曙 [shǔ]
　名 break of day;daybreak;dawn
曙光 the first light of morning;dawn
曙色 the light of early dawn

癙 [shǔ]
　动 fall ill from worry and distress
癙忧 depressed;illness caused by anxiety

<h2 style="text-align:center">shù(ㄕㄨ)</h2>

术 [shù]
　名 ①art;skill;craft; technique ②method; tactics;trick ➡ zhú
术科 technical courses offered in military (or physical) training
术士 ①a Confucian scholar ②magician
术语 technical term;terminology

戍 [shù]
　动 defend;garrison
戍边 defend the frontiers
戍楼 garrison watchtower
戍守 defend;garrison
戍卒 garrison soldiers (at the frontiers)

束 [shù]
　I 动 ①bind; tie; bundle up ②control;contain;restrain Ⅱ 量 bundle;bunch;sheaf;一束

红玫瑰 a bouquet of red roses Ⅲ 名 beam
束带 bridle;girding;spanner band;lacing
束缚 tie; bind up;fetter; bound; rigid control; bound;rigid control
束紧 stricture;bind up
束身 ① control oneself; restrain oneself ② bind oneself
束手 have one's hands tied;be helpless
束脩 private tutor's remuneration
束装 pack up (for a journey)
束发带 snood;fillet;bandeau
束射管 beam tube
束身自爱 treasure one's own good name and act within the bounds of propriety
束手待毙 fold one's hands and await destruction;helplessly wait for death;resign oneself to extinction
束手就擒 allow oneself to be seized without putting up a fight
束手束脚 be over-cautious
束手无策 be at a loss what to do;feel quite helpless;be at one's wit's end
束之高阁 tie sth up and place it on the top shelf—lay aside and neglect; shelve; pigeonhole

述 [shù]
　动 state;relate;narrate;recount
述评 review;commentary
述说 state;recount;narrate
述语 predicate
述职 report on one's work;report
述职报告 duty report;progress report

树 [shù]
　I 名 tree Ⅱ 动 ①plant;cultivate ②hold up;set up;establish
树杈 crotch (of a tree)
树丛 grove;thicket
树敌 make an enemy of sb;set others against oneself;antagonize
树顶 the top end of a trunk;treetop
树墩 tree stump;stump
树蜂 wood wasp
树干 tree trunk;trunk
树根 tree stump;tree root
树挂 (soft) rime
树冠 crown (of a tree)
树胶 gum (of a tree)
树懒 sloth
树篱 quickset hedge;quick-fence;brush hurdle
树立 set up;establish
树林 woods;grove
树苗 sapling
树木 trees
树皮 bark
树鼩 tree shrew
树梢 the tip of a tree;treetop

树身 tree trunk;trunk
树蛙 tree frog
树丫 crotch (of a tree)
树叶 leaf;leafage;foliage
树阴 the shade of a tree
树影 shadow of the tree
树葬 arbour burial
树枝 branch;twig
树脂 resin
树种 ①kinds of trees ②seeds of trees
树桩 tree stump;stump
树籽 seeds of trees
树榜样 set an example
树典型 hold sb up as model
树行子 grove;rows of trees;woods
树皮画 bark picture
树栽子 sapling
树脂酸 resinic acid
树碑立传 build up sb's public image;sing the praises of sb;place sb on the pedestal
树大根深 a big tree with deep roots (said of an influential person or a huge organization)
树大招风 a tall tree catches the wind—a person in a high position is liable to be attacked
树敌招怨 arouse a nest of hornets;make enemy;stir up a nest of hornets
树脂镜片 colophony glass
树脂整理 resin finishing
树倒猢狲散 Once the tree falls, the monkeys on it will disperse;When the chief falls from fortune or power, his followers disperse all at once.
树雄心,立壮志 cherish lofty aspirations;aim high and have lofty ambitions
树欲静而风不止 the tree may crave calm, but the wind will not drop—things take their own course regardless of one's will
树高千丈,叶落归根 a tree may grow a thousand *zhang* high, but its leaves fall back to the roots—a person residing away from home eventually returns to his native soil

竖 [shù]
I 形 vertical;straight up;upright;perpendicular II 动 set upright;put up;erect;stand III 名 ① vertical stroke (in Chinese characters) ②young servant
竖笛 recorder
竖钩 flute
竖井 (vertical) shaft
竖立 erect;set upright;stand
竖起 hold up;erect
竖琴 harp
竖着 endways
竖直 upright;vertical
竖柱 upright post
竖子 ①boy;lad ②mean fellow;fellow

竖蜻蜓 handstand
竖式钢琴 upright piano

恕 [shù]
I 名 forbearance (as advocated by Confucius);consideration for others II 动 ① forgive;pardon;excuse;allow for ②excuse me;beg your pardon
恕道 principle of reciprocity;do unto others as you wish others to do unto you
恕罪 pardon an offence;forgive a sin;forgive a mistake
恕不奉陪 excuse me (for not keeping you company)
恕不退货 non-refundable;all sale final
恕不远送 I am sorry I cannot escort you farther.
恕难从命 We regret that we cannot comply with your wishes.
恕我打扰 Excuse my troubling you.
恕我无知 Please forgive my ignorance.
恕我直言 Excuse me for being blunt,but...

庶 [shù]
I 形 multitudinous; numerous; myriad II 名 ①common people;the populace ②children born of (*or* by) the concubine (as distinguished from the wife) III 连 so that;so as to;in order to
庶保 in order to ensure...
庶出 be born of a concubine
庶多 very much
庶类 various kinds of animals;various things of life
庶民 the common people;the multitude
庶母 concubine of one's father
庶人 commoner;the common people
庶务 ① general affairs;business matters ②a person in charge of business matters
庶物 every kind of creature;all things of the universe
庶几乎 so that;so as to
庶不致误 so as to keep away from mistakes

腧 [shù]
名 acupuncture points on the human body
腧穴 acupuncture points on the human body

数 [shù]
I 名 ①number;figure ②number ③inexorable doom;fate;destiny II 数 several;a few ⇒ shǔ;shuò
数词 numeral
数额 a fixed number;a definite amount
数据 data
数控 numerical control (NC)
数量 quantity;amount
数列 an ordered series of numbers
数论 number theory
数码 ① numeral code ②number;amount ③ digital

S

数目 number；amount
数位 digit；numerical digit；digit position
数系 number system
数序 number sequence
数学 mathematics
数域 number field
数值 numerical value
数制 a system of computation
数轴 number axis
数珠 beads
数字 ① numeral；figure；digit ② quantity；a-mount
数据库 database；data bank
数据源 data source
数理化 mathematics，physics，and chemistry
数量词 numeral-classifier compound
数目字 ①numeral；figure；digit ②quantity；a-mount
数字化 digitalization
数据保护 data protection
数据处理 data processing
数据传输 data communications；data transfer
数据分析 data analysis
数据恢复 data recovery
数据加密 data encryption
数据模型 data model
数据通信 data communication
数据信号 data signal
数理逻辑 mathematical logic
数码磁带 digital tape
数码电视 digital television
数以万计 number in the tens of thousands
数字编码 digital coding；numeric coding
数字唱片 digital disk；digital disc
数字城市 digital city
数字地球 digital earth
数字电视 digital television
数字鸿沟 digital divide
数字控制 numerical control（NC）
数字通信 digital communication
数字显示 digital display（or presentation）
数字相机 digital camera
数罪并罚 cumulative punishment；combined punishment for more than one crime
数据工作站 data workbench
数据接收器 data sink
数理统计学 mathematical statistics
数码摄像机 digital video camera
数码照相机 digital camera
数字化部队 digital troops
数字化世界 digitalized world
数字化战场 digital battlefield
数字计算机 digital computer
数字式电视 digital television
数字图书馆 digital library
数字小键盘 numeric keypad
数据存储系统 data-storage system

数据终端设备 data terminal equipment
数值天气预报 numerical weather forecast
数字控制系统 numerical control system
数字视频技术 digital sound compression coding
数字移动电话 digital mobile telephone
数据库管理系统 database management system （DBMS）
数字程控交换机 digital program-controlled switchboards
数字高级移动电话系统 digital advanced mobile phone system（DAMPS）

墅 [shù]
图 villa

漱 [shù]
勋 gargle；rinse
漱口 rinse the mouth；gargle
漱出液 gargling
漱口杯 tooth glass
漱口剂 gargle
漱口药 mouth-wash
漱口液 gargle

澍 [shù]
图 timely rain

shuā（ㄕㄨㄚ）

刷 [shuā]
I 图 brush Ⅱ 勋 ①brush；scrub；clean ②daub；varnish；paint；paste ③expel；discharge；eliminate（through selection or competition） Ⅲ 象 swish；rustle；树叶被风吹得刷刷地响。The leaves rustled in the wind. → shuà
刷卡 punch the card；use a card（for payment）
刷啦 swish
刷洗 scrub；scour
刷新 ① renovate；refurbish ② outdo；surpass ③refresh
刷牙 brush（or clean）one's teeth
刷子 brush
刷标语 paste on posters

shuǎ（ㄕㄨㄚˇ）

耍 [shuǎ]
勋 ①play ②play with；juggle with；manipulate ③give play to；behave（in an unsavoury manner）④play with
耍逗 play with；tease
耍奸 try to shirk（work or responsibility）；act in a slick way
耍闹 have horseplay
耍弄 make fun of；make a fool of；deceive
耍钱 gamble
耍枪 playing with a spear
耍人 make fun of others；poke fun at others；make a fool of sb
耍笑 ①joke；have fun ②make fun of；play a joke on

耍把戏 ①give an acrobatic performance;perform juggling feats ②play tricks

耍笔杆 wield a pen; be skilled in literary tricks

耍狗熊 perform tricks with a bear; put on a bear show

耍猴儿 ①put on a monkey show ②make fun of sb;tease;kid

耍花腔 cheat by glib talk;speak guilefully

耍花招 ① display showy movements in *wushu*,etc. ②play (*or* get up to) tricks

耍滑(头) try to shirk (work or responsibility);act in a slick way

耍赖(皮) act shamelessly;be perverse

耍流氓 behave like a hoodlum; take liberties with women;act indecently

耍女人 play with the affections of a woman; womanize

耍排场 parade one's wealth;go in for ostentation and extravagance

耍派头 make a show of importance;put on airs

耍盘子 plate-spinning;disc-spinning

耍脾气 get into a huff;put on a show of bad temper

耍贫嘴 be garrulous

耍狮子 perform lion dance

耍手腕 use artifices;play tricks

耍手艺 make a living as a craftsman

耍态度 lose one's temper;get into a huff

耍坛子 juggling with jars;jar balancing act

耍威风 make a show of authority;throw one's weight about;be overbearing

耍无赖 make scene;create mischief;act perversely;be perverse

耍阴谋 hatch a conspiracy;brew a plot;conspire

耍鬼把戏 play a dirty trick;be up to mischief

耍两面派 resort to double-dealing tactics;be Janus-faced;play a double game;be double faced

耍心眼儿 exercise one's wits for personal gain;be calculating;pull a smart trick

耍嘴皮子 ① talk glibly;be a slick talker ② mere empty talk;lip service

shuà(ㄕㄨㄚˋ)

刷 [shuà]
〔动〕 select;pick;pick and choose ➡ shuā

刷白 white;pale

shuāi(ㄕㄨㄞ)

衰 [shuāi]
〔动〕 decline

衰败 decline;wane;be at a low ebb

衰惫 feeble and exhausted

衰敝 decline;wane;be at a low ebb

衰变 decay

衰草 withering grass

衰减 ①weaken;fail;diminish ②attenuation

衰竭 exhaustion;prostration

衰老 old and feeble;decrepit;senile

衰落 decline;be on the wane;go downhill

衰弱 ① weak; feeble ② weaken; diminish in strength

衰颓 weak and degenerate

衰退 fail;decline

衰亡 become feeble and die;decline and fall;wither away

衰微 decline;wane

衰萎 shrivel;wither

衰朽 feeble and decaying;decrepit

摔 [shuāi]
〔动〕 ① fall; tumble (after losing one's balance) ② hurtle down; plunge; crash; drop quickly ③(cause to) fall and break ④throw; cast;hurl;fling ⑤beat;knock

摔打 ①beat;knock ②rough it

摔跤 ①tumble;trip and fall ②trip up;come a cropper;make a blunder ③wrestling

摔跟头 ①tumble;trip and fall ②trip up;come a cropper;make a blunder

摔耙子 throw away one's job

shuǎi(ㄕㄨㄞˇ)

甩 [shuǎi]
〔动〕 ① swing; sway; wave ② throw; fling; hurl;toss ③throw off;leave behind

甩车 uncouple railway coaches from the locomotive;uncouple

甩掉 throw off;cast off;shake off;get rid of

甩干 spin-dry (laundry in an automatic washing machine);tumble-dry

甩卖 clearance sale; be on sale; disposal of goods at reduced prices;markdown sale;reduction sale

甩腔 dragged tune

甩手 ①swing one's arms ②refuse to do;wash one's hands of

甩线 fishing line

甩站 does not stop at scheduled stops

甩子 [shuǎizǐ] (of fish, insects, etc.) lay eggs

甩子 [shuǎizi] fly whisk;whisk

甩包袱 cast off burden; get a load off one's back

甩干机 spin-dryer

甩脸子 pull a long face

甩卖品 clearance goods

甩开膀子 go all out;go full steam ahead

甩手掌柜 "hand-off" boss—boss who merely gives general instructions but keeps his hands off any practical work; "do-noting" guy

shuài（ㄕㄨㄞˋ）

帅 ［shuài］
名 commander-in-chief Ⅱ 形 handsome; graceful; smart
帅才 born commander
帅哥 dashing guy
帅旗 flag of a commander in chief
帅气 handsome; elegant
帅印 seal of a commander in chief

率 ［shuài］
Ⅰ 动 ① lead; command ② follow; comply; conform Ⅱ 形 ① hasty; rash; impetuous ② frank; straightforward; forthright Ⅲ 副 in general; generally; usually ➡lǜ
率常 usually; generally
率尔 rashly; hastily
率领 lead; head; command
率然 hastily; rashly
率先 take the lead in doing sth; be the first to do sth
率性 ① so; fearfully ② wilfully; do whatever one pleases
率真 forthright and sincere
率直 straightforward; unreserved; blunt
率尔操觚 write at random
率忽应战 engage the enemy in haste
率由旧章 act in accordance with set rules; follow the beaten track

蟀 ［shuài］
◇蟋蟀 cricket (an insect)

shuān（ㄕㄨㄢ）

闩 ［shuān］
Ⅰ 名 bolt; latch; beam used to bar a door Ⅱ 动 fasten with a bolt (or latch)
闩锁 breech lock; latch

拴 ［shuān］
动 ①tie; bind; fasten ②be bogged down
拴绑 tie up; bind up
拴缚 tie up; bind up
拴马索 lariat

栓 ［shuān］
名 ①bolt; plug ②rifle bolt ③stopper; cork; anything resembling a cork or stopper
栓剂 suppository
栓皮 cork (the outer bark of a kind of oak tree)
栓塞 embolism
栓子 embolus
栓皮栎 oriental oak

shuàn（ㄕㄨㄢˋ）

涮 ［shuàn］
动 ①rinse ②scald thin slices of meat, etc. in boiling water; dip-boil ③cheat; trick; fool; deceive
涮手 rinse one's hands
涮锅子 instant-boil slices of meat and vegetables in a chafing dish
涮海鲜 dip-boil sea food
涮羊肉 ① instant-boil slices of mutton in a chafing dish ②instant-boiled mutton; Mongolian fire pot

shuāng（ㄕㄨㄤ）

双 ［shuāng］
Ⅰ 形 ① two; twin; both; dual ② even ③ double; twofold Ⅱ 量 pair; 一双手 a pair of hands
双倍 twofold; double
双边 bilateral
双层 double-deck; two-layers
双重 double; dual; twofold
双打 doubles
双方 both sides; the two parties
双飞 round trip flight
双幅 double width
双杠 parallel bars
双工 duplex operation; duplex; duplexing
双关 having a double meaning
双管 double-barrelled
双规 the prescribed time and place
双轨 double track
双号 even numbers (of tickets, seats, etc.)
双簧 a two-man act, with one acting in pantomime and another hiding behind him doing all the speaking or singing
双交 double cross
双联 duplex
双料 of reinforced material; extra quality
双轮 ①double round ②two-wheeled
双面 two-sided; double-edged; double-faced; reversible
双名 two-character given name
双抢 double rush for harvesting and sowing; rush planting and harvesting
双亲 (both) parents; father and mother
双全 be complete in both respects; possess both
双日 even-numbered days (of the month)
双生 twin
双声 alliterative compound
双手 both hands
双数 even numbers
双双 in pairs
双胎 twins
双态 bifurcation
双糖 disaccharide
双喜 double happiness
双响 double-bang firecracker (which goes off twice—once on the ground, and then again

in the air)
双向 two-way
双效 economic benefits and social benefits
双薪 double pay
双星 ①double star ②Altair and Vega
双姓 two-character surname
双选 two-way selection
双赢 win-win
双绉 crêpe de Chine
双座 two-seater;double-seater
双棒儿 twins
双胞胎 twins
双宾语 double object
双车道 dual-lane;two-lane;double lane
双唇音 bilabial consonant;bilabial (i.e. p,b, m in Chinese)
双份儿 double portion
双峰驼 two-humped camel;Bactrian camel
双宫丝 doupion silk
双挂号 registered mail requiring the receivers receipt
双关语 pun
双轨制 double system;dual-track system;two-tier system
双铧犁 double plow;two-bottom plow
双簧管 oboe
双季稻 double cropping of rice;double-harvest rice
双面绣 double-faced embroidery
双球菌 diplococcus
双曲面 hyperboloid
双曲线 hyperbola
双人舱 double cabin
双人床 double bed
双人房 double-bedded room; twin-bedded room
双人舞 dance for two performers;pas de deux
双刃剑 double-edged sword
双身子 a pregnant woman
双声道 double audio frequency line
双体船 catamaran
双下巴 double chin
双行道 two-way road (*or* street)
双休日 two-day weekend; double rest day; two-day day off
双学位 double major;double BA degree
双眼井 a twin-mouthed well
双眼皮 double-edged eyelid
双氧水 hydrogen peroxide solution
双翼机 biplane
双鱼座 Pisces
双语制 bilingualism
双元音 diphthong
双月刊 bimonthly (magazine)
双折射 double refraction
双职工 man and wife both at work;working couple

双周刊 biweekly (magazine);fortnightly
双子座 Gemini
双百方针 policy of letting a hundred flowers blossom and a hundred schools of thought contend
双倍赔偿 double refund
双边贸易 bilateral trade;two-way trade
双重保险 belt and braces;double insurance
双重标准 dual standard
双重承认 dual recognition
双重国籍 dual (*or* double) nationality
双重汇率 two-tier exchange rate
双重间谍 double agent
双重领导 double leadership; dual leadership; duel authority
双重人格 dual personality
双工控制 duplex control
双管齐下 paint a picture with two brushes at the same time—work along both lines; double-barreled
双机牵引 dual-locomotive traction
双联汇票 drafts in duplicate
双面织物 reversible cloth
双目失明 blind in both eyes;lose the sight of both eyes
双喜临门 Double blessings have descended upon the house.
双向付费 pay the air time for incoming calls as well as outgoing
双向交流 two-way exchanges
双向开关 two-way switch
双向选择 two-way selection
双音节词 disyllabic word;disyllable
双语教育 bilingual education
双重代表权 dual representation
双重税率制 dual tariff system
双缸洗衣机 twin-tub washer
双肩挑干部 cadres working on two different jobs
双轮双铧犁 two-wheeled double-shared plough
双面摇纱机 double reeling frame
双面印刷机 perfecting press;perfector
双目显微镜 binocular microscope
双筒望远镜 binoculars;field glasses
双向合同制 double-direction contract system
双子叶植物 dicotyledon
双层公共汽车 double deck bus;double decker
双方对等原则 principle of being equitable to both parties
双推力发动机 dual-thrust motor
双向飞碟射击 skeet shooting
双引擎战斗机 twin-engined fighter plane
双镜头反光照相机 twin-lens reflex

霜 [shuāng]
Ⅰ 名 ①frost ②frostlike powder Ⅱ 形 ① white;silver;hoary
霜冰 rime ice

霜晨 frosty morning
霜冻 frost (the frozen condition)
霜锋 shining edge of a knife
霜害 frost injury;frost
霜花 ①frostwork ②(soft) rime
霜降 ① Frost's Descent—the 18th of the 24 solar terms ② the day marking the beginning of the 18th solar term (Oct. 23 or 24, when hoarfrost descends and is likely to bring the first film of ice)
霜期 frost season
霜天 frosty day
霜雪 frost and snow
霜叶 frosty leaves—autumn maple leaves
霜灾 frost hazard
霜霉病 downy mildew

孀 [shuāng]
[名] widow
孀妇 widow
孀居 be a widow;live in widowhood

shuǎng(ㄕㄨㄤˇ)

爽 [shuǎng]
I [形] ①bright;clear;fresh;crisp ②frank;straightforward;forthright;open-hearted ③feel well II [动] make a mistake;deviate
爽脆 ①(of sounds or voices) sharp and clear ②frank;straightforward ③quick;brisk ④(of food) crisp and tasty
爽口 tasty and refreshing
爽快 ① refreshed;comfortable ② frank;outright;straightforward ③ with alacrity;readily
爽朗 ① bright and clear ② hearty;candid;frank and open;straightforward
爽利 brisk and neat;efficient and able
爽亮 ① loud and clear;resounding;sonorous ②cheerful;sanguine
爽目 pleasing to the eye
爽然 at a loss
爽声 (in) a loud and clear voice
爽信 fail to keep one's promise;break one's promise;go back on one's word
爽性 may just as well
爽约 fail to keep an appointment;break an appointment
爽直 frank;straightforward;candid
爽滑剂 slipping agent
爽身粉 talcum powder
爽然若失 not know what to do;be at a loss

shuǐ(ㄕㄨㄟˇ)

水 [shuǐ]
I [名] ①water ②river ③general term for rivers,lakes,seas,etc.;water ④liquid ⑤additional cost;extra income II [量] times of

washing:洗过两水 be washed twice
水吧 water bar
水坝 dam
水泵 water pump
水笔 ①a stiff-haired writing brush (or water-colour paintbrush) ②fountain pen
水边 water's edge;waterside;waterfront
水标 water gauge
水表 water meter
水鳖 frogbit
水滨 waterside;waterfront
水兵 seaman;sailor;bluejacket
水波 wave;ripple
水彩 watercolour
水仓 sump
水槽 water channel
水草 ① water and grass ② waterweed;water plants
水趸 the nymph of the dragonfly,etc.
水产 aquatic products
水车 ①waterwheel (for raising water or driving machinery) ②watercart;water waggon
水城 waterside town
水程 journey by boat;voyage
水池 pond;pool;cistern
水尺 water gauge
水床 water bed
水袋 water bag
水道 ①water course ②waterway;water route ③lanes in a swimming pool
水稻 paddy (rice);rice
水地 ①irrigated land ②paddy field
水电 ① hydraulic power generation ② water and electricity
水貂 mink
水洞 water-tunnel
水痘 varicella;chicken pox;water pox
水肥 liquid manure
水肺 aqualung
水粉 ①soaked noodles made from beans (or sweet potatoes) ②a cosmetic made from face powder and glycerine
水分 ①moisture content ②exaggeration
水缸 water vat
水拱 water bridge
水沟 ditch;drain;gutter
水垢 scale;incrustation
水臌 ascites
水管 waterpipe
水罐 water pot;water tank
水龟 terrapin
水柜 ① water tank ② cistern;reservoir ③ counter (in a shop)
水锅 boiler
水果 fruit
水合 hydration
水红 bright pink;cerise

水壶 ①kettle ②canteen ③watering can
水花 spray
水华 water bloom；algal bloom
水患 flood；inundation
水荒 water shortage
水毁 destroyed by flood
水火 ①fire and water—two things diametrically opposed to each other ②extreme misery
水货 smuggled goods；"parallel goods"
水鸡 ①water bird ②frog ③a drenched chicken；a drowned rat
水碱 scale；incrustation
水礁 water-powered trip-hammer (for husking rice)
水饺 boiled dumplings
水解 hydrolysis
水晶 crystal；rock crystal
水井 well
水景 waterscape
水警 water police；coastal guard；river patrol
水酒 watery wine
水具 glassware for drinking water
水军 waterborne troops；navy
水坑 puddle；pool；water hole
水口 water gap
水库 reservoir
水裤 wader
水牢 water dungeon
水涝 waterlogging
水雷 (submarine) mine
水冷 water-cooling
水力 waterpower；hydraulic power
水利 ① water conservancy ② irrigation works；water conservancy project
水帘 cascade；waterfall
水疗 hydropathy；hydrotherapy
水灵 ①(of fruit, greens, etc.) fresh and juicy ②(of appearance) bright and beautiful；radiant and vivacious
水溜 eaves gutter
水流 ① rivers；streams；waters ② current；flow
水龙 fire hose；hose
水陆 ①land and water ②delicacies from land and sea
水路 waterway；water route
水绿 light green
水轮 waterwheel
水门 water valve
水密 watertight
水面 ①the surface of the water ②the area of a body of water
水磨 [shuǐmó] ①polish with a water stone ②grind grain, etc. fine while adding water
水磨 [shuǐmò] watermill
水母 jellyfish；medusa

水幕 water screen
水难 shipwreck
水泥 cement
水碾 water-powered roller (for grinding grain)
水鸟 aquatic bird；water bird
水牛 (water) buffalo
水暖 ①hot water central heating system ②water supply and heating
水泡 bubble
水疱 blister
水盆 basin
水瓢 (gourd) water ladle
水平 ①horizontal；level ②standard；level
水汽 water vapour；steam
水枪 giant；(hydraulic) monitor
水橇 water ski
水禽 waterfowl；water bird
水情 regimen
水球 water polo
水渠 ditch；canal
水圈 hydrosphere
水杉 metasequoia
水上 on (or above) water
水笪 a pail made of wood (or bamboo) strips；bucket
水蛇 water snake
水师 waterborne forces (in former times)
水虱 beach louse
水蚀 erosion by the action of running water
水势 the flow of water；the rise and fall of flood-water
水手 seaman；sailor
水松 China cypress (Glyptostrobus pensilis)
水塔 water tower
水獭 otter
水潭 puddle；pool
水塘 pool；pond
水体 waters；body of water
水田 paddy field；paddy
水桶 pail；bucket
水头 ①head ②flood peak；peak of flow
水土 ①water and soil ②natural environment and climate
水洼 paddles of water
水弯 arm；brace
水网 a network of rivers, rivulets, lakes and ponds
水位 water level
水文 hydrology
水螅 hydra
水系 river system；hydrographic net
水下 under water
水仙 narcissus (the plant and its flower)
水险 marine insurance
水线 waterline
水乡 a region of rivers and lakes

水箱 water tank
水泻 watery diarrhoea
水榭 waterside pavilion
水星 Mercury
水性 ①ability in swimming ②the depth, currents and other characteristics of a river, lake, etc. ③(of a woman) of easy virtue
水袖 water sleeves
水锈 ① scale; incrustation ② watermark (in water vessels)
水选 seed or ore selection by immersion
水靴 water boots
水压 hydraulic (*or* water) pressure
水烟 shredded tobacco for water pipes
水样 water sample
水银 mercury; quicksilver
水域 waters; water area; a body of water
水源 ①the source of a river; headwaters; waterhead ②source of water
水运 water transport
水灾 flood; inundation
水葬 water burial
水蚤 water flea
水藻 algae
水泽 a region of rivers, lakes and marshes
水闸 sluice; water gate
水战 a battle on water
水质 water quality
水蛭 leech
水肿 oedema; dropsy
水珠 a drop of water
水柱 water column
水准 level; standard
水族 aquatic animals
水半球 water hemisphere
水饱儿 feel bloated after eating much liquid food
水玻璃 water glass
水彩画 watercolour (painting)
水产品 aquatic product
水产业 aquatic industry
水池子 ①pond; pool; cistern ②sink
水处理 water treatment
水稻土 rice (*or* paddy) soil
水电费 charges for water and electricity
水电机 water motor
水电站 hydroelectric (power) station; hydropower station
水飞蓟 milk thistle
水粉画 painting gouache
水果刀 fruit knife
水果糖 fruit drops
水合水 hydrate water
水合物 hydrate
水葫芦 water hyacinth
水火地 an area afflicted alternately with drought and waterlogging

水浇地 irrigated land
水解质 hydrolyte
水晶包 a steamed dumpling stuffed with diced pig fat and sugar
水晶宫 the Crystal Palace (of the Dragon King)
水晶棺 crystal sarcophagus
水晶体 crystalline lens
水净化 water purification
水老鸦 cormorant
水涝地 waterlogged land
水力学 hydraulics
水利化 bring all farmland under irrigation
水疗法 hydrotherapy
水淋淋 dripping wet
水流星 spinning bowls of water; water meteors
水龙骨 wall fern; golden locks
水龙卷 waterspout
水龙头 (water) tap; faucet; bibcock
水漉漉 wet; damp
水铝矿 gibbsite (a mineral)
水轮泵 (water) turbine pump
水轮机 hydraulic (*or* water) turbine
水落管 downspout; water-spout
水煤气 water gas
水锰矿 manganite (a mineral)
水蜜桃 honey peach
水磨石 terrazzo
水墨画 ink and wash; wash painting
水泥厂 cement plant
水泥船 concrete boat; plastered boat
水泥浆 cement wash; cement paste
水泥瓦 cement tile
水牛儿 snail
水暖工 plumber
水培法 water culture; hydroponics
水平面 level surface; level
水平线 level line; level
水平仪 level; spirit level
水曲柳 Manchurian ash
水溶液 aqueous solution
水蛇腰 a very slender waist
水声学 marine acoustics
水手长 boatswain
水刷石 granitic plaster
水田犁 paddy plough
水田耙 paddy harrow
水汪汪 ① full of water; very wet ② (of children's or young women's eyes) bright and intelligent
水位计 fluviograph
水文队 hydrological team
水文图 hydrological map
水文学 hydrology
水文站 hydrometric station; hydrologic station
水污染 water pollution; water contamination

水循环 hydrologic cycle; water cycle
水压机 hydraulic press
水烟袋 water pipe
水舀子 dipper; ladle; scoop (for water)
水翼船 hydrofoil
水翼艇 hydrofoil boat
水银灯 mercury-vapour lamp
水银柱 mercury column
水莹莹 (of eyes, etc.) radiant and crystal-clear; bright and clear
水硬度 hardness of water
水源林 shelter belts to protect the headwaters of rivers
水栽法 water culture; hydroponics
水栽培 hydroponics; water culture
水蒸气 steam; water vapour
水准点 bench mark
水准面 level surface; level plane
水准器 level; spirit level
水准仪 surveyor's level
水资源 water resource
水渍险 with particular average (W.P.A.)
水族馆 aquarium
水族箱 aquarium
水彩颜料 watercolour
水产养殖 aquaculture
水到渠成 when the water comes, a channel is formed—when conditions are ripe, success is achieved
水滴石穿 Dripping water wears through rock; Little strokes fell great oaks.
水底电缆 submarine cable; subaqueous cable
水电资源 hydroelectric resource
水果罐头 tinned (or canned) fruit
水果软糖 fruit jelly
水火无情 Floods and fires have no mercy.
水解产物 hydrolysate
水解蛋白 protein hydrolysate
水晶玻璃 crystal (glass)
水力发电 hydraulic power generation
水力开采 hydraulic mining
水力资源 hydroelectric resources (or potential); waterpower resources
水利工程 irrigation works; water conservancy project (or works)
水利设施 water conservancy facilities
水利枢纽 key water control project
水利资源 water resources
水陆联运 land-and-water coordinated transport; water-land transshipment
水陆两用 amphibious; able to live on land and in the water
水陆坦克 amphibious tank
水陆运输 transportation by land and water
水轮泵站 (water) turbine-pump station
水落石出 when the water subsides the rocks emerge—the whole thing comes to light

水门事件 Watergate Incident
水米无交 ① have no relations (or contact) with each other ② (of officials) be upright and accept no gifts from the people
水磨功夫 patient and precise work; painstaking work
水泥标号 strength of cement; cement grade
水泥森林 forest of skyscrapers
水平飞行 horizontal (or level) flight
水平轰炸 horizontal (or level) bombing
水平贸易 horizontal trade
水平扫描 horizontal sweep; horizontal scanning
水平输出 horizontal output
水汽浓度 vapour concentration
水乳交融 as well blended as milk and water—in complete harmony
水上芭蕾 water ballet
水上飞机 seaplane; hydroplane
水上居民 boat dwellers
水上人家 boat dwellers
水上运动 aquatic sports; water sports
水深火热 deep water and scorching fire—an abyss of suffering; extreme misery
水生动物 aquatic animal
水生植物 water (or aquatic) plant; hydrophyte
水体污染 contamination of water bodies
水天一色 The water and the sky blended in one colour (said of a vast body of water).
水土保持 water and soil conservation
水土不服 not acclimatized
水土流失 water loss and soil erosion
水文年鉴 Water Year Book
水文预报 hydrologic forecast
水下发射 underwater launching
水泄不通 not even a drop of water could trickle through; be watertight
水性杨花 (of a woman) have easy virtue; have loose morals; easy to seduce
水印木刻 watercolour block printing; watermark
水运码头 a port handling river (or ocean) cargo
水涨船高 When the river rises the boat goes up.
水针疗法 acupuncture therapy with medicinal injection; liquid acupuncture
水质保护 water quality protection
水质污染 water pollution
水中捞月 fish for the moon—make impractical or vain efforts
水稻插秧机 rice (or paddy) transplanter
水工建筑物 hydraulic structure
水火不相容 be incompatible as fire and water
水力发电站 hydroelectric (power) station; hydropower station

S

水利工程学 hydraulic engineering
水利灌溉网 irrigation network
水陆交通线 land and water communication lines
水陆两用车 amphibious vehicle
水轮发电机 water turbogenerator
水文地理学 hydrography
水文地质学 hydrogeology
水文气象学 hydrometeorology
水银气压表 mercury (*or* mercurial) barometer
水银温度计 mercury (*or* mercurial) thermometer
水资源保护 water resource protection
水陆联运码头 a dock for joint land and water transport service
水陆两用飞机 amphibious aircraft
水有源,树有根 every river has its source and every tree its roots—everything has its origin
水能载舟,亦能覆舟 While the waters can bear the boat,they can also sink it.
水至清则无鱼,人至察则无徒 water which is too clean has few fish;he who is too critical has few friends—one should not demand absolute purity

shuì(ㄕㄨㄟˋ)

说 [shuì]
动 persuade;bring round ➡ shuō

悦 [shuì]
名 shawl

税 [shuì]
名 tax;duty;revenue
税单 tax list
税额 the amount of tax to be paid
税法 taxation regulations;tax law
税负 tax burdens
税改 tax reform;reform of tax system
税号 duty paragraph
税后 after-tax
税基 tax base
税金 tax payment;taxation
税款 tax payment;taxation
税率 tax rate;rate of taxation;tariff rate
税目 tax items;taxable items
税前 pre-tax;before tax
税收 tax revenue
税源 source of taxes
税则 tax regulations
税政 tax administration
税制 tax system;taxation
税种 items of taxation;tax category
税后利 after-tax profits
税务局 tax bureau
税务员 tax collector
税后净利 net profit after tax

税后所得 income after taxes
税率封顶 rate-capping
税前利润 pre-tax profits
税收抵免 tax credit
税收功能 taxation functions
税收鼓励 tax incentive
税收流失 tax losses
税收征管 tax administration;tax collection and management
税收政策 tax policy
税务机关 tax authorities
税务人员 tax collector
税制改革 taxation reform;reform in the tax system
税收管理权 tax jurisdiction
税务稽查员 inspector of taxes

睡 [shuì]
动 sleep
睡袋 sleeping bag
睡觉 sleep
睡裤 pyjama trousers
睡莲 water lily;candock
睡帽 nightcap
睡梦 sleep;slumber
睡眠 sleep
睡魔 extreme sleepiness
睡袍 nightgown;nightdress
睡狮 sleeping lion
睡乡 dreamland
睡醒 wake up
睡衣 nightclothes;pyjamas
睡椅 reclining chair;deck chair
睡意 sleepiness;drowsiness
睡着 [shuìzháo] get to sleep;doze off
睡美人 sleeping beauty
睡眠疗法 physiological sleep therapy
睡眼惺忪 eyes still heavy with sleep;eyes still fogged with sleep
睡眠呼吸暂停综合征 sleep apnea syndrome

shǔn(ㄕㄨㄣˇ)

吮 [shǔn]
动 suck
吮乳 suck milk
吮吸 suck
吮痈舐痔 lick sb's ulcers and piles—debase oneself in trying to please sb important or powerful

shùn(ㄕㄨㄣˋ)

顺 [shùn]
Ⅰ 动 ①obey;yield to;submit to ②arrange;sort out;put in order ③ be suitable;be agreeable ④act at one's convenience;take the opportunity Ⅱ 形 ①lucky;smooth;successful ②harmonious Ⅲ 介 along

顺坝 longitudinal dike
顺变 conform to changes（*or* unforeseen events）
顺便 (do sth) in addition to what one is already doing；without much extra effort
顺差 favourable balance；surplus
顺产 natural labour
顺畅 smooth and easy；unhindered
顺磁 paramagnetic
顺次 in order；in succession；in proper sequence
顺从 be obedient to；submit to；yield to
顺带 (do sth) in addition to what one is already doing，without much extra effort
顺当 smooth；without a hitch；plain sailing
顺导 guide（*or* steer）（a movement, etc.）along its proper course
顺耳 pleasing to the ear
顺访 visit (a place, person, etc.) on the way
顺风 ①have a favourable wind；have a tail wind ②favourable wind；tail wind
顺服 obey；be obedient；be docile
顺和 genial；gentle；affable
顺价 earning price
顺脚 ①(do sth) on the way；without going out of one's way ②be a direct route
顺境 favourable circumstances
顺口 ①read smoothly ②say offhandedly；say without thinking ③suit one's taste
顺利 smooth；successful；without a hitch
顺路 ①on the way ②be a direct route
顺民 abjectly obedient citizens
顺市 confirm to market tendency
顺势 ①take advantage of an opportunity（as provided by an opponent's reckless move）②conveniently；in passing
顺手 ①smooth；without a hitch；without difficulty ②conveniently；without extra trouble ③(do sth) as a natural sequence or simultaneously ④handy；convenient and easy to use
顺水 downstream；with the stream
顺遂 (of things) go well；go smoothly
顺心 be satisfactory
顺行 direct motion
顺序 ①sequence；order ②in proper order；in turn
顺延 postpone
顺眼 pleasing to the eye
顺应 comply with；conform to
顺着 [shùnzhe] along with
顺证 a serious case which improves steadily
顺嘴 ①read smoothly ②say offhandedly ③suit one's taste
顺道儿 ①on the way ②be a direct route
顺风耳 ①a person in traditional Chinese novels who can hear voices a long way off ②a

well-informed person
顺口溜 doggerel；jingle
顺时针 clockwise
顺丁橡胶 butadiene rubber
顺风吹火 take advantage of favourable conditions
顺风转舵 bend with wind；tack with wind；trim one's sails；take one's cue from changing conditions
顺竿儿爬 take one's cue from sb and say everything to please him
顺乎民意 conform to the popular will
顺口搭音 echo what others say；chime in with others
顺理成章 (of a statement, argument, etc.) logical；well reasoned
顺其自然 let nature take its course；in accordance with its natural tendency
顺势疗法 homoeopathy
顺手牵羊 lead off a goat in passing—pick up sth on the sly；walk off with sth
顺水人情 a favour done at little or no cost
顺水推舟 push the boat along with the current—make use of an opportunity to gain one's end
顺顺当当 by a happy chance；win in a canter；easily；smoothly
顺藤摸瓜 follow the vine to get the melon—track down sb or sth by following clues
顺序入场 enter the hall one by one
顺应民心 comply with the wishes（*or* aspirations）of the people；bow to the will of the people
顺应时代潮流 be in keeping with the tide of the times
顺之者昌, 逆之者亡 Those who submit will prosper, those who resist shall perish.

瞬 [shùn]
〔名〕 wink；twinkling
瞬间 in the twinkling of an eye
瞬时 instantaneous
瞬息 twinkling
瞬时性 instantaneity
瞬时值 instantaneous value
瞬时速度 instantaneous velocity
瞬息万变 undergoing a myriad changes in the twinkling of an eye；change rapidly

shuō（ㄕㄨㄛ）

说 I 〔动〕 ①speak；talk；say；express oneself by words ②give an explanation；explain ③scold；criticise ④act as go-between；act as matchmaker；introduce ⑤hint；indicate；refer to II 〔名〕 theory；views；doctrine ➡shuì
说白 spoken parts in an opera
说唱 ballard-singing

说穿　tell what sth really is;reveal;disclose
说辞　excuse;pretext
说道　[shuōdào] say (the words quoted)
说道　[shuōdao] ①say;tell ②talk over;discuss ③what lies behind sth;reason
说定　settle;agree on
说法　[shuōfǎ] expound Buddhist teachings
说法　[shuōfa] ①way of saying a thing;wording;formulation ② statement;version;argument
说服　persuade;convince;prevail on; talk sb over
说好　come to an agreement (or understanding)
说合　①bring two (or more) parties together ②talk over;discuss
说和　mediate a settlement;compose a quarrel
说话　① speak;talk;say ② chat;talk ③ censure;gossip;talk ④very soon;in a minute
说谎　tell a lie;lie
说教　①deliver a sermon;preach ②preachify
说开　①explain clearly ②(of words or expressions) be in current use
说客　①a person often sent to win sb over (or enlist his support through persuasion) ②a persuasive talker
说来　come to speak of it
说理　① argue; reason things out ②(usu. used in the negative) listen to reason;be reasonable
说媒　act as a matchmaker
说明　① explain;illustrate ② show;prove ③ explanation;directions;caption
说破　lay bare;reveal
说亲　act as a matchmaker
说情　plead for mercy for sb;intercede for sb
说啥　no matter what one says
说是　be said to;be supposed to;they say
说书　storytelling
说死　fix definitely;make it definite
说妥　come to an agreement
说戏　(of a film or play director) explain (to one or more actors) how a part or a scene is to be acted
说项　put in a good word for;intercede for
说笑　chat and laugh
说嘴　①brag;boast ②argue;quarrel
说不得　①unspeakable;unmentionable ②scandalous ③have no say;have to comply
说不定　perhaps;maybe
说不过　cannot match sb's eloquence
说不好　be unable to say for certain;not be certain;can't say
说不来　①cannot get along (with sb) ②not know how to put it
说不清　be unable to explain clearly
说不上　①cannot say;cannot tell ②not worth

mentioning
说大话　brag;boast;talk big
说到底　in the final analysis;at bottom
说得来　①can get along;be on good terms ②have a glib tongue
说漏嘴　let slip a remark;make a slip of the tongue
说梦话　talk in one's dream;talk nonsense;talk in sleep
说明书　(a booklet of) directions;(technical) manual;synopsis (of a play or film)
说明文　expository writing;exposition
说婆家　find a husband
说破嘴　talk till one is hoarse; talk oneself hoarse
说起来　in fact;as a matter of fact
说头儿　①sth to talk about ②excuse
说闲话　①gossip;grumble ②chat
说笑话　①tell a joke ②joke
说不过去　cannot be justified (or explained) away
说不下去　be unable to finish what one is saying
说长道短　talk about right and wrong of other people;gossip
说到做到　do what one says;match one's deeds to one's words;live up to one's word
说得过去　be justifiable;be passable
说东道西　chatter away on a variety of things
说短论长　gossip
说好说歹　use every possible argument to convince sb
说黑道白　criticize irresponsibly (or thoughtlessly)
说话算话　fit one's deeds to one's words;abide by one's promise
说黄道黑　talk irresponsibly;gossip
说来话长　it's a long story
说来说去　repeat over and over again
说良心话　be fair
说漂亮话　offer lip service;pay lip service to
说千道万　keep on stating one's point
说三道四　make irresponsible remarks
说一不二　mean what one says;stand by one's word
说着玩儿　be joking;not be serious in saying sth
说得多做得少　much talk but little action;a giant in word but a dwarf in deed
说到钱,便无缘　To speak of a loan is to put an end to friendship.
说时迟,那时快　in the twinkling of an eye;in an instant
说曹操曹操就到　mention Cao Cao and there he is;talk of the devil and he will appear

shuò（ㄕㄨㄛˋ）

妁 [shuò]
◇媒妁 matchmaker

烁 [shuò]
〔形〕bright；brilliant；shining
烁亮 dazzling；brilliant；resplendent
烁烁 glitter；sparkle

铄 [shuò]
〔动〕① melt（metal，etc.）② waste away；weaken
铄石流金（hot enough to）make rocks and metals melt—sweltering

朔 [shuò]
〔名〕① new moon ② first day of the lunar month ③ north
朔方 north
朔风 north wind
朔日 the first day of the lunar month
朔望 the first and the fifteenth day of the lunar month；syzygy
朔月 new moon
朔望月 lunar month；lunation；synodic month
朔风呼啸 The north wind is whistling.

硕 [shuò]
〔形〕big；large
硕导 supervisor of postgraduate students
硕果 rich fruits；great achievements
硕士 master
硕大无朋 of enormous size；huge；gigantic
硕果仅存 sole survival；rare survival
硕学通儒 a wise and learned scholar

蒴 [shuò]
〔名〕sesame；capsule
蒴果 capsule

搠 [shuò]
〔动〕stab；poke；thrust

数 [shuò]
〔副〕often；frequently；repeatedly ➡ shǔ；shù
数脉 rapid pulse
数见不鲜 be a common occurrence；be nothing new

槊 [shuò]
〔名〕*shuo*，ancient spear，which has a fairly long pole

sī（ㄙ）

司 [sī]
Ⅰ〔动〕take charge of；attend to；operate；manage Ⅱ〔名〕① department（under a ministry）② official in charge of a department；official
司舵 ① be at the helm；steer a boat ② helmsman；steersman
司法 administration of justice；judicature
司号 ① sound a bugle ② bugler；trumpeter
司机 driver；chauffeur

司考 national judicial examination
司库 cashier；treasure；keeper of treasure vaults
司令 commander；commanding officer
司炉 stoker；fireman
司务 ① petty official in charge of miscellaneous duties ② craftsman；workman
司药 pharmacist；druggist；chemist
司仪 master of ceremonies
司职 take up a position（*or* responsibility）
司钻 (head) driller
司泵员 pump man；pumper
司法权 judicial powers
司号员 bugler；trumpeter
司令部 headquarters command
司令台 review stand
司令员 commander；commanding officer
司务长 mess officer；company quartermaster
司线员 linesman
司乘人员 drivers and attendants（on a bus or train）
司法部门 judicial department；judiciary
司法独立 have an independent judiciary
司法腐败 judicial corruption
司法机关 judicial organ
司法鉴定 expert testimony（*or* evidence）
司法救助 judicial aid
司法人员 judicial and law-enforcement personnel
司空见惯 common sight；common occurrence
司售人员 bus drivers and conductors（ticket collectors）
司马昭之心，路人皆知 Sima Zhao's ill intent is known to all—the villain's design is obvious

丝 [sī]
Ⅰ〔名〕① silk ② anything threadlike ③ one ten-thousandth of certain units of measure ④ unit of weight（= 0.0005 grams）⑤ unit of length（= 0.0033 millimetres）Ⅱ〔量〕tiny bit；least bit：露出一丝笑容 reveal（*or* betray）a trace of smile
丝虫 filaria（a parasitic worm）
丝绸 silk cloth；silk
丝带 silk ribbon；silk braid；silk sash
丝杠 guide screw；leading screw
丝糕 steamed millet；steamed corn cake
丝瓜 towel gourd；dishcloth gourd
丝光 the silky lustre of mercerized cotton fabrics
丝毫 the slightest amount（*or* degree）；a bit；a particle；a shred；an iota
丝极 filament
丝萝 the bond of marriage
丝米 decimillimetre
丝绵 silk floss；silk wadding
丝绒 velvet；velour
丝袜 silk stockings（*or* socks）

S

丝网 silk screen
丝弦 ①silk string ②a Hebei provincial opera
丝线 silk thread; silk yarn
丝质 silk quality
丝竹 ①traditional stringed and woodwind instruments ②music
丝状 filiform
丝锥 tap
丝虫病 filariasis
丝瓜络 loofah; vegetable sponge
丝光机 mercerizing range
丝织品 ①silk fabrics ②silk knit goods
丝绸之路 the Silk Road
丝杠车床 leading screw lathe
丝光纱线 mercerized yarn
丝丝拉拉 off and on; intermittently
丝丝入扣 (done) with meticulous care and flawless artistry
丝网印刷 screen printing
丝网印刷机 screen process press

私 [sī]
形 ①personal; private ②selfish ③secret; stealthy; private ④illicit; illegal; unlawful
私奔 elope
私弊 corrupt practices
私藏 ①a private collection ②keep (or possess) illegally
私产 private property
私娼 unlicensed (or unregistered) prostitute
私仇 personal enmity (or grudge)
私处 private parts; genitals
私党 personal clique or faction
私邸 private residence (of a high-ranking official)
私法 private law
私贩 smuggle; traffic in contraband goods
私房 [sīfáng] a privately owned house; private residence
私访 (of officials) go incognito among the people to make investigations
私房 [sīfang] ①private savings ②confidential
私愤 personal spite
私股 private shares (in a joint state-private enterprise)
私函 private letter
私活 private job done during work hours instead of in one's spare time
私货 run goods; smuggled goods; contraband goods
私家 privately owned (or engaged)
私见 ①personal prejudice ②personal opinion
私交 personal friendship
私酒 bootleg liquor; moonshine
私立 privately run; private
私利 private (or selfish) interests; personal gain

私了 settle a case out of court; reconcile before going public
私密 privacy; private
私囊 private purse
私念 selfish motives (or ideas)
私企 privately-run enterprise
私情 personal relationships
私人 ①private; personal ②one's own man
私商 ①privately owned shop ②businessman; merchant; trader
私事 private (or personal) affairs
私塾 old-style private school
私逃 abscond
私通 ① have secret communication with ② have illicit intercourse; commit adultery
私图 one's personal scheme (or attempt)
私下 in private; in secret
私心 selfish motives (or ideas); selfishness
私信 private letter; personal letter
私刑 illegal punishment (meted out by a kangaroo court); lynching
私行 do sth in a private capacity (or on one's own initiative)
私蓄 personal (or private) savings
私盐 smuggled salt; contraband salt
私营 privately owned; privately run (or operated); private
私有 privately owned; private
私语 ①whisper ②confidence
私欲 selfish desire
私运 smuggle
私章 personal seal; signet
私自 privately; secretly; without permission
私底下 in private; in secret
私生活 private life
私生子 a child born out of wedlock; illegitimate child
私有化 privatization; denationalization
私有制 private ownership (of means of production)
私藏武器 unlawful possession of weapons
私订终身 pledge to marry without the permission of parents
私人代表 personal representative
私人经济 private sector of the economy
私人劳动 individual labour
私人秘书 private secretary
私人企业 individual enterprise; private enterprise
私设公堂 set up an illegal court; get up a kangaroo court
私相授受 privately give and accept; illegally pass things between individuals; make an illicit transfer
私心杂念 selfish ideas and personal considerations; selfish considerations
私营经济 private sector of the economy

私营企业 private enterprises; self-employed businesses
私有财产 private property
私有观念 private ownership mentality
私有经济 private economy

唑 [sī]
象 (of shells and bullets) whistle

思 [sī]
I 动 ①think; consider; ponder ②think of; long for; miss ③wish; hope; desire II 名 train of thought
思潮 ①trend of thought; ideological trend ②thoughts
思忖 ponder; consider
思凡 (of an immortal or of a monk or a nun) long for the world; yearn for the company of the opposite sex
思归 wish to go home; be homesick
思过 ponder over one's mistakes; make an introspection into one's faults
思旧 think fondly of past times (*or* old acquaintances)
思考 think deeply; ponder over; reflect on
思恋 think fondly of; long for
思量 consider
思路 train of thought; thinking
思虑 consider; contemplate; deliberate
思慕 think of sb with respect; admire
思念 think of; long for; miss
思索 think deeply; ponder
思维 ①thought; thinking ②think; consider
思乡 be homesick
思想 thought; thinking; idea; ideology
思绪 ①train of thought; thinking ②feeling
思想家 thinker
思想库 think bank; brain trust
思想性 ideological content (*or* level)
思前虑后 ponder over the cause and effect of a thing
思如泉涌 ideas teeming in one's mind
思贤若渴 (of a ruler) thirst for (*or* long for) the assistance of wise men
思想包袱 sth weighing on one's mind
思想动态 trends of thoughts
思想动向 ideological trend
思想斗争 mental struggle; ideological struggle
思想方法 method (*or* mode, way) of thinking
思想负担 load on one's mind; mental burden
思想改造 ideological remoulding
思想高度 ideological plane; intellectual level
思想疙瘩 mental block; hang-up
思想根源 underlying causes of words and deeds
思想工作 ideological work
思想回潮 an ideological relapse (*or* retrogression)
思想汇报 (give an) account of one's ideolog-

ical progress and problems
思想检查 check on one's thinking; examine one's wrong ideas
思想见面 have frank exchange of ideas
思想僵化 fossilized concept; thinking world become rigid
思想交流 traffic in ideas
思想教育 ideological education
思想禁锢 ideological shackles
思想禁区 ideologically forbidden zone
思想境界 ideological level
思想觉悟 political consciousness (*or* awareness)
思想烙印 ideological imprint; deep influences on (one's) thinking
思想路线 ideological line
思想体系 ideological system; ideology
思想问题 a problem arising from erroneous thinking; ideological problem
思想武装 ideological weapon
思想修养 ideological cultivation (degree of ideological sophistication)
思想意识 ideology
思想战线 ideological front
思想作风 one's way of thinking, work-style, and life-style
思想道德建设 construction of ideology and morality; raise people's ideological and moral standards
思想道德素质 ideological and ethical quality (*or* standards)
思想政治工作 ideological and political work (in guiding or directing people's way of thinking)

斯 [sī]
I 代 this; here II 连 then; thus
斯时 this time (*or* moment)
斯文 [sīwén] ①culture ②men of letters; scholars; literati
斯文 [sīwen] refined; gentle
斯文败类 scum of the literati
斯文扫地 disgrace one's scholarly dignity; scholarly dignity swept into the dust

厮 [sī]
I 名 ①male servant ②fellow; guy II 副 each other; together
厮缠 pester
厮打 wrestle; grapple; tussle
厮混 fool around (*or* about) with sb; play around (*or* about) with sb
厮闹 play; romp; frolic
厮拼 fight; battle it out
厮杀 fight at close quarters (with weapons)
厮熟 be well acquainted; know each other well; become close
厮敬厮爱 love and respect each other

澌 [sī]
〈名〉 floating ice (as on a river during the spring thaw); ice floe

撕 [sī]
〈动〉 tear; rend; rip
撕毁 tear up; tear to shreds
撕票 (of kidnappers) kill the hostage
撕破 tear; rip
撕碎 rive; destroy
撕咬 bait; worry
撕纸 paper-tear picture (folk art)
撕破脸 put aside all considerations of face; not spare sb's sensibilities
撕毁合同 tear up a contract; scrap a contract
撕心裂肺 grieved

嘶 [sī]
I 〈动〉 (of horses) neigh II 〈形〉 hoarse III 〈象〉 whistle
嘶喊 shout; yell
嘶叫 ① shout; yell; scream ② neigh; whinny; (of donkeys) bray
嘶鸣 neigh; whinny; bray
嘶哑 hoarse

澌 [sī]
〈副〉 totally; completely

SǏ(ㄙˇ)

死 [sī]
I 〈动〉 die; cease to live; be dead II 〈副〉 ① to the death ② determinedly; adamantly; unyieldingly ③ very; extremely III 〈形〉 ① implacable; deadly; irreconcilable ② fixed; rigid; stereotyped; inflexible ③ impassable; closed
死板 rigid; stiff; inflexible
死别 be parted by death; part forever
死产 stillbirth
死沉 silent as the grave; still as death
死党 sworn follower; diehard follower
死等 wait indefinitely
死敌 deadly enemy; mortal enemy; implacable foe
死地 a fatal position; deathtrap
死光 ① death ray ② all die
死鬼 devil
死海 the Dead Sea
死耗 news of sb's death
死后 after death; posthumous
死缓 death sentence with a two-year reprieve and forced labour; stay of execution
死灰 cold ashes (of an extinguished fire); dead ashes; burnt-out cinders
死活 ① life or death; fate ② anyway; simply
死机 system halted; hang; hang-up; crash, down
死忌 death anniversary
死寂 deathly stillness
死角 ① dead angle; dead space ② a spot as yet untouched by a trend, political movement, etc.

死结 a fast knot
死静 deathly silent; deathly still
死牢 dead cell
死力 ① all one's strength ② with all one's strength
死路 ① blind alley ② the road to ruin (or destruction)
死面 unleavened dough
死命 ① doom; death ② desperately
死难 die in an accident; die in a political incident (esp. for a just cause)
死期 the time of death; date of doom
死棋 ① a dead piece in a game of chess ② a hopeless case; a stupid move
死契 irrevocable title deed
死囚 convict sentenced to death; convict awaiting execution
死球 dead ball
死人 dead person
死伤 the dead and the wounded; casualties
死神 Death (personified)
死尸 corpse; dead body
死守 ① defend to the death; defend to the last; make a last-ditch defence ② obstinately cling to; rigidly adhere to
死水 stagnant water
死胎 stillborn foetus; stillbirth
死土 dead soil
死亡 death; doom
死巷 blind pass
死心 drop the idea forever; have no more illusions about the matter
死信 ① dead letter ② news of sb's death
死刑 death penalty; death sentence; capital punishment
死讯 news of sb's death
死因 cause of death
死硬 ① stiff; inflexible ② very obstinate; diehard
死战 ① a life-and-death struggle (or battle) ② fight to the death
死仗 tough (or hard-fought) battle
死账 dead loan; dead account
死者 the dead; the deceased; the departed
死症 incurable disease
死罪 capital offence (or crime)
死沉沉 ① heavy as lead; extremely heavy ② silent as the grave; still as death ③ glum; sullen; gloomy
死读书 study mechanically; rely on book learning rather than practical experience; be bookish
死对头 deadly enemy; irreconcilable opponent
死工夫 hard persevering work; sheer hard work

死工资 fixed salary (*or* wages)
死规矩 hard and fast rule
死胡同 blind alley; dead end
死魂灵 Dead Souls
死火山 extinct volcano
死教条 lifeless dogma
死劲儿 ①all one's strength; all one's might ② with all one's strength (*or* might); with might and main; for all one's worth
死扣儿 a fast knot
死库容 minimum volume of water a reservoir must have for normal operation
死老虎 a dead tiger—a man who has lost his power and influence
死脑筋 one-track mind
死亡率 death rate; mortality
死硬派 diehards
死不改悔 die impenitent; be absolutely unrepentant (*or* incorrigible)
死不回头 wilfully refuse to mend one's ways; remain absolutely unrepentant
死不讲理 stubbornly refuse to listen to reason; be impervious (*or* dead) to reason
死不瞑目 not close one's eyes when one dies—die with a grievance or everlasting regret; die discontent
死不要脸 be dead to all sense of shame; be utterly shameless; have no sense of shame
死不足惜 death is not too high a price (for sth); (sb) deserves death
死得其所 die a worthy death
死而不僵 dead but not yet showing signs of rigor mortis; retaining remnants of former influence, power or wealth
死而复生 revive; return to life after death; come back to life
死而后已 until one's dying day; to the end of one's days
死而无憾 die without regret
死而有知 if the dead should know
死灰复燃 dying cinders glowing again—resurgence; revival
死啃书本 try to memorize what one reads without thinking
死拉活拽 drag sb along against his will; drag by force
死里逃生 escape by the skin of one's teeth; have a narrow escape; barely escape with one's life
死皮赖脸 thick-skinned and hard to shake off; brazen and unreasonable
死乞白赖 pester endlessly
死气沉沉 lifeless; spiritless; stagnant
死去活来 half dead; only half alive; hovering between life and death
死说活说 beg and beg; try every means to persuade

死亡教育 death education
死无对证 be totally devoid of evidence (because of the death of the principal witness, etc.); The witness, if any, is dead; Dead men tell no tales.
死无牵挂 die content; rest content in one's grave
死心塌地 be dead set; be hell-bent
死心眼儿 ① stubborn; as obstinate as a mule ②a person with a one-track mind
死要面子 be extremely anxious to keep up appearances
死有余辜 Even death would be too good for him; Even death would not expiate all his crimes.
死于非命 die an unnatural (*or* a violent) death
死记(硬背) memorize mechanically; learn by rote; learn without comprehension
死无葬身之地 die without a place for burial—come to a bad end
死不死,活不活 ① those that should die, do not, those that are alive live poorly; benefit no one ②neither dead nor living; dejected; listless; dispirited
死马当做活马医 doctor a dead horse as if it were still alive—make every possible effort; not give up for lost
死要面子活受罪 suffer excruciatingly from trying hard to save face
死猪不怕开水烫 a dead pig fears not scalding water—be impervious to; oblivious of; know no better
死生有命,富贵在天 Life and death are a matter of Destiny; Wealth and honour depend on Heaven.
死了张屠夫,不吃浑毛猪 Even if Butcher Zhang dies, we won't have to eat the hog with its hair; No man is indispensable.

sì(厶)

巳 [sì]
巳时 the period of the day from 9 a.m. to 11 a.m.

四 [sì]
四 four
四边 (on) four sides
四出 go hither and thither; go from place to place; go around
四处 all around; in all directions; everywhere
四大 the four elements—earth, water, fire, and wind
四方 ①the four directions; all sides; all quarters ②square; cubic
四顾 look around (*or* about)
四海 the four seas; the whole country; the

whole world
四害 the four pests
四呼 the four classes of syllables
四胡 *sihu*, a four-stringed bowed instrument
四化 the Four Modernizations
四季 the four seasons
四近 neighbourhood; vicinity
四开 quarto
四邻 one's near neighbours
四面 (on) four sides; (on) all sides
四旁 ①back and front ②the "four sides"
四起 rise from all directions
四散 scatter (*or* disperse) in all directions
四声 the four tones of modern standard Chinese pronunciation
四时 the four seasons
四书 *the Four Books* (namely, The Great Learning (《大学》), The Doctrine of the Mean (《中庸》), The Analects of Confucius (《论语》), and The Mencius (《孟子》))
四外 all around (esp. in the open)
四围 on all sides; all around
四维 ① the four directions (i.e. northeast, southeast, northwest and southwest) ②the four limbs ③four-dimensional
四野 the surrounding country; a vast expanse of open ground
四月 ①April ②the fourth month of the lunar year; the fourth moon
四则 the four fundamental operations of arithmetic
四诊 the four methods of diagnosis
四肢 the four limbs; arms and legs
四周 all around; on all sides
四座 all the people present
四倍体 tetraploid
四边形 quadrilateral
四不像 ①David's deer; *milu* ②non-descript; neither fish nor fowl
四重唱 (vocal) quartet
四重奏 (instrumental) quartet
四叠体 corpora quadrigemina
四方步 leisurely and measured steps
四环素 tetracycline
四级风 force 4 wind; moderate breeze
四极管 tetrode
四脚蛇 lizard
四开本 quarto
四六风 umbilical tetanus of newborn babies (frequently occurring on the 4th to 6th day after birth)
四面体 tetrahedron
四拍子 four beat
四人帮 the Gang of Four
四人舞 dance for four people
四下里 all around
四言诗 four-character verse

四分五裂 fall apart; be rent by disunity; be all split up; disintegrate
四分音符 crotchet; quarter note
四海升平 peace in the world
四海为家 make one's home wherever one is
四合院儿 *siheyuanr*, a compound with houses around a square courtyard; quadrangle
四角号码 the four-corner system (a system of classifying Chinese characters)
四脚朝天 (fall) on one's back
四邻八舍 all the neighbours; whole neighbourhood
四面八方 all directions; all quarters; all around; far and near
四面出击 hit out in all directions
四面楚歌 be besieged on all sides; be utterly isolated; be in desperate straits; find oneself under fire from all quarters
四面受敌 be exposed to enemy attacks on all sides
四平八稳 ① very steady; well balanced ② overcautious and lacking in initiative
四舍五入 round up or down; round off
四时八节 the four seasons and the eight periods——throughout the year
四世同堂 four generations under one roof
四通八达 extend in all directions
四维空间 space-time; space-time continuum
四仰八叉 (lie) sprawling
"四有"新人 people of a new socialist type with lofty aspirations, high moral principles, a high sense of discipline; educated persons with high ideals, moral integrity and a strong sense of discipline
四战之地 a place open to attack from all directions
四足动物 quadruped; tetrapod
四个现代化 the Four Modernizations
四项基本原则 the Four Cardinal Principles (i.e. keeping to the socialist road, and upholding the people's democratic dictatorship, leadership by the Communist Party, and Marxism-Leninism and Mao Zedong Thought)
四海之内皆兄弟 Within the four seas all men are brothers.
四体不勤, 五谷不分 can neither toil with one's four limbs nor tell five cereals apart

寺 [sì]
图 ① central government organ; ministry ②temple; mosque; monastery
寺产 property (*or* real estate) owned by a monastery (*or* temple, mosque)
寺舍 temple (*or* mosque, etc.) premises
寺院 temple; monastery

似 [sì]
Ⅰ 动 ①be similar; be like; approximate ②

look;seem;appear Ⅱ 助 *indicating superiority* ➡shì
似乎 as if;seemingly
似曾相识 seem to have met before
似懂非懂 not fully understand;have only a hazy notion;knowing a subject half well
似是而非 apparently right but actually wrong;specious;plausible
似水流年 Time passes swiftly like flowing water;Youth slips away like flowing water.

咒 [sì]
名 female rhinoceros

伺 [sì]
动 keep watch;await;observe ➡cì
伺服 servo
伺机 watch for one's chance
伺隙 wait for a chance;watch for an opportunity

祀 [sì]
动 offer sacrifices to gods or ancestors
祀孔 hold a memorial ceremony for Confucius
祀祖 offer sacrifices to the spirits of one's ancestors

姒 [sì]
名 ①elder sister ②wife of husband's elder brother

饲 [sì]
Ⅰ 动 raise;breed;rear Ⅱ 名 forage;feed
饲槽 feeding trough
饲草 forage grass
饲料 forage;fodder;feed
饲喂 feed;raise (animals)
饲养 raise;rear
饲养场 feed lot;dry lot;farm
饲养业 animal husbandry
饲养员 stockman;poultry raiser;animal keeper
饲料作物 forage (*or* fodder,feed) crop
饲料粉碎机 feed (*or* fodder) grinder
饲料添加剂 feed additive

泗 [sì]
名 nasal mucus;snivel

驷 [sì]
名 ①a team of four horses ②horse
驷马 a team of four horses
驷不及舌 a team of four horses cannot overtake the tongue—what is said cannot be unsaid

俟 [sì]
动 wait
俟机出击 wait for the right moment to attack
俟河之清,人寿几何 How long does a man live,that he can wait for the River to run clear?

食 [sì]
动 bring food to;feed ➡shí

肆 [sì]
Ⅰ 形 wanton;wilful;unbridled Ⅱ 名 shop
肆虐 indulge in wanton massacre (*or* perse-

cution);wreak havoc
肆意 wantonly;recklessly;wilfully
肆口大骂 swear like a trooper;use profane language freely;let loose a torrent of abuse
肆无忌惮 unbridled;unscrupulous;impertinent

嗣 [sì]
Ⅰ 动 succeed;inherit Ⅱ 名 heir;inheritor;descendant
嗣承 succeed in line
嗣后 hereafter;subsequently;afterwards;later on
嗣君 succeed to the throne

sōng(ㄙㄨㄥ)

松 [sōng]
Ⅰ 名 ① pine ② dried meat floss;dried minced meat Ⅱ 形 ①not firm;loose;slack ②not hard up;well off ③light and flaky;fluffy;soft Ⅲ 动 ①loosen;relax;relieve;slacken ②untie
松绑 ①untie a person ②relax restrictions
松弛 ①limp;flabby;slack ②lax
松脆 friability
松貂 pine marten
松动 ①become less crowded ②not hard up ③become flexible;show flexibility;relax
松果 deal apple
松缓 relax;ease up;mitigate
松鸡 capercaillie;grouse
松紧 ①degree of tightness ②elasticity
松劲 relax one's efforts;slacken (off)
松口 ①relax one's bite and release what is held ②be less unyielding;soften;relent
松快 ①be less crowded ②feel relieved ③relax
松林 pinery;pinewood
松明 pine torch
松气 relax one's efforts
松球 pinecone
松雀 grosbeak
松仁 pine nut kernel
松软 soft;spongy;loose
松散 [sōngsǎn] ① loose;porous ② inattentive
松散 [sōngsan] relax;take one's ease
松手 loosen one's grip;let go
松鼠 squirrel
松树 pine tree;pine
松塔 ①pinecone ②the cone of lacebark pine
松涛 the soughing of the wind in the pines
松土 loosen the soil;scarify the soil
松闲 not busy;slack
松香 rosin;colophony
松懈 ①lax;slack ②relax;slacken
松蕈 pine mushroom
松鸦 jaybird;jay
松烟 pine soot

松针 pine needle
松脂 rosin;pine resin
松子 ①pine nut ②pine nut kernel
松嘴 ①relax one's bite and release what is held ②be less unyielding;soften;relent
松糕鞋 platforms
松花蛋 preserved egg
松焦油 pine tar
松节油 turpentine (oil)
松紧带 elastic cord;elastic
松毛虫 pine moth
松土机 scarifier
松香油 retinol;rosin oil
松烟墨 Chinese ink (*or* ink stick) made from pine soot;pine-soot ink (*or* ink stick)
松柏常青 remain evergreen as the pine and cypress; the pine and cypress stay evergreen
松鹤延年 live as long as the pine and crane
松松垮垮 ①not solid;loose;unsteady ②slack;sluggish
松散型联营 loosely-jointed venture

凇 [sōng]
◇雾凇 (soft) rime

菘 [sōng]
名 Chinese cabbage

嵩 [sōng]
Ⅰ名 high mountain Ⅱ形 (of mountains) high;lofty

sǒng(ㄙㄨㄥˇ)

悚 [sǒng]
形 frightened
悚兢 alarmed;scared;panic-stricken
悚恿 instigate;incite;egg sb on;abet

耸 [sǒng]
Ⅰ形 towering;high;lofty Ⅱ动 alarm;attract (attention)
耸动 ①raise (one's shoulders);shrug ②stir up;rouse
耸肩 shrug one's shoulders
耸立 tower aloft
耸身 jump;leap
耸听 deliberately exaggerate so as to create a sensation
耸耳倾听 prick up one's ears
耸人听闻 deliberately exaggerate so as to create a sensation
耸入云霄 tower to the skies

悚 [sǒng]
形 terrified;horrified
悚然 terrified;horrified

竦 [sǒng]
形 ①respectful; deferential ②terrified;horrified
竦然起敬 hold somebody in high esteem

sòng(ㄙㄨㄥˋ)

讼 [sòng]
动 ①bring a case to court ②debate;dispute;argue
讼案 lawsuit
讼词 legal cases
讼棍 legal pettifogger;shyster
讼师 legal pettifogger
讼事 lawsuit;litigation
讼状 plaint;indictment

宋 [Sòng]
宋词 *ci*,poetry of the Song Dynasty
宋锦 Song brocade
宋体字 Song typeface,a standard typeface

送 [sòng]
动 ①send;deliver;carry ②give as a present;offer;give ③see sb off (*or* out);go along with;accompany
送别 ①see sb off;wish sb bon voyage ②give a send-off party
送殡 attend a funeral;take part in a funeral procession
送达 deliver
送电 power transmission
送还 give back;return
送货 deliver goods
送检 submit (products) for inspection to product-testing authorities
送交 deliver to;hand over to
送客 see a visitor out
送礼 give sb a present;present a gift to sb
送命 lose one's life; get killed; go to one's doom
送气 aspirated
送亲 (of the bride's kinsfolk) escort the bride to the groom's home (*or* the wedding hall)
送人 give away;present someone with
送丧 attend a funeral;take part in a funeral procession
送审 submit to a higher level for approval or revision
送死 court death
送行 ①see sb off;wish sb bon voyage ②give a send-off party
送修 send for repair
送葬 take part in a funeral procession
送展 (send and) put on display
送终 attend upon a dying parent or other senior member of one's family;bury a parent
送风机 forced draught blower;blower
送话器 microphone
送气音 aspirated sound;aspirate
送人情 ①do favours at no great cost to oneself ②make a gift of sth
送上门 deliver to the doorstep

送瘟神 send away the god of plague—get rid of sb or sth undesirable
送信儿 send word;go and tell
送养人 donors for adoption
送货上门 door-to-door delivery;home delivery service;deliver goods to the doorstep;render a door-to-door service
送旧迎新 see out the old and welcome the new
送上西天 send sb to heaven
送书下乡 bring books to the countryside
送往迎来 see off those who depart and welcome those who arrive;speed the parting guests and welcome the new arrivals
送温暖工程 heart-warming project

诵 [sòng]
动 ①read aloud;declaim;chant ②recite ③state;relate;narrate
诵读 read aloud;chant
诵习 chant and study

颂 [sòng]
I 动 ①praise;extol;acclaim;laud ②express good wishes (usu. in letters) II 名 ① one of the three sections in *The Book of Songs* (诗经) consisting of sacrificial songs ② ode;paean;panegyric;eulogy;《橘颂》*Ode to the Tangerine*
颂词 ①complimentary address;panegyric;eulogy ②a speech delivered by an ambassador on presentation of his credentials
颂歌 song;ode
颂扬 sing praises of;laud;extol;eulogize
颂古非今 extol the ancient and negate the present;eulogize the past and condemn the present

sōu(ㄙㄡ)

搜 [sōu]
动 ①look for;collect;gather ②search
搜捕 track down and arrest
搜查 search;ransack;rummage
搜刮 extort;plunder;expropriate;fleece
搜集 hunt high and low for;collect;gather
搜剿 track down and exterminate
搜救 search-and-rescue
搜罗 round up;collect;gather;recruit
搜求 seek;search for;hunt for
搜身 make a body search;give sb a toss
搜索 search for;hunt for;scout around
搜寻 search for;look for;hunt for;seek
搜查证 search warrant
搜腰包 search sb's pockets;search sb for money and valuables
搜肠刮肚 rack one's brains
搜索飞行 scouting flight
搜索引擎 search engine
搜索枯肠 rack one's brains (for fresh ideas or apt expressions)

嗖 [sōu]
象 whiz

馊 [sōu]
形 sour;spoiled
馊点子 stupid suggestion;lousy idea
馊主意 stupid suggestion;lousy idea

飕 [sōu]
I 动 (of wind) make sth dry (*or* cool)
II 象 whiz

艘 [sōu]
量 (of ships):五艘货轮 five freighters; five cargo ships;five cargo vessels
艘次 vessel-time (total number of operations in which vessels or ships are involved)

sǒu(ㄙㄡ)

叟 [sǒu]
名 old man

瞍 [sǒu]
I 形 pupilless;blind II 名 blind person

嗾 [sǒu]
I 象 sounds made to incite a dog II 动 ① incite (a dog) by making such sounds ②instigate;abet
嗾使 instigate
嗾犬伤人 set a dog on sb

薮 [sǒu]
名 ①lake overgrown with grass ②gathering place (of fish,beasts,etc.);den;haunt

擞 [sǒu]
⇒ sòu
◇抖擞 enliven;rouse

sòu(ㄙㄡ)

嗽 [sòu]
动 cough

擞 [sòu]
动 poke the fire (to make the ashes fall through the grating);rake ⇒ sǒu

sū(ㄙㄨ)

苏 [sū]
I 名 ①perilla ②threads hanging down ③Soviet II 动 revive;come to;become conscious
苏打 soda;soda ash;sodium carbonate
苏醒 revive;regain consciousness;come to;come round
苏子 perilla-seed
苏门羚 serow
苏伊士运河 the Suez Canal

酥 [sū]
I 名 ①butter (made from cow's or mare's milk) ②shortbread;shortcake II 形 ①crisp;fluffy ②limp;weak;frail;soft
酥脆 crisp
酥麻 limp and numb
酥软 (of the body) limp;languid

酥松（of soil, etc.）loose; porous;（of pastries, etc.）flaky; crisp
酥糖 crunchy candy
酥胸 soft and white breasts（of a woman）
酥油 butter
酥油茶 buttered tea
酥皮点心 crisp-skinned pastry

稣 [sū]
〔动〕 revive; come to

sú（ㄙㄨˊ）

俗 [sú]
Ⅰ〔名〕①custom; practice; convention ②secular; lay Ⅱ〔形〕① popular; common; ordinary ②vulgar; boorish
俗白 simple and clear
俗话 common saying; proverb
俗家 ①my parents' home ②layman
俗名 popular name; local name
俗气 vulgar; in poor taste
俗人 ①layman ②vulgar person; philistine
俗套 conventional pattern; convention
俗务 everyday matters; routine business
俗物 a vulgar（or uncouth）person
俗语 common saying; folk adage
俗体字 nonstandard forms of characters
俗文学 popular literature
俗不可耐 unbearably vulgar
俗缘未了 The time has not yet come for entering monastery.

sù（ㄙㄨˋ）

夙 [sù]
〔形〕①early in the morning ②long-standing; of yore; old
夙仇 ①long-time enemy ②long-standing enmity
夙敌 old enemy
夙日 generally; usually; ordinarily
夙世 previous incarnation
夙夜 morning and night; day and night
夙怨 old grudge
夙愿 long-cherished wish
夙兴夜寐 rise early and retire late—hard at work night and day
夙夜匪懈 work tirelessly day and night

诉 [sù]
〔动〕①tell; narrate; relate ②complain; speak out what is on one's mind ③accuse; sue
诉苦 complain; vent one's grievances; pour out one's woes
诉求 petition; pursue
诉说 tell; relate; recount
诉讼 lawsuit; litigation
诉冤 complain of injustice; air one's grievances
诉状 bill; extract; petition; writ

诉讼法 procedural law
诉讼费 costs
诉讼地点 venue of trial
诉讼豁免 immunity from suit
诉讼离婚 divorce by litigation
诉讼权利 procedural rights
诉讼条例 rules of procedure
诉诸法律 go to law; have recourse to law; start（or take）（legal）proceedings
诉诸武力 resort to force; appeal to arms
诉讼代理人 agent ad litem; legal representative
诉讼当事人 litigant

肃 [sù]
Ⅰ〔形〕 respectful; solemn; sombre Ⅱ〔动〕eliminate; eradicate
肃毒 eliminate drug addiction, drug trafficking and other related illegal activities
肃反 elimination of counterrevolutionaries
肃静 solemn silence
肃立 stand as a mark of respect
肃穆 ①solemn and quiet; solemn and respectful ②respectful and congenial
肃清 eliminate; clean up; mop up
肃杀 （of autumn or winter）stern; harsh
肃贪 eliminate corruption; root out corruption
肃清贪污 purge of corrupt
肃然起敬 be filled with deep veneration

素 [sù]
Ⅰ〔形〕① white ② plain; simple; quiet ③ native Ⅱ〔名〕①vegetables, fruits, etc. ②basic element Ⅲ〔副〕habitually; of long standing
素白 plain and white
素材 source material（of literature and art）; material
素菜 vegetable dish
素餐 ①a vegetarian meal ②be a vegetarian ③not work for one's living; eat the bread of idleness
素常 usually; habitually; ordinarily
素淡 plain; quiet
素点 vegetarian light refreshments; cakes and pastries made to Muslim taste
素服 plain white clothes（esp. as mourning apparel）
素洁 white and pure
素净 plain and neat; quiet
素酒 ①wine served with vegetarian food ②a vegetarian feast
素来 always; usually
素面 ①vegetarian noodles; noodles with vegetable trimmings ② in one's natural state（or features）
素描 ①sketch ②literary sketch
素日 generally; usually
素食 ①vegetarian food; vegetarian diet ②be a vegetarian

S

素数 prime number
素望 (one's) usual (*or* customary) reputation
素席 vegetarian feast
素心 ①one's real intention;one's true will ② clean and honest;pure in heart
素馨 jasmine
素性 one's natural instincts;one's true disposition (*or* temperament)
素雅 simple but elegant;plain and in good taste
素养 accomplishment;attainment
素油 vegetable oil
素愿 a long-cherished desire (*or* wish,aspiration)
素质 quality;intrinsic qualifications
素香肠 prosage
素因子 prime factor
素不相识 have never met;not be acquainted with each other
素混凝土 plain concrete
素昧平生 have never met before;have never made sb's acquaintance
素面朝天 (of a woman) wear no make-up
素衣素服 white clothing
素质教育 ①quality-oriented education;education aimed at all-round development (of students) ②diathesis
素妆淡描 simple make-up

速 [sù] Ⅰ 形 fast;rapid;swift;quick Ⅱ 名 speed;velocity;tempo Ⅲ 动 invite
速成 attain a goal in a much shorter time than usual;gain a quick mastery (of a course or subject)
速递 deliver directly and rapidly;send out by express mail;express delivery;express mail service
速冻 quick-freeze
速度 ① speed;velocity ② tempo ③ speed;rate;pace;tempo
速记 shorthand;stenography
速决 quick decision
速率 speed;rate
速溶 instant
速射 rapid fire
速胜 quick victory;immediate success
速效 ①quick results ②quick-acting
速写 ①sketch ②literary sketch
速成班 accelerated course;crash course;crash program;intensive class;intensive program
速度计 speed indicator;speedometer
速记员 stenographer
速决战 a quick battle
速射炮 quick-firing gun;quick-firer
速生林 fast-growing woods (*or* timber forests)
速食面 instant noodles

速调管 klystron
速冻食品 frozen food
速度滑冰 speed skating
速溶咖啡 instant coffee
速溶奶粉 fast-melting milk powder;instant milk powder
速效肥料 quick-acting fertilizer
速战速决 fight a quick battle to force a quick decision
速生丰产林 fast-growing,high-yield woods (*or* timber forests)
速效洗涤剂 quick-acting detergent
速效感冒胶囊 quick-cold-relieving capsule

宿 [sù] Ⅰ 动 put up for the night;stay overnight Ⅱ 形 ①long-standing ②old;veteran ➡ xiǔ;xiù
宿弊 a long-standing abuse
宿娼 go whoring;visit prostitutes
宿仇 long-standing enmity
宿处 lodgings;accommodation
宿敌 old enemy
宿根 ①perennial root ②biennial root
宿疾 chronic complaint;old trouble
宿将 veteran general
宿舍 hostel;living quarters;dormitory
宿营 (of troops) take up quarters;camp
宿缘 predestined relationship
宿怨 old grudges;old scores
宿愿 long-cherished wish
宿主 host
宿命论 fatalism
宿营车 ①trailer caravan;home on wheels ②dormitory car (of a long-distance train for its attendants to sleep in)

粟 [sù] 名 millet
粟米 maize;Indian corn;corn
粟子 millet

谡 [sù] 动 rise;stand up

嗉 [sù] 名 crop (of a bird)
嗉子 ①crop (of a bird) ②tin (*or* porcelain) wine flask

塑 [sù] Ⅰ 动 model;sculpture;mould Ⅱ 名 plastic
塑封 plastic-coated
塑钢 plastic and steel frame
塑胶 plastic cement
塑炼 plasticate
塑料 plastics
塑身 get into shape;shape
塑像 statue
塑性 plasticity
塑造 ①model;mould ②portray
塑炼机 plasticator
塑料袋 baggie;plastic bag

塑料薄膜 plastic film; plastic sheeting
塑料大棚 plastic tent; plastic greenhouse
塑料地膜 framed plastic sheets; plastic groundcover
塑料印版 plastic (printing) plate
塑料炸弹 plastic bomb
塑像揭幕 unveil a statue
塑性炸药 plastic bomb; high-explosive plastics
塑料胶布带 plastic adhesive tape
塑料热合机 plastic welder
塑料贴面板 plastic veneer

溯 [sù]
动 ①go up (a stream, etc.) ②trace back; recall; recollect
溯源 trace (back) to the source
溯本追源 trace to the beginnings; go back to the source
溯流而上 go up a river or stream; go upstream

愫 [sù]
名 true feeling; sincerity

蔌 [sù]
名 vegetable

簌 [sù]

簌簌 ①rustle ②(of tears) streaming down

suān(ㄙㄨㄢ)

酸 [suān]
I 名 acid II 形 ① sour; vinegary; tart ② sick at heart; sad; grieved ③of impoverished pedantic scholars in the old days III 动 ache
酸鼻 have a sting in the nose; feel like crying
酸菜 pickled Chinese cabbage; Chinese sauerkraut
酸楚 grieved; distressed; miserable
酸度 acidity
酸酐 acid anhydride
酸根 acid radical
酸解 acidolysis
酸刻 sharp-tongued; sarcastic
酸苦 bitterness; misery; hardship
酸麻 (of limbs) limp and numb
酸梅 smoked plum; dark plum
酸奶 yoghurt; sour milk
酸软 aching and limp
酸涩 ①(of smell, taste, feeling) sour and bitter ②sad; grieved; sick at heart
酸疼 (of muscles) ache
酸甜 sweet and sour
酸痛 ache
酸味 tart flavour; acidity
酸洗 pickling; acid pickling
酸心 ① be grieved; feel sad ② suffer from heartburn
酸性 acidity
酸雨 acid rain
酸枣 wild jujube
酸值 acid value
酸不唧 ①slightly sour (*or* tart); sourish ② tired and feeling weak; exhausted; worn-out
酸沉降 acid deposition
酸处理 acid treatment
酸辣酱 chutney, an Indian condiment made of fruits or vegetables, vinegar, spices, sugar, etc.
酸辣汤 vinegar-pepper soup
酸溜溜 ①sour; pungent ②tingle; ache ③sad; mournful ④envious; green with envy ⑤pedantic; priggish
酸马奶 koumiss
酸梅汤 sweet-sour plum juice
酸泡菜 sauerkraut
酸式盐 acid salt
酸杏儿 sour apricot
酸性岩 acidic rock
酸中毒 acidism; acid poisoning
酸不拉唧 unpleasantly sour
酸不溜丢 unpleasantly sour
酸劲大作 burn with jealousy
酸甜苦辣 sour, sweet, bitter, hot—joys and sorrows of life
酸文假醋 priggish; prudish
酸洗试验 acid washing test
酸性反应 acid reaction
酸性试验 acid test

suàn(ㄙㄨㄢ)

蒜 [suàn]
名 ①garlic ②bulb of this plant
蒜黄 blanched garlic leaves
蒜苗 garlic bolt
蒜泥 mashed garlic
蒜薹 the flower stalk of garlic (edible when tender)
蒜头 the head (*or* bulb) of garlic
蒜瓣儿 garlic clove
蒜(味)肠 garlic sausage

算 [suàn]
I 动 ① calculate; estimate; reckon ② count; include; figure in ③plan; figure; calculate ④ think; suppose; reckon ⑤ regard as; consider; count as; take for ⑥ count; carry weight; be effective ⑦ (followed by 了) come, come; let it be II 副 due to; on account of; in the end; finally
算尺 slide rule
算得 regard as; count as
算法 algorithm
算卦 tell sb's fortune by using the Eight Trigrams
算计 ①calculate; reckon ②consider; plan ③ expect; figure ④scheme; plot
算进 figure in; reckon in
算命 tell sb's fortune

S

算盘 ①abacus ②calculation;plan;scheme
算式 mathematical formula or equation
算是 at last
算术 arithmetic
算数 count;hold;stand
算题 arithmetic problem;mathematical exercise
算学 ①mathematics ②arithmetic
算账 ①do (*or* work out) accounts;balance the books;make out bills ②square (*or* settle) accounts with sb;get even with sb
算子 operator
算旧账 settle an old account;settle an old score
算老账 settle an old score
算法语言 algorithmic language
算来算去 contrive this and that;count over and over
算命先生 fortune-teller
算盘子儿 beads of an abacus
算术级数 arithmetic progression;arithmetic series
算术平均值 arithmetic mean

suī(ㄙㄨㄟ)

尿 [suī] 〖名〗 urine ➡niào
尿脬 bladder

虽 [suī] 〖连〗 ① though;although ② even if;even though
虽然 though;although
虽说 though;although
虽则 though;although
虽死犹生 live on in spirit

荽 [suī]
◇芫荽 coriander

睢 [suī] 〖动〗 gaze thoughtfully at
睢然而视 gaze intently at

suí(ㄙㄨㄟ)

绥 [suí] Ⅰ〖形〗 peaceful Ⅱ〖动〗 bring peace to;pacify
绥靖 pacify;appease
绥靖政策 appeasement policy;policy of appeasement

随 [suí] Ⅰ〖动〗①follow ②comply with;adapt to;go along with ③let (sb do as he likes);do at one's convenience;act at one's discretion ④look like;be similar;resemble Ⅱ〖介〗 along with (some other action)
随笔 ①informal essay ②jottings
随便 ①do as one pleases ②casual;random;informal ③careless;slipshod ④wanton;wilful;arbitrary ⑤anyhow;any
随常 ordinary;common;everyday
随处 everywhere;anywhere
随从 ①accompany;follow (one's superior);attend ②retinue;suite;entourage
随带 ①going along with ②have sth taken along with one
随地 anywhere;everywhere
随访 (of doctors,etc.) follow up a case (by regular visits to or correspondence with a patient)
随感 random thoughts
随和 amiable;easy-going
随后 soon afterwards
随机 ①random ②stochastic ③act according to circumstances
随即 soon after that;immediately;presently
随军 go along with an army
随口 speak thoughtlessly (*or* casually);blurt out whatever comes into one's head
随迁 (of spouse or dependents) change and register permanent residence along with the head of the household when this person moves to a new locality;trail
随群 do as everybody else does;follow the crowd
随身 (carry) on one's person;(take) with one
随时 ①at any time;at all times ②whenever necessary;as the occasion demands
随侍 ①attend (*or* wait) upon one's elders and betters ②personal attendant
随手 conveniently (when doing sth);without extra trouble
随顺 be obedient to;comply with;yield to
随俗 comply with convention;follow the customs;do as everybody else does
随同 be in company with;be accompanying
随喜 ①join in charitable and pious deeds ②join in an enjoyable activity ③visit a temple
随心 ①follow one's inclinations ②find sth satisfactory;be gratified
随行 ①accompany (*or* follow) sb on a trip ②retinue;suite;entourage
随宜 as one sees fit
随意 at will;as one pleases
随员 ①suite;retinue;entourage ②diplomacy attaché
随展 (of staff) travel with the exhibits on an exhibition tour
随着 along with;in the wake of;in pace with
随大溜 drift (*or* swim) with the stream;follow (*or* conform to) the trend;do as others do
随动件 follower
随份子 ①contribute one's share of a group gift ②present a gift of money for a wed-

ding,funeral,etc.
随风倒 bend with the wind—be easily swayed
随身听 walkman; personal stereo; portable player
随想曲 caprice;capriccio
随意肌 voluntary muscle
随葬物 funerary objects;burial articles
随波逐流 drift with the tide (*or* current);go with the stream
随处可见 can be seen everywhere
随风而舞 dance in the wind
随风转舵 trim one's sails;take one's cue from changing conditions
随行就市 fluctuate along with market changes;fluctuate in line with market conditions
随机变数 random variable
随机抽样 random sampling; sampling by chance
随机过程 stochastic process
随机应变 do as the changing circumstances demand;suit one's actions to changing conditions;act according to circumstances
随军记者 war correspondent
随军家属 camp family
随人俯仰 be at sb's beck and call
随身行李 accompanying luggage; carry-on items
随声附和 echo others;echo what others say; chime in with others
随时随地 at all times and all places
随随便便 ①be rather casual;be careless about things ②free and easy;in an easygoing way ③without order
随乡入乡 wherever you are,follow local customs;when in Rome do as the Romans do
随心所欲 follow one's inclinations;have one's own way;do as one pleases
随行人员 entourage;suite;party
随遇而安 fit in anywhere;feel at home wherever one is;be able to adapt oneself to different circumstances
随遇平衡 indifferent equilibrium
随员领事 diplomacy attaché consul
随机存取存储器 random access memory (RAM)

遂 [suí]
➡ suì
◇半身不遂 hemiplegia

suǐ(ㄙㄨㄟˇ)

髓 [suǐ]
图 ①marrow ②sth like marrow ③pith
髓室 pulp chamber
髓体 corpus medullae
髓脓肿 pulp abscess
髓组织 myeloid tissue

suì(ㄙㄨㄟˋ)

岁 [suì]
图 ①year ②year (of age) ③age ④time ⑤year's harvest
岁差 precession of the equinoxes
岁出 annual expenditure
岁除 New Year's Eve
岁暮 the close of the year
岁入 annual income;revenue
岁首 the beginning of the year; the first month of the lunar year
岁数 age;years
岁月 years
岁不我与 Time and tide wait for no man.
岁寒三友 the three plant friends who thrive in cold weather—the pine, the bamboo, and the plum
岁寒知松柏 Only when the year grows cold do we see the qualities of the pine and the cypress;adversity reveals virtue.

祟 [suì]
Ⅰ 图 evil spirit;ghost Ⅱ 动 act like an evil spirit;haunt;plague

谇 [suì]
动 ①scold; berate ②counsel a sovereign against a royal decision

遂 [suì]
Ⅰ 动 ① gratify; satisfy; fulfil ② succeed Ⅱ 副 then;thereupon;hence ➡ suí
遂心 after one's own heart;to one's liking
遂意 to one's liking
遂愿 have one's wish fulfilled;meet one's wishes

碎 [suì]
Ⅰ 图 broken pieces Ⅱ 动 break Ⅲ 形 ① broken; fragmentary; scattered ② garrulous; gabby; talkative
碎波 broken sea;surf
碎块 fragment;shiver
碎料 crushed aggregates
碎裂 splintering;fragmentation
碎片 fragment;patch;debris;segment
碎石 crushed stone;broken stone;macadam
碎音 acciaccatura
碎布片 oddments of cloth
碎步儿 quick short step
碎石机 stone crusher
碎石路 broken stone road; macadam road; macadam
碎土地 broken clod
碎屑岩 clastic rock
碎纸机 shredder
碎纸屑 scraps of paper
碎嘴子 ①chatter; jabber; prate ②a garrulous person;chatterbox
碎金屑玉 bits of gold and powder of jade—

fragmentary pieces of excellent literature
碎尸万段 tear the body to thousands of pieces
碎石混凝土 crushed stone concrete

隧 [suì]
名 tunnel
隧道 tunnel
隧洞 tunnel
隧道管 tunneltron
隧道效应 tunnel effect

燧 [suì]
名 ①flint ②beacon fire
燧石 flint
燧石玻璃 flint glass

穗 [suì]
名 ①ear of grain；spike ②tassel；fringe ③ another name for Guangzhou
穗选 ear selection
穗子 ①the ear of grain；spike ②tassel；fringe
穗状花序 spike

sūn（ㄙㄨㄣ）

孙 [sūn]
名 ①grandson ②generations below that of the grandchild ③ relative belonging to grandchild's generation ④ second growth of plants
孙儿 grandchild
孙女 son's daughter；granddaughter
孙竹 new shoots of bamboo from the old stump
孙子 son's son；grandson
孙女婿 granddaughter's husband；grandson-in-law
孙媳妇 grandson's wife；granddaughter-in-law
孙子兵法 The Art of War by Sunzi

荪 [sūn]
名 aromatic plant referred to in ancient Chinese books

猻 [sūn]
◇猢猻 macaque；monkey

飧 [sūn]
名 supper；dinner

sǔn（ㄙㄨㄣˇ）

损 [sǔn]
Ⅰ动 ①decrease；diminish；lose ②harm；injure ③damage Ⅱ形 ①mean；shabby；vicious ②sarcastic；biting；caustic；cutting
损德 injure one's virtue（by misdeeds）
损害 ①do harm to；damage；impair ②harm；injury；damage
损耗 ①loss；wear and tear ②wastage；spoilage
损坏 damage（objects）
损毁 damage；destroy
损伤 ①harm；damage；injure ②loss

损失 ①lose ②loss；damage
损益 ① increase and decrease ② profit and loss；gains and losses
损耗费 cost of wear and tear
损耗率 proportion of goods damaged
损益比 profit and loss ratio
损益表 profit and loss account
损兵折将 suffer heavy casualties
损公肥私 injure the public interest to benefit one's private interests；seek private gain at public expense；profit at public expense；feather one's nest at public expense
损人利己 harm others to benefit oneself；benefit oneself at the expense of others
损益计算书 profit and loss statement
损有余而补不足 cut the unnecessary surplus to make up for the deficiency

笋 [sǔn]
名 bamboo shoot
笋鞭 the subterranean stem of bamboo
笋干 air-dried（cooked）bamboo shoots
笋瓜 winter squash
笋鸡 young chicken；broiler
笋尖 tender tips of bamboo shoots

隼 [sǔn]
名 falcon
隼形目 falconiformes

榫 [sǔn]
名 tenon
榫刨 dovetailing plane
榫槽 tongue-and-groove；mortise
榫头 tenon
榫眼 mortise
榫凿 framing chisel；heading chisel；mortise chisel
榫子 tenon

suō（ㄙㄨㄛ）

莎 [suō]
莎草 nutgrass flatsedge

唆 [suō]
动 instigate；abet；incite
唆弄 incite；instigate
唆使 instigate；abet

梭 [suō]
名 shuttle
梭镖 spear
梭箱 shuttle box
梭芯 cop latch
梭巡 move around to watch and guard；patrol to and fro
梭鱼 （redeye）mullet
梭子 ①weaver's shuttle ②cartridge clip ③a clip（of bullets）
梭子蟹 swimming crab
梭子鱼 barracuda

挲 ［suō］
➡ sā
◇ 摩挲 ［mósuō］ caress;stroke

睃 ［suō］
〔动〕 look askance at;cast a sidelong glance at

蓑 ［suō］
蓑草 Chinese alpine rush
蓑衣 alpine rush or palm-bark rain coat

嗦 ［suō］
◇ 哆嗦 tremble;shiver

嗍 ［suō］
〔动〕 suck

羧 ［suō］
〔名〕 carboxyl
羧基 carboxyl;carboxyl group
羧酸 carboxylic acid

缩 ［suō］
〔动〕 ① become smaller;contract;shrink ② draw back;withdraw ③ withdraw;fall back; retreat
缩编 (of troops,government organs,etc.) reduce the staff
缩尺 reduced scale;scale
缩短 shorten;cut down;cut short
缩合 condensation
缩减 reduce;cut;trim;retrench
缩聚 condensation polymerization
缩口 throat
缩率 shrinkage
缩手 ①draw back one's hand ②shrink (from doing sth)
缩水 (of cloth through wetting) shrink
缩微 microform
缩小 ① reduce;lessen;narrow;shrink ② be reduced;shrink
缩写 ①abbreviation ②abridge
缩印 reprint books in a reduced format
缩影 epitome;miniature
缩编本 abridged edition
缩脖子 draw back one's neck—draw back; shrink back
缩尺图 scale drawing
缩放仪 pantograph
缩合物 condensation compound
缩聚物 condensation polymer
缩略语 abbreviation;abbreviated expression
缩水率 shrinkage
缩头虫 bamboo worm
缩写本 abridged edition (or version)
缩成一团 huddle oneself up
缩短战线 contract the front—narrow the scope of an activity
缩合反应 condensation reaction
缩手缩脚 ① shrink with cold ② be overcautious
缩头缩脑 ①be timid;be fainthearted ②shrink

from responsibility
缩微技术 microphotography
缩微胶卷 microfilm
缩微胶片 microfiche;microfilm;microcopy
缩微照片 microfilm;microphotograph
缩微制品 microform
缩位拨号 abbreviated dialling
缩写签字 initials

suǒ（ㄙㄨㄛˇ）

所 ［suǒ］
I 〔名〕①place ②place of garrison during the Ming Dynasty ③(*used as a name of an institution or other organization*) II 〔量〕 of house, school, buildings, etc.：两所民宅 two civilian houses III 〔助〕①*used together with* 为 *or* 被, *to indicate passive construction*)：被他的谎言所欺骗 be taken in by his lies ②(*used before a verb followed by a noun which is the receiver of the action*)：大家所谈的看法 the views expressed by various people/他所采取的行动 the actions he has taken ③(*used in the* "是…的" *sentence structure for emphasis*) ④(*used before a verb to form a compound object*)：为好奇心所驱使 be driven by one's curiosity ⑤(*used after* 有 *or* 无 *to form* "有所…" *meaning to some extent or* "无所…" *meaning all-inclusive structure*)：有所发明 have some inventions to one's credit
所部 troops under one's command
所长 ［suǒcháng］ what one is good at; one's strong point;one's forte
所得 what one has gained (*or* acquired); gains;earnings;income
所好 inclination
所属 ① what is subordinate to one or under one's command ②what one belongs to (*or* is affiliated with)
所谓 ①what is called;what is known as ②so-called
所以 ①as a result;so;therefore ②the reason why ③that's why ④that's just the reason; that's just the point
所有 ①own;possess ②possessions ③all
所在 ①place;location ②where sb or sth is
所长 ［suǒzhǎng］ the head of institute
所致 be caused by;be the result of
所得税 income tax
所以然 the reason why;the whys and wherefores
所有格 the possessive case
所有权 proprietary rights;ownership;title
所有制 system of ownership;ownership
所在地 location;seat;site
所见略同 have similar views;hit on the same

idea
所剩无几 There is not much left.
所向披靡 (of troops) carry all before one; sweep away all obstacles; send the enemy fleeing helter-skelter
所向无敌 be all-conquering; be ever-victorious; break all enemy resistance
所向无前 carry all before one; be irresistible
所作所为 one's behaviour (or conduct)
所答非所问 not give a direct answer to a question; not answer to the point; give an irrelevant answer
所学非所用 be employed in a job not in one's line

索 [suǒ]
Ⅰ 名 large rope (or chain) Ⅱ 动 ①search; look for ②demand; ask Ⅲ 形 ①solitary; all by oneself ②dull; insipid
索偿 claim damages
索酬 demand reward
索道 cableway; ropeway
索贿 extort bribes
索价 ask (or demand) a price; charge
索解 seek an answer (or explanation)
索具 rigging; gear
索寞 ①down-hearted; dejected; dispirited ②lonely; desolate
索赔 contract claims; make a claim; claim for damages; claim for compensation
索桥 chain bridge; cable bridge
索取 ask for; demand; exact; extort
索然 dull; dry; insipid
索索 ①a rustling sound ②trembling
索性 simply; just; might as well
索要 ask for; claim; demand
索引 index
索债 demand debt payment

索赔人 claimant
索赔信 letter of claims
索债人 claimant
索贿受贿 solicit or accept bribes
索赔条款 claim clause
索赔通知 notice of claim
索取回扣 demand kickbacks; acquire kickbacks
索然无味 flat and insipid

唢 [suǒ]
唢呐 *suona* horn, a woodwind instrument

琐 [suǒ]
形 ① trivial; insignificant; petty ② lowly; humble
琐事 trifles; trivial matters
琐碎 trifling; trivial
琐闻 bits of news; scraps of information
琐细 trifling; trivial
琐屑 trifling; trivial
琐杂 petty and involved

锁 [suǒ]
Ⅰ 名 ①lock ②sth which resembles a lock ③chains Ⅱ 动 ①lock (up) ②lockstitch
锁定 lock
锁骨 clavicle; collarbone
锁国 cut off one's country from the outside world
锁簧 locking spring
锁键 locking key
锁匠 locksmith
锁紧 locking
锁孔 lockhole; keyhole
锁链 ①chain ②shackles; fetters; chains
锁眼 lockhole
锁阳 Chinese cynomorium
锁钥 ①key ②strategic gateway

S

 Tt

tā（ㄊㄚ）

他 [tā]
代 ①(*referring to the third person singular, now usu. male*) ②(*used between a verb and a numeral as a form word*)：咬他一口 have a bite ③other；another；some other
他方 ①the other party ②other places
他律 heteronomy
他们 ① they；them (referring to people) ② (*used before or after a noun or nouns for emphasis*) ③(*used after the name or title of a person to mean "and the others"*)
他年 another year；sometime in future
他人 another person；other people；others
他日 some other time；some other day
他杀 homicide
他乡 a place far away from home；an alien land
他动词 transitive verb
他妈的 damn it；blast it；to hell with it
他乡遇故知 meet an old friend in a distant land

它 [tā]
代 (*referring to the third person singular and nonhuman*)
它们 they；them

她 [tā]
代 ①referring to the third person singular of female gender ②reference to sth beloved
她们 they；them

趿 [tā]
趿拉 wear cloth shoes with the backs turned in；shuffle about with the backs of one's shoes trodden down
趿拉儿 slippers
趿拉板儿 wooden slippers；clogs

铊 [tā]
名 thallium（Tl）

塌 [tā]
动 ①collapse；crumble；fall down ②sink；subside；droop ③ease；calm down；settle down
塌崩 breakdown
塌方 ①cave in；collapse ②landslide；landslip
塌架 ①(of a building, etc.) collapse；topple down ②fall from power
塌落 cave in；collapse
塌台 fall from power；collapse
塌陷 subside；sink；cave in
塌鼻子 flat nose；snubby nose

遢 [tā]
◇邋遢 slovenly；sloppy

溻 [tā]
动 (of clothes, etc.) become soaked with sweat；(of sweat) soak (clothes)

踏 [tā]
➡ tà
踏实 ① steady and sure；dependable ② free from anxiety；having peace of mind

褟 [tā]
动 hem；sew (lace or tassel)

tǎ（ㄊㄚˇ）

塔 [tǎ]
名 ①Buddhist pagoda；pagoda ②tower
塔吊 tower crane
塔楼 ①tower ②turret
塔轮 cone pulley；stepped pulley
塔台 control tower
塔糖 sugarloaf
塔钟 tower clock；turret clock
塔柱 pylon
塔桌 tier table
塔夫绸 taffeta
塔式起重机 tower crane

獭 [tǎ]
名 otter

tà（ㄊㄚˋ）

拓 [tà]
动 make rubbings from (inscriptions, pictures, etc. on stone tablets or bronze vessels)

➡tuò
拓本 a book of rubbings
拓片 rubbing (from a stone tablet or bronze vessel)
拓印 monotype;rubbing

沓 [tà]
动 crowded;repeated ➡dá
沓乱 numerous and disorderly

挞 [tà]
动 flog;whip
挞伐 send armed forces to suppress;send a punitive expedition against
挞罚 punishment by whipping

嗒 [tà]
➡dā
嗒然 dejected;despondent;depressed
嗒丧 in low spirits;dejected;despondent
嗒然若丧 deeply despondent;mournful and dejected

榻 [tà]
名 long,narrow and low bed;couch
榻榻米 tatami—Japanese mattress placed on the floor

踏 [tà]
动 ①step on;tread;stamp ②go to the spot
➡tā
踏板 ①treadle;footboard;footrest ②footstool ③pedal (of a piano,etc.)
踏步 ①mark time;march in place ②a flight of steps;steps leading up to a house,etc.
踏歌 singing accompanied by stamping of feet (*or* rhythmic dancing)
踏勘 ①make an on-the-spot survey ②make a personal investigation on the spot
踏看 go to the spot to make an investigation
踏青 walk on the green grass—go for an outing in early spring
踏雪 walk in the snow
踏月 walk in the moonlight
踏脚板 running board
踏胜寻幽 choose places of scenic beauty
踏破铁鞋无觅处,得来全不费工夫 you can wear out iron shoes in fruitless searching, and yet by a lucky chance you may find the lost thing without even looking for it; fancy finding by sheer luck what one has searched for far and wide

蹋 [tà]
动 ①tread;stamp ②kick
蹋鞠 kick the ball

tāi（ㄊㄞ）

苔 [tāi]
➡tái
◇**舌苔** coating on the tongue;fur

胎 [tāi]
名 ①foetus;embryo ②birth;farrow ③pad-

ding;stuffing;wadding ④roughcast ⑤tyre
胎动 movement of the foetus which can be felt by the mother
胎儿 (human) foetus
胎发 foetal hair;lanugo
胎记 birthmark
胎教 prenatal influence; pre-birth braining; foetal training
胎毛 foetal hair;lanugo
胎膜 foetal membrane
胎盘 placenta
胎气 nausea,vomiting and oedema of legs during pregnancy;pregnancy complications
胎生 viviparity
胎室 proloculum
胎位 position of a foetus
胎衣 afterbirth
胎痣 birthmark
胎座 placenta
胎里坏 a born villain
胎毛笔 brush made with foetal hair
胎死腹中 nip sth in the bud

tái（ㄊㄞ）

台 [tái]
Ⅰ名 ①tower ②platform;stage;terrace ③stand;support ④anything shaped like a platform,stage or terrace ⑤table;desk ⑥station;service ⑦Taiwan Ⅱ量 ①(of a stage performance or properties on a stage):两台刨床 two planers/一台布景 a setting ②(of a mechanical device or a machine):一台电扇 an eletric fan Ⅲ代 you;your
台胞 compatriots in or from Taiwan
台本 a playscript with stage directions
台布 tablecloth
台步 (in traditional opera) stage walk
台车 trolley;bogie;tompkins
台秤 ① platform scale; platform balance ② counter scale
台词 actor's lines
台灯 desk lamp;table lamp;reading lamp
台地 ①platform;tableland ②mesa
"台独" "independence of Taiwan"
台风 ① typhoon ② an actor's demeanour on the stage
台甫 your honoured style
台海 Taiwan Straits
台驾 your presence
台教 your advice
台阶 ①a flight of steps;steps leading up to a house,etc. ② chance to extricate oneself from an awkward position ③bench
台坎 banquette
台历 desk calendar
台面 ① mesa ② on the table; aboveboard; in

public ③winnings and losses (in gambling)

台钳 bench clamp

台球 ①billiards ②billiard ball

台扇 desk fan

台商 businessman from Taiwan

台钟 desk clock

台资 capital from Taiwan; Taiwan capital; investment from Taiwan

台子 ①platform; stage ②table; desk ③billiard table ④table tennis table; ping-pong table

台钻 bench drill

台虎钳 bench vice

台柱子 ① leading member (of a theatrical troupe) ② soul member (of an organization); mainstay; pillar

"台独"势力 the forces which demand "Taiwan Independence"

台资企业 Tanwanese-funded enterprises; Tanwanese-funded businesses

台风警戒线 typhoon detective line

苔 [tái]
[名] liverwort; moss; lichen ⟹ tāi

苔原 tundra

苔藓动物 bryozoan

苔藓植物 bryophyte

抬 [tái]
Ⅰ [动] ①lift; raise ②(of two or more persons) carry; move ③argue for the sake of arguing Ⅱ [量] (of what is carried by two persons): 三抬嫁妆 three trunkfuls of dowry

抬秤 huge steelyard

抬杠 ①argue for the sake of arguing; bicker; wrangle ②carry a coffin on stout poles

抬高 raise; heighten; enhance

抬价 jack up (or raise) prices; force up commodity prices

抬肩 half the circumference of the sleeve where it joins the shoulder

抬举 praise or promote sb to show favour; favour sb

抬升 rise

抬手 ①raise one's hand ②be magnanimous; not be too hard on sb; make an exception in sb's favour

抬头 ①raise one's head ②gain ground; look up; rise ③begin a new line, as a mark of respect, when mentioning the addressee in letters, official correspondence, etc. ④(on receipts, bills, etc.) name of the buyer or payee; space for filling in such a name

抬轿子 carry sb in a sedan chair—flatter (rich and influential people); sing the praises of; boost

抬头纹 wrinkles on one's forehead

抬高身价 raise one's status; boost one's prestige; put a higher value on oneself

抬头挺胸 raise one's head and throw out one's chest; chin up and chest out

tài (ㄊㄞˋ)

太 [tài]
Ⅰ [形] ①highest; greatest; remotest ②extreme; most ③most senior; great Ⅱ [副] ①over; too; excessively ②extremely; terribly; very ③very; quite; too

太公 great-grandfather

太古 remote antiquity

太后 mother of an emperor; empress dowager; queen mother

太极 the Supreme Ultimate

太监 (court) eunuch

太空 the firmament; outer space

太庙 the Imperial Ancestral Temple

太平 peaceful and tranquil; having good social order and without war

太婆 great-grandmother

太甚 too far; to the extreme

太岁 ①the Master of the Year ②Taisui; the God of the Year ③a nickname for the most powerful man in a locality

太太 ① Mrs.; madame ② the mistress of a household; madam; lady ③ wife ④ (paternal) great-grandmother or great-grandfather

太虚 the great void; the universe

太学 the Imperial College

太阳 ① the sun ② the sun's rays; sunshine; sunlight

太爷 ① (paternal) grandfather ② (paternal) great-grandfather

太医 ①an imperial physician ②medical man; doctor

太阴 ①the moon ②lunar

太子 prince; crown prince

太祖 the first founder of a dynasty

太白星 Grand White

太妃糖 taffy; toffee

太古代 the Archean (or Archaeozoic) Era

太极拳 taijiquan

太极图 Diagram of the Supreme Ultimate

太空步 moonwalk; space walk dance (imitation of walking in space)

太空城 cosmograd

太空船 a space craft; space ship

太空服 spacesuit

太空人 astronauts; cosmonauts

太空学 spatiography

太空葬 space burial

太空战 space warfare

太空站 space station

太平官 cadres who are satisfied with the existing state of affairs and do not want to change

太平花 Beijing mock orange
太平间 mortuary
太平门 exit（of a building，etc.）
太平鸟 waxwing
太平梯 fire escape
太平洋 the Pacific（Ocean）
太上皇 ①a title assumed by an emperor's father who abdicated in favour of his son ②overlord；super-sovereign；backstage ruler
太师椅 an old-fashioned wooden armchair
太阳灯 sunlamp；sunlight lamp
太阳风 solar wind
太阳光 sunlight
太阳镜 sunglasses
太阳历 solar calendar
太阳炉 solar furnace
太阳帽 sun helmet；topee
太阳能 solar energy
太阳年 tropical year；solar year
太阳鸟 sunbird
太阳系 the solar system
太阳穴 the temples
太阳灶 solar energy stove；solar cooker
太阴历 lunar calendar
太阴年 lunar year
太阴月 lunar month；lunation
太仓一粟 a grain of millet in a granary—a drop in the ocean
太阿倒持 hold the sword by the blade—surrender one's power to another at one's own peril
太空垃圾 space trash
太空行走 space-walk
太平盛世 times of peace and prosperity
太平天国 the Taiping Heavenly Kingdom
太平无事 All is well.
太上老君 Most Exalted Lord Lao
太虚幻境 in a state of visionary and emptiness
太阳常数 solar constant
太阳地儿 a place where there is sunshine；sunny spot
太阳电池 solar cell
太阳风暴 solar storm
太阳辐射 solar radiation
太阳光谱 solar spectrum
太阳黑子 sunspot
太阳活动 solar activity
太阳活动周 solar cycle
太阳目视镜 helioscope
太阳能汽车 car running on soar-energy battery
太岁头上动土 provoke sb far more powerful
太阳同步轨道 sun-synchronous orbit
太公钓鱼，愿者上钩 like the fish rising to Jiang Taigong's hookless and baitless line—a willing victim letting himself be caught

汰 ［tài］
动 discard；eliminate

态 ［tài］
名 ①form；state；condition；appearance ②voice
态度 ①manner；bearing ②attitude；approach
态势 state；situation；posture

肽 ［tài］
名 peptide

钛 ［tài］
名 titanium（Ti）
钛白粉 titanium white；titanium dioxide
钛铁矿 ilmenite

泰 ［tài］
形 ① safe；secure；peaceful ② extreme；most ③excessive；too much
泰斗 Mount Tai and the North Star—an eminent scholar，musician，artist，etc.
泰古 remote antiquity
泰然 calm；composed；self-possessed
泰山 ①Mount Tai ②a symbol of great weight（or import）③wife's father；father-in-law
泰然处之 take sth calmly；bear sth with equanimity
泰然自若 behave with perfect composure；be self-possessed
泰山北斗 Mount Tai and the North Star（a respectful epithet for a person of distinction）
泰山压顶 be overwhelmed；bear down on one with the weight of Mount Tai
泰山压卵 like Mount Tai bearing down on an egg—with overwhelmingly superior force

酞 ［tài］
名 phthalein

tān（ㄊㄢ）

坍 ［tān］
动 collapse；fall；crumble；cave in
坍方 ①cave in；collapse ②landslide；landslip
坍塌 cave in；collapse
坍台 ①（of enterprises，etc.）collapse；fold ②fall into disgrace；lose face

贪 ［tān］
动 ① corrupt；venal ② have an insatiable desire for；be greedy ③covet；seek；hanker after
贪杯 be excessively fond of drinking；love a drop too much
贪财 be greedy for money；be a money-grubber
贪婪 avaricious；greedy；rapacious
贪恋 be reluctant to part with；hate to leave；cling to
贪色 be fond of women；be a womanizer
贪图 seek；hanker after；covet
贪玩 be too fond of play
贪污 embezzle；practise graft；be corrupt
贪心 ①greed；avarice；rapacity ②greedy；ava-

ricious;insatiable;voracious
贪赃 take bribes;practise graft
贪嘴 greedy (for food);gluttonous
贪内助 wife of a corrupt official
贪便宜 bargain-hunt; seek petty advantages; eager to get things on the cheap; keen on gaining petty advantages
贪大求全 go in for grandiose projects
贪大求洋 concentrate on grandiose projects and advanced technologies without considering actual conditions
贪得无厌 be insatiably avaricious
贪多务得 greedy and acquisitive
贪官污吏 corrupt officials;venal officials
贪婪成性 Avarice becomes a second nature.
贪生怕死 cravenly cling to life instead of braving death; care for nothing but saving one's skin;be mortally afraid of death
贪天之功 arrogate to oneself the merits of others; claim credit for other people's achievements
贪图富贵 desire wealth and honour greatly
贪污盗窃 graft and embezzlement
贪污腐化 corruption and degeneration; corruption
贪污受贿 embezzlement and bribe-taking;corruption
贪小失大 covet a little and lose a lot; seek small gains but incur big losses
贪赃枉法 take bribes and bend the law; pervert justice for a bribe
贪多嚼不烂 bite off more than one can chew
贪污腐化分子 person guilty of corruption; grafter;embezzler

摊 I 〔动〕 ①spread out;unfold ②fry batter in a thin layer ③take a share in;share ④(usu. of sth unpleasant) befall; happen to Ⅱ〔名〕 vendor's stand;booth;stall Ⅲ〔量〕 (of sth, usu. pasty or liquid, that is spread out):一摊工作 a whole lot of work
摊车 pedlar's stand and cart
摊床 vendor's stand
摊点 stand;booth
摊贩 street pedlar
摊开 spread out
摊牌 lay one's cards on the table;show one's hand (or cards);have a showdown
摊派 apportion (expenses,work,etc.)
摊手 loosen one's grip;let go
摊售 (of a vendor's stand) sell goods;set up a stall
摊位 vendor's stand;booth;stall
摊子 ① vendor's stand; booth; stall ② the structure of an organization;setup
摊晒机 tedder

滩 〔名〕 ①beach;sands ②shoal
滩羊 a kind of sheep known for its fine thick wool
滩头堡 beachhead

瘫 〔动〕 be paralysed
瘫痪 ①paralysis;palsy ②(of transportation, etc.) be paralysed; break down; be at a standstill
瘫软 (of arms, legs, etc.) become weak and limp
瘫子 a person suffering from paralysis;paralytic

tán(ㄊㄢˊ)

坛 I 〔名〕 ①altar;platform ②raised plot of land for planting flowers,etc.;terrace ③organization set up by a secret society to worship gods in a rally ④(sports or literary) circles;world ⑤earthen jar;jug Ⅱ〔量〕:一坛酒 a jug of wine
坛子 earthen jar;jug
坛坛罐罐 pots and pans—personal possessions

昙 〔形〕 covered with clouds;cloudy
昙花 broad-leaved epiphyllum
昙花一现 flower briefly as the broad-leaved epiphyllum; last briefly; be a flash in the pan

倓 〔形〕 calm;tranquil

谈 I 〔动〕 talk;speak;chat;discuss Ⅱ〔名〕 what is said or talked about;tale;story
谈锋 volubility;eloquence
谈话 ①talk;chat;discuss ②statement
谈论 discuss;talk about
谈判 negotiate;hold talks
谈天 chat;make conversation
谈吐 style of conversation
谈笑 talk (or chat) and laugh
谈心 heart-to-heart talk
谈兴 mood for conversation
谈资 matter for gossip;subject of a conversation
谈不到 out of the question
谈不来 not get along well
谈不上 out of the question;far from being
谈得到 take into consideration
谈得来 get along well
谈家常 talk about everyday (or commonplace) matters; engage in small talk; chit-chat
谈何容易 easier said than done; by no means easy
谈虎色变 turn pale at the mention of the ti-

ger—turn pale at the mere mention of sth terrifying

谈话节目 talk show；chat show；talking show
谈判筹码 bargain chip
谈情说爱 be courting；talk love
谈天说地 talk of everything under the sun
谈笑风生 talk and laugh cheerfully（*or* merrily）
谈笑自若 go on talking and laughing as if nothing had happened
谈言微中 speak tactfully but to the point；make one's point through hints

弹 I 动 ① catapult；spring；bounce ② fluff；tease ③flick；flip ④ play（a stringed musical instrument）；pluck ⑤ assail；attack（with words）；lash out at II 形 elastic；resilient；springy ➡ dàn
弹拨 play；pluck
弹词 ① storytelling（esp. in Suzhou dialect）to the accompaniment of stringed instruments ②script for this kind of storytelling
弹劾 impeach（a public official）
弹簧 spring
弹力 elastic force；elasticity；resilience；spring
弹球（play）marbles
弹射 ①launch（as with a catapult）；catapult；shoot off；eject ②pick faults and criticize；censure
弹升 bounce
弹跳 bounce；spring
弹性 elasticity；resilience；spring
弹压 suppress by force；quell
弹指 snap one's fingers—（of time）quickly pass
弹奏 play；pluck
弹花机 cotton fluffer
弹簧秤 spring balance
弹簧床 spring bed
弹簧钢 spring steel
弹簧门 swing door
弹簧圈 spring coil
弹簧锁 spring lock
弹力纱 stretch yarn
弹力袜 stretch socks
弹射器 ejector；catapult
弹跳板 springboard
弹涂鱼 mudskipper
弹性计 elastometer
弹性抗 elastic reactance
弹性体 elastomer
弹拨乐器 plucked string（*or* stringed）instrument；plucked instrument
弹唱自如 play and sing as one pleases
弹冠相庆 congratulate each other in anticipation of fat jobs（upon hearing of a mutual friend's appointment to a high post）；con-

gratulate each other on the prospect of getting good appointments

弹簧铰链 spring hinge
弹力尼龙 stretch nylon；elastic nylon
弹射座舱 ejection capsule
弹射座椅 ejection（*or* ejector）seat
弹性分析 elasticity analysis；elastic analysis
弹性极限 elastic limit
弹性塑料 elastoplastic
弹性外交 elastic diplomacy
弹指之间 during the snapping of the fingers—in a flash；in the twinkling of an eye；in an instant
弹性工时制 flexible work hours system；elastic work schedule system
弹指一挥间 in a fillip of the finger

痰 ［tán］
名 phlegm；sputum
痰桶 spittoon
痰盂 spittoon；cuspidor
痰迷心窍 blinded judgement

潭 ［tán］
名 ①deep pool；pond ②pit；depression
潭第 your house
潭府 ①deep pool ②your house

檀 ［tán］
名 wingceltis
檀板 hardwood clappers
檀香 white sandalwood；sandalwood
檀香木 sandalwood
檀香扇 sandalwood fan
檀香油 sandalwood oil
檀香皂 sandal soap
檀香山 Honolulu
檀口樱唇 cherry lips and sandalwood mouth；small and reddish mouth of a woman

tǎn（ㄊㄢˇ）

忐 ［tǎn］
忐忑 perturbed；mentally disturbed
忐忑不安 uneasy；fidgety；restless

坦 ［tǎn］
形 ① level；even；smooth ② open；frank；candid ③calm；collected；composed
坦白 ①honest；frank；candid ②confess；make a confession；own up（to）
坦陈 state frankly
坦承 admit candidly
坦诚 frank and sincere；frank and open
坦荡 ①broad and level ②magnanimous；big-hearted
坦克 tank
坦然 calm；unperturbed；having no misgivings
坦率 candid；frank；straightforward
坦途 level road；highway
坦言 ① be straightforward about；say frankly

②straightforward remarks

坦挚 frank and sincere;frank and open

坦诚布公 nail one's colours to the mast

坦诚相见 deal with sb in all sincerity;treat sb open-heartedly

坦然自若 calm and confident;completely at ease

钽 [tǎn]
[名] tantalum (Ta)

袒 [tǎn]
[动] ①leave (the upper part of the body) uncovered; be stripped to the waist; have one's shirt unbuttoned ②be biased towards; shield;shelter

袒护 give unprincipled protection to; be partial to;shield

袒露 expose;uncover

袒露心声 reveal one's inner world

袒裼裸裎 stand completely naked

袒胸露臂 bare one's bosom and arms; expose one's neck and shoulders;be décolleté

荽 [tǎn]
[名] Miscanthus sacchariflorus,a kind of reed

毯 [tǎn]
[名] blanket;rug;carpet 满铺的地毯 wall-to-wall carpet

毯子 blanket

tàn（ㄊㄢˋ）

叹 [tàn]
[动] ①sigh ②recite (poetry) with a cadence; chant ③exclaim in admiration; acclaim;praise

叹词 interjection;exclamation

叹服 gasp in admiration

叹气 sigh;heave a sigh

叹赏 admire;express admiration for

叹息 heave a sigh

叹为观止 acclaim (a work of art,etc.) as the acme of perfection

炭 [tàn]
[名] ①charcoal;carbon ②charcoal-like thing ③coal

炭笔 charcoal pencil

炭厂 charcoal works;charcoal mill

炭化 carbonize

炭画 charcoal drawing;charcoal

炭火 charcoal fire

炭精 ①(general name for) charcoal products ②(general name for) artificial charcoal and graphite

炭疽 anthrax

炭盆 charcoal brazier

炭窑 charcoal kiln

炭精棒 carbon stick

炭精灯 arc lamp;arc light

炭疽病 anthracnose

炭疽热 anthrax

探 [tàn]
Ⅰ [动] ①try to find out; explore; sound; prospect ②visit; call on ③stretch forward; crane ④concern oneself with; take an interest in Ⅱ [名] scout;agent;spy;detective

探宝 ①hunt for treasure ②prospect for mineral deposits

探病 visit a sick person (or a patient)

探测 survey;sound;probe

探查 look over;examine;scout

探察 watch;look carefully at;observe

探访 ①seek by inquiry (or search) ②pay a visit to;visit

探风 make inquiries about sb or sth;fish for information

探戈 tango (a transliteration)

探花 title conferred on the one who won third place in the highest imperial examination in the Ming and Qing Dynasties

探家 make a brief trip home

探监 visit a prisoner (usu. a relative or a friend)

探井 ①prospect (or test) pit;exploring (or exploratory) shaft ②test well;exploratory well

探究 make a thorough inquiry;probe into

探看 ①visit ②look about;watch

探空 sounding

探孔 hand-hole;manhole

探矿 go prospecting;prospect

探雷 detect (or locate) a mine

探路 explore the way

探明 ①ascertain; verify ②get a clear understanding of sth;find out

探亲 go to visit one's family;go to visit one's relatives

探求 seek;pursue;search after (or for)

探伤 detect a flaw (or crack)

探身 lean forward

探视 visit

探索 explore;probe

探讨 inquire into;probe into;delve into

探听 try to find out;make inquiries

探头 pop one's head in;crane one's neck

探望 ①look about ②call on sb (usu. from afar);visit;see

探问 ①make cautious inquiries about ②inquire after

探悉 ascertain;learn;find out

探险 explore; make explorations; venture into the unknown

探信 make inquiries about sb or sth;fish for information

探寻 seek;pursue;search after (or for)

探询 make cautious inquiries about

探针 probe

探知 get to know;find out;learn
探子 ① scout ② a thin tube used to extract samples of food grains,etc.
探测器 sounder;probe;detector
探空仪 sounding device
探口气 ascertain (*or* find out) sb's opinions or feelings;sound sb out
探亲假 home leave
探望权 right of visiting
探险队 exploring (*or* exploration) party;expedition
探险家 explorer
探鱼仪 fish detector;fish-finder
探照灯 searchlight
探测气球 sounding balloon
探端知绪 investigate the beginning and know the end
探明储量 verified deposits;verified reserves
探囊取物 (like) taking sth out of one's pocket—as easy as winking;as easy as falling off a log
探亲外交 family-visit diplomacy;relative-visiting diplomacy
探视时间 visiting hours (in a hospital)
探听虚实 spy out the strength of
探头探脑 pop one's head in and look about
探头张望 crane one's neck and look around
探幽寻胜 visit scenic spots

碳 [tàn]
名 carbon (C)
碳酐 carbonic anhydride
碳黑 carbon black
碳酸 carbonic acid
碳化钙 calcium carbide
碳化硅 carborundum;silicon carbide
碳化物 carbide
碳酸钙 calcium carbonate
碳酸钠 sodium carbonate;soda
碳酸气 carbon dioxide;chokedamp
碳酸盐 carbonate
碳纤维 carbon fibre
碳原子 carbon atom
碳三植物 C_3 plant
碳四植物 C_4 plant
碳酸氢钠 sodium bicarbonate;baking soda
碳氢化合物 hydrocarbon
碳 14 测年法 C14 dating
碳水化合物 carbohydrate

tāng（ㄊㄤ）

汤 [tāng]
名 ① hot water;boiling water ② hot spring ③ water in which sth has been boiled ④ soup;broth ⑤ liquid preparation of medical herbs;decoction
汤包 steamed dumplings filled with minced meat and gravy

汤池 ① ramparts of metal and a moat of boiling water—an impregnable fortress ② hot water bathing pool (in a public bath-house)
汤匙 tablespoon;soupspoon
汤罐 a jug (fitted in an old-style kitchen range) used for heating up water
汤锅 ① a butcher's cauldron in a slaughterhouse ② slaughterhouse
汤壶 metal (*or* earthenware) hot-water bottle
汤剂 decoction (of herbal medicine)
汤料 soup stock
汤面 noodles in soup
汤盘 soup plate
汤泉 hot spring
汤勺 soup ladle
汤头 a prescription for a medical decoction
汤碗 soup bowl
汤药 a decoction of medicinal ingredients
汤圆 (usu. stuffed) dumplings made of glutinous rice flour served in soup
汤泉沐浴 bathe in a hot spring

耥 [tāng]
动 weed and loosen the soil (in a paddy field)

嘡 [tāng]
象 loud ringing sound (of gongs, shots, etc.)

趟 [tāng]
动 ① wade;ford ② turn the soil and dig up weeds (with a hoe,etc.) ➡ tàng

táng（ㄊㄤ）

唐 [táng]
形 ① exaggerative;bombastic;boastful ② in vain;for nothing;to no avail
唐花 hothouse flower
唐突 ① rudely offend sb;blaspheme;profane ② pass oneself off as;pass sth off as
唐装 Chinese-style costume;dress of the Tang Dynasty style
唐人街 Chinatown
唐三彩 trio-coloured glazed pottery of the Tang Dynasty;Tang tricolour
唐大无验 sheer bragging;braggadocio
唐唐大国 a great powerful nation
唐突陈说 make a statement unceremoniously

堂 [táng]
Ⅰ 名 ① main room of a house ② hall or room for a specific purpose ③ court of law;principal hall in a *yamen*：大堂之上 in the court ④（ *used in a hall's name* ）⑤（ *used in a shop's name* ）⑥（ *used to indicate relationship between cousins*, *etc*. *with the same paternal grandfather*;*great-grandfather* ）Ⅱ 量 ①（for sets of furniture）：一堂西式家具 a set of western-styled furniture ②

(for classes in school) ③(for appearances in court):过了两堂 appear twice in court (to be tried);have been through two sessions (of a trial) ④(for mural paintings,stage scenes, etc.):两堂内景 two indoor scenes
堂伯 uncle who is older than one's father on the paternal side
堂弟 younger male cousin with the same surname
堂哥 elder male cousin with the same surname
堂鼓 barrel-shaped drum
堂倌 waiter
堂皇 grand;stately;magnificent
堂会 entertainment party with hired performers held at home on auspicious occasions
堂姐 elder female cousin with the same surname
堂妹 younger female cousin with the same surname
堂上 ①one's parents ②(a term of address to magistrates or judges) Your Honour
堂堂 ① dignified;impressive ②(of a man) having high aspirations and boldness of vision ③imposing;awe-inspiring;formidable
堂屋 ①central room ②principal rooms
堂兄妹 cousins on the paternal side;cousins
堂侄子 nephews on the paternal side;nephews
堂而皇之 ① openly and legally ② do sth in grand style
堂堂正正 ①impressive;dignified ②open and above-board

棠 [táng]
 图 birchleaf pear
棠棣 ①Chinese bush cherry ②a kind of white poplar
棠梨 birchleaf pear

塘 [táng]
 图 ① dyke;embankment ② pool;pond ③ hot-water bathing pool ④stove chamber
塘肥 pond sludge used as manure
塘醅 sleeper
塘泥 pond sludge;pond silt
塘堰 a small reservoir (in a hilly area)
塘鱼 pond fish

搪 [táng]
 动 ①ward off;fend off;keep out:设一道篱障给地里的菜搪搪风 build up a fence for vegetables in the fields to ward off the wind ②evade;shirk;do perfunctorily:搪事 do sth perfunctorily ③ spread (clay,paint,etc.) over;daub:搪炉子 line a stove with clay
搪瓷 enamel
搪塞 stall sb off;do sth perfunctorily;put sb off
搪瓷钢板 enamelled pressed steel
搪瓷器皿 enamelware

溏 [táng]
 形 half congealed;viscous

膛 [táng]
 图 ①thorax;chest ②enclosed space inside sth;chamber
膛线 rifling

糖 [táng]
 图 ①a kind of organic compound ②sugar ③sweets;candy
糖包 steamed bun stuffed with sugar
糖厂 sugar refinery
糖醋 sugar and vinegar;sweet and sour
糖果 sweets;candy;sweetmeats
糖化 saccharification
糖姜 sugared ginger;ginger in syrup
糖浆 ①medicinal syrup ②syrup
糖精 saccharin;gluside
糖类 carbohydrate
糖酶 carbohydrase
糖蜜 molasses;treacle
糖食 sweet food;sweets
糖水 syrup
糖蒜 garlic in syrup;sweetened garlic
糖稀 malt sugar;maltose
糖衣 sugarcoating
糖元 glycogen
糖醋鱼 fish in sweet and sour sauce
糖葫芦 sugarcoated haws on a stick
糖量计 saccharometer;saccharimeter
糖萝卜 ①beet ②preserved carrot
糖尿病 diabetes
糖人儿 sugar figurine
糖三角 steamed bun in triangular shape stuffed with sugar
糖醋排骨 sweet and sour spareribs
糖料作物 sugar crop
糖衣炮弹 sugarcoated bullet

糖 [táng]
 形 red

螳 [táng]
 图 mantis
螳螂 mantis
螳臂当车 a mantis trying to obstruct a chariot—overrate oneself and try to hold back an overwhelmingly superior force
螳螂捕蝉,黄雀在后 the mantis stalks the cicada,unaware of the oriole behind—covet gains ahead,unaware of danger behind

tǎng（ㄊㄤ）

帑 [tǎng]
 图 funds in the state treasury

倘 [tǎng]
 连 if;supposing;in case
倘或 it;supposing;in case
倘若 if;supposing;in case
倘使 if;supposing;in case
倘来之物 an unexpected gain;windfall
倘能如此 if this can be done

倘能如愿 if one can satisfy his wishes

淌
[tǎng] 劢 drip;trickle;shed

傥
[tǎng]
◇倜傥 elegant;free and easy

躺
[tǎng] 劢 lie;recline;rest
躺柜 a long low box with a lid on top;chest
躺椅 deck chair;sling chair
躺倒不干 stay in bed—refuse to shoulder responsibilities any longer
躺在功劳簿上 rest on one's laurels

tàng(ㄊㄤ)

烫
[tàng] Ⅰ 劢 ① scald;burn ② iron;heat up in hot water;warm ③ perm;have one's hair permed Ⅱ 形 very hot;scalding;steaming hot
烫发 give (or have) a permanent wave;perm
烫金 gild;bronze
烫蜡 polish with melted wax;wax (a floor, etc.)
烫面 dough made with boiling water
烫伤 scald
烫手 ① burn (or scald) the hand ② troublesome;knotty
烫金机 gilding press;bronzing machine
烫洗工 scalder
烫洗机 scalder

趟
[tàng] Ⅰ 量 ① (of a trip, etc., or a vehicle that makes a trip):昨晚上我找了你三趟。Yesterday evening I went three times to look for you. ② (of sth that stands or is arranged in a row):两趟桌子 two rows of tables Ⅱ 名 (marching) ranks:差一点儿跟不上趟 almost lag behind ➡ tāng

tāo(ㄊㄠ)

叨
[tāo] 劢 be favoured with;get the benefit of;receive ➡ dāo;dáo
叨光 be much obliged to you
叨教 thank you for your advice
叨扰 thank you for your hospitality

涛
[tāo] 名 great waves;billows

绦
[tāo] 名 silk ribbon;silk braid
绦虫 tapeworm;cestode
绦子 silk ribbon;silk braid

掏
[tāo] 劢 ① take out;draw out;pull out;fish out ② dig (a hole, etc.);hollow out;scoop out
掏槽 cutting
掏底 try to find out the real intention (or situation)
掏腰包 ① pay out of one's own pocket;foot a bill ② pick sb's pocket
掏心(窝子) from bottom of one's heart

滔
[tāo] 劢 inundate;flood
滔滔 ① torrential; surging ② keeping up a constant flow of words
滔天 ① (of billows, etc.) dash to the skies ② heinous;monstrous
滔滔不绝 pouring out words in a steady flow
滔天大罪 a monstrous crime;a heinous crime; a towering crime

韬
[tāo] Ⅰ 名 ① sheath;bow case ② art of war Ⅱ 劢 hide;conceal
韬晦 conceal one's true features (or intentions);lie low
韬迹 lie low;hide one's light
韬略 military strategy
韬光养晦 hide one's capacities and bide one's time

táo(ㄊㄠ)

咷
[táo] 劢 scream;yell

逃
[táo] 劢 ① run away;escape;flee;take to one's heels ② evade;dodge;shirk;escape
逃奔 run away to (another place)
逃避 escape;evade;shirk
逃兵 army deserter;deserter
逃窜 run away;flee in disorder
逃遁 flee;escape;evade
逃犯 escaped criminal (or convict)
逃荒 flee from famine;get away from a famine-stricken area
逃汇 evade foreign exchange;evade foreign exchange control;avoid the foreign exchange controls of the state;illegal dealings in foreign currency
逃婚 run away from an arranged marriage
逃课 play truant;cut a class
逃命 run (or flee, fly) for one's life
逃难 flee from a calamity (esp. a war);be a refugee
逃匿 escape and hide;go into hiding
逃跑 run away;flee;take flight;take to one's heels
逃票 steal rides
逃散 become separated in flight
逃生 flee (or run, fly) for one's life;escape with one's life
逃税 evade (or dodge) a tax;tax evasion
逃脱 succeed in escaping;make good one's escape;get clear of
逃亡 become a fugitive;flee from home;go in-

to exile
逃学 play truant;cut class
逃逸 escape;run away;abscond
逃债 dun(for debts);claim a debt;demand the payment of a debt
逃走 run away;flee;take flight;take to one's heels
逃罪 escape responsibility for an offence (*or* crime);get away with it
逃税人 tax dodger
逃避斗争 evade struggle
逃避现实 escape reality
逃避责任 shirk responsibility
逃跑主义 flightism (the advocacy or practice of running away from the battlefield or from difficulties in revolutionary struggle)
逃税手段 tax shelter
逃逸速度 space escape velocity
逃之夭夭 decamp;make one's get-away;slip away;show a clean pair of heels

桃 [táo]
图 ①peach ②peach-shaped thing ③walnut
桃脯 preserved peach
桃红 pink
桃花 peach blossom
桃李 peaches and plums—one's pupils or disciples
桃仁 ①peach kernel ②walnut meat;shelled walnut
桃色 ①pink colour ②illicit love and sex
桃酥 walnut shortbread
桃树 peach (tree)
桃花汛 spring flood
桃花鱼 minnow
桃花运 ①a man's luck in love affairs ②good luck
桃红柳绿 red peach flowers and green willows—a spring scene
桃花心木 mahogany
桃腮杏眼 peach-like cheeks and almond-shaped eyes—the beauty of a woman
桃色新闻 reports of love affairs and sex scandals
桃李满天下 have pupils everywhere;have students all over the country (*or* world)
桃李不言,下自成蹊 the peach and the plum do not speak, yet a path is worn beneath them—a man of true worth attracts admiration

陶 [táo]
Ⅰ图 pottery;earthenware Ⅱ动 ① make pottery ② cultivate;mould;nurture;educate Ⅲ形 contented;happy
陶瓷 pottery and porcelain;ceramics
陶管 earthenware pipe
陶匠 potter
陶钧 ①potter's wheel ②train (talents)

陶器 pottery;earthenware
陶然 happy and carefree
陶陶 happy;carefree
陶土 potter's clay;pottery clay;kaolin
陶文 inscription on pottery
陶冶 ①make pottery and smelt metal ②exert a favourable influence (on a person's character,etc.);mould
陶艺 ceramic art;ceramic handicraft
陶俑 pottery figurine
陶铸 ①mould;cast ②train (talents)
陶醉 be intoxicated (with happiness, etc.);revel in
陶瓷片 potsherd
陶瓷学 ceramics
陶情养性 cleanse one's spirit
陶冶情操 refine a person's sentiment

葡 [táo]
图 grapes

啕 [táo]
动 cry loudly;wail

淘 [táo]
Ⅰ动 ①wash in a pan or basket ②seek or buy sth in a second-hand shop or a flea market ③clean out;dredge ④tax (a person's energy) Ⅱ形 naughty;mischievous
淘金 wash (for gold);pan
淘箩 a basket for washing rice in
淘气 ①naughty;mischievous ②get angry
淘汰 ①eliminate through selection (*or* competition) ②die out;fall into disuse
淘汰赛 elimination series
淘沙拣金 wash the sand for gold;search for the very best

tǎo(ㄊㄠˇ)

讨 [tǎo]
动 ①send armed forces to suppress;send a punitive expedition;fight ②denounce;decry;condemn ③demand;ask for;beg for ④marry (a woman) ⑤incur;court;invite ⑥discuss;discourse;study
讨伐 send armed forces to suppress;send a punitive expedition against
讨饭 beg for food;be a beggar
讨好 ①ingratiate oneself with;fawn on;toady to;curry favour with ②be rewarded with a fruitful result;have one's labour rewarded
讨还 get sth back
讨价 ask (*or* name) a price
讨教 ask for advice
讨论 discuss;talk over
讨巧 act artfully to get what one wants;get the best for oneself at the least expense;choose the easy way out
讨情 plead for sb;beg sb off
讨扰 trespass on sb's hospitality

讨嫌 disagreeable;annoying
讨厌 ① disagreeable; disgusting; repugnant; repulsive ② hard to handle; troublesome; nasty ③dislike;loathe;be disgusted with
讨债 demand the payment of a debt (*or* loan)
讨论会 discussion;symposium
讨便宜 seek undue advantage;try to gain sth at the expense of others;look for a bargain
讨债鬼 ①a child dying young ②a person difficult to deal with (*or* shake off)
讨好上司 carry favour with one's superior
讨还血债 demand payment of a blood debt; make sb pay for his bloody crimes
讨价还价 bargain;haggle over;drive a bargain
讨债公司 debt-recovery firm

tào(ㄊㄠˋ)

套 [tào]
Ⅰ 动 ①cover with; slip over (*or* on); encase in ② overlap; interlock; interlink ③ put cotton,silk wadding,etc. into bedclothes and sew up ④ harness (an animal); hitch up (an animal to a cart) ⑤illegally purchase (state-controlled commodities) ⑥ model on (*or* after);copy;imitate ⑦coax a secret out of sb; pump sb about sth; sound out ⑧ try to win (sb's friendship); draw over to one's side ⑨ use the tap or screw die to cut a thread Ⅱ 名 ①sheath; case; cover; slipcover ②that which covers (garments, shoes, etc.) ③ bend of a river; curve in a mountain range ④ cotton padding (*or* wadding); batting ⑤traces;harness ⑥knot;loop;noose ⑦convention;formula;stereotype ⑧set;suit;suite Ⅲ 量 (of series or sets of things):新出版的一套儿童读物 a set of newly published children's books
套版 ①register ②process plate;colourplate
套包 collar (for a horse)
套裁 make suitable arrangements on one piece of cloth so that two or more jackets, dresses,etc. can be cut out of it
套菜 semi-finished dish
套餐 table d'hote; set meal; package product or service
套车 harness a draught animal to a cart
套服 suit (of clothes)
套购 fraudulently purchase (state-controlled commodities);illegally buy up
套管 casing pipe;casing
套话 ①polite formula;conventionality ②stereotyped expressions
套换 buy or get (goods,etc.) by illegal means
套汇 ①arbitrage;buy foreign exchange by illegal means ②engage in arbitrage (of foreign exchange);arbitrage
套间 ①a small room opening off another;inner room ②apartment;flat
套裤 trouser legs worn over one's trousers; leggings
套牢 hung up
套路 a series of skills and tricks in *wushu*
套马 lasso a horse
套曲 divertimento
套裙 overskirt;petticoat
套色 chromatography;colour process
套衫 pullover
套书 book series
套数 ①a sequence of songs,dramatic or non-dramatic,with one rhyme and a common set of melodies ②a series of skills and tricks in *wushu*, etc. ③ conventional (*or* stereotyped) remark;conventionality
套索 lasso;noose
套套 ways;tricks
套筒 sleeve;muff
套头 pullover
套鞋 overshoes;rubbers;galoshes
套袖 oversleeve
套印 chromatography
套用 apply mechanically;use indiscriminately
套语 polite formula;conventionality
套种 interplanting
套装 suit (of clothes)
套子 ① sheath; case; cover ② conventional (*or* stereotyped) remark;conventionality ③cotton padding (*or* wadding);batting ④ snare;trap
套交情 try to get in good with sb
套近乎 carry favour with;cotton up to;try to form ties with;cotton up to
套口供 trap suspect into revealing information
套色版 process plate;colourplate
套购外汇 arbitrage; illegally procure foreign exchange with state authorization
套购证券 arbitrage of stocks and shares
套汇汇率 arbitrage rate
套汇交易 arbitrage transaction
套期保值 hedge
套色木刻 coloured woodcut

tè(ㄊㄜˋ)

忑 [tè]
◇忐忑 perturbed;mentally disturbed

忒 [tè]
名 error;mistake ➡ tuī

特 [tè]
Ⅰ 形 special; unusual; exceptional; extraordinary Ⅱ 副 for a special purpose; specially Ⅲ 名 ① secret agent; spy ② tesla, unit of magnetic flux density Ⅳ 连 but;only
特别 ①special;particular;out of the ordinary; distinctive ②especially;particularly ③for a

special purpose；specially
特菜 special vegetable
特产 special local product；speciality
特长 what one is skilled in；strong point；speciality
特此 hereby
特大 especially （*or* exceptionally） big；the most
特等 special grade （*or* class）；top grade
特地 for a special purpose；specially
特点 characteristic；distinguishing feature；peculiarity；trait
特定 ① specially designated （*or* appointed） ②specific；specified；given
特工 secret service
特行 special trade
特惠 indulgence；special offer
特级 ①special grade （*or* class） ②superfine
特急 extra urgent
特辑 ①special number （*or* issue） of a periodical ②a special collection of short films
特技 ①stunt；trick ②film special effects
特价 special offer；red tag；special price；bargain price
特教 special education
特警 special police；special policeman；special police force
特刊 special issue （*or* number）；special
特快 ① express ② express train；special express
特困 in great hardship
特例 a special case
特卖 red tag sale
特派 specially appoint
特批 give special approval to；specially approve
特聘 specially engage
特勤 ①special duty，such as security and traffic control on special occasions ②person on a special mission
特区 special zone；special administrative region （SAR）
特权 privilege；prerogative
特色 characteristic；distinguishing feature （*or* quality）
特设 ad hoc
特赦 ①grant a special pardon ②grant a special amnesty
特使 special envoy
特殊 special；particular；peculiar；exceptional
特务 ①special task （*or* duties） ②special （*or* secret） agent；spy
特效 specially good effect；special efficacy
特写 ①feature article or story；feature ②film close-up
特性 specific property （*or* characteristic）
特需 special need

特许 specially permit
特压 extreme pressure
特邀 specially invite
特异 ① exceptionally good；excellent；superfine ②peculiar；distinctive
特意 for a special purpose；specially
特有 peculiar；characteristic
特约 engage by special arrangement
特召 special admission to （an organization or team）；exceptional admittance
特征 characteristic；feature；trait
特指 refer in particular to
特制 specially made （for specific purpose or by special process）
特质 special quality
特种 special type；particular kind
特别法 special law
特长生 students with special skills
特氟隆 teflon
特警队 Special Weapons and Tactics(SWAT)
特困户 destitute household；household with special difficulties
特困生 financially-handicapped students
特派员 special commissioner
特屈儿 tetryl
特赦令 decree of special pardon （*or* amnesty）
特殊钢 special steel
特殊化 （esp. of leading cadres） become privileged
特殊性 particularity；peculiarity；specific characteristics
特斯拉 tesla
特许权 chartered right
特约稿 special contribution （to a publication）
特招生 specially enrolled student
特种兵 special technical troops
特别背书 special endorsement
特别股息 special dividend
特别会议 special meeting；special session
特别津贴 extra allowance；special subsidy
特别快车 express train；express；special express
特别条款 special clause
特惠待遇 preferential treatment
特惠关税 preferential tariff
特混舰队 （naval） task force
特级教师 star teacher；teacher of a special classification
特技飞行 stunt flying；aerobatics
特技演员 stunt man；stunt woman
特价出售 sell at a bargain price
特快专递 express mail service （EMS）
特立独行 independent in mind and action
特派记者 special correspondent；accredited journalist
特遣部队 task force；commando
特权阶层 privileged stratum；the privileged

特权思想 " special privilege " mentality; thought of the privileged

特色产业 business (*or* trade) with special features

特色行业 business (*or* trade) with special features

特赦战犯 grant a special amnesty to war criminals

特殊教育 special education (for disabled or mentally retarded people)

特殊津贴 special allowance

特务机关 secret service; espionage agency

特务组织 secret service; spy organization

特写镜头 close-up(film shot)

特型演员 typecast actor

特邀代表 specially-invited delegate

特异功能 supernatural abilities; extrasensory perception; extrasensory powers

特异(体)质 idiosyncrasy

特约记者 special correspondent

特约商店 appointed store

特约演员 guest actor

特种部队 special technical units; special forces; task forces; commando

特种工艺 special arts and crafts; special handicraft products (of a particular place)

特种蔬菜 special vegetable

特种提议 privileged motion

特种债券 special bonds

特种战争 special warfare

特别公诉人 special prosecutor

特别提款权 special drawing rights(SDRs); paper gold

特别委员会 special committee; ad hoc committee

特别行政区 special administrative region

特别许可证 special license

特色电话机 feature phone

特殊防卫权 right of special defences

特约经售处 special sales agency

特约评论员 special commentator

特约维修店 special repair shop

特约撰稿人 special contributor

特别监护病房 intensive care unit (ICU)

特命全权大使 ambassador extraordinary and plenipotentiary

特命全权公使 envoy extraordinary and minister plenipotentiary

特许经营商店 franchise store

téng(ㄊㄥˊ)

疼 [téng]
囫 ①ache; pain; hurt; be sore ②love dearly; adore; be fond of; dote on

疼爱 love dearly; be fond of; dote on

疼痛 pain; ache; soreness

疼惜 love tenderly; have tender affection for

腾 [téng]
囫 ①gallop; jump; bound; prance ②rise; ascend; soar ③make room; clear out; release; vacate ④(*used after a verb denoting repeated action*): 这些想法一直在脑子里翻腾。 These ideas have been tossing about in my mind.

腾达 ① rise; soar ② make rapid advances in one's career; rise to power and position

腾飞 ①fly swiftly upward; soar ②make rapid advance; develop rapidly

腾空 soar; rise high into the air; rise to the sky

腾挪 ①transfer (funds, etc.) to other use ② move sth to make room

腾腾 steaming; seething

腾越 jump over

腾云驾雾 ① (of mythical beings) ride the clouds and mount the mist ②feel giddy (*or* dizzy)

誊 [téng]
囫 transcribe; copy out

誊录 transcribe (by hand); copy out

誊清 make a clean copy of

誊写 transcribe (by hand); copy out

誊写版 stencil

誊印社 mimeograph service

誊写钢版 steel plate for cutting stencils

誊写蜡纸 stencil paper

誊写油墨 stencil ink

滕 [téng]
Ⅰ囫 seal off; restrain Ⅱ囵 rope

藤 [téng]
囵 ①vine ②cane; rattan

藤黄 ①garcinia ②gamboge

藤篮 rattan basket

藤萝 Chinese wistaria

藤牌 cane (*or* rattan) shield; shield

藤条 rattan

藤箱 cane suitcase; rattan trunk

藤椅 cane chair; rattan chair

藤本植物 liana; vine

tǐ(ㄊㄧ)

体 [tǐ]
➡tǐ

体己 ①intimate; confidential ②private (savings)

剔 [tǐ]
Ⅰ囫 ①clean with a pointed instrument; pick (meat from bones) ②pick (as from a crack or fissure) ③pick out and reject; get rid of Ⅱ囵 rising stroke (in Chinese characters)

剔除 reject; get rid of

剔红 carved lacquerware

梯 [tǐ]
囵 ① ladder; steps; stairs ② equipment

which functions as a ladder or stairs ③ anything shaped like a staircase;terraced

梯次 step-by-step

梯度 gradient;step-by-step

梯队 ①echelon formation;echelon ②a group of persons of one level or grade in an organization,kept for use if needed

梯级 stair;step

梯田 terraced fields;terrace

梯形 ①trapezoid;trapezium ②ladder-shaped

梯子 ladder;stepladder

梯恩梯 trinitrotoluene (TNT)

梯形翼 trapezoidal wing;tapered airfoil

梯次队形 echelon formation

梯田建设 terrace construction

锑 [tī] 名 antimony;stibium (Sb)

踢 [tī] 动 kick;play (football)

踢腾 ①kick at random ②spend money freely

踢腿 split kick;extension;kick a leg

tí（ㄊí）

莫 [tí] 名 ①(of grass) sprouts ②tare ➡yí

提 [tí] Ⅰ 动 ①carry (in hand with arm hanging down) ②move upward;lift;raise;promote ③ move to an earlier date or time;move up (a date);advance ④offer for consideration;put forward;raise ⑤draw;take out;withdraw; extract ⑥bring or take out from prison under escort;summon ⑦speak about;bring up;mention;refer to Ⅱ 名 ①dipper;ladle ②rising stroke (in Chinese characters) ➡dī

提案 motion;proposal;draft resolution

提拔 promote

提包 handbag;shopping bag;bag;valise

提笔 take up one's pen;start writing

提倡 advocate;promote;encourage;recommend

提成 deduct a percentage (from a sum of money,etc.);draw a percentage

提出 put forward;advance;pose;raise

提纯 purify;refine;deposit

提词 prompt

提单 bill of lading (B/L)

提兜 handbag;bag;valise

提督 a provincial commander in imperial China

提法 the way sth is put;formulation;wording

提干 ①make sb a cadre ②promote a cadre to a higher position

提纲 outline

提高 raise;heighten;enhance;increase;improve

提供 provide;supply;furnish;offer

提灌 irrigate by lifting water to a higher level with a water pump,etc.

提行 begin a new line (in writing or printing)

提盒 a tiered lunchbox with several round compartments one above the other and a handle

提花 jacquard weave

提货 pick up goods;take delivery of goods

提及 speak of;talk about;refer to;mention

提级 advance in rank or salary

提价 raise the price,markup

提交 submit (a problem,etc.) to;refer to

提款 draw money (from a bank)

提篮 hand-basket

提炼 extract and purify;abstract;refine

提留 retain part of total revenue or resources for use in one's own unit

提名 nominate (for election)

提起 ① mention; speak of ② raise; arouse; brace up

提前 ① shift to an earlier date;move up (a date);advance ②do sth in advance (or ahead of time)

提挈 ① lead; take with one; marshal ② guide and support;give guidance and help to

提亲 propose a marriage alliance

提琴 the violin family

提请 submit sth to

提取 ①draw; pick up; collect ② extract; abstract;recover

提神 refresh oneself;give oneself a lift

提审 ①bring (a prisoner) before the court; bring (sb in custody) to trial;fetch (a detainee) for interrogation ②review (a case tried by a lower court)

提升 ①promote;lift ②hoist;elevate

提示 point out;prompt

提速 speed up

提味 render palatable (by adding condiments);season

提问 (esp. of a teacher) put question to;quiz

提现 cash drawing

提箱 suitcase

提携 ①lead (a child) by the hand ②guide and support;give guidance and help to

提醒 remind;warn;call attention to

提选 select;choose

提要 précis;summary;abstract;epitome;synopsis

提议 ① propose; suggest; move ② proposal; motion

提早 shift to an earlier time;be earlier than planned or expected

提制 obtain through refining;distil;extract

提案国 sponsor;sponsor country (of a resolution)

提成额 unit

提成费 royalties
提货单 bill of lading（B/L）
提名权 right of nomination
提前量 lead
提取器 extractor
提取塔 extraction column
提升机 windlass；hoister；elevator
提示符 prompt
提出辞呈 submit（*or* hand）in one's resignation
提出抗议 lodge protest
提出上诉 entry of appeal
提纯复壮 purification and rejuvenation
提纲挈领 take a net by the head rope or a coat by the collar—concentrate on the main points；bring out the essentials
提高效益 raise efficiency and profits
提线木偶 marionette
提心吊胆 have one's heart in one's mouth；be on tenterhooks
提成工资制 deduction wage system
提高业务水平 improve one's professional skills；raise one's vocational level
提案审查委员会 motions examination committee

啼 ［tí］
圆 ①cry；weep aloud ②crow；caw
啼号 cry loudly；wail
啼哭 cry；wail
啼鸣 （of birds）crow；caw
啼饥号寒 wail with hunger and cold；cry out from hunger and cold
啼天哭地 wail with great sorrow
啼笑皆非 not know whether to laugh or cry；find sth both funny and annoying

题 ［tí］
Ⅰ 名 topic；subject；title；problem Ⅱ 动 write；inscribe
题跋 ①preface and postscript ②short comments, annotations, etc. on a scroll（of painting or calligraphy）；colophon
题材 subject matter；theme
题词 ①write a few words of encouragement, appreciation or commemoration ②inscription；dedication ③foreword
题花 title design
题解 ①explanatory notes on the title or background of a book ②key to exercises or problems
题库 test item bank；item pool；examination question bank
题名 ①inscribe one's name；autograph ②autograph ③title（of an article, etc.）
题目 ① title；subject；topic ②exercise problems；examination questions
题签 ①write the title of a book on a label to be stuck on the cover ②a label with the title of a book on it
题旨 ①the meaning of the title of an article ②the theme of a literary work
题字 ①write a few words of commemoration（on an autograph album, etc.）② inscription；autograph
题外话 digression；what is mentioned in passing
题海战术 exercises-stuffed teaching method
题名留念 give autograph as memento

醒 ［tí］
醒醐 clarified butter；ghee
醒醐灌顶 ①be filled with wisdom；be enlightened ②suddenly feel refreshed

蹄 ［tí］
名 hoof
蹄膀 the upper part of a leg of pork
蹄筋 tendons of beef, mutton or pork
蹄铁 shoe
蹄印 hoof print
蹄子 ①hoof ②upper part of a leg of pork

<h3 align="center">tǐ（ㄊㄧˇ）</h3>

体 ［tǐ］
Ⅰ 名 ①body；part of the body；limb ②substance；state of a substance ③style；form ④system；regime ⑤aspect（of a verb）Ⅱ 动 personally do（*or* experience）sth；put oneself in another's position ➡ tī
体壁 body wall
体裁 type（*or* form）of literature
体彩 sports lotteries
体操 gymnastics
体测 testing of physical strength
体察 experience and observe
体罚 corporal（*or* physical）punishment
体格 physique；build
体会 ①know（*or* learn）from experience；realize ②knowledge；understanding
体绘 body painting
体积 volume；bulk
体检 physical examination；health checkup
体力 physical（*or* bodily）strength；stamina；physical power
体例 stylistic rules and layout；style
体谅 show understanding and sympathy for；make allowances for
体貌 one's figure and features—general physical appearance
体面 ①dignity；face ②honourable；creditable ③good-looking
体能 physical strength
体念 give sympathetic consideration to
体魄 physique
体腔 body cavity
体虱 body louse

体式 ① form of characters (*or* letters) ② form of literary works
体饰 body piercing
体视 stereo
体态 posture; carriage
体坛 athletic circles; world of sports; sports world
体贴 show consideration for; give every care to
体统 decorum; propriety; decency
体温 (body) temperature
体悟 comprehend
体系 system; setup
体现 embody; incarnate; reflect; give expression to
体形 bodily form; build
体型 ① build; figure ② somatotype
体恤 understand and sympathize with; show solicitude for
体癣 ringworm of the body
体验 learn through practice; learn through one's personal experience
体液 body fluid; humour
体育 ① physical culture; physical training ② sports
体征 sign
体制 system (of organization); structure
体质 physique; constitution
体重 (body) weight
体操服 gym outfit (*or* clothes, suit)
体操馆 gymnastic stick
体温计 (clinical) thermometer
体恤衫 T-shirt
体循环 systemic circulation; greater circulation
体育场 stadium
体育界 sports circles; the sporting world
体操表演 gymnastic exhibition (*or* display)
体操器械 gymnastic apparatus
体格检查 physical examination; health check-up
体积膨胀 volume expansion
体力劳动 physical (*or* manual) labour
体弱多病 weak and ill; valetudinarian
体贴入微 look after with great care; care for with great solicitude; show every possible consideration; be extremely thoughtful
体外受精 in vitro fertilization; external fertilization
体无完肤 ① have cuts and bruises all over the body; be a mass of bruises ② be thoroughly refuted (*or* exposed); be scathingly criticized; be torn to pieces (*or* shreds)
体验生活 observe and learn from real life
体育彩票 sports lottery; lottery tickets for sports games
体育疗法 physical exercise therapy

体育人口 sports population
体育设施 sports facilities
体育外交 sports diplomacy
体育舞蹈 sports dancing
体育用品 sports goods (*or* requisites)
体育运动 sports
体育中心 sports centre
体制改革 structural reform; organizational reform; restructuring
体操运动员 gymnast
体育节目主持人 sportscaster

tì (去ì)

屉 [tì] 名 ① food steamer with several trays; steamer tray ② drawer
屉子 ① (one of) a set of removable trays (in furniture or a utensil) ② drawer

剃 [tì] 动 shave
剃刀 razor
剃度 tonsure
剃头 ① have one's head shaved ② have one's hair cut; have a haircut
剃光头 have one's head shaved—score no points (in games)
剃须膏 shaving cream

倜 [tì]
倜傥 elegant; free and easy

逖 [tì] 形 far away; distant

涕 [tì] 名 ① tear ② mucus of the nose; snivel
涕泪 ① tears ② tears and snivel
涕零 shed tears
涕泣 weep
涕泗 tears and snivel
涕泗交流 tears and snivel streaming down at the same time—crying piteously
涕泗滂沱 be drenched with tears and snivel

悌 [tì] 动 love and respect for one's elder brother

惕 [tì] 形 cautious; watchful

替 [tì] I 动 take the place of; replace; substitute for II 介 for; on behalf of III 形 declining; falling
替班 take sb else's place (in a work shift)
替补 substitute for
替代 substitute for; replace; supersede
替工 ① work as a temporary substitute ② a temporary substitute (worker)
替换 replace; substitute for; displace; take the place of
替身 ① substitute; replacement; stand-in ② scapegoat

替角儿 understudy
替死鬼 scapegoat;fall guy
替罪羊 scapegoat
替补队员 second-stringer; bench warmer; scrub
替身母亲 surrogate mother
替身演员 stunt man;stunt woman
替天行道 right wrongs in accordance with heaven's decree

嚏 [tì]
囫 sneeze

趯 [tì]
囫 jump;leap

tiān（ㄊㄧㄢ）

天 [tiān]
I 名 ①sky;heaven ②overhead ③day ④period of time in a day;time of day ⑤season ⑥weather ⑦nature ⑧Heaven;God ⑨celestial abode of gods;heaven;paradise Ⅱ 形 inborn;innate;inherent;natural
天边 horizon;the ends of the earth;remotest places
天兵 troops from heaven—an invincible army
天才 genius;talent;gift;endowment
天蚕 giant silkworm;wild silkworm
天车 overhead travelling crane;shop traveller
天窗 skylight
天赐 be bestowed by heaven
天大 as large as the heavens;extremely big
天道 ①the natural laws; heavenly laws ②weather
天敌 natural enemy
天底 nadir
天地 ①heaven and earth;world;universe ②field of activity;scope of operation
天帝 the Lord of Heaven
天电 atmospherics;static
天顶 zenith
天鹅 swan
天蛾 hawkmoth;sphinx
天分 natural gift;talent;special endowments
天赋 ①inborn;innate;endowed by nature ②natural gift;talent;endowments
天干 the ten Heavenly Stems, used as serial numbers and also in combination with the twelve Earthly Branches（地支）to designate years,months,days and hours
天罡 ①the Big Dipper ②the handle of the Big Dipper
天公 the ruler of heaven;God
天宫 heavenly palace (in mythology)
天沟 gutter
天国 ①the Kingdom of Heaven;paradise ②utopia
天河 the Milky Way
天黑 ①deepening dusk;dusk ②dark

天候 weather
天花 smallpox
天皇 ①the Son of Heaven—the emperor ②the emperor of Japan;Mikado
天机 ①nature's mystery;sth inexplicable ②God's design;secret
天极 celestial pole
天际 horizon
天价 sky-high price
天骄 proud son of heaven
天井 ①small yard;courtyard ②skylight ③raise
天军 space forces
天空 the sky;the heavens
天籁 sounds of nature
天蓝 sky blue;azure
天理 ①heavenly principles—feudal ethics as propounded by the Song Confucianist ②(divine) justice
天良 conscience
天亮 daybreak;dawn
天量 staggering amount
天伦 the natural bonds and ethical relationships between members of a family
天麻 the tuber of elevated gastrodia
天明 daybreak;dawn
天命 God's will;the mandate of heaven;destiny;fate
天幕 ①the canopy of the heavens ②backdrop (of a stage)
天年 ①a natural span of life;one's allotted span ②the year's harvest ③times;age;era
天牛 long-horned beetle
天女 a female deva;a heavenly maiden
天棚 ①ceiling ②awning;canopy (usu. made of reed matting and bamboo poles)
天平 balance;scales
天气 weather
天谴 the wrath of heaven; God's punishing hands
天堑 natural moat
天桥 platform bridge;overhead walkway
天青 reddish black
天穹 the vault of heaven
天球 celestial sphere
天然 natural
天日 the sky and the sunlight
天色 colour of the sky; time of the day as shown by the colour of the sky;weather
天神 god;deity
天生 born;inborn;inherent;innate
天时 ①weather;climate ②timeliness;opportunity
天使 angel
天书 ①a book from heaven—abstruse or illegible writing ②imperial edict (in ancient China)

天数 predestination;fate
天坛 the Temple of Heaven (in Beijing)
天堂 paradise;heaven
天梯 very tall ladder on high buildings and structures
天体 celestial body
天天 every day
天条 Heaven's commandments
天庭 the middle of the forehead
天头 the top (*or* upper) margin of a page
天图 sky maps
天外 beyond the highest heavens—far, far away
天王 heavenly king
天威 heavenly might
天文 astronomy
天下 ①land under heaven—the world ②rule; domination
天仙 ①goddess ②a beautiful young woman;a beauty
天险 natural barrier
天线 aerial;antenna
天象 astronomical phenomena;celestial phenomena
天幸 a providential escape;a close shave (*or* call)
天性 natural instincts;nature
天涯 the world's end;the remotest corner of the earth
天意 God's will;the will of Heaven
天宇 ① the sky; the heavens ② land under heaven—the world
天渊 high heaven and deep sea;poles apart
天缘 predestined friendship or marriage;predestination
天灾 catastrophe;natural disaster;act of God
天葬 celestial burial (by which bodies are exposed to birds of prey)
天真 innocent;simple and unaffected;artless; naive
天职 bounden duty;vocation
天轴 ①line shaft ②celestial axis
天资 natural gift;talent;natural endowments
天子 the Son of Heaven—the emperor
天尊 celestial worthy
天才论 the theory of innate genius
天蚕蛾 giant silkworm moth
天秤座 Libra
天底下 in the world;on earth
天地头 top and bottom margins of a page;upper and lower margins of a page
天鹅绒 velvet
天鹅座 Cygnus
天罡星 the Big Dipper
天花板 ceiling (of a room)
天花粉 the root of Chinese trichosanthes
天狼星 Sirius

天灵盖 top of the skull;crown (of the head)
天龙座 Draco
天疱疮 pemphigus
天平动 libration
天气图 weather map;synoptic chart
天气学 synoptic meteorology
天琴座 Lyra
天球仪 celestial globe
天然堤 natural levee
天然港 natural harbour
天然气 natural gas
天生桥 natural bridge
天王星 Uranus
天文馆 planetarium
天文时 astronomical time
天文台 (astronomical) observatory
天文学 astronomy
天文钟 astronomical clock
天仙子 henbane seed
天象仪 planetarium
天晓得 God (*or* Heaven) knows
天蝎座 Scorpio;Scorpius
天鹰座 Aquila
天知道 God (*or* Heaven) knows
天竺鲷 cardinal fish
天竺葵 fish pelargonium
天竺鼠 guinea pig;cavy
天主教 Catholicism
天崩地裂 heaven felling and earth rending—violent political or social upheavals
天不作美 The weather is not too good.
天长地久 enduring as the universe;everlasting and unchanging
天长日久 long lasting
天成佳偶 a good match as of made in heaven
天从人愿 Heaven grants man's wish;by the grace of God
天地不容 neither god nor men can forgive
天地良心 can say in all honesty;must point out in all fairness
天恩浩荡 grace in abundance
天翻地覆 heaven and earth turning upside down
天方夜谭 ①The Arabian Nights ②a cock-and-bull story;a most fantastic tale
天府之国 (usu. referring to Sichuan Province) Nature's storehouse—a land of abundance;a land of plenty
天赋人权 natural right;inalienable right
天高地厚 as high as the heavens and as deep as the earth—①(of kindness) profound; deep ②complexity of things
天高气爽 the sky is clear and the air is crisp—fine autumn weather
天各一方 (of relatives or friends) each in a different corner of the world
天公地道 absolutely fair

天寒地冻 The weather is cold and the ground is frozen.

天花乱坠 flowers cascading from the sky—an extravagantly colourful description

天荒地老 when the earth and heaven get old—a long, long time

天昏地暗 ①murky heavens over a dark earth; dark all round ②in a state of chaos and darkness

天经地义 perfectly justified; perfectly proper; truth pure and simple in the nature of things

天朗气清 The sky is clear and the air is fresh.

天理难容 an intolerable injustice

天理昭彰 Heaven's laws are fully manifest.

天伦之乐 family happiness

天罗地网 nets above and snares below—tight encirclement

天马行空 a heavenly steed soaring across the skies—a powerful and unconstrained style (of writing, calligraphy, etc.)

天南地北 ①far apart ②from different places (or areas)

天南海北 ①all over the country ②discursive; rambling

天怒人怨 the wrath of God and the anger of men; widespread indignation and discontent

天气预报 weather forecast

天球赤道 celestial equator

天球坐标 celestial coordinates

天然更新 forestry natural regeneration

天然免疫 innate immunity; native immunity; natural immunity

天然牧地 natural pasture

天壤之别 worlds apart; poles apart; world of difference; as a part as heaven and earth

天人合一 theory that man is an integral part of nature

天生丽质 be born a beauty

天塌地陷 ① heaven felling and earth rending—violent political or social upheavals ②serious; grave; critical

天体力学 celestial mechanics

天王老子 emperor

天文单位 astronomical unit

天文导航 astronavigation; celestial navigation

天文年历 astronomical yearbook; astronomical almanac

天文数字 astronomical figure; enormous figure

天文制导 celestial guidance

天下大乱 great disorder under heaven; state of great confusion; great disorder throughout world

天下大势 the momentum of history; historical trends

天下大治 great order throughout the land; a well-ordered world

天下第一 the first under heaven—unequalled; peerless

天下奇闻 a most fantastic tale; a very strange story; the most absurd thing in the world

天下太平 Peace reigns under heaven; The world (or the country) is at peace.

天下为公 the whole world as one community

天下无敌 invincible; ever-victorious; all-conquering

天下无双 unparalleled in the world; unique; without equal; matchless

天行赤目 red and swollen eyes; conjunctivitis

天旋地转 (feel as if) the sky and earth were spinning round; dizzy

天涯海角 the ends of the earth; the remotest corners of the earth

天衣无缝 a seamless heavenly robe—flawless

天渊之别 as far apart as heaven and earth; worlds (or poles) apart; a world of difference

天灾人祸 natural and man-made calamities

天造地设 created by nature; heavenly; ideal

天真烂漫 innocent and artless; simple and unaffected

天真无邪 innocent and pure

天之骄子 God's favoured one—an unusually lucky person

天诛地灭 be destroyed by heaven and earth; stand condemned by God

天姿国色 reigning beauty; a woman of matchless beauty

天作之合 heaven-made match

天赋人权论 the theory of natural rights

天高皇帝远 heaven is high and the emperor far away—①justice is tardy ②one may do whatever one wishes without fear of interference

天公不作美 Heaven is not cooperative; The weather isn't cooperating.

天球子午圈 celestial meridian

天然深水港 natural deep-water harbour

天体光谱学 astrospectroscopy

天体物理学 astrophysics

天体演化学 cosmogony

天体照相仪 astrograph

天文望远镜 astronomical telescope

天文照相术 astrophotography

天字第一号 number one; A1

天机不可泄漏 God's design must not be revealed to mortal ears; Heaven's secrets must not be divulged; Don't say a word about it to a soul.

天气形势预报 weather prognostics

天无绝人之路 Heaven never seals off all the exits—there is always a way out

天有不测风云 a storm may arise from a clear

sky—sth unexpected may happen any time

天不怕,地不怕 fear neither Heaven nor Earth;fear nothing on earth;nothing daunted

天翻地覆的变化 earthshaking changes; tremendous changes

天若有情天亦老 If Heaven has feelings,Heaven too will become aged.

天下文章一大抄 All writings under heaven are nothing but copies.

天下乌鸦一般黑 all crows under the sun are black—evil people are bad all over the world

天下无不散的宴席 there never was a feast but the guests had to depart—all good things must come to an end

天网恢恢,疏而不漏 the net of Heaven has large meshes,but it lets nothing through; the mills of God grind slowly,but they grind exceedingly small;Justice has a long arm;The guilty can never escape Heaven's justice.

天无二日,民无二王 There cannot be two kings for the people just as there cannot be two suns in the heavens.

天下无难事,只怕有心人 Nothing in the world is difficult for one who sets his mind on it.

天作孽,犹可违;自作孽,不可活 When Heaven sends down calamities, there is hope of weathering them;When man brings them upon himself,there is no hope of escapes.

添 [tiān]
劢 ①add;get (or give) more;increase ② have (a baby)

添补 replenish;get more

添丁 have a baby (esp. a boy) born into the family

添置 add to one's possessions;acquire

添加剂 additive

添油加醋 add colour and emphasis to (a narration);add highly coloured details to (a story);embellish (a story)

添枝加叶 add colour and emphasis to (a narration);add highly coloured details to (a story);embellish (a story)

添砖加瓦 do one's little bit to do sth;get one's two cents in

tián (ㄊㄧㄢ)

田 [tián]
Ⅰ 名 ①(cultivated) land;farmland;cropland;field ②field (of ores, etc.) Ⅱ 劢 go hunting

田鳖 giant water bug;fish killer

田产 (property in the form of) land;landed property;estate

田地 ① field;farmland;cropland ② wretched

situation;plight

田凫 lapwing

田埂 a low bank of earth between fields;ridge

田鸡 ①sora rail ②frog

田间 ①field;farm ②countryside

田菁 sesbania

田径 track and field;athletics

田猎 go hunting

田鹨 paddy-field pipti

田螺 river snail

田亩 field;farmland

田契 title deed for farmland;land deed

田赛 field events

田舍 ①farm ②farmhouse ③a farming family

田鼠 vole

田野 field;open country

田园 fields and gardens;countryside

田庄 country estate

田租 farm rent

田径队 track and field team

田径赛 track and field meet

田园诗 idyll;pastoral poetry

田间管理 field management

田间劳动 field labour;farm work

田径运动 track and field sports;athletics

田园诗人 pastoral poet

田间持水量 field capacity

田径赛项目 track and field events

田径运动员 athlete

佃 [tián]
劢 till;cultivate ➡ diàn

畋 [tián]
劢 go hunting

恬 [tián]
形 ① quiet;tranquil;peaceful;calm ② not caring at all;indifferent;unperturbed

恬淡 indifferent to fame (or gain)

恬和 quiet and gentle

恬静 quiet;peaceful;tranquil

恬美 quiet and happy

恬谧 quiet;peaceful;tranquil

恬然 unperturbed;calm;nonchalant

恬适 quiet and comfortable

恬不为意 remain unruffled (or unperturbed); be indifferent (or nonchalant);could not care less

恬不知耻 not feel ashamed;have no sense of shame;be shameless

恬然自若 calm and at ease;nonchalant and composed

钿 [tián]
名 ①coin ② money ③ sum of money ➡ diàn

甜 [tián]
形 ①sweet;honeyed ②(of sleep) sound

甜菜 ①beet ②beetroot

甜点 sweet snacks;sweets

甜羹 sweet custard

甜瓜 muskmelon
甜酒 sweet wine
甜美 ①sweet;luscious ②pleasant;refreshing
甜蜜 sweet;happy
甜食 sweet food;sweets
甜水 ① fresh water ② sugar water—happiness;comfort
甜睡 sleep soundly;be fast asleep
甜头 ①sweet taste;pleasant flavour ②good;benefit (as an inducement)
甜味 sweet taste
甜妹子 sweet girl;charming girl
甜面酱 a sweet sauce made of fermented flour
甜丝丝 ① pleasantly sweet ② quite pleased;gratified;happy
甜滋滋 ① pleasantly sweet ② quite pleased;gratified;happy
甜而不腻 sweet but not cloying;agreeably sweet
甜情蜜意 sweet feelings and honeyed sentiment—affection
甜言蜜语 sweet words and honeyed phrases;fine-sounding words

填 [tián]
囫 ①fill;stuff;stop up ②replenish;supplement;complement ③write;fill in;fill out
填报 fill in a form and submit it to the leadership
填补 fill (a vacancy,gap,etc.)
填充 ①fill up;stuff ②fill in the blanks (in a test paper)
填词 fill in the words to fit a given tune—compose a *ci* poem by choosing a tune and then writing words to it
填方 fill
填房 [tiánfáng] marry a widower
填房 [tiánfang] second wife after one's first wife's death;woman who marries a widower
填空 ①fill a vacant position;fill a vacancy ②fill in the blanks (in a test paper)
填料 packing;stuffing;filling;filler
填密 packing
填平 fill and level up
填权 trading price of a stock after ex rights and ex dividends is higher than the ex rights and ex dividends price
填塞 stop up;block up
填写 fill in;write
填鸭 ①force-feed a duck ②a force-fed duck
填充塔 packed column (*or* tower)
填充物 filler;infilling;pack
填补空白 fill in the gap;fill in the void
填补真空 fill up the vacuum
填海造田 reclaim arable land from the sea
填字游戏 crossword puzzle
填鸭式教学 forced-feeding;cramming method

of teaching
填鸭式教学法 cramming (*or* forced-feeding) method of teaching

tiǎn(ㄊㄧㄢˇ)

忝 [tiǎn]
囫 be unworthy of the honour;have the honour (though not worthy of it)
殄 [tiǎn]
囫 extirpate;exterminate
觍 [tiǎn]
I 囮 ashamed II 囫 brazen
腆 [tiǎn]
I 囮 rich;sumptuous;plentiful II 囫 protrude;stick out;thrust out
舔 [tiǎn]
囫 lick;lap
舔屁股 lick one's ass;lick sb's boot;fawn servilely
舔犊情深 very affectionate toward one's children

tiāo(ㄊㄧㄠ)

佻 [tiāo]
囮 frivolous;flippant;giddy
挑 [tiāo]
I 囫 ①choose;select;pick ②find (fault);pick (holes);be fastidious ③ carry on the shoulder with a pole;shoulder II 囵 carrying pole with its load;load carried on a shoulder pole III 囶 (of loads carried on the shoulder pole):一挑子新鲜蔬菜 two baskets of fresh vegetables carried on a shoulder pole ⇒ tiǎo
挑拣 pick;pick and choose
挑礼 quibble about etiquette;reproach sb with a faux pas
挑食 be very choosy about what one eats
挑剔 nitpick;be hypercritical;be fastidious
挑选 choose;select;pick out
挑眼 be fastidious (about etiquette,etc.)
挑子 carrying pole with its load;load carried on a shoulder pole
挑剌儿 find fault;pick holes;be captious
挑肥拣瘦 pick the fat or choose the lean—choose whatever is to one's personal advantage
挑三拣四 ①pick and choose;be choosy ②nitpick;be hypercritical;be fastidious
挑五嫌六 pick and choose
挑字眼儿 find fault with the choice of words;quibble

tiáo(ㄊㄧㄠˊ)

条 [tiáo]
I 囵 ① twig ② long narrow piece;strip;slip ③item;article ④ order II 囶 ①(of sth narrow or thin and long):两条鱼 two fish ②

(of bar-shaped objects)：一条肥皂 a bar of soap/一条香烟 a carton of cigarettes ③(of itemized or abstract nouns)：几条建议 several proposals (*or* suggestions)/一条心 be of one mind/一条新闻 a piece (*or* an item) of news ④(of towels, quilts, clothes, etc.)：一条床单 a sheet

条案 a long narrow table
条播 drilling
条凳 bench
条幅 a vertically-hung scroll (of painting or calligraphy)；a wall scroll
条钢 bar iron
条规 rules；regulations
条痕 streak
条几 long narrow table
条件 ① condition；term；factor ② requirement；prerequisite；qualification
条款 clause (in a formal document)；article；provision
条理 proper arrangement (*or* presentation)；orderliness；method
条例 rules and regulations；ordinances
条令 regulations
条码 bar code
条目 ① clauses and sub-clauses (in a formal document) ②entry (in a dictionary)
条绒 corduroy
条饰 cover fillet
条鳎 striped sole
条文 article (in laws and regulations)；clause
条纹 stripe；streak
条约 treaty；pact
条子 ① strip ② a brief informal note ③ gold bar
条播机 seed drill；drill
条件句 conditional clause
条纹布 striped cloth；stripe
条形码 bar code；(U.S.) Universal Product Code (UPC)
条锈病 stripe rust；yellow rust
条分缕析 make a careful and detailed analysis
条件刺激 conditioned stimulus
条件反射 conditioned reflex
条块分割 barriers existed between different departments and between different regions；create barriers between central ministries and local governments；sever links between various departments and regions
条条框框 rules and regulations；regulations and restrictions；conventions and taboos；restrictions and fetters

苕 [tiáo]
〈名〉Chinese trumpet creeper ➡sháo

迢 [tiáo]

迢迢 far away；remote

调 [tiáo]
〈动〉①suit well；fit in perfectly；be harmonious (*or* propitious) ②mix；regulate；adjust ③mediate；reconcile；arbitrate ④ tease；provoke；dally ⑤abet；instigate；incite ➡diào
调处 mediate；arbitrate
调挡 gear shift
调房 ①adjust housing ②housing exchange
调服 be taken after mixing with liquid
调幅 amplitude modulation；AM
调羹 spoon
调和 ①be in harmonious proportion ②mediate；reconcile ③compromise；make concessions
调护 take care of a patient during convalescence；nurse
调级 adjust a wage scale (usu. upwards)
调剂 ①make up (*or* fill) a prescription ②adjust；regulate
调价 ① price adjustment ② readjust prices；modify prices
调减 adjust and reduce
调浆 size mixing
调焦 focusing
调教 ①look after and guide (children) ②feed and train (domestic animals)
调节 regulate；adjust
调解 mediate；make peace
调经 regulate the menstrual function
调侃 ridicule；jeer at；deride
调控 regulate and control
调理 ①nurse one's health；recuperate ②take care of；look after ③subject sb to discipline ④make fun of；play tricks on；tease
调料 condiment；seasoning；flavouring
调弄 ① make fun of；tease ② arrange；adjust ③instigate；stir up
调配 mix；blend
调皮 ①naughty；mischievous ②unruly；tricky ③insincere；scheming
调频 frequency modulation；FM
调情 flirt
调色 mix colours
调试 debug
调适 modulate
调唆 incite；instigate
调停 mediate；intervene；act as an intermediary
调味 flavour；season
调温 thermoregulation
调息 regulation of breathing
调戏 take liberties with (a woman)；assail (a woman) with obscenities
调弦 tune a stringed instrument
调笑 make fun of；poke fun at；tease
调协 coordinate；harmonize；bring into line
调谐 ①harmonious ②radio tune

调养 take good care of oneself（as in poor health or after an illness）；build up one's health by rest and by taking nourishing food；be nursed back to health
调音 tune
调匀 mix well
调整 adjust；regulate；revise
调制 modulation
调治 recuperate under medical treatment
调节器 regulator；conditioner
调节税 adjustable tax；regulatory business tax
调色板 palette
调色刀 palette knife；painting knife
调色碟 colour mixing tray
调色剂 toner
调速器 governor
调味品 condiment；seasoning；flavouring
调压器 voltage regulator
调整杆 adjusting rod
调整器 adjuster
调剂库存 buffer stock
调皮捣蛋 mischievous；troublesome；making trouble
调资工作 salary adjustment work
调制解调器 modem，modulator-demodulator
调整、改革、整顿、提高 readjustment，reform，rectification and improvement

笤 ［tiáo］

笤帚 whisk broom；small broom

tiǎo（ㄊㄧㄠˇ）

挑 Ⅰ［动］①hold up with a pole（*or* stick）；raise ②poke；prick ③（in embroidery）cross-stitch ④stir up；instigate；foment Ⅱ［名］rising stroke（one of the basic strokes of Chinese characters）➡ tiāo

挑拨 instigate；incite；sow discord
挑灯 ①raise the wick of an oil lamp ②hang a lantern from a pole
挑动 ①give rise to；lead to；touch off；arouse ②provoke；stir up；incite
挑逗 provoke；tease；tantalize
挑花 cross-stitch work
挑明 no longer keep it back；let it all out；bring it out into the open
挑起 provoke；stir up；instigate
挑唆 incite；abet；instigate
挑头 take the lead；be the first to do sth
挑衅 provoke
挑战 ①throw down the gauntlet；challenge to battle ②challenge to a contest
挑大梁 play a leading role；shoulder the main responsibility
挑战书 written challenge；a letter of challenge
挑棒游戏 jackstraws

挑拨离间 make mischief；whip up disputes；play off against one another；sow discord；foment dissension；incite one against the other；drive a wedge between
挑拨是非 foment discord
挑动是非 give rise to a dispute；touch off a dispute
挑起争端 provoke a dispute

朓 ［tiǎo］
［名］appearance of the moon in the west at the end of a lunar month

窕 ［tiǎo］
◇窈窕 ①（of a woman）gentle and graceful ②（of a palace，landscape，etc.）secluded

斛 ［tiǎo］
［动］exchange；swap；change

tiào（ㄊㄧㄠˋ）

眺 ［tiào］
［动］look into the distance from a high place
眺望 look into the distance from a high place

粜 ［tiào］
［动］sell（grain）

跳 ［tiào］
［动］①jump；leap；bounce；spring ②move up and down；beat；pulsate ③skip（over）；make omissions
跳班 （of pupils）skip a grade
跳板 ①gangplank ②springboard；diving board
跳槽 jump the manger—①（of a horse，etc.）leave its own manger to eat at another ②throw up one job and take on another；job-hop
跳虫 springtail
跳弹 ricochet
跳动 move up and down；beat；pulsate
跳高 high jump
跳行 ①skip a line（in reading or transcribing）②start a new paragraph ③change one's profession（*or* occupation，trade）
跳级 （of pupils）skip a grade
跳脚 stamp one's foot
跳井 drown oneself in a well
跳栏 hurdle race；the hurdles
跳雷 bounding mine
跳羚 springbok
跳马 ①vault horse ②horse-vaulting
跳棋 Chinese checkers；Chinese draughts
跳球 jump ball
跳伞 ①parachute；bale（*or* bail）out ②parachute jumping
跳绳 ①rope skipping ②jump rope
跳蚤 flea
跳鼠 jerboa
跳水 dive；diving
跳台 diving tower；diving platform

跳舞 ①dance（as a performance）②dance（socially or in a ballroom）

跳箱 ①box horse；vaulting box ②jump over the box horse

跳鞋 a kind of leather shoes specially made for high jumping or long jumping

跳远 long jump；broad jump

跳月 moon dance（a festive dance performed in the moonlight by young people of the Miao and Yi ethnic groups）

跳蚤 flea

跳闸 trip；tripping

跳发球 jump-serving

跳房子 ①play hopscotch ②hopscotch

跳龙门 pass civil examinations successfully

跳楼货 distress merchandise

跳楼价 rock-bottom price；end-of-world sale

跳伞区 parachute drop zone

跳伞塔 parachute tower

跳舞毯 dancing mat

跳板跳水 springboard diving

跳出火坑 leap from the fiery pit—as a girl who is freed from prostitution

跳梁小丑 buffoon；clown；a contemptible scoundrel

跳皮筋儿 rubber band skipping；skipping and dancing over a chain of rubber bands

跳台跳水 platform diving

跳跃着陆 rebound landing

跳蚤市场 flea market；swap market

跳跃式发展 development by leaps and bounds

跳到黄河洗不清 be unable to cleanse oneself even if one plunges into the Yellow River—find it hard to clear oneself (of a charge)

tiē（ㄊ丨ㄝ）

帖 [tiē] 形 ①submissive；pliant；obedient ②proper；steady；secure ➡tiě；tiè

帖子 post

帖 [tiē] 动 suppress；put down

贴 [tiē] Ⅰ 动 ①paste；stick；glue；attach ②cling to；keep close to；press（or nestle）closely to ③subsidize；help（out）financially Ⅱ 名 subsidy；allowance；grant Ⅲ 量（used of medicated plaster）：一贴膏药 a piece of medicated plaster

贴边 hem（of a garment）

贴补 ①subsidize（one's relatives or friends）；help（out）financially ②use stored material or savings（to cover daily needs or expenses）

贴兜 patch pocket

贴花 appliqué

贴画 ①pinup picture（e.g. a New Year picture，a picture poster，etc.）②matchbox picture

贴换 trade sth in（for）；trade in

贴己 ①intimate；close；confidential ②private savings

贴金 ①cover with gold leaf（or gold foil）；gild ②touch up；prettify

贴近 press close to；nestle up against

贴牌 production of appointed trademark products

贴钱 pay out of one's own pocket

贴切 （of words）apt；suitable；appropriate；proper

贴权 trading price of stock after ex rights and ex dividends is lower than the ex rights and ex dividends price

贴身 ①next to the skin ②constantly accompanying

贴水 ①pay an agio ②agio

贴题 relevant；pertinent；to the point

贴体 （of clothes）fit

贴息 ①pay interest in the form of a deduction when selling a bill of exchange，etc. ②interest so deducted；discount

贴现 discount（on a promissory note）

贴心 intimate；close

贴饼子 ①bake corn（or millet）cakes on a pan ②corn（or millet）cakes so baked

贴金漆 gold size

贴面舞 cheek-to-cheek dancing

贴面砖 furring brick

贴现率 discount rate；discount

贴心话 words spoken in confidence

贴身保镖 personal bodyguard

贴身警卫 body-guard

贴现市场 discount market

贴现银行 discount bank

贴现经纪人 discount broker

萜 [tiē] 名 terpene

tiě（ㄊ丨ㄝˇ）

铁 [tiě] Ⅰ 名 ①iron；ferrum（Fe）②arms；weapon Ⅱ 形 ①hard（or strong）as iron ②violent；harsh；cruel ③ironclad；indisputable；unalterable ④serious；solemn

铁板 iron plate；sheet iron

铁笔 ①cutting tool used in carving seals，etc. ②stylus for cutting stencils；stencil pen

铁饼 ①discus throw ②discus

铁窗 ①window with iron grating ②prison bars；prison

铁搭 an iron rake with three to six teeth

铁打 iron-forged—unshakable

铁道 railway；railroad

铁定 ironclad；fixed；unalterable

铁锭 ingot iron
铁工 ①ironwork ②ironworker;blacksmith
铁钩 cleek;hasp iron
铁箍 iron hoop
铁管 iron pipe;iron tube
铁轨 rail(s) (for trains,etc.);tracks
铁柜 strongbox;safe
铁锅 iron wok
铁黑 ①iron oxide black ②iron black
铁红 iron oxide red
铁花 ornamental work of iron;iron openwork
铁画 iron picture
铁环 iron hoop
铁活 ironwork
铁甲 ① mail;armour ② armour for vessels, vehicles,etc.
铁匠 blacksmith;ironsmith
铁警 railway police
铁军 iron army—invincible army
铁铠 mail;armour
铁矿 iron ore;iron mine
铁链 iron chain;shackles
铁路 railway;railroad
铁马 iron-clad (*or* armoured) horses—strong mounted forces
铁门 iron gate;grille
铁皮 iron sheet
铁骑 armoured horses—strong cavalry
铁器 ironware
铁锹 spade;shovel
铁青 ashen;livid;ghastly pale
铁拳 iron fist—powerful striking force
铁人 iron man—a person of exceptional physical and moral strength
铁纱 wire gauze;wire cloth
铁砂 ①iron sand ②shot (in a shotgun cartridge);pellets
铁杉 Chinese hemlock
铁树 sago cycas
铁水 molten iron
铁丝 iron wire
铁索 iron chain;cable
铁塔 ① iron tower; iron pagoda ② pylon; transmission tower
铁蹄 iron heel—cruel oppression of the people
铁桶 metal pail (*or* bucket);drum
铁腕 ①iron hand ②strong rule (over a country)
铁锨 shovel;spade
铁屑 ①iron filings ②iron chippings and shavings
铁心 ① be unshakable in one's determination ②(iron) core
铁锈 rust
铁盐 molysite
铁栅 iron railings;iron bars;grill
铁砧 anvil

铁证 ironclad evidence;incontestable proof
铁箅子 ①grate (of a stove) ②gridiron;grill
铁蚕豆 roasted broad bean
铁磁性 ferromagnetism
铁道兵 railway corps
铁饭碗 iron rice bowl;lifelong job;secure job
铁杆儿 ① stubborn; inveterate; dyed-in-the-wool ②of guaranteed high yield;surefire
铁哥们 very close friends (usu. young men)
铁工资 iron salary;fixed salary
铁公鸡 iron cock (from which no feathers can be plucked)—a stingy person;miser
铁观音 *Yieguanyin*,a variety of oolong tea
铁合金 ferroalloy
铁蒺藜 caltrop
铁甲车 armoured car;armoured vehicle
铁甲舰 ironclad (a warship)
铁匠铺 smithy;blacksmith's shop
铁交椅 iron posts; lifetime posts; guaranteed leading posts;lifetime tenure of office
铁脚板 iron soles—toughened feet
铁矿石 iron ore
铁了心 resolve to do sth in desperation;be bound and determined
铁路网 railway network
铁路线 railway line
铁娘子 iron lady
铁丝网 wire netting;wire meshes;wire entanglement
铁素体 ferrite
铁算盘 iron abacus—①careful calculation and strict budgeting ②an astute businessman;a financial wizard
铁索桥 chain bridge
铁线蕨 venus-hair fern
铁线莲 cream clematis
铁椅子 secured official
铁陨石 iron meteorite
铁案如山 case borne out by ironclad evidence; ironclad case
铁板钉钉 that clinches it;that's final;no two ways about it
铁板一块 monolithic bloc
铁壁铜墙 (like an) iron wall;bastion of iron; impregnable fortress
铁窗风味 prison life;life behind bars
铁磁共振 ferromagnetic resonance
铁道炮兵 railway artillery
铁电现象 ferroelectricity
铁骨铮铮 firm and unyielding
铁路复线 alternated railway lines
铁路干线 trunk railway
铁路路基 railway bed
铁面无私 impartial and incorruptible;strictly impartial
铁器时代 the Iron Age
铁人精神 iron-man spirit

铁人三项 triathlon
铁石心肠 be ironhearted; have a heart of stone; be hardhearted; be heartless
铁树开花 the iron tree in blossom—sth seldom seen or hardly possible
铁索吊车 cable car
铁腕人物 ironhanded person; despotic person; tyrannical person; strong man or iron lady
铁血宰相 iron-and-blood prime minister
铁血政策 blood-and-iron policy
铁证如山 a mass of ironclad evidence; irrefutable, conclusive evidence
铁中铮铮 the finest of metals—an outstanding person
铁杵磨成针 If you work at it hard enough, you can grind an iron rod into a needle; Perseverance spells success.
铁将军把门 General Iron guarding the door—the door is padlocked
铁线订书机 wire stitcher; wire stitching machine
铁路公路两用桥 (railway and highway) combined bridge; road and rail bridge

帖 [tiě]
Ⅰ 〈名〉① invitation ② card on which are written the hour, date, month and year of one's birth (traditionally used for betrothal, etc.); age card ③ note; card Ⅱ 〈量〉(of Chinese herbal medicine): 几帖草药 a few doses (or draughts) of herbal medicine ➡tiē; tiè
帖子 ①invitation ②note; card

tiè (ㄊㄧㄝˋ)

帖 [tiè]
〈名〉book containing models of handwriting or painting for learners to copy ➡tiē; tiě

tīng (ㄊㄧㄥ)

厅 [tīng]
〈名〉①hall ②office ③department under the provincial government
厅堂 hall
厅长 head of a department (under a provincial government)

汀 [tīng]
〈名〉low, level land along a river; spit of land

听 [tīng]
Ⅰ 〈动〉①listen; hear ②heed; obey ③administer; manage ④let be; allow Ⅱ 〈名〉tin; can
听便 do as one pleases
听残 hearing impairment
听差 manservant; office attendant
听从 obey; heed; comply with
听懂 understand; take
听骨 ear bones
听候 wait for (a decision, settlement, etc. from higher authorities)

听话 heed what an elder or superior says; be obedient
听见 hear
听讲 listen to a talk; attend a lecture
听觉 sense of hearing
听课 ①visit (or sit in on) a class ②attend a lecture
听力 ①hearing (ability) ②aural comprehension (in language teaching)
听命 ①take orders from; be at sb's command ②submit to the will of Heaven; resign oneself to one's fate; trust to luck
听凭 allow; let (sb do as he pleases)
听取 listen to
听任 allow; let (sb do as he pleases)
听说 ①be told; hear of ②heed what an elder or superior says; be obedient
听筒 ① (telephone) receiver ② headphone; earphone ③stethoscope
听戏 go to the opera (esp. Beijing opera)
听写 dictation
听信 ① wait for information ② believe what one hears (usu. sth incorrect or one-sided); believe
听诊 auscultation
听政 (of a monarch or regent) hold court; administer affairs of state
听众 audience; listeners
听装 tinned; canned
听话儿 wait for a reply
听起来 strike one's ear; sound
听墙根 eavesdrop
听神经 auditory (or acoustic) nerve
听头儿 worth listening to
听诊器 stethoscope
听证会 hearing
听而不闻 hear but pay no attention; turn a deaf ear to
听风是雨 hear the wind and mistake it for the rain—believe rumours
听凭处理 put oneself into sb's hands
听其自然 let things take their own course; let matters slide
听天由命 leave things to chance; resign oneself to one's fate; trust to luck; at the mercy of natural; bow to necessity
听之任之 let sth (undesirable, evil, etc.) go unchecked; take a laissez-faire attitude; let sb have his own way; let matters drift
听众热线节目 call-in (show); phone-in (show); talk-in (show)
听其言而观其行 listen to a person's words and watch his deeds; judge people by their deeds, not just by their words

烃 [tīng]
〈名〉hydrocarbon
烃气 hydrocarbon gas

烃转化 hydrocarbon conversion
烃聚合油 hydrocarbon polymer oil
烃类树脂 hydrocarbon resin

tíng（ㄊㄧㄥˊ）

廷 [tíng]
［名］court of a monarch; seat of a monarchical government
廷杖 flogging with a big stick at court (a punishment in ancient China)

莛 [tíng]
［名］stem of a herb, etc.

亭 [tíng]
Ⅰ［名］① pavilion; kiosk ② stall; stand; booth; kiosk Ⅱ［形］well-proportioned; well-balanced
亭子 pavilion (in a park or beside a road for people to rest)
亭台楼阁 pavilions, terraces and open halls; airy pavilions and pagodas
亭亭如盖 (of a tree) standing straight with a canopy of leaves
亭亭玉立 ①(of a girl) fair, slim and graceful ②(of a tree, etc.) tall and straight

庭 [tíng]
［名］①hall ②front courtyard; front yard ③law court
庭训 paternal instructions and admonitions
庭园 flower garden; grounds
庭院 courtyard
庭长 the president of a law court; presiding judge
庭审笔录 minutes of a court trial
庭外和解 imparlance; extrajudicial settlement; settle out of court
庭院经济 courtyard economy

停 [tíng]
Ⅰ［动］① stop; cease; halt; pause ② stop over; stay ③(of cars) be parked; (of ships) lie at anchor Ⅱ［形］ready; settled Ⅲ［量］part (of a total); portion：三停人马损了一停。 One third of the troops were lost.
停摆 (of a pendulum) come to a standstill; stop
停办 stop (a business); close down
停播 break; close down
停泊 anchor; berth
停产 stop production
停车 ①stop; pull up ②park (a car) ③(of a machine) stall; stop working
停当 ready; settled
停电 ①cut off the power supply; have a power failure ②power cut; power failure; blackout
停顿 ①stop; halt; pause; be at a standstill ② pause (in speaking)
停放 ①park (a vehicle) ②place (a coffin)
停飞 grounding of aircraft

停工 stop work; shut down
停航 suspend flight; suspend air (or shipping) service
停火 cease fire
停建 suspend the project
停刊 stop publication (of a newspaper, magazine, etc.)
停靠 (of a train) stop; (of a ship) berth
停课 suspend classes
停灵 keep a coffin in a temporary shelter before burial; rest the coffin temporarily
停留 stay for a time; stop; remain
停牌 stop listing
停球 stop the ball
停赛 ①(of a match or sports meet) stop; halt ②be temporarily disqualified from contests
停食 gastric disorder; indigestion
停售 suspend sale of
停水 cut off the water supply; cut off the water
停妥 be well arranged; be in order
停息 stop; cease
停歇 ①close a business; go out of business ② stop; cease ③stop for a rest; rest
停学 stop going to school; drop out of school
停业 ① stop doing business ② close a business; go out of business
停运 off-stream; off-the-line
停战 armistice; truce; cessation of hostilities
停职 suspend sb from his duties
停止 stop; cease; halt; suspend; call off
停滞 stagnate; be at a standstill; bog down
停住 stop; halt; anchor
停泊处 berth; anchorage; roads; roadstead
停车场 car park; parking lot; parking area
停机坪 aircraft parking area; parking apron
停靠港 port of call
停产整顿 suspended for restructuring; straighten things up by stopping (or ceasing) production
停工待料 suspend work to await materials
停火协议 cease fire agreement
停留时间 retention period
停薪留职 remain employed without wage; retain the job but suspend the salary; take an unpaid leave of absence; leave without pay
停战谈判 armistice talks (or negotiations)
停战协定 armistice; truce agreement
停职反省 be temporarily relieved of one's post for self-examination
停滞不前 remain stagnant; be at a standstill; bog down

蜓 [tíng]
◇蜻蜓 dragonfly

渟 [tíng]
［动］(of water) stagnate

霆 ［tǐng］
名 thunderbolt

tǐng（ㄊㄧㄥˇ）

町 ［tǐng］
Ⅰ 名 ①raised path as border between farm fields ②farmland; field Ⅱ 量 Japanese measure of length (＝119 yards)

侹 ［tǐng］
形 level and straight

挺 ［tǐng］
Ⅰ 动 ① straighten up (physically); stick out; protrude ② endure; bear; hold out; stick out Ⅱ 形 ① hard and straight; erect; stiff ② outstanding; striking; prominent Ⅲ 副 very; rather; quite Ⅳ 量 (used of machine guns): 一挺机枪 a machine gun
挺拔 ①tall and straight ②forceful
挺杆 tappet
挺括 stiff and smooth
挺进 (of troops) boldly drive on; press onward; push forward
挺举 clean and jerk
挺立 stand upright; stand firm
挺身 straighten one's back
挺尸 lie sleeping like a corpse
挺秀 tall and graceful
挺直 ①straighten (the body or a part of it) ②straight; erect
挺然不群 be distinguished from fellow men
挺身而出 step forward bravely; come out boldly; stride boldly forward

铤 ［tǐng］
副 (walk or run) quickly ➡dìng
铤而走险 take a risk in desperation; make a reckless move

艇 ［tǐng］
名 ① (light) boat; skiff ② (light) naval vessel
艇索 boat-lashing
艇长 coxswain

tìng（ㄊㄧㄥˋ）

梃 ［tìng］
Ⅰ 动 poke Ⅱ 名 iron rod or bar used for the above purpose

tōng（ㄊㄨㄥ）

恫 ［tōng］
名 disease; sickness; pain ➡dòng

通 ［tōng］
Ⅰ 动 ①open; through ②open up (or clear) out by poking; poke ③lead to; head for; go to ④ connect; link; communicate ⑤ notify; inform; tell ⑥ know; understand; comprehend Ⅱ 名 authority; expert Ⅲ 形 ①logical; coherent; correct ② general; ordinary; common ③ all; entire; whole Ⅳ 量 (of documents, letters, telegrams, etc.): 手书两通 two letters hand-written by sb ➡tòng
通报 ①circulate a notice ②circular ③bulletin; journal ④notify; report to (one's superior or master)
通病 common failing; common fault
通才 all-round (or versatile) person; universal genius
通常 ①general; usual; normal ②generally; usually; ordinarily; as a rule
通畅 ①unobstructed; clear ②easy and smooth
通车 ①(of a railway or highway) be open to traffic ②have transport service
通称 ① be generally called; be generally known as ②a general (or common) term
通达 understand things; be sensible; be reasonable
通道 thoroughfare; passageway; passage
通敌 collude (or collaborate) with the enemy; have illicit relations with the enemy
通电 ①set up an electric circuit; electrify; energize ②publish an open telegram (making known one's political views) ③circular (or open) telegram
通牒 diplomatic note
通读 ①read over (or through) ②acquire a good knowledge of; have a good grasp of
通兑 circulate; exchange
通分 reduction of fractions to a common denominator
通风 ①ventilate; aerate ②be well ventilated ③divulge information
通告 ①give public notice; announce ②public notice; announcement; circular
通共 in all; altogether; all told
通关 ①play a finger-guessing game with each other in sequence ②clear the customs
通过 ① pass through; get past; traverse ② adopt; pass; carry ③ ask the consent (or approval) of ④by means of; by way of; by; through
通航 be open to navigation (or air traffic)
通红 very red; red through and through
通话 ①converse ②communicate by telephone
通婚 be (or become) related by marriage; intermarry
通货 currency; current money
通缉 order the arrest of a criminal at large; list (sb) as wanted; put (sb) on the wanted list
通奸 commit adultery; have illicit sexual intercourse
通经 ①stimulate the menstrual flow (by emmenagogue or acupuncture) ② be well versed in Confucian classics
通栏 the layout of a page of a book (or a peri-

odical) without columns
通览 take an overall view of (a situation, etc.)
通力 put in a concerted effort
通例 ①general rule;usual practice ②universal law
通亮 well-illuminated;brightly lit
通量 flux
通令 ①issue a circular (or general) order ②circular (or general) order
通路 ① thoroughfare;passageway;route ② way;channel
通论 ① a well-rounded argument ② (usu. used in book titles) a general survey
通脉 ①promote blood circulation by invigorating vital energy ②promote lactation
通门 open gate
通名 ①introduce oneself ②general (or common) term
通明 well-illuminated;brightly lit
通年 throughout the year;all the year round
通盘 overall;all-round;comprehensive
通票 all-inclusive ticket;through ticket
通铺 a wide bed for a number of people (as in barracks,hostels,etc.)
通气 ① ventilate;aerate ② be in touch (or communication) with each other;keep each other informed
通窍 understand things;be sensible;be reasonable
通情 ① understanding and considerate;reasonable ② communicate the affection between a man and a woman
通融 ①stretch rules;get around regulations, etc.,to accommodate sb;make an exception in sb's favour ② accommodate sb with a short-term loan
通商 (of nations) have trade relations
通身 the whole body
通史 comprehensive history;general history
通式 general formula
通顺 (of writing) clear and coherent;smooth
通俗 popular;common
通缩 deflation
通体 the entire body;entire mass
通天 ①exceedingly high (or great) ②direct access to the highest authorities
通条 ①(stove) poker ②cleaning rod (for a gun)
通通 all;entirely;completely
通途 thoroughfare
通宵 all night;the whole night;throughout the night
通晓 thoroughly understand;be well versed in;be proficient in
通信 communicate by letter;correspond
通行 ①pass (or go) through ②current;general

eral
通性 general character;generality
通讯 ① communication ② news report;news dispatch;correspondence;newsletter
通用 ①in common use;current;general ②interchangeable
通邮 accessible by postal communication
通则 general rule
通胀 inflation
通知 ① notify;inform;give notice ② notice; circular
通便剂 laxative;cathartic
通风道 air-duct;fan drift;vent gutter
通风机 ventilator;fanner
通风井 ventilation shaft;air shaft
通风口 air vent;vent
通关节 get round (laws,rules,etc.) by bribery
通缉令 wanted circular;order for arrest
通气孔 air vent;vent
通勤车 common bus (or train) for staff
通俗化 popularize
通脱木 rice-paper plant
通心粉 macaroni
通信兵 signal corps (or unit,troops);signalman
通信处 mailing address
通信鸽 homing pigeon;carrier pigeon
通信连 signal company
通信犬 messenger dog
通信员 messenger;orderly
通行费 toll
通行权 right of way; pass; permit; laissez-passer
通行税 transit duty
通行证 pass; permit; safe-conduct; laissez-passer
通讯录 address book
通讯社 news agency;news (or press) service
通讯网 communication network
通讯员 reporter;(press) correspondent
通知书 notice;advice note
通才教育 liberal arts education
通存通兑 banking procedure where deposits and withdrawals are processed at any branch bank
通都大邑 a large city;metropolis
通风报信 furnish secret information;tip sb off
通观全局 take an overall view of the situation
通过验收 pass inspection
通话时间 air time
通货贬值 devaluation of currency
通货紧缩 (of money) deflation;expansion of the currency
通货膨胀 inflation
通今博古 be conversant with things present and past;be versed in ancient and modern

通力合作 act with united strength; give full cooperation to
通情达理 showing good sense; understanding and reasonable; sensible
通权达变 act as the occasion requires; adapt oneself to circumstances; follow a flexible course of action
通商口岸 trading port
通俗读物 books for popular consumption; popular literature
通俗歌曲 pop song; popular song
通俗音乐 popular music
通脱不羁 be free from petty formalisms and unrestrained
通宵达旦 all night long; all through the night
通晓世故 be perfectly familiar with the ways of the world
通信保密 communication (or traffic) security
通信联络 signal communication; communications and liaison
通信枢纽 signal (or communication) centre
通信卫星 communications satellite; telecommunication satellite
通行能力 traffic capacity
通讯线路 communication line
通用货币 current money
通用设备 flexible unit; general equipment
通用月票 a monthly ticket for all urban and suburban lines
通话计时器 peg count meter
通货膨胀率 rate of inflation
通用机械厂 universal machine works
通用计算机 general-purpose computer
通用货币单位 current money unit
通用商业语言 common business oriented language

嗵 [tōng]
拟 thump; thud: 嗵嗵的脚步声 thudding footfalls; heavy footsteps

tóng(ㄊㄨㄥˊ)

同 [tóng]
Ⅰ 形 same; identical; alike; similar Ⅱ 动 be the same as; be similar to; be alike Ⅲ 介 ① with: 理论同实践相结合 combine theory and practice ② as…as; like; as ③ for Ⅳ 连 and; as well as Ⅴ 副 share; do together; have in common: 一同前往 go (or set out) together ➡ tòng
同班 ①be in the same class ②classmate
同伴 companion
同胞 ① born of the same parents ② fellow countryman; compatriot
同辈 of the same generation
同比 compared to the same period of the previous year
同步 ① synchronism ② in step with; in pace with
同窗 ①study in the same school ②schoolmate
同党 ① belong to the same political faction (or party) ②fellow member of a political faction (or party)
同道 ①people cherishing the same ideals and following the same path; people having a common goal ② people of the same trade (or occupation)
同等 on an equal basis (or footing)
同犯 accomplice
同房 ①(of husband and wife) sleep together; have sexual intercourse ② of the same branch of a family
同感 the same feeling (or impression)
同庚 of the same age
同行 [tóngháng] ①of the same trade (or occupation) ②people of the same trade (or occupation)
同好 people having similar interests (or tastes)
同化 ①assimilate (ethnic groups, etc.) ②assimilation
同伙 ①work in partnership; collude (in doing evil) ②partner; confederate
同居 ①live together ②cohabit
同类 of the same kind
同僚 colleague; fellow official
同龄 of the same age; about the same age
同路 go the same way
同门 ① pupils of the same master ② match gate; equivalence gate
同盟 alliance; league
同名 of the same title (or name)
同谋 ①conspire (with sb) ②confederate; accomplice
同年 ① the same year ② of the same age ③ candidates who passed the imperial examinations in the same year
同期 ① the corresponding period ② the same term (in school, etc.)
同前 ditto; idem
同情 sympathize with; show sympathy for
同人 colleagues
同仁 colleagues
同上 ditto; idem
同声 in chorus; in unison
同时 ① at the same time; simultaneously; meanwhile; in the meantime ② moreover; besides; furthermore
同事 ①work in the same place; work together ②colleague; fellow worker
同岁 of the same age
同榻 sleep in the same bed; share a bed
同屋 ①share a room ②roommate
同喜 Thank you for your congratulation.
同乡 a person from the same village (or

town, province); a fellow villager (*or* townsman, provincial)

同心 ①concentric ②with one heart

同行 [tóngxíng] travel together

同性 ①of the same sex ②of the same nature (*or* character)

同姓 of the same surname

同学 ①be in the same school; be a schoolmate of sb ②fellow student; schoolmate ③a form of address used in speaking to a student

同样 same; equal; similar

同业 ①the same trade (*or* business) ②a person of the same trade (*or* business)

同一 same; identical

同意 agree; consent; approve

同余 congruence

同志 comrade

同种 of the same race

同轴 coaxial

同宗 of the same clan; have common ancestry

同族 ①of the same clan; have common ancestry ②of the same race

同辈人 contemporary

同根词 conjugate

同功酶 isoenzyme

同进退 (of colleagues taking the same stand over an issue) advance or withdraw together; stay on or quit together

同龄人 contemporary

同路人 fellow traveller

同盟国 ① ally; allied nations ② the Central Powers (during World War I) ③ the Allies (during World War II)

同盟军 allied forces; allies

同谋犯 accessory

同情心 sympathy; fellow feeling

同位角 corresponding angles

同位素 isotope

同位语 appositive

同温层 stratosphere

同系物 homologue

同乡会 an association of fellow provincials or townsmen

同心度 concentricity

同心圆 concentric circles

同性恋 homo; homosexuality; homosexual

同学录 schoolmates' address book

同一律 the law of identity

同一性 identity

同义词 synonym

同音词 homonym; homophone

同病相怜 those who have the same illness sympathize with each other—fellow sufferers commiserate with each other

同步轨道 a synchronous orbit

同步技术 synchronization

同步卫星 geostationary satellite; synchronous satellite

同步增长 grow simultaneously; increase simultaneously; grow in step (*or* phase) with

同仇敌忾 share a bitter hatred of the enemy; be bound by a common hatred for the enemy

同出一辙 be of an identical nature

同床异梦 share the same bed but dream different dreams—be strange bedfellows

同等学力 the same educational level

同等学历 equivalent scholarship; comparable educational background; comparable record of formal schooling

同恶相济 The wicked help the wicked.

同甘共苦 share weal and woe (*or* comforts and hardships, joys and sorrows)

同工同酬 equal pay for equal work; equal remuneration for work of equal value

同归于尽 perish together; end up in common ruin

同化政策 the policy of national assimilation (as pursued by reactionary rulers)

同化作用 assimilation

同类相残 cannibalism; kill one's own kind

同流合污 wallow in the mire with sb; associate with an evil person; go along with sb in his evil deeds

同盟罢工 joint strike

同盟条约 treaty of alliance

同衾共枕 (of husband and wife) share the same quilt and pillow—sleep together

同日而语 be mentioned in the same breath; be named on the same day

同声传译 simultaneous interpretation

同室操戈 members of one family drawing swords on each other—fratricidal strife; internal strife; internecine feud

同素异形 allotropy

同心同德 be of one heart and one mind; be dedicated heart and soul to the same cause

同心协力 work in full cooperation and with unity of purpose; work together with one heart; make concerted efforts

同业拆借 inter-bank borrowing

同业公会 trade council; trade association; guild

同业竞争 horizontal trade competition

同舟共济 cross a river in the same boat—pull together in times of trouble

同步电动机 synchronous motor

同步计算机 synchronous computer

同步加速器 synchrotron

同分异构体 isomer

同源多倍体 autopolyploid

同步通信卫星 synchronous communications satellite; syncom

同呼吸，共命运 share a common fate; throw in

one's lot with sb
同生死,共患难 share weal and woe
同步回旋加速器 synchrocyclotron
同声相应,同气相求 like attracts like
同呼吸,共命运,心连心 share weal and woe and unite as one

彤 [tóng]
形 red
彤弓 red-painted bow
彤云 ①red clouds ②dark clouds

侗 [tóng]
形 childish;ignorant ➡ dòng

茼 [tóng]
茼蒿 crown daisy

桐 [tóng]
名 ①paulownia ②tung tree ③phoenix tree
桐油 tung oil
桐油树 tung oil tree;tung tree

铜 [tóng]
名 copper (Cu)
铜板 copper coin;copper
铜版 copperplate
铜币 copper coin;copper
铜臭 the stink of money—profits-before-everything mentality
铜锭 copper ingot
铜鼓 bronze drum
铜号 brass trumpet
铜婚 Copper Wedding
铜活 ①brass or copper fittings,accessories,etc. ②work in copper
铜匠 coppersmith
铜镜 bronze mirror
铜蓝 covellite;indigo copper
铜绿 verdigris
铜锣 gong
铜模 matrix;(copper) mould
铜牌 bronze medal;bronze
铜器 bronze,brass or copper ware
铜钱 copper cash
铜丝 copper wire
铜像 bronze statue
铜元 copper coin;copper
铜氨液 cuprammonia
铜版画 copperplate etching (or engraving);copperplate
铜版纸 art (printing) paper
铜管乐 music for (or played by) a brass band
铜子儿 copper coin;copper
铜版印刷 copperplate printing
铜管乐队 brass band
铜管乐器 brass-wind instrument;brass instrument;brass wind;brass
铜壶滴漏 copper clepsydra
铜筋铁骨 copper muscles and iron bones—strongly built;robust
铜器时代 the Bronze Age

铜墙铁壁 a bastion of iron—an impregnable fortress
铜溶金属 copper-soluble metal
铜铵人造丝 cuprammonium (or copper) rayon
铜版印刷机 copperplate press;etching press
铜模雕刻机 matrix cutting machine

童 [tóng]
Ⅰ 名 ①child ②virgin ③page-boy Ⅱ 形 bare;bald;barren
童便 boys' urine (the urine of boys under 12,used in cases of hemorrhage and extravasated blood)
童车 bassinet
童工 ①child labour ②child labourer
童话 children's stories;fairy tales
童婚 child marriage
童枯 dried up and barren;bleak and desolate
童伶 boy actor (in traditional opera)
童男 virgin boy
童年 childhood
童女 maiden;virgin
童仆 ①houseboy ②menservant;servant
童山 bare hills
童声 child's voice
童书 children's book
童叟 children and old men—the old and the young
童心 child's heart;childlike innocence
童星 child star
童谣 children's folk rhymes
童贞 virginity (esp. of a woman);chastity
童真 child's simplicity (or innocence)
童稚 ①child ②child's naivety
童装 children's wear (or clothing)
童子 boy;lad
童养媳 a girl taken into the family as a daughter-in-law-to-be; child daughter-in-law;child bride
童子鸡 young chicken;broiler
童子军 boy scouts
童山濯濯 bare and barren hills;hills denuded of vegetation
童叟无欺 (a shop sign) neither old nor young cheated (i.e. honest with all customers)
童心未泯 (of a grown-up,esp. an aged person) still preserve traces of childishness (or childlike innocence)
童言无忌 Children say what they think (without fear); Children and fools speak the truth;take no offence at a child's babble
童颜皓首 ruddy complexion and hoary head

酮 [tóng]
名 ketone
酮胺 ketoamine
酮醇 keto-alcohol;acyloin
酮基 ketone group

酮酸 ketonic acid

橦 [tóng]
名 silk cotton tree; kapok tree

瞳 [tóng]
名 pupil (of the eye)
瞳孔 pupil
瞳仁 pupil
瞳孔开大 mydriasis
瞳孔缩小 myosis

tǒng（ㄊㄨㄥˇ）

统 [tǒng]
Ⅰ 名 ①continuum (*or* order) of interrelated things; system; genealogy ②series ③tube-shaped part of an article of clothing, etc. Ⅱ 动 lead; command; control Ⅲ 副 all; entirely; together
统舱 steerage (passenger accommodation)
统称 ①be called by a joint name ②a general designation; a general term (*or* name)
统筹 plan as a whole
统共 altogether; in all
统合 uniform
统计 ①statistics ②add up; count
统建 construct in a systematic way
统考 a general examination with a common test paper for all students from different schools
统领 ①command; lead ②commander; leader
统配 state controlled allocation of vital commodities (grain, oil, coal, etc.)
统铺 a wide bed for a number of people (as in barracks, hostels, etc.)
统摄 exercise control over; govern
统属 subordination
统帅 ① commander in chief; commander ② command
统率 command
统统 all; entirely; completely
统辖 have under one's command; exercise control over; govern
统销 state monopoly of marketing of vital commodities
统一 ① unify; unite; integrate ② unified; unitary; centralized
统战 united front
统制 control
统治 rule; dominate
统计学 statistics
统计员 statistician
统帅部 supreme command
统一税 flat tax; consolidated tax
统一体 entity; unity
统一性 unity
统包统揽 monopolize the management of every thing; take on the entire responsibility for sth

统编教材 state-designated textbook; unified teaching materials
统筹安排 comprehensive arrangement; give overall consideration
统筹兼顾 overall planning and all-round consideration; unified planning with due consideration for all concerned; take all factors into consideration and make overall plans
统得过死 rigid and excessive control
统购包销 unified state purchasing and marketing
统购统销 unified purchase and sales system; state monopoly for purchase and marketing; unified purchase of farm products by the state according to fixed quotas
统计地图 statistical map
统计力学 statistical mechanics
统计数字 statistical figures; statistics
统计图表 statistical graph (*or* chart, table)
统计推断 statistical inference
统收统支 unified collection and allocation of funds by the state
统一发票 uniform invoice
统一分配 unified distribution
统一价格 price on a uniform basis; uniform price
统一考试 a general examination with a common test paper for all students from different schools
统一口径 agree on a uniform version (*or* account)
统一领导 unified leadership
统一认识 share the same understanding
统一市场 single market
统一思想 reach a common understanding; seek unity of thinking; unify one's thoughts
统一行动 co-ordinate action; act in unison; seek unity of action
统一战线 united front
统战对象 candidates for united front recruitment
统治阶级 ruling class

捅 [tǒng]
① poke, stab ② touch; nudge; push (with one's hand or elbow) ③ disclose; leak; give away; let out
捅娄子 get (oneself *or* others) into trouble through a blunder; make a blunder; make a mess of sth
捅马蜂窝 stir up a hornet's nest; bring a hornets' nest about one's ears

桶 [tǒng]
名 tub; pail; bucket; keg; barrel

筒 [tǒng]
名 ①section of thick bamboo ②thick tube-shaped object ③tube-shaped part of clothing or accessories

简管 bobbin
简裤 cuffless trousers; trousers without turn-ups
简裙 tight skirt
简子 tube; tube-shaped object
简状花 tubular flower
简子楼 dormitory building; tube-shaped apartment; non-self-contained apartment building

tòng（ㄊㄨㄥˋ）

同 [tòng]
➡ tóng
◇胡同 lane; alley

恸 [tòng]
Ⅰ 动 feel deep sorrow Ⅱ 副 bitterly; sorrowfully
恸哭 wail; cry one's heart out

通 [tòng]
量 (*referring to action*)：发了一通议论 make a torrent of comments ➡ tōng

痛 [tòng]
Ⅰ 动 ache; pain Ⅱ 名 sadness; grief; sorrow Ⅲ 副 extremely; deeply; thoroughly; bitterly
痛陈 state (*or* present) in strong terms
痛斥 bitterly attack; scathingly denounce
痛楚 pain; anguish; suffering
痛处 sore spot; tender spot
痛打 give a good thrashing; beat soundly
痛风 gout
痛感 keenly feel
痛恨 hate bitterly; utterly detest
痛悔 bitterly repent; deeply regret; be filled with remorse
痛击 deal a severe blow; deliver a telling blow
痛歼 wipe out; annihilate
痛经 menorrhalgia; menalgia; dysmenorrhea
痛觉 sense of pain
痛哭 cry (*or* weep) bitterly; wail
痛苦 pain; suffering; agony
痛快 ① very happy; delighted; joyful ② to one's heart's content; to one's great satisfaction ③ simple and direct; forthright; straightforward
痛骂 severely scold; roundly curse
痛切 with intense sorrow; most sorrowfully
痛诉 give a bitter account
痛惜 deeply regret; deplore
痛心 pained; distressed; grieved
痛痒 ① sufferings; difficulties ② importance; consequence
痛饮 drink one's fill; drink to one's heart's content
痛阈 threshold of pain
痛责 severely rebuke; castigate
痛不可支 unbearably painful
痛不欲生 be so grieved as to wish one were dead
痛彻肺腑 cut sb to the heart; feel deep grief
痛定思痛 recall a painful experience; draw a lesson from a bitter experience
痛改前非 sincerely mend one's ways; thoroughly rectify one's errors
痛加斥责 denounce sharply; reproach deeply; haul over the coals
痛哭流涕 weep bitter tears; cry one's heart out
痛快淋漓 impassioned and forceful
痛入心髓 ache in the heart and bones
痛心疾首 with bitter hatred
痛痒相关 share a common lot

tōu（ㄊㄡ）

偷 [tōu]
Ⅰ 动 ① steal; pilfer; pinch; filch ② take (time) off; find (time) ③ seek temporary ease; muddle along Ⅱ 副 stealthily; secretly; on the sly; surreptitiously Ⅲ 名 thief; pilferer; burglar
偷安 seek temporary ease
偷盗 steal; pilfer
偷渡 slip out of a blockade in a water area; run a blockade
偷换 substitute one thing for another surreptitiously
偷看 steal a glance; peek; peep
偷空 take time off (from work to do sth else); snatch a moment
偷懒 loaf on the job; be lazy
偷垒 (in baseball and softball) steal a base; steal
偷漏 evade tax; defraud of taxes
偷拍 use a hidden camera (in an undercover interview, etc.)
偷跑 jump the gun
偷窃 steal; pilfer
偷情 carry on a clandestine love affair
偷生 drag out an ignoble existence
偷税 evade taxes
偷听 eavesdrop
偷偷 stealthily; secretly; covertly; on the sly
偷袭 sneak attack; sneak raid; surprise attack
偷闲 ① snatch a moment of leisure ② loaf on the job; be idle
偷眼 steal a glance; take a furtive glance
偷营 make a surprise attack on an enemy camp; raid an enemy camp
偷越 cross (a border, etc.) illegally (*or* stealthily)
偷嘴 take food on the sly
偷渡者 smuggler; stowaway
偷汉子 (of a married woman) have illicit relations with a man; commit adultery

偷老婆 (of a man) have an affair with sb's wife;commit adultery

偷工减料 scamp work;jerry-build;do shoddy work and use inferior material;scamp work and stint material;do shortcut workmanship

偷鸡摸狗 ①steal chickens and dogs—pilfer ②(of a man) always having affairs with women

偷奸取巧 seize every chance to gain advantage by trickery;be opportunistic

偷梁换柱 steal the beams and change the pillars—perpetrate a fraud

偷龙换凤 secretly steal a male child and substitute a female child

偷天换日 steal the sky and put up a sham sun—perpetrate a gigantic fraud

偷偷摸摸 furtively;surreptitiously;covertly

偷香窃玉 indulge in secret relations with women;have illicit sexual relations;pick up loose women

偷鸡不着蚀把米 try to steal a chicken only to end up losing the rice;go for wool and come back shorn

tóu(ㄊㄡˊ)

头 [tóu]
Ⅰ 〈名〉①head ②hair;hair style ③top;tip;end ④beginning;end ⑤remnant;leftover;end ⑥chief;head;boss ⑦side;aspect Ⅱ 〈数〉number one;first Ⅲ 〈量〉①(of domestic animals):两头驴 two donkeys/十头牛 ten heads of cattle ②(of garlic):两头蒜 two bulbs of garlic Ⅳ 〈形〉①leading ②first ③previous;last Ⅴ 〈介〉right before;prior to

头版 front page (of a newspaper)
头彩 first prize in a lottery
头筹 first;championship
头寸 ①money market;money supply ②cash
头灯 head lamp
头等 first-class;first-rate
头顶 the top (or crown) of the head
头儿 head;chief;leader;boss
头发 hair (on the human head)
头伏 ①the first of the three periods of the hot season ②the first day of the first period of the hot season
头功 greatest service;highest merit
头骨 skull;cranium
头号 ①number one;size one ②first-rate;top quality
头花 headdress flower
头回 for the first time
头昏 dizzy;giddy
头奖 first prize (in a contest,etc.)
头角 brilliance (of a young person);talent

头巾 scarf;kerchief
头盔 (steel) helmet
头里 ①in front;ahead ②in advance;beforehand ③before;ago
头脸 ①head and face ②face;features ③reputation;prestige
头领 leader;head
头颅 head
头马 lead horse
头面 [tóumian] woman's head-ornaments
头名 first place (in a contest,etc.)
头目 head of a gang;ringleader;chieftain
头脑 ①brains;mind ②main threads;clue ③chieftain;leader;head
头年 ①the first year ②last year or the previous year
头帕 scarf;kerchief
头皮 ①scalp ②dandruff;scurf
头纱 gauze kerchief worn on a woman's head
头生 firstborn
头虱 head louse
头式 hair style;hairdo;coiffure
头饰 head ornaments
头水 ①(of goods) of the best quality;top-quality ②(of utensils) be used for the first time ③be washed for the first time
头胎 firstborn
头套 actor's headgear
头疼 (have a) headache
头痛 (have a) headache
头陀 mendicant Buddhist monk
头衔 title (a sign of rank,profession,etc.)
头像 head (portrait or sculpture)
头屑 dandruff;scurf
头绪 main threads (of a complicated affair)
头癣 favus of the scalp
头雁 the wild goose that leads the flock flying in formation
头羊 bellwether
头油 hair oil;pomade
头晕 dizzy;giddy
头胀 feeling of fullness in the head
头子 chieftain;chief;boss
头半天 forenoon;morning
头盖骨 cranium;skull
头鲈鱼 silver-spotted grunt
头头儿 [tóutour] head;chief;leader;boss
头版头条 first line in the first edition
头道贩子 one who purchases goods directly from the producer and sells them to the retailer at a profit;
头等大事 cardinal task;major event of paramount importance;issue of prime importance;matter of primary signifcance
头发夹子 hairpin
头号标题 banner heading;the banner
头昏脑胀 feel giddy (or dizzy);feel one's

head swimming

头昏眼花 feel giddy (*or* dizzy); feel one's head swimming

头角峥嵘 (of a youth) brilliant; very promising; outstanding

头面人物 a prominent figure; a big shot; a bigwig

头破血流 one's head covered with bumps and bruises—be badly battered; be beaten; be crushed

头球攻门 head goal

头疼脑热 a headache and a slight fever; a slight illness

头条新闻 front-page headline

头头是道 clear and logical; systematic and orderly; closely reasoned and well argued; coherent and cogent

头针疗法 head-acupuncture therapy

头重脚轻 top-heavy and unsteady

头状花序 capitulum; head

头足动物 cephalopod

头号通缉犯 most wanted man

头痛医头,脚痛医脚 treat the head when the head aches, treat the foot when the foot hurts—treat the symptoms but not the disease; take stopgap measures; apply palliative remedies

头上长疮,脚底流脓——坏透了 with boils on the head and feet running with pus—rotten from head to foot; rotten to the core

投 [tóu]
Ⅰ 动 ① throw; toss; fling; hurl ② put in; drop ③ throw oneself into (a river, well, etc. to commit suicide) ④ project; cast; fling ⑤ send; dispatch; deliver ⑥ go to; enter; join ⑦ fit in with; agree with; be congenial to Ⅱ 介 approaching; before

投案 give oneself up (*or* surrender oneself) to the police

投保 insure; take out an insurance policy; offer to buy insurance from the insurer

投奔 go to (a friend or a place) for shelter

投标 make a bid; submit a tender; enter a tender

投镖 ① dart; dart throwing ② throw a dart

投产 (of a factory) go into operation; put into production

投诚 (of enemy troops, rebels, bandits, etc.) surrender; cross over; switch loyalty

投弹 ① drop a bomb ② throw a hand grenade

投档 submit students' files

投敌 go over to the enemy; defect to the enemy

投递 deliver

投放 ① throw in; put in ② put (money) into circulation; put (goods) on the market

投稿 submit a piece of writing for publication;

contribute (to a newspaper or magazine)

投合 ① agree; get along ② cater to

投河 drown oneself in a river

投机 ① congenial; agreeable ② speculate ③ seize a chance to seek private gain; be opportunistic

投寄 send (a letter, etc.) by post; post

投井 drown oneself in a well

投考 sign up for an examination

投靠 go and seek refuge (with sb)

投篮 shoot (a basket)

投拍 start shooting

投票 vote; cast a vote

投枪 javelin; (throwing) spear

投亲 go and live with relatives; seek refuge with relatives

投入 ① be absorbed in ② input ③ put into; throw into

投射 ① throw (a projectile, etc.); cast ② project (a ray of light); cast

投身 throw oneself into; join

投生 ① be reincarnated in a new body; be reborn ② seek a livelihood outside one's hometown

投师 seek instruction from a master

投手 (in baseball and softball) pitcher

投诉 ① appeal ② (of a customer) complain

投宿 seek temporary lodging; put up for the night

投胎 reincarnation

投纬 picking

投降 surrender; capitulate

投药 offer medicine (to take)

投医 seek medical advice; go to a doctor

投影 projection

投缘 find each other congenial; hit it off

投运 go into operation

投掷 throw; hurl

投置 throw oneself into; join

投注 throw (energy, etc.) into

投资 ① invest ② money invested; investment

投保单 insurance application (from); insurance cover note

投保方 policy-holder

投保人 applicant; policy holder

投标价 tender price

投标书 tender form

投弹角 dropping angle

投弹器 bomb rack control; bomb release mechanism

投弹手 bombardier; grenadier

投递员 postman; letter (*or* mail) carrier; mailman

投机商 speculator; profiteer

投票日 polling day

投票箱 ballot box

投票站 polling booth (*or* station); the polls

投降派 capitulator;capitulationist
投影图 projection drawing
投资额 amount of capital invested
投案自首 give oneself up to (the government);go to the police and confess;surrender oneself to justice(the police)
投保价值 insured value
投奔自由 flee for freedom
投笔从戎 cast aside the pen and join the army—renounce the pen for the sword;give up intellectual pursuits for a military career
投币电话 coin telephone
投鞭断流 (of a vast and mighty army) could fling its whips into a river and stem its flow
投标保函 tender guarantee;band's guarantee for bid bond
投标担保 tender security
投标广告 tender advertisement
投弹高度 release altitude
投反对票 cast opposing votes
投机倒把 speculation and profiteering;play the market;engage in speculation and profiteering
投机分子 opportunist; political speculator; someone who practises opportunism
投机取巧 wheel and deal;seize every chance to seek private gain;be opportunistic;seek private gain by dishonest;gain by trickery; take advantage of the moment;seize every change to gain advantage by trickery
投票表决 decide by ballot
投其所好 cater to sb's likes (or tastes)
投入生产 put into production;go into operation
投身革命 join the revolutionary ranks;join in the revolutions
投石问路 throw a stone to clear the road
投鼠忌器 hesitate to pelt a rat for fear of smashing the dishes—hold back from taking action against an evil-doer for fear of involving or harming good people
投桃报李 give a plum in return for a peach—return present for present;exchange gifts
投降主义 capitulationism
投影电视 projection TV
投资保护 investment protection
投资场所 outlet for investment
投资方向 investment orientation
投资风险 investment risk
投资公司 investment company
投资规模 investment scale
投资环境 investment environment; investment climate
投资基金 investment funds
投资激励 investment incentives
投资结构 investment structure
投资决策 investment decision

投资市场 investment market
投资收益 income from (or on) investment
投资限额 size of investment
投资效益 investment results
投资银行 investment bank
投资债券 investment bond
投资主体 major investor;principal for investment
投资转让 investment grants
投资资金 investment funds
投标保证金 tender bond
投标人须知 Instruction of Tenders
投影几何学 projective geometry
投资多元化 diversified investment
投资回收率 return on investment
投资回收期 payback period
投机倒把分子 speculator;profiteer
投诉热线电话 dial-a-cheat hotline
投资理想场所 ideal place for investment
投资连结寿险 investment-linked life insurance
投资倾斜制度 measures which favour investment in
投资税收减让 tax incentives for investment
投资少,见效快 less investment but yield quicker returns
投融资体制改革 reform of investment and financing systems
投身到事业中去 throw oneself into a career
投币式自动售货机 slot machine
投资主体法人责任制 system of responsibility for the legal person-main investor

tòu(ㄊㄡˋ)

透 [tòu]
Ⅰ 动 ① penetrate; pass through; seep through leak through ②tell secretly;leak ③ appear;look; show Ⅱ 副 ① thoroughly; in a penetrating way; clearly ② to saturation; to the extreme;fully;completely
透彻 penetrating;thorough
透底 reveal the exact details
透顶 thoroughly;downright; in the extreme; through and through
透风 ①let in air;ventilate ②dry in the air;air ③divulge a secret;leak
透骨 ①(of cold air) chill one to the bone;be piercing ②deep;profound;penetrating
透汗 a good sweat
透话 drop a hint;hint;suggest
透镜 lens
透亮 [tòuliang] ①bright;transparent ②perfectly clear
透漏 divulge;leak;reveal
透露 ①divulge;leak ②appear;disclose;reveal
透绿 reveal the green
透明 transparent;diaphanous

透辟 penetrating;incisive;thorough
透气 ①ventilate ②breathe freely ③leak (*or* disclose) information;drop a hint;tip off
透射 ①(of light) pass through ②transmission
透视 ① perspective ② fluoroscopy;roentgenoscopy ③see through
透水 leaky
透析 analyse penetratingly
透信 leak (*or* disclose) information;drop a hint;tip off
透雨 saturating (*or* soaking) rain;soaker
透支 ①banking overdraw;make an overdraft ②expenditure exceeds revenue;overspend ③draw one's salary in advance
透翅蛾 clearwing (moth)
透亮儿 allow light to pass through
透明度 openness;transparency
透明计 diaphanometer
透明胶 adhesive tape
透明漆 celluloid paint;clear lacquer
透明体 transparent body
透明纸 cellophane paper;cellophane
透热性 diathermancy
透视图 perspective drawing
透水层 pervious bed;permeable stratum
透心儿 to the core;to the marrow
透心凉 ①penetrating coolness ②utterly disappointing
透过现象看本质 see through the appearance to perceive the essence

tū（ㄊㄨ）

凸 [tū]
形 protruding;bulging;raised;convex
凸岸 convex bank
凸版 relief printing plate
凸镜 convex mirror;convex lens
凸轮 cam
凸纹 raised carving or design
凸显 present clearly
凸现 show distinctively
凸缘 flange
凸面镜 convex mirror
凸透镜 convex lens

秃 [tū]
形 ①bald;bare ②barren;bare ③blunt ④incomplete;deficient;unsatisfactory
秃笔 bald writing brush—poor writing ability;low skill at composition
秃疮 favus of the scalp
秃顶 ①bald ②bald head
秃鹫 cinereous vulture
秃树 bare trees;defoliated trees
秃头 ① bareheaded;hatless ② bald head ③ shaven head
秃鹰 bald eagle
秃子 ①baldhead;baldpate ②favus of the scalp

秃发病 alopecia

突 [tū]
Ⅰ 动 ①dash forward;charge;sprint ②project;protrude;stick out Ⅱ 副 all of a sudden;abruptly;unexpectedly Ⅲ 名 chimney
突变 ①sudden change ②leap ③mutation
突出 ① break through ② protruding;projecting;sticking out ③ outstanding;prominent ④give prominence to;stress;highlight
突击 ①make a sudden and violent attack;assault ②make a concentrated effort to finish a job quickly;do a crash job
突破 ① break through;make (*or* effect) a breakthrough ②surmount;break;top ③(in football,etc.) break through a defence
突起 ① break out;suddenly appear ② rise high;tower
突然 ①sudden;abrupt;unexpected ②suddenly;abruptly;unexpectedly
突围 break out of an encirclement
突兀 ①lofty;towering ②sudden;abrupt;unexpected
突袭 surprise attack
突显 make apparent
突出部 salient
突击点 point of assault
突击队 shock brigade
突击手 shock worker
突破点 breakthrough point;point of penetration
突破口 breach;gap
突发案件 emergency;contingency;eventuality
突飞猛进 advance by leaps and bounds;advance with seven-league strides;make giant strides
突击花钱 rush to expend surplus funds;go on buying spree;deliberately spend money with no consideration of discipline
突击检查 spot check
突击战术 shock tactics
突破地区 area of penetration (*or* breakthrough)
突然袭击 surprise attack;sudden onslaught
突如其来 arise suddenly;come all of a sudden;appear out of nowhere
突击上项目 rush into a project
突然死亡法 sudden death(overtime)

tú（ㄊㄨ）

图 [tú]
Ⅰ 名 ①picture;drawing;diagram;chart ②intention;intent Ⅱ 动 ①scheme;plan;seek;pursue ②covet;desire;be after ③draw;paint
图案 pattern;design
图板 drawing board
图版 plate (for printing photos,maps,illustrations,etc.)

图报 seek ways to return sb's kindness
图表 chart;diagram;graph
图册 atlas
图钉 drawing pin;thumbtack
图符 icon
图画 drawing;picture;painting
图鉴 illustrated (*or* pictorial) handbook
图解 ①diagram;graph;figure ②graphic solution
图景 view;prospect
图卷 picture scroll
图利 desire to make money (*or* profit);plan to make money
图例 legend (of a map,etc.);key
图谋 plot;scheme;conspire
图片 picture;photograph
图谱 a collection of illustrative plates;atlas
图示 graphic; diagrammatic presentation; graphic expression
图书 books
图腾 totem
图像 picture;image
图形 ①graph;figure ②geometric figure
图样 pattern;design;draft;drawing
图章 seal;stamp
图纸 blueprint;drawing
图案操 callisthenic performance forming patterns
图画纸 drawing paper
图书馆 library
图书室 reading room
图书学 bibliology
图财害命 murder sb for his money
图画文字 picture writing;pictography
图名图利 seek fame and wealth
图谋不轨 hatch a sinister plot;plot sth unlawful;engage in conspiratorial activities
图书馆学 library science
图书目录 catalogue of books;library catalogue
图腾崇拜 totem worship;totemism
图文并茂 Picture and accompanying essay are both excellent.
图文传真 fax
图文电视 teletext
图文资讯 Ceefax
图像识别 image recognition;pattern recognition
图穷匕首见 when the map was unrolled,the dagger was revealed—hidden intentions are revealed in the end

荼 [tú]
名 ①bitter edible plant ②white flower of reeds,etc.
荼毒 afflict with great suffering;torment
荼蘼 roseleaf raspberry
荼毒生灵 plunge the people into the depths of suffering

徒 [tú]
Ⅰ 形 bare;empty Ⅱ 副 ①on foot ②merely;just only ③in vain;to no avail Ⅲ 名 ①apprentice;pupil;disciple ②(of a religion) believer;follower ③clique member ④person;fellow ⑤(prison) sentence;imprisonment
徒步 on foot
徒弟 apprentice;disciple
徒工 apprentice
徒劳 make a futile effort;work fruitlessly
徒然 ①in vain;for nothing;to no avail ②merely;only
徒手 bare-handed;unarmed
徒孙 disciple's disciple
徒刑 imprisonment;(prison) sentence
徒长 excessive growth (of branches and leaves);spindling
徒手操 free-standing exercises
徒费唇舌 waste one's breath
徒费精力 waste one's energy;make futile efforts
徒唤奈何 utter bootless cries;utter unavailing cries of despair
徒具虚名 exist only in name;have an undeserved reputation
徒劳往返 make a futile journey;hurry back and forth for nothing
徒劳无功 make a futile effort;work to no avail
徒劳无益 work in vain
徒乱人意 can only confuse people's minds
徒有其表 have a good appearance only;be reduced to pure form
徒有其名 in name only
徒有虚名 have a false (*or* unearned, undeserved) reputation
徒子徒孙 ①disciples and followers ②hangers-on and their spawn
徒自惊扰 frighten oneself without reason;become needlessly alarmed

途 [tú]
名 way;road;route;path
途程 road;way;course
途经 by way of;via
途径 way;channel
途穷 at the end of one's resources
途中 on the way;en route

涂 [tú]
涂层 coat;coating
涂改 alter
涂画 scribble;scrawl;daub
涂料 coating;paint
涂抹 ①daub;smear;paint ②scribble;scrawl
涂片 smear
涂饰 ① cover with paint, lacquer, colour wash, etc. ② daub (plaster, etc.) on a wall;whitewash
涂刷 apply paint,etc. with a brush

涂炭 mud and ashes—utter misery; great affliction; misery and suffering
涂写 scribble; scrawl; doodle
涂鸦 poor handwriting; scrawl; chicken tracks
涂泽 gloss over; whitewash
涂改液 correction fluid
涂改痕迹 sign of erasure
涂改支票 tamper with check
涂写污染 graffiti pollution
涂脂抹粉 apply powder and paint—prettify; whitewash

屠 [tú]

〔动〕①slaughter (animals for food) ②massacre; butcher
屠场 slaughterhouse
屠刀 butcher's knife
屠夫 ①butcher ②ruthless ruler
屠户 butcher; butcher's
屠戮 massacre; butcher; slaughter
屠杀 massacre; butcher; slaughter
屠宰 butcher; slaughter
屠宰场 slaughterhouse
屠宰率 dressing percentage
屠宰税 tax on slaughtering animals
屠宰业 butchery
屠龙之技 the art of butchering dragons—an art of a high order but of little value

tǔ (ㄊㄨˇ)

土 [tǔ]

Ⅰ〔名〕①soil; earth; dust ②land; ground; territory ③(raw) opium Ⅱ〔形〕①local; native; indigenous ②home-made; local; indigenous ③unrefined; unenlightened; crude; rustic
土坝 earth-filled dam; earth dam
土豹 buzzard
土表 soil surface
土鳖 ground beetle
土布 handwoven cloth; home-spun cloth
土层 pedosphere; soil horizon; soil layer
土产 ①produced in a locality ②local (or native) product
土地 ①land; soil ②territory
土豆 potato
土法 indigenous method; local method
土方 ①cubic metre of earth ②earthwork ③folk recipe
土房 an adobe house
土匪 bandit; brigand
土豪 local tyrant
土话 local, colloquial expressions; local dialect
土黄 colour of loess; yellowish brown
土货 local product; native produce
土炕 heatable adobe sleeping platform; adobe *kang*
土路 dirt road
土木 building; construction

土坯 sun-dried mud brick; adobe
土气 ①rustic style ②rustic; uncouth; countrified
土丘 mound; hillock
土壤 soil
土人 natives; aborigines
土司 ①system of appointing national minority hereditary headmen in the Yuan, Ming and Qing Dynasties ②such a headman
土豚 earth pig
土卫 satellite of Saturn; Saturnian satellite
土温 soil temperature
土星 Saturn
土音 local accent
土语 local, colloquial expressions; local dialect
土葬 burial (of the dead) in the ground
土造 make sth with local methods
土质 the quality and composition of the soil
土冢 grave mound
土著 original inhabitants; aborigines
土霸王 cock of the dunghill
土办法 indigenous methods
土包子 clodhopper; (country) bumpkin
土拨鼠 marmot
土地法 land law; agrarian law
土地税 land tax
土地爷 local god of the land; village god
土地证 land certificate; land deed
土方子 handed-down recipe; home remedy
土皇帝 local despot; local tyrant
土霉素 terramycin; oxytetracycline
土壤学 soil science; pedology
土设备 crude, home-made equipment
土石方 cubic metre of earth and stone
土特产 special local product; speciality
土腥气 the smell of soil
土政策 local policy
土专家 self-taught expert; local expert
土崩瓦解 disintegrate; crumble; fall apart; collapse
土地板结 hardening (or crusting) of soil
土地承包 land contract
土地分红 dividend on land shares
土地复垦 land reclamation
土地改革 land reform; agrarian reform
土地集中 concentration of landholdings
土地入股 pooling of land
土地沙化 desertification of land; desert encroachment
土地闲置 vacant land; idle land
土地征用 expropriation of land
土地制度 land system
土地转租 land release
土地资源 land resources
土地租赁 land lease
土法上马 do sth using native methods
土豪劣绅 local tyrants (or bullies) and evil

gentry
土老冒儿 clodhopper;(country) bumpkin
土里土气 rustic;uncouth;countrified
土木工程 civil engineering
土生土长 locally born and bred;born and brought up in the locality
土头土脑 rustic;uncouth;countrified
土洋并举 use both indigenous and foreign methods;use both traditional and modern methods;use both simple and sophisticated methods
土洋结合 combine indigenous (*or* native) and foreign methods;combine traditional and modern methods;combine simple and sophisticated methods
土族元素 earthy element
土地承包期 land contract period
土地利用率 the land use efficiency
土地使用费 land use charge
土地使用权 right of land use;land-use rights
土地使用税 land-use tax
土地增值税 land value-added tax
土地二级市场 secondary land market
土地经营管理 land business management
土地一级市场 primary land market
土地有偿使用 paid land use
土地报酬递减律 the law of diminishing returns

吐 [tǔ] 动 ① spit;force sth out of one's mouth ② emit;send out;put forth ③ say;tell;pour out ➡tù
吐翠 look fresh and green
吐根 ipecac
吐口 ① tell truth ② put forward a claim;make a demand
吐露 reveal;tell
吐气 ① feel elated after unburdening oneself of resentment;feel elated and exultant ② aspirated
吐弃 spurn;cast aside;reject
吐穗 earing (up);heading (of cereal plants)
吐痰 spit;expectorate
吐絮 opening of bolls;boll opening
吐字 (of an actor in traditional opera) enunciate
吐根素 emetine
吐苦水 pour out one's grievances (*or* bitterness)
吐舌头 put (*or* stick) out one's tongue
吐绶鸡 turkey
吐刚茹柔 bully the weak and fear the strong
吐故纳新 exhale the old and inhale the new;get rid of the stale and take in the fresh
吐露真情 unbosom oneself;come out with the truth
吐露衷曲 pour out one's heart;come out with the truth;unbosom oneself
吐字清楚 enunciate clearly

tù(ㄊㄨˋ)

吐 [tù] 动 ① vomit;retch;throw up ② disgorge;give up unwillingly ➡tù
吐沫 saliva;spittle;spit
吐血 spitting blood;haematemesis
吐泻 vomiting and diarrhoea
吐赃 disgorge ill-gotten gains
吐酒石 tartar emetic

兔 [tù] 名 hare;rabbit
兔唇 harelip
兔毫 a writing brush made of rabbit's hair
兔狲 steppe cat
兔脱 run away like a hare;escape;flee
兔子 hare;rabbit
兔儿爷 clay figurine with the head of a rabbit (children's toy at the Mid-Autumn Festival)
兔崽子 brat;bastard
兔死狗烹 kill the hounds for food once the hares are bagged—eliminate trusted aids when they have outlived their usefulness
兔死狐悲 the fox mourns the death of the hare—like feels for like
兔子不吃窝边草 a rabbit doesn't eat the grass near its own hole (for its own protection)—a villain doesn't harm his next-door neighbours
兔子尾巴长不了 the tail of a rabbit can't be long—won't last long

tuān(ㄊㄨㄢ)

湍 [tuān] Ⅰ 形 (of a current) rapid;swift;torrential Ⅱ 名 rapids;rushing waters
湍急 (of a current) rapid;torrential
湍流 ① swift current;rushing waters;torrent;rapids ② turbulent flow;turbulence
湍滩 sault

tuán(ㄊㄨㄢˊ)

团 [tuán] Ⅰ 形 round;circular Ⅱ 动 ① roll into a ball;roll ② unite;assemble ③ conglomerate Ⅲ 名 ① dumpling ② sth shaped like a ball or a circle;roundish mass ③ group;circle;organization ④ regiment ⑤ (short for 中国共产主义青年团) the Communist Youth League of China;the League ⑥ village-level government Ⅳ 量:一团废纸 a ball of waste paper
团拜 gather together to exchange greetings (as on New Year's Day)

团城 round city
团队 group；corps；team
团费 League membership dues
团粉 cooking starch
团徽 emblem of the Communist Youth League；League emblem
团伙 gang；band；clique
团籍 League membership
团结 unite；rally
团聚 ①reunite ②unite and gather
团课 League class；League lecture
团矿 nodulizing；briquetting
团粒 granule
团脐 ① broad and rounded abdomen of a female crab ②female crab
团旗 flag of the Communist Youth League；League flag
团扇 a round fan
团体 organization；group；team
团团 round and round；all round
团委 committee of the Communist Youth League（at a college, etc.）；League committee
团险 group insurance
团鱼 soft-shelled turtle
团员 ①member ②a member of the Communist Youth League of China；League member
团圆 ①reunion（of family members）②round
团藻 volvox
团长 ① regimental commander ② head（or chief, chairman）of a delegation, troupe, etc.
团子 dumpling
团坐 （of a group of people）sit in a circle
团拜会 group greetings；group congratulations；mass greetings；mass congratulations
团体操 group callisthenics
团体票 group ticket
团体赛 team competition
团团转 round and round
团圆饭 family reunion dinner；reunion dinner
团圆节 Family Reunion Festival
团支部 Youth League branch
团队精神 team spirit
团结互助 unity and mutual aid
团结友爱 solidarity and friendship
团体冠军 team title
团体旅游 package tour
团团坐下 sit down in a circle

抟 ［tuán］
囫 ①hover；circle；spiral ②roll sth into a ball；roll

tuǎn（ㄊㄨㄢˇ）

疃 ［tuǎn］
图 village

tuàn（ㄊㄨㄢˋ）

象 ［tuàn］
囫 judge；assert

tuī（ㄊㄨㄟ）

忒 ［tuī］
圖 too；awfully ➡ tè

推 ［tuī］
囫 ①push；shove；thrust ②turn a mill（or grindstone）；grind ③cut；pare；plane；mow ④ push forward；promote；advance；apply ⑤infer；deduce；consider all aspects of a situation ⑥ decline；yield；give ⑦ push away；shift；shirk ⑧put off；delay；postpone ⑨hold in esteem；praise highly ⑩ elect；choose；recommend
推刨 plane（a carpenter's tool）
推测 infer；conjecture；guess
推迟 put off；postpone；defer
推斥 repulsion
推崇 hold in esteem；praise highly
推出 introduce；put out；present
推辞 decline（an appointment, invitation, etc.）；derive（sth from sth）
推戴 support sb assuming leadership
推挡 half volley with push
推导 ①derivation（in math, physics, etc.）② derive（sth from sth）
推倒 ①push over；overturn ②repudiate；cancel；reverse
推定 ①elect；choose ②infer；deduce
推动 promote；give a push to
推度 infer；conjecture；guess
推断 infer；deduce
推翻 ①overthrow；overturn；topple ②repudiate；cancel；reverse
推杆 push rod
推故 give（or find）a pretext；make an excuse
推广 popularize；spread；extend
推及 spread to；reach by analogy
推挤 ① push and shove ② push out；squeeze out；elbow out
推荐 recommend
推介 introduce
推进 ①push on；carry forward；advance；give impetus to ②move forward；push；drive
推究 examine；study
推举 ①elect；choose ②clean and press；press
推拉 push-and-pull
推理 inference；reasoning
推力 thrust
推论 inference；deduction；corollary
推磨 turn a millstone
推拿 massage
推敲 weigh；deliberate

推求 inquire into;ascertain
推却 refuse;decline
推让 decline (a position,favour,etc. out of modesty)
推说 ①offer as an excuse (for not doing sth); plead ②infer;deduce
推算 calculate;reckon
推头 ①cut sb's hair (with clippers) ②have a haircut
推托 offer as an excuse (for not doing sth); plead
推脱 evade;shirk
推挽 ①recommend (sb for a post) ②push-pull
推诿 shift (or shirk) responsibility to others
推问 investigate;cross-examine
推想 imagine;guess;reckon
推销 promote sales;market;peddle
推卸 shirk (responsibility)
推行 carry out;pursue;practise
推选 elect;choose
推延 put off;postpone
推移 ①(of time) elapse;pass ②(of a situation,etc.) develop;evolve
推展 propel;promotional exhibition
推知 know by inference;deduce
推重 have a high regard for;hold in esteem
推子 hair-clippers;clippers
推草机 mowing machine;mower
推广站 centre for spreading (or introducing) sth
推进剂 propellant
推进力 propulsive force;driving power
推进器 propeller
推土机 bulldozer
推销术 salesmanship;selling techniques
推销员 salesman;promotion worker
推移质 bed load
推本溯源 trace the origin;ascertain the cause
推波助澜 make a stormy sea stormier;add fuel to the flames
推陈出新 weed through the old to bring forth the new
推诚相见 deal with sb in good faith;treat sb with sincerity
推而广之 likewise;in the same way
推广经验 spread the experience
推广项目 spreading projects
推己及人 put oneself in the place of another; treat other people as you would like to be treated;be considerate
推荐产品 recommended products
推来推去 each pushes sth away to the other; give the runaround
推梨让枣 decline the pears and jujubes (in favour of one's brothers,etc.)
推情度理 consider the circumstances and infer

the reasons
推人犯规 pushing (in basketball,etc.)
推三阻四 decline with all sorts of excuses; give the runaround
推涛作浪 stir up (or make) trouble;create disturbances
推推搡搡 push and shove
推诿责任 pass buck;shift responsibility;shirk responsibility
推贤让能 recommend the worthy and make way for the talented
推向市场 push onto the market
推心置腹 repose full confidence in sb;confide in sb
推广普通话 popularize the common spoken Chinese;encourage the wide use of Putonghua
推倒油瓶不扶 be unwilling to right an oil bottle that's been knocked over—be lazy in the extreme
推广科研成果 spread the use of scientific and technological achievements;turn laboratory achievements into commercial production

萩 [tuī]
名 motherwort

tuí（ㄊㄨㄟˊ）

颓 [tuí]
形 ①dilapidated;ruined ②declining;decadent;decayed ③dejected;dispirited
颓败 decay;decline;decadent;declining;become corrupt
颓废 dispirited;decadent
颓风 depraved customs;corrupt morals
颓坏 ruined;dilapidated
颓靡 downcast;dejected;crestfallen
颓然 dejected;disappointed
颓丧 dejected;dispirited;listless
颓势 declining tendency
颓唐 dejected;dispirited
颓朽 rotten;decayed
颓运 adversity;misfortune
颓井残垣 ruined wells and crumbling walls

tuǐ（ㄊㄨㄟˇ）

腿 [tuǐ]
名 ①leg ②leg-like support ③ham
腿带 bottom bands of trouser legs;leg wrappings
腿箍 leg band
腿脚 legs and feet—ability to walk
腿快 quick-footed;swift-footed
腿懒 disinclined to move about;lazy about paying visits
腿勤 be tireless in running around;love to run around

腿酸　have stiff legs
腿痛　leg pain；skelalgia
腿肚子　calf (of the leg)
腿弯子　back of the joint connecting the thigh and calf
腿腕子　ankle
腿勤手快　deft of hand and tireless in running around

tui(ㄊㄨㄟˋ)

侻　[tuì]
〔形〕　handsome；beautiful；agreeable；suitable

退　[tuì]
〔动〕　①move backwards；draw back；back up；retreat ②cause to move back；withdraw；remove ③retire from；quit；adjourn ④decline；recede；decrease；ebb ⑤return；give back；refund ⑥cancel；retract；break off

退保　surrender；withdraw one's guaranty；cease to act as guarantor
退避　withdraw and keep off；keep out of the way
退兵　①retreat；withdrawal ②force the enemy to retreat
退步　① lag (or fall) behind；retrogress ② room for manoeuvre；leeway
退场　①(of athletes) withdraw from the arena (as after the opening ceremony)；march off the arena ②(of an audience) leave the theatre (as when a play ends)
退潮　ebb tide；ebb；falling tide
退出　withdraw from；secede；quit
退磁　demagnetize
退党　withdraw from (or resign，quit) a political party
退敌　get the enemy to retreat (or withdraw)；repulse the enemy
退稿　send back the manuscript
退耕　convert farmland to other purpose
退股　withdraw share(from company)
退关　(of an exporter，etc.) cancel a declaration (of goods already cleared by customs)
退汗　arrest perspiration；stop sweating
退化　① degeneration ② degenerate；deteriorate；retrograde
退还　return
退换　exchange (or replace) a purchase
退回　①return；send (or give) back ②go (or turn) back
退婚　break off an engagement
退火　annealing
退伙　①withdraw from a secret society (or underworld gang) ②cancel an arrangement to eat at a mess；withdraw from a mess
退货　return goods (or merchandise)
退居　①retire from a prominent position and take (a less important one) ②be reduced to (a lower rank)
退款　refund；reimburse
退路　①route of retreat ②room for manoeuvre；leeway
退赔　pay compensation for what one has unlawfully taken；restitute；pay compensation；return sth misappropriated
退票　①return a ticket；get a refund for a ticket ②returned (or unused) ticket
退钱　refund
退亲　break off an engagement
退却　①retreat；withdraw ②hang back；shrink back；flinch
退让　make a concession；yield；give in
退热　①bring down (or allay) a fever ②(of a person's temperature) come down
退色　fade
退烧　①bring down (or allay) a fever ②(of a person's temperature) come down
退市　quit from market
退守　withdraw and stand on the defensive
退税　tax rebate；tax refund；tax reimbursement
退缩　shrink back；flinch；cower
退庭　withdraw from the court
退团　withdraw from a youth league；give up league membership
退位　give up the throne；abdicate
退伍　retire (or be discharged) from active military service；be demobilized；leave the army
退席　① leave a banquet (or a meeting) ② walk out
退闲　go into retirement
退省　introspection；self-questioning；self-examination
退休　retire
退学　leave school；discontinue one's schooling
退养　early retirement
退役　retire (or be released) from military service (on completing the term of reserve)
退隐　retire from public life；go into retirement
退赃　disgorge ill-gotten gains；give up ill-gotten gains；surrender ill-gotten gains
退职　resign (or be discharge)d from office；quit working
退走　retreat；withdraw
退格键　backspace key
退烧药　antipyretic
退休金　retirement pay；pension
退避三舍　retreat ninety *li*—give way to avoid a conflict
退而让贤　withdraw in favour of more competent people
退耕还林　grain for green
退归林下　retire from public life

退还公物 return public property
退居二线 retire from the leading post; retire from active duty; retreat to the back line to take an advisory post
退居幕后 retire backstage
退思补过 quit one's position in order to repair the wrong one has done; retire to amend one's error
退田还林 restore the reclaimed land to forest
退无可退 be left with no room for retreat; there is no place to retreat to
退休工人 retired worker
退休年龄 retirement age
退职经商 quit one's regular work to engage in business
退而求其次 have to take the second best; settle for one's second choice
退还公积金 retiring allowance reserve
退耕还林还草 grain for green; Terraced fields on steep slopes should be returned to forests or pastures.
退耕还林还牧 convert the land for forestry and posture

蜕 [tuì]
Ⅰ〔动〕① slough off; exuviate ②(of birds) moult ③ shed one's body; pass away Ⅱ〔名〕slough; (of snakes, cicadas, etc.) skin that has been shed
蜕变 ①change qualitatively; transform; transmute ②decay
蜕化 ①slough off; exuviate ②degenerate
蜕皮 cast off (or shed) a skin; exuviate
蜕化变质 become morally degenerate

煺 [tuì]
〔动〕scald (a pig, chicken, etc.) in order to remove hairs or feathers

褪 [tuì]
〔动〕①take off (clothes); shed(feathers) ②(of colour) fade ➡ tùn
褪色 fade
褪黑素 melatonin

tūn(ㄊㄨㄣ)

吞 [tūn]
〔动〕①swallow; devour; gulp down ②seize; take (illegal) possession of; annex
吞并 annex; gobble (or swallow) up
吞吃 ①swallow; gulp down ②embezzle; misappropriate
吞服 swallow; take; go down
吞金 swallow gold (to commit suicide)
吞灭 conquer and annex (a country)
吞没 ① embezzle; misappropriate ② swallow up; engulf
吞声 gulp down one's sobs; dare not cry out
吞食 swallow; devour
吞蚀 ①embezzle; misappropriate ②corrode; erode
吞噬 swallow; gobble up; engulf
吞吐 swallow and spit—take in and send out in large quantities
吞咽 swallow; gulp down
吞占 ① embezzle; misappropriate ② invade and occupy; seize
吞吐量 handling capacity(of a harbour); volume of freight handled; cargo handling capacity; loading and unloading capacity
吞刀吐火 (in magic) swallow knives and spit fire
吞敌之势 so overwhelming as to make the enemy cower
吞饵上钩 swallow the bait
吞公肥己 swallow public and fatten oneself
吞声饮泣 choke down one's tears; repress one's tears and keep silent; swallow the voice and tears; weep silent tears; sob bitterly
吞噬细胞 phagocyte
吞噬作用 phagocytosis
吞吞吐吐 hesitate in speech; hem and haw; mutter and mumble
吞云吐雾 swallow clouds and blow out fog—smoke (opium or cigarette)

暾 [tūn]
〔名〕newly-risen sun

tún(ㄊㄨㄣ)

屯 [tún]
Ⅰ〔动〕① gather; collect; store up ② station (troops); quarter (troops) Ⅱ〔名〕village
屯兵 station troops
屯集 assemble; collect
屯聚 (of troops, etc.) concentrate; assemble
屯垦 station troops to open up wasteland
屯落 village
屯田 have garrison troops or peasants open up wasteland and grow food grain
屯扎 station (troops); quarter (troops)
屯驻 be stationed; be quartered

囤 [tún]
〔动〕store up; hoard up; collect ➡ dùn
囤货 store goods
囤积 hoard for speculation; corner (the market)
囤聚 store up (goods)
囤粮 hoard grain
囤积居奇 hoarding and cornering; hoarding and profiteering

豚 [tún]
〔名〕suckling pig; pig

臀 [tún]
〔名〕buttock; rump
臀部 buttocks
臀尖 pork rump

臀鳍 anal fin
臀围 hipline
臀疣 monkey's ischial callosities; monkey's seat pads
臀锥 anal cone

tǔn(ㄊㄨㄣˇ)

氽 [tǔn] 动 ①float; drift ②deep-fry

tùn(ㄊㄨㄣˋ)

褪 [tùn] 动 ①(as of one's limbs) slip out of sth: 褪下手镯子 slip off a bracelet ②keep (*or* hide) in the sleeve ➡tuì
褪去 take off (clothes, etc.)
褪套儿 ①break loose; free oneself; get oneself free ②shake off responsibility

tuō(ㄊㄨㄛ)

托 [tuō] Ⅰ 动 ①hold up; hold in the palm; support with the hand (*or* palm) ②serve as a foil; set off ③ask; beg; entrust ④give as a pretext; plead ⑤count upon; rely on; owe to Ⅱ 名 sth serving as a support
托儿 a partner of a street pedlar or shopkeeper who pretends to be a customer and lures people into buying; salesperson's decoy
托板 couch; layer board; supporting board
托庇 rely upon one's elder or an influential person for protection
托病 plead illness
托词 ①find a pretext; make an excuse ②pretext; excuse; subterfuge
托大 ①give oneself airs; be self-important; be conceited and arrogant ②careless; negligent
托带 send through others; girdle
托福 ①(usu. responding to greetings) thanks to you ②rely upon; owe to
托付 entrust; commit sth to sb's care
托孤 (usu. of a dying emperor) entrust his young son to the care of a minister
托故 give (*or* find) a pretext; make an excuse
托汇 apply for remittance
托架 bracket
托梦 (of the ghost of one's kith and kin) appear in one's dream and make a request
托名 do sth in sb else's name
托盘 (serving) tray
托身 ①find a place to live in ②seek a living
托生 reincarnation; transmigration
托收 collection of payment
托叶 stipule
托运 consign for shipment; check
托嘱 entrust
托子 base; support
托儿所 nursery; child-care centre
托管国 trustee state; trustee
托管区 trust area
托管制 trusteeship
托灰板 hawk
托拉斯 trust
托老所 nursing home for the aged
托门子 solicit help from potential backers; gain one's end through pull
托人情 ask an influential person to help arrange sth; gain one's end through pull; seek the good offices of sb
托运单 booking note
托运人 consignor
托运物 consignment
"托福"考试 Test of English as a Foreign Language(TOEFL)
托古改制 carry out reforms in the name of ancient precedents; quote classical principles to institute a reform
托管领土 trustee territory
托管制度 trusteeship system; trusteeship
托足无门 cannot find a place to stay
托管理事会 Trusteeship Council

拖 [tuō] 动 ①pull; tug; drag; haul ②drag behind one ③drag on; delay; postpone; procrastinate
拖把 mop
拖布 mop
拖长 ①lengthen ②drag on
拖车 trailer
拖船 ①tugboat; tug; towboat ②a wooden boat (towed by a tugboat)
拖带 traction; pulling; towing
拖拉 dilatory; slow; sluggish
拖累 ①encumber; be a burden on ②implicate; involve
拖轮 towboat; tugboat
拖锚 dragging anchor
拖欠 be behind in payment; be in arrears; default
拖沓 dilatory; sluggish; laggard
拖堂 (of a teacher) not dismiss class when time is up
拖网 trawlnet; trawl; dragnet
拖鞋 slippers
拖延 delay; put off; procrastinate
拖曳 pull; tow; draw
拖运 haulage; towage
拖债 be behind in paying one's debt; be in arrears with one's debt
拖后腿 hinder (*or* impede) sb; hold sb back; be a drag on sb
拖拉机 tractor
拖尾巴 ①hinder (*or* impede) sb; hold sb

back;be a drag on sb ②leave a project,etc. unfinished;leave loose ends

拖油瓶 ①(of a widow) remarry and take her children to her second husband's home ② such children

拖运费 haulage

拖儿带女 be burdened with children; be tied down by children

拖家带口 be burdened with a family

拖泥带水 messy;sloppy;slovenly

拖欠工资 delay salaries;owe salaries

拖人下水 involve sb in evildoing

拖三拉四 put off one's work with all sorts of excuses;give the runaround

拖拖拉拉 drag one's feet; be sluggish; delay action

拖延战术 dilatory tactics; delaying tactics; stalling tactics

挩 [tuō]
囫 ①free (or extricate) oneself;release ②omit;err

脱 [tuō]
Ⅰ囫 ①shed (hair, skin, etc.); lose; come off ②take off; cast off ③escape from; extricate oneself from; get out of ④miss out (words); omit; elide ⑤neglect; slight Ⅱ囵 supposing;in case

脱靶 miss the target in shooting practice

脱班 ①be late for work ②(of a bus, train, etc.) be behind schedule

脱产 be leased from one's regular work to take on other duties

脱出 deviate from;shake off;break away from

脱党 leave a political party; give up party membership

脱发 loss of the hair;alopecia

脱肛 prolapse of the anus

脱稿 (of a manuscript) be completed

脱钩 break off relations; cut ties; sever ties with

脱轨 be derailed

脱滑 try to shirk work or responsibility;act in a slick way

脱货 be in short supply;be out of stock

脱胶 ①(of parts joined with gum or glue) come unglued;come unstuck ②degum

脱节 come apart; be disjointed; be out of line with

脱臼 dislocation

脱空 ①come to nothing;fail;fall through ② tell a lie;lie;resort to deception

脱困 get out of difficulty

脱蜡 dewaxing

脱离 separate oneself from; break away from; be divorced from

脱粒 ①threshing ②shelling

脱磷 dephosphorization

脱硫 desulphurization;sweetening

脱漏 be left out;be omitted;be missing

脱落 drop;fall off (or away);come off

脱盲 become literate

脱毛 lose hair (or feathers);moult;shed

脱帽 take off (or raise) one's hat (in respect)

脱模 drawing of patterns

脱坯 mould adobe blocks

脱皮 peel;decrustation

脱贫 poverty eradication; poverty relief; get rid of poverty;lift oneself out of poverty

脱期 (of a periodical) fail to come out on time

脱氢 dehydrogenation

脱色 ①decolour;decolourize ②fade

脱涩 take away the puckery taste (from persimmons)

脱身 get away;get free;extricate oneself

脱手 ①slip out of the hand ②get off one's hands;dispose of;sell

脱水 ①deprivation (or loss) of body fluids; dehydration ②dewatering

脱俗 free from vulgarity;refined

脱榫 be out of joint

脱胎 ①emerge from the womb of; be born out of ②a process of making bodiless lacquerware

脱逃 run away;escape;flee

脱兔 a fleeing hare—fast speed

脱位 dislocation

脱险 escape (or be out of) danger

脱销 out of stock;sold out

脱卸 shirk (responsibility)

脱氧 deoxidation;deoxidization

脱羽 (of birds) moult

脱证 exhaustion of vital energy at the critical stage of an illness

脱脂 de-fat;degrease

脱壳机 huller;sheller

脱口秀 talk show

脱粒机 thresher;sheller

脱水机 hydroextractor

脱水剂 dehydrator

脱衣舞 striptease

脱脂剂 degreasing agent

脱脂棉 pledget;absorbent cotton

脱脂乳 skimmed milk

脱产干部 cadre released from production

脱产学习 off-the-job study

脱出樊笼 get out of the cage; shake off the yoke

脱弓之箭 arrow shot from a bow

脱缰之马 a runaway horse—uncontrollable; running wild

脱口而出 say sth unwittingly;blurt out

脱扣落襷 miss this and that;deal with sth in a careless way

脱离关系 break off relations;cut ties
脱离苦海 escape from the human world of woes;get rid of this troublesome life
脱离群众 cut oneself off from the masses;be divorced from the masses
脱离实际 lose contact with reality;be divorced from reality
脱离速度 second cosmic velocity
脱帽致敬 take off one's hat to sb
脱皮掉肉 work with all one's might
脱贫致富 cast (*or* shake, throw) off poverty and set out on a road to prosperity
脱身之计 plan of escape;plan that helps one to slip away
脱水蔬菜 dehydrated vegetables
脱胎换骨 be reborn;cast off one's old self;thoroughly remould oneself
脱氧核糖 deoxyribose
脱颖而出 the point of an awl sticking out through a bag—talent revealing itself
脱脂奶粉 de-fatted milk powder;nonfat dried milk
脱脂纱布 absorbent gauze
脱氧核糖核酸 deoxyribonucleic acid (DNA)

tuó(ㄊㄨㄛˊ)

驮 [tuó]
动 carry (*or* bear) on the back ➡ duò
驮畜 pack animal
驮筐 pannier
驮马 pack horse

佗 [tuó]
动 carry (*or* bear) on the back

陀 [tuó]
名 hill;hillock
陀螺 top (a toy)
陀螺仪 gyroscope;gyro

坨 [tuó]
Ⅰ 动 (of food made of flour) stick together
Ⅱ 名 lump;heap
坨子 ①lump ②heap

沱 [tuó]
Ⅰ 名 small bay in a river Ⅱ 动 (of tears) stream down like rain
沱茶 a bowl-shaped compressed mass of tea leaves

驼 [tuó]
Ⅰ 名 camel Ⅱ 形 hunchbacked; humpbacked
驼背 ①hunchback;humpback ②hunchbacked; humpbacked
驼峰 ①hump(of a camel) ②hump
驼铃 camel bells
驼毛 camel's hair
驼绒 ①camel's hair ②camel hair cloth
驼子 hunchback;humpback

鸵 [tuó]
名 ostrich

鸵鸟 ostrich
鸵鸟政策 ostrich policy

跎 [tuó]
◇蹉跎 waste time

tuǒ(ㄊㄨㄛˇ)

妥 [tuǒ]
形 ①appropriate;suitable;sound;proper ②ready;settled;resolved;finished
妥当 appropriate;proper
妥靠 reliable;dependable
妥善 appropriate;proper;well arranged
妥帖 appropriate;fitting;proper
妥协 come to terms;compromise
妥协条例 compromise act

椭 [tuǒ]
名 ellipse
椭率 ellipticity
椭面 ellipsoid
椭圆 ellipse
椭圆形 oval;ellipse;elliptocytosis
椭圆截面 oval cross section
椭圆星云 elliptical nebula
椭圆柱面 elliptic cylinder
椭圆锥面 elliptic cone

tuò(ㄊㄨㄛˋ)

拓 [tuò]
动 open up;develop;reclaim ➡ tà
拓地 extend (*or* expand) territory
拓荒 open up virgin soil;reclaim wasteland
拓宽 widen
拓落 ① be frustrated; be disappointed ② broad;extensive;vast
拓销 expand the market
拓展 expand;spread;extend;develop
拓殖 plant a colony;colonize
拓扑学 topology
拓宽业务 extend one's business
拓展业务 branch out

唾 [tuò]
Ⅰ 名 saliva;spittle Ⅱ 动 ①spit;expectorate ②show one's contempt (by spitting)
唾骂 spit on and curse;revile
唾沫 saliva;spittle
唾弃 cast aside;spurn
唾涎 saliva;spittle
唾液 saliva;spittle
唾余 idle talk;casual remarks
唾液腺 salivary gland
唾沫星子 a spray of saliva
唾手可得 extremely easy to obtain

箨 [tuò]
名 sheaths of bamboo shoots

wā(ㄨㄚ)

凹 [wā] 图 concave;hollow ➡āo

挖 [wā] 团 ①dig;excavate;scoop ②scratch;claw
挖补 mend by replacing a damaged part
挖兜 inset pocket
挖耳 ①pick one's ears (to get rid of the wax) ②earpick
挖方 ①excavation (of earth or stone) ②cubage of excavation
挖掘 excavate;unearth
挖苦 speak sarcastically (*or* ironically)
挖潜 tap potential;tap the latent power
挖槽机 groover
挖沟机 ditcher;trencher;trench digger
挖掘机 excavator;navvy
挖苦话 ironical remarks;verbal thrusts
挖泥船 dredger;dredge
挖墙脚 sap the wall; undermine the foundation;cut the ground from under sb's feet
挖人才 headhunt talents; scoop out qualified personnel
挖树机 tree mover
挖土机 excavator;shovelling machine
挖空心思 rack one's brains
挖肉补疮 cut out a piece of flesh to cure a boil—resort to a remedy worse than the ailment;resort to a stopgap measure detrimental to long-term interests
挖东墙补西墙 digging the eastern wall to repair the western one;keep up in one place at the expense of others

哇 [wā] Ⅰ 叹 (*used to indicate sound of crying, etc.*);哇地哭出声来 cry out loud;burst out crying Ⅱ 形 decadent ➡wa
哇啦 hullabaloo;uproar;din
哇哇 the crying of a child; the cawing of a crow,etc.

洼 [wā] Ⅰ 形 low-lying;hollow;depressed Ⅱ 图 depression;low-lying area
洼地 depression;low-lying land
洼陷 (of ground) be sunken;be low-lying

窊 [wā] 图 concave;hollow

蛙 [wā] 图 frog
蛙人 frogman
蛙泳 breaststroke
蛙科动物 ranid
蛙式打夯机 frog rammer

wá(ㄨㄚˊ)

娃 [wá] 图 ①baby;child ②newborn animal
娃娃 baby;child
娃娃床 crib;cot
娃娃亲 the betrothal of a little boy and a little girl arranged by parents of both sides
娃娃鱼 giant salamander

wǎ(ㄨㄚˇ)

瓦 [wǎ] Ⅰ 图 tile Ⅱ 形 made of baked clay;earthen Ⅲ 量 watt ➡wà
瓦房 tile-roofed house
瓦工 ① bricklaying, tiling or plastering ② bricklayer;tiler;plasterer
瓦棺 earthen coffin
瓦罐 earthen jar
瓦匠 bricklayer;tiler;plasterer
瓦解 disintegrate;collapse;crumble
瓦块 fragments of tiles;broken tiles
瓦楞 ①rows of tiles on a roof ②corrugated
瓦砾 rubble;debris
瓦亮 very bright
瓦盆 earthen basin
瓦圈 rim (of a bicycle wheel, cart wheel, etc.)

瓦舍 ① tile-roofed house ② pleasure quarters in cities in Song and Yuan times
瓦时 watt-hour
瓦斯 gas
瓦特 watt
瓦头 hanging edge of a dripping tile
瓦砚 tile inkslab
瓦窑 tile kiln
瓦碴儿 broken tiles
瓦楞纸 corrugated paper
瓦楞子 blood clam
瓦釜雷鸣 an earthen crock sounding like thunder—an unworthy man in a high position
瓦楞铁皮 corrugated sheet iron

wà(ㄨㄚˋ)

瓦 [wà] 动 cover (a roof) with tiles; tile ➡ wǎ
瓦刀 (bricklayer's) cleaver

袜 [wà] 名 socks; stockings; hose
袜带 suspenders; garters
袜口 welt; blank
袜裤 pantyhose; pantihose
袜套 ankle socks; socks
袜筒 the leg of a stocking
袜子 socks; stockings; hose
袜底儿 sole of a sock
袜底子 (usu. with hand-stitched patches) reinforced soles of socks

wa(·ㄨㄚ)

哇 [wa] 助 variant of 啊 when preceded by words ending phonetically in u or ao ➡ wā

wāi(ㄨㄞ)

歪 [wāi] I 形 ① inclined; slanting; askew; tilted; off-centre ② improper; devious; crooked; evil ③ domineering; despotic II 动 lie on one's side to rest
歪才 talent for intrigue; person with unique talent (in a specialized field or activity)
歪缠 pester unjustifiably
歪道 ① evil ways; depraved life; vice ② evil ideas; devil's advice
歪风 evil wind; unhealthy trend
歪理 false reasoning
歪路 crooked ways; underhand ways; dishonest practices
歪扭 twisted; awry
歪曲 ① distort; misrepresent; twist ② crooked; askew; aslant
歪诗 inelegant verses; doggerel
歪斜 crooked; askew; aslant

歪词儿 worthless talk; defamatory talk
歪打正着 hit the mark by a fluke; score a lucky hit
歪风邪气 evil trends; perverse trends; unhealthy trends and evil practices
歪门邪道 crooked ways; underhand means; dishonest practices (or methods)
歪七扭八 crooked; askew; shapeless and twisted
歪曲报道 managed news; distorted news
歪歪倒倒 ① rickety; shaky ② uneven; irregular; untidy
歪歪扭扭 crooked; askew; shapeless and twisted

wǎi(ㄨㄞˇ)

崴 [wǎi] I 形 rugged (mountain path) II 动 ① bend (in a river or mountain range) ② sprain; twist

wài(ㄨㄞˋ)

外 [wài] I 形 ① outer; outside ② other (than one's own) ③ foreign; external; alien ④ (relatives) of one's mother, sisters or daughters ⑤ not of the same family, class, organization, etc.; not closely related ⑥ unofficial II 副 besides; moreover; in addition; beyond III 名 role of an elderly man
外邦 foreign country
外币 foreign currency
外边 ① outside; out ② a place other than where one lives (or works) ③ exterior; outside
外表 outward appearance; exterior; surface
外宾 foreign guest (or visitor)
外部 ① outside; external ② exterior; surface
外埠 towns (or cities) other than where one is
外财 extra income
外侧 outboard
外差 heterodyne
外场 ① sociable ② outfield (in baseball and softball)
外钞 foreign bank note
外城 outer city
外出 go out
外村 other village
外带 ① outer cover (of a tyre); tyre ② as well; besides; into the bargain
外待 treat sb as a stranger (or an outsider)
外道 [wàidao] over-polite
外敌 foreign enemy
外地 parts of the country other than where one is
外电 dispatches from foreign news agencies

W

外调 ① transfer（materials or personnel）to other localities ② go out to another work unit to make investigations
外耳 external ear
外藩 vassal state
外敷 apply（ointment,etc.）
外感 diseases caused by external factors
外港 outport
外公 （maternal）grandfather
外功 exercises to benefit the muscles and bones
外姑 wife's mother;mother-in-law
外观 outward appearance;exterior
外国 foreign country
外行 ① layman; outsider; nonprofessional ② lay;unprofessional
外壕 outer trench
外号 nickname
外话 unduly polite words that a friend is not expected to say
外患 foreign aggression
外汇 foreign exchange
外货 foreign goods;imported goods
外祸 foreign aggression
外籍 foreign nationality
外加 more;additional;extra
外家 ① maternal grandparents' home ② mistress;concubine;kept woman ③house for a mistress or concubine
外嫁 marry abroad;marry out
外间 ①outer room ②the external world;outside circles
外交 diplomacy;foreign affairs
外角 exterior angle
外教 foreign teacher
外界 ① the external（or outside）world ② outside
外借 lend out
外景 outdoor scene;a scene shot on location; exterior
外径 external diameter;outside（or outer）diameter
外舅 wife's father;father-in-law
外卡 wild card
外科 surgical department
外客 visitor（who is not a relative or friend）; guest
外寇 invading army;aggressor troops
外快 gravy train;side money;pin money;extra income
外来 outside;external;foreign
外力 ①outside force ②external force
外流 outflow;drain
外路 from outside;not local
外露 reveal;show
外轮 foreign steamer;foreign ship（or vessel）

外卖 takeout;takeaway;carry-out
外贸 foreign trade;external trade
外貌 appearance;exterior;looks
外面 ［wàimiàn］ outward appearance;exterior;surface
外面 ［wàimian］ outside;out
外膜 outer membrane
外脑 outside brainpower
外皮 sheath;outer bark;crust
外婆 （maternal）grandmother
外戚 relatives of a king（or emperor）on the side of his mother or wife
外墙 exposed wall
外壳 outer covering（or casing）;shell;case
外亲 wife's or mother's relatives;relatives on mother's or wife's side
外勤 ① work done outside the office（or in the field）（as surveying,prospecting,news gathering,etc.）②field personnel
外倾 extroversion
外圈 outer lane;outside lane
外人 ①stranger;outsider ②foreigner;alien
外伤 an injury;wound;trauma
外商 foreign businessman;foreign merchant
外设 peripheral device
外甥 ① sister's son; nephew ② daughter's son;grandson
外省 provinces other than where one is;other provinces
外史 unofficial history;informal history
外事 foreign affairs;external affairs
外室 ① mistress; concubine; kept woman ② house for a mistress（or concubine）
外孙 daughter's son;grandson
外胎 outer cover（of a tyre）;tyre
外逃 ①flee to some other place ②flee the country
外套 ①overcoat ②loose coat;outer garment
外头 outside;out
外围 periphery
外文 foreign language
外屋 outer room
外侮 foreign aggression;external aggression
外务 ①matters outside one's job ②foreign affairs;external affairs
外县 counties other than where one is;other counties
外线 ①exterior lines ②outside（telephone）connections
外乡 another part of the country;some other place
外向 extroversion
外销 for sale abroad（or in another part of the country）
外心 ① unfaithful intentions（of husband or wife）②circumcentre
外形 appearance;external form;contour

W

外姓 (people) not of the same surname
外需 overseas market demand
外延 extension
外焰 outer flame
外衣 ①coat; jacket; outer clothing; outer garment ②semblance; appearance; garb
外因 external cause
外阴 vulva
外用 external use; external application
外语 foreign language
外域 foreign land
外遇 extramarital relations
外援 foreign player; foreign aid; outside help; external assistance
外源 external source
外运 transport out to other places or countries
外在 external; extrinsic
外债 external loan; foreign loan; foreign debt; loan from foreign countries; loan from outside
外罩 outer garment; dustcoat; overall
外痔 external piles (or haemorrhoids)
外智 outside brainpower
外传 unofficial life history; unauthorized biography
外资 foreign funds; foreign capital
外子 my husband
外族 ①people not of the same clan ②foreigner; alien ③other nationalities
外包装 outer packing; external packing
外出血 external haemorrhage
外道儿 stranger; outsider
外毒素 exotoxin
外耳道 external auditory meatus
外耳炎 otitis externa
外翻足 talipes valgus
外分泌 exocrine; external secretion
外敷药 medicine for external application
外骨骼 dermoskeleton; ectoskeleton
外国货 foreign goods; imported goods
外国人 foreigner; alien
外国语 foreign language
外果皮 exocarp
外汇率 foreign exchange rate
外活儿 ①orders taken by factories or craftsmen ②work taken in by housewives
外交部 ministry of foreign affairs; foreign ministry
外交法 diplomatic law
外交官 diplomat
外交家 diplomat
外交界 diplomatic circles
外交团 diplomatic corps
外交衔 diplomatic rank
外接圆 circumscribed circle; circumcircle
外景队 camera crew on location
外科学 surgery

外来户 a household from another place; non-native
外来语 word of foreign origin; foreign word; loanword
外卖袋 take-out bag
外贸部 ministry of foreign trade
外胚层 ectoblast; ectoderm; epiblast
外切形 circumscribed figure
外燃机 external-combustion engine
外伤学 traumatology
外甥女 ① sister's daughter; niece ② daughter's daughter; granddaughter
外事局 bureau of foreign affairs, foreign affairs bureau
外事口 a collective name for all government organs that have to do with foreign affairs
外事组 ① foreign affairs section ② section dealing with foreign personnel and foreign visitors
外孙女 daughter's daughter; granddaughter
外听道 external auditory meatus
外围赛 outside match
外务省 the Ministry of Foreign Affairs (as in Japan)
外务相 minister of foreign affairs
外星人 extra-terrestrial (E. T.); extraterrestrial being; alien planet dweller; people from outside the earth; people from other planets; man from outer space
外阴炎 vulvitis
外在性 externalism
外置式 outboard
外祖父 (maternal) grandfather
外祖母 (maternal) grandmother
外部环境 external environment; external condition
外部资金 external sources of finance
外层空间 outer space
外出谋生 leave home to seek a living
外脆里嫩 crisp on the outside but tender within
外调物资 materials allocated for transfer to other places
外公切线 external common tangent
外国侨民 foreign national; alien
外国专家 foreign expert; foreign specialist
外国租界 foreign settlement; foreign concession
外汇储备 foreign exchange reserve
外汇负债 foreign exchange liabilities
外汇管制 foreign exchange control; foreign exchange restrictions
外汇行情 exchange quotations
外汇交易 foreign exchange transactions
外汇结存 foreign exchange balance; foreign exchange surplus
外汇留成 retention of a share of foreign ex-

change earned; proportional foreign exchange retention
外汇流失 foreign exchange rate
外汇牌价 list of exchange rate quotations; quotation of exchange rate; official exchange rate
外汇倾销 exchange dumping
外汇升水 exchange premium
外汇市场 foreign exchange market
外汇收入 foreign exchange earnings (*or* income)
外汇体制 foreign exchange system
外汇调剂 regulation of foreign exchange
外汇贴水 exchange discount
外汇业务 foreign exchange transaction; foreign exchange policy
外汇预算 foreign exchange budget
外汇政策 foreign exchange policy
外汇资产 foreign exchange assets
外籍教师 foreign teacher
外籍教员 foreign teacher (*or* coach)
外寄生物 ectoparasite
外加电压 applied voltage
外交庇护 diplomatic asylum
外交部长 minister of (*or* for) foreign affairs; foreign minister
外交程序 diplomatic procedure
外交辞令 diplomatic language (*or* parlance)
外交大臣 Foreign Secretary (in Britain)
外交代表 diplomatic agent (*or* representative)
外交格局 pattern of a country's foreign affairs
外交关系 diplomatic relations
外交惯例 diplomatic practice; diplomatic usage; customary diplomatic practice
外交行话 diplomat-speak
外交护照 diplomatic passport
外交机关 diplomatic establishments
外交礼节 diplomatic protocol (*or* etiquette)
外交签证 diplomatic visa
外交使节 diplomatic envoy
外交使团 diplomatic mission
外交谈判 diplomatic negotiation
外交特权 diplomatic prerogative (*or* privilege)
外交途径 diplomatic channels
外交文书 diplomatic papers
外交信使 diplomatic courier
外交阴谋 a diplomatic intrigue
外交邮袋 diplomatic pouch; diplomatic bag
外交邮件 diplomatic mail
外交语言 diplomatese; diplomatic language
外交照会 diplomatic note
外交政策 foreign policy
外交制裁 diplomatic sanction
外来干涉 foreign intervention; external intervention; outside intervention

外卖服务 takeout service; carryout service
外贸经营 foreign trade management
外贸逆差 import surplus
外贸中心 foreign trade centres
外面儿光 deceptively smooth appearance; outward show
外强中干 outwardly strong but inwardly weak; strong in appearance but weak in reality
外侨身份 alienism
外柔内刚 soft outside but hard inside—outwardly yielding but inwardly firm
外生殖器 external genital organs
外事往来 dealings with foreign nationals (*or* organizations)
外为中用 make foreign things serve China
外围防线 outer defence line
外围设备 peripheral equipment
外围组织 peripheral organization
外务大臣 minister of (*or* for) foreign affairs; foreign minister
外销产品 product for export; article for sale in other areas
外溢效应 spillover effect
外引内联 introduce foreign capital and technology and establish domestic connections; introduce investment from abroad and establish lateral ties at home
外圆内方 round outside but square inside—outwardly gentle but inwardly stern
外债偿付 external debt servicing; external debt repayment
外资流入 foreign capital inflow
外资企业 foreign-funded enterprise; invested enterprise
外资项目 foreign-funded project
外国管辖权 foreign jurisdiction
外国留学生 foreign student; international student
外汇单轨制 single-tier exchange system
外汇兑换率 rate of exchange
外汇兑换券 foreign exchange certificate (FEC)
外汇交易厅 foreign exchange dealing room
外汇调剂价 foreign exchange regulation price
外交豁免权 diplomatic immunity
外径千分尺 outside micrometer
外贸代理制 proxy system in foreign trade; agency system in foreign trade
外贸经营权 power to engage in foreign trade
外贸自主权 autonomy in foreign trade
外事办公室 office of foreign affairs; foreign affairs office
外向型经济 export-oriented economy
外向型企业 export-oriented enterprises
外向型人才 talents applicable to foreign affairs

外国军事基地 foreign military base
外国驻华机构 foreign institutions in China
外汇管制法规 foreign exchange control regulations
外汇平准基金 exchange stabilization fund
外汇期货交易 forward exchange transaction
外商独资企业 exclusively foreign-owned enterprises
外商来料加工 process materials for foreign businessman
外国驻华使领馆 foreign diplomatic and consular missions in China
外汇营业许可证 foreign-exchange business licence
外甥打灯笼——照舅(旧) the nephew carrying a lantern to give light to his uncle—the same as before

wān (ㄨㄢ)

弯 [wān]
Ⅰ 〔形〕 curved; roundabout; tortuous; crooked Ⅱ 〔动〕 ①make crooked (*or* curved); bend; flex ②turn; curve ③bend; draw
弯度 curvature
弯弓 draw a bow; bend a bow
弯路 ①crooked road; tortuous path ②roundabout way; detour
弯曲 winding; meandering; zigzag; crooked; curved
弯头 angle head
弯子 bend; turn; curve
弯嘴钳 angle jaw tongs

剜 [wān]
〔动〕 cut out; gouge out; scoop out
剜肉补疮 cut out a piece of flesh to cure a boil—resort to a remedy worse than the ailment; resort to a stopgap measure detrimental to long-term interests

塆 [wān]
〔名〕 glen

湾 [wān]
Ⅰ 〔名〕 ①bend in a stream ②gulf; bay; estuary Ⅱ 〔动〕 cast anchor; anchor; moor
湾泊 anchor; berth
湾流 gulf stream

蜿 [wān]
蜿蜒 ①(of snakes, etc.) wriggle ②wind; zigzag; meander

豌 [wān]
豌豆 pea
豌豆黄 pea-flour cake
豌豆象 pea weevil

wán (ㄨㄢ)

丸 [wán]
〔名〕 ①ball; pellet ②pill; bolus
丸剂 pill
丸药 pill (*or* bolus) of Chinese medicine
丸子 ①a round mass of food; ball ②pill; bolus

纨 [wán]
〔名〕 fine silk fabrics
纨绔 silk clothes—a rich family
纨扇 round silk fan
纨素 white, fine gauze
纨绔子弟 profligate son of rich parents; fop; dandy; playboy

抏 [wán]
〔动〕 frustrate; consume; exhaust

完 [wán]
Ⅰ 〔动〕 ①exhaust; finish; use up; run out ②end; finish; be over; be through ③fulfil; complete ④pay Ⅱ 〔形〕 intact; entire; whole
完备 complete; perfect
完毕 finish; complete; end
完成 accomplish; complete; fulfil; bring to success (*or* fruition)
完蛋 be done for; be finished
完稿 finish a piece of writing; complete the manuscript
完工 complete a project, etc.; finish doing sth; get through
完好 intact; whole; in good condition
完婚 (of a man) get married; marry; consummate a marriage
完结 end; be over; finish
完了 come to ah end; be over
完满 satisfactory; successful
完美 perfect; consummate
完密 careful; meticulous; deliberate
完全 ①complete; whole ②completely; fully; wholly; entirely; absolutely
完人 perfect man
完善 ①perfect; consummate ②make perfect; improve
完胜 win a perfect of complete victory (over sb); thoroughly defeat
完事 finish; get through; come to an end
完税 pay taxes
完整 complete; integrated; intact
完全叶 complete leaf
完璧归赵 return the jade intact to the State of Zhao—return sth to its owner in perfect condition
完好无损 excellent without damage
完美无缺 perfect; flawless
完全变态 complete metamorphosis
完全燃烧 complete combustion
完税凭证 proof of tax paid; receipt of tax paid; certificate of tax paid

玩 [wán]
Ⅰ 〔动〕 ①play; have fun; joke; amuse (*or* enjoy) oneself ②play (a game or instrument);

be engaged in cultural or sporting activity ③ use;employ; resort to（improper means, tricks, etc.）④ trifle with; toy with; mess about; treat lightly ⑤ enjoy; appreciate; find pleasure in Ⅱ〔名〕object for appreciation; curio
玩法 trifle with the law
玩忽 neglect; trifle with
玩话 joking remarks; joke
玩火 play with fire
玩具 toy; plaything
玩弄 ①dally with ②play with; juggle with ③ resort to; employ
玩偶 doll; toy figurine
玩赏 enjoy; take pleasure（*or* delight）in
玩耍 play; have fun; amuse oneself
玩味 ponder; ruminate
玩物 plaything; toy
玩笑 ① joke with; play a prank on ② joke; jest; prank
玩儿坏 be up to mischief; play a dirty trick
玩儿命 ①gamble（*or* play）with one's life; risk one's life needlessly ②exerting the utmost strength; for all one is worth; with all one's might
玩儿票 play a role in Beijing opera as an amateur
玩儿去 get away; clear off
玩儿完 ①be done for; be finished ②dead
玩意儿 ① toy; plaything ② acrobatics, cross talks, ballad singing, magic, etc. ③thing
玩儿不转 can't handle; can't manage of duty; flop at a job; be neglectful of one's duties; be remiss in one's duty
玩忽职守 dereliction; neglect; negligence
玩火自焚 He who plays with fire will get burnt; Whoever plays with fire will perish by fire.
玩弄权术 play politics
玩人丧德 denigrate one's virtues by playing tricks on others
玩世不恭 thumb one's nose at the world; be cynical
玩物丧志 riding a hobby saps one's will to make progress; pursuit of petty pleasures thwarts high aims

顽 〔wán〕
〔形〕① stupid; foolish; dense; insensate ② stubborn; persistent ③naughty; mischievous
顽磁 magnetic retentivity
顽敌 stubborn enemy; inveterate
顽钝 ①dull and obtuse; stupid; thickheaded ② lacking moral courage ③blunt
顽梗 obstinate; perverse
顽固 ①obstinate; stubborn; headstrong ②bitterly opposed to change; diehard
顽疾 chronic and stubborn disease; persistent ailment

顽抗 stubbornly resist
顽劣 stubborn and stupid; stubborn and obstreperous
顽皮 naughty; mischievous
顽强 indomitable; staunch; tenacious
顽石 hard rock; insensate stone
顽童 naughty boy; urchin
顽癣 stubborn dermatitis（e. g. neurodermatitis）
顽症 chronic and stubborn disease; persistent ailment
顽固派 the diehards
顽固不化 incorrigibly obstinate
顽固分子 diehard; diehard element
顽石点头 the insensate stones nodding in agreement（said of persuasive powers）

烷 〔wán〕
〔名〕alkane
烷化 alkylation
烷基 alkyl

wǎn（ㄨㄢˇ）

宛 〔wǎn〕
Ⅰ〔形〕winding; circuitous; tortuous Ⅱ〔连〕as if
宛然 as if
宛如 just like
宛似 just like
宛若 just like

挽 〔wǎn〕
〔动〕①draw; hold; pull ②reverse; retrieve ③ roll up ④ tow; draw ⑤ lament; elegise（the deceased）⑥coil up
挽词 memorial speech
挽歌 dirge; elegy
挽回 retrieve; redeem
挽救 save; remedy; rescue
挽具 harness
挽联 elegiac couplet
挽留 urge（*or* persuade）sb to stay
挽马 draught horse
挽诗 elegy
挽幛 large, oblong sheet of silk
挽回损失 retrieve a loss

莞 〔wǎn〕
➡guān
莞尔 smile

菀 〔wǎn〕
➡yù
◇紫菀 aster

晚 〔wǎn〕
Ⅰ〔名〕evening; night; night time Ⅱ〔形〕①far on in time; late ②upper; neo- ③behind time; late（for sth）④ succeeding; junior ⑤ your humbly
晚安 good night
晚班 night shift
晚报 evening paper

W

晚辈 the younger generation;one's juniors
晚餐 supper;dinner
晚场 evening show;evening performance
晚车 night train
晚春 deep spring
晚稻 late rice
晚弟 your humble younger brother;I;me
晚点 (of a train, ship, etc.) late; behind schedule
晚饭 supper;dinner
晚会 evening of entertainment; soirée; social evening;evening party
晚婚 ①marry late ②late marriage
晚间 (in the) evening;(at) night
晚节 integrity in one's later years
晚景 ①evening scene ②one's circumstances in old age
晚年 old age;one's later (or remaining) years
晚娘 stepmother
晚期 late period
晚秋 ①late autumn;late in the autumn ②late-autumn crops
晚上 (in the) evening;(at) night
晚生 I
晚熟 late-maturing
晚霜 late frost
晚霞 sunset glow;sunset clouds
晚宴 dinner party
晚育 late childbirth
晚礼服 evening dress;evening clothes
晚香玉 tuberose
晚奥陶世 Upper Ordovician
晚白垩世 Upper Cretaceous
晚秋作物 late-autumn crops
晚侏罗世 Upper Jurassic
晚婚晚育,少生优生 late marriage, later birth; fewer and healthier births

悗 [wǎn]
〔动〕 heave a sigh;sigh
悗伤 heave a sigh of grief
悗叹 sigh mournfully;lament
悗惜 feel sorry for sb (or about) sth;regret

婉 [wǎn]
〔形〕 ① mild; restrained; tactful ② gentle; meek ③graceful;elegant;charming;beautiful
婉词 gentle words;euphemism
婉辞 ①graciously decline;politely refuse
婉丽 beautiful;lovely;charming
婉劝 plead (with sb) tactfully
婉容 lovely features;graceful manners
婉谢 graciously decline;politely refuse
婉言 gentle words;tactful expressions
婉约 ① graceful and restrained ② subtle and concise
婉转 ①mild and indirect;tactful ②sweet and agreeable
婉言谢绝 graciously decline;politely refuse

碗 [wǎn]
〔名〕①bowl ②bowl-like vessel or object
碗橱 cupboard
碗柜 kitchen cupboard
碗盏 crockery;chinaware

wàn(ㄨㄢˋ)

万 [wàn]
Ⅰ〔数〕 ten thousand Ⅱ〔量〕 very great number;multitude;myriad Ⅲ〔副〕 absolutely;under all circumstances
万般 ①all the different kinds ②utterly;extremely
万邦 all countries;all nations
万倍 ten thousand times;ten thousand-fold
万代 generation after generation
万端 multifarious
万恶 extremely evil;absolutely vicious
万方 ①all places ②extremely;incomparably
万分 very much;extremely
万福 a woman's bow;curtsy
万古 through the ages;eternally;forever
万贯 ten thousand strings of cash—great wealth
万机 numerous state affairs
万钧 ten thousand *jun*—very heavy; very powerful
万类 all creation;all living things
万难 ①extremely difficult;utterly impossible ②all sorts of difficulties
万能 ①omnipotent;all-powerful ②universal; all-purpose
万年 ten thousand years;all ages;eternity
万千 multifarious;myriad
万全 perfectly sound;surefire
万世 all ages;generation after generation
万事 all things;everything
万死 die ten thousand deaths
万岁 ①long live ②the emperor;Your Majesty;His Majesty
万万 ①absolutely ②hundred million
万物 the ten thousand things of creation;all things of creation all things on the earth
万向 universal
万象 every phenomenon on earth;all manifestations of nature
万幸 very lucky (or fortunate);by sheer luck
万一 ①just in case;if by any chance ②what if ③contingency;eventuality ④one ten thousandth;a very small percentage
万丈 lofty;bottomless
万众 millions of people;the multitude
万状 in the extreme;extremely
万把人 some ten thousand people
万不能 absolutely cannot; can by no means; must not on any account
万户侯 a marquis with a fief of 10,000 fami-

lies—a high noble;a high official
万花筒 kaleidoscope
万金油 ①a balm for treating headaches,scalds and other minor ailments ② Jack of all trades and master of none
万年历 perpetual calendar
万年青 ①evergreen ②Japanese rohdea
万人坑 a pit of ten thousand corpses—a mass grave
万事通 know-all
万维网 World Wide Web (WWW)
万元户 ten-thousand *yuan* income family (*or* household)
万儿八千 ten thousand or a bit less
万般无奈 have no alternative (but to)
万不得已 out of absolute necessity;as a last resort
万恶之源 root of all evil
万分之一 one ten-thousandth
万夫莫当 more than a match for ten thousand men (said of a brave warrior)
万夫之勇 brave enough to match ten thousand warriors
万古长存 last forever;be everlasting
万古长青 remain fresh forever;be everlasting
万古流芳 leave a good name that will live forever;achieve immortal fame
万古千秋 through unnumbered ages;for eons
万家灯火 a myriad twinkling lights (of a city)
万箭穿心 (as if) ten thousand arrows have pierced the heart—in extreme grief
万劫不复 lost forever;beyond redemption
万籁俱寂 All is quiet and still;Silence reigns supreme.
万里长城 the Great Wall
万里长空 boundless sky
万里长征 a long march of ten thousand *li*
万里挑一 one in ten thousand
万马奔腾 ten thousand horses galloping ahead—all going full steam ahead
万马齐喑 ten thousand horses standing mute—a lifeless atmosphere
万木争荣 All trees and shrubs vie in splendour.
万能钥匙 skeleton key;master key
万念俱灰 abandon oneself to despair;be in the slough of despond
万全之计 a completely safe plan;a surefire plan
万人空巷 the whole town turns out (to celebrate or to welcome sb)
万世师表 the Model Teacher of a Myriad Ages
万事大吉 Everything is just fine;Everything goes off without a hitch;Everything's O.K.
万事亨通 Everything goes well.
万事如意 have all one's wishes;good luck in everything;Everything is as one wishes.

万寿无疆 (may you enjoy) boundless longevity
万水千山 ten thousand torrents and a thousand crags—the trials of a long and arduous journey
万死不辞 willing to risk any danger (to fulfil a task)
万无此理 cannot be true under any circumstances
万无一失 no danger of anything going wrong;no risk at all;perfectly safe
万象更新 All things take on a new aspect;Everything looks new and fresh.
万应灵丹 cure-all;panacea
万用电表 avometer;multimeter
万有引力 (universal) gravitation;gravitational attraction
万丈深渊 a bottomless chasm;abyss
万众一心 millions of people all of one mind
万紫千红 a riot (*or* blaze) of colour
万国博览会 World's Fair
万事开头难 Everything's hard in the beginning;The first step is always difficult.
万变不离其宗 change ten thousand times without leaving the original aim or stand;change time and again,yet stay much the same
万国邮政联盟 Universal Postal Union
万有引力定律 the law of universal gravitation
万丈高楼平地起 The loftiest towers are built up from the ground;Great oaks grow from little acorns.
万国邮政联盟大会 the Universal Postal Union Congress
万事俱备,只欠东风 everything is ready,all we need is an east wind—all is ready except what is crucial
万般皆上品,唯有读书糟 All other callings now rank first,the study of books is last and worst.
万般皆下品,唯有读书高 The worth of other pursuits is small,the study of books excels them all.

腕 [wàn]
名 wrist
腕儿 big shot
腕力 wrist strength
腕子 wrist
腕足动物 brachiopod

蔓 [wàn]
名 tendrilled vine ➡ mán;màn

wāng（ㄨㄤ）

汪 [wāng]
Ⅰ 形 (of water) deep and wide Ⅱ 动 (of liquids) collect;gather;accumulate Ⅲ 名 puddle Ⅳ 量 (*used for liquid*) Ⅴ 象 bark;yap;

bow-wow

汪汪 ①tears welling up; tearful ②bark; yap; bowwow ③(of a body of water) vast; boundless

汪洋 (of a body of water) vast; boundless

汪洋大海 a vast (*or* boundless) ocean

wáng（ㄨㄤˊ）

亡 [wáng]
Ⅰ 〔动〕①flee; escape; run away ②lose; be lost ③die; pass away; perish ④fall; subjugate Ⅱ 〔形〕 deceased; dead

亡故 die; pass away; decease

亡国 ①subjugate a nation; let a state perish ②a conquered nation

亡魂 soul of the newly deceased; ghost

亡灵 soul of a deceased person; ghost; spectre

亡命 ①flee; seek refuge; go into exile ②desperate

亡友 deceased friend

亡者 the deceased

亡国奴 a slave without a country; a conquered people

亡国灭种 national doom and racial extinction

亡戟得矛 lose a halberd and get a spear—the gains offset the losses

亡命之徒 desperado

亡羊补牢 mend the fold after the sheep is lost

王 [wáng]
Ⅰ 〔名〕①king; monarch; sovereign ②duke; prince ③head; chief ④first (*or* largest) of its kind Ⅱ 〔形〕① senior; grand ② best; strongest ➡wàng

王八 ①tortoise ②cuckold

王朝 ①imperial court; royal court ②dynasty

王储 crown prince

王道 kingly way; benevolent government

王法 the law of the land; state law

王妃 princess; consort of a prince

王府 palace of a prince

王父 grandfather

王公 princes and dukes; the nobility

王宫 (imperial) palace

王冠 imperial crown; royal crown

王国 ①kingdom ②realm; domain

王侯 princes and marquises; the nobility

王后 queen consort; queen

王浆 royal jelly

王母 grandmother

王牌 trump card

王权 monarchical power

王室 ① royal family ② imperial court; royal court

王水 aqua regia

王孙 prince's descendants; offspring of the nobility

王位 throne

王爷 Your Royal Highness

王子 king's son; prince

王族 persons of royal lineage; imperial kinsmen

王八蛋 bastard; son of a bitch

王牌军 elite troops; crack units

王八羔子 bastard; son of a bitch

王母娘娘 the Lady Queen Mother

wǎng（ㄨㄤˇ）

网 [wǎng]
Ⅰ 〔名〕①net (for fishing or catching birds) ②net-like object ③network ④network; web; (esp.) Internet Ⅱ 〔动〕①catch with a net; net ②cover (*or* enclose) as with a net; enmesh

网吧 cyber café; Internet café; Internet bar; cyberbar

网虫 Internet buff; web enthusiast; Internet geek

网德 network ethics

网点 a network of commercial establishments

网兜 string bag

网格 great global grid (GGG)

网关 gateway

网管 network management; network administrator

网规 netiquette

网教 internet education

网巾 hairnet

网警 net police

网卡 network interface card (NIC)

网篮 a basket with netting on top

网恋 cyber love; online love affair

网龄 standing (*or* seniority) on Internet

网路 network

网罗 ①a net for catching fish or birds; trap ② enlist the services of

网络 ①network ②network ③Internet

网迷 cyber head; cyber cult; cyber jock; cyber addict; web fan; Internet buff

网民 netizen; net citizen; cyber citizen; nethead

网目 mesh

网屏 screen

网球 ①tennis ②tennis ball

网坛 tennis circles

网校 network school

网眼 mesh

网页 web page

网友 net partner; net acquaintance; net friend

网站 website; Website; cyber station; network station

网址 NA, network address; web site

网子 ①net ②hairnet

网获量 haul

网络战 network war

网评家 cyber critic
网状脉 netted (*or* reticulated) veins
网开一面 give the wrongdoer a way out;leave one side of the net open
网罗人才 enlist able men
网络安全 security on internet
网络出版 publishing on internet;online publishing
网络电话 Internet phone
网络犯罪 cybercrime;net-criminal
网络分析 network analysis
网络公司 dot. com
网络黄页 online Yellow Pages
网络会议 net meeting
网络结构 net structure
网络经济 cybereconomy
网络警察 net police
网络空间 cyberspace
网络漫游 cybersurf
网络色情 cybersex
网络文学 net literature
网络新闻 cyber journalism
网络银行 network bank
网络营销 online marketing
网络用户 cybernaut;on(-)liner;webster
网络用语 cyberspeak;cyber word
网络资源 network resource
网上爱情 e-mail affair;on-line affair
网上采购 shopping on Internet;web (*or* Internet) shopping
网上超市 cyber mall
网上冲浪 surf on the Internet
网上购物 on-line shopping;E-shopping
网上交易 online transaction
网上聊天 cyber chat
网上录取 on-line enrollment;enrolment on internet
网上拍卖 Internet auction;online auction
网上营销 web (*or* Internet) marketing
网上招聘 e-recruiting
网状结构 netted texture
网络服务器 network server
网络管理员 network administrator
网络综合征 network syndrome
网上购物者 E-shopper
网络文明工程 net civilization project
网上交易平台 online trading platform

枉 [wǎng]
Ⅰ 形 warped Ⅱ 动 ① twist;bend;pervert ② treat unjustly (*or* badly);wrong Ⅲ 副 in vain;to no avail;uselessly;vainly
枉道 ① make a detour;go by a roundabout route ②curry favour by crooked means
枉法 pervert (*or* bend) the law
枉费 waste;try in vain;be of no avail
枉驾 I am honoured by your visit.
枉然 futile;in vain;to no purpose

枉死 die uncleared of a false charge;die a victim of injustice
枉自 futile;in vain;to no purpose
枉尺直寻 bend the foot in order to straighten the yard—lose a little in order to gain a great deal
枉费唇舌 waste one's breath
枉费心机 hatch plots in vain;scheme to no avail
枉己正人 be crooked yet try to set others straight

罔 [wǎng]
Ⅰ 动 deceive Ⅱ 副 no;not

往 [wǎng]
Ⅰ 动 go Ⅱ 介 in the direction of;towards Ⅲ 形 former;past;previous
往常 habitually in the past;as one used to do formerly
往返 go there and back;journey to and fro
往复 ① move back and forth;reciprocate ② contact;dealings;intercourse
往后 from now on;later on;in the future
往还 contact;dealings;intercourse
往来 ① come and go ② contact;dealings;intercourse
往年 (in) former years
往前 before;formerly;in the past
往日 (in) former days;(in) bygone days
往事 past events;the past
往往 often;frequently;more often than not
往昔 in the past;in former times
往返票 return ticket;round-trip ticket
往来账 current (*or* open,running) account
往来银行 correspondent bank
往事如烟 Past events have vanished like smoke.

惘 [wǎng]
动 feel frustrated;be in a trance
惘然 frustrated;disappointed
惘然若失 feel lost

辋 [wǎng]
名 wheel rim (of a cart)

魍 [wǎng]
魍魉 demons and monsters

wàng（ㄨㄤˋ）

王 [wàng]
动 (of a monarch) reign over (a kingdom)
➡wáng

妄 [wàng]
形 ① absurd;ridiculous;preposterous ② presumptuous;excessive;rash
妄称 declare falsely (*or* presumptuously)
妄动 rash (*or* reckless,ill-considered) action
妄断 draw a rash conclusion;jump to a conclusion
妄念 wild fancy;improper thought

妄求 inappropriate request; presumptuous demand

妄取 take sth without authorization (*or* permission)

妄说 talk irresponsibly; talk nonsense

妄图 try in vain; vainly attempt

妄为 act recklessly (*or* wildly)

妄想 ①vainly hope to do sth ②vain hope (*or* attempt); wishful thinking ③delusion

妄言 ①talk tactlessly; speak carelessly; make irresponsible remarks ②wild talk; rant

妄语 ① tell lies; talk nonsense ② wild talk; rant

妄想狂 paranoia

妄加猜测 make wild guesses

妄加指责 make rash criticism

妄下雌黄 ①make irresponsible comments ② make wrong corrections

妄言妄听 loose talk not to be taken seriously

妄语虚词 wild talks and vain words

妄自菲薄 belittle oneself; be unduly humble

妄自尊大 have too high an opinion of oneself; be overweening; be self-important

忘 [wàng]
动 forget; escape one's memory; neglect

忘本 forget one's past suffering; forget where one's happiness comes from

忘掉 forget; let slip from one's mind

忘怀 forget; dismiss from one's mind

忘记 ①forget ②overlook; neglect

忘旧 forget old friends (after making new friends)

忘情 ①be unruffled by emotion; be unmoved; be indifferent ②let oneself go

忘却 forget

忘我 oblivious of oneself; selfless

忘形 be beside oneself (with glee, etc.); have one's head turned

忘性 forgetfulness

忘年交 ①friendship between generations ② good friends despite great difference in age

忘恩负义 devoid of gratitude; ungrateful

忘乎所以 forget oneself

旺 [wàng]
形 ①prosperous; thriving; flourishing; vigorous ②plenty; abundant

旺炽 flaming; blazing

旺季 midseason; the peak season; peak period; busy season

旺期 most productive period

旺盛 vigorous; exuberant

旺市 brisk market

旺势 prosperity

旺销 be in great demand; sell well

旺汛 best fishing period

旺月 busy month (in business)

望 [wàng]
I 动 ①look (*or* gaze) into the distance; look far ahead ②call on; pay a visit; visit ③ hope; expect; look forward to ④hate II 名 ① reputation; fame; prestige ② hatred ③ sign flag ④full moon ⑤15th (occasionally 16th or 17th) day of the lunar month III 介 to; towards IV 副 (of age) approaching; near; almost

望板 roof boarding

望断 watch sth in the distance until it vanishes

望风 be on the lookout (while conducting secret activities); keep watch

望楼 watchtower; lookout tower

望日 the 15th day of a lunar month

望月 full moon

望诊 observation

望族 distinguished family; prominent family

望天田 fields on hill tops which depend on rains for water

望远镜 telescope

望尘莫及 so far behind that one can only see the dust of the rider ahead—too far behind to catch up; too inferior to bear comparison

望穿秋水 keep gazing anxiously till one's eyes are strained; await with great anxiety

望而却步 shrink back at the sight of (sth dangerous or difficult); flinch; hang back

望而生畏 be terrified (*or* awed) by the sight of sb or sth

望风而逃 flee at the mere sight of the oncoming force

望风披靡 scatter at the mere sight of the oncoming force

望风引领 gazing at the wind and stretch-ing out the neck—anxiously expecting sb

望梅止渴 quench one's thirst by thinking of plums—console oneself with false hopes; feed on fancies

望文生义 misinterpret words through taking them too literally

望闻问切 look, listen, question and feel the pulse

望眼欲穿 keep gazing anxiously till one's eyes are strained; have long been looking forward with eager expectancy

望洋兴叹 lament one's littleness before the vast ocean—bemoan one's inadequacy in the face of a great task

望子成龙 long to see one's son become a dragon (i.e. win success in the world); long to see one's son succeed in life

wēi (ㄨㄟ)

危 [wēi]
I 名 ①danger; hazard; peril ② twelfth of

the twenty-eight constellations in ancient astronomy Ⅱ 动 endanger; jeopardize; imperil Ⅲ 形 ①dying ②high; precipitous; sheer ③proper; erect; upright

危殆 in great danger; in jeopardy; in a critical condition

危笃 critically ill; on the point of death

危房 buildings that are ready to collapse; unsafe buildings; dilapidated building

危峰 precipitous peak

危改 reconstructure dilapidated buildings

危害 harm; endanger; jeopardize

危机 crisis

危及 endanger

危急 critical; in imminent danger; in a desperate situation

危境 a desperate situation

危局 a dangerous (or critical, desperate) situation

危惧 worry and fear; be apprehensive

危楼 a high building; a high tower

危难 danger and disaster; calamity

危迫 critical; in imminent danger; in a desperate situation

危亡 in peril; at stake

危险 dangerous; perilous

危重 critically ill

危坐 sit bolt upright; sit properly

危害性 harmfulness; perniciousness

危机感 crisis awareness; sense of crisis

危险品 dangerous articles; dangerous goods

危险期 on the verge of death; critical days

危险区 danger area; danger zone; caution area

危险性 dangerous nature; danger

危机四伏 danger lurks on every side

危急存亡 danger and crisis

危陋平房 deteriorating and unsafe houses

危然高坐 sit high

危如累卵 as precarious as a pile of eggs; in an extremely precarious situation

危危欲坠 crumbling; ramshackle; on the verge of collapse

危险废物 hazardous waste

危险因素 hazardous factor

危言耸听 say frightening things just to cause alarm; exaggerate just to scare people

危在旦夕 in imminent danger; on the verge of death or destruction

危旧房改革 re-development of condemned housing

危害公共利益 harm the public interest

危害国家安全 jeopardize state security

危害社会治安 jeopardize public security

危急存亡之秋 a most critical moment (for a nation)

威 ［wēi］
Ⅰ 名 impressive strength; mighty force; prowess Ⅱ 动 threaten by force (or by sheer strength)

威逼 threaten by force; coerce; intimidate

威风 power and prestige; might

威吓 intimidate; threaten; bully

威力 power; might

威猛 brave and fierce

威名 fame (based on great strength or military exploits); mighty name; mighty reputation

威迫 threaten by force; coerce; intimidate

威慑 terrorize with military force; deter

威势 power and influence

威望 prestige

威武 ① might; force; power ② powerful; mighty

威胁 threaten; menace; imperil

威信 prestige; popular trust

威严 ①dignified; stately; majestic; awe-inspiring ②prestige; dignity

威仪 impressive and dignified manner

威士忌 whisky

威逼利诱 alternate intimidation and bribery; combine threats with inducements; use carrot and stick

威风凛凛 have an awesome bearing; have a commanding presence

威风扫地 with every shred of one's prestige swept away—completely discredited

威慑力量 deterrent power

威武不屈 not to be subdued by force; unyielding in the face of force

威信扫地 with every shred of prestige swept away—completely discredited

威震群雄 domineer over other gallant men with power and prestige

威武之师，文明之师 mighty force and civilized force

逶 ［wēi］

逶迤 winding; meandering

偎 ［wēi］
动 snuggle up to; nestle in; lean close to

偎抱 hug; cuddle

偎贴 lean close to; snuggle up to

偎依 snuggle up to; lean close to

微 ［wēi］
Ⅰ 形 ①minute; tiny ②profound; abstruse; esoteric Ⅱ 动 decline; weaken Ⅲ 量 one millionth part; micro-

微安 microampere

微波 ①ripples ②microwave

微薄 meagre; scanty

微差 tiny difference

微词 veiled criticism; complaints

微雕 miniature sculpture

微分 differential

微风 ①gentle breeze ②breeze
微伏 microvolt
微服 (of officials) in disguise;in incognito
微观 microcosmic
微光 glim;gleam;shimmer
微火 slow fire;gentle heat
微机 microcomputer
微贱 humble;lowly
微刻 miniature carving
微利 meager profit
微粒 ①particle ②corpuscle
微量 trace;micro-
微码 microcode
微米 micron
微妙 delicate;subtle
微末 trifling;insignificant
微热 low-grade fever
微弱 faint;feeble;weak
微调 fine tuning;trimming
微微 ①slightly;faintly ②pico-
微细 very small;tiny
微小 small;little
微笑 smile
微行 travel incognito
微型 miniature;mini-
微恙 slight illness;indisposition
微震 ①slight shock ②microseism
微波炉 microwave oven
微代码 microcode
微法拉 microfarad
微分学 differential calculus
微利房 houses for micro (or minimum) profit
  only;economic houses;houses being sold at
  preferential (or very low) price
微粒体 microsome
微生物 microorganism;microbe
微血管 (blood) capillary
微音器 microphone
微波武器 microwave weapon
微不足道 too trivial (or insignificant) to
  mention;insignificant;inconsiderable;neg-
  ligible
微处理机 microprocessor
微创手术 minimally invasive surgery
微服出访 make a tour in disguise
微观世界 microworld;microcosm
微观调控 micro regulating;micro regulation
微观现象 microphenomenon
微乎其微 very little;next to nothing
微积分学 infinitesimal calculus;calculus
微利行业 trade that makes only small profits
微量化学 microchemistry
微量天平 microbalance
微量元素 trace element
微软公司 Microsoft Corporation
微生物学 microbiology
微缩景观 miniature landscape

微笑服务 service with a smile
微型小说 mini-story
微言大义 sublime words with profound meaning
微程序设计 microprogramming;microcoding
微电子技术 micro-electronic technology
微观经济学 microeconomics
微观物理学 microphysics
微调电容器 trimmer;trimmer capacitor;trim-
  mer condenser
微型计算机 microcomputer
微型照相机 micro-camera
微型公共汽车 minibus

煨 [wēi] 动 ①cook over a slow fire;stew;simmer
②roast in fresh cinders

潋 [wēi] 名 drizzle

薇 [wēi] 名 common vetch

巍 [wēi] 形 towering;soaring;lofty
巍峨 towering;lofty
巍然 towering;lofty;majestic;imposing
巍巍 towering;lofty
巍然屹立 stand lofty and firm;stand rock-firm

wéi(xǐ)

韦 [wéi] 名 leather;hide
韦伯 weber (Wb)
韦编三绝 be diligent in one's studies

为 [wéi] Ⅰ 动 ①do;act;perform ② take as;serve
as;act as;work as ③ become;turn ④ be;
mean;make Ⅱ 介 (often used together with
所):为风雪所阻 be held up by a snowstorm;
be snowed up Ⅲ 动 why;what for:何后期为?
Why come after the scheduled time? Ⅳ 副 ①
(used after certain single character adjectives to form adverbs to indicate "extent"
"scope",etc.):大为增加 increase greatly ②
(used after certain single-character adverbs to strengthen the tone):极为幸福 extremely happy ➡wèi
为害 cause harm;cause damage
为患 bring trouble
为难 ① feel embarrassed;feel awkward ②
  make things difficult for
为期 (to be completed) by a definite date
为人 behave;conduct oneself
为生 make a living
为首 with sb as the leader;headed (or led) by
为数 amount to;number
为伍 associate with
为限 be within the limit of;not exceed
为止 up to;till

为重 attach most importance to
为主 give first place to;give priority to
为非作歹 do evil;commit crimes;perpetrate outrages
为富不仁 be rich and cruel;be one of the heartless rich
为官清正 be an incorrupt official;be a pure and upright officer
为期不远 The day is not far off.
为人处世 the way one conducts oneself in society;one's attitude towards life
为人师表 be worthy of the name of teacher;be a paragon of virtue and learning
为人之道 the rules of conduct
为时过早 premature;too early;too soon
为所欲为 act wilfully;do whatever one likes;have one's own way

圩 [wéi]
图 dike;embankment ➡xū

圩埂 earth dike
圩田 ① low-lying paddy fields surrounded with dykes ②polder
圩垸 protective embankments in lakeside areas
圩子 protective embankments surrounding low-lying fields

违 [wéi]
囫 ①oppose;disobey;violate ②part with;leave

违碍 taboo;prohibition
违拗 defy (one's superiors or elders);disobey
违背 violate;go against;run counter to
违法 break the law;be illegal
违反 violate;run counter to;transgress;infringe
违犯 violate;infringe;act contrary to
违建 squatter building
违禁 violate a ban
违抗 disobey;defy
违例 breach of rules;violation
违令 disobey orders
违逆 violate;go against;run counter to
违误 disobey orders and cause delay
违宪 violate the constitution;unconstitutional;be unconstitutional
违心 against one's will;contrary to one's convictions
违约 ① break a contract;violate a treaty ② break one's promise;break off an engagement
违章 ①breach of regulation ②break rules and regulations
违禁品 contraband
违约金 penal sum;default fine
违法必究 ensure that law breakers be prosecuted;Violations of the law must be prosecuted.

违法分包 illegal subcontracting
违法乱纪 violations of the law and lack of discipline;break (or infringe) and violate discipline;violate law and discipline (or regulations);break law and violate discipline
违法失职 transgression of the law and neglect of duty
违法行为 illegal activities;unlawful practice
违反规定 be against regulations
违反合同 breach of contract
违反事实 fly in the face of facts
违反刑法 commit a criminal offence
违反政策 run counter to the policy
违禁贸易 illicit trade;contraband of trade
违宪行为 unconstitutional act
违心之论 words uttered against one's conscience;insincere talk
违约成本 penalty cost
违约责任 liability for breach of contract
违章操作 operate a machine contrary to the instructions
违章建筑 non-conforming (or unlicensed, squatter) building;building put up in defiance of rules and regulations;unauthorized construction
违章行驶 drive against traffic regulations
违约当事人 delinquent party
违章肇事人 delinquent
违法违纪案件 violations of laws and rules of official conducts
违反社会发展规律 go against the laws of social development

围 [wéi]
Ⅰ 囫 enclose;surround;besiege Ⅱ 图 ①all round;around ②measurement of certain parts of body Ⅲ 量 ①hand span:腰大十围 waist of ten hand spans ②arm span

围捕 surround and seize;round up
围场 hunting grounds
围城 ① encircle (or besiege) a city ② besieged city
围攻 ① besiege;lay siege to ② jointly speak (or write) against sb;jointly attack sb
围观 (of a crowd of people) watch;look on
围护 go along with sb to guard him
围击 besiege;lay siege to
围歼 surround and annihilate
围剿 encircle and suppress
围巾 muffler;scarf
围聚 crowd around;gather round
围垦 (build dykes to) reclaim land from marshes;enclose tideland for cultivation
围困 besiege;hem in;pin down
围栏 rail;impalement;grate;enclosure
围猎 round up and hunt
围拢 crowd around;gather round
围棋 *weiqi*, a game played with black and

white pieces on a board of 361 crosses; *go*
围墙 enclosure; enclosing wall
围裙 apron
围绕 ①encircle; go round ②centre on
围网 purse seine; purse net
围岩 country rock; surrounding rock
围堰 cofferdam; coffer
围子 ①defensive wall or stockade surrounding a village ②curtain ③protective embankments surrounding low-lying fields
围坐 sit around sb or sth
围脖儿 muffler; scarf
围嘴儿 bib
围城打援 lay siege to a city to annihilate the enemy relief force; besiege the enemy in order to strike at his reinforcements
围湖造田 (build dykes to) reclaim land from a lake; reclaim lake bottom land and plant it to crops
围魏救赵 besiege Wei to rescue Zhao—relieve the besieged by besieging the base of the besiegers
围追堵截 encirclement, pursuit, obstruction and interception

帏 [wéi]
㊅ ①curtain ②perfume bag

闱 [wéi]
㊅ ①palace's side gate ②hall of the imperial (civil service) examination

桅 [wéi]
㊅ mast
桅灯 ①mast head light; range light ②barn lantern
桅顶 masthead
桅杆 mast
桅樯 mast

唯 [wéi]
㊎ only; solely; alone ➡ wěi
唯独 only; alone
唯恐 for fear that; lest
唯其 precisely because
唯实 base oneself only on reality; proceed from objective realities
唯书 rely solely on books and documents
唯一 only; sole
唯有 only; alone
唯理论 rationalism
唯名论 nominalism
唯能说 energetics
唯物论 materialism
唯心论 idealism
唯成分论 the theory of the unique importance of class origin
唯利是图 be bent on profit; be intent on nothing but profit; put profit-making before anything else
唯美主义 aestheticism

唯命是从 be at sb's bidding; be obedient to sb
唯条件论 view that everything depends entirely on conditions
唯我独尊 overweening; extremely conceited; assume air of self-importance
唯我主义 solipsism
唯武器论 the theory that weapons alone decide the outcome of war
唯物主义 materialism
唯心主义 idealism
唯一无二 only one
唯意志论 theory that the will of men determines everything in economic work
唯生产力论 theory that overemphasizes development of forces of production (ultra-left distortion of any attempts to increase production)
唯物辩证法 materialist dialectics
唯恐天下不乱 crave nothing short of nation-wide chaos; desire to see the world plunged into chaos; desire to stir up trouble

帷 [wéi]
㊅ curtain
帷幔 heavy curtain
帷幕 heavy curtain
帷幄 army tent
帷帐 bed-curtain
帷子 curtain

惟 [wéi]
㊅ thinking; thought; idea
惟妙惟肖 remarkably true to life; absolutely lifelike

维 [wéi]
Ⅰ㊐ ①bind; tie up; hold together ②keep; maintain; safeguard; uphold Ⅱ㊅ ①thought; thinking ②dimension
维持 keep; maintain; preserve
维和 peace-keeping
维护 safeguard; defend; uphold
维纶 polyvinyl alcohol fibre
维棉 vinylon and cotton blend
维权 safeguard legal rights
维数 dimension; dimensionality
维系 hold together; maintain
维新 reform; modernization
维修 keep in (good) repair; service; maintain
维管束 vascular bundle
维尼纶 vinylon
维生素 vitamin
维他命 Vitamin(e)
维持现状 let things go on as they are; maintain the status quo; maintain the present situation
维持原判 affirm the original judgement; uphold the decision
维和部队 peace-keeping troops
维持性价格 support price

W

维持和平部队 peace-keeping force

嵬 [wéi]
囫 tower aloft;rise up
嵬然 towering;loftily

wěi(xǐ)

伟 [wěi]
囫 ①great ②strong and handsome
伟岸 tall and sturdy;stalwart;husky;strapping
伟大 great;mighty
伟哥 Viagra
伟观 a grand (*or* magnificent) sight
伟绩 great feats; great exploits; brilliant achievements
伟男 big muscular man
伟人 a great man;a great personage
伟业 great cause;exploit
伟丈夫 strong and handsome man

伪 [wěi]
囫 ①false;counterfeit;fake;bogus ②puppet;collaborationist;quisling
伪币 ① counterfeit money; counterfeit (*or* forged) bank note;spurious coin ②money issued by a puppet government
伪钞 counterfeit (*or* forged) bank note
伪军 puppet army (*or* soldier)
伪劣 (of goods) fake,shoddy,of poor quality
伪善 hypocritical
伪书 ancient books found to have been incorrectly dated, forged, or attributed to a wrong author;ancient books of dubious authenticity
伪托 forge ancient literary or art works,or pass off modern works as ancient ones
伪造 forge;falsify;fabricate;counterfeit
伪证 false testimony;perjury
伪撰 write an essay under sb else's name (esp. that of a writer of the past)
伪装 ①pretend;feign ②disguise;guise;mask ③camouflage
伪足 pseudopodium
伪作 counterfeit
伪君子 hypocrite;a wolf in sheep's clothing
伪科学 pseudoscience
伪造品 counterfeit;forgery
伪造罪 forgery
伪政府 illegitimate government
伪政权 puppet government;puppet regime
伪劣产品 counterfeit; fake; shoddy products; low-quality goods;fake and shoddy products
伪造签字 forged signature
伪造文件 falsification of document
伪造账目 falsify accounts
伪造证件 forge certificates;forge diplomas
伪币辨别仪 currency detector
伪造证件者 certificate forger

苇 [wěi]
囵 reed
苇箔 reed matting
苇丛 a clump of reeds
苇塘 reed pond
苇席 reed mat
苇子 reed

尾 [wěi]
Ⅰ 囵 ①tail;rear ②sixth of the 28 constellations into which the celestial sphere was divided in ancient Chinese astronomy ③end ④remaining part;remainder;remnant Ⅱ 囵 (of fish):有鱼数百尾。There are hundreds of fish. ➡yǐ
尾巴 ① tail ② tail-like part ③ servile adherent;appendage ④ remaining part ⑤ a person shadowing sb
尾灯 tail light;tail lamp
尾骨 coccyx
尾矿 tailings
尾轮 tail-wheel (of an aircraft)
尾期 last stage;last phase;final phase
尾鳍 tail fin;caudal fin
尾气 tail-gas;exhaust
尾欠 ①owe a small balance ②balance due
尾声 ①coda ②epilogue ③end
尾市 end of the market
尾数 odd amount in addition to the round number (usu. of a credit balance)
尾水 tail water
尾随 tail behind;tag along after;follow at sb's heels
尾箱 rear trunk;car trunk;boot;luggage boot
尾须 cercus
尾翼 tail surface (of an aircraft);empennage
尾音 last (*or* end) syllable
尾蚴 cercaria
尾追 in hot pursuit;hot on the trail of
尾座 tailstock
尾巴工程 dragging-on construction project
尾巴主义 tailism
尾大不掉 ①leadership rendered ineffectual by recalcitrant subordinates ②(of an organization) too cumbersome to be effective
尾气污染 vehicle tail emission
尾气排放标准 waste gas emission standard

纬 [wěi]
囵 ① weft; woof ② latitude ③ augury (book)
纬编 weft knitting
纬度 latitude
纬密 weft density
纬纱 ①weft (yarn);woof;filling ②pick
纬线 ①parallel ②weft
纬世之才 the ability to rule the state

委 [wěi]
委顿 tired;exhausted;weary

委令 appointment
委派 appoint;delegate;designate
委弃 abandon;forsake;cast aside
委曲 ①(of roads,rivers,etc.) winding;tortuous ②ins and outs;all the details
委屈 ①feel wronged;nurse a grievance ②put sb to great inconvenience
委任 appoint
委身 submit to;give oneself to
委实 really;indeed
委琐 ①petty;trifling ②of wretched appearance
委托 entrust;trust
委婉 mild and roundabout;tactful
委员 committee member;member of a committee
委罪 put the blame on sb else
委培生 trainee on a contracted training program
委任书 certificate of appointment
委任状 certificate of appointment
委托书 trust deed;power of attorney
委婉语 euphemism
委员会 committee;commission;council
委员长 chairman of a committee
委决不下 hesitate to make a decision;be undecided
委靡不振 dejected and apathetic;dispirited;in low spirits
委曲求全 make concessions to achieve one's aim;compromise for the sake of the general interest
委任统治 mandate
委托代理 agency by agreement
委托培养 sponsored training;consign the training of personnel to a certain school
委托商店 commission shop;commission house
委托销售 sales on commission
委托责任 fiduciary duty
委婉其辞 speak in a mild and roundabout way;be tactful in wording
委以要职 appoint sb to an important post
委以重任 entrust sb with an important post (or task)
委任统治地 mandated territory

炜 [wěi]
形 bright

诿 [wěi]
动 shift (the responsibility or blame) to sb else;shirk
诿过 put the blame on sb else;shift the blame on to sb else
诿过于人 lay one's faults at other people's door;try to impute it to others

娓 [wěi]
娓娓 (talk) tirelessly

娓娓动听 speak most interestingly
娓娓而谈 talk in a kindly and informal fashion

萎 [wěi]
动 ①wither;wilt;fade ②decline
萎靡 listless;dispirited;dejected
萎蔫 wilting
萎缩 ① wither;shrivel ② listless;dispirited;dejected ③ (of a market, economy, etc.) shrink;sag ④atrophy
萎谢 wither;fade
萎陷疗法 collapse therapy

唯 [wěi]
叹 yea ➡ wéi
唯唯诺诺 be a yes-man;mumble "yes,yes";"yes,yes" repeatedly

骪 [wěi]
动 bend;crook;pervert
骪法 pervert the law
骪曲 stoop to compromise

猥 [wěi]
形 ①numerous;multifarious;miscellaneous ②base;lewd;lascivious;salacious
猥词 obscenities;obscene (or dirty,foul) language;salacious words
猥贱 lowly;humble
猥滥 excessively numerous
猥劣 abject;base;mean
猥陋 base;mean;despicable
猥琐 of wretched appearance
猥屑 base;mean;despicable
猥亵 ①obscene;salacious ②act indecently towards (a woman)
猥杂 miscellaneous

瘘 [wěi]
名 paralysis

wèi(xì)

卫 [wèi]
I 动 defend;guard;protect II 名 place for stationing troops in the Ming Dynasty
卫兵 guard;bodyguard
卫道 defend traditional moral principles
卫队 squad of bodyguards;armed escort
卫护 protect;guard
卫矛 winged euonymus
卫冕 defend one's championship;defend one's title
卫生 hygiene;health;sanitation
卫士 bodyguard
卫视 satellite television
卫戍 garrison
卫星 ① satellite;moon ② artificial satellite;man-made satellite
卫道士 apologist
卫护者 guardian
卫生带 sanitary belt;sanitary napkin
卫生队 medical unit;medical team

卫生间 toilet (room)
卫生巾 feminine napkin
卫生局 health department; public health bureau
卫生科 health section
卫生裤 sweat pants
卫生筷 hygienic chopsticks
卫生棉 cotton wool
卫生球 camphor ball; mothball
卫生室 clinic
卫生学 hygiene; hygienics
卫生衣 sweat shirt
卫生员 health worker; medical orderly; medic
卫生院 small hospital
卫生纸 toilet paper
卫星城 satellite town
卫星国 satellite state; satellite country
卫生保健 health care
卫生城市 hygienic city
卫生检查 sanitary inspection
卫生检疫 health quarantine
卫生教育 hygienic education
卫生设备 sanitary equipment
卫星导航 satellite navigation
卫星电视 television programs transmitted by satellite; satellite TV
卫星广播 satellite broadcast
卫星天线 satellite antenna
卫星通信 satellite communications
卫星云图 satellite cloud picture
卫生防疫站 sanitation and antiepidemic station
卫星处理机 satellite processor
卫星地面站 ground satellite station
卫星测控中心 satellite control centre
卫星遥感技术 satellite remote sensing technology
卫星导航地面站 satellite navigation earth station

为 ［wèi］
Ⅰ 动 be on the side of; help; support Ⅱ 介 ①on behalf of; for the benefit of; in the interest of ②for (the purpose or sake of) ③to：此事请勿为外人道。 Please say nothing of this (or Don't breathe a word about it) to other people. ④because; for; on account of：为什么如此激动？ Why get so worked up? ➡wéi
为此 to this end; for this reason (or purpose); in this connection
为何 why; for what reason
为了 for; for the sake of; in order to
为什么 why; why (or how) is it that
为国捐躯 lay down one's life for one's country
为国增光 do credit to one's country
为虎添翼 give wings to a tiger—aid an evildoer
为虎作伥 play the jackal to the tiger—help a villain do evil

为民除害 eliminate a public scourge; rid the people of an evil; rid the people of a scourge
为民请命 plead in the name of the people; plead for the people
为人作嫁 sew sb else's trousseau—do work for others with no benefit to oneself
为我之物 thing-for-us
为之动容 become interested and show so in one's facial expression
为之心碎 break one's heart
为用户着想 user-oriented
为艺术而艺术 art for art's sake
为亲友非法牟利罪 crime of seeking illegal profits for the family members and friends
为渊驱鱼，为丛驱雀 drive the fish into deep waters and the sparrows into the thickets—drive friends over to the side of the enemy

未 ［wèi］
副 ①not yet ②not; no：前途未可限量 have boundless prospects
未必 may not; not necessarily
未便 not be in a position to; find it hard to
未曾 have not; did not
未尝 ①have not; did not ②(*used before a negative word*, *in making a guarded assertion*)
未定 uncertain; undecided; undefined
未婚 unmarried; single
未及 ①there's not enough time (to do sth); it's too late (to do sth) ②not touch upon; leave unmentioned
未竟 unfulfilled; unaccomplished
未决 unsettled; outstanding
未可 cannot
未来 ①coming; approaching; next; future ②future; tomorrow
未了 unfinished; outstanding
未免 ①rather; a bit too; truly ②unavoidable
未能 fail to; cannot
未时 the period of the day from 1 p. m. to 3 p. m.
未遂 not accomplished; abortive
未完 unfinished
未详 unknown
未爆弹 dud
未成年 ①infancy; nonage; minority ②not yet of age; under age
未定稿 manuscript not yet finalized; draft
未定界 undefined boundary
未婚夫 fiancé
未婚妻 fiancée
未来派 futurism
未来学 futurology
未遂犯 one who attempts to commit a crime
未遂罪 attempted crime; attempt
未亡人 the bereaved one (a form of self-address formerly used by a widow)

未知量 unknown quantity
未知数 ① unknown number ② unknown;uncertain
未必如此 be not necessarily so;may not necessarily turn out that way
未卜先知 know without consulting the oracle—have foreknowledge
未成年人 minor
未定之天 an unknown factor
未敢苟同 beg to differ;cannot agree
未婚同居 domestic partnership;live in sin
未婚先寡 woman who remains unmarried after the death of her fiancé
未竟之业 unaccomplished task
未可厚非 not be altogether unjustifiable;give little cause for criticism
未可乐观 give no cause for optimism;there is nothing to be optimistic about
未来主义 futurism
未老先衰 frail and failing before one's time
未能免俗 be unable to rise above the convention;cannot but follow conventional practice
未遂政变 abortive coup détat
未完待续 be continued
未雨绸缪 repair the house before it rains;provide for a rainy day;take precautions
未知可否 uncertain of feasibility
未置可否 neither "yes" nor "no";non-committal

位 [wèi]
Ⅰ 名 ① place;location;seat ② position;rank;status ③throne ④place;figure;digit ⑤bit Ⅱ 量 *used in deferential reference to people*:各位女士 Ladies
位次 ① precedence;seating arrangement ② rank
位能 potential energy
位移 displacement;shifting
位于 be located;be situated;lie
位置 ①seat;place ②place;position
位子 seat;place
位势米 geopotential metre
位极人臣 get (*or* rise) to the highest official position
位居要津 occupy a key position

味 [wèi]
Ⅰ 名 ①taste;flavour ②smell;scent;odour ③interest;relish ④dishes;food ⑤distinguish the flavour of;reflect on Ⅱ 量 ingredient (of a Chinese medicine prescription):这个方子里共有八味药。This prescription specifies eight medical herbs.
味道 taste;flavour
味精 monosodium glutamate;gourmet powder;MSG
味觉 sense of taste

味蕾 taste bud
味素 gourmet powder
味同嚼蜡 like chewing wax—insipid

畏 [wèi]
动 ①fear;dread ②admire
畏避 avoid sth out of fear;recoil from;flinch from
畏光 photophobia
畏忌 have scruples;fear;dread
畏惧 fear;dread
畏难 be afraid of difficulty
畏怯 cowardly;timid;chickenhearted
畏缩 recoil;shrink;flinch
畏途 a dangerous road—a perilous undertaking
畏友 an esteemed friend
畏罪 dread punishment for one's crime
畏首畏尾 be full of misgivings;be over-cautious
畏缩不前 recoil in fear;hesitate to press forward;hang back
畏之如虎 fear sth (*or* sb) as if it were a tiger
畏罪潜逃 abscond to avoid punishment
畏罪自杀 commit suicide to escape punishment

胃 [wèi]
名 stomach
胃癌 cancer of the stomach;gastric carcinoma
胃病 stomach trouble;gastric disease;gastropathy
胃寒 stomach cold
胃镜 gastroscope
胃口 ①appetite ②liking
胃酸 hydrochloric acid in gastric juice
胃痛 stomachache;gastralgia
胃腺 gastric gland
胃炎 gastritis
胃液 gastric juice
胃肠炎 gastroenteritis
胃出血 gastric bleeding;gastric hemorrhage;gastrorrhagia
胃穿孔 gastric perforation;stomach perforation
胃痉挛 gastrospasm
胃溃疡 gastric ulcer
胃扩张 dilatation of the stomach
胃黏膜 gastric mucosa
胃舒平 gastropine
胃下垂 ptosis of the stomach;gastroptosis
胃蛋白酶 pepsin
胃切除术 gastrectomy
胃黏膜疾病 gastric mucosa disease
胃十二指肠 gastroduodenal
胃十二指肠溃疡 gastroduodenal ulcer

谓 [wèi]
动 ①say ②call;name;mean
谓词 predicate

谓语 predicate

尉 ［wèi］
［名］①ancient official title ②(military rank) junior officer
尉官 a military officer above the rank of warrant officer and below that of major; a junior officer

遗 ［wèi］
［动］offer as a gift; make a present of ➡yí

喂 ［wèi］
Ⅰ［叹］(of greeting) hello; hey Ⅱ［动］①give food to; feed ②spoon-feed
喂料 feed (draught animals)
喂奶 breast-feed; suckle; nurse
喂养 feed; raise; keep

猬 ［wèi］
［名］hedgehog

渭 ［wèi］
［名］Weihe River, a tributary of the Yellow River

蔚 ［wèi］
［形］① luxuriant; grand; magnificent ② colourful
蔚蓝 azure; sky blue
蔚然成风 become common practice; become the order of the day
蔚为大观 present a splendid sight; afford a magnificent view
蔚为大国 great country in all its magnificence

碨 ［wèi］
［名］millstone

慰 ［wèi］
［动］① console; soothe; comfort ② feel relieved
慰抚 comfort; console; soothe
慰藉 comfort; console
慰劳 bring gifts to (or send one's best wishes to)in recognition of services rendered
慰留 urge sb to stay on
慰勉 comfort and encourage
慰问 express sympathy and solicitude for; extend one's regards to; convey greetings to; salute
慰唁 condole with sb
慰安妇 comfort woman
慰问袋 gift bag
慰问团 a group sent to convey greetings and appreciation
慰问信 a letter expressing one's appreciation or sympathy
慰情胜无 A little comfort is better than none.
慰问演出 a special performance as an expression of gratitude (or appreciation)

wēn（ㄨㄣ）

温 ［wēn］
Ⅰ［形］① warm; lukewarm; tepid ②gentle; meek; tender Ⅱ［名］①temperature ②seasonal febrile disease Ⅲ［动］①warm up; heat up (to a moderate degree) ②review; revise
温饱 adequate (or ample) food and clothing; dress warmly and eat one's fill; have adequate food and clothing; have enough to eat and wear
温标 thermometric scale
温差 difference in temperature; range of temperature
温床 ①hotbed ②breeding ground; hotbed
温存 ①attentive (usu. to a person of the opposite sex) ②gentle; kind
温带 temperate zone
温度 temperature
温和 ［wēnhé］ ① temperate; mild; moderate ②gentle; mild
温厚 gentle and kind; good-natured
温乎 warm; lukewarm
温和 ［wēnhuo］ warm; lukewarm
温觉 sense of heat
温良 gentle and kindhearted
温暖 warm
温情 ①tender feeling ②too soft-hearted
温泉 hot spring
温柔 (usu. of a woman) gentle and soft
温润 ①gentle; kindly ②mild (or temperate) and moist
温室 greenhouse; glasshouse; hothouse; forcing house; conservatory
温淑 (of a woman) gentle and kind
温水 lukewarm water; warm water
温顺 docile; meek
温汤 ①lukewarm water ②hot spring
温吞 ①lukewarm; tepid ②(of language) not to the point; irrelevant
温习 review; revise
温馨 soft and sweet; warm
温驯 (of animals) docile; meek; tame
温雅 gentle and refined
温饱型 simply having adequate food and clothing
温差电 thermoelectricity
温度表 thermometer
温度计 thermograph; thermometer
温和派 the moderates
温乎乎 warm; lukewarm
温柔乡 the land of warmth and tenderness—a place where a man can find solace in feminine charms
温湿计 hygrothermograph; thermohygrograph
温饱工程 program for adequate food and clothing
温饱问题 problem of adequate (ample) food and clothing
温差电偶 thermoelectric couple; thermocouple
温带气候 temperate climate
温故知新 ①gain new knowledge by reviewing

old ②understand the present by reviewing the past
温暖如春 as warm as spring
温情脉脉 full of tenderness
温情主义 undue leniency
温柔敦厚 gentle and kind
温室效应 greenhouse effect
温汤浸种 hot water treatment of seeds
温文尔雅 refined and cultivated
温血动物 warm-blooded animal
温良恭俭让 temperate, kind, courteous, restrained and magnanimous
温差电检波器 thermodetector

瘟 [wēn] Ⅰ 〔名〕 acute communicable disease Ⅱ 〔形〕 (of traditional operas) dull; insipid; vapid
瘟病 seasonal febrile diseases
瘟神 god of plague
瘟疫 pestilence; plague

wén (ㄨㄣˊ)

文 [wén] Ⅰ 〔名〕 ① character; writing; inscription; script ② language ③ literary composition; article; writing ④ literary (or classical) language ⑤ culture; civilization ⑥ liberal arts; humanities ⑦ etiquette; formal ritual: 虚文 mere formality ⑧ (used to refer to certain natural phenomena): 水文 hydrology Ⅱ 〔形〕 ①civilian; civil ②soft; mild; refined Ⅲ 〔动〕 ① tattoo ②cover up; paint over; explain away Ⅳ 〔量〕 unit of ancient coins: 一文不名 penniless
文案 ①official documents and correspondence ②secretary; clerk
文本 text; version
文笔 style of writing
文才 literary talent; aptitude for writing
文采 ① rich and bright colours ② literary grace; literary talent
文丑 (in traditional opera) a comedian in civil plays
文唇 lip tattooing
文辞 diction; language
文斗 verbal struggle; nonviolent struggle
文牍 ①official documents and correspondence ②secretary; clerk
文法 ① rules of composition and rhetoric ② grammar
文房 study (a room)
文风 style of writing
文稿 manuscript; draft
文告 proclamation; statement; message
文官 civil official
文蛤 clam
文豪 literary giant; great writer; eminent writer
文化 ① civilization; culture ② education; cul-

ture; schooling; literacy
文火 slow fire; gentle heat
文集 collected works
文件 documents; papers; instruments; file
文教 culture and education
文静 gentle and quiet
文句 diction; language
文具 writing materials; stationery
文据 written pledge
文科 liberal arts
文库 a series of books issued in a single format by a publisher; library
文侩 literary prostitute
文理 unity and coherence in writing
文盲 an illiterate person; illiterate
文眉 eyebrow tattooing
文庙 Confucian temple
文明 ①civilization; culture ②civilized
文墨 writing
文鸟 mannikin
文痞 literary prostitute
文凭 diploma
文气 [wénqì] vigour of style
文契 contracts concerning the buying and selling of real estate, etc.
文气 [wénqi] gentle and quiet
文人 man of letters; scholar; literati
文弱 gentle and frail-looking
文身 tattoo
文史 literature and history
文饰 ① polish (a piece of writing) ② gloss over (one's mistakes); cover up
文书 ① document; official dispatch ② copy clerk
文思 the thread of ideas in writing; the train of thought in writing
文坛 the literary world (or arena, circles); the world of letters
文体 ①type of writing; literary form; style ② recreation and sports
文武 civil and military
文物 cultural relic; historical relic
文戏 (in traditional opera) civil plays
文献 document; literature
文胸 bra tattooing
文选 selected works; literary selections
文学 literature
文雅 elegant; refined; cultured; polished
文言 classical Chinese
文艺 literature and art
文友 literary friend
文娱 cultural recreation; entertainment
文员 clerk
文苑 ①the literary world (or arena, circles); the world of letters ②literary and art circles; the world of literature and art
文约 contract; deed

文责 the responsibility an author should assume for his own writings; author's responsibility

文摘 abstract; digest

文章 ① essay; article ② literary works; writings ③ hidden meaning; implied meaning

文职 civilian post

文治 civil administration

文竹 asparagus fern

文字 ① characters; script; writing ② written language ③ writing (as regards form or style)

文宗 outstanding literary figure; one whose writings are modelled after

文昌鱼 lancelet

文抄公 plagiarist

文工团 song and dance ensemble; art troupe; cultural troupe

文冠果 shiny-leaved yellowhorn

文化宫 palace of culture; cultural palace

文化馆 cultural centre

文化街 street with many cultural institutions and facilities

文化界 cultural circles

文化热 cultural craze

文化人 intellectual

文教界 cultural and educational circles

文盲率 illiteracy rate

文明棍 walking stick; stick

文明戏 early form of spoken drama

文人画 literati painting

文史馆 Research Institute of Culture and History

文学士 bachelor of arts (B. A.)

文言文 writings in classical Chinese; classical style of writing

文艺界 literary and art circles; the world of literature and art

文绉绉 genteel

文字交 pen friends; literary friends

文字学 philology

文字狱 imprisonment or execution of an author for writing sth considered offensive by the imperial court; literary inquisition

文本编辑 text editing

文笔流畅 write in an easy and fluent style; wield a facile pen

文不对题 irrelevant; beside the point (or mark); wide of the mark

文不加点 never make the slightest change in one's writing; have a facile pen

文从字顺 readable and fluent

文牍主义 red tape

文房四宝 the four treasures of the study

"文革"遗风 customs remaining from the "Cultural Revolution"

文过饰非 conceal faults and gloss over wrongs; gloss over one's faults; cover up (or explain away) one's errors

文化参赞 cultural counsellor; cultural attaché

文化产业 culture industry

文化程度 cultural level; cultural standard

文化互渗 acculturation

文化机关 cultural institution

文化快餐 cultural fast food

文化模式 cultural pattern

文化偶像 culture icon

文化品位 standing of culture; cultural level

文化沙漠 cultural desert

文化渗透 cultural aggression; cultural infiltration

文化市场 cultural market

文化素养 artistic appreciation

文化污染 cultural pollution

文化遗产 cultural heritage; cultural legacy

文化用品 stationery

文化娱乐 relish of culture

文化中心 cultural centre

文化专员 cultural attaché

文教事业 culture and education

文君新寡 newly widowed woman

文明单位 unit sited for cultural and ideological progress; model establishment; civilized establishment; culturally advanced department

文明古国 country with an ancient civilization

文明经商 trade in accordance with work ethic; do business with civility; do business in courteous and proper way

文明生产 carry out production strictly in line with rules and regulations

文凭至上 credentialism

文情并茂 (of writing) elegant in style and rich in sentiment

文人无行 Men of letters are lacking in moral character.

文人相轻 Scholars tend to look down upon each other.

文人学士 scholars; men of letters

文如其人 The writing mirrors the writer; The style is the man.

文山会海 a mountain of papers and a sea of meetings—the intricate routine that a leading cadre gets bogged down in

文韬武略 military expertise; military strategy

文恬武嬉 (of a corrupt regime) the officials are indolent and the officers frivolous

文武双全 be well versed in both polite letters and martial arts; adept with both pen and sword

文物保护 preservation of cultural relics; protection of historical relics

文学语言 standard speech; literary language

文以载道 The function of literature is to convey the Tao.

文艺创作 literary and artistic

文艺复兴 the Renaissance

文艺会演 theatrical festival

文艺节目 programme of entertainment；theatrical items；theatrical performance

文艺批评 literary (*or* art) criticism

文责自负 The author takes sole responsibility for his views.

文职总统 civilian President

文质彬彬 gentle；urbane；suave

文治武功 cultural and military achievements

文字方程 literal equation

文字改革 reform of a writing system (as in China)

文字游戏 play with words；juggle with terms

文化寻根热 cultural root-seeking craze

文件缓冲区 file buffers

文明礼貌月 Ethics and Courtesy Month；the Civic Virtues Month；Civic Pride and Courtesy Month

文献记录片 documentary film

文艺工作者 literary and art workers；writers ad artists

文字处理机 word processor

文化扶贫工程 project of aiding the poor areas in developing culture

文化专制主义 cultural tyranny

纹 ［wén］
名 ①pattern ②line；vein；grain

纹理 veins；grain

纹饰 decorative pattern (on utensils)；figure

纹银 fine silver

纹路 lines；grain

纹丝不动 absolutely still

炆 ［wén］
动 cook food on a slow fire

闻 ［wén］
I 动 ①hear ②smell Ⅱ 名 ①news；story；anecdote ② repute；reputation Ⅲ 形 well-known；renowned；famous

闻达 illustrious and influential；eminent

闻见 ［wénjiàn］ what one sees and hears；knowledge；information

闻见 ［wénjian］ ①notice by smell；smell ②hear

闻名 ① well-known；famous；renowned ② be familiar with sb's name；know sb by repute

闻人 well-known figure；famous man；celebrity

闻悉 hear；learn；be informed

闻讯 hear the news

闻风而动 act without delay upon hearing the news；immediately respond to a call；go into action without delay

闻风丧胆 become terror-stricken (*or* panic-stricken，terrified) at the news

闻过则喜 be glad to have one's errors pointed out

闻鸡起舞 rise at cock's crow—diligent and self-disciplined

闻名遐迩 be known to all，far and near；enjoy widespread renown

闻所未闻 hear what one has never heard before；unheard-of

闻一知十 learn one thing and know ten things—very intelligent

闻名不如见面 knowing a person by repute is not as good as meeting him face to face

蚊 ［wén］
名 mosquito

蚊虫 mosquito

蚊香 mosquito-repellent incense

蚊帐 mosquito net

蚊子 mosquito

<h2 style="text-align:center">wěn（ㄨㄣˇ）</h2>

刎 ［wěn］
动 cut one's throat

刎颈之交 friends that are ready to die for each other

刎颈自戮 commit suicide by cutting one's throat

抆 ［wěn］
动 wipe

吻 ［wěn］
I 名 lips Ⅱ 动 ①touch by the lips；kiss ② muzzle；snout

吻别 kiss sb goodbye

吻合 ①be identical；coincide；tally ②connect by anastomosis

吻合术 anastomosis

紊 ［wěn］
形 dishevelled；disorderly；confused

紊流 turbulence；turbulent flow

紊乱 disorder；chaos；confusion

稳 ［wěn］
I 形 ① steady；firm；steadfast ② calm；staid；sedate Ⅱ 动 stabilize；calm；put at ease Ⅲ 副 surely；certainly

稳步 with steady steps；steadily

稳产 stable yields

稳当 ①reliable；secure；safe ②steady；stable

稳定 ①stable；steady ②stabilize；steady

稳固 ①firm；stable ②stabilize

稳健 firm；steady

稳流 steady flow

稳拿 be certain to win，achieve，etc.

稳妥 safe；reliable

稳重 steady；staid；sedate

稳定剂 stabilizer

稳健派 moderates

稳压器 voltage stabilizer；voltage regulator

"稳、准、狠" "sure，accurate and relentless"

稳操胜券 be certain (*or* confident) of success
稳产高产 high and stable yields
稳定货币 stabilize the value of the currency
稳定平衡 stable equilibrium
稳定情绪 set sb's mind at rest;reassure sb
稳定装置 stabilization plant;stabilizer
稳如泰山 as stable as Mount Tai
稳扎稳打 ①go ahead steadily and strike sure blows (in war) ②go about things steadily and surely
稳中求进 seek progress amid stability;seek further progress on the basis of stability
稳住阵脚 maintain (*or* secure) one's position;hold one's ground

wèn(ㄨㄣˋ)

问 [wèn]
Ⅰ 〔动〕①seek information from;ask;inquire ②ask after;inquire after ③interrogate;question;examine ④ hold responsible;intervene Ⅱ 〔介〕from
问安 pay one's respects (usu. to elders);wish sb good health
问案 try (*or* hear) a case
问卜 divine by the Eight Trigrams
问答 questions and answers
问鼎 ①inquire about the tripods—aspire after the throne;have monarchic ambitions ② compete for a championship;try to carry off the first prize
问好 send one's regards to;say hello to
问号 ①question mark;interrogation mark (*or* point) (?) ② unknown factor;unsolved problem
问候 send one's respects (*or* regards) to;extend greetings to
问话 ask about;inquire
问津 make inquiries (as about prices or the situation)
问荆 meadow pine
问卷 questionnaire
问难 raise difficult questions for discussion
问世 be published;come out
问事 ①inquire;ask ②run affairs;be in charge
问题 ① question;problem;issue ② trouble;mishap
问讯 inquire;ask
问斩 behead;decapitate
问诊 inquiry;diagnose through interrogation
问住 stump sb with a question
问罪 denounce;condemn
问事处 inquiry office;information desk
问讯处 inquiry office;information desk
问长问短 make detailed inquiries;inquire with concern about sb's well-being;ask about this and that

问道于盲 ask a blind man the way—seek advice from one who can offer none
问东问西 ask all sorts of questions
问寒问暖 inquire with concern about sb's wellbeing;be solicitous for sb's welfare
问题少年 problem child
问心无愧 feel no qualms upon self-examination;have a clear conscience
问心有愧 feel a twinge of conscience;have a guilty conscience
问这问那 ask about this and that

wēng(ㄨㄥ)

翁 [wēng]
〔名〕①old man ②father ③husband's father;(woman's) father-in-law ④wife's father
翁姑 a woman's parents-in-law
翁婿 father-in-law and son-in-law
翁仲 stone statue placed in front of a tomb

嗡 [wēng]
〔象〕buzz;hum;drone;蚊子老是在耳边嗡叫。 Mosquitoes were buzzing around my ears.

鹟 [wēng]
〔名〕flycatcher

wèng(ㄨㄥˋ)

瓮 [wèng]
〔名〕earthen jar
瓮城 the enceinte of a city gate;a barbican entrance to a city
瓮声瓮气 in a low,muffled voice
瓮中之鳖 like a turtle in a jar—bottled up;trapped
瓮中捉鳖 catch a turtle in a jar—go after an easy prey

蕹 [wèng]
蕹菜 water spinach

wō(ㄨㄛ)

莴 [wō]
莴苣 lettuce
莴笋 asparagus lettuce

倭 [wō]
〔名〕Japan
倭瓜 pumpkin;cushaw
倭寇 Japanese pirates

涡 [wō]
〔名〕whirlpool;maelstrom;eddy
涡虫 turbellarian worm;turbellarian
涡流 ①the circular movement of a fluid;whirling fluid;eddy ②eddy current;vortex flow
涡轮 turbine
涡旋 vortex
涡轮机 turbine

涡轮发电机 turbogenerator
涡轮喷气发动机 turbojet (engine)
涡轮螺旋桨发动机 turboprop (engine)

喔 [wō]
〔象〕 cock's crow

窝 [wō]
Ⅰ 〔名〕①nest ②lair;den;haunt ③place (*or* space) occupied ④hollow part of the human body (*or* a place);pit Ⅱ 〔动〕①harbour;shelter;shield ②huddle up;curl up;stay still ③hold in;check ④bend Ⅲ 〔量〕 litter;brood:一窝下了四只猫 bear four kittens at a litter
窝憋 ①feel frustrated ②shut oneself indoors; stay at home ③narrow and small;poky
窝藏 harbour;shelter
窝匪 give shelter to (*or* harbour) a bandit
窝工 enforced idleness due to poor organization of work;holdup in the work through poor organization
窝火 be filled with anger
窝囊 ① feel vexed; be annoyed ② good-for-nothing;hopelessly stupid
窝棚 shack;shed;shanty
窝铺 shack;shed
窝气 choke with resentment;feel injured and resentful
窝赃 harbour stolen goods;conceal booty
窝主 a person who harbours criminals,loot or contraband goods
窝脖儿 meet with a rebuff;strike a snag;be crossed
窝囊废 good-for-nothing;worthless wretch
窝窝头 steamed bread of corn,sorghum,etc.
窝藏罪犯 give shelter to a criminal;harbour a criminal
窝儿里斗 internal struggle;internal quarrels and fights
窝儿里反 internal strife;family quarrel
窝儿里横 a terror at home (but a coward outside)

蜗 [wō]
蜗杆 worm
蜗居 humble abode
蜗牛 snail
蜗旋 spiral;helix

踒 [wō]
〔动〕 sprain;strain

WǑ (ㄨㄛˇ)

我 [wǒ]
〔代〕①I;me;my ②we;us;our ③one;people ④self
我辈 we;us
我见 my opinion
我们 we;us
我见犹怜 Even I cannot help loving her upon seeing her.

我行我素 persist in one's old ways (no matter what others say);stick to one's old way of doing things

WÒ (ㄨㄛˋ)

肟 [wò]
〔名〕 oxime

沃 [wò]
Ⅰ 〔动〕 irrigate;pour (water) Ⅱ 〔形〕 (of soil) fertile;rich
沃土 fertile soil;rich soil
沃野千里 a thousand *li* of fertile fields;a vast expanse of fertile land

卧 [wò]
Ⅰ 〔动〕①lie ②get babies to lie down ③(of animals or birds) crouch;sit ④poach Ⅱ 〔形〕 for sleeping in
卧病 be confined to bed;be laid up
卧舱 sleeping cabin
卧车 ①sleeping car;sleeping carriage;sleeper ②automobile;car;limousine;sedan
卧床 ①(of the old or the sick) lie in bed;be confined to bed ②bed
卧倒 drop to the ground;take a prone position
卧底 be a planted agent
卧房 bedroom
卧佛 reclining Buddha (a huge statue of a recumbent Buddha)
卧轨 lay oneself on the railway tracks
卧具 bedding (provided on a train or ship)
卧龙 sleeping dragon—a talent in obscurity
卧铺 sleeping berth;sleeper
卧射 prone fire
卧式 horizontal
卧室 bedroom
卧榻 bed
卧姿 prone position
卧铺票 sleeper ticket;berth
卧床不起 remain in bed;take to one's bed and be likely to die
卧轨自杀 kill oneself on the railway
卧薪尝胆 sleep on brushwood and taste gall—undergo self-imposed hardships

涴 [wò]
〔动〕 stain;make dirty

握 [wò]
〔动〕① take in one's hand;hold;grasp ② have;possess
握别 shake hands at parting;part
握力 the power of gripping;grip
握拳 make a fist;clench one's fist
握手 shake hands;clasp hands
握力器 spring-grip dumb-bells
握手言欢 hold hands and chat cheerfully (esp. in making up a quarrel)

幄 [wò]
〔名〕 tent

渥 ［wò］
Ⅰ 动 wet;moisten Ⅱ 形 deep;profound
渥恩 great kindness

斡 ［wò］
动 revolve;gyrate;rotate
斡旋 ①mediate ②good offices

WŪ（ㄨ）

乌 ［wū］
乌鲳 black pomfret
乌龟 ①tortoise ②cuckold
乌黑 pitch-black;jet-black
乌桕 Chinese tallow tree
乌鳢 snakehead
乌亮 glossy black;jet-black
乌梅 smoked plum;dark plum
乌木 ebony
乌头 the rhizome of Chinese monkshood
乌涂 ①（of drinking water）lukewarm;tepid ②not clear-cut
乌鸦 crow
乌药 the root of three-nerved spicebush
乌有 nothing;naught
乌鱼 snakehead
乌云 black clouds;dark clouds
乌枣 smoked jujube;black jujube
乌贼 cuttlefish;inkfish
乌饭树 oriental blueberry
乌龟壳 tortoiseshell; enemy's pillbox （or tank）
乌溜溜 （of eyes）dark and liquid
乌龙茶 oolong（tea）
乌龙球 own goal（in football）
乌纱帽 ①black gauze cap（worn by feudal officials）②official post
乌托邦 Utopia
乌油油 shiny black
乌合之众 disorderly band;motley crowd;rabble;mob
乌七八糟 ①in a horrible mess;in great disorder ②obscene;dirty;filthy
乌烟瘴气 a foul（or pestilential）atmosphere

圬 ［wū］
Ⅰ 名 trowel used by a bricklayer Ⅱ 动 plaster a wall

污 ［wū］
Ⅰ 名 dirt;muck;filth Ⅱ 形 ①dirty;filthy;foul ②corrupt;dishonest Ⅲ 动 defile;vilify;smear
污点 stain;spot;blemish;smirch
污毒 dirty and noxious
污垢 dirt;filth
污秽 filthy;foul
污迹 stain;smear;smudge
污蔑 slander;vilify;calumniate;smear
污名 bad name
污泥 mud;mire;sludge

污染 pollute;contaminate
污辱 ①humiliate;insult ②defile;sully;tarnish
污水 foul（or polluted,waste）water;sewage;slops;dirty water
污浊 （of air,water,etc.）dirty;muddy;foul;filthy
污染源 pollution source
污泥浊水 filth and mire
污七八糟 in a filthy mess
污染环境 environmental-hostile
污染控制 pollution control
污染排除 pollutant discharge
污染企业 enterprises responsible for pollution;enviromental-unfriendly（or hostile）enterprises
污染转移 pollution transportation
污水处理 sewage disposal;sewage treatment
污水工厂 sewage works
污水灌溉 sewage irrigation
污水净化 sewage purification
污染计数管 contamination counter
污染监测器 contamination monitor
污染控制物 pollutant;contaminant
污染气象学 air pollution meteorology;pollution meteorology
污水源治理 prevention and control of pollution source
污染报警系统 pollution warning system
污染集中控制 centralized pollution control
污染社会风气 debase the standards of social conduct
污染限期治理 deadline for eliminating pollution
污染指示生物 pollution indicating organism
污水处理系统 sewage disposal system
污水排放标准 sewage discharge standard
污染物排放标准 pollutant discharge（or emission）standards

巫 ［wū］
名 shaman;witch;wizard
巫婆 witch;sorceress
巫师 wizard;sorcerer
巫术 witchcraft;sorcery
巫医 witch doctor
巫山云雨 unite in sexual intercourse

呜 ［wū］
图 hoot;toot;雾中汽笛在呜呜叫。A horn hooted in the fog.
呜呼 ①alas;alack ②die
呜咽 sob;whimper
呜呼哀哉 ①alas ②dead and gone;all is lost

於 ［wū］
叹 sigh

钨 ［wū］
名 tungsten;wolfram（W）
钨钢 wolfram steel;tungsten steel
钨砂 tungsten ore

钨丝 tungsten filament
钨铁 ferrotungsten
钨合金 tungsten alloy
钨锰矿 huebnerite
钨铁矿 ferberite

湾 [wū] Ⅰ 名 low-lying land Ⅱ 动 dig a pond (*or* a pool)
湾池 low-lying pond

诬 [wū] 动 accuse falsely; slander
诬告 lodge a false accusation against; bring a false charge against; trump up a charge against
诬害 injure by spreading false reports about; calumniate; malign
诬赖 falsely incriminate
诬蔑 slander; vilify; calumniate; smear
诬陷 frame a case against; frame sb up; make a false charge against sb
诬告罪 false witness; false accusation
诬良为盗 accuse innocent people of stealing; falsely charge people with robbery

屋 [wū] 名 ①house ②room
屋顶 roof; housetop
屋脊 ridge (of a roof)
屋架 roof truss
屋面 roofing
屋檐 eaves
屋宇 house
屋子 room
屋顶花园 roof garden
屋顶平台 roof-deck
屋上架屋 build one house on top of another—needless duplication

恶 [wū] Ⅰ 代 what; how Ⅱ 叹 (*used to indicate surprise*): 恶，是何言也！ Oh! What a remark is this? ➡ ě; è; wù

wú (ㄨ)

无 [wú] Ⅰ 动 not have; be without; have nothing or nil; 从无到有 grow out of nothing; start from scratch Ⅱ 副 ①not; un-; a-; in-; 无须重申 not necessary to reiterate ②do not; most not Ⅲ 连 regardless of; irrespective of; no matter whether, what, etc.; 国无大小，一律平等。All nations, big or small, are equal. ➡ mó
无比 incomparable; unparalleled; matchless
无补 of no help; of no avail
无不 all without exception; invariably
无常 ①a demon regarded as the messenger of death ②die ③variable; changeable
无偿 free; gratis; gratuitous
无成 accomplish nothing

无耻 shameless; brazen; impudent
无从 have no way (of doing sth); not be in a position (to do sth)
无道 not follow the way; be without principles
无敌 unmatched; invincible; unconquerable
无度 immoderate; excessive
无端 for no reason
无法 unable; incapable
无方 not in the proper way; in the wrong way; not knowing way
无妨 there's no harm; may (*or* might) as well
无非 nothing but; no more than; simply; only
无风 calm
无干 have nothing to do with
无辜 ① not guilty; innocent ② an innocent person
无故 without cause or reason
无关 have nothing to do with
无规 random
无害 harmless
无何 ①soon; before long ②nothing else
无核 nuclear-free; nonnuclear
无后 without male offspring; without issue
无华 simple and unadorned
无机 inorganic
无稽 unfounded; fantastic; absurd
无及 it's too late (to do sth); there's not enough time (to do sth)
无级 stepless
无几 very few; very little; hardly any
无际 boundless; limitless; vast
无间 ①not keeping anything from each other; very close to each other ② continuously; without interruption
无疆 boundless; limitless
无菌 asepsis
无愧 feel no qualms; have a clear conscience
无赖 ①rascally; scoundrelly; blackguardly ② rascal
无理 unreasonable; unjustifiable
无力 ①lack strength; feel weak ②unable; incapable; powerless
无量 measureless; immeasurable; boundless
无聊 ①bored; in extreme depression ②senseless; uninteresting
无虑 worry about nothing; be free from care
无论 no matter what, how, etc.; regardless of
无名 ①nameless; unknown ②indefinable; indescribable
无奈 ①cannot help but; have no alternative; have no choice ②but; however
无能 incompetent; incapable
无前 ① unmatched; invincible; unconquerable ②unprecedented
无情 merciless; ruthless; heartless
无穷 infinite; endless; boundless; inexhaustible
无权 have no right

无缺　intact;whole
无人　①unmanned ②depopulated ③self-serv-ice
无任　extremely;immensely
无日　①all the time;not a single day ②soon;before long
无上　supreme;paramount;highest
无声　noiseless;silent
无视　ignore;disregard;defy
无数　①innumerable;countless ②not know for certain;be uncertain
无双　unparalleled;unrivalled;matchless
无水　anhydrous
无私　selfless;disinterested;unselfish
无损　① cannot harm; be harmless; will not lessen ②intact;whole;in good condition
无题　no title
无望　hopeless
无为　("do nothing") inaction
无味　① tasteless;unpalatable ②dull;insipid;uninteresting
无畏　fearless;dauntless
无谓　meaningless;pointless;senseless
无物　empty;devoid of substance
无误　no mistake;errorless
无息　interest-free
无瑕　flawless
无暇　have no time;be too busy
无限　infinite;limitless;boundless;immeasurable
无线　wireless
无效　of (or to) no avail;invalid;null and void
无心　①not be in the mood for ②not intentionally;unwittingly;inadvertently
无行　be a man of loose conduct
无形　invisible;intangible
无性　asexual
无需　need not
无涯　boundless;limitless
无恙　in good health;well;safe
无业　①be out of work;be unemployed ②have no property
无遗　nothing left
无疑　beyond doubt;undoubtedly
无已　①endlessly;incessantly ②have no alternative but to;have to
无异　not different from; tantamount to; as good as
无益　unprofitable;useless;no good
无意　①have no intention (of doing sth);not be inclined to ②inadvertently;unwittingly;accidentally
无垠　boundless;vast
无用　useless;of no use
无由　not be in a position (to do sth);have no way (of doing sth)
无余　nothing left

无援　have no support;be cut off from help
无缘　①have not the chance (or luck) (to do sth) ②have no way (of doing sth);not be in a position (to do sth)
无源　passive
无照　without a licence
无知　ignorant
无着　①nowhere ②unassured
无阻　without hindrance;unimpeded
无罪　innocent;not guilty
无柄叶　sessile leaf
无产者　proletarian
无党派　without party affiliation;nonparty
无底洞　bottomless pit
无风带　calm belt;calm zone
无公害　environmentally harmless; socially harmless
无国籍　absent nationality;stateless
无核化　denuclearize
无核区　nuclear-free zone;non-nuclear zone
无花果　fig
无机酸　inorganic acid
无机盐　inorganic salts
无机物　inorganic substance;inorganic matter
无记名　①secret ②bearer
无厘头　wulitou culture
无理式　irrational expression
无理数　irrational number
无名火　unaccountable anger
无名氏　an anonymous person
无名帖　poison-pen letter
无名指　the third finger;ring finger
无明火　flames of anger
无奈何　can do nothing about it
无穷大　infinitely great;infinity
无穷小　infinitely small;infinitesimal
无人区　depopulated zone;no man's land
无神论　atheism
无生代　the Azoic Era
无生物　inanimate object;nonliving matter
无声片　silent film
无事忙　busy oneself over nothing;make much ado about nothing
无霜期　frost-free period
无所谓　① cannot be called; not deserve the name of ②be indifferent;not matter
无条件　unconditional;without preconditions
无限大　infinitely great;infinity
无限期　indefinite duration
无限小　infinitely small;infinitesimal
无限制　unrestricted;unbridled;unlimited
无线电　radio;wireless
无形中　imperceptibly;virtually
无休止　ceaseless;endless
无须(乎)　need not;not have to
无怪(乎)　no wonder;not to be wondered at
无烟煤　anthracite

无烟区 a smokeless zone
无意识 unconscious
无翼鸟 kiwi
无影灯 shadowless lamp
无用能 unavailable energy
无原则 unprincipled
无韵诗 blank verse
无止境 have no limits;know no end
无重力 space agravic
无边无际 boundless;limitless;vast
无病而死 die without illness
无病呻吟 ①moan and groan without being ill; make a fuss about an imaginary illness ② adopt a sentimental pose (in writing or speech)
无补于事 of no avail
无产阶级 the proletariat
无偿献血 non-remunerated blood donation
无偿援助 aid without repayment;aid given gratis
无耻之徒 a person who has lost all sense of shame;a shameless person
无耻之尤 brazen in the extreme;the height of shamelessness
无酬劳动 unpaid labour
无出其右 second to none;matchless;unequalled
无处藏身 have nowhere to hide oneself
无处容身 have no place of refuge;have nowhere to rest
无地自容 can find no place to hide oneself for shame;feel too ashamed to show one's face;look for a hole to crawl into
无的放矢 shoot an arrow without a target; shoot at random
无冬无夏 throughout the year;all the year round
无动于衷 aloof and indifferent;unmoved;untouched;unconcerned
无独有偶 It is not unique,but has its counterpart.
无恶不作 stop at nothing in doing evil;stop at no evil;commit all manner of crimes
无法无天 defy laws human and divine;become absolutely lawless;run wild
无纺织物 adhesive-bonded fabric
无缝钢管 seamless steel tube (or pipe)
无氟冰箱 Freon-free refrigerator
无福消受 not have the luck to enjoy;be unable to take advantage of
无功受禄 get a reward without deserving it
无关大局 not affecting (or having no bearing on) the general situation;insignificant;of little account
无关宏旨 insignificant;minor;immaterial
无关紧要 of no importance;immaterial
无关痛痒 of no consequence;immaterial

无轨电车 trackless trolley;trolleybus
无害通过 innocent passage;inoffensive passage
无话不谈 keep no secrets from each other;be in each other's confidence
无机化肥 inorganic fertilizer;mineral fertilizer
无机化学 inorganic chemistry
无稽之谈 an unfounded statement;fantastic talk;sheer nonsense
无疾而终 (of an old person) pass peacefully away
无计可施 have exhausted one's whole bag of tricks;at one's wits' end;at the end of one's resources
无济于事 not help matters;of no help;of no avail;to no effect
无家可归 wander about with no home to go to;be homeless
无价之宝 a priceless treasure;an invaluable asset
无坚不摧 overrun all fortifications;carry all before one;be all-conquering
无精打采 listless;in low spirits;out of sorts; lackadaisical
无拘无束 unrestrained;unconstrained;free and easy
无菌包装 aseptic packaging
无菌装罐 aseptic canning process
无可比拟 incomparable;unparalleled;matchless;beyond compare
无可辩驳 irrefutable;indisputable;beyond all dispute
无可非议 irreproachable;blameless;beyond (or above) reproach;above criticism
无可奉告 no-comment;I take the fifth
无可厚非 not be altogether unjustifiable;give little cause for criticism
无可讳言 There is no hiding (or denying) the fact.
无可救药 incurable;beyond cure;incorrigible
无可名状 unable to describe;indescribable
无可奈何 have no way out;be utterly helpless;have no alternative
无可挽回 irretrievable;irredeemable;irrevocable
无可争辩 indisputable;irrefutable
无可置疑 indubitable;unquestionable
无孔不入 get in by every opening;seize every opportunity
无理方程 irrational equation;radical equation
无理取闹 wilfully make trouble;be deliberately provocative
无理指责 unwarranted accusation;groundless charges
无脸见人 have no face to show to any man; feel too ashamed to face people

无论如何　in any case；at any rate；whatever happens；at all events

无米之炊　cook a meal without rice；make bricks without straw

无冕之王　crownless king—reporter

无名高地　an unnamed hill

无名鼠辈　be a pack of worthless rats

无名小卒　nobody；nonentity

无名英雄　①unknown hero；unsung hero ②unknown soldier

无名肿毒　nameless sore（*or* boil）

无能为力　powerless；helpless；incapable of action

无期徒刑　life imprisonment

无奇不有　There is no lack of strange things.

无牵无挂　have no cares；be free from care

无铅汽油　clear gasoline；unleaded gasoline；unleaded petrol

无巧不巧　by coincidence；as it happens；as luck would have it

无穷无尽　inexhaustible；endless

无权追索　without recourse

无人地带　no man's land

无人问津　nobody troubles to ask；nobody is interested

无伤大雅　not matter much；not affect things as a whole

无声电影　silent film

无声手枪　pistol with silencer

无声无息　unknown；obscure

无绳电话　cordless（phone）；cordless telephone

无师自通　learn sth without a teacher；be self-taught

无时无刻　all the time；incessantly

无事生非　make trouble out of nothing；be deliberately provocative

无事自扰　make a fuss about nothing；worry oneself over nothing

无税货物　non-dutiable goods

无丝分裂　amitosis

无所不包　all-embracing；all-inclusive；all-encompassing

无所不能　①omnipotent ②versatile

无所不为　do all manner of evil；stop at nothing

无所不在　omnipresent；ubiquitous

无所不知　omniscient

无所不至　①penetrate everywhere ②spare no pains（usu. to do evil）；be capable of anything；stop at nothing

无所事事　be occupied with nothing；have nothing to do；idle away one's time

无所适从　not know what to do；not know whom to turn to

无所畏惧　fearless；dauntless；undaunted

无所用心　not give serious thought to anything

无所作为　attempt nothing and accomplish nothing；be in a state of inertia

无头公案　an intricate case without a clue；an unsolved mystery

无土栽培　soiless cultivation；tank farming

无往不利　go smoothly everywhere；be ever successful

无往不胜　ever-victorious；invincible

无妄之灾　an unexpected calamity；an undeserved ill turn

无微不至　meticulously；in every possible way

无为而治　govern by doing nothing that is against nature；govern by non-interference

无尾礼服　dinner jacket；tuxedo

无息贷款　interest-free loan

无隙可乘　no crack to get in by；no loophole to exploit；no weakness to take advantage of；no chink in one's armour

无限公司　unlimited company

无限花序　indefinite inflorescence

无线电报　wireless telegram；radiotelegram

无线电话　radiotelephone；radiophone

无线寻呼　radio paging

无效分蘖　ineffective tillering

无效合同　void contract

无效婚姻　invalid marriage

无效劳动　fruitless labour；labour lost

无懈可击　with no chink in one's armour；unassailable；invulnerable

无形财产　incorporeal assets；invisible assets；intangible assets；immaterial assets；incorporeal assets；non-physical assets

无形贸易　invisible trade

无形资本　incorporeal capital

无性繁殖　vegetative propagation；cloning

无性生殖　asexual reproduction

无性世代　asexual generation

无性杂交　asexual（*or* vegetative）hybridization

无烟工业　smokeless industry

无烟火药　smokeless powder；ballistite

无言以对　have nothing to say in reply

无氧运动　anaerobic exercise

无业游民　vagrant

无依无靠　have no one to depend on（*or* to turn to）；be helpless

无以复加　in the extreme

无以为生　have no means of livelihood；have no means of support

无影无踪　without a trace

无忧无虑　free from care；free from all anxieties；carefree

无与伦比　incomparable；unparalleled；peerless；unique；without equal

无缘无故　without cause（*or* reason）；without rhyme（*or* reason）；for no reason at all

无纸贸易　electronic data interchange（EDI）

无中生有　make（*or* create）sth out of nothing

无足轻重　of little importance（*or* conse-

quence)；insignificant；negligible
无罪推定 presumption of innocence
无伴奏合唱 a cappella
无被害人罪 crime without victims
无被选举权 ineligible
无偿付能力 bankruptcy
无偿还义务 without recourse
无偿债能力 insolvency
无党派人士 nonpartisan；personages without party affiliation
无敌于天下 unmatched anywhere in the world；invincible
无毒不丈夫 Every real man has his venom；All great men are ruthless.
无风不起浪 There are no waves without wind；There's no smoke without fire.
无公害蔬菜 "green" vegetable
无官一身轻 Happy is the man who is relieved of his official duties.
无过错责任 liability without fault
无核武器区 nuclear-weapon-free zone
无后顾之忧 without fear of an attack from the rear；have no worries about the rear
无机化合物 inorganic compound
无脊椎动物 invertebrate
无记名股票 bearer shares；stock to bearer
无记名投票 secret ballot；unsigned vote
无记名债券 bearer bond；unregistered bond
无记名支票 bearer check；bearer cheque
无菌操作法 aseptic manipulation
无可无不可 not care one way or the other
无巧不成书 without coincidences there would be no stories
无人售票车 pay-to-driver bus；self-service bus
无熟料水泥 clinker-free cement
无添加剂的 E-free
无条件反射 unconditional reflex
无条件服从 complete obedience
无条件接受 unconditional acceptance
无条件谈判 hold negotiations without preconditions
无条件投降 unconditional surrender
无条件转让 absolute conveyance
无线电导航 radio navigation
无线电干扰 radio jamming
无线电跟踪 radio tracking
无线电通信 radio communication；wireless communication
无线电遥测 radio telemetry
无线电遥控 wireless remote control
无线电装置 radio device；wireless device
无线因特网 wireless internet
无行为能力 incompetence；legal to go by
无原则纠纷 unprincipled dispute
无增长经济 nil-growth economy
无障碍设计 barrier-free design
无政府主义 anarchism

无政府状态 state of anarchy
无纸办公室 paperless office
无保护的工业 unsheltered industry
无产阶级专政 dictatorship of the proletariat；proletarian dictatorship
无核武器国家 nonnuclear country
无后(坐)力炮 recoilless gun
无所不用其极 resort to every conceivable means；stop at nothing；go to any extreme；go to any length(s)
无线电测向器 radio direction finder；radio goniometer
无线电发射机 radio transmitter
无线电收音机 radio receiver
无线电探空仪 radiosonde
无线电天文学 radio astronomy
无线电转播台 radio relaying station
无线应用协议 wireless application protocol (WAP)
无人驾驶飞行器 unmanned vehicle
无事不登三宝殿 One never goes to the temple for no reason；I wouldn't come to you if I hadn't sth to ask of you.
无颜见江东父老 cannot bear to see again the elders east of the river—be ashamed to go back to one's people after a defeat or failure
无线电收发两用机 transceiver
无源之水,无本之木 water without a source, a tree without roots

毋 [wú]
副 no；not
毋宁 rather…(than)；(no so much…) as
毋庸 need not
毋庸讳言 no need for reticence
毋庸赘述 There is no need to go into details；It is pointless to belabour the obvious.

芜 [wú]
I 形 ① overgrown with weeds ② mixed and disorderly；superfluous；useless II 名 land overgrown with weeds
芜词 superfluous words
芜菁 turnip
芜杂 (of writing) mixed and disorderly；jumbled

吾 [wú]
代 I；we
吾辈 we；us
吾人 we；us
吾友 my friend

唔 [wú]
◇咿唔 the sound of reading aloud

梧 [wú]
名 Chinese parasol
梧桐 Chinese parasol (tree)；phoenix tree

Wǔ(ㄨˇ)

五 [wǔ]
（数） five

五爱 five loves—love for the motherland, for the people, for physical labour, for science, and for socialism

五彩 ① the five colours (blue, yellow, red, white and black) ②multicoloured

五毒 ① the five poisonous creatures (scorpion, viper, centipede, house lizard and toad) ②the "five evils"

五方 the five directions (i. e. the four cardinal points and the centre)

五更 ①the five watches (or periods) of the night ② the fifth watch of the night; just before dawn

五谷 ① the five cereals (rice, two kinds of millet, wheat and beans) ②food crops

五官 ①the five sense organs (ears, eyes, lips, nose and tongue) ②facial features

五加 slender acanthopanax

五金 ①the five metals ②metals; hardware

五经 *the Five Classics*

五伦 the five human relationships

五内 viscera

五色 ① the five colours (blue, yellow, red, white and black) ②multicoloured

五味 ①the five flavours (sweet, sour, bitter, pungent and salty) ②all sorts of flavours

五香 ①the five spices ②spices

五行 the five elements

五音 the five notes of the ancient Chinese five-tone scale

五月 ① May ② the fifth month of the lunar year; the fifth moon

五脏 the five internal organs

五指 the five fingers

五洲 the five continents; the whole world

五保户 a household enjoying the five guarantees

五倍子 Chinese gall; gallnut

五边形 pentagon

五重唱 (vocal) quintet

五重奏 (instrumental) quintet

五大生 students (or graduates) from five types of universities

五斗柜 chest of drawers

五分制 the five-grade marking system

五合板 five-ply board; plywood

五花肉 streaky pork

五环旗 the five-ring flag

五级风 force 5 wind; fresh breeze

五极管 pentode

五加皮 ①bark of the slender acanthopanax ② a medicinal wine made by soaking the bark of the slender acanthopanax in liquor

五角星 five-pointed star

五里雾 thick fog—bewilderment

五敛子 carambola

五味子 the fruit of Chinese magnoliavine

五线谱 staff; stave

五香豆 spiced beans

五星级 five-star

五言诗 a poem with five characters to a line

五月节 the Dragon Boat Festival

五子棋 gobang

五倍子虫 gall makers

五笔字型 one way for entering Chinese characters by numbered strokes

五彩缤纷 colourful, blazing with colour

五大三粗 big and tall; tall and stalwart; strapping

五短身材 (of a man) squat

五方杂处 (of a big city) be inhabited by people from all parts; have a mixed (or cosmopolitan) population

五谷丰登 an abundant harvest of all food crops; a bumper grain harvest

五官端正 have regular features

五光十色 ① multicoloured; bright with many colours ②of great variety; of all kinds; multifarious

五好家庭 five virtue family; "five good" family

五湖四海 all corners of the land

五花八门 multifarious; of a wide (or rich) variety

五花大绑 tie a person's hands behind his back with a rope that is looped round his neck

五讲四美 Five Stresses and Four Points of Beauty

五角大楼 the Pentagon

五劳七伤 general debility

五雷轰顶 be struck by lightning; be struck by thunderbolts

五马分尸 dismemberment by five horses—dividing up; sharing out

五内如焚 one's heart rent with grief; one's heart torn by anxiety

五年计划 Five-Year Plan

五日京兆 (of an official) not expecting to remain long in office; holding office only for a brief period

五卅运动 the May 30th Movement

五色斑斓 a riot of colour

五声音阶 five-tone scale; pentatonic scale

五四运动 The May 4th Movement of 1919

五体投地 prostrate oneself before sb

五星红旗 the Five-Starred Red Flag (the national flag of the People's Republic of China)

五星上将 five-star general

五言绝句 pentasyllabic quatrain
五言律诗 pentasyllabic (*or* five-syllable) regulated verse
五颜六色 of various (*or* all) colours; multicoloured; colourful
五脏六腑 the internal organs of the body; the viscera
五个一工程 Five-One Program (*or* Project) (one good book, one good play, one good film, one good TV drama, and one or several creative and persuasive or convincing articles)
五局三胜制 best of give games; three out of five sets
五氯硝基苯 pentachloronitrobenzene; PCNB
五四青年节 Youth Day (May 4)
五天工作制 five-day workweek
五星级宾馆 five-star(hotel)
五十步笑百步 one who retreats fifty paces mocks one who retreats a hundred—the pot calls the kettle black
五项全能运动 sports pentathlon
五一国际劳动节 May 1, International Labour Day; May Day

午 ［wǔ］
［名］noon; midday
午安 good afternoon
午餐 midday meal; lunch
午饭 midday meal; lunch
午后 afternoon
午间 noon; midday
午觉 afternoon nap; noontime snooze
午前 forenoon; before noon; morning
午时 the period of the day from 11 a.m. to 1 p.m.
午睡 ① afternoon nap; noontime snooze ② take (*or* have) a nap after lunch
午休 noon break; midday rest; noontime rest; lunch hour
午宴 luncheon
午夜 midnight
午餐肉 (pork) luncheon meat

伍 ［wǔ］
Ⅰ［名］① basic five-man unit of the army in ancient China; army ②company Ⅱ［数］five

仵 ［wǔ］
［名］coroner

连 ［wǔ］
［动］①encounter ②be disobedient; be defiant

庑 ［wǔ］
［名］side room or building in a traditional compound house; wing

怃 ［wǔ］
［名］①tender affection ②frustration; disappointment

忤 ［wǔ］
［形］①disobedient; unfilial ②on bad terms; uncongenial

忤逆 disobedient (to parents)

妩 ［wǔ］
妩媚 (of a woman) lovely; charming

武 ［wǔ］
武备 defence preparations, specifically the condition of the armed forces and armaments
武场 percussion instruments in Chinese operas
武丑 (in traditional opera) a comedian in military plays
武打 acrobatic fighting in Chinese opera or dance
武旦 female character type versed in shadowboxing, swordplay, etc. in Chinese operas
武斗 resort to violence (in a debate, dispute, etc.)
武断 arbitrary; subjective assertion
武夫 ①a man of great physical prowess ②soldier; military man
武功 military accomplishments (*or* achievements)
武官 ①military officer ②military attaché
武行 (in traditional opera) specialists in acrobatics (actors who take minor parts in military combats)
武火 high heat (in cooking)
武将 military officer; general
武警 armed police
武力 ①force ②military force; armed might; armed strength; force of arms
武林 martial arts circles
武器 weapon; arms
武生 actor playing a martial role in Chinese operas
武师 a man versed in martial arts; martial arts master
武士 ①palace guards in ancient times ②man of prowess; warrior; knight
武术 *wushu*
武戏 (in traditional opera) military plays
武侠 a person adept in martial arts and given to chivalrous conduct (in olden times)
武艺 skill in *wushu*
武职 military post
武装 ①arms; military equipment; battle outfit ②armed forces ③equip (*or* supply) with arms; arm
武昌鱼 blunt-snout bream
武打片 martial arts film; Kung-fu film
武官处 military attaché's office
武器库 arsenal; armoury
武士俑 warrior figure
武装带 Sam Browne belt
武器禁运 embargo on arms shipment
武器装备 weaponry

武士债券 samurai bond
武侠小说 martial arts fiction; martial novels; swordsman fiction; knight-errant fiction
武装部队 armed forces
武装冲突 armed clash
武装斗争 armed struggle
武装对峙 military confrontation
武装干涉 armed interference; armed interventions
武装警察 armed police
武装力量 armed power; armed forces
武装起义 armed uprising (*or* insurrection)
武装泅渡 swim with one's weapons; swim in battle gear
武装挑衅 armed provocation
武装巡逻 armed patrol
武装到牙齿 be armed to teeth
武装直升机 gunship; helicopter gunship
武装夺取政权 seizure of power by armed force
武装警察部队 armed police forces

侮 [wǔ]
〔动〕 insult; humiliate; bully
侮骂 abuse; call sb names; hurl insults
侮慢 slight; treat disrespectfully
侮蔑 despise; look down on
侮辱 insult; humiliate; subject sb to indignities

捂 [wǔ]
〔动〕 cover; seal; hide; muffle
捂盖子 keep the lid on—try to cover up the truth (about a crime, etc.)

牾 [wǔ]
〔动〕 contradict; go against; run counter to
牾意 go against sb's wish

鹉 [wǔ]
◇鹦鹉 parrot

舞 [wǔ]
I 〔名〕 dance II 〔动〕 ①move about as if in a dance; dance ②dance with sth in one's hands ③flourish; wave; brandish; wield ④play with ⑤get
舞伴 dancing partner
舞弊 fraudulent practices; malpractices; irregularities; embezzlement
舞步 step (in dancing)
舞场 dance hall; ballroom
舞池 dancing floor
舞蹈 dance
舞动 wave; brandish
舞会 dance; ball
舞姬 dancing girl
舞技 dancing skill
舞剑 perform; a sword-dance; (perform) swordplay
舞剧 dance drama; ballet
舞客 dance hall customer
舞迷 habitual dancer
舞弄 wave; wield; brandish

舞女 dancing girl; dance-hostess; taxi dancer
舞曲 dance music; dance
舞台 stage; arena
舞厅 dance hall; ballroom
舞艺 dancing skill
舞姿 a dancer's posture and movements
舞蹈病 chorea
舞龙灯 (perform) the dragon lantern dance
舞狮子 (perform) the lion dance
舞台艺术 stagecraft
舞文弄法 pervert the law by playing with legal phraseology
舞文弄墨 engage in phrase-mongering; show off one's literary skill; juggle with words
舞榭歌台 entertainment setups
舞台纪录片 stage documentary

wù (ㄨˋ)

兀 [wù]
〔形〕 ①rising to a height; lofty; towering ②(of a hill) barren; bald
兀鹫 griffon vulture
兀立 stand upright
兀鹰 buzzard
兀自 still
兀然不动 immovable and steadfast; very determined

勿 [wù]
〔副〕 no; not
勿忘草 forget-me-not (Myosotis sylvatica)
勿谓言之不预 Do not say that you have not been forewarned; Do not blame us for not having forewarned you
勿以善小而不为, 勿以恶小而为之 Don't fail to do good even if it's small; Don't engage in evil even if it's small

务 [wù]
I 〔名〕 ①task; affair; business ②outpost of a tax office II 〔动〕 apply oneself to; be engaged in; go in for III 〔副〕 must; be sure to
务必 must; be sure to
务农 be engaged in agriculture; be a farmer
务求 must; be sure to
务商 go in for commerce; go into business
务实 deal with concrete matters relating to work; be pragmatic
务使 make sure; ensure
务虚 discuss principles (*or* ideological guidelines) alone
"务实外交" "pragmatic diplomacy"
务实作风 practical style of work
务实的政府 a pragmatically-inclined government
务实的政治家 a pragmatic politician

屼 [wù]
〔形〕 (of a hill etc.) barren; bald

坞 ［wù］
名 ① depressed place; hollow ② structure tall on all sides that keep out the wind ③ small castle; fort

芴 ［wù］
名 fluorene

杌 ［wù］
名 (usu. small) stool
杌子 a square stool

物 ［wù］
名 ① thing; creature; matter; material ② outside world as distinct from oneself; people other than oneself; other people ③ content; essence; substance
物产 product; produce
物故 pass away; die
物化 pass away; die
物价 special offer; special price
物件 thing; article
物镜 objective (lens)
物理 ① innate laws of things ② physics
物力 material resources; materiel
物流 material circulation
物品 article; goods
物权 real right
物色 look for; seek out; choose
物体 body; substance; object
物象 ① image ② visible phenomena
物业 property
物语 story
物欲 material desires
物证 material evidence
物质 ① matter; substance ② material
物种 species
物主 owner
物资 goods and materials
物候学 phenology
物理学 physics
物品袋 carrier bag
物质性 materiality
物腐虫生 worms breed in decaying matter
物归原主 return sth to its rightful owner
物换星移 things change and the stars move—change of the seasons
物极必反 things turn into their opposites when they reach the extreme
物价波动 price fluctuation
物价补贴 subsidies paid out to compensate for price rises
物价冻结 price freeze
物价飞涨 steep increase in prices; skyrocketing prices; soaring prices; rocketing prices
物价趋涨 prices tend upwards
物价上涨 inflation of price; price rise
物价失控 runaway prices; prices out of control
物价统计 statistic of prices
物价稳定 stable price
物价政策 pricing policy

物价指数 price index
物尽其用 make the best use of everything; let all things serve their proper purpose
物竞天择 survival of the fittest in natural selection
物理变化 physical change
物理化学 physical chemistry
物理疗法 physical therapy; physiotherapy
物理性质 physical property
物理学家 physicist
物理诊断 physical diagnosis
物美价廉 (of a commodity) cheap but good; inexpensive but elegant
物色人才 headhunt qualified personnel
物伤其类 like feels for like
物业公司 property company; real estate company
物业管理 property management; estate management
物质报酬 material reward
物质刺激 material incentive
物质鼓励 material reward; material incentive
物质基础 material base
物质名词 material noun
物质生活 material life
物质世界 the material (or physical) world
物质文明 material civilization
物质运动 the motion of matter
物质资源 material resources; physical resources
物资流通 materials circulation
物资调剂 regulation and coordination of materials
物价大检查 price inspection
物以稀为贵 When a thing is scarce, it is precious.
物价上涨幅度 increase rate of commodity price
物价上涨指数 index of price rises
物质不灭定律 the law of conservation of matter
物以类聚，人以群分 Things of a kind come together, people of a mind fall into the same group; Like attracts like; Birds of a feather flock together.

误 ［wù］
I 动 ① miss; delay ② harm; damage II 副 by mistake; accidentally III 名 mistake; error
误差 error
误场 (of an actor) fail to turn up for the show
误传 false information
误导 mislead; lead astray
误点 late; overdue; behind schedule
误工 ① delay one's work ② loss of working time
误国 endanger the realm
误会 ① misunderstand; mistake; misconstrue

②misunderstanding
误解 ① misread；misunderstand ② misunder-
　standing
误期 exceed the time limit；be behind schedule
误区 misunderstandings；the wrong region
误杀 manslaughter
误伤 ①accidentally injure ②accidental injury
误事 ① cause delay（in work or business）；
　hold things up ②bungle matters
误信 be wrongly believed；be misled
误诊 make a wrong diagnosis
误差率 error rate
误工费 compensation for one's absence from
　work
误差函数 error function
误触忌讳 break a taboo by mistake
误导宣传 mislead publicity
误人不浅 do no little harm to other people
误人子弟 （of a teacher） harm the younger
　generation；lead young people astray
误入歧途 go astray

恶 ［wù］
Ⅰ 劢 dislike；loathe；detest；hate　Ⅱ 名
aversion ➡ě；è；wū
恶风 aversion to wind
恶寒 aversion to cold
恶食 aversion to food

悟 ［wù］
劢 realize；become aware；awaken
悟道 awake to the truth；attain enlightenment
悟解 understand；comprehend；grasp
悟性 power of understanding；comprehension

晤 ［wù］
劢 meet；encounter；interview；see
晤面 meet；see

晤谈 meet and talk；have a talk；interview

焐 ［wù］
劢 warm up

靰 ［wù］
靰鞡 leather boots lined with wula sedge
靰鞡草 wula sedge

鹜 ［wù］
劢 ①move about freely and quickly ② go
after；seek for；pursue

雾 ［wù］
名 ①fog；mist ②fine spray
雾霭 fog；mist；vapour
雾标 fog buoy
雾滴 droplet
雾虹 fogbow
雾化 atomize
雾气 fog；mist；vapour
雾凇 （soft） rime
雾天 greasy weather
雾沉沉 misty；foggy
雾化器 atomizer
雾茫茫 misty；foggy
雾腾腾 misty；foggy
雾里看花 look at flowers in a fog—a blurred
　vision

寤 ［wù］
劢 wake up

鹜 ［wù］
名 duck

鋈 ［wù］
Ⅰ 名 copper-nickel alloy；white copper　Ⅱ
形 plating；gilding
鋈器 gilded ware；gold-plated utensil

W

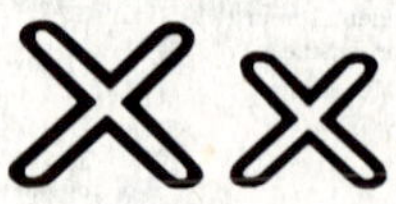

夕 [xī]
〔名〕①sunset；dusk ②evening；night
夕晖 evening twilight
夕烟 evening mist
夕阳 the evening sun；the setting sun
夕照 the glow of the setting sun；evening glow
夕阳产业 sunset industry；declining industry
夕阳职业 sunset job

兮 [xī]
〔助〕：风萧萧兮易水寒。 The wind soughs and sighs while the water in the Yi River chills.

西 [xī]
〔名〕①west ②the Occident；the West
西北 ① northwest ② northwest China；the Northwest
西边 west
西部 west
西菜 Western-style food；foreign food
西餐 Western-style (or European) food
西点 Western-style pastry
西法 Western method
西方 ①the west ②the West；the Occident
西非 West Africa
西风 ① west wind；westerly wind ② autumn wind ③decaying influences
西服 Western-style clothes；suit
西宫 ①the palace for concubines of the king (or emperor) ②imperial concubine；concubines of the king (or emperor)
西瓜 watermelon
西湖 the West Lake
西化 be westernized
西经 west longitude
西历 the Gregorian calendar
西米 sago
西面 west
西南 ① southwest ② southwest China；the Southwest
西欧 Western Europe

西皮 one of the two chief types of music in traditional Chinese operas
西晒 (of a room) have a western exposure (hot on summer afternoons)
西施 ① the name of a famous beauty in the late Spring and Autumn Period ②beautiful woman；beauty
西式 Western style
西天 ①Western Heaven ②Western Paradise
西学 Western learning
西洋 the West；the Western world
西药 Western medicine
西医 ① Western medicine (as distinguished from traditional Chinese medicine) ②doctor trained in Western medicine
西语 ① Western languages ② Spanish (language)
西乐 Western music
西岳 the Western Mountain
西藏 Tibet
西装 Western-style clothes；suit
西半球 the Western Hemisphere
西北风 northwest wind；northwesterly wind
西部片 bang-bang；western film；cowboy movie
西餐馆 a restaurant which serves Western food
西番莲 ①passionflower ②dahlia
西服料 suiting
西瓜子 watermelon seed
西红柿 tomato
西葫芦 pumpkin；summer squash
西南风 southwest wind；southwesterly wind
西南亚 Southwest Asia
西洋参 American ginseng
西洋画 Western painting
西洋景 peep show
西洋镜 hanky-panky；trickery
西洋人 Westerner
西洋史 history of the Western world (or Western countries)
西伯利亚 Siberia

西电东送 transmission of electricity from the western to the eastern region
西府海棠 midget crabapple
西气东输 transport the natural gas from the West to the East
西部大开发 West Development; Western Region Development
西藏自治区 the Tibet Autonomous Region
西方七国首脑会议 summit meeting of the seven industrial nations

吸 [xī] 劢 ① inhale; breathe in; draw ② absorb; suck up ③ attract; draw to oneself
吸虫 fluke
吸储 attract savings
吸毒 ① drug taking; drug abuse; dope-taking ② take addictive drugs; be addicted to a narcotic
吸附 adsorb
吸管 straw
吸力 suction; attraction
吸纳 absorb; draw; attract
吸盘 sucking disc (of certain animals); sucker
吸取 absorb; draw; assimilate
吸热 absorption of heat
吸声 sound-absorbing; acoustic
吸湿 moisture-absorbing
吸食 suck; take in (liquid foods; narcotic drugs, etc.)
吸收 ① absorb; suck up; assimilate; imbibe; draw ② recruit; enrol; admit
吸吮 suck; absorb
吸烟 smoke
吸引 attract; draw; fascinate
吸滞 (of plants) absorb and retain
吸嘴 suction nozzle
吸尘器 dust catcher; dust collector
吸毒犯 drug addict
吸毒窝 drug den; drug haven; acid house
吸毒者 drug user; drug abuser; drug addict; dope addict; drug-dependent; drugster; druggie
吸附剂 adsorbent
吸附器 absorber
吸附水 adsorbed water
吸力计 suction gauge
吸墨纸 blotting paper
吸奶器 breast pump
吸泥泵 dredge pump
吸气泵 aspirator pump
吸湿剂 hygroscopic agent; moisture absorbent
吸湿性 hygroscopicity; moisture absorbency
吸收剂 absorbent
吸收率 absorptivity
吸收塔 absorption tower
吸铁石 magnet; lodestone
吸血鬼 bloodsucker; vampire

吸烟室 smoking room
吸音板 acoustic board
吸音器 aspirator
吸毒贩毒 drug abuse and trafficking
吸风饮露 inhale wind and drink dew——(of Taoist priest, etc.) abstain from food
吸热反应 endothermic reaction
吸收光谱 absorption spectrum
吸收作用 absorption

汐 [xī] 名 tide during the night; night tide

希 [xī] 劢 hope
希冀 hope for; wish for; aspire after
希求 ① hope for; wish for ② what one hopes or wishes for
希图 harbour the intention of; intend to; attempt to
希望 ① hope; wish; expect ② hope; wish; expectation ③ a person or thing on which hope is placed
希腊字母 the Greek alphabet
希望工程 Project Hope; Hope Project

昔 [xī] 名 the past; former times
昔酒 old wine; mellow wine
昔年 (in) former years
昔日 (in) former days (or times)
昔时 (in) former days (or times)

析 [xī] 劢 ① divide; separate; resolve ② analyse; dissect
析产 divide property
析出 ① find (results) on analysis ② separate out
析疑 resolve a doubt; clear up a doubtful point
析义 analyse the meaning (of a word, etc.)
析箸 break up the household; split up the family
析像管 image dissector

唏 [xī] I 劢 sigh II 叹 (*used to show surprise*): 唏! 你这出的什么洋相! Hey! What a fool you are making of yourself!

牺 [xī] 名 beast of pure colour used for sacrifice; sacrifice
牺牲 ① a beast slaughtered for sacrifice; sacrifice ② sacrifice oneself; die a martyr's death; lay down one's life ③ sacrifice; give up; do sth at the expense of
牺牲品 victim; prey
牺牲个人利益 sacrifice one's personal interests

息 [xī] I 名 ① breath ② news ③ rest; break ④ interest ⑤ one's children II 劢 ① cease; stop; end ② grow; breed; multiply

X

息兵　cease fire
息鼓　①stop beating the drum ②(of sports competition) end
息怒　cease to be angry;calm one's anger
息票　interest coupon
息钱　interest (money)
息肉　polyp;polypus
息影　retire into private life;quit the screen
息战　cease fire;stop fighting
息交绝游　shut oneself in and cut oneself off from social life
息事宁人　①patch up a quarrel ②give way to avoid trouble;gloss things over to stay on good terms
息息相关　be closely linked;be closely bound up
息息相通　one's heart beats as one with sb's

奚 [xī] 代 interrogative word meaning why, how, where, what, etc.
奚落　scoff at;taunt;gibe at

悉 [xī] Ⅰ 形 all;entirely Ⅱ 动 know;understand; learn;be informed
悉力　go all out;spare no effort
悉数　all;every single one
悉听尊便　You are free to try anything you like.

烯 [xī] 名 alkene
烯烃　alkene

淅 [xī] 动 wash rice
淅沥　the sound of a light rain, a breeze, falling leaves,etc.
淅飒　the sound of a light wind,rain,etc.

惜 [xī] 动 ①value;cherish;appreciate ②regret; have pity;feel sorry ③stint;spare;grudge
惜别　be reluctant to part;hate to see sb go
惜贷　unwillingness to make loans
惜力　be sparing of one's energy;not do one's best
惜怜　feel sorry for;pity;sympathize;regret
惜赔　reluctance to pay full compensation
惜老怜贫　have compassion for the old and the poor
惜墨如金　(of a painter,calligrapher,or writer) use ink as if it were gold-work with scrupulous care
惜指失掌　stint a finger and lose a hand—try to save a little only to lose a lot;spoil the ship for a ha'p'orth of tar

晰 [xī] 形 clear;distinct;explicit

稀 [xī] Ⅰ 形 ①rare;scarce;unusual;uncommon ②sparse; thinly scattered ③ watery; diluted;

thin Ⅱ 副 very;extremely Ⅲ 名 sth watery; sth thin
稀薄　thin;rare
稀饭　rice (or millet) gruel;porridge
稀罕　①rare;scarce;uncommon ②value as a rarity;cherish ③rare thing;rarity
稀客　a rare visitor
稀拉　①sparse; scanty; thinly scattered ② slovenly;sloppy;slack
稀烂　①completely mashed;pulpy ②smashed to pieces (or smithereens);broken to bits
稀泥　thin mud;slime
稀奇　rare;strange;curious
稀缺　in short supply;scarce;in pressing demand
稀少　few;rare;scarce
稀释　dilute
稀疏　(of objects,sounds,etc.) few and scattered;few and far between;thin;sparse
稀松　①sloppy;lax ②unimportant;trivial ③ loose;porous
稀有　rare;unusual
稀粥　watery porridge;gruel
稀巴烂　smashed to pieces (or smithereens); broken to bits
稀释剂　diluent;thinner
稀里呼噜　the sound of snoring,guzzling porridge,etc.
稀里糊涂　①not knowing what one is about; muddleheaded ②careless;casual;perfunctory
稀里哗啦　①the sound of rain or of sth falling down ②badly battered;broken to pieces; utterly shattered
稀世之宝　extremely rare treasure
稀世之才　the supramundane power of intellect
稀世之珍　rare treasure
稀释测定　dilution metering
稀汤寡水　(of porridge, soup, etc.) watery; thin and tasteless
稀土金属　rare-earth metal
稀土元素　rare-earth element
稀稀拉拉　①sparse;thinly scattered ②slack; remiss
稀稀落落　①become sparse; be thinning ② sparse;scattered;thin
稀有金属　rare metal
稀有元素　rare element

翕 [xī] Ⅰ 形 amiable;docile Ⅱ 动 fold;close;furl
翕动　(of lips,nostrils,etc.) open and close; quiver
翕然　(of opinions,actions,etc.) be in unison; be in harmony

粞 [xī] 名 ①broken rice ②chaff;husk

犀 [xī]
名 rhinoceros
犀角 rhinoceros horn
犀利 sharp;incisive;trenchant
犀鸟 hornbill
犀牛 rhinoceros

皙 [xī]
形 light-complexioned;fair-shinned

锡 [xī]
I 名 tin;stannum (Sn) II 动 bestow;grant
锡箔 tinfoil paper (formerly used as funeral offerings)
锡恩 grant a favour
锡福 bestow happiness
锡罐 tin can;tin
锡壶 tinpot
锡匠 tinsmith
锡金 Sikkim
锡矿 tin ore
锡命 give an order
锡器 tinware
锡石 cassiterite;tinstone
锡杖 Buddhist abbot's staff
锡纸 tinfoil;silver paper
锡兰肉桂 Ceylon cinnamon

溪 [xī]
名 small stream;brook;rivulet
溪谷 small valley
溪涧 mountain stream
溪流 brook;rivulet
溪水潺潺 gurgling stream

熙 [xī]
形 ①bright;sunny ②happy and content ③amiable;lovely;pleasant ④prosperous;flourishing
熙春 happy spring;lovely spring
熙和 ① congenial and happy ② pleasantly warm;genial
熙事 auspicious (*or* happy) event
熙笑 happy and contented smile
熙朝 prosperous reign or age;prosperous and peaceful reign
熙来攘往 the hustle and bustle of large crowds;coming and going in crowds
熙熙攘攘 bustling with activity;with people bustling about

蜥 [xī]
名 lizard
蜥蜴 lizard

僖 [xī]
形 happy and joyous

熄 [xī]
动 extinguish (a fire);put out (a light)
熄风 relieve dizziness, high fever, infantile convulsions,epilepsy,etc.
熄火 ①(of fuel,a stove,etc.) stop burning;die out ②(of an engine,etc.) stop working;go dead ③stop (fuel) from burning;stop (an engine,etc.)
熄灭 (of a fire,light,etc.) go out;die out
熄灯号 lights-out;taps

嘻 [xī]
I 叹 (used to show one's surprise) II 拟 sound of laughing
嘻嘻哈哈 laughing and joking;laughing merrily;mirthful

膝 [xī]
名 knee
膝盖 knee
膝腱 patellar tendon
膝下 at one's knees
膝盖骨 kneecap
膝关节 knee joint
膝内翻 out knee;bowleg
膝外翻 in knee;knock knee
膝腱反射 patellar reflex;knee jerk
膝上电脑 laptop computer
膝下无子 have no little son to rock on one's knee
膝痒搔背 not scratch at the itch;not scratch where it itches—fail to handle a matter properly;miss the point;miss fire

嬉 [xī]
动 play;have fun
嬉闹 laugh and frolic
嬉耍 play;sport;frolic
嬉戏 play;sport
嬉笑 be laughing and playing
嬉皮士 hippie;hippy
嬉游曲 divertimento
嬉皮笑脸 grinning cheekily;smiling and grimacing
嬉笑怒骂 laughing merrily or cursing angrily

熹 [xī]
名 ①dawn;daybreak ②brightness

樨 [xī]
◇木樨 ①sweet-scented osmanthus ②egg beaten and then cooked

螅 [xī]
名 hydra

蹊 [xī]
名 footpath ➡ qī
蹊径 path;way

螅 [xī]
螅蟀 cricket (an insect)
螅蟀草 yard grass

曦 [xī]
名 sunlight
曦光 morning sunlight

X

XÍ (ＴＩ)

习 [xī]
I 动 ①study;learn;review;practise ②be accustomed to;be used to;be inured to;be fa-

miliar with Ⅱ 〔名〕 habit; custom; convention; usual practice

习惯 ①be accustomed to; be used to; be inured to ②habit; custom; usual practice

习见 commonly seen (thing or sight)

习气 a bad habit; bad practice

习尚 custom; common practice

习俗 custom; convention

习题 exercises (in school work)

习习 (of a wind) blow gently

习性 habits and characteristics

习艺 learn a trade, skill, handicraft, etc.

习用 habitually use

习语 idiom

习字 practise penmanship; do exercises in calligraphy

习作 ①do exercises in composition ②an exercise in composition, drawing, etc.

习惯法 common law; customary law

习字帖 copybook; calligraphy model

习非成是 get used to what is wrong and regard it as right

习以为常 be used (or accustomed, inured) to sth

习与性成 Habit becomes second nature.

习惯成自然 Once you form a habit, it comes natural to you; Habit becomes second nature.

席 〔xí〕
Ⅰ 〔名〕 ①mat ②seat; place; box ③seat in parliament ④feast; banquet; dinner Ⅱ 〔量〕: 一席话 a talk

席次 the order of seats; seating arrangement; one's place among the seats arranged

席地 have a mat on the ground; (sit or lie) on the ground

席间 at or during the feast

席卷 ①roll up like a mat; carry everything with one; take away everything ②sweep across; engulf

席面 the dishes served at a feast

席棚 mat shed; mat hoarding

席位 seat

席子 mat

席梦思 Simmons (a transliteration); innerspring mattress

席卷一空 abscond with everything

觋 〔xí〕
〔名〕 wizard; sorcerer

袭 〔xí〕
Ⅰ 〔动〕 ①raid; attack ②follow the pattern of; carry on as before; copy Ⅱ 〔量〕: 一袭棉衣 a suit of cotton-padded clothes

袭击 ①make a surprise attack on; attack by surprise ②a surprise attack; raid

袭取 ①take by surprise ②take over

袭扰 harass; attack repeatedly

袭用 take over (sth that has long been used in the past)

袭占 capture (a place) by a surprise attack

媳 〔xí〕
〔名〕 daughter-in-law

媳妇 ①son's wife; daughter-in-law ②the wife of a relative of the younger generation

媳妇儿 ①wife ②a young married woman

檄 〔xí〕
Ⅰ 〔名〕 official summons to arms; official proclamation Ⅱ 〔动〕 announce (or denounce) in such a call (or proclamation)

檄讨 issue an official denunciation

檄文 war proclamation

檄喻 issue an official announcement

xǐ(ㄒㄧ)

洗 〔xǐ〕
Ⅰ 〔动〕 ①wash; bathe; clean ②baptize ③redress; remedy; right ④clear away; eliminate ⑤kill and loot; sack ⑥develop (a film) ⑦erase (a recording) ⑧shuffle (cards, etc.) Ⅱ 〔名〕 small vessel or tray for washing (writing) brushes

洗肠 intestinal lavage

洗尘 give a dinner of welcome (to a visitor from afar)

洗涤 wash; cleanse

洗剂 lotion; wash

洗劫 loot; sack

洗井 flushing

洗礼 ①baptism ②a severe test

洗练 succinct; clear

洗煤 coal washing

洗牌 shuffle cards; make the pack; shuffle

洗片 develop a film; process a photo

洗钱 launder money; money laundering

洗漱 wash one's face and rinse one's mouth

洗刷 ①wash and brush; scrub ②wash off; clear oneself of (opprobrium, stigma, guilt, etc.)

洗涮 rinse

洗头 wash one's hair; shampoo one's hair; have a shampoo

洗胃 gastric lavage

洗选 ore dressing (by washing)

洗雪 wipe out (a disgrace); redress (a wrong)

洗盐 desalinization of soil by flooding or leaching

洗衣 wash clothes

洗印 develop and print (photos); process

洗冤 right a wrong; remedy an injustice

洗澡 have (or take) a bath; bathe

洗濯 wash; cleanse

洗不掉 can't be washed off; can't wash out

洗涤槽 washing tank; sink

洗涤剂 detergent
洗涤器 washing appliance;washer;scrubber
洗涤塔 washing tower
洗发剂 shampoo
洗脸盆 washbasin;washbowl
洗煤厂 coal washery;coal cleaning plant
洗面膏 (facial) cleansing cream
洗脑(筋) ①wash brains;brainwash ②ideological remoulding
洗片机 developing machine
洗钱罪 crime of money laundering
洗染店 cleaners and dyers;laundering and dyeing shop
洗手间 toilet;lavatory;washroom;rest room
洗碗机 dishwasher
洗眼杯 eyecup
洗眼剂 eyewash
洗衣板 washboard
洗衣店 laundry
洗衣房 washhouse;laundry
洗衣粉 laundry detergent (powder);washing powder
洗衣机 washing machine
洗衣刷 wash brush
洗印机 (film) processor
洗澡间 bathroom
洗澡盆 bathtub
洗澡堂 bath pool
洗耳恭听 listen with respectful attention
洗劫一空 robbed of everything one had
洗手不干 ①(of a thief, etc.) stop doing wrong and reform oneself ②wash one's hands of sth
洗洗涮涮 laundering, washing of utensils and other household cleaning jobs
洗心革面 turn over a new leaf;thoroughly reform oneself

枲 [xǐ] 名 male nettle-hemp;hemp

玺 [xǐ] 名 imperial seal;royal seal
玺书 document with imperial (or royal) seal

铣 [xǐ] 动 mill ➡xiǎn
铣床 milling machine;miller
铣刀 milling cutter
铣工 ①milling (work) ②miller;milling machine operator

徙 [xǐ] 动 ①move (from one place to another);migrate ②be transferred to another official post
徙居 move house
徙迁之累 fatigue of moving from one place to another

喜 [xǐ] I 形 happy;delighted;joyful;pleased II 名 ①happy event (esp. wedding);auspicious occasion ②pregnancy III 动 ①be fond of;love;like;have a partiality for ②be prone to;agree with;require
喜爱 like;love;be fond of;be keen on
喜报 a bulletin of glad tidings
喜好 like;love;be fond of;be keen on
喜欢 ①like;love;be fond of;be keen on ②happy;elated;filled with joy
喜酒 drinks offered to guests at a wedding;wedding feast
喜剧 comedy
喜联 antithetical couplet hung on walls at wedding
喜期 the happy occasion—wedding day
喜气 a cheerful atmosphere (or countenance)
喜庆 ①joyous;jubilant ②a happy event (or occasion)
喜鹊 magpie
喜人 give pleasure and satisfaction;be gratifying or satisfactory
喜色 a happy expression;a joyful look
喜事 ①a happy event;a joyous occasion ②marriage;wedding
喜糖 wedding sweets (or candies)
喜讯 happy news;good news;glad tidings
喜筵 wedding feast
喜雨 a seasonable rain;a welcome fall of rain
喜悦 happy;joyous
喜冲冲 look exhilarated;be in a joyful mood
喜洋洋 beaming with joy;radiant
喜滋滋 feeling greatly pleased;filled with joy
喜不自胜 be beside oneself with joy;be delighted beyond measure
喜出望外 be overjoyed (at an unexpected gain, good news, etc.);be pleasantly surprised
喜从天降 a heaven-sent fortune;a heavenly blessing—an unexpected piece of good fortune;a gift from the gods
喜结良缘 consummate a marriage happily;tie the nuptial knot
喜剧演员 comedian
喜眉笑眼 be all smiles;be smiling all over
喜怒哀乐 happiness,anger,grief and joy—the gamut of human feeling
喜怒无常 be subject to changing moods
喜气洋洋 full of joy;jubilant
喜迁新居 happily move into new housing
喜上眉梢 [xǐshàngméishāo] be radiant with joy;look very happy
喜上加喜 [xǐshangjiāxǐ] two happy events come one after the other
喜闻乐见 love to see and hear
喜笑颜开 a face wreathed in smiles;a face lit up with pleasure
喜新厌旧 love the new and loathe the old—be fickle in one's affections

喜形于色 a face lit up with pleasure; visibly pleased; beaming with happiness

喜溢眉梢 be radiant with joy; eyes lit up with joy

喜忧参半 mingled hope and fear; be torn between joy and sorrow; be partly glad and partly worried

葹 [xī] 名 fivefold increase

屣 [xī] 名 shoes; slippers; sandals

禧 [xī] 名 auspiciousness; happiness; jubilation

xì (丅ì)

戏 [xì] I 动 ①play; sport; have fun ②make fun of; joke with II 名 drama; opera; play; show

戏词 actor's part (or lines)

戏单 theatrical bill

戏法 conjuring; juggling; tricks; magic

戏歌 opera-pop

戏剧 drama; play; theatre

戏迷 theatre fan

戏目 (theatrical) programme

戏弄 make fun of; play tricks on; tease; kid

戏票 theatre ticket

戏评 a review of a play

戏曲 traditional opera

戏耍 tease; play tricks on

戏说 playful narrative

戏台 stage

戏文 actor's part (or lines)

戏谑 banter; crack jokes

戏言 joking remarks; pleasantries

戏衣 stage costume

戏院 theatre

戏装 theatrical (or stage) costume

戏子 opera singer; actor

戏剧化 dramatize; theatricalize

戏剧家 playwright; dramatist

戏剧界 theatrical circles

戏剧性 dramatic

戏曲片 a screen adaptation of a traditional (or local) opera

戏班(子) theatrical troupe

戏路(子) the range of character types that an actor can portray

饩 [xì] I 名 ①grain; fodder; provisions ②living animal; animal for sacrifice; raw meat II 动 present (food) as a gift

系 [xì] I 名 ①system; series; line ②department; faculty ③system II 动 ①relate to; rely on ②be concerned; feel solicitous ③tie up and carry; fasten and pull up; fasten and lower down ④tie; fasten ⑤take into custody; jail ⑥be ➡

jì

系词 ①copula ②copulative verb; linking verb

系缚 tie; fasten; bind up

系恋 be reluctant to leave; can't bear to part (from sb or with sth)

系列 series; set

系念 be anxious about; worry about; feel concerned about

系谱 family; genealogy

系数 coefficient

系统 ①system ②systematic

系列化 serialize; come out in serial form

系列片 serial

系谱树 family tree

系统化 systematize; systemize

系统论 systems theory

系统盘 system disk

系统性 systematic nature; system

系列产品 a series of products; line extensions

系列小说 novel series

系统测试 system testing

系统分析 systems analysis

系统工程 systems engineering

系统集成 system integration

系统科学 system science

系统支持 system support

系统装置命令 system configuration commands

细 [xì] 形 ①thin; slender; fine ②narrow; thin ③in small particles; fine ④(of one's voice) thin and soft ⑤fine; superb; exquisite; delicate ⑥careful; prudent; meticulous; detailed ⑦minute; tiny; trivial; trifling ⑧young; little

细胞 cell

细布 muslin

细部 detail (of a drawing)

细察 investigate (or examine) carefully

细长 long and thin; tall and slender

细齿 serration

细瓷 fine porcelain

细纺 finespun

细工 fine workmanship

细故 trifle; trivial matter

细化 specify

细活 a job requiring fine workmanship (or meticulous care); skilled work

细火 slow fire; gentle heat

细节 details; particulars

细菌 germ; bacterium

细粮 fine food grain

细流 thread; trickle

细脉 thready pulse

细毛 fine, soft fur

细密 ①fine and closely woven; close ②meticulous; detailed

细面 fine flour

细目 ①detailed catalogue ②specific item;detail
细嫩 delicate;tender
细腻 ①fine and smooth ②exquisite;minute
细巧 exquisite;dainty;delicate
细情 details
细柔 fine and soft; gentle and slender; fine-textured
细软 jewelry, expensive clothing and other valuables
细润 fine and glossy
细弱 thin and delicate;slim and fragile
细沙 fine sand
细纱 spun yarn
细说 recount (*or* describe) in detail; tell at length
细碎 in small,broken bits
细谈 recount (*or* describe) in detail; tell at length
细挑 tall and slender
细微 slight;fine;subtle
细小 very small;tiny;fine;trivial
细心 careful;attentive
细辛 the root of Chinese wild ginger
细腰 slender waist(esp. of a woman)
细雨 drizzle;fine rain
细语 speak softly;whisper
细则 detailed rules and regulations
细账 itemized account
细致 careful;meticulous;painstaking
细作 spy;secret agent
细胞壁 cell wall
细胞核 cell nucleus
细胞膜 cell membrane
细胞学 cytology
细胞质 cytoplasm
细菌弹 B-bomb;bacteria bomb
细菌学 bacteriology
细菌战 bacteriological warfare;germ warfare
细毛线 thin knitting wool
细毛羊 fine-wool sheep
细妹子 little girl
细木工 ①joinery ②joiner;cabinetmaker
细绒线 fingering yarn
细纱机 spinning frame
细石器 microlith
细娃子 little boy
细纹木 fine-grained wood
细细儿 ①very thin;very fine ②very careful
细支纱 fine-count yarn
细胞分裂 cell division
细胞移植 cell transplantation
细大不捐 reject nothing,big or small
细高挑儿 ① tall and slender figure ② tall, slender person
细嚼慢咽 chew carefully and swallow slowly; chew one's food well before swallowing it

细菌肥料 bacterial fertilizer
细菌农药 bacterial pesticide
细菌武器 bacteriological weapon;germ weapon
细菌学家 bacteriologist
细皮嫩肉 delicate skin and fair complexion
细如发丝 as thin as a hair
细声细气 in a soft voice;soft-spoken
细水长流 ①economize to avoid running short ②go about sth little by little without a let-up
细说详情 relate all this in elaborate detail
细针密缕 in fine,close stitches—(work) in a meticulous way
细枝末节 minor details;nonessentials
细菌性痢疾 bacillary dysentery
细石器文化 microlithic culture

隙 [xì]
名 ①crack; rift; chink; crevice ② gap; interval ③loophole;opening;opportunity ④discord;rift;grudge
隙地 unoccupied place;open space

虩 [xì]
名 red (colour)

潟 [xì]
名 saline soil
潟湖 lagoon

xiā(ㄒ丨ㄚ)

呷 [xiā]
动 sip;drink

虾 [xiā]
名 shrimp
虾干 dried shrimp
虾蛄 mantis shrimp
虾酱 salted shrimp paste
虾米 ①dried,shelled shrimp ②small shrimp
虾皮 dried,unshelled small shrimp
虾片 prawn slices;shrimp cracker
虾仁 shelled fresh shrimp;shrimp meat
虾油 shrimp sauce
虾子 shrimp roe (*or* eggs)
虾米皮 dried,unshelled small shrimps
虾兵蟹将 shrimp soldiers and crab generals—ineffective troops;hopeless soldiers
虾荒蟹乱 panic among shrimps and crabs—omen of war and great disturbance

瞎 [xiā]
Ⅰ 动 ①be blind ②(as of seeds) fail to sprout (*or* bud) ③waste;spoil;lose Ⅱ 副 groundlessly;foolishly;to no avail Ⅲ 形 ①fail to detonate (*or* explode);misfire;go dud ②(as of thread,etc.) become tangled
瞎掰 ①talk nonsense ②do stupid things
瞎扯 ①talk groundlessly (*or* irresponsibly); talk nonsense ② talk at random about anything under the sun;waffle;natter

瞎吹 boast in the most fantastic of terms
瞎干 go it blind;fly blind
瞎话 untruth;lie
瞎混 muddle along
瞎聊 chat at random about anything under the sun;chat idly
瞎蒙 make a wild guess
瞎闹 ① act senselessly; mess about ② fool around;be mischievous
瞎炮 ignited dynamite (*or* fired) artillery shell) that fails to explode;dud
瞎说 talk groundlessly (*or* irresponsibly); talk nonsense
瞎诌 make up wild stories;tell cock-and-bull stories
瞎抓 do things without a plan;go about sth in a haphazard way
瞎子 a blind person
瞎操心 worry for nothing
瞎胡闹 ① act senselessly; mess about ② fool around;be mischievous
瞎忙(活) make a fuss about nothing
瞎指挥 give arbitrary and impracticable directions;mess things up by giving wrong orders;blindly order others about;issue confused (*or* wrong) orders
瞎蹦乱跳 be on the scamper
瞎猜一通 make wild (*or* random) guesses
瞎搞一通 make a mess of;act without a plan
瞎讲一气 talk groundlessly;shoot one's mouth off
瞎子摸象 the blind men sizing up the elephant—take a part for the whole
瞎子摸鱼 a blind person groping for fish—act blindly
瞎字儿不识 cannot read a single word;be completely illiterate
瞎猫碰上死耗子 A blind cat caught a dead rat; A dead rat fell into a blind cat's clutches—sheer luck.
瞎子点灯白费蜡 a blind person lighting a candle—a sheer waste

xiá(ㄒㄧㄚˊ)

匣 [xiá]
[名] small box (*or* case);casket
匣子 a small box (*or* case);casket

侠 [xiá]
Ⅰ [名] person adept in martial arts and given to chivalrous conduct;chivalrous swordsman Ⅱ [形] chivalrous
侠骨 chivalry;chivalrous frame of mind
侠客 a person adept in martial arts and given to chivalrous conduct (in olden times)
侠气 lofty sense of honour and courage;heroic spirit
侠士 a person adept in martial arts and given to chivalrous conduct (in olden times)
侠义 having a strong sense of justice and ready to help the weak;chivalrous

狎 [xiá]
[动] be improperly familiar;indulge in flirtations or intimacies
狎妓 visit prostitutes;go whoring
狎近 take liberties with
狎客 a frequenter of brothels
狎昵 be improperly familiar with
狎弄 treat with improper intimacy

柙 [xiá]
[名] cage for wild beasts,formerly also used for felons

峡 [xiá]
[名] gorge
峡谷 gorge;canyon
峡湾 fiord

狭 [xiá]
[形] of small width;narrow
狭隘 ①narrow ②(of mind,views,etc.) narrow and limited;parochial
狭长 long and narrow
狭小 narrow and small;narrow
狭义 narrow sense
狭窄 ①narrow;cramped ②(of mind,experience,etc.) narrow and limited;narrow ③ stricture
狭路相逢 (of adversaries) meet face to face on a narrow path—come into unavoidable confrontation
狭隘民族主义 narrow nationalism

遐 [xiá]
[形] ① far;remote;distant ② lasting;durable;long
遐布 spread far and wide
遐福 enduring blessing (*or* happiness)
遐思 reverie;daydreaming
遐眺 look as far as the eye can see
遐想 reverie;daydreaming
遐迩闻名 be known far and wide;enjoy widespread renown

瑕 [xiá]
[名] flaw (in a piece of jade);defect;drawback;shortcoming
瑕疵 flaw;blemish
瑕玷 blemish;stain;defect
瑕不掩瑜 one flaw cannot mar the jade—small defects cannot obscure great virtues
瑕瑜互见 have defects as well as merits;have both strong and weak points

暇 [xiá]
[名] free time;spare moment;leisure
暇日 days of leisure
暇时 at leisure;at one's leisure;in one's leisure

辖 [xiá]
Ⅰ [名] linchpin Ⅱ [动] have jurisdiction over;

be under one's command;administer;govern

辖区 administered area;area of jurisdiction

辖制 control

辖治 govern;rule

霞 [xiá]

〖名〗 rosy clouds;morning (*or* evening) glow

霞光 rays of morning (*or* evening) sunlight

霞帔 scarf over ceremonial robe for ladies of nobles

霞石 nepheline

黠 [xiá]

〖形〗 sly;crafty;cunning

黠智 crafty;cunning

xià（ㄒㄧㄚˋ）

下 [xià]

Ⅰ〖名〗①(*used in collocations indicating circumstances, extent, situation, etc.*):名下 under sb's name ②(*used in collocations indicating a particular time or season*):节下 during a holiday (*or* festival) ③(*used after a numeral to indicate orientation or position*):两下里都愿意 both sides are willing Ⅱ〖形〗①lower;inferior;poor ②next;latter;later Ⅲ〖副〗①below;under;underneath ②down;downward Ⅳ〖动〗①go down;descend;alight;get off:顺河而下 go down a river;go downstream ②(of rain,snow,etc.) fall ③issue;deliver;send:下战书 deliver a letter of challenge ④go (down) to:上山下乡 go and work in the countryside or mountainous areas ⑤exit;leave:下火线 leave the front (*or* battlefield) ⑥put in;cast:舍得下作料 not stint the condiments ⑦play (board) games:咱俩下两盘。Let's play chess for a while. ⑧take away;take off;unload;dismantle:把门下下来 take down the door ⑨form (an opinion);draw (a conclusion);give (a definition):下保证 make a pledge ⑩apply;use:下筷子吃饭 use one's chopsticks and start eating ⑪(of animals) give birth to;lay ⑫capture;seize;take ⑬give in;yield ⑭finish (work,etc.);leave off:下早班 come off morning shift ⑮be less than:不下十次 no less than ten times Ⅴ〖量〗又作"下子"①(*used to indicate repetition of action*):敲了两下门 give a couple of knocks on the door ②(*used to indicate the volume of a container*):杯子里装了半下白酒。The glass of liquor was half-full. ③(*used after* 两 *or* 几 *to indicate one's ability or skill*):他真有两下! He really can show you a thing or two! He is really capable!

下巴 ①the lower jaw ②chin

下摆 the lower hem (of a gown,jacket or shirt)

下拜 make obeisance;kneel down to pay respect;kowtow

下班 get off work;knock off

下辈 ①future generations;offspring ②the younger generation of a family

下笔 put pen to paper;begin to write (*or* paint)

下边 under

下拨 (of governments or other organizations at higher levels) allocate and transfer (goods or funds) to units at lower levels

下部 ①the lower part ②the lower part of the body

下操 ①have drills ②finish drilling

下策 a bad plan;an unwise decision;the worst thing to do;a stupid move

下层 ①lower levels ②lower strata

下场 [xiàchǎng] ①go off stage;exit ②leave the playing field (*or* court)

下场 [xiàchang] an end that a person comes to,usu. bad;fate

下沉 sink;subside;submerge

下乘 ①Little Vehicle (a school of Buddhism);Hinayana ②low order;inferior quality

下处 one's temporary lodging during a trip

下船 ①go ashore;disembark ②get down into a junk;go aboard

下垂 ①hang down;droop ②prolapse

下次 next time;next

下挫 decrease

下达 make known (*or* transmit) to lower levels

下蛋 lay eggs

下等 of low grade or caste;inferior

下地 ①go to the fields ②leave a sickbed

下店 put up at an inn

下调 [xiàdiào] transfer to a lower-level work unit

下跌 (of water level,prices,etc.) fall;drop

下碇 cast anchor

下毒 put in poison

下蹲 crouch;squat

下颚 ①maxilla (of certain arthropods) ②the lower jaw;mandible (of vertebrates)

下发 give (instructions,notice,etc.) to subordinates

下法 laxative (*or* purgative) remedy

下凡 (of gods or immortals) descend to the world

下饭 ①go with rice ②go well with rice

下放 ① transfer to a lower level ② transfer (cadres,etc.) to work at the grass-roots level or to do manual labour in the countryside or in a factory

下风 ①leeward ②disadvantageous position

下浮 drop

下岗 ①come or go off sentry duty ②lay off

下工 come or go off work;stop work;knock

off

下跪 kneel down; go down on one's knees

下锅 put food in the pot or pan (ready to be cooked)

下海 ①go to sea ②(of fishermen) go fishing on the sea; put out to sea ③(of people from other walks of life) go in for business; become a businessman; plunge into the commercial sea

下颔 the lower jaw

下滑 glide; gliding; letting down

下怀 one's heart's desire

下回 next time

下级 ①lower level ②subordinate

下家 (in mah-jong, card games, or in wine games) the player whose turn comes next

下嫁 (of a girl of high birth) marry a man of lower social status

下贱 ①of humble origin; low in social status ②low; mean; degrading

下降 descend; go or come down; drop; fall; decline

下焦 the part of the body cavity below the umbilicus, housing the bladder, kidneys and bowels

下脚 ①get a foothold; plant one's foot ②leftover bits and pieces

下届 the next session of a regular meeting; next (graduating class, etc.)

下界 ①the world of mortals; the world of man ②(of gods or immortals) descend to the world

下劲 exert oneself; go all out

下酒 ①go with wine ②go well with wine

下课 ①get out of class; finish class ②lay off; be removed from a post; be made redundant

下款 ①the name of the donor ②the signature at the end of a letter

下来 ① come down ② come down to a place regarded as being lower or below ③ (of farm crops) be harvested ④(of a period of time) be over; come to an end ⑤ (indicating motion toward a lower or nearer position) down (here) ⑥up to the present; till the end (or finish) ⑦(used after a verb, expressing completion or finality of an action) ⑧(used after an adjective, indicating increasing degree)

下联 the second (or latter) line of a couplet

下列 listed below; following

下令 give orders; order

下流 ① lower reaches (of a river) ② low down; mean; obscene; dirty

下落 ①whereabouts ②drop; fall

下马 ①get down (or dismount) from a horse ②(of a project, plan, etc.) be discontinued; be given up

下面 ① below; under; underneath ② the next in order; following ③ lower level; subordinate

下奶 stimulate (or increase) the secretion of milk (of nursing mothers)

下品 of the lowest grade (or quality)

下聘 (of the bridegroom-to-be's family) send betrothal gifts and money over to the bride

下铺 lower berth; bottom berth

下棋 play chess; have a game of chess

下欠 ①still owe (after paying part of one's debt) ②a sum still owing

下情 ①conditions at the lower levels; feelings (or wishes) of the masses or one's subordinates ②the situation I am in; my feelings or wishes

下去 ① go down; descend ② go down to a place regarded as lower or below; step down (from the stage, platform, etc.) ③ lessen; be reduced; go down ④ (indicating motion toward a lower or farther position) down (there) ⑤go on (doing sth); continue ⑥develop; grow

下人 servant

下山 ①go down a hill (or mountain) ②(of the sun) set; sink below the horizon

下身 ①the lower part of the body ②private parts; genitals

下生 be born

下士 corporal; petty officer third class; petty officer second class

下世 ①next life ②leave this world—die

下手 ①right hand side (or seat); seat of lower priority ②(in mah-jong, card games, or in wine games) the player whose turn comes next ③put one's hand to; start doing sth; set about; set to ④assistant; helper

下首 right hand side or seat; seat of lower priority

下书 deliver a letter

下属 subordinate

下水 [xiàshuǐ] ① enter the water; be launched ② soak in water to shrink cloth (or fabrics) before use ③take to evil-doing; fall into evil ways ④ going downstream; downriver

下水 [xiàshuǐ] tripe; chitterlings

下榻 stay (at a place during a trip)

下台 ①step down from the stage or platform ②fall out of power; leave office ③(usu. used in the negative) get out of a predicament (or an embarrassing situation)

下体 ①the lower part of the body ②private parts; genitals

下调 [xiàtiáo] adjust (prices, standards, quotas, etc.) downward

下帖 send an invitation card

下同 similarly hereinafter; the same below
下头 ①below; under; underneath ②lower level; subordinate
下网 off-line
下文 ① what follows in the passage, paragraph, article, etc. ② later development; outcome; sequel
下午 afternoon
下弦 last (*or* third) quarter (of the moon)
下限 the latest (*or* minimum) permissible; lower limit; prescribed minimum; floor level; floor
下陷 be sunken; be hollow; form a depression
下乡 go to the countryside
下泻 ①(of water) flow down ②(of prices, etc.) drop sharply ③have loose bowels
下行 ①(of trains) going from the capital to any other part of the country; down ②(of boats) going downstream; downriver ③(of documents) being issued to the lower levels
下旋 underspin; backspin
下学 finish classes and leave school (for the day)
下旬 the last ten-day period of a month
下咽 swallow (food or other things)
下药 ①prescribe medicine ②put in poison
下野 (of a ruler) retire from the political arena; be forced to relinquish power
下游 ①lower reaches (of a river) ②backward position
下余 be left
下狱 throw into prison; imprison
下载 download
下葬 be interred; be buried
下诏 issue an imperial edict
下肢 lower limbs; legs
下种 sow (seeds)
下注 lay down a stake (in gambling)
下箸 apply one's chopsticks to the food—start eating
下装 remove theatrical makeup and costume
下坠 straining (at stool); tenesmus
下子 what one is good at (*or* capable of)
下钻 run the drilling tool into a well
下作 low-down; mean; obscene; dirty
下半场 second half (of a game, concert, etc.)
下半旗 fly flag at half-mast; haul down (*or* lower) the flag half-mast
下半晌 afternoon
下半身 the lower part of the body; below the waist
下半天 afternoon
下半夜 the time after midnight; the latter half of the night
下辈子 the next life
下本儿 put in time, money and effort; make an investment

下本钱 put in time, money and effort; make an investment
下不来 ①cannot come down ②cannot be accomplished; won't do ③feel embarrassed
下厨房 go to the kitchen (i.e. to cook or to prepare a meal)
下等人 a person belonging to one of the lower social strata
下毒手 resort to cruel treachery; strike a vicious blow; lay murderous hands on sb
下工夫 put in time and energy; concentrate one's efforts
下颌骨 lower jawbone
下基层 go to a grassroots level (*or* unit)
下脚货 unsalable leftover goods of inferior quality
下脚料 leftover bits and pieces (of industrial material, etc.); scrap
下酒菜 a dish that goes with alcoholic drinks
下决心 make up one's mind; make a firm decision
下马威 severity shown by an official on assuming office; the severity of a newly-appointed official
下坡路 ①a downhill path; a downhill journey ②decline
下水道 sewer
下台阶 get out of a predicament or an embarrassing situation
下弦月 the moon at the last (*or* third) quarter
下议院 ① lower house; lower chamber ② the House of Commons
下意识 subconsciousness
下中农 lower-middle peasant
下巴颏儿 chin
下半辈子 the latter half of one's life; the rest of one's life
下笔成章 produce a piece of writing as soon as the pen is put to paper (said of a good and fast writer)
下笔如神 write like an angel; write quickly and powerfully
下不来台 be unable to get out of an embarrassing situation; be unable to back down with good grace; be on the spot; feel embarrassed
下不为例 special one-time case; not serve as a precedent; not be taken as a precedent; not be repeated
下车伊始 the moment one alights from the official carriage—the moment one takes up a post; immediately on arrival at a new post
下穿交叉 underpass
下放干部 cadre transferred to a lower level to work in the countryside or in a factory
下岗分流 lay off works and reposition redun-

dant personnel
下岗工人 layoff;laid-off worker
下级机关 a lower-level government office
下级组织 a subordinate organization
下拉列表 drop-down list
下马观花 get off one's horse to look at the flowers—go deep into the realities of life and make thorough investigations
下马看花 get off one's horse to look at the flowers—go deep into the realities of life and make thorough investigations
下游行业 downstream industry
下拉式选单 pull-down menu;drop-down menu
下马中上马 start a new project amid suspension of the previous ones
下岗人员分流 redirect (*or* divert) laid-off workers
下岗工人再就业 re-employment of laid-off workers
下笔千言,离题万里 a thousand words flow from the pen, but ten thousand *li* away from the theme—write fast and at length but not to the point;long-winded and irrelevant

吓 [xià]
　囫 frighten;terrify;scare;intimidate ➡hè
吓唬 frighten;scare;intimidate
吓跑 scare (sb) away
吓人 be frightening
吓得发抖 shake (*or* tremble) with fear;shake in one's shoes
吓得要死 be scared to death;be nearly frightened to death
吓人一跳 give sb a start
吓得屁滚尿流 frighten the pants off (sb);be terror-stricken

夏 [xià]
　囵 summer
夏播 summer sowing
夏布 grass linen;grass cloth
夏锄 summer hoeing and weeding
夏管 field management in summer
夏洪 full in summer
夏季 summer (season)
夏历 the traditional Chinese calendar;the lunar calendar
夏粮 summer grain crops
夏令 ①summertime ②summer weather
夏眠 aestivation (of certain animals)
夏末 end of summer;late summer
夏收 summer harvest
夏熟 ripen in summer
夏天 summer
夏娃 Eve (the first woman according to the Bible)
夏汛 summer floods
夏衣 summer clothing;summer wear

夏至 ①the Summer Solstice—the 10th of the 24 solar terms ②the day marking the beginning of the 10th solar term
夏种 summer sowing
夏装 summer clothing;summer wear
夏候鸟 summer resident
夏枯草 selfheal
夏令时 summer time;daylight-saving time
夏令营 summer camp
夏时制 daylight-saving summer;summer time system;day-saving time
夏至点 the Summer Solstice
夏炉冬扇 stoves in summer and fans in winter—things that do not meet the needs of the time

罅 [xià]
　囵 crack;chink;crevice;rift
罅隙 crack;rift;loose seam

xià(·ㄒㄧㄚ)

下 [xia]
　剾 (*used after a verb*)①(*indicate downward motion*):跳下卡车 jump off the truck ②(*indicate room or space*):这间教室起码能坐下八十人。This classroom can seat (*or* hold) at least eighty people. ③(*indicate completion or consequence of an action*):定下锦囊妙计 work out a wise plan (for an emergency,etc.)/准备下各种应变方案 get ready plans for all eventualities

xiān(ㄒㄧㄢ)

仙 [xiān]
　囵 celestial being;immortal;fairy:仙才 genius;immortal talent
仙丹 elixir of life
仙姑 ①female immortal (*or* celestial) ②sorceress
仙鹤 ①red-crowned crane ②white crane
仙境 fairyland;wonderland;paradise
仙女 female celestial;fairy maiden
仙人 celestial being;immortal
仙逝 pass away
仙术 magic arts
仙姿 fairy-like beauty
仙子 ①female celestial ②celestial being;immortal
仙鹤草 hairyvein agrimony
仙后座 Cassiopeia
仙客来 cyclamen
仙女座 Andromeda
仙人果 prickly-pear cactus;prickly pear
仙人球 ball cactus
仙人掌 cactus
仙王座 Cepheus
仙风道骨 the demeanour of a transcendent be-

ing

仙山琼阁 a jewelled palace on the mountain of the immortals

仙童玉女 boy and girl servants in fairyland

先 [xiān]
I 副 ①early;earlier;before;in advance ②earlier on;before II 名 older generation;ancestor;forefather III 形 deceased;late

先辈 elder generation;ancestor

先导 guide;forerunner;precursor

先锋 vanguard;van

先河 the beginning of sth

先后 ①being early or late;priority;order ②successively;one after another

先机 the initiative

先进 advanced

先决 prerequisite

先觉 one who becomes awakened earlier in politics and social reforms

先例 precedent

先烈 martyr

先令 ① shilling (a monetary unit of Britain until 1971) ②shilling (a monetary unit of Uganda, Kenya, Somalia and Tanzania) ③schilling (a monetary unit of Austria)

先期 earlier than the date scheduled;earlier on;in advance

先前 before;previously

先遣 sent in advance

先驱 pioneer;forerunner;harbinger

先人 ①ancestor;forefather ②my late father

先生 ① teacher ②Mister (Mr.);gentleman;sir ③husband ④doctor ⑤(usu. used in 账房先生 bookkeeper/算命先生 fortune-teller)

先声 first signs;herald;harbinger

先师 teacher of the older generation

先是 before this;originally

先手 offensive position (in chess)

先天 ①congenital;inborn ②priori;innate

先头 ①ahead;in front;in advance ②before;formerly;in the past

先行 ①go ahead of the rest;start off before the others ②beforehand;in advance

先验 priori

先兆 omen;portent;sign;indication

先哲 a great thinker of the past;sage

先知 ①a person of foresight ②religion prophet

先锋队 vanguard

先行官 commander of an advance unit (or vanguard)

先行者 forerunner

先验论 apriorism

先睹为快 consider it a pleasure to be among the first to read (a poem, article, etc.) or see (a play, ballet, etc.)

先发制人 gain the initiative by striking the first blow;forestall the enemy

先公后私 Public interest comes before private (or personal) interests.

先国后家 The state comes before the family.

先见之明 prophetic vision;foresight

先进集体 advanced group (or collective)

先进人物 advanced person

先决条件 presupposition;precondition;premise

先来后到 in the order of arrival;first come, first served

先礼后兵 take strong measures only after courteous ones fail;try peaceful means before resorting to force

先遣部队 advance force

先人后己 put others before oneself;put other people's interest ahead of one's own

先入为主 First impressions are strongest;prejudices die hard

先入之见 preconception;preconceived idea;prejudice

先声夺人 demoralize one's opponent by a show of strength;overawe people by displaying one's strength

先天不足 congenital deficiency;inborn weakness

先验方法 transcendental method

先斩后奏 execute sb first and report to the emperor afterwards—act first and report afterwards

先兆流产 early signs of miscarriage;threatened miscarriage

先兆子痫 preeclampsia

先知先觉 ① a person of foresight ② having foresight

先进工作者 advanced worker

先天性疾病 congenital disorders

先天性缺陷 birth defects

先下手为强 He who strikes first gains the advantage;To take the initiative is to gain the upper hand.

先天性心脏病 congenital heart disease

先小人后君子 let's allow impoliteness to precede courtesy (said when discussing the terms of a deal)

先天下之忧而忧,后天下之乐而乐 be the first to become concerned with the world's troubles and the last to rejoice in its happiness;be concerned before anyone else and enjoy oneself only after everyone else finds enjoyment

纤 [xiān]
形 fine;tiny;minute ➡qiàn

纤尘 fine dust

纤度 fibre number;size

纤毛 cilium

纤巧 dainty;delicate
纤弱 slim and fragile;delicate
纤手 dainty (*or* delicate) hands (of a woman)
纤体 slenderize
纤维 fibre;staple
纤细 very thin;slender;fine;tenuous
纤小 fine;tenuous
纤毛虫 ciliate;infusorian
纤维板 fibreboard
纤维瘤 fibroma
纤维束 tow
纤维素 cellulose
纤尘不染 ①without a speck of dust ②untainted with evil thoughts or bad habits
纤毫不爽 be extremely accurate;be free from the slightest error
纤维蛋白 fibrin
纤维光学 fibre optics
纤维集束 collection of filaments
纤维植物 fibre plant
纤悉无遗 with not a single detail left out
纤纤玉手 fine and slim hands of a young woman;delicately formed hands
纤维蛋白原 fibrinogen
纤维素分解菌 cellulose-decomposing bacterium

氙 [xiān]
　名 xenon (Xe)
氙灯 xenon lamp

忺 [xiān]
　形 pleased;gratified;happy

籼 [xiān]

籼稻 long-grained nonglutinous rice; indica rice
籼米 polished long-grained nonglutinous rice; polished indica rice

掀 [xiān]
　动 ①lift (a cover,lid,etc.);open up;turn over ②convulse;rock;shake
掀动 ①launch (a war) ②lift;start;set in motion
掀开 open;lift;draw
掀起 ①lift;raise ②surge;cause to surge ③set off (a movement,etc.);start
掀风鼓浪 raise a storm—stir up trouble

锨 [xiān]
　名 shovel;spade

鲜 [xiān]
Ⅰ 形 ① fresh;new ② bright-coloured; bright ③delicious;tasty:这鸡汤很鲜。This chicken broth is delicious. Ⅱ 名 ①delicacy ②aquatic food ➡xiǎn
鲜脆 (of fruits,melons and gourds) fresh and crisp
鲜果 fresh fruit
鲜红 bright red;scarlet
鲜花 fresh flower;flower

鲜活 ①fresh and alive (of aquatic products, flowers,etc.) ②vivacious;lively
鲜货 fresh fruit,vegetables,or seafood,etc.
鲜亮 (of colour) shining bright
鲜美 ①delicious;tasty ②fresh and pleasing
鲜明 ① (of colour) bright ② clear-cut; distinct;distinctive
鲜嫩 fresh and tender
鲜血 (red) blood
鲜艳 bright-coloured;gaily-coloured
鲜牛肉 fresh beef
鲜啤酒 fresh (*or* new) beer
鲜艳夺目 dazzlingly beautiful;resplendent
鲜衣怒马 be dressed in fine clothes and ride on well-groomed horses—lead a luxurious life

xián(ㄒㄧㄢˊ)

闲 [xián]
Ⅰ 形 ①not busy;idle;leisurely;unoccupied ②not in use;unoccupied;free;lying idle ③informal; irrelevant; random; idle Ⅱ 名 spare time;leisure
闲扯 chat;engage in chitchat
闲荡 stroll;loaf about
闲逛 saunter;stroll
闲话 ①digression ②complaint;gossip ③talk casually about;chat about
闲空 free time;spare time;leisure
闲聊 chat
闲气 anger about trifles
闲钱 spare cash
闲人 ①an unoccupied person;idler ②person not concerned
闲散 ①free and at leisure;at loose ends ②unused;idle
闲时 leisure;free time
闲事 ①a matter that does not concern one; other people's business ②an unimportant matter
闲书 light reading
闲谈 chat;engage in chitchat
闲暇 leisure
闲心 leisurely mood
闲杂 without fixed duties
闲职 unoccupied post; extremely light and easy job;sinecure
闲置 leave unused;let sth lie idle;gather dust
闲不住 refuse to stay idle;always keep oneself busy
闲工夫 spare time;leisure
闲来无事 be free and at leisure;be unoccupied and have nothing to do
闲情逸致 (be in) a leisurely and carefree mood;(have) the leisure and (be in the) mood for enjoyment

闲散人员 idle people; idlers; unoccupied persons
闲散资金 scattered funds
闲是闲非 idle gossip
闲言碎语 ① idle chatter; irrelevancies ② gossip; backbiting; groundless rumour; slander
闲云野鹤 (like) drifting clouds and wild storks—free and unrestrained
闲置设备 standby equipment; idle equipment

贤 Ⅰ 〔形〕 ① virtuous; worthy; able ② worthy Ⅱ 〔名〕 able and virtuous person; wise man [xián]
贤达 a prominent and worthy personage
贤德 ① good and honest virtue ② (of a woman) virtuous
贤弟 my worthy brother; your good self
贤惠 (of a woman) virtuous; genial and prudent; kindhearted and understanding
贤良 ①(of a man) able and virtuous ② able and virtuous men
贤明 wise and able; sagacious
贤能 a virtuous and talented person
贤妻 (a term of respect) my good (or worthy) wife
贤人 a person of virtue (or merit); a person of outstanding worth
贤淑 (of a woman) virtuous, kind and genial
贤侄 my good nephew; your nephew
贤昆仲 your worthy brothers
贤内助 ①(said of another person's wife) a good wife ② my better half; my good wife
贤妻良母 a good wife and loving mother

弦 〔名〕 ① bowstring ② string of a musical instrument; chord ③ spring (of a watch, etc.) ④ chord ⑤ hypotenuse [xián]
弦月 crescent; half moon
弦乐队 string orchestra (or band); string ensemble
弦乐器 stringed instrument
弦外之音 overtone; implication

咸 Ⅰ 〔副〕 all Ⅱ 〔形〕 salted; salty [xián]
咸菜 salted vegetables; pickles
咸淡 degree of saltiness
咸肉 salted meat; bacon
咸涩 salty and bitter
咸水 salt water
咸味 saline taste
咸盐 table salt; salt
咸水湖 saltwater lake
咸水鱼 saltwater fish

挦 〔动〕 tear; pull [xián]

涎 〔名〕 saliva [xián]
涎剂 sialagogue
涎水 saliva

涎着脸 be brazenfaced; be cheeky
涎皮赖脸 brazen; cheeky; shameless and loathsome

娴 〔形〕 ① refined; elegant ② adept; skilled; well-versed [xián]
娴静 gentle and refined
娴熟 adept; skilled
娴雅 (of a woman) refined; elegant
娴于辞令 be skilled in the use of words; be gifted with a silver tongue
娴于交际 be a good mixer; be sociable

衔 Ⅰ 〔动〕 ① hold in the mouth ② cherish; harbour; bear ③ accept (instructions or orders) ④ connect; link Ⅱ 〔名〕 rank; title [xián]
衔恩 cherish a kindness
衔恨 harbour resentment; bear a grudge
衔接 link up; join
衔命 carry out an order
衔铁 armature
衔头 title
衔冤 nurse a bitter sense of wrong; have a simmering sense of injustice
衔诏讨逆 launch an expedition against the rebels on imperial instructions

舷 〔名〕 side of a ship or plane; board [xián]
舷边 gunwale; gunnel
舷窗 porthole
舷梯 ① gangway ladder; accommodation ladder ②(boarding) ramp

嫌 Ⅰ 〔名〕 ① suspicion ② ill will; hard feeling; spite; grudge Ⅱ 〔动〕 dislike; loathe; complain [xián]
嫌烦 find sth annoying or trying
嫌犯 criminal suspect
嫌弃 dislike and avoid; cold-shoulder
嫌恶 detest; loathe
嫌隙 feeling of animosity; enmity; ill will; grudge
嫌疑 suspicion
嫌怨 grudge; resentment; enmity
嫌疑犯 suspect
嫌贫爱富 dislike the poor and cherish the rich; despise the poor and curry favour with the rich
嫌疑分子 suspect

xiǎn(ㄒㄧㄢˇ)

显 Ⅰ 〔形〕 ① apparent; evident; obvious; noticeable ② illustrious and influential Ⅱ 〔动〕 show; reveal; display; manifest [xián]
显出 show; reveal
显达 illustrious and influential
显得 look; seem; appear

显贵 eminence; high officials; influential officials
显赫 illustrious; celebrated
显见 be obvious; be self-evident; be apparent
显灵 (of a ghost or spirit) make its presence (*or* power) felt
显露 become visible; appear; manifest itself
显明 obvious; manifest; distinct; marked
显目 conspicuous
显能 show off one's talent (*or* competence)
显然 obviously; evidently; clearly
显圣 (of the ghost of a saintly person) make its presence (*or* power) felt
显示 ① show; display; demonstrate; manifest ②show; indication
显现 manifest (*or* reveal) oneself; appear; show
显效 ①produce effects ②tangible results
显形 show one's (true) colours; betray oneself
显性 dominance
显眼 conspicuous; showy
显要 ①powerful and influential ②an influential figure; an important personage; VIP
显耀 ①show off ②be of high repute
显影 develop
显著 notable; marked; striking; remarkable; outstanding
显身手 display one's talent (*or* skill)
显示管 display tube
显示器 display; indicator
显微镜 microscope
显微术 microscopy
显像管 picture-tube; kinescope
显影机 developing machine
显影剂 developer
显影盘 developing dish
显影纸 developing-out paper
显而易见 obviously; evidently; clearly
显赫一时 be far famed for a time; have renown and influence for a time
显花植物 phanerogam
显露原形 show its original shape; show its real form
显色染料 developing dye
显身扬名 show one's mettle and make a name
显微胶片 microfilm; microfiche; bibliofilm
显微外科 microsurgery
显微照片 micrograph
显微组织 microscopic structure
显著变化 noticeable changes
显微望远镜 micro-telescope
显微阅读机 microfilm viewer (*or* reader)
显微照相术 microphotography; photomicrography

险 [xiǎn]
I 形 ①(of terrain, etc.) dangerous; perilous; difficult of access ② sinister; perfidious; vicious; venomous II 名 ① place difficult of access ②danger; peril; risk III 副 by a hair's breadth; by inches; almost nearly
险隘 a strategic pass; defile
险毒 sinister and vicious
险恶 ① dangerous; perilous; ominous ② sinister; vicious; malicious; treacherous
险峰 a perilous peak
险境 dangerous situation
险峻 dangerously steep; precipitous
险情 dangerous state (*or* situation)
险球 (mostly football) a near miss (goal)
险区 danger zone
险胜 cliff-hanging win; narrow victory; nose out; win by a narrow margin
险滩 dangerous shoal; rapids
险些 narrowly (escape from sth untoward); just barely; nearly
险要 strategically located and difficult of access
险诈 sinister and crafty
险症 dangerous illness
险阻 (of roads) dangerous and difficult
险象环生 dangers lurking on all sides; beset (*or* surrounded) by perils
险遭不测 have a near (*or* narrow) escape
险遭毒手 nearly fall a victim to sb's treachery; escape sb's plot by a hair's breadth

铣 [xiǎn]
➡ xǐ
铣铁 cast iron

跣 [xiǎn]
形 bare-footed

鲜 [xiǎn]
副 little; rare ➡ xiān
鲜见 rarely seen; rare; seldom met with
鲜有 rarely available; rare
鲜为人知 be little known

xiàn(ㄒㄧㄢ)

县 [xiàn]
名 county; (Japan) prefecture
县城 county seat; county town
县官 county magistrate
县委 county Party committee
县长 the head of a county; county magistrate
县志 general records of a county; county annals
县改市 county upgraded to city
县级市 county-level city
县政府 county government

现 [xiàn]
I 形 ①present; present-day; current; existing ②on hand; ready; available II 副 as the occasion arises; impromptu; extempore III 名 cash; ready money IV 动 show; reveal; appear

现案 recent case
现场 ①scene (of an incident) ②site;spot
现成 ready-made
现存 extant;in stock
现代 ① modern times;the contemporary age ②modern;contemporary
现房 spot building
现汇 spot exchange
现货 merchandise on hand;spot goods
现浇 cast-in-place;cast-in-situ
现今 nowadays;these days
现金 ①ready money;cash ②cash reserve in a bank
现款 ready money;cash
现况 present (*or* current) state of affairs
现钱 ready money;cash
现任 ① at present hold the office of ② currently in office;incumbent
现时 now;at present
现实 ①reality;actuality ②real;actual
现世 ① this life ② lose face; be disgraced; bring shame on oneself
现玩 modern antiques
现下 now;at present
现象 appearance (of things);phenomenon
现行 ①currently in effect;in force;in operation ②(of a criminal) active
现形 reveal one's true features;betray oneself
现眼 make a spectacle (*or* fool) of oneself; lose face
现役 ①active service;active duty ②on active service;on active duty;active
现有 now available;existing
现在 now;at present;today
现状 present (*or* current) situation; status quo;existing state of affairs
现成饭 food ready for the table;unearned gain
现成话 an onlooker's unsolicited comments;a kibitzer's comments
现代化 modernize
现代派 modernist school
现代史 contemporary history
现代舞 modern dance
现代戏 drama with a contemporary theme
现金账 cash account;cash book
现世报 retribution in this life
现行犯 active criminal (a criminal caught in, or immediately before or after the act)
现场办公 on-the-spot handling of official business;on-site handling of matters
现场报导 on-the-scene report
现场采访 spot coverage
现场会议　on-the-spot meeting; in-the-field meeting;on-site meeting
现场勘验 inspection of the scene (of a crime or accident)
现场求助 on-line help

现炒现卖 sell what one has just make ready; use what one has just learned
现代农业 modern agriculture
现代艺术 modern art
现货市场 spot market
现身说法 advise sb (*or* explain sth) by citing one's own experience;expound by using one's own experience as example
现实主义 realism
现行法令 decrees in effect
现行利率 prevailing rate of interest
现行政策 present policies
现役军人 serviceman; member of the armed forces in active service
现有人员 assigned personnel
现代服务业 modern service industry
现浇混凝土 cast-in-place concrete;cast-in-site concrete
现金出纳机 cash register
现场访问节目 talk show;chat show
现代金融体系 modern financial system
现代企业制度 modern enterprise (*or* corporate) system

限 [xiàn]
　I 名 ①limits;bounds;confines ②threshold
　II 动 restrict;limit;prescribe;allow
限电 restrict use of electricity
限定 prescribe (*or* set) a limit to;limit;restrict
限度 limit;limitation
限额 norm;quota
限价 ①fix the official price ②the (officially) fixed price
限量 limit the quantity of;set bounds to
限令 order sb to do sth within a certain time
限期 ①prescribe (*or* set) a time limit ②time limit;deadline
限行 traffic restriction
限养 pet-raising restriction
限于 be confined to;be limited to
限制 ①place (*or* impose) restrictions on;restrict; limit; confine ② restriction; limit; confinement
限制性 restricted;restrictive
限量供应 supply in limited quantities
限期外交 deadline diplomacy
限时抢购 flash sale
限时专送 special delivery
限制性多边条约 restrictive multilateral treaty
限制战略武器会谈 strategic arms limitation talks (SAL)

线 [xiàn]
　I 名 ① thread; string; wire ② line ③ sth shaped like a line or thread;ray ④route;line ⑤(political) line ⑥demarcation line;dividing line; boundary ⑦ brink; verge; line ⑧ clue; lead;thread II 量 (*used after — to indicate*

a tiny amount)：一线光明 a gleam of light
线虫 nematode
线段 line segment
线规 wire gauge
线间 space
线脚 ①stitch ②mold
线路 ① circuit；line ② communication line；route
线呢 cotton suiting
线圈 coil
线人 an inner connection；spy；informer
线绳 cotton rope
线索 clue；thread
线毯 a blanket woven of thick cotton yarn；cotton（thread）blanket
线条 line；contour；figure
线头 ①the end of a thread ②an odd piece of thread；a bit of thread
线团 knob；a ball of string；a reel of incense
线性 linear
线衣 cotton knitwear
线装 traditional thread binding（of Chinese books）
线虫病 nematodiasis
线电压 line voltage
线路图 circuit diagram
线膨胀 linear expansion
线手套 knit cotton gloves
线速度 linear velocity
线务员 lineman
线形叶 linear leaf
线轴儿 ①a reel for thread；bobbin ②a reel （*or* spool）of thread
线装书 thread-bound book
线上项目 above-the-line item；above-the-line
线形动物 roundworm
线下商贸运作 offline business operation

宪 [xiàn]
〔名〕①statute；law ②constitution
宪兵 military police；military policeman；gendarme
宪法 constitution；charter
宪章 ①follow the example of；model oneself on；learn from ② institutions，decrees and regulations ③charter
宪政 constitutional government；constitutionalism
宪法草案 draft constitution
宪法修正草案 draft amendment of the constitution

陷 [xiàn]
Ⅰ〔名〕①pitfall；snare；trap ②defect；flaw；deficiency Ⅱ〔动〕① get stuck（*or* bogged down）；sink into ② sink；cave in ③ frame （up）；set up ④（of a town，etc.）be captured；be taken；fall
陷害 frame（up）；make a false charge against

陷阱 pitfall；pit；trap；snare
陷坑 pitfall；pit
陷落 ①subside；sink in；cave in ②sink（*or* fall）into；land oneself in ③（of territory）fall into enemy hands
陷入 ①sink（*or* fall）into；land oneself in；be caught in；get bogged down in ②be lost in；be immersed in；be deep in
陷身 fall into；land in
陷于 fall into（an unfavourable position）
陷阵 break enemy ranks
陷入僵局 be bogged down on a question；reach an impasse；come to a deadlock
陷入困境 be cornered；be caught in a dilemma；be confronted with a predicament

馅 [xiàn]
〔名〕filling；stuffing
馅儿饼 meat pie

羡 [xiàn]
Ⅰ〔动〕admire；envy；covet Ⅱ〔形〕plentiful；surplus
羡财 surplus money
羡力 spare energy
羡慕 admire；envy
羡叹 praise

献 [xiàn]
〔动〕① offer；present；dedicate；donate ②show；display
献宝 ①present a treasure ②offer a valuable piece of advice（*or* one's valuable experience）③show off what one treasures
献策 offer advice；give advice；make suggestions
献丑 （speaking of one's own performance） show oneself up；show one's incompetence （*or* inadequacy）
献词 congratulatory message
献花 present flowers（*or* bouquets）
献计 offer advice；make suggestion
献技 show one's skill（in a performance）
献礼 present a gift；offer a present
献媚 try to ingratiate oneself with；make up to
献身 devote（*or* dedicate）oneself to；give one's life for
献血 blood donation；donate blood
献演 give a performance
献艺 （of actors，singers，etc.） show one's skill；give a performance
献殷勤 do everything to please；pay attentions to；pay one's addresses to
献计献策 offer adivce；make suggestion；give one's valuable experience；come up with new and better ways to do things；contribute ideas and exert efforts for
献身精神 spirit of dedication

腺 [xiàn]
〔名〕gland；aden
腺癌 glandular cancer

X

腺瘤 adenoma
腺热 glandular fever

xiāng（ㄒㄧ尤）

乡 [xiāng]
　〔名〕① country; countryside; rural area; village ② native place; home village (*or* town); birthplace ③ township—rural administrative unit under county or district
乡愁 homesickness
乡村 village; countryside; rural area
乡间 in the village; in the country
乡里 ① home village (*or* town) ② fellow villagers (*or* townsmen)
乡民 villagers; country people
乡气 rustic; countrified; uncouth
乡企 township and village enterprises
乡亲 ① a person from the same village (*or* town); fellow villager; fellow townsman ② local people; villagers; folks
乡绅 country gentleman; squire
乡思 homesickness; nostalgia
乡俗 local customs; village customs
乡土 native soil; one's native land; local
乡下 countryside; village
乡音 accent of one's native place; local accent
乡邮 rural postal service
乡长 township head
乡镇 ① villages and towns ② small towns in general
乡巴佬 (country) bumpkin
乡公所 township office
乡土志 local records or annals
乡下人 country folk; country cousin; rustic
乡邮员 rural postman
乡政府 township government
乡规民约 rules set by villagers; written pledges (*or* common pledges) drawn up by farmers; village regulations and folk conventions; written rules drawn up by villagers for self-regulation
乡土风味 local flavour
乡土观念 provincialism
乡土教材 teaching material on rural life and landscape
乡土气息 country flavour
乡土文学 literary style that draws heavily on local subjects, customs and language
乡镇企业 rural and township enterprises; township and village enterprises; township enterprises

芗 [xiāng]
　〔名〕aromatic herbs mentioned in ancient books as a condiment

相 [xiāng]
　Ⅰ〔副〕① each other; one another; reciprocally; mutually ② (*used to indicate an action* one side does to the other）：好言相劝 offer well-meant advice Ⅱ〔动〕see and evaluate in person; choose for oneself; choose for sb close to oneself ➡ xiàng
相爱 be in love with each other
相比 compare
相差 differ
相称 [xiāngchèn] match; suit
相称 [xiāngchēng] call each other; address each other (as…)
相持 be locked in a stalemate
相处 get along (with one another)
相传 ① tradition has it that… ; according to legend ② hand down (*or* pass on) from one to another
相待 treat
相当 ① match; balance; correspond to; be about equal to; be commensurate with ② suitable; fit; appropriate ③ quite; fairly; considerably
相等 be equal
相抵 offset; balance; counterbalance
相对 ① opposite to each other; face to face ② relative ③ relatively; comparatively
相反 ① contrary; opposite ② on the contrary
相仿 be similar; resemble each other; be more or less the same
相逢 meet (by chance); come across
相符 conform to; tally (*or* agree) with; correspond to (*or* with)
相干 ① have sth to do with; be concerned with ② coherent
相告 inform (*or* tell) you
相隔 be separated by; be apart; be at a distance of
相关 be mutually related; be interrelated
相好 ① be on intimate terms ② an intimate friend ③ have an affair with ④ lover; mistress
相互 ① mutual; reciprocal ② mutually; reciprocally; each other
相会 meet
相继 in succession; one after another
相间 alternate with
相交 ① intersect ② make friends with
相近 ① close; near ② similar; about the same
相救 come to sb's rescue; save sb from danger
相距 be separated by (a distance of…); be… apart; be… away from
相连 be linked together; be joined
相配 be well-matched; be a good match
相亲 size up a prospective mate in an arranged meeting
相劝 try to persuade sb; offer advice to sb
相商 ① consult each other ② consult you
相识 ① be acquainted with each other ② an acquaintance

相思 pine with love; yearn for sb's love; languish with lovesickness
相似 resemble; be similar; be alike
相通 communicate with each other; be interlinked
相同 identical; the same; alike
相投 be congenial; agree with each other
相违 disagree; be opposed to each other
相像 resemble; be similar; be alike
相信 believe in; be convinced of; trust; have faith in
相依 depend on each other; be interdependent
相宜 suitable; fitting; appropriate
相异 different
相迎 welcome sb
相应 corresponding; relevant; fitting; appropriate
相与 ① get along with sb; deal with sb ② with each other; together
相遇 meet
相约 agree (on meeting place, date, etc.); reach agreement; make an appointment
相赠 present to sb; give as a present
相争 argue (or wrangle) with each other
相知 ① be well acquainted with each other; know each other well ② a bosom friend; a great friend
相中 take a fancy to; settle on
相助 come to sb's help; aid
相撞 collide
相左 ① fail to meet each other ② conflict with each other; fail to agree; be at odds with
相对论 the theory of relativity; relativity
相对性 relativity
相对值 relative value
相干性 coherence; coherency
相思病 lovesickness
相思鸟 red-billed leiothrix
相思子 ① jequirity (the plant) ② jequirity bean; love pea ③ ormosia seed
相似形 similar figures
相安无事 live in peace with each other
相抱而哭 weep in each other's arms
相持不下 each sticks to his own stand; be locked in a stalemate
相得益彰 each shining more brilliantly in the other's company; bring out the best in each other; complement each other
相对高度 relative altitude (or height)
相对论性 relativistic
相对湿度 relative humidity
相对速度 relative velocity
相对无言 sit facing each other in silence; fall silent with each other
相对误差 relative error
相对运动 relative motion
相对真理 relative truth

相对主义 relativism
相反相成 ① things that oppose each other also complement each other ② be both opposite and complementary to each other; oppose each other and yet also complement each other
相辅而行 be complementary to each other; proceed in coordination; go together
相辅相成 supplement and complement each other
相互参股 purchase each other's shares
相互作用 interaction
相见恨晚 regret not having met earlier
相较见长 gain by contrast (or comparison)
相敬如宾 (of husband and wife) treat each other with the respect due to a guest
相聚一堂 get together in a hall
相亲相爱 be friendly; be on intimate terms
相去无几 there is not much difference; pretty much the same
相忍为安 When you bear with each other you'll have peace; Peace means live and let-live.
相濡以沫 (of stranded fish) moisten each other with spit—give one's meagre resources to help another in time of need
相生相克 mutual promotion and restraint between the five elements
相视而笑 smile at each other; smile into each other's eyes
相提并论 mention in the same breath; place on a par
相形见绌 prove inferior by comparison; pale by comparison; be outshone
相形失色 show apparently a great difference by comparison
相形之下 by contrast; by comparison
相沿成习 become common practice through long usage
相依为命 depend on each other for survival
相映成趣 set each other off and form a pleasing contrast; contrast pleasingly with each other
相与愕然 stare at each other astounded
相知恨晚 regret that one has not got to know sb sooner
相对多数选举制 plurality system; first-past-the-post system
相骂无好言,相打无好拳 There are no quarrels with nice words nor fights with weak blows.

香 [xiāng]
I 形 ① fragrant; scented; sweet-smelling; aromatic ② savoury; palatable; appetizing; delicious ③ with relish; with good appetite ④ (sleep) soundly ⑤ in vogue; popular; welcome
II 名 ① perfume; scent; spice ② incense; joss

stick ③ (*used as a complimentary attribute; esp. of women in traditional literature*)

香案 a long altar on which incense burners are placed; incense burner table
香波 shampoo
香菜 coriander
香草 vanilla
香肠 sausage
香椿 ① Chinese toon ② the tender, edible leaves and stems of Chinese toon
香醇 fragrant, rich (smell or taste)
香醋 aromatic vinegar
香袋 sachet
香榧 Chinese torreya
香粉 cosmetic powder
香干 smoked bean curd
香菇 fragrant mushroom
香瓜 muskmelon
香魂 woman's departed soul (*or* ghost)
香柬 woman's letter
香蕉 banana
香精 essence
香客 worshipper at a Buddhist temple; Buddhist pilgrim
香料 ①perfume ②spice
香炉 incense burner
香茅 lemongrass
香莓 flowering raspberry
香墨 fragrant ink stick
香囊 perfume satchel
香片 scented tea
香蒲 cattail
香气 a sweet smell; fragrance; aroma
香水 perfume; scent
香甜 ①fragrant and sweet ②(of sleep) sound
香蕈 fragrant mushroom
香烟 ①incense smoke ②cigarette
香艳 amorous; erotic
香油 sesame oil
香鼬 alpine weasel
香橼 citron
香皂 perfumed (*or* scented) soap; toilet soap
香脂 ①face cream ②balm; balsam
香烛 joss sticks and candles
香槟酒 champagne
香草醛 vanillic aldehyde; vanillin; vanilla
香榧子 Chinese torreya nut
香馥馥 strongly scented; richly fragrant
香蕉球 ① curling ball ② (of soccer) curved shot
香蕉人 banana
香蕉水 banana oil
香料厂 perfumery
香茅醛 citronellal
香茅油 citronella oil
香喷喷 ① sweet-smelling ② savoury; appetizing

香云纱 gambiered Guangdong gauze
香獐子 musk deer
香风习习 caressed by a scented wind; with a scented wind gently blowing
香格里拉 Shangri-La
香闺绣阁 lady's chamber
香蕉苹果 a species of apple with a bananalike odour
香醪佳酿 delicious (*or* mellow) vintage wine
香港基本法 Hong Kong Basic Law
香港特别行政区 the Hong Kong Special Administrative Region (HKSAR)

厢 [xiāng]
㊣ ①wing; wing-room ②compartment; box ③areas just outside a city gate ④(often used in the early vernacular) side
厢房 wing (usu. of one-storeyed house); wing-room

箱 [xiāng]
㊣ ① box; case; chest; trunk ② box-like thing
箱底 ① the bottom of a chest ② valuables stowed away at the bottom of the chest; one's store of valuables
箱子 chest; box; case; trunk

襄 [xiāng]
㊢ assist; aid; help
襄办 help manage; act as assistant (*or* deputy)
襄理 assistant manager
襄助 assist

镶 [xiāng]
㊢ ①inlay; set; mount ②rim; edge; border
镶板 panelling
镶边 edge; border; rim
镶嵌 ①inlay; set; mount ②mosaic; tessellate
镶牙 put in a false tooth; insert an artificial tooth
镶嵌画 a picture (*or* design) made of mosaic; mosaic

xiáng (ㄒㄧㄤ)

详 [xiáng]
I ㊠ detailed; minute II ㊢ ① explain in detail; elaborate ②clear
详备 detailed, complete
详解 explain in detail; detailed annotation
详尽 detailed and complete; exhaustive; thorough
详密 elaborate; meticulous
详明 full and clear
详情 detailed information; details; particulars
详实 full and accurate
详述 explain; discuss
详谈 talk out; expand on
详图 detail drawing

详细 detailed;minute
详注 ①annotate fully ②detailed annotations
详征博引 quote extensively and at (great) length

降 [xiáng]
〔动〕①surrender;capitulate;show the white flag ② subdue;conquer;vanquish;tame ➡ jiàng
降伏 subdue;vanquish;tame
降服 yield;surrender and acknowledge allegiance
降旗 flag of surrender;white flag
降顺 yield and pledge allegiance to
降龙伏虎 subdue the dragon and tame the tiger—overcome powerful adversaries
降妖伏魔 subdue demons and monsters

庠 [xiáng]
〔名〕school

祥 [xiáng]
〔形〕auspicious;propitious;promising;lucky
祥和 ①happy and auspicious ②kind;benign
祥云 auspicious clouds
祥兆 good omen

翔 [xiáng]
〔动〕circle in the air;fly
翔实 full and accurate

xiǎng(ㄒㄧㄤˇ)

享 [xiǎng]
〔动〕enjoy;share
享福 enjoy a happy life;live in ease and comfort
享乐 lead a life of pleasure;indulge in creature comforts
享年 (of a deceased, generally old person) die at the age of;live to the age of
享受 ①enjoy ②enjoyment;treat
享用 enjoy the use of;enjoy
享有 enjoy (rights,prestige,etc.)
享誉 enjoy good fame
享乐主义 hedonism;pleasure-seeking
享受特权 enjoy privileges
享受公费医疗 enjoy public health services
享受公民权利 enjoy equal rights

响 [xiǎng]
Ⅰ〔名〕sound;noise Ⅱ〔动〕①echo;resound ② sound;ring;beat;fire Ⅲ〔形〕loud;noisy
响板 castanets
响鼻 snort (of a horse,mule,etc.)
响动 the sound of sth astir
响度 degree of loudness;volume
响雷 ①be thundering ②a crash of thunder;thunderclap
响亮 loud and clear;resounding;resonant;sonorous
响铃 jingle bell;cascabel
响锣 beat (or sound) a gong

响器 Chinese percussion instruments
响枪 fire a gun
响晴 (of sky) clear and bright
响声 sound;noise
响吻 smack
响音 ①resonant ②sonorant
响应 ①echo correspondingly ② respond,answer
响当当 ① (of the sound made by a bell, a gong, etc.) loud and resounding ② (of a person) of resounding fame;outstanding;worthy
响尾蛇 rattlesnake
响彻云霄 resound (or reverberate) across the heavens
响鼓还得重锤敲 a loud drum takes a heavy stick to beat it—even talented people require meticulous (or intensive) training

饷 [xiǎng]
Ⅰ〔动〕entertain (with food and drink) Ⅱ〔名〕(usu. of soldiers,policemen,etc.) pay

飨 [xiǎng]
〔动〕treat to food and drink;entertain
飨客 entertain a guest

想 [xiǎng]
〔动〕① think;reflect;mull over ② suppose;consider;think;reckon ③ want;would like feel like (doing sth);intend to ④ remember with longing;pine for;miss
想必 presumably;most probably (or likely)
想出 (object obligatory) think out;think up
想到 ①think of;call to mind ②expect sth to happen;expect that sth will happen
想法 [xiǎngfǎ] think of a way;do what one can;try
想法 [xiǎngfa] idea;opinion;what one has in mind
想家 be homesick
想见 infer;gather
想来 it may be assumed that;presumably
想念 remember with longing; long to see again;miss
想起 remember;recollect;recall;think of;call to mind
想通 straighten out one's thinking;become convinced;come round
想头 ①idea ②hope
想望 ①desire;long for;yearn for ②admire;look up to
想象 ①imagination ②imagine;fancy;visualize
想不到 never expect;be unexpected
想不开 take things too hard;take a matter to heart
想不通 can't follow the reasoning
想出来 think out;think up
想当然 assume sth as a matter of course;take

sth for granted
想得到 think; imagine; expect
想得开 not take to heart; take philosophically; try to look on the bright side of things
想起来 remember; recollect; recall; think of; call to mind
想象力 the power (*or* faculty) of imagination; imagination
想方设法 do everything possible; try every means; try by hook or by crook
想来想去 think it over and over again; turn over in one's mind
想入非非 indulge in fantasy; allow one's fancy to run wild

xiàng(ㄒㄧㄤˋ)

向 [xiàng]
Ⅰ 名 direction; orientation; trend Ⅱ 动 ① face; turn towards ② take sb's part; side with; favour; be partial to Ⅲ 副 always; all along Ⅳ 介 to; towards; against
向背 support or oppose
向导 ① show sb the way; lead sb somewhere; act as a guide ② a guide; an escort
向后 towards the back; backward
向来 always; all along
向例 convention; usual practice
向量 vector
向前 forward; onward; ahead
向上 upward; up
向往 yearn for; look forward to
向下 downward; down
向斜 syncline
向性 tropism
向学 be determined to learn
向阳 be exposed to the sun; have a sunny exposure
向右 towards the right
向着 ① turn towards; face ② take sb's part; side with; be partial to
向左 towards the left
向光性 phototropism
向前看 look to the future; be forward-looking; be optimistic about one's future; eyes front
向钱看 mammonism, put money above all; be money grubbing; be money oriented; be money conscious
向日葵 sunflower
向日性 heliotropism
向上爬 ① climb (up) ② seek personal advancement; be a social climber; be a careerist
向水性 hydrotropism
向斜谷 synclinal valley
向心力 centripetal force
向阳花 sunflower
向壁虚构 make up out of one's head; fabricate
向隅而泣 weep all alone in a corner; be left to grieve in the cold

项 [xiàng]
Ⅰ 名 ① nape (of the neck) ② sum (of money) ③ term Ⅱ 量 (of itemized things): 三项规定 three regulations
项背 a person's back
项链 necklace
项目 item
项圈 neckband (a band of gold or silver, worn around the neck as an ornament); necklet
项背相望 walk one after another in close succession
项目报批 submit a project for approval
项目管理 project management
项目经理 project manager
项目立项 approve and initiate a project
项目评估 projects appraisal
项目融资 project financing
项目预算 project budget
项上枷锁 chain round one's neck
项目建议书 project proposals
项目鉴定报告 project evaluation report
项目资金筹措 project financing
项目法人责任制 system whereby a legal person is held responsible for a project
项庄舞剑，意在沛公 performed the sword dance as a cover for his attempt on Liu Bang's life—act with a hidden motive
项目管理专业人员资格认证制度 Project Management Professional(PMP)

巷 [xiàng]
名 narrow street; lane; alley ➡ hàng
巷口 entrance to a lane
巷尾 end of a lane
巷战 street fighting

相 [xiàng]
Ⅰ 名 ① looks; countenance; appearance ② appearance of things; facies ③ bearing; carriage; posture ④ phase position ⑤ phase ⑥ form; image; picture ⑦ state of element; phase state ⑧ chief minister; prime minister; chancellor ⑨ minister (in some countries) ⑩ minister, one of the pieces in Chinese chess ⑪ attendant; usher Ⅱ 动 ① look at and appraise; examine the physiognomy of ② assist; help ➡ xiāng
相货 examine the goods
相机 ① camera ② watch for an opportunity
相马 look at a horse to judge its worth
相貌 facial features; looks; appearance
相面 tell sb's fortune by reading his face; practise physiognomy
相片 photo (of a person); snapshot
相扑 sumo (wrestling)
相声 comic dialogue; cross talk

相术 fortune-telling by studying facial features;physiognomy
相位 phase position;phase
相印 chief minister's seal of office
相纸 (photographic) printing paper; photographic paper
相手术 palmistry
相夫教子 assist one's husband and bring up the children
相机行事 act as the occasion demands;do as one sees fit
相体裁衣 cut the dress in accordance with one's shape

象 [xiàng]
I 名 ①elephant ②(Chinese chess) elephant ③appearance;look;shape;image II 动 imitate;mimic
象鼻 trunk;proboscis
象棋 chess
象限 quadrant
象牙 elephant's tusk;ivory
象征 ①symbolize;signify;stand for ②symbol;emblem;token
象鼻虫 weevil;snout beetle
象皮病 elephantiasis
象声词 onomatopoeia
象限仪 quadrant
象形字 pictographic character
象牙塔 ①ivory tower ②aloofness from practical life;separation from the harsh realities of ordinary life
象牙质 ①ivory ②dentine
象征性 symbolic;emblematic;token
象形食品 shaped food products,e.g. animal cookies
象形文字 pictograph;hieroglyph
象牙海岸 the Ivory Coast

像 [xiàng]
I 名 ①likeness (of sb);portrait;statue;picture ②image II 动 ①be alike;resemble;take after;look like ②look as if;appear;seem III 介 such as;like
像册 photo album
像差 aberration
像话 reasonable;proper;right
像散 astigmatism
像样 up to the mark;presentable;decent;sound
像章 badge (or button) with sb's likeness on it
像散镜 astigmatoscope
像模像样 up to the mark;presentable;decent
像散透镜 astigmatic lens

橡 [xiàng]
名 ①oak ②rubber tree
橡浆 rubber latex
橡胶 rubber

橡皮 ①(vulcanized) rubber ②eraser;rubber
橡实 acorn
橡子 acorn nut
橡胶草 Russian dandelion;koksaghyz
橡皮版 rubber plate
橡皮船 rubber boat
橡皮膏 adhesive plaster
橡皮筋 rubber band
橡皮泥 plasticine
橡皮圈 ①inflatable life preserver (for swimming learners) ②rubber ring or band (for binding or tying things together)
橡皮线 rubber-sheathed wire
橡实管 acorn tube
橡皮图章 rubber stamp

xiāo(ㄒㄧㄠ)

枭 [xiāo]
I 名 ①owl; legendary bird said to eat its own mother ②chief;chieftain;ringleader ③salt smuggler II 形 fierce and brave III 动 hang (severed heads)
枭鸟 owl
枭骑 elite cavalry unit
枭示 hang (sb's decapitated head) as a warning (for others)
枭雄 a fierce and ambitious person;a formidable man
枭首示众 cut off a person's head and hang it up as a warning to all

枵 [xiāo]
形 empty;hollow
枵肠辘辘 have an empty stomach;be starving

削 [xiāo]
动 ①pare (or peel) with a knife;scrape;whittle ②cut;chop ➡xuē
削皮 pare;peel
削球 chop;cut

哓 [xiāo]
哓哓不休 argue (or talk) endlessly

骁 [xiāo]
形 valiant;valorous;brave
骁将 a valiant general
骁卫 imperial guard
骁勇 brave;valiant

逍 [xiāo]
逍遥 free and unfettered
逍遥法外 get off scot-free;remain at large
逍遥自在 free and unfettered; leisurely and carefree

鸮 [xiāo]
名 owl

消 [xiāo]
动 ①disappear;vanish;melt ②eliminate;dispel;reduce;remove ③pass the time in a leisurely way;idle away (the time) ④(after

不，只，何 etc.）need；require；take
消沉 downhearted；low-spirited；dejected；depressed
消愁 dispel（*or* allay）worries
消除 eliminate；dispel；remove；clear up
消毒 ①disinfect；sterilize ②disinfected；sterilized；pasteurized
消法 consumer protection law
消防 ① fire fighting ② fire prevention and control
消费 consume
消耗 consume；use up；deplete；expend
消化 ①absorb；digest（food）②think over and absorb；digest（knowledge）
消极 ①negative ②passive；inactive
消解 clear up；dispel；remove
消弭 put an end to（an evil）；prevent
消灭 ① perish；die out；pass away ② eliminate；abolish；exterminate；wipe out
消磨 ① wear down；fritter away ② while away；idle away
消纳 dispose
消气 cool down；be mollified
消遣 ①divert oneself；while away the time ② diversion；pastime
消融（of ice or snow）melt；thaw
消散 scatter and disappear；dissipate
消声 diminish（*or* eliminate）noises
消失 disappear；vanish；dissolve；die（*or* fade）away
消食 help digestion
消逝 die（*or* fade）away；vanish；elapse
消释 dispel；clear up；dissipate
消受 ① enjoy（having sth）② endure；bear；stand（hardship，ill treatment，etc.）
消瘦 emaciated；thinning down
消暑 ① spend a summer holiday ② relieve summer heat
消损 ① reduce bit by bit；decrease ② fritter away
消停 silent；steady
消亡 wither away；die out
消息 ①news；information ②tidings；news
消夏 spend a summer holiday
消闲 fill one's spare time；while away the time
消炎 diminish（*or* counteract，reduce）inflammation；dephlogisticate
消灾 rid calamities
消长 decrease and increase；growth and decline；wax and wane
消肿 ①cause a swelling to go down ②detumescence；streamline
消毒剂 disinfectant
消防车 fire engine
消防队 fire brigade；fire department
消防艇 fireboat
消防站 fire station

消费品 consumer goods
消费税 consumption tax
消费者 consumer
消耗热 hectic fever
消耗战 war of attrition
消化道 alimentary canal；digestive tract
消化酶 digestive enzyme；digestive ferment
消化液 digestive juice
消火栓 fire hydrant
消色差 achromatism
消声器 muffler
消声室 anechoic chamber
消炎剂 antiphlogistic
消炎片 antiphlogistic tablets
消音器 bumper；muffler；noise suppressor
消愁解闷 divert oneself from boredom；dispel depression（*or* melancholy）
消除病毒 ①debug；devirus（as in computer）②disinfect；sterilize；sanitize；listerize；antisepsis（as hospital）
消除隐患 remove a hidden danger
消费潮流 consume trend
消费城市 consume city
消费过热 overheated consumption
消费基金 funds for consumption
消费结构 consumption patterns
消费膨胀 inflated consumption；over-expanded consumption
消费水平 level of consumption
消费心理 consumer psychology
消费心态 psychographics
消费信贷 consumer credit
消费资料 means of subsistence；consumer goods
消化不良 ①indigestion ②dyspepsia
消化器官 digestive organ
消化系统 digestive system
消极怠工 sabotage
消遣读物 escape book；entertainment
消费合作社 consumer cooperative
消费品换代 updating and upgrading of consumer goods
消费者协会 consumer association
消化性溃疡 peptic ulcer
消色差透镜 achromatic lens；achromat
消费价格指数 consumer price
消费者权益法 consumer law
消费者权益日 Consumers' Right Day
消息灵通人士 well-informed circles；well-informed sources；informed guesswork；hipster
消费品价格指数 consumer price index
消费者物价指数 consumer price index（CPI）；cost of living index

宵 ［xiāo］
〖名〗night
宵禁 curfew

宵夜 food (*or* refreshments) taken late at night; midnight snack

绡 [xiāo]
名 ①raw silk ②fabric made of unprocessed or raw silk

萧 [xiāo]
形 deserted and miserable; desolate; dreary

萧墙 the screen wall facing the gate of a Chinese house

萧瑟 ①rustling in the air; soughing ②bleak; desolate

萧森 dreary and desolate

萧索 ①bleak and dreary; dull and desolate ② (of a person's mood) melancholy; depressed

萧条 ①desolate; bleak ②depression

萧萧 ① the sound of a horse neighing (*or* whinnying) ② the sound of a whistling wind, pattering rain, etc.

萧墙之祸 trouble behind the screen wall— trouble at home; trouble from within; internal strife

硝 [xiāo]
I 名 nitre; saltpetre II 动 taw; tan

硝化 nitrify

硝石 nitre; saltpetre

硝水 glass gall

硝酸 nitric acid

硝烟 smoke of gunpowder

硝盐 salt made from earth containing a comparatively high percentage of sodium chloride

硝酸铵 ammonium nitrate

硝酸钾 potassium nitrate

硝酸钠 sodium nitrate

硝酸盐 nitrate

硝化甘油 nitroglycerine

硝酸甘油片 nitroglycerine tablets

硝酸纤维素 nitrocellulose; cellulose nitrate

销 [xiāo]
I 动 ①melt (metal) ②cancel; annul; cross out ③put on sale; sell; market ④pay out; expend; spend ⑤fasten with a latch II 名 pin

销案 close a case; bring a case to a close

销钉 pin; peg; plug; dowel

销毁 destroy (by melting, burning, etc.)

销魂 be overwhelmed (with sorrow or joy); feel transported

销货 sales; merchandise sales

销假 report back after leave of absence

销量 the quantity (of goods) sold; sales made

销路 outlet; sale; market

销蚀 corrode

销势 sale; sales momentum

销售 sell; market

销行 sell; be on sale

销赃 dispose of stolen goods

销账 cancel (*or* remove) from an account; write off

销子 pin; peg; dowel; bolt

销户口 cancel one's residence registration

销金窟 money squandering den (e. g. a brothel, gambling house, etc.)

销蚀剂 corrodent

销售税 sales tax

销声匿迹 keep silent and lie low; disappear from the scene

销售疲软 sluggish market

销售渠道 sales channels

销售特色 selling point

销售网点 sales outlets

销售组合 sales mix

销售者市场 seller's market

箫 [xiāo]
名 *xiao*, a vertical bamboo flute

潇 [xiāo]
形 ①(of water) deep and clear ②(of wind and rain) beating; driving

潇洒 (of a person's appearance, demeanour, carriage, etc.) natural and unrestrained

潇潇 ①(of wind and rain) driving; whistling and pattering ②drizzling; drizzly

潇洒自如 with an easy grace; casual and elegant

霄 [xiāo]
名 clouds; sky; heaven

霄汉 the sky; the firmament

霄壤 heaven and earth

霄壤之别 as far apart (*or* as different) as heaven and earth; a world of difference

嚣 [xiāo]
动 clamour; hubbub; din

嚣张 rampant; arrogant; aggressive

XIÁO (ㄒㄧㄠˊ)

淆 [xiáo]
动 confuse; mix

淆惑 confuse; bewilder

淆乱 ① mixed and disorderly ② confuse; befuddle

XIĂO (ㄒㄧㄠˇ)

小 [xiǎo]
I 形 ①small; little; tiny; minor ②I; me; my ③(*used before* (a surname) *to refer to a young person*, *or before a given name to refer to a child*): 小军 Xiao Jun; Little Jun ④youngest: 小孙子 youngest grandson II 副 ①for a short while; for a little time ②a little; a bit; slightly ③a little less than; almost III 名 ①young children; little ones ②lesser (*or* minor) wife; concubine

小报 small-sized newspaper; tabloid

小辈 junior members of a family or of families more or less related

小便 ①urinate;pass (*or* make) water;empty one's bladder ②urine ③penis

小病 minor illness;indisposition

小菜 ① pickled vegetables; pickles ② dial; meat,fish and vegetable dishes;common dishes

小产 have a miscarriage

小肠 small intestine

小潮 neap tide

小炒 stir-fry dish cooked in a small wok

小车 ① wheelbarrow; handbarrow; handcart; pushcart ②car;sedan

小乘 Little Vehicle (a school of Buddhism); Hinayana

小吃 ①snacks;refreshments ②cold dishes (of western food)

小丑 ① clown; buffoon ② contemptible wretch;vile character

小葱 shallot;spring onion

小刀 pocket knife

小道 small lane;path

小调 ①ditty;tune ②minor

小队 the lowest-level unit of a group organized for a particular purpose;team;squad

小额 small amount

小儿 ①children ②my son

小二 young waiter in a wineshop or an inn

小贩 pedlar;vendor;hawker

小费 tip;gratuity

小腹 underbelly;lower abdomen

小工 unskilled labourer

小鼓 side drum;snare drum

小褂 Chinese-style shirt (worn next to the skin)

小鬼 ①little devil;demon servant in Hell ②child;imp (a term of endearment used in addressing a child)

小国 small country;microstate

小号 ①small size (of clothes,etc.) ②my (*or* our) store ③trumpet

小蓟 field thistle

小脚 bound feet (of women in the old days)

小节 ①a small matter;trifle ②bar;measure

小结 ①a brief sum-up;a preliminary (*or* interim) summary ②summarize briefly

小姐 ①a young (unmarried) lady ②Miss

小看 look down upon;underestimate;belittle

小康 comfortable level of living; better-off life;moderate prosperity

小考 minor examination

小路 path;trail

小麦 wheat

小米 millet

小蜜 a young lover

小名 pet name for a child;childhood name

小命 life

小脑 cerebellum

小农 small farmer

小跑 trot;jog

小品 skit;one-act play;sketch

小气 ① stingy; niggardly; mean ② narrow-minded;petty

小憩 take a short rest

小瞧 look down upon;underestimate

小区 residence district;small residential district, with shopping centers and various other amenities

小觑 despise;look down upon;underestimate

小人 ①a small man ②I ③a base person;a vile character;villain

小山 little hill;hillock

小舌 uvula

小时 hour

小事 trifle;petty thing;minor matter

小树 sapling

小数 decimal

小睡 nap;beauty sleep

小说 novel;fiction

小厮 ①young male servant;page boy;page ②boy;young lad

小艇 small boat;dinghy;skiff (rowed or sailed by one person)

小偷 petty (*or* sneak) thief;pilferer

小腿 shank;lower leg

小巷 alley;holing-through

小鞋 tight shoes—difficulties created,or unfair treatment given,by one's boss or superior when he cannot punish openly

小写 ①the ordinary form of a Chinese numeral ②small letter;minuscule

小心 take care;be careful;be cautious

小型 small-size;small-scale;miniature

小学 ① primary (*or* elementary) school ②philological studies

小样 galley proof

小姨 mother's youngest sister—aunt

小引 a brief (*or* short) introductory note (to a poem,essay,etc.);foreword

小雨 light rain;drizzle

小灶 small mess—a mess hall where higher-grade food is prepared and served to a restricted group of diners

小账 tip;gratuity

小照 a small-sized photograph of oneself

小指 little finger or toe

小众 minority

小传 brief biography;biographical sketch;profile

小资 petty bourgeoisie

小子 [xiǎozǐ] ①the younger male generation ②a term of address used by seniors to juniors ③I

小字 ①handwritten small characters ②childhood name

小子 [xiǎozi] ①boy ②bloke;fellow;guy
小卒 foot soldier
小组 small group
小白菜 a variety of Chinese cabbage
小白领 young white-collar worker
小百货 sundries;notions;smalls;small articles of daily use
小摆设 little curios, handicrafts, statuettes, etc. placed on shelves and desks for decoration; bric-a-bracs; ornamental knick-knacks
小报告 a little report—a secret report to the higher authority on the shortcomings or wrongdoings of sb
小扁豆 lentil
小便池 urinal
小辫儿 short braid;pigtail
小辫子 a mistake (*or* shortcoming) that may be exploited by others;vulnerable point; handle
小标题 subheading;subhead
小部分 small;fraction
小菜儿 sth extremely easy (to do or manage)
小册子 booklet;pamphlet
小吃部 snack counter
小吃店 snack bar
小吃街 snack street;food street
小聪明 cleverness in trivial matters; petty trick
小道理 minor principle
小动作 ①mean and petty action;little trick or manoeuvre ②fidgety movements (made by schoolchildren in class)
小豆蔻 cardamom;cardamum
小肚子 underbelly;lower abdomen
小儿科 ①(department of) paediatrics ②trivial;insignificant;petty;kid's stuff
小儿子 youngest son
小而全 small and all inclusive
小分队 small group;squad;detachment
小个子 short person;small fellow
小姑(子) ①husband's younger sister;sister-in-law ②one's youngest paternal aunt
小广播 spreading of hearsay information;grapevine;bush telegraph
小广告 handbill
小孩儿 child
小环境 ① micro-environment ② local social environment
小皇帝 pampered offspring of the one-child-family
小黄鱼 little yellow croaker
小伙子 young man; lad; young fellow (*or* chap);youngster
小集团 clique;faction;sect
小家伙 kid
小家庭 small family

小轿车 sedan;car
小金库 private gold storage;self-concerned exchequer;unit-owned exchequer
小景气 boomlet
小舅子 wife's younger brother;brother-in-law
小剧场 mini theatre
小客车 minibus
小口径 small-bore;small-calibre
小老婆 concubine
小两口 a young (married) couple
小灵通 little smart
小流域 micro-watersheds
小萝卜 radish
小买卖 small business
小麦粉 wheat-meal
小麦穗 wheatear
小卖部 ①a small shop attached to a school, factory, theatre, etc. (selling cigarettes, confectionery,cold drinks,etc.) ②buffet; snack counter
小猫熊 lesser panda
小拇指 little finger
小妞儿 a young girl
小牛肉 veal
小朋友 ①children ②little friend;little boy or girl
小便宜 small gain;petty advantage
小品文 familiar essay;essay
小评论 a short comment
小气鬼 miser;penny pincher
小气候 microclimate;local conditions;specific political or economic climate
小前提 minor premise (in a syllogism)
小青年 young people;boys and girls
小青瓦 small black tile
小球藻 chlorella
小曲儿 ditty;popular tune
小圈子 ①a small social circle;a narrow area of activity ②a small circle (*or* set) of people;a small clique
小犬座 Canis Minor
小人书 children's picture-story book
小人物 an unimportant person;a nobody;cipher;nonentity
小日子 the easy life of a small family (esp. of a young couple)
小商品 small commodities
小生产 small (*or* small-scale) production
小狮座 Leo Minor
小时工 hourly paid worker
小时候 in one's childhood; when one was young
小市民 a town-dweller of the lower middle class;urban petty bourgeois;plebeian;philistine
小叔子 husband's younger brother;brother-in-law

小数点 decimal point
小说家 novelist;writer of fiction
小苏打 sodium bicarbonate
小算盘 small abacus-selfish calculations
小提琴 violin
小天地 one's own little world
小五金 metal fittings (e.g. nails,wires,hinges,bolts,locks.etc.);hardware
小先生 little teacher—a student playing the role of a teacher to his classmates
小小说 short story
小行星 minor planet
小型张 small sheet
小熊猫 lesser panda
小熊座 Ursa Minor
小学生 primary school pupil;schoolchild;schoolboy or schoolgirl
小循环 pulmonary circulation
小妖精 coquettish young girl
小业主 small (or petty) proprietor
小夜曲 serenade
小姨子 wife's younger sister;sister-in-law
小意思 ①a small token of one's regard ②a mere trifle;nothing important
小音阶 minor scale
小字辈 juniors;younger members;persons of lower status
小白脸儿 a young fair face—a handsome,effeminate young man
小本经营 do business with little capital—go in for sth in a small way
小本生意 business with a small capital;go in for sth in a small way
小别重逢 meet again after a short interval
小步舞曲 minuet (the music)
小不点儿 ①very small;tiny ②tiny tot
小打小闹 on a small scale;in a small way
小肚鸡肠 petty;narrow-minded
小额存款 small savings account
小额贷款 petty loan
小额优惠 fringe benefits
小额支票 small check
小恩小惠 bounty;small mercies;little favours;small favours;economic sops or bait
小户(人家) ①a poor,humble family;a family of limited means and without powerful connections ②a small family
小家碧玉 a pretty girl of humble birth
小家子气 small-minded;petty
小康社会 society in which people enjoy a fairly comfortable life;well-off society
小康之家 family with a modest competence;comfortably-off family;well-off family
小麦线虫 nematode of wheat (Anguina tritici)
小门小户 poor and humble family
小鸟依人 an endearing little bird (said of a lovely young girl)

小农经济 small-scale peasant economy;small-scale farming by individual owners
小巧玲珑 small and exquisite
小人得志 small man intoxicated by success;a small man having greatness thrust upon him;villains holding sway
小生产者 small producer
小试锋芒 display only a small part of one's talent or capability
小手小脚 ①stingy;mean ②lacking boldness;timid;niggling
小提琴手 violinist
小题大做 make a fuss over a trifle;make a mountain out of a molehill
小偷小摸 pilfering
小玩意儿 knickknack;trinket
小心谨慎 careful;cautious;discreet;prudent
小心眼儿 narrow-minded;petty
小心翼翼 with the greatest of care;very cautiously
小型飞机 aviette;light aeroplane
小型跑车 kart
小有才干 of some ability
小百科全书 micropaedia
小城镇建设 construction of small towns and cities
小儿麻痹症 infantile paralysis;poliomyelitis;polio
小规模战争 miniwar
小麦赤霉病 wheat scab
小麦吸浆虫 wheat midge
小商品经济 small commodity economy
小手工业者 small handicraftsman
小团体主义 cliquism;small-group mentality
小巫见大巫 a minor magician in the presence of a great one—feel dwarfed;pale into insignificance by comparison
小型核武器 mini-nukes
小型张邮票 souvenir sheet (or card)
小资产阶级 petty bourgeoisie
小组循环赛 group round robin
小道(儿)消息 hearsay;grapevine;gossip;alley news;bush telegraph;side-street news
小土地出租者 a lessor of small plots of land
小型公共汽车 minibus
小机构,大服务 minimum institution,maximum service
小政府,大社会 small government,big society
小不忍则乱大谋 lack of forbearance in small matters upsets great plans
小商品批发市场 wholesale market for small commodities
小型电视连续剧 mini-series

晓 [xiǎo]
Ⅰ 名 dawn;daybreak Ⅱ 动 ①know ②let sb know;inform;tell
晓畅 ①be familiar with;have a deep under-

standing of ② (of a piece of writing) smooth and explicit
晓得 know
晓示 tell explicitly；notify
晓谕 give explicit instructions
晓行夜宿 (of a person on a long journey) start at dawn and stop at dusk
晓以大义 instil in sb's mind the righteousness of a cause
晓以利害 warn sb of the possible consequences；impress on sb the gains and losses involved
晓之以理 try to persuade sb with reason；reason things out with sb

筱 ［xiǎo］
名 ①thin bamboo ②substitute for 小

xiào（ㄒㄧㄠ）

孝 ［xiào］
名 ① filial piety ② mourning period ③ mourning dress
孝道 filial duty
孝服 ① mourning apparel ② a conventional period of mourning
孝敬 ① show filial respect to (one's elders) ②give presents to (one's elders or superiors) to show one's respect；pay a tribute of respect to
孝顺 show filial obedience
孝心 filial sentiment；filial devotion
孝衣 mourning dress
孝子 ①filial son；dutiful son ②son in mourning
孝子贤孙 worthy progeny；a fine son

肖 ［xiào］
动 resemble；be similar；be like
肖像 portrait；portraiture
肖像画 portrait-painting
肖像权 portraiture right

校 ［xiào］
名 ①school ②field officer ➡jiào
校车 school bus
校风 school spirit
校服 school uniform
校官 field officer；field grade officer
校规 school regulations
校花 campus belle
校徽 school badge
校刊 school publication；college journal
校历 school calendar
校内 on (the) campus
校庆 the anniversary of the founding of a school or college
校舍 schoolhouse；school building
校外 outside school；outside the campus
校务 administrative affairs of a school or college

校训 school motto
校医 school doctor
校友 alumnus or alumna
校园 campus；school grounds
校长 ① headmaster (of a middle or primary school)；principal ② president (of a university，college，etc.)；chancellor
校址 the location of a school or college；school or college address
校办企业 school-run enterprise
校外活动 after-school activities
校外辅导员 guest counsellor for school children's activities；afterschool activities counsellor

哮 ［xiào］
动 ① heavy breathing；wheeze；cough ② roar；howl；yell
哮喘 asthma
哮吼 yell and scream
哮声如雷 thunderous howl

笑 ［xiào］
动 ① smile；laugh ② ridicule；laugh at；deride
笑柄 laughing stock；butt；joke
笑话 ①joke；jest ②laugh at；ridicule
笑脸 smiling face
笑料 sth funny (or laughable)；laughing stock；joke
笑骂 ① deride and upbraid；taunt ② scold in jest (or jokingly)
笑纳 kindly accept (this small gift of mine)
笑气 laughing gas；nitrous oxide
笑容 smiling expression；smile
笑谈 ① laughing stock；object of ridicule ② funny remark；joke；jest
笑纹 laugh line
笑星 comic star，usu. outstanding comic dialogue performer
笑颜 smiling face
笑靥 ①dimple ②smiling face
笑哈哈 laughingly；with a laugh
笑眯眯 smiling；with a genial smile on one's face
笑面虎 smiling tiger—an outwardly kind but inwardly cruel person
笑嘻嘻 grinning；smiling broadly
笑掉大牙 laugh one's head off
笑而不答 only smile but not reply
笑话百出 make many stupid mistakes；make oneself utterly ridiculous
笑口常开 grinning all the time
笑里藏刀 hide a dagger behind a smile—with murderous intent behind one's smiles
笑破肚皮 split one's sides with laughter
笑容可掬 be radiant with smiles
笑逐颜开 beam with smiles；wreath in smiles

效 [xiào]
I 〔名〕 effect; result; efficiency; 生效 come into effect (*or* force) II 〔动〕 ①imitate; follow the example of; follow suit ②devote (one's energy or life); dedicate (oneself); render (a service)
效法 follow the example of; model oneself on; learn from
效仿 imitate; follow the example of
效果 ① effect; result ② sound and lighting effects
效劳 work in the service of; work for
效力 ①render a service to; serve ②effect
效率 efficiency
效命 go all out to serve sb regardless of the consequences
效能 efficacy; usefulness
效验 intended effect; desired result
效益 beneficial result; benefit
效应 (physical or chemical) effect
效用 effectiveness; usefulness
效尤 knowingly follow the example of a wrongdoer
效忠 pledge loyalty to; devote oneself heart and soul to
效率优先 give priority to efficiency
效益工资 efficiency-related wages; wages based on economic performance
效犬马之劳 serve sb faithfully

啸 [xiào]
〔动〕 ①(of people) whistle ②(of birds or animals) scream; roar; howl ③sound of some natural phenomena ④whirring; buzzing; hissing; whizzing
啸聚 holler to each other; band together; gang up
啸鸣 ① whistle; whizz; screech; howl ② a loud, shrill and long sound
啸聚山林 holler to each other, form a band and take to the greenwood

xiē(ㄒㄧㄝ)

些 [xiē]
〔量〕 ①a few; some ②a little; a bit; rather; somewhat
些微 slightly; a little; a bit
些许 a little; a few

揳 [xiē]
〔动〕 drive (a wedge, etc.)

楔 [xiē]
I 〔名〕 wedge; peg II 〔动〕 drive (a wedge, etc.)
楔子 ①wedge ②peg ③prologue or interlude in Yuan Dynasty drama ④prologue in some modern novels
楔形文字 cuneiform characters; sphenogram

歇 [xiē]
I 〔动〕 ① rest; take a rest ② stop (work, etc.); knock off; quit ③ go to bed II 〔名〕 a short time; a little while; a moment
歇班 be off duty; have time off
歇顶 get a bit thin on top; be balding
歇伏 stop work during the hottest days of the year
歇工 stop work; knock off
歇脚 rest the feet—stop on the way for a rest
歇气 have a short break
歇晌 take a midday nap (*or* rest)
歇宿 put up somewhere for the night; make an overnight stop
歇息 ①have a rest ②put up for the night; go to bed
歇业 withdrawl from business; close a business; go out of business
歇后语 a two-part allegorical saying, of which the first part, always stated, is descriptive, while the second part, sometimes unstated, carries the message
歇斯底里 ① hysteria ② unnaturally excited (*or* emotional); hysterical

蝎 [xiē]
〔名〕 scorpion
蝎毒 scorpion venom; buthotoxin
蝎子 scorpion
蝎虎(子) gecko; house lizard

xié(ㄒㄧㄝ)

叶 [xié]
〔名〕 rhyme; concordance ➡yè

协 [xié]
I 〔名〕 harmony; concord; coordination II 〔形〕 joint; concerted; common III 〔动〕 aid; assist
协办 help sponsor; assist in holding
协捕 assist in catching (*or* capturing) a criminal
协查 help investigate (crime)
协定 ① agreement; accord ② reach an agreement on sth; conclude a convention
协会 association; society
协理 ①assist in the management (of an enterprise, etc.) ②assistant manager (in a bank, business enterprise, etc.)
协力 unite efforts; join in a common effort
协商 consult; talk things over
协调 ① coordinate; concert; harmonize; bring into line ②in a concerted way; balanced; harmonious; in tune
协同 work in coordination with; cooperate with
协议 ①agree on ②agreement
协助 assist; help; give assistance; provide help
协作 cooperate; coordinate; combine (in efforts)

协定价 agreement price
协议工 contract worker
协奏曲 concerto
协定边界 conventional boundary
协定关税 conventional tariff
协商对话 consultation and dialogue (*or* discussion)
协商会议 consultative conference
协调发展 harmonious development (*or* growth);coordinated and balanced development
协同作战 fight in coordination
协议离婚 divorce by agreement; mutual-agreed divorce;divorce on contract
协作精神 communist spirit of cooperation
协商委员会 consultative committee (*or* commission)
协调委员会 coordination committee
协议投资额 committed investment volume
协约国际法 conventional international law
协商一致的原则 principle of reaching unanimity through consultation;principle of consensus
协议外商投资额 volume of agreed foreign investment;contractual value of foreign investment;committed amount of foreign investment

邪 [xié] I 形 ①evil;heresy ②irregular;abnormal;strange II 名 ①unhealthy environmental influence that causes disease; miasma ② evil spirits that bring disasters
邪道 evil ways;a depraved life;vice
邪恶 evil;wicked;vicious
邪乎 extraordinary;severe
邪教 (evil) cult;heretic sect;heathendom
邪路 evil ways;vice
邪魔 evil spirit;demon
邪念 an evil thought;a wicked idea
邪气 a perverse trend;an evil influence
邪术 black magic;sorcery;witchcraft
邪说 heresy;heretical ideas;fallacy
邪心 an evil thought;a wicked idea
邪门儿 ① strange; odd; abnormal ② crooked ways;underhand means;dishonest practices (*or* methods)
邪不侵正 The evil will not triumph over the virtuous.
邪不压正 The evil with not triumph over the virtuous.
邪恶轴心 axis of evil
邪教组织 evil organizations with the pretext
邪门歪道 crooked ways; underhand means; dishonest practices (*or* methods)
邪魔外道 ①evil demons and heretics ②unorthodox ways;crooked ways and means

胁 [xié] I 名 flank;side of the human body from the armpit to the waist II 动 compel;coerce;force
胁从 be an accomplice under duress
胁迫 coerce;force
胁肩谄笑 cringe and smile obsequiously;bow and scrape

挟 [xié] 动 ①hold under the arm ②coerce;compel;force sb to submit (*or* yield) ③bear;harbour (resentment,etc.)
挟持 ①seize sb on both sides by the arms ② hold sb under duress
挟仇 harbour a grudge
挟带 carry under one's arms
挟恨 harbour intense hatred
挟嫌 harbour resentment;bear a grudge
挟制 take advantage of sb's weakness to enforce obedience;force sb to do one's bidding
挟势弄权 abuse one's position and power
挟天子以令诸侯 have the emperor in one's power and order the nobles about in his name;control the emperor and command the nobles

偕 [xié] 副 together with;accompanied by;in the company of
偕老 (used in blessing newly-weds) live together to a ripe old age
偕同 in the company of;accompanied by;along with
偕行 ①travel (*or* go) together ②coexist

斜 [xié] 形 oblique;slanting;tilted;askew
斜边 ①hypotenuse ②bevel edge
斜度 degree of inclination;gradient
斜高 slant height
斜角 ①oblique angle ②bevel angle
斜井 ① inclined shaft; slope ② petroleum inclined well;slant hole
斜路 wrong path
斜率 slope
斜面 ①inclined plane ②oblique plane;bevel (face)
斜坡 slope
斜射 ①cast oblique rays (*or* beams) on ②oblique fire
斜视 ① strabismus ② look sideways; cast a sidelong glance
斜躺 recline
斜纹 twill (weave)
斜线 oblique line
斜眼 ① strabismus ② wall-eye; cross-eye; squint ③a wall-eyed (*or* cross-eyed) person
斜阳 the setting sun
斜照 ①cast oblique rays (*or* beams) on ②the

setting sun
斜长石 plagioclase (a mineral)
斜度标 gradient sign
斜对面 opposite slightly to the right or left
斜角规 bevel square
斜拉桥 cable-stayed bridge
斜视图 oblique drawing
斜体字 italics
斜纹布 twill;drill
斜线号 slant (/)
斜线球 diagonal shot;cross-court shot
斜轴线 oblique axis
斜风细雨 gentle wind and light rain

谐 [xié]
Ⅰ 形 ①harmony;accord ②humorous Ⅱ 动
come to an agreement;agree with;settle
谐和 harmonious;concordant
谐调 harmonious;well-balanced
谐星 comic star
谐谑 banter
谐音 ①euphony ②partials ③homophony
谐振 resonance
谐谑曲 scherzo
谐振腔 resonant cavity

絜 [xié]
动 ① measure the circumference of ②
measure ➡jié

颉 [xié]
动 (of birds) fly upwards;soar

携 [xié]
动 ①carry;take (or bring) along ②take
(or hold) by the hand
携带 carry;take along
携手 join hands
携款潜逃 abscond with an amount of money;
run off with money
携款外逃 flee abroad with funds
携手并进 go forward hand in hand

鞋 [xié]
名 shoe
鞋帮 upper (of a shoe)
鞋带 shoelace;shoestring
鞋底 sole (of a shoe)
鞋垫 shoe-pad;insole
鞋跟 heel (of a shoe)
鞋尖 toe cap
鞋匠 shoemaker;cobbler
鞋扣 shoe buckle
鞋刷 shoe brush
鞋样 shoe pattern;outline of a shoe's upper
and sole
鞋油 shoe polish (or cream)
鞋掌 heelpiece;plate
鞋拔子 shoehorn

撷 [xié]
动 pick;pluck

鳃 [xié]
名 harmony;concord (usu. used in person-

al names)

缬 [xié]
名 patterned silk fabric

xiě(ㄒㄧㄝˇ)

写 [xiě]
动 ① write ② compose;write ③ describe;
portray;depict ④paint;sketch;draw
写法 ①style of writing;literary style ②style
of handwriting;penmanship
写稿 write for (or contribute to) a magazine,
etc.
写生 sketch from life;do a still life painting;
paint (or sketch) from nature
写实 write (or paint) realistically
写意 freehand brushwork in traditional Chinese painting
写照 ① portray (a person or character) ②
portrayal;portraiture
写真 ① portray a person;draw a portrait ②
portrait ③ true-to-life depiction;faithful
representation ④photograph
写作 writing
写生画 sketch
写真集 photo album
写字间 office
写字楼 office building
写字台 writing desk;desk;bureau
写作班子 writing group

血 [xiě]
➡xuè
血块 blood clot;clot
血丝 a trace of blood
血晕 [xiěyùn] contusion;bruise
血淋淋 ①dripping with blood;bloody;gory ②
grim;bitter;cruel

xiè(ㄒㄧㄝˋ)

泄 [xiè]
动 ①let out;discharge;deflate;release ②
divulge;let out;leak;disclose ③give vent to;
vent
泄底 reveal (or expose) what is at the bottom
of sth
泄愤 give vent to one's pent-up anger
泄洪 flood discharge;release floodwater
泄劲 lose heart;feel discouraged;be disheartened;slacken one's efforts
泄漏 ①(of a fluid or gas) leak;escape ②(of a
secret, etc.) leak; let out; divulge; give
away
泄露 let out;reveal
泄密 divulge a secret;betray confidential matters
泄气 ① lose heart; feel discouraged; be disheartened ② disappointing; frustrating; pathetic

泄水 sluicing
泄洪道 flood-relief channel;floodway
泄水道 sluiceway
泄水孔 outlet
泄水闸 sluice gate;sluice
泄殖腔 cloacal chamber;cloaca
泄洪隧道 flood-discharge tunnel
泄漏秘密 let out a secret;divulge a secret; give away a secret
泄密事件 case of leakage of a secret
泄私愤,图报复 revenge a personal grudge

泻 [xiè]
囫 ①flow swiftly;rush down;pour out ② loose bowels;diarrhoea;(as in cattle) scour ③purge;quench
泻肚 have loose bowels;have diarrhoea
泻肺 purge the lungs of pathogenic fire
泻火 purge (the body of) pathogenic fire; quench pathogenic fire
泻盐 Epsom salts;salts
泻药 laxative;cathartic;purgative

绁 [xiè]
I 图 rope;bonds II 囫 fasten;bind;tie

卸 [xiè]
囫 ①unload;discharge ②remove;take off ③unhitch;unharness (draught animals,etc.) ④remove;strip;dismantle ⑤lay down;shirk
卸鞍 remove the saddle;unsaddle
卸车 unload (goods,etc.) from a vehicle;un-load a truck,car,etc.
卸过 shirk one's responsibility for an error
卸货 unload (or discharge) a cargo;unload
卸任 be relieved of one's office
卸责 shirk responsibility and shift the blame onto others
卸妆 (of a female) remove ornaments and formal dress
卸装 (of an actor or actress) remove stage makeup and costume
卸货港 port of discharge;unloading port
卸甲归田 take off one's armour and go home—retire from office
卸磨杀驴 kill the donkey the moment it leaves the millstone—get rid of sb as soon as he has done his job

屑 [xiè]
I 图 bits;scraps;fragments;crumbs II 彤 trifling;trivial III 囫 (mostly used in the neg-ative) deign;consider worthwhile
屑子 crumb

械 [xiè]
图 ①tool;device;instrument ②weapon; arms ③fetters;shackles
械斗 a fight with weapons between groups of people
械系 put fetters on sb

亵 [xiè]
I 囫 treat with irreverence;slight;be dis-respectful II 彤 lewd;obscene;indecent
亵渎 blaspheme;profane;pollute
亵近 be intimate with (a woman);treat with familiarity
亵器 chamber pot
亵衣 underwear;underclothes
亵语 salacious language;dirty words;obsceni-ties
亵渎神明 blasphemy against gods

渫 [xiè]
囫 ①remove;get rid of ②discharge; dredge

谢 [xiè]
囫 ①thank ②make an apology;apologize ③decline;refuse ④(of flowers,leaves,etc.) wither
谢忱 gratitude;thankfulness
谢词 a thank-you speech
谢顶 get a bit thin on top;be balding
谢恩 (usually of a minister to an emperor) express gratitude for a favour
谢过 apologize for having done sth wrong;a-pologize for one's mistake (or error)
谢绝 politely refuse;decline;deny oneself to
谢客 ①decline to receive visitors;not be see-ing any visitors ②thank a guest for his visit
谢礼 a gift in token of gratitude;a return present
谢幕 answer (or respond to) a curtain call
谢世 pass away;die
谢谢 thanks
谢意 gratitude;thankfulness
谢罪 apologize for an offence;offer one's apol-ogy for a fault
谢绝参观 No visitors allowed;Not open to vis-itors.
谢天谢地 thank goodness;thank heaven

媟 [xiè]
彤 dally (with a woman);be familiar
媟渎 blaspheme;profane
媟慢 treat cheaply or immodestly;dally with; take liberties with
媟狎 behave in a licentious manner;philander

解 [xiè]
I 囫 get the point;get wise to (sth);be clear about;see II 图 acrobatic performance, especially on horseback ➡jiě;jiè

榭 [xiè]
图 pavilion (or house) on a terrace

邂 [xiè]
邂逅 meet (a relative,friend,etc.) unexpect-edly;run into sb;meet by chance

懈 [xiè]
彤 slack;lax;remiss
懈怠 slack;sluggish
懈劲 relax one's exertions;lose one's drive; slack off

懈气 relax one's exertions; lose one's drive; slack off

蟹 [xiè]
名 crab

蟹黄 the reddish-yellow crab meat (made up of the ovary and digestive glands)
蟹钳 the crab's claws
蟹青 greenish-grey (colour)

XīN（ㄒ１ㄣ）

心 [xīn]
名 ① heart ② mind; feeling; moral nature (or character); intention ③ centre; core ④ fifth of the 28 constellations in ancient Chinese astronomy

心爱 loved; treasured; dear to one's heart
心包 pericardium
心病 ① worry; anxiety ② sore point; secret trouble
心搏 heartbeat
心裁 idea; conception; mental plan
心肠 ①heart; intention ②state of mind; mood
心潮 a tidal surge of emotion; surging thoughts and emotions
心得 what one has learned from work, study, etc.
心底 the bottom of one's heart
心地 a (person's) mind; character; moral nature
心动 ①heartbeat ②one's mind is perturbed; one's desire, enthusiasm or interest is aroused
心耳 auricle (of the heart); auricular appendage
心烦 be vexed; be perturbed
心房 atrium (of the heart)
心扉 the door of one's heart
心服 be genuinely convinced; acknowledge (one's defeat, mistake, etc.) sincerely
心浮 flighty and impatient; unstable
心腹 ①trusted subordinate; reliable agent ②confidential
心肝 ① conscience ② darling; dear; sweetheart; honey
心寒 be bitterly disappointed
心狠 cruel; merciless
心怀 ① intention; purpose ② state of mind; mood ③harbour; entertain; cherish
心慌 ①be flustered; be nervous; get alarmed ②(of the heart) palpitate
心机 thinking; scheming
心肌 cardiac muscle; myocardium
心急 impatient; short-tempered
心计 calculation; scheming; planning
心迹 the true state of one's mind; true motives; true feelings
心悸 ①palpitation ②be scared

心件 heart ware
心焦 anxious; worried
心静 calm
心境 state (or frame) of mind; mental state; mood
心坎 ①the pit of the stomach ②the bottom of one's heart
心口 the pit of the stomach
心宽 not lend oneself to worry and anxiety
心里 in the heart; at heart; in (the) mind
心理 mentality; psychology
心力 mental and physical efforts
心灵 ① clever; intelligent; quick-witted ② heart; soul; spirit
心律 rhythm of the heartbeat
心率 heart rate
心目 ① mood; frame of mind ② memory ③ mind; mental view
心皮 carpel
心窍 capacity for clear thinking
心切 eager; impatient; anxious
心情 frame (or state) of mind; mood
心软 be softhearted; be tenderhearted
心上 in the heart
心神 mind; state of mind
心声 heartfelt wishes; aspirations; thinking
心事 sth weighing on one's mind; a load on one's mind; worry
心室 ventricle
心术 ① intention; design ② calculation; scheming; planning
心思 ① thought; idea ② thinking ③ state of mind; mood
心死 one's will dies within one—see the futility of one's attempt
心酸 be grieved; feel sad
心算 mental arithmetic; doing sums in one's head
心碎 be heartbroken
心态 mindset; mentality; psychology
心疼 ①love dearly ②feel sorry; be distressed
心田 ①heart ②intention
心跳 palpitation
心痛 cardialgia; cardiodynia
心头 mind; heart
心细 careful; scrupulous
心弦 heartstrings
心想 think to oneself; think
心性 disposition; temperament
心胸 ①breadth of mind ②aspiration; ambition
心虚 ①afraid of being found out; with a guilty conscience ②lacking in self-confidence; diffident
心绪 state of mind
心血 painstaking care (or effort)
心痒 have an itch for
心仪 admire; respect

心疑 become (*or* be) suspicious
心意 ① regard; kindly feelings ② intention; purpose
心音 heart sounds; cardiac sounds
心硬 hard-hearted; stony-hearted; callous; unfeeling
心语 inner voice
心愿 cherished desire; aspiration; wish; dream
心脏 ① the heart ② the central (*or* most vital) part of anything
心照 understand without being told
心智 intelligence; wisdom; mentality
心中 in the heart; in the mind
心轴 mandrel
心子 ① centre (of sth); heart; core ② the heart of a pig, sheep, etc. as food
心醉 be charmed; be enchanted; be fascinated
心瓣膜 heart valve
心包炎 pericarditis
心电图 electrocardiogram
心肌炎 myocarditis
心绞痛 angina pectoris
心静脉 cardiac vein
心里话 one's innermost thoughts and feelings
心理学 psychology
心理战 psychological warfare
心连心 heart linked to heart
心灵美 beautification of the mind
心上人 person of one's heart; one's beloved
心头肉 a dearly loved person; a treasured possession
心窝儿 ① the pit of the heart (*or* stomach) ② deep down in one's heart
心眼儿 ① heart; mind ② intention; a person's mind ③ intelligence; cleverness ④ unfounded doubts; unnecessary misgivings ⑤ tolerance
心杂音 heart murmur
心脏病 heart disease
心安理得 feel at ease and justified; have an easy conscience; with mind at rest and conscience clear
心不在焉 absent-minded; inattentive; preoccupied (with sth else)
心潮澎湃 feel an upsurge of emotion
心驰神往 one's thoughts fly to (a place or person); have a deep longing for
心慈面软 kind heart and soft countenance
心慈手软 softhearted
心粗气浮 hotheaded; thoughtless and impetuous
心存芥蒂 bear sb a grudge; nurse a grievance
心胆俱裂 be frightened out of one's wits; be terror-stricken
心荡神驰 be distracted; feel excited
心动过速 tachycardia
心动徐缓 bradycardia

心动周期 cardiac cycle
心烦意乱 be terribly upset; be perturbed
心房纤颤 atrial fibrillation
心服口服 be sincerely convinced
心浮气躁 flighty and impetuous
心腹大患 be a mortal malady
心腹之患 disease in one's vital organs—danger from within; serious hidden trouble or danger
心甘情愿 be most willing to; be perfectly happy to
心肝宝贝 sweetheart; be all in all to sb—the person (*or* thing) that one loves most
心高气傲 ambitious and proud
心广体胖 carefree and contented; fit and happy
心狠手辣 cruel and ruthless; wicked and merciless
心花怒放 burst with joy; be wild with joy; be elated
心怀二意 have two faces; harbour disloyal sentiments
心怀鬼胎 have evil intentions; have sinister motives
心怀叵测 harbour unfathomable evil designs; have sinister intentions
心慌意乱 be alarmed and confused; be nervous and flustered
心灰意懒 be downhearted; be dispirited
心肌梗死 myocardial infarction
心急火燎 burning with impatience; in a nervous state
心急如焚 burning with impatience
心惊胆战 tremble with terror; shake with fright; quake with fear
心惊肉跳 be jumpy; have the jitters
心口如一 say what one thinks; speak from the heart; be frank and forthright
心旷神怡 relaxed and joyful; carefree and happy
心劳日拙 fare worse and worse for all one's scheming
心理病态 morbid state of mind
心理分析 psychoanalysis
心理距离 psychological gap
心理疗法 psychotherapy
心理素质 psychological quality
心理卫生 mental hygiene
心理训练 psychological training
心理医生 psychotherapist
心理障碍 psychogenic disorder
心理治疗 psychotherapy
心理咨询 psychological counselling
心力交瘁 be mentally and physically exhausted
心力衰竭 heart failure
心灵手巧 have clever hands and good sense;

clever in mind and skilful in hand

心领神会 understand tacitly; readily take a hint

心律不齐 arrhythmia

心乱如麻 have one's mind all in a tangle; be utterly confused and disconcerted; be terribly upset

心满意足 be perfectly content (*or* satisfied)

心明眼亮 see and think clearly; be sharp-eyed and clear-headed

心平气和 even-tempered and good-humoured; calm

心如刀割 feel as if a knife were piercing one's heart

心如火焚 with one's heart afire; burning with anxiety

心如蛇蝎 with one's heart as poisonous as a viper or scorpion; having the heart of the devil

心如死灰 one's heart is like dead ashes—hopelessly apathetic

心身疾病 psychosomatic disease

心神不定 have no peace of mind; feel restless; be distracted

心神恍惚 be ill at ease and full of dread; perturbed in mind

心事重重 be laden with anxiety; be weighed down with care

心室纤颤 ventricular fibrillation

心输出量 cardiac output

心输入量 cardiac input

心术不正 evil intentions

心无二用 one cannot keep one's mind on two things at the same time; one should concentrate on one thing at a time

心向往之 yearning for sb or sth

心心相印 have mutual affinity; be kindred spirits

心胸开阔 broad-minded; unprejudiced

心胸狭窄 narrow-minded; intolerant; insular

心绪不宁 in a disturbed state of mind; in a flutter

心血来潮 be prompted by a sudden impulse; be seized by a whim

心有余悸 one's heart still fluttering with fear; have a lingering fear

心猿意马 a heart like a capering monkey and a mind like a galloping horse—restless; perturbed

心悦诚服 be completely convinced; feel a heartfelt admiration

心脏导管 cardiac catheter

心脏地带 heartland

心脏死亡 heart death

心脏移植 heart transplant

心照不宣 have a tacit understanding

心直口快 frank and outspoken; straightforward and plain-spoken

心中无数 have no idea of how things stand; not know for certain

心中有愧 have a guilty conscience

心中有数 know the score; have a pretty good idea of how things stand; know fairly well; know what's what

心拙口笨 dull-witted and slow-tongued

心醉神迷 be in ecstasies; in an ecstasy of delight

心电描记器 electrocardiograph

心理测验学 psychometry

心血管系统 cardiovascular system

心血管造影 angiocardiography

心脏起搏器 (cardiac) pacemaker

心有灵犀一点通 hearts which beat in unison are linked

心有余而力不足 one's ability falls short of one's wishes; the spirit is willing, but the flesh is weak

心之系之，口则含之 What the mind thinks, the tongue speaks.

心往一处想，劲往一处使 think with one mind and work with one heart

芯 [xīn]

〔名〕 rush pith ➡ xìn

芯片 chip

辛 [xīn]

〔形〕① (as in flavour) hot; pungent ② hard; difficult; laborious ③ bitter; distressing; painful

辛苦 ① hard; strenuous; toilsome; laborious ② work hard; go to great trouble; go through hardships

辛辣 pungent; hot; bitter

辛劳 work hard; toil

辛勤 industrious; hardworking

辛酸 sad; bitter; miserable

辛迪加 syndicate

辛苦费 reward for help; lobbying commission; service charge; trouble fee

辛烷值 octane number (*or* value)

辛辛苦苦 take a lot of trouble; take great pains; work laboriously

忻 [xīn]

〔形〕 glad; happy; elated; joyful

昕 [xīn]

〔名〕 time just before the sun rises; dawn

欣 [xīn]

〔形〕 glad; happy; elated; joyful

欣然 joyfully; with pleasure

欣赏 appreciate; enjoy; admire

欣慰 be gratified

欣悉 be glad (*or* happy) to learn

欣喜 glad; joyful; happy

欣羡 admire

欣幸 be glad and thankful

欣逢盛世 happy to live in a prosperous (*or*

flourishing) age
欣然从命 obey without reluctance
欣然允诺 readily consent
欣生恶死 covet life and fear death；be afraid of death and cling to life
欣喜若狂 be wild with joy；go into raptures
欣欣向荣 thriving；flourishing；prosperous

炘 ［xīn］
〔形〕 intense heat

锌 ［xīn］
〔名〕 zinc（Zn）
锌白 zinc white
锌板 sheet zinc；rolled tin
锌版 zinc plate；zincograph
锌粉 zinc powder
锌矿 zinc ore
锌钡白 lithopone
锌版印刷术 zincography

新 ［xīn］
I 〔形〕 ①occurring for the first time；new；fresh；modern ②just begun；unused；new ③newly（or recently）married ④renewed；improved；new；neo- Ⅱ 〔名〕 sth new；new things；new people Ⅲ 〔副〕 newly；just
新版 new edition
新编 newly organized
新兵 recruit；（Brit. Navy）ordinary seaman；（Brit. Air Force）aircraftsman
新茶 newly picked and processed tea leaves
新潮 new trend；new fashion
新宠 new favourite
新词 new word；new expression
新村 new residential quarter；new housing development（or estate）
新低 new low
新房 bridal chamber
新妇 bride
新高 new high
新贵 upstart
新欢 new sweetheart（esp. a woman）
新婚 newly-married
新交 new acquaintance；new friend
新教 Protestantism
新近 recently；lately；in recent times
新居 new home；new residence
新军 new force
新郎 bridegroom
新历 the new calendar—the Gregorian calender
新马 Singapore and Malaysia
新貌 new look
新苗 ① young plant；seedling ② newly emerging，vigorous and promising talent
新年 New Year
新盘 fresh building
新奇 strange；novel；new
新秋 early autumn

新区 newly developed area；newly added district
新人 ①people of a new type ②new personality；new talent ③bride and bridegroom ④bride
新任 ①newly appointed ②new post
新锐 novel；new talent
新生 ① newborn；newly born ② new life；rebirth；regeneration ③a new student or pupil
新诗 new poetry；free verse written in the vernacular
新式 new type；latest type；new style
新手 new hand；raw recruit
新书 ①new book ②new title
新闻 news
新禧 good fortune for the new year
新鲜 ①fresh ②new；novel；strange
新兴 new and developing；rising；burgeoning
新星 ①nova ②new star
新型 new type；new pattern
新秀 rising star；promising young talent；up-and-coming stars
新义 new meaning
新意 new meaning；new conception
新颖 new and original；novel
新约 the New Testament
新月 ①crescent（moon）②new moon
新正 the first month of the lunar year
新制 new system
新装 new clothes
新产品 new product
新大陆 the New World—the Americas
新风尚 new custom（or habit）
新格局 new pattern
新华社 the Xinhua News Agency
新纪录 new record
新纪元 new era；new epoch
新教徒 Protestant
新局面 new situation；fresh progress
新举措 new measures
新名词 ①new term；new expression ②vogue word；newfangled phrase
新娘(子) bride
新篇章 new page
新品种 new variety（or strain）
新气象 new atmosphere；new look
新上市 new arrival；garden-fresh
新社会 the new society
新生代 ①the Cenozoic Era ②new generation
新生界 the Cenozoic Erathem
新四军 the New Fourth Army
新文学 new-vernacular literature
新闻处 office of information；information service
新闻稿 press（or news）release
新闻界 press circles；the press

新闻片 newsreel；news film
新闻司 department of information（of the Foreign Ministry）
新闻业 journalism
新闻纸 newsprint
新小说 nouveau roman
新安全观 new security theory
新潮人物 swinger
新潮新款 new fashion and new style
新车展览 Motorama
新陈代谢 ① metabolism ② the new superseding the old
新仇旧恨 new hatred piled on old；old scores and new
新婚燕尔 happy wedding couple；the couple joy in their marriage
新旧交替 the transition from the old to the new
新来乍到 newly arrived
新老交替 succession（*or* replacement）of the old by the new；replace old cadres with new ones
新人新事 new people and new things
新生力量 newly emerging force；new rising force；new force
新生事物 newly emerging things；new things
新闻导向 the guiding role of mass media
新闻道德 journalistic code of ethics；ethics of journalism
新闻封锁 news blockout
新闻公报 press communiqué
新闻广播 newscast
新闻记者 newsman；newspaperman；reporter；journalist
新闻检查 press censorship
新闻联播 news hookup
新闻人物 newsmaker
新闻通讯 newsletter
新闻嗅觉 nose for news；journalistic nose
新闻自由 press freedom
新闻综述 situationer；wrap-up
新媳妇儿 bride
新鲜血液 fresh blood；new addition to the membership；new blood
新新人类 New Human Being；X Generation
新兴产业 infant industry；new industry；rising industry；burgeoning industry
新兴力量 newly emerging forces
新兴市场 emerging market
新兴势力 the rising forces；the forces in the ascendant
新兴学科 new branches of science
新增贷款 incremental credit；loan increment；credit growth；credit expansion
新材料技术 new material technology
新产品开发 new products development
新发行证券 new issue

新概念武器 new concept weapon
新古典主义 neoclassicism
新经济政策 New Economic policy
新旧约全书 the Old and New Testaments
新民主主义 new democracy
新瓶装旧酒 old wine in a new bottle—the same old stuff with a new label
新石器时代 the Neolithic Age；the New Stone Age
新闻吹风会 backgrounder
新闻发布会 press conference；news releasing
新闻发言权 press spokesperson
新闻发言人 spokesman for news release
新闻工作者 journalist
新闻评论员 news analyst
新闻图片栏 news window
新闻主持人 anchor
新殖民主义 neocolonialism；new colonialism
新自由主义 neoliberalism
新长征突击手 pace-setter in the modernization drive；pacesetters in the long march；shock worker of the new Long March
新古典经济学 neoclassical economics
新技术开发区 new technology industrial area
新旧体制接轨 dovetailing of the old and new systems
新兴带头学科 rising and leading disciplines
新增固定资产 newly acquired（*or* increased）fixed assets
新增生产能力 new productive capacity
新殖民主义者 neocolonialist
新官上任三把火 A new official applies strict measures；A new broom sweeps clean.
新民主主义革命 new-democratic revolution

歆 ［xīn］
勋 envy；admire；adore
薪 ［xīn］
名 ①firewood；fuel；faggot ②salary
薪俸 salary；pay
薪金 pay in money；salary
薪水 earning；salary；pay；wages；compensation
薪饷 soldier's pay and rations
薪炭林 fuel forest
薪尽火传 as one piece of fuel is consumed，the flame passes on to another—the torch of learning is passed on from teacher to student
馨 ［xīn］
名 strong and pervasive fragrance
馨香 ①fragrance ②the sweet smell of burning incense
鑫 ［xīn］
勋 prosper in business

xīn（ㄒㄧㄣ）

囟 [xìn]

囟门 fontanel

芯 [xìn]

名 core ➡ xīn

芯子 ①fuse (as in a firecracker); wick (as in a candle) ②the forked tongue of a snake

信 [xìn]

Ⅰ 形 true; truthful Ⅱ 名 ①pledge; token; sign; evidence ② letter; mail ③ message; news; word ④fuse ⑤faith; trust; confidence; reputation ⑥core ⑦arsenic Ⅲ 动 ①believe; trust ② profess faith in; embrace; believe in Ⅲ 副 at will; at random; casually; without plan

信笔 write freely without hesitation or as fancy dictates

信步 take a leisurely walk; stroll; walk aimlessly

信差 ①courier ②postman

信贷 credit

信道 information channel

信访 correspondence and visitation; letters and calls

信风 trade winds; trades

信封 envelope

信奉 believe in

信服 completely accept; be convinced

信鸽 carrier pigeon; homing pigeon; homer

信管 fuse

信函 letters

信号 signal

信汇 mail transfer (M/T)

信笺 letter paper; notepaper

信件 letters, papers, printed matter, etc. (sent either by post or by messenger)

信教 profess a religion; be religious

信口 speak thoughtlessly or casually

信赖 trust; count on; have faith in

信念 faith; belief; conviction

信女 female believer

信皮 envelope

信任 trust; have confidence in

信使 courier; messenger

信手 do sth spontaneously or without much thought or effort

信守 abide by; stand by

信条 article of creed (or faith); creed; precept; tenet

信筒 pillar-box; mailbox

信徒 believer; disciple; follower; adherent; devotee

信托 trust; entrust

信物 authenticating object; token; keepsake

信息 ① information; news; message ② information

信箱 ①letter box; mailbox ② post-office box (P.O.B.)

信邪 believe in dishonest practices or yield to evil forces

信心 confidence; faith

信仰 faith; belief; conviction

信义 good faith; faith

信用 ①trustworthiness ②credit

信誉 prestige; credit; reputation

信札 letters

信纸 letter paper; writing paper

信标灯 beacon light

信不过 distrust; have no trust in

信达雅 fidelity, fluency, fairness

信得过 ①trust ②trustworthy; dependable

信访办 public access office; correspondence and visitation department

信风带 trade wind zone

信号兵 signalman

信号弹 signal flare

信号灯 signal lamp; semaphore

信号机 annunciator; semaphore

信号旗 signal flag; semaphore

信号枪 flare pistol; signal pistol

信任状 credential

信骚扰 mail harassment

信天翁 albatross

信息港 cyber port

信息化 informationalize the national economy and society

信息库 information base

信息量 amount of information; information content

信息论 information theory

信息台 information broadcasting station

信息体 informosome

信息网 information network

信息学 information science; informatics

信息战 information war

信用卡 credit card

信用社 credit office

信用证 letter of credit (L/C)

信噪比 signal-to-noise ratio (SNR)

信贷担保 credit guarantee

信贷支持 credit aid

信道容量 channel capacity

信而不疑 believe without the slightest doubt

信而有征 borne out by evidence

信孚中外 have the confidence of foreigners and Chinese alike; enjoy a good reputation both at home and abroad

信号刺激 signal stimulus

信及豚鱼 one's sincerity (or truthfulness) extends even to the lowest creatures

信口雌黄 make irresponsible remarks; wag one's tongue too freely

信口开河 talk irresponsibly; wag one's tongue too freely; talk at random

信马由缰 ①ride a horse without holding the

reins ②stroll about aimlessly; act or do as one pleases

信任投票 vote of confidence

信任危机 credibility crisis; crisis of confidence

信赏必罚 due rewards and punishments will be meted out without fail

信誓旦旦 pledge in all sincerity; vow solemnly

信手拈来 have the words at hand; have materials, etc. at one's fingertips

信守不渝 be unswervingly true (to one's promise, etc.)

信托公司 trust company

信托基金 trust fund

信托商店 commercial shop (*or* house, agent)

信息安全 information security

信息爆炸 information explosion

信息编码 information encoding

信息产业 information industry

信息处理 information processing

信息传播 information dissemination

信息反馈 information feedback

信息服务 information service

信息革命 information revolution

信息技术 information technology

信息家电 information appliance

信息检索 information retrieval

信息交换 information interchange; information switching

信息交流 information exchange

信息科学 information science

信息社会 information society

信息载体 information carrier

信息资源 information resources

信仰危机 belief crisis; credibility crisis; crisis in moral convictions; crisis of belief

信以为真 accept sth as true

信用报告 credit report

信用紧缩 credit crunch

信用债券 debenture stock

"信得过"单位 trustable work-unit

"信得过"企业 "Trusted by the masses" enterprise

信息发布会 information conference

信息工程学 information engineering

信用合作社 credit cooperative

信托投资公司 trust and investment corporation

信息高速公路 information superhighway; data (super) highway; infobahn; info highway; digital highway; electronic highway; info pike

信用卡诈骗案 credit card fraud

信言不美, 美言不信 Truthful words are not pleasant to the ear, while pleasant words are not truthful.

信则全信, 否则不信 trust sb completely or not at all

衅 [xìn]
图 quarrel; row; dispute

衅端 a cause for a quarrel (*or* dispute)

焮 [xìn]
动 ①burn; scorch ②(of skin, etc.) be inflamed and swollen

xīng (ㄒㄧㄥ)

兴 [xīng]
Ⅰ 动 ①rise; flourish; prevail; become popular ② encourage; foster; promote ③ begin; start; found ④get up; rise ⑤(usu. used in the negative) allow; let; permit Ⅱ 副 probably; maybe; perhaps ➡xìng

兴办 initiate; set up

兴奋 ①be excited ②excitation

兴工 start construction

兴建 build; construct

兴隆 prosperous; thriving; flourishing; brisk

兴起 ①rise; spring up; be on the upgrade ② rise in excitement; be aroused

兴盛 prosper; flourish; thrive; be in the ascendant

兴衰 rise and decline; rise and fall

兴替 rise and fall; rise of a power and its supersession by another

兴亡 rise and fall (of a nation)

兴旺 prosper; flourish; thrive

兴修 start construction; start building

兴许 perhaps; maybe

兴奋剂 excitant; stimulant; dope; ecstasy; upper; uppie; performance drug; pick-me-up

兴奋性 excitability

兴风作浪 stir up trouble; make trouble; fan the flames of disorder

兴利除弊 promote the beneficial, abolish the harmful; promote what is beneficial and abolish what is harmful

兴师动众 move troops and stir up people-draw in many people (to do sth)

兴师问罪 send a punitive expedition

兴修水利 build water conservancy (*or* irrigation) projects; undertake new water conservancy projects; engage in water conservancy projects

兴妖作怪 conjure up demons to make trouble—stir up trouble

兴奋剂检测中心 doping control centre; drug-testing centre; steroid-testing lab

星 [xīng]
图 ① star ② any heavenly body ③ bit; piece; particle ④ marks (resembling asterisks) on the arm of a steelyard indicating *jin* and its fractions ⑤famous performer; star

星表 star catalogue

星辰 stars and constellations

星等 magnitude

星斗 stars
星光 star light
星号 asterisk (*)
星河 the Milky Way
星火 ①spark ②shooting star；meteor
星级 star；high-grade；starry
星际 interplanetary；interstellar
星空 starry sky；star-studded sky；starlit sky
星期 ①week ②day of the week ③Sunday
星球 celestial body；heavenly body
星鲨 gummy shark
星探 talent scout
星体 celestial body；heavenly body
星图 star chart；star map；star atlas
星团 star cluster
星系 galaxy
星相 horoscope
星象 configurations of the stars
星星 [xīngxīng] tiny spot；speck
星星 [xīngxing] star
星宿 constellation
星夜 starlit (or starry) night
星云 nebula
星运 luck to become a star
星占 divine by astrology；cast a horoscope
星震 starquake
星座 constellation
星期二 Tuesday (Tues.)
星期六 Saturday (Sat.)
星期日 Sunday (Sun.)
星期三 Wednesday (Wed.)
星期四 Thursday (Thur. or Thurs.)
星期五 Friday (Fri.)
星期一 Monday (Mon.)
星条旗 Stars and Stripes；the Star-Spangled Banner
星系晕 galactic halo
星占术 astrology
星火计划 the Spark(le) Plan；the Spark(le) Program
星火燎原 A single spark can start a prairie fire.
星级饭店 star-grade hotel
星际飞船 spaceship
星际航行 interplanetary flight (or travel)；interstellar flight (or travel)；space flight (or travel)
星际物质 interstellar medium
星罗棋布 scattered all over like stars in the sky or men on a chessboard；spread all over the place
星球大战 Star-War
星星点点 tiny spots；bits and pieces
星移斗转 change in the positions of the stars—change of the seasons；passage of time
星月无光 Both the moon and the stars were dim；The moon and the stars lost their brightness.
星系天文学 extragalactic astronomy
星期日工程师 Sunday engineer
星球大战计划 Strategic Defence Initiative (SDI)
星星之火，可以燎原 A single spark can start a prairie fire.

骍 [xīng]
彤 (of horse or cattle) red

猩 [xīng]
名 orangutan
猩红 scarlet；bloodred
猩猩 orangutan
猩红热 scarlet fever；scarlatina
猩猩草 painted euphorbia (Euphorbia heterophylla)

惺 [xīng]
形 ① intelligent；clever ② come to one's senses；be sober
惺忪 ①(of eyes) not yet fully open on waking up ②awake；conscious；clearheaded
惺惺 ①clearheaded；awake ②wise；intelligent ③an intelligent person；a wise man
惺惺作态 be affected；simulate (friendship, innocence, etc.)

腥 [xīng]
名 ①raw meat or fish (as food) ②having the smell of fish，seafood，etc.；rank
腥臭 stinking smell as of rotten fish；stench
腥气 ①the smell of fish，seafood，etc. ②stinking；fishy
腥臊 stench
腥膻 the smell of fish，mutton，etc.
腥味儿 the foul smell of fish；a fishy smell
腥风血雨 a foul wind and a rain of blood—reign of terror

xíng（ㄒㄧㄥˊ）

刑 [xíng]
名 ①punishment；sentence ② torture；corporal punishment
刑场 execution ground
刑罚 penalty (for a criminal offence)；punishment
刑法 ① penal code；criminal law ② corporal punishment；torture
刑警 criminal policeman；police handling criminal matters
刑拘 criminal detention
刑具 instruments of torture；implements of punishment
刑律 criminal law
刑期 term of imprisonment；prison term
刑事 criminal；penal
刑释 release from imprisonment
刑讯 inquisition by torture

刑种 kinds of punishment
刑事犯 criminal offender；criminal
刑满释放 be released upon completion of a sentence（*or* one's term）
刑事案件 criminal case
刑事法庭 criminal court
刑事犯罪 criminal offence；criminal act
刑事警察 criminal police
刑事拘留 criminal detention
刑事诉讼 criminal procedure；criminal suit
刑事责任 criminal responsibility
刑事侦查 criminal investigation
刑讯逼供 extort a confession by torture；use torture to coerce a statement
刑在禁恶 Punishment is aimed at deterring wrongdoing.
刑事管辖权 criminal jurisdiction
刑事诉讼法 code of criminal procedure；criminal procedure law
刑不上大夫，礼不下庶人 "Punishment according to the law" does not apply to the nobility，while etiquette is not meant for the commoners.

行 ［xíng］ I 团 ①go；walk；travel ②be current；prevail；circulate ③do；act；practise；implement ④（*used before a two-character verb to express the performance of the action*）：即行查复 check and reply promptly ⑤will do；be all right ⑥（of medicine）take effect II 名 ①journey；road ②travel ③behaviour；conduct；deeds III 形 ①temporary；makeshift ②able；capable；competent IV 副 presently；shortly；soon ➡háng；héng
行板 andante
行车 drive a vehicle
行程 ①route or distance of travel ②stroke；throw；travel
行船 sail a boat；navigate
行刺 assassinate
行道 preach one's doctrine；propagate one's belief
行动 ①move（*or* get）about ②act；take action ③action；operation
行房 （of husband and wife）sleep together；have sexual intercourse
行宫 imperial palace for short stays away from the capital；temporary dwelling place of an emperor when away from the capital
行好 act charitably；be merciful；be charitable；do a good turn
行贿 bribe；offer a bribe；resort to bribery
行迹 trace；track；trackway
行将 be about to；be just going to；be on the verge of
行劫 commit robbery；rob
行进 （usu. of troops）march forward；advance

行经 ①menstruate；be in the period ②go（*or* pass）by
行径 act；action；move
行军 （of troops）march
行乐 indulge in pleasures；seek amusement；make merry
行礼 ①salute ②present gifts
行李 luggage；baggage
行令 play drinker's wager game
行囊 travelling bag
行骗 practise fraud；swindle；cheat
行期 date of departure
行乞 beg one's bread；beg alms；beg
行窃 steal；thieve
行人 pedestrian；foot traveller
行色 circumstances（*or* style）of departure
行善 do good；do kind deeds；practise philanthropy
行商 itinerant trader；travelling merchant；pedlar
行赏 give awards；dispense rewards or honours
行时 ①（of a thing）be in vogue；be all the rage ②（of a person）be in the ascendant
行使 exercise；perform
行驶 （of a vehicle，ship，etc.）go；ply；travel
行事 ①act；handle matters ②behaviour；conduct
行书 cursive handwriting；running hand
行署 administrative office（within a province）
行头 ①actor's costumes and paraphernalia ②dress；clothing；apparel；outfit
行为 action；behaviour；conduct
行文 ①style or manner of writing ②（of a government office）send an official communication to other organizations
行销 be on sale；sell
行星 planet
行刑 carry out a death sentence；execute
行凶 commit physical assault or murder；do violence
行医 practise medicine（usu. on one's own）
行营 field headquarters
行灶 makeshift（*or* portable）cooking stove
行者 ①pedestrian ②Buddhist monk prior to his tonsure
行政 administration
行止 ①whereabouts ②behaviour；conduct
行装 outfit for a journey；luggage
行踪 whereabouts；track
行走 walk
行不开 won't work；will get nowhere
行不通 won't do（*or* work）；will get nowhere
行道树 roadside trees；sidewalk trees；trees that line a street
行得通 will do（*or* work）；be practicable
行方便 make things convenient for sb；be ac-

commodating

行军床 camp bed; camp cot; a lightweight folding bed

行军锅 field cauldron

行军壶 canteen

行军灶 field kitchen

行李车 ①luggage van; baggage car ②luggage cart

行李架 luggage rack; baggage rack

行李票 luggage (*or* baggage) check

行星际 interplanetary

行刑队 executioners; firing squad

行政区 administrative area

行政院 the Executive Yuan

行不逾方 never exceed what is proper in one's behaviour; behave in a fit and proper way

行成于思 A deed is accomplished through taking thought; Success depends on forethought.

行动纲领 programme of action

行将毕业 will graduate shortly (*or* soon)

行将就木 be getting closer and closer to the coffin—be fast approaching death; have one foot in the grave

行将灭亡 will soon perish; be on one's last legs

行李标签 baggage tags

行李卷儿 bedroll; bedding roll; bedding pack

行若无事 behave as if nothing had happened

行色匆匆 be in a hurry to set out

行尸走肉 a walking corpse—one who vegetates; an utterly worthless person

行使职权 exercise one's functions and powers

行同狗彘 behave like dogs and pigs

行为不轨 act against the law; engage in conspiratorial activities

行为干预 behaviour intervention

行为规范 behavioural norm; standards of social conduct

行为科学 behavioural science

行为疗法 behaviour therapy

行为模式 behaviour pattern

行为医学 behavioural medicine

行为主义 behaviourism

行侠仗义 have a strong sense of justice and ready to help the weak

行云流水 (of style of writing) like floating clouds and flowing water—natural and spontaneous

行政部门 administrative department; executive branch; administration

行政处罚 administrative sanction

行政处分 administrative sanction; disciplinary sanction

行政单位 administrative unit

行政法规 administrative regulations (*or* statutes, rules, laws)

行政费用 expenses of administration

行政复议 administrative reconsideration

行政干预 administrative intervention

行政公署 administrative office (within a province)

行政管理 administration

行政纠纷 administrative dispute

行政拘留 administrative detention

行政命令 administrative decree (*or* order)

行政区划 division into administrative districts

行政人员 administrative personnel (*or* staff)

行政手段 administrative measures

行政诉讼 administrative litigation

行政长官 chief executive

行政制裁 administrative sanction

行之有效 effective (in practice); effectual

行李寄存处 left-luggage office; checkroom

行使否决权 exercise (*or* use) the power of veto over

行政负责制 administrative responsibility system

行政复议条例 regulations on administrative reconsideration

行政事业单位 government departments and state institutions

行百里者半九十 ninety *li* is only half of a hundred-*li* journey—the going is toughest towards the end of a journey; one must sustain one's effort when a task is nearing completion

行政首长负责制 system under which administrative heads assume full responsibility

行不更名,坐不改姓 Whether I travel or stay at home, I never change my name.

饧 [xíng]
Ⅰ 〈名〉 treacle made from malt Ⅱ 〈动〉 (of candy, dough, etc.) become sticky and soft Ⅲ 〈形〉 be in low spirits or half asleep with one's eyes about to close

形 [xíng]
Ⅰ 〈名〉 ①form; appearance; shape ②body; entity Ⅱ 〈动〉 ①appear; seem; look ②compare; contrast

形变 deformation

形成 take shape; form

形骸 the human skeleton; the human body

形迹 ①a person's movements and expression ②formality

形容 ①appearance; countenance ②describe

形式 form; shape

形势 ① terrain; topographical features ② situation; circumstances

形似 likeness in form (*or* appearance); formal likeness (*or* resemblance)

形态 ①form; shape; pattern ②morphology

形体 ①shape (of a person's body); physique; body ②form and structure

形象 ①image;form;figure ②literary or artistic image;imagery
形状 form;appearance;shape
形成层 cambium
形容词 adjective
形式上 in form;formal
形态学 ①morphology ②morphology
形体装 shapewear
形丑心善 look ugly but be kind at heart
形单影只 a solitary form, a single shadow—extremely lonely;solitary
形而上学 metaphysics
形迹可疑 of suspicious appearance;suspicious-looking
形容憔悴 wan-looking;thin and pallid
形式逻辑 formal logic
形式主义 formalism
形势逼人 pressing situation
形势喜人 gratifying situation
形似实非 similar in appearance but different in essence
形同虚设 be nothing but an empty shell;perform practically no function
形象大使 image representative
形象工程 CI engineering;image project
形象设计 image building
形象思维 thinking in (terms of) images
形象塑造 image-building
形销骨立 be all (or mere) skin and bones;be worn to a shadow of one's former self;be just a skeleton
形形色色 of every hue;of all shades;of all forms;of every description
形影不离 be inseparable as body and shadow;be always together
形影相吊 body and shadow comforting each other—extremely lonely;sad and solitary
形影相随 be as close as body and shadow;be always together
形于辞色 show in one's words and expression
形诸笔墨 put down in black and white
形"左"实右 "Left" in form but Right in essence
形象代言人 image spokesman
形象设计师 image-spinner;image craftsman

型 [xíng]
名 ①mould ②model;type;variety;pattern
型板 template;templet
型材 section bar;structural section
型钢 section steel;shape
型号 model;type
型宽 moulded breadth
型砂 moulding sand
型深 moulded depth
型心 core
型钢轧机 shape rolling mill

xǐng(ㄒㄧㄥˇ)

省 [xǐng]
动 ①examine oneself critically;introspect ②visit (esp. one'parents or elders) ③come to realize;become conscious (or aware) ⇒ shěng
省察 examine oneself critically;examine one's thoughts and conduct
省亲 pay a visit to one's parents or elders (living at another place)
省视 ① call upon;pay a visit to ② examine carefully;inspect

醒 [xǐng]
动 ①regain consciousness;sober up;come round ②wake up;awaken;be awake ③keep dough (after mixing it) till water and flour are well mixed ④clear in mind;alert;aware ⑤striking to the eye;eye-catching;conspicuous
醒酒 dispel the effects of alcohol;sober up
醒木 attention-catching block
醒目 (of written words or pictures) catch the eye;attract attention;be striking to the eye
醒世 rouse the public;awaken the world
醒悟 come to realize (or see) (the truth, one's error,etc.);wake up to reality

擤 [xǐng]
动 blow (one's nose)

xìng(ㄒㄧㄥˋ)

兴 [xìng]
名 passion or appetite for sth;mood or desire to do sth;interest;excitement ⇒xīng
兴会 a sudden flash of inspiration;brain wave
兴趣 interest
兴头 enthusiasm;keen interest
兴味 interest
兴致 interest;mood to enjoy
兴冲冲 (do sth) with joy and expedition;excitedly
兴高采烈 in high spirits;excited;jubilant
兴趣相投 have similar tastes and interests;find each other congenial
兴味索然 have lost all interest in sth;be bored stiff
兴之所至 when one is in high spirits…;when the fit is on sb (for sth)…
兴致勃勃 full of zest;in high spirits

杏 [xìng]
名 apricot;almond
杏红 yellowish pink;apricot pink
杏黄 pinkish yellow;apricot (colour)
杏脯 sun-dried sweetened apricot;preserved sweetened apricot
杏仁 apricot kernel;almond
杏子 apricot

杏核儿 apricot stone
杏仁眼 almond-eyed
杏眼柳腰 apricot-like eyes and soft waistline of a beauty
杏眼秀眉 girl with almond-shaped eyes and long eyebrows
杏眼圆睁 almond-shaped eyes glaring round with rage

幸 [xìng]
I 名 ① good fortune; happiness ② favour II 动 ①rejoice; be happy ②I hope; I trust ③ (of a monarch) come; arrive: 巡幸江南 go south of the Yangtze on an imperial tour of inspection III 副 fortuitously; fortunately; luckily
幸而 luckily; fortunately
幸福 ①happiness; well-being ②happy
幸好 fortunately; luckily
幸会 (a rather formal greeting) very pleased to meet you
幸亏 fortunately; luckily
幸免 escape by sheer luck; have a narrow escape
幸事 a piece of good fortune; a stroke of luck; blessing
幸喜 fortunately; luckily
幸运 ① good fortune; good luck ② fortunate; lucky
幸存者 survivor; survival
幸运儿 fortune's favourite; lucky fellow
幸免于难 escape death by sheer luck; escape death by a hair's breadth
幸运号码 lucky number
幸灾乐祸 take pleasure in (or gloat over) other people's misfortune

性 [xìng]
I 名 ① nature; character; inclination; disposition ②property; quality; characteristic ③ sex ④sexual distinction; gender ⑤gender: 中性名词 neutral noun II ① (noun-forming suffix used to express ideology, emotion, etc.) ②(noun-forming suffix used to denote a category)
性爱 love between the sexes; sexual love; love
性别 sexual distinction; sex
性病 venereal disease(V. D.)
性感 sex appeal; sexiness
性格 nature; disposition; temperament
性急 impatient; short-tempered
性交 ①sexual intercourse ②make love; have sex
性灵 ① personality; temperament; character ②intelligent; bright; brilliant
性命 life (of a man or animal)
性能 function (of a machine, etc.); performance; property
性情 disposition; temperament; temper

性腺 sexual (or sex) gland
性学 sexology
性欲 sexual desire (or urge)
性征 sex character; sexuality
性质 quality; nature; character
性状 shape and properties; properties; character
性子 [xìngzi] ①temper ②strength; potency
性变态 sexual deviation
性冲动 the sexual impulse
性道德 sex morality
性泛滥 sexploitation
性观念 concept of sex
性贿赂 sex bribe
性激素 sex hormone
性价比 cost performance
性教育 sex education
性解放 sexual liberation; blue revolution
性糜乱 sexual promiscuity
性奴役 sexual enslavement
性器官 sexual organs; genitals
性骚扰 sexual harassment; sexual disturbance
性生活 sexual life
性卫生 sex hygiene
性行为 sexual behaviour; sex act
性学家 sexologist
性早熟 sexual precocity
性知识 sex knowledge
性自由 free love; sexual freedom
性别平等 gender equality
性别歧视 sexism; sexual discrimination; discrimination against women
性感明星 sexy star; sexy symbol
性感女郎 sex kitten; sexpot
性格刻画 characterization
性格演员 character actor; character actress
性好清高 be of exalted and proud nature
性命攸关 (a matter) of life and death; of vital importance
性能数据 performance data
性能指标 performance standards (or indicators)
性虐待狂 sadism
性染色体 heterosome; sex chromosome
性心理学 sexual psychology
性传播疾病 sexually transmitted disease (STD)
性功能障碍 sex dysfunction

姓 [xìng]
名 family or clan name; surname
姓名 surname and personal name; full name
姓氏 surname
姓名权 right of personal name

悻 [xìng]

悻然 enraged
悻悻 angry; resentful

X

xiōng(ㄒㄩㄥ)

凶 [xiōng]
Ⅰ 形 ①inauspicious; unlucky; ominous ② crop failure; famine ③fierce; menacing; ferocious ④ terrible; violent; fearful ⑤ efficient; effective; tough Ⅱ 名 ①act of violence; murder ②evildoer; criminal; murderer

凶暴 fierce and brutal

凶残 ①fierce and cruel; savage and cruel ②a fierce and cruel person

凶恶 （of temper, appearance or behaviour） fierce; ferocious; fiendish

凶犯 one who has committed homicide or mayhem; murderer

凶悍 fierce and tough

凶狠 ①fierce and malicious ②powerful; vigorous

凶狂 fierce; savage; ferocious

凶猛 violent; ferocious

凶气 fierce manner; ferocious expression

凶器 a tool or weapon for criminal purposes; a lethal weapon

凶杀 homicide; murder

凶神 demon; fiend

凶手 murderer; assassin; assailant

凶徒 villain; murderer

凶险 ①dangerous; perilous; critical ②ruthless and treacherous

凶相 ferocious features; fierce look; fiendish look

凶信 news of sb's death

凶焰 ferocity; aggressive arrogance

凶宅 a haunted house; an unlucky abode

凶兆 ill omen; boding of evil

凶多吉少 bode ill rather than well; be fraught with grim possibilities

凶如猛虎 with the ferocity of tigers

凶神恶煞 devils; fiends

凶相毕露 look thoroughly ferocious; unleash all one's ferocity

兄 [xiōng]
名 ①elder brother ②elder male relative of one's own generation ③courteous form of address between men

兄弟 ① brothers ② fraternal; brotherly ③ younger brother ④ a familiar form of address for a man younger than oneself ⑤I

兄嫂 elder brother and his wife

兄长 ① a respectful form of address for an elder brother ② a respectful form of address for a male friend

兄弟民族 fraternal ethnic groups

汹 [xiōng]
名 rush of water; tumult

汹汹 ① the sound of turbulent waves ② violent; truculent ③tumultuous; agitated

汹涌 surging; turbulent; tempestuous

汹涌澎湃 surging; turbulent; tempestuous

恟 [xiōng]
形 in terror; panic-stricken

胸 [xiōng]
名 ①chest; breast; bosom; thorax ②mind; heart

胸靶 chest silhouette

胸部 thorax; chest

胸骨 sternum; breastbone

胸怀 ①mind; heart ②keep in the mind; cherish

胸襟 mind; breadth of mind

胸卡 name tag

胸口 the pit of the stomach; chest

胸膜 pleura

胸脯 chest; breast

胸鳍 pectoral fin

胸腔 thoracic cavity; chest cavity

胸墙 breastwork; parapet

胸膛 chest

胸围 chest measurement; bust

胸像 (sculptured) bust

胸臆 thought; heart; one's feelings

胸章 badge

胸罩 brassiere; bra

胸针 brooch

胸椎 thoracic vertebra

胸膜炎 pleurisy

胸怀大志 cherish high ideals; have lofty aspirations

胸无城府 artless; simple and candid

胸无点墨 unlearned; unlettered

胸有成竹 have a well-thought-out plan, stratagem, etc.

xióng(ㄒㄩㄥˊ)

雄 [xióng]
Ⅰ 形 ①male ②grand; imposing; commanding; majestic ③virile; powerful; mighty Ⅱ 名 person or state having great power and influence

雄辩 ①convincing argument; eloquent speech ②convincing; eloquent

雄兵 a powerful army

雄蜂 drone; male bee

雄关 an impregnable pass

雄厚 （of strength, resources, etc.） ample; rich; solid; abundant

雄花 male flower; staminate flower

雄黄 realgar; red orpiment

雄浑 vigorous and firm; forceful

雄鸡 cock; rooster

雄健 robust; vigorous; powerful

雄劲 vigorous and powerful

雄跨 straddle; bestride

雄起 bravo

雄蕊 stamen
雄师 a powerful army; a mighty army
雄图 a great ambition; a grandiose plan
雄威 full of power and grandeur; strong and imposing; awe-inspiring
雄伟 grand; imposing
雄文 profound and powerful writing; great works
雄心 great ambitions; lofty aspirations
雄性 male
雄蚁 male ant
雄主 a ruler of great talent and bold vision
雄壮 full of power and grandeur; magnificent; majestic
雄姿 majestic appearance; heroic posture
雄激素 androgen
雄赳赳 valiant; gallant
雄霸一方 act the tyrant in a locality; hold a part of the country and exercise undisputed authority
雄才大略 (a man of) great talent and bold vision; (a statesman or general of) rare gifts and bold strategy
雄心勃勃 very ambitious
雄心壮志 lofty aspirations and high ideals
雄性不育 male sterility
雄姿英发 majestic and spirited; dashing and debonair

熊 [xióng]
I 〈名〉 bear II 〈动〉 rebuke; upbraid; abuse; scold III 〈形〉 impotent; timid; faint-hearted
熊胆 bear gall
熊蜂 bumblebee
熊猴 Assamese macaque
熊猫 panda
熊市 bear market; bearish market
熊熊 flaming; ablaze; raging
熊掌 bear's paw (a rare delicacy)
熊心豹胆 bear's heart and leopard's gall—fearlessness; courage; guts
熊腰虎背 with a bear's loin and a tiger's back; thick powerful back and shoulder tough and strong

xiòng (ㄒㄩㄥˋ)

诇 [xiòng]
〈动〉 detect; spy on
诇察 brown bearprobe into sth; spy out sth

夐 [xiòng]
〈形〉 ①remote; distant ②far back; long long ago

xiū (ㄒㄧㄡ)

休 [xiū]
I 〈动〉 ①stop; end; cease; give up ②rest; repose ③divorce one's wife and send her home II 〈副〉 don't III 〈名〉 good fortune; rejoicing

休耕 fallow; lie fallow
休怪 don't blame
休会 adjourn meeting
休假 (of workers, students, etc.) have (or take, go on) a holiday or vacation; (of soldiers, personnel working abroad, etc.) be on leave
休刊 (of newspapers or magazines) cease to publish; suspend publication
休克 shock
休眠 dormancy
休牧 grazing-off
休妻 divorce and send one's wife away
休戚 weal and woe; joys and sorrows
休憩 have (or take) a rest; rest
休市 off business; market closed; business suspended; break
休庭 adjourn
休息 have (or take) a rest; rest
休闲 lie fallow; leisure
休想 don't imagine that it's possible
休学 suspend one's schooling without losing one's status as a student
休养 recuperate; convalesce
休业 ①suspend business; be closed down ② (of a short-term course, etc.) come to an end; wind up
休渔 suspend fishing; fishing-off
休战 truce; cease-fire; armistice
休征 auspicious omen
休整 rest and reorganization (of troops, etc.)
休止 stop; cease
休病假 on sick leave
休眠期 rest period
休眠芽 resting (or dormant) bud
休息室 lounge; lobby; vestibule; foyer
休闲服 casual clothes
休闲装 sportswear; slack suit; casual clothes
休养所 sanatorium; rest home
休止符 rest
休得多问 Don't ask too many questions.
休克疗法 shock therapy
休眠火山 dormant volcano
休戚相关 share joys and sorrows; be bound together by common interests
休戚与共 share weal and woe; stand together through thick and thin
休闲消费 leisure consumption
休养生息 (of a nation) recuperate and multiply; rest and build up strength; rehabilitate

咻 [xiū]
〈动〉 make a din

修 [xiū]
I 〈动〉 ①embellish; decorate; adorn ②repair; mend; fix; overhaul ③write; compile ④study; learn; cultivate ⑤ (superstition) practise Buddhism or Taoism ⑥build; construct ⑦

trim；pare；prune Ⅱ 形 long；tall and slim
修补 ①mend；patch up；repair；revamp ②repair
修长 tall and thin；slender
修辞 rhetoric
修道 cultivate oneself according to a religious doctrine
修订 revise
修复 ①repair；restore；renovate ②repair（of destroyed cells or tissues）
修改 revise；modify；amend；alter
修盖 build
修函 write a letter
修好 ①foster cordial relations between states ②do good works
修剪 prune；trim；clip
修建 build；construct；erect
修脚 pedicure
修浚 dredge
修理 ① repair；mend；overhaul；fix ② prune；trim
修炼 practise austerities；practise asceticism
修面 shave；have a shave
修女 nun（of the Roman Catholic and Greek Orthodox churches）；sister
修配 make repairs and supply replacements
修葺 repair；renovate
修缮 repair；renovate
修身 cultivate one's moral character
修史 compile（or write）history
修士 monk；brother；friar
修饰 ①decorate；adorn；embellish ②make up and dress up ③polish（a piece of writing）④qualify；modify
修书 ①compile a book ②write a letter
修行 practise Buddhism or Taoism
修养 ①accomplishment；training；mastery ②accomplishment in self-cultivation；self-possession
修业 study at school
修造 build as well as repair
修整 ①repair and maintain ②prune；trim
修正 ① revise；amend；correct ② mutilate（Marxism-Leninism）；revise
修枝 prune
修竹 tall bamboo
修筑 build；construct；put up
修船厂 shipyard；dockyard
修辞格 figures of speech
修辞学 rhetoric
修道院 monastery or convent
修订本 revised edition
修脚师 pedicure
修理厂 fix-it shop；repair shop
修面膏 shaving cream
修面刷 shaving brush
修饰剂 dressing agent

修饰语 modifier
修正案 amendment
修正角 aviation correction angle
修枝剪 pruning scissors；pruning shears
修地方志 write annals of local history
修旧利度 repair and utilize old or discarded things
修理行业 repairing trades
修缮工程 renovation project
修身养性 cultivate oneself through meditation
修修补补 patch up；tinker
修业证书 certificate for the completion of a course of study；certificate showing courses attended
修正主义 revisionism

麻 [xiū]
动 shield（sb）；shelter；protect

脩 [xiū]
名 ①dried meat ②private tutor's remuneration

羞 [xiū]
Ⅰ 形 shy；coy；bashful Ⅱ 动 ①embarrass；shame ②feel ashamed Ⅲ 名 shame；mortification；disgrace
羞惭 be ashamed
羞耻 sense of shame；shame
羞愤 ashamed and resentful
羞愧 ashamed；abashed
羞明 photophobia
羞恼 be angry and ashamed
羞怯 shy；timid；sheepish
羞人 feel embarrassed（or ashamed）
羞辱 ① shame；dishonour；humiliation ② humiliate；put sb to shame
羞涩 shy；bashful；embarrassed
羞花闭月 so beautiful as to cause the flowers to bush and the moon to hide
羞羞答答 coy；shy；bashful
羞于启齿 be too shy to speak out
羞与为伍 feel ashamed to associate with sb；think it beneath one to associate with sb
羞与为友 feel ashamed to have such a friend

xiǔ（ㄒ丨ㄡˇ）

朽 [xiǔ]
形 ①（mostly of wood）rotten；decayed ②senile
朽败 decayed；rotten
朽坏 decayed；rotten
朽烂 rotten
朽木 ①rotten wood（or tree）②a hopeless case；a good-for-nothing
朽木粪土 rotten wood and worthless soil—a worthless person；useless stuff

宿 [xiǔ]
量（used to count nights）➡ sù；xiù

X

xiù(ㄒㄧㄡˋ)

秀 [xiù] Ⅰ 动 (of grain crops) put forth flowers or ears Ⅱ 形 ① elegant; beautiful; pretty and delicate ② clever; smart; intelligent ③ excellent; superb Ⅲ 名 excellent person; outstanding talent

秀拔 beautiful and forceful

秀才 ① xiucai, one who passed the imperial examination at the county level ② scholar; skilful writer

秀丽 beautiful; handsome; pretty

秀美 graceful; elegant

秀气 ① delicate; elegant; fine ② (of manners) refined; urbane ③ (of articles of use) delicate and well-made; exquisite

秀雅 tasteful and refined; graceful; elegant

秀逸 (of style) free, easy and beautiful

秀而不实 flowering but bearing no fruit—fine in appearance but empty in substance

秀色可餐 be a feast to the eye (usu. said of a very attractive woman, sometimes of beautiful scenery)

秀外慧中 beautiful and intelligent

秀才不出门, 能知天下事 Without stepping outside his gate the scholar knows all the wide world's affairs.

岫 [xiù] 名 ① cave; cavern ② mountain; mountain peak

臭 [xiù] 名 odour; smell ➡chòu

臭腺 scent gland

袖 [xiù] Ⅰ 名 sleeve Ⅱ 动 tuck or hide inside the sleeve

袖标 armband (or badge) worn on the sleeve for identification

袖管 ① sleeve ② cuff

袖口 cuff (of a sleeve)

袖扣 cuff links

袖套 oversleeve

袖筒 sleeve

袖章 armband; sleeve badge

袖珍 pocket-size; pocket

袖子 sleeve

袖珍本 pocket edition

袖手而立 stand there, tucking one's hands in one's sleeves

袖手旁观 look on (or stand by) with folded arms; look on unconcerned

袖珍词典 pocket dictionary

绣 [xiù] Ⅰ 动 embroider Ⅱ 名 embroidery

绣房 young girl's bedroom

绣工 ① embroidery worker ② embroidery; embroidery work

绣花 embroider; do embroidery

绣品 embroidery

绣球 a ball made of rolled coloured silk

绣像 ① tapestry portrait; embroidered portrait ② exquisitely drawn portrait

绣花鞋 embroidered shoes

绣花针 embroidery needle

绣球花 big-leaf hydrangea

绣花丝线 floss silk; embroidery silk

绣花枕头 ① pillow with an embroidered case ② outwardly attractive but worthless person

宿 [xiù] 名 constellation ➡sù; xiǔ

锈 [xiù] Ⅰ 名 ① rust ② rust (disease) Ⅱ 动 become rusty

锈斑 rust; rusty spot; pitting

锈病 rust

锈蚀 corroded by rust; spoilt by rust

锈损 corrode

嗅 [xiù] 动 scent; smell; sniff

嗅觉 (sense of) smell; scent

嗅神经 olfactory nerve

溴 [xiù] 名 bromine (Br)

溴水 bromine water

溴酸 bromic acid

溴化物 bromide

xū(ㄒㄩ)

圩 [xū] 名 country fair ➡wéi

圩场 country fair; market

吁 [xū] Ⅰ 动 sigh Ⅱ 叹 (expressing surprise) why; oh ➡yū; yù

吁吁 sound of breathing hard

盱 [xū] 动 look up with eyes wide open; stare upwards

盱盱然 glowering

须 [xū] Ⅰ 动 ① must; have to ② wait; await Ⅱ 名 ① beard; mustache ② palpus; feeler; tassel

须发 beard and hair

须根 fibrous root

须鲸 baleen whale

须眉 beard and eyebrows—a man

须要 must; have to

须臾 moment; instant

须知 ① one should know that; it must be understood (or borne in mind) that ② points for attention; notice

须子 ① palpus; feeler ② tassel

胥 [xū]
Ⅰ 名 petty official Ⅱ 副 all;each and every

虚 [xū]
Ⅰ 名 ① void;emptiness ② guiding principles;theory Ⅱ 形 ①empty;void;vacant;unoccupied ②diffident;timid;cowardly ③false;deceitful;nominal ④ humble;unassuming;modest ⑤weak;feeble;in poor health Ⅲ 副 in vain;futilely Ⅳ 动 reserve space

虚报 make a false report;report untruthfully
虚词 function word;form word
虚度 spend time in vain;waste
虚浮 impractical;superficial
虚高 empty high
虚根 imaginary root
虚构 fabricate;make up
虚汗 abnormal sweating due to general debility
虚幻 unreal;illusory
虚假 false;sham
虚价 nominal price
虚惊 false alarm
虚空 vacant space;hollow;void
虚夸 exaggerative;bombastic;boastful
虚名 false reputation;undeserved reputation
虚拟 ①invented;fictitious ②suppositional
虚胖 puffiness
虚弱 ① in poor health;weak;debilitated ② weak;feeble
虚设 nominal;existing in name only
虚实 ①false or true—the actual situation (as of the opposing side) ② theoretical and practical
虚饰 ①cover up;modify with false words ② flashy;without substance
虚数 ①unreliable figure ②imaginary number
虚岁 nominal age
虚土 ploughed,soft soil
虚脱 collapse;prostration
虚妄 unfounded;fabricated;invented
虚伪 sham;false;hypocritical
虚文 ① rules and regulations that have become a dead letter; dead letter ② empty forms
虚无 nihility;nothingness
虚线 ①dotted line;line of dashes ②imaginary line
虚像 virtual image
虚心 open-minded;modest
虚职 nominal position without authority or specific duties;redundant
虚字 empty word;function word;form word
虚焦点 virtual focus
虚拟网 virtual net
虚荣(心) vanity
虚报冒领 make a fraudulent application and claim

虚不掩实 false appearance can never cover up reality
虚度光阴 fritter away one's time
虚度年华 idle away one's time;waste one's life
虚高价格 empty high price
虚怀若谷 have a mind as open as a valley—be extremely modest;be open-minded
虚晃一枪 feint a thrust with one's spear;make a feint
虚假报道 false report;mendacious report
虚假繁荣 bubble boom
虚假广告 sham publicity; sham promotion; false advertisements;deceptive advertisements
虚拟地址 virtual address
虚拟经济 virtual economy
虚拟市场 dummy market
虚拟现实 VR,virtual reality
虚拟语气 the subjunctive mood
虚情假意 a false display of affection;a hypocritical show of friendship
虚实并举 pay attention to both theory and practical work
虚位以待 leave a seat vacant (or save a seat) for sb
虚无缥缈 purely imaginary; entirely unreal; visionary;illusory
虚无主义 nihilism
虚虚实实 the true mingled with the false;a mixture of truth and falsehood
虚应故事 do sth perfunctorily as a mere form or routine
虚有其表 look impressive but lack real worth;appear better than it is
虚与委蛇 deal with sb courteously but without sincerity; pretend politeness and compliance
虚张声势 make an empty show of strength; bluff and bluster;be swashbuckling
虚拟存储器 virtual memory
虚拟主持人 virtual compère
虚开增值税发票 fake value-added tax forms

墟 [xū]
名 ①ruins ②country fair

需 [xū]
Ⅰ 动 need;want;demand;require Ⅱ 名 necessities;needs
需求 requirement;demand
需要 ①need;want;require;demand ②needs
需求膨胀 demand pull
需求疲软 weak in demand
需求曲线 demand curve
需求弹性 demand elasticity
需求拉动型通货膨胀 demand-pull inflation

嘘 [xū]
Ⅰ 动 ①breathe out slowly ②utter a sigh;

sigh ③(of cooking fire,steam,etc.) come into contact with;scald;sear;burn ④hiss;boo;
give a Bronx cheer Ⅱ 叹 sh;hush ➡ shī
嘘气 exhale slowly
嘘寒问暖 inquire after sb's well-being;be solicitous about sb's health

XÚ(ㄒㄨˊ)

徐 副 slowly;gently
徐步 walk slowly (or leisurely);stroll
徐缓 slow
徐徐 slowly;gently
徐娘半老,风韵犹存 in middle age, attractive
all the same—an attractive middle-aged
woman

XǓ(ㄒㄨˇ)

许 Ⅰ 动 ①praise;commend ②make a promise;promise ③betroth;be betrothed to ④al-
low;permit;consent Ⅱ 副 ①perhaps;proba-
bly; maybe ② (expressing extent or a-
mount) ③about;approximately Ⅲ 名 place
许多 many;much;a great deal of;a lot of
许久 for a long time;for ages
许可 permit;allow
许诺 make a promise;promise
许配 (of a girl) be betrothed to sb (in an arranged match)
许愿 ①make a vow to a god ②promise sb a
reward
许可证 license;permit
许许多多 lots and lots of
许可证贸易 licence trade
诩 [xǔ] 动 brag;boast;blow one's own horn
栩 [xǔ] 名 oak
栩栩 vivid;lively
栩栩如生 lifelike;to the life
湑 [xǔ] 形 ①clear ②luxuriant
糈 [xǔ] 名 grain
醑 [xǔ] 名 ①mellow wine ②spirit;essence
醑剂 spirit;essence

XÙ(ㄒㄨˋ)

旭 [xù] 名 brilliance of the rising sun
旭日 the rising sun
旭日东升 the sun rising in the eastern sky—a
display of youthful vigour and vitality
芧 [xù] 名 acorn ➡ zhù

序 [xù]
Ⅰ 名 ①order;sequence ②preface ③wing-
room ④type of local school Ⅱ 动 arrange in
order;order Ⅲ 形 initial;opening;introducto-
ry
序跋 preface and postscript
序列 alignment;array
序幕 ①prologue (to a play) ②prologue (to a
major event,etc.);prelude
序曲 ①overture ②prelude (to an event, action,etc.)
序数 ordinal number;ordinal
序文 preface;foreword
序言 preface;foreword
序时账 accounting journal
序列分析 sequential analysis
序列记录 chronological record
序列账簿 chronological book;book of chronological entry

叙 [xù] 动 ① talk;chitchat;chat ②narrate;re-
count;relate ③assess;evaluate;appraise
叙别 have a farewell talk
叙旧 talk about the old days
叙事 narrate (in writing);recount
叙述 narrate (in speech or writing);recount;
relate
叙说 tell;narrate (in speech)
叙谈 chat;chitchat
叙事剧 epic theatre
叙事曲 ballade
叙事诗 narrative poem;ballade
叙事体 descriptive style
叙事文 narrative;narrative prose
叙多论少 more narrating than theorizing
叙事歌剧 ballad opera

洫 [xù] 名 water duct in a field;ditch

恤 [xù] 动 ①pity;sympathize;commiserate ②give
relief;compensate
恤金 pension for a person disabled while on
duty;pension for the dependants of a person who died while on duty

堷 [xù] 名 east or west wall of a house

畜 [xù] 动 raise (domestic animals);breed;rear ➡
chù
畜产 livestock (or animal) products
畜牧 raise (or rear) livestock (or poultry)
畜养 raise (domestic animals)
畜产品 animal by-products
畜牧场 animal farm;livestock (or stock) farm
畜牧业 animal husbandry;livestock husbandry;livestock farming

酗 [xù]

酗酒 indulge in excessive drinking

绪 [xù]
〈名〉①end of a silk thread ②beginning of a matter ③remnants ④mental or emotional state;mood ⑤task;cause;enterprise;undertaking
绪风 remnants of a social trend
绪论 introduction
绪言 introduction

续 [xù]
Ⅰ〈形〉continuous;successive;one after another Ⅱ〈动〉①continue;resume;extend ②add;increase;supply more;续煤 add coal
续编 continuation (of a book);sequel
续订 renew one's subscription (to a newspaper or magazine)
续读 resume studies
续断 teasel root
续航 (of an airplane or ship) continue (or pursue) a journey without refuelling
续会 resume a meeting
续集 continuation (of a book);sequel
续假 extend one's leave of absence;extend leave
续借 renew (a library book)
续篇 sequel
续聘 renew (contract)
续闻 follow-up news
续弦 ①remarry after the death of one's wife ②a second wife (after the death of one's first wife)
续约 ①renew a treaty (or contract) ②a renewed treaty or contract;a supplementary contract
续航力 endurance;flying range (of an airplane);cruising radius (of a ship)

絮 [xù]
Ⅰ〈名〉①(cotton) wadding;padding ②sth resembling cotton ③coarse silk floss Ⅱ〈动〉wad or pad (as with cotton);絮棉衣 line (or wad) one's clothes with cotton Ⅲ〈形〉①long-winded;loquacious;talkative;garrulous ②bored;fed up
絮叨 be long-winded;be garrulous;be wordy
絮烦 wordy;long winded
絮棉 cotton for wadding
絮片 flocculus
絮语 incessantly chatter;be wordy;garrulity

婿 [xù]
〈名〉①son-in-law ②husband

蓄 [xù]
〈动〉①store up;save up ②cause to grow;grow ③harbour;cherish;entertain (ideas)
蓄藏 save and preserve;lay in;lay up;store
蓄洪 store floodwater
蓄积 store up;save up
蓄谋 premeditate
蓄能 energy storage
蓄水 retain (or store) water
蓄须 grow a beard
蓄养 build up;accumulate
蓄意 premeditated;deliberate
蓄志 harbour an ambition
蓄电池 storage battery;accumulator
蓄洪区 flood containment area;flood control area
蓄水池 cistern;reservoir
蓄电池车 accumulator vehicle
蓄发明志 wear one's hair long to show one's resolve
蓄势已久 long premeditated
蓄水工程 water storage project
蓄意伤害 wounding with intent
蓄意挑衅 premeditated provocation

昫 [xù]
〈形〉warm;balmy

xu(·ㄒㄩ)

蓿 [xu]
◇苜蓿 lucerne;alfalfa

xuān(ㄒㄩㄢ)

轩 [xuān]
Ⅰ〈形〉high;lofty;dignified Ⅱ〈名〉①small room or veranda with windows;open corridor or pavilion ②high-fronted,curtained carriage ③window or door
轩昂 dignified;imposing
轩敞 spacious and bright
轩车 carriage used by senior officials in dynastic China
轩帘 curtain;door drape
轩轾 high and low chariots—high or low;good or bad
轩然大波 a great disturbance;a mighty uproar

宣 [xuān]
〈动〉①announce;declare;proclaim;promulgate ②drain;lead off (liquids)
宣布 declare;proclaim;announce
宣称 assert;declare;profess
宣传 conduct propaganda;propagate;disseminate;give publicity to
宣读 read out (in public)
宣告 declare;proclaim
宣讲 ① explain and publicize (a policy, decree,etc.) ②preach (a religious doctrine)
宣教 propaganda and education
宣判 pronounce judgment
宣赦 proclaim a general amnesty
宣示 declare;announce
宣誓 take (or swear) an oath;make a vow;make a pledge
宣泄 ①lead off (liquids);drain ②get sth off one's chest;unbosom oneself

X

宣言 declaration;manifesto
宣扬 publicise;propagate;advocate;advertise
宣战 declare war
宣纸 rice paper;*xuan* paper
宣传车 sound truck;sound ear;sound van
宣传队 propaganda team
宣传画 picture poster
宣传品 propaganda (*or* publicity) material
宣传网 propaganda network
宣传员 propagandist
宣叙调 recitative
宣战书 a declaration of war
宣布戒严 proclaim martial law
宣传副页 tip-on
宣传工具 instrument (*or* means) of propaganda (*or* publicity)
宣传工作 publicity work;propaganda work
宣传机构 propaganda organ
宣传机器 propaganda machine
宣誓就职 take an oath of office;be sworn into office
宣传工作者 propagandist
宣传推广资料 promotional literature
宣传舆论工作 publicity work and guidance for public opinion
宣誓就职典礼 swearing-in ceremony

谖 [xuān]
动 ①forget ②cheat;swindle;trick

萱 [xuān]
名 ①tawny daylily ②(your) mother
萱草 daylily
萱堂 formal honour your mother

揎 [xuān]
动 ①roll up sleeves ②push ③hit;strike
揎拳捋袖 roll up one's sleeves and raise one's fists (to fight)

喧 [xuān]
形 noisy
喧哗 ① confused noise;hubbub;uproar ② make an uproar;make a racket
喧闹 noise and excitement;bustle;racket
喧嚷 make an uproar;make a racket
喧扰 stir up a disturbance;make a commotion
喧腾 noise and excitement;hubbub
喧天 make a deafening sound
喧嚣 ①noisy ②make a clamour;make a hullabaloo;raise a din
喧笑 ①laugh loudly ②loud laughter
喧宾夺主 A presumptuous guest usurps the role of the host;The secondary supersedes the primary.

暄 [xuān]
Ⅰ 名 warmth (of the sun);genial warmth
Ⅱ 形 fluffy;soft
暄腾 fluffy;soft
暄土 soft soil

煖 [xuān]
形 warm

煊 [xuān]
煊赫 of great renown and influence

儇 [xuān]
形 ①frivolous;flighty;light ②crafty;cunning;sly
儇薄 frivolous

xuán (ㄒㄩㄢˊ)

玄 [xuán]
形 ① black;dark ② profound;subtle;abstruse ③ unreliable;mysterious;far-fetched;incredible:你说得也太玄了。What you said is a pretty tall story.
玄奥 profound;abstruse
玄服 black gown
玄鹤 black crane
玄乎 fantastic;incredible
玄机 arcane truth
玄略 subtle strategy
玄妙 mysterious;abstruse
玄青 deep black
玄孙 great-great-grandson;grandson of one's grandson
玄想 fancy;imagination
玄虚 deceitful trick;mystery
玄学 metaphysics
玄武岩 basalt
玄之又玄 the mystery of mysteries—extremely mysterious and abstruse

悬 [xuán]
Ⅰ 动 ① hang;suspend;fly ② announce openly;make known to the public ③raise;lift ④miss;be concerned about ⑤imagine Ⅱ 形 ① unresolved;unsettled;outstanding ② far apart ③dangerous;precarious;perilous
悬案 ①an unsettled law case ②an outstanding issue;an unsettled question
悬臂 cantilever
悬垂 overhang
悬吊 be suspended;hang
悬浮 suspension
悬隔 be separated by a great distance;be far apart
悬挂 ①hang;suspend;fly (a flag) ②suspension (of a motor vehicle)
悬壶 practise medicine
悬乎 dangerous;unsafe
悬胶 suspensoid
悬空 hang in the air—be unsettled;be impractical
悬梁 hang oneself from a beam
悬拟 fabricate;make up
悬念 ①be concerned about (sb who is elsewhere) ②suspense (felt as a story, play, etc. builds to a climax)
悬赏 offer (*or* post) a reward

悬殊 a great disparity；a wide gap
悬梯 hanging ladder
悬腕 suspend the wrist
悬想 imagine；fancy
悬心 be on tenterhooks
悬崖 overhanging (*or* steep) cliff；precipice
悬账 unsettled account
悬臂梁 cantilever (beam)
悬臂桥 cantilever bridge
悬浮体 suspended substance；suspension
悬挂犁 mounted plough
悬铃木 plane tree
悬索桥 suspension bridge
悬雍垂 uvula
悬浊液 turbid liquid
悬灯结彩 hang up lanterns and festoons；adorn with lanterns and coloured streamers
悬而未决 outstanding；unresolved
悬浮固体 suspended solid
悬挂国旗 fly the national flag
悬河泻水 a hanging river in flood—a flood of eloquence
悬空通道 skywalk
悬梁刺股 tie one's hair to a beam to keep from nodding off，or prod oneself awake with an awl in the thigh—study assiduously
悬赏缉拿 set a price on sb
悬首示众 display sb's chopped-off head at a public place as a warning to all
悬索结构 suspended-cable structure
悬心吊胆 have one's heart in one's mouth；be on tenterhooks
悬崖勒马 rein in at the brink of the precipice—wake up to danger at the last moment
悬崖峭壁 sheer precipices and overhanging rocks；(perilous) cliffs and precipices
悬臂起重机 cantilever crane
悬挂式滑翔 hang gliding
悬索斜拉桥 cable suspension bridge
悬挂式滑翔机 hang glider
悬赏缉拿罪犯 offer a reward for the capture of a runaway criminal；set a price for a runaway criminal's head

旋 ［xuán］
I 动 ①revolve；circle；spin；wheel ②return；go back；come back II 名 part of the scalp where the hair is whorled III 副 soon；quickly ➡ xuàn
旋耕 rotary tillage
旋悔 regret it soon after
旋即 soon；before long；quickly
旋律 melody
旋钮 knob
旋桥 swing bridge
旋绕 curl up；wind around
旋塞 cock

旋涡 eddy；vortex
旋踵 in the brief time it takes to turn round on one's heel—in an instant
旋转 revolve；gyrate；rotate；spin
旋耕机 rotary cultivator
旋光性 optical rotation
旋毛虫 trichina
旋木雀 tree creeper
旋翼机 rotary-wing aircraft；rotorcraft
旋涡星云 spiral nebula
旋转餐厅 revolving restaurant
旋转天线 rotary antenna
旋转乾坤 effect a drastic change in nature or the established order of a country；be earth-shaking

漩 ［xuán］
名 whirlpool；eddy
漩涡 whirlpool；vortex；eddy

xuǎn （ㄒㄩㄢˇ）

选 ［xuǎn］
I 动 ①select；choose；pick ②elect II 名 ①those who are elected or chosen ②selection；anthology
选拔 select；choose
选本 anthology；selected works
选材 ①select a suitable person ②select suitable materials
选单 menu
选调 recruit
选定 decide on；fix
选读 ①pick out (pieces or passages) to read；read excerpts ②selected readings
选段 aria；selected parts
选购 pick out and buy；choose from a variety of goods
选集 selected works (*or* writings)；selections；anthology
选辑 ①select and compile ②selected works；selected writings
选举 elect
选刊 ①publish ②periodicals exclusively carrying selected writings
选矿 ore dressing；mineral separation；beneficiation
选录 select
选美 pageant；beauty contest
选民 voter；elector
选派 select；detail
选配 ①provide ②select better breeds for reproduction；selective breeding
选票 vote；ballot
选聘 appoint to a position；engage or employ；select and employ
选区 precinct；electoral district；election district；election ward；constituency
选曲 selected songs (*or* tunes)

选取 select;choose
选任 select (a suitable person) for a post
选手 an athlete selected for a sports meet; (selected) contestant;player
选送 select and recommend sb (for a position or for admission to a school,etc.)
选题 ① select a title,subject or topic (for writing or research) ② the title,subject or topic selected
选修 take as an elective course
选秀 draft
选样 sampling;sample
选用 select for employment or for use
选育 ① seed selection ② animal husbandry breeding
选择 select;choose;opt
选种 seed selection
选中 pick on;decide on;settle on
选拔赛 (selective) trial
选举法 electoral law
选举权 the right to vote;franchise
选举人 voter
选民榜 list of eligible voters
选民证 elector's certificate;voter registration card
选修课 selective course;optional course;elective
选择税 alternative duty
选择题 multiple-choice question;multiple-choice test
选拔考试 competitive examination
选举舞弊 corrupt practice
选料精良 superior materials
选贤举能 appoint the good and able men to office
选择场地 choice of ends
选择问句 alternative question
选址原则 site selection principle
选拔委员会 selection board

烜 [xuǎn]
形 grand;magnificent
烜赫 of great renown and influence
烜赫一时 have renown and influence for a time

癣 [xuǎn]
名 tinea;ringworm

xuàn(ㄒㄩㄢˋ)

券 [xuàn]
名 arch ⇒ quàn

泫 [xuàn]
动 fall in drops;drip;trickle

眩 [xuàn]
名 sunshine;sunlight

炫 [xuàn]
动 ①daze;dazzle;blaze ②show off;display
炫目 dazzling

炫弄 show off;display;parade
炫示 show off;display;parade
炫耀 make a display of;show off;flaunt
炫人耳目 confuse the ears and eyes of the people

绚 [xuàn]
形 gorgeous;(of colour) prismatic
绚烂 splendid;gorgeous
绚丽 gorgeous;magnificent
绚丽多彩 bright and colourful;gorgeous

眩 [xuàn]
形 ① dizzy;giddy;vertiginous ② dazzled;bewildered
眩光 dazzling light
眩目 dazzle the eyes
眩晕 ①dizziness ②vertigo

铉 [xuàn]
名 hook-like instrument to carry an ancient tripod by catching its rings or ears

旋 [xuàn]
Ⅰ 动 ①whirl ②turn on a lathe;lathe;pare Ⅱ 副 at the time when sth is needed;at the last moment ⇒ xuán
旋床 (turning) lathe
旋风 whirlwind
旋工 turner
旋子 ① copper plate (for making sheets of bean-starch jelly) ② hot water container for warming wine
旋用旋买 buy sth when you need it;buy for immediate use

渲 [xuàn]
动 wash (a piece of drawing paper) with watercolours
渲染 ①(in Chinese painting) add washes of ink or colour to a drawing ②play up;exaggerate;pile it on

楦 [xuàn]
Ⅰ 名 (shoe) last;(hat) block Ⅱ 动 ① stuff;fill up ②shape with a last or block
楦子 shoe last;shoe tree;hat block

碹 [xuàn]
动 build arches with bricks or stones

xuē(ㄒㄩㄝ)

削 [xuē]
动 (used only in compound words) scrape;pare;whittle;cut ⇒ xiāo
削壁 precipice;cliff
削发 tonsure;cut off one's hair
削价 cut the price;lower the price
削肩 sloping shoulders;drooping shoulders
削减 cut (down);reduce;slash;whittle down
削平 wipe out;suppress;subdue
削弱 weaken;cripple
削瘦 lean;gaunt;very thin
削职 remove from office
削价处理 be disposed of at reduced price

削价商品 cut-rate commodities
削减关税 reduction in tariff
削铁如泥 cut through iron as if it were mud (said of an exceptionally sharp sword)
削足适履 cut the feet to fit the shoes
削减战略核武器会谈 strategic arms reduction talks(START)

靴 [xuē]
　名 boots
靴筒 the leg of a boot;bootleg
靴子 boots

xué(ㄒㄩㄝ)

穴 [xué]
　名 ①cave;hole ②den;lair;nest ③grave; coffin pit;tomb ④acupuncture point;acupoint
穴道 acupuncture point;acupoint
穴居 live in a cave
穴头 illicit broker
穴位 acupuncture point;acupoint
穴居人 cave dweller;troglodyte

荥 [xué]
　团 store grain by enclosing it with coarse mat
荥子 matting;coarse mat

学 [xué]
　Ⅰ 动 ①study;learn:学技术 learn a skill ② imitate;mimic;copy:学狗叫 mimic the barking of a dog Ⅱ 名 ①learning;knowledge; scholarship ②subject of study;field or branch of learning ③school;college
学报 learned journal;journal
学潮 student strike; student unrest; campus upheaval
学阀 scholar-tyrant
学费 ①tuition fee;tuition ②a price for what one has learned to one's cost
学分 credit
学风 ①academic atmosphere;academic discipline ②style of study
学府 seat of learning; institution of higher learning
学工 learning industrial production
学好 learn from good examples;emulate good
学坏 ①follow bad examples ②(used with 了) be corrupted by bad examples
学会 ①learn;master ②learned society;society;institute
学籍 one's status as a student;one's name on the school roll
学监 visitor
学界 academic circles
学究 pedant
学军 learning military affairs
学科 ① a branch of learning; discipline ② a school subject;a course of study ③theoretical courses offered in military or physical training

学理 scientific principle (or theory)
学历 résumé of sb's education;education status; academic qualifications; record of formal schooling
学龄 school age
学路 ①ways to run a school ②ways of learning
学名 ①scientific name (e.g. Latin name for plants,etc.) ②formal name used at school (as distinguished from infant name or pet name at home)
学年 school (or academic) year
学农 learning agricultural production
学派 school of thought;school
学期 school term;term;semester
学舌 ① mechanically repeat other people's words; parrot; ape ② wag one's tongue spreading hearsay
学生 ①student;pupil ②disciple;follower ③ boy;lad
学时 class hour;period
学识 learning; knowledge; scholarly attainments
学士 ①scholar ②a holder of the bachelor's degree;bachelor
学术 systematic learning;science
学说 theory;doctrine
学堂 school
学徒 ①apprentice;trainee ②serve an apprenticeship
学位 academic degree;degree
学问 ① systematic learning; a branch of knowledge ②learning;knowledge;scholarship
学习 study;learn;emulate
学衔 academic rank (or title)
学校 school;educational institution
学业 one's studies;school work
学艺 ①learn a craft (or trade) ②knowledge and skills
学员 student (usu. of a college or a training course)
学院 college;academy;institute
学长 fellow student
学者 scholar;a learned man;a man of learning
学制 ① educational (or school) system ② length of schooling
学子 student
学分制 credit system
学生处 students' affairs division
学生会 student union;student association
学生证 student's identity card
学术界 academic circles
学徒工 apprentice
学而不厌 have an insatiable desire to learn;be insatiable in learning

学非所用 what one is doing has nothing to do with one's training

学富五车 have read five cartloads of books—be very learned

学籍管理 administration of student records; registrar's work

学科渗透 infiltration of disciplines

学前教育 preschool education; infant school education

学生生源 source of students

学生运动 student movement

学术气氛 academic atmosphere

学位制度 academic degree system

学无止境 Knowledge is infinite; There is no limit to knowledge.

学习动机 academic motivation

学习目的 aim of learning

学习系统 learning system

学以致用 study for the sake (*or* purpose) of application; study sth in order to apply it

学科带头人 pace-setter in scientific research; academic leader

学然后知不足 the more you learn, the less you feel you know

学得快,忘得快 soon learnt, soon forgotten

学而不思则罔,思而不学则殆 Learning without thinking will give rise to confusion; Thinking without learning will lead people astray.

趐 [xué]

㔟 pace up and down; walk to and fro; turn back half way

趐来趐去 walk back and forth

xué(ㄒㄩㄝˇ)

雪 [xuě]

I 名 ①snow ②snow-like II 动 wipe out (a humiliation, disgrace, etc.); avenge (a wrong)

雪白 snow-white; snowy white

雪板 skis

雪豹 snow leopard

雪暴 snowstorm; blizzard

雪崩 snowslide; avalanche

雪藏 refrigerate; hold in store

雪车 sled; sledge; sleigh

雪耻 avenge an insult; wipe out a disgrace or humiliation

雪地 snowfield

雪雕 snow sculpture

雪堆 snowbank; snow drift

雪糕 ice cream

雪恨 wreak vengeance; avenge

雪花 snowflake

雪鸡 snow cock

雪茄 cigar

雪景 snow-covered landscape

雪莲 snow lotus

雪亮 bright as snow; shiny

雪盲 snow blindness

雪片 snowflake

雪橇 sled; sledge; sleigh

雪青 lilac (colour)

雪球 snowball

雪人 ①snowman ②the Abominable Snowman (a hairy manlike creature reported to live in the snows of the Himalayas)

雪山 snow-capped mountain; snowy mountain

雪松 cedar

雪条 ice-lolly; frozen sucker; popsicle

雪兔 snow hare

雪冤 clear sb of a false charge; redress a wrong

雪原 snowfield

雪杖 ski pole; ski stick

雪纺绸 chiffon

雪花膏 vanishing cream

雪花莲 snowdrop

雪里蕻 potherb mustard

雪利酒 sherry

雪崩效应 avalanche effect

雪花石膏 alabaster

雪里送炭 send charcoal in snowy weather—provide timely help

雪泥鸿爪 marks left by goose claws in the snow—traces of past events

雪上加霜 snow plus frost—one disaster after another

雪上汽车 snowmobile

雪中送炭 send charcoal in snowy weather—provide timely help

雪上汽车运动 snowmobiling

xuè(ㄒㄩㄝˋ)

血 [xuè]

I 名 ① blood: 血 的 教训 lesson paid for with blood; lesson written in blood ②zeal; ardour; courage ③ menstruation; period II 形 related by blood ⇒xiě

血癌 leukaemia

血案 a murder case; a bloody incident

血本 principal; original capital

血沉 erythrocyte sedimentation rate (ESR)

血防 the prevention and cure of schistosomiasis (*or* snail fever)

血钙 blood calcium

血管 blood vessel

血海 a sea of blood; bloodbath

血汗 blood and sweat; sweat and toil

血花 spattered drops of blood

血迹 bloodstain

血痂 scab

血检 blood testing

血浆 (blood) plasma
血库 blood bank
血亏 anaemia
血路 a bloody path; an escape route
血脉 ① blood vessels; blood circulation ② blood relationship; blood lineage
血尿 haematuria; blood in the urine
血泊 a pool of blood
血气 ① animal spirits; sap; vigour ② courage and uprightness
血亲 blood relations
血清 (blood) serum
血球 blood cell; blood corpuscle
血肉 flesh and blood; the human body
血色 redness of the face; colour
血书 a letter (expressing one's determination, last wish, etc.) written in one's own blood
血栓 thrombus
血糖 blood sugar
血统 blood relationship; blood lineage; extraction
血头 organizer of illegal blood donation
血污 bloodstain
血洗 bloodbath
血像 blood picture; hemogram
血腥 reeking of blood; bloody; sanguinary
血型 blood group; blood type
血性 courage and uprightness
血胸 haemothorax
血压 blood pressure
血样 blood sample; blood specimen
血液 ① (human) blood ② lifeblood; lifeline
血衣 a bloodstained garment; clothes covered with gore
血印 bloodstain
血缘 ties of blood; consanguinity; blood relationship
血晕 [xuèyùn] coma after childbirth due to excessive loss of blood
血债 a debt of blood
血战 ① a bloody (or sanguinary) battle ② fight a very fierce battle
血肿 haematoma
血崩症 metrorrhagia
血管瘤 haemangioma; angioma
血泪仇 vengeful feelings nurtured by blood and tears
血淋淋 dripping with blood; bloody
血清病 serum sickness; serum disease
血色素 haemochrome
血吸虫 blood fluke; schistosome
血小板 (blood) platelet
血循环 blood circulation
血压计 sphygmomanometer
血液病 blood diseases
血友病 haemophilia

血管硬化 vascular sclerosis
血管造影 angiography
血海深仇 a huge debt of blood; intense and deep-seated hatred
血红蛋白 haemoglobin
血口喷人 make unfounded and malicious attacks upon sb; venomously slander
血泪斑斑 full of blood and tears
血流成河 blood flowing like a river—bloodbath
血流如注 blood streaming down
血浓于水 Blood is thicker than water.
血气方刚 full of animal spirits; full of sap; full of vigour and vitality
血亲婚配 incest
血染沙场 stain the battlefield with blood—die in battle
血肉横飞 blood and flesh flying in every direction
血肉模糊 be badly mangled
血肉相连 as close as flesh and blood
血肉之躯 the human body; flesh and blood
血栓形成 thrombosis
血吸虫病 schistosomiasis; snail fever
血小板病 thrombocytopathy
血液透析 haemodialysis
血雨腥风 wind and rain reeking of blood—a reign of terror; a bloodbath on a battlefield
血债累累 have a mountain of blood debts
血战到底 fight to the last drop of one's blood; fight to the bitter end
血细胞计数 blood count

谑 [xuè]
〔动〕 joke; banter; tease; jest
谑而不虐 tease without hurting (or embarrassing); banter

xūn (ㄒㄩㄣ)

勋 [xūn]
〔名〕 ① merit; meritorious service; exploit; achievement ② medal; decoration
勋绩 meritorious service; outstanding contribution
勋爵 ① a feudal title of nobility conferred for meritorious service ② Lord (in Great Britain)
勋劳 meritorious service
勋业 contribution; merit; exploit
勋章 medal; decoration

埙 [xūn]
〔名〕 xun, ancient Chinese wind instrument, made of porcelain with one to six holes and shaped like an egg

熏 [xūn]
I 〔动〕 ① smoke; fumigate ② treat (meat, fish, etc.) with smoke; smoke II 〔形〕 pleasantly warm; genial ➡ xùn

X

熏风 warm, southerly breeze
熏干 smoke-dried beancurd
熏鸡 smoked chicken
熏笼 a frame placed over a brazier for drying things (*or* over a censer for scenting clothes)
熏炉 censer
熏染 exert a gradual, corrupting influence on
熏肉 smoked meat
熏陶 exert a gradual, uplifting influence on; nurture; edify
熏鱼 smoked fish
熏蒸 ①sultry; sweltering; stifling; suffocating ② fuming or steaming—treating diseases with fumes as in moxibustion or with steam generated by boiling medicinal herbs ③fumigate
熏制 cure (meat, etc.) by smoking; smoke
熏衣草 lavender
熏蒸剂 fumigant

薰 [xūn]
名 fragrance
薰花茶 scented tea
薰衣草 lavender

曛 [xūn]
名 ①dim glow of the setting sun ②dusk; nightfall
曛黄 dusk
曛暮 dusk; nightfall

醺 [xūn]
形 drunk

xún (ㄒㄩㄣˊ)

旬 [xún]
名 ① period of ten days ② period of ten years in an old person's age
旬刊 a publication appearing once every ten days
旬日 ten-day

寻 [xún]
动 try to find; look for; search; seek
寻常 ordinary; usual; common
寻的 target-seeking; homing
寻访 look for (sb whose whereabouts is unknown); try to locate; make inquiries about
寻呼 page; bleep
寻觅 seek; look for
寻求 seek; explore; go in quest of
寻声 follow the sound (to find sb or sth)
寻思 think to oneself; think
寻死 ①try to commit suicide; attempt suicide ②commit suicide
寻味 chew sth over; ruminate; think over
寻衅 pick a quarrel; provoke
寻找 seek; look for
寻短见 commit suicide; take one's own life
寻呼机 pager; bleeper; beeper

寻呼台 beeper station
寻开心 make fun of; poke fun at; joke
寻的导弹 homing missile
寻根究底 get to the bottom (*or* root) of things; inquire deeply into
寻呼服务 paging services
寻呼小姐 operators who work with paging centres
寻呼信息 beeper message
寻呼用户 pager user
寻花问柳 sport with flowers and willows—① enjoy a beautiful spring scene ②dally with prostitutes; visit houses of ill repute
寻欢作乐 roister; skylark; seek pleasure and make merry
寻亲访友 call on relatives and friends
寻人启事 notice for looking for sb
寻事生非 seek a quarrel; stir up or make trouble
寻死觅活 attempt suicide (usu. as a threat)
寻幽览胜 travel around visiting quiet and secluded scenic spots
寻章摘句 cull phrases and cite passages; write in clichés
寻租活动 rent seeking activities

巡 [xún]
I 动 patrol; inspect; make one's rounds II 量 round of drinks: 酒过三巡, 主人起立致辞。 When the wine had gone round three times, the host stood up to make a speech.
巡捕 police; policeman
巡查 go on a tour of inspection; make one's rounds
巡航 cruise
巡回 go the rounds; tour; make a circuit of
巡警 patrol police; policeman
巡礼 ①visit a sacred land; go on a pilgrimage ②tour; sight-seeing
巡逻 go on patrol; patrol
巡哨 scout; conduct reconnaissance
巡视 ①make (*or* be on) an inspection tour; tour ②cast one's eyes around
巡天 tour the heavens
巡行 go the rounds; make a circuit of
巡演 performing tour
巡夜 go on night patrol; keep night watch
巡弋 (of a warship) cruise
巡游 cruise
巡展 exhibition tour
巡诊 make a round of visits
巡边员 linesman
巡捕房 Police Station
巡道工 trackwalker
巡逻车 cruising vehicle
巡逻队 patrol party
巡逻哨 roving sentry; patrol; patrol boat
巡逻线 patrol route

巡洋舰 cruiser
巡航导弹 cruise missile;stand-off bomb
巡回采访 itinerating coverage
巡回大使 roving ambassador
巡回剧团 touring theatrical troupe; touring company
巡回演出 on the circuit
巡回招聘 milk round
巡回放映队 mobile film projection unit
巡回医疗队 mobile medical team
巡逻护卫舰 partrol escort

询 [xún]
劻 ask;inquire;consult
询价 enquiry
询问 ① ask about; inquire about ② examination ③ inquiry; question; interrogation

荨 [xún]
➡ qián
荨麻疹 nettle rash;urticaria

峋 [xún]
◇ 嶙峋 ① (of mountain rocks, cliffs, etc.) jagged; rugged; craggy ② (of a person) bony; thin

洵 [xún]
副 really;truly;indeed
洵美且仁 truly handsome and kind
洵属可贵 truly precious; indeed praiseworthy; really valuable

浔 [xún]
名 waterside;water margin

恂 [xún]
形 ① honest;respectful ② fearful
恂谨 respectful and circumspect
恂然 in fear

循 [xún]
劻 follow;abide by;act in accordance with
循法 abide by the law
循环 circulate;cycle
循例 follow the usual practice;follow a precedent
循序 in proper order or sequence
循环赛 round robin
循规蹈矩 observe rules, obey orders, etc. docilely; conform to convention; toe the line
循环经济 circular economy
循环论证 argue in a circle
循环往复 move in cycles
循环系统 the circulatory system
循环小数 recurring decimal
循阶而上 go up by the steps
循流而下 sail down the river
循名责实 see that the reality matches the name
循途守辙 follow the track and keep to the rut
循序渐进 follow in order and advance step by step; proceed in an orderly way and step by step

循循善诱 be good at giving systematic guidance; teach with skill and patience
循环信用证 revolving letter of credit

xùn（ㄒㄩㄣˋ）

训 [xùn]
Ⅰ 劻 ① lecture; instruct; teach; admonish ② train; drill　Ⅱ 名 ① teachings; precept; maxim ② standard; rule; guideline; model; paragon; example ③ explanation of words
训斥 reprimand; rebuke; dress down
训词 admonition; instructions
训导 instruct and guide
训诂 exegetical studies (esp. of ancient texts); exegesis
训话 give an admonitory talk to subordinates
训诫 ① advise; admonish ② rebuke; reprimand
训练 train; drill
训令 mandate; ordinance
训示 allocution
训育 moral education at school
训喻 instruct; teach
训导长 (formerly in college) the dean of students
训诂学 exegetics
训练班 training class; training course
训练有素 have received a regular and thorough training; be well-trained

讯 [xùn]
Ⅰ 劻 ① ask; inquire ② interrogate; question　Ⅱ 名 message; dispatch; news; information
讯号 radio signal; signal
讯问 ① ask about; inquire about ② interrogate; question

汛 [xùn]
名 ① seasonal flood; high water ② season when fish schools emerge; fishing season
汛期 flood (or high-water) season
汛情 flood situation

迅 [xùn]
形 fast; swift
迅步 walk fast; hurry
迅即 immediately; at once
迅疾 swift; rapid
迅捷 fast; agile; quick
迅猛 swift and violent
迅速 rapid; swift; speedy; prompt
迅若流矢 fast as a flying arrow
迅逝如飞 vanish rapidly into thin air
迅雷不及掩耳 a sudden peal of thunder leaves no time to cover the ears—as sudden as a flash of lightning

驯 [xùn]
Ⅰ 形 tame and docile; gentle; obedient　Ⅱ 劻 tame; domesticate
驯服 ① docile; tame; tractable ② tame; break; domesticate

驯化 domesticate；tame
驯良 tractable；docile；tame and gentle
驯鹿 reindeer
驯兽 tame animals
驯顺 tame and docile；submissive
驯养 raise and train (animals)；domesticate
驯虎女郎 female tamer of tigers

徇 ［xùn］
〈动〉① comply with；give in to；submit to；yield to ② declare to the public；announce publicly
徇情 act wrongly out of personal considerations；practise favouritism
徇私 act wrongly out of personal considerations；practise favouritism
徇从人意 act in compliance with popular wishes or feelings
徇情枉法 bend law for relatives (*or* friends)；bend the law for the benefit of relatives or friends
徇私舞弊 play favouritism and practise fraud；practise favouritism and engage in irregularities；resort to fraudulent practices for personal gain

逊 ［xùn］
Ⅰ〈动〉abdicate Ⅱ〈形〉① unassuming；modest ② inferior to

逊色 ① be inferior ② not good；badly
逊位 abdicate
逊言恭色 be modest in language and respectful and submissive in manner

殉 ［xùn］
〈动〉① be buried alive with the dead ② sacrifice one's life for；die for
殉道 die for a cause
殉国 die (*or* give one's life) for one's country
殉教 die for a religious cause
殉节 ① die out of loyalty to one's country ② die in defence of one's chastity ③ (of a woman) commit suicide rather than remarry
殉难 die for a just cause or for one's country
殉情 die for love
殉葬 be buried alive with the dead
殉职 die at one's post；die in the course of performing one's duty；die in line of duty
殉道者 martyr
殉葬品 funerary object；sacrificial object

熏 ［xùn］
〈动〉be poisoned or suffocated by coal gas ⇒ xūn

噀 ［xùn］
〈动〉keep in the mouth so as to spurt
噀水 spurt water

X

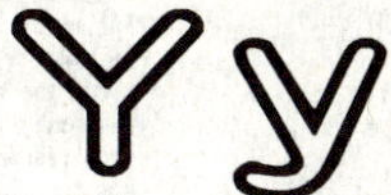

yā（ㄧㄚ）

丫 **[yā]**
〈名〉①bifurcation (at top end)；fork ②girl
丫杈 fork；clotch
丫鬟 slave girl；servant girl
丫髻 girl's coiffure with a loop on either side of the head
丫头 ①girl ②slave girl

压 **[yā]**
Ⅰ〈动〉① press; crush; push down; hold down; weigh down ② surpass; outdo; exceed ③stabilize; keep under control; hold down or back; keep (sb or sth) still or calm; repress ④ bring pressure to bear on; force; awe; intimidate ⑤ approach; get closer; near; draw near ⑥ pigeonhole; shelve; set aside; defer Ⅱ〈名〉 pressure ➡yà
压宝 stake
压扁 battering；press flat
压产 force to reduce the production
压场 ①have a meeting, an audience, etc. well under one's control ②present a theatrical performance as the last item on a programme
压秤 ①be relatively heavy per unit volume ② deduct a certain weight from the scale-weight for agricultural products such as cotton, food grains because of claimed excessive water content
压船 ships backed up in the port due to delays in loading and unloading
压床 press (machine)
压倒 overwhelm；overpower；prevail over
压低 lower；drop
压电 piezoelectricity
压顶 bear down on one；weigh heavily on one
压锭 reduce the spindles
压锻 press forging
压队 bring up the rear
压服 force (*or* compel) sb to submit
压盖 gland

压港 cargo or ships being held up at a harbour
压坏 crush；squash
压级 arbitrarily downgrade (by government purchase departments when assessing and buying farm produce or goods from farmers)
压挤 extrude
压价 force prices down；demand a lower price
压紧 compact；clamp；compress tightly
压惊 help sb get over a shock (by entertaining him, etc.)
压井 kill the well
压境 (of enemy troops) press on to the border
压库 ①overstock ②reduce the stocks
压力 ①pressure ②overwhelming force；pressure
压裂 fracture
压平 smashing；crushing；nipping；even；flatten
压迫 ①oppress；repress ②constrict
压气 calm sb's anger
压强 intensity of pressure；pressure
压青 green dressing
压实 compaction；ramming；densification
压塑 compression moulding
压碎 squashing；crushing；bruising
压缩 ① compress ② condense；reduce；cut down
压台 present a theatrical performance as the last item on a programme
压堂 run overtime
压条 layering
压痛 tenderness
压线 line ball
压延 mangle；roll；calender
压抑 constrain；inhibit；depress；hold back
压榨 ① extract (juice, etc.) by pressure；press；squeeze ②oppress and exploit；extort (*or* exact) money from；squeeze；bleed
压阵 ①bring up the rear ②keep a situation well under one's control
压植 layer；propagate (a plant) by layering

Y

（burying plant stem in the ground to root）

压制 ① suppress; stifle; inhibit; repress ② neutralize（enemy fire by massive bombardment, etc.）③ pressing

压铸 die-cast

压不住 cannot keep under control

压仓物 ballast

压得住 can keep under control

压根儿 ever; at all

压力锅 pressure cooker

压力计 pressure gauge; manometer

压裂车 fracturing unit truck

压路机 road roller; roller

压强计 pressure gauge

压舌板 tongue depressor

压岁钱 money given to children as a lunar New Year gift

压缩机 compressor

压台戏 the last item on a theatrical programme

压下去 subdue; suppress; stifle; muffle

压载舱 ballast tank

压榨机 squeezer; mangle

压制板 pressboard

压轴戏 grand finale; last and best item on a theatrical program

压倒多数 overwhelming majority

压倒一切 overriding; all-conquering

压电晶体 piezocrystal; piezoelectric crystal

压电效应 piezoelectric effect

压盖填料 gland packing

压花玻璃 pattern glass

压级压价 press down the grade and price

压挤成形 extrusion moulding

压热效应 piezocaloric effect

压缩饼干 hardtack; ship biscuit（or bread）; pilot biscuit（or bread）

压缩开支（practise）retrench expenditures

压缩空气 compressed air

压寨夫人 mistress of the fort（a sobriquet for the wife of a brigand chief）; the wife of a brigand chief

压制民主 suppress democracy

压制自由 crush freedom

压住阵脚 hold in battle array; finish setting out in battle array

压倒性胜利 landslide victory; overwhelming victory

压电拾音器 piezoelectric pickup

呀 ［yā］
Ⅰ 叹（indicating surprise）ah; oh: 呀, 屋子里怎么这么多烟气! Oh, how come the room is full of smoke? Ⅱ 象 creak ➡ ya

押 ［yā］
Ⅰ 动 ① give as security; mortgage; pawn; pledge ② detain; take away; take into custody ③ accompany as an escort; escort ④ sign a written statement; put one's mark on Ⅱ 名 signature; mark made on a written statement in place of signature

押宝 gambling game, played with dice under a bowl; stake

押车 escort goods on a train, truck, etc.

押队 bring up the rear

押赴 send

押汇 loan secured from a bank by an exporter with the waybill of the export as mortgage

押解 send（a criminal or captive）under escort; escort

押金 deposit; security; cash pledge

押款 ① borrow money on security; raise a mortgage ② mortgage loan; loan on security; secured loan

押送 ① send（a prisoner or captive）under escort; escort ② escort（goods）in transportation

押尾 sign（or mark）in lieu of signature at the end of a document

押运 escort（goods）in transportation

押韵 rhyme

押账 leave sth as security for a loan; offer sth as security for a loan

押租 rent deposit

押赌注 stake

押汇汇票 documentary bill（draft）

押解出境 deport under escort

垭 ［yā］
名 strip of land or pass between hills

鸦 ［yā］
名 crow

鸦片 opium

鸦雀 crow tit（a bird）

鸦片战争 the Opium War

鸦雀无声 not a crow or sparrow is heard—silence reigns; all is quiet; no birds sing

哑 ［yā］
➡ yǎ

哑哑 ① caw ② babble

桠 ［yā］
名 fork（of a tree）

桠杈 ① fork（of a tree）; crotch ② crotched; forked

鸭 ［yā］
名 duck

鸭蛋 ① duck's egg ② zero（as a score or mark）; nought; goose egg

鸭绒 duck's down; eiderdown; down

鸭掌 duck's web（a delicacy）

鸭胗 duck's gizzard（a delicacy）

鸭子 duck

鸭蛋脸 oval face

鸭蛋青 pale blue

鸭蛋圆 oval

鸭绒被 duck's down quilt; eiderdown quilt

鸭舌帽 peaked cap

Y

鸭跖草 dayflower (Commelina communis)
鸭嘴笔 drawing pen;ruling pen
鸭嘴兽 platypus;duckbill
鸭绒背心 duck's down waistcoat
鸭行鹅步 walk in a slow, rocking manner; waddle

yá(ㅣㄚ)

牙 [yá]
〔名〕① tooth ② ivory ③ sth shaped like a tooth
牙碜 ①(of food) gritty ②(of language) coarse;jarring
牙齿 tooth
牙床 ① gum ② a richly carved ivory-in-laid bed
牙雕 ivory carving
牙粉 tooth powder
牙缝 space between the teeth
牙缸 a mug for mouth-rinsing or tooth-cleaning;tooth mug
牙膏 toothpaste
牙根 gum
牙垢 tartar;dental calculus
牙关 mandibular joint
牙冠 crown (of a tooth)
牙祭 an unusually good meal (with plenty of meat)
牙具 tooth-cleaners
牙科 (department of) dentistry
牙口 ①the age of a draught animal as shown by the number of its teeth ②the condition of an old person's teeth
牙筷 ivory chopsticks
牙轮 gear wheel;gear
牙签 toothpick
牙刷 toothbrush
牙髓 dental pulp
牙套 facing
牙痛 toothache
牙线 dental floss
牙牙 the sound of baby talk;babble
牙医 dentist;dental surgeon
牙龈 gum;gingiva
牙质 ①made of ivory ②dentine
牙子 ①serrated edge ②middleman
牙本质 dentine
牙骨扇 ivory fan
牙骨质 cementum;cement
牙花子 ①tartar;dental calculus ②gum
牙科学 dentistry
牙髓炎 pulpitis
牙龈炎 gingivitis
牙釉质 enamel
牙周病 periodontosis
牙周炎 periodontitis

牙科医生 dentist;dental surgeon
牙牙学语 babble one's first sounds; learn to speak
牙科治疗机 dental units

伢 [yá]
〔名〕child;kid

芽 [yá]
〔名〕①bud;sprout;shoot ②sth resembling a bud or sprout
芽孢 gemma (of a fungus)
芽变 bud mutation
芽茶 young tea leaves;bud-tea
芽豆 sprouted broad bean
芽接 bud grafting;budding
芽眼 eye

蚜 [yá]
〔名〕aphid;aphis;plant louse
蚜虫 aphid;aphis;plant louse

崖 [yá]
〔名〕① precipice; cliff; crag ② limit; bound; boundary;margin
崖岸 scarp
崖壁 precipice;cliff
崖略 outline;general idea
崖墓 rock-tombs

涯 [yá]
〔名〕①shore;bank ②margin;bound;limit

睚 [yá]
〔名〕corner of the eye
睚眦 ①angry stare ②small grievance
睚眦必报 seek revenge just for an angry look

衙 [yá]
〔名〕yamen
衙门 yamen,government office in feudal China
衙门作风 bureaucracy; bureaucratic work-style

yǎ(ㅣㄚ)

哑 [yǎ]
〔形〕①incapable of speech;mute;dumb ②(of voice) hoarse;husky ③(of artillery shell or bullet) ineffective;dud;unexploded ➡yā
哑巴 ①a dumb person;mute ②be dumb;keep mum
哑场 an awkward silence at a meeting
哑剧 dumb show;pantomime
哑铃 dumbbell
哑谜 a puzzling remark;enigma;riddle
哑然 ①soundless;silent ②the sound of laughing
哑人 mute
哑语 sign language;dactylology
哑巴亏 grievance that one has to keep to oneself
哑嗓子 hoarse voice;husky voice
哑口无言 be left without an argument; be reduced to silence;be rendered speechless

哑巴吃黄连,有苦说不出 a dumb person tasting bitter herbs—be unable to express one's discomfort; be forced to suffer in silence

雅 [yǎ] I 〔形〕①standard; orthodox; proper; correct ②refined; polished; elegant; graceful; stylish ③your II 〔名〕①ode; court hymns of Western Zhou, one of the three genres of *The Book of Songs* ②acquaintance; friendship III 〔副〕①usually; customarily; often ②very; extremely

雅淡 simple and tasteful; quietly elegant

雅观 (usu. used in the negative) refined (in manner, etc.); in good taste

雅号 ①your elegant name ②nickname

雅虎 Yahoo (Yet Another Hierarchical Officious Oracle)

雅教 your esteemed opinion; your excellent advice

雅静 ①tastefully quiet ②gentle and quiet

雅量 ①magnanimity; generosity ②great capacity for liquor

雅趣 refined (*or* cultivated) tastes

雅儒 orthodox Confucian scholar

雅士 a refined scholar

雅思 International English Language Testing System (IELTS)

雅兴 an aesthetic mood

雅意 ①kindly thoughts ②your kindness; your kind offer

雅音 refined music; standard pronunciation

雅乐 (in ancient times) ceremonial music; court music

雅正 ①standard; correct ②upright; righteous ③(said when presenting sb with a specimen of one's calligraphy, a copy of one's book, etc.) would you kindly point out my inadequacies

雅致 refined; tasteful

雅座 private room (in a restaurant, etc.)

雅皮士 yuppie

雅善鼓琴 usually play the harp well

雅思考试 International English Language Testing System(IELTS)

雅俗共赏 (of a work of art or literature) appeal to all; suit both refined and popular tastes

雅以为美 consider sth very beautiful

雅鲁藏布江 the Yarlung Zangbo (Yalu Tsangpo) River

yà(丨丫)

轧 [yà] I 〔动〕①flatten with a roller; roll; run over ②eject; throw out; squeeze out; push out ③jostle; push against II 〔象〕(of a machine) click; rumble ➡gá; zhá

轧场 ①thresh grain on a threshing ground with a stone roller ②level a threshing floor with a stone roller

轧光 calendering

轧花 cotton ginning

轧板机 mangle

轧道车 line inspection trolley; track-testing trolley

轧光机 calender

轧花机 cotton gin

亚 [yà] I 〔形〕①of lower quality; inferior; second; shabby ②substandard ③of lower (atomic) valence II 〔名〕(short for 亚洲) Asia

亚当 Adam (the first man according to the Bible)

亚砜 sulphoxide

亚军 second place (in a sports contest); runner-up

亚科 subfamily

亚麻 flax

亚太 Asia-Pacific

亚铁 ferrous

亚种 subspecies

亚洲 Asia

亚氨基 imino group

亚急性 subacute

亚硫酸 sulphurous acid

亚麻布 linen (cloth)

亚麻籽 linseed; flaxseed

亚热带 subtropical zone; subtropics; semitropics

亚细亚 Asia

亚硝酸 nitrous acid

亚音速 subsonic speed

亚油酸 linoleic acid

亚运村 Asia Games Village (now a housing neighbourhood in Beijing)

亚麻籽油 linseed oil

亚太地区 the Asia-Pacific region

亚文化群 subculture

亚原子学 subatomics

亚麻精纺机 flax spinning frame

亚欧大陆桥 the Eurasian Continental Bridge

亚热带气候 subtropical climate

亚洲四小龙 four little dragons of Asia—Taiwan, Hong Kong, the Republic of Korea and Singapore

亚洲运动会 the Asian Games; the Asiad

亚太经合组织 APEC (Asia-Pacific Economic Cooperation) group

亚太经济一体化 Asia-Pacific economic integration

亚非经济合作组织 Afro-Asian Organization for Economic Co-operation

亚太经济合作论坛 APEC Forum

亚洲议会和平协会 Association of Asian Parliament for Peace(AAPP)

亚太经合组织部长级会议 APEC ministerial meeting

压 [yà]
➡yā

压板 seesaw; teeterboard; teeter-totter

压根儿 from the start; in the first place; altogether

讶 [yà]
动 be surprised; be astonished; be amazed

讶然 be surprised; be astonished

迓 [yà]
动 welcome; greet; meet

砑 [yà]
动 press and smooth; calender

砑光 calendering; mangling

砑光机 calender; mangle

挜 [yà]
动 force sb to take or buy sth

氩 [yà]
名 argon (Ar)

揠 [yà]
动 pull up; tug upward

揠苗助长 try to help shoots grow by pulling them up—spoil things by excessive enthusiasm

ya (・丨Y)

呀 [ya]
助 (*variant of* 啊 *used after a word ending phonetically in* a, e, i, o *or* u): 他搞了这么多发明，真了不起呀。What a terrific man he is with so many inventions to his credit.
➡yā

yān (丨ㄢ)

咽 [yān]
名 pharynx ➡yàn; yè

咽喉 ①pharynx and larynx; throat ②strategic (*or* vital) passage; key junction (*or* link)

咽痛 pharyngalgia

咽炎 pharyngitis

咽鼓管 Eustachian tube

咽喉炎 sore throat

咽峡炎 angina

咽喉要地 strategic (*or* vital) passage; key junction (*or* link)

恹 [yān]

恹恹 weak and weary through illness; rundown

殷 [yān]
形 blackish red ➡yīn; yǐn

殷红 blackish red; dark red

胭 [yān]
名 rouge

胭脂 rouge

胭脂红 carmine; famille rose

烟 [yān]
Ⅰ 名 ①smoke ②mist; thin fog; vapour ③tobacco; cigarette: 一袋烟 a pipeful of tobacco ④opium ⑤soot Ⅱ 动 (of eyes) be irritated by smoke

烟波 mist-covered waters

烟草 the tobacco plant; tobacco

烟尘 smoke and dust

烟囱 chimney; funnel; stovepipe

烟袋 a long-stemmed pipe

烟道 flue

烟蒂 cigarette end (*or* stub, butt, stump)

烟斗 (tobacco) pipe

烟缸 ashtray

烟膏 prepared opium paste

烟鬼 ①opium addict ②heavy smoker

烟锅 pipe bowl

烟海 a sea of fog or mist—vast and voluminous

烟盒 cigarette case

烟花 ①a lovely spring scene ②prostitution ③fireworks

烟灰 tobacco (*or* cigarette) ash

烟火 ①smoke and fire ②cooked food ③fireworks

烟碱 nicotine

烟具 smoking paraphernalia; smoking set

烟煤 bituminous coal; soft coal

烟民 smoker; tobacco user

烟幕 smoke screen

烟枪 opium pipe

烟圈 smoke ring

烟色 dark brown

烟丝 cut tobacco; pipe tobacco

烟酸 nicotinic acid; niacin

烟筒 chimney; funnel; stovepipe

烟头 cigarette end (*or* stub, butt, stump)

烟土 crude opium

烟雾 ①smoke, mist, or vapour; a mixture of smoke and vapour ②smog

烟叶 tobacco leaf; leaf tobacco

烟瘾 a craving for opium; a craving for tobacco

烟雨 misty rain

烟云 smoke, mists and clouds

烟柱 a column of smoke

烟子 soot

烟袋锅 ①the bowl of a long-stemmed pipe; pipe bowl ②a long-stemmed pipe

烟斗架 pipe rack

烟斗丝 pipe tobacco

烟灰缸 ashtray

烟火食 cooked food

烟酒税 wine and tobacco tax

烟卷儿 cigarette

烟幕弹 smoke shell; smoke bomb; smoke screen

烟屁股 cigarette end (*or* stub,butt,stump)
烟油子 tobacco tar;cigarette tar
烟嘴儿 cigarette holder
烟波浩渺 a vast expanse of misty, rolling waters
烟袋杆儿 the stem of a pipe
烟袋荷包 tobacco pouch
烟袋嘴儿 the mouth-piece of a long-stemmed pipe
烟花爆竹 fireworks
烟酒不分 smoke and drink together;hobnob;hang together
烟雾弥漫 be full of smoke;be enveloped in mist
烟消云散 vanish like smoke and disperse like clouds—completely vanish
烟草专卖局 tobacco monopoly bureau
烟火探测器 smoke detector
烟酸缺乏症 pellagra
烟草专卖管理 tobacco monopoly administration
烟草专卖计划 plans for monopoly on tobacco

焉 [yān]
I 代 here; this II 副 ①how; why ②only then III 助 (*used at the end of a sentence for emphasis*)：吾行将就木焉。I already have one foot in the grave.

阉 [yān]
动 ①castrate;spay ②eunuch
阉割 ①castrate;spay ②deprive a theory,etc. of its essence;emasculate
阉鸡 capon
阉马 gelding
阉牛 bullock;steer
阉人 ①castrated person ②eunuch
阉羊 wether
阉猪 castrated boar;spayed sow;hog;barrow

淹 [yān]
I 动 ①cover with a flood;flood;inundate;submerge ② be tingling or smarting from sweat ③delay;tarry II 形 wide;extensive
淹博 wide;broad
淹灌 basin irrigation
淹留 stay for a long period
淹埋 (of mud, sand, etc.) flow (*or* blow) over and cover completely
淹没 submerge;flood;inundate;drown
淹溺 drowning
淹死 be drowned
淹通古今 be thoroughly acquainted with the ancient and the modern

腌 [yān]
动 preserve in salt,sugar,etc.;salt;pickle;cure ➡ā
腌菜 sauerkraut;pickled vegetables
腌肉 salted meat;bacon
腌熏 bloat

腌鱼 salted fish;cured fish
腌制 make by pickling (*or* salting)
腌渍 preserve in brine,vinegar,etc.;pickle
腌黄瓜 pickled cucumber

湮 [yān]
动 ①sink into oblivion;bury in obscurity ②silt up;clog up;stop
湮灭 bury in oblivion;annihilate
湮没 ①fall into oblivion;be neglected;be forgotten ②annihilation
湮没无闻 sink into oblivion;fall into obscurity

嫣 [yān]
形 pretty;beautiful;handsome
嫣红 bright red
嫣然 beautiful;sweet
嫣然一笑 give a pleasant (*or* sweet, charming, winsome, soft) smile;smile gently

yán (l ㄢˊ)

延 [yán]
动 ① prolong; extend; lengthen ② postpone;put off;delay ③engage;employ
延挨 delay;stall
延长 lengthen;prolong;extend
延迟 delay;defer;postpone
延宕 procrastinate;delay;keep putting off
延发 delayed action
延搁 delay;procrastinate
延后 postpone;put off;defer
延缓 delay;postpone;put off
延揽 enlist the services of
延聘 extension of employment;continue to employ;continue to hire
延期 postpone;defer;put off
延请 invite (sb to do a particular job);engage
延伸 extend;stretch;elongate
延师 hire a teacher
延时 delay
延寿 lengthen (*or* prolong) one's life
延髓 medulla oblongata
延误 incur loss through delay
延性 ductility
延续 continue;go on;last
延医 send for a doctor
延展 extension
延长号 pause
延长线 extension (*or* extended) line
延胡索 ①yanhusuo ②tuber of yanhusuo
延伸率 percentage elongation
延绳钓 longline fishing;long-lining
延续性 continuity
延爆炸弹 delayed action bomb
延长时间 extra period
延迟电路 delay circuit
延迟失真 delay distortion
延发引信 delayed-action fuse;delay fuse
延年益寿 (of tonics,etc.) prolong life;prom-

ise longevity
延期交货 back order
延伸火力 creeping fire;lift fire
延时摄影 time-lapse photography
延首远望 stretch one's neck and look far a-
  head
延误时机 miss an opportunity because of a delay
延迟继电器 delayed relay
延期偿付权 moratorium
延期交货通知单 back order memo

芫 [yán]
  ⟹yuán
芫荽 coriander

严 [yán]
Ⅰ 形 ①tight ②strict;stern;exacting;rig-
orous ③heavy;severe;acute;extreme Ⅱ 名
father
严惩 punish severely
严办 deal with severely;punish with severity
严词 strong terms;stern words
严打 crackdown on crime;strike-hard campaign
严冬 a severe winter;a hard winter
严防 be strictly on guard against;take strict
  precautions against
严格 ①strict;rigorous;rigid;stringent ②rig-
  orously enforce
严寒 severe cold;bitter cold
严紧 tight;close
严谨 ①rigorous;strict;careful and precise ②
  compact;well-knit
严禁 strictly forbid (or prohibit)
严峻 stern;severe;rigorous;grim
严酷 ①harsh;bitter;grim ②cruel;ruthless
严厉 stern;severe
严令 give strict orders
严密 tight;close
严明 ①strict and impartial ②strictly enforce
  (discipline)
严判 severe judgement
严师 a strict teacher
严实 ①tight;close ②(hide) safely
严守 ①observe strictly ②guard closely
严霜 a severe (or heavy) frost
严肃 ①serious;solemn;earnest ②strictly enforce
严刑 cruel torture
严整 (usu. of troops) be in neat formation
严正 solemn and just;serious and principled
严重 serious;grave;critical
严惩不贷 punish severely and strictly;punish
  without leniency;punish without mercy
严词拒绝 give a stern rebuff;sternly refuse
严词谴责 denounce in strong terms;sternly
  condemn
严打斗争 Strike-Hard Operation;strike-hard

war on crimes;campaign to crack down relentlessly on criminal activities
严而不苛 exacting but not harsh
严防死守 make one's utmost efforts to ensure
the safety of the embankments;fight until
death to ensure the safety of the dyke (or
embankments);safeguard (the embankment) under the "fight-to-death" call;make
a desperate/last-ditch attempt to safeguard
(the embankment)
严父慈母 stern father and compassionate
mother
严格把关 make strict checks to guarantee
quality
严加管束 bring under stern discipline
严密拦网 wall blocking (in volleyball)
严声厉色 stern in voice and countenance
严师诤友 a strict teacher and a friend who will
give unpalatable advice
严守中立 remain strictly neutral;observe
strict neutrality
严丝合缝 fit together perfectly;join tightly;
dovetail
严肃党纪 enforce Party discipline
严肃法纪 strictly enforce law and discipline
严肃法制 maintain the legal system
严肃音乐 serious music
严刑拷打 subject sb to severe torture;cruelly
beat up
严阵以待 be in full battle array;stand in combat readiness
严重警告 serious warning
严以律己,宽以待人 be strict with oneself and
lenient towards others

言 [yán]
Ⅰ 名 ①speech;remark;word ②character;
word Ⅱ 动 say;talk;speak
言传 explain in words
言辞 one's words;what one says
言和 make peace;become reconciled;bury the
hatchet
言教 teach by word of mouth;give verbal directions
言路 channels through which criticisms and
suggestions may be communicated to the
leadership
言论 opinion on public affairs;expression of
one's political views;speech
言说 put into words;say
言谈 the way one speaks;what one says
言行 words and deeds;statements and actions
言语 [yányǔ] spoken language;speech
言语 [yányu] speak;talk;answer
言责 ① a subject's responsibility of offering
advice to the ruler ② responsibility for
what one says
言重 overstate;exaggerate

言情片 film with a romantic story;sentimental movie
言声儿 utter a sound or a word
言行录 records of the words and deeds (of a famous person)
言必有信 be as good as one's word
言必有中 When one speaks,one speaks to the point;Whenever one says something one hits the mark.
言不及义 never say anything serious; talk frivolously
言不尽意 I should like to say more (but I must bring my letter to a close)
言不由衷 speak insincerely;speak with one's tongue in one's cheek
言差语错 mistakes (or slips) in speaking
言传身教 teach by personal example as well as verbal instruction;teach by precept and example
言辞恳切 be sincere in what one says
言多语失 He who talks too much is prone to error.
言而无信 fail to keep faith;go back on one's word
言而有信 be true to one's word;be as good as one's word
言归于好 make it up (with sb);become reconciled
言归正传 come back to our story;return to the subject
言过其实 exaggerate;overstate
言简意赅 concise and comprehensive;compendious
言近旨远 simple words but deep meaning; simple in language but profound in meaning
言情小说 a romantic (or sentimental) novel
言人人殊 different people,different versions; each person tells a different story
言三语四 make irresponsible remarks
言谈举止 speech and deportment;manner of speech and behaviour
言听计从 listen to sb's words and follow his counsels;always follow sb's advice;act upon whatever sb says;have implicit faith in sb
言外之意 what is actually meant; the real meaning;implication
言为心声 Words are the voice of the mind; Speech is the picture of the mind;What the heart thinks the tongue speaks.
言行不一 The deeds do not match the words; One's actions do not square with one's promises.
言行一致 The deeds match (or square with) the words; One's actions are in keeping with one's promises;One's deeds are consistent with one's words; be as good as

one's word
言犹在耳 The words still ring (or reverberate) in one's ears.
言之不预 haven't been forewarned;not have been told beforehand
言之成理 speak in a rational and convincing way;sound reasonable
言之无物 (of speech or writing) be devoid of substance;be mere verbiage;be empty talk
言之有据 speak on good grounds (or on good authority)
言之凿凿 say sth with certainty
言必信,行必果 insist on keeping one's word and seeing one's actions through to the end;always stand by one's word, and undertake nothing that one does not bring to achievement
言有尽而意无穷 The words come to an end, but the meaning is inexhaustible.
言者无心,听者有意 A casual remark sounds significant to a suspicious listener;A careless word may reveal much to an attentive listener.
言者无罪,闻者足戒 blame not the speaker but be warned by his words;blame not the critic,heed what he says
言者谆谆,听者藐藐 The speaker is earnest but the hearer is casual;The words are earnest but they fall on deaf ears.

妍 [yán]
形 beautiful;enchanting;charming

岩 [yán]
名 ①rock;stone ②cliff;crag
岩岸 rocky coast
岩壁 crag;cliff
岩层 rock stratum;rock formation
岩洞 grotto
岩鸽 rock dove;rock pigeon
岩画 rock painting
岩浆 magma
岩墙 dike;rib;cog
岩溶 karst
岩石 rock
岩相 lithofacies
岩心 (drill) core
岩穴 cavern;cave
岩崖 cliff
岩盐 rock salt;halite
岩羊 blue sheep;bharal
岩样 ①rock specimen ②core sample
岩浆岩 magmatic rock
岩羚羊 chamois
岩美人 rock beauty
岩石圈 lithosphere
岩石学 petrology
岩心筒 core barrel
岩性学 lithology

岩溶地貌 karst features;karst topography
岩石力学 rock mechanics

炎 [yán]
Ⅰ 形 scorching;extremely hot Ⅱ 名 ①inflammation ②power;influence ③ *Yan Di*
炎帝 *Yan Di*,also known as Shen Nong（神农）,a legendary ruler
炎旱 hot and dry
炎黄 *Yan Di* and *Huang Di*（*or* the Yellow Emperor）,two legendary rulers of remote antiquity
炎凉 warmth or coldness is the way of the world—people are friendly or unfriendly,depending on whether one is successful or not
炎热 （of weather）scorching;blazing;burning hot
炎日 burning sun;scorching sun
炎暑 hot summer;sweltering summer days;dog days
炎威 fierce heat
炎夏 a torrid（*or* scorching）summer
炎炎 scorching;sweltering;blazing
炎症 inflammation
炎黄子孙 descendants of *Yan Di* and *Huang Di*—the Chinese people

沿 [yán]
Ⅰ 介 along Ⅱ 动 ①follow;conform to（a tradition,pattern,etc.）②trim（with tape,ribbon,etc.）Ⅲ 名 edge;brim;border
沿岸 along the bank or coast;littoral or riparian
沿革 the course of change and development;evolution
沿海 along the coast;coastal;littoral
沿江 along the river;riparian;riverine
沿例 follow the usual practice;follow the established precedents
沿路 along the road;on the way
沿途 on the way;throughout a journey
沿袭 carry on as before;follow
沿线 along the line（i.e. a railway,highway,air or shipping line）
沿用 continue to use（an old method,etc.）
沿着 [yánzhe] along
沿边儿 trim（with tape,ribbon,etc.）
沿阶草 dwarf lilyturf
沿边地区 the areas along the borders
沿海地区 foreland;seaboard;coastland;coastal regions;coastal areas
沿街叫卖 hawk one's wares in the streets
沿街乞讨 beg in the streets
沿门挨户 from door to door
沿途贸易 way-port trade
沿海开放城市 open coastal cities
沿海沿边地区 coastal and border areas
沿江开放城市 open cities along rivers

沿海经济开发区 open coastal economic development areas

研 [yán]
动 ①grind;rub;pestle ②study;research
研钵 mortar（a vessel）
研杵 pestle;grinder;pulverizer
研订 develop
研读 study carefully
研发 R&D,research and development
研究 ① study;research ② consider;discuss;deliberate
研磨 ①grind;pestle ②abrade;polish
研墨 rub an ink stick on an inkslab（to make ink for writing with a brush）
研拟 discuss and formulate;develop
研判 study and judge
研评 examine;appraise
研讨 deliberate;study and discuss
研习 study;research
研修 do research work;research and advanced studies
研药 grind medicine
研制 ①develop（drugs,weapons,etc.）②prepare medicinal powder by pestling
研究生 postgraduate（student）;graduate student
研究室 research room
研究所 research institute
研究员 research fellow;full professor（at research institutes）
研究院 research institute;graduate school
研讨会 symposium;seminar
研修生 researcher
研究成果 research results;research payoffs;research fruits
研究开发 research and development;R&D
研究热点 hot topics of research
研究生院 graduate school
研讨小组 research group
研究工作者 research worker
研究密集型 research-intensive
研究生毕业证 graduate diploma
研究生学位证 graduate degree's diploma
研究生入学考试 Graduate Record Examination（GRE）

盐 [yán]
名 salt
盐巴 table salt;salt
盐层 salt deposit;salt bed
盐场 saltern;saltworks
盐池 salt pond
盐分 salt content
盐罐 saltcellar;saltshaker
盐湖 salt lake
盐花 a little salt;a pinch of salt
盐井 salt well;brine pit
盐矿 salt mine

盐卤 bitter

盐瓶 saltcellar;saltshaker

盐泉 brine (*or* salt) spring

盐霜 salt efflorescence

盐水 salt solution;brine

盐酸 hydrochloric acid

盐滩 a beach for making sea salt

盐田 salt pan;salina

盐土 solonchak;saline soil

盐析 salt out

盐业 salt industry

盐液 saline solution

盐沼 salt marsh;salt cure

盐肤木 Chinese sumac

盐碱地 saline or alkaline land

盐碱化 salinization or alkalinization (of soil); salinization of alkaline soil;alkalinization of saline soil

盐碱土 saline or alkaline soil;alkalinized saline soil;saline-alkaline soil

盐汽水 salt soda water

盐水鸭 salted duck

盐水输液 saline infusion

盐水选种 seed sorting by salt water

盐肤木根皮 the root bark of Chinese sumac

盐液比重计 salinometer;salimeter

阎 [yán] 名 gate of a lane

阎罗 Yama,King of Hell

阎王 ① Yama,King of Hell ② an extremely cruel and violent person

阎王殿 the Palace of the King of Hell

阎王账 usurious loan;shark's loan

筵 [yán] 名 ①bamboo mat spread on the floor for people to sit on ②banquet;feast

筵席 ①seats arranged at a banquet ②feast; banquet

颜 [yán] 名 ①face;look;countenance ②grace;decency;face ③dye;colour

颜料 pigment;colouring

颜面 ①face ②prestige;face

颜容 facial expression;complexion;countenance

颜色 ① colour ② countenance;facial expression ③ facial expression ④ stern look on one's face as a warning

颜体 the *Yan* style

檐 [yán] 名 ①eaves;projecting ②ledge;brim

檐沟 eaves gutter

檐口 cornice;end sprout of an eaves gutter

檐前 in front of the eaves

檐下 under the eaves

檐子 eaves

yǎn（|ㄢˇ）

奄 [yǎn] I 动 cover;overspread;include II 副 suddenly;all of a sudden

奄忽 suddenly;all of a sudden;all at once

奄然 quickly;suddenly

奄奄 breathing feebly

奄奄一息 at one's last gasp;on the verge of death

俨 [yǎn] I 形 majestic;solemn;serious;dignified II 副 just as;like

俨然 ①solemn;dignified ②neatly arranged ③just like

俨如 just like

衍 [yǎn] I 动 spread out;extend;develop;enfold II 形 redundant;superfluous;tautological III 名 ①low-lying flatland ②marsh;swamp;bog

衍变 develop;evolve

衍化 evolve;develop

衍射 diffraction

衍生 ①derive ②evolve;produce

衍文 redundancy due to misprinting or miscopying

衍生物 derivative

弇 [yǎn] 动 cover

剡 [yǎn] I 动 sharpen II 形 sharp;sharp-pointed

掩 [yǎn] 动 ①cover;conceal;hide ②close;shut ③get squeezed when closing a door,lid,etc. ④attack by surprise;launch a surprise attack

掩鼻 hold one's nose;detest

掩蔽 screen;shelter;cover

掩藏 hide;conceal

掩盖 ①cover;overspread ②conceal;cover up

掩护 screen;shield;cover

掩埋 bury

掩泣 cover one's face with one's hands and start weeping

掩杀 make a surprise attack;pounce on (the enemy)

掩饰 cover up (faults,mistakes,etc.);gloss over;conceal

掩体 blindage;bunker

掩星 occultation

掩映 (of things screening part of each other from view) show off (each other);set off (one another)

掩眼法 cover-up;camouflage

掩蔽阵地 covered position

掩耳盗铃 plug one's ears while stealing a bell—deceive oneself;bury one's head in the sand

掩盖真相 cover up the facts
掩护部队 covering force
掩护火力 covering fire
掩人耳目 deceive the public；hoodwink people

眼 [yǎn]
Ⅰ 〔名〕①eye ②small hole ③key point；crux ④(in *weiqi*) trap ⑤unaccented beat in traditional Chinese music Ⅱ 〔量〕(of a well or cave-dwelling)：打一眼井 sink a well
眼白 the white of the eye
眼波 glances
眼馋 cast covetous eyes at sth；eye sth covetously
眼眵 gum (in the eyes)
眼底 ①eyeground；the fundus of the eye (fundus oculi) ②in one's eyes；in sight
眼点 eyespot (of a protozoan)；stigma
眼福 the good fortune of seeing sth rare or beautiful
眼光 ①eye ②sight；foresight；insight；vision
眼黑 pupil
眼红 ①covet；be envious；be jealous ②eyes burning with fury；be furious
眼花 have dim eyesight；have blurred vision
眼尖 be sharp-eyed；have sharp eyes；have keen sight
眼睑 eyelid
眼见 soon；in no time
眼角 canthus；the corner of the eye
眼界 field of vision (*or* view)；outlook
眼镜 eyeglasses；glasses；spectacles
眼睛 eye
眼看 ①soon；in a moment ②watch helplessly；look on passively
眼科 (department of) ophthalmology
眼库 eye bank
眼快 be sharp-eyed (*or* sharp-sighted)；have sharp eyes；have keen sight
眼眶 ①eye socket；eyehole；orbit ②rim of the eye
眼泪 tears
眼离 have hallucinations；see things
眼里 in one's eyes；in one's view
眼力 ①eyesight；vision ②judgment；discrimination
眼帘 eyes
眼量 perceptiveness
眼眉 eyebrow
眼目 ①eyes ②spy
眼泡 upper eyelid
眼皮 eyelid
眼前 ①before one's eyes ②at the moment；at present；now
眼浅 short-sighted
眼球 eyeball；attention
眼圈 ①eye socket；orbit ②rim of the eye
眼热 cast covetous eyes at sth；eye sth covetously

ously
眼色 a hint given with the eyes；a meaningful glance；wink
眼梢 corner of the eye close to the temple
眼神 ①expression in one's eyes ②eyesight
眼生 look unfamiliar
眼屎 gum (in the eyes)
眼熟 look familiar
眼跳 twitching of the eyelid
眼窝 eye socket；eyehole；orbit
眼下 at the moment；at present；now
眼线 [yǎnxiàn] eye-liner
眼线 [yǎnxian] informer；stool-pigeon；finger man
眼压 intraocular pressure
眼药 medicament for the eyes；eye ointment；eyedrops
眼影 eye-shadow
眼晕 dizziness (owing to defective vision)
眼拙 my bad eyes；my bad memory
眼巴巴 ①(expecting) eagerly；anxiously ②helplessly (watching sth unpleasant happen)
眼虫藻 euglena (a green flagellate protozoan having a reddish eyespot)
眼瞅着 ①see sth happen ②soon；in no time
眼底镜 funduscope
眼底下 ①right before one's eyes ②at the moment
眼干症 xerophthalmia
眼见得 (of sth unpleasant) be evident
眼睫毛 eyelash
眼镜猴 tarsier
眼镜框 rims (of spectacles)；spectacles frame
眼镜蛇 cobra
眼科学 ophthalmology
眼内压 intraocular pressure
眼皮高 fastidious；hard to please
眼皮浅 short-sighted；shallow
眼前欢 pleasure of the moment
眼前亏 trouble right before the eyes
眼药水 eyedrops
眼影粉 eye-shadow power；eye-shadow
眼罩儿 ①eyeshade ②blinkers (for a horse，donkey，etc.)
眼睁睁 looking on helplessly (*or* unfeelingly)
眼中钉 thorn in one's side
眼珠儿 ①eyeball ②the apple of sb's eye
眼保健操 ocular exercises
眼底检查 funduscopy
眼高手低 have high standards but little ability；be fastidious but incompetent
眼花缭乱 be dazzled
眼犄角儿 the corner of the eye；canthus
眼疾手快 quick of eye and deft of hand
眼科医生 oculist；ophthalmologist；eye-doctor
眼泪汪汪 eyes brimming with tears；in tears

Y

眼力见儿 sensible；able to see what's happening

眼明手快 quick of eye and deft of hand；sharp-eyed and deft-handed

眼皮底下 right before one's eyes

眼弦赤烂 blepharitis

眼底照相机 fundus camera

眼不见，心不烦 What the eye doesn't see the heart doesn't grieve for.

眼中钉、肉中刺 a thorn in one's flesh (*or* side)

眼观六路，耳听八方 have sharp eyes and keen ears；be observant and alert

偃 [yǎn]

团 ①fall on one's back；lie down ②desist；stop；cease

偃卧 lie supine；lie on one's back

偃旗息鼓 lower the banners and muffle the drums—cease all activities

偃武修文 desist from war and encourage the arts of peace；desist from military activities and encourage culture and education

罨 [yǎn]

Ⅰ 名 net for catching birds or fish Ⅱ 团 cover；apply

演 [yǎn]

团 ①develop；evolve ②elaborate；deduce；exert ③drill；practise ④perform；play；act；stage

演变 develop；evolve

演播 telecast (a play，performance，etc.)

演唱 sing (in a performance)

演出 perform；show；put on a show

演化 evolution

演技 acting；stage performance

演讲 give a lecture；make a speech；lecture

演进 gradual progress；evolution

演剧 act in a play

演练 drill

演示 demonstrate

演说 ①deliver a speech；make an address ② speech

演算 perform mathematical calculations

演替 succession

演武 practise traditional martial arts

演习 manoeuvre；exercise；drill；practice

演戏 ①put on a play；act in a play ②playact；pretend

演义 historical novel；historical romance

演艺 performing arts

演绎 deduce；demonstrate

演员 actor or actress；performer

演奏 give an instrumental performance；play a musical instrument (in a performance)

演兵场 parade ground

演播室 broadcast studio；television studio

演唱会 vocal recital；concert

演出本 acting version；playscript；script

演出队 troupe

演电影 show a film

演说家 speaker；orator

演说术 oratory

演艺界 performing arts circles；performing arts sector

演绎法 the deductive method；deduction

演杂技 perform acrobatics

演职员 general term for the performers and supporting staff of an artistic troupe

演奏家 an accomplished performer (of a musical instrument)

演出单位 producer

演示程序 demonstration program

魇 [yǎn]

团 ① have a nightmare ② talk in one's sleep；somniloquy

yàn(1ㄢ)

厌 [yàn]

团 ①be satisfied；be satiated ②be sick of；be bored with；be tired of ③ be disgusted with；dislike intensely；detest

厌读 tired of school

厌烦 be sick of；be fed up with

厌恨 abhor；loathe

厌倦 be weary of；be tired of

厌腻 be bored with；be tired of；be fed up with

厌弃 detest and reject；detest；loathe

厌世 be world-weary；be pessimistic

厌恶 detest；abhor；abominate；be disgusted with

厌学 tired of school

厌战 be weary of war；be war-weary

厌食症 (esp. in young women) anorexia；anorexia nervosa

厌恶疗法 aversion therapy

厌氧微生物 anaerobe

砚 [yàn]

名 ① inkstone；inkslab ② fellow student；classmate

砚池 inkstone；inkslab

砚台 inkstone；inkslab

砚友 classmate

咽 [yàn]

团 swallow；devour ➡ yān；yè

咽气 breathe one's last；die

彦 [yàn]

名 man of virtue and ability

艳 [yàn]

Ⅰ 形 ①bright；colourful；fresh and attractive；gorgeous ②amorous；romantic Ⅱ 团 admire；envy

艳福 a man's good fortune in love affairs

艳红 bright red

艳丽 bright-coloured and beautiful；gorgeous

艳情 erotic

艳诗 erotic poetry
艳史 erotic adventures;amorous adventures
艳事 love affair;romance
艳羡 admire immensely
艳遇 affair;one's romantic history
艳冶 pretty and coquettish
艳装 gaudy attire
艳阳天 bright spring day;bright sunny skies
艳如桃李,冷若冰霜 (of a woman) as beautiful as peach and plum blossoms,but as cold as frost and ice

晏 〔yàn〕
形 ①behind time;late ②of ease and comfort
晏驾 pass away
晏起 get up late

唁 〔yàn〕
名 extend condolences
唁电 telegram (*or* cable) of condolence;message of condolence
唁函 letter (*or* message) of condolence

宴 〔yàn〕
Ⅰ 动 entertain to dinner;fete Ⅱ 名 feast;banquet;spread Ⅲ 形 ease and comfort
宴会 banquet;feast;dinner party
宴客 entertain guests with a feast;host a dinner in honour of visitors
宴请 entertain (to dinner);fête
宴席 banquet;feast
宴会服 dinner clothes
宴会厅 banquet hall
宴安鸩毒 seeking pleasure is like drinking poisoned wine;voluptuous comfort is poison

验 〔yàn〕
Ⅰ 动 ① examine; check; verify; test ② prove effective; produce the expected result Ⅱ 名 intended effect;desired result
验方 proved recipe
验关 customs examination
验光 optometry
验核 check;verify
验货 examine goods
验看 examine;inspect
验尿 test the urine
验讫 checked;examined
验枪 inspect arms
验墒 check the moisture of the soil
验尸 postmortem;autopsy
验收 check and accept;check before acceptance;check upon delivery
验算 checking computations
验血 blood test
验证 verify
验资 check the assets;check the capital of a business or organization
验钞机 a machine for checking paper money for counterfeits;money detector
验潮器 tide gauge

验电器 electroscope
验护照 examine (*or* check) a passport
验尸官 coroner
验明正身 identify;prove through examination
验证数据 verify data
验收合格证 acceptance certificate

谚 〔yàn〕
名 proverb;saying;saw
谚语 proverb;saying;adage;saw

堰 〔yàn〕
名 weir;dam;barrage
堰塞湖 barrier lake

雁 〔yàn〕
名 wild goose
雁来红 tricolour amaranth
雁过拔毛 pluck feathers from each goose as it passes by—squeeze whenever possible

喭 〔yàn〕
Ⅰ 形 rude;boorish Ⅱ 名 condolence

焰 〔yàn〕
名 flame;blaze
焰火 fireworks

焱 〔yàn〕
名 spark;flame

滟 〔yàn〕

◇ 潋滟 ① overflowing; inundating ② billowing; rippling

燕 〔yàn〕
名 swallow
燕好 (of husband and wife) be very fond of each other;be happily married
燕鸻 pratincole;swallow plover
燕麦 oats
燕鸥 tern
燕雀 brambling;bramble
燕隼 hobby
燕窝 edible bird's nest
燕鱼 Spanish mackerel
燕子 swallow
燕尾服 swallowtail; swallow-tailed coat; tailcoat;tails
燕巢幕上 a swallow nesting on a canopy—in a precarious position
燕尔新婚 marital happiness;joy of new marriage;conjugal bliss
燕颔虎颈 a majestic and awe-inspiring appearance
燕雀处堂 swallows nesting in a hall that is about to be on fire—unaware of one's danger
燕雀安知鸿鹄之志 how could a sparrow understand the ambitions of a swan? —the lofty aims of the great are beyond the understanding of the lowly

赝 〔yàn〕
形 counterfeit;spurious;fake;pseudo-
赝本 spurious edition (*or* copy)
赝币 counterfeit coin

赝品 phony; postiche; snide; imitation; shoddy; art forgery
赝晶体 pseudocrystal
赝真难辨 hard to distinguish the false from the true (*or* the fake from the authentic)

yāng(丨尢)

央 [yāng]
Ⅰ 动 ①entreat; beg; earnestly ask ②end; finish Ⅱ 名 centre
央告 beg; plead; implore
央行 central bank
央求 beg; plead; implore
央视 CCTV, China Central Television
央托 entreat sb to do sth

泱 [yāng]
泱泱 ①(of waters) vast ②grand; great; magnificent; glorious
泱泱大国 great and proud country

殃 [yāng]
Ⅰ 名 scourge; disaster; calamity; misfortune Ⅱ 动 bring disaster to; spell calamity for
殃及 bring disaster to
殃及无辜 trouble involves the innocent people

鸯 [yāng]
◇鸳鸯 ①mandarin duck ②affectionate couple

秧 [yāng]
Ⅰ 名 ①seedling; sprout ②rice seedling ③vine; stem ④(of some domestic animals) young; fry Ⅱ 动 cultivate; raise
秧歌 *yangge* (dance), a popular rural folk dance
秧瓜 grow melons
秧鸡 rail
秧龄 the length of time rice seedlings grow in seedling beds until they are transplanted
秧苗 rice shoot; rice seedling
秧畦 rice seedling bed
秧田 rice seedling bed
秧子 vine

鞅 [yāng]
名 halter strap

yáng(丨尢́)

扬 [yáng]
动 ①raise; hoist ②throw up and scatter; winnow ③spread; publicize; make known ④be good-looking; be of distinguished appearance
扬场 winnowing
扬尘 ①raise dust to the air ②flying dust
扬程 lift
扬帆 hoist the sails; set sail
扬谷 winnow the chaff from the grain
扬花 (of cereal crops) be flowering
扬厉 develop
扬名 make a name for oneself; become famous
扬旗 semaphore
扬弃 ①develop what is useful or healthy and discard what is not ②sublate
扬琴 dulcimer
扬升 increase
扬声 ①raise one's voice ②make public; disclose ③make a name for oneself; become famous
扬水 pump up water
扬言 threaten (that one is going to take action)
扬誉 become famous; make a name for oneself
扬州 Yangzhou (in Jiangsu Province)
扬场机 winnowing machine; winnower
扬声器 loudspeaker
扬水泵 lift pump
扬水站 pumping station
扬子鳄 Chinese alligator
扬长避短 exploit to the full one's favourable conditions and avoid unfavourable ones; make best use of the advantages and bypass the disadvantages; maximize favourable factors and minimize unfavourable ones
扬长补短 bring out one's strengths to make up for one's weaknesses
扬长而去 stalk off; swagger off
扬幡招魂 fly a funeral banner to summon the soul—try to revive what is obsolete
扬基债券 Yankee bond
扬眉吐气 feel proud and elated
扬汤止沸 try to stop water from boiling by skimming it off and pouring it back—apply a palliative

羊 [yáng]
名 sheep; goat
羊齿 bracken; fern
羊痘 sheep pox
羊羔 ①lamb ②the name of a wine
羊倌 shepherd
羊毫 writing brush made of goat's hair
羊叫 baa; bleat
羊圈 sheepfold; sheep pen
羊栏 fold yard; sheepcote
羊毛 sheep's wool; wool; fleece
羊膜 amnion
羊奶 ewe's milk
羊排 mutton chop; lamb chop
羊皮 sheepskin
羊绒 cashmere
羊肉 mutton
羊水 amniotic fluid
羊驼 alpaca
羊脂 suet; serum
羊肠线 catgut suture
羊癫风 epilepsy

羊肚蕈 morel
羊角锤 claw hammer
羊角风 epilepsy
羊毛婚 wool wedding
羊毛衫 woollen sweater;cardigan
羊毛袜 woollen socks (*or* stockings)
羊毛脂 lanolin;wool fat
羊皮纸 parchment
羊绒衫 cashmere sweater
羊肉串 mutton cubes roasted on a skewer; shish kebab (*or* kabob);shashlik
羊驼毛 alpaca fibre
羊痫风 epilepsy
羊肠小道 a narrow winding trail;a meandering footpath
羊角面包 croissant;crescent-shaped roll;crescent
羊毛套衫 pullover
羊质虎皮 a sheep in a tiger's skin—outwardly strong,inwardly weak
羊肚儿手巾 towel
羊毛出在羊身上 after all,the wool still comes from the sheep's back—in the long run, whatever you're given,you pay for
羊群里头出骆驼 stand out like a camel in a flock of sheep

阳 [yáng]
Ⅰ 名 ①(in Chinese philosophy, medicine, etc.) *yang*, the masculine or positive principle in nature ②sun ③south of a hill or north of a river ④male genitals Ⅱ 形 ①in relief; convex ② open; overt; outward ③ of this world; of this life; concerned with living beings ④positive
阳春 spring (season)
阳电 positive electricity
阳刚 manly;virile
阳沟 open drain;ditch
阳光 sunny;sunlight;sunshine
阳极 positive pole;positive electrode;anode
阳间 this world
阳历 ①solar calendar ② the Gregorian calendar
阳面 sunny side
阳平 rising tone
阳畦 seed bed with windbreaks;cold bed
阳伞 parasol;sunshade
阳世 this world
阳台 balcony;veranda
阳痿 impotence
阳文 characters (*or* designs) cut in relief;relief
阳线 upward slope curve
阳性 ①positive ②masculine gender
阳虚 deficiency of *yang*;lack of vital energy
阳春面 noodles in a simple sauce
阳电荷 positive charges

阳电子 positive electron;positron
阳光权 right of lighting
阳离子 positive ion;cation
阳起石 actinolite (a mineral)
阳春白雪 Spring Snow—highbrow art and literature
阳地植物 sun plant
阳奉阴违 overtly agree but covertly oppose; comply in public but oppose in private; feign compliance
阳关大道 a broad highway;a broad road;thoroughfare
阳光采购 sunshine purchase
阳光操作 sunshine case work
阳光明媚 The sun is shining brightly.
阳伞效应 parasol effect
阳性植物 sun plant

杨 [yáng]
名 poplar
杨柳 ①poplar and willow ②willow
杨梅 red bayberry
杨树 poplar
杨桃 carambola
杨梅疮 syphilis
杨枝鱼 pipefish

佯 [yáng]
动 pretend;feign;fake;sham
佯嗔 pretend to be angry or displeased
佯称 allege falsely;tell lies;lie;pretend
佯动 make a feint
佯攻 feign (*or* simulate) attack;make a feint
佯狂 feign madness;pretend to be mad
佯死 play dead;feign death;play possum
佯羞 pretend to be shy
佯言 allege falsely;tell lies;lie;pretend
佯装 pretend;feign
佯作 bogus

疡 [yáng]
名 ①sore ②ulcer

垟 [yáng]
名 field

洋 [yáng]
Ⅰ 形 ① vast; abundant; multitudinous ② foreign;imported ③modern Ⅱ 名 ①ocean ② silver dollar
洋财 an unexpected big fortune;windfall money
洋菜 agar-agar;agar
洋场 metropolis infested with foreign adventurers (usu. referring to preliberation Shanghai)
洋车 rickshaw
洋瓷 enamel
洋葱 onion
洋房 foreign-style house
洋粉 agar-agar;agar
洋服 Western-style clothes
洋镐 pick;pickaxe;mattock

Y

洋行 foreign firm (in preliberation China)
洋红 carmine;crimson pigment
洋槐 locust tree
洋灰 cement
洋火 matches
洋货 foreign goods;imported goods
洋姜 Jerusalem artichoke
洋流 ocean current
洋楼 Western-style building
洋奴 slave of a foreign master;flunkey of imperialism;worshipper of everything foreign
洋气 ①foreign flavour;Western style ②in an ostentatious Western style
洋钱 silver dollar
洋人 foreigner (usu. a Westerner)
洋文 foreign language
洋务 foreign affairs
洋相 make an exhibition of oneself;make a spectacle of oneself
洋烟 imported cigarette
洋洋 numerous;copious
洋溢 be permeated with;brim with
洋油 ①imported oil ②kerosene
洋装 Western-style clothes
洋八股 foreign stereotyped writing;foreign stereotypes
洋白菜 cabbage
洋办法 modern methods
洋博士 foreign-trained Ph. D. ;doctor educated abroad
洋插队 settle in a foreign country for further education (implying hardship)
洋地黄 digitalis
洋橄榄 olive
洋鬼子 foreign devil
洋教条 ①foreign tenets (doctrines,dogmas, creeds) ②dogmatic assertion or blind worship of foreign doctrines,theories or rules
洋金花 datura flower
洋泾浜 pidgin English;pidgin
洋娃娃 (Western-style) doll
洋里洋气 in an ostentatious Western style
洋奴哲学 blind worship of everything foreign
洋腔怪调 exotic accent;outlandish way of talking
洋为中用 make foreign things serve China
洋务运动 Westernization Movement
洋洋大观 spectacular;grandiose;imposing
洋洋得意 be immensely proud with success; look triumphant
洋洋洒洒 voluminous;of great length
洋洋自得 be very pleased with oneself;be complacent

烊 [yáng]
　动 melt;dissolve ➡yàng

蚌 [yáng]
　名 insects such as the rice weevil

yǎng(1㤅)

仰 [yǎng]
　动 ① look up;face upward ② admire;revere;look up to ③rely on;depend on ④hope
仰给 count on sb for support
仰角 angle of elevation
仰赖 rely on
仰面 face upward
仰慕 admire;look up to
仰食 depend on another for food (or for one's living)
仰视 look up
仰首 raise one's head
仰天 look up to heaven
仰望 ① look up at ② respectfully seek guidance (or help) from;look up to
仰卧 lie on one's back;lie supine
仰泳 backstroke
仰仗 rely on;look to sb for backing (or support)
仰八叉 (fall) on one's back
仰即遵照 please comply immediately with this
仰请即示 looking forward to your prompt instructions
仰人鼻息 be dependent on the whims of others;be slavishly dependent
仰韶文化 the Yangshao culture (a Neolithic culture)
仰首伸眉 hold one's head high,feeling proud and elated
仰天长啸 cry into the air;make a long wheezing noise in the open air
仰卧起坐 sit-up
仰屋兴叹 look up at the ceiling and sigh—be at the end of one's resources

养 [yǎng]
　Ⅰ 动 ①support;keep;provide for ②raise; keep;grow;rear ③ give birth to ④form;acquire;contract ⑤nourish;rest;convalesce;recuperate ⑥cultivate;refine ⑦maintain;keep in good repair ⑧(of hair) grow long ⑨foster;support Ⅱ 形 adoptive;foster
养兵 maintain an army
养病 take rest and nourishment to regain one's health;recuperate
养蚕 engage in sericulture
养成 develop;cultivate
养地 increase soil fertility (by fertilization, crop rotation,etc.)
养分 nutrient
养蜂 raise (or keep) bees;engage in apiculture (or beekeeping)
养父 foster father
养汉 (of a woman) have a lover
养护 ①maintain;conserve ②curing
养花 grow flowers

养活 ① support; feed ② raise（animals）③ give birth to
养鸡 raise chickens
养老 ①provide for the aged（usu. one's parents）②live out one's life in retirement
养廉 （of government officials）nourish honesty—refrain from squeeze and graft
养料 nutriment; nourishment
养路 maintain a road（or railway）
养母 foster mother
养鸟 keep pet birds
养女 adopted daughter
养伤 nurse one's injuries（or wounds）
养神 rest to attain mental tranquility; repose
养生 care for life; conserve one's vital powers; preserve one's health; keep in good health
养息 rest and take nourishing food to build up one's health; recuperate
养性 nourish one's nature
养鸭 raise ducks
养眼 please one's eyes
养鱼 breed fish; engage in pisciculture
养育 bring up; rear
养殖 breed（aquatics）
养猪 raise hogs or pigs
养子 adopted son
养蚕业 sericulture
养蜂场 apiary; bee farm
养蜂业 apiculture; beekeeping
养鸡场 chicken run; chicken farm
养老金 old-age pension; annuity; annuities
养老院 home for the old
养路费 road toll; road maintenance expense
养马场 （horse）ranch
养身体 recuperate
养兔场 rabbit warren
养鱼池 fishpond
养殖业 breeding industry
养猪场 pig farm; piggery
养虎遗患 to rear a tiger is to court calamity—appeasement brings disaster
养家活口 support one's family
养精蓄锐 conserve strength and store up energy
养老保险 endowment insurance
养老送终 look after one's parents in their old age and give them a proper burial after they die
养生之道 how to care for life（or conserve one's vital powers）; how to maintain good health
养痈遗患 a boil neglected becomes the bane of one's life—leaving evil unchecked spells ruin
养殖基地 raising and breeding base（or farm）
养殖珍珠 cultured pearl

养尊处优 enjoy high position and live in comfort; live in clover
养兵千日,用兵一时 maintain an army for a thousand days to use it for an hour
养儿防老,积谷防荒 just as one stores up grain against lean years, one rears children against old age

氧 ［yǎng］
名 oxygen（O）
氧吧 oxygen bar（for oxygen therapy）
氧化 oxidize; oxidate
氧疗 oxygen therapy
氧气 oxygen
氧化剂 oxidizer; oxidant
氧化数 oxidation number; oxidation state
氧化态 oxidation state; oxidation number
氧化铁 ferric oxide
氧化物 oxide
氧化焰 outer flame
氧气袋 oxygen bag
氧气瓶 oxygen cylinder
氧气枪 oxygen lance
氧气帐 oxygen tent
氧气罩 oxygen mask
氧切割 oxygen cutting
氧合作用 oxygenation
氧气面具 oxygen mask
氧化还原酶 oxido-reducing enzyme; oxidoreductase
氧化抑制剂 oxidation retarder（or inhibitor）
氧乙炔吹管 oxyacetylene blowpipe
氧化还原反应 oxidation-reduction reaction
氧气顶吹转炉 oxygen top-blown convertor

痒 ［yǎng］
名 itch; tickle
痒痒 itch; tickle
痒疹 prurigo

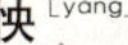

怏 ［yàng］
怏怏 disgruntled; sullen
怏怏而归 come back quite crestfallen; go home sadly

样 ［yàng］
Ⅰ 名 ①shape ②appearance; expression ③sample; model; pattern ④trend; situation Ⅱ 量 kind; type; variety: 几样儿风味菜 a few local delicacies
样板 ①sample plate ②templet ③model; prototype; example
样本 ①sample book ②sample; specimen
样稿 sample manuscript
样机 ①prototype ②sample machine
样件 sample
样款 pattern; style; sample
样片 the sample copy of a film;（of a film）

rushes
样品 sample (product);specimen
样式 pattern;type;style;form
样书 final proof;sample book
样图 master drawing
样样 every kind;each and every;all
样张 specimen page
样子 ① appearance;shape ② manner;air ③ sample;model;pattern ④ tendency;likelihood
样板房 show flat
样板田 demonstration field;model plot
样板戏 model opera

恙 〔yàng〕
〔名〕 ailment;illness;indisposition
恙虫 tsutsugamushi mite
恙虫热 tsutsugamushi disease;scrub typhus

烊 〔yàng〕
➡ yáng-
◇打烊 (of shops) put up the shutters;close for the night

漾 〔yàng〕
Ⅰ〔动〕①ripple ②brim over;overflow Ⅱ〔名〕 small lake;lakelet
漾动 ripple;flutter
漾奶 (of a baby) throw up milk

yāo (丨幺)

幺 〔yāo〕
Ⅰ〔数〕 one Ⅱ〔形〕①youngest ②small;thin
幺妹 youngest sister
幺叔 youngest uncle
幺小 petite;small
幺蛾子 wicked idea;devilish trick

夭 〔yāo〕
Ⅰ〔动〕 die young Ⅱ〔形〕 luxuriant;exuberant
夭殇 die young
夭亡 die young
夭折 ①die young ②come to a premature end

吆 〔yāo〕
〔动〕 bawl;shout;cry out
吆喊 cry out;call
吆喝 ①cry out;call;shout ②cry one's wares ③loudly urge on (an animal)
吆唤 cry out;call

约 〔yāo〕
〔动〕 weigh on a balance (or scale) ➡ yuē
约克夏猪 Yorkshire (hog)

妖 〔yāo〕
Ⅰ〔名〕 monster;goblin;demon;evil spirit Ⅱ〔形〕①evil and bewitching ②(of a woman) coquettish;seductive ③beautiful;charming
妖道 Taoist sorcerer (or witch)
妖风 evil wind;noxious trend
妖怪 monster;bogy;goblin;demon
妖精 ①evil spirit;demon ②seductress;siren
妖媚 seductively charming;bewitching;sexy
妖魔 evil spirit;demon
妖孽 ①person or event associated with evil or misfortune ②evildoer
妖娆 enchanting;fascinating;bewitching
妖人 sorcerer;enchanter
妖术 sorcery;witchcraft;black art
妖妄 fantastic;absurd
妖物 evil spirit;monster
妖言 heresy;fallacy
妖艳 seductive;bewitching
妖冶 seductive;bewitching
妖里妖气 seductive;sexy
妖魔鬼怪 demons and ghosts;monsters of every description;all forces of evil
妖声妖气 speak in an affected voice and manner
妖言惑众 spread fallacies to deceive people

要 〔yāo〕
〔动〕①demand;claim;ask ②force;compel;coerce ➡ yào
要求 ①ask;demand;require;claim;call for ②requirement;demand;claim
要挟 coerce;put pressure on;threaten

腰 〔yāo〕
〔名〕①waist;small of the back ②waist (of a garment) ③pocket;purse;wallet ④middle ⑤ waist-like terrain
腰包 belt bag;purse;pocket
腰部 waist;the small of the back
腰带 belt;girdle
腰鼓 ①waist drum ②waist drum dance
腰果 cashew nut;cashew
腰花 scalloped pork (or lamb kidneys)
腰牌 sign fixed to the sides of public transport
腰身 waistline;waist;waist measurement;girth
腰痛 lumbago
腰围 ①waistline;waist measurement ②girdle
腰眼 either side of the small of the back
腰斩 ①cutting sb in two at the waist (a capital punishment in ancient China) ②cut sth in half
腰肢 waist
腰椎 lumbar vertebra
腰子 kidney
腰板儿 ①back ②physique;build
腰带包 bum-bag
腰杆子 ①back ②backing;support
腰果树 cashew (tree)
腰缠万贯 be loaded;be very rich
腰肌劳损 strain of lumbar muscles
腰酸背痛 have a sore waist and an aching back—be aching all over
腰椎穿刺 lumbar puncture

邀 〔yāo〕
〔动〕①invite;ask;request ②gain;receive;seek ③intercept
邀宠 try to win sb's favour;curry favour with

sb

邀功 take credit for someone else's achievements

邀击 intercept (the enemy);waylay

邀集 invite to meet together;call together

邀请 invite

邀赏 ask to be rewarded for service rendered

邀游 invite to an excursion

邀请国 host country

邀请赛 invitational tournament

邀请信 letter of invitation

邀买人心 buy popular support;court popularity

yáo(l幺)

爻 [yáo]

◇阳爻 whole line

阴爻 broke line

尧 [yáo]

[名] Yao,a legendary monarch and model for all rulers in ancient China

尧舜 Yao and Shun,legendary sage kings in ancient China—ancient sages

尧天舜日 the days of Yao and Shun—the golden age of Chinese history (according to the Confucianists)

肴 [yáo]

[名] meat and fish dishes

肴肉 a kind of cured pork

肴馔 sumptuous courses at a meal

窑 [yáo]

[名] ①kiln ②pit ③cave dwelling ④brothel

窑变 kiln transmutation—the technique of making iridescent chinaware by the irregular application of glaze

窑洞 cave dwelling

窑子 brothel

窑姐儿 prostitute

窑灰钾肥 flue ash potash

谣 [yáo]

[名] ①ballad;rhyme ②rumour;hearsay

谣传 ① rumour; hearsay ② it is rumoured that;rumour has it that

谣俗 customs and habits;folkways

谣言 rumour;unfounded report;groundless allegation

摇 [yáo]

[动] shake;wave;wag;rock

摇把 cranking bar

摇摆 sway;swing;rock;vacillate

摇臂 rocker (or rock,rocking) arm

摇船 row a boat;scull a boat

摇床 table

摇荡 rock;sway

摇动 ①wave;shake ②sway;rock

摇撼 give a violent shake to;shake to the root

(or foundation);rock

摇晃 rock;sway;shake

摇奖 ①lottery ②lot cast

摇篮 cradle

摇蜜 extract honey

摇旗 wave a flag

摇手 shake one's hand in admonition or disapproval

摇头 shake one's hand

摇曳 flicker;sway

摇椅 rocking chair

摇钻 brace;bit-stock

摇摆舞 swing;rock and roll;rock

摇摆乐 swing;swing music

摇纺车 turn a spinning wheel

摇滚乐 rock and roll;rock (music)

摇奖机 lottery wheel; lottery-drawing machine

摇篮曲 cradle-song;lullaby;berceuse

摇蜜机 honey extractor

摇钱树 a legendary tree that sheds coins when shaken—a ready source of money

摇纱机 reeling frame

摇头丸 ecstasy;dancing outreach

摇唇鼓舌 flap one's lips and beat one's tongue—wag one's tongue;engage in loose talk (to stir up trouble)

摇旗呐喊 wave flags and shout battle cries—bang the drum for sb

摇身一变 give oneself a shake and change into another form—suddenly change one's identity

摇头摆尾 shake the head and wag the tail—assume an air of complacency or levity

摇头晃脑 wag one's head—look pleased with oneself;assume an air of self-approbation (or self-satisfaction)

摇尾乞怜 wag the tail ingratiatingly—fawn obsequiously

摇摇欲坠 tottering;crumbling;on the verge of collapse

徭 [yáo]

[名] forced labour; compulsory service; corvée

遥 [yáo]

[形] distant;remote;faraway

遥测 telemetering

遥感 remote sensing

遥控 remote control;telecontrol

遥望 look into the distance

遥想 recall;recollect;reminisce

遥遥 far away;a long way off

遥远 distant;remote;faraway

遥测计 telemeter

遥测器 remote detector

遥测术 telemetry

遥感卫星 remote sensing satellite

Y

遥控力学 telemechanics
遥相呼应 echo each other at a distance；coordinate with each other from afar
遥遥领先 be far ahead；hold a safe lead
遥遥无期 not（realizable，etc.）within the foreseeable future
遥测温度计 telethermometer

瑶 [yáo]
Ⅰ 名 precious jade Ⅱ 形 precious；wonderful
瑶池 Jasper Lake
瑶浆 good wine
瑶族 Yao ethnic group；the Yaos；the Yao nationality

鳐 [yáo]
动 ray；skate

yǎo（丨ㄠ）

杳 [yǎo]
形 too far away to be readily accessible
杳渺 distant and indistinct
杳然 quiet；still
杳如黄鹤 leave like the yellow crane—leave never to return；be gone for ever
杳无人烟 not a single soul can be seen
杳无音信 there has been no news whatsoever about sb；never been heard of since

咬 [yǎo]
动 ①bite；gnaw；snap at ②grip；bite ③（of a dog）bark ④incriminate another person（usu. innocent）；implicate ⑤pronounce；enunciate；articulate ⑥be fastidious or nitpicking（about the use of words）⑦follow closely；close in；advance on
咬定 assert emphatically；insist
咬钩 bite
咬合（of gear wheels，etc.）interlock；engage；mesh
咬啮 gnaw
咬破 break by the teeth；bite through
咬伤 bite
咬牙 ① grit（or set，clench，gnash）one's teeth ②grind one's teeth（in sleep）
咬住 ①bite into；grip with one's teeth ②grip；take firm hold of；refuse to let go of
咬嘴 be difficult to articulate；be awkward-sounding
咬耳朵 whisper in sb's ear；whisper
咬舌儿 ①lisp ②lisper
咬字儿 pronounce；articulate
咬紧牙关 grit（or clench）one's teeth；endure with dogged will
咬文嚼字 pay excessive attention to wording
咬牙切齿 gnash one's teeth
咬字眼儿 be nitpicking on words

舀 [yǎo]
动 ladle out；spoon up；scoop up

舀子 dipper；ladle；scoop

窈 [yǎo]
形 ①deep；profound ②dim
窈冥 ①dim；dusky ②deep；profound；abstruse
窈窕 ①（of a woman）gentle and graceful ②（of a palace，landscape，etc.）secluded
窈窕淑女 quiet and modest maiden；gentle and graceful young woman

yào（丨ㄠ）

疟 [yào]
➡nüè
疟子 malaria

药 [yào]
Ⅰ 名 ①medicine；drug；remedy ②certain chemicals Ⅱ 动 ①cure with medicine ②kill with poison
药补 build up one's health by taking tonic
药材 medicinal materials；crude drugs
药草 medicinal herbs
药茶 herb tea；medicated tea
药厂 pharmaceutical factory
药袋 medicine bag
药单（medical）prescription
药典 pharmacopoeia
药店 drugstore；chemist's shop；pharmacy
药方 prescription
药房 ① drugstore；chemist's shop；pharmacy ②hospital pharmacy；dispensary
药费 expenses for medicine；charges for medicine
药粉（medicinal）powder
药膏 ointment；salve
药谷 medicine valley
药害 environmental damage caused by improper use of insecticides
药衡 apothecaries' measure or weight
药剂 medicament；drug
药检 drug test
药箭 a poisoned arrow
药酒 medicinal liquor
药局 officina
药具 medication and device（for contraception）；contraceptives
药理 ①pharmacodynamics ②pharmacology
药力 efficacy of a drug（or medicine）
药麻 drug anaesthesia
药棉 absorbent cotton
药农 a peasant who cultivates or collects medicinal herbs；medicinal herb grower（or collector）；herbalist
药片（medicinal）tablet
药品 medicines and chemical reagents
药瓶 medicine bottle
药铺 herbal medicine shop
药签 swab
药膳 medicated food；food cooked with medici-

nal herbs

药石 medicines and stone needles for acupuncture—remedies

药水 ①liquid medicine;medicinal liquid ②lotion

药丸 pill

药味 ①herbal medicines in a prescription ②flavour of a drug

药物 pharmaceuticals;materia medica;medicines;drugs

药箱 medical kit;medicine-chest

药效 efficacy of a drug (*or* medicine)

药性 property of a medicine

药学 pharmacy

药瘾 dopy;drug addiction;drug dependence;drug-habit

药浴 dipping

药皂 medicated soap

药渣 dregs of a decoction

药枕 medical pillow

药疹 drug rash;drug eruption

药政 pharmaceutical control and administration

药罐子 ①a pot for decocting herbal medicine ②a chronic invalid

药剂师 pharmacist;pharmaceutist;druggist

药剂学 pharmaceutics;pharmacy

药劲儿 efficacy of a drug (*or* medicine)

药理学 pharmacology

药面儿 (medicinal) powder

药捻儿 ① fuse (for igniting an explosive charge) ②a slender roll of medicated paper (*or* gauze) (to be inserted into wounds, boils,etc.)

药捻子 a slender roll of medicated paper or gauze (to be inserted into wounds, boils, etc.)

药物学 materia medica;pharmacognosy

药引子 an ingredient added to enhance the efficacy of a dose of medicine;a medical supplement

药石之言 unpalatable but salutary advice

药物过敏 drug allergy

药物化学 pharmaceutical chemistry

药物检查 dope control;drug testing

药物牙膏 medicated toothpaste

药物中毒 drug poisoning

药用植物 medicinal plant

要 [yào]
Ⅰ 形 important;significant Ⅱ 名 important substance; essentials Ⅲ 动 ① want; desire; need;like to keep ②demand;claim ③ask for; ask sb to do sth;request ④want to;wish to; desire ⑤ must; should; have to ⑥ require; need;take ⑦will;be going to;be about to ⑧ (*used to indicate an estimation in comparisons*)might;must Ⅳ 连 ①if;suppose;in case ②or;either...or... ➡ yāo

要隘 strategic pass

要案 important case

要不 ①otherwise;or else;or ②either...or...

要冲 communications centre (*or* hub)

要道 thoroughfare

要得 good;fine;desirable

要地 important place;strategic point

要点 ① main points; essentials; gist ② key strongpoint

要犯 an important criminal

要饭 beg (for food or money)

要害 ① vital part; crucial point ② strategic point

要好 ①be on good terms;be close friends ② be eager to improve oneself; try hard to make progress

要谎 ask an exorbitant price

要价 ask a price;charge

要件 ①an important document ②an important condition

要津 ①key place ②key post

要紧 ① important; essential ② be critical; be serious;matter ③be in a hurry to;be anxious to

要诀 important tricks of the trade;knack

要脸 be keen on face-saving;care much about one's reputation

要领 ①main points;gist ②essentials (of an exercise in military or athletic training)

要略 outline;summary

要么 or;either...or...

要命 ①drive sb to his death;kill ②confoundedly;extremely;awfully;terribly ③a nuisance

要钱 charge

要强 be eager to excel;be anxious to outdo others

要人 very important person (VIP);important personage

要塞 fort;fortress;fortification

要事 an important matter

要是 if;suppose;in case

要死 extremely;awfully;terribly

要素 essential factor;key element

要图 an important plan (*or* programme)

要闻 important news;front-page story

要务 important business;urgent business

要义 essentials

要员 important official

要债 demand payment of a debt

要账 demand payment of a debt;press for repayment of a loan;dun

要职 an important post

要旨 main idea;gist

要不得 be no good;be intolerable

要不然 otherwise;or else;or

要不是 if it were not for;but for
要回扣 demand commissions
要面子 be keen on face-saving;be anxious to keep up appearances
要害部门 key department
要价过高 place excessive (*or* exorbitant) demands
要价还价 bargain;haggle
要言不烦 terse;succinct;pithy

钥 [yào]
➡yuè

钥匙 key

鞠 [yào]
名 leg of a boot (*or* stocking)

鹞 [yào]
名 ①harrier ②sparrow hawk

鹞鹰 sparrow hawk
鹞子 ①sparrow hawk ②kite

曜 [yào]
I 名 ①sunlight ②(*used to refer to the sun , the moon and the stars*) Ⅱ 动 shine;radiate;illuminate

耀 [yào]
I 动 ①shine;radiate;illuminate;dazzle ②vaunt;show off;boast of Ⅱ 名 ①brilliance;glow ②glory;honour;credit

耀斑 solar flare
耀眼 dazzling
耀武扬威 make a show of one's strength;swagger around;throw one's weight around

yē(lㅓ)

耶 [yē]
➡yé

耶稣 Jesus;Jesus Christ
耶和华 Jehovah
耶稣会 the Society of Jesus;the Jesuits
耶稣教 Protestantism

掖 [yē]
动 tuck in (*or* up);thrust in between ➡yè

椰 [yē]
名 coconut palm;coconut tree;coco

椰雕 coconut-shell carving
椰干 desiccated coconut;copra
椰壳 coconut husk
椰仁 coconut kernel;coconut meat
椰蓉 fine coconut mash (used as a filling for cakes)
椰树 coconut palm;coconut tree
椰丝 shredded coconut meat
椰油 coconut oil;coconut butter
椰枣 date palm;date
椰子 ①coconut palm;coconut tree;coco ②coconut (the fruit)
椰仁干 desiccated coconut;copra
椰壳纤维 coir fibre;coir

噎 [yē]
动 ①choke ②be choked by wind ③render

sb speechless by saying sth blunt (*or* rude);interrupt rudely;choke off
噎嗝 cancer of the esophagus

yé(lㅓ)

爷 [yé]
名 ① father ② grandfather ③ respectful form of address for a man of the older generation ④form of address for an official (*or* rich man) ⑤form of address for god,used by superstitious people

爷儿 (often followed by 俩,几个,etc.) a senior male member of a family together with one or more junior members
爷娘 father and mother
爷爷 ①(paternal) grandfather ②grandpa
爷儿们 a collective term for men of two or more generations
爷们儿 ①man (*or* menfolk) ②husband;a collective term for men of two or more generations

耶 [yé]
助 *used to indicate the interrogative* :是耶,非耶? Yes or no?;Is it or isn't it?;Is it true or is it not? ➡yē

揶 [yé]

揶揄 ridicule;deride

yě(lㅓ)

也 [yě]
I 助 ①(*used at the end of a sentence indicating explanation or judgement*):师者,所以传道授业解惑也。A teacher is one who propagates the doctrines of ancient sages,passes on knowledge and helps to clear up doubts. ②(*used at the end of a question or counter question*):是可忍也,孰不可忍也? If this can be tolerated,then what cannot be? ③(*used in the middle of a sentence indicating a pause*):是日也,天朗气清,惠风和畅。It was a bright sunny day with gentle breeze. Ⅱ 副 ① also; too; as well; either ② both... and... ;as well as ③either... or... ;whether... or... ;no matter whether ④(*used to indicate concession*):宁可牺牲,也绝不向敌人投降。We'd rather die than surrender to the enemy. ⑤(*used to indicate resignation*):也只好如此了。We'll have to leave it at that. ⑥(*often used together with* 一点,连,*etc.* *to indicate emphasis*):天空连一丝云也没有。There's not even a single trace of a cloud in the sky.

也罢 ① well; all right ② (reduplicated) whether... or... ;no matter whether
也好 ①it may not be a bad idea;may as well ②(reduplicated) whether... or... ;no mat-

Y

ter whether

也许 perhaps;probably;maybe

也…也… ①both... and... ; either ... or... ②no matter（whether,who,etc.）

冶 ［yě］

I 动 smelt（metal）Ⅱ 形 （of a woman）seductively dressed（*or* made up）

冶荡 lewd;lascivious

冶金 metallurgy

冶炼 smelt

冶艳 pretty and coquettish

冶游 visit prostitutes

冶金学 metallurgy

冶炼厂 smelter;smeltery

野 ［yě］

I 名 ① open country; wild land ② limit; boundary ③not being in power;being out of office Ⅱ 形 ① wild; uncultivated; undomesticated ②rude;rough;wild ③unrestrained;unruly;undisciplined

野菜 edible wild herbs

野餐 picnic

野草 weeds

野炊 cook in the open air

野地 wild country;wilderness

野狗 stray dog;wild dog

野果 wild fruit

野合 have illicit sexual relations;commit adultery

野花 wild flower

野火 prairie fire;bush fire

野鸡 ① pheasant ② streetwalker; unlicensed prostitute

野景 wild scenery

野驴 Asiatic wild ass;kiang

野麻 wild flax;wild hemp

野马 wild horse;untamed horse

野蛮 ① uncivilized; savage ② barbarous; cruel;brutal

野猫 ①wildcat ②a stray cat ③hare

野牛 wild ox

野炮 field gun;field artillery

野趣 rustic charm

野人 ①an uncouth person;rustic ②savage; barbarian

野生 wild;undomesticated;uncultivated;feral

野史 unofficial history

野兽 wild beast;wild animal

野兔 hare

野外 open country;field

野味 game（as food）

野心 wild ambition;careerism

野性 wild nature;unruliness

野鸭 wild duck

野营 camp;bivouac

野战 field operations;field battle

野猪 wild boar

野汉子 a woman's lover

野狐禅 heresy

野菊花 mother chrysanthemum

野葡萄 bryony;wild grape

野蔷薇 multiflora rose

野食儿 ①animals' food picked up in the wilds ②ill-gotten（*or* illicit）gains

野兽派 fauvism;brutalism

野豌豆 vetch

野心家 careerist

野心狼 a vicious wolf—a person of evil ambitions

野营车 camper

野战军 field army

野战炮 fieldpiece;field gun

野草闲花 ① weeds and wild flowers ② mistress ③prostitute

野鸡大学 diploma mill

野蛮行为 barbarous act;brutal act;savage behaviour

野生动物 wildlife

野心勃勃 be obsessed with ambition

野战演习 field exercise

野战医院 field hospital

野生动物园 animal safari park

野火烧不尽,春风吹又生 even a prairie fire cannot destroy the grass; it grows again when the spring breeze blows（said of what cannot be suppressed）

yè（lㄝ）

业 ［yè］

I 名 ① course of study; course ② occupation; profession; employment ③ trade; industry;business ④cause;enterprise;undertaking ⑤ estate; property ⑥ karma; deed; action Ⅱ 动 engage in;go in for Ⅲ 副 already

业报 retribution for sins

业海 sea of retribution

业绩 outstanding achievement;track record

业界 business circles;in field

业经 already

业内 in the business

业商 engage in commerce;be in business

业师 one's（former）teacher

业态 type of operation

业外 beyond the scope of certain trade,business or profession

业务 vocational work;professional work;business

业已 already

业余 ① spare time; after-hours ②nonprofessional;amateur

业障 ①retribution in this life for the sins of a previous existence ②（said to one's children）medium of retribution

业者 practitioner of a certain business
业种 ①the bane of one's existence ②(said to one's descendant) vile spawn; unfilial son
业主 owner (of an enterprise or estate); proprietor
业精于勤 mastery of work comes from diligent application; a subject is mastered through diligent study
业内公司 people in the line (*or* business); professional quarters; in-group sources
业内人士 insider
业务班子 professional team; business team
业务范围 scope of business
业务挂帅 put professional work in command; professional work comes first
业务尖子 top-notch professional
业务能力 professional ability (*or* proficiency)
业务水平 professional skill; vocational level
业务协定 business agreement
业务学习 vocational study
业务知识 professional knowledge
业务总裁 chief operating officer
业余教育 spare-time education
业余学校 spare-time school
业余补习学校 spare-time continuation school

叶 [yè]
名 ①leaf; blade; foliage ②leaf-like thing ③page; leaf ④part of a historical period ➡ xié
叶柄 petiole; leafstalk
叶蝉 leafhopper (an insect)
叶蜂 sawfly (an insect)
叶猴 leaf monkey
叶轮 impeller; vane wheel
叶脉 leaf vein
叶片 ①leaf blade ②vane
叶鞘 leaf sheath
叶肉 mesophyll
叶酸 folic acid; folacin
叶序 phyllotaxy; leaf arrangement
叶芽 leaf bud
叶子 leaf
叶斑病 leaf spot
叶红素 carotene
叶黄素 xanthophyll; lutein
叶蜡石 pyrophyllite (a mineral)
叶绿素 chlorophyll
叶绿体 chloroplast
叶锈病 leaf rust
叶子烟 dried tobacco leaves
叶公好龙 Lord Ye's love of dragons—professed love of what one really fears
叶落归根 the falling leaves settle on the roots—a person residing elsewhere finally returns to his ancestral home

Y

页 [yè]
名 ①leaf; sheet ②page
页边 margin

页理 the laminated structure of shale
页码 page number
页面 page layout; webpage
页心 type page
页岩 shale
页岩油 shale oil

曳 [yè]
动 drag; haul; tug; pull; tow
曳白 hand in a blank paper in an imperial examination
曳光 train
曳力 drag force
曳引 tow; tug
曳光弹 tracer bullet (*or* shell); tracer
曳绳钓 trolling
曳光穿甲弹 armour-piercing tracer

夜 [yè]
Ⅰ 名 night; nighttime; evening Ⅱ 动 get (*or* grow) dark; evening falls
夜班 night shift
夜半 midnight
夜餐 midnight snack
夜叉 ①yaksa (a malevolent spirit) ②hideous, ferocious person
夜娼 night walker
夜场 evening show; evening performance
夜车 night train
夜盗 burglar
夜饭 supper; dinner
夜工 night work; night job
夜光 noctilucent
夜航 night flight (*or* navigation)
夜合 ①silk tree ②the tuber of multiflower knotweed
夜壶 chamber pot
夜间 night; nighttime; at night
夜禁 curfew
夜景 night scene (*or* view)
夜课 evening class
夜空 the night sky
夜里 at night
夜盲 nyctalopia; night blindness
夜幕 curtain (*or* veil) of night; gathering darkness
夜勤 night duty
夜曲 nocturne
夜色 the dim light of night
夜深 in the dead of night; late at night
夜市 night market; night fair
夜啼 morbid night crying of babies
夜晚 night
夜袭 night attack (*or* raid)
夜宵 food (*or* refreshments) taken late at night; midnight snack
夜校 night (*or* evening) school
夜行 ①go out walking in the night; travel by night ②night flight (*or* navigation)

夜夜 every night
夜莺 nightingale
夜鹰 nightjar;goatsucker
夜战 ①night fighting ②night work
夜大学 evening university
夜光杯 a cup of phosphorescent jade
夜光表 luminous watch
夜光虫 noctiluca
夜光螺 green snail
夜交藤 the vine of multiflower knotweed
夜来香 cordate telosma
夜猫子 ① owl ② a person who goes to bed late;night owl
夜明珠 night-luminescent pearl
夜尿症 enuresis;bed-wetting
夜生活 night life
夜视仪 night vision device (*or* instrument)
夜望镜 snooperscope
夜行军 night march
夜游神 the legendary god on patrol at night—a person who is up and about at night;night owl
夜总会 nightclub;cabaret
夜不闭户 doors are not bolted at night—law and order prevail
夜长梦多 a long night is fraught with dreams—a long delay means trouble
夜出动物 nocturnal animal
夜静更深 in the still of night;in the dead of night
夜阑人静 in the dead of night;in the still (*or* quiet) of the night
夜郎自大 ludicrous conceit of the King of Yelang—parochial arrogance
夜以继日 day and night;round the clock
夜入私宅罪 burglary

咽 [yè]
〔形〕(of sound) obstructed and therefore low ➡yān;yàn

晔 [yè]
〔形〕(of light) bright

烨 [yè]
Ⅰ〔名〕firelight; sunlight Ⅱ〔形〕(of light) brilliant

掖 [yè]
〔动〕support sb by the arm;support;assist;promote ➡yē

液 [yè]
〔名〕liquid;fluid;juice
液肥 liquid manure (*or* fertilizer)
液化 liquefaction
液晶 liquid crystal
液冷 liquid cooling (*or* cooled)
液力 hydraulic
液泡 vacuole
液态 liquid state
液体 liquid
液压 hydraulic pressure

液化气 liquefied gas
液化器 liquefier
液体镜 liquid mirror
液压泵 hydraulic pump
液压表 hydraulic pressure gauge
液压机 hydraulic press
液化气罐 gas bottle
液晶电视 liquid crystal TV
液晶显示 liquid crystal display (LCD)
液体燃料 liquid fuel
液化石油气 liquefied petroleum gas (LPG)
液化天然气 liquefied natural gas (LNG)
液晶显示屏 liquid crystal display (LCD)
液体比重计 hydrometer
液压传动装置 hydraulic transmission device

谒 [yè]
〔动〕call on (a superior or an elder person);pay homage to;pay one's respects to
谒见 call on (a superior or a senior in the clan hierarchy);have an audience with
谒陵 pay homage at sb's mausoleum

腋 [yè]
〔名〕①axilla;armpit ②axil
腋臭 underarm odour
腋毛 armpit hair
腋窝 armpit
腋芽 axillary bud

馌 [yè]
〔动〕deliver a meal to the field

yī(1)

一 [yī]
Ⅰ〔数〕one Ⅱ〔形〕①same ②whole;entire;all ③concentrated;wholehearted ④another Ⅲ〔副〕①also;otherwise ②once;now that Ⅳ〔助〕①(*used to indicate that an action occurs just once, or lasts for a short time;or is being attempted*) (a) (*used between reduplicated often monosyllabic verbs*):唱一唱 sing/笑一笑 give a smile (b) (*used after a verb and before a verbal classifier*):跑一趟 make a trip/哭一场 have a cry ②(*used for emphasis*):一何速也! How fast it is!
一把 handful;bundle;bunch
一百 hundred
一般 ①same as;just like ②general;ordinary;common
一斑 one spot (on a leopard);one of a number of similar things
一半 one half;half;in part
一帮 a gang;a band
一杯 a cup of
一边 ①one side;side ②either side ③at the same time;simultaneously
一并 along with all the others;in the lump
一餐 a meal
一刹 in an instant;in a split second;in the

twinkling of an eye
一匙 a spoon;a spoonful
一传 first pass
一串 a string;a hand of
一次 once
一代 ①a dynasty ②an era;the present age ③ all one's life;a lifetime;a generation
一带 the area around a particular place
一旦 ①in a single day;in a very short time ② once;in case;now that
一道 together;side by side;alongside
一等 first-class; first-rate; top-grade; top-notch
一定 ① fixed; specified; definite; regular ② certainly;surely ③given;particular;certain ④proper;fair;due
一动 ①a move;a jerk ②easily;frequently;at every turn
一度 ①once ②on one occasion;for a time
一端 one aspect (or side) of the matter
一段 ① one paragraph;one passage ②a section;a length of
一堆 a pile;a heap;a ruck
一对 duad;twain;a pair;a couple
一顿 a meal
一二 one or two;just a few;just a little
一发 ①all the more;even more ② together; along with all the others
一份 a part;a portion;a share
一服 a dose
一副 a pair;a set
一概 one and all; without exception; totally; categorically
一干 all those involved
一共 altogether;in all;all told
一贯 consistent;persistent;all along
一行 a row;a line;a single file
一盒 a box of
一晃 [yīhuǎng] flash
一晃 ([yīhuàng])(of time) pass in a flash
一伙 a gang of;a band of
一己 oneself
一截 a section;a length
一节 ①a lesson ②bus
一经 as soon as;once
一径 straight;directly;straightaway
一…就… no sooner... than... ;the moment...; as soon as;at once
一举 one action;one stroke;one fell swoop
一口 ① a mouthful; a bite ② a manner of speech ③with certainty;readily;flatly
一览 general survey;bird's-eye view
一类 of the same class;of the same species
一力 do one's best;do all one can
一例 same;alike
一连 in a row;in succession;running
一流 ①a kind; the same kind ② first-class;

first-rate;top-notch
一楼 〈英〉the ground floor;〈美〉the first floor
一路 ①all the way;throughout the journey ② of the same kind ③go the same way;take the same route ④single file
一律 ①same;alike;uniform ②all;without exception
一秘 first secretary
一面 ①one side ②one aspect ③at the same time;simultaneously ④have met once before
一旁 one side
一篇 a piece of
一片 ①a slice;a fardel;a tablet ②a stretch (of land);a sheet of (water) ③a scene (of rejoicing);a patter (of footsteps)
一瞥 ①a quick glance ②a glimpse;a brief survey
一品 the highest official rank in imperial China
一齐 at the same time;simultaneously;in unison
一起 ①in the same place ②together;in company ③altogether;in all ④a batch of people
一气 ①at one go;without a break;at a stretch ②of the same gang;hand in glove ③a spell;a fit
一千 a thousand
一腔 be full of (zeal,grievances,etc.)
一切 ①all;every ②everything;all
一群 a group;a crowd;a herd;a flock
一任 allow
一如 just like;the same as
一色 ① of the same colour ② of the same type;uniform
一霎 in an instant;in a moment
一晌 ①a short time;a little while ②earlier on;lately;consistently;all along ③a period of time
一身 ①the whole body;all over the body ②a suit ③a single person
一审 first instance
一生 all one's life;throughout one's life
一时 ①a period of time ②for a short while; temporary; momentary ③ now... , now... ; one moment... ,the next...
一世 ①all one's life;a lifetime ②age;era; times
一式 the same form
一手 ① proficiency; skill ② trick; move ③ single-handed;all by oneself;all alone
一束 a bunch;a head;a bob
一双 a couple;a pair;duad;twain
一瞬 an instant; a flash; the twinkling of an eye
一体 ①an organic (or integral) whole ②all

people concerned;to a man
一天 ①a day ②one day (in the past) ③the whole day;all (the) day;from morning till night
一同 together;at the same time and place
一统 unify (a country)
一头 ①at the same time;simultaneously ②all of a sudden;all at once ③directly;headlong ④a head ⑤one end ⑥in a group;together
一味 blindly
一线 ①a ray of;a gleam of ②units or job directly involved in production and scientific research
一箱 a boxful
一向 ① earlier on; lately ② consistently; all along
一些 a number of;certain;some;a few;a little
一心 ① wholeheartedly; heart and soul ② of one mind;at one
一新 become sth entirely new
一行 a group travelling together;party
一宿 one night
一样 the same;alike;as... as...
一一 one by one;one after another
一应 all;everything
一隅 a corner
一月 January
一再 time and again;again and again;repeatedly
一…再… (*used with two identical verbs*) repeatedly
一早 early in the morning
一朝 ①in one day ②once
一直 ① straight ② continuously; all along; always;all the way
一致 showing no difference; identical; unanimous;consistent
一准 sure;surely;certainly
一总 ①altogether;all told;in all ②all
一把手 ①a party to an undertaking;a member;a hand ②very capable person ③(of an institution) first in command, head, chief ④a good hand ⑤first in command;number one man;a person holding primary responsibility
一把抓 ① take everything into one's own hands ②try to tackle all problems at once regardless of their relative importance
一班人 members of a squad—a small body of people working together
一般化 vague generalization
一半天 in a day or two
一辈子 all one's life;throughout one's life;as long as one lives;a lifetime
一边倒 ①lean to one side;side with sb without reservation ②predominate;enjoy overwhelming superiority

一步裙 one-step skirt
一部分 a part;a portion;partial;partially
一刹那 in a moment;in a split second
一长制 system of one-man leadership; one-man authority
一场空 all in vain;futile
一程子 a number of days
一次性 ①once only (without a second time) ②disposable
一大块 a bulk
一大片 a sheet
一大群 a crowd of
一大早 early in the morning
一党制 one-partyism
一刀切 cut it even at one stroke—make everything rigidly uniform;impose uniformity in all cases;prescribe a single solution for diverse problems
一道菜 course
一等兵 (U.S. Army) private first class; (Brit. Army) lance corporal;(U.S. Navy) seaman first class;(Brit. Navy) leading seaman; (U.S. Air Force) airman first class;(Brit. Air Force) senior aircraftsman;(U.S. Marine Corps) private first class;(Brit. Marine Corps) marine first class
一等功 Merit Citation, First Class; first-class merit
一点儿 ①a bit;a little ②the least bit
一点论 the doctrine that everything has only one aspect;the doctrine affirming only one aspect
一肚子 a stomachful of;full of
一多半 the greater part
一方面 ① one side ② on the one hand... , on the other hand... ; for one thing... , for another...
一风吹 scatter to the winds—dismiss all charges,etc. ;cancel the whole thing
一贯制 ①continuous education through junior and senior divisions without examinations between the two ②unchanged for a long time
一锅端 ① hold in a pot ② bring everything out;speak out without reservation ③eliminate,eradicate completely
一锅粥 a pot of porridge—a complete mess;all in a muddle
一锅煮 cook all things in one pot—treat different persons or things alike (*or* indiscriminately);cook different foods in one pot;treat identically
一忽儿 ①a little while ②in a moment;presently ③ now... now... ; one moment... the next...
一回事 ① one and the same (thing) ② one

thing
一会儿 ①a little while ②in a moment; presently ③ now... now... ; one moment... the next...
一级风 force 1 wind; light air
一家子 ①a family ②the whole family
一句话 in a word; in short
一卡通 universal credit card; all-purpose card
一口气 ①one breath ②in one breath; without a break; at one go; at a stretch
一块儿 ①at the same place ②together
一览表 table; schedule
一揽子 wholesale; package
一连串 a succession of; a series of; a string of; a chain of
一溜儿 ①a row ②neighbourhood; vicinity ③a short period of activity
一溜风 like a gust of wind—very quickly
一溜烟 like a streak of smoke—very quickly
一麻黑 pitch-dark
一米线 one-metre mark
一抹平 ①the same; equal ②level; smooth
一年生 (of plants) annual
一盘棋 ①chess game ②overall situation
一票通 one ticket (or bill) for all; one single inclusive fee for all
一品红 poinsettia
一切险 all risk
一清早 early in the morning
一闪念 a fleeting thought
一上来 at first; at the beginning
一神论 monotheism
一顺儿 in the same direction (or order)
一体化 integration
一条龙 ①one continuous line ②a connected sequence; a coordinated process
一条心 be of one mind; be at one
一团糟 a complete mess; a chaotic state
一位数 one-digit number
一窝蜂 like a swarm of bees
一席话 what one says during a conversation
一系列 a series of
一下子 ①one time; once ②in a short while; all at once; all of a sudden
一线通 N-ISDN, narrow integrated services digital network
一小撮 a handful
一小时 an hour; one hour
一言堂 a conference hall where one person has all the say—what I say goes; one person alone has the say; one person lays down the law
一夜情 one-night stand
一元化 centralized; unified
一元论 monism
一元酸 monoacid; monoatomic acid
一院制 unicameral (or one chamber) legisla-

ture
一阵风 ①gust of wind ②short-lived (of work in general and a campaign in particular); capricious; unsteady
一阵子 ①a burst; a fit; a peal ②a period of time; a spell
一字儿 in a row; in a line
一字师 one's single-correction teacher
一败涂地 fail completely; suffer a crushing defeat; be routed
一般见识 (lower oneself to) the same level as sb
一板一眼 following a prescribed (or set) pattern in speech (or action); scrupulous and methodical
一暴十寒 — 一曝十寒 have one day's sun and then ten days' cold—work by fits and starts
一本万利 make big profits with a small capital; a small investment that brings big profits
一本正经 in all seriousness; in dead earnest
一笔勾销 write off at one stroke; cancel
一笔抹杀 blot out at one stroke; condemn out of hand; totally negate
一臂之力 a helping hand
一表人才 a man of striking appearance
一病不起 take to one's bed and never leave it again; fall ill and die
一波三折 full of twists and turns (or ups and downs)
一步到位 accomplish a task at one stroke; achieve a goal in one leap; get it settled once for all; get to the right position with only one move
一步登天 reach the sky in a single bound—attain the highest level in one step; have a meteoric rise
一差二错 a possible mistake or mishap
一场春梦 a spring dream—a fleeting illusion
一唱百和 when one starts singing, the others join in—meet with general approval
一唱一和 sing a duet; sing the same tune; echo each other
一尘不染 not soiled by a speck of dust; spotless
一成不变 immutable and frozen; invariable; unalterable
一筹莫展 can find no way out; be at one's wits' end; be at the end of one's tether
一触即发 may break out at any moment; be on the verge of breaking out
一触即溃 collapse at the first encounter
一锤定音 set the tune with one beat of the gong—give the final word
一词多义 polysemy
一次方程 linear equation
一次付清 pay in one lump sum; pay a round

sum
一次函数 linear function
一次能源 primary energy
一次消费 one-time consumption
一蹴而就 reach the goal in one step; accomplish one's aim in one move
一搭两用 one thing serving two purposes
一打一拉 strike and stroke alternately; alternate hard and soft tactics; use the carrot and the stick
一刀两断 sever at one stroke—make a clean break
一得之功 just an occasional, minor success
一得之愚 my humble opinion
一等秘书 first secretary
一点一滴 every little bit
一丁点儿 a wee bit
一定之规 ①a fixed pattern; a set rule ②one's own way
一二报数 By twos, number!
一发千钧 a hundredweight hanging by a hair—in imminent peril
一帆风顺 plain sailing; smooth sailing
一反常态 depart from one's normal behaviour; act out of character
一分为二 one divides into two—everything has its good and bad sides; there are two sides to everything
一概而论 treat (different matters) as the same
一干二净 thoroughly; completely
一个劲儿 continuously; persistently
一股劲儿 without a break; at one go; at a stretch
一股脑儿 completely; lock, stock and barrel; root and branch
一鼓作气 press on to the finish without letup; get sth done in one sustained effort
一官半职 some official post or other
"一国两府" one country, two governments
一国两制 one country, two systems
一国三公 a state with three rulers—a divided leadership
一哄而起 (of a group of people) be roused to precipitate action; rush headlong into mass action
一哄而散 break up (or disperse) in a hubbub
一哄而上 impulsive; unthinking
一呼百诺 have hundreds at one's beck and call
一呼百应 hundreds respond to a single call
一挥而就 a flourish of the pen and it's done
一级市场 primary market
一级战备 first-degree combat readiness
一级准尉 (Brit. Army, Navy, Air Force & Marine Corps) warrant officer (Class I); (U.S. Army & Air Force) chief warrant officer; (U.S. Navy & Marine Corps) com-

missioned warrant officer
一技之长 proficiency in a particular line (or field); professional skill; speciality
一家之言 a distinctive doctrine (or theory); an original system of thought
一见倾心 fall in love at first sight
一见如故 feel like old friends at the first meeting; hit it off well right from the start
一见钟情 fall in love at first sight
一箭双雕 hit two hawks with one arrow; kill two birds with one stone
一箭之仇 the wrong of an arrow shot—a loss or defeat to be retrieved
一箭之地 as far as the arrow flies—a short distance
一举两得 gain two ends at once; kill two birds with one stone
一举一动 every act and every move; every action
一决雌雄 fight to see who is the stronger; fight it out
一蹶不振 collapse after a single setback; be unable to recover after a setback
一刻千金 one moment is worth a thousand pieces of gold—time is gold
一孔之见 a peephole view; a narrow view; a very limited outlook
一口咬定 state categorically; assert positively; insist emphatically
一来二去 in the course of frequent contact; in the course of time
一览无余 take in everything at a glance
一劳永逸 by one supreme effort gain lasting repose—settle a matter once and for all
一连气儿 in a row; in succession; running
一了百了 all troubles end when the main trouble ends
一鳞半爪 odd bits; fragments
一溜歪斜 (walk, etc.) unsteadily in a zigzag
一路货(色) the same sort of stuff; one of a kind; birds of a feather
一路平安 have a pleasant journey; have a good trip; bon voyage
一路顺风 have a pleasant journey; have a good trip; bon voyage
一落千丈 drop a thousand *zhang* in one fall—suffer a drastic decline
一马当先 gallop at the head—take the lead; be in the forefront
一马平川 a wide expanse of flat land; a wide stretch of flat country
一脉相承 come down in one continuous line; can be traced to the same origin; in direct line of descent (or succession)
一毛不拔 unwilling to give up even a hair—very stingy
一门心思 heart and soul; wholeheartedly

一面之词 the statement of only one of the parties

一面之交 have met only once; be casually acquainted

一面之缘 having met once (as ordained by fate)

一鸣惊人 (of an obscure person) amaze the world with a single brilliant feat; set the world on fire

一命归天 quit this world; pass away; die

一命呜呼 die; kick the bucket; give up the ghost

一模活脱 cast in the same mould—exactly alike; as like as two peas

一模一样 exactly alike; as like as two peas

一木难支 one log can't prop up a tottering building—one person alone can't save the situation

一目了然 be clear at a glance

一目十行 take in ten lines at a glance—read rapidly

一男半女 a son or a daughter; a child or two

一年半载 in a year or so; in about a year

一年到头 throughout the year; all the year round

一年四季 throughout (the four seasons of) the year; all the year round

一念之差 a wrong decision made in a moment of weakness; a momentary slip with serious consequences

一诺千金 a promise worth a thousand pieces of gold—a promise that can be counted on

一拍即合 fit in readily; chime in easily

一盘散沙 a sheet of loose sand—a state of disunity (formerly said of a country)

一贫如洗 penniless; utterly destitute

一平二调 equalitarianism and indiscriminate transfer of resources

一抔黄土 a handful of yellow earth—sth utterly insignificant

一曝十寒 have one day's sun and then ten days' cold—work by fits and starts

一气呵成 ① (of an essay) form a coherent whole; make smooth reading ② get sth done at one go; carry sth through without stopping

一气之下 in a fury; in a fit of anger

一钱不值 not worth a penny; utterly worthless; mere trash

一窍不通 know nothing about (a subject); lack the slightest knowledge of; be utterly ignorant of

一切从简 dispense with all unnecessary formalities

一清二白 perfectly clean; blameless; unimpeachable

一清二楚 perfectly clear

一穷二白 poor and blank

一丘之貉 jackals from the same lair; birds of a feather

一仍旧贯 stick to the old practice; follow the old routine

一日千里 a thousand *li* a day—at a tremendous pace; with giant strides

一日之长 a slight superiority

一如既往 just as in the past; as before; as always

一扫而光 make a clean sweep of; clear off; finish off; get rid of sth lock, stock and barrel

一身两役 hold two jobs at the same time; serve in a dual capacity

一身是胆 one's whole body is all pluck—know no fear; be absolutely fearless

一生一世 all one's life; throughout one's life

一声不响 not say a word; not utter a sound

一时半刻 a short time; a little while

一时三刻 a short time; a little while

一时一刻 every moment

一式两份 (receipt or invoice) in duplicate

一式三份 triplicate

一式四份 quadruplicate

一式五份 quintuplicate

一事无成 accomplish nothing; get nowhere

一视同仁 treat equally without discrimination

一手包办 do sth all by oneself; keep everything in one's own hands; take everything on oneself

一手遮天 shut out the heavens with one hand—hide the truth from the masses; hoodwink the public

一丝不苟 not be the least bit negligent; be scrupulous about every detail; be conscientious and meticulous

一丝不挂 not have a stitch on; be stark naked

一丝一毫 a tiny bit; an iota; a trace

一塌糊涂 in a complete mess; in an awful (*or* terrible) state

一潭死水 a pool of stagnant water—a stagnant or lifeless condition

一天到晚 from morning till night; from dawn to dusk; all day long

一通百通 master one and you'll master a hundred; grasp this and you'll grasp everything

一统天下 the whole empire under one ruler

一头儿沉 ① heavy-at-one-end, a desk with a cupboard or drawers at one end ② be partial (in mediation)

一头雾水 puzzled

一吐为快 cannot rest until one has one's say; feel relief after getting it all out

一团和气 keep on good terms with everyone (at the expense of principle); keep on the right side of everyone

一团漆黑 ① pitch-dark—utterly hopeless ② be

entirely ignorant of; be in the dark
一湾秋水 an arch of autumnal water
一网打尽 catch the whole lot in a dragnet; round up the whole gang at one fell swoop
一往情深 be deeply attached; be passionately devoted; be head over heels in love
一往无前 press forward with an indomitable will
一望无际 stretch as far as the eye can see; stretch to the horizon
一位论派 Unitarianism
一文不名 not have a penny to one's name; be penniless
一文不值 not worth a farthing; utterly worthless; mere trash
一无可取 have nothing to recommend one; be worthless
一无是处 without a single redeeming feature; devoid of any merit; having no saving grace
一无所长 have no special skill
一无所有 not own a thing in the world; not have a thing to one's name
一无所知 know nothing about; not have the least inkling of; be absolutely ignorant of
一五一十 (narrate) systematically and in full detail
一误再误 ① make one error after another; keep on making mistakes ② make things worse by repeated delays
一息尚存 so long as one still has a breath left; till one's last gasp
一线员工 worker at the production line
一厢情愿 one-sided wish; one's own wishful thinking
一笑置之 dismiss with a laugh (or smile); laugh off
一泻千里 ①(of a river) rush down a thousand *li*—flow powerfully ②(of a writer's style) bold and flowing
一心为公 devote oneself to the public interests; be wholehearted for the public interests
一心一德 be of one heart and one mind; be dedicated to the same cause
一心一意 heart and soul; whole-heartedly
一星半点 a tiny bit; a very small amount
一言不发 not say (or utter) a word; keep one's mouth shut
一言难尽 it's hard to explain in a few words; it's a long story
一言为定 that's settled then
一氧化碳 carbon monoxide
一氧化物 monoxide
一叶扁舟 a tiny boat; a skiff; a small rowboat
一叶知秋 the falling of one leaf heralds the autumn; a small sign can indicate a great trend

一衣带水 a narrow strip of water
一意孤行 cling obstinately to one's course; act wilfully; insist on having one's own way
一应俱全 everything needed is there
一拥而上 rush up in a crowd
一语道破 lay bare the truth with one remark; hit the nail on the head
一语破的 hit the mark with a single comment
一语双关 a single phrase with a double meaning
一元方程 equation with one unknown
一张一弛 tension alternating with relaxation
一朝一夕 in one morning or evening; overnight
一针见血 pierce to the truth with one pertinent remark; hit the nail on the head
一枕黄粱 Golden Millet Dream—a brief dream (or delusion) of grandeur
一知半解 have a smattering of knowledge; have scanty (or half-baked) knowledge
一纸空文 a mere scrap of paper; empty words on a sheet of paper
一掷千金 stake a thousand pieces of gold on one throw—throw away money like dirt; spend money like water
一柱擎天 one pillar supporting the sky—shouldering the heavy responsibility of high office
一专多能 versatile talents who have their own specialities to master many skills while specializing in one; be expert in one thing and good at many
一字褒贬 one word clearly expressing praise or censure—a strict, deliberate choice of words
一字千金 each word worth a thousand pieces of gold—a highly finished literary product
一字一板 (speak) calmly and clearly
一走了之 pack off and leave an obligation
一报还一报 retribution paid out in kind
一鼻孔出气 breathe through the same nostrils—sing the same tune
一锤子买卖 "once-for-all" deal—the one and only business deal to be made with sb (from which the greatest possible advantage is to be derived)
一次性变动 once-and-for-all change
一次性筷子 throwaway chopsticks; disposable chopsticks
一次性收入 lump-sum payment
一次用包装 non-returnable container
一次用货品 single-use goods
一分钟小说 one-minute story
一夫多妻制 polygyny; polygamy
一夫一妻制 monogyny; monogamy
一竿子到底 carry (a task or directive) right down to the grass-roots level; carry sth

through to the end

一个心眼儿 ①have one's heart set on sth;devotedly;stubbornly ②be of one mind

一棍子打死 knock sb down at one stroke;finish off with one blow;completely negate

一环扣一环 one ring linked with another—a closely linked succession

一揽子计划 package program;total plans

一揽子价格 blanket price;flat price;package price

一揽子建议 package proposal

一揽子交易 package deal

一浪接一浪 wave upon wave

一门式服务 one-stop service

一妻多夫制 polyandry

一去不复返 gone never to return;gone for ever

一体化经营 unified operation; coordinated management;do things in unison and comprehensively;operate holistically with every aspect well considered

一条龙服务 connected sequence; coordinated process;one package service

一退六二五 evade (or deny) all responsibility

一碗水端平 hold a bowl of water level—be impartial

一问三不知 say "I don't know" to every question—not know a thing;be entirely ignorant

一物降一物 one thing conquers another;everything has its superior

一言抄百总 to make a long story short;in a word;in short;in brief

一言以蔽之 in a nutshell;sum up in a word

一元化管理 unified management

一站式服务 one-stop service

一站式购物 one-stop shopping

一支笔审批 one-chop approval

一字长蛇阵 single-line battle array

一步一个脚印 every step leaves its print—work steadily and make solid progress

一次成像照片 Polaroid picture

一动不如一静 to stay put is better than to move (said when questioning the necessity of a move)

一分钱一分货 the higher the price,the better the quality;what price,what goods

一客不烦二主 one guest should not bother two hosts (said when asking an additional favour of sb)

一块石头落地 the mind is at last set at rest

一蟹不如一蟹 each crab is smaller than the one before—each one is worse than the last

一不做,二不休 carry it through,whatever the consequences;in for a penny,in for a pound

一传十,十传百 (of news) spread from one to ten,and from ten to a hundred—pass quickly from mouth to mouth;get around quickly

一而再,再而三 again and again; time and again;repeatedly

一回生,二回熟 strangers at the first meeting,friends at the second;ill at ease the first time,at home the second;difficult the first time,easy the second

一场秋雨一场寒 a spell of autumn rain,and a spell of cold

一朝天子一朝臣 every new sovereign brings his own courtiers—a new chief brings in new aides

一次使用信用证 straight letter of credit

一次性解决问题 solve the problem once and for all

一寸光阴一寸金 time is gold;time is precious

一个巴掌拍不响 one hand alone can't clap—it takes two to make a quarrel

一个萝卜一个坑 one radish,one hole—①each has his own task,and nobody is dispensable ②steady and reliable

一级方程式赛车 Formula One (car racing)

一口吃不成胖子 you can't get fat on one mouthful—you must keep at it

一慢二看三通过 first slow down,then look around,and then cross (rhyme to remind drivers of safety when crossing an intersection)

一年之计在于春 the whole year's work depends on a good start in spring

一失足成千古恨 one false step brings everlasting grief;a single slip may cause lasting sorrow;a moment's error can bring a lifelong regret

一条道儿跑到黑 follow one road until it's dark—cling obstinately to one course

一夜夫妻百夜恩 husband and wife for one night,love lingers on for a hundred nights

一把钥匙开一把锁 open different locks with different keys—use different methods to solve different problems

一波未平,一波又起 hardly has one wave subsided when another rises—one trouble follows another

一不怕苦,二不怕死 fear neither hardship nor death

一方有难,八方支援 When disaster strikes,help comes from all quarters.

一夫当关,万夫莫开 if one man guards the pass,ten thousand cannot get through

一犬吠影,百犬吠声 when one dog barks at a shadow a hundred others join in—blindly follow others

一人得道,鸡犬升天 when a man attains the Tao,even his pets ascend to heaven—when a man gets to the top,all his friends and relations get there with him

一日不见,如隔三秋 one day apart seems like three years—miss sb very much

一日为师,终身为父 a teacher for a day is a father for a lifetime

一手交钱,一手交货 give me the case, and I'll give you the goods;COD (cash on delivery)

一言既出,驷马难追 a word once spoken cannot be taken back even by a team of four horses—what is said cannot be unsaid

一要吃饭,二要建设 first, feed the people; and second, build the country

一叶障目,不见泰山 a leaf before the eye shuts out Mount Tai—have one's view of the important overshadowed by the trivial

一着不慎,满盘皆输 one careless move and the whole game is lost

一瓶子不响,半瓶子晃荡 the half-filled bottle sloshes, the full bottle makes no sound—the dabbler in knowledge chatters away, the wise man stays silent

一朝被蛇咬,十年怕井绳 once bitten by a snake, one shies at coiled rope for ten years; once bitten, twice shy

伊 [yī]

Ⅰ 助 *used before a phrase*:伊谁之力? To whom should the credit go? Ⅱ 代 he;she

伊人 that person (referring esp. to a woman)

伊始 beginning

伊蚊 yellow-fever mosquito

伊甸园 the Garden of Eden;paradise

伊斯兰教 Islam;Islamism

伊斯兰教历 the Moslem Calendar

伊斯兰教徒 Moslem

衣 [yī]

名 ① clothing; clothes; garment; dress ② coating; covering ③ afterbirth

衣胞 (human) afterbirth

衣钵 a Buddhist monk's mantle and alms bowl which he hands down to his favourite disciple;legacy

衣橱 wardrobe

衣兜 pocket

衣蛾 casemaking clothes moth

衣分 ginning outturn;gin turnout

衣服 clothing;clothes

衣钩 clothes hook

衣冠 hat and clothes;dress

衣柜 wardrobe

衣架 ① coat hanger; clothes-rack ② clothes tree;clothes stand

衣襟 the front of a Chinese jacket

衣料 material for clothing;dress material

衣领 collar

衣衾 burial clothes

衣衫 clothes

衣裳 clothing;clothes

衣饰 dress and personal adornment;dress

衣物 clothing and other articles of daily use

衣箱 trunk;suitcase

衣鱼 silverfish;fish moth;bookworm

衣装 ①dress;attire ②clothes and luggage

衣着 clothing,headgear and footwear

衣冠冢 a tomb containing personal effects of the deceased, whose remains are either missing or buried elsewhere

衣帽架 clothes tree;clothes stand

衣帽间 cloakroom

衣不蔽体 be dressed in rags;have nothing but rags on one's back

衣冠楚楚 be immaculately dressed

衣冠禽兽 a beast in human clothing;brute

衣锦还乡 go back to one's old home in silken robes

衣衫褴褛 shabbily dressed; out at elbows; in rags

衣食住行 food, clothing, shelter and transportation; basic necessities of life; clothing, shelter and transportation

衣食足而知荣辱 when food and clothing are enough, men have a sense of honour and shame

医 [yī]

Ⅰ 名 ①doctor (of medicine);medical practitioner ② medical science; medical service; medicine Ⅱ 动 treat;cure;heal

医道 art of healing; medical knowledge; physician's skill

医德 medical ethics; professional morality of medical workers

医风 style of work,medical practice

医改 reform of the medicare system

医护 give medical treatment and nursing

医家 physician

医经 ancient Chinese medical classics

医科 medical courses in general;medicine

医理 principles of medical science; medical knowledge

医疗 medical treatment

医密 confidentiality of medical records

医生 doctor;medical man

医师 (qualified) doctor

医士 practitioner with secondary medical school education

医书 medical book

医术 medical skill;art of healing

医坛 medical circle

医托 doctor's decoy

医务 medical matters

医学 medical science;medicine

医药 medicine

医院 hospital

医治 cure;treat;heal

医嘱 doctor's advice (*or* orders)

医助 assistant doctor (in the army)

医疗队 medical team
医疗站 medical station;health centre
医务室 grassroots health clinic，often small and equipped with basic facilities
医务所 health clinic
医学界 medical community
医疗保险 medical insurance
医疗事故 malpractice;therapeutical accident
医疗体育 medico-athletics
医学文献 medical literature
医学学士 Bachelor of Medicine
医学遗产 medical heritage
医助自杀 doctor-assisted suicide;physician-assisted suicide
医疗辐射学 atomic (*or* radiological) medicine
医务工作者 medical worker;medic
医学科学院 academy of medical sciences
医疗保险制度 medical insurance system
医疗事故损害赔偿 medical malpractice compensation

依 〔yī〕
Ⅰ 劲 ①depend on;rely on;count on;look to ②obey;comply with;listen to;yield to Ⅱ 介 according to;in the light of;judging by;on the basis of
依傍 ①depend on;rely on ②imitate;model oneself on
依次 in proper order;successively
依从 comply with;yield to
依存 depend on sb or sth for existence
依法 according to law;in conformity with legal provisions;in accordance with the law
依附 depend on;attach oneself to;become an appendage to
依借 use;turn to advantage;draw on
依旧 as before;still
依据 ①according to;in the light of;on the basis of;judging by ②basis;foundation
依靠 ①rely on;depend on ②sth to fall back on;support;backing
依赖 rely on;be dependent on
依恋 be reluctant to leave;feel regret at parting from
依凭 rely on;depend on
依然 still;as before
依顺 be obedient
依随 agree to;yield to;comply with
依托 ①rely on;depend on ②support;prop;backing
依偎 snuggle up to;lean close to
依稀 vaguely;dimly
依循 follow;abide by
依依 ①luxuriant ②reluctant to part
依允 assent;consent
依仗 count on;rely on
依照 according to;in accordance with;in the light of

依此类推 the rest may be inferred;and so on and so forth
依法惩办 punish according to law
依法治国 administer (*or* govern) the country according to law;rule the country by law
依然故我 I'm still my same old self;I'm just the same as before
依然如故 remain as before;remain the same
依山傍水 at the foot of a hill and beside a stream
依稀可见 faintly visible
依依不舍 be reluctant to part;cannot bear to part
依样画葫芦 draw a gourd according to the model—copy mechanically

祎 〔yī〕
形 glorious;fine

咿 〔yī〕
咿唔 recite (*or* intone) in reading
咿呀 ①squeak;creak ②prattle;babble

猗 〔yī〕
Ⅰ 助 (*often used at the end of a sentence with similar function as* 啊)：河水清且涟漪。The river is clear and rippling. Ⅱ 叹 (*used for praise*)：猗欤盛哉！Magnificent! (*or* Superb!)

揖 〔yī〕
劲 (make a) bow with hands clasped

yí（í）

匜 〔yí〕
名 ladle shaped like a gourd;gourd-shaped ladle

仪 〔yí〕
Ⅰ 名 ①appearance;bearing;looks ②ceremony;rite;protocol ③present;gift ④apparatus;instrument Ⅱ 劲 admire;yearn for;look forward to
仪表 ①appearance;bearing ②meter
仪器 instrument;apparatus
仪容 looks;appearance
仪式 ceremony;rite;function
仪态 bearing;deportment
仪仗 ①insignia carried before the emperor ②flags,weapons,etc. carried by a guard of honour
仪仗队 honour guard;guard of honour
仪表堂堂 dignified in appearance;impressive-looking
仪态万方 (of a beauty) appear in all her glory

圯 〔yí〕
名 bridge

夷 〔yí〕
Ⅰ 形 level;smooth;safe Ⅱ 劲 ①raze;level (to the ground) ② exterminate;wipe out Ⅲ 名 ①name for ancient tribes in the east of China;barbarians ②foreign country;foreigner

夷族 extermination of an entire family
夷为平地 level to the ground;raze

迤 [yí]
➡ yǐ
◇ 逶迤 winding;meandering

饴 [yí]
名 maltose
饴糖 maltose;malt sugar
饴糖果 barley sugar;barley candy

怡 [yí]
形 happy;joyful;cheerful
怡和 affable;genial
怡然 happy and contented
怡神 soothe the spirit
怡悦 happy;joyous
怡情悦性 cheer the heart and compose the mind
怡然自得 be happy and pleased with oneself; feel a glow of happiness
怡神养性 soothe one's spirit and nourish one's nature
怡声下气 speak with a pleasing voice and in a respectful and submissive manner

宜 [yí]
I 形 suitable;appropriate;desirable;fitting II 动 should;ought to III 副 of course;certainly;with no doubt
宜人 pleasant;delightful
宜于 be suitable for

荑 [yí]
动 clear the fields of weeds;weed ➡ tí

咦 [yí]
叹 (*indicating surprise*) well;why

贻 [yí]
动 ①send sb a gift;make sb a present of sth ②bequeath;leave behind;hand down
贻贝 mussel
贻害 leave a legacy of trouble
贻患 leave a legacy of trouble
贻误 mislead bungle;spoil disrupt
贻训 teachings of the deceased
贻赠 make a gift of sth;present
贻害无穷 entail untold troubles;involve endless trouble
贻人口实 provide one's critics with a handle; give occasion for talk
贻误战机 bungle the chance of winning a battle;forfeit a chance for combat
贻笑大方 make a laughingstock of oneself before experts;incur the ridicule of experts

姨 [yí]
名 ①one's mother's sister; aunt ②one's wife's sister;sister-in-law
姨表 the relationship between the children of sisters (*or* maternal cousins);cousinship
姨夫 the husband of mother's sister (*or* one's maternal aunt);uncle
姨妈 (married) maternal aunt;aunt
姨母 (married) maternal aunt;aunt
姨娘 ①a term of address for father's concubine ②(married) maternal aunt;aunt
姨丈 husband of one's maternal aunt;uncle
姨姥姥 sister of one's maternal grandmother; great-aunt
姨奶奶 ①sister of one's paternal grandmother;great-aunt ②concubine
姨太太 concubine

胰 [yí]
名 pancreas
胰岛 pancreas islet
胰酶 pancreatin
胰腺 pancreas
胰液 pancreatic juice
胰皂 soap
胰子 ①pancreas (of pigs,sheep,etc.) ②soap
胰岛素 insulin
胰腺炎 pancreatitis
胰脂酶 pancreatic lipase;steapsin
胰蛋白酶 trypsin
胰淀粉酶 amylopsin

宧 [yí]
名 northeast corner of a room

蛇 [yí]
➡ shé
◇ 虚与委蛇 deal with sb courteously but without sincerity; pretend politeness and compliance

移 [yí]
动 ①move;remove;divert;shift ②change; alter;transform
移调 transposition
移动 move;shift
移防 be shifted elsewhere for garrison duty
移行 [yíháng] divide a word with a hyphen at the end of a line
移交 ①turn over;transfer;deliver into sb's custody ②hand over one's job to a successor
移解 transfer a prisoner from one place to another under escort
移居 move one's residence;migrate
移苗 transplant seedlings
移民 ①migrate;emigrate (*or* immigrate) ②emigrant;immigrant
移师 move the troops
移时 after a short while
移送 turn over (suspects,legal files,etc.) to (appropriate judicial organs)
移位 shift
移徙 move;migrate
移项 transposition
移易 change;alter;transform
移用 divert from one use to another
移栽 transplant
移植 ① transplant ② transplant; graft ③

Y

adapt; transfer
移动 PC mobile PC
移民点 settlement
移民法 immigration laws
移民局 immigration service (*or* office)
移位键 shift key
移相器 phase shifter
移动电话 cellular telephone; mobile phone; mobile telephone
移动基期 shifting base period
移动均衡 moving equilibrium
移动通信 mobile communications
移风易俗 change prevailing habits and customs; transform outmoded habits and customs; reform the ways and manners of the people
移花接木 graft one twig on another—stealthily substitute one thing for another
移民签证 immigrant visa
移山倒海 move mountains and drain seas—exercise magic powers; transform nature
移天换日 move the sky and change the sun—perpetrate a gigantic fraud
移樽就教 take one's wine cup and go to sb's table to ask his advice—go to sb for advice
移动存储器 mobile storage
移动因特网 mobile Internet
移动交换中心 mobile switching centre (MSC)
移动加权平均法 moving weighted average method
移动电话双向收费 two-way charges for cellular phones

痍 [yí]
名 wound; trauma

遗 [yí]
I 动 ①lose ②omit; forget ③leave behind; keep back; stint ④ leave behind at one's death; bequeath; hand down ⑤ (involuntary) discharge II 名 sth lost ⇒ wèi
遗案 unsolved case; cases left over
遗笔 writings left behind by the deceased
遗产 legacy; inheritance; heritage
遗传 heredity; inheritance
遗存 ①be left over; be handed down ②remnants; remains
遗毒 evil legacy; harmful tradition; pernicious influence
遗范 the example set by the deceased
遗风 customs which have been handed down
遗稿 a manuscript left unpublished by the author at his death; a posthumous manuscript
遗孤 orphan
遗骨 remains (of the dead)
遗骸 remains (of the dead)
遗害 leave a legacy of trouble
遗憾 regret; pity
遗恨 eternal regret

遗患 leave a legacy of trouble
遗祸 leave a legacy of trouble
遗迹 historical remains; traces; vestiges
遗教 teachings of the deceased
遗精 (seminal) emission
遗老 ①a surviving adherent of a former dynasty; an old fogy; an old diehard ②old people who have witnessed big social changes
遗留 leave over; hand down
遗漏 omit; leave out
遗命 last will; final charge
遗墨 letters, manuscripts, scrolls of painting or calligraphy, etc. left behind by the deceased
遗尿 enuresis; bed-wetting
遗篇 writings left behind by the deceased
遗弃 ①abandon; forsake; desert; walk out on ②leave behind; cast away; abandon
遗容 ①the looks of the deceased ②a portrait of the deceased
遗撒 litter and leak
遗少 a young man with the mentality of an old fogy; a young diehard
遗失 lose
遗矢 empty one's bowels; defecate
遗事 ①incidents of past ages ②deeds of those now dead
遗书 ① surviving works; posthumous works; collected writings published after the author's death ②a letter (*or* note) left by one immediately before death (*or* suicide) ③lost books
遗属 members of the deceased's family; family dependants of the deceased
遗孀 widow; relict
遗体 remains (of the dead)
遗蜕 remains (esp. of a Taoist priest)
遗忘 forget
遗闻 tales of old times
遗物 ①things left behind by the deceased ②relic
遗像 a portrait of the deceased
遗训 teachings of the deceased
遗言 words of the deceased; (a person's) last words
遗业 work left unfinished by one's predecessor or ancestor
遗愿 unfulfilled wish of the deceased; last wish; behest
遗赠 bequeath
遗诏 testamentary edict left by a dying emperor
遗照 a photograph of the deceased
遗址 site (where sth was)
遗志 unfulfilled wish; behest; work bequeathed by the deceased
遗嘱 testament; will; dying words

遗著 posthumous work (of an author)
遗族 family of the deceased
遗作 posthumous work (of art or literature)
遗产税 inheritance tax; succession duty
遗传病 hereditary disease
遗传学 genetics
遗腹子 a posthumous child
遗忘症 amnesia
遗臭万年 leave a name that will stink to eternity; go down in history as a byword for infamy
遗传工程 genetic engineering
遗传基因 genetic genes
遗传密码 genetic code
遗传信息 hereditary (or genetic) information
遗传学家 geneticist
遗传因子 genetic factor
遗老遗少 old fogies and young diehards; diehards old and young
遗嘱继承 inherit by will
遗产承受人 legatee
遗传字母表 genetic alphabet
遗传指纹鉴别 genetic fingerprinting

颐 [yí] I 名 chin; cheek II 动 keep fit; take good care of one's health; preserve
颐养 keep fit; take good care of oneself
颐和园 the Summer Palace (in Beijing)
颐神养性 preserve one's vital energy
颐指气使 order people about by gestures; be insufferably arrogant

疑 [yí] I 动 doubt; disbelieve; suspect II 形 doubtful; suspicious; uncertain
疑案 doubtful (or disputed) case; an open question; mystery
疑兵 troops deployed to mislead the enemy; deceptive deployment (of soldiers)
疑病 hypochondriasis
疑存 existence doubtful
疑点 doubtful (or questionable) point; an uncertain (or unclear) point
疑窦 cause for suspicion; suspicion
疑犯 criminal suspect
疑惑 feel uncertain; not be convinced
疑忌 be suspicious and jealous of
疑惧 apprehensions; misgivings
疑虑 misgivings; doubts
疑难 difficult; knotty
疑念 suspicions; doubts
疑事 suspicious matter
疑似 doubtful
疑团 doubts and suspicions
疑问 query; question; doubt
疑心 suspicion
疑凶 murderer suspect
疑义 doubt; doubtful point

疑云 misgivings or suspicions clouding one's mind
疑阵 deceptive battle array to mislead the enemy; stratagem
疑问句 interrogative sentence
疑心病 a suspicious frame of mind
疑难杂症 cases (of illness) that are both hard to diagnose and to cure; difficult and complicated problems
疑神疑鬼 be terribly suspicious; be even afraid of one's own shadow
疑心生暗鬼 suspicions create fantastic fears

簃 [yí] 名 small cabin (or hut) beside a storeyed building (or a pavilion)

彝 [yí] 名 ①wine vessel ②law; rule ③Yi nationality
彝典 common code
彝器 sacrificial vessel
彝准 common law

yǐ(ǐ)

乙 [yǐ] I 数 second II 代 used for an unspecified person or thing
乙胺 ethylamine; aminoethane
乙苯 ethylbenzene; phenylethane
乙醇 ethyl alcohol; ethanol; alcohol
乙等 second grade; Grade B
乙方 the second party
乙醚 ether
乙醛 acetaldehyde; ethanal
乙炔 acetylene; ethyne
乙烷 ethane
乙烯 ethylene
乙酰 acetyl
乙夜 the second watch (the second of the five two-hour periods into which the night was formerly divided, corresponding to around 10 p.m.)
乙烯基 vinyl
乙酰基 the acetyl group
乙级联赛 minor league
乙酰唑胺 acetazolamide; diamox
乙型肝炎 hepatitis B; viral hepatitis type B
乙种粒子 beta particle
乙种射线 beta ray
乙状结肠 sigmoid; sigmoid colon
乙酰水杨酸 acetylsalicylic acid; aspirin
乙型超声波 B-mode ultrasound

已 [yǐ] I 动 stop; halt; cease; end II 副 ①already ②thereafter; later on; afterwards ③too; excessively
已而 ①then; afterwards ②that's all; simply that; no more

Y

已故 deceased;late
已极 to the utmost;in the extreme
已经 already
已然 be already so;have already become a fact
已往 before;previously;in the past
已知 known number
已决犯 convicted prisoner;convict
已知数 known number

以 [yǐ]
I 介 ①with;by means of ②according to; in order of ③because of;for;by ④at (a certain time);at;on (a fixed date) ⑤(*used before words of locality to indicate the limits of time, place, direction or number*):松花江以南 south of the Songhua River Ⅱ 连 ① and;as well as ②in order to;so as to
以便 so that;in order to;so as to;with the aim of;for the purpose of
以此 for this reason;on this account
以次 ①in proper order;in turn ②the following
以后 after;afterwards;later;hereafter
以及 as well as;along with;and
以近 up to
以来 since
以免 in order to avoid;so as not to;lest
以内 within;less than
以期 in the hope of
以前 before;formerly;previously
以求 in the hope of;in an attempt to
以上 ①more than;over;above ②the above; the foregoing;the above-mentioned
以太 ether
以外 beyond;outside;other than
以往 before;formerly;in the past
以为 think;believe;consider
以…为… take... as... ;regard... as...
以下 ①below;under ②the following;hereafter
以远 beyond
以至 down to;up to
以致 so that;with the result that;consequently;as a result
以资 as a means of
以…告终 end in
以…名义 in the name of
以太网 Ethernet
以远权 the right to extend a flying route;the right to fly beyond designated points
以至于 to such an extent as to... ;so... that...
以暴易暴 replace one tyranny by another
以备不虞 be prepared for any contingency
以博一笑 in order to elicit a smile;so as to amuse sb
以诚相待 treat people with sincerity
以词害意 let the words interfere with the sense

以此为戒 take this as a lesson;take warning from this
以次充好 use the bad to take place of the good;use the inferior stuff rather than quality goods
以大欺小 the strong bullies the weak
以党代政 substitution of the Party for the government
以德报怨 return good for evil;repay evil with good;requite ingratitude with kindness
以德服人 win people by virtue;overcome people with virtue
以德治国 run (*or* govern) the country by the rule of virtue
以点带面 fan out from point to area;use the experience of selected units to promote work in the entire area
以毒攻毒 fight poison with poison;use poison as an antidote for poison
以讹传讹 incorrectly relay an erroneous message (so that it becomes increasingly distorted);spread an error (*or* a falsehood)
以耳代目 rely upon hearsay instead of seeing for oneself
以罚代刑 substitute administrative for legal penalties;mete out administrative penalties instead of prosecuting
以法治国 govern (*or* run) the country according to law
以防万一 be prepared for all contingencies;be ready for any eventuality
以丰补歉 store up in fat years to make up for lean ones;have high-yield areas help low-yield areas
以丰养廉 foster clean government by giving better pay to civil servants
以副养农 support agriculture with non-agricultural (*or* sideline) production
以干带学 use practical experience to promote learning
以工补农 use industry to supplement (*or* subsidize) agriculture;have industry help agriculture
以工代干 when a worker does a cadre's job
以工代赈 exchange relief for work;relief-in-exchange-for-work program;provide work as a form of relief
以攻为守 use attack as a means of defence;attack in order to defend
以古非今 disparage the present by extolling the past
以寡敌众 pit few against many;fight against heavy odds
以观后效 (lighten a punishment and) see how the offender behaves
以己度人 judge others by oneself;measure others' corn with one's own bushel

以假充真 pass fake imitations for genuine; pass off the false as genuine

以假乱真 mix the false with the true; mix the spurious with the genuine

以解倒悬 so as to relieve sb's distress

以进养出 promote exports by attracting foreign investment (through various forms of cooperation with foreign businessmen)

以儆效尤 to warn others against following a bad example; as a warning to others

以旧换新 trade in the old one for a new one

以泪洗面 have a tearful face; wear a woebegone look

以蠡测海 measure the sea with an oyster shell—make an appraisal in the light of limited knowledge

以礼相待 treat sb with due respect

以理服人 convince by reasoning

以力服人 force people to submit; dominate others by force

以邻为壑 use one's neighbour's field as a drain—shift one's troubles onto others

以卵击石 throw an egg against a rock—court defeat by fighting against overwhelming odds

以貌取人 judge people solely by their appearance

以偏概全 take a part for the whole; draw a conclusion without an overall assessments of sth or sb

以强凌弱 oppress the weak by sheer strength

以屈求伸 bend in order to straighten up—retreat in order to advance; make concessions to gain advantages

以权代法 handle a case by using one's power instead of using legal channels (or proceedings)

以权谋私 influence peddling; exploit one's position and power to seek personal gain; abuse one's power for personal gains; seek personal gain by abusing one's position and authority

以权压法 use power to suppress law

以权易法 use the power of one's position to change the law

以人为本 people oriented; people foremost

以商养教 support education through doing business; support education with profits from a business; support cultural activities with profits from a business

以身试法 violate (or defy) the law; defy (or challenge) the law personally

以身相许 (of a girl) pledge to marry sb

以身殉职 die at one's post; die in harness; die on duty; die a martyr at one's post

以身作则 set a good example with one's own conduct; set an example

以售其奸 in order to carry out an evil plot; to achieve a treacherous purpose

以税代利 (of a state enterprise) replace profit delivery to the state by taxation; substitute taxation for profit delivery to the state

以汤沃雪 melting snow with hot water—easily done

以汤止沸 trying to stop water from boiling by adding boiling water to it—an ineffective measure

以退为进 retreat in order to advance; make concessions in order to gain advantages

以文会友 make friends through literary activities

以销定产 fix production quota on the basis of sales or how much has been sold

以虚带实 have political and ideological work promote the professional work

以一当十 pit one against ten

以逸待劳 wait at one's ease for an exhausted enemy

以怨报德 return evil for good; repay good with evil; requite kindness with ingratitude; bite the hand that feeds one

以正视听 in order to ensure a correct understanding of the facts; so as to set the record straight; so as to ensure correct understanding of the facts

以直报怨 meet resentment with upright dealing

以大局为重 set store by the overall situation (or interests)

以谋略制胜 outmaneuver

以色列议会 Knesset

以失败告终 end in a fiasco

以不变应万变 meet all changes by remaining unchanged—cope with a constantly changing situation by sticking to a fixed principle or policy

以私人的身份 in a private capacity

以经济建设为中心 focus on the central task of economic construction; take economic development as the central task; centre (or focus) on economic development

以其昏昏,使人昭昭 try to enlighten others while in darkness oneself

以眼还眼,以牙还牙 an eye for an eye and a tooth for a tooth

以子之矛,攻子之盾 set a person's own spear against his own shield—refute sb with his own argument

以小人之心,度君子之腹 gauge the heart of a gentleman with one's own mean measure

以其人之道,还治其人之身 deal with a man as he deals with you; pay sb back in his own coin

钇 [yǐ]
〈名〉 yttrium (Y)
钇合金 yttrium alloy

苡 [yǐ]
〈名〉 Job's tears
苡米 seed of Job's tears
苡仁 seed of Job's tears

尾 [yǐ]
〈名〉 ①hairs on a horsetail ②spikelets on a cricket's tail ➡wěi

矣 [yǐ]
〈助〉 ①(*used at the end of a sentence like* 了):由来久矣。It dated way back. ②(*used in exclamation*)how;what

迤 [yǐ]
〈动〉 stretch (*or* extend) towards ➡yí
迤逦 winding;tortuous;meandering

蚁 [yǐ]
〈名〉 ant
蚁巢 ant nest
蚁后 queen (of an ant colony);ant queen
蚁丘 ant hill
蚁行感 formication

舣 [yǐ]
〈动〉 pull in a boat to shore

醯 [yǐ]
〈名〉 ①wine made of broomcorn millet ②thin gruel ③elixir
醯剂 elixir

倚 [yǐ]
Ⅰ〈动〉 ①lean on (*or* against);rest on (*or* against) ②rely on;depend on;count on Ⅱ〈形〉 biased;prejudiced;partial
倚傍 ①depend on;rely on ②imitate;model oneself on
倚靠 ① lean on (*or* against);rest on (*or* against) ② rely on;depend on;sth to fall back on;support;backing
倚赖 rely on;be dependent on
倚音 appoggiatura
倚仗 rely on;count on
倚重 rely heavily on sb's service
倚财仗势 exploit one's wealth and power
倚官仗势 rely on one's power and position; count on one's powerful connections; take advantage of one's power and position; count on one's powerful connections
倚老卖老 take advantage of one's seniority (*or* old age) (to ignore manners, regulations,etc.);flaunt one's seniority
倚马可待 can write at the side of a horse—can write very fast
倚马千言 dash off a thousand words at the side of a horse—write with great facility
倚门而望 lean on the door and gaze into the distance
倚势欺人 take advantage of one's position to bully people

倚树而立 stand leaning against a tree

椅 [yǐ]
〈名〉 chair
椅背 the back of a chair
椅垫 chair cushion
椅披 a colourful silk chair cover
椅套 a slipcover for a chair
椅子 chair
椅子顶 balancing on a pyramid of chairs

yì(ì)

弋 [yì]
Ⅰ〈动〉 shoot with a retrievable arrow with a string attached to it Ⅱ〈名〉 such retrievable arrow

亿 [yì]
〈数〉 ①hundred million ②hundred thousand
亿万 hundreds of millions;millions upon millions
亿万富翁 billionaire;multi-millionaire
亿万斯年 (for) billions of years;time without end;eternity

义 [yì]
Ⅰ〈名〉 ① justice; righteousness ② friendly feeling or affection involved in human ties or relationship ③ meaning; sense; significance Ⅱ〈形〉 ①righteous;equitable;fair ②adopted; adoptive ③artificial;false
义兵 a righteous army
义齿 false tooth;artificial tooth
义地 cemetery
义发 wig
义愤 righteous indignation;moral indignation
义父 adoptive father
义工 volunteer
义举 a magnanimous act undertaken for the public good;an undertaking in public interests
义捐 donations for public welfare
义理 ①reason and good sense ②argumentation (of a speech or essay)
义卖 a sale of goods for charity or other worthy causes;(charity) bazaar
义母 adoptive mother
义女 adopted daughter;foster daughter
义拍 charitable auction;fund-raising auction
义旗 the banner of an army fighting a just war;banner of righteousness
义气 code of brotherhood;personal loyalty
义犬 a faithful dog
义赛 benefit competition
义师 an army fighting a just war;a righteous army
义士 a high-minded (*or* chivalrous) person;a person who upholds justice; a righteous man
义手 artificial hand

义素 sememe
义位 glosseme
义务 ①duty; obligation ②volunteer; voluntary
义项 senses of a dictionary entry
义学 (in former times) a private or community run school charging no tuition; free school
义演 benefit show; variety show; variety performance
义诊 (of doctors) give free outpatient service to raise funds for charity or other worthy causes; benefit outpatient service
义肢 artificial limb
义冢 (in former times) a burial ground for the remains of unidentified persons
义子 adopted son
义务兵 conscripted army; compulsory serviceman
义勇军 army of volunteers; volunteers
义不容辞 be duty-bound; have an unshirkable duty
义愤填膺 be filled with indignation
义无反顾 honour permits no turning back; be duty-bound not to turn back
义务教育 compulsory education; mandatory education
义务劳动 voluntary labour; volunteer labour
义务年限 obligatory term
义务献血 blood donation
义务植树 voluntary tree planting; voluntary tree afforestation
义形于色 with righteous indignation written on one's face
义正词严 speak out sternly from a sense of justice; speak with the force of justice
义和团运动 the Yihetuan Movement
义务兵役制 compulsory military service; conscription
义务植树运动 voluntary afforestation campaign
义勇军进行曲 March of the Volunteers (the national anthem of the People's Republic of China)

艺 [yì]
〈名〉①skill; technique ②art ③norm; criterion; limit
艺妓 geisha (in Japan)
艺林 the world of art; art circles
艺龄 length of sb's stage career
艺名 stage name (of an actor or actress)
艺能 mastery of a skill or technique; technical ability; skill
艺人 ①actor (or entertainer) (in local drama, storytelling, acrobatics, etc.) ② artisan; handicraftsman
艺术 ①art ②skill; art; craft ③ conforming to good taste
艺坛 art circles
艺徒 apprentice
艺员 actor or actress
艺苑 the realm of art and literature; art and literary circles
艺术家 artist
艺术节 arts festival
艺术界 art circles
艺术片 movie placing emphasis on artistic quality
艺术品 work of art
艺术团 art ensemble; art troupe
艺术性 artistic quality; artistry
艺术风格 artistic style
艺术构思 artistic conception
艺术化妆 artistic make-up
艺术体操 sports rhythmic gymnastics
艺术造型 artistic design
艺术造诣 artistic attainments
艺术指导 art director
艺高人胆大 boldness of execution stems from superb skill

刈 [yì]
〈动〉mow; cut down
刈草 mow grass
刈除 cut off; root out; eradicate
刈麦 cut wheat
刈草机 mowing machine; mower

艾 [yì]
〈动〉punish; penalize ⇒ ài

忆 [yì]
〈动〉recall; recollect
忆及 call to mind; remember
忆旧 recollect the past; recall the bygone days with nostalgia
忆起 call to mind; recall; remember
忆想 recall; recollect; call to mind
忆苦思甜 recall the sorrows of the past and savour the joys of the present; tell of one's sufferings in the old society and one's happiness in the new; contrast past misery with present happiness
忆昔抚今 recall the past and compare it with the present; reflect on the past in the light of the present

议 [yì]
Ⅰ〈名〉opinion; view; proposal Ⅱ〈动〉① discuss; deliberate; exchange views on; talk over ②comment; remark; debate
议案 proposal; motion
议程 agenda
议订 negotiate
议定 decide through consultation; agree on
议付 negotiation
议购 buy at negotiated prices
议和 negotiate peace; carry on peace negotia-

tions

议会 parliament；congress；legislative assembly

议价 ①negotiate a price ②negotiated price

议决 resolve after deliberation；pass a resolution

议论 comment；talk；discuss

议事 discuss official business

议题 item on the agenda；subject under discussion；topic for discussion

议席 seat in a legislative assembly

议销 sell at negotiated prices

议员 member of a legislative assembly；assemblyman；(in Great Britain) Member of Parliament (MP)；(in U.S.) Congressman；Congresswoman

议院 legislative assembly；parliament；congress

议长 speaker (of a legislative body)；president

议政 discuss affairs of government

议定书 protocol

议会制 parliamentarism

议论文 argumentative writing；argumentation

议而不决 discuss sth without reaching a decision；have a fruitless discussion

议会走廊 lobby

议价采购 negotiated purchase；purchase at negotiated price

议论纷纷 all sorts of comments；widespread comment

议事日程 agenda；order of the day

屹 [yì]

形 towering like a mountain peak

屹立 stand towering like a giant；stand erect

屹然 towering；majestic

屹立不动 stand rock-firm；immovable；standing mighty；stand stock-still

亦 [yì]

副 also；too；as well as

亦即 that is；i.e.；namely

亦且 moreover

亦步亦趋 ape sb at every step；imitate sb's every move；blindly follow suit

亦复如是 It's also the same.

亦工亦农 take part both in industry and agriculture

亦庄亦谐 serious and comical at the same time；seriocomic

异 [yì]

Ⅰ形 ① not the same；different；dissimilar ②strange；bizarre；unusual；extraordinary ③other；another Ⅱ动 ① surprise；astonish ② separate；part；divide

异邦 a foreign country

异步 asynchronous

异才 exceptional talents

异彩 extraordinary (or radiant) splendour

异常 ① unusual；abnormal ② extremely；exceedingly；particularly

异词 dissenting words

异地 a place far away from home；a strange land

异读 variant pronunciation

异端 heterodoxy；heresy

异国 a foreign country (or land)

异化 ①alienation ②dissimilation

异己 dissident；alien

异教 paganism；heathenism

异客 stranger

异类 ①foreign peoples ②a different class or species (of plants or animals)

异名 different name；variant name；synonym

异趣 difference of tastes and interests

异人 ①an extraordinary person (referring to a supernatural being or an immortal) ②another person

异日 some other day

异事 strange happening

异兽 strange animals；rare animals

异说 ① dissenting views；different views ② absurd remarks

异体 allosome

异同 ① similarities and differences ② objection；dissent

异外 unusual；exceptional

异位 dystopy；allotopia

异味 ①a rare delicacy ②a peculiar smell

异物 ① foreign matter；a foreign body ② a dead person；ghost ③a rare object

异乡 a foreign land；a strange land

异香 an unusually sweet smell；a rare perfume

异心 infidelity；disloyalty

异型 abnormal shape；allotype

异性 ①opposite sex ②different in nature

异姓 different family names

异言 dissenting words

异样 ①difference ②unusual；peculiar

异议 objection；dissent

异域 ① a foreign country ②an alien land；a strange land

异兆 strange omen

异质 alloplasm

异族 a different race (or nation)

异常期 anomalistic period

异构化 isomerization

异教徒 pagan；heathen

异体字 a variant form of a Chinese character

异形管 special pipe

异性恋 heterosex

异重流 density current

异地安置 resettle at a different place

异地结算 settlement between different cities

异端邪说 heresies；heretical beliefs；unorthodox opinions

异乎寻常 unusual;extraordinary
异花传粉 cross pollination
异花受精 allogamy;cross fertilization
异化作用 dissimilation
异军突起 a new force suddenly coming to the fore
异口同声 with one voice;in unison
异曲同工 different tunes sung with equal skill—different approaches but equally satisfactory results
异体受精 ① cross-fertilization ② allogamy;cross-fertilization
异想天开 indulge in the wildest fantasy;have a most fantastic idea
异形钢材 special-shaped steel
异性按摩 massage by the opposite sex;massage delivered by an opposite sex
异域情调 exotic romance
异步电动机 induction motor
异步发电机 asynchronous generator
异步计算机 asynchronous computer
异源多倍体 allopolyploid
异步传输方式 asynchronous transfer mode (ATM)
异步通信接口 asynchronous communication interface

抑 [yì] I 动 press down;suppress;restrain;curb II 连 ①or ②but;however ③besides;moreover ④then
抑或 or
抑且 also;moreover;furthermore
抑扬 (of sound) rise and fall;modulate
抑郁 depressed;despondent;gloomy
抑止 hold in check;hold back
抑制 ①restrain;control;check ②inhibition
抑郁症 depression
抑制剂 inhibitor
抑恶扬善 suppress the bad and commend the good
抑菌作用 bacteriostasis
抑强扶弱 curb the strong and help the weak;uphold the weak against the strong
抑扬顿挫 cadence;modulation in tone
抑制神经 inhibitory nerve

呓 [yì] 动 talk in one's sleep
呓语 ①talk in one's sleep ②crazy talk;ravings

邑 [yì] 名 ①city;town ②county
邑境 county area
邑宰 county magistrate

佚 [yì] I 动 ①live in seclusion (or solitude) ②be lost II 形 dissolute
佚文 ancient essay no longer extant

役 [yì] I 名 ① labour;service ② military service ③servant ④battle;campaign II 动 work;use as a servant
役畜 draught animal;beast of burden
役龄 enlistment age
役使 work (an animal);use

译 [yì] 动 translate;interpret
译本 translated version (of a book);translation
译笔 the quality (or style) of a translation
译成 translate into;turn into;put into
译电 ①encode (or encipher) a telegram ② decode (or decipher) a telegram
译稿 the manuscript of a translation
译解 decipher
译介 translate and write an introduction to (a book)
译码 decode;decipher
译名 a translated term (or name)
译配 translate and dub
译审 first-grade translator (or interpreter)
译述 translate (or render) freely
译文 translated text;translation
译音 transliteration
译员 interpreter
译者 translator
译制 dub (a film,etc.)
译注 translate and annotate
译著 translations
译作 translations
译电员 decoder;code clerk;cryptographer
译电组 code and cipher section
译码器 decoder;decipherer
译意风 simultaneous interpretation installation
译制片 a dubbed film

易 [yì] I 形 ①easy ②amiable II 动 ①change;alter ② exchange ③ despise;look down upon;underestimate
易货 barter
易经 *The Book of Changes*
易手 change hands
易碎 breakable;fragile
易于 be easy to
易辙 change one's course;strike out on a new path
易帜 change one's banner—change one's principles (or allegiance)
易爆物 explosive substance
易感者 susceptible person;susceptible
易拉罐 easy-open tin; pop-top; pull-top; flip-top
易燃物 combustibles;inflammables
易熔点 eutectic point

Y

易性癖 transsexualism
易装癖 transvestite
易货汇兑 barter exchange
易货经济 barter economy
易货贸易 barter;barter trade
易货协定 an agreement on the exchange of commodities;barter agreement
易熔合金 fusible alloy
易如反掌 as easy as turning one's hand over; as easy as falling off a log
易货贸易制 barter system
易货贸易协定 barter trade agreement

怿 〔yì〕
动 rejoice;be happy

诣 〔yì〕
Ⅰ 动 call on;visit Ⅱ 名 (academic or technical) attainments

驿 〔yì〕
名 post station
驿道 post road
驿站 post station;courier station

绎 〔yì〕
动 unravel;sort out

轶 〔yì〕
动 ①be lost ②excel
轶材 talents above the average
轶伦 tower above one's generation;surpass one's contemporaries
轶事 anecdote
轶闻 anecdote

疫 〔yì〕
名 epidemic disease;pestilence
疫病 epidemic disease
疫苗 vaccine
疫情 information about and appraisal of an epidemic;epidemic situation
疫区 an epidemic-stricken area

弈 〔yì〕
Ⅰ 名 *weiqi*,a game played with black and white pieces on a board of 361 intersections; *go* Ⅱ 动 play chess
弈林 chess-playing circles
弈棋 play chess

奕 〔yì〕
形 grand;magnificent
奕奕 ①grand;great ②radiating power and vitality

挹 〔yì〕
动 ①scoop up;ladle out ②pull

悒 〔yì〕
形 sad;worried;in low spirits
悒闷 depressed;dejected;in low spirits
悒郁 depressed;despondent;gloomy

Y

益 〔yì〕
Ⅰ 名 good;benefit;profit;advantage Ⅱ 形 beneficial;helpful Ⅲ 动 increase;add to Ⅳ 副 all the more;still more;increasingly
益兵 reinforce the troops
益虫 beneficial insect

益处 benefit;profit;good
益发 all the more;even more
益加 all the more;even more
益鸟 beneficial bird
益寿 lengthen one's life
益友 friend and mentor
益智 enhance intelligence
益母草 motherwort

浥 〔yì〕
动 wet;soak

谊 〔yì〕
名 friendship

埸 〔yì〕
名 ①low bank of earth between fields; ridge ②boundary;border

逸 〔yì〕
Ⅰ 名 ease;leisure;rest Ⅱ 动 ①escape; flee;run away ②live in seclusion (*or* solitude) ③be lost ④surpass;excel
逸居 hermit;recluse
逸乐 comfort and pleasure
逸民 hermit;recluse
逸趣 refined interests (*or* tastes)
逸散 escape;lose;disperse
逸史 unofficial history
逸致 a carefree mood
逸散电子 escaped electron

翊 〔yì〕
动 assist (a ruler)
翊戴 assist and support (a ruler)
翊卫 assist in safeguarding sth
翊赞 assist (a monarch)

翌 〔yì〕
形 immediately following in time;next
翌晨 the next morning
翌年 next year
翌日 next day

嗌 〔yì〕
名 throat

肄 〔yì〕
动 study
肄习 study
肄业 study in school (*or* at college)

裔 〔yì〕
名 ①descendants;posterity ②distant land
裔孙 remote descendants

意 〔yì〕
Ⅰ 名 ①meaning;idea;thought ②wish;desire;intention Ⅱ 动 believe what is going to happen;anticipate;expect
意表 expectation;what one expects
意会 perceive by intuition;sense
意见 ①idea;view;opinion;suggestion ②objection;differing opinion;complaint
意境 the mood of a literary work or a work of art
意料 anticipate;expect
意念 idea;thought
意气 ①will and spirit ②temperament ③per-

sonal feelings (*or* prejudice)
意趣 interest and charm; temperament and taste; mood
意识 ① consciousness; awareness ② be conscious (*or* aware) of; awake to; realize
意思 ① meaning; idea ② opinion; wish; desire ③ interest; fun ④ token of affection, appreciation, gratitude, etc. ⑤ suggestion; hint; trace ⑥ (reduplicated) as a mere token
意态 mien; demeanor; bearing
意图 intention; intent
意外 ① unexpected; unforeseen ② accident; mishap
意味 ① meaning; significance; implication ② interest; overtone; flavour
意下 ① in the mind; in the heart ② opinion; idea; view
意想 imagine; expect
意向 intention; purpose
意象 images; imagery
意兴 interest; enthusiasm
意义 meaning; sense; significance
意译 free translation
意欲 intend to; want to
意愿 wish; desire; aspiration
意蕴 meaning; implication; connotation
意旨 intention; wish; will
意志 will; willpower; determination
意见簿 visitors' book, customers' book, etc.
意见箱 suggestion box
意识流 stream of consciousness
意识域 sphere of consciousness
意味着 signify; mean; imply
意向书 letter of intent
意中人 the person one is in love with; the person of one's heart; the beloved one
意中事 sth that is to be expected
意简言赅 simple ideas expressed succinctly
意气风发 high-spirited and vigorous; daring and energetic
意气相投 be alike in temperament; be congenial
意气用事 be swayed by personal feelings
意识形态 ideology
意外风险 emergency risk
意外利润 windfall profit
意味深长 having deep meaning; pregnant with meaning; of profound significance
意意思思 hesitate in speech
意在笔先 have an idea in the mind before starting writing or painting
意在言外 the meaning is implied
意大利肉饼 pizza
意向性协议 agreement of intent

溢 [yì]
Ⅰ 动 overflow; spill Ⅱ 形 excessive; exaggerated

溢出 spill over; overflow
溢额 surplus
溢价 premium
溢流 overflow; brim over
溢美 excessive praise; fulsome praise; undeserved praise
溢水 overflow; overfall
溢洪道 spillway
溢流坝 water conservancy overfall dam; spillway dam
溢额部分 surplus share
溢美之词 adulatory speech
溢于言表 (of feelings) show clearly in one's words and manner
溢额再保险 surplus reinsurance

缢 [yì]
动 hang
缢杀 strangle to death; kill by strangling

蜴 [yì]

◇蜥蜴 lizard

毅 [yì]
形 firm; resolute; steadfast
毅力 willpower; will; stamina; tenacity
毅然 resolutely; firmly; determinedly
毅然决然 resolutely; determinedly

臆 [yì]
Ⅰ 名 chest Ⅱ 副 subjectively
臆测 conjecture; surmise; guess
臆断 form a subjective judgment; assume
臆度 conjecture; surmise; guess
臆见 a subjective view
臆说 assumption; supposition
臆想 wishful imagination
臆造 fabricate (a story, reason, etc.); concoct

翼 [yì]
Ⅰ 名 ① wing of a bird, etc. ② wing of an aeroplane ③ side; flank Ⅱ 动 assist (a ruler); aid
翼庇 protect; patronize
翼蔽 shield; protect; screen
翼侧 flank
翼翅 wing
翼护 shield sb with one's own body
翼型 wing section; aerofoil
翼翼 ① reverent and cautious ② in neat formation; in orderly array ③ thriving; abundant
翼展 span; wingspan; tip-to-tip
翼手目 Chiroptera
翼指龙 pterodactyl (an extinct reptile)
翼手动物 chiropter (e.g. the bat)
翼状胬肉 pterygium

懿 [yì]
形 exemplary
懿德 admirable virtue; moral excellence
懿范 virtuous example
懿旨 decree of an empress; empress dowager

Y

yīn（ㄧㄣ）

因 [yīn]
I 〔动〕 follow; carry on II 〔名〕 cause; reason; grounds III 〔介〕 ①because; due to; as a result of ②on the basis of; in accordance with; in the light of

因此 so; therefore; for this reason; consequently

因次 dimension

因而 thus; as a result; therefore

因果 ①cause and effect ②karma; preordained fate

因明 a system of Hindu logic

因式 factor (which is an algebraic expression)

因数 factor (which is a whole number)

因素 factor; element

因为 ①because ②because of; on account of; owing to

因袭 follow (old customs, methods, rules, etc.); copy

因循 ①follow (old customs, etc.); continue in the same old rut ②procrastinate

因应 ①keep up with; conform to; comply with ②take measures to cope with

因由 reason; cause; origin

因缘 ①principal and subsidiary causes; cause ②predestined relationship

因果律 the law of cause and effect; the law of causality (or causation)

因果论 causationism

因素论 theory of factors

因特网 Internet

因病下药 prescribe for a patient according to the symptoms

因材施教 teach students according to their aptitude; suit the instruction to the student's level

因地制宜 suit measures to local conditions; take measures suited to local conditions; work out measures to suit local conditions

因工负伤 work-related injury

因工殉职 death in line of duty

因公负伤 getting injured while on duty; work-related injury

因公牺牲 die while on duty; die at one's post

因果报应 retribution; karma

因祸得福 derive gain from misfortune; profit by misfortune

因利乘便 take advantage of the opening; exploit the opportunity

因陋就简 make do with whatever is available; do things simply and thriftily

因人成事 rely on others of success in work; create a job to accommodate a person; set up posts simply to create jobs

因人而异 vary with each individual

因人设事 create a job to accommodate a person

因人制宜 do what is suited to each individual; take measures suited to each person

因时制宜 do what is suited to the occasion; take measures suited to the time

因势利导 guide a matter along its course of development; adroitly guide action according to circumstances

因小失大 try to save a little only to lose a lot

因循守旧 stick to old ways; follow the beaten track

因噎废食 give up eating for fear of choking—refrain from doing what one should for fear of running a risk

因特网用户 Internaut

阴 [yīn]
I 〔名〕 ①principle of Yin; feminine or negative principle in nature ②moon ③shade ④north of a hill or south of a river ⑤back ⑥private parts (esp. of the female) II 〔形〕 ①(of weather) overcast; cloudy; gloomy ②in intaglio ③hidden; secret; underhand ④sinister; perfidious; foul ⑤of the nether world ⑥negative

阴暗 dark; gloomy

阴部 private parts; genitals; pudenda

阴沉 cloudy; overcast; gloomy

阴唇 labia (of the vulva)

阴道 vagina

阴德 good deeds done in secret; hidden acts of merit

阴地 a shaded place; shade

阴蒂 clitoris

阴电 negative electricity

阴毒 insidious; sinister and ruthless

阴风 ①a cold wind ②an ill (or evil) wind

阴干 be placed in the shade to dry; dry in the shade

阴功 good deeds done in secret; hidden acts of merit

阴沟 sewer; covered drain

阴河 underground river

阴黑 dark and gloomy; murky; sombre

阴户 vaginal orifice

阴魂 ghost; spirit; apparition

阴极 negative pole; negative electrode; cathode

阴间 the nether world; the Hades

阴茎 penis

阴冷 ①(of weather) gloomy and cold; raw ②(of a person's look) sombre; glum

阴历 lunar calendar

阴凉 ①shady and cool ②a cool place; shade

阴霾 haze

阴毛 pubes; pubic hair

阴门 vaginal orifice;vulva
阴面 the shady side;the back side
阴谋 ① conspire;plot;scheme ② conspiracy;plot;scheme
阴囊 scrotum
阴平 high and level tone
阴燃 glow;smoulder
阴森 gloomy;gruesome;ghastly
阴虱 crab louse
阴湿 dark and damp
阴私 shameful secret;privacy
阴天 an overcast sky;a cloudy day
阴文 characters (*or* designs) cut in intaglio; intaglio
阴险 sinister;insidious;treacherous
阴线 downward slope curve
阴笑 a sinister smile
阴性 ①negative ②feminine gender
阴虚 deficiency of *yin* (insufficiency of body fluid),with irritability,thirst,constipation, etc. as symptoms
阴阳 ① *yin* and *yang*,the two opposing principles in nature,the former feminine and negative,the latter masculine and positive ②ancient Chinese astronomy ③occult arts ④ *yin-yang* adept
阴翳 ①be shaded or hidden by foliage ②with luxuriant foliage
阴影 shadow
阴雨 overcast and rainy
阴郁 gloomy;dismal;depressed
阴云 dark clouds
阴宅 grave;tomb
阴暗面 the dark (*or* seamy) side of things
阴沉木 hard wood which has long been buried in earth
阴道炎 vaginitis
阴电子 negatron;negative electron
阴茎套 condom
阴离子 anion
阴谋家 schemer;intriguer;conspirator
阴阳家 ① geomancer ② the Yin-Yang School or School of Naturalists
阴阳历 lunisolar calendar
阴阳人 a bisexual person;hermaphrodite
阴阳生 *yin-yang* adept
阴阳水 *yin-yang* water
阴着儿 a treacherous act
阴差阳错 a mistake or error due to a strange combination of circumstances
阴错阳差 a mistake or error due to a strange combination of circumstances
阴丹士林 ①indanthrone (a deep blue dye) ② a cotton cloth dyed with indanthrone
阴地植物 shade plant
阴魂不散 the ghost lingers on—the evil influence remains

阴极射线 cathode ray
阴谋篡权 scheme to usurp power
阴谋诡计 schemes and intrigues
阴谋集团 conspiratorial clique (*or* group)
阴谋破坏 plot sabotage
阴谋手段 conspiratorial means
阴生植物 shade plant
阴盛阳衰 ① *yin* rises while *yang* declines; the *yang* forces recede in favour of the *yin* forces ② the female being stronger and more powerful,or more numerous than the male
阴阳怪气 ①mystifying;enigmatic;deliberately ambiguous ②eccentric;queer;cynical
阴阳交错 The Yin and Yang forces are opposing but complementary to each other.
阴阳先生 geomancer
阴曹(地府) the nether world;the Hades
阴一套,阳一套 act one way in public and another in private;be engaged in double-dealing

茵 [yīn]
〈名〉mattress
茵陈 capillary artemisia (Artemisia capillaris)
茵褥 mattress
茵茵 (of grass,etc.) lush;luxuriant

音 [yīn]
〈名〉①sound;voice ②news ③syllable ④pronunciation ⑤tone
音爆 sonic boom
音标 phonetic symbol;phonetic transcription
音波 sound wave
音叉 tuning fork
音长 the duration of a sound
音程 interval
音带 audiotape
音调 tone
音读 pronunciation (of a character)
音段 segment;stretch
音符 note
音高 pitch
音阶 scale
音节 syllable
音量 volume (of sound)
音律 temperament
音名 musical alphabet
音频 audio frequency
音强 intensity of sound
音容 voice and face (of sb as recalled after his death)
音色 tone colour;timbre
音诗 tone poem
音素 phoneme
音速 velocity (*or* speed) of sound
音位 phoneme
音箱 speaker;loudspeaker;amplifier;sound box

音响 sound; acoustics
音像 audiovisual; audio-video; sound and video recording
音信 mail; message; news
音型 figure
音讯 mail; message; news
音译 transliteration
音域 range; compass; register
音乐 music
音韵 ①harmonious sounds; rhyme and rhythm ②the initial, final and tone of a Chinese character
音障 sound (*or* sonic) barrier
音值 value
音质 ①tone quality ②acoustic fidelity
音准 accuracy in pitch
音节表 syllabary
音位学 phonemics; phonology
音响师 sound engineer
音像业 recording and video industry
音效卡 audio card; sound card
音乐盒 music box
音乐会 concert
音乐家 musician
音乐节 musical festival
音乐剧 musical comedy
音乐片 musical (film)
音乐厅 concert hall
音乐学 musicology
音韵学 phonology
音调失真 tonal distortion
音节文字 syllabic language
音控开关 voice-operated switch
音频电话 tone telephone
音频调制 voice modulation
音容宛在 the same voice and face seem still there
音容笑貌 one's voice and expression; one's lovely voice and happy countenance
音素文字 phonemic writing
音位文字 phonemic writing
音像市场 tape market
音像制品 audiovisual (*or* -video) products; audio and video tapes and disks; sound and video product
音乐茶座 music teahouse
音乐电视 MTV; music TV
音乐疗法 music therapy
音乐门铃 music bell; music door-bell
音乐学院 conservatory (of music)
音像出版社 audiovisual press (*or* publishing house)
音像同步装置 moviola

Y

姻 [yīn]
名 ①marriage ②relation by marriage
姻亲 relation by marriage
姻缘 the happy fate which brings lovers together

骃 [yīn]
名 black horse with streaks of white hair

殷 [yīn]
形 ①rich; plentiful; abundant ②eager; ardent ③hospitable; cordial ➡ yān; yǐn
殷富 wealthy; well-off
殷钢 invar
殷切 ardent; eager
殷勤 eagerly attentive; solicitous
殷实 well-off; substantial
殷殷 ardent; sincere
殷切期望 ardent expectations
殷勤备至 be all attention
殷殷嘱咐 enjoin sincerely

yín (1ㄣ)

吟 [yín]
I 动 ①intone; recite; chant ②groan; lament; sigh II 名 ①song (as a type of classical poetry):《江上吟》(李白) *Song on the River* (by Li Bai) ②cry of certain animals
吟唱 sing; chant
吟哦 recite (poetry) with a cadence; chant
吟诵 chant; recite
吟味 recite with relish; recite with appreciation
吟咏 recite (poetry) with a cadence; chant
吟风弄月 sing of the moon and the wind—write sentimental verse
吟诗作画 recite (*or* compose) poetry and do brush-work

垠 [yín]
名 boundary; limit

银 [yín]
I 名 ①silver; argentum (Ag) ②money; currency II 形 silver-coloured
银白 silvery white
银杯 silver cup
银币 silver coin
银弹 silver bullet
银锭 silver ingot
银耳 tremella (Tremella fuciformis)
银发 silver (*or* silvery) hair
银根 money market; money supply
银行 bank
银号 banking house
银河 the Milky Way
银狐 silver fox
银灰 silver grey
银婚 silver wedding
银奖 silver award
银匠 silversmith
银卡 silver card
银库 treasury
银矿 silver mine; silver ore
银两 silver (used as currency)

银幕 （motion-picture） screen; projection screen
银鸥 herring gull
银牌 silver medal
银票 silver draft
银屏 ① fluorescent screen; luminescent screen; telescreen ② television; television circles
银器 silverware
银钱 money
银鼠 snow weasel
银条 silver bar
银团 financial group formed by banks; bank association; banking consortium
银线 silver thread
银箱 cash box
银杏 ginkgo; gingko
银燕 silver swallow—aeroplane
银洋 silver dollar
银鱼 whitebait
银圆 silver dollar
银针 acupuncture needle
银朱 vermilion
银装 snow cover
银子 silver; money
银白杨 white poplar
银本位 silver standard
银汉鱼 silverside
银行家 banker
银行卡 bank card
银河系 the Milky Way Galaxy
银灰色 silver grey; silvery
银联卡 interchangeable card
银项链 silver necklace
银屑病 psoriasis
银质奖 silver medal
"银弹"外交 "silver bullet" diplomacy; dollar diplomacy
银根紧缩 money squeeze; tighten the money market
银行承兑 banker's acceptance
银行倒闭 bank failure; bank close-up
银行电汇 bank telegraph transfer （B.T.T.）
银行利率 bank rate
银行破产 bank failure
银行信贷 bank credit
银河星团 galactic cluster
银团贷款 bank consortium loan
银行承兑票 banker's acceptance bill
银行间贷款 interbank loan
银样镴枪头 a pewter spearhead that shines like silver—an impressive-looking but useless person
银河-Ⅲ巨型计算机 Galaxy-Ⅲ Super computer

淫 [yín]
圈 ①excessive; extreme ②adulterous; promiscuous; dissolute ③ lewd; obscene; pornographic
淫词 ① extravagant speech ② obscene language; lewd expressions
淫荡 loose in morals; lascivious; licentious; lewd
淫风 wanton customs; lascivious practices
淫妇 a wanton woman; adulteress
淫棍 libertine; womanizer; wolf
淫话 obscene language; dirty remark
淫秽 obscene; salacious; bawdy
淫乐 [yínlè] in sensual pleasures; gratify carnal desires
淫乱 （sexually） promiscuous; licentious
淫靡 ①obscene; decadent ②extravagant
淫威 abuse of power; despotic power
淫猥 obscene
淫笑 lewd （or lustful） smile
淫邪 obscene and wicked; lewd and vicious
淫亵 ①obscene; salacious ②act indecently towards （a woman）
淫刑 ①mete out excessive punishments ②excessive punishments
淫雨 excessive rains
淫欲 sexual desire; lust
淫乐 [yínyuè] decadent music; obscene music
淫羊霍 longspur epimedium
淫秽作品 pornography

寅 [yín]
寅时 the period of the day from 3 a.m. to 5 a.m.
寅吃卯粮 eat next year's food; anticipate one's income

龈 [yín]
名 gum; gingiva

yǐn（ㄧㄣˇ）

尹 [yǐn]
名 ancient official title：京兆尹 magistrate of the capital city

引 [yǐn]
Ⅰ 动 ① draw; pull; stretch ② draw; lead; guide ③ leave ④ stretch; crane; extend ⑤ attract; draw; induce ⑥ cause; arouse; trigger; set off ⑦ quote; cite：援引名言警句 quote well-known proverbs and adages Ⅱ 名 ① white cloth used to drape over the coffin in a funeral procession ② unit of length （= 33⅓ metres）
引爆 ignite; detonate
引柴 kindling
引产 induce labour
引出 draw forth; lead to
引导 guide; lead
引逗 ①tantalize; tease ②lure; entice
引渡 extradition; extradite

引发 initiate;touch off;spark off;trigger off
引港 ①pilot a ship（into or out of a harbour）②pilot（of a ship）
引航 pilot a ship（into or out of a harbour）
引号 quotation marks（" "）
引河 ①irrigation channel ②diversion canal
引火 light a fire
引见 present（a person）to another;introduce
引荐 recommend（a person）
引介 introduce
引进 ①recommend（a person）② introduce from elsewhere
引颈 crane one's neck
引咎 hold oneself responsible for a serious mistake;take the blame
引理 lemma
引力 gravitation;gravitational force;attraction
引领 crane one's neck to look into the distance—eagerly look forward to sth
引流 drainage
引路 lead the way
引起 give rise to;lead to;set off;touch off;cause;arouse
引桥 bridge approach;approach bridge
引擎 engine
引入 lead into;draw into;introduce from elsewhere
引申 extend（the meaning of a word,etc.）
引首 raise one's head;crane one's neck
引述 quote sb's words;quote from sb's speech
引水 ①pilot a ship（through difficult waters, or into or out of a harbour）②draw（or channel）water
引头 take the lead
引退 retire from office;resign
引文 quoted passage;quotation
引线 ①fuse ②go-between ③sewing needle
引信 detonator;fuse
引言 foreword;introduction
引用 ①quote;cite ②recommend;appoint
引诱 lure;entice;seduce
引语 quotation;citation
引证 quote（or cite）as proof or evidence
引智 import outside brainpower
引种 ［yǐnzhǒng］introduce a fine variety
引种 ［yǐnzhòng］plant an introduced variety
引资 introduce investment; import outside funds
引子 ①an actor's opening words（either spoken or sung）②introductory music ③introductory remarks;introduction ④ an added ingredient（to enhance the efficacy of medicines）
引座 usher
引发剂 initiator
引航员 pilot（of a ship）

引火线 fuse
引流管 drainage tube
引燃管 ignitron
引燃物 tinder
引申义 extended meaning
引水渠 feed canal;diversion canal
引水员 pilot（of a ship）
引座员 usher
引而不发（of a teacher of archery）draw the bow but not release the arrow—show people what to do without doing it for them
引发价格 trigger price
引火烧身 draw fire against oneself—bring trouble on oneself
引进技术 import technology;introduce technology
引进人才 employ competent persons;invite competent persons;recruit competent persons
引进外资 introduce overseas capital
引进项目 projects introduced
引经据典 quote the classics;quote authoritative works
引咎辞职 take the blame and resign;hold oneself responsible for a serious mistake and send in one's resignation
引吭高歌 sing joyfully in a loud voice;sing heartily
引狼入室 invite a wolf into the house—open the door to an enemy
引领而望 crane one's neck to see;eagerly look forward to
引起公愤 provoke general rage;stir up a hornet's nest
引起轰动 cause a sensation
引起骚乱 cause turbulence
引起争端 give rise to（or lead to）a dispute
引人入胜（of scenery,literary works,etc.）fascinating;enchanting;bewitching
引人注目 noticeable;conspicuous;spectacular
引入歧途 lead sb onto a wrong path;lead sb astray
引蛇出洞 lure the snake out of the hole
引水工程 water diversion project;diversion works
引水灌田 channel water into the fields
引为鉴戒 draw a lesson（from a mistake, etc.）;take warning
引以为耻 regard it as a disgrace;regard as a shame;consider it shameful
引以为憾 deem it regrettable
引以为戒 draw a lesson（from a mistake, etc.）;take warning
引以为荣 regard it as an honour;take it as an honour
引玉之砖 a brick cast to attract jade
引渡劫机犯 delivery of the plane hijacker

饮 [yǐn]
I 动 ①drink;drink wine (*or* other liquor) ②keep in the heart;nurse;bottle up;bite down hard (usu. of hatred) II 名 ① sth to drink;drink ②decoction of Chinese medicine to be taken cold ③watery sputum ➡yìn
饮弹 be hit by a bullet
饮恨 nurse a grievance
饮酒 drink wine;have a drink
饮料 beverage;drink (esp. a soft drink)
饮片 prepared herbal medicine in small pieces ready for decoction
饮品 drink
饮泣 weep in silence
饮辱 nurse humiliation;bury one's humiliation deep
饮食 food and drink;diet
饮水 drinking water;potable water
饮誉 have a good reputation;enjoy popularity
饮子 decoction of Chinese medicine to be taken cold
饮食店 eating house;café;snack bar
饮食业 the catering trade
饮水器 drinking bowl;drinker
饮用水 drinking water;potable water
饮恨而终 die with bottled-up grievance
饮恨吞声 swallow one's resentment and choke back one's sobs;endure insults and injuries
饮恨终身 harbour hatred all one's life
饮食疗法 dietotherapy
饮食男女 food, drink and sex—human prime wants
饮食卫生 dietetic hygiene
饮水思源 when drinking water, think of its source—bear in mind where one's happiness comes from
饮鸩止渴 drink poison to quench thirst—seek quick relief regardless of the consequences
饮水不忘掘井人 When you drink the water, think of those who dug the well.

蚓 [yǐn]
名 earthworm

殷 [yǐn]
拟 sound of thunder;thundering:殷其雷 loud crashes of thunder ➡yān;yīn

隐 [yǐn]
I 动 hide (from view);conceal II 形 latent;dormant;lurking III 名 privacy;secret
隐蔽 conceal;take cover
隐才 dormant talent
隐藏 hide;conceal;remain under cover
隐伏 lie concealed (*or* hidden);lie low
隐含 imply
隐患 hidden trouble;hidden danger;snake in the grass
隐讳 avoid mentioning;cover up
隐晦 obscure;veiled

隐疾 unmentionable disease
隐居 live in seclusion;withdraw from society and live in solitude;be a hermit
隐瞒 conceal;hide;hold back;cover up
隐秘 ①conceal;hide ②secret
隐没 [yǐnmò] hide and disappear
隐匿 conceal;hide;go into hiding;lie low
隐情 facts (*or* circumstances) one wishes to hide;secrets
隐然 dim;faint
隐忍 bear patiently;forbear
隐射 insinuate;hint;throw out innuendoes
隐士 recluse;hermit
隐私 one's secrets;private matters one wants to hide
隐痛 secret anguish
隐退 go and live in seclusion;retire from political life
隐现 be now visible, now invisible;be dimly visible
隐性 recessiveness
隐血 occult blood
隐隐 indistinct;faint
隐忧 secret worry
隐语 enigmatic language; insinuating language;riddle
隐喻 metaphor
隐约 indistinct;faint
隐衷 feelings (*or* troubles) one wishes to keep to onself
隐蔽色 cryptic colour (*or* coloration)
隐睾症 cryptorchidism
隐函数 implicit function
隐君子 ①recluse;hermit ②opium addict
隐身草 a person (*or* thing) acting as cover
隐身术 art of making oneself invisible;disappearing act;vanishing act
隐私权 privacy;right to privacy;right of privacy
隐恶扬善 cover up sb's faults and publicize his merits;hide sb's evil deeds and praise his good ones
隐花植物 cryptogam
隐晦曲折 (of a statement) veiled and roundabout
隐名捐赠 silent contribution
隐身技术 stealth technology
隐显墨水 invisible ink
隐形飞机 stealth fighter; stealth aircraft; radar-avoiding fighter plane;Nighthawk
隐形技术 stealth technology
隐形就业 unregistered employment; veiled employment
隐形失业 recessive unemployment
隐形收入 invisible income;off-payroll income
隐形眼镜 contact lens
隐性就业 unregistered employment

Y

隐性杀手 hidden killer
隐性失业 recessive unemployment
隐性收入 invisible income
隐姓埋名 conceal one's identity; keep one's identity hidden; live incognito
隐隐绰绰 indistinct; faint
隐约可见 may be seen indistinctly
隐约其词 use ambiguous language; speak in equivocal terms
隐形轰炸机 stealth bomber

瘾 [yǐn] 名 ①addiction; habitual craving: 打牌上瘾了 become addicted to card playing; have formed a habit of playing cards ②strong interest; passion
瘾头 addiction; strong interest
瘾君子 retired scholar—drug addict; opium addict

yìn(ㄧㄣˋ)

印 [yìn] I 名 ① seal; chop ② print; mark II 动 ① print; engrave: 复印几份文件 photocopy a few documents ②tally; conform; accord with
印版 printing plate
印本 printed copy
印鼻 the knob (or handle) of a seal
印次 impression
印发 print and distribute
印盒 seal box
印痕 mark; trace
印花 ①printing ②revenue stamp; fiscal stamp
印迹 trace; mark; vestige
印记 ①the seal or stamp of a government organization in old China ②the impression of a seal; trace; mark ③ impress deeply on one's mind
印鉴 specimen seal impression for checking when marking payments
印泥 red ink paste used for seals; Chinese vermilion seal paste
印纽 the knob (or handle) of a seal
印染 printing and dyeing (of textiles)
印绶 an official seal and the ribbon attached to it; an official seal
印数 the number of copies of a book printed at one impression; impression
印刷 printing
印台 ink pad; stamp pad
印玺 imperial seal
印象 impression
印行 print and distribute; publish
印油 stamp-pad ink
印张 printed sheet (equal to a half sheet of printing paper)
印章 seal; signet; stamp
印证 confirm; corroborate; verify

印制 print; duplicate (a painting, etc.)
印把子 seal of authority; power
印花税 stamp duty; stamp tax
印刷厂 printing house
印刷机 printing machine; press
印刷品 printed matter
印刷术 art of printing; printing
印刷体 block letter; print hand
印刷纸 printing paper
印相纸 photographic paper
印象派 impressionist school; impressionist
印章学 sigillography; sphragistics
印花税票 revenue stamp; fiscal stamp
印刷错误 misprint; typographic error
印刷电路 printed circuit
印刷工人 printing worker; printer
印刷合金 type metal
印象主义 impressionism
印刷电路板 printed circuit board (PCB)
印纹陶文化 Stamped Pottery Culture

饮 [yìn] 动 water (an animal) ➡ yǐn

茚 [yìn] 名 (transliteration) indene

萌 [yìn] I 形 shady and damp II 动 shelter; protect III 名 privileges given to one's descendants because of one's meritorious service
荫庇 shelter; protect; bless
荫蔽 ①be shaded (or hidden) by foliage ② cover; conceal
荫凉 shady and cool

yīng(ㄧㄥ)

应 [yīng] 动 ① answer; reply; respond ② promise; agree; accept ③should; ought to ➡ yìng
应当 should; ought to
应得 (well) deserved; due
应分 part of one's job
应该 should; ought to
应声 answer; respond
应许 ①agree; promise ②permit; allow
应有 due; proper; deserved
应允 assent; consent
应名儿 ①hold a title but have no real power or responsibility ②only in name; nominally
应付票据 note payable
应付押款 mortgage payable
应付账款 account payable
应收税款 tax receivable
应收押款 mortgage receivable
应收账款 account receivable
应税商品 taxable good; dutiable commodity
应有尽有 have everything that one could wish for
应届毕业生 graduating students (or pupils);

this year's graduates
应纳税收入 taxable income

英 [yīng]
　[名] ①blossom; bloom; petal ②hero; man of valour; outstanding person ③Britain; England
英镑 pound sterling
英才 a person of outstanding ability; a person of superior talents
英尺 foot (a measure)
英寸 inch
英吨 long ton; gross ton
英豪 heroes; outstanding figures
英魂 spirit of the brave departed; spirit of a martyr
英杰 heroes; outstanding figures
英俊 ①eminently talented; brilliant ②handsome and spirited; smart
英里 mile
英两 ounce
英烈 ①heroic; valiant ②heroic martyr ③brilliant achievement
英灵 ①spirit of the brave departed; spirit of a martyr ②a person of outstanding ability
英名 heroic name; illustrious name
英明 wise; brilliant
英模 heroic model; heroes and models; one who sets an example
英亩 acre
英年 youthful years; youth
英气 heroic spirit
英武 of soldierly (*or* martial) bearing
英雄 ①hero ②heroic
英寻 fathom (= 6 feet)
英勇 heroic; valiant; brave; gallant
英语 English (language)
英制 the English system
英姿 heroic bearing
英镑区 the sterling area
英仙座 Perseus
英语热 popular enthusiasm for learning English
英才教育 meritocracy
英雄本色 true colour of a hero; true quality of a hero
英雄模范 heroic model; one who sets an example
英雄气短 brief is the spirit of a hero
英姿焕发 dashing and spirited
英姿飒爽 valiant and heroic in bearing; bold and brave
英雄所见略同 great minds think alike
英语水平考试 English Proficiency Test (EPT)
英雄无用武之地 a hero with no place to display his prowess—have no scope for the exercise of one's abilities
英语专业八级考试 Test for English Majors Band Eight (TEM8)

英语专业四级考试 Test for English Majors Band Four (TEM4)

莺 [yīng]
　[名] warbler; oriole
莺歌燕舞 orioles sing and swallows dart—the joy of spring; a scene of prosperity
莺簧婉转 talk as glibly and eloquently as a chirping oriole
莺声燕语 like an oriole trilling or a swallow twittering (said of a woman speaking in a sweet, delicate voice)

婴 [yīng]
　Ⅰ [名] baby; infant Ⅱ [动] touch; contract; surround; entangle
婴儿 baby; infant
婴孩 baby; infant
婴疾 contract a disease
婴儿车 pram; baby carriage; stroller; pushchair
婴儿床 crib; cot; cradle
婴幼儿 infants and young children
婴城固守 fortify the city to beef up its defence
婴儿死亡率 infant mortality rate

撄 [yīng]
　[动] ①butt against; arouse; oppose; challenge ②disturb; harass
撄怒 arouse one's anger

嘤 [yīng]
　[拟] chirp
嘤鸣 ①(of birds) trill; chirp ②friend seeking friend
嘤泣 sob
嘤嘤 the sound of chirping, whispering, or sobbing
嘤其鸣矣,求其友声 a bird sings to call forth a mate's response

罂 [yīng]
　[名] small-mouthed jar
罂粟 opium poppy

缨 [yīng]
　[名] ①ribbon or band used to fasten the hat in ancient times ②tassel ③sth shaped like a tassel
缨帽 red-tasselled official hat
缨子 ①ornamental tassels ②sth shaped like a tassel

樱 [yīng]
　[名] ①cherry ②oriental cherry
樱唇 cherry lips
樱花 oriental cherry
樱桃 cherry

鹦 [yīng]
鹦哥 parrot
鹦鹉 parrot
鹦哥绿 parrot green
鹦鹉螺 nautilus
鹦鹉热 psittacosis; parrot fever

鹦嘴鱼 parrot fish
鹦鹉学舌 repeat another person's words like a parrot;parrot

膺 [yīng]
Ⅰ 名 chest;breast Ⅱ 动 ①bear;shoulder;receive ②send a punitive expedition against;attack;smite

鹰 [yīng]
名 hawk;eagle
鹰犬 falcons and hounds—lackeys;hired thugs
鹰隼 hawks and falcons—brutal or fierce people
鹰洋 Mexican silver dollar
鹰鼻鹞眼 hawk-nosed and vulture-eyed—sinister and fierce-looking
鹰钩鼻子 aquiline nose
鹰爪毛儿 a kind of curly sheep's wool

yíng（１ㄥ）

迎 [yíng]
动 ① meet;greet;welcome;receive ② go (*or* move) towards;meet face to face;face
迎宾 receive visitors
迎风 ①facing (*or* against) the wind ②down the wind;with the wind
迎合 cater to;pander to
迎候 await the arrival of
迎击 meet (an approaching enemy) head-on
迎接 meet;welcome;greet
迎面 head-on;in one's face
迎亲 (of the bridegroom) send a party to meet the bride at the bride's home and escort her to the bridegroom's home for the wedding
迎娶 (of a man) get married
迎头 head-on;directly
迎新 ①see the New Year in ②welcome new arrivals
迎战 ①meet (an approaching enemy) head-on ②(of sports) play;meet in competition;take on
迎宾曲 music of welcome for the guests
迎宾员 doorman
迎春花 winter jasmine
迎客松 The Pine Greeting Guests
迎新会 party to welcome newcomers
迎来送往 receive and see off guests
迎刃而解 (bamboo) splits as it meets the edge of the knife—(of a problem) be readily solved
迎头赶上 strive to catch up with the foremost;try hard to catch up;catch up forth with
迎头痛击 deal a head-on blow

茔 [yíng]
名 grave;cemetery
茔地 graveyard

荧 [yíng]
形 ①glimmering;gleaming;dim
荧光 fluorescence;fluorescent light
荧惑 ①bewilder;confuse ②the Sparkling Deluder
荧屏 ①fluorescent screen ②television
荧荧 (of stars, lights, etc.) twinkling;glimmering
荧光灯 fluorescent lamp;daylight lamp
荧光粉 fluorescent powder
荧光管 fluorescent tube
荧光镜 fluoroscope
荧光屏 fluorescent screen

盈 [yíng]
动 ①fill;pack;throng ②gain
盈亏 ① profit and loss ② the waxing and waning of the moon
盈利 profit;gain
盈溢 brim over
盈盈 ①clear;lucid ②delicate;dainty ③brimming over ④graceful
盈余 surplus;profit
盈月 full moon;waxing moon
盈利能力 profitability
盈千累万 thousands and tens of thousands;thousands upon thousands
盈盈秋水 young lady's sad look

莹 [yíng]
Ⅰ 名 jade-like stone Ⅱ 形 lustrous and transparent
莹白 shining and white
莹澈 lustrous and transparent;sparkling and crystal
莹洁 shining and clean
莹莹 sparkling;glistening

萤 [yíng]
名 firefly;glowworm
萤石 fluorite;fluorspar
萤火虫 firefly;glowworm;lightning bug

营 [yíng]
Ⅰ 动 ① seek;pursue ② operate;manage;run Ⅱ 名 ①camp;barracks ②battalion
营巢 (of birds) build a nest
营地 campsite;camping ground
营房 barracks
营火 campfire
营建 construct;build
营救 succour;rescue
营垒 ① barracks and the enclosing walls ② camp
营利 seek profits
营盘 military camp;barracks
营舍 barracks
营生 earn a living;make a living
营收 business income
营私 seek private gain;feather one's nest
营销 sell;market;marketing
营养 nutrition;nourishment

营业 do business
营员 participant in a summer (*or* winter) camp
营运 operation
营造 construct;build
营寨 military camp;barracks
营长 battalion commander
营帐 tent
营火会 campfire party;campfire
营养钵 nutritive cube
营养餐 nutritious food
营养级 trophic level
营养链 food chain
营养品 nourishment;nutriment
营养师 dietitian;dietician;nutritionist
营养霜 nourishing cream
营养素 nutrient
营养学 nutriology
营养液 nourishing oral liquid
营业额 turnover;volume of business
营业税 business tax; transactions tax; turnover tax;sales tax
营业员 shop employees (including buyers, travelling salespersons and shop assistants)
营私舞弊 embezzle;engage in fraud (*or* malpractice) of selfish ends;practise graft
营销经理 marketing manager
营养不良 dystrophy;malnutrition;undernourishment
营养价值 nutritive (*or* nutritional) value
营业范围 business activities range; scope of business;line of business
营业时间 business hours;banking hours (of a bank)
营业执照 business license (*or* permit)

萦 [yíng]
劢 entwine;entangle;encompass
萦怀 occupy one's mind
萦回 hover;linger
萦念 think of;long for
萦绕 hover;linger

蝇 [yíng]
名 housefly;fly
蝇虎 a kind of spider that feeds on flies (Menemerus)
蝇拍 flyswatter;flyflap
蝇头 fly's head—very small;tiny
蝇子 fly;housefly
蝇头小利 a fly's head of profit; a pittance of profit;a petty profit
蝇头小字 very small character
蝇营狗苟 shamelessly seek personal gain

赢 [yíng]
劢 ①win;beat;defeat ②gain (*or* obtain) (profit)
赢得 win;gain
赢面 chance to win

赢得市场 gain a larger share of the market; carve a niche in the market
赢利性的 for-profit

yǐng (讠ㄥˇ)

颖 [yǐng]
Ⅰ 名 ①glume;grain husk ②tip (of a writing brush,etc.);point Ⅱ 形 clever;bright
颖果 caryopsis
颖慧 (of a teenager) clever;bright;intelligent
颖悟 (of a teenager) clever;bright

影 [yǐng]
Ⅰ 名 ① shadow ② reflection;image ③ trace;vestige;vague impression ④ photograph;picture ⑤portrait of one's ancestor ⑥ motion picture;film;movie ⑦ leather silhouette show;shadow play;galanty show Ⅱ 劢 ①hide;cover;conceal ②trace;copy
影壁 ①screen wall ②a wall with carved murals
影城 video city
影带 videotape of a TV programme,film, etc.;MTV tape
影帝 king of the silver screen—most popular male movie star
影碟 video compact disc (VCD); VCR disk; video disc
影后 movie queen;most popular female movie star
影集 photograph (*or* picture,photo) album
影楼 portrait studio
影迷 film (*or* movie) fan
影片 film;movie
影评 film review
影射 allude to;hint obliquely at;insinuate
影视 film and television
影坛 film (*or* movie) circles
影条 shadow stripes
影戏 ① leather-silhouette show; shadow play ②film;movie
影响 ①influence;effect;impact ②affect;influence ③hearsay;gossip
影像 ①image ②portrait
影协 Chinese Association of Film Artists
影星 film star;movie star
影业 the film industry;the motion picture industry;the cinema
影印 photomechanical printing; photo-offset process
影院 cinema;movie (house)
影展 ①photo exhibition ②film exhibition
影子 ① shadow ② reflection ③ trace;sign; vague impression
影剧界 film and drama circles
影剧院 theatre
影视界 film and TV circles
影视音乐 movie and TV music

Y

影影绰绰 vague;dim;indistinct
影子价格 shadow price
影子内阁 shadow cabinet
影子项目 project still on the drawing board
影迷俱乐部 cineclub

瘿 [yǐng]
〔名〕①goitre ②gall
瘿虫 gall insect

yìng（1之）

应 [yìng]
〔动〕① answer;reply;respond;echo ②comply with;grant;concede ③ suit;conform to;accord with ④deal with;cope with;meet ⮕ yīng
应变 ①meet an emergency (or contingency) ②strain
应标 respond to offer of tender
应承 agree (to do sth);promise;consent
应酬 ① have social intercourse with;treat with courtesy ②social engagement
应从 assent to;comply with
应答 reply;answer
应对 reply;answer;respond to
应付 ①deal with;cope with;handle ②do sth perfunctorily;do sth after a fashion ③make do
应合 ①meet;suit;agree (of words,action) ② accompany with sound (or movement);echo;respond in concert with
应和 echo;work in concert with
应机 take an opportunity when it offers (or presents itself)
应急 meet an urgent need;meet an emergency (or contingency)
应景 do sth for the occasion
应考 take (or sit for) an entrance examination
应力 stress
应卯 answer the roll call at *maoshi*—put in a routine appearance
应门 be in charge of the opening and closing of the door
应募 respond to a call for recruits;enlist;join up
应诺 agree (to do sth);promise;undertake
应拍 accept an offer at auction
应聘 accept an offer of employment
应声 happen right at the sound of sth
应时 ①seasonable;in season ②at once;immediately
应市 put marketable products on the market
应试 take an exam;take (or sit for) an entrance examination
应诉 respond to a charge
应许 promise;agree;permit
应选 be a candidate for election;be an election candidate;run for election
应验 come true;be confirmed;be fulfilled
应邀 at sb's invitation;on invitation
应用 ①apply;use ②applied
应援 make a move to reinforce
应战 ①meet an enemy attack ② accept (or take up) a challenge
应召 respond to a call (or summons)
应招 respond to a call for recruits or candidates
应诏 do sth in response to an imperial decree
应诊 (of a doctor) see patients
应征 ① be recruited ②respond to a call for contributions (to a publication)
应准 approve
应变规 strain gauge
应变计 strainometer
应酬话 social chitchat
应电流 induced current
应活儿 take on service jobs (e.g. repairs, processing,etc.)
应声虫 yesman;echo
应用文 practical writing
应战书 a letter accepting a challenge
应答如流 reply readily and fluently
应付考试 cram for an examination
应付自如 handle the situation with ease;be equal to the occasion;be master of the situation
应急措施 emergency measure
应急计划 contingency plan;crash program
应接不暇 have more (visitors or business) than one can attend to
应试教育 exam-dominated (or oriented) education;education solely for the preparation of examination
应用程序 application program
应用科学 applied science
应用软件 application software
应用研究 application study;applied scientific research
应运而生 arise at the historic moment;emerge as the times demand
应召女郎 call girl
应征入伍 be called to active duty in the army
应用性人才 practical personnel

映 [yìng]
〔动〕 reflect;mirror;image;shine
映衬 ①set off ②antithesis
映带 enhance each other's beauty;set off each other
映射 shine upon;cast light upon
映托 set off;serve as a foil to
映现 appear before one's eyes;show,manifest
映像 image;map;mapping
映照 shine upon;cast light upon
映山红 azalea

映像管 kinescope
映入眼帘 heave in sight;leap to the eyes

硬 [yìng]
Ⅰ 〔形〕①hard;solid;stiff;tough ②strong;firm;tough;rigid ③good;able;capable Ⅱ 〔动〕manage to do sth with effort
硬笔 hard-tipped pen;pen with a hard point—writing tools other than the traditional Chinese writing brush
硬币 ①coin;specie ②hard currency
硬撑 hold out (or keep on) in spite of difficulties
硬瓷 hard porcelain
硬顶 ①resist stubbornly ②contradict rudely
硬度 hardness
硬腭 hard palate
硬化 ①harden ②sclerosis ③become rigid or inflexible in attitudes,opinions,etc.;ossify
硬货 hard goods
硬件 hardware;material conditions
硬结 ①indurate;harden ②scleroma
硬朗 hale and hearty
硬领 stiff collar
硬煤 hard coal;anthracite
硬面 ①stiff dough ②hard-face;hard-surface
硬模 die
硬木 hardwood
硬盘 hard disk
硬磐 hardpan
硬拼 fight recklessly
硬气 ① strong-willed;firm;staunch;unyielding ②have no qualms;have an easy conscience
硬驱 disc drive
硬实 strong;sturdy;robust
硬是 ① actually (accomplish sth extremely difficult) ②just;simply
硬手 a skilled (or good) hand
硬水 hard water
硬说 stubbornly insist;obstinately assert;allege
硬挺 endure with all one's will;hold out with all one's might
硬席 hard seats (or berths) (on a train)
硬性 rigid;stiff;inflexible
硬玉 jadeite
硬仗 a tough (or hard-fought) battle;a formidable task
硬脂 tristearin;stearin
硬座 hard seat
硬邦邦 very hard;very stiff
硬包装 ① hard packaging ② hard packaging material,such as tinplate can,glass bottle,etc.
硬衬布 crinoline
硬磁盘 hard disks
硬道理 absolute principle;cardinal principle;

top priority
硬度计 sclerometer
硬功夫 great proficiency;masterly skill
硬骨头 hard bone—a dauntless,unyielding person
硬骨鱼 bony fish
硬广告 hard advertisement
硬汉(子) a dauntless,unyielding man;a man of iron
硬环境 material environment;infrastructure,spec. geographical conditions,buildings,communications,living facilities,etc.;hard environment
硬货币 hard currency
硬拷贝 hard copy
硬科学 hard science
硬锰矿 psilomelane
硬碰硬 ①confront the tough with toughness;meet force with force ②(of a job) demanding solid,painstaking work or real skill
硬皮病 scleroderma
硬皮书 hardback
硬任务 indispensable and demanding task (with a pressing deadline)
硬砂岩 greywacke
硬石膏 anhydrite
硬通货 hard currency
硬橡胶 hard rubber;ebonite;vulcanite
硬脂酸 stearic acid
硬脂油 stearine oil
硬纸板 hardboard;cardboard
硬指标 unalterable quota;definable (or non-negotiable) target
硬着陆 ①hard-land ②hard landing
硬笔书法 calligraphical works by hard-tipped pens
硬边绘画 hard-edge
硬充大方 feign generosity
硬充内行 deck oneself out as an expert
硬头硬脑 stubborn
硬席卧铺 sleeping carriage with hard berths;hard sleeper
硬性规定 rigid rules
硬性指标 brass-tag indices
硬着头皮 toughen one's scalp—brace oneself;force oneself to do sth against one's will
硬脂酸盐 stearate
硬质合金 hard alloy;hard metal
硬质塑料 rigid plastics

媵 [yìng]
Ⅰ 〔动〕accompany a bride to her new home Ⅱ 〔名〕①servants accompanying a bride to her new home ②concubine

yōng（ㄩㄥ）

佣 [yōng]
Ⅰ 〔动〕hire;employ Ⅱ 〔名〕servant

佣妇 woman servant;maid
佣工 hired labourer;servant
佣人 (domestic) servant

拥 [yōng]
囵 ①clasp (*or* hold) in one's arms;embrace;hug ②surround;gather around ③crowd;throng;flock;swarm ④support;uphold ⑤have;possess;boast
拥抱 embrace;hug;hold in one's arms
拥戴 support (sb as leader)
拥堵 jam
拥趸 fan
拥护 support;uphold;endorse
拥挤 ①be crowded;be packed ②push and squeeze
拥进 crowd into;swarm into
拥塞 jam;congest
拥吻 hug and kiss
拥有 possess;have;own
拥有率 possession rate
拥兵自重 build up one's power by dint of one's army;assume importance by raising an army
拥军优属 support the army and give preferential treatment to families of revolutionary armymen and martyrs;support the army and give preferential treatment to families of revolutionary soldiers and martyrs;support soldiers and their dependents
拥政爱民 (of the army) support the government and cherish the people

庸 [yōng]
Ⅰ 囵 ①commonplace;ordinary;mediocre ②inferior;second-rate;incompetent Ⅱ 囵 need Ⅲ 囵 how;in what way
庸才 a mediocre person;a person of mediocre ability;mediocrity
庸常 commonplace;mediocre
庸夫 a mediocre person
庸劣 inferior;low-grade
庸碌 mediocre and unambitious
庸人 a mediocre person
庸俗 vulgar;philistine;low
庸言 trite remark
庸医 medicaster;charlatan;quack
庸人自扰 bark at the moon;worry about imaginary troubles;alarm oneself needlessly
庸中佼佼 a giant among dwarfs

雍 [yōng]
囵 harmony
雍和 harmony
雍容 natural,graceful and poised
雍容大雅 display poise and refinement
雍容华贵 elegant and poised;stately

慵 [yōng]
囵 weary;lethargic;languid
慵惰 lazy;indolent

慵倦 tired and sleepy
慵懒 sluggish;indolent;lethargic

镛 [yōng]
囵 big bell used in ancient China to keep other musical instruments in tune

壅 [yōng]
囵 ①stop up;bar;obstruct ②heap soil (*or* fertilizer) over and around the roots (of plants and trees)
壅蔽 hide from view;cover;conceal
壅塞 be clogged up;be jammed;be congested

臃 [yōng]
囵 swollen
臃肿 ①too fat to move ②overstaffed

yóng (ㄩㄥˊ)

喁 [yóng]
囵 fish sticking its mouth out of the water ⇒yú
喁喁 ①everyone looking up to sb ②whisper

yǒng (ㄩㄥˇ)

永 [yǒng]
囵 perpetually;forever;for good;always
永别 part never to meet again;part forever;be parted by death
永磁 permanent magnetism
永存 ①eternal;lasting forever ②remain forever
永恒 eternal;perpetual
永久 permanent;perpetual;everlasting;forever;for good (and all)
永诀 part forever;be separated by death
永眠 die;be dead
永生 ①eternal life ②(usu. used in mourning for the dead) be immortal;live forever
永世 forever
永远 always;forever;ever
永磁体 permanent magnet
永冻层 permafrost horizon
永葆青春 always keep one's spirit young;keep alive the fervour of youth
永垂不朽 sb's memory will live forever;be immortal
永恒运动 perpetual motion
永结秦晋 ensure perpetual alliance between two families by a marriage
永久磁铁 permanent magnet
永久地址 permanent address
永久冻土 permafrost
永久和平 perpetual (*or* everlasting) peace
永久会员 permanent member
永久雪线 firn line
永久中立 permanent neutrality
永久主权 permanent sovereignty
永生永世 for ever and ever
永无宁日 never will there be days of peace

永志不忘 will forever bear in mind; will always cherish the memory of sb or sth
永磁发电机 magneto
永久性居民身份证 permanent identity card
永久正常贸易关系 Permanent Normal Trade Relations（PNTR）

甬 ［yǒng］
甬道 ①a paved path leading to a main hall or a tomb ②corridor

咏 ［yǒng］
劲 ①chant;recite;intone ②express or narrate in poetic form
咏唱 chant;sing
咏怀 singing from one's heart（a literary subgenre）
咏叹 intone;chant;sing
咏赞 sing the praises of;praise
咏叹调 aria

泳 ［yǒng］
劲 swim
泳道 lane（in a swimming race）
泳坛 swimming circles
泳装 swimsuit;swimwear;beach wear

俑 ［yǒng］
名 wooden or earthen human figurine buried with the dead in ancient times; tomb figure;figurine

勇 ［yǒng］
Ⅰ 形 brave;valiant;courageous;dauntless Ⅱ 名 temporary recruits in times of war during the Qing Dynasty
勇敢 brave;courageous
勇猛 bold and powerful;full of valour and vigour
勇气 courage;nerve
勇士 a brave and strong man;warrior
勇武 valiant
勇毅 brave and steadfast
勇于 be brave in;be bold in;have the courage to
勇不可挡 too courageous to be met with
勇冠三军 the bravest of the brave in the whole army;distinguish oneself by peerless valour
勇往直前 march forward courageously; advance bravely
勇于创新 be brave（or bold）in making innovations;have the courage to bring forth new ideas
勇于负责 be brave in shouldering responsibilities

涌 ［yǒng］
Ⅰ 劲 ① gush; well; pour; surge ② rise; surge;emerge Ⅱ 名 mountainous wave ⇒ chōng
涌潮 tidal bore
涌动 surge;billow
涌进 pour into
涌浪 turbulent waves
涌流 flow rapidly;pour
涌泉 fountain
涌现 emerge in large numbers;spring up; come to the fore
涌溢 gush out

愿 ［yǒng］
◇怂愿 instigate;incite;egg sb on;abet

蛹 ［yǒng］
名 pupa;chrysalis

踊 ［yǒng］
劲 leap up;jump up
踊跃 ①leap;jump ②vying with one another; eagerly ③enthusiastically

yòng（ㄩㄥ）

用 ［yòng］
Ⅰ 劲 ①use;utilize;employ;apply ②need; have to ③eat;drink;have Ⅱ 名 ①expense; spending; outlay ② use; usefulness; utility Ⅲ 副 hence;therefore
用兵 use military forces;resort to arms
用场 use
用处 use;good
用词 wording
用掉 used up;suck away
用度 expenditure;expense;outlay
用法 use;usage
用费 expense;cost
用工 recruit and use（workers）
用功 hardworking;diligent;studious
用惯 be accustomed to the use of
用户 consumer;user
用劲 exert oneself（physically）; put forth one's strength
用具 utensil;apparatus;appliance
用开 be widely used;become popular
用力 exert oneself（physically）; put forth one's strength
用品 articles for use
用人 ①choose a person for a job;make use of personnel ②need hands ③servant
用膳 have one's meals
用上 be made use of;be put to use
用事 ①act ②be in power ③make literary allusions
用途 use
用武 use force;display one's abilities or talents
用项 items of expenditure;expenditures
用心 ① diligently; attentively; with concentrated attention ②motive;intention
用刑 put sb to torture;torture
用以 in order to;so as to
用意 intention;purpose

用印 affix an official seal (to a document); seal (a document)

用语 ①choice of words; wording ②phraseology; term

用不了 ①have more than is needed ②less than

用不着 ①not need; have no use for ②there is no need to; it is not worthwhile to

用材林 commercial forest; timber forest

用出来 ①use; exert ②become easier to handle with use; be broken in

用得了 need that much (*or* many)

用得着 ①find sth useful; need ②there is need to; it is necessary to; it is worthwhile to

用工夫 study (*or* work) hard; spend time and energy

用户名 user name; user ID

用兵如神 direct military operations with miraculous skill; be a superb military commander

用非所长 unable to put one's specialized skill to best use; be engaged in an occupation having nothing to do with one's specialty

用非所学 be engaged in an occupation not related to one's training; What one is doing has nothing to do with one's training.

用工制度 system of recruitment (*or* employment)

用户电报 telex

用户界面 user interface

用户手册 user's manual

用户指南 user's guide

用户至上 customers first; clients first

用户终端 user terminal

用脑过度 overstrain one's nerves

用舍行藏 go forward when employed and stay out of sight when set aside

用特函达 Hence the present letter.

用心良苦 have really given much thought to the matter; have expended much care and thought on sth

用足政策 carry out policies from above to the fullest extent

佣 [yòng] 名 commission ➡ yōng

佣金 commission; brokerage; middleman's fee

yōu(ㄧㄡ)

优 [yōu] Ⅰ 形 ①good; excellent ②adequate; plentiful; affluent Ⅱ 动 give preferential treatment Ⅲ 名 actor; actress

优待 ①give preferential (*or* favoured, special) treatment ②preferential (*or* favoured, special) treatment

优等 high-class; first-rate; excellent

优点 merit; strong (*or* good) point; advan-

tage; virtue

优厚 munificent; liberal; favourable

优弧 major arc

优化 optimize

优惠 preferential; favourable

优价 ①favorable (*or* concessional) rates; preferential prices; favorable prices ②higher prices

优教 good education

优良 fine; good

优劣 good and bad; superior and inferior

优伶 actor; actress

优美 graceful; fine; exquisite

优俳 farce

优盘 only disc

优人 actor; actress

优柔 ①leisurely; unhurried ②gentle; amiable ③weak in character; hesitant

优胜 winning; superior

优势 superiority; preponderance; dominant position

优死 healthy death

优先 have priority; take precedence

优秀 outstanding; excellent; splendid; fine

优雅 graceful; elegant; in good taste

优异 excellent; outstanding; exceedingly good

优游 leisurely and carefree

优遇 give special treatment

优裕 affluent; abundant

优越 superior; advantageous

优质 high (*or* top) quality; high grade

优待券 complimentary ticket

优惠国 favoured nation

优惠权 preferential rights

优惠券 discount shopping coupon

优生学 eugenics

优胜旗 challenge flag; championship red banner

优先股 referred stock; preference share; preference stocks

优先权 priority; preference

优选法 optimization; optimum seeking method

优越感 sense of superiority; superiority complex

优越性 superiority; advantage

优抚安置 special care for disabled servicemen and families of revolutionary martyr and servicemen with jobs for demobilized soldiers

优抚对象 object of preferential treatment

优厚待遇 excellent pay and conditions; top reward

优化管理 optimize management

优化结构 optimize structure

优化组合 optimization; optimized composite; optimization regrouping; optional regrouping

优惠差额 margin of preference
优惠贷款 loan on favorable terms
优惠待遇 preferential treatment; favoured treatment
优惠价格 favoured price
优惠利率 prime rate
优惠期间 grace period
优惠条件 favourable terms; concessional terms
优惠条款 preferential clause
优惠政策 preferential policy; favorable policy
优良作风 exemplary working style
优孟衣冠 the actor Meng in costume—act on the stage; imitate others
优柔寡断 irresolute and hesitant; indecisive
优生优育 good pregnancy and good rearing; sound child-rearing; prenatal and postnatal care; bear and rear better children; raise healthier, better educated children
优胜劣败 the good prevailing over the bad
优胜劣汰 survival of the fittest; keep the superior and eliminate the inferior; pick out the good and leave the bad
优势兵力 superior force
优势产业 superior industry; strong industry
优势互补 take advantage of each other's strengths
优先录取 priority of admission
优哉游哉 leisurely and carefree; leisurely and unhurried
优质产品 superior quality products
优质服务 excellent service; superior service; first-rate service; first-class service; top quality service
优质高产 good quality and high output; high quality and high yield
优质优价 high quality and high price
优惠购货券 voucher
优惠贴现率 preferential exchange rate
优先认股权 stock option
优秀企业家 outstanding entrepreneur
优惠关税协定 preferential tariff agreement
优质名牌产品 high-quality famous-brand products

忧 [yōu]
Ⅰ 形 worried; sad; depressed Ⅱ 名 ① sorrow; anxiety; concern; care ② funeral of one's parent Ⅲ 动 worry; concern oneself
忧愁 worried; troubled; depressed
忧烦 worried; vexed
忧愤 worried and indignant
忧患 suffering; misery; hardship
忧惧 worried and apprehensive
忧劳 care-laden and overworked
忧虑 ① be worried; be anxious; be concerned ② worry; anxiety
忧闷 depressed; feeling low; weighed down with cares
忧戚 distressed; weighed down with sorrow; laden with grief
忧容 a worried look
忧伤 distressed; weighed down with sorrow; laden with grief
忧思 ① be worried; be anxious ② troubled thoughts
忧心 a troubled heart
忧悒 anxious and restless
忧郁 melancholy; heavyhearted; dejected
忧郁症 melancholia
忧国忧民 be concerned about one's country and one's people
忧患意识 consciousness (or awareness) of difficult times and disasters
忧患余生 a person who has known adversity and sorrow
忧喜参半 be half downcast and half glad
忧心忡忡 heavy-hearted; care-laden; weighed down with anxieties
忧心如焚 burning with anxiety; extremely worried

呦 [yōu]
叹 used to express surprise, astonishment, etc.: 呦! 电视机怎么坏了? Why, the television no longer works.
呦呦 the cry of a deer

幽 [yōu]
Ⅰ 形 ① deep and remote; out-of-the-way; secluded; dim ② secret; hidden; covert ③ quiet; tranquil; serene Ⅱ 动 imprison; place in confinement Ⅲ 名 ① name of an ancient prefecture covering present northern Hebei and southern Liaoning provinces ② nether world
幽暗 dim; dark; gloomy
幽闭 ① put under house arrest ② confine oneself indoors
幽愤 hidden resentment
幽谷 deep and secluded valley
幽会 a secret meeting of lovers; a lovers' rendezvous; tryst
幽寂 secluded and lonely
幽禁 put under house arrest; imprison
幽静 quiet and secluded; peaceful
幽居 ① live in seclusion ② a place of seclusion
幽兰 orchid
幽蓝 dull blue
幽灵 ghost; spectre; spirit
幽美 secluded and beautiful
幽门 pylorus
幽冥 ① dark; gloomy; sombre ② the nether world
幽默 humour
幽期 a secret meeting of lovers; a lover's rendezvous; tryst
幽情 exquisite feelings

幽囚 imprison；put in jail；keep in captivity
幽趣 the delightful serenity of seclusion
幽深 （of forests，palaces，etc.）deep and serene；deep and quiet
幽思 ①ponder；muse；meditate ②deep contemplation；melancholy brooding
幽婉 profound and complicated
幽娴 gentle and serene
幽香 a delicate（or faint）fragrance
幽雅 （of a place）quiet and tastefully laid out
幽幽 ①（of light or sound）faint ②looming in the distance
幽远 deep and distant（or far away）
幽怨 hidden bitterness（of a young woman thwarted in love）
幽默感 a sense of humour
幽默曲 humoresque
幽门梗阻 pyloric stenosis
幽默大师 humourist
幽默小说 humorous story；joke book

悠 [yōu]
I 形 ①remote in time or space；long；far ②leisurely；unhurried Ⅱ 动 swing；sway
悠长 long；long-drawn-out
悠荡 swing（to and fro）；sway（back and forth）
悠久 long；long-standing；age-old
悠然 carefree and leisurely
悠闲 leisurely and carefree
悠扬 （of music，etc.）rising and falling；melodious；mellifluous
悠悠 ①long；long-drawn-out；remote ②leisurely；unhurried ③absurd；preposterous
悠游 ①move about unhurriedly ②leisurely and carefree
悠远 ①a long time ago；long ago；distant ②far off（or away）；remote；distant
悠着 take things easy
悠久文明 time-honoured civilization
悠然自得 be carefree and content
悠悠荡荡 floating about；swinging to and fro
悠悠忽忽 ①loitering languidly；lounging around ②be in a trance

yóu（ㄧㄡˊ）

尤 [yóu]
I 形 remarkable；conspicuous；outstanding Ⅱ 副 particularly；especially；in particular：尤妙 even better；all the better Ⅲ 名 fault；error；wrongdoing Ⅳ 动 have a grudge against；resent；blame
尤其 especially；particularly
尤甚 more so；especially so
尤物 ①a rare thing ②an extraordinary person；a woman of great beauty
尤异 excellent；outstanding
尤伯杯 Uber Cup

由 [yóu]
I 名 cause；reason；grounds Ⅱ 介 ①because of；owing to；due to ②to or for（sb）；by（sb）③by means of ④（starting）from Ⅲ 动 ①pass by or through ②follow；obey
由此 from this；therefrom；hence；thus
由来 ①origin；source ②up to now；so far
由头 pretext
由于 ①owing to；thanks to；as a result of；due to；in virtue of ②because；since
由衷 ①from the bottom of one's heart ②sincere；heartfelt
由不得 ①not be up to sb to decide；be beyond the control of ②cannot help
由表及里 from the outside to the inside；from the surface to the centre
由此及彼 from one to the other
由此可见 thus it can be seen；this shows；that proves
由此类推 be parity of reasoning；by the same token
由点到面 take the experience gained at one unit and popularize it in a whole area
由简及繁 from the simple to the complex
由近及远 from the near to the distant
由来已久 long-standing；time-honoured
由浅入深 from the easy to the difficult；from the elementary to the profound
由易到难 from the easier to the more advanced
由衷之言 words from the bottom of one's heart；sincere words
由乱到治的过程 transition from disorder to rule
由俭入奢易，由奢入俭难 it is easy to go from frugality to extravagance，but difficult to go from extravagance to frugality

邮 [yóu]
I 动 post；mail Ⅱ 名 ①post；mail ②stamps Ⅲ 形 postal
邮包 postal parcel；parcel
邮差 postman
邮车 postal（or mail）car
邮船 ocean liner；liner；packet ship
邮戳 postmark
邮袋 mailbag；postbag；(mail) pouch
邮递 ①send by post（or mail）②postal（or mail）delivery
邮电 post and telecommunications
邮发 distributed and delivered by the post office
邮费 postage
邮购 mail-order
邮汇 remit by post
邮寄 send by post；post
邮件 postal matter；post；mail
邮局 post office

邮路 postal (*or* mail) route
邮轮 ocean liner;liner;packet ship
邮票 postage stamp;stamp
邮品 philatelic items (such as stamps,miniature sheets,first-day covers,etc.)
邮市 philatelic market
邮亭 postal kiosk
邮筒 pillar-box;postbox;mailbox
邮箱 postbox;mailbox
邮展 philatelic exhibition;stamp exhibition
邮政 postal service
邮资 postage
邮递员 postman;mailman
邮电局 post and telecommunications office
邮政局 post office
邮政网 postal network
邮递协议 post office protocol(POP)
邮件炸弹 mail bomb
邮政包裹 postal parcel
邮政编码 postal code (PC); postcode; zip code;zip
邮政储蓄 postal savings deposit
邮政汇票 postal money order;postal order
邮政局长 postmaster
邮政信箱 post-office box (P.O.B.)
邮件服务器 mail server
邮政代办所 postal agency
邮件传输协定 simple mail transfer protocol (SMTP)

犹 [yóu]
Ⅰ 〔副〕 still;even Ⅱ 〔介〕 just as;like
犹然 still;just as before
犹如 just as;like;as if
犹疑 hesitate
犹豫 hesitate;be irresolute
犹自 still
犹太教 Judaism
犹豫不决 hesitate;remain undecided;be irresolute
犹太复国主义 Zionism
犹太人定居点 Jewish settlements

油 [yóu]
Ⅰ 〔名〕 oil;fat;grease Ⅱ 〔动〕 ①apply tung oil (*or* varnish);paint ②be stained with oil (*or* grease) Ⅲ 〔形〕 oily;glib
油泵 oil pump
油饼 ①oilcake (as animal feed or fertilizer) ②deep-fried dough cake
油驳 oil barge
油布 oilcloth;oilskin;tarpaulin
油彩 greasepaint
油菜 ①rape (Brassica napus) ②Chinese cabbage (Brassica chinensis)
油藏 oil deposit;oil pool
油层 oil reservoir;oil layer;oil horizon
油茶 ①tea-oil tree;oil-tea camellia (Camellia oleifera) ② a gruel of sweetened, fried flour
油船 oil tanker;tanker;oil carrier
油灯 oil lamp
油坊 oil mill
油封 oil seal
油膏 ointment
油垢 greasy filth;greasy dirt
油管 ①oil pipe ②oil tube
油罐 oil tank;storage tank
油光 glossy;shiny;varnished
油耗 oil consumption
油黑 glossy black
油壶 oilcan
油滑 slippery;foxy
油画 oil painting
油灰 putty
油鸡 a fine breed of chicken with thick brownish feathers
油迹 oil stains;grease spots
油匠 painter
油井 oil well
油锯 chain saw
油库 oil depot;tank farm
油矿 ①oil deposit ②oilfield
油亮 (often reduplicated) glossy;shiny
油料 oil-bearing seed;oilseed
油绿 glossy dark green
油轮 oil tanker;tanker;oil carrier
油门 ①throttle ②accelerator
油焖 braise
油苗 oil seepage
油墨 printing ink
油泥 greasy filth
油腻 ①greasy;fatty;oily ②greasy food;fatty food;oily food
油盘 food tray
油票 ①cooking oil coupon ②gasoline coupon
油漆 ①paint ②cover with paint;paint
油气 associated gas
油枪 oil gun
油裙 kitchen apron;apron
油然 ① spontaneously; involuntarily ② (of clouds) gathering
油润 glossy and sleek;wet and smooth
油色 oil colours;oils
油砂 oil sand
油石 oilstone (for sharpening cutting tools)
油饰 cover (*or* decorate) with paint;paint;varnish
油柿 wild kaki persimmon
油刷 cover with paint (*or* varnish);paint
油水 [yóushuǐ] oil-water
油水 [yóushui] ①grease ②pickings;profit
油松 Chinese pine
油酥 short;crisp;flaky
油酸 oleic acid
油提 oil-dipper

Y

油田 oilfield
油条 deep-fried twisted dough sticks
油桐 tung oil tree; tung tree
油桶 oil drum
油位 oil level
油污 greasy dirt
油香 a salted cake fried in sesame oil
油箱 fuel tank
油鞋 oiled shoes (for wet weather)
油星 drops of oil on the surface of soup; blobs of fat
油性 oiliness; greasiness
油靴 oiled boots (for wet weather)
油压 oil pressure
油衣 oilskins
油印 mimeograph
油油 ① glossy; shiny ② flowing smoothly and incessantly ③ luxuriant and dense
油浴 oil bath
油渣 ① dregs of fat ② petroleum oil residue
油炸 deep-fry
油毡 asphalt felt
油脂 oil; fat
油纸 oilpaper
油子 ① black sticky substance ② a foxy old hand
油棕 oil palm
油嘴 ① glib ② a glib talker ③ spray nozzle; spray head
油槽车 tank truck
油淬火 oil hardening; oil quenching
油底子 oil dregs
油豆腐 fried bean curd
油橄榄 olive
油乎乎 oily; greasy
油葫芦 a kind of field cricket
油花儿 drops of oil on the surface of soup; blobs of fat
油画色 oil colours; oils
油码头 oil jetty; oil wharf; tanker (loading) terminal
油毛毡 asphalt felt
油漆工 painter
油气比 oil-gas ratio
油气田 oil and gas field
油汪汪 ① dripping with oil; full of grease ② glossy; shiny
油位表 oil (level) gauge
油压泵 oil pressure pump
油压表 oil pressure gauge
油压机 hydraulic press; oil press
油烟(子) lampblack; soot
油椰子 oil palm
油页岩 oil-shale
油印机 mimeograph
油炸鬼 deep-fried dough strips (or rings)
油茶面儿 flour fried in beef fat with sugar and sesame

油光水滑 smooth and shining; sleek
油画颜料 oil colours; oils
油煎火燎 in a state of great agitation; in a stew
油料作物 oil-bearing crops; oil crops
油母页岩 oil-shale
油气界面 the interface of oil and gas; oil-gas interface
油腔滑调 glib
油然而生 (of a feeling) rise of itself; be produced of itself
油头粉面 sleek-haired and creamy-faced—heavily made-up; dressy or foppish
油头滑脑 slick; smooth; oily
油压传动 hydraulic transmission
油印蜡纸 stencil; stencil paper
油质颜料 oil pigment
油嘴滑舌 glib-tongued
油溶性染料 oil-soluble dyes
油压千斤顶 hydraulic jack; oil jack

柚 ［yòu］
➡ yòu
柚木 teak; teakwood

疣 ［yóu］
疣赘 ① wart ② anything superfluous or useless

莜 ［yóu］
莜麦 naked oats

莸 ［yóu］
〈名〉① common bluebeard ② stinking grass; stinking personality

铀 ［yóu］
〈名〉uranium (U)
铀矿石 uranium ore
铀后元素 transuranium element; transuranium

游 ［yóu］
I 〈动〉① swim ② stroll (or rove) about; travel; tour ③ associate with II 〈形〉roving; migrating; unsettled III 〈名〉part of a river; reach
游伴 travel companion
游标 vernier; vernier scale
游程 ① distance of swimming ② route of travel ③ itinerary
游船 pleasure-boat
游春 go on a spring outing
游词 ① unfounded remarks; a groundless statement ② joke; jest
游荡 loaf about; loiter; wander
游动 ① move about; go from place to place ② mobile; moving; roving
游逛 go sightseeing; stroll about
游魂 a wandering ghost
游击 guerrilla warfare
游记 travel notes; travels
游街 parade sb through the streets

游客 visitor (to a park, etc.); tourist; excursionist; sightseer
游览 go sightseeing; tour; visit
游廊 covered corridor (linking two or more buildings); veranda
游乐 make merry; amuse oneself
游离 ①dissociate; drift away ②free
游历 travel for pleasure; travel; tour
游猎 go on a hunting trip
游民 vagrant; vagabond
游牧 move about in search of pasture; rove around as a nomad
游禽 natatorial bird
游人 visitor (to a park, etc.); sightseer; tourist
游蛇 water snake; ringed snake
游水 swim
游说 go about selling an idea; go about drumming up support for an idea; go canvassing
游丝 ①gossamer ②hairspring
游艇 yacht; pleasure-boat
游玩 ①amuse oneself; play ②go sightseeing; stroll about
游戏 ①recreation; game ②play
游侠 (in former times) roving brave; knight-errant
游行 parade; march; demonstration
游兴 interest in going on an excursion (or sightseeing)
游医 itinerant doctor
游移 (of attitude, policy, etc.) waver; vacillate; wobble
游弋 cruise
游艺 entertainment; recreation
游泳 swim
游勇 stragglers and disbanded soldiers
游园 ①visit a garden (or park) ②mass celebrations in parks
游资 idle fund; idle money; floating capital; unemployed capital
游子 man travelling or residing in a place far away from home
游踪 the whereabouts of a traveller
游动哨 a roving sentry; patrol
游击队 guerrilla forces; a guerrilla detachment
游击区 guerrilla area
游击战 guerrilla war; guerrilla warfare
游览车 tourist coach
游览地 place for sightseeing; excursion centre
游览区 tourist area
游览图 tourist map
游乐场 play field; amusement centre
游乐车 funabout
游乐厅 pleasure-house
游乐园 amusement park; pleasure ground (or garden)
游离基 free radical

游戏机 video game machine; computer video game
游艺会 entertainment gathering
游艺室 recreation room
游泳池 swimming pool
游泳馆 natatorium
游泳裤 bathing (or swimming) trunks
游泳帽 bathing (or swimming) cap
游泳衣 swimsuit; swimming suit (or costume); bathing suit (or costume)
游园会 garden gathering; garden carnival; garden party
游离电子 free electron
游目骋怀 look as far as one's eyes can see and give free rein to one's thoughts and feelings
游刃有余 handle a cleaver with skill—do a job with skill and ease; be more than equal to a task
游山玩水 go on scenic; travel from one beauty spot to another; visit various scenic spots
游手好闲 idle about; loaf

yǒu(1ㄡˇ)

友 Ⅰ 名 friend Ⅱ 动 be on intimate terms; be close to Ⅲ 形 friendly
友爱 friendly affection; fraternal love
友邦 friendly nation (or country)
友好 ①close friend; friend ②friendly; amicable
友军 friendly forces
友邻 friendly neighbours; good neighbours
友朋 friends
友情 friendly sentiments; friendship
友人 friend
友善 friendly; amicable
友谊 friendship
友谊杯 cup of friendship
友谊赛 friendly match
友好城市 twin cities; sister cities; sibling cities; cities of friendship
友好相处 keep in with; live on friendly terms with
友情出演 friendship performance
友谊商店 friendship store
友好邀请赛 friendship invitational tournament

有 Ⅰ 动 ①have; own; possess ②there is; exist ③(used for estimation or comparison): 你有一米八吧? You are about 1.80 metres tall, aren't you? ④(used to indicate that sth takes place or appears): 情况有了新的变化。There was a new change in the situation. ⑤(used to indicate ample amount): 他管理很有经验。He is very experienced in management. ⑥(used in a gener-

al sense, similar to the meaning of 某）：有些事还需要从长计议。Certain things need to be given further thought and deliberation. ⑦（*used before people, time, or place to indicate a part*）：有人赞成，有人反对。Some are for it, others are against it. Ⅱ 劻（*used before certain verbs to form polite formulae*）Ⅲ（*prefix used before the names of dynasties*）：有宋一代 Song Dynasty ➡ yòu

有碍 be a hindrance to; get in the way of; obstruct

有偿 with compensation; compensated; paid

有成 achieve success

有待 remain (to be done); await

有道 have attained the Way; be accomplished in the Way; adhere to principles of truth and right

有得 [yǒudé] have learned sth; have gained some knowledge

有的 [yǒude] some

有底 know how things stand and feel confident of handling them; be fully prepared for what is coming

有方 with the proper method; in the right way

有感 thoughts on sth (usu. used in the title of a literary sketch)

有功 have rendered great service; have performed meritorious service

有关 ① have sth to do with; have a bearing on; relate to; concern ② related; concerned; relevant; pertinent

有光 ① glazed ② bright

有鬼 there's something fishy

有害 harmful; pernicious; detrimental

有恒 persevering

有机 ① organic ② organic

有救 can be saved (*or* cured, remedied)

有愧 feel qualms about sth; have a guilty conscience

有赖 depend on; rest on

有劳 may I trouble you; sorry to bother you

有理 ① reasonable; justified; in the right ② rational

有力 strong; powerful; forceful; energetic; vigorous

有利 advantageous; beneficial; favourable

有脸 ① have prestige; command respect ② have the face

有了 ①（said when hitting upon an idea）I've got it. ② be pregnant

有零 (used after round numbers) odd

有名 well-known; famous; celebrated

有气 be or get angry; take offence

有钱 rich; wealthy

有情 be in love

有请 ask the visitor in

有趣 interesting; fascinating; amusing

有染 have illicit sexual relations

有扰 thanks for your hospitality

有如 just like; as if; as though

有色 coloured

有时 sometimes; at times; now and then

有事 ① have a job; be employed ② be occupied; be busy ③ have sth happen; meet with an accident; get into trouble ④（*used with* 心里）have sth on one's mind; be anxious; worry

有数 ① know exactly how things stand; have a definite idea of what one's doing ② not many; only a few

有所 to some extent; somewhat

有望 hopeful

有为 promising

有喜 be pregnant; be expecting; be in the family way

有戏 hopeful

有隙 ① bear a grudge ② there is a loophole

有闲 have leisure

有限 limited; finite

有线 wired

有效 efficacious; effective; valid

有些 ① some ② somewhat; rather

有心 ① have a mind to; set one's mind on ② intentionally; purposely

有形 tangible; visible; physical

有幸 be lucky to; have the good fortune to

有性 sexual

有益 profitable; beneficial; useful

有意 ① have a mind to; be inclined (*or* disposed) to ② intentionally; deliberately; purposely

有余 ① have a surplus; have enough and to spare ② odd

有缘 be predetermined by fate; be predestined; have a bond; have an affinity

有源 active

有种 have guts; be plucky; be gritty

有罪 be guilty of a crime; be guilty

有把握 confident of success

有奔头 have bright prospects

有成果 productive; fruitful

有袋类 marsupial

有的是 have plenty of; there's no lack of

有点儿 ① some; a little ② somewhat; rather; a bit

有份儿 have a share; have taken a part in

有会子 quite a long while; quite some time

有机酸 organic acid

有机体 organism

有机物 organic matter (*or* substance)

有计划 in a planned way; according to plan

有理式 rational formula

有理数 rational number

有门儿 ① find the beginning of a solution; be

hopeful (of success) ②get the hang

有门路 have a way out;have powerful connections

有你的 ①you really are something;good for you ②you'll get your deserts;you'll suffer for this

有盼头 hopeful

有谱儿 have sth to go by;have confidence

有气儿 be breathing

有情人 lovers

有求于 have to look to sb for help;have a favour to ask of sb

有日子 ①for quite a few days;for days ② have fixed a date

有神论 theism

有声片 sound film;talkie

有味儿 ①(of food) be tasty;be delicious ② (of food) smell bad;be off ③be interesting;be meaningful

有效票 valid ballot paper

有效期 term (or period) of validity;time of efficacy

有心人 a person who sets his mind on doing sth useful;a person with high aspirations and determination;an observant and conscientious person

有眼光 have good taste

有意识 consciously

有意思 ①significant;meaningful ②interesting;enjoyable

有助于 contribute to;be conducive to;conduce to

有碍观瞻 be unsightly;offend the eye;be an eyesore

有案可稽 be a matter of record;be on record; be documented

有板有眼 rhythmical;measured;orderly

有备无患 Where there is precaution,there is no danger;Preparedness averts peril.

有悖事实 not square with the facts;be at variance with the facts

有财有势 have plenty of money and pull;be rich and powerful

有产阶级 propertied class

有偿服务 paid service;compensable service

有偿使用 paid use

有偿新闻 payable news;newswriting for illicit payments;illicit paid news coverage;pay-off-aimed journalism; kickback-oriented journalism

有偿转让 transfer for money;re-sales for reward;paid transfer(of technology)

有吃有喝 have plenty to eat and drink

有酬劳动 paid labour

有错必纠 Every wrong will be righted.

有胆有识 be courageous and knowledgeable

有的放矢 shoot the arrow at the target—have

an object in view

有毒大米 poisonous rice

有法必依 ensure that laws are observed

有法不依 laws are ignored

有关当局 the authorities concerned;the proper authorities

有关规定 pertinent regulations

有轨电车 tramcar;streetcar

有行无市 (of a market) have only quotations but no actual trading

有机玻璃 polymethyl methacrylate;plexiglass

有机肥料 organic fertilizer;manure

有机耕作 organic farming;organic gardening

有机合成 organic synthesis

有机化学 organic chemistry

有机可乘 There's an opportunity to take advantage of;There's a loophole that can be used.

有机农业 organic agriculture

有机染料 organic dyestuff

有机食品 organic food

有价证券 negotiable securities;securities

有奖储蓄 prize-giving savings deposits;premium savings account;savings deposit account which offers premiums; savings account with prizes

有奖购物 lottery shopping

有奖销售 prize-giving sales;sales with give-a-ways; comeback premium; sale with rewards;offer a premium with the sale of an item;sell goods with prize

有奖债券 premium bond

有奖征文 reward for written works

有教无类 in education there should be no class distinctions

有借无还 borrow without returning

有禁不止 disregard prohibitions;ignore an interdiction

有禁则止 observe a prohibition strictly;respect a taboo

有惊无险 be more scared than hurt;threatening but not dangerous

有口皆碑 win universal praise;be universally acclaimed

有口难辩 find it hard to defend (or vindicate) oneself

有口难言 cannot bring oneself to mention sth; find it hard (or embarrassing) to bring up a matter

有口无心 be sharp-tongued but not malicious

有来有往 give-and-take;reciprocal

有理分式 rational fraction

有理函数 rational function

有理无情 ①stick to the principle and disregard personal feelings ②for no apparent reason;without rhyme or reason

有利可图 have good prospects of profit;stand

Y

to gain; be profitable
有利时机 opportune time
有利条件 favourable conditions (*or* terms)
有利无弊 have every advantage and not a single disadvantage; be advantageous in every respect
有利有弊 There are both advantages and disadvantages.
有例在先 there is a precedent for that
有两下子 have real skill; know one's stuff
有令则行 obey orders strictly
有名无实 in name but not in reality; merely nominal; titular
有名有姓 identifiable by both given name and surname—of established identity
有目共睹 be obvious to anyone who has eyes; be perfectly obvious
有目共赏 have a universal appeal; appeal to all alike
有难同当 join in with sb to take a risk
有凭有据 fully substantiated; well-documented
有期徒刑 fixed-term imprisonment
有气无力 feeble; weak; faint; listless
有钱有势 have wealth and influence; rich and powerful
有求必应 respond to every plea; grant whatever is requested
有去无还 gone never to return; gone forever
有人家儿 (of a girl) be engaged
有辱家门 be a scandal to the family
有色金属 nonferrous metal
有色人种 coloured race (*or* people)
有啥吃啥 eat whatever is available
有伤风化 be harmful to society's morals; be destructive to the morals
有生力量 effective strength; effectives
有生以来 ever since one's birth
有生之年 one's remaining years
有声读物 audiobook
有声书籍 audiobook
有声有色 full of sound and colour—vivid and dramatic
有声资料 voice data
有失身份 beneath one's dignity
有识之士 a person with breadth of vision; a man of insight
有史以来 since the beginning (*or* dawn) of history; throughout history
有始无终 start sth but not carry it through
有始有终 carry sth through to the end
有恃无恐 when one has something to fall back upon one has nothing to fear; feel secure in the knowledge that one has strong backing
有说有笑 talk and laugh
有丝分裂 mitosis
有所侧重 emphasis (laid) on one particular field

有蹄动物 ungulate
有天没日 ① wanton; unbridled; outrageous ② complete darkness—total absence of justice
有条不紊 in an orderly way; methodically; systematically
有条有理 methodical; systematic; orderly
有头无尾 have a beginning but no end; start sth but not finish it; leave sth unfinished; give up sth halfway
有头有脸 have prestige; command respect
有头有尾 have a beginning and an end; do sth from beginning to end; start sth and finish it
有闻必录 record whatever one hears
有隙可乘 there is a crack to squeeze through—there is a loophole to exploit
有限公司 limited company; limited-liability company
有限花序 definite inflorescence
有限级数 finite progression; finite series
有限战争 limited war
有线传真 wirephoto
有线电报 wire telegraph
有线电话 wire (*or* wired) telephone
有线电视 cable TV; community antenna television (CATV)
有线广播 wire (*or* wired) broadcasting; rediffusion on wire
有效分蘖 effective tillering
有效功率 effective power; useful power
有效供给 efficiency of supply
有效荷载 useful load
有效库容 effective storage
有效射程 effective range
有效数字 significant digits
有形财产 corporeal property; material property
有形贸易 visible trade
有形损耗 material loss
有形资本 material capital
有形资产 tangible assets; visible assets; tangibles
有性生殖 sexual reproduction; zoogamy
有性世代 sexual generation
有性杂交 sexual hybridization
有血有肉 lifelike; true to life; vivid
有言在先 make clear beforehand; forewarn
有眼无珠 have eyes but see not; possess no true discernment
有氧运动 aerobic exercise
有一得一 no more, no less; just that much
有意无意 wittingly or unwittingly; consciously or unconsciously; by accident or design
有影没影 groundless; unfounded
有勇无谋 have valour but lack strategy; be brave but not resourceful; be foolhardy
有增无已 ever-increasing; increasingly

Y

有朝一日 should the day come when...; if by chance...

有职无权 hold a post but have no real power or authority; be a figurehead

有职有权 hold both the post and the power; have the authority that goes with one's post; exercise the power that goes with one's post

有志之士 a person of noble aspirations; a person with lofty ideals

有滋有味 ① tasty; delicious ② with relish; avidly

有机化合物 organic compound

有奶便是娘 whoever suckles me is my mother; submit to whoever feeds one; lick the hand of anyone who throws a few crumbs

有政治眼光 have a political foresight

有组织犯罪 organized crimes

有鼻子有眼儿 with every detail described

有偿土地使用 paid land use

有过之无不及 go even farther than; outdo

有条件的援助 aid with attached strings

有线电视广播 cable television

有眼不识泰山 have eyes but not see Mount Tai; entertain an angel unawares

有一搭没一搭 ① trying to engage sb in small talk; conversing for the sake of conversing ② not essential; not indispensable

有志者事竟成 Where there's a will there's a way.

有利可图的市场 a juicy (or lucrative) market

有钱能使鬼推磨 with money you can make the devil turn the millstone; money makes the mare go

有情人终成眷属 lovers will be married; Jack shall have Jill, all shall be well.

有限责任制公司 limited liability company

有其父,必有其子 like father; like son

有法可依,有章可循 There are laws and regulations to go by.

有福同享,有祸同当 share joys and sorrows; share weal and woe; stick together through thick and thin

有令不行,有禁不止 go one's own way in disregard of orders and prohibitions; flout the rules

有一分热,发一分光 give as much light as the fuel can produce—do one's best, however little it may be

有则改之,无则加勉 correct mistakes if you have made any and guard against them if you have not

有中国特色的社会主义 socialism with Chinese characteristics

有朋自远方来,不亦乐乎 Is it not a joy to have friends come from afar?

有所不为而后可以有所为 you must leave some things undone if you want to get others done; refrain from doing some things in order to be able to do other things

有理走遍天下,无理寸步难行 With justice on your side, you can go anywhere; Without it, you can't take a step.

有缘千里能相会,无缘对面不相逢 If there is a bond between them, the two will meet across a thousand *li*; Without a bond, they will not meet though face to face.

酉 [yǒu]

酉时 the period of the day from 5 p.m. to 7 p.m.

莠 [yǒu]

Ⅰ 名 green bristlegrass Ⅱ 形 bad (people)

黝 [yǒu]

形 black; dark

黝黑 dark; swarthy

yòu(ㅣㄡˋ)

又 [yòu]

副 ① (*used to indicate repetition or continuation*): 过了一天又一天 day after day ② (*used to indicate that several conditions or qualities exist at the same time*): 又聪明又能干 be intelligent as well as capable/又方便又安全 be both convenient and safe ③ furthermore; in addition; moreover ④ besides; apart from ⑤ (*used to indicate that an odd number is added to a whole number*): 两小时又十分 two hours and ten minutes ⑥ (*used often in parallel to indicate two contradictory things*): 今晚这场电影,她又想看,又不想看,一时还拿不定主意。 She couldn't make up her mind whether or not to see the film tonight. ⑦ but; yet; however: 她想吃冰淇淋,可又怕发胖。 She loves ice cream but is afraid of getting fat. ⑧ (*used for emphasis in negative sentences or rhetorical questions*): 你又不是第一次上台,紧张什么? Why so nervous? This is not the first time you've appeared on the stage.

又及 postscript (PS)

又名 also called; alias; also known as

又打又拉 strike and stroke alternately; use both the carrot and the stick

又红又专 both socialist-minded and professionally proficient; both politically conscious and professionally competent

又惊又喜 be both startled and delighted; be pleasantly surprised

又想当婊子,又想立牌坊 lead the life of a whore and want a monument put up to one's chastity

又要马儿跑,又要马儿不吃草 expect the horse to run fast but not let it graze; eat one's

cake and have it

右 [yòu]
I 名 ① right side; right ② west ③ right side as the side of precedence Ⅱ 动 ①uphold; advocate ② help; protect; defend; bless Ⅲ 形 conservative; the Right

右边 ① the right (*or* right-hand) side ② the right

右侧 ① the right (*or* right-hand) side ② the right

右舵 right standard rudder; right rudder

右锋 right forward

右面 ① the right (*or* right-hand) side ② the right

右派 the Right; the right wing; Rightist

右倾 Right deviation

右手 ①the right hand ②the right-hand side; the right

右首 the right-hand side; the right

右袒 take sides with; be partial to

右武 advocate a military (*or* martial) spirit

右舷 starboard (of a ship)

右旋 dextrorotation

右翼 ① right wing; right flank ② the right wing; the Right

右边锋 outside right; right wing

右后卫 right back

右内锋 inside right

右前轮 off-front wheel (of a car)

右前卫 right halfback; right half

右旋糖 dextrose; glucose; grape sugar

右手定则 the right-hand rule

右翼分子 rightist; Right-winger

右翼政府 right-wing government

右倾机会主义 Right opportunism

幼 [yòu]
I 形 young; minor; under age Ⅱ 名 children; the young

幼虫 larva

幼雏 young bird; baby bird; nestling

幼儿 child; infant

幼功 skills (of actors, acrobats, etc.) acquired during childhood

幼教 preschool education

幼苗 seedling

幼嫩 ①tender; delicate ②immature; naive

幼年 childhood; infancy

幼女 a young girl

幼弱 young and delicate

幼师 preschool teachers training school

幼时 childhood; infancy

幼树 sapling

幼体 the young; larva

幼童 child

幼小 young and small; immature

幼芽 young shoot; bud

幼稚 ①young ②childish; puerile; naive

幼株 young plant; seedling

幼子 ①the youngest son ②young (and immature) son

幼儿园 kindergarten; nursery school; infant school

幼龄林 young growth

幼稚病 ①infantilism ②infantile disorder

幼稚园 kindergarten; nursery school; infant school

幼儿教育 preschool education

幼稚产业 infant industry

幼稚工业 infant industry

幼儿保健诊所 well-child clinic

幼儿家庭教师 baby tutor

幼儿师范学校 preschool teachers training school

有 [yòu]
副 (*used to add an odd number to a whole number*) ⇒ yǒu

佑 [yòu]
动 help; protect; defend; bless

佑护 protect; bless

佑助 help; aid; assist

侑 [yòu]
动 press (sb to eat or drink); press

侑食 urge sb to have food

侑饮 press sb to drink

狖 [yòu]
名 a kind of monkey

柚 [yòu]
名 ①Rangoon teak; Burma teak ②fruit of Rangoon teak commonly known as shaddock or pomelo ⇒ yóu

柚子 shaddocks

囿 [yòu]
I 名 animal farm; enclosure; park Ⅱ 动 limited; constrained; hampered

囿于成见 be blinded by prejudice

囿于传统陋习 constrained by corrupt traditional customs

诱 [yòu]
动 ① guide; direct; lead; induce ② lure; tempt; seduce; entice

诱逼 cajole and coerce

诱变 mutagenesis; mutagenicity

诱捕 lure criminal out of hiding and arrest him; trap (animals)

诱导 ①guide; lead; induce ②induce

诱饵 bait

诱发 bring out (sth potential or latent); induce; cause to happen

诱供 trap a person into a confession; induce a person to make a confession

诱拐 abduct; carry off (a woman) by fraud; kidnap (a child)

诱惑 ①entice; tempt; seduce; lure ②attract; allure

诱奸 entice into unlawful sexual intercourse;

seduce
诱骗 inveigle;cajole;trap;trick
诱迫 cajole and coerce
诱人 alluring; fascination; captivating; enchanting
诱杀 trap and kill;lure to destruction
诱使 trick into;inveigle into;lure into
诱降 lure into surrender
诱胁 cajole and coerce
诱因 cause (esp. of an illness)
诱致 lead to;cause
诱变剂 mutagen;mutagenic agent
诱虫灯 moth-killing lamp
诱蛾灯 moth-killing lamp
诱售法 bait-and-switch
诱癌因素 carcinogen
诱变处理 mutagenize
诱变基因 mutator;mutator gene
诱变物质 mutagen matter
诱变因素 mutagen
诱变因子 mutagen;mutagenic agent
诱变育种 mutation breeding
诱导反应 induced reaction
诱敌深入 lure the enemy in deep
诱售广告 bait-and-switch advertising
诱致流动 induced flow
诱致投资 induced investment

蚴 〔yòu〕
〈名〉 larva of a tapeworm or cercaria of a schistosome

釉 〔yòu〕
〈名〉 glaze
釉工 glazer
釉料 frit;slag
釉陶 glazed pottery
釉质 enamel
釉子 glaze
釉面砖 glazed tile
釉彩玻璃 enameled glass

鼬 〔yòu〕
〈名〉 weasel
鼬獾 ferret badger

yū〔ㄩ〕

迂 〔yū〕
Ⅰ 〈动〉 go round; take a detour; wind one's way Ⅱ 〈形〉 given to outworn rules and ideas; pedantic;impractical
迂腐 stubbornly clinging to outworn rules and ideas;pedantic
迂缓 slow in movement;dilatory
迂回 ① circuitous; tortuous; roundabout ② outflank
迂见 pedantic ideas
迂阔 high-sounding and impracticable
迂论 impractical views
迂曲 tortuous;circuitous

迂儒 a pedantic scholar;pedant
迂拙 impractical and stupid
迂夫子 pedant
迂回曲折 full of twists and turns;circuitous;tortuous
迂回战术 outflanking tactics

吁 〔yū〕
〈叹〉 call to an animal to halt;whoa ⇒ xū;yù

纡 〔yū〕
Ⅰ 〈形〉 tortuous; circuitous; winding Ⅱ 〈动〉 tie;bind

淤 〔yū〕
Ⅰ 〈动〉 ①silt up ②spill;overflow Ⅱ 〈形〉 silted (up) Ⅲ 〈名〉 ①silt;sediment;mud ②stasis
淤地 alluvial plain
淤淀 silt up
淤灌 warping
淤积 silt up;deposit
淤泥 silt;sludge;ooze
淤塞 silt up;be choked with silt
淤血 extravasated blood
淤滞 ①(of the flow of a river,etc.) be retarded by silt;silt up ②stasis (of blood or other bodily fluids)
淤地坝 silt arrester
淤浊不清 muddy and unclear

瘀 〔yū〕
〈名〉 stasis of blood
瘀斑 ecchymosis
瘀点 petechiae

yú〔ㄩˊ〕

于 〔yú〕
Ⅰ 〈介〉 ①in;at;on;黄河发源于青海。 The Yellow River originates in Qinghai. ② towards;to;求救于人 ask people for help③to; onto;嫁祸于人 shift the blame onto others④ for;to;习惯于这种生活 be used to this kind of life/忠于人民 be loyal to the people ⑤ from;out of;出于好心 out of good will/出于自愿 of one's own free will;of one's own accord/青出于蓝而胜于蓝。 Blue comes from the indigo plant but is bluer than the plant itself.⑥than;出发时间不能晚于上午8点。 The start-off time should not be later than eight o'clock in the morning. /参加者不得多于20人。 The number of attendants should not exceed twenty. /为人民而死,重于泰山。 It is weightier than Mount Tai to die for the people.⑦(used in the passive voice) by;见笑于人 be laughed at by others/限于水平 be restricted by one's ability Ⅱ (used as a suffix after a verb or after an adjective);敢于斗争 dare to fight/善于斗争 be good at fighting
于今 ①up to the present;since ②nowadays;today;now

于是 so；then；thereupon；hence
于事无补 It would not help matters；It doesn't help the situation.
于心不忍 not have the heart to；can't bear to
于心有愧 have a guilty conscience；have sth on one's conscience；feel ashamed
于愿已足 have nothing left to wish for

予 [yú]
氏 I；me ➡ yǔ

余 [yú]
Ⅰ 氏 I；me；my Ⅱ 形 ①surplus；spare；left；remaining ②more than；odd；over Ⅲ 名 ①remainder ②time after（an event）
余波 the swell after a storm—repercussions
余存 balance；remainder
余党 remnants of an overthrown clique（or gang）；remaining confederates
余地 leeway；margin；room；latitude
余毒 pernicious influence；leftover poison
余额 ①vacancies yet to be filled ②remaining sum；balance
余割 cosecant
余晖 sunset glow；evening glow
余悸 lingering fear
余角 complementary angle
余烬 ashes；embers
余款 spare money（or cash）
余力 surplus energy（or strength）
余粮 surplus grain
余量 remnant；leftover
余年 one's remaining years
余孽 remaining evil element；leftover evil；surviving supporter of an evil cause
余切 cotangent
余缺 surplus and deficiency
余热 ①surplus energy ②old people's capacity for work
余生 ①the remainder of one's life；one's remaining years ②survival（after a disaster）
余矢 coversed sine（covers）
余数 remainder（after division）
余头 remainder
余威 remaining prestige（or influence）
余味 agreeable aftertaste；pleasant impression
余隙 clearance
余暇 spare time；leisure time；leisure
余下 remaining
余弦 cosine
余兴 ①lingering interest；a wish to prolong a pleasant diversion ②entertainment after a meeting（or a dinner party）
余音 lingering sound（of music or singing）
余韵 lingering charm
余震 aftershock
余函数 complementary function
余因子 complementary divisor
余额承前 balance brought forward

余可类推 The rest may be inferred by analogy.
余怒未消 be still angry；be still fuming
余音绕梁 the music lingering around the beams；the music lingering in the air long after the performance
余勇可贾 with plenty of fight left in one；with strength yet to spare

欤 [yú]
欤 ①（expressing doubt or used in rhetorical questions）：子非三闾大夫欤？ Aren't you the cabinet minister Qu Yuan？ ②（used in an exclamation）：论者之言，一似管窥虎欤！ Indeed，the speaker's argument was as one-sided as looking at a tiger through a bamboo tube！

盂 [yú]
名 broad-mouthed receptacle；jar
盂兰盆会 the Buddhist name of the Ghost Festival（on the 15th of the seventh lunar month）

鱼 [yú]
名 fish
鱼白 ①fish sperm；milt ②the whitish colour of a fish's belly—grey dawn
鱼鳔 air bladder（of fish）；swim bladder
鱼叉 fish spear；fish fork
鱼场 fish farm
鱼池 fish pond
鱼翅 shark's fin（a delicacy）
鱼虫 water flea（used as fish feed）
鱼唇 shark's lip（as food）
鱼刺 fishbone
鱼肚 fish maw（as food）
鱼饵 （fish）bait
鱼贩 fishmonger
鱼粉 fish meal
鱼腹 fish belly
鱼竿 fish pole；fishing rod
鱼缸 fish bowl；fish tank
鱼钩 fishhook；angle
鱼狗 kingfisher
鱼贯 one following the other；in single file
鱼胶 ①fish glue；isinglass ②air bladder；swim bladder
鱼口 lymphogranuloma inguinale；climatic（or tropical）bubo
鱼雷 torpedo
鱼鳞 fish scale；scale
鱼龙 ichthyosaur
鱼篓 bamboo fish hamper
鱼露 fish sauce
鱼卵 （fish）roe
鱼苗 （fish）fry
鱼片 sliced fish meat
鱼漂 cork on a fishing line；float
鱼鳍 fin

Y

鱼群 a shoal of fish
鱼肉 ①the flesh of fish ②fish and meat ③cut up like fish and meat—cruelly oppress
鱼市 fish market
鱼水 fish and water
鱼塘 fish pond
鱼汛 fishing season
鱼雁 ①fish and wild geese ②letters (from the legends of fish and wild geese as bearers of letters)
鱼鹰 ①a large hawk that feeds on fish; fish hawk ②a diving bird leashed by fishermen to catch fish; cormorant
鱼油 fish oil
鱼圆 fish ball
鱼源 source of fish; breeding ground for fish
鱼跃 fish dive
鱼闸 fish lock
鱼种 fingerling
鱼子 (fish) roe
鱼肚白 the whitish colour of a fish's belly—grey dawn
鱼肝油 cod-liver oil
鱼类学 ichthyology
鱼鳞病 ichthyosis; fishskin disease
鱼鳞坑 pits arranged like fish scales, dug on mountain slopes for holding water or planting trees; fish-scale pits
鱼石脂 ichthammol; ichthyol
鱼水情 relationship between fish and water—close relationship
鱼藤精 derris extract
鱼藤酮 rotenone
鱼丸子 fish ball
鱼尾号 boldface square brackets (
鱼尾纹 crow's feet
鱼腥草 cordate houttuynia (Houttuynia cordata)
鱼秧子 fingerling
鱼子酱 caviare
鱼大水小 a big fish in shallow water—a ponderous apparatus without sufficient resources for maintenance
鱼贯而入 enter in single file; file in
鱼龙混杂 dragons and fishes jumbled together—good and bad people mixed up
鱼米之乡 a land of fish and rice—a well-watered place where fish and rice are abundant
鱼目混珠 pass off fish eyes as pearls—pass off sth sham as genuine
鱼肉人民 oppress the people
鱼水情深 be close as fish and water
鱼死网破 either the fish dies or the net gets torn—a life-and-death struggle
鱼香肉丝 fish-flavoured shredded pork
鱼游釜中 like fish swimming in a cooking pot—in imminent peril
鱼雷(快)艇 torpedo boat

禺
[yú]
名 a kind of monkey

竽
[yú]
名 *yu*, ancient Chinese windpipe (made of a number of reed pipes blown through a single mouth piece): 吹竽 blow *yu*

谀
[yú]
动 fawn on; curry favour; flatter
谀词 flattering words; flattery

娱
[yú]
I 动 give pleasure to; entertain; amuse: 以娱宾客 entertain the guests II 名 joy; pleasure; amusement
娱乐 amusement; entertainment; recreation
娱记 paparazzo
娱乐界 show biz; show business
娱乐片 non-serious film; film or TV program for entertainment
娱乐设施 leisure facilities

萸
[yú]
◇ 山茱萸 the fruit of medicinal cornel (Cornus officinalis)
食茱萸 ailanthus prickly ash

雩
[yú]
名 sacrificial rites in quest of rain

渔
[yú]
动 ①fish ②take sth one has no right to
渔产 aquatic products
渔场 fishing ground; fishery
渔船 fishing boat
渔村 fishing village
渔夫 fisherman
渔竿 fishing tod
渔港 fishing port (*or* harbour)
渔歌 fisherman's song
渔鼓 ①a percussion instrument made of bamboo, used to accompany the chanting of folk tales ②chanting of folk tales to the accompaniment of a bamboo percussion instrument
渔火 lights on fishing boats
渔家 fisherman's family
渔具 fishing tackle (*or* gear)
渔况 fishing condition
渔捞 fishery
渔利 ①reap unfair gains; profit at others' expense ②easy gains; spoils
渔猎 fishing and hunting
渔轮 fishing vessel
渔民 fisherman; fisherfolk
渔区 fishing zone
渔人 fisherman; fisherfolk
渔网 fishnet; fishing net
渔翁 an old fisherman
渔线 fishing line; fishline

Y

渔乡 fish-farming area；fishing village
渔汛 fishing season
渔业 fishery
渔政 fish-farming operation
渔获量 a catch（of fish）
渔鼓道情 chanting of folk tales to the accompaniment of a bamboo percussion instrument
渔人之利 the fisherman's gains—profit reaped by a third party
渔事纠纷 fishing disputes
渔业资源 fishery resources

隅 ［yú］
名 ①corner；nook ②outlying area；border

揄 ［yú］
动 raise；tow；draw

喁 ［yú］
名 echo ➡ yóng

嵎 ［yú］
名 ①mountain curve ②corner；nook；outlying area；border

逾 ［yú］
Ⅰ 动 surpass；exceed；go beyond Ⅱ 副 even more
逾常 out of the ordinary；unusual
逾分 excessive；undue
逾恒 out of the common；unusual
逾期 exceed the time limit；be overdue
逾限 exceed the time limit；be overdue
逾越 exceed；go beyond
逾越节 Passover—a holiday in memory of the escape of the Jews from Egypt

腴 ［yú］
形 ①fat；plump；rounded out ②fertile

渝 ［yú］
动 change（of faith，oath，etc.）

愉 ［yú］
形 pleased；happy；delighted；overjoyed
愉快 happy；joyful；cheerful
愉乐 happy；joyful；cheerful
愉悦 joyful；cheerful；delighted

瑜 ［yú］
名 ①beautiful jade ②splendour or lustre of jade ③virtues；strong points
瑜伽 yoga

榆 ［yú］
名 elm
榆荚 elm seeds
榆树 elm tree；elm
榆钱儿 elm seeds
榆叶梅 flowering plum

虞 ［yú］
Ⅰ 动 ① speculate；suppose；expect；predict ②deceive；cheat；dupe Ⅱ 名 anxiety；misgiving；worry
虞美人 corn poppy

愚 ［yú］
Ⅰ 形 foolish；doltish；stupid Ⅱ 动 make a fool of；fool Ⅲ 代 humble

愚笨 foolish；stupid；clumsy
愚蠢 stupid；foolish；silly
愚钝 slow-witted people in ignorance
愚见 my humble opinion
愚昧 ignorant；benighted
愚民 ①ignorant people ②try to keep the people in ignorance；try to prevent the people from knowing the truth
愚弄 deceive；hoodwink；make a fool of；dupe
愚人 fool；simpleton
愚顽 ignorant and stubborn
愚妄 ignorant but self-important；stupid but conceited
愚意 my humble opinion
愚忠 blind devotion（to a master，ruler，etc.）
愚拙 stupid and clumsy
愚人节 All Fools' Day；April Fools'（or Fool's）Day
愚不可及 couldn't be more foolish；be hopelessly stupid
愚公精神 indomitable spirit
愚公移山 like the Foolish Old Man who removed the mountains—with dogged perseverance
愚昧无知 benighted；unenlightened；ignorant
愚民政策 policy of keeping the people in ignorance；obscurantist policy；obscurantism
愚者千虑，必有一得 The greatest fool，in a thousand schemes，must hit once on the truth；Even a fool occasionally hits on a good idea.

觎 ［yú］
◇觊觎 covet；cast greedy eyes on

歈 ［yú］
Ⅰ 名 song Ⅱ 形 pleased

舆 ［yú］
Ⅰ 名 ①cart；coach；carriage ②coach body ③palanquin；palankeen；sedan chair ④land；area；territory Ⅱ 形 public；popular
舆地 land；territory
舆论 public opinion
舆情 public sentiment；popular feelings
舆图 map
舆论界 the media；press circles
舆论导向 direction of public opinion；orientation of public opinion；guidance of public opinion
舆论工具 mass media；the media
舆论监督 supervision by public opinion

yǔ（ǔ）

与 ［yǔ］
Ⅰ 动 ①give；offer；grant ②associate with；be in friendly contact with ③ praise；commend；support；assist ④wait for；await Ⅱ 介 with；against；together with Ⅲ 连 and ➡ yù

与其 rather than;better than
与虎谋皮 ask a tiger for its skin—expect sb (usu. an evil person) to act against his own interests
与会期间 on-going meeting
与人为善 well-intentioned;well-meaning
与日俱增 grow with each passing day;be steadily on the increase
与时俱进 advance with the times
与世长辞 depart from the world for ever;pass away
与世浮沉 drift with the current of the times;swim with the tide
与世隔绝 be cut off from the outside world;live in solitude
与世无争 stand aloof from worldly strife;hold oneself aloof from the world
与众不同 out of the ordinary;different from the common run
与人民为敌 set oneself against the people
与日月同辉 shine as long and brightly as the sun and moon;shine forever
与人方便,自己方便 He who helps others helps himself.
与君一席话,胜读十年书 I have learnt much more from this evening's talk with you than I could have learnt from ten years of study.

予 ［yǔ］
动 give;grant;bestow;award ➡ yú
予夺 ①(the power) to give and take away ②commend and depreciate
予以 give;grant
予人口实 give people a handle

屿 ［yǔ］
名 small island;islet

伛 ［yǔ］
Ⅰ名 hunchback Ⅱ动 bow to show respect
伛偻 ①hunchbacked;humpbacked ②bow (to show respect)

宇 ［yǔ］
名 ①eaves;house ②space;universe;world ③manner;bearing;temperament
宇称 parity
宇航 space flight;space travel
宇宙 universe;cosmos
宇航员 astronaut;spaceman;cosmonaut
宇航站 space station
宇宙尘 cosmic dust
宇宙服 spacesuit
宇宙观 world view;world outlook
宇宙学 cosmology
宇宙站 space station
宇宙飞船 spaceship;spacecraft
宇宙飞行 space flight;space travel
宇宙航行 space flight;space travel
宇宙火箭 space rocket
宇宙空间 cosmic space;outer space

宇宙射线 cosmic rays;cosmic radiation
宇宙速度 cosmic velocity (or speed)
宇宙飞行员 astronaut;spaceman;cosmonaut
宇宙航行学 astronautics;cosmonautics
宇宙航行员 astronaut;spaceman;cosmonaut
宇宙生物学 exobiology

羽 ［yǔ］
Ⅰ名 ①feather;plume ②(of birds, etc.) wing Ⅱ量 (of birds):一羽信鸽 a carrier pigeon
羽缎 sateen
羽冠 crest (of a bird)
羽化 ①sprout wings—become an immortal ②pass away;die ③eclosion
羽翎 plume
羽毛 feather;plume
羽绒 fine soft feathers;eiderdown;down
羽纱 camlet
羽扇 feather fan
羽坛 badminton circles;the badminton world
羽衣 ①garment (or robe) made of feathers ②robe worn by a Taoist priest ③Taoist priest
羽翼 ①wing ②assistant
羽族 birds
羽毛画 feather patchwork;feather picture
羽毛球 ①badminton ②shuttlecock
羽毛扇 feather fan
羽毛丰满 become full-fledged;mature
羽毛未丰 unfledged;young and immature
羽扇纶巾 calm and leisurely;(of a man's manners) natural and restrained

雨 ［yǔ］
名 rain ➡ yù
雨暴 rainstorm
雨布 waterproof cloth;waterproof
雨带 rain band
雨滴 raindrop
雨点 raindrop
雨刮 windscreen (or windshield) wiper (of a car)
雨季 rainy season
雨具 rain gear (i.e. umbrella,raincoat,etc.)
雨帘 a curtain of rain—a thick rain
雨量 rainfall
雨林 rainforest
雨露 ①rain and dew ②favour;grace;bounty
雨帽 ①rain cap ②hood
雨幕 a curtain of rain—a thick rain
雨棚 canopy
雨披 rain cape
雨期 rain spell
雨情 rainfall (in a given area)
雨区 rain area;rain field
雨伞 umbrella
雨势 the force of rain
雨刷 windshield wiper

Y

雨水 ① rainwater; rainfall; rain ② Rain Water—the 2nd of the 24 solar terms ③ the day marking the beginning of the 2nd solar term

雨丝 a very light rain

雨蛙 tree toad

雨雾 misty rain

雨鞋 galoshes; rubbers

雨靴 rubber boots; rain boots

雨烟 misty rain

雨燕 swift

雨衣 raincoat; waterproof

雨意 signs of approaching rain

雨云 nimbus

雨珠 raindrop

雨层云 nimbostratus

雨花石 *yuhua* pebbles (colourful fine-grained pebbles found in the Yuhuatai 雨花台 area at Nanjing)

雨夹雪 sleet; rain and snow mixed

雨量计 rain gauge; udometer

雨水管 downspout; water-spout

雨过天晴 the sun shines again after the rain—after gloom comes brightness

雨后春笋 (spring up like) bamboo shoots after a spring rain

雨后送伞 give sb an umbrella after the rain has stopped—offer help when it's too late; offer help when it's no longer needed

雨过地皮湿 do sth as a mere formality; go through the motions; do sth perfunctorily or superficially

语 [yǔ]
Ⅰ 名 ① language; tongue; words ② adage; proverb; saying; idiom ③ nonlinguistic means of communicating ideas; sign; signal Ⅱ 动 speak; say ➡ yù

语病 faulty wording

语词 words and phrases

语调 intonation

语法 grammar

语感 an instinctive feel for the language

语汇 vocabulary

语境 ① language environment; speech environment ② context

语句 sentence

语料 linguistic material

语流 flow of speech

语录 recorded utterance; quotation

语气 ① tone; manner of speaking ② mood

语塞 be unable to utter a word (due to excitement, anger, etc.)

语失 make an indiscreet remark

语素 morpheme

语态 voice

语体 type of writing; style

语文 ① Chinese (as a subject of study or a

means of communication) ② language and literature

语系 family of languages; language family

语序 word order

语训 speech therapy

语言 language

语义 semantic meaning

语意 meaning of one's words

语音 ① speech sounds ② pronunciation

语域 register (in stylistics)

语种 categories (*or* families) of languages

语族 branch

语料库 language database; corpus

语气词 an auxiliary word that indicates mood

语体文 prose written in the vernacular

语言学 linguistics

语义学 semantics

语音学 phonetics

语用学 pragmatics

语源学 etymology

语助词 an auxiliary word that indicates mood

语惊四座 The words startle all present.

语妙天下 speak with inimitable wit

语无伦次 speak incoherently

语焉不详 ① not speak in detail; be not elaborate ② (of a statement) be rather too brief (*or* sketchy)

语言隔阂 language barrier

语言科学 linguistic science

语言学家 linguist; philologist

语音合成 speech synthesis

语音识别 speech recognition

语音信箱 voice mailbox

语重心长 sincere words and earnest wishes

语言规范化 standardization of speech

语言与文字 spoken and written language

yù(ㄩ)

与 [yù]
动 join in; participate in ➡ yǔ

与会 participate in a conference

与闻 have a participant's knowledge of; be let into (a secret, etc.)

玉 [yù]
Ⅰ 名 jade; jade-like stone Ⅱ 形 pure; fair; handsome; beautiful Ⅲ 代 your

玉帛 jade objects and silk fabrics (used as state gifts in ancient China)

玉成 kindly help secure the success of sth

玉带 jade belt

玉雕 jade carving; jade sculpture

玉钩 ① jade hook ② the crescent moon; the new moon

玉洁 pure as jade

玉兰 *yulan* magnolia

玉立 ① slim and graceful ② steadfast to principles

玉米 ① maize; Indian corn; corn ② ear of maize (*or* corn)
玉女 the Jade Maiden
玉盘 ①jade plate ②a bright full moon
玉佩 jade pendant; jade ornament (tied usu. on the waistband in ancient times)
玉器 jade article; jade object; jadeware
玉人 ①jade worker ②jade figure ③a handsome man or (esp.) a beautiful woman
玉容 beautiful face (usu. of a woman); good looks; fair looks
玉色 jade green; light bluish green
玉石 jade
玉手 jade hands—slender white hands (of a pretty woman)
玉树 eucalyptus
玉碎 be like a broken piece of jade—die in glory
玉体 ① your person; your health ② jade-like frame—the naked body of a beautiful woman
玉兔 the Jade Hare—the moon
玉玺 imperial jade seal
玉言 your words
玉颜 beautiful features
玉液 jade-like wine; good wine
玉宇 ① residence of the immortals ② the universe
玉簪 ①jade hairpin ②fragrant plantain lily
玉照 your photograph
玉版纸 a fine-quality writing paper
玉兰片 dried slices of tender bamboo shoots
玉米饼 johnnycake; hoecake
玉米面 maize flour; cornmeal
玉米螟 corn borer
玉米芯 corncob; cob
玉米粥 maize gruel
玉蜀黍 ① maize; Indian corn; corn ② ear of maize (*or* corn)
玉成其事 kindly help make a success of it
玉皇大帝 the Jade Emperor
玉洁冰清 pure as jade and chaste as ice; pure and noble
玉米花儿 popcorn
玉米粒儿 kernel of corn; grain of corn
玉米穗儿 corncob
玉石俱焚 jade and stone burned together—destruction of good and bad alike
玉碎珠沉 death of a beauty
玉米大斑病 leaf blight of corn
玉米黑粉病 corn smut
玉米脱粒机 maize sheller
玉不琢,不成器 jade cannot be made into anything without being cut and polished—one cannot become useful without being educated

驭 [yù]
〈动〉①drive ②command; master
驭手 soldier in charge of pack animals; driver of a military pack train

芋 [yù]
〈名〉①taro; dasheen ②similar tuber crop
芋艿 taro
芋头 ①taro ②sweet potato
芋头白菜 cabbage and taro

吁 [yù]
〈动〉appeal; plead; call on ➡ xū; yū
吁请 implore; plead; petition
吁求 implore; plead; petition

饫 [yù]
〈形〉be full

妪 [yù]
〈名〉old woman; old lady

雨 [yù]
〈动〉(of rain, snow, etc.) fall ➡ yǔ

郁 [yù]
〈形〉①(of plants) teeming; luxuriant; lush ②(of sorrow, anger, etc.) pent-up; gloomy; depressed ③of powerful or strong fragrance; strongly fragrant
郁闭 closing
郁愤 worried and indignant
郁积 pent up
郁结 pent up
郁金 the root-tuber of aromatic turmeric (Curcuma aromatica)
郁闷 gloomy; depressed
郁血 stagnation of the blood; venous stasis
郁郁 ① elegant; refined ② strongly fragrant ③lush; luxuriant
郁蒸 hot and suffocating; sultry; muggy
郁金香 tulip
郁郁不乐 depressed; melancholy; gloomy
郁郁葱葱 lush and green
郁郁寡欢 depressed; melancholy; joyless

育 [yù]
〈动〉①give birth to; bear ②rear; raise; bring up; grow ③educate; cultivate
育才 cultivate (*or* educate) people of ability
育雏 raise young fowl
育林 afforest
育龄 child-bearing age
育苗 grow (*or* raise) seedlings
育人 cultivate (*or* foster) talent; educate
育性 fertility
育幼 raise an infant; child care
育种 breeding
育珠 grow cultured pearls
育雏器 brooder
育儿袋 brood pouch; marsupium
育婴堂 foundling hospital
育成品种 improved variety
育龄夫妇 couples of child-bearing age
育龄妇女 women of child-bearing age; fertile

Y

昱 [yù] I 名 sunshine; sunlight; daylight II 动 shine

狱 [yù] 名 ①prison; jail ②lawsuit; case
狱警 prison guard; jailer

语 [yù] 动 tell; inform; let sb know ➡ yǔ

峪 [yù] 名 (often used in place names) ravine; valley

钰 [yù] 名 treasure

浴 [yù] 动 have a bath; bathe
浴场 outdoor bathing place
浴池 ① common bathing pool (in a public bathhouse) ②public bathhouse; public baths
浴缸 bathtub
浴巾 bath towel
浴具 bathroom facilities
浴疗 balneation
浴女 woman at her bath
浴盆 bathtub
浴室 bathroom; shower room
浴血 bathed in blood; bloody
浴液 liquid soap
浴衣 bathrobe
浴皂 toilet soap
浴罩 plastic bathtub cover
浴血奋战 fight bloody battle

预 [yù] 副 in advance; beforehand
预案 reserve plan
预报 forecast
预备 prepare; get ready
预卜 augur; foretell
预测 calculate; forecast
预订 subscribe; book; place an order
预定 fix in advance; predetermine; schedule
预防 prevent; take precautions against; guard against
预付 pay in advance
预感 ① premonition; presentiment ② have a premonition
预告 ① announce in advance; herald ② advance notice
预购 place an order (*or* purchase) in advance
预后 prognosis
预计 calculate in advance; estimate
预减 estimated profit squeeze
预见 ①foresee; predict ②foresight; prevision
预警 early warning
预科 preparatory course (in a college)
预亏 estimated loss
预料 expect; predict; anticipate
预谋 premeditate; plan beforehand

预期 expect; anticipate
预热 preheat; warm-up
预赛 preliminary contest; preliminary heats; preliminary; trial match
预审 preliminary (*or* first) hearing
预示 betoken; indicate; presage; forebode
预收 collect money in advance
预售 (usu. train tickets) be available for booking; sell in advance
预算 budget
预习 (of students) prepare lessons before class
预先 in advance; beforehand
预想 anticipate; expect
预选 preliminary election; primary election
预言 ① prophesy; predict; foretell ② prophecy; prediction
预研 advance research
预演 preview (of a performance or motion picture)
预赢 estimated earnings
预约 make an appointment
预增 estimated profit increase
预兆 omen; presage; sign; harbinger
预支 ①pay in advance ②get payment in advance
预知 know beforehand
预制 prefabricate
预祝 congratulate beforehand; wish
预备队 reserve force; reserves
预备金 reserve fund
预备军 reserve army
预备期 probationary period
预备役 reserve duty; reserve service; preliminary service
预产期 expected date of childbirth
预处理 pretreatment
预付款 advance payment; down payment
预警机 early-warning aircraft
预科班 pre-college class; preparatory class
预选赛 preliminary heat; qualifying round
预言家 prophet
预言者 predictor
预应力 prestressing force
预制板 prefabricated board
预制件 prefab
预备党员 probationary Party member
预备会议 preparatory meeting or conference
预定轨道 designated orbit
预防接种 preventive (*or* prophylactic) inoculation
预防为主 put prevention first
预防医学 preventive medicine
预计投资 projected investment
预警飞机 early warning system
预期效果 desired result; due result
预算编制 budget lay-out (*or* preparation, for-

mulation)

预算拨款 budget allocation
预算赤字 budget deficit
预算收入 budgetary receipts
预制构件 prefabricated components
预备役部队 reserve units
预备役军人 reservist
预防性拘留 preventive detention
预付保证金 advance bond
预决算制度 budget and final account system
预算内拨款 budgetary appropriations
预算外投资 extra-budgetary investment; investment outside the State plan
预算外支出 off-budget expenditure
预算外资金 extra-budgetary funds
预计到达时间 estimated time of arrival (E. T. A.)

域 〔yù〕
名 ①land within certain boundaries; territory; area; region ②domain; sphere; range
域名 domain name
域外 outside the country
域中 inside the country

堉 〔yù〕
名 rich or fertile soil

菀 〔yù〕
形 flourishing; luxuriant ➡ wǎn

欲 〔yù〕
Ⅰ 名 desire; longing; yearning; wish Ⅱ 动 ①wish; want; yearn; desire ②need; should ③ be about to; be just going to; be on the point of
欲火 the fire of lust; lewd desire
欲念 desire; wish; lust
欲求 desire; wish; lust
欲望 desire; wish; lust
欲罢不能 unable to stop even though one wants to; try to stop but cannot; cannot refrain from going on
欲盖弥彰 The more one tries to hide, the more one is exposed; try to cover up a misdeed, only to make it more conspicuous; protest too much
欲壑难填 Greed is a valley that can never be filled; Avarice knows no bounds.
欲哭无泪 with no tears to shed even though one is in deep sorrow
欲擒故纵 leave sb at large the better to apprehend him; allow sb more latitude first to keep a tighter rein on him afterwards
欲取姑与 give in order to take; make concessions for the sake of future gains
欲言又止 began to speak and then hesitated; about to speak, but saying nothing
欲益反损 good intentions end up in harm
欲速则不达 Haste brings no success; more haste, less speed
欲加之罪, 何患无辞 If you are out to condemn

sb, you can always trump up a charge.
欲穷千里目, 更上一层楼 ascend another storey to see a thousand *li* ahead

阈 〔yù〕
名 doorsill; threshold; limits; confines
阈限 threshold
阈值 threshold value
阈电流 threshold current
阈调整 threshold adjustment

谕 〔yù〕
动 decree; instruct; order
谕告 (of superiors or elders) give explicit instructions (*or* directions); tell
谕令 order
谕示 (of seniors or elders) instruct
谕旨 imperial edict

遇 〔yù〕
Ⅰ 动 ①meet; encounter ②treat; receive Ⅱ 名 chance; opportunity
遇便 when it's convenient; at sb's convenience
遇刺 be attacked by an assassin
遇到 run into; encounter; come across
遇害 be murdered
遇见 meet; come across
遇救 be rescued; be saved
遇难 ①die (*or* be killed) in an accident ②be murdered
遇事 when anything crops (*or* comes) up
遇险 meet with a mishap; be in danger; be in distress
遇缘 as luck would have it; by chance; by a lucky coincidence
遇事生风 sow discord whenever possible
遇险船只 ship in distress
遇险信号 distress signal; SOS

喻 〔yù〕
Ⅰ 动 ①explain; tell; inform ②understand; know; be aware of Ⅱ 名 analogy; figure of speech

御 〔yù〕
Ⅰ 动 ①drive; ride ②control; dominate ③ defend (against sb); resist; keep out Ⅱ 形 related to the emperor or king; imperial
御宝 imperial seal
御笔 imperial brush—handwriting or painting of the emperor
御赐 bestowed by the emperor
御道 a road for the imperial carriage
御敌 resist the enemy
御寒 keep out the cold
御驾 imperial carriage
御览 ①for the emperor's inspection ②books for the emperor's inspection
御前 in his majesty's presence
御膳 the food of the imperial household
御侮 resist foreign aggression
御医 imperial physician; court physician
御用 ①for the use of an emperor ②serve as a

Y

tool;be in the pay of

御苑 imperial garden or park

御旨 imperial decree (*or* edict)

御制 made by the emperor (*or* by imperial order)

御准 royal assent

御夫座 Auriga

御花园 imperial garden

御林军 ①imperial guards ②elite troops;crack units

御膳房 imperial kitchen

寓 [yù] Ⅰ 劢 ①inhabit;reside;live ②imply;place;contain Ⅱ 名 residence;dwelling;abode

寓居 make one's home in (a place other than one's native place)

寓所 residence;abode;dwelling place

寓言 fable;allegory;parable

寓意 implied meaning;moral;message;import

寓于 be contained in;reside in

寓教于乐 combine education with recreation;edutainment

寓庄于谐 seriousness (*or* serious intent) contained in humour (*or* facetious remarks)

裕 [yù] Ⅰ 形 abundant;plentiful;ample Ⅱ 劢 enrich;make affluent

裕如 effortlessly;with ease

粥 [yù] 劢 ①give birth to (a child);bear ②sell ➡ zhōu

愈 [yù] Ⅰ 劢 ①be cured;heal;recover ②be better than;overtake;surpass Ⅱ 副 the more... the more;more and more

愈合 (of a wound) heal

愈加 all the more;even more;further

愈演愈烈 grow in intensity;become increasingly intense

煜 [yù] 劢 shine;illuminate

誉 [yù] Ⅰ 名 reputation; renown; fame Ⅱ 劢 praise;comment;extol

誉不绝口 be full of praise;praise (*or* extol) to the skies

誉满全球 of world renown;famed the world over

誉满天下 be famed all over the world

豫 [yù] Ⅰ 形 pleased;happy;glad Ⅱ 名 comfort;contentment

鹬 [yù] 名 sandpiper;snipe

鹬鸵 kiwi

鹬蚌相争,渔人得利 when the snipe and the clam grapple,it's the fisherman who stands to benefit—it's the third party that benefits from the tussle

yuān (ㄩㄢ)

鸢 [yuān] 名 kite;hawk

鸢尾 iris

鸢飞鱼跃 (with) kites hovering and fish diving

眢 [yuān] 形 ①(of eyes) dry and sunken ②drained dry

鸳 [yuān] 名 mandarin duck

鸳侣 husband and wife

鸳衾 quilt shared by husband and wife

鸳鸯 ①mandarin duck ②an affectionate couple

鸳鸯房 ① mandarin duck room (*or* apartment) ② room (*or* apartment) reserved for newly married couples to rent temporarily before they find their own place

鸳鸯楼 ①mandarin duck building ②commercial apartment building specially reserved for newly-weds

鸳鸯座 love seat

鸳梦重温 reunion of old lovers after a long separation

冤 [yuān] Ⅰ 名 ① wrong; grievance; injustice ② hatred;enmity;feud Ⅱ 形 not commensurate with the effort or money;not worthwhile;in vain;for nothing Ⅲ 劢 kid;fool;pull sb's leg

冤案 a case in which a person is unjustly charged or sentenced;an unjust case

冤仇 rancour;enmity

冤魂 the ghost of one who was wrongly put to death (*or* was murdered)

冤家 ①enemy;foe ②(usu. used in dramas or folk songs) one's destined love; sweetheart;lover

冤气 resentment;rancour

冤情 facts of an injustice

冤屈 ① treat unjustly; wrong ② wrongful treatment;injustice

冤枉 ① treat unjustly; wrong ② not worthwhile;not repaying the effort

冤狱 an unjust charge or verdict; a miscarriage of justice;frame-up

冤大头 a person who spends money wastefully and foolishly;squanderer;wastrel

冤枉路 a longer way;a roundabout way

冤枉气 unjust treatment;mistreatment

冤家对头 opponent and foe

冤家路窄 enemies are bound to meet on a narrow road—one can't avoid one's enemy (much as one wants to)

冤假错案 cases in which people were unjustly, falsely or wrongly charged or denounced;unjust,false and erroneous cases

冤冤相报 injury for injury

冤有头,债有主 Every injustice has its perpetrator,every debt has its debtor.

冤家宜解不宜结 better make friends than make enemies

渊 [yuān]
Ⅰ 〈名〉deep pool Ⅱ 〈形〉deep

渊博 broad and profound;erudite

渊默 profound (*or* deep) silence

渊泉 deep spring

渊深 profound;deep;erudite

渊薮 a gathering place of fish or beasts;den; haunt

渊源 origin;source

渊识博学 profound knowledge and extensive learning

蜎 [yuān]
〈名〉wiggler;wriggler

yuán (ㄩㄢ)

元 [yuán]
Ⅰ 〈形〉①first;initial;primary ②arch;chief; principal ③basic;essential;fundamental Ⅱ 〈名〉① element ② unit; component Ⅲ 〈量〉unit of money:两元五角 two *yuan* and fifty *fen*

元宝 a shoe-shaped gold or silver ingot used as money in feudal China

元旦 New Year's Day

元件 element;component;cell

元老 senior statesman;founding member

元麦 highland barley

元年 the first year of an era (*or* of the reign of an emperor)

元配 first wife

元气 vitality;vigour

元曲 ①Yuan songs ②Yuan drama

元日 the first day of the first lunar month;the lunar New Year's Day

元首 head of state

元帅 ①marshal;(Brit. Army) Field Marshal; (Brit. Air Force) Marshal of the Royal Air Force;(Brit. Navy) Admiral of the Fleet ②supreme commander (in ancient times)

元素 element

元宵 ①the night of the 15th of the 1st lunar month ② sweet dumplings made of glutinous rice flour (for the Lantern Festival)

元凶 prime culprit;chief culprit;arch-criminal

元勋 a man of great merit;founding father

元音 vowel

元鱼 soft-shelled turtle

元月 ①January ②the first month of the lunar year;the first moon

元宝铁 V-block

元古代 the Proterozoic Era

元古界 the Proterozoic Erathem

元器件 components and parts (of an apparatus,etc.)

元宵节 the Lantern Festival (the 15th of the 1st lunar month)

元语言 metalanguage

元素周期表 periodic table of elements

芫 [yuán]
➡yán

芫花 lilac daphne

园 [yuán]
〈名〉① garden; plot; plantation ② place of recreation;park;garden

园地 ①garden plot ②field;scope

园丁 ①gardener ②school teacher

园林 gardens;park

园陵 tombs surrounded by a park;cemetery

园圃 garden;ground used for growing vegetables,flowers or fruit

园区 park

园田 vegetable garden

园亭 arbour

园艺 horticulture;gardening

园子 orchard;garden

园艺师 horticulturist

园艺学 horticulture;gardening

员 [yuán]
Ⅰ 〈名〉①person engaged in a certain field of activity ②member (of an organization) Ⅱ 〈量〉: 一员猛将 a valiant general;a vigorous man

员额 specified number of personnel

员工 staff;personnel

垣 [yuán]
〈名〉①wall ②town;city

爰 [yuán]
Ⅰ 〈代〉where Ⅱ 〈连〉thus;then;accordingly

原 [yuán]
Ⅰ 〈形〉①primary; initial; inceptive ② original;former ③ unprocessed;crude;raw Ⅱ 〈名〉① plain;level;open country ②terrace;tableland Ⅲ 〈动〉excuse;forgive;pardon:情有可原 excusable;pardonable

原版 original edition (of a book,etc.)

原本 ① original manuscript; master copy ② the original (from which a translation is made) ③originally;formerly

原肠 primitive gut;archenteron

原虫 protozoon

原初 originally;formerly;at first

原创 original

原防 place where troops were originally stationed; original station or position (of a unit)

原封 with the seal unbroken;intact

原稿 original manuscript;master copy

原告 (in civil cases) plaintiff;(in criminal cases) prosecutor

原故 cause;reason

原画 original painting
原级 positive degree
原籍 ancestral home
原价 original price
原件 ①original manuscript (of a document); master copy ②the original (from which a replica is made)
原来 ①original; former ②originally; formerly; at first ③as a matter of fact; as it turns out; actually
原理 principle; tenet
原谅 excuse; forgive; pardon
原料 raw material
原貌 original appearance (of things)
原煤 raw coal
原棉 raw cotton
原木 log
原判 original sentence; original judgment
原配 first wife
原品 original
原任 ①formerly held the post of ②predecessor
原色 primary colours
原审 first trial
原始 ①original; firsthand ②primeval; primitive
原诉 plaintiff's or prosecutor's accusation
原糖 raw sugar
原委 how a thing happened from beginning to end; the whole story; all the details
原文 ①the original (from which a translation is made) ②original text
原物 the original thing
原先 ①original; former ②originally; formerly; at first
原形 original shape; the true shape under the disguise
原型 model; prototype
原盐 crude salt
原样 ① the same old way ② original state; previous condition
原野 open country; champaign
原义 original (or primary) meaning (of a word or phrase)
原意 meaning; original intention
原因 cause; reason
原由 cause; reason
原油 crude oil; crude
原则 principle
原汁 normal juice; stock
原职 former post
原址 former address
原主 original owner (or proprietor)
原注 original annotation
原著 original work; original
原装 intact; unopened; in the original package
原状 original state; previous condition; status

quo ante
原子 atom
原罪 original sin
原作 original work; original
原材料 raw materials; raw and semi-finished materials
原动力 motive power (or force); motivity
原生林 primeval forest; virgin forest
原生质 protoplasm
原声带 original sound tape; master tape (as made by an orchestra)
原始股 initial public offering(IPO)
原始群 primitive horde
原始人 primitive man
原线圈 primary coil
原子笔 ball-point pen
原子尘 fallout
原子弹 atom bomb; atomic bomb; A-bomb
原子核 atomic nucleus
原子价 valence; atomicity
原子键 atomic bond
原子量 atomicweight
原子论 atomic theory; atomism
原子能 atomic energy
原子炮 atomic gun
原子团 atomic group
原子序 atomic number
原子钟 atomic clock
原作者 original writer
原班人马 same troupe; old cast; former staff
原版磁带 original tape; master
原地不动 remain where one is; stay put
原地待命 stay where one is pending orders
原封不动 be left intact; remain untouched
原来如此 so that's how it is; so that's what's happened; I see
原生动物 protozoon
原生矿物 primary mineral
原生生物 protist
原生植物 protophyte
原始档案 raw file
原始公社 primitive commune
原始积累 primitive accumulation
原始森林 virgin forest
原始社会 primitive society
原索动物 protochordate
原形毕露 be revealed for what one is; show one's true colours
原有人数 former number of persons
原原本本 from beginning to end
原子辐射 atomic radiation
原子结构 atomic structure
原子时代 atomic age
原子武器 atomic weapon
原子战争 atomic war (or warfare)
原教旨主义 fundamentalism
原子动力船 atomic-powered ship

原子反应堆 atomic reactor;atomic pile
原子物理学 atomic physics
原教旨主义者 fundie;fundy;Fundi

圆 [yuán]
Ⅰ 形 ①round;circular;spherical ②tactful;
satisfactory Ⅱ 名 ①circle ②ball-shaped ③a
unit of currency Ⅲ 动 justify;make perfect or
complete
圆材 roundwood;log
圆场 mediate;help to effect a compromise
圆成 help sb to attain his aim
圆顶 dome
圆房 consummate of a marriage between a
　child bride and her husband when they
　come of age
圆钢 steel strip
圆功 achieve the desired results;complete a
　project,etc.
圆规 compasses
圆号 French horn;horn
圆和 ①mediate (a dispute);help to effect a
　compromise ②flexible; accommodating ③
　mellow and full
圆滑 smooth and evasive;slick and sly
圆谎 patch up a lie
圆浑 ①(of voice) round and mellow ②(of
　writing) natural and spontaneous
圆活 ①flexible;smooth ②mellow and full
圆寂 (of Buddhist monks or nuns) pass away;
　die
圆锯 circular saw
圆脸 round face
圆满 satisfactory
圆梦 prognostication by dreams;oneiromancy
圆盘 disc
圆圈 circle;ring
圆润 mellow and full
圆鲹 round scad
圆熟 skilful;proficient;dexterous
圆说 speak in defence of;argue in favour of;
　defend
圆通 flexible;accommodating
圆筒 barrel;cylinder;drum
圆心 the centre of a circle
圆形 round;circular
圆鱼 soft-shelled turtle
圆周 circumference
圆柱 cylinder
圆锥 circular cone;taper
圆桌 round table
圆子 ① dumpling (made of glutinous rice
　flour) ②(meat,fish,etc.) ball
圆白菜 cabbage
圆嘟嘟 full and plump;chubby
圆墩墩 full and plump;chubby
圆骨碌 good and round;rounded
圆鼓鼓 rounded and bulging

圆滚滚 good and round;rounded
圆乎(乎) roundish
圆滑线 slur
圆括号 parentheses;curves (())
圆溜溜 good and round;rounded
圆盘犁 disc plough
圆盘耙 disc harrow
圆舞曲 waltz
圆心角 central angle
圆周角 angle in a circular segment
圆周率 ratio of the circumference of a circle
　to its diameter (π)
圆珠笔 ball-point pen;ball-pen
圆柱根 cylindrical root
圆柱体 cylinder
圆柱形 cylinder;cylindrical;cylinder-shaped
圆锥根 conical root
圆锥台 frustum of a cone
圆锥体 conicalness
圆桌面 a detachable round tabletop (which
　can be put on a square table)
圆唇元音 round vowel
圆颅方趾 round skull and square feet—human
　being
圆形建筑 rotunda
圆形剧场 amphitheatre
圆凿方枘 like a square tenon for a round mor-
　tise—at variance with each other
圆周接缝 circumferential seam
圆周运动 circular motion
圆锥花序 panicle
圆锥曲线 conic section
圆桌会议 round-table conference

鼋 [yuán]
名 soft-shelled turtle
鼋鱼 soft-shelled turtle

援 [yuán]
动 ① pull by hand;hold ② quote;cite ③
help;aid;assist;rescue
援笔 take up a pen
援兵 relief troops;reinforcements
援建 give construction aid (to foreign coun-
　tries or other work units)
援救 rescue;save;deliver from danger
援军 relief troops;reinforcements
援款 aid fund
援例 quote (*or* cite) a precedent
援手 aid;save;rescue;helping hand
援外 foreign aid
援引 ①quote;cite ②recommend;appoint
援用 quote;cite;invoke
援助 help;support;aid
援经引典 quote from classics and canons
援外物资 materials in aid of a foreign country
援外项目 foreign aid project

缘 [yuán]
Ⅰ 名 ①reason ②happy fate or chance ③

rim;brink;edge;fringe Ⅱ〔介〕along Ⅲ〔连〕because

缘分 lot（*or* luck）by which people are brought together
缘故 reason;cause
缘膜 velum
缘起 genesis;origin
缘由 cause;reason
缘木求鱼 climb a tree to catch fish—a fruitless approach
缘悭一面 It was never my good fortune to meet him.

塬 ［yuán］〔名〕tableland;terrace

猿 ［yuán］〔名〕ape
猿猴 apes and monkeys
猿人 ape-man

源 ［yuán］〔名〕①water source;fountainhead ②source;cause;root
源流 source and course（of a river,etc.）;origin and development
源泉 source;fountainhead;well-spring
源头 fountainhead;source
源源 in a steady stream;continuously
源程序 source program
源代码 source code
源源不绝 in an endless stream;continuously
源源而来 come in a steady（*or* continuous）stream
源远流长 distant source and long stream—of long standing and well established

辕 ［yuán］〔名〕①shafts（of a cart,palanquin,etc.）②outer gate of a government office or barracks;government office
辕杆 hitch pole;tongue tree
辕马 horse in the shafts;shaft-horse
辕门 the outer gate of a government office in ancient times
辕子 shafts of a cart（*or* carriage）

yuǎn（ㄩㄢˇ）

远 ［yuǎn］Ⅰ〔形〕①(of time and space) far;distant;remote ②(of blood relationship) distant Ⅱ〔副〕(of differences) by far Ⅲ〔动〕be not intimate
远程 long-range;long-distance
远处 distant point or place
远大 long-range;broad;ambitious
远道 long way
远东 the Far East
远渡 travel across a vast expanse of water
远方 distant place
远房 distantly related
远古 remote antiquity;ancient times

远海 distant sea waters
远航 take a long（sea）voyage;sail to a distant place
远话 stranger's words
远见 foresight;vision
远郊 the outer suburbs;the remoter outskirts of a city
远近 ①far and near ②distance
远景 distant view;long-range perspective;prospect
远距 long distance
远客 a guest from afar
远路 ①long way ②longer way;roundabout way
远虑 foresight;long view
远门 far away from home
远谋 long-term plan
远年 many years ago;of long standing
远期 at a specified future date;forward
远亲 distant relative（*or* relation）;remote kinsfolk
远山 distant mountain
远涉 make a long, arduous journey（esp. across the sea）
远识 foresight;vision
远视 long sight;farsightedness;hyperopia;hypermetropia
远台 far from the table
远眺 look far into the distance（from a high place）
远图 long-term plan
远销 sell goods to distant places
远行 go on a long journey
远扬（of fame, reputation, etc.）spread far and wide
远洋 ①ocean ②of the open sea beyond the littoral zone;oceanic
远因 remote cause
远游 travel faraway
远征 expedition
远志 ①great and far-reaching ambition;high aspiration ②the root of the narrow-leaved polygala（polygala tenuifolia）
远足 pleasure trip on foot;hike;walking tour
远祖 remote ancestor
远地点 apogee
远距离 remote
远日点 aphelion
远月点 apocynthion
远征军 expeditionary force
远程导弹 far-ranging missile;long-range missile
远程登录 telenet;remote login
远程访问 remote access
远程航行 long（sea）voyage
远程火箭 long-range rocket
远程教育 distance learning;distance education

远程医疗 telemedicine
远房表亲 distant cousin
远非如此 far from it; far from being so
远隔重洋 be separated by vast oceans
远见卓识 foresight and sagacity
远交近攻 befriend distant states while attacking those nearby
远景计划 long-term development targets
远离家乡 far away from one's home village (*or* homeland, *or* native country)
远期汇票 long draft; term draft; period bill; time bill
远期票据 long note
远射程炮 long-range gun
远摄镜头 ①film long shot ②telephoto lens
远事记忆 long term memory
远洋航行 oceangoing voyage
远洋货轮 oceangoing freighter
远洋客轮 ocean liner
远洋渔业 deep-sea (*or* pelagic) fishing
远洋运输 ocean carriage; ocean shipping; ocean transportation
远缘杂交 distant hybridization
远走高飞 fly far and high; be off to distant parts; flee to faraway places
远走他乡 travel in distant parts
远程轰炸机 long-range bomber
远程巡航导弹 long-range cruise missile
远亲不如近邻 A relative far off is less help than a neighbour close by; Neighbours are dearer than distant relatives.
远水不解近渴 distant water can't quench present thirst—the aid is too slow in coming to be of any help
远洋救助拖轮 oceangoing salvage tug
远水救不了近火 distant water won't put out a fire close at hand—a slow remedy cannot meet an urgency
远在天边,近在眼前 seemingly far away, actually close at hand (said playfully to call attention to sb or sth right in front of sb's eyes)

yuàn(ㄩㄢˋ)

苑 [yuàn]
图 ①enclosed ground for growing trees, keeping animals, etc.; imperial garden; park ②centre (of art and literature, etc.)
苑囿 animal farm (*or* park)

怨 [yuàn]
Ⅰ 图 resentment; hatred; grudge Ⅱ 动 blame
怨愤 discontented and indignant
怨怪 blame
怨恨 ①have a grudge against sb; hate ②resentment; grudge; enmity
怨悔 repent remorsefully

怨懑 discontented and indignant; resentful
怨偶 unhappy couple
怨气 grievance; complaint; resentment
怨言 complaint; grumble
怨尤 resentment; grudge
怨不得 ①cannot blame ②no wonder; so that's why
怨声载道 Cries of discontent rise all round; complaints (*or* voices of discontent) are heard everywhere.
怨天尤人 blame god and man—blame everyone and everything but oneself

院 [yuàn]
图 ①yard; courtyard; compound ②designation for certain government institutions and public places ③institute of higher learning; college ④hospital
院落 courtyard; yard; compound
院墙 the walls that surround a house
院士 academician
院校 institutions of higher learning; colleges, universities and academic institutes
院长 president
院址 institute
院子 courtyard; yard; compound
院线制 cinema chain system
院外调解 out-of-court settlement

垸 [yuàn]
图 protective embankment in a riverside or lakeside area; levee

掾 [yuàn]
图 subordinate; petty official; clerk

嫒 [yuàn]
图 beautiful woman

愿 [yuàn]
Ⅰ 形 honest and prudent Ⅱ 图 ① wish; hope; desire ②vow; declare solemnly Ⅲ 动 be willing; be ready; be glad
愿望 desire; wish; aspiration
愿心 a vow made to a god or Buddha
愿意 ①be willing; be ready ②wish; like; want
愿供差遣 willingly put oneself at sb's disposal
愿伺箕帚 be glad to be sb's wife
愿效犬马之劳 be willing to do what little one can; wish to render one's service

yuē(ㄩㄝ)

曰 [yuē]
动 ①say ②call; name

约 [yuē]
Ⅰ 动 ① make an appointment; agree; arrange ②invite (in advance); engage ③check; restrict; restrain Ⅱ 图 ① pact; treaty; agreement; appointment ②reduction of a fraction Ⅲ 形 ①economical; thrifty; frugal ②simple; brief; succinct Ⅳ 副 about; around; or so; approximately ➡ yāo
约定 agree on; appoint; arrange

约法 provisional constitution
约访 request to discuss
约分 reduction of a fraction
约稿 make an arrangement in advance with sb for his contribution
约合 invite to meet together; call together
约会 ①arrange a meeting; make an appointment ②appointment; engagement; date
约集 invite to meet together; call together
约计 count roughly; come roughly to
约见 make an appointment to meet (esp. a foreign diplomatic official); ask for (or request) an appointment with
约略 ① rough; approximate ② roughly; approximately; about
约莫 about; roughly
约期 ①fix a date; appoint a time ②appointment; engagement; the appointed time ③ the term (or duration) of an agreement
约请 invite; ask
约束 keep within bounds; restrain; bind
约数 ①approximate number ②divisor
约谈 arrange talks
约言 promise; word; pledge
约束力 binding force
约定俗成 established (or sanctioned) by popular usage; accepted through common practice
约法三章 make a few simple rules to be observed by all concerned

yuě（ㄩㄝˇ）

哕 [yuě]　I 〈象〉 sound of vomiting II 〈动〉 vomit; throw up ➡huì

yuè（ㄩㄝˋ）

月 [yuè]　I 〈名〉①moon ②month II 〈形〉①monthly ② full-moon shaped; round
月白 bluish white; very pale blue
月半 the 15th day of a month (esp. of a lunar month)
月报 ①monthly magazine; monthly ②monthly report
月饼 moon cake
月尘 lunar dust
月初 the beginning of the month
月底 the end of the month
月度 monthly
月份 month
月工 a labourer hired by the month
月宫 the Lunar Palace
月光 moonlight; moonbeam
月晷 lunar dial
月海 lunar maria

月华 ①moonlight ②lunar corona
月季 Chinese rose
月经 menses; menstruation; period
月均 monthly average
月刊 monthly magazine; monthly
月蓝 pale blue
月老 ① the Old Man of the Moon ② matchmaker
月历 monthly calendar
月利 monthly interest
月亮 the moon
月龄 the moon's age; age of the moon
月轮 full moon
月门 moon gate
月末 the end of the month
月票 monthly ticket
月钱 monthly payment
月琴 a four-stringed plucked instrument with a full-moon-shaped sound box
月球 the moon
月嫂 confinement-caring woman
月色 moonlight
月石 borax
月食 lunar eclipse
月台 railway platform
月尾 the end of the month
月息 monthly interest
月相 phases of the moon
月薪 monthly pay
月牙 crescent moon
月岩 moon rock
月夜 moonlit (or moonlight) night
月晕 lunar halo
月震 moonquake
月中 the middle of the month
月终 the end of the month
月子 ① month of confinement after giving birth to a child ② time of childbirth; confinement
月长石 moonstone
月洞门 moon gate
月份牌 calendar
月光花 large moonflower
月桂树 laurel; bay tree; bay
月黑天 a moonless night
月经带 sanitary belt (or napkin)
月经期 menstrual period
月亮门 moon gate
月偏食 partial lunar eclipse
月球学 selenology
月全食 total lunar eclipse
月月红 Chinese rose
月中人 the man (or woman) in the moon
月子病 puerperal fever
月白风清 a bright moon and a gentle breeze— a beautiful night
月经不调 menoxenia; abnormal menstruation

月经过多 menorrhagia; excessive menstruation

月经过少 hypomenorrhea

月经失调 menstrual disorder

月经周期 menstrual cycle

月亮地儿 a place where there is moonlight; moonlit spot

月面行走 moonwalk

月球探测 moon exploration

月下老人 ① the Old Man of the Moon ② matchmaker

月到中秋分外明 The mid-autumn moon is exceptionally bright.

月晕而风，础润而雨 a halo round the moon means wind; a damp plinth means rain—premonitory signs of future events

乐 [yuè]　名 music：配乐朗诵 poem recitation with musical accompaniment ➡lè

乐池 orchestra pit; orchestra

乐段 period

乐队 orchestra; band

乐感 musicality; musical feeling; musical texture; tonal quality; music aptitude; sense of music

乐句 phrase

乐理 music theory

乐律 temperament

乐迷 music lover

乐谱 music score; music

乐器 musical instrument; instrument

乐曲 musical composition; composition; music

乐师 musician (who performs on a musical instrument)

乐坛 the musical world; music circles

乐团 ① philharmonic society ② philharmonic orchestra

乐舞 a dance with accompaniment

乐音 musical sound; tone

乐章 movement

乐谱架 music stand

乐队指挥 conductor; bandmaster

乐控喷泉 fountain display electronically synchronized to music

玥 [yuè]　动 ①shake ②break

玥 [yuè]　名 legendary magic pearl

岳 [yuè]　名 ① high mountain ② wife's parents and paternal uncles

岳父 wife's father; father-in-law

岳家 wife's parents' home

岳母 wife's mother; mother-in-law

岳丈 wife's father; father-in-law

钥 [yuè]　名 key ➡yào

钺 [yuè]　名 ancient weapon made of bronze or iron and shaped like a broad axe; ancient battle-axe

阅 [yuè]　动 ①read; go over; scan ②review; inspect ③experience; undergo; pass through

阅兵 review troops

阅操 review soldiers at drill

阅读 read

阅卷 go over examination papers

阅览 read

阅历 ①see, hear or do for oneself ② experience

阅批 (of leading cadres) review and make written comments and instructions on an official document; read official papers

阅世 see the world

阅报栏 public information board; showcase or bulletin board, erected in the street or parks where newspapers are displayed for the public to read

阅兵场 parade ground

阅兵式 military review (or parade)

阅览室 reading room

悦 [yuè]　Ⅰ 形 happy; glad; pleased; delighted：心情不悦 unhappy; displeased Ⅱ 动 please; delight

悦耳 pleasing to the ear; sweet-sounding

悦服 heartily admire

悦目 pleasing to the eye; good-looking

跃 [yuè]　动 jump; leap; spring

跃动 move up and down; quiver

跃进 make (or take) a leap; leap forward

跃居 jump or leap to a higher ranking

跃马 spur the horse on

跃迁 transition

跃然 appear vividly

跃然纸上 show forth in one's writing

跃跃欲试 be eager to have a try; itch to have a go

跃层式住宅 duplex house

越 [yuè]　Ⅰ 动 ① get over; jump over; cross ② exceed; pass; overstep ③ (of voice or emotion) be at a high pitch; vigorous ④ loot：杀人越货 kill a person and seize his belongings; rob and kill Ⅱ ① (used in duplicates "越…越…")：越多越好。The more, the better. / 雨越下越大。The rain is getting heavier. ② (used in "越来越…")：他的进步越来越大。He is making greater and greater progress.

越冬 live through (or survive) the winter

越发 ①all the more; even more ②(the more. ..) the more...

越轨 exceed the bounds; transgress

越过 cross; surmount; negotiate

越级 ①bypass the immediate leadership ②(of

personnel promotion) skip a grade or rank

越加 all the more;even more

越界 overstep the boundary;cross the border

越境 cross the boundary illegally;sneak in or out of a country

越橘 cowberry

越礼 improper;indecorous

越理 unreasonable

越权 ①ultra vires;excess of authority ②exceed one's authority;overstep one's power

越位 offside

越野 cross-country

越狱 escape from prison;break prison

越来越… more and more

越狱犯 prison escapee;prison breaker

越冬作物 winter crop;overwintering crop

越轨行为 behaviour out of bounds;impermissible behaviour;outre behaviour

越级提升 promote sb more than one grade at a time;appoint sb by bypassing the conventional rules

越权审批 do the examination and approval without consúltation with above;approve sth without the permission of the authority;approve sth which could have been done by the people above

越野赛跑 cross-country race

越铀元素 transuranic element

越俎代庖 exceed one's functions and meddle in other people's affairs;take sb else's job into one's own hands

越雷池一步 transgress the bounds

越权减免税 unauthorized tax reduction

yūn（ㄩㄣ）

晕 [yūn]
I 〔形〕dizzy;giddy;faint II 〔动〕swoon;faint;lose consciousness;pass out ⇒ yùn

晕倒 fall in a faint;pass out

晕糊 dizzy;giddy

晕厥 syncope;faint

晕头晕脑 ①dizzy;giddy ②muddleheaded

晕头转向 confused and disoriented

晕晕忽忽 ①dizzy;giddy ②muddleheaded

赟 [yūn]
〔形〕fine;glorious

yún（ㄩㄣ）

云 [yún]
I 〔动〕say;utter II 〔动〕*auxiliary word in classical Chinese*:云谁之思? Whose idea is it? /岁云暮矣。It is late in the year. III 〔名〕①cloud ②Yunnan (Province)

云鬓 lady's thick and beautiful hair

云彩 cloud

云层 cloud layer

云顶 cloud top

云端 high in the clouds

云朵 flaky clouds

云海 a sea of clouds

云集 come together in crowds;gather;converge

云量 cloudiness

云幂 ceiling

云母 mica

云霓 rain clouds

云气 thin,floating clouds

云雀 skylark

云散 disperse like the clouds

云杉 dragon spruce (Picea asperata)

云室 cloud chamber

云梯 scaling ladder

云天 the skies

云图 cloud atlas;cloud chart;cloud picture

云团 cloud cluster

云雾 cloud and mist;mist

云系 cloud system

云霞 rosy clouds

云霄 the skies

云崖 high cliff

云烟 ①cloud and mist;mist ②cigarettes made in Yunnan

云涌 like surging clouds—in large numbers;in force

云游 (of a Buddhist monk or a Taoist priest) wander about;roam about

云雨 the sport of cloud and rain—sexual intercourse;making love

云云 and so on

云雾天 soupy weather

云贵高原 the Yunnan-Guizhou Plateau

云谲波诡 bewilderingly changeable

云开见日 the clouds disperse and the sun shines forth—①darkness recedes and light dawns ②all misunderstanding has been dispelled

云泥之别 as far apart as clouds and mud—worlds (*or* poles) apart;a world of difference

云起龙骧 dragons rise as clouds gather—great men come to the fore when opportunity offers

云山雾罩 ① be enveloped in mist;misty ② rambling;discursive ③ dazed;confused;muddled

云上轰炸 overcast bombing

云天高谊 great kindness and friendship

云消雾散 the clouds melt and the mists disperse—vanish into thin air

云遮雾障 enveloped in mist;blurred;indistinct;hazy

云蒸霞蔚 (of scenery) magnificent

匀 [yún]
I 形 even; equitable II 动 ① even up; divide evenly：这两份苹果多少不等，应该再匀一匀。 The two portions of apples are not equal and need evening up. ② take from sth and give to sb；take from sth for some other purpose；spare
匀称 well-proportioned；well-balanced；symmetrical
匀度 evenness
匀兑 spare；share
匀和 even；neat；uniform
匀净 uniform；even；neat
匀脸 rub powder and paint evenly on one's face
匀溜 of the right size，thickness，consistency，etc.
匀染 level dyeing
匀实 even；neat；uniform
匀调 even；well-proportioned
匀妥 even；equitable
匀细 even and fine；even and light
匀圆 nicely rounded
匀整 neat and well spaced；even and orderly
匀速度 uniform velocity
匀速运动 uniform motion

芸 [yún]
名 ① rue ② rape
芸豆 kidney bean
芸薹 rape
芸香 rue
芸芸 numerous；multitudinous
芸芸众生 all living things；all mortal beings

沄 [yún]
名 great waves

昀 [yún]
名 sunlight；sunshine

耘 [yún]
动 weed
耘锄 hoe (a farm tool)
耘田 weed the fields

筼 [yún]
名 ① green bamboo skin ② bamboo

yǔn （ㄩㄣˇ）

允 [yǔn]
I 动 consent；grant；allow；permit II 形 just；fair；impartial
允差 permissible margin of error or disparity
允承 agree (or promise) to do sth；undertake
允从 consent to；assent to
允当 proper；suitable
允诺 promise；consent；undertake
允许 permit；allow
允准 approve；permit；allow
允许速度 permissible velocity
允许误差 allowable (or permissible) error
允许载荷 allowable load

陨 [yǔn]
动 fall from the sky or outer space
陨落 (of a meteorite, etc.) fall from the sky or outer space
陨灭 ① fall from outer space and burn up ② meet one's death；perish
陨石 aerolite；stony meteorite
陨铁 meteoric iron；iron meteorite；siderite
陨星 meteorite

殒 [yǔn]
动 perish；die；pass away
殒灭 meet one's death；perish
殒命 meet one's death；perish

yùn （ㄩㄣˋ）

孕 [yùn]
动 pregnant
孕妇 pregnant woman
孕期 pregnancy；gestation
孕穗 booting
孕吐 vomiting during pregnancy；morning sickness
孕育 give birth to；be pregnant with；breed
孕震 tectonic stress；buildup of stress along a fault line that may eventually induce an earthquake

运 [yùn]
I 名 ① motion；movement ② luck；fortune；destiny；fate II 动 ① transport；haul；carry ② use；wield；utilize
运笔 wield the pen (in writing or painting)
运材 cart-load of woods；log transportation
运程 haul
运筹 draw up plans；devise strategies
运动 ① motion；movement ② sports；athletics；exercise ③ (political) movement；campaign；drive
运费 transportation expenses；freight；carriage
运河 canal
运货 freight
运价 transport price
运距 load distance hauled；distance carried
运力 ① transportation facilities ② transport capacity；carrying capacity
运量 freight volume；traffic
运能 transport capacity；carrying capacity
运气 [yùnqì] (the art of) directing one's strength, through concentration, to a part of the body
运气 [yùnqi] fortune；luck
运球 dribble
运输 transport；carriage；conveyance
运送 transport；ship；convey
运算 operation
运销 (commodity) transportation and sale
运行 ① move；be in motion ② operate；func-

Y

tion

运营 (of buses,ships,etc.) run;ply
运用 use;wield;apply
运载 deliver;carry
运转 ①revolve;turn round ②work;operate
运作 function
运筹学 operational research;operations research
运动病 motion sickness (carsickness,seasickness,etc.)
运动场 sports (*or* athletic) ground;playground;stadium
运动服 sportswear
运动会 sports meet;athletic meeting;games
运动裤 knickers
运动量 amount of (physical) exercises
运动衫 sports shirt
运动鞋 sport footwear
运动学 kinematics
运动员 sportsman or sportswoman;athlete;player
运动战 mobile war (*or* warfare)
运费表 freight list
运费单 freight note
运费吨 freight ton
运费率 freight rate
运货车 waggon;truckline
运煤船 coal carrier;collier
运输船 cargo ship;transport ship
运输队 transport corps (*or* team)
运输机 ①transport plane;air-freighter ②conveyor
运输舰 transport ship;naval transport
运输量 freight volume
运输网 transport network
运输线 landline;supplyline
运输业 transport service;carrying trade;transportation
运算器 arithmetic unit
运笔如神 wield a pen with miraculous skill
运筹帷幄 plan strategies within a command tent
运动处方 exercise prescription
运动健将 master of sports
运动神经 efferent nerve
运动医学 sports medicine
运动知觉 consciousness of motion
运费付讫 carriage paid
运费免付 carriage free
运费条款 freight clause
运费已付 freight (*or* carriage) paid
运费预付 freight prepaid;advanced freight
运斤成风 whirl the hatchet with a noise like the wind—an uncanny feat
运输部队 transportation troops
运输方式 modes of transport
运输工具 means of transport;conveyance

运输公司 transport company
运输里程 transport mileage
运输力量 transportation facilities
运输能力 transport capacity;carrying capacity
运算分析 operational analysis
运算误差 arithmeticerror
运行机制 operating mechanism;operational mechanism
运用自如 handle very skilfully;have a perfect command of
运载工具 means of delivery
运载火箭 carrier rocket;launch vehicle
运载技术 delivery technology
运算微积分 operational calculus
运载飞行器 carrier vehicle
运用之妙,存乎一心 Ingenuity in varying tactics depends on mother wit.

晕 [yùn]
Ⅰ 形 dizzy;giddy;faint;sick Ⅱ 名 ① halo ②haze or halo round some colour or light ➡ yūn
晕场 have stage fright;feel nervous and dizzy at an examination
晕车 carsickness
晕船 suffer from seasickness
晕机 suffer from airsickness
晕针 have a fainting spell during acupuncture treatment
晕高儿 feel giddy when on a height

酝 [yùn]
Ⅰ 动 make wine;brew beer Ⅱ 名 wine
酝酿 ① brew;ferment ② have a preliminary informal discussion;deliberate on

愠 [yùn]
形 angry;annoyed;irritated
愠恼 angry;indignant;furious
愠怒 be inwardly angry
愠容 angry look;irritated look
愠色 angry look;irritated look

缊 [yùn]
名 ① bits of hemp, flax, jute, etc. ② silk wadding
缊袍 silk-padded robe

韫 [yùn]
动 include;contain
韫椟 hidden in a box—unrecognized talents

韵 [yùn]
名 ①beautiful or sweet sound;sound pleasant to the ear ②simple or compound vowel (of a Chinese syllable) ③appeal;charm
韵白 ① spoken parts in Beijing opera where the traditional pronunciation of certain words is slightly different from that in current Beijing dialect ②rhyming spoken parts in traditional opera
韵调 musical tone
韵腹 the head vowel of a final
韵脚 the rhyming word that ends a line of

verse;rhyme

韵律 ①metre (in verse) ②rules of rhyming; rhyme scheme

韵母 the final of a syllable

韵目 rhyme classes (in traditional rhyming dictionaries)

韵事 ①literary or artistic pursuits, often with pretence to good taste and refinement ② romantic affair

韵书 (traditional) rhyming dictionary

韵头 another name for head vowel

韵尾 the ending of a final

韵味 lingering charm;lasting appeal

韵文 literary composition in rhyme;verse

韵语 rhymes

韵致 charm;beauty

韵律操 rhythmic gymnastics

韵律学 prosody

蕴 [yùn] I 动 contain;hold in store Ⅱ 名 profoundness

蕴藏 hold in store;contain

蕴含 contain

蕴涵 implication

蕴藉 temperate and refined;cultured and restrained

蕴蓄 lie hidden and undeveloped;be latent

熨 [yùn] 动 iron;press

熨斗 flatiron;iron

熨衣板 ironing board

Zz

zā（ㄗㄚ）

扎 [zā] Ⅰ 〔动〕 tie；bind；fasten Ⅱ 〔量〕 bundle：一扎钞票 a bundle of banknotes ➡ zhā
扎彩 hang up festoons
扎线 bundle
扎制 make sth by trussing or tying together
扎束机 bundling press

匝 [zā] Ⅰ 〔量〕 circle；circumference Ⅱ 〔动〕 surround；encircle Ⅲ 〔形〕 whole；full
匝道 ring road
匝数 number of turns；number of windings
匝月 a full month

咂 [zā] 〔动〕 ①sip；suck ②smack one's lips (in admiration, praise, etc.) ③ taste (*or* savour) carefully
咂嘴 make clicks (of admiration, praise, surprise, etc.)

拶 [zā] 〔动〕 force；coerce ➡ zǎn

zá（ㄗㄚˊ）

杂 [zá] Ⅰ 〔形〕 ① varied；diverse；mixed；sundry ② extra；irregular Ⅱ 〔动〕 mix；combine；mingle
杂草 weeds；rank grass
杂处 (of people from different places) live together
杂肥 miscellaneous fertilizers (e. g. urban refuse)
杂费 ①incidental (*or* miscellaneous) expenses；incidentals ② sundry fees (*or* charges)；extras
杂感 ①random (*or* stray) thoughts ②a type of literature recording such thoughts
杂工 backman
杂股 miscellaneous share
杂环 heterocycle；heterocyclic ring
杂烩 ①a stew of various ingredients；mixed stew；hotchpotch ② mixture；miscellany；medley；hotchpotch
杂婚 mixed marriage；promiscuity
杂货 fancy goods；sundry goods；general merchandise
杂记 ① jottings；notes ② miscellanies (as a type of literature)
杂技 acrobatics
杂家 the Eclectics, a school of thought flourishing at the end of the Warring States Period and the beginning of the Han Dynasty
杂交 hybridize；cross
杂居 (of people of two or more nationalities) live together
杂粮 mixed grain；food grains other than wheat and rice
杂乱 mixed and disorderly；in a jumble；in a muddle
杂念 distracting thoughts
杂牌 a less known and inferior brand
杂品 sundry goods；groceries
杂散 stray
杂色 ①variegated；motley ②an inferior brand
杂史 unofficial history
杂耍 variety show；vaudeville
杂税 miscellaneous levies
杂碎 chopped cooked entrails of sheep or oxen
杂坛 acrobatics circles
杂谈 tittle-tattle
杂文 essay
杂务 odd jobs；sundry duties
杂音 ①noise ②static ③murmur
杂症 miscellaneous diseases
杂志 ①magazine ②miscellaneous notes；notes
杂质 ① impurity ② foreign matter (*or* substance)
杂种 ①hybrid；crossbreed ②bastard；son of a bitch
杂拌儿 ① assorted preserved fruits；mixed sweetmeats ② mixture；miscellany；medley；hotchpotch
杂活儿 odd jobs

杂货店 grocery;sundry store;general store
杂和菜 [záhuocài] mixed stew (of left-
杂技团 acrobatic troupe
杂牌货 goods of an inferior brand
杂牌机 off-brand computer;kludge;kluge
杂牌军 miscellaneous troops;troops of miscel-
　laneous brands
杂院儿 a compound occupied by many house-
　holds
杂志架 magazine rack
杂和面儿 [záhuomiànr] maize flour mixed
　with a little soya bean flour
杂技演员 acrobat
杂交后代 filial generation
杂交水稻 hybrid paddy rice
杂交玉米 hybrid (or crossbred) maize
杂交育种 crossbreeding
杂乱无章 disorderly and unsystematic;confus-
　ed and disorderly;chaotic
杂乱信号 hash (in radio,radar or TV recep-
　tion)
杂七杂八 mixed;assorted;miscellaneous
杂食动物 omnivorous animal
杂种优势 hybrid vigour;heterosis
杂交高产稻 miracle rice
杂种不育性 hybrid sterility

砸 [zá]
动 ①pound;crush;tamp ②break;shatter;
smash ③fail;fall through;foul up;be bungled
砸锅 fail;fall through;be bungled
砸伤 injured by a crashing object
砸碎 break into pieces;smash;shatter
砸饭碗 smash sb's rice bowl—make sb lose his
　job;dismiss sb from his job
砸牌子 have the reputation ruined;lose one's
　reputation
砸锅卖铁 give away all one has

zǎ (ㄗㄚˇ)

咋 [zǎ]
代 what;how;why ➡zé;zhā
咋个 how;why

zāi (ㄗㄞ)

灾 [zāi]
名 ①calamity;disaster;catastrophe ②personal misfortune;ill luck;mishap
灾变 natural calamity;disaster
灾害 calamity;disaster
灾患 calamity;disaster
灾荒 famine due to crop failures
灾毁 destroyed by calamity
灾祸 disaster;calamity;catastrophe
灾民 victims of a natural calamity
灾难 suffering;calamity;disaster;catastrophe
灾年 famine (or lean) year

灾歉 crop failure due to natural disasters
灾情 the condition of a disaster
灾区 disaster area
灾星 the star of calamity—sb or sth that
　brings disaster
灾变说 catastrophism
灾连祸结 succession of disasters
灾难深重 disaster-ridden;calamity-ridden

甾 [zāi]
名 steroid

哉 [zāi]
助 ①(indicating exclamation):呜呼哀
哉! Alas! ②(used together with an interrogative to express doubt or form a rhetorical question):如此而已,岂有他哉! That's
all there is to it!

栽 [zāi]
Ⅰ 动 ①plant;grow ②insert;erect;plant ③
impose sth on sb ④tumble;topple;fall ⑤be
set;be back;frustrate Ⅱ 名 young plant;
seedling
栽培 ①cultivate;grow ②foster;train;educate
　③help advance sb's career;patronize
栽诬 falsely accuse;slander
栽秧 transplant seedlings (as of tomatoes or
　eggplants)
栽养 plant and cultivate
栽赃 ①plant stolen or banned goods on sb ②
　frame sb;fabricate a charge against sb
栽植 plant;transplant
栽种 plant;grow
栽子 young plant;seedling
栽跟头 ①tumble;fall ②come to grief;come a
　cropper
栽培技术 cultivation technique
栽培品种 cultivar
栽培植物 cultivated plant
栽赃陷害 trump up charges against sb;plant
　stolen goods on sb to implicate him;lay
　one's own crimes at sb's door

zǎi (ㄗㄞˇ)

仔 [zǎi]
名 young man ➡zǐ

载 [zǎi]
Ⅰ 名 year Ⅱ 动 put down in writing;enter
(in a register);record ➡zài
载入记录 place on record;record in the mi-
　nutes
载入史册 be written into the annals of histo-
　ry;go down in history

宰 [zǎi]
Ⅰ 动 ①slaughter;butcher ②force to pay
through the nose;overcharge;fleece ③be in
charge of;head Ⅱ 名 government official (in
ancient China)
宰割 invade,oppress and exploit

Z

宰客 fleece customers
宰人 rip off; rob sb blind; put the bite (*or* lug) on
宰杀 slaughter; butcher
宰相 prime minister (in feudal China); chancellor
宰牲节 animal-slaughtering day
宰相肚里能撑船 a prime minister's heart is big enough to pole a boat in—a great person is largehearted or magnanimous

崽 [zǎi]

[名] ①son ②young animal; whelp
崽子 whelp; bastard

zài (ㄗㄞˋ)

再 [zài]

Ⅰ [副] ①again; once more; another time ②to a greater extent or degree ③(*indicating what will happen if things are allowed to continue*): 再不快点，我们上课就要迟到了。 We'll be late for class if we don't hurry up. ④(*indicating that one action takes place after the completion of another*): 先到重庆，再去成都 first go to Chongqing and then Chengdu ⑤(*indicating additional information*): 参加会议的有编辑、记者，再就是学生代表。 Present at the meeting were editors, reporters and also representatives of the students. ⑥(*often followed by 也 for emphasis*): 再贵也得买。 We'll have to buy it no matter how expensive it is. Ⅱ [动] continue; return
再版 ①second edition ②reprint; second impression
再不 or else; or
再次 once more; a second time; once again
再度 once more; a second time; once again
再会 goodbye; see you again
再婚 remarry; marry again
再嫁 (of a woman) remarry
再见 goodbye; see you again
再起 recurrence; resurgence; revival
再三 over and over again; time and again; again and again; repeatedly
再审 ①review ②retrial
再生 ①be a second so-and-so (a well-known figure already dead) ②regeneration ③reprocess; regenerate
再说 ①put off until some time later ②what's more; besides
再现 (of a past event) reappear; be reproduced
再造 ①give sb a new lease of life ②restore lost limbs or any other body part implants made from macro-molecular materials
再则 moreover; furthermore; besides
再者 moreover; furthermore; besides

再保险 reinsurance
再出口 reexport
再处理 retreatment; reprocessing
再贷款 re-lending
再分配 redistribution
再教育 reeducation
再进口 reimport
再就业 re-employment; re-employment after being laid off
再生产 reproduction
再生水 recycled water
再贴现 rediscount
再投资 reinvest; plough back
再接再厉 make persistent efforts; continue to exert oneself
再生父母 one's second parent (said with gratitude of a person who has saved or spared one's life)
再生之德 the grace of rebirth; one's grateful acknowledgment
再生资源 regenerative resources
再造之恩 the grace of rebirth
再就业工程 re-employment project
再生检波器 regenerative detector
再生障碍性贫血 aplastic anemia

在 [zài]

Ⅰ [动] ① exist; be living ②(*indicating where a person or thing is*): 我今晚不在家。 I won't be in this evening. ③remain: 在校学生 in-school student; student ④ belong to an organization ⑤ consist in; rest with; rely on ⑥(*used together with 所 and often followed by 不 to indicate emphasis*): 成败在所不计。 I don't care whether this will lead to success or end up in failure. Ⅱ [介] (*indicating time, place, condition, scope, etc.*): 在此期间 during this period Ⅲ [副] (*indicating an action in progress*): 在任期间 while in office
在案 be on record
在编 (of personnel) be on the permanent staff; be on the regular payroll
在场 be on the scene; be on the spot; be present
在读 in-school
在岗 be at one's post; on duty
在行 be expert at sth; know a job (*or* trade, etc.) well
在乎 ①depend on; rest with ②lie in; consist in ③care about; mind; take to heart
在即 near at hand; shortly; soon
在家 ① be at home; be in ② have not renounced the family and become a monk or nun
在建 under construction
在理 reasonable; sensible; right
在内 included

Z

在前 before;beforehand;in front;ahead
在世 be living
在逃 has escaped;be at large
在外 excluded
在望 ①be visible;be in sight;be in view ② will soon materialize;be in sight;be in the offing
在位 ①be on the throne;reign ②be at one's post
在握 be in one's hands;be within one's grasp; be under one's control
在下 I
在先 formerly;in the past;before
在线 be on line
在心 feel concerned;mind;be attentive
在学 be at school
在押 be under detention;be in custody;be in prison
在野 not be in office;be out of office
在业 employed;having a job
在意 take notice of;care about;mind;take to heart
在于 ①depend on;rest with;be determined by ②lie in;consist in
在职 be on the job;be at one's post
在座 be present (at a meeting,banquet,etc.)
在朝党 party in power;ruling party
在逃犯 escaped criminal;criminal at large;fugitive
在押犯 remand;criminal in custody;prisoner
在野党 party not in office; non-government party
在编人员 personnel on the permanent staff; personnel on the regular payroll
在此一举 hang upon this single action;depend upon this one movement
在家办公 telecommuting
在建项目 construction work in process;project under construction
在劫难逃 If you're doomed,you're doomed; There's no escape.
在所不辞 will not refuse under any circumstances;will not hesitate to
在所不惜 will not grudge;will never balk at
在所难免 can hardly be avoided;be unavoidable
在天之灵 sb's soul in heaven (said when thinking fondly of a dead person)
在校学生 in-school student;student
在职干部 cadres at their posts;cadres at work
在职培训 on-the-job training;in-service training
在职总统 incumbent president
在职无业者 idled employee (from overstaffing,or from improved efficiency)
在职研究生 cadres admitted to a postgraduate programme

载 [zài]
Ⅰ 动 ①carry;bring;be loaded with;搭载 carry (on the side) ②(the road) be filled with;风雪载途。The snowstorm has blocked the road. Ⅱ 连 and;moreover;at the same time:载笑载言 talking and laughing at the same time ⇒zǎi
载波 carrier wave;carrier
载荷 load
载货 carry cargo (or freight)
载客 carry passengers
载量 carrying capacity;loading capacity;bearing capacity
载频 carrier frequency
载体 ①carrier ②vehicle;medium
载途 ①encounter during a journey ②route
载誉 win honour or award
载运 convey by vehicles,ships,etc.;transport;carry
载重 load;carrying capacity
载流子 carrier;charge carrier
载重量 loading capacity;deadweight capacity (of a ship,etc.)
载重线 load line;load waterline
载歌载舞 festively singing and dancing
载誉而归 come back winning high praise
载重标尺 deadweight scale
载重吨位 deadweight tonnage
载重汽车 lorry;truck
载人飞行器 manned vehicle
载重线标志 load line mark;freeboard mark; Plimsoll mark
载舟之水足以覆舟 The water that bears the boat is the same that swallows it.

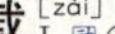

zān(ㄗㄢ)

糌 [zān]

糌粑 *zanba*, staple food for Tibetans, prepared by mixing roasted barlay flour with buttered tea or barly wine into small balls

簪 [zān]
Ⅰ 名 hairpin Ⅱ 动 wear in one's hair
簪子 hair clasp

zán(ㄗㄢˊ)

咱 [zán]
代 ①we:咱大伙儿一条心。We are all of one heart and one mind. ②I ⇒zan
咱们 ①we;us ②I;me ③you

zǎn(ㄗㄢˇ)

拶 [zǎn]
动 press hard;squeeze forcibly ⇒zā
攒 [zǎn]
动 accumulate;collect;save ⇒cuán

攒钱 save up

zàn（ㄗㄢˋ）

暂 [zàn]
Ⅰ 〔形〕of short duration; transient; brief：人生是短暂的。Life is short (*or* fleeting).
Ⅱ 〔副〕for the time being; for the moment; momentarily：暂停营业 business suspended
暂定 arranged for the time being; tentative; provisional
暂缓 postpone; put off; defer
暂且 for the time being; for the moment
暂缺 ①(of a post) be left vacant for the time being ②(of a commodity) be out of stock at the moment
暂时 ① temporary; transient ② temporarily; for the time being; for the moment
暂停 ①suspend ②sports time-out
暂行 provisional; temporary; interim
暂记账 suspense account
暂住权 right for temporary stay
暂住证 certificate (*or* card) for temporary stay
暂定议程 provisional measures; tentative measures; tentative agenda
暂缓执行 stay of execution
暂住人口 temporary residents; transit populace

錾 [zàn]
Ⅰ 〔动〕engrave on gold or silver; carve; incise; chisel Ⅱ 〔名〕engraving tool; chisel; graver
錾刀 (engraver's) burin; graver
錾子 chisel (for cutting stone)

赞 [zàn]
Ⅰ 〔动〕①support; aid; assist ②praise; laud; commend Ⅱ 〔名〕eulogy
赞成 ① approve of; favour; agree with; endorse ②help sb accomplish sth
赞服 appreciate; admire
赞歌 song of praise; paean
赞夸 praise; commend
赞礼 master of ceremonies; serve as the master of ceremonies
赞美 praise; eulogize
赞赏 appreciate; admire
赞颂 extol; eulogize; sing the praises of
赞叹 gasp in (*or* with) admiration; highly praise
赞同 approve of; agree with; endorse
赞许 speak favourably of; praise; commend
赞扬 speak highly of; praise; commend
赞诩 extravagant, exaggerated praise
赞语 words of praise; praise
赞誉 praise; acclaim; commend
赞助 support; assistance
赞成票 affirmative vote
赞美诗 hymn; psalm

赞不绝口 be profuse in praise; be full of praise

zan（·ㄗㄢ）

咱 [zan]
〔副〕(*used in* 这咱,那咱 *and* 多咱, *as a combined pronunciation of* 早 *and* 晚)：他多咱来的？When did he come？/你多咱走？When are you leaving？ ➡zán

zāng（ㄗㄤ）

赃 [zāng]
〔名〕①stolen goods; booty; loot; spoils ②embezzled money or goods; bribes
赃官 corrupt official
赃款 money stolen, embezzled or received in bribes; illicit money
赃物 ①stolen goods; booty; spoils ②bribes
赃款赃物 proceeds of crime

脏 [zāng]
〔形〕dirty; filthy; unclean ➡zàng
脏病 venereal disease
脏弹 dirty bomb
脏话 obscene (*or* dirty, foul) language; obscenities
脏乱 (of a place) dirty and messy
脏钱 ill-gotten money
脏土 rubbish; garbage
脏污 ①dirty ②stain; soil
脏物 foul
脏字 obscene word; swearword; dirty word
脏活儿 dirty work

牂 [zāng]
〔名〕ewe

臧 [zāng]
〔形〕good; right
臧否 pass; judgement (on people)

zǎng（ㄗㄤˇ）

驵 [zǎng]
〔名〕fine horse; steed

zàng（ㄗㄤˋ）

脏 [zàng]
〔名〕internal organs of the body(such as the heart, liver, spleen, lungs and kidneys); viscera ➡zāng
脏寒 cold syndrome in infant
脏器 internal organs of the body; viscera

奘 [zàng]
〔形〕① strong; robust ② rough; boorish in manner and speech ➡zhuǎng

葬 [zàng]
〔动〕consign to the grave; bury; inter
葬礼 funeral (*or* burial) rites; funeral
葬身 be buried
葬送 ruin; spell an end to

葬仪 funeral
葬身火海 be engulfed in a sea of flames；be buried in flames
葬身鱼腹 become food for the fishes；be swept to a watery grave；be drowned

藏 [zàng]
[名] ①storage；depository ②Buddhist or Taoist scriptures ③Xizang（*or* Tibet）Autonomous Region ④ Zang or Tibetan nationality ➡cáng

藏蓝 purplish blue
藏青 dark blue
藏医 ①Tibetan medicine ②physician practicing traditional Tibetan medicine
藏族 the Zang（*or* Tibetan）nationality
藏旱獭 Himalayan marmot
藏红花 ①saffron crocus ②saffron
藏羚羊 Tibetan chamois
藏传佛教 Tibetan Buddhism

zāo（ㄗㄠ）

遭 [zāo]
I [动] meet with（disaster，misfortune，etc.）；sustain；suffer：遭险 run into（*or* meet with）danger II [量] ①time；turn：来回走了好几遭 walk back and forth several times ② round：沿城墙跑了两遭 run round the city wall twice

遭到 suffer；meet with；encounter
遭逢 meet with；come across；encounter
遭际 ①circumstances；lot ②meet with；encounter；run up against
遭劫 meet with catastrophe
遭难 meet with misfortune；suffer disaster
遭受 suffer；be subjected to；sustain
遭殃 suffer disaster；suffer
遭遇 ①meet with；encounter；run up against ②（bitter）experience；（hard）lot
遭灾 be hit by a natural calamity
遭罪 endure hardships（*or* tortures，rough conditions，etc.）；have a hard time
遭遇战 meeting engagement；encounter（action）；contact battle

糟 [zāo]
I [名] distillers' grains；brewers' grains；grains II [动] be pickled with grains or in wine III [形] ① rotten；worn out ② in a wretched state；in a mess：别把邻里关系搞糟了。Don't mess up your relations with your neighbours./这孩子身体糟得很。He is a very frail child.

糟坊 distillery
糟糕 how terrible；what bad luck；too bad
糟行 distillery
糟践 ①waste；ruin；spoil ②insult；trample on；ravage ③violate（a woman）；rape
糟糠 distillers' grains，husks，chaff，etc.—foodstuffs for the poor
糟烂 decomposed
糟粕 waste matter；dross；dregs
糟蹋 ①waste；ruin；spoil ②insult；trample on；ravage ③violate（a woman）；rape
糟心 vexed；annoyed；dejected
糟朽 decayed；crumbled；disintegrated
糟鱼 pickled fish
糟糠夫妻 bread-and-cheese marriage；love in a cottage
糟糠之妻不下堂 The wife of one's "chaff and husks" days shall never go down from the hall；A wife who has shared her husband's hard lot must never be cast aside.

záo（ㄗㄠ）

凿 [záo]
I [名] ①chisel ②mortise；hole II [动] bore a hole；chisel；dig：用大理石凿一尊雕像 chisel a statue out of（*or* from）the marble/在门上凿个窟窿 bore a hole in the door/凿冰 cut（*or* make）a hole in the ice/凿地道 dig a tunnel/凿一条隧道穿过这岩石 tunnel through the rock III [形] certain；sure；authentic；irrefutable

凿刀 chisel
凿缝 staking
凿井 ①dig（*or* sink，bore）a well ②shaft sinking；pit sinking
凿空 forced；farfetched
凿密 caulking
凿岩（rock）drilling
凿子 chisel
凿孔机 puncher；mortising machine
凿榫机 mortiser；mortising machine
凿死理儿 obstinate；stubborn；dogged

zǎo（ㄗㄠ）

早 [zǎo]
I [名] morning：从早到晚 from morning to night；from dawn till dusk/一大早就出发 set out before dawn II [副] long time ago；as early as：他早就毕业了。It has been a long time since he graduated；He graduated long ago./我早就想和你聊聊了。I have been wanting to have a chat with you. III [形] ①（as in a time sequence）former；previous；early ②earlier（than scheduled or expected）；beforehand；in advance；early：早睡早起 go to bed early and get up early；early to bed and early to rise/你早来两天就好了。If only you had come two days earlier./请尽早答复。Please reply at your earliest convenience；An early reply would be appreciated. ③（word of greeting）good morning：先生早！Good morning，sir!

早安 good morning
早班 morning shift

早播 early sowing
早餐 breakfast
早操 morning (setting-up) exercises
早茶 morning tea
早产 premature delivery;premature birth
早场 morning show (at a cinema, theatre, etc.)
早车 morning train or coach
早晨 (early) morning
早春 early spring;early in spring
早稻 early (season) rice
早点 (light) breakfast
早饭 breakfast
早花 early blossoming
早慧 (of a child) precocious
早婚 marry too early
早就 long since
早恋 love at an early age
早年 one's early years
早期 early stage;early phase;early days;initial stage
早起 get up early;rise early
早秋 early autumn;early in autumn
早日 at an early date;early;soon
早上 (early) morning
早市 ①morning market ②morning business
早逝 early death
早熟 ①precocity ②early-maturing;early-ripe
早衰 premature senility (or decrepitude); early ageing
早霜 early frost
早退 leave earlier than one should;leave early
早晚 ①morning and evening ②sooner or later ③time ④some time in the future;some day
早先 previously;before;in the past
早泄 premature ejaculation
早已 long ago;for a long time
早育 early childbearing
早产儿 premature baby;premature infant
早早儿 as early as possible;well in advance
早出晚归 leave early in the morning and return late at night
早婚早育 early marriage,early birth (discouraged in China for the sake of population control)

枣 [zǎo]
　图 jujube;(Chinese) date
枣红 purplish red;claret
枣林 jujube grove
枣泥 jujube paste
枣树 jujube tree
枣椰 date palm
枣子 Chinese date

蚤 [zǎo]
　图 flea

澡 [zǎo]
　图 bath:给婴儿洗澡 give the baby a bath/

洗个凉水澡 take a cold bath
澡盆 bathtub
澡堂 public baths;bathhouse
澡塘 common bathing pool (in a bathhouse)

璪 [zǎo]
　图 silk tassels threaded with jades hanging from a crown

藻 [zǎo]
　图 ① algae ② aquatic plants ③ literary adornment
藻花 water bloom
藻礁 algal reef
藻井 sunk panel;caisson ceiling
藻饰 embellishments in writing
藻类学 algology
藻类植物 algae

ZÀO（ㄗㄠˋ）

皂 [zào]
　Ⅰ 形 black:皂衣 black coat Ⅱ 图 ①office boy;*yamen* runner ②soap
皂白 black and white—right and wrong
皂化 saponification
皂荚 Chinese honey locust
皂角 Chinese honey locust
皂片 soap flakes
皂石 soapstone;soaprock;saponite
皂素 saponin
皂洗机 soaper

灶 [zào]
　图 ①kitchen range;cooking stove ②kitchen;mess;canteen;cafeteria ③kitchen god
灶间 kitchen
灶具 cooking utensils
灶君 kitchen god
灶鸟 ovenbird
灶神 kitchen god
灶台 the top of a kitchen range
灶膛 chamber of a kitchen range
灶头 kitchen range;cooking stove
灶王爷 kitchen god
灶性感染 focal infection

造 [zào]
　Ⅰ 动 ①make;build;construct;create:生造词语 coin words and expressions/通过传媒大造舆论 whip up public opinion through mass media/造花名册 compile a register (of names)/造机器 make (or manufacture) machines/造预算 draw up (or make) a budget ②fabricate;cook up;concoct:造假象 create a false image;put up a facade ③go to;arrive at;reach:造门迎宾 meet the guest at the door ④train;educate;cultivate Ⅱ 图 ①one of the two parties to a legal agreement or in a lawsuit:甲造 first party/两造具备 both parties are present ②crop:早造 early crops/一年三造皆丰收。We reaped three bumper crops

this year. ③ achievement; accomplishment; success
造成 create; cause; give rise to; bring about
造船 shipbuilding
造次 ①hurried; hasty ②rash; impetuous
造反 rise in rebellion; rebel; revolt
造访 pay a visit (*or* call); call on
造福 bring benefit to; benefit
造化 [zàohuà] the Creator; Nature; Creation
造化 [zàohua] good luck; good fortune
造假 manufacture fake products; forge; counterfeit
造价 cost (of building or manufacture)
造就 ① bring up; train ② achievements; attainments (usu. of young people)
造句 make a sentence
造块 agglomeration
造林 afforestation
造孽 do evil; commit a sin
造市 marketing
造势 promote
造物 the divine force that created the universe; Nature
造像 statue
造型 ① modelling; mould-making ② model; mould ③moulding
造血 internal functions to revitalize oneself
造谣 cook up a story and spread it around; start a rumour
造诣 (academic or artistic) attainments
造影 radiography
造渣 slag making; slag formation
造纸 papermaking
造作 [zàozuò] make; manufacture
造作 [zàozuo] affected; artificial
造币厂 mint (a place where money is made)
造船厂 shipyard; dockyard
造船业 shipbuilding industry
造假账 falsified accounts; draw up false accounts
造林学 silviculture
造山带 orogenic zone
造物主 God; the Creator
造型板 mould board
造纸厂 paper mill
造纸机 paper machine
造纸业 paper industry
造就人才 make useful citizens through education; train qualified personnel
造陆运动 epeirogenic movement; epeirogeny; epeirogenesis
造山运动 orogenic movement; orogeny; orogenesis
造型美观 attractive appearance; handsome appearance
造型艺术 plastic arts
造谣惑众 spread rumours to confuse people; fabricate rumours to mislead people
造谣生事 spread rumours to create trouble; start a rumour to create trouble; stir up trouble by rumour-mongering
造谣诬蔑 rumour-mongering and mudslinging; calumny and slander
造谣中伤 spread slanderous rumours; spread rumours to defame others

噪 [zào]
动 ①(of birds, insects, etc.) chirp: 群鸦乱噪。Numerous crows are cawing. ②make an uproar; clamour ③become well known
噪鹃 Chinese koel
噪鹛 laughing thrush
噪闹 noisy; noise; racket; din
噪嚷 cry; shout
噪声 noise; din
噪音 noise
噪声级 noise level
噪声污染 noise pollution
噪音污染 noise pollution
噪音抑制 noise suppression
噪声污染防治 prevention and control of noise pollution

簉 [zào]
形 secondary; subsidiary

燥 [zào]
形 dry
燥剂 drying prescription; desicating prescription
燥裂 crack from dryness; chap
燥热 hot and dry

躁 [zào]
形 rash; impetuous; impulsive: 他的脾气太躁。He is too hot-tempered (*or* quick-tempered).
躁动 move restlessly
躁急 restless; uneasy
躁狂 mania

zé(ㄗㄜˊ)

则 [zé]
I 名 ①standard; gauge; norm; criterion ②rule; decree; regulation II 动 ① take as a model; imitate; follow: 则先烈之言行 follow the example of the martyrs in word and deed ②be: 此则意料中之事也! That's to be expected! III 量 item (of news); paragraph or piece (of writing): 一则新闻 an item of news IV 连 ①(*indicating that one action follows another*): 每首歌曲唱完, 则掌声四起。Each song was greeted by loud applause. ②(*indicating cause and effect, condition, etc.*) ③(*indicating contrast*): 夜深了, 人们都已入睡, 而他则在紧张备课。It was late at night, and everyone was asleep, but he was still busy preparing his lessons. ④(*used between two*

Z

identical words to indicate concession）：你的方法好则好，却不易学会。Though your method is good, it is difficult to learn. Ⅴ 连 (*used together with* 一，二，三 *to enumerate causes or reasons*)：他没有考上大学，一则基础差，二则复习时间短，三则临考时发高烧。He failed the matriculation (*or* college entrance) examination because, first, he lacked a good grounding in the subjects; second, he didn't have enough time for revision; and third, he was running a high fever when the examination was close at hand.
则声 make a sound; utter a word

责 [zé] Ⅰ 名 duty; obligation; responsibility Ⅱ 动 ①demand; exact; require：责人宽，责己严 be strict with oneself and generous towards others ②interrogate; question closely; call sb to account ③criticize; reproach; blame; reprove ④punish
责备 reproach; blame; reprove; take sb to task
责成 instruct (sb to fulfil a task); charge (sb with a task); enjoin (sb to do sth)
责打 punish by beating
责罚 punish
责怪 blame
责令 order; instruct; charge
责骂 scold; rebuke; dress down
责难 censure; blame
责任 ① duty; responsibility ② responsibility for a fault or wrong; blame
责问 call (*or* bring) sb to account
责任感 sense of responsibility (*or* duty)
责任田 farmland covered by contract; responsibility field
责任心 sense of responsibility (*or* duty)
责任制 responsibility system; system of job responsibility
责任状 responsibility contract
责任保险 liability insurance
责任编辑 ① executive editor ② be an editor-in-charge; be in charge of editing
责任事故 accident due to negligence; accident involving criminal or civil liability
责任限额 liability limit
责任预算 responsibility budget
责无旁贷 there is no shirking the responsibility; be duty-bound
责有攸归 Responsibility must rest somewhere.
责任追究制 system of accountability

择 [zé] 动 select; choose; opt for; pick ➡ zhái
择伐 selective cutting (*or* felling)
择吉 select (*or* choose) an auspicious day (for a marriage, funeral, etc.)
择交 choose friends

择偶 choose a spouse
择期 pick a day; select a day or time
择校 select a school
择业 choose an occupation; select a job
择优 select the superior ones
择校生 students choosing to attend a particular school
择肥而噬 select the rich for extortion; victimize the rich; take a lion's share
择日动工 fix a date to begin construction
择善而从 choose and follow what is good
择婿嫁女 choose a worthy husband for one's daughter
择业观念 job-seeking ideas
择优录取 admit the best of the examinees

咋 [zé] 动 bite ➡ zǎ; zhā

迮 [zé] 形 narrow

泽 [zé] Ⅰ 名 ① pool; pond; swamp ② lustre (of metals, pearls, etc.) ③ favour; largesse; beneficence Ⅱ 形 wet; moist; damp
泽国 ①a land that abounds in rivers and lakes ②inundated area
泽泻 ①oriental water plantain ②the rhizome of such a plant

啧 [zé] Ⅰ 形 subtle; abstruse Ⅱ 动 dispute; compete for a chance to speak Ⅲ 象 click of the tongue
啧啧 ①clicking the tongue; chattering ②chirping
啧有烦言 There are a lot of complaints.
啧啧称羡 click the tongue in admiration

赜 [zé] 形 subtle; profound; abstruse

zè (ㄗㄜˋ)

仄 [zè] Ⅰ 形 ①narrow ②uneasy; sorry Ⅱ 名 oblique tones
仄声 oblique tones

昃 [zè] 动 (sun) incline to the west：日中则昃 The sun will incline towards the west after midday.

zéi (ㄗㄟˊ)

贼 [zéi] Ⅰ 名 ① thief; burglar ② traitor; enemy Ⅱ 形 ① wicked; crooked; evil ② wily; sly; cunning：那小子贼得厉害，一肚子鬼心眼儿。That guy is very crafty and full of tricks. Ⅲ 动 injure; harm; maim Ⅲ 副 extremely; exceedingly; disagreeably：贼冷 terribly cold
贼巢 thieves' den; thieves' lair

贼船 pirate ship
贼死 extremely；utterly
贼窝 thieves' den
贼相 thievish-looking
贼心 wicked heart；evil designs；evil intentions
贼星 meteor；shooting star
贼赃 stolen goods；booty；spoils
贼喊捉贼 a thief crying" Stop thief "
贼眉鼠眼 shifty-eyed；thievish-looking
贼去关门 lock the door after the thief has gone；lock the stable door after the horse is stolen
贼头贼脑 behaving stealthily like a thief；stealthy；furtive
贼心不死 refuse to give up one's evil designs
贼性不改 A thief cannot change his nature.

zěn(ㄗㄣˇ)

怎 [zěn]
疑 why；what；how：这事该怎办? What's to be done about it?
怎么 ①how；what；why ②in a certain way；in any way；no matter how ③(not) very；(not) much；(not) quite；(not) too ④what
怎样 ①how；what ②in a certain way；in any way；no matter how
怎么样 ①how；what ②what's it like；how are things；what do you think ③in a certain way；in any way；no matter how ④(not) up to much
怎么着 ①what to do；what ②no matter what；whatever ③what
怎么得了 where will it all end；what a terrible thing it would be；this is one hell of a mess

zèn(ㄗㄣˋ)

谮 [zèn]
动 falsely charge；defame；slander；calumniate
谮言 calumny；defamation

zēng(ㄗㄥ)

曾 [zēng]
形 relationship between great-grandchildren and great-grandparents ➡céng
曾孙 great-grandson
曾祖 (paternal) great-grandfather
曾孙女 great-granddaughter
曾祖母 (paternal) great-grandmother

增 [zēng]
动 increase；enhance；grow；gain：信心倍增 with redoubled confidence
增白 brighten
增补 augment；supplement
增产 increase production

增订 revise and enlarge (a book)
增多 grow in number or quantity；increase
增防 strengthen defences
增幅 degree of increase；rate of growth；range of increase
增高 ① get higher；rise；increase ② make higher；heighten；raise；increase
增光 add lustre to；do credit to；add to the prestige of
增加 increase；raise；add
增减 increase and decrease；fluctuate
增进 enhance；promote；further
增刊 supplement (to a newspaper or periodical)；supplementary issue
增量 ① increase ② increment；incremental quantity
增绿 enlarge afforested area
增强 strengthen；heighten；enhance
增色 add colour to；add beauty to
增删 additions and deletions
增设 establish an additional or new (organization, unit, course, etc.)
增生 hyperplasia；proliferation；multiplication
增收 increase income；increase revenues
增添 add；increase
增选 elect more
增页 text or pictures added to a periodical；supplement
增益 ①increase；raise；add ②gain
增盈 increase profit or profitability
增援 reinforce
增长 increase；rise；grow
增支 increase expenditure
增值 ①increase or rise in value；add value；increment ② appreciate；appreciation；increase in production or value ③increase in value
增殖 ① hyperplasia；proliferation；multiplication ② breed；reproduce；multiply；propagate
增资 increase salary
增白剂 brightening agent；brightener
增白霜 fair complexion cream；skin whitener
增补本 an enlarged edition
增充剂 extender
增订版 enlarged edition
增订本 a revised and enlarged edition
增加值 value-added output
增塑剂 plasticizer
增效剂 synergist
增长点 growth engine
增长率 rate of increase；growth rate
增长税 value-added tax；increment value duty
增值税 value-added tax (VAT)；accelerated profit tax
增殖率 animal husbandry rate of increase
增产节约 increase production and practise

economy
增进食欲 whet one's appetite
增强党性 enhance Party spirit
增强经济 galvanize the economy; boost the economy; invigorate the economy; enliven the economy; stimulate the economy
增强塑料 reinforced plastics
增强体质 get one's body together physically
增援部队 reinforcements; reinforcing units
增长过猛 hasty increase; excessive growth
增砖添瓦 ①add bricks and tiles (to the construction of a building) ②make whatever contribution one can (to a cause)
增加透明度 increase the transparency
增强竞争力 sharpen the competitiveness; make more competitive
增强战斗力 strengthen fighting capacity; increase combat effectiveness
增进相互了解 promote mutual understanding
增强防御能力 enhance (or strengthen) one's defense capabilities
增强国防实力 strengthen the defense capabilities
增强企业活力 enliven enterprises
增收节支运动 campaign to raise revenues and reduce expenditures; drive to increase income and save unnecessary expenses

憎 [zēng]
囫 hate; loathe; abhor
憎称 derogatory name for sb one hates or loathes
憎恨 hate; detest
憎恶 abhor; loathe; abominate
憎厌 dislike

zèng(ㄗㄥˋ)

综 [zèng]
囵 heddle; heald ➡zōng
综框 heald frame
综丝 heddle; harness wire

锃 [zèng]
囮 (of utensils, etc.) polished
锃光 shiny
锃亮 shiny
锃光瓦亮 shiny

赠 [zèng]
囫 send as a gift; give as a present: 互赠礼品 exchange (or present each other with) gifts
赠别 present a friend with gifts, poems, etc. at parting
赠答 present each other with gifts, poems, etc.
赠款 grant
赠礼 ①present sb with a gift ②gift; present
赠品 (complimentary) gift; free gift; free offer; feebie; giveaway

赠券 gift coupons
赠书 ①present sb with a book ②complimentary copy
赠送 give as a present; present as a gift
赠言 words of advice or encouragement given to a friend at parting
赠予 present to; donate to
赠阅 (of a book, periodical, etc.) given free by the publisher
赠款人 donor
赠予国 donor country
赠阅本 complimentary copy
赠送仪式 presentation ceremony

zhā(ㄓㄚ)

扎 [zhā]
囫 ①prick; needle into: 扎得相当疼 prick rather badly/背后被扎了一刀 be stabbed in the back/在纸板上扎洞 punch holes in the cardboard ②plunge into; dive into; get into: 树根深深地扎在泥土里。 The tree has taken root deeply in the earth. ③(of troops) be stationed; be quartered ➡zā
扎根 take root
扎花 embroider
扎啤 draught beer
扎实 ①sturdy; strong ②solid; sound; down-to-earth
扎手 ①prick the hand ②difficult to handle; thorny
扎眼 ① dazzling; offending to the eye; loud; garish ②offensively conspicuous
扎针 give (or have) an acupuncture treatment
扎堆儿 get together
扎猛子 dive; swim with the head kept submerged in water
扎耳朵眼儿 pierce the earlobe (in order to wear earrings)

咋 [zhā]
➡zǎ; zé
咋呼 ①shout blusteringly ②show off; make a fuss

揸 [zhā]
囫 ①pick up sth with the fingers: 揸一点盐 take a pinch of salt ②spread one's fingers

喳 [zhā]
Ⅰ 囡 yes, sir Ⅱ 囨 chatter: 麻雀叽叽喳喳叫个不停。 Sparrow are twittering nonstop. ➡chā

渣 [zhā]
囵 ①dregs; slag; sediment; residue ②broken bits
渣车 slag car; slag wagon
渣罐 slag ladle; slag pot
渣油 residual oil; residuum
渣泽 dregs; sediment; residue

渣子 ①dregs;sediment;residue ②broken bits

楂 [zhā]
➡chá
◇山楂 ①(Chinese) hawthorn ②haw

zhá(ㄓㄚˊ)

札 [zhá]
〔名〕①thin pieces of wood used for writing on in ancient China ②letter
札记 reading notes

轧 [zhá]
〔动〕roll (steel):轧钢板 roll out in plates ➡yà;gá
轧钢 steel rolling
轧辊 roll;roller
轧焊 roller welding
轧机 rolling mill
轧件 rolled piece
轧制 rolling
轧钢厂 steel rolling mill

闸 [zhá]
Ⅰ〔名〕①floodgate;sluice;sluice gate:开闸放水 open (or let loose) the sluices ②brake ③electric switch Ⅱ〔动〕dam up water
闸盒 fuse box
闸轮 brake wheel;brake pulley
闸门 ① sluice gate ②(ship) lock gate ③ throttle valve
闸瓦 brake shoe
闸流管 thyratron

炸 [zhá]
〔动〕①fry in deep fat or oil;deep-fry:软炸鱼 soft-fried fish/炸鸡蛋 fried egg/炸肉丸子 fried meat balls/炸油条 deep-fried twisted dough sticks ②dip in boiling water;scald (as a way of cooking):把菠菜放在开水里炸一下。Scald the spinach in boiling water. ➡zhà
炸酱 fried bean sauce (usu. with minced meat)
炸酱面 noodles served with fried bean sauce
炸薯条 chips;French fries
炸鱼丸 croquette

铡 [zhá]
Ⅰ〔名〕hand hay cutter;fodder chopper Ⅱ〔动〕cut up with a hay cutter;铡草 chop hay
铡刀 hand hay (or straw） cutter; fodder chopper
铡草机 hay cutter;chaffcutter

zhǎ(ㄓㄚˇ)

拃 [zhǎ]
Ⅰ〔动〕measure by stretching one's hand across in one span;span Ⅱ〔量〕span;这块布有三拃宽。This cloth is three spans wide.

眨 [zhǎ]
〔动〕blink;wink;bat (the eyes):眼睛也不眨一眨 without even batting an eyelid/眨了一

眼 give a wink
眨巴 blink
眨眼 very short time;wink;twinkle

zhà(ㄓㄚˋ)

乍 [zhà]
Ⅰ〔副〕①first;at first;for the first time:乍一看 at first glance ②all of a sudden;suddenly;abruptly Ⅱ〔动〕open out;spread;extend:乍翅 stretch wings
乍暖还寒 After suddenly getting warmer, it's turned cold again.

诈 [zhà]
〔动〕① cheat; swindle; deceive:到处行诈 practise extortion everywhere ② pretend; feign;fake ③bluff sb into giving information; feel out:你不要拿话来诈我。Don't try to draw me out.
诈病 malinger;malingering;feign illness;pretend sickness
诈称 jactitation
诈唬 bluff;bluster
诈骗 defraud;swindle
诈死 feign death;play possum
诈降 pretend to surrender;feign surrender
诈语 lie;falsehood;fabrication
诈病者 malingerer
诈骗犯 swindler
诈骗钱财 defraud sb of money;swindle money out of sb;get money by fraud
诈巧虚伪 cunning and hypocritic
诈人钱财 cheat (or swindle） people out of their money;get money by fraud

栅 [zhà]
〔名〕railings;palisade;paling;bars ➡shān
栅栏 ①railings;paling;bars ②boom
栅篱 hedgerow
栅门 fence gate

咤 [zhà]
◇叱咤 shout or bawl angrily

炸 [zhà]
〔动〕①explode;break;burst:炸得粉碎 explode into pieces ②blow up;blast;bomb:从山中炸出一条隧道 blast a tunnel through a mountain/在墙上炸出了一个洞 blow a hole through the wall/炸碉堡 blow up the blockhouse ③fly into a rage;explode with anger; flare up:他一听这话就炸了。He flew into a towering rage when he heard it. ④scamper; scurry away;flee in terror ➡zhá
炸弹 bomb
炸锅 ①oil spattering when food is fried ②unrestrained anger;great dissatisfaction
炸胶 blasting gelatine
炸雷 a clap of thunder
炸窝 scamper;flee in terror

Z

炸响 explode；make cracking noise
炸药 explosive（charges）；dynamite
炸弹舱 bomb bay
炸药包 pack（*or* satchel）of dynamite；explosive package；satchel charges
炸弹气球 balloon with bomb（often for propaganda）

蚱 ［zhà］

蚱蜢 grasshopper

榨 ［zhà］
［动］press；extract；squeeze out：榨出水分 squeeze the water out/榨干血汗 bleed sb white；wring every ounce of sweat and blood out of sb /榨橘子汁 squeeze juice from an orange
榨菜 ①mustard tuber ②hot pickled mustard tuber
榨取 squeeze；extort
榨油 extract oil
榨干机 wringer；drying press
榨棉机 cotton press
榨汁机 juicer

zhāi（ㄓㄞ）

侧 ［zhāi］
［动］tilt；incline；slant ➡cè

斋 ［zhāi］
I［名］① vegetarian diet adopted by Buddhists and Taoists ②room or building II［动］①abstain from meat，wine，etc.；fast ②give alms（to a monk）
斋饭 food given to Buddhist monks as alms
斋祭 offer sacrifices（to gods *or* ancestors）while refraining from wine and meat
斋戒 abstain from meat，wine，etc.（when offering sacrifices to gods or ancestors）；fast
斋期 fast days；fast
斋僧 give alms to monks
斋堂 dining hall in a Buddhist temple
斋月 Ramadan；the month of fast
斋戒节 Ramadan；the fast of Ramadan
斋戒日 fast day
斋戒沐浴 fast and ablution；fast and take a bath before a religious observance

摘 ［zhāi］
［动］① pick；pluck；remove；take off：摘花 pluck flowers/摘下面具 tear off the mask；unmask/摘葡萄 pick grapes/摘眼镜 take off one's glasses ②select；pick out；make extracts from：摘喜欢的段落朗读 read aloud excerpts one likes best ③borrow money when in urgent need
摘报 make a summary report
摘编 ① select and edit；make extracts ②extracts
摘抄 ①take passages；make extracts；extract；excerpt ②extracts；excerpts
摘除 excise
摘登 publish excerpts（*or* extracts）of sth
摘发 publish an abstract of sth
摘桂 take the crown；win the title
摘记 ①take notes ②extracts；excerpts
摘借 borrow money when in urgent need
摘录 ①take passages；make extracts；extract；excerpt ②extracts；excerpts
摘牌 delist；win the prize
摘取 ①obtain；get ②quote
摘要 ① make a summary ② summary；abstract；précis
摘译 ①translate selected passages ②translations of selected passages
摘引 quote
摘由 key extracts（of a document）；résumé
摘桃子 ① pick peaches ② steal the fruit of other's labour
摘东补西 take from one and make up another；pluck from one end to repair the other
摘棉铃机 cotton stripper

zhái（ㄓㄞˊ）

宅 ［zhái］
［名］residence；dwelling；house
宅第 large house；mansion
宅基 the foundations of a house；the site of a house
宅门 ①gate of an old-style big house ②family living in such a house
宅区 quarter
宅院 house with a courtyard；house
宅子 residence；house
宅急送 express delivery company
宅心仁厚 be of a kindly disposition；settle the mind with benevolence and honesty

择 ［zhái］
［动］①select；choose ②pick：择鸡毛 pick a chicken ➡zé
择菜 trim vegetables for cooking
择床 be unable to sleep well in a new place
择席 be unable to sleep well in a new place
择不开 ①unable to disentangle（*or* undo）② cannot get away from

zhǎi（ㄓㄞˇ）

窄 ［zhǎi］
［形］① narrow ② petty；small-minded：心眼儿窄 narrow-minded ③hard up；badly off；on the rocks
窄带 narrow band
窄道 narrow path
窄缝 narrow slit；small clearance space
窄小 narrow and small
窄轨铁路 narrow-gauge railway

zhài（ㄓㄞˋ）

债 [zhài]
〔名〕debt
债额 amount of debt
债户 debtor
债款 loan
债权 creditor's rights
债券 bond;debenture
债市 bond market
债务 debt;liabilities
债息 debt service
债项 amount due
债主 creditor
债权国 creditor nation
债权人 creditor
债务国 debtor nation
债务率 debt ratio
债务期 debt duration
债务人 debtor
债转股 debt-to-equity swap;transformation of debt into equity rights;debt-equity swap
债权担保 security for debt
债权抵押 pledge of obligation
债券兑回 bond redemption
债券发行 the issuance of debentures
债券价格 bond price
债券价值 bond value
债券交易 bond exchange
债券市场 bond market
债券投资 bond investment
债券息票 bond coupons;coupon
债券溢价 bond premium
债券转让 transfer of bonds
债台高筑 be heavily in debt;be up to one's ears in debt;be debt-ridden
债务公司 debtor corporation
债务纠纷 dispute over obligation
债务证券 debt instrument
债务咨询 debt counselling
债主权益 creditor's equity
债券担保人 bond underwriter
债券发行人 floater

砦 [zhài]
〔名〕stockade;enclosures for deer

寨 [zhài]
〔名〕①stockade;fence ②camp ③móuntain stronghold ④stockaded village;fenced hamlet:村村寨寨 all the villages
寨墙 bulwark
寨主 (in former times) brigand chief
寨子 stockaded village

zhān（ㄓㄢ）

占 [zhān]
〔动〕practise divination;divine ➡zhàn

占卜 practise divination;divine
占卦 divine by means of the Eight Diagrams
占课 divine by tossing coins
占梦 prognostication by dreams;oneiromancy
占星 divine by astrology;cast a horoscope
占星术 astrology
占断吉凶 try to find out one's lot by divination;tell one's fortune
占卦问卜 consult the oracle;inquire about by divination

沾 [zhān]
〔动〕①moisten;wet;damp:沾满泪痕 be blotted with tears ②be stained with;be soiled with:沾有油渍 stained with grease/沾满了泥 covered with mud stains ③touch:脚不沾地 one's feet do not touch the ground—walk very fast;run very fast;be extremely busy ④gain by association with sb or sth;benefit from some sort of relationship:沾点便宜 gain some advantages
沾边 ①touch on (or upon) only lightly ②be close to what it should be;be relevant
沾光 benefit from one's association
沾染 be infected with;be contaminated by;be tainted with
沾手 ①touch with one's hand ②have a hand in
沾污 ①make dirty;dirty;soil ②contaminate
沾染区 contaminated area
沾亲带故 have ties of kinship;be related somehow or other
沾沾自喜 feel complacent;be pleased with oneself

毡 [zhān]
〔名〕felt
毡衬 packing felt
毡垫 felt pan;felted mattress
毡帽 felt cap;felt hat
毡子 felt;felt rug;felt blanket

粘 [zhān]
〔动〕glue;stick;paste:粘信封 seal up an envelope/把椅子腿粘上 glue the leg on to the chair
粘接 splice
粘连 adhesion
粘贴 paste;stick

谵 [zhān]
〔动〕rave;rant;be delirious
谵妄 delirium
谵言 delirious speech;ravings;wild talk
谵语 delirious speech;wild talk;ravings

瞻 [zhān]
〔动〕look up;look forward
瞻顾 look ahead and behind
瞻念 look to;think of
瞻赏 enjoy the sight of
瞻望 look forward;look far ahead
瞻仰 look at with reverence

Z

瞻前顾后 peer ahead and look behind—① think over carefully ②be over-cautious and indecisive

zhǎn（ㄓㄢˇ）

斩 [zhǎn]
〔动〕①chop;cut;kill ②fleece;blackmail
斩仓 sell out all one's securities at a price lower than that when they are bought
斩获 capture
斩首 behead;decapitate
斩波器 chopper;lopper
斩假石 artificial stone;imitation stone
斩草除根 destroy root and branch;cut the weeds and dig up the roots—stamp out the source of trouble
斩钉截铁 resolute and decisive;categorical
斩风劈浪 speed through wind and waves
斩关夺隘 capture many strategic points;take pass after pass
斩尽杀绝 kill all;wipe out;exterminate
斩头去尾 chop the head and tail off

盏 [zhǎn]
Ⅰ〔名〕small cup Ⅱ〔量〕：一盏花灯 a festive lantern/两盏电灯 two electric lamps

展 [zhǎn]
Ⅰ〔动〕①stretch;unfold;display;spread out;open up ②put to good use;give free play to：施展鸿才 give full play to one's talent;put one's talent to use ③ postpone;extend;prolong;put off Ⅱ〔名〕exhibition;show
展播 ①special TV programme (to show the best productions);run (on TV,as in a festival) ②arrange and broadcast programmes
展翅 spread the wings;get ready for flight
展出 put on display;be on show (or view);exhibit
展地 site of an exhibition
展度 latitude of emulsion
展观 unroll and view a scroll painting
展馆 exhibition centre;exhibition hall
展柜 showcase;display window
展缓 postpone;extend;prolong
展会 exhibition
展绘 plotting
展开 ①spread out;unfold;open up ②launch;unfold;develop;carry out
展览 put on display;exhibit;show
展廊 exhibition gallery
展露 reveal;show
展卖 exhibit for sale
展品 exhibit;item on display
展评 display and appraise;exhibit and compare
展期 ①extend a time limit;postpone ②duration of an exhibition;exhibition period
展区 exhibition area;place of exhibition;display zone (set up in a museum or sales exhibition according to content or geographical division)
展示 open up before one's eyes;reveal;show;lay bare
展事 exhibition activities
展室 exhibition room;show room
展售 exhibition sale
展诵 open a book and read
展台 showcase;booth;display counter
展厅 demonstration room
展望 ①look into the distance ②look into the future;look ahead ③forecast;prospect
展现 unfold before one's eyes;emerge;develop
展销 exhibit (or display) and sell(goods)
展性 malleability
展演 performance;exhibition performance
展业 develop the business
展映 film festival;festival;exhibition show
展阅 open and read
展览馆 exhibition centre (or hall)
展览会 exhibition
展览品 exhibit;item on display
展览室 exhibition room;show room
展览亭 exhibition booth
展示会 exhibition;show
展销会 trunk show;commodities fair
展眉舒目 stretch the eyes and relax the brows;beam with joy

崭 [zhǎn]
〔形〕①rise high;towering (over) ②fine;superb;swell
崭新 brand-new;completely new
崭岩 (of peaks) steep and towering;(of rocks) overhanging
崭露头角 (of a young person) begin to show one's brilliant talents;display remarkable ability or talent

揞 [zhǎn]
〔动〕wipe or dab with a soft dry object to sop up liquid
揞布 dishcloth;dish towel

辗 [zhǎn]
辗转 ①pass through many hands (or places) ②toss about (in bed)
辗转反侧 toss about (in bed);toss and turn
辗转流传 pass through many hands;spread from place to place
辗转相除法 division algorithm

zhàn（ㄓㄢˋ）

占 [zhàn]
〔动〕① take possession of; occupy; seize; take：占座位 occupy seats ②constitute;form;hold;make up；占第一位 take the first place;

rank first/占绝大多数 constitute an over-whelming (*or* absolute) majority ➡zhān

占地 (of a garden,farm,etc.)cover an area of
占据 occupy;hold
占理 reasonable;sensible;right
占领 capture;occupy;seize
占先 take precedence;take the lead;get ahead of
占线 The line (of a telephone) is busy (*or* engaged).
占用 occupy and use;take up (time)
占有 ①own;possess;have ②occupy;hold
占鳌头 come out first;tower above the rest
占领军 occupation army
占领区 occupied area
占便宜 ① gain extra advantage by unfair means;profit at other people's expense ② advantageous;favourable
占上风 get the upper hand;win an advantage;prevail
占下风 be at a disadvantage
占优势 gain the upper hand;hold preponderance;prevailing
占线通道 active channel
占小便宜 gain petty advantages;secure small advantages at other people's expense;make small gains at other people's expense
占着茅坑不拉屎 sit on the (toilet) seat but not shit—hold on to a post without doing any work and not let anyone else take over;be a dog in the manger

栈 [zhàn]
〔名〕 ①shed;pen;fold ②warehouse ③plank road built on sides of cliffs for army
栈道 a plank roadway built along perpendicular rock-faces by means of wooden brackets fixed into the cliff
栈房 ①warehouse;storehouse ②inn
栈桥 landing stage (in a port);loading bridge (at a railway station)
栈租 storage charges

战 [zhàn]
Ⅰ〔名〕war;warfare;combat;armed conflict
Ⅱ〔动〕①fight;battle:为和平而战 fight for peace/战死沙场 die on the battlefield ② tremble;shiver;shake;shudder:冷得打寒战 shiver with cold
战败 ① be defeated;be vanquished;suffer a defeat;lose (a battle or war) ②defeat;vanquish;beat
战报 war communiqué;battlefield report
战备 war preparedness;combat readiness
战场 battlefield;battleground;battlefront
战车 war chariot
战船 man-of-war;naval vessel;warship
战刀 sabre
战地 battlefield;battleground;combat zone

战抖 tremble;shiver;shudder
战斗 ① fight;battle;combat;action ② militant;fighting
战端 the beginning of a war
战法 strategies and tactics of war
战犯 war criminal
战俘 prisoner of war (P.O.W.)
战斧 battle-ax(e)
战歌 battle song;fighting song
战功 meritorious military service;outstanding military exploit;battle achievement
战鼓 war drum;battle drum
战国 the Warring States
战果 results of battle;combat success;victory
战壕 trench;entrenchment
战后 postwar
战火 flames of war
战祸 disaster of war
战机 opportunity for combat
战绩 military successes (*or* exploits,feats);combat gains
战舰 warship
战将 warrior
战局 war situation
战况 battlefield situation;situation on the battlefield;progress of a battle
战例 object-lesson battles;a specific example of a battle (in military science)
战栗 tremble;shiver;shudder
战乱 chaos caused by war;war
战略 strategy
战马 battle steed;war-horse
战幕 war curtain
战袍 (in former times) war robe;soldier's garb
战前 prewar
战区 war zone;theatre of operations
战胜 defeat;triumph over;vanquish;overcome
战时 wartime
战史 military history;war history
战士 ① soldier;man ② champion;warrior;fighter
战事 war;hostilities
战书 written challenge to war;letter of challenge
战术 (military) tactics
战死 die (*or* be killed) in battle
战位 battle station
战线 battle line;battlefront;front
战役 campaign;battle
战鹰 fighting eagle (an affectionate term for a fighter plane)
战友 comrade-in-arms;battle companion
战云 war cloud
战阵 battle array;battle scene
战争 war;warfare

Z

战败国 vanquished (*or* defeated) nation
战备粮 grain stockpiled in case of war
战斗力 combat effectiveness (*or* strength, capability); fighting capacity
战斗员 fighter
战俘营 prisoner of war camp
战利品 spoils of war; captured equipment; war trophies (*or* booty)
战列舰 battleship
战略家 strategist
战略学 science of strategy
战胜国 victorious nation
战术学 science of tactics
战役学 science of campaigns
战争狂 war mania; war hysteria
战争学 polemology
战备等级 degree of combat readiness
战备工作 preparations against war
战备行军 tactical march; tactical movement
战备训练 military training in preparation for the eventuality of war
战备状态 combat readiness
战地记者 war correspondent
战斗减员 depletion of combat strength
战斗英雄 combat hero
战火纷飞 flames of war raging everywhere
战略储备 strategic reserves; strategic stockpiles
战略反攻 strategic counterattack
战略防御 strategic defense
战略决策 strategic policy decision
战略态势 strategic situation
战略物资 strategic goods and materials
战略转移 strategic shift
战时联盟 war-born alliance
战天斗地 fight against heaven and earth; combat nature; brave the elements
战无不胜 invincible; ever-victorious; all-conquering
战战兢兢 trembling with fear; with fear and trepidation; gingerly
战争保险 war insurance
战争贩子 warmonger
战争机器 war machine; war apparatus
战争赔偿 war indemnity; war reparations
战争状态 state of war
战斗轰炸机 fighter-bomber
战列巡洋舰 battle cruiser
战略性考虑 strategic approach
战术核武器 tactical nuclear weapons
战斗堡垒作用 function of a fortress; role of fighting bastions
战略防御计划 Strategic Defense Initiative (SDI)
战略伙伴关系 strategic partnership
战区导弹防御 Theater Missile Defense (TMD)

战役战术导弹 tactical operational missiles
战争边缘政策 brink of war policy; brinkmanship; policy of brink-of-war; brink-or-war policy
战斧式巡航导弹 Tomahawk cruise missile

站 [zhàn]
I 〔动〕①stand; get up; be on one's feet: 并排站着 stand side by side/站起来发言 rise to speak/站在人民的立场上 uphold the stand of the people ②stop; come to a halt II 〔名〕①station; stop ② station or centre for rendering certain services
站点 website
站队 line up; fall in; stand in line
站岗 stand (*or* mount) guard; be on sentry duty; stand sentry
站立 stand; be on one's feet
站票 ticket for standing room; standing ticket
站哨 stand (*or* mount) guard; be on sentry duty; stand sentry
站台 platform (in a railway station)
站位 court position; playing position
站稳 ①come to a stop ②stand firm; take a firm stand
站长 head of a station, centre, etc.
站住 ①stop; halt ②stand firmly on one's feet; keep one's feet ③stand (*or* hold) one's ground; consolidate one's position ④hold water; be tenable
站柜台 serve as a shop assistant; a serve behind the counter
站台票 platform ticket
站住脚 ①stop; halt ②stand (*or* hold) one's ground; consolidate one's position ③stay put ④hold water; be tenable
站不住脚 unable to stand one's ground; cannot be justified; impossible to defend
站在时代前列 stand at the forefront of the times
站得高,看得远 stand taller and see farther; stand high and see far; have vision; be far-sighted

绽 [zhàn]
〔动〕split; tear; burst: 他的上衣绽线了。His coat has split at the seams.
绽放 (of flowers) burst forth; burst into bloom
绽裂 split open; burst open
绽露 show; appear

湛 [zhàn]
〔形〕① profound; thorough; deep ② crystal clear; limpid
湛蓝 (of the sky, the sea, a lake, etc.) azure blue; azure
湛清 limpid; clear

蘸 [zhàn]
〔动〕dip in (ink, sauce, etc.): 蘸酱油 dip in soy sauce

zhāng（ㄓㄤ）

张 [zhāng]
Ⅰ〔动〕①open;spread;draw;stretch:张弓射箭 draw a bow to shoot/张开嘴 open one's mouth/张网捕鱼 spread a net to catch fish ②lay on;display ③magnify;amplify;exaggerate ④look;glance ⑤open a new shop:择日开张 choose an auspicious day for the opening of the shop Ⅱ〔量〕①(of paper,paintings,tickets,etc.):两张火车票 two train tickets/一张报纸 a piece of paper②(of articles such as bed,table,etc.):一张沙发 a sofa/一张写字台 a writing desk③(of human face,mouth,etc.):一张利嘴 a sharp tongue/一张笑脸 a smiling face④(of bow,plough,etc.):一张弓 a bow/一张犁 a plough Ⅲ〔名〕one of the twenty-eight constellations

张榜 put up a notice;post a notice

张本 ①anticipatory action ②hint foreshadowing later developments in a story;anticipatory remark

张弛 tension and relaxation;tightness and looseness

张大 magnify;exaggerate;publicize widely

张挂 hang up (a picture,curtain,etc.)

张皇 alarmed;scared;flurried;flustered

张狂 flippant and impudent;insolent

张力 ①tension ②pulling force

张量 tensor

张罗 ①take care of;get busy about ②raise (funds); get together (money, etc.) ③greet and entertain (guests); attend to (customers,etc.)

张目 open one's eyes wide

张幕 pitch a tent

张贴 put up (a notice,poster,etc.)

张望 ①peep (through a crack,etc.) ②look around

张扬 make widely known;make public;publicize

张嘴 ①open one's mouth (to say sth) ②ask for a loan or a favour

张力计 tensiometer

张应力 tensile stress

张灯结彩 be decorated with lanterns and coloured streamers; be decked with lanterns and bunting; be decked out and hung with lanterns; be gay with lanterns and decorations

张冠李戴 put Zhang's hat on Li's head—attribute sth to the wrong person or confuse one thing with another

张皇失措 be in a flurry of alarm; lose one's head; get into a panic

张口结舌 be agape and tongue-tied; be at a loss for words

张三李四 Zhang, Li or anybody—any Tom, Dick or Harry

张牙舞爪 bare fangs and brandish claws—make threatening gestures; engage in sabre rattling

张家长,李家短 idle gossip; gossip about this or that family

章 [zhāng]
〔名〕① chapter; section; division ② clause; sub-clause:《土地法》第二章 second clause of the *Land Law* ③ order; orderliness ④ rule; regulation; charter; constitution ⑤ memorial to the throne ⑥seal; signet; stamp:刻一枚图章 engrave a seal ⑦badge; insignia; medal

章程 [zhāngchéng] rules; regulations; constitution

章程 [zhāngcheng] solution; way

章法 ① presentation of ideas in a piece of writing; art of composition ②orderly ways; methodicalness

章节 chapters and sections

章句 ① chapters, sections, sentences and phrases in ancient texts ②syntactic and semantic analysis of ancient texts

章鱼 octopus

章则 rules and regulations

章回小说 a type of traditional Chinese novel with each chapter headed by a couplet giving the gist of its content

獐 [zhāng]
〔名〕river deer;Chinese water deer

獐子 river deer

獐头鼠目 with the head of a buck and the eyes of a rat—repulsively ugly and sly-looking

彰 [zhāng]
Ⅰ〔形〕obvious; evident; conspicuous Ⅱ〔动〕cite (in dispatches);commend

彰显 ① conspicuous; outstanding; well know ②show to advantage; bring out conspicuously

彰彰 clear;evident;conspicuous

彰明较著 very obvious; conspicuous; easily seen

彰其德威 display one's virtue and dignity

彰善瘅恶 praise good and denounce evil; uphold virtue and condemn vice

樟 [zhāng]
〔名〕camphor tree

樟蚕 a kind of wild silkworm

樟木 camphorwood

樟脑 camphor

樟树 camphor tree

樟脑丸 camphor ball;moth-ball

樟脑油 camphor oil

蟑 [zhāng]

蟑螂 cockroach;roach

zhǎng（ㄓㄤˇ）

长 [zhǎng]
Ⅰ 形 ①older; elder; senior ②eldest; oldest
Ⅱ 名 ①older generation ②chief; head; leader
Ⅲ 动 ①come into being; spring up; form ②grow; develop: 孩子长得真胖。 What a chubby child! ③boost; enhance; increase: 长信心 boost one's confidence/长学问 increase one's learning (*or* knowledge) ➡cháng
长辈 elder member of a family; elder; senior
长膘 (of a domestic animal) get fat; put on flesh; flesh out
长大 grow up; be brought up
长房 the eldest branch of a family
长官 senior officer (*or* official); commanding officer
长机 lead aircraft; leader
长进 progress
长老 elder
长毛 [zhǎngmáo] become mildewed; be covered with mildew
长肉 put on flesh; fill out
长势 the way a crop is growing
长孙 ①eldest son's eldest son ②eldest grandson
长相 looks; features; appearance
长者 ①elder; senior ②venerable elder
长子 eldest son
长个儿 grow taller
长见识 gain experience; increase one's knowledge
长老会 the Presbyterian Church
长子继承权 (right of) primogeniture; birthright

涨 [zhǎng]
动 (of water, prices, etc.) rise; go up; become higher ➡zhàng
涨潮 rising tide; flood tide
涨风 upward trend of prices
涨幅 growth margin; extent of price increase
涨价 rise in price
涨落 (of water, prices, etc.) rise and fall; fluctuate
涨水 (of a river) rise; (of price) rise
涨落线 advance balance line
涨停板 limit up

掌 [zhǎng]
Ⅰ 名 ①palm ②bottom of certain animals' feet; pad; sole ③horseshoe ④shoe sole or heel: 钉鞋掌 have a shoe soled Ⅱ 动 ①strike with the palm of the hand; slap ②hold in one's hand; take charge of; control; wield ③mend the sole of a shoe ④add; put in (cooking oil, salt, etc.): 掌点醋 add a bit of vinegar Ⅲ 介 (*used in the same way as* 把): 掌门关上 close the door

掌厨 be the chief cook; be in charge of cooking
掌灯 ①hold a lamp in one's hand ②light an oil lamp
掌舵 ①be at the helm; operate the rudder; take the tiller; steer a boat ②helmsman; steersman
掌骨 metacarpal bone
掌故 anecdotes
掌管 be in charge of; administer
掌颊 slap sb on the face
掌控 control
掌权 be in power; wield (*or* hold) power; exercise control
掌声 clapping; applause
掌纹 palm print; friction ridge
掌握 ①grasp; master; know well ②have in hand; take into one's hands; control
掌鞋 mend the sole of a shoe
掌心 ①the centre (*or* hollow) of the palm ②control; influence
掌印 keep the seal—be in power
掌灶 be the chef
掌子 ①face; work area ②horseshoe
掌嘴 slap sb's face; box sb's ears
掌柜的 ①shopkeeper; manager (of a shop) ②husband
掌勺儿 be the chef
掌子面 face
掌上电脑 palm computer; handheld computer; palmtop; hand-held
掌上明珠 a pearl in the palm—a beloved daughter
掌声雷动 thunderous applause
掌握分寸 exercise sound judgment; act or speak properly
掌上型电脑 palm computer; palm held computer
掌握主动权 have the initiative in one's hands

zhàng（ㄓㄤˋ）

丈 [zhàng]
Ⅰ 量 *zhang*, a unit of length (= 3⅓ metres) Ⅱ 动 measure (land): 清丈 make an exact measurement of the land Ⅲ 名 ①respectful form of address for an old man in ancient times ②form of address for certain male relatives by marriage
丈夫 ①man ②husband
丈量 measure (land)
丈人 wife's father; father-in-law
丈母娘 wife's mother; mother-in-law
丈二和尚，摸不着头脑 you can't touch the head of the ten-foot monk—you can't make head or tail of it; be very much in the dark

仗 [zhàng]
Ⅰ 名 ①weaponry; weapons; arms ②fight; battle; war Ⅱ 动 ①hold (a weapon) ②rely

on;depend on;on the strength of
仗剑 hold a sword
仗恃 rely on (an advantage)
仗义 ① uphold justice ② be loyal (to one's friends)
仗势欺人 take advantage of one's own (*or* sb else's power) to bully people;bully people on the strength of one's powerful connections or position;abuse one's power and bully people
仗势作恶 use power to do evil
仗义疏财 be generous in aiding needy people
仗义执言 stand up for the weak;speak out from a sense of justice

杖 [zhàng]
名 ① cane;stick:挂**杖**而立 stand with a cane under one's arm ②rod or staff used for a specific purpose

帐 [zhàng]
名 curtain;tent;canopy
帐钩 bed-curtain (*or* mosquito net) hook
帐幕 tent
帐篷 tent
帐子 ①bed-curtain ②mosquito net
帐篷拖车 tent-trailer

账 [zhàng]
名 ①account:记在我的**账**上 put it on my account;charge it to my account ② account book:一摞**账** stack of account books ③debt;credit
账本 account book
账册 account book
账单 bill;check
账房 ①accountant's office ②accountant
账号 number of a bank account
账户 account
账款 funds on account;credit
账面 as shown in an account book
账目 items of an account;accounts
账项 accounting item
账外资产 invisible assets;unlisted property

胀 [zhàng]
动 ①grow in size;expand;distend ②swell;be bloated
胀大 swell
胀管 expand tube
胀闸 hub brake

涨 [zhàng]
动 ①swell after absorbing water,etc. ②be swelled by a rush of blood;redden ③(of weights and measures,etc.) be more,longer,etc. than expected ➡zhǎng

障 [zhàng]
Ⅰ 动 hinder;impede;obstruct Ⅱ 名 screen;barrier;block
障碍 ① hinder;obstruct ② obstacle;obstruction;barrier;impediment
障蔽 block;obstruct;shut out

障幕 screen;covering veil
障子 a barrier made of reeds;sorghum stalks;closely planted shrubs;hedge
障碍船 blockship
障碍物 obstacle;obstruction;barrier
障眼法 cover-up;camouflage
障碍赛跑 steeplechase;obstacle race

幛 [zhàng]
名 large,oblong sheet of silk with an inscription presented at a wedding,birthday or funeral

嶂 [zhàng]
名 screen-like mountain peak

瘴 [zhàng]
名 miasma
瘴疠 communicable subtropical diseases,such as pernicious malaria,etc.
瘴气 miasma
瘴雨蛮烟 miasmatic rain and harmful fog

zhāo（ㄓㄠ）

钊 [zhāo]
动 encourage;urge;spur;exhort

招 [zhāo]
Ⅰ 动 ①beckon;gesture ②recruit;engage;enlist;enrol:**招**临时工 recruit temporary workers ③attract;invite;incur;court:**招**蚊子 attract mosquitoes ④ offend;provoke;tease ⑤draw;cause:**招**人嫉恨 rouse envy and hatred/**招**人注意 draw people's attention ⑥infect;be catching ⑦ confess;admit;own up Ⅱ 名 trick;device;move
招安 (of feudal rulers) offer amnesty and enlistment to rebels
招办 admissions office
招标 invitation for bid;invite (to) bid;call for bid;call for tender
招兵 recruit soldiers;raise troops
招待 receive (guests);entertain;serve (customers)
招风 catch the wind—attract too much attention and invite trouble
招干 recruit cadres
招工 advertise for workers;recruit workers
招供 make a confession of one's crime;confess
招股 raise capital by floating shares
招雇 recruit;employ
招呼 ①call ②hail;greet;say hello to ③notify;tell ④take care of ⑤mind;take care
招幌 shop sign
招魂 call back the spirit of the dead
招祸 court disaster
招集 call together;convene
招架 ward off blows;hold one's own
招考 give public notice of entrance examination;admit (students,applicants,etc.) by

Z

examination

招徕 solicit (customers or business);canvass

招揽 solicit (customers or business);canvass

招领 announce the finding of lost property

招录 recruit;employ

招募 recruit;enlist

招纳 recruit

招牌 shop sign;signboard

招聘 ① give public notice of vacancies to be filled;invite applications for jobs;advertise for (a secretary,teacher,etc.) ② want ad;wanted (for a job)

招亲 ① take a man into the family as a son-in-law ② marry into and live with one's bride's family

招请 ① hire help ② invite

招惹 ① provoke;incur;court ② (usu. used in the negative) tease;provoke

招认 confess one's crime;plead guilty

招商 invite outside investment;attract investment or business through advertising,exhibition,etc.

招生 enrol new students;recruit students

招式 movements (in martial arts or traditional opera)

招事 bring trouble on oneself;invite trouble

招收 recruit;take in

招手 beckon;wave

招数 ① a move in chess ② a movement in *wushu* ③ trick;device

招贴 poster;placard;bill

招贤 ① (of a ruler) summon men of worth to serve their country ② call the able to service

招降 summon sb to surrender

招训 recruit and train

招眼 eye-catching

招摇 act ostentatiously

招引 attract;induce

招怨 incur hatred

招展 ① flutter;wave ② invite (institutes) to rent exhibition positions;invite exhibitors

招致 ① recruit (followers); scout about for (talents,etc.) ② incur;bring about;lead to

招赘 take a man into the family as a son-in-law

招租 (house) for rent

招标制 competitive-bidding system

招待会 reception

招待券 complimentary ticket

招待所 guest house;hostel

招风耳 protruding ears;flappy ears

招股书 prospectus (stocks and shares)

招女婿 take a man into the family as a son-in-law

招商会 meeting to invite investments

招贴画 pictorial poster (*or* placard)

招降书 demand to surrender

招标承包 make a contract through public bidding

招标公告 announcement of tender

招兵买马 recruit men and buy horses—raise or enlarge an army;recruit followers

招财进宝 let riches and treasures come into the house

招蜂引蝶 attract bees and butterflies—(of a woman) flirtatious

招工提干 recruit workers and promote personnel

招股章程 prospectus

招揽生意 canvass (*or* seek) business orders; solicit (for) business;drum up trade

招聘广告 want ad

招聘面试 job interview

招聘外援 sign foreign player

招惹是非 bring trouble on oneself

招商银行 China Merchants Bank

招商引资 bid for investments; invite investments (form overseas)

招生简章 school admission brochure

招降纳叛 recruit deserters and traitors

招摇过市 swagger through the streets—blatantly seek publicity

招摇撞骗 swindle and bluff;bluff one's way around

招灾惹祸 court disaster;invite trouble

招之即来 come at sb's beck (*or* sb's beck and call)

招标投标制 system of public bidding

招生就业指导办公室 enrollment and vocation guidance office

昭 [zhāo] I 〔形〕 clear; evident; obvious II 〔动〕 show; demonstrate

昭告 declare to the public

昭然 clear;obvious

昭示 make clear to all;declare publicly

昭苏 come to life;wake up

昭雪 exonerate;rehabilitate

昭彰 clear;manifest;evident

昭著 clear;evident;obvious

昭然若揭 abundantly clear;all too clear

着 [zhāo] I 〔名〕 ① move in chess;只因一着错,输却满盘棋。 One wrong move and the whole game is lost. ② trick;device;tactic II 〔动〕 put in; add;着点儿醋 add a bit vinegar/着些糖 put some sugar III 〔副〕 all right;okay;着,你们就么办吧! Okay, go ahead as (has been) agreed. ➡ zháo;zhe;zhuó

着数 ① a move in chess ② a movement in *wushu* ③ trick;device

朝 [zhāo] 〔名〕 ① early morning;dawn;morning ② day

➡cháo

朝晖　morning sunlight

朝气　youthful spirit;vigour;vitality

朝夕　①morning and evening;from morning to night;day and night;daily ②a very short time

朝霞　rosy clouds of dawn;rosy dawn

朝阳　[zhāoyáng] the rising sun;the morning sun

朝不保夕　not know at dawn what may happen by dusk;be in a precarious state

朝不谋夕　be unable to plan one's day;be in a precarious state

朝发夕至　start at dawn and arrive at dusk——a day's journey

朝令夕改　issue an order at dawn and rescind it at dusk;make unpredictable changes in policy

朝气蓬勃　full of youthful spirit;full of vigour and vitality;imbued with vitality

朝秦暮楚　serve (the State of) Qin in the morning and (the State of) Chu in the evening——be quick to switch sides;be fickle;be inconstant

朝三暮四　blow hot and cold;chop and change

朝思暮想　yearn day and night

朝夕相处　be together morning and night;be closely associated

朝阳产业　sunrise industry;industry with bright future

zháo（ㄓㄠˊ）

着 [zháo]

动 ①touch;contact:不着边际 not to the point ②feel;suffer ③burn:房子着火了！The house is on fire! ④(*used after a verb to indicate the result of the action*):谜语猜着了 have guessed a riddle right/我没见着他。I haven't seen him. ⑤fall asleep ➡zhāo;zhe;zhuó

着风　be chilled by the wind

着慌　get nervous;get alarmed;become flustered (*or* jittery);be thrown into a panic

着火　catch fire;be on fire

着急　get worried;get excited;feel anxious

着凉　catch cold;catch a chill

着忙　be in a hurry;be in a rush

着迷　be fascinated;be captivated

着魔　be bewitched;be possessed;crazy

着色　coloration

zhǎo（ㄓㄠˇ）

爪 [zhǎo]

名 claw;talon ➡zhuǎ

爪片　clavus

爪牙　talons and fangs——lackeys;underlings

找 [zhǎo]

动 ①look for;hunt for;try to discover;want to see:找原因 try to find out the cause/我下次来时一定再来找你。I'll surely call on you again when I come next time. ②give change:这是找给你的钱。Here is your change./你少找钱了。You have short-changed me.

找补　make up a deficiency

找平　make level;level up or down

找齐　①make uniform;even up ②make up a deficiency

找事　①look (*or* hunt) for a job ②pick a quarrel

找死　court death

找头　change (from money paid)

找赎　small change

找寻　①look for;seek ②find fault with;pick on

找不开　have no small change for (money of a higher denomination)

找茬儿　find fault;pick holes;pick a quarrel

找对象　look for a partner in marriage

找饭碗　look for a job

找借口　seek pretext

找麻烦　①look for trouble;ask for trouble ②cause sb trouble

找婆家　look for a husband

找窍门　find better techniques;find out the secret to success

找不自在　ask for trouble;borrow trouble;bring trouble upon oneself

找米下锅　①search for rice to cook ②look for supplies of raw materials instead of waiting for state allocations

沼 [zhǎo]

名 natural pond

沼矿　bog ore;bog mine ore

沼泥　cripple

沼气　marsh gas;firedamp;methane;sewage gas;sludge gas

沼泽　marsh;swamp;bog

zhào（ㄓㄠˋ）

召 [zhào]

动 call together;gather;convene;summon

召唤　call

召回　recall

召集　call together;convene

召见　①call in (a subordinate) ②diplomacy summon (an envoy) to an interview

召开　convene;convoke

召集人　convener

兆 [zhào]

Ⅰ 名 sign;omen;foreboding Ⅱ 动 augur;portend;foretell Ⅲ 数 ①million;mega- ②million million;trillion

兆赫　megahertz (MHz);megacycle per second

Z

兆头 sign;omen;portent
兆位 megabit (Mb)
兆周 megacycle
兆字节 megabyte

诏 [zhào]

Ⅰ 动 instruct;admonish;warn;exhort Ⅱ 名 imperial edict
诏令 imperial edict
诏书 imperial edict

照 [zhào]

Ⅰ 动 ①shine;radiate;illuminate;light up：往远处照 light the way far ahead/用手电筒照一照 light up with a torch ②reflect;mirror：照镜子 look in the mirror ③take a picture;photograph;shoot ④ take care of;look after;attend to：照看老人 look after old people/照料家务 manage household affairs ⑤inform;notify;关照一声 notify sb;let sb know ⑥ compare;contrast ⑦make out;understand Ⅱ 名 ①photograph;picture ②licence;permit Ⅲ 介 ①in the direction of;towards：照那边看 look in that direction ②according to;in conformity with：照此办理 handle it accordingly
照搬 indiscriminately imitate;copy
照办 act accordingly;act in accordance with;act upon;comply with;follow
照壁 a screen wall facing the gate of a house
照常 as usual
照抄 ①copy word for word ②indiscriminately imitate;copy
照登 publish sth as it is (i.e. without alterations)
照度 intensity of illumination;illuminance
照发 ①issue as before ②approved for distribution
照拂 look after;care for;attend to
照顾 ①give consideration to;show consideration for;make allowance(s) for ②look after;care for;attend to ③(of a customer) patronize
照管 look after;tend;be in charge of
照护 look after (patients;the wounded,etc.)
照会 ①present (or deliver,address) a note to (a government) ②note
照价 according to the set (or arranged) price
照旧 as before;as usual;as of old
照看 look after;attend to;keep an eye on
照理 according to reason;in the ordinary course of events;normally
照例 as a rule;as usual;usually
照料 take care of;attend to
照临 shine on;illuminate;light up
照明 illumination;lighting
照排 image composition;imaging
照片 [zhàopiàn] photograph;picture
照射 shine;illuminate;light up;irradiate
照实 according to the facts

照说 ordinarily;as a rule
照相 take a picture (or photograph);photograph
照样 ①after a pattern (or model) ②in the same old way;as before;as usual
照耀 shine;illuminate
照引 illuminate the way
照应 ①coordinate;correlate ②look after;take care of
照章 in accordance with rules (or regulations)
照直 ①(go) straight on ②straight-forward;direct
照准 ①(used in official documents) request granted ②aim at
照面儿 ①put in an appearance;show up;turn up ②encounter;come across
照明弹 flare;star shell
照片儿 [zhàopiānr] photo
照片子 take an X-ray;X-ray
照相版 process plate
照相簿 photo album
照相弹 photo-flash bomb;flash bomb
照相馆 photo studio
照相机 camera
照相枪 gun camera
照相纸 photographic paper
照妖镜 monster-revealing mirror
照准仪 alidade
照本宣科 parrot a text;read entirely from the text;echo what the book says
照常营业 business as usual;Our business is carried on as usual.
照方抓药 have prescription filled at a pharmacy
照价赔偿 compensate according to the cost
照猫画虎 draw a tiger with a cat as a model—copy sth without catching its spirit
照明电路 lighting circuit
照明炮弹 illuminating shell
照相复制 photocopy
照相排字 filmsetting;phototype setting
照相制版 photomechanical process
照相制图 photomap
照章办事 act in compliance with the rules (or law);proceed according to regulations
照章罚款 be fined strictly in accordance with the relevant regulations
照章纳税 pay taxes as required
照葫芦画瓢 draw a dipper with a gourd as a model—copy;imitate

罩 [zhào]

Ⅰ 动 cover;envelop;overspread;wrap：烟雾笼罩着江面。The lake is shrouded in mist. Ⅱ 名 ①cover;shade;hood;casing ②outer garment;dustcoat;overall：袍罩儿 outer garment of a robe (or gown);dust-robe;dust-gown;overall ③small cage or coop for raising chickens ④bamboo fish trap

罩垫 hood pad

罩袍 dust-robe;dust-gown;overall

罩棚 an awning over a gateway or a courtyard

罩裙 tunic

罩衫 overall;dustcoat

罩袖 oversleeve;sleevelet

罩衣 dustcoat;overall

罩子 cover;shade;hood;casing

肇 [zhào]

⟨动⟩ ①cause (trouble, etc.); lead to ②begin;commence;initiate

肇端 beginning

肇祸 cause trouble;cause an accident

肇始 start;commence;initiate

肇事 cause trouble;create a disturbance

肇事者 troublemaker

肇事生非 create an incident

肇事逃跑司机 hit-run driver

zhē（ㄓㄜ）

折 [zhē]

⟨动⟩ ①roll over;turn over and over ②pour back and forth between two containers ➡ shé;zhé

折腾 ①turn from side to side;toss about ②do sth over and over again ③cause physical or mental suffering; get sb down ④ spend freely;squander

折跟头 turn a somersault

蜇 [zhē]

⟨动⟩ ①prick with a sting;sting ②cause sharp pain;smart;sting ➡ zhé

蜇针 sting;stinger

遮 [zhē]

⟨动⟩ ①cover;conceal;hide;screen ②hinder; obstruct;impede ③cover up;cloak：遮不住真实感情 unable to conceal one's true feelings

遮蔽 ①hide from view;cover;screen ②obstruct;block ③defilade

遮藏 hide;conceal;cover up

遮丑 gloss over one's blemishes;hide one's shame;cover up one's defect

遮挡 ①shelter from;keep out ②a shelter;a cover

遮断 interdict

遮盖 ①cover;overspread ②hide;conceal;cover up

遮拦 block;obstruct;impede

遮没 hide from view;cover;screen

遮篷 awning

遮羞 hush up a scandal;cover up one's embarrassment

遮掩 ①cover;overspread;envelop ②cover up;hide;conceal

遮阳 sunshade

遮阴 shelter from heat or light;shade

遮光罩 lens hood

遮护板 shield

遮护物 baffle

遮羞布 fig leaf

遮眼法 cover-up;camouflage

遮阳帘 sunshade;sunbonnet

遮阳罩 sky shade

遮幅电影 a masked wide-screen film

遮人耳目 throw dust in people's eyes;hoodwink (or fool) the public

遮天蔽日 blot out the sky and the sun (said of a dense forest)

遮天盖地 blot out the sky and cover up the earth (said of a snowstorm or sandstorm or of an invading army)

zhé（ㄓㄜ）

折 [zhé]

Ⅰ⟨动⟩ ①fracture; break; snap：大腿骨折 have a fracture in the thigh;fracture one's thigh/折颈而死 break one's neck ②be deprived of; lose ③ bend; turn; twist ④ turn back;change direction ⑤be filled with admiration;be won over;be convinced ⑥convert into;change into;amount to：折价 convert into money;evaluate in terms of money ⑦discount; rebate：打七折 give 30% discount; charge 70% of the original (or full) price ⑧fold：折衬衣 fold a shirt Ⅱ⟨名⟩ ①(of a musical drama) act ②book or booklet used for keeping accounts,etc. ➡ shé;zhé

折半 reduce (a price) by half;give 50% discount

折变 sell off (one's property)

折尺 folding rule

折冲 repulse (or subdue) the enemy

折纯 (of chemical products) count only the active ingredients

折凳 camp stool

折叠 fold

折兑 exchange (gold or silver) for money; convert

折返 return;turn back (halfway)

折缝 scarf;welt seam

折服 ①subdue; bring into submission; convince ②be convinced;be filled with admiration

折光 (of water,glass,etc.) refract light

折桂 pluck the cassia—① pass the imperial examinations ② carry off the first prize; win a championship

折合 convert into;amount to

折回 turn back (halfway)

折痕 line made by folding

折价 convert into money;evaluate in terms of

money
折旧 depreciation（in value of property）
折扣 discount；rebate
折门 folding door；accordion door
折磨 cause physical or mental suffering；torment
折让 allowance
折辱 humiliate
折杀 You overwhelm me with more than what I deserve.
折扇 folding fan
折射 refraction
折实 ①reckon the actual amount after a discount ②adjust payment in accordance with the price index of certain commodities
折寿 have one's allotted portion of life reduced by having or getting more than one deserves
折算 convert
折梯 folding stair
折线 broken line
折腰 bend one's back—bow in obeisance；cringe
折页 folding
折账 pay a debt in kind
折纸 paper folding
折中 compromise
折子 booklet in accordion form with a slipcase，used for keeping accounts，etc.
折布机 folding machine
折叠床 folding bed
折叠剪 folding scissors
折叠伞 folding umbrella
折叠椅 folding chair
折光度 dioptre
折子戏 highlights from operas
折板结构 folded plate structure
折戟沉沙 broken halberds embedded in sand—reminder of a fierce battle or a beaten army
折旧资金 depreciation funds
折中措施 middle-of-the-road measure；half measure
折中方案 compromise（proposal）；middle way；golden mean；method of meeting half way
折中主义 eclecticism
折叠翼飞机 folding-wing aircraft

哲 ［zhé］
Ⅰ 〔形〕 intelligent；wise；sagacious Ⅱ 〔名〕 wise man；sage
哲理 philosophic theory；philosophy
哲人 sage；philosopher
哲学 philosophy
哲学家 philosopher
哲学系 philosophy department

辄 ［zhé］
〔副〕 ①always；often；regularly ②as soon as；soon after：稍饮辄醉 get drunk after a few drops

皙 ［zhé］
〔形〕 bright；shining：皙皙明星 bright stars；twinkling stars

謺 ［zhé］
〔名〕 fear；awe；apprehension；dread
謺服 surrender（or yield）in fear

蛰 ［zhé］
〔动〕 hibernate
蛰伏 ①dormancy；hibernation ②live in seclusion
蛰居 live in seclusion

谪 ［zhé］
〔动〕 ①（as a punishment in feudal China）relegate a high official to a minor post in a remote border town；banish from the court；exile ②（of an immortal，etc.）be banished from Heaven ③blame；rebuke；censure
谪居 （of officials in former times）live in banishment

摺 ［zhé］
摺尺 folding rule
摺扇 folding fan

辙 ［zhé］
〔名〕 ①track of a wheel；groove；rut ②direction of traffic：上下辙 up the road，down the road ③rhyme（of a song，poetic drama，etc.）④way；idea；wit
辙叉 frog
辙口 rhyme（of a song，poetic drama，etc.）
辙乱旗靡 crisscross chariot tracks and drooping banners（said of an army in headlong flight）

---

zhě（ㄓㄜˇ）

者 ［zhě］
〔助〕 ①person or thing；-er；-or ②follower of a doctrine，etc.；-ist ③（used after such numerals as 二，三 or 数 to refer to things mentioned above）：二者必居其一。 It must be one or the other. ④（indicating a rhetorical pause）：光阴者，百代之过客。 Time is a passer-by that never stops for any generation. ⑤（often used in the early vernacular to give force to a command）：路上小心在意者！ Do take care while on your way.

锗 ［zhě］
〔名〕 germanium（Ge）
锗石 germanite
锗烷 germane
锗酸盐 germanate

赭 ［zhě］
〔形〕 burnt ochre；reddish brown
赭石 ochre

褶 ［zhě］
〔动〕 pleat；crease；fold；wrinkle

褶边 ruffle;catch selvedge
褶皱 ①fold ②wrinkle (in the skin)
褶子 ①pleat ②crease;fold;wrinkle ③wrinkle (on the face)

zhè（ㄓㄜˋ）

这 [zhè]
  代 ①this;these ②now;then ➡ zhèi
这儿 ①here ②now;then
这般 such;so;like this
这边 this side;here
这次 this time;present;current
这等 like this;so;such
这番 this;these
这个 ①this one;this ②so;such ③(repeated to show hesitation)
这里 here
这么 so;such;this way;like this
这些 these
这样 so;such;like this;this way
这号人 people of this sort
这会儿 now;at the moment;at present
这么些 so much;so many
这么样 so;such;like this;this way
这么着 like this;so
这阵儿 now;at the moment
这还了得 That is really going too far!
这么点儿 such a little bit
这样那样 this or that;of one kind or another;in one way or another
这早晚儿 so late
这山望着那山高 It's always the other mountain that looks higher;always think the grass is greener on the other side of the hill;never be happy where one is

柘 [zhè]
  名 three-bristle cudrania

蔗 [zhè]
  名 sugarcane
蔗螟 sugarcane borer
蔗农 sugarcane grower
蔗糖 ①sucrose ②cane sugar
蔗田 sugarcane field
蔗渣 bagasse

嗻 [zhè]
  叹 yes;alright;yeah

鹧 [zhè]
鹧鸪 Chinese francolin;partridge

zhe（·ㄓㄜ）

着 [zhe]
  助 ①be doing:坐着怎么也比站着好。Anyway, sitting is better than standing. ②(*used to indicate a state*):桌上放着很多书。There are a lot of books on the desk. ③(*used to give force to a verb or adjective*):

你仔细听着。Just listen. ④(*used in forming a preposition*) ➡ zhāo;zháo;zhuó
着哩 very (much);quite;awfully
着呢 very (much);quite;awfully

zhèi（ㄓㄟˋ）

这 [zhèi]
  代 this;these:这封信 this letter ➡ zhè

zhēn（ㄓㄣ）

贞 [zhēn]
  I 形 loyal;staunch;faithful II 名 ①chastity;virginity ②divination
贞操 ①chastity;virginity ②loyalty;moral integrity
贞妇 chaste woman
贞节 ①loyalty;constancy ②chastity;virginity
贞洁 chaste and undefiled
贞烈 ready to die to preserve one's chastity
贞女 a chaste girl;virgin
贞淑 chaste and gentle

针 [zhēn]
  名 ①needle ②stitch:在外衣上缝两针 sew (*or* put) a couple of stitches in one's jacket ③anything like a needle ④injection;inoculation;shot:打了一针 have (*or* give) an injection ⑤acupuncture
针布 card clothing
针刺 needling;acupuncture
针打 stylus printer
针对 ① be directed against; be aimed at; counter ② in the light of; in accordance with;in connection with
针箍 thimble
针剂 injection
针尖 the point of a needle;pinpoint
针脚 stitch
针灸 acupuncture and moxibustion
针筒 syringe
针头 syringe needle
针线 needlework
针绣 needlework
针眼 ①the eye of a needle ②pinprick ③sty
针鼹 echidna;spiny anteater
针药 medicine administered by injection
针织 knitting
针黹 needlework
针鼻儿 the eye of a needle
针对性 focus;focalization
针梳机 gill box
针尾鸭 pintail
针线包 sewing kit
针叶树 coniferous tree;conifer
针织厂 knitting mill;knit goods mill
针织品 knit goods;knitwear;hosiery
针刺疗法 acupuncture treatment

Z

针刺麻醉 acupuncture anaesthesia
针锋相对 give tit for tat;be diametrically opposed to
针灸医生 acupuncturist;doctor of acupuncture and moxibustion
针头线脑 odds and ends needed for sewing;needle and thread;sewing kit
针尖对麦芒 a pin against an awl;diamond cut diamond
针式打印机 stylus printer
针插不进,水泼不进 impenetrable and watertight (said of an exclusive group,etc.)
针尖大的窟窿,斗大的风 A big wind can blow through a small hole;A little leak can sink a great ship.

侦 [zhēn]
劭 investigate;explore;scout;detect
侦办 investigate and prosecute
侦测 listen;monitor (e.g. radio communications)
侦查 investigate (a crime)
侦察 reconnoitre;scout
侦错 debug;debugger
侦获 capture after investigation (criminal,etc.)
侦缉 track down and arrest
侦结 end of criminal investigation
侦控 track down;track and monitor
侦破 investigate and crack;break (a criminal case)
侦探 ①do detective work ②detective;spy
侦听 intercept (enemy radio communications);monitor
侦训 investigation and interrogation
侦察兵 scout
侦察机 reconnaissance plane;spy plane;scout
侦察员 scout
侦察站 intelligence platform
侦察部队 reconnaissance troops (or unit);scouting force
侦察卫星 reconnaissance (or spy) satellite
侦探小说 detective story;detective fiction;crime novel

珍 [zhēn]
I 名 treasure;riches II 形 treasured;precious;rare;valuable III 劭 value highly;set great store by
珍爱 treasure;love dearly;be very fond of
珍宝 jewellery;treasure
珍本 rare edition;rare book
珍藏 collect (rare books,art treasures,etc.)
珍贵 valuable;precious
珍品 treasure
珍奇 rare
珍赏 treasure and delight in (curios,etc.);highly value and appreciate
珍视 value;prize;cherish;treasure

珍玩 rare curios
珍味 rare delicacies;dainties
珍闻 news titbits;fillers
珍惜 treasure;value;cherish
珍稀 rare and precious
珍馐 delicacies;dainties
珍重 ①highly value;treasure;set great store by ②take good care of yourself
珍珠 pearl
珍珠贝 pearl shell;pearl oyster
珍珠粉 pearl powder
珍珠港 Pearl Harbour
珍珠鸡 guinea fowl
珍珠梅 false spiraea
珍珠米 maize;(Indian) corn
珍珠岩 pearlite
珍禽异兽 rare birds and animals
珍稀动物 rare animal
珍稀植物 rare plant
珍稀濒危物种 rare and endangered species

帧 [zhēn]
量 of paintings and calligraphy,etc. :一帧画 a painting
帧频 TV frame frequency;picture frequency
帧脉冲发生器 framing pulse generator

胗 [zhēn]
名 gizzard:鸡胗儿 chicken's gizzard/鸭胗儿 duck's gizzard
胗肝儿 gizzard and liver (esp. chicken's or duck's)

真 [zhēn]
I 形 true;real;factual;genuine II 副 ①really;truly;indeed ②clearly;distinctly;unmistakably III 名 ①(in Chinese calligraphy) regular script ②portrait;image ③nature;natural state
真北 true north
真唱 really sing
真诚 sincere;genuine;true
真传 be handed down in a direct line from the master
真谛 true essence;true meaning
真鲷 genuine porgy;red porgy
真个 really;truly;indeed
真果 true fruit
真话 the truth
真迹 authentic work (of painting or calligraphy)
真菌 fungus
真空 vacuum
真理 truth
真命 ordained by Heaven
真皮 ①derma ②genuine leather
真漆 lacquer
真切 vivid;clear;distinct
真情 ①the real (or true) situation;the facts;the actual state of affairs;truth ②true feel-

ings;real sentiments

真确 ①true;real;authentic ②clear;distinct

真人 ①real person ②true man (i.e. a man who has attained enlightenment or immortality;used esp. in official Taoist titles)

真实 true;real;authentic

真书 (in Chinese calligraphy) regular script

真率 sincere;unaffected;straightforward

真髓 essence

真相 the real (*or* true) situation;the real (*or* actual) facts; the actual state of affairs; truth

真心 whole-hearted;heartfelt;sincere

真性 genuine

真正 genuine;true;real

真知 genuine (*or* real) knowledge

真挚 sincere;cordial

真主 Allah

真地平 true horizon

真分数 proper fraction

真格的 real;true

真见鬼 Shiver my timbers!

真菌学 mycology

真空表 vacuum meter

真空舱 vacuum chamber

真空管 electron tube;valve

真面目 true features;true colours

真命题 true statement

真善美 the true, the good and the beautiful; truth,goodness and beauty

真实性 realness; authenticity; factuality; truthfulness

真糟糕 Damn it all!

真值表 truth table

真珠层 pearly (*or* nacreous) layer

真才实学 real ability and learning; genuine talent

真诚无私 be sincere and selfless

真刀真枪 real swords and spears—the real thing

真假难分 The true is mingled with the false; find it hard to tell truth from falsehood

真空包装 vacuum packaging

真空地带 no-man's-land

真名实姓 real name

真凭实据 genuine evidence; hard evidence; conclusive proof

真枪实弹 real guns and bullets;live ammunition

真情实感 one's real feelings;real sentiments; true feelings

真人真事 real people and real events; actual persons and events

真相大白 The whole truth has come out;The whole affair is now out in the open.

真心实意 genuinely and sincerely; truly and wholeheartedly

真真假假 the true mingled with the false; a mixture of truth and falsehood

真知灼见 real knowledge and deep insight; penetrating judgment

真空成型机 a vacuum forming machine

真金不怕火炼 true gold fears no fire—a person of integrity can stand severest tests

桢 [zhēn]
〔名〕 terminal posts used in building a wall in ancient times

桢干 core member;backbone (element)

砧 [zhēn]
〔名〕 hammering block;anvil

砧板 chopping block

砧骨 incus;anvil

砧木 stock

砧子 hammering block;anvil

祯 [zhēn]
〔形〕 auspicious

斟 [zhēn]
〔动〕 pour (tea or wine)

斟酌 consider;deliberate

斟字酌句 weigh one's words; refine on the words;weigh each sentence and each word

甄 [zhēn]
〔动〕 draw a distinction;distinguish;discriminate;examine

甄拔 select

甄别 ①examine and distinguish; screen; discriminate ②reexamine a case

甄录 examine and employ

甄选 select

甄用 select for appointment

榛 [zhēn]
〔名〕 ①hazel ②hazelnut;filbert

榛果 filbert

榛鸡 hazel grouse

榛莽 luxuriant vegetation

榛实 hazelnut

榛子 ①hazel ②hazelnut

箴 Ⅰ〔动〕 advise;exhort;admonish Ⅱ〔名〕 didactic literary style

箴言 admonition;exhortation;maxim

臻 [zhēn]
〔动〕 ①attain (a higher level);become (better) ②arrive;come

zhěn (ㄓㄣˇ)

诊 [zhěn]
〔动〕 examine (a patient)

诊病 diagnose a disease

诊察 examine (a patient)

诊断 diagnose

诊金 consultation fee;hospital fee

诊疗 make a diagnosis and give treatment

诊脉 feel the pulse

诊室 consulting room

Z

诊所 clinic;dispensary
诊台 diagnostic table;examination table
诊治 make a diagnosis and give treatment
诊断书 medical certificate
诊断程序 diagnostic program
诊断记录 diagnostic record
诊断医师 diagnostician
诊断性测试 diagnostic test
诊断性评价 diagnostic evaluation

枕 [zhěn]
Ⅰ 名 pillow Ⅱ 动 rest one's head on
枕骨 occipital bone
枕巾 a towel used to cover a pillow
枕木 railway sleeper;tie
枕套 pillowcase;pillowslip
枕头 pillow
枕席 ①a mat used to cover a pillow;pillow mat ②bed
枕心 pillow (without the pillowcase)
枕头箱 pillow casket (a small box for valuables)
枕戈待旦 lie with one's head pillowed on a spear,waiting for day to break—be ready for battle;maintain combat readiness
枕戈待命 await eagerly the order for;all set to start the battle
枕席自荐 be willing to become a concubine to sb

轸 [zhěn]
Ⅰ 名 ①cross board at the rear of an ancient carriage;carriage ②one of the 28 constellations Ⅱ 形 sorrowful;grieved
轸悼 grieve (or mourn) over sb's death
轸怀 sorrowfully cherish the memory of sb
轸念 sorrowfully cherish the memory of sb; think anxiously about
轸子 tuning peg

畛 [zhěn]
名 low bank of earth between fields

疹 [zhěn]
名 bleb;rash
疹子 measles

袗 [zhěn]
Ⅰ 名 unlined garment Ⅱ 形 (of clothes) gorgeous

缜 [zhěn]
形 careful;painstaking;meticulous
缜密 careful;meticulous;deliberate

zhèn（ㄓㄣ）

圳 [zhèn]
名 ditch (between fields)

阵 [zhèn]
Ⅰ 名 ①battle array;battle formation ②position;front lines;front ③ period of time; some time Ⅱ 量：一阵大笑 a fit (or burst) of laughter/一阵恶心 a spell (or fit) of vomiting;a vomiting spell/一阵欢呼 a burst of cheers/一阵咳嗽 a fit (or spasm) of coughing/一阵雨 a spatter of rain/阵阵北风 blasts of the north wind/阵阵狂风 gusts of wind
阵地 position;front
阵点 lattice point
阵发 paroxysm
阵法 tactical deployment of troops
阵风 a gust of wind
阵脚 ① front line ② position; situation; circumstances
阵列 array
阵容 ①battle array (or formation),②lineup
阵势 ①battle array (or formation);a disposition of combat forces ② situation; condition;circumstances
阵痛 ①labour pains;throes (of childbirth) ② growing pains; problems and discomfort caused by social dislocation as a result of rapid change
阵图 a system of battle formations
阵亡 be killed in action;fall in battle
阵线 front;ranks;alignment
阵型 formation
阵雪 snow shower
阵营 a group of people who pursue a common interest;camp
阵雨 shower
阵地战 positional warfare
阵列天线 array antenna
阵列处理机 array processor
阵列机语言 array machine language (AML)

纼 [zhèn]
名 tether for tying domestic animals

鸩 [zhèn]
Ⅰ 名 ① legendary bird with poisonous feathers ②poisoned wine Ⅱ 动 kill with poisoned wine
鸩毒 poisoned wine
鸩酒 poisoned wine

振 [zhèn]
动 ①shake;flutter;flap ② vibrate ③ rise with force and spirit;brace up;boost：大振官兵的士气 greatly boost the morale of both officers and men
振臂 raise one's arm
振荡 ①vibration ②oscillation
振动 vibration
振奋 ①rouse oneself;rise with force and spirit;be inspired with enthusiasm ②inspire; stimulate
振幅 amplitude (of vibration)
振兴 develop vigorously;promote
振作 bestir (or exert) oneself;display vigour
振荡器 generator;oscillator
振捣器 vibrator
振笔疾书 write with flying strokes; wield one's pen furiously

振笔直书 write with flying strokes; wield the pen furiously

振臂一呼 raise one's arm and cry for action—issue a call for action; sound the trumpet call of action

振翅高飞 flutter and soar high

振奋人心 inspire people; fill people with enthusiasm

振铃呼叫 silent call alert

振聋发聩 rouse the deaf, enlighten the benighted

振兴中华 achieve China's rejuvenation; rejuvenate China

振振有词 speak plausibly and volubly (in self-justification)

振作精神 brace up; pluck up the spirits; bestir oneself; keep up one's spirits; get up steam

朕 [zhèn]
Ⅰ 代 I, the sovereign; we Ⅱ 名 sign; omen
朕兆 sign; omen; portent

赈 [zhèn]
动 bring relief to; relieve; aid
赈济 relieve; aid
赈款 relief fund
赈贫 aid the poor
赈灾 disaster relief; relieve the people in stricken areas
赈济灾民 relieve the people in stricken areas aid the victims of natural calamities
赈灾义演 benefit performance for the people in stricken areas

揕 [zhèn]
动 stab

震 [zhèn]
动 ①shake; quake; shock ②be shocked; be greatly excited: 感到震惊 be astonished (or stunned); be taken aback
震波 seismic wave; earthquake wave
震颤 tremble; quiver
震荡 shake; shock; vibrate; quake
震动 shake; shock; vibrate; quake
震感 sensation of vibration and quaking (esp. earthquake)
震骇 shock; appal; astonish
震撼 shake; shock; vibrate
震级 magnitude (of an earthquake)
震惊 shock; amaze; astonish; stun
震怒 be enraged; be furious
震情 situation after an earthquake
震区 earthquake region
震慑 awe; frighten
震悚 tremble with fear; be terrified; be frightened
震音 tremolo
震源 earthquake focus; focus (of an earthquake)
震灾 disaster caused by earthquake
震中 an epicentre

震旦纪 the Sinian Period
震撼价 stirring price
震耳欲聋 deafening
震古烁今 surpassing the ancients and amazing contemporaries
震撼人心 stirring; thrilling
震天动地 shake heaven and earth
震天价响 sound great enough to shake the heavens
震颤性麻痹 paralysis agitans

镇 [zhèn]
Ⅰ 动 ①press down; force down; ease ②calm; tranquil; stable; at ease ③keep peace by force; garrison ④cool with cold water or ice; ice: 镇一镇这瓶啤酒 ice the bottle of beer Ⅱ 名 ①garrison post ②township: 乡镇企业 township and village enterprises ③relatively large town Ⅲ 副 ①often; time and again; frequently: 十年镇相随 frequently accompanying sb for ten years. ②all the time
镇尺 paperweight (in the shape of a ruler)
镇定 calm; cool; composed; unruffled
镇服 force sb into submission
镇静 calm; cool; composed; unruffled
镇守 guard (a strategically important place); garrison
镇痛 ①ease pain; relieve pain ②analgesia
镇压 ①suppress; repress; put down ②execute (a counterrevolutionary) ③ rolling; compacting; tamping
镇长 town head
镇纸 paperweight
镇住 bring (or keep) sb under control; reduce sb to submission
镇子 town; market town
镇公所 town hall
镇静钢 killed steel
镇静剂 sedative; tranquillizer
镇流管 ballast tube
镇流器 ballast
镇痛剂 anodyne; analgesic; pain-killer
镇痛药 analgesic
镇压器 (land) roller

zhēng（ㄓㄥ）

正 [zhēng]
名 first month of the lunar year; first moon
➡ zhèng
正旦 the lunar New Year's Day
正月 the first month of the lunar year; the first moon

争 [zhēng]
动 ① contend; compete; vie; strive ② argue; dispute; wrangle: 意气之争 dispute caused by personal grudges ③be short of; be shy; want
争霸 contend (or struggle) for hegemony;

scramble (*or* strive) for supremacy
争辩 argue;debate;contend
争吵 quarrel;wrangle;squabble
争持 refuse to give in;stick to one's guns
争宠 strive for sb's favour
争斗 ①fight ②struggle;contend
争端 dispute; conflict; controversial issues; contentious issues
争夺 fight (*or* contend,scramble) for;enter into rivalry with sb over sth;vie with sb for sth
争锋 fight for mastery;strive for a decisive victory
争购 rush to purchase;snap up (goods)
争光 win honour (*or* glory) for
争脸 try to win credit (*or* honour)
争论 controversy;dispute;debate;contention
争鸣 contend
争奈 but;however;nevertheless
争气 try to make a good showing;try to win credit for;try to bring credit to
争抢 fight for;scramble for
争取 strive for;fight for;win over
争权 contend for power
争胜 compete for first place
争讼 contest a lawsuit
争先 try to be the first to do sth
争雄 contend for supremacy
争议 dispute;controversy
争战 fight;war
争执 disagree;dispute;stick to one's position (*or* guns)
争地位 scramble (*or* jockey) for position
争名誉 strive for fame
争霸世界 contend for world domination (*or* hegemony)
争长论短 squabble;argue
争夺市场 seize markets;contend for markets
争分夺秒 race (*or* work) against time;make every minute and second count
争风吃醋 fight for the affections (of a man or woman)
争名夺利 scramble for power and profit;be on the make;struggle for power
争奇斗艳 (of flowers, etc.) compete with each other for beauty of looks
争强好胜 seek to prevail over others;desire to excel over others
争权夺利 scramble for power and profit; struggle for power
争先恐后 strive to be the first and fear to lag behind;vie with each other in doing sth
争执不下 each stands (*or* holds) his ground; each sticks to his own stand;each sticks to his guns

Z

征 [zhēng]
I 〔动〕①make a long journey ②go on an ex-
pedition：举兵北征 make an expedition to the north ③levy (troops);recruit;call up;draft：应征服役 be drafted into the army ④levy (taxes);collect;extort;impose ⑤solicit;ask for II 〔名〕①evidence;proof ②sign;portent; phenomenon
征兵 conscription;draft;call-up
征尘 dust which settles on one during a journey
征程 journey;march
征答 question and answer game
征调 requisition;call up
征伐 go on a punitive expedition
征帆 a ship on a long voyage
征服 conquer;subjugate
征稿 solicit contributions (to a journal,etc.)
征歌 invitation to compose songs on a specific theme
征管 levy (*or* collect) and administer (taxes)
征候 sign
征婚 seek a marriage partner
征集 ①collect ②draft;call up;recruit
征借 seek to borrow
征粮 impose grain levies;collect grain taxes
征马 battle steed;war horse
征募 enlist;recruit
征聘 advertise for; solicit applications for a job;recruit
征迁 relocate residents from locations to be used for construction of new buildings or factories
征求 solicit;seek;ask for
征收 levy;collect;impose
征税 ①levy (*or* collect) taxes;impose a tax; make a levy ②taxation
征讨 go on a punitive expedition
征途 the road to be travelled;journey
征文 solicit articles (*or* essays)
征象 sign;symptom
征信 collect credit information
征询 seek the opinion of;consult
征引 quote;cite
征用 take over for use;commandeer;requisition
征战 go on an expedition (*or* a campaign)
征召 ① call up; enlist; draft; conscript ②appoint to an official position
征兆 sign;omen;portent;indication
征租 collect a land tax
征兵法 conscription (*or* draft) law
征兵制 universal military service;conscription system
征信所 credit information bureau;credit information service
征购任务 task of requisition (*or* public) purchase
征购土地 land acquisition

征聘广告 want ads

征求意见 solicit opinions; seek opinions; ask for criticisms

征文启事 notice soliciting articles or essays on a chosen subject (for a special issue, etc.)

怔 [zhēng]
形 terror-stricken; panicked ➡zhèng

怔忡 palpitation

怔营 in a state of alarm (*or* trepidation)

怔忪 alarmed and panicky; terrified; panic-stricken; seized with terror

挣 [zhēng]
➡zhèng

挣扎 struggle

峥 [zhēng]

峥嵘 ①lofty and steep; towering ②outstanding; extraordinary

峥嵘岁月 memorable years (of one's life)

狰 [zhēng]

狰狞 ferocious; savage; hideous

狰狞面目 ferocious features; a vile visage

钲 [zhēng]
名 bell-shaped percussion instrument with a handle

症 [zhēng]
名 lump in the abdomen; abdominal agglomerate or mass ➡zhèng

症结 crux; crucial reason

症瘕积聚 a lump in the abdomen causing distension and pain

睁 [zhēng]
动 open (the eyes): 半睁着眼 with one's eyes half open/眼睛睁得大大的 with one's eyes wide open

睁眼瞎 a blind person with eyes wide open—an illiterate

睁目怒眉 dart fierce looks of hate

睁着眼睛说瞎话 tell a bare-faced (*or* out-and-out) lie

睁一只眼,闭一只眼 turn a blind eye to sth; wink at sth

铮 [zhēng]
➡zhèng

铮铮 clank; clang

筝 [zhēng]
名 ①Chinese zither with 21 or 25 strings ②kite

蒸 [zhēng]
动 ①evaporate ②steam: 蒸米饭 steam rice

蒸饼 steamed cake

蒸发 evaporate

蒸锅 a pot for steaming food; steamer

蒸饺 steamed dumpling (with meat and vegetable stuffing)

蒸烤 scorch; roast

蒸馏 distillation

蒸笼 ①food steamer (usu. made of bamboo) ②(of room etc.) very hot and sultry

蒸馍 steamed bun

蒸气 vapour

蒸汽 steam

蒸球 paper making rotary spherical digester

蒸腾 (of steam) rising

蒸煮 cook; digest; boil down; stewing

蒸发计 evaporimeter

蒸馏瓶 cucurbit

蒸馏室 distillery

蒸馏水 distilled water

蒸气浴 sauna

蒸汽锤 steam hammer

蒸汽机 steam engine

蒸汽浴 steam bath

蒸气软件 vapourware

蒸腾作用 transpiration

蒸蒸日上 becoming more prosperous every day; flourishing; thriving

鲭 [zhēng]
名 fish cooked together with meat ➡qīng

zhěng（ㄓㄥ）

拯 [zhěng]
动 save; rescue; free; deliver: 拯民于水深火热之中 save the people from untold miseries

拯救 save; rescue; deliver

整 [zhěng]
Ⅰ 形 ①whole; complete; total; entire: 八点整 eight o'clock sharp/两年整 two solid years/整套卧室用家具 bedroom suite ②in good order; orderly; tidy; neat: 仪容不整 untidy in appearance Ⅱ 动 ①put in order; straighten; rectify: 整顿校纪 strengthen school discipline ②repair; fix; mend; renovate ③punish; castigate; make sb suffer ④make; do; work

整备 reorganize and outfit (troops)

整编 reorganize (troops)

整饬 ①put in order; strengthen ②in good order; neat; tidy

整除 be divided with no remainder; divide exactly

整存 whole deposit; full storage

整党 consolidate the Party organization

整地 soil preparation (i.e. preparation of land for sowing or planting by ploughing, harrowing, levelling, etc.)

整点 integral point

整队 dress the ranks; get (*or* bring) the ranks into orderly alignment; line up

整顿 rectify; consolidate; reorganize

整风 rectification of incorrect styles of work or thinking

整复 restore; restitution

Z

整改 ①rectification and reform (*or* consolidation) ②rectify and reform
整个 whole；entire
整固 readjust and consolidate
整合 ①conformity ②integrate；consolidate；unify；unite；regroup
整机 assembled machinery
整纪 tighten discipline
整洁 clean and tidy；neat；trim
整经 warping
整理 put in order；straighten out；arrange；sort out
整料 material all in one piece for a given job
整流 rectification
整齐 ①in good order；neat；tidy ②even；regular
整人 take measures against；give people hurdles to jump；create troublesome problems for people；make sb suffer；fix sb
整容 ①tidy oneself up (i.e. have a haircut, a shave,etc.) ②face-lifting
整数 ①integer；whole number ②round number；round figure
整肃 ①strict；rigid ②rectify；consolidate
整套 a complete (*or* whole) set of
整体 whole；entirety
整天 the whole day；all day；all day long
整托 put one's child in a boarding nursery
整形 plastic
整修 rebuild；renovate；recondition
整训 train and consolidate (troops,etc.)
整整 whole；full
整枝 training；pruning
整治 ① renovate；repair；dredge (a river, etc.) ②punish；fix ③do；work at
整装 get one's things ready (for a journey, etc.)
整流器 rectifier
整容术 cosmetic operation；face-lifting
整顿纪律 strengthen discipline；improve discipline
整风运动 rectification campaign；rectification movement
整齐划一 uniform
整容手术 vanity surgery
整体吊装 integral hoisting
整体观念 ① the concept of viewing the situation as a whole ②an organic conception of the human body,viewing its various parts as forming an organic whole
整体素质 integrated quality
整体推进 push forward in union
整体优化 overall optimization
整装待发 get ready for (a journey or a march)；be ready to start out
整顿工作作风 rectify the style of work
整顿经济秩序 rectify economic order

整顿领导班子 consolidate (*or* reorganize) the leading body
整顿音像工作 straighten out irregularities in the audiovisual industry

zhèng（ㄓㄥˋ）

正 ［zhèng］
I 形 ①straight；upright；perpendicular：在正前方 directly ahead/正西 due west ②situated in the middle；main：正门 main entrance/正院儿 main courtyard ③(of time) sharp；on time；punctual ④front；obverse；right (side)：钱币的正面 obverse side of a coin ⑤upright；impartial；honest ⑥correct；right；proper：走正道儿 follow the correct path ⑦(of colour and flavour) pure；right：正红 pure red/这菜的味儿正。The dish is of the right flavour. ⑧regular；normal：五官端正 have regular features/正楷 regular script ⑨chief；prime；principal ⑩(of figures,designs,etc.) regular ⑪positive；plus ⑫positive：正电 positive electricity II 动 ①set right；put straight：把帽子正一正 put one's hat straight ②set to rights；rectify ③correct (mistakes) III 副 ① just；right；exactly；precisely：正好赶上 arrive in the nick of time ②be doing：我正在听广播。I'm listening to the radio. ➡zhēng
正版 original edition；copyrighted edition；genuine edition
正本 ①original (of a document) ②reserved copy (of a library book)
正比 direct ratio
正步 parade step；goose step
正餐 ①a regular meal served in a restaurant ②dinner
正册 regular register
正茬 the main crop (in crop rotation)
正常 normal；regular
正大 upright；honest；aboveboard
正当 ［zhèngdāng］ just when；just the time for
正当 ［zhèngdàng］ ①proper；appropriate；legitimate ②(of behaviour, etc.) correct；proper
正道 ①the right way (*or* course)；the correct path ② the correct principle；the correct way
正点 (of ships, trains, etc.) on schedule；on time；punctually
正电 positive electricity
正殿 main hall (in a palace or temple)
正法 execute (a criminal)
正反 positive and negative
正方 square
正房 ①principal rooms ②legal wife
正风 righteous style and practice

正告 earnestly admonish; warn sternly; warn in all seriousness

正割 secant

正宫 ①empress's palace ②empress

正骨 bonesetting

正规 regular; standard

正轨 the right (*or* correct) path

正果 the right fruit—the proper consequence of a regulated life in this world

正好 ①just in time; just right; just enough ②happen to; chance to; as it happens

正号 positive sign; plus sign

正话 ① serious words ② what one really means

正火 normalizing

正极 positive electrode; positive pole; anode

正角 leading role; lead; protagonist

正经 ①decent; respectable; honest ②serious ③standard ④really; truly; indeed

正剧 serious drama

正楷 (in Chinese calligraphy) regular script

正课 required courses (in college)

正理 correct principle; valid reason (*or* argument); the right thing to do

正梁 ridge purlin

正路 the right way (*or* course); the correct path

正论 just opinion

正门 front door (*or* gate); main entrance

正面 ①front; frontage; facade ② the obverse side; the right side ③positive ④directly; openly

正名 rectification of name

正派 upright; honest; decent

正片 ①positive ②copy ③feature (film)

正品 certified products (*or* goods); quality products (*or* goods)

正气 ①healthy atmosphere (*or* tendency) ②vital energy

正桥 the main structure of a bridge

正巧 ①happen to; chance to; as it happens ②just in time; in the nick of time; just at the right time

正切 tangent

正确 correct; right; proper

正如 just as; exactly as

正色 ①pure colours ②adopt a stern countenance

正身 in person; not by proxy

正史 history books written in biographical style

正式 formal; official; regular

正事 one's proper business

正视 face squarely; face up to; look squarely at

正室 ①legal wife ②the wife's eldest son

正手 forehand

正数 positive number

正税 regular tax

正题 ①subject; topic (of a talk or essay) ②thesis

正体 ①standardized form of Chinese characters ②regular script ③block letter

正厅 ①main hall (in the middle) ②stalls (in a theatre)

正统 ①legitimism ②orthodox

正文 main body (of a book, etc.); text

正屋 principal rooms (in a courtyard, usu. facing south)

正午 high noon

正误 correct (typographical) errors

正弦 sine

正像 positive; erect image

正凶 principal murderer

正选 (of athletes) key player on a team

正盐 normal salt

正眼 look straight

正业 regular occupation; proper duties

正义 ①justice ②just; righteous ③(formerly often used in book titles) orthodox or rectified interpretation (of ancient texts)

正音 ①correct one's pronunciation ②standard pronunciation

正用 proper use

正在 in process of; in course of

正直 honest; upright; fair-minded

正职 ①the position of the chief of an office, department, etc. ②full-time job; main occupation

正治 normal treatment, i.e. administering medicines of a cold nature to treat a febrile disease

正中 right in the middle (*or* centre)

正传 main story (of a novel, etc.); subject under discussion

正字 ①correct a wrongly written character or a misspelt word ②regular script ③standardized form of Chinese characters

正宗 ①orthodox school ②genuine

正座 central seats that directly face the stage; stalls

正比例 direct proportion

正长石 orthoclase

正长岩 syenite

正厂长 factory manager

正当年 in the prime of life; in one's prime

正当时 the right season (*or* time)

正电荷 positive charge

正电子 positive electron; positron

正方体 cube

正方形 square

正规军 regular army

正规战 regular warfare

正教授 full professor

正面图 front view; elevation

正牌货 standard brand of goods
正视图 front view;elevation
正手球 forehand;forehand ball
正投影 orthographic projection
正误表 errata;corrigenda
正弦波 sine wave
正义感 a sense of what is right;a sense of justice (*or* righteousness)
正音法 orthoepy
正应力 direct stress
正院儿 main courtyard
正字法 orthography
正儿八经 serious;earnest
正本清源 thoroughly overhaul;effect radical reform
正大光明 open and aboveboard;just and honourable
正当防卫 legitimate defence; justified defence;self-defence;legal defence;justifiable defence
正多边形 regular polygon
正规教育 education by positive examples
正合吾意 suit me down to the ground
正驾驶员 first pilot
正襟危坐 straighten one's clothes and sit properly
正经八百 serious;earnest
正六边形 regular hexagon
正六面体 regular hexahedron
正面进攻 frontal attack
正面人物 positive character
正人君子 a man of honour;a man of integrity; gentleman
正三角形 equilateral triangle
正式开业 formally start business
正式声明 official statement
正式照会 formal note
正手抽球 forehand drive
正手击球 forehand stroke
正手快抽 forehand fast drive
正手切击 forehand cut
正手握拍 forehand grip
正手削球 forehand chop
正手远抽 forehand long drive
正态分布 statistics normal distribution
正邪相争 struggle between the vital energy and the pathogenic factor
正颜厉色 serious and severe;with a stern look
正义之师 armed forces with a just cause; troops representing a just cause;army dedicated to a just cause
正中下怀 be just what one hopes for;fit in exactly with one's wishes;be precisely to one's liking
正人先正己 These who wish to make others upright must be upright themselves first.
正式友好访问 official goodwill (*or* friendly) visit

正负电子对撞机 electron-positron collider
正反两方面的理由 pros and cons

证 [zhèng]
Ⅰ 动 testify to;prove;demonstrate:出庭作证 give evidence (*or* bear witness) in a law court;serve as a witness at court Ⅱ 名 certificate;card
证词 testimony
证件 credentials;papers;certificate
证据 evidence;proof;testimony
证明 ①prove;testify;bear out ②certificate; identification;testimonial
证券 bond;security;negotiable securities
证人 witness;evidence;rapper
证实 confirm;verify;bear out
证书 certificate;credentials
证物 exhibit (produced in court as evidence)
证言 testimony
证章 badge
证照 certificate;license
证婚人 chief witness at a wedding ceremony
证监会 Securities Supervision Commission
证明书 certificate;testimonial
证明信 certificate
证券镑 security sterling
证券纸 loan;security paper
证人席 witness box;witness stand
证券存款 certificate deposit
证券兑换 exchange of securities
证券公司 securities company
证券交易 dealing in securities;stock swap
证券借款 security loan
证券市场 stock market; bond market,market of (for) securities;security market
证券投资 investment securities; portfolio investment
证券包销人 underwriter
证券持有人 securities holder
证券抵押品 collateral security
证券分析家 securities analyst
证券及投资 securities and investments
证券交易所 bourse;stock exchange;securities exchange
证券经纪人 underwriter;bill broker
证券推销所 boiler room
证券销售书 prospectus
证券营业部 stock exchange;security exchange
证券金融公司 securities finance company
证券投资分析 securities analysis
证券投资基金 stock investment fund;mutual fund
证券及投资损益 profit and loss on securities and investment
证券价格平均数 stock price average
证券交易所交易 stock exchange transactions
证券交易所牌价 stock exchange list

证券买卖人协会 association of securities dealers

证券交易所委员会 stock exchange committee

郑 [zhèng]

郑重 serious;solemn;earnest

郑重声明 solemnly declare

怔 [zhèng]
囫 stare blankly;be in a daze;be in a trance
➡ zhēng

怔怔 stare blankly;be in a daze;be in a trance

怔神儿 stare blankly;be in a daze

诤 [zhèng]
囫 criticise frankly;expostulate;remonstrate;admonish

诤谏 criticize sb's faults frankly

诤言 forthright admonition

诤友 a friend who will give forthright admonition

政 [zhèng]
囵 ①politics;government;political affairs;军政领导 heads of government and army ② administrative affairs of certain government departments;财政部长 Minister of Finance/市政当局 municipal authorities ③affairs of a family or an organization

政变 coup d'état;coup

政策 policy

政党 political party

政敌 political opponent

政法 politics and law

政风 atmosphere in government bodies;the ideological and work styles of government officials;the attitude and efficiency of government functions

政府 government

政纲 political programme;platform

政工 political and ideological work

政绩 administrative merits; achievements in one's political career

政纪 government discipline;administrative regulation's

政见 political view

政界 political circles;government circles

政局 political situation;political scene

政客 politician

政令 government decree (or order)

政论 political comment

政情 political situation

政权 political (or state) power;regime

政审 ①examine sb's political behaviour or record ② political investigation;background check

政坛 political circles

政体 system (or form) of government

政委 political commissar (of a PLA regiment and above);commissar

政务 government affairs;government administration

政协 political consultative conference

政治 politics;political affairs

政策性 ①adherence to policy ②policy-related;involving policy considerations

政工师 intermediate rank for people engaged in political work

政监会 The China Securities Regulatory Commission

政务院 the Government Administration Council

政治部 political department

政治犯 political offender;political prisoner

政治家 statesman

政治局 the Political Bureau

政治权 political rights

政治学 political science;government

政变阴谋 coup plot

政策兑现 materialize a policy

政策攻心 try to win over or obtain a confession from a person by explaining the Party's policy

政策专家 policy wonk

政出多门 multiple leadership;conflicting policies resulting from clashing departmental interests;each department acting on its own;too many branches of an administration making decisions

政法机构 procuratorial,judicial and public security organizations

政法学院 institute of political science and law

政府补贴 government subsidy

政府采购 government procurement

政府贷款 government loans

政府干预 government intervention

政府换届 election of a new leadership of the government

政府债券 government bonds

政府职能 government functions

政工干部 cadres responsible for political work;political cadre

政教分离 separation of religion from politics;separation of the church from the state

政教合一 unification of church and state;temporal and religious administration

政企不分 integration of government administration with enterprise;government department's running without a clear line between the functions of the government and enterprises;functions of the government and enterprises mixed up

政企分开 draw a clear line between (or separate) the functions of the government and enterprise

政权机关 organs of state (or political) power

政权交接 transfer of government

Z

政务公开 make government affairs public; keep the public informed of the political activities

政治庇护 political asylum

政治避难 political refuge; political asylum

政治待遇 political treatment

政治地位 political position; political standing

政治动乱 political unrest; political turmoil; political disturbance

政治风波 political disturbances

政治纲领 political programme; platform

政治工作 political work

政治攻势 political offensive

政治挂帅 put politics in command

政治捐款 political contributions

政治觉悟 political conciousness

政治立场 political stand

政治面目 political affiliation; political background

政治迫害 political prosecution

政治欺诈 political skulduggery

政治掮客 political broker

政治倾向 political inclination

政治清洗 political purge

政治权利 political rights

政治审查 ① examine sb's political behaviour or record ② political investigation; background check

政治素质 political caliber

政治体制 political structure

政治委员 political commissar (of a PLA regiment and above); commissar

政治文明 political civilization

政治稳定 political situation

政治舞台 political stage

政治信仰 political conviction; political belief

政治嗅觉 political acumen; political sensitiveness; political sense of smell

政治资本 political capital

政策性补贴 policy-related subsidies; subsidies granted for policy consideration

政策性计划 plan for policy consideration; policy-related plan

政策性亏损 policy-related losses; losses incurred due to policy decisions

政策性住房 policy-related house; policy-based house

政府间贷款 inter-government loans

政治庇护所 political asylum; safe house; sanctuary

政治多元化 political pluralism

政治教导员 political instructor (of a PLA battalion)

政治经济学 political economy

政治社会学 political sociology

政治协理员 political assistant (of a PLA regiment and above)

政治指导员 political instructor (of a PLA company)

政治追随者 henchmen

政府采购制度 system of government procurement; procedures of government procurement

政府工作报告 government work report; report on the work of the government

政府机构改革 reorganization of institutions; institutional restructuring; reform of government organizations

政府上网工程 Government Online Project; government networking

政府特殊津贴 special government allowance; special government subsidies

政府贴息贷款 government concessional (or interest) -subsidized loan

政府职能部门 functional government departments

政治思想工作 political and ideological work

政治协商会议 political consultative conference

政策性金融银行 non-commercial bank; policy-related bank

挣 [zhèng]

⃝动 ①struggle to get free; try to shake off ②get by one's labour; earn; make; 挣生活费 earn money to cover one's living expenses/挣碗饭吃 earn (or make) a living; make (or earn) one's bread ➡ zhēng

挣揣 struggle; strive hard

挣命 struggle to save one's life

挣钱 earn (or make) money

挣脱 struggle to free oneself; shake off; get rid of

症 [zhèng]

⃝名 disease; malady; illness ➡ zhēng

症候 ①disease ②symptom

症状 symptom

铮 [zhèng]

⃝形 dazzling; shining ➡ zhēng

zhī (业)

之 [zhī]

Ⅰ 动 go to: 由沪之宁 leave Shanghai for Nanjing Ⅱ 代 ①(used in place of a person or thing as an object): 求之不得的好机会 most welcome opportunity ②(without actual reference): 我最喜欢喝茶,咖啡次之。 I like tea best and coffee second best. ③this; that Ⅲ 助 ①(used to connect the modifier and the word modified): 以其人之道,还治其人之身 pay somebody back in his own coin; do unto somebody as he does unto others ② (placed between the subject and the predicate to express subordination): 世界之大,无奇不有。 Nothing is too strange in this big world.

之后 later;after;afterwards
之前 before;prior to;ago
之乎者也 particles of literary Chinese—pedantic terms;literary jargon;archaisms

支 [zhī]

Ⅰ 〔动〕①prop up;set up:把布景支起来 prop the stage scenery ②protrude;raise;prick up:两颗大牙朝外支着 with two protruding teeth ③sustain;stand;bear ④send away;put sb off;order about ⑤pay out;draw (money):预支两个月工资 get two months' pay in advance Ⅱ 〔名〕① branch;offshoot ② twelve earthly branches Ⅲ 〔量〕①(of army units):一支军队 an army contingent ②(of songs):唱一支民歌 sing a folk song/一支动人的乐曲 a melodious musical composition ③(of watts):二十五支光的灯泡 a 25-watt bulb ④(textile counts):细支棉纱 fine count yarn ⑤(for long,thin,inflexible objects):一支铅笔 a pencil

支边 support the border areas
支部 branch
支撑 ① prop up;sustain;support ② strut;brace
支承 support;bear
支持 ① sustain;hold out;bear ② support;back;stand by
支出 ①pay (money);expend;disburse ②expenses;expenditure;outlay;disbursement
支点 fulcrum
支店 branch store;branch shop
支队 detachment
支付 pay (money);defray
支行 subbranch (of a bank)
支护 strut;support (tunnels,walls)
支唤 order about
支架 support;stand;trestle
支局 substation
支棱 hold up;stick up
支离 ① fragmented;broken;disorganized ② (of writing) trivial and jumbled;incoherent
支流 ① tributary;affluent ② minor aspects;nonessentials
支脉 offshoot (of a mountain range);branch range
支派 ① branch;sect;offshoot ② order;send;dispatch
支配 ① arrange;allocate;budget ② control;dominate;govern
支票 cheque;check
支前 support the front
支渠 branch (irrigation) canal
支取 draw (money)
支使 ①order about ②send away;put sb off
支书 secretary of a Party or League branch;branch secretary
支枢 pivot

支数 number (of yarn);count
支吾 prevaricate;equivocate;hum and haw
支线 branch line;feeder (line)
支援 support;assist;help
支柱 pillar;prop;mainstay
支撑点 strong point;centre of resistance
支持率 favorability rating
支墩坝 buttress dam
支气管 bronchus
支柱根 prop root
支部书记 secretary of a Party or League branch;branch secretary
支撑门面 maintain the front;keep up appearance
支离破碎 torn to pieces;broken up;fragmented
支农产品 products for agricultural use
支票挂失 registration of lost check;report the loss of one's checks
支气管炎 bronchitis
支吾其词 speak evasively;hum and haw
支援部队 support unit;supporting troops
支柱产业 pillar industry;cornerstone industry
支气管扩张 bronchiectasis
支气管性气喘 bronchial asthma

只 [zhī]

Ⅰ 〔形〕isolated;single;one only Ⅱ 〔量〕①(for one of a pair):两只耳朵 two ears/一只手套 one glove ②(for certain animals,birds):六只燕子 six swallows/一只猫 one cat ③(for certain containers):四只皮箱 four leather suitcases (or trunks) ④(for certain boats):一只橡皮筏 a rubber raft/一只小船 a boat ➡ zhǐ
只身 alone;by oneself
只身在外 be away from home all by oneself
只言片语 a word or two;a few isolated words and phrases
只字不提 not say a single word about sth;not so much as mention sth

汁 [zhī]

〔名〕juice
汁水 juice
汁液 juice

芝 [zhī]

〔名〕①glossy ganoderma ②root of Dahurian angelica
芝兰 irises and orchids
芝麻 ①sesame ②sesame seed
芝麻官 sesame official—petty official
芝麻酱 sesame paste
芝麻油 sesame-seed oil;sesame oil
芝麻开花节节高 sesame stalks putting forth flowers notch by notch,higher and higher—(of living standards,etc.) rising steadily

吱 [zhī]

〔拟〕creak:嘎吱作响的竹椅 creaky bamboo

chair/楼梯的嘎吱嘎吱声 creak in the stairs ➡zī

枝 [zhī]

Ⅰ 〈名〉branch; twig：插枝 plant (willows, etc.) by sticking branches into the soil Ⅱ 〈量〉(for flowers with stems intact)：一枝樱花 a spray of cherry blossoms

枝桠 branch; twig
枝接 scion grafting
枝节 ①branches and knots—minor matters ②complication; unexpected difficulty
枝蔓 branches and tendrils—complicated and confused
枝条 branch; twig
枝头 on a branch
枝丫 branch; twig
枝叶 ①branches and leaves ②nonessentials; minor details
枝子 branch; twig
枝繁叶茂 (of trees) with luxuriant foliage and spreading branches

知 [zhī]

Ⅰ 〈动〉①know; be aware (of)：略知兵法 have some knowledge of the art of war ②inform; notify; tell; learn ③ administer; be in charge of Ⅱ 〈名〉①knowledge; learning ②intimate friend

知耻 have a sense of shame
知道 know; realize; be aware of
知底 know the inside story; be in the know
知府 (in former times) prefect
知会 tell (orally)
知己 ①intimate; understanding ②bosom (or intimate) friend
知交 bosom (or intimate) friend
知觉 ①consciousness ②perception
知了 cicada
知名 well-known; noted; celebrated; famous
知命 understand the Decree of Heaven
知母 ①wind-weed ②rhizome of wind-weed
知青 school leavers; school graduates; educated youth
知情 ①know the facts of a case (or the details of an incident); be in the know ②feel grateful to sb; appreciate the kindness
知趣 know how to behave in a delicate situation; be sensible; be tactful
知事 (in former times) county magistrate
知识 knowledge; intellect
知悉 know; learn; be informed of
知县 (in former times) county magistrate
知晓 know; be aware of; understand
知心 intimate; understanding
知行 knowing and doing
知音 a friend keenly appreciative of one's talents; an understanding friend
知遇 have found a patron (or superior appreciative) of one's ability

知政 knowledge of major state policies and activities
知足 be content with one's lot
知罪 admit one's guilt
知本家 knowledge-capitalist
知更鸟 robin; redbreast
知己话 intimate words; heart-to-heart talk
知名度 degree of fame; degree of popularity; extent to which a person is known to the public
知情权 right to inform
知情人 insider; person in the know
知识界 intellectual circles; the intelligentsia
知法犯法 deliberately break the law; violate the law knowingly
知根知底 know sb's background; know sb thoroughly
知过必改 always correct an error when one becomes aware of it
知冷知热 love sb (esp. one's husband or wife) tenderly
知命之年 the age of fifty
知难而进 press forward despite difficulties; advance in the face of difficulties
知难而退 beat a retreat in the face of difficulties; shrink back from difficulties
知情达理 reasonable; sensible
知人善任 know one's subordinates well enough to assign them suitable jobs; know how to judge and use people
知人之明 ability to appreciate a person's character and capability; a keen insight into a person's character
知识爆炸 knowledge explosion
知识产权 intellectual property rights
知识产业 knowledge industry
知识分子 intellectual; the intelligentsia
知识更新 upgrading of one's knowledge
知识结构 structure of knowledge
知识经济 knowledge economy; knowledge-based economy
知识老化 process of knowledge becoming outdated
知识青年 school leavers; school graduates; educated youth
知识水平 know-how
知识渊博 have a wide range of knowledge
知书达理 be well-educated and reasonable; highly cultured and steeped in propriety
知疼着热 love sb (esp. one's husband or wife) tenderly
知无不言 say all you know
知行合一 the unity of knowledge and practice
知足常乐 contentment brings happiness
知耻近乎勇 To know the things of shame is to be near to fortitude.

知识密集型 knowledge intensive; knowledge concentrated

知子莫若父 No one knows a son better than his father.

知识创新工程 knowledge innovation project

知识分子政策 policy towards intellectuals

知识就是力量 knowledge is power

知人知面不知心 You may know a person's face but not his heart; One may know a person for a long time without understanding his true nature.

知识密集型产业 knowledge-intensive industry

知其一,不知其二 know only one aspect of a thing; have a one-sided view

知其不可为而为之 know it's no use, but keep on doing it; do what one knows is impossible

知彼知己,百战不殆 Know the enemy and know yourself, and you can fight a hundred battles without defeat.

知无不言,言无不尽 say all you know and say it without reserve

知其然,不知其所以然 know that sth is so but not why it is so; know the hows but not the whys

知之为知之,不知为不知,是知也 To say you know when you know, and to say you do not when you do not, that is knowledge.

肢 [zhī]
名 limb

肢解 dismemberment

肢体 ①limbs ②limbs and trunk

肢障 physical disability; handicap (of the limbs)

织 [zhī]
动 ①weave: 织地毯 weave rugs ②knit: 织围巾 knit a scarf

织补 darning; invisible mending

织布 weaving cotton cloth; weaving

织机 loom

织锦 ①brocade ②picture-weaving in silk

织女 ① weaving-girl; weaving-maid; girl weaver ②the Weaving-girl

织品 textile; fabric

织物 fabric

织造 weaving

织针 knitting needle

织轴 beam (of a loom)

织布鸟 weaverbird

织锦厂 brocade mill

织锦缎 tapestry satin

织女星 the Weaving-girl star—Vega

织袜机 hosiery machine

织造厂 weaving mill

脂 [zhī]
名 ①fat; grease; tallow; resin ②rouge

脂肪 fat

脂粉 rouge and powder; cosmetics

脂膏 ①fat; grease ②fruits of the people's labour; wealth of the people

脂瘤 lipoma

脂肪肝 fatty liver

脂肪酶 lipase

脂肪酸 fatty acid

脂粉气 womanlike ways; femininity

脂血症 lipemia; lipidemia

脂眼鲱 Pacific round herring

脂肪组织 adipose tissue

稙 [zhī]
形 (of crops) early-planting; early-maturing: 稙庄稼 early-planting crops

蜘 [zhī]

蜘蛛 spider

蜘蛛人 spiderman

蜘蛛丝 cobweb; thread of a spider web

蜘蛛网 web; cobweb; spider web

蜘蛛抱蛋 (common) aspidistra

zhí (虫)

执 [zhí]
I 动 ①hold; grip; grasp ②take charge of; control; manage ③stick to; adhere to; persist in ④carry out; execute; observe: 执弟子礼 treat sb as one's teacher (*or* mentor) ⑤catch; seize; capture Ⅱ 名 ①written acknowledgement ②intimate friend

执棒 hold the baton; conduct music

执笔 write; do the actual writing

执鞭 hold the teacher's pointer—be a teacher

执炊 cook; prepare meals

执导 direct a film or a play

执法 enforce (*or* execute) the law

执管 be in charge of

执纪 enforce discipline

执教 be a teacher; teach

执拗 stubborn; pigheaded; wilful

执判 referee a contest

执勤 be on duty

执行 carry out; execute; implement

执业 practice

执意 insist on; be determined to; be bent on

执掌 wield; be in control of

执照 license; permit

执政 be in power; be in office; be at the helm of the state

执著 persistent; persevering

执行官 action officer

执行员 marshal

执照税 tax on licenses

执政党 the party in power (*or* in office); the ruling (*or* governing) party

执法必严 enforce law rigorously

执法不严 laws are not strictly enforced; lax

Z

enforcement of laws
执法部门 law-enforcing departments
执法队伍 the ranks of law-enforcing personnel
执法犯法 violation of the law enforcement officials
执法检查 law-enforcement inspection
执法人员 law enforcement officer
执法如山 enforce the law strictly
执迷不悟 obstinately stick to a wrong course; be perverse; refuse to come to one's senses
执手同行 walk together hand in hand
执行董事 executive director
执行机构 executive body
执行机关 executive organ
执行秘书 executive secretary
执行主席 executive (*or* presiding) chairman
执行委员会 executive committee

直 [zhí] I 形 ①straight ②vertical; upright ③perpendicular ④ just; upright ⑤ candid; frank; straightforward II 动 straighten: 把铁丝拉直 straighten a piece of wire III 名 vertical stroke (in Chinese characters) IV 副 ①directly; direct; straight: 直飞巴黎 fly nonstop to Paris ②continuously; straight ③just; simply; exactly: 疼得直像针扎似的 feel a piercing pain
直白 ①frank and honest ②boring; flat
直播 ① direct seeding ②live (radio or TV) transmission; broadcast live
直肠 rectum
直尺 straightedge
直刺 ①straight thrust (in fencing) ②perpendicular inserting (in acupuncture)
直达 through; nonstop
直捣 drive straight on to
直到 ①until ②up to
直根 taproot
直观 directly perceived through the senses; audio-visual
直航 direct voyage; straight flight; fly nonstop; direct route
直话 straightforward talk
直击 live broadcast
直角 right angle
直接 direct; immediate
直径 diameter
直觉 intuition
直露 forthright; explicit
直属 directly under; directly subordinate (*or* affiliated) to
直率 frank; candid; straightforward
直爽 frank; candid; straightforward; forthright
直说 say out
直投 deliver directly
直辖 directly under the jurisdiction of
直线 ① straight line ② steep; sharp (rise or

fall)
直销 direct marketing; door-to-door sale; direct sale
直选 direct election
直言 speak bluntly; state outright
直译 word-for-word translation; literal translation
直至 ①until ②up to
直肠癌 carcinoma of the rectum
直肠镜 proctoscope
直肠炎 proctitis; rectitis
直肠子 ① straightforward; downright; forthright ②a straightforward person
直陈句 narrative sentence
直齿轮 straight gear
直贡呢 venetian
直勾勾 (stare) fixedly
直角尺 square
直接税 direct tax
直立茎 erect stern
直流电 direct current (D.C.)
直升机 helicopter; copter
直挺挺 straight; stiff; bolt upright
直辖市 municipality directly under the Central Government
直性子 ① straightforward; downright; forthright ②a straightforward person
直展云 cloud with vertical development
直拨电话 direct-dial telephone
直肠直肚 straightforward; frank
直达快车 through express train
直捣黄龙 drive straight on to Huanglong (i.e. the enemy stronghold)
直道而行 follow the straight path—act with rectitude
直观教学 object teaching
直呼其名 address sb disrespectfully by name; address a person without an honorific title
直接宾语 direct object
直接费用 direct cost; direct charge; direct expense
直接经验 direct experience
直接起飞 rolling (*or* follow-through) takeoff; rolling start
直接染料 direct dyes
直接融资 direct financing
直接投资 direct investment
直接推理 immediate reasoning
直接选举 direct election
直接着陆 straight-in landing
直截了当 straightforward; blunt; point-blank
直觉主义 intuitionism
直来直去 frank and outspoken; blunt
直眉瞪眼 ① stare in anger; fume ② stare blankly; be in a daze; be stupefied
直拍握法 pen-hold grip
直上云霄 soar straight up into the sky

直射距离 battle-sight range; point-blank range
直抒己见 state one's views frankly; be plain-spoken
直系亲属 directly-related members of one's family—parents, spouse and children
直线运动 rectilinear motion
直心眼儿 open; frank; straightforward
直言不讳 speak without reservation; not mince words; call a spade a spade
直翅目昆虫 orthopteran
直角三角形 right (*or* right-angled) triangle
直接任意球 free kick (in soccer)
直线加速器 linear accelerator
"直通车"计划 "through train" plan (*or* arrangement)

侄 ［zhí］
［名］brother's son; nephew
侄女 brother's daughter; niece
侄孙 brother's grandson; grandnephew
侄子 brother's son; nephew
侄女婿 husband of brother's daughter; niece's husband
侄孙女 brother's granddaughter; grandniece
侄媳妇 wife of brother's son; nephew's wife

值 ［zhí］
Ⅰ［名］value Ⅱ［动］①what a specified sum of money can buy ② be worth; worthwhile ③ happen to; chance to: 值此国家危急之秋 at this time of national crisis ④ be on duty; take one's turn at sth
值班 ① be on duty ② unsold merchandise on the shelf
值乘 (attendants) attend to needs of passengers (on plane, ship, train, etc.)
值得 be worth; merit; deserve
值钱 costly; valuable
值勤 (of armymen, policemen, etc.) be on duty; be on point duty
值日 be on duty for the day; be one's turn to be on duty
值守 guard; watch over; be on duty and on guard
值星 (of army officers) be on duty for the week
值夜 be on night duty; be on the night shift
值班室 guards' room; night shift room
值班员 person on duty
值不当 not be worthwhile
值日表 duty roster
值日生 student on duty
值班经理 shift manager
值分布理论 value distribution theory

埴 ［zhí］
［名］clay

职 ［zhí］
Ⅰ［名］①duty; job: 做好本职工作 do one's job well ②position; post; office ③your subordinate Ⅱ［动］be in charge of; administer; man-

age Ⅲ［公］for: 职是之故 for this reason
职别 level of position; official rank
职称 the title of a technical or professional post (such as engineer, professor, lecturer, academician, etc.); professional title
职大 workers' college
职分 ①duty ②official post; position
职高 vocational high school
职工 ① staff and workers; workers and staff members ②workers; labour
职级 rank
职教 vocational schooling; vocational education
职能 function
职权 powers (*or* authority) of office
职守 post; duty
职位 position; post
职务 post; duties; job
职衔 post and rank
职业 occupation; profession; vocation
职员 office worker; staff member; functionary
职责 duty; obligation; responsibility
职掌 ①be in charge of ②duty; charge
职代会 meeting of employee representatives
职业病 employment (*or* occupational) disease
职称等级 professional qualification
职称改革 the reform in professional titles
职称评定 the evaluation of professional titles
职能部门 functional department
职前教育 pre-job training
职权范围 limits (*or* scope) of one's functions and powers; terms of reference
职务发明 service invention
职务工资 wages related to specific work posts
职业道德 professional ethics; work ethics; occupational ethics
职业妇女 career woman
职业高中 vocational high school
职业过失 malpractice
职业教育 vocational schooling; vocational education
职业女装 career woman's wear
职业培训 vocational training; occupational training
职业杀手 hit man
职业团体 professional organization
职业学校 vocational school
职业训练 vocational training
职务侵占罪 functionary embezzlement
职业介绍所 job centre; career service centre; employment agency
职业外交官 career diplomat
职业运动员 professional athlete; professional
职工代表大会 congress of employees; congress of workers and staff
职业技术教育 job (*or* vocational) education
职业资格证书制度 professional qualification

Z

certificate system

植 [zhí]

Ⅰ 〔动〕①plant; grow ②set up; build; establish Ⅱ 〔名〕plant; flora

植保 plant (*or* crop) protection
植被 vegetation
植根 ①take root ②lay a solid basis
植苗 plant seedlings
植皮 skin grafting
植绒 flocking
植树 tree planting
植物 plant; flora
植株 plant
植树节 Afforestation Day; Arbour Day; National Tree-planting Day
植树葬 arbour burial
植物胶 vegetable gum (*or* glue)
植物界 plant kingdom; vegetable kingdom
植物人 vegetable (a human being); comatose person; person in vegetative state
植物学 botany
植物油 vegetable oil
植物园 botanical garden
植物志 flora
植党营私 set up a clique for one's own selfish interests
植树造林 plant trees and make into forest land
植物保护 plant (*or* crop) protection
植物病害 plant disease
植物检疫 plant quarantine
植物净化 plant purification
植物区系 flora
植物群落 plant community
植物纤维 plant fibre
植物育种 plant breeding
植物性神经 autonomic nerve
植物生长调节剂 plant growth regulator

殖 [zhí]

〔动〕breed; multiply; propagate

殖民 establish a colony; colonize
殖民地 colony
殖民国家 colonialist power
殖民政策 colonial policy
殖民主义 colonialism

絷 [zhí]

Ⅰ 〔动〕①bind; tie; bundle up ②take into custody Ⅱ 〔名〕reins; halter

跖 [zhí]

〔名〕①metatarsus ②sole of the foot ③tread

摭 [zhí]

〔动〕pick up; collect

蹠 [zhí]

蹢躅 walk to and fro; loiter around

蹢 [zhí]

Ⅰ 〔名〕①metatarsus ②sole of the foot Ⅱ 〔动〕tread; step on

蹢骨 metatarsal bones

zhǐ（止）

止 [zhǐ]

Ⅰ 〔动〕①stop; halt; cease; desist ②prohibit; check; hold back ③close; end; 到目前为止 to date; up to now Ⅱ 〔副〕only; sole; 不止一次 not just once; more than once

止步 halt; stop; go no further
止跌 stop dropping
止付 banking stop payment
止境 end; limit
止咳 relieve a cough
止渴 quench one's thirst
止痛 relieve pain; stop pain
止血 stop bleeding; stanch bleeding
止痒 relieve itching
止住 stop; halt
止车器 train stop
止动闸 fixing brake; holding brake; stopping brake
止痛药 anodyne; analgesic; pain-killer
止泻药 antidiarrheal
止血带 tourniquet
止血器 haemostat
止血药 haemostatic
止动机构 stop motion (mechanism)
止咳糖浆 cough syrup

只 [zhǐ]

〔副〕①only; merely ②all that there is; only
➡ zhī

只得 have no alternative but to; be obliged to; have to
只顾 ①be only concerned with; just think of ②(do sth) single-mindedly; just (do sth)
只管 ①by all means ②simply; just
只好 have to; be forced to
只怕 be afraid of only one thing
只是 ①only; just; merely ②except that; only; but
只消 all one has to do is; you only need to
只要 if only; as long as; provided
只有 ①only; alone ②have to; be forced to
只不过 only; just; merely
只看不买 eye shopping
只说不做 be all talk and no deed
只争朝夕 seize the day, seize the hour; seize every minute; race against time
只读存储器 read-only memory (ROM)
只重衣衫不重人 only value the clothes and not the man himself; judge people by their clothes, not their qualities
只此一家,别无分店 the only shop of this name—no branches anywhere (a shop sign warning of sham goods)
只可意会,不可言传 can be sensed, but not explained in words; can be apprehended but not expressed

只听楼梯响,不见人下来 the stairs creak but no one comes down—much talk but no action

只要功夫深,铁杵磨成针 if you work at it hard enough,you can grind an iron rod into a needle—perseverance spells success

只许州官放火,不许百姓点灯 The magistrates are free to burn down houses,while the common people are forbidden even to light lamps;One may steal a horse while another may not look over the hedge.

旨 [zhǐ] Ⅰ〔形〕 tasty;delicious;delectable Ⅱ〔名〕①purport;purpose ②intention;wish;decree

旨酒 excellent wine

旨趣 purport;objective

旨要 main idea;gist

旨意 decree;order

址 [zhǐ] 〔名〕 site;location;ground

抵 [zhǐ] 〔动〕 attack with one's hand

沚 [zhǐ] 〔名〕 islet;small piece of land in a pond

纸 [zhǐ] Ⅰ〔名〕 paper Ⅱ〔量〕:一纸家书 a letter from home/一纸空文 a mere scrap of paper

纸板 paperboard

纸版 paper mould;paper matrix

纸币 paper money;paper currency;note

纸锭 paper ingots (burned as offerings to the dead)

纸花 paper flower

纸婚 first wedding anniversary

纸浆 paper pulp;pulp

纸巾 paper towel;towel;tissue paper;napkin

纸媒 paper media

纸捻 spill of rolled paper used to light a pipe,etc.;(paper) spill

纸牌 playing cards

纸钱 paper made to resemble money and burned as an offering to the dead

纸绳 paper string

纸条 paper tape

纸屑 scraps of paper

纸型 paper mould;paper matrix

纸烟 cigarette

纸样 outturn sheet

纸鱼 silverfish;fish moth

纸鸢 kite

纸张 paper

纸饭碗 ①paper rice bowl ②unstable job

纸老虎 paper tiger

纸上谈兵 fight only on paper;be an armchair strategist;engage in idle theorizing

纸醉金迷 (a life of) luxury and dissipation

纸包不住火 you can't wrap fire in paper—there is no concealing the truth;truth will out

祉 [zhǐ] 〔名〕 happiness;felicity;blessedness

枳 [zhǐ] 〔名〕 trifoliate orange

枳橙 citrange

枳壳 dried fruit of citron or trifoliate orange

枳实 dried immature fruit of citron or trifoliate orange

枳机草 splendid achnatherum

轵 [zhǐ] 〔名〕 axletree terminal

指 [zhǐ] Ⅰ〔名〕①finger:六指儿 six-finger hand;one whose hand has six fingers/指如玉葱 have slim,delicate fingers ②fingerbreadth;digit:两指宽的贴边 hem (of a dress,etc.) two finger breadths wide Ⅱ〔动〕①show the direction of;point to ②(of hair) stand;bristle ③direct;point out ④refer to ⑤depend on;rely on;count on

指标 target;quota;norm;index

指称 ①point out;profess;claim ②call

指斥 reprove;denounce

指出 point out;lay one's finger on

指导 guide;direct

指点 ①give directions (or pointers,advice);show how (to do sth) ②gossip about sb's faults

指定 appoint;assign

指法 fingering

指供 force the accused to describe or admit to an offense that match the assumptions of the interrogator;lead the accused in to a confession;ask leading questions in an interrogation

指骨 phalanx

指航 navigate;guide the course

指画 ①point at;point to ②finger drawing

指环 (finger) ring

指挥 ① command;direct;conduct ② commander;director ③conductor

指甲 nail

指尖 fingertip

指教 give advice (or comments)

指靠 depend on (for one's livelihood);look to (for help);count on

指控 accuse (sb of);charge(sb with)

指令 ①instruct;order;direct ②instructions;order;directive ③computer instruction

指名 mention by name;name

指明 show clearly;demonstrate;point out

指模 finger print or thumb print

指墨 finger writing or painting

指南 guide;guidebook

指派 appoint;name;designate

指认 point out;identify

指使 instigate;incite;put sb up to sth

指示 ①indicate;point out ②instruct ③direc-

Z

tive;instructions

指事 self-explanatory characters,e. g. 上（above) and 下(below)—one of the six categories of Chinese characters（六书）

指数 index number;index

指头 ①finger ②toe

指望 ①look to;count on ②prospect;hope

指纹 ①loops and whorls on a finger ②fingerprint

指向 directional

指要 main idea;gist

指引 point（the way）;guide;show

指印 fingerprint;finger mark

指责 censure;criticize;find fault with

指摘 censure;criticize;find fault with

指针 ① indicator; pointer; needle ② guiding principle;guide ③ pressing with a finger（on an acupuncture point）;finger-pressing

指正 ①point out mistakes so that they can be corrected;point out and prove ② make a comment or criticism

指北针 compass

指不定 perhaps;maybe

指导员 instructor

指挥棒 ①conductor's baton ②baton used by a policeman to direct traffic ③direction and control

指挥部 command post;headquarters

指挥舱 space command module

指挥车 command car

指挥刀 officer's sword

指挥官 commanding officer;commander

指挥所 command post

指挥员 commander

指甲刀 nail clippers

指甲油 nail polish

指路牌 signpost;fingerpost;guidepost

指南车 an ancient Chinese vehicle with a wooden figure always pointing to the south

指南针 compass

指示板 indicator board

指示灯 pilot lamp（*or* light）;indicator lamp

指示剂 indicator

指示器 indicator

指数律 index law

指纹学 dactylography

指战员 officers and men（of the PLA）

指不胜屈 too many to be counted on the fingers;a great many

指点迷津 show sb how to get onto the right path;point out the right way to sb when he goes astray

指东话西 point to the east and talk west—make pointless comments;be irrelevant

指腹为婚 an antenatal（*or* prenatal）betrothal

指挥若定 direct（work, etc.）with perfect ease;give competent leadership

指挥塔台 aviation control tower

指挥系统 command system

指鸡骂狗 point at the chicken and abuse the dog—point at one but abuse another;make oblique accusations

指甲锉刀 nail file

指甲盖儿 nail

指甲心儿 nail

指鹿为马 call a stag a horse—deliberately misrepresent

指路明灯 beacon light;beacon

指名道姓 mention sb's name;name names

指日可待 can be expected soon;be just round the corner

指桑骂槐 point at the mulberry and abuse the locust—point at one but abuse another;make oblique accusations

指示代词 demonstrative pronoun

指示功率 indicated power

指示生物 indicator organism

指示植物 indicator plant

指手画脚 ① make gestures; gesticulate ② make indiscreet remarks or criticisms

指数函数 exponential function

指天画地 gesticulate excitedly;speak without restraint

指头肚儿 face of the fingertip

指导性计划 guideline plan;indicative plan

指定分包人 nominated subcontractor

指令性计划 mandatory plans

指令性指标 mandatory target

指纹鉴定法 dactyloscopy

咫 [zhǐ]
ancient measure of length,equal to eight *cun*（寸）

咫尺 very close

咫尺天涯 so near and yet so far—see little of each other though living close together

趾 [zhǐ]
①toe ②foot

趾骨 metatarsal bones

趾甲 toenail

趾关节 toe joint

趾高气扬 strut about and give oneself airs;be swollen with arrogance

酯 [zhǐ]
ester

酯化 esterify

酯酶 esterase

酯油 ester oil

酯交换 ester exchange

酯缩合(作用) ester condensation

zhì（至）

至 [zhì]
I reaching;to;until:从头至尾 from beginning to end/截至今日为止 up to today/自

夏至冬 from summer to winter Ⅱ 〔副〕①go so far as;go to the extent of ②extremely;very;most:不胜感激之至 be deeply grateful;be very much obliged

至宝 most valuable treasure

至诚 ①complete sincerity ②sincere;straightforward

至迟 at (the) latest

至此 up to this point;at this stage

至多 at (the) most

至好 most intimate friend;best friend

至极 to the utmost point;extremely

至交 most intimate friend;best friend

至今 up to now;to this day;so far

至亲 very close relative;close kin

至情 true feelings;real sentiments

至若 as for;as to

至上 supreme;the highest

至少 at (the) least

至圣 the greatest sage—Confucius

至死 unto death;till death

至言 pertinent remarks;profound words

至友 most intimate friend;best friend

至于 ①as for;as to ②go so far as to

至尊 the most revered and respected—the emperor

至高无上 most lofty;paramount;supreme

至关紧要 the most important;of the utmost importance

至理名言 famous dictum;maxim;axiom

至亲好友 close relatives and good friends

至圣先师 the greatest sage and teacher—Confucius

至死不变 will not change even unto death;stick to one's course until the end of one's days

至死不悟 remain benighted to the end of one's days;be incorrigibly stubborn

至死方休 not to stop until death;be released only by death

志 〔zhì〕 Ⅰ 〔名〕①will;aspiration;ambition;ideal:人穷志不穷 be poor materially but not in willpower/有志于此 be bent upon this ②records;chronicles;annals:《三国志》*History of the Three Kingdoms* ③mark;sign Ⅱ 〔动〕①ascertain the weight, length, size, etc.;weigh;measure ②remember;keep in mind

志哀 indicate mourning

志气 aspiration;ambition

志庆 congratulate;celebrate

志趣 aspiration and interest;inclination;bent

志士 person of ideals and integrity

志书 district annals;local histories

志喜 offer congratulations (as on sb's wedding day)

志向 aspiration;ideal;ambition

志愿 ①aspiration;wish;ideal ②do sth of one's own free will;volunteer

志留纪 the Silurian Period

志留系 Silurian

志愿兵 volunteer (soldier)

志愿军 people who volunteer to fight in another country;volunteers

志愿书 application form

志愿者 volunteer

志大才疏 have great ambition but little talent;have high aspirations but little ability

志得意满 enormously proud of one's success;smug;complacent

志士仁人 people with high ideals

志同道合 cherish the same ideals and follow the same path;have a common goal

志在必得 determined to get

志愿兵役制 voluntary enlistment in the army

志愿者助残行动 volunteer helping the disabled activities

郅 〔zhì〕 〔副〕 most;very

郅盛 great prosperity

郅治 best administration;supreme order

帜 〔zhì〕 〔名〕①flag;streamer;banner ②sign;mark

帙 〔zhì〕 Ⅰ 〔名〕 cloth slip-case for a book Ⅱ 〔量〕 slip-case (of thread-bound Chinese books):一帙宋版书 a slip-case of thread bound Chinese books published in the Song Dynasty

制 〔zhì〕 Ⅰ 〔动〕①make;manufacture:缝制书包 sew a school satchel/自制教具 make teaching aids oneself ②work out;draw up;formulate:制礼作乐 set up rites and compose music (for the occasion) ③restrict;check;control Ⅱ 〔名〕 system

制版 plate making

制备 prepare

制币 standard national currency

制表 ①draw up a form or list ②statistics tabulation

制裁 sanction;punish

制导 control and guide (a missile,etc.)

制订 work (*or* map) out;formulate

制定 lay down;draw up;formulate;draft

制动 apply the brake;brake

制度 system;institution

制服 ①subdue;check;bring under control ②uniform

制革 process hides;tan

制衡 check and balance

制剂 preparation

制假 counterfeit

制冷 refrigeration

制帽 uniform cap

制片 produce (a film)

Z

制品 products;goods
制胜 get the upper hand of;subdue
制式 ①standard model;prescribed method ② system
制售 make and sell
制糖 refine sugar
制图 charting;map-making;drafting
制宪 draw up a constitution
制销 cotter
制药 pharmacy
制约 restrict;condition
制造 ① make; manufacture ② engineer;create;fabricate
制止 check;curb;prevent;stop
制种 develop new seed strains
制作 make;manufacture
制成品 finished products; manufactured goods;manufactures
制钉厂 nailery
制动器 brake
制动液 brake fluid
制动闸 damper brake
制服呢 uniform suiting (or coating)
制高点 commanding elevation (or point, ground,height)
制海权 command of the sea;sea control;sea mastery
制空权 command (or control) of the air;air supremacy;air mastery;air domination
制粒机 granulator
制图学 cartography
制药厂 pharmaceutical factory
制药学 pharmaceutics
制音器 damper
制造厂 manufactory;manufacturing plant
制造商 manufacturer
制造业 manufacturing industry
制动火箭 retrorocket
制动距离 transportation braking (or stopping) distance
制霉菌素 nystatin
制导导弹防御系统 guided missile defense system

质 [zhì]
Ⅰ 名 ①nature;character;essence ②quality ③matter;substance:铝质壶 kettle made of aluminium/木质纤维 wood fibre/铁质器皿 iron utensils ④pledge;security:以祖传珍宝为质 with the family heirloom as a pledge Ⅱ 形 simple;natural;plain Ⅲ 动 ①ask;question ② pawn;pledge
质变 qualitative change
质地 ①quality of a material;texture;grain ② character;disposition
质点 particle
质感 (art) sense of reality;real
质检 quality testing;quality inspection;quali-

ty control
质粒 plasmid
质量 ①quality ②mass
质料 material
质难 blame;censure;reproach
质朴 simple and unadorned;unaffected;plain
质谱 mass spectra
质数 prime number
质问 question;interrogate;call to account
质心 centre of mass
质询 address inquiries to;ask for an explanation;request explanation
质言 truthful words
质疑 call in question;query
质子 ① (in feudal times) a prince sent to a neighbouring state to be held as hostage ② proton
质量比 mass ratio
质量数 mass number;nuclear number;nucleon number
质谱仪 mass spectrometer;mass spectrograph
质因数 prime (number) factor
质量把关 guarantee the quality of the finished products;make the final check on products
质量标准 quality specification
质量低劣 inferior quality
质量第一 quality first
质量管理 quality management;quality control
质量监督 quality supervision
质量检验 quality inspection
质量鉴定 quality determination
质量控制 quality control
质量立业 base the development on quality
质量认证 quality verification
质量审查 quality review
质量守恒 conservation of mass
质疑问难 raise doubts and difficult questions for discussion
质量否定权 qualitative veto power
质能关系式 mass-energy relation
质量保障体系 quality assurance systems
质量分级标准 quality classification standard
质量高于数量 quality over (or before) quantity
质量体系认证 quality system certification
质量作用定律 law of mass action
质量品种效益年 Quality, Variety, and Benefit Year

炙 [zhì]
Ⅰ 动 broil;grill;roast:炙肉 broil meat;barbecue;barbeque Ⅱ 名 roast meat
炙烤 scorch
炙酷 extremely hot (weather)
炙晒 expose to the hot sun
炙烧 roast;burn
炙手可热 if you stretch out your hand you feel the heat (said of the imperative manner of

a person with power)

治 [zhì]
I 动 ①rule;govern;harness;control:整治运河 dredge a canal ②treat (a disease);heal;cure:治好伤 heal a wound ③eliminate;stamp out:治虫子 eliminate harmful insects/治蟑螂 exterminate cockroaches ④ punish ⑤ pursue one's studies;study;research Ⅱ 名 ①stability;order;peace ②seat of a local government
治安 public order;public security
治保 maintain law and order
治本 effect a permanent cure;get at the root (of a problem,etc.);take radical measures
治标 merely alleviate the symptoms of an illness;bring about a temporary solution (of a problem,etc.);take stopgap measures
治国 administer (or run) a country;manage state affairs
治淮 harness the Huai River
治家 manage a household
治假 punish counterfeiters
治经 study classics
治理 ① administer;govern ② harness;bring under control;put in order
治疗 treat;cure
治丧 make funeral arrangements
治沙 control sand
治史 specialize in history
治世 times of peace and prosperity
治水 regulate rivers and watercourses;prevent floods by water control
治所 seat of local government
治校 run a school
治学 pursue study;do scholarly research
治愚 rid people of ignorance and backwardness
治装 purchase things necessary (esp. clothes) for a long journey
治罪 punish sb for a crime
治疗学 therapeutics
治愈率 cure rate
治安处罚 public security penalty
治病救人 cure the sickness to save the patient
治国安民 run the country well and give the people peace and security
治理国家 administer a country;run a state
治理河流 harness a river;bring a river under control;clean up polluted rivers
治理整顿 improvement and rectification;improve the economic environment and rectify the economic order
治山驯水 tame rivers and mountains
治山治水 transform mountains and harness rivers;bring the water under control and improve the soil
治土改水 bring the water under control and improve the soil

治外法权 extraterritoriality;exterritoriality;extrality
治标不治本 cure the symptoms,not the diseases—temporary medical relief;palliatives
治国平天下 manage state affairs and put the country in order
治理环境污染 control and prevent environmental pollution
治理经济环境 improve the economic environment

栉 [zhì]
动 ①comb:手执巾栉 have the towel and comb in hand ②comb (hair)
栉比 placed closely side by side (like the teeth of a comb)
栉沐 wash and dress
栉风沐雨 be combed by the wind and washed by the rain—travel or work in the open despite wind and rain

峙 [zhì]
动 stand erect;rise aloft;tower
峙立 stand towering

庤 [zhì]
动 store up

陟 [zhì]
动 ① climb;ascend a height:陟山 climb mountains ②promote
陟黜 promotion and dismissal (of officials)

桎 [zhì]
名 fetters
桎梏 fetters and handcuffs;shackles

挚 [zhì]
形 sincere;earnest;heartfelt:真挚的友谊 true friendship
挚爱 true love
挚诚 sincere;earnest
挚厚 true,deep (feeling)
挚切 sincere;earnest;cordial
挚情 deep emotion;deep feeling
挚热 sincere and warm;fervent
挚深 true;genuine
挚意 ①sincere wish ②sincerely;genuinely
挚友 intimate friend;bosom friend

致 [zhì]
I 动 ①send;extend;make;deliver:致以热烈的祝贺 extend warm congratulations ②concentrate;devote ③ achieve;attain;apply ④bring about;incur;result in;lead to:招致杀身大祸 incur a fatal disaster Ⅱ 名 manner or style that attracts attention or arouses interest;interest Ⅲ 形 fine;delicate;exquisite
致哀 pay one's respects to the dead
致癌 cause (or produce) cancer;be carcinogenic
致病 cause a disease
致残 cause disability;become disabled
致辞 make (or deliver) a speech
致电 send a telegram

Z

致富 become rich;make a fortune
致函 write (a letter) to
致贺 extend one's congratulations
致敬 salute;pay one's respects to;pay tribute
to
致力 devote oneself to;work for
致密 fine and close;compact
致命 causing death;fatal;mortal;deadly
致使 cause;result in
致死 cause death;die
致谢 express one's thanks (or gratitude);extend thanks to
致意 give one's regards (or best wishes);
present one's compliments; send one's
greetings
致知 pursue knowledge;attain (or acquire)
knowledge
致敬电 a message of greeting
致癌物质 carcinogen;carcinogenic substance
致密结构 compact texture
致命要害 Achilles' heel
致命一击 strike a deadly blow;give the finishing blow
致死性毒气 lethal gas
致富思源,富而思进 think of the source of getting rich and of making progress after becoming affluence

轺 ［zhì］
◇轺轻 high and low chariots—high or low;good
or bad

秩 ［zhì］
［名］①order ②official salary;in good order
③decade:七秩寿辰 seventy birthday
秩序 order;sequence
秩序井然 in perfect order

狾 ［zhì］
［形］(of dog) mad;rabid

掷 ［zhì］
［动］throw;cast;fling;hurl:掷杯为号 give a
signal by throwing one's wine cup on the floor
掷还 please return (to the writer,etc.)
掷弃 throw away;abandon;cast away
掷扔 throw;cast
掷标枪 javelin throw
掷弹兵 grenadier
掷弹筒 grenade discharger;grenade launcher
掷骰子 cast the dice;play dice
掷铁饼 discus throw
掷地有声 (of speech) forceful and impressive
掷界外球 throw-in (in football)

痔 ［zhì］
［名］haemorrhoids;piles
痔疮 haemorrhoids;piles
痔漏 anal fistula

窒 ［zhì］
［动］stop up;block;obstruct
窒闷 close;stuffy

窒热 stuffy;oppressive
窒塞 stop up;block
窒息 stifle;suffocate
窒欲 suppress one's desire
窒息弹 stifling bomb
窒息性毒气 asphyxiating (or choking) gas

蛭 ［zhì］
［名］leech
蛭石 vermiculite (a mineral)

智 ［zhì］
［名］wisdom;intelligence;resourcefulness
智齿 wisdom tooth
智慧 wisdom;intelligence
智库 think-tank
智力 intelligence;intellect
智略 wisdom and resourcefulness
智谋 resourcefulness
智囊 big think (or Big) Think;brain truster;
brainpower
智能 ①intellectual power;intellectual ability
②things that have intellect and ability of
man
智巧 brains and tact
智取 take (a fort,town,etc.) by strategy
智商 intelligence quotient (IQ)
智童 child prodigy
智牙 wisdom tooth
智育 intellectual education;intellectual development
智障 person afflicted with a mental deficiency;mentally retarded
智残人 mentally-retarded person; mentally
handicapped
智多星 wizard—resourceful person; mastermind
智囊团 brain trust; brainstorming trust; think
tank;think company
智能卡 smart card
智力剥削 intellectual exploitation;brain drain
智力产业 white collar occupations where people do not engage in manual labour and resources are knowledge and expertise
智力结构 structure of talent in an institution
智力开发 intellectual development; development of intellectual resources
智力年龄 intellectual age
智力投资 investment in human capital
智力引进 bringing in talent from outside;hiring external scientific;technical, managerial and professional talent; introduction of foreign brainpower
智力支持 intellectual support
智能材料 intelligent material
智能测验 aptitude test;intelligence test
智能大厦 intelligent building
智能电话 smart phone
智能科学 intellectual science

Z

智能武器 intelligent weapon

智穷才尽 at the end of one's resources; at one's wits' end

智勇双全 both intelligent and courageous; both brave and resourceful

智圆行方 resourceful and upright; flexible and principled

智珠在握 be endowed with high native intelligence

智力密集型 knowledge-intensive

智能机器人 intelligent robot

智能型犯罪 intellective crimes

智能交通系统 intelligent transportation system(ITS)

智者千虑，必有一失 The wisest man, in a thousand schemes, must make at least one mistake; Even the wise are not free from error.

痣 [zhì]
〈名〉 nevus; mole

滞 [zhì]
I 〈形〉 stagnant; sluggish II 〈动〉 be at a standstill

滞碍 block (up); obstruct

滞尘 lay the dust; hold the dust down

滞呆 dull

滞洪 flood detention; slow down flood waters

滞后 ①hysteresis ②lag; delay

滞缓 slow; tardy; sluggish

滞留 be detained; be held up

滞闷 have pent-up feeling

滞泥 ①be a sticker for (form, etc.); rigidly adhere to (formalities, etc.) ②slow (in speech or action)

滞塞 block; obstruct; clog

滞涩 ①slow; dull ②(of writing) unsmooth; obscure

滞水 stagnant water

滞销 unsalable; unmarketable; slow-selling; slow-moving; be dull of sale

滞育 diapause

滞胀 stagflation

滞纳金 overdue fine; fine for delaying payment; fine for paying late; overdue fine

滞期费 demurrage charges

滞外法 extraterritoriality; extrality

滞销货 unsalable (or slow-selling) goods

滞销产品 poor seller; unsalable/slow-selling goods; sleeping stock

置 [zhì]
〈动〉 ①place; set; put ②set up; form; establish; install ③buy; purchase

置办 buy (durables); purchase

置备 purchase (equipment, furniture, etc.)

置产 buy property (esp. an estate)

置放 put; lay up

置换 displacement; replacement

置买 purchase; buy

置评 comment on; discuss

置身 place oneself; stay

置信 believe

置业 buy property

置疑 doubt

置家立室 get married and set up a home

置若罔闻 turn a deaf ear to; pay no heed to

置身事外 stay aloof from the affair; keep out of the business; refuse to be drawn into the matter

置之不顾 leave out of account; ignore; disregard

置之不理 ignore; brush aside; pay no attention to

置之度外 give no thought to; have no regard for

置之高阁 put sth on the shelf; shelve

置之脑后 banish from one's mind; ignore and forget; turn one's back on

置之一笑 laugh out of court; carry off with a laugh

置之死地而后快 will be content with nothing less than sb's destruction

置之死地而后生 confront a person with the danger of death and he will fight to live

雉 [zhì]
〈名〉 ①pheasant ②parapet section of a city wall (approximately 10 ft. high and 30 ft. long)

雉堞 crenelation

雉鸡 pheasant

雉鸠 turtledove

雉尾扇 fan made of pheasant's tail feather

雉尾鸭 pheasant-tailed widgeon

稚 [zhì]
〈形〉 young; childish

稚虫 naiad

稚嫩 ①young and tender ②immature

稚气 childishness

稚趣 childlike; innocent

稚弱 childish and tender

稚童 child

稚拙 uncomplicated; unsophisticated

稚子 (innocent) child

稚气未脱 still possessing the innocence of childhood

寘 [zhì]
〈动〉 place; put; 寘之于怀 keep in mind

踬 [zhì]
〈动〉 ①trip; fall; stumble ②suffer a setback and fall; 中年遭踬 suffer a setback at middle age

zhōng (ㄓㄨㄥ)

中 [zhōng]
I 〈名〉 ①centre; middle ②China ③inside; 半

空中 in midair/铭记心中 keep firmly in mind ④middle；mid；八月中 in the middle of August ⑤medium；intermediate ⑥intermediary ⑦in the process of；in the course of Ⅱ 劢 be suitable for；be fit for；good for：不中用 no good；good for nothing Ⅲ 形 ①all right；okay②impartial；mean；between two extremes ➡ zhòng

中巴 medium-sized bus or coach；minibus

中班 ①middle shift；swing shift ②the middle class in a kindergarten

中板 ①medium plate ②moderato

中保 middleman and guarantor

中表 first cousin（child of father's sister or mother's sister or brother）

中波 medium wave

中部 central section；middle part

中餐 Chinese meal；Chinese food

中策 the second best plan

中层 middle-level

中场 midfield

中程 intermediate range；medium range

中词 middle term

中档 medium quality at middling price

中道 ①halfway；midway ②the golden mean（of the Confucian school）

中稻 semilate rice；middle-season rice

中等 ①medium；moderate；middling ②secondary

中点 midpoint

中东 the Middle East

中端 medium-end

中断 suspend；break off；discontinue

中队 ①military unit corresponding to a company；squadron ②a unit composed of several groups

中耳 auris media；middle ear

中幡 flagpole-waving

中饭 midday meal；lunch

中分 ①divide sth equally into two halves ②part hair in the middle

中锋 centre forward（as in football）；centre

中缝 ①the column on the folding line of a newspaper，usu. reserved for advertisements or notices ②the line sewn down the back of a jacket

中伏 ①the middle or second *fu*—the second hottest period of the year（10 or 20 days）②the first day of the middle or second *fu*（falling in late July）

中耕 intertill

中古 ①the middle ancient times（in Chinese history，from the 3rd to the 9th century）②medieval times；Middle Ages

中国 China

中号 medium size

中和 neutralization

中华 ①the Chinese nation ②China

中级 middle rank；intermediate

中继 relay

中坚 nucleus；hard core；backbone

中间 ①among；between ②centre；middle

中将 （U. S. & Brit. Army，U. S. Air Force，U. S. & Brit. Marine Corps）lieutenant general；（U. S. & Brit. Navy）vice admiral；（Brit. Air Force）air marshal

中焦 the part of the body cavity between the diaphragm and the umbilicus housing the spleen，stomach，etc.

中觉 afternoon nap；noontime snooze

中介 intermediary；medium

中景 film medium shot

中看 be pleasant to the eye

中考 entrance examinations to secondary school，senior middle school，technical school and vocational high school；senior middle school or senior middle technical school entrance examination

中栏 intermediate hurdles

中立 neutrality

中林 middle forest

中流 midstream

中路 ①mediocre in quality ②halfway；midway

中落 （of family fortunes）decline；ebb

中脑 mesencephalon；midbrain

中年 middle age

中跑 middle-distance race

中频 intermediate frequency

中期 middle period

中人 ①middleman；go-between；mediator；intermediary ②one of ordinary stature，appearance，ability，etc. ；an average man

中师 secondary normal school

中士 （U. S. & Brit. Army，Brit. Air Force，U. S. & Brit. Marine Corps）sergeant；（U. S. Navy）petty officer second class；（Brit. Navy）petty officer first class；（U. S. Air Force）staff sergeant

中式 Chinese style

中试 pre-production test

中枢 centre

中水 recycled water

中速 intermediate speed

中堂 ①central room（of a one-storey Chinese traditional house consisting of several rooms in a row）；principal rooms（in a courtyard，usu. facing south）②central scroll of painting or calligraphy（hung in the middle of the wall of the main room）

中天 ①in the sky ②culmination；meridian passage（*or* transit）

中听 pleasant to the ear；agreeable to the hearer

中途 halfway；midway
中土 ①Central Plains（comprising the middle and lower reaches of the Huanghe River）②China
中外 China and foreign countries
中卫 centre halfback
中尉 （U. S. Army，Air Force & Marine Corps）first lieutenant；（Brit. Army & Marine Corps）lieutenant；（U. S. Navy）lieutenant junior grade；（Brit. Navy）sublieutenant；senior commissioned branch officer；（Brit. Air Force）flying officer
中文 the Chinese language；Chinese
中午 noon；midday
中西 Chinese and Western
中线 ①centre line（in basketball and volleyball）；halfway line（in football）② central line
中校 （U. S. & Brit. Army，U. S. Air Force，U. S. & Brit. Marine Corps）lieutenant colonel；（U. S. & Brit. Navy）commander；（Brit. Air Force）wing commander
中心 centre；heart；core；hub
中兴 resurgence（of a nation）；restoration（of a dynasty）
中型 medium-sized；middle-sized
中性 ①neutral ②Neuter
中学 middle school；high school
中旬 the middle ten days of a month
中央 ① centre；middle ② central authorities（of a state，party，etc.）
中药 traditional Chinese medicine
中叶 middle period
中衣 underpants；pants
中医 ①traditional Chinese medical science ② doctor of traditional Chinese medicine；practitioner of Chinese medicine
中庸 ① the golden mean（of the Confucian school）②of ordinary talent；common；mediocre
中用 of use；useful
中游 ① middle reaches（of a river）② the state of being middling
中雨 moderate rain
中原 Central Plains（comprising the middle and lower reaches of the Huanghe River）
中岳 the Central Mountain
中云 medium cloud
中支 medium-counts
中止 discontinue；suspend；break off
中指 middle finger
中专 secondary specialized school；polytechnic school
中转 change trains
中子 neutron
中草药 Chinese herbal medicine
中成药 Chinese patent drug

中垂线 perpendicular bisector
中短波 intermediate wave；medium-short wave
中耳炎 otitis media
中国画 traditional Chinese painting
中国话 the Chinese language；Chinese
中国结 traditional Chinese knot
中国热 Sinomania
中国人 Chinese
中国通 old China hand；sinologue
中国字 Chinese characters；the Chinese written language
中果皮 mesocarp
中华鲟 Chinese sturgeon
中继器 repeater
中继线 trunk line
中继站 relay station；repeat station
中间派 middle-of-the-roaders；middle elements；intermediate sections（or forces）
中间人 middleman；go-between；mediator；intermediary
中间商 middleman；jobber
中间税 intermediate tax
中间体 intermediate
中间线 medium line
中介人 broker；matchmaker；intermediary；medium
中介子 neutretto
中距离 middle distance
中立国 neutral state
中量级 middleweight
中胚层 mesoderm；mesoblast
中青年 adultescent
中秋节 the Mid-autumn Festival（15th day of the 8th lunar month）
中山狼 the Zhongshan wolf in the fable—one who repays good with evil
中山装 Chinese tunic suit
中生代 the Mesozoic Era；the Mesozoic
中生界 the Mesozoic Erathem
中世纪 Middle Ages
中式盐 neutral salt
中碳钢 medium carbon steel
中提琴 viola
中途岛 Midway Island
中微子 neutrino
中位数 median
中纬度 middle latitudes
中心规 centre gauge
中心角 central angle
中心线 centre line
中心项 central term
中新世 the Miocene Epoch
中性人 gender bender
中性土 neutral soil
中性盐 neutral salt
中学生 middle school student

Z

中央税　state tax;central tax
中药铺　shop (*or* store) or traditional Chinese medicines;Chinese pharmacy
中药学　traditional Chinese pharmacology
中医学　traditional Chinese medicine
中音号　althorn;alto horn
中硬钢　medium steel
中元节　the Festival of the Dead Spirits (15th day of the seventh lunar month when sacrifices are offered to the dead)
中注管　running-gate
中专生　secondary specialized (*or* technical) school student
中转港　entrepot
中转站　transfer station
中子弹　neutron bomb
中子态　neutron state
中子星　neutron star
中子源　neutron source
中饱私囊　batten on money entrusted to one's care;line one's pockets with public funds or other people's money;embezzle
中不溜儿　fair to middling;middling
中产阶级　middle class;middle bourgeoisie
中程导弹　intermediate range missile;medium range missile
中档产品　medium products;medium goods
中等教育　secondary school education
中等身材　of medium height
中低产田　farmland that provides low or medium yields
中国特色　Chinese characteristics;Sinicism
中华民族　the Chinese nation
中间阶层　intermediate strata
中间力量　middle-of-the-road forces;intermediate forces
中间路线　middle-of-the-road
中间盘剥　exploitation by middlemen
中介机构　intermediary agency; brokerage; brokering organ;intermediary organ
中立政策　policy of neutrality
中立主义　neutralism
中流砥柱　mainstay;chief corner stone
中年妇女　middle-aged woman
中篇小说　medium-length novel;novelette
中枢神经　central nervous system
中外合资　joint ventures involving Chinese and foreign investment
中西合璧　good combination of Chinese and Western elements; combination of Chinese and Western content
中心城市　key city
中心发言　main speech
中心工作　central task
中心环节　key link;central link
中心思想　central idea;gist
中心问题　central issue;crucial question

中性反应　neutral reaction
中性名词　neuter noun
中性树脂　neutral resin
中央党校　the Party School of the (CPC) Central Committee
中央机构　central organs (*or* institutions)
中央集权　centralism;centralization(of authority)
中央全会　plenary session of the Central Committee
中央委员　member of the Central Committee (of the Chinese Communist Party)
中央银行　central bank;national bank
中医学院　college of traditional Chinese medicine
中庸之道　the doctrine of the Golden Mean
中止发行　discontinue publishing
中止射击　lift fire
中止谈判　suspend (*or* break off) negotiations
中低档消费　low and medium-grade goods
中高层住宅　semi-high-rise housing
中国共产党　the Communist Party of China (CPC);the Chinese Communist Party
中国科学院　the Chinese Academy of Sciences; Academia Sinica
中华老字号　China's time-honoured brand (shop)
中华世纪坛　China Millennium Monument;China Century Platform
中间消费者　intermediate consumer
中看不中吃　look nice but taste nasty;be pleasing to the eye but not to the taste
中石器时代　Mesolithic Period;Middle Stone Age
中西药结合　combine traditional Chinese and Western medicine;the integration of traditional Chinese and Western medicine
中小型企业　small and medium-size enterprise
中央处理器　central processing unit (CPU)
中央电视台　China Central Television (CCTV)
中央各部门　departments under the Party's Central Committee and the State Council
中央情报局　the (U. S.) Central Intelligence Agency (CIA)
中央商务区　CBD,central business district
中医研究院　academy of traditional Chinese medicine
中子反应堆　neutron reactor
中子物理学　neutronics
中等发达国家　moderately developed countries
中等技术学校　secondary technical school
中等师范学校　secondary normal school
中等专科学校　secondary specialized school; polytechnic school
中东和平进程　the Middle East peace process
中国问题专家　China watcher;China expert
中外合资法律　Sino-foreign joint venture law

中外合资经营 joint ventures involving Chinese and foreign investment
中外合作企业 Sino-foreign cooperative enterprises
中外文化交流 Sino-foreign cultural exchanges
中文信息处理 Chinese information processing
中央工作会议 the Central Working Conference
中央候补委员 alternate member of the Central Committee (of the Chinese Communist Party)
中央计划经济 central government planned economy
中央条约组织 the Central Treaty Organization (CENTO)
中央直属机关 departments under the Party Central committee
中止外交关系 suspend diplomatic relations
中国人民解放军 the Chinese People's Liberation Army
中国人民志愿军 the Chinese People's Volunteers
中国社会科学院 the Chinese Academy of Social Sciences
中国新经济峰会 China New Economy Summit
中华人民共和国 the People's Republic of China
中日邦交正常化 normalization of Sino-Japanese relations
中西部对口帮助 counterpart assistance to the West by the East
中型便携式电脑 luggable computer
中央顾问委员会 the Central Advisory Commission
中央军事委员会 the Central Military Commission
中等职业技术教育 secondary vocational and technical education
中外商业股份公司 Sino-foreign commercial shareholding company
中央大型企业工委 Central Work Committee for Large Enterprises
中央经济工作会议 the Central Economic Working Conference
中央人民广播电台 Central People's Broadcasting Station of China (CPBS)
中英联合联络小组 the Sino-British Joint Liaison Group
中英香港交接仪式 the Sino-British Hong Kong handover ceremony
中共十一届三中全会 the Third Plenary Session of the 11th CPC Central Committee
中国常驻联合国代表 Chinese Permanent Representative to the UN
中国共产主义青年团 the Communist Youth League of China
中国人权状况白皮书 white paper on China's human rights conditions
中华全国妇女联合会 the All-China Women's Federation
中央纪律检查委员会 the Central Commission for Discipline Inspection
中国爱国民主统一战线 the Chinese Patriotic and Democratic United Front
中国共产党中央委员会 the Central Committee of the Communist Party of China
中国人民政治协商会议 the Chinese People's Political Consultative Conference (CPPCC)
中华见义勇为奖励基金 the China foundation for Heroism Award
中国共产党全国代表大会 the National Congress of the Communist Party of China
中国改革开放政策的总设计师 the chief architect of China's reform and opening policy
中英(关于香港问题的)联合声明 the Sino-British Joint Declaration(on the question of Hong Kong)

忪 ［zhōng］

◇ 怔忪 alarmed and panicky; terrified; panic-stricken; seized with terror

忠 ［zhōng］
形 loyal; staunch; faithful; devoted
忠臣 official loyal to his sovereign
忠诚 loyal; faithful; staunch
忠告 ① sincerely advise; admonish ② sincere advice; advice
忠厚 honest and tolerant; sincere and kindly
忠君 loyal to the throne (or sovereign)
忠实 loyal; true; faithful
忠顺 loyal and obedient; obedient
忠孝 loyalty and filial piety
忠心 loyalty; devotion
忠言 sincere advice; earnest advice
忠义 loyal and righteous
忠勇 loyal and brave; faithful and courageous
忠于 true to; loyal to; faithful to; devoted to
忠贞 loyal and steadfast
忠肝义胆 having good faith, virtue and patriotism
忠君爱国 be loyal to the sovereign and devoted to the country
忠心耿耿 loyal and devoted; most faithful and true
忠言逆耳 Faithful words offend the ear; Good advice jars on the ear.
忠义之士 honest and righteous man
忠于职守 be devoted to one's duty; be faithful in the discharge of one's duties
忠贞不渝 unswervingly loyal

终 ［zhōng］
Ⅰ 名 ①end; close; finish：年终总结 sum up one's work at the end of the year ②death; end
Ⅱ 副 eventually; ultimately; in the end; after

Z

all Ⅲ 形 whole;full;entire;all
终场 ①end of a performance or game ②final session in an examination
终点 ①terminal point;destination ②finish
终端 terminal
终归 eventually;in the end;after all
终极 ultimate
终结 end;final stage
终究 eventually;in the end;after all
终局 end;outcome
终老 spend one's remaining years till death
终了 end (of a period)
终年 ①(all) the year round;throughout the year ②the age at which one dies
终曲 finale
终日 all day long;all day
终身 lifelong;all one's life
终审 last instance;final judgment
终生 all one's life
终霜 latest frost
终岁 whole year;throughout the year
终席 (of a dinner party or meeting) end;come to a close
终须 have to in the end
终夜 all night long;the whole night
终于 af (long) last;in the end;finally
终止 ① stop;end ② termination;annulment;abrogation ③cadence
终点站 terminus;terminal
终端局 terminal station (in postal service)
终审权 power of final adjudication;right of adjudication;right of giving final approval
终成眷属 get married eventually
终成泡影 come to naught;come to nothing;end up in smoke;vanish like a bubble
终底于成 succeed in the end
终南捷径 a short cut to high office;the high road to fame or success
终身伴侣 lifelong companion—one's husband or wife
终身保险 perpetual insurance
终身保修 whole life service
终身不嫁 (women) remain unmarried all one's life
终身大事 a great event in one's life (usu. referring to marriage)
终身服务 lifelong service
终身教授 tenured professor
终身教育 lifelong education
终身年金 life annuity
终审法院 court of last instance
终审判决 final judgement
终天之恨 lifelong regret;eternal regret
终夜不眠 lie awake all night
终有一日 One day there will happen.
终止合同 terminate a contract
终身职务制 lifelong tenure;lifelong position

终身人寿保险 whole life insurance

盅 ［zhōng］
名 handleless cup

钟 ［zhōng］
Ⅰ 名 ①bell ②clock ③time (as measured in hours and minutes) Ⅱ 动 concentrate (one's affections,etc.);focus on
钟爱 dote on (a child);cherish
钟摆 pendulum (of a clock)
钟表 clocks and watches;timepiece
钟点 ①a time for sth to be done (or to happen) ②hour
钟楼 ①bell tower;belfry ②clock tower
钟琴 carillon
钟情 be deeply in love
钟头 hour
钟罩 bell jar;immersion bell
钟点房 hourly paid hotel
钟点工 accommodator;daily help;hourly paid worker
钟鼎文 inscriptions on ancient bronze objects
钟乳石 stalactite
钟灵毓秀 (of a place) pregnant with beauty and productive of talent
钟鸣鼎食 partake of rich food in *ding* vessels to the accompaniment of music—affluency;extravagance
钟鸣漏尽 the morning bell is striking and the night is waning—be in one's declining years

衷 ［zhōng］
名 innermost feelings
衷肠 words right from one's heart
衷情 heartfelt emotion;inner feelings
衷曲 heartfelt emotion;inner feelings
衷心 heartfelt;wholehearted;cordial

zhǒng（ㄓㄨㄥˇ）

肿 ［zhǒng］
动 swell;be swollen
肿块 bossing;lump;swelling
肿瘤 tumour
肿胀 ①swelling ②oedema and abdominal distension
肿骨鹿 palaeontology thick-jawed deer

种 ［zhǒng］
Ⅰ 名 ①species ②race ③seed;strain;breed ④ guts;grit;nerve;pluck Ⅱ 量 kind;style;sort;type：两种不同的思想 two different ideas (or views)/十五种灯具 fifteen types of lights/这种人 this sort of people ➡ zhòng
种畜 breeding stock;stud stock
种蛋 breeding eggs (allowed to hatch)
种肥 seed manure
种类 kind;type;variety
种马 stud
种牛 bull kept for covering

种禽 breeding fowl
种仁 kernel
种系 germ line
种姓 caste (of India)
种源 place of origin
种种 all sorts (*or* kinds) of;a variety of
种子 ①seed ②seeded player;seed
种族 race
种子队 seeded team
种间杂交 interspecific hybridization (*or* cross)
种内杂交 intraspecific hybridization (*or* cross)
种子选手 seeded player
种族隔离 racial segregation;apartheid
种族灭绝 genocide
种族歧视 racial discrimination
种族清洗 ethnic cleaning;tribal cleaning
种族主义 racism;racialism

冢 [zhǒng]
名 tomb;grave

踵 [zhǒng]
Ⅰ 名 heel Ⅱ 动 ①call in person ②follow on sb's heels;follow close behind
踵武 follow in sb's footsteps;imitate;follow suit
踵至 arrive upon the heels of another;arrive immediately after sb
踵门相告 call in person to pass the news
踵事增华 carry on a predecessor's task and make a greater success of it;take over and carry forward
踵趾相接 follow the footsteps;one after another;in succession

zhòng(ㄓㄨㄥˋ)

中 [zhòng]
动 ①hit;fit exactly;be just right ②fall into;sustain;suffer:中了圈套 walk into a trap/中埋伏 fall into an ambush/中煤气 be gassed ➡ zhōng
中标 win the bid;be the successor (*or* winner) of the bid
中彩 draw a prizewinning ticket in a lottery
中弹 be hit by a bullet;get shot
中的 hit the mark;hit the nail on the head
中毒 ①be poisoned (usu. accidentally) ②poisoning;toxicosis
中风 suffer from a stroke of apoplexy
中寒 catch a cold
中计 play into sb's hands;fall into a trap;be taken in
中奖 draw a prizewinning ticket (*or* win a prize) in a lottery;get the winning number in a bond
中举 pass the provincial civil service examination

中肯 ①apropos;pertinent;to the point ②critical
中签 be the lucky number (in drawing lots, etc.)
中伤 slander;malign;vilify
中试 pass a test,etc.
中暑 ①suffer heatstroke (*or* sunstroke);be affected by the heat ② heatstroke;sunstroke
中听 agreeable to the ear;pleasing to listener
中邪 be bewitched
中选 be chosen;be selected
中意 be to one's liking;take (*or* catch) the fancy of
中规中矩 straight and narrow

仲 [zhòng]
形 ①middle;intermediate ②(of the three months in a season) second:《仲夏夜之梦》 *Midsummer Night's Dream* ③(of brothers) second in order of birth
仲裁 arbitration;arbitrate
仲春 second month of spring;the middle of spring
仲冬 second month of winter;midwinter
仲父 father's younger brother
仲秋 second month of autumn
仲夏 second month of summer;midsummer
仲裁人 arbiter;arbitrator;referee
仲裁员 arbiter;arbitrator;referee
仲裁条款 arbitration clause
仲裁协定 arbitration agreement
仲裁申请书 application for arbitration
仲裁通知书 arbitration notice
仲裁委员会 arbitration committee;board of arbitration

众 [zhòng]
Ⅰ 形 many;numerous;innumerable Ⅱ 名 large number of people;crowd;multitude
众多 multitudinous;numerous
众人 everybody
众生 all living creatures
众数 mode
众望 people's expectations;popular confidence
众议员 representative (in Congress);member of the House of Representatives;Congressman or Congresswoman
众议院 House of Representatives (in the United States,Australia,Japan,etc.);Chamber of Deputies (in Italy,Mexico,Chile,etc.)
众寡悬殊 a great disparity in numerical strength
众口难调 It is difficult to cater for all tastes.
众口铄金 Public clamour can confound right and wrong.
众口一词 with one voice;unanimously
众目睽睽 with everybody watching

Z

众目昭彰 seen clearly by everyone; clear to all
众怒难犯 One cannot afford to incur public wrath; It is dangerous to incur the anger of the masses.
众叛亲离 with the masses rising in rebellion and one's friends deserting; be opposed by the masses and deserted by one's followers; be utterly isolated
众擎易举 with many people it's easy to lift a load—many hands make light work
众矢之的 a target of public criticism (*or* censure)
众说纷纭 Opinions vary; Opinions are widely divided.
众所周知 as everyone knows; as is known to all; it is common knowledge that
众望所归 enjoy popular confidence; command popular support
众星拱月 a myriad of stars surrounding the moon—a host of lesser lights around the leading one
众志成城 unity of will is an impregnable stronghold; unity is strength
众人拾柴火焰高 when everybody adds fuel the flames rise high—the more people, the more strength

种 [zhòng]
〔名〕sow; grow; plant; cultivate ➡zhǒng
种地 till (*or* cultivate) land; go in for farming
种痘 vaccinate sb against smallpox
种花 ①cultivate (*or* grow) flowers ②vaccinate sb against smallpox ③grow cotton
种田 till (*or* cultivate) land; go in for farming
种养 grow; cultivate
种因 do things that will entail grave consequences
种植 plant; grow
种植园 plantation
种植面积 acreage
种瓜得瓜, 种豆得豆 plant melons and you get melons, sow beans and you get beans—as you sow, so will you reap

重 [zhòng]
Ⅰ 〔名〕weight: 超重信件 overweight letter/ 加重自行车 heavy duty bike Ⅱ 〔形〕①heavy; weighty; considerable in amount or value ② deep; serious: 案情很重 very serious case/口味重 have a heavily seasoned taste ③important ④prudent; discreet Ⅲ 〔动〕lay stress on; set store by; attach importance to: 以友谊为重 set store by friendship; value friendship/重基础教育 lay stress on basic education ➡ chóng
重办 severely punish (a criminal)
重兵 a large number of troops; massive forces
重柄 great political power
重病 serious disease (*or* illness)

重臣 minister (of a monarchy) holding an important post or shouldering heavy responsibilities; important official
重惩 severely punish; punish without leniency
重酬 ①generously reward ②a high (*or* handsome) reward
重创 inflict heavy losses (*or* casualties) on; maul (heavily)
重挫 frustrate
重大 great; weighty; major; significant
重担 heavy burden; difficult task
重地 important place (usu. not open to the public)
重典 ①severe punishment; heavy sentence ② important ancient books and records
重点 ①weight ②focal point; stress; emphasis
重读 stress
重罚 grave punishment; impose heavy penalties on
重犯 major criminal
重负 heavy burden; heavy load
重荷 heavy burden; heavy responsibilities
重话 hard words; harsh words
重活 heavy work
重价 high price
重奖 handsomely reward; give ample rewards to
重金 a huge sum (of money)
重力 gravity; gravitational force
重利 ①high interest ②huge profit
重量 weight
重炮 heavy artillery; heavy artillery piece; heavy gun
重氢 heavy hydrogen; deuterium
重任 important task; heavy responsibility
重伤 a severe injury
重赏 a high (*or* handsome) reward
重视 attach importance to; pay attention to; think highly of; take sth seriously; value
重水 heavy water
重税 heavy (*or* oppressive) taxation
重听 hard of hearing
重头 ①significant; weighty ②important part
重托 great trust
重望 ① good reputation ② high hopes; great expectations
重孝 deep mourning
重心 ①centre of gravity ②heart; core; focus
重刑 severe punishment; heavy sentence
重型 heavy-duty; heavy
重压 heavy (*or* strong) pressure
重要 important; significant; major
重音 ①stress ②accent
重用 put sb in an important position
重油 heavy oil
重枣 reddish brown (like dried dates)
重责 ① heavy responsibility; important task

②severely reprimand or punish
重镇 place of strategic importance
重子 baryon
重罪 serious crime;felony
重病号 severely sick person
重工业 heavy industry
重金属 heavy metal
重晶石 barite;heavy spar (a mineral)
重力坝 gravity dam
重力场 gravitational field
重力秤 gravity balance
重力水 gravitational water;free water
重力仪 gravity meter;gravimeter
重量级 heavyweight
重切削 heavy cut
重水堆 heavy water reactor
重头戏 traditional opera involving much singing and action;significant part
重武器 heavy weapons
重元素 heavy element
重大过失 gross negligence
重点发展 prioritize
重点扶植 priority support
重点工程 major project;key project;priority project
重点行业 key trades
重点学科 priority fields of study;key disciplinary areas
重点学校 key school,institute,or university
重轰炸机 heavy bomber
重机关枪 heavy machine gun
重金新闻 checkbook journalism
重力选矿 gravity separation (or concentration)
重力异常 gravity anomaly
重男轻女 ①regard men as superior to women ②prefer sons to daughters;preference of boys to girls
重农主义 agrarianism
重商主义 mercantilism
重头厂家 important factory plant
重头作品 significant work;opus magnum
重型机床 heavy-duty machine tool
重型卡车 heavy-duty truck;heavy truck
重义轻利 value justice more than material gains
重在参与 emphasize on participating in
重在建设 lay emphasis on progress
重中之重 top of all priorities
重过磷酸钙 double superphosphate
重力加速度 acceleration of gravity
重大技术装备 important technical equipments
重大体育比赛 blue-ribbon event
重合同,守信用 honour contracts and keep promise; honour contracts and maintain commercial integrity; stand by the contracts and keep promise

重点文物保护单位 major historical and cultural sites under state protection
重赏之下,必有勇夫 When a high reward is offered,brave fellows are bound to come forward.
重于泰山,轻于鸿毛 (of one's death) weightier than Mount Tai or lighter than a feather
重大环境污染事故罪 crime of severe environmental pollution

zhōu（ㄓㄡ）

舟 [zhōu]
图 boat
舟车 ①vessel and vehicle ②journey
舟楫 vessels
舟桥 bridge of boats
舟子 boatman
舟状窝 fossa navicularis;fossa scaphoidea
舟车劳顿 fatigued by a long journey;travel-worn

州 [zhōu]
图 ① administrative division ② (autonomous) prefecture ③(US) state

诌 [zhōu]
动 spin (a yarn);cook up

周 [zhōu]
I 图 ① circumference; perimeter; circuit; periphery ② week ③ cycle: 820 千周 820 kc
II 动 ①circle; make a circuit; move in a circular course ②help out (the needy);assist; relieve III 形 ①all; whole ② thoughtful; considerate;attentive
周报 a weekly newspaper or periodical;weekly
周边 ①periphery ②neighboring;surrounding
周波 cycle
周长 girth;circumference;perimeter
周到 attentive and satisfactory; thoughtful; considerate
周济 help out (the needy);relieve
周角 round angle;perigon
周刊 weekly publication
周流 circulate
周率 frequency
周密 careful;thorough
周末 weekend
周年 anniversary
周期 period;cycle
周全 ①thorough;comprehensive ②help sb attain his aim
周身 the whole body;all over the body
周岁 one full year of life
周围 around;round;about
周详 comprehensive;complete;careful
周旋 ①circle round;spiral ②mix with other people;socialize ③deal with;contend with
周延 distribution

Z

周游 travel round; journey round
周遭 the surrounding area
周章 ①be scared ②trouble; effort
周折 twists and turns; setbacks
周正 straight; regular
周知 everybody knows; make known to all
周转 ①turnover ②have enough to meet the need
周期表 periodic table
周期律 periodic law
周期性 periodicity; cyclicity
周转金 revolving fund; working fund .
周边国家 surrounding countries; neighboring countries
周边环境 peripheral environment
周而复始 go round and begin again; go round and round; move in cycles
周身温暖 be warm all over
周围神经 peripheral nerves

洲 [zhōu]
图 ①continent ②islet in a river; sandbar
洲际 intercontinental
洲际导弹 intercontinental ballistic missile
洲际弹道导弹 intercontinental ballistic missile

粥 [zhōu]
图 gruel; porridge; congee ⇒ yù
粥少僧多 little gruel and many monks—not enough to go round

zhóu(ㄓㄡˊ)

妯 [zhóu]
妯娌 wives of brothers; sisters-in-law

轴 [zhóu]
I 图 ①axle; shaft ②axis; pivot ③spool; roller; rod II 量 几轴字画 several scrolls of calligraphy／两轴棉线 two spools of thread ⇒ zhòu
轴承 bearing
轴距 wheelbase (of a vehicle)
轴套 axle sleeve
轴瓦 axle bush
轴线 ①axis ②spool thread; spool contton
轴箱 axle box; axle housing; step box
轴向 axial
轴心 ①axle centre ②axis
轴子 ①roller (for a scroll of calligraphy or painting) ②(tuning) peg (or pin)
轴对称 axial symmetry
轴流泵 axial-flow pump; axial pump
轴心国 Axis powers; the Axis

zhǒu(ㄓㄡˇ)

肘 [zhǒu]
图 ①elbow ②upper part of a leg of pork
肘板 bracket; toggle plate; wrist plate
肘节 toggle
肘窝 crook of the arm
肘腋 elbow and armpit—close at hand
肘子 ①upper part of a leg of pork ②elbow
肘接 toggle (or elbow) joint
肘腋之患 trouble coming from those closest

帚 [zhǒu]
图 broom

zhòu(ㄓㄡˋ)

纣 [zhòu]
图 canvas or leather strap round the rump of a shaft-horse; crupper

咒 [zhòu]
I 图 incantation II 动 curse; swear; damn
咒骂 curse; swear; abuse; revile
咒人 curse people
咒语 incantation

宙 [zhòu]
图 time

绉 [zhòu]
图 crape; crepe
绉布 cotton crepe; crepe
绉缎 crepe-back satin
绉呢 crape; crepe
绉纱 crape
绉纹 crinkle
绉纸 crepe paper; twisting paper

菷 [zhòu]
I 动 wrap sth up with straw II 量 a bundle (of bowls, dishes, etc. tied with straw rope)

胄 [zhòu]
图 ① progeny; descendants; offspring ② helmet

咮 [zhòu]
图 beak; bill

昼 [zhòu]
图 daylight; daytime; day
昼夜 day and night; round the clock
昼出动物 diurnal animal
昼伏夜出 hide by day and come out by night

酎 [zhòu]
图 double-fermented wine

皱 [zhòu]
I 动 wrinkle; crease; 眉头一皱，计上心来。Knit the brows and a stratagem comes to one's mind. II 图 crease; crinkle; wrinkle
皱襞 fold; plica; wrinkles; lines
皱痕 fine wrinkle
皱皮 cockles; wrinkled skin
皱缩 shrinking; buckling; crimp
皱胃 abomasum
皱纹 wrinkles; creases; lines
皱褶 fold; crease; wrinkle
皱纸 wadding
皱眉头 knit (or contract) one's brows; frown
皱纹革 shrink leather
皱纹纸 crepe paper
皱皱巴巴 wrinkled; crumpled

Z

皱纹法兰绒 crepe flannel

骤 [zhòu]
Ⅰ 动 (of a horse) trot Ⅱ 形 rapid;hurried Ⅲ 副 suddenly;abruptly
骤变 cataclysm
骤冷 shock cooling
骤然 suddenly;abruptly
骤热 shock heating
骤雨 brash;heavy shower;sudden downpour
骤止 quick stoppage
骤不及防 be taken by surprise

籀 [zhòu]
动 read aloud;chant;recite

zhū(ㄓㄨ)

朱 [zhū]
Ⅰ 形 vermilion;bright red Ⅱ 名 cinnabar; vermilion
朱笔 writing brush dipped in red ink
朱红 vermilion;bright red
朱鹮 Japanese crested ibis
朱门 vermilion gates—red-lacquered doors of wealthy homes
朱墨 ①red and black ②ink made of cinnabar
朱批 comments written in red with a brush
朱雀 rosefinch
朱砂 cinnabar
朱文 characters on a seal carved in relief
朱颜 ①beautiful face (of a woman) ②youthful colour
朱顶雀 redpoll (linnet)
朱古力 chocolate
朱陈之好 the union of two families
朱唇皓齿 red lips and shining teeth—very pretty or handsome
朱门酒肉臭,路有冻死骨 behind the red doors meat and wine go to waste while out on the road lie the bones of the frozen

侏 [zhū]
名 dwarf
侏儒 dwarf;midget;pygmy
侏罗纪 Jurassic Period
侏罗系 Jurassic system

诛 [zhū]
动 ①put (a criminal) to death;execute ② condemn;punish
诛戮 kill;put to death
诛求 make exorbitant demands;extort;exact
诛锄异己 wipe out (or liquidate) dissenters
诛求无已 make endless exorbitant demands
诛杀无辜 kill the innocent
诛心之论 penetrating criticism;exposure of sb's ulterior motives

珠 [zhū]
名 ①pearl ②bead
珠蚌 pearl oyster
珠宝 pearls and jewels;jewelry

珠茶 a kind of green tea (the tea leaves looking like beads)
珠翠 pearls and jade;ornaments made with pearls and jade
珠花 pearl head-ornaments
珠玑 ①pearl;gem ②exquisite (or excellent) wording of a writing
珠江 the Zhujiang River;the Pearl River
珠帘 pearl-decorated screen or curtain;bead curtain
珠母 pearl oyster
珠算 reckoning by the abacus;calculation with an abacus
珠子 ①pearl ②bead
珠光体 pearlite
珠母贝 pearl shell
珠光宝气 resplendent with jewels;bedecked with jewels
珠联璧合 strings of pearls and girdles of jade—a perfect pair;a happy combination
珠围翠绕 ①(of a woman) be gorgeously dressed and richly ornamented ②be surrounded by attending maids
珠圆玉润 round as pearls and smooth as jade—excellent singing or polished writing
珠穆朗玛峰 Mount Qomolangma (known to the West as Mount Everest)

株 [zhū]
Ⅰ 名 ①base of a tree;stump ②individual plant;plant Ⅱ 量 (of plants and trees):三株枣树 three jujube trees
株距 spacing in the rows
株连 involve (others) in a criminal case;implicate
株式会社 Kabuskiki Kaisha;limited-liability company;limited company

诸 [zhū]
Ⅰ 形 all;numerous;various Ⅱ 代 (mixed pronunciation of 之于 or 之乎):有诸？ Is this true?
诸多 a good deal;a lot of
诸公 gentlemen
诸侯 dukes or princes under an emperor
诸君 ladies and gentlemen;you
诸如 such as
诸色 various;all kinds
诸事 everything;every matter
诸位 ladies and gentlemen;you
诸兵种 various arms of the services
诸恶莫作 Every form of evil cannot be done.
诸如此类 things of that sort;and such like;and what not
诸事顺遂 Everything went smoothly.
诸子百家 the various schools of thought and their exponents during the period from pre-Qin times to the early years of the Han Dynasty

铢 [zhū]
量 *zhu*, ancient unit of weight, equal to 1/24 *liang* (两)

铢积寸累 accumulate little by little; build up bit by bit

铢两悉称 carry the same weight; be exactly equal

铢锱必较 stand on weight and measure

猪 [zhū]
名 pig; hog; swine; porker

猪草 greenfeed for pigs

猪场 pig farm; piggery

猪肚 pork tripe

猪肝 pork liver

猪倌 swineherd

猪獾 sand badger

猪圈 pigsty; pigpen; hogpen

猪栏 swinery; hogcote; pigsty

猪苓 umbellate pore fungus

猪猡 pig; swine

猪苗 piglet; pigling

猪排 pork chop

猪皮 pigskin; hogskin

猪群 swinery

猪肉 pork

猪舍 pig (*or* hog) house

猪食 pig feed; pigwash; swill

猪蹄 pig's trotters

猪头 pig's head

猪腿 leg of pork; ham

猪瘟 swine fever; hog cholera

猪窝 pigsty

猪血 coagulated pig's blood used as a food

猪油 lard

猪仔 porkling; piglet

猪鬃 (hog) bristles

猪丹毒 swine erysipelas; diamond-skin disease

猪肝色 liver-coloured; purplish red

猪笼草 common nepenthes

猪腰子 pork kidney

猪囊虫病 pork measles

猪气喘病 swine enzootic pneumonia

猪八戒倒打一耙 Pigsy striking backwards with his rake—make a counterattack or countercharge

蛛 [zhū]
名 spider

蛛网 spider web; cobweb

蛛蛛 spider

蛛丝马迹 the thread of a spider and the trail of a horse—clues; traces

蛛形动物 arachnid

zhú (ㄓㄨˊ)

Z

术 [zhú]
➡ shù

◇苍术 ①Chinese atractylodes ②the rhizome of Chinese atractylodes

竹 [zhú]
名 bamboo

竹板 bamboo clappers

竹编 bamboo woven articles

竹帛 bamboo slips and silk; ancient books

竹布 light blue or white cotton cloth for making summer clothes

竹材 bamboo used as lumber

竹蛏 razor clam; razor shell

竹筹 bamboo chip

竹雕 bamboo carving

竹筏 bamboo raft

竹竿 bamboo pole; bamboo

竹黄 handicraft articles made from bamboo with its green covering removed

竹鸡 bamboo partridge

竹简 bamboo slip

竹节 bamboo joint

竹刻 bamboo carving; bamboo engraving

竹帘 bamboo screen or curtain

竹林 bamboo forest; groves of bamboo

竹马 ①bamboo stick used as a toy horse ②a bamboo horse used in a folk dance

竹排 bamboo raft

竹器 articles made of bamboo

竹扦 bamboo spike

竹笋 shoots of *mao* bamboo

竹筒 thick bamboo tube

竹席 bamboo mat

竹椅 bamboo chair

竹芋 arrowroot

竹园 bamboo garden

竹纸 paper made from young bamboo

竹子 bamboo

竹板书 story recited to the rhythm of bamboo clappers

竹算子 bamboo grid (to be put in a pot for steaming food)

竹黄菌 bamboo parasitic fungus

竹节虫 stick insect; walkingstick

竹帘画 painting on a bamboo curtain

竹叶青 ①green bamboo snake ②a kind of liquor

竹枝词 ①ancient folk songs with love as their main theme ②occasional poems in the classical style devoted to local topics

竹篱茅舍 thatched cottage with bamboo fence—simple dwelling of a hermit

竹马之交 friends from childhood days

竹头木屑 bamboo ends and wood shavings—things not of much value but of some use

竹筒倒豆子 pour beans out of a bamboo tube—withhold nothing

竹篮打水一场空 draw water with a bamboo basket—achieve nothing; all in vain

逐 [zhú]
Ⅰ 动 ①pursue；seek；chase ②expel；oust；drive out Ⅱ 副 one by one；in turn：按情况逐项处理 address each case on its merits
逐步 step by step；progressively
逐出 drive out；expel；eject；kick out；oust
逐处 everywhere；in all respects
逐次 each time；gradually；successive
逐格 frame by frame
逐个 one by one
逐渐 gradually；by degrees
逐鹿 chase the deer—fight for the throne；bid for state power
逐年 year by year；year after year
逐日 day by day；every day
逐水 relieve oedema or abdominal distension through diuresis or purgation
逐条 item by item；point by point
逐一 one by one
逐字 word for word；verbatim
逐客令 order for guests to leave
逐步到位 phased implementation；phase in
逐步取消 phase out
逐步推行 phase in
逐臭之夫 ①eccentric person；eccentric ②person of depraved tastes—striving after fame and gain
逐段修改 revise (an essay，etc.) paragraph by paragraph
逐格放映 stop frame projection
逐格摄影 single frame photography
逐行扫描 line by line scan；progressive scanning
逐鹿中原 chase the deer on the Central Plains—try to seize control of the empire
逐日保费 annual premium
逐条讲解 explain point by point
逐项定价 item pricing
逐月检查 examine every month
逐字逐句 word by word and sentence by sentence；word for word
逐行倒相制 phase-alternation

烛 [zhú]
Ⅰ 名 candle Ⅱ 动 make bright with light；illuminate；light up Ⅲ 量 watt：一百烛灯泡 100-watt bulb
烛光 candlepower；candle
烛花 snuff
烛泪 gutterings of a candle
烛台 candlestick
烛芯 candlewick

舳 [zhú]
名 stern (of a ship，etc.)

瘃 [zhú]
名 chilblain

蠋 [zhú]
名 larva of a butterfly or moth

zhǔ (ㄓㄨˇ)

主 [zhǔ]
Ⅰ 名 ①host ②owner；lord；master ③God；Lord；the Master：求主保佑！ God bless me! ④person or party concerned ⑤Allah ⑥memorial tablet Ⅱ 形 principal；main Ⅲ 动 ①be in charge of；preside over；manage ②advocate；favour ③hold a definite view about sth：这事儿该怎么办，我实在没主。 I have no idea at all how to deal with this matter. ④foretell；indicate；signify：早霞主雨，晚霞主晴。 Rosy morning clouds mean rain and a rosy sunset fine weather. ⑤be of one's own accord；take the initiative
主儿 ①master；employer ②husband ③person of a specified type
主板 motherboard；mainboard
主办 direct；sponsor
主笔 ①editor in chief ②chief commentator
主币 standard currency；standard money
主编 ① chief editor (or compiler)；editor in chief ② supervise the publication of (a newspaper，magazine，etc.)；edit
主宾 guest of honour
主场 home court；host arena
主持 ①take charge (or care) of；manage；direct ②preside over；chair ③uphold；stand for
主厨 ①be the chef ②chef
主创 principal creators
主词 subject term；subject
主次 primary and secondary
主从 principal and subordinate
主打 leading
主刀 ①perform an operation ②operator
主导 leading；dominant；guiding
主调 ①top melody of a homophonic piece ②keynote (of a speech，etc.)
主动 ①take the initiative；do sth of one's own accord ②driving
主队 home team；host team
主儿 ①master；employer ②person of a specified type ③husband or fiancé
主伐 final felling (or cutting)
主犯 prime culprit；principal criminal (or offender)；principal
主峰 the highest peak in a mountain range
主妇 housewife；hostess
主干 ①trunk ②main force；mainstay
主稿 be responsible for the first draft；be the chief writer (of a joint work)
主格 the nominative case
主根 main root；taproot
主攻 main attack
主顾 customer；client

主观 subjective
主管 ①be responsible for; be in charge of ② person in charge
主和 advocate peace; be for a peaceful settlement
主婚 (usu. of the parents of the bride and the bride groom) preside over a wedding ceremony
主机 ① main engine; main processor ② lead plane; leader ③ main body of a computer (compared with display and peripherals) ④ host computer
主见 ideas (*or* thoughts) of one's own; one's own judgment; definite view
主将 chief commander; commanding general
主讲 be the speaker; give a lecture
主教 bishop
主井 main shaft
主句 main (*or* principal) clause
主角 leading role; lead; protagonist
主考 ①be in charge of an examination ②chief examiner (in a school, etc.)
主客 ①host and guest ②guest of honour
主课 main subject; major course
主力 main force; main strength of an army
主梁 girder
主粮 staple food grain
主流 ①trunk stream; mainstream ②essential or main aspect; main trend
主楼 main building in a complex
主麻 Djumah (Friday)
主谋 ①head a conspiracy; be the chief plotter ②chief instigator
主脑 ①control centre; centre of operation ② leader; chief
主仆 master and servant; master and man
主权 sovereign rights; sovereignty
主人 ①master ②host ③owner
主任 director; head; chairman
主食 staple food; principal food
主使 instigate; incite; abet
主事 be in charge; take charge
主帅 chief commander; commanding general
主诉 patient's description of symptoms
主题 theme; subject; motif; leitmotiv
主体 ①main body; main part; principal part ② subject
主位 ① status of a sovereign ② seat of the host (at table)
主文 main body of a court verdict
主席 ①chairman (of a meeting) ②chairman; president (of an organization or a state)
主线 thread (of a novel, etc.)
主项 main project; main event
主星 primary (component)
主刑 principal penalty
主凶 prime (*or* chief) culprit (in a murder

case); principal
主修 ① specialize (in a subject); major ②be responsible for the repair or overhaul (of a machine)
主演 act the leading role (in a play or film); star
主要 main; chief; principal; major
主页 home page
主义 doctrine; -ism
主意 ①idea; plan ②decision; definite view
主因 main cause; main reason; major cause
主音 keynote; tonic
主语 subject
主宰 dominate; dictate; decide
主战 advocate war
主张 ① advocate; stand for; maintain; hold ② view; position; stand; proposition
主政 head the government
主旨 purport; substance; gist
主治 indications
主轴 main shaft; spindle
主子 master; boss
主裁判 chief referee; head referee
主菜单 main menu
主持人 compère; host; hostess; interviewer; moderator; anchorman, anchorperson (of a news or talkshow program)
主单位 basic unit (as a standard of measurement)
主导风 prevailing wind
主动脉 aorta
主攻手 ace spiker (in volleyball)
主和派 peace party
主焦点 prime (*or* principal) focus
主教练 principal coach
主考官 official in charge of an imperial examination; chief examiner
主力舰 capital ship
主力军 main (*or* principal) force
主渠道 main channel
主人公 leading character in a novel, etc.; hero or heroine; protagonist
主人翁 ①master ②leading character in a novel, etc.; hero or heroine; protagonist
主视图 front view; elevation
主题词 theme word; catch phrase
主题歌 theme song
主谓句 subject-predicate sentence
主文件 master file
主席台 rostrum; platform
主席团 presidium; bureau
主心骨 ①backbone; mainstay; pillar ②a definite view; one's own judgment
主星序 main sequence
主旋律 main melody; top melody; theme
主战派 war faction; war party; war hawk
主板市场 major market; leading market; main

board of the stock market
主导力量 the leading force;the main force
主导思想 dominant ideas;guiding ideology
主导主题 leitmotiv
主调音乐 homophony
主动脉弓 arch of aorta
主动脉炎 aortitis
主动语态 active voice
主发动机 sustainer
主攻部队 main attack force
主攻方面 main phase of attack
主攻方向 main direction of attack
主观主义 subjectivism
主管官员 officer-in-charge
主管机关 authorities concerned
主计算机 host computer
主力兵团 main formations
主力队员 top players of a team
主任委员 head member of a committee
主随客便 what the guest wishes,the host will oblige
主题公园 theme park
主题音乐 theme music
主体工程 principal part of a project
主体经济 principal sector of the economy;mainstay of the economy
主谓词组 subject-predicate word group
主要矛盾 principal contradiction
主旨演讲 keynote speech
主治医生　physician-in-charge; doctor in charge of a case
主观能动性 subjective initiative;conscious activity;dynamism
主流和支流 principal and secondary aspects
主权换治权 sovereignty for right to rule
主观唯心主义 subjective idealism
主权共享,治权分属 sharing sovereignty and separated administration

拄 ［zhǔ］
囡 lean on (a stick,etc.):拄拐棍儿 use a walking stick;with a stick

渚 ［zhǔ］
囝 small piece of land surrounded by water;islet

煮 ［zhǔ］
囡 boil;stew;cook:煮面条 cook noodles/水煮开了。The water is boiling.
煮饭 cook rice;cook meals
煮沸 boiling;elixation;coction;boil
煮呢 potting
煮熟 cook thoroughly
煮粥 cook congee
煮豆燃萁 burn beanstalks to cook beans—fratricidal strife

属 ［zhǔ］
囡 ① join; connect; combine ② centre (one's attention,etc.) upon;concentrate on

⟹ shǔ
属草 draft (or draw up) a document
属望 centre one's hope on; look forward to; expect
属文 compose a piece of prose writing
属意 fix one's mind on sb (as one's choice, favourite,etc.)
属垣有耳 walls have ears; beware of eavesdroppers

褚 ［zhǔ］
Ⅰ 囝 ①silk floss ②bag;satchel;sack Ⅱ 囡 pad with silk wadding ⟹ chǔ

嘱 ［zhǔ］
囡 exhort;advise;urge;entrust
嘱咐 enjoin;tell;exhort
嘱托 entrust

瞩 ［zhǔ］
囡 fasten one's look on;look steadily;gaze; focus eyes on
瞩目 fix one's eyes upon;focus one's attention upon
瞩望 ① look forward to ② gaze at;look long and steadily upon

zhù(ㄓㄨˋ)

伫 ［zhù］
囡 stand for a long time
伫候 stand waiting
伫立 stand still for a long while

苎 ［zhù］
苎麻 ramie

芧 ［zhù］
囝 ramie ⟹ xù

助 ［zhù］
囡 give help to;help;assist;aid;support:助她一臂之力 lend (or give) her a (helping) hand
助残 help the handicapped
助产 practise midwifery
助词 auxiliary word
助耕 help in farmwork
助攻 holding (or secondary) attack
助剂 auxiliary
助教 assistant professor (of a college faculty)
助老 help the elderly
助理 assistant
助力 a helping hand;help;assistance
助跑 approach run,run-up
助燃 combustion-supporting
助手 assistant;helper;aide
助推 promote
助威 boost the morale of;cheer (for)
助兴 liven things up;add to the fun
助学 give financial aid to students
助养 help to foster
助益 benefit;help

Z

助战 ①assist in fighting ②bolster sb's morale
助长 encourage;abet;foster;foment
助爆药 booster charge;booster
助残日 Day to Help the Disabled
助产士 midwife
助动词 auxiliary verb
助力车 bicycle fitted with a small motor,using mechanical power to replace pedalling
助熔剂 flux
助色团 auxochrome
助听器 audiphone;hearing aid;deaf-aid
助推级 space booster
助学金 stipend;grant-in-aid
助桀为虐 aid King Jie in his tyrannical rule—aid and abet the evil-doer
助理编辑 assistant editor
助理导演 assistant director (of a film or play)
助人为乐 find it a pleasure to help others;take pleasure in helping people
助纣为虐 aid King Zhou in his tyrannical rule—aid and abet the evil-doer
助理工程师 assistant engineer

住 [zhù]
〔动〕①live;stay;reside;dwell:住进新房 move into a new house ②stop;end;cease:风停雨住。 The wind died down and the rain stopped. ③(used after some verbs as a complement indicating a halt, stillness, fastness, etc.):记住 remember/接住! Catch it! /站住! Halt! /他没被吓住。 He was not intimidated.
住持 abbot
住处 residence;dwelling (place);lodging; quarters
住读 (of a student) board at school
住房 housing;lodgings
住户 household;resident
住家 ①(of one's family) live;reside in ② household;resident
住口 shut up;stop talking
住声 stop talking (or laughing,crying)
住手 stay one's hand;stop
住宿 stay;put up;get accommodation
住所 dwelling place;residence;domicile
住校 (of a student) board at school
住院 be in hospital;be hospitalized
住宅 residence;dwelling
住址 address;dwelling (place);lodging
住嘴 stop talking
住院部 inpatient department
住院处 admission office (in a hospital)
住宅区 residential quarters (or district)
住房改革 housing reform
住房津贴 house allowance
住房面积 floor space
住房汽车 motor home
住房质量 quality of residential building

住院病人 inpatient
住院医生 resident (physician)
住宅保险 residence insurance
住宅建设 housing construction
住宅设计 housing design
住宅小区 dwelling districts;housing district
住房公积金 collective housing funds; public accumulation funds for housing;housing reserve
住房零首付 zero-*yuan* first payment (for apartment)
住房商品化 housing commercialization;commercialization of housing
住房制度改革 housing (system) reform
住宅小区建设 construction of neighbourhoods
住房分配货币化 monetize housing distribution

纻 [zhù]
〔名〕cloth made from ramie
纻衣 ramie clothes

杼 [zhù]
〔名〕①reed ②shuttle

贮 [zhù]
〔动〕store;save;keep;lay aside
贮备 store up;have in reserve;lay aside
贮藏 store up;lay in
贮存 store;keep in storage
贮蓄 ①store up;lay in;conserve ②storage or saving
贮运 storage and transportation
贮木场 timber depot;timber yard;lumber yard
贮粮备荒 store up grain against a lean year; store away grain against famine

注 [zhù]
I〔动〕①pour;fill ②pay full attention;concentrate;fix ③make annotations;explain with notes;annotate ④put on record;record;register II〔名〕①stakes ②notes III〔量〕(often used of money or business transactions):两注买卖 two business transactions/一注交易 a deal
注册 ①register ②log-in
注带 casting
注定 be doomed;be destined
注脚 footnote
注解 ①annotate;explain with notes ②(explanatory) note;annotation
注明 give clear indication of
注目 gaze at;fix one's eyes on
注入 ①pour into;empty into ②petroleum injection
注射 inject
注视 look attentively at;gaze at
注释 explanatory note;annotation
注疏 commentary and sub-commentary
注水 petroleum water flooding
注塑 mould plastics
注文 explanatory notes;notes
注销 cancel;write off
注意 pay attention to;take note (or notice) of

注音 phonetic notation
注油 ①oiling;greasing ②fuel-injection
注重 lay stress on;pay attention to;attach importance to
注资 capital infusion
注册处 registration office;registrar's office
注目礼 salute with eyes
注入式 injection type
注射剂 injection
注射器 injector;syringe
注水肉 water-injected meat
注意力 attention
注油枪 grease gun;oil gun
注册商标 registered trademark
注册证书 registration certificate
注册资本 registered capital
注销支票 cancel check
注意广度 attention span;range of attention
注意事项 matters needing attention;points for attention
注音字母 the national phonetic alphabet
注册会计师 certified public account(CPA)
注入新的活力 inject new vigour
注意力缺乏症 attention deficit disorder

驻 [zhù]
㪇 ①stop;halt;stay ②be stationed;be posted;encamp:常驻代表 permanent representative
驻兵 station troops
驻波 standing wave
驻地 ①place where troops,etc. are stationed ②seat (of a local administrative organ)
驻防 be on garrison duty;garrison
驻军 ①station troops ②garrison troops;garrison
驻守 garrison;defend
驻屯 (of troops) be stationed;be quartered
驻颜 preserve youthful looks
驻扎 (of troops) be stationed;be quartered
驻足 halt;stop;go no further
驻在国 state to which a diplomatic envoy is accredited
驻港部队 People's Liberation Army garrison in Hong Kong
驻外机构 institution functioning (or stationed) abroad

柱 [zhù]
㝯 ①post;pillar;column:大理石圆柱 marble column ②column-like thing ③cylinder
柱础 stone base of a column;plinth
柱顶 capital
柱基 stylopodium
柱脚 shoe;zocle;stylopodium;stand;heel;foot stall
柱廊 colonnade
柱面 cylinder
柱身 shaft

柱石 pillar;mainstay
柱头 ①stigma ②column cap;column head ③ post;pillar
柱子 post;pillar
柱座 column base;plinth
柱状剖面 columnar section;geologic column

炷 [zhù]
Ⅰ 㝯 wick (of an oil lamp) Ⅱ 㪇 incense;burn Ⅲ 㝱:三炷香 three burning joss sticks
炷香 burn a joss stick

祝 [zhù]
㪇 ①offer good wishes;wish;blesh:祝你早日康复。 I wish you a speedy recovery. /祝你生日快乐! Happy birthday to you! /祝你一路顺风。 Have a pleasant journey;Bon voyage! /祝你俩顺利。 Good luck to you both. /祝您长寿! (greeting on sb's birthday) Many happy returns (of the day)! /祝贵国繁荣昌盛。 May your country enjoy prosperity! /祝你成功! Wish you success!;May success wait upon your efforts! /祝你新年快乐! Happy New Year to you! ②cut
祝词 ①congratulatory speech (at a ceremony,etc.);congratulations ②prayers at sacrificial rites in ancient times
祝祷 pray;say one's prayers
祝福 blessing;benediction
祝贺 congratulate
祝捷 celebrate a victory
祝酒 drink a toast;toast
祝寿 congratulate (an elderly person) on his or her birthday
祝文 congratulatory message
祝愿 wish
祝发为僧 cut off one's hair and become a monk

疰 [zhù]
疰夏 ①a summer disease,usu. contracted by children with symptoms of fever,loss of appetite,lassitude,etc. ②loss of appetite and weight in summer

著 [zhù]
Ⅰ 㓝 marked;conspicuous;outstanding;notable Ⅱ 㪇 ① show;display;prove ② write;compose Ⅲ 㝯 work;book ➡ zhuó
著称 celebrated;famous
著录 put down in writing;record
著名 famous;celebrated;well-known
著书 author (or compile) a book
著述 ①write;compile ②book;work
著者 author;writer
著作 ①work;book;writings ②write
著作权 copyright (of the author)
著书立说 write books to expound a theory; write scholarly works
著述等身 one's writings piled up to one's own

Z

height—be a prolific writer

蛀 [zhù]

Ⅰ 〔名〕moth; borer Ⅱ 〔动〕(of moths, etc.) eat into; bore through: 木头已遭虫蛀。The wood was worm-eaten.

蛀齿 decayed tooth; dental caries

蛀虫 insect that eats books, clothes or wood; moth; borer

蛀空 worm-eaten hollow

蛀眼 pinworm holes; worm channel

蛀心虫 borer

铸 [zhù]

〔动〕cast; coin; found: 铜铸的古钟 bronze bell

铸币 coin; specie

铸成 cast into

铸错 commit blunders; make grave mistakes

铸锭 ingot casting

铸钢 cast steel

铸工 ① foundry work ② foundry worker; founder

铸件 cast; casting

铸就 cast into

铸模 mould for casting; matrix

铸钱 mint money; coin money

铸石 cast stone; molten-rock casting; stone casting

铸铁 ①iron casting ②cast iron

铸铜 cast copper

铸型 casting mould

铸造 casting; founding

铸币权 mintage

铸成大错 make a gross error; make a stupendous mistake

铸工车间 foundry (shop)

铸工鼓风机 foundry fan

筑 [zhù]

〔动〕build; construct: 构筑工事 build defences (or fortifications)

筑坝 damming

筑巢 ①build nest ②build infrastructure

筑堤 fill; embank; banking; dike; construct a dam

筑路 construct a road; pave a road; build a road

筑埂机 ridger

筑巢引凤 attract talented people by providing them with good working conditions and fanciful living facilities; make facilities available first to attract people of talent

筑室道谋 ask every passerby how to build one's house—have no idea or plan of one's own (and accomplish nothing)

zhuā (ㄓㄨㄚ)

Z ## 抓 [zhuā]

〔动〕①seize; clutch; grab; grasp: 抓住一点小事大做文章 seize on a trifle and make an is-

sue of it; make a fuss over sth trivial; make a mountain out of a molehill ② scratch ③ arrest; catch; pressgang ④vie for (work) ⑤lay stress on; stress: 抓主要矛盾 identify and tackle the principal contradiction ⑥ be in charge of; be responsible for; 她是抓人事的。She is in charge of personnel matters. ⑦attract; grip or hold attention

抓膘 fatten

抓兵 pressgang a man into military service

抓捕 arrest; catch

抓茬 find fault; pick holes; pick a quarrel

抓差 draft sb for a particular task; press sb into service

抓点 concentrate on work at selected units

抓丁 pressgang able-bodied men

抓赌 (of police) break up a gambling party and arrest the participants

抓夫 pressgang; press people into service

抓哏 (of a comedian, etc.) throw in impromptu lines

抓好 do a good job of; make great efforts to

抓获 catch (a criminal, etc.); capture; seize

抓紧 firmly grasp; pay close attention to; rush in

抓举 snatch

抓挠 ① scratch ② mess about ③ come to blows; fight ④prepare sth hastily ⑤sb or sth that one can rely on ⑥solution to a difficulty

抓拍 ①take a candid photograph (or picture) ②a candid photograph (or picture); candid

抓破 injure (or damage) by scratching (or clawing)

抓钱 grab money; raise money

抓人 arrest sb; take sb into custody

抓瞎 find oneself at a loss; be in a rush and muddle; be thrown off balance

抓痒 scratch an itch; relieve the itching

抓药 ① make up (or fill) a prescription of Chinese herbal medicine ②have a prescription of Chinese herbal medicine made up (or filled)

抓住 ①catch (or seize) hold of; grip ②catch; capture ③grip sb's attention

抓本质 grasp the essence

抓大事 concentrate on major issues

抓福利 pay special attention to the welfare

抓工夫 make good use of one's time; find time (to do sth)

抓机遇 seize a good opportunity

抓阄儿 draw lots

抓空子 find time (to do sth)

抓苗头 watch out for the first signs (or the symptoms of a trend)

抓破脸 scratch each other's face—quarrel openly

抓要点 grasp the main points
抓壮丁 pressgang able-bodied men
抓不起来 ① cannot get hold of or lift sth ② cannot manage sth （because of inability, etc.）
抓大放小 manage large enterprises while adopt a flexible policy toward small ones; focus on large enterprises while give a free hand to small ones
抓点带面 draw experience from selected units to promote overall work
抓耳挠腮 tweak one's ears and scratch one's cheeks （as a sign of anxiety or delight）
抓尖儿卖块 go out of one's way to curry favour
抓两头,带中间 grasp the two ends to bring along the middle—sustain the advanced and help the backward so as to encourage the vast majority to move along

挝 [zhuā]
动 strike; beat (a drum)
挝鼓 beat a drum

zhuǎ（ㄓㄨㄚˇ）

爪 [zhuǎ]
名 claw; talon; paw ⇒ zhǎo
爪儿 ① paw of a small animal ② foot of a utensil
爪子 claw; paw; talon
爪尖儿 pig's trotters; pettitoes

zhuāi（ㄓㄨㄞ）

拽 [zhuāi]
动 fling; cast; throw; hurl; 把球拽给我。Fling me the ball; Throw the ball to me. ⇒ zhuài

zhuǎi（ㄓㄨㄞˇ）

转 [zhuǎi]
⇒ zhuǎn; zhuàn
转文 lard one's speech with literary allusions; use flowery language

跩 [zhuǎi]
动 waddle; 那胖子一跩一跩地走到塘边。The stout man waddled to the pond.

zhuài（ㄓㄨㄞˋ）

拽 [zhuài]
动 pull; drag; haul ⇒ zhuāi

zhuān（ㄓㄨㄢ）

专 [zhuān]
Ⅰ 形 concentrated on; special; devoted Ⅱ 名 ① expert ② college for professional training Ⅲ 动 have a monopoly of; monopolize

专案 special case for investigation; case
专长 speciality; special skill (or knowledge)
专场 special performance; show intended for a limited audience
专车 special train (or car)
专诚 for a particular purpose; specially
专程 special trip
专电 special dispatch (sent by a reporter to a newspaper)
专断 make an arbitrary decision; act arbitrarily
专访 exclusive interview on a specific topic
专攻 specialize in; do special research on
专柜 special counter in shop (for specific products)
专函 special letter
专号 special issue (of a periodical)
专横 imperious; peremptory; domineering
专机 ① special plane ② private plane
专辑 special edition
专家 expert; specialist
专刊 ① special issue or column ② monograph
专科 ① special field of study; specialized subject; specialty ② college for professional training; training school
专款 special fund
专栏 special column
专力 with concentrated effort
专利 patent
专列 a special train; chartered trains for special uses
专论 monograph
专卖 exclusive possession of the trade in some commodity; monopoly
专门 special; specialized
专名 proper name
专区 prefecture
专权 arrogate all powers to oneself; monopolize power
专人 person specially assigned for a task or job
专任 full-time; regular
专属 exclusive
专署 prefectural commissioner's office
专题 special subject; special topic
专线 ① special railway line ② special telephone line; line for special use
专项 assigned (to a use); dedicated; specialized
专心 concentrate one's attention; be absorbed
专修 specialize in
专业 ① special field of study; specialized subject; speciality; discipline ② specialized trade (or profession); special line
专一 single-minded; concentrated
专营 exclusive sale rights; monopoly under exclusive government control

Z

专用 for a special purpose
专有 related to a particular person or thing
专员 ① assistant director; (administrative) commissioner ② person specially assigned for a job
专约 convention
专责 specific responsibility
专政 dictatorship
专职 ①sole duty; specific duty ②full-time
专制 ①autocracy ②autocratic; despotic
专注 concentrate one's attention on; be absorbed in; devote one's mind to
专著 monograph; treatise; a book on a special subject
专案组 special group for the examination of a case; special case section (or division)
专利法 patent law
专利费 patent fee
专利局 patent bureau
专利品 patent; patented article
专利权 patent right; patent
专利税 patent tax
专卖店 exclusive agency; franchised store; speciality store
专卖权 patent right
专名号 a line under (or beside) a word to show that it is a proper noun (e.g. 西安, 诸葛亮)
专升本 upgrade from junior college student to university student
专修科 special (training) course
专业户 professional household; specialized household
专业课 specialized course
专案材料 material connected with a case; dossier
专案人员 person engaged in the examination of a case
专横跋扈 imperious and despotic; arrogant and domineering
专家门诊 outpatient consultation by a specialist
专家系统 expert system
专科学校 college for professional training; training school
专科医生 (medical) specialist
专控商品 goods under special control (or regulation); controlled commodities (commodities controlled by the government)
专款专用 earmark a fund for its specified purpose only; the funds used for specified purposes
专栏作家 columnist
专利技术 patent technology
专利配方 patented formula
专利申请 patent application
专利证书 letter of patent

专门机构 special agency; special organ
专门列车 a special train; chartered trains for special uses
专门人材 people with professional skill; specialized personnel
专门术语 technical terms; nomenclature
专门知识 specialized knowledge; expertise; technical know-how
专属渔区 exclusive fishing zone
专属主权 exclusive sovereignty
专题报告 report (or lecture) on a special topic
专题调查 investigation of a special subject
专题论文 disquisition
专题讨论 seminar
专题研究 monographic study
专题著作 monograph; treatise
专项清理 cleanup as a special project
专项训练 specialized training
专项资金 special funds
专心致志 wholly absorbed; with single-hearted devotion
专业队伍 professional contingent
专业分工 division of labour based on specialization
专业人员 personnel in a specific field
专业学校 vocational school; specialized school
专业银行 specialist bank; specialized bank
专业知识 professional knowledge
专用款项 control account
专用线路 private line
专有技术 proprietary technology; know-how
专政机关 organ of dictatorship
专制君主 autocrat
专制政府 autocratic government
专制政体 autocracy
专家鉴定书 expert statement; written testimony
专属管辖权 exclusive jurisdiction
专属经济区 exclusive economic zone
专题广告片 informercial
专题研讨会 symposium
专门人民法院 special people's court
专项审计制度 separate item auditing system
专业技术证书 certificate of vocational skill
专业生产会议 a conference on specialized trades
专项粮食储备制度 special grain reserve system

砖 [zhuān]

①brick ②brick-like thing
砖茶 brick tea
砖厂 brickfield; brickyard
砖雕 carved brick; brick carving
砖房 brick house
砖坯 unfired brick
砖墙 brick wall

砖头 ［zhuāntóu］ fragment of a brick
砖头 ［zhuāntou］ brick
砖窑 brickkiln
砖红壤 laterite
砖块儿 fragment of a brick
砖红壤性土 lateritic soil

颛 ［zhuān］
囮 ①ignorant；benighted ②good and honest

zhuǎn（ㄓㄨㄢˇ）

转 ［zhuǎn］
囝 ①turn；shift；change；transform：向右转 turn to the right；right face；right turn ②pass on；forward；transfer：请把这本书转寄到新地址。Please forward the book to the new address. ➡zhuǎi；zhuàn
转包 pass-contract
转变 change；transform
转播 relay (a radio or TV broadcast)
转产 (of a factory) switch to the manufacture of another line of products；change the line of production
转车 change trains (*or* buses)；transfer to another train (*or* bus)
转船 change to another ship；transship
转达 pass on；convey；communicate
转道 make a detour；go by way of
转递 pass on；transmit
转调 ①modulation ②(of a government employee, etc.) be transferred to another post；transfer
转动 turn；move；turn round
转发 transmit
转法 facing
转干 (of workers) be promoted to the position of a cadre (usu. administrative position)
转岗 transfer (*or* switch) to another job；change jobs；be transferred to a new job
转港 route through one port to another
转告 pass on (word)；communicate；transmit
转轨 ①shift from one track to another；retrack ②undergo a fundamental change
转行 change profession；change jobs
转化 change；transform
转换 change；transform
转会 transfer
转机 ①a favourable turn；a turn for the better ②change plane
转嫁 ①(of women) marry again；remarry ②shift；transfer
转交 pass on；transmit
转角 street corner；corner
转借 lend sth (*or* one's personal certificate) to sb else
转口 transit
转脸 ①turn one's face ②in no time；in the twinkling of an eye

转录 make a copy of a pre-recorded cassette tape or videotape；copy；dub
转卖 resell
转年 ①coming year；next year ②following year
转念 reconsider and give up an idea；think better of
转让 transfer the ownership of；make over
转入 change over to；shift to；switch to
转身 (of a person) turn round；face about
转生 reincarnation；transmigration
转世 reincarnation；transmigration
转手 ①pass on ②sell what one has bought
转述 report；relate sth as told by another
转瞬 in the twinkling of an eye；in an instant；in a flash
转送 ①pass on；transmit on ②make a present of what one has been given
转体 truck rotation，turn，twist
转头 ①(of a person) turn round；face about ②(of a car, etc.) make a U-turn ③repent
转托 ask someone else to do what is asked of one
转弯 turn a corner；make a turn
转系 (of a college student) transfer from one department to another
转向 ①change direction ②change one's political stand
转型 transformation；change the mode of production
转学 (of a student) transfer from one school to another
转眼 in the twinkling of an eye；in an instant；in a flash
转业 ①(of an armyman) be transferred to civilian work ②(of laid-off worker) transfer to a new occupation；move to a new area
转移 ①shift；transfer；divert ②change；transform ③metastasis
转义 transferred meaning (a collective name for extended meaning and metaphorical meaning)
转译 re-translation
转引 quote from a secondary source
转院 (of a patient) transfer from one hospital to another
转运 ①have a change of luck；luck turns in one's favour ②transport；transfer；transship
转韵 change rhyme (in a classic poem)
转载 reprint sth that has been published elsewhere；reprint
转赠 make a present of what one has been given
转战 fight in one place after another
转账 transfer accounts

转折 ①a turn in the course of events ②transition（of an essay）

转正 ①（of a probationary member of the Communist Party of China）become a full member after completion of the probationary period ②（of a temporary worker）become a regular worker

转制 transform the system

转租 sublet；sublease

转氨酶 glutamic-pyruvic transaminase（GPT）

转发器 transponder

转关系 transfer the registration of Party membership，etc. from one unit to another

转换债 roll-over bonds

转会费 transfer fee

转基因 transgenetic；fenetically modified

转接器 adapter

转让方 assignor

转让费 royalty

转让人 assignor

转体跳 turning leap；turning jump

转弯子 change one's position or get one's thinking straightened out

转向架 bogie（fitted under a railway carriage）

转载权 right of reprint

转折点 turning point

转辙器 switch

转败为胜 turn defeat into victory

转轨措施 changeover measures

转轨经济 transition economy

转化机制 shift to new management mechanism

转口贸易 carrying trade；entrepot trade

转亏为盈 turn loss into gain；show a turn from loss to profit

转怒为喜 one's anger gives way to delight

转让作价 transfer pricing

转生来世 next reincarnation

转体动作 rotational movement

转体两周 double turn

转体跳水 twist dive

转弯抹角 ①full of twists and turns ②beat about the bush；speak in a roundabout way

转危为安 take a turn for the better and be out of danger；pull through

转业培训 vocational training for re-employment

转账支票 deposit check；check for deposit only

转基因技术 transgenesis

转基因食品 genetically-engineered plant and food；genetically-altered food；Franken food

转变政府职能 transform the governmental function

传 ［zhuàn］
（名）①commentaries on classics ②biography　为他立传 write his biography ③novel or story written in historical style ⇒chuán

传记 biography

传略 brief biography；biographical sketch

转 ［zhuàn］
Ⅰ（动）①rotate；revolve；spin ②turn round；move about；circle：他绕着湖转了两圈。He walked twice round the lake. Ⅱ（名）revolution：这台发动机每分钟三千转。The engine turns over at 3000 revolutions per minute（or at 3000 rpm）. ⇒zhuǎn；zhuǎi

转碟 plate-spinning

转动 turn；revolve；rotate

转筋 ①have a cramp（esp. in the leg）；have a twisted muscle ②convulsion；spasm

转铃 revolving bell

转炉 converter

转门 revolving door

转盘 ①turntable（as of a record player）②sports giant stride ③disc-spinning ④petroleum rotary table

转圈 circle；go round and round

转数 revolution

转速 rotational speed

转台 revolving stage

转梯 spiral stairs

转向 lose one's bearings；get lost

转椅 swivel chair；revolving chair

转悠 ①turn；move from side to side ②stroll；saunter；take a leisurely walk

转轴 axle

转转 take a short walk；go for a stroll

转子 rotor

转笔刀 pencil sharpener

转速计 tachometer

转弯子 beat about the bush；speak in a roundabout way

转轮手枪 revolver

赚 ［zhuàn］
Ⅰ（动）①make a profit；gain ②earn Ⅱ（名）profit ⇒zuàn

赚钱 make money；make a profit

赚头 profit

撰 ［zhuàn］
（动）write；compose

撰稿 contribute

撰述 ①write；compile ②book；work

撰文 write an article

撰写 write（usu. short articles）

撰著 write；compose

篆 ［zhuàn］
Ⅰ（名）①seal character ②seal Ⅱ（动）write seal characters

篆额 write seal characters on the top part of a tablet

Z zhuàn（ㄓㄨㄢˋ）

篆刻 seal cutting
篆书 seal character
篆体 seal script
篆字 seal character

馔 [zhuàn]
名 food

zhuāng（ㄓㄨㄤ）

妆 [zhuāng]
Ⅰ 动 make up;wear makeup;apply makeup Ⅱ 名 ①woman's personal adornments or ornaments ②trousseau;dowry
妆扮 dress up;attire;deck out
妆点 decorate;dress up;deck out
妆奁 trousseau;dowry
妆饰 ①adorn;dress up;deck out ②makeup
妆梳 make up and dress up
妆台 dressing table

庄 [zhuāng]
Ⅰ 名 ①village;hamlet ②manor;estate ③place of business ④banker Ⅱ 形 serious;sober;solemn;grave
庄户 peasant household
庄家 ①banker (in a gambling game) ②investor who has abundant capital,buy and sell huge amounts of shares and can affect the stock market trend
庄稼 crops
庄严 solemn;dignified;stately
庄园 manor
庄重 serious;grave;solemn;sedate
庄子 village;hamlet
庄稼地 cropland;fields
庄稼汉 farmer;peasant
庄稼人 peasant;farmer
庄户人家 peasant family
庄稼活儿 farm work

桩 [zhuāng]
Ⅰ 名 stake;pile;post Ⅱ 量 一桩丑闻 a scandal/一桩错案 a mishandled case;a miscarriage of justice/一桩小事 a trifle
桩墩 pile pier
桩砦 post obstacles
桩子 stake;pile

装 [zhuāng]
Ⅰ 动 ①dress up;attire;deck;act;play the part (or role) of ②pretend;feign;fake;make believe ③load;pack;fill;hold:装车 load a truck (or train, or cart) ④install;fit;assemble:装保险锁 fit a safety lock/装电话 have a telephone installed/装收音机 assemble a radio ⑤bind;bookbind Ⅱ 名 ①clothing;dress;suit;coufit ②outfit for a journey;luggage:轻装旅行 travel light ③stage makeup and costume
装扮 ①dress up;attire;deck out ②disguise;masquerade

装备 ①equip;fit out ②equipment;outfit
装裱 mount (a picture,etc.)
装病 pretend sickness;feign illness;malinger
装舱 stow the hold (with cargo)
装船 shipment
装点 decorate;dress;deck
装订 binding;bookbinding
装潢 ① mount (a picture, etc.); decorate;dress ②decoration;mounting;packaging
装货 load (cargo)
装甲 ①plate armour ②armoured
装假 pretend;feign;make believe
装殓 dress and lay a corpse in a coffin
装料 ①feed (a machine) ②loading;charging
装配 assemble;fit together
装腔 behave affectedly;be artificial
装傻 act dumb;pretend not to know;pretend to be naive or stupid
装设 install;fix;fit
装饰 decorate;adorn;ornament;deck
装束 ①dress;attire ②pack up (for a journey)
装睡 pretend sleep;sham sleep
装死 feign death;sham dead
装蒜 pretend not to know;feign ignorance;play dumb
装填 load;ram
装相 pretend;put on an act
装卸 ①load and unload ②assemble and disassemble
装修 fit up (a house,etc.)
装药 powder charge;filling
装运 load and transport;ship
装载 loading
装帧 binding and layout (of a book,magazine,etc.)
装置 ①install;fit ②installation;unit;device;plant
装作 pretend to be;disguise as
装糊涂 pretend not to know;feign ignorance;play the fool
装幌子 put up a front;maintain an outward show;keep up appearances
装货单 shipping order
装货港 port of shipment;port of loading
装甲兵 armoured force (or troops)
装甲车 armoured car;armoured vehicle
装甲舰 ironclad (a warship)
装甲师 armoured division
装门面 put up a front;maintain an outward show;keep up appearances
装配工 assembler;fitter
装配件 assembly parts
装配线 assembly line
装饰布 upholstery fabrics
装饰品 ornament
装饰音 grace note;grace;ornament
装孙子 ①pretend to be helpless and miserable

Z

②pretend not to know;feign ignorance
装卸工 loader;stevedore
装样子 put on an act;do sth for appearance sake
装备精良 well equipped
装疯卖傻 feign madness and act like an idiot
装潢门面 do window dressing;put up a facade;keep up appearances
装机容量 installed capacity
装聋作哑 pretend to be deaf and dumb;feign ignorance
装模作样 be affected;attitudinize;put on an act;behave in an affected way
装配车间 assembly shop;fitting shop
装腔作势 be affected (*or* pretentious);strike a pose;put on airs
装神弄鬼 purposely make a mystery of simple things;be deliberately mystifying
装饰艺术 art deco
装卸时间 lay day
装甲输送车 armoured carrier

zhuǎng（ㄓㄨㄤˇ）

奘 [zhuǎng]
形 big and thick;thickset;stout;robust：他长得又高又奘。He is tall and burly;He is of great stature. ➡zàng

zhuàng（ㄓㄨㄤˋ）

壮 [zhuàng]
Ⅰ 形 ①having great strength;strong;robust ② magnificent;splendid;grand Ⅱ 动 strengthen;improve;make better
壮大 ①grow in strength;expand;strengthen ②thick and strong;bulky
壮胆 build up sb's courage;boost sb's courage
壮丁 able-bodied man (subject to conscription)
壮工 unskilled labourer
壮观 grand (*or* magnificent) sight
壮健 strong and healthy;sturdy;sthenia
壮举 magnificent feat;heroic undertaking
壮阔 vast;grand;magnificent;grandiose
壮丽 majestic;magnificent;glorious
壮烈 heroic;brave
壮美 majestic;magnificent
壮苗 strong sprout
壮年 the more robust years of a person's life (between thirty and fifty);prime of life
壮士 brave man;heroic man;hero;warrior
壮实 sturdy;robust
壮伟 grand;lofty;magnificent
壮心 great aspiration;lofty ideal
壮志 great aspiration;lofty ideal
壮族 the Zhuang (*or* Chuang) nationality
壮军威 add to military prowess

壮劳力 ①strong labour power ②an able-bodied adult (esp. for farming)
壮声势 lend impetus and strength;enhance fame and influence
壮志凌云 with soaring (*or* high) aspirations
壮志未酬 with one's lofty aspirations unrealized

状 [zhuàng]
Ⅰ 名 ①shape;form;appearance：呈衰老状 old and feeble;senile;decrepit ②state of affairs;situation;condition ③account;record ④written complaint;lawsuit ⑤certificate Ⅱ 动 describe;depict
状词 written complaint;plaint;indictment
状况 condition;state;state of affairs
状貌 appearance;form
状态 state;condition;state of affairs
状语 adverbial modifier;adverbial
状元 ① Number One Scholar, title conferred on the one who came first in the highest imperial examination ② the very best (in any field)
状纸 official form for filing a lawsuit
状子 written complaint;plaint;indictment
状态图 state diagram
状元秀 top pick

撞 [zhuàng]
动 ①bump against;knock down;crash;collide：把门撞开 ram the door open/头撞在路灯杆子上 bump one's head into a lamppost ② meet by chance;run into;come across：今儿个真是撞鬼了，干什么都不顺利。What bad luck! Nothing is going on well today. ③ probe;try ④barge;dash;rush
撞车 ① collision of vehicles ② clash of opinions (*or* interests) ③（of two meetings,etc.) clash
撞击 ram;dash against;strike
撞见 meet (*or* discover) by chance;run across;catch sb in the act
撞骗 look about for a chance to swindle;swindle
撞墙 run up against a wall;be rebuffed
撞衫 resemblance in wearing
撞锁 ①spring lock ②find that sb is not home
撞针 firing pin (in a firearm)
撞运气 try one's luck
撞机事件 air (*or* plane) collision incident

幢 [zhuàng]
量 (for buildings)：一幢八层楼房 a eight-storeyed building ➡chuáng

zhuī（ㄓㄨㄟ）

隹 [zhuī]
名 (in ancient books) bird with a short tail
追 [zhuī]
动 ① chase after;run after;pursue;catch

up with ②trace;look into;try to find out;get the bottom of ③ seek;go after;woo ④ bring back to mind;recall;reminisce ⑤act posthumously;do retroactively

追逼 ①pursue closely (a fleeing enemy) ② press for (repayment);extort (a confession)

追兵 pursuing troops

追补 ①add to (the original amount) ②make up;remedy;make good

追捕 pursue and capture

追查 investigate;trace;find out

追偿 ①make compensation afterwards ②recover

追悼 mourn over a person's death

追访 make a follow-up visit;follow-up reporting

追肥 top application;topdressing

追赶 quicken one's pace to catch up;run after;pursue

追根 get to the root (or bottom) of sth

追怀 call to mind;recall;reminisce

追回 recover

追悔 repent;regret

追击 pursue and attack;follow up

追辑 pursue and capture (an escaped criminal)

追记 write immediate record of an event　award posthumously

追加 add to (the original amount)

追歼 pursue and wipe out

追剿 pursue and wipe out

追缴 ① demand payment (of tax arrears, etc.) ②recover

追究 look into;find out;investigate

追念 think back;recall

追捧 follow

追求 ①seek;pursue ②court (a woman);woo

追认 ①subsequently confirm (or endorse); recognize retroactively ② admit (or confer) posthumously

追授 be posthumously awarded;confer a posthumous honour on

追思 recall;reminisce

追述 tell about the past;relate;recount

追诉 prosecute

追溯 trace back to;date from

追随 follow

追索 ① seek;pursue;explore ② demand;exact;extort

追逃 manhunt

追讨 demand payment of an old debt

追尾 tailgate

追问 question closely;make a detailed inquiry;examine minutely

追叙 ①tell about the past;relate;recount ② narration of earlier episodes;flashback

追寻 pursue;search;track down

追询 inquire persistently;question closely; make a detailed inquiry;examine minutely

追忆 recollect;recall;look back

追赃 make sb disgorge spoils;order the return of stolen money or goods;recover stolen money or goods

追赠 confer posthumously (a title)

追债 claim repayment of a debt

追逐 ①pursue;chase ②seek;quest

追踪 follow the trail of;track;trace

追悼会 memorial meeting

追随者 follower;adherent

追索权 recourse;right of recourse

追星热 craze of chasing after stars

追星族 star fan

追奔逐北 give chase to a routed enemy

追本溯源 trace to its source;get to the root of the matter

追风逐电 chase after wind and lightning—(of a train,etc.) run swiftly

追回款项 recoveries

追回赃物 recover stolen property;recover stolen money;recover stolen goods

追加保险 supplementary insurance

追加拨款 supplementary appropriations

追加条款 rider clause;supplemental clause

追加预算 supplement a budget

追加支出 make an additional expenditure

追缴税款 demand tax areas

追究责任 ascertain where the responsibility lies

追名逐利 seek (or be after) fame and wealth

追索办法 means of recourse

追索诉讼 recovery action

追忆往昔 recall the past

追逐利润 profit-seeking;quest for profit

追踪报道 follow-up (report); development story;developing story;follow-up story

追索财产者 recoverer

追赶型和跨越式发展 pursuant and leap-forward development

骓 [zhuī] 名 horse with white and black hair

椎 [zhuī] 名 vertebra ➡chuí

椎骨 vertebra

椎间盘 intervertebral disc

椎间盘凸出症 protrusion of the intervertebral disc

锥 [zhuī] Ⅰ 名 ①awl ②awl-like thing;cone ③cone Ⅱ 动 bore;drill

锥度 ①coning;taper ②taper ratio

锥孔 make a hole with an awl

锥栗 chinquapin

锥面 ①conical surface ②pyramidal face

Z

锥形 conical contour;cone;taper;pyramid
锥指 have a meagre knowledge of sth;have a limited view of sth
锥子 awl
锥尖儿 point of an awl
锥处囊中 an awl in a bag—talent will reveal itself despite temporary obscurity
锥刀之末 petty profits;small gains

zhuì(ㄓㄨㄟ)

坠 [zhuì]
Ⅰ 动 ① fall;tumble;drop ② weigh down;droop:累累果实把树枝坠得弯弯的。Heavy fruit weighed the branches down. Ⅱ 名 weight;hanging object
坠地 (of a child) be born
坠毁 (of a plane,etc.) fall and break;crash
坠楼 ①fall off a building ②commit suicide by jumping off a building
坠落 fall;drop
坠马 fall off a horse
坠胎 have a miscarriage;have an abortion
坠子 ①weight;plummet;pendant ②ear pendant

缀 [zhuì]
动 ①sew;stitch;mend ②put words together correctly;compose;write ③ embellish;adorn;decorate:缀满繁星的天空 sky studded with stars
缀合 put together;make up;compose
缀辑 compile;edit
缀饰 decoration
缀文 compose an essay;write a composition
缀句成文 put sentences together to make an essay
缀字成句 put words together to make a sentence

惴 [zhuì]
动 be anxious and afraid
惴恐 be anxious and frightened
惴栗 tremble with fear;shudder
惴惴不安 be anxious and fearful;be alarmed;be on tenterhooks

缒 [zhuì]
动 let down (with a rope)

腄 [zhuì]
名 (of foot) swelling

赘 [zhuì]
Ⅰ 形 superfluous;tautological;redundant Ⅱ 动 ①(of a man) go to live in the household of one's in-laws upon marriage;(of the bride's parents) gain a son-in-law in such a manner ② be a drag on;be burdensome;be cumbersome:这些孩子实在赘人。These children are really burdensome.
赘词 superfluous words;redundancy
赘瘤 anything superfluous or useless

赘述 give unnecessary details;say more than is needed
赘婿 a son-in-law who lives in the home of his wife's parents
赘言 ① give unnecessary details;say more than needed ② superfluous words;redundancy
赘疣 ① wart ② anything superfluous or useless

醊 [zhuì]
动 hold a memorial ceremony for

zhūn(ㄓㄨㄣ)

肫 [zhūn]
Ⅰ 形 sincere;earnest;genuine Ⅱ 名 gizzard (of a fowl)
肫挚 sincere

谆 [zhūn]
副 sincerely;warmly;earnestly and tirelessly
谆嘱 advise (or enjoin) earnestly
谆谆 earnest and tireless
谆谆告诫 repeatedly admonish;tirelessly exhort
谆谆教导 earnestly and tirelessly instruct

zhǔn(ㄓㄨㄣ)

准 [zhǔn]
Ⅰ 动 ①allow;permit;approve;grant:不准入内! No admittance! ②in line with;in accordance with;follow Ⅱ 名 standard;norm;criterion;yardstick Ⅲ 形 ① accurate;exact;precise:放之四海而皆准 valid everywhere;universally applicable ② quasi-;para- Ⅳ 副 definitely;surely;certainly:他不准能来。He may be unable to come.
准儿 certain;sure
准保 certainly;for sure
准备 ①prepare;get ready ②intend;plan
准得 certainly;for sure
准点 on time;on the dot
准定 certainly;for sure
准话 definite message or answer
准将 (U.S. Army,Air Force & Marine Corps) brigadier general;(Brit. Army & Marine Corps) brigadier;(U.S. & Brit. Navy) commodore;(Brit. Air Force) air commodore
准确 accurate;exact;precise
准绳 criterion;yardstick
准时 punctual;on time;on schedule
准头 accuracy (in speech, marksmanship, etc.)
准尉 warrant officer
准线 neat line
准信 definite message or answer
准星 front sight (of a gun)

准行 there won't be any problem
准许 permit;allow
准予 grant;approve;permit
准则 norm;standard;criterion
准直 collimation
准博士 all but dissertation(ABD)
准光波 quasi-optical waves
准考证 examination card (*or* pass)
准粒子 quasi-particle
准平原 paraplain
准谱儿 certain;sure
准运证 navicert
准直仪 collimator
准租金 quasi-rent
准备活动 warming-up exercise;limbering-
准不动产 chattel real
准此办理 be handled in the same manner
准单色光 quasi-monochromatic light
准国际法 quasi-international law
准直透镜 collimating lens
准分子激光 quasi-molecular laser
准国际协定 quasi-international agreement
准国家实体 entité paraétatique
准军事组织 paramilitary organization
准上市公司 pro-listed company
准司法团体 quasi-judicial body
准战争状态 quasi-state of war
准中立地位 quasi-neutral status
准契约性义务 quasi-contractual obligation

墫 [zhǔn]
〈名〉 bull's eye (of a target)

zhuō（ㄓㄨㄛ）

拙 [zhuō]
〈形〉 ①clumsy;awkward;unskilful;dull;stupid ②my
拙笨 clumsy;dull;unskilful
拙笔 my (poor) writing or painting
拙稿 my (poor) writing;my (poor) work
拙见 my (humble) opinion
拙荆 my wife
拙劣 clumsy;inferior
拙朴 simple and unadorned
拙涩 clumsy and obscure
拙译 my translation
拙直 straightforward and good-natured;simple and frank
拙著 my (poor) writing;my (poor) work
拙作 my (poor) writing, painting, etc.; my (poor) work
拙于言辞 inarticulate;unable to communicate one's ideas adequately
拙嘴笨腮 clumsy-tongued;inarticulate

捉 [zhuō]
〈动〉 ①clutch;hold firmly;grab;grasp：捉住他的手臂 grab him by the arm ②catch;seize;capture

捉刀 write (an article, etc.) for sb else;ghostwrite
捉奸 catch adulterers in the act
捉摸 fathom;ascertain
捉拿 arrest;catch
捉弄 tease;make fun of;play tricks on
捉住 get sb by the neck
捉刀人 ghostwriter
捉迷藏 ①hide-and-seek;blindman's buff ②be tricky and evasive;play hide-and-seek
捉笔赋诗 pick up a brush (*or* pen) to write a poem
捉襟见肘 when one pulls together one's lapels; one's elbows poke through the sleeves—have too many difficulties (esp. financial) to cope with

桌 [zhuō]
Ⅰ〈名〉table;desk Ⅱ〈量〉(of a feast table, etc.)：两桌酒菜 two tables of wine and dishes/五桌客人 five tables of guests
桌布 tablecloth
桌菜 prepared meals (fresh prepared foods which can be bought and cooked at home)
桌面 top of a table;tabletop
桌子 table;desk
桌挡儿 cross bar of a desk (*or* table)
桌面儿上 ①on the table;aboveboard ②in public
桌椅板凳 tables, chairs and benches—household furniture generally
桌面计算机 desktop computer
桌子下交易 under-the-table trade
桌面办公系统 desktop system
桌面出版系统 desktop publishing (DTP);desktop

zhuó（ㄓㄨㄛ）

灼 [zhuó]
Ⅰ〈动〉burn;sear;scorch Ⅱ〈形〉bright;shining;luminous
灼急 anxious;worried
灼见 profound view;penetrating view
灼烤 burn;bake;scorch
灼亮 bright;shining
灼然 quite obvious;fairly clear
灼热 scorching hot
灼伤 (of fire,acid,etc.) burn
灼烧 firing
灼灼 shining;brilliant

茁 [zhuó]
〈动〉 grow vigorously;grow healthily
茁实 healthy and strong;sturdy
茁壮 healthy and strong;sturdy;vigorous
茁壮成长 grow up strong and sturdy

卓 [zhuó]
〈形〉 ①tall and upright ②remarkable;outstanding;eminent

Z

卓见 excellent opinion; brilliant idea

卓绝 unsurpassed; extreme; of the highest degree

卓立 stand upright

卓然 outstanding; splendid; remarkable

卓识 judicious judgment; sagacity

卓午 high noon

卓异 out of the ordinary; outstanding; unique; preeminent

卓越 outstanding; brilliant; remarkable

卓著 distinguished; outstanding; eminent

卓尔不群 stand head and shoulders above all others; be preeminent

卓有成效 fruitful; highly effective

斫 [zhuó]

〔动〕 cut; chop; hack: 斫柴 cut fireword/斫树 hack (*or* cut, *or* chop) down a tree

浊 [zhuó]

〔形〕 ① muddy; murky; turbid ②（of voices）deep and thick: 说话浊声浊气 speak in a deep, raucous voice ③ chaotic; confused; disorderly

浊点 cloud point

浊酒 unstrained wine or liquor

浊流 turbidity current

浊气 foul smell

浊世 ① the corrupted world; chaotic times ② the mortal world

浊水 turbid water

浊物 absurd creature; insensitive creature; ignoramus

浊音 voiced sound

酌 [zhuó]

Ⅰ 〔动〕 ① pour out（wine）; drink ② deliberate; weigh and consider; mull over; use one's discretion Ⅱ 〔名〕 meal with wine or spirits

酌办 act according to one's judgment; act at one's discretion; do as one thinks fit

酌定 make a decision as one thinks fit; decide according to one's judgment

酌减 discretionary reduction

酌量 consider; deliberate; use one's judgment

酌情 take into consideration the circumstances; exercise discretion in the light of the circumstances; use one's discretion

酌予 give sth as one thinks fit

酌情处理 act at one's discretion; settle a matter as one sees fit

浞 [zhuó]

〔动〕 drench: 被雨浞了 be drenched (*or* soaked) with rain

著 [zhuó]

➡zhù

◇执著 persistent; perservering; rigid; work unflaggingly

啄 [zhuó]

〔动〕 peck

啄食 peck at food

啄木鸟 woodpecker

着 [zhuó]

Ⅰ 〔动〕 ① touch; contact ② attach; apply; use ③ wear（clothes）; be dressed ④ send; dispatch: 请着人前去联系。 Please send someone to contact them. ⑤（*of documentary usage*, *indicating an imperative tone of voice*）: 着即缉拿凶手。 The criminal must be arrested immediately. Ⅱ 〔名〕 whereabouts; assured source ➡zhāo; zháo; zhe

着笔 put（*or* set）pen to paper; begin to write or paint

着力 put forth effort; exert oneself

着陆 land; touch down

着落 ① whereabouts ② assured source ③ fall to sb; rest with sb ④ settle

着墨 apply ink to paper—write or paint

着色 put colour on; colour

着实 ① really; indeed ② severely

着手 put one's hand to; set about

着想 consider（the interests of sb or sth）

着眼 have sth in mind; see（*or* view）from the angle of

着意 act with care and effort; take pains

着重 stress; emphasize

着装 ① put on; wear ② clothing, headgear and footwear

着陆舱 space landing module

着先鞭 take precedence; take the lead; get ahead of

着眼点 starting point; focus of attention; object in mind

着重号 mark of emphasis（as in 正是他本人）

琢 [zhuó]

〔动〕 chisel; cut; carve ➡zuó

琢磨 [zhuómó] ① carve and polish（jade）② improve（literary works）; polish; refine

斫 [zhuó]

〔动〕 chop; cut

缴 [zhuó]

〔名〕 raw silk string tied to an arrow for shooting birds ➡jiǎo

擢 [zhuó]

〔动〕 ① pull out; extract ② advance in rank; raise; promote

擢拔 select; promote

擢升 promote; raise

擢用 promote to a post

濯 [zhuó]

〔动〕 wash

濯足 wash one's feet

镯 [zhuó]

〔名〕 bracelet

镯子 bracelet

Zī（ㄗ）

吱 [zī]

〔名〕 ① squeak: 老鼠在墙角吱吱叫。 The

mouse squeaked in the corner. ②（of small birds) chirp;cheep;peep ➡ zhī

吱声 utter sth;make a sound;speak

孜 [zī]

孜孜 diligent;industrious;hardworking
孜孜不倦 diligently;assiduously;indefatigably

咨 [zī]

〔动〕consult;seek advice;take counsel
咨文 ①official communication（between government offices of equal rank) ②report delivered by the head of a government on affairs of state;message
咨问 seek advice;consult
咨询 seek advice from;hold counsel with;consult
咨询业 consultive service;advisory works
咨询服务 consultancy service
咨询公司 consultant firm;consulting company
咨询会议 executive council
咨询活动 information service
咨询热线 helpline

姿 [zī]

〔名〕① looks;countenance;appearance;aspect;mien ② gesture;carriage;bearing;posture
姿容 looks;appearance
姿色 good looks（of a woman)
姿势 posture;gesture
姿态 ①posture;carriage ②attitude;pose

兹 [zī]

Ⅰ〔代〕this Ⅱ〔副〕now;at present;at this time:自兹以后 from now on/兹将获奖人员名单公布如下。Below is a list of the prize-winners. Ⅲ〔名〕year

赀 [zī]

Ⅰ〔动〕reckon;calculate;estimate Ⅱ〔名〕fund;money;expense

资 [zī]

Ⅰ〔名〕① fund;money;expenses;capital:劳资双方 labour and capital ② natural ability;endowment;aptitude ③ qualifications;seniority;record of service Ⅱ〔动〕①help;subsidize;support ②serve;provide;supply
资本 ① capital ② what is capitalized on;sth used to one's own advantage
资材 goods,materials and equipments
资财 capital and goods;assets
资产 ①property ②capital fund;capital ③assets
资方 those representing capital;capital
资费 expenses;fee
资格 ①qualifications ②seniority
资金 fund;capital
资力 financial strength
资历 qualifications and record of service
资料 ①means ②data;material
资深 senior

资送 send sb away with money provided
资信 credit strength;capital and credit
资讯 date;information
资用 available
资源 natural resources;resources
资质 aptitude; natural endowments; intelligence;credentials and ability of a designing and engineering enterprise
资助 aid financially;subsidize
资本家 capitalist
《资本论》 *Das Kapital*
资料库 data bank;data base;database
资源税 resources tax
资本过剩 surplus of capital
资本货物 capital goods
资本市场 capital market
资本主义 capitalism
资不抵债 unable to pay one's debt with all his assets;insolvent
资产重组 assets reorganization
资产冻结 freezing of asset
资产阶级 the capitalist class;the bourgeoisie
资产评估 assets evaluation; assets appraisal; make an appraisal one's assets
资产组合 asset portfolio
资格认定 qualifications verification
资格预审 prequalifications
资格证书 credentials
资金拆借 capital-borrowing
资金筹措 financing;fund raising
资金倒流 reverse flow of funds
资金到位 full supply of funds;fully funded
资金短缺 capital shortage
资金积累 the capital accumulation
资金流通 fund circulation
资金缺口 shortage（*or* insufficiency）of capital;financing gap
资金外流 capital flight; capital drain; capital outflow;capital exodus
资金雄厚 abundant funds
资金占压 funds tied up
资金周转 capital turnover;capital circulation
资料处理 data processing
资浅齿少 of a young age and with little work experience
资深望重 one's reputation is distinguished
资深元老 senior statesmen
资深院士 senior academician
资信可靠 creditworthy
资信状况 credit worthiness
资源共享 share of resources;resource sharing
资源开发 resources development
资源配置 distribution of resources; allocation of resources
资源优势 resource advantages
资本金制度 capital system; system capital funds

资产负债表 statement of assets and liabilities; balance sheet
资产阶级化 become bourgeoisified
资本帝国主义 capitalist-imperialism
资本运作效率 efficiency of the operation of capital
资本主义道路 the capitalist road
资本主义倾向 tendencies towards capitalism
资本主义社会 capitalist society
资本主义制度 capitalist system
资产保值增值 maintain and increase the value of assets; maintenance and appreciation of assets value
资产阶级分子 bourgeois element
资产阶级革命 bourgeois revolution
资产阶级民主 bourgeois democracy
资产阶级权利 bourgeois right
资产阶级思想 bourgeois ideas; bourgeois ideology
资产阶级专政 the dictatorship of the bourgeoisie
资源富集地区 areas richly endowed with resources
资源优化配置 optimum distribution of resources
资产阶级世界观 bourgeois world outlook
资产阶级自由化 bourgeois liberalization
资格审查委员会 credentials committee
资本主义经济成份 capitalist sector of the economy
资本主义生产方式 capitalist mode of production
资本主义自发势力 spontaneous capitalist forces
资产阶级个人主义 bourgeois individualism
资产阶级民主革命 bourgeois-democratic revolution
资源有偿使用制度 system of paid use of resources

缁 [zī]
〈形〉 black
缁衣 black coat

辎 [zī]
〈名〉 ancient covered wagon
辎重 impedimenta; supplies and gear of an army; baggage

嗞 [zī]
〈象〉 squeak; chirp; peep

孳 [zī]
〈动〉 multiply; propagate
孳乳 ①breed; propaqate; multiply ②derive
孳生 multiply; breed; propagate
孳衍 grow and multiply

滋 [zī]
Ⅰ〈动〉 ①grow; multiply; breed ②increase; wax ③spurt; spout; burst Ⅱ〈名〉 taste; flavour
滋补 nourishing; nutritious
滋蔓 grow and spread; grow vigorously; grow quickly
滋茂 (of plants) grow vigorously; thrive
滋润 ①moist; humid ②moisten ③comfortable; well off
滋生 ①multiply; breed; propagate ②cause; create; provoke
滋事 make (*or* stir up) trouble
滋味 taste; flavour
滋养 ①nourish ②nutriment; nourishment
滋阴 method of treating *yin* deficiency by reinforcing body fluid and nourishing the blood
滋育 grow; multiply; breed
滋长 grow; develop
滋补品 tonic
滋养品 nourishing food; nutriment; nourishment

訾 [zī]
〈动〉 estimate; measure ➡ zǐ

锱 [zī]
〈量〉 *zi*, ancient unit of weight, equal to one fourth of a *liang*
锱铢 small amount of money; trifle; farthing
锱铢必较 haggle over every penny; dispute over every detail

龇 [zī]
〈动〉 bare; show
龇露 (of teeth) protrude
龇牙咧嘴 ①show one's teeth; look fierce ② contort one's face (in agony); grimace (with pain)

ZǏ(ㄗ)

子 [zǐ]
Ⅰ〈名〉 ①child; son: 母子候车室 waiting room (as in a railway station) for mothers with babies ②person ③ancient title of respect for a learned or virtuous man or a man in general ④philosophy ⑤seed ⑥egg: 鸭子儿 duck's egg ⑦sth small and hard ⑧copper coin; copper: 半个子儿都不值 not worth half a copper; worthless ⑨viscount Ⅱ〈量〉: 一子儿挂面 a bundle of fine dried noodles/一子儿毛线 a hank of knitting wool Ⅲ〈代〉 you Ⅳ〈形〉 ① young; small; tender ②subsidiary
子部 philosophy
子城 a small city within a larger one
子代 filial generation
子弹 bullet; cartridge
子弟 ①sons and younger brothers ②young generation; juniors; children
子房 ovary
子宫 uterus; womb
子规 cuckoo
子金 interest
子爵 viscount
子母 ①son and mother ②of similar relation-

ship like a son and mother
子目 specific item;subtitle
子囊 ascus
子女 sons and daughters;children;offspring
子时 the period of the day from 11 p.m. to 1 a.m.
子书 philosophical works—one of the four traditional divisions of a Chinese library
子嗣 son;male offspring
子孙 children and grandchildren;descendants
子息 ①son;male offspring ②interest
子痫 eclampsia
子虚 fictitious;unreal
子婿 son-in-law
子叶 cotyledon
子夜 midnight
子音 consonant
子猪 pigling
子菜单 submenu
子弹带 cartridge belt;bandoleer
子弹箱 cartridge box
子弟兵 army made up of the sons of the people;our own army
子公司 subsidiary company;subsidiary
子宫颈 cervix (of womb)
子宫帽 cervical cap
子母船 bargecarrier; lighter aboard ship (LASH)
子母弹 sharpnel;canister
子母机 composite aircraft
子母钟 synchronized clock
子午圈 meridian (line)
子午线 meridian (line)
子午仪 meridian instrument
子宫颈炎 cervicitis
子宫脱垂 metroptosis;prolapse of uterus
子宫外孕 ectopic (or extrauterine) pregnancy
子爵夫人 viscountess
子母电话 composite telephone
子母扣儿 snap fastener;popper
子孙后代 descendants;posterity;coming generations
子孙满堂 (of a person) be blessed with many children
子午卯酉 from midnight to noon and from sunrise to sunset—① from beginning to end;from start to finish ② reason;argument ③result;achievement
子虚乌有 it is sheer fiction;without foundation in fact;nonexistent;unreal;imaginary
子宫切除术 uterectomy

仔 [zǐ]
囮 ①(of domestic animals or fowl) young ②closely woven;close ➡zǎi
仔畜 newborn animal;young animal
仔鸡 chick

仔密 (of knitwear) close-knitted;(of textiles) close-woven
仔兽 newborn animal;young animal
仔细 ① careful; attentive ② be careful; look out ③frugal;economical
仔鸭 duckling
仔鱼 spawn;newborn fish
仔猪 piglet;pigling

姊 [zǐ]
囵 elder sister;sister
姊妹 elder and younger sisters;sisters
姊妹城 sister city
姊妹船 sister ship
姊妹花 the two sisters
姊妹篇 companion volume (or piece)

籽 [zǐ]
囫 hill up;earth up

秭 [zǐ]
囵 billion;thousand billion or trillion

籽 [zǐ]
囵 seed
籽粒 seed;grain;kernel;bean
籽棉 unginned cotton
籽实 seed;grain;kernel;bean

第 [zǐ]
囵 mat made of thin bamboo strips

梓 [zǐ]
Ⅰ囵 Chinese catalpa Ⅱ囫 cut blocks for printing

紫 [zǐ]
囮 purple;violet
紫菜 laver
紫草 Asian puccoon;Chinese gromwell
紫貂 sable
紫毫 writing brush made of rabbit's hair
紫绀 cyanosis
紫红 purplish red
紫花 pale reddish brown
紫胶 shellac;lac
紫荆 Chinese redbud
紫堇 corydalis
紫萍 duckweed
紫砂 boccaro ware
紫杉 (Japanese) yew
紫苏 purple perilla
紫檀 red sandalwood;padauk
紫藤 Chinese wistaria
紫铜 red copper
紫菀 aster
紫葳 Chinese trumpet creeper
紫薇 crape myrtle
紫涨 flushed;red in the face
紫竹 black bamboo
紫草茸 shellac;lac
紫丁香 (early) lilac
紫河车 dried human placenta
紫胶虫 lac insect
紫荆花 bauhinia;flower of the Chinese redbud

Z

紫金牛 Japanese ardisia
紫禁城 the Forbidden City
紫羚羊 bongo
紫罗兰 violet;common stock
紫茉莉 four-o'clock
紫石英 amethyst
紫穗槐 false indigo
紫外线 ultraviolet ray
紫药水 gentian violet
紫云英 Chinese milk vetch
紫花地丁 Chinese violet
紫花苜蓿 alfalfa

訾 [zǐ]
〔动〕slander;smear;calumniate ➡ zī
訾毁 vilify;defame

滓 [zǐ]
I 〔名〕sediment;dregs;lees Ⅱ 〔形〕muddy;
dirty

ZÌ(ｐ)

自 [zì]
I 〔代〕self;oneself;one's own:自顾自 give
consideration only to oneself;be selfregar-
ding;be selfish Ⅱ 〔副〕naturally;certainly;as a
matter of course:自当如此. It should be so
as a matter of course. Ⅲ 〔介〕from;since:自此
以后 since then;from then on
自爱 regard for oneself;self-respect
自傲 ①arrogant;conceited ②be proud of sth;
take pride in sth
自拔 free oneself（from pain or evildoing）;
extricate oneself
自白 make clear one's meaning;vindicate oneself
自卑 feel oneself inferior;be self-abased
自备 provide for oneself
自便 at one's convenience;as one pleases
自裁 commit suicide;take one's own life
自残 injure oneself;kill each other（in the
same group）
自惭 feel ashamed
自测 test oneself;self-test
自差 autodyne
自嘲 laugh at oneself
自沉 drown oneself
自称 call oneself;claim to be;profess
自乘 involution;squaring
自持 ①control oneself;restrain oneself;exer-
cise self-restraint ② reserved; self-possessed
自筹 collect or raise（funds,etc.）independ-
ently
自从 from;since
自打 from;since
自大 self-important;arrogant
自得 contented;self-satisfied
自动 ①voluntarily;of one's own accord ②au-

tomatic
自渎 self-abuse;masturbation
自发 spontaneous
自肥 fatten oneself;enrich oneself by misap-
propriating funds or materials; feather
one's nest
自费 at one's own expense
自焚 burn oneself to death
自封 ①proclaim（or style）oneself ②confine
oneself;isolate oneself
自奉 provide the necessities of life for oneself
自负 ①be responsible for one's own action,
etc. ②think highly of oneself;be conceited
自割 autotomy
自供 confess
自古 since ancient times;from time immemorial
自汗 spontaneous perspiration（or sweating）
自豪 have a proper sense of pride or dignity;
be proud of sth
自毁 self-destruction
自己 ①referring to the person mentioned earlier in the sentence ②oneself ③closely related;own
自给 self-sufficient;self-supporting
自家 one or oneself
自荐 recommend oneself（for a job）;offer
one's services
自尽 commit suicide;take one's own life
自刭 cut one's own throat;commit suicide by
cutting one's throat
自净 self-purification
自咎 blame oneself;rebuke oneself
自疚 feel compunction;have qualms of conscience
自救 save oneself;provide for and help oneself
自居 consider oneself to be;pose as
自决 self-determination
自觉 ①be conscious;aware of ②on one's own
initiative;conscious
自绝 alienate oneself
自考 self-taught examination
自控 ①automatic control ②self-control
自夸 sing one's own praises;crack oneself up
自宽 comfort oneself;console oneself
自来 from the beginning;in the first place;o-
riginally
自理 take care of or provide for oneself
自力 do sth through one's own efforts;rely on
oneself
自立 stand on one's own feet;support oneself;
earn one's own living
自励 self-excitation;auto-excitation
自量 estimate one's own ability or strength
自留 reserve sth for one's own use
自流 ①（of water,etc.）flow automatically;
flow by itself ②（of a thing）take its natural

course；(of a person) do as one pleases
自律 exercise self-discipline；self-management
自满 complacent；self-satisfied
自明 self-evident；self-explanatory；obvious
自命 consider oneself；regard oneself as
自馁 lose confidence；be discouraged
自弃 give oneself up as hopeless；have no urge to make progress
自谦 be modest
自戕 kill oneself；commit suicide；take one's own life
自强 strive to become stronger
自然 [zìrán] ①natural world；nature ②natural ③naturally；in the ordinary course of events ④of course；naturally
自燃 spontaneous combustion (*or* ignition)
自然 [zìran] at ease；natural；free from affectation
自认 accept as unavoidable；resign oneself to
自如 freely；smoothly；with facility
自若 self-possessed；composed；calm and at ease
自杀 commit suicide；take one's own life
自伤 self-inflicted injury；self-injury
自身 self；oneself
自视 consider (*or* think，imagine) oneself
自是 ①naturally；of course ②consider oneself always in the right
自恃 ① over confident and conceited ② be self-assured for having sth or sb to rely on；count on；capitalize on
自首 ①(of a criminal) voluntarily surrender oneself；confess one's crime；give oneself up ②make a political recantation；surrender to the enemy
自赎 redeem oneself；tone for one's crime
自述 an account in one's own words
自私 selfish；self-centred
自诉 private prosecution；action initiated by an injured party without the participation of the public prosecutor
自卫 defend oneself；self-defence
自慰 ①console onself ②masturbate
自刎 commit suicide by cutting one's throat；cut one's throat
自问 ①ask oneself；examine oneself ②reach a conclusion after weighing a matter
自我 self；oneself
自习 (of students) study by oneself in scheduled time or free time
自销 (of a factory，etc.) sell goods through one's own channels
自小 since childhood
自新 turn over a new leaf；make a fresh start
自信 self-confident；confident
自行 ①by oneself ②of oneself；of one's own accord；voluntarily ③proper motion

自省 examine oneself；examine one's ability，conduct，etc.
自修 ①(of students) study by oneself；have selfstudy ②study on one's own；study independently
自许 ①take pride in；pride oneself on ②call oneself；claim to be
自诩 praise oneself；crack oneself up；brag
自序 author's preface；preface
自叙 autobiographic note；brief account of oneself
自选 free；optional
自学 study on one's own；study independently；teach oneself
自己 control one's emotions
自缢 hang oneself
自用 ① obstinately holding to one's own views；self-opinionated；self-willed ② for private use；personal
自由 ① freedom；liberty ② freedom ③ free；unrestrained
自幼 since childhood
自娱 please oneself；amuse oneself
自育 self-fertile
自愿 voluntary；of one's own accord；of one's own free will
自在 [zìzài] free；unrestrained
自在 [zìzai] comfortable；at ease
自责 blame oneself；reprove oneself
自找 suffer from one's own actions；ask for it
自制 ① made by oneself ② self-control；self-restraint
自治 autonomy；self-government
自重 ① conduct oneself with dignity；be self-possessed ②dead weight
自主 act on one's own；decide for oneself；keep the initiative in one's own hands
自传 autobiography
自转 rotation
自足 self-satisfied；complacent；smug
自尊 self-respect；self-esteem；proper pride
自白书 a written confession
自卑感 inferiority complex；a sense of inferiority
自变量 independent variable
自变数 independent variable
自大狂 megalomania
自动词 verb intransitive
自动档 (car) automatic gearshift；automatic transmission
自动化 automate
自动炮 automatic gun
自动线 transfer machine
自感应 self-induction
自个儿 oneself；by oneself
自耕农 owner-peasant；land-holding peasant
自供状 confession

Z

自画像 self-portrait
自己人 people on one's own side;one of us
自家人 people on one's own side;one of us
自决权 right to self-determination
自觉性 (level of political) consciousness
自来火 ①matches ②cigarette lighter
自来水 running water;tap water
自留畜 livestock for personal needs;privately owned livestock
自留地 private lot; plot for one's personal needs;family plot
自流井 artesian well
自鸣钟 striking clock;chime clock
自捻纱 self-twisted yarn
自拍机 self-timer
自喷井 flowing well;gusher well
自喷期 flush stage;flowing life
自然村 natural village
自然法 natural law;law of nature
自然光 natural light
自然界 natural world;nature
自然力 natural forces
自然人 natural person
自然数 natural number
自然铜 native copper
自然物 unprocessed thing
自杀学 suicidology
自首书 confession
自卫队 Self-Defence Force
自卫军 self-defence corps
自行车 bicycle;bike
自由港 free-trade port,free port
自由化 liberalize
自由民 freeman
自由能 free energy
自由诗 free verse;unorthodox verse;vers libre
自由泳 freestyle (swimming);crawl
自治领 self-governing dominion;dominion
自治区 autonomous region
自治权 autonomy
自治县 autonomous county
自治州 autonomous prefecture
自主权 the decision-making power;power to make one's own decisions
自助餐 buffet dinner
自助游 self-service travel
自转轴 axis of rotation
自走式 self-propelled
自暴自弃 give oneself up as hopeless;have no urge to make progress;be resigned to one's backwardness
自不待言 be self-evident; that goes without saying;that is taken for granted
自不量力 overrate oneself;overestimate one's strength or oneself; not know one's own limitations

自惭形秽 feel unworthy (of others' company);have a sense of inferiority or inadequacy
自成一家 have a style of one's own;have a unique or original style
自筹资金 self finance;funds collected by localities
自出机杼 (of literary compositions) be original in conception
自出心裁 think up an idea of one's own;make new departure
自吹自擂 blow one's own trumpet;crack oneself up
自得其乐 derive pleasure from sth;find enjoyment in sth
自动补胎 tubeless seal tire
自动步枪 automatic rifle
自动传呼 auto call
自动电话 automatic telephone
自动电梯 self-service elevator
自动扶梯 escalator
自动呼叫 auto-call
自动控制 automatic control
自动门锁 autolock
自动免疫 active immunity
自动铅笔 propelling pencil
自动消磁 autodegauss
自动应答 automatic answer
自费出版 vanity publication
自负盈亏 assume sole responsibility for one's profits or losses
自甘堕落 wallow in degeneration; abandon oneself to vice
自高自大 self-important;conceited;arrogant
自告奋勇 offer to undertake (a difficult or dangerous task);volunteer (to do sth difficult)
自古以来 from time immemorial;since ancient times
自顾不暇 be unable even to fend for oneself (much less look after others); be busy enough with one's own affairs
自花传粉 self-pollination
自给自足 autarchy; autarky; self-sufficiency; be able to support oneself and supply one's own needs
自净作用 self-purification
自觉症状 subjective symptoms
自觉自愿 voluntarily; willingly; of one's own free will
自掘坟墓 dig one's own grave;work for one's own destruction
自宽自解 comfort and relieve oneself
自愧弗如 feel ashamed of one's inferiority
自拉自唱 ①accompany one's own singing ② hold forth all alone in defence of one's own views or proposals;second one's own mo-

tion
自来水笔 fountain pen
自力更生 self-reliance; rely on one's own efforts; stand on one's own feet; under one's own steam
自力霉素 mitomycin C
自励励人 encourage oneself and others
自流灌溉 gravity irrigation
自律机制 self-restraining (*or* -discipline) system
自卖自夸 praise the goods one sells; indulge in self-glorification; blow one's own trumpet
自鸣得意 show self-satisfaction; be very pleased with oneself; preen oneself
自鸣清高 profess to be above politics and worldly considerations
自命不凡 consider oneself no ordinary being; have an unduly high opinion of oneself; think no end of oneself
自谋出路 find one's own means of livelihood
自谋职业 individual search for jobs; search for a job oneself; seek a job on one's own (as opposed being assigned by the government)
自欺欺人 deceive oneself as well as others
自强不息 constantly strive to become stronger; make unremitting (*or* unceasing) efforts to improve oneself
自轻自贱 demean oneself; belittle oneself; lack self-confidence and self-respect
自取灭亡 court (*or* invite) destruction; take the road to one's doom
自取其咎 bring blame on oneself; have only oneself to blame
自然地理 physical geography
自然而然 naturally; automatically; spontaneously; of oneself
自然规律 natural law; law of nature
自然环境 natural environment
自然键盘 natural keyboard
自然金属 native metal
自然经济 natural economy
自然科学 natural science
自然类群 natural group
自然免疫 innate immunity; native immunity; natural immunity
自然区域 natural regions
自然神论 deism
自然死亡 natural death
自然现象 natural phenomena
自然形态 natural form
自然选择 natural selection
自然灾害 natural calamity (*or* disaster)
自然主义 naturalism
自然资源 natural resources (*or* wealth)
自上而下 from above to below; from top to bottom
自身难保 be unable even to protect or fend for

oneself
自生自灭 (of a thing) emerge of itself and perish of itself; run its course
自食其果 eat one's own bitter fruit—reap what one has sown
自食其力 support oneself by one's own labour; earn one's own living
自食其言 go back on one's word; break one's promise; break faith with sb
自始至终 from beginning to end; from start to finish
自说自话 ①act on one's own; decide for oneself ② talk to oneself; think aloud; soliloquize
自私自利 selfish
自讨苦吃 ask for trouble; bring trouble upon oneself
自讨没趣 ask for a snub; court a rebuff
自投罗网 cast oneself into the net; walk right into the trap; bite the hook; leap at the bait
自为阶级 class-for-itself
自卫反击 fight (*or* strike) back in self-defence
自我安慰 self-consolation
自我暗示 self-suggestion
自我暴露 self-betrayal; self-exposure
自我辩解 self-justification
自我标榜 blow one's own trumpet
自我表现 self-expression; sing one's own praises
自我吹嘘 self-glorification
自我催眠 autohypnosis
自我发展 self-development
自我改造 self-remoulding
自我观察 self-observation
自我检查 self-examination; introspection
自我教育 self-education
自我解嘲 find excuses to console oneself
自我介绍 introduce oneself
自我克制 self-alonegation
自我批评 self-criticism
自我陶醉 be intoxicated with self-satisfaction
自我完善 self-improvement
自我牺牲 self-sacrifice
自我欣赏 self-appreciation; self-admiration
自我作古 be the founder (*or* originator) of sth
自下而上 from below
自相残杀 fratricide; (of persons within a group, party, etc.) kill each other; cause one another's death
自相惊扰 alarm one's own group, etc.; create a disturbance within one's ranks; raise false alarms
自相矛盾 contradict oneself; be self-contradictory
自卸卡车 dump truck; tip truck

Z

自行车架 ①bicycle frame ②bicycle stand (*or* rack)
自行车棚 bicycle shed
自行车赛 cycle racing;cycling
自行火炮 self-propelled gun
自行其是 go one's own way;act wilfully
自选动作 optional exercise
自选商场 supermarket;self-service market
自选市场 supermarket
自学成才 be self-taught
自学考试 examination for self-taught students;self-taught examination
自学课本 teach-yourself book
自寻烦恼 worry oneself needlessly;bring vexation on oneself
自寻死路 bring about one's own destruction
自言自语 talk to oneself;think aloud;soliloquize
自养生物 autotroph
自养殖物 autophyte;autotrophic plant
自以为非 consider oneself in the wrong;recognize one's own fallibility
自以为是 consider oneself (always) in the right;regard oneself as infallible;be self-opinionated
自由电子 free electron
自由兑换 convertibility
自由泛滥 (of erroneous ideas,etc.) spread unchecked;run wild
自由放任 let people do what they like;let things go their own way;follow one's own inclinations
自由汇率 free exchange rate
自由价格 free price
自由竞争 free competition
自由联想 free (*or* uncontrolled) association
自由恋爱 freedom to arrange one's own marriage;free courtship
自由贸易 free trade
自由软件 freeware;free software
自由散漫 slack;lax in discipline
自由市场 free (*or* open) market
自由体操 free exercise;floor exercise;free callisthenics
自由王国 realm of freedom
自由意志 free will
自由职业 profession
自由主义 liberalism
自由自在 leisurely and carefree;free and unrestrained
自圆其说 make one's statement valid;justify oneself
自怨自艾 be full of remorse;repent
自在阶级 class-in-itself
自在之物 thing-in-itself
自知之明 knowledge of oneself
自治机关 organ of self-government

自主创新 independent innovation;independent creation
自主关税 autonomous tariff
自主经营 be independent in management
自主决策 enjoy decision-making autonomy
自助餐厅 cafeteria
自作聪明 think oneself clever (in making suggestions,etc.);try to be smart (by acting on one's own,etc.)
自作多情 proffer a love (*or* affection) which is not reciprocated
自作主张 act on one's own;decide for oneself
自作自受 suffer from one's own actions;stew in one's own juice
自动柜员机 automatic teller machine(ATM);cash machine
自动取款机 cashpoint;automatic teller machine(ATM);sidewalk bank
自动售货机 vending machine;vendor;slot machine
自动售票机 ticket vendor
自动饲喂器 self-feeder
自动提款机 ATM (automatic teller machine);cash machine
自动饮水器 automatic drinking bowl
自动装配线 automatic assembly line
自动装填炮 autoloading gun
自花不稔性 self-sterility
自然保护区 nature reserve;nature preservation zone;wilderness area
自然辩证法 dialectics of nature
自然博物馆 museum of natural history
自然增长率 natural growth
自体不育性 self-sterility
自以为得计 be pleased with one's own scheming;think oneself smart
自营出口权 power to engage in export independently
自由关税区 tariff-free zone
自由贸易区 free trade zone;free trade area
自由职业者 professional
自由撰稿人 free writer
自动报价系统 automated quotation system
自动出口限制 voluntary restraint export
自动除霜系统 automatic defrosting system
自动换梭织机 automatic shuttle-changing loom
自动音量控制 automatic volume control
自动增益控制 automatic gain control
自动诊断程序 automated conversion routine
自我保护意识 self-protection awareness
自由放任主义 laissez-faire
自由落体运动 free fall
自由职业人员 free-lance professional
自由资本主义 non-monopoly capitalism;laissez-faire capitalism
自由资产阶级 non-monopoly bourgeoisie;lib-

eral bourgeoisie

自由组合规律 law of independent assortment

自主知识产权 own intellectual property

自动绢网印花机 automatic screen printing machine

自杀性爆炸事件 suicide bombing

自由、平等、博爱 liberty, equality and fraternity

自走式联合收割机 self-propelled combine harvester

自我约束，自我发展 practice self-restraint and develop on their own initiative

自尊、自信、自立、自强 self-respect, self-confidence, self-reliance and self-improving

字 [zì]
Ⅰ 名 ① word; character ② pronunciation (of a word or character)：吐字清楚 pronounce every word clearly; have clear articulation (*or* enunciation) ③form of a written or printed character; style of handwriting ④scripts; writings; calligraphy：他只藏画，不藏字。He only collects paintings, not scripts. ⑤wording; diction ⑥receipt; voucher; written pledge ⑦another name derived from the meaning of one's original name：诸葛亮字孔明。Zhuge Liang styled himself Kongming. ⑧ number shown on an electric meter, water meter, etc. Ⅱ 动 (of a girl) be betrothed; be engaged：许字于人 be betrothed

字标 slogan written in large characters

字典 character dictionary (which defines only single characters, though including compounds as illustrative examples)

字调 tones of Chinese characters

字段 field

字符 character

字幅 horizontal or vertical scroll of calligraphy

字号 [zìhào] type size; word size

字号 [zìhao] name of a shop

字盒 (type) mould

字画 calligraphy and painting

字汇 glossary; wordbook; lexicon

字迹 handwriting; writing

字节 byte

字句 words and expressions; writing

字据 written pledge (e.g. receipt, IOU, contract, etc.)

字库 ①word bank ②font bank; font collection

字码 character code

字谜 a riddle about a character (*or* word)

字面 literal

字模 matrix; typehead; nib

字母 ① letters of an alphabet; letter ② (in phonology) a character representing an initial consonant

字幕 captions (of motion pictures, etc.); sub-

titles

字数 word number

字素 grapheme

字体 ①form of a written or printed character; script; typeface ②style of calligraphy ③font; typeface

字条 brief note; note

字帖 brief note

字眼 wording; diction

字样 ①model of written characters ②printed or written words

字义 literal meaning

字纸 wastepaper with characters written or printed on it

字典纸 India paper; Bible paper

字段名 field name

字符串 string

字码儿 ①numberal ②number amount

字母表 alphabet

字纸篓 wastepaper basket

字段标记 fieldmark

字段位移 field shifting

字里行间 between the lines

字斟句酌 choose one's words with care; weigh every word

字字珠玑 each word a gem (said in praise of sb's writing)

恣 [zì]
Ⅰ 动 be self-indulgent; do as one pleases; throw off all restraint Ⅱ 形 comfortable; at ease

恣情 ①to one's heart's content; as much as one likes ②wanton; arbitrary; willful

恣意 unscrupulous; reckless; unbridled; wilful

恣纵 induldge in sensual pleasures

恣情放纵 indulge in passions and run wild

恣行无忌 act wilfully and unscrupulously; behave recklessly

恣意妄为 act wilfully and wildly; behave unscrupulously

眦 [zì]
名 corner of the eye; canthus

渍 [zì]
Ⅰ 动 ①soak; steep; ret：汗水把白衬衣渍黄了。The white shirt has yellowed with sweat. ②be soiled or stained (with grease, etc.)：渍满油泥的工作服 work clothes stained with grease/他的鞋上渍满了泥。His shoes were caked with mud. Ⅱ 名 ①floodwater on low-lying land; waterlogging ②stain; smear; sludge

渍涝 waterlogging

渍染 dye

渍水 accumulated water

子 [zǐ]
I （*used after a noun, adjective or verb as a noun suffix*） II （*used after a classifier as a suffix*）：忙了一阵子 be busily occupied （*or* busy） for some time／我一下子就认出了她。 I recognized her at first glance.

zōng（ㄗㄨㄥ）

宗 [zōng]
I 〈名〉①ancestor; forefather ②clan ③faction; sect; school ④principal aim; purpose; objective ⑤ *zong*, an old administrative unit in Tibet, roughly corresponding to the county ⑥ great master; exmaple; model II 〈动〉（in academic or artistic work） model on：他的唱腔宗马派。 His singing belongs to the Ma School. III 〈量〉：大宗货物 a large quantity of goods／一宗刑事案件 a criminal case／一宗心事 a cause for worry
宗祠 ancestral hall （*or* temple）
宗法 patriarchal clan system
宗教 religion
宗筋 penis
宗庙 ancestral temple （*or* shrine） of a ruling house
宗派 faction; sect
宗谱 family tree; genealogical tree; genealogy
宗亲 members of the same clan; clansmen
宗师 master of great learning and integrity
宗室 ①imperial （*or* royal） clan ②imperial （*or* royal） clansman
宗仰 hold in esteem
宗旨 aim; purpose
宗族 ①patriarchal clan ②clansman
宗教界 religious circles
宗主国 suzerain （state）; metropolitan state
宗主权 suzerainty
宗教法庭 the Inquisition （in European history）
宗教改革 the Reformation （in European history）
宗教戒律 religious taboo
宗教派别 religious sect
宗教团体 religious organization; religious body
宗教信仰 religious beliefs
宗教仪式 religious rites; ritual
宗派斗争 factional strife
宗派活动 factional activities; sectarian activities
宗派主义 sectarianism; factionalism
宗兄宗弟 brothers of the same clan

综 [zōng]
〈动〉sum up; put together; combine ➡ zèng
综观 make a comprehensive survey
综合 ①synthesize ②synthetical; comprehensive; multiple; composite
综计 sum up; add up
综括 sum up
综述 summarize; sum up
综艺 comprehensive arts
综合语 synthetic language
综合征 syndrome
综合保险 comprehensive insurance
综合报道 comprehensive （*or* composite） dispatch; news roundup
综合报告 comprehensive report; summing-up report
综合大学 university
综合防治 integrated control
综合服务 comprehension service
综合规划 unified plan
综合国力 overall national strength; a country's overall （*or* comprehensive, aggregate） strength
综合教学 integrated teaching
综合考察 comprehensive survey
综合利用 comprehensive utilization; multipurpose use
综合平衡 overall balance
综合素质 comprehensive quality; all the good qualities combined
综合效益 comprehensive benefits
综合银行 universal bank
综合整治 comprehensive improvement
综合指数 composite index
综合治理 comprehensive administration; tackle a problem in a comprehensive way; adopt an integrated and holistic approach
综理万机 manage a myriad of affairs
综艺大观 display of all arts
综合保险单 comprehensive policy
综合性工厂 multiple-producing factory
综合业务数字网 integrated service digital network（ISDN）

棕 [zōng]
〈名〉①palm ②palm fibre; coir
棕绷 wooden bed frame strung with crisscross coir ropes
棕编 coir-woven articles
棕黑 dark brown
棕红 reddish brown
棕黄 pale brown
棕榈 palm
棕毛 palm fibre
棕壤 brown earth
棕色 brown
棕绳 coir rope
棕树 palm
棕刷 coir brush
棕毯 coir-woven blanket
棕熊 brown bear
棕叶 palm leaf
棕衣 palm-bark rain cape
棕竹 bamboo palm; lady palm

棕榈酸 palmitic (*or* palmic) acid
棕榈油 palm oil;palm butter
棕色云团 brown cloud

腙 [zōng]
　图 hydrazone

踪 [zōng]
　图 track;trail;trace;footprint
踪迹 trace;track
踪影 trace;sign

鬃 [zōng]
　图 hair (on the neck of a pig,horse,etc.):
红鬃烈马 spirited steed with a red mane
鬃毛 horsehair;acicula
鬃刷 bristle brush

zǒng（ㄗㄨㄥ）

总 [zǒng]
　Ⅰ 动 assemble;gather;put together;sum
up:总起来说 to sum up Ⅱ 形 ①general;o-
verall;gross;total:抓总 assume overall responsibility ②chief;leading;general Ⅲ 副 ①
without exception;always;invariably:我总忘
记带钥匙。I invariably forgets to take my
keys. ②anyway;after all;eventually;sooner
or later:人总是要死的。Death is inevitable;
We must go the way of all flesh;Everyone
must die. ③at least;surely:你嫁给他总该有
十年了吧。It must have been ten years at
least since you married him./她总该给我个
解释。She should at any rate give me an explanation.
总部 general headquarters
总裁 director-general (of a political party);
president (of a company);governor (of a
bank)
总称 general term
总成 assembly
总得 must;have to;be bound to
总店 main store (of a business)
总督 ①(in the Qing Dynasty) governor-gen-
eral ②(in British colonies and dominions)
viceroy;governor-general;governor
总队 general detachment
总额 total
总纲 general programme;general principles
总攻 general offensive
总共 in all;altogether;in the aggregate
总管 ①take overall responsibility ②steward;
butler
总归 anyway;after all;eventually
总行 head office (of a bank)
总合 sum up;add up
总和 sum;total;sum total
总汇 ①(of streams) come or flow together ②
confluence;concourse;aggregate
总机 ① switchboard; telephone exchange ②
operator

总集 sylloge
总计 ①grand total ②amount to;add up to;to-
tal
总监 inspector general;chief inspector
总角 a child's hair twisted in a knot—childhood
总结 ①sum up;summarize ②summary;sum-
ming-up
总括 sum up
总览 overview;take an overall view
总揽 assume overall responsibility; take on
everything
总理 premier;prime minister
总量 aggregate;total supply and demand
总论 introduction (at the beginning of a book)
总目 general table of contents;general catalogue
总评 general comment;overall appraisal
总谱 score
总是 always;invariably
总数 total;sum total
总算 ①at long last;finally ②considering everything;all things considered;on the whole
总体 overall;total
总统 president (of a republic)
总务 ①general affairs ②person in charge of
general affairs
总线 highway;bus;trunk
总则 general rules;general principles;general
provisions
总站 master station
总长 ①cabinet minister ②chief of the general
staff
总账 general ledger
总之 ①in a word;in short;in brief ②anyway;
anyhow
总支 general branch
总值 total (*or* gross) value
总装 assemble a machine
总罢工 general strike
总编辑 editor in chief
总裁判 chief referee
总产值 gross output value;total output value
总成本 total cost;overall cost
总赤字 total deficit
总代表 chief representative
总代理 general agent
总调度 chief dispatcher
总动员 general (*or* total) mobilization
总方针 general policy;general principle
总干事 secretary-general
总根源 root cause
总工长 general foreman;section chief
总工会 federation of trade unions
总公司 head office (of a corporation)
总供给 aggregate supply
总后方 rear area (in wartime)

Z

总教练 head coach
总结会 summing-up meeting
总经理 chief executive officer;general manager;managing director
总经销 exclusive distribution
总开关 master switch
总利润 gross profits
总领事 consul general
总路线 general line
总趋势 the general (*or* predominant) trend
总收益 total revenue;gross income
总书记 secretary-general;general secretary
总司令 commander in chief
总统府 presidential palace;the residence and office of a president
总统制 presidential government;presidential system
总危机 general crisis
总务处 general affairs department
总务科 general affairs section
总务司 general service department
总需求 aggregate demand
总闸门 petroleum master valve;master gate
总账单 master bill
总支出 total expenditure
总指挥 ① commander in chief ② general director
总指数 combined index
总资本 total capital
总资产 total assets
总参谋部 the Headquarters of the General Staff
总参谋长 chief of the general staff
总承包商 general contractor
总而言之 in short;in a word;in brief;to make a long story short
总工程师 chief engineer
总后勤部 the General Logistics Department
总检查官 procurator general
总角之交 childhood friend
总结报告 summing-up report;summary report
总会计师 general accountant;chief accountant
总揽全局 grasp the overall situation;assume overall control of a situation
总量控制 control aggregate supply and demand;control of aggregates
总量平衡 overall balance
总量调控 control total supply and total demand
总领事馆 consulate general
总平面图 general layout
总设计师 chief architect
总司令部 general headquarters
总体规划 overall plans;master plans;general planning
总体设计 master design
总体水平 overall quality level

总体外交 total diplomacy
总体战略 total strategy
总体战争 total war;general war;total warfare
总统选举 presidential election
总政治部 the General Political Department
总指挥部 general headquarters
总状花序 raceme
总统选举团 electoral college
总悬浮颗粒物 total suspended particles

zòng（ㄗㄨㄥˋ）

纵 [zòng]
Ⅰ 形 ① from north to south ② from the front to the back ③ vertical;horizontal ④ wrinkled;creased;crumpled Ⅱ 连 even if;even though;though：纵死不悔 refuse to repent even to the end of one's life Ⅲ 动 ①release;set free;let go ②indulge;let loose;let oneself go ③jump up;jump into the air
纵波 longitudinal wave
纵步 ①stride ②jump;bound
纵队 ① column;file ② a military unit during the War of Liberation,equivalent to an army;column
纵隔 mediastinum
纵观 take a sweeping view;make a general survey
纵贯 pass through from north to south or from south to north
纵横 ① in length and breadth;vertically and horizontally ② with great ease;freely ③ sweep over;march over unhindered
纵火 set on fire;commit arson
纵酒 drink to excess
纵览 look far and wide;scan
纵论 talk freely;have a wide-ranging discussion
纵目 look as far as one's eyes can see
纵情 to one's heart's content;as much as one likes
纵然 even if;even though
纵容 connive;wink at
纵射 enfilade
纵身 jump;leap
纵深 depth
纵声 at the top of one's voice
纵使 even if;even though
纵谈 talk freely
纵眺 look as far as one's eyes can see
纵向 vertical;longitudinal;lengthwise
纵欲 give way to one's carnal desires;indulge in sensual pleasures
纵恣 self-indulgent;undisciplined;wanton
纵断面 vertical section
纵剖面 vertical section
纵切面 vertical section

纵视图 longitudinal view
纵坐标 ordinate
纵观全局 make a general survey of the situation
纵横捭阖 manoeuvre among various states or political groupings
纵横驰骋 （of an army） move about freely and quickly; sweep through the length and breadth of
纵横交错 crisscross
纵虎归山 let the tiger return to the mountains—cause calamity for the future
纵向合并 vertical consolidating; vertical merger
纵向结合 vertical integration （as of enterprises）

棕 [zòng]

棕子 glutinous rice dumpling

ZŌU（ㄗㄡ）

驺 [zōu]
名 groom

ZǑU（ㄗㄡˇ）

走 [zǒu]
动 ①walk; go; follow: 边走边唱 sing while walking ②run; rush about ③（of cars, boats, etc.）move; operate ④leave; be off; go away: 他搬走了。 He has moved out. ⑤go; die ⑥（of friends and relatives）call on; pay a visit; visit ⑦leak; reveal; let out: 说走了嘴 make a slip of the tongue; give away the secret; let the cat out of the bag ⑧be different from the original; lose shape, flavour, etc.: 这茶叶走味了。 The tea has lost its flavour.
走板 ①be out of tune; be off the beat ②digress from the subject; stray from the point
走笔 write rapidly
走步 walking
走道 ① pavement; sidewalk ② path; walk; footpath
走低 go down
走电 leakage of electricity
走调 out of tune
走跌 go down
走动 ①walk about; stretch one's legs ②（of relatives and friends）visit each other
走读 attend a day school
走访 ①interview; have an interview with ②pay a visit to; go and see
走风 let out a secret; leak out
走高 go up
走狗 running dog; lackey; flunkey; stooge; servile follower
走好 go well

走合 run in
走红 become famous （or popular）; rise in fame or reputation
走火 ① sparking ②（of firearms）discharge accidentally ③go too far in what one says; put sth too strongly; overstate ④catch fire; be on fire
走廊 corridor; passage; passageway
走漏 ①leak out; divulge ②smuggling and tax evasion
走路 ①walk; go on foot ②leave; go away
走马 gallop along a horseback
走牛 bullish
走强 go strong
走俏 （of goods）sell well; be in great demand
走禽 Cursores; cursorial birds
走热 become popular
走人 go away; leave
走软 go weak
走弱 go weak
走色 lose colour; fade
走扇 （of a door or window）won't shut properly （due to warping）
走墒 evaporation of water in soil
走神 （of one's attention）wander; be absent-minded
走绳 ropedancing; ropewalking
走失 ① wander away; be lost; be missing ② fail to keep; lose
走势 tendency
走兽 four-footed animals; quadrupeds; beasts
走水 ①leak water ②（of water）flow; run ③ be on fire; catch fire
走私 smuggle
走索 ropedancing; ropewalking
走台 rehearse; walk-through
走题 （of a speech, etc.）digress from the subject; stray from the point
走险 take a risk; make a reckless move
走相 become deformed
走向 ①run; trend; alignment ②strike ③move towards; head for; be on the way to
走形 be out of shape
走熊 bearish
走穴 perform for outside salary income without approval by the unit they belong to
走眼 see wrong
走样 lose shape; go out of form; be different from what is expected or intended
走油 （of oily food）go rancid
走运 have good luck; be in luck
走账 charge a sum to account; enter a sum in the account book
走走 ①take a stroll ②come or go in a general sense
走卒 pawn; cat's-paw; lackey; stooge
走嘴 make a slip of the tongue; let slip an in-

advertent remark
走错路 take a wrong path;mistake a road;go astray
走刀量 feed
走道儿 walk
走读生 commuter;day student;non-resident student
走钢丝 ①wirewalking ②take risks
走关节 get in through the back door;get round (laws,rules,etc.) by bribery
走过场 do sth as a mere formality;go through the motions;do sth perfunctorily or superficially
走红运 have good luck;be in luck
走后门 get in by (*or* through) the back door—get sth done through pull;secure advantages through influence
走江湖 wander from place to place and earn a living by juggling,fortune-telling,etc.;become a vagrant
走老路 follow a set routine;move in a rut;stick to the old path
走轮包 suitcase with wheels
走马灯 running horse lantern (a lantern on the top band of which are decorative figures,which revolve as the hot air ascends)
走马疳 noma;gangrenous stomatitis
走门子 solicit help from potential backers;gain one's end through pull
走内线 take the inner line—use private influence to achieve one's end (e.g. seek sb's favour by approaching his confidants or members of his family);go through private channels
走娘家 (of a married woman) visit her parents' home
走亲戚 call on relatives
走时运 have good luck;be in luck
走私船 runner
走私犯 smuggler;owler
走私货 contraband goods
走弯路 take a wrong path;follow a zigzag course
走味儿 lose flavour
走形式 do sth as a mere formality;go through the motions
走着瞧 wait and see
走村串寨 go from village to village
走读大学 private,self-financing day college
走火入魔 possessed by the Devil
走马观花 look at flowers while riding a horse—gain a shallow understanding from a fleeting glance
走马换将 change of command;reshuffle of personnel
走马上任 go to one's post;take up (*or* assume) office

走南闯北 journey north and south;travel widely
走亲访友 call on relatives and friends
走上正轨 be on the right track
走投无路 have no way out;be in an impasse;come to a dead end
走下坡路 go downhill;be on the decline
走乡随乡 when in Rome do as the Romans do
走中间道路 steer a middle course
走一步,看一步 take one step and look around before taking another—proceed without a plan,or with caution

zòu(ㄗㄡˋ)

奏 [zòu]
𛰃 ①play;strike up;perform (on a musical instrument):奏国歌 play the national anthem/奏迎宾曲 strike up a tune of welcome ②achieve;attain;produce ③present a memorial to an emperor
奏本 present a memorial to an emperor (*or* the throne)
奏功 achieve success
奏捷 win a battle;score a success
奏效 prove effective;be successful;get the desired result
奏乐 play music;strike up a tune
奏章 memorial to the throne (*or* an emperor)
奏折 memorial to the throne (*or* an emperor) (as written on paper folded in accordion form)
奏鸣曲 sonata
奏鸣曲式 sonata form

揍 [zòu]
𛰃 ①beat;hit;strike:揍揍 get a thrashing (*or* beating) ②break;smash:小心别把瓶子揍了。Take care not to break the bottle.

zū(ㄗㄨ)

租 [zū]
Ⅰ 𛰃 ①rent;hire;lease;charter:按小时租自行车 hire a bicycle by the hour ②rent out;let out;hire out;lease:此房出租。House to let. Ⅱ 名 ①rent ②land tax
租船 chartering
租佃 (of a landlord) rent out land to tenants
租户 ①tenant;lessee;leaseholder ②hirer (of a thing)
租价 rent;rental
租界 concession;settlement
租借 rent;hire;lease
租金 rent;rental
租赁 rent;lease;hire
租让 lease
租税 (in former times) land tax and other levies

租用 rent;hire;take on lease
租约 lease
租债 rent and debt
租子 land rent;ground rent;rent
租船人 charterer
租借地 leased territory;leasehold
租借人 leaseholder;lessee;tenant;hirer
租赁业 leasing trade
租赁制 contractual and leasing system
租书处 book rental
租船代理 chartering agent
租船契约 charter party;charter
租船市场 chartering market
租佃关系 tenancy relationship
租佃制度 tenancy system
租赁承包 contract lease
租赁合同 contract for lease
租赁经营 leasing business
租赁贸易 the rent trade

莸 [zǔ] Ⅰ 名 ①marshland ②pickled Chinese cabbage;Chinese sauerkraut Ⅱ 动 cut or chop up（meat or vegetables）into very small pieces;mince;shred

ZÚ（ㄗㄨˊ）

足 [zú] Ⅰ 名 ①foot;leg ②leg-shaped support of utensils or instruments:三足凳 three-legged stool Ⅱ 形 enough;adequate;sufficient;ample:资金不足 inadequate fund Ⅲ 副 as much（or many）as necessary
足本 an unabridged version（of a novel,etc.）
足彩 football lottery
足赤 pure gold;solid gold
足够 enough;ample;sufficient
足迹 footmark;footprint;track
足价 full price
足见 it serves to show;one can well perceive
足金 pure gold;solid gold
足球 ①soccer;football ②football
足色 （of gold or silver）of standard purity
足岁 actual age
足坛 the football world
足下 a polite form of address between friends
足以 enough;sufficiently
足音 （sound of）footsteps
足银 pure silver
足月 （of a foetus）born after the normal period of gestation;mature
足球队 football team;eleven
足球迷 football fan
足不出户 never leave one's home
足谋寡断 resourceful but irresolute
足球宝贝 football baby
足球彩票 football lottery
足球流氓 football hooligan;soccer hooligan

足球先生 footballer;player of the year
足智多谋 wise and full of stratagems;wise and resourceful
足球运动员 footballer

卒 [zú] Ⅰ 名 ①soldier;private ②servant;attendant ③pawn,one of the pieces in Chinese chess Ⅱ 动 ①finish;end:有始有卒 begin well and end well ②die:生卒年月不详。The dates of birth and death are unknown. Ⅲ 副 at last;in the end;finally:卒偿素愿 had one's wishes fulfilled at long last ➡cù
卒岁 get through the year
卒业 graduate;finish a course of study
卒子 ①rank-and-file soldier ②pawn,one of the pieces in Chinese chess

崒 [zú] 形 steep;perilous

族 [zú] 名 ①clan ②death penalty in ancient China,imposed on an offender and his whole family,or even the families of his mother and wife ③nationality;race;ethnic group ④class or group of things or people with common features:芳香族化合物 aromatic compound;aromatic
族徽 emblem for a clan,tribe or nation
族际 between nations
族居 live together as a clan
族类 the same clan（tribe,nation）
族谱 family tree;genealogical tree;pedigree of a clan
族亲 members of a clan;clansmen
族权 clan authority;clan power
族群 certain group of people or things
族人 clansman
族长 clan elder;the head of a clan

ZǓ（ㄗㄨˇ）

诅 [zǔ] 动 ①curse;swear;abuse ②take an oath;make a vow;swear
诅骂 curse;swear;abuse;revile
诅盟 swear to form an alliance
诅咒 curse;swear;wish sb evil;imprecate

阻 [zǔ] 动 block;impede;hinder;obstruct
阻碍 hinder;block;impede
阻车 hold up traffic;traffic jam
阻挡 stop;stem;resist;obstruct
阻断 stop;obstruct;block;cut off
阻遏 check;stem;stop;repression;baffling
阻隔 separate;cut off
阻击 block;check
阻截 stop;obstruct;bar the way
阻抗 impedance
阻拦 stop;obstruct;bar the way

Z

阻力 ①obstruction; resistance ②resistance; drag
阻流 choked flow
阻留 be detained; be held up
阻挠 obstruct; thwart; stand in the way; put a spoke in sb's wheel
阻尼 damping
阻塞 block; obstruct; clog
阻援 hold off (*or* delay) enemy reinforcements
阻止 prevent; stop; hold back
阻击战 blocking action in a battle
阻挡犯规 blocking
阻抗匹配 impedance matching
阻塞振荡器 blocking oscillator

组 [zǔ] I 动 organize; build; form II 名 group; team III 量 ①set; series; battery; group: 两组透镜 two batteries of lenses/四组人 four groups of people/一组纪念邮票 a set of commemorative stamps ②(of literary works) suite; series
组胺 histamine
组办 organize; run
组编 put together (material); fit together
组成 form; make up; compose
组队 form a team (usu. to take part in a competition)
组分 component; constituents
组稿 (of editors) commission authors to write on given topics; solicit contributions
组歌 suite of songs
组阁 organize a cabinet
组合 ①make up; compose; constitute ②association; combination ③combination
组画 a series of paintings
组件 package; module
组建 put together (a group); form
组接 film montage; film editing
组曲 suite
组诗 set of poems
组台 organize a performance
组态 configuration
组团 organize a performance group, touring group, etc.
组长 group (*or* team) leader; headman; chargehand; chargeman
组织 ①organize; form ②organization; organized system ③weave ④tissue
组装 put together; assemble
组合柜 large multi-use cabinet (for sound system, TV, books, etc.)
组合体 assembly
组委会 organizing committee
组织法 rules of organization; organic law; constituent act
组织学 histology

组织液 tissue fluid
组装机 kludge; kluge
组成部分 component part; component; ingredient
组合车床 combined lathe
组合贷款 loan portfolio
组合家具 composite furniture; component furniture
组合理论 combinatorial theory
组合音响 hi-fi stereo component system; hi-fi (system, set, equipment)
组合钻床 combination drilling machine
组织关系 credentials showing membership in an organization; membership credentials
组织疗法 tissue therapy; histotherapy
组织生活 regular activities of an organization
组织实施 initiate and put into operation
组织条例 organizational rules
组织原则 principle of organazition
组字游戏 crossword puzzle
组织纪律性 sense of organizational discipline
组织行为学 organizational behaviourism

俎 [zǔ] 名 ①sacrificial vessel ②chopping block
俎上肉 meat on a chopping block

祖 [zǔ] 名 ①grandfather ②ancestor ③founder (of a craft, religious sect, etc.); originator
祖辈 ancestors; forefathers; ancestry
祖本 first edition (of a block-printed book); first rubbing (taken from a stone inscription)
祖产 property handed down from one's ancestors; ancestral estate
祖传 handed down from one's ancestors
祖坟 ancestral grave
祖父 (paternal) grandfather
祖国 one's country; homeland; native land; motherland; fatherland
祖籍 original family home; ancestral home; the land of one's ancestors
祖居 ① ancestral home ② original family home; ancestral home; the land of one's ancestors ③have one's ancestral home at; be a native of
祖母 (paternal) grandmother
祖上 ancestors; forefathers; forbears
祖孙 grandparent and grandchild
祖先 ancestry; ancestors; forbears; forefathers
祖业 property handed down from one's ancestors; ancestral estate
祖茔 ancestral grave
祖宗 forefathers; ancestry; forbears
祖母绿 emerald
祖师(爷) ①the founder of a school of learning, a craft, etc. ②the founder of a sect of Buddhism or Taoism

祖传秘方 a secret prescription handed down in the family from generation to generation

祖祖辈辈 for generations;from generation to generation

zuān（ㄗㄨㄢ）

钻 ［zuān］
劲 ① drill；bore ② get into；sneak into；make one's way into：钻进地窖 go down into the cellar/钻进人群 be lost（*or* vanish）in the crowd ③make a thorough study of；study intensively；dig into：钻书本 bury oneself in books；dig into books ④curry favour with sb in authority；secure personal gain ➡ zuàn

钻劲 application to studies；studiousness

钻井 well drilling

钻孔 drill；bore

钻圈 jumping（*or* plunging）through hoops

钻探（exploration）drilling

钻心 ①（of pain,itching,etc.）unbearable ② sneak in；infiltrate

钻研 study intensively；dig into

钻营 curry favour with sb in authority for personal gain；secure personal gain

钻井船 oil rig

钻井队 drilling crew（*or* team）

钻空子 avail oneself of loopholes（in a law,contract,etc.）；exploit an advantage

钻门子 jockey for favours；manoeuvre for advantage

钻探工 driller

钻探机 drilling machine

钻天柳 lombardy poplar（Populus nigra var. italica）

钻天杨 Chosenia macrolepis

钻心虫 borer

钻故纸堆 bury oneself in outdated writings；delve into musty old books

钻井工人 driller

钻井记录 drill log

钻木取火 drill wood to make fire

钻牛角尖 ① take unnecessary pains to study an insignificant or insoluble problem；split hairs ②get into a dead end（*or* a blind alley）

钻探设备 drilling equipment

钻头觅缝 worm oneself into every crack and crevice—try all possible means

zuǎn（ㄗㄨㄢ）

缵 ［zuǎn］
劲 inherit

纂 ［zuǎn］
Ⅰ 劲 compile；edit Ⅱ 名 large knot or roll of hair worn at the back of the head by women；bun；chignon

纂辑 compile

纂修 compile；edit；prepare

zuàn（ㄗㄨㄢ）

钻 ［zuàn］
Ⅰ 名 ①drill；auger ②diamond；jewel：十七钻的手表 17-jewel watch Ⅱ 劲 drill（*or* bore）with auger（*or* drill）➡ zuān

钻床 drilling machine；driller

钻杆 drill rod（*or* pipe）

钻机（drilling）rig；drilling machine

钻戒 diamond ring

钻具 drilling tool；drilling rig

钻模（drill）jig

钻石 ①diamond ②jewel

钻塔 boring tower；derrick

钻台 drilling platform

钻铤 drill collar

钻头 bit（of a drill）

钻压 bit pressure；bit weight

赚 ［zuàn］
劲 deceive；hoax；fool；kid ➡ zhuàn

攥 ［zuàn］
劲 grip；grasp；clasp；hold：手里攥着一把刀 hold a knife in one's hand

攥拳 clench one's fist

zuǐ（ㄗㄨㄟ）

嘴 ［zuǐ］
Ⅰ 名 ①mouth ②anything shaped（*or* functioning）like a mouth Ⅱ 劲 speak；talk：堵他的嘴 tie his tongue；stop（*or* shut）his mouth

嘴巴 mouth

嘴笨 inarticulate；clumsy of speech

嘴馋 fond of good food；greedy；voracious

嘴唇 lip

嘴臭 having a sinking mouth

嘴刁 ①be choosy about what one eat；be particular about food ②cunning tricky

嘴乖（of children）clever and pleasant when speaking to elders

嘴尖 ①sharp-tongued；cutting in speech ②be choosy about what one eats ③have a keen sense of taste

嘴角 corners of the mouth

嘴紧 tight-lipped；closemouthed

嘴快 have a loose tongue

嘴懒 not inclined to talk much

嘴脸 face；features；countenance

嘴贫 loquacious；garrulous

嘴勤 fond of talking；chatty

嘴软 afraid to speak out

嘴松 have a loose tongue

嘴碎 loquacious；garrulous

嘴损 sharptongued；sarcastic

嘴甜 ingratiating in speech；smooth-tongued；

honeymouthed
嘴稳 discreet in speech;able to keep a secret
嘴严 tight-lipped;closemouthed
嘴硬 stubborn and reluctant to admit mistakes or defeats
嘴直 outspoken;plainspoken
嘴子 ①anything shaped or functioning like a mouth ② mouthpiece (of a wind instrument)
嘴啃泥 fall on one's face
嘴皮子 lips (of a glib talker)
嘴不饶人 fond of making sarcastic remarks
嘴上没毛,办事不牢 A man too young to grow a beard is not dependable;A man with downy lips is bound to make slips.

zuì(ㄗㄨㄟˋ)

最 [zuì]
Ⅰ 副 ①most;least;best;to the highest or lowest degree:跑得最快 run the fastest;be the fastest runner/时间最短 take the shortest time/质量最差 of the poorest quality ②farthest to;nearest Ⅱ 名 best;top
最爱 favourite
最初 initial;first
最大 the biggest;the largest;the greatest;maximum
最低 lowest;minimum
最多 most;at (the) most;maximum
最高 highest;supreme;tallest
最好 ①best;first-rate ②had better;it would be best
最后 final;last;ultimate
最佳 ①optimum ②the best
最近 ①recently;lately;of late ②in the near future;soon
最少 least;at (the) least;minimum
最为 most;extremely
最先 the first;the earliest
最小 the smallest;the tiniest;minimal
最新 latest;up-to-date
最优 optimal;optimum
最终 final;ultimate
最北边 farthest to the north;northernmost
最大值 maximum (value)
最高点 statistics peak
最高级 ①highest;summit ②the superlative degree
最惠国 most-favoured-nation
最困难 most difficult;hardest
最里头 innermost
最便宜 cheapest;least expensive
最前线 nearest the front;forefront
最下层 nearest the bottom;at the very bottom;bottommost
最要紧 most crucial;most important

最不中用 out of the least use
最低纲领 minimum programme
最低价格 lowest price;bottom price;bedrock price
最低税率 minimum tariff
最低温度 minimum temperature
最低限额 zero norm;nil norm
最低限价 lowest (or floor) price limit
最高纲领 maximum programme
最高关税 maximum tariff
最高权力 supreme power
最高税率 maximum tariff
最高速度 maximum speed
最高统帅 supreme commander
最高温度 maximum temperature
最高限额 ceiling
最高限价 price ceiling;ceiling price
最好成绩 best result
最后冲刺 final spurt
最后条款 final provisions;final articles
最后通牒 ultimatum
最佳服务 optimum services;best services
最轻量级 bantamweight
最新产品 latest product;newest product
最新工艺 latest technology
最新技术 up-to-date technology
最新款式 latest fashion
最新消息 latest (or red-hot, stop-press) news;up-to-the-minute information
最优方法 optimization method
最大公约数 greatest common divisor
最高级会议 summit conference (or meeting)
最高年产量 peak annual output
最后议定书 final protocol
最后议事录 precés-verbal final
最惠国待遇 most-favoured-nation (MFN) treatment;MFN trading status
最惠国税率 most-favoured-nation rate
最惠国条款 most-favoured-nation clause
最小二乘法 least square method
最小公倍数 least (or lowest) common multiple
最新流行品 last cry
最终消费者 ultimate consumer
最不发达国家 least developed countries
最高国务会议 the Supreme State Conference
最高人民法院 supreme people's court
最佳竞技状态 career-best times
最佳男主角奖 Best Male Lead Award
最佳女主角奖 Best Female Lead Award
最简单派艺术 minimal art
最简单派艺术家 minimal artist;minimalist
最低生活保障制度 system for ensuring a minimum standard of living

晬 [zuì]
名 child's first birthday

罪 [zuì]
Ⅰ 〔名〕① guilt; offence; crime ② fault; failing; blame: 是我之罪。It's my fault; I'm to blame. ③ suffering; hardship; pain Ⅱ 〔动〕 put the blame on; blame
罪案 details of a criminal case; case
罪错 criminal offenses and errors
罪恶 crime; evil
罪犯 criminal; offender; culprit
罪过 ① fault; offence; sin ② thanks, but this is really more than I deserve
罪己 blame oneself for wrongdoing; take the blame on oneself
罪魁 chief criminal (or culprit, offender); archcriminal
罪名 charge; accusation
罪孽 wrongdoing that brings retribution; sin
罪人 guilty person; offender; sinner
罪嫌 suspect
罪刑 crime and punishment
罪行 crime; guilt; offence
罪责 responsibility for an offence
罪证 evidence of a crime; proof of one's guilt
罪状 facts about a crime; charges in an indictment
罪不容诛 even death cannot atone for the offence; be guilty of crimes for which even death is insufficient punishment
罪大恶极 be guilty of the most heinous crimes
罪恶昭彰 have committed flagrant crimes
罪该万死 be guilty of a crime for which one deserves to die ten thousand deaths; be guilty of a crime for which even death cannot atone
罪加一等 be doubly guilty
罪魁祸首 chief criminal (or culprit, offender); ringleader; archcriminal
罪莫大焉 There is no greater crime than this.
罪刑法定 Crimes shall be punished only under the law.
罪有应得 One deserves one's punishment; The punishment fits the crime.
罪行和过错 criminal offenses and errors

醉 [zuì]
Ⅰ 〔形〕① drunk; intoxicated; inebriated; tipsy: 把他灌醉 drink him down ② (of certain food or fruits) liquor-saturated; soaked or steeped in liquor Ⅱ 〔动〕 be drunk with; indulge in: 美丽的夜色使她心醉。She was enchanted by (or with) the beauty of the night.
醉鬼 drunkard; sot; inebriate
醉汉 drunkard; drunken man
醉话 words uttered when a person becomes drunk
醉酒 drunk; intoxicated
醉拳 drunken boxing (a form of boxing with movements suggesting a drunken man reeling along)
醉人 ① make drunk; intoxicate ② in toxicating; enchanting; fascinating
醉态 drunkenness
醉蟹 liquor-saturated crab
醉心 be bent on; be wrapped up in
醉眼 eyes showing the effects of drink
醉意 signs (or feeling) of getting drunk
醉枣 wine-soaked dates
醉醺醺 sottish; drunk; tipsy
醉生梦死 live as if drunk or dreaming; lead a befuddled life
醉言不较 do not find fault with drunken talk
醉翁之意不在酒 the Old Tippler's delight does not reside in wine—have other things in mind; have ulterior motives

zūn（ㄗㄨㄣ）

尊 [zūn]
Ⅰ 〔形〕① of a senior generation; senior; elder ② your Ⅱ 〔动〕 esteem; respect; honour; venerate: 尊他为老师 look up to him as one's teacher Ⅲ 〔量〕: 二十尊大炮 twenty artillery pieces/一尊佛像 a statue of a Buddha Ⅳ 〔名〕 wine vessel
尊称 ① a respectful form of address; honorific title ② address sb respectfully
尊崇 worship; revere; venerate
尊府 ① your residence; your home ② your father
尊贵 honourable; respectable; respected
尊驾 you
尊敬 respect; honour; esteem
尊命 your instructions
尊容 distinguished face
尊严 dignity; honour
尊意 your opinion
尊长 elders and betters
尊重 ① respect; value; esteem ② serious; proper
尊卑有序 proper regard for precedence (or priority in place or rank); proper order of seniority
尊德乐道 honour virtue and keep to (or abide by) moral principles
尊而不敬 show courtesy but no respect
尊老爱幼 respect the old and cherish the young
尊师爱生 respect the teacher and love the student; students respecting teachers and teachers loving students
尊师重道 honour the teacher and revere his teachings
尊姓大名 your name

遵 [zūn]
〔动〕 abide by; obey; adhere to; observe; follow

Z

遵办 act in compliance with instructions
遵从 defer to;comply with;follow
遵命 comply with your wish;obey your command
遵守 observe;abide by;comply with
遵行 act on;follow
遵循 follow;abide by;adhere to
遵照 obey;conform to;comply with;act in accordance with
遵纪守法 observe law and discipline;abide by the law and observe discipline
遵令而行 act according to orders
遵守诺言 honour one's promise

樽 [zūn] 名 wine vessel used in ancient times

鳟 [zūn] 名 trout

zǔn(ㄗㄨㄣˇ)

撙 [zǔn] 劲 save

撙节 save;retrench

zùn(ㄗㄨㄣˋ)

拨 [zùn] 劲 press with one's finger

zuō(ㄗㄨㄛ)

作 [zuō] 名 workshop ⇒ zuò

作坊 workshop

嘬 [zuō] 劲 suck:让她嘬一口 let her have a suck/嘬奶的婴儿 baby sucking at its mother's breast ⇒ chuài

嘬瘪子 feel embarrassed;be nonplussed

zuó(ㄗㄨㄛˊ)

昨 [zuó] 名 ①yesterday ②the past
昨日 yesterday
昨天 yesterday
昨晚 yesterday evening;last night
昨夜 yesterday evening;last night
昨儿个 yesterday

捽 [zuó] 劲 seize;hold tight;grasp

笮 [zuó] 名 rope made of thin bamboo strips

琢 [zuó] ⇒ zhuó

琢磨 [zuómo] think over;turn over in one's mind;ponder

zuǒ(ㄗㄨㄛˇ)

左 [zuǒ] Ⅰ 名 ①left;left side ②east ③"left" deviation Ⅱ 形 ①eccentric;heretical;unorthodox ②wrong;erroneous;incorrect ③contrary;opposite;different ④ progressive;revolutionary;the left
左边 [zuǒbian] the left;the left (or left-hand) side
左侧 the left;the left (or left-hand) side
左舵 left standard rudder;left rudder
左锋 left forward
左近 in the vicinity (or neighbourhood);nearby
左面 the left (or left-hand) side;the left
左派 ①the Left;the left wing ②Leftist
左倾 ① left-leaning;progressive;inclined towards the revolution ②" Left "deviation
左手 the left hand
左首 the left-hand side;the left
左舷 port (of a ship)
左…右… over and over again
左翼 ①left wing;left flank ②the left wing;the Left
左右 ①the left and right sides ②about;or so ③ master;control;influence ④ those in close attendance;retinue ⑤ anyway;anyhow;in any case
左边锋 outside left;left wing
左不过 ①anyway;anyhow;in any event ②only;merely;just
左后卫 left back
左内锋 inside left
左撇子 left-handed person;left-hander;lefty
左前卫 left halfback;left half
左性子 stubborn;pigheaded;wilful
左右手 right-hand man;capable assistant
左膀右臂 right-hand man;a capable assistant
左道旁门 ① heretical sect;heterodox school ②heresy;heterodoxy
左顾右盼 glance right and left;look around
左邻右舍 neighbours
左思右想 think over from different angles;turn sth over in one's mind
左提右挈 ①help each other;give mutual help ② guide and support;give guidance and help to
左翼阵线 leftist front
左右逢源 ① be able to achieve success one way or another ②gain advantage from both sides
左右开弓 shoot first with one hand,then with the other;use both hands alternately in quick succession;be ambidextrous
左右为难 in a dilemma;in an awkward predicament
左支右绌 find it hard to cover expenses;be in straitened circumstances; have too many

problems to cope with
左轮(手枪) bulldog;revolver
"左"倾空谈 "Left" phrasemongering
"左"倾机会主义 "Left" opportunism
"左"倾冒险主义 "Left" adventurism
"左"的和右的干扰 interference from both the "Left" and the Right

佐 [zuǒ]
I 动 assist;help II 名 assistant
佐餐 ①be eaten together with rice or bread; go with rice or bread ②appetizing
佐酒 ① drink with sb ②(of food) go with wine
佐理 assist sb in management;assist sb with a task
佐药 adjuvant
佐证 evidence;proof

撮 [zuǒ]
量 (for a bunch of hair):一撮白毛 a tuft of white hair/一撮胡子 a tuft of beard ⟹cuō
撮子 tuft (of hair)

ZUÒ(ㄗㄨㄛ)

作 [zuò]
I 动 ① make; manufacture; produce ② rise;get up:枪声大作。Heavy fighting broke out. ③do;work at;engage in:作报告 deliver a speech;give a talk;make a talk;make a report/作长期打算 plan on a long-term basis ④ take sb or sth for;regard as;consider to be:把她当作亲闺女 treat her as one's own daughter ⑤write;compose ⑥pretend;feign;affect ⑦act as;be;become ⑧feel;have II 名 writings;work ⟹zuō
作案 commit a crime;carry out criminal activities
作罢 drop;relinquish;give up
作伴 keep company
作保 be sb's guarantor;go bail for sb;sponsor sb
作弊 practise fraud;cheat;indulge in corrupt practices
作别 bid farewell;take one's leave
作成 help (sb to achieve his or her aim)
作词 write words (for a song)
作答 answer
作对 ①set oneself against;oppose ②pair off in marriage
作恶 ①do evil ②gloomy;melancholy
作伐 act as matchmaker
作法 ①exercise magic ②technique of writing
作废 become invalid
作风 style;style of work;way
作复 write in reply;write back
作梗 obstruct;hinder;create difficulties
作古 die;pass away
作怪 do mischief;make trouble

作画 paint
作害 (of birds and beasts) damage (crops, etc.);make havoc of
作家 writer;author
作价 fix a price for sth;evaluate
作假 ①counterfeit;falsify ②cheat;play tricks ③behave affectedly
作践 ①spoil;waste ②run sb down;disparage ③humiliate;insult
作客 sojourn
作乐 make merry;enjoy oneself;have a good time
作脸 win honour for;win glory for;try to make a good showing
作料 condiments;seasonings;dressings
作乱 stage an armed rebellion
作美 (of weather,etc.) help;cooperate;make things easy for sb
作难 [zuònán] ①feel embarrassed;feel awkward;find oneself in a predicament ②make things difficult for sb
作难 [zuònàn] start a revolt;rise in revolt
作孽 do evil;commit a sin
作弄 tease;make a fool of;play a trick on; poke fun at
作呕 feel sick;feel like vomiting;be overcome by nausea
作陪 help entertain the guest of honour;be invited along with the chief guest
作品 works (of literature and art)
作畦 bedding
作情 ①admire ②send gifts;make a gift of sth ③mediate;arbitrate ④feel grateful to sb; appreciate the kindness ⑤be affected (or pretentious);strike a pose
作曲 ① write music;compose ② write music (for a song)
作色 show signs of anger;get worked up
作声 make a sound
作诗 compose (or write) a poem
作势 assume a posture;attitudinize
作数 count;be valid
作死 seek death;take the road to ruin;look for trouble
作速 lose no time;hasten
作祟 ① (of ghosts, spirits, etc.) haunt ② make mischief;cause trouble;exercise evil influence
作态 pose;affect;strike an attitude
作痛 have a pain;ache
作为 ① conduct; deed; action ② accomplishment;achievement ③scope for one's abilities (or talents) ④act;regard as;look on as;take as ⑤in the role and character of;as
作伪 fake (works of art,cultural relics,etc.); make an imitation;forge
作文 ① (of students) write a composition ②

Z

composition
作物 crop
作息 work and rest
作响 make a sound
作兴 ①there's reason to; it's justifiable (*or* permissible) to ②perhaps; possibly; maybe
作秀 perform; show
作痒 have an itch; itch all over
作业 ①school assignment ②work; task; operation; production
作揖 make a slight bow with hands folded in front
作艺 perform; put on a show
作俑 ①make idols to be buried with the dead ②initiate an immoral and bad practice; create a bad precedent
作用 ① act on; affect ② action; function ③ effect ④purpose; intention; motive
作乐 ① write music; compose music ② play music
作战 fight; conduct operations; do battle
作者 author; writer
作证 ①be used as evidence ②testify; give evidence; bear witness
作主 ① decide; take the responsibility for a decision ②back up; support
作准 ①count; be valid ②approve; recognize; acknowledge
作表率 serve as an example
作调查 investigate
作斗争 wage a struggle; fight against; combat
作功课 do one's homework
作假账 falsify accounts
作结论 reach a conclusion; pass a verdict
作曲家 composer
作文章 write an essay (*or* article)
作向导 act as a guide
作用力 acting force
作战线 battle line
作案现场 scene of a crime
作壁上观 watch the fighting from the ramparts—sit by and watch; be an onlooker (*or* bystander)
作法自毙 make a law only to fall foul of it oneself; be hoist with one's own petard; get caught in one's own trap
作废支票 spoilaged check
作风正派 be honest and upright
作家协会 the Writers' Union
作奸犯科 violate the law and commit crimes; commit offences against law and discipline
作茧自缚 spin a cocoon around oneself; get enmeshed in a web of one's own spinning
作客思想 feeling of not belonging; guest mentality
作困兽斗 fight like a cornered beast; fight back at bay

作鸟兽散 scatter like birds and beasts; flee helter-skelter; stampede
作如是观 view the matter in this light
作威作福 act tyrannically; tyrannically abuse one's power; ride roughshod over others; act like a tyrant
作战部队 combat (*or* fighting) troops
作战部署 operational preparations
作战地图 battle map; operation map
作战方案 battle plan; line of action
作战方法 method of fighting; tactics in operations
作战方式 mode of operations
作战方针 concept of operations; operational principles; operational policy
作战基地 operational base; base of operations
作战技术 fighting technique
作战命令 combat (*or* operation) order
作战区域 theatre of war
作战效能 fighting efficiency
作息时间表 daily schedule; work schedule; timetable
作战直升机 gunship
作战指挥部 operational headquarters

坐 [zuò]
Ⅰ〔动〕①sit; be seated; take a seat ②travel by (bus, train, plane, etc.) ③(of a building) have its back towards: 这幢大楼坐北朝南。 This building faces south. ④put (a kettle, pot, pan, etc.) on a fire: 把这壶水坐上 put the kettle of water on the fire ⑤(of guns, etc.) recoil; kick; kick back ⑥(of a building) sink; sag; subside: 这堵墙向后坐了。 This wall is beginning to slope backwards. ⑦(of fruit, melon, gourd, etc.) bear fruit ⑧be punished ⑨result in a disease; develop into a disease: 坐下了腰疼病 gradually get lumbago Ⅱ〔名〕seat; place Ⅲ〔副〕for no reason at all; without cause
坐班 keep office hours; keep set office hours (where staff are required to be in their offices during certain hours)
坐标 coordinate
坐禅 sit in meditation
坐船 by boat; embark (on a ship)
坐待 sit back and wait
坐等 sit back and wait
坐垫 cushion
坐骨 ischium
坐果 bear fruit; fructify; fruit setting; fruition
坐化 (of Buddhist monks) pass away (*or* die) in a sitting posture
坐具 a thing to sit on; seat
坐困 be confined; be walled in; be shut up
坐蜡 land in a predicament; be cornered; be put in a tight spot
坐牢 be in prison; be in jail; be imprisoned

坐力 recoil (of a gun);kick
坐落 (of a building) be situated;be located
坐坡 kick-back
坐骑 saddle horse;mount
坐蓐 confinement in child-birth;lying-in
坐商 tradesman;shopkeeper
坐失 let sth slip by
坐探 an enemy agent planted within one's own ranks
坐位 ①place to sit;seat ②thing to sit on;seat
坐席 ①take one's seat at a banquet table ② attend a banquet
坐药 suppository
坐椅 seat
坐浴 a hip bath
坐诊 sitin doctor
坐镇 (of a commander) personally attend to garrison duty;assume personal command
坐正 sit properly
坐庄 ①be a resident buyer of a business firm ②be the banker or dealer (in a gambling game)
坐班房 be in prison
坐不下 (of a vehicle, table, room, etc.) have not enough seats for (a certain number of people);cannot seat
坐不住 cannot sit still;be restless;fidget
坐得下 (of a vehicle, table, room, etc.) have seats for (a certain number of people);seat
坐得住 can sit still;can sit for long
坐飞机 by air
坐监(狱) be in prison;be in jail;be imprisoned
坐禁闭 be confined;be placed in confinement (as a disciplinary measure)
坐山雕 cinereous vulture
坐月子 confinement in childbirth;lying-in
坐吃山空 fritter away a great fortune;if left to sit idle, one can even consume a mountain;sit idle and eat, and in time your whole fortune will be used up
坐地分赃 (of a ringleader, criminal, receiver of stolen goods, etc.) take a share of the spoils without participating in the robbery
坐而论道 sit and talk idly;sit back and pontificate
坐骨神经 sciatic nerve
坐观成败 wait to see what will come of another's venture;look on coldly;be a mere onlooker
坐怀不乱 be not disturbed with a woman in one's lap;wear Joseph's coat
坐井观天 look at the sky from the bottom of a well—have a very narrow view
坐困愁城 be walled in by one's own worries
坐冷板凳 sit on a cold bench—hold an unimportant post and be neglected;be kept waiting for an assignment or an audience with a VIP
坐立不安 feel uneasy whether sitting or standing;be fidgety;be on tenterhooks
坐失良机 let slip a golden opportunity;miss the bus (or boat);fail to take the tide at the flood
坐视不救 sit back and watch without going to the rescue
坐收渔利 reap the spoils of victory without lifting a finger;profit from others' conflict;reap third party profit
坐卧不安 be unable to sit down or sleep at ease;feel restless;be on tenterhooks
坐享其成 enjoy fruits of others' work;sit idle and enjoy the fruits of others' work;reap where one has not sown
坐以待毙 sit still waiting for death;await one's doom;resign oneself to death
坐以待旦 sit up and wait for daybreak
坐山观虎斗 sit on top of the mountain to watch the tigers fight—watch in safety while others fight, then reap the spoils when both sides are exhausted

怍 [zuò]
〔形〕 ashamed

柞 [zuò]
〔名〕 oak
柞蚕 tussah
柞树 oaks;oak tree
柞蚕丝 tussah silk;wild silk;antherea silk
柞丝绸 lustrous, tussah silk fabric with a plain weave, suitable for making summer dresses;pongee

祚 [zuò]
〔名〕 ①good fortune;blessing ②throne

唑 [zuò]
◇咔唑 carbazole
噻唑 thiazole

座 [zuò]
Ⅰ〔名〕① seat; place：请入座。Please be seated. ②stand; base;pedetal ③constellation ④ form of address to high-ranking officials Ⅱ〔量〕(of large and solid thing)：两座摩天大楼 two skyscrapers/一座大理石雕像 a statue in marble/一座水库 a reservoir
座儿 patron;passenger
座舱 ① passenger cabin (in an airliner) ② cockpit (of a fighter)
座次 order of seats;seating arrangements
座号 seat number
座机 sb's private plane
座谈 have an informal discussion
座位 a place to sit;seat
座席 ①take one's seat at a banquet table ② attend a banquet
座椅 seat
座钟 desk clock

Z

座子 ①stand;pedestal;base ②saddle
座上客 guest of honour;honoured guest
座谈会 forum;symposium;informal discussion
座右铭 motto;maxim
座无虚席 all seats are occupied;there are no empty seats

做 [zuò]
动 ①do;act;undertake;engage in:做前人没有做过的事情 be engaged in a cause never undertaken by one's forefathers (or before)/说得好不如做得好. Action speaks louder than words. ②make;manufacture;produce:做鞋 make shoes ③write;compose ④hold a family celebration ⑤be;become ⑥be used as;serve as:这雨伞也可以做拐杖。The umbrella can serve as a walking stick. ⑦form (or contract) a relationship ⑧pretend;feign;make believe;do sth for appearance sake
做爱 make love
做操 do gymnastics;do callisthenics;do exercises
做大 put on airs;give oneself airs
做到 accomplish;achieve
做东 play the host;host sb;act as host to sb
做法 way of doing or making a thing;method of work;practice
做饭 do the cooking;prepare a meal
做工 ①do manual work;work ②charge for the making of sth ③workmanship
做功 acting;apply work;business
做官 be an official;secure an official position
做鬼 play tricks;play an underhand game;get up to mischief
做绝 leave no room for manoeuvre
做媒 be a matchmaker (or go-between)
做梦 ①have a dream;dream ②have a pipe dream;daydream
做亲 ①(of two families) become related by marriage ②get married
做人 ①conduct oneself;behave ②be an upright person
做事 ①do work;do a deed;handle affairs ②work;have a job
做寿 celebrate the birthday (usu. of elderly people);hold a birthday party
做戏 ①put on a play;act in a play ②playact;pretend

做作 affected;artificial
做对头 set oneself against sb;be hostile to sb
做翻译 act as an interpreter;interpret for sb
做好人 try to be a good fellow;try to get along with everyone
做活儿 do manual labour;work
做假账 salt an account;tamper with accounting records
做礼拜 go to church;be at church
做买卖 do business;carry on trade
做满月 celebrate a baby's birth when he is one month old
做朋友 make friends (with sb);become friends
做圈套 set a trap (to deceive sb)
做人情 do sb a favour
做生日 celebrate sb's birthday;hold (or throw) a birthday party for sb
做生意 do business;carry on trade
做手脚 juggle things;put up a job
做文章 ①write a composition;write an article ②make an issue of sth;make a fuss about sth
做学问 engage in scholarship;do research
做样子 make a show;go through the motions;for appearance sake;for the sake of appearance
做针线 do needlework;sew
做字典 compile a dictionary
做好做歹 try every possible way to persuade sb or to mediate
做老实人 be an honest person
做零活儿 do odd jobs
做贼心虚 have a guilty conscience like a thief;have sth on one's conscience
做两手准备 prepare for two eventualities
做一天和尚撞一天钟 go on tolling the bell as long as one is a monk—do the least that is expected of one;take a passive attitude towards one's work

酢 [zuò]
动 (of a guest) propose a toast to the host
➡cù

西文字母开头的词语

B 超 ①ultrasonic diagnosis B ②ultrasonograph B
B 股 B-share
C 值 DNA content
K 金 carat gold
X 刀 X-ray knife
X 光 X-ray
γ 刀 gamma knife
A 股 A-share
AB 角 two actors playing the same role in a theatrical work
AB 制 system in which two actors play the same role in a theatrical work
BP 机 wireless beeper；pager
CD 机 CD (compact disk) player
CT 机 CT (computerized tomography) apparatus
e 化 electronic
H 股 H-share
IC 卡 IC card
IP 卡 IP telephone card
Ma 数 Mach number
PC 机 personal computer
pH 计 pH meter
pH 值 pH value
A 型血 blood type A
AA 制 going Dutch；Dutch treat
ATM 机 automated teller machine
B 夸克 beauty quark，a drug
B 型血 blood type B
DVD 机 DVD (digital video disk) player
O 型血 blood type O
POS 机 ①POS terminal ②cash register in a store
SIM 卡 SIM card
T 型台 catwalk

T 恤衫 T-shirt
VCD 机 VCD (video compact disk) player
X 射线 X-ray
α 射线 α (particle) ray；alpha ray
α 衰变 α-decay
γ 射线 γ ray；gamma ray
AB 型血 blood type AB
CT 扫描 computerized tomography
IP 地址 Internet protocol address；IP address
IP 电话 IP telephone
IT 产业 IT (information technology)
ABC 武器 atomic，bacteriological and chemical weapons
DNA 芯片 DNA chip
DNA 指纹 DNA fingerprint
PTC 陶瓷 PTC (positive temperature coefficient) porcelain
SPF 动物 SPF animal
X 射线源 X-ray source；X-ray burster
α 粒子 α particle；alpha particle
F-1 赛车 Fomular One racing (car)；F-1 racing
B 淋巴细胞 bone marrow lymphocyte
DNA 基因图 DNA (deoxyribonucleic acid) profile
n 型半导体 negative semiconductor；N-semiconductor
p 型半导体 positive semiconductor；P-semiconductor
SOS 儿童村 SOS children's village
T 淋巴细胞 thymus lymphocyte
DNA 指纹鉴定 DNA fingerprinting
β 粒子 β particle；beta particle
β 射线 β ray；beta ray
β 衰变 β-decay

中国各民族

阿昌族	Achang	Achang	傈僳族	Lisu	Lisu
白族	Bai	Bai	珞巴族	Luoba	Lhoba
保安族	Bao'an	Bonan	满族	Man	Manchu
布朗族	Bulang	Blang	毛南族	Maonan	Maonan
布依族	Buyi	Bouyei	门巴族	Menba	Monba
朝鲜族	Chaoxian	Korean	蒙古族	Menggu	Mongol
达斡尔族	Dawo'er	Daur	苗族	Miao	Miao
傣族	Dai	Dai	仫佬族	Mulao	Mulam
德昂族	De'ang	De'ang	纳西族	Naxi	Naxi
东乡族	Dongxiang	Dongxiang	怒族	Nu	Nu
侗族	Dong	Dong	普米族	Pumi	Primi
独龙族	Dulong	Derung	羌族	Qiang	Qiang
俄罗斯族	Eluosi	Russian	撒拉族	Sala	Salar
鄂伦春族	Elunchun	Oroqen	畲族	She	She
鄂温克族	Ewenke	Ewenki	水族	Shui	Sui
高山族	Gaoshan	Gaoshan	塔吉克族	Tajike	Tajik
仡佬族	Gelao	Gelao	塔塔尔族	Tata'er	Tatar
哈尼族	Hani	Hani	土族	Tu	Tu
哈萨克族	Hasake	Kazak	土家族	Tujia	Tujia
汉族	Han	Han	佤族	Wa	Va
赫哲族	Hezhe	Hezhen	维吾尔族	Weiwu'er	Uygur
回族	Hui	Hui	乌孜别克族	Wuzibieke	Uzbek
基诺族	Jinuo	Jino	锡伯族	Xibo	Xibe
京族	Jing	Gin	彝族	Yi	Yi
景颇族	Jingpo	Jingpo	瑶族	Yao	Yao
柯尔克孜族	Ke'erkezi	Kirgiz	裕固族	Yugu	Yugur
拉祜族	Lahu	Lahu	藏族	Zang	Tibetan
黎族	Li	Li	壮族	Zhuang	Zhuang

附录二

中国法定假日和主要传统节日

法定假日 Official Holidays

元旦	New Year's Day (1 January, 1 day off)
国际劳动妇女节	International Working Women's Day (8 March, 1/2 day off for women)
国际劳动节	International Labour Day (1 May, 1 day off)
中国青年节	Chinese Youth Day (4 May, 1/2 day off for youths of and above 14)
国际儿童节	International Children's Day (1 June, 1 day off for those below 14)
中国人民解放军建军节	Army Day (Anniversary of the Founding of the Chinese People's Liberation Army, 1 August, 1/2 day off for those in active service)
国庆节	National Day (1 October, 3 days off)
春节	Spring Festival(*or* Chinese New Year's Day, 1st of the first lunar month, 3 days off)
元宵节	Lantern Festival (15th of the first lunar month, marking the end of Chinese New Year celebrations with a display of colourful lanterns and eating of *yuanxiao*)
清明节	Pure Brightness Festival (marking the 5th seasonal division point and usually falling on the 4th or 6th of April, a traditional festival for commemorating the dead, 1 day off)
端午节	Dragon Boat Festival (5th of the fifth lunar month, celebrated by eating *zongzi* and holding dragon boat races, 1 day off)
中秋节	Mid-Autumn Festival (15th of the eighth lunar month, a traditional festival for family reunion, celebrated by eating moon cakes and enjoying the full moon, 1 day off)
重阳节	Double Ninth Festival (9 th of the ninth lunar month, celebrated by climbing heights to enjoy nature and honouring elderly people)

附录三

中国人民解放军军衔

陆　军 Army

一级上将	General First Class	中尉	First Lieutenant
上将	General	少尉	Second Lieutenant
中将	Lieutenant General	军士长	Master Sergeant
少将	Major General	专业军士	Specialist Sergeant
大校	Senior Colonel	上士	Sergeant, First Class
上校	Colonel	中士	Sergeant
中校	Lieutenant Colonel	下士	Corporal
少校	Major	上等兵	Private, First Class
上尉	Captain	列兵	Private

海　军 Navy

一级上将	Admiral, First Class	中尉	Lieutenant, Junior Grade
上将	Admiral	少尉	Ensign
中将	Vice Admiral	军士长	Chief Petty Officer
少将	Rear Admiral	专业军士	Specialist Petty Officer
大校	Senior Captain	上士	Petty Officer, First Class
上校	Captain	中士	Petty Officer, Second Class
中校	Commander	下士	Petty Officer, Third Class
少校	Lieutenant Commander	上等兵	Seaman, First Class
上尉	Lieutenant	列兵	Seaman, Second Class

空　军 Air Force

一级上将	General, First Class	中尉	First Lieutenant
上将	General	少尉	Second Lieutenant
中将	Lieutenant General	军士长	Master Sergeant
少将	Major General	专业军士	Specialist Sergeant
大校	Senior Colonel	上士	Technical Sergeant
上校	Colonel	中士	Staff Sergeant
中校	Lieutenant Colonel	下士	Sergeant
少校	Major	上等兵	Airman, First Class
上尉	Captain	列兵	Airman, Second Class

附录四

诞生石与结婚周年纪念日

诞生石 Birthstones

1 月	石榴石	Garnet	7 月	红宝石	Ruby
2 月	紫晶	Amethyst	8 月	缠丝玛瑙	Sardonyx
3 月	海蓝宝石	Aquamarine	9 月	蓝宝石	Sapphire
4 月	钻石	Diamond	10 月	猫眼石	Opal
5 月	绿宝石	Emerald	11 月	黄玉	Topaz
6 月	珍珠	Pearl	12 月	绿松石	Turquoise

结婚周年纪念日 Wedding Anniversaries

第 1 周年	纸婚	Paper Wedding
第 2 周年	棉婚	Cotton Wedding
第 3 周年	皮革婚	Leather Wedding
第 4 周年	水果婚	Fruit Wedding
第 4 周年	花卉婚	Flowers Wedding
第 5 周年	木婚	Wooden Wedding
第 6 周年	糖婚	Candy Wedding
第 6 周年	铁婚	Iron Wedding
第 7 周年	羊毛婚	Wool Wedding
第 7 周年	铜婚	Copper Wedding
第 8 周年	青铜婚	Bronze Wedding
第 9 周年	陶器婚	Pottery Wedding
第 10 周年	锡婚	Tin Wedding
第 10 周年	铝婚	Aluminum Wedding
第 11 周年	钢婚	Steel Wedding
第 12 周年	丝婚	Silk Wedding
第 12 周年	亚麻婚	Linen Wedding
第 13 周年	花边婚	Lace Wedding
第 14 周年	象牙婚	Ivory Wedding
第 15 周年	水晶婚	Crystal Wedding
第 20 周年	瓷器婚	China Wedding
第 25 周年	银婚	Silver Wedding
第 30 周年	珍珠婚	Pearl Wedding
第 35 周年	珊瑚婚	Coral Wedding
第 40 周年	红宝石婚	Ruby Wedding
第 45 周年	蓝宝石婚	Sapphire Wedding
第 50 周年	金婚	Golden Wedding
第 55 周年	绿宝石婚	Emerald Wedding
第 60 周年	钻石婚	Diamond Wedding
第 75 周年	钻石婚	Diamond Wedding

附录五

二十四节气与天干地支

二十四节气 The Twenty-four Seasonal Division Points

立春	Beginning of Spring	立秋	Beginning of Autumn
雨水	Rain Water	处暑	Limit of Heat
惊蛰	Waking of Insects	白露	White Dew
春分	Vernal Equinox	秋分	Autumnal Equinox
清明	Pure Brightness	寒露	Cold Dew
谷雨	Grain Rain	霜降	Frost's Descent
立夏	Beginning of Summer	立冬	Beginning of Winter
小满	Grain Budding	小雪	Slight Snow
芒种	Grain in Ear	大雪	Great Snow
夏至	Summer Solstice	冬至	Winter Solstice
小暑	Slight Heat	小寒	Slight Cold
大暑	Great Heat	大寒	Great Cold

天　干 Heavenly Stems

甲	(jiǎ)	Heavenly Stem One	己	(jǐ)	Heavenly Stem Six
乙	(yǐ)	Heavenly Stem Two	庚	(gēng)	Heavenly Stem Seven
丙	(bǐng)	Heavenly Stem Three	辛	(xīn)	Heavenly Stem Eight
丁	(dīng)	Heavenly Stem Four	壬	(rén)	Heavenly Stem Nine
戊	(wù)	Heavenly Stem Five	癸	(guǐ)	Heavenly Stem Ten

地　支 Earthly Branches

子	(zǐ)	Earthly Branch One	午	(wǔ)	Earthly Branch Seven
丑	(chǒu)	Earthly Branch Two	未	(wèi)	Earthly Branch Eight
寅	(yín)	Earthly Branch Three	申	(shēn)	Earthly Branch Nine
卯	(mǎo)	Earthly Branch Four	酉	(yǒu)	Earthly Branch Ten
辰	(chén)	Earthly Branch Five	戌	(xū)	Earthly Branch Eleven
巳	(sì)	Earthly Branch Six	亥	(hài)	Earthly Branch Twelve

附录六

中国历史纪元表

五帝时代 Period of the Five Legendary Rulers c. 30th century~c. 21st century BC	黄帝 Huangdi（Yellow Emperor）		
	颛顼 Zhuanxu		
	帝喾 Diku(Emperor Ku)		
	唐尧 Yao of Tang		
	虞舜 Shun of Yu		
夏 Xia Dynasty	2070BC~1600BC		
商 Shang Dynasty	1600BC~1046BC		
西周 Western Zhou Dynasty	1046BC~771BC		
东周 Eastern Zhou Dynasty 770BC~256BC	春秋 Spring and Autumn Period	770BC~476BC	
	战国 Warring States Period	475BC~221BC	
秦 Qin Dynasty	221BC~206BC		
汉 Han Dynasty 206BC~220AD	西汉 Western Han	206BC~25AD	
	东汉 Eastern Han	25~220	
三国 Three Kingdoms 220~280	魏 Wei	220~265	
	蜀汉 Shu Han	221~263	
	吴 Wu	222~280	
晋 Jin Dynasty 265~420	西晋 Western Jin	265~317	
	东晋 Eastern Jin	317~420	
南北朝 Northern and Southern Dynasties 420~589	南朝 Southern Dynasties	宋 Song	420~479
		齐 Qi	479~502
		梁 Liang	502~557
		陈 Chen	557~589
	北朝 Northern Dynasties	北魏 Northern Wei	386~534
		东魏 Eastern Wei	534~550
		北齐 Northern Qi	550~577
		西魏 Western Wei	535~556
		北周 Northern Zhou	557~581

隋 Sui Dynasty		581～618		
唐 Tang Dynasty		618～907		
五代十国 Five Dynasties and Ten States Period	五代 Five Dynasties 907～960	后梁 Later Liang	907～923	
		后唐 Later Tang	923～936	
		后晋 Later Jin	936～947	
		后汉 Later Han	947～950	
		后周 Later Zhou	951～960	
	十国 Ten States Period 902～979	北汉 Northern Han	951～979	
		吴 Wu	902～937	
		南唐 Southern Tang	937～975	
		吴越 Wuyue	907～978	
		闽 Min	909～945	
		南汉 Southern Han	917～971	
		楚 Chu	927～951	
		荆南 Jingnan	924～963	
		前蜀 Former Shu	907～925	
		后蜀 Later Shu	934～965	
宋 Song Dynasty 960～1279	北宋 Northern Song	960～1126		
	南宋 Southern Song	1127～1279		
辽 Liao		907～1125		
金 Jin		1115～1234		
西夏 Xixia		1038～1227		
元 Yuan Dynasty		1206～1368		
明 Ming Dynasty		1368～1644		
清 Qing Dynasty		1616～1911		
中华民国 Republic of China		1912～1949		
中华人民共和国 The People's Republic of China		1949～		

附录七

联合国及其他国际组织

联合国主要机构

联合国大会　General Assembly (GA)
安全理事会　Security Council (SC)
经济及社会理事会　Economic and Social Council (ECONSOC)
托管理事会　Trusteeship Council
国际法院　International Court of Justice
秘书处　Secretariat

政府间组织及专门机构

国际电信联盟　International Telecommunication Union (ITU)
国际复兴开发银行　International Bank for Reconstruction and Development (IBRD)
国际海事组织　International Maritime Organization (IMO)
国际货币基金组织　International Monetary Fund (IMF)
国际金融公司　International Finance Corporation (IFC)
国际开发协会　International Development Association (IDA)
国际劳工组织　International Labour Organization (ILO)
国际民用航空组织　International Civil Aviation Organization (ICAO)
联合国教育、科学及文化组织　United Nations Educational, Scientific and Cultural Organization (UNESCO)
联合国粮食及农业组织　Food and Agriculture Organization of the United Nations (FAO)
世界气象组织　World Meteorological Organization (WMO)
世界卫生组织　World Health Organization (WHO)
万国邮政联盟　Universal Postal Union (UPU)

其他组织及专门机构

国际麻醉品管理局　International Narcotics Control Board (INCB)
国际农业发展基金　International Fund for Agricultural Development (IFAD)
国际提高妇女地位研究所　International Research and Training Institute for the Advancement of Women
联合国巴勒斯坦和解委员会　United Nations Conciliation Commission for Palestine (UNCCP)
联合国巴勒斯坦难民救济组织　United Nations Relief for Palestine Refugees (UNRPR)
联合国裁军会议　United Nations Conference on Disarmament (UNCD)
联合国裁军审议委员会　United Nations Disarmament Commission (UNDC)
联合国裁军中心　United Nations Center for Disarmament
联合国大学　United Nations University (UNU)
联合国地区经济委员会　United Nations Regional Economic Commission
联合国儿童基金会　United Nations Children Fund (UNICEF)
联合国非殖民化特别委员会　United Nations Special Committee on Decolonization
联合国非洲经济委员会　United Nations Economic Commission for Africa (UNECA)
联合国妇女地位委员会　United Nations Commission on the Status of Women
联合国工业发展组织　United Nations Industrial Development Organization (UNIDO)
联合国脱离接触观察员部队　United Nations Disengagement Observer Force (UNDOF)
联合国国际法委员会　United Nations International Law Commission (UNILC)
联合国国际贸易法委员会　United Nations Commission on International Trade Law (UNCITRAL)
联合国国际刑事管辖问题委员会　United Nations Committee on International Criminal Jurisdiction
联合国环境规划署　United Nations Environment Programme (UNEP)
联合国环境基金　United Nations Environment Fund (UNEF)

联合国环境与发展大会　United Nations Conference on Environment and Development（UNCED）
联合国货币金融会议　United Nations Monetary and Financial Conference
联合国控制毒品滥用基金组织　United Nations Fund for Drug Abuse Control（UNFDAC）
联合国经济发展特别基金　Special United Nations' Fund for Economic Development（SUNFED）
联合国经济发展总署　United Nations Economic Development Administration（UNEDA）
联合国经济合作行动计划署　United Nations Action Programme for Ecomomic Cooperation
联合国开发公司　United Nations Development Corporation（UNDC）
联合国救灾协调专员办事处　Office of United Nations Disaster Relief Co-ordinator（UNDRO）
联合国开发计划署　United Nations Development Programme（UNDP）
联合国跨国公司委员会　United Nations Economic Commission on Transnational Corporations
联合国跨国公司中心　United Nations Centre on Transnational Corporations（UNCTC）
联合国拉丁美洲经济委员会　United Nations Economic Commission for Latin America（UNECLA）
联合国麻醉品管制署　United Nations International Drug Control Programme（UNIDCP）
联合国贸易促进中心　Trade Promotion Centre of the United Nations（UNTPC）
联合国贸易和发展会议　United Nations Conference on Trade and Development（UNCTAD）
联合国贸易与发展理事会　United Nations Trade and Development Board（UNTDB）
联合国难民事务高级专员办事处　Office of the United Nations High Commissioner for Refugees
　（UNHCR）
联合国区域发展中心　United Nations Center for Regional Development（UNCRD）
联合国人口活动基金　United Nations Fund for Population Activities（UNFPA）
联合国人口奖委员会　Committee for the United Nations Population Award
联合国人口委员会　Population Commission of the United Nations
联合国人类环境会议　United Nations Conference on the Human Environment
联合国人类住区会议　United Nations Conference on the Human Settlements
联合国人类住区中心　United Nations Centre for Human Settlements（HABITAT）
联合国人权委员会　United Nations Commission on Human Rights
联合国人权中心　United Nations Centre for Human Rights
联合国善后救济总署　United Nations Relief and Rehabilitation Administration（UNRRA）
联合国社会发展和人道主义事务中心　United Nations Centre for Social Development and Hu-
　manitarian Affairs（UNCSDHA）
联合国社会发展首脑会议　World Summit for Social Development（Socail Summit）
联合国社会发展研究所　United Nations Research Institute for Social Development（UNRISD）
联合国特别基金　United Nations Special Fund
联合国停战监督组织　United Nations Truce Supervision Organization（UNTSO）
联合国统计局　United Nations Statistical Office
联合国宪章问题委员会　Committee on the Charter of the United Nations
联合国协会世界联合会　World Federation of United Nations Associations（WFUNA）
联合国行政法庭　United Nations Administrative Tribunal
联合国行政和预算问题咨询委员会　UN Advisory Committee on Administrative and Budgetary
　Questions（UNACABQ）
联合国训练研究所　United Nations Institute for Training and Research（UNITAR）
联合国亚洲及太平洋经济和社会委员会　United Nations Economic and Social Commission for A-
　sia and the Pacific（ESCAP）
联合国印度巴基斯坦委员会　United Nations Commission for India and Pakistan（UNCIP）
联合国预防和控制犯罪委员会　United Nations Committee on Crime Prevention and Control
联合国殖民主义问题特别委员会　United Nations Special Committee on Colonialism
联合国周转基金　United Nations Revolving Fund
联合国资本开发基金　United Nations Capital Development Fund（UNCDF）
世界粮食理事会　World Food Council（WFC）
世界知识产权组织　World Intellectual Property Organization（WIPO）

其他国际与区域组织

阿拉伯共同市场　Arab Common Market（ACM）
阿拉伯国家联盟（阿盟）　League of Arab States（Arab League；LAS）
阿拉伯货币基金组织　Arab Monetary Fund（AMF）
阿拉伯经济统一委员会　Council of Arab Economic Unity（CAEU）

阿拉伯联盟教科文组织　Arab League Educational, Cultural, and Scientific Organization (ALEC-SO)

阿拉伯石油输出国组织　Organization of Arab Petroleum Exporting Countries (OAPEC)

安第斯共同市场　Andean Common Market (ANCOM)

安第斯共同体　Andean Community

安第斯条约组织　Andean Pact Organization (APO); Pacto Andino (PA)

八国集团　Group of Eight (G8)

巴黎俱乐部　Paris Club (Group of Ten)

巴黎联盟（国际保护工业产权联盟）　Paris Convention (International Union for the Protection of Industrial Property)

巴黎统筹委员会　Coordinating Committee on Export Control (COCOM); Coordinating Committee for Export to Communist Countries

北大西洋公约组织　North Atlantic Treaty Organization (NATO)

北大西洋合作理事会　North Atlantic Cooperation Council

北美自由贸易区　North American Free Trade Area (NAFTA)

北南核控制联合委员会　North-South Nuclear Joint Committee

北欧理事会　Nordic Council

北欧邮政联盟　Nordic Postal Union (NPU)

北太平洋海洋科学组织　North Pacific Marine Science Organization (PICES)

伯尔尼联盟　Berne Union

不结盟运动　Non-Aligned Movement (NAM)

朝鲜半岛能源开发组织　Korean Peninsula Energy Development Organization (KEDO)

船长协会国际联合会　International Federation of Shipmasters' Associations (IFSMA)

促进种族平等公民协会　Citizen's Association for Racial Equality

大陆架界限委员会　Commission on the Limits of the Continental Shelf

大气科学委员会　Commission of Atmospheric Sciences (CAS)

大气污染管制委员会　Air Pollution Control Commission (APCC)

大气污染控制管理局　Air Pollution Control Administration (APCA)

大赦国际　Amnesty International

大西洋自由贸易区　Atlantic Free Trade Area (AFTA)

第三世界科学院　Academy of Sciences for the Third World

东非共同体　East African Community (EAC)

东加勒比共同市场　East Caribbean Common Market (ECCM)

东加勒比组织　Organizaiton of the Eastern Caribbean States

东盟各国议会组织　ASEAN Inter-Parliamentary Organization

东盟自由贸易区　ASEAN Free Trade Area (AFTA)

东南非共同市场　Common Market for Eastern and Southern Africa (COMESA)

东南亚国家联盟　Association of Southeast Asian Nations (ASEAN)

发展工业产权和有关权力合作常设委员会　Permanent Committee for Development Cooperation Related to Industrial Property

发展中国家间经济合作委员会　Committee on Economic Cooperation Among Developing Countries

发展著作权和邻接权利合作常设委员会　Permanent Committee for Development Cooperation Related to Copyright and Neighbouring Rights

法语国家首脑会议　Somet de la francophonie; Summit of Francophone Countries

反对原子弹氢弹会议　Conference Against Atomic and Hydrogen Bombs

泛非电信联盟　Pan-African Telecommunication Union (PATU)

泛非妇女组织　Organization Panafricaine des Femmes (OPF); Pan-African Women's Organization (PAWO)

防止空气污染协会国际联合会　International Union of Air Pollution Prevention Associations (IU-APPA)

防止歧视和保护少数小组委员会　Sub-Commission on prevention of Discrimination and Protection of Minorities

防止外层空间军备竞赛特设委员会　Ad Hoc Committee on the Prevention of Arms Race in Outer Space

非殖民化委员会　Commission on Decolonization

非洲、加勒比和太平洋地区国家集团　Group of African, Caribbean and Pacific Region Countries (ACP Group)

非洲经济共同体　African Economic Community

非洲人权和民族权委员会　African Committee on Human and People's Rights

非洲统一组织　Organization of African Unity (OAU)

非洲邮政联盟　African Postal Union (APU)

扶轮社国际　Rotary International

各国议会联盟　Inter-Parliamentary Union (IPU)

国际奥林匹克委员会　International Olympic Committee (IOC)

国际版权协会　International Copyright Society

国际保护工业产权联盟　International Union for the Protection of Industrial Property

国际保护工业产权协会　International Association for the Protection of Industrial Property (IA-PIP)

国际保护知识产权联合局　United International Bureau for the Protection of Intellectual Property (BIRPI)

国际保护自然与自然资源联盟　International Union for Conservation of Nature and Natural Resources (IUCN)

国际笔会　International PEN

国际标准化组织　International Standardization Organization (ISO)

国际材料物理中心　International Center for Materials Physics (ICMP)

国际船东协会　International Shipping Federation (ISF)

国际船级社协会　International Association of Classification Societies (IACS)

国际纯粹和应用化学联盟　International Union of Pure and Applied Chemistry (IUPAC)

国际纯粹和应用生物物理学联盟　International Union of Pure and Applied Biophysics (IUPAB)

国际大坝委员会　International Commission on Large Dams (ICOLD)

国际大学生体育联合会　Fédération International du Sport Universitaire (FISU)

国际地球科学信息网络集团　Consortium for International Earth Science Information Network (CIESIN)

国际地球学联盟　International Geographical Union (IGU)

国际地震中心　International Seismological Centre (ISC)

国际地质大会　International Geological Congress (IGC)

国际地质科学联盟　International Union of Geological Sciences (IUGS)

国际冻土协会　International Permafrost Association (IPA)

国际独立油船东协会　International Association of Independent Tanker Owners (INTERTANKO)

国际度量衡局　International Bureau of Weight and Measurements (IBWM)

国际儿童福利联合会　International Union for Child Welfare (IUCW)

国际法官联合会　International Union of Judges

国际法协会　International Law Association

国际法学家委员会　International Commission of Jurists (ICJ)

国际法学协会　International Association of Legal Science (IALS)

国际纺织学会　International Textile Institute (ITI)

国际辐射防护协会　International Radiation Protection Association (IRPA)

国际妇女同盟　International Alliance of Women (IAW)

国际妇女协会　International Women Society

国际港口协会　International Association of Ports and Harbours (IAPH)

国际公务员协会联合会　Federation of International Civil Servants Associations (FICSA)

国际公务员制度委员会　International Civil Service Commission (ICSC)

国际古生物协会　International Palaeontological Association (IPA)

国际雇主组织　International Organization of Employers (IOE)

国际广播协会　International Association of Broadcasting (IAB)

国际海道测量组织　International Hydrographic Organization (IHO)

国际海底管理局　International Sea-Bed Authority

国际海事卫星组织　International Maritime Satellite Organization (INMARSAT)

国际海运联盟　International Shipping Federation

国际航标协会　International Association of Lighthouse Authorities (IALA)

国际航空科学理事会　International Council of Aeronautical Sciences (ICAS)

国际航空联合会　Aeronautic International Federation (FAI)
国际航空运输协会　International Air Transport Association (IATA)
国际航运会议常设协会　Permanent International Association of Navigation Congresses (PIANC)
国际航运协会　International Chamber of Shipping
国际和平利用原子能会议　International Conference on the Peaceful Use of Atomic Energy
国际和平学会　International Peace Academy (IPA)
国际核数据委员会　International Nuclear Data Committee (INDC)
国际红十字会　International Red Cross (IRC)
国际环境法理事会　International Council of Environmental Law
国际环境事务研究所　International Institute for Environmental Affairs
国际计划生育联合会　International Planned Parenthood Federation (IPPF)
国际建筑师协会　International Union of Architects (IUA)
国际救济联合会　International Relief Union (IRU)
国际军事体育理事会　International Military Sports Council (IMSC)
国际开发委员会　Commission on International Development (CID)
国际科学基金会　International Foundation of Sciences (IFS)
国际科学联盟理事会　International Council of Scientific Unions (ICSU)
国际空间研究委员会　International Committee on Space Research (ICSR)
国际空运协会　International Air Transport Association (IATA)
国际理论和应用力学联盟　International Union of Theoretical and Applied Mechanics
国际理论物理中心　International Centre for Theoretical Physics (ICTP)
国际律师协会　International Bar Association (IBA)
国际毛纺组织　International Wool Textile Organization (IWTO)
国际民主妇女联合会　Women's International Democratic Federation (WIDF)
国际难民组织　International Refugee Organization (IRO)
国际能源机构　International Energy Agency (IEA)
国际欧亚科学院　International Academy for Europe and Asia (IAEA)
国际清算银行　Bank for International Settlements (BIS)
国际人口问题科学研究联合会　International Union for the Scientific Study of Population (IU-SSP)
国际人权法院　International Court of Human Rights
国际人权联合会　International Federation of Human Rights
国际人与生物圈保护区网络　International Man and Biosphere Reserve Network
国际商会　International Chamber of Commerce (ICC)
国际商业仲裁委员会　International Council for Commercial Arbitration
国际生态学协会　International Association for Ecology
国际生物化学与分子生物学联盟　International Union of Biochemistry and Molecular Biology (IUBMB)
国际生物科学联合会　International Union of Biological Sciences (IUBS)
国际圣经协会　International Bible Society (IBS)
国际世界语协会　Universala Esperanto-Asocio; Universal Esperanto Association (UEA)
国际数学联盟　International Mathematical Union (IMU)
国际水资源协会　International Water Resources Association (IWRA)
国际丝绸协会　International Silk Association (ISA)
国际体操联合会　Fédération Internationale de Gymnastique (FIG); International Federation of Gymnastics
国际天文学联合会　International Astronomical Union (IAU)
国际通讯卫星组织　International Telecommunications Satellite Organization (INTELSAT)
国际投资银行　International Investment Bank (IIB)
国际土壤协会　International Society of Soil Science (ISSS)
国际细胞生物学联合会　International Federation for Cell Biology (IFCB)
国际心理科学联盟　International Union of Psychological Science
国际新闻工作者协会　International Federation of Journalists
国际信息和文献联合会　International Federation for Information and Documentation
国际刑法协会　International Association on Penal Law (IAPL)
国际刑警组织　International Criminal Police Organization (INTERPOL; ICPO)

国际刑事学会　International Association of Criminal Science
国际宣教协会　International Missionary Council（IMC）
国际学生联合会　International Union of Students（IUS）
国际移民组织　International Organization for Migration（IOM）
国际遗传学联合会　International Genetics Federation（IGF）
国际译联　International Federation of Translators
国际音乐理事会　International Music Council（IMC）
国际应用心理学协会　International Association of Applied Psychology（IAAP）
国际有线发行联盟　International Alliance for Distribution by Cable
国际宇航科学院　International Academy of Astronautics（IAA）
国际植物生理学家协会　International Association for Plant Physiologists（IAPP）
国际自动控制联合会　International Federation of Automatic Control（IFAC）
国际自由工会联合会　International Confederation of Free Trade Unions（ICFTU）
国际足球联合会　International Football Federation（FIFA）
海湾合作委员会　Cooperation Council for the Arab States of the Gulf；Gulf Cooperation Council（GCC）
海洋研究科学委员会　Scientific Committee on Oceanic Research（SCOR）
海洋研究气象委员会　Commission on Maritime Meteorology（CMM）
海洋资源研究咨询委员会　Advisory Committee on Marine Resources Research
和平利用外层空间委员会　Committee of Peaceful Uses of Outer Space
和平利用原子能国际会议咨询委员会　Advisory Committee of the International Conference on the Peaceful Uses of Atomic Energy
和平利用原子能委员会　Committee on the Use of Atomic Energy for Peaceful Purposes（CUAEPP）
红十字会与红新月会国际联合会　International Federation of Red Cross and Red Crescent Societies（IFRCS）
环境问题科学委员会　Scientific Committee on Problems of the Environment（SCOPE）
环境与发展国际研究中心　Centre for International Research of Environment and Development（CIRED）
环太平洋论坛　Pacific Rim Forum（PRF）
基督教会联合会　World Council of Churches（WCC）
基督教女青年会　Young Women's Christian Association（YWCA）
基督教青年会　Young Men's Christian Association（YMCA）
计划生育－世界人口组织　Planned Parenthood-World Population
加勒比共同体和共同市场　Caribbean Community and Common Market（CARICOM）
经济合作与发展组织　Organization for Economic Cooperation and Development（OECD）
孔塔多拉集团　Contadora Group
拉丁美洲共同市场　Latin American Common Market（LACM）
拉丁美洲和加勒比禁止核武器组织　Organization for the Prohibition of Nuclear Weapons in Latin America and the Caribbean
拉丁美洲货币同盟　Latin American Monetary Union
拉丁美洲经济体系　Latin American Economic System（LAES）
拉丁美洲经济委员会　Economic commission of Latin American（ECLA）
拉丁美洲开发金融机构协会　Latin American Association of Development of Financing Institutions
拉丁美洲能源组织　Latin American Energy Organization（OLAE）
拉丁美洲社会学会　Association of Latin American Sociology（ALAS）
拉丁美洲协调特别委员会　Special Committee on Latin American Coordination
拉丁美洲一体化协会　Latin American Integration Association（LAIA）
拉丁美洲自由贸易区　Latin American Free Trade Area（LAFTA）
拉丁美洲自由贸易市场　Latin American Free Trade Market
拉丁美洲自由贸易协会　Latin American Free Trade Association
联合国协会世界联和会　World Federation of United Nations Associations（WFUNA）
伦敦核供应国俱乐部　Lodon Suppliers' Club
马格里布联盟　Union du Maghreb（UMA）
美洲出口贸易促进中心　Inter-American Export Promotion Centre

美洲储蓄和贷款银行　Inter-American Savings and Loans Bank
美洲国家间人权委员会　Inter-American Commission on Human Rights
美洲国家组织　Organization of American States (OAS)
美洲经济及社会理事会　Inter-American Economic and Social Council
美洲开发银行　Inter-American Development Bank
美洲人权委员会　Inter-American Commission on Human Rights (IACHR)
南北协调委员会　North-South Coordinating Committee
南部非洲发展共同体　Southern African Development Community (SADC)
南部非洲关税同盟　Southern African Customs Union (SACU)
南方共同市场　South Common Market
南南会议　South-South Conference
南太平洋论坛　South Pacific Forum (SPF)
南亚区域合作联盟　South Asian Association for Regional Cooperation (SAARC)
欧洲安全与合作组织　Organization for Security and Cooperation in Europe (OSCE)
欧洲裁军会议　Conference on Disarmament in Europe (CDE)
欧洲复兴开发银行　European Bank of Reconstruction and Development
欧洲经济合作组织　Organization for European Economic Cooperation (OEEC)
欧洲联盟　European Union (EU)
欧洲人权法院　European Court of Human Rights
欧洲人权委员会　European Commission of Human Rights
欧洲原子能委员会　European Atomic Commission (EAC)
欧洲原子能学会　European Atomic Energy Society (EAES)
欧洲自由贸易联盟　European Free Trade Association (EFTA)
七国集团　Group of Seven (G7)
七十七国集团　Group of 77
区域合作发展组织　Regional Cooperation Organization for Development (RCOD)
三边委员会　Trilateral Commission of Japan, North America and Europe (TC)
社会党国际　Socialist International
石油输出国组织　Organization of Petroleum Exporting Countries (OPEC)
世界残疾人组织理事会　Council of World Organizations Interested in the Handicapped (CWOIH)
世界动物保护联合会　World Federation for the Protection of Animals
世界佛教徒联谊会　World Fellowship of Buddhists (WFB)
世界工会联合会　World Federation of Trade Unions (WFTU)
世界海关组织　World Customs Organization
世界和平理事会　World Peace Council (WPC)
世界基督教联合会　World Council of Churches (WCC)
世界教师工会协进会　World Federation of Teachers' Unions (WFTU)
世界科学工作者联合会　World Federation of Scientific Workers (WFSW)
世界劳工联合会　World Confederation of Labour (WCL)
世界旅游组织　World Tourism Organization (WTO)
世界贸易组织　World Trade Organization (WTO)
世界穆斯林联盟　Muslim World League (MWL)
世界青年大会　World Assembly of Youth (MAY)
世界人权大会　World Conference on Human Rights
世界野生动物基金会　World Wildlife Fund (WWF)
世界医学协会　World Medical Association
世界艺术与科学学会　World Academy of Art and Science
世界犹太人大会　World Jewish Congress
世界幼儿教育组织　World Organization for Early Children's Education
世界针灸学会联合会　World Federation of Acupuncture and Moxibustion Societies
世界自然保护联盟　World Conservation Union
世界宗教和平大会　World Conference on Religion and Peace (WCRP)
太平洋经济合作理事会　Pacific Economic Cooperation Council (PECC)
西方七国首脑会议　Seven-Nation Economic Summit; Group of Seven Summit (G7 Summit)
西非国家经济共同体　Economic Community of West African States (ECOWAS)
西欧联盟　Western European Union (WEU)

亚大邮联　Asian-Oceanic Postal Union (AOPU;UPAO)
亚非法律协商委员会　Asian-African Legal Consultative Committee (AALCC)
亚非会议　Asian-African Conference
亚非拉人民团结组织　Organization of Solidarity of the Peoples of Africa,Asia and Latin America (OSPAALA)
亚非人民团结组织　Afro-Asian People's Solidarity Organization (AAPSO)
亚非新闻工作者协会　Afro-Asian Journalists' Association (AAJA)
亚欧合作理事会　Council for Asian-Europe Cooperation (CACE)
亚欧环境技术中心　Asia-Europe Environmental Technology Center
亚太安全合作理事会　Council on Security Cooperation in Asia and Pacific Region (CSCAP)
亚太经合组织　Asian-Pacific Economic Cooperation (APEC)
亚太空间技术与应用多边合作会议　Asia-Pacific Conference on Multilateral Cooperation in Space Technology and Applications (APC-MCSTA Conference)
亚洲－大洋洲邮政联盟　Asian-Oceanic Postal Union (AOPU;UPAO)
亚洲化学学会联合会　Federation of Asian Chemical Societies (FACS)
亚洲环境问题协会　Asian Environmental Society (AES)
亚洲基督教会议　Christian Conference of Asia (CCA)
亚洲及太平洋和平与裁军区域中心　Regional Centre for Peace and Disarmament in Asia and the Pacific
亚洲及太平洋理事会　Asian and Pacific Council (ASPAC)
亚洲开发银行　Asian Development Bank (ADB)
亚洲科学联合会　Federation of Asian Scientific Academies and Societies
亚洲青年理事会　Asian Youth Council (AYC)
亚洲生产力组织　Asian Productivity Organization
亚洲－太平洋广播联盟　Asian-Pacific Broadcasting Union (ABU)
亚洲－太平洋通讯社组织　Organization of Asia-Pacific News Agencies (OANA)
亚洲－太平洋邮政联盟　Asian-Pacific Postal Union
亚洲遥感协会　Asian Association on Remote Sensing (AARS)
印度洋特设委员会　Ad Hoc Committee on the Indian Ocean
英联邦　British Commonwealth of Nations (Commonwealth)
中非国家经济共同体　Economic Community of Central African States (CEEAC)
中非国家联盟　Union of Central African States (UEAC)
中美洲共同市场　Central American Common Market
中美洲国家组织　Organization of Central American States

Team Competition
盛装舞步团体
Individual Competition
盛装舞步个人

Jumping
场地障碍

Team Competition
场地障碍团体
Individual Competition
场地障碍个人

Fencing
击剑

Men's Foil Individual
男子花剑个人
Men's Epee Individual
男子重剑个人
Men's Epee Team
男子重剑团体
Men's Sabre Individual
男子佩剑个人
Men's Sabre Team
男子佩剑团体
Women's Foil Individual
女子花剑个人
Women's Foil Team
女子花剑团体
Women's Epee Individual
女子重剑个人
Women's Sabre Team
女子佩剑团体
Women's Sabre Individual
女子佩剑个人

Football
足球

Men
男子
Women
女子

Gymnastics
体操

Artistic Gymnastics
体操

Men's Team Competition
男子团体
Men's Individual Competition
男子个人全能
Men's Floor
男子自由体操
Men's Pommel Horse
男子鞍马
Men's Rings
男子吊环
Men's Vault
男子跳马
Men's Parallel Bars
男子双杠
Men's Horizontal Bar
男子单杠
Women's Team Competition
女子团体
Women's Individual Competition
女子个人全能
Women's Vault
女子跳马
Women's Uneven Bars
女子高低杠
Women's Balance Beam
女子平衡木
Women's Floor
女子自由体操

Rhythmic Gymnastics
艺术体操

Individual Competition
女子个人全能
Group Competition
女子集体全能

Trampoline
蹦床

Men's Individual Event
男子个人赛
Women's Individual Event
女子个人赛

Handball
手球

Men
男子
Women
女子

Hockey
曲棍球

Men
男子
Women
女子

Judo
柔道

Men's Up to 60kg
男子－60公斤级
Men's 60 to 66kg
男子60－66公斤级
Men's 66 to 73kg
男子66－73公斤级
Men's 73 to 81kg
男子73－81公斤级
Men's 81 to 90kg
男子81－90公斤级
Men's 90 to 100kg
男子90－100公斤级
Men's Over 100kg
男子＋100公斤级
Women's Up to 48kg
女子－48公斤级
Women's 48 to 52kg
女子48－52公斤级

Women's 52 to 57kg

女子52-57公斤级

Women's 57 to 63kg

女子57-63公斤级

Women's 63 to 70kg

女子63-70公斤级

Women's 70 to 78kg

女子70-78公斤级

Women's Over 78kg

女子+78公斤级

Modern Pentathlon
现代五项

Men's Individual Competition

男子个人赛

Women's Individual Competition

女子个人赛

Rowing
赛艇

Men's Single Sculls (1×)

男子单人双桨

Men's Pairs (2 -)

男子双人单桨无舵手

Men's Double Sculls (2×)

男子双人双桨无舵手

Men's Fours (4 −)

男子四人单桨无舵手

Men's Quadruple Sculls (4×)

男子四人双桨无舵手

Men's Eights (8 +)

男子八人单桨有舵手

Men's Lightweight Double Sculls (2×)

男子轻量级双人双桨无舵手

Men's Lightweight Fours (4 -)

男子轻量级四人单桨无舵手

Women's Single Sculls (1×)

女子单人双桨

Women's Pairs (2 -)

女子双人单桨无舵手

Women's Double Sculls (2×)

女子双人双桨无舵手

Women's Quadruple Sculls (4×)

女子四人双桨无舵手

Women's Eights (8 +)

女子八人单桨有舵手

Women's Lightweight Double Sculls (2×)

女子轻量级双人双桨无舵手

Sailing
帆船

470-Men's Two Person Dinghy

男子双人艇470级

Laser-Men's One Person Dinghy

男子单人艇激光级

Star-Men's Keelboat

男子龙骨船星级

RS:X-Men's Windsurfer

男子帆板RS：X

470-Women's Two Person Dinghy

女子双人艇470级

Yngling-Women's Keelboat

女子龙骨船英凌级

Laser Radial-Women's One Person Dinghy

女子单人艇激光雷迪尔级

RS:X-Women's Windsurfer

女子帆板RS：X

Finn-Heavyweight Dinghy

重量级艇芬兰人级

49er-Skiff

快船49人级

Tornado-Multihull

多体船托纳多级

Shooting
射击

Men's 10m Air Pistol

男子10米气手枪

Men's 25m Rapid Fire Pistol

男子25米手枪速射

Men's 50m Pistol

男子50米手枪

Men's 10m Air Rifle

男子10米气步枪

Men's 50m Rifle 3 posisitons

男子50米步枪3种姿势

Men's 50m Rifle Prone

男子50米步枪卧射

Men's Double Trap

男子飞碟双多向

Men's Trap

男子飞碟多向

Men's Skeet

男子飞碟双向

Women's 10m Air Pistol

女子10米气手枪

Women's 25m Pistol

女子25米手枪

Women's 10m Air Rifle

女子10米气步枪

Women's 50m Rifle 3 Positions

女子50米步枪3种姿势

Women's Trap

女子飞碟多向

Women's Skeet

女子飞碟双向

Softball
垒球

Women

女子

Table Tennis
乒乓球

Men's Singles

男子单打

Men's Teams

男子团体

Women's Singles

女子单打

Women's Teams

女子团体

Taekwondo
跆拳道

Boxing
拳击

Men's Light Fly Weight

男子-48公斤级

Men's Fly Weight

男子48-51公斤级

Men's Bantam Weight

男子51-54公斤级

Men's Feather Weight

男子54-57公斤级

Men's Light Weight

男子57-60公斤级

Men's Light Welter Weight

男子60-64公斤级

Men's Welter Weight

男子64-69公斤级

Men's Middle Weight

男子69-75公斤级

Men's Light Heavy Weight

男子75-81公斤级

Men's Heavy Weight

男子81-91公斤级

Men's Super Heavy Weight

男子+91公斤级

Canoe/Kayak
皮划艇

Flatwater
静水

Men's K-1 500m

男子单人皮艇500米

Men's K-1 1000m

男子单人皮艇1000米

Men's K-2 500m

男子双人皮艇500米

Men's K-2 1000m

男子双人皮艇1000米

Men's K-4 1000m

男子四人皮艇1000米

Men's C-1 500m

男子单人划艇500米

Men's C-1 1000m

男子单人划艇1000米

Men's C-2 500m

男子双人划艇500米

Men's C-2 1000m

男子双人划艇1000米

Women's K-1 500m

女子单人皮艇500米

Women's K-2 500m

女子双人皮艇500米

Women's k-4 500m

女子四人皮艇500米

Slalom
激流回旋

Men's K-1 Kayak Single

男子单人皮艇

Men's C-1 Canoe Single

男子单人划艇

Men's C-2 Canoe Double

男子双人划艇

Women's K-1 Kayak Single

女子单人皮艇

Cycling
自行车

Track
场地

Men's Sprint

男子争先赛

Men's Team Sprint

男子团体竞速赛

Men's Individual Pursuit

男子4公里个人追逐赛

Men's Team Pursuit

男子4公里团体追逐赛

Men's Points Race

男子记分赛

Men's Madison

男子麦迪逊赛

Men's Keirin

男子凯林赛

Women's Sprint

女子争先赛

Women's Individual Pursuit

女子3公里个人追逐赛

Women's Points Race

女子记分赛

Road
公路

Men's Mass Start Event

男子公路个人赛

Men's Time Trial Event

男子公路个人计时赛

Women's Mass Start Event

女子公路个人赛

Women's Time Trial Event

女子公路个人计时赛

Mountain Bike
山地车

Men's Cross-Country

男子越野赛

Women's Cross-Country

女子越野赛

BMX
BMX 小轮车

Men's Race

男子BMX个人赛

Women's Race

女子BMX个人赛

Equestrian
马术

Eventing
三项赛

Team Competition

三项赛团体

Individual Competition

三项赛个人

Dressage
盛装舞步

Athletics
田径

Men's 100m
男子100米

Men's 200m
男子200米

Men's 400m
男子400米

Men's 800m
男子800米

Men's 1500m
男子1500米

Men's 5000m
男子5000米

Men's 10000m
男子10000米

Men's 110m Hurdles
男子110米栏

Men's 400m Hurdles
男子400米栏

Men's 3000m Steeplechase
男子3000米障碍

Men's 20km Race Walk
男子20公里竞走

Men's 50km Race Walk
男子50公里竞走

Men's 4×100m Relay
男子4×100米接力

Men's 4×400m Relay
男子4×400米接力

Men's Marathon
男子马拉松

Men's High Jump
男子跳高

Men's Long Jump
男子跳远

Men's Triple Jump
男子三级跳远

Men's Pole Vault
男子撑竿跳高

Men's Shot Put
男子铅球

Men's Discus Throw
男子铁饼

Men's Javelin Throw
男子标枪

Men's Hammer Throw
男子链球

Men's Decathlon
男子十项全能

Women's 100m
女子100米

Women's 200m
女子200米

Women's 400m
女子400米

Women's 800m
女子800米

Women's 1500m
女子1500米

Women's 5000m
女子5000米

Women's 10000m
女子10000米

Women's 100m Hurdles
女子100米栏

Women's 400m Hurdles
女子400米栏

Women's 3000m Steeplechase
女子3000米障碍

Women's 20km Race Walk
女子20公里竞走

Women's 4×100m Relay
女子4×100米接力

Women's 4×400m Relay
女子4×400米接力

Women's Marathon
女子马拉松

Women's High Jump
女子跳高

Women's Long Jump
女子跳远

Women's Triple Jump
女子三级跳远

Women's Pole Vault
女子撑竿跳高

Women's Shot Put
女子铅球

Women's Discus Throw
女子铁饼

Women's Javelin Throw
女子标枪

Women's Hammer Throw
女子链球

Women's Heptathlon
女子七项全能

Badminton
羽毛球

Men's Singles
男子单打

Men's Doubles
男子双打

Women's Singles
女子单打

Women's Doubles
女子双打

Mixed Doubles
混合双打

Baseball
棒球

Men
男子

Basketball
篮球

Men
男子

Women
女子